Oxford School Dictionary & Thesaurus

Editor: Robert Allen

OXFORD
UNIVERSITY PRESS

OXFORD
UNIVERSITY PRESS

Great Clarendon Street, Oxford OX2 6DP

Oxford University Press is a department of the University of Oxford. It furthers the University's objective of excellence in research, scholarship, and education by publishing worldwide in

Oxford New York
Auckland Cape Town Dar es Salaam Hong Kong Karachi
Kuala Lumpur Madrid Melbourne Mexico City Nairobi New Delhi
Shanghai Taipei Toronto

with offices in

Argentina Austria Brazil Chile Czech Republic France Greece
Guatemala Hungary Italy Japan Poland Portugal Singapore
South Korea Switzerland Thailand Turkey Ukraine Vietnam

Oxford is a registered trade mark of Oxford University Press in the UK and in certain other countries

First published 2005
This edition 2007

Database right Oxford University Press (maker)

This title is comprised of the *Oxford Concise School Dictionary* and the *Oxford Concise School Thesaurus*

British Library cataloguing in Publication Data available

Hardback ISBN 978-0-19-911536-5

Paperback ISBN 978-0-19-911537-2

10 9 8 7 6 5 4 3 2 1

Typeset in OUP Argo and OUP Swift

by The Read Setter, Oxford

Printed in Italy by Rotolito Lombarda

Dictionary and Thesaurus Features

Pronunciations are given for difficult words

Parts of speech (word classes) are given for all headwords and derivatives

plaintiff *NOUN* **plaintiffs** the person who brings a complaint against somebody else to a lawcourt COMPARE **defendant**

Cross-references are given to other words of interest

plaintive *ADJECTIVE* sounding sad • *a plaintive cry*

plait (plat) *VERB* **plaits, plaiting, plaited** weave three or more strands of hair or rope to form one length

Plurals of nouns are given

plait *NOUN* **plaits** a length of hair or rope that has been plaited

Definitions are clear and accurate

plan *NOUN* **plans** **1** a way of doing something thought out in advance **2** a drawing showing the arrangement of parts of something **3** a map of a town or district

plan *VERB* **plans, planning, planned** make a plan for something
▷ **planner** *NOUN*

Headwords are numbered when they have different meanings or origins

plane[1] *NOUN* **planes** **1** an aeroplane **2** a tool for making wood smooth by scraping its surface **3** a flat or level surface

Headwords in the dictionary and the thesaurus are on the same page to make access quick and easy

plane *VERB* **planes, planing, planed** smooth wood with a plane

plane *ADJECTIVE* flat or level • *a plane surface*
USAGE Do not confuse with **plain**.

plane[2] *NOUN* **planes** a tall tree with broad leaves

Usage notes in the dictionary give grammar and language support

planet *NOUN* **planets** one of the bodies that move in an orbit round the sun. The main planets are Mercury, Venus, Earth, Mars, Jupiter, Saturn, Uranus, Neptune, and Pluto
▷ **planetary** *ADJECTIVE*

---

plan *NOUN* **1** (*informal*) *a plan of the building*
► chart, diagram, map, layout, blueprint, representation **2** *a clever plan for raising money*
► scheme, idea, proposal, project, programme, strategy, suggestion, proposition

Register labels help users to select appropriate vocabulary

Over 100,000 synonyms are listed with the most appropriate coming first

plan *VERB* **1** *She began planning tomorrow's journey.* ► organize, arrange, work out, think out, prepare **2** *some tips for anyone planning a new garden* ► design, devise, contrive, sketch out **3** *We plan to go abroad this year.* ► intend, propose, aim, mean, envisage, contemplate, be thinking of USAGE If you use any of the last three synonyms, you need to say *going* instead of *to go*, e.g. *We envisage going abroad this year.*

Usage notes in the thesaurus give language and grammar support

plane *NOUN* **1** *The plane rose gently in the air.*
► aeroplane, aircraft, jet, airliner, craft **2** *The thought that came to her now was on a more creative plane.* ► level, stage, degree, position

Up-to-date example sentences and phrases show how words are used in context

planet *NOUN* *the population of the planet*
► globe, world, orb

Aa

a *ADJECTIVE* (called the *indefinite article* and changing to **an** before most vowel sounds) **1** one (but not any special one) • *Can you lend me a book?* **2** each; per • *We see it once a day* or *once an hour.*

aback *ADVERB*
taken aback surprised
[from Old English *on baec* = backwards]

abacus (ab- a- kus) *NOUN* **abacuses** a frame used for counting with beads sliding on wires [from a Greek word *abax* meaning 'slab'. An early form of abacus was a slab of wood with a coating of dust, for writing on and adding up figures]

abandon *VERB* **abandons, abandoning, abandoned** **1** give up • *We never abandoned hope.* **2** leave something without intending to return • *Abandon ship!*
▷ **abandonment** *NOUN*

abandon *NOUN* a careless and uncontrolled manner • *She was dancing with great abandon.*

abbey *NOUN* **abbeys** **1** a monastery or convent **2** a church that was once part of a monastery • *Westminster Abbey.*

abbot *NOUN* **abbots** the head of an abbey

abbreviate *VERB* **abbreviates, abbreviating, abbreviated** shorten something

abbreviation *NOUN* **abbreviations** **1** a shortened form of a word or words, especially one using the initial letters, such as GCSE, St, USA **2** abbreviating something [from Latin *brevis* = short]

abdicate *VERB* **abdicates, abdicating, abdicated** **1** resign from a throne **2** give up an important responsibility
▷ **abdication** *NOUN*

abdomen (ab- dom- en) *NOUN* **abdomens** **1** the lower front part of a person's or animal's body, containing the stomach, intestines, and other digestive organs **2** the rear section of an insect's body
▷ **abdominal** (ab- dom- in- al) *ADJECTIVE*

abduct *VERB* **abducts, abducting, abducted** take a person away illegally; kidnap
▷ **abduction** *NOUN* **abductor** *NOUN*

abhor *VERB* **abhors, abhorring, abhorred** (*formal*) hate something very much
▷ **abhorrent** *ADJECTIVE* **abhorrence** *NOUN*

abide *VERB* **abides, abiding, abided** **1** (*old use; past tense* **abode**) remain or dwell somewhere **2** bear or tolerate • *I can't abide wasps.*
abide by keep a promise etc.
[from Old English]

ability *NOUN* **abilities** **1** being able to do something **2** cleverness or talent

ablaze *ADJECTIVE* blazing; on fire

able *ADJECTIVE* **1** having the power or skill or opportunity to do something **2** skilful or clever
▷ **ably** *ADVERB*

-able *SUFFIX* (also **-ble, -ible**, and **-uble**) forms adjectives (e.g. *readable, legible*) The nouns formed from these end in **-bility** (e.g. *readability, legibility*)

Thesaurus

abandon *VERB* **1** *The children had been abandoned in the war.* ► desert, leave behind, leave stranded, strand, forsake, leave in the lurch **2** *The car was abandoned near the motorway.* ► leave, (*more informal*) dump, (*more informal*) ditch **3** *The entire project had to be abandoned.* ► cancel, drop, discontinue, (*more informal*) give up, (*more informal*) scrap, (*very informal*) ditch **4** *The company abandoned its claims to the money.* ► drop, give up, renounce, waive, (*more formal*) relinquish

abbreviate *VERB* *The medium is known as a digital versatile disc, usually abbreviated to DVD.* ► shorten

abhorrent *ADJECTIVE* *Racial abuse is abhorrent to most people.* ► hateful, loathsome, detested (by), detestable, repugnant, repellent, obnoxious, odious, offensive, horrifying, repulsive, revolting

abide *VERB* **1** *I cannot abide grown men walking around in trainers.* ► bear, stand, endure, tolerate, (*more informal*) stomach, (*more informal*) put up with **2** **abide by** *The company expects its employees to abide by its rules.* ► obey, observe, follow, accept, keep to, carry out, conform to, stick to, adhere to, act in accordance with, stand by, submit to

ability *NOUN* **1** *An unexpected inheritance gave him the ability to travel the world.* ► power, resources, capability, capacity, means, opportunity, potential, wherewithal **2** *Jane's new employers had received good reports of her ability.* ► capability, competence, aptitude, expertise, proficiency, (*more informal*) know-how **3** *You have the ability to do well in life.* ► capacity, talent, intelligence, skill, aptitude, flair **4** *He has many unusual abilities.* ► talent, skill, accomplishment, gift, qualification

able *ADJECTIVE* **1** *a group of the most able students* ► talented, accomplished, proficient, efficient, gifted, capable, clever, skilled, competent, intelligent, effective AN OPPOSITE IS incompetent **2** **able to** *Are you able to come?* ► allowed to, free to, prepared to, in a position to, (*more informal*) up to (coming)

abnormal *ADJECTIVE* not normal; unusual
▷ **abnormally** *ADVERB* **abnormality** *NOUN*

aboard *ADVERB, PREPOSITION* on or into a ship or aircraft or train

abolish *VERB* **abolishes, abolishing, abolished** put an end to a law or custom etc.
▷ **abolition** (ab- ol- **ish**- on) *NOUN*

abominable *ADJECTIVE* very bad or unpleasant
▷ **abominably** *ADVERB* **abomination** *NOUN*

aborigine (ab- er- **ij**- in- ee) *NOUN* **aborigines** one of the original inhabitants of a country
▷ **aboriginal** *ADJECTIVE, NOUN*
Aborigine one of the original inhabitants of Australia who lived there before the Europeans arrived
[from Latin *ab origine* = from the beginning]

abort *VERB* **aborts, aborting, aborted** put an end to something before it has been completed • *They aborted the space flight because of problems.*

abortion *NOUN* **abortions** an operation to remove an unborn child from the womb before it has developed enough to survive

abortive *ADJECTIVE* unsuccessful • *an abortive attempt.*

abound *VERB* **abounds, abounding, abounded** **1** be plentiful or abundant • *Fish abound in the river.* **2** have something in great quantities • *The river abounds in fish.*

about *PREPOSITION* **1** near in amount or size or time etc. • *It costs about £5.* • *Come about two o'clock.* **2** on the subject of; in connection with • *Tell me about your holiday.* **3** all round; in various parts of • *They ran about the playground.*

about *ADVERB* **1** in various directions • *They were running about.* **2** not far away • *He is somewhere about.*
be about to be going to do something

above *PREPOSITION* **1** higher than **2** more than

above *ADVERB* at or to a higher place

abrasive *ADJECTIVE* **1** that scrapes things away • *an abrasive wheel.* **2** harsh • *an abrasive manner.*

abreast *ADVERB* **1** side by side **2** keeping up with something

abridge *VERB* **abridges, abridging, abridged** shorten a book etc. by using fewer words • *an abridged edition.*
▷ **abridgement** *NOUN*

abroad *ADVERB* in or to another country

abrupt *ADJECTIVE* **1** sudden or hasty • *his abrupt departure.* **2** rather rude and unfriendly; curt • *She has quite an abrupt manner.*
▷ **abruptly** *ADVERB* **abruptness** *NOUN*

abscess (ab- sis) *NOUN* **abscesses** an inflamed place where pus has formed in the body

abscond *VERB* **absconds, absconding, absconded** go away secretly • *The cashier had absconded with the money.*

absent *ADJECTIVE* not here; not present • *absent from school.*
▷ **absence** *NOUN*

absent (ab- **sent**) *VERB* **absents, absenting, absented**
absent yourself stay away

Thesaurus

abnormal *ADJECTIVE* **1** *The tests produced some abnormal results.* ► unusual, untypical, uncommon, extraordinary, exceptional, unrepresentative, aberrant, anomalous, freak **2** *He was surprised by her abnormal beliefs and behaviour.* ► strange, peculiar, odd, weird, curious, eccentric, wayward, perverse, erratic, queer, bizarre AN OPPOSITE IS normal

abnormality *NOUN* **1** *The study gave evidence of some abnormality.* ► strangeness, peculiarity, irregularity, oddity, oddness, aberration, anomaly, deviation, eccentricity, idiosyncrasy, waywardness, singularity **2** *The baby was born with several abnormalities.* ► deformity, malformation

abolish *VERB a decision to abolish the community charge* ► end, cancel, put an end to, (*more informal*) get rid of, (*more informal*) do away with, (*technical*) abrogate, annul, repeal, remove, rescind, revoke, quash, suppress, terminate, eliminate, eradicate, overturn, withdraw AN OPPOSITE IS create

abominable *ADJECTIVE The revolt was suppressed with abominable cruelty.* ► atrocious, appalling, detestable, hateful, odious, detestable, vile, obnoxious, brutal, dreadful, abhorrent, diabolical, disgusting, repellent, horrifying AN OPPOSITE IS humane

about-turn *NOUN The change in policy amounted to a complete about-turn.* ► reversal, U-turn, volte face, change of direction, change of course, change of mind, sea change

abrupt *ADJECTIVE* **1** *She gave a cry and came to an abrupt halt.* ► sudden, hurried, unexpected, quick, hasty, rapid, swift, precipitate, unforeseen, unpredicted **2** *Beyond the cliff edge they could see an abrupt drop.* ► sheer, sharp, steep, precipitous AN OPPOSITE IS gradual **3** *He had a decidedly abrupt manner.* ► blunt, harsh, curt, terse, gruff, rude, offhand, brusque, insensitive, outspoken, plain-spoken OPPOSITES ARE polite, courteous

absent *ADJECTIVE* **1** *The man had been absent from work all week.* ► away, off, missing, (*more informal*) skiving AN OPPOSITE IS present **2** *Her*

absentee *NOUN* **absentees** a person who is absent
▷ **absenteeism** *NOUN*

absent-minded *ADJECTIVE* having your mind on other things; forgetful

absolute *ADJECTIVE* complete; not restricted
• *absolute power.*
▷ **absolutely** *ADVERB*

absolute zero *NOUN* the lowest possible temperature, calculated as -27,315°C

absolve *VERB* **absolves, absolving, absolved**
1 clear a person of blame or guilt **2** release a person from a promise or obligation

absorb *VERB* **absorbs, absorbing, absorbed**
1 soak up a liquid or gas **2** receive something and reduce its effects • *The buffers absorbed most of the shock.* **3** take up a person's attention or time
▷ **absorption** *NOUN*

absorbent *ADJECTIVE* able to soak up liquids easily • *absorbent paper.*

abstain *VERB* **abstains, abstaining, abstained**
1 keep yourself from doing something; refrain
2 choose not to use your vote
▷ **abstention** *NOUN*

abstinence *NOUN* abstaining, especially from alcohol
▷ **abstinent** *ADJECTIVE*

abstract (ab- strakt) *ADJECTIVE* **1** concerned with ideas, not solid objects • *Truth, hope, and danger are all abstract.* **2** (said about a painting or sculpture) showing the artist's ideas or feelings, not showing a recognizable person or thing

absurd *ADJECTIVE* ridiculous or foolish
▷ **absurdly** *ADVERB* **absurdity** *NOUN*

abundance *NOUN* a large amount, plenty

abundant *ADJECTIVE* plentiful
▷ **abundantly** *ADVERB*

abuse (ab- yooz) *VERB* **abuses, abusing, abused** **1** use something badly or wrongly;

Thesaurus

eyes had an absent look. ► distracted, dreamy, far-away, absorbed, inattentive, preoccupied, absent-minded OPPOSITES ARE attentive, alert

absent-minded *ADJECTIVE* *Stephen looked absent-minded as he hurried off.* ► forgetful, distracted, preoccupied, inattentive, absorbed, scatterbrained OPPOSITES ARE attentive, alert

absolute *ADJECTIVE* **1** *The house was an absolute mess.* ► complete, total, utter, sheer, perfect, downright, unmitigated **2** *The venture had been an absolute success.* ► complete, total, outright, categorical, out-and-out, unqualified **3** *Speak only the absolute truth.* ► definite, positive, categorical, undoubted, unquestioned **4** *The country had known only absolute rulers.*
► autocratic, despotic, dictatorial, tyrannical, omnipotent, sovereign, totalitarian, unrestricted, undemocratic

absolutely *ADVERB* *You are absolutely right.*
► completely, totally, utterly, perfectly, quite, unquestionably, unreservedly

absorb *VERB* **1** *Wood absorbs wetness and expands.* ► soak up, suck up, assimilate, take in AN OPPOSITE IS emit **2** *It is difficult to absorb so much information at once.* ► assimilate, take in, soak up, digest, comprehend **3** *Getting through the day absorbed all her energies.* ► consume, drain, exhaust, use up, take up, swallow up **4** *Special buffers absorb the impact.* ► cushion, deaden, soften, reduce, lessen **5** *The children were absorbed by their game.* ► preoccupy, engross, captivate, occupy, enthral, fascinate, interest, involve, rivet

abstain *VERB* **abstain from** *They agreed to abstain from violent action for the time being.*
► go without, give up, forgo, refrain from, eschew, avoid, reject, renounce, deny yourself, desist from AN OPPOSITE IS indulge (yourself)

abstemious *ADJECTIVE* *They lead an abstemious life.* ► frugal, temperate, austere, ascetic, restrained, sparing, puritanical, strict, spartan, sober AN OPPOSITE IS self-indulgent

abstract *ADJECTIVE* **1** *Abstract concepts are hard to define.* ► theoretical, conceptual, hypothetical, academic, notional, metaphysical, philosophical, intangible, intellectual, indefinite AN OPPOSITE IS concrete **2** *The pieces are stitched together to form a large abstract design.* ► symbolic, non-pictorial, non-representational AN OPPOSITE IS representational

abstruse *ADJECTIVE* *He had spent a lifetime poring over abstruse codes.* ► obscure, cryptic, complex, difficult, hard, puzzling, incomprehensible, perplexing, mysterious, unfathomable AN OPPOSITE IS obvious

absurd *ADJECTIVE* *It was an absurd suggestion.*
► ridiculous, preposterous, ludicrous, unreasonable, nonsensical, incredible, irrational, senseless, insane, mad, anomalous, silly, stupid, illogical, incongruous, meaningless, paradoxical, untenable, laughable, (*more informal*) crazy, (*more informal*) daft, (*more informal*) barmy, (*more informal*) zany OPPOSITES ARE reasonable, sensible

abundant *ADJECTIVE* *Luckily, there was an abundant supply of things to do.* ► plentiful, copious, ample, liberal, profuse, generous, lavish, rich, bountiful, prolific, inexhaustible OPPOSITES ARE scarce, sparse

misuse **2** hurt someone or treat them cruelly **3** say unpleasant things about a person or thing

abuse (ab- yooss) *NOUN* **abuses 1** a misuse • *the abuse of power.* **2** ill-treatment **3** physical harm or cruelty done to someone

abusive *ADJECTIVE* rude and insulting • *abusive remarks.*

abysmal (ab- iz- mal) *ADJECTIVE* extremely bad • *abysmal ignorance.*

abyss (ab- iss) *NOUN* **abysses** an extremely deep pit [from Greek *abyssos* = bottomless]

AC *ABBREVIATION* alternating current

academic *ADJECTIVE* **1** to do with education or studying, especially at a school or college or university **2** theoretical; having no practical use • *an academic point.*

academic *NOUN* **academics** a university or college teacher

academy *NOUN* **academies 1** a school or college, especially one for specialized training **2** a society of scholars or artists • *The Royal Academy.* [from Greek *Akademeia*, the name of the garden where the Greek philosopher Plato taught his pupils The garden was named after *Akademos*, one of the ancient heroes of Athens]

accelerate *VERB* **accelerates, accelerating, accelerated** make or become quicker; increase speed

acceleration *NOUN* **accelerations 1** the rate at which the speed of something increases **2** the rate of change of velocity

accelerator *NOUN* **accelerators 1** the pedal that a driver presses to make a motor vehicle go faster **2** a thing used to increase the speed of something

accent (ak- sent) *NOUN* **accents 1** the way a person pronounces the words of a language • *She has a French accent.* **2** the main emphasis or stress in a word • *In 'strawberry', the accent is on 'straw-'.* **3** a mark placed over a letter to show how it is pronounced, e.g. on *fête*

Thesaurus

abuse *NOUN* **1** *The action amounted to a serious abuse of authority.* ► misuse, misapplication **2** *No society can tolerate the abuse of children.* ► maltreatment, mistreatment, ill-treatment, misuse, (sexual) assault, molestation **3** *A group of mothers yelled abuse.* ► insults, invective, obscenities, curses, slanders

abuse *VERB* **1** *Players on both sides were abusing the referee.* ► insult, be rude to, curse, swear at, call someone names, malign, revile, defame, slander **2** *He was accused of abusing children.* ► mistreat, maltreat, ill-treat, (sexually) assault, molest, interfere with, batter, harm, hurt **3** *The judge had abused his authority in his directions to the jury.* ► misuse, misapply, exploit

abusive *ADJECTIVE* *He was thrown out of the hall for yelling abusive remarks.* ► insulting, derogatory, rude, offensive, opprobrious, pejorative, defamatory, disparaging, scathing, hurtful, impolite, libellous, obscene, scurrilous, slanderous, vituperative OPPOSITES ARE friendly, polite

abysmal *ADJECTIVE* **1** *The service was abysmal.* ► poor, very bad, awful, appalling, dreadful, disgraceful, terrible, worthless **2** *the abysmal ignorance of science in Britain* ► profound, extreme, utter, complete, deep, unfathomable, immeasurable, incalculable, infinite

abyss *NOUN* *There is still a deep abyss to be crossed.* ► chasm, pit, void, gulf, crater, fissure, gap, hole, opening, rift

academic *ADJECTIVE* **1** *She had spent her entire life in an academic environment.* ► educational, scholastic, scholarly, pedagogical **2** *They are academic historians and not writers for the popular market.* ► scholarly, studious, learned, intellectual, erudite, educated, cultured, bookish, clever, highbrow, intelligent, well-read, (*more informal*) brainy **3** *The point is of more than academic interest.* ► theoretical, notional, conceptual, conjectural, hypothetical, speculative AN OPPOSITE IS practical

academic *NOUN* *a group of visiting academics* ► scholar, intellectual, professor, lecturer, thinker, (*more informal*) egghead, (*more informal*) highbrow

academy *NOUN* *The students of the academy were involved in a project to catalogue the papers.* ► college, educational institution, training establishment, conservatory, conservatoire, university, institute

accede *VERB* **accede to** *He acceded to all her demands.* ► agree to, consent to, accept, grant, comply with, concur with

accelerate *VERB* **1** *The vehicle accelerated sharply.* ► go faster, speed up, pick up speed, quicken speed OPPOSITES ARE decelerate, slow down **2** *The oil-producing countries have agreed to accelerate production.* ► increase, step up, stimulate, expedite, promote, spur on

accent *NOUN* **1** *She spoke with a distinct Welsh accent.* ► pronunciation, intonation, inflection, tone, cadence, enunciation **2** *There is an accent on the first syllable.* ► stress, emphasis, accentuation, force **3** *The accent is on economy.* ► emphasis, stress

accept *VERB* **accepts, accepting, accepted** **1** take a thing that is offered or presented **2** say yes to an invitation, offer, etc.
▷ **acceptance** *NOUN*
USAGE Do not confuse with **except**.

acceptable *ADJECTIVE* good enough to accept; pleasing
▷ **acceptably** *ADVERB* **acceptability** *NOUN*

access (ak- sess) *NOUN* **1** a way to enter or reach something **2** the right to use or look at something

access *VERB* **accesses, accessing, accessed** find information that has been stored in a computer

accessible *ADJECTIVE* **1** able to be reached **2** able to be understood easily
▷ **accessibly** *ADVERB* **accessibility** *NOUN*

accessory (ak- sess- er- ee) *NOUN* **accessories** **1** an extra thing that goes with something **2** a person who helps another with a crime

accident *NOUN* **accidents** an unexpected happening, especially one causing injury or damage
▷ **accidental** *ADJECTIVE* **accidentally** *ADVERB*
by accident by chance; without its being arranged in advance

acclaim *VERB* **acclaims, acclaiming, acclaimed** welcome or applaud
▷ **acclaim** *NOUN* **acclamation** *NOUN*

accommodate *VERB* **accommodates, accommodating, accommodated** **1** provide somebody with a place to live, work, or sleep overnight **2** help by providing something • *We can accommodate you with skis.*

Thesaurus

accept *VERB* **1** *I decided to accept the offer.* ► receive, take, get, welcome, (*more informal*) jump at **2** *The council does not accept responsibility.* ► admit, acknowledge, bear, assume, undertake **3** *Reluctantly, he had to accept the decision.* ► agree to, go along with, accede to, acquiesce in, defer to, comply with, consent to, concur with, abide by, acknowledge, be reconciled to, recognize, resign yourself to, submit to, yield to
AN OPPOSITE IS reject

acceptable *ADJECTIVE* **1** *The agreement was acceptable to the majority.* ► welcome, agreeable, appreciated, gratifying, pleasant, pleasing, worthwhile **2** *The courses fell below an acceptable standard.* ► adequate, satisfactory, reasonable, tolerable, admissible, appropriate, passable, suitable AN OPPOSITE IS unacceptable

acceptance *NOUN* **1** *The plan found wide acceptance.* ► approval, consent, acquiescence, agreement, welcome
AN OPPOSITE IS refusal **2** *Their acceptance of the explanation came as some relief.* ► belief (in), confidence (in)

access *NOUN* **1** *The away fans could not gain access to that end of the stadium.* ► entry, admission, admittance, right of entry **2** *The building has no access at the front.* ► entrance, entry, way in, approach

accessible *ADJECTIVE* **1** *The library has been made accessible for wheelchairs.* ► reachable, within reach, at hand, available, convenient, (*more informal*) get-at-able, (*more informal*) handy
AN OPPOSITE IS inaccessible **2** *Ministers want to be more accessible.* ► approachable, available, informal, welcoming

accessory *NOUN* **1** *Accessories include a remote control.* ► attachment, fitting, extra, addition, appendage, extension **2** *He might be charged with being an accessory to the crime.* ► accomplice, associate, collaborator (in)

accident *NOUN* **1** *He died in an accident while working on his boat.* ► misfortune, mishap, disaster, calamity, catastrophe, misadventure **2** *She had witnessed a traffic accident.* ► collision, smash, (*more informal*) pile-up **3** *It was pure accident that we met that day.* ► chance, luck, coincidence, fate, a fluke
by accident *I found it by accident.* ► by chance, accidentally, fortuitously, unwittingly, coincidentally

accidental *ADJECTIVE* *Make sure you avoid accidental erasure of the tape.* ► unintentional, chance, coincidental, fortuitous, inadvertent, unintended, adventitious, arbitrary, casual, lucky, random AN OPPOSITE IS intentional

accidentally *ADVERB* *We met accidentally.* ► by accident, by chance, fortuitously, unintentionally, unwittingly AN OPPOSITE IS intentionally

acclaim *VERB* *The film has been widely acclaimed in the press.* ► praise, applaud, commend, cheer, congratulate, celebrate

acclimatize *VERB* *They soon became acclimatized to their new surroundings.* ► accustom, adjust, familiarize

accolade *NOUN* *He received the accolade of a knighthood.* ► praise, honour, tribute, recognition, admiration, acclamation, plaudits

accommodate *VERB* **1** *We will do our best to accommodate your wishes.* ► serve, help, aid, assist, supply, oblige, provide **2** *The lodge accommodates nine residents.* ► house, lodge, provide for, cater for, shelter, board, take in, hold, (*more informal*) put up

accommodating *ADJECTIVE* *The local tourist office is very accommodating.* ► helpful, obliging, cooperative, considerate

accommodation *NOUN* somewhere to live, work, or sleep overnight

accompanist *NOUN* **accompanists** a pianist etc. who accompanies a singer or another musician

accompany *VERB* **accompanies, accompanying, accompanied** **1** go somewhere with somebody **2** be present with something • *Thunder accompanied the storm.* **3** play music, especially on a piano, that supports a singer or another player etc.
▷ **accompaniment** *NOUN*

accomplice (a- kum- pliss) *NOUN* **accomplices** a person who helps another in a crime etc.

accomplish *VERB* **accomplishes, accomplishing, accomplished** do something successfully
▷ **accomplishment** *NOUN*

accomplished *ADJECTIVE* skilled

accord *NOUN* agreement; consent
of your own accord without being asked or compelled

according *ADVERB*
according to **1** as stated by • *According to him, we are stupid.* **2** in relation to • *Price the apples according to their size.*

accordingly *ADVERB* **1** in the way that is required • *I've given you your instructions and I expect you to act accordingly.* **2** therefore

accordion *NOUN* **accordions** a portable musical instrument like a large concertina with a set of piano-type keys at one end, played by squeezing it in and out and pressing the keys

account *NOUN* **accounts** **1** a statement of money owed, spent, or received; a bill **2** an arrangement to keep money in a bank etc. **3** a description or report
on account of because of
on no account under no circumstances; certainly not
take something into account consider or include it when making a decision or calculation

account *VERB* **accounts, accounting, accounted**
account for make it clear why something happens
[from early French *conter* = to count]

accountable *ADJECTIVE* responsible; having to explain why you have done something
▷ **accountability** *NOUN*

accountant *NOUN* **accountants** a person whose job is keeping or inspecting financial accounts
▷ **accountancy** *NOUN*

accumulate *VERB* **accumulates, accumulating, accumulated** pile up or increase
▷ **accumulation** *NOUN*

Thesaurus

accommodation *NOUN* *The cost includes three days' accommodation in Bruges.* ► board, lodging, shelter, housing, rooms

accompany *VERB* **1** *She regularly accompanied groups of her students.* ► go with, escort, travel with, attend, follow, chaperone, look after, partner, (*more informal*) tag along with **2** *A note accompanied the flowers.* ► go with, occur with, coincide with, be present with, coexist with, complement, belong with, supplement

accomplice *NOUN* *An accomplice stood at the door on lookout.* ► associate, partner, accessory, abetter, confederate, collaborator, co-conspirator

accomplish *VERB* *Brady believes his side can accomplish the awesome task.* ► achieve, fulfil, succeed in, realize, complete, conclude, bring off, carry out, discharge, attain, effect, execute, finish, perform

accomplished *ADJECTIVE* *Diana is an accomplished pianist.* ► expert, talented, able, skilled, gifted, capable, clever, competent, proficient

accomplishment *NOUN* *This was quite an accomplishment and she was duly rewarded.* ► achievement, attainment, ability, talent, skill, gift

account *NOUN* **1** *Write down a full account of what you saw.* ► description, report, statement, report, record, explanation, narrative, version, commentary, (*more informal*) write-up **2** *An account for the work has come in the post.* ► invoice, statement, bill **3** *The damage done to the vehicles is of little account.* ► importance, significance, consequence, concern, moment, interest, worth, value, use
on account of *They stayed indoors on account of the bad weather.* ► because of, in view of, owing to, due to, as a result of, as a consequence of, considering

account *VERB* **account for** *It is difficult to account for such a sudden change in their attitude.* ► explain, justify, clarify, elucidate, answer for, give reasons for, excuse, make excuses for, rationalize, vindicate

accountable *ADJECTIVE* *The Minister is accountable to Parliament.* ► responsible, answerable, subject, liable

accrue *VERB* *The honour that is supposed to accrue from being unpaid.* ► result, follow, ensue, arise, stem, spring, emanate, be produced

accumulate *VERB* **1** *He accumulated information from different sources.* ► gather, collect, amass,

accurate *ADJECTIVE* correct or exact
▷ **accurately** *ADVERB* **accuracy** *NOUN*

accuse *VERB* **accuses, accusing, accused** say that a person has committed a crime etc.; blame
▷ **accusation** *NOUN* **accuser** *NOUN*

ace *NOUN* **aces 1** a playing card with one spot **2** a very skilful person or thing **3** (in tennis) a serve that is too good for the other player to reach

ache *NOUN* **aches** a dull continuous pain

ache *VERB* **aches, aching, ached** have an ache

achieve *VERB* **achieves, achieving, achieved** succeed in doing or producing something
▷ **achievable** *ADJECTIVE* **achievement** *NOUN*

acid *NOUN* **acids** a chemical substance that contains hydrogen and neutralizes alkalis. The hydrogen can be replaced by a metal to form a salt
▷ **acidic** *ADJECTIVE* **acidity** *NOUN*

acid *ADJECTIVE* **1** sharp-tasting; sour **2** looking or sounding bitter • *an acid reply*
▷ **acidly** *ADVERB*

acid rain *NOUN* rain made acidic by mixing with waste gases from factories etc.

acknowledge *VERB* **acknowledges, acknowledging, acknowledged 1** admit that something is true **2** state that you have received or noticed something • *The college wrote back to acknowledge my letter.* **3** express thanks or appreciation for something
▷ **acknowledgement** *NOUN*

acne (ak- nee) *NOUN* inflamed red pimples on the face and neck

acorn *NOUN* **acorns** the seed of the oak tree

Thesaurus

assemble, bring together, heap up, mass, pile up, hoard, store up, (*more informal*) stash away AN OPPOSITE IS disperse **2** *Leaves tend to accumulate in the gullies.* ► build up, increase, multiply, grow, accrue AN OPPOSITE IS decrease.

accumulation *NOUN* *The book is an accumulation of work by many scholars.* ► collection, build-up, mass, store, supply, heap, pile, hoard, stock, conglomeration

accuracy *NOUN* *Can we trust the accuracy of these figures?* ► precision, correctness, exactness, validity, reliability

accurate *ADJECTIVE* **1** *It was an accurate account of what had happened.* ► faithful, factual, authentic, true, truthful, close, exact, precise, reliable **2** *She took accurate notes during the meeting.* ► exact, precise, correct, careful, faultless, errorless, error-free, meticulous, minute, perfect, scrupulous **3** *His aim was steady and accurate.* ► certain, unerring, sure, (*more informal*) spot-on AN OPPOSITE IS inaccurate

accusation *NOUN* *There had been several accusations of cheating.* ► allegation, charge, complaint, indictment, alleged offence

accuse *VERB* **1 accuse of** *The men were accused of disorderly behaviour.* ► charge with, blame for, put on trial for, take to court for, indict for **2 accuse of** *The banks are accused of creating confusion among customers.* ► blame for, hold responsible for, criticize for, condemn for, denounce for AN OPPOSITE IS defend

accustomed *ADJECTIVE* *Wars remove whole populations from their accustomed ways of life.* ► normal, customary, familiar, habitual, established, usual, common, conventional, traditional, ordinary, regular, routine, set
become *or* **get accustomed to** *The family soon became accustomed to life in the country.* ► get used to, adapt to, adjust to, acclimatize to, become conditioned to, become inured to, familiarize yourself with, (*more informal*) feel at home in

ache *NOUN* *A nagging stomach ache spoiled the evening.* ► pain, pang, soreness, hurt, discomfort, twinge

ache *VERB* *His tooth was beginning to ache.* ► hurt, smart, be painful, be sore, throb, sting

achieve *VERB* **1** *Students who achieve their goals will be promised jobs.* ► succeed in, accomplish, fulfil, complete, carry out, attain, manage, bring about, bring off **2** *They worked hard to achieve success.* ► acquire, win, gain, earn, get, obtain, procure, reach, score

achievement *NOUN* **1** *They are proud of their achievement.* ► accomplishment, attainment, success, deed, exploit **2** *We hoped for the achievement of all our aims.* ► attainment, realization, accomplishment, fulfilment, reaching, gaining, winning, conclusion

acknowledge *VERB* **1** *They acknowledged their obligation to their predecessors.* ► admit, concede, accept, grant, recognize, allow AN OPPOSITE IS deny **2** *No one has acknowledged my letter.* ► answer, reply to, respond to, react to, notice **3** *She acknowledged him with a nod.* ► greet, salute, hail, recognize, respond to, (*more informal*) say hello to

acknowledgement *NOUN* **1** *There was an acknowledgement of a need for action.* ► admission, acceptance, agreement, realization, concession **2** *Tom gave a smile of acknowledgement.* ► greeting, recognition, welcome, (*more formal*) salutation

acoustic (a- koo- stik) *ADJECTIVE* **1** to do with sound or hearing **2** (said about a musical instrument) not electronic • *an acoustic guitar.*
▷ **acoustically** *ADVERB*
[from Greek *akouein* = hear]

acoustics (a- koo- stiks) *PLURAL NOUN* **1** the qualities of a hall etc. that make it good or bad for carrying sound **2** the properties of sound

acquaint *VERB* **acquaints, acquainting, acquainted** tell somebody about something • *Acquaint him with the facts.*
be acquainted with know slightly

acquaintance *NOUN* **acquaintances 1** a person you know slightly **2** familiarity with someone or something

acquire *VERB* **acquires, acquiring, acquired** obtain

acquisition *NOUN* something you have obtained

acquit *VERB* **acquits, acquitting, acquitted** decide that somebody is not guilty • *The jury acquitted her.*
▷ **acquittal** *NOUN*
acquit yourself well perform or do something well

acre (ay- ker) *NOUN* **acres** an area of land measuring 4,840 square yards or 0405 hectares
▷ **acreage** *NOUN*
[from Old English *aecer* = field]

acrobat *NOUN* **acrobats** a person who performs spectacular gymnastic stunts for entertainment
▷ **acrobatic** *ADJECTIVE* **acrobatics** *PLURAL NOUN*

acronym (ak- ron- im) *NOUN* **acronyms** a word or name that is formed from the initial letters of other words and pronounced as a word in its own right • *Nato is an acronym of North Atlantic Treaty Organization.*

across *PREPOSITION, ADVERB* **1** from one side to the other • *Swim across the river.* • *Are you across yet?* **2** on the opposite side • *the house across the street.*

acrylic (a- kril- ik) *NOUN* a kind of fibre, plastic, or resin made from an organic acid

act *NOUN* **acts 1** something someone does **2** a pretence • *She is only putting on an act.* **3** one of the main divisions of a play or opera **4** each short performance in a programme of entertainment • *a juggling act.* **5** a law passed by a parliament

act *VERB* **acts, acting, acted 1** do something; perform actions **2** perform a part in a play or film etc. **3** function; have an effect

action *NOUN* **actions 1** doing something **2** something done **3** a battle; fighting • *He was killed in action.* **4** a lawsuit
out of action not working or functioning
take action do something

Thesaurus

acquaint *VERB* **be acquainted with** *Lorna is acquainted with several European languages.* ► be familiar with, be conversant with, be versed in, be informed about AN OPPOSITE IS be ignorant of

acquaintance *NOUN* *Philip was just a business acquaintance.* ► associate, colleague, contact

acquire *VERB* *His father had acquired some shares in a freight company.* ► obtain, get, receive, come by, gain, appropriate

acquit *VERB* *The jury acquitted all three of the accused.* ► absolve, clear, exonerate, find innocent, find not guilty, free, discharge, excuse, (*more informal*) let off

acrimonious *ADJECTIVE* *The meetings were acrimonious and badly managed.* ► bitter, hostile, abusive, peevish, acerbic, caustic, angry, petulant, bad-tempered, ill-tempered, ill-natured, venomous, biting, sharp
AN OPPOSITE IS peaceable

acrobat *NOUN* *An acrobat performed a back somersault.* ► gymnast, tumbler, contortionist

act *NOUN* **1** *It needed an act of great courage.* ► deed, feat, action, exploit, undertaking, effort, enterprise, operation, proceeding **2** *The next act will be a juggler.* ► item, turn, performance, routine, sketch
put on an act ► pretend, dissemble, play a part

act *VERB* **1** *Jim was beginning to act strangely.* ► behave, conduct yourself **2** *The large table also acted as a work area. The medicine will soon begin to act.* ► function, operate, serve, work, take effect, have an effect **3** *He has always wanted to act the role of a villain.* ► play, portray, appear (as), perform, represent, assume the character of, characterize, enact, impersonate **4** *It was obvious that they were only acting.* ► pretend, sham, fake, pose, (*more informal*) kid

action *NOUN* **1** *It was a decisive action and very effective.* ► act, deed, step, feat, exploit, endeavour, enterprise, proceeding, effort, measure, performance, process, undertaking **2** *Write a story with plenty of action.* ► activity, drama, excitement, vitality, movement, energy, liveliness, vigour **3** *The action of the play is set in medieval France.* ► story, plot, events, happenings, incidents **4** *The clock has a mechanical action.* ► working, works, mechanism, functioning, operation **5** *McLeish led his troops into action.* ► battle, engagement

activate *VERB* **activates, activating, activated** start something working
▷ **activation** *NOUN* **activator** *NOUN*

active *ADJECTIVE* **1** taking part in many activities; energetic **2** functioning or working; in operation • *an active volcano.* **3** radioactive **4** (said about a form of a verb) used when the subject of the verb is performing the action In 'The shop *sells* videos' the verb is active; in 'Videos *are sold* by the shop' the verb is passive
▷ **actively** *ADVERB* **activeness** *NOUN*

activist *NOUN* **activists** a person who is active and energetic, especially in politics

activity *NOUN* **activities 1** an action or occupation • *outdoor activities.* **2** being active or lively

actor *NOUN* **actors** a person who acts a part in a play or film etc.

actress *NOUN* **actresses** a woman who acts a part in a play or film etc.

actual *ADJECTIVE* real
▷ **actually** *ADVERB* **actuality** *NOUN*

acupuncture (ak- yoo- punk- cher) *NOUN* pricking parts of the body with needles to relieve pain or cure disease
▷ **acupuncturist** *NOUN*

acute *ADJECTIVE* **1** sharp or strong • *acute pain.* **2** having a sharp mind
▷ **acutely** *ADVERB* **acuteness** *NOUN*
[from Latin *acus* = needle]

acute accent *NOUN* **acute accents** a mark over a vowel, as over *é* in *fiancé*

acute angle *NOUN* **acute angles** an angle of less than 90°

AD *ABBREVIATION* Anno Domini (Latin = in the year of Our Lord), used in dates counted from the birth of Jesus Christ

adamant (ad- am- ant) *ADJECTIVE* firm and not giving way to requests

adapt *VERB* **adapts, adapting, adapted 1** change something so that it is suitable for a new purpose **2** to become used to a new situation
▷ **adaptable** *ADJECTIVE* **adaptation** *NOUN*

adaptor *NOUN* **adaptors** a device to connect pieces of electrical or other equipment

add *VERB* **adds, adding, added 1** put one thing with another **2** make another remark
add up 1 make or find a total **2** (*informal*) make sense; seem reasonable

Thesaurus

activate *VERB* *The smaller button activates the reboot function.* ► operate, start, initiate, mobilize, actuate, trigger off, set in motion

active *ADJECTIVE* **1** *They were having an active time.* ► busy, lively, eventful, energetic, vivacious OPPOSITES ARE inactive, uneventful **2** *She is very active for her age.* ► energetic, agile, sprightly, lively, spry, frisky, (*more informal*) on the go, (*more informal*) full of beans OPPOSITES ARE inactive, lethargic **3** *Yvonne is an active member of the society.* ► diligent, hard-working, dedicated, enthusiastic, assiduous, industrious, committed, devoted, staunch, zealous OPPOSITES ARE inactive, unenthusiastic **4** *Part of the old factory was still active.* ► functional, functioning, operative, working, in operation OPPOSITES ARE inactive, defunct

activity *NOUN* **1** *At weekends the house is always a scene of great activity.* ► liveliness, action, commotion, bustle, life, hustle, animation, movement, excitement **2** *Marketing is an activity in which all staff can be involved.* ► job, task, venture, enterprise, undertaking, project, scheme **3** *She enjoyed many leisure activities.* ► interest, pursuit, hobby, pastime, occupation

actor *NOUN* *He was the actor who played James Bond.* ► player, performer, stage performer, artist, (*female*) actress, (*female*) artiste

actual *ADJECTIVE* *Have you seen the actual damage done?* ► real, true, physical, genuine, definite, certain, concrete OPPOSITES ARE imaginary, supposed, notional, non-existent

acute *ADJECTIVE* **1** *The pain was acute.* ► sharp, severe, stabbing, burning, intense, piercing, fierce AN OPPOSITE IS mild **2** *There is an acute shortage of teachers.* ► severe, drastic, extreme, serious, dire, grave AN OPPOSITE IS continual **3** *He was suffering from an acute illness.* ► critical, sudden **4** *Jenna has an acute mind.* ► sharp, keen, astute, shrewd, penetrating, perceptive, quick, discerning OPPOSITES ARE dull, stupid

adapt *VERB* **1 adapt to** *The children have adapted well to their new surroundings.* ► adjust to, acclimatize yourself to, get used to, reconcile yourself to **2** *The vans are all adapted to carry dangerous substances.* ► modify, alter, convert, change, rearrange, reorganize, reconstruct, customize, tailor, prepare, transform **3** *The story has been adapted for television.* ► edit, modify, prepare, alter

adaptable *ADJECTIVE* **1** *The tool is adaptable to many tasks.* ► adjustable, versatile, convertible **2** *Michael is always willing and very adaptable.* ► flexible, versatile, resilient, amenable

add *VERB* **1** *Add all the numbers in the first column.* ► add up, count, count up, calculate, total, find the sum of, work out, (*more informal*) tot up OPPOSITES ARE deduct, subtract **2** *A conservatory was added in the 1930s.* ► build on, attach, add on, integrate, join, (*more informal*) tack on OPPOSITES ARE remove, demolish **3 add to** *Our*

A
B
C
D
E
F
G
H
I
J
K
L
M
N
O
P
Q
R
S
T
U
V
W
X
Y
Z

adder NOUN **adders** a small poisonous snake [from Old English; originally called *a nadder*, which became *an adder* The same change happened to other Old English words, e.g. *apron*]

addict NOUN **addicts** a person who does or uses something that he or she cannot give up ▷ **addicted** ADJECTIVE **addiction** NOUN

addictive ADJECTIVE causing a habit that people cannot give up ● *an addictive drug.*

addition NOUN **additions** **1** the process of adding **2** something added ▷ **additional** ADJECTIVE **additionally** ADVERB **in addition** also; as an extra thing

additive NOUN **additives** a substance added to another in small amounts for a special purpose, e.g. as a flavouring

address NOUN **addresses** **1** the details of the place where someone lives or of where letters etc. should be delivered to a person or firm **2** (in computing) the part of an instruction that shows where a piece of information is stored in a computer's memory **3** a speech to an audience

address VERB **addresses, addressing, addressed** **1** write an address on a letter etc. **2** make a speech or remark etc. to somebody

adenoids PLURAL NOUN thick spongy flesh at the back of the nose and throat, which may hinder breathing

adept (a- dept) ADJECTIVE very skilful

adequate ADJECTIVE enough or good enough ▷ **adequately** ADVERB **adequacy** NOUN

adhere VERB **adheres, adhering, adhered** stick to something ▷ **adhesion** NOUN

adhesive ADJECTIVE sticky; causing things to stick together

adhesive NOUN **adhesives** a substance used to stick things together; glue

adjacent ADJECTIVE near or next to ● *I waited in an adjacent room.*

adjective NOUN **adjectives** a word that describes a noun or adds to its meaning, e.g. *big, honest, strange, our* ▷ **adjectival** ADJECTIVE **adjectivally** ADVERB

adjourn (a- jern) VERB **adjourns, adjourning, adjourned** **1** break off a meeting etc. until a

Thesaurus

shouts only added to the confusion. ► increase, intensify, amplify, augment, enlarge, supplement

add up **1** *It was time to add up the scores.* ► count, count up, calculate, total, find the sum of, work out, (*more informal*) tot up **2** (*more informal*) *The story didn't add up.* ► make sense, be convincing, be reasonable, (*more informal*) hold water, (*more informal*) ring true

add up to *The costs added up to many thousands.* ► total, amount to, come to, make

addiction NOUN *An addiction to crisps was putting cellulite on her thighs.* ► dependence, compulsion, craving, fixation, habit, obsession

addition NOUN **1** *I'm not very good at addition.* ► adding, adding up, counting, calculating, totalling **2** *The porch is a nineteenth-century addition.* ► supplement, appendage, extension, attachment, afterthought, (*more informal*) add-on

additional ADJECTIVE *The railways need additional resources.* ► extra, added, further, supplementary, increased, more, new, other, spare

address NOUN **1** *They live at a smart address in town.* ► residence, location, locality, home, abode **2** *The president gave a short address to the press.* ► speech, talk, discourse, lecture, monologue, (*more formal*) oration, (*more formal*) disquisition

address VERB *A man came up and addressed me.* ► greet, hail, salute, speak to, talk to, accost, approach, engage in conversation, (*more informal*) buttonhole

adequate ADJECTIVE **1** *The work must be of an adequate standard.* ► satisfactory, acceptable, sufficient, suitable, tolerable, competent, fair, good enough, passable, presentable, respectable AN OPPOSITE IS inadequate **2** *The hospital lacks adequate resources.* ► sufficient, enough, suitable, appropriate

adhere VERB **1** *A piece of fluff adhered to his collar.* ► stick, cling, be fixed, be fastened **2** **adhere to** *We must adhere to our principles.* ► maintain, observe, follow, respect, stick to, abide by, stand by, comply with

adjacent ADJECTIVE **adjacent to** *the area adjacent to the fire station* ► adjoining, bordering, abutting, neighbouring, alongside, touching, next to, close by, next door to, (*more formal*) contiguous with

adjoin VERB *The house adjoins an old warehouse.* ► be next to, abut, border on, connect with, link up with, be next door to, touch, (*more formal*) be contiguous with

adjourn VERB *The meeting was adjourned for a week.* ► suspend, break off, discontinue, defer, dissolve, postpone, interrupt, put off

adjournment NOUN *The reason for the adjournment of the meeting will become clear in time.* ► suspension, postponement, putting

later time **2** break off and go somewhere else • *They adjourned to the library.*
▷ **adjournment** NOUN

adjudicate (a-joo-dik-ayt) VERB **adjudicates, adjudicating, adjudicated** act as judge in a competition etc.
▷ **adjudication** NOUN **adjudicator** NOUN

adjust VERB **adjusts, adjusting, adjusted** **1** put a thing into its proper position or order **2** alter something so that it fits or is suitable
▷ **adjustable** ADJECTIVE **adjustment** NOUN

ad-lib VERB **ad-libs, ad-libbing, ad-libbed** say or do something without any rehearsal or preparation

administer VERB **administers, administering, administered** **1** give or provide something • *He administered medicine.* **2** manage business affairs

admirable ADJECTIVE worth admiring; excellent
▷ **admirably** ADVERB

admiral NOUN **admirals** a naval officer of high rank [from Arabic *amir* = commander. The full title was *amir-al bahr* = commander of the sea (bahr = sea) Early Christian writers thought that *amir-al* was one word meaning commander, whereas it meant 'commander of the ']

admire VERB **admires, admiring, admired** **1** look at something and enjoy it **2** think that someone or something is very good
▷ **admiration** NOUN **admirer** NOUN

admission NOUN **admissions** **1** admitting **2** the charge for being allowed to go in **3** a statement admitting something; a confession

admit VERB **admits, admitting, admitted** **1** allow someone or something to come in **2** state reluctantly that something is true; confess • *We admit that the task is difficult.* • *He admitted his crime.*

admittance NOUN being allowed to go in, especially to a private place

admonish VERB **admonishes, admonishing, admonished** advise or warn someone firmly
▷ **admonition** NOUN

adolescent NOUN **adolescents** a young person at the age between being a child

Thesaurus

off, break (in), pause (in), interruption, discontinuation, deferment

adjust VERB **1** *You need to adjust the picture.* ► modify, alter, regulate, rectify, tune, vary, change, balance, amend, arrange, position, put right **2 adjust to** *The workforce have had to adjust to new procedures.* ► adapt to, acclimatize yourself to, accommodate yourself to, familiarize yourself with, get used to, reconcile yourself to, harmonize yourself with

ad-lib ADJECTIVE *The chairperson made a few ad-lib remarks.* ► impromptu, extempore, improvised, spontaneous, unplanned, unprepared, unrehearsed, made-up, (*more informal*) off the cuff, (*more informal*) off the top of your head

ad-lib VERB *She ad-libbed a large part of her speech.* ► improvise, extemporize, make it up, (*more informal*) play it by ear

administer VERB **1** *The director administers an organization of two hundred people.* ► regulate, run, manage, direct, preside over, conduct the affairs of, control, supervise, govern, head, lead, look after, command, organize, oversee **2** *A nurse administered medicines throughout the ward.* ► dispense, hand out, deal out, give, provide, supply, apply, distribute, dole out, measure out, mete out (a punishment)

admirable ADJECTIVE *Their aims are admirable but will be difficult to achieve.* ► laudable, praiseworthy, worthy, fine, commendable, creditable, estimable, excellent, pleasing, exemplary, honourable, wonderful, marvellous, enjoyable, likeable AN OPPOSITE IS deplorable

admiration NOUN *Their achievement won much admiration.* ► esteem, acclaim, commendation, high regard, honour, praise, respect, appreciation, approval AN OPPOSITE IS contempt

admire VERB **1** *Jill is much admired for her efficiency.* ► applaud, approve of, respect, praise, revere, esteem, value, look up to, marvel at, think highly of, (*more formal*) laud AN OPPOSITE IS despise **2** *Come and admire the view.* ► enjoy, appreciate, be delighted by

admirer NOUN *He is a great admirer of Napoleon.* ► fan, devotee, supporter, adherent, enthusiast

admission NOUN **1** *Admission to the gallery is free.* ► entrance, entry, admittance, access **2** *The statement sounded like an admission of guilt.* ► confession, declaration, acknowledgement, profession, revelation, affirmation, avowal, acceptance AN OPPOSITE IS denial

admit VERB **1** *Some of the people were not admitted to the house.* ► let in, allow in, grant access, receive, take in AN OPPOSITE IS exclude **2** *She admitted she had been to the house that morning.* ► acknowledge, concede, confess, reveal, declare, disclose, divulge, agree, grant, accept, allow, own up, profess, recognize AN OPPOSITE IS deny

adolescence NOUN *The problems are the normal ones of adolescence and will pass in time.*

and being an adult
▷ **adolescence** *NOUN* **adolescent** *ADJECTIVE*
adopt *VERB* **adopts, adopting, adopted 1** take someone into your family as your own child **2** accept something; take something and use it • *They adopted new methods of working.*
▷ **adoption** *NOUN*
adore *VERB* **adores, adoring, adored** love a person or thing very much
▷ **adorable** *ADJECTIVE* **adoration** *NOUN*
adorn *VERB* **adorns, adorning, adorned** decorate
▷ **adornment** *NOUN*
adrenalin (a- dren- al- in) *NOUN* a hormone that stimulates the nervous system, making your heart beat faster and increasing your energy and your ability to move quickly
adrift *ADJECTIVE*, *ADVERB* drifting
adulation *NOUN* very great flattery
adult (ad- ult) *NOUN* **adults** a fully grown or mature person
adultery *NOUN* being unfaithful to your wife or husband by having sexual intercourse with someone else
▷ **adulterer** *NOUN* **adulterous** *ADJECTIVE*
advance *NOUN* **advances 1** a forward movement; progress **2** an increase **3** a loan; payment made before it is due
in advance beforehand; ahead
advance *VERB* **advances, advancing, advanced 1** move forward; make progress **2** lend or pay money ahead of the proper time • *Can you advance me a month's salary?*
▷ **advancement** *NOUN*
advantage *NOUN* **advantages 1** something useful or helpful **2** the next point won after deuce in tennis
▷ **advantageous** *ADJECTIVE*
take advantage of use a person or thing profitably or unfairly
to advantage making a good effect • *The painting can be seen to its best advantage here.*
to your advantage profitable or helpful to you
Advent *NOUN* the period just before Christmas, when Christians celebrate the coming of Christ
advent *NOUN* the arrival of a new person or thing • *the advent of computers*

Thesaurus

► puberty, teens, youth, boyhood, girlhood, growing-up
adopt *VERB* **1** *The blue shirt was adopted as the official uniform in the 1930s. He asked them to adopt a more professional approach.* ► take up, choose, support, follow, accept, approve, back, embrace, espouse, endorse, (*more informal*) go for **2** *She already knew that she had been adopted.* ► foster, take in
adorable *ADJECTIVE* *What an adorable little cat!* ► lovable, delightful, charming, appealing, enchanting
adore *VERB* **1** *Neil obviously still adores you.* ► love, be fond of, dote on, idolize, worship, cherish, admire **2** *We all adore shopping.* ► love, like OPPOSITES ARE hate, detest
adorn *VERB* *The room was adorned with tapestries.* ► decorate, embellish, enhance, beautify, furnish, trim
adult *ADJECTIVE* *a medical problem associated with adult males* ► grown-up, of age, fully grown, full-grown, developed, mature AN OPPOSITE IS immature
advance *NOUN* *There has been a considerable advance in cancer treatments.* ► progress, development, improvement, headway, step, stride
advance *VERB* **1** *The column of soldiers began to advance.* ► move forward, go forward, proceed, press ahead, press on, progress, approach, come near, gain ground, forge ahead, make headway, make progress, (*more informal*) make strides, (*more informal*) push on AN OPPOSITE IS retreat **2** *Computer technology has advanced in the last few years.* ► develop, evolve, improve, increase, grow, thrive AN OPPOSITE IS regress **3** *Good qualifications will advance your career.* ► benefit, boost, further, promote, foster, assist, expedite, facilitate, accelerate AN OPPOSITE IS hinder **4** *The Bank has agreed to advance the money.* ► lend, loan, pay in advance, provide, supply **5** *He advanced some interesting ideas.* ► present, propose, submit, suggest, adduce, cite, furnish, give
advanced *ADJECTIVE* **1** *Advanced techniques have solved many of these problems.* ► progressive, leading, modern, sophisticated, up-to-date, forward, latest AN OPPOSITE IS obsolete **2** *Their ideas were very advanced for the time.* ► forward-looking, innovative, pioneering, progressive, revolutionary, trend-setting, leading, futuristic, avant-garde, new, novel, original AN OPPOSITE IS old-fashioned **3** *a course in advanced mathematics* ► higher, complex, complicated, difficult, hard AN OPPOSITE IS elementary **4** *Jamie appears quite advanced for his age.* ► mature, grown-up, sophisticated, well-developed
advantage *NOUN* *There is an advantage in having a bank account.* ► benefit, asset, help, assistance, aid, blessing, convenience, boon, favour, gain, use, service
take advantage of *His friends all took advantage of him.* ► exploit, make use of, utilize, profit by, manipulate

adventure *NOUN* **adventures 1** an exciting or dangerous experience **2** willingness to take risks
▷ **adventurer** *NOUN* **adventurous** *ADJECTIVE*

adverb *NOUN* **adverbs** a word that adds to the meaning of a verb or adjective or another adverb and tells how, when, or where something happens, e.g. *gently*, *soon*, and *upstairs*
▷ **adverbial** *ADJECTIVE* **adverbially** *ADVERB*

adversary (ad- ver- ser- ee) *NOUN* **adversaries** an opponent or enemy

adverse *ADJECTIVE* unfavourable or harmful
• *adverse effects.*
▷ **adversely** *ADVERB*

adversity *NOUN* **adversities** trouble or misfortune

advert *NOUN* **adverts** (*informal*) an advertisement

advertise *VERB* **advertises, advertising, advertised 1** praise goods etc. in order to encourage people to buy or use them **2** make something publicly known • *advertise a meeting* **3** ask or offer by a public notice
• *advertise for a secretary*
▷ **advertiser** *NOUN*

advertisement *NOUN* **advertisements** a public notice or announcement, especially one advertising goods or services in newspapers, on posters, or in broadcasts

advice *NOUN* **1** telling a person what you think he or she should do **2** a piece of information
• *We received advice that the goods had been dispatched.*
USAGE Do not confuse with the verb **advise**.

advisable *ADJECTIVE* to be recommended; sensible
▷ **advisability** *NOUN*

advise *VERB* **advises, advising, advised 1** give somebody advice; recommend **2** inform
▷ **adviser** *NOUN* **advisory** *ADJECTIVE*

aerial *ADJECTIVE* **1** in or from the air **2** to do with aircraft

aerial *NOUN* **aerials** a wire or rod etc. for receiving or transmitting radio or television signals

aerobics *PLURAL NOUN* exercises to stimulate breathing and strengthen the heart and lungs
▷ **aerobic** *ADJECTIVE*

aerodrome *NOUN* **aerodromes** an airfield

aerodynamic *ADJECTIVE* designed to move through the air quickly and easily

aeronautics *NOUN* the study of aircraft and flying
▷ **aeronautic** *ADJECTIVE* **aeronautical** *ADJECTIVE*

aeroplane *NOUN* **aeroplanes** a flying machine with wings

aerosol *NOUN* **aerosols** a container that holds a liquid under pressure and can let it out in a fine spray

Thesaurus

adventure *NOUN* **1** *His adventures had already turned him into a local hero.* ► exploit, escapade, venture, enterprise, undertaking, deed, feat **2** *They travelled the world together in search of adventure.* ► excitement, danger, interesting times, fun, stimulation

adventurous *ADJECTIVE* **1** *an adventurous child* ► daring, enterprising, bold, venturesome, heroic, intrepid, valiant **2** *an adventurous time* ► eventful, exciting, challenging, dangerous, perilous, risky AN OPPOSITE IS unadventurous

adverse *ADJECTIVE* **1** *The request brought an adverse response.* ► hostile, unfriendly, unfavourable, critical, antagonistic, negative, uncomplimentary, derogatory, disapproving, censorious **2** *The treatment can produce adverse side effects.* ► harmful, unfavourable, disadvantageous, unfortunate, inauspicious, uncongenial, unpropitious, contrary
AN OPPOSITE IS favourable

adversity *NOUN* *Peter showed he was stable in adversity.* ► misfortune, bad luck, hardship, difficulty, affliction, tribulation, suffering, sorrow, misery, hard times

advertise *VERB* *The job will be advertised in national newspapers.* ► publicize, promote, make known, market, announce, broadcast, display, flaunt, show off, (*more informal*) push, (*more informal*) spotlight, (*more informal*) tout, (*more informal*) plug

advertisement *NOUN* **1** *There are far more advertisements on television now.* ► commercial, (*more informal*) ad, (*more informal*) advert **2** *Let's put an advertisement in the local newsagent.* ► announcement, notice, (*more informal*) ad, (*more informal*) advert **3** *There are advertisements all along the main road.* ► hoarding, placard

advice *NOUN* *I could do with some advice.* ► guidance, counselling, counsel, directions, suggestions, recommendations, tips, pointers

advisable *ADJECTIVE* *It is advisable to arrive early.* ► wise, sensible, prudent, desirable, a good idea, recommended AN OPPOSITE IS inadvisable

advise *VERB* **1** *He advised her to go the police.* ► recommend, counsel, instruct, encourage, admonish, caution, warn, (*more formal*) enjoin, (*more formal*) exhort **2** *The doctor advised a period of rest.* ► suggest, prescribe, urge, advocate **3** *Visitors are advised that the house will close at six o'clock.* ► inform, notify, warn

aesthetic (iss- thet- ik) ADJECTIVE to do with the appreciation of beautiful things

afar ADVERB far away • *The din was heard from afar.*

affair NOUN **affairs 1** an event or matter • *The party was a grand affair.* **2** a temporary sexual relationship between two people who are not married to each other

affairs PLURAL NOUN the business and activities that are part of private or public life • *Keep out of my affairs* • *current affairs*

affect VERB **affects, affecting, affected 1** have an effect on; influence **2** pretend • *She affected ignorance.*
USAGE The word **affect** is a verb. Do not confuse it with the noun **effect**.

affectation NOUN **affectations** unnatural behaviour that is intended to impress other people

affected ADJECTIVE pretended and unnatural

affection NOUN **affections** a strong liking for a person

affectionate ADJECTIVE showing affection; loving
▷ **affectionately** ADVERB

affirm VERB **affirms, affirming, affirmed** state something definitely or firmly
▷ **affirmation** NOUN

affirmative ADJECTIVE that says 'yes' • *an affirmative reply* COMPARE **negative**

afflict VERB **afflicts, afflicting, afflicted** cause somebody to suffer • *He is afflicted with arthritis.*
▷ **affliction** NOUN

affluent (af- loo- ent) ADJECTIVE rich
▷ **affluence** NOUN

afford VERB **affords, affording, afforded**
1 have enough money to pay for something **2** have enough time or resources etc. to do something **3** to be able to do something without a risk • *We can't afford to complain.*

affront VERB **affronts, affronting, affronted** insult or offend someone

affront NOUN **affronts** an insult

afloat ADJECTIVE, ADVERB floating; on the sea

afraid ADJECTIVE frightened or alarmed
I'm afraid I regret • *I'm afraid I'm late.*

afresh ADVERB again; in a new way • *We must start afresh.*

African ADJECTIVE to do with Africa or its people

African NOUN **Africans** an African person

aft ADVERB at or towards the back of a ship or aircraft

after PREPOSITION **1** later than • *Come after tea.* **2** behind in place or order • *Which letter comes after H?* **3** trying to catch; pursuing • *Run after him.* **4** in spite of • *We can come after all.* **5** in imitation or honour of • *She is named after her aunt.* **6** about or concerning • *He asked after you.*

Thesaurus

affair NOUN **1** *The meeting was an odd affair.* ► incident, event, happening, episode, occurrence, circumstance, occasion, (*more informal*) business **2** *She suspected her husband was having an affair.* ► relationship, love affair, romance, (*more informal*) fling **3 affairs** *They need to put their financial affairs in order.* ► business, activities, concerns, transactions, operations, undertakings, interests, matters

affect VERB **1** *Alcohol affects women and men differently.* ► have an effect on, have an impact on, influence, impinge on, modify, act on, alter, attack, change, transform, (*more informal*) hit **2** *The sad news affected all of us.* ► upset, disturb, trouble, concern, move, perturb, sadden, distress, agitate, grieve, impress, stir, touch **3** *The man affects a Glasgow accent.* ► assume, feign, put on

affected ADJECTIVE *He assumed an affected voice, as though coming from God.* ► artificial, sham, insincere, pretentious, assumed, (*more informal*) put-on

affection NOUN *The friends show obvious affection for one another.* ► fondness, friendship, friendliness, attachment, devotion, tenderness, warmth, feeling, liking, love, (*more informal*) soft spot AN OPPOSITE IS hatred

affectionate ADJECTIVE *an affectionate smile* ► fond, loving, devoted, tender, friendly, kind, kind-hearted, warm-hearted, sympathetic

afflict VERB *The family has been afflicted by illness.* ► trouble, bother, torment, beset, burden, strike, distress, oppress, harass, vex, plague

affliction NOUN *He bore his affliction with great dignity.* ► suffering, distress, misfortune, hardship, misery, torment, ordeal, pain, trouble, tribulation, adversity

affluence NOUN *In recent years the country has shown signs of greater affluence.* ► wealth, prosperity, opulence, fortune, richness

affluent ADJECTIVE *The more affluent houses had compost heaps in their large gardens.* ► prosperous, rich, well-off, wealthy, opulent, (*more informal*) flush OPPOSITES ARE poor, impoverished

afford VERB *We can't afford a holiday this year.* ► have enough money for, pay for, manage

afraid ADJECTIVE **1** *The younger children were afraid of the dark.* ► frightened, scared, terrified, alarmed (at, by), fearful, intimidated (by), anxious, nervous OPPOSITES ARE unafraid, brave, bold, confident **2** *I'm afraid all the food has gone.* ► sorry, regretful, unhappy **3** *Don't*

after *ADVERB* **1** behind • *Jill came tumbling after.* **2** later • *It came a week after.*

afternoon *NOUN* **afternoons** the time from noon or lunchtime to evening

aftershave *NOUN* a pleasant-smelling lotion that men put on their skin after shaving

afterwards *ADVERB* at a later time

again *ADVERB* **1** another time; once more • *try again.* **2** as before • *You will soon be well again.* **3** besides; moreover

against *PREPOSITION* **1** touching or hitting • *He leant against the wall.* **2** in opposition to; not in favour of • *They voted against the proposal.* **3** in preparation for • *Protect them against the cold.*

age *NOUN* **ages 1** the length of time a person has lived or a thing has existed **2** a special period of history or geology • *the ice age*
ages *PLURAL NOUN* (*informal*) a very long time • *We've been waiting for ages.*
come of age reach the age at which you have an adult's legal rights and obligations (now at 18 years; formerly 21)

age *VERB* **ages, ageing, aged** make or become old

aged *ADJECTIVE* **1** (ayjd) having the age of • *a girl aged 9* **2** (ay-jid) very old • *an aged man*

agency *NOUN* **agencies 1** the office or business of an agent • *a travel agency* **2** the means by which something is done • *Flowers are pollinated by the agency of bees.*

agenda (a-**jen**-da) *NOUN* **agendas** a list of things to be done or discussed • *The agenda is rather long.*

agent *NOUN* **agents 1** a person who organizes things for other people **2** a spy • *a secret agent*

aggravate *VERB* **aggravates, aggravating, aggravated 1** make a thing worse or more serious **2** (*informal*) annoy
▷ **aggravation** *NOUN*
[from Latin *gravis* = heavy]

aggregate *NOUN* **aggregates** a total amount or score

aggression *NOUN* starting an attack or war etc.; aggressive behaviour

aggressive *ADJECTIVE* likely to attack people; forceful
▷ **aggressively** *ADVERB* **aggressiveness** *NOUN*
aggressor *NOUN*

aggrieved (a-**greevd**) *ADJECTIVE* resentful because of being treated unfairly

aghast *ADJECTIVE* horrified

agile *ADJECTIVE* moving quickly or easily
▷ **agilely** *ADVERB* **agility** *NOUN*

agitate *VERB* **agitates, agitating, agitated 1** make someone feel upset or anxious **2** stir up public interest or concern; campaign • *They*

Thesaurus

be afraid to ask. ► reluctant, hesitant, shy, slow, chary (of)

age *NOUN* **1** *The grandparents were showing signs of age.* ► old age, senility, elderliness, decrepitude, dotage, decline AN OPPOSITE IS youth **2** *the Elizabethan age* ► era, period, epoch, days, generation, time, years **3** (*more informal*) *It's an age since you were last here. We've had to wait for ages.* ► lifetime, long time, aeon

age *VERB* **1** *Frank had aged in the last few years.* ► decline, degenerate, look older, fade **2** *A good wine needs to age.* ► mature, mellow, ripen, develop, grow older

aged *ADJECTIVE* *an aged relative* ► elderly, old, senile

agent *NOUN* *When she became a writer she needed an agent.* ► representative, mediator, intermediary, broker, delegate, emissary, go-between, middleman, negotiator, trustee

aggravate 1 *The delays only aggravated the situation.* ► worsen, exacerbate, increase, intensify, magnify, add to, make more serious, make worse, augment, compound, heighten, inflame, exaggerate AN OPPOSITE IS alleviate **2** (*informal*) *Their flippant remarks aggravated us.* ► annoy, irritate, bother, exasperate, incense, vex, irk, anger, nettle, provoke, trouble, (*more informal*) needle, (*more informal*) peeve

aggravation *NOUN* *It's not worth all the aggravation.* ► bother, annoyance, nuisance, trouble, hassle, irritation, difficulty

aggression *NOUN* *an act of aggression* ► hostility, aggressiveness, provocation, militancy, violence

aggressive *ADJECTIVE* *Lily was in one of her aggressive moods.* ► hostile, provocative, pugnacious, antagonistic, militant, belligerent, bellicose, argumentative, quarrelsome, attacking, violent, warlike, assertive, bullying, (*more informal*) pushy, (*more informal*) macho AN OPPOSITE IS friendly

aggrieved *ADJECTIVE* *He sounded aggrieved and astonished.* ► offended, indignant, resentful, wronged, distressed, discontented, piqued, riled

aghast *ADJECTIVE* *They were aghast at the news.* ► horrified, appalled, shocked, dismayed, astounded, astonished, amazed

agile *ADJECTIVE* *The child was as agile as a monkey.* ► nimble, lithe, spry, deft, graceful, fleet, adroit, sprightly, supple, lively, acrobatic, active, limber, lissom, mobile, quick-moving, swift OPPOSITES ARE clumsy, slow

agitate *VERB* **1** *A special device agitates the clothes.* ► stir, disturb, shake, ruffle, stimulate,

A B C D E F G H I J K L M N O P Q R S T U V W X Y Z

agitated for a new bypass. **3** shake something about
▷ **agitation** *NOUN* **agitator** *NOUN*

agnostic (ag- nost- ik) *NOUN* **agnostics** a person who believes that it is impossible to know whether God exists
▷ **agnosticism** *NOUN*
[from *a-* = not + Greek *gnostikos* = knowing The word was invented by the biologist Thomas Huxley in the 19th century He based it on the word *gnostic* which meant 'relating to knowledge']

ago *ADVERB* in the past • *long ago*

agog *ADJECTIVE* eager and excited

agony *NOUN* **agonies** extremely great pain or suffering
▷ **agonizing** *ADJECTIVE*

agree *VERB* **agrees, agreeing, agreed** **1** think or say the same as another person etc. **2** consent • *She agreed to come.* **3** suit a person's health or digestion • *Curry doesn't agree with me.* **4** correspond in grammatical number, gender, or person In 'They were good teachers' *they* agrees with *teachers* (both are plural forms) and *were* agrees with *they*; *was* would be incorrect because it is singular

agreeable *ADJECTIVE* **1** willing • *We shall go if you are agreeable.* **2** pleasant • *an agreeable place*
▷ **agreeably** *ADVERB*

agreement *NOUN* **agreements** **1** agreeing **2** an arrangement that people have agreed on

agriculture *NOUN* cultivating land on a large scale and rearing livestock; farming
▷ **agricultural** *ADJECTIVE*

aground *ADVERB*, *ADJECTIVE* stranded on the bottom in shallow water

ahead *ADVERB* **1** further forward; in front **2** forwards • *Full steam ahead!*

aid *NOUN* **aids** **1** help **2** something that helps • *a hearing aid* **3** money, food, etc. sent to another country to help it • *overseas aid*
in aid of for the purpose of; to help something

aid *VERB* **aids, aiding, aided** help

Aids *NOUN* a disease that greatly weakens a person's ability to resist infections [from the initial letters of 'acquired immune deficiency syndrome']

ailing *ADJECTIVE* **1** ill; in poor health **2** in difficulties; not successful • *the ailing ship industry*

ailment *NOUN* **ailments** a slight illness

aim *VERB* **aims, aiming, aimed** **1** point a gun etc. **2** throw or kick in a particular direction **3** try or intend to do something

Thesaurus

beat, churn, convulse, toss **2** *Her remark seemed to agitate her guest.* ► upset, alarm, rouse, unsettle, disquiet, disturb, excite, worry, confuse, trouble, disconcert, fluster, perturb, stir up AN OPPOSITE IS calm

agitated *ADJECTIVE* *She became agitated when they did not appear.* ► upset, unsettled, anxious, confused, disturbed, ruffled, edgy, excited, distraught, flustered, nervous, restive, restless, fidgety, feverish, (*more informal*) tin a tizzy OPPOSITES ARE calm, relaxed

agonize *VERB* *We agonized for hours over the decision.* ► worry, fret, fuss, struggle, labour, suffer, wrestle, be anxious

agonizing *ADJECTIVE* *an agonizing pain* ► excruciating, acute, intense, severe, extreme, piercing, painful

agony *NOUN* *The victims died in agony.* ► pain, torment, torture, suffering, anguish, distress, suffering

agree *VERB* **1** *I'll have a word with your father, and I'm sure he'll agree.* ► approve, consent, be willing **2** *You must agree to take six books in the first year of membership.* ► be willing, consent, undertake, promise **3** *I think we all agree on the action needed.* ► concur, be unanimous, be united, (*more informal*) see eye to eye **4** *No two versions of the story seem to agree.* ► match, accord, correspond, tally, coincide, conform, harmonize, fit OPPOSITES ARE disagree, conflict
agree on *We should agree on a price.* ► fix, settle, decide on, establish, choose
agree to *He agreed to their requests.* ► accept, consent to, acquiesce in, accede to, assent to, grant, allow
agree with *I don't agree with the decision to go to war.* ► support, advocate, defend, argue for, (*more informal*) back

agreeable *ADJECTIVE* *I spent an agreeable day with their family.* ► pleasant, likeable, pleasing, delightful, congenial, appealing OPPOSITES ARE disagreeable, unpleasant

agreement *NOUN* **1** *There's a large measure of agreement between them.* ► accord, concord, concurrence, unanimity, consensus, harmony, unity, affinity, similarity, sympathy, conformity, consistency, correspondence AN OPPOSITE IS disagreement **2** *The two sides reached an agreement.* ► settlement, deal, compact, accord, pact, understanding, pledge, arrangement

aid *NOUN* *The project was largely financed from foreign aid.* ► help, support, assistance, relief, favour, patronage

aid *VERB* **1** *an agreement to aid the poorest countries* ► help, assist, support, sustain, relieve, subsidize **2** *These measures will aid the process.* ► encourage, support, promote, facilitate, expedite

aim *NOUN* **aims** **1** aiming a gun etc. **2** a purpose or intention

aimless *ADJECTIVE* without a purpose
▷ **aimlessly** *ADVERB*

air *NOUN* **airs** **1** the mixture of gases that surrounds the earth and which everyone breathes **2** the open space above the earth **3** a tune or melody **4** an appearance or impression of something • *an air of mystery* **5** an impressive or haughty manner • *He puts on airs.*
by air in or by aircraft
on the air on radio or television

air *VERB* **airs, airing, aired** **1** put clothes etc. in a warm place to finish drying **2** ventilate a room **3** express • *He aired his opinions.*

air bag *NOUN* **air bags** a safety device in a vehicle, which inflates in front of the driver or passenger to reduce the impact in a collision

air-conditioning *NOUN* a system for controlling the temperature, purity, etc. of the air in a room or building
▷ **air-conditioned** *ADJECTIVE*

aircraft *NOUN* **aircraft** an aeroplane, glider, or helicopter etc.

aircraft carrier *NOUN* **aircraft carriers** a large ship with a long deck where aircraft can take off and land

airfield *NOUN* **airfields** an area equipped with runways etc. where aircraft can take off and land

air force *NOUN* **air forces** the part of a country's armed forces that is equipped with aircraft

airline *NOUN* **airlines** a company that provides a regular service of transport by aircraft

airliner *NOUN* **airliners** a large aircraft for carrying passengers

airlock *NOUN* **airlocks** **1** a compartment with an airtight door at each end, through which people can go in and out of a pressurized chamber **2** a bubble of air that stops liquid flowing through a pipe

airmail *NOUN* mail carried by air

airman *NOUN* **airmen** a man who is a member of an air force or of the crew of an aircraft

airport *NOUN* **airports** a place where aircraft land and take off, with passenger terminals and other buildings

air raid *NOUN* **air raids** an attack by aircraft

airstrip *NOUN* **airstrips** a strip of ground prepared for aircraft to land and take off

airtight *ADJECTIVE* not letting air in or out

airy *ADJECTIVE* **1** with plenty of fresh air **2** light as air **3** vague and insincere • *airy promises*
▷ **airily** *ADVERB*

aisle (I'll) *NOUN* **aisles** **1** a passage between or beside rows of seats or pews **2** a side part of a church

ajar *ADVERB, ADJECTIVE* slightly open • *Leave the door ajar.*

akin *ADJECTIVE* related or similar to • *a feeling akin to regret*

alarm *NOUN* **alarms** **1** a warning sound or signal; a piece of equipment for giving this **2** a feeling of fear or worry **3** an alarm clock

alarm *VERB* **alarms, alarming, alarmed** make someone frightened or anxious

Thesaurus

aim *NOUN* *Our aim is to win the championship.*
► ambition, goal, objective, object, aspiration, plan, purpose, intention, target, wish, end, dream, hope, desire, design

aim *VERB* **1** *He aimed a gun at her.* ► point, direct, level, train, focus **2** *We aim to meet our targets in full next year.* ► intend, aspire, resolve, want, wish, seek, plan, strive, try, endeavour, attempt

aimless *ADJECTIVE* *an aimless existence*
► pointless, purposeless, undirected, haphazard, random, meaningless, senseless, fruitless

air *NOUN* **1** *the air around us* ► sky, atmosphere, ether, heavens, airspace **2** *Open the window and let some air in.* ► breeze, draught, breath of air, oxygen, waft, wind **3** *She showed an air of defiance.* ► appearance, look, aura, manner, impression, bearing, aspect, ambience, character, demeanour, effect, feeling

air *VERB* **1** *You will need to air the room.*
► ventilate, aerate, freshen **2** *an opportunity to air your opinions* ► express , voice, utter, disclose, divulge, vent, declare, make known

airy *ADJECTIVE* **1** *The room was light and airy.*
► fresh, well ventilated, spacious, roomy, breezy OPPOSITES ARE stuffy, airless, close, oppressive **2** *He looked at them with an airy confidence.* ► cheerful, cheery, light-hearted, nonchalant, lively OPPOSITES ARE serious, solemn

aisle *NOUN* *The cinema had several aisles.*
► gangway, passage, passageway, corridor, lane

alarm *NOUN* **1** *The woman looked round in alarm.*
► fear, fright, panic, terror, trepidation, apprehension, consternation, dismay, anxiety, distress, nervousness, uneasiness **2** *Suddenly the alarm sounded.* ► signal, alarm signal, warning signal, distress signal, siren

alarm *VERB* *The news had alarmed us* ► frighten, scare, startle, unnerve, agitate, shock, disturb, fluster, surprise, terrify, upset, daunt, dismay, distress, panic, (*more informal*) put the wind up AN OPPOSITE IS reassure

▷ **alarming** *ADJECTIVE*
[from Italian *all' arme!* = to arms!]

alarm clock *NOUN* **alarm clocks** a clock that can be set to make a sound at a fixed time to wake a sleeping person

alas *INTERJECTION* an exclamation of sorrow

albatross *NOUN* **albatrosses** a large seabird with very long wings

albino (al- been- oh) *NOUN* **albinos** a person or animal with no colour in the skin and hair (which are white)

album *NOUN* **albums 1** a book with blank pages in which to keep a collection of photographs, stamps, autographs, etc. **2** a collection of songs on a CD, record, or tape

alcohol *NOUN* **1** a colourless liquid made by fermenting sugar or starch **2** drinks containing this liquid (e.g. wine, beer, whisky), that can make people drunk [The original meaning was a powdered cosmetic, and it came from an Arabic word *al-kuhul*. The meaning changed to any powder and then to a refined liquid produced by purifying, as alcohol is]

alcoholic *ADJECTIVE* containing alcohol

alcoholic *NOUN* **alcoholics** a person who is seriously addicted to alcohol
▷ **alcoholism** *NOUN*

ale *NOUN* **ales** beer

alert *ADJECTIVE* watching for something; ready to act
▷ **alertly** *ADVERB* **alertness** *NOUN*

alert *NOUN* **alerts** a warning or alarm
on the alert on the lookout; watchful

alert *VERB* **alerts, alerting, alerted** warn someone of danger etc.; make someone aware of something [from Italian *all' erta!* = to the watchtower!]

A level *NOUN* **A levels** advanced level in GCSE

algae (al- jee) *PLURAL NOUN* plants that grow in water, with no true stems or leaves

algebra (al- jib- ra) *NOUN* mathematics in which letters and symbols are used to represent quantities
▷ **algebraic** (al- jib- ray- ik) *ADJECTIVE*
[from Arabic *al-jabr* = putting together broken parts It was part of the name of an Arabic mathematical work written in the 9th century]

alias (ay- lee- as) *NOUN* **aliases** a false or different name

alias *ADVERB* also named • *Clark Kent, alias Superman.*

alibi (al- ib- I) *NOUN* **alibis** evidence that a person accused of a crime was somewhere else when it was committed

alien (ay- lee- en) *NOUN* **aliens 1** a person who is not a citizen of the country where he or she is living; a foreigner **2** a being from another world

alien *ADJECTIVE* **1** foreign **2** unnatural • *Cruelty is alien to her nature.*

alienate (ay- lee- en- ayt) *VERB* **alienates, alienating, alienated** make a person become unfriendly or not willing to help you
▷ **alienation** *NOUN*

alight *ADJECTIVE* **1** on fire **2** lit up

alike *ADJECTIVE*, *ADVERB* like one another; in the same way • *The twins are very alike.* • *Treat them alike.*

alimony *NOUN* money paid by someone to their wife or husband after they are separated or divorced; maintenance

Thesaurus

alert *ADJECTIVE* **1** *We need to stay alert driving in the dark.* ► attentive, vigilant, watchful, aware, circumspect, wide awake, on the lookout, on the ball, on your guard, (*more informal*) on the qui vive AN OPPOSITE IS inattentive **2** *mentally alert* ► sharp, quick-witted, alive, active, acute

alert *VERB* *We alerted them to the problem.* ► warn (of), notify (of), tip off (about), inform (about)

alias *NOUN* *Jack was not his real name, only an alias.* ► pseudonym, false name, assumed name, (*said of a writer*) pen name, (*said of an actor*) stage name

alibi *NOUN* *She has a cast-iron alibi for that evening.* ► excuse , pretext, story, defence, explanation

alien *ADJECTIVE* **1** *an alien landscape* ► strange, unfamiliar, outlandish, exotic, foreign, remote **2** *alien beings* ► foreign, extra-terrestrial, remote

alien *NOUN* *illegal aliens* ► foreigner, immigrant, stranger, outsider

alight *ADJECTIVE* *The house was well and truly alight.* ► on fire, ablaze, burning, blazing, in flames, ignited, lit up

alight *VERB* **1** *Three passengers alighted from the train.* ► get off, get down, descend, disembark, dismount **2** *The bird alighted on a branch.* ► land, settle, perch, come to rest, touch down, come down

align *VERB* **1** *The shelves are aligned in rows.* ► place in line, arrange in line, line up, straighten up **2** *He aligns himself with the workers.* ► associate, affiliate, side, sympathize, agree, ally, cooperate, join

alike *ADJECTIVE* *All the houses looked alike.* ► similar, identical, indistinguishable, the same, uniform, comparable, interchangeable

alive *ADJECTIVE* **1** living **2** alert • *Be alive to the possible dangers.*

alkali (alk- al- I) *NOUN* **alkalis** a chemical substance that neutralizes an acid to form a salt
▷ **alkaline** *ADJECTIVE*
[from Arabic *al-kali* = the ashes (because alkalis were first obtained from the ashes of seaweed)]

all *ADJECTIVE* the whole number or amount of • *All my books are here.* • *all day*

all *NOUN* **1** everything • *That is all I know.* **2** everybody • *All are agreed.*

all *ADVERB* **1** completely • *She was dressed all in white.* **2** to each team or competitor • *The score is fifteen all.*
all in (*informal*) exhausted • *I'm all in.*
all-in *ADJECTIVE* including or allowing everything • *an all-in price*
all there (*informal*) having an alert mind
all the same in spite of this; making no difference • *I like him, all the same.*

Allah *NOUN* the Muslim name of God

allegation (al- ig- ay- shon) *NOUN* **allegations** a statement made without proof

allege (a- lej) *VERB* **alleges, alleging, alleged** say something without being able to prove it • *He alleged that I had cheated.*
▷ **allegedly** (a- lej- id- lee) *ADVERB*

allegiance (a- lee- jans) *NOUN* **allegiances** loyalty

allegory (al- ig- er- ee) *NOUN* **allegories** a story in which the characters and events represent or symbolize a deeper meaning, e.g. to teach a moral lesson
▷ **allegorical** (al- ig- o- rik- al) *ADJECTIVE*

alleluia *INTERJECTION* praise to God

allergy (al- er- jee) *NOUN* **allergies** something that a person is sensitive to and that can make them ill • *He has an allergy to cats.*
▷ **allergic** (al- er- jik) *ADJECTIVE*

alley *NOUN* **alleys** **1** a narrow street or passage **2** a place where you can play bowls or skittles

alliance (a- leye- ans) *NOUN* **alliances** an association formed by countries or groups who wish to support each other

allied *ADJECTIVE* **1** joined as allies; on the same side **2** of the same kind

alligator *NOUN* **alligators** a large reptile of the crocodile family [from Spanish *el lagarto* = the lizard]

alliteration *NOUN* the repetition of the same letter or sound at the beginning of several words to make a special effect, e.g. in • *Whisper words of wisdom.*

allotment *NOUN* **allotments** **1** a small rented piece of public land used for growing vegetables, fruit, or flowers **2** allotting; the amount allotted

allow *VERB* **allows, allowing, allowed** **1** permit • *Smoking is not allowed.* **2** permit someone to have something; provide with • *She was allowed £10 for books.* **3** agree • *I allow that you have been patient.*
▷ **allowable** *ADJECTIVE*

Thesaurus

alive *ADJECTIVE* **1** *She was last seen alive a week ago.* ► living, live, breathing, animate, existing AN OPPOSITE IS dead **2** *Many of the old customs of the country are kept alive.* ► active, in existence, current, functioning, flourishing, surviving OPPOSITES ARE obsolete, inactive **3** *The company is alive to recent developments.* ► alert, sensitive, aware (of), conscious (of), apprised (of), cognizant (of)

allegation *NOUN* *There were the usual allegations of police brutality.* ► accusation, charge, claim, assertion, declaration, statement, testimony

allege *VERB* *She alleged that he had attacked her.* ► assert, affirm, maintain, claim, contend, declare, insist, state

allegiance *NOUN* *an oath of allegiance to the king* ► loyalty, fidelity, obedience, devotion, duty, faithfulness, (*historical*) fealty

allergic *ADJECTIVE* **1** *If you are allergic to foods, you'll know what these are.* ► sensitive **2** (*more informal*) *I think I must be allergic to hard work.* ► averse, opposed, hostile, resistant, disinclined, antagonistic, unsympathetic, antipathetic

alleviate *VERB* *Medicines can help alleviate the pain.* ► ease, relieve, calm, soothe, diminish, reduce, lessen, dull, assuage, moderate AN OPPOSITE IS aggravate

alliance *NOUN* **1** *a political alliance* ► association, confederation, federation, compact, league, bloc, treaty, pact **2** *a business alliance* ► partnership, relationship, consortium, affiliation

allocate *VERB* *Funds are allocated to each project.* ► allot, assign, apportion, grant, award, distribute, set aside (for), allow, dispense, give out, share out

allow *VERB* **1** *Smoking is only allowed in certain parts of the hotel.* ► permit, approve, authorize, tolerate, bear, (*more informal*) put up with AN OPPOSITE IS forbid **2** *The teacher allowed him to go home.* ► permit, let, authorize, give permission, enable **3** *We need to allow more time for the journey.* ► provide, set aside, grant, allot, allocate, give

A B C D E F G H I J K L M N O P Q R S T U V W X Y Z

allowance *NOUN* **allowances** an amount of money that is given regularly for a particular purpose
make allowances be considerate; excuse • *Make allowances for his age.*

alloy *NOUN* **alloys** a metal formed by mixing two or more metals etc.

all right *ADJECTIVE, ADVERB* **1** satisfactory **2** in good condition **3** as desired **4** yes, I consent

all-round *ADJECTIVE* general; not specialist • *an all-round athlete*
▷ **all-rounder** *NOUN*

allude *VERB* **alludes, alluding, alluded** refer to something without naming it
▷ **allusion** *NOUN*
USAGE Do not confuse with **elude**.

allure *VERB* **allures, alluring, allured** attract or fascinate someone
▷ **allure** *NOUN* **alluring** *ADJECTIVE*

ally (al- eye) *NOUN* **allies** **1** a country in alliance with another **2** a person who cooperates with another

ally *VERB* **allies, allying, allied** form an alliance

almighty *ADJECTIVE* **1** having complete power **2** (*informal*) very great • *an almighty din*

almond (ah- mond) *NOUN* **almonds** an oval edible nut

almost *ADVERB* near to being something but not quite • *almost ready*

alone *ADJECTIVE* without any other people or things; without help

along *PREPOSITION* following the length of something • *Walk along the path.*

along *ADVERB* **1** on or onwards • *Push it along.* **2** accompanying somebody • *I've brought my brother along.*
along with as well as; together with

alongside *PREPOSITION, ADVERB* next to something; beside

aloof *ADVERB* apart; not taking part • *We stayed aloof from their quarrels.*

aloof *ADJECTIVE* distant and not friendly in manner • *She seemed aloof.*

aloud *ADVERB* in a voice that can be heard

alpha *NOUN* the first letter of the Greek alphabet, = a

alphabet *NOUN* **alphabets** the letters used in a language, usually arranged in a set order
▷ **alphabetical** *ADJECTIVE* **alphabetically** *ADVERB*
[from *alpha* and *beta*, the first two letters of the Greek alphabet The Hebrew names *aleph* and *beth* are related to the Greek words]

already *ADVERB* by now; before now

Thesaurus

allowance *NOUN* **1** *A weekly allowance is provided for each prisoner.* ► allocation, portion, measure, quota, ration, share, amount **2** *He received an allowance from his father.* ► remittance, payment, pocket money, subsistence, annuity, grant, stipend, pension **3** *The shop will offer you an allowance for your old appliance.* ► discount, rebate, reduction, deduction
make allowances for *You have to make allowances for possible delays on the journey.* ► take into account, consider, bear in mind, keep in mind, remember, have regard for

all right *ADJECTIVE* **1** *She seemed all right.* ► well, unhurt, unharmed, uninjured, in good health, safe, secure **2** *The food's all right, though not very exciting.* ► satisfactory, acceptable, adequate, reasonable, tolerable, passable
OPPOSITES ARE unsatisfactory, unacceptable

allude *VERB* **allude to** *Several speakers alluded to the problem.* ► refer to, hint at, make an allusion to, mention, touch on, speak of, suggest

ally *NOUN* *a political ally* ► associate, colleague, collaborator, partner, companion, confederate, supporter, friend, helper, accomplice, helpmate AN OPPOSITE IS enemy

ally *VERB* *Bruce again allied himself with the English.* ► unite, join, band together, join forces, side, team up, form an alliance, make common cause

almighty *ADJECTIVE* **1** *Almighty God* ► all-powerful, omnipotent, supreme, pre-eminent **2** *an almighty explosion* ► huge, enormous, tremendous, mighty, overpowering, overwhelming, big

almost *ADVERB* *The riders had almost reached her. He was earning nearly a million a year by now. I was almost tempted to ask why they had come.* ► nearly, not quite, practically, virtually, about, just about, all but, around, as good as, approximately

alone *ADJECTIVE* **1** *The man was alone in the house at the time.* ► on your own, by yourself, solitary, single, unaccompanied, apart, separate, solo **2** *She said she often felt very alone.* ► lonely, isolated, lonesome, solitary, friendless, forlorn, desolate

aloof *ADJECTIVE* *Michele seemed aloof and oddly tense.* ► distant, remote, haughty, supercilious, forbidding, cold, unfriendly, reserved, standoffish, austere, scornful, unsympathetic, unforthcoming, inaccessible, detached OPPOSITES ARE friendly, approachable

aloud *ADVERB* *Madge read the letter aloud.* ► out loud, audibly, clearly, distinctly, plainly, loudly
AN OPPOSITE IS silently

Alsatian (al- say- shan) *NOUN* **Alsatians** a German shepherd dog
also *ADVERB* in addition; besides
altar *NOUN* **altars** a table or similar structure used in religious ceremonies
USAGE Do not confuse with the verb **alter**.
alter *VERB* **alters, altering, altered** make or become different; change
▷ **alteration** *NOUN*
USAGE Do not confuse with the noun **altar**.
alternate (ol- tern- at) *ADJECTIVE* **1** happening or coming one after the other • *alternate layers of sponge and cream* **2** one in every two • *We meet up on alternate Fridays.*
▷ **alternately** *ADVERB*
USAGE See the note at **alternative**.
alternate (ol- tern- ayt) *VERB* **alternates, alternating, alternated** use or come alternately
▷ **alternation** *NOUN*
alternating current *NOUN* **alternating currents** electric current that keeps reversing its direction at regular intervals
alternative *ADJECTIVE* available instead of something else
▷ **alternatively** *ADVERB*
USAGE Do not confuse **alternative** with **alternate**. If there are *alternative colours* it means that there is a choice of two or more colours, but *alternate colours* means that there is first one colour and then the other.
alternative *NOUN* **alternatives** one of two or more possibilities
no alternative no choice
alternative energy *NOUN* any form of energy that does not use up the earth's resources or harm the environment
alternative medicine *NOUN* types of medical treatment that are not based on ordinary medicine
alternator *NOUN* **alternators** a dynamo that generates an alternating current
although *CONJUNCTION* though
altitude *NOUN* **altitudes** the height of something, especially above sea level
alto *NOUN* **altos** **1** an adult male singer with a very high voice **2** a contralto
altogether *ADVERB* **1** with all included; in total • *The outfit costs £20 altogether.* **2** completely • *The stream dries up altogether in summer.* **3** on the whole • *Altogether, it was a good concert.*
USAGE Do not confuse **altogether** and *all together*.
aluminium *NOUN* a lightweight silver-coloured metal
always *ADVERB* **1** at all times **2** often • *You are always crying.* **3** whatever happens • *You can always sleep on the floor.*
Alzheimer's disease *NOUN* a serious disease of the brain which affects some old people and makes them confused and forgetful
a.m. *ABBREVIATION* before noon
amalgamate *VERB* **amalgamates, amalgamating, amalgamated** mix or combine
▷ **amalgamation** *NOUN*
amateur (am- at- er) *NOUN* **amateurs** a person who does something as a hobby, not as a professional
amateurish *ADJECTIVE* not done or made very well; not skilful

Thesaurus

also *ADVERB* *His married sister also lives nearby.* ► too, additionally, in addition, as well, besides, furthermore, moreover

alter *VERB* *The text of the speech had been altered to take account of the recent events.* ► change, adjust, modify, vary, adapt, convert, transform, amend, re-form

alteration *NOUN* *After a few alterations the typescript was ready for publication.* ► change, modification, variation, adaptation, adjustment, amendment, reorganization, transformation

alternate *VERB* *In a democratic system political parties alternate in office.* ► take turns, interchange, act alternately, swap round, replace each other, rotate

alternative *NOUN* *There is no alternative.* ► choice, option, other possibility, substitute, replacement

altogether *ADVERB* *We are not altogether satisfied.* ► completely, entirely, fully, wholly, totally, perfectly, absolutely, quite, thoroughly, utterly

always *ADVERB* **1** *You are always late.* ► every time, constantly, repeatedly, habitually, invariably, regularly **2** *He is always complaining.* ► forever, constantly, incessantly, endlessly **3** *I will always remember you.* ► for ever, permanently, perpetually, evermore

amateur *ADJECTIVE* *The band was made up entirely of amateur musicians.* ► unpaid, unqualified, untrained, inexperienced AN OPPOSITE IS professional

amateur *NOUN* *The players were all amateurs.* ► non-professional, layman, layperson, enthusiast, devotee, dabbler AN OPPOSITE IS professional

amateurish *ADJECTIVE* *There are some very poor amateurish productions around.* ► unskilful,

amaze *VERB* **amazes, amazing, amazed** surprise somebody greatly; fill with wonder
▷ **amazement** *NOUN*

amazing *ADJECTIVE* very surprising or remarkable

amazon *NOUN* **amazons** a strong or athletic woman [The Amazons were a mythical race of women warriors The Greeks thought that the name came from *a-* = without + *mazos* = breast, believing that the Amazons used to cut off their right breast in order to hold a bow better]

ambassador *NOUN* **ambassadors** a person sent to a foreign country to represent his or her own government

amber *NOUN* **1** a hard clear yellowish substance used for making ornaments **2** a yellow traffic light shown as a signal for caution, placed between red (= stop) and green (= go)

ambidextrous *ADJECTIVE* able to use either your left hand or your right hand equally well

ambiguous *ADJECTIVE* having more than one possible meaning; unclear
▷ **ambiguously** *ADVERB* **ambiguity** *NOUN*

ambition *NOUN* **ambitions** **1** a strong desire to achieve something **2** the thing desired

ambitious *ADJECTIVE* full of ambition

ambivalent (am- biv- al- ent) *ADJECTIVE* having mixed feelings about something (e.g. liking and disliking it)
▷ **ambivalence** *NOUN*

amble *VERB* **ambles, ambling, ambled** walk at a slow easy pace

ambulance *NOUN* **ambulances** a vehicle equipped to carry sick or injured people

ambush *NOUN* **ambushes** a surprise attack from troops etc. who have concealed themselves

ambush *VERB* **ambushes, ambushing, ambushed** attack someone after lying in wait for them

amen *INTERJECTION* a word used at the end of a prayer or hymn, meaning 'may it be so'

amend *VERB* **amends, amending, amended** alter something in order to improve it
▷ **amendment** *NOUN*
make amends make up for having done something wrong; atone

American *ADJECTIVE* **1** to do with the continent of America **2** to do with the United States of America
▷ **American** *NOUN*

amino acid (a- meen- oh) *NOUN* **amino acids** an acid found in proteins

Thesaurus

incompetent, inept, inexpert, crude, bumbling, amateur AN OPPOSITE IS skilled

amaze *VERB* *It always amazes me how dirty the place is.* ► astonish, astound, surprise, stagger, startle, disconcert, dumbfound, shock, flabbergast, perplex, stun, stupefy, bewilder, confound

amazing *ADJECTIVE* *an amazing sight*
► astonishing, astounding, extraordinary, remarkable, staggering, startling, stunning, breathtaking, fantastic, wonderful, magnificent, phenomenal, incredible
AN OPPOSITE IS unimpressive

ambiguous *ADJECTIVE* *The replies were ambiguous and misleading.* ► confusing, obscure, enigmatic, ambivalent, uncertain, unclear, equivocal, indefinite, indeterminate, puzzling, vague, woolly AN OPPOSITE IS definite

ambition *NOUN* **1** *young people with a lot of ambition* ► drive, enthusiasm, enterprise, self-assertion, zeal, (*more informal*) push **2** *Her ambition is to become a model.* ► aim, dream, hope, goal, aspiration, objective, object, target, wish, desire, ideal, intention

ambitious *ADJECTIVE* **1** *an ambitious politician*
► aspiring, assertive, determined, enthusiastic, (*more informal*) go-ahead, (*more informal*) pushy AN OPPOSITE IS apathetic.
2 *ambitious ideas* ► grand, grandiose, large-scale, big, far-reaching, unrealistic
OPPOSITES ARE modest, realistic

ambivalent *ADJECTIVE* *an ambivalent attitude towards the new technology* ► equivocal, uncertain, hesitant, fluctuating, contradictory, inconsistent, vacillating, wavering, ambiguous, confused, muddled

ambush *NOUN* *The fighters set up an ambush.*
► surprise attack, trap, snare, ambuscade

ambush *VERB* *The gang specialized in ambushing unsuspecting passers-by.* ► waylay, pounce on, surprise, swoop on, trap, entrap, ensnare, intercept, attack

amends *NOUN* **make amends to** *It's not too late to make amends to them for the trouble you caused.* ► recompense, compensate, make it up to

amenity *NOUN* *an old house with few amenities*
► facility, service, benefit, provision

amiable *ADJECTIVE* *an amiable old fellow*
► friendly, amicable, agreeable, affable, likeable, pleasant, congenial

ammunition *NOUN* **1** *The house was full of ammunition.* ► bullets, cartridges, shells, bombs, missiles, shrapnel **2** *The blunder provided ammunition for the opposition.*
► evidence, arguments, material, information

amok or **amuck** *ADVERB* **run amok** *Some of the animals had broken loose and run amok.* ► go

amiss *ADJECTIVE* wrong or faulty • *She knew something was amiss.*

ammonia *NOUN* a colourless gas or liquid with a strong smell

ammunition *NOUN* a supply of bullets, shells, grenades, etc. for use in fighting

amnesia (am- nee- zee- a) *NOUN* loss of memory

amnesty *NOUN* **amnesties** a general pardon for people who have committed a crime

amoeba (a- mee- ba) *NOUN* **amoebas** a microscopic creature consisting of a single cell which constantly changes shape and can split itself in two

among or **amongst** *PREPOSITION* **1** surrounded by; in • *There were weeds among the flowers.* **2** between • *Divide the sweets among the children.*

amount *NOUN* **amounts** **1** a quantity **2** a total

amount *VERB* **amounts, amounting, amounted**
amount to **1** add up to **2** be equivalent to • *Their reply amounts to a refusal.*

amp *NOUN* **amps** **1** an ampere **2** (*informal*) an amplifier

ampere (am- pair) *NOUN* **amperes** a unit for measuring electric current

amphibian *NOUN* **amphibians** **1** an animal able to live both on land and in water, such as a frog, toad, or newt **2** a vehicle that can move on both land and water

amphibious *ADJECTIVE* able to live or move on both land and in water

ample *ADJECTIVE* **1** quite enough • *ample provisions* **2** large
▷ **amply** *ADVERB*

amplifier *NOUN* **amplifiers** a piece of equipment for making a sound or electrical signal louder or stronger

amplify *VERB* **amplifies, amplifying, amplified** **1** make a sound or electrical signal louder or stronger **2** give more details about something • *Could you amplify that point?*

amplitude *NOUN* **1** (in science) the strength of a sound wave or electronic signal **2** largeness or abundance

amputate *VERB* **amputates, amputating, amputated** cut off an arm or leg by a surgical operation
▷ **amputation** *NOUN*

amuse *VERB* **amuses, amusing, amused** **1** make a person laugh or smile **2** make time pass pleasantly for someone
▷ **amusing** *ADJECTIVE*

amusement *NOUN* **amusements** **1** being amused **2** a way of passing time pleasantly

an *ADJECTIVE* SEE **a**

anachronism (an- ak- ron- izm) *NOUN* **anachronisms** something wrongly placed in a particular historical period, or regarded as out of date • *Bows and arrows would be an*

Thesaurus

berserk, go on the rampage, run riot, go out of control, go crazy

amoral *ADJECTIVE* *Guy was greedy, amoral, and obsessed with power.* ► unprincipled, loose, lax, unethical AN OPPOSITE IS moral.

amorous *ADJECTIVE* *Her employer had made amorous advances.* ► sexual, romantic, lustful, erotic, carnal, passionate, impassioned OPPOSITES ARE unloving, frigid

amount *NOUN* **1** *He wrote out a cheque for the whole amount.* ► quantity, sum, total, lot, whole **2** *The program needs a large amount of computer memory.* ► quantity, volume, bulk, lot, mass, expanse, extent, measure, supply

amount *VERB* **amount to** *The cost amounted to several thousands.* ► add up to, come to, total, aggregate, be equivalent to, equal, make

ample *ADJECTIVE* **1** *an ample supply of books and magazines* ► plentiful, abundant, copious, lavish, generous, liberal, rich AN OPPOSITE IS meagre **2** *ample space for several cars* ► enough, adequate, sufficient, plenty of OPPOSITES ARE inadequate, insufficient

amplify *VERB* **1** *A good acoustic will amplify the sound.* ► louden, magnify, boost, intensify, heighten, increase, make louder, raise the volume of AN OPPOSITE IS decrease **2** *The following notes amplify the position.* ► expand, enlarge on, elaborate on, develop, supplement, augment, add to, flesh out, broaden AN OPPOSITE IS condense

amuse *VERB* *Their comments amused him.* ► entertain, delight, divert, enliven, gladden, cheer up, make laugh, raise a smile, (*more informal*) tickle
amuse yourself *He amused himself by writing postcards.* ► occupy yourself, pass the time, engage yourself, interest yourself, immerse yourself (in)

amusement *NOUN* **1** *We read the article with amusement.* ► mirth, hilarity, delight, merriment, enjoyment, laughter **2** *A theme park with a wide range of amusements for all the family.* ► entertainment, activity, leisure activity, recreation, diversion, interest, delight, distraction, enjoyment, game, hobby, pastime, sport

amusing *ADJECTIVE* *an amusing story* ► entertaining, enjoyable, witty, funny, diverting, pleasing

A B C D E F G H I J K L M N O P Q R S T U V W X Y Z

anachronism in modern warfare. [from Greek *chronos* = time]

anaemia (a- nee- mee- a) NOUN a poor condition of the blood that makes a person pale
▷ **anaemic** ADJECTIVE

anaesthetic (an- iss- thet- ik) NOUN **anaesthetics** a substance or gas that makes you unable to feel pain
▷ **anaesthesia** NOUN

anaesthetist (an- ees- thet- ist) NOUN **anaesthetists** a person trained to give anaesthetics
▷ **anaesthetize** VERB

anagram NOUN **anagrams** a word or phrase made by rearranging the letters of another • *'Trap' is an anagram of 'part'.*

anal (ay- nal) ADJECTIVE to do with the anus

analogy (a- nal- oj- ee) NOUN **analogies** a comparison between things that are alike in some ways • *the analogy between the human heart and a pump*
▷ **analogous** ADJECTIVE

analyse VERB **analyses, analysing, analysed** **1** examine and interpret something • *The book analyses the causes of the war.* **2** separate something into its parts

analysis NOUN **analyses** **1** a separation of something into its parts **2** a detailed examination of something
▷ **analytic** ADJECTIVE **analytical** ADJECTIVE

anarchist (an- er- kist) NOUN **anarchists** a person who believes that all forms of government are bad and should be abolished

anarchy (an- er- kee) NOUN **1** lack of government or control, resulting in lawlessness **2** complete disorder

anatomy (an- at- om- ee) NOUN the study of the structure of the bodies of humans or animals
▷ **anatomical** ADJECTIVE **anatomist** NOUN

ancestor NOUN **ancestors** anyone from whom a person is descended
▷ **ancestral** ADJECTIVE **ancestry** NOUN

anchor NOUN **anchors** a heavy object joined to a ship by a chain or rope and dropped to the bottom of the sea to stop the ship from moving

anchor VERB **anchors, anchoring, anchored** **1** fix or be fixed by an anchor **2** fix something firmly

ancient ADJECTIVE **1** very old **2** belonging to the distant past • *ancient history*

and CONJUNCTION **1** together with; in addition to • *We had cakes and buns.* **2** so that; with this result • *Work hard and you will pass.* **3** to • *Go and buy a pen.*

android NOUN **androids** (in science fiction) a robot that looks like a human being

anecdote NOUN **anecdotes** a short amusing or interesting story about a real person or thing

angel NOUN **angels** **1** an attendant or messenger of God **2** a very kind or beautiful person

Thesaurus

analogy NOUN *There is an analogy between the human brain and a computer.* ► similarity, parallel, resemblance, comparison, likeness, correspondence, correlation

analyse VERB *You need to analyse your motives.* ► examine, evaluate, review, scrutinize, consider, study, interpret, investigate

analysis NOUN *an analysis of the unemployment figures* ► examination, breakdown, evaluation, study, scrutiny, research (into), enquiry (into), interpretation, investigation, test

analytical ADJECTIVE *an analytical approach to the problem* ► systematic, logical, methodical, rational, critical, rigorous, searching, inquiring, investigative, penetrating, questioning AN OPPOSITE IS unsystematic

anarchy NOUN *The country is threatened with anarchy.* ► lawlessness, disorder, bedlam, disorganization, insurrection, chaos, confusion, misgovernment, misrule, mutiny, pandemonium, riot

ancestor NOUN *We can trace our ancestors back to the Stuarts.* ► forebear, forefather, antecedent, predecessor, progenitor AN OPPOSITE IS descendant RELATED ADJECTIVE atavistic

ancestry NOUN *The family has a Spanish ancestry.* ► lineage, origin, pedigree, roots, stock, pedigree, parentage, ancestors, forebears

anchor VERB **1** *Several ships had anchored in the harbour.* ► berth, moor, tie up, make fast **2** *The lid was anchored to the sides with screws.* ► fasten, attach, fix

ancient ADJECTIVE **1** *the ancient buildings at Pompeii* ► old, historic, early, classical **2** *ancient civilizations* ► early, old, historic, prehistoric (= before the time of written records), archaic, bygone AN OPPOSITE IS modern

angel NOUN **1** *a depiction of angels with wings and beautiful faces* ► archangel, divine messenger, cherub, seraph **2** *She was an absolute angel during my illness.* ► dear, darling, treasure, gem, (*more informal*) brick

angelic ADJECTIVE **1** *angelic beings* ► heavenly, celestial, divine, ethereal **2** *an angelic expression* ► beautiful, lovely, heavenly, enchanting **3** *angelic behaviour* ► innocent, virtuous,

▷ **angelic** (an-jel-ik) ADJECTIVE
[from Greek *angelos* = messenger]

anger NOUN a strong feeling that you have towards someone who has done wrong or has done something you do not like

anger VERB **angers, angering, angered** make a person angry

angle NOUN **angles** **1** the space between two lines or surfaces that meet; the amount by which a line or surface must be turned to make it lie along another **2** a point of view

angle VERB **angles, angling, angled** **1** put something in a slanting position **2** present news etc. from one point of view

angler NOUN **anglers** a person who fishes with a fishing rod and line
▷ **angling** NOUN

Anglican ADJECTIVE to do with the Church of England
▷ **Anglican** NOUN

Anglo-Saxon NOUN **Anglo-Saxons** **1** an English person, especially of the time before the Norman conquest in 1066 **2** the form of English spoken from about 700 to 1150; Old English

angry ADJECTIVE **angrier, angriest** feeling anger
▷ **angrily** ADVERB

angular ADJECTIVE **1** having angles or sharp corners **2** (said about a person) bony, not plump

animal NOUN **animals** **1** a living thing that can feel and usually move about • *Horses, birds, fish, bees, and people are all animals.* **2** a cruel or uncivilized person

animate VERB **animates, animating, animated** make a thing lively
▷ **animation** NOUN

animated ADJECTIVE **1** lively and excited **2** (said about a film) made by photographing a series of still pictures and showing them rapidly one after another, so they appear to move

ankle NOUN **ankles** the part of the leg where it joins the foot

annihilate (an-I-il-ayt) VERB **annihilates, annihilating, annihilated** destroy something

Thesaurus

exemplary, pure, saintly, pious, unworldly
AN OPPOSITE IS devilish.

anger NOUN *Anger surged through him.*
► annoyance, irritation, crossness, exasperation, displeasure, fury, rage, indignation, temper, vexation, bitterness, hostility, outrage, resentment, passion, pique, (*more formal*) rancour, (*literary*) wrath, (*literary*) ire

anger VERB *Their rudeness angered all of us.*
► enrage, annoy, irritate, infuriate, exasperate, incense, vex, madden, aggravate, antagonize, displease, incite, inflame, make angry, (*more informal*) needle, (*more informal*) rile, (*more informal*) bug, (*more informal*) rub up the wrong way OPPOSITES ARE pacify, placate, appease

angle NOUN **1** *a cupboard built into the angle of the two walls* ► corner, intersection, recess **2** *We need to look at the problem from another angle.* ► perspective, point of view, standpoint, viewpoint, position, slant, approach, outlook

angry ADJECTIVE *John looked angry and started to shout. She gave us all an angry look.* ► annoyed, enraged, angered, cross, displeased, furious, irritated, irate, infuriated, incensed, indignant, outraged OPPOSITES ARE pleased, calm
become angry *Eventually the witch became angry.* ► lose your temper, go into a rage, fly into a rage, flare up, (*more informal*) see red, (*more informal*) fly off the handle, (*more informal*) hit the roof, (*more informal*) go off the deep end, (*very informal*) freak out, (*very informal*) go ballistic

anguish NOUN *a cry of anguish* ► agony, pain, distress, torment, torture, sorrow, suffering, anxiety, grief, misery, tribulation, heartache, (*literary*) woe

animal NOUN **1** *Like many animals they hibernate in winter.* ► living being, creature, beast, being, brute **2 animals** ► wildlife

animate VERB *A feeling of excitement animated the whole team.* ► invigorate, enliven, vitalize, revitalize, energize, stimulate, hearten, activate, revive, liven up, excite, encourage, exhilarate, fire, inspire, arouse, rejuvenate, galvanize, (*more informal*) buck up, (*more informal*) pep up, (*more informal*) give a buzz

animated ADJECTIVE *There was a sound of animated conversation in the next room.* ► lively, spirited, excited, enthusiastic, exuberant, heated, vivacious, high-spirited, passionate, impassioned OPPOSITES ARE lethargic, lifeless

animation NOUN *They arrived full of animation and determination.* ► liveliness, energy, vitality, spirit, enthusiasm, excitement, activity OPPOSITES ARE lethargy, inertia

animosity NOUN *There was a strong animosity between the two brothers.* ► hostility, ill-feeling, antagonism, enmity, acrimony, antipathy, rancour, bitterness, hate, hatred, loathing, venom OPPOSITES ARE goodwill, rapport, friendship

annihilate VERB *The army set about annihilating the whole population.* ► destroy, wipe out, eliminate, eradicate, exterminate, extinguish,

completely
▷ **annihilation** NOUN

anniversary NOUN **anniversaries** a day when you remember something special that happened on the same day in a previous year

announce VERB **announces, announcing, announced** make something known, especially by saying it publicly or to an audience
▷ **announcement** NOUN **announcer** NOUN

annoy VERB **annoys, annoying, annoyed** **1** make a person slightly angry **2** be troublesome to someone
▷ **annoyance** NOUN

annual ADJECTIVE **1** happening once a year • *her annual visit* **2** calculated over one year • *our annual income* **3** living for one year or one season • *an annual plant*
▷ **annually** ADVERB

annual NOUN **annuals** **1** a book that comes out once a year **2** an annual plant [from Latin *annus* = year]

anode NOUN **anodes** the electrode by which electric current enters a device COMPARE **cathode**

anoint VERB **anoints, anointing, anointed** put oil or ointment on something, especially in a religious ceremony

anon ADVERB (*old use*) soon • *I will say more about this anon.*

anon. ABBREVIATION anonymous

anonymous (an- on- im- us) ADJECTIVE without the name of the person responsible being known or made public • *an anonymous donor.*
▷ **anonymously** ADVERB **anonymity** (an- on- im- it- ee) NOUN

anorak NOUN **anoraks** a thick warm jacket with a hood [from an Inuit word]

anorexia (an- er- eks- ee- a) NOUN an illness that makes a person so anxious to lose weight that he or she refuses to eat
▷ **anorexic** ADJECTIVE

another ADJECTIVE, PRONOUN a different or extra person or thing • *another day* • *choose another*

answer NOUN **answers** **1** a reply **2** the solution to a problem

answer VERB **answers, answering, answered** **1** give or find an answer to; reply **2** respond to a signal • *Answer the telephone.*
answer back reply cheekily
answer for be responsible for
answer to correspond to • *This answers to the description of the stolen bag.*

ant NOUN **ants** a very small insect that lives as one of an organized group

Thesaurus

obliterate, slaughter, raze, abolish, erase, liquidate, (*more formal*) extirpate, (*more informal*) kill off

announce VERB **1** *The government will announce its plans next week.* ► make public, make known, declare, reveal, disclose, divulge, publish, publicize, broadcast, advertise OPPOSITES ARE conceal, suppress **2** *The presenter announced the next act.* ► introduce, present

announcement NOUN **1** *There will be an announcement from the Palace this afternoon.* ► statement, declaration, communiqué, pronouncement, proclamation, bulletin, dispatch **2** *We are still waiting for an announcement of the decision.* ► declaration, notification, intimation, disclosure

announcer NOUN *The announcer gave details of the programme changes.* ► presenter, anchorman, anchorwoman, newscaster, newsreader, broadcaster, commentator, compère, master of ceremonies

annoy VERB *The comments had clearly annoyed her.* ► irritate, displease, anger, infuriate, enrage, exasperate, incense, vex, madden, aggravate, nettle, antagonize, inflame, make angry, (*more informal*) needle, (*more informal*) rile, (*more informal*) bug, (*more informal*) rub up the wrong way OPPOSITES ARE please, gratify

annoyance NOUN **1** *Much to her annoyance, Mike had taken the car.* ► irritation, indignation, displeasure, exasperation, pique, chagrin, vexation **2** *The animals in the road proved quite an annoyance.* ► irritant, irritation, nuisance, bother, worry, (*more informal*) aggravation

annoyed ADJECTIVE *His mother was beginning to look annoyed.* ► irritated, angry, cross, displeased, vexed, peeved, infuriated, incensed, enraged, (*more informal*) miffed, (*more informal*) put out AN OPPOSITE IS pleased

annoying ADJECTIVE *His mouth curled into an annoying smile.* ► irritating, infuriating, exasperating, maddening, irksome, bothersome, tiresome OPPOSITES ARE pleasant, agreeable

anonymous ADJECTIVE **1** *The author was anonymous.* ► unnamed, nameless, incognito, unacknowledged, unidentified, unknown, unspecified, (*literary*) unsung **2** *an anonymous letter* ► unattributed, unsigned **3** *an anonymous way of writing* ► impersonal, nondescript, characterless, faceless, unremarkable

answer NOUN **1** *Our letter brought a quick answer.* ► reply, response, reaction, acknowledgement, riposte **2** *The answer to the question was far from clear.* ► solution, explanation **3** *Violence is no answer.* ► solution,

antagonism (an- tag- on- izm) *NOUN* an unfriendly feeling; hostility
▷ **antagonist** *NOUN* **antagonistic** *ADJECTIVE*

antagonize *VERB* **antagonizes, antagonizing, antagonized** make a person feel hostile or angry

antelope *NOUN* **antelope** *or* **antelopes** a fast-running animal like a deer, found in Africa and parts of Asia

antenatal (an- tee- nay- tal) *ADJECTIVE* before birth; during pregnancy

antenna *NOUN* **1** (**antennae**) a feeler on the head of an insect or crustacean **2** (**antennas**) an aerial

anthem *NOUN* **anthems** a religious or patriotic song, usually sung by a choir or group of people

anthology *NOUN* **anthologies** a collection of poems, stories, songs, etc. in one book [from Greek *anthos* = flower + *logia* = collection: early collections of poems were regarded as including the 'flowers', ie the most beautiful examples]

anthropoid *ADJECTIVE* like a human being • *Gorillas are anthropoid apes.*

anthropology *NOUN* the study of human beings and their customs
▷ **anthropological** *ADJECTIVE* **anthropologist** *NOUN*

antibiotic *NOUN* **antibiotics** a substance (e.g. penicillin) that destroys bacteria or prevents them from growing

antibody *NOUN* **antibodies** a protein that forms in the blood as a defence against certain substances which it then attacks and destroys

anticipate *VERB* **anticipates, anticipating, anticipated** **1** take action in advance about something you are aware of • *A good teacher learns to anticipate what students will ask.* **2** act before someone else does • *Others may have anticipated Columbus in discovering America.* **3** expect • *We anticipate that it will rain.*
▷ **anticipation** *NOUN* **anticipatory** *ADJECTIVE*
USAGE Many people regard use 3 as incorrect; it is better to avoid it and use 'expect'.

anticlimax *NOUN* **anticlimaxes** a disappointing ending or result where something exciting had been expected

anticlockwise *ADVERB, ADJECTIVE* moving in the direction opposite to clockwise

antics *PLURAL NOUN* funny or foolish actions

Thesaurus

remedy, way out **4** *his answer to the charge* ► defence, plea, vindication

answer *VERB* **1** *Please answer my question. Will nobody answer me?* ► reply to, respond to, acknowledge, give an answer to, react to **2** *'I'm not feeling well,' she answered.* ► rejoin, reply, respond, retort, return **3** *A good encyclopedia will answer your problem.* ► resolve, solve, explain **4** *The accused could answer all but one of the charges.* ► refute, rebut, defend yourself against **5** *We have enough money to answer our present needs.* ► satisfy, serve, fulfil, meet, correspond to, echo, fit, match up to, suffice, suit **6** *The police have arrested a man answering the description.* ► match, fit, correspond to, conform to
answer someone back *It was unwise to answer the teacher back in those days, however provoked you felt.* ► talk back to, be impertinent to, be cheeky to, contradict, (*more informal*) cheek

answerable *ADJECTIVE* *Ministers are answerable to Parliament.* ► responsible, accountable, subject

antagonism *NOUN* *She was pleased, despite her antagonism to him.* ► hostility, ill-feeling, animosity, enmity, acrimony, antipathy, rancour, bitterness, hate, hatred, loathing, venom OPPOSITES ARE goodwill, rapport, friendship

antagonistic *ADJECTIVE* *The march threatened to attract an antagonistic rival mob.* ► hostile, opposed, ill-disposed, antipathetic

antagonize *VERB* *They seem to be trying to antagonize us.* ► alienate, provoke, make an enemy of, offend, anger, annoy, embitter, estrange, irritate, upset OPPOSITES ARE pacify, placate

anthology *NOUN* *an anthology of short stories* ► collection, selection, treasury, compilation, compendium, miscellany, digest

anticipate *VERB* **1** *It was impossible to anticipate all the possible moves.* ► forestall, pre-empt, intercept, prevent **2** *I anticipate that the result will be a draw.* ► expect, foresee, predict, forecast, foretell, hope

anticlimax *NOUN* *After all the excitement, the journey proved to be rather an anticlimax.* ► let-down, comedown, disappointment

antics *PLURAL NOUN* *He was reminded of his childhood antics.* ► foolery, tricks, capers, buffoonery, tomfoolery, clowning, escapades, fooling, pranks, (*more informal*) larking about, (*more informal*) skylarking

antidote *NOUN* *The poison has no known antidote.* ► antitoxin, cure, remedy, neutralizing agent

antipathy *NOUN* *He expressed his antipathy to institutions of any kind.* ► hostility, ill-feeling, animosity, enmity, acrimony, antagonism, rancour, bitterness, hate, hatred, loathing, venom OPPOSITES ARE fondness, goodwill, liking

a b c d e f g h i j k l m n o p q r s t u v w x y z

A B C D E F G H I J K L M N O P Q R S T U V W X Y Z

anticyclone NOUN **anticyclones** an area where air pressure is high, usually producing fine settled weather

antidote NOUN **antidotes** something that acts against the effects of a poison or disease

antifreeze NOUN a liquid added to water to make it less likely to freeze

antihistamine NOUN **antihistamines** a drug that protects people against unpleasant effects when they are allergic to something

antimony NOUN a brittle silvery metal

antiquarian (an- ti- kwair- ee- an) ADJECTIVE to do with the study of antiques

antiquated ADJECTIVE old-fashioned

antique (an- teek) ADJECTIVE very old; belonging to the distant past

antique NOUN **antiques** something that is valuable because it is very old

antiquity (an- tik- wit- ee) NOUN ancient times

anti-Semitic (an- ti- sim- it- ik) ADJECTIVE hostile or prejudiced towards Jews
▷ **anti-Semitism** (an- ti- sem- it- izm) NOUN

antiseptic ADJECTIVE **1** able to destroy bacteria, especially those that cause things to become septic or to decay **2** thoroughly clean and free from germs

antiseptic NOUN **antiseptics** a substance with an antiseptic effect

antisocial ADJECTIVE unfriendly or inconsiderate towards other people

antler NOUN **antlers** the branching horn of a deer

anus (ay- nus) NOUN **anuses** the opening at the lower end of the alimentary canal, through which solid waste matter is passed out of the body

anvil NOUN **anvils** a large block of iron on which a blacksmith hammers metal into shape

anxious ADJECTIVE **1** worried **2** eager • *She is anxious to please us.*
▷ **anxiously** ADVERB **anxiety** NOUN

any ADJECTIVE, PRONOUN **1** one or some • *Have you any wool?* • *There isn't any.* **2** no matter which • *Come any day you like.* **3** every • *Any fool knows that!*

any ADVERB at all; in some degree • *Is that any better?*

anybody NOUN, PRONOUN any person

anyhow ADVERB **1** anyway **2** (*informal*) carelessly • *He does his work anyhow.*

anyone NOUN, PRONOUN anybody

anything NOUN, PRONOUN any thing

anyway ADVERB whatever happens; whatever the situation may be

anywhere ADVERB in or to any place

anywhere PRONOUN any place • *Anywhere will do.*

aorta (ay- or- ta) NOUN **aortas** the main artery that carries blood away from the left side of the heart

apart ADVERB **1** away from each other; separately • *Keep your desks apart.* **2** into pieces • *It fell apart.* **3** excluded • *Joking apart, what do you*

Thesaurus

antiquated ADJECTIVE *Their ideas seem antiquated these days. an antiquated typewriter* ► old-fashioned, out-dated, outmoded, out-of-date, obsolete, ancient, antediluvian, antique, archaic, dated, anachronistic, old, passé, (*more informal*) past it, (*more informal*) prehistoric, primitive, quaint, (*humorous*) superannuated, unfashionable OPPOSITES ARE up to date, modern, current, new

antique ADJECTIVE *Amanda has an eye for good antique furniture.* ► old, ancient, antiquarian, antiquated, historic, old-fashioned, traditional, veteran (car), vintage (car) OPPOSITES ARE modern, new

antique NOUN *a sale of antiques* ► collector's item, curio, curiosity, rarity

antiquity NOUN **1** *The place had been a harbour in antiquity.* ► ancient times, the ancient past, past times **2** *a site of great antiquity* ► age, oldness, elderliness

antisocial ADJECTIVE *Most people show some signs of antisocial behaviour.* ► asocial, unsociable, unacceptable, objectionable, undisciplined, offensive, disorderly, disruptive, obnoxious, uncooperative, unfriendly, troublesome, unruly, alienated, anarchic, disagreeable, nasty, rebellious, rude OPPOSITES ARE friendly, sociable

anxiety NOUN **1** *anxiety about money* ► concern, apprehension, unease, worry, disquiet, foreboding, nervousness, tension, distress, doubt, dread, fear, fretfulness, misgiving, qualm, scruple, strain, stress, uncertainty AN OPPOSITE IS calmness **2** *She showed a strong anxiety to please.* ► eagerness, enthusiasm, desire, keenness, impatience, willingness OPPOSITES ARE reluctance, unwillingness

anxious ADJECTIVE **1** *Anxious relatives were waiting for further news. Everyone is anxious about the next few weeks.* ► worried, concerned, nervous, apprehensive, fearful, uneasy, troubled, distressed, agitated, tense, restless AN OPPOSITE IS calm **2** *She always seems anxious to please.* ► eager, keen, enthusiastic, willing, impatient
be anxious *He was anxious about his work.* ► worry, fret

think of it?
apart from excluding, other than

apartheid (a- part- hayt) NOUN the political policy that used to be practised in South Africa, of keeping people of different races apart [Afrikaans, = being apart]

apartment NOUN **apartments** **1** a set of rooms **2** (*American*) a flat

apathy (ap- ath- ee) NOUN not being interested in something or caring much about it
▷ **apathetic** (ap- a- thet- ik) ADJECTIVE

ape NOUN **apes** any of the four kinds of monkey (gorillas, chimpanzees, orang-utans, and gibbons) that do not have a tail

ape VERB **apes, aping, aped** imitate or mimic

aperture NOUN **apertures** an opening

apex (ay- peks) NOUN **apexes** the tip or highest point

aplomb (a- plom) NOUN dignity and confidence • *She handled the press conference with aplomb.*

apologetic ADJECTIVE making an apology
▷ **apologetically** ADVERB

apologize VERB **apologizes, apologizing, apologized** make an apology

apology NOUN **apologies** **1** a statement saying that you are sorry for having done something wrong or badly **2** something very poor • *this feeble apology for a meal.*

apoplexy (ap- op- lek- see) NOUN **1** (*old use*) sudden loss of the ability to feel and move, caused by the blocking or breaking of a blood vessel in the brain **2** (*informal*) rage or anger
▷ **apoplectic** ADJECTIVE

Apostle NOUN **Apostles** any of the twelve men sent out by Christ to preach the Gospel

apostrophe (a- poss- trof- ee) NOUN **apostrophes** the punctuation mark ' used to show that letters have been missed out (as in *I can't* = I cannot) or to show possession (as in *the boy's book; the boys' books*)

appalling ADJECTIVE shocking; very unpleasant

apparatus NOUN the equipment for a particular experiment or job etc.

apparent ADJECTIVE **1** clear or obvious • *His embarrassment was apparent to everyone.* **2** seeming; appearing to be true but not really so • *I could not understand her apparent indifference.*
▷ **apparently** ADVERB

apparition NOUN **apparitions** **1** a ghost **2** something strange or surprising that appears

Thesaurus

apart ADVERB *Their parents are now living apart.*
► separately, independently, on your own
apart from *Everyone came apart from him.*
► except (for), but for, aside from, besides, excepting, excluding

apathetic ADJECTIVE *They seem apathetic about the whole idea.* ► uninterested (in), indifferent (to), unconcerned, unenthusiastic, uncommitted, unfeeling, uninvolved, unmotivated (by)
OPPOSITES ARE enthusiastic, eager, keen (on)

apathy NOUN *At the general election the voters showed more than usual apathy.* ► indifference, coolness, lack of interest, unconcern, lassitude, lethargy, listlessness, passivity, inertia, inactivity AN OPPOSITE IS enthusiasm

aperture NOUN *There was a strange window-like aperture in one wall.* ► opening, hole, gap, slit, vent, fissure, (*technical*) orifice

apologetic ADJECTIVE *They don't sound too apologetic considering it was their fault.*
► regretful, repentant, sorry, contrite, penitent, remorseful, rueful OPPOSITES ARE unrepentant, defiant

apologize VERB *He apologized for his mistake.*
► say sorry, express regret, ask for forgiveness, be penitent, make an apology, repent

apology NOUN *We all owe you an apology.*
► expression of regret, acknowledgement, confession, explanation, justification, defence, excuse, plea

appal VERB *The level of violence appals most people.*
► horrify, shock, alarm, outrage, dismay, scandalize, repel, offend, disgust, sicken, revolt

appalling ADJECTIVE **1** *Their attitude was appalling in its callousness.* ► horrifying, horrific, shocking, outrageous, revolting, repellent, repulsive, terrifying, terrible, dreadful, awful, unnerving, sickening, nauseating, horrible **2** *an appalling piece of work* ► dreadful, awful, terrible, atrocious, abysmal

apparatus NOUN **1** *an apparatus for processing sea water* ► device, appliance, gadget, instrument, machine, mechanism, system, tool, (*usually disapproving*) contraption, (*more informal*) set-up **2** *Laboratory apparatus can be extremely expensive.* ► equipment, implements, materials, machinery, (*more informal*) tackle, (*more informal*) gear

apparent ADJECTIVE *There was no apparent motive for the crime. A sense of relief was all too apparent.*
► evident, discernible, ostensible, perceptible, recognizable, noticeable, observable, obvious, clear, manifest, conspicuous, detectable, overt, patent, visible, self-explanatory
OPPOSITES ARE obscure, hidden, concealed

appeal *VERB* **appeals, appealing, appealed** **1** ask for something earnestly or formally • *They appealed for funds.* **2** ask for a decision to be changed • *He appealed against the prison sentence.* **3** seem attractive or interesting • *Cricket doesn't appeal to me.*

appeal *NOUN* **appeals** **1** asking for something you badly need **2** asking for a decision to be changed **3** attraction or interest

appear *VERB* **appears, appearing, appeared** **1** come into sight **2** seem **3** take part in a play, film, or show etc.

appearance *NOUN* **appearances** **1** appearing **2** what somebody looks like; what something appears to be

appease *VERB* **appeases, appeasing, appeased** calm or pacify someone, especially by giving in to demands
▷ **appeasement** *NOUN*

appendage *NOUN* **appendages** something added or attached; a thing that forms a natural part of something larger

appendicitis *NOUN* inflammation of the appendix

appendix *NOUN* **1** (**appendixes**) a small tube leading off from the intestine **2** (**appendices**) a section added at the end of a book

appetite *NOUN* **appetites** **1** desire for food **2** an enthusiasm for something • *an appetite for violent films*

appetizing *ADJECTIVE* (said about food) looking and smelling good to eat

applaud *VERB* **applauds, applauding, applauded** show that you like something, especially by clapping your hands

applause *NOUN* clapping

apple *NOUN* **apples** a round fruit with a red, yellow, or green skin

appliance *NOUN* **appliances** a device or piece of equipment • *electrical appliances*

applicable (ap- lik- a- bul) *ADJECTIVE* able to be applied; suitable or relevant

Thesaurus

apparently *ADVERB* *Apparently satisfied, the man leaned back.* ► seemingly, evidently, ostensibly

appeal *NOUN* **1** *The radio station broadcast an appeal for calm.* ► call, request, cry, entreaty, petition, supplication, prayer **2** *Packaging is an important part of a product's appeal.* ► attraction, attractiveness, charm, allure, charisma, seductiveness, (*more informal*) pull

appeal *VERB* **1 appeal for** *Detectives are appealing for information about the incident.* ► call for, cry out for, beg for, plead for, ask earnestly for, request, solicit **2 appeal to** *Hoskins said that at first the film role didn't appeal to him.* ► attract, interest, please, entice, tempt

appealing *ADJECTIVE* *The prospect of a whole day with Jemima was rather appealing.* ► attractive, agreeable, engaging, captivating, charming, delightful, lovely, enchanting OPPOSITES ARE unappealing, disagreeable

appear *VERB* **1** *A large building appeared in the distance.* ► come into view, come into sight, be seen, arise, loom up OPPOSITES ARE disappear, vanish **2** *By lunch time the twins still hadn't appeared.* ► arrive, come, make an appearance, put in an appearance, (*more informal*) show your face, (*more informal*) show up, (*more informal*) turn up **3** *A few problems have appeared since we last met.* ► emerge, arise, develop, come to light, materialize, occur, (*more informal*) crop up, (*more informal*) turn up **4** *The road did not appear to lead anywhere.* ► seem, look, turn out **5** *Jake's sister was appearing in the school play for the first time.* ► perform, take part, act

appearance *NOUN* **1** *His scruffy appearance took us by surprise.* ► look, looks, aspect, bearing, demeanour, impression **2** *an appearance of friendliness* ► semblance, air, pretence, illusion, facade, guise, veneer

appetite *NOUN* **1** *A long walk will sharpen our appetites.* ► hunger, need for food, taste buds **2** *Her appetite for information was phenomenal.* ► craving, longing, yearning, eagerness, hankering (after), desire, passion, thirst, relish, zest, demand

appetizing *ADJECTIVE* *The woman brought in a large appetizing meal.* ► tasty, delicious, inviting, palatable, (*more informal*) mouth-watering

applaud *VERB* **1** *The audience applauded loudly.* ► clap, cheer, give an ovation, acclaim, show your approval, (*more informal*) bring the house down OPPOSITES ARE boo, hiss **2** *They were watching and applauding the youngsters' efforts.* ► acclaim, commend, praise, salute, congratulate, compliment, eulogize, extol, (*more formal*) laud AN OPPOSITE IS criticize

applause *NOUN* **1** *There was a great round of applause when the dance ended.* ► clapping, cheering, acclamation, (an) ovation, plaudits, approval **2** *The author wins universal applause from his followers.* ► praise, acclaim, approval, acclamation, plaudits, accolades, admiration

appliance *NOUN* **1** *There's no reason why you shouldn't use individual heating appliances.* ► device, apparatus, gadget, instrument, machine, mechanism, system, tool, (*usually disapproving*) contraption, (*more informal*) setup

applicant *NOUN* **applicants** a person who applies for a job or position

application *NOUN* **applications** **1** the action of applying **2** a formal request **3** the ability to apply yourself **4** (in computing) a program or piece of software designed for a particular purpose

applied *ADJECTIVE* put to practical use • *applied maths*

apply *VERB* **applies, applying, applied** **1** put one thing on another **2** start using something **3** concern; be relevant • *This rule does not apply to you.* **4** make a formal request • *apply for a job*
apply yourself give all your attention to a job; work diligently

appoint *VERB* **appoints, appointing, appointed** **1** choose a person for a job **2** arrange something officially • *They appointed a time for the meeting.*

appointment *NOUN* **appointments** **1** an arrangement to meet or visit somebody at a particular time **2** choosing somebody for a job **3** a job or position

apposition *NOUN* placing things together, especially nouns and phrases in a grammatical relationship In *the reign of Elizabeth, our Queen,* 'our Queen' is in apposition to 'Elizabeth'

appreciable *ADJECTIVE* enough to be noticed or felt; perceptible
▷ **appreciably** *ADVERB*

appreciate *VERB* **appreciates, appreciating, appreciated** **1** enjoy or value something **2** understand **3** increase in value
▷ **appreciation** *NOUN* **appreciative** *ADJECTIVE*

apprehend *VERB* **apprehends, apprehending, apprehended** **1** seize or arrest someone **2** understand

apprehension *NOUN* **1** fear or worry **2** understanding **3** the arrest of a person

apprehensive *ADJECTIVE* anxious or worried

Thesaurus

applicant *NOUN The best applicant was a female graduate with fresh ideas.* ► candidate, contender, interviewee, competitor, entrant, participant, aspirant

application *NOUN* **1** *an application for a grant* ► request, appeal, claim **2** *the application of new solutions to old problems* ► implementation, employment, use, exercise

apply *VERB* **1** *Apply antiseptic cream to the cut.* ► administer, bring into contact, lay on, put on, spread **2** *Contestants will need to apply all their skill and experience.* ► employ, exercise, use, utilize, bring into use, implement, practise **3 apply for** *More than a hundred people have applied for the job.* ► put in an application for, seek, request, (*more informal*) put in for **4 apply to** *The rules only apply to England and Wales.* ► be relevant to, pertain to, refer to, relate to, appertain to, concern, affect, involve **apply yourself** ► concentrate, exert yourself, be diligent, be assiduous, be industrious, work hard, make an effort, persevere, (*more informal*) buckle down

appoint *VERB Amanda had been appointed store manager.* ► name, nominate, designate, choose (to be), engage (as), take on (as), install (as)

appointment *NOUN* **1** *June had to rush to keep her five o'clock appointment.* ► engagement, assignation, arrangement, consultation, session, date, fixture, meeting, rendezvous, (*in poetry*) tryst **2** *the appointment of new members of staff* ► nomination, selection, choice, choosing, commissioning, election, naming **3** *Frank held an appointment at the University.* ► position, post, job, situation, office, place

appraisal *NOUN The article is an honest appraisal of the problems.* ► assessment, evaluation, estimation, valuation, review, rating, consideration, appreciation

appraise *VERB They stood back to appraise the work they had done.* ► assess, evaluate, estimate, review, consider, (*more informal*) size up

appreciable *ADJECTIVE an appreciable sum of money* ► considerable, substantial, significant, sizeable, large, (*more informal*) tidy

appreciate *VERB* **1** *I'd appreciate any help you can give me.* ► be grateful for, value, welcome, prize, regard highly, esteem OPPOSITES ARE think little of, despise, disparage **2** *We appreciate good music.* ► enjoy, value, cherish, respect, treasure, like, think highly of OPPOSITES ARE despise, dislike **3** *I appreciate that you cannot stay long.* ► recognize, realize, understand, acknowledge, comprehend, know, apprehend, see OPPOSITES ARE be unaware of, disregard **4** *Most properties in the area have appreciated in value.* ► increase, gain, rise, go up, grow, improve, build up, escalate, mount, soar, strengthen OPPOSITES ARE depreciate, decrease, fall, go down, weaken

appreciation *NOUN* **1** *They showed their appreciation by taking us out to dinner.* ► gratitude, indebtedness, thanks, obligation, thankfulness **2** *an appreciation of good literature* ► enjoyment, understanding

apprehensive *ADJECTIVE Polly was apprehensive about going back up on deck.* ► anxious, worried, concerned, nervous, fearful, uneasy, troubled, distressed, agitated, tense, restless

apprentice *NOUN* **apprentices** a person who is learning a trade or craft by a legal agreement with an employer
▷ **apprenticeship** *NOUN*

apprentice *VERB* **apprentices, apprenticing, apprenticed** place a person as an apprentice

approach *VERB* **approaches, approaching, approached** **1** come near **2** go to someone with a request or offer • *They approached me for help.* **3** set about doing something or tackling a problem

approach *NOUN* **approaches** **1** approaching **2** a way or road

appropriate (a- proh- pree- at) *ADJECTIVE* suitable
▷ **appropriately** *ADVERB*

appropriate (a- proh- pree- ayt) *VERB* **appropriates, appropriating, appropriated** take something and use it as your own
▷ **appropriation** *NOUN*

approval *NOUN* approving somebody or something
on approval received by a customer to examine before deciding to buy

approve *VERB* **approves, approving, approved** **1** say or think that a person or thing is good or suitable **2** agree formally to something • *The committee has approved the expenditure.*

approximate (a- proks- im- at) *ADJECTIVE* almost exact or correct but not completely so
▷ **approximately** *ADVERB*

approximate (a- proks- im- ayt) *VERB* **approximates, approximating, approximated** make or be almost the same as something

apricot *NOUN* **apricots** a juicy orange-coloured fruit with a stone in it [from Spanish or Portuguese]

April *NOUN* the fourth month of the year [from Latin *Aprilis*]

Thesaurus

approach *NOUN* **1** *Flowers in the park announced the approach of spring.* ► arrival, coming, advance, appearance, nearing, imminence, advent OPPOSITES ARE retreat, departure **2** *The most beautiful approach to the city is from the south.* ► access, passage, road, way in, entry, entrance, drive **3** *His approach was to try out new ideas on other people.* ► method, procedure, technique, way, system, course, manner, means, style, mode **4** *We need an international approach to problems such as global warming.* ► attitude, perspective, policy (for, regarding), outlook (on), point of view (on), viewpoint (on) **5** *I made an informal approach to the bank manager.* ► appeal, application, invitation, offer, overture, proposal, proposition

approach *VERB* **1** *A grinning dark-haired youth approached them, holding out his hand.* ► move towards, proceed towards, come towards, go towards, come near, draw near, advance on, bear down on, near **2** *The committee approached its task with determination.* ► set about, tackle, embark on, make a start on, begin, undertake, get down to **3** *Should we approach the bank manager about a loan?* ► contact , speak to, sound out, appeal to **4** *The likely cost was now approaching several millions.* ► border on, get near, get close to, verge on, approximate, (*more informal*) get on for

approachable *ADJECTIVE* *She looked younger and more approachable.* ► friendly, welcoming, well-disposed, congenial, cordial, agreeable, pleasant, obliging, communicative, accessible, affable, informal, kind, open, sociable, sympathetic, (*more informal*) unstuffy, (*more informal*) matey OPPOSITES ARE aloof, formal

appropriate *ADJECTIVE* **1** *This isn't an appropriate time to ask questions.* ► suitable, fitting, proper, apt **2** *The form should be completed with any appropriate comments.* ► relevant, apposite, pertinent, applicable, germane OPPOSITES ARE inappropriate, irrelevant

approval *NOUN* **1** *Jane looked at them with approval.* ► favour, approbation, admiration, support, appreciation, commendation, acclaim, acclamation, applause, respect, regard, esteem, liking OPPOSITES ARE disapproval, disfavour **2** *Congress had given final approval to the bill in October.* ► consent, assent, support, agreement, endorsement, acceptance, authorization, acquiescence, (*more informal*) blessing, (*more informal*) (the) go-ahead, (*more informal*) (the) green light, (*more informal*) OK, (*more informal*) thumbs up OPPOSITES ARE refusal, veto

approve *VERB* **1** *Some members are thought to have approved the plan.* ► support, accept, agree to, assent to, consent to, acquiesce in, accede to, endorse, back, subscribe to, authorize OPPOSITES ARE refuse, veto
2 approve of *Some parents and teachers still do not approve of the use of calculators.* ► welcome, favour, endorse, advocate, support, hold with, countenance, tolerate, recommend, (*more informal*) go along with OPPOSITES ARE disapprove of, condemn, reject

approximate *ADJECTIVE* *All measurements are approximate.* ► rough, estimated, close, inexact, near AN OPPOSITE IS exact

approximately *ADVERB* *Homework should last approximately an hour.* ► roughly, about, round about, around, more or less, nearly, in

apron NOUN **aprons** **1** a piece of clothing worn over the front of the body, especially to protect other clothes **2** a hard-surfaced area on an airfield where aircraft are loaded and unloaded

apt ADJECTIVE **1** likely • *He is apt to be careless.* **2** suitable • *an apt quotation*
▷ **aptly** ADVERB **aptness** NOUN

aptitude NOUN a talent or skill • *an aptitude for languages*

aquarium NOUN **aquariums** a tank or building in which live fish and other water animals are displayed

aquatic ADJECTIVE to do with water • *aquatic sports*

aqueduct NOUN **aqueducts** a bridge carrying a water channel across low ground or a valley

Arab NOUN **Arabs** a member of a Semitic people living in parts of the Middle East and North Africa
▷ **Arabian** ADJECTIVE

Arabic ADJECTIVE to do with the Arabs or their language

Arabic NOUN the language of the Arabs

arabic numerals PLURAL NOUN the symbols 1, 2, 3, 4, etc. COMPARE **Roman numerals**

arable ADJECTIVE suitable for ploughing or growing crops on • *arable land*

arbitrary (ar- bit- rer- ee) ADJECTIVE chosen or done on an impulse, not according to a rule or law • *an arbitrary decision.*
▷ **arbitrarily** ADVERB

arbitration NOUN settling a dispute by calling in someone from outside to make a decision
▷ **arbitrate** VERB **arbitrator** NOUN

arbour (ar- ber) NOUN **arbours** a shady place among trees

arc NOUN **arcs** **1** a curve; part of the circumference of a circle **2** a luminous electric current passing between two electrodes

arcade NOUN **arcades** a covered passage or area, especially for shopping

arch[1] NOUN **arches** **1** a curved structure that helps to support a bridge or other building etc. **2** something shaped like this

arch VERB **arches, arching, arched** form something into an arch; curve • *The cat arched its back and hissed.*

arch[2] ADJECTIVE pretending to be playful; mischievous • *an arch smile*
▷ **archly** ADVERB

archaeology (ar- kee- ol- oj- ee) NOUN the study of ancient civilizations by digging for the remains of their buildings, tools, coins, etc. and examining them
▷ **archaeological** ADJECTIVE **archaeologist** NOUN

archaic (ar- kay- ik) ADJECTIVE belonging to former or ancient times

archangel NOUN **archangels** an angel of the highest rank

archbishop NOUN **archbishops** the chief bishop of a region

arch-enemy NOUN **arch-enemies** the chief enemy

archer NOUN **archers** a person who shoots with a bow and arrows

archery NOUN the sport of shooting at a target with a bow and arrows

archetype (ark- i- typ) NOUN **archetypes** the original form or model from which others are copied

archipelago (ark- i- pel- ag- oh) NOUN **archipelagos** a large group of islands, or the sea containing these

Thesaurus

the region of, in the order of, approaching, (*more informal*) something like, (*more informal*) ... or so, (*more informal*) ... or thereabouts, (*much more informal*) pushing, (*literary*) nigh on

apt ADJECTIVE **1** *He tried to think of an apt reply.* ▸ appropriate , suitable, fitting, proper **2** *The old man is apt to fall asleep in the evening.* ▸ inclined, liable, prone, likely

aptitude NOUN *an aptitude for dancing* ▸ talent, gift, flair, ability, genius, faculty, capacity

arbitrary ADJECTIVE **1** *Decisions can appear arbitrary without all the information.* ▸ random, irrational, indiscriminate, capricious, unreasonable, unpredictable, whimsical, wilful, casual, chance, fanciful, illogical, subjective OPPOSITES ARE methodical, rational **2** *the exercise of arbitrary power* ▸ autocratic, despotic, dictatorial, absolute, unrestrained, high-handed, oppressive, repressive, imperious, summary, tyrannical, tyrannous

arbitrate VERB *The ambassador offered to arbitrate in the dispute.* ▸ adjudicate, judge, intercede, mediate, negotiate, pass judgement, referee, umpire, settle, make peace, decide the outcome

arbitration NOUN *The county court will automatically refer the matter to arbitration.* ▸ mediation, negotiation, conciliation, adjudication, judgement, settlement

archaic ADJECTIVE **1** *archaic Greek sculpture* ▸ ancient, old, primitive **2** *He arrived in a top hat and morning coat, already a somewhat archaic form of working dress.* ▸ old-fashioned, antiquated, outmoded, obsolete

architect (ark- i- tekt) *NOUN* **architects** a person who designs buildings [from Greek *arch-* = chief + Greek *tekton* = builder]

architecture *NOUN* **1** the process of designing buildings **2** a particular style of building • *Elizabethan architecture.*
▷ **architectural** *ADJECTIVE*

archives (ark- I'vz) *PLURAL NOUN* the historical documents etc. of an organization or community

archway *NOUN* **archways** an arched passage or entrance

arc lamp or **arc light** *NOUN* **arc lamps** or **arc lights** a light using an electric arc

arctic *ADJECTIVE* very cold • *The weather was arctic.*

ardour (ar- der) *NOUN* enthusiasm or passion

arduous *ADJECTIVE* needing much effort; laborious
▷ **arduously** *ADVERB*

area *NOUN* **areas** **1** the measurement of a surface, or the amount of space a surface covers • *The area of the room is 20 square metres.* **2** a particular region or piece of land **3** a subject or activity

arena (a- reen- a) *NOUN* **arenas** the level area in the centre of an amphitheatre or sports stadium [from Latin, = sand: the floors of Roman arenas were covered with sand to soak up the blood that was spilt in fighting between gladiators]

aren't (*mainly spoken*) are not
aren't I? (*informal*) am I not?

arguable *ADJECTIVE* possible but not certain
▷ **arguably** *ADVERB*

argue *VERB* **argues, arguing, argued** **1** say that you disagree; exchange angry comments **2** state that something is true and give reasons

argument *NOUN* **arguments** **1** a disagreement or quarrel **2** a reason or series of reasons put forward

argumentative *ADJECTIVE* fond of arguing

aria (ar- ee- a) *NOUN* **arias** a solo in an opera or oratorio

arid *ADJECTIVE* dry and barren

arise *VERB* **arises, arising, arose, arisen** **1** come into existence; come to people's notice • *Problems arose.* **2** (*old use*) rise; stand up • *Arise, Sir Francis.*

aristocracy (a- ris- tok- ra- see) *NOUN* people of the highest social rank; members of the nobility

Thesaurus

architect *NOUN* *Ictinus, architect of the Parthenon*
► builder, master builder, designer, planner

ardent *ADJECTIVE* *ardent admirers of good music*
► passionate, avid, fervent, zealous, eager, keen, enthusiastic

arduous *ADJECTIVE* *an arduous journey over the hills* ► exhausting, tiring, punishing, onerous, demanding, daunting, rigorous, tough
OPPOSITES ARE easy, effortless

area *NOUN* **1** *They came to an open area of land.*
► expanse, extent, stretch, patch, tract, sector, sheet, space, surface, width, breadth
2 *More money is needed for deprived urban areas.*
► district, region, sector, locality, neighbourhood, precinct, vicinity, zone, environment, environs, province, territory **3** *an area of study* ► field, domain, sphere, subject

arguable *ADJECTIVE* *It is arguable that the official figures exaggerate the unemployment problem.*
► possible, conceivable, tenable, credible, defensible

argue *VERB* **1** *The children do seem to argue a lot.*
► quarrel, squabble, wrangle, bicker, row
2 *The group argued late into the night.*
► deliberate, discuss, debate, dispute **3** *Some people argue that all ownership is theft.*
► contend, maintain, postulate, assert, claim, submit, suggest, reason, insist, show, demonstrate, prove

argument *NOUN* **1** *A fierce argument followed.*
► quarrel, disagreement, squabble, row, wrangle, altercation, difference, dispute, dissension, clash, controversy, feud, fight, remonstration, expostulation, (*more informal*) set-to **2** *a long argument about politics*
► discussion, debate, consultation, deliberation **3** *No convincing argument has been offered.* ► case, line of reasoning, demonstration, hypothesis, defence, gist, idea, summary, synopsis, view **4** *the principal argument of the book* ► thesis, contention, theme, topic, plot

argumentative *ADJECTIVE* *He could be difficult and argumentative at times.* ► quarrelsome, combative, contentious, disputatious, truculent, aggressive

arid *ADJECTIVE* *an arid landscape* ► barren, parched, desert, dry, waste, waterless, infertile, lifeless, sterile, torrid, unproductive
OPPOSITES ARE fertile, lush

arise *VERB* **1** *If any problems arise go and see your doctor.* ► emerge, develop, appear, come to light, materialize, occur, (*more informal*) crop up, (*more informal*) turn up **2** *The misunderstanding arose from poor communications.* ► result, originate, stem, derive, spring, follow, ensue, proceed

aristocrat (a- ris- tok- rat) *NOUN* **aristocrats** a member of the aristocracy
▷ **aristocratic** *ADJECTIVE*

arithmetic *NOUN* the science or study of numbers; calculating with numbers
▷ **arithmetical** *ADJECTIVE*

ark *NOUN* **arks** **1** (in the Bible) the ship in which Noah and his family escaped the Flood **2** a wooden box in which the writings of the Jewish Law were kept

arm[1] *NOUN* **arms** **1** either of the two upper limbs of the body, between the shoulder and the hand **2** a sleeve **3** something shaped like an arm or jutting out from a main part **4** the raised side part of a chair
▷ **armful** *NOUN*

arm[2] *VERB* **arms, arming, armed** **1** supply someone with weapons **2** prepare for war

armada (ar- mah- da) *NOUN* **armadas** a fleet of warships
the Armada or **Spanish Armada** the warships sent by Spain to invade England in 1588

armadillo *NOUN* **armadillos** a small burrowing South American animal whose body is covered with a shell of bony plates

armature *NOUN* **armatures** the current-carrying part of a dynamo or electric motor

armchair *NOUN* **armchairs** a chair with arms

armed forces or **armed services** *PLURAL NOUN* a country's army, navy, and air force

armistice *NOUN* **armistices** an agreement to stop fighting in a war or battle

armour *NOUN* **1** a protective covering for the body, formerly worn in fighting **2** a metal covering on a warship, tank, or car to protect it from missiles
▷ **armoured** *ADJECTIVE*

armpit *NOUN* **armpits** the hollow underneath the top of the arm, below the shoulder

arms *PLURAL NOUN* **1** weapons **2** a coat of arms
up in arms protesting vigorously

arms race *NOUN* competition between nations in building up supplies of weapons, especially nuclear weapons

army *NOUN* **armies** **1** a large number of people trained to fight on land **2** a large group

aroma (a- roh- ma) *NOUN* **aromas** a smell, especially a pleasant one
▷ **aromatic** (a- ro- mat- ik) *ADJECTIVE*

around *ADVERB, PREPOSITION* all round; about

arouse *VERB* **arouses, arousing, aroused** **1** stir up a feeling in someone • *You've aroused my curiosity.* **2** wake someone up

arpeggio (ar- pej- ee- oh) *NOUN* **arpeggios** the notes of a musical chord played one after the other instead of together

arrange *VERB* **arranges, arranging, arranged** **1** put things into a certain order; adjust **2** form plans for something • *We arranged to be there.* **3** prepare music for a particular purpose
▷ **arrangement** *NOUN*

array *NOUN* **arrays** **1** a display **2** an orderly arrangement

Thesaurus

aristocrat *NOUN* *an aristocrat from an old family* ► noble, nobleman, noblewoman, lord, lady, peer, peeress, patrician, grandee, titled person, (*more informal*) toff, (*more informal*) nob

aristocratic *ADJECTIVE* *a member of an aristocratic family* ► noble, upper-class, high-born, titled, patrician, blue-blooded, lordly, princely, royal, courtly, élite, thoroughbred

arm *VERB* *The woman had gone downstairs, armed with an empty bottle.* ► equip, provide, protect, supply, fortify, furnish

army *NOUN* **1** *The king raised an army of ten thousand foot soldiers.* ► armed force, fighting force, force, militia, horde RELATED ADJECTIVE military **2** *an army of tourists* ► crowd, swarm, throng, horde, stream, mass, herd, host, multitude

aroma *NOUN* *an aroma of fresh coffee* ► smell, fragrance, odour, bouquet, perfume, scent, whiff

arouse *VERB* *The proposals aroused strong public hostility.* ► rouse, cause, kindle, prompt, provoke, instigate, spark off, stimulate, stir up, (*more informal*) whip up AN OPPOSITE IS allay

arrange *VERB* **1** *It was time to arrange the seating for dinner.* ► organize, set out, lay out, sort out, put in order, plan, fix, order, spread out, dispose **2** *We hope to arrange an outing for next week.* ► organize, fix, fix up, plan, set up, make arrangements for, devise, schedule, contrive, coordinate, manage, prepare, see to, settle **3** *Ravel arranged the music for an orchestra.* ► adapt, score, set, harmonize, orchestrate

arrangement *NOUN* **1** *They've changed the arrangement of the furniture.* ► positioning, layout, placing, planning, spacing, disposition, distribution, organization, setting out, alignment, display, grouping, design **2** *an arrangement to share the costs* ► agreement, understanding, settlement, compact, contract, deal, pact, scheme, terms **3** *a musical arrangement* ► adaptation, setting, harmonization, orchestration, version

array *NOUN* *a gleaming array of vintage cars* ► arrangement, display, presentation, show, exhibition, parade, collection, muster, (*more informal*) line-up

arrears *PLURAL NOUN* **1** money that is owing and ought to have been paid earlier **2** a backlog of work etc.
in arrears behind with payments

arrest *VERB* **arrests, arresting, arrested** **1** seize a person by authority of the law **2** stop a process or movement

arrest *NOUN* **arrests** **1** arresting somebody • *The police made several arrests.* **2** stopping something

arrive *VERB* **arrives, arriving, arrived** **1** reach the end of a journey or a point on it **2** come • *The great day arrived.*
▷ **arrival** *NOUN*

arrogant *ADJECTIVE* behaving in an unpleasantly proud way because you think you are superior to other people
▷ **arrogantly** *ADVERB* **arrogance** *NOUN*

arrow *NOUN* **arrows** **1** a pointed stick to be shot from a bow **2** a sign with an outward-pointing V at the end, used to show direction or position
▷ **arrowhead** *NOUN*
[from Old Norse]

arsenic *NOUN* a very poisonous metallic substance

arson *NOUN* the crime of deliberately setting fire to a house or building
▷ **arsonist** *NOUN*

art *NOUN* **arts** **1** producing something beautiful, especially by painting or drawing; things produced in this way **2** a skill • *the art of sailing*

artefact *NOUN* **artefacts** an object made by humans, especially one from the past that is studied by archaeologists

artery *NOUN* **arteries** **1** one of the tubes that carry blood away from the heart to all parts of the body COMPARE **vein** **2** an important road or route
▷ **arterial** (ar- teer- ee- al) *ADJECTIVE*

artesian well *NOUN* **artesian wells** a well that is bored straight down into a place where water will rise easily to the surface

artful *ADJECTIVE* crafty
▷ **artfully** *ADVERB*

arthritis (arth- ry- tiss) *NOUN* a disease that makes joints in the body stiff and painful
▷ **arthritic** (arth- rit- ik) *ADJECTIVE*

arthropod *NOUN* **arthropods** an animal of the group that includes insects, spiders, crabs, and centipedes

artichoke *NOUN* **artichokes** a kind of plant with a flower head used as a vegetable [from Arabic]

article *NOUN* **articles** **1** a piece of writing published in a newspaper or magazine **2** an object
definite article the word 'the'
indefinite article the word 'a' or 'an'

articulate (ar- tik- yoo- lat) *ADJECTIVE* able to express things clearly and fluently

articulate (ar- tik- yoo- layt) *VERB* **articulates, articulating, articulated** **1** say or speak clearly **2** connect by a joint
▷ **articulation** *NOUN*

Thesaurus

arrest *VERB* **1** *Police arrested him for shoplifting.* ► apprehend, detain, take into custody, take in, (*more informal*) book, (*more informal*) pull in, (*more informal*) pick up, (*more informal*) nick, (*more informal*) nab **2** *Recent measures have arrested the spread of disease.* ► check, stop, end, halt, prevent, retard, slow, stem, impede, slow down, block, inhibit, interrupt, delay, hinder, obstruct

arrival *NOUN* **1** *A crowd awaited the Queen's arrival.* ► coming, appearance, approach, entrance, homecoming, landing, return, touchdown **2** *Pretty girls greeted the new arrivals.* ► comer, caller, newcomer, visitor

arrive *VERB* **1** *Guests started to arrive at around six o'clock.* ► come, come along, appear, enter, present yourself, (*more informal*) turn up, (*more informal*) roll up, (*more informal*) show up **2** (*informal*) *When they got the invitation they knew they had arrived.* ► succeed, be successful, reach the top, break through, (*more informal*) make it **3 arrive at** *We arrived at the bus station.* ► reach, come to, get to, (*more informal*) make

arrogance *NOUN* *His arrogance took her breath away.* ► haughtiness, conceit, self-importance, high-handedness, condescension, disdain, insolence

arrogant *ADJECTIVE* *He was proud, and had an arrogant manner.* ► haughty, conceited, self-important, high-handed, lordly, overbearing, boastful, scornful, condescending, supercilious, superior, bumptious, disdainful, cavalier, imperious, insolent, pompous, presumptuous, proud, snobbish, vain, (*more informal*) hoity-toity, (*more informal*) cocky, (*more informal*) high and mighty, (*more informal*) stuck-up AN OPPOSITE IS modest

art *NOUN* **1** *She had done an art course.* ► fine art, painting, sculpture, drawing, artistry, artwork, craft, craftsmanship, draughtsmanship **2** *the art of writing* ► skill, craft, talent, technique, aptitude, gift, knack, expertise, facility, knack, proficiency, trick, cleverness, dexterity

article *NOUN* **1** *various household articles* ► object, item, thing, commodity, product, (*in plural*) goods **2** *I read an article on the subject.* ► essay, report, paper, study, feature, review, account, piece

articulated *ADJECTIVE* (said about a vehicle) in two sections that are connected by a flexible joint • *an articulated lorry.*

artificial *ADJECTIVE* not natural; made by human beings in imitation of a natural thing
▷ **artificially** *ADVERB* **artificiality** *NOUN*

artificial intelligence *NOUN* the use of computers to perform tasks normally requiring human intelligence, e.g. decision-making

artificial respiration *NOUN* helping somebody to start breathing again after their breathing has stopped

artillery *NOUN* **1** large guns **2** the part of the army that uses large guns

artist *NOUN* **artists 1** a person who produces works of art, especially a painter **2** an entertainer
▷ **artistry** *NOUN*

artistic *ADJECTIVE* **1** to do with art or artists **2** having a talent for art
▷ **artistically** *ADVERB*

arts *PLURAL NOUN* subjects (e.g. languages, literature, or history) in which opinion and understanding are very important, as opposed to sciences where measurements and calculations are used
the arts painting, music, and writing etc., considered together

as *ADVERB* equally or similarly • *This is just as easy.*

as *PREPOSITION* in the function or role of • *Use it as a handle.*

as *CONJUNCTION* **1** when or while • *She slipped as she got off the bus.* **2** because • *As he was late, we missed the train.* **3** in a way that • *Leave it as it is.*
as for with regard to • *As for you, I despise you.*
as it were in a way • *She became, as it were, her own enemy.*
as well also

A/S *ABBREVIATION* advanced subsidiary level in GCSE

asbestos *NOUN* a fireproof material made up of fine soft fibres

ascend *VERB* **ascends, ascending, ascended** go up
ascend the throne become king or queen

ascent *NOUN* **ascents 1** ascending **2** a way up; an upward path or slope

ascertain (as- er- tayn) *VERB* **ascertains, ascertaining, ascertained** find something out by asking
▷ **ascertainable** *ADJECTIVE*

ascetic (a- set- ik) *ADJECTIVE* not allowing yourself pleasure and luxuries
▷ **asceticism** *NOUN*

ascribe *VERB* **ascribes, ascribing, ascribed** regard something as belonging to or caused by; attribute • *She ascribes her success to good luck.*

asexual *ADJECTIVE* (in biology) not involving sexual activity • *asexual reproduction*

ash[1] *NOUN* **ashes** the powder that is left after something has been burned
▷ **ashy** *ADJECTIVE*

ash[2] *NOUN* **ashes** a tree with silver-grey bark

ashamed *ADJECTIVE* feeling shame

Asian *ADJECTIVE* to do with Asia or its people

Thesaurus

artificial *ADJECTIVE* **1** *artificial light; artificial trees* ► synthetic, imitation, simulated, unnatural, man-made, manufactured, false, fake, substitute AN OPPOSITE IS natural **2** *an artificial smile* ► false, spurious, affected, fake, feigned, assumed, pretended, bogus, contrived, counterfeit, factitious, pseudo, sham, simulated, unreal, (*more informal*) phoney, (*more informal*) put-on AN OPPOSITE IS genuine

artist *NOUN* **1** *The artist used a wide range of colour.* ► painter, sculptor, craftsman, craftswoman, designer **2** *a music-hall artist* ► performer

artistic *ADJECTIVE* *Desktop publishing requires artistic skills. The designs looked very artistic.* ► creative, imaginative, aesthetic, decorative, ornamental, tasteful, stylish, elegant, beautiful, attractive, cultured OPPOSITES ARE crude, ugly

ascend *VERB* **1** *He ascended the stairs.* ► climb, climb up, go up, come up, mount, move up, scale **2** *The little plane began slowly to ascend.* ► rise, soar, take off, lift off, fly up **3** *An unmade road ascends to the church.* ► climb, slope up AN OPPOSITE IS descend

ascent *NOUN* *A gradual ascent made the walk more arduous.* ► rise, slope, gradient, hill, incline, climb, elevation, ramp AN OPPOSITE IS descent

ascertain *VERB* *The police had to ascertain whether Darren had actually entered the room.* ► find out, establish, confirm, determine, discover, learn, make certain, make sure, settle, verify, identify

ascribe *VERB* *The inquest ascribed his death to natural causes.* ► attribute, assign, put down, blame (on), connect (with), associate (with)

ashamed *ADJECTIVE* **1** *She was ashamed of her outburst of bad temper.* ► sorry (for), apologetic (about), remorseful (about), contrite (about), repentant (about), shamefaced (about), abashed (about), penitent (about), embarrassed (about), distressed (about), upset (about), conscience-stricken (about), discomfited (about), mortified (about), red-faced (about), chastened (about), rueful (about) OPPOSITES ARE unrepentant, unabashed **2** *He seemed too ashamed to admit his mistake.* ► reticent, reluctant, loath, unwilling, bashful, shy, diffident, hesitant, embarrassed, modest,

Asian NOUN **Asians** an Asian person

Asiatic ADJECTIVE to do with Asia

aside ADVERB **1** to or at one side • *pull it aside* **2** away; in reserve

aside NOUN **asides** words spoken so that only certain people will hear

ask VERB **asks, asking, asked 1** speak so as to find out or get something **2** invite • *Ask her to the party.*

asleep ADVERB, ADJECTIVE sleeping

asparagus NOUN a plant whose young shoots are eaten as a vegetable

aspect NOUN **aspects 1** one part of a problem or situation • *Violence was the worst aspect of the crime.* **2** a person's or thing's appearance • *The forest had a sinister aspect.* **3** the direction a house etc. faces • *This room has a southern aspect.*

asphalt (ass- falt) NOUN a sticky black substance like tar, often mixed with gravel to surface roads etc.

asphyxiate (ass- fiks- ee- ayt) VERB **asphyxiates, asphyxiating, asphyxiated** suffocate
▷ **asphyxiation** NOUN

aspidistra NOUN **aspidistras** a house plant with broad leaves

aspirate (asp- er- at) NOUN **aspirates** the sound of 'h'

aspiration NOUN **aspirations** ambition; strong desire

aspire VERB **aspires, aspiring, aspired** have an ambition to achieve something • *He aspired to be world champion.*

aspirin NOUN **aspirins** a medicinal drug used to relieve pain or reduce fever

ass NOUN **asses 1** a donkey **2** (*informal*) a stupid person

assassin NOUN **assassins** a person who assassinates somebody [from Arabic *hashishi* = hashish-takers: the word was used as a name for a group of Muslims at the time of the Crusades, who were believed to take hashish before going out to kill Christian leaders]

assassinate VERB **assassinates, assassinating, assassinated** kill an important person deliberately and violently, especially for political reasons
▷ **assassination** NOUN

assault NOUN **assaults** a violent or illegal attack

assault VERB **assaults, assaulting, assaulted** make an assault on someone

assemble VERB **assembles, assembling, assembled 1** bring or come together **2** fit or put together the parts of something
▷ **assemblage** NOUN

Thesaurus

prudish, self-conscious, sheepish OPPOSITES ARE proud, shameless

ask VERB **1** *I'll ask him what he means.* ► enquire (of somebody), quiz (somebody about) **2** *They want to ask a few questions.* ► pose, put, raise, submit **3** *Ask them to fetch help.* ► entreat, request, implore, beg, solicit, exhort, urge, plead with, (*literary*) beseech, (*literary*) enjoin **4** *We could ask them to dinner.* ► invite, summon, (*more formal*) request the pleasure of the company of **5 ask for** *Don't hesitate to ask for anything you need.* ► request, demand, seek **6 ask for** *The remarks were asking for trouble.* ► look for, provoke, invite, attract, court, incite, tempt, cause, encourage, generate, (*more informal*) stir up

asleep ADJECTIVE *The girls were asleep in bed.* ► sleeping, slumbering, dozing, napping, (*more informal*) out like a light, (*more informal*) dead to the world

aspect NOUN **1** *The article describes every aspect of life in deprived areas.* ► feature, facet, characteristic, side, angle, respect, particular, circumstance, detail, standpoint **2** *Dark stone gave the facade a grim aspect.* ► appearance, look, air **3** *The house has a southern aspect.* ► outlook, view, prospect, exposure, orientation, direction, position, situation

aspersions NOUN **cast aspersions on** *The remarks are not intended to cast any aspersions on your honesty.* ► criticize, disparage, denigrate, belittle, vilify, deprecate, poor scorn on, decry, condemn, malign, discredit, stigmatize, denounce

aspire VERB **aspire to** *They aspired to be back in the city to which they belonged. We can aspire to a higher and fuller life.* ► aim to *or* for, wish to *or* for, want, yearn to *or* for, strive (after), seek (to), long to *or* for, desire to, crave to *or* for, dream of, hope to *or* for, pursue, set your sights on, have ambitions to *or* for

aspiring ADJECTIVE *aspiring young writers* ► would-be, intending, aspirant, budding, hopeful, eager, potential

assault VERB *He was prosecuted for assaulting a police officer.* ► attack , hit, strike, set upon, beat up, fall on, molest, (*more informal*) rough up

assault NOUN *an assault on the enemy position* ► attack , onslaught, strike, offensive, raid, foray, sortie, charge

assemble VERB **1** *A crowd began to assemble.* ► gather, congregate, come together, collect, converge, convene, crowd together, rally, rally round, meet, flock together, join up, swarm, muster, throng round, accumulate **2** *We*

assembly *NOUN* **assemblies** **1** assembling **2** a regular meeting, such as when everybody in a school meets together **3** people who regularly meet for a special purpose; a parliament

assent *VERB* **assents, assenting, assented** consent; say you agree

assent *NOUN* consent or approval

assert *VERB* **asserts, asserting, asserted** state something firmly
▷ **assertion** *NOUN*
assert yourself use firmness or forcefulness

assertive *ADJECTIVE* acting forcefully and with confidence

assess *VERB* **assesses, assessing, assessed** decide or estimate the value or quality of a person or thing
▷ **assessment** *NOUN* **assessor** *NOUN*

asset *NOUN* **assets** something useful

assets *PLURAL NOUN* a person's or company's property that could be sold to pay debts or raise money

assign *VERB* **assigns, assigning, assigned** **1** give or allot **2** appoint a person to perform a task

assignment *NOUN* **assignments** **1** assigning **2** something assigned; a task given to someone

assimilate *VERB* **assimilates, assimilating, assimilated** take in and absorb something, e.g. nourishment into the body or knowledge into the mind
▷ **assimilation** *NOUN*

assist *VERB* **assists, assisting, assisted** help
▷ **assistance** *NOUN*

Thesaurus

assembled our belongings in the hall. The general assembled his forces. ► gather, collect together, bring together, amass, convene, get together, round up, marshal, mobilize, muster, pile up, rally OPPOSITES ARE disperse, scatter **3** *Few cars are now assembled in Britain.* ► build, construct, manufacture, produce, put together, erect, fabricate, fit together, make, piece together AN OPPOSITE IS dismantle

assembly *NOUN* **1** *a political assembly, an assembly of bishops* ► gathering, meeting, congress, convocation, assemblage, council, (church) synod **2** *An assembly of spectators waited at the gates.* ► crowd, gathering, throng, rally, meeting, (*literary*) multitude **3** *The special glue is used in the assembly of model aircraft.* ► construction, building, making, putting together, manufacture, erection (of buildings)

assent *NOUN* *Parents need to give their assent to attendance on field trips.* ► agreement, approval, consent, permission, authorization, blessing, (*more informal*) go-ahead AN OPPOSITE IS refusal

assert *VERB* **1** *She asserted that multinational companies should not be blamed for damage to the environment.* ► declare, maintain, contend, submit, insist, argue, proclaim, profess, claim, emphasize, affirm, allege, protest, state, stress **2** *It is not always easy for people to assert their rights.* ► insist on, claim, stand up for, make use of, uphold
assert yourself *Some of the newer committee members began to assert themselves at meetings.* ► be assertive, behave confidently, be resolute, make yourself felt, exert your influence, make demands, persist, stand firm, (*more informal*) stick to your guns

assertive *ADJECTIVE* *You will need to be assertive in this job.* ► forceful, determined, resolute, confident, decisive, firm, assured, self-assured, authoritative, strong-willed, bold, positive, aggressive, domineering, strong, (*usually disapproving*) pushy OPPOSITES ARE submissive, reticent, retiring

assess *VERB* **1** *The hospital used a scanner to assess the extent of their head injuries.* ► evaluate, gauge, judge, determine, review, reckon, estimate, appraise, calculate, work out, value **2** *All pupils are assessed and graded at the end of their first term.* ► rate, judge, appraise, check, review

asset *NOUN* **1** *A good sense of humour can be an asset.* ► benefit, advantage, blessing, boon, strength, virtue, help, aid, support, good, (*more informal*) plus, (*more informal*) godsend **2** **assets** *The family's assets were reckoned at over two million dollars.* ► capital, resources, possessions, reserves, property, estate, funds, goods, holdings, means, money, savings, securities, wealth, (*more informal*) worldly goods

assign *VERB* **1** *Tasks are assigned on the basis of experience.* ► allocate, distribute, allot, apportion, dispense, give out, hand over, share out **2** *Kathryn was told she would be assigned to the case.* ► appoint, consign, delegate, designate, nominate, put down, choose (for), select (for)

assignment *NOUN* **1** *I have a difficult assignment to finish.* ► task, piece of work, exercise, project, job, duty **2** *the assignment of responsibilities* ► allocation, issuing, granting

assist *VERB* *Could you assist us for a while?* ► help, aid, support, give a hand to, lend a (helping) hand to, oblige OPPOSITES ARE hinder, impede

assistance *NOUN* *They said they would not need any assistance.* ► help, support, aid, encouragement, reinforcement, backing, collaboration, cooperation, contribution,

assistant *NOUN* **assistants** **1** a person who assists another; a helper **2** a person who serves customers in a shop

assistant *ADJECTIVE* helping a person and ranking next below him or her • *the assistant manager*

associate *VERB* **associates, associating, associated** **1** connect things in your mind • *I don't associate Ryan with fitness and healthy living.* **2** spend time or have dealings with a group of people

associate *NOUN* **associates** a colleague or companion; a partner
▷ **associate** *ADJECTIVE*

association *NOUN* **associations** **1** an organization of people; a society **2** associating **3** a connection or link in your mind

Association football *NOUN* a form of football using a round ball that may not be handled during play except by the goalkeeper

assonance (ass- on- ans) *NOUN* similarity of vowel sounds, e.g. in *vermin* and *furnish*

assorted *ADJECTIVE* of various sorts put together; mixed • *assorted sweets*

assortment *NOUN* **assortments** a mixed collection of things

assume *VERB* **assumes, assuming, assumed** **1** accept (without proof or question) that something is true or sure to happen **2** take on; undertake • *She assumed the extra responsibility.* **3** put on • *He assumed an innocent expression.*
▷ **assumption** *NOUN*
assumed name a false name

assurance *NOUN* **assurances** **1** a promise or guarantee that something is true or will happen **2** a kind of life insurance **3** confidence in yourself

assure *VERB* **assures, assuring, assured** **1** tell somebody confidently; promise **2** make certain

asterisk *NOUN* **asterisks** a star-shaped sign * used to draw attention to something

asteroid *NOUN* **asteroids** one of the small planets found mainly between the orbits of Mars and Jupiter

asthma (ass- ma) *NOUN* a disease that makes breathing difficult
▷ **asthmatic** *ADJECTIVE, NOUN*

astonish *VERB* **astonishes, astonishing, astonished** surprise somebody greatly
▷ **astonishment** *NOUN*

Thesaurus

patronage, sponsorship, subsidy AN OPPOSITE IS hindrance

assistant *NOUN* *The team leader has three assistants.* ► helper, subordinate, supporter, associate, deputy, colleague, underling, junior, ancillary, collaborator

associate *VERB* **1** *Stephen had been associating with dropouts and oddballs.* ► mix, keep company, go about, consort, socialize, fraternize, mingle, (*more informal*) hang about AN OPPOSITE IS dissociate **2** *Patience was not a quality I associated at all with him.* ► connect, link, identify, equate, relate (to)

association *NOUN* **1** *They enjoyed several years of friendly association.* ► relationship, connection, link, bond, ties, friendship, attachment, union **2** *an association of sports clubs* ► organization, confederation, federation, coalition, society, league, partnership, alliance, syndicate, group

assorted *ADJECTIVE* *a collection of assorted objects* ► miscellaneous, mixed, different, sundry, varied, various, differing, diverse, diversified, heterogeneous, manifold, motley, multifarious, several, (*old-fashioned*) divers

assortment *NOUN* *an assortment of dog-eared paperbacks* ► mixture, selection, collection, variety, array, miscellany, choice, diversity, medley, mélange

assume *VERB* **1** *I assumed the book was a gift.* ► presume, suppose, infer, deduce, take for granted, surmise, conjecture, reckon, imagine, come to the conclusion, guess, suspect, believe, imagine, deduce, expect, think, understand, (*more informal*) have a hunch **2** *The children should be encouraged to assume responsibilities.* ► take on, undertake, accept, embrace **3** *To play the part she had to assume a Scottish accent.* ► adopt, put on, feign, acquire

assumption *NOUN* *The assumption is that prices will stay the same.* ► supposition, presumption, conjecture, expectation, belief, guess, hypothesis, premise, surmise, theory

assurance *NOUN* *She had an air of complete assurance.* ► confidence, composure, self-confidence, poise, aplomb, level-headedness, self-possession, self-reliance

assure *VERB* **1** *He assured me he would arrive in time.* ► promise, reassure, convince, persuade, satisfy **2** *The win assured them a place in the finals.* ► ensure, secure, guarantee, make certain, confirm, establish

assured *ADJECTIVE* *an assured manner* ► confident, self-confident, self-assured, positive, assertive, composed, collected, calm, level-headed

astonish *VERB* *We were astonished at how much the place had changed.* ► amaze, astound, surprise, stagger, startle, disconcert, dumbfound, shock, flabbergast, perplex, stun, stupefy, bewilder

astound *VERB* **astounds, astounding, astounded** astonish; shock somebody greatly

astray *ADVERB, ADJECTIVE* away from the right path or place or course of action
go astray be lost or mislaid
lead astray make someone do something wrong

astride *ADVERB, PREPOSITION* with one leg on each side of something

astringent *ADJECTIVE* **1** causing skin or body tissue to contract **2** harsh or severe • *astringent criticism*

astrology *NOUN* the study of how the stars and planets may influence people's lives
▷ **astrologer** *NOUN* **astrological** *ADJECTIVE*

astronaut *NOUN* **astronauts** a person who travels in a spacecraft
▷ **astronautics** *NOUN*

astronomical *ADJECTIVE* **1** to do with astronomy **2** extremely large • *The restaurant's prices are astronomical.*

astronomy *NOUN* the study of the stars and planets and their movements
▷ **astronomer** *NOUN*

astute *ADJECTIVE* clever and good at understanding situations quickly; shrewd
▷ **astutely** *ADVERB* **astuteness** *NOUN*

asylum *NOUN* **asylums** **1** refuge and safety offered by one country to political refugees from another **2** (*old use*) a hospital for mentally ill people

asymmetrical (ay- sim- et- rik- al) *ADJECTIVE* not symmetrical
▷ **asymmetrically** *ADVERB*

at *PREPOSITION* This word is used to show **1** position (*at the top*), **2** time (*at midnight*), **3** condition (*Stand at ease*), **4** direction towards something (*Aim at the target*), **5** level or price etc. (*Sell them at £1 each*), **6** cause (*We were annoyed at his failure*)
at all in any way
at it doing or working at something
at once **1** immediately **2** at the same time • *It all came out at once.*

atheist (ayth- ee- ist) *NOUN* **atheists** a person who believes that there is no God
▷ **atheism** *NOUN*

athlete *NOUN* **athletes** a person who is good at sport, especially athletics

athletic *ADJECTIVE* **1** physically strong and active **2** to do with athletes
▷ **athletically** *ADVERB*

athletics *PLURAL NOUN* physical exercises and sports, e.g. running, jumping, and throwing

atlas *NOUN* **atlases** a book of maps [named after Atlas, a giant in Greek mythology who was punished for taking part in a revolt against the gods by being made to support the sky on his shoulders. *Atlas* was used as the title of a 17th-century Flemish book of maps which had a picture of Atlas at the front]

atmosphere *NOUN* **atmospheres** **1** the air round the earth **2** a feeling or mood given by surroundings • *the happy atmosphere of the fairground* **3** (in science) a unit of pressure, equal to the pressure of the atmosphere at sea level
▷ **atmospheric** *ADJECTIVE*

atom *NOUN* **atoms** the smallest particle of a substance [from Greek *atomos* = indivisible: people used to think that an atom could not be divided]

atom bomb or **atomic bomb** *NOUN* **atom bombs** *or* **atomic bombs** a bomb that explodes from the energy produced by splitting atoms

atomic *ADJECTIVE* **1** to do with an atom or atoms **2** to do with the energy produced by splitting atoms

atomic number *NOUN* **atomic numbers** (in science) the number of protons in the nucleus of the atom of a chemical element

Thesaurus

astound *VERB* *His arrogance astounded her.*
► astonish, amaze, surprise, stagger, startle, disconcert, dumbfound, shock, flabbergast, perplex, stun, stupefy, bewilder

astray *ADVERB* *Several missiles had gone astray and hit civilian targets.* ► off course, adrift, amiss, awry, lost, wide of the mark

astute *ADJECTIVE* *an astute manager, some astute remarks* ► shrewd, sharp, acute, canny, prudent, clever, intelligent, quick-witted, perceptive, discerning, crafty, wily
AN OPPOSITE IS stupid

asylum *NOUN* *Spain refused to hand over four men who had sought asylum in their embassy.*
► haven, shelter, refuge, retreat, safety, sanctuary

athletic *ADJECTIVE* *an athletic physique*
► muscular, fit, well-built, powerful, strong, sturdy, acrobatic, active, energetic, robust, sinewy, vigorous, wiry, (*more informal*) sporty, (*more informal*) strapping OPPOSITES ARE frail, weak

atmosphere *NOUN* **1** *Harmful gases are escaping into the atmosphere.* ► air, sky, ether, (*literary*) heavens **2** *the warm cosy atmosphere of the kitchen* ► ambience, aura, environment, surroundings, quality, character, climate, mood, feeling, (*more informal*) vibes

atom *NOUN* *There is not an atom of truth in the story.* ► scrap, speck, spot, trace, morsel, bit, crumb, grain, iota, jot, molecule, particle

atrocity (a-tross-it-ee) *NOUN* **atrocities** something extremely bad or wicked; wickedness

attach *VERB* **attaches, attaching, attached** **1** fix or join to something else **2** think that something is an important part of something else • *We attach great importance to fitness.*
▷ **attachment** *NOUN*
attached to fond of

attack *NOUN* **attacks** **1** a violent attempt to hurt or overcome somebody **2** a piece of strong criticism **3** sudden illness or pain **4** an attempt to score a goal in a game

attack *VERB* **attacks, attacking, attacked** make an attack
▷ **attacker** *NOUN*

attain *VERB* **attains, attaining, attained** accomplish; succeed in doing or getting something
▷ **attainable** *ADJECTIVE* **attainment** *NOUN*

attempt *VERB* **attempts, attempting, attempted** make an effort to do something; try

attempt *NOUN* **attempts** an effort to do something; a try

attend *VERB* **attends, attending, attended** **1** give care and thought to something; look and listen • *Why don't you attend to your teacher?* **2** be present somewhere; go often to a place **3** look after someone; be an attendant
▷ **attendance** *NOUN*

Thesaurus

atrocious *ADJECTIVE* *They were guilty of atrocious brutality.* ► abominable, appalling, brutal, vicious, detestable, hateful, odious, detestable, vile, obnoxious, dreadful, abhorrent, diabolical, disgusting, repellent, horrifying AN OPPOSITE IS humane

atrocity *NOUN* *Further atrocities have been reported.* ► outrage, enormity, cruelty, act of brutality

attach *VERB* **1** *The brackets are attached to the wall with a pair of small screws.* ► fix, fasten, secure, affix, join, link, stick, bond, couple, anchor, connect, tie, add, append OPPOSITES ARE detach, remove **2** *We attach great importance to punctuality.* ► attribute, ascribe, assign, apply, put (on), place (on), associate (with), impute

attached *ADJECTIVE* **attached to** *The sisters seem very attached to each other.* ► fond of, close to, devoted to, dear to, affectionate to *or* towards, friendly to *or* towards, loving to *or* towards, loyal to *or* towards, warm to *or* towards

attack *NOUN* **1** *An attack on the enemy was planned for the next day.* ► assault, onslaught, strike, offensive, raid, charge, ambush, foray, sortie, rush, blitz, bombardment, broadside, cannonade, counter-attack **2** *Their attack on her honesty upset her very much.* ► criticism (of), tirade (against), outburst (against), vilification (of), abuse (of), censure (of), denunciation (of), diatribe (against), revilement (of), invective (against) **3** *an attack of coughing* ► fit, bout, spasm, convulsion, outbreak, paroxysm, seizure, stroke, (*more informal*) turn

attack *VERB* **1** *We attack the enemy position at dawn.* ► charge, bombard, assault, ambush, raid, rush, descend on, storm, strike at, (*more informal*) blast, (*more informal*) pitch into, (*more informal*) wade into **2** *A bunch of youths attacked him in the street on his way home.* ► assault, mob, mug, pounce on, ambush, set about, set on, jump on, (*more informal*) beat up, (*more informal*) do over, (*more informal*) lay into **3** *The clergy regularly attack government policy.* ► criticize, find fault with, censure, denounce, condemn, impugn, vilify, inveigh against, malign, round on, snipe at AN OPPOSITE IS defend **4** *We need to attack the problem of poverty.* ► confront, address, focus on, attend to, apply yourself to, deal with, (*more informal*) have a go at

attacker *NOUN* **1** *The little force fought bravely against its attackers.* ► aggressor, assailant, invader, opponent, raider, enemy **2** *The attacker ran off empty-handed.* ► assailant, mugger, aggressor, intruder, rapist **3** *The journal agreed to publish a defence against her attackers.* ► critic, detractor, persecutor, opponent, enemy

attain *VERB* *He did not attain this honour until the reign of Queen Victoria.* ► achieve, accomplish, obtain, gain, win, earn, get, acquire, secure, reach, (*more informal*) clinch, (*more informal*) carry off, (*more informal*) pull off

attempt *NOUN* *a brave attempt* ► try, effort, endeavour, venture, (*more informal*) shot

attempt *VERB* **1** *We attempted to visit all three sites in one day.* ► try, endeavour, aim, aspire, strive, undertake, set out, make an effort *or* every effort, do your best, do your utmost, venture, seek, (*more informal*) have a go (at), (*more informal*) have a stab (at), (*more informal*) bend over backwards **2** *Candidates should attempt three questions.* ► undertake, try, choose, answer

attend *VERB* **1** *Frances had to attend an interview the following week.* ► go to *or* for, present yourself at, appear at, be present at **2** *The bride was attended by two bridesmaids.* ► escort, assist, accompany, chaperone, follow, guard, usher, wait on **3** **attend to** *A nurse attended to*

attendant NOUN **attendants** a person who helps or accompanies someone

attention NOUN **1** giving concentration and careful thought • *Pay attention to what I'm saying.* **2** a position in which a soldier etc. stands with feet together and arms straight downwards

attentive ADJECTIVE giving attention to something
▷ **attentively** ADVERB **attentiveness** NOUN

attic NOUN **attics** a room in the roof of a house

attitude NOUN **attitudes** **1** the way a person thinks or behaves **2** the position of the body; posture

attract VERB **attracts, attracting, attracted** **1** get someone's attention or interest; seem pleasant to someone **2** pull something by an invisible force • *Magnets attract metal pins.*

attraction NOUN **1** something that attracts visitors • *a tourist attraction* **2** what is pleasant or appealing about something • *City life has many attractions.*

attractive ADJECTIVE **1** pleasant or good-looking **2** interesting or appealing • *an attractive plan*
▷ **attractively** ADVERB **attractiveness** NOUN

attribute (a- trib- yoot) VERB **attributes, attributing, attributed** regard something as belonging to or created by • *We attribute his success to hard work.*
▷ **attribution** NOUN

attribute (at- rib- yoot) NOUN **attributes** a quality or characteristic • *Kindness is one of his attributes.*

attributive (a- trib- yoo- tiv) ADJECTIVE expressing an attribute and placed before the word it describes, e.g. *old* in *the old dog* COMPARE **predicative**
▷ **attributively** ADVERB

auburn ADJECTIVE (said about hair) reddish-brown

auction NOUN **auctions** a public sale where things are sold to the person who offers the most money for them

auction VERB **auctions, auctioning, auctioned** sell something by auction
▷ **auctioneer** NOUN

audacious (aw- day- shus) ADJECTIVE bold or daring
▷ **audaciously** ADVERB **audacity** NOUN

Thesaurus

the injured. ► look after, care for, tend, treat, help, deal with, (*more formal*) minister to **4 attend to** *Frank said he would attend to the details of the trip.* ► deal with, take care of, look after, see to, manage, organize, make arrangements for, take responsibility for **5 attend to** *Please attend to what I say.* ► listen to, pay attention to, heed, mark, mind, concentrate on, follow carefully, hear, note, notice, observe, think about

attendant NOUN *The Queen had three attendants.* ► assistant, aide, retainer, companion, escort, equerry, servant, bodyguard

attention NOUN *Please give the matter your full attention.* ► concentration, observation, regard, consideration, scrutiny, notice, thought, concern, care, diligence, heed, recognition

attentive ADJECTIVE **1** *Julian was standing silent and attentive in the shadows.* ► alert, vigilant, watchful, aware, circumspect, wide awake, on the lookout, on the ball, on your guard, (*more informal*) on the qui vive **2** *Helen was patient and attentive, holding my hand to calm me.* ► thoughtful, considerate, kind, caring, understanding, tender, devoted

attitude NOUN *a positive, joyful attitude* ► outlook, approach, air, manner, demeanour, disposition, inclination, position, bearing, frame of mind, mien, mood, posture, stance, behaviour

attract VERB **1** *The recent lecture attracted a good turnout.* ► draw, bring, bring in, produce, cause, generate **2** *They were attracted by the beauty of the place.* ► enchant, entrance, excite, captivate, lure, entice, allure, tempt, charm, fascinate, beguile, bewitch AN OPPOSITE IS repel

attractive ADJECTIVE **1** *an attractive young woman* ► good-looking, nice-looking, pretty, striking, fetching, beautiful, gorgeous, lovely, charming, engaging, appealing, delightful, glamorous, stunning AN OPPOSITE IS repulsive **2** *an attractive offer* ► appealing, agreeable, tempting, interesting, difficult to resist *or* refuse

attribute VERB *A cool head is not the first quality I would attribute to the colonel.* ► ascribe, associate (with), connect (with), assign, put down, blame (on)

audacious ADJECTIVE *an audacious decision* ► bold, daring, brave, courageous, adventurous, enterprising

audacity NOUN **1** *His sheer audacity was enough to carry the day.* ► bravery, daring, boldness, courage, enterprise **2** (*usually disapproving*) *Then they had the audacity to ask for money.* ► effrontery, cheek, nerve, boldness, temerity, impertinence, impudence, insolence, presumptuousness, shamelessness, (*more informal*) sauce

audible *ADJECTIVE* loud enough to be heard
▷ **audibly** *ADVERB* **audibility** *NOUN*

audience *NOUN* **audiences** **1** people who have gathered to hear or watch something **2** a formal interview with an important person

audio *NOUN* reproduced sounds

audio-visual *ADJECTIVE* using both sound and pictures to give information

audit *NOUN* **audits** an official examination of financial accounts to see that they are correct

audit *VERB* **audits**, **auditing**, **audited** make an audit of accounts
▷ **auditor** *NOUN*

audition *NOUN* **auditions** a test to see if an actor or musician is suitable for a job
▷ **audition** *VERB*

auditorium *NOUN* **auditoriums** the part of a theatre or hall where the audience sits

August *NOUN* the eighth month of the year [named after Augustus Caesar, the first Roman emperor]

aunt *NOUN* **aunts** the sister of your father or mother; your uncle's wife

au pair (oh pair) *NOUN* **au pairs** a person from abroad, usually a young woman, who works for a time in someone's home

aura (or- a) *NOUN* **auras** a general feeling surrounding a person or thing • *an aura of happiness*

aural (or- al) *ADJECTIVE* to do with the ear or hearing
▷ **aurally** *ADVERB*
USAGE Do not confuse with **oral**.

aurora (aw- raw- ra) *NOUN* **auroras** bands of coloured light appearing in the sky at night, the **aurora borealis** (bor- ee- ay- liss) in the northern hemisphere and the **aurora australis** (aw- stray- liss) in the southern hemisphere

auspices (aw- spiss- eez) *PLURAL NOUN* protection or support • *under the auspices of the Red Cross*

auspicious (aw- **spish**- us) *ADJECTIVE* fortunate or favourable • *an auspicious start*

austere (aw- **steer**) *ADJECTIVE* very simple and plain; without luxuries
▷ **austerely** *ADVERB* **austerity** *NOUN*

authentic *ADJECTIVE* genuine • *an authentic signature*
▷ **authentically** *ADVERB* **authenticity** *NOUN*

author *NOUN* **authors** the writer of a book, play, poem, etc.
▷ **authorship** *NOUN*

authoritative *ADJECTIVE* having proper authority or expert knowledge; official

authority *NOUN* **authorities** **1** the right or power to give orders to other people **2** a person or organization with the right to give orders **3** an expert; a book etc. that gives reliable information • *an authority on spiders*

Thesaurus

audible *ADJECTIVE* *Her words were hardly audible above the noise of the traffic.* ► perceptible, discernible, recognizable, clear, distinct, detectable, high, loud, noisy, strong
AN OPPOSITE IS inaudible

audience *NOUN* *There was a more lively audience on the Saturday.* ► spectators, onlookers, crowd, gathering, turnout, (*television*) viewers, (*radio*) listeners

austere *ADJECTIVE* **1** *Their lives tended to be short and austere.* ► severe, sober, frugal, strict, spartan, restrained, abstemious, ascetic, temperate, simple, chaste OPPOSITES ARE indulgent, elaborate **2** *She seemed austere but had a great deal of charm, once you got to know her.* ► stern, severe, strict, grave, solemn, forbidding, dour, formal, remote, distant, aloof AN OPPOSITE IS genial **3** *Dark windows gave the house an austere appearance.* ► stark, grim, bleak, forbidding OPPOSITES ARE bright, ornate

authentic *ADJECTIVE* **1** *an authentic painting by Rembrandt* ► actual, bona fide, certain, genuine, legitimate, original, real, true, valid AN OPPOSITE IS fake **2** *an authentic story* ► accurate, authoritative, dependable, factual, honest, reliable, truthful, veracious AN OPPOSITE IS false

author *NOUN* **1** *modern American authors* ► writer, novelist, dramatist, composer, creator, playwright, poet, scriptwriter **2** *the author of the plan* ► originator, creator, initiator, instigator, architect, producer, begetter, designer, inventor

authoritative *ADJECTIVE* **1** *an authoritative edition of the text* ► definitive, authorized, classic, standard **2** *an authoritative source of information* ► reliable, dependable, sound, authentic, trustworthy

authority *NOUN* **1** *The salesperson does not always have the authority to deal with a complaint.* ► authorization, power, right, prerogative, consent, licence, mandate, permission **2** *I was convinced that she would never accept a challenge to her authority.* ► power, sovereignty, control, jurisdiction, domination, supremacy, charge, command, force, influence, might, prerogative, right, sway, weight **3** *He is the world's foremost authority on the subject.* ► expert, specialist, pundit, boffin, connoisseur (of)
the authorities *The matter was reported to the authorities.* ► officials, officialdom, government, management, administration,

authorize *VERB* **authorizes, authorizing, authorized** give official permission for something
▷ **authorization** *NOUN*

autistic (aw- tist- ik) *ADJECTIVE* having a disability that makes someone unable to communicate with other people or respond to surroundings
▷ **autism** *NOUN*

autobiography *NOUN* **autobiographies** the story of a person's life written by himself or herself
▷ **autobiographical** *ADJECTIVE*

autocrat *NOUN* **autocrats** a ruler with unlimited power
▷ **autocratic** *ADJECTIVE* **autocratically** *ADVERB*

autocue *NOUN* **autocues** (*trade mark*) a device that displays the script for a television presenter or newsreader to read

autograph *NOUN* **autographs** the signature of a famous person

autograph *VERB* **autographs, autographing, autographed** sign your name in a book etc.

automatic *ADJECTIVE* **1** working on its own without continuous attention or control by people **2** done without thinking
▷ **automatically** *ADVERB*

automation *NOUN* making processes automatic; using machines instead of people to do jobs

automaton (aw- tom- at- on) *NOUN* **automatons** **1** a robot **2** a person who seems to act mechanically without thinking

autonomy (aw- ton- om- ee) *NOUN* **1** self-government **2** the right to act independently without being told what to do
▷ **autonomous** *ADJECTIVE*

autumn *NOUN* **autumns** the season between summer and winter
▷ **autumnal** *ADJECTIVE*

auxiliary *ADJECTIVE* giving help and support
• *auxiliary services.*

auxiliary *NOUN* **auxiliaries** a helper

auxiliary verb *NOUN* **auxiliary verbs** a verb such as *do, have,* and *will,* which is used to form parts of other verbs, e.g. *have* in *I have finished*

avail *NOUN*
to no avail without any success

available *ADJECTIVE* ready or able to be used; obtainable
▷ **availability** *NOUN*

avalanche *NOUN* **avalanches** a mass of snow or rock falling down the side of a mountain

avenge *VERB* **avenges, avenging, avenged** take vengeance for something done to harm you
▷ **avenger** *NOUN*

avenue *NOUN* **avenues** **1** a wide street **2** a road with trees along both sides

average *NOUN* **averages** **1** the value obtained by adding several quantities together and dividing by the number of quantities **2** the usual or ordinary standard

average *ADJECTIVE* **1** worked out as an average • *Their average age is ten.* **2** of the usual or ordinary standard

average *VERB* **averages, averaging, averaged** work out, produce, or amount to as an average

Thesaurus

people in charge, (*more informal*) the powers that be

authorize *VERB* *The government has authorized a further billion pounds of spending on health.* ► approve, permit, allow, agree to, enable, sanction, back, accede to, consent to, (*more informal*) OK, ratify, (*more informal*) rubber-stamp, (*more informal*) give the go-ahead for

automatic *ADJECTIVE* **1** *His reaction was automatic.* ► instinctive, spontaneous, involuntary, unconscious, reflex, unthinking, unintentional, natural, mechanical, habitual, impulsive **2** *automatic windows* ► mechanical, automated, computerized, programmed, robotic, self-regulating, unmanned

autonomous *ADJECTIVE* *an autonomous nation* ► independent, self-governing, sovereign, free, self-ruling, self-determining
AN OPPOSITE IS subject

auxiliary *ADJECTIVE* **1** *an auxiliary power supply* ► supplementary, additional, ancillary, reserve, secondary, spare, subsidiary, emergency, extra, (*more informal*) back-up

available *ADJECTIVE* *Camping facilities will be available on site.* ► obtainable, accessible, procurable, ready, at *or* on *or* to hand, to be had, usable, disposable AN OPPOSITE IS unavailable

avenge *VERB* *We shall avenge their deaths a thousand times.* ► take revenge for, take vengeance for, punish, exact punishment for, exact retribution for, repay, (*more informal*) get your own back for

average *ADJECTIVE* **1** *Few of us have any idea how much water we use on an average day.* ► typical, normal, ordinary, usual, regular, standard **2** *He is only an average golfer.* ► mediocre, undistinguished, unremarkable, indifferent, unexceptional, run-of-the-mill, second-rate, passable, tolerable, mainstream OPPOSITES ARE exceptional, outstanding **3** *The average summer temperature is 18 degrees.* ► mean, medial, standard

average *NOUN* *Prices of new cars will rise by an average of 3 per cent.* ► mean, median, mid-point

aversion *NOUN* a strong dislike

avert *VERB* **averts, averting, averted** **1** turn something away • *People averted their eyes from the accident.* **2** prevent • *We averted a disaster.*

aviary *NOUN* **aviaries** a large cage or building for keeping birds

aviation *NOUN* the flying of aircraft
▷ **aviator** *NOUN*

avocado (av- ok- **ah**- doh) *NOUN* **avocados** a pear-shaped tropical fruit [via Spanish from Nahuatl (a Central American language)]

avoid *VERB* **avoids, avoiding, avoided** **1** keep yourself away from someone or something **2** keep yourself from doing something; refrain from • *Avoid rash promises.*
▷ **avoidable** *ADJECTIVE* **avoidance** *NOUN*

avoirdupois (av- wah- dew- **pwah**) *NOUN* a system of weights using the unit of 16 ounces = 1 pound

await *VERB* **awaits, awaiting, awaited** wait for

awake *VERB* **awakes, awaking, awoke, awoken** wake up

awake *ADJECTIVE* not asleep

award *VERB* **awards, awarding, awarded** give something officially as a prize, payment, or penalty

award *NOUN* **awards** something awarded, such as a prize or a sum of money

aware *ADJECTIVE* knowing or realizing something • *Were you aware of the danger?*
▷ **awareness** *NOUN*

away *ADVERB* **1** to or at a distance; not at the usual place **2** out of existence • *The water had boiled away.* **3** continuously or persistently • *We worked away at it.*

away *ADJECTIVE* played on an opponent's ground • *an away match*

awe *NOUN* fearful or deeply respectful wonder • *The mountains always fill me with awe.*
▷ **awed** *ADJECTIVE* **awesome** *ADJECTIVE* **awestricken** *ADJECTIVE* **awestruck** *ADJECTIVE*

Thesaurus

avid *ADJECTIVE* *avid fans of the movies* ► keen, eager, enthusiastic, ardent, passionate, fervent, devoted, dedicated, zealous
OPPOSITES ARE uninterested, apathetic

avoid *VERB* **1** *I try to avoid arguments.* ► refrain from, stay clear of, steer clear of, eschew, circumvent OPPOSITES ARE seek, confront **2** *You cannot avoid responsibility for the decision.* ► evade, escape, dodge, shirk, sidestep, (*more informal*) get out of, (*more informal*) duck AN OPPOSITE IS face up to **3** *She had to swerve to avoid a collision.* ► prevent, avert, circumvent **4** *There was a woman at the party he was anxious to avoid.* ► ignore, shun, keep away from, hide from, stay clear of, steer clear of AN OPPOSITE IS seek out **5** *Women should avoid alcohol during pregnancy.* ► refrain from, desist from, abstain from, eschew AN OPPOSITE IS indulge in

awake *ADJECTIVE* *They are often not awake until ten or eleven. She felt too awake to go back to sleep again.* ► conscious, alert, sleepless, wakeful, wide awake, lively, restless AN OPPOSITE IS asleep

awake *VERB* **1** *The alarm awoke her at six.* ► wake (up), waken, awaken, rouse, arouse **2** *James awoke with a start.* ► wake (up), waken, awaken, stir, come to **3** *The accident awoke old fears about passenger safety.* ► awaken, waken, rouse, arouse, stir up, revive, stimulate, trigger, bring back
USAGE The normal word to use for the main meanings is *wake* or *wake up*. There are three other words, *awake, awaken*, and *waken*, but you cannot use *up* with any of these. All four words can be transitive (i.e. can take an object, as in the first example in this entry) or intransitive (i.e. can have no object, as in the second example). *Awaken* and *waken* are rather more formal or literary in effect than *awake* and *wake*.

awaken *VERB* **1** *The noise outside awakened us. We awakened early.* ► wake (up), waken, awake, stir, come to **2** *The incident awakened strong feelings in her.* ► awake, waken, rouse, arouse, stir up, revive, stimulate, trigger, bring back

award *NOUN* **1** *By his third year he had won three awards.* ► prize, trophy, decoration, medal **2** *an award of £5,000* ► payment, grant, subsidy, subvention, bursary **3** *the award of an honour* ► granting, bestowal, conferment, conferral

award *VERB* **1** *MPs plan to award themselves a four per cent pay rise. Referee Hart did not even award a free kick.* ► grant, give, present, accord, allot, assign **2** *The college awarded her a scholarship.* ► grant, present, (*more formal*) endow, (*more formal*) confer, (*more formal*) bestow
USAGE If you use *present* or *endow*, you say *The college presented* (or *endowed*) her with a scholarship. If you use *bestow* or *confer*, you say *They bestowed* (or *conferred*) *a scholarship on her*. These words are much more formal in effect and are mainly used in official language.

aware *ADJECTIVE* **aware of** *The children were aware of the dangers.* ► conscious of, acquainted with, alive to, appreciative of, mindful of, informed about, knowledgeable about, sensitive to, familiar with, attentive to, conversant with, heedful of, observant of,

awful *ADJECTIVE* **1** very bad • *an awful accident.* **2** (*informal*) very great • *That's an awful lot of money.*
▷ **awfully** *ADVERB*

awkward *ADJECTIVE* **1** difficult to use or deal with; not convenient **2** clumsy; not skilful
▷ **awkwardly** *ADVERB* **awkwardness** *NOUN*
[from Old Norse *afugr* = turned the wrong way]

awning *NOUN* **awnings** a roof-like shelter made of canvas etc.

axe *NOUN* **axes 1** a tool for chopping things **2** (*informal*) being axed

have an axe to grind have a personal interest in something and want to take care of it

axe *VERB* **axes, axing, axed 1** cancel or abolish something **2** reduce something greatly

axis *NOUN* **axes 1** a line through the centre of a spinning object **2** a line dividing a thing in half **3** the horizontal or vertical line on a graph

axle *NOUN* **axles** the rod through the centre of a wheel, on which the wheel turns

ayatollah (I- a- tol- a) *NOUN* **ayatollahs** a Muslim religious leader in Iran

aye (I) *ADVERB* yes

azure *ADJECTIVE* sky-blue

Thesaurus

responsive to OPPOSITES ARE unaware, ignorant, insensitive (to)

awe-inspiring *ADJECTIVE The stained-glass windows were awe-inspiring in gold and blue.* ► awesome, breathtaking, dramatic, stunning, stupendous, spectacular, astonishing, grand, imposing, impressive, magnificent, amazing, marvellous, overwhelming, wonderful, fearsome, (*poetic*) wondrous OPPOSITES ARE insignificant, unimpressive

awful *ADJECTIVE* **1** *awful weather* ► bad, terrible, dreadful, atrocious, appalling, frightful, poor, (*more informal*) lousy OPPOSITES ARE wonderful, lovely **2** *an awful smell* ► unpleasant, disgusting, nasty, dreadful, terrible, horrible, horrid, foul, frightful, obnoxious OPPOSITES ARE pleasant, lovely **3** *awful news, an awful illness* ► grave, serious, bad, terrible, dreadful AN OPPOSITE IS excellent **4** *I felt awful for losing my temper.* ► guilty, remorseful, regretful, ashamed, sorry

awkward *ADJECTIVE* **1** *The case was an awkward object to carry.* ► cumbersome, bulky, unmanageable, unwieldy, inconvenient AN OPPOSITE IS convenient **2** *He ran with awkward movements.* ► clumsy, ungainly, inept, inexpert, unskilful, uncoordinated, graceless, blundering, bungling, gauche, gawky, ham-fisted, maladroit OPPOSITES ARE skilful, dexterous, adroit **3** *This is an awkward situation to be in.* ► difficult, troublesome, trying, vexatious, vexing, annoying, perplexing AN OPPOSITE IS straightforward **4** *There was an awkward pause in the conversation.* ► embarrassing, uncomfortable, uneasy, delicate, tricky, unwelcome AN OPPOSITE IS comfortable **5** *He thought she was being extremely awkward.* ► unreasonable, unhelpful, uncooperative, stubborn, obstinate, perverse, tiresome, exasperating, wayward, (*more informal*) bloody-minded, (*more informal*) bolshie OPPOSITES ARE cooperative, obliging, amenable

axe *VERB The company will axe thousands of jobs.* ► terminate, discontinue, eliminate, cut, cancel, drop, get rid of, remove, withdraw

axis *NOUN The earth spins on its axis once a day.* ► centre line, central line, pivot

axle *NOUN Something had broken the car's back axle.* ► rod, shaft, spindle

A B C D E F G H I J K L M N O P Q R S T U V W X Y Z

Bb

babble *VERB* **babbles, babbling, babbled** **1** talk very quickly without making sense **2** make a murmuring sound
▷ **babble** *NOUN* **babbler** *NOUN*

baboon *NOUN* **baboons** a kind of large monkey from Africa and Asia Baboons have long muzzles and short tails

baby *NOUN* **babies** a very young child or animal
▷ **babyish** *ADJECTIVE*

babysitter *NOUN* **babysitters** someone who looks after a child while the parents are out

bachelor *NOUN* **bachelors** a man who has not married
Bachelor of Arts *or* **Science** a person who has taken a first degree in arts or science

back *NOUN* **backs** **1** the part that is furthest from the front **2** the back part of the body from the shoulders to the buttocks **3** the part of a chair etc. that your back rests against **4** a defending player near the goal in football, hockey, etc.

back *ADJECTIVE* **1** placed at or near the back **2** to do with the back • *back pain*

back *ADVERB* **1** to or towards the back **2** to the place you have come from • *Go back home.* **3** to an earlier time or position • *Put the clocks back one hour.*

back *VERB* **backs, backing, backed** **1** move backwards **2** give someone support or help **3** bet on something **4** cover the back of something • *Back the rug with canvas.*
▷ **backer** *NOUN*
back out refuse to do what you agreed to do
back up **1** give support or help to a person or thing **2** (in computing) make a spare copy of a file or data **back-up** *NOUN*

backbencher *NOUN* **backbenchers** a Member of Parliament who does not hold an important position

backbone *NOUN* **backbones** the column of small bones down the centre of the back; the spine

backfire *VERB* **backfires, backfiring, backfired** **1** if a car backfires, it makes a loud noise, caused by an explosion in the exhaust pipe **2** if a plan backfires, it goes wrong

background *NOUN* **1** the back part of a picture, scene, or view etc. **2** the conditions influencing something **3** a person's family, upbringing, and education
in the background not noticeable or obvious

Thesaurus

baby *NOUN* **1** *The woman was holding a baby.* ► babe, infant, toddler, child **2** *a baby car* ► miniature, mini, small-scale, midget, diminutive

babyish *ADJECTIVE* *Older children are usually told that it is babyish to cry.* ► childish, juvenile, puerile, immature, infantile AN OPPOSITE IS mature

back *NOUN* **1** *a person's back* ► spine, backbone, spinal column RELATED ADJECTIVE dorsal (upper side of an animal), lumbar (lower back) **2** *the back of the vehicle* ► end, rear, tail-end AN OPPOSITE IS front **3** *the back of the building* ► rear, rear side OPPOSITES ARE front, facade **4** *the back of the ship* ► stern OPPOSITES ARE front, bow **5** *the back of an envelope* ► reverse, verso AN OPPOSITE IS front **6** *the back of an animal* ► rear, tail, hindquarters, posterior AN OPPOSITE IS front

back *ADJECTIVE* **1** *the back door* ► rear AN OPPOSITE IS front **2** *an animal's back legs* ► rear, hind, hindmost AN OPPOSITE IS front **3** *the back row of the hall* ► end, rearmost AN OPPOSITE IS front **4** *a bird's back feathers; the back fin of a fish* ► (*technical*) dorsal **5** *back issues of a journal* ► past, previous OPPOSITES ARE forthcoming, future

back *VERB* **1** *He decided to back his van into the space. The car backed slowly up the drive.* ► reverse, go backwards, move back **2** *We would like them to back our plan.* ► support, endorse, approve of, stand behind, sponsor, patronize **3** *He backed a horse at 3–1.* ► bet on, place a bet on, put money on
back down *The government has had to back down on tax increases.* ► withdraw, concede, yield, give way, retreat, change your mind, (*more informal*) do a U-turn
back out of *Mr James wanted to back out of the deal.* ► withdraw from, give up, pull out of

backbone *NOUN* **1** *She has an injured backbone.* ► spine, spinal column, vertebrae RELATED ADJECTIVE spinal **2** *The backbone of a good team is a good manager.* ► mainstay, foundation, cornerstone, chief support **3** *Drivers need to have some backbone to sustain pole position.* ► courage, nerve, spirit, mettle, determination, strength of character, firmness of purpose

backfire *VERB* *The plan backfired.* ► miscarry, misfire, fail, flop, rebound

background *NOUN* **1** *You can see a steeple in the background.* ► distance, (on the) horizon AN OPPOSITE IS foreground **2** *the background to the war* ► circumstances (of), context (of), history, (*informal*) lead-up **3** *students from different backgrounds* ► environment, social circumstances, breeding, culture, (*formal*) milieu, tradition, upbringing

backing NOUN **1** support **2** material that is used to line the back of something **3** musical accompaniment

backlash NOUN **backlashes** a violent reaction to an event

backlog NOUN **backlogs** an amount of work that should have been finished but is still waiting to be done

backstroke NOUN a way of swimming lying on your back

backward ADJECTIVE **1** going backwards **2** slow at learning or developing
▷ **backwardness** NOUN

backward ADVERB backwards
USAGE The adverb **backward** is mainly used in American English.

backwards ADVERB **1** to or towards the back **2** with the back end going first **3** in reverse order • *Count backwards.*
backwards and forwards in each direction alternately; to and fro

bacon NOUN smoked or salted meat from the back or sides of a pig

bacterium NOUN **bacteria** a microscopic organism that can cause disease
▷ **bacterial** ADJECTIVE
USAGE Note that it is a mistake to use the plural form **bacteria** as if it were the singular. It is incorrect to say 'a bacteria' or 'this bacteria'; correct usage is *this bacterium* or *these bacteria*.

bad ADJECTIVE **worse, worst 1** not having the right qualities; not good **2** wicked or evil **3** serious or severe • *a bad accident* **4** ill or unhealthy **5** harmful • *Sweets are bad for your teeth.* **6** decayed or rotten • *This meat has gone bad.*
▷ **badness** NOUN
not bad quite good

badge NOUN **badges** a button or sign that you wear to show people who you are or what school or club etc. you belong to

badger NOUN **badgers** a grey burrowing animal with a black and white head

badger VERB **badgers, badgering, badgered** keep asking someone to do something; pester

badly ADVERB **worse, worst 1** in a bad way; not well **2** severely; causing much injury • *He was badly wounded.* **3** very much • *She badly wanted to win.*

baffle VERB **baffles, baffling, baffled** puzzle or confuse somebody
▷ **bafflement** NOUN

Thesaurus

backing NOUN **1** *We need the backing of the unions.* ► support, agreement, endorsement, assistance, encouragement, help **2** *financial backing* ► support, funding, patronage, subsidy, sponsorship **3** *a musical backing* ► accompaniment, orchestration, scoring

backward ADJECTIVE **1** *a backward movement* ► reverse, rearward, regressive, retrograde, retrogressive AN OPPOSITE IS forward **2** *Don't be backward if you need to ask for help.* ► reticent, bashful, coy, diffident, shy, timid, unforthcoming, hesitant, inhibited, afraid, modest, reluctant, reserved, self-effacing AN OPPOSITE IS confident **3** *The decision was a backward step.* ► retrograde, regressive, negative **4** *a backward learner* ► subnormal, (*offensive*) retarded

bad ADJECTIVE **1** *bad work* ► poor, inferior, substandard, second-rate, unsatisfactory, inadequate, deficient, awful, terrible, dreadful, (*more informal*) shoddy, (*more informal*) ropy OPPOSITES ARE excellent, outstanding, good **2** *a bad driver* ► incompetent, poor, awful, terrible, dreadful **3** *a bad effect* ► harmful, damaging, detrimental, injurious, undesirable OPPOSITES ARE beneficial, good **4** *leading a bad life* ► wicked, sinful, immoral, depraved, degenerate, dissolute OPPOSITES ARE virtuous, good **5** *a bad child* ► naughty, badly behaved, disobedient, mischievous OPPOSITES ARE well behaved, good **6** *bad language* ► vulgar, crude, foul, coarse, indecent, offensive, profane, blasphemous **7** *bad news* ► unpleasant, disagreeable, unwelcome OPPOSITES ARE good, welcome **8** *a bad time to buy a house* ► unsuitable, inappropriate, difficult, unfavourable, unfortunate, inauspicious OPPOSITES ARE favourable, suitable, good **9** *a bad accident, a bad toothache* ► serious, severe, acute, grave, critical OPPOSITES ARE minor, slight **10** *the meat is bad* ► rotten, off, putrid, decomposing, decomposed, mouldy, contaminated, sour (milk), rancid (butter) AN OPPOSITE IS fresh **11** *feeling bad* ► unwell, ill, sick OPPOSITES ARE well, healthy **12** *a bad leg* ► injured, wounded, diseased **13** *I felt bad after losing my temper.* ► guilty, remorseful, ashamed, conscience-stricken OPPOSITES ARE proud, unrepentant

bad-tempered ADJECTIVE *She was a thoroughly selfish, bad-tempered litle girl.* ► irritable, irascible, grumpy, testy, grouchy, touchy, crotchety, cantankerous, peevish, fractious, cross, (*more informal*) stroppy, (*more informal*) shirty OPPOSITES ARE good-tempered, good-humoured, affable

baffle VERB *Her answer baffled him.* ► perplex, bewilder, puzzle, mystify, confuse, bemuse, disconcert, confound, fox, (*more informal*) flummox, (*more informal*) floor

baffling ADJECTIVE *a baffling response* ► puzzling, bewildering, perplexing, confusing,

a **b** c d e f g h i j k l m n o p q r s t u v w x y z

bag *NOUN* **bags** a container made of a soft material, for holding or carrying things **bags** (*informal*) plenty • *bags of room*

bag *VERB* **bags, bagging, bagged** **1** (*informal*) catch or claim something **2** put something into bags

baggage *NOUN* luggage

baggy *ADJECTIVE* (said about clothes) large and loose

bagpipes *PLURAL NOUN* a musical instrument in which air is squeezed out of a bag into pipes Bagpipes are played especially in Scotland

bail[1] *NOUN* money that is paid or promised as a guarantee that a person who is accused of a crime will return for trial if he or she is released in the meantime

bail *VERB* **bails, bailing, bailed** provide bail for a person

bail[2] *NOUN* **bails** one of the two small pieces of wood placed on top of the stumps in cricket

bail[3] *VERB* **bails, bailing, bailed** scoop out water that has got into a boat

bailiff *NOUN* **bailiffs** **1** a law officer who serves writs and performs arrests **2** an official who takes people's property when they owe money

bait *NOUN* **1** food that is put on a hook or in a trap to catch fish or animals **2** something that is meant to tempt someone

bait *VERB* **baits, baiting, baited** **1** put bait on a hook or in a trap **2** try to make someone angry by teasing them

baize *NOUN* the thick green cloth that is used for covering snooker tables

bake *VERB* **bakes, baking, baked** **1** cook in an oven **2** make or become very hot **3** make a thing hard by heating it

baker *NOUN* **bakers** a person who bakes and sells bread or cakes
▷ **bakery** *NOUN*

balance *NOUN* **balances** **1** a steady position, with the weight or amount evenly distributed **2** a person's feeling of being steady **3** a device for weighing things, with two containers hanging from a bar **4** the difference between money paid into an account and money taken out **5** the amount of money that someone still has to pay

balance *VERB* **balances, balancing, balanced** make or be steady or equal

balcony *NOUN* **balconies** **1** a platform that sticks out from an outside wall of a building **2** the upstairs part of a theatre or cinema

Thesaurus

mystifying, mysterious, inexplicable, inscrutable, insoluble, unfathomable, extraordinary, frustrating OPPOSITES ARE clear, straightforward, comprehensible

bag *NOUN* **1** *I'll put these things in a bag.* ► container, carrier bag, carrier **2** *We'd better go and pack our bags* ► case, suitcase **3** *She always carried a bag.* ► handbag, shoulder bag **4** *The walkers had bags on their backs.* ► backpack, rucksack

bag *VERB* **1** *You need to get there early and bag a good seat.* ► secure, obtain, reserve, acquire, get **2** *He bagged four pheasants.* ► catch, shoot, kill, capture

baggage *NOUN* *She put her baggage in and climbed aboard.* ► luggage, bags, cases, suitcases, trunks, belongings, paraphernalia, (*informal*) gear, (*informal*) stuff

bait *NOUN* *The offer was meant to be a bait.* ► enticement, inducement, lure, bribe, allurement, attraction

bait *VERB* *The boys wouldn't stop baiting her.* ► tease, torment, annoy, goad, persecute, pester, provoke, hound, jeer at, (*more informal*) needle

bake *VERB* *The hot sun was baking the earth.* ► scorch, burn, parch, sear

balance *NOUN* **1** *You can weigh the fruit in the balance.* ► scales, weighing machine **2** *It is easy to stumble and lose your balance.* ► equilibrium, stability, equipoise, poise, steadiness **3** *a balance between fairness and firmness* ► parity, correspondence, symmetry, evenness, equality, equivalence **4** *a sense of personal balance* ► composure, self-assurance, equanimity, self-possession **5** *The balance of the payment is due in July.* ► remainder, difference, rest, residue
on balance *On balance it is a good scheme.* ► overall, all in all, by and large

balance *VERB* **1** *If I carry one bag in each hand, they balance each other.* ► counteract, counterbalance, neutralize, offset, equalize, match, stabilize, steady **2** *He tried to eat by balancing a plate on his knee.* ► support, keep, keep balanced, steady **3** *You have to balance the advantages and disadvantages.* ► weigh, weigh up, compare, assess, appraise, consider, estimate

balanced *ADJECTIVE* **1** *a balanced view of the issues* ► fair, objective, impartial, equitable, even-handed, impartial, disinterested OPPOSITES ARE partial, biased **2** *a balanced individual* ► level-headed, equable, sensible, sane, stable, practical OPPOSITES ARE unbalanced, neurotic **3** *a balanced diet* ► mixed, varied, well-planned, healthy OPPOSITES ARE unbalanced, unhealthy

bald *ADJECTIVE* **1** without hair on the top of the head **2** with no details; blunt • *a bald statement*
▷ **baldly** *ADVERB* **baldness** *NOUN*

ball[1] *NOUN* **balls** **1** a round object used in many games **2** anything that has a round shape • *a ball of string*
ball of the foot the rounded part of the foot at the base of the big toe

ball[2] *NOUN* **balls** a formal party where people dance

ballad *NOUN* **ballads** a simple song or poem that tells a story

ballast (bal- ast) *NOUN* heavy material that is carried in a ship to keep it steady

ball bearings *PLURAL NOUN* small steel balls rolling in a groove on which machine parts can move easily

ballerina (bal- er- een- a) *NOUN* **ballerinas** a female ballet dancer

ballet (bal- ay) *NOUN* **ballets** a stage entertainment that tells a story with dancing, mime, and music

ballistic missile *NOUN* **ballistic missiles** a missile that is initially powered and guided and then falls under gravity on its target

balloon *NOUN* **balloons** **1** a bag made of thin rubber that can be inflated and used as a toy or decoration **2** a large round bag inflated with hot air or light gases to make it rise in the air, often carrying a basket for passengers to ride in **3** an outline round spoken words in a strip cartoon

ballot *NOUN* **ballots** **1** a secret method of voting, usually by making a mark on a piece of paper **2** a piece of paper on which a vote is made

ballot *VERB* **ballots, balloting, balloted** invite people to vote for something by a ballot

ballpoint pen *NOUN* **ballpoint pens** a pen with a tiny ball round which the ink flows

balm *NOUN* **1** a sweet-scented ointment **2** something that soothes you

balmy *ADJECTIVE* **1** sweet-scented like balm **2** soft and warm • *a balmy breeze*

bamboo *NOUN* **bamboos** **1** a tall plant with hard hollow stems **2** a stem of the bamboo plant

ban *VERB* **bans, banning, banned** forbid something officially

ban *NOUN* **bans** an order that bans something

banana *NOUN* **bananas** a long curved fruit with a yellow or green skin

band[1] *NOUN* **bands** **1** a strip or loop of something **2** a range of values, wavelengths, etc.

band[2] *NOUN* **bands** **1** an organized group of people doing something together • *a band of robbers* **2** a group of people playing music together

band *VERB* **bands, banding, banded** form an organized group

bandage *NOUN* **bandages** a strip of material for binding up a wound
▷ **bandage** *VERB*

bandit *NOUN* **bandits** a member of a gang of robbers who attack travellers

bandwagon *NOUN*
jump *or* **climb on the bandwagon** join other people in something that is successful

Thesaurus

bald *ADJECTIVE* **1** *a bald man* ► bald-headed, hairless, (*euphemistic*) thin on top **2** *bald tyres* ► bare, smooth **3** *a bald statement* ► plain, direct, forthright, plain, simple, stark, straightforward, unadorned, uncompromising

ball *NOUN* **1** *a ball of string, The little animal curled itself into a ball.* ► sphere, globe, globule, orb, spheroid **2** *a ball of food* ► pellet, globule, slug **3** *a fancy-dress ball* ► dance, party, disco, social

ballot *NOUN* *a ballot for the party leadership* ► election, vote, poll, plebiscite, referendum

ban *NOUN* *a ban on smoking* ► embargo, prohibition, bar, moratorium, veto

ban *VERB* *The government wants to ban some blood sports.* ► prohibit, forbid, bar, disallow, proscribe, suppress, make illegal, stop, restrict
OPPOSITES ARE permit, allow

banal *ADJECTIVE* *a banal image of the perfect married couple* ► trite, hackneyed, commonplace, stereotypical, stock, humdrum, clichéd, dull, unimaginative, tired, boring, tedious, (*more informal*) corny
OPPOSITES ARE original, interesting

band *NOUN* **1** *red with a blue band along the top* ► strip, stripe, streak, belt, line, loop, ribbon, ring **2** *a band of followers* ► troop, body, company, group, gang, horde, party, association, clique, club, crew, flock, herd, society **3** *A band was playing.* ► orchestra, ensemble, group

band *VERB* **band together** *The village banded together to repel their attackers.* ► gather, group, unite, cooperate, join together, work together, fight together, collaborate

bandage *NOUN* *The nurse put a bandage on his wound.* ► dressing, plaster, gauze, lint

bandit *NOUN* *The camp was attacked by bandits.* ► robber, brigand, thief, outlaw, desperado, gangster, gunman, marauder, highwayman, pirate, hijacker

A B C D E F G H I J K L M N O P Q R S T U V W X Y Z

bandy *VERB* **bandies, bandying, bandied** if a word or story is bandied about, it is mentioned or told by a lot of different people

bane *NOUN* a cause of trouble or worry etc. • *Exams are the bane of our lives!*

bang *NOUN* **bangs 1** a sudden loud noise like that of an explosion **2** a sharp blow or knock

bang *VERB* **bangs, banging, banged 1** hit or shut something noisily **2** make a sudden loud noise

bang *ADVERB* **1** with a bang; suddenly **2** (*informal*) exactly • *bang in the middle*

banish *VERB* **banishes, banishing, banished 1** punish a person by ordering them to leave a place **2** drive away doubts or fears ▷ **banishment** *NOUN*

banisters *PLURAL NOUN* a handrail with upright supports beside a staircase

banjo *NOUN* **banjos** an instrument like a guitar with a round body

bank[1] *NOUN* **banks 1** a slope **2** a long piled-up mass of sand, snow, cloud, etc. **3** a row of lights or switches etc.

bank *VERB* **banks, banking, banked 1** build or form a bank **2** tilt sideways while changing direction • *The plane banked as it prepared to land.*

bank[2] *NOUN* **banks 1** a business that looks after people's money **2** a reserve supply • *a blood bank*

bank *VERB* **banks, banking, banked** put money in a bank
bank on rely on

banker *NOUN* **bankers** a person who runs a bank

bank holiday *NOUN* **bank holidays** a public holiday, when banks are officially closed

bankrupt *ADJECTIVE* unable to pay your debts ▷ **bankruptcy** *NOUN*

banner *NOUN* **banners 1** a flag **2** a strip of cloth with a design or slogan on it, carried on a pole or two poles in a procession or demonstration

banquet *NOUN* **banquets** a formal public meal ▷ **banqueting** *NOUN*

banter *NOUN* playful teasing or joking ▷ **banter** *VERB*

baptism *NOUN* **baptisms** the ceremony of baptizing someone

Baptist *NOUN* **Baptists** a member of a group of Christians who believe that a person should not be baptized until he or she is old enough to understand what baptism means

baptize *VERB* **baptizes, baptizing, baptized** receive a person into the Christian Church in a ceremony in which he or she is sprinkled with or dipped in water, and usually given a name or names

bar *NOUN* **bars 1** a long piece of something hard • *a gold bar* **2** a counter or room where refreshments, especially alcoholic drinks, are

Thesaurus

bang *NOUN* **1** *He had got a bang on the head.* ► blow, hit, smack, knock, thump, rap, clout, punch, whack, cuff, bump, collision, slam, stroke, (*more informal*) wallop **2** *Suddenly there was a loud bang.* ► blast, report, boom, crack, thud, thump, explosion, clap, crash, pop

bang *VERB* *He banged the table with his fist.* ► hit, thump, strike, whack, (*more informal*) bash, (*more informal*) clout

banish *VERB* **1** *The authorities banished him as a traitor.* ► exile, expel, deport, send away, eject, evict, expatriate, outlaw, ship away, transport **2** *Her look banished any remainng fears.* ► dispel, remove, dismiss, disperse, allay, scatter, dissipate, drive away *or* out

bank *NOUN* **1** *a grassy bank* ► slope, rise, incline, earthwork, embankment, mound, ridge, dike, rampart **2** *the bank of the lake* ► edge, border, margin, shore, side, brink **3** *a steep bank on the curve* ► camber, gradient, incline, slope, tilt, ramp, rise, (*formal*) declivity **4** *a bank of dials and switches* ► array, row, panel, tier, console, collection, series, display, file, group, line **5** *a blood bank* ► store, reserve, stock, supply, fund, depository

bank *VERB* **1** *The little plane banked to the left.* ► tilt, lean, slant, pitch, tip, incline, cant, heel, list, slope **2** *Bank the cheque immediately.* ► deposit, pay in

bankrupt *ADJECTIVE* **1** *The business was soon bankrupt.* ► insolvent, failed, ruined, in liquidation, (*more informal*) bust AN OPPOSITE IS solvent

banner *NOUN* *A banner was flying from a tall building.* ► flag, pennant, pennon, standard, streamer, ensign, colours (plural)

banter *NOUN* *good-humoured banter* ► joking, jesting, repartee, badinage, raillery, ribbing, jocularity, teasing, word play, chaffing, pleasantry

bar *NOUN* **1** *an iron bar* ► rod, pole, stake, shaft, batten, stick, strut, beam, girder, rail, railing **2** *a bar of chocolate, a bar of soap* ► block, slab, cake, tablet, chunk, wedge, piece, hunk, ingot, lump, nugget **3** *a bar to progress* ► obstacle, barrier, obstruction, hindrance, impediment, block, hurdle, check, deterrent, barricade **4** *eating and drinking at bars* ► pub, public house, saloon, cafe, tavern

bar *VERB* **1** *The people were barred from entering the country.* ► ban, prohibit, forbid, exclude,

served **3** a barrier or obstruction **4** one of the small equal sections into which music is divided • *three beats to the bar.*
the Bar barristers

bar *VERB* **bars, barring, barred** **1** fasten something with a bar or bars **2** block or obstruct • *A man with a dog barred the way.* **3** forbid or ban

barb *NOUN* **barbs** the backward-pointing spike of a spear, arrow, or fish hook, which makes the point stay in

barbarian *NOUN* **barbarians** an uncivilized or brutal person

barbaric *ADJECTIVE* savage and cruel
▷ **barbarity** *NOUN* **barbarism** *NOUN*

barbecue *NOUN* **barbecues** **1** a metal frame for grilling food over an open fire outdoors **2** a party where food is cooked in this way

barbecue *VERB* **barbecues, barbecuing, barbecued** cook food on a barbecue [via American Spanish from a Caribbean word It originally meant a wooden frame for drying fish and meat]

barbed *ADJECTIVE* **1** having a barb or barbs **2** a barbed comment or remark is deliberately hurtful

barbed wire *NOUN* wire with small spikes in it, used to make fences

barber *NOUN* **barbers** a men's hairdresser

bar chart *NOUN* **bar charts** a diagram that shows amounts as bars of varying width or height

bar code *NOUN* **bar codes** a set of black lines that are printed on goods, library books, etc., and can be read by a computer to give information about the goods, books, etc.

bard *NOUN* **bards** a poet or travelling singer [from a Celtic word used in Scottish, Irish, and Welsh]

bare *ADJECTIVE* **1** without clothing or covering **2** empty • *The cupboard was bare.* **3** plain; without details • *the bare facts* **4** only just enough • *the bare necessities of life*
▷ **bareness** *NOUN*

bare *VERB* **bares, baring, bared** uncover or reveal • *The dog bared its teeth in a snarl.*

barely *ADVERB* only just; with difficulty • *We barely reached home in time.*

bargain *NOUN* **bargains** **1** an agreement about buying or selling or exchanging something **2** something that you buy cheaply

bargain *VERB* **bargains, bargaining, bargained** argue over the price to be paid or what you will do in return for something
bargain for be prepared for or expect • *He got more than he bargained for.*

barge *NOUN* **barges** a long flat-bottomed boat used on canals

barge *VERB* **barges, barging, barged** push or knock against roughly
barge in rush into a room rudely

baritone *NOUN* **baritones** a male singer with a voice between a tenor and a bass

barium (bair- ee- um) *NOUN* a soft silvery-white metal

bark[1] *NOUN* **barks** the short harsh sound made by a dog or fox

Thesaurus

debar, forbid to enter, prevent from entering, keep out **2** *An angry crowd barred the way.* ► block, obstruct, hinder, impede, check, halt, prevent, stop, thwart

barbaric *ADJECTIVE* *a barbaric attack* ► barbarous, brutal, cruel, cold-blooded, inhuman, primitive, savage, uncivilized, wild OPPOSITES ARE civilized, humane

bare *ADJECTIVE* **1** *bare flesh* ► naked, unclothed, uncovered, nude, stark-naked, exposed, stripped, unclad, undressed, bald OPPOSITES ARE clothed, covered **2** *a bare landscape* ► barren, bleak, desolate, exposed, featureless, treeless, stark, empty, open, windswept OPPOSITES ARE lush, fertile **3** *bare trees* ► leafless, defoliated AN OPPOSITE IS leafy **4** *a bare room* ► empty, unfurnished, vacant, cleared, plain, simple, austere **5** *a bare wall* ► blank, clean, uncovered, unadorned, undecorated, unmarked, stripped **6** *the bare facts* ► straightforward, plain, simple, basic, pure, essential, fundamental, hard, bald, literal, unadorned, unambiguous, unembellished, unconcealed, undisguised **7** *the bare necessities* ► basic, essential, minimum, mere, just adequate, just sufficient

bare *VERB* *She bared her arm for the injection.* ► uncover, expose, unclothe, strip

bargain *NOUN* **1** *The government has made a bargain with the other parties.* ► agreement, deal, understanding, arrangement, pact, pledge, compact, contract, negotiation, promise, settlement, transaction, treaty **2** *a bargain at £12.99* ► good buy, good value, (*more informal*) snip, (*more informal*) steal

bargain *VERB* *The union is trying to bargain with the employers.* ► negotiate, do a deal, barter, discuss terms, hold talks, argue, haggle
bargain on *or* **for** *The crush at the doors was something I hadn't bargained for.* ► expect, foresee, imagine, plan for, allow for, reckon on, anticipate, be prepared for, contemplate, consider

bark *VERB* **1** *The dog barked.* ► woof, yap, yelp **2** *The sergeant barked an order.* ► shout, snap, growl, snarl

A B C D E F G H I J K L M N O P Q R S T U V W X Y Z

▷ **bark** *VERB*
[from Old English *beorc*, imitating the sound]

bark² *NOUN* the outer covering of a tree's branches or trunk

barley *NOUN* a cereal plant from which malt is made

bar mitzvah *NOUN* **bar mitzvahs** a religious ceremony for Jewish boys aged 13

barn *NOUN* **barns** a farm building for storing hay or grain etc.
▷ **barnyard** *NOUN*

barnacle *NOUN* **barnacles** a shellfish that attaches itself to rocks and the bottoms of ships

barometer (ba- rom- it- er) *NOUN* **barometers** an instrument that measures air pressure, used in forecasting the weather

baron *NOUN* **barons** **1** a member of the lowest rank of noblemen **2** a powerful owner of an industry or business • *a newspaper baron*
▷ **barony** *NOUN* **baronial** (ba- roh- nee- al) *ADJECTIVE*

baroness *NOUN* **baronesses** a female baron or a baron's wife

baronet *NOUN* **baronets** a nobleman ranking below a baron but above a knight
▷ **baronetcy** *NOUN*

baroque (ba- rok) *NOUN* an elaborately decorated style of architecture used in the 17th and 18th centuries

barracks *NOUN* a large building or group of buildings for soldiers to live in

barrage (ba- rahzh) *NOUN* **barrages** **1** a dam built across a river **2** heavy gunfire **3** a large amount of something • *a barrage of questions*

barrel *NOUN* **barrels** **1** a large rounded container with flat ends **2** the metal tube of a gun, through which the shot is fired

barrel organ *NOUN* **barrel organs** a musical instrument which you play by turning a handle

barren *ADJECTIVE* **1** (said about a woman) not able to have children **2** (said about land) not fertile

barricade *NOUN* **barricades** a barrier, especially one put up hastily across a street or door

barricade *VERB* **barricades, barricading, barricaded** block a street or door with a barricade

barrier *NOUN* **barriers** **1** a fence or wall that prevents people from getting past
2 something that stops you doing something

barrister *NOUN* **barristers** a lawyer who represents people in the higher lawcourts

barrow *NOUN* **barrows** **1** a wheelbarrow **2** a small cart that is pushed or pulled by hand

barter *VERB* **barters, bartering, bartered** trade by exchanging goods for other goods, not for money
USAGE This word does not mean 'to bargain'.

barter *NOUN* the system of bartering

basalt (bas- awlt) *NOUN* a kind of dark volcanic rock

base¹ *NOUN* **bases** **1** the lowest part of something; the part on which a thing stands **2** a starting point or foundation; a basis **3** a headquarters **4** each of the four corners that must be reached by a runner in baseball **5** a substance that can combine with an acid to form a salt **6** the number in terms of which other numbers can be expressed in a number

Thesaurus

bark *NOUN* *the dog's bark* ▸ woof, yap, yelp

barmy *ADJECTIVE* *(informal) You must be barmy. a barmy idea* ▸ mad, crazy, foolish

barn *NOUN* *The farm vehicles were kept in a barn.* ▸ shed, outbuilding

barrage *NOUN* **1** *a barrage across a river* ▸ dam, barrier, embankment, wall **2** *a barrage of gunfire* ▸ bombardment, salvo, battery, cannonade, fusillade, storm, volley, assault, attack, onslaught **3** *a barrage of criticism* ▸ stream, deluge, flood, onslaught, torrent, shower, mass

barrel *NOUN* *a barrel of beer* ▸ cask, butt, keg, tub, tun, drum, canister, hogshead, water-butt

barren *ADJECTIVE* **1** *barren desert* ▸ infertile, lifeless, arid, parched, desert, dry, waste, waterless, sterile, torrid, unproductive
OPPOSITES ARE fertile, lush **2** *a barren woman* ▸ infertile, sterile, childless, sterilized
AN OPPOSITE IS fertile

barricade *NOUN* *barricades across the road* ▸ barrier, obstruction, obstacle, blockade, bulwark, fence, palisade, stockade

barrier *NOUN* **1** *Police put up barriers to keep out the crowd.* ▸ barricade, fence, obstacle, obstruction, railing, fencing, wall, bar, hurdle **2** *a barrier to progress* ▸ obstacle, hindrance, impediment, check, drawback, handicap, limitation, restriction, stumbling block

base *NOUN* **1** *the base of the tower* ▸ foot, bottom, foundation, pedestal **2** *The hut was used as a base for the expedition.* ▸ headquarters, centre, station, camp, depot, post

base *VERB* **1** *The company is based in Paris.* ▸ locate, establish, set up, station **2** *Base your*

system 10 is the base of the decimal system and 2 is the base of the binary system

base VERB **bases, basing, based** use something as a starting point or foundation • *The story is based on facts.*

base[2] ADJECTIVE **1** dishonourable • *base motives* **2** not of great value • *base metals*
▷ **basely** ADVERB **baseness** NOUN

baseball NOUN **baseballs** **1** an American game in which runs are scored by hitting a ball and running round a series of four bases **2** the ball used in this game

basement NOUN **basements** a room or rooms below ground level

bash VERB **bashes, bashing, bashed** hit hard

bash NOUN **bashes** **1** a hard hit **2** (*informal*) a try • *Have a bash at it.*

bashful ADJECTIVE shy and self-conscious
▷ **bashfully** ADVERB

basic ADJECTIVE forming a basis or starting point • *Bread is a basic food.*

basin NOUN **basins** **1** a deep bowl **2** a washbasin **3** a sheltered area of water for mooring boats **4** the area from which water drains into a river • *the Amazon basin*

basis NOUN **bases** something to start from or add to; the main principle or ingredient

bask VERB **basks, basking, basked** sit or lie comfortably warming yourself in the sun

basket NOUN **baskets** a container for holding or carrying things, made of strips of flexible material or wire woven together

basketball NOUN **basketballs** **1** a game in which goals are scored by putting a ball through high nets **2** the ball used in this game

bass (bayss) ADJECTIVE deep-sounding; the bass part of a piece of music is the lowest part

bass NOUN **basses** **1** a male singer with a very deep voice **2** a bass instrument or part

bassoon NOUN **bassoons** a bass woodwind instrument

bastard NOUN **bastards** **1** (*old use*) an illegitimate child **2** (*slang*) an unpleasant or difficult person or thing
▷ **bastardy** NOUN

bat[1] NOUN **bats** **1** a shaped piece of wood used to hit the ball in cricket, baseball, etc. **2** a batsman • *their opening bat*
off your own bat without help from other people

bat VERB **bats, batting, batted** use a bat in cricket etc.

bat[2] NOUN **bats** a flying animal that looks like a mouse with wings

batch NOUN **batches** a set of things or people dealt with together

bath NOUN **baths** **1** washing your whole body while sitting in water **2** a large container for water in which to wash your whole body; this water • *Your bath is getting cold.* **3** a liquid in which something is placed • *an acid bath*

bath VERB **baths, bathing, bathed** wash in a bath

bathe VERB **bathes, bathing, bathed** **1** go swimming **2** wash something gently
▷ **bathe** NOUN **bather** NOUN **bathing suit** NOUN

bathroom NOUN **bathrooms** a room containing a bath

baths PLURAL NOUN **1** a building with rooms where people can bath **2** a public swimming pool

Thesaurus

story on events in the news. ► build, construct, establish, found, ground

bash VERB **1** *She could hardly avoid bashing him in the stomach.* ► hit, strike, knock, smack, clout, (*more informal*) biff **2 bash into** *The car bashed into a lamp post.* ► collide with, crash into, run into, bang into, bump into

bashful ADJECTIVE *Men tend to be bashful about their feelings.* ► shy, coy, reserved, diffident, embarrassed, inhibited, modest, self-conscious, hesitant, timid, reserved, retiring OPPOSITES ARE assertive, forward, bold, confident

basic ADJECTIVE **1** *You must first learn the basic principles of the subject.* ► fundamental, chief, main, key, crucial, principal, central, primary, elementary AN OPPOSITE IS secondary **2** *Washing facilities at the camp are very basic.* ► plain, simple, crude, modest, stark, sparse, spartan, unsophisticated OPPOSITES ARE elaborate, sophisticated

basin NOUN *She poured some water into the basin.* ► bowl, dish, sink, stoup

basis NOUN *The accusations had no factual basis.* ► foundation, justification, support, rationale, base

basket NOUN *a basket of fruit* ► hamper, pannier, creel, punnet, trug

bass ADJECTIVE *a bass note* ► low, deep, bottom

batch NOUN *a batch of cakes* ► consignment, group, quantity, assortment, lot, set

bath NOUN **1** *I'm going to have a bath.* ► wash, douche, jacuzzi (*trademark*), sauna, shower, (*more informal*) soak

bathe VERB **1** *Holiday-makers were bathing in the sea.* ► swim, paddle, plunge, splash about, (*more informal*) take a dip **2** *The wound must be carefully bathed.* ► cleanse, clean, wash, rinse, immerse, moisten, soak, steep, swill

a b c d e f g h i j k l m n o p q r s t u v w x y z

batsman *NOUN* **batsmen** a player who uses a bat in cricket etc.

battalion *NOUN* **battalions** an army unit containing two or more companies

batten *VERB* **battens, battening, battened** fasten something down firmly

batter *VERB* **batters, battering, battered** hit hard and often

batter *NOUN* **batters** **1** a beaten mixture of flour, eggs, and milk, used for making pancakes etc. **2** a player who is batting in baseball

battery *NOUN* **batteries** **1** a device for storing and supplying electricity **2** a set of similar pieces of equipment; a group of large guns **3** a series of cages in which poultry or animals are kept close together • *battery farming*

battle *NOUN* **battles** **1** a fight between two armies **2** a struggle
▷ **battlefield** *NOUN* **battleground** *NOUN*

battle *VERB* **battles, battling, battled** fight or struggle

battlements *PLURAL NOUN* the top of a castle wall, often with gaps from which the defenders could fire at the enemy

battleship *NOUN* **battleships** a heavily armed warship

bawl *VERB* **bawls, bawling, bawled** **1** shout **2** cry noisily

bay[1] *NOUN* **bays** a place where the shore curves inwards

bay[2] *NOUN* **bays** a compartment or small area set aside for something • *a parking bay*

bay[3] *NOUN* **bays** the long deep cry of a hunting hound or other large dog
at bay cornered but defiantly facing attackers • *a stag at bay*
keep at bay prevent something from coming near or causing harm • *We need laws to keep poverty at bay.*

bayonet *NOUN* **bayonets** a blade that can be fixed to the end of a rifle and used for stabbing

bay window *NOUN* **bay windows** a window that sticks out from the main wall of a house

bazaar *NOUN* **bazaars** **1** a market place in an Eastern country **2** a sale to raise money for a charity etc.

BBC *ABBREVIATION* British Broadcasting Corporation

BC *ABBREVIATION* before Christ (used with dates counting back from the birth of Jesus Christ)

be *VERB* **am, are, is; was, were; being, been**
1 exist; occupy a position • *The shop is on the corner.* **2** happen; take place • *The wedding is tomorrow.* This verb is also used **1** to join subject and complement (*He is my teacher*) **2** to form parts of other verbs (*It is raining. He was killed*)
have been have gone to or come to as a visitor etc. • *We have been to Rome.*

beach *NOUN* **beaches** the part of the seashore nearest to the water

beacon *NOUN* **beacons** a light or fire used as a signal or warning

bead *NOUN* **beads** **1** a small piece of a hard substance with a hole in it for threading with

Thesaurus

batter *VERB* **1** *Someone battered on the door.* ► pound, beat, knock **2** *Winds were battering the waterfront.* ► pound, buffet, lash, pummel **3** *He was battered into submission.* ► beat, pummel, thump

battered *ADJECTIVE* *help for battered wives* ► beaten, abused, assaulted, maltreated, victimized

battle *NOUN* **1** *The battle took place a few miles north of the city.* ► fight, engagement, action, clash, encounter, conflict **2** *a legal battle for ownership of the club* ► conflict, struggle, dispute **3** *a battle to save the library from closure* ► campaign, crusade

battle *VERB* *They battled to control the fire.* ► fight, struggle, strive

baulk *VERB* **baulk at** *Some farmers baulk at using pesticides.* ► resist, (*more formal*) eschew, be reluctant to

bawdy *ADJECTIVE* *bawdy stories* ► rude, indecent, crude, ribald, naughty, improper, risqué, lewd, vulgar, obscene

bawl *VERB* **1** *The child sat on its bed bawling.* ► cry, sob, weep, blubber **2** *'Get out,' she bawled.* ► yell, shout, roar, bellow, shriek, scream

bay *NOUN* **1** *a large bay on the coast* ► cove, inlet, gulf, bight **2** *a loading bay* ► recess, alcove, booth, compartment, niche, nook, opening

bazaar *NOUN* *the church bazaar* ► sale, fair, fête, jumble sale, car boot sale, bring-and-buy, market, auction

be *VERB* **1** *There was a young family next door.* ► exist, live **2** *After he'd been there a while he ordered a drink.* ► remain, stay, wait, linger, (*more informal*) hang on **3** *The next performance of the play will be tomorrow.* ► take place, occur, happen, come about

beach *NOUN* *a picnic on the beach* ► shore, sand, sands, seashore, coast, (*poetic*) strand

beacon *NOUN* *a beacon on the hill* ► flare, signal, bonfire, beam

bead *NOUN* *beads of sweat* ► drop, droplet, globule, blob, drip, pearl

others on a string or wire, e.g. to make a necklace **2** a drop of liquid • *a bead of sweat* [from Old English *gebed* The original meaning was 'prayer': people kept count of the prayers they said by moving the beads on a rosary, to which the meaning of *bead* was transferred.]

beady *ADJECTIVE* (said about eyes) small and bright

beak *NOUN* **beaks** the hard horny part of a bird's mouth [via early French from Latin *beccus*]

beaker *NOUN* **beakers 1** a tall drinking mug, often without a handle **2** a glass container used for pouring liquids in a laboratory

beam *NOUN* **beams 1** a long thick bar of wood or metal **2** a ray or stream of light or other radiation **3** a happy smile

beam *VERB* **beams, beaming, beamed 1** smile happily **2** send out a beam of light or other radiation

bean *NOUN* **beans 1** a kind of plant with seeds growing in pods **2** its seed or pod eaten as food **3** the seed of coffee

bear[1] *NOUN* **bears** a large heavy animal with thick fur and large teeth and claws

bear[2] *VERB* **bears, bearing, bore, borne 1** carry or support **2** have or show a mark etc. • *She still bears the scar.* **3** endure or stand • *I can't bear this pain.* **4** produce or give birth to • *She bore him two sons.*

▷ **bearer** *NOUN*

bear in mind remember something and take it into account

bear out support or confirm

bearable *ADJECTIVE* able to be endured; tolerable

beard *NOUN* **beards** hair on a man's chin

▷ **bearded** *ADJECTIVE*

beard *VERB* **beards, bearding, bearded** come face to face with a person and challenge him or her boldly

bearing *NOUN* **bearings 1** the way a person stands, walks, behaves, etc. **2** relevance • *My friendship with Tom has no bearing on his selection for the team.* **3** the direction or position of one thing in relation to another **4** a device for preventing friction in a machine • *ball bearings*

get your bearings work out where you are in relation to things

beast *NOUN* **beasts 1** any large four-footed animal **2** (*informal*) a cruel or vicious person

▷ **beastly** *ADJECTIVE*

beat *VERB* **beats, beating, beat, beaten 1** hit often, especially with a stick **2** shape or flatten something by beating it **3** stir vigorously **4** make repeated movements • *His heart beat faster.* **5** do better than somebody; overcome

▷ **beater** *NOUN*

beat *NOUN* **beats 1** a regular rhythm or stroke • *the beat of your heart* **2** emphasis in rhythm;

Thesaurus

beaker *NOUN* *a beaker of water* ► mug, tumbler, goblet, cup, glass, jar, tankard

beam *NOUN* **1** *a house with wooden beams* ► timber, joist, girder, spar, bar, plank, post, rafter, support, stanchion, boom **2** *a beam of light* ► ray, shaft, gleam, stream

beam *VERB* **1** *Satellites beam radio waves to rooftop aerials.* ► broadcast, transmit, direct, emit, radiate, send out, aim **2** *Daphne beamed happily.* ► smile, grin OPPOSITES ARE glower, frown

bear *VERB* **1** *The rope would no longer bear his weight.* ► support, carry, hold, sustain, prop up, take **2** *The document bore a signature.* ► display, possess, show, exhibit, have **3** *The postman arrived, bearing a large parcel.* ► carry, bring, convey, transport, deliver, fetch, move, take, transfer **4** *I cannot bear pain. We found the noise hard to bear.* ► put up with, endure, tolerate, stand, stomach, abide, accept, cope with, live with, suffer, sustain, undergo, brook **5** *The woman bore a child.* ► give birth to, produce, mother, bring forth

bear down on *A huge vehicle was bearing down on them.* ► approach, advance on, close in on

bear out *The report bears out what I was saying.* ► confirm, endorse, corroborate

bearable *ADJECTIVE* *The pain was only just bearable.* ► tolerable, endurable, acceptable

bearing *NOUN* **1** *The Baroness had a regal bearing.* ► demeanour, air, manner, look, appearance, behaviour, presence, carriage, deportment, mien, poise, posture, style **2** *The discovery could have some bearing on the mystery.* ► connection (with), relevance (to), significance (for), import (for), pertinence (to), reference (to), relationship (with)

bearings *PLURAL NOUN* *When it got dark we began to lose our bearings.* ► sense of direction, orientation, whereabouts, position, situation, way

beast *NOUN* **1** *the roars of wild beasts* ► animal, creature, brute **2** *Her husband was a beast.* ► brute, monster, fiend, demon RELATED ADJECTIVE bestial

beastly *ADJECTIVE* *Derek had been beastly to them.* ► unkind, cruel, mean, nasty, horrible, spiteful

beat *NOUN* **1** *music with a strong beat* ► rhythm, pulse, throb, accent, stress **2** *a policeman's beat* ► circuit, rounds, route, itinerary, journey, path, way

beat *VERB* **1** *The man was beating a dog with a stick.* ► hit, strike, thrash, whip, attack, assault, (*more informal*) wallop, (*more informal*) whack **2** *Molly was beating eggs for her omelette.*

the strong rhythm of pop music **3** a policeman's regular route

beautiful *ADJECTIVE* attractive to your senses or your mind
▷ **beautifully** *ADVERB*

beautify *VERB* **beautifies, beautifying, beautified** make someone beautiful
▷ **beautification** *NOUN*

beauty *NOUN* **beauties 1** a quality that gives pleasure to your senses or your mind **2** a person or thing that has beauty **3** an excellent example of something

beaver *NOUN* **beavers** an animal with soft brown fur and strong teeth; it builds its home in a deep pool which it makes by damming a stream

beaver *VERB* **beavers, beavering, beavered** work hard • *He's beavering away on the computer.*

because *CONJUNCTION* for the reason that
because of for the reason of • *He limped because of his bad leg.*

beck *NOUN*
at someone's beck and call always ready and waiting to do what he or she asks

beckon *VERB* **beckons, beckoning, beckoned** make a sign to a person asking him or her to come

become *VERB* **becomes, becoming, became, become 1** come or grow to be; begin to be • *It became dark.* **2** be suitable for; make a person look attractive
become of happen to • *What became of it?*

bed *NOUN* **beds 1** a piece of furniture that you sleep or rest on, especially one with a mattress and coverings **2** a piece of a garden where plants are grown **3** the bottom of the sea or of a river **4** a flat base; a foundation **5** a layer of rock or soil

bedclothes *PLURAL NOUN* sheets, blankets, etc.

bedpan *NOUN* **bedpans** a container for use as a lavatory by a bedridden person

bedraggled (bid- rag- eld) *ADJECTIVE* very untidy; wet and dirty

bedridden *ADJECTIVE* too weak or ill to get out of bed

bedrock *NOUN* solid rock beneath soil

bedroom *NOUN* **bedrooms** a room for sleeping in

bedtime *NOUN* **bedtimes** the time for going to bed

bee *NOUN* **bees** a stinging insect with four wings that makes honey

beech *NOUN* **beeches** a tree with smooth bark and glossy leaves

beef *NOUN* meat from an ox, bull, or cow [via early French from Latin *bos bovis* = head of cattle]

Thesaurus

► whip, agitate, blend, froth up, mix, stir **3** *His heart was beating faster.* ► pound, pulsate, race, thump, flutter, palpitate **4** *William of Normandy beat the English at the Battle of Hastings. The visitors beat the home team decisively.* ► defeat, overcome, conquer, vanquish, subdue, crush, overpower, overwhelm, rout, trounce, win against, get the better of, (*more informal*) thrash
beat about the bush *Let's not beat about the bush.* ► prevaricate, vacillate, hedge, (*more informal*) flannel
beat up *They went into town and got beaten up.* ► assault, attack

beautiful *ADJECTIVE* *a beautiful young woman, a beautiful garden* ► attractive, pretty, good-looking, nice-looking, lovely, glamorous, gorgeous, stunning AN OPPOSITE IS ugly

beauty *NOUN* *the beauty of the scene* ► attractiveness, prettiness, loveliness, charm, allure, magnificence, radiance, splendour, appeal, glamour, glory, grace, handsomeness AN OPPOSITE IS ugliness RELATED ADJECTIVE aesthetic

because *CONJUNCTION*
because of *He missed most of the season because of injury.* ► on account of, owing to, due to, as a result of, as a consequence of, in view of

beckon *VERB* *She beckoned him to go over to her.* ► signal, gesture, motion, gesticulate, invite

become *VERB* **1** *Caterpillars become butterflies.* ► grow into, turn into, change into, develop into **2** *The family soon became rich.* ► grow, come to be, turn **3** *She wants to become the second woman prime minister.* ► be appointed, be elected, be chosen, be made **4** *Dark colours become you.* ► suit, flatter, befit, grace, set off, enhance, harmonize with

becoming *ADJECTIVE* *The dress is very becoming.* ► attractive, elegant, fetching, pretty, comely

bed *NOUN* **1** *A cat lay on the bed.* ► divan, bunk, couch **2** *a flower bed* ► plot, patch, area **3** *the bed of a river* ► bottom, floor, course **4** *posts set in a bed of concrete* ► base, foundation, support, setting

bedraggled *ADJECTIVE* *The heavy rain had left him looking bedraggled.* ► dishevelled, unkempt, untidy, sodden, messy, scruffy, dirty, soiled, stained, wet OPPOSITES ARE neat, clean, spruce

bee *NOUN* *Bees hovered round the flowers.* ► drone, worker, bumblebee, honeybee, queen
a bee in your bonnet *He had a bee in his bonnet about queues.* ► obsession, preoccupation, fixation, compulsion, (*more informal*) hang-up

beefy ADJECTIVE having a solid muscular body
▷ **beefiness** NOUN

beehive NOUN **beehives** a box or other container for bees to live in

beeline NOUN
make a beeline for go straight or quickly towards something

beer NOUN **beers** an alcoholic drink made from malt and hops
▷ **beery** ADJECTIVE

beet NOUN **beet** or **beets** a plant with a thick root used as a vegetable or for making sugar

beetle NOUN **beetles** an insect with hard shiny wing covers

beetroot NOUN **beetroot** the dark red root of beet used as a vegetable

before ADVERB at an earlier time • *Have you been here before?*

before PREPOSITION, CONJUNCTION **1** earlier than • *I was here before you!* **2** in front of • *He came before the judge.*

beforehand ADVERB earlier; in readiness

befriend VERB **befriends, befriending, befriended** make friends with someone

beg VERB **begs, begging, begged** **1** ask to be given money, food, etc. **2** ask formally or desperately
beg the question argue in an illogical way by relying on the result that you are trying to prove
go begging be available

I beg your pardon I apologize; I did not hear what you said

beggar NOUN **beggars** **1** a person who lives by begging **2** (*informal*) a person • *You lucky beggar!*
▷ **beggary** NOUN

begin VERB **begins, beginning, began, begun** **1** do the earliest or first part of something; start speaking **2** come into existence • *The problem began last year.* **3** have something as its first part • *The word begins with B.*

beginner NOUN **beginners** a person who is just beginning to learn a subject

beginning NOUN **beginnings** the start or first part of something

begrudge VERB **begrudges, begrudging, begrudged** resent having to give or allow something; grudge

beguile (big- I'll) VERB **beguiles, beguiling, beguiled** **1** amuse or fascinate **2** deceive

behalf NOUN
on behalf of for the benefit of someone else or as their representative • *We are collecting money on behalf of cancer research.*
on my behalf for me
USAGE Do not use *on behalf of* (= for someone else) when you mean *on the part of* (= by someone). For example, do not say: *This was the worst performance on behalf of Arsenal that I can remember.*

behave VERB **behaves, behaving, behaved** **1** act in a particular way • *They behaved badly.*

Thesaurus

beefy ADJECTIVE *A beefy man sat at the bar.*
► muscular, brawny, burly, hefty, stocky, fat, portly

before ADVERB *She had called the day before.*
► earlier, in advance, previously, sooner

befriend VERB *He had tried to befriend the new boy.* ► make friends with, get to know, look after, stand by, help, support, take under your wing

beg VERB **1** *A man on the pavement was begging.* ► ask for money, solicit money, (*more informal*) cadge, (*more informal*) scrounge **2** *Do we have to beg for a favour?* ► plead, entreat, implore, ask, beseech, crave, importune, petition, pray, request, (*formal*) supplicate

beggar NOUN *He always gave money to beggars he met in the street.* ► tramp, vagrant, destitute person, down-and-out, homeless person, (*more formal*) mendicant, pauper, poor person

begin VERB **1** *We will begin work tomorrow.* ► start, embark on, set about, get down to, (*more formal*) commence AN OPPOSITE IS finish **2** *The interviewer began with a few quick questions.* ► start, start off, open, lead off, get going AN OPPOSITE IS conclude **3** *Where did the rumour begin?* ► start, originate, spring up, emerge, (*more formal*) commence
AN OPPOSITE IS end RELATED ADJECTIVE incipient

beginner NOUN **1** *The course is for beginners.* ► novice, initiate, learner, starter, new recruit, trainee, apprentice, tiro

beginning NOUN **1** *the beginning of a new era* ► birth, dawn, start, starting point, inception, establishment, origin, onset, emergence **2** *She had been opposed to the idea from the beginning* ► outset, start **3** *the beginning of the story* ► opening, start, prelude

begrudge VERB *Kate didn't seem to begrudge Harry all his wealth.* ► resent, grudge, mind, object to, be bitter about, covet, envy, be jealous of, be envious of

behave VERB **1** *The children worked hard and behaved well.* ► conduct yourself, act, react, respond, run, acquit yourself **2** **behave yourself** *Try to behave yourself.* ► be good, act correctly, be on your best behaviour

A
B
C
D
E
F
G
H
I
J
K
L
M
N
O
P
Q
R
S
T
U
V
W
X
Y
Z

2 show good manners • *Behave yourself!*
▷ **behaviour** NOUN **behavioural** ADJECTIVE

behead VERB **beheads, beheading, beheaded** cut the head off a person or thing; execute a person in this way

behind ADVERB **1** at or to the back; at a place people have left • *Don't leave it behind.* **2** not making good progress; late • *I'm behind with my rent.*

behind PREPOSITION **1** at or to the back of; on the further side of **2** having made less progress than • *He is behind the others in French.* **3** supporting; causing • *What is behind all this trouble?*
behind a person's back kept secret from him or her deceitfully
behind the times out of date

behind NOUN **behinds** (*informal*) a person's bottom

behindhand ADVERB, ADJECTIVE late or slow in doing something

beige (bayzh) NOUN, ADJECTIVE a very light brown colour

being NOUN **beings 1** existence **2** a creature

belated ADJECTIVE coming very late or too late
▷ **belatedly** ADVERB

belch VERB **belches, belching, belched 1** send out wind from your stomach through your mouth noisily **2** send out fire or smoke etc. from an opening
▷ **belch** NOUN

belief NOUN **beliefs 1** believing **2** something a person believes

believe VERB **believes, believing, believed** think that something is true or that someone is telling the truth
▷ **believable** ADJECTIVE **believer** NOUN
believe in think that something exists or is good or can be relied on

belittle VERB **belittles, belittling, belittled** make something seem of little value • *Do not belittle their success.*
▷ **belittlement** NOUN

bell NOUN **bells 1** a cup-shaped metal instrument that makes a ringing sound when struck by the clapper hanging inside it **2** any device that makes a ringing or buzzing sound to attract attention **3** a bell-shaped object

belligerent (bil- ij- er- ent) ADJECTIVE **1** aggressive; eager to fight **2** fighting; engaged in a war
▷ **belligerently** ADVERB **belligerence** NOUN

bellow NOUN **bellows 1** the loud deep sound made by a bull or other large animal **2** a deep shout

bellow VERB **bellows, bellowing, bellowed** give a deep shout

belly NOUN **bellies** the abdomen; the stomach

belong VERB **belongs, belonging, belonged** have a proper place • *The pans belong in the kitchen.*

Thesaurus

behaviour NOUN *Their behaviour was disgusting.*
► conduct, manners, attitude, demeanour, deportment, bearing

behead VERB *The king was beheaded.*
► decapitate, execute, guillotine

being NOUN **1** *She loves him with all her being.*
► existence, soul, spirit, essence, actuality, life, living, reality, solidity, substance **2** *a mortal being* ► person, creature, individual, animal, entity

belch VERB **1** *Laurence belched behind his hand.* ► burp, emit wind **2** *The vehicle was belching black smoke.* ► emit, give out, discharge, send out, smoke, spew out, erupt, fume, gush

belief NOUN **1** *She had a strong belief that he was innocent.* ► conviction, confidence, opinion, certainty, credence, sureness OPPOSITES ARE disbelief, doubt **2** *a belief in the benefits of a good diet* ► trust, reliance (on), credence **3** *religious belief* ► faith, ideology, principle, creed, dogma AN OPPOSITE IS scepticism

believe VERB **1** *I find that hard to believe.*
► accept, be certain about, be convinced by, regard as true, (*more informal*) swallow
AN OPPOSITE IS disbelieve RELATED ADJECTIVE credible **2** *I believe several people have cheated.*
► think, consider, maintain, conclude, be of the opinion, think it likely, feel, imagine, judge, suppose, take it for granted

believer NOUN *a religious believer* ► devotee, disciple, follower, adherent, fanatic, proselyte, supporter, upholder, zealot OPPOSITES ARE sceptic, agnostic, atheist

bell NOUN *I can hear the bell.* ► chime, gong, alarm, carillon, knell, peal, signal

belligerent ADJECTIVE **1** *She stared in a belligerent manner.* ► aggressive, hostile, antagonistic, confrontational, argumentative, quarrelsome, militant, combative, provocative, contentious, pugnacious **2** *a belligerent nation* ► warlike, bellicose, militant, militaristic, violent
AN OPPOSITE IS peaceable

bellow VERB *He bellowed something in her ear.*
► shout, yell, bawl, roar, boom, shriek

belly NOUN *He stood scratching his belly.*
► stomach, abdomen, middle, (*usually disapproving*) paunch, (*more informal*) tummy, (*much more informal*) tum

belong VERB **1 belong to** *The house belongs to his mother.* ► be owned by, be the property of **2 belong to** *I belong to a sports club.* ► be a member of, be affiliated with, be connected

belong to be the property of; be a member of • *We belong to the same club.*

belongings PLURAL NOUN a person's possessions

beloved ADJECTIVE dearly loved

below ADVERB at or to a lower position; underneath • *There's fire down below.*

below PREPOSITION lower than; under • *The temperature was ten degrees below zero.*

belt NOUN **belts** **1** a strip of cloth or leather etc. worn round the waist **2** a band of flexible material used in machinery **3** a long narrow area • *a belt of rain*

belt VERB **belts, belting, belted** **1** put a belt round something **2** (*slang*) hit or beat **3** (*slang*) rush along

bench NOUN **benches** **1** a long seat **2** a long table for working at **3** the seat where judges or magistrates sit; the judges or magistrates hearing a lawsuit

bend VERB **bends, bending, bent** **1** change from being straight **2** turn downwards; stoop • *She bent to pick it up.*

bend NOUN **bends** a place where something bends; a curve or turn • *a bend in the road*

beneath PREPOSITION **1** under **2** unworthy of • *Cheating is beneath you.*

beneath ADVERB underneath

benefactor NOUN **benefactors** a person who gives money or other help

beneficial ADJECTIVE having a good or helpful effect; advantageous

beneficiary (ben- if- ish- er- ee) NOUN **beneficiaries** a person who receives benefits, especially from a will

benefit NOUN **benefits** **1** something that is helpful or profitable **2** a payment to which a person is entitled from government funds or from an insurance policy

benefit VERB **benefits, benefiting, benefited** **1** do good to a person or thing **2** receive a benefit

benevolent ADJECTIVE **1** kind and helpful **2** formed for charitable purposes • *a benevolent fund*
▷ **benevolently** ADVERB **benevolence** NOUN

benign (bin- I'n) ADJECTIVE **1** kindly **2** favourable **3** (said about a disease) mild, not malignant
▷ **benignly** ADVERB

benignant (bin- ig- nant) ADJECTIVE kindly

Thesaurus

with **3** *They felt they did not belong there.* ► feel welcome, have a place, be at home **4** *The book belongs on the top shelf.* ► be located, have a place, go

belongings PLURAL NOUN *Remember to take all your belongings with you.* ► possessions, property, personal effects, (*more informal*) stuff

beloved ADJECTIVE *her beloved father* ► dear, dearest, darling, loved, much loved, cherished

belt NOUN **1** *a raincoat tied with a belt* ► girdle, sash, strap, waistband, (*of a man's evening suit*) cummerbund **2** *a spindle driven by a belt* ► band, loop, circle **3** *a belt of woodland* ► strip, stretch, area, tract, zone, region, district, line, swathe

belt VERB **belt along** (*informal*) *They all belted along to the bus station.* ► hurry, rush, speed

bemused ADJECTIVE *She sat there with a bemused expression.* ► bewildered, confused, distracted, puzzled, muddled, baffled, perplexed

bench NOUN *The children sat in a row on a bench.* ► pew, long seat, form, stall

bend NOUN *We came to a bend in the road.* ► curve, turn, angle, corner, twist, zigzag

bend VERB **1** *You can bend the pipe round the tank.* ► curve, curl, angle, turn **2** *The road bends ahead.* ► curve, turn, veer, deviate, twist
bend down *He bent down to pick up the piece of paper.* ► stoop, bow, crouch, duck, kneel, lean

beneficial ADJECTIVE *A good diet is beneficial to health.* ► good (for), advantageous, favourable, useful, valuable, helpful, salutary, wholesome AN OPPOSITE IS harmful

benefit NOUN **1** *the benefits of a healthy diet* ► advantage, reward, strength, blessing, convenience, gain, asset, service AN OPPOSITE IS disadvantage **2** *We are doing it for your benefit.* ► good, sake, interest, welfare, advantage **3** *the unemployed who are on benefit* ► social security, welfare, assistance, allowance, income support

benefit VERB *The tax cuts will benefit those on a low income.* ► help, advantage, assist, aid, advance, be beneficial to, do good to, profit, serve AN OPPOSITE IS hinder

benevolence NOUN *The hospital is dependent on the benevolence of local businesses.* ► kindness, generosity, goodness, goodwill, consideration, charity, magnanimity

benevolent ADJECTIVE *She smiled a benevolent smile.* ► kind, generous, helpful, caring, benign, friendly, magnanimous, sympathetic, considerate, philanthropic AN OPPOSITE IS unkind

benign ADJECTIVE **1** *a benign smile* ► friendly, kind, benevolent **2** *a benign influence* ► favourable, beneficial, advantageous, propitious

A B C D E F G H I J K L M N O P Q R S T U V W X Y Z

bent *ADJECTIVE* curved or crooked
bent on intending to do something

bent *NOUN* a talent for something

bequeath *VERB* **bequeaths, bequeathing, bequeathed** leave something to a person, especially in a will

bequest *NOUN* **bequests** something left to a person, especially in a will

bereaved *ADJECTIVE* extremely sad because a relative or friend has died
▷ **bereavement** *NOUN*

berry *NOUN* **berries** any small round juicy fruit without a stone

berserk (ber- serk) *ADJECTIVE*
go berserk become uncontrollably violent

berth *NOUN* **berths** **1** a sleeping place on a ship or train **2** a place where a ship can moor
give a wide berth to keep at a safe distance from a person or thing

berth *VERB* **berths, berthing, berthed** moor in a berth

beseech *VERB* **beseeches, beseeching, beseeched** *or* **besought** ask earnestly; implore

beside *PREPOSITION* **1** by the side of; near **2** compared with
be beside himself *or* **herself** *etc.* be very excited or upset

besides *PREPOSITION, ADVERB* in addition to; also • *Who came besides you?* • *And besides, it's the wrong colour.*

besiege *VERB* **besieges, besieging, besieged** **1** surround a place in order to capture it **2** crowd round • *Fans besieged the singer after the concert.*

besotted *ADJECTIVE* too fond of something; fond in a silly way

besought *past tense of* **beseech**

best *ADJECTIVE* of the most excellent kind; most able to do something

best *ADVERB* **1** in the best way; most **2** most usefully; most wisely • *We had best go.*

best man *NOUN* the bridegroom's chief attendant at a wedding

bestow *VERB* **bestows, bestowing, bestowed** present to someone
▷ **bestowal** *NOUN*

best-seller *NOUN* **best-sellers** a book that sells in large numbers

bet *NOUN* **bets** **1** an agreement that you will receive money if you are correct in choosing the winner of a race, game, etc. or in saying something will happen, and will lose money if you are not correct **2** the money you risk losing in a bet

bet *VERB* **bets, betting, bet** *or* **betted** **1** make a bet **2** (*informal*) think most likely; predict • *I bet he will forget.*

beta (beet- a) *NOUN* the second letter of the Greek alphabet, = b

betray *VERB* **betrays, betraying, betrayed** **1** be disloyal to a person or country etc.

Thesaurus

bent *ADJECTIVE* **1** *a bent nail* ► crooked, twisted, misshapen, angled, buckled, distorted, folded, looped, warped AN OPPOSITE IS straight **2** *a man with a bent back* ► crooked, hunched, arched, bowed, curved **3** (*informal*) *bent politicians* ► corrupt, criminal, dishonest, fraudulent, immoral, untrustworthy, wicked AN OPPOSITE IS honest

berserk *ADJECTIVE* **go berserk** *reports of a man who went berserk in the street and was hit by a car* ► go crazy, go mad, become demented, become frantic, become hysterical, go out of your mind, rave, become deranged, run amok, (*more informal*) freak out

besiege *VERB* **1** *Alexander besieged the city for two years.* ► lay siege to, blockade, surround, encircle, confine, beleaguer, (*old use*) invest **2** *She spent a whole day besieged by reporters outside her London home.* ► surround, mob, plague, harass, pester, overwhelm

best *ADJECTIVE* **1** *one of the best bookshops in London* ► foremost, leading, top, finest, pre-eminent, supreme, premier, optimum, outstanding, unsurpassed, unequalled, unrivalled AN OPPOSITE IS worst **2** *Do whatever you think best.* ► most suitable, most appropriate, most fitting, most sensible

bestow *VERB* *The college bestowed a scholarship on her.* ► award, confer, endow, (*less formal*) present, (*less formal*) give
USAGE If you use *award*, you say *The college awarded her a scholarship*. This is a much less formal and more ordinary word. If you use *present* or *endow*, you say *The college presented* (or *endowed*) *her with a scholarship*. If you use *confer*, you say *The college conferred a scholarship on her*.

bet *NOUN* **1** *a £10 bet* ► gamble, wager, (*informal*) punt **2** *My bet is they won't come.* ► opinion, forecast, prediction, feeling, hunch

bet *VERB* **1** *She bet all her savings and won.* ► wager, gamble, stake, risk **2** (*informal*) *I bet I'm right.* ► (*less informal*) be sure, (*less informal*) be confident, (*less informal*) be convinced, (*less informal*) expect

betray *VERB* **1** *We trusted him and he betrayed us.* ► let down, break your promise to, be unfaithful to, double-cross, deceive **2** *They were betrayed to the authorities.* ► inform on,

2 reveal something without meaning to
▷ **betrayal** NOUN **betrayer** NOUN

betrothed ADJECTIVE (*formal*) engaged to be married
▷ **betroth** VERB **betrothal** NOUN

better ADJECTIVE **1** more excellent; more satisfactory **2** recovered from illness

better ADVERB **1** in a better way; more **2** more usefully; more wisely • *We had better go.*
get the better of defeat or outwit

better VERB **betters, bettering, bettered**
1 improve something **2** do better than
▷ **betterment** NOUN

between PREPOSITION, ADVERB **1** within two or more given limits • *between the walls*
2 connecting two or more people, places, or things • *The train runs between London and Glasgow.* **3** shared by • *Divide this money between you.* **4** separating; comparing • *Can you tell the difference between them?*
USAGE The preposition **between** should be followed by the object form of the pronoun (**me, her, him, them,** or **us**). The expression 'between you and I' is incorrect; say *between you and me.*

beverage NOUN **beverages** any kind of drink

bewail VERB **bewails, bewailing, bewailed** mourn for something

beware VERB be careful • *Beware of pickpockets.*

bewilder VERB **bewilders, bewildering, bewildered** puzzle someone hopelessly
▷ **bewilderment** NOUN

bewitch VERB **bewitches, bewitching, bewitched** **1** put a magic spell on someone **2** delight someone very much

beyond PREPOSITION, ADVERB **1** further than; further on • *Don't go beyond the fence.* **2** outside the range of; too difficult for • *The problem is beyond me.*

bias NOUN **biases** **1** a feeling or influence for or against someone or something; a prejudice **2** a tendency to swerve **3** a slanting direction

biased ADJECTIVE prejudiced

bib NOUN **bibs** **1** a cloth or covering put under a baby's chin during meals **2** the part of an apron above the waist

Bible NOUN **Bibles** the sacred book of the Jews (the Old Testament) and of the Christians (the Old and New Testament) [from Greek *biblia* = books. The word originally meant rolls of papyrus from Byblos, a port now in Lebanon.]

biblical ADJECTIVE to do with or in the Bible

bibliography (bib- lee- og- ra- fee) NOUN **bibliographies** **1** a list of books about a subject or by a particular author **2** the study of books and their history
▷ **bibliographical** ADJECTIVE

bicentenary (by- sen- teen- er- ee) NOUN **bicentenaries** a 200th anniversary
▷ **bicentennial** (by- sen- ten- ee- al) ADJECTIVE

biceps (by- seps) NOUN **biceps** the large muscle at the front of the arm above the elbow

bicker VERB **bickers, bickering, bickered** quarrel over unimportant things; squabble

bicycle NOUN **bicycles** a two-wheeled vehicle driven by pedals
▷ **bicyclist** NOUN

bid[1] NOUN **bids** **1** the offer of an amount you are willing to pay for something, especially at an auction **2** an attempt

Thesaurus

denounce **3** *Please don't betray my secret. He found it hard not to betray his feelings.* ► reveal, give away, manifest, show, indicate, disclose, divulge, expose, let out, let slip, tell

better ADJECTIVE **1** *We are looking for better facilities.* ► superior, finer, preferable **2** *Are you feeling better?* ► healthier, fitter, stronger, recovered, (*more informal*) on the mend

better VERB *The idea cannot be bettered.* ► improve on, surpass, outdo

beware VERB **1** *There are landmines in the fields so beware.* ► watch out, look out, be careful, take care, be on the lookout, be on the alert **2** *Beware of the dog.* ► watch out for, mind, avoid, steer clear of

bewilder VERB *His remarks had bewildered her.* ► puzzle, perplex, baffle, mystify, confuse, bemuse, disconcert, confound, (*more informal*) flummox, (*more informal*) floor

bewildered ADJECTIVE *Harry looked quite bewildered.* ► puzzled, perplexed, baffled, mystified, confused, bemused, disconcerted, (*more informal*) flummoxed

bewitch VERB *We were bewitched by the beauty of the place.* ► captivate, charm, enchant, entrance, enthral, delight, mesmerize
AN OPPOSITE IS repel

bias NOUN *The management was accused of bias.* ► prejudice, partiality, discrimination, unfairness, injustice, partisanship, favouritism, bigotry, intolerance, chauvinism, racism, sexism

biased ADJECTIVE *a biased attitude The judge was clearly biased.* ► prejudiced, partial, one-sided, partisan, subjective, bigoted, chauvinistic, racist, sexist OPPOSITES ARE unbiased, impartial

bicker VERB *I don't want to stand here all day bickering about it.* ► quarrel, squabble, wrangle, argue, scrap, row

bid NOUN **1** *a bid of £5,000* ► offer, tender, proposal, price, proposition **2** *a bid to discover the truth* ► attempt, effort, endeavour, try (at), (*informal*) go (at), (*informal*) crack (at)

bid *VERB* **bids, bidding, bid** make a bid
▷ **bidder** *NOUN*

bid[2] *VERB* **bids, bidding, bid** or (*old use*) **bade bid** or **bidden** **1** say as a greeting or farewell • *I bid you all good night.* **2** command • *Do as you are bid* or *bidden*

bidding *NOUN* if you do someone's bidding, you do what they tell you to do

bide *VERB* **bides, biding, bided**
bide your time wait patiently for the right time to do something

biennial *NOUN* **biennials** a plant that lives for two years, flowering and dying in the second year

bier (beer) *NOUN* **biers** a movable stand on which a coffin or a dead body is placed before it is buried

bifocal (by- **foh**- kal) *ADJECTIVE* (said about lenses for glasses) made in two sections, with the upper part for looking at distant objects and the lower part for reading

bifocals *PLURAL NOUN* bifocal glasses

big *ADJECTIVE* **bigger, biggest** **1** large **2** important • *the big match* **3** more grown-up; elder • *my big sister*

bigamy (**big**- a- mee) *NOUN* the crime of marrying a person when you are already married to someone else
▷ **bigamous** *ADJECTIVE* **bigamist** *NOUN*

bigot *NOUN* **bigots** a bigoted person

bigoted *ADJECTIVE* narrow-minded and intolerant
▷ **bigotry** *NOUN*

bike *NOUN* **bikes** (*informal*) a bicycle or motorcycle

bikini *NOUN* **bikinis** a woman's two-piece swimsuit [named after the island of Bikini in the Pacific Ocean, where an atomic bomb test was carried out in 1946, at about the time the bikini was first worn (both caused great excitement)]

bilateral *ADJECTIVE* **1** of or on two sides **2** between two people or groups • *a bilateral agreement*

bile *NOUN* a bitter liquid produced by the liver, helping to digest fats

bilingual (by- **ling**- wal) *ADJECTIVE* **1** able to speak two languages well **2** written in two languages

bilious *ADJECTIVE* feeling sick; sickly
▷ **biliousness** *NOUN*

bill[1] *NOUN* **bills** **1** a written statement of charges for goods or services that have been supplied **2** a poster **3** a list; a programme of entertainment **4** the draft of a proposed law to be discussed by Parliament **5** (*American*) a banknote
bill of fare a menu

bill[2] *NOUN* **bills** a bird's beak

billabong *NOUN* **billabongs** (in Australia) a backwater

billboard *NOUN* **billboards** a tall fence or hoarding for advertisements

billiards *NOUN* a game in which three balls are struck with cues on a cloth-covered table (**billiard table**)

billion *NOUN* **billions** **1** a thousand million (1,000,000,000) **2** a million million (1,000,000,000,000)
▷ **billionth** *ADJECTIVE, NOUN*
USAGE Although the word originally meant a million million, nowadays it usually means a thousand million.

billow *NOUN* **billows** a huge wave

bin *NOUN* **bins** a large or deep container, especially one for rubbish or litter [via Old English from a Celtic word]

binary (**by**- ner- ee) *ADJECTIVE* involving sets of two; consisting of two parts

binary digit *NOUN* **binary digits** either of the two digits (0 and 1) used in the binary system

binary system or **binary notation** *NOUN* (in computing) a system of expressing numbers by using the digits 0 and 1 only

Thesaurus

bid *VERB* *A buyer bid a record price at the auction.* ► offer, make an offer of, put in a bid of, tender, proffer, propose

biff *VERB* (*informal*) *He had biffed her by mistake.* ► hit, strike, knock, smack, bash, clout

big *ADJECTIVE* **1** *a big house, The bill was very big.* ► large, great, huge, enormous, colossal, immense **2** *a big difference* ► significant, important, substantial, considerable, sizeable **3** *big ideas* ► ambitious, grand, grandiose, far-reaching **4** *That was big of you.* ► generous, considerate, magnanimous, kind, gracious

bigoted *ADJECTIVE* *He disliked people who held such bigoted views.* ► prejudiced, biased, partial, intolerant, narrow-minded
USAGE Note that *bigoted* is a much stronger word than the alternatives given here.

bill *NOUN* **1** *The bill came to over a thousand pounds.* ► account, invoice, statement, list of charges **2** *a bill advertising a sale* ► poster, notice, advertisement, placard, sheet, leaflet, broadsheet, circular, handout, bulletin **3** *a bill in parliament* ► draft law, proposed law

billow *VERB* **1** *Her dress billowed out in the wind.* ► balloon, blow, puff, swell, bulge **2** *Smoke billowed from the chimney.* ► pour, swirl, spiral

bin *NOUN* *a row of storage bins* ► container, canister, receptacle, drum

bind *VERB* **binds, binding, bound** **1** fasten material round something **2** fasten the pages of a book into a cover **3** tie up or tie together **4** make somebody agree to do something
▷ **binder** *NOUN*
bind a person over make him or her agree not to break the law

bind *NOUN* (*slang*) a nuisance; a bore

binding *NOUN* **bindings** something that binds, especially the covers, glue, etc. of a book

binding *ADJECTIVE* (said about an agreement or promise) that must be carried out or obeyed

binge *NOUN* **binges** (*slang*) a time spent eating a lot of food

bingo *NOUN* a game using cards on which numbered squares are crossed out as the numbers are called out at random

binoculars *PLURAL NOUN* a device with lenses for both eyes, making distant objects seem nearer

biochemistry *NOUN* the study of the chemical composition and processes of living things
▷ **biochemical** *ADJECTIVE* **biochemist** *NOUN*

biodegradable *ADJECTIVE* able to be broken down by bacteria in the environment • *All our packaging is biodegradable.*

biography (by- og- ra- fee) *NOUN* **biographies** the story of a person's life
▷ **biographical** *ADJECTIVE* **biographer** *NOUN*

biology *NOUN* the study of the life and structure of living things
▷ **biological** *ADJECTIVE* **biologist** *NOUN*

bionic (by- on- ik) *ADJECTIVE* (said about a person or parts of the body) operated by electronic devices

biopsy (by- op- see) *NOUN* **biopsies** examination of tissue from a living body

biped (by- ped) *NOUN* **bipeds** a two-footed animal

birch *NOUN* **birches** **1** a deciduous tree with slender branches **2** a bundle of birch branches for flogging people

bird *NOUN* **birds** **1** an animal with feathers, two wings, and two legs **2** (*slang*) a young woman
bird's-eye view a view from above

bird of prey *NOUN* **birds of prey** a bird that feeds on animal flesh, such as an eagle or hawk

birth *NOUN* **births** **1** the process by which a baby or young animal comes out from its mother's body **2** origin; parentage • *He is of noble birth.*

birth control *NOUN* ways of avoiding conceiving a baby

birthday *NOUN* **birthdays** the anniversary of the day a person was born

birth rate *NOUN* **birth rates** the number of children born in one year for every 1,000 people

birthright *NOUN* a right or privilege to which a person is entitled through being born into a particular family or country

biscuit *NOUN* **biscuits** a small flat kind of cake that has been baked until it is crisp [from Latin *bis* = twice + *coctus* = cooked: originally they were baked and then dried out in a cool oven to make them keep longer]

bisect (by- sekt) *VERB* **bisects, bisecting, bisected** divide something into two equal parts
▷ **bisection** *NOUN* **bisector** *NOUN*

bishop *NOUN* **bishops** **1** an important member of the clergy in charge of all the churches in a city or district **2** a chess piece shaped like a bishop's mitre

bismuth *NOUN* a greyish-white metal

bison (by- son) *NOUN* **bison** a wild ox found in North America and Europe, with a large shaggy head

bit[1] *NOUN* **bits** **1** a small piece or amount of something **2** the metal part of a horse's bridle that is put into its mouth **3** the part of a tool that cuts or grips things when twisted
a bit **1** a short distance or time • *Wait a bit.* **2** slightly • *I'm a bit worried.*
bit by bit gradually

bit[2] *past tense of* **bite**

Thesaurus

bind *VERB* **1** *I'll bind the two pieces with string.* ► fasten, tie, secure, attach, clamp, stick, connect, join, lash, link, rope, strap, truss, hitch **2** *A nurse bound their wounds.* ► bandage, dress, cover, wrap, swathe **3** *They were bound by a solemn oath not to reveal their secret.* ► oblige, require, compel, constrain, force, necessitate **4** *Their sufferings had bound them together.* ► unite, join, draw, hold

birth *NOUN* **1** *the birth of a child* ► delivery, childbirth, (*technical*) parturition RELATED ADJECTIVE natal **2** *of noble birth* ► ancestry, descent, origin, parentage, lineage, pedigree, breeding, background, blood, extraction, family, genealogy, line, race, stock, strain **3** *the birth of socialism* ► beginning, origin, emergence, advent, dawn

bit *NOUN* *a bit of chocolate, a bit of stone* ► piece, portion, chunk, lump, hunk, fragment, morsel, particle, slice
a bit *That was a bit hard.* ► rather, fairly, slightly, somewhat, a little, (*more informal*) pretty
a bit of *a bit of a shame* ► rather
bit by bit *Bit by bit she began to understand.* ► gradually, slowly, little by little

bit[3] *NOUN* **bits** the smallest unit of information in a computer, expressed as a choice between two possibilities

bitch *NOUN* **bitches** **1** a female dog, fox, or wolf **2** (*informal*) a spiteful woman
▷ **bitchy** *ADJECTIVE*

bite *VERB* **bites, biting, bit, bitten** **1** cut or take something with your teeth **2** penetrate; sting **3** accept bait • *The fish are biting.*
bite the dust die or be killed

bite *NOUN* **bites** **1** an act of biting • *She took a bite.* **2** a wound or mark made by biting • *an insect bite* **3** a snack

bitter *ADJECTIVE* **1** tasting sharp, not sweet **2** feeling or causing mental pain or resentment • *a bitter disappointment* **3** very cold
▷ **bitterly** *ADVERB* **bitterness** *NOUN*

bivalve *NOUN* **bivalves** a shellfish (e.g. an oyster) that has a shell with two hinged parts

bizarre (biz- ar) *ADJECTIVE* very odd in appearance or effect

black *NOUN* **blacks** **1** the very darkest colour, like coal or soot **2** a person with a very dark or black skin

black *ADJECTIVE* **1** of the colour black **2** (said about a person) having dark skin **3** dismal; not hopeful • *The outlook is black.* **4** hostile; disapproving • *He gave me a black look.* **5** very dirty **6** (said about coffee or tea) without milk
▷ **blackly** *ADVERB* **blackness** *NOUN*

black *VERB* **blacks, blacking, blacked** make a thing black
black out **1** cover windows etc. so that no light can penetrate **2** faint, lose consciousness

blackberry *NOUN* **blackberries** a sweet black berry

blackbird *NOUN* **blackbirds** a European songbird, the male of which is black

blackboard *NOUN* **blackboards** a dark board for writing on with chalk

black box *NOUN* **black boxes** a flight recorder

blacken *VERB* **blackens, blackening, blackened** make or become black

black eye *NOUN* **black eyes** an eye with a bruise round it

blackguard (blag- erd) *NOUN* **blackguards** (*old use*) a wicked person

black hole *NOUN* **black holes** a region in outer space with such a strong gravitational field that no matter or radiation can escape from it

black ice *NOUN* thin transparent ice on roads

blacklist *VERB* **blacklists, blacklisting, blacklisted** put someone on a list of those who are disapproved of

blackmail *VERB* **blackmails, blackmailing, blackmailed** demand money etc. from someone by threats
▷ **blackmail** *NOUN* **blackmailer** *NOUN*

black market *NOUN* **black markets** illegal trading

black sheep *NOUN* a member of a family who behaves badly or has a bad reputation

blacksmith *NOUN* **blacksmiths** a person who makes and repairs iron things, especially one who makes and fits horseshoes

black spot *NOUN* **black spots** a dangerous place

Thesaurus

bite *NOUN* **1** *a bite on the arm* ► nip, sting, pinch, wound **2** *a bite to eat* ► mouthful, snack, morsel, bit, nibble, piece, taste

bite *VERB* **1** *He bit a chunk out of an apple.* ► munch, nibble, chew, crunch, gnaw, nip, champ, (*formal*) masticate **2** *She had been bitten by an insect.* ► sting, pierce **3** *Tax increases will begin to bite in the new tax year.* ► take effect, have an effect, take hold **4** **bite into** *Acid starts to bite into the metal.* ► eat into, corrode, erode, wear away

biting *ADJECTIVE* **1** *a biting wind* ► bitterly cold, bitter, freezing, icy, raw, piercing, perishing, arctic **2** *a biting remark* ► caustic, harsh, cutting, incisive, bitter, penetrating, stinging, hurtful, cruel, sharp

bitter *ADJECTIVE* **1** *a bitter taste* ► sour, sharp, acid, acrid, tart, harsh OPPOSITES ARE mild, sweet **2** *The decision was seen as a bitter disappointment.* ► cruel, distressing, painful, unpleasant **3** *bitter remarks* ► harsh, cutting, caustic, incisive, biting, penetrating, stinging, hurtful, cruel, sharp **4** *She felt bitter about what had happened.* ► resentful, embittered, cynical, aggrieved, disgruntled **5** *a bitter quarrel* ► acrimonious, rancorous, angry, vitriolic **6** *a bitter wind* ► biting, freezing, icy, raw, piercing, perishing, bitterly cold, arctic
AN OPPOSITE IS gentle

bizarre *ADJECTIVE* *a bizarre story of survival in wartime* ► strange, weird, odd, extraordinary, eccentric, peculiar, curious, queer, unusual, grotesque AN OPPOSITE IS ordinary

black *ADJECTIVE* **1** *black ink* ► jet-black, coal-black **2** *a black night* ► dark, unlit, moonless, starless, gloomy **3** *hands black from mending the mower* ► filthy, dirty, grimy, grubby, soiled AN OPPOSITE IS spotless **4** *in a black mood* ► melancholy, miserable, glum, wretched, unhappy, despondent

black *VERB* *I blacked my shoes.* ► blacken, polish

blacken *VERB* *She decided to blacken her hair.* ► darken, make black

bladder *NOUN* **bladders** **1** the bag-like part of the body in which urine collects **2** the inflatable bag inside a football

blade *NOUN* **blades** **1** the flat cutting edge of a knife, sword, axe, etc. **2** the flat wide part of an oar, spade, propeller, etc. **3** a flat narrow leaf • *blades of grass* **4** a broad flat bone • *shoulder blade*

blame *VERB* **blames, blaming, blamed** **1** say that somebody or something has caused what is wrong • *They blamed me.* **2** find fault with someone • *We can't blame them for wanting a holiday.*

blame *NOUN* responsibility for what is wrong

blancmange (bla-**monj**) *NOUN* **blancmanges** a jelly-like pudding made with milk

bland *ADJECTIVE* **1** having a mild flavour rather than a strong one **2** lacking any interesting featues or qualities • *a bland manner*
▷ **blandly** *ADVERB* **blandness** *NOUN*

blank *ADJECTIVE* **1** not written or printed on; unmarked **2** without interest or expression • *a blank look.* **3** empty of thoughts • *My mind's gone blank.*
▷ **blankly** *ADVERB* **blankness** *NOUN*

blank *NOUN* **blanks** **1** an empty space **2** a blank cartridge

blanket *NOUN* **blankets** **1** a warm cloth covering used on a bed etc. **2** any thick soft covering • *a blanket of snow*

blanket *ADJECTIVE* covering all cases or instances • *a blanket ban*

blank verse *NOUN* poetry without rhyme, usually in lines of ten syllables

blare *VERB* **blares, blaring, blared** make a loud harsh sound
▷ **blare** *NOUN*

blaspheme (blas-**feem**) *VERB* **blasphemes, blaspheming, blasphemed** talk or write irreverently about sacred things

blasphemy (**blas**-fim-ee) *NOUN* **blasphemies** irreverent talk about sacred things
▷ **blasphemous** *ADJECTIVE*

blast *NOUN* **blasts** **1** a strong rush of wind or air **2** a loud noise • *the blast of the trumpets*

blast *VERB* **blasts, blasting, blasted** blow up with explosives
blast off launch by the firing of rockets **blast-off** *NOUN*

blatant (**blay**-tant) *ADJECTIVE* very obvious • *a blatant lie*
▷ **blatantly** *ADVERB*

blaze *NOUN* **blazes** a very bright flame, fire, or light

blaze *VERB* **blazes, blazing, blazed** **1** burn or shine brightly **2** show great feeling • *He was blazing with anger.*

blazer *NOUN* **blazers** a kind of jacket, often with a badge or in the colours of a school or team etc.

bleach *VERB* **bleaches, bleaching, bleached** make or become white

bleach *NOUN* **bleaches** a substance used to bleach things

Thesaurus

blame *NOUN* **1** *They were cleared of all blame.* ► responsibility, guilt, liability, culpability **2** *Who got the blame for it?* ► criticism, censure, condemnation, (*more informal*) rap

blame *VERB* *The report blamed the driver for the accident.* ► hold responsible, hold accountable, condemn, censure, criticize, reprove, reprimand, accuse (of), charge (with) AN OPPOSITE IS excuse

blameless *ADJECTIVE* *a blameless life* ► innocent, guiltless, faultless, exemplary, irreproachable, upright, virtuous, unblemished OPPOSITES ARE blameworthy, guilty

bland *ADJECTIVE* **1** *a bland taste* ► insipid, uninteresting, dull, weak, nondescript, watery, mild, boring, flat OPPOSITES ARE sharp, strong **2** *a bland personality, bland remarks* ► dull, tedious, uninteresting, unexciting, monotonous, drab, dreary, feeble, vapid, weak, (*informal*) wishy-washy OPPOSITES ARE interesting, stimulating

blank *ADJECTIVE* **1** *a blank page* ► empty, unused, unfilled, clear, bare, void, unmarked AN OPPOSITE IS used **2** *a blank look* ► expressionless, featureless, impassive, vacant, deadpan, inscrutable, unresponsive AN OPPOSITE IS expressive

blanket *NOUN* *a blanket of fog* ► covering, layer, film, shroud, cloak, mantle, mask, sheet, cover

blare *VERB* *Sirens were blaring.* ► blast, resound, screech, shriek

blast *NOUN* **1** *a blast of cold air* ► gust, rush, blow, draught, squall **2** *Hundreds were injured in the blast.* ► explosion, discharge, shock

blast *VERB* **1** *A series of missiles blasted the building.* ► blow up, bomb, demolish, raze **2** *radios blasting out rock music* ► blare, boom, roar, thunder, bellow

blatant *ADJECTIVE* *a blatant lie* ► flagrant, brazen, barefaced, glaring, shameless, unconcealed AN OPPOSITE IS inconspicuous

blaze *NOUN* **1** *It took firefighters all night to control the blaze.* ► fire, flames **2** *a blaze of light* ► burst, flash, gleam, streak, beam, glitter

blaze *VERB* **1** *The fire began to blaze.* ► burn, flare up, be alight **2** *Lights blazed from the top floor.* ► shine, beam, flare, flash, gleam, glitter

bleak *ADJECTIVE* **1** bare and cold • *a bleak hillside* **2** dreary or miserable • *a bleak future*
▷ **bleakly** *ADVERB* **bleakness** *NOUN*

bleary *ADJECTIVE* watery and not seeing clearly • *bleary eyes*
▷ **blearily** *ADVERB*

bleat *NOUN* **bleats** the cry of a lamb, goat, or calf

bleat *VERB* **bleats, bleating, bleated** make a bleat

bleed *VERB* **bleeds, bleeding, bled 1** lose blood **2** draw blood or fluid from

blemish *NOUN* **blemishes** a flaw; a mark that spoils a thing's appearance
▷ **blemish** *VERB*

blench *VERB* **blenches, blenching, blenched** flinch

blend *VERB* **blends, blending, blended** mix smoothly or easily

blend *NOUN* **blends** a mixture

blender *NOUN* **blenders** an electric machine used to mix food or turn it into liquid

bless *VERB* **blesses, blessing, blessed 1** make sacred or holy **2** bring God's favour on a person or thing

blessing *NOUN* **blessings 1** a prayer that blesses a person or thing; being blessed **2** something that people are glad of

blight *NOUN* **blights 1** a disease that makes plants wither **2** something that does a lot of harm • *Vandalism is a blight on our community.*

blight *VERB* **blights, blighting, blighted 1** affect with blight **2** spoil or damage something • *Injuries have blighted his career.*

blind *ADJECTIVE* **1** without the ability to see **2** without any thought or understanding • *blind obedience.* **3** (said about a tube, passage, or road) closed at one end
▷ **blindly** *ADVERB* **blindness** *NOUN*

blind *VERB* **blinds, blinding, blinded** make a person blind

blind *NOUN* **blinds 1** a screen for a window **2** a deception; something used to hide the truth • *His journey was a blind.*

blind date *NOUN* **blind dates** a date between a man and woman who have not met before

blindfold *NOUN* **blindfolds** a strip of cloth tied round someone's eyes so that they cannot see

blindfold *VERB* **blindfolds, blindfolding, blindfolded** cover someone's eyes with a blindfold

Thesaurus

bleak *ADJECTIVE a bleak landscape* ► bare, barren, desolate, exposed, featureless, treeless, stark, empty, open, windswept

bleary *ADJECTIVE bleary eyes, bleary vision* ► blurred, blurry, unfocused, clouded, cloudy, fogged, foggy, hazy, murky AN OPPOSITE IS clear

bleed *VERB The wound began to bleed.* ► lose blood, haemorrhage, weep, seep

blemish *NOUN a beautiful rose bloom without a single blemish* ► imperfection, flaw, fault, defect, spot, mark, stain, speck, taint

blend *NOUN a blend of several ingredients* ► mixture, mix, combination, mingling, amalgam, fusion, synthesis

blend *VERB* **1** *Blend the ingredients carefully.* ► mix, combine, mingle, merge, stir together, beat, fold in, integrate, whip, whisk **2** *The colours blend well.* ► harmonize, match, fit

bless *VERB The couple were blessed with a child.* ► favour, grace, endow

blessed *ADJECTIVE a blessed place* ► holy, sacred, sanctified, adored, divine, hallowed, revered

blessing *NOUN* **1** *The priest gave a blessing.* ► benediction, grace, prayer **2** *The manager gave the scheme his blessing.* ► approval, backing, support, consent, approbation, leave, permission AN OPPOSITE IS disapproval **3** *Central heating is a blessing in the winter.* ► benefit, advantage, asset, boon, comfort, convenience, godsend, help AN OPPOSITE IS affliction

blight *NOUN* **1** *potato blight* ► disease, rot, decay, (*more formal*) infestation **2** *the blight of traffic noise* ► affliction, curse, plague, menace, nuisance, tribulation, trial, misfortune AN OPPOSITE IS blessing

blight *VERB Their lives were blighted by troublesome neighbours.* ► ruin, wreck, spoil, afflict, shatter, disrupt

blind *ADJECTIVE* **1** *She had been blind from birth.* ► sightless, unsighted, visually impaired, partially sighted, unseeing **2** *blind to all dangers* ► oblivious, imperceptive, heedless (of), unaware (of), inattentive, indifferent, insensible, insensitive, ignorant (of), blinkered (from) OPPOSITES ARE aware, perceptive **3** *showing a blind acceptance of criticism* ► uncritical, reckless, impulsive, indiscriminate, unreasoning, mindless **4** *a blind corner* ► concealed, hidden, obscure, obstructed

blind *NOUN She pulled down a blind.* ► screen, shade, cover, curtain, shutter

blind *VERB* **1** *The light blinded her for a few moments.* ► dazzle **2** *They are trying to blind us all with science.* ► confuse, deceive, overawe, intimidate, disconcert, unsettle, (*more informal*) put off

blind spot *NOUN* **blind spots** a subject that you do not understand or know much about

blink *VERB* **blinks, blinking, blinked** shut and open your eyes rapidly
▷ **blink** *NOUN*

bliss *NOUN* perfect happiness
▷ **blissful** *ADJECTIVE* **blissfully** *ADVERB*

blister *NOUN* **blisters** a swelling like a bubble, especially on skin
▷ **blister** *VERB*

blizzard *NOUN* **blizzards** a severe snowstorm

bloated *ADJECTIVE* swollen by fat, gas, or liquid

blob *NOUN* **blobs** a small round mass of something • *blobs of paint*

block *NOUN* **blocks** **1** a solid piece of something **2** an obstruction **3** a large building divided into flats or offices **4** a group of buildings

block *VERB* **blocks, blocking, blocked** obstruct; prevent something from moving or being used
▷ **blockage** *NOUN*

blockade *NOUN* **blockades** the blocking of a city or port etc. in order to prevent people and goods from going in or out

blockade *VERB* **blockades, blockading, blockaded** set up a blockade of a place

block letters *PLURAL NOUN* plain capital letters

bloke *NOUN* **blokes** (*informal*) a man

blond or **blonde** *ADJECTIVE* fair-haired; fair

blonde *NOUN* **blondes** a fair-haired girl or woman

blood *NOUN* **1** the red liquid that flows through veins and arteries **2** family relationship; ancestry • *He is of royal blood.*
in cold blood deliberately and cruelly

blood bank *NOUN* **blood banks** a supply of blood and plasma for transfusions

bloodbath *NOUN* **bloodbaths** a massacre

blood donor *NOUN* **blood donors** a person who gives blood for use in transfusions

blood group *NOUN* **blood groups** any of the classes or types of human blood

bloodhound *NOUN* **bloodhounds** a large dog that tracks people by their scent

bloodshed *NOUN* the killing or wounding of people

bloodshot *ADJECTIVE* (said about eyes) streaked with red

blood sport *NOUN* **blood sports** a sport that involves wounding or killing animals

bloodstream *NOUN* the blood circulating in the body

bloodthirsty *ADJECTIVE* eager for bloodshed

blood vessel *NOUN* **blood vessels** a tube carrying blood in the body; an artery, vein, or capillary

bloody *ADJECTIVE* **bloodier, bloodiest**
1 bloodstained **2** with much bloodshed • *a bloody battle*
bloody-minded *ADJECTIVE* deliberately awkward and not helpful

Thesaurus

blink *VERB* *A light on the control panel began to blink.* ► flash, wink, flicker, twinkle, flutter, gleam, glimmer

bliss *NOUN* *a life of bliss* ► joy, delight, pleasure, rapture, ecstasy, euphoria, felicity, gladness, happiness, heaven, paradise AN OPPOSITE IS misery

blissful *ADJECTIVE* *They spent a blissful week together.* ► ecstatic, joyful, rapturous, euphoric, elated, happy AN OPPOSITE IS miserable

blizzard *NOUN* *They were kept indoors by blizzards.* ► snowstorm, squall

bloated *ADJECTIVE* *a bloated stomach* ► swollen, dilated, distended, enlarged, inflated OPPOSITES ARE shrunken, shrivelled

blob *NOUN* *a blob of ice cream* ► drop, droplet, globule, lump

block *NOUN* **1** *a block of chocolate, a block of stone* ► chunk, hunk, slab, bar, brick, cake, lump, mass, piece **2** *The pipe had a block in it.* ► blockage, obstruction, stoppage **3** *Lack of funds proved a block to progress.* ► barrier, hindrance, impediment, obstacle

block *VERB* **1** *The drain was blocked with leaves* ► (*informal*) bung up, choke, clog, close, congest, constrict, dam, fill, jam, obstruct, plug, stop up **2** *A parked van was blocking access to the house.* ► obstruct, bar, impede, inhibit, restrict, limit **3** *The scheme was blocked by the directors.* ► stop, prevent, halt, thwart

blockage *NOUN* *The drain has a blockage.* ► obstruction, stoppage, block, constriction, jam, obstacle, resistance, barrier, bottleneck, congestion

bloke *NOUN* (*informal*) *He's a funny bloke, isn't he?* ► chap, fellow, guy, man, boy, individual

blond, blonde *ADJECTIVE* *blond hair* ► fair, flaxen, golden, light, yellow, bleached

blood *NOUN* *a person of noble blood* ► ancestry, descent, origin, parentage, lineage, pedigree, breeding, background, birth, extraction, family, genealogy, line, race, stock, strain

bloodshed *NOUN* *The government were anxious to avoid further bloodshed.* ► killing, slaughter, carnage, butchery, violence

bloody *ADJECTIVE* **1** *a bloody wound* ► bleeding, blood-stained, raw, gaping **2** *a bloody battle* ► fierce, gory, bloodthirsty, violent

A B C D E F G H I J K L M N O P Q R S T U V W X Y Z

bloom NOUN **blooms** **1** a flower **2** the fine powder on fresh ripe grapes etc.

bloom VERB **blooms, blooming, bloomed** produce flowers

blossom NOUN **blossoms** a flower or mass of flowers, especially on a fruit tree

blossom VERB **blossoms, blossoming, blossomed** **1** produce flowers **2** develop into something • *She blossomed into a fine singer.*

blot NOUN **blots** **1** a spot of ink **2** a flaw or fault; something ugly • *a blot on the landscape*

blot VERB **blots, blotting, blotted** **1** make a blot or blots on something **2** dry with blotting paper
blot out **1** cross out thickly **2** obscure • *Fog blotted out the view.*

blotch NOUN **blotches** an untidy patch of colour
▷ **blotchy** ADJECTIVE

blotting paper NOUN absorbent paper for soaking up ink from writing

blouse NOUN **blouses** a loose piece of clothing like a shirt, worn by women

blow[1] VERB **blows, blowing, blew, blown** **1** send out a current of air **2** move in or with a current of air • *His hat blew off.* **3** make or sound something by blowing • *blow bubbles* • *blow the whistle* **4** melt with too strong an electric current • *A fuse has blown.* **5** (*slang*) damn • *Blow you!*
blow up **1** inflate **2** explode **3** shatter by an explosion

blow NOUN **blows** the action of blowing

blow[2] NOUN **blows** **1** a hard knock or hit **2** a shock; a disaster

blowlamp or **blowtorch** NOUN **blowlamps** or **blowtorches** a device used for directing a very hot flame at a surface

blubber NOUN the fat of whales

bludgeon (**bluj**-on) NOUN **bludgeons** a short stick with a thickened end, used as a weapon

bludgeon VERB **bludgeons, bludgeoning, bludgeoned** hit someone several times with a heavy stick or other object

blue NOUN **blues** the colour of a cloudless sky
out of the blue unexpectedly

blue ADJECTIVE **1** of the colour blue **2** unhappy; depressed • *feeling blue* **3** indecent; obscene • *blue films*
▷ **blueness** NOUN

bluebottle NOUN **bluebottles** a large bluish fly

blueprint NOUN **blueprints** a detailed plan

Thesaurus

bloom NOUN **1** *rose blooms* ► blossom, flower, bud **2** *the bloom of youth* ► prime, peak, glow, flush, acme

bloom VERB **1** *The roses have all bloomed now.* ► blossom, flower, open AN OPPOSITE IS fade **2** *The children had bloomed in the country air.* ► flourish, thrive, prosper, blossom, develop

blossom NOUN *apple blossom* ► blooms, buds, florets, flowers

blossom VERB **1** *The trees have started to blossom.* ► bloom, flower, open AN OPPOSITE IS fade **2** *The scheme can blossom with the right support.* ► flourish, thrive, prosper, bloom, develop

blot NOUN **1** *a blot of ink* ► spot, blotch, mark, smear, smudge, stain, splodge, blob **2** *a blot on the landscape* ► eyesore, blemish, defect, fault, flaw

blot VERB *Ink blotted the page.* ► smudge, mark, spoil, spot, stain, bespatter, mar
blot out *A tall building blotted out the view* ► conceal, hide, mask, obliterate, obscure, cover, delete, eclipse, erase, expunge, rub out, wipe out, cancel

blotch NOUN *The walls had damp blotches down them.* ► patch, smudge, speck, speckle, blot, mark

blotchy ADJECTIVE *a blotchy skin* ► spotty, spotted, blemished, marked, patchy, smudged, uneven

blow NOUN **1** *a blow on the head* ► knock, bang, hit, thump, smack **2** *The news was a terrible blow.* ► shock, surprise, reverse, setback, upset, disappointment, calamity, disaster

blow VERB **1** *The storm blew the ship on the rocks.* ► drive, sweep, force, blast, fling, whisk **2** *Leaves were blowing across the drive.* ► drift, flutter, whirl, stream
blow out *The heater blows out hot air.* ► puff out, blast out, exhale, breathe, fan, waft
blow up **1** *I'll blow up the tyres.* ► inflate, pump up, fill, dilate, expand OPPOSITES ARE let down, deflate **2** *The photograph can be blown up.* ► enlarge **3** *A bomb blew up the building.* ► bomb, blast, detonate, dynamite, explode **4** (*informal*) *When he heard what we had done he blew up.* ► grow angry, lose your temper, rage

blue ADJECTIVE **1** *a pretty blue colour* ► sky-blue, turquoise, ultramarine, aquamarine, azure, cerulean, cobalt, indigo, navy, sapphire **2** *a blue movie* ► indecent, coarse, obscene, salacious, risqué **3** (*informal*) *Jake was feeling blue that day.* ► sad, depressed, dejected

blueprint NOUN **1** *blueprints of the new aircraft* ► design, plan, drawing, draft, outline, pattern, layout, prototype **2** *a blueprint for political reform* ► model, plan, scheme, framework, basis, pattern, guide, proposal

blues *NOUN* a slow sad jazz song or tune
the blues a very sad feeling; depression

bluff[1] *VERB* **bluffs, bluffing, bluffed** deceive someone, especially by pretending to be someone else or to be able to do something

bluff *NOUN* **bluffs** the act of bluffing; a threat that you make but do not intend to carry out

bluff[2] *ADJECTIVE* frank and hearty in manner
▷ **bluffness** *NOUN*

blunder *NOUN* **blunders** a stupid mistake

blunder *VERB* **blunders, blundering, blundered** **1** make a blunder **2** move clumsily and uncertainly

blunt *ADJECTIVE* **1** not sharp **2** speaking in plain terms; straightforward • *a blunt refusal*
▷ **bluntly** *ADVERB* **bluntness** *NOUN*

blunt *VERB* **blunts, blunting, blunted** make a thing blunt

blur *VERB* **blurs, blurring, blurred** make or become indistinct or smeared

blur *NOUN* **blurs** an indistinct appearance • *Without his glasses on, everything was a blur.*

blurt *VERB* **blurts, blurting, blurted** say something suddenly or tactlessly • *He blurted it out.*

blush *VERB* **blushes, blushing, blushed** become red in the face because you are ashamed or embarrassed

blush *NOUN* **blushes** reddening in the face

bluster *VERB* **blusters, blustering, blustered** **1** blow in gusts; be windy **2** talk loudly and aggressively
▷ **blustery** *ADJECTIVE*

BMX *ABBREVIATION* a kind of bicycle for use in racing on a dirt track

boar *NOUN* **boars** **1** a wild pig **2** a male pig

board *NOUN* **boards** **1** a flat piece of wood **2** a flat piece of stiff material, e.g. a chessboard **3** daily meals supplied in return for payment or work • *board and lodging.* **4** a committee
on board on or in a ship, aircraft, etc.

board *VERB* **boards, boarding, boarded** **1** go on board a ship etc. **2** give or get meals and accommodation
board up block with fixed boards

boarder *NOUN* **boarders** **1** a pupil who lives at a boarding school during the term **2** a lodger who receives meals

boarding school *NOUN* **boarding schools** a school where pupils live during the term

boast *VERB* **boasts, boasting, boasted** **1** speak with great pride and try to impress people **2** have something to be proud of • *The town boasts a fine park.*
▷ **boaster** *NOUN* **boastful** *ADJECTIVE* **boastfully** *ADVERB*

boast *NOUN* **boasts** a boastful statement

Thesaurus

blues *PLURAL NOUN* **the blues** *I woke up with the blues just like you did.* ▸ depression, sadness, melancholy, dejection, despondency, low spirits, misery, gloom

bluff *NOUN* *The offer is regarded as a crude bluff.* ▸ deception, subterfuge, sham, pretence, fake, fraud, ruse, artifice, trick

bluff *VERB* **1** *We think they must be bluffing us.* ▸ deceive, delude, mislead, hoodwink, trick **2** *I am sure they are only bluffing.* ▸ pretend, sham, put on an act, lie, (*more informal*) kid

blunder *NOUN* *Harry shook his head at his own blunder.* ▸ mistake, error, gaffe, slip, faux pas, (*more informal*) howler, (*much more informal*) cock-up

blunder *VERB* **1** *The security officer had blundered by letting the men into the building.* ▸ make a mistake, bungle, err, be in error, misjudge, miscalculate, slip up, (*more informal*) put your foot in it, (*more informal*) goof, (*much more informal*) screw up, (*much more informal*) cock up

blunt *ADJECTIVE* **1** *a blunt knife* ▸ dull, rounded, thick, unpointed, unsharpened AN OPPOSITE IS sharp **2** *a blunt reply* ▸ abrupt, harsh, curt, terse, gruff, rude, offhand, brusque, insensitive, outspoken, plain-spoken OPPOSITES ARE polite, tactful

blunt *VERB* *A series of snacks blunted my appetite.* ▸ dull, reduce, dampen, take the edge off, weaken OPPOSITES ARE sharpen, intensify

blur *VERB* *The steam had blurred her glasses.* ▸ cloud, fog, mask, obscure, befog, blear, dim, smear

blurred *ADJECTIVE* *When he lifted his head everything looked blurred.* ▸ indistinct, blurry, bleary, fuzzy, hazy, misty

blush *VERB* *She blushed as he kissed her hand.* ▸ go red, flush, glow, colour

board *NOUN* **1** *a wooden board* ▸ plank, panel, beam, length of timber, lath **2** *the board of directors* ▸ committee, council, panel

board *VERB* **1** *Passengers may now board the aircraft.* ▸ get on, go on board, enter, embark, ascend **2** *His wife boarded students in a spare room.* ▸ accommodate, house, lodge, put up, billet, quarter

boast *VERB* *His mother had been boasting about how clever he was.* ▸ brag, crow, bluster, swank, show off, gloat, sing someone's praises, (*more informal*) talk big

boastful *ADJECTIVE* *He was constantly boastful of all his achievements.* ▸ bragging, conceited, big-headed, bumptious, proud, puffed-up, swaggering, swollen-headed, vain, egotistical,

boat *NOUN* **boats** a vehicle built to travel on water and carry people etc.
in the same boat in the same situation; suffering the same difficulties

bob *VERB* **bobs, bobbing, bobbed** move quickly up and down

bobsleigh or **bobsled** *NOUN* **bobsleighs** or **bobsleds** a sledge with two sets of runners

bodice *NOUN* **bodices** the upper part of a dress

bodily *ADJECTIVE* to do with your body • *bodily functions*

bodily *ADVERB* by taking hold of someone • *He was picked up bodily and bundled into a car.*

body *NOUN* **bodies** **1** the structure consisting of bones and flesh etc. of a person or animal; the main part of this apart from the head and limbs **2** a corpse **3** the main part of something **4** a group or quantity regarded as a unit • *the school's governing body* **5** a distinct object or piece of matter • *Stars and planets are heavenly bodies.*
▷ **bodily** *ADJECTIVE, ADVERB*

bodyguard *NOUN* **bodyguards** a guard to protect a person's life

bog *NOUN* **bogs** an area of wet spongy ground
▷ **boggy** *ADJECTIVE*
bogged down stuck and unable to make any progress

bogus *ADJECTIVE* not real; sham

boil[1] *VERB* **boils, boiling, boiled** **1** make or become hot enough to bubble and give off steam **2** cook or wash something in boiling water **3** be very hot

boil *NOUN* boiling point • *Bring the milk to the boil.* [via early French *boillir* from Latin *bullire* = to bubble]

boil[2] *NOUN* **boils** an inflamed swelling under the skin

boiler *NOUN* **boilers** a container in which water is heated

boisterous *ADJECTIVE* noisy and lively

bold *ADJECTIVE* **1** confident and courageous **2** impudent **3** (said about colours, designs, etc.) strong and bright
▷ **boldly** *ADVERB* **boldness** *NOUN*

bolster *NOUN* **bolsters** a long pillow for placing across a bed under other pillows

bolster *VERB* **bolsters, bolstering, bolstered** add extra support

Thesaurus

(*informal*) cocky, (*informal*) swanky
AN OPPOSITE IS modest

boat *NOUN* *boats in the little harbour* ► craft, vessel, ship

bob *VERB* *Little boats were bobbing in the water.* ► bounce, move up and down, dance, toss about, skip about, oscillate
bob up *A woman at the back bobbed up to ask a question.* ► jump up, leap up, spring up, rise (up), appear

bodily *ADJECTIVE* *bodily contact* ► physical, corporeal

body *NOUN* **1** *the human body* ► frame, figure, form, physique, shape, anatomy, being, build RELATED ADJECTIVES corporal, somatic **2** *a blow to the body* ► trunk, torso **3** *a body floating in the river* ► corpse, cadaver, carcass, mortal remains, (*more informal*) stiff **4** *the managing body* ► committee, company, association, corporation, society, band **5** *a large body of evidence* ► quantity, collection, volume, mass, accumulation, agglomeration, corpus

bog *NOUN* *The ground became wetter, and eventually they were on the edge of a bog.* ► marsh, marshland, swamp, mire, morass, fen, quicksands, mudflats, quagmire
bogged down *bogged down with all the work* ► encumbered, hindered, impeded, slowed down, in difficulties, stuck, sunk

bogus *ADJECTIVE* *The man had given a bogus address.* ► fake, false, spurious, fraudulent, counterfeit, pretended

bogy *NOUN* *bogies and other beings of the night* ► evil spirit, ghost, spectre, phantom

boil *NOUN* *a boil on the skin* ► swelling, pustule, pimple, abscess, blister, spot, tumour

boil *VERB* **1** *Boil the potatoes in water.* ► bring to boiling point, bring to the boil, cook, heat, simmer **2** *The water was beginning to boil.* ► bubble, effervesce, foam, seethe, steam **3** *She was boiling with anger.* ► seethe, be angry, lose your temper, go into a rage, fly into a rage, flare up, (*more informal*) see red

boisterous *ADJECTIVE* *a boisterous beach game* ► lively, spirited, animated, exuberant, rough, rowdy OPPOSITES ARE restrained, calm

bold *ADJECTIVE* **1** *a bold move, a bold traveller* ► brave, courageous, daring, adventurous, audacious, confident, dauntless, enterprising, fearless, forceful, gallant, heroic, intrepid, self-confident, valiant, valorous, venturesome, (*more informal*) plucky AN OPPOSITE IS cowardly **2** *bold remarks* ► brazen, forward, cheeky, brash, impertinent, impudent, insolent, presumptuous, fresh, pert, rude, saucy, shameless, unashamed OPPOSITES ARE polite, reticent **3** *a bold pattern, bold colours* ► striking, strong, bright, clear, conspicuous, eye-catching, prominent, pronounced, showy, vivid AN OPPOSITE IS inconspicuous

bolt NOUN **bolts** **1** a sliding bar for fastening a door **2** a thick metal pin for fastening things together **3** a sliding bar that opens and closes the breech of a rifle **4** a shaft of lightning **5** an arrow shot from a crossbow **6** the action of bolting
a bolt from the blue a surprise, usually an unpleasant one
bolt upright quite upright

bolt VERB **bolts, bolting, bolted** **1** fasten with a bolt or bolts **2** run away or escape **3** swallow food quickly

bomb NOUN **bombs** an explosive device
the bomb an atomic or hydrogen bomb

bomb VERB **bombs, bombing, bombed** attack a place with bombs

bombard VERB **bombards, bombarding, bombarded** **1** attack with gunfire or many missiles **2** direct a large number of questions or comments etc. at somebody
▷ **bombardment** NOUN

bomber NOUN **bombers** **1** someone who plants or sets off a bomb **2** an aeroplane from which bombs are dropped

bombshell NOUN **bombshells** a great shock

bonanza (bon-an-za) NOUN **bonanzas** sudden great wealth or luck

bond NOUN **bonds** **1** a close friendship or connection between two or more people **2 bonds** ropes or chains used to tie someone up **3** a document stating an agreement

bond VERB **bonds, bonding, bonded** become closely linked or connected

bondage NOUN slavery; captivity

bone NOUN **bones** one of the hard parts that make up the skeleton of a person's or animal's body

bone VERB **bones, boning, boned** remove the bones from meat or fish

bonfire NOUN **bonfires** an outdoor fire to burn rubbish or celebrate something [originally *bone fire* = a fire to dispose of people's or animals' bones]

bonnet NOUN **bonnets** **1** a hat with strings that tie under the chin **2** a Scottish beret **3** the hinged cover over a car engine

bonus (boh-nus) NOUN **bonuses** **1** an extra payment in addition to a person's normal wages **2** an extra benefit

bony ADJECTIVE **1** with large bones; having bones with little flesh on them **2** full of bones **3** like bones

boo VERB **boos, booing, booed** shout 'boo' in disapproval
▷ **boo** NOUN

booby NOUN **boobies** a babyish or stupid person

booby prize NOUN **booby prizes** a prize given as a joke to someone who comes last in a contest

booby trap NOUN **booby traps** something designed to hit or injure someone unexpectedly

book NOUN **books** a set of sheets of paper, usually with printing or writing on them, fastened together inside a cover
▷ **bookseller** NOUN **bookshop** NOUN **bookstall** NOUN

Thesaurus

bolt NOUN **1** *The door bolt was stuck.* ► catch, bar, latch, lock, fastening **2** *Put a nut on the bolt.* ► pin, rivet, rod, screw
a bolt from the blue ► shock, surprise, (*more informal*) bombshell

bolt VERB **1** *We'd better bolt the door.* ► fasten, latch, lock, secure, bar **2** *She bolted from the room.* ► dash, dart, flee, fly, rush, hurry, sprint, run, escape **3** *He was in such a rush he had to bolt his food.* ► gobble, gulp, wolf, guzzle, stuff, scoff down

bomb NOUN *The building was destroyed by bombs.* ► explosive, missile

bomb VERB *The city was bombed for days on end.* ► bombard, drop bombs on, shell

bombard VERB **1** *Offshore ships bombarded the city all night.* ► shell, pound, blast, strafe, assault, attack, beset, bomb, fire at, pelt, shoot at, assail **2** *The speaker was bombarded with questions.* ► overwhelm, inundate, swamp, flood, deluge, pester, plague

bombardment NOUN *The city was practically demolished by the bombardment.* ► barrage, blast, shelling, attack, cannonade, discharge, fusillade, hail, salvo, volley

bond NOUN **1** *There was a close bond between the two brothers.* ► attachment, connection, tie, link, relationship, affinity, unity, affiliation **2** *By running away he had broken his bond* ► promise, pledge, word, agreement, compact, contract, covenant, guarantee **3 bonds** *The prisoner struggled to undo his bonds.* ► chains, fetters, manacles, shackles, restraints, fastenings

bonus NOUN **1** *no Christmas bonus this year* ► extra payment, handout, reward **2** *A meal out was an unexpected bonus.* ► benefit, extra, addition, advantage, (*informal*) plus

bony ADJECTIVE *a bony figure* ► thin, angular, gawky, lanky, gaunt, emaciated, gangling, lean, scraggy, scrawny, skinny AN OPPOSITE IS plump

book NOUN *a book to read and enjoy* ► volume, tome, publication, tract, booklet

A B C D E F G H I J K L M N O P Q R S T U V W X Y Z

book *VERB* **books, booking, booked 1** reserve a place in a theatre, hotel, train, etc. **2** enter a person in a police record • *The police booked him for speeding.*

bookcase *NOUN* **bookcases** a piece of furniture with shelves for books

bookkeeping *NOUN* recording details of the money that is spent and received by a business ▷ **bookkeeper** *NOUN*

booklet *NOUN* **booklets** a small thin book

bookmaker *NOUN* **bookmakers** a person whose business is taking bets

bookmark *NOUN* **bookmarks** something to mark a place in a book

bookworm *NOUN* **bookworms** a person who loves reading

boom *VERB* **booms, booming, boomed 1** make a deep hollow sound **2** be growing and prospering • *Business is booming.*

boom *NOUN* **booms 1** a deep hollow sound **2** prosperity; growth

boomerang *NOUN* **boomerangs** a curved piece of wood that can be thrown so that it returns to the thrower, originally used by Australian Aborigines [from an Australian Aborginal word]

boor *NOUN* **boors** an ill-mannered person ▷ **boorish** *ADJECTIVE*

boost *VERB* **boosts, boosting, boosted 1** increase the strength, value, or reputation of a person or thing **2** push something upwards ▷ **booster** *NOUN*

boost *NOUN* **boosts 1** an increase **2** an upward push

boot *NOUN* **boots 1** a shoe that covers the foot and ankle or leg **2** the compartment for luggage in a car ▷ **booted** *ADJECTIVE*

boot *VERB* **boots, booting, booted 1** kick hard **2** switch on a computer

booty *NOUN* valuable goods taken away by soldiers after a battle

booze *VERB* **boozes, boozing, boozed** (*slang*) drink alcohol

booze *NOUN* (*slang*) alcoholic drink

border *NOUN* **borders 1** the boundary of a country; the part near this **2** an edge **3** something placed round an edge to strengthen or decorate it **4** a strip of ground round a garden or part of it

border *VERB* **borders, bordering, bordered** put or be a border to something

borderline *ADJECTIVE* only just belonging to a particular group or category • *a borderline case*

bore[1] *VERB* **bores, boring, bored 1** drill a hole **2** get through by pushing

Thesaurus

book *VERB* **1** *On his way to the hospital he was booked for speeding.* ► arrest, take your name, write down details **2** *We booked tickets for the concert.* ► reserve, order, arrange for, prearrange, buy **3** *Will you book a disco for the party?* ► engage, organize, sign up, arrange

booklet *NOUN* *a booklet of travel advice* ► pamphlet, brochure, leaflet, paperback

boom *NOUN* **1** *Suddenly there was the boom of the one o'clock gun.* ► bang, reverberation, roar, sound, blast **2** *a boom in trade* ► upturn, upsurge, upswing, boost, growth, improvement, expansion, increase, spurt AN OPPOSITE IS slump

boom *VERB* **1** *The guns began to boom.* ► rumble, thunder, crash, reverberate, resound, echo **2** *Business is booming.* ► thrive, prosper, flourish, do well, (*more informal*) pick up OPPOSITES ARE decline, slump

boon *NOUN* *Cheap travel is such a boon.* ► benefit, blessing, help, asset, advantage, (*more informal*) piece of luck

boost *NOUN* **1** *a boost to morale* ► impetus, stimulus, lift, uplift, (*more informal*) shot in the arm **2** *a boost in sales* ► increase, expansion, growth, improvement, boom, upturn, upsurge, upswing, spurt OPPOSITES ARE decrease, decline

boost *VERB* *The award boosted everyone's morale.* ► raise, uplift, heighten, stimulate, bolster, increase, enhance OPPOSITES ARE depress, hinder

boot *NOUN* *He had lost his left boot in the mud.* ► gumboot, wellington, (*more informal*) welly

booth *NOUN* *a telephone booth, a voting booth* ► cubicle, kiosk, stall, compartment, enclosure, carrel, hut, stand

booze *NOUN* (*informal*) *Lunch had to include lots of booze.* ► alcohol, drink, alcoholic drink, liquor, spirits

booze *VERB* (*informal*) *They had been boozing all night.* ► drink, have a drink, indulge, imbibe, (*also informal*) tipple

border *NOUN* **1** *the border of a tablecloth; the border of a lake* ► edge, margin, perimeter, fringe, verge **2** *the border between Italy and Slovenia* ► frontier, boundary, borderline

border *VERB* *The park borders a housing estate.* ► skirt, adjoin, be adjacent to, be alongside, abut on, join, share a border with, touch

borderline *ADJECTIVE* *a borderline case* ► marginal, indeterminate, uncertain, ambivalent

bore *VERB* **1** *You need to bore a hole in the wall.* ► drill, punch, cut, pierce, sink **2** *Long films*

bore[2] *VERB* **bores, boring, bored** make somebody feel uninterested by being dull

bore *NOUN* **bores** a boring person or thing
▷ **boredom** *NOUN*

bore[3] *past tense of* **bear**[2]

bored *ADJECTIVE* weary and uninterested because something is so dull

boring *ADJECTIVE* dull or tedious

born *ADJECTIVE* **1** having come into existence by birth (See the note on **borne**) **2** having a certain natural quality or ability • *a born leader*

borne *past participle of* **bear**[2]
USAGE The word **borne** is used before **by** or after **have, has,** or **had**, e.g. *children borne by Eve; she had borne him a son.* The word **born** is used e.g. in *a son was born.*

bosom *NOUN* **bosoms** a woman's breasts

boss *NOUN* **bosses** (*informal*) a manager; a person whose job is to give orders to workers etc.

boss *VERB* **bosses, bossing, bossed** (*informal*) order someone about

bossy *ADJECTIVE* fond of ordering people about
▷ **bossiness** *NOUN*

botany *NOUN* the study of plants
▷ **botanical** *ADJECTIVE* **botanist** *NOUN*

both *ADJECTIVE, PRONOUN* the two; not only one • *Are both films good?* • *Both are old.*

both *ADVERB*
both ... and not only ... but also • *The house is both small and ugly.*

bother *VERB* **bothers, bothering, bothered**
1 cause somebody trouble or worry; pester
2 take trouble; feel concern • *Don't bother to reply.*

bother *NOUN* trouble or worry

bottle *NOUN* **bottles** **1** a narrow-necked container for liquids **2** (*slang*) courage • *She showed a lot of bottle.*

bottle *VERB* **bottles, bottling, bottled** put or store something in bottles
bottle up if you bottle up your feelings, you keep them to yourself
[via early French *botaille* from Latin *buttis* = cask]

bottle bank *NOUN* **bottle banks** a large container in which used glass bottles are collected for recycling

Thesaurus

tend to bore him. ► weary, tire, (*more informal*) turn off OPPOSITES ARE interest, entertain

bore *NOUN* *What a bore to have to wait another hour.* ► nuisance, bother, annoyance, (*more informal*) drag, (*more informal*) pain, (*more informal*) pest

boring *ADJECTIVE* *What a boring book. The work turned out to be very boring.* ► tedious, dull, monotonous, dreary, humdrum, routine, uninteresting, unexciting, insipid, vapid, jejune OPPOSITES ARE interesting, stimulating

born *ADJECTIVE* *a born comic* ► natural, untaught, instinctive, genuine

borrow *VERB* *I need to borrow a pen.* ► loan, have use of, obtain, acquire, (*more informal*) cadge, (*more informal*) scrounge AN OPPOSITE IS lend

bosom *NOUN* **1** *The dress was cut high over her bosom.* ► bust, chest, breasts **2** *The family took her into its bosom.* ► care, protection, shelter

boss *NOUN* (*informal*) *The boss would be away all that week.* ► head, chief, manager, leader

boss *VERB* *You have no right to boss me about like this.* ► order, dictate to, push around, lord it over, bully, domineer

bossy *ADJECTIVE* *Why do you treat us in such a bossy manner?* ► domineering, officious, overbearing, high-handed, imperious, dictatorial, authoritarian, autocratic, aggressive, bullying, despotic, lordly, oppressive, peremptory, tyrannical
AN OPPOSITE IS submissive

botch *VERB* *They managed to botch the next job as well.* ► bungle, make a mess of, mismanage, mishandle, do badly, spoil, mess up, (*more informal*) screw up AN OPPOSITE IS succeed in

bother *NOUN* **1** *There was some bother at the disco.* ► disorder, trouble, disturbance, difficulty, fuss, (*more informal*) hassle, (*more informal*) aggro **2** *It was a bother to keep the food hot.* ► nuisance, annoyance, irritation, inconvenience, palaver, pest, trouble, worry, trial, job

bother *VERB* **1** *We found a quiet spot where no one would be able to bother us.* ► disturb, trouble, pester, molest, annoy, vex, worry, concern, dismay, exasperate, harass, (*informal*) hassle, inconvenience, irk, irritate, nag, plague, upset **2** *The accident was too minor to bother about.* ► concern yourself, be concerned, be worried, care, mind

bottle *NOUN* **1** *a bottle of wine; water in bottles* ► flask, carafe, decanter, flagon, jar, pitcher **2** (*informal*) *She had bottle to stand up to him, they had to admit.* ► courage, nerve, pluck, spirit, mettle, daring, audacity, boldness, bravery

bottle *VERB* **bottle up** *He had bottled up his problems for too long.* ► suppress, repress, hold in, keep in, stifle

a b c d e f g h i j k l m n o p q r s t u v w x y z

bottleneck *NOUN* **bottlenecks** a narrow place where something, especially traffic, cannot flow freely

bottom *NOUN* **bottoms 1** the lowest part; the base **2** the part furthest away • *the bottom of the garden* **3** a person's buttocks

bottom *ADJECTIVE* lowest • *the bottom shelf*

bough *NOUN* **boughs** a large branch coming from the trunk of a tree

boulder *NOUN* **boulders** a very large smooth stone

bounce *VERB* **bounces, bouncing, bounced 1** spring back when thrown against something **2** make a ball etc. bounce **3** (said about a cheque) be sent back by the bank because there is not enough money in the account **4** jump suddenly; move in a lively manner

bounce *NOUN* **bounces 1** the action or power of bouncing **2** a lively confident manner • *full of bounce*
▷ **bouncy** *ADJECTIVE*

bound[1] *VERB* **bounds, bounding, bounded** jump or spring; run with jumping movements • *The dogs were bounding along.*

bound *NOUN* **bounds** a bounding movement

bound[2] *past tense of* **bind**

bound *ADJECTIVE*
bound to certain to • *He is bound to fail.*
bound up with closely connected with • *Happiness is bound up with success.*

bound[3] *ADJECTIVE* going towards something • *We are bound for Spain.*

bound[4] *VERB* **bounds, bounding, bounded** limit; be the boundary of • *Their land is bounded by the river.*

boundary *NOUN* **boundaries 1** a line that marks a limit **2** a hit to the boundary of a cricket field

bounds *PLURAL NOUN* limits • *This was beyond the bounds of possibility.*
out of bounds where you are not allowed to go

bouquet (boh- kay) *NOUN* **bouquets** a bunch of flowers

bout *NOUN* **bouts 1** a boxing or wrestling contest **2** a period of exercise or work or illness • *a bout of flu*

boutique (boo- teek) *NOUN* **boutiques** a small shop selling fashionable clothes

Thesaurus

bottleneck *NOUN There was a bottleneck ahead at the old bridge.* ► blockage, hold-up, traffic jam, tailback

bottom *ADJECTIVE* **1** *the bottom rung of a ladder* ► deepest, lowest AN OPPOSITE IS top **2** *bottom marks* ► least, minimum AN OPPOSITE IS top

bottom *NOUN* **1** *the bottom of the stairs* ► foot, base AN OPPOSITE IS top **2** *the bottom of the wall* ► foot, base, foundation AN OPPOSITE IS top **3** *the bottom of the car* ► underside, underneath AN OPPOSITE IS topside **4** *the bottom of the sea* ► bed, depths, floor AN OPPOSITE IS surface **5** *They were at the bottom of their fortunes* ► lowest point, nadir AN OPPOSITE IS peak **6** *It is very hard to get to the bottom of the problem.* ► origin, root, source, heart, essence, grounds **7** *She said she had a tattoo on her bottom.* ► buttocks, rear, rump, seat, (*more informal*) behind, (*more informal*) backside, (*more informal*) bum, (*humorous*) sit-upon, (*formal or humorous*) posterior

bounce *VERB The ball hit the ground and bounced up.* ► rebound, spring up, bob up, bound, leap up, recoil, ricochet

bounce *NOUN She was exhausted and had lost much of her bounce.* ► vitality, energy, vigour, liveliness, vivacity, verve, exuberance

bound *ADJECTIVE* **1** *Our friends are bound to help.* ► certain, sure, very likely, liable, obliged, destined, fated **2** *bound by an oath* ► obligated, committed, obliged, duty-bound, pledged, compelled **3** *His wrists and ankles were bound with rope.* ► tied, tied up, shackled, fettered, secured, trussed up, strapped **4 bound for** *a train bound for the north* ► going to, heading for, making for, off to, travelling towards

bound *VERB A dog bounded across the lawn.* ► leap, jump, skip, spring, bounce, gambol, bob, caper, frisk

boundary *NOUN* **1** *A wire fence marks the boundary.* ► border, frontier, borderline, dividing line **2** *the boundary of the estate* ► bounds, confines, circumference, perimeter, extremity, outer edge, fringe, limit, margin

boundless *ADJECTIVE The boys seemed to have boundless energy.* ► unlimited, limitless, unbounded, untold, endless, immeasurable, incalculable, inexhaustible, infinite, unflagging, vast AN OPPOSITE IS limited

bouquet *NOUN* **1** *a bouquet of flowers* ► bunch, spray, posy, sprig, nosegay, corsage, garland **2** *The white wine had a sweet bouquet.* ► aroma, fragrance, nose, scent

bourgeois *ADJECTIVE a bourgeois family* ► middle-class, suburban, conventional, traditional, conservative

bout *NOUN* **1** *a bout of coughing* ► attack, fit, spasm, outburst, burst, convulsion **2** *a boxing bout* ► contest, match, round, fight, encounter, engagement, struggle, combat, competition

bow[1] (rhymes with *go*) NOUN **bows 1** a strip of wood curved by a tight string joining its ends, used for shooting arrows **2** a wooden rod with horsehair stretched between its ends, used for playing a violin etc. **3** a knot made with loops

bow[2] (rhymes with *cow*) VERB **bows, bowing, bowed 1** bend your body forwards to show respect or as a greeting **2** bend downwards • *bowed by the weight*

bow NOUN **bows** bowing your body

bow[3] (rhymes with *cow*) NOUN **bows** the front part of a ship

bowels PLURAL NOUN the intestines

bowl[1] NOUN **bowls 1** a rounded deep container for food or liquid **2** the rounded part of a spoon or tobacco pipe etc.

bowl[2] NOUN **bowls** a ball used in the game of **bowls** or in bowling, when heavy balls are rolled towards skittles

bowl VERB **bowls, bowling, bowled 1** send a ball to be played by a batsman **2** get a batsman out by bowling **3** send a ball etc. rolling

bow-legged ADJECTIVE having legs that curve outwards at the knees; bandy

bowling NOUN **1** the game of bowls **2** the game of knocking down skittles with a heavy ball

bow tie NOUN **bow ties** a man's necktie tied into a bow

bow window NOUN **bow windows** a curved window

box[1] NOUN **boxes 1** a container made of wood, cardboard, etc., usually with a top or lid **2** a rectangular space to be filled in on a form, computer screen, etc. **3** a compartment in a theatre, lawcourt, etc. • *the witness box* **4** a hut or shelter • *a sentry box* **5** a small evergreen shrub

the box (*informal*) television

box[2] VERB **boxes, boxing, boxed** fight with the fists as a sport

boxer NOUN **boxers 1** a person who boxes **2** a dog that looks like a bulldog

Boxing Day NOUN the first weekday after Christmas Day

box office NOUN **box offices** an office for booking seats at a theatre or cinema

boy NOUN **boys 1** a male child **2** a young man
▷ **boyhood** NOUN **boyish** ADJECTIVE

boycott VERB **boycotts, boycotting, boycotted** refuse to use or have anything to do with • *They boycotted the buses when the fares went up.*
▷ **boycott** NOUN

boyfriend NOUN **boyfriends** a person's regular male companion in a romantic or sexual relationship

bra NOUN **bras** a piece of underwear worn by women to support their breasts

brace VERB **braces, bracing, braced** support; make a thing firm against something

bracelet NOUN **bracelets** an ornament worn round the wrist

braces PLURAL NOUN straps to hold trousers up, passing over the shoulders

bracing ADJECTIVE making you feel refreshed and healthy • *the bracing sea breeze.*

bracken NOUN a type of large fern that grows in open country; a mass of these ferns

bracket NOUN **brackets 1** a mark used in pairs to enclose words or figures • *There are round brackets ( ) and square brackets [ ].* **2** a support attached to a wall etc. **3** a group or range between certain limits • *a high income bracket.*

bracket VERB **brackets, bracketing, bracketed 1** enclose in brackets **2** put things together because they are similar

Thesaurus

bow VERB (rhymes with *cow*) **1** *The man bowed his head.* ► incline, lower, bend **2** *In the end they had to bow to pressure.* ► yield, succumb, submit, surrender, give way, give in

bow NOUN (rhymes with *cow*) *the bow of a ship* ► front, prow, fore-end

bow NOUN (rhymes with *go*) *She tied the ribbon into a neat bow.* ► loop, knot

bowl NOUN *a bowl of soup* ► dish, basin, tureen, vessel

bowl VERB *He bowled three fast balls in a row.* ► throw, toss, fling, hurl, pitch, lob

box NOUN *a box of coloured pencils* ► carton, pack, packet, case, casket, chest

boy NOUN *He had loved reading as a boy.* ► lad, youngster, (*more informal*) kid, (*more informal*) nipper

boyish ADJECTIVE *He had a boyish sense of fun.* ► youthful, childlike, young, (*disapproving*) childish, (*disapproving*) puerile OPPOSITES ARE manly, mature, adult

bracing ADJECTIVE *The sea air is very bracing.* ► invigorating, stimulating, refreshing, exhilarating, fortifying AN OPPOSITE IS debilitating

brag VERB *He was bragging about all the friends he had.* ► boast, crow, bluster, swank, show off, gloat, sing someone's praises, (*more informal*) talk big

brahmin *NOUN* **brahmins** a member of the highest Hindu class, originally priests

Braille (rhymes with *mail*) *NOUN* a system of representing letters etc. by raised dots which blind people can read by feeling them

brain *NOUN* **brains 1** the organ inside the top of the head that controls the body **2** the mind; intelligence

brainwash *VERB* **brainwashes, brainwashing, brainwashed** force a person to give up one set of ideas or beliefs and accept new ones; indoctrinate

brainwave *NOUN* **brainwaves** a sudden bright idea

brainy *ADJECTIVE* clever; intelligent

brake *NOUN* **brakes** a device for slowing or stopping something

brake *VERB* **brakes, braking, braked** use a brake

bramble *NOUN* **brambles** a blackberry bush or a prickly bush like it

bran *NOUN* ground-up husks of corn

branch *NOUN* **branches 1** a woody arm-like part of a tree or shrub **2** a part of a railway, road, or river etc. that leads off from the main part **3** a shop or office etc. that belongs to a large organization

branch *VERB* **branches, branching, branched** form a branch

branch out start something new

brand *NOUN* **brands** a particular make of goods

brandish *VERB* **brandishes, brandishing, brandished** wave something about

brand new *ADJECTIVE* completely new

brandy *NOUN* **brandies** a strong alcoholic drink, usually made from wine

brash *ADJECTIVE* **1** impudent **2** reckless

brass *NOUN* **brasses 1** a metal that is an alloy of copper and zinc **2** wind instruments made of brass, e.g. trumpets and trombones
▷ **brass** *ADJECTIVE*

brassy *ADJECTIVE* **brassier, brassiest 1** resembling brass in colour **2** loud or showy

bravado (brav- ah- doh) *NOUN* a display of boldness

brave *ADJECTIVE* having or showing courage
▷ **bravely** *ADVERB* **bravery** *NOUN*

brave *VERB* **braves, braving, braved** face and endure something bravely

brawl *NOUN* **brawls** a noisy quarrel or fight

Thesaurus

brain *NOUN* **1** *You need brains to succeed in this job.* ► intelligence, intellect, sense, common sense, understanding, a good mind, a good head, (*informal*) grey matter, (*informal*) nous **2** *the brains of the family* ► intellectual, clever one, clever person, mastermind, (*more informal*) egghead RELATED ADJECTIVE cerebral

brainwash *VERB He likes to brainwash people into thinking they need help.* ► indoctrinate, condition, re-educate

brainy *ADJECTIVE a brainy child* ► intelligent, clever, bright, gifted, brilliant, intellectual, highbrow, (*more informal*) smart OPPOSITES ARE stupid, unintelligent

brake *VERB She saw a child step out and braked quickly.* ► slow down, reduce speed, put on the brakes, (*more formal*) decelerate AN OPPOSITE IS accelerate

branch *NOUN* **1** *a branch of a tree* ► bough, limb, arm, offshoot, sprig **2** *the executive branch of government* ► department, section, division, subdivision, wing, part **3** *The firm has closed several overseas branches.* ► office, bureau, agency

branch *VERB The road branches ahead.* ► divide, fork

branch out *She wanted to branch out into another career.* ► diversify, develop, expand, extend, enlarge, broaden out

brand *NOUN a new brand of margarine* ► make, kind, type, variety, brand-name, trademark, label, line, sort

brand *VERB* **1** *The cattle are branded with hot irons.* ► mark, stamp, burn, identify, label, scar **2** *The men are all branded as troublemakers.* ► stigmatize, vilify, censure, denounce, discredit, disgrace, taint, give (someone) the reputation of

brash *ADJECTIVE a group of brash youths* ► brazen, forward, insolent, (*more informal*) cocky OPPOSITES ARE meek, shy

brave *ADJECTIVE He was a good fighter and a brave man. They put up a brave fight.* ► courageous, valiant, daring, audacious, spirited, intrepid, plucky, adventurous, fearless AN OPPOSITE IS cowardly

bravery *NOUN Everyone praised their bravery.* ► courage, audacity, boldness, daring, nerve, gallantry, determination, fearlessness, fortitude, heroism, (*more informal*) bottle, (*more informal*) grit, (*more informal*) guts, (*more informal*) pluck, (*much more informal*) spunk AN OPPOSITE IS cowardice

brawl *NOUN The argument rapidly grew into a drunken brawl.* ► fight , affray, melee, wrangle, altercation, fracas, clash, fray, scrap, scuffle, tussle, (*informal*) punch-up, (*more informal*) set-to, (*more informal*) bust-up

brawl *VERB* **brawls, brawling, brawled** take part in a brawl

brawny *ADJECTIVE* strong and muscular

brazen *VERB* **brazens, brazening, brazened**
brazen it out behave as if there is nothing to be ashamed of when you have done wrong

breach *NOUN* **breaches 1** the breaking of an agreement or rule etc. **2** a broken place; a gap

bread *NOUN* **breads** a food made by baking flour and water, usually with yeast
▷ **breadcrumbs** *PLURAL NOUN*

breadth *NOUN* width; broadness

break *VERB* **breaks, breaking, broke, broken 1** divide or fall into pieces by hitting or pressing **2** damage; stop working properly **3** fail to keep a promise or law etc. **4** stop for a time; end • *She broke her silence.* **5** change • *the weather broke* **6** (said about waves) fall in foam **7** go suddenly or with force • *They broke through.* **8** appear suddenly • *Dawn had broken.*
▷ **breakage** *NOUN*
break a record do better than anyone else has done before
break down 1 stop working properly **2** collapse
break out 1 begin suddenly **2** escape
break the news make something known
break up 1 break into small parts **2** leave for the holidays at the end of a school term

break *NOUN* **breaks 1** a broken place; a gap **2** an escape; a sudden dash **3** a short rest from work **4** a number of points scored continuously in snooker etc. **5** (*informal*) a piece of luck; a fair chance • *Give me a break.*
break of day dawn

breakdown *NOUN* **breakdowns 1** breaking down; failure • *the breakdown of law and order* **2** a period of mental illness caused by anxiety or depression **3** an analysis of accounts or statistics **4** a sudden failure to work, especially by a car • *We had a breakdown on the motorway.*

breakfast *NOUN* **breakfasts** the first meal of the day

Thesaurus

brawl *VERB grown men brawling in the street* ► fight, scuffle, scrap, tussle, wrestle, exchange blows

brazen *ADJECTIVE a brazen lie* ► blatant, barefaced, flagrant, shameless, unashamed, unabashed, audacious, cheeky, defiant, impertinent, impudent, insolent, rude OPPOSITES ARE modest, shamefaced

breach *NOUN* **1** *a breach of the rules* ► breaking, infringement, violation, contravention, offence (against), transgression **2** *a breach between the king and his chancellor* ► rift, break, split, difference, disagreement, drifting apart, estrangement, quarrel, separation, alienation **3** *a breach in the sea wall* ► break, split, fissure, gap, crack, fracture, rupture, aperture, chasm, hole, opening

bread *NOUN* **1** *She was responsible for keeping a roof over their heads and bread in their mouths.* ► food, nourishment, sustenance, subsistence

break *NOUN* **1** *a break in a pipe* ► breach, split, fissure, gap, crack, fracture, rupture, aperture, chasm, hole, opening **2** *a break in work* ► pause, respite, rest, breathing space, intermission, interval, hiatus, interlude, (*informal*) let-up, lull, (*informal*) breather **3** *He had listened to thirty new songs without a break.* ► interruption, disruption, halt, stop, lapse, suspension

break *VERB* **1** *The cup fell to the floor and broke.* ► shatter, smash, crack, split, fragment, splinter, (*more informal*) bust **2** *He broke the stick into three pieces.* ► split, cut, divide, sever, (*more informal*) bust OPPOSITES ARE repair, mend **3** *It would be unwise to break the law.* ► contravene, violate, disobey, flout, infringe OPPOSITES ARE obey, respect, abide by **4** *Let's break for lunch.* ► pause, stop, take a break, (*more informal*) knock off **5** *She was determined to break the power of the unions.* ► subdue, tame, defeat, crush, smash, suppress, undermine
break down 1 *The car broke down near the border.* ► stop working, go wrong, (*more informal*) pack up, (*more informal*) conk out **2** *Negotiations broke down without an agreement.* ► fail, collapse, fall through, come to nothing
break in 1 *His mother then broke in with a question about the arrangements.* ► interrupt, butt in, intrude **2** *Thieves had broken in during the night.* ► commit burglary, force your way in, make a raid
break off *It was hard to break off before finishing the chapter.* ► discontinue, pause, stop
break out of *Several prisoners were able to break out of the detention centre.* ► escape from, abscond from, break loose from
break up 1 *A dump where they break up old cars.* ► demolish, dismantle, take apart **2** *The meeting broke up after several hours.* ► adjourn, finish, end, come to an end, (*more formal*) terminate **3** *The crowd began to break up.* ► disperse, scatter, disband, go their separate ways **4** *Jane and her boyfriend had recently broken up.* ► separate, split up, stop living together, get divorced

breakdown *NOUN* **1** *The system has experienced a complete breakdown.* ► malfunction, failure, collapse **2** *a breakdown in the peace talks* ► failure, collapse **3** *a breakdown of the figures* ► analysis, classification, itemization

break-in *NOUN a break-in at the bank* ► burglary, robbery, theft, raid

A B C D E F G H I J K L M N O P Q R S T U V W X Y Z

breakneck *ADJECTIVE* dangerously fast • *He had to drive at breakneck speed to get there on time.*

breakthrough *NOUN* **breakthroughs** an important advance or achievement

breast *NOUN* **breasts 1** one of the two fleshy parts on the upper front of a woman's body that produce milk to feed a baby **2** a person's or animal's chest

breastplate *NOUN* **breastplates** a piece of armour covering the chest

breath (breth) *NOUN* **breaths 1** air drawn into the lungs and sent out again **2** a gentle blowing • *a breath of wind*
out of breath panting
take your breath away surprise or delight you greatly
under your breath in a whisper

breathalyser *NOUN* **breathalysers** a device for measuring the amount of alcohol in a person's breath
▷ **breathalyse** *VERB*

breathe (breeth) *VERB* **breathes, breathing, breathed 1** take air into the body and send it out again **2** speak or utter • *Don't breathe a word of this.*

breather (bree-ther) *NOUN* **breathers** a pause for rest • *Let's take a breather.*

breathless *ADJECTIVE* out of breath

breed *VERB* **breeds, breeding, bred 1** produce young creatures **2** keep animals in order to produce young ones from them **3** bring up or train **4** create or produce • *Poverty breeds illness.*
▷ **breeder** *NOUN*

breed *NOUN* **breeds** a variety of animals with qualities inherited from their parents

breeze *NOUN* **breezes** a wind
▷ **breezy** *ADJECTIVE*

brevity *NOUN* shortness; briefness

brew *VERB* **brews, brewing, brewed 1** make beer or tea **2** develop • *Trouble is brewing.*

brew *NOUN* **brews** a brewed drink

brewery *NOUN* **breweries** a place where beer is brewed

bribe *NOUN* **bribes** money or a gift offered to a person to influence him or her

Thesaurus

breakneck *ADJECTIVE* *driving at breakneck speed* ► headlong, dangerous, reckless, fast, hasty, suicidal

breakthrough *NOUN* *a breakthrough in the search for a cure* ► advance, leap forward, discovery, development, revolution, progress, find, improvement, innovation, invention, success

breast *NOUN* *a woman's breast* ► bosom(s), bust, chest, front RELATED ADJECTIVE mammary

breath *NOUN* **1** *Take a deep breath.* ► gulp of air, (*technical*) inhalation **2** *a breath of wind* ► puff, waft, whiff, whisper, breeze, sigh

breathe *VERB* **1** *It is lovely to breathe fresh air again.* ► inhale, exhale, respire, puff, pant **2** *Try not to breathe a word of what happened.* ► speak, whisper, hint, let out

breathless *ADJECTIVE* *They arrived breathless and red in the face.* ► out of breath, gasping, panting, puffing, tired out, wheezy, exhausted

breathtaking *ADJECTIVE* *The view was breathtaking.* ► spectacular, magnificent, stunning, amazing, astonishing, astounding, staggering, startling, fantastic, wonderful, phenomenal AN OPPOSITE IS unimpressive

breed *NOUN* **1** *a rare breed of dog* ► variety, type, kind, sort, strain, family, pedigree **2** *a new breed of writer* ► type, kind, sort, class, variety, genre, order

breed *VERB* **1** *Rabbits have a reputation for breeding rapidly.* ► reproduce, produce young, bear young, multiply, procreate, increase **2** *Familiarity breeds contempt.* ► produce, cause, create, arouse, engender, foster, cultivate, develop, generate, induce, nourish, nurture, occasion

breeze *NOUN* *A slight breeze made the tall grass tremble.* ► gentle wind, breath of air, puff of air, flurry

breezy *ADJECTIVE* **1** *a breezy afternoon* ► windy, blowy, fresh, brisk, airy, draughty, fresh OPPOSITES ARE still, windless **2** *She walked in with a breezy air.* ► cheerful, jaunty, lively, bright, animated, carefree, light-hearted OPPOSITES ARE sombre, serious

brevity *NOUN* *Everyone who had to read it welcomed the brevity of the report.* ► conciseness, shortness, succinctness, economy, briefness, compression, incisiveness, pithiness, terseness, crispness, curtness OPPOSITES ARE verbosity, long-windedness

brew *NOUN* *a strong brew made with fruit juices* ► mixture, blend, concoction, compound, infusion, potion, preparation, punch, drink, liquor

brew *VERB* **1** *Southerners just can't brew good beer.* ► ferment, make **2** *Christopher and Francis disappeared to brew coffee.* ► make, prepare, heat **3** *Someone is brewing mischief for us.* ► plot, stir up, foment, threaten, concoct, contrive, hatch, plan, prepare, scheme, (*more informal*) cook up **4** *Trouble is brewing.* ► develop, loom, build up, threaten, gather

bribe *NOUN* *He was accused of accepting bribes.* ► inducement, enticement, incentive, (*more*

bribe *VERB* **bribes, bribing, bribed** give someone a bribe
▷ **bribery** *NOUN*

brick *NOUN* **bricks 1** a small hard block of baked clay etc. used to build walls **2** a rectangular block of something

brick *VERB* **bricks, bricking, bricked** close something with bricks • *We bricked up the gap in the wall.*

bricklayer *NOUN* **bricklayers** a worker who builds with bricks

bride *NOUN* **brides** a woman on her wedding day
▷ **bridal** *ADJECTIVE*

bridegroom *NOUN* **bridegrooms** a man on his wedding day

bridesmaid *NOUN* **bridesmaids** a girl or unmarried woman who attends the bride at a wedding

bridge[1] *NOUN* **bridges 1** a structure built over and across a river, railway, or road etc. to allow people to cross it **2** a high platform above a ship's deck, for the officer in charge **3** the bony upper part of the nose **4** something that connects things

bridge *VERB* **bridges, bridging, bridged** make or form a bridge over something

bridge[2] *NOUN* a card game rather like whist

bridle *NOUN* **bridles** the part of a horse's harness that fits over its head

bridleway or **bridle path** *NOUN* **bridleways** or **bridle paths** a road suitable for horses but not for vehicles

brief *ADJECTIVE* short
▷ **briefly** *ADVERB* **briefness** *NOUN*
in brief in a few words

brief *NOUN* **briefs** instructions and information given to someone, especially to a barrister

brief *VERB* **briefs, briefing, briefed 1** give a brief to a barrister **2** instruct or inform someone concisely in advance

briefcase *NOUN* **briefcases** a flat case for carrying documents etc.

briefing *NOUN* **briefings** a meeting to give someone concise instructions or information

briefs *PLURAL NOUN* very short knickers or underpants

brigade *NOUN* **brigades 1** a large unit of an army **2** a group of people organized for a special purpose • *the fire brigade*

bright *ADJECTIVE* **1** giving a strong light; shining **2** clever **3** cheerful
▷ **brightly** *ADVERB* **brightness** *NOUN*

brighten *VERB* **brightens, brightening, brightened** make or become brighter

Thesaurus

informal) sweetener, (*more informal)* backhander, (*more informal)* carrot

bribe *VERB They had tried to bribe an official.* ► offer a bribe to, buy off, pay off, corrupt, entice, influence, pervert, (*more formal)* suborn

brick *NOUN an outhouse made of bricks* ► block, building block, breeze-block

bridge *NOUN a bridge over the river* ► viaduct, aqueduct (carrying water), arch, crossing, span, way over

bridge *VERB A footpath bridged the motorway.* ► span, cross, straddle, traverse, go over, extend across, reach across

brief *ADJECTIVE* **1** *a brief visit* ► short, cursory, fleeting, passing, quick, hasty, limited, little, momentary, sharp, short-lived, temporary, transient OPPOSITES ARE long, prolonged **2** *a brief account of the incident* ► short, concise, succinct, pithy, crisp, incisive, compact, condensed, curt, terse, thumbnail OPPOSITES ARE wordy, verbose, lengthy

brief *NOUN* **1** *Here is a detailed brief for the assignment.* ► (set of) instructions, (set of) orders, (set of) directions, (set of) guidelines, set of information, outline, plan **2** *a barrister's brief* ► case, defence, argument, dossier, summary

brief *VERB Staff will be briefed about the changes.* ► inform, advise, direct, instruct, prime, apprise of, give the facts, guide, prepare, (*more informal)* fill in, (*more informal)* put in the picture

briefs *PLURAL NOUN He stood in the doorway in nothing but briefs.* ► underpants, pants, knickers, panties, shorts, trunks

brigand *NOUN The travellers were robbed by brigands.* ► bandit, robber, thief, outlaw, desperado, gangster, gunman, marauder, highwayman, footpad, pirate, hijacker

bright *ADJECTIVE* **1** *bright colours; bright sunshine* ► shining, luminous, brilliant, vivid, radiant, dazzling, glaring, blazing, sparkling, twinkling OPPOSITES ARE dark, dull **2** *a bright morning* ► sunny, fine, fair, clear, cloudless OPPOSITES ARE dull, cloudy **3** *a bright manner* ► cheerful, jaunty, lively, breezy, animated AN OPPOSITE IS subdued **4** *a bright student* ► clever, intelligent, gifted, sharp, quick, quick-witted, smart, brilliant OPPOSITES ARE dull, stupid, unintelligent

brighten *VERB The weather brightened* ► become sunny, become bright, clear up, lighten AN OPPOSITE IS darken
brighten up *Some pictures will brighten the place up.* ► cheer up, smarten up, embellish,

A B C D E F G H I J K L M N O P Q R S T U V W X Y Z

brilliant ADJECTIVE **1** very bright; sparkling **2** very clever
▷ **brilliantly** ADVERB **brilliance** NOUN

brim NOUN **brims 1** the edge of a cup etc. **2** the bottom part of a hat that sticks out

brim VERB **brims, brimming, brimmed** be full to the brim
brim over overflow

brimful ADJECTIVE full to the brim

bring VERB **brings, bringing, brought** cause a person or thing to come; lead; carry
bring about cause to happen
bring off achieve; do something successfully
bring up 1 look after and train growing children **2** mention a subject **3** vomit **4** cause to stop suddenly

brisk ADJECTIVE quick and lively
▷ **briskly** ADVERB **briskness** NOUN

bristle NOUN **bristles 1** a short stiff hair **2** one of the stiff pieces of hair, wire, or plastic etc. in a brush
▷ **bristly** ADJECTIVE

bristle VERB **bristles, bristling, bristled 1** (said about an animal) raise its bristles in anger or fear **2** show indignation
bristle with be full of • *The roof bristled with aerials.*

brittle ADJECTIVE hard but easy to break or snap
▷ **brittleness** NOUN

broad ADJECTIVE **1** large across; wide **2** full and complete • *broad daylight* **3** in general terms; not detailed • *We are in broad agreement.* **4** strong and unmistakable • *a broad hint* • *a broad accent*
▷ **broadly** ADVERB **broadness** NOUN

broad bean NOUN **broad beans** a bean with large flat seeds

Thesaurus

enhance, enliven, gladden, illuminate, light up, revitalize AN OPPOSITE IS darken

brilliant ADJECTIVE **1** *brilliant light* ► blazing, bright, dazzling, glaring, gleaming, glittering, glorious, resplendent, scintillating, shining, showy, sparkling, splendid, vivid AN OPPOSITE IS dull **2** *a brilliant student* ► clever, intelligent, outstanding, gifted, sharp, quick, quick-witted, smart, bright OPPOSITES ARE dull, stupid **3** (*informal*) *a brilliant game* ► excellent, marvellous, wonderful, superb, exceptional

brim NOUN *full to the brim* ► top, rim, edge, limit, lip, brink, circumference, margin, perimeter, periphery

bring VERB **1** *She brought me a mug of tea.* ► fetch, carry, convey, bear, deliver, take, transfer, transport **2** *Bring your friends into the garden.* ► escort, accompany, conduct, guide, lead, usher **3** *Their success brought a great deal of great attention.* ► draw, attract, produce, cause, engender, generate
bring about *The new manager brought about many changes.* ► cause, effect, achieve, create, engineer, manage
bring in 1 *The appeal brought in a huge response.* ► result in, lead to, realize, yield, earn, gross **2** *The company is bringing in a new product* ► introduce, initiate, start, make available
bring off *It was a difficult play to bring off.* ► achieve, accomplish, be successful in, do successfully, succeed in
bring on *The shock brought on his asthma.* ► cause, give rise to, induce, trigger, lead to, precipitate, provoke, aggravate
bring out 1 *The publishers are to bring out a new edition.* ► publish, release, issue, produce, print **2** *The description brings out the comical side of the story.* ► emphasize, accentuate, underline, highlight, stress, dwell on, feature, make obvious, play up, point up, show clearly, spotlight
bring up 1 *As a young child she was brought up in Poland.* ► raise, rear, educate, care for, look after, nurture, teach, train **2** *The baby brought up his dinner.* ► vomit, sick up **3** *There's a small matter I want to bring up.* ► mention, raise, broach, touch on, refer to

brink NOUN **1** *The children stood at the brink staring into the water.* ► edge, verge, margin, bank, brim, border **2** *We were on the brink of a major discovery.* ► verge, point, threshold, start

brisk ADJECTIVE **1** *walking at a brisk pace* ► quick, rapid, fast, lively, energetic, speedy, swift, hurried OPPOSITES ARE leisurely, slow **2** *brisk exercise* ► vigorous, energetic, bracing, refreshing **3** *The hotel was doing a brisk trade.* ► busy, bustling, lively, hectic, good OPPOSITES ARE quiet, slack

bristle NOUN *John rubbed a hand over his bristles.* ► stubble, facial hair, whisker, prickle, spine, wire

brittle ADJECTIVE *brittle bones* ► breakable, fragile, frail, delicate, splintery, crackly OPPOSITES ARE flexible, resilient

broad ADJECTIVE **1** *They were walking along a broad path.* ► wide, large, big, ample, capacious, expansive, extensive, great, large, open, roomy, spacious, sweeping, vast OPPOSITES ARE narrow, small **2** *a broad sweep of countryside* ► wide, spacious, ample, extensive, vast, rolling **3** *the broad outline of the story* ► general, rough, vague, loose, imprecise, indefinite, inexact, undetailed OPPOSITES ARE detailed, precise **4** *She had broad tastes in music* ► comprehensive, eclectic, catholic, wide-ranging, all-embracing, encyclopedic, universal OPPOSITES ARE

broadcast *NOUN* **broadcasts** a programme sent out on the radio or on television

broadcast *VERB* **broadcasts, broadcasting, broadcast** send out a programme on the radio or on television
▷ **broadcaster** *NOUN*

broaden *VERB* **broadens, broadening, broadened** make or become broader

broad-minded *ADJECTIVE* tolerant; not easily shocked

broccoli *NOUN* **broccoli** a kind of cauliflower with greenish flower heads

brochure (broh-shoor) *NOUN* **brochures** a booklet or pamphlet containing information

broke *ADJECTIVE* (*informal*) having spent all your money

broken-hearted *ADJECTIVE* extremely sad or upset about something

broken home *NOUN* **broken homes** a family lacking one parent through divorce or separation

bronchitis (bronk-I-tiss) *NOUN* a disease with bronchial inflammation, which makes you cough a lot

bronze *NOUN* **bronzes** **1** a metal that is an alloy of copper and tin **2** something made of bronze **3** a bronze medal, awarded as third prize **4** yellowish-brown
▷ **bronze** *ADJECTIVE*

Bronze Age *NOUN* the time when tools and weapons were made of bronze

brooch *NOUN* **brooches** an ornament with a hinged pin for fastening it on to clothes

brood *NOUN* **broods** young birds that were hatched together

brood *VERB* **broods, brooding, brooded** **1** sit on eggs to hatch them **2** keep thinking and worrying about something

brook *NOUN* **brooks** a small stream

broom *NOUN* **brooms** **1** a brush with a long handle, for sweeping **2** a shrub with yellow, white, or pink flowers

broomstick *NOUN* **broomsticks** the handle of a broom

broth *NOUN* **broths** a kind of thin soup

brother *NOUN* **brothers** **1** a son of the same parents as another person **2** a man who is a fellow member of a Church, trade union, etc.
▷ **brotherly** *ADJECTIVE*
[from Old English]

brother-in-law *NOUN* **brothers-in-law** the brother of a married person's husband or wife; the husband of a person's sister

Thesaurus

restricted, limited, narrow **5** *broad humour* ► coarse, earthy, racy, ribald, indecent, vulgar, indelicate, bawdy, suggestive, improper, impure, (*more informal*) blue **6** *a broad local accent* ► pronounced, strong, marked, noticeable **7** *You'll need to drop a broad hint.* ► clear, direct, obvious, unmistakeable

broadcast *NOUN* *a radio broadcast* ► transmission, relay, programme

broadcast *VERB* **1** *The concert was broadcast worldwide on television.* ► transmit, relay, send out, televise, show, (*more informal*) screen, (*more informal*) air **2** *This is sensitive information and should not be broadcast too widely.* ► report, publicize, circulate, spread, make known, make public, proclaim, advertise, announce, (*more formal*) disseminate, (*more formal*) promulgate

broad-minded *ADJECTIVE* *Their language would offend the most broad-minded of people.* ► liberal, tolerant, enlightened, permissive, forbearing, open-minded, unbiased, receptive OPPOSITES ARE narrow-minded, intolerant

broke *ADJECTIVE* (*informal*) *He reached home completely broke.* ► impoverished, penniless, poor, insolvent, destitute, ruined

broken *ADJECTIVE* **1** *A waitress was picking up the broken plates.* ► smashed, shattered, cracked, split OPPOSITES ARE whole, unbroken **2** *The television is broken.* ► faulty, defective, out of order, not working, (*more formal*) inoperative OPPOSITES ARE working, fixed **3** *The failure of the company left him a broken man.* ► defeated, crushed, beaten, overwhelmed **4** *a broken marriage* ► failed, ended **5** *a few hours of broken sleep* ► interrupted, disturbed, disrupted, fitful, troubled OPPOSITES ARE continuous, uninterrupted

broken-hearted *ADJECTIVE* *The little girl was broken-hearted at the loss of her doll.* ► heartbroken, inconsolable, devastated, grief-stricken, desolate, despairing AN OPPOSITE IS happy

brood *NOUN* **1** *a mother hen and her brood* ► young, offspring, clutch, family **2** *Felicity was the eldest of a large brood.* ► family, household

brood *VERB* **1** *A hen was brooding her eggs.* ► hatch, incubate, sit on **2** *It's a mistake to brood over past mistakes.* ► dwell (on), agonize, muse (on), ponder, reflect (on), think (about), sulk (about), fret, meditate (on), mope, mull over

brother *NOUN* *Freddie was Margaret's brother.* ► sibling RELATED ADJECTIVE fraternal

A B C D E F G H I J K L M N O P Q R S T U V W X Y Z

brow *NOUN* **brows** **1** an eyebrow **2** the forehead **3** the ridge at the top of a hill; the edge of a cliff

brown *NOUN* **browns** the colour of earth

brown *ADJECTIVE* **1** of the colour brown **2** having a brown skin; suntanned

Brownie *NOUN* **Brownies** a member of a junior branch of the Guides

browse *VERB* **browses, browsing, browsed** **1** read or look at something casually **2** feed on grass or leaves **3** (in computing) to look through files or data, especially on the Internet

browser *NOUN* **browsers** (in computing) a program for searching the Internet

bruise *NOUN* **bruises** a dark mark made on the skin by hitting it

bruise *VERB* **bruises, bruising, bruised** give or get a bruise or bruises

brunette *NOUN* **brunettes** a woman with brown hair

brunt *NOUN* the chief impact or strain • *They bore the brunt of the attack.*

brush *NOUN* **brushes** **1** an implement used for cleaning or painting things or for smoothing the hair, usually with pieces of hair, wire, or plastic etc. set in a solid base **2** a fox's bushy tail **3** brushing • *Give it a good brush.* **4** a short fight • *They had a brush with the enemy.*

brush *VERB* **brushes, brushing, brushed** **1** use a brush on something **2** touch gently in passing
brush up revise a subject

brusque (bruusk) *ADJECTIVE* curt and offhand in manner
▷ **brusquely** *ADVERB*

Brussels sprouts *PLURAL NOUN* the edible buds of a kind of cabbage

brutal *ADJECTIVE* very cruel
▷ **brutally** *ADVERB* **brutality** *NOUN*

brute *NOUN* **brutes** **1** a brutal person **2** an animal
▷ **brutish** *ADJECTIVE*

BSE *ABBREVIATION* bovine spongiform encephalopathy; a fatal disease of cattle that affects the nervous system and makes the cow stagger about BSE is sometimes known as 'mad cow disease'

bubble *NOUN* **bubbles** **1** a thin transparent ball of liquid filled with air or gas **2** a small ball of air in something
▷ **bubbly** *ADJECTIVE*

Thesaurus

brow *NOUN the brow of the hill* ► peak, crest, summit, crown, top OPPOSITES ARE foot, bottom

brown *ADJECTIVE* **1** *brown hair* ► brunette, auburn, bronze, chestnut, chocolate-coloured **2** *a brown coat* ► fawn, beige, buff, tan, tawny, biscuit, terracotta, dun, khaki, ochre, russet, sepia, umber

browned off *ADJECTIVE (informal) He was feeling tired and browned off.* ► fed up, dispirited, depressed, peeved, disgruntled, disheartened

browse *VERB* **1** *I was browsing in a book.* ► flick through, leaf through, look through, scan, skim, thumb through, dip in, (*more formal*) peruse **2** *Cattle browsed in a field.* ► graze, pasture, crop grass, feed, eat

bruise *NOUN He had a bruise on his leg.* ► swelling, bump, contusion, lesion, discoloration

bruise *VERB The blow bruised her arm.* ► mark, discolour, injure, hurt

brush *NOUN* **1** *Use a brush to sweep up.* ► broom, besom **2** *a brush with the law* ► clash, encounter, altercation, quarrel, wrangle

brush *VERB Wait while I brush my hair.* ► tidy, comb, groom
brush aside *The minister tried to brush aside the objections.* ► discount, dismiss, disregard, ignore, shrug off, put aside, (*more informal*) pooh-pooh
brush off *He was trying to be friendly but they brushed him off.* ► spurn, rebuff, snub, cold-shoulder, reject, disregard, ignore, slight
brush up *Are you going to brush up your French?* ► revise, improve, read up, go over, refresh your memory of, relearn, study, (*more informal*) swot up

brutal *ADJECTIVE a brutal attack* ► savage, cruel, vicious, fierce, ferocious, barbaric, callous, heartless, cold-blooded, pitiless, ruthless, merciless, vile, sadistic, brutish OPPOSITES ARE gentle, humane

brutality *NOUN The crime was committed with staggering brutality.* ► savagery, cruelty, viciousness, ferocity, barbarity, callousness, heartlessness, cold-bloodedness, ruthlessness AN OPPOSITE IS gentleness

brute *NOUN He began behaving like the brute he was.* ► beast, animal, monster, fiend, demon

brute *ADJECTIVE brute force* ► physical, crude, rough, unthinking

bubble *NOUN* **1** *bubbles rising to the ceiling* ► globule, ball, blister, hollow, (*more formal*) vesicle **2** **bubbles** *soap bubbles* ► foam, froth, lather, suds **3** **bubbles** *bubbles of champagne* ► effervescence, fizz

bubble *VERB The water was bubbling.* ► boil, gurgle, seethe, sparkle

bubble *VERB* **bubbles, bubbling, bubbled**
1 send up bubbles; rise in bubbles **2** show great liveliness

buccaneer *NOUN* **buccaneers** a pirate

buck *NOUN* **bucks** a male deer, rabbit, or hare

buck *VERB* **bucks, bucking, bucked** (said about a horse) jump with its back arched
buck up (*informal*) **1** hurry **2** cheer up

bucket *NOUN* **buckets** a container with a handle, for carrying liquids etc.
▷ **bucketful** *NOUN*

buckle *NOUN* **buckles** a device through which a belt or strap is threaded to fasten it

buckle *VERB* **buckles, buckling, buckled** fasten something with a buckle

bud *NOUN* **buds** a flower or leaf before it opens

Buddhism (buud- izm) *NOUN* a faith that started in Asia and follows the teachings of the Indian philosopher Gautama Buddha, who lived in the 5th century BC
▷ **Buddhist** *NOUN*

budge *VERB* **budges, budging, budged** if you cannot budge something, you cannot move it at all

budgerigar *NOUN* **budgerigars** an Australian bird often kept as a pet in a cage [from Australian Aboriginal *budgeri* = good + *gar* = cockatoo]

budget *NOUN* **budgets 1** a plan for spending money wisely **2** an amount of money set aside for a purpose
▷ **budgetary** *ADJECTIVE*
the Budget the Chancellor of the Exchequer's statement of plans to raise money (e.g. by taxes)
[via early French *bougette* = little leather bag, from Latin *bulga* = leather bag In the 18th century, the Chancellor presented his statement by 'opening the budget']

buffalo *NOUN* **buffalo** or **buffaloes** a large ox Different kinds are found in Asia, Africa, and North America (where they are also called **bison**)

buffer *NOUN* **buffers 1** something that softens a blow, especially a device on a railway engine or wagon or at the end of a track **2** (in computing) a memory in which text or data can be stored for a time

buffet[1] (buu- fay) *NOUN* **buffets 1** a cafe at a station **2** a meal where guests serve themselves to food

buffet[2] (buf- it) *NOUN* **buffets** a hit, especially with the hand

buffet *VERB* **buffets, buffeting, buffeted** hit or knock • *Strong winds buffeted the aircraft.*

buffoon *NOUN* **buffoons** a person who plays the fool
▷ **buffoonery** *NOUN*

bug *NOUN* **bugs 1** an insect **2** an error in a computer program that prevents it working properly **3** (*informal*) a germ or virus **4** (*informal*) a secret hidden microphone

Thesaurus

bubbly *ADJECTIVE* **1** *a bubbly drink* ► fizzy, carbonated, foaming, seething, sparkling, effervescent OPPOSITES ARE still, flat **2** *a bubbly personality* ► vivacious, animated, spirited, vibrant, lively AN OPPOSITE IS dull

buck *VERB* *The horse began to buck.* ► jump, leap, prance, bound, jerk, spring
buck up (*informal*) **1** *We'll have to buck up if we're going to catch the train.* ► hurry, speed up, get a move on **2** *She did her best to buck me up but I still felt miserable.* ► cheer up, encourage, rally, hearten, enliven, inspire, make cheerful, please, revitalize, revive

bucket *NOUN* *a bucket of water* ► pail, can, tub, pitcher

buckle *NOUN* *a belt buckle* ► clasp, clip, fastener, fastening, hasp, catch

buckle *VERB* **1** *He quickly buckled his coat.* ► fasten, do up, clasp, hook up, secure, clip **2** *The bridge began to buckle under the weight.* ► bend, warp, twist, crumple, distort, fold, bulge, collapse, contort, curve, dent

budding *ADJECTIVE* *a budding young singer* ► promising, aspiring, developing, (*informal*) hopeful, inexperienced, intending, new, potential, (*more informal*) would-be OPPOSITES ARE established, experienced

budge *VERB* **1** *The window was stuck and wouldn't budge.* ► give way, move, shift, change position **2** *The solution is a compromise but no one will budge.* ► change your mind, give way, yield, compromise, influence, move, persuade, propel, push, remove, shift, sway **3** *They are much too stubborn and won't be be budged.* ► persuade, influence, sway, induce, cajole

budget *NOUN* *The hospital had not spent all its budget for the year.* ► allowance, allocation of funds, quota, estimate, resources, funds, means

buffet *VERB* *The sea front was buffeted by the wind and spray.* ► batter, pound, lash, dash

buffoon *NOUN* *She thought her cousin was a complete buffoon.* ► fool, idiot, clown, ass, dolt, blockhead, (*more informal*) prat, (*more informal*) halfwit, (*more informal*) chump

bug *NOUN* **1** *The plants were covered in tiny bugs.* ► insect, pest, mite **2** *a stomach bug* ► illness, disease, upset, ailment, complaint, disorder **3** *The computer software developed a bug.* ► fault, error, defect, flaw, (*more informal*) gremlin

a b c d e f g h i j k l m n o p q r s t u v w x y z

A B C D E F G H I J K L M N O P Q R S T U V W X Y Z

bug *VERB* **bugs, bugging, bugged** (*informal*) **1** fit with a secret hidden microphone **2** annoy

bugbear *NOUN* **bugbears** something that you fear or dislike

buggy *NOUN* **buggies** a pushchair for young children

build *VERB* **builds, building, built** make something by putting parts together
build in include
build up 1 establish gradually **2** accumulate **3** cover an area with buildings **4** make stronger or more famous • *build up a reputation*

build *NOUN* **builds** the shape of someone's body • *of slender build.*

builder *NOUN* **builders** someone who puts up buildings

building *NOUN* **buildings 1** the process of making houses and other structures **2** a structure with walls and a roof that people can go into

building society *NOUN* **building societies** an organization that people can pay money into and that lends money to people who want to buy houses

bulb *NOUN* **bulbs 1** a thick rounded part of a plant from which a stem grows up and roots grow down **2** a rounded part of something • *the bulb of a thermometer* **3** a glass globe that produces electric light
▷ **bulbous** *ADJECTIVE*

bulge *NOUN* **bulges** a rounded swelling; an outward curve
▷ **bulgy** *ADJECTIVE*

bulge *VERB* **bulges, bulging, bulged** form or cause to form a bulge

bulimia (buu- **lim**- ia) *NOUN* an illness that makes someone eat too much and then too little People who suffer from bulimia often makes themselves vomit after eating
▷ **bulimic** *ADJECTIVE*

bulk *NOUN* **bulks 1** the size of something, especially when it is large **2** the greater portion; the majority • *The bulk of the population voted for it.*
in bulk in large amounts

bulk *VERB* **bulks, bulking, bulked** increase the size or thickness of something • *bulk it out*

bulky *ADJECTIVE* **bulkier, bulkiest** taking up a lot of space
▷ **bulkiness** *NOUN*

bull *NOUN* **bulls 1** a fully grown male of the cow family **2** an adult male seal, whale, or elephant

bulldog *NOUN* **bulldogs** a dog of a powerful courageous breed with a short thick neck

bulldozer *NOUN* **bulldozers** a powerful tractor with a wide metal blade or scoop in front, used for shifting soil or clearing ground

bullet *NOUN* **bullets** a small piece of metal shot from a rifle or revolver

bulletin *NOUN* **bulletins 1** a brief news report on radio or television **2** a regular letter or

Thesaurus

bug *VERB* **1** *The telephone had been bugged.* ► intercept, tap, interfere with, listen in to **2** (*informal*) *Her constant whining was bugging me.* ► annoy, irritate, anger, infuriate, needle, rile

build *VERB* **1** *There are plans to build a new apartment block on the site.* ► construct, erect, raise, put up, set up, assemble, fabricate
OPPOSITES ARE demolish, destroy
build up 1 *He has built up a thriving business.* ► establish, develop, create, enlarge, expand, raise, accumulate, amass, assemble, begin, bring together, collect **2** *Traffic is building up in the city centre.* ► increase, intensify, escalate, grow, mount up, strengthen, rise, augment

build *NOUN* *a man of slim build* ► physique, form, frame, body

building *NOUN* *a large grim building with few windows* ► structure, construction, premises, erection, establishment, place, piece of architecture, (*more formal*) edifice, (*more informal*) pile

build-up *NOUN* *a steady military build-up on the border* ► increase, growth, escalation, expansion, development, accumulation, proliferation

bulge *NOUN* *There was a strange bulge at the bottom of the bed.* ► bump, swelling, protuberance, hump, lump, projection, (*more formal*) protrusion

bulge *VERB* *The sheets bulged in the breeze.* ► swell, billow, puff out, balloon out, dilate, distend, expand, belly, enlarge, project, protrude, stick out

bulk *NOUN* **1** *The sheer bulk of the containers was staggering.* ► size, volume, dimensions, proportions, extent, magnitude, mass, substance, amplitude, body, immensity, largeness **2** *We did the bulk of the work ourselves.* ► most, best part, most part, greater part, preponderance, majority

bulky *ADJECTIVE* *a bulky parcel* ► sizeable, large, substantial, cumbersome, unwieldy, massive, immense, enormous OPPOSITES ARE small, compact, manageable

bulletin *NOUN* **1** *a television news bulletin* ► report, statement, announcement, communication, communiqué, dispatch, message, newsflash, notice, proclamation

report giving information about an organization

bullfight *NOUN* **bullfights** a public entertainment in which bulls are tormented and killed in an arena
▷ **bullfighter** *NOUN*

bullock *NOUN* **bullocks** a young castrated bull

bullseye *NOUN* **bullseyes** the centre of a target

bully *VERB* **bullies, bullying, bullied 1** use strength or power to hurt or frighten a weaker person **2** start play in hockey, when two opponents tap the ground and each other's stick • *bully off*

bully *NOUN* **bullies** someone who bullies people

bulwark *NOUN* **bulwarks** a wall of earth built as a defence; a protection

bumblebee *NOUN* **bumblebees** a large bee with a loud hum

bump *VERB* **bumps, bumping, bumped**
1 knock against something **2** move along with jolts
bump into (*informal*) meet by chance
bump off (*slang*) kill

bump *NOUN* **bumps 1** the action or sound of bumping **2** a swelling or lump
▷ **bumpy** *ADJECTIVE*

bumper[1] *NOUN* **bumpers** a bar along the front or back of a motor vehicle to protect it in collisions

bumper[2] *ADJECTIVE* unusually large or plentiful
• *a bumper crop*

bumpkin *NOUN* **bumpkins** a country person with awkward manners

bun *NOUN* **buns 1** a small round sweet cake **2** hair twisted into a round bunch at the back of the head

bunch *NOUN* **bunches** a number of things joined or fastened together

bundle *NOUN* **bundles** a number of things tied or wrapped together

bundle *VERB* **bundles, bundling, bundled**
1 make a number of things into a bundle
2 push hurriedly or carelessly • *They bundled him into a taxi.*

bungalow *NOUN* **bungalows** a house without any upstairs rooms [from Hindi *bangla* = to do with Bengal, where there were houses of this kind]

bungle *VERB* **bungles, bungling, bungled** make a mess of doing something
▷ **bungler** *NOUN*

bunion *NOUN* **bunions** a swelling at the side of the joint where the big toe joins the foot

bunk *NOUN* **bunks** a bed built like a shelf

Thesaurus

2 *The club's monthly bulletin* ► newsletter, news-sheet, gazette

bully *NOUN the well-known school bullies*
► tormentor, persecutor, oppressor, thug, tough, (*more informal*) heavy

bully *VERB Some of the other children used to bully him.* ► persecute, torment, intimidate, oppress, tyrannnize, (*more informal*) push around

bump *NOUN* **1** *The man fell on the floor with a bump.* ► thud, thump, smack, crash, bang, blow, collision, hit, knock, smash **2** *When he got up he had a bump on the head.* ► swelling, lump, bulge, (*technical*) contusion, protuberance

bump *VERB* **1** *Chris bumped his head while snorkelling.* ► hit, strike, knock, bang **2 bump into** *A lorry had bumped into a parked car.*
► collide with, run into, crash into, bang into, smash into, knock into, knock, hit, ram, slam, strike **3** *We were bumping up and down on the rough road.* ► bounce, shake, jerk, jolt
bump off (*informal*) *He became president by bumping off all his rivals.* ► kill, murder, assassinate, eliminate

bumpy *ADJECTIVE* **1** *a bumpy ride* ► bouncy, rough, jerky, jolting, lurching **2** *a bumpy surface*
► uneven, rough, irregular, pitted, knobbly, lumpy OPPOSITES ARE even, smooth

bunch *NOUN* **1** *a bunch of carrots; a bunch of keys*
► bundle, cluster, clump, collection, heap, batch, set, lot, number, quantity **2** *a bunch of flowers* ► bouquet, posy, spray, garland **3** *a friendly bunch of people* ► group, set, circle, band, (*more informal*) gang, (*more informal*) crowd

bunch *VERB The friends had bunched together in a corner.* ► gather, assemble, cluster, huddle, collect, congregate, crowd, flock, group, herd AN OPPOSITE IS scatter

bundle *NOUN a bundle of papers* ► bunch, sheaf, carton, collection, pack, package, packet, parcel, bag, bale

bundle *VERB* **1** *He quickly bundled up the remaining papers.* ► tie, bind, wrap, bale, truss, fasten, pack, roll **2** *The kidnappers bundled their victim into the back of the car.* ► hustle, jostle, shove, sweep

bung *VERB* (*informal*) *You'd better bung that in the bin.* ► throw, chuck, toss, stick, put

bungle *VERB Two prisoners bungled an escape bid after running either side of a lamp-post while handcuffed.* ► mishandle, mismanage, botch, ruin, spoil, fluff, muff, mess up, make a mess of,

A B C D E F G H I J K L M N O P Q R S T U V W X Y Z

bunker *NOUN* **bunkers 1** a container for storing fuel **2** a sandy hollow built as an obstacle on a golf course **3** an underground shelter

bunny *NOUN* **bunnies** (*informal*) a rabbit

Bunsen burner *NOUN* **Bunsen burners** a small gas burner used in scientific work

bunting[1] *NOUN* **buntings** a kind of small bird

bunting[2] *NOUN* strips of small flags hung up to decorate streets and buildings

buoy (boi) *NOUN* **buoys** a floating object anchored to mark a channel or underwater rocks etc.

buoyant (boi- ant) *ADJECTIVE* **1** able to float **2** light-hearted; cheerful
▷ **buoyantly** *ADVERB* **buoyancy** *NOUN*

bur *NOUN* **burs** a different spelling of **burr** (seed case)

burden *NOUN* **burdens 1** a heavy load that you have to carry **2** something troublesome that you have to bear • *Exams are a burden.*
▷ **burdensome** *ADJECTIVE*

burden *VERB* **burdens, burdening, burdened** cause someone work or trouble

bureau (bewr- oh) *NOUN* **bureaux 1** a writing desk **2** a business office • *They will tell you at the Information Bureau.*

bureaucracy (bewr- ok- ra- see) *NOUN* the use of too many rules and forms by officials, especially in government departments
▷ **bureaucratic** (bewr- ok- rat- ik) *ADJECTIVE*

burger *NOUN* **burgers** a hamburger

burglar *NOUN* **burglars** a person who breaks into a building in order to steal things
▷ **burglary** *NOUN*

burgle *VERB* **burgles, burgling, burgled** rob a place as a burglar

burial *NOUN* **burials** burying somebody

burlesque (ber- lesk) *NOUN* **burlesques** a comical imitation

burly *ADJECTIVE* **burlier, burliest** having a strong heavy body

burn *VERB* **burns, burning, burned** *or* **burnt 1** blaze or glow with fire; produce heat or light by combustion **2** damage or destroy something by fire, heat, or chemicals **3** be damaged or destroyed by fire etc. **4** feel very hot

USAGE The word **burnt** (not **burned**) is always used when an adjective is required, e.g. in *burnt wood*. As parts of the verb, either **burned** or **burnt** may be used, e.g. *the wood had burned* or *had burnt completely*.

burn *NOUN* **burns 1** a mark or injury made by burning **2** the firing of a spacecraft's rockets

burning *ADJECTIVE* **1** intense • *a burning ambition.* **2** very important; hotly discussed • *a burning question*

Thesaurus

(*more informal*) make a hash of, (*much more informal*) cock up, (*much more informal*) screw up OPPOSITES ARE succeed in, bring off

buoyant *ADJECTIVE* **1** *a buoyant material* ► floating, light **2** *in a buoyant mood* ► cheerful, happy, cheery, carefree, light-hearted, lively, optimistic, animated, sunny OPPOSITES ARE depressed, pessimistic

burden *NOUN* **1** *donkeys carrying heavy burdens* ► load, weight, encumbrance, pack, bundle, cargo **2** *a large financial burden* ► responsibility, obligation, liability, duty, onus, charge, affliction, anxiety, worry, care, handicap, problem, millstone

burden *VERB For years she was burdened by family worries.* ► afflict, oppress, bother, beset, torment, distress, strain, tax, trouble, worry, encumber, hamper, handicap, load (with), (*informal*) lumber (with), (*informal*) saddle (with)

bureau *an information bureau* ► agency, office, service, department, organization, counter

bureaucracy *NOUN hampered by regulations and bureaucracy* ► administration, government, officialdom, paperwork, (*more informal*) red tape

burglar *NOUN Burglars stole jewellery worth thousands of pounds.* ► housebreaker, robber, thief, intruder

burglary *NOUN Barry had been convicted of burglary.* ► housebreaking, breaking and entering, robbery, theft, forcible entry, larceny, pilfering, stealing, thieving, break-in

burial *NOUN a burial service* ► burying, entombment, funeral, interment, obsequies

burly *ADJECTIVE a burly figure* ► hefty, beefy, sturdy, well-built, strapping, brawny, hulking, muscular, powerful, stocky, stout, athletic, big, heavy OPPOSITES ARE slight, thin

burn *VERB* **1** *The bonfire burned all day.* ► be alight, be on fire, be ablaze, flare, blaze, flicker, glow, smoke, smoulder **2** *An incinerator will burn anything.* ► ignite, kindle, incinerate, cremate, consume **3** *The heat began to burn our skin.* ► scald, scorch, blister, brand, toast, char, sear, singe, sting

burning *ADJECTIVE* **1** *a burning building* ► blazing, flaming, glowing, ablaze, afire, alight, incandescent, lit up, on fire, raging, smouldering **2** *a burning pain* ► scalding, searing, acute, stinging, biting **3** *a burning desire* ► intense, extreme, fervent, passionate, eager, ardent, profound, consuming **4** *a burning question* ► urgent, crucial, vital,

burr *NOUN* **burrs** **1** a plant's seed case or flower that clings to hair or clothes **2** a whirring sound **3** a soft country accent

burrow *NOUN* **burrows** a hole or tunnel dug by a rabbit or fox etc. as a dwelling

burrow *VERB* **burrows, burrowing, burrowed** **1** dig a burrow **2** push your way through or into something; search deeply • *She burrowed in her handbag.*

bursar *NOUN* **bursars** a person who manages the finances and other business of a school or college

burst *VERB* **bursts, bursting, burst** **1** break or force apart **2** come or start suddenly • *It burst into flame.* • *They burst out laughing.* **3** be very full • *bursting with energy*

burst *NOUN* **bursts** **1** a split caused by something bursting **2** something short and forceful • *a burst of gunfire*

bury *VERB* **buries, burying, buried** **1** place a dead body in the earth, a tomb, or the sea **2** put underground; cover up

bus *NOUN* **buses** a large vehicle for passengers to travel in

bush *NOUN* **bushes** **1** a shrub **2** wild uncultivated land, especially in Africa and Australia
▷ **bushy** *ADJECTIVE*

bushel *NOUN* **bushels** a measure for grain and fruit (8 gallons or 4 pecks)

business (biz- niss) *NOUN* **businesses** **1** a person's concern or responsibilities • *Mind your own business.* **2** an affair or subject • *I'm tired of the whole business.* **3** a shop or firm **4** buying and selling things; trade
▷ **businessman** *NOUN* **businesswoman** *NOUN*

busking *NOUN* playing music for money in the street
▷ **busker** *NOUN*

bust *NOUN* **busts** **1** a sculpture of a person's head, shoulders, and chest **2** the upper front part of a woman's body

bustle *VERB* **bustles, bustling, bustled** hurry in a busy or excited way

bustle *NOUN* hurried or excited activity

busy *ADJECTIVE* **busier, busiest** **1** having a lot to do; occupied **2** full of activity **3** (said about a telephone line) engaged
▷ **busily** *ADVERB* **busyness** *NOUN*

Thesaurus

essential, pressing, important, pertinent, relevant

burrow *VERB* *A rabbit could burrow under the fence.* ► tunnel, excavate, dig, mine, delve

burst *VERB* **1** *The impact cause a tyre to burst.* ► rupture, split open **2** *Water burst through the hole.* ► gush, surge, stream, pour, spurt, cascade **3** *A man suddenly burst into the room.* ► rush, run, charge, plunge, shove your way

bury *VERB* **1** *The dog buried its bone in the ground.* ► hide, conceal, cover, sink, embed AN OPPOSITE IS uncover **2** *The dead are buried in the local cemetery.* ► inter, lay to rest, entomb **3** *She buried herself in her work.* ► absorb, engross, engage, occupy, immerse

business *NOUN* **1** *It proved to be quite a tricky business.* ► matter, affair, issue, problem, point, question, concern **2** *What sort of business do you want to go into?* ► work, job, occupation, employment, career, line of work, profession, pursuit, trade, vocation, calling, craft, industry **3** *The new supermarket has taken a lot of business from the local shops.* ► trade, trading, buying and selling, selling, merchandising, transactions, commerce, dealings, industry, marketing **4** *He wants to run his own business.* ► firm, company, establishment, enterprise, organization, concern, venture, corporation, practice, (*more informal*) outfit, (*more informal*) set-up

businesslike *ADJECTIVE* *The office was run in a businesslike way.* ► efficient, professional, competent, methodical, well organized, systematic, practical, pragmatic, orderly

businessman, businesswoman *NOUN* *a shrewd businesswoman* ► entrepreneur, executive, industrialist, dealer, financier, manager, merchant, trader, tycoon, magnate

bust *NOUN* *a woman's bust* ► bosom, chest, breast, breasts

bust *VERB* *Be careful with that or you'll bust it.* ► break, snap, crack, split, burst

bustle *NOUN* *The air terminal was full of bustle.* ► activity, hustle, commotion, stir, excitement, flurry, fuss, haste, hurly-burly, hurry, movement, restlessness, scurry, agitation

bustle *VERB* *People were bustling about looking for their friends.* ► rush, dash, scurry, scamper, scuttle, hurry, hustle, dart, fuss, move busily, scramble, whirl, hasten, (*more informal*) tear

busy *ADJECTIVE* **1** *Are you very busy at work?* ► active, occupied, hard-pressed, (*more informal*) rushed off your feet AN OPPOSITE IS idle **2** *She's a very busy person.* ► active, energetic, diligent, industrious OPPOSITES ARE lazy, idle **3** *The manager is busy at the moment but can see you this afternoon.* ► engaged, unavailable, occupied, (*more informal*) tied up AN OPPOSITE IS free **4** *Her mother leads a busy life.* ► active, hectic, lively, strenuous, demanding, exacting **5** *The committee members are busy organizing the next conference.* ► occupied (with), working (at), engaged (in), hard at work (on), wrapped

A B C D E F G H I J K L M N O P Q R S T U V W X Y Z

busy *VERB* **busies, busying, busied**
busy yourself occupy yourself; keep busy

busybody *NOUN* **busybodies** a person who meddles or interferes

but *CONJUNCTION* however; nevertheless • *I wanted to go, but I couldn't.*

but *PREPOSITION* except • *There is no one here but me.*

but *ADVERB* only; no more than • *We can but try.*

butcher *NOUN* **butchers 1** a person who cuts up meat and sells it **2** a person who kills cruelly or needlessly
▷ **butchery** *NOUN*

butcher *VERB* **butchers, butchering, butchered** kill cruelly or needlessly

butler *NOUN* **butlers** a male servant in charge of other servants in a large private house [from early French *bouteillier* = someone who carried the bottles]

butt[1] *NOUN* **butts 1** the thicker end of a weapon or tool **2** a stub • *cigarette butts*

butt[2] *NOUN* **butts** a large cask or barrel

butt[3] *NOUN* **butts** a person or thing that is a target for ridicule or teasing • *He was the butt of their jokes.*

butt[4] *VERB* **butts, butting, butted 1** push or hit with the head as a ram or goat does **2** place the edges of things together
butt in interrupt or meddle

butter *NOUN* a soft fatty food made by churning cream
▷ **buttery** *ADJECTIVE*

buttercup *NOUN* **buttercups** a wild plant with bright yellow cup-shaped flowers

butterfly *NOUN* **butterflies 1** an insect with large white or coloured wings **2** a swimming stroke in which both arms are lifted at the same time

buttock *NOUN* **buttocks** either of the two fleshy rounded parts of your bottom

button *NOUN* **buttons 1** a knob or disc sewn on clothes as a fastening or ornament **2** a small knob pressed to work an electric device

button *VERB* **buttons, buttoning, buttoned** fasten something with a button or buttons

buttonhole *NOUN* **buttonholes 1** a slit through which a button passes to fasten clothes **2** a flower worn on a lapel

buttonhole *VERB* **buttonholes, buttonholing, buttonholed** stop somebody so that you can talk to him or her

buttress *NOUN* **buttresses** a support built against a wall

buy *VERB* **buys, buying, bought** get something by paying for it
▷ **buyer** *NOUN*

buy *NOUN* **buys** something that is bought

buzz *NOUN* **buzzes** a vibrating humming sound

buzz *VERB* **buzzes, buzzing, buzzed 1** make a buzz **2** threaten an aircraft by deliberately flying close to it

by *PREPOSITION* This word is used to show **1** closeness (*Sit by me*), **2** direction or route (*We got here by a short cut*), **3** time (*They came by night*), **4** manner or method (*cooking by gas*), **5** amount (*You missed it by inches*)
by the way incidentally
by yourself alone; without help

by *ADVERB* **1** past • *I can't get by.* **2** in reserve; for future use • *Put it by.*
by and by soon; later on
by and large on the whole

Thesaurus

up (in) **6** *The shopping malls were busy all day.* ► crowded, hectic, lively, teeming, bustling, swarming, thronging, frantic, full of people
AN OPPOSITE IS quiet

busybody *NOUN* *Pry was an inquisitive busybody.* ► meddler, interferer, gossip, scandalmonger, snooper, eavesdropper, (*more informal*) nosy parker, (*more informal*) gawper

butch *ADJECTIVE* (*informal*) *a butch builder* ► masculine, manly, virile OPPOSITES ARE effeminate, feminine

butt *NOUN* **1** *the butt of a rifle* ► stock, shaft, shank, handle, hilt, haft **2** *a water butt* ► barrel, cask, keg, vat **3** *a cigarette butt* ► stub, end, stump, remnant, (*more informal*) fag end **4** *the butt of a joke* ► target, victim, object, subject, mark

butt *VERB* *He butted her playfully with his head.* ► hit, ram, bump, knock, jab, prod, poke
butt in *Nick didn't want to butt in, so he waited patiently.* ► interrupt, break in, cut in, (*more informal*) chip in

buttocks *PLURAL NOUN* *He knelt with his heels against his buttocks.* ► bottom, behind, backside, rear, rump, seat, haunches, hindquarters, (*more informal*) bum, (*usually humorous*) posterior

buy *VERB* **1** *I will buy the drinks.* ► get, pay for, obtain, acquire, (*more formal*) purchase
AN OPPOSITE IS sell **2** *a man who could not be bought* ► bribe, buy off, suborn, corrupt

buy *NOUN* *A well-looked-after used car can be a good buy.* ► acquisition, deal, bargain, (*more formal*) purchase

by-election *NOUN* **by-elections** an election to replace a Member of Parliament who has died or resigned

bygone *ADJECTIVE* belonging to the past
let bygones be bygones forgive and forget

bypass *NOUN* **bypasses 1** a road taking traffic round a city or congested area **2** a channel that allows something to flow when the main route is blocked

bypass *VERB* **bypasses, bypassing, bypassed** avoid something by means of a bypass

by-product *NOUN* **by-products** something useful produced while something else is being made

byroad *NOUN* **byroads** a minor road

bystander *NOUN* **bystanders** a person standing near but taking no part when something happens

byte *NOUN* **bytes** a fixed number of bits (= binary digits) in a computer, often representing a single character

byword *NOUN* **bywords** a person or thing spoken of as a famous example • *Their firm became a byword for quality.*

Thesaurus

bypass *VERB* **1** *To speed things up we can bypass the usual checking process.* ► ignore, omit, avoid, circumvent, sidestep, neglect, find a way round, get out of, go round, dodge, evade

by-product *NOUN* *Temporary deafness was a by-product of her illness.* ► side effect, consequence, repercussion, result, complement, corollary, (*more informal*) knock-on effect, (*more informal*) spin-off (from), (*more informal*) fallout (from)

bystander *NOUN* *The man had assaulted a bystander and smashed windows.* ► onlooker, passer-by, observer, spectator, watcher, witness, eyewitness

a b c d e f g h i j k l m n o p q r s t u v w x y z

Cc

A B C D E F G H I J K L M N O P Q R S T U V W X Y Z

cab *NOUN* **cabs** **1** a taxi **2** a compartment for the driver of a lorry, train, bus, or crane

cabaret (kab- er- ay) *NOUN* **cabarets** an entertainment provided for the customers in a restaurant or nightclub [from early French *cabaret* = wooden inn or hut]

cabbage *NOUN* **cabbages** a vegetable with green or purple leaves [from early French *caboche* = head]

cabin *NOUN* **cabins** **1** a hut or shelter **2** a room for sleeping on a ship **3** the part of an aircraft in which passengers sit **4** a driver's cab

Cabinet *NOUN* the group of chief ministers, chosen by the Prime Minister, who meet to decide government policy

cabinet *NOUN* **cabinets** a cupboard or container with drawers or shelves

cable *NOUN* **cables** **1** a thick rope of fibre or wire; a thick chain **2** a covered group of wires laid underground for transmitting electrical signals **3** a telegram sent overseas

cable television *NOUN* a system of television programmes transmitted by cables to people who have paid for themd

cackle *NOUN* **cackles** **1** a loud silly laugh **2** noisy chatter **3** the loud clucking noise a hen makes
▷ **cackle** *VERB*

cactus *NOUN* **cacti** a fleshy plant, usually with prickles, from a hot dry climate

cad *NOUN* **cads** a dishonourable man

cadaverous (kad- av- er- us) *ADJECTIVE* pale and gaunt

caddie *NOUN* **caddies** a person who carries a golfer's clubs during a game

cadence (kay- denss) *NOUN* **cadences** **1** rhythm; the rise and fall of the voice in speaking **2** the final notes of a musical phrase

cadenza (ka- den- za) *NOUN* **cadenzas** an elaborate passage for a solo instrument or singer, to show the performer's skill

cadet *NOUN* **cadets** a young person being trained for the armed forces or the police

cadge *VERB* **cadges, cadging, cadged** get something by begging for it
▷ **cadger** *NOUN*

cadmium *NOUN* a metal that looks like tin

Caesarean or **Caesarean section** (siz- air- ee- an) *NOUN* **Caesareans** or **Caesarean sections** a surgical operation for taking a baby out of the mother's womb

cafe (kaf- ay) *NOUN* **cafes** a small restaurant

caffeine (kaf- een) *NOUN* a stimulant substance found in tea and coffee

cage *NOUN* **cages** **1** a container with bars or wires, in which birds or animals are kept **2** the enclosed platform of a lift

cairn *NOUN* **cairns** a pile of loose stones set up as a landmark or monument

cajole *VERB* **cajoles, cajoling, cajoled** persuade someone to do something by flattering them; coax

cake *NOUN* **cakes** **1** a baked food made from a mixture of flour, fat, eggs, sugar, etc. **2** a shaped or hardened mass • *a cake of soap* • *fish cakes*

caked *ADJECTIVE* covered with dried mud etc.

calamine *NOUN* a pink powder used to make a soothing lotion for the skin

calamity *NOUN* **calamities** a disaster
▷ **calamitous** *ADJECTIVE*

Thesaurus

cabaret *NOUN* *a cabaret at a nightclub in town*
► floor show, revue, entertainment

cabin *NOUN* **1** *a cabin by the river* ► hut, lodge, chalet, shack, shanty, shed, shelter **2** *a cabin on the lower deck* ► berth, compartment, sleeping quarters **3** *the driver's cabin* ► cab, compartment

cabinet *NOUN* *a glass-fronted cabinet for china*
► cupboard, dresser, closet, chest

cable *NOUN* **1** *The ship was moored by means of thick cables.* ► rope, cord, hawser, line, chain, mooring **2** *Watch out for the power cable.*
► wire, lead, line

cache *NOUN* *a cache of weapons; a cache of gold*
► hoard, store, stock, stockpile, depot, dump, repository, storehouse, supply

cafe *NOUN* *We could have a snack at a local cafe.*
► snack bar, cafeteria, coffee bar, coffee shop, tea shop, buffet, canteen, bistro

cage *NOUN* *an animal's cage* ► enclosure, pen, pound, coop, hutch USAGE A large cage for birds is called an *aviary*

cagey *ADJECTIVE* *He was being very cagey about what he had been up to.* ► secretive, guarded, cautious, tight-lipped, reticent, evasive, wary, chary OPPOSITES ARE open, frank

cake *NOUN* **1** *There are cakes for tea today.* ► bun, gateau **2** *a cake of soap* ► bar, tablet, block, lump, piece, slab

cake *VERB* *Finn's shoes were caked with mud.*
► cover, coat, clog, encrust

calamity *NOUN* *Disobedience will bring calamity on the nation.* ► disaster, catastrophe, tragedy, misfortune, affliction, blow, cataclysm, tribulation, mishap

calcium *NOUN* a chemical substance found in teeth, bones, and lime

calculate *VERB* **calculates, calculating, calculated 1** work something out by using mathematics **2** plan something deliberately; intend • *Her remarks were calculated to hurt me.*
▷ **calculable** *ADJECTIVE* **calculation** *NOUN*

calculator *NOUN* **calculators** a small electronic device for making calculations

calculus *NOUN* mathematics for working out problems about rates of change

calendar *NOUN* **calendars** a chart or set of pages showing the dates of the month or year

calf[1] *NOUN* **calves** a young cow, whale, seal, etc.

calf[2] *NOUN* **calves** the fleshy back part of the leg below the knee

calibre (kal- ib- er) *NOUN* **calibres 1** the diameter of a tube or gun barrel, or of a bullet etc. **2** ability; importance • *someone of your calibre*

call *NOUN* **calls 1** a shout or cry **2** a visit **3** telephoning somebody **4** a summons

call *VERB* **calls, calling, called 1** shout or speak loudly, e.g. to attract someone's attention **2** telephone somebody **3** name a person or thing • *They've decided to call the baby Alexander.* **4** tell somebody to come to you; summon **5** make a short visit
▷ **caller** *NOUN*
call a person's bluff challenge a person to do what was threatened, and expose the fact that it was a bluff
call for 1 come and collect **2** require • *The scandal calls for investigation.*
call off cancel or postpone
call up summon to join the armed forces

calligraphy (kal- ig- raf- ee) *NOUN* the art of beautiful handwriting

calling *NOUN* **callings** an occupation; a profession or trade

callous (kal- us) *ADJECTIVE* hard-hearted; unsympathetic
▷ **callously** *ADVERB* **callousness** *NOUN*

calm *ADJECTIVE* **1** quiet and still; not windy **2** not excited or agitated
▷ **calmly** *ADVERB* **calmness** *NOUN*

Thesaurus

calculate *VERB* *Interest on the loan is calculated monthly.* ► work out, compute, reckon, assess, count, determine, add up

calibre *NOUN* *People of this calibre are not something you come across every day.* ► quality, ability, distinction, excellence, capacity, standard, talent, stature, character

call *VERB* **1** *'Come here!,' she called.* ► cry, cry out, shout, yell, exclaim **2** *I'll call you this evening.* ► phone, telephone, ring, ring up, give someone a call **3** *What did they call him?* ► baptize, christen, dub, name **4** *Why did you call your cat Albert?* ► name **5** *His mother said she would call him early next morning.* ► wake, wake up, waken, awaken, get someone up, arouse, rouse **6** *The headteacher called me to her office.* ► summon, invite, order **7** *We'd better call the doctor.* ► send for, fetch, summon, ask to come **8** *We need to call a meeting.* ► convene, organize, gather **9** *Harriet's mother called the next day.* ► visit, pay a visit, (*more informal*) drop in, (*more informal*) drop by
call for 1 *The assignment calls for careful planning.* ► require, need, demand, necessitate, make necessary, involve, entail, warrant **2** *Shall we call for you about six o'clock?* ► fetch, pick up, come for, collect
call off *The barbecue was called off because of bad weather.* ► cancel, abandon, postpone, adjourn, discontinue, drop, end, halt USAGE You use *cancel* if you mean calling off for good, and *postpone* if you mean calling off until a later date. You often use *abandon* to refer to things that have been started but cannot be completed.
call on *I might call on my friends this afternoon.* ► visit, go and see, (*more informal*) drop in on, (*more informal*) look up

call *NOUN* **1** *a call for help* ► cry, exclamation, shout, yell, scream **2** *a call for strike action* ► appeal, plea, summons, demand, request **3** *He decided to pay a call on his old father.* ► visit, stop **4** *There's little call for caviar here.* ► demand, market, need **5** *There's no call for that kind of talk.* ► need, necessity, occasion, reason, justification, excuse

calling *NOUN* *He thought that the law was the right calling.* ► profession, career, line of work, occupation, vocation, business, employment, walk of life, job, trade, work

callous *ADJECTIVE* *a callous remark* ► heartless, hard-hearted, unfeeling, uncaring, indifferent, insensitive, cruel, brutal, ruthless OPPOSITES ARE kind, considerate

calm *ADJECTIVE* **1** *a calm sunny day* ► still, tranquil, quiet, peaceful, balmy OPPOSITES ARE stormy, windy **2** *The sea was calm.* ► smooth, tranquil, still, flat, waveless **3** *He remained calm despite the difficulties.* ► composed, collected, self-possessed, cool, poised, dispassionate, unperturbed, imperturbable, unruffled, unflustered, unbothered, untroubled, unemotional, (*more informal*) unflappable, (*more informal*) laid-back OPPOSITES ARE

A B C D E F G H I J K L M N O P Q R S T U V W X Y Z

calm *VERB* **calms, calming, calmed** make or become calm

calorie *NOUN* **calories** a unit for measuring an amount of heat or the energy produced by food
▷ **calorific** *ADJECTIVE*

calypso *NOUN* **calypsos** a West Indian song about current happenings, made up as the singer goes along

calyx (kay- liks) *NOUN* **calyces** a ring of leaves (**sepals**) forming the outer case of a bud

camcorder *NOUN* **camcorders** a combined video camera and sound recorder

camel *NOUN* **camels** a large animal with a long neck and either one or two humps on its back, used in desert countries for riding and for carrying goods

cameo (kam- ee- oh) *NOUN* **cameos** **1** a small hard piece of stone carved with a raised design in its upper layer **2** a short part in a play or film, usually one played by a well-known actor

camera *NOUN* **cameras** a device for taking photographs, films, or television pictures
▷ **cameraman** *NOUN*
in camera in a judge's private room; in private

camouflage (kam- off- lah*zh*) *NOUN* a way of hiding things by making them look like part of their surroundings

camouflage *VERB* **camouflages, camouflaging, camouflaged** hide by camouflage

camp *NOUN* **camps** a place where people live in tents or huts etc.

camp *VERB* **camps, camping, camped** have a holiday in a tent
▷ **camper** *NOUN*

campaign *NOUN* **campaigns** **1** a series of battles in one area or with one purpose **2** a planned series of actions, usually to arouse interest in something • *an advertising campaign*

campaign *VERB* **campaigns, campaigning, campaigned** take part in a campaign
▷ **campaigner** *NOUN*
[via French from Latin *campania* = a piece of open ground (where armies camped and had exercises)]

camphor *NOUN* a strong-smelling white substance used in medicine, mothballs, and making plastics
▷ **camphorated** *ADJECTIVE*

campsite *NOUN* **campsites** a place where people can have a camping holiday

campus *NOUN* **campuses** the grounds of a university or college

can[1] *NOUN* **cans** **1** a sealed tin in which food or drink is preserved **2** a metal or plastic container for liquids

can *VERB* **cans, canning, canned** preserve in a sealed can
▷ **canner** *NOUN*

can[2] *AUXILIARY VERB* *past tense* **could** **1** be able to • *He can play the violin.* **2** have permission to • *You can go.*

USAGE Some people object to **can** being used with the meaning 'have permission to' and insist that you should only use **may** for this meaning. **Can** is widely used in this meaning, however, and in most situations there is little reason to prefer **may**. **May** is appropriate, though, in formal or official writing.

canal *NOUN* **canals** **1** an artificial river cut through land so that boats can sail along it or so that it can drain or irrigate an area **2** a tube through which something passes in the body • *the alimentary canal*

canary *NOUN* **canaries** a small yellow bird that sings

cancel *VERB* **cancels, cancelling, cancelled** **1** say that something planned will not be done or will not take place **2** stop an order or instruction for something **3** mark a stamp or ticket etc. so that it cannot be used again
▷ **cancellation** *NOUN*
cancel out stop each other's effect • *The good and harm cancel each other out.*

Thesaurus

anxious, upset, excited **4** *a calm temperament* ► serene, placid, phlegmatic, tranquil, relaxed

calm *NOUN* **1** *the calm of a summer afternoon* ► tranquillity, calmness, quietness, stillness, peace, quiet, quietude AN OPPOSITE IS storm **2** *I had to admire her calm.* ► composure, calmness, self-possession, equanimity

calm *VERB* *He was so upset it was impossible to calm him.* ► soothe, placate, quieten, mollify, pacify, settle down, sober down, tranquillize, appease, compose, control, cool down, lull OPPOSITES ARE agitate, upset

camouflage *NOUN* **1** *The foliage made good camouflage.* ► disguise, concealment, cover, screen, veil, blind, cloak, front, guise, mask **2** *an animal's camouflage* ► protective colouring **3** *Their friendly manner was only camouflage.* ► facade, front, disguise, mask, pretence

camp *NOUN* *an army camp* ► encampment, camping ground, campsite, base

campaign *NOUN* **1** *a military campaign* ► operation, offensive, action, engagement, advance, battle, push **2** *a campaign to save the environment* ► crusade, movement, drive, effort, struggle, fight, push

can *NOUN* *a can of orange juice* ► tin, canister, jar

cancel *VERB* **1** *The family had to cancel their holiday.* ► call off, abandon, drop, end, (*more*

cancer *NOUN* **cancers** **1** a disease in which harmful growths form in the body **2** a tumour, especially a harmful one
▷ **cancerous** *ADJECTIVE*

candid *ADJECTIVE* frank and honest
▷ **candidly** *ADVERB* **candour** *NOUN*

candidate *NOUN* **candidates** **1** a person who wants to be elected or chosen for a particular job or position etc. **2** a person taking an examination
▷ **candidacy** *NOUN* **candidature** *NOUN*

candle *NOUN* **candles** a stick of wax with a wick through it, giving light when burning
▷ **candlelight** *NOUN*

candyfloss *NOUN* **candyflosses** a fluffy mass of very thin strands of spun sugar

cane *NOUN* **canes** **1** the stem of a reed or tall grass etc. **2** a thin stick

cane *VERB* **canes, caning, caned** beat someone with a cane

canine (kayn- I'n) *ADJECTIVE* to do with dogs
canine tooth a pointed tooth at the front of the mouth

canine *NOUN* **canines** **1** a dog **2** a canine tooth

canker *NOUN* a disease that rots the wood of trees and plants or causes ulcers and sores on animals

cannabis *NOUN* hemp, especially when smoked as a drug

cannibal *NOUN* **cannibals** **1** a person who eats human flesh **2** an animal that eats animals of its own kind
▷ **cannibalism** *NOUN*

cannon *NOUN* **1** (**cannon**) a large heavy gun **2** (**cannons**) the hitting of two balls in billiards by the third ball

cannon *VERB* **cannons, cannoning, cannoned** bump into something heavily
USAGE Do not confuse with **canon.**

cannon ball *NOUN* **cannon balls** a large solid ball fired from a cannon

cannot can not

canoe *NOUN* **canoes** a narrow lightweight boat, moved forwards with paddles

canoe *VERB* **canoes, canoeing, canoed** travel in a canoe
▷ **canoeist** *NOUN*

canon *NOUN* **canons** **1** a general principle or rule **2** a clergyman of a cathedral
USAGE Do not confuse with **cannon.**

canopy *NOUN* **canopies** **1** a hanging cover forming a shelter above a throne, bed, or person etc. **2** the part of a parachute that spreads in the air

cant *NOUN* **1** insincere talk **2** jargon

can't (*mainly spoken*) cannot

cantankerous *ADJECTIVE* bad-tempered

canteen *NOUN* **canteens** **1** a restaurant for workers in a factory, office, etc. **2** a case or box containing a set of cutlery **3** a soldier's or camper's water flask

canter *NOUN* a gentle gallop

canter *VERB* **canters, cantering, cantered** go or ride at a canter

cantilever *NOUN* **cantilevers** a beam or girder fixed at one end only and used to support a bridge etc.

canvas *NOUN* **canvases** **1** a kind of strong coarse cloth **2** a piece of canvas for painting on; a painting

canvass *VERB* **canvasses, canvassing, canvassed** visit people to ask them for their support, especially in an election
▷ **canvasser** *NOUN*

canyon *NOUN* **canyons** a deep valley, usually with a river running through it

Thesaurus

informal) axe **2** *They agreed to cancel the debt.* ► revoke, annul, nullify, rescind, erase, expunge, set aside, withdraw
cancel out *One small mistake could cancel out all our hard work.* ► counterbalance, neutralize, wipe out, offset, outweigh, make up for, compensate for

candid *ADJECTIVE* *a candid reply* ► frank, honest, open, sincere, straightforward, blunt, truthful, outspoken, forthright, unequivocal
OPPOSITES ARE insincere, guarded, devious

canny *ADJECTIVE* *a canny businessman* ► shrewd, astute, sharp, acute, perceptive, clever, prudent USAGE *Canny* is a generally favourable word. Other words that are less favourable, because they imply a kind of dishonesty, are *cunning*, *crafty*, and *wily*

cantankerous *ADJECTIVE* *The heat had made him especially cantankerous.* ► bad-tempered, irritable, irascible, grumpy, testy, grouchy, touchy, crotchety, peevish, fractious, cross, (*more informal*) stroppy, (*more informal*) shirty
OPPOSITES ARE good-tempered, good-humoured, affable

canteen *NOUN* *Let's have a quick lunch in the canteen.* ► snack bar, cafeteria, cafe, coffee bar, coffee shop, tea shop, buffet, bistro

canyon *NOUN* *The army moved through a deep canyon.* ► gorge, ravine, defile

cap *NOUN* **caps** **1** a soft hat without a brim but often with a peak **2** a special headdress, e.g. that worn by a nurse **3** a cap showing membership of a sports team **4** a cap-like cover or top **5** something that makes a bang when fired in a toy pistol

cap *VERB* **caps, capping, capped** **1** put a cap or cover on something; cover **2** award a sports cap to someone chosen to be in a team **3** do better than something • *Can you cap that joke?*

capable *ADJECTIVE* able to do something
▷ **capably** *ADVERB* **capability** *NOUN*

capacious (ka- pay- shus) *ADJECTIVE* roomy; able to hold a large amount

capacity *NOUN* **capacities** **1** the amount that something can hold **2** ability; capability **3** the position that someone occupies • *In my capacity as your guardian I am responsible for you.*

cape[1] *NOUN* **capes** a cloak

cape[2] *NOUN* **capes** a large piece of high land that sticks out into the sea

caper *VERB* **capers, capering, capered** jump or run about playfully

caper *NOUN* **capers** **1** jumping about playfully **2** (*slang*) an activity or adventure

capillary (ka- pil- er- ee) *NOUN* **capillaries** any of the very fine blood vessels that connect veins and arteries

capital *ADJECTIVE* **1** important **2** (*informal*) excellent

capital *NOUN* **capitals** **1** a capital city **2** a capital letter **3** the top part of a pillar **4** money or property that can be used to produce more wealth

capital city *NOUN* **capital cities** the most important city in a country

capitalism (kap- it- al- izm) *NOUN* an economic system in which trade and industry are controlled by private owners for profit, and not by the state COMPARE **communism**

capitalist (kap- it- al- ist) *NOUN* **capitalists** **1** a person who has a lot of wealth invested; a rich person **2** a person who is in favour of capitalism

capitalize (kap- it- al- I'z) *VERB* **capitalizes, capitalizing, capitalized** **1** write or print as a capital letter **2** change something into capital; provide something with capital (= money)
▷ **capitalization** *NOUN*
capitalize on profit by something; use it to your own advantage • *You could capitalize on your skill at drawing.*

capital letter *NOUN* **capital letters** a large letter of the kind used at the start of a name or sentence

capital punishment *NOUN* punishing criminals by putting them to death

capitulate *VERB* **capitulates, capitulating, capitulated** admit that you are defeated and surrender
▷ **capitulation** *NOUN*

capricious (ka- prish- us) *ADJECTIVE* deciding or changing your mind in an impulsive way
▷ **capriciously** *ADVERB* **capriciousness** *NOUN*

Thesaurus

cap *VERB* *The mountains were capped with snow.*
► cover, top, crown, blanket

capable *ADJECTIVE* *a capable young woman*
► competent, able, accomplished, proficient, efficient, talented, gifted, clever, skilled, intelligent, effective AN OPPOSITE IS incompetent
be capable of *He's capable of doing any of these tasks.* ► have the ability (to do), be competent (to do), be adept (at doing), be equal (to doing) AN OPPOSITE IS be incapable of

capacity *NOUN* **1** *The tank's capacity is 30 litres.*
► size, volume, magnitude, extent, space
2 *You need the capacity to motivate yourself.*
► ability, power, potential, capability, competence, aptitude, faculty, skill, talent
3 *He acted in his capacity as commander-in-chief of the army.* ► position, function, role, office

cape *NOUN* **1** *She was wearing a waterproof cape.*
► cloak, mantle, shawl, wrap, stole **2** *The ship rounded the cape at dawn.* ► headland, promontory, head, point, foreland

caper *VERB* *The children capered about the room.*
► skip, bound, dance, leap, cavort, jump, spring, bounce, gambol, bob, frisk

capital *ADJECTIVE* **1** *a capital city* ► chief, principal, leading, main, first, foremost **2** *in capital letters* ► upper-case, large, big, block

capital *NOUN* **1** *Rome is the capital of Italy.*
► chief city, first city, seat of government, centre of government **2** *In three years he had enough capital to start his own business.* ► funds, finance, money, cash, assets, savings, means, wherewithal

capitalize *VERB* **capitalize on** *The opposition capitalized on the government's mistakes.*
► exploit, take advantage of, profit from, make capital out of

capitulate *VERB* *The enemy capitulated after a siege of ten months.* ► surrender, give in, submit, succumb, admit defeat, yield, (*more informal*) throw in the towel OPPOSITES ARE resist, hold out

capsize *VERB* **capsizes, capsizing, capsized** overturn • *The boat capsized.*

capsule *NOUN* **capsules 1** a hollow pill containing medicine **2** a plant's seed case that splits open when ripe **3** a compartment of a spacecraft that can be separated from the main part

captain *NOUN* **captains 1** a person in command of a ship or aircraft **2** the leader in a sports team **3** an army officer ranking next below a major; a naval officer ranking next below a commodore
▷ **captaincy** *NOUN*

caption *NOUN* **captions 1** the words printed with a picture to describe it **2** a short title or heading in a newspaper or magazine

captious (kap- shus) *ADJECTIVE* pointing out small mistakes or faults

captivate *VERB* **captivates, captivating, captivated** charm or delight someone
▷ **captivation** *NOUN*

captive *NOUN* **captives** someone taken prisoner

captive *ADJECTIVE* taken prisoner; unable to escape
▷ **captivity** *NOUN*

capture *VERB* **captures, capturing, captured 1** take someone prisoner **2** take or obtain by force, trickery, skill, or attraction • *He captured her heart.* **3** (in computing) put data in a form that can be stored in a computer

capture *NOUN* taking or obtaining by force; capturing

car *NOUN* **cars 1** a motor car **2** a carriage of a train • *the dining car*

caramel *NOUN* **caramels 1** a kind of toffee tasting like burnt sugar **2** burnt sugar used for colouring and flavouring food

carat *NOUN* **carats 1** a measure of weight for precious stones **2** a measure of the purity of gold • *Pure gold is 24 carats.*

caravan *NOUN* **caravans 1** a vehicle towed by a car and used for living in **2** a group of people travelling together across desert country
▷ **caravanning** *NOUN*

carbohydrate *NOUN* **carbohydrates** a compound of carbon, oxygen, and hydrogen (e.g. sugar or starch)

carbolic *NOUN* a kind of disinfectant

carbon *NOUN* **carbons 1** a substance that is present in all living things and that occurs in its pure form as diamond and graphite **2** carbon paper **3** a carbon copy

carbonate *NOUN* **carbonates** a compound that gives off carbon dioxide when mixed with acid

carbon dioxide *NOUN* a gas formed when things burn, or breathed out by humans and animals

carburettor *NOUN* **carburettors** a device for mixing fuel and air in an engine

carcass *NOUN* **carcasses 1** the dead body of an animal **2** the bony part of a bird's body after the meat has been eaten

carcinogen *NOUN* **carcinogens** any substance that produces cancer

card *NOUN* **cards 1** thick stiff paper or thin cardboard **2** a small piece of stiff paper for writing or printing on, especially to send

Thesaurus

capsize *VERB* *Some of the boats capsized.*
► overturn, tip over, turn over, turn upside down, flip over, keel over, (*more informal*) turn turtle

captain *NOUN* **1** *the captain of the winning team* ► leader, chief player, head, boss **2** *the ship's captain* ► commander, master, officer in charge, skipper **3** *a captain of industry* ► magnate, mogul, tycoon, mandarin, baron

captivate *VERB* *The beauty of the scene captivates all visitors.* ► charm, enchant, delight, entrance, enthral, fascinate, bewitch, beguile, engross, excite, mesmerize OPPOSITES ARE repel, disgust

captive *ADJECTIVE* **1** *captive animals* ► confined, caged, captured, incarcerated, chained, detained, enslaved, ensnared, fettered, gaoled, imprisoned, jailed, restricted, secure, taken prisoner **2** *The men had been held captive for several weeks.* ► locked up, imprisoned, jailed, detained, under lock and key AN OPPOSITE IS free

captive *NOUN* *The captives all wore handcuffs.* ► prisoner, convict, detainee, inmate, internee, hostage

captivity *NOUN* *Years of captivity had ruined his health.* ► imprisonment, confinement, internment, incarceration, detention, custody AN OPPOSITE IS freedom

capture *VERB* **1** *He was captured boarding a ship for France.* ► catch, arrest, apprehend, seize, take prisoner, take into custody, (*more informal*) nab, (*more informal*) pull in, (*much more informal*) nick **2** *The building was captured by stormtroopers.* ► occupy, take, seize, secure

car *NOUN* *A lot of the students arrived in cars.* ► motor car, automobile, motor, vehicle

card *NOUN* **1** *a piece of stiff card* ► cardboard, pasteboard, board **2** *Let's play cards.* ► card game, game of cards
USAGE *Card* is often short for *playing card*, *greetings* (or *birthday* or *Christmas*) *card*, and *credit card*
on the cards (*informal*) • *A marriage was always on the cards.* ► possible, a possibility,

messages or greetings or to record information **3** a small, oblong piece of plastic issued to a customer by a bank or building society, giving details of their account and allowing them to use cash machines etc. **4** a playing card
cards *PLURAL NOUN* a game using playing cards
on the cards likely; possible

cardboard *NOUN* a kind of thin board made of layers of paper or wood fibre

cardiac (**kard**- ee- ak) *ADJECTIVE* to do with the heart

cardigan *NOUN* **cardigans** a knitted jersey fastened with buttons down the front [named after the Earl of Cardigan, a commander in the Crimean War in the 19th century, whose troops wore this kind of jersey]

cardinal *NOUN* **cardinals** a senior priest in the Roman Catholic Church

cardinal *ADJECTIVE* **1** chief; most important • *the cardinal features of our plan.* **2** deep scarlet (like a cardinal's cassock)

cardinal number *NOUN* **cardinal numbers** a number for counting things, e.g. one, two, three, etc. COMPARE **ordinal number**

cardinal points *PLURAL NOUN* the four main points of the compass (North, South, East, and West)

care *NOUN* **cares 1** serious attention and thought • *Plan your holiday with care.* **2** caution to avoid damage or loss • *Glass—handle with care.* **3** protection or supervision • *Leave the child in my care.* **4** worry or anxiety • *freedom from care*
take care be especially careful
take care of look after

care *VERB* **cares, caring, cared 1** feel interested or concerned **2** feel affection
care for 1 have in your care **2** be fond of

career *NOUN* **careers** a series of jobs that mark a person's progress in the profession or work they choose to do • *a career in journalism*

career *VERB* **careers, careering, careered** rush along wildly

carefree *ADJECTIVE* without worries or responsibilities

careful *ADJECTIVE* **1** giving serious thought and attention to something **2** avoiding damage or danger etc.; cautious
▷ **carefully** *ADVERB* **carefulness** *NOUN*

careless *ADJECTIVE* not careful
▷ **carelessly** *ADVERB* **carelessness** *NOUN*

Thesaurus

likely, a likelihood, probable, a probability, in the offing AN OPPOSITE IS out of the question

cardboard *NOUN* *a cardboard cutout* ► card, pasteboard

care *NOUN* **1** *We need to proceed with care.* ► caution, carefulness, vigilance, watchfulness, awareness, prudence, circumspection, concentration, attention, concern, diligence, heed AN OPPOSITE IS carelessness **2** *The job needs to be done with great care.* ► discretion, thought, attention, thoroughness, meticulousness, concentration **3** *You need to escape from all your cares.* ► worry, anxiety, trouble, concern, burden, problem, difficulty, hardship, responsibility, sorrow, stress, tribulation, vexation, woe AN OPPOSITE IS joy **4** *She left the baby in the care of a minder.* ► charge, safe-keeping, keeping, custody, control, supervision, protection

care *VERB* **care about** *She obviously cares about her staff.* ► interest yourself in, concern yourself about, mind about , bother about, worry about, be troubled by
care for 1 *The hospice cares for sick children.* ► look after, take care of, tend, attend to, provide for, nurse, supervise, watch over, (*more informal*) keep an eye on **2** *He cares for his grandchildren.* ► love, be fond of, adore, cherish, hold dear, dote on, think the world of **3** *I don't really care for those biscuits.* ► like, fancy, feel like, be keen on, enjoy, want

career *NOUN* *a career in teaching* ► profession, occupation, job, calling, position

carefree *ADJECTIVE* **1** *a carefree young girl* ► unworried, untroubled, cheerful, cheery, light-hearted, easy-going, casual, relaxed, (*more informal*) laid-back OPPOSITES ARE anxious, tense **2** *a carefree time* ► relaxing, restful, trouble-free, untroubled, peaceful, quiet OPPOSITES ARE hectic, nerve-wracking

careful *ADJECTIVE* **1** *Be careful walking through the park at night.* ► alert, vigilant, heedful, attentive, watchful AN OPPOSITE IS careless **2** *You must be careful with your spending.* ► prudent, cautious, circumspect, economical, thrifty, canny OPPOSITES ARE careless, extravagant, reckless **3** *Such a long journey needs careful planning.* ► detailed, thorough, meticulous, conscientious, scrupulous **4** *She's a very careful driver.* ► attentive, diligent, conscientious OPPOSITES ARE careless, inattentive

careless *ADJECTIVE* **1** *a careless driver; careless remarks* ► inattentive, thoughtless, inconsiderate, negligent, absent-minded, heedless, irresponsible, reckless OPPOSITES ARE careful, attentive **2** *There is no excuse for careless work.* ► slipshod, shoddy, slapdash, slovenly, inaccurate, scrappy, incorrect OPPOSITES ARE

caress NOUN **caresses** a gentle loving touch

caress VERB **caresses, caressing, caressed** touch lovingly

caretaker NOUN **caretakers** a person employed to look after a school, block of flats, etc.

cargo NOUN **cargoes** goods carried in a ship or aircraft

Caribbean ADJECTIVE to do with or from the Caribbean Sea, a part of the Atlantic Ocean east of Central America

caricature NOUN **caricatures** an amusing or exaggerated picture of someone

carnage NOUN the killing of many people

carnival NOUN **carnivals** a festival, often with a procession in fancy dress [from Latin *carnis* = of flesh: originally this meant the festivities before Lent, when meat was given up until Easter]

carnivorous (kar- **niv**- er- us) ADJECTIVE meat-eating COMPARE **herbivorous**
▷ **carnivore** NOUN

carol NOUN **carols** a Christmas hymn
▷ **caroller** NOUN **carolling** NOUN

carp [1] NOUN **carp** an edible freshwater fish

carp [2] VERB **carps, carping, carped** keep finding fault

car park NOUN **car parks** an area where cars may be parked

carpenter NOUN **carpenters** a person who makes things out of wood
▷ **carpentry** NOUN

carpet NOUN **carpets** a thick soft covering for a floor
▷ **carpeted** ADJECTIVE **carpeting** NOUN
[from early Italian *carpita*, from Latin *carpere* = to pluck]

carriage NOUN **carriages 1** one of the separate parts of a train, where passengers sit **2** a passenger vehicle pulled by horses **3** carrying goods from one place to another; the cost of carrying goods • *Carriage is extra.* **4** a moving part carrying or holding something in a machine

carrier NOUN **carriers** a person or thing that carries something

carrot NOUN **carrots** a plant with a thick orange-coloured root used as a vegetable

carry VERB **carries, carrying, carried 1** take something from one place to another **2** support the weight of something **3** take an amount into the next column when adding figures **4** be heard a long way away • *Sound carries in the mountains.* **5** if a proposal at a meeting is carried, it is approved by most people at the meeting • *The motion was carried by ten votes to six.*
be carried away be very excited
carry on 1 continue **2** (*informal*) behave excitedly **3** (*informal*) complain
carry out put into practice

cart NOUN **carts** an open vehicle for carrying loads

Thesaurus

careful, accurate **3** *She has always been rather careless about money.* ► extravagant, reckless
OPPOSITES ARE careful, prudent

carelessness NOUN *The accident was caused by carelessness.* ► inattention, inattentiveness, absent-mindedness, negligence, recklessness, irresponsibility, slovenliness, thoughtlessness, untidiness, haste, (*more informal*) sloppiness
OPPOSITES ARE care, carefulness

caretaker NOUN *the caretaker at the village hall* ► janitor, warden, custodian, attendant, keeper, porter, superintendent, watchman

cargo NOUN *a ship's cargo* ► freight, load, haul, payload, consignment, merchandise, shipment, goods

caricature VERB *She caricatured the movements of a ballerina.* ► parody, mimic, imitate, lampoon, mock, ridicule, satirize, burlesque, make fun of, exaggerate, (*more informal*) send up, (*more informal*) take off

carnival NOUN *the town's annual carnival* ► festival, gala, jamboree, fiesta, fete, fair, celebration, revelry

carriage NOUN *a railway carriage* ► coach, wagon

carry VERB **1** *We will have to carry our own luggage.* ► convey, take, transfer, bring, fetch, haul, lift, manhandle, move, remove, shoulder, (*more informal*) lug **2** *The channel ships carry passengers and freight.* ► transport, convey, handle, ferry, ship **3** *Telegraph wires carry signals.* ► communicate, relay, transmit **4** *The bridge would not carry the weight of a large vehicle.* ► support, bear, hold up **5** *The job carries many responsibilities.* ► demand, entail, involve, require, lead to, result in
carry on 1 *We carried on for as long as we could.* ► persevere, persist, continue, go on, keep on, last, remain, stay, (*informal*) stick it out **2** *She has been carrying on her own business for several years.* ► run, engage in, maintain, manage, operate, administer **3** (*informal*) *Tell them to stop carrying on like that!* ► misbehave, behave badly, cause trouble
carry out *They were just carrying out orders.* ► obey, follow, discharge, implement, execute, finish, perform, complete

a b c d e f g h i j k l m n o p q r s t u v w x y z

A B C D E F G H I J K L M N O P Q R S T U V W X Y Z

cart *VERB* **carts, carting, carted 1** carry in a cart **2** (*informal*) carry something heavy or tiring • *I've carted these books all round the school.*

carthorse *NOUN* **carthorses** a large strong horse used for pulling heavy loads

cartilage *NOUN* tough white flexible tissue attached to a bone

carton *NOUN* **cartons** a cardboard or plastic container

cartoon *NOUN* **cartoons 1** an amusing drawing **2** a series of drawings that tell a story; a comic strip **3** an animated film
▷ **cartoonist** *NOUN*

cartridge *NOUN* **cartridges 1** a case containing the explosive for a bullet or shell **2** a container holding film for a camera, ink for a pen, etc. **3** the device that holds the stylus of a record player

cartwheel *NOUN* **cartwheels 1** the wheel of a cart **2** a handstand balancing on each hand in turn with arms and legs spread like spokes of a wheel

carve *VERB* **carves, carving, carved 1** make something by cutting wood or stone etc. **2** cut cooked meat into slices
▷ **carver** *NOUN*

case[1] *NOUN* **cases 1** a container **2** a suitcase

case[2] *NOUN* **cases 1** an example of something existing or occurring; a situation • *In every case we found that someone had cheated.* **2** something investigated by police etc. or by a lawcourt • *a murder case* **3** a set of facts or arguments to support something • *She put forward a good case for equality.* **4** the form of a word that shows how it is related to other words. *Fred's* is the possessive case of *Fred; him* is the objective case of *he*
in any case anyway
in case because something may happen

cash *NOUN* **1** money in coin or notes **2** immediate payment for goods etc.

cash *VERB* **cashes, cashing, cashed** change a cheque etc. for cash

cashew *NOUN* **cashews** a small kidney-shaped nut [via Portuguese from Tupi (a South American language)]

cashier *NOUN* **cashiers** a person who takes in and pays out money in a bank or takes payments in a shop

cash machine or **cash dispenser** *NOUN* **cash machines** or **cash dispensers** a machine, usually outside a bank or building society, from which people can draw out cash by using a bank card

cashpoint *NOUN* **cashpoints** a cash machine

cash register *NOUN* **cash registers** a machine that records and stores the money received in a shop

casing *NOUN* **casings** a protective covering

casino *NOUN* **casinos** a public building or room for gambling

cask *NOUN* **casks** a barrel

casket *NOUN* **caskets** a small box for jewellery etc.

casserole *NOUN* **casseroles 1** a covered dish in which food is cooked and served **2** food cooked in a casserole

cassette *NOUN* **cassettes** a small sealed case containing recording tape, film, etc.

Thesaurus

cart *NOUN The fruit was taken to the barns in carts.* ► barrow, wheelbarrow, handcart, trolley, truck

cart *VERB* (*informal*) *The books were too bulky to cart around.* ► carry, move, take, haul, (*informal*) lug

cartoon *NOUN* **1** *The story is in the form of a cartoon.* ► comic strip, drawing, caricature, sketch **2** *a film cartoon* ► animation **3** *a political cartoon* ► caricature, parody, lampoon

carve *VERB* **1** *It was time to carve the meat.* ► cut, slice, chop **2** *a tool for carving wood* ► chisel, hew, sculpt, fashion, form, shape

case *NOUN* **1** *She hurriedly threw a few clothes into a case.* ► suitcase, bag, travel bag, trunk **2** *The books were still in their packing cases.* ► box, chest, canister, carton, crate, container **3** *The videotape was spilling out of its case.* ► shell, cartridge, cassette, container, capsule, cover **4** *The china was kept in a handsome display case.* ► cabinet, cupboard, showcase, sideboard **5** *a classic case of misunderstanding* ► instance, example, occurrence, occasion, manifestation, illustration **6** *If that's the case we'll have to think of an another way.* ► situation, position, state of affairs, event, circumstances **7** *Police from several forces are involved in the case.* ► investigation, inquiry **8** *The lawyers agreed it was a difficult case.* ► lawsuit, action, legal action, suit, trial

cash *NOUN a purse full of cash* ► money, notes, banknotes, coins, change, ready money

cash *VERB I need to cash a cheque.* ► exchange, change, get money for, get cash for
cash in on *I don't like to cash in on your bad luck.* ► take advantage of, profit by, exploit

casing *NOUN The hard disk has its own protective casing.* ► case, shell, cover, sheath, housing, sleeve

cask *NOUN a cask of wine* ► barrel, keg, butt, vat, tun, hogshead, firkin

cast *VERB* **casts, casting, cast 1** throw **2** shed or throw off **3** make a vote **4** make something of metal or plaster in a mould **5** choose performers for a play or film etc.

cast *NOUN* **casts 1** a shape made by pouring liquid metal or plaster into a mould **2** all the performers in a play or film

castaway *NOUN* **castaways** a shipwrecked person

caste *NOUN* **castes** (in India) one of the social classes into which Hindus are born

casting vote *NOUN* **casting votes** the vote that decides which group wins when the votes on each side are equal

castle *NOUN* **castles 1** a large old fortified building **2** a piece in chess, also called a **rook**
castles in the air daydreams

castor *NOUN* **castors** a small wheel on the leg of a table, chair, etc.

castor sugar *NOUN* finely ground white sugar

castrate *VERB* **castrates, castrating, castrated** remove the testicles of a male animal COMPARE **spay**
▷ **castration** *NOUN*

casual *ADJECTIVE* **1** happening by chance; not planned **2** not careful; not methodical **3** informal; suitable for informal occasions • *casual clothes* **4** not permanent • *casual work*
▷ **casually** *ADVERB* **casualness** *NOUN*

casualty *NOUN* **casualties 1** a person who is killed or injured in war or in an accident **2** a department of a hospital that deals with emergency patients

cat *NOUN* **cats 1** a small furry domestic animal **2** a wild animal of the same family as a domestic cat, e.g. a lion, tiger, or leopard **3** (*informal*) a spiteful girl or woman
let the cat out of the bag reveal a secret

cataclysm (kat- a- klizm) *NOUN* **cataclysms** a violent upheaval or disaster

catalogue *NOUN* **catalogues 1** a list of things (e.g. of books in a library), usually arranged in order **2** a book containing a list of things that can be bought • *a Christmas catalogue*

catalogue *VERB* **catalogues, cataloguing, catalogued** enter something in a catalogue

catalyst (kat- a- list) *NOUN* **catalysts 1** (in science) something that starts or speeds up a chemical reaction **2** something that causes a change

catalytic converter *NOUN* **catalytic converters** a device fitted to a car's exhaust system, with a catalyst for converting pollutant gases into less harmful ones

catapult *NOUN* **catapults 1** a device with elastic for shooting small stones **2** an ancient military weapon for hurling stones etc.

catapult *VERB* **catapults, catapulting, catapulted** hurl or rush violently

cataract *NOUN* **cataracts 1** a large waterfall or rush of water **2** a cloudy area that forms in the eye and prevents a person from seeing clearly

catastrophe (ka- tass- trof- ee) *NOUN* **catastrophes** a sudden great disaster
▷ **catastrophic** (kat- a- strof- ik) *ADJECTIVE* **catastrophically** *ADVERB*

catch *VERB* **catches, catching, caught 1** take and hold something **2** arrest or capture **3** overtake **4** be in time to get on a bus or train etc. **5** be infected with an illness **6** hear • *I didn't catch what he said.* **7** discover someone

Thesaurus

cast *VERB* **1** *He cast a coin into the fountain.* ► throw, toss, fling, flip, sling, (*more informal*) chuck, hurl **2** *The statue is cast entirely in bronze.* ► mould, form, shape, model, sculpture
cast down *They all felt cast down at the news.* ► dejected, depressed, saddened, upset, disheartened

casual *ADJECTIVE* **1** *a casual encounter with an old friend* ► chance, unexpected, unforeseen, unintentional, unplanned, fortuitous, accidental, random OPPOSITES ARE deliberate, intentional **2** *a casual remark* ► offhand, spontaneous, impromptu, unconsidered, random OPPOSITES ARE committed, enthusiastic **3** *a casual acquaintance* ► slight, vague OPPOSITES ARE close, intimate **4** *a casual approach to life* ► relaxed, nonchalant, lackadaisical, indifferent, carefree, easy-going, offhand, apathetic, flippant, (*more informal*) laid-back OPPOSITES ARE concerned, serious **5** *He gave her a casual glance.* ► cursory, fleeting, passing, hasty, quick, perfunctory OPPOSITES ARE thorough, careful **6** *casual clothes* ► informal AN OPPOSITE IS formal

casualty *NOUN* *The bombing led to many casualties.* ► death, fatality, injury, loss, victim, (*in plural*) dead and wounded

cat *NOUN* *People thought he was odd for talking to his cat.* ► tom, tomcat, tabby, kitten, (*more informal*) moggy, (*more informal*) pussy RELATED ADJECTIVE feline

catalogue *NOUN* **1** *a library catalogue* ► inventory, list, record, register, directory, index, roll, schedule, table **2** *a catalogue of mistakes* ► series, sequence, string, long list

catastrophe *NOUN* *The floods were a catastrophe for the area.* ► calamity, tragedy, misfortune, mishap, tragedy, affliction, cataclysm, blow

catch *VERB* **1** *Josh caught the ball.* ► seize, grab, take hold of, grip, clutch, intercept **2** *They hadn't managed to catch any fish.* ► hook, net, land, trap **3** *Do you think they will catch the thief?*

doing something wrong • *They were caught smoking in the playground.* **8** make or become fixed or unable to move; entangle • *I caught my dress on a nail.* **9** hit; strike • *The blow caught him on the nose.*
catch fire start burning
catch it (*informal*) be scolded or punished
catch on (*informal*) **1** become popular **2** understand
catch out discover someone in a mistake

catch NOUN **catches** **1** catching something **2** something caught or worth catching **3** a hidden difficulty **4** a device for fastening something

catching ADJECTIVE infectious

catchment area NOUN **catchment areas** **1** the area from which a school takes pupils or a hospital takes patients **2** the whole area from which water drains into a river or reservoir

catchphrase NOUN **catchphrases** a popular phrase

catchy ADJECTIVE easy to remember; soon becoming popular • *a catchy tune*

category NOUN **categories** a set of people or things classified as being similar to each other

cater VERB **caters, catering, catered** **1** provide food, especially for a lot of people **2** provide what is needed
▷ **caterer** NOUN

caterpillar NOUN **caterpillars** the creeping worm-like creature that will turn into a butterfly or moth

cathedral NOUN **cathedrals** the most important church of a district, usually containing the bishop's throne

Catherine wheel NOUN **Catherine wheels** a firework that spins round

cathode NOUN **cathodes** the electrode by which electric current leaves a device COMPARE **anode**

Catholic ADJECTIVE **1** belonging to the Roman Catholic Church **2** of all Christians • *the Holy Catholic Church*
▷ **Catholicism** NOUN

Catholic NOUN **Catholics** a Roman Catholic

catholic ADJECTIVE including most things • *Her taste in literature is catholic.*

cattle PLURAL NOUN animals with horns and hoofs, kept by farmers for their milk and beef

catty ADJECTIVE **cattier, cattiest** speaking or spoken spitefully

catwalk NOUN **catwalks** a long platform that models walk along at a fashion show

cauldron NOUN **cauldrons** a large deep pot for boiling things in

cauliflower NOUN **cauliflowers** a cabbage with a large head of white flowers

Thesaurus

► capture, arrest, apprehend **4** *We have a train to catch.* ► board, be in time for, get to, reach **5** *He caught a rare virus on a business trip.* ► contract, be infected with, develop, get, go down with, become sick with, become ill with **6** *She caught them in the act.* ► discover, detect, find, find out, surprise, expose **7** *A trip to Paris caught their fancy.* ► capture, attract, appeal to, seize, win, absorb, engross **8** *I didn't catch what you said.* ► hear, perceive, discern, make out, recognize
catch up *If we hurry we can catch them up.* ► reach, overtake, draw level with

catch NOUN **1** *The fishermen returned with their catch over their shoulders.* ► haul, net, bag, booty, prize **2** *The price is so good there must be a catch.* ► snag, disadvantage, difficulty, drawback, obstacle, problem, trap, trick **3** *He tried to slip the catch on the window.* ► latch, lock, fastener, fastening, bolt, clasp

catching ADJECTIVE *Fortunately the disease is not catching.* ► infectious, contagious, communicable, transmittable, spreading

catchy ADJECTIVE *a catchy tune* ► memorable, tuneful, haunting, attractive, popular, singable

categorical ADJECTIVE *a categorical assurance* ► absolute, unqualified, unconditional, unequivocal, unreserved, outright, complete, definite, express

category NOUN *There is a maximum penalty for each category of offence. Non-fiction books fall into several categories.* ► class, type, classification, kind, sort, division, group, grade, heading

cater VERB **1 cater for** *The hotel will cater for vegetarians.* ► provide for, make arrangements for, supply, feed, cook for **2 cater for** *A simple barrow will cater for most of your gardening needs.* ► serve, satisfy, answer, provide for, cope with, take care of

cause NOUN **1** *Police are still trying to find the cause of the explosion.* ► source, origin, root, basis, reason (for), beginning, genesis, grounds, motivation, motive, occasion, spring, stimulus **2** *The older boys were the cause of much of the trouble.* ► initiator, instigator, originator, producer, agent **3** *There is no cause for alarm.* ► reason, grounds, justification, call, need, necessity, occasion, excuse, pretext **4** *a worthy cause* ► purpose, object, end, aim, ideal, undertaking, enterprise

cause *NOUN* **causes** **1** a person or thing that makes something happen or produces an effect **2** a reason • *There is no cause for worry.* **3** a purpose for which people work; an organization or charity

cause *VERB* **causes, causing, caused** be the cause of; make something happen

causeway *NOUN* **causeways** a raised road across low or marshy ground

caustic *ADJECTIVE* **1** able to burn or wear things away by chemical action **2** sarcastic
▷ **caustically** *ADVERB*

caution *NOUN* **cautions** **1** care taken in order to avoid danger etc. **2** a warning

caution *VERB* **cautions, cautioning, cautioned** warn someone

cautionary *ADJECTIVE* giving a warning

cautious *ADJECTIVE* showing caution
▷ **cautiously** *ADVERB* **cautiousness** *NOUN*

Cavalier *NOUN* **Cavaliers** a supporter of King Charles I in the English Civil War (1642–9)

cavalry *NOUN* soldiers who fight on horseback or in armoured vehicles COMPARE **infantry**

cave *NOUN* **caves** a large hollow place in the side of a hill or cliff, or underground

cave *VERB* **caves, caving, caved**
cave in **1** fall inwards **2** give way in an argument

cavern *NOUN* **caverns** a large cave
▷ **cavernous** *ADJECTIVE*

cavity *NOUN* **cavities** a hollow or hole

cavort (ka- **vort**) *VERB* **cavorts, cavorting, cavorted** jump or run about excitedly

caw *NOUN* **caws** the harsh cry of a crow etc.

cc *ABBREVIATION* cubic centimetre(s)

CCTV *ABBREVIATION* closed circuit television, a security device

CD *ABBREVIATION* compact disc

CD-ROM *ABBREVIATION* compact disc read-only memory; a compact disc on which large amounts of data can be stored and then displayed on a computer screen

cease *VERB* **ceases, ceasing, ceased** stop or end

cease *NOUN*
without cease not ceasing

ceasefire *NOUN* **ceasefires** a signal to stop firing

ceaseless *ADJECTIVE* not ceasing

cedar *NOUN* **cedars** an evergreen tree with hard fragrant wood
▷ **cedarwood** *NOUN*

cedilla (sid- **il**- a) *NOUN* **cedillas** a mark under *c* in certain languages to show that it is pronounced as *s*, e.g. in *façade*

ceiling *NOUN* **ceilings** **1** the flat surface under the top of a room **2** the highest limit that something can reach

celebrate *VERB* **celebrates, celebrating, celebrated** **1** do something special or enjoyable to show that a day or event is

Thesaurus

cause *VERB* **1** *The bad weather has caused many delays.* ► bring about, result in, give rise to, lead to, produce, generate, create, precipitate, induce, entail, stimulate **2** *Poor health caused him to give up work.* ► force, compel, lead, encourage, induce, make

caustic *ADJECTIVE* **1** *a caustic substance* ► corrosive, acid, astringent, burning **2** *caustic remarks* ► sharp, sarcastic, scathing, hurtful, acid, acerbic, cutting, bitter, spiteful, vicious, abrasive

caution *NOUN* **1** *Drivers were advised to proceed with extreme caution.* ► care, alertness, attentiveness, carefulness, wariness, watchfulness, vigilance, restraint, discretion, circumspection, heed, heedfulness, prudence AN OPPOSITE IS recklessness **2** *A first offender is usually let off with a caution.* ► reprimand, warning, admonition

cautious *ADJECTIVE* **1** *He was a cautious man and avoided risks.* ► careful, attentive, vigilant, circumspect, heedful, alert, prudent, scrupulous, watchful OPPOSITES ARE careless, reckless **2** *Their response was cautious.* ► guarded, discreet, wary, chary, tactful OPPOSITES ARE forthright, impetuous

cave *NOUN* *There are caves at the foot of the cliffs.* ► cavern, grotto, hollow, cavity, underground chamber, den, hole, pothole

cave *VERB* **1** **cave in** *The roof caved in* ► collapse, fall in, give way, disintegrate, crumble **2** **cave in** *The government refused to cave in to the protesters' demands.* ► yield, surrender, comply (with)

cavity *NOUN* *a secret cavity in the wall* ► space, chamber, hollow, hole, pit, cave, crater, dent

cavort *VERB* *The children cavorted about the room.* ► skip, bound, dance, leap, caper, jump, spring, bounce, gambol, bob, frisk

cease *VERB* *Hostilities will cease at midnight. Both armies have ceased military activity.* ► end, stop, finish, halt, come *or* bring to an end, conclude, terminate AN OPPOSITE IS commence

ceaseless *ADJECTIVE* *ceaseless activity* ► continuous, continual, constant, incessant, endless, unceasing, interminable, non-stop OPPOSITES ARE temporary, intermittent

celebrate *VERB* **1** *They celebrated with a bottle of champagne.* ► enjoy yourself, have fun, have a good time, make merry **2** *The couple celebrate their golden wedding this week.*

important **2** perform a religious ceremony
▷ **celebrant** *NOUN* **celebration** *NOUN*

celebrated *ADJECTIVE* famous

celebrity *NOUN* **celebrities** **1** a famous person **2** fame; being famous

celery *NOUN* a vegetable with crisp white or green stems

celestial (sil- est- ee- al) *ADJECTIVE* **1** to do with the sky **2** to do with heaven; divine
celestial bodies *PLURAL NOUN* stars etc.

cell *NOUN* **cells** **1** a small room where a prisoner is locked up **2** a small room in a monastery **3** a microscopic unit of living matter **4** a compartment of a honeycomb **5** a device for producing electric current chemically **6** a small group or unit in an organization etc.

cellar *NOUN* **cellars** an underground room

cello (chel- oh) *NOUN* **cellos** a musical instrument like a large violin, placed between the knees of a player
▷ **cellist** *NOUN*

cellular *ADJECTIVE* **1** consisting of living cells **2** (said about a mobile telephone system) using a number of short-range radio stations to cover the area it serves

cellulose *NOUN* **1** tissue that forms the main part of all plants and trees **2** paint made from cellulose

Celsius (sel- see- us) *ADJECTIVE* measuring temperature on a scale using 100 degrees, where water freezes at 0° and boils at 100° *[named after A. Celsius, a Swedish astronomer, who invented it]*

Celtic *ADJECTIVE* to do with the Celts, a group of peoples living in parts of Europe and Asia before Roman times, or to the languages spoken by them, including Irish, Scottish Gaelic, and Welsh

cement *NOUN* **1** a mixture of lime and clay used in building, to join bricks together, etc. **2** a strong glue

cement *VERB* **cements, cementing, cemented** **1** put cement on something **2** join firmly; strengthen

cemetery (sem- et- ree) *NOUN* **cemeteries** a place where people are buried

censor *NOUN* **censors** a person who examines films, books, letters, etc. and removes or bans anything that seems harmful
▷ **censor** *VERB* **censorship** *NOUN*
USAGE Do not confuse with **censure**.

censure (sen- sher) *NOUN* strong criticism or disapproval of something
▷ **censure** *VERB*
USAGE Do not confuse with **censor**.

census *NOUN* **censuses** an official count or survey of the population of a country or area

cent *NOUN* **cents** a coin worth one-hundredth of a dollar

centenary (sen- teen- er- ee) *NOUN* **centenaries** a 100th anniversary
▷ **centennial** (sen- ten- ee- al) *ADJECTIVE*

centigrade *ADJECTIVE* measuring temperature on a scale using 100 degrees, where water freezes at 0° and boils at 100° Celsius

centimetre *NOUN* **centimetres** one-hundredth of a metre, about four-tenths of an inch

centipede *NOUN* **centipedes** a small crawling creature with a long body and many legs

central *ADJECTIVE* **1** to do with or at the centre **2** most important
▷ **centrally** *ADVERB*

central heating *NOUN* a system of heating a building from one source by circulating hot water or hot air or steam in pipes or by linked radiators

Thesaurus

► commemorate, observe, mark, recognize, honour, remember, keep

celebration *NOUN* **1** *a birthday celebration* ► party, function, festivity, (*more informal*) binge **2** *a cause for celebration* ► festivities, jollification, merrymaking, enjoying yourself, partying

celebrity *NOUN* **1** *a team made up of celebrities* ► star, famous person, public figure, dignitary, idol, personality, luminary **2** *The group seemed to be enjoying their celebrity.* ► fame, stardom, prominence, popularity, glory, reputation, renown

cell *NOUN* **1** *a prison cell* ► room, cubicle, chamber, compartment, enclosure, unit **2** *cells of a honeycomb* ► compartment, cavity, chamber, hollow, section **3** *a terrorist cell* ► unit, group, faction, caucus, section, arm, wing

censure *NOUN* *Her voice had a note of censure.* ► criticism, disapproval, reproach, rebuke, condemnation, reproof

censure *VERB* *Shareholders censured the bank.* ► criticize, reprimand, condemn, rebuke, reproach

central *ADJECTIVE* **1** *the central chamber of the temple* ► innermost, inner, interior, middle, focal **2** *the central issues* ► chief, key, main, essential, pivotal, primary, principal, vital,

centre *NOUN* **centres 1** the middle point or part **2** an important place • *a centre of the film industry* **3** a building or place for a special purpose • *a sports centre*

centre *VERB* **centres, centring, centred** place something at the centre
centre on or **centre around 1** be concentrated in **2** have as its main subject or concern

centre of gravity *NOUN* **centres of gravity** the point in an object around which its mass is perfectly balanced

century *NOUN* **centuries 1** a period of one hundred years **2** a hundred runs scored by a batsman in an innings at cricket

ceramic *ADJECTIVE* to do with or made of pottery

cereal *NOUN* **cereals 1** a grass producing seeds which are used as food, e.g. wheat, barley, or rice **2** a breakfast food made from these seeds
USAGE Do not confuse with **serial**.

cerebral (se- rib- ral) *ADJECTIVE* to do with the brain

cerebral palsy *NOUN* a condition caused by brain damage before birth that makes a person suffer from spasms of the muscles and jerky movements

ceremonial *ADJECTIVE* to do with or used in a ceremony; formal
▷ **ceremonially** *ADVERB*

ceremonious *ADJECTIVE* full of ceremony; elaborately performed

ceremony *NOUN* **ceremonies** the formal actions carried out on an important occasion, e.g. at a wedding or a funeral

certain *ADJECTIVE* sure; without doubt
a certain person *or* **thing** a person or thing that is known but not named
▷ **certainly** *ADVERB*

certainty *NOUN* **certainties 1** something that is sure to happen **2** being sure

certificate *NOUN* **certificates** an official written or printed statement giving information about a person etc. • *a birth certificate*

certitude *NOUN* a feeling of certainty

cervix *NOUN* **cervices** (ser- vis- ees) the entrance to the womb
▷ **cervical** *ADJECTIVE*

cesspit or **cesspool** *NOUN* **cesspits** or **cesspools** a covered pit where liquid waste or sewage is stored temporarily

CFC *ABBREVIATION* chlorofluorocarbon; a gas containing chlorine and fluorine that is thought to be harmful to the ozone layer in the Earth's atmosphere

chaff[1] *NOUN* husks of corn, separated from the seed

chaff[2] *VERB* tease someone

chain *NOUN* **chains 1** a row of metal rings fastened together **2** a connected series of things • *a chain of mountains* • *a chain of events* **3** a number of shops, hotels, or other businesses owned by the same company

Thesaurus

fundamental, crucial, major, overriding, important AN OPPOSITE IS peripheral

centre *NOUN* **1** *the centre of a circle* ► middle, mid-point, heart, core, eye, bullseye **2** *the centre of the city* ► middle, heart, nucleus

cereal *NOUN* *farmers who prefer cereal production to livestock* ► corn, grain

ceremony *NOUN* **1** *a wedding ceremony* ► rite, ritual, service, observance, celebration **2** *a grand occasion with all due ceremony* ► formality, pomp, protocol, propriety, ritual, solemnity

certain *ADJECTIVE* **1** *I was certain they did it.* ► sure, confident, positive, convinced, assured, satisfied OPPOSITES ARE uncertain (whether), doubtful (whether) **2** *It is certain that there will be reprisals.* ► definite, undeniable, indubitable, unquestionable, clear, plain, evident, obvious, conclusive OPPOSITES ARE uncertain (whether), doubtful **3** *She faced certain failure.* ► inevitable, assured, inescapable, unavoidable **4** *They are certain to win.* ► sure, bound, assured (of winning) AN OPPOSITE IS unlikely **5** *A certain person has been here.* ► particular, specific, definite, unnamed, individual

certainly *ADVERB* *It was certainly a beautiful building.* ► undoubtedly, unquestionably, surely, undeniably, definitely, without question, without doubt

certainty *NOUN* **1** *The answers may never be known with certainty.* ► assurance, assuredness, confidence, conviction, certitude OPPOSITES ARE uncertainty, doubt **2** *A high-scoring match seemed a certainty.* ► inevitability, certain fact, foregone conclusion, matter of course, necessity, (*more informal*) sure thing AN OPPOSITE IS impossibility

certify *VERB* *You have to sign the form to certify that the information is true.* ► verify, guarantee, confirm, affirm, testify, warrant, declare, demonstrate

chain *NOUN* **1** *The prisoners were held in chains.* ► fetters, shackles, bonds, irons, manacles, coupling, handcuffs, links **2** *a chain of events* ► series, sequence, succession, string, course, train, progression **3** *a chain of supermarkets* ► group, firm, series

A B C D E F G H I J K L M N O P Q R S T U V W X Y Z

chain *VERB* **chains, chaining, chained** fasten something with a chain or chains

chain letter *NOUN* **chain letters** a letter that you are asked to copy and send to several other people, who are supposed to do the same

chain reaction *NOUN* **chain reactions** a series of happenings in which each causes the next

chain store *NOUN* **chain stores** one of a number of similar shops owned by the same firm

chair *NOUN* **chairs 1** a movable seat, with a back, for one person **2** the person in charge at a meeting

chair *VERB* **chairs, chairing, chaired** be in control of a meeting • *Who will chair this meeting?*

chairman *NOUN* **chairmen** the person who is in control of a meeting
▷ **chairmanship** *NOUN*
USAGE The word **chairman** may be used of a man or of a woman; they are addressed formally as *Mr Chairman* and *Madam Chairman*

chairperson *NOUN* **chairpersons** a chairman

chalk *NOUN* **chalks 1** a soft white or coloured stick used for writing on blackboards or for drawing **2** soft white limestone
▷ **chalky** *ADJECTIVE*

challenge *NOUN* **challenges 1** a call to someone to take part in a contest **2** a task or activity that is new and exciting but also difficult

challenge *VERB* **challenges, challenging, challenged 1** make a challenge to someone **2** be a challenge to someone **3** question whether something is true or correct
▷ **challenger** *NOUN*

chamber *NOUN* **chambers 1** (*old use*) a room **2** a hall used for meetings of a parliament etc.; the members of the group using it **3** a compartment in machinery etc.

chambermaid *NOUN* **chambermaids** a woman employed to clean bedrooms at a hotel etc.

chamber music *NOUN* classical music for a small group of players

chamber pot *NOUN* **chamber pots** a receptacle for urine etc., used in a bedroom

chameleon (kam- ee- lee- on) *NOUN* **chameleons** a small lizard that can change its colour to that of its surroundings

champagne (sham- payn) *NOUN* a bubbly white wine, especially from the Champagne region in France

champion *NOUN* **champions 1** a person or thing that has defeated all the others in a sport or competition etc. **2** someone who supports a cause by fighting, speaking, etc.
▷ **championship** *NOUN*

champion *VERB* **champions, championing, championed** support a cause by fighting or speaking for it

chance *NOUN* **chances 1** an opportunity or possibility • *Now is your chance to escape.* **2** the way things happen without being planned • *I met her by chance.*
take a chance take a risk

chancellor *NOUN* **chancellors 1** an important government or legal official **2** the chief minister of the government in some European countries
Chancellor of the Exchequer the government minister in charge of a country's finances
[from Latin *cancellarius* = secretary]

Thesaurus

chain *VERB* *The bicycle was chained to a fence.* ► tie, fasten, secure, hitch, tether, manacle, fetter

challenge *VERB* **1** *The woman had challenged an intruder.* ► accost, confront, take on **2** *It was a job that would challenge their abilities.* ► test, tax, try, stretch **3** *He challenged one of the men to a duel.* ► dare, summon, invite, defy, provoke **4** *We will have to challenge the decision.* ► dispute, oppose, object to, protest against, query, question, disagree with, argue against, dissent from

champion *NOUN* **1** *the world champion* ► title-holder, victor, conqueror, winner **2** *a champion of reform* ► supporter, advocate, defender, upholder, patron, backer, guardian, protector

champion *VERB* *a charity championing the rights of asylum-seekers* ► support, promote, uphold, defend, campaign for, fight for, stand up for, advance, espouse, protect

chance *ADJECTIVE* *a chance discovery* ► accidental, fortuitous, coincidental, casual, incidental, unintentional, unforeseen, random
OPPOSITES ARE intentional, planned

chance *NOUN* **1** *There is a slight chance of snow.* ► possibility, likelihood, probability, prospect, risk, danger **2** *Give them a chance to answer.* ► opportunity, time, turn, occasion **3** *We were taking an awful chance.* ► risk, gamble
by chance *I found the earring by chance.* ► by accident, accidentally, fortuitously, inadvertently, unwittingly

chancy *ADJECTIVE* (*informal*) *It was chancy taking a shortcut across the meadow in the dark.* ► risky, dangerous, hazardous, unsafe, precarious, insecure, tricky, uncertain, unpredictable,

change *VERB* **changes, changing, changed** **1** make or become different **2** exchange **3** put on different clothes **4** go from one train or bus etc. to another **5** give smaller units of money, or money in another currency, for an amount of money • *Can you change £20?*

change *NOUN* **changes** **1** changing; a difference in doing something **2** coins or notes of small values **3** money given back to the payer when the price is less than the amount handed over **4** a fresh set of clothes **5** a variation in routine • *Let's walk home for a change.*

changeable *ADJECTIVE* likely to change; changing frequently • *changeable weather*

channel *NOUN* **channels** **1** a stretch of water connecting two seas **2** a broadcasting wavelength **3** a way for water to flow along **4** the part of a river or sea etc. that is deep enough for ships

channel *VERB* **channels, channelling, channelled** **1** make a channel in something **2** direct something through a channel or other route

chant *NOUN* **chants** **1** a tune to which words with no regular rhythm are fitted, especially one used in church music **2** a rhythmic call or shout

chant *VERB* **chants, chanting, chanted** **1** sing **2** call out words in a rhythm

chaos (kay- oss) *NOUN* great disorder
▷ **chaotic** *ADJECTIVE* **chaotically** *ADVERB*
[from Greek, = vast chasm or pit]

chap *NOUN* **chaps** (*informal*) a man

chapatti *NOUN* **chapattis** a flat cake of unleavened bread, used in Indian cookery

chapel *NOUN* **chapels** **1** a small building or room used for Christian worship **2** a section of a large church, with its own altar [via early French *chapele* from Latin *capella* = little cloak: the first chapel had as a relic the cloak of St Martin]

chaplain *NOUN* **chaplains** a member of the clergy who regularly works in a college, hospital, prison, regiment, etc.

chapped *ADJECTIVE* with skin split or cracked from cold etc.

chapter *NOUN* **chapters** **1** a division of a book **2** the clergy of a cathedral or members of a monastery. The room where they meet is called a **chapter house**

character *NOUN* **characters** **1** a person in a story, film, or play **2** all the qualities that make

Thesaurus

(*more informal*) dicey OPPOSITES ARE safe, predictable

change *NOUN* **1** *a change of plan* ► alteration, modification, variation, revision, amendment (to), replacement (for) **2** *We'd like a change.* ► diversion, novelty, innovation, variety **3** *I've got no change for the bus.* ► coins, small change, loose change

change *VERB* **1** *These events have changed the world for ever.* ► alter, make different, transform, modify, reshape, refashion, reorder **2** *Things have changed a lot since we were last here.* ► alter, become different, develop, fluctuate, (*more informal*) move on **3** *I need to change my library book.* ► exchange, swap, substitute, switch, replace

changeable *ADJECTIVE* *The weather is very changeable.* ► variable, unsettled, unpredictable, unreliable, temperamental, volatile

channel *NOUN* **1** *a water channel* ► duct, conduit, gully, gutter, furrow, flume **2** *a channel of communication* ► medium, avenue, means, route, path, way **3** *a television channel* ► station, waveband, wavelength

chaos *NOUN* *When we arrived on the scene there was total chaos.* ► confusion, disorder, mayhem, muddle, bedlam, pandemonium, anarchy, disorganization, lawlessness, shambles, tumult AN OPPOSITE IS order

chaotic *ADJECTIVE* **1** *A good party is a chaotic jumble of noise and movement.* ► disorderly, confused, disorganized, disordered, topsy-turvy, uncontrolled, muddled, tumultuous OPPOSITES ARE organized, orderly **2** *The country was in a chaotic state for years.* ► anarchic, lawless, unruly, uncontrolled AN OPPOSITE IS orderly

chap *NOUN* (*informal*) *Some chap gave it to me.* ► man, boy, individual, bloke

chapter *NOUN* **1** *a chapter of a book* ► section, part, division **2** *a new chapter in the nation's history* ► stage, phase, period, era, epoch

character *NOUN* **1** *Jane has a forceful character.* ► personality, temperament, nature, temper **2** *The trees and parks add a special character to the town.* ► distinctiveness, individuality, uniqueness, stamp, feature **3** *He was acquitted without a stain on his character.* ► reputation, name, standing, stature, position **4** (*informal*) *The new doctor is a charming character.* ► person, individual, being, sort, type, fellow, (*more informal*) bloke, (*more informal*) chap **5** (*informal*) *Her father is something of a character.* ► eccentric, oddity, (*more informal*) oddball, (*more informal*) case **6** *a woman of character* ► integrity, honour, quality **7** *She has played several characters in the same play.* ► part, role **8** *The sign was printed in Greek characters.* ► letter, figure, symbol

a person or thing what he, she, or it is **3** a letter of the alphabet or other written symbol

characteristic *NOUN* **characteristics** a quality that forms part of a person's or thing's character

characteristic *ADJECTIVE* typical of a person or thing
▷ **characteristically** *ADVERB*

charade (sha-rahd) *NOUN* **charades 1** a scene in the game of **charades**, in which people try to guess a word from other people's acting **2** a pretence

charcoal *NOUN* a black substance made by burning wood slowly. Charcoal can be used for drawing with.

charge *NOUN* **charges 1** the price asked for something **2** a rushing attack **3** the amount of explosive needed to fire a gun etc. **4** electricity in something **5** an accusation that someone has committed a crime **6** a person or thing in someone's care
in charge in control; deciding what shall happen to a person or thing

charge *VERB* **charges, charging, charged 1** ask a particular price **2** rush forward in an attack **3** give an electric charge to something **4** accuse someone of committing a crime **5** entrust someone with a responsibility or task

chariot *NOUN* **chariots** a horse-drawn vehicle with two wheels, used in ancient times for fighting, racing, etc.
▷ **charioteer** *NOUN*

charity *NOUN* **charities 1** an organization set up to help people who are poor, ill, or disabled or have suffered a disaster **2** giving money or help etc. to the needy **3** kindness and sympathy towards others; being unwilling to think badly of people
▷ **charitable** *ADJECTIVE* **charitably** *ADVERB*

charm *NOUN* **charms 1** the power to please or delight people; attractiveness **2** a magic spell **3** a small object believed to bring good luck **4** an ornament worn on a bracelet etc.

charm *VERB* **charms, charming, charmed 1** give pleasure or delight to people **2** put a

Thesaurus

characteristic *ADJECTIVE He spoke with his characteristic eloquence.* ► typical, distinctive, usual, normal, particular, singular, special, individual, peculiar, recognizable, specific, unique, distinguishing, essential, idiosyncratic

characteristic *NOUN The building has some interesting characteristics.* ► feature, peculiarity, trait, attribute, distinguishing feature, property, aspect, hallmark, idiosyncrasy

characterize *VERB* **1** *The film characterizes the king as a cruel dictator.* ► portray, depict, represent, describe, categorize, delineate, draw, present **2** *The period after the War was characterized by great social hardship.* ► distinguish, mark, identify, set apart, brand, differentiate, individualize, recognize, typify

charge *NOUN* **1** *Our charges will increase from next April.* ► fee, price, cost, tariff **2** *The children were left in their sister's charge.* ► care, protection, custody, keeping, surveillance, command, control, responsibility, safe-keeping, trust **3** *The company's directors face criminal charges.* ► accusation, allegation, indictment, imputation **4** *The infantry suffered heavy casualties in the charge.* ► assault, attack, onslaught, offensive, rush, sortie, raid
in charge of *He was in charge of the factory during his father's absence.* ► responsible for, in control of, managing, running, looking after

charge *VERB* **1** *What do they charge for a coffee?* ► ask for, ask in payment, make you pay, exact, levy, require **2** *They charged him with producing a video of the event.* ► entrust, burden, saddle, tax, empower **3** *The witness was later charged with perjury.* ► accuse (of), prosecute (for), indict (for), put on trial (for) **4** *The mounted cavalry charged the enemy line.* ► attack, storm, rush, assault, assail, fall on, set on

charitable *ADJECTIVE* **1** *a charitable activity* ► philanthropic, humanitarian, benevolent **2** *a charitable attitude* ► generous, magnanimous, friendly, liberal, benign, considerate, compassionate, understanding, broad-minded

charity *NOUN* **1** *Show some charity towards those in need.* ► goodwill, generosity, consideration, kindness, sympathy, compassion, fellow feeling AN OPPOSITE IS selfishness **2** *The church depends on the charity of parishioners.* ► financial assistance, generosity, donations, contributions, subsidies, patronage

charm *NOUN* **1** *As he relaxed, his charm and humour returned.* ► attractiveness, appeal, allure, lure, charisma, desirability, fascination, enchantment **2** *magical charms* ► spell, incantation, **3** *a lucky charm* ► trinket, talisman, amulet, mascot, idol

charm *VERB He charmed everyone with his stories.* ► delight, please, captivate, bewitch, enchant, entrance, enthral, mesmerize OPPOSITES ARE repel, disgust

charming *ADJECTIVE My mother tells me that I was a charming baby.* ► delightful, attractive, pleasant, pleasing, endearing, alluring, disarming, likeable

spell on someone; bewitch
▷ **charmer** *NOUN*

chart *NOUN* **charts** **1** a map for people sailing ships or flying aircraft **2** an outline map showing special information • *a weather chart* **3** a diagram, list, or table giving information in an orderly way
the charts a list of the records that are most popular

chart *VERB* **charts, charting, charted** make a chart of something; map

charter *NOUN* **charters** **1** an official document giving somebody certain rights etc. **2** chartering an aircraft, ship, or vehicle

charter *VERB* **charters, chartering, chartered** **1** hire an aircraft, ship, or vehicle **2** give a charter to someone

charwoman *NOUN* **charwomen** a woman employed as a cleaner

chase *VERB* **chases, chasing, chased** go quickly after a person or thing in order to capture or catch them up or drive them away
▷ **chase** *NOUN*

chasm (kazm) *NOUN* **chasms** a deep opening in the ground

chassis (shas- ee) *NOUN* **chassis** the framework under a car etc., on which other parts are mounted

chaste *ADJECTIVE* not having sexual intercourse at all, or only with the person you are married to
▷ **chastity** *NOUN*

chat *NOUN* **chats** a friendly conversation

chat *VERB* **chats, chatting, chatted** have a friendly conversation

chatter *VERB* **chatters, chattering, chattered** **1** talk quickly about unimportant things; keep on talking **2** (said about the teeth) make a rattling sound because you are cold or frightened
▷ **chatterer** *NOUN*

chatter *NOUN* chattering talk or sound

chauvinism (shoh- vin- izm) *NOUN* **1** prejudiced belief that your own country is superior to others **2** the belief of some men that men are superior to women
▷ **chauvinist** *NOUN* **chauvinistic** *ADJECTIVE*

cheap *ADJECTIVE* **1** low in price; not expensive **2** of poor quality; of low value
▷ **cheaply** *ADVERB* **cheapness** *NOUN*

cheapen *VERB* **cheapens, cheapening, cheapened** make cheap

cheat *VERB* **cheats, cheating, cheated** **1** try to do well in an examination or game by breaking the rules **2** trick or deceive somebody so they lose something

cheat *NOUN* **cheats** a person who cheats

check[1] *VERB* **checks, checking, checked** **1** make sure that something is correct or in

Thesaurus

chart *NOUN* **1** *a flow chart* ► diagram, graph, plan, table **2** *a weather chart* ► map

chary *ADJECTIVE* *She was chary about lending him any more money.* ► wary, cautious, doubtful, dubious, careful, hesitant, guarded
AN OPPOSITE IS heedless

chase *VERB* *The farmer chased the intruders across a field.* ► pursue, run after, track, trail, drive, follow, hound, hunt
chase around *I've been chasing around all morning trying to finish my work.* ► rush, hurry, bustle, scamper

chat *VERB* *We spent hours chatting about nothing in particular.* ► talk, gossip, chatter, (*more informal*) jabber, (*more informal*) babble
chat up (*informal*) • *He tried to chat Jenny up in the bus queue.* ► flirt with, make up to, make advances to

chat *NOUN* *I needed to have a chat with her.* ► talk, conversation, chatter, (*more informal*) natter, (*more informal*) chinwag

chatter *VERB* *Some of the people stayed chattering at one end of the room.* ► talk, gossip, chat, (*more informal*) jabber, (*more informal*) babble

chatty *ADJECTIVE* (*informal*) *She seemed to be in a chatty mood.* ► talkative, communicative, effusive, expansive, open, friendly

cheap *ADJECTIVE* **1** *a cheap edition of Shakespeare's works* ► inexpensive, economical, low-priced, affordable, reasonable **2** *racks of cheap digital watches* ► inferior, second-rate, shoddy, vulgar, tawdry, (*more informal*) tatty, (*more informal*) tacky **3** *cheap tabloid journalism* ► mean, despicable, low, contemptible, tasteless **4** *They made us feel cheap.* ► ashamed, embarrassed, humiliated, degraded

cheat *VERB* *Some dealers are cheating their customers.* ► swindle, defraud, deceive, exploit, hoodwink, short-change, dupe, (*more informal*) con, (*more informal*) rip off

cheat *NOUN* **1** *He called his brother a cheat.* ► swindler, deceiver, fraud, charlatan, impostor, (*more informal*) phoney **2** *The scheme was really a bit of a cheat.* ► deception, deceit, fraud, pretence, hoax, trick, (*more informal*) racket, (*more informal*) fiddle

check *VERB* **1** *Police were checking vehicles at roadblocks.* ► examine, inspect, test, look over, scrutinize, scan, investigate **2** *I'll check the answers against this list.* ► verify, confirm, test, compare **3** *He checked an impulse to look round.* ► resist, control, suppress, restrain, curb, repress, stifle **4** *Extensive flooding checked their*

a b c d e f g h i j k l m n o p q r s t u v w x y z

good condition **2** make something stop or go slower **3** in chess, put an opponent's king in check

check *NOUN* **checks 1** checking something **2** stopping or slowing; a pause **3** a receipt; a bill in a restaurant **4** in chess, the situation in which a king is threatened with capture [via early French from a Persian word meaning 'king': the chess meaning is the oldest]

check[2] *NOUN* **checks** a pattern of squares
▷ **checked** *ADJECTIVE*

checkmate *NOUN* the winning situation in chess
▷ **checkmate** *VERB*

checkout *NOUN* **checkouts** a place where goods are paid for in a self-service shop

check-up *NOUN* **check-ups** a routine medical or dental examination

cheek *NOUN* **cheeks 1** the side of the face below the eye **2** rude or disrespectful behaviour; impudence

cheeky *ADJECTIVE* rude or disrespectful; impudent
▷ **cheekily** *ADVERB* **cheekiness** *NOUN*

cheer *NOUN* **cheers 1** a shout of praise or pleasure or encouragement **2** cheerfulness
• *full of good cheer*

cheer *VERB* **cheers, cheering, cheered 1** give a cheer **2** gladden or encourage somebody
cheer up make or become cheerful

cheerful *ADJECTIVE* **1** looking or sounding happy **2** pleasantly bright or colourful
▷ **cheerfully** *ADVERB* **cheerfulness** *NOUN*

cheerless *ADJECTIVE* gloomy or dreary

cheery *ADJECTIVE* bright and cheerful

cheese *NOUN* **cheeses** a solid food made from milk

cheetah *NOUN* **cheetahs** a large spotted animal of the cat family that can run extremely fast

chemical *ADJECTIVE* to do with or produced by chemistry

chemical *NOUN* **chemicals** a substance obtained by or used in chemistry

chemist *NOUN* **chemists 1** a person who makes or sells medicines **2** a shop selling medicines, cosmetics, etc. **3** an expert in chemistry

chemistry *NOUN* **1** the way that substances combine and react with one another **2** the study of substances and their reactions etc.

chemotherapy *NOUN* the treatment of disease, especially cancer, by the use of chemical substances

cheque *NOUN* **cheques** a printed form on which you write instructions to a bank to pay out money from your account

cherish *VERB* **cherishes, cherishing, cherished 1** look after a person or thing lovingly **2** be fond of

cherry *NOUN* **cherries** a small soft round fruit with a stone

Thesaurus

progress. ► hinder, obstruct, hamper, impede, restrict, inhibit, frustrate

check *NOUN* **1** *There will be an official check of documents at the border.* ► inspection, examination, scrutiny, perusal, investigation **2** *a check on the abuse of power* ► curb, restraint, control

check-up *NOUN* *The car goes for a check-up next week.* ► check, inspection, examination, overhaul

cheek *NOUN* (*informal*) *He had the cheek to tell me to leave.* ► audacity, effrontery, nerve, temerity, impertinence, impudence, insolence, presumptuousness, shamelessness, (*more informal*) sauce

cheeky *ADJECTIVE* *A cheeky boy from down the road called after him.* ► impudent, impertinent, insolent, impolite, disrespectful, brazen, audacious, forward, pert

cheer *VERB* **1** *We'll be there to cheer our team.* ► applaud, acclaim, clap, shout **2** *The good news cheered them a great deal.* ► comfort, console, gladden, delight, encourage, uplift, exhilarate, make cheerful, please, solace
AN OPPOSITE IS sadden
cheer up *As I reached home I began to cheer up.* ► take heart, become more cheerful, perk up, brighten, rally, revive

cheer *NOUN* *The spectators gave her a cheer.* ► hurrah, cry of approval, shout of approval, ovation, acclamation, applause, encouragement

cheerful *ADJECTIVE* *They arrived looking cheerful. It was a cheerful occasion.* ► happy, jolly, glad, joyful, joyous, lively, elated, animated, contented, buoyant, good-humoured, light-hearted, chirpy OPPOSITES ARE sad, dejected

cheerless *ADJECTIVE* *The town was a nondescript cheerless place.* ► dreary, dull, gloomy, bleak, dismal, grim, sombre, dingy, drab, stark, desolate AN OPPOSITE IS cheerful

cheery *ADJECTIVE* *She answered the phone with a cheery 'Good morning'.* ► cheerful, jolly, merry, spirited, jaunty, carefree, happy, sunny, joyful, joyous

cherish *VERB* **1** *His friends all cherished him.* ► adore, love, be devoted to, be fond of, hold dear, care for, foster, keep safe, look after, nourish, nurse, protect **2** *I shall cherish this gift all my life.* ► treasure, value, prize

chess *NOUN* a game for two players with sixteen pieces each (called **chessmen**) on a board of 64 squares (a **chessboard**)

chest *NOUN* **chests** **1** the front part of the body between the neck and the waist **2** a large strong box for storing things in

chestnut *NOUN* **chestnuts** **1** a tree that produces hard brown nuts **2** the nut of this tree **3** an old joke or story

chest of drawers *NOUN* **chests of drawers** a piece of furniture with drawers for storing clothes etc.

chew *VERB* **chews, chewing, chewed** grind food between the teeth
▷ **chewy** *ADJECTIVE*

chewing gum *NOUN* a sticky flavoured type of sweet for chewing

chick *NOUN* **chicks** a very young bird

chicken *NOUN* **chickens** **1** a young hen **2** a hen's flesh used as food

chicken *ADJECTIVE* (*slang*) afraid to do something; cowardly

chicken *VERB* **chickens, chickening, chickened**
chicken out (*slang*) not take part in something because you are afraid

chickenpox *NOUN* a disease that produces red spots on the skin

chief *NOUN* **chiefs** **1** a leader or ruler of a people, especially of a Native American tribe **2** a person with the highest rank or authority

chief *ADJECTIVE* most important; main
▷ **chiefly** *ADVERB*

chieftain *NOUN* **chieftains** the chief of a tribe or clan

child *NOUN* **children** **1** a young person; a boy or girl **2** someone's son or daughter

childhood *NOUN* **childhoods** the time when a person is a child

childish *ADJECTIVE* **1** like a child; unsuitable for a grown person **2** silly and immature
▷ **childishly** *ADVERB*

childminder *NOUN* **childminders** a person who is paid to look after children while their parents are out at work

chill *NOUN* **chills** **1** unpleasant coldness **2** an illness that makes you shiver

chill *VERB* **chills, chilling, chilled** make a person or thing cold

chilli *NOUN* **chillies** the hot-tasting pod of a red pepper [via Spanish from Nahuatl (a Central American language)]

chilly *ADJECTIVE* **1** rather cold **2** unfriendly • *We got a chilly reception.*
▷ **chilliness** *NOUN*

chime *NOUN* **chimes** a series of notes sounded by a set of bells each making a different musical sound

Thesaurus

chest *NOUN* **1** *The ball hit him in the chest.* ► breast, ribcage RELATED ADJECTIVE pectoral **2** *a large chest of tools* ► case, crate, box, casket, coffer, strongbox, trunk

chew *VERB* *Claire was chewing a piece of bread.* ► eat, munch, nibble, champ, bite, crunch, gnaw, (*more formal*) masticate

chief *ADJECTIVE* **1** *Money was the chief problem.* ► main, principal, primary, prime, most important, overriding, foremost, fundamental, key, crucial, central, paramount, predominant, basic, essential **2** *the chief cook* ► head, senior, principal, leading

chief *NOUN* *He is the chief of a merchant bank.* ► head, principal, president, chairman, chief executive

chiefly *ADVERB* *Dogs were chiefly to blame for the damage.* ► mainly, mostly, primarily, principally, predominantly, especially, essentially

child *NOUN* **1** *She was only a child when I last saw her.* ► youngster, girl (or boy), baby, infant, little one, (*more informal*) kid, (*more informal*) nipper, (*more informal*) tot RELATED ADJECTIVE juvenile **2** *She is the child of Greek parents.* ► offspring, progeny, daughter (or son), descendant, heir, issue

childish *ADJECTIVE* *It was childish of him to say that.* ► immature, babyish, puerile, infantile, juvenile, silly, foolish AN OPPOSITE IS mature
USAGE Note that *childish* is normally an unfavourable word, whereas *childlike* is favourable or neutral in tone.

childlike *ADJECTIVE* *a world of childlike simplicity* ► innocent, naive, artless, guileless, ingenuous, trusting OPPOSITES ARE artful, disingenuous

chill *NOUN* **1** *We felt a distinct chill in the air.* ► coldness, chilliness, coolness, crispness, rawness, bite, nip **2** *She decided to stay at home because of her chill.* ► cold, flu

chill *VERB* *The drinks need to be chilled.* ► cool, refrigerate, ice, freeze, make cold
AN OPPOSITE IS warm

chilly *ADJECTIVE* **1** *a chilly evening in March* ► cold, crisp, sharp, fresh, cool, frosty, icy, raw, (*more informal*) nippy, (*more informal*) parky
AN OPPOSITE IS warm **2** *You may get a chilly reception.* ► unfriendly, cool, lukewarm, unwelcoming, frigid, hostile, unsympathetic, reserved, aloof, (*informal*) standoffish
OPPOSITES ARE warm, friendly, enthusiastic

chimney *NOUN* **chimneys** a tall pipe or structure that carries smoke away from a fire

chimney pot *NOUN* **chimney pots** a pipe fitted to the top of a chimney

chimpanzee *NOUN* **chimpanzees** an African ape, smaller than a gorilla

chin *NOUN* **chins** the lower part of the face below the mouth

china *NOUN* thin delicate pottery

chink *NOUN* **chinks** **1** a narrow opening • *a chink in the curtains* **2** a chinking sound

chink *VERB* **chinks, chinking, chinked** make a sound like glasses or coins being struck together

chip *NOUN* **chips** **1** a thin piece cut or broken off something hard **2** a fried oblong strip of potato **3** a place where a small piece has been knocked off something **4** a small counter used in games **5** a microchip
a chip off the old block a child who is very like their father or mother
have a chip on your shoulder feel resentful or defensive about something

chip *VERB* **chips, chipping, chipped** **1** knock small pieces off something **2** cut a potato into chips

chipolata *NOUN* **chipolatas** a small spicy sausage

chiropody (ki- rop- od- ee) *NOUN* medical treatment of the feet, e.g. corns
▷ **chiropodist** *NOUN*

chirp *VERB* **chirps, chirping, chirped** make short sharp sounds like a small bird
▷ **chirp** *NOUN*

chisel *NOUN* **chisels** a tool with a sharp end for shaping wood, stone, etc.

chisel *VERB* **chisels, chiselling, chiselled** shape or cut something with a chisel

chivalrous (shiv- al- rus) *ADJECTIVE* being considerate and helpful towards people less strong than yourself
▷ **chivalry** *NOUN*

chlorine (klor- een) *NOUN* a greenish-yellow gas used to disinfect water etc.

chloroform (klo- ro- form) *NOUN* a liquid that gives off a vapour that makes people unconscious

chlorophyll (klo- ro- fil) *NOUN* the substance that makes plants green

chock-full *ADJECTIVE* crammed full

chocolate *NOUN* **chocolates** **1** a solid brown food or powder made from roasted cacao seeds **2** a drink made with this powder **3** a sweet made of or covered with chocolate [via French or Spanish from Nahuatl (a Central American language)]

choice *NOUN* **choices** **1** choosing between things **2** the range of things from which someone can choose • *There is a wide choice of holidays.* **3** a person or thing chosen

choice *ADJECTIVE* of the best quality • *choice bananas*

choir *NOUN* **choirs** a group of people trained to sing together, especially in a church
▷ **choirboy** *NOUN* **choirgirl** *NOUN*

choke *VERB* **chokes, choking, choked** **1** cause somebody to stop breathing properly **2** be unable to breathe properly **3** clog

choke *NOUN* **chokes** a device controlling the flow of air into the engine of a motor vehicle

cholera (kol- er- a) *NOUN* an infectious disease that is often fatal

cholesterol (kol- est- er- ol) *NOUN* a fatty substance that can clog the arteries

choose *VERB* **chooses, choosing, chose, chosen** decide which you are going to take

Thesaurus

chip *NOUN* **1** *a chip of wood* ► fragment, piece, bit, sliver, splinter, slice, flake, fleck, scrap, shaving **2** *The cup had a chip in it.* ► crack, nick, flaw, scratch, gash, notch, snick

chip *VERB* *Someone had chipped the teapot.* ► crack, nick, scratch, splinter, notch, damage

chirpy *ADJECTIVE* *She came in with a chirpy grin.* ► cheerful, happy, jolly, glad, joyful, joyous, lively, elated

chivalrous *ADJECTIVE* *He treated everyone in the same chivalrous manner.* ► gallant, courteous, polite, honorable, considerate, gracious, thoughtful OPPOSITES ARE dishonourable, rude

chivalry *NOUN* *Where is your sense of chivalry Roger?* ► gallantry, courtesy, politeness, consideration, graciousness, thoughtfulness

choice *NOUN* **1** *We have no other choice now.* ► option, alternative, possibility, answer **2** *the viewers' choice of programmes* ► selection, choosing, preference, election **3** *Write in with your choice.* ► decision, selection, vote, nomination **4** *a wide choice of good food* ► range, variety, selection, array, assortment, display

choke *VERB* **1** *The dust was nearly choking them.* ► suffocate, asphyxiate, smother, stifle **2** *There was a danger of the necklace choking her to death.* ► strangle, throttle, suffocate, asphyxiate **3** *Oliver choked and had to be thumped on the back.* ► gag, gasp, retch, suffocate **4** *The motorways are constantly choked with traffic.* ► clog, congest, constrict, block, obstruct
choke back *Sandra choked back the tears as she tried to answer.* ► stifle, suppress, fight back, hold back

from among a number of people or things
▷ **choosy** *ADJECTIVE*

chop *VERB* **chops, chopping, chopped** cut or hit something with a heavy blow

chop *NOUN* **chops 1** a chopping blow **2** a small thick slice of meat, usually on a rib

choppy *ADJECTIVE* **choppier, choppiest** (said about the sea) not smooth; full of small waves
▷ **choppiness** *NOUN*

chopsticks *PLURAL NOUN* a pair of thin sticks used for lifting Chinese and Japanese food to your mouth

choral *ADJECTIVE* to do with or sung by a choir or chorus

chord[1] (kord) *NOUN* **chords** a number of musical notes sounded together

chord[2] (kord) *NOUN* **chords** a straight line joining two points on a curve
USAGE Do not confuse with **cord**.

chore (chor) *NOUN* **chores** a regular or dull task

choreography (ko- ree- og- ra- fee) *NOUN* the art of writing the steps for ballets or stage dances
▷ **choreographer** *NOUN*

chorus *NOUN* **choruses 1** the words repeated after each verse of a song or poem **2** music sung by a group of people **3** a group singing together

chorus *VERB* **choruses, chorusing, chorused** sing or speak in chorus

christen *VERB* **christens, christening, christened 1** baptize **2** give a name or nickname to a person or thing
▷ **christening** *NOUN*

Christian *NOUN* **Christians** a person who believes in Jesus Christ and his teachings

Christian *ADJECTIVE* to do with Christians or their beliefs
▷ **Christianity** *NOUN*

Christian name *NOUN* **Christian names** a name given to a person at his or her christening; a person's first name

Christmas *NOUN* **Christmases** the day (25 December) when Christians commemorate the birth of Jesus Christ; the days round it

Christmas pudding *NOUN* **Christmas puddings** a dark pudding containing dried fruit etc., eaten at Christmas

Christmas tree *NOUN* **Christmas trees** an evergreen or artificial tree decorated at Christmas

chromatic (krom- at- ik) *ADJECTIVE* to do with colours
chromatic scale *NOUN* a musical scale going up or down in semitones

chromium (kroh- mee- um) *NOUN* a shiny silvery metal

chromosome (kroh- mos- ohm) *NOUN* **chromosomes** a tiny thread-like part of an animal cell or plant cell, carrying genes

chronic *ADJECTIVE* lasting for a long time • *a chronic illness*
▷ **chronically** *ADVERB*

chronicle *NOUN* **chronicles** a record of events in the order that they happened

chronology (kron- ol- oj- ee) *NOUN* the order of events in the sequence in which they happened, e.g. in history
▷ **chronological** *ADJECTIVE*

chrysalis *NOUN* **chrysalises** the hard cover a caterpillar makes round itself before it changes into a butterfly or moth

chrysanthemum *NOUN* **chrysanthemums** a garden flower that blooms in autumn

chubby *ADJECTIVE* **chubbier, chubbiest** plump
▷ **chubbiness** *NOUN*

Thesaurus

choose *VERB* **1** *We chose a quiet spot by the river.* ► pick, pick out, select, opt for, plump for, go for, settle on, fix on, decide on **2** *Mark chose to go in first.* ► decide, elect, make up your mind, determine, prefer, resolve, see fit

chop *VERB* **1** *He was in the yard chopping wood.* ► cut, hew **2** *Chop the vegetables into small chunks.* ► cut up, slice, split, dice
chop down *The tree should be chopped down.* ► cut down, fell
chop off *His arm had been chopped off in an accident.* ► sever, amputate, detach, lop off

chopper *NOUN* *He cut up the logs with a chopper.* ► axe, cleaver

chore *NOUN* *I spent the day cooking and doing household chores.* ► task, job, duty, burden, errand

chorus *NOUN* **1** *The chorus sang well.* ► choir, choral group, choral society, vocal ensemble **2** *Everyone can join in the choruses.* ► refrain, response

christen *VERB* **1** *The church in which Tania was christened.* ► baptize, name **2** *His friends christened him 'The King'* ► name, dub, style, designate

chronic *ADJECTIVE* **1** *a chronic illness* ► persistent, long-standing, lifelong, lingering, incurable
OPPOSITES ARE acute, temporary **2** *chronic food shortages* ► constant, persistent, continuous, continual

chubby *ADJECTIVE* *a chubby little baby* ► plump, tubby, podgy, round, dumpy, portly, rotund, stout, buxom

a b c d e f g h i j k l m n o p q r s t u v w x y z

chuckle *NOUN* **chuckles** a quiet laugh

chuckle *VERB* **chuckles, chuckling, chuckled** laugh quietly

chum *NOUN* **chums** (*informal*) a friend
▷ **chummy** *ADJECTIVE*

chunk *NOUN* **chunks** a thick piece of something
▷ **chunky** *ADJECTIVE*

church *NOUN* **churches** **1** a public building for Christian worship **2** a religious service in a church • *I will see you after church.* **3** a particular Christian religion, e.g. the Church of England

churlish *ADJECTIVE* ill-mannered and unfriendly; surly

churn *NOUN* **churns** **1** a large can in which milk is carried from a farm **2** a machine in which milk is beaten to make butter

churn *VERB* **churns, churning, churned** **1** make butter in a churn **2** stir or swirl vigorously
churn out produce something in large quantities

chute (shoot) *NOUN* **chutes** a steep channel for people or things to slide down

chutney *NOUN* **chutneys** a strong-tasting mixture of fruit, peppers, etc., eaten with meat [from Hindi *chatni*]

cider *NOUN* **ciders** an alcoholic drink made from apples

cigar *NOUN* **cigars** a roll of compressed tobacco leaves for smoking

cigarette *NOUN* **cigarettes** a small roll of shredded tobacco in thin paper for smoking

cinder *NOUN* **cinders** a small piece of partly burnt coal or wood

cine-camera (sin- ee) *NOUN* **cine-cameras** a camera used for taking moving pictures

cinema *NOUN* **cinemas** **1** a place where films are shown **2** the business or art of making films

cipher (sy- fer) *NOUN* **ciphers** **1** a kind of code **2** the symbol 0, representing nought or zero

circle *NOUN* **circles** **1** a perfectly round flat shape or thing **2** a number of people with similar interests **3** the balcony of a cinema or theatre

circle *VERB* **circles, circling, circled** move in a circle; go round something

circuit (ser- kit) *NOUN* **circuits** **1** a circular line or journey **2** a track for motor racing **3** the path of an electric current

circular *ADJECTIVE* **1** shaped like a circle; round **2** moving round a circle
▷ **circularity** *NOUN*

circular *NOUN* **circulars** a letter or advertisement etc. sent to a number of people

circulate *VERB* **circulates, circulating, circulated** **1** go round something continuously • *Blood circulates in the body.* **2** pass from place to place **3** send something round to a number of people

circulation *NOUN* **circulations** **1** the movement of blood around the body **2** the number of copies of each issue of a newspaper or magazine that are sold or distributed

circumcise *VERB* **circumcises, circumcising, circumcised** cut off the fold of skin at the tip of the penis
▷ **circumcision** *NOUN*

Thesaurus

chuck *VERB* (*informal*) *I'll chuck the letter in the bin.* ► throw, toss, fling, hurl, dump, sling
chuck out *There are a lot of old clothes to chuck out.* ► throw away, discard, dispose of, reject, scrap

chuckle *VERB* *Andrew chuckled as he left the room.* ► chortle, snigger, giggle, laugh

chunk *NOUN* *little chunks of cheese on a plate; a chunk of wood* ► lump, hunk, block, wedge, piece, portion, slab

churn *VERB*
churn up *The propellers churned up the water.* ► agitate, stir up, disturb
churn out *When he was young he churned out poem after poem.* ► produce, turn out

circle *NOUN* **1** *The children stood in a circle* ► ring, round RELATED ADJECTIVE circular **2** *He has a new circle of friends.* ► group, set, band, body, company, society, association, gang, party

circle *VERB* **1** *The birds circled over his head.* ► wheel, fly round, spiral **2** *Satellites circle the earth.* ► orbit, go round, circumnavigate, revolve round **3** *The grass was circled by trees.* ► surround, enclose, encircle, ring, skirt, girdle, hem in

circuit *NOUN* **1** *two circuits of the playing field* ► lap, turn, round, revolution **2** *a racing circuit* ► track, course

circular *ADJECTIVE* *a circular window* ► round, disc-shaped, ring-shaped USAGE You can also use *oval* and *elliptical* to describe a shape that is nearly circular but slightly flattened

circular *NOUN* *an advertising circular* ► advertisement, leaflet, letter, notice, pamphlet

circulate *VERB* *We circulated a notice about our sale.* ► send round, distribute, issue, publicize, publish, spread about, disseminate

circulation *NOUN* **1** *air circulation* ► flow, motion, movement, course **2** *the circulation of information* ► dissemination, distribution, spread, transmission, broadcasting **3** *a*

circumference *NOUN* **circumferences** the line or distance round something, especially round a circle

circumflex accent *NOUN* **circumflex accents** a mark over a vowel, as over *e* in *fête*

circumnavigate *VERB* **circumnavigates, circumnavigating, circumnavigated** sail completely round something
▷ **circumnavigation** *NOUN*

circumscribe *VERB* **circumscribes, circumscribing, circumscribed** **1** draw a line round something **2** limit or restrict something
• *Her powers are circumscribed by many regulations.*

circumspect *ADJECTIVE* cautious and watchful
▷ **circumspection** *NOUN*

circumstance *NOUN* **circumstances** a fact or condition connected with an event or person or action

circumstantial (ser- kum- stan- shal) *ADJECTIVE* consisting of facts that strongly suggest something but do not actually prove it
• *circumstantial evidence*

circus *NOUN* **circuses** a travelling show usually performed in a tent, with clowns, acrobats, and sometimes trained animals [from Latin, = ring; related to *circle*]

cistern *NOUN* **cisterns** a tank for storing water

citizen *NOUN* **citizens** a person belonging to a particular city or country
▷ **citizenship** *NOUN*

citrus fruit *NOUN* **citrus fruits** a lemon, orange, grapefruit, or other sharp-tasting fruit

city *NOUN* **cities** a large important town, usually with special rights given by a charter

civic *ADJECTIVE* **1** to do with a city or town **2** to do with citizens

civil *ADJECTIVE* **1** polite and courteous **2** to do with citizens **3** to do with civilians; not military
• *civil aviation*
▷ **civilly** *ADVERB*

civilian *NOUN* **civilians** a person who is not serving in the armed forces

civility *NOUN* **civilities** politeness

civilization *NOUN* **civilizations** **1** a society or culture at a particular time in history • *ancient civilizations.* **2** a developed or organized way of life • *We were far from civilization.*

civilize *VERB* **civilizes, civilizing, civilized** bring culture and education to a primitive community

Civil Service *NOUN* people employed by the government in various departments other than the armed forces

civil war *NOUN* **civil wars** war between groups of people of the same country

claim *VERB* **claims, claiming, claimed** **1** ask for something to which you believe you have a right **2** declare; state something without being able to prove it
▷ **claimant** *NOUN*

claim *NOUN* **claims** **1** claiming **2** something claimed **3** a piece of ground claimed or assigned to someone for mining etc.

clairvoyant *NOUN* **clairvoyants** a person who is said to be able to predict future events or communicate mentally with people who are dead or far away
▷ **clairvoyance** *NOUN*

Thesaurus

newspaper's circulation ► distribution, readership, sales figures

circumstances PLURAL NOUN **1** *the right economic circumstances* ► situation, conditions, state of affairs, factors, position, background **2** *The police wanted to know all the circumstances.* ► facts, details, particulars, incidents, events

citizen *NOUN* **1** *a British citizen* ► subject, national, taxpayer, voter RELATED ADJECTIVES civic, civil, civilian **2** *the citizens of Glasgow* ► inhabitant, resident, native, townsperson, householder

city *NOUN* *a large city north of the river* ► town, metropolis, conurbation RELATED ADJECTIVES civic, urban

civil *ADJECTIVE* **1** *I know you don't like her but try to be civil.* ► polite, respectful, well mannered, courteous, considerate, affable, civilized, refined, obliging OPPOSITES ARE impolite, rude **2** *a civil wedding* ► secular, non-religious **3** *civil rights* ► social, state, communal, national, public **4** *civil politics* ► domestic, home, internal, national, local

civilization *NOUN* **1** *ancient civilizations* ► culture, society, people **2** *advances in civilization* ► human development, human achievements, human attainments, enlightenment

civilized *ADJECTIVE* **1** *a civilized nation* ► advanced, developed, enlightened, cultured, refined AN OPPOSITE IS uncivilized **2** *civilized behaviour* ► polite, orderly

claim *VERB* **1** *You can claim a refund at the office.* ► ask for, request, demand, collect, require, take **2** *He claimed the witness had been lying.* ► allege, maintain, contend, assert, avow, protest, insist

claim *NOUN* **1** *a claim for damages; an insurance claim* ► application, demand, request **2** *Their*

clamber *VERB* **clambers, clambering, clambered** climb with difficulty

clammy *ADJECTIVE* damp and slimy

clamour *NOUN* **clamours 1** a loud confused noise **2** an outcry; a loud protest or demand
▷ **clamorous** *ADJECTIVE*

clamour *VERB* **clamours, clamouring, clamoured** make a loud protest or demand

clamp *NOUN* **clamps** a device for holding things tightly

clamp *VERB* **clamps, clamping, clamped 1** fix something with a clamp **2** fix something firmly **clamp down on** become stricter about something or put a stop to it

clan *NOUN* **clans** a group sharing the same ancestor, especially in Scotland

clang *NOUN* **clangs** a loud ringing sound
▷ **clang** *VERB*

clank *NOUN* **clanks** a sound like heavy pieces of metal banging together
▷ **clank** *VERB*

clap *VERB* **claps, clapping, clapped 1** strike the palms of the hands together loudly, especially as applause **2** slap in a friendly way • *She clapped him on the shoulder.* **3** put quickly • *They clapped him in gaol.*

clap *NOUN* **claps 1** a sudden sharp noise • *a clap of thunder.* **2** a round of clapping • *Give the winners a clap.* **3** a friendly slap

claret *NOUN* **clarets** a kind of red wine

clarify *VERB* **clarifies, clarifying, clarified** make something clear or easier to understand
▷ **clarification** *NOUN*

clarinet *NOUN* **clarinets** a woodwind instrument
▷ **clarinettist** *NOUN*

clarity *NOUN* clearness

clash *VERB* **clashes, clashing, clashed 1** make a loud sound like that of cymbals banging together **2** conflict **3** (said about two or more events) happen inconveniently at the same time **4** (said about colours) look unpleasant together
▷ **clash** *NOUN*

clasp *NOUN* **clasps 1** a device for fastening things, with parts that lock together **2** a tight grasp

clasp *VERB* **clasps, clasping, clasped 1** grasp or hold tightly **2** fasten with a clasp

class *NOUN* **classes 1** a group of children, students, etc. who are taught together **2** a group of similar people, animals, or things **3** people of the same social or economic level **4** level of quality • *first class*

Thesaurus

claim is hardly credible. ► assertion, allegation, contention, declaration

clammy *ADJECTIVE* **1** *They sat waiting with clammy hands for an hour and a half.* ► moist, sticky, sweaty, damp **2** *The atmosphere was cold and clammy.* ► dank, humid, damp, moist, muggy, slimy, sticky

clamp *VERB* *Each shelf is clamped to three brackets.* ► fasten, fix, secure, attach, clip
clamp down on *a plan to clamp down on illegal parking* ► reduce, suppress, end, stop, eradicate, get tough on, crack down on

clap *NOUN* **1** *a clap of thunder* ► crash, crack, boom, bang, thunderclap **2** *a clap on the shoulder* ► slap, thump, smack, blow

clap *VERB* **1** *The audience clapped her performance.* ► applaud, cheer, acclaim **2** *Someone clapped me on the shoulder.* ► slap, hit, pat, smack

claptrap *NOUN* (*informal*) *He was speaking claptrap.* ► nonsense, rubbish, gibberish, drivel, (*informal*) poppycock

clarify *VERB* *To clarify matters, let us ask some basic questions.* ► explain, throw light on, elucidate, make clear, gloss, illuminate, define
AN OPPOSITE IS confuse

clarity *NOUN* *She explained the problem with great clarity.* ► clearness, lucidity, transparency, intelligibility, simplicity, precision, coherence

clash *NOUN* **1** *There was a metallic clash as the two vehicles came together.* ► crash, striking, bang **2** *Clashes followed between students and riot police.* ► fight, conflict, hostilities, collision **3** *a clash between the president and his secretary of state* ► disagreement, altercation, argument, quarrel, exchange

clash *VERB* **1** *The cymbals clashed.* ► crash, strike, resound, bang **2** *The violence began outside a chip shop, when rival gangs clashed.* ► disagree, conflict, quarrel, wrangle, fight **3** *The interview clashes with my holiday.* ► coincide, conflict, come at the same time (as)

clasp *NOUN* **1** *The bracelet needs a strong clasp.* ► fastener, fastening, catch, hook, buckle, clip, hasp, pin **2** *His clasp loosened a bit, but he didn't let her go.* ► hold, grasp, grip, embrace, squeeze, hug, cuddle

clasp *VERB* **1** *John clasped the woman in his arms.* ► hug, hold, embrace, squeeze, cling to, clutch, enfold, grasp, grip **2** *Before leaving she clasped his hand for a few moments.* ► grasp, hold, grip, clutch

class *NOUN* **1** *Our hotel is quite good for its class.* ► category, grade, classification, group, section, division, status **2** *a new class of medicine* ► type, kind, sort, genre, species, genus **3** *discrimination on the basis of social class* ► status, standing, position, station, caste,

class *VERB* **classes, classing, classed** arrange things in classes or groups; classify

classic *ADJECTIVE* generally agreed to be excellent or important

classic *NOUN* **classics** a classic book, film, writer, etc.

classical *ADJECTIVE* **1** to do with ancient Greek or Roman literature, art, or history **2** serious or conventional in style • *classical music*

classified *ADJECTIVE* **1** put into classes or groups **2** (said about information) declared officially to be secret and available only to certain people

classify *VERB* **classifies, classifying, classified** arrange things in classes or groups
▷ **classification** *NOUN*

classroom *NOUN* **classrooms** a room where a class of children or students is taught

clatter *VERB* **clatters, clattering, clattered** make a sound like hard objects rattling together
▷ **clatter** *NOUN*

clause *NOUN* **clauses** **1** a single part of a treaty, law, or contract **2** part of a complex sentence, with its own verb • *There are two clauses in 'We choose what we want'.*

claustrophobia *NOUN* fear of being inside an enclosed space

claw *NOUN* **claws** **1** a sharp nail on a bird's or animal's foot **2** a claw-like part or device used for grasping

clay *NOUN* a kind of stiff sticky earth that becomes hard when baked, used for making bricks and pottery
▷ **clayey** *ADJECTIVE*

clean *ADJECTIVE* **1** without any dirt or marks or stains **2** fresh; not yet used **3** honourable; not unfair • *a clean fight* **4** not indecent **5** a clean catch is one made skilfully with no fumbling
▷ **cleanness** *NOUN*

clean *VERB* **cleans, cleaning, cleaned** make a thing clean

clean *ADVERB* completely • *I clean forgot*

Thesaurus

grouping **4** *a history class* ► form, set, group, stream

class *VERB* *Her performance was classed as a distinction.* ► classify, categorize, group, grade, designate, rank, label

classic *ADJECTIVE* **1** *the classic book on the subject; classic works of literature* ► definitive, outstanding, established, best, ideal, time-honoured, abiding, enduring **2** *a classic example of how a good idea has gone wrong* ► typical, characteristic, quintessential, archetypal, perfect

classic *NOUN* *The film has good points but is certainly not a classic.* ► masterpiece, masterwork, model

classical *ADJECTIVE* **1** *classical civilizations* ► ancient, Greek and Roman **2** *a classical style* ► traditional, simple, pure, restrained, elegant, well-proportioned **3** *classical music; classical ballet* ► traditional, established, harmonious, highbrow AN OPPOSITE IS modern

classification *NOUN* *the classification of volcanoes into active, dormant, and extinct; a system of classification* ► categorization, division, grading, ordering, organization, codification, taxonomy

classify *VERB* *We can classify the plants according to the shape of their leaves.* ► categorize, class, group, organize, grade, sort, catalogue, order

classy *ADJECTIVE* *a classy outfit* ► stylish, elegant, smart, chic, sophisticated, fashionable, high-class, (*more informal*) posh, (*more informal*) snazzy

clatter *VERB* *Something in the engine began to clatter.* ► rattle, clank, clunk

clause *NOUN* *There is an extra clause in the new contract.* ► section, article, condition, provision, proviso, subsection, paragraph, item, part, passage

claw *NOUN* **1** *a bird's claws* ► talon, nail **2** *a crab's claw* ► pincer, nipper

clean *ADJECTIVE* **1** *She went in to put on clean clothes.* ► washed, cleaned, laundered, pristine **2** *Keep the wound clean.* ► sterile, sterilized, healthy, uncontaminated **3** *Write your details on a clean sheet of paper.* ► blank, unused, empty, plain, fresh, bare **4** *The air is clean in the mountains.* ► pure, clear, fresh, untainted **5** *The family all led a clean life.* ► virtuous, honest, moral, decent, respectable, exemplary, blameless, upright, pure, innocent **6** *We hope for a clean fight.* ► fair, honest, sporting **7** *Make a clean cut with a sharp knife.* ► smooth, neat, tidy, straight, accurate **8** *I decided to make a clean break with the place.* ► complete, total, thorough, decisive, final

clean *VERB* **1** *I'll go and clean the car.* ► wash, sponge, hose down, shampoo, polish **2** *We'll have to clean the bathroom floor.* ► wash, wipe, sponge, scrub, sweep, mop, swab **3** *Put out the clothes you want to be cleaned.* ► launder, dry-clean **4** *The whole room needs cleaning.* ► dust, brush, spruce up **5** *Make sure you clean the wound.* ► cleanse, wash, bathe, disinfect, sanitize, purify

A B C D E F G H I J K L M N O P Q R S T U V W X Y Z

clear *ADJECTIVE* **1** transparent; not muddy or cloudy **2** easy to see or hear or understand; distinct **3** free from obstacles or unwanted things **4** free from guilt • *a clear conscience* **5** complete • *Give three clear days' notice.*
▷ **clearly** *ADVERB* **clearness** *NOUN*

clear *ADVERB* **1** distinctly; clearly • *We heard you loud and clear.* **2** completely • *He got clear away.* **3** apart; not in contact • *Stand clear of the doors.*

clear *VERB* **clears, clearing, cleared 1** make or become clear **2** show that someone is innocent or reliable **3** jump over something without touching it **4** get approval or authorization for something • *Clear this with the headmaster.*
clear away remove used plates etc. after a meal
clear off or **out** (*informal*) go away
clear up 1 make things tidy **2** become better or brighter **3** solve • *clear up the mystery*

clearing *NOUN* **clearings** an open space in a forest

clef *NOUN* **clefs** a symbol on a stave in music, showing the pitch of the notes • *treble clef* • *bass clef*

cleft *NOUN* **clefts** a split in something

clemency *NOUN* gentleness or mildness; mercy

clench *VERB* **clenches, clenching, clenched** close your teeth or fingers tightly

clergy *NOUN* the people who have been ordained as priests or ministers of the Christian Church
▷ **clergyman** *NOUN* **clergywoman** *NOUN*

clerical *ADJECTIVE* **1** to do with the routine work in an office, such as filing and writing letters **2** to do with the clergy

clerk (klark) *NOUN* **clerks** a person employed to keep records or accounts, deal with papers in an office, etc.

clever *ADJECTIVE* **1** quick at learning and understanding things **2** skilful
▷ **cleverly** *ADVERB* **cleverness** *NOUN*

cliché (klee-shay) *NOUN* **clichés** a phrase or idea that is used so often that it has little meaning

click *NOUN* **clicks** a short sharp sound
▷ **click** *VERB*

client *NOUN* **clients** a person who gets help or advice from a professional person such as a lawyer, accountant, architect, etc.; a customer

cliff *NOUN* **cliffs** a steep rock face, especially on a coast

climate *NOUN* **climates** the regular weather conditions of an area
▷ **climatic** (kly-mat-ik) *ADJECTIVE*

Thesaurus

clear *ADJECTIVE* **1** *clear instructions* ► plain, understandable, easy, direct, logical **2** *It was clear we would have to wait. a clear case of discrimination* ► evident, obvious, plain, apparent, patent, blatant, glaring, manifest **3** *a pool of clear water* ► transparent, translucent, crystalline **4** *a clear blue sky* ► bright, cloudless, unclouded, sunny, fair, fine **5** *a clear complexion* ► fresh, unblemished **6** *a clear voice* ► pure, distinct **7** *The motorway was clear again by the afternoon.* ► open, unobstructed, unblocked, unrestricted, passable **8** *a clear conscience* ► untroubled, undisturbed, easy, calm, guiltless, blameless **9** *a clear month's notice* ► full, whole, entire, complete, total

clear *VERB* **1** *The weather seemed to be clearing.* ► brighten, become brighter, turn fine, lighten OPPOSITES ARE darken, get worse **2** *Rain will slowly clear from the south.* ► disappear, fade out, dwindle, disperse, recede, diminish, peter out, wear off, dry out **3** *We should clear the backlog of work by Friday.* ► complete, eliminate, deal with, get rid of **4** *a special tool for clearing drains* ► unblock, unclog, free, loosen AN OPPOSITE IS block **5** *I have cleared most of the weeds.* ► tidy, remove, get rid of, eliminate, disentangle **6** *Staff were told to clear the building immediately.* ► evacuate, empty, leave **7** *The ball cleared the bar easily.* ► go over, pass over, go above **8** *The appeal judges are expected to clear him this week.* ► acquit, exonerate, free AN OPPOSITE IS condemn
clear up 1 *I'll stay here and clear up the mess.* ► tidy (up), clean (up) **2** *I'm glad we've cleared up the misunderstanding.* ► resolve, explain, straighten out, get to the bottom of

clearly *ADVERB* **1** *Clearly we will need to make some changes.* ► obviously, evidently, surely, plainly, undoubtedly, patently **2** *It is important to write clearly.* ► legibly, distinctly, intelligibly

clench *VERB* **1** *She clenched her hands to stop them shaking.* ► squeeze (tightly), press (together) **2** *He looked ridiculous, clenching a rose in his teeth.* ► hold, clasp, grasp, grip

clergymanclergywoman *NOUN* *an elderly clergyman in a cassock* ► cleric, churchman, churchwoman, man *or* woman of God, minister, priest, vicar, pastor, parson, chaplain usage Special ranks of clerics include *canon, curate, deacon, dean, rector*

clever *ADJECTIVE* *a clever young student; It was clever of you to work that out.* ► intelligent, bright, gifted, brilliant, intellectual, talented, capable, (*more informal*) smart

climate *NOUN* **1** *countries with a temperate climate* ► weather, weather conditions, weather pattern **2** *a changed political climate*

climax *NOUN* **climaxes** the most interesting or important point of a story, series of events, etc.

climb *VERB* **climbs, climbing, climbed 1** go up or over or down something **2** grow upwards **3** go higher
▷ **climb** *NOUN* **climber** *NOUN*
climb down admit that you have been wrong

clinch *VERB* **clinches, clinching, clinched 1** settle something definitely • *We hope to clinch the deal today.* **2** (said about boxers) be clasping each other
▷ **clinch** *NOUN*

cling *VERB* **clings, clinging, clung** hold on tightly

clinic *NOUN* **clinics** a place where people see doctors etc. for treatment or advice

clinical *ADJECTIVE* **1** to do with the medical treatment of patients **2** coldly efficient or aloof

clink *NOUN* **clinks** a thin sharp sound like glasses being struck together
▷ **clink** *VERB*

clip[1] *NOUN* **clips** a fastener for keeping things together, usually worked by a spring

clip *VERB* **clips, clipping, clipped** fasten with a clip

clip[2] *VERB* **clips, clipping, clipped 1** cut with shears or scissors etc. **2** (*informal*) hit

clip *NOUN* **clips 1** a short piece of film shown on its own **2** (*informal*) a hit on the head

clippers *PLURAL NOUN* an instrument for cutting hair

clique (kleek) *NOUN* **cliques** a small group of people who stick together and keep others out

cloak *NOUN* **cloaks** a sleeveless piece of outdoor clothing that hangs loosely from the shoulders

cloak *VERB* **cloaks, cloaking, cloaked** cover or conceal

cloakroom *NOUN* **cloakrooms 1** a place where people can leave outdoor clothes, luggage, etc. **2** a toilet

clock *NOUN* **clocks 1** a device that shows what the time is **2** a measuring device with a dial or digital display

clock *VERB* **clocks, clocking, clocked**
clock in *or* **out** register the time you arrive at work or leave work
clock up reach a certain speed

clockwise *ADVERB, ADJECTIVE* moving round a circle in the same direction as a clock's hands

clockwork *NOUN* a mechanism with a spring that has to be wound up
like clockwork very regularly

clod *NOUN* **clods** a lump of earth or clay

clog *NOUN* **clogs** a shoe with a wooden sole

clog *VERB* **clogs, clogging, clogged** block up

cloister *NOUN* **cloisters** a covered path along the side of a church or monastery etc., round a courtyard

clone *NOUN* **clones** an animal or plant made from the cells of another animal or plant and therefore exactly like it

clone *VERB* **clones, cloning, cloned** produce a clone of an animal or plant

close[1] (klohss) *ADJECTIVE* **1** near **2** detailed or concentrated • *with close attention* **3** tight; with little empty space • *a close fit* **4** in which competitors are nearly equal • *a close contest* **5** stuffy
▷ **closely** *ADVERB* **closeness** *NOUN*

Thesaurus

▶ atmosphere, mood, spirit, ambience, temper, trend, environment, feeling

climax *NOUN The appointment marked the climax of her career.* ▶ peak, summit, acme, zenith, highlight, high point, head AN OPPOSITE IS nadir

climb *VERB* **1** *She climbed the stairs.* ▶ ascend, go up, mount, move up, scale, clamber up **2** *The plane climbed to 30,000 feet.* ▶ rise, ascend, fly up, soar **3** *The road climbs steeply into the hills.* ▶ rise, ascend, slope up **4** *They climbed the mountain in three days.* ▶ conquer, reach the top of
climb down *The Government has had to climb down on the issue.* ▶ give way, back down, yield, retreat, capitulate

clinch *VERB eager to clinch a deal* ▶ conclude, agree, settle, sign, close, ratify, confirm, decide, make certain of, shake hands on, verify

cling *VERB* **1 cling to** *Climbing plants cling to the walls.* ▶ adhere to, fasten on, stick to **2 cling to** *Charles took her hand and clung to it.* ▶ clasp, clutch, embrace, grasp, hug **3 cling to** *I still cling to the hope that I'm mistaken.* ▶ adhere to, stand by, abide by, have faith in, cherish

clip *NOUN* **1** *He undid the clip and opened the case.* ▶ fastener, clasp, catch, hook **2** *a clip from a film* ▶ excerpt, extract, section, fragment

clip *VERB* **1** *It's my job to clip the hedge.* ▶ cut, trim, snip, prune, crop **2** *Clip the coupon and send it to the address below.* ▶ cut out, remove, detach, tear out **3** *She clipped him on the head and made him yell.* ▶ slap, smack, hit, cuff

cloak *NOUN* **1** *She threw her cloak over her shoulder.* ▶ cape, wrap, mantle, coat, cope, robe **2** *a cloak of secrecy* ▶ screen, mask, shield, cover, veneer

clog *VERB Wet leaves had clogged the drains.* ▶ block, bung up, stop up, obstruct, choke

close *ADJECTIVE* **1 close to** *A large proportion of the world's population lives close to rivers.* ▶ near, near to, adjacent to, alongside, not far from, in the vicinity of, within reach of **2 close to** *He*

close *ADVERB* closely • *close behind*

close *NOUN* **closes** **1** a street that is closed at one end **2** an enclosed area, especially round a cathedral

close[2] (klohz) *VERB* **closes, closing, closed** **1** shut **2** end
close in **1** get nearer **2** if the days are closing in, they are getting shorter

close *NOUN* end • *at the close of play*

close-up *NOUN* **close-ups** a photograph or piece of film taken at close range

closure *NOUN* **closures** closing

clot *NOUN* **clots** **1** a small mass of blood, cream, etc. that has become solid **2** (*slang*) a stupid person

clot *VERB* **clots, clotting, clotted** form clots

cloth *NOUN* **cloths** **1** woven material or felt **2** a piece of this material **3** a tablecloth

clothes *PLURAL NOUN* things worn to cover the body

clothing *NOUN* clothes

cloud *NOUN* **clouds** **1** a mass of condensed water vapour floating in the sky **2** a mass of smoke, dust, etc., in the air

cloudy *ADJECTIVE* **cloudier, cloudiest** **1** full of clouds **2** not transparent • *The liquid became cloudy.*
▷ **cloudiness** *NOUN*

clover *NOUN* a small plant usually with three leaves on each stalk
in clover in ease and luxury

clown *NOUN* **clowns** **1** a performer who does amusing tricks and actions, especially in a circus **2** a person who does silly things

cloying *ADJECTIVE* sickeningly sweet

club *NOUN* **clubs** **1** a heavy stick used as a weapon **2** a stick with a shaped head used to hit the ball in golf **3** a group of people who meet because they are interested in the same thing; the building where they meet **4** a playing card with black clover leaves on it **5** a nightclub

Thesaurus

seemed to be close to tears as he told the story. ► near to, on the verge of, on the brink of, on the point of **3** *The house is fairly close.* ► near, nearby **4** *At last an agreement seemed close.* ► imminent, impending, at hand **5** *It was a very close contest.* ► even, level, evenly matched, evenly balanced, hard-fought **6** *The aircraft were flying in a close formation.* ► tight, dense, concentrated, compact **7** *They are close friends.* ► intimate, dear, devoted, loving, constant **8** *The problem needs our close attention.* ► careful, thorough, fixed, concentrated, keen, intense **9** *The weather had become somewhat close.* ► humid, muggy, stuffy, airless, heavy, sticky, clammy, oppressive

close *VERB* **1** *Come in and close the door.* ► shut, lock, secure, fasten, bolt **2** *The road was closed at the far end.* ► block off, cordon off, bar, barricade, obstruct **3** *The chairman closed the meeting at this point.* ► conclude, end, finish, stop, terminate, discontinue, wind up, complete **4** *The hole had been closed with a wad of paper.* ► fill, stop, seal, plug, bung **5** *a plan to close the gap between rich and poor* ► narrow, reduce, lessen, shorten, fill, make smaller

close *NOUN* *At the close of polling, the votes are collected in a central area.* ► end, finish, completion, conclusion, cessation, termination

clot *NOUN* **1** *a clot of blood* ► lump, mass, (*in an artery or vein*) embolism, thrombosis **2** (*informal*) *I felt a real clot.* ► fool, idiot

clot *VERB* *a substance to make the blood clot* ► coagulate, congeal, set, thicken, solidify, stiffen

cloth *NOUN* *a length of cloth* ► fabric, material, textile

clothe *VERB* **1** *Despite the war she was able to clothe herself well.* ► dress, fit out, attire **2 be clothed in** *He was clothed in a long striped garment.* ► be dressed in, be attired in, wear

clothes *PLURAL NOUN* *She wore lovely clothes, beautifully made from fine materials.* ► clothing, garments, attire, garb, dress, (*more informal*) gear RELATED ADJECTIVE sartorial

cloud *NOUN* **1** *Visibility was affected by cloud.* ► haze, vapour, mist **2** *a cloud of steam* ► mass, billow, haze, mist, puff

cloud *VERB* **1** *A light haze clouded the view.* ► obscure, shade, hide, conceal, shroud, mist, dim **2** *Anger clouded their judgement.* ► confuse, obscure, blur, muddle, obfuscate

cloudy *ADJECTIVE* **1** *a cloudy sky* ► overcast, dull, grey, gloomy, hazy, leaden OPPOSITES ARE clear, bright **2** *The water went cloudy.* ► hazy, milky, murky, muddy AN OPPOSITE IS clear

clout *VERB* *His mother clouted him on the ear.* ► hit, slap, thump, bash, box, smack, cuff, strike

clout *NOUN* *She threatened him with another clout on the ear.* ► slap, smack, thump, bash

clown *NOUN* *They regarded him as the clown of the group.* ► joker, jester, comedian, comic, fool, funny man *or* woman, buffoon

club *NOUN* **1** *He had been hit with a heavy club.* ► cosh, cudgel, bat, bludgeon, truncheon, baton, stick **2** *She belonged to a local book club.*

club *VERB* **clubs, clubbing, clubbed** hit with a heavy stick

club together join with other people in order to pay for something • *club together to buy a boat*

cluck *VERB* **clucks, clucking, clucked** make a hen's throaty cry
▷ **cluck** *NOUN*

clue *NOUN* **clues** something that helps a person to solve a puzzle or a mystery

not have a clue (*informal*) be stupid or helpless

clump *NOUN* **clumps** **1** a cluster or mass of things **2** a clumping sound

clump *VERB* **clumps, clumping, clumped** **1** form a cluster or mass **2** walk with a heavy tread

clumsy *ADJECTIVE* **clumsier, clumsiest** **1** heavy and ungraceful; likely to knock things over or drop things **2** not skilful; not tactful • *a clumsy apology*
▷ **clumsily** *ADVERB* **clumsiness** *NOUN*

cluster *NOUN* **clusters** a small close group

cluster *VERB* **clusters, clustering, clustered** form a cluster

clutch *VERB* **clutches, clutching, clutched** grasp tightly

clutch *NOUN* **clutches** **1** a tight grasp **2** a device for connecting and disconnecting the engine of a motor vehicle from its gears

clutter *NOUN* things lying about untidily

clutter *VERB* **clutters, cluttering, cluttered** fill with clutter • *Piles of papers cluttered her desk.*

Co. *ABBREVIATION* Company

c/o *ABBREVIATION* care of

co- *PREFIX* **1** together, jointly (as in *coexistence, cooperate*) **2** joint (as in *co-pilot*)

coach *NOUN* **coaches** **1** a bus used for long journeys **2** a carriage of a railway train **3** a large horse-drawn carriage with four wheels **4** an instructor in sports **5** a teacher giving private specialized tuition

coach *VERB* **coaches, coaching, coached** instruct or train somebody, especially in sports

coagulate *VERB* **coagulates, coagulating, coagulated** change from liquid to semi-solid; clot
▷ **coagulation** *NOUN*

coal *NOUN* **coals** a hard black mineral substance used for burning to supply heat; a piece of this

coalesce (koh- a- less) *VERB* **coalesces, coalescing, coalesced** combine and form one whole thing
▷ **coalescence** *NOUN*

coalition *NOUN* **coalitions** a temporary alliance, especially of two or more political parties in order to form a government

coarse *ADJECTIVE* **1** not smooth or delicate; rough **2** composed of large particles **3** not refined; vulgar
▷ **coarsely** *ADVERB* **coarseness** *NOUN*

Thesaurus

► society, association, circle, group, union, organization, league, set

club *VERB* *The man had been clubbed almost to death.* ► beat, batter, cosh, cudgel, hit, strike, (*more informal*) clobber

clue *NOUN* **1** *Give me a clue what it's all about.* ► hint, indication, sign, pointer, inkling, tip, idea, suggestion, key **2** *Police are looking for clues in the immediate area of the crime.* ► piece of evidence, lead, evidence

not have a clue (*informal*) *I didn't have a clue what to do next.* ► have no idea, be baffled, be completely stuck, be at a loss, (*more informal*) not have the faintest idea

clump *NOUN* **1** *a clump of trees* ► cluster, group, mass, thicket, bunch, bundle, collection **2** *a clump of grass* ► tuft, bundle, bunch **3** *a clump of earth* ► lump, clod, mass

clumsy *ADJECTIVE* **1** *She was clumsy and spilt most of the milk.* ► inept, bungling, bumbling, blundering, fumbling, uncoordinated, unskilful OPPOSITES ARE careful, adroit **2** *His movements looked clumsy.* ► awkward, ungainly, graceless, ungraceful, gawky, gangling, fumbling OPPOSITES ARE graceful, elegant

cluster *NOUN* **1** *a cluster of buildings* ► group, bunch, collection **2** *a cluster of people* ► crowd, group, gathering, body, throng, assembly

clutch *VERB* *They were all clutching beer mugs.* ► grip, grasp, clasp, hold

clutter *NOUN* *It's difficult to work with all this clutter around.* ► mess, muddle, confusion, untidiness, disorder, jumble, junk, litter, lumber, mix-up, odds and ends, rubbish

clutter *VERB* *Bits of broken machinery cluttered the yard.* ► litter, fill, cover, bestrew, mess up

coach *NOUN* **1** *The coach takes the motorway.* ► bus, motor coach **2** *a railway coach* ► carriage, wagon, van **3** *a sports coach* ► trainer, instructor, teacher

coach *VERB* *Michael coached her to an international standard.* ► train, instruct, tutor, teach, prepare

coalition *NOUN* *a coalition from the three main political parties* ► combination, alliance, union, partnership

coarse *ADJECTIVE* **1** *coarse sand; coarse cloth* ► rough, unrefined, unprocessed, lumpy, gritty OPPOSITES ARE fine, soft **2** *coarse language* ► crude, vulgar, offensive, bawdy, lewd, foul,

coarsen *VERB* **coarsens, coarsening, coarsened** make or become coarse

coast *NOUN* **coasts** the seashore or the land close to it
▷ **coastal** *ADJECTIVE* **coastline** *NOUN*
the coast is clear there is no chance of being seen or hindered

coastguard *NOUN* **coastguards** a person whose job is to keep watch on the coast, detect or prevent smuggling, etc.

coat *NOUN* **coats** **1** a piece of clothing with sleeves, worn over other clothes **2** the hair or fur on an animal's body **3** a covering layer • *a coat of paint*

coat *VERB* **coats, coating, coated** cover something with a coating

coating *NOUN* **coatings** a thin covering or layer

coat of arms *NOUN* **coats of arms** a design on a shield, used as an emblem by a family or institution

coax *VERB* **coaxes, coaxing, coaxed** persuade someone gently or patiently

cobalt *NOUN* a hard silvery-white metal

cobble *NOUN* **cobbles** a rounded stone used for paving streets etc.
▷ **cobbled** *ADJECTIVE* **cobblestone** *NOUN*

cobra (**koh**- bra) *NOUN* **cobras** a poisonous snake that can rear up

cobweb *NOUN* **cobwebs** the thin sticky net made by a spider to trap insects

cocaine *NOUN* a drug made from the leaves of a tropical plant called *coca*

cock *NOUN* **cocks** **1** a male chicken **2** a male bird **3** a stopcock **4** a lever in a gun

cock *VERB* **cocks, cocking, cocked** **1** make a gun ready to fire by raising the cock **2** turn something upwards or in a particular direction • *The dog cocked its ears.*

cockatoo *NOUN* **cockatoos** a crested parrot

cockerel *NOUN* **cockerels** a young male chicken

cocker spaniel *NOUN* **cocker spaniels** a kind of small spaniel

cockpit *NOUN* **cockpits** the compartment where the pilot of an aircraft sits

cockroach *NOUN* **cockroaches** a dark brown beetle-like insect, often found in dirty houses

cocksure *ADJECTIVE* very sure; too confident

cocoa *NOUN* **cocoas** **1** a hot drink made from a powder of crushed cacao seeds **2** this powder

coconut *NOUN* **coconuts** **1** a large round nut that grows on a kind of palm tree **2** its white lining, used in sweets and cookery

cocoon *NOUN* **cocoons** **1** the covering round a chrysalis **2** a protective wrapping

cod *NOUN* **cod** a large edible sea fish

code *NOUN* **codes** **1** a word or phrase used to represent a message in order to keep its meaning secret **2** a set of signs used in sending messages by machine etc. • *the Morse code* **3** a set of numbers that represents an area in telephoning • *Do you know the code for Norwich?* **4** a set of laws or rules • *the Highway Code*

code *VERB* **codes, coding, coded** put a message into code

coeducation *NOUN* educating boys and girls together
▷ **coeducational** *ADJECTIVE*

coefficient *NOUN* **coefficients** a number by which another number is multiplied; a factor

coexist *VERB* **coexists, coexisting, coexisted** exist together or at the same time
▷ **coexistence** *NOUN* **coexistent** *ADJECTIVE*

coffee *NOUN* **coffees** **1** a hot drink made from the roasted ground seeds (**coffee beans**) of a tropical plant **2** these seeds

coffin *NOUN* **coffins** a long box in which a body is buried or cremated

cog *NOUN* **cogs** one of a number of tooth-like parts round the edge of a wheel, fitting into and pushing those on another wheel

cogent (**koh**- jent) *ADJECTIVE* convincing • *a cogent argument*

cogitate *VERB* **cogitates, cogitating, cogitated** think deeply about something
▷ **cogitation** *NOUN*

Thesaurus

dirty, smutty, indecent, indelicate, improper, obscene, ribald OPPOSITES ARE refined, polite

coast *NOUN* *a house by the coast* ► seaside, seashore, sea, shore, beach, coastline, seaboard

coat *NOUN* **1** *Put on a coat if you go out.* ► overcoat, jacket **2** *the coat of an animal* ► fur, hair, hide, pelt, skin, fleece **3** *a coat of paint* ► layer, coating, covering, veneer

coat *VERB* *Coat the surface with varnish.* ► cover, paint, glaze, varnish, laminate, smear

coax *VERB* *It was impossible to coax them back home.* ► persuade, tempt, cajole, allure, entice, induce, wheedle, beguile, inveigle, woo

code *NOUN* **1** *a code of conduct; a social code* ► system, set of rules, set of principles **2** *The message was written in code.* ► cipher, secret language

coerce *VERB* *He was coerced into signing an agreement.* ► pressure, pressurize, force (to), compel (to), constrain (to), bully, browbeat, intimidate

coherent (koh- heer- ent) *ADJECTIVE* clear, reasonable, and making sense
▷ **coherently** *ADVERB*

coil *NOUN* **coils** something wound into a spiral

coil *VERB* **coils, coiling, coiled** wind something into a coil

coin *NOUN* **coins** a piece of metal, usually round, used as money

coin *VERB* **coins, coining, coined**
1 manufacture coins **2** invent a word or phrase

coincide *VERB* **coincides, coinciding, coincided** **1** happen at the same time as something else **2** be in the same place **3** be the same • *My opinion coincided with hers.*

coincidence *NOUN* **coincidences** the happening of similar events at the same time by chance

colander *NOUN* **colanders** a bowl-shaped container with holes in it, used for straining water from vegetables etc. after cooking

cold *ADJECTIVE* **1** having a low temperature; not warm **2** not friendly or loving; not enthusiastic
▷ **coldly** *ADVERB* **coldness** *NOUN*
get cold feet have doubts about doing something bold or ambitious
give someone the cold shoulder be deliberately unfriendly

cold *NOUN* **colds** **1** lack of warmth; low temperature; cold weather **2** an infectious illness that makes your nose run, your throat sore, etc.

cold-blooded *ADJECTIVE* **1** having a body temperature that changes according to the surroundings **2** callous; deliberately cruel

collaborate *VERB* **collaborates, collaborating, collaborated** work together on a job
▷ **collaboration** *NOUN* **collaborator** *NOUN*

collapse *VERB* **collapses, collapsing, collapsed** **1** break or fall to pieces; fall in **2** become very weak or ill **3** fold up

Thesaurus

coercion *NOUN* *Some form of coercion is needed to get them to start work.* ► compulsion, pressure, force, constraint, intimidation, duress, harassment

coherent *ADJECTIVE* *a coherent argument* ► logical, reasonable, rational, lucid, clear, sound, cogent, compelling, persuasive OPPOSITES ARE incoherent, illogical

coil *NOUN* *coils of rope* ► loop, twist, ring, spiral, roll, turn

coil *VERB* *He coiled her hair round his finger.* ► curl, wind, twine, loop, roll

coin *NOUN* **1** *a pile of silver coins* ► piece, bit **2** *large quantities of coin* ► change, loose change, small change, coppers, silver

coin *VERB* **1** *The city began to coin silver money at this time.* ► mint, make, mould, stamp RELATED ADJECTIVE numismatic **2** *A Czech writer coined the word 'robot'.* ► invent, devise, make up, create, originate, think up, conceive

coincide *VERB* **1** *It was a nuisance that the two programmes coincided.* ► come together, occur simultaneously, happen at the same time, overlap, clash **2 coincide with** *His life coincides with the decline of the Empire.* ► clash, coexist, fall together, happen together, synchronize **3** *Your interests and ours do not always coincide.* ► correspond, tally, agree, match, accord, harmonize

coincidence *NOUN* *The resemblance was just coincidence.* ► accident, chance, fluke, luck, providence

coincidental *ADJECTIVE* *Any resemblance is purely coincidental.* ► accidental, fortuitous, by chance, unintentional

cold *ADJECTIVE* **1** *a cold day; cold weather* ► chilly, cool, fresh, freezing, icy, raw, bitter, biting, perishing, wintry, (*more informal*) nippy, (*more informal*) parky AN OPPOSITE IS hot **2** *I was feeling cold.* ► chilly, chilled, shivery, freezing, frozen AN OPPOSITE IS hot **3** *a cold reception* ► unfriendly, unsympathetic, unwelcoming, cool, frosty, lukewarm, forbidding, indifferent, unenthusiastic OPPOSITES ARE warm, friendly

cold *NOUN* *We all feel the cold in winter.* ► coldness, chill, chilliness

cold-blooded *ADJECTIVE* *cold-blooded murder* ► cruel, brutal, savage, barbaric, callous, inhuman, pitiless, merciless, sadistic AN OPPOSITE IS humane

collaborate *VERB* **1** *Several companies have collaborated to develop a new vaccine.* ► cooperate, combine, unite, work together, join forces, team up **2** *Several villagers were accused of collaborating with the enemy.* ► conspire, fraternize, collude, consort, cooperate

collaboration *NOUN* **1** *The work was done in collaboration with a British firm.* ► association, cooperation, partnership, combination, alliance, tandem **2** *collaboration with the enemy* ► collusion, connivance, conspiring

collaborator *NOUN* **1** *She wrote the book with the help of a collaborator.* ► associate, colleague, partner, co-worker, co-author **2** *After the war he was accused of being a collaborator.* ► traitor, fraternizer, colluder, defector, fifth-columnist, quisling

collapse *VERB* **1** *Part of the floor collapsed.* ► fall in, cave in, fall down, give way, crumble,

a b c d e f g h i j k l m n o p q r s t u v w x y z

A B C D E F G H I J K L M N O P Q R S T U V W X Y Z

collapse *NOUN* **collapses** **1** collapsing **2** a breakdown

collapsible *ADJECTIVE* able to be folded up • *a collapsible bed*

collar *NOUN* **collars** **1** the part of a piece of clothing that goes round your neck **2** a band that goes round the neck of a dog, cat, horse, etc.

colleague *NOUN* **colleagues** a person you work with

collect (kol- ekt) *VERB* **collects, collecting, collected** **1** bring people or things together from various places **2** obtain examples of things as a hobby • *She collects stamps.* **3** come together **4** ask for money or contributions etc. from people **5** fetch • *Collect your coat from the cleaners.*
▷ **collector** *NOUN*

collection *NOUN* **collections** **1** collecting **2** things collected **3** money collected for a charity etc.

collective noun *NOUN* **collective nouns** a noun that is singular in form but refers to many individuals taken as a unit, e.g. *army, herd*

college *NOUN* **colleges** a place where people can continue learning something after they have left school

collide *VERB* **collides, colliding, collided** crash into something
▷ **collision** *NOUN*

colloquial (col- oh- kwee- al) *ADJECTIVE* suitable for conversation but not for formal speech or writing
▷ **colloquially** *ADVERB* **colloquialism** *NOUN*

colon[1] *NOUN* **colons** a punctuation mark (:), often used to introduce lists

colon[2] *NOUN* **colons** the largest part of the intestine

colonel (ker- nel) *NOUN* **colonels** an army officer in charge of a regiment

colonial *ADJECTIVE* to do with a colony

colonize *VERB* **colonizes, colonizing, colonized** establish a colony in a country
▷ **colonist** *NOUN* **colonization** *NOUN*

colony *NOUN* **colonies** **1** an area of land that the people of another country settle in and control **2** the people of a colony **3** a group of people or animals of the same kind living close together

colossal *ADJECTIVE* immense; enormous [from *colossus* = huge statue, from the bronze statue of Apollo at Rhodes, called the *Colossus of Rhodes*]

colour *NOUN* **colours** **1** the effect produced by waves of light of a particular wavelength **2** the

Thesaurus

crumple, tumble down, buckle, disintegrate **2** *People were collapsing in the heat.* ► faint, pass out, lose consciousness, black out, keel over, (*more informal*) flake out **3** *Harriet collapsed exhausted in her chair.* ► fall, sink, slump **4** *The banking system was about to collapse.* ► fail, break down, founder, come to grief

collapse *NOUN* **1** *the collapse of part of the floor* ► cave-in, disintegration, subsidence **2** *the collapse of peace talks* ► breakdown, failure, foundering

collect *VERB* **1** *He collected data from over fifty countries.* ► accumulate, gather, assemble, amass, accrue, bring together **2** *The squirrels scurried round collecting nuts.* ► gather, heap, hoard, lay up, pile up, put by, reserve, save, scrape together, stockpile, store AN OPPOSITE IS scatter **3** *People collected to watch the fireworks.* ► assemble, gather, come together, congregate, crowd round, convene, converge, flock, group, muster AN OPPOSITE IS disperse **4** *We are collecting money for charity.* ► raise, appeal for, ask for, seek, solicit **5** *I must collect the children from school.* ► fetch, get, meet, go and get, bring, call for OPPOSITES ARE take, drop off

collection *NOUN* **1** *a collection of strange objects* ► assortment, accumulation, hoard, array, cluster, conglomeration, heap, mass, pile, supply, stock, set, stack **2** *a collection of people outside the ground* ► group, crowd, gathering, band, accumulation **3** *a collection of poems* ► anthology, selection, compilation, treasury, miscellany

college *NOUN* *a college of art* ► school, academy, institute, conservatory

collide *VERB* **1 collide with** *A van collided head on with the stolen vehicle.* ► crash into, smash into, hit, strike **2** *The two vehicles collided head on.* ► crash, hit each other, run into each other, meet

collision *NOUN* *a collision on the motorway* ► crash, accident, smash, pile-up

colloquial *ADJECTIVE* *colloquial language* ► informal, conversational, everyday, casual, vernacular AN OPPOSITE IS formal

colony *NOUN* **1** *Britain's former colonies in the region* ► territory, possession, dependency, dominion, protectorate, province, settlement, outpost **2** *the British colony in New York* ► population, community

colossal *ADJECTIVE* *a colossal building* ► huge, massive, enormous, gigantic, immense, vast, giant, towering, mammoth, monumental, elephantine AN OPPOSITE IS tiny

colour *NOUN* **1** *You can choose from over thirty beautiful colours.* ► hue, shade, tint, tone, tinge, pigment, tincture, colouring **2** *The exercise put some colour back in her cheeks.*

use of various colours, not only black and white **3** the colour of someone's skin **4** a substance used to colour things **5** the special flag of a ship or regiment

colour *VERB* **colours, colouring, coloured** **1** put colour on; paint or stain **2** blush **3** influence what someone says or believes
▷ **colouring** *NOUN*

colour-blind *ADJECTIVE* unable to see the difference between certain colours

coloured *ADJECTIVE* **1** having colour **2** having a dark skin
USAGE The word **coloured**, used to describe people, is often considered to be insulting. It is better to use **black**.

colourful *ADJECTIVE* **1** full of colour **2** lively; with vivid details

column *NOUN* **columns** **1** a pillar **2** something long or tall and narrow • *a column of smoke* **3** a vertical section of a page • *There are two columns on this page.* **4** a regular article in a newspaper
▷ **columnist** *NOUN*

coma (koh- ma) *NOUN* **comas** a state of deep unconsciousness, especially in someone who is ill or injured [from Greek *koma* = deep sleep]

comb *NOUN* **combs** **1** a strip of wood or plastic etc. with teeth, used to tidy hair or hold it in place **2** something used like this, e.g. to separate strands of wool **3** the red crest on a fowl's head **4** a honeycomb

comb *VERB* **combs, combing, combed** **1** tidy hair with a comb **2** search thoroughly

combat *NOUN*, *VERB* **combats, combating, combated** fight
▷ **combatant** (kom- ba- tant) *NOUN*

combination *NOUN* **combinations** **1** combining **2** a number of people or things that are combined
combination lock a lock that is opened by using a special sequence of numbers or letters

combine (komb- I'n) *VERB* **combines, combining, combined** join or mix together

Thesaurus

► bloom, redness, pinkness, glow, rosiness, ruddiness **3 colours** *the team's new colours* ► strip, kit, uniform, livery, outfit **4 colours** *the regimental colours* ► banner, ensign, flag, standard

colour *VERB* **1** *Why not colour it blue?* ► paint, tint, tinge, dye, stain, shade, colourwash **2** *Her face began to colour.* ► blush, flush, redden, go red OPPOSITES ARE fade, go pale **3** *The experience had coloured his judgement.* ► influence, affect, prejudice, sway, impinge on, slant, bias, distort, pervert

colourful *ADJECTIVE* **1** *a colourful bunch of flowers* ► brilliant, bright, showy, radiant, vibrant, gaudy, iridescent, multicoloured, psychedelic OPPOSITES ARE colourless, dull **2** *a colourful account of the incident* ► graphic, vivid, dramatic, picturesque, animated, exciting, stimulating, striking, florid, picturesque, rich OPPOSITES ARE dull, plain **3** *music and colourful dancing* ► lively, flamboyant, glamorous, energetic, dashing, vigorous, flashy AN OPPOSITE IS restrained

colourless *ADJECTIVE* **1** *a bottle of colourless liquid* ► transparent, uncoloured, neutral, watery **2** *a colourless complexion* ► pale, pallid, wan, anaemic, sickly **3** *a colourless personality* ► dull, uninteresting, unexciting, boring, tedious, insipid, dismal, drab, characterless, dreary, vapid, lacklustre, monotonous AN OPPOSITE IS colourful

column *NOUN* **1** *The temple stood on massive columns.* ► pillar, support, pilaster, post, upright **2** *His sister writes a column in the local newspaper.* ► article, report, feature, review, editorial **3** *a column of figures* ► list, line, string **4** *The troops advanced in three columns.* ► line, row, rank

comb *VERB* **1** *He looked for a mirror to comb his hair.* ► groom, tidy, neaten, arrange, smarten up, smooth out, untangle **2** *Police combed the house and garden for signs of a struggle.* ► search, scour, explore, rake, ransack, hunt, sweep

combat *NOUN* *Many men were killed in the combat that followed.* ► action, battle, fight, fighting, hostilities, warfare, engagement, encounter, armed conflict, contest, clash

combat *VERB* *new measures to combat crime* ► fight, battle against, tackle, contest, counter, contend against, stand up to, strive against, struggle against, withstand, face up to, grapple with, oppose, resist

combination *NOUN* **1** *a combination of luck and good judgement* ► blend, mixture, amalgamation, fusion, synthesis **2** *The evidence was considered in combination with other factors.* ► conjunction, association

combine *VERB* **1** *His father combines a social visit with a trip to the laundry.* ► merge, amalgamate, join (to) **2** *Several drivers combined to get everyone home.* ► cooperate,

A B C D E F G H I J K L M N O P Q R S T U V W X Y Z

combustion *NOUN* the process of burning, a chemical process (accompanied by heat) in which substances combine with oxygen in air

come *VERB* **comes, coming, came, come**
1 move towards somewhere • *Come here!*
2 arrive at or reach a place or condition or result • *They came to a city.* • *We came to a decision.*
3 happen • *How did you come to lose it?* **4** occur or be present • *It comes on the next page.*
5 result • *That's what comes of being careless.*
come by obtain
come in for receive a share of
come to **1** amount to **2** become conscious again
come to pass (*old use*) happen

comedian *NOUN* **comedians** someone who entertains people by making them laugh

comedy *NOUN* **comedies** **1** a play or film etc. that makes people laugh **2** humour [from Greek *komos* = noisy fun + *oide* = song]

comet *NOUN* **comets** an object moving across the sky with a bright tail of light

comfort *NOUN* **comforts** **1** a comfortable feeling or condition **2** soothing somebody who is unhappy or in pain **3** a person or thing that gives comfort

comfort *VERB* **comforts, comforting, comforted** make a person less unhappy; soothe

comfortable *ADJECTIVE* **1** (said about a person) physically relaxed and feeling good **2** making someone physically relaxed • *a comfortable chair*
▷ **comfortably** *ADVERB*

comic *ADJECTIVE* making people laugh
▷ **comical** *ADJECTIVE* **comically** *ADVERB*
comic strip a series of drawings telling a story, especially a funny one

comic *NOUN* **comics** **1** a paper full of comic strips **2** a comedian

comma *NOUN* **commas** a punctuation mark (,) used to mark a pause in a sentence or to separate items in a list

Thesaurus

collaborate, join forces, pool resources, come together, get together, link up, unite

come *VERB* **1** *Our friends came last night.* ► arrive, appear, visit, (*more informal*) turn up **2** *Spring came early this year.* ► occur, happen **3** **come to** *Eventually they came to a river.* ► reach, arrive at, get to, come across, happen on, approach, near **4** **come to** *The shirt came to his knees.* ► reach, extend to
come about ► happen, occur, (*more formal*) come to pass
come across *I came across an old friend.* ► find, encounter, discover, chance upon, meet, (*more informal*) bump into
come apart *One of my shoes came apart.* ► disintegrate, fall to pieces, break up
come clean *You'd better come clean before they find out.* ► confess, own up
come out with *Goodness knows what he'll come out with next.* ► say, let out, utter, disclose
come round *It took nearly an hour for her to come round after the operation.* ► recover, wake, awake
come up *Something has come up and she has had to leave.* ► arise, occur, happen, crop up
come upon *He came upon a little hut in the wood.* ► find, discover, (*more informal*) bump into

comeback *NOUN* *The band has achieved an amazing comeback.* ► recovery, revival, resurgence, rally, upturn

comedian *NOUN* *a well-known television comedian* ► comic, entertainer, humorist, wit, jester, buffoon, clown, fool, joker, wag

comedy *NOUN* *The show contained a great deal of comedy.* ► humour, farce, wit, jesting, facetiousness, clowning, satire, slapstick, fun, joking, buffoonery, hilarity

comfort *NOUN* **1** *They like to live in comfort.* ► ease, tranquillity, luxury, opulence, prosperity, relaxation, well-being
OPPOSITES ARE discomfort, hardship **2** *We tried to offer the unfortunate woman some words of comfort.* ► consolation, sympathy, condolence, commiseration, encouragement, moral support, reassurance, solace, succour, support, aid, help OPPOSITES ARE misery, grief

comfort *VERB* *Her sister tried to comfort her.* ► console, soothe, cheer, assuage, hearten, encourage, reassure, solace, sympathize with

comfortable *ADJECTIVE* **1** *a comfortable chair; a comfortable house* ► snug, cosy, relaxing, convenient, pleasant, easy, enjoyable, roomy, plush, soft, well furnished, warm, (*more informal*) comfy AN OPPOSITE IS uncomfortable **2** *comfortable shoes* ► well fitting, well made, snug **3** *a comfortable lifestyle* ► prosperous, affluent, pleasant, well off, luxurious, agreeable

comic *ADJECTIVE* *The effect of the speech was almost comic.* ► comical, humorous, funny, amusing, entertaining, diverting, laughable, facetious, hilarious, absurd, ridiculous, ludicrous

comic *NOUN* **1** *The show included a rather feeble comic.* ► comedian, entertainer, jester, clown, humorist **2** *A girl was buying a comic to read on the train.* ► magazine, cartoon paper

command *NOUN* **commands** **1** a statement telling somebody to do something; an order **2** authority; control **3** ability to use something; mastery • *She has a good command of Spanish.*

command *VERB* **commands, commanding, commanded** **1** give a command to somebody; order **2** have authority over **3** deserve and get • *They command our respect.*
▷ **commander** *NOUN*

commandeer *VERB* **commandeers, commandeering, commandeered** take or seize something for military purposes or for your own use

commandment *NOUN* **commandments** a sacred command, especially one of the Ten Commandments given to Moses

commando *NOUN* **commandos** a soldier trained for making dangerous raids

commemorate *VERB* **commemorates, commemorating, commemorated** be a celebration or reminder of some past event or person etc.
▷ **commemoration** *NOUN* **commemorative** *ADJECTIVE*

commence *VERB* **commences, commencing, commenced** begin
▷ **commencement** *NOUN*

commend *VERB* **commends, commending, commended** **1** praise • *He was commended for bravery.* **2** entrust • *We commend him to your care.*
▷ **commendation** *NOUN*

comment *NOUN* **comments** an opinion given about an event etc. or to explain something

comment *VERB* **comments, commenting, commented** make a comment

commentary *VERB* **commentaries** a description of an event by someone who is watching it, especially for radio or television
▷ **commentate** *VERB* **commentator** *NOUN*

commercial *ADJECTIVE* **1** to do with commerce **2** paid for by firms etc. whose advertisements are included • *commercial radio* **3** profitable
▷ **commercially** *ADVERB*

commercial *NOUN* **commercials** a broadcast advertisement

commiserate *VERB* **commiserates, commiserating, commiserated** sympathize
▷ **commiseration** *NOUN*

Thesaurus

command *NOUN* **1** *Officers shouted commands.* ► order, instruction, directive, direction, requirement **2** *He has twenty men under his command.* ► authority, control, direction, charge, leadership, supervision, jurisdiction **3** *She has a good command of French and German.* ► knowledge, mastery, grasp, understanding, comprehension, grip, fluency (in)

command *VERB* **1** *He commanded his men to advance.* ► order, instruct, direct, tell, call on, require, bid **2** *Meredith commands a squadron.* ► be in charge of, be in command of, have charge of, lead, head, manage, supervise, rule, control, govern

commander *NOUN* *Army commanders were discouraged from getting involved in politics.* ► chief , leader, officer, general, head, captain, commanding officer

commemorate *VERB* *The ceremony commemorated those who died in war.* ► celebrate, honour, salute, remember, be a memorial to, be a reminder of, pay respects to, pay tribute to

commence *VERB* **1** *Work will commence in the spring.* ► begin, start, get under way **2** *He has now commenced his contract with an Italian club.* ► begin, start, inaugurate, launch, open, get under way

commend *VERB* **1** *The committee commended her for a thorough and useful report.* ► praise, compliment, congratulate, applaud, salute, acclaim AN OPPOSITE IS criticize **2** *They have done well and I commend them unreservedly.* ► recommend, endorse, support, vouch for

comment *NOUN* **1** *I have had some very positive comments about it.* ► remark, opinion, criticism, observation, reference, statement, mention **2** *He added a few comments at the end of the paper.* ► note, annotation, footnote, gloss **3** *The news caused a lot of comment in the press.* ► discussion, debate, interest, consideration

comment *VERB* **comment on** *The article commented on the problems of travel in the area.* ► mention, discuss, refer to, allude to, remark on, touch on, speak about

commentary *NOUN* **1** *a commentary on the test match* ► description, report, narration, account **2** *The second part contains a commentary on the text.* ► analysis, criticism, critique, explanation, review, interpretation, treatise, discourse, elucidation, notes

commerce *NOUN* *Settlers came to Gaul for the sake of commerce.* ► trade, trading, buying and selling, business, dealing, traffic, (*old-fashioned*) merchandising

commercial *ADJECTIVE* **1** *The ships were built for commercial use.* ► trading, trade, business, economic, financial, mercantile **2** *She turned to writing as a commercial venture.* ► business, monetary, financial, profitable, profit-making, viable, lucrative

a b c d e f g h i j k l m n o p q r s t u v w x y z

commission *NOUN* **commissions** **1** a task formally given to someone • *a commission to paint a portrait* **2** an appointment to be an officer in the armed forces **3** a group of people given authority to do or investigate something **4** payment to someone for selling your goods etc.

commission *VERB* **commissions, commissioning, commissioned** give a commission to a person or for a task etc.

commit *VERB* **commits, committing, committed** **1** do or perform • *commit a crime* **2** place in someone's care or custody • *He was committed to prison.* **3** promise that you will make your time etc. available for a particular purpose • *Don't commit all your spare time to helping him.*

commitment *NOUN* **commitments** something you have agreed to do or to be involved in; an obligation

committee *NOUN* **committees** a group of people appointed to deal with something

commodity *NOUN* **commodities** a useful thing; a product

commodore *NOUN* **commodores** **1** a naval officer ranking next below a rear admiral **2** the commander of part of a fleet

common *ADJECTIVE* **1** ordinary; usual; found or occurring frequently • *a common weed* **2** of all or most people • *They worked for the common good.* **3** shared • *Music is their common interest.* **4** vulgar

▷ **commonly** *ADVERB* **commonness** *NOUN*

in common shared by two or more people or things

Common Market *NOUN* a group of European countries that trade freely together

commonplace *ADJECTIVE* ordinary; usual

common sense *NOUN* normal good sense in thinking or behaviour

commonwealth *NOUN* **1** a group of countries cooperating together **2** a country made up of an association of states • *the Commonwealth of Australia*

the Commonwealth **1** an association of Britain and various other countries that used to be part of the British Empire, including Canada, Australia, and New Zealand **2** the republic set up in Britain by Oliver Cromwell, lasting from 1649 to 1660

commotion *NOUN* an uproar; a fuss

Thesaurus

commission *NOUN* **1** *a commission to paint the family's portraits* ► assignment, appointment, contract, order, mandate, charge, instruction, project, undertaking, task

commission *VERB* *They went on to commission him to build a palace for the queen.* ► appoint, engage, contract, recruit, employ, hire, retain, delegate, select, nominate

commit *VERB* **1** *He swore he had not committed any crime.* ► carry out, be guilty of, be responsible for, perform, perpetrate, do, effect, enact, execute, (*more informal*) pull off **2** *The child was committed to her care.* ► entrust, consign, hand over, give over, turn over, deliver, deposit

commit yourself to *Students often have to commit themselves to long leases on lodgings.* ► undertake, pledge, guarantee, promise, contract

commitment *NOUN* **1** *The contract included a commitment to complete the work by the end of the year.* ► promise, pledge, undertaking, guarantee, assurance, liability, duty **2** *The team felt a commitment to continue the search.* ► determination, resolution, obligation, responsibility, dedication, devotion **3** *There are only a few commitments this week.* ► engagement, duty, appointment

committee *NOUN* *A committee will be set up to supervise the project.* ► board, panel, council, supervisory body, advisory group, task force

common *ADJECTIVE* **1** *This is a common question. Accidents are quite common on this stretch of road.* ► frequent, regular, usual, normal, habitual, customary, familiar, standard, typical, routine, everyday **2** *Her parents had thought some of her friends were too common for her.* ► inferior, low-class, ill-bred, vulgar, coarse, crude **3** *There is a common belief in these superstitions.* ► widespread, general, popular, universal, prevalent, conventional, established, accepted **4** *working for the common good* ► collective, communal, public, shared, joint

commonplace *ADJECTIVE* **1** *a commonplace occurrence* ► common, regular, normal, typical, familiar, routine, standard, everyday, typical, unremarkable AN OPPOSITE IS unusual **2** *a commonplace style of writing* ► ordinary, plain, simple, unremarkable, undistinguished, average, indifferent, humdrum, pedestrian, prosaic OPPOSITES ARE remarkable, original

commotion *NOUN* *She was distracted by the commotion across the street.* ► disturbance, uproar, racket, tumult, hullabaloo, hubbub, rumpus, fracas, furore, upheaval, agitation, excitement

communal *ADJECTIVE* *communal washing facilities* ► collective, shared, joint, common, public, general, mutual, open AN OPPOSITE IS private

commune (kom-yoon) *NOUN* **communes** **1** a group of people living together and sharing everything **2** a district of local government in France and some other countries

communicate *VERB* **communicates, communicating, communicated** **1** pass news, information, etc. to other people **2** (said about rooms etc.) have a connecting door

communication *NOUN* **communications** **1** communicating **2** something communicated; a message
communications *PLURAL NOUN* links between places (e.g. roads, railways, telephones, or radio)

communicative *ADJECTIVE* willing to talk

communion *NOUN* the act of sharing thoughts or feelings
Communion or **Holy Communion** the Christian ceremony in which consecrated bread and wine are given to worshippers

communism *NOUN* a political system where the state controls property, production, trade, etc. COMPARE **capitalism**
▷ **communist** *NOUN*

community *NOUN* **communities** **1** the people living in one area **2** a group with similar interests or origins

commute *VERB* **commutes, commuting, commuted** **1** travel a fairly long way by train, bus, or car to and from your daily work **2** alter a punishment to something less severe

commuter *NOUN* **commuters** a person who commutes to and from work

compact *ADJECTIVE* **1** closely or neatly packed together **2** concise
▷ **compactly** *ADVERB* **compactness** *NOUN*

compact *NOUN* **compacts** a small flat container for face powder

compact disc *NOUN* **compact discs** a small plastic disc on which music, information, etc. is stored as digital signals and is read by a laser beam

companion *NOUN* **companions** **1** a person you spend time with or travel with **2** one of a matching pair of things **3** (in book titles) a guidebook or reference book • *The Oxford Companion to Music*
▷ **companionship** *NOUN*

company *NOUN* **companies** **1** a number of people together **2** a business firm **3** having

Thesaurus

commune *NOUN* *She lived for several years in a commune in Chicago.* ► community, collective, settlement, colony, fellowship, kibbutz

communicate *VERB* **1** *Somebody has to communicate the bad news to her.* ► convey, announce, report, reveal, declare, disclose, impart, pass on, relate USAGE You can also say *Somebody has to tell her the bad news*, or *Somebody has to inform her of the bad news*, or *Somebody has to acquaint her with the bad news* **2 communicate with** *Parents and teachers need to communicate with one another regularly.* ► speak to, talk to, make contact with, liaise with **3 communicate with** *Each bedroom communicates with its own bathroom.* ► connect with, adjoin, lead to **4** *It is possible to communicate the disease through ordinary contact.* ► transmit, pass on, infect someone with, spread, transfer, give

communication *NOUN* **1** *She received an official communication from the tax office.* ► message, letter, correspondence, advice **2** *There has been little communication between them for several years.* ► contact, dealings, association, relations, correspondence, intercourse **3** *The newsletters are used for the communication of information.* ► transmission, imparting, disclosure, dissemination, reporting, imparting, passing on

communicative *ADJECTIVE* *They are always friendly and communicative.* ► forthcoming, outgoing, informative, candid, uninhibited, frank, open, sociable, talkative OPPOSITES ARE uncommunicative, secretive

community *NOUN* **1** *He had the interests of the community in mind.* ► population, populace, society, people, residents, inhabitants, local people, general public **2** *a small farming community in the Borders* ► district, region, locality, neighbourhood **3** *a community of gay men* ► group, colony, commune, coterie, band, society

commute *VERB* **1** *The death sentence will be commuted to life imprisonment.* ► reduce, lessen, cut , lighten, remit, moderate, adjust **2** *Her husband commutes to the city every day.* ► travel, journey, shuttle

compact *ADJECTIVE* **1** *a compact machine that will fit in a small suitcase* ► small, little, petite, portable **2** *a compact encyclopedia* ► concise, succinct, condensed, brief

companion *NOUN* *He turned to speak to his companions.* ► friend, associate, comrade, colleague, partner, mate, escort

company *NOUN* **1** *I miss her company.* ► companionship, fellowship, society, presence, friendship **2** *We are expecting company tomorrow evening.* ► visitors, guests, callers **3** *He works for an insurance company.* ► firm, business, corporation, establishment, concern, enterprise, office, bureau **4** *a performance by the local theatre company*

people with you; companionship **4** visitors • *We've got company.* **5** a section of a battalion

comparative ADJECTIVE comparing a thing with something else • *They live in comparative comfort.*
▷ **comparatively** ADVERB

comparative NOUN **comparatives** the form of an adjective or adverb that expresses 'more' • *The comparative of 'big' is 'bigger'.*

compare VERB **compares, comparing, compared** put things together so as to tell in what ways they are similar or different
compare notes share information
compare with **1** be similar to **2** be as good as • *Our art gallery cannot compare with Tate Modern.*
USAGE When **compare** is used with an object, it can be followed by either *to* or *with*. Traditionally *to* is used when you are showing the similarity between two things: *She compared me to a pig.* *With* is used when you are looking at the similarities and differences between things: *Just compare this year's profits with last year's.*

comparison NOUN **comparisons** the act of comparing things

compartment NOUN **compartments** **1** one of the spaces into which something is divided; a separate room or enclosed space **2** a division of a railway carriage

compass NOUN **compasses** a device that shows direction, with a magnetized needle pointing to the north
compasses or **pair of compasses** a device for drawing circles, usually with two rods hinged together at one end

compassion NOUN pity or mercy
▷ **compassionate** ADJECTIVE **compassionately** ADVERB

compel VERB **compels, compelling, compelled** force somebody to do something

compensate VERB **compensates, compensating, compensated** **1** give a person money etc. to make up for a loss or injury **2** have a balancing effect • *This victory compensates for our earlier defeats.*
▷ **compensation** NOUN **compensatory** ADJECTIVE

compete VERB **competes, competing, competed** take part in a competition

Thesaurus

► group, troupe, society, ensemble, association **5** *a company of friends* ► group, circle, community, band, gang, gathering

comparable ADJECTIVE *Customers will look elsewhere for better service at comparable prices. Interest rates are not comparable to those in the rest of Europe.* ► similar, equivalent, corresponding, proportionate, commensurate (with), analogous, parallel, compatible (with), equal, related AN OPPOSITE IS dissimilar

compare VERB **1** *We have to compare this year's results with last year's.* ► check (against), contrast, correlate, juxtapose, set side by side, weigh, draw parallels between, make connections between, match, relate **2** *You can't compare the book to the video.* ► liken, equate, draw a parallel between (*the book and the video*), regard (*the book*) as the same as (*the video*) **3** **compare with** *Our achievements hardly compare with yours.* ► match, equal, compete with, emulate, rival, vie with

comparison NOUN **1** *There is no comparison between the two versions of the story.* ► resemblance, likeness, similarity, correspondence, parallel, correlation, equivalence, analogy **2** *The conclusions are based on a comparison of Hackney and Westminster.* ► analysis, collation, correlation, juxtaposition, contrast

compartment NOUN **1** *He then discovered that the case had a secret compartment.* ► section, space, pocket, cavity, recess **2** *The shed has a small compartment at the back for tools.* ► alcove, space, niche, cubby hole, chamber, division

compel VERB **1** *The court could compel him to give evidence.* ► force, oblige, coerce, constrain, order, pressure, pressurize **2** **be compelled to** *In the end Jem was compelled to admit the truth.* ► have to, be obliged to, be bound to, have no choice but to

compensate VERB **1** *If you have lost money you will be compensated for it.* ► recompense, repay, reimburse, pay back, remunerate **2** **compensate for** *Nothing can compensate for such a dreadful loss.* ► make up for, make amends for, balance, offset, counteract, cancel out, neutralize, redress, atone for

compensation NOUN **1** *You will receive compensation for any loss.* ► reparation, recompense, reimbursement, repayment, restitution, amends **2** *The balmy evening was some compensation for the unpleasantness of the day.* ► consolation, recompense, comfort

compete VERB **1** *The boys were competing in a five-a-side tournament.* ► take part, participate, perform, enter, go in for **2** *You will have to compete with children over twice your age.* ► contend, vie **3** **compete with** *No one can compete with him when he's on good form.* ► match, rival, compare with, equal, challenge, emulate, keep up with

competent *ADJECTIVE* able to do a particular thing
▷ **competently** *ADVERB* **competence** *NOUN*

competition *NOUN* **competitions 1** a game or race or other contest in which people try to win **2** competing **3** the people competing with yourself
▷ **competitive** *ADJECTIVE*

competitor *NOUN* **competitors** someone who competes; a rival

compile *VERB* **compiles, compiling, compiled** put things together into a list or collection, e.g. to form a book
▷ **compiler** *NOUN* **compilation** *NOUN*

complacent *ADJECTIVE* smugly satisfied with the way things are, and feeling that no change or action is necessary
▷ **complacently** *ADVERB* **complacency** *NOUN*

complain *VERB* **complains, complaining, complained** say that you are annoyed or unhappy about something

complaint *NOUN* **complaints 1** a statement complaining about something **2** an illness

complement *NOUN* **complements 1** the quantity needed to fill or complete something • *The ship had its full complement of sailors.* **2** the word or words used after verbs such as *be* and *become* to complete the sense. In *She was brave* and *He became king of England*, the complements are *brave* and *king of England*
USAGE Do not confuse with **compliment**.

complementary *ADJECTIVE* completing; forming a complement

complementary angle *NOUN* **complementary angles** either of two angles that add up to 90°

complete *ADJECTIVE* **1** having all its parts **2** finished **3** thorough; in every way • *a complete stranger*
▷ **completely** *ADVERB* **completeness** *NOUN*

complete *VERB* **completes, completing, completed** make a thing complete; add what

Thesaurus

competent *ADJECTIVE* **1** *a competent builder* ► capable, proficient, accomplished, qualified, able, skilful, efficient, adept AN OPPOSITE IS incompetent **2** *a competent performance* ► adequate, satisfactory, acceptable, decent, reasonable

competition *NOUN* **1** *We face some fierce competition this year.* ► opposition, rivalry, contention, struggle, contest **2** *Lisa came third in the competition.* ► contest, match, tournament, game, championship, race

competitive *ADJECTIVE* **1** *a competitive sport* ► combative, contentious, aggressive, antagonistic **2** *a competitive player* ► ambitious, aggressive, combative **3** *Banking is a highly competitive business.* ► ruthless, aggressive, contentious, fierce, cut-throat **4** *top quality at competitive prices* ► reasonable, moderate, affordable, keen, economical OPPOSITES ARE exorbitant, uncompetitive

competitor *NOUN* **1** *Every competitor has to take a blood test.* ► candidate, contestant, entrant, participant, contender **2** *We have to improve on our business competitors.* ► rival, challenger, adversary, opponent

complacent *ADJECTIVE* *We are doing a good job but we must not be complacent.* ► smug, self-satisfied, overconfident, oversatisfied, pleased with yourself, self-congratulatory, self-righteous, unconcerned, contented, untroubled AN OPPOSITE IS dissatisfied

complain *VERB* **1** *We'll wait till we get home before complaining.* ► protest, make a complaint, grumble **2 complain about** *The neighbours complained about the noise.* ► protest about, grumble about, make a fuss about, object to, carp about, find fault with, criticize, condemn, (*more informal*) whinge about, (*more informal*) go on about

complaint *NOUN* **1** *After a series of complaints about his behaviour he was sent back to England.* ► protest, objection (to), criticism (of), accusation, grumble, censure, fault-finding, (*more informal*) gripe **2** *Supporters have little cause for complaint.* ► grievance, dissatisfaction, disapproval, criticism, grumbling, fuss **3** *Her breathing difficulty was due to a lung complaint.* ► disorder, disease, illness, infection, sickness, upset, affliction, ailment, indisposition, malady, malaise

complement *VERB* *The restaurant's wine list complements its good food perfectly.* ► accompany, complete, go with, round off, enhance, make complete, make perfect
USAGE Do not confuse **complement** with **compliment**

complete *ADJECTIVE* **1** *The complete report will be published tomorrow.* ► whole, full, entire, unabridged, unedited, unexpurgated, total, unabbreviated AN OPPOSITE IS incomplete **2** *The exercise is now complete.* ► completed, finished, concluded, ended, accomplished, achieved AN OPPOSITE IS incomplete **3** *He was acting like a complete fool.* ► absolute, utter, out-and-out, thorough, thoroughgoing, outright OPPOSITES ARE qualified, partial **4** *The story was complete rubbish.* ► utter, absolute, downright, sheer, pure, total, unqualified, unmitigated

complete *VERB* **1** *She will complete her training in two years.* ► finish, end, conclude, terminate, finalize, fulfil, round off, accomplish, achieve,

is needed
▷ **completion** NOUN

complex ADJECTIVE **1** made up of parts **2** complicated
▷ **complexity** NOUN

complex NOUN **complexes** **1** a set of buildings made up of related parts • *a sports complex* **2** a group of feelings or ideas that influence a person's behaviour etc. • *a persecution complex*

complexion NOUN **complexions** **1** the natural colour and appearance of the skin of the face **2** the way things seem • *That puts a different complexion on the matter.*

complicated ADJECTIVE **1** made up of many parts **2** difficult to understand or do

complication NOUN **complications** **1** something that complicates things or adds difficulties **2** a complicated condition

compliment NOUN **compliments** something said or done to show that you approve of a person or thing • *He paid me a compliment.*

compliments PLURAL NOUN formal greetings given in a message

compliment VERB **compliments, complimenting, complimented** pay someone a compliment; congratulate
USAGE Do not confuse with **complement**.

complimentary ADJECTIVE **1** expressing a compliment **2** given free of charge • *complimentary tickets*

component NOUN **components** each of the parts of which a thing is made up

compose VERB **composes, composing, composed** **1** form or make up • *The class is composed of 20 students.* **2** write music or poetry etc. **3** arrange in good order **4** make calm • *compose yourself*

composer NOUN **composers** a person who composes music etc.

composite (kom- poz- it) ADJECTIVE made up of a number of parts or different styles

Thesaurus

carry out, clinch, close, do, perfect, perform, (*informal*) wind up **2** *Please complete the application form attached.* ► fill in, fill out, fill up, answer

completely ADVERB *He was completely honest about what had happened.* ► totally, absolutely, utterly, entirely, perfectly, quite

completion NOUN *the completion of the project* ► finish, conclusion, realization, achievement, fulfilment

complex ADJECTIVE *a complex subject* ► complicated, intricate, involved, elaborate, convoluted, tortuous, tangled, diverse, manifold OPPOSITES ARE simple, straightforward

complexion NOUN **1** *a young girl with a pale complexion* ► colouring, colour, appearance, skin, skin colour **2** *The latest revelation put a new complexion on things.* ► perspective, angle, slant **3** *political views of different complexions* ► type, kind, sort, nature, character

complicated ADJECTIVE *a complicated story; a complicated set of rules* ► complex, intricate, involved, elaborate, convoluted, tortuous, tangled, diverse, manifold OPPOSITES ARE simple, straightforward

complication NOUN **1** *Patients can leave hospital after three days if no complications occur.* ► problem, setback, repercussion, difficulty, drawback, snag, complexity, ramification **2** *the complication of modern city life* ► intricacy, complexity, confusion

compliment NOUN *She blushed at the unexpected compliment.* ► praise, flattery, tribute, accolade, approval, eulogy, (*more informal*) pat on the back AN OPPOSITE IS insult
USAGE Do not confuse **compliment** with **complement**. *Flattery* usually means insincere praise.

compliment VERB *He complimented her on the performance.* ► praise, applaud, commend, congratulate, flatter OPPOSITES ARE criticize, insult USAGE See the note at the previous entry.

complimentary ADJECTIVE **1** *The comments were all complimentary.* ► appreciative, approving, favourable, congratulatory, laudatory, admiring, commendatory, eulogistic, flattering, fulsome, generous, rapturous, supportive OPPOSITES ARE critical, insulting **2** *You get a complimentary lunch on the day of arrival.* ► free, gratis, courtesy

comply VERB **comply with** *He was anxious to comply with their wishes.* ► abide by, accede to, observe, obey, follow, fulfil, acquiesce in, submit to, yield to, agree to, assent to, conform to, consent to, defer to, fall in with, perform, satisfy OPPOSITES ARE ignore, defy

component NOUN *a store full of components for computers* ► part, piece, bit, constituent part, spare part, unit, element, ingredient, item, (*more informal*) spare

compose VERB **1** *The village was composed of small huts.* ► build, compile, constitute, construct, fashion, form, frame, make, put together **2** *That year he composed mainly film music. She sat down to compose a letter.* ► write, create, arrange, devise, imagine, make up, produce **3** **compose yourself** *He began to tremble and tried to compose himself.* ► calm down, control yourself, settle down, pull yourself together
be composed of *The government was composed*

composition *NOUN* **compositions**
1 composing **2** something composed, especially a piece of music **3** an essay or story written as a school exercise **4** the parts that make something • *the composition of the soil*

compost *NOUN* **1** decayed leaves and grass etc. used as a fertilizer **2** a soil-like mixture for growing seedlings, cuttings, etc.

composure *NOUN* calmness of manner

compound *ADJECTIVE* made of two or more parts or ingredients

compound *NOUN* **compounds** a compound substance

compound *VERB* **compounds, compounding, compounded** put together; combine

comprehensible *ADJECTIVE* understandable

comprehensive *ADJECTIVE* including all or many kinds of people or things

comprehensive *NOUN* **comprehensives** a comprehensive school

comprehensive school *NOUN* **comprehensive schools** a secondary school for all or most of the children of an area

compress (kom- press) *VERB* **compresses, compressing, compressed** press together or into a smaller space
▷ **compression** *NOUN* **compressor** *NOUN*

compromise (kom- prom- I'z) *NOUN* **compromises** an agreement reached by each side accepting less than it asked for

compromise *VERB* **compromises, compromising, compromised** **1** settle a dispute by a compromise **2** expose someone to danger or suspicion etc. • *His confession compromises his sister.*

compulsion *NOUN* **compulsions** a strong and uncontrollable desire to do something

compulsory *ADJECTIVE* required by law or rule; not optional • *Wearing seat belts is compulsory.*

compunction *NOUN* a guilty feeling • *She felt no compunction about hitting the burglar.*

Thesaurus

of individuals rather than parties. ► consist of, comprise, contain, embody, incorporate, involve, comprehend, embrace, include

composition *NOUN* **1** *the composition of the new team* ► structure, make-up, formation, constitution, content, establishment, formulation **2** *the composition of a group of poems* ► writing, creation, devising, production **3** *a musical composition* ► piece, work, (*technical*) opus

composure *NOUN* *She acted with great composure.* ► self-control, dignity, calmness, coolness, tranquillity, (*more informal*) cool

compound *VERB* *The bad weather compounded our difficulties.* ► aggravate, exacerbate, intensify, increase, worsen, complicate

comprehend *VERB* *I tried to comprehend what he was saying.* ► understand, grasp, conceive, fathom, make sense of, appreciate, discern, fathom, follow, perceive

comprehensive *ADJECTIVE* *a comprehensive account of the topic* ► inclusive, complete, full, broad, exhaustive, compendious, wide-ranging, detailed, extensive, all-embracing, thorough, total, universal, encyclopedic
OPPOSITES ARE selective, partial

compress *VERB* **1** *The activities can be compressed into an eight-hour day.* ► squeeze, press, squash, jam **2** *The text has been compressed into a mere ten pages.* ► condense, abridge, shorten, cut, summarize

comprise *VERB* *The building comprises several apartments.* ► consist of, contain, be composed of, include, incorporate, embody, embrace, involve

compromise *NOUN* *Eventually the two sides reached a compromise.* ► understanding, accommodation, settlement, agreement, middle course, middle way

compromise *VERB* **1** *In the end we had to compromise.* ► make concessions, meet halfway, strike a balance, concede a point, negotiate, settle **2** *The scandal has severely compromised his reputation.* ► undermine, discredit, jeopardize, weaken, prejudice, risk, dishonour, imperil

compromising *ADJECTIVE* *Before he left he tore up the compromising letter.* ► embarrassing, damaging, scandalous, discreditable, dishonourable, improper

compulsion *NOUN* **1** *There is no compulsion to go.* ► obligation, necessity, constraint, pressure **2** *She felt a strong compulsion to tell the whole story.* ► urge, impulse, desire, longing, obsession

compulsive *ADJECTIVE* **1** *He felt a compulsive urge to jump out.* ► irresistible, uncontrollable, overpowering, overwhelming, besetting, compelling, driving, involuntary, powerful **2** *Not all fat people are compulsive over-eaters.* ► habitual, obsessive, addicted, persistent, incorrigible, incurable

compulsory *ADJECTIVE* *Each exam paper has one compulsory question. Carrying an identity card is now compulsory.* ► obligatory, mandatory,

compute *VERB* **computes**, **computing**, **computed** calculate
▷ **computation** *NOUN*

computer *NOUN* **computers** an electronic machine for making calculations, storing and analysing information put into it, or controlling machinery automatically

comrade *NOUN* **comrades** a companion who shares in your activities
▷ **comradeship** *NOUN*

concave *ADJECTIVE* curved like the inside of a ball or circle (The opposite is **convex**)
▷ **concavity** *NOUN*

conceal *VERB* **conceals**, **concealing**, **concealed** hide; keep something secret
▷ **concealment** *NOUN*

concede *VERB* **concedes**, **conceding**, **conceded** **1** admit that something is true **2** grant or allow something • *They conceded us the right to cross their land.* **3** admit that you have been defeated

conceit *NOUN* being too proud of yourself; vanity
▷ **conceited** *ADJECTIVE*

conceive *VERB* **conceives**, **conceiving**, **conceived** **1** become pregnant; form a baby in the womb **2** form an idea or plan; imagine • *I can't conceive why you want to come.*

concentrate *VERB* **concentrates**, **concentrating**, **concentrated** **1** give your full attention or effort to something **2** bring or come together in one place **3** make a liquid etc. less dilute

concentration *NOUN* **concentrations** **1** concentrating **2** the amount dissolved in each part of a liquid

concentric *ADJECTIVE* having the same centre • *concentric circles*

concept *NOUN* **concepts** an idea

conception *NOUN* **conceptions** **1** the conceiving of a baby **2** an idea

concern *VERB* **concerns**, **concerning**, **concerned** **1** be important to or affect somebody **2** worry somebody **3** be about; have as its subject • *The story concerns a group of rabbits.*

Thesaurus

binding, required, stipulated, unavoidable, de rigueur, imperative, imposed, incumbent, inescapable, official AN OPPOSITE IS optional

con *NOUN* *The offer proved to be just a con.* ► trick, cheat, swindle, deception, fraud

con *VERB* *They conned the couple out of their life savings.* ► trick, cheat, swindle, dupe, deceive, inveigle, hoodwink, (*more informal*) bamboozle

conceal *VERB* **1** *She concealed the device in her camera. A mass of cloud concealed the sun.* ► hide, cover up, disguise, secrete, blot out, mask, obscure, screen, veil, bury, cloak, envelop, camouflage OPPOSITES ARE reveal, expose, uncover **2** *He could barely conceal his frustration.* ► hide, suppress, keep secret, hush up, keep dark, keep quiet AN OPPOSITE IS reveal

concealed *ADJECTIVE* *The house stood behind a concealed entrance.* ► hidden, invisible, camouflaged, disguised, secret, cloaked, furtive, unobtrusive OPPOSITES ARE obvious, visible

concede *VERB* **1** *I conceded that I might have been wrong.* ► admit, acknowledge, accept, grant, agree, recognize, allow, confess AN OPPOSITE IS deny **2** *The country conceded some of the territory to its neighbour.* ► surrender, yield, give up, relinquish, cede, hand over, submit

conceit *NOUN* *She said it without conceit, simply as a fact.* ► vanity, arrogance, pride, boastfulness

conceited *ADJECTIVE* *Without sounding conceited, I think we offer the best service.* ► vain, boastful, immodest, arrogant, haughty, self-satisfied, proud, complacent, (*more informal*) cocky AN OPPOSITE IS modest

conceive *VERB* **1** *She was unable to conceive.* ► get pregnant, become pregnant, have a baby **2** *The plan was conceived after the war.* ► think up, devise, originate, create, form, formulate, invent, design **3** *It is hard to conceive what it must have been like for them.* ► imagine, envisage, visualize, picture, appreciate, comprehend, apprehend, grasp

concentrate *VERB* **1** **concentrate on** *Sharon was concentrating on the video.* ► pay attention to, keep your mind on, put your mind to, apply yourself to, focus on, be engrossed in, be absorbed in, attend to, think about **2** *Troops concentrated on the border.* ► gather, mass, collect, congregate, converge, crowd, accumulate AN OPPOSITE IS disperse **3** *We need to concentrate our efforts on improving public services.* ► focus, direct (to), aim (at), intensify OPPOSITES ARE reduce, dilute

concentrated *ADJECTIVE* **1** *concentrated fruit juice* ► condensed, undiluted, reduced, rich, dense, strong, evaporated AN OPPOSITE IS diluted **2** *making concentrated efforts* ► intense, strenuous, intensive, concerted, vigorous, committed, thorough, hard, (*more informal*) all-out AN OPPOSITE IS half-hearted

concept *NOUN* *It's not an easy concept to grasp.* ► idea, notion, principle, theory, thought, hypothesis, image, conception

concern *VERB* **1** *What I have to say concerns everyone.* ► affect, involve, apply to, refer to,

concern *NOUN* **concerns** **1** something that concerns you; a responsibility **2** worry **3** a business

concert *NOUN* **concerts** a musical entertainment

concerto (kon-chert-oh) *NOUN* **concertos** a piece of music for a solo instrument and an orchestra

concession *NOUN* **concessions** **1** conceding **2** something conceded **3** a reduction in price for a certain category of person
▷ **concessionary** *ADJECTIVE*

conciliate *VERB* **conciliates, conciliating, conciliated** **1** win over an angry or hostile person by friendliness **2** help people who disagree to come to an agreement
▷ **conciliation** *NOUN*

concise *ADJECTIVE* brief; giving much information in a few words
▷ **concisely** *ADVERB* **conciseness** *NOUN*

conclude *VERB* **concludes, concluding, concluded** **1** bring or come to an end **2** decide; form an opinion by reasoning • *The jury concluded that he was guilty.*

conclusion *NOUN* **conclusions** **1** an ending **2** an opinion formed by reasoning

conclusive *ADJECTIVE* putting an end to all doubt
▷ **conclusively** *ADVERB*

concoct *VERB* **concocts, concocting, concocted** **1** make something by putting ingredients together **2** invent • *We'll have to concoct an excuse.*
▷ **concoction** *NOUN*

concord *NOUN* friendly agreement or harmony

concrete *NOUN* cement mixed with sand and gravel, used in building

concrete *ADJECTIVE* **1** able to be touched and felt; not abstract **2** definite • *We need concrete evidence, not theories.*

concurrent *ADJECTIVE* happening or existing at the same time

concussion *NOUN* a temporary injury to the brain caused by a hard knock
▷ **concussed** *ADJECTIVE*

condemn *VERB* **condemns, condemning, condemned** **1** say that you strongly disapprove of something **2** convict or sentence a criminal • *He was condemned to death.* **3** make

Thesaurus

relate to, be relevant to, be important to, interest, matter to, (*more formal*) pertain to **2** *The book concerns various aspects of the subject.* ► deal with, be about, treat, describe, review, relate to **3** *Her news concerned us deeply.* ► worry, disturb, upset, trouble, distress, bother

concern *NOUN* **1** *concern for others* ► regard, consideration, thought, care, attention (to), interest (in) **2** *It's no concern of ours.* ► affair, business, matter, responsibility, problem **3** *a cause for great concern* ► anxiety, worry, disquiet, unease, distress, apprehension **4** *a publishing concern* ► company, firm, business, enterprise, establishment, organization, corporation

concerned *ADJECTIVE* **1** *His parents looked concerned.* ► worried, anxious, troubled, bothered, disturbed, distressed, fearful, upset
AN OPPOSITE IS unconcerned **2** *If you want more information, talk to the people concerned.* ► connected, interested, involved, relevant

concise *ADJECTIVE* *a concise account of events in the war* ► brief, succinct, compact, short, condensed, concentrated, compressed, abridged, abbreviated, pithy, terse
OPPOSITES ARE lengthy, diffuse

conclude *VERB* **1** *Hostilities concluded at midnight.* ► finish, end, stop, cease, terminate, be over, come to a close, be brought to an end
OPPOSITES ARE start, commence **2** *The jury concluded that the witness had been lying.* ► infer, deduce, decide, gather, judge, suppose, think, reckon, surmise, assume **3** *an attempt to conclude a treaty* ► negotiate, agree, come to terms on, arrange, effect, bring about, broker

conclusion *NOUN* **1** *A few gentle jokes formed the conclusion of her speech.* ► end, finish, close, completion, termination, culmination, finale, rounding-off, peroration **2** *The court's original conclusion in the case has been proved correct.* ► deduction, decision, judgement, verdict, opinion, interpretation, inference, resolution, belief, conjecture, assumption, presumption, surmise

conclusive *ADJECTIVE* *It will be difficult to provide conclusive proof.* ► decisive, definitive, definite, indisputable, incontrovertible, irrefutable, unequivocal, unambiguous, unarguable, convincing, persuasive, unanswerable
AN OPPOSITE IS inconclusive

concoct *VERB* *She didn't have much time to concoct her story.* ► make up, think up, invent, fabricate, contrive, formulate, prepare, devise, create, develop, (*more informal*) cook up

concrete *ADJECTIVE* **1** *concrete objects* ► solid, physical, material, palpable, substantial, tactile, touchable, visible **2** *The case lacks concrete evidence. The proposals are not yet concrete.* ► firm, solid, objective, tangible, material, physical, factual, real, actual, definite, existing OPPOSITES ARE abstract, theoretical

condemn *VERB* **1** *He condemned all forms of violence.* ► deplore, denounce, castigate, criticize, censure OPPOSITES ARE commend,

someone suffer something unpleasant • *They were condemned to a life of poverty.* **4** declare that houses etc. are not fit to be used
▷ **condemnation** NOUN

condense VERB **condenses, condensing, condensed** **1** make a liquid denser or more compact **2** put something into fewer words **3** change from gas or vapour to liquid • *Steam condenses on windows.*
▷ **condensation** NOUN **condenser** NOUN

condescend VERB **condescends, condescending, condescended** **1** behave in a way which shows that you feel superior to others **2** allow yourself to do something that seems unsuitable for a person of your high rank
▷ **condescension** NOUN

condition NOUN **conditions** **1** the state or fitness of a person or thing • *This bicycle is in good condition.* **2** the situation or surroundings etc. that affect something • *working conditions* **3** something required as part of an agreement
on condition that only if; on the understanding that something will be done

condition VERB **conditions, conditioning, conditioned** **1** put something into a good or proper condition **2** train someone to behave in a particular way or become used to a particular situation

conditional ADJECTIVE depending on a condition or requirement being met • *a conditional offer*
▷ **conditionally** ADVERB

condom NOUN **condoms** a rubber sheath worn on the penis during sexual intercourse as a contraceptive and as a protection against disease

condone VERB **condones, condoning, condoned** forgive or ignore wrongdoing • *We do not condone violence.*

conduct (kon-**dukt**) VERB **conducts, conducting, conducted** **1** lead or guide **2** be the conductor of an orchestra or choir **3** manage or direct something • *conduct an experiment* **4** allow heat, light, sound, or electricity to pass along or through **5** behave • *They conducted themselves with dignity.*

conduction NOUN the conducting of heat or electricity etc.

conductor NOUN **conductors** **1** a person who directs the performance of an orchestra or choir by movements of the arms **2** a person who collects the fares on a bus etc. **3** something that conducts heat or electricity etc.
▷ **conductress** NOUN

cone NOUN **cones** **1** an object that is circular at one end and narrows to a point at the other end **2** an ice cream cornet **3** the dry cone-shaped fruit of a pine, fir, or cedar tree

confectionery NOUN sweets, cakes, and sweet biscuits

Thesaurus

approve of **2** *The committee condemned them for their behaviour.* ► criticize, censure, denounce, reprehend, deprecate, disparage, berate, revile **3** *After a lengthy trial the court finally condemned them.* ► convict, find guilty, sentence, pass judgement, prove guilty, punish, judge
AN OPPOSITE IS acquit

condense VERB **1** *She condensed the ten episodes into a single hour-long drama.* ► shorten, reduce, abridge, compress, cut, contract, telescope, summarize AN OPPOSITE IS expand **2** *The liquid is slowly condensed.* ► distil, reduce, concentrate, solidify, thicken AN OPPOSITE IS dilute

condescend VERB *Eventually an official condescended to see us.* ► deign, consent, see fit, vouchsafe, stoop, lower yourself

condescending ADJECTIVE *She narrowed her eyes at us in a condescending manner.* ► superior, supercilious, disdainful, patronizing, haughty, imperious, lofty, (*more informal*) snooty

condition NOUN **1** *Check that your vehicle is in good condition.* ► order, state, shape, (*more informal*) trim, (*more informal*) nick USAGE If you use *state* you have to say *in a good state* **2** *She was told she had a medical condition.* ► disorder, illness, disease, complaint, ailment, infirmity **3** *There are some conditions attached to membership.* ► requirement, proviso, term, qualification, restriction, stipulation, limitation, obligation

conditional ADJECTIVE *The offer of a place was a conditional one.* ► provisional, qualified, dependent, limited, restricted AN OPPOSITE IS unconditional

condone VERB *We cannot condone this sort of behaviour.* ► tolerate, endorse, disregard, overlook, pardon, forgive, ignore, allow, connive at, excuse, let someone off
OPPOSITES ARE condemn, punish

conduct NOUN **1** *good conduct* ► behaviour, demeanour, attitude, bearing, manner, ways, actions **2** *the conduct of the nation's affairs* ► management, direction, handling, organization, running, supervision, administration, control, discharge

conduct VERB **1** *Visitors are conducted round the building in small groups.* ► escort, guide, accompany, take, usher, lead, convey, shepherd **2** *The group conducted a survey into children's eating habits.* ► organize, administer, coordinate, carry out, manage, direct, run, handle, preside over
conduct yourself *He conducted himself in a*

confederate *ADJECTIVE* allied; joined by an agreement or treaty

confederate *NOUN* **confederates** **1** a member of a confederacy **2** an ally; an accomplice

confederation *NOUN* **confederations** **1** the process of joining in an alliance **2** a group of people, organizations, or states joined together by an agreement or treaty

conference *NOUN* **conferences** a meeting for holding a discussion

confess *VERB* **confesses, confessing, confessed** say openly that you have done something wrong or have a weakness; admit

confession *NOUN* **confessions** saying that you have done something wrong

confetti *NOUN* tiny pieces of coloured paper thrown by wedding guests at the bride and bridegroom

confide *VERB* **confides, confiding, confided** **1** tell someone a secret • *I decided to confide in my sister.* **2** entrust something to someone

confidence *NOUN* **confidences** **1** firm trust **2** a feeling of certainty or boldness; being sure that you can do something **3** something told confidentially

in confidence as a secret

in a person's confidence trusted with his or her secrets

confidence trick *NOUN* **confidence tricks** swindling a person after persuading him or her to trust you

confident *ADJECTIVE* showing or feeling confidence; bold

▷ **confidently** *ADVERB*

confidential *ADJECTIVE* meant to be kept secret

▷ **confidentially** *ADVERB* **confidentiality** *NOUN*

confine *VERB* **confines, confining, confined** **1** keep something within limits; restrict • *Please confine your remarks to the subject being discussed.* **2** keep somebody in a place

confirm *VERB* **confirms, confirming, confirmed** **1** prove that something is true or correct **2** make a thing definite • *Please write to*

Thesaurus

typically high-handed manner. ► behave, act, carry on, acquit yourself

confer *VERB* **1** *The King conferred a knighthood on him.* ► bestow, award, accord, give, grant, honour with, invest USAGE Note that with all the alternatives apart from *bestow*, you say (for example) *The King awarded him a knighthood.* If you use *bestow* you follow the same pattern as for *confer.* **2** *He asked for a pause to confer with his colleagues.* ► consult, discuss things, have a discussion, speak, communicate, deliberate

conference *NOUN* **1** *an international conference on the environment.* ► congress, convention, meeting, symposium, summit **2** *They gathered round the table for a conference.* ► discussion, consultation, deliberation, exchange of views, talks

confess *VERB* **1** *Several of the suspects later confessed.* ► admit guilt, plead guilty, own up, accept blame, (*more informal*) come clean **2** *She confessed that she had broken the man's window.* ► own up, admit, acknowledge, concede **3** *I confess I agree with all they have said.* ► admit, concede, grant, allow

confession *NOUN* *The interrogators failed to get a confession out of him.* ► admission of guilt, acknowledgement of guilt, declaration, disclosure, profession, revelation

confide *VERB* *He confided his fears to his wife.* ► reveal, disclose, divulge, admit, declare

confide in *He is not easy to confide in.* ► unburden yourself to, tell all to, trust in

confidence *NOUN* **1** *We can face the future with confidence. She shows a lot of confidence.* ► optimism, assurance, positiveness, conviction, certainty, credence, faith, hope, reliance, trust OPPOSITES ARE doubt, scepticism, diffidence

have confidence in *They have confidence in your abilities.* ► trust, believe in, be sure of

confident *ADJECTIVE* **1** *We are confident that the money can be found.* ► optimistic, hopeful, sure, certain, convinced, sanguine, positive, trusting AN OPPOSITE IS doubtful **2** *She lifted her head in a confident gesture.* ► self-assured, self-confident, assertive, assured, self-possessed, self-reliant, positive, bold, composed, definite, fearless, secure, unafraid AN OPPOSITE IS diffident

confidential *ADJECTIVE* **1** *All conversations are strictly confidential.* ► secret, top secret, private, personal, classified, restricted, suppressed, intimate, (*more informal*) hush-hush, (*more informal*) off the record **2** *a confidential secretary* ► personal, private, trusted

confine *VERB* **1** *She confined her writing to poems and short stories.* ► restrict, limit, keep **2** *During the winter months the animals are confined in a small field near the buildings. He was confined in the Tower to await his trial.* ► enclose, imprison, keep, shut, close, fence, box, cage, incarcerate, intern, isolate

confinement *NOUN* **1** *a period of confinement* ► imprisonment, incarceration, detention, internment, custody, captivity, restraint OPPOSITES ARE freedom, liberty **2** *She was admitted to hospital for her confinement.* ► labour, delivery, childbirth

confirm *VERB* **1** *What happened next day confirmed her suspicions about the place.* ► support, corroborate, bear out, back up,

confirm your booking. **3** make a person a full member of the Christian Church
▷ **confirmation** NOUN **confirmatory** ADJECTIVE

confiscate VERB **confiscates, confiscating, confiscated** take something away as a punishment
▷ **confiscation** NOUN

conflagration NOUN **conflagrations** a great and destructive fire

conflict (kon-flikt) NOUN **conflicts** a fight, struggle, or disagreement

conflict (kon-flikt) VERB **conflicts, conflicting, conflicted** have a conflict; differ or disagree

conform VERB **conforms, conforming, conformed** keep to accepted rules, customs, or ideas
▷ **conformist** NOUN **conformity** NOUN

confound VERB **confounds, confounding, confounded** **1** astonish or puzzle someone **2** confuse

confront VERB **confronts, confronting, confronted** **1** come or bring face to face, especially in a hostile way **2** be present and have to be dealt with • *Problems confront us.*
▷ **confrontation** NOUN

confuse VERB **confuses, confusing, confused** **1** make a person puzzled or muddled

Thesaurus

upheld, validate, approve, give credence to, substantiate OPPOSITES ARE contradict, disprove **2** *The hotel will need a deposit to confirm the booking.* ► verify, guarantee, clinch, endorse, validate, ratify, formalize, make legal, make official AN OPPOSITE IS cancel **3** *I confirm that I will be arriving on Saturday.* ► affirm, assert, assure you, give an assurance

confirmation NOUN **1** *The DNA evidence provided confirmation of his guilt.* ► proof, corroboration, verification, testimony, substantiation **2** *Confirmation of the appointment will follow shortly.* ► ratification, endorsement, approval, validation, formalization

conflict NOUN **1** *conflict between management and workers* ► dispute, disagreement, discord, contention, confrontation, dissension, antagonism, hostility, friction, strife, clash AN OPPOSITE IS harmony **2** *a military conflict* ► war, struggle, confrontation, contest, clash, campaign, encounter, engagement, action, battle, combat, feud, fight, quarrel, skirmish, warfare

conflict VERB *This fact conflicts with statements made back in September.* ► clash, disagree, differ (from), be incompatible, be inconsistent, be at variance, be at odds OPPOSITES ARE support, agree with

conform VERB **1** *I conform because I think it gives a good impression.* ► comply, acquiesce, follow convention, fit in, obey the rules, play by the rules, keep in step OPPOSITES ARE rebel, disobey, differ **2 conform to** *You have to conform to strict rules of etiquette.* ► comply with, follow, obey, abide by, accept, accede to, fit in with, uphold, fulfil **3 conform to** *Our experiences do no always conform to our beliefs.* ► match, fit, suit, correspond to, agree with, tally with, harmonize with, accord with, compare with, square with

conformity NOUN *There is a lot of conformity among young people.* ► conventionality, orthodoxy, uniformity, compliance, obedience, submission OPPOSITES ARE eccentricity, rebellion

confront VERB **1** *He confronted an intruder in the hallway.* ► challenge, accost, approach, stand up to, take on, tackle, defy, face, meet, oppose, withstand, argue with, brave AN OPPOSITE IS avoid **2** *He realized he had to confront his problems and sort himself out.* ► tackle, face up to, address, deal with, cope with

confrontation NOUN *a serious confrontation with the authorities* ► conflict, dispute, disagreement, discord, contention, dissension, antagonism, hostility, friction, strife, clash

confuse VERB **1** *All these comments only confuse the issue.* ► complicate, muddle, obscure, cloud, obfuscate **2** *Too much detail will confuse us.* ► bewilder, perplex, baffle, puzzle, mystify, bemuse, disconcert, confound, (*more informal*) flummox, (*more informal*) floor

confused ADJECTIVE **1** *The children were very confused about what was happening.* ► bewildered, perplexed, baffled, puzzled, mystified, bemused, disconcerted, confounded, (*more informal*) flummoxed AN OPPOSITE IS clear **2** *Her clothes lay in a confused pile on the floor.* ► untidy, disorderly, disorganized, muddled, jumbled OPPOSITES ARE tidy, organized **3** *confused accounts of the incident* ► vague, muddled, unclear, indistinct AN OPPOSITE IS clear

confusion NOUN **1** *a lot of confusion about which system to buy* ► uncertainty, indecision, misunderstanding, hesitation, doubt, ignorance **2** *People were wandering about in confusion.* ► bewilderment, perplexity, bafflement, mystification, shock **3** *The kitchen was in a terrible state of confusion.* ► disorder, disorganization, untidiness, clutter, chaos, mayhem, disarray, muddle, jumble, mess, shambles

2 mistake one thing for another
▷ **confusion** NOUN

confute VERB **confutes, confuting, confuted** prove a person or statement to be wrong
▷ **confutation** NOUN

congeal (kon-jeel) VERB **congeals, congealing, congealed** become jelly-like instead of liquid, especially in cooling
• *congealed blood.*

congenital (kon-jen-it-al) ADJECTIVE existing in a person from birth
▷ **congenitally** ADVERB

congested ADJECTIVE crowded or blocked up
• *congested streets* • *congested lungs*
▷ **congestion** NOUN

conglomeration NOUN **conglomerations** a mass of different things put together

congratulate VERB **congratulates, congratulating, congratulated** tell a person that you are pleased about his or her success or good fortune
▷ **congratulation** NOUN **congratulatory** ADJECTIVE

congregate VERB **congregates, congregating, congregated** assemble; flock together

congregation NOUN **congregations** a group of people who have come together to take part in religious worship

Congress NOUN the parliament of the USA

congruent ADJECTIVE congruent triangles have exactly the same shape and size
▷ **congruence** NOUN

conic ADJECTIVE to do with a cone

conical ADJECTIVE cone-shaped
▷ **conically** ADVERB

conifer (kon-if-er) NOUN **conifers** an evergreen tree with cones
▷ **coniferous** ADJECTIVE

conjecture NOUN **conjectures** guesswork or a guess
▷ **conjecture** VERB **conjectural** ADJECTIVE

conjugate VERB **conjugates, conjugating, conjugated** give all the different forms of a verb
▷ **conjugation** NOUN

conjunction NOUN **conjunctions** 1 a word that joins words or phrases or sentences, e.g. *and, but* 2 combination or union • *The four armies acted in conjunction.*

conjure VERB **conjures, conjuring, conjured** perform tricks that look like magic
▷ **conjuror** NOUN
conjure up produce in your mind • *Mention of the Arctic conjures up visions of snow.*

connect VERB **connects, connecting, connected** 1 join together; link 2 think of things or people as being associated with each other

connection NOUN **connections** 1 a point where two things are connected; a link • *We all know there is a connection between smoking and cancer.* 2 a train, bus, etc. that leaves a station soon after another arrives, so that passengers can change from one to the other

connoisseur (kon-a-ser) NOUN **connoisseurs** a person with great experience and appreciation of something • *a connoisseur of wine*

conquer VERB **conquers, conquering, conquered** defeat or overcome
▷ **conqueror** NOUN

Thesaurus

congratulate VERB *I must congratulate Freda on her success.* ► praise, compliment, commend, applaud, acclaim

congratulations PLURAL NOUN 1 *We sent our congratulations on their wedding.* ► compliments, good wishes, greetings, felicitations 2 *You all deserve warm congratulations on the success of the enterprise.* ► praise, commendation, applause

congregate VERB *A large crowd had congregated in the town square.* ► gather, assemble, come together, collect, converge, convene, crowd together, rally, rally round, meet, flock together, join up, swarm, muster, throng round, accumulate

connect VERB 1 *The speakers are connected to a powerful amplifier.* ► link, attach, couple, join, fasten AN OPPOSITE IS disconnect. 2 *Police believe the two crimes could be connected.* ► associate, link, relate, couple, compare, tie up, bracket together, put together AN OPPOSITE IS dissociate

connection NOUN *There is a connection between money and power.* ► relationship, link, association, correlation, correspondence, bond, affinity, coherence, contact, interrelationship, join, unity, (*more informal*) tie-up AN OPPOSITE IS distinction

conquer VERB 1 *Napoleon's attempt to conquer Europe* ► seize, capture, overrun, occupy, invade, take possession of, subjugate, take, win, annex, subject 2 *William of Normandy conquered the English at the Battle of Hastings.* ► defeat, beat, overcome, conquer, vanquish, subdue, crush, overpower, rout 3 *With a great effort she conquered her fears.* ► overcome, suppress, master, control, curb, surmount, prevail over

conqueror NOUN *He entered the capital of Bengal as a conqueror.* ► victor, subjugator, defeater, winner, champion, master

conquest *NOUN* **conquests** **1** a victory over someone **2** conquered territory

conscience (kon- shens) *NOUN* **consciences** knowing what is right and wrong, especially in your own actions

conscientious (kon- shee- en- shus) *ADJECTIVE* careful and honest about doing your work properly
▷ **conscientiously** *ADVERB*

conscientious objector *NOUN* **conscientious objectors** a person who refuses to serve in the armed forces because he or she believes it is morally wrong

conscious (kon- shus) *ADJECTIVE* **1** awake and knowing what is happening **2** aware of something • *I was not conscious of the time.* **3** done deliberately • *a conscious decision*
▷ **consciously** *ADVERB* **consciousness** *NOUN*

conscript (kon- skript) *VERB* **conscripts, conscripting, conscripted** make a person join the armed forces
▷ **conscription** *NOUN*

conscript (kon- skript) *NOUN* **conscripts** a conscripted person

consecrate *VERB* **consecrates, consecrating, consecrated** officially say that a thing, especially a building, is holy
▷ **consecration** *NOUN*

consecutive *ADJECTIVE* following one after another
▷ **consecutively** *ADVERB*

consensus *NOUN* **consensuses** general agreement; the opinion of most people

consent *NOUN* agreement to what someone wishes; permission

consent *VERB* **consents, consenting, consented** say that you are willing to do or allow what someone wishes

consequence *NOUN* **consequences** **1** something that happens as the result of an event or action **2** importance • *It is of no consequence.*

consequent *ADJECTIVE* happening as a result
▷ **consequently** *ADVERB*

conservation *NOUN* conserving; preservation, especially of the natural environment
▷ **conservationist** *NOUN*

conservative *ADJECTIVE* **1** liking traditional ways and disliking changes **2** moderate or cautious; not extreme • *a conservative estimate*
▷ **conservatively** *ADVERB* **conservatism** *NOUN*

Thesaurus

conquest *NOUN* *Alexander's conquest of the Persian Empire* ► defeat, subjection, subjugation, capture, invasion, occupation, annexation, appropriation, overthrow, triumph (over), victory (over), (*more informal*) takeover

conscience *NOUN* **1** *His conscience forced him to admit the truth in the end.* ► moral sense, principles, morals, ethics, standards **2** *Large organizations have no conscience about getting rid of people.* ► scruples, compunction, misgivings, qualms, reservations

conscientious *ADJECTIVE* *a conscientious worker* ► hard-working, diligent, industrious, painstaking, thorough, meticulous, punctilious, accurate, attentive, dedicated, rigorous, careful, dutiful, unflagging, assiduous, scrupulous OPPOSITES ARE careless, irresponsible, lazy

conscious *ADJECTIVE* **1** *Despite the blow to his head, he remained conscious.* ► awake, aware, alert, compos mentis, sensible AN OPPOSITE IS unconscious **2** *It was a conscious attempt to deceive us.* ► deliberate, intended, intentional, calculated, knowing, planned, premeditated, studied, wilful AN OPPOSITE IS accidental

consecutive *ADJECTIVE* *Interest rates have remained unchanged for six consecutive months.* ► continuous, successive, uninterrupted, running (*six months running*), in succession (*six months in succession*), in a row (*six months in a row*)

consent *VERB* **1** *In the end she consented to do something about it.* ► agree, be willing, undertake OPPOSITES ARE refuse, decline **2** **consent to** *He said the girl had consented to his advances.* ► agree to, allow, approve, concede, grant, authorize, permit, comply with OPPOSITES ARE refuse, forbid

consent *NOUN* *The authorities refused their consent.* ► agreement, assent, permission, authorization, approval, backing, endorsement, (*more informal*) go-ahead

consequence *NOUN* **1** *Cooling of the stratosphere was seen as a consequence of the greenhouse effect.* ► result, effect, outcome, aftermath, by-product, corollary, repercussion, sequel, side-effect, upshot **2** *These small losses are of little consequence.* ► importance, significance, account, concern, moment, note, value, weight

conservation *NOUN* *the conservation of energy and resources* ► preservation, protection, safeguarding, saving, careful management, economy, maintenance, upkeep AN OPPOSITE IS destruction

conservative *ADJECTIVE* **1** *conservative ideas; his conservative father* ► traditional, conventional, orthodox, reactionary, old-fashioned, die-hard, hidebound, moderate, narrow-minded,

Conservative *NOUN* **Conservatives** a person who supports the Conservative Party, a political party that favours private enterprise and freedom from state control
▷ **Conservative** *ADJECTIVE*

conserve *VERB* **conserves, conserving, conserved** prevent something valuable from being changed, spoilt, or wasted

consider *VERB* **considers, considering, considered** **1** think carefully about or give attention to something, especially in order to make a decision **2** have an opinion; think to be • *Consider yourself lucky.*

considerable *ADJECTIVE* fairly great • *a considerable amount*
▷ **considerably** *ADVERB*

considerate *ADJECTIVE* taking care not to inconvenience or hurt others
▷ **considerately** *ADVERB*

consideration *NOUN* **considerations** **1** being considerate **2** careful thought or attention **3** a fact that must be kept in mind **4** payment given as a reward
take into consideration allow for

considering *PREPOSITION* taking something into consideration • *The car runs well, considering its age.*

consist *VERB* **consists, consisting, consisted** be made up or composed of • *The flat consists of three rooms.*

consistency *NOUN* **consistencies** **1** being consistent **2** thickness or stiffness, especially of a liquid

consistent *ADJECTIVE* **1** keeping to a regular pattern or style; not changing **2** not contradictory
▷ **consistently** *ADVERB*

consolation *NOUN* **consolations** **1** consoling **2** something that consoles someone

console [1] (kon-sohl) *VERB* **consoles, consoling, consoled** comfort someone who is unhappy or disappointed

console [2] (kon-sohl) *NOUN* **consoles** a panel or unit containing the controls for equipment

consolidate *VERB* **consolidates, consolidating, consolidated** **1** make or become secure and strong **2** combine two or more organizations, funds, etc. into one
▷ **consolidation** *NOUN*

Thesaurus

sober, unadventurous OPPOSITES ARE progressive, radical **2** *the conservative section of the party* ► right-wing, right-of-centre, reactionary, traditionalist, Tory OPPOSITES ARE radical, socialist **3** *Fifty pounds is a conservative estimate.* ► cautious, moderate, reasonable, understated, unexaggerated AN OPPOSITE IS extreme

conserve *VERB* *It is important to conserve energy.* ► save, preserve, protect, sustain, maintain, safeguard, be economical with, use sparingly, keep, look after, store up OPPOSITES ARE waste, squander

consider *VERB* **1** *Donna paused to consider the possibilities.* ► think about, contemplate, ponder, reflect on, weigh up, mull over, cogitate, deliberate, muse, meditate on, discuss, examine, ruminate, study, (*informal*) turn over **2** *I consider it a privilege.* ► regard (as), deem, count, think, judge, reckon, believe (to be)

considerable *ADJECTIVE* *There was a considerable amount of traffic on the road. He had inherited a considerable sum from his grandparents.* ► substantial, sizeable, appreciable, significant, reasonable, respectable, tolerable, worthwhile, large, comfortable, noteworthy, noticeable, perceptible AN OPPOSITE IS negligible

considerate *ADJECTIVE* *We are encouraged to be polite, modest, and considerate to others.* ► kind, thoughtful, attentive, helpful, caring, obliging, generous, sensitive, accommodating OPPOSITES ARE inconsiderate, selfish

consideration *NOUN* *The matter needs careful consideration.* ► thought, attention, deliberation, reflection, examination, contemplation, meditation, scrutiny, review

consist *VERB* **consist of** *Audiences consist of very different types of people.* ► be composed of, comprise, be made of, include, contain, incorporate, involve

consistent *ADJECTIVE* **1** *a consistent pattern of behaviour* ► steady, uniform, stable, regular, even, uniform, constant, unchanging, unvarying, dependable, reliable, predictable, unfailing **2** *The theory is consistent with recent research.* ► compatible, in accordance, in agreement, in harmony AN OPPOSITE IS inconsistent

consolation *NOUN* *I tried to offer her some consolation for her loss.* ► comfort, solace, sympathy, commiseration, compassion, reassurance, support, succour, encouragement, cheer, ease, help, relief

console *VERB* *His friends tried to console him.* ► comfort, solace, hearten, encourage, relieve, soothe, sympathize with, calm, cheer

consolidate *VERB* **1** *attempts to consolidate their reputation in Europe* ► strengthen, reinforce, fortify, enhance, stabilize, make secure, make strong AN OPPOSITE IS weaken **2** *All the resources need to be consolidated.* ► amalgamate,

consonant *NOUN* **consonants** a letter that is not a vowel • *b, c, d, f, etc. are consonants.*

conspicuous *ADJECTIVE* easily seen; noticeable ▷ **conspicuously** *ADVERB* **conspicuousness** *NOUN*

conspiracy *NOUN* **conspiracies** planning with others to do something illegal; a plot ▷ **conspirator** *NOUN*

constable *NOUN* **constables** a police officer of the lowest rank

constant *ADJECTIVE* **1** not changing; happening all the time **2** faithful or loyal ▷ **constantly** *ADVERB* **constancy** *NOUN*

constant *NOUN* **constants** **1** a thing that does not vary **2** (in science and mathematics) a number or value that does not change

constellation *NOUN* **constellations** a group of stars

constipated *ADJECTIVE* unable to empty the bowels easily or regularly ▷ **constipation** *NOUN*

constituency *NOUN* **constituencies** a district represented by a Member of Parliament elected by the people who live there

constituent *NOUN* **constituents** **1** one of the parts that form a whole thing **2** someone who lives in a particular constituency ▷ **constituent** *ADJECTIVE*

constitute *VERB* **constitutes, constituting, constituted** make up or form something • *Twelve months constitute a year.*

constitution *NOUN* **constitutions** **1** the group of laws or principles that state how a country is to be organized and governed **2** the nature of the body in regard to healthiness • *She has a strong constitution.* **3** constituting **4** the composition of something ▷ **constitutional** *ADJECTIVE*

constrict *VERB* **constricts, constricting, constricted** squeeze or tighten something by making it narrower ▷ **constriction** *NOUN*

construct *VERB* **constructs, constructing, constructed** make something by placing parts together; build ▷ **constructor** *NOUN*

construction *NOUN* **constructions** **1** constructing **2** something constructed; a building **3** two or more words put together to form a phrase or clause or sentence **4** an

Thesaurus

combine, integrate, merge, unify, bring together, fuse

consort *VERB* **consort with** *consorting with the opposition* ► associate with, socialize with, have dealings with, befriend, fraternize with, keep company with, mix with, be friends with, be seen with

conspicuous *ADJECTIVE* **1** *Her bright clothes made her conspicuous.* ► prominent, distinct, clearly visible, easily seen, noticeable, apparent, perceptible AN OPPOSITE IS inconspicuous **2** *The infantry showed conspicuous bravery that day.* ► obvious, manifest, evident, outstanding, exceptional, marked, pronounced, unmistakable

conspiracy *NOUN* *They were involved in a conspiracy to kill the king.* ► plot, scheme, intrigue, machination, plan, stratagem

conspire *VERB* *They twice conspired to overthrow the dictatorship.* ► plot, scheme, intrigue, plan, hatch a plot, collude, connive, collaborate, consort, be in league

constant *ADJECTIVE* **1** *the constant hum of traffic on the bypass* ► continuous, continual, persistent, ceaseless, incessant, endless, unending OPPOSITES ARE changeable, irregular **2** *The wheel should turn at a constant speed* ► steady, regular, stable, uniform, even, invariable, fixed **3** *She proved to be a constant friend.* ► faithful, loyal, devoted, staunch, true, firm, dependable, reliable, dedicated OPPOSITES ARE fickle, unreliable

constantly *ADVERB* *The train times are constantly changing.* ► always, continually, repeatedly, all the time, forever

constitute *VERB* **1** *Their attitude constitutes a form of discrimination.* ► amount to, be equivalent to, be tantamount to, compose, comprise, form, make up **2** *A Scottish Parliament was constituted in 1999.* ► establish, set up, inaugurate, create, found, appoint

constraint *NOUN* *Political constraints prevented him from speaking his mind.* ► restriction, restraint, limitation, inhibition, control, hindrance, check

constriction *NOUN* *He felt a constriction in his throat.* ► tightening, tightness, narrowing, pressure, stricture

construct *VERB* **1** *The local council wants to construct a new bridge over the railway line.* ► build, erect, put up, set up, assemble **2** *We must construct a new form of society.* ► create, devise, develop, formulate, fashion, design, invent

construction *NOUN* **1** *In 1858 the construction of the present chapel was put in hand.* ► building, erection, assembly, creation, establishment, putting-up, setting-up, erecting **2** *The new building was a mainly timber construction.* ► building, edifice, erection, structure, framework

explanation or interpretation • *They put a bad construction on our refusal.*

constructive *ADJECTIVE* helpful and positive • *constructive suggestions*

consult *VERB* **consults, consulting, consulted** go to a person or book etc. for information or advice
▷ **consultation** *NOUN*

consultant *NOUN* **consultants** a person who is qualified to give expert advice

consume *VERB* **consumes, consuming, consumed** **1** eat or drink something **2** use up • *Much time was consumed in waiting.* **3** destroy • *Fire consumed the building.*

consumer *NOUN* **consumers** a person who buys or uses goods or services

consummate (kon- sum- at) *ADJECTIVE* perfect; highly skilled • *a consummate artist*

consumption *NOUN* **1** consuming **2** (*old use*) tuberculosis of the lungs

contact *NOUN* **contacts** **1** touching **2** being in touch; communication **3** a person to communicate with when you need information or help

contact *VERB* **contacts, contacting, contacted** get in touch with a person

contact lens *NOUN* **contact lenses** a tiny lens worn against the eyeball, instead of glasses

contagious *ADJECTIVE* spreading by contact with an infected person • *a contagious disease*

contain *VERB* **contains, containing, contained** **1** have inside • *The box contains chocolates.* **2** consist of • *A gallon contains 8 pints.* **3** restrain; hold back • *Try to contain your laughter.*

container *NOUN* **containers** **1** a box or bottle etc. designed to contain something **2** a large box-like object of standard design in which goods are transported

contaminate *VERB* **contaminates, contaminating, contaminated** make a thing dirty or impure or diseased etc.; pollute
▷ **contamination** *NOUN*

contemplate *VERB* **contemplates, contemplating, contemplated** **1** look at something thoughtfully **2** consider or think about doing something • *We are contemplating a visit to London.*
▷ **contemplation** *NOUN* **contemplative** *ADJECTIVE*

Thesaurus

constructive *ADJECTIVE* *The talks proved to be helpful and constructive.* ► positive, useful, worthwhile, beneficial, advantageous, creative, helpful, practical, valuable
AN OPPOSITE IS destructive

consult *VERB* **1** *He wanted to consult the workforce before introducing any changes.* ► speak to, confer with, refer to, seek advice from, debate with, discuss matters with, exchange views with **2** *Consult your doctor before attempting these exercises.* ► see, ask, get advice from, refer to **3** *He consulted a list pinned to the wall.* ► refer to, turn to, look something up in

consume *VERB* **1** *A lot of food and drink was consumed that day.* ► eat, drink, devour, digest, swallow, feast on, (*more informal*) gobble up **2** *The factory consumes thousands of tons of fuel each year.* ► use, use up, utilize, expend, absorb, swallow up, deplete, drain, eat into, employ, exhaust **3** *Fire consumed a row of buildings.* ► destroy, demolish, devastate, wipe out, annihilate, wreck, ravage, ruin **4** *George was consumed by guilt.* ► overcome, overwhelm, preoccupy, obsess, absorb

contact *NOUN* **1** *He had been avoiding physical contact with her all day.* ► touch, touching, proximity **2** *Contact between Europe and Africa can be traced back hundreds of years.* ► communication, connection, association **3** *Make sure all electrical contacts are secure.* ► connection, join **4** *I will ask one of my contacts in Italy.* ► associate, connection, acquaintance, liaison

contact *VERB* *I'll contact them when I have more information.* ► notify, communicate with, get in touch with, get hold of, approach, correspond with, call, call on, phone, ring, speak to, talk to, (*more informal*) drop a line to

contain *VERB* **1** *The box contained bottles of red wine.* ► hold, accommodate **2** *The atlas contains photographs taken from space.* ► include, incorporate, comprise, consist of, be composed of **3** *You will have to contain your impatience.* ► restrain, curb, suppress, control, hold back, keep back, repress, check, stifle, limit

container *NOUN* *a watertight container* ► receptacle, vessel, holder, repository, canister, case

contaminate *VERB* *Farming contaminates watercourses every day.* ► pollute, adulterate, defile, infect, poison, foul, soil, taint
AN OPPOSITE IS purify

contemplate *VERB* **1** *He contemplated her over his glasses.* ► look at, view, observe, regard, survey, watch, eye, gaze at, stare at, (*in literature*) behold **2** *She could not even contemplate what might happen.* ► think about, consider, cogitate, deliberate, examine, mull over, plan, reflect on, study, work out **3** *He contemplated leaving.* ► consider, think about, envisage, have in mind, intend (to), propose

contemporary ADJECTIVE **1** belonging to the same period • *Dickens was contemporary with Thackeray.* **2** modern; up-to-date • *contemporary furniture*

contemporary NOUN **contemporaries** a person who is contemporary with another or who is about the same age • *She was my contemporary at college.*

contempt NOUN a feeling of despising a person or thing

contemptible ADJECTIVE deserving contempt • *Hurting her feelings like that was a contemptible thing to do.*

contemptuous ADJECTIVE feeling or showing contempt • *She gave me a contemptuous look.*
▷ **contemptuously** ADVERB

content[1] (kon- tent) ADJECTIVE contented
▷ **contentment** NOUN

content[2] (kon- tent) NOUN or **contents** PLURAL NOUN what something contains

contented ADJECTIVE happy with what you have; satisfied
▷ **contentedly** ADVERB

contest (kon- test) NOUN **contests** a competition; a struggle in which rivals try to obtain something or to do best

Thesaurus

4 *She sat quietly and contemplated.* ► ponder, reflect, ruminate, think, meditate, muse

contemporary ADJECTIVE **1** *The historical information comes from contemporary accounts.* ► contemporaneous, concurrent, synchronous, coinciding, simultaneous, coexistent, of the time **2** *a concert of contemporary music* ► modern, current, present-day, recent, fashionable, the latest, newest

contempt NOUN *She had nothing but contempt for them.* ► disgust, scorn, disdain, loathing, abhorrence, derision, disparagement, detestation, dislike, disrespect, hatred, ridicule AN OPPOSITE IS admiration
feel or **show contempt for** *He felt contempt for their extreme views.* ► despise, spurn, revile, detest

contemptible ADJECTIVE *a contemptible insult* ► despicable, shameful, disgraceful, detestable, hateful, deplorable, ignominious, loathsome, odious, mean, vile, low, cheap AN OPPOSITE IS admirable

contemptuous ADJECTIVE *a contemptuous tone of voice* ► scornful, disdainful, scathing, disrespectful, insulting, derisive, dismissive, supercilious, condescending, insolent, haughty, mocking, withering, arrogant AN OPPOSITE IS admiring
be contemptuous of ► denigrate, disparage, revile, malign, belittle, decry, impugn, abuse

contend VERB **1** *political parties contending for power* ► compete, struggle, vie, strive, fight, grapple, oppose one another, rival one another, contest, dispute **2** *She contended that she had been given bad advice.* ► claim, declare, maintain, aver, hold, assert, allege, argue, affirm, plead **3 contend with** *They have a lot to contend with.* ► cope with, deal with, put up with, sort out, manage, organize

content ADJECTIVE *He seems content now that he's got his way.* ► happy, contented, satisfied, pleased, gratified, glad, cheerful, smug

content NOUN **1** *The article is admired more for its content than its style.* ► subject matter, subject, theme, substance, argument, message **2** *Butter has a high fat content.* ► element, ingredient, substance **3** *She smiled with content.* ► happiness, contentment, satisfaction, pleasure

content VERB *The answer seemed to content him.* ► satisfy, please, placate, appease, pacify, soothe

contented ADJECTIVE *a contented feeling* ► happy, content, satisfied, pleased, gratified, glad, cheerful, smug OPPOSITES ARE discontented, dissatisfied

contention NOUN *Her contention is that the action would be illegal.* ► argument, claim, opinion, view, assertion, submission, belief, position

contentious ADJECTIVE **1** *a contentious issue* ► controversial, debatable, disputed, disputable, vexed **2** *a contentious group of people* ► quarrelsome, argumentative, disputatious, difficult

contentment NOUN *They achieved contentment in the country.* ► happiness, well-being, comfort, pleasure, content, contentedness, gratification, satisfaction, peace of mind, tranquillity, ease, fulfilment, relaxation, serenity OPPOSITES ARE dissatisfaction, unhappiness

contest NOUN **1** *a song contest; a boxing contest* ► competition, tournament, match, bout, encounter, fight, battle, dispute **2** *a contest for the leadership* ► struggle, challenge, confrontation, duel

contest VERB **1** *Seven candidates will contest the election.* ► enter, compete in, take part in, participate in, contend in, fight in, (*informal*) make a bid for, strive for, struggle for, take up the challenge of, vie for **2** *They decided to contest the decision.* ► oppose, challenge, dispute, object to, argue against, take issue with, query, refute, resist, debate, doubt, question

contestant *NOUN* **contestants** a person taking part in a contest; a competitor

context *NOUN* **contexts** **1** the words that come before and after a particular word or phrase and help to fix its meaning **2** the background to an event that helps to explain it

continent *NOUN* **continents** one of the main masses of land in the world • *The continents are Europe, Asia, Africa, North America, South America, Australia, and Antarctica.*
▷ **continental** *ADJECTIVE*
the Continent the mainland of Europe, not including the British Isles

continual *ADJECTIVE* happening all the time, usually with breaks in between • *Stop this continual quarrelling!*
▷ **continually** *ADVERB*
USAGE Do not confuse with **continuous**. **Continual** is used to describe something that happens very frequently (*there were continual interruptions*) while **continuous** is used to describe something that happens without a pause (*there was continuous rain all day*).

continue *VERB* **continues, continuing, continued** **1** do something without stopping **2** begin again after stopping • *The game will continue after lunch.*
▷ **continuation** *NOUN*

continuous *ADJECTIVE* going on and on; without a break
▷ **continuously** *ADVERB* **continuity** *NOUN*
USAGE See note at **continual**.

contort *VERB* **contorts, contorting, contorted** twist or force out of the usual shape or meaning
▷ **contortion** *NOUN*

contortionist *NOUN* **contortionists** a person who can twist his or her body into unusual positions

contour *NOUN* **contours** **1** a line on a map joining the points that are the same height above sea level **2** an outline

contraband *NOUN* smuggled goods

contraception *NOUN* a way of preventing pregnancy; birth control

contraceptive *NOUN* **contraceptives** a substance or device that prevents pregnancy

contract (kon- trakt) *NOUN* **contracts** **1** a formal agreement to do something **2** a document stating the terms of an agreement

contract (kon- trakt) *VERB* **contracts, contracting, contracted** **1** make or become smaller **2** make a contract **3** get an illness • *She contracted measles.*

contraction *NOUN* **contractions** **1** contracting **2** a shortened form of a word or words. *Can't* is a contraction of *cannot*

contractor *NOUN* **contractors** a person who makes a contract, especially for building

Thesaurus

context *NOUN* *The events have to be put in their historical context.* ► background, circumstances, surroundings, framework, situation, ambience, frame of reference, milieu, position

continual *ADJECTIVE* *She needed continual reassurance. The service is affected by continual breakdowns.* ► constant, repeated, frequent, regular, perpetual, ceaseless, incessant, persistent OPPOSITES ARE occasional, sporadic

continuation *NOUN* **1** *He returned to the clinic for the continuation of his treatment.* ► resumption, maintenance, continuing, continuance, carrying on, extension, prolongation **2** *the continuation of a story* ► sequel, supplement, addition, appendix, postscript

continue *VERB* **1** *Police continued the search until dark.* ► carry on, maintain, keep up, keep going, persevere with, proceed with, prolong, pursue, (*more informal*) stick at **2** *Shall we continue after lunch?* ► resume, restart, begin again, recommence **3** *Talks continued all week.* ► last, carry on, go on, endure, persist, keep on, linger, live on, remain, stay, survive

continuous *ADJECTIVE* *three days of continuous rain* ► uninterrupted, unbroken, constant, steady, ceaseless, endless, incessant, persistent, non-stop OPPOSITES ARE intermittent, sporadic

contract *NOUN* *A contract is legally binding.* ► agreement, settlement, covenant, compact, commitment, deal, bond, pact, concordat, bargain, indenture, lease, treaty, understanding, undertaking

contract *VERB* **1** *The glass contracts as it cools. Labour markets contracted in this area.* ► shrink, lessen, diminish, reduce, become smaller, condense, shrivel, decrease, dwindle, wither, close up, draw together, fall away, narrow, slim down, thin out OPPOSITES ARE expand, enlarge **2** *The company contracted to build an extension to the house.* ► sign an agreement, undertake, covenant, make a deal, promise, agree, arrange **3** *The woman might have contracted smallpox.* ► develop, catch, get, become infected by, be taken ill with

contraction *NOUN* **1** *a contraction of overseas markets* ► shrinking, shrivelling, diminution, decline, decrease **2** *'Goodbye' is a contraction of 'God be with you'.* ► abbreviation, diminutive, short form, shortened form

a b c d e f g h i j k l m n o p q r s t u v w x y z

contradict *VERB* **contradicts, contradicting, contradicted** **1** say that something said is not true or that someone is wrong **2** say the opposite of • *These rumours contradict previous ones.*
▷ **contradiction** *NOUN* **contradictory** *ADJECTIVE*

contraflow *NOUN* **contraflows** a flow of road traffic travelling in the opposite direction to the usual flow and close beside it

contralto *NOUN* **contraltos** a female singer with a low voice

contraption *NOUN* **contraptions** a strange-looking device or machine

contrary *ADJECTIVE* **1** (kon- tra- ree) of the opposite kind or direction etc.; opposed; unfavourable **2** (kon- trair- ee) awkward and obstinate

contrary (kon- tra- ree) *NOUN* the opposite
on the contrary the opposite is true

contrast *NOUN* **contrasts** **1** a difference clearly seen when things are compared **2** something showing a clear difference

contrast *VERB* **contrasts, contrasting, contrasted** **1** compare or oppose two things in order to show that they are clearly different **2** be clearly different when compared

contravene *VERB* **contravenes, contravening, contravened** act against a rule or law
▷ **contravention** *NOUN*

contribute *VERB* **contributes, contributing, contributed** **1** give money or help along with other people **2** write something for a newspaper or magazine etc. **3** help to cause something • *Tiredness contributed to the accident.*
▷ **contribution** *NOUN* **contributor** *NOUN* **contributory** *ADJECTIVE*

contrite *ADJECTIVE* very sorry for having done wrong

Thesaurus

contradict *VERB* **1** *I didn't like to contradict him but I really didn't agree.* ► disagree with, challenge, oppose, speak against, impugn **2** *The new evidence contradicts earlier conclusions.* ► conflict with, be at odds with, be inconsistent with, run counter to, challenge, disprove **3** *The statement was later contradicted by the Prime Minister.* ► deny, repudiate, rebut, dispute, counter AN OPPOSITE IS confirm

contradictory *ADJECTIVE* *The two points of view are completely contradictory.* ► opposite, opposed, conflicting, contrary, incompatible, inconsistent, irreconcilable, different, discrepant, antithetical OPPOSITES ARE consistent, compatible

contraption *NOUN* *Above his head was a contraption consisting of springs and wires.* ► device, contrivance, gadget, apparatus, mechanism, invention, machine

contrary *ADJECTIVE* **1** (with the stress on *con*) *Other may take the contrary view.* ► opposite, opposing, opposed, contradictory, conflicting, contrasting, reverse, converse, different, other AN OPPOSITE IS similar **2** (with the stress on *-trary*, pronounced like *Mary*) *a contrary child* ► perverse, awkward, difficult, uncooperative, obstinate, unhelpful, tiresome, disobedient, vexatious, (*more informal*) bolshie, (*more informal*) stroppy AN OPPOSITE IS cooperative **3** **contrary to** *The result was contrary to all expectations.* ► in conflict with, at odds with, at variance with, counter to

contrast *NOUN* *a noticeable contrast between what they say and what they do* ► difference, dissimilarity, disparity, variance, divergence, contradiction, opposition AN OPPOSITE IS similarity

contrast *VERB* **1** *People contrast the two brothers.* ► differentiate, distinguish, make distinctions between, discriminate between, compare **2** **contrast with** *Her fair hair contrasted with her dark dress.* ► set off, complement, clash with

contrasting *ADJECTIVE* *contrasting colours; contrasting opinions* ► complementary, conflicting, different, opposing, opposite AN OPPOSITE IS similar

contribute *VERB* **1** *Employers have to contribute a set amount to the fund.* ► give, subscribe, donate, provide, put up, supply, add, grant, bestow **2** **contribute to** *The weather contributed to the success of the occasion.* ► play a part in, add to, be a factor in, have a hand in, make for, enhance, help, reinforce, support, encourage

contribution *NOUN* *All income comes from charitable contributions.* ► donation, benefaction, payment, gift, subscription, allowance, endowment, grant, offering, sponsorship, (*more informal*) handout

contributor *NOUN* **1** *The charity has acquired several new contributors.* ► donor, benefactor, subscriber, supporter, patron, sponsor, giver, backer, helper **2** *a regular contributor to the magazine* ► writer, columnist, correspondent, freelance, journalist, reporter

contrive VERB **contrives, contriving, contrived** plan cleverly; find a way of doing or making something

control VERB **controls, controlling, controlled** **1** have the power to make someone or something do what you want **2** hold something, especially anger, in check; restrain
▷ **controller** NOUN

control NOUN controlling a person or thing; authority
in control having control of something
out of control no longer able to be controlled

controls PLURAL NOUN the switches etc. used to control a machine

controversial ADJECTIVE causing controversy

controversy (kon- tro- ver- see, kon- trov- er- see) NOUN **controversies** a long argument or disagreement

conundrum NOUN **conundrums** a riddle; a hard question

convalesce VERB **convalesces, convalescing, convalesced** be recovering from an illness
▷ **convalescence** NOUN **convalescent** ADJECTIVE, NOUN

convection NOUN the passing on of heat within liquid, air, or gas by circulation of the warmed parts

convenience NOUN **conveniences** **1** being convenient **2** something that is convenient **3** a public toilet
at your convenience whenever you find convenient; as it suits you

convenient ADJECTIVE easy to use or deal with or reach
▷ **conveniently** ADVERB

conventional ADJECTIVE **1** done or doing things in the accepted way; traditional **2** (said about weapons) not nuclear
▷ **conventionally** ADVERB **conventionality** NOUN

Thesaurus

contrivance NOUN *The blinds were opened by a strange contrivance at the side.* ► device, contraption, gadget, apparatus, mechanism, invention, machine

control NOUN **1** *this theme of giving back control over civic affairs to the local people* ► jurisdiction, administration, management, regulation, authority, charge, power, government, supervision, command, direction, oversight, organization, guidance, influence **2** *He needs to exercise a little more control and not lose his temper so much.* ► restraint, self-control, self-command, self-possession, composure **3** *Some of the controls were difficult to reach.* ► switch, knob, button, lever, handle, dial
gain control of *The Portuguese had gained control of the Indian Ocean a century earlier.* ► take over, dominate, usurp, win, annex, seize, steal

control VERB **1** *You have to be able to control all the resources.* ► be in charge of, manage, administer, have authority over, supervise, govern, oversee, run, operate, look after **2** *He found it hard to control his temper.* ► restrain, check, contain, curb, confine, keep in check, master, repress, subdue, suppress

controversial ADJECTIVE *He wrote a controversial article on the death penalty.* ► contentious, controvertible, debatable, disputable, questionable, doubtful, polemical, problematical, arguable OPPOSITES ARE uncontroversial, straightforward

convene VERB **1** *The chairman convened a meeting.* ► call, summon, assemble, bring together, (*more formal*) convoke **2** *The committee convened at two o'clock.* ► assemble, meet, gather, come together

convenient ADJECTIVE **1** *He asked when it would be convenient to interview her.* ► suitable, appropriate, opportune, fitting, agreeable, neat, timely, usable OPPOSITES ARE inconvenient, awkward **2** *Fast foods are often the most convenient option.* ► practical, handy, useful, helpful, labour-saving **3** *There is a regular bus service and convenient shops.* ► nearby, accessible, handy, at hand, available **4 convenient for** *The house was so convenient for London.* ► accessible to, within easy reach of, well situated for, handy for AN OPPOSITE IS inconvenient

convention NOUN **1** *All these social conventions can become tedious.* ► custom, practice, tradition, rule, protocol, canon, formality, matter of form, matter of etiquette **2** *American-style political conventions* ► conference, meeting, congress, assembly, symposium **3** *a convention signed by all the countries of the area* ► agreement, treaty, accord, compact, understanding

conventional ADJECTIVE **1** *He was willing to follow conventional ideas.* ► orthodox, established, traditional, customary, prevalent, mainstream, commonplace, routine, unoriginal, hackneyed OPPOSITES ARE unconventional, unorthodox **2** *Kevin was a conventional man.* ► conservative, hidebound, traditional, traditionalist, conformist, formal, correct, proper, bourgeois, stereotyped, unadventurous, unimaginative, unoriginal, (*more informal*) stuffy, (*more informal*) fuddy-duddy OPPOSITES ARE unconventional, radical

A B C D E F G H I J K L M N O P Q R S T U V W X Y Z

conversation *NOUN* **conversations** talk between people
▷ **conversational** *ADJECTIVE*

convert (kon- vert) *VERB* **converts, converting, converted** **1** change **2** cause a person to change his or her beliefs **3** kick a goal after scoring a try at rugby football
▷ **converter** *NOUN* **conversion** *NOUN*

convex *ADJECTIVE* curved like the outside of a ball or circle (The opposite is **concave**)
▷ **convexity** *NOUN*

convey *VERB* **conveys, conveying, conveyed** **1** transport **2** communicate a message or idea etc.
▷ **conveyor** *NOUN*

conveyor belt *NOUN* **conveyor belts** a continuous moving belt for moving objects from one place to another

convict (kon- vikt) *VERB* **convicts, convicting, convicted** prove or declare that a certain person is guilty of a crime

convict (kon- vikt) *NOUN* **convicts** a convicted person who is in prison

conviction *NOUN* **convictions** **1** convicting or being convicted of a crime **2** being convinced **3** a firm opinion or belief
carry conviction be convincing

convince *VERB* **convinces, convincing, convinced** make a person feel certain that something is true

convoy *NOUN* **convoys** a group of ships or lorries travelling together

convulsion *NOUN* **convulsions** **1** a violent movement of the body **2** a violent upheaval

coo *VERB* **coos, cooing, cooed** make a dove's soft murmuring sound
▷ **coo** *NOUN*

cook *VERB* **cooks, cooking, cooked** make food ready to eat by heating it
cook up (*informal*) if you cook up a story or plan, you invent it

cook *NOUN* **cooks** a person who cooks

Thesaurus

3 *A conventional telephone can be a lot less fiddly than many mobiles.* ► standard, normal, regular, traditional, ordinary

converge *VERB* *The light rays converge to form a sharp image.* ► merge, combine, meet, join, come together, coincide OPPOSITES ARE separate, diverge

conversation *NOUN* *The rest of the conversation was in French.* ► discussion, talk, discourse, dialogue, exchange, consultation, (*more informal*) chat

conversion *NOUN* **1** *the conversion of waste into forms of energy* ► change, changing, turning, transformation **2** *The house has had a loft conversion.* ► adaptation, alteration, renovation, reconstruction, rebuilding, modification

convert *VERB* **1** *We plan to convert the loft into a workroom. Most of her novels have now been converted into films.* ► adapt, change, turn, rebuild, reconstruct, renovate, modify, reorganize **2** *a device for converting digital data into audio signals* ► turn, change, transform, translate

convey *VERB* **1** *A shuttle service conveys passengers from the city to the suburbs.* ► transport, carry, take, transfer, deliver, bring, fetch, move **2** *The dancer's movements can convey a variety of meanings.* ► communicate, signify, indicate, impart, disclose, relate, imply, mean, reveal, put across, get across

convict *NOUN* (with the stress on *con-*) *He looked like an convict in his striped pyjamas.* ► prisoner, criminal, condemned person

convict *VERB* (with the stress on *-vict*) *A jury had earlier convicted Duncan of assault.* ► condemn, declare guilty, find guilty OPPOSITES ARE acquit, clear

conviction *NOUN* **1** *He spoke with complete conviction.* ► confidence, assurance, certainty, sureness, positiveness, firmness AN OPPOSITE IS uncertainty **2** *She has keenly felt political convictions.* ► belief, opinion, view, principle, persuasion, creed, faith, tenet

convince *VERB* *It will be difficult to convince them. She tried to convince herself that nobody would have heard her.* ► persuade, assure, prove to, reassure, satisfy, sway, win over, bring round

convincing *ADJECTIVE* **1** *a convincing argument* ► strong, powerful, conclusive, cogent, decisive, compelling, definite, persuasive, unambiguous, unarguable, unequivocal AN OPPOSITE IS inconclusive **2** *a convincing victory* ► decisive, conclusive, resounding, emphatic, impressive

convoy *NOUN* *a convoy of ships* ► group, fleet, armada, procession

convulsion *NOUN* **1** *The convulsions stopped and Charles lay back exhausted.* ► fit, seizure, spasm, attack, paroxysm **2** *seismic convulsions; a political convulsion* ► upheaval, disturbance, tremor, turbulence, eruption, outburst

convulsive *ADJECTIVE* *convulsive movements* ► spasmodic, jerky, shaking, uncontrolled, uncoordinated, violent, (*more informal*) twitchy

cook *NOUN* *the hotel's new cook* ► chef

cook *VERB* *She cooked them both a romantic dinner.* ► prepare, make, get, put together, (*more*

cookery NOUN the skill of cooking food

cool ADJECTIVE **1** fairly cold; not hot or warm **2** calm; not enthusiastic
▷ **coolly** ADVERB **coolness** NOUN

cool VERB **cools, cooling, cooled** make or become cool
▷ **cooler** NOUN

cooped up ADJECTIVE having to stay in a place which is small and uncomfortable

cooperate VERB **cooperates, cooperating, cooperated** work helpfully with other people
▷ **cooperation** NOUN **cooperative** ADJECTIVE

coordinate VERB **coordinates, coordinating, coordinated** organize people or things to work properly together
▷ **coordination** NOUN **coordinator** NOUN

coordinate NOUN **coordinates** either of the pair of numbers or letters used to fix the position of a point on a graph or map

cope VERB **copes, coping, coped** manage or deal with something successfully

copious ADJECTIVE plentiful; in large amounts
▷ **copiously** ADVERB

copper NOUN **coppers** **1** a reddish-brown metal used to make wire, coins, etc. **2** a reddish-brown colour **3** a coin made of copper or metal of this colour
▷ **copper** ADJECTIVE

copse NOUN **copses** a small group of trees

copulate VERB **copulates, copulating, copulated** have sexual intercourse with someone
▷ **copulation** NOUN

copy NOUN **copies** **1** a thing made to look like another **2** something written or typed out again from its original form **3** one of a number of specimens of the same book or newspaper etc.

Thesaurus

informal) fix RELATED ADJECTIVE culinary
cook something up *He cooked up an idea for getting her to go with him.* ► concoct, devise, contrive, plot, scheme

cool ADJECTIVE **1** *the cool air of early morning* ► fresh, bracing, crisp, brisk, chilly, chilled, (*more informal*) nippy OPPOSITES ARE warm, balmy **2** *We got a cool response.* ► unfriendly, chilly, lukewarm, unwelcoming, frigid, hostile, unsympathetic, reserved, aloof, (*informal*) standoffish OPPOSITES ARE warm, friendly, enthusiastic **3** *He was determined to keep cool in the crisis.* ► calm, composed, collected, clear-headed, self-controlled, self-possessed, unflustered, unruffled **4** (*informal*) *She seems to think she's so cool.* ► fashionable, trendy, stylish, sophisticated, chic **5** (*informal*) *It's a cool song.* ► good, excellent, super, superb

cool NOUN *He finally lost his cool and started shouting.* ► composure, self-control, self-possession, calm, calmness

cool VERB **1** *He threw open the shutters to cool the room.* ► chill, make cooler, lower the temperature of **2** *Cool the mixture in the fridge for about an hour.* ► chill, refrigerate, make cold **3** *Their enthusiasm had begun to cool. Recent events had cooled their enthusiasm.* ► lessen, reduce, moderate, dampen, diminish, abate, take the edge off *or* lose its edge

cooped up ADJECTIVE *She doesn't like being cooped up at home all day.* ► confined, shut in, shut up, caged, trapped, locked up, imprisoned, incarcerated

cooperate VERB **1** *Several police forces cooperated in the operation.* ► collaborate, combine, unite, work together, join forces, team up **2 cooperate with** *He absolutely refused to cooperate with them.* ► assist, help, support, work with

cooperation NOUN **1** *wise cooperation between management and workers* ► collaboration, coordination, joint action, teamwork, unity, mutual support OPPOSITES ARE conflict, rivalry **2** *She thanked them all for their cooperation.* ► assistance, help, helpfulness, support, backing

cooperative ADJECTIVE **1** *The staff were pleasant and cooperative.* ► helpful, obliging, accommodating, supportive, constructive, willing, keen AN OPPOSITE IS uncooperative **2** *The project was achieved by a cooperative effort.* ► joint, combined, collective, concerted, coordinated, corporate, shared, communal AN OPPOSITE IS individual

coordinate VERB *A committee will coordinate all the sporting activities.* ► harmonize, organize, bring together, synchronize, systematize

cope VERB **1** *She is too old now to cope by herself.* ► manage, survive, carry on, get by, fend for yourself, make do **2 cope with** *We found so many problems at once difficult to cope with.* ► deal with, handle, manage, contend with, endure, tolerate

copious ADJECTIVE *They sat listening and writing copious notes. a long breakfast of croissants and copious coffee* ► plenty of, abundant, plentiful, extensive, substantial, profuse, lavish, generous, ample, numerous, full OPPOSITES ARE sparse, meagre

copy NOUN **1** *Keep a copy of your letter.* ► duplicate, photocopy, (*trademark*) Xerox, facsimile, transcript, clone, double, pattern, print, representation, tracing **2** *The painting is*

a b c d e f g h i j k l m n o p q r s t u v w x y z

A B C D E F G H I J K L M N O P Q R S T U V W X Y Z

copy *VERB* **copies, copying, copied** **1** make a copy of something **2** do the same as someone else; imitate

copyright *NOUN* the legal right to print a book, reproduce a picture, record a piece of music, etc.

coral *NOUN* **1** a hard red, pink, or white substance formed by the skeletons of tiny sea creatures massed together **2** a pink colour

cord *NOUN* **cords** **1** a long thin flexible strip of twisted threads or strands **2** a piece of flex **3** a cord-like structure in the body • *the spinal cord* **4** corduroy
USAGE Do not confuse with **chord**.

cordial *ADJECTIVE* warm and friendly
▷ **cordially** *ADVERB* **cordiality** *NOUN*

corduroy *NOUN* cotton cloth with velvety ridges

core *NOUN* **cores** **1** the part in the middle of something **2** the hard central part of an apple or pear etc., containing the seeds

corgi *NOUN* **corgis** a small dog with short legs and upright ears

cork *NOUN* **corks** **1** the lightweight bark of a kind of oak tree **2** a stopper for a bottle, made of cork or other material

cork *VERB* **corks, corking, corked** close something with a cork

corkscrew *NOUN* **corkscrews** **1** a device for removing corks from bottles **2** a spiral

corn [1] *NOUN* **1** the seed of wheat and similar plants **2** a plant, such as wheat, grown for its grain

corn [2] *NOUN* **corns** a small hard painful lump on the foot

cornea *NOUN* **corneas** the transparent covering over the pupil of the eye
▷ **corneal** *ADJECTIVE*

corner *NOUN* **corners** **1** the angle or area where two lines or sides or walls meet or where two streets join **2** a free hit or kick from the corner of a hockey or football field **3** a region • *a quiet corner of the world*

corner *VERB* **corners, cornering, cornered** **1** drive someone into a corner or other position from which it is difficult to escape **2** travel round a corner **3** obtain possession of all or most of something • *corner the market*

cornet *NOUN* **cornets** **1** a cone-shaped wafer etc. holding ice cream **2** a musical instrument rather like a trumpet

cornflakes *PLURAL NOUN* toasted maize flakes eaten as a breakfast cereal

cornucopia *NOUN* **1** a horn-shaped container overflowing with fruit and flowers **2** a plentiful supply of good things

corny *ADJECTIVE* **cornier, corniest** (*informal*) **1** repeated so often that people are tired of it • *a corny joke.* **2** sentimental

corollary (ker-ol-er-ee) *NOUN* **corollaries** a fact etc. that logically results from another • *The work is difficult and, as a corollary, tiring.*

coronary *NOUN* **coronaries** short for **coronary thrombosis**, blockage of an artery carrying blood to the heart [from Latin *corona* = crown: the coronary arteries encircle the heart like a crown]

coronation *NOUN* **coronations** the crowning of a king or queen

Thesaurus

only a copy. ► reproduction, replica, imitation, likeness, model, fake, forgery, twin USAGE You use *fake* or *forgery* when you mean a copy that is intended to deceive people. AN OPPOSITE IS original

copy *VERB* **1** *Copy the passage from the book.* ► write out, reproduce, make a copy of, duplicate, repeat **2** *He copied several drawings by Hogarth.* ► reproduce, make a copy of, forge, fake, plagiarize, counterfeit, crib, follow usage You use *fake* or *forge* or *counterfeit* when you mean make a copy that is intended to deceive people. **3** *A lot of musicians have tried to copy their sound.* ► imitate, mimic, reproduce, emulate, ape, impersonate, parrot, poach

cord *NOUN* *I tightened the cord on the hood of my jacket.* ► string, thread, strap, tape, rope, strand, cable

core *NOUN* **1** *the earth's core* ► centre, nucleus, heart, middle, inside **2** *the core of the problem* ► heart, essence, crux, nub, central issue, kernel, (*more informal*) nitty-gritty

corn *NOUN* *a field of corn* ► grain, cereal, cereal crop, wheat, barley

corner *NOUN* **1** *Turn left at the corner.* ► bend, curve, turning **2** *Three women sat in a corner of the room.* ► nook, niche, recess, alcove **3** *Stuart felt he was in a bit of a corner.* ► predicament, plight, quandary, dilemma, awkward situation, mess, (*more informal*) spot, (*more informal*) scrape, (*more informal*) stew
round the corner *The shops are round the corner.* ► nearby, close at hand, not far away, within reach

corner *VERB* *The animal had cornered its prey.* ► trap, shut in, bring to bay, run to ground, capture, catch

corny *ADJECTIVE* *corny jokes* ► hackneyed, banal, stereotyped, stale, feeble, tired

corporation *NOUN* **1** *a business corporation* ► company, firm, organization, concern, enterprise **2** *a city corporation* ► council, town council, local authority

corporal *NOUN* **corporals** a soldier ranking next below a sergeant

corporal punishment *NOUN* punishment on the body, such as spanking or caning

corps (kor) *NOUN* **corps** (korz) **1** a special army unit • *the Medical Corps* **2** a large group of soldiers **3** a set of people doing the same job • *the diplomatic corps* [from French, from Latin *corpus* = body]

corpse *NOUN* **corpses** a dead body

corpuscle *NOUN* **corpuscles** one of the red or white cells in blood

correct *ADJECTIVE* **1** true; accurate; without any mistakes **2** proper; done or said in an approved way
▷ **correctly** *ADVERB* **correctness** *NOUN*

correct *VERB* **corrects, correcting, corrected** **1** make a thing correct by altering or adjusting it **2** mark the mistakes in something **3** point out or punish a person's faults
▷ **correction** *NOUN* **corrective** *ADJECTIVE*

correspond *VERB* **corresponds, corresponding, corresponded** **1** write letters to each other **2** agree; match • *Your story corresponds with his.* **3** be similar or equivalent • *Their assembly corresponds to our parliament.*

correspondence *NOUN* **1** letters; writing letters **2** similarity; agreement

corridor *NOUN* **corridors** a passage in a building

corroborate *VERB* **corroborates, corroborating, corroborated** help to confirm a statement etc.
▷ **corroboration** *NOUN*

corrode *VERB* **corrodes, corroding, corroded** destroy metal gradually by chemical action
▷ **corrosion** *NOUN* **corrosive** *ADJECTIVE*

corrugated *ADJECTIVE* shaped into alternate ridges and grooves • *corrugated iron*

corrupt *ADJECTIVE* **1** dishonest; accepting bribes **2** wicked **3** decaying

corrupt *VERB* **corrupts, corrupting, corrupted** **1** cause someone to become dishonest or wicked **2** spoil; cause something to decay
▷ **corruption** *NOUN* **corruptible** *ADJECTIVE*

Thesaurus

corpse *NOUN Police found the corpse under the floorboards.* ► body, dead body, remains, cadaver, carcass, skeleton

correct *ADJECTIVE* **1** *What is the correct time? Not all the information proved correct.* ► right, accurate, exact, true, precise, genuine, authentic, reliable, factual, faithful, faultless, flawless, strict OPPOSITES ARE inaccurate, wrong **2** *She wanted to know the correct course of action.* ► right, proper, appropriate, fitting, suitable, acceptable, just OPPOSITES ARE inappropriate, wrong **3** *correct behaviour* ► proper, decent, well mannered, tactful, unexceptionable

correct *VERB* **1** *Please correct your mistakes.* ► rectify, put right, make good, amend, remedy, cure, redress, adjust, alter, repair, right **2** *Your work will be corrected within two days.* ► mark, assess, evaluate, appraise **3** *She corrected him for his rudeness.* ► scold, admonish, rebuke, chastise, punish

correction *NOUN the correction of errors* ► rectification, righting, putting right, resolution, adjustment, amendment

correspond *VERB* **1 correspond to** *The translator must choose words that correspond to the sense of the original.* ► match, fit, conform to, accord with, agree with, be consistent with, parallel, concur with, harmonize with, square with, tally with, convey **2** *Emma and I corresponded for many years.* ► communicate, exchange letters, write to each other

correspondence *NOUN* **1** *a collection of the composer's published correspondence* ► letters, communications, memoranda, notes **2** *There is some correspondence between the two ideas.* ► correlation, similarity, resemblance, comparability, agreement

corresponding *ADJECTIVE Climate change brings a corresponding change in average temperature.* ► matching, equivalent, commensurate, related, analogous, appropriate, complementary, parallel

corrupt *ADJECTIVE* **1** *The government is accused of being corrupt and incompetent.* ► dishonest, dishonourable, unprincipled, unscrupulous, untrustworthy, underhand, disreputable, discreditable, bribable, unsound, false, (*more informal*) bent OPPOSITES ARE honest, reputable **2** *They were involved in some form of corrupt practice.* ► dishonest, crooked, criminal, fraudulent, unethical **3** *Some people say society is getting more corrupt.* ► sinful, immoral, decadent, degenerate, depraved, dissolute, debauched, rotten, wicked, evil, iniquitous, low, perverted, profligate, venal AN OPPOSITE IS moral

corrupt *VERB* **1** *Some firms even try to corrupt local officials.* ► bribe, suborn, buy off, pay off, influence, (*more informal*) fix **2** *Pornography corrupts the innocent.* ► pervert, deprave, debauch, lead astray, make corrupt, contaminate, degrade, tempt, seduce

corruption *NOUN* **1** *He was found guilty of treason, espionage, and corruption.* ► dishonesty, deception, misconduct, bribery, fraud AN OPPOSITE IS honesty **2** *all kinds of moral*

a b c d e f g h i j k l m n o p q r s t u v w x y z

cosine *NOUN* **cosines** (in a right-angled triangle) the ratio of the length of a side adjacent to one of the acute angles to the length of the hypotenuse COMPARE **sine**

cosmetic *NOUN* **cosmetics** a substance (e.g. face powder or lipstick) put on the skin to make it look more attractive

cosmetic surgery *NOUN* surgery carried out to make people look more attractive

cosmic *ADJECTIVE* **1** to do with the universe **2** to do with outer space • *cosmic rays*

cosmopolitan *ADJECTIVE* from many countries; containing people from many countries

cosmos (koz-moss) *NOUN* the universe

cost *NOUN* **costs** **1** the amount of money needed to buy, do, or make something **2** the effort or loss needed to achieve something
at all costs or **at any cost** no matter what the cost or difficulty may be

cost *VERB* **costs, costing, cost** **1** have a certain amount as its price or charge **2** cause the loss of • *This war has cost many lives.* **3** (*past tense* is **costed**) estimate the cost of something

costly *ADJECTIVE* **costlier, costliest** expensive
▷ **costliness** *NOUN*

costume *NOUN* **costumes** clothes, especially for a particular purpose or of a particular place or period

cosy *ADJECTIVE* **cosier, cosiest** warm and comfortable
▷ **cosily** *ADVERB* **cosiness** *NOUN*

cot *NOUN* **cots** a baby's bed with high sides [from Hindi *khat* = framework of a bed]

cottage *NOUN* **cottages** a small simple house, especially in the country

cotton *NOUN* **1** a soft white substance covering the seeds of a tropical plant; the plant itself **2** thread made from this substance **3** cloth made from cotton thread

cotton wool *NOUN* soft fluffy material originally made from cotton

couch *NOUN* **couches** **1** a long soft seat like a sofa but with only one end raised **2** a sofa or settee

couch *VERB* **couches, couching, couched** express in words of a certain kind • *The request was couched in polite terms.*

cough (kof) *VERB* **coughs, coughing, coughed** send out air from the lungs with a sudden sharp sound

cough *NOUN* **coughs** **1** the act or sound of coughing **2** an illness that makes you cough

could *past tense* of **can** ²

couldn't (*mainly spoken*) could not

council *NOUN* **councils** a group of people chosen or elected to organize or discuss something, especially those elected to organize the affairs of a town or county
USAGE Do not confuse with **counsel**.

councillor *NOUN* **councillors** a member of a town or county council

council tax *NOUN* **council taxes** a tax paid to a local authority to pay for local services, based on the estimated value of someone's house or flat

Thesaurus

corruption ► sin, immorality, degradation, depravity, degeneracy, impurity OPPOSITES ARE morality, purity

cosmopolitan *ADJECTIVE* **1** *a large city with a cosmopolitan atmosphere* ► international, multicultural, sophisticated AN OPPOSITE IS provincial **2** *cosmopolitan attitudes* ► worldly, well travelled, sophisticated, urbane, liberal

cost *NOUN* **1** *The cost of a ticket has increased.* ► price, charge (for), expense, amount, payment (for), levy (on), tariff (on), outlay (on), expenditure (on), rate (for), value, fare, figure **2** *The cost in human lives is too great.* ► sacrifice, loss, penalty, price, suffering

cost *VERB* **1** *Each item on this shelf costs a pound.* ► be priced at, sell for, go for, come to, fetch, realize, (*more informal*) set you back

costly *ADJECTIVE* *The five-star service is very costly.* ► expensive, dear, overpriced, exorbitant, (*more informal*) pricey

costume *NOUN* *a prize for the best costume* ► outfit, dress, ensemble, clothing, suit, attire, (*informal*) get-up

cosy *ADJECTIVE* *They lived in a cosy little house.* ► snug, comfortable, warm, homely, restful, secure, intimate, reassuring, relaxing, soft, (*more informal*) comfy AN OPPOSITE IS uncomfortable

cottage *NOUN* *a cottage in the country* ► little house, bungalow, cabin, chalet, (*mainly Scottish*) bothy

couch *NOUN* *A cat sat next to her on the couch.* ► sofa, settee, chesterfield, ottoman, divan

council *NOUN* **1** *The council is responsible for maintaining the roads.* ► local authority, legislature, corporation, assembly **2** *a meeting*

counsel *NOUN* **counsels** **1** advice • *give counsel* **2** a barrister or group of barristers representing someone in a lawsuit
take counsel with consult
USAGE Do not confuse with **council**.

counsel *VERB* **counsels, counselling, counselled** give advice to someone; recommend

count[1] *VERB* **counts, counting, counted** **1** say numbers in their proper order **2** find the total of something by using numbers **3** include in a total • *There are six of us, counting the dog.* **4** be important • *It's what you do that counts.* **5** regard; consider • *I should count it an honour to be invited.*
count on rely on

count *NOUN* **counts** **1** counting **2** a number reached by counting; a total **3** any of the points being considered, e.g. in accusing someone of crimes • *guilty on all counts*

count[2] *NOUN* **counts** a foreign nobleman

countdown *NOUN* **countdowns** counting numbers backwards to zero before an event, especially the launching of a space rocket

counter[1] *NOUN* **counters** **1** a flat surface over which customers are served in a shop, bank, etc. **2** a small round playing piece used in board games **3** a device for counting things

counter[2] *VERB* **counters, countering, countered** **1** counteract **2** counter-attack; return an opponent's blow by hitting back

counteract *VERB* **counteracts, counteracting, counteracted** act against something and reduce or prevent its effects
▷ **counteraction** *NOUN*

counterbalance *NOUN* **counterbalances** a weight or influence that balances another
▷ **counterbalance** *VERB*

counterfeit (kownt- er- feet) *ADJECTIVE* fake; not genuine

counterfeit *VERB* **counterfeits, counterfeiting, counterfeited** forge or make an imitation of something

counterfoil *NOUN* **counterfoils** a section of a cheque or receipt etc. that is torn off and kept as a record

counterpart *NOUN* **counterparts** a person or thing that corresponds to another • *Their President is the counterpart of our Prime Minister.*

countless *ADJECTIVE* too many to count

country *NOUN* **countries** **1** the land occupied by a nation **2** all the people of a country **3** the countryside

countryside *NOUN* an area with fields, woods, villages, etc. away from towns

county *NOUN* **counties** each of the main areas that a country is divided into for local government

coup (koo) *NOUN* **coups** a sudden action taken to win power; a clever victory

couple *NOUN* **couples** two people or things considered together; a pair

couple *VERB* **couples, coupling, coupled** fasten or link two things together

couplet *NOUN* **couplets** a pair of lines in rhyming verse

coupon *NOUN* **coupons** a piece of paper that gives you the right to receive or do something

Thesaurus

of the society's administrative council ► board, committee, commission, panel

count *VERB* **1** *He was counting the number of cars parked along the street.* ► add up, total, calculate, work out, reckon, check, (*more informal*) tot up **2** *It's important for people to feel that they count.* ► matter, be important, have significance, signify **3** **count on** *You can count on my support.* ► rely on, depend on, bank on, be sure of, trust, believe in, expect, have faith in

counteract *VERB* *new laws to counteract terrorism* ► prevent, resist, oppose, curb, forestall, fight against, act against, work against, thwart, frustrate, foil, reduce, neutralize, withstand

countless *ADJECTIVE* *They have to make countless decisions every day.* ► innumerable, untold, myriad, numerous, numberless, unnumbered, endless, immeasurable, incalculable, infinite, many, measureless, limitless AN OPPOSITE IS few

country *NOUN* **1** *a country of warlike people* ► nation, land, state, territory, realm **2** *They could return to their own country at last.* ► homeland, home, native land, native soil, mother country, country of origin, birthplace **3** *The prime minister would appeal to the country in an election.* ► people, nation, public, populace, population, community **4** *You drive through lovely open country.* ► terrain, landscape, countryside, scenery, surroundings, environment RELATED ADJECTIVE rural

couple *NOUN* **1** *A couple were dancing on the balcony.* ► pair, twosome, partners, duo, husband and wife **2** *Let me know if you see him in the next couple of days.* ► few, two or three
USAGE You can also say *in the next day or so*

couple *VERB* *A second locomotive is coupled to the train at Crewe.* ► connect, attach, join, link, fasten, hitch, yoke, unite (with), combine (with), pair

coupon *NOUN* **1** *The offer includes money-saving coupons.* ► voucher, token, ticket, certificate

A B C D E F G H I J K L M N O P Q R S T U V W X Y Z

courage *NOUN* the ability to face danger or difficulty or pain even when you are afraid; bravery
▷ **courageous** *ADJECTIVE*

courier (koor- ee- er) *NOUN* **couriers** **1** a messenger **2** a person employed to guide and help a group of tourists

course *NOUN* **courses** **1** the direction in which something goes; a route • *the ship's course* **2** a series of events or actions etc. • *Your best course is to start again.* **3** a series of lessons, exercises, etc. **4** part of a meal • *the meat course* **5** a racecourse **6** a golf course
of course without a doubt; as we expected

court *NOUN* **courts** **1** the royal household **2** a lawcourt; the judges etc. in a lawcourt **3** an enclosed area for games such as tennis or netball **4** a courtyard

court *VERB* **courts, courting, courted** try to win somebody's love or support [from early French, from Latin *cohors* = a crowd of people]

courteous (ker- tee- us) *ADJECTIVE* polite
▷ **courteously** *ADVERB* **courtesy** *NOUN*

courtier *NOUN* **courtiers** (*old use*) one of a king's or queen's companions at court

courtly *ADJECTIVE* dignified and polite

courtship *NOUN* **1** courting someone, especially a boyfriend or girlfriend **2** the mating ritual of some birds and animals

courtyard *NOUN* **courtyards** a space surrounded by walls or buildings

cousin *NOUN* **cousins** a child of your uncle or aunt

cover *VERB* **covers, covering, covered** **1** place one thing over or round another; conceal **2** travel a certain distance • *We covered ten miles a day.* **3** aim a gun at somebody • *I've got you covered.* **4** protect by insurance or a guarantee • *These goods are covered against fire or theft.* **5** be enough money to pay for something • *£10 should cover my fare.* **6** deal with or include • *The book covers all kinds of farming.*
▷ **coverage** *NOUN*
cover up conceal something, especially an awkward fact or piece of information

cover *NOUN* **covers** **1** a thing used for covering something else; a lid, wrapper, envelope, etc. **2** the binding of a book **3** something that hides or shelters or protects you

Thesaurus

2 *For more information fill in the coupon below.* ► form, tear-off slip, slip

courage *NOUN* *It needs courage to argue with them.* ► bravery, audacity, boldness, daring, nerve, pluck, gallantry, determination, fearlessness, fortitude, heroism, (*more informal*) bottle, (*more informal*) grit, (*more informal*) guts, (*much more informal*) spunk
AN OPPOSITE IS cowardice

courageous *ADJECTIVE* *It was a courageous attempt against all the odds.* ► brave, valiant, daring, audacious, spirited, intrepid, plucky, adventurous, fearless AN OPPOSITE IS cowardly

course *NOUN* **1** *a beginner's course in German* ► programme of study, course of study, educational programme, classes, lessons, studies **2** *The aircraft had changed its course again.* ► direction, route, way, tack, path, flight path, bearing, itinerary **3** *an event that changed the course of history* ► progress, progression, development, advance, evolution, flow, unfolding, future **4** *the best course to adopt* ► plan, plan of action, procedure, approach, method, programme, policy **5** *They had only just started the main course.* ► dish, part of a meal, menu item **6** *six laps of the course* ► track, circuit, ground, stadium

court *NOUN* **1** *The court acquitted them all.* ► lawcourt, court of law, bench, tribunal **2** *entertainment for the Queen's court* ► entourage, followers, royal household, establishment **3** *a court for ball games* ► enclosure, playing area, ground, field

courteous *ADJECTIVE* *The staff are always helpful and courteous.* ► polite, civil, obliging, considerate, respectful, well mannered, affable, civilized, refined

courtesy *NOUN* *Everyone is entitled to the same level of courtesy.* ► politeness, consideration, civility, respect, attention

cover *NOUN* **1** *The computer screen has its own plastic cover.* ► covering, envelope, wrapper, case **2** *Lift the cover and look inside.* ► lid, top, cap **3** *The book has a blue cover.* ► jacket, dust jacket, dust cover, wrapper **4** *a thick cover of snow* ► covering, layer, coat, coating, blanket, carpet, cloak, overlay **5** *The trees provide some sort of cover.* ► shelter, protection, refuge, shield, haven, defence **6** *The business is a cover for spying activities.* ► front, facade, pretext, disguise, screen

cover *VERB* **1** *She covered her knees with a blanket.* ► envelop, enclose, protect, overlay USAGE You can also say *She put* (*or placed*) *a blanket over her knees.* **2** *The car was covered in mud.* ► coat, cake, encrust, plaster, smother, spread **3** *The book covers most of the main topics.* ► deal with, treat, consider, include, contain, comprise,

cow *NOUN* **cows** the fully grown female of cattle or of certain other large animals (e.g. elephant, whale, or seal)

coward *NOUN* **cowards** a person who has no courage and shows fear in a shameful way
▷ **cowardice** *NOUN* **cowardly** *ADJECTIVE*

cowboy *NOUN* **cowboys** a man in charge of grazing cattle on a ranch in the USA

cower *VERB* **cowers, cowering, cowered** crouch or shrink back in fear

coy *ADJECTIVE* pretending to be shy or modest; bashful
▷ **coyly** *ADVERB* **coyness** *NOUN*

crab *NOUN* **crabs** a shellfish with ten legs, the first pair being a set of pincers

crab apple *NOUN* **crab apples** a small sour apple

crack *NOUN* **cracks** **1** a line on the surface of something where it has broken but not come completely apart **2** a narrow gap **3** a sudden sharp noise **4** a knock • *a crack on the head* **5** (*informal*) a joke; a wisecrack **6** a drug made from cocaine

crack *ADJECTIVE* (*informal*) first-class • *He is a crack shot.*

crack *VERB* **cracks, cracking, cracked** **1** make or get a crack; split **2** make a sudden sharp noise **3** break down • *He cracked under the strain.*
crack a joke tell a joke
crack down on (*informal*) stop something that is illegal or against rules
get cracking (*informal*) get busy

cracker *NOUN* **crackers** **1** a paper tube that bangs when pulled apart **2** a thin biscuit

crackle *VERB* **crackles, crackling, crackled** make small cracking sounds • *The fire crackled in the grate.*
▷ **crackle** *NOUN*

cradle *NOUN* **cradles** **1** a small cot for a baby **2** a supporting framework

cradle *VERB* **cradles, cradling, cradled** hold gently

craft *NOUN* **crafts** **1** a job that needs skill, especially with the hands **2** skill **3** cunning; trickery **4** (**craft**) a ship or boat; an aircraft or spacecraft

Thesaurus

encompass, embrace, provide for, incorporate **4** *The money should cover most of our needs.* ► cater for, be enough for, meet, suffice for, pay for

covering *NOUN* *a light covering of snow* ► cover, layer, coat, coating, blanket, carpet, cloak, overlay

coward *NOUN* *He accused them of being cheats and cowards.* ► weakling, faint-heart, (*more informal*) chicken, (*more informal*) wimp
AN OPPOSITE IS hero

cowardice *NOUN* *Her husband had been executed for cowardice.* ► cowardliness, faint-heartedness, spinelessness, timorousness, timidity OPPOSITES ARE bravery, courage

cowardly *ADJECTIVE* *The thieves ran off, showing how cowardly they are. The decision was feeble and cowardly.* ► faint-hearted, lily-livered, spineless, craven, weak, timid, pusillanimous, (*more informal*) gutless, (*more informal*) yellow
OPPOSITES ARE brave, courageous

coy *ADJECTIVE* *Don't be coy: come and be introduced* ► shy, bashful, reserved, diffident, embarrassed, inhibited, self-conscious, hesitant, timid, retiring OPPOSITES ARE assertive, forward, bold

crack *NOUN* **1** *a plate with a crack in it* ► break, chip, chink, split, fracture, fissure, gap **2** *a crack on the head* ► blow, bang, knock, smack, hit, punch, (*more informal*) bash **3** *the crack of a rifle; a crack of thunder* ► bang, report, crash, explosion, burst, snap, pop **4** *a cheap crack* ► joke, jest, quip, wisecrack, gibe, dig, (*more informal*) gag **5** *have a crack at it* ► try, attempt, (*more informal*) go, (*more informal*) shot, (*more informal*) stab

crack *VERB* **1** *She dropped a cup and cracked it.* ► break, split, shatter, splinter, chip, fracture **2** *Guns cracked in the distance.* ► burst, bang, go bang, explode, thump, boom, pop, crackle, crash **3** *She cracked him round the head.* ► strike, smack, thump, slap, hit, (*more informal*) bash, (*more informal*) whack **4** *The problem proved hard to crack.* ► solve, resolve, work out, puzzle out, fathom, decipher, break **5** *A suspect finally cracked and confessed.* ► break down, give in, give way, collapse, yield
crack down on *a drive to crack down on street crime* ► reduce, suppress, end, stop, eradicate, get tough on, clamp down on
crack up (*informal*) **1** *I'm so anxious I could be cracking up.* ► break down, have a breakdown, lose control, go to pieces, go mad, go crazy **2** *The remark made everyone want to crack up.* ► burst out laughing, roar with laughter, laugh uncontrollably

crackle *VERB* *The fire began to crackle.* ► sizzle, fizzle, crack, fizz, hiss, sputter

cradle *NOUN* *a baby's cradle* ► cot, crib, bed

craft *NOUN* **1** *the traditional craft of hand weaving* ► handicraft, trade, business, pursuit, activity, occupation, profession, work, job **2** *Pete demonstrated the blacksmith's craft.* ► skill, art, technique, expertise, mastery, talent, ability

A B C D E F G H I J K L M N O P Q R S T U V W X Y Z

craftsman *NOUN* **craftsmen** a person who is good at a craft
▷ **craftsmanship** *NOUN*

crafty *ADJECTIVE* **craftier, craftiest** cunning
▷ **craftily** *ADVERB* **craftiness** *NOUN*

crag *NOUN* **crags** a steep piece of rough rock
▷ **craggy** *ADJECTIVE* **cragginess** *NOUN*
[from a Celtic word]

cram *VERB* **crams, cramming, crammed** **1** push many things into something so that it is very full **2** learn as many facts as you can in a short time just before an examination

cramp *NOUN* **cramps** pain caused by a muscle tightening suddenly

cramp *VERB* **cramps, cramping, cramped** hinder someone's freedom or growth etc.

cramped *ADJECTIVE* in a space that is too small or tight

crane *NOUN* **cranes** **1** a machine for lifting and moving heavy objects **2** a large wading bird with long legs and neck

crane *VERB* **cranes, craning, craned** stretch your neck to try to see something

crank *NOUN* **cranks** **1** an L-shaped part used for changing the direction of movement in machinery **2** a person with strange or fanatical ideas
▷ **cranky** *ADJECTIVE*

cranny *NOUN* **crannies** a crevice

crash *NOUN* **crashes** **1** the loud noise of something breaking or colliding **2** a violent collision or fall **3** a sudden drop or failure

crash *VERB* **crashes, crashing, crashed** **1** make or have a crash; cause to crash **2** move with a crash **3** (said about a computer) stop working suddenly

crash *ADJECTIVE* intensive • *a crash course*

crash helmet *NOUN* **crash helmets** a padded helmet worn by cyclists and motorcyclists to protect the head

crass *ADJECTIVE* **1** very obvious or shocking; gross • *crass ignorance* **2** very stupid

crate *NOUN* **crates** **1** a packing case made of strips of wood **2** an open container with compartments for carrying bottles

crater *NOUN* **craters** **1** the mouth of a volcano **2** a bowl-shaped cavity or hollow caused by an explosion or impact

craving *NOUN* **cravings** a strong desire; a longing

crawl *VERB* **crawls, crawling, crawled** **1** move with the body close to the ground or other surface, or on hands and knees **2** move slowly

Thesaurus

3 *The harbour was teeming with river craft.* ► vessels, ships, boats

craftsman *NOUN* *Passers-by could watch the craftsmen at work.* ► artisan, artist, craftsperson, master

craftsmanship *NOUN* *an age when craftsmanship in building reached a peak* ► skill, technique, expertise, workmanship, artistry, ability, dexterity, handiwork, (*more informal*) know-how

crafty *ADJECTIVE* *That's a crafty way of avoiding the problem.* ► cunning, clever, shrewd, ingenious, wily, artful, canny

cram *VERB* **1** *They were busy cramming burgers into their mouths. The shelves were crammed with books.* ► stuff, force, press, squeeze, jam, pack, overfill **2** *I'll never know how we managed to cram into such a tiny car.* ► crowd, crush, squeeze, pack **3** *Many of the students are still cramming for tomorrow's exam.* ► study hard, (*more informal*) swot, (*more informal*) mug up

cramped *ADJECTIVE* *It was hard to sleep in the cramped quarters of the submarine.* ► restricted, confined, poky, constricted, narrow, tight, uncomfortable AN OPPOSITE IS roomy

crash *NOUN* **1** *There was a loud crash in the kitchen.* ► bang, smash, clash, clatter, clang, racket, thump, thud, boom **2** *She had been injured in a car crash.* ► accident, collision, smash, bump, pile-up, derailment, disaster, impact, knock, wreck **3** *a stock-market crash* ► collapse, failure, depression, fall, ruin

crash *VERB* **1 crash into** *The car crashed into a tree.* ► hit, strike, smash into, collide with, bump into, knock into, lurch into, pitch into **2** *The company had crashed in the recession.* ► fail, collapse, fold, go under, founder, become bankrupt **3** *Parts of the roof crashed to the ground.* ► collapse, fall, plunge, topple, hurtle

crate *NOUN* *Three crates of books stood by the door.* ► case, packing case, box, carton, tea chest

crave *VERB* *The chapel might provide the privacy she craved.* ► long for, yearn for, hunger for, dream of, hanker after, desire, seek

craving *NOUN* *the body's natural craving for food* ► longing, desire, hankering, hunger, thirst, appetite

crawl *VERB* **1** *He escaped by crawling out of the back of the house.* ► creep, edge, inch, slither, clamber **2** (*informal*) *You can get their support without having to crawl to them all the time.* ► grovel, pander, kowtow, fawn (over), be obsequious, (*more informal*) suck up
be crawling with *The place is crawling with visitors in the summer months.* ► be full of, be

3 be covered with crawling things
▷ **crawler** NOUN

crawl NOUN **1** a crawling movement **2** a very slow pace **3** an overarm swimming stroke

crayon NOUN **crayons** a stick or pencil of coloured wax etc. for drawing

craze NOUN **crazes** a temporary enthusiasm

crazy ADJECTIVE **crazier, craziest 1** insane **2** very foolish • *this crazy idea*
▷ **crazily** ADVERB **craziness** NOUN

crazy paving NOUN paving made of oddly shaped pieces of stone etc.

creak NOUN **creaks** a harsh squeak like that of a stiff door hinge
▷ **creaky** ADJECTIVE

creak VERB **creaks, creaking, creaked** make a creak

cream NOUN **creams 1** the fatty part of milk **2** a yellowish-white colour **3** a food containing or looking like cream • *chocolate cream* **4** a soft substance • *face cream* **5** the best part
▷ **creamy** ADJECTIVE

cream VERB **creams, creaming, creamed** make creamy; beat butter etc. until it is soft like cream
cream off remove the best part of something

crease NOUN **creases 1** a line made in something by folding, pressing, or crushing it **2** a line on a cricket pitch marking a batsman's or bowler's position

crease VERB **creases, creasing, creased** make a crease or creases in something

create VERB **creates, creating, created 1** bring into existence; make or produce, especially something that no one has made before **2** (*slang*) make a fuss; grumble
▷ **creation** NOUN **creator** NOUN

creative ADJECTIVE showing imagination and thought • *a creative use of language*
▷ **creativity** NOUN

creature NOUN **creatures** a living being, especially an animal

crèche (kresh) NOUN **crèches** a place where babies and young children are looked after while their parents are at work

Thesaurus

overrun by, be teeming with, be packed with, be crowded with

craze NOUN *the latest craze to sweep the country* ► fad, trend, vogue, fashion, rage, mania, diversion, enthusiasm, infatuation, novelty, obsession, passion, pastime

crazy ADJECTIVE **1** *It was crazy to expect them to agree.* ► absurd, ridiculous, ludicrous, preposterous, foolish, idiotic, stupid, foolhardy, unwise, (*more informal*) barmy **2** *She was going crazy with all the work.* ► mad, insane, out of your mind, off your head, unbalanced, demented, deranged **3** *The whole family are crazy about golf.* ► mad, passionate, keen (on), devoted (to), smitten (with), taken (with), (*more informal*) potty

creak VERB *The door began to creak.* ► squeak, grate, groan, scrape, grind, rasp

cream NOUN **1** *Rub in some skin cream.* ► lotion, ointment, rub, salve, moisturizer **2** *the cream of the country's jockeys* ► pick, elite, choice, finest, best AN OPPOSITE IS dregs

creamy ADJECTIVE *The powder makes a creamy paste when mixed with water.* ► smooth, thick, rich, velvety, milky, oily

crease NOUN *The cloth was full of creases and would have to be ironed.* ► wrinkle, crinkle, pucker, fold, furrow, groove, line, pleat, ridge, ruck, tuck, corrugation

crease VERB *I tried not to crease my clothes.* ► crumple, crinkle, wrinkle, pucker, crush, crimp, rumple, ruck, fold, furrow, pleat, ridge

create VERB **1** *A new work had to be created from scratch.* ► produce, make, generate, develop, compose, devise, design **2** *His father had created the business fifty years before.* ► set up, start, begin, found, establish, institute, initiate **3** *The appointment created a lot of resentment.* ► cause, bring about, lead to, engender, prompt, produce, result in, give rise to

creation NOUN **1** *the creation of a modern industrial society* ► making, formation, foundation, fashioning, establishment, institution, conception, birth, development, origination, production OPPOSITES ARE disintegration, destruction **2** *The decor was entirely her creation.* ► work, effort, conception, invention, design, devising, achievement, handiwork, brainchild, product, work of art

creative ADJECTIVE *Students need to be creative in their thinking.* ► imaginative, inventive, expressive, resourceful, original, productive, fertile, artistic, positive, ingenious, clever, inspired, talented, visionary AN OPPOSITE IS destructive

creator NOUN **1** *the creator of many good novels* ► writer, author, producer, composer, designer, deviser, initiator, inventor, maker, manufacturer, parent **2** *the creators of the Assyrian Empire* ► architect, builder, originator, begetter

creature NOUN **1** *Whales are the largest living creatures.* ► animal, living thing, beast, being, brute **2** *The poor creature had been out in the*

A B C D E F G H I J K L M N O P Q R S T U V W X Y Z

credentials *PLURAL NOUN* documents showing a person's identity, qualifications, etc.

credible *ADJECTIVE* able to be believed; convincing

▷ **credibly** *ADVERB* **credibility** *NOUN*

USAGE Do not confuse with **creditable** or **credulous**.

credit *NOUN* **credits** **1** a source of pride or honour • *a credit to the school* **2** praise or acknowledgement given for some achievement or good quality • *I must give you credit for persistence.* **3** an arrangement trusting a person to pay for something later on **4** an amount of money in an account at a bank etc., or entered in a financial account as paid in COMPARE **debit** **5** belief or trust • *I put no credit in this rumour.*

credits a list of people who have helped to produce a film or television programme

credit *VERB* **credits**, **crediting**, **credited** **1** believe **2** attribute; say that a person has done or achieved something • *Columbus is credited with the discovery of America.* **3** enter something as a credit in a financial account COMPARE **debit**

creditable *ADJECTIVE* deserving praise

USAGE Do not confuse with **credible** or **credulous**.

credit card *NOUN* **credit cards** a card authorizing a person to buy on credit

creditor *NOUN* **creditors** a person to whom money is owed

credulous *ADJECTIVE* too ready to believe things; gullible

USAGE Do not confuse with **credible** or **creditable**.

creed *NOUN* **creeds** a set or formal statement of beliefs

creep *VERB* **creeps**, **creeping**, **crept** **1** move along close to the ground **2** move quietly **3** come gradually **4** prickle with fear • *It makes my flesh creep*

creep *NOUN* **creeps** **1** a creeping movement **2** (*informal*) an unpleasant person, especially one who seeks to win favour

the creeps (*informal*) a nervous feeling caused by fear or dislike

creeper *NOUN* **creepers** a plant that grows along the ground or up a wall etc.

creepy *ADJECTIVE* **creepier**, **creepiest** frightening and sinister

cremate *VERB* **cremates**, **cremating**, **cremated** burn a dead body to ashes

▷ **cremation** *NOUN*

crematorium *NOUN* **crematoria** a place where dead bodies are cremated

crescendo (krish- end- oh) *NOUN* **crescendos** a gradual increase in loudness

crescent *NOUN* **crescents** **1** a narrow curved shape coming to a point at each end **2** a curved street

cress *NOUN* a plant with hot-tasting leaves, used in salads and sandwiches

crest *NOUN* **crests** **1** a tuft of hair, skin, or feathers on an animal's or bird's head **2** the top of a hill or wave etc. **3** a design used on notepaper etc.

▷ **crested** *ADJECTIVE*

Thesaurus

rain all night. ► fellow, individual, person, wretch, beggar, chap

credibility *NOUN* *The details give credibility to the story.* ► plausibility, conviction, integrity, believability, reliability, probability, trustworthiness

credible *ADJECTIVE* *The man was unable to give any credible explanation for his presence there.* ► believable, plausible, reasonable, tenable, conceivable, possible, convincing, imaginable, likely, persuasive AN OPPOSITE IS incredible

credit *NOUN* **1** *Gary helped him with his chemistry and deserves a lot of the credit for the good grades he got.* ► praise, acclaim, approval, recognition, acknowledgement, commendation, distinction, prestige, merit, esteem, fame, glory, honour, (*more informal*) kudos, reputation, status AN OPPOSITE IS dishonour **2** *Kate had better taste than she'd been given credit for.* ► recognition, acknowledgement, approval

credit *VERB* **1** *It is difficult to credit such an unlikely story.* ► accept, believe, subscribe to, trust, have confidence in, have faith in, rely on, depend on, count on, endorse, reckon on, (*more informal*) swallow, (*informal*) buy AN OPPOSITE IS disbelieve **2** *The idea is credited to Aristotle.* ► attribute to, ascribe to, assign to, attach to, associate (with)

creditable *ADJECTIVE* *The team were on good form and put on a creditable performance.* ► commendable, laudable, respectable, estimable, admirable, praiseworthy, worthy, excellent, good, honourable, meritorious, well thought of AN OPPOSITE IS unworthy

creep *VERB* **1** *She watched him creep under the table.* ► crawl, slither, slink, wriggle, worm your way, writhe, edge, inch, move slowly **2** *Gilly packed a suitcase and crept down the stairs.* ► slip, sneak, steal, move quietly, tiptoe

creepy *ADJECTIVE* *The place gave her creepy feelings.* ► frightening, eerie, spooky, scary, weird, sinister, uncanny, unearthly, macabre, ominous AN OPPOSITE IS pleasant

crest *NOUN* **1** *a bird with a bright crest* ► plume, tuft, comb **2** *We reached the crest of the hill.*

crestfallen *ADJECTIVE* disappointed or dejected

crevasse (kri- vass) *NOUN* **crevasses** a deep open crack, especially in a glacier

crevice *NOUN* **crevices** a narrow opening, especially in a rock or wall

crew [1] *NOUN* **crews** **1** the people working in a ship or aircraft **2** a group working together • *the camera crew*

crew [2] *past tense of* **crow** [2]

crib *NOUN* **cribs** **1** a baby's cot **2** a framework holding fodder for animals **3** a model representing the Nativity of Jesus Christ **4** something cribbed **5** a translation for use by students

crib *VERB* **cribs, cribbing, cribbed** copy someone else's work

crick *NOUN* **cricks** painful stiffness in the neck or back

cricket [1] *NOUN* a game played outdoors between teams with a ball, bats, and two wickets
▷ **cricketer** *NOUN*

cricket [2] *NOUN* **crickets** a brown insect like a grasshopper

crime *NOUN* **crimes** **1** an action that breaks the law **2** lawbreaking

criminal *NOUN* **criminals** a person who has committed a crime or crimes
▷ **criminal** *ADJECTIVE* **criminally** *ADVERB*

crimson *ADJECTIVE* deep-red
▷ **crimson** *NOUN*

cringe *VERB* **cringes, cringing, cringed** shrink back in fear; cower

cripple *NOUN* **cripples** a person who is permanently lame

cripple *VERB* **cripples, crippling, crippled** **1** make a person lame **2** weaken or damage something seriously

crisis *NOUN* **crises** an important and dangerous or difficult situation

crisp *ADJECTIVE* **1** very dry so that it breaks with a snap **2** fresh and stiff • *a crisp £5 note* **3** cold and dry • *a crisp morning* **4** brisk and sharp • *a crisp manner*
▷ **crisply** *ADVERB* **crispness** *NOUN*

crisp *NOUN* **crisps** a very thin fried slice of potato, usually sold in packets

criss-cross *ADJECTIVE, ADVERB* with crossing lines

criterion (kry- teer- ee- on) *NOUN* **criteria** a standard by which something is judged or decided

critic *NOUN* **critics** **1** a person who gives opinions on books, plays, films, music, etc. **2** a person who criticizes

Thesaurus

► peak, crown, brow, ridge, summit, top, apex **3** *the royal crest* ► insignia, regalia, emblem, badge, seal, sign, symbol

crew *NOUN* **1** *a ship's crew* ► company, complement, sailors, seamen **2** *a road-mending crew* ► team, gang, unit, party, squad

crime *NOUN* **1** *The report shows a decrease in street crime.* ► lawbreaking, lawlessness, delinquency, wrongdoing, transgression, misconduct, dishonesty, illegality **2** *Blackmail is a serious crime.* ► offence, misdeed, misdemeanour, transgression, illegal act, unlawful act, (*more informal*) racket, (*old use*) felony

criminal *NOUN* *His friends were criminals, working with the smugglers.* ► lawbreaker, offender, villain, wrongdoer, delinquent, miscreant, convict, culprit, (*more informal*) crook

criminal *ADJECTIVE* *Hardship can never justify criminal behaviour.* ► illegal, unlawful, illicit, dishonest, corrupt, nefarious, (*more informal*) crooked, (*more informal*) bent OPPOSITES ARE legal, honest

cringe *VERB* **1** *The old man cringed, his hands shaking.* ► cower, shrink back, draw back, recoil, flinch, shy away, quail, tremble, crouch, quiver, dodge, duck, grovel **2** *I cringe when I hear those songs these days.* ► wince, blench, squirm, blush

cripple *VERB* **1** *The car hit her, crippling her for life.* ► disable, incapacitate, maim, injure, lame, damage, paralyse **2** *Industry was crippled by a series of strikes.* ► ruin, destroy, crush, paralyse, scupper, bring to a standstill, put out of action, spoil

crippled *ADJECTIVE* **1** *His crippled right leg is bent back at the knee.* ► disabled, deformed, lame, incapacitated, physically impaired, injured, maimed, paralysed, handicapped, hurt, invalid, mutilated **2** *Witnesses watched the crippled car being winched on to the Relay tender.* ► immobilized, damaged, incapacitated, out of action, sabotaged, useless

crisis *NOUN* **1** *Events in Europe were reaching a crisis.* ► climax, critical point, turning point, moment of truth **2** *The following year there was another economic crisis.* ► emergency, predicament, problem, danger, difficulty

crisp *ADJECTIVE* **1** *crisp biscuits* ► crunchy, crispy, brittle, crackly, fragile, crumbly AN OPPOSITE IS soft **2** *a crisp morning in November* ► fresh, brisk, bracing, exhilarating, refreshing **3** *a crisp style of writing* ► terse, incisive, pithy, succinct, sparing, laconic

critic *NOUN* **1** *the most famous music critic of the time* ► commentator, reviewer, authority,

A B C D E F G H I J K L M N O P Q R S T U V W X Y Z

critical *ADJECTIVE* **1** criticizing **2** to do with critics or criticism **3** to do with or at a crisis; very serious
▷ **critically** *ADVERB*

criticism *NOUN* **criticisms** **1** criticizing; pointing out faults **2** the work of a critic

criticize *VERB* **criticizes, criticizing, criticized** say that a person or thing has faults

croak *NOUN* **croaks** a deep hoarse sound like that of a frog
▷ **croak** *VERB*

crockery *NOUN* household china

crocodile *NOUN* **crocodiles** **1** a large tropical reptile with a thick skin, long tail, and huge jaws **2** a long line of schoolchildren walking in pairs
crocodile tears sorrow that is not sincere (so called because the crocodile was said to weep while it ate its victim)

crocus *NOUN* **crocuses** a small plant with yellow, purple, or white flowers

crony *NOUN* **cronies** a close friend or companion

crook *NOUN* **crooks** **1** a shepherd's stick with a curved end **2** something bent or curved **3** (*informal*) a person who makes a living dishonestly

crooked *ADJECTIVE* **1** bent or twisted; not straight **2** dishonest

croon *VERB* **croons, crooning, crooned** sing softly and gently

crop *NOUN* **crops** **1** something grown for food • *a good crop of wheat* **2** a whip with a loop instead of a lash **3** part of a bird's throat **4** a very short haircut

crop *VERB* **crops, cropping, cropped** **1** cut or bite off • *Sheep were cropping the grass.* **2** produce a crop
crop up happen unexpectedly

croquet (kroh-kay) *NOUN* a game played with wooden balls and mallets

cross *NOUN* **crosses** **1** a mark or shape made like + or x **2** an upright post with another piece of wood across it, used in ancient times for crucifixion; (**the Cross**) the cross on which

Thesaurus

expert, pundit, judge, analyst **2** *a major critic of government policy* ► detractor, attacker

critical *ADJECTIVE* **1** *a critical assessment of the available literature* ► analytical, objective, evaluative, discerning, perceptive **2** *He is highly critical of American foreign policy.* ► disapproving, censorious, derogatory (about), disparaging (about), scathing (about), uncomplimentary (about) OPPOSITES ARE appreciative, complimentary (about) **3** *He only escaped death by moving his head at the critical moment.* ► crucial, vital, decisive, essential, all-important **4** *She was taken to hospital where her condition is described as critical.* ► serious, grave, dangerous, precarious AN OPPOSITE IS safe

criticism *NOUN* **1** *The management have come in for a lot of criticism.* ► disapproval, blame, censure, disparagement, fault-finding, reproach, stricture, tirade, verbal attack, (*more informal*) flak **2** *Their work will be submitted for criticism.* ► evaluation, assessment, appraisal, analysis, judgement, appreciation

criticize *VERB* **1** *Police criticized motorists for using mobile phones while driving.* ► condemn, censure, find fault with, denounce, blame, castigate, disparage, denigrate, deprecate, (*more informal*) knock, (*more informal*) slam, (*more informal*) pan AN OPPOSITE IS praise **2** *a review criticizing the work of four modern poets* ► appraise, assess, evaluate, analyse, judge, review

crockery *NOUN* *The table had been laid and the crockery brought out.* ► dishes, plates, tableware, china, crocks, earthenware, porcelain, pottery, ceramics

crook *NOUN* **1** *His head was lying in the crook of her arm.* ► bend, curve, angle **2** *She accused them of being crooks.* ► criminal, lawbreaker, villain, wrongdoer

crooked *ADJECTIVE* **1** *The picture looks slightly crooked.* ► askew, awry, lopsided, off-centre, slanting, angled, (*more informal*) skew-whiff **2** *The garden was a maze of crooked paths.* ► winding, twisting, tortuous, twisty, zigzag **3** *She put a crooked finger to her lips.* ► bent, misshapen, deformed, bowed, curved, curving **4** *Several officials were probably crooked.* ► criminal, dishonest, corrupt, nefarious, (*more informal*) bent

crop *NOUN* *My crop of Brussels sprouts are ready to eat.* ► harvest, yield, produce, gathering

crop *VERB* **1** *Sheep cropped grass in the fields.* ► graze on, browse on, eat, nibble, bite off **2** *She had to crop her long blonde hair.* ► cut short, cut, clip, trim, snip, shear
crop up *The same names keep cropping up over the years.* ► occur, arise, appear, come up, turn up, emerge, spring up, happen

cross *ADJECTIVE* *Dad got cross and said I was setting a bad example.* ► angry, annoyed, testy, tetchy, upset, vexed, irate, bad-tempered, cantankerous, crotchety, ill-tempered, irascible, irritable, peevish, short-tempered, (*more informal*) grumpy AN OPPOSITE IS good-humoured

cross *NOUN* **1** *a difficult cross to bear* ► burden, problem, difficulty, misfortune, trial,

Christ was crucified, used as a symbol of Christianity **3** a mixture of two different things

cross VERB **crosses, crossing, crossed 1** go across something **2** draw a line or lines across something **3** make the sign or shape of a cross • *Cross your fingers for luck.* **4** produce something from two different kinds
cross out draw a line across something because it is unwanted, wrong, etc.

cross ADJECTIVE **1** annoyed or bad-tempered **2** going from one side to another • *There were cross winds on the bridge.*
▷ **crossly** ADVERB **crossness** NOUN

crossbar NOUN **crossbars** a horizontal bar, especially between two uprights

cross-breed VERB **cross-breeds, cross-breeding, cross-bred** breed by mating an animal with one of a different kind
▷ **cross-breed** NOUN COMPARE **hybrid**

cross-examine VERB **cross-examines, cross-examining, cross-examined** cross-question someone, especially in a lawcourt
▷ **cross-examination** NOUN

cross-eyed ADJECTIVE with eyes that look or seem to look towards the nose

crossing NOUN **crossings** a place where people can cross a road or railway

cross-legged ADJECTIVE, ADVERB with ankles crossed and knees spread apart

cross-question VERB **cross-questions, cross-questioning, cross-questioned** question someone carefully in order to test answers given to previous questions

cross-reference NOUN **cross-references** a note telling people to look at another part of a book etc. for more information

crossroads NOUN **crossroads** a place where two or more roads cross one another

cross-section NOUN **cross-sections 1** a drawing of something as if it has been cut through **2** a typical sample

crossword NOUN **crosswords** a puzzle in which words have to be guessed from clues and then written into the blank squares in a diagram

crotchet NOUN **crotchets** a note in music, which usually represents one beat (written ♩)

crouch VERB **crouches, crouching, crouched** lower your body, with your arms and legs bent

crow[1] NOUN **crows** a large black bird
as the crow flies in a straight line

crow[2] VERB **crows, crowing, crowed** *or* **crew 1** make a shrill cry as a cock does **2** boast; be triumphant
▷ **crow** NOUN

crowbar NOUN **crowbars** an iron bar used as a lever

crowd NOUN **crowds** a large number of people in one place

crowd VERB **crowds, crowding, crowded 1** come together in a crowd **2** cram; fill uncomfortably full

crown NOUN **crowns 1** an ornamental headdress worn by a king or queen **2** (often **Crown**) the sovereign • *This land belongs to the Crown.* **3** the highest part • *the crown of the*

Thesaurus

tribulation, trouble, worry, grief, sorrow, affliction **2** *a cross between a yak and a cow* ► hybrid, cross-breed, amalgam (of), blend (of), combination (of), half-way house, mixture (of)

cross VERB **1** *The roads cross north of the town.* ► intersect, intertwine, meet **2** *There is only one place you can cross the river.* ► go across, pass over, ford, traverse **3** *It's better not to cross the common in the dark.* ► go across, walk across, traverse **4** *A stone bridge crossed the stream.* ► span, bridge, arch, go across, extend across, pass across **5** *He blew up if anyone crossed him.* ► oppose, annoy, defy, argue with, obstruct, thwart
cross out *He crossed out part of the sentence and rewrote it.* ► delete, strike out, erase, cancel

crouch VERB *The boys crouched behind a large tree.* ► squat, kneel, stoop, bend, bob down, bow down, cower, cringe, duck, hunch, huddle

crowd NOUN **1** *The crowd dispersed quickly.* ► throng, multitude, mob, masses, horde, gathering, company, rabble, crush **2** *a large crowd at the ground* ► gate, attendance, audience, spectators

crowd VERB **1** *Some of them had crowded round a drinks machine.* ► gather, collect, cluster, congregate, huddle, muster, mass, swarm, surge **2** *The guests were crowding into the dining room.* ► stream, push, pile, pack, squeeze, swarm, flock, surge, jostle

crowded ADJECTIVE *It was hard to find a space on the crowded beach.* ► packed, congested, overcrowded, swarming, teeming, thronging, cramped, full, busy, jammed, jostling, overflowing OPPOSITES ARE empty, deserted

crown NOUN **1** *The Queen was wearing her crown.* ► coronet, diadem, tiara **2** *He paused at the crown of the hill.* ► brow, crest, top, summit, peak, ridge, head, apex

crown VERB **1** *William was crowned in Westminster Abbey on Christmas Day.* ► install, enthrone, anoint **2** *He crowned his career with a diplomatic post in America.* ► cap, round off, top off, complete, conclude, consummate, fulfil, finish off, perfect

road **4** a former coin worth 5 shillings (25p)
Crown Prince or **Crown Princess** the heir to the throne

crown VERB **crowns**, **crowning**, **crowned** **1** place a crown on someone as a symbol of royal power or victory **2** form or cover or decorate the top of something **3** reward; make a successful end to something • *Our efforts were crowned with victory.* **4** (*slang*) hit someone on the head

crucial (kroo- shal) ADJECTIVE most important
▷ **crucially** ADVERB

crucifix NOUN **crucifixes** a model of the Cross or of Jesus Christ on the Cross

crucify VERB **crucifies**, **crucifying**, **crucified** put a person to death by nailing or binding the hands and feet to a cross
▷ **crucifixion** NOUN

crude ADJECTIVE **1** in a natural state; not yet refined • *crude oil* **2** not well finished; rough • *a crude carving* **3** vulgar
▷ **crudely** ADVERB **crudity** NOUN

cruel ADJECTIVE **crueller**, **cruellest** causing pain or suffering
▷ **cruelly** ADVERB **cruelty** NOUN

cruise NOUN **cruises** a pleasure trip in a ship

cruise VERB **cruises**, **cruising**, **cruised** **1** sail or travel at a moderate speed **2** have a cruise

cruiser NOUN **cruisers** **1** a fast warship **2** a large motor boat

crumb NOUN **crumbs** a tiny piece of bread etc.

crumble VERB **crumbles**, **crumbling**, **crumbled** break or fall into small fragments
▷ **crumbly** ADJECTIVE

crumpet NOUN **crumpets** a soft flat cake made with yeast, eaten toasted with butter

crumple VERB **crumples**, **crumpling**, **crumpled** **1** crush or become crushed into creases **2** collapse loosely

crunch VERB **crunches**, **crunching**, **crunched** crush something noisily, for example between your teeth

crunch NOUN **crunches** a crunching sound
▷ **crunchy** ADJECTIVE
the crunch (*informal*) a crucial event or turning point

Crusade NOUN **Crusades** a military expedition made by Christians in the Middle Ages to recover Palestine from the Muslims who had conquered it
▷ **Crusader** NOUN

crusade NOUN **crusades** a campaign against something bad

Thesaurus

crucial ADJECTIVE **1** *Police investigation plays a crucial role in the criminal process.* ► major, central, pivotal, decisive, critical, important, momentous, serious OPPOSITES ARE minor, unimportant **2** *Secrecy is crucial in this matter.* ► paramount, essential, vital, critical, indispensable

crude ADJECTIVE **1** *increased production of crude oil* ► unrefined, unpurified, unprocessed, natural, raw AN OPPOSITE IS refined **2** *a crude method of counting votes* ► primitive, simple, basic, rudimentary, rough, makeshift, improvised, homespun, clumsy, unrefined, amateurish, awkward, inelegant, inept OPPOSITES ARE sophisticated, advanced **3** *He went in for a very crude type of humour.* ► coarse, indecent, vulgar, bawdy, lewd, offensive, obscene
USAGE *Obscene* is a very strong word and often implies an intention to offend or corrupt people.

cruel ADJECTIVE **1** *Their opponents were huge cruel men. Hunting is widely regarded as a cruel sport.* ► brutal, savage, vicious, fierce, ferocious, barbaric, callous, heartless, cold-blooded, pitiless, ruthless, merciless, vile, sadistic, brutish OPPOSITES ARE gentle, humane, kind, compassionate **2** *Her father's sudden death was a cruel blow.* ► severe, harsh, bitter, grim, painful OPPOSITES ARE mild, gentle

cruelty NOUN *The rebellion was put down with great cruelty.* ► brutality, savagery, viciousness, ferocity, barbarity, callousness, heartlessness, cold-bloodedness, ruthlessness

crumb NOUN *crumbs of bread; a small crumb of comfort* ► fragment, grain, morsel, scrap, bit, speck, particle, shred

crumble VERB **1** *The damaged buildings were beginning to crumble.* ► disintegrate, break up, collapse, fall apart, fall down, decay, decompose, deteriorate **2** *He crumbled the soil into a fine powder.* ► crush, grind, pound, powder, pulverize, break into pieces, fragment

crumple VERB *It's hard not to crumple your clothes in such a tiny car.* ► crease, crush, crinkle, wrinkle, squash

crunch VERB **1** *She sat there crunching biscuits.* ► munch, chomp, champ, masticate, devour **2** *He was fed up with getting his head crunched in rugby matches.* ► crush, pound, pulverize, grind, smash

crush *VERB* **crushes, crushing, crushed** **1** press something so that it gets broken or harmed **2** squeeze tightly **3** defeat

crush *NOUN* **crushes** **1** a crowd of people pressed together **2** a drink made with crushed fruit

crust *NOUN* **crusts** **1** the hard outer layer of something, especially bread **2** the rocky outer layer of the earth

crustacean (krust- ay- shon) *NOUN* **crustaceans** an animal with a shell, e.g. a crab, lobster, or shrimp

crutch *NOUN* **crutches** a support like a long walking stick for helping a lame person to walk

cry *NOUN* **cries** **1** a loud wordless sound expressing pain, grief, joy, etc. **2** a shout **3** crying • *Have a good cry.*

cry *VERB* **cries, crying, cried** **1** shed tears; weep **2** call out loudly

cryptic *ADJECTIVE* hiding its meaning in a puzzling way
▷ **cryptically** *ADVERB*

crystal *NOUN* **crystals** **1** a transparent colourless mineral rather like glass **2** very clear high-quality glass **3** a small solid piece of a substance with a symmetrical shape • *ice crystals*
▷ **crystalline** *ADJECTIVE*

crystallize *VERB* **crystallizes, crystallizing, crystallized** **1** form into crystals **2** become definite in form
▷ **crystallization** *NOUN*

cub *NOUN* **cubs** a young lion, tiger, fox, bear, etc.

Cub or **Cub Scout** *NOUN* **Cubs** or **Cub Scouts** a member of the junior branch of the Scout Association

cubby hole *NOUN* **cubby holes** a small compartment

cube *NOUN* **cubes** **1** an object that has six equal square sides, e.g. a box or dice **2** the number produced by multiplying something by itself twice • *The cube of 3 is 3 x 3 x 3 = 27.*

cube *VERB* **cubes, cubing, cubed** **1** multiply a number by itself twice • *4 cubed is 4 x 4 x 4 = 64.* **2** cut something into small cubes

cube root *NOUN* **cube roots** the number that gives a particular number if it is multiplied by itself twice • *The cube root of 27 is 3.*

cubic *ADJECTIVE* three-dimensional
cubic metre, cubic foot, etc., the volume of a cube with sides one metre, foot, etc. long, used as a unit of measurement for volume

cubicle *NOUN* **cubicles** a compartment of a room

cuckoo *NOUN* **cuckoos** a bird that makes a sound like 'cuck-oo'

cucumber *NOUN* **cucumbers** a long green-skinned vegetable eaten raw or pickled

cuddle *VERB* **cuddles, cuddling, cuddled** put your arms closely round a person or animal that you love
▷ **cuddle** *NOUN*

cuddly *ADJECTIVE* pleasantly soft and plump; nice to cuddle

cue [1] *NOUN* **cues** something said or done that acts as a signal for an actor etc. to say or do something

cue [2] *NOUN* **cues** a long stick for striking the ball in billiards or snooker

cuff *NOUN* **cuffs** **1** the end of a sleeve that fits round the wrist **2** hitting somebody with your hand; a slap
off the cuff without rehearsal or preparation

cuff *VERB* **cuffs, cuffing, cuffed** hit somebody with your hand

Thesaurus

crush *VERB* **1** *He nearly crushed his arm in the lift doors.* ► squash, squeeze, mangle, crunch, scrunch, compress, mash, break, bruise, grind **2** *She was afraid she would crush her dress.* ► crease, crumple, crinkle, wrinkle, squash **3** *The army crushed the rebellion in a short time.* ► suppress, subdue, quell, quash, put down, defeat, vanquish, overcome

crush *NOUN* *There was quite a crush by the doors.* ► crowd, throng, congestion, jam, press, multitude, mob

crust *NOUN* *The paint left in the pot had formed a hard crust.* ► covering, skin, surface, shell, exterior, outside

crusty *ADJECTIVE* **1** *a meal of dry crusty bread and cheese* ► crisp, crispy, brittle, crunchy **2** *He seems so crusty these days.* ► irritable, grumpy, gruff, grouchy, tetchy, testy, bad-tempered, irascible, fractious

cry *VERB* **1** *Debbie looked upset and about to cry.* ► weep, shed tears, sob, howl, whimper, snivel, blubber, bawl, wail USAGE The last six synonyms are unfriendly or disapproving, and *sob* means to cry uncontrollably and unattractively. *Weep* and *shed tears* are more neutral in tone, although *weep* is more literary. **2** *'Come on!' cried Sam.* ► call, yell, exclaim, shout, shriek, scream, bawl
cry off *The game was cancelled when three players cried off.* ► withdraw, back out, cancel, excuse yourself
cry out *Somebody was crying out in the darkness.* ► call out, yell, scream, screech, shout, shriek

a b c d e f g h i j k l m n o p q r s t u v w x y z

cul-de-sac NOUN **cul-de-sacs** a street with an opening at one end only; a dead end

cull VERB **culls, culling, culled** **1** pick out and kill surplus animals from a flock **2** select and use • *I've culled lines from several poems.*
▷ **cull** NOUN

culpable ADJECTIVE deserving blame

culprit NOUN **culprits** the person who has done something wrong

cult NOUN **cults** **1** a religious sect **2** a film, TV programme, rock group, etc. that is very popular with a particular group of people

cultivate VERB **cultivates, cultivating, cultivated** **1** use land to grow crops **2** grow or develop things by looking after them
▷ **cultivation** NOUN **cultivator** NOUN

culture NOUN **cultures** **1** appreciation and understanding of literature, art, music, etc. **2** the customs and traditions of a people • *West Indian culture* **3** (in science) a quantity of bacteria or cells grown for study **4** improvement by care and training • *physical culture* **5** cultivating things
▷ **cultural** ADJECTIVE

cumbersome ADJECTIVE clumsy to carry or manage

cumulative ADJECTIVE accumulating; increasing by continuous additions

cunning ADJECTIVE **1** clever at deceiving people **2** cleverly designed or planned

cunning NOUN **1** skill in deceiving people; craftiness **2** skill or ingenuity [originally = clever, skilful: perhaps from an Old Norse word meaning 'knowledge']

cup NOUN **cups** **1** a small bowl-shaped container for drinking from **2** anything shaped like a cup **3** a goblet-shaped ornament given as a prize
▷ **cupful** NOUN

cup VERB **cups, cupping, cupped** form into the shape of a cup • *cup your hands*

cupboard NOUN **cupboards** a piece of furniture with a door, for storing things

cur NOUN **curs** a scruffy or bad-tempered dog

curate NOUN **curates** a member of the clergy who helps a vicar

curator (kewr- ay- ter) NOUN **curators** a person in charge of a museum or other collection

curb VERB **curbs, curbing, curbed** restrain • *You need to curb your impatience*

Thesaurus

cry NOUN **1** *a cry of pain* ► call, shout, yell, shriek, scream, screech, roar, bellow **2** *a cry for help* ► appeal, plea, entreaty

cuddle VERB *So far he had only kissed and cuddled her.* ► hug, caress, embrace, hold, clasp, pet, fondle, huddle against, snuggle against

culprit NOUN *New evidence showed that he was not the culprit after all.* ► guilty party, person responsible, offender, criminal, wrongdoer, miscreant, transgressor

cultivate VERB **1** *Peasants cultivated the land.* ► farm, till, dig, work, plough **2** *They helped with cultivating food crops.* ► grow, raise, rear, sow, plant, tend, produce **3** *We need to cultivate a better attitude to work.* ► develop, foster, nurture, encourage, promote, pursue, try to achieve, cherish, further, improve

cultural ADJECTIVE *a country's cultural heritage* ► artistic, intellectual, aesthetic, educational, elevating, enlightening, improving

culture NOUN **1** *modern popular culture* ► civilization, society, intellectual activity, arts, traditions, customs, education, learning **2** *a person of culture* ► intellectual awareness, achievement, enlightenment, education, discernment, good taste

cultured ADJECTIVE *a pleasant, cultured man* ► cultivated, educated, well educated, well read, enlightened, civilized, erudite, artistic, refined, urbane, highbrow, knowledgeable, scholarly AN OPPOSITE IS ignorant

cumbersome ADJECTIVE *The suitcases were cumbersome rather than heavy.* ► unwieldy, awkward, bulky, clumsy, hefty, burdensome

cunning ADJECTIVE **1** *a cunning plan* ► crafty, wily, artful, sly, devious, knowing, guileful, disingenuous, machiavellian OPPOSITES ARE ingenuous, guileless **2** *The crime was solved by cunning detective work.* ► skilful, clever, shrewd, astute, adroit, subtle, ingenious

cunning NOUN *The defence counsel will need quite a bit of cunning.* ► guile, craftiness, artfulness, shrewdness, astuteness, adroitness, deviousness

cup NOUN **1** *They were drinking tea from pretty cups.* ► teacup, coffee cup, mug, tankard **2** *a silver cup for the winner* ► trophy, award, prize

cupboard NOUN *The tools and nails were kept in a cupboard.* ► cabinet, closet, locker, dresser, *(for clothes)* wardrobe, *(for food)* larder

curb VERB *He tried to curb his temper.* ► restrain, suppress, control, contain, check, hold back, stifle AN OPPOSITE IS release

curb *NOUN* **curbs** a restraint • *Put a curb on spending*
USAGE Do not confuse with **kerb**.

curd *NOUN* or **curds** *PLURAL NOUN* a thick substance formed when milk turns sour

curdle *VERB* **curdles, curdling, curdled** form into curds
make someone's blood curdle horrify or terrify them

cure *VERB* **cures, curing, cured** **1** get rid of someone's illness **2** stop something bad **3** treat food in order to preserve it

cure *NOUN* **cures** **1** something that cures a person or thing; a remedy **2** curing; being cured • *We cannot promise a cure.*

curfew *NOUN* **curfews** a time or signal after which people must remain indoors until the next day

curiosity *NOUN* **curiosities** **1** being curious **2** something unusual and interesting

curious *ADJECTIVE* **1** wanting to find out about things; inquisitive **2** strange; unusual
▷ **curiously** *ADVERB*

curl *NOUN* **curls** a curve or coil, e.g. of hair

curl *VERB* **curls, curling, curled** form into curls
curl up sit or lie with your knees drawn up

curly *ADJECTIVE* having curls

currant *NOUN* **currants** **1** a small black dried grape used in cookery **2** a small round red, black, or white berry
USAGE Do not confuse with **current**.

currency *NOUN* **currencies** **1** the money in use in a country **2** the general use of something • *Some words have no currency now.*

current *ADJECTIVE* happening now; used now
▷ **currently** *ADVERB*

current *NOUN* **currents** **1** water or air etc. moving in one direction **2** the flow of electricity along a wire etc. or through something
USAGE Do not confuse with **currant**.

curriculum *NOUN* **curricula** a course of study in a school or university

curry[1] *NOUN* **curries** food cooked with spices that taste hot
▷ **curried** *ADJECTIVE*

Thesaurus

cure *VERB* **1** *A long period of rest will cure his ailment.* ► heal, remedy, treat, alleviate, counteract, ease, help, palliate, relieve OPPOSITES ARE aggravate, worsen **2** *The fault may be difficult to cure.* ► correct, rectify, mend, repair, put right, solve, (*more informal*) fix

cure *NOUN* **1** *a cure for cancer* ► remedy, treatment, antidote, medicine, prescription, restorative, panacea, palliative, therapy **2** *Her unexpected cure amazed the doctors.* ► recovery, healing, restoration to health

curiosity *NOUN* **1** *I found it hard to contain my curiosity.* ► inquisitiveness, interest, nosiness, prying, meddling, snooping USAGE The last four synonyms are unfavourable in tone, whereas the first two are neutral. **2** *He had an elephant's head displayed as a curiosity in his house.* ► novelty, oddity, curio, rarity, collector's item

curious *ADJECTIVE* **1** *I was curious about the reason for this unexpected visit.* ► inquisitive, intrigued, interested, puzzled, eager to know, agog OPPOSITES ARE incurious, unconcerned, indifferent. **2** *He walked off with a curious jerking motion.* ► strange, odd, peculiar, queer, funny, bizarre, unusual, extraordinary, eccentric AN OPPOSITE IS normal

curl *NOUN* **1** *Her hair was a mass of curls.* ► ringlet, wave, coil, loop, kink **2** *a pattern with repeated curls* ► loop, spiral, swirl, twist, bend, circle, curve, scroll, turn **3** *There was a curl of smoke in the distance.* ► spiral, coil, swirl, twirl, whorl, corkscrew

curl *VERB* **1** *Smoke curled from the tall chimney.* ► coil, spiral, twirl, swirl, furl **2** *The path curls round old tree trunks.* ► wind, twist, curve, meander, snake, writhe, zigzag **3** *Sarah curled an arm round his waist.* ► wind, twine, entwine, wrap, twist **4** *a treatment to curl the hair* ► crimp, wave, frizz, perm

curly *ADJECTIVE* *thick curly hair* ► wavy, curled, curling, crinkly, kinky, frizzy, fuzzy, crimped, permed AN OPPOSITE IS straight

currency *NOUN* *The euro simplifies the business of getting foreign currency.* ► money, legal tender, coinage, cash, coins, banknotes

current *ADJECTIVE* **1** *keeping abreast of current events* ► modern, contemporary, present-day, topical AN OPPOSITE IS past **2** *The opinion is still current.* ► common, prevalent, prevailing, widespread, popular, accepted AN OPPOSITE IS obsolete **3** *a current driving licence* ► valid, usable, up to date OPPOSITES ARE out of date, expired **4** *the current administration in the White House* ► present, incumbent, existing, extant, reigning OPPOSITES ARE past, former

current *NOUN* **1** *a current of air* ► stream, flow, draught, jet, course **2** *The girls were in danger from the strong currents.* ► tide, undertow, drift

a b c d e f g h i j k l m n o p q r s t u v w x y z

curry [2] *VERB* **curries, currying, curried**
curry favour seek to win favour by flattering someone

curse *NOUN* **curses** **1** a call or prayer for a person or thing to be harmed; the evil produced by this **2** something very unpleasant **3** an angry word or words

curse *VERB* **curses, cursing, cursed** **1** make a curse **2** use a curse against a person or thing
be cursed with something suffer from it

cursor *NOUN* **cursors** a movable indicator, usually a flashing light, on a computer screen, showing where new data will go

curt *ADJECTIVE* brief and hasty or rude • *a curt reply*
▷ **curtly** *ADVERB* **curtness** *NOUN*

curtain *NOUN* **curtains** **1** a piece of material hung at a window or door **2** the large cloth screen hung at the front of a stage

curtsy *NOUN* **curtsies** a movement of respect made by women and girls, putting one foot behind the other and bending the knees

curtsy *VERB* **curtsies, curtsying, curtsied** make a curtsy

curvature *NOUN* **curvatures** curving; a curved shape

curve *VERB* **curves, curving, curved** bend smoothly

curve *NOUN* **curves** a curved line or shape
▷ **curvy** *ADJECTIVE*

cushion *NOUN* **cushions** **1** a bag, usually of cloth, filled with soft material so that it is comfortable to sit on or lean against **2** anything soft or springy that protects or supports something • *The hovercraft travels on a cushion of air.*

cushion *VERB* **cushions, cushioning, cushioned** protect from the effects of a knock or shock etc. • *A pile of boxes cushioned his fall.*

custard *NOUN* **custards** **1** a sweet yellow sauce made with milk **2** a pudding made with beaten eggs and milk

custody *NOUN* **1** care and supervision; guardianship **2** imprisonment
take into custody arrest
[from Latin *custos* = guardian]

custom *NOUN* **customs** **1** the usual way of behaving or doing something **2** regular business from customers

Thesaurus

curse *NOUN* **1** *John caught his finger in the door and let out a curse.* ► swear word, oath, expletive, profanity, obscenity, blasphemy, exclamation **2** *The witch had put a curse on them.* ► malediction, imprecation, jinx **3** *the curse of unemployment* ► affliction, blight, scourge, plague, bane, misfortune, torment, evil

curse *VERB* *I listened to him cursing and shouting.* ► swear, utter profanities, blaspheme, damn, fulminate

be cursed with *The family was cursed for years with sickness and poverty.* ► be afflicted with, be blighted with, be plagued with, be troubled by, be burdened with

curt *ADJECTIVE* *Carl dismissed the idea with a curt grunt.* ► abrupt, blunt, harsh, terse, gruff, rude, offhand, brusque, insensitive, outspoken, plain-spoken OPPOSITES ARE polite, courteous

curtain *NOUN* *Clive closed the curtains.* ► drape, drapery, hanging, blind, screen

curve *NOUN* **1** *a series of curves in the road* ► bend, turn, twist, loop **2** *a tall window with a curve at the top* ► arch, arc, bow, crescent

curve *VERB* *The river curved to the west.* ► bend, twist, wind, loop, snake, turn, swerve

curved *ADJECTIVE* **1** *a tall building with a curved roof* ► arched, bowed, rounded, humped, crescent, vaulted, convex, bent OPPOSITES ARE flat, straight **2** *The road was narrow and curved.* ► twisty, twisted, sinuous, meandering, serpentine, sweeping AN OPPOSITE IS straight

cushion *NOUN* **1** *She put a cushion behind her and leaned back.* ► pillow, bolster, headrest, hassock, pad, beanbag **2** *a cushion against inflation* ► protection, buffer, shield, defence

custom *NOUN* **1** *local customs dating back to the thirteenth century* ► tradition, practice, usage, institution, convention, procedure, observance, form, habit, way, etiquette, manner, formality, routine **2** *It is our custom to visit relatives at the weekends.* ► practice, habit, routine, way, rule, policy, wont **3** *The shop offers discounts to attract custom* ► business, trade, customers, buyers, patronage, support

customary *ADJECTIVE* **1** *It is customary to stand during the playing of the anthem. the customary rules of behaviour* ► traditional, normal, usual, common, conventional, established, expected, general, ordinary, popular, prevailing, routine, fashionable AN OPPOSITE IS unusual **2** *Dr Ali fell once again into his customary silence.* ► usual, accustomed, regular, wonted, habitual, typical

customary ADJECTIVE according to custom; usual
▷ **customarily** ADVERB

customer NOUN **customers** a person who uses a shop, bank, or other business

customs PLURAL NOUN **1** taxes charged on goods brought into a country **2** the place at a port or airport where officials examine your luggage

cut VERB **cuts, cutting, cut** **1** divide or wound or separate something by using a knife, axe, scissors, etc. **2** make a thing shorter or smaller; remove part of something • *They are cutting all their prices.* **3** divide a pack of playing cards **4** hit a ball with a chopping movement **5** go through or across something **6** switch off electrical power or an engine etc. **7** (in a film) move to another shot or scene **8** make a sound recording
cut a corner pass round it very closely
cut and dried already decided
cut in interrupt

cut NOUN **cuts** **1** cutting; the result of cutting **2** a small wound **3** (*slang*) a share
be a cut above something be superior

cute ADJECTIVE (*informal*) **1** attractive **2** clever
▷ **cutely** ADVERB **cuteness** NOUN

cutlass NOUN **cutlasses** a short sword with a broad curved blade

cutlery NOUN knives, forks, and spoons

cutlet NOUN **cutlets** a thick slice of meat for cooking

cutting NOUN **cuttings** **1** a steep-sided passage cut through high ground for a road or railway **2** something cut out of a newspaper or magazine **3** a piece cut from a plant to form a new plant

cycle NOUN **cycles** **1** a bicycle or motorcycle **2** a series of events that are regularly repeated in the same order
▷ **cyclic** ADJECTIVE **cyclical** ADJECTIVE

cycle VERB **cycles, cycling, cycled** ride a bicycle or tricycle
▷ **cyclist** NOUN

cyclone NOUN **cyclones** a wind that rotates round a calm central area
▷ **cyclonic** ADJECTIVE

Thesaurus

customer NOUN *The business is trying to attract younger customers.* ► shopper, buyer, purchaser, client, consumer, patron
AN OPPOSITE IS seller

cut NOUN **1** *He had a cut on his hand.* ► gash, wound, injury, nick, incision, scratch, graze
USAGE *Scratch* and *graze* do not normally involve breaking of the skin and escape of blood. **2** *She had to accept a small cut in pay.* ► reduction, decrease, lowering (of), lessening (of) **3** *The leader of the gang demanded a higher cut.* ► share, portion, slice, (*more informal*) whack

cut VERB **1** *He had cut his finger with a kitchen knife.* ► gash, pierce, wound, injure, slash, nick, incise, scratch, graze USAGE *Scratch* and *graze* do not normally involve breaking of the skin and escape of blood. **2** *Cut the vegetables into small pieces.* ► slice, chop, dice, cube, divide, pare **3** *She was going to have her hair cut. It will soon be time to start cutting the grass again.* ► trim, clip, crop, mow **4** *The supermarkets have cut prices on a wide range of goods.* ► reduce, lower, lessen, (*more informal*) slash **5** *Parts of the story were cut to make the film version.* ► omit, remove, delete, excise, take out, edit out **6** *You will have to cut your essay by about a third.* ► shorten, abridge, condense, reduce, precis, truncate **7** *The remarks were spiteful and cut her deeply.* ► hurt, offend, upset, wound

cut down **1** *Men are cutting the trees down.* ► fell, hew, lop **2** *I'm trying to cut down some of these expenses.* ► reduce, decrease, lower, lessen
cut in *Tessa cut in with a remark that made everyone laugh.* ► interrupt, butt in, break in, interject, intervene, intrude
cut off **1** *The blade nearly cut off her finger.* ► sever, chop off, amputate, hack off, remove **2** *The Gas Board threatened to cut off the supply.* ► disconnect, discontinue, interrupt, suspend
OPPOSITES ARE restore, reconnect **3** *Storms cut off the village for several days.* ► isolate, separate, seclude **4** *Her family had cut her off without a penny.* ► disinherit, disown, reject, repudiate, cast aside
cut out *The report mentioned several ways in which we could cut out inefficiencies.* ► remove, eliminate, excise, get rid of
cut up *Cut up the meat into small cubes.* ► chop, slice, dice, carve

cute ADJECTIVE *When I was young I had a cute little collie dog.* ► appealing, lovely, delightful, attractive, pretty, endearing, adorable, engaging

cycle NOUN *a cycle of growth and decline lasting 75 years* ► pattern, sequence, round, circle, series, era, period, revolution, rotation

A B **C** D E F G H I J K L M N O P Q R S T U V W X Y Z

cygnet (sig- nit) *NOUN* **cygnets** a young swan

cylinder *NOUN* **cylinders** an object with straight sides and circular ends
▷ **cylindrical** *ADJECTIVE*

cymbal *NOUN* **cymbals** a percussion instrument consisting of a metal plate that is hit to make a ringing sound
USAGE Do not confuse with **symbol**.

cynic (sin- ik) *NOUN* **cynics** a person who believes that people's reasons for doing things are selfish or bad, and shows this by sneering at them
▷ **cynical** *ADJECTIVE* **cynically** *ADVERB* **cynicism** *NOUN*
[from Greek *kynikos* = surly: probably from the name *Kynosarges*, the gymnasium where the Greek philosopher Aristotle taught, but popularly associated with the Greek word *kuon* = dog]

cypress *NOUN* **cypresses** an evergreen tree with dark leaves

Thesaurus

cynical *ADJECTIVE* *I may be unduly cynical in thinking they are only in it for the money.*
► sceptical, distrustful, suspicious, disbelieving, pessimistic, negative, doubting, questioning AN OPPOSITE IS optimistic

Dd

dab *NOUN* **dabs** **1** a quick gentle touch, usually with something wet **2** a small lump • *a dab of butter*

dab *VERB* **dabs, dabbing, dabbed** touch something quickly and gently

dabble *VERB* **dabbles, dabbling, dabbled** **1** splash something about in water **2** do something as a hobby • *dabble in chemistry*

dachshund (daks- huund) *NOUN* **dachshunds** a small dog with a long body and very short legs

daffodil *NOUN* **daffodils** a yellow flower that grows from a bulb

daft *ADJECTIVE* (*informal*) silly or stupid

dagger *NOUN* **daggers** a pointed knife with two sharp edges, used as a weapon

daily *ADVERB, ADJECTIVE* every day

dainty *ADJECTIVE* **daintier, daintiest** small, delicate, and pretty
▷ **daintily** *ADVERB* **daintiness** *NOUN*

dairy *NOUN* **dairies** a place where milk, butter, etc. are produced or sold

daisy *NOUN* **daisies** a small flower with white petals and a yellow centre

dam [1] *NOUN* **dams** a wall built to hold water back

dam *VERB* **dams, damming, dammed** hold water back with a dam

dam [2] *NOUN* **dams** the mother of a horse or dog etc. COMPARE **sire**

damage *NOUN* harm or injury done to something

damage *VERB* **damages, damaging, damaged** harm or spoil something

damages *PLURAL NOUN* money paid as compensation for an injury or loss

Dame *NOUN* **Dames** the title of a woman who has been given the equivalent of a knighthood

dame *NOUN* **dames** a comic middle-aged woman in a pantomime, usually played by a man

damn *VERB* **damns, damning, damned** curse or condemn

damnation *NOUN* being condemned to hell

damned *ADJECTIVE* hateful or annoying

damp *ADJECTIVE* slightly wet; not quite dry
▷ **damply** *ADVERB* **dampness** *NOUN*

damp *NOUN* moisture in the air or on a surface or all through something

damp course *NOUN* **damp courses** a layer of material built into a wall to prevent dampness in the ground from rising

dampen *VERB* **dampens, dampening, dampened** **1** make something damp **2** reduce the strength of something

damsel *NOUN* **damsels** (*old use*) a young woman

Thesaurus

dab *VERB* *He dabbed paint on the scratch.* ► pat, daub, touch, apply (to)

dabble *VERB* **1** *The children dabbled their feet in the water.* ► dip, paddle, splash, wet **2 dabble in** *She began to dabble in astrology.* ► toy with, dip into, tinker with, trifle with

daft *ADJECTIVE* *a daft idea* ► silly, stupid, absurd, foolish, crazy, unwise, idiotic

daily *ADJECTIVE* *a daily occurrence* ► everyday, day-to-day, regular

dainty *ADJECTIVE* **1** *a dainty lace handkerchief* ► delicate, elegant, exquisite, neat, charming, fine, graceful, pretty OPPOSITES ARE clumsy, crude **2** *a dainty eater* ► fastidious, choosy, fussy, finicky, discriminating, careful AN OPPOSITE IS gross

dally *VERB* *There's not enough time to dally.* ► dawdle, delay, linger, loiter, waste time, idle, loaf, play about, procrastinate, (*more informal*) hang about, (*informal*) dilly-dally, (*literary*) tarry

damage *NOUN* *Fortunately the thieves caused little damage.* ► harm, injury, destruction, devastation, havoc, hurt, mutilation

damage *VERB* *High winds damaged properties along the sea front.* ► harm, hurt, injure, spoil, wreck, blemish, disfigure, deface, mutilate

damn *VERB* **1** *The voices damned him to hell.* ► curse, put a curse on, (*more formal*) execrate **2** *They had been damned for something that was not their fault.* ► condemn, censure, blame, abuse, revile, criticize, denounce, castigate, reprove

damp *ADJECTIVE* **1** *Someone had applied a damp cloth to her head.* ► moist, dampened, moistened, wet, wetted, soggy **2** *The air was damp and cold.* ► wet, drizzly, muggy, humid

dampen *VERB* **1** *Dampen a soft cloth.* ► moisten, wet, damp **2** *Nothing could dampen their enthusiasm now.* ► lessen, diminish, deaden, dull, stifle, muffle, restrain, smother, discourage, dishearten

dance *VERB* **dances, dancing, danced** move about in time to music

dance *NOUN* **dances 1** a set of movements used in dancing **2** a piece of music for dancing to **3** a party or gathering where people dance
▷ **dancer** *NOUN*

dandelion *NOUN* **dandelions** a yellow wild flower with jagged leaves

dandruff *NOUN* tiny white flakes of dead skin in a person's hair

D and T *ABBREVIATION* design and technology

danger *NOUN* **dangers 1** something that is not safe or could harm you **2** the possibility of suffering harm or death

dangerous *ADJECTIVE* likely to kill or harm you
▷ **dangerously** *ADVERB*

dangle *VERB* **dangles, dangling, dangled** hang or swing loosely

dappled *ADJECTIVE* marked with patches of a different colour

dare *VERB* **dares, daring, dared 1** be brave or bold enough to do something **2** challenge a person to do something risky

dare *NOUN* **dares** a challenge to do something risky

dark *ADJECTIVE* **1** with little or no light **2** not light in colour • *a dark suit* **3** having dark hair **4** sinister or evil
▷ **darkly** *ADVERB* **darkness** *NOUN*

dark *NOUN* **1** absence of light • *Cats can see in the dark.* **2** the time when darkness has come • *She went out after dark.*

darken *VERB* **darkens, darkening, darkened** make or become dark

darling *NOUN* **darlings** someone who is loved very much

darn *VERB* **darns, darning, darned** mend a hole by weaving threads across it

darn *NOUN* **darns** a place that has been darned

dart *NOUN* **darts 1** an object with a sharp point, thrown at a target **2** a darting movement **3** a tapering tuck stitched in something to make it fit

dart *VERB* **darts, darting, darted** run suddenly and quickly

Thesaurus

dance *NOUN* *He was going to take her to the dance next week.* ► ball, disco, (*more informal*) hop RELATED ADJECTIVE choreographic RELATED NOUN choreography

dance *VERB* *Children danced around playfully.* ► caper, cavort, frisk, frolic, skip, prance, leap, gambol, hop, jig, jump

danger *NOUN* **1** *There is a danger of flooding on low ground.* ► risk, threat, chance, probability, possibility, likelihood, prospect, liability **2** *The contamination could become a danger to public health.* ► threat, hazard, menace, risk **3** *There was a real sense of danger about the place.* ► insecurity, vulnerability, uncertainty, precariousness **4** *Their very lives were in danger.* ► peril, jeopardy, (at) risk AN OPPOSITE IS safety

dangerous *ADJECTIVE* **1** *Building at such a height can be dangerous work.* ► hazardous, perilous, risky, unsafe, precarious, insecure, tricky **2** *He was charged with dangerous driving.* ► reckless, careless **3** *a dangerous criminal* ► ruthless, violent, vicious, desperate

dangle *VERB* **1** *There were curtains dangling above my head.* ► hang, droop, swing, flap, sway, trail, be suspended, wave about **2** *She dangled the keys in his face.* ► wave, swing, brandish, flourish, hold

dare *VERB* **1** *No one dared to say anything.* ► have the courage, be brave enough, take the risk (of), take a chance, venture **2** *She dared him to jump.* ► challenge, defy, provoke, goad, taunt

daring *ADJECTIVE* *a daring attack* ► bold, brave, courageous, adventurous, audacious, intrepid, gallant, confident, dauntless, enterprising, heroic, valiant, (*more informal*) plucky
AN OPPOSITE IS timid

dark *ADJECTIVE* **1** *a dark room* ► dim, dingy, dull, gloomy, unlit, unilluminated, shadowy OPPOSITES ARE light, bright **2** *a dark night* ► black, pitch-black, starless, moonless, unlit, unilluminated OPPOSITES ARE light, bright **3** *a dark colour* ► deep, strong, heavy OPPOSITES ARE pale, light **4** *a dark secret* ► mysterious, enigmatic, hidden, obscure, impenetrable, cryptic **5** *dark thoughts* ► pessimistic, gloomy, sinister, sombre, grim, dismal, bleak, cheerless, fatalistic
AN OPPOSITE IS optimistic

dark *NOUN* *afraid of the dark* ► darkness, blackness, gloom, night, night-time
AN OPPOSITE IS light

darken *VERB* **1** *The sky darkened.* ► become dark, become overcast, cloud over
OPPOSITES ARE lighten, brighten **2** *These fears darkened his life for many years.* ► overshadow, shadow, blacken, threaten, dim, make gloomy
OPPOSITES ARE lighten, brighten

darling *ADJECTIVE* *his darling wife* ► dear, dearest, beloved, adored, cherished, treasured

darling *NOUN* **1** *Jane had always been his darling.* ► beloved, loved one, love, sweetheart, dear, dearest **2** *the darling of the gods* ► favourite, pet, idol

dart *VERB* *Children were darting about everywhere.* ► dash, rush, hurtle, leap, shoot, spring,

darts *NOUN* a game in which darts are thrown at a circular board (**dartboard**)

dash *VERB* **dashes, dashing, dashed** **1** run quickly; rush **2** throw a thing violently against something • *The storm dashed the ship against the rocks.*

dash *NOUN* **dashes** **1** a short quick run; a rush **2** energy or liveliness **3** a small amount • *Add a dash of brandy.* **4** a short line (-) used in writing or printing

dashboard *NOUN* **dashboards** a panel fitted in a vehicle in front of the driver, with dials and controls

dashing *ADJECTIVE* lively and showy

data (day- ta) *NOUN* pieces of information

USAGE Strictly speaking, this word is a plural noun (the singular is *datum*), so it should be used with a plural verb: *Here are the data.* However, the word is widely used nowadays as if it were a singular noun and most people do not regard this as wrong: *Here is the data.*

database *NOUN* **databases** a store of information held in a computer

date [1] *NOUN* **dates** **1** the time when something happens or happened or was written, stated as the day, month, and year (or any of these) **2** an appointment to meet someone, especially someone of the opposite sex

date *VERB* **dates, dating, dated** **1** give a date to something **2** have existed from a particular time • *The church dates from 1684.* **3** seem old-fashioned

date [2] *NOUN* **dates** a small sweet brown fruit that grows on a kind of palm tree

daub *VERB* **daubs, daubing, daubed** paint or smear something clumsily
▷ **daub** *NOUN*

daughter *NOUN* **daughters** a girl or woman who is someone's child

daughter-in-law *NOUN* **daughters-in-law** a son's wife

daunt *VERB* **daunts, daunting, daunted** make somebody afraid or discouraged
▷ **daunting** *ADJECTIVE*

dawdle *VERB* **dawdles, dawdling, dawdled** go slowly and lazily
▷ **dawdler** *NOUN*

dawn *NOUN* **dawns** the time when the sun rises

dawn *VERB* **dawns, dawning, dawned** **1** begin to grow light in the morning **2** begin to be realized • *The truth dawned on them.*

day *NOUN* **days** **1** the 24 hours between midnight and the next midnight **2** the light part of this time **3** a particular day • *sports day* **4** a period of time • *in Queen Victoria's day*

daybreak *NOUN* dawn

daydream *NOUN* **daydreams** pleasant thoughts of something you would like to happen

daydream *VERB* **daydreams, daydreaming, daydreamed** have daydreams

day-to-day *ADJECTIVE* ordinary; happening every day

Thesaurus

bound, flit, fly, move suddenly, (*more informal*) whiz, (*more informal*) zip

dash *NOUN* *They made a dash for the door.* ► rush, bolt, leap, sprint, spurt, race, run, chase

dash *VERB* **1** *We dashed home as soon as we could.* ► rush, race, bolt, tear, hasten, hurry, speed, shoot, run, sprint, chase, dart, fly, hasten, (*informal*) zoom **2** *He dashed the plate against the wall.* ► smash, crash, hurl, strike, throw, knock

data *NOUN* *a group collecting data on teenage pregnancies* ► information, details, particulars, facts and figures, statistics, evidence, material

date *NOUN* **1** *coins and pottery from a very early date* ► time, age, era, period **2** *She was in danger of missing her date with Paul.* ► meeting, appointment, rendezvous, engagement, assignation, fixture **3** *Mary was his date for the evening.* ► partner, escort, girlfriend (or boyfriend)

dawdle *VERB* *Ruth dawdled back through the wood, reluctant to return.* ► linger, dally, take your time, delay, idle, (*more informal*) dilly-dally
AN OPPOSITE IS hurry

dawn *NOUN* **1** *We got up at dawn.* ► daybreak, sunrise, break of day, first light, (*more informal*) first thing AN OPPOSITE IS dusk **2** *the dawn of modern civilization* ► beginning, start, birth, origin, genesis, advent, emergence

day *NOUN* **1** *He looked after Lucy during the day while I was at work.* ► daytime, daylight
AN OPPOSITE IS night **2** *The girls are required to plan their own day.* ► working day, working time, work time, period of work **3** *He was the leading musician of the day.* ► age, period, time, era, epoch

daydream *NOUN* *She tried to shake off her daydreams.* ► reverie, fantasy, trance, fancy, dream, vision, imagining, absent-mindedness, meditation, musing, illusion, pipe dream

daydream *VERB* *He went out, leaving me to dress and daydream.* ► fantasize, dream, muse, meditate, be lost in thought, imagine

daylight *NOUN* *Until eight o'clock there is no daylight in our room.* ► sunlight, light of day, natural light

dazed ADJECTIVE unable to think or see clearly
▷ **daze** NOUN
[from Old Norse *dasathr* = weary]

dazzle VERB **dazzles**, **dazzling**, **dazzled** **1** make a person unable to see clearly because of too much bright light **2** amaze or impress a person by a splendid display

DC ABBREVIATION direct current

de- PREFIX **1** removing (as in *defrost*) **2** down, away (as in *descend*) **3** completely (as in *denude*)

dead ADJECTIVE **1** no longer alive **2** not lively **3** not functioning; no longer in use **4** exact or complete • *a dead loss*

deaden VERB **deadens**, **deadening**, **deadened** make pain or noise etc. weaker

dead end NOUN **dead ends** **1** a road or passage with one end closed **2** a situation where there is no chance of making progress

dead heat NOUN **dead heats** a race in which two or more winners finish exactly together

deadline NOUN **deadlines** a time limit [originally this meant a line round an American military prison. If prisoners went beyond it they could be shot]

deadlock NOUN **deadlocks** a situation in which no progress can be made

deadly ADJECTIVE **deadlier**, **deadliest** likely to kill

deaf ADJECTIVE **1** unable to hear **2** unwilling to hear
▷ **deafness** NOUN

deafen VERB **deafens**, **deafening**, **deafened** make somebody become deaf, especially by a very loud noise
▷ **deafening** ADJECTIVE

deal VERB **deals**, **dealing**, **dealt** **1** hand something out; give **2** give out cards for a card game **3** do business; buy and sell • *He deals in scrap metal*
▷ **dealer** NOUN
deal with **1** be concerned with • *This book deals with words and meanings.* **2** do what is needed • *I'll deal with the washing-up.*

deal NOUN **deals** **1** an agreement or bargain **2** someone's turn to deal at cards

Thesaurus

daze VERB **1** *The fall dazed him for a few minutes.* ► stun, stupefy, shock **2** *She was dazed by the news.* ► astound, amaze, astonish, startle, dumbfound, bewilder, stagger

dazzle VERB **1** *The sunlight burst through the window and dazzled him.* ► daze, blind **2** *The beauty of the place dazzled her.* ► overpower, overwhelm, overawe, impress, amaze, astonish

dead ADJECTIVE **1** *Both her parents were dead.* ► deceased, departed, passed on, gone OPPOSITES ARE alive, living **2** *There was a dead animal on the road.* ► lifeless, killed, inanimate **3** *Latin is a dead language.* ► extinct, obsolete, defunct, disused, died out
AN OPPOSITE IS existing **4** *My feet were dead with cold.* ► numb, deadened, insensitive, paralysed, without feeling
AN OPPOSITE IS sensitive **5** *The battery was dead.* ► flat, unresponsive, defunct, inoperative, not working, burnt out, used up, useless, worn out
AN OPPOSITE IS operational **6** *When Sheila picked up the phone again the line was dead.* ► not working, inoperative, out of order, unresponsive **7** *The place is dead on a Friday night.* ► lifeless, dreary, uninteresting, boring, dull, moribund, slow OPPOSITES ARE lively, exciting **8** (*informal*) *He felt dead by the time he got home.* ► exhausted, worn out, drained, tired **9** *He is the dead image of his brother.* ► exact, absolute, perfect, complete, utter, downright

dead ADVERB *The road ahead was dead straight.* ► completely, absolutely, perfectly, utterly

deaden VERB **1** *Mufflers deaden the noise.* ► muffle, soften, mute, damp, reduce, quieten, smother, stifle, suppress, weaken, cushion, lessen, check, hush
OPPOSITES ARE amplify, sharpen **2** *A local anaesthetic will deaden the pain.* ► numb, stifle, dull, blunt, suppress, alleviate, soothe, desensitize, anaesthetize
OPPOSITES ARE intensify, aggravate

deadly ADJECTIVE **1** *a deadly poison* ► lethal, noxious, harmful, mortal, dangerous
AN OPPOSITE IS harmless **2** *a deadly disease* ► terminal, fatal, life-threatening, destructive
AN OPPOSITE IS mild **3** (*informal*) *The party turned out to be deadly.* ► dull, boring, dreary, tedious, unexciting, uninteresting OPPOSITES ARE lively, exciting **4** *He fired an arrow with a deadly aim.* ► unerring, unfailing, true, perfect

deaf ADJECTIVE **1** *By this time he was deaf and nearly blind.* ► hard of hearing **2** **deaf to** *They were deaf to all our pleas.* ► indifferent to, unmoved by, heedless of, oblivious to, unconcerned with

deafening ADJECTIVE *a deafening roar* ► loud, noisy, piercing, ear-splitting, booming, thunderous, overpowering

deal NOUN **1** *He was good at business deals and not much more.* ► agreement, arrangement, negotiation, transaction, settlement, contract, bargain, understanding **2** *Shoppers should look around for the best deal.* ► buy, bargain, transaction
a good deal *or* **a great deal** *We have already*

a good deal or **a great deal** a large amount

dear *ADJECTIVE* **1** loved very much **2** a polite greeting in letters • *Dear Sir* **3** expensive
▷ **dearly** *ADVERB*

death *NOUN* **deaths** dying; the end of life

debatable *ADJECTIVE* questionable; that can be argued against

debate *NOUN* **debates** a formal discussion

debate *VERB* **debates, debating, debated** hold a debate
▷ **debater** *NOUN*

debilitating *ADJECTIVE* causing weakness

debit *NOUN* **debits** an entry in an account showing how much money is owed

debit *VERB* **debits, debiting, debited** enter something as a debit in a financial account
[from Latin *debitum* = something owed]

debris (deb- ree) *NOUN* scattered fragments or wreckage

debt (det) *NOUN* **debts** something that you owe someone
in debt owing money etc.
[from Latin *debitum* = something owed]

debtor (det- or) *NOUN* **debtors** a person who owes money to someone

decade (dek- ayd) *NOUN* **decades** a period of ten years

decadent (dek- a- dent) *ADJECTIVE* falling to lower moral standards, especially in order to enjoy pleasure
▷ **decadence** *NOUN*

Thesaurus

achieved a great deal. ► a lot, much, plenty, a large amount, a large quantity

deal *VERB* **1** *She dealt the cards for another round.* ► give out, distribute, share out, dispense, apportion, allot, assign, divide, (*informal*) dole out **2** *The man dealt him a blow on the head.* ► deliver, inflict, give, administer, apply, mete out **3** *He deals in stocks and shares.* ► trade, do business, buy and sell, traffic **4 deal with** *a difficult issue to deal with* ► handle, manage, tackle, cope with, attend to, come to grips with, resolve, control, consider, grapple with, look after, see to, sort out, take action on **5 deal with** *The book deals with several important topics.* ► be concerned with, treat, cover, tackle, explain

dealer *NOUN* *an antique dealer; a dealer in second-hand cars* ► trader, supplier, merchant, wholesaler, retailer, merchandiser, shopkeeper, stockist, tradesman

dear *ADJECTIVE* **1** *They soon became dear friends.* ► beloved, close, intimate, lovable, loved, valued, darling AN OPPOSITE IS hated **2** *Fruit is dear at this time of year.* ► expensive, costly, high-priced, overpriced, exorbitant, (*more informal*) pricey AN OPPOSITE IS cheap

dear *NOUN* *Everyone agrees he's a dear.* ► darling, lovable person, treasure, pet

dearly *ADVERB* *She loved Simon dearly.* ► deeply, intensely, profoundly, fondly, tenderly, very much, a great deal

death *NOUN* **1** *Charles phoned to tell her of her uncle's death.* ► dying, passing, passing away, end RELATED ADJECTIVE mortal **2** *The disaster caused many deaths.* ► casualty, fatality RELATED ADJECTIVE fatal **3** *The news meant the death of all their dreams.* ► end, ending, finish, collapse, ruin, destruction, termination, cessation

put to death *The king put all the conspirators to death.* ► execute, kill, have killed

debatable *ADJECTIVE* *It is debatable whether the public wants this sort of sensationalism.*
► arguable, questionable, disputable, doubtful, dubious, a moot point, open to doubt, open to question, contentious, controversial, controvertible, problematical, uncertain AN OPPOSITE IS indisputable

debate *NOUN* *a debate about personal freedom* ► discussion, argument, exchange of views, controversy, deliberation, contention, dialogue, dispute, (*more formal*) dialectic, (*more formal*) disputation

debate *VERB* **1** *Parliament will debate schemes for reducing traffic in cities.* ► discuss, consider, deliberate, confer about, exchange views on, dispute, argue, weigh up **2** *I am debating whether to get in touch with them.* ► consider, think over, ponder, deliberate, contemplate, reflect, (*more informal*) mull over

debris *NOUN* **1** *There was debris all around from the collapsed buildings.* ► rubbish, rubble, ruins, remains, wreckage **2** *Use rubber gloves to clean out debris from the gutters.* ► waste, remains, detritus, refuse, litter, bits, dregs, scraps

debt *NOUN* **1** *It is easy for students to build up large debts.* ► money owed, arrears, financial obligation, financial commitment, bill **2** *I owe you a great debt for your kindness.* ► duty, indebtedness, obligation

in debt *By the end of the year he was heavily in debt.* ► owing money, in arrears, insolvent

in someone's debt *I shall be forever in your debt.* ► grateful to, indebted to, obliged to, beholden to

debtor *NOUN* *Debtors who fail to pay their hotel bill are not usually sent to prison any more.*
► bankrupt, defaulter

decadent *ADJECTIVE* *a decadent society*
► immoral, dissolute, degenerate, dissipated,

A B C D E F G H I J K L M N O P Q R S T U V W X Y Z

decaffeinated ADJECTIVE (said about coffee or tea) with the caffeine removed

decapitate VERB **decapitates, decapitating, decapitated** cut someone's head off; behead
▷ **decapitation** NOUN

decathlon NOUN **decathlons** an athletic contest in which each competitor takes part in ten events

decay VERB **decays, decaying, decayed** **1** go bad; rot **2** become less good or less strong
▷ **decay** NOUN

deceased ADJECTIVE dead

deceit (dis-eet) NOUN **deceits** making a person believe something that is not true
▷ **deceitful** ADJECTIVE **deceitfully** ADVERB

deceive VERB **deceives, deceiving, deceived** make a person believe something that is not true
▷ **deceiver** NOUN

December NOUN the twelfth month of the year [from Latin *decem* = ten, because it was the tenth month of the ancient Roman calendar]

decent ADJECTIVE **1** respectable and honest **2** reasonable or adequate **3** (*informal*) kind
▷ **decently** ADVERB **decency** NOUN

deception NOUN **deceptions** deceiving someone
▷ **deceptive** ADJECTIVE **deceptively** ADVERB

decibel (dess-ib-el) NOUN **decibels** a unit for measuring the loudness of sound

decide VERB **decides, deciding, decided** **1** make up your mind; make a choice **2** settle a contest or argument
▷ **decider** NOUN

decided ADJECTIVE **1** having clear and definite opinions **2** noticeable • *a decided difference*
▷ **decidedly** ADVERB

deciduous (dis-id-yoo-us) ADJECTIVE a deciduous tree is one that loses its leaves in autumn

decimal ADJECTIVE using tens or tenths

decimal NOUN **decimals** a decimal fraction

decimal currency NOUN **decimal currencies** a currency in which each unit is ten or one hundred times the value of the one next below it

decimal fraction NOUN **decimal fractions** a fraction with tenths shown as numbers after a dot ($\frac{3}{10}$ is 0.3; $1\frac{1}{2}$ is 1.5)

decimal point NOUN **decimal points** the dot in a decimal fraction

Thesaurus

corrupt, depraved, declining
AN OPPOSITE IS moral

decay VERB **1** *The skulls were in good condition but the bones had decayed.* ► decompose, rot, putrefy, go bad, waste away, perish, deteriorate, degrade, disintegrate **2** *Inner cities had been allowed to decay.* ► decline, deteriorate, degenerate, crumble, corrode, disintegrate, wither, fall apart, go downhill

decay NOUN **1** *Today I found a dead blackbird in an advanced state of decay.* ► decomposition, rotting, festering, putrefaction **2** *Television is often blamed for the so-called decay in social values.* ► deterioration, decline, degradation, collapse, fall, disintegration

deceit NOUN *They achieved much by lies and deceit.* ► deception, duplicity, trickery, pretence, cheating, misrepresentation, fraud, guile, subterfuge, artifice, ruse
OPPOSITES ARE honesty, openness

deceitful ADJECTIVE *George got used to the fact that I was deceitful and irresponsible.* ► dishonest, untruthful, insincere, untrustworthy, deceptive, duplicitous, underhand, false, fraudulent, (*more informal*) two-faced

deceive VERB *It had not been too difficult to deceive him.* ► trick, fool, mislead, hoodwink, delude, dupe, cheat, swindle, (*more informal*) take in

decent ADJECTIVE **1** *Mum always said it wasn't decent to watch people undress.* ► proper, respectable, appropriate, suitable, fitting, seemly, becoming, nice, modest, decorous, tasteful AN OPPOSITE IS indecent **2** *Apart from that, he seemed a decent enough bloke.* ► obliging, courteous, honest, trustworthy, reliable, dependable, upright, polite, honourable **3** *It was her first decent meal of the day.* ► good, satisfactory, nice, pleasant, agreeable AN OPPOSITE IS unsatisfactory

deception NOUN *For a spy, I'm not very good at deception.* ► deceit, duplicity, trickery, pretence, cheating, misrepresentation, fraud, guile, subterfuge, artifice, ruse
OPPOSITES ARE honesty, openness

deceptive ADJECTIVE **1** *Similarities can be deceptive.* ► misleading, illusory, false, unreliable, delusive, fallacious, fraudulent, insincere, specious, spurious, treacherous
AN OPPOSITE IS genuine **2** *deceptive practices* ► dishonest, deceitful, fraudulent, underhand, duplicitous, sham, bogus AN OPPOSITE IS honest

decide VERB **1** *He decided to become a journalist.* ► resolve, determine, make up your mind, choose, reach a decision, opt, plan, aim **2** *We don't have enough evidence to decide the issue.* ► determine, judge, adjudicate on, make a judgement on, pronounce on

decipher (dis-I-fer) *VERB* **deciphers, deciphering, deciphered** **1** work out the meaning of a coded message **2** work out the meaning of something written badly
▷ **decipherment** *NOUN*

decision *NOUN* **decisions** **1** deciding; what you have decided **2** determination

decisive (dis-I-siv) *ADJECTIVE* **1** that settles or ends something • *a decisive battle* **2** able to make decisions quickly and firmly
▷ **decisively** *ADVERB* **decisiveness** *NOUN*

deck *NOUN* **decks** **1** a floor on a ship or bus **2** a pack of playing cards **3** a turntable on a record player

deckchair *NOUN* **deckchairs** a folding chair with a canvas or plastic seat

declaim *VERB* **declaims, declaiming, declaimed** make a speech etc. loudly and dramatically
▷ **declamation** *NOUN*

declare *VERB* **declares, declaring, declared** **1** say something clearly or firmly **2** tell customs officials that you have goods on which you ought to pay duty **3** end a cricket innings before all the batsmen are out
▷ **declaration** *NOUN*
declare war announce that you are starting a war against someone

decline *VERB* **declines, declining, declined** **1** refuse **2** become weaker or smaller **3** slope downwards **4** state the forms of a noun, pronoun, or adjective that correspond to particular cases, numbers, and genders

decline *NOUN* **declines** a gradual decrease or loss of strength

decode *VERB* **decodes, decoding, decoded** work out the meaning of something written in code
▷ **decoder** *NOUN*

decompose *VERB* **decomposes, decomposing, decomposed** decay or rot
▷ **decomposition** *NOUN*

decorate *VERB* **decorates, decorating, decorated** **1** make something look more beautiful or colourful **2** put fresh paint or paper on walls **3** give somebody a medal
▷ **decoration** *NOUN* **decorator** *NOUN* **decorative** *ADJECTIVE*

Thesaurus

decision *NOUN* **1** *the jury's decision on damages* ► verdict, finding, ruling, conclusion, judgement, pronouncement, adjudication **2** *The King agreed with this decision.* ► resolution, conclusion, outcome, result, recommendation, resolve, determination

decisive *ADJECTIVE* **1** *The car's faster speed proved to be a decisive advantage.* ► conclusive, definite, significant, crucial, critical, positive, deciding, determining, convincing, final, influential OPPOSITES ARE inconclusive, insignificant **2** *His decisive no-nonsense manner had given him quite a reputation. They showed themselves capable of decisive action.* ► resolute, determined, firm, strong-willed, strong-minded, forceful, forthright, unhesitating, incisive, decided, definite OPPOSITES ARE indecisive, hesitant

declaration *NOUN* **1** *a joint declaration by the four heads of state* ► announcement, proclamation, notification, promulgation, edict, manifesto **2** *a declaration of trust in the government* ► affirmation, assertion, acknowledgement, profession, confirmation, pledge, avowal

declare *VERB* **1** *Both sides declared their intentions.* ► announce, proclaim, express, voice, affirm, reveal, divulge **2** *He declared that he was ready to do a deal.* ► assert, insist, maintain, announce, aver, state, claim, certify, vow, avow

decline *NOUN* **1** *a decline in profits* ► reduction, decrease, drop, fall, downturn, falling off, recession, slump, diminution (of), loss (of), failing (of) **2** *a decline in their fortunes* ► deterioration, degeneration, worsening (of)

decline *VERB* **1** *He declined all our invitations.* ► refuse, reject, dismiss, turn down, pass up, forgo AN OPPOSITE IS accept **2** *After the accident her health declined.* ► worsen, deteriorate, weaken, degenerate, flag, die away, fail, fall off, sink, wane, wilt AN OPPOSITE IS improve **3** *Profits have declined for the third year in succession.* ► decrease, diminish, be reduced, lessen, go down, drop away, dwindle, ebb

decode *VERB* *The messages were quickly decoded.* ► decipher, unscramble, interpret, make sense of, understand, construe, solve, read, (*more informal*) crack, (*more informal*) make out, (*more informal*) figure out OPPOSITES ARE code, encode

decorate *VERB* **1** *a nursery chair decorated with little rabbits* ► adorn, ornament, embellish, trim, beautify, enhance **2** *We will decorate the house before moving in.* ► paint, renovate, smarten up, refurbish, redecorate, paper, wallpaper, (*more informal*) do up **3** *He was decorated for bravery at the end of the war.* ► honour, reward, give a medal to, mention in dispatches

decoration **1** *a tall ceiling with elaborate decoration* ► ornamentation, adornment, embellishment, trimmings, filigree, tracery, frill, scroll **2** *a decoration for bravery* ► award, badge, medal, ribbon, star, (*more informal*) gong

decorous (dek- er- us) *ADJECTIVE* polite and dignified
▷ **decorously** *ADVERB*

decoy (dee- koi) *NOUN* **decoys** something used to tempt a person or animal into a trap or into danger

decoy (dik- oi) *VERB* **decoys, decoying, decoyed** tempt a person or animal into a trap etc.

decrease *VERB* **decreases, decreasing, decreased** make or become smaller or fewer

decrease *NOUN* **decreases** decreasing; the amount by which something decreases

decree *NOUN* **decrees** an official order or decision

decree *VERB* **decrees, decreeing, decreed** make a decree

decrepit (dik- rep- it) *ADJECTIVE* old and weak
▷ **decrepitude** *NOUN*

dedicate *VERB* **dedicates, dedicating, dedicated** **1** devote all your time or energy to something • *She dedicated her life to nursing.* **2** name a person as a mark of respect, e.g. at the beginning of a book
▷ **dedication** *NOUN*

deduce *VERB* **deduces, deducing, deduced** work something out by reasoning from facts that you know are true
▷ **deducible** *ADJECTIVE*

deduct *VERB* **deducts, deducting, deducted** subtract part of something

deduction *NOUN* **deductions** **1** deducting; something deducted **2** deducing; something deduced

deed *NOUN* **deeds** **1** something that someone has done; an act **2** a legal document

deep *ADJECTIVE* **1** going a long way down or back or in • *a deep well* • *deep cupboards* **2** measured from top to bottom or front to back • *a hole six feet deep* **3** intense or strong • *deep colours* • *deep feelings* **4** low-pitched, not shrill • *a deep voice*
▷ **deeply** *ADVERB* **deepness** *NOUN*

Thesaurus

decorative *ADJECTIVE* *a decorative mirror in a frame* ► ornamental, ornate, fancy, adorning, embellishing, enhancing, elaborate, non-functional AN OPPOSITE IS functional

decoy *NOUN* *They set up a decoy to distract our attention.* ► lure, bait, trap, enticement

decoy *VERB* *His enemies had decoyed him to another part of the country.* ► lure, entice, induce, inveigle, ensnare, seduce, tempt, bait, draw, lead

decrease *NOUN* *a decrease in crime levels* ► reduction, decline, lessening (of), falling off, drop, downturn AN OPPOSITE IS increase

decrease *VERB* **1** *We need to decrease our costs.* ► reduce, lessen, lower, cut, cut down, curtail AN OPPOSITE IS increase **2** *The aircraft's speed was rapidly decreasing.* ► diminish, lessen, reduce, fall off, dwindle AN OPPOSITE IS increase

decree *NOUN* *a presidential decree banning all protest meetings* ► order, edict, command, mandate, proclamation, dictum, enactment

decree *VERB* *The law decreed that Sunday should be a day of rest.* ► order, command, declare, prescribe, ordain, proclaim, pronounce, direct, rule, decide, determine, dictate

decrepit *ADJECTIVE* **1** *He lived in a decrepit old cottage.* ► dilapidated, battered, ramshackle, tumbledown, worn out, broken down, derelict **2** *a decrepit old woman* ► feeble, frail, weak, infirm

dedicated *ADJECTIVE* *a dedicated musician* ► devoted, committed, keen, staunch, steadfast, fervent, loyal, enthusiastic, zealous, whole-hearted, single-minded, faithful

dedication *NOUN* **1** *She appreciated all his hard work and dedication.* ► devotion, commitment, allegiance, faithfulness, loyalty, adherence, single-mindedness **2** *The book bore a dedication to his wife.* ► inscription

deduce *VERB* *He deduced that she must be a good cook.* ► conclude, come to the conclusion, reason, work out, gather, infer, surmise, glean

deduct *VERB* *The cost of the breakage will be deducted from his allowance.* ► subtract, knock off, take away, debit (to) OPPOSITES ARE add (to), credit (to)

deduction *NOUN* **1** USAGE from the verb **deduct** *Income is subject to the deduction of tax.* ► subtraction, taking away, taking off, removal, stoppage **2** USAGE from the verb **deduce** *Her deduction was quite correct.* ► conclusion, inference, reasoning

deed *NOUN* *a heroic deed* ► act, action, feat, exploit, endeavour, enterprise, achievement, adventure, effort, performance, undertaking

deep *ADJECTIVE* **1** *The well is deep.* ► bottomless, fathomless, cavernous, yawning AN OPPOSITE IS shallow **2** *a deep disappointment* ► intense, profound, extreme, serious **3** *a deep mystery* ► obscure, secret, mysterious, unfathomable, fathomless, arcane **4** *deep affection* ► intense, heartfelt, fervent, ardent, deep-seated **5** *a deep thinker* ► wise, intelligent, profound, perceptive, learned, discerning **6** *They were deep in conversation.* ► rapt, absorbed, engrossed, immersed, preoccupied, riveted **7** *a deep sound* ► low, low-pitched, bass, resonant, booming **8** *a deep colour* ► dark, rich, vivid, strong, intense

deepen *VERB* **deepens, deepening, deepened** make or become deeper

deer *NOUN* **deer** a fast-running graceful animal, the male of which usually has antlers

deface *VERB* **defaces, defacing, defaced** spoil the surface of something, e.g. by scribbling on it
▷ **defacement** *NOUN*

default *VERB* **defaults, defaulting, defaulted** fail to do what you have agreed to do, especially to pay back a loan
▷ **defaulter** *NOUN*

default *NOUN* **defaults** **1** failure to do something **2** (in computing) what a computer does unless you give it another command
by default because something has failed to happen

defeat *VERB* **defeats, defeating, defeated** **1** win a victory over someone **2** baffle; be too difficult for someone

defeat *NOUN* **defeats** **1** defeating someone **2** being defeated; a lost game or battle

defect (dee- fekt) *NOUN* **defects** a flaw

defect (dif- ekt) *VERB* **defects, defecting, defected** desert your own country etc. and join the enemy
▷ **defection** *NOUN* **defector** *NOUN*

defective *ADJECTIVE* having defects; incomplete
▷ **defectiveness** *NOUN*

defence *NOUN* **defences** **1** defending something **2** something that defends or protects **3** a reply put forward by a defendant

defend *VERB* **defends, defending, defended** **1** protect, especially against an attack **2** try to prove that a statement is true or that an accused person is not guilty
▷ **defender** *NOUN*

defendant *NOUN* **defendants** a person accused of something in a lawcourt

defensive *ADJECTIVE* used or done for defence; protective
▷ **defensively** *ADVERB*
on the defensive ready to defend yourself

defer [1] *VERB* **defers, deferring, deferred** postpone
▷ **deferment** *NOUN* **deferral** *NOUN*

defer [2] *VERB* **defers, deferring, deferred** give way to a person's wishes or authority; yield

deference (def- er- ens) *NOUN* polite respect
▷ **deferential** (def- er- en- shal) *ADJECTIVE*
deferentially *ADVERB*

defiant *ADJECTIVE* defying; openly disobedient
▷ **defiantly** *ADVERB* **defiance** *NOUN*

Thesaurus

deepen *VERB* **1** *Their love had deepened over the years.* ▸ increase, intensify, grow, grow stronger **2** *The hole had been deepened.* ▸ dig out, make deeper, hollow, scoop out

defeat *NOUN* **1** *the defeat of Napoleon at Waterloo* ▸ conquest, subjugation, overthrow, beating, victory (over) **2** *The home side faced defeat.* ▸ failure, loss, setback, humiliation, disappointment, reverse, trouncing
AN OPPOSITE IS victory

defeat *VERB* **1** *The French army defeated the enemy in a long engagement.* ▸ overcome, beat, conquer, overpower, subdue, vanquish, subjugate, quell, rout **2** *The complexity of the task defeated them.* ▸ confound, baffle, frustrate, fox, (*more informal*) flummox

defect *NOUN* (with the stress on *de-*) *The machinery showed several defects.* ▸ fault, flaw, imperfection, deficiency, weakness, failing, inadequacy, blemish, error, (*more informal*) bug

defect *VERB* (with the stress on *-fect*) *MPs might defect to other parties.* ▸ desert, go over, change sides, revolt

defective *ADJECTIVE* *The car's brakes were defective.* ▸ faulty, out of order, deficient, broken, malfunctioning, inoperative

defence *NOUN* **1** *Several friends spoke in defence of his actions.* ▸ support, vindication, justification, endorsement **2** *a defence against attack* ▸ protection, resistance (to), shield, deterrent, barricade, bulwark

defend *VERB* **1** *An air squadron helped to defend the country against enemy attack.* ▸ protect, guard, safeguard, secure, shield, shelter, screen, cover **2** *He found it hard to defend his actions.* ▸ justify, vindicate, make a case for

defensive *ADJECTIVE* **1** *The aircraft formed a defensive circle.* ▸ defending, protective, protecting, guarding AN OPPOSITE IS aggressive **2** *Her attitude seemed nervous and defensive.* ▸ wary, watchful, cautious, apologetic, self-justifying AN OPPOSITE IS assertive

defer *VERB* **1** *She had decided to defer unpacking to the following day.* ▸ postpone, put off, delay, adjourn, hold over, suspend, (*more informal*) shelve **2** **defer to** *He agreed to defer to his parents' wishes.* ▸ yield to, submit to, respect, accede to, give way to, agree to, surrender to

defiance *NOUN* *Her dark eyes were ablaze with defiance.* ▸ opposition, confrontation, resistance, challenge, audacity, bravado, contempt

defiant *ADJECTIVE* *He remained defiant in spite of the threats.* ▸ obstinate, determined, intransigent, resistant, confrontational, recalcitrant, unyielding
OPPOSITES ARE cooperative, apologetic

deficiency NOUN **deficiencies** **1** a lack or shortage **2** a defect
▷ **deficient** ADJECTIVE

defile VERB **defiles, defiling, defiled** make a thing dirty or impure
▷ **defilement** NOUN

define VERB **defines, defining, defined** **1** explain what a word or phrase means **2** show clearly what something is; specify **3** show a thing's outline
▷ **definable** ADJECTIVE

definite ADJECTIVE **1** clearly stated; exact • *Fix a definite time.* **2** certain or settled • *Is it definite that we are to move?*

definite article NOUN **definite articles** (in grammar) the word 'the'

definitely ADVERB certainly; without doubt

definition NOUN **definitions** **1** a statement of what a word or phrase means or of what a thing is **2** being distinct; clearness of outline (e.g. in a photograph)

deflate VERB **deflates, deflating, deflated** **1** let out air from a tyre or balloon etc. **2** make someone feel less proud or less confident **3** reduce or reverse inflation
▷ **deflation** NOUN **deflationary** ADJECTIVE

deflect VERB **deflects, deflecting, deflected** make something turn aside
▷ **deflection** NOUN **deflector** NOUN

deforest VERB **deforests, deforesting, deforested** clear away the trees from an area
▷ **deforestation** NOUN

deform VERB **deforms, deforming, deformed** spoil a thing's shape or appearance
▷ **deformation** NOUN

deft ADJECTIVE skilful and quick
▷ **deftly** ADVERB **deftness** NOUN

defuse VERB **defuses, defusing, defused** **1** remove the fuse from a bomb so that it cannot explode **2** make a situation less dangerous or tense

defy VERB **defies, defying, defied** **1** resist something openly; refuse to obey • *They defied the law.* **2** challenge a person to do something you believe cannot be done • *I defy you to prove this.* **3** prevent something being done • *The door defied all efforts to open it.*

Thesaurus

deficiency NOUN *a vitamin deficiency* ► insufficiency, shortage, inadequacy, lack, deficit, shortfall

deficient ADJECTIVE **1** *a diet deficient in vitamins* ► lacking, wanting, defective, inadequate, insufficient OPPOSITES ARE adequate, excessive **2** *deficient leadersip* ► defective, flawed, faulty, unsound, imperfect, inadequate, (*more informal*) duff AN OPPOSITE IS perfect

deficit NOUN *a deficit in the budget* ► loss, shortfall, deficiency, lack AN OPPOSITE IS surplus

define VERB **1** *We can define evidence as information about whether a particular thing is true or not.* ► explain, interpret, clarify, formulate, give the meaning of **2** *The fence defines the boundary of the estate.* ► mark, mark out, indicate, set, determine, demarcate, outline

definite ADJECTIVE **1** *She came to some definite conclusions.* ► clear, clear-cut, explicit, express, precise, established, fixed, concrete, plain, hard AN OPPOSITE IS indefinite **2** *There are definite signs of improvement.* ► distinct, clear, plain, discernible, obvious, perceptible, noticeable, positive, unmistakable, marked, pronounced, apparent AN OPPOSITE IS imperceptible

definitely ADVERB *She definitely hadn't been there before.* ► certainly, positively, surely, unquestionably, beyond doubt, assuredly, for certain, indubitably, doubtless, without doubt, without fail

definition NOUN **1** *It is hard to write a good definition of 'left' and 'right'.* ► explanation, description, elucidation, interpretation, meaning **2** *The photograph lacked definition.* ► clarity, clearness, sharpness, precision, focus

definitive ADJECTIVE **1** *the definitive film guide* ► authoritative, standard, classic, recognized, accepted, official, ultimate, complete, reliable **2** *a definitive reply* ► decisive, conclusive, categorical, final AN OPPOSITE IS provisional

deflate VERB **1** *Someone had deflated two of the tyres.* ► let down, let the air out of, flatten AN OPPOSITE IS inflate. **2** *The news deflated him.* ► subdue, humble, humiliate, dishearten, dispirit, dismay, chasten, mortify OPPOSITES ARE encourage, boost

deflect VERB *He managed to deflect the blow.* ► divert, turn aside, parry, fend off, intercept, avert, head off, prevent, ward off

deformed ADJECTIVE *He was so deformed the gods took pity on him.* ► misshapen, contorted, crippled, crooked, distorted, disfigured, twisted, malformed, maimed, bent, warped, mutilated, buckled, mangled, defaced, gnarled, grotesque, ugly

defy VERB **1** *He was arrested for defying a court order to hand over the property.* ► disobey, refuse to obey, flout, disregard, violate, contravene, infringe, breach, resist AN OPPOSITE IS obey **2** *She defied Robin to admit the truth.* ► challenge, dare **3** *The situation defied all attempts at rational explanation.*

A B C D E F G H I J K L M N O P Q R S T U V W X Y Z

degenerate (di- jen- e- rayt) *VERB* **degenerates, degenerating, degenerated** become worse or lower in standard
▷ **degeneration** *NOUN*

degenerate (di- jen- e- ret) *ADJECTIVE* having become immoral or bad
▷ **degeneracy** *NOUN*

degrade *VERB* **degrades, degrading, degraded** **1** humiliate or dishonour someone **2** reduce to a simpler molecular form
▷ **degradation** (deg- ra- day- shon) *NOUN*

degree *NOUN* **degrees** **1** a unit for measuring temperature **2** a unit for measuring angles **3** extent • *to some degree* **4** an award to someone at a university or college who has successfully finished a course

dehydrated *ADJECTIVE* dried up, with all moisture removed
▷ **dehydration** *NOUN*

deity (dee- it- ee, day- it- ee) *NOUN* **deities** a god or goddess

dejected *ADJECTIVE* sad or depressed
▷ **dejectedly** *ADVERB* **dejection** *NOUN*

delay *VERB* **delays, delaying, delayed** **1** make someone or something late **2** postpone

delay *NOUN* **delays** delaying; the time for which something is delayed • *a two-hour delay*

delegate (del- ig- at) *NOUN* **delegates** a person who represents others and acts on their instructions

delegate (del- ig- ayt) *VERB* **delegates, delegating, delegated** **1** give someone a task or duty to do on your behalf • *I'm going to delegate this job to my assistant.* **2** appoint someone as a delegate • *We delegated Jones to represent us.*

delegation (del- ig- ay- shon) *NOUN* **delegations** **1** delegating **2** a group of delegates

delete (dil- eet) *VERB* **deletes, deleting, deleted** cross out or remove something written or printed or stored on a computer
▷ **deletion** *NOUN*

deliberate (dil- ib- er- at) *ADJECTIVE* **1** done on purpose; intentional **2** slow and careful
▷ **deliberately** *ADVERB*

deliberate (dil- ib- er- ayt) *VERB* **deliberates, deliberating, deliberated** discuss or think carefully
▷ **deliberation** *NOUN*

delicacy *NOUN* **delicacies** **1** being delicate **2** a delicious food

Thesaurus

► elude, escape, defeat, frustrate, thwart, resist

degree *NOUN* *The work involves a high degree of trust.* ► level, order, measure, extent, range, stage, intensity, standard
to some degree *The risk will still be present to some degree.* ► partly, to some extent, up to a point

deign *VERB* *She practised all the things she would say to him when he deigned to contact her.* ► condescend, see fit, consent, descend, stoop

dejected *ADJECTIVE* *Lisa was looking dejected.* ► downcast, depressed, despondent, dispirited, disheartened, downhearted, unhappy, fed up, sad, down, glum, melancholy, miserable, cast down
OPPOSITES ARE cheerful, happy

delay *NOUN* **1** *Traffic is subject to long delays.* ► hold-up, wait, waiting period, stoppage, obstruction **2** *A delay in the proceedings followed.* ► deferment, postponement, suspension

delay *VERB* **1** *Heavy traffic delayed many of the guests.* ► detain, hold up, make late, hamper, impede **2** *We might have to delay the start of the game.* ► postpone, put off, defer, suspend, adjourn, hold over OPPOSITES ARE advance, bring forward **3** *There is no time to delay.* ► linger, dally, take your time, (*more formal*) procrastinate, (*more informal*) drag your feet, (*more informal*) hang about

delegate *VERB* **1** *The council delegated a member to speak to the press.* ► appoint, authorize, commission, nominate, designate, empower, mandate **2** *She delegates routine tasks to an assistant.* ► assign, entrust, pass on, hand over, devolve, consign

delegation *NOUN* *There was a delegation from Nigeria.* ► deputation, commission, legation, delegacy, mission, representative group, contingent

delete *VERB* *One paragraph was deleted from the article.* ► remove, cut out, take out, erase, expunge, cross out

deliberate *ADJECTIVE* **1** *The disaster may have been an accident rather than deliberate sabotage.* ► intentional, calculated, conscious, planned, culpable, premeditated, wilful
OPPOSITES ARE unplanned, accidental, fortuitous
2 *She could hear the slow deliberate footsteps.* ► careful, measured, steady, cautious, unhurried, considered, methodical
AN OPPOSITE IS hasty

delicacy *NOUN* **1** *lacework of great delicacy* ► fineness, exquisiteness, daintiness, fragility, intricacy, precision, accuracy, care **2** *It was an unpleasant matter that called for some delicacy.* ► sensitivity, subtlety, tact, discrimination,

A B C D E F G H I J K L M N O P Q R S T U V W X Y Z

delicate *ADJECTIVE* **1** fine and graceful • *delicate embroidery* **2** fragile and easily damaged **3** pleasant and not strong or intense **4** becoming ill easily **5** using or needing great care • *a delicate situation*
▷ **delicately** *ADVERB* **delicateness** *NOUN*

delicious *ADJECTIVE* tasting or smelling very pleasant
▷ **deliciously** *ADVERB*

delight *VERB* **delights, delighting, delighted** **1** please someone greatly **2** take great pleasure in something

delight *NOUN* **delights** great pleasure
▷ **delightful** *ADJECTIVE* **delightfully** *ADVERB*

delinquent (dil- ing- kwent) *NOUN* **delinquents** a young person who breaks the law
▷ **delinquent** *ADJECTIVE* **delinquency** *NOUN*

delirious (di- li- ri- us) *ADJECTIVE* **1** affected with delirium **2** extremely excited or enthusiastic
▷ **deliriously** *ADVERB*

delirium (dil- irri- um) *NOUN* **1** a state of mental confusion and agitation during a feverish illness **2** wild excitement

deliver *VERB* **delivers, delivering, delivered** **1** take letters or goods etc. to someone's house or place of work **2** give a speech or lecture etc. **3** help with the birth of a baby **4** aim or strike a blow or an attack **5** rescue; set free

Thesaurus

finesse **3** *Several plates of delicacies were brought in.* ► titbit, rarity, speciality, treat

delicate *ADJECTIVE* **1** *The tablecloths were made of beautiful, delicate fabrics.* ► fine, exquisite, elegant, intricate, graceful, flimsy, fragile OPPOSITES ARE coarse, crude **2** *He awoke feeling somewhat delicate, after his night on the town.* ► unwell, sickly, ill, unfit, poorly, frail, weak OPPOSITES ARE healthy, fit, robust **3** *The old clock had a delicate mechanism.* ► precise, intricate, accurate, exact **4** *a delicate shade of blue* ► subtle, muted, soft, pale, gentle, pastel, subdued **5** *Angie made a tiny, delicate gesture with her hand.* ► gentle, deft, adroit, neat, skilful **6** *The next issue to come up was delicate, to put it mildly.* ► difficult, tricky, sensitive, awkward, embarrassing, problematical **7** *The matter called for delicate handling.* ► sensitive, careful, discriminating **8** *It would not be easy to cater for their delicate taste in food.* ► fastidious, discriminating, fussy, (*more informal*) choosy, (*more informal*) pernickety, (*more informal*) faddy, (*more informal*) picky

delicious *ADJECTIVE* *You can have a delicious meal at the local pub.* ► tasty, appetizing, palatable, delectable, enjoyable, luscious, succulent, choice, savoury, (*more informal*) mouth-watering, (*more informal*) scrumptious, (*more informal*) yummy opposites are unpleasant, uneatable

delight *NOUN* *Florence laughed with delight.* ► pleasure, happiness, joy, enjoyment, bliss, rapture, ecstasy

delight *VERB* **1** *She delighted her father by singing for him.* ► please, charm, thrill, gratify, enchant, captivate, enthral, entrance, amuse, (*more informal*) bowl over OPPOSITES ARE displease, disgust **2 delight in** *Fran delighted in the flowers he gave her.* ► relish, enjoy, love, savour, revel in OPPOSITES ARE hate, dislike, loathe

delighted *ADJECTIVE* *He was delighted to see that Jenny had arrived.* ► pleased, happy, glad, thrilled, overjoyed, gratified, excited, ecstatic OPPOSITES ARE dismayed, disappointed

delightful *ADJECTIVE* *He told Julie how delightful it had been to meet her.* ► pleasant, lovely, enjoyable, pleasing, pleasurable, gratifying, satisfying, marvellous, wonderful

delinquency *NOUN* *attacking the root causes of delinquency* ► crime, wrongdoing, criminality, lawbreaking, misconduct, misbehaviour

delinquent *ADJECTIVE* *She was quite good with delinquent adolescents.* ► lawless, lawbreaking, errant, unruly, offending, criminal, unmanageable, uncontrollable

delinquent *NOUN* *It was not fair to label them delinquents.* ► offender, lawbreaker, wrongdoer, young offender, criminal, hooligan, hoodlum, miscreant, (*informal*) tearaway

delirious *ADJECTIVE* **1** *The illness made Luke delirious for days on end.* ► demented, raving, incoherent, hysterical, irrational, feverish, frenzied **2** *She was delirious with joy.* ► ecstatic, elated, thrilled, beside yourself, exultant, wild

deliver *VERB* **1** *The books will be delivered to your address within the next week.* ► send, convey, transport, bring, supply, take, dispatch **2** *The court delivered its verdict.* ► utter, give, make, read, announce, declare, pronounce, speak **3** *He delivered a powerful blow to the back of the head.* ► administer, deal, launch, aim, strike, hit **4** *The hostages were all delivered from their captors.* ► rescue, save, set free, liberate, release, redeem, ransom

delivery *NOUN* **1** *There is a daily delivery of fresh vegetables.* ► consignment, batch, shipment, distribution **2** *The delivery of the message was timed at 3.30.* ► dispatch, transmission, conveyance

▷ **deliverer** *NOUN* **deliverance** *NOUN* **delivery** *NOUN*

delta *NOUN* **deltas** a triangular area at the mouth of a river where it spreads into branches

delude *VERB* **deludes, deluding, deluded** deceive or mislead someone

deluge *NOUN* **deluges** **1** a large flood **2** a heavy fall of rain **3** something coming in great numbers • *a deluge of questions*

deluge *VERB* **deluges, deluging, deluged** overwhelm by a deluge

delusion *NOUN* **delusions** a false belief

demagogue (dem- a- gog) *NOUN* **demagogues** a leader who wins support by making emotional speeches rather than by careful reasoning

demand *VERB* **demands, demanding, demanded** **1** ask for something firmly or forcefully **2** need • *This work demands great skill*

demand *NOUN* **demands** **1** a firm or forceful request **2** a desire to have or buy something • *There is a great demand for computers*
in demand wanted or needed

demanding *ADJECTIVE* needing a lot of effort or attention • *a demanding job*; • *a demanding child*

demarcation (dee- mar- kay- shon) *NOUN* marking the boundary or limits of something

demented *ADJECTIVE* driven mad; crazy

demigod *NOUN* **demigods** a partly divine being

democracy *NOUN* **democracies** **1** government of a country by representatives elected by the whole people **2** a country governed in this way
▷ **democrat** *NOUN* **democratic** *ADJECTIVE* **democratically** *ADVERB*

Democrat *NOUN* **Democrats** a member of the Democratic Party in the USA

demolish *VERB* **demolishes, demolishing, demolished** **1** knock a building down and break it up **2** destroy something completely
▷ **demolition** *NOUN*

demon *NOUN* **demons** **1** a devil; an evil spirit **2** a fierce or forceful person
▷ **demonic** (dim- on- ik) *ADJECTIVE*

demonstrate *VERB* **demonstrates, demonstrating, demonstrated** **1** show or prove something **2** take part in a demonstration
▷ **demonstrator** *NOUN*

demonstration *NOUN* **demonstrations** **1** demonstrating; showing how to do or work something **2** a march or meeting held to show everyone what you think about something

demonstrative (dim- on- strat- iv) *ADJECTIVE* **1** showing or proving something **2** showing feelings or affections openly **3** (in grammar) pointing out the person or thing referred to. *This, that, these,* and *those* are demonstrative adjectives and pronouns
▷ **demonstratively** *ADVERB* **demonstrativeness** *NOUN*

Thesaurus

delude *VERB* *You are deluding yourself if you think that.* ► deceive, mislead, fool, take in, hoodwink, beguile, bamboozle, trick

demand *NOUN* **1** *She refused to give way to their demands.* ► request, requirement, claim, ultimatum, stipulation, insistence **2** *There is much less demand for hardback books.* ► call, market, need, necessity

demand *VERB* **1** *The workers demanded a 10% pay rise.* ► call for, ask for, claim, want, insist on, require, request, expect **2** *'Where are they?' he demanded.* ► ask, enquire, challenge, question

demanding *ADJECTIVE* **1** *a demanding child* ► insistent, trying, tiresome, importunate, nagging **2** *a demanding task* ► difficult, challenging, testing, exacting, taxing, hard, tough, onerous, arduous, formidable

demeanour *NOUN* *an anxious and nervous demeanour* ► attitude, bearing, manner, disposition

demise *NOUN* *the demise of the Assyrian Empire* ► downfall, collapse, end, disappearance, failure

democratic *ADJECTIVE* *a democratic government* ► elected, elective, popular, representative, chosen, egalitarian AN OPPOSITE IS undemocratic

demolish *VERB* *The explosion demolished a row of houses.* ► destroy, wreck, flatten, level, knock down, tear down, break down, obliterate, reduce to ruins OPPOSITES ARE construct, assemble

demolition *NOUN* *The houses face demolition.* ► destruction, dismantling, levelling, pulling down, flattening, clearance

demon *NOUN* *demons from hell* ► devil, fiend, spirit, goblin, imp

demonstrate *VERB* **1** *The evidence demonstrates a major change in the role of women.* ► show, indicate, establish, display, exhibit, point to, prove, substantiate, verify, exemplify, illustrate, manifest, represent **2** *People demonstrated in the streets.* ► protest, rally, hold a rally, lobby, march, parade, picket

demonstration *NOUN* **1** *a demonstration of skill and creativity* ► display, exhibition, manifestation, indication, revelation, expression, presentation, embodiment **2** *a*

A B C D E F G H I J K L M N O P Q R S T U V W X Y Z

demoralize *VERB* **demoralizes, demoralizing, demoralized** dishearten someone; weaken someone's confidence or morale
▷ **demoralization** *NOUN*

demote *VERB* **demotes, demoting, demoted** reduce a person to a lower position or rank
▷ **demotion** *NOUN*

demure *ADJECTIVE* shy and modest
▷ **demurely** *ADVERB* **demureness** *NOUN*

den *NOUN* **dens** **1** a lair **2** a person's private room **3** a place where something illegal happens • *a gambling den*

denial *NOUN* **denials** denying or refusing something

denim *NOUN* a kind of strong, usually blue, cotton cloth used to make jeans etc.

denomination *NOUN* **denominations** **1** a name or title **2** a religious group with a special name • *Baptists, Methodists, and other denominations* **3** a unit of weight or of money • *coins of small denomination*

denominator *NOUN* **denominators** the number below the line in a fraction, showing how many parts the whole is divided into, e.g. 4 in $\frac{1}{4}$ COMPARE **numerator**

denounce *VERB* **denounces, denouncing, denounced** speak strongly against something; accuse • *They denounced him as a spy.*
▷ **denunciation** *NOUN*

dense *ADJECTIVE* **1** thick; packed close together • *dense fog* • *dense crowds* **2** (*informal*) stupid
▷ **densely** *ADVERB*

density *NOUN* **densities** **1** thickness **2** (in science) the proportion of mass to volume

dent *NOUN* **dents** a hollow left in a surface where something has pressed or hit it

dent *VERB* **dents, denting, dented** make a dent in something

dental *ADJECTIVE* to do with the teeth or with dentistry

dentist *NOUN* **dentists** a person who is trained to treat teeth, fill or extract them, fit false ones, etc.
▷ **dentistry** *NOUN*

denture *NOUN* **dentures** a set of false teeth

denude *VERB* **denudes, denuding, denuded** make bare or naked; strip something away
▷ **denudation** *NOUN*

denunciation *NOUN* **denunciations** denouncing

deny *VERB* **denies, denying, denied** **1** say that something is not true **2** refuse to give or allow something • *deny a request*

deodorant (dee-*oh*-der-ant) *NOUN* **deodorants** a substance that removes smells

depart *VERB* **departs, departing, departed** go away; leave
▷ **departure** *NOUN*
[from early French *départir* = separate]

Thesaurus

demonstration against the war ► protest, (*informal*) demo, rally, march, parade, sit-in, vigil

demoralize *VERB* *Poor pay demoralized the staff.* ► discourage, dishearten, depress, deject, dispirit, disconcert

den *NOUN* *He worked all evening in his den upstairs.* ► study, retreat, sanctum, hideaway, hideout, lair, sanctuary, private place, secret place

denial *NOUN* **1** *Reports of a threatened strike met with a firm denial.* ► contradiction, renunciation, repudiation, disavowal, dismissal, abnegation, disclaimer, negation, rejection AN OPPOSITE IS admission **2** *the denial of rights to certain minorities* ► refusal, withholding, withdrawal, veto

denote *VERB* *A snort from the corner denoted disagreement.* ► indicate, mean, express, signify, stand for, represent, symbolize, be the sign for

denounce *VERB* *He denounced them for their dishonesty.* ► condemn, censure, find fault with, criticize, blame, castigate, disparage, denigrate, deprecate, (*more informal*) knock, (*more informal*) slam, (*more informal*) pan

dense *ADJECTIVE* **1** *a dense crowd; dense undergrowth* ► thick, closely packed, tightly packed, impenetrable, massed AN OPPOSITE IS sparse **2** *dense smoke* ► thick, heavy, concentrated OPPOSITES ARE thin, light **3** *too dense to understand the point* ► stupid, foolish, crass, dull, slow, slow-witted, unintelligent OPPOSITES ARE clever, intelligent

dent *NOUN* *There were several small dents in the side of the vehicle.* ► indentation, dint, dimple, dip, concavity, depression, hollow, pit

dent *VERB* **1** *He dropped the saucepan and dented it.* ► make a dent in, push in, knock in, buckle, depress **2** *Nothing much could dent her confidence.* ► diminish, reduce, impair, damage, harm, affect

deny *VERB* **1** *The story was denied by the Prime Minister's office. The accused denied all the charges.* ► contradict, repudiate, rebut, reject, dismiss, contest, oppose, refute USAGE Note that *refute* means 'to disprove by using arguments' **2** *The authorities have denied them their basic rights.* ► refuse, forbid, withhold

depart *VERB* **1** *The officials departed after lunch.* ► leave, go, go away, go off, withdraw, make

department *NOUN* **departments** one section of a large organization or shop
▷ **departmental** *ADJECTIVE*

depend *VERB* **depends, depending, depended**
depend on 1 rely on • *We depend on your help* **2** be controlled by something else • *It all depends on the weather.*

dependant *NOUN* **dependants** a person who depends on another, especially financially • *She has two dependants*
USAGE Note that the spelling ends in **-ant** for this noun but **-ent** for the adjective **dependent**.

dependent *ADJECTIVE* depending • *She has two dependent children* • *they are dependent on her*
▷ **dependence** *NOUN*

deplore *VERB* **deplores, deploring, deplored** be very upset or annoyed by something
▷ **deplorable** *ADJECTIVE* **deplorably** *ADVERB*

deport *VERB* **deports, deporting, deported** send an unwanted foreign person out of a country
▷ **deportation** *NOUN*

depose *VERB* **deposes, deposing, deposed** remove a person from power

Thesaurus

off, retire, quit, (*old-fashioned*) take your leave, (*old-fashioned*) decamp AN OPPOSITE IS arrive **2** *At this point the speaker departed from his notes.* ► deviate, digress, differ, diverge, drift AN OPPOSITE IS stick to

department *NOUN* **1** *He works in a government department.* ► division, section, sector, unit, branch, subdivision, office, bureau, agency, ministry **2** (*informal*) *I'm afraid travel arrangements are not my department.* ► domain, responsibility, business, affair, concern, field, area, sphere, line, province, function, job, specialism, (*more informal*) pigeon, (*more informal*) baby

departure *NOUN* **1** *Our departure has been delayed by half an hour.* ► leaving, setting off, going, exit, withdrawal, disappearance, embarkation, escape, exodus, retirement, retreat AN OPPOSITE IS arrival **2** *The book represents a departure from the author's familiar style.* ► change, change of direction, deviation, digression, shift, variation, innovation, branching out

depend *VERB* **1 depend on** *Choice of university can depend a lot on expected exam grades.* ► be dependent on, hinge on, hang on, rest on, revolve around **2 depend on** *I shall depend on you to help me.* ► rely on, count on, need, bank on, trust

dependable *ADJECTIVE* *She looked at Roland: so strong and dependable.* ► reliable, trustworthy, faithful, true, loyal, constant, unswerving, sensible, responsible, conscientious, sound, steady, unfailing AN OPPOSITE IS unreliable

dependence *NOUN* **1** *Trevor was determined to reduce his dependence on his family.* ► reliance, need (for), trust (in), confidence (in) **2** *a rise in drug dependence* ► addiction, dependency, reliance, craving, abuse

dependent *ADJECTIVE* **1 dependent on** *A lot is dependent on their decision.* ► conditional on, contingent on, connected with, controlled by, determined by, liable to, relative to, subject to, vulnerable to AN OPPOSITE IS independent **2 dependent on** *Prisoners remain dependent on what visitors bring for them.* ► reliant on, supported by, sustained by, needful of **3 dependent on** *Some of these people are dependent on drugs.* ► addicted to, reliant on, enslaved by, (*more informal*) hooked on

depict *VERB* **1** *The painting depicts a village in winter.* ► show, portray, represent, picture, illustrate, reproduce, delineate, describe, draw, narrate, outline, paint, sketch **2** *The author depicts his own childhood in the story.* ► describe, relate, narrate, recount, present, record, outline, delineate, portray, characterize

deplete *VERB* *Local wars have depleted the food supply.* ► exhaust, use up, consume, expend, reduce, decrease, lessen, drain, cut OPPOSITES ARE increase, augment, boost

deplorable *ADJECTIVE* **1** *Their behaviour had been deplorable.* ► disgraceful, shameful, inexcusable, unforgivable, disreputable, lamentable, shocking, blameworthy, discreditable, reprehensible, scandalous, unfortunate, unworthy OPPOSITES ARE admirable, praiseworthy **2** *The troops lived in deplorable conditions.* ► lamentable, regrettable, awful, wretched, terrible, miserable, atrocious

deplore *VERB* **1** *We deplore all forms of violence.* ► condemn, disapprove of, denounce, abhor, decry, deprecate **2** *He deplored the past difficulties and promised a brighter future.* ► regret, lament, bemoan, express regret for

deploy *VERB* **1** *The government deployed troops to prevent demonstrations.* ► position, station, post, install, establish, bring into action **2** *You will need to deploy all your personal and social skills.* ► use, make use of, utilize, employ, exploit, take advantage of

deport *VERB* *Illegal immigrants were deported.* ► expel, banish, exile, expatriate, transport, extradite

depose *VERB* *A military coup deposed the government.* ► overthrow, overturn, bring down, oust, get rid of, remove, displace, (*more informal*) topple AN OPPOSITE IS enthrone

deposit *NOUN* **deposits** **1** an amount of money paid into a bank etc. **2** money paid as a first instalment **3** a layer of solid matter in or on the earth

deposit *VERB* **deposits, depositing, deposited** **1** put something down **2** pay money as a deposit
▷ **depositor** *NOUN*

depot (dep-oh) *NOUN* **depots** **1** a place where things are stored **2** a place where buses or trains are kept and repaired **3** a headquarters

depraved *ADJECTIVE* behaving wickedly; of bad character
▷ **depravity** *NOUN*

depress *VERB* **depresses, depressing, depressed** **1** make somebody sad **2** lower the value of something • *Threat of war depressed prices.* **3** press down • *Depress the lever.*
▷ **depressive** *ADJECTIVE*

depression *NOUN* **depressions** **1** a feeling of great sadness or hopelessness **2** a long period when trade is very slack because many people cannot afford to buy things, with widespread unemployment **3** a shallow hollow in the ground or on a surface **4** an area of low air pressure which may bring rain **5** pressing something down

deprive *VERB* **deprives, depriving, deprived** take or keep something away from somebody
▷ **deprival** *NOUN* **deprivation** *NOUN*

depth *NOUN* **depths** **1** being deep; how deep something is **2** the deepest or lowest part
in depth thoroughly
out of your depth **1** in water that is too deep to stand in **2** trying to do something that is too difficult for you

deputation *NOUN* **deputations** a group of people sent as representatives of others

Thesaurus

deposit *NOUN* **1** *You will need to pay a deposit to clinch the booking.* ► down payment, advance payment, part payment, security, retainer, first payment **2** *a thick deposit of mud* ► layer, covering, coating, accumulation, sediment, silt, sludge, dregs, lees, precipitate **3** *a deposit at the bottom of the bottle* ► sediment, accumulation, dregs, silt

deposit *VERB* **1** *She deposited a pile of papers on the desk.* ► put down, set down, lay down, place, leave, (*more informal*) dump, (*more informal*) stick, (*more informal*) plonk, (*more informal*) park **2** *The money is deposited each Friday.* ► pay in, bank, lodge, save **3** *The flood water deposited layers of mud.* ► precipitate, wash up

depot *NOUN* **1** *a military depot* ► store, storehouse, base, cache, depository, arsenal, dump, hoard **2** *a bus depot* ► garage, station, terminus, headquarters

depreciate *VERB* *The value of property is not likely to depreciate.* ► drop, fall, become less, lessen, lower, reduce, decrease, go down, deflate, slump, weaken AN OPPOSITE IS appreciate

depress *VERB* **1** *The latest news depressed everyone.* ► sadden, deject, dishearten, dispirit, upset, discourage, grieve, lower the spirits of, oppress, make sad
AN OPPOSITE IS cheer **2** *Aid tends to depress local markets.* ► undermine, weaken, impair, inhibit, check, make less active, slow down, bring down, push down, deflate AN OPPOSITE IS boost

depressed *ADJECTIVE* *Sam looked tired and depressed.* ► dejected, downcast, despondent, dispirited, disheartened, downhearted, disconsolate, unhappy, sad, down, glum, melancholy, miserable, cast down
OPPOSITES ARE cheerful, happy

depressing *ADJECTIVE* **1** *Tuesday was a cold, depressing day.* ► gloomy, bleak, dreary, dismal, grim, drab, sombre, dingy, cheerless **2** *He tried to get rid of all such depressing thoughts.* ► dispiriting, disheartening, upsetting, distressing, melancholy, painful, morbid

depression *NOUN* **1** *A sudden feeling of depression took hold of him.* ► sadness, dejection, melancholy, sorrow, despondency, unhappiness, low spirits, glumness, desolation, despair, pessimism, (*more informal*) the blues, (*more informal*) the dumps
AN OPPOSITE IS cheerfulness **2** *an economic depression* ► recession, slump, decline, downturn, slowdown, stagnation, hard times
AN OPPOSITE IS boom **3** *a meteorological depression* ► area of low pressure, cyclone, low
AN OPPOSITE IS anticyclone **4** *The wheel hit a depression in the ground.* ► hollow, indentation, dent, cavity, hole, pothole, dip, dimple, concavity OPPOSITES ARE bump, protuberance

deprive *VERB* **deprive of** *The war deprived her of her income.* ► deny, dispossess of, rob of, divest of, strip of, take away, starve of, refuse, prevent from having

deprived *ADJECTIVE* *deprived sections of society* ► disadvantaged, underprivileged, needy, poor, badly off, destitute

depth *NOUN* **1** *They tried to measure the depth of the water.* ► deepness, distance to the bottom, vertical extent, drop **2** *The orchestra's playing showed a great depth of feeling.* ► extent, degree, range, breadth, scope

deputy *NOUN* **deputies** a person appointed to act as a substitute for another

deranged *ADJECTIVE* insane
▷ **derangement** *NOUN*

derby (dar- bi) *NOUN* **derbies** a sports match between two teams from the same city or area [from the name of the Earl of Derby, who in 1780 founded the famous horse race called the Derby which is run at Epsom in Surrey]

derelict (derri- likt) *ADJECTIVE* abandoned and left to fall into ruin
▷ **dereliction** *NOUN*

deride *VERB* **derides, deriding, derided** laugh at with contempt or scorn; ridicule
▷ **derision** *NOUN*

derive *VERB* **derives, deriving, derived** **1** obtain something from a source • *She derived great enjoyment from music.* **2** form or originate from something • *Some English words are derived from Latin words.*
▷ **derivation** *NOUN* **derivative** *ADJECTIVE*

descend *VERB* **descends, descending, descended** go down
▷ **descent** *NOUN*
be descended from have as an ancestor; come by birth from a certain person or family

descendant *NOUN* **descendants** a person who is descended from someone

describe *VERB* **describes, describing, described** **1** say what someone or something is like **2** draw in outline; move in a pattern • *The orbit of the Earth around the Sun describes an ellipse.*
▷ **description** *NOUN* **descriptive** *ADJECTIVE*

desert (dez- ert) *NOUN* **deserts** a large area of dry often sandy land

desert (diz- ert) *VERB* **deserts, deserting, deserted** leave a person or place without

Thesaurus

deputy *NOUN* *During her absence her duties are done by a deputy.* ► second in command, number two, substitute, assistant, stand-in, representative, understudy USAGE Note that *understudy* normally means an actor who takes the place of the main actor when they are ill or indisposed.

derelict *ADJECTIVE* *The car passed a row of derelict buildings.* ► dilapidated, ramshackle, run down, tumbledown, ruined, deserted, abandoned, neglected, broken down, decrepit

derivation *NOUN* **1** *the derivation of the word 'posh'* ► origin, etymology, root, provenance, source **2** *a family of noble derivation* ► ancestry, origin, genealogy, descent, provenance

derive *VERB* **1** *She derived some comfort from the fact that she knew the truth.* ► gain, receive, obtain, draw, acquire, get **2** *The family's wealth derives from oil.* ► originate (in), stem, arise, spring, flow, emanate **3** **be derived from** *The word 'yacht' is derived from Dutch.* ► come from, originate in, stem from, descend from

descend *VERB* **1** *The little plane descended towards the runway.* ► come down, go down, drop, subside, fall, move down, sink, dive, plummet OPPOSITES ARE ascend, climb **2** *The road descends to a small village.* ► slope, dip, drop, fall, incline, slant AN OPPOSITE IS ascend
be descended from *We are descended from an Italian family.* ► come from, originate in, spring from, stem from
descend from *He watched her descend from the train.* ► get off, alight from, disembark from, dismount from
descend on *A coach party descended on the local pub.* ► engulf, overwhelm, invade
descend to *In the end they descended to trickery.* ► condescend to, stoop to, lower yourself to, resort to, be reduced to, go as far as

descendants *PLURAL NOUN* *descendants of J. S. Bach* ► line, lineage, heirs, family, successors, offspring, progeny, children, issue, posterity AN OPPOSITE IS ancestors

descent *NOUN* **1** *the descent into Dentdale from Newby Head* ► way down, drop, incline, dip, declivity, slant, slope, fall AN OPPOSITE IS ascent **2** *a person of British descent* ► ancestry, parentage, origin, lineage, extraction, heredity, blood, pedigree, genealogy, background, derivation, family, stock, strain

describe *VERB* **1** *A witness described the incident in detail.* ► report, narrate, relate, set out, explain, recount **2** **describe as** *I would never describe him as 'charming'.* ► call, speak of, refer to, classify, categorize, characterize as, portray, present, represent **3** *The pencil described a circle.* ► draw, mark out, trace

description *NOUN* **1** *She launched into a detailed description of her day.* ► account, explanation, report, narration, commentary (on) **2** *The room was crammed with furniture of every description.* ► sort, kind, variety, type, category, class, order

descriptive *ADJECTIVE* *an exercise using descriptive language* ► expressive, graphic, colourful, detailed, pictorial, vivid, striking, explanatory, illustrative

desert *NOUN* (with the stress on *des-*) *lost in the desert* ► wasteland, wilderness, waste, wilds

desert *ADJECTIVE* (with the stress on *des-*) **1** *desert conditions* ► arid, dry, waterless, parched, barren, infertile, sterile, uncultivated, wild AN OPPOSITE IS fertile **2** *a desert island*

intending to return
▷ **deserter** *NOUN* **desertion** *NOUN*

desert island *NOUN* **desert islands** an uninhabited island

deserve *VERB* **deserves, deserving, deserved** have a right to something; be worthy of something
▷ **deservedly** *ADVERB*

design *NOUN* **designs** **1** a drawing that shows how something is to be made **2** the way something is made or arranged **3** lines and shapes that form a decoration; a pattern **4** a mental plan or scheme
have designs on plan to get hold of

design *VERB* **designs, designing, designed** **1** draw a design for something **2** plan or intend something for a special purpose
▷ **designer** *NOUN*

desirable *ADJECTIVE* **1** causing people to desire it; worth having **2** worth doing; advisable
▷ **desirability** *NOUN*

desire *NOUN* **desires** a feeling of wanting something very much
▷ **desirous** *ADJECTIVE*

desire *VERB* **desires, desiring, desired** have a desire for something

desk *NOUN* **desks** **1** a piece of furniture with a flat top and often drawers, used when writing or doing work **2** a counter at which a cashier or receptionist sits

desktop *ADJECTIVE* suitable to be used on a desk
• *a desktop computer*

desolate *ADJECTIVE* **1** lonely and sad **2** uninhabited ▷ **desolation** *NOUN*

despair *NOUN* a feeling of hopelessness

despair *VERB* **despairs, despairing, despaired** feel despair

Thesaurus

► uninhabited, solitary, lonely, desolate, isolated, unfrequented AN OPPOSITE IS inhabited

desert *VERB* (with the stress on *-sert*) **1** *Her husband had deserted her.* ► abandon, leave, strand, forsake, give up, jilt, renounce, betray, (*more informal*) dump, (*more informal*) walk out on, (*more informal*) leave in the lurch **2** *He had decided to desert the party and join the opposition.* ► renounce, abandon, leave, quit, disavow, forsake, (*more informal*) have done with **3** *Soldiers were deserting in large numbers.* ► abscond, defect, decamp, make off, go absent, turn tail, run away

deserted *ADJECTIVE* **1** *a deserted village* ► uninhabited, empty, unoccupied, evacuated, neglected, desolate, vacant **2** *a deserted wife* ► abandoned, stranded, forsaken, jilted, cast off, betrayed

deserve *VERB* **1** *You deserve a holiday.* ► be entitled to, be worthy of, have earned, have a right to, be good enough for **2** *The work deserves the highest praise.* ► merit, justify, warrant, rate

design *NOUN* **1** *a design for the new building* ► plan, blueprint, drawing, outline, pattern, prototype, sketch, draft, model **2** *furniture of a fresh bright design* ► pattern, style, form, composition, arrangement, configuration **3** *His design was to travel and enjoy life.* ► intention, ambition, aim, aspiration, goal, object, objective, purpose, end, scheme

design *VERB* **1** *Wren designed several London churches.* ► plan, draw plans of, map out, outline, draw, sketch **2** *an engineer who designed a new kind of aero engine* ► create, invent, develop, devise, originate, conceive, think up

desirable *ADJECTIVE* **1** *a very desirable woman* ► attractive, beautiful, alluring, appealing, (*more informal*) sexy **2** *It would be desirable for them to express their support.* ► advantageous, advisable, helpful, beneficial, worthwhile, preferable, sensible, prudent

desire *NOUN* **1** *Ed has always had a desire to travel.* ► wish, longing, yearning, craving, inclination, eagerness, enthusiasm, impulse, appetite (for), (*more informal*) yen **2** *She saw that his eyes were dark with desire.* ► lust, passion, ardour, lasciviousness, libido, love

desire *VERB* **1** *We all desire peace.* ► want, wish for, yearn for, long for, covet, crave, need, hanker after, hunger for, thirst for, pine for, ache for, fancy, like, prefer, (*informal*) set your heart on, (*informal*) itch for, (*informal*) have a yen for **2** *He knew she desired him too.* ► be attracted to, be captivated by, be infatuated by, lust after, (*more informal*) have a crush on

desolate *ADJECTIVE* **1** *They reached a desolate spot near the coast.* ► deserted, uninhabited, abandoned, barren, bare, bleak, gloomy, dismal, dreary, godforsaken **2** *Feeling desolate, she asked him to forgive her.* ► miserable, sad, unhappy, forlorn, depressed, dejected, downcast, despondent, disconsolate
AN OPPOSITE IS cheerful

despair *NOUN* *Stephen was in a state of despair.* ► hopelessness, desperation, despondency, anguish, pessimism, melancholy, gloom, misery, wretchedness, dejection, depression
AN OPPOSITE IS hope

despair *VERB* *At times like this you can easily despair.* ► lose hope, give up hope, lose heart, be demoralized AN OPPOSITE IS hope

desperate *ADJECTIVE* **1** extremely serious or hopeless • *a desperate situation* **2** having a great need or desire for something • *She is desperate to get a ticket* **3** reckless and ready to do anything
▷ **desperately** *ADVERB* **desperation** *NOUN*

despise *VERB* **despises, despising, despised** think someone or something is inferior or worthless

despite *PREPOSITION* in spite of

despondent *ADJECTIVE* sad or gloomy
▷ **despondently** *ADVERB* **despondency** *NOUN*

dessert (diz- ert) *NOUN* **desserts** fruit or a sweet food served as the last course of a meal

destination *NOUN* **destinations** the place to which a person or thing is travelling

destined *ADJECTIVE* having as a destiny; intended

destiny *NOUN* **destinies** what will happen or has happened to somebody or something; fate

destitute *ADJECTIVE* left without anything; living in extreme poverty
▷ **destitution** *NOUN*

destroy *VERB* **destroys, destroying, destroyed** ruin or put an end to something
▷ **destruction** *NOUN* **destructive** *ADJECTIVE*

destroyer *NOUN* **destroyers** a fast warship

detach *VERB* **detaches, detaching, detached** unfasten or separate
▷ **detachable** *ADJECTIVE* **detachment** *NOUN*

detached *ADJECTIVE* **1** separated **2** (said about a house) not joined to another **3** impartial; not involved in something

Thesaurus

desperate *ADJECTIVE* **1** *He tried not to listen to the desperate cries outside.* ▶ despairing, hopeless, anguished, inconsolable, distraught, distressed, miserable, wretched **2** *There was a desperate shortage of food.* ▶ acute, critical, severe, serious, grave, dire, urgent **3** *a band of desperate criminals* ▶ violent, wild, dangerous, reckless, impetuous

desperation *NOUN* **1** *In desperation, she decided to go back to London to find him.* ▶ despair, hopelessness, anguish, despondency, distress **2** *The robbery seemed like an act of desperation.* ▶ recklessness, rashness, impetuosity, foolhardiness, frenzy

despicable *ADJECTIVE* *guilty of despicable crimes* ▶ contemptible, loathsome, hateful, vile, shameful, detestable, abhorrent

despise *VERB* *She despised the methods he used in business.* ▶ scorn, disdain, look down on, deride, condemn, deplore, revile, detest, loathe, feel contempt for AN OPPOSITE IS admire

despondent *ADJECTIVE* *Perhaps he was feeling despondent about his exam results.* ▶ disheartened, dejected, depressed, downhearted, downcast, gloomy, upset, down, miserable, sad

destiny *NOUN* **1** *Destiny had intervened to help them.* ▶ fate, fortune, chance, luck, providence, karma **2** *He seemed once more in control of his destiny.* ▶ future, fortune, fate, lot

destitute *ADJECTIVE* *He had left her destitute with two children to care for.* ▶ penniless, impoverished, poverty-stricken, impecunious, homeless, indigent, deprived, down and out, insolvent, needy, poor, (*informal*) skint
AN OPPOSITE IS wealthy

destroy *VERB* **1** *A bomb had destroyed the building.* ▶ demolish, ruin, wreck, obliterate, devastate, shatter, blow up **2** *Disease destroyed all hopes of an economic recovery.* ▶ wreck, ruin, spoil, obliterate, disrupt, upset, put an end to, frustrate, thwart, undermine
OPPOSITES ARE raise, revive **3** *Their intention was to destroy the enemy.* ▶ kill, slaughter, annihilate, slay, eradicate

destruction *NOUN* **1** *Fires caused widespread destruction.* ▶ devastation, damage, demolition, ruination, havoc **2** *much wildlife faces destruction* ▶ annihilation, obliteration, elimination, extinction, extermination

destructive *ADJECTIVE* **1** *a destructive storm* ▶ devastating, damaging, ruinous, catastrophic, violent, ravaging **2** *destructive criticism* ▶ hostile, antagonistic, vicious, negative, fierce, disparaging
AN OPPOSITE IS constructive

detach *VERB* *You can detach the printing head for cleaning.* ▶ remove, unfasten, disconnect, take off, separate, disengage, unfix, free
AN OPPOSITE IS attach

detached *ADJECTIVE* **1** *detached houses set back from the road* ▶ free-standing, separate, unconnected **2** *Her face expressed detached amusement.* ▶ dispassionate, disinterested, impartial, aloof, distant, objective
AN OPPOSITE IS committed

detachment *NOUN* **1** *He regarded the matter with detachment.* ▶ dispassion, objectivity, disinterest, impartiality, neutrality, unconcern, aloofness, remoteness **2** *a detachment of soldiers* ▶ unit, squad, force, troop, corps, brigade, task force

A B C D E F G H I J K L M N O P Q R S T U V W X Y Z

detail *NOUN* **details** **1** a very small part of a design or plan or decoration etc. **2** a small piece of information
▷ **detailed** *ADJECTIVE*
in detail describing or dealing with everything fully

detain *VERB* **detains, detaining, detained** **1** keep someone waiting **2** keep someone at a place

detect *VERB* **detects, detecting, detected** discover
▷ **detection** *NOUN* **detector** *NOUN*

detective *NOUN* **detectives** a person who investigates crimes

detention *NOUN* **detentions** **1** detaining; being detained **2** being made to stay late in school as a punishment

deter *VERB* **deters, deterring, deterred** discourage or prevent a person from doing something

detergent *NOUN* **detergents** a substance used for cleaning or washing things

deteriorate (dit- eer- ee- er- ayt) *VERB* **deteriorates, deteriorating, deteriorated** become worse
▷ **deterioration** *NOUN*

determination *NOUN* **1** the firm intention to achieve what you have decided to achieve **2** determining or deciding something

determine *VERB* **determines, determining, determined** **1** decide • *determine what is to be done* **2** find out; calculate • *determine the height of the mountain*

determined *ADJECTIVE* full of determination; with your mind firmly made up

determiner *NOUN* **determiners** (in grammar) a word (such as *a*, *the*, *many*) that modifies a noun

Thesaurus

detail *NOUN* **1** *The copy of the painting was accurate in every detail.* ► feature, particular, aspect, characteristic, circumstance, respect, item, point, factor, specific, fact, ingredient
usage You can also use *minutiae*, which is a Latin plural word meaning 'details'. **2** *She has an eye for detail.* ► precision, exactness, accuracy, rigour, thoroughness
in detail *They commented on the proposals in detail.* ► in depth, thoroughly, closely, methodically, minutely, meticulously, point by point, item by item

detail *VERB* **1** *An appendix details the sources used in the book.* ► describe, list, present, explain, recount, spell out **2** *The head boy was detailed to look after the visitors.* ► appoint, assign, delegate, commission, nominate, choose

detailed *ADJECTIVE* *a detailed description of the scene* ► precise, exact, comprehensive, complete, elaborate, exhaustive, minute, intricate, specific OPPOSITES ARE general, summary

detain *VERB* **1** *The authorities wanted to detain them for questioning.* ► hold, arrest, apprehend, hold in custody, confine, restrain, intern, imprison, gaol, capture
AN OPPOSITE IS release **2** *Something must have detained them.* ► delay, hold up, impede, hinder, keep, check, prevent, keep waiting, retard, slow, stop, waylay

detect *VERB* **1** *We detected slight patches of rust.* ► notice, become aware of, perceive, discern, make out, recognize, identify, spot **2** *The crime was detected with the help of DNA evidence.* ► discover, uncover, expose, reveal, unearth, find out, root out, unmask, track down

deter *VERB* **1** *It was mainly the expense that deterred them.* ► discourage, put off, inhibit, dissuade, intimidate, prevent, exclude
AN OPPOSITE IS encourage **2** *measures to deter crime* ► prevent, stop, check, put a stop to, reduce, discourage, counteract

deteriorate *VERB* **1** *His health deteriorated rapidly after his wife's death.* ► worsen, weaken, decline, lapse, fail, fade, fall off, get worse, relapse, slip, collapse, depreciate, (*more informal*) go downhill AN OPPOSITE IS improve
2 *These materials deteriorate if they are not stored correctly.* ► decay, degenerate, disintegrate, decompose, crumble

determination *NOUN* **1** *His determination to win grew daily stronger.* ► resolution, resolve, will, strength of will, intentness **2** *You will need a lot of determination.* ► resolve, firmness of purpose, tenacity, persistence, dedication, drive

determine *VERB* **1** *It can be difficult to determine the sex of pandas.* ► find out, discover, ascertain, decide, establish, identify, verify
2 *Certain chromosomes determine the sex of an embryo.* ► control, regulate, decide, direct, dictate, govern, influence, affect

determined *ADJECTIVE* **1** *He is determined he will have his way.* ► adamant, resolute, insistent, convinced, bent (on having), resolved (to have), intent (on having)
AN OPPOSITE IS doubtful **2** *a determined young woman* ► resolute, purposeful, strong-willed, single-minded, strong-minded, steadfast, tenacious, dogged AN OPPOSITE IS irresolute

deterrent *NOUN* **deterrents** something that deters people, such as a powerful weapon or a threat of punishment

detest *VERB* **detests, detesting, detested** dislike something very much; loathe
▷ **detestable** *ADJECTIVE* **detestation** *NOUN*

detonate (det- on- ayt) *VERB* **detonates, detonating, detonated** explode or cause something to explode
▷ **detonation** *NOUN* **detonator** *NOUN*

detour (dee- toor) *NOUN* **detours** a roundabout route instead of the normal one

detriment (det- rim- ent) *NOUN* harm or disadvantage • *She worked long hours, to the detriment of her health.*

detrimental (det- rim- en- tal) *ADJECTIVE* harmful or disadvantageous
▷ **detrimentally** *ADVERB*

deuce *NOUN* **deuces** a score in tennis where both sides have 40 points and must gain two consecutive points to win

devalue *VERB* **devalues, devaluing, devalued** **1** reduce a thing's value **2** reduce the value of a country's currency in relation to other currencies or to gold
▷ **devaluation** *NOUN*

devastate *VERB* **devastates, devastating, devastated** **1** ruin or cause great destruction to something **2** cause great shock or grief to someone
▷ **devastating** *ADJECTIVE* **devastation** *NOUN*

develop *VERB* **develops, developing, developed** **1** make or become bigger or better **2** come gradually into existence • *Storms developed.* **3** begin to have or use • *They developed bad habits.* **4** use an area of land for building houses, shops, factories, etc. **5** treat photographic film with chemicals so that pictures appear
▷ **developer** *NOUN* **development** *NOUN*

deviate (dee- vee- ayt) *VERB* **deviates, deviating, deviated** turn aside from a course or from what is usual or true
▷ **deviation** *NOUN*

device *NOUN* **devices** **1** something made for a particular purpose • *a device for opening tins* **2** a design used as a decoration or emblem
leave someone to their own devices leave them to do as they wish

devil *NOUN* **devils** **1** an evil spirit **2** a wicked, cruel, or annoying person
▷ **devilish** *ADJECTIVE* **devilry** *NOUN*

devilment *NOUN* mischief

Thesaurus

deterrent *NOUN* *Penalties need to serve as a deterrent to those tempted to offend.*
► discouragement, disincentive, impediment, warning, caution, brake, check, curb, obstacle, restraint, threat, (*more informal*) turn-off
AN OPPOSITE IS encouragement

detest *VERB* *I detest that kind of talk.* ► hate, abhor, loathe, despise, dislike, deplore, recoil from

devastate *VERB* **1** *Storms have devastated the region.* ► destroy, damage severely, ravage, demolish, flatten, ruin, wreck, lay waste, level, overwhelm, raze **2** *He was clearly devastated by the news.* ► shatter, shock, dismay, stun, distress, overwhelm, upset

develop *VERB* **1** *Our plans have developed rapidly in the last few weeks.* ► progress, advance, evolve, grow, flourish, get better, improve, mature, thrive, move on AN OPPOSITE IS regress **2** *An argument developed.* ► arise, ensue, result, emerge, start, begin, erupt, come about, (*informal*) blow up **3** *The company wants to develop its overseas business.* ► expand, extend, diversify, build up, enlarge, increase, swell **4** *Children develop their reading skills at this age.* ► evolve, expand, advance, cultivate, acquire **5** *Let's see if we can develop these ideas.* ► amplify, augment, elaborate, enlarge on **6** *People were developing the disease at an early age.* ► contract, catch, get, succumb to, be infected with, come down with

development *NOUN* **1** *the development of a national road network* ► evolution, growth, advance, furtherance, expansion, spread, enlargement, promotion, improvement **2** *The Cabinet met to discuss recent developments in the Middle East.* ► event, happening, occurrence, outcome, result, change, incident **3** *The land has been set aside for industrial development.* ► exploitation, building, conversion, use

deviate *VERB* *politicians who deviate from the party policy* ► diverge, depart, digress, drift, stray, wander, turn aside, differ, part, veer, vary, err

deviation *NOUN* *Any deviation from the normal routine caused chaos.* ► departure, divergence, digression, variation, variance, deflection, alteration, fluctuation, change, shift, disparity

device *NOUN* **1** *a device for converting digital data into audio signals* ► implement, apparatus, appliance, contraption, contrivance, tool, utensil, gadget, instrument, invention, machine **2** *a device to avoid prosecution* ► ploy, tactic, plan, ruse, scheme, stratagem, manoeuvre, contrivance, trick, stunt, expedient, wile, gambit, gimmick, (*more informal*) dodge **3** *a shield with a device showing the family arms* ► emblem, symbol, motif, badge, crest, insignia, seal, figure, logo

devil *NOUN* **1** *a sermon on the Devil and his works* ► Satan, Lucifer, the Evil One, the Prince of Darkness, the Adversary **2** *a painting with*

devious (dee- vee- us) *ADJECTIVE* **1** roundabout; not direct • *a devious route* **2** not straightforward; underhand
▷ **deviously** *ADVERB* **deviousness** *NOUN*

devise *VERB* **devises, devising, devised** invent or plan

devoid *ADJECTIVE* lacking or without something • *His work is devoid of merit.*

devolution *NOUN* handing over power from central government to local or regional government

devolve *VERB* **devolves, devolving, devolved** pass or be passed to a deputy or successor

devote *VERB* **devotes, devoting, devoted** give completely • *He devoted his time to sport.*

devoted *ADJECTIVE* very loving or loyal

devotee (dev- o- tee) *NOUN* **devotees** a person who is devoted to something; an enthusiast

devotion *NOUN* great love or loyalty

devotions *PLURAL NOUN* prayers

devour *VERB* **devours, devouring, devoured** eat or swallow something hungrily or greedily

devout *ADJECTIVE* earnestly religious or sincere
▷ **devoutly** *ADVERB* **devoutness** *NOUN*

dew *NOUN* tiny drops of water that form during the night on surfaces of things in the open air
▷ **dewdrop** *NOUN* **dewy** *ADJECTIVE*

dexterity (deks- terri- tee) *NOUN* skill in handling things

dhoti *NOUN* **dhotis** the loincloth worn by male Hindus

diabetes (dy- a- bee- teez) *NOUN* a disease in which there is too much sugar in a person's blood
▷ **diabetic** (dy- a- bet- ik) *ADJECTIVE, NOUN*

diabolical *ADJECTIVE* **1** like a devil; very wicked **2** very clever or annoying

diadem (dy- a- dem) *NOUN* **diadems** a crown or headband worn by a royal person

diagnose *VERB* **diagnoses, diagnosing, diagnosed** find out what disease a person has or what is wrong
▷ **diagnosis** *NOUN* **diagnostic** *ADJECTIVE*

diagonal (dy- ag- on- al) *NOUN* **diagonals** a straight line joining opposite corners
▷ **diagonal** *ADJECTIVE* **diagonally** *ADVERB*

diagram *NOUN* **diagrams** a kind of drawing or picture that shows the parts of something or how it works

Thesaurus

green-skinned devils holding tridents ► demon, fiend, imp, spirit **3** *The poor devil looked frozen and soaked through.* ► wretch, fellow, soul **4** *cheeky young devils* ► rascal, rogue, monkey, scamp

devious *ADJECTIVE* **1** *a devious route round the hills* ► circuitous, indirect, winding, rambling, meandering, tortuous, roundabout, erratic, deviating, wandering, crooked
AN OPPOSITE IS direct **2** *devious methods; a devious person* ► underhand, deceitful, dishonest, scheming, calculating, cunning, treacherous, evasive, insincere, misleading, sly, sneaky, wily AN OPPOSITE IS straightforward

devise *VERB* *Devise a history project that includes role play.* ► conceive, think up, think out, work out, invent, make up, plan, form, prepare, design, concoct, contrive, scheme, formulate, imagine, plot

devote *VERB* *He claimed he wanted to devote more time to his family.* ► set aside, dedicate, assign, allot, commit, give yourself

devoted *ADJECTIVE* *a devoted wife and mother* ► loyal, faithful, dedicated, staunch, fond, loving, caring, committed, devout, steadfast, true

devotion *NOUN* **1** *her devotion to her family* ► loyalty, dedication, commitment, faithfulness, staunchness, steadfastness, fondness (for) **2** *a life of religious devotion* ► piety, spirituality, devoutness, holiness, sanctity

devour *VERB* **1** *She watched him as he devoured his meal.* ► eat, consume, guzzle, gobble, wolf down, bolt down, (*more informal*) scoff, (*more informal*) demolish **2** *Flames devoured the barn.* ► destroy, consume, engulf, envelop, demolish, ravage, wreck, dispatch

devout *ADJECTIVE* *a devout Muslim* ► pious, devoted, dedicated, reverent, faithful, dutiful, true

diabolical *ADJECTIVE* **1** *The soldiers showed diabolical cruelty.* ► outrageous, appalling, atrocious, wicked, vile, shocking, fiendish, devilish **2** (*informal*) *The standard of driving was diabolical.* ► dreadful, awful, frightful, terrible, poor, bad

diagnose *VERB* *The consultant diagnosed a tumour.* ► identify, detect, recognize, spot, determine, isolate, distinguish, find, pinpoint

diagnosis *NOUN* *The original diagnosis proved to be incorrect.* ► identification, explanation, pronouncement, opinion, verdict, analysis, conclusion, interpretation

diagram *NOUN* *a diagram showing the workings of the digestive system* ► chart, plan, drawing, outline, representation, sketch, schematic representation, figure, table, flowchart, graph, illustration, picture

dial *NOUN* **dials** a circular object with numbers or letters round it
dial *VERB* **dials, dialling, dialled** telephone a number by turning a telephone dial or pressing numbered buttons
dialect *NOUN* **dialects** the words and pronunciations used by people in one district but not in the rest of a country
dialogue *NOUN* **dialogues** **1** the words spoken by characters in a play, film, or story **2** a conversation
dialysis (dy- al- iss- iss) *NOUN* a way of removing harmful substances from the blood by letting it flow through a machine
diameter (dy- am- it- er) *NOUN* **diameters** **1** a line drawn straight across a circle or sphere and passing through its centre **2** the length of this line
diametrically *ADVERB* completely • *diametrically opposite*
diamond *NOUN* **diamonds** **1** a very hard precious stone, a form of carbon, that looks like clear glass **2** a shape with four equal sides and four angles that are not right angles **3** a playing card with red diamond shapes on it
diaper *NOUN* **diapers** (*American*) a baby's nappy
diaphanous (dy- af- an- us) *ADJECTIVE* (said about fabric) almost transparent
diaphragm (dy- a- fram) *NOUN* **diaphragms** **1** the muscular layer inside the body that separates the chest from the abdomen and is used in breathing **2** a dome-shaped contraceptive device that fits over the cervix
diarist *NOUN* **diarists** a person who keeps a diary
diarrhoea (dy- a- ree- a) *NOUN* too frequent and too watery emptying of the bowels
diary *NOUN* **diaries** a book in which someone writes down what happens each day
diatribe *NOUN* **diatribes** a strong verbal attack
dice *NOUN* (strictly this is the plural of **die** [2], but it is often used as a singular, plural **dice**) a small cube marked with dots (1 to 6) on its sides, used in games
dice *VERB* **dices, dicing, diced** **1** cut meat, vegetables, etc. into small cubes **2** gamble or take risks with • *dice with death*
dictate *VERB* **dictates, dictating, dictated** **1** speak or read something aloud for someone else to write down **2** give orders in a bossy way
▷ **dictation** *NOUN*
dictates (dik- tayts) *PLURAL NOUN* orders or commands
dictator *NOUN* **dictators** a ruler who has unlimited power
▷ **dictatorial** (dik- ta- tor- ee- al) *ADJECTIVE*
dictatorship *NOUN*
diction *NOUN* **1** a person's way of speaking words • *clear diction* **2** a writer's choice of words
dictionary *NOUN* **dictionaries** a book that contains words in alphabetical order so that you can find out how to spell them and what they mean
didactic (dy- dak- tik) *ADJECTIVE* having the manner of someone who is lecturing people
▷ **didactically** *ADVERB*
diddle *VERB* **diddles, diddling, diddled** (*slang*) cheat or swindle
didn't (*mainly spoken*) did not
die [1] *VERB* **dies, dying, died** **1** stop living or existing **2** stop burning or functioning • *The fire had died down.*
be dying for *or* **to** (*informal*) want to have or

Thesaurus

diary *NOUN* **1** *She kept a diary from the age of ten.* ► journal, chronicle, daily record, log **2** *Put the date in your diary.* ► appointment book, engagement book, organizer, personal organizer

dicey *ADJECTIVE* (*informal*) *Crossing the bridge can be dicey in high winds.* ► risky, chancy, dangerous, hazardous, unsafe, precarious, insecure, tricky, uncertain, unpredictable
AN OPPOSITE IS safe

dictate *VERB* **1** *He dictated a letter to his secretary.* ► read out, say aloud, recite, utter **2** *She wasn't going to let him dictate how she wore her hair.* ► prescribe, lay down, direct, order, ordain, impose, command, decree, enforce, give orders about, make the rules about, (*informal*) lay down the law about **3 dictate to** *He does rather tend to dictate to his friends.* ► order about, boss, tyrannize, bully, domineer, lord it over, (*more informal*) push around, (*more informal*) walk all over

dictator *NOUN* *what I would do if I were dictator for a day* ► tyrant, despot, autocrat, oppressor, (*more informal*) Big Brother

dictatorial *ADJECTIVE* *a dictatorial regime* ► autocratic, authoritarian, (*informal*) bossy, despotic, totalitarian, tyrannical, domineering, oppressive, absolute, intolerant, overbearing, repressive, undemocratic
AN OPPOSITE IS democratic

dictionary *NOUN* *a word that was not in their dictionary* ► lexicon, glossary, vocabulary, wordbook, wordfinder, thesaurus

die *VERB* **1** *He was sixteen when his father died.* ► pass away, pass on, lose your life, meet your end, breathe your last, expire, (*more formal*) decease, (*more informal*) snuff it, (*more informal*) bite the dust, (*more informal*) kick the bucket **2** *Hopes of a peaceful settlement are*

do something very much • *We are all dying to see you again.*

die[2] *NOUN* singular of **dice**

die[3] *NOUN* **dies** a device that stamps a design on coins etc. or that cuts or moulds metal

diehard *NOUN* **diehards** a person who obstinately refuses to give up old ideas or policies

diesel (dee- zel) *NOUN* **diesels 1** an engine that works by burning oil in compressed air **2** fuel for this kind of engine

diet[1] *NOUN* **diets 1** special meals that someone eats in order to be healthy or to lose weight **2** the sort of foods usually eaten by a person or animal

diet *VERB* **diets, dieting, dieted** keep to a diet

diet[2] *NOUN* **diets** the parliament of certain countries (e.g. Japan)

dietitian (dy- it- ish- an) *NOUN* **dietitians** an expert in diet and nutrition

differ *VERB* **differs, differing, differed 1** be different **2** disagree

difference *NOUN* **differences 1** being different; the way in which things differ **2** the remainder left after one number is subtracted from another • *The difference between 8 and 3 is 5.* **3** a disagreement

different *ADJECTIVE* unlike; not the same
▷ **differently** *ADVERB*

USAGE It is regarded as more acceptable to say *different from* rather than *different to*, which is common in less formal use. The phrase *different than* is used in American English but not in standard British English.

differential *NOUN* **differentials 1** a difference in wages between one group of workers and another **2** a differential gear

differential gear *NOUN* **differential gears** a system of gears that makes a vehicle's driving wheels revolve at different speeds when going round corners

differentiate *VERB* **differentiates, differentiating, differentiated 1** be a difference between things; make one thing different from another • *What are the features that differentiate one breed from another?* **2** distinguish; recognize differences • *We do not differentiate between them.*
▷ **differentiation** *NOUN*

difficult *ADJECTIVE* needing a lot of effort or skill; not easy

Thesaurus

dying. ► fade, dwindle, sink, disappear, vanish, wither, melt away, dissolve **3** *The engine spluttered and died.* ► fail, cut out, stall

diet *NOUN* **1** *You need a healthy diet.* ► nutrition, nourishment, nutriment, food, fare **2** *His doctor put him on a diet.* ► dietary regime, regimen, abstinence, fast

differ *VERB* **1** *Opinions on the matter differed.* ► vary, diverge, be different **2** *Our beliefs differ from those of other religious groups.* ► diverge, vary, deviate, be different, contrast (with) AN OPPOSITE IS conform (to) **3** *The ministers differed about what to do next.* ► disagree, argue, dispute, dissent, clash, conflict, be at odds, oppose each other, contradict each other, fall out, quarrel AN OPPOSITE IS agree

difference *NOUN* *There is a big difference in their ages.* ► dissimilarity, divergence, contrast, disparity, discrepancy, distinction, diversity, gap, variety, inconsistency, incompatibility, differential, differentiation, incongruity
an opposite is similarity

difference of opinion *The brothers were trying to resolve their difference of opinion.*
► disagreement, misunderstanding, dispute, argument, clash, conflict, controversy, debate, disharmony, dissent, quarrel, strife, tiff, wrangle

different *ADJECTIVE* **1** *There were many different answers to the question.* ► dissimilar, unlike, unalike, diverging, divergent, varying, deviating, opposed, inconsistent, incompatible, contradictory, contrary, clashing OPPOSITES ARE identical, similar **2** *Everything about the house looked different.* ► changed, altered, transformed, strange, unfamiliar AN OPPOSITE IS unchanging **3** *We want to try something different.* ► unusual, unorthodox, uncommon, new, fresh, original, unconventional, unique, abnormal, extraordinary, irregular
AN OPPOSITE IS conventional **4** *Every person's fingerprint is different.* ► distinct, unique, distinctive, individual, special, peculiar, personal, particular, specific
OPPOSITES ARE identical, indistinguishable

differentiate *VERB* *It was hard to differentiate fact from fiction.* ► distinguish, tell apart, tell the difference between, discriminate between

difficult *ADJECTIVE* **1** *a difficult problem* ► complicated, complex, hard, intricate, involved, intractable, abstruse, obscure, advanced, perplexing, problematical, baffling, deep, enigmatic, (*more informal*) thorny, (*more informal*) tricky OPPOSITES ARE easy, straightforward **2** *a difficult climb; a difficult task* ► hard, arduous, laborious, demanding, strenuous, tough, formidable, wearisome, burdensome, exacting, challenging
OPPOSITES ARE easy, light **3** *difficult neighbours; a difficult child* ► unmanageable, troublesome, trying, tiresome, uncooperative, intractable,

difficulty *NOUN* **difficulties** **1** being difficult **2** something that causes a problem

diffident (dif- id- ent) *ADJECTIVE* shy and not self-confident; hesitating to put yourself or your ideas forward
▷ **diffidently** *ADVERB* **diffidence** *NOUN*

diffract *VERB* **diffracts, diffracting, diffracted** break up a beam of light etc.
▷ **diffraction** *NOUN*

diffuse (dif- yooz) *VERB* **diffuses, diffusing, diffused** **1** spread something widely or thinly • *diffused lighting* **2** mix slowly • *diffusing gases*
▷ **diffusion** *NOUN*

diffuse (dif- yooss) *ADJECTIVE* **1** spread widely; not concentrated **2** using many words; not concise
▷ **diffusely** *ADVERB* **diffuseness** *NOUN*

dig *VERB* **digs, digging, dug** **1** break up soil and move it; make a hole or tunnel by moving soil **2** poke something in • *Dig a knife into it.* **3** seek or discover by investigating • *We dug up some facts.*
▷ **digger** *NOUN*

dig *NOUN* **digs** **1** a piece of digging, especially an archaeological excavation **2** a poke **3** a critical remark

digest (dy- jest) *VERB* **digests, digesting, digested** **1** soften and change food in the stomach etc. so that the body can absorb it **2** take information into your mind and think it over
▷ **digestible** *ADJECTIVE* **digestion** *NOUN*

digest (dy- jest) *NOUN* **digests** a summary of news, information, etc.

digestive *ADJECTIVE* to do with digestion • *the digestive system*

digestive biscuit *NOUN* **digestive biscuits** a wholemeal biscuit (because it is supposed to be easy to digest)

digit (dij- it) *NOUN* **digits** **1** any of the numbers from 0 to 9 **2** a finger or toe

digital *ADJECTIVE* **1** to do with or using digits **2** (said about a watch or clock) showing the time with a row of figures **3** (said about a computer, recording, etc.) storing the data or sound as a series of binary digits

dignified *ADJECTIVE* having dignity

dignitary *NOUN* **dignitaries** an important official

dignity *NOUN* a calm and serious manner
beneath your dignity not considered worthy enough for you to do

dilapidated *ADJECTIVE* falling to pieces
▷ **dilapidation** *NOUN*

Thesaurus

unruly, unhelpful, perverse
OPPOSITES ARE manageable, tractable, accommodating

difficulty *NOUN* **1** *They found themselves in some difficulty.* ► trouble, distress, hardship, adversity, need, predicament, embarrassment, (*more informal*) fix, (*more informal*) mess **2** *The cost of the holiday might be a difficulty.* ► problem, complication, snag, obstacle, hindrance, stumbling block, hurdle, pitfall, (*more informal*) headache, (*more informal*) hiccup

diffidence *NOUN* *She replied with some diffidence.* ► reserve, shyness, bashfulness, timidity, modesty, humility, hesitancy, uncertainty, unassertiveness, self-consciousness

diffident *ADJECTIVE* *a diffident smile* ► shy, coy, reserved, bashful, sheepish, inhibited, embarrassed, modest, self-conscious, hesitant, timid, retiring OPPOSITES ARE assertive, forward, bold, confident

dig *VERB* **1** *The little dog was digging a hole in the garden.* ► burrow, excavate, scoop, tunnel, gouge out, hollow out, mine, quarry, delve **2** *Dinah dug him in the ribs.* ► poke, prod, jab, nudge, shove
dig up **1** *The police dug up the remains.* ► disinter, extricate, exhume **2** *Can you dig up some more information?* ► uncover, find out, discover

digest *VERB* **1** *The food is stodgy and difficult to digest.* ► absorb, assimilate, process, dissolve, break down **2** *There is a lot of information to digest.* ► take in, consider, absorb, ponder, study, understand

digit *NOUN* **1** *Add up the digits.* ► numeral, figure, number, integer **2** *We tried to bring the blood back to our frozen digits.* ► finger, toe, extremity

dignified *ADJECTIVE* *Dr McNab combined an air of authority with a calm and dignified manner.* ► stately, solemn, noble, majestic, imposing, distinguished, honourable, becoming, august, proper, grand, grave, decorous, sedate
AN OPPOSITE IS undignified

dignity *NOUN* **1** *They accepted their misfortune with great dignity.* ► calmness, decorum, gravity, propriety, self-respect, eminence **2** *the dignity of a state occasion* ► majesty, grandeur, formality, solemnity, stateliness, magnificence, glory, greatness, honour, importance, nobility, pride, respectability, seriousness

digs *PLURAL NOUN* (*informal*) *My father paid for my digs in Paddington.* ► lodgings, room(s), accommodation, living quarters, bedsit, flat, (*more informal*) place, (*more informal*) pad

dilemma (dil- em- a) *NOUN* **dilemmas** a situation where someone has to choose between two or more possible actions, each of which will bring difficulties
USAGE Do not use **dilemma** to mean simply a problem or difficult situation. There should be some idea of choosing between two (or perhaps more) things.

diligent (dil- ij- ent) *ADJECTIVE* hard-working
▷ **diligently** *ADVERB* **diligence** *NOUN*

dilute *VERB* **dilutes, diluting, diluted** make a liquid weaker by adding water or other liquid
▷ **dilution** *NOUN*

dilute *ADJECTIVE* diluted • *a dilute acid*

dim *ADJECTIVE* **dimmer, dimmest** **1** not bright or clear; only faintly lit **2** (*informal*) stupid
▷ **dimly** *ADVERB* **dimness** *NOUN*

dim *VERB* **dims, dimming, dimmed** make or become dim
▷ **dimmer** *NOUN*

dimension *NOUN* **dimensions** **1** a measurement such as length, width, area, or volume **2** size or extent
▷ **dimensional** *ADJECTIVE*

diminish *VERB* **diminishes, diminishing, diminished** make or become smaller
▷ **diminution** *NOUN*

diminutive (dim- in- yoo- tiv) *ADJECTIVE* very small

dimple *NOUN* **dimples** a small hollow or dent, especially in the skin
▷ **dimpled** *ADJECTIVE*

din *NOUN* a loud annoying noise

dine *VERB* **dines, dining, dined** (*formal*) have dinner
▷ **diner** *NOUN*

dinghy (ding- ee) *NOUN* **dinghies** a kind of small boat [from Hindi *dingi* = a small river boat]

dingy (din- jee) *ADJECTIVE* dirty-looking
▷ **dingily** *ADVERB* **dinginess** *NOUN*

dinner *NOUN* **dinners** **1** the main meal of the day, either at midday or in the evening **2** a formal evening meal in honour of something

dinosaur (dy- noss- or) *NOUN* **dinosaurs** a prehistoric reptile, often of enormous size

diocese (dy- oss- iss) *NOUN* **dioceses** a district under the care of a bishop

dioxide *NOUN* an oxide with two atoms of oxygen to one of another element • *carbon dioxide*

dip *VERB* **dips, dipping, dipped** put down or go down, especially into a liquid

Thesaurus

dilapidated *ADJECTIVE* *a row of dilapidated Victorian houses* ► rundown, ramshackle, decrepit, tumbledown, rickety, derelict, broken down, crumbling, neglected, ruined, decayed, tottering, uncared for
OPPOSITES ARE smart, well maintained

dilemma *NOUN* *The need to earn money while still studying placed him in a dilemma.* ► quandary, difficulty, predicament, awkward situation, (*more informal*) catch-22

diligent *ADJECTIVE* *She had been diligent about her piano lessons.* ► conscientious, industrious, hard-working, painstaking, thorough, meticulous, punctilious, accurate, attentive, dedicated, rigorous, careful, dutiful, unflagging, assiduous, scrupulous
OPPOSITES ARE careless, irresponsible, lazy

dim *ADJECTIVE* **1** *dim shapes in the distance; dim memories of their childhood* ► vague, indistinct, shadowy, unclear, fuzzy, blurred
OPPOSITES ARE distinct, clear **2** *a dim room* ► dark, sombre, dingy, gloomy, murky, dismal
AN OPPOSITE IS bright **3** (*informal*) *You probably think I'm awfully dim.* ► stupid, dense, obtuse, (*more informal*) thick

dim *VERB* **1** *The sky slowly dimmed.* ► grow dark, darken, blacken, dull, cloud over **2** *He insisted on dimming the lights.* ► turn down, fade, lower, dip, shade, obscure OPPOSITES ARE turn up, brighten

dimensions *PLURAL NOUN* *a palace of huge dimensions* ► proportions, magnitude, size, scale, capacity, extent, scope

diminish *VERB* **1** *His angry feelings diminished in time.* ► decrease, reduce, lessen, decline, subside, wane, become less, depreciate, dwindle, peter out, shrink, shrivel, contract
AN OPPOSITE IS increase **2** *We must not diminish their achievement.* ► belittle, disparage, demean, minimize, undervalue, devalue
OPPOSITES ARE exaggerate, magnify

dimple *NOUN* *Her smile produced an instant dimple in each cheek.* ► hollow, dip, depression, dint, cleft

din *NOUN* *It was hard to hear anything above the din.* ► uproar, racket, rumpus, commotion, hubbub, clamour, tumult, hullabaloo, noise, outcry, pandemonium, row, shouting

dingy *ADJECTIVE* *The front door opened on to a dingy hallway.* ► gloomy, dismal, dim, dreary, sombre, dark, drab, dull, murky
OPPOSITES ARE bright, cheerful

dip *VERB* **1** *She dipped her hand in the water.* ► immerse, lower, plunge, submerge, douse, dunk, drop, duck **2** *The path dips towards the village.* ► descend, slope down, go down,

dip *NOUN* **dips** **1** dipping **2** a downward slope **3** a quick swim **4** a substance into which things are dipped

diploma *NOUN* **diplomas** a certificate awarded by a college etc. for skill in a particular subject

diplomacy *NOUN* **1** the work of making agreements with other countries **2** skill in dealing with people and gently persuading them to agree to things; tact

diplomat *NOUN* **diplomats** **1** a person employed in diplomacy on behalf of his or her country **2** a tactful person
▷ **diplomatic** *ADJECTIVE*

direct *ADJECTIVE* **1** as straight as possible **2** going straight to the point; frank **3** exact • *the direct opposite*

direct *VERB* **directs, directing, directed** **1** tell someone the way **2** guide or aim in a certain direction **3** control or manage **4** order • *He directed his troops to advance.*

direct current *NOUN* electric current flowing only in one direction

direction *NOUN* **directions** **1** directing **2** the line along which something moves or faces
▷ **directional** *ADJECTIVE*

directly *ADVERB* immediately; by a direct route

direct object *NOUN* **direct objects** the word that receives the action of the verb In *'she hit him'*, 'him' is the direct object

director *NOUN* **directors** **1** a person who is in charge of something **2** a person who decides how a film, programme, or play should be made or performed

directory *NOUN* **directories** a book containing a list of people with their telephone numbers, addresses, etc.

direct speech *NOUN* someone's words written down exactly in the way they were said

dirge *NOUN* **dirges** a slow sad song

dirt *NOUN* earth, soil; anything that is not clean [from an Old Norse word meaning 'excrement']

Thesaurus

subside, dive, slump **3** *He would just smile and dip his head a little.* ► lower, drop

dip *NOUN* **1** *We reached a dip in the ground.* ► slope, incline, depression, declivity, dent, hollow, fall, hole, concavity **2** *There will be a dip in sales after Christmas.* ► decrease, fall, decline, downturn, falling off **3** *He likes a quick dip in the river.* ► bathe, swim, dive, plunge, splash, paddle

diplomacy *NOUN* **1** *They gave up the war and tried diplomacy.* ► negotiation, discussion, consultation, dialogue, statesmanship, statecraft **2** *Her answer combined honesty and diplomacy.* ► tact, tactfulness, sensitivity, politeness, discretion, delicacy

diplomatic *ADJECTIVE* *He tried to be diplomatic but the news was not good.* ► tactful, sensitive, considerate, discreet, subtle, polite, understanding, politic, careful, delicate, judicious, prudent, thoughtful
OPPOSITES ARE tactless, outspoken

dire *ADJECTIVE* **1** *The economy was in a dire state.* ► terrible, dreadful, awful, appalling, disastrous, catastrophic **2** *a dire warning* ► ominous, portentous, dreadful, gloomy, grim **3** *in dire need of help* ► urgent, desperate, pressing, sore, serious, grave

direct *ADJECTIVE* **1** *Travel by the direct route.* ► straight, undeviating, shortest, quickest, nonstop, unswerving AN OPPOSITE IS indirect **2** *We want a direct answer.* ► straightforward, honest, frank, candid, unequivocal, sincere, blunt AN OPPOSITE IS evasive **3** *The sisters are direct opposites in character.* ► absolute, exact, complete, diametrical, downright, thorough, utter, head-on, (*informal*) out-and-out

direct *VERB* **1** *Earlier in her career she directed a child-growth project.* ► manage, run, administer, be in charge of, be responsible for, control, preside over, lead, organize **2** *An official directed them to the meeting room.* ► show the way, tell the way, indicate the way, give directions to, guide, point, route **3** *The books are mainly directed at teenagers.* ► target, aim, point, design (for), orient (towards) **4** *The judge directed the jury to return a verdict of not guilty.* ► instruct, order, tell, command, require, advise, charge, bid, enjoin

direction *NOUN* **1** *She left an hour later and went off in another direction.* ► route, way, course, line, bearing, orientation **2** (**directions**) *The nursing staff receive regular directions on new medicines.* ► instructions, guidelines, guidance, indications, briefing, plans, orders

directly *ADVERB* **1** *She will join us directly.* ► immediately, at once, instantly, right away, straight away, in a moment, forthwith, presently **2** *You can fly directly from here to Montreal.* ► straight, immediately, by a direct route

director *NOUN* *the directors of the main London museums* ► head, chief, manager, administrator, principal, (*more informal*) boss

dirt *NOUN* **1** *The area in front of the house was covered in dirt.* ► grime, filth, muck, refuse, rubbish, garbage, dust, slime, sludge, mess, mire, pollution **2** *Chickens were scratching about in the dirt.* ► earth, soil, mud, loam, clay

dirty ADJECTIVE **dirtier, dirtiest 1** not clean; soiled **2** unfair; dishonourable • *a dirty trick* **3** indecent; obscene
▷ **dirtily** ADVERB **dirtiness** NOUN

dis- PREFIX (changing to **dif-** before words beginning with *f*, and to **di-** before some consonants) **1** not; the reverse of (as in *dishonest*) **2** apart; separated (as in *disarm, disperse*)

disabled ADJECTIVE unable to use part of your body properly because of illness or injury
▷ **disability** NOUN **disablement** NOUN

disadvantage NOUN **disadvantages** something that hinders or is unhelpful

disagree VERB **disagrees, disagreeing, disagreed 1** have or express a different opinion from someone **2** have a bad effect • *Rich food disagrees with me.*
▷ **disagreement** NOUN

disagreeable ADJECTIVE unpleasant

disappear VERB **disappears, disappearing, disappeared** stop being visible; vanish
▷ **disappearance** NOUN

disappoint VERB **disappoints, disappointing, disappointed** fail to do what someone hopes for
▷ **disappointment** NOUN

Thesaurus

dirty ADJECTIVE **1** *a dirty room; dirty clothes* ► filthy, grimy, grubby, soiled, stained, mucky, dingy, unwashed, squalid AN OPPOSITE IS clean **2** *dirty water* ► impure, muddy, murky, polluted, untreated, cloudy AN OPPOSITE IS pure **3** *dirty tricks* ► corrupt, dishonest, illegal, mean, treacherous, unfair, ungentlemanly, unsporting, (*more informal*) low-down OPPOSITES ARE honest, sporting **4** *a dirty joke* ► rude, indecent, obscene, coarse, crude, smutty, suggestive, improper, risqué, offensive, vulgar AN OPPOSITE IS clean **5** *a dirty look* ► angry, hostile, resentful, peeved, black

dirty VERB *Try not to dirty the towels.* ► soil, stain, mess up, spoil, taint, tarnish AN OPPOSITE IS clean

disability NOUN *A disability can make the most routine tasks extremely difficult.* ► handicap, incapacity, infirmity, disablement, impairment, affliction, complaint, abnormality, weakness

disable VERB **1** *The injury disabled her for several months.* ► incapacitate, injure, immobilize, cripple, debilitate, enfeeble, handicap, impair, lame, maim, paralyse, weaken, (*informal*) hamstring **2** *The army succeeded in disabling the device.* ► incapacitate, put out of action, deactivate, disarm, make useless, stop working OPPOSITES ARE restore, repair

disabled ADJECTIVE *The house caters well for disabled visitors.* ► handicapped, physically handicapped, physically impaired, incapacitated, immobilized, bedridden, crippled, deformed, lame, paralysed AN OPPOSITE IS able-bodied

disadvantage NOUN *Heavy traffic is a major disadvantage of road travel.* ► drawback, snag, downside, inconvenience, weakness, nuisance, handicap, hardship, liability, privation, trouble, hindrance, impediment, (*more informal*) minus

disagree VERB **1** *We constantly disagree.* ► dissent, differ, argue, conflict, clash, fall out, quarrel, squabble, wrangle, bicker AN OPPOSITE IS agree **2 disagree with** *She disagrees with everything he says.* ► oppose, contradict, counter, argue with, dissent from, object to, take issue with, be at variance with, deviate from **3 disagree with** *Onions disagree with me.* ► make ill, make unwell, upset

disagreeable ADJECTIVE *a disagreeable taste; a disagreeable person* ► unpleasant, nasty, horrible, horrid, offensive, repugnant, revolting, repellent

disagreement NOUN **1** *The two brothers had a disagreement.* ► argument, altercation, clash, quarrel, dispute, contretemps, misunderstanding, squabble, wrangle, (*more informal*) tiff, (*more informal*) barney AN OPPOSITE IS agreement **2** *There is some disagreement between the two versions of the story.* ► difference, disparity, variance, dissimilarity, discrepancy, incompatibility, divergence

disappear VERB **1** *The crowd rapidly disappeared.* ► vanish, disperse, recede, clear, evaporate, fade, melt away, wane, dissolve, dwindle, cease to exist, ebb **2** *She disappeared round a corner.* ► go, pass, withdraw, run away, walk away, depart, retire, escape, flee, fly AN OPPOSITE IS appear **3** *a way of life that has almost disappeared* ► die out, become extinct, vanish, perish OPPOSITES ARE emerge, appear

disappoint VERB **1** *We will try not to disappoint you.* ► let down, fail, dissatisfy, disillusion, disenchant, dishearten AN OPPOSITE IS satisfy **2** *In the end their hopes were disappointed.* ► thwart, frustrate, dash, defeat, foil

disappointed ADJECTIVE *I was disappointed when you didn't come.* ► saddened, unhappy, upset, let down, dissatisfied, dejected, despondent, downcast, downhearted, crestfallen, discontented, disenchanted, disgruntled, disillusioned, frustrated OPPOSITES ARE satisfied, contented

disappointment NOUN **1** *She could not hide her feeling of disappointment.* ► regret, sorrow, sadness, displeasure, dissatisfaction, disapproval, dismay, disillusionment,

disapprove *VERB* **disapproves, disapproving, disapproved** have an unfavourable opinion of something; not approve
▷ **disapproval** *NOUN*

disarm *VERB* **disarms, disarming, disarmed** **1** reduce the size of armed forces **2** take away someone's weapons **3** overcome a person's anger or doubt • *Her friendliness disarmed their suspicions.*
▷ **disarming** *ADJECTIVE*

disarmament *NOUN* reduction of a country's armed forces or weapons

disaster *NOUN* **disasters** **1** a very bad accident or misfortune **2** a complete failure
▷ **disastrous** *ADJECTIVE* **disastrously** *ADVERB*

disbelief *NOUN* refusal or unwillingness to believe something
▷ **disbelieve** *VERB*

disc *NOUN* **discs** **1** any round flat object **2** a layer of cartilage between vertebrae in the spine **3** a CD or record

discerning *ADJECTIVE* perceptive; showing good judgement

discharge *VERB* **discharges, discharging, discharged** **1** release a person **2** send something out • *discharge smoke* **3** pay or do what was agreed • *discharge the debt*

disciple *NOUN* **disciples** **1** a person who accepts the teachings of another whom he or she regards as a leader **2** any of the original followers of Jesus Christ

Thesaurus

discontent **2** *The exam result had been a disappointment.* ► let-down, setback, misfortune, blow, anticlimax

disapproval *NOUN* *Her face clearly showed her disapproval.* ► dislike, displeasure, dissatisfaction, criticism, anger, disapprobation, disfavour, dissent, reproach, hostility, censure, condemnation, reprimand AN OPPOSITE IS approval

disapprove *VERB* **disapprove of** *They disapprove of gambling.* ► dislike, condemn, deplore, deprecate, object to, frown on, look askance at, be displeased by, take exception to, reject, criticize, denounce, censure, disparage, make unwelcome, regret, (*more informal*) take a dim view of AN OPPOSITE IS approve of

disarray *NOUN* *The room was by now in some disarray. The opposition parties were in disarray.* ► disorder, confusion, chaos, mess, muddle

disaster *NOUN* **1** *the world's worst air disaster* ► catastrophe, calamity, tragedy, misfortune, mishap, affliction, cataclysm, blow **2** (*informal*) *It would be a complete disaster for him if she came back.* ► failure, fiasco, catastrophe, setback, reversal AN OPPOSITE IS success

disastrous *ADJECTIVE* *a disastrous fire; a disastrous choice* ► catastrophic, calamitous, cataclysmic, devastating, ruinous, terrible, tragic, crippling, destructive, dire, dreadful, fatal, bad OPPOSITES ARE fortunate, successful

disband *VERB* *The team disbanded once the work was done.* ► break up, disperse, scatter, separate, part company, go your own way

disbelief *NOUN* *He looked at her in disbelief.* ► incredulity, distrust, scepticism, doubt, mistrust, suspicion OPPOSITES ARE belief, credence

disbelieve *VERB* *He disbelieved everything we said.* ► doubt, mistrust, reject, suspect, discount, discredit, have no faith in, be sceptical of AN OPPOSITE IS believe

disc *NOUN* **1** *the disc of the sun* ► circle, round, ring **2** *a new disc from the same band* ► CD, compact disc, record, album, single

discard *VERB* *I decided to discard some old clothes.* ► get rid of, dispose of, dispense with, throw away, cast off, reject, eliminate, jettison, scrap, shed, dump, (*more informal*) chuck away, (*more informal*) ditch

discern *VERB* *We discerned a tower in the distance.* ► perceive, spot, make out, pick out, detect, recognize, distinguish, become aware of

discernible *ADJECTIVE* *His face was clearly discernible to her all the time.* ► visible, perceptible, observable, noticeable, distinct, manifest, conspicuous

discharge *VERB* **1** *Factories along the river were discharging thick smoke.* ► emit, give out, pour out, give off, exude, belch, release, secrete, produce, send out, eject, expel **2** *He discharged the gun by accident.* ► fire, shoot, detonate, let off, explode **3** *Three employees were discharged on the same day.* ► dismiss, fire, make redundant, remove, sack, throw out **4** *The authorities discharged him from prison on a Sunday.* ► release, liberate, free, allow to leave, dismiss, excuse

discharge *NOUN* **1** *discharge from prison* ► release, liberation **2** *the discharge of a duty* ► accomplishment, execution, completion, fulfilment, achievement

disciple *NOUN* *a disciple of Aristotle* ► follower, pupil, adherent, devotee, student, supporter, acolyte, admirer, apostle

discipline *NOUN* **disciplines** **1** orderly and obedient behaviour **2** a subject for study
▷ **disciplinary** (dis- ip- lin- er- ee) *ADJECTIVE*

disc jockey *NOUN* **disc jockeys** a person who plays recorded music on the radio or at a disco or nightclub

disco *NOUN* **discos** a place where CDs or records are played for dancing

discolour *VERB* **discolours, discolouring, discoloured** spoil a thing's colour; stain
▷ **discoloration** *NOUN*

disconcert (dis- kon- sert) *VERB* **disconcerts, disconcerting, disconcerted** make a person feel uneasy

disconnect *VERB* **disconnects, disconnecting, disconnected** break a connection; detach
• *The phone has been disconnected.*
▷ **disconnection** *NOUN*

disconsolate (dis- **kon**- sol- at) *ADJECTIVE* disappointed

discontent *NOUN* lack of contentment; dissatisfaction
▷ **discontented** *ADJECTIVE* **discontentment** *NOUN*

discontinue *VERB* **discontinues, discontinuing, discontinued** put an end to something

discord *NOUN* **discords** **1** disagreement; quarrelling **2** musical notes sounded together and producing a harsh or unpleasant sound
▷ **discordant** *ADJECTIVE*

discount *NOUN* **discounts** an amount by which a price is reduced

discount *VERB* **discounts, discounting, discounted** ignore or disregard something
• *We cannot discount the possibility.*

discourage *VERB* **discourages, discouraging, discouraged** **1** take away someone's enthusiasm or confidence **2** try to persuade someone not to do something
▷ **discouragement** *NOUN*

Thesaurus

discipline *NOUN* **1** *Good financial discipline is important.* ► control, regulation, order, authority, orderliness, management, self-control, strictness, system, training, obedience **2** *Their mother had been responsible for administering discipline.* ► punishment, chastisement, correction **3** *Sociology is a fairly new discipline.* ► field of study, field, branch of knowledge, speciality

discipline *VERB* **1** *Families have different ways of disciplining their children.* ► train, control, instruct, educate, restrain, break in, drill **2** *Several staff have been disciplined.* ► punish, reprimand, reprove, penalize, chasten, chastise

disclaim *VERB* *The company disclaimed all responsibility for the pollution.* ► deny, reject, renounce, repudiate, disown, forswear OPPOSITES ARE acknowledge, accept, admit

disclose *VERB* *This information should not be disclosed to anyone outside this room.* ► divulge, reveal, communicate, make known, pass on

discomfort *NOUN* *Her arm felt numb but she managed to hide the discomfort.* ► pain, soreness, ache, irritation, distress, hardship AN OPPOSITE IS comfort

disconcerting *ADJECTIVE* *He answered all the questions with disconcerting honesty.* ► unsettling, unnerving, off-putting, confusing, disturbing, perplexing, upsetting, worrying AN OPPOSITE IS reassuring

disconnect *VERB* **1** *The power company had disconnected the supply.* ► cut off, break off, stop OPPOSITES ARE reconnect, restore **2** *The engine was disconnected at Crewe.* ► uncouple, detach, disengage, decouple, separate OPPOSITES ARE attach, connect **3** *Televisions should be disconnected at night.* ► unplug, deactivate OPPOSITES ARE connect, plug in

disconnected *ADJECTIVE* *a disconnected argument* ► incoherent, disjointed, garbled, confused, disorganized, rambling, uncoordinated OPPOSITES ARE coherent, logical

discount *NOUN* *a £5 discount on the sticker price* ► reduction, deduction, concession, cut, allowance, rebate, (*more informal*) markdown

discount *VERB* *We discounted all these rumours.* ► disregard, reject, disbelieve, overlook, ignore

discourage *VERB* **1** *The audience was discouraged from asking questions.* ► deter, dissuade, restrain, prevent, hinder, put off, warn off **2** *Her cool response discouraged them.* ► dishearten, dispirit, demoralize, disappoint, dismay, depress, unnerve, intimidate

discouragement *NOUN* *Strong police presence is a discouragement to crime.* ► deterrent, disincentive, constraint, hindrance, impediment, restraint, obstacle, setback, (*informal*) damper (on) AN OPPOSITE IS encouragement

discouraging *ADJECTIVE* *The latest news is discouraging.* ► depressing, dispiriting, disheartening, demoralizing, disappointing, daunting

discourse *NOUN* (with the stress on *dis-*) **1** *They continued their discourse well into the night.* ► conversation, disquisition, literature, speech **2** *a discourse on semantics* ► dissertation, essay, treatise, monograph, thesis, paper

discover *VERB* **discovers, discovering, discovered** **1** find or find out **2** be the first person to find something
▷ **discoverer** *NOUN* **discovery** *NOUN*

discredit *VERB* **discredits, discrediting, discredited** **1** cause something to be doubted **2** damage someone's reputation

discredit *NOUN* damage to someone's reputation
▷ **discreditable** *ADJECTIVE*

discreet *ADJECTIVE* **1** not giving away secrets **2** not showy
▷ **discreetly** *ADVERB*
USAGE Do not confuse with **discrete**.

discrepancy (dis- **krep**- an- see) *NOUN* **discrepancies** lack of agreement between things which should be the same • *There are several discrepancies in the two accounts.*

discrete *ADJECTIVE* separate; distinct from each other
USAGE Do not confuse with **discreet**.

discretion (dis- **kresh**- on) *NOUN* **1** being discreet; keeping secrets • *I hope I can count on your discretion.* **2** freedom to decide things and take action according to your own judgement • *You can use your discretion.*

discriminate *VERB* **discriminates, discriminating, discriminated** **1** notice the differences between things; distinguish; prefer one thing to another **2** treat people differently or unfairly, e.g. because of their race, sex, or religion
▷ **discrimination** *NOUN*

Thesaurus

discourse *VERB* (with the stress on *-course*) *He likes to discourse on his favourite topics.* ► speak, hold forth, expatiate, pontificate

discourteous *ADJECTIVE* *It would be discourteous to refuse.* ► rude, impolite, bad-mannered, ill-mannered, disrespectful, uncivil, churlish, ungracious, boorish

discourtesy *NOUN* *He had committed the grave discourtesy of not turning up for the speech.* ► rudeness, bad manners, ill manners, disrespect, incivility, churlishness

discover *VERB* **1** *The children had discovered a secret door at the bottom of the garden.* ► find, locate, come across, uncover, chance on, stumble on **2** *We discovered that he had been lying.* ► find out, learn, realize, come to know, come to realize, work out, perceive **3** *Faraday discovered electricity.* ► originate, develop, pioneer, invent USAGE Note that *discover* and *invent* do not mean quite the same: you discover something natural that was always there (e.g. electricity), and you invent something new that did not exist before (e.g. television)

discovery *NOUN* **1** *a major new discovery* ► invention, innovation, revelation, breakthrough, disclosure, exploration, (*more informal*) find **2** *the discovery of the body* ► finding, location, locating, detection, uncovering, unearthing

discredit *VERB* **1** *His enemies are looking for information that might discredit him.* ► disparage, defame, disgrace, smear, slander, dishonour, ruin the reputation of, slur, vilify **2** *The new evidence discredits the witness's story.* ► disprove, prove false, invalidate, challenge, refute, raise doubts about, (*more informal*) explode, (*more informal*) show up

discreet *ADJECTIVE* USAGE Do not confuse this word with *discrete*, which means 'distinct' or 'separate'. *I made a few discreet enquiries.* ► careful, circumspect, cautious, guarded, wary, tactful, judicious, prudent, considerate, delicate, diplomatic, sensitive, thoughtful, polite, politic OPPOSITES ARE indiscreet, rash

discrepancy *NOUN* *There is a discrepancy between the two versions of the story.* ► inconsistency, difference, disparity, variance, conflict, dissimilarity, divergence, incompatibility, incongruity
AN OPPOSITE IS similarity

discrete *ADJECTIVE* USAGE Do not confuse this word with *discreet*, which means 'careful' or 'cautious'. *teaching the course in discrete units* ► distinct, separate, individual, detached

discretion *NOUN* **1** *The police conducted their enquiries with discretion.* ► diplomacy, tact, sensitivity, good sense, judgement, maturity, prudence, responsibility, wisdom
AN OPPOSITE IS indiscretion **2** *Payment of interest is at the Bank's discretion.* ► choice, option, judgement, will, wish, preference

discriminate *VERB* **1** *It is hard to discriminate between the two theories.* ► differentiate, distinguish, make a distinction, tell the difference **2** *Some employment practices still discriminate against women.* ► be biased, be prejudiced, show discrimination, be intolerant (towards)

discriminating *ADJECTIVE* *a discriminating art collector* ► discerning, perceptive, astute, judicious, fastidious, critical, particular, selective, (*more informal*) choosy
AN OPPOSITE IS undiscriminating

discrimination *NOUN* **1** *She shows discrimination in her choice of music.* ► discernment, good taste, insight,

discus *NOUN* **discuses** a thick heavy disc thrown in athletic contests

discuss *VERB* **discusses, discussing, discussed** talk with other people about a subject
▷ **discussion** *NOUN*

disease *NOUN* **diseases** an unhealthy condition; an illness
▷ **diseased** *ADJECTIVE*

disembark *VERB* **disembarks, disembarking, disembarked** get off a ship or aircraft
▷ **disembarkation** *NOUN*

disentangle *VERB* **disentangles, disentangling, disentangled** free from tangles or confusion

disfigure *VERB* **disfigures, disfiguring, disfigured** spoil the appearance of a person or thing
▷ **disfigurement** *NOUN*

disgrace *NOUN* **1** shame; loss of approval or respect **2** something that causes shame
▷ **disgraceful** *ADJECTIVE* **disgracefully** *ADVERB*

disgrace *VERB* **disgraces, disgracing, disgraced** bring disgrace on someone

disguise *VERB* **disguises, disguising, disguised** **1** make a person or thing look different in order to deceive people **2** conceal your feelings

disguise *NOUN* **disguises** something used for disguising

disgust *NOUN* a feeling that something is very unpleasant or disgraceful

disgust *VERB* **disgusts, disgusting, disgusted** give someone a feeling of disgust
▷ **disgusted** *ADJECTIVE* **disgusting** *ADJECTIVE*

Thesaurus

judgement, perceptiveness, refinement, selectivity, subtlety, taste **2** *victims of discrimination* ► prejudice, bias, bigotry, intolerance, chauvinism, favouritism, male chauvinism, racism, sexism, unfairness
AN OPPOSITE IS impartiality

discuss *VERB* *It was good to discuss other people's problems.* ► debate, consider, talk about, confer about, consult about, deliberate, examine, deal with

discussion *NOUN* *a lively discussion about funding universities* ► debate, deliberation, conference, dialogue, consultation, conversation, argument, discourse, consideration, examination, exchange of views, symposium, talk

disease *NOUN* *suffering from a disease; a country afflicted by disease* ► illness, sickness, bad health, ailment, malady, disorder, infirmity
RELATED ADJECTIVE morbid

disentangle *VERB* **1** *The cord had a knot that was difficult to disentangle.* ► untangle, undo, untie, untwist, sort out, straighten, unknot, unravel AN OPPOSITE IS entangle **2** *She disentangled his hand from her twisted clothing.* ► free, release, extricate, extract, remove, disengage, liberate, separate
AN OPPOSITE IS enmesh

disfigure *VERB* *A new motorway will disfigure the landscape.* ► mar, scar, deface, deform, mutilate, spoil, damage OPPOSITES ARE enhance, beautify

disgrace *NOUN* **1** *the public disgrace of being prosecuted for shoplifting* ► dishonour, shame, humiliation, ignominy, degradation, slur, stain, stigma, discredit, embarrassment, opprobrium, scandal AN OPPOSITE IS honour **2** (*informal*) *The local facilities for children were a disgrace.* ► outrage, scandal, affront, insult
OPPOSITES ARE credit, asset

disgrace *VERB* *He very nearly disgraced his friends by reciting an improper poem.* ► shame, bring shame on, defame, humiliate, scandalize

disgraceful *ADJECTIVE* *Their behaviour had been disgraceful.* ► shameful, deplorable, shocking, dreadful, despicable, dishonourable, reprehensible, appalling, bad

disguise *NOUN* *She looked quite convincing in her nun's disguise.* ► costume, outfit, impersonation, camouflage, concealment, pretence, cloak, cover, fancy dress, make-up, front, mask, (*more informal*) get-up

disguise *VERB* **1** *Her long sleeves disguised her burns.* ► hide, conceal, cover, mask, screen, shroud, veil, camouflage, dress up, make inconspicuous **2** *He made no attempt to disguise his anger.* ► hide, conceal, cover up, gloss over, misrepresent
disguise yourself as *I changed my identity and disguised myself as one of the locals.* ► dress up as, impersonate, pretend to be, pose as, counterfeit, imitate, mimic, (*more informal*) take off

disgust *NOUN* *I couldn't hide my disgust at his behaviour.* ► revulsion, repugnance, repulsion, abhorrence, distaste, aversion, antipathy, contempt, loathing, detestation, nausea, dislike, hatred OPPOSITES ARE liking, relish

disgust *VERB* *The hospital food disgusted me.* ► revolt, nauseate, offend, appal, repel, sicken, be distasteful to, displease, horrify, outrage, put off, shock, (*more informal*) turn your stomach OPPOSITES ARE please, appeal to

disgusting *ADJECTIVE* *The smell was disgusting. They showed disgusting bigotry.* ► revolting, nauseating, offensive, sickening, loathsome, repugnant, repulsive, unpleasant
OPPOSITES ARE pleasant, appealing, attractive

dish *NOUN* **dishes** **1** a plate or bowl for food **2** food prepared for eating **3** a satellite dish

dish *VERB* **dishes, dishing, dished** (*informal*)
dish out give out portions of something to people

dishevelled (dish- ev- eld) *ADJECTIVE* ruffled and untidy
▷ **dishevelment** *NOUN*

dishonest *ADJECTIVE* not honest
▷ **dishonestly** *ADVERB* **dishonesty** *NOUN*

dishonour *VERB* **dishonours, dishonouring, dishonoured** disgrace someone
▷ **dishonour** *NOUN* **dishonourable** *ADJECTIVE*

disillusion *VERB* **disillusions, disillusioning, disillusioned** get rid of someone's wrong beliefs
▷ **disillusionment** *NOUN*

disinclined *ADJECTIVE* unwilling to do something

disinfect *VERB* **disinfects, disinfecting, disinfected** destroy the germs in something
▷ **disinfection** *NOUN*

disinfectant *NOUN* **disinfectants** a substance used for disinfecting things

disintegrate *VERB* **disintegrates, disintegrating, disintegrated** break up into small parts or pieces
▷ **disintegration** *NOUN*

disinterested *ADJECTIVE* impartial; not influenced by the hope of gaining something yourself • *She gave us some disinterested advice.*
USAGE It is not accepted as part of standard English to use this word as if it meant 'not interested' or 'bored'. If this is what you mean, use **uninterested**.

disjointed *ADJECTIVE* (said about talk or writing) not having parts that fit together well and so difficult to understand

disk *NOUN* **disks** a computer storage device consisting of magnetically coated plates

dislike *VERB* **dislikes, disliking, disliked** not like somebody or something

Thesaurus

dish *NOUN* **1** *He tipped the pasta into a dish.* ► plate, bowl, platter **2** *a nutritious vegetarian dish* ► food, recipe

dish *VERB* (*informal*)
dish out *The children helped by dishing out piles of books.* ► distribute, give out, hand round, deal out, issue
dish up *Shirley was busy dishing up burgers and hot dogs.* ► serve, serve up, provide, dispense

dishearten *VERB* *The result disheartened them so much they almost gave up.* ► discourage, dispirit, dismay, depress, disappoint, deter, put off, sadden OPPOSITES ARE hearten, encourage

dishevelled *ADJECTIVE* *She ran a hand through her dishevelled hair.* ► untidy, bedraggled, disordered, unkempt, scruffy, disarranged, tangled, ruffled, rumpled, slovenly, tousled, uncombed, messy OPPOSITES ARE neat, tidy

dishonest *ADJECTIVE* *Their solicitor proved to be dishonest. a dishonest statement* ► deceitful, untruthful, lying, fraudulent, false, double-dealing, cheating, swindling, corrupt, underhand, untrustworthy, (*more informal*) crooked OPPOSITES ARE honest, truthful

dishonesty *NOUN* *a charge of dishonesty against former colleagues* ► corruption, fraud, fraudulence, cheating, deceit, deception, deviousness, lying, falsity, falsehood, (*more informal*) crookedness, (*more informal*) shadiness AN OPPOSITE IS honesty

dishonour *NOUN* *I have no wish to bring dishonour on you or your family.* ► disgrace, shame, discredit, degradation, humiliation, ignominy, stigma, opprobrium, indignity OPPOSITES ARE honour , credit

dishonourable *ADJECTIVE* *It would be dishonourable to refuse to pay.* ► disgraceful, shameful, discreditable, ignominious, contemptible, reprehensible

dishy *ADJECTIVE* (*informal*) *Judging by the photograph, the author's dishy, too.* ► attractive, good-looking, charming, sexy, appealing

disinfect *VERB* *An aromatic plant is used to disinfect houses where malaria is present.* ► sterilize, sanitize, clean, cleanse, purify, fumigate OPPOSITES ARE infect, contaminate

disinfectant *NOUN* *She wiped the surface down with disinfectant.* ► antiseptic, sterilizer, germicide, carbolic, cleaner

disintegrate *VERB* *The aircraft caught fire and disintegrated in the air.* ► break up, fall apart, fall to pieces, explode, come apart, decompose

disinterested *ADJECTIVE* *Her advice would always be disinterested.* ► impartial, neutral, unbiased, unprejudiced, dispassionate, open-minded, even-handed AN OPPOSITE IS biased
USAGE Note that *disinterested* means 'impartial' and does not mean the same as *uninterested*.

disjointed *ADJECTIVE* *She turned her disjointed thoughts over in her mind.* ► disconnected, incoherent, confused, disordered, unconnected, disorganized, jumbled, rambling, fitful, erratic AN OPPOSITE IS coherent

dislike *VERB* *She dislikes me because I won't do what she says.* ► not like, detest, hate, object to, abhor, disapprove of, despise
AN OPPOSITE IS like

dislike *NOUN* *He had a fear and dislike of big cities.* ► aversion (to), distaste (for), antagonism (to), antipathy (to), contempt (for), disgust (for),

A B C D E F G H I J K L M N O P Q R S T U V W X Y Z

dislocate VERB **dislocates, dislocating, dislocated** **1** move or force a bone from its proper position in one of the joints **2** disrupt • *Fog dislocated the traffic.*
▷ **dislocation** NOUN

dislodge VERB **dislodges, dislodging, dislodged** move or force something from its place

disloyal ADJECTIVE not loyal
▷ **disloyally** ADVERB **disloyalty** NOUN

dismal ADJECTIVE **1** gloomy **2** of poor quality
▷ **dismally** ADVERB

dismantle VERB **dismantles, dismantling, dismantled** take something to pieces

dismay NOUN a feeling of surprise and discouragement
▷ **dismayed** ADJECTIVE

dismiss VERB **dismisses, dismissing, dismissed** **1** send someone away **2** tell a person that you will no longer employ him or her **3** put something out of your thoughts because it is not worth thinking about **4** get a batsman or cricket side out
▷ **dismissal** NOUN **dismissive** ADJECTIVE

dismount VERB **dismounts, dismounting, dismounted** get off a horse or bicycle

disobey VERB **disobeys, disobeying, disobeyed** not obey; disregard orders
▷ **disobedient** ADJECTIVE **disobedience** NOUN

disorder NOUN **disorders** **1** untidiness **2** a disturbance **3** an illness
▷ **disorderly** ADJECTIVE

Thesaurus

revulsion (from), detestation, disapproval, hatred, loathing AN OPPOSITE IS liking

dislodge VERB *Several stones had been dislodged, causing a hazard to passers-by.* ► displace, disarrange, dislocate, disturb, misplace, move, shift, remove, knock out of place, knock out of position

disloyal ADJECTIVE *His colleagues criticized him for being disloyal in his comments.* ► unfaithful, faithless, treacherous, subversive, seditious, dissident, false, traitorous OPPOSITES ARE loyal, faithful

disloyalty NOUN *She felt a sense of guilt, of disloyalty.* ► unfaithfulness, infidelity, betrayal, duplicity, faithlessness, falseness, inconstancy, perfidy, treachery, treason, double-dealing AN OPPOSITE IS loyalty

dismal ADJECTIVE **1** *She led them into a dismal little room.* ► gloomy, dingy, dim, dreary, sombre, dark, drab, dull, murky OPPOSITES ARE bright, cheerful **2** (*informal*) *a row of dismal performances* ► dreadful, awful, terrible, feeble, disgraceful **3** *We looked at the dismal faces around us.* ► glum, gloomy, sad, miserable, melancholy, sombre, forlorn, despondent, downcast, sorrowful, mournful, woeful

dismantle VERB *Before they left, the soldiers dismantled the row of huts.* ► take apart, take to pieces, take down, knock down, break up, demolish, strip down OPPOSITES ARE assemble, build

dismay NOUN *Laura gave a yelp of dismay as she caught sight of the time on her watch.* ► alarm, shock, surprise, consternation, concern, distress, apprehension, agitation, trepidation, fright, horror

dismay VERB *You should not be dismayed by these comments.* ► alarm, daunt, horrify, shock, appal, discourage, dishearten, dispirit, distress, deject, depress, devastate, disappoint, unnerve, frighten, scare AN OPPOSITE IS encourage

dismiss VERB **1** *Elaine dismissed her husband with a wave of her hand.* ► send away, discharge, free, let go, release **2** *Three employees were dismissed on the spot.* ► give someone notice, discharge, lay off, (*more informal*) sack, (*more informal*) fire **3** *She had dismissed Nina's allegations as rubbish.* ► reject, discount, disregard, set aside, repudiate, discard, spurn, drop, get rid of, give up, shelve, wave aside, (*more informal*) pooh-pooh **4** *He tried to dismiss these thoughts from his mind.* ► banish, dispel, remove, reject, shrug off

disobedience NOUN *They were punished for their disobedience.* ► insubordination, naughtiness, misbehaviour, bad behaviour, misconduct, unruliness, rebelliousness, wilfulness

disobedient ADJECTIVE *The children had been disobedient and demanding.* ► naughty, badly behaved, insubordinate, troublesome, disorderly, disruptive, fractious, rebellious, unruly, wayward, intractable, obstreperous, wilful, contrary AN OPPOSITE IS obedient

disobey VERB **1** *The Queen was angry that so many people had disobeyed her orders.* ► defy, flout, rebel against, contravene, disregard, ignore, infringe, break, resist, transgress, violate **2** *Remember never to disobey.* ► be disobedient, rebel, revolt AN OPPOSITE IS obey

disorder NOUN **1** *They were arrested for acts of public disorder.* ► disturbance, unrest, agitation, disruption, upheaval, tumult, insurrection, rebellion OPPOSITES ARE order, peace **2** *The house is in total disorder.* ► untidiness, disarray, disorganization, confusion, chaos, a jumble, a mess, a muddle, a shambles OPPOSITES ARE order, tidiness

disorganized *ADJECTIVE* muddled and badly organized
▷ **disorganization** *NOUN*

dispatch *VERB* **dispatches, dispatching, dispatched** **1** send off to a destination **2** kill

dispatch *NOUN* **dispatches** **1** dispatching **2** a report or message sent **3** promptness; speed

dispel *VERB* **dispels, dispelling, dispelled** drive away; scatter • *Wind dispels fog.*

dispensary *NOUN* **dispensaries** a place where medicines are dispensed

dispense *VERB* **dispenses, dispensing, dispensed** **1** distribute; deal out **2** prepare medicine according to prescriptions
▷ **dispensation** *NOUN*
dispense with do without something

dispenser *NOUN* **dispensers** a device that supplies a quantity of something • *a cash dispenser*

disperse *VERB* **disperses, dispersing, dispersed** scatter
▷ **dispersal** *NOUN* **dispersion** *NOUN*

displace *VERB* **displaces, displacing, displaced** **1** shift from its place **2** take a person's or thing's place
▷ **displacement** *NOUN*

display *VERB* **displays, displaying, displayed** show; arrange something so that it can be clearly seen

display *NOUN* **displays** **1** the displaying of something; an exhibition **2** something displayed **3** (in computing) an electronic device for visually presenting data

Thesaurus

disorderly *ADJECTIVE* **1** *behaving in a disorderly manner* ► unruly, rowdy, rebellious, disruptive, undisciplined, disobedient, boisterous, rough, wild OPPOSITES ARE orderly, disciplined **2** *a disorderly arrangement* ► untidy, disorganized, messy, muddled, confused, chaotic OPPOSITES ARE orderly, tidy

disorganized *ADJECTIVE* **1** *The room looked completely disorganized.* ► untidy, disorderly, messy, muddled, confused, chaotic OPPOSITES ARE neat, systematic **2** *I was accused of being careless and disorganized.* ► unmethodical, slapdash, slovenly, absent-minded, scatterbrained, inefficient

disown *VERB* *Her family disowned her when she married Jem.* ► reject, renounce, repudiate, cast off, abandon, end relations with

dispatch *NOUN* *A messenger brought dispatches.* ► bulletin, communiqué, letter, message, report

dispatch *VERB* **1** *Reminders will be dispatched next week.* ► send, post, transmit, consign, convey, forward **2** *In the film the good guy has to dispatch a host of vicious villains.* ► kill, put an end to, put to death, dispose of, finish off

dispense *VERB* **1** *Waiters were there to dispense drinks.* ► distribute, give out, pass round, mete out, provide, allocate, allot, apportion, deal out, dole out, share **2** *The local chemist dispenses medicines.* ► supply, prepare, make up
3 dispense with *We can dispense with the formalities.* ► waive, disregard, ignore, forgo, do without, pass over, drop, omit, cancel, dispose of, get rid of

disperse *VERB* **1** *Troops arrived to disperse the demonstrators.* ► break up, split up, separate, scatter, drive away, send away, disband, dispel, dismiss OPPOSITES ARE assemble, collect **2** *The crowd dispersed quickly.* ► break up, split up, disband, separate, scatter, dissolve, disappear, vanish, melt away OPPOSITES ARE collect, gather, assemble **3** *Birds disperse the seed.* ► scatter, spread, disseminate, distribute, strew AN OPPOSITE IS centralize

dispirited *ADJECTIVE* *He felt tired and dispirited.* ► disheartened, depressed, dejected, downcast, despondent, downhearted, disconsolate, unhappy, sad, down, glum, melancholy, miserable, cast down OPPOSITES ARE cheerful, happy

displace *VERB* **1** *The gales have displaced many roof tiles.* ► dislodge, disarrange, dislocate, disturb, misplace, move, shift, remove, knock out of place, knock out of position **2** *The recent land reforms have displaced thousands of people.* ► force out, drive out, eject, expel, oust, remove, supplant

display *NOUN* *an air display a display of horsemanship* ► exhibition, demonstration, show, spectacle, pageant, presentation, parade

display *VERB* **1** *A room will be built to display the marbles.* ► exhibit, show, put on show, present **2** *He displayed a good knowledge of the subject.* ► show, reveal, demonstrate, manifest, flaunt, produce, betray, air, evince

displease *VERB* *The decision clearly displeased him.* ► annoy, irritate, infuriate, incense, anger, enrage, vex, exasperate, madden, aggravate, antagonize, inflame, make angry, (*more informal*) needle, (*more informal*) rile, (*more informal*) bug, (*more informal*) rub up the wrong way

disposal *NOUN* **1** *the disposal of troops for battle* ► arrangement, disposition, order, grouping, mustering **2** *the disposal of radioactive waste* ► removal, elimination, discarding, destruction, riddance

a b c d e f g h i j k l m n o p q r s t u v w x y z

disposable *ADJECTIVE* made to be thrown away after it has been used • *disposable nappies*

dispose *VERB* **disposes, disposing, disposed** **1** make a person ready or willing to do something • *I feel disposed to help him.* **2** place in position; arrange • *Dispose your troops in two lines.*
be well disposed be friendly
dispose of get rid of

disposition *NOUN* **dispositions** **1** a person's nature or qualities **2** arrangement

disproportionate *ADJECTIVE* out of proportion; too large or too small

disprove *VERB* **disproves, disproving, disproved** show that something is not true

dispute *VERB* **disputes, disputing, disputed** **1** argue; debate **2** quarrel **3** raise an objection to • *We dispute their claim.*

dispute *NOUN* **disputes** **1** an argument or debate **2** a quarrel
in dispute being argued about

disqualify *VERB* **disqualifies, disqualifying, disqualified** bar someone from a competition etc. because he or she has broken the rules or is not properly qualified to take part
▷ **disqualification** *NOUN*

disregard *VERB* **disregards, disregarding, disregarded** ignore

disregard *NOUN* the act of ignoring something

disrepair *NOUN* bad condition caused by not doing repairs • *The old mill is in a state of disrepair.*

disreputable *ADJECTIVE* not respectable

disrespect *NOUN* lack of respect; rudeness
▷ **disrespectful** *ADJECTIVE* **disrespectfully** *ADVERB*

disrupt *VERB* **disrupts, disrupting, disrupted** put into disorder; interrupt a continuous flow • *Fog disrupted traffic.*
▷ **disruption** *NOUN* **disruptive** *ADJECTIVE*

dissatisfied *ADJECTIVE* not satisfied
▷ **dissatisfaction** *NOUN*

dissect (dis- **sekt**) *VERB* **dissects, dissecting, dissected** cut something up in order to examine it
▷ **dissection** *NOUN*

dissent *NOUN* disagreement over an idea, proposal, etc.

dissent *VERB* **dissents, dissenting, dissented** disagree

Thesaurus

dispose *VERB* **1** *A general disposes his troops for battle.* ► arrange, array, group, place, position, set out **2 dispose of** *Equipment was needed to dispose of soiled nappies.* ► deal with, get rid of, destroy, discard, jettison, scrap, sell, throw away, (*more informal*) dump
be disposed to *Brian was not disposed to question this idea.* ► be inclined to, be ready to, be willing to, be liable to, be likely to

disproportionate *ADJECTIVE* *Small tasks can take up a disproportionate amount of time.* ► undue, uneven, unequal, unreasonable, inordinate, excessive, unbalanced OPPOSITES ARE proportional, reasonable

disprove *VERB* *New evidence has disproved the original verdicts.* ► invalidate, refute, overturn, confute, contradict, controvert, discredit, negate, rebut, expose, (*more informal*) explode OPPOSITES ARE prove, confirm

dispute *NOUN* *a matter of great dispute* ► debate, discussion, controversy, contention, argument, disagreement, conflict, dissension

dispute *VERB* **1** *We disputed with them deep into the night.* ► debate, argue, contend, exchange views, quarrel **2** *No one can dispute their claim.* ► challenge, contest, question, oppose, deny, doubt, contradict, controvert, impugn, argue against, quarrel with AN OPPOSITE IS accept

disqualify *VERB* *He was disqualified from driving for a year.* ► ban, bar, debar, prohibit, forbid (to drive), preclude

disregard *VERB* *Anne tried to disregard the noise.* ► ignore, take no notice of, pay no attention to, discount, overlook, pass over, make light of, brush aside AN OPPOSITE IS heed

disrespectful *ADJECTIVE* *He was often disrespectful towards his elders.* ► rude, discourteous, impertinent, impolite, insolent, impudent, cheeky OPPOSITES ARE respectful, polite

disrupt *VERB* *A strike of air-traffic controllers has disrupted holiday travel.* ► interrupt, break up, dislocate, disturb, upset, interfere with, throw into disorder, break the routine of

dissatisfaction *NOUN* *There is widespread dissatisfaction with the quality of service.* ► discontent, discontentment, disappointment, disquiet, disgruntlement, frustration, annoyance, irritation, unhappiness, displeasure, anger, exasperation, chagrin, dismay, regret AN OPPOSITE IS satisfaction

dissatisfied *ADJECTIVE* *They were clearly dissatisfied with our answer.* ► discontented, disappointed, unsatisfied, unhappy, disgruntled, displeased, aggrieved (by), disaffected (by), frustrated (by), (*more informal*) fed up, unfulfilled OPPOSITES ARE satisfied, contented

dissident *NOUN* **dissidents** a person who disagrees, especially someone who opposes their government
▷ **dissident** *ADJECTIVE* **dissidence** *NOUN*

dissolute *ADJECTIVE* having an immoral way of life

dissolution *NOUN* **dissolutions 1** putting an end to a marriage or partnership etc. **2** the formal ending of a parliament or assembly

dissolve *VERB* **dissolves, dissolving, dissolved 1** mix something with a liquid so that it becomes part of the liquid **2** make or become liquid; melt **3** put an end to a marriage or partnership etc. **4** formally end a parliament, assembly, or other gathering • *Parliament was dissolved and a general election was held.*

dissuade *VERB* **dissuades, dissuading, dissuaded** persuade somebody not to do something
▷ **dissuasion** *NOUN*

distance *NOUN* **distances** the amount of space between two places
in the distance far away but visible

distant *ADJECTIVE* **1** far away **2** not friendly; not sociable **3** not closely related • *distant cousins*
▷ **distantly** *ADVERB*

distaste *NOUN* dislike

distasteful *ADJECTIVE* unpleasant

distemper *NOUN* **1** a disease of dogs and certain other animals **2** a kind of paint

distil *VERB* **distils, distilling, distilled** purify a liquid by boiling it and condensing the vapour
▷ **distillation** *NOUN* **distiller** *NOUN*

distinct *ADJECTIVE* **1** easily heard or seen; noticeable **2** clearly separate or different
▷ **distinctly** *ADVERB* **distinctness** *NOUN*
USAGE See the note at **distinctive**.

distinction *NOUN* **distinctions 1** a difference **2** excellence or honour **3** an award for excellence; a high mark in an examination

Thesaurus

dissimilar *ADJECTIVE* **1** *a wide range of dissimilar tasks* ► different, differing, diverse, distinct, unrelated, varying, unlike, disparate, heterogeneous **2 dissimilar to** *This catfish shows a parental care not dissimilar to that of the cuckoo.* ► unlike, different from *or* to, unrelated to AN OPPOSITE IS similar

dissociate *VERB* *We decided to dissociate ourselves from the more extravagant claims being made.* ► break away, back away, detach, distance, separate , cut off, divorce, isolate
AN OPPOSITE IS associate

dissolve *VERB* **1** *The acids dissolve in water.* ► liquefy, become liquid, diffuse, disperse, melt, deliquesce, disappear, disintegrate **2** *Dissolve salts in the water to keep it pure.* ► liquefy, melt, disintegrate, disperse **3** *His anger began to dissolve.* ► disappear, vanish, evaporate, dissipate, subside, disperse
OPPOSITES ARE grow, develop **4** *The Assembly was dissolved after the revolution.* ► disband, terminate, abolish, close down, suspend, break up, dismiss, end, bring to an end, cancel, (*more informal*) wind up

dissuade *VERB* **dissuade from** *He dissuaded his colleagues from taking strike action.* ► discourage from, prevent from, deter from, divert from, disincline (to take), talk out of, urge against, advise against, persuade not (to take) AN OPPOSITE IS persuade (to)

distance *NOUN* **1** *the distance between the two vehicles* ► space, interval, gap, extent, length, range, reach, separation **2** *She keeps her distance.* ► aloofness, reserve, detachment, reticence, coolness, remoteness, coldness
AN OPPOSITE IS closeness

in the distance *a church spire visible in the distance* ► far away, far off, in the background, on the horizon, yonder

distant *ADJECTIVE* **1** *distant countries* ► far-off, faraway, remote, outlying, isolated
AN OPPOSITE IS close **2** *a distant memory* ► vague, dim, faint, indistinct, obscure, indefinite **3** *a distant manner* ► aloof, detached, impersonal, reserved, reticent, unfriendly, withdrawn, cool
OPPOSITES ARE friendly, warm

distaste *NOUN* **1** *George looked with distaste at the man sitting opposite.* ► disgust, revulsion, abhorrence, repugnance, disdain, disfavour, dislike **2** *a distaste for politics* ► dislike (of), aversion (to), repugnance (for), disapproval (of)

distasteful *ADJECTIVE* *The day was hot and their work distasteful.* ► unpleasant, disagreeable, offensive, repulsive, objectionable, unappealing, unpalatable, repugnant, abhorrent, unsavoury

distinct *ADJECTIVE* **1** *four distinct categories* ► discrete, separate, individual, detached
OPPOSITES ARE indistinct, fuzzy **2** *a distinct improvement* ► clear, definite, marked, sharp, decided, unmistakable, obvious, plain

distinction *NOUN* **1** *There is a clear distinction between politicians and the rest of us.* ► difference, contrast, dissimilarity, divergence, variance, variation, differentiation, discrimination, distinctiveness
AN OPPOSITE IS similarity **2** *a writer of distinction* ► importance, significance, note, consequence, account, greatness, renown, celebrity, eminence, fame, reputation, repute,

a b c d e f g h i j k l m n o p q r s t u v w x y z

distinctive *ADJECTIVE* that distinguishes one thing from another or others • *The school has a distinctive uniform.*
▷ **distinctively** *ADVERB*
USAGE Do not confuse this word with **distinct**. A **distinct** mark is a clear mark; a **distinctive** mark is one that is not found anywhere else.

distinguish *VERB* **distinguishes, distinguishing, distinguished** **1** make or notice differences between things **2** see or hear something clearly **3** bring honour to • *He distinguished himself by his bravery.*
▷ **distinguishable** *ADJECTIVE*

distinguished *ADJECTIVE* **1** important and famous **2** dignified in appearance

distort *VERB* **distorts, distorting, distorted** **1** pull or twist out of its normal shape **2** misrepresent; give a false account of something • *distort the truth*
▷ **distortion** *NOUN*

distract *VERB* **distracts, distracting, distracted** take a person's attention away from something

distraction *NOUN* **distractions** **1** something that distracts attention **2** an amusement **3** great worry or distress

distress *NOUN* **distresses** great sorrow, pain, or trouble

distribute *VERB* **distributes, distributing, distributed** **1** deal or share out **2** spread or scatter
▷ **distribution** *NOUN* **distributor** *NOUN*

district *NOUN* **districts** part of a town or country

Thesaurus

prestige, honour AN OPPOSITE IS mediocrity **3** *treating people without distinction of race, age, creed, or sex* ► differentiation, discrimination (between) **4** *He served with distinction in the war.* ► honour, credit, merit, courage, valour

distinctive *ADJECTIVE* *This duck has a distinctive white neck.* ► distinguishing, characteristic, typical, individual, peculiar, unique, special, singular, different, original, idiosyncratic, unusual

distinguish *VERB* **1** *the capacity to distinguish between good and bad in literature* ► differentiate, discriminate, decide, tell the difference, pick out (good and bad), determine (what is good and bad) **2** *We could distinguish a line of trees in the darkness.* ► make out, identify, discern, perceive, recognize, observe, notice, glimpse

distinguished *ADJECTIVE* *a distinguished statesman* ► eminent, famous, prominent, well known, celebrated, acclaimed, renowned, illustrious, famed, notable, noteworthy, esteemed, respected, honoured, outstanding

distort *VERB* **1** *His face was distorted with pain.* ► twist, contort, warp, deform, misshape, bend, wrench **2** *That explanation distorts the truth.* ► twist, misrepresent, pervert, slant, falsify, misstate, garble, put a slant on, (*more informal*) put a spin on

distorted *ADJECTIVE* *a distorted version of the events* ► twisted, slanted, perverted, coloured, false, biased, one-sided, prejudiced, inaccurate

distract *VERB* **1** *A noise across the street distracted him.* ► divert, sidetrack, disturb **2** *Helen appeared to be distracted by the back of the cereal packet.* ► puzzle, bewilder, disconcert, confuse, perplex, trouble, worry

distraction *NOUN* **1** *the distractions of life in a big city* ► amusement, entertainment, diversion, pleasure, recreation, enjoyment, fun, interest, pastime **2** *The baby's crying drove her to distraction.* ► frenzy, distress, insanity, madness, delirium

distraught *ADJECTIVE* *The poor woman looked distraught.* ► upset, overwrought, distressed, distracted, agitated, frantic, (*more informal*) beside yourself

distress *NOUN* **1** *She put her hand over her mouth to hide her distress.* ► anguish, suffering, misery, torment, discomfort, wretchedness, unhappiness, disquiet, despair, desolation, agony, grief OPPOSITES ARE happiness, comfort **2** *the distress of extreme poverty* ► hardship, adversity, tribulation, destitution, privation, trial AN OPPOSITE IS prosperity

distress *VERB* *I was distressed by the fact that everyone seemed to turn against him.* ► upset, perturb, disturb, trouble, bother, worry, sadden, afflict, torment OPPOSITES ARE comfort, soothe

distribute *VERB* **1** *They spent the day distributing pamphlets.* ► circulate, issue, spread, disperse, hand out, make available **2** *The house was sold and the money distributed among his heirs.* ► share out, divide up, apportion, allocate **3** *The seed should be distributed evenly.* ► scatter, spread, disperse, strew, disseminate, arrange

district *NOUN* *the shopping district of the town* ► area, region, quarter, locality, zone, neighbourhood, sector, vicinity, part

distrust *VERB* *On the whole the public distrusts politicians.* ► mistrust, suspect, be suspicious of, be sceptical about, have misgivings about, have qualms about, be wary of, disbelieve, doubt, question AN OPPOSITE IS trust

distrust *NOUN* lack of trust; suspicion
▷ **distrustful** *ADJECTIVE*

distrust *VERB* **distrusts, distrusting, distrusted** have little trust in

disturb *VERB* **disturbs, disturbing, disturbed** **1** spoil someone's peace or rest **2** cause someone to worry **3** move a thing from its position
▷ **disturbance** *NOUN*

disuse *NOUN* the state of being no longer used
▷ **disused** *ADJECTIVE*

ditch *NOUN* **ditches** a trench dug to hold water or carry it away, or to serve as a boundary [from Old English]

ditto *NOUN* (used in lists) the same again

dive *VERB* **dives, diving, dived** **1** go under water, especially head first **2** move down quickly
▷ **dive** *NOUN*

diverse (dy-**verss**) *ADJECTIVE* varied; of several different kinds
▷ **diversity** *NOUN*

diversify *VERB* **diversifies, diversifying, diversified** make or become varied; involve yourself in different kinds of things
▷ **diversification** *NOUN*

diversion *NOUN* **diversions** **1** diverting something from its course **2** an alternative route for traffic when a road is closed **3** a recreation or entertainment

divert *VERB* **diverts, diverting, diverted** **1** turn something aside from its course **2** entertain or amuse
▷ **diverting** *ADJECTIVE*

divide *VERB* **divides, dividing, divided** **1** separate from something or into smaller parts; split up **2** find how many times one number is contained in another • *Divide six by three* $(6 \div 3 = 2)$
▷ **divider** *NOUN*

divine *ADJECTIVE* **1** belonging to or coming from God **2** like a god **3** (*informal*) excellent; extremely beautiful
▷ **divinely** *ADVERB* **divinity** *NOUN*

Thesaurus

disturb *VERB* **1** *He crept into the house quietly so as not to disturb his sleeping parents.* ► bother, annoy, interrupt, intrude on, disrupt, upset, alarm, wake **2** *Try not to disturb the books and papers.* ► muddle, mix up, disarrange, disorganize, confuse

disturbance *NOUN* *People were injured in violent disturbances in the capital.* ► commotion, uproar, racket, tumult, hullabaloo, hubbub, rumpus, fracas, furore, upheaval, agitation, excitement

ditch *NOUN* *Some sheep had fallen into a ditch and had to be rescued.* ► trench, channel, gully, watercourse, conduit, dike, drain, gutter, moat

ditch *VERB* (*informal*) *We will have to ditch that idea.* ► abandon, drop, scrap, jettison, throw out, shelve, discard, forget, (*more informal*) dump, (*more informal*) pull the plug on

dither *VERB* *He dithered over which suit to wear that day.* ► hesitate, waver, be in two minds, vacillate, (*more informal*) shilly-shally

dive *VERB* **1** *A young girl dived into the water.* ► plunge, leap, jump, drop **2** *The hawk dived rapidly towards its prey.* ► swoop, plunge, plummet, descend, nose-dive, drop, pitch

diverge *VERB* **1** *The roads diverged at this point.* ► separate, divide, part, split, branch, deviate, fork OPPOSITES ARE converge, come together, join **2** *Clearly our opinions diverge.* ► differ, disagree, clash, be different
OPPOSITES ARE agree, coincide

diverse *ADJECTIVE* *information from diverse sources* ► various, varying, different, sundry, assorted, miscellaneous, mixed, distinct, (*more formal*) manifold

diversion *NOUN* **1** *a traffic diversion* ► detour, deviation, alternative route **2** *a large city with plenty of diversions* ► entertainment, amusement, recreation, relaxation, distraction, pastime, game, hobby, play, sport

diversity *NOUN* *a great diversity of fruit and vegetables* ► variety, assortment, miscellany, mixture, range, array, multiplicity
OPPOSITES ARE uniformity, similarity

divert *VERB* **1** *The plane was diverted to another airport.* ► redirect, reroute, deflect, turn aside, switch **2** *We tried to divert them with funny stories.* ► amuse, entertain, distract, occupy, interest, cheer up, delight, keep happy, regale

divide *VERB* **1** *The river divides north of the city. We divided into two groups.* ► separate, diverge, split, split in two, fork, branch
AN OPPOSITE IS converge **2** *We divided the food between us* ► share out, allocate, allot, apportion, distribute, pass round **3** *We divide the eggs according to size.* ► sort, classify, grade, group, arrange, organize, categorize, sort out, separate, subdivide AN OPPOSITE IS combine

divine *ADJECTIVE* **1** *divine worship* ► holy, sacred, religious **2** *a divine being* ► supernatural, godlike, superhuman, heavenly, spiritual, immortal

A B C D E F G H I J K L M N O P Q R S T U V W X Y Z

division *NOUN* **divisions** **1** dividing **2** a dividing line; a partition **3** one of the parts into which something is divided **4** (in Parliament) separation of members into two sections for counting votes
▷ **divisional** *ADJECTIVE*

divisive (div-I-siv) *ADJECTIVE* causing disagreement within a group

divorce *NOUN* **divorces** the legal ending of a marriage

divorce *VERB* **divorces**, **divorcing**, **divorced** **1** end a marriage by divorce **2** separate; think of things separately

Diwali (di-wah-lee) *NOUN* a Hindu religious festival at which lamps are lit, held in October or November

DIY *ABBREVIATION* do-it-yourself

dizzy *ADJECTIVE* **dizzier**, **dizziest** having or causing the feeling that everything is spinning round; giddy
▷ **dizzily** *ADVERB* **dizziness** *NOUN*

DJ *ABBREVIATION* disc jockey

DNA *ABBREVIATION* deoxyribonucleic acid; a substance in chromosomes that stores genetic information

do *VERB* **does**, **doing**, **did**, **done** This word has many different uses, most of which mean performing or dealing with something (*Do your best. I can't do this. She is doing well at school.*) or being suitable or enough (*This will do.*) The verb is also used with other verbs **1** in questions (*Do you want this?*), **2** in statements with 'not' (*He does not want it.*), **3** for emphasis (*I do like nuts.*), **4** to avoid repeating a verb that has just been used (*We work as hard as they do.*)
do away with get rid of
do up **1** fasten • *Do your coat up.* **2** repair or redecorate • *Do up the spare room.*

dock[1] *NOUN* **docks** a part of a harbour where ships are loaded, unloaded, or repaired

dock *VERB* **docks**, **docking**, **docked** **1** bring or come into a dock **2** when two spacecraft dock, they join together in space

dock[2] *NOUN* an enclosure for the prisoner on trial in a lawcourt

dock[3] *NOUN* a weed with broad leaves

dock[4] *VERB* **docks**, **docking**, **docked** **1** cut short an animal's tail **2** reduce or take away part of someone's wages or supplies etc.

docker *NOUN* **dockers** a labourer who loads and unloads ships

Thesaurus

division *NOUN* **1** *divisions in modern society* ▶ split, disunity, rupture, breach, disunion, schism, disagreement, conflict **2** *the division of Germany after the war* ▶ dividing, splitting, partitioning, separation **3** *the overseas division of the company* ▶ department, branch, arm, sector, office, bureau, subsidiary **4** *the division of the spoils* ▶ distribution, dividing up, sharing out, allocation, apportionment, allotment

divorce *NOUN* *One in three marriages ends in divorce.* ▶ separation, annulment, (*more informal*) break-up, (*more informal*) split-up

divorce *VERB* *Her parents divorced last year.* ▶ separate, end a marriage, (*more informal*) split up

divulge *VERB* *The article did not divulge the whereabouts of the individuals.* ▶ disclose, reveal, communicate, make known, pass on

dizzy *ADJECTIVE* *All that leaping about made her feel dizzy.* ▶ giddy, faint, shaky, wobbly, light-headed, (*more informal*) woozy

do *VERB* **1** *I have a lot of work to do.* ▶ carry out, undertake, perform, achieve, fulfil, complete, discharge **2** *You can do as you please.* ▶ behave, act, conduct yourself **3** *If there's no tea, a glass of water will do.* ▶ suffice, satisfy, serve, be enough, be adequate **4** *Shall I do the lunch now?* ▶ prepare, make, get ready, fix, organize, provide **5** *She went upstairs to do her hair.* ▶ arrange, groom, style, brush, comb, wash, fix **6** *He will be doing languages at university.* ▶ study, read, learn, take a course in **7** *She has been doing very well in the new job.* ▶ get on, progress, succeed
do away with **1** *We want to do away with outdated practices.* ▶ abolish, get rid of, discontinue, put an end to, dispense with, terminate, suppress **2** *I was afraid his enemies might want to do away with him.* ▶ kill, murder, put to death, assassinate, eliminate, exterminate
do up **1** *He stopped to do up his laces.* ▶ tie, fasten, secure **2** *They have bought an old farmhouse to do up.* ▶ renovate, restore, refurbish, decorate, revamp, (*more informal*) make over
do without *I cannot do without my eight hours' sleep.* ▶ forgo, dispense with, give up, renounce, abstain from

docile *ADJECTIVE* *Hannah has a docile nature.* ▶ gentle, compliant, meek, mild, obedient, amenable, cooperative, submissive, deferential

dock *NOUN* *The boat was moored at the end of the dock.* ▶ harbour, quay, wharf, jetty, landing stage, marina, dockyard, waterfront

dock *VERB* **1** *The ship docked the next morning.* ▶ moor, berth, tie up, put in, anchor, drop anchor **2** *The dog's tail had been docked.* ▶ cut short, cut off, crop, shorten **3** *The company will*

doctor *NOUN* **doctors** **1** a person who is trained to treat sick or injured people **2** a person who holds an advanced degree (a **doctorate**) at a university • *Doctor of Music*

doctrine *NOUN* **doctrines** a belief held by a religious, political, or other group
▷ **doctrinal** *ADJECTIVE*

document *NOUN* **documents** a written or printed paper giving information or evidence about something
▷ **documentation** *NOUN*

documentary *ADJECTIVE* **1** consisting of documents • *documentary evidence* **2** showing real events or situations

documentary *NOUN* **documentaries** a film giving information about real events

dodge *VERB* **dodges, dodging, dodged** move quickly to avoid someone or something

dodge *NOUN* **dodges** **1** a dodging movement **2** (*informal*) a trick; a clever way of doing something

dodgy *ADJECTIVE* (*informal*) **1** awkward or tricky **2** not working properly **3** dishonest

dodo *NOUN* **dodos** a large heavy bird that used to live on an island in the Indian Ocean but has been extinct for over 200 years

doe *NOUN* **does** a female deer, rabbit, or hare

doesn't (*mainly spoken*) does not

dog *NOUN* **dogs** a four-legged animal that barks, often kept as a pet

dog *VERB* **dogs, dogging, dogged** follow closely or persistently • *Reporters dogged his footsteps.* [from Old English]

dog-eared *ADJECTIVE* (said about a book) having the corners of the pages bent from constant use

dogged (dog- id) *ADJECTIVE* persistent or obstinate
▷ **doggedly** *ADVERB*

dogma *NOUN* **dogmas** a belief or principle that a Church or other authority declares is true and must be accepted

dogmatic *ADJECTIVE* expressing ideas in a very firm authoritative way
▷ **dogmatically** *ADVERB*

do-it-yourself *ADJECTIVE* suitable for an amateur to do or make at home

dole *VERB* **doles, doling, doled**
dole out distribute

dole *NOUN* (*informal*) money paid by the state to unemployed people

doll *NOUN* **dolls** a toy model of a person

dollar *NOUN* **dollars** a unit of money in the USA and some other countries

dolphin *NOUN* **dolphins** a sea animal like a small whale with a beak-like snout [via early French from Greek *delphis*]

domain (dom- **ayn**) *NOUN* **domains** **1** a kingdom **2** an area of knowledge, interest, etc.

Thesaurus

dock your wages for any misdemeanour. ► reduce, cut, lessen, decrease

doctor *NOUN* *Jane is unwell and should see a doctor.* ► GP, physician, medical officer, consultant, (*more informal*) medic RELATED ADJECTIVE medical

document *NOUN* *a legal document* ► paper, certificate, contract, deed, record, charter, (*technical*) instrument

dodge *NOUN* (*informal*) *a clever dodge* ► ruse, ploy, trick, device, scheme, tactic, manoeuvre, stratagem, (*informal*) wheeze

dodge *VERB* **1** *He flicked his head to one side as if dodging a blow.* ► avoid, duck, fend off, evade, move out of the way of, swerve away from, turn away from, veer away from **2** *The Minister may try to dodge the issue.* ► avoid, evade, shun, equivocate over, get out of, fudge, sidestep, (*more informal*) duck **3** *He managed to dodge between parked cars.* ► dart, dive, duck, leap, swerve, jump

dodgy *ADJECTIVE* (*informal*) **1** *Avoid dodgy travel agents at all costs.* ► dishonest, suspect, unreliable, underhand **2** *He took out a dodgy-looking sausage sandwich.* ► suspicious, suspect, dubious, unappealing, inferior, nasty

dog *NOUN* *She was walking her dog along the beach.* ► hound, mongrel, pedigree, pup, puppy, whelp, bitch, dingo

dogged *ADJECTIVE* *She was found again by the dogged efforts of her father.* ► determined, persistent, resolute, persevering, tenacious, steadfast, single-minded, unflagging, relentless

dogma *NOUN* *religious dogma* ► belief, creed, doctrine, teaching, tenet, principle, conviction, orthodoxy, set of beliefs

dogmatic *ADJECTIVE* *He was far too dogmatic to argue with.* ► opinionated, doctrinaire, assertive, peremptory, insistent, arrogant, categorical, overbearing AN OPPOSITE IS open-minded

dole *NOUN* (*informal*) *He lived on the dole for three years.* ► unemployment benefit, state benefit, benefit, social security, income support

dole *VERB*
dole out *Mum started doling out cornflakes.* ► distribute, give out, share out, hand round, dish up, issue

dome *NOUN* **domes** a roof shaped like the top half of a ball
▷ **domed** *ADJECTIVE*

domestic *ADJECTIVE* **1** to do with the home or household **2** (said about animals) kept by people, not wild
▷ **domestically** *ADVERB* **domesticated** *ADJECTIVE*

dominate *VERB* **dominates, dominating, dominated** **1** control by being stronger or more powerful **2** be conspicuous or prominent • *The mountain dominated the whole landscape.*
▷ **dominant** *ADJECTIVE* **dominance** *NOUN* **domination** *NOUN*

domineer *VERB* **domineers, domineering, domineered** behave in a dominating way
▷ **domineering** *ADJECTIVE*

dominion *NOUN* **dominions** **1** authority to rule others; control **2** an area over which someone rules; a domain

domino *NOUN* **dominoes** a small flat oblong piece of wood or plastic with dots (1 to 6) or a blank space at each end, used in the game of dominoes

donkey *NOUN* **donkeys** an animal that looks like a small horse with long ears

donor *NOUN* **donors** someone who gives something • *a blood donor*

don't (*mainly spoken*) do not

doom *NOUN* a grim fate that you cannot avoid, especially death or destruction • *a sense of impending doom*

doomed *ADJECTIVE* destined to fail or be destroyed

door *NOUN* **doors** a movable barrier on hinges (or one that slides or revolves), used to open or close an entrance
▷ **doorknob** *NOUN* **doormat** *NOUN*

doorstep *NOUN* **doorsteps** the step or piece of ground just outside a door

doorway *NOUN* **doorways** the opening into which a door fits

dope *NOUN* **dopes** **1** (*informal*) a drug, especially one taken or given illegally **2** (*informal*) a stupid person
▷ **dopey** *ADJECTIVE*

dope *VERB* **dopes, doping, doped** (*informal*) give a drug to a person or animal [from Dutch *doop* = sauce]

dormant *ADJECTIVE* **1** sleeping **2** living or existing but not active; not extinct • *a dormant volcano*

dormitory *NOUN* **dormitories** a room for several people to sleep in, especially in a school or institution
dormitory town or **suburb** a place from which people travel to work elsewhere

dormouse *NOUN* **dormice** an animal like a large mouse that hibernates in winter

Thesaurus

domain *NOUN* **1** *the king's domain* ► realm, kingdom, empire, dominion, territory, country **2** *the domain of science education* ► field, sphere, area, concern, speciality, department

domestic *ADJECTIVE* **1** *fuel for domestic use* ► household, home, family, private AN OPPOSITE IS public **2** *goods for the domestic market* ► national, inland, internal, local, state AN OPPOSITE IS foreign **3** *a domestic type of person* ► home-loving, homely, domesticated

domesticated *ADJECTIVE* *domesticated animals* ► tame, tamed, domestic, house-trained, trained AN OPPOSITE IS wild

dominant *ADJECTIVE* **1** *She was the dominant member of the partnership.* ► leading, primary, prime, main, principal, foremost, uppermost, prominent, pre-eminent **2** *The leader plays a dominant role.* ► controlling, leading, authoritative, powerful, influential, assertive **3** *the dominant feature of the landscape* ► conspicuous, prominent, imposing

dominate *VERB* *London no longer dominates the British arts scene.* ► control, monopolize, govern, rule, direct, overshadow, predominate in

domineering *ADJECTIVE* *He had a domineering mother.* ► overbearing, authoritarian, autocratic, tyrannical, dictatorial, despotic, oppressive, harsh, strict

donation *NOUN* *The organization depends on voluntary donations.* ► gift, contribution, subscription, benefaction

donor *NOUN* *a large gift from an anonymous donor* ► benefactor, contributor, philanthropist, provider, sponsor, giver AN OPPOSITE IS recipient

doom *NOUN* *There was a feeling of doom about the place.* ► ruin, downfall, catastrophe, destruction, disaster

doomed *ADJECTIVE* *The project seemed doomed from the start.* ► ill-fated, ill-omened, condemned, damned, fated, cursed, jinxed, hopeless, hapless

doomsday *NOUN* *He kept bomb-making equipment for a doomsday scenario.* ► apocalypse, end of the world, judgement day

door *NOUN* *She walked out through the door.* ► doorway, entrance, exit

dope *NOUN* **1** (*informal*) *smuggling dope* ► drugs, narcotics, cannabis, heroin **2** (*informal*) *He must*

dose *NOUN* **doses** an amount of medicine etc. taken at one time

dot *NOUN* **dots** a tiny spot

dot *VERB* **dots, dotting, dotted** mark something with dots

double *ADJECTIVE* **1** twice as much; twice as many **2** having two things or parts that form a pair • *a double-barrelled gun* **3** suitable for two people • *a double bed*
▷ **doubly** *ADVERB*

double *NOUN* **doubles 1** a double quantity or thing **2** a person or thing that looks exactly like another

double *VERB* **doubles, doubling, doubled 1** make or become twice as much or as many **2** bend or fold in two **3** turn back sharply • *The fox doubled back on its tracks.* [via early French from Latin *duplus*]

double bass *NOUN* **double basses** a musical instrument with strings, like a large cello

double-cross *VERB* **double-crosses, double-crossing, double-crossed** deceive or cheat someone who thinks you are working with them

double-decker *NOUN* **double-deckers** a bus with two floors, one above the other

doubt *NOUN* **doubts** a feeling of not being sure about something

doubt *VERB* **doubts, doubting, doubted** feel doubt
▷ **doubter** *NOUN*

doubtful *ADJECTIVE* **1** feeling doubt **2** making you feel doubt
▷ **doubtfully** *ADVERB*

dough *NOUN* **1** a thick mixture of flour and water used for making bread, pastry, etc. **2** (*slang*) money
▷ **doughy** *ADJECTIVE*

doughnut *NOUN* **doughnuts** a round bun that has been fried and covered in sugar

dour (doo-er) *ADJECTIVE* stern and gloomy-looking
▷ **dourly** *ADVERB*

dove *NOUN* **doves** a kind of pigeon

dovetail *NOUN* **dovetails** a wedge-shaped joint used to join two pieces of wood

dovetail *VERB* **dovetails, dovetailing, dovetailed 1** join pieces of wood with a dovetail **2** fit neatly together • *My plans dovetailed with hers.*

dowager *NOUN* **dowagers** a woman who holds a title or property after her husband has died • *the dowager duchess*

dowdy *ADJECTIVE* **dowdier, dowdiest** shabby; unfashionable
▷ **dowdily** *ADVERB*

down[1] *ADVERB* **1** to or in a lower place or position or level • *She fell down.* **2** to a source or place

Thesaurus

have looked a real dope. ► fool, idiot, dolt, dimwit, nincompoop

dopey *ADJECTIVE* (*informal*) *He grew dopey and fell asleep.* ► dazed, groggy, befuddled, drowsy

dose *NOUN* *a dose of cough mixture* ► measure, prescribed amount, dosage, portion, quantity

dot *NOUN* *The picture consists of tiny dots.* ► spot, speck, point, mark, particle

double *ADJECTIVE* *double yellow lines on the road* ► dual, twin, duplicate, matched, matching, twofold, duple AN OPPOSITE IS single

double *NOUN* *It was either you or your double.* ► lookalike, clone, replica, spitting image

double *VERB* *We must double our efforts.* ► increase, multiply, magnify, enlarge, repeat
double back *He doubled back, crossed the bridge, and reached home.* ► turn back, backtrack, retrace your steps, return
double up *She doubled up with pain.* ► collapse, crumple up, fold over, fold up, bend over

double-cross *VERB* *He was double-crossing his friends.* ► cheat, betray, deceive, defraud, (*more informal*) two-time

doubt *NOUN* **1** *There was some doubt about the identity of the father.* ► uncertainty, hesitation, confusion, difficulty **2** *I was plagued by doubt.* ► indecision, uncertainty, misgiving, lack of confidence, distrust, mistrust, suspicion, reservation, qualm

doubt *VERB* **1** *I doubt whether they will be there.* ► question, think it unlikely **2** *I do not doubt their motives.* ► disbelieve, distrust, question, query, suspect

doubtful *ADJECTIVE* **1** *At first I was doubtful about taking him with me. The woman sounded doubtful.* ► hesitant, uncertain, unsure, undecided, dubious, irresolute, ambivalent, wavering, tentative, sceptical, in two minds OPPOSITES ARE confident, assured **2** *It was doubtful whether the witness would back him up.* ► dubious, uncertain, questionable, debatable, in doubt, open to question AN OPPOSITE IS certain **3** *We are very doubtful of the conclusions they reached.* ► suspicious, distrustful, mistrustful, cautious, wary, uneasy (about), sceptical, unsure OPPOSITES ARE confident, trusting **4** *The chances of success are fairly doubtful.* ► unlikely, improbable, uncertain, dubious, remote OPPOSITES ARE probable, likely

down *ADJECTIVE* *He felt down all day.* ► depressed, dejected, sad, unhappy,

a b c d e f g h i j k l m n o p q r s t u v w x y z

etc. • *Track them down* **3** in writing • *Take down these instructions.* **4** as a payment • *We will pay £5 down and the rest later.* **5** unhappy or depressed
be down on disapprove of • *She is down on smoking.*

down PREPOSITION downwards through or along or into • *Pour it down the drain.*

down ² NOUN very fine soft feathers or hair
▷ **downy** ADJECTIVE

down ³ NOUN **downs** a grass-covered hill • *the South Downs*
▷ **downland** NOUN

downhill ADVERB, ADJECTIVE down a slope

download VERB **downloads, downloading, downloaded** transfer data from a large computer system to a smaller one

downpour NOUN **downpours** a heavy fall of rain

downright ADVERB & ADJECTIVE complete or completely • *a downright lie*

Down's syndrome NOUN a medical condition caused by a chromosome defect that causes intellectual impairment and physical abnormalities such as short stature and a broad flattened skull

down-to-earth ADJECTIVE sensible and practical

downward ADJECTIVE, ADVERB going towards what is lower
▷ **downwards** ADVERB

dowry NOUN **dowries** property or money brought by a bride to her husband when she marries him

doze VERB **dozes, dozing, dozed** sleep lightly

doze NOUN a light sleep
▷ **dozy** ADJECTIVE

dozen NOUN **dozens** a set of twelve
USAGE Correct use is *ten dozen* (not *ten dozens*).

drab ADJECTIVE **drabber, drabbest** **1** not colourful **2** dull or uninteresting • *a drab life*
▷ **drably** ADVERB **drabness** NOUN

draft NOUN **drafts** **1** a rough sketch or plan **2** a written order for a bank to pay out money

draft VERB **drafts, drafting, drafted** **1** prepare a draft **2** select for a special duty • *She was drafted to our office in Paris.*
USAGE This is also the American spelling of **draught**.

drag VERB **drags, dragging, dragged** **1** pull something heavy along **2** search a river or lake etc. with nets and hooks **3** continue slowly and tediously

drag NOUN **1** something that is tedious or a nuisance **2** (*slang*) women's clothes worn by men

dragon NOUN **dragons** **1** a mythological monster, usually with wings and able to

Thesaurus

miserable, downcast, despondent, dispirited, disheartened, disconsolate, glum, melancholy, cast down OPPOSITES ARE cheerful, happy

down and out ADJECTIVE *down and out in the streets of a big city* ► destitute, homeless, penniless, vagrant, living rough
OPPOSITES ARE prosperous, affluent, well off

downcast ADJECTIVE *Their mother often looked downcast.* ► dejected, depressed, despondent, dispirited, disheartened, downhearted, unhappy, sad, down, glum, melancholy, miserable, cast down OPPOSITES ARE cheerful, happy

downhearted ADJECTIVE *Steve tried not to look too downhearted.* ► dejected, depressed, despondent, dispirited, disheartened, downcast, unhappy, sad, down, glum, melancholy, miserable, cast down
OPPOSITES ARE cheerful, happy

downpour NOUN *On the way home we were caught in a downpour.* ► rainstorm, cloudburst, deluge

downright ADJECTIVE *They were telling half-truths and downright lies.* ► utter, absolute, total, complete, out-and-out, outright, positive, categorical, sheer, unmitigated

doze VERB *He began to doze by the fire.* ► sleep lightly, nap, catnap, drowse, (*more informal*) snooze, (*more informal*) have a snooze, (*more informal*) have forty winks

doze NOUN *She needed a short doze before her guests arrived.* ► nap, catnap, light sleep, siesta, (*more informal*) snooze, (*more informal*) forty winks

drab ADJECTIVE *The room had a few pieces of drab furniture.* ► dowdy, shabby, dreary, dingy, dull, shabby, sombre, lacklustre, unattractive, uninteresting, (*more informal*) tatty
OPPOSITES ARE bright, colourful

draft NOUN USAGE Do not confuse this word with **draught** *a draft of a speech* ► outline, sketch, abstract, first version, rough version, plan

drag VERB **1** *She dragged another chair over to the table.* ► pull, draw, haul, heave, (*more informal*) yank AN OPPOSITE IS push **2** *Time began to drag.* ► become tedious, crawl, go slowly, move slowly, pass slowly OPPOSITES ARE fly, pass quickly

drag NOUN (*informal*) *Working six days a week can become a drag.* ► bore, nuisance, bother, pest, annoyance, trial, (*informal*) pain in the neck

breathe out fire **2** a fierce person, especially a woman

dragonfly NOUN **dragonflies** an insect with a long thin body and two pairs of transparent wings

drain NOUN **drains** **1** a pipe or ditch etc. for taking away water or other liquid **2** something that takes away strength or resources
▷ **drainpipe** NOUN

drain VERB **drains, draining, drained** **1** take away water etc. through a drain **2** flow or trickle away **3** empty liquid out of a container **4** take away strength etc.; exhaust
▷ **drainage** NOUN

drake NOUN **drakes** a male duck

drama NOUN **dramas** **1** a play **2** writing or performing plays **3** a series of exciting events
▷ **dramatic** ADJECTIVE **dramatist** NOUN **dramatize** VERB
[from Greek *drama*, from *dran* = to do, to act]

drape VERB **drapes, draping, draped** hang cloth etc. loosely over something

draper NOUN **drapers** (*old use*) a shopkeeper who sells cloth or clothes
▷ **drapery** NOUN

drastic ADJECTIVE having a strong or violent effect
▷ **drastically** ADVERB

draught (drahft) NOUN **draughts** **1** a current of usually cold air indoors **2** the depth of water needed to float a ship **3** a swallow of liquid
▷ **draughty** ADJECTIVE

draught (drahft) ADJECTIVE (said about beer) served from a cask or barrel rather than a bottle or can

draughts NOUN a game played with 24 round pieces on a chessboard

draw VERB **draws, drawing, drew, drawn** **1** produce a picture or outline by making marks on a surface **2** pull **3** take out • *draw water* **4** attract • *The fair drew large crowds.* **5** end a game or contest with the same score on both sides **6** move or come • *The ship drew nearer.* **7** write out a cheque to be cashed
draw a conclusion form an opinion about something by thinking about the evidence

draw NOUN **draws** **1** the drawing of lots (SEE **lot**) **2** the drawing out of a gun etc. • *He was quick on the draw.* **3** an attraction **4** a drawn game
USAGE Do not confuse this word with **drawer**.

Thesaurus

drain NOUN *The drain had become clogged with leaves.* ▸ channel, conduit, culvert, pipe, drainpipe, outlet, duct, gutter, sewer, watercourse

drain VERB **1** *There is a tap to drain water from the tank.* ▸ draw off, empty, remove, bleed, clear, take off **2** *Lisa drained the cocoa from her mug.* ▸ empty, drink up, quaff, gulp, swallow, finish off, polish off **3** *The water drains through into the river.* ▸ seep, leak out, ooze, strain, trickle **4** *The colour had drained from her face.* ▸ fade, vanish, disappear, wane, evaporate **5** *The expense drained all my funds.* ▸ exhaust, consume, deplete, use up, sap, spend

drama NOUN **1** *Ruth is studying drama.* ▸ acting, dramatics, dramatic art, the theatre, the stage, stagecraft **2** *Hardly a day goes by without some family drama or other.* ▸ scene, incident, excitement, spectacle, crisis, commotion, disturbance, fracas

dramatic ADJECTIVE **1** *a dramatic production* ▸ theatrical, stage **2** *a dramatic rescue at sea* ▸ exciting, striking, thrilling, stirring
OPPOSITES ARE unexciting, routine **3** *a dramatic change in the weather* ▸ substantial, significant, marked, pronounced
AN OPPOSITE IS insignificant

dramatize VERB **1** *The novel has been dramatized for television.* ▸ adapt, make into a play, rewrite **2** *He tends to dramatize small difficulties.* ▸ exaggerate, overplay, overstate, overdo, make too much of

drastic ADJECTIVE *drastic measures to reduce pollution* ▸ extreme, harsh, severe, radical, rigorous, draconian, desperate, dire

draught NOUN USAGE Do not confuse this word with *draft*. **1** *The draught made her shiver.* ▸ current of air, puff, wind, breeze **2** *He took another draught of his beer.* ▸ drink, gulp, swallow, mouthful, (*more informal*) swig

draw NOUN *She won a prize in the office draw.* ▸ raffle, lottery

draw VERB **1** *Neil drew a shape on his beer mat.* ▸ sketch, depict, trace, outline, mark out, pencil, map out, (*more formal*) delineate **2** *The secretary drew another chair up to the desk.* ▸ pull, drag, haul, heave, (*more informal*) yank **3** *His aunt went over to draw the curtains.* ▸ close, shut, pull together, open, part USAGE Note that *draw* can mean either 'close' or 'open' when referring to curtains. **4** *By Saturday the show was drawing huge audiences.* ▸ attract, bring in, win, entice, allure, persuade **5** *That is the conclusion I drew.* ▸ reach, arrive at, deduce, infer **6** *The teams drew after extra time.* ▸ tie, be even, be equal
draw out *We could draw out the conversation for hours.* ▸ prolong, extend, protract, stretch, lengthen
draw up **1** *The lawyers will draw up a contract.* ▸ formulate, compose, prepare, write, draft **2** *A car drew up outside the house.* ▸ stop, pull up, come to a halt, come to a standstill

A B C D E F G H I J K L M N O P Q R S T U V W X Y Z

drawback *NOUN* **drawbacks** a disadvantage

drawbridge *NOUN* **drawbridges** a bridge over a moat, hinged at one end so that it can be raised or lowered

drawer *NOUN* **drawers** **1** a sliding box-like compartment in a piece of furniture **2** a person who draws something **3** someone who draws (= writes out) a cheque

drawing *NOUN* **drawings** a picture or outline drawn

drawing pin *NOUN* **drawing pins** a short pin with a flat top to be pressed with your thumb, used for fastening paper etc. to a surface

drawing room *NOUN* **drawing rooms** a sitting room

drawl *VERB* **drawls, drawling, drawled** speak very slowly or lazily

drawl *NOUN* **drawls** a drawling way of speaking

dread *NOUN* great fear

dread *VERB* **dreads, dreading, dreaded** fear something very much

dreadful *ADJECTIVE* very bad • *dreadful weather*
▷ **dreadfully** *ADVERB*

dreadlocks *PLURAL NOUN* hair worn in many ringlets or plaits, especially by Rastafarians

dream *NOUN* **dreams** **1** a series of pictures or events in a sleeping person's mind **2** something imagined; an ambition or ideal
▷ **dreamy** *ADJECTIVE* **dreamily** *ADVERB*

dream *VERB* **dreams, dreaming, dreamt** *or* **dreamed** **1** have a dream or dreams **2** have an ambition **3** think something might happen • *I never dreamt she would leave.*
▷ **dreamer** *NOUN*
dream up invent or imagine a plan, idea, etc.

dreary *ADJECTIVE* **drearier, dreariest** **1** dull or boring **2** gloomy
▷ **drearily** *ADVERB* **dreariness** *NOUN*

dredge *VERB* **dredges, dredging, dredged** drag something up, especially by scooping at the bottom of a river or the sea
▷ **dredger** *NOUN*

dregs *PLURAL NOUN* the last drops of a liquid at the bottom of a glass, barrel, etc., together with any sediment

drench *VERB* **drenches, drenching, drenched** make wet all through; soak

dress *NOUN* **dresses** **1** a woman's or girl's piece of clothing with a bodice and skirt **2** clothes; costume • *fancy dress*

dress *VERB* **dresses, dressing, dressed** **1** put clothes on **2** arrange a display in a window etc.; decorate • *dress the shop windows* **3** prepare food for cooking or eating **4** put a dressing on a wound
▷ **dresser** *NOUN*

Thesaurus

drawback *NOUN* *The weather was rather a drawback.* ► disadvantage, snag, hitch, nuisance, weakness, (*more informal*) fly in the ointment OPPOSITES ARE advantage, benefit

drawing *NOUN* *She made drawings of the children.* ► sketch, picture , illustration, study, portrayal, design, outline

dread *VERB* *He dreaded the telephone call that might take her away from him.* ► fear, be afraid of, shrink from, be anxious about, worry about

dread *NOUN* *With a mounting feeling of dread I went to answer the door.* ► fear, trepidation, apprehension, foreboding, anxiety

dreadful *ADJECTIVE* **1** *a dreadful accident; a dreadful mistake* ► terrible, frightful, horrible, awful, fearful, ghastly, hideous, shocking, frightening, terrifying **2** *a dreadful person* ► unpleasant, disagreeable, nasty, awful, deplorable

dream *NOUN* **1** *I had a dream about lizards.* ► fantasy, nightmare, delusion, vision, hallucination, illusion, reverie, trance **2** *She was walking around in a dream.* ► daydream, reverie, trance, daze **3** *It had always been his dream to run a country pub.* ► ambition, wish, desire, yearning, aspiration, pipedream, daydream, ideal

dream *VERB* **1** *She dreamed she was on a journey.* ► have a dream, imagine, fantasize, fancy **2** *I have always dreamt of playing for England.* ► long (to play), yearn (to play), hanker (after), fantasize (about)
dream up *There's not much time to dream up an excuse.* ► invent, devise, think up, concoct, contrive, work out

dreary *ADJECTIVE* **1** *a dreary story* ► dull, uninteresting, drab, tedious, boring, monotonous, unexciting
OPPOSITES ARE exciting, interesting **2** *dreary countryside* ► gloomy, dismal, bleak, drab, sombre, murky

dress *NOUN* **1** *Guests must wear formal dress.* ► clothes, clothing, costume, attire, apparel, garb, garments, ensemble, outfit, (*more informal*) gear RELATED ADJECTIVE sartorial **2** *She wore a beautiful red dress.* ► frock, gown, robe, shift USAGE A *robe* is usually a long dress, and a *shift* is usually a short one.

dress *VERB* **1** *She had to dress her disabled husband.* ► clothe, provide clothes for, put clothes on AN OPPOSITE IS undress **2** *He dressed quickly and left the house.* ► put on clothes, get dressed **3** *A nurse dressed the wound.* ► bandage, put a dressing on, bind up, tend, treat, attend to

dresser *NOUN* **dressers** a sideboard with shelves at the top for dishes etc.

dressing *NOUN* **dressings** **1** a bandage, plaster, or ointment etc. for a wound **2** a sauce of oil, vinegar, etc. for a salad **3** manure or other fertilizer for spreading on the soil

dressing gown *NOUN* **dressing gowns** a loose garment for wearing when you are not fully dressed

dress rehearsal *NOUN* **dress rehearsals** a rehearsal at which the cast wear their costumes

dribble *VERB* **dribbles, dribbling, dribbled** **1** let saliva trickle out of your mouth **2** (said about a liquid) flow in drops **3** move the ball forward in football or hockey with slight touches of your feet or stick

drift *VERB* **drifts, drifting, drifted** **1** be carried gently along by water or air **2** move along slowly and casually **3** live casually with no definite objective
▷ **drifter** *NOUN*

drift *NOUN* **drifts** **1** a drifting movement **2** a mass of snow or sand piled up by the wind **3** the general meaning of what someone says

driftwood *NOUN* wood floating on the sea or washed ashore by it

drill *NOUN* **drills** **1** a tool for making holes; a machine for boring holes or wells **2** repeated exercises, e.g. in military training

drill *VERB* **drills, drilling, drilled** **1** make a hole etc. with a drill **2** teach someone to do something by making them do repeated exercises

drink *VERB* **drinks, drinking, drank, drunk** **1** swallow liquid **2** drink a lot of alcoholic drinks
▷ **drinker** *NOUN*

drink *NOUN* **drinks** **1** a liquid for drinking; an amount of liquid swallowed **2** an alcoholic drink

drip *VERB* **drips, dripping, dripped** fall or let something fall in drops

drip *NOUN* **drips** **1** liquid falling in drops; the sound it makes **2** apparatus for dripping liquid into the veins of a sick person

drip-dry *ADJECTIVE* made of material that dries easily and does not need ironing

dripping *NOUN* fat melted from roasted meat and allowed to set

drive *VERB* **drives, driving, drove, driven** **1** make something or someone move **2** operate a motor vehicle or a train etc. **3** force or compel someone to do something • *Hunger drove them to steal* **4** force someone into a state

Thesaurus

dribble *VERB* **1** *A dog lay in the hearth dribbling.* ► drool, slaver, slobber, salivate **2** *Water dribbled from the end of the hose.* ► trickle, seep, drip, ooze, flow, leak, run

drift *NOUN* **1** *a drift of deep snow* ► pile, heap, bank, mass, mound, ridge, accumulation **2** *the drift of the story* ► gist, essence, core, substance, thrust, import, tenor, purport

drift *VERB* **1** *The boat began to drift downstream.* ► be carried, be borne, float, stray, coast, move slowly **2** *People drifted out into the gardens.* ► wander, ramble, stray, meander, move casually, dawdle, potter **3** *The snow had drifted across the road.* ► pile up, bank up, heap up, accumulate, gather, form drifts

drill *NOUN* **1** *three months of military drill* ► training, instruction, discipline, exercise, practice **2** *Everyone knows the drill.* ► routine, procedure, system

drill *VERB* **1** *He filed the edges and drilled a series of holes.* ► bore, make, pierce, penetrate **2** *A sergeant was drilling the new recruits.* ► train, instruct, coach, teach, exercise

drink *NOUN* **1** *She had another drink of her coffee.* ► sip, swallow, gulp, swill, (*more informal*) swig **2** *In the end he turned to drink.* ► alcohol, liquor, alcoholic drink, strong drink, (*more informal*) booze

drink *VERB* **1** *She drank her tea.* ► swallow, sip, gulp down, quaff, swill **2** *an upright citizen who never drank* ► take alcohol, indulge, (*more informal*) tipple, (*more informal*) booze

drip *NOUN* **1** *You could hear the drips from the blocked gutters.* ► drop, dribble, splash, plop, trickle **2** (*informal*) *He thought he must have seemed a complete drip.* ► weakling, idiot, (*informal*) ninny, (*informal*) wimp, (*informal*) weed, (*informal*) wally

drip *VERB* *Water was dripping on the floor.* ► drop, plop, splash, dribble, leak, drizzle, fall in drips, sprinkle, trickle

drive *NOUN* **1** *a short drive into town* ► trip, run, ride, excursion, journey, outing, jaunt **2** *a young woman with plenty of drive* ► motivation, ambition, initiative, enterprise, determination, enthusiasm, energy, keenness, persistence, zeal, (*more informal*) push **3** *a drive to recruit blood donors* ► campaign, crusade, effort, appeal

drive *VERB* **1** *I'll drive them to the station.* ► take, transport, ferry, carry **2** *Can you drive a tractor?* ► operate, control, manage, handle **3** *She drives everywhere.* ► go by car, travel by car, (*old-fashioned*) motor **4** *Most teachers drove their students very hard.* ► work, push, urge, direct **5** *Poverty drove them to crime.* ► force, compel, urge, push **6** *He drove a nail into the wall.* ► hammer, bang, ram
drive at *What was he driving at?* ► imply,

• *She is driving me crazy.* **5** rush; move rapidly • *Rain drove against the window.*
▷ **driver** NOUN

drive NOUN **drives** **1** a journey in a vehicle **2** a hard stroke in cricket or golf etc. **3** the transmitting of power to machinery • *four-wheel drive* **4** energy or enthusiasm **5** an organized effort • *a sales drive* **6** a track for vehicles through the grounds of a house

drive-in ADJECTIVE that you can use without getting out of your car

drivel NOUN silly talk; nonsense

drizzle NOUN very fine rain

drone VERB **drones, droning, droned** **1** make a deep humming sound **2** talk in a boring voice

drone NOUN **drones** **1** a droning sound **2** a male bee

drool VERB **drools, drooling, drooled** dribble
drool over be very emotional about liking something

droop VERB **droops, drooping, drooped** hang down weakly

drop NOUN **drops** **1** a tiny amount of liquid **2** a fall or decrease **3** a descent **4** a small round sweet **5** a hanging ornament

drop VERB **drops, dropping, dropped** **1** fall **2** let something fall **3** become lower or less **4** put down a passenger etc. • *Drop me at the station*
drop in visit someone casually

dropout NOUN **dropouts** a person who has dropped out of society or a course of study

droppings PLURAL NOUN the dung of animals or birds

drought (drout) NOUN **droughts** a long period of dry weather

drown VERB **drowns, drowning, drowned** **1** die or kill by suffocation under water **2** flood or drench **3** make so much noise that another sound cannot be heard

drowsy ADJECTIVE sleepy
▷ **drowsily** ADVERB **drowsiness** NOUN

drudge NOUN **drudges** a person who does hard or tedious work
▷ **drudgery** NOUN

drug NOUN **drugs** **1** a substance used in medicine **2** a substance that affects your senses or your mind, especially one causing addiction

drug VERB **drugs, drugging, drugged** give a drug to someone, especially to make them unconscious

drum NOUN **drums** **1** a musical instrument made of a cylinder with a skin or parchment stretched over one or both ends **2** a cylindrical object or container • *an oil drum*

drum VERB **drums, drumming, drummed** **1** play a drum or drums **2** tap repeatedly on something
▷ **drummer** NOUN
drum into drive a lesson, facts etc. into a person's mind by constant repetition

drumstick NOUN **drumsticks** **1** a stick for beating a drum **2** the lower part of a cooked bird's leg

Thesaurus

suggest, intimate, insinuate, allude to, refer to, hint at, (*more informal*) get at

droop VERB *The flowers began to droop.* ► wither, wilt, flop, sag, slump, go limp, hang, bend, dangle, fall

drop NOUN **1** *a drop of water* ► droplet, drip, globule, bead, bubble **2** *It needs a drop of glue.* ► dash, spot, dab, trace, pinch, small amount **3** *a drop of 100 metres* ► descent, fall, dive, plunge **4** *She walked to the edge of the cliff and peered at the drop below her.* ► precipice, chasm, gorge, abyss, slope **5** *a drop in prices* ► reduction, decrease, cut, falling off, downturn, slump AN OPPOSITE IS rise

drop VERB **1** *A maid had dropped a tray in the hallway.* ► let fall, let go of **2** *They all dropped to their knees.* ► sink, fall, go down **3** *The union decided to drop some of its claims.* ► abandon, give up, relinquish, discontinue **4** *She dropped many of her friends after leaving university.* ► desert, abandon, renounce, give up, disown, reject, discard **5** *Many outlets have dropped their prices.* ► reduce, lower, cut **6** *He was dropped from the team.* ► exclude, leave out (of), discard, expel **7** *The aeroplane dropped a thousand feet.* ► descend, fall, plunge, plummet, dive, nosedive, sink

drown VERB **1** *He fell into the water and nearly drowned.* ► submerge, sink, go under **2** *Noises from the street drowned our conversation.* ► overwhelm, overpower, drown out, engulf, make inaudible, silence

drowsy ADJECTIVE *We became drowsy in the heat.* ► sleepy, dozy, lethargic, somnolent, (*more informal*) snoozy

drug NOUN **1** *Her doctor prescribed a new drug.* ► medicine, medication, medicament, remedy, potion **2** *under the influence of drugs* ► narcotic, hallucinogen, stimulant, (*more informal*) dope, (*more informal*) junk

drug VERB *The victim seems to have been drugged before being driven off.* ► anaesthetize, knock out, stupefy, (*more informal*) dope

drum NOUN *a drum of oil* ► barrel, canister, cask, butt, keg, tub, tun

drunk *ADJECTIVE* not able to control your behaviour through drinking too much alcohol

drunk *NOUN* **drunks** a person who is drunk

drunkard *NOUN* **drunkards** a person who is often drunk

drunken *ADJECTIVE* **1** drunk • *a drunken man* **2** caused by drinking alcohol • *a drunken brawl*

dry *ADJECTIVE* **drier, driest 1** without water or moisture **2** thirsty **3** boring or dull **4** (said about remarks or humour) said in a matter-of-fact or ironical way • *dry wit*
▷ **drily** *ADVERB* **dryness** *NOUN*

dry *VERB* **dries, drying, dried** make or become dry

dry-cleaning *NOUN* a method of cleaning clothes etc. using a liquid that evaporates quickly

dual carriageway *NOUN* **dual carriageways** a road with a dividing strip between lanes of traffic in opposite directions

dub *VERB* **dubs, dubbing, dubbed** change or add new sound to the soundtrack of a film or to a recording

dubious (dew- bee- us) *ADJECTIVE* doubtful
▷ **dubiously** *ADVERB*

duchess *NOUN* **duchesses** a duke's wife or widow

duchy *NOUN* **duchies** the territory of a duke • *the duchy of Cornwall*

duck *NOUN* **ducks 1** a swimming bird with a flat beak; the female of this **2** a batsman's score of nought at cricket **3** a ducking movement

duck *VERB* **ducks, ducking, ducked 1** bend down quickly to avoid something **2** go or push quickly under water **3** dodge; avoid doing something

duckling *NOUN* **ducklings** a young duck

duct *NOUN* **ducts** a tube or channel through which liquid, gas, air, or cables can pass

ductile *ADJECTIVE* (said about metal) able to be drawn out into fine strands

due *ADJECTIVE* **1** expected; scheduled to do something or to arrive • *The train is due in ten minutes.* **2** owing; needing to be paid **3** that ought to be given; rightful • *Treat her with due respect.*
due to as a result of
USAGE Traditionally, correct use is as in *His lateness was due to an accident.* Some people object to the use of 'due to' without a preceding noun (e.g. 'lateness') to which it refers. However, such uses as *He was late, due to an accident* are nowadays widely regarded as acceptable. But if you prefer, you can use *because of* or *owing to* instead.

due *ADVERB* exactly • *We sailed due east.*

due *NOUN* **dues 1** something you deserve or have a right to; proper respect • *Give him his due.* **2** a fee • *harbour dues*

duel *NOUN* **duels** a fight between two people, especially with pistols or swords
▷ **duelling** *NOUN* **duellist** *NOUN*

duet *NOUN* **duets** a piece of music for two players or singers

Thesaurus

drunk *ADJECTIVE* *The men got drunk and waved bottles around.* ▶ intoxicated, inebriated, tipsy, drunken, under the influence, (*more informal*) plastered, (*more informal*) tight, (*more informal*) sloshed

dry *ADJECTIVE* **1** *Ahead lay miles of dry desert.* ▶ arid, parched, barren, waterless, desiccated, scorched, torrid **2** *a dry story* ▶ dull, tedious, boring, dreary, monotonous **3** *dry humour* ▶ droll, ironic, wry, sardonic, subtle

dry *VERB* *It wasn't easy drying clothes in such a wet climate.* ▶ get dry, make dry

dubious *ADJECTIVE* **1** *I was dubious about the idea.* ▶ doubtful, hesitant, uncertain, unsure, undecided, irresolute, ambivalent, wavering, tentative, sceptical, in two minds
OPPOSITES ARE confident, assured **2** *a dubious excuse* ▶ suspect, suspicious, untrustworthy, unreliable, (*more informal*) fishy, (*more informal*) shady

duck *VERB* **1** *The boys ducked behind a bush.* ▶ crouch, stoop, bob down **2** *I ducked to avoid an overhanging branch.* ▶ dodge, sidestep, bend, swerve, bob down **3** *They ducked him in the river.* ▶ dip, immerse, plunge, submerge, lower

dud *ADJECTIVE* (*informal*) *The light bulb was dud.* ▶ faulty, defective, useless

dud *NOUN* (*informal*) *Some of the fireworks were duds.* ▶ failure, flop, disappointment

due *ADJECTIVE* **1** *Your subscription is due this week.* ▶ owing, owed, payable, outstanding **2** *She drove with due care.* ▶ proper, rightful, fitting, appropriate, necessary, suitable, adequate **3** *the respect due to an eminent statesman* ▶ deserved (by), merited (by), earned (by), fitting, appropriate, suitable (for)
due to 1 *Death was due to a heart attack.* ▶ caused by, the result of, attributable to **2** *The game was cancelled due to bad weather.* ▶ owing to, because of, on account of, as a consequence of, as a result of, in view of, thanks to

due *NOUN* *We must give them their due.* ▶ deserts, entitlement, rightful treatment, rights, merits, reward

A B C D E F G H I J K L M N O P Q R S T U V W X Y Z

duffel coat *NOUN* **duffel coats** a thick overcoat with a hood, fastened with toggles

duffer *NOUN* **duffers** a person who is stupid or not good at doing something

duke *NOUN* **dukes** a member of the highest rank of noblemen
▷ **dukedom** *NOUN*
[via early French from Latin *dux* = leader]

dull *ADJECTIVE* **1** not bright or clear • *dull weather* **2** stupid **3** boring • *a dull concert* **4** not sharp • *a dull pain;* • *a dull thud*
▷ **dully** *ADVERB* **dullness** *NOUN*

dumb *ADJECTIVE* **1** without the ability to speak **2** silent **3** (*informal*) stupid
▷ **dumbly** *ADVERB* **dumbness** *NOUN*

dumbfound *VERB* **dumbfounds, dumbfounding, dumbfounded** astonish; strike a person dumb with surprise

dummy *NOUN* **dummies** **1** something made to look like a person or thing **2** an imitation teat given to a baby to suck

dump *NOUN* **dumps** **1** a place where something (especially rubbish) is left or stored **2** (*informal*) a dull or unattractive place

dump *VERB* **dumps, dumping, dumped** **1** get rid of something that is not wanted **2** put something down carelessly

dumpling *NOUN* **dumplings** a lump of dough cooked in a stew etc. or baked with fruit inside

dumpy *ADJECTIVE* short and fat

dunce *NOUN* **dunces** a person who is slow at learning [from John Duns Scotus, a Scottish philosopher in the Middle Ages. His opponents said that his followers could not understand new ideas]

dune *NOUN* **dunes** a mound of loose sand shaped by the wind

dung *NOUN* solid waste matter excreted by an animal

dungarees *PLURAL NOUN* overalls made of thick strong cloth [from Hindi *dungri* = the cloth they were made of]

dungeon (**dun**-jon) *NOUN* **dungeons** an underground cell for prisoners

duo (**dew**-oh) *NOUN* **duos** a pair of people, especially playing music

duodenum (dew-o-**deen**-um) *NOUN* **duodenums** the part of the small intestine that is just below the stomach
▷ **duodenal** *ADJECTIVE*

dupe *VERB* **dupes, duping, duped** deceive

duplicate (**dyoop**-lik-at) *NOUN* **duplicates** **1** something that is exactly the same as something else **2** an exact copy

duplicate (**dyoop**-lik-ayt) *VERB* **duplicates, duplicating, duplicated** make or be a duplicate
▷ **duplication** *NOUN* **duplicator** *NOUN*

duplicity (dew-**plis**-it-ee) *NOUN* deceitfulness

durable *ADJECTIVE* strong and likely to last
▷ **durably** *ADVERB* **durability** *NOUN*

during *PREPOSITION* while something else is going on

dusk *NOUN* **dusks** twilight in the evening

Thesaurus

dull *ADJECTIVE* **1** *dull colours* ▸ drab, dreary, sombre, dark, lacklustre AN OPPOSITE IS bright **2** *a dull winter morning* ▸ gloomy, overcast, dark, dim, dismal, bleak, murky, sunless OPPOSITES ARE sunny, bright **3** *The report makes dull reading.* ▸ boring, tedious, uninteresting, unexciting, monotonous, tiresome, insipid OPPOSITES ARE interesting, exciting **4** *a dull pupil* ▸ stupid, slow, unintelligent, dim, slow-witted, dense OPPOSITES ARE clever, bright

dumb *ADJECTIVE* **1** *He kept dumb while the others argued.* ▸ mute, silent, speechless, tongue-tied, unable to speak **2** (*informal*) *He's not as dumb as he makes out.* ▸ stupid, unintelligent, foolish, slow-witted, dull, dim

dumbfounded *ADJECTIVE* *I gazed back at him, dumbfounded.* ▸ astonished, astounded, amazed, surprised, staggered, startled, nonplussed, disconcerted, speechless, shocked, flabbergasted, perplexed, stunned, stupefied, bewildered, (*more informal*) thunderstruck

dummy *NOUN* **1** *The gun was only a dummy.* ▸ imitation, fake, sham, substitute, toy, copy, model, counterfeit **2** *a ventriloquist's dummy* ▸ doll, puppet, manikin, figure

dummy *ADJECTIVE* *a dummy attack* ▸ simulated, pretended, trial, mock, practice, bogus, (*more informal*) pretend

dump *NOUN* **1** *We've a lot to take to the dump.* ▸ tip, refuse dump, rubbish heap, junk yard **2** *an ammunition dump* ▸ cache, depot, hoard, store

dump *VERB* **1** *Worn-out cars had been dumped at the side of the road.* ▸ dispose of, discard, get rid of, jettison, reject, scrap, (*more informal*) ditch **2** *She dumped her shopping by the door.* ▸ put down, set down, throw down, deposit, drop, tip, place, unload, (*more informal*) park

duplicate *ADJECTIVE* *The manager opened his room with a duplicate key.* ▸ matching, identical, twin, second, alternative, copied, corresponding

duplicate *NOUN* *The document in the file is a duplicate.* ▸ copy, facsimile, photocopy, carbon copy, reproduction, replica

dust *NOUN* tiny particles of earth or other solid material

dust *VERB* **dusts, dusting, dusted 1** wipe away dust **2** sprinkle with dust or something powdery

dustbin *NOUN* **dustbins** a bin for household rubbish

dustman *NOUN* **dustmen** a person employed to empty dustbins and take away rubbish

dustpan *NOUN* **dustpans** a pan into which dust is brushed from a floor

dusty *ADJECTIVE* **dustier, dustiest 1** covered with dust **2** like dust

dutiful *ADJECTIVE* doing your duty; obedient
▷ **dutifully** *ADVERB*

duty *NOUN* **duties 1** what you ought to do or must do **2** a task that must be done **3** a tax charged on imports and on certain other things
on *or* **off duty** actually doing (or not doing) what is your regular work

duvet (doo- vay) *NOUN* **duvets** a kind of quilt used instead of other bedclothes

DVD *ABBREVIATION* digital versatile disc (formerly digital videodisc); a disc used for storing large amounts of audio or video information, especially films

dwarf *NOUN* **dwarfs** or **dwarves** a very small person or thing

dwarf *VERB* **dwarfs, dwarfing, dwarfed** make something seem small by contrast • *The ocean liner dwarfed the tugs that were towing it.*

dwelling *NOUN* **dwellings** a house etc. to live in

dwindle *VERB* **dwindles, dwindling, dwindled** get smaller gradually

dye *VERB* **dyes, dyeing, dyed** colour something by putting it into a liquid
▷ **dyer** *NOUN*

dye *NOUN* **dyes** a substance used to dye things

dynamic *ADJECTIVE* **1** energetic or forceful **2** (said about a force) producing motion
▷ **dynamically** *ADVERB*

dynamics *NOUN* the scientific study of force and motion

dynamite *NOUN* **1** a powerful explosive **2** something likely to make people very excited or angry

dynamo *NOUN* **dynamos** a machine that makes electricity

dynasty (din- a- stee) *NOUN* **dynasties** a line of rulers or powerful people all from the same family
▷ **dynastic** *ADJECTIVE*

dyslexia (dis- leks- ee- a) *NOUN* special difficulty in being able to read and spell, caused by a brain condition
▷ **dyslexic** *ADJECTIVE*

dystrophy (dis- trof- ee) *NOUN* a disease that weakens the muscles

Thesaurus

dust *NOUN* *The surfaces were covered in dust.* ► dirt, grime, grit, filth, smut, particles, powder

dusty *ADJECTIVE* **1** *The tables were dusty.* ► dirty, filthy, grubby **2** *a light dusty substance* ► powdery, chalky, crumbly, granular, sandy

duty *NOUN* **1** *He felt a strong sense of duty.* ► responsibility, loyalty, obligation, allegiance, faithfulness, obedience, service **2** *One of his duties was to make the afternoon tea.* ► job, role, task, assignment, function, (*more informal*) chore **3** *an increased duty on cigarettes* ► tax, levy, tariff, excise, toll, dues

dwarf *ADJECTIVE* *a dwarf cactus* ► miniature, small, little, undersized, diminutive

dwarf *VERB* *The tower blocks dwarf the old cathedral.* ► dominate, tower over, overshadow

dwell *VERB* **dwell in** *Hermits used to dwell in these caves.* ► inhabit, live in, populate, lodge in, (*more formal*) reside in

dwindle *VERB* *After the war the population dwindled.* ► decrease, decline, diminish, shrink, contract, peter out, wane, fall off, die out

dye *NOUN* *a yellow dye* ► colouring, colourant, pigment, stain, tint, tinge

dye *VERB* *She dyed the curtains to match the new paint.* ► colour, tint, stain, pigment, colour-wash

dynamic *ADJECTIVE* *The country needs dynamic leadership.* ► energetic, vigorous, forceful, spirited, positive, effective, bold, vital, active

dynasty *NOUN* *The ruling dynasty went back to medieval times.* ► family, house, line, bloodline, succession, regime

Ee

E. ABBREVIATION east; eastern

each ADJECTIVE, PRONOUN every; every one • *each child;* • *each of you*
USAGE In standard English, the pronoun **each** should be used with a singular verb and singular pronouns: *Each has chosen her own outfit.*

eager ADJECTIVE strongly wanting to do something; enthusiastic
▷ **eagerly** ADVERB **eagerness** NOUN

eagle NOUN **eagles** a large bird of prey with very strong sight

ear[1] NOUN **ears** **1** the organ of the body that is used for hearing **2** hearing ability • *She has a good ear for music.*

ear[2] NOUN **ears** the spike of seeds at the top of a stalk of corn

eardrum NOUN **eardrums** a membrane in the ear that vibrates when sounds reach it

earl NOUN **earls** a British nobleman
▷ **earldom** NOUN

early ADJECTIVE, ADVERB **earlier**, **earliest** **1** before the usual or expected time **2** near the beginning • *early in the book*
▷ **earliness** NOUN

earmark VERB **earmarks**, **earmarking**, **earmarked** put something aside for a particular purpose

earn VERB **earns**, **earning**, **earned** get something by working or in return for what you have done

earnest ADJECTIVE showing serious feelings or intentions
▷ **earnestly** ADVERB **earnestness** NOUN
in earnest **1** more seriously or with more determination • *We began to shovel the snow in earnest.* **2** meaning what you say

earshot NOUN the distance within which a sound can be heard

earth NOUN **earths** **1** the planet (**Earth**) that we live on **2** the ground; soil **3** the hole where a fox or badger lives **4** connection to the ground to complete an electrical circuit

earth VERB **earths**, **earthing**, **earthed** connect an electrical circuit to the ground

earthenware NOUN pottery made of coarse baked clay

earthly ADJECTIVE concerned with life on earth rather than with life after death

earthquake NOUN **earthquakes** a violent movement of part of the earth's surface

earthy ADJECTIVE **1** like earth or soil **2** direct and unembarrassed about bodily functions or sexual subjects

earwig NOUN **earwigs** a crawling insect with pincers at the end of its body [called this because it was thought to crawl into people's ears]

Thesaurus

eager ADJECTIVE **1** *It was good to see smiling, eager faces.* ► keen, enthusiastic, avid, fervent, zealous OPPOSITES ARE apathetic, unenthusiastic **2** *They were eager to find a seat near the front.* ► keen, anxious, determined **3** *The young ones are eager for more adventure.* ► longing, yearning, intent (on)

eagerness NOUN *Her eyes shone with eagerness.* ► enthusiasm, keenness, fervour, ardour, earnestness, excitement, intentness, longing, passion OPPOSITES ARE apathy, indifference

ear NOUN *He had the ear of the President.* ► attention, heed, notice, consideration, regard RELATED ADJECTIVE aural

early ADJECTIVE **1** *early symptoms of the disease* ► initial, first, advance, preliminary, forward AN OPPOSITE IS late **2** *early civilizations* ► ancient, primitive, prehistoric
USAGE Note that *prehistoric* means 'before the time of written records. *Primitive* means 'early in history', but can also mean 'not advanced, simple', and so it is not always a good choice for the meaning shown here.

earn VERB **1** *She earns a six-figure salary.* ► receive, be paid, make, (*more informal*) bring in, (*more informal*) take home **2** *They have all earned our gratitude.* ► deserve, merit, warrant, justify, be worthy of, gain, secure, obtain OPPOSITES ARE lose, forfeit

earnest ADJECTIVE **1** *an earnest attempt to help* ► committed, determined, resolute, conscientious, devoted, diligent, purposeful, eager, industrious, involved OPPOSITES ARE casual, flippant **2** *He was an earnest, church-going man.* ► serious, serious-minded, thoughtful, solemn, grave, sober, staid, humourless OPPOSITES ARE casual, half-hearted

earnings PLURAL NOUN *He looked for ways to supplement his earnings.* ► income, pay, salary, wages, remuneration

earth NOUN **1** *life on earth* ► this world, the planet, the globe RELATED ADJECTIVE terrestrial **2** *The fork turned the soft earth.* ► soil, topsoil, loam, clay, sod, ground, humus, land

ease *NOUN* freedom from trouble or effort or pain • *She climbed the tree with ease.*
at ease relaxed

ease *VERB* **eases, easing, eased** **1** make less painful or less tight or troublesome **2** move gently into position **3** become less severe • *The pressure eased.*

easel *NOUN* **easels** a stand for supporting a blackboard or a painting

easily *ADVERB* **1** without difficulty; with ease **2** by far • *easily the best* **3** very likely • *He could easily be lying.*

east *NOUN* **1** the direction where the sun rises **2** the eastern part of a country, city, etc.

east *ADJECTIVE, ADVERB* towards or in the east; coming from the east
▷ **easterly** *ADJECTIVE* **eastern** *ADJECTIVE* **easterner** *NOUN* **easternmost** *ADJECTIVE*

Easter *NOUN* the Sunday (in March or April) when Christians commemorate the resurrection of Christ; the days around it

eastward *ADJECTIVE, ADVERB* towards the east
▷ **eastwards** *ADVERB*

easy *ADJECTIVE* **easier, easiest** able to be done or used or understood without trouble
▷ **easiness** *NOUN*

easy *ADVERB* with ease; comfortably • *Take it easy!*

eat *VERB* **eats, eating, ate, eaten** **1** chew and swallow as food **2** have a meal • *When do we eat?* **3** use up; destroy gradually • *Extra expenses ate up our savings.* [from Old English]

eaves *PLURAL NOUN* the overhanging edges of a roof

eavesdrop *VERB* **eavesdrops, eavesdropping, eavesdropped** listen secretly to a private conversation
▷ **eavesdropper** *NOUN*

Thesaurus

ease *NOUN* **1** *Most people can recognize road symbols with ease.* ► effortlessness, straightforwardness, no trouble, no problem, facility, simplicity AN OPPOSITE IS difficulty **2** *Notice the ease with which he completed the task.* ► skill, dexterity, facility, naturalness, deftness, mastery, cleverness **3** *a life of ease* ► affluence, comfort, contentment, enjoyment, relaxation, luxury, leisure, wealth, prosperity AN OPPOSITE IS stress

ease *VERB* **1** *The medicine will ease the pain.* ► relieve, alleviate, mitigate, soothe, assuage, allay, lessen, deaden, dull, calm, lighten, moderate, quell, comfort
OPPOSITES ARE aggravate, worsen **2** *measures taken to ease the tension* ► reduce, relax, decrease, slacken, take off
AN OPPOSITE IS increase **3** *He eased the stopper out of the bottle.* ► guide, slide, slip, edge, inch, manoeuvre, move gradually
ease off *The rain eased off.* ► abate, subside, let up, slacken off, die out, lessen

easily *ADVERB* **1** *She is easily the brightest student of her year.* ► by far, without doubt, undoubtedly, indubitably, indisputably, undeniably, definitely, certainly, patently **2** *In the end I managed the work easily.*
► effortlessly, comfortably, with ease, simply, straightforwardly, with no difficulty

easy *ADJECTIVE* **1** *an easy task* ► straightforward, undemanding, effortless, light, pleasant, painless, (*more informal*) cushy
OPPOSITES ARE difficult, heavy **2** *easy instructions to follow* ► simple, straightforward, elementary, clear, uncomplicated, understandable, plain, user-friendly, foolproof, manageable OPPOSITES ARE complicated, difficult **3** *an easy manner* ► relaxed, easy-going, affable, natural, friendly, tolerant, informal, open, docile, amenable, accommodating, undemanding, (*more informal*) laid-back OPPOSITES ARE difficult, intolerant **4** *I long for an easy life.*
► comfortable, carefree, untroubled, leisurely, peaceful, restful, serene, relaxed, contented, cosy, tranquil AN OPPOSITE IS stressful

easy-going *ADJECTIVE* *Despite his easy-going nature he was extraordinarily energetic.*
► relaxed, easy, affable, natural, friendly, tolerant, informal, open, docile, amenable, accommodating, undemanding, (*more informal*) laid-back

eat *VERB* **1** *The condemned man ate a hearty breakfast.* ► consume, devour, swallow, (*more informal*) put away, (*more informal*) tuck into, (*more informal*) scoff, (*more informal*) polish off, (*more informal*) get stuck into RELATED ADJECTIVE edible **2** *Where shall we eat tonight?* ► have a meal, have dinner, dine, (*more informal*) feed **3** **eat into** *Rust was eating into the bodywork.*
► corrode, erode, wear away, wear through, rot, decay

eatable *ADJECTIVE* *The food is a little overcooked, but still eatable.* ► palatable, wholesome, edible, fit to eat, safe to eat, digestible
OPPOSITES ARE uneatable, inedible USAGE Note that *edible* does not mean quite the same as *eatable*. You say that something is *edible* when you mean it is suitable as food and is not (for example) poisonous, whereas you use *eatable* about food that is good enough to eat and not (for example) burnt or undercooked.

A B C D E F G H I J K L M N O P Q R S T U V W X Y Z

ebb *NOUN* **ebbs 1** the movement of the tide when it is going out, away from the land **2** a low point • *Our courage was at a low ebb.*

eccentric (ik- sen- trik) *ADJECTIVE* behaving strangely
▷ **eccentrically** *ADVERB* **eccentricity** (ek- sen- triss- it- ee) *NOUN*

ecclesiastical (ik- lee- zee- ast- ik- al) *ADJECTIVE* to do with the Church or the clergy

echo *NOUN* **echoes** a sound that is heard again as it is reflected off something

echo *VERB* **echoes, echoing, echoed 1** make an echo **2** repeat a sound or saying

eclair (ay- klair) *NOUN* **eclairs** a finger-shaped cake of pastry with a creamy filling

eclipse *NOUN* **eclipses** the blocking of the sun's or moon's light when the moon or the earth is in the way

ecology (ee- kol- o- jee) *NOUN* the study of living things in relation to each other and to where they live
▷ **ecological** *ADJECTIVE* **ecologically** *ADVERB* **ecologist** *NOUN*

economic (ee- kon- om- ik) *ADJECTIVE* **1** to do with economy or economics **2** profitable

economical *ADJECTIVE* using as little of something as possible
▷ **economically** *ADVERB*

economics *NOUN* the study of how money is used and how goods and services are provided and used
▷ **economist** *NOUN*

economize *VERB* **economizes, economizing, economized** be economical; use or spend less • *We need to economize on fuel.*

economy *NOUN* **economies 1** a country's or household's income (e.g. from what it sells or earns) and the way this is spent (e.g. on goods and services) **2** being economical **3** a saving • *You need to make economies.*

ecstasy (ek- sta- see) *NOUN* **1** a feeling of great delight **2** an illegal drug that makes people feel very energetic and can cause hallucinations
▷ **ecstatic** (ik- stat- ik) *ADJECTIVE* **ecstatically** *ADVERB*

Thesaurus

ebb *VERB* **1** *The tide ebbed late in the morning.* ► go out, recede, fall back, flow back, retreat AN OPPOSITE IS come in **2** *Her strength was beginning to ebb.* ► dwindle, decline, fade, wane, diminish, disappear, vanish, weaken OPPOSITES ARE increase, revive

eccentric *ADJECTIVE* *His eccentric behaviour was worrying.* ► unconventional, abnormal, irregular, odd, strange, peculiar, weird, bizarre, extraordinary, idiosyncratic, capricious, quirky, erratic OPPOSITES ARE ordinary, conventional

eccentric *NOUN* *She had a reputation as an eccentric.* ► individualist, nonconformist, oddity, (*more informal*) oddball, (*more informal*) weirdo, (*more informal*) crackpot

echo *NOUN* *The mountains are full of strange echoes.* ► reverberation, reiteration, reflection of sound

echo *VERB* **1** *The slightest sound echoes across the hall. The words echoed in Isabel's head.* ► reverberate, resound, ring, resonate **2** *These thoughts were echoed by another speaker.* ► repeat, reiterate, reproduce, say again, ape, copy, imitate, mimic

eclipse *VERB* **1** *The sun is eclipsed by the moon.* ► blot out, block out, obscure, veil, cloud, cover, shade, darken, extinguish **2** *This achievement eclipsed all previous attempts.* ► overshadow, outshine, surpass, excel, outdo, put into the shade, dim

economic *ADJECTIVE* USAGE The main meanings of *economic* are 'to do with economics or use of money' (the first meaning below) and 'providing good value or profit' (the second meaning below). If you mean 'careful in using money' you should use *economical* or its synonyms. **1** *an outline of the government's economic policies* ► financial, monetary, commercial, fiscal, budgetary, business, money-making, trading **2** *The railway line was closed because it was no longer economic.* ► profitable, lucrative, fruitful, productive

economical *ADJECTIVE* USAGE See the note at the entry for **economic**. **1** *It may be more economical to use an alternative form of fuel.* ► inexpensive, cost-effective, reasonable OPPOSITES ARE wasteful, expensive **2** *She is very economical with what money she has.* ► thrifty, careful, prudent, provident, sensible, canny AN OPPOSITE IS extravagant

economize *VERB* *One way of economizing is to grow your own vegetables.* ► save, save money, cut back, cut costs, cut expenditure, spend less, (*more informal*) tighten your belt AN OPPOSITE IS be extravagant

economy *NOUN* **1** *You can enjoy life and still exercise economy.* ► thrift, frugality, prudence, parsimony, providence AN OPPOSITE IS wastefulness **2** *To avoid debt we had to make some economies.* ► saving, cut **3** *the country's economy* ► financial system, wealth, budget

ecstasy *NOUN* *He ran out in ecstasy, doing cartwheels across the grass.* ► rapture, bliss, joy, delight , elation, euphoria, exultation

ecstatic *ADJECTIVE* *They were ecstatic as they returned with the good news.* ► elated,

eddy *NOUN* **eddies** a swirling patch of water or air or smoke etc.

edge *NOUN* **edges** **1** the part along the side or end of something **2** the sharp part of a knife or axe or other cutting instrument
be on edge be tense and irritable

edgy *ADJECTIVE* tense and irritable
▷ **edginess** *NOUN*

edible *ADJECTIVE* suitable for eating, not poisonous • *edible fruits*

edit *VERB* **edits, editing, edited** **1** be the editor of a newspaper or other publication **2** make written material ready for publishing **3** choose and put the parts of a film or tape recording etc. into order

edition *NOUN* **editions** **1** the form in which something is published • *a paperback edition* **2** all the copies of a book etc. issued at the same time • *the first edition* **3** an individual television or radio programme in a series

editor *NOUN* **editors** **1** the person in charge of a newspaper or a section of it **2** a person who edits something

editorial *ADJECTIVE* to do with editing or editors

editorial *NOUN* **editorials** a newspaper article giving the editor's comments on something

educate *VERB* **educates, educating, educated** provide people with education
▷ **educative** *ADJECTIVE* **educator** *NOUN*

educated *ADJECTIVE* showing a high standard of knowledge and culture, as a result of a good education

education *NOUN* the process of training people's minds and abilities so that they acquire knowledge and develop skills
▷ **educational** *ADJECTIVE* **educationally** *ADVERB* **educationist** *NOUN*

EEC *ABBREVIATION* European Economic Community (= the Common Market)

eel *NOUN* **eels** a long fish that looks like a snake

eerie *ADJECTIVE* **eerier, eeriest** strange in a frightening or mysterious way
▷ **eerily** *ADVERB* **eeriness** *NOUN*

effect *NOUN* **effects** **1** a change that is produced by an action or cause; a result **2** an impression that is produced by something • *a cheerful effect*
USAGE Do not confuse with **affect**.

Thesaurus

rapturous, exultant, delighted, euphoric, enraptured, joyful, overjoyed, blissful, delirious, gleeful, happy, (*more informal*) over the moon, (*more informal*) on top of the world

edge *NOUN* **1** *We sat by the edge of the lake.* ▸ border, bank, fringe, extremity, verge, perimeter **2** *They now have the edge over their competitors.* ▸ advantage, upper hand, superiority

edge *VERB* **1** *a dress edged with lace* ▸ trim, decorate, finish, fringe, border **2** *She edged closer to the table.* ▸ creep, inch, slink, steal, sidle, move stealthily

edible *ADJECTIVE* USAGE See the note at the entry for *eatable. The decorations on the tree were all edible.* ▸ fit to eat, safe to eat, eatable, wholesome AN OPPOSITE IS inedible

edict *NOUN* *a royal edict* ▸ decree, order, command, mandate, proclamation, dictum, enactment

educate *VERB* *They hired a tutor to educate the children at home.* ▸ teach, tutor, instruct, coach, train, drill, cultivate, school

educated *ADJECTIVE* *an educated woman named Fiona* ▸ learned, knowledgeable, cultivated, cultured, well read, informed, refined, enlightened, civilized, erudite, literate, numerate, sophisticated
AN OPPOSITE IS uneducated

education *NOUN* *He had received a first-class education.* ▸ schooling, training, teaching, instruction, tuition, coaching, curriculum, enlightenment, guidance

eerie *ADJECTIVE* *an eerie silence* ▸ weird, strange, uncanny, sinister, frightening, (*more informal*) spooky, (*more informal*) creepy, (*more informal*) scary

effect *NOUN* **1** *The effect of all these announcements was to confuse everyone.* ▸ result, consequence, upshot, outcome, conclusion **2** *Sandy and I were feeling the effect of our long day.* ▸ consequence, repercussion, result, influence, aftermath **3** *The violence of those years had a profound effect on people.* ▸ impression, impact **4** *The drug was losing its effect.* ▸ effectiveness, efficacy, power, potency
in effect *He was now in effect a figurehead with little real power.* ▸ in fact, effectively, really, actually, in truth, to all intents and purposes
take effect *The change takes effect next April.* ▸ come into force, be effective, become operative, become valid, be implemented
AN OPPOSITE IS lapse

effect *VERB* USAGE Do not confuse this word, which means 'to achieve or bring about', with *affect*, which means 'to cause a change in'. *We need to effect a compromise.* ▸ achieve, accomplish, bring about, carry out, initiate, make, put into effect, cause, create, execute, implement

effective ADJECTIVE **1** producing the effect that is wanted **2** impressive and striking
▷ **effectively** ADVERB **effectiveness** NOUN

effeminate ADJECTIVE (said about a man) having qualities that are thought to be feminine
▷ **effeminacy** NOUN

efficient ADJECTIVE doing work well; effective
▷ **efficiently** ADVERB **efficiency** NOUN

effort NOUN **efforts 1** the use of energy; the energy used **2** something difficult or tiring **3** an attempt • *This painting is a good effort.*

e.g. ABBREVIATION for example
USAGE Do not confuse with **i.e.**

egg[1] NOUN **eggs 1** a more or less round object produced by the female of birds, fish, reptiles, and insects, which may develop into a new individual if fertilized **2** a hen's or duck's egg used as food **3** an ovum

egg[2] VERB **eggs, egging, egged** encourage someone with taunts or dares etc. • *We egged him on.*

ego (eeg- oh) NOUN **egos** a person's self or self-respect

Eid (eed) NOUN a Muslim festival marking the end of the fast of Ramadan

eiderdown NOUN **eiderdowns** a quilt stuffed with soft material

eight ADJECTIVE, NOUN **eights** the number 8
▷ **eighth** ADJECTIVE, NOUN

eighteen ADJECTIVE, NOUN the number 18
▷ **eighteenth** ADJECTIVE, NOUN

eighty ADJECTIVE, NOUN **eighties** the number 80
▷ **eightieth** ADJECTIVE, NOUN

either ADJECTIVE, PRONOUN **1** one or the other of two • *Either team can win.* • *either of them* **2** both of two • *There are fields on either side of the river.*

either ADVERB also; similarly • *If you won't go, I won't either*

either CONJUNCTION *(used with or)* the first of two possibilities • *He is either ill or drunk.* • *Either come right in or go away.*

ejaculate VERB **ejaculates, ejaculating, ejaculated 1** (said about a man) produce semen from the penis **2** (*formal*) suddenly say something
▷ **ejaculation** NOUN

eject VERB **ejects, ejecting, ejected 1** send something out forcefully **2** force someone to leave **3** (said about a pilot) be thrown out of an aircraft in a special seat in an emergency
▷ **ejection** NOUN **ejector** NOUN

elaborate (il- ab- er- at) ADJECTIVE having many parts or details; complicated
▷ **elaborately** ADVERB **elaborateness** NOUN

elaborate (il- ab- er- ayt) VERB **elaborates, elaborating, elaborated** explain or work something out in detail
▷ **elaboration** NOUN

elastic NOUN cord or material woven with strands of rubber etc. so that it can stretch

elastic ADJECTIVE able to be stretched or squeezed and then go back to its original length or shape
▷ **elasticity** NOUN

Thesaurus

effective ADJECTIVE **1** *There is no effective alternative.* ► useful, workable, successful, fruitful, productive, worthwhile, potent, powerful, effectual, efficient, real, strong, (*more formal*) efficacious
AN OPPOSITE IS ineffective **2** *The government still lacks an effective opposition.* ► capable, competent, able, proficient, useful **3** *He produced several effective arguments.* ► convincing, cogent, persuasive, compelling, telling, striking, meaningful
OPPOSITES ARE weak, unconvincing **4** *The changes will be effective from midnight.* ► operative, in force, valid
OPPOSITES ARE inoperative, invalid

efficient ADJECTIVE **1** *The housekeeping was extremely efficient.* ► methodical, systematic, well organized, cost-effective
AN OPPOSITE IS inefficient **2** *She was lucky to have found such an efficient young assistant.* ► capable, competent, proficient, able, well-organized, businesslike

effort NOUN **1** *We will make an effort to complete the task in time.* ► attempt, endeavour, try, (*more informal*) shot, (*more informal*) stab **2** *It took considerable effort to get the boiler working again.* ► exertion, energy, trouble, force, application, pains **3** *It was a tremendous team effort.* ► achievement, accomplishment, performance, feat, undertaking, success

egg VERB **egg on** *One of the group was egging the others on.* ► urge, goad, drive, provoke, incite, encourage

eject VERB **1** *Two heavy bouncers arrived to eject him from the club.* ► expel, throw out, evict, remove, dismiss, (*more informal*) kick out **2** *A tall chimney was ejecting black smoke.* ► emit, discharge, send out, pour out, spew out, give off, belch, disgorge

elaborate ADJECTIVE **1** *elaborate schemes to raise money* ► complicated, complex, intricate, detailed, extensive, well worked out, involved
AN OPPOSITE IS simple **2** *elaborate wood carvings* ► ornate, decorative, ornamental, intricate, fancy, baroque, rococo, showy
OPPOSITES ARE simple, plain

elastic ADJECTIVE **1** *An elastic cord is tied to an ankle.* ► flexible, plastic, pliable, pliant,

elbow *NOUN* **elbows** the joint in the middle of the arm

elbow *VERB* **elbows, elbowing, elbowed** push with the elbow

elder[1] *ADJECTIVE* older • *my elder brother*

elder *NOUN* **elders** **1** an older person • *Respect your elders!* **2** an official in certain Churches

elder[2] *NOUN* **elders** a tree with white flowers and black berries
▷ **elderberry** *NOUN*

elderly *ADJECTIVE* rather old

eldest *ADJECTIVE* oldest

elect *VERB* **elects, electing, elected** **1** choose by voting **2** choose to do something; decide

election *NOUN* **elections** electing; the process of electing Members of Parliament

electorate *NOUN* **electorates** all the electors

electric *ADJECTIVE* **1** to do with or worked by electricity **2** causing sudden excitement • *The news had an electric effect*
▷ **electrical** *ADJECTIVE* **electrically** *ADVERB*

electric chair *NOUN* an electrified chair used for capital punishment in the USA

electrician *NOUN* **electricians** a person whose job is to deal with electrical equipment

electricity *NOUN* a form of energy carried by certain particles of matter (electrons and protons), used for lighting and heating and for making machines work

electrify *VERB* **electrifies, electrifying, electrified** **1** give an electric charge to something **2** supply something with electric power; cause something to work with electricity **3** thrill with sudden excitement
▷ **electrification** *NOUN*

electrocute *VERB* **electrocutes, electrocuting, electrocuted** kill by electricity
▷ **electrocution** *NOUN*

electrode *NOUN* **electrodes** a solid conductor through which electricity enters or leaves a vacuum tube

electromagnet *NOUN* **electromagnets** a magnet worked by electricity
▷ **electromagnetic** *ADJECTIVE*

electron *NOUN* **electrons** a particle of matter with a negative electric charge

electronic *ADJECTIVE* produced or worked by a flow of electrons
▷ **electronically** *ADVERB*

electronic mail *NOUN* a system of sending messages and data from one computer to another by means of a network

electronics *NOUN* the use or study of electronic devices

elegant *ADJECTIVE* graceful and dignified
▷ **elegantly** *ADVERB* **elegance** *NOUN*

element *NOUN* **elements** **1** each of the parts that make up a whole thing **2** each of about 100 substances composed of atoms that have the same number of protons **3** a basic or elementary principle • *the elements of algebra* **4** a wire or coil that gives out heat in an electric fire or cooker etc. **5** the environment or circumstances that suit you best • *Karen is really in her element at parties.*
the elements the forces of weather, such as rain, wind, and cold

Thesaurus

rubbery, bendy, ductile, yielding, (*more informal*) bouncy, (*more informal*) springy, (*more informal*) stretchy AN OPPOSITE IS rigid
2 *The arrangements can be made more elastic if you wish.* ► flexible, adaptable, adjustable, variable, accommodating OPPOSITES ARE rigid, fixed

elated *ADJECTIVE* *Her huge win left her feeling elated.* ► thrilled, exhilarated, ecstatic, exultant, delighted, euphoric, overjoyed, (*more informal*) over the moon, (*more informal*) on top of the world

elderly *ADJECTIVE* *the increase in the number of elderly people* ► aged, ageing, old, senile

elect *VERB* *The Party elects a leader every four years.* ► choose, select, vote for, pick, adopt, appoint, decide on, name, nominate

election *NOUN* **1** *the election of a president* ► selection, choosing, ballot (for), poll (for), vote (for) **2** *She became an MP in the 1997 election.* ► poll, vote, ballot RELATED NOUN psephology

electric *ADJECTIVE* *The atmosphere in the room was electric.* ► electrifying, exciting, dramatic, thrilling, tense, charged

electrifying *ADJECTIVE* *an electrifying performance* ► thrilling, exciting, astounding, hair-raising, stimulating, amazing, astonishing, electric

elegant *ADJECTIVE* **1** *Fire destroyed an elegant building in the Old Town.* ► handsome, stylish, graceful, gracious, smart, tasteful AN OPPOSITE IS inelegant **2** *A tall elegant woman walked in.* ► graceful, fashionable, beautiful, chic, smart **3** *an elegant solution to an awkward problem* ► neat, ingenious, clever, deft, effective

element *NOUN* **1** *That is only one element of the situation.* ► component, factor, part, ingredient, constituent, piece, strand, aspect **2** *There is an element of truth in the story.* ► trace, hint, touch, suspicion, smattering, soupçon **3** *James was in his element messing about with old cars.* ► environment, domain, habitat, sphere

A B C D E F G H I J K L M N O P Q R S T U V W X Y Z

elementary *ADJECTIVE* dealing with the simplest stages of something; easy

elephant *NOUN* **elephants** a very large animal with a trunk and tusks

elevate *VERB* **elevates, elevating, elevated** lift or raise something to a higher position
▷ **elevation** *NOUN*

eleven *ADJECTIVE, NOUN* **elevens** the number 11
▷ **eleventh** *ADJECTIVE, NOUN*

elicit (ill- iss- it) *VERB* **elicits, eliciting, elicited** draw out information by reasoning or questioning

eligible (el- ij- ib- ul) *ADJECTIVE* qualified or suitable for something
▷ **eligibility** *NOUN*

eliminate *VERB* **eliminates, eliminating, eliminated** get rid of something
▷ **elimination** *NOUN*

elision (il- li*zh*- on) *NOUN* omitting part of a word in pronouncing it, e.g. in saying *I'm* for *I am*

elite (ay- leet) *NOUN* a group of people given privileges which are not given to others

ellipse (il- ips) *NOUN* **ellipses** an oval shape

elliptical (il- ip- tik- al) *ADJECTIVE* **1** shaped like an ellipse **2** with some words omitted • *an elliptical phrase*
▷ **elliptically** *ADVERB*

elm *NOUN* **elms** a tall tree with rough leaves

elocution (el- o- kew- shon) *NOUN* the art of speaking clearly and correctly

elongated *ADJECTIVE* made longer; lengthened
▷ **elongation** *NOUN*

elope *VERB* **elopes, eloping, eloped** run away secretly to get married
▷ **elopement** *NOUN*

eloquent *ADJECTIVE* speaking fluently and expressing ideas vividly
▷ **eloquently** *ADVERB* **eloquence** *NOUN*

else *ADVERB* **1** besides; other • *Nobody else knows.* **2** otherwise; if not • *Run or else you'll be late.*

elsewhere *ADVERB* somewhere else

elude (il- ood) *VERB* **eludes, eluding, eluded** avoid being caught by someone • *The fox eluded the hounds.*
▷ **elusive** *ADJECTIVE*
USAGE Do not confuse with **allude**.

email *NOUN* electronic mail
▷ **email** *VERB*

emancipate (im- an- sip- ayt) *VERB* **emancipates, emancipating, emancipated** set free from slavery or other restraints
▷ **emancipation** *NOUN*

embalm *VERB* **embalms, embalming, embalmed** preserve a dead body from decay by using spices or chemicals

embankment *NOUN* **embankments** a long bank of earth or stone to hold back water or support a road or railway

embargo *NOUN* **embargoes** an official ban, especially on trade with a country

embark *VERB* **embarks, embarking, embarked** put or go on board a ship or aircraft
▷ **embarkation** *NOUN*
embark on begin • *They embarked on a dangerous exercise.*

embarrass *VERB* **embarrasses, embarrassing, embarrassed** make someone feel awkward or ashamed
▷ **embarrassment** *NOUN*

Thesaurus

the elements *We could brave the elements in our cagoules.* ► the weather, the wind and rain

elementary *ADJECTIVE* **1** *an elementary maths course* ► basic, rudimentary, fundamental, introductory, primary AN OPPOSITE IS advanced **2** *The answer to the question is elementary.* ► simple, easy, straightforward, uncomplicated

elevated *ADJECTIVE* **1** *an elevated roadway* ► raised, overhead, high **2** *elevated discussions* ► grand, dignified, noble, superior, exalted, lofty

eligible *ADJECTIVE* **be eligible for** *You would be eligible for tax relief on donations.* ► be entitled to, qualify for, be allowed, be permitted AN OPPOSITE IS ineligible

eliminate *VERB* **1** *We can eliminate sabotage as a cause of the accident.* ► exclude, discount, disregard, remove **2** *The junta went on to eliminate many of their opponents.* ► get rid of, do away with, eradicate, exterminate, kill, murder, stamp out

eloquent *ADJECTIVE* *After dinner he made an eloquent speech.* ► expressive, articulate, fluent, moving, stirring, forceful, potent, persuasive, powerful, unfaltering AN OPPOSITE IS inarticulate

embark *VERB* **1** *Passengers may embark from eight o'clock this evening.* ► board, go aboard, go on board OPPOSITES ARE disembark, land **2 embark on** *He was ready to embark on a career in medicine.* ► begin, start, enter on, commence, undertake, take up, set about

embarrass *VERB* *He gazed at her until he realized he was embarrassing her.* ► make (someone) uncomfortable, make (someone) feel embarrassed, disconcert, distress, upset, shame, mortify, fluster, nonplus, humiliate

embassy *NOUN* **embassies** **1** an ambassador and his or her staff **2** the building where they work

embellish *VERB* **embellishes**, **embellishing**, **embellished** ornament something; add details to it
▷ **embellishment** *NOUN*

embers *PLURAL NOUN* small pieces of glowing coal or wood in a dying fire

embezzle *VERB* **embezzles**, **embezzling**, **embezzled** take dishonestly money that was left in your care
▷ **embezzlement** *NOUN*

emblem *NOUN* **emblems** a symbol that represents something • *The crown is a royal emblem.*
▷ **emblematic** *ADJECTIVE*

embody *VERB* **embodies**, **embodying**, **embodied** **1** express principles or ideas in a visible form • *The house embodies our idea of a modern home.* **2** include or contain • *Parts of the old treaty are embodied in the new one.*
▷ **embodiment** *NOUN*

embrace *VERB* **embraces**, **embracing**, **embraced** **1** hold someone closely in your arms **2** include a number of things **3** accept or adopt a cause or belief

embrace *NOUN* **embraces** a hug

embroider *VERB* **embroiders**, **embroidering**, **embroidered** **1** decorate cloth with needlework **2** add made-up details to a story to make it more interesting
▷ **embroidery** *NOUN*

embryo (em- bree- oh) *NOUN* **embryos** **1** a baby or young animal as it starts to grow in the womb; a young bird growing in an egg **2** anything in its earliest stages of development
▷ **embryonic** (em- bree- on- ik) *ADJECTIVE*

emend *VERB* **emends**, **emending**, **emended** remove errors from a piece of writing

emerald *NOUN* **emeralds** **1** a bright-green precious stone **2** its colour

emerge *VERB* **emerges**, **emerging**, **emerged** **1** come out or appear **2** become known
▷ **emergence** *NOUN* **emergent** *ADJECTIVE*

emergency *NOUN* **emergencies** a sudden serious happening needing prompt action

emigrate *VERB* **emigrates**, **emigrating**, **emigrated** leave your own country and go and live in another
▷ **emigration** *NOUN* **emigrant** *NOUN*
USAGE People are *emigrants* from the country they leave and *immigrants* in the country where they settle.

eminent *ADJECTIVE* **1** famous and respected **2** outstanding and conspicuous
▷ **eminently** *ADVERB* **eminence** *NOUN*

emit *VERB* **emits**, **emitting**, **emitted** send out light, heat, fumes, etc.
▷ **emission** *NOUN*

Thesaurus

embarrassed *ADJECTIVE* *Geoff's outspoken remarks left him feeling embarrassed.*
► awkward, self-conscious, disconcerted, uncomfortable, abashed, mortified, ashamed, confused, distressed, flustered, nonplussed, humiliated, shamed, upset, (*more informal*) red in the face

embarrassing *ADJECTIVE* *She was afraid of making an embarrassing mistake.* ► awkward, humiliating, shaming, shameful, disconcerting, distressing, mortifying, upsetting

embarrassment *NOUN* *Jane tried to hide her embarrassment.* ► awkwardness, self-consciousness, discomfort, unease, mortification, humiliation, distress

emblem *NOUN* *America's national emblem, the bald eagle* ► symbol, sign, token, mark, insignia, badge, crest, device, image, regalia, seal

embrace *VERB* **1** *The old man got up and embraced his son.* ► hug, clasp, hold, cuddle, grasp, squeeze **2** *Imelda could not embrace the idea of life without a husband.* ► accept, espouse, welcome, take on, receive **3** *The county embraces the best part of two national parks.* ► comprise, embody, include, incorporate, bring together, contain, assimilate, take in

emerge *VERB* **1** *A cyclist emerged from the entrance.* ► come out, appear, come into view, issue, emanate AN OPPOSITE IS disappear
2 *Another version of the story later emerged.*
► become known, become evident, be revealed, come to light, surface, unfold, (*more informal*) crop up

emergency *NOUN* *She offered a helping hand in an emergency.* ► crisis, danger, difficulty, predicament, urgent situation, extremity, (*more informal*) tight spot

eminent *ADJECTIVE* *an eminent scientist and scholar* ► distinguished, famous, prominent, well known, celebrated, acclaimed, renowned, illustrious, famed, notable, noteworthy, esteemed, respected, honoured, outstanding

emission *NOUN* *carbon dioxide emissions*
► discharge, release, issue, outpouring, emanation

emit *VERB* *Vehicle exhausts emit hydrocarbons.*
► discharge, release, give off, give out, pour out, radiate

emotion *NOUN* **emotions** a strong feeling in the mind, such as love or hate
▷ **emotional** *ADJECTIVE* **emotionally** *ADVERB*

emperor *NOUN* **emperors** a man who rules an empire

emphasis (em- fa- sis) *NOUN* **emphases** **1** special importance given to something **2** stress put on a word or part of a word
▷ **emphasize** *VERB*

emphatic (im- fat- ik) *ADJECTIVE* using emphasis
▷ **emphatically** *ADVERB*

empire *NOUN* **empires** **1** a group of countries controlled by one person or government **2** a large business organization controlled by one person or group

employ *VERB* **employs, employing, employed** **1** pay a person to work for you **2** make use of
• *Our doctor employs the most modern methods.*
▷ **employment** *NOUN*

employee *NOUN* **employees** a person employed by someone

employer *NOUN* **employers** a person or organization that employs people

empress *NOUN* **empresses** **1** a woman who rules an empire **2** an emperor's wife

empty *ADJECTIVE* **1** with nothing in it **2** with nobody in it **3** with no meaning or no effect
• *empty promises*
▷ **emptily** *ADVERB* **emptiness** *NOUN*

empty *VERB* **empties, emptying, emptied** make or become empty

emulsion *NOUN* **emulsions** **1** a creamy or slightly oily liquid **2** a kind of water-based paint **3** the coating on photographic film which is sensitive to light

enable *VERB* **enables, enabling, enabled** give the means or ability to do something

enamel *NOUN* **enamels** **1** a shiny substance for coating metal **2** paint that dries hard and shiny **3** the hard shiny surface of teeth

encamp *VERB* **encamps, encamping, encamped** settle in a camp

encampment *NOUN* **encampments** a camp

Thesaurus

emotion *NOUN* *He spoke with a voice full of emotion.* ► feeling, passion, sentiment, intensity, warmth, agitation, excitement, fervour AN OPPOSITE IS indifference

emotional *ADJECTIVE* **1** *an emotional tribute* ► poignant, passionate, impassioned, intense, moving, touching, warm-hearted **2** *an emotional woman* ► passionate, demonstrative, fervent, sensitive, temperamental, excitable, romantic

emphasis *NOUN* *This year there is a special emphasis given to creative writing.* ► importance, significance, prominence, priority, urgency, weight, stress, attention

emphasize *VERB* *The spokesman emphasized the need to remain calm.* ► stress, underline, focus on, highlight, point up, draw attention to, play up, make a point of OPPOSITES ARE understate, play down

emphatic *ADJECTIVE* *an emphatic refusal* ► absolute, firm, forceful, vehement, vigorous, definite, unequivocal, direct, positive, energetic, out-and-out

employ *VERB* **1** *The business employs over a hundred people.* ► engage, hire, pay, take on, retain, use the services of, give work to, have on the payroll **2** *This medical practice employs the most modern techniques.* ► use, utilize, apply

employee *NOUN* *He was an employee of his own brother's bank.* ► worker, member of staff, member of the workforce

employees *measures to improve working conditions for the employees* ► staff, workforce

employer *NOUN* **1** *His employer was younger than he was.* ► boss, manager, manageress, proprietor, chief executive, head **2** *The Health Service is the country's largest employer.* ► business, management, company, organization

employment *NOUN* *She found employment as a bank clerk.* ► work, a job, a post, a position, a situation, a livelihood

empty *ADJECTIVE* **1** *The house had been empty for years.* ► vacant, unoccupied, uninhabited, abandoned, deserted **2** *Without him her life felt empty.* ► aimless, futile, worthless, purposeless, unimportant, hollow **3** *These warnings were not just empty threats.* ► vain, idle, meaningless, ineffectual

empty *VERB* **1** *No one had troubled to empty the washing machine.* ► unload, unpack, clear OPPOSITES ARE fill, load **2** *He emptied the glass for a second time.* ► drain, exhaust, drink up AN OPPOSITE IS fill

enable *VERB* **1** *The new law will enable individuals to own shares in these companies.* ► authorize, permit, allow, qualify, empower, equip, aid, assist **2** *Wells took time off work to enable him to train twice a day.* ► allow, permit, let, help, make it possible for, provide the means for AN OPPOSITE IS prevent

enchant *VERB* **enchants, enchanting, enchanted** **1** put someone under a magic spell **2** fill someone with intense delight
▷ **enchanter** *NOUN* **enchantment** *NOUN* **enchantress** *NOUN*

encircle *VERB* **encircles, encircling, encircled** surround
▷ **encirclement** *NOUN*

enclose *VERB* **encloses, enclosing, enclosed** **1** put a wall or fence round; shut in on all sides **2** put something into a box or envelope etc.

enclosure *NOUN* **enclosures** **1** enclosing **2** an enclosed area **3** something enclosed with a letter or parcel

encore (on- kor) *NOUN* **encores** an extra item performed at a concert etc. after previous items have been applauded

encounter *VERB* **encounters, encountering, encountered** **1** meet someone unexpectedly **2** experience • *We encountered some difficulties.*

encounter *NOUN* **encounters** **1** an unexpected meeting **2** a battle

encourage *VERB* **encourages, encouraging, encouraged** **1** give confidence or hope; hearten **2** try to persuade; urge **3** stimulate; help to develop • *We need to encourage healthy eating.*
▷ **encouragement** *NOUN*

encroach *VERB* **encroaches, encroaching, encroached** intrude upon someone's rights; go further than the proper limits • *The extra work would encroach on their free time.*
▷ **encroachment** *NOUN*

encrust *VERB* **encrusts, encrusting, encrusted** cover with a crust or layer
▷ **encrustation** *NOUN*

encumber *VERB* **encumbers, encumbering, encumbered** be a burden to; hamper
▷ **encumbrance** *NOUN*

encyclopedia *NOUN* **encyclopedias** a book or set of books containing all kinds of information
▷ **encyclopedic** *ADJECTIVE*

end *NOUN* **ends** **1** the last part or extreme point of something **2** the half of a sports pitch or court defended or occupied by one team or player **3** destruction or death **4** a purpose • *She did it to gain her own ends.*

end *VERB* **ends, ending, ended** bring or come to an end

endanger *VERB* **endangers, endangering, endangered** cause danger to

Thesaurus

enchant *VERB* *The scenery never ceased to enchant me.* ► delight, please, captivate, bewitch, charm, entrance, enthral, mesmerize
OPPOSITES ARE repel, disgust

enclose *VERB* **1** *A tall fence enclosed the garden.* ► surround, circle, encircle, bound, border, skirt, encompass, shut in, fence in, confine, contain **2** *Please enclose payment with your order.* ► include, insert, put in

encounter *VERB* **1** *One day, they encountered their friends.* ► meet, run into, come across, chance on, (*more informal*) bump into **2** *You may encounter a few problems.* ► experience, be faced with, come up against, suffer, undergo

encourage *VERB* **1** *The cries of support encouraged the players.* ► hearten, cheer, inspire, buoy up, uplift, motivate, stimulate, animate, invigorate, spur, rally, reassure **2** *The government is keen to encourage small businesses.* ► support, promote, endorse, stimulate, aid, advance, assist, foster, strengthen **3** *Clever marketing encourages sales.* ► promote, increase, boost, generate, foster, further, be conducive to, be an incentive to, engender, help, induce **4** *Her mother encouraged her to take up medicine.* ► persuade, prompt, urge, invite
AN OPPOSITE IS discourage

encouragement *NOUN* *All they need is a little encouragement.* ► reassurance, support, inspiration, stimulation, cheering up

encouraging *ADJECTIVE* *The first results were very encouraging.* ► reassuring, heartening, promising, favourable, gratifying, hopeful, auspicious, cheering, comforting, optimistic

end *NOUN* **1** *The shed was at the end of the garden.* ► extremity, edge, boundary, limit **2** *The end of the story is confusing.* ► conclusion, ending, culmination, climax, denouement
AN OPPOSITE IS beginning **3** *His end came when he contracted pneumonia.* ► death, demise, passing on, expiry, downfall **4** *The plan was just a means to achieve an end.* ► aim, goal, purpose, objective

end *VERB* **1** *The programme ends at midnight. The bus route ends at this point.* ► finish, conclude, terminate, come to an end, close
OPPOSITES ARE start, begin **2** *He wanted to end his relationship with Greta.* ► break off, stop, halt, discontinue, wind up OPPOSITES ARE maintain, continue **3** *The government plans to end the benefit next year.* ► abolish, terminate, finish, extinguish, put an end to

ending *NOUN* *The story has an exciting ending.* ► end, conclusion, finish, close, resolution, completion, climax, denouement

a b c d e f g h i j k l m n o p q r s t u v w x y z

endless ADJECTIVE **1** never stopping **2** with the ends joined to make a continuous strip for use in machinery etc. • *an endless belt*
▷ **endlessly** ADVERB

endow VERB **endows, endowing, endowed**
1 provide a source of income to establish something • *She endowed a scholarship.*
2 provide with an ability or quality • *He was endowed with great talent.*
▷ **endowment** NOUN

endure VERB **endures, enduring, endured**
1 suffer or put up with pain or hardship etc.
2 continue to exist; last
▷ **endurable** ADJECTIVE **endurance** NOUN

enemy NOUN **enemies 1** one who hates and opposes or seeks to harm another **2** a nation or army etc. at war with another

energetic ADJECTIVE full of energy
▷ **energetically** ADVERB

energy NOUN **energies 1** strength to do things, liveliness **2** the ability of matter or radiation to do work. Energy is measured in joules **3** power obtained from fuel and other resources and used for light and heat, the operation of machinery, etc.

enforce VERB **enforces, enforcing, enforced** compel people to obey a law or rule
▷ **enforcement** NOUN **enforceable** ADJECTIVE

engage VERB **engages, engaging, engaged**
1 arrange to employ or use • *Engage a typist.*
2 occupy the attention of • *They engaged her in conversation.* **3** begin a battle with • *We engaged the enemy.*

engaged ADJECTIVE **1** having promised to marry somebody **2** in use; occupied

engagement NOUN **engagements**
1 engaging something **2** a promise to marry somebody **3** an arrangement to meet somebody or do something **4** a battle

engaging ADJECTIVE attractive or charming

engine NOUN **engines 1** a machine that provides power **2** a vehicle that pulls a railway train; a locomotive [from old French: it originally meant 'cleverness' and is related to *ingenious*]

Thesaurus

endless ADJECTIVE **1** *an endless source of good ideas*
► boundless, infinite, unlimited, unbounded
2 *He sipped endless cups of strong coffee.*
► ceaseless, countless, innumerable, constant, perpetual, interminable, eternal

endurance NOUN **1** *The race is a test of endurance.* ► stamina, staying power, fortitude, perseverance, determination, tenacity, resoluteness, resolution, strength, (*more informal*) grit, (*more informal*) bottle
2 *Such suffering is beyond anyone's endurance.*
► toleration, tolerance, bearing, sufferance, forbearance

endure VERB **1** *The pain is greater than anyone could endure.* ► tolerate, bear, withstand, suffer, cope with, undergo, submit to **2** *Their love will endure for ever.* ► last, survive, abide, persist, prevail, continue, remain, stay

enemy NOUN *The country faces a new and more dangerous enemy.* ► foe, adversary, opponent, antagonist, opposition OPPOSITES ARE friend, ally

energetic ADJECTIVE **1** *an energetic young person*
► dynamic, active, lively, spirited, animated, enthusiastic, indefatigable, tireless, unflagging OPPOSITES ARE inactive, lethargic, lazy
2 *energetic exercises* ► strenuous, vigorous, rigorous, arduous, brisk **3** *an energetic sales promotion* ► forceful, vigorous, aggressive, determined, powerful OPPOSITES ARE feeble, half-hearted

energy NOUN **1** *She felt full of energy.* ► vitality, vigour, drive, liveliness, spirit, verve, zest, zeal, exuberance, strength, (*more informal*) zip AN OPPOSITE IS lethargy **2** *new and cleaner sources of energy* ► power, fuel

engage VERB **1 engage in** *She is always eager to engage in conversation.* ► participate in, take part in, become involved in, go in for, enter into, share in **2** *They decided to engage a nanny for the younger children.* ► employ, hire, recruit, take on, appoint, retain **3** *These activities do not always engage the imagination very well.*
► occupy, absorb, engross, attract, interest, capture, captivate, grip **4** *The infantry engaged the enemy early the next day.* ► fight, do battle with, clash with, encounter, enter into battle with **5** *The lowest gear did not engage properly.*
► connect, mesh, interlock

engaged ADJECTIVE **1** *an engaged couple*
► betrothed, affianced, attached **2** *He was engaged in his work.* ► occupied, busy, engrossed, absorbed, immersed, preoccupied

engagement 1 *They have broken off their engagement.* ► betrothal, promise to marry
2 *He had a business engagement that afternoon.*
► appointment, arrangement, commitment, obligation, meeting, date **3** *A series of military engagements followed.* ► battle, conflict, encounter, fight, clash, skirmish, offensive

engaging ADJECTIVE *an engaging little girl*
► charming, attractive, appealing, delightful, lovely, pleasing, likeable, lovable

engine NOUN **1** *a car engine* ► motor, power unit, mechanism **2** *a railway engine*
► locomotive

engineer *NOUN* **engineers** an expert in engineering

engineer *VERB* **engineers, engineering, engineered** plan and construct or cause to happen • *He engineered a meeting between them.*

engineering *NOUN* the design and building or control of machinery or of structures such as roads and bridges

engrave *VERB* **engraves, engraving, engraved** carve words or lines etc. on a surface
▷ **engraver** *NOUN* **engraving** *NOUN*

enigma (in-ig-ma) *NOUN* **enigmas** something very difficult to understand; a puzzle

enigmatic (en-ig-mat-ik) *ADJECTIVE* mysterious and puzzling
▷ **enigmatically** *ADVERB*

enjoy *VERB* **enjoys, enjoying, enjoyed** get pleasure from something
▷ **enjoyable** *ADJECTIVE* **enjoyment** *NOUN*

enlarge *VERB* **enlarges, enlarging, enlarged** make bigger
▷ **enlargement** *NOUN*

enlighten *VERB* **enlightens, enlightening, enlightened** give more knowledge or information to a person
▷ **enlightenment** *NOUN*

enlist *VERB* **enlists, enlisting, enlisted** **1** join the armed forces **2** obtain someone's support or services etc. • *enlist their help*
▷ **enlistment** *NOUN*

enmity *NOUN* being somebody's enemy; hostility

enormous *ADJECTIVE* very large; huge
▷ **enormously** *ADVERB* **enormousness** *NOUN*

enough *ADJECTIVE, NOUN, ADVERB* as much or as many as necessary • *enough food* • *I have had enough.* • *Are you warm enough?*

enquire *VERB* **enquires, enquiring, enquired** **1** ask for information • *He enquired if I was well.*

Thesaurus

engineer *NOUN the engineer's drawings*
► designer, planner, inventor, architect

engraving *NOUN an engraving of the two younger children* ► etching, print, impression, woodcut, carving

engrossed *ADJECTIVE Fran was engrossed in her book.* ► absorbed, immersed, involved, interested, engaged, preoccupied (by), gripped (by), captivated (by), occupied (by), enthralled (by), fascinated (by), riveted (by)

enhance *VERB These successes enhanced his reputation.* ► improve, further, increase, heighten, reinforce, boost, intensify, strengthen, build up

enjoy *VERB* **1** *We all enjoy our outings. She enjoyed playing the piano.* ► like, love, appreciate, be fond of, be keen on, be pleased by, take pleasure from *or* in, delight in, indulge in, rejoice in, relish, revel in, savour
OPPOSITES ARE dislike, hate **2** *Visitors enjoy many privileges.* ► benefit from, have the benefit of, have the advantage of, experience, use
enjoy yourself ► have fun, have a good time, celebrate, (*informal*) have a ball, (*informal*) let your hair down

enjoyable *ADJECTIVE You can have a good meal in enjoyable surroundings.* ► agreeable, pleasant, delightful, gratifying, likeable, satisfying, delicious, pleasurable, rewarding, entertaining, amusing OPPOSITES ARE unpleasant, disagreeable

enlarge *VERB* **1** *The new emperor sought to enlarge his territory to the east.* ► increase, expand, augment, develop, add to, stretch
2 enlarge on *He didn't want to enlarge on his remarks.* ► elaborate on, expand on, amplify, develop, broaden, supplement, flesh out

enlightened *ADJECTIVE an enlightened attitude to funding the arts* ► informed, educated, liberal, sophisticated, knowledgeable, civilized, cultivated, refined, open-minded

enlist *VERB* **1** *Arafat enlisted thousands of young people in his army.* ► recruit, enrol, conscript, engage, muster **2 enlist in** *The brothers enlisted in the Royal Engineers.* ► enrol in, sign up for, join, enter, join up for, volunteer (for) **3** *In Paris, he enlisted the aid of an influential American physician.* ► obtain, secure, procure, engage, win

enmity *NOUN people who live in a state of enmity with one another* ► hostility, antagonism, animosity, strife, opposition (towards), antipathy (towards), acrimony (towards)
AN OPPOSITE IS friendship

enormity *NOUN* **1** *the enormities of the Nazi years*
► atrocity, outrage, horror, crime, abomination, wickedness **2** *the enormity of the task* ► immensity, hugeness, magnitude, vastness, seriousness, enormousness USAGE Note that *enormity* is not correct when the reference is simply to physical size, e.g. *the enormity of the building*. It's better to say *the huge size of the building* or use one of the synonyms given above.

enormous *ADJECTIVE An enormous insect crept across the floor.* ► huge, gigantic, immense, massive, colossal, (*more informal*) whopping, (*more informal*) ginormous

enough *ADJECTIVE Do you have enough food?*
► sufficient, adequate, ample, as much (food) as you need

enquire *VERB She enquired about times of the trains home.* ► ask, make enquiries, seek information, want to know USAGE Note that

A B C D E F G H I J K L M N O P Q R S T U V W X Y Z

2 investigate something carefully
USAGE See the note at **inquire**.

enquiry *NOUN* **enquiries** **1** a question **2** an investigation

enrage *VERB* **enrages, enraging, enraged** make someone very angry

enrich *VERB* **enriches, enriching, enriched** make richer
▷ **enrichment** *NOUN*

enrol *VERB* **enrols, enrolling, enrolled** **1** become a member of a society etc. **2** make someone into a member
▷ **enrolment** *NOUN*

ensemble (on-sombl) *NOUN* **ensembles** **1** a group of things that go together **2** a group of musicians **3** a matching outfit of clothes

enslave *VERB* **enslaves, enslaving, enslaved** make a slave of someone; force someone into slavery
▷ **enslavement** *NOUN*

ensure *VERB* **ensures, ensuring, ensured** make certain of; guarantee • *Good food will ensure good health.*
USAGE Do not confuse with **insure**.

entail *VERB* **entails, entailing, entailed** make a thing necessary; involve • *This plan entails danger.*
▷ **entailment** *NOUN*

entangle *VERB* **entangles, entangling, entangled** tangle
▷ **entanglement** *NOUN*

enter *VERB* **enters, entering, entered** **1** come in or go in **2** put something into a list or book **3** type something into a computer **4** register as a competitor

enterprise *NOUN* **enterprises** **1** being enterprising; adventurous spirit **2** an undertaking or project **3** business activity • *private enterprise*

enterprising *ADJECTIVE* willing to undertake new or adventurous projects

entertain *VERB* **entertains, entertaining, entertained** **1** amuse **2** have people as guests and give them food and drink **3** consider • *He refused to entertain the idea.*
▷ **entertainer** *NOUN*

entertainment *NOUN* **entertainments** **1** entertaining; being entertained **2** something performed before an audience to amuse or interest them

Thesaurus

inquire is normally used in the meaning 'to make an official investigation', as in *a committee appointed to inquire into the incident.*

enquiry *NOUN* *routine telephone enquiries* ► query, question USAGE Note that *inquiry* is normally used in the meaning 'official investigation', as in *The opposition called for a public inquiry into the incident.*

enrage *VERB* *Such a casual attitude enraged her.* ► anger, annoy, irritate, infuriate, exasperate, incense, vex, madden, aggravate, antagonize, displease, incite, inflame, make angry, (*more informal*) needle, (*more informal*) rile, (*more informal*) bug, (*more informal*) rub up the wrong way OPPOSITES ARE pacify, placate

ensure *VERB* USAGE Note that *ensure* means 'to make sure' whereas *insure* means 'to take out insurance'. *A mild sedative ensured a good night's sleep.* ► guarantee, make sure, secure, confirm, make certain

enter *VERB* **1** *Soldiers entered the building.* ► go in *or* into, come in *or* into, gain access to, set foot in, pass into AN OPPOSITE IS leave **2** *While the sign is up please do not enter.* ► go in, come in AN OPPOSITE IS leave **3** *A bullet had entered his chest.* ► penetrate, pierce, puncture, perforate, make a hole in **4** *That year the Americans entered the war.* ► join, take part in, participate in **5** *I'm going to enter a competition.* ► go in for, become a contestant in, enrol for **6** *Please enter your details on the form.* ► record, register, note, write down

enterprise *NOUN* **1** *a dangerous enterprise* ► undertaking, endeavour, venture, pursuit, operation, project, adventure, business, effort **2** *a charitable enterprise* ► organization, business, establishment, company, firm **3** *Success in the job calls for considerable enterprise.* ► initiative, resourcefulness, resource, adventurousness, spirit, drive, determination, imagination

enterprising *ADJECTIVE* *An enterprising buyer can get quite a bargain at this time of year.* ► adventurous, resourceful, daring, bold, enthusiastic, energetic, imaginative, inventive, creative AN OPPOSITE IS unadventurous

entertain *VERB* **1** *He told stories to entertain his children.* ► amuse, divert, delight, gladden, cheer up, make laugh, raise a smile, (*more informal*) tickle **2** *We will be entertaining friends this Christmas.* ► receive, play host to, cater for, welcome **3** *She refused to entertain the idea.* ► consider, contemplate, countenance, accept, agree to

entertainer *NOUN* *a television entertainer* ► performer, artiste, artist

entertaining *ADJECTIVE* *an entertaining story* ► amusing, enjoyable, witty, funny, diverting, pleasing

entertainment *NOUN* *The holiday includes free evening entertainment.* ► amusement, diversion, enjoyment, recreation, pastime, play, fun, pleasure, sport, distraction

enthusiasm NOUN **enthusiasms** a strong liking, interest, or excitement
▷ **enthusiast** NOUN **enthusiastic** ADJECTIVE

entire ADJECTIVE whole or complete
▷ **entirely** ADVERB

entirety (int- I- rit- ee) NOUN the whole of something
in its entirety in its complete form

entitle VERB **entitles, entitling, entitled** give the right to have something • *This coupon entitles you to a ticket.*
▷ **entitlement** NOUN

entitled ADJECTIVE having as a title • *a short poem entitled 'Spring'*

entomology (en- tom- ol- o- jee) NOUN the study of insects
▷ **entomologist** NOUN

entrance[1] (en- trans) NOUN **entrances 1** the way into a place **2** entering • *Her entrance is the signal for applause.*

entrance[2] (in- trahns) VERB **entrances, entrancing, entranced** fill with intense delight; enchant

entrant NOUN **entrants** someone who enters for an examination or contest etc.

entrench VERB **entrenches, entrenching, entrenched 1** fix or establish firmly • *These ideas are entrenched in his mind.* **2** settle in a well-defended position
▷ **entrenchment** NOUN

entrust VERB **entrusts, entrusting, entrusted** place a person or thing in someone's care

entry NOUN **entries 1** an entrance **2** something entered in a list, diary, or reference book **3** something entered in a competition • *Send your entries to this address.*

entwine VERB **entwines, entwining, entwined** twine round

enumerate VERB **enumerates, enumerating, enumerated** count; list one by one

envelop (en- vel- op) VERB **envelops, enveloping, enveloped** cover or wrap round something completely

envelope (en- vel- ohp) NOUN **envelopes** a wrapper or covering, especially a folded cover for a letter

Thesaurus

enthralling ADJECTIVE *They watched an enthralling series of singles matches.* ► exciting, fascinating, engrossing, captivating, dazzling

enthusiasm NOUN **1** *They will take on their new role with enthusiasm. He has a new-found enthusiasm for the game.* ► eagerness, excitement, keenness, ardour, relish, commitment, zeal, zest, fervour, ambition, drive, panache, spirit, verve
AN OPPOSITE IS apathy **2** *Their latest enthusiasm is swimming.* ► interest, pursuit, pastime, diversion, hobby, passion, craze, (*informal*) fad

enthusiast NOUN *an amateur radio enthusiast* ► devotee, fan, fanatic, aficionado, follower, lover, (*more informal*) buff

enthusiastic ADJECTIVE *The visitors got an enthusiastic reception; a group of enthusiastic supporters* ► eager, keen, ardent, fervent, devoted, passionate, fervent, whole-hearted
OPPOSITES ARE unenthusiastic, apathetic

entice VERB *A friend of mine enticed me to go to a club with him.* ► persuade, tempt, lure (into going), induce, coax

entire ADJECTIVE **1** *He spent his entire life on the island.* ► whole, complete, total, full **2** *The arch of one of the gates is entire.* ► intact, complete, undamaged

entirely ADVERB *I entirely agree with you.* ► completely, absolutely, fully, totally, utterly, thoroughly

entitle VERB **1 entitle to** *The voucher entitles you to free entrance to the gallery.* ► qualify for, authorize to, allow, permit, warrant **2** *The story is entitled 'A Day in the Life of My Dog'.* ► call, name, title, designate

entrance NOUN **1** *The main entrance to the building is round the corner.* ► entry, way in, access, door, doorway, gateway, approach **2** *At the entrance of the hosts a silence fell on the room.* ► entry, appearance, arrival, approach, coming in, going in, (*more formal*) ingress **3** *Several people were refused entrance.* ► admission, admittance, entry, access

entrust VERB **1** *She entrusted her brother with the task.* ► charge, give responsibility for, put in charge of, trust, (*more informal*) saddle **2** *She entrusted the task to her brother.* ► assign, allocate, commit, delegate, confer (on), turn over

entry NOUN **1** *The entry to the grounds was closed.* ► entrance, way in, access, door, doorway, gateway, approach **2** *They were allowed entry on production of a passport.* ► admission, admittance, entrance, access **3** *the entry in the diary* ► item, record, statement, note, insertion **4** *an entry in a competition* ► candidate, competitor, contender, contestant, entrant, participant, player

envelop VERB *A poison gas enveloped the place.* ► cover, surround, enfold, blanket, enwrap, engulf, cloak, cocoon

envelope NOUN *He put the money in an envelope.* ► wrapper, wrapping, cover, sleeve

a b c d e f g h i j k l m n o p q r s t u v w x y z

A B C D E F G H I J K L M N O P Q R S T U V W X Y Z

envious *ADJECTIVE* feeling envy
▷ **enviously** *ADVERB*

environment *NOUN* **environments**
1 surroundings, especially as they affect people's lives **2** the natural world of the land, sea, and air
▷ **environmental** *ADJECTIVE* **environmentally** *ADVERB*

environmentalist *NOUN* **environmentalists** a person who wants to protect or improve the environment

environmentally friendly *ADJECTIVE* not harmful to the environment

envy *NOUN* **1** a feeling of discontent you have when someone possesses things that you would like to have for yourself **2** something causing this • *Their car is the envy of all their friends.*

envy *VERB* **envies, envying, envied** feel envy towards someone

enzyme *NOUN* **enzymes** a kind of substance that assists chemical processes

epic *NOUN* **epics** **1** a long poem or story about heroic deeds or history **2** a spectacular film

epicentre *NOUN* **epicentres** the point where an earthquake reaches the earth's surface

epidemic *NOUN* **epidemics** an outbreak of a disease that spreads quickly among the people of an area

epigram *NOUN* **epigrams** a short witty saying

epilepsy *NOUN* a disease of the nervous system, causing convulsions
▷ **epileptic** *ADJECTIVE, NOUN*

epilogue (ep-il-og) *NOUN* **epilogues** a short section at the end of a book or play etc.

episode *NOUN* **episodes** **1** one event in a series of happenings **2** one programme in a radio or television serial

epitaph *NOUN* **epitaphs** words written on a tomb or describing a person who has died

epithet *NOUN* **epithets** an adjective; words expressing something special about a person or thing, e.g. 'the Great' in *Alfred the Great*

equal *ADJECTIVE* **1** the same in amount, size, or value etc. **2** having the necessary strength, courage, or ability etc. • *She was equal to the task*.
▷ **equally** *ADVERB*

equal *NOUN* **equals** a person or thing that is equal to another • *She has no equal*

equal *VERB* **equals, equalling, equalled** **1** be the same in amount, size, or value etc. **2** match or be as good as • *No one has yet equalled this score.*

equality *NOUN* being equal

equalize *VERB* **equalizes, equalizing, equalized** make things equal
▷ **equalization** *NOUN*

Thesaurus

enviable *ADJECTIVE* *She has the enviable job of entertaining celebrities.* ► attractive, desirable, favourable

envious *ADJECTIVE* *He was envious of his brother's success.* ► jealous, resentful, grudging, begrudging, bitter (about), covetous, dissatisfied, (*more informal*) green with envy (about *or* over)

environment *NOUN* **1** *a natural environment for wild birds* ► habitat, location, setting, surroundings, conditions, situation, milieu, territory **2 the environment** *industrial activities that threaten the environment* ► the natural world, the earth, the planet, the world we live in

envy *NOUN* *He could not help feeling envy at her good luck.* ► jealousy, bitterness, resentment, covetousness, cupidity, dissatisfaction, ill-will

envy *VERB* *He envied her success.* ► be jealous of, be envious of, begrudge, grudge, resent

episode *NOUN* **1** *a happy episode in my life* ► incident, event, occurrence, happening, occasion, circumstance **2** *the final episode of the series* ► instalment, part, section, programme

equal *ADJECTIVE* **1** *a row of houses of equal size* ► identical, similar, uniform, the same, like, corresponding, comparable, commensurate
OPPOSITES ARE unequal, different, varying **2** *an equal contest* ► even, balanced, level, evenly matched OPPOSITES ARE unequal, uneven
3 equal to *We thought he was equal to the task.* ► capable of, fit for, adequate for, good enough for, suitable for, suited for
AN OPPOSITE IS incapable of

equal *NOUN* *They treated him as their equal.* ► peer, equivalent, counterpart, fellow

equal *VERB* **1** *Her performance almost equalled the world record.* ► match, reach, be as good as, compete with, rival **2** *Three and ten equals thirteen.* ► total, amount to

equality *NOUN* **1** *an equality of supply and demand* ► evenness, similarity, balance (between), parity, uniformity, correspondence, identity **2** *equality before the law* ► fairness, justice, equal rights, impartiality

equalize *VERB* **1** *The law equalizes pay for men and women.* ► balance, make equal, level, match, even up, (*more informal*) square **2** *Celtic equalized after ten minutes.* ► level the score, draw level

equation *NOUN* **equations** (in mathematics) a statement that two amounts etc. are equal, e.g. 3 + 4 = 2 + 5
equator *NOUN* **equators** an imaginary line round the Earth at an equal distance from the North and South Poles
equatorial (ek- wa- tor- ee- al) *ADJECTIVE* to do with or near the equator
equilateral (ee- kwi- lat- er- al) *ADJECTIVE* (said about a triangle) having all sides equal
equilibrium (ee- kwi- lib- ree- um) *NOUN* **1** a balance between different forces, influences, etc. **2** a balanced state of mind
equinox (ek- win- oks) *NOUN* **equinoxes** the time of year when day and night are equal in length (about 20 March in spring, about 22 September in autumn)
▷ **equinoctial** *ADJECTIVE*
equip *VERB* **equips, equipping, equipped** supply with what is needed
equipment *NOUN* the things needed for a particular purpose
equivalent *ADJECTIVE* equal in importance, meaning, value, etc.
▷ **equivalence** *NOUN*
-er [1] *and* **-ier** *SUFFIX* can form the comparative of adjectives and adverbs (e.g. *high/higher, lazy/lazier*)
-er [2] *SUFFIX* can form nouns meaning 'a person or thing that does something' (e.g. *farmer, computer*)
era (eer- a) *NOUN* **eras** a period of history
eradicate *VERB* **eradicates, eradicating, eradicated** get rid of something; remove all traces of it
▷ **eradication** *NOUN*
erase *VERB* **erases, erasing, erased** **1** rub something out **2** wipe out a recording on magnetic tape
▷ **eraser** *NOUN*
erect *ADJECTIVE* standing straight up
erect *VERB* **erects, erecting, erected** set up or build something
▷ **erection** *NOUN* **erector** *NOUN*
erosion *NOUN* the wearing away of the earth's surface by the action of water, wind, etc.
erotic *ADJECTIVE* arousing sexual feelings
▷ **erotically** *ADVERB*
errand *NOUN* **errands** a short journey to take a message or fetch goods etc.
erratic (ir- at- ik) *ADJECTIVE* **1** not regular **2** not reliable
▷ **erratically** *ADVERB*
error *NOUN* **errors** a mistake
erupt *VERB* **erupts, erupting, erupted** **1** burst out **2** when a volcano erupts, it shoots out lava
▷ **eruption** *NOUN*
escalate *VERB* **escalates, escalating, escalated** make or become greater, more serious, or more intense • *The riots escalated into a war*
▷ **escalation** *NOUN*

Thesaurus

equip *VERB* **1** *Each seat is equipped with a set of headphones.* ► provide, supply, furnish, fit, fit up **2** *qualifications that will equip you for your careers* ► qualify, prepare
equipment *NOUN* *equipment needed to record the concert* ► apparatus, appliances, tools, gear
equivalent *ADJECTIVE* *a degree or an equivalent qualification* ► comparable, similar, identical, corresponding
era *NOUN* *a new era of peace* ► age, period, epoch
erase *VERB* *They erased a sentence that might cause offence.* ► delete, remove, rub out
erect *ADJECTIVE* *an erect posture* ► upright, rigid, stiff
erect *VERB* *They will erect a walkway to join the two buildings.* ► build, construct, assemble, put up
erode *VERB* *Rainwater has eroded the soil.* ► wear away, wear down, eat away, corrode
erotic *ADJECTIVE* *erotic art* ► sensual, sexual, amatory, carnal, titillating, (*disapproving*) pornographic, (*disapproving*) salacious, (*disapproving*) lewd, (*disapproving*) suggestive
err *VERB* **1** *The authorities had erred in not making the information known.* ► be wrong, make a mistake, misjudge, miscalculate, blunder, slip up **2** *They were punished if they erred.* ► misbehave, do wrong, be bad, be naughty, disobey, transgress
errand *NOUN* *They did errands for their parents.* ► task, job, duty, assignment, commission, mission
erratic *ADJECTIVE* *It is hard to explain such erratic behaviour.* ► changeable, unpredictable, inconstant, irregular, unstable, variable
OPPOSITES ARE consistent, stable
error *NOUN* *The report contained many factual errors.* ► mistake, inaccuracy, slip, blunder, fault, flaw, miscalculation
erupt *VERB* **1** *Lava continued to erupt from the volcano.* ► spew, spout, spurt, gush, issue, pour out, shoot out, belch, be discharged, be emitted, be expelled **2** *Violence erupted on the streets of the city.* ► break out, flare up
eruption *NOUN* **1** *an eruption of Vesuvius; an eruption of violence* ► outbreak, outburst, discharge, burst, explosion **2** *a skin eruption* ► rash, inflammation
escalate *VERB* *The dispute might escalate into an all-out war.* ► grow, develop, build up, heighten, intensify, accelerate

A B C D E F G H I J K L M N O P Q R S T U V W X Y Z

escalator *NOUN* **escalators** a staircase with an endless line of steps moving up or down

escapade (es- ka- payd) *NOUN* **escapades** a reckless adventure

escape *VERB* **escapes, escaping, escaped 1** get yourself free; get out or away **2** avoid something • *He escaped punishment* **3** be forgotten by someone • *Her name escapes me for the moment*

escape *NOUN* **escapes 1** escaping **2** a way to escape

escapism *NOUN* escaping from the difficulties of life by thinking about or doing more pleasant things
▷ **escapist** *ADJECTIVE*

escort (ess- kort) *NOUN* **escorts** a person or group accompanying a person or thing, especially to give protection

escort (iss- kort) *VERB* **escorts, escorting, escorted** act as an escort to somebody or something

especially *ADVERB* **1** in particular **2** to a great extent

espionage (ess- pee- on- ah*zh*) *NOUN* spying

espresso *NOUN* **espressos** coffee made by forcing steam through ground coffee beans

Esq. *ABBREVIATION* (short for **Esquire**) a title written after a man's surname where no title is used before his name

-ess *SUFFIX* forms feminine nouns (e.g. *lioness, princess*)

essay (ess- ay) *NOUN* **essays 1** a short piece of writing in prose **2** an attempt

essence *NOUN* **essences 1** the most important quality or element of something **2** a concentrated liquid

essential *ADJECTIVE* not able to be done without
▷ **essentially** *ADVERB*

essential *NOUN* **essentials** an essential thing

-est or **-iest** *SUFFIX* can form the superlative of adjectives and adverbs (e.g. *high/highest, lazy/laziest*)

establish *VERB* **establishes, establishing, established 1** set up a business, government, or relationship etc. on a firm basis **2** show something to be true; prove • *He established his innocence.*
the established Church a country's national Church, officially recognized as such by law

establishment *NOUN* **establishments**
1 establishing something **2** a business firm or other institution
the Establishment people who are established in positions of power and influence

Thesaurus

escapade *NOUN a dangerous escapade*
► adventure, exploit, prank, caper, mischief, romp, antic, spree, fling, scrape, stunt, (*more informal*) lark

escape *NOUN* **1** *an escape from prison*
► breakout, getaway, absconding, bolt, flight, flit, retreat, running away **2** *an escape of gas*
► leak, leakage, emission, seepage, discharge **3** *an escape from life's troubles* ► distraction, diversion, relief, avoidance, relaxation

escape *VERB* **1** *They must have had help to escape.*
► get away, break free, break out, break loose, run away, abscond, make a break for it **2** *Oil was escaping from a crack in the hull.* ► leak, seep, ooze, discharge, drain, pour out, run out **3** *The passengers all escaped serious injury. We managed to escape a lot of the work.* ► avoid, evade, elude, dodge, miss

escort *NOUN* **1** *The police provided an escort.*
► guard, guide, bodyguard, convoy **2** *a royal escort* ► attendant, entourage, train, retinue

escort *VERB A representative will escort you to your seat.* ► accompany, conduct, guide, lead, take, show, usher

especially *ADVERB* **1** *Property is especially expensive in the central area of the city.*
► particularly, exceptionally, extremely, peculiarly, extraordinarily, remarkably, uncommonly **2** *Patients, especially those with head injuries, become disoriented.* ► chiefly, mainly, principally, particularly, in particular, above all, primarily

essay *NOUN I have to write an essay by the end of the week.* ► article, piece of writing, composition, assignment, study

essence *NOUN* **1** *The essence of good detective work is patience.* ► nature, substance, quintessence, core, kernel, basis, crux, essential part **2** *Add a little vanilla essence.*
► extract, concentrate

essential *ADJECTIVE The leaflet provides essential travel information.* ► necessary, basic, vital, important, indispensable, crucial, fundamental, principal, key, primary, requisite, main AN OPPOSITE IS inessential

establish *VERB* **1** *The new evidence established their guilt.* ► prove, demonstrate, substantiate, confirm, indicate, affirm, verify, certify, authenticate **2** *The Bank aims to establish branches throughout the world.* ► set up, install, found, initiate, institute, organize, inaugurate, create, base

established *ADJECTIVE an established practice*
► accepted, confirmed, orthodox, traditional, customary, prevailing, well known, well tried, familiar, entrenched, long-standing, routine

estate *NOUN* **estates** **1** an area of land with a set of houses or factories on it **2** a large area of land owned by one person **3** all that a person owns when he or she dies **4** (*old use*) a condition or status • *the holy estate of matrimony*

estate agent *NOUN* **estate agents** a person whose business is selling or letting houses and land

esteem *VERB* **esteems, esteeming, esteemed** think that a person or thing is excellent

esteem *NOUN* respect and admiration

estimable *ADJECTIVE* worthy of esteem

estimate (ess- tim- at) *NOUN* **estimates** a rough calculation or guess about an amount or value

estimate (ess- tim- ayt) *VERB* **estimates, estimating, estimated** make an estimate
▷ **estimation** *NOUN*

estuary (ess- tew- er- ee) *NOUN* **estuaries** the mouth of a river where it reaches the sea and the tide flows in and out

etc. *ABBREVIATION* (short for **et cetera**) and other similar things; and so on

etch *VERB* **etches, etching, etched** **1** engrave a picture with acid on a metal plate, especially for printing **2** if something is etched on your mind or memory, it has made a deep impression and you will never forget it
▷ **etcher** *NOUN*

eternal *ADJECTIVE* lasting for ever; not ending or changing
▷ **eternally** *ADVERB* **eternity** *NOUN*

ether (ee- ther) *NOUN* **1** a colourless liquid that evaporates easily into fumes that are used as an anaesthetic **2** the upper air

ethereal (ith- eer- ee- al) *ADJECTIVE* light and delicate
▷ **ethereally** *ADVERB*

ethical (eth- ik- al) *ADJECTIVE* **1** to do with ethics **2** morally right; honourable
▷ **ethically** *ADVERB*

ethics (eth- iks) *PLURAL NOUN* standards of right behaviour; moral principles

ethnic *ADJECTIVE* belonging to a particular racial group within a larger set of people

ethnic cleansing *NOUN* the mass expulsion or killing of one ethnic group by another in an area

etiquette (et- ik- et) *NOUN* the rules of correct behaviour

etymology (et- im- ol- o- jee) *NOUN* **etymologies** **1** an account of the origin of a word and its meaning **2** the study of the origins of words
▷ **etymological** *ADJECTIVE*

EU *ABBREVIATION* European Union

eucalyptus (yoo- kal- ip- tus) *NOUN* **eucalyptuses** **1** a kind of evergreen tree **2** a strong-smelling oil obtained from its leaves

Eucharist (yoo- ker- ist) *NOUN* the Christian sacrament in which bread and wine are consecrated and swallowed, commemorating the Last Supper of Christ and his disciples

eulogy (yoo- loj- ee) *NOUN* **eulogies** a piece of praise for a person or thing

Thesaurus

establishment *NOUN* **1** *the establishment of a new republic* ▸ creation, institution, introduction, constitution, formation, foundation, inauguration, inception, composition **2** *an old publishing establishment* ▸ business, concern, enterprise, venture, undertaking, company

estate *NOUN* **1** *The family lived in a housing estate.* ▸ development, area, land **2** *Her grandfather had left an estate worth several millions.* ▸ assets, possessions, wealth, property, belongings, holdings

esteem *NOUN* *She was held in high esteem by all her friends.* ▸ respect, admiration, favour, honour, regard, opinion, acclaim, estimation, credit, reverence, veneration

estimate *NOUN* **1** *Our estimate of the situation is fairly dire.* ▸ assessment, appraisal, evaluation, estimation, judgement, opinion, view **2** *The painter will let us have an estimate.* ▸ price, quotation, reckoning, specification, valuation, calculation

estimate *VERB* *The agents estimated the selling price of the house at over a million pounds.* ▸ reckon, consider, assess, evaluate, calculate, gauge, work out

eternal *ADJECTIVE* **1** *eternal happiness* ▸ everlasting, never-ending, unending, undying, enduring, abiding, timeless, infinite
OPPOSITES ARE transient, ephemeral **2** *I'm tired of your eternal complaining.* ▸ constant, continual, interminable, ceaseless, unceasing, incessant, everlasting, never-ending, perpetual, persistent, unremitting
OPPOSITES ARE occasional, intermittent

eternity *NOUN* **1** *the eternity after death* ▸ afterlife, eternal life, infinity, perpetuity, immortality **2 an eternity** (*informal*) *We waited an eternity for a train.* ▸ ages, hours, a long time, for ever

ethics *PLURAL NOUN* *the ethics of medical research* ▸ morality, moral code, morals, principles, propriety, standards, values, ideals, rights and wrongs

a b c d e f g h i j k l m n o p q r s t u v w x y z

A B C D E F G H I J K L M N O P Q R S T U V W X Y Z

euphemism (yoo- fim- izm) NOUN **euphemisms** a mild word or phrase used instead of an offensive or frank one; *'to pass away'* is a euphemism for *'to die'*.
▷ **euphemistic** ADJECTIVE **euphemistically** ADVERB

euro NOUN **euros** or **euro** the currency which replaced the national currencies of several EU states in 2002

European ADJECTIVE to do with Europe or its people
▷ **European** NOUN

euthanasia (yooth- an- ay- zee- a) NOUN causing somebody to die gently and without pain, especially when they are suffering from a painful incurable disease

evacuate VERB **evacuates, evacuating, evacuated** **1** move people away from a dangerous place **2** make a thing empty of air or other contents
▷ **evacuation** NOUN

evacuee NOUN **evacuees** a person who has been evacuated

evade VERB **evades, evading, evaded** avoid a person or thing by cleverness or trickery

evaluate VERB **evaluates, evaluating, evaluated** estimate the value of something; assess
▷ **evaluation** NOUN

evaporate VERB **evaporates, evaporating, evaporated** **1** change from liquid into steam or vapour **2** cease to exist • *Their enthusiasm had evaporated.*
▷ **evaporation** NOUN

evasion NOUN **evasions** **1** evading **2** an evasive answer or excuse

evasive ADJECTIVE trying to avoid answering something; not frank or straightforward
▷ **evasively** ADVERB **evasiveness** NOUN

even ADJECTIVE **1** level and smooth **2** not varying **3** calm; not easily upset • *an even temper* **4** equal • *Our scores were even* **5** able to be divided exactly by two • *Six and fourteen are even numbers*. COMPARE **odd**
▷ **evenly** ADVERB **evenness** NOUN
get even take revenge

even VERB **evens, evening, evened** make or become even

even ADVERB (used to emphasize a word or statement) • *She ran even faster*
even so although that is correct

even-handed ADJECTIVE fair and impartial

evening NOUN **evenings** the time at the end of the day before most people go to bed

event NOUN **events** **1** something that happens, especially something important **2** a race or competition that forms part of a sports contest

Thesaurus

ethnic ADJECTIVE **1** *people with different ethnic backgrounds* ► cultural, national, indigenous, genetic, tribal, racial **2** *men and women in ethnic dress* ► local, traditional, national, folk

evacuate VERB **1** *It is essential to evacuate everybody from the building.* ► remove, clear, move out, send away **2** *Police decided to evacuate the area.* ► vacate, leave, quit, relinquish, withdraw from, abandon, decamp from, desert, empty

evacuation NOUN **1** *the evacuation of buildings* ► clearance, vacation, abandonment **2** *the evacuation of civilians* ► removal, clearance, eviction

evade VERB **1** *Charlie was clearly guilty of evading his responsibilities.* ► avoid, shirk, shun, dodge, duck, sidestep, steer clear of, turn your back on AN OPPOSITE IS accept **2** *They did all they could do to evade capture.* ► avoid, elude, escape, escape from, fend off, circumvent

evaluate VERB *A panel of doctors will evaluate the treatment.* ► assess, value, gauge, appraise, rate, calculate

evaporate VERB **1** *The water quickly evaporates.* ► disperse, dry up, vaporize AN OPPOSITE IS condense **2** *With this news all their hopes evaporated.* ► disappear, fade, vanish, melt away, come to an end, dissolve, dissipate AN OPPOSITE IS materialize

even ADJECTIVE **1** *an even surface* ► flat, smooth, level, flush, true, unbroken AN OPPOSITE IS rough **2** *an even temperament* ► calm, stable, equable, even-tempered, placid, composed, serene, steady OPPOSITES ARE moody, excitable **3** *the even ticking of the clock* ► steady, regular, constant, uniform, unvarying AN OPPOSITE IS irregular **4** *The scores were even.* ► level, equal, identical, balanced, the same AN OPPOSITE IS unequal

even VERB
even out *I tried to even out the wrinkled carpet.* ► smooth, straighten, flatten, level
even up *Another point will even up the scores* ► level, balance, equalize, (*more informal*) square

evening NOUN *It was evening when we reached home.* ► dusk, sunset, sundown, nightfall, twilight, (*poetic*) eventide, (*poetic*) gloaming

event NOUN **1** *an annual event* ► occurrence, happening, occasion, affair, episode, experience, activity, function, business, circumstance, contingency, eventuality, incident, chance **2** *a sporting event* ► game, match, competition, tournament
in the event *In the event, the plan was abandoned.* ► as it turned out, as it happened, in the end, in actual fact, as a result, as a consequence

eventful *ADJECTIVE* full of happenings

eventual *ADJECTIVE* happening at last • *his eventual success*
▷ **eventually** *ADVERB*

ever *ADVERB* **1** at any time • *the best thing I ever did* **2** always • *ever hopeful* **3** (*informal*, used for emphasis) • *Why ever didn't you tell me?*

evergreen *ADJECTIVE* having green leaves all the year
▷ **evergreen** *NOUN*

every *ADJECTIVE* each without any exceptions • *We enjoyed every minute*
every one each one
every other day or **week** etc., each alternate one; every second one
USAGE Follow with a singular verb, e.g. *Every one of them is growing* (not 'are growing').

everybody *PRONOUN* every person

everyday *ADJECTIVE* ordinary; usual • *everyday clothes*

everyone *PRONOUN* everybody

everything *PRONOUN* **1** all things; all **2** the only or most important thing • *Beauty is not everything.*

everywhere *ADVERB* in every place

evict *VERB* **evicts, evicting, evicted** make people move out from where they are living
▷ **eviction** *NOUN*

evidence *NOUN* **1** anything that gives people reason to believe something **2** statements made or objects produced in a lawcourt to prove something

evident *ADJECTIVE* obvious; clearly seen
▷ **evidently** *ADVERB*

evil *ADJECTIVE* morally bad; wicked
▷ **evilly** *ADVERB*

evil *NOUN* **evils** **1** wickedness **2** something unpleasant or harmful

evolution (ee-vol-oo-shon) *NOUN* **1** gradual change into something different **2** the development of animals and plants from earlier or simpler forms
▷ **evolutionary** *ADJECTIVE*

evolve *VERB* **evolves, evolving, evolved** develop gradually or naturally

ewe (yoo) *NOUN* **ewes** a female sheep

ex- *PREFIX* (changing to **ef-** before words beginning with *f*; shortened to **e-** before many consonants) **1** out; away (as in *extract*) **2** up, upwards; thoroughly (as in *extol*) **3** formerly (as in *ex-president*)

Thesaurus

eventful *ADJECTIVE It had been a long and eventful week.* ► busy, lively, active, full, action-packed, remarkable, noteworthy, momentous
OPPOSITES ARE routine, uneventful, dull

eventual *ADJECTIVE We will have to wait for the eventual verdict.* ► final, ultimate, ensuing, resulting, prospective, future

eventually *ADVERB Eventually they agreed.* ► in the end, by and by, finally, at length

everlasting *ADJECTIVE The gift would be an everlasting reminder of her evening.* ► eternal, never-ending, unending, undying, enduring, abiding, timeless, infinite
OPPOSITES ARE transient, ephemeral

everyday *ADJECTIVE Road accidents were an everyday occurrence.* ► commonplace, common, frequent, ordinary, regular, familiar

everyone *PRONOUN She was afraid everyone would know by now.* ► everybody, the whole world, every person, one and all, (*more informal*) every Tom, Dick, and Harry

everywhere *ADVERB He looked everywhere for his keys.* ► all over, in every place, far and wide, high and low

evidence *NOUN* **1** *evidence of life on other planets* ► confirmation, verification, proof, corroboration, substantiation, authentication **2** *Her evidence helped convict all four of them.* ► testimony, statement, information

evident *ADJECTIVE It was evident that he didn't like her.* ► obvious, apparent, clear, plain, noticeable, observable, transparent, discernible AN OPPOSITE IS unclear

evil *ADJECTIVE* **1** *an evil act; the most evil person he had met* ► wicked, bad, wrong, sinful, vile, immoral, depraved OPPOSITES ARE good, virtuous **2** *An evil smell came from the drains.* ► nasty, foul, noxious, unpleasant, offensive, unspeakable, vile, pestilential, poisonous, troublesome AN OPPOSITE IS pleasant **3** *an evil influence* ► harmful, hurtful, pernicious, destructive, deadly, poisonous

evil *NOUN* **1** *a crime of the utmost evil* ► wickedness, wrong, sinfulness, depravity, immorality, vileness, vice, iniquity **2** *a great social evil* ► catastrophe, affliction, disaster, enormity, calamity, curse, misfortune

evoke *VERB The scene evoked memories of her childhood.* ► arouse, stir up, summon up, bring to mind, call to mind, call up, raise, stimulate, inspire, awaken, conjure up, elicit, excite, kindle, produce, provoke, suggest

evolution *NOUN the evolution of scientific methods* ► development, emergence, growth, improvement, maturing, progress, unfolding

exact *ADJECTIVE* **1** correct **2** clearly stated; giving all details • *exact instructions*
▷ **exactly** *ADVERB* **exactness** *NOUN*

exact *VERB* **exacts, exacting, exacted** insist on something and obtain it • *He exacted obedience from the recruits*
▷ **exaction** *NOUN*

exaggerate *VERB* **exaggerates, exaggerating, exaggerated** make something seem bigger, better, or worse etc. than it really is
▷ **exaggeration** *NOUN*

examination *NOUN* **examinations** **1** a test of a person's knowledge or skill **2** examining something; an inspection • *a medical examination*

examine *VERB* **examines, examining, examined** **1** test a person's knowledge or skill **2** look at something closely or in detail
▷ **examiner** *NOUN*

example *NOUN* **examples** **1** anything that shows what others of the same kind are like or how they work **2** a person or thing good enough to be worth imitating

exasperate *VERB* **exasperates, exasperating, exasperated** annoy someone
▷ **exasperation** *NOUN*

excavate *VERB* **excavates, excavating, excavated** dig out; uncover by digging
▷ **excavation** *NOUN* **excavator** *NOUN*

exceed *VERB* **exceeds, exceeding, exceeded** **1** be greater than; surpass **2** do more than you need or ought to do; go beyond a thing's limits • *He has exceeded his authority.*

excel *VERB* **excels, excelling, excelled** be better than others at doing something

Excellency *NOUN* **Excellencies** the title of high officials such as ambassadors and governors

excellent *ADJECTIVE* extremely good
▷ **excellently** *ADVERB* **excellence** *NOUN*

Thesaurus

evolve *VERB* *The plan evolved from quite a simple idea.* ► develop, grow, derive, progress, mature, emerge, expand

exact *ADJECTIVE* **1** *Stacey likes to be exact in her work.* ► careful, precise, accurate, meticulous, methodical, painstaking, rigorous **2** *These are the exact measurements of the room.* ► precise, accurate, correct, definite **3** *Is this an exact copy?* ► identical, faithful, close

exactly *ADVERB* **1** *She looks exactly like her mother at that age.* ► precisely, entirely, absolutely, completely, totally, utterly, every inch **2** *Describe the scene exactly.* ► accurately, precisely, faithfully, in detail

exaggerate *VERB* *The press reports exaggerated the scale of the fire.* ► overstate, overemphasize, overestimate, overstress, overdo, inflate, magnify, make too much of, amplify, enlarge, maximize, (*more informal*) play up opposites are understate, underestimate

examination *NOUN* **1** *the annual examination of the accounts* ► inspection, scrutiny, study, scanning, analysis, appraisal **2** *a written examination in history* ► exam, test, paper **3** *a medical examination* ► check-up, check, inspection, review

examine *VERB* **1** *The Fraud Squad will examine the company accounts for the last ten years.* ► inspect, scrutinize, study, investigate, check, analyse, review, scan, probe **2** *Students are examined at the end of each year.* ► test, assess, appraise **3** *The defence counsel will examine the witness tomorrow.* ► cross-examine, interrogate, cross-question

example *NOUN* **1** *a fine example of a Tudor building* ► specimen, sample, case, exemplar, illustration, instance, occurrence **2** *We ought to follow their example.* ► precedent, model, pattern, ideal, standard **3** *They were convicted as an example to others.* ► warning, lesson, deterrent, caution

exasperate *VERB* *This stupid behaviour exasperated us.* ► infuriate, incense, anger, annoy, irritate, enrage, vex, (*more informal*) rile

excavate *VERB* **1** *Moles had excavated tunnels under the grass.* ► dig, bore, burrow, hollow out **2** *A coin hoard was excavated from the ancient site.* ► unearth, dig up, uncover, discover, reveal

exceed *VERB* **1** *Total luggage weight must not exceed 300 kilos.* ► be more than, be greater than, go over **2** *Police stopped her for exceeding the speed limit.* ► break, go beyond, go faster than **3** *The amount exceeded all our expectations.* ► surpass, beat, outstrip, better, outdo, excel, pass, top

exceedingly *ADVERB* *an exceedingly good meal* ► extremely, exceptionally, especially, supremely, outstandingly, immensely, amazingly, unusually, extraordinarily, tremendously, really, very

excel *VERB* **1** *One choir excelled all the others and was invited back for next year.* ► surpass, outdo, outclass, outstrip, do better than, beat, exceed **2** *He excels at most things he turns his hand to.* ► shine, do well, be good, stand out, be outstanding

excellent *ADJECTIVE* *an excellent idea; The book is excellent.* ► outstanding, very good, first-class,

except *PREPOSITION* excluding; not including • *They all left except me.*

except *VERB* **excepts**, **excepting**, **excepted** exclude; leave out • *I blame you all, no one is excepted.*
USAGE Do not confuse with **accept**.

exception *NOUN* **exceptions** a person or thing that is left out or does not follow the general rule
take exception raise objections to something
with the exception of except

exceptional *ADJECTIVE* **1** very unusual **2** outstandingly good
▷ **exceptionally** *ADVERB*

excess *NOUN* **excesses** too much of something
in excess of more than

excessive *ADJECTIVE* too much or too great • *Do not use excessive force.*
▷ **excessively** *ADVERB*

exchange *VERB* **exchanges**, **exchanging**, **exchanged** give something and receive something else for it
▷ **exchangeable** *ADJECTIVE*

exchange *NOUN* **exchanges** **1** exchanging **2** a place where things (especially stocks and shares) are bought and sold • *a stock exchange* **3** a place where telephone lines are connected to each other when a call is made

exchequer *NOUN* **exchequers** a national treasury into which public funds (such as taxes) are paid

excitable *ADJECTIVE* easily excited

excite *VERB* **excites**, **exciting**, **excited** **1** make someone eager and enthusiastic about something • *The thought of finding gold excited them.* **2** cause a feeling or reaction • *The invention excited great interest.*
▷ **excited** *ADJECTIVE* **excitedly** *ADVERB*

excitement *NOUN* **excitements** a strong feeling of eagerness or pleasure

exclaim *VERB* **exclaims**, **exclaiming**, **exclaimed** shout or cry out in eagerness or surprise

exclamation *NOUN* **exclamations** **1** exclaiming **2** a word or words cried out expressing joy or pain or surprise etc.

Thesaurus

first-rate, superlative, superb, remarkable, exceptional, splendid, wonderful, marvellous, tremendous

except *PREPOSITION* *The restaurant is open every evening except Monday.* ► excluding, except for, apart from, other than, besides

exception *NOUN* *Most countries are represented, although there are a few exceptions.* ► abnormality, irregularity, oddity, peculiarity, deviation, anomaly, departure, eccentricity, special case, freak, quirk, rarity
take exception to *She takes exception to people smoking in the house.* ► object to, disapprove of, complain about, demur at, resent, be offended by

exceptional *ADJECTIVE* **1** *a woman of exceptional ability* ► outstanding, excellent, very good, first-class, first-rate, superlative, superb, remarkable **2** *exceptional weather patterns* ► unusual, abnormal, untypical, extraordinary, strange, irregular, peculiar, freakish

excess *NOUN* **1** *an excess of vitamin E* ► surplus, surfeit, superfluity, oversufficiency, superabundance, abundance, glut
OPPOSITES ARE scarcity, deficit **2** *a lifestyle characterized by excess* ► extravagance, overindulgence, intemperance, lavishness, prodigality

excessive *ADJECTIVE* **1** *excessive drinking* ► immoderate, inordinate, extreme, extravagant, disproportionate, superfluous **2** *The cost proved excessive.* ► unreasonable, exorbitant, inordinate, (*more informal*) steep

exchange *NOUN* **1** *The two sides agreed to an exchange of prisoners.* ► switch, interchange, replacement, substitution, (*informal*) swap **2** *This misunderstanding led to a series of bitter exchanges.* ► argument, altercation, recrimination, war of words **3** *Archaeological evidence points to an exchange of goods between the two areas.* ► trade, traffic, barter, dealing

exchange *VERB* **1** *The players exchanged shirts at the end of the game.* ► swap, change, switch, interchange **2** *I exchanged my old bike for a smart new one.* ► swap, barter, trade, substitute

excite *VERB* *The prospect of a day out excited them.* ► thrill, exhilarate, elate, enliven, stimulate
AN OPPOSITE IS bore

excited *ADJECTIVE* *The children were becoming excited.* ► animated, stimulated, worked up, boisterous, lively, elated, restless, overwrought, vivacious

excitement *NOUN* **1** *They could hardly conceal their excitement.* ► enthusiasm, exhilaration, agitation, elation, eagerness, stimulation **2** *There will be a lot of excitement at the party this afternoon.* ► commotion, activity, adventure

exciting *ADJECTIVE* *an exciting story* ► thrilling, stirring, exhilarating, rousing, stimulating, invigorating, enthralling, gripping, dramatic, sensational OPPOSITES ARE dull, boring

exclaim *VERB* *He exclaimed that he had never been there.* ► cry, cry out, call, yell, shout, shriek, scream

exclamation *NOUN* *With an exclamation of horror she rushed upstairs.* ► cry, yell, call,

A B C D E F G H I J K L M N O P Q R S T U V W X Y Z

exclamation mark NOUN **exclamation marks** the punctuation mark (!) placed after an exclamation

exclude VERB **excludes, excluding, excluded** **1** keep somebody or something out **2** leave something out • *Do not exclude the possibility of rain.*
▷ **exclusion** NOUN

exclusive ADJECTIVE **1** allowing only certain people to be members etc. • *an exclusive club* **2** not shared with others • *This newspaper has an exclusive report.*
▷ **exclusively** ADVERB **exclusiveness** NOUN
exclusive of excluding, not including • *This is the price exclusive of meals.*

excrement (eks- kri- ment) NOUN waste matter from the body

excrete VERB **excretes, excreting, excreted** get rid of waste matter from the body
▷ **excretion** NOUN **excretory** ADJECTIVE
[from *ex-* = out + Latin *cretum* = separated]

excruciating (iks- kroo- shee- ayt- ing) ADJECTIVE extremely painful; agonizing
▷ **excruciatingly** ADVERB
[from *ex-* = out + Latin *cruciatum* = tortured]

excursion NOUN **excursions** a short journey made for pleasure [from *ex-* = out + Latin *cursus* = course]

excuse (iks- kewz) VERB **excuses, excusing, excused** **1** forgive **2** allow someone not to do something or to leave a room etc. • *Please may I be excused swimming?*

excuse (iks- kewss) NOUN **excuses** a reason given to explain why something wrong has been done

execute VERB **executes, executing, executed** **1** put someone to death as a punishment **2** perform or produce something • *She executed the somersault perfectly.*
▷ **execution** NOUN
[from Latin *executare* = to carry out, to punish]

executive (ig- zek- yoo- tiv) NOUN **executives** a senior person with authority in a business or government organization

exempt ADJECTIVE not having to do something that others have to do • *Charities are exempt from paying tax.*
▷ **exemption** NOUN

exercise NOUN **exercises** **1** using your body to make it strong and healthy **2** a piece of work done for practice

exercise VERB **exercises, exercising, exercised** **1** do exercises **2** give exercise to an animal etc. **3** use • *You must exercise more patience.*

exert VERB **exerts, exerting, exerted** use power or influence etc. • *He exerted all his strength.*
▷ **exertion** NOUN
exert yourself make an effort

exhale VERB **exhales, exhaling, exhaled** breathe out
▷ **exhalation** NOUN

Thesaurus

shout, shriek, interjection, (*old-fashioned*) ejaculation

exclude VERB **1** *They were anxious to exclude the inevitable gatecrashers from the house.* ► keep out, deny access to, ban, disallow, prevent, prohibit, deter, debar, reject **2** *He excluded his own name from the list.* ► omit, leave out, miss out, fail to include, rule out **3** *These figures exclude any allowance for inflation.* ► omit, be exclusive of, not include

exclusive ADJECTIVE **1** *The room is for your exclusive use.* ► sole, unique, private, unshared, undivided, unrestricted **2** *one of London's most exclusive clubs* ► select, elite, fashionable, restrictive, private, premier, (*more informal*) classy, (*more informal*) posh

excursion NOUN *an excursion to Brighton* ► trip, outing, jaunt, journey, expedition, day out, drive, run

excuse NOUN **1** *He trotted out the usual feeble excuses.* ► defence, pretext, explanation, alibi, plea, reason **2** *There is no excuse for what you did.* ► justification, vindication

excuse VERB **1** *We cannot excuse bad behaviour.* ► justify, defend, condone, tolerate, overlook, ignore, sanction, mitigate **2** *She found it hard to excuse them this time.* ► forgive, pardon, absolve

execute VERB **1** *The manoeuvre is particularly hard to execute in heavy traffic.* ► carry out, implement, perform, complete, accomplish, achieve, do, effect **2** *The State no longer executes convicted murderers.* ► put to death, apply the death penalty to, hang, behead, electrocute

exercise NOUN **1** *Regular exercise will keep you fit.* ► physical activity, working out, exertion, training **2** *the exercise of authority* ► use, application, practice **3** **exercises** *army exercises* ► operations, manoeuvres

exercise VERB **1** *She exercises every day.* ► work out, do exercises, keep fit **2** *Please exercise a little patience.* ► use, have, employ, apply **3** *The problem continues to exercise us.* ► trouble, worry, bother, make anxious

exert VERB **1** *She exerts a considerable influence on the children.* ► exercise, wield, bring to bear, apply **2** **exert yourself** *He exerted himself to get*

exhaust *VERB* **exhausts, exhausting, exhausted** **1** make somebody very tired **2** use up something completely
▷ **exhaustion** *NOUN*

exhaust *NOUN* **exhausts** **1** the waste gases or steam from an engine **2** the pipe etc. through which they are sent out

exhaustive *ADJECTIVE* thorough; trying everything possible • *We made an exhaustive search.*
▷ **exhaustively** *ADVERB*

exhibit *VERB* **exhibits, exhibiting, exhibited** show or display something in public
▷ **exhibitor** *NOUN*

exhibit *NOUN* **exhibits** something on display in a gallery or museum

exhibition *NOUN* **exhibitions** a collection of things put on display for people to look at

exhilarate (ig- zil- er- ayt) *VERB* **exhilarates, exhilarating, exhilarated** make someone very happy and excited
▷ **exhilaration** *NOUN*

exhort (ig- zort) *VERB* **exhorts, exhorting, exhorted** try hard to persuade someone to do something
▷ **exhortation** *NOUN*

exile *VERB* **exiles, exiling, exiled** banish

exile *NOUN* **exiles** **1** having to live away from your own country • *He was in exile for ten years* **2** a banished person

exist *VERB* **exists, existing, existed** **1** be present as part of what is real • *Do ghosts exist?* **2** stay alive • *We cannot exist without food.*
▷ **existence** *NOUN* **existent** *ADJECTIVE*

exit *NOUN* **exits** **1** the way out of a building **2** going off the stage • *The actress made her exit.*

exit *VERB* (in stage directions) he or she leaves the stage [from Latin *exit*, = he or she goes out]

Thesaurus

the job done on time. ► strive, endeavour, try hard, make an effort, go to some trouble

exhaust *VERB* **1** *We exhausted the fuel supply after only a week.* ► use up, consume, drain, empty, deplete, dry up, finish off, go through, spend, sap, void **2** *Her day out had exhausted her.* ► tire out, wear out, fatigue, weary, tax, strain

exhausted *ADJECTIVE* **1** *They went to bed exhausted that night.* ► tired out, worn out, weary, fatigued, (*more informal*) shattered, (*more informal*) dead tired, (*more informal*) played out, (*more informal*) washed out **2** *exhausted money reserves* ► depleted, used up, spent

exhausting *ADJECTIVE* *an exhausting journey* ► tiring, wearying, fatiguing, wearing, arduous, strenuous, taxing, gruelling, demanding, laborious, punishing, sapping, difficult, hard, severe AN OPPOSITE IS refreshing

exhaustion *NOUN* *He had to stop from sheer exhaustion.* ► fatigue, weariness, tiredness, debility, weakness AN OPPOSITE IS vigour

exhibit *VERB* **1** *The gallery will exhibit a collection of new paintings.* ► show, display, put on display, present, set up **2** *He exhibited great pride in his family.* ► show, reveal, display, demonstrate, manifest, disclose, express OPPOSITES ARE hide, conceal

exhibition *NOUN* *an exhibition of Greek sculpture* ► display, presentation, show, showing, demonstration

exhilarated *ADJECTIVE* *The day's events left them feeling exhilarated.* ► excited, elated, thrilled, animated, stimulated, worked up AN OPPOSITE IS dejected

exhilarating *ADJECTIVE* *The ride was an exhilarating experience.* ► exciting, thrilling, stirring, rousing, stimulating, invigorating, enthralling, gripping, dramatic, sensational OPPOSITES ARE dull, boring

exhilaration *NOUN* *a feeling of exhilaration* ► excitement, enthusiasm, elation, eagerness, stimulation

exile *NOUN* **1** *The poet was punished with exile.* ► banishment, expulsion, deportation, expatriation, extradition **2** *a group of political exiles* ► émigré, exiled person, displaced person, deportee, expatriate, outcast, refugee

exile *VERB* *The new regime immediately exiled the dictators.* ► expel, banish, deport, drive out, eject, expatriate, send away

exist *VERB* **1** *animals that no longer exist* ► live, occur, be alive, be in existence **2** *They had to exist for years on a meagre income.* ► survive, subsist, live, hold out, keep going, continue, endure, last

existence *NOUN* **1** *The new law threatens the very existence of these old institutions.* ► survival, continuance, continuation, being, actuality, life, living, reality AN OPPOSITE IS non-existence **2** *a dreary existence in a remote part of the country* ► way of life, livelihood, lifestyle

existing *ADJECTIVE* *The existing arrangements were proving inadequate.* ► current, present, available, prevailing, actual, existent, extant
usage You can also say *the arrangements already in place* or *the arrangements already in force.*

exit *NOUN* **1** *A passage on the right leads to the exit.* ► way out, door, doorway, egress, gate, gateway AN OPPOSITE IS entrance **2** *They made a quick exit.* ► departure, withdrawal, retreat,

a b c d e f g h i j k l m n o p q r s t u v w x y z

A B C D E F G H I J K L M N O P Q R S T U V W X Y Z

exorcize *VERB* **exorcizes, exorcizing, exorcized** drive out an evil spirit
▷ **exorcism** *NOUN* **exorcist** *NOUN*

exotic *ADJECTIVE* **1** very unusual • *exotic clothes* **2** from another part of the world • *exotic plants*
▷ **exotically** *ADVERB*

expand *VERB* **expands, expanding, expanded** make or become larger or fuller
▷ **expansion** *NOUN* **expansive** *ADJECTIVE*

expect *VERB* **expects, expecting, expected** **1** think or believe that something will happen or that someone will come **2** think that something ought to happen • *She expects obedience.*

expectant *ADJECTIVE* **1** expecting something to happen; hopeful **2** an expectant mother is a woman who is pregnant
▷ **expectantly** *ADVERB* **expectancy** *NOUN*

expectation *NOUN* **expectations** **1** expecting something; being hopeful **2** something you expect to happen or get

expedient (iks- pee- dee- ent) *ADJECTIVE* **1** suitable or convenient **2** useful and practical though perhaps unfair
▷ **expediently** *ADVERB* **expediency** *NOUN*

expedient *NOUN* **expedients** a means of doing something, especially when in difficulty

expedition *NOUN* **expeditions** **1** a journey made in order to do something • *a climbing expedition* **2** speed or promptness
▷ **expeditionary** *ADJECTIVE*

expel *VERB* **expels, expelling, expelled** **1** send or force something out • *This fan expels stale air.* **2** make a person leave a school or country etc.

expendable *ADJECTIVE* able to be sacrificed or got rid of in order to gain something

expenditure *NOUN* **expenditures** the spending or using up of money or effort etc.

expense *NOUN* **expenses** the cost of doing something

expensive *ADJECTIVE* costing a lot
▷ **expensively** *ADVERB* **expensiveness** *NOUN*

experience *NOUN* **experiences** **1** what you learn from doing or seeing things **2** something that has happened to you

experience *VERB* **experiences, experiencing, experienced** have something happen to you

experienced *ADJECTIVE* having great skill or knowledge from much experience

Thesaurus

leaving, exodus OPPOSITES ARE entrance, arrival **3** *Take the exit marked Leeds.* ► turning, turn-off, turn, road

exotic *ADJECTIVE* **1** *exotic places in the Far East* ► faraway, distant, remote, foreign, romantic, unfamiliar, alien AN OPPOSITE IS familiar **2** *an exhibition of exotic birds* ► foreign, non-native, tropical, alien, unnaturalized, imported AN OPPOSITE IS native **3** *exotic dress* ► colourful, striking, unusual, unfamiliar, unconventional, outlandish AN OPPOSITE IS conventional

expand *VERB* **1** *a good opportunity to expand the business* ► develop, enlarge, extend, broaden, build up, diversify, increase, amplify, augment, elaborate, fill out, make bigger OPPOSITES ARE contract, reduce **2** *Metal expands when heated.* ► increase in size, become larger, swell, dilate, grow, stretch, thicken, widen AN OPPOSITE IS contract

expansive *ADJECTIVE* *After a few drinks he became quite expansive.* ► talkative, communicative, forthcoming, outgoing, sociable, unreserved, uninhibited, voluble, conversational, open OPPOSITES ARE curt, unfriendly

expect *VERB* **1** *We expect a large number of visitors this year.* ► hope for, look for, look forward to, envisage, predict, anticipate, await, bank on **2** *We expect complete discretion.* ► demand, insist on, require, call for, count on, rely on, want **3** *I expect they missed the train.* ► suppose, assume, presume, imagine, believe, guess, judge, think, (*more informal*) reckon

expel *VERB* **1** *He was expelled from the country.* ► banish, exile, deport, drive out, throw out, cast out, evict, expatriate **2** *The machinery was expelling thick smoke.* ► discharge, emit, let out, release, disgorge, spew out

expense *NOUN* **1** *the increasing expense of running a car* ► cost, price, spending **2** *unexpected expenses* ► expenditure, outlay, charges, outgoings, overheads, payment

expensive *ADJECTIVE* *an expensive holiday* ► costly, dear, high-priced, extravagant, lavish, exorbitant, (*more informal*) pricey OPPOSITES ARE cheap, inexpensive

experience *NOUN* **1** *You learn by experience* ► practice, involvement, participation, familiarity, observation, taking part **2** *Salary will depend partly on experience.* ► skill, knowledge, background, understanding, (*more informal*) know-how **3** *a terrifying experience* ► incident, event, episode, affair, happening, occurrence, ordeal, adventure

experience *VERB* *She experienced some harassment at work.* ► meet, encounter, undergo, face, run into, suffer

experienced *ADJECTIVE* **1** *an experienced actor* ► expert, skilled, skilful, qualified, trained, practised, knowledgeable, professional, specialized, well versed

experiment *NOUN* **experiments** a test made in order to find out what happens or to prove something
▷ **experimental** *ADJECTIVE* **experimentally** *ADVERB*

experiment *VERB* **experiments, experimenting, experimented** carry out an experiment
▷ **experimentation** *NOUN*

expert *NOUN* **experts** a person with great knowledge or skill in something

expert *ADJECTIVE* having great knowledge or skill
▷ **expertly** *ADVERB* **expertness** *NOUN*

expire *VERB* **expires, expiring, expired** **1** come to an end; stop being usable • *Your season ticket has expired.* **2** die **3** breathe out air
▷ **expiration** *NOUN* **expiry** *NOUN*

explain *VERB* **explains, explaining, explained** **1** make something clear to somebody else; show its meaning **2** account for something • *That explains his absence.*
▷ **explanation** *NOUN*

explicit (iks- pliss- it) *ADJECTIVE* stated or stating something openly and exactly COMPARE **implicit**
▷ **explicitly** *ADVERB*

explode *VERB* **explodes, exploding, exploded** **1** burst or suddenly release energy with a loud noise **2** cause a bomb to go off **3** increase suddenly or quickly

exploit (iks- **ploit**) *VERB* **exploits, exploiting, exploited** **1** use or develop resources **2** use a person or thing selfishly
▷ **exploitation** *NOUN*

Thesaurus

AN OPPOSITE IS inexperienced **2** *an experienced man of the world* ► mature, seasoned, sophisticated, worldly wise, knowing, wise OPPOSITES ARE innocent, naive

experiment *NOUN* **1** *She conducted experiments using laser technology.* ► test, investigation, trial, enquiry, demonstration, observation, analysis, piece of research **2** *The new library hours are an experiment.* ► trial, trial run, try-out

experiment *VERB* **experiment with** *You need to experiment with the camera's different settings.* ► test, try out, investigate, explore, do tests on, conduct an experiment on, do research on

experimental *ADJECTIVE* **1** *The new designs are still at an experimental stage.* ► exploratory, investigatory, provisional, tentative, preliminary, speculative, trial, test **2** *experimental forms of music* ► innovative, innovatory, radical, avant-garde, original

expert *ADJECTIVE* **1** *You can get independent expert advice quite cheaply.* ► skilled, professional, qualified, specialist **2** *I am an expert swimmer.* ► skilful, skilled, accomplished, proficient, competent, talented, outstanding, exceptional, formidable

expert *NOUN* **1** *You need to get advice from an expert.* ► specialist, professional, authority, (*more informal*) pro **2** *He is an expert at board games.* ► authority, master, past master, connoisseur, genius, virtuoso, (*more informal*) ace, (*more informal*) whizz, (*more informal*) wizard, (*more informal*) dab hand, (*disapproving*) know-all AN OPPOSITE IS novice

expertise *NOUN* *A high level of expertise is required.* ► skill, competence, proficiency, ability, knowledge, capability, professionalism

expire *VERB* **1** *The animals were expiring in the heat.* ► die, perish, pass away **2** *Our television licence has expired.* ► run out, become invalid, lapse, finish

explain *VERB* **1** *I will try to explain the problem.* ► describe, clarify, make clear, spell out, elucidate, interpret, demonstrate, express, put into words **2** *It is hard to explain such stupidity.* ► account for, justify, excuse, defend, vindicate, give reasons for, make excuses for, rationalize

explanation *NOUN* **1** *I owe you an explanation for what happened.* ► justification, reason, account, excuse, defence, rationale **2** *What on earth can the explanation be?* ► cause, motive, reason **3** *The summary at the end gives a brief explanation of the ideas discussed.* ► account, clarification, elucidation, interpretation, demonstration

explicit *ADJECTIVE* **1** *The advance party had received explicit instructions to turn back.* ► clear, plain, direct, definite, express, precise, distinct, exact, emphatic, specific, positive, categorical, unambiguous, unmistakable, unequivocal AN OPPOSITE IS vague **2** *The film contains a number of sexually explicit scenes.* ► candid, open, direct, frank, unreserved, undisguised, plain OPPOSITES ARE implicit, suggestive

explode *VERB* **1** *A bomb exploded in the centre of the city.* ► go off, blow up, detonate **2** *The findings explode a number of myths about cancer treatment.* ► disprove, rebut, refute, expose, debunk, discredit, destroy, put an end to

exploit *NOUN* (with the stress on *ex-*) *Their exploits gave them a fearsome reputation.* ► feat, deed, adventure, accomplishment, achievement

exploit *VERB* (with the stress on *-ploit*) **1** *The newcomers exploited the land's mineral resources.* ► make use of, utilize, use, take advantage of, draw on, benefit from, capitalize on **2** *They are*

A B C D **E** F G H I J K L M N O P Q R S T U V W X Y Z

explore *VERB* **explores, exploring, explored** **1** travel through a country etc. in order to learn about it **2** examine a subject or idea carefully • *We explored the possibilities.*
▷ **exploration** *NOUN* **explorer** *NOUN* **exploratory** *ADJECTIVE*

explosion *NOUN* **explosions** **1** the exploding of a bomb etc.; the noise made by exploding **2** a sudden great increase

explosive *ADJECTIVE* able to explode

explosive *NOUN* **explosives** an explosive substance

exponent *NOUN* **exponents** **1** a person who puts forward an idea etc. **2** someone who is good at an activity **3** (in mathematics) the raised number etc. written to the right of another (e.g. 3 in 2^3) showing how many times the first one is to be multiplied by itself; the index

export *VERB* **exports, exporting, exported** send goods abroad to be sold
▷ **exportation** *NOUN* **exporter** *NOUN*

export *NOUN* **exports** **1** exporting things **2** something exported

expose *VERB* **exposes, exposing, exposed** **1** reveal or uncover **2** allow light to reach a photographic film so as to take a picture
▷ **exposure** *NOUN*

express *ADJECTIVE* **1** going or sent quickly **2** clearly stated • *This was done against my express orders.*

express *NOUN* **expresses** a fast train stopping at only a few stations

express *VERB* **expresses, expressing, expressed** **1** put ideas etc. into words; make your feelings known **2** press or squeeze out • *Express the juice.*

expression *NOUN* **expressions** **1** the look on a person's face that shows his or her feelings **2** a word or phrase etc. **3** a way of speaking or of playing music etc. so as to show your feelings **4** expressing • *this expression of opinion*

expressive *ADJECTIVE* full of expression

expulsion *NOUN* **expulsions** expelling or being expelled

exquisite (eks- kwiz- it) *ADJECTIVE* very beautiful
▷ **exquisitely** *ADVERB*

extend *VERB* **extends, extending, extended** **1** stretch out **2** make something become longer or larger **3** offer or give • *Extend a warm welcome to our friends.*
▷ **extendible** *ADJECTIVE*

extension *NOUN* **extensions** **1** extending or being extended **2** something added on; an

Thesaurus

accused of exploiting an impoverished workforce. ► take advantage of, mistreat, ill-treat, abuse, oppress, manipulate, cheat, swindle, (*more informal*) fleece

explore *VERB* **1** *an outing to explore the neighbourhood* ► tour, travel through, reconnoitre, survey, inspect, take a look at **2** *We'd like to explore the possibility of working together.* ► investigate, examine, look into, consider, study, review, probe, analyse

explosion *NOUN* *A loud explosion shook the building.* ► blast, bang, boom, burst, crash, report, detonation, discharge

explosive *ADJECTIVE* **1** *explosive substances* ► volatile, inflammable, combustible, unstable **2** *an explosive situation* ► tense, highly charged, critical, fraught, hazardous, dangerous, perilous, sensitive
AN OPPOSITE IS stable

expose *VERB* **1** *The investigation exposed many faults.* ► reveal, uncover, bring to light, disclose, unveil, unmask **2 expose someone to** *They were exposed to serious danger.* ► put at risk of, subject to, lay open to

express *VERB* *They expressed their wishes clearly.* ► communicate, articulate, utter, convey, voice, vent, give vent to, release, air, phrase, put into words, ventilate

express *ADJECTIVE* **1** *It was his express wish.* ► explicit, clear, plain, direct, definite, precise, distinct, exact, emphatic, specific, positive, categorical, unambiguous, unmistakable, unequivocal **2** *an express train* ► fast, rapid, high-speed, non-stop

expression *NOUN* **1** *He liked to use old-fashioned expressions.* ► phrase, idiom, statement, saying, turn of phrase, phraseology, wording, cliché, formula, remark, term **2** *She had a puzzled expression.* ► look, countenance, aspect, air, face, appearance, mien **3** *She read the letter without expression.* ► emotion, feeling, passion, intensity, poignancy, sensibility, sensitivity, sympathy, understanding **4** *The regime forbids the expression of opposing ideas.* ► utterance, uttering, voicing, assertion

exquisite *ADJECTIVE* **1** *a ring with exquisite little jewels* ► beautiful, lovely, delicate, dainty **2** *She always showed exquisite taste.* ► refined, discriminating, discerning, sensitive, impeccable

extend *VERB* **1** *The emperor sought to extend his power.* ► expand, enlarge, develop, build up, broaden, spread AN OPPOSITE IS reduce **2** *The meeting was extended to allow for questions.* ► prolong, lengthen, continue, protract, draw out, make longer **3** *We extend our thanks to all contributors.* ► offer, proffer, advance, bestow,

addition to a building **3** one of a set of telephones in an office or house etc.

extensive ADJECTIVE covering a large area or range • *extensive gardens*
▷ **extensively** ADVERB **extensiveness** NOUN

extent NOUN **extents** **1** the area or length over which something extends **2** the amount, level, or scope of something • *the full extent of his power*

exterior ADJECTIVE outer

exterior NOUN **exteriors** the outside of something

exterminate VERB **exterminates, exterminating, exterminated** destroy or kill all the members or examples
▷ **extermination** NOUN **exterminator** NOUN

external ADJECTIVE outside
▷ **externally** ADVERB

extinct ADJECTIVE **1** not existing any more • *The dodo is an extinct bird* **2** not burning; not active • *an extinct volcano*

extinction NOUN **1** making or becoming extinct **2** extinguishing; being extinguished

extinguish VERB **extinguishes, extinguishing, extinguished** **1** put out a fire or light **2** put an end to; destroy • *Our hopes of victory were extinguished.*

extort VERB **extorts, extorting, extorted** obtain something by force or threats
▷ **extortion** NOUN

extortionate ADJECTIVE charging or demanding far too much

extra ADJECTIVE additional; more than is usual • *extra strength*

extra ADVERB more than usually • *extra strong*

extra NOUN **extras** **1** an extra person or thing **2** a person acting as part of a crowd in a film or play

extract (iks- trakt) VERB **extracts, extracting, extracted** take out; remove
▷ **extractor** NOUN

extract (eks- trakt) NOUN **extracts** **1** a passage taken from a book, speech, film, etc. **2** a substance separated or obtained from another

extraction NOUN **1** extracting **2** someone's descent • *He is of Chinese extraction.*

extraordinary ADJECTIVE very unusual or strange
▷ **extraordinarily** ADVERB

extrasensory ADJECTIVE outside the range of the known human senses

extraterrestrial ADJECTIVE from beyond the earth's atmosphere; from outer space

extraterrestrial NOUN **extraterrestrials** a being from outer space

Thesaurus

confer, hold out, present, accord **4** *The fields extend as far as the river.* ► reach, go, continue, carry on, spread

extension NOUN **1** *The new owners built a huge extension to the house.* ► addition, annexe, wing **2** *We needed an extension of the deadline.* ► postponement, deferral, delay **3** *the extension of the royal territories; the extension of knowledge* ► enlargement, increase, expansion, broadening, development, growth

extent NOUN **1** *The estate is about three acres in extent.* ► area, size, expanse, scope, dimensions, spread, distance **2** *It was only later that we saw the extent of the damage.* ► degree, scale, scope, size, magnitude, amount, measure, quantity, range

external ADJECTIVE *an external surface* ► outer, outside, exterior, outermost

extinct ADJECTIVE **1** *an extinct volcano* ► inactive, extinguished OPPOSITES ARE active, dormant **2** *an extinct species* ► lost, vanished, defunct, died out, dead, destroyed, obsolete, exterminated OPPOSITES ARE extant, living, surviving

extra ADJECTIVE **1** *She had a second job to bring in extra money.* ► additional, more, further, added, increased, supplementary, fresh **2** *There was a lot of extra food in the house.* ► spare, excess, surplus, superfluous, unused, leftover **3** *The large stores take on extra staff before Christmas.* ► temporary, ancillary, auxiliary, supernumerary

extra ADVERB *He worked extra hard just before the exams.* ► especially, exceptionally, particularly, extremely, unusually

extra NOUN *The Monday holiday was a welcome extra.* ► addition, supplement, bonus, extension

extract VERB **1** *The dentist extracted her tooth.* ► pull out, take out, draw out, remove, withdraw AN OPPOSITE IS insert **2** *It was difficult to extract any information from them.* ► obtain, wrest, draw, glean, elicit, derive, gather, get

extraordinary ADJECTIVE *What an extraordinary story! Their behaviour was quite extraordinary.* ► remarkable, exceptional, amazing, astonishing, astounding, wonderful, startling, staggering, stunning, breathtaking, fantastic, phenomenal, incredible AN OPPOSITE IS ordinary

A B C D E F G H I J K L M N O P Q R S T U V W X Y Z

extravagant *ADJECTIVE* spending or using too much
▷ **extravagantly** *ADVERB* **extravagance** *NOUN*

extreme *ADJECTIVE* **1** very great or intense • *extreme cold* **2** furthest away • *the extreme north* **3** going to great lengths in actions or opinions; not moderate
▷ **extremely** *ADVERB*

extreme *NOUN* **extremes 1** something extreme **2** either end of something

extricate (eks- trik- ayt) *VERB* **extricates, extricating, extricated** free someone or something from a difficult position or situation
▷ **extrication** *NOUN*

extrovert *NOUN* **extroverts** a person who is generally friendly and likes company (The opposite is **introvert**)

exuberant (ig- zew- ber- ant) *ADJECTIVE* very lively and cheerful
▷ **exuberantly** *ADVERB* **exuberance** *NOUN*

exude *VERB* **exudes, exuding, exuded 1** give off moisture, a smell, etc. **2** display a feeling or quality openly • *She exuded confidence.*

exult *VERB* **exults, exulting, exulted** rejoice greatly
▷ **exultant** *ADJECTIVE* **exultation** *NOUN*

eye *NOUN* **eyes 1** the organ of the body that is used for seeing **2** the power of seeing • *She has sharp eyes* **3** the small hole in a needle **4** the centre of a storm

eye *VERB* **eyes, eyeing, eyed** look at something with interest [from Old English]

eyeball *NOUN* **eyeballs** the ball-shaped part of the eye inside the eyelids

eyebrow *NOUN* **eyebrows** the fringe of hair growing on the face above the eye

eyelash *NOUN* **eyelashes** one of the short hairs that grow on an eyelid

eyelid *NOUN* **eyelids** either of the two folds of skin that can close over the eyeball

eyepiece *NOUN* **eyepieces** the lens of a telescope or microscope etc. that you put to your eye

eyesight *NOUN* the ability to see

eyewitness *NOUN* **eyewitnesses** a person who actually saw an accident or crime etc.

Thesaurus

extravagance *NOUN* *The new outfit was bought in a fit of extravagance.* ► indulgence, lavishness, prodigality, profligacy, excess, squandering, improvidence, wastefulness
AN OPPOSITE IS thrift

extravagant *ADJECTIVE* *an extravagant lifestyle* ► indulgent, lavish, spendthrift, improvident, squandering, wasteful AN OPPOSITE IS thrifty

extreme *ADJECTIVE* **1** *a sure sign of extreme tiredness* ► great, intense, exceptional, extraordinary, utter, acute, downright
AN OPPOSITE IS slight **2** *The situation called for extreme measures.* ► drastic, serious, radical, dire, desperate, severe, tough, harsh, strict
AN OPPOSITE IS mild **3** *in the extreme north of the country* ► farthest, furthest, far-off, distant, remotest, faraway **4** *a person of extreme political opinions* ► radical, extremist, fanatical, diehard, zealous
AN OPPOSITE IS moderate

extreme *NOUN* *These theories go from one extreme to the other. an attitude pushed to its extreme* ► limit, extremity, height, end

extremity *NOUN* **1** *at the southern extremity of the island* ► limit, edge, end, tip, boundary, margin

extrovert *NOUN* *Most of the volunteers are extroverts by nature.* ► socializer, outgoing person, mixer AN OPPOSITE IS introvert

extrovert *ADJECTIVE* *an extrovert personality* ► outgoing, extroverted, sociable, gregarious, positive, active, confident
AN OPPOSITE IS introvert

eye *NOUN* **1** *He has a sharp eye.* ► eyesight, vision, power of sight, visual perception RELATED ADJECTIVES ocular, ophthalmic **2** *Not much escaped her attentive eye.* ► watch, observation, vigilance, notice **3 eyes** *It was a dreadful mistake in our eyes.* ► opinion, view, judgement, way of thinking, viewpoint, (to our) mind
an eye for *an eye for detail* ► an appreciation of, an awareness of, an understanding of, a perception of, a sensitivity for, an instinct for

eye *VERB* *He eyed the visitors carefully.* ► look at, watch, observe, view, gaze at, glance at, scrutinize, examine

Ff

fable *NOUN* **fables** a short story that teaches about behaviour, often with animals as characters [from Latin *fabula* = story]

fabric *NOUN* **fabrics** **1** cloth **2** the basic framework of something, especially the walls, floors, and roof of a building

fabricate *VERB* **fabricates, fabricating, fabricated** **1** construct or manufacture something **2** invent • *fabricate an excuse*
▷ **fabrication** *NOUN*

fabulous *ADJECTIVE* **1** wonderful **2** incredibly great • *fabulous wealth* **3** told of in fables and myths
▷ **fabulously** *ADVERB*

façade (fas- ahd) *NOUN* **façades** **1** the front of a building **2** an outward appearance, especially a deceptive one

face *NOUN* **faces** **1** the front part of the head **2** the expression on a person's face **3** the front or upper side of something **4** a surface • *A cube has six faces.*

face *VERB* **faces, facing, faced** **1** look or have the front towards something • *Our room faced the sea.* **2** meet and have to deal with something; encounter • *Explorers face many dangers.* **3** cover a surface with a layer of different material

facetious (fas- ee- shus) *ADJECTIVE* trying to be funny at an unsuitable time • *facetious remarks*
▷ **facetiously** *ADVERB*

facilitate (fas- il- it- ayt) *VERB* **facilitates, facilitating, facilitated** make something easier to do
▷ **facilitation** *NOUN*

facility (fas- il- it- ee) *NOUN* **facilities** **1** something that provides you with the means to do things • *There are sports facilities.* **2** ease or skill in doing something • *She reads music with great facility.*

facsimile (fak- sim- il- ee) *NOUN* **facsimiles** **1** an exact reproduction of a document etc. **2** a fax

fact *NOUN* **facts** something that is certainly true
the facts of life information about how babies are conceived

faction *NOUN* **factions** a small united group within a larger one, especially in politics

factor *NOUN* **factors** **1** something that helps to bring about a result • *Hard work was a factor in her success.* **2** a number by which a larger number can be divided exactly • *2 and 3 are factors of 6.*

factory *NOUN* **factories** a large building where machines are used to make things

Thesaurus

fable *NOUN* *the fable of the fox and the crow*
► story, tale, parable, moral tale

fabric *NOUN* **1** *Special fabrics are often used for the seats.* ► cloth, material, stuff, textile **2** *The bomb did some damage to the fabric of the building.* ► structure, framework, frame, construction, make-up

fabricate *VERB* *The witness had fabricated his evidence.* ► invent, falsify, make up, concoct, trump up

fabulous *ADJECTIVE* **1** *They had a fabulous time in Morocco.* ► wonderful, marvellous, fantastic, splendid, magnificent **2** *fabulous places you read about in stories* ► legendary, mythical, imaginary, fictitious, fantastic

face *NOUN* **1** *She has a lovely face.* ► features, countenance, visage, profile, physiognomy **2** *His face became angry.* ► expression, look, appearance, manner, bearing, countenance **3** *A cube has six faces.* ► side, surface, plane, aspect **4** *the north face of the house* ► aspect, façade **5** *He put on a brave face for the sake of his visitors.* ► front, show, display, act

face *VERB* **1** *The hotel faces the lake.* ► overlook, be opposite (to), front, give on to **2** *You will face a lot of criticism.* ► meet, encounter, experience, confront
face up to *She faced up to all her obligations.* ► accept, come to terms with, recognize, acknowledge, deal with, cope with

facet *NOUN* *every facet of the situation* ► aspect, feature, characteristic, detail, particular

facility *NOUN* **1** *She has a great facility for singing.* ► aptitude, talent, flair, faculty, adeptness, skill (in), expertise (in) **2** *This facility is used for copying music to a CD.* ► function, device, provision **3 facilities** *the use of a sauna and sports facilities* ► amenities, resources, services, equipment, provisions

fact *NOUN* *It is a fact that car use has risen steeply in the last decade.* ► reality, truth, actuality, certainty, fait accompli AN OPPOSITE IS fiction
the facts *The jury has to take all the facts into account.* ► evidence, information, details, data, circumstances, particulars, aspects

factor *NOUN* *Cost was a key factor in the decision.* ► circumstance, element, feature, component, ingredient, influence, aspect, determinant

factory *NOUN* *I worked in a factory that made parts for tractors.* ► manufacturing plant, workshop, works, assembly line

A B C D E F G H I J K L M N O P Q R S T U V W X Y Z

faculty NOUN **faculties** **1** any of the powers of the body or mind (e.g. sight, speech, or understanding) **2** a department teaching a particular subject in a university or college • *the faculty of music*

fad NOUN **fads** **1** a person's particular like or dislike **2** a temporary fashion or craze
▷ **faddy** ADJECTIVE

fade VERB **fades, fading, faded** **1** lose colour or freshness or strength **2** disappear gradually **3** make a sound etc. become gradually weaker (*fade it out*) or stronger (*fade it in* or *up*)

faeces (fee- seez) PLURAL NOUN solid waste matter passed out of the body

Fahrenheit ADJECTIVE measuring temperature on a scale where water freezes at 32° and boils at 212° [named after G. D. Fahrenheit, a German scientist, who invented the mercury thermometer]

fail VERB **fails, failing, failed** **1** try to do something but be unable to do it **2** become weak or useless; break down • *The brakes failed.* **3** not do something • *He failed to warn me.* **4** not get enough marks to pass an examination **5** judge that someone has not passed an examination

fail NOUN
without fail for certain; whatever happens

failing NOUN **failings** a weakness or a fault

failure NOUN **failures** **1** not being able to do something **2** a person or thing that has failed

faint ADJECTIVE **1** pale or dim; not distinct **2** weak or giddy; nearly unconscious **3** slight • *a faint hope.*
▷ **faintly** ADVERB **faintness** NOUN

faint VERB **faints, fainting, fainted** become unconscious for a short time
USAGE Do not confuse with **feint**.

fair[1] ADJECTIVE **1** right or just; according to the rules • *a fair fight* **2** (said about hair or skin) light in colour; (said about a person) having fair hair **3** (*old use*) beautiful **4** fine or favourable • *fair weather* **5** moderate; quite good • *a fair number of people*
▷ **fairness** NOUN

Thesaurus

factual ADJECTIVE *a factual description of the events* ► truthful, accurate, historical, authentic, genuine, realistic, faithful, objective

faculty NOUN **1** *the faculty of speech* ► power, capability, capacity, facility **2** *a faculty for settling disputes* ► aptitude, talent, facility, flair, adeptness, skill (in), expertise (in) **3 faculties** ► senses, wits, intelligence, reason, powers

fad NOUN *Rap music was not just a passing fad.* ► craze, fashion, trend, vogue, whim, passion, enthusiasm, obsession, compulsion, (*more informal*) rage, (*more informal*) thing

fade VERB **1** *The light has faded the colours.* ► blanch, bleach, discolour, whiten AN OPPOSITE IS brighten **2** *The music began to fade.* ► weaken, decline, decrease, diminish, dwindle, dim, wane, disappear, evanesce, fail, melt away, pale, vanish AN OPPOSITE IS intensify **3** *The flowers had faded by now.* ► wither, wilt, droop, flag, perish, shrivel AN OPPOSITE IS bloom **4** *Their enthusiasm was fading.* ► decline, diminish, dwindle, fail, flag, sink, disappear

fail VERB **1** *In the end all attempts failed.* ► be unsuccessful, go wrong, miscarry, fall through, come to grief, collapse AN OPPOSITE IS succeed **2** *The business had failed and the family faced ruin.* ► collapse, founder, go under, go bankrupt, (*more informal*) fold AN OPPOSITE IS prosper **3** *She was angry with her daughter who had failed to contact her.* ► neglect, forget, omit **4** *Her health was failing.* ► deteriorate, decline, weaken, sink, collapse AN OPPOSITE IS improve **5** *They believe we have failed them.* ► let down, disappoint, betray, desert AN OPPOSITE IS support **6** *He failed one of his exams.* ► be unsuccessful in, not pass AN OPPOSITE IS pass

failing NOUN *She loved him despite his failings.* ► fault, weakness, shortcoming, flaw, defect OPPOSITES ARE strength, strong point

failure NOUN **1** *The negotiations ended in failure.* ► disappointment, lack of success, defeat, disaster **2** *The plan proved to be a failure.* ► disaster, catastrophe, fiasco, debacle, blunder, mistake, (*more informal*) flop, (*more informal*) damp squib **3** *a failure in the power supply* ► breakdown, fault, malfunction **4** *To do nothing might be regarded as a failure of duty.* ► dereliction, neglect, omission, deficiency

faint ADJECTIVE **1** *There was a faint smell of gas.* ► slight, indistinct, vague, weak AN OPPOSITE IS strong **2** *The sky had a faint pink colour.* ► pale, light, hazy, weak AN OPPOSITE IS bright **3** *We heard a faint cry from the next room.* ► quiet, muted, muffled, feeble, weak AN OPPOSITE IS loud **4** *There is a faint possibility of an improvement in the weather.* ► slight, slim, slender, remote, small, vague, doubtful AN OPPOSITE IS strong **5** *She was feeling faint and had to lie down.* ► dizzy, giddy, light-headed, weak, (*more informal*) woozy

faint VERB *He grew pale and seemed about to faint.* ► pass out, lose consciousness, black out, collapse, (*more informal*) flake out, (*literary*) swoon

fair ADJECTIVE **1** *It doesn't seem fair to blame the children.* ► just, equitable, reasonable, honourable AN OPPOSITE IS unfair **2** *They gave a fair assessment of the situation.* ► honest,

fair *ADVERB* fairly • *Play fair!*

fair² *NOUN* **fairs 1** a group of outdoor entertainments such as roundabouts, sideshows, and stalls **2** an exhibition or market
▷ **fairground** *NOUN*

fairly *ADVERB* **1** justly; according to the rules **2** moderately • *It is fairly hard.*

fairy *NOUN* **fairies** an imaginary very small creature with magic powers
▷ **fairyland** *NOUN* **fairy tale** *NOUN*

faith *NOUN* **faiths** strong belief or trust
in good faith with honest intentions

faithful *ADJECTIVE* **1** loyal and trustworthy **2** true to the facts • *a faithful account* **3** sexually loyal to one partner
▷ **faithfully** *ADVERB* **faithfulness** *NOUN*
Yours faithfully see **yours**

fake *NOUN* **fakes** something that looks genuine but is not; a forgery

fake *VERB* **fakes, faking, faked 1** make something that looks genuine, in order to deceive people **2** pretend to have or be something • *He used to fake illness to miss games.*
▷ **faker** *NOUN*

falcon *NOUN* **falcons** a kind of hawk often used in the sport of hunting other birds or game
▷ **falconry** *NOUN*

fall *VERB* **falls, falling, fell, fallen 1** come or go down without being pushed or thrown etc. **2** decrease; become lower • *Prices fell.* **3** be captured or overthrown • *The city fell.* **4** die in battle **5** happen • *Silence fell.* **6** become • *She fell asleep.*
fall back retreat
fall back on use for support or in an emergency
fall for 1 be attracted by a person **2** be taken in by a deception
fall out quarrel
fall through fail • *plans fell through*

fall *NOUN* **falls 1** the action of falling **2** (*American*) autumn, when leaves fall

fallacy (fal- a- see) *NOUN* **fallacies** a false or mistaken idea or belief
▷ **fallacious** (fal- ay- shus) *ADJECTIVE*

Fallopian tube *NOUN* **Fallopian tubes** one of the two tubes in a woman's body along which the eggs travel from the ovaries to the uterus

fallout *NOUN* particles of radioactive material carried in the air after a nuclear explosion

Thesaurus

impartial, reasonable, objective, dispassionate, neutral, even-handed
OPPOSITES ARE unreasonable, biased **3** *She believes she has a fair chance of success. He had achieved a fair result in his exams.* ► moderate, reasonable, average, satisfactory, adequate, acceptable, tolerable, respectable, decent
OPPOSITES ARE excellent, outstanding **4** *There was a fair amount of traffic going past.* ► considerable, moderate, average **5** *She had blue eyes and fair hair.* ► blond(e), light, pale, yellow **6** *It was a good match played in fair weather.* ► fine, dry, bright, clear, sunny, warm
OPPOSITES ARE bad, wet, inclement

fair *NOUN* **1** *a country fair* ► fête, gala, carnival, funfair, festival **2** *an antiques fair* ► market, sale, mart, bazaar **3** *a book fair* ► exhibition, display, show, presentation

fairly *ADVERB* *The news is fairly good.* ► reasonably, moderately, tolerably, quite, rather, somewhat, (*more informal*) pretty
AN OPPOSITE IS extremely

fairy tale or **fairy story** *NOUN* *fairy tales about witches and dragons* ► folk tale, legend, myth, story

faith *NOUN* **1** *His employers had complete faith in him.* ► trust, confidence, hope, belief, reliance **2** *Her faith is very precious to her.* ► religion, belief, religious conviction

faithful *ADJECTIVE* **1** *He wondered if Clara had a faithful partner waiting for her at home.* ► loyal, devoted, constant, dependable, dutiful, reliable, staunch, steadfast, trusty, trustworthy, close, consistent, unswerving
OPPOSITES ARE unfaithful, disloyal **2** *He kept a faithful record of the events of that day.* ► accurate, true, truthful, precise, exact, authentic AN OPPOSITE IS inaccurate

fake *ADJECTIVE* **1** *You could tell the diamonds were fake.* ► imitation, artificial, simulated, synthetic, unreal, false, bogus, sham, (*more informal*) phoney **2** *He brought out a wad of fake banknotes.* ► counterfeit, forged, false, sham, bogus, fraudulent, (*more informal*) phoney
AN OPPOSITE IS genuine

fake *NOUN* **1** *One of the paintings was a fake.* ► forgery, copy, imitation, reproduction, replica, duplicate, hoax, sham, simulation, (*more informal*) phoney **2** *The man who claimed to be a surgeon is a fake.* ► fraud, charlatan, impostor, cheat, (*more informal*) quack, (*more informal*) phoney

fake *VERB* *They would have to fake a death certificate.* ► forge, fabricate, counterfeit, falsify, (*more informal*) fiddle

fall *VERB* **1** *He stumbled and fell.* ► tumble, fall over, topple, trip over, keel over, collapse
AN OPPOSITE IS get up **2** *Flood levels began to fall at last.* ► drop, go down, subside, recede
AN OPPOSITE IS rise **3** *Bombs continued to fall all night.* ► drop, descend, plummet, rain down **4** *Prices are expected to fall soon.* ► go down, decrease, decline, diminish OPPOSITES ARE rise, increase **5** *The Empire in the East did not fall for*

A B C D E F G H I J K L M N O P Q R S T U V W X Y Z

false *ADJECTIVE* **1** untrue or incorrect **2** not genuine; artificial • *false teeth* **3** treacherous or deceitful
▷ **falsely** *ADVERB* **falseness** *NOUN* **falsity** *NOUN*

falter *VERB* **falters, faltering, faltered**
1 hesitate when you move or speak **2** become weaker; begin to give way • *His courage began to falter.*

fame *NOUN* being famous
▷ **famed** *ADJECTIVE*

familiar *ADJECTIVE* **1** well known; often seen or experienced **2** knowing something well • *Are you familiar with this book?* **3** very friendly
▷ **familiarly** *ADVERB* **familiarity** *NOUN*

family *NOUN* **families 1** parents and their children, sometimes including grandchildren and other relations **2** a group of things that are alike in some way **3** a group of related plants or animals • *Lions belong to the cat family.*

family planning *NOUN* birth control

family tree *NOUN* **family trees** a diagram showing how people in a family are related

famine *NOUN* **famines** a very bad shortage of food in an area

famished *ADJECTIVE* very hungry

famous *ADJECTIVE* known to very many people

famously *ADVERB* (*informal*) very well • *They get on famously.*

Thesaurus

several more centuries. ► decline, collapse, disintegrate, deteriorate AN OPPOSITE IS flourish **6** *Thousands fell in the war.* ► die, be killed, be lost, lose your life, perish, (*literary*) be slain **7** *Her birthday falls on a Saturday this year.* ► occur, come, happen, take place
fall apart *The sheds fell apart in the high winds.* ► collapse, disintegrate, break up, fragment, crumble, fall to pieces, shatter
fall asleep *She couldn't help falling asleep.* ► doze off, drop off, go to sleep, (*more informal*) nod off
fall in *The roof has fallen in.* ► collapse, come down, cave in
fall off *Demand for these products has fallen off lately.* ► decline, slacken, decrease, lessen, drop off
fall out *They fell out over money.* ► quarrel, argue, disagree, fight, squabble, bicker, clash
fall through *In the end the plan fell through.* ► come to nothing, fail, miscarry, founder, collapse OPPOSITES ARE go ahead, succeed

fall *NOUN* **1** *He was hurt in a fall.* ► tumble, spill, topple, stumble **2** *Economists expect a fall in house prices.* ► drop, decline, fall-off, decrease, dip, lessening, reduction, slump
OPPOSITES ARE rise, increase **3** *an epic poem on the fall of Troy* ► surrender, capitulation, submission, defeat **4** *the fall of the Roman Empire* ► downfall, collapse, ruin, failure, demise, destruction

false *ADJECTIVE* **1** *a false alibi* ► untrue, fictitious, invented, concocted, fabricated, invalid, spurious AN OPPOSITE IS genuine **2** *a false friend* ► unfaithful, disloyal, unreliable, dishonourable, untrustworthy
AN OPPOSITE IS faithful **3** *false hair* ► artificial, unreal, imitation, synthetic, simulated, fake, sham AN OPPOSITE IS real **4** *a false belief* ► incorrect, erroneous, mistaken, fallacious, wrong AN OPPOSITE IS correct

falter *VERB* **1** *The country must not falter in the face of such danger.* ► hesitate, waver, delay, vacillate, flinch, hold back, lose confidence, be indecisive, get cold feet
AN OPPOSITE IS persevere **2** *He faltered for a moment over an awkward name.* ► stammer, stumble, stutter

fame *NOUN* *Their fame spread all over the world.* ► renown, celebrity, stardom, popularity, notability, prestige, reputation, glory, name, stature, standing, prominence

familiar *ADJECTIVE* **1** *The room was full of familiar faces.* ► well known, recognizable, accustomed, everyday, commonplace **2** *a familiar friend* ► close, intimate, dear **3** *The atmosphere in the house was friendly and familiar.* ► informal, casual, relaxed, natural, open, unreserved, free and easy, unceremonious

familiarity *NOUN* **1** *A familiarity with at least one European language is needed.* ► acquaintance, knowledge (of), understanding (of) **2** *They spoke to one another with a great deal of familiarity.* ► informality, intimacy, closeness, friendliness, naturalness, casualness

family *NOUN* **1** *a large house divided to accommodate two families* ► household **2** *She sends a yearly newsletter to family and friends.* ► relatives, relations, kin, kinsmen, clan
USAGE *Kin* and *kinsmen* are words you normally find only in stories and literature **3** *parents clearly devoted to their family* ► children, offspring, sons and daughters

famine *NOUN* *a country constantly threatened by famine* ► hunger, malnutrition, scarcity, shortage, starvation, dearth, want
AN OPPOSITE IS plenty

famous *ADJECTIVE* *a famous singer* ► well known, celebrated, renowned, acclaimed, admired, prominent, revered, distinguished, honoured, eminent, exalted, illustrious, great, notable, noted OPPOSITES ARE unknown, obscure

fan[1] *NOUN* **fans** an object or machine for making air move about so as to cool people or things

fan *VERB* **fans, fanning, fanned** send a current of air on something
fan out spread out in the shape of a fan

fan[2] *NOUN* **fans** an enthusiastic admirer or supporter

fanatic *NOUN* **fanatics** a person who is very enthusiastic or too enthusiastic about something
▷ **fanatical** *ADJECTIVE* **fanatically** *ADVERB* **fanaticism** *NOUN*

fanciful *ADJECTIVE* **1** imagining things **2** imaginary

fancy *NOUN* **fancies 1** a liking or desire for something **2** imagination

fancy *ADJECTIVE* decorated or elaborate; not plain

fancy *VERB* **fancies, fancying, fancied 1** have a liking or desire for something **2** imagine **3** believe • *I fancy it's raining.*

fancy dress *NOUN* unusual costume worn for a party, often to make you look like a famous person

fantastic *ADJECTIVE* **1** (*informal*) excellent **2** strange or unusual **3** designed in a very fanciful way
▷ **fantastically** *ADVERB*

fantasy *NOUN* **fantasies** something imaginary or fantastic

far *ADVERB* **1** at or to a great distance • *We didn't go far.* **2** much; by a great amount • *This is far better.*

far *ADJECTIVE* distant or remote • *On the far side of the river.*

farce *NOUN* **farces 1** an exaggerated comedy **2** a situation or series of events that is ridiculous or a pretence • *The trial was a complete farce.*
▷ **farcical** *ADJECTIVE*

fare *NOUN* **fares 1** the price charged for a passenger to travel **2** food and drink • *There was only very plain fare.*

farewell *INTERJECTION, NOUN* **farewells** goodbye

farm *NOUN* **farms 1** an area of land where someone grows crops or keeps animals for food or other use **2** the farmer's house
▷ **farmhouse** *NOUN* **farmyard** *NOUN*

farm *VERB* **farms, farming, farmed 1** grow crops or keep animals for food etc. **2** use land for growing crops; cultivate

farmer *NOUN* **farmers** a person who owns or manages a farm

farther *ADVERB, ADJECTIVE* at or to a greater distance; more distant
USAGE **Farther** and **farthest** are used only in connection with distance (e.g. *She lives farther from the school than I do*), but even in such cases many people prefer to use **further**. Only **further** can be used to mean 'additional', e.g. in *We must make further inquiries.* If you are not sure which is right, use **further**.

farthest *ADVERB, ADJECTIVE* at or to the greatest distance; most distant
USAGE See the note at **farther**.

farthing *NOUN* **farthings** a former British coin worth one-quarter of a penny

fascinate *VERB* **fascinates, fascinating, fascinated** be very attractive or interesting to somebody
▷ **fascination** *NOUN* **fascinator** *NOUN*

Thesaurus

fan *NOUN* **1** *a fan of rock music* ► devotee, enthusiast, admirer, lover, fanatic, addict, aficionado, (*more informal*) freak **2** *A ceiling fan cooled the room.* ► ventilator, blower, extractor, air conditioner

fanatic *NOUN* **1** *a religious fanatic* ► extremist, zealot, militant, activist, diehard **2** *a fitness fanatic* ► enthusiast, devotee, admirer, lover, fan, addict, aficionado, (*more informal*) freak

fanciful *ADJECTIVE* *full of fanciful ideas* ► unrealistic, far-fetched, fantastic, imaginary, whimsical, illusory, visionary, romantic

fancy *ADJECTIVE* **1** *The belts are decorated with fancy patterns.* ► elaborate, decorative, ornamental, ornate **2** *They don't like wearing fancy clothes.* ► showy, ostentatious, gaudy

fancy *NOUN* **1** *The little cottage caught our fancy.* ► imagination, ingenuity, whim **2** *I had a fancy they might be there.* ► notion, idea, belief, impression, suspicion, hunch

fancy *VERB* **1** *I fancied I could see a light in the sky.* ► imagine, think, suppose, believe, suspect **2** *I fancy a doughnut.* ► feel like, wish for, want, desire **3** *This was the boy she had fancied for so long.* ► be attracted to, find attractive, have a crush on, desire, want

fantastic *ADJECTIVE* **1** *We had a fantastic time.* ► wonderful, marvellous, fabulous, splendid, magnificent **2** *It's a fantastic idea.* ► fanciful, extraordinary, incredible, unbelievable

fantasy *NOUN* *a fantasy about living on a desert island* ► dream, daydream, pipe dream, delusion, fancy

far *ADJECTIVE* *He'd been to many far places.* ► distant, faraway, far off, remote, out of the way, outlying

fare *NOUN* *a standard-class rail fare* ► price, charge, cost, payment, fee

farm *NOUN* *a farm of 200 acres* ► smallholding, farmstead, estate, grange

fascinate *VERB* *Most people are fascinated by the way words change their meaning.* ► interest (in),

a b c d e f g h i j k l m n o p q r s t u v w x y z

A B C D E **F** G H I J K L M N O P Q R S T U V W X Y Z

fascist *NOUN* **fascists** someone who believes in or practises very oppressive and nationalistic forms of government
▷ **fascism** *NOUN*
[from *fasces*, the rods of office in ancient Rome, used as an emblem by the Italian Fascist party in the 1920s]

fashion *NOUN* **fashions** **1** the style of clothes or other things that most people like at a particular time **2** a way of doing something • *Continue in the same fashion.*

fashionable *ADJECTIVE* following the fashion of the time; popular
▷ **fashionably** *ADVERB*

fast[1] *ADJECTIVE* **1** moving or done quickly; rapid **2** allowing fast movement • *a fast road* **3** showing a time later than the correct time • *Your watch is fast* **4** firmly fixed or attached **5** not likely to fade • *fast colours*
▷ **fastness** *NOUN*

fast *ADVERB* **1** quickly • *Run fast!* **2** firmly • *His leg was stuck fast in the mud.*
fast asleep in a deep sleep

fast[2] *VERB* **fasts**, **fasting**, **fasted** go without food
▷ **fast** *NOUN*

fasten *VERB* **fastens**, **fastening**, **fastened** fix one thing firmly to another
▷ **fastener** *NOUN* **fastening** *NOUN*

fat *NOUN* **fats** **1** the white greasy part of meat **2** oil or grease used in cooking
the fat of the land the best food

fat *ADJECTIVE* **fatter**, **fattest** **1** having a very thick round body **2** thick • *a fat book* **3** full of fat
▷ **fatness** *NOUN*

fatal *ADJECTIVE* causing death or disaster • *a fatal accident*
▷ **fatally** *ADVERB*

fate *NOUN* **fates** **1** a power that is thought to make things happen **2** what will happen or has happened to somebody or something; destiny
[from Latin *fatum* = what has been spoken]

father *NOUN* **fathers** **1** a male parent **2** the title of certain priests
▷ **fatherly** *ADJECTIVE*
[from Old English]

Thesaurus

engross, captivate, enthral, absorb, beguile, entrance, attract, charm

fascinating *ADJECTIVE a fascinating book about the invention of the camera* ► interesting, engrossing, intriguing, captivating, enthralling, absorbing, beguiling, entrancing, attractive, charming

fashion *NOUN* **1** *the fashion for long dresses* ► trend, vogue, craze **2** *She was behaving in a very odd fashion.* ► way, manner, mode, method

fashionable *ADJECTIVE a fashionable hotel in central London* ► stylish, popular, chic, elegant, modish, (*more informal*) trendy
AN OPPOSITE IS unfashionable

fast *ADJECTIVE She drives a fast car. The race was run at a fast pace. Delivery is always fast.* ► quick, rapid, speedy, swift, brisk, lively, sprightly, flying, high-speed, (*more informal*) nippy
an opposite is slow

fast *ADVERB* **1** *The train was travelling fast towards the tunnel.* ► quickly, rapidly, swiftly, speedily, at full speed, at full tilt, briskly
AN OPPOSITE IS slowly **2** *The wheels were stuck fast in the mud.* ► tightly, securely, immovably **3** *By now she was fast asleep.* ► deeply, sound, completely

fast *VERB a month in which many people are fasting* ► go without food, abstain, deny yourself
AN OPPOSITE IS overeat

fasten *VERB* **1** *a sleeveless jacket that you fasten at the back* ► do up, tie, close, button up
OPPOSITES ARE unfasten, undo **2** *We were told to fasten all windows.* ► close, secure, lock, bolt
AN OPPOSITE IS unfasten **3** *Brackets are fastened to the wall.* ► fix, attach, secure, bolt
AN OPPOSITE IS remove

fat *ADJECTIVE* **1** *A fat woman came into the room.* ► plump, stout, large, overweight, corpulent, rotund, podgy, obese, tubby, portly
OPPOSITES ARE thin, slim **2** *He was reading a fat book.* ► thick, bulky, chunky, substantial **3** (*informal*) *A fat cheque arrived just before Christmas.* ► large, substantial, sizeable, generous

fat *NOUN He has a lot of fat to get rid of.* ► fatness, obesity, blubber, (*technical*) adipose tissue, (*more informal*) flab

fatal *ADJECTIVE* **1** *He delivered a fatal blow with the axe.* ► deadly, mortal, lethal **2** *She contracted a fatal illness in the Far East.* ► deadly, terminal, mortal, incurable, malignant **3** *That decision proved to be a fatal mistake.* ► disastrous, catastrophic, calamitous, destructive

fate *NOUN* **1** *I am ready for whatever fate has to offer.* ► destiny, chance, providence, fortune, the future, luck, the stars, karma, kismet **2** *He was to meet a terrible fate.* ► death, demise, end, ruin, doom

fated *ADJECTIVE They were fated not to meet again.* ► destined, doomed, predestined, preordained, predetermined, meant, bound, certain, intended

father *NOUN His father was now living in Bristol.* ► male parent, (*more informal*) dad, (*more*

father-in-law *NOUN* **fathers-in-law** the father of a married person's husband or wife

fatigue *NOUN* **1** tiredness **2** weakness in metals, caused by stress
▷ **fatigued** *ADJECTIVE*

fatten *VERB* **fattens, fattening, fattened** make or become fat

fatty *ADJECTIVE* like fat; containing fat

fatuous *ADJECTIVE* silly or foolish
▷ **fatuously** *ADVERB* **fatuousness** *NOUN* **fatuity** *NOUN*

fault *NOUN* **faults** **1** anything that makes a person or thing imperfect; a flaw or mistake **2** the responsibility for something wrong • *It wasn't your fault.* **3** a break in a layer of rock, caused by movement of the earth's crust
▷ **faulty** *ADJECTIVE*
at fault responsible for a mistake or failure

fault *VERB* **faults, faulting, faulted** find faults in something

fauna *NOUN* the animals of a certain area or period of time COMPARE **flora**

favour *NOUN* **favours** **1** a kind or helpful act **2** friendly support or approval • *The visitors soon won the favour of the local people.*
be in favour of like or support

favour *VERB* **favours, favouring, favoured** be in favour of something; show favour to a person

favourable *ADJECTIVE* **1** helpful or advantageous **2** showing approval
▷ **favourably** *ADVERB*

favourite *ADJECTIVE* liked more than others

favourite *NOUN* **1** a person or thing that someone likes most **2** a competitor that is generally expected to win

fax *NOUN* **faxes** **1** a machine that sends an exact copy of a document electronically **2** a copy produced by this

fax *VERB* **faxes, faxing, faxed** send a copy of a document using a fax machine [a shortening of *facsimile*]

fear *NOUN* **fears** a feeling that something unpleasant may happen

fear *VERB* **fears, fearing, feared** feel fear; be afraid of somebody or something

fearful *ADJECTIVE* **1** feeling fear; afraid **2** causing fear or horror • *a fearful monster* **3** (*informal*) very great or bad
▷ **fearfully** *ADVERB*

fearsome *ADJECTIVE* frightening

Thesaurus

informal) daddy, (*more informal*) pop, (*old-fashioned*) pater RELATED ADJECTIVE paternal

fatty *ADJECTIVE* *fatty food* ► greasy, oily, fat, (*technical*) oleaginous

fault *NOUN* **1** *a fault in the manufacturing process* ► defect, deficiency, failure, failing, flaw, weakness, imperfection, shortcoming, blemish, malfunction, snag **2** *There is a fault in their argument.* ► flaw, error, fallacy, inaccuracy, miscalculation, mistake **3** *He had his faults, but carelessness was not one of them.* ► failing, weakness, shortcoming, flaw, defect OPPOSITES ARE strength, strong point **4** *The problem was my fault.* ► responsibility, liability, mistake, error

faulty *ADJECTIVE* *The light bulb was faulty.* ► broken, defective, not working, malfunctioning, inoperative, out of order, deficient

favour *NOUN* **1** *She regards us with great favour.* ► approval, approbation, commendation, goodwill, kindness, friendliness, benevolence, esteem OPPOSITES ARE disfavour, disapproval **2** *Could you do me a favour?* ► good turn, benefit, kindness, kind act, courtesy, indulgence, good deed

favour *VERB* **1** *I favour casual clothes.* ► prefer, choose, opt for, approve of, like **2** *The government favours a policy of peace.* ► recommend, support, back, subscribe to, promote, advocate, espouse, endorse, champion

favourable *ADJECTIVE* **1** *CDs at favourable prices* ► advantageous, beneficial, competitive, convenient **2** *a favourable assessment of their ability* ► positive, encouraging, enthusiastic, complimentary, sympathetic, approving, agreeable

favourite *ADJECTIVE* *John was her favourite nephew.* ► best-loved, most-liked, preferred, favoured, treasured, dearest, special, chosen, pet

favourite *NOUN* *Sarah had always been one of his favourites.* ► first choice, preference, darling, pet, idol, apple of your eye

fear *NOUN* **1** *I remember the shock of fear when I heard her scream.* ► terror, fright, horror, alarm, panic, dread, trepidation **2** *He found it hard to overcome his fears.* ► anxiety, concern, foreboding, unease, misgiving

fear *VERB* **1** *They all feared Ted and kept away from him.* ► be afraid of, be scared of, dread, be terrified of, tremble at, worry about **2** *We fear a bad outcome. I fear you may be right.* ► suspect, expect, foresee, anticipate

fearful *ADJECTIVE* **1** *The generals were fearful of enemy reprisals.* ► afraid, frightened, scared, nervous, apprehensive (about), anxious (about), uneasy (about), (*more informal*) jittery (about) **2** (*informal*) *She felt a fearful pain in her leg.* ► terrible, dreadful, frightful, horrible, awful **3** (*informal*) *There would be a fearful row if anyone found out.* ► major, very great, dreadful, terrible, awful

A B C D E F G H I J K L M N O P Q R S T U V W X Y Z

feasible ADJECTIVE **1** able to be done; possible **2** likely or probable • *a feasible explanation*
▷ **feasibly** ADVERB **feasibility** NOUN
USAGE The use of **feasible** to mean 'likely or probable' has not become generally accepted in standard English, so it is better to avoid it in writing or formal situations.

feast NOUN **feasts** **1** a large splendid meal **2** a religious festival
▷ **feast** VERB
[from old French; related to *fête*]

feather NOUN **feathers** one of the very light coverings that grow from a bird's skin
▷ **feathery** ADJECTIVE

feather VERB **feathers, feathering, feathered** cover or line something with feathers

feature NOUN **features** **1** any part of the face (e.g. the mouth, nose, or eyes) **2** an important or noticeable part; a characteristic **3** a special newspaper article or programme that deals with a particular subject **4** the main film in a cinema programme

February NOUN the second month of the year [named after *februa*, the ancient Roman feast of purification held in this month]

fed *past tense of* **feed**
fed up (*informal*) discontented

federal ADJECTIVE to do with a system in which several states are ruled by a central government but are responsible for their own internal affairs

federation NOUN **federations** a group of federal states

fee NOUN **fees** a charge for something

feeble ADJECTIVE weak; without strength
▷ **feebly** ADVERB **feebleness** NOUN

feed VERB **feeds, feeding, fed** **1** give food to a person or animal **2** take food **3** supply something to a machine etc.
▷ **feeder** NOUN

feed NOUN food for animals or babies

feedback NOUN **1** the response you get from people to something you have done **2** the harsh noise produced when some of the sound from an amplifier goes back into it

feel VERB **feels, feeling, felt** **1** touch something to find out what it is like **2** be aware of something; have an opinion **3** experience an emotion **4** give a certain sensation • *the sand feels warm*
feel like want

feeler NOUN **feelers** **1** a long thin projection on an insect's or crustacean's body, used for

Thesaurus

feasible ADJECTIVE *With luck the plan might be feasible.* ► practicable, practical, workable, achievable, realizable, attainable, possible, viable OPPOSITES ARE impractical, impossible

feast NOUN *a feast fit for a king* ► banquet, meal, dinner, (*more formal*) repast, (*more informal*) spread, (*more informal*) binge

feat NOUN *a feat of great daring* ► deed, exploit, act, accomplishment, achievement, undertaking, action, attainment, performance

feature NOUN **1** *This latest incident has some notable features.* ► characteristic, circumstance, aspect, point, facet, detail, peculiarity, quality, trait **2** *a magazine feature* ► article, report, story, item, piece, column
features *Her coiled hair accentuated her fine features.* ► face, countenance, expression, lineaments, look, (*more formal*) physiognomy

fed up ADJECTIVE **1** (*informal*) *You look tired and fed up.* ► depressed, dejected, dispirited, despondent, disheartened, miserable, cast down, sad, down, glum **2** (*informal*) **be fed up with** *I was totally fed up with all their whinging.* ► be sick of, be tired of, be weary of, have had enough of

feeble ADJECTIVE **1** *My feeble attempts to protest were ignored.* ► weak, ineffective, inadequate, tame, poor, flimsy, shallow **2** *The illness left him too feeble to stand.* ► weak, weakened, frail, delicate, sickly, poorly, infirm, incapacitated, helpless **3** *Her brother was a feeble character.* ► spineless, timid, weak, ineffective, ineffectual

feed VERB **1** *She has a large family to feed.* ► nourish, sustain, provide for, cater for **2** *He was feeding information to the enemy.* ► supply, provide, deliver, present **3** *They spend all their time feeding and sleeping.* ► eat, take food, have a meal, dine **4** **feed on** *The local wildlife feeds on these plants.* ► eat, live on, exist on, consume, devour

feel VERB **1** *He felt the back of his head with his hand.* ► touch, stroke, finger, handle, caress, fondle **2** *She felt a hand on her shoulder.* ► sense, perceive, detect, be aware of, be conscious of, discern **3** *Did you feel any pain?* ► experience, suffer, undergo, endure, go through **4** *We feel you should apologize to her.* ► believe, think, consider, consider it right, reckon, judge **5** *The fabric feels soft.* ► seem, appear, strike you as
feel for *She had had a bad time and I felt for her.* ► feel sorry for, sympathize with, pity, commiserate with
feel like *Do you feel like a drink?* ► fancy, wish for, want, desire

feel NOUN **1** *The wood had a warm feel.* ► texture, quality, surface, touch, impression **2** *She has a good feel for the music.* ► aptitude, flair, talent, gift, knack

feeling; an antenna **2** a cautious question or suggestion etc. to test people's reactions

feeling *NOUN* **feelings** **1** the ability to feel things; the sense of touch **2** what a person feels in the mind; emotion • *I didn't mean to hurt your feelings.* **3** what you think about something • *I have a feeling that we are going to win.*

feint (faynt) *NOUN* **feints** a pretended attack or punch meant to deceive an opponent

feint *VERB* **feints, feinting, feinted** make a feint
USAGE Do not confuse with **faint**.

fell[1] *past tense of* **fall**

fell[2] *VERB* **fells, felling, felled** make something fall; cut or knock down • *They were felling the trees.*

fellow *NOUN* **fellows** **1** a friend or companion; one who belongs to the same group **2** a man or boy **3** a member of a learned society

fellow *ADJECTIVE* of the same group or kind • *Her fellow teachers supported her.*

fellowship *NOUN* **fellowships** **1** friendship **2** a group of friends; a society

felt[1] *past tense of* **feel**

felt[2] *NOUN* a thick fabric made of fibres of wool or fur etc. pressed together

female *ADJECTIVE* of the sex that can bear offspring or produce eggs or fruit

female *NOUN* **females** a female person, animal, or plant

feminine *ADJECTIVE* **1** to do with or like women; suitable for women **2** (in some languages) belonging to the class of words which includes the words referring to women
▷ **femininity** *NOUN*

feminist *NOUN* **feminists** a person who believes that women should have the same rights and status as men
▷ **feminism** *NOUN*

fence *NOUN* **fences** **1** a barrier made of wood or wire etc. round an area **2** a structure for a horse to jump over **3** a person who buys stolen goods and sells them again

fence *VERB* **fences, fencing, fenced** **1** put a fence round or along something **2** fight with long narrow swords (called **foils**) as a sport
▷ **fencer** *NOUN*

fend *VERB* **fends, fending, fended**
fend for yourself take care of yourself
fend off keep a person or thing away from you

ferment (fer- ment) *VERB* **ferments, fermenting, fermented** bubble and change chemically by the action of a substance such as yeast
▷ **fermentation** *NOUN*

ferment (fer- ment) *NOUN* **1** fermenting **2** an excited or agitated condition

fern *NOUN* **ferns** a plant with feathery leaves and no flowers

ferocious *ADJECTIVE* fierce or savage
▷ **ferociously** *ADVERB* **ferocity** *NOUN*

ferry *VERB* **ferries, ferrying, ferried** transport people or things, especially across water

ferry *NOUN* **ferries** a boat or ship used for transporting people or things across a short stretch of water

Thesaurus

feeling *NOUN* **1** *They enjoyed the feeling of power and superiority.* ▶ sensation, sense, awareness, consciousness, perception **2** *I had a feeling she wouldn't be coming.* ▶ suspicion, inkling, notion, idea, hunch, fancy, premonition **3** *There was a friendly feeling about the place.* ▶ atmosphere, aura, air, ambience, climate, quality, mood **4** *She spoke with great feeling.* ▶ emotion, passion, intensity, concern, tenderness, warmth, ardour **5** *He had lost all feeling in his arm.* ▶ sensation, perception, sense of touch

fell *VERB* **1** *A guard felled him with a single blow.* ▶ knock down, knock over, bring down, flatten, prostrate, (*more informal*) floor **2** *Dead trees have to be felled fairly quickly.* ▶ chop down, cut down

fellow *NOUN* *He's a decent fellow, always ready to help out.* ▶ chap, man, boy, individual, (*more informal*) bloke, (*more informal*) guy

fence *NOUN* *The area was surrounded by a tall fence.* ▶ railing, enclosure, barrier, wall, paling, hedge

fence *VERB*
fence in *You will need to fence in the hens.* ▶ confine, pen in, coop up, shut in, close in, hedge in
fence off *More land would be fenced off.* ▶ enclose, surround, encircle, separate off, section off, partition off, cut off

fend *VERB*
fend for yourself *They can fend for themselves for a few days.* ▶ look after yourself, care for yourself, take care of yourself, manage, cope, (*more informal*) get by
fend off *A small force might not be enough to fend off an attack.* ▶ repel, repulse, resist, ward off, beat off, fight off, hold back, thwart

ferocious *ADJECTIVE* *He was the victim of a ferocious attack.* ▶ fierce, brutal, violent, savage, cruel, vicious, barbaric, callous, heartless, cold-blooded, pitiless, ruthless, merciless, vile, sadistic, brutish
OPPOSITES ARE gentle, humane

ferocity *NOUN* *The police were surprised by the ferocity of the attack.* ▶ savagery, brutality, cruelty, viciousness, fierceness, barbarity,

A B C D E F G H I J K L M N O P Q R S T U V W X Y Z

fertile *ADJECTIVE* **1** producing good crops • *fertile soil* **2** able to produce offspring **3** able to produce ideas • *a fertile imagination*
▷ **fertility** *NOUN*

fertilize *VERB* **fertilizes, fertilizing, fertilized** **1** add substances to the soil to make it more fertile **2** put pollen into a plant or sperm into an egg or female animal so that it develops seed or young
▷ **fertilization** *NOUN*

fertilizer *NOUN* **fertilizers** chemicals or manure added to the soil to make it more fertile

fervent *ADJECTIVE* strongly passionate

festival *NOUN* **festivals** **1** a time of celebration, especially for religious reasons **2** an organized series of concerts, films, performances, etc., especially one held every year

festivity *NOUN* **festivities** a festive occasion or celebration

festoon *NOUN* **festoons** a chain of flowers or ribbons etc. hung as a decoration

festoon *VERB* **festoons, festooning, festooned** decorate something with ornaments

fetch *VERB* **fetches, fetching, fetched** **1** go for and bring back • *fetch some milk* • *fetch a doctor* **2** be sold for a particular price • *The chairs fetched £20.*

fête (fayt) *NOUN* **fêtes** an outdoor entertainment with stalls and sideshows

fetter *NOUN* **fetters** a chain or shackle put round a prisoner's ankle

fetus or **foetus** (fee- tus) *NOUN* **fetuses** or **foetuses** a developing embryo, especially an unborn human baby
▷ **fetal** *ADJECTIVE*
[from Latin, = offspring]

feud (fewd) *NOUN* **feuds** a long-lasting quarrel, especially between two families

feudal (few- dal) *ADJECTIVE* to do with the system used in the Middle Ages in which people could farm land in exchange for work done for the owner
▷ **feudalism** *NOUN*

fever *NOUN* **fevers** **1** an abnormally high body temperature, usually with an illness **2** excitement or agitation
▷ **fevered** *ADJECTIVE* **feverish** *ADJECTIVE* **feverishly** *ADVERB*

few *ADJECTIVE* not many

Thesaurus

callousness, heartlessness, cold-bloodedness, ruthlessness AN OPPOSITE IS gentleness

fertile *ADJECTIVE* **1** *fertile soil* ► fruitful, productive, prolific, rich, fecund AN OPPOSITE IS infertile **2** *a fertile mind* ► imaginative, inventive, creative, resourceful, ingenious

fervent *ADJECTIVE* **1** *a fervent hope that we can be friends* ► heartfelt, earnest, eager, intense, keen, strong **2** *a fervent cricket supporter* ► eager, ardent, passionate, impassioned, avid, zealous, keen, enthusiastic

festival *NOUN* *The city has a music festival in the spring.* ► jubilee, pageant, carnival, gala, fête, jamboree, celebration, festivities, anniversary

festive *ADJECTIVE* *A festive atmosphere encourages the children to have a good time.* ► jolly, joyous, joyful, happy, merry, cheerful, cheery, jubilant, convivial, celebratory, gay, gleeful, jovial, light-hearted OPPOSITES ARE gloomy, sombre

festivities *PLURAL NOUN* *The family returned home in time for the New Year festivities.* ► celebrations, revels, revelry, festival, party, entertainments, amusements, fun, jollification

fetch *VERB* **1** *She went to fetch a bucket from the cupboard.* ► get, bring, collect, pick up, retrieve, obtain, bear, call for, carry, convey, import, transfer, transport **2** *Will you fetch your brother from the station?* ► collect, pick up, transport, bring, get, convey, conduct **3** *We had better fetch the doctor.* ► send for, call for, summon, go for, get, bring **4** *By this time he reckoned the house might fetch a cool million.* ► sell for, be sold for, be bought for, raise, realize, bring in, earn, go for, make, produce

fête *NOUN* *a village fête* ► gala, fair, festival, pageant, bazaar, garden party, jubilee, carnival

feud *NOUN* *The family feud came to a head this week.* ► vendetta, dispute, conflict, rivalry, strife, quarrel , antagonism, hostility, enmity, animosity

fever *NOUN* **1** *He caught some sort of fever and never got over it.* ► feverishness, high temperature, delirium **2** *We were in a fever of impatience waiting for them to return.* ► frenzy, ferment **3** *World Cup football fever* ► excitement, agitation, passion, frenzy

feverish *ADJECTIVE* **1** *She looked flushed and feverish.* ► fevered, burning, hot, febrile, inflamed, delirious **2** *The house was a scene of feverish activity.* ► frenzied, frantic, frenetic, excited, hectic, agitated, hurried, hasty, impatient, restless OPPOSITES ARE calm, gentle

few *ADJECTIVE* **1** *Few details are available about the crash. A few people had gathered at the gates.* ► not many, hardly any, a small number of, a handful of AN OPPOSITE IS many **2** *Buses are few at this time of night.* ► scarce, scant, meagre, in short supply, thin on the ground, few and far between

few *NOUN* a small number of people or things **quite a few** or **a good few** a fairly large number
USAGE See the note at **less**.

fiancé (fee- ahn- say) *NOUN* **fiancés** a man who is engaged to be married

fiancée (fee- ahn- say) *NOUN* **fiancées** a woman who is engaged to be married

fiasco (fee- as- koh) *NOUN* **fiascos** a complete failure

fibre *NOUN* **fibres** **1** a very thin thread **2** a substance made of thin threads **3** indigestible material in certain foods that stimulates the action of the intestines
▷ **fibrous** *ADJECTIVE*

fibreglass *NOUN* **1** fabric made from glass fibres **2** plastic containing glass fibres

fickle *ADJECTIVE* constantly changing; not loyal to one person or group etc.
▷ **fickleness** *NOUN*

fiction *NOUN* **fictions** **1** writings about events that have not really happened; stories and novels **2** something imagined or untrue
▷ **fictional** *ADJECTIVE*

fiddle *NOUN* **fiddles** **1** a violin **2** (*informal*) a swindle

fiddle *VERB* **fiddles, fiddling, fiddled** **1** play the violin **2** fidget or tinker with something, using your fingers **3** (*informal*) alter accounts or records dishonestly
▷ **fiddler** *NOUN*

fidget *VERB* **fidgets, fidgeting, fidgeted** make small restless movements
▷ **fidgety** *ADJECTIVE*

field *NOUN* **fields** **1** a piece of land with grass or crops growing on it **2** an area of interest or study • *recent advances in the field of genetics* **3** those who are taking part in a race or outdoor game etc.

field *VERB* **fields, fielding, fielded** **1** stop or catch the ball in cricket etc. **2** be on the side not batting in cricket etc. **3** put a team into a match, contest, etc. • *They fielded their best players for the final.*
▷ **fielder** *NOUN* **fieldsman** *NOUN*

fieldwork *NOUN* practical work or research done in various places, not in a library or museum or laboratory etc.

fiend (feend) *NOUN* **fiends** **1** an evil spirit; a devil **2** a very wicked or cruel person **3** an enthusiast • *a fresh-air fiend*

fiendish *ADJECTIVE* **1** very wicked or cruel **2** extremely difficult or complicated
▷ **fiendishly** *ADVERB*

fierce *ADJECTIVE* **1** angry and violent or cruel **2** intense • *fierce heat*
▷ **fiercely** *ADVERB* **fierceness** *NOUN*

Thesaurus

few *NOUN* *I only have a few left.* ► small number, handful, sprinkling, couple, one or two
AN OPPOSITE IS lot

fib *NOUN* (*informal*) *It was obvious that he was telling fibs.* ► lie, untruth, story, falsehood

fibre *NOUN* **1** *The fibres are then spun, either by hand or by machine.* ► thread, strand, hair, filament **2** *clothes in natural fibres* ► cloth, fabric, stuff, material, substance **3** *a diet low in fat and high in fibre* ► roughage, bulk, fibrous material **4** *a person of great moral fibre* ► character, backbone, toughness, courage, determination, spirit, tenacity

fickle *ADJECTIVE* *His fickle supporters soon deserted him.* ► changeable, disloyal, unfaithful, inconstant, changing, erratic, faithless, variable, unreliable, unstable, vacillating, volatile, unpredictable OPPOSITES ARE loyal, faithful, constant

fiction *NOUN* **1** *a course in twentieth-century fiction* ► novels, stories, creative writing
AN OPPOSITE IS non-fiction **2** *The allegations were a total fiction.* ► invention, fabrication, concoction, deception, fantasy, figment, flight of fancy, pack of lies, (*more informal*) tall story
OPPOSITES ARE fact, truth

fiddle *NOUN* **1** *a group of fiddle players* ► violin **2** (*informal*) *He was involved in a huge tax fiddle.* ► fraud, swindle, cheat, trick

fiddle *VERB* **1** **fiddle with** *Stephen was fiddling with the CD player.* ► tinker with, play about with, tamper with, meddle with, twiddle, finger **2** (*informal*) *The auditors will find out if anyone has fiddled the accounts.* ► falsify, misrepresent, rig, alter, interfere with, tamper with, (*more informal*) doctor, (*more informal*) cook

fidget *VERB* *The heat in the room made me fidget.* ► wriggle, twitch, jiggle, shuffle about, be jittery

field *NOUN* **1** *There was a bull in the next field.* ► enclosure, paddock, pasture **2** *The field was too wet to play on.* ► pitch, ground, sports field, playing field, (*more informal*) park **3** *great names in the field of medicine* ► sphere, domain, area, speciality, subject, discipline **4** *The house lay outside our field of vision.* ► range, scope, extent

fierce *ADJECTIVE* **1** *a fierce dog* ► ferocious, vicious, savage, wild, brutal
OPPOSITES ARE gentle, tame **2** *fierce competition* ► strong, intense, powerful, keen, aggressive, cutthroat AN OPPOSITE IS mild **3** *fierce resentment*

fifteen *ADJECTIVE, NOUN* **1** the number 15 **2** a team in rugby union football
▷ **fifteenth** *ADJECTIVE, NOUN*

fifth *ADJECTIVE, NOUN* **fifths** next after the fourth
▷ **fifthly** *ADVERB*

fifty *ADJECTIVE, NOUN* **fifties** the number 50
▷ **fiftieth** *ADJECTIVE, NOUN*

fifty-fifty *ADJECTIVE, ADVERB* **1** shared equally between two people or groups • *We'll split the money fifty-fifty.* **2** evenly balanced • *a fifty-fifty chance*

fig *NOUN* **figs** a soft fruit full of small seeds

fight *NOUN* **fights** **1** a struggle against somebody using hands, weapons, etc. **2** an attempt to achieve or overcome something • *the fight against poverty*

fight *VERB* **fights, fighting, fought** **1** have a fight **2** attempt to achieve or overcome something
▷ **fighter** *NOUN*

figure *NOUN* **figures** **1** the symbol of a number **2** an amount or value **3** a diagram or illustration **4** a shape **5** the shape of a person's, especially a woman's, body **6** a person **7** a representation of a person or animal in painting, sculpture, etc.

figure *VERB* **figures, figuring, figured** appear or take part in something • *She figures in some of the stories about King Arthur*
figure out work something out

figurehead *NOUN* **figureheads** **1** a carved figure decorating the prow of a sailing ship **2** a person who is head of a country or organization but has no real power

figure of speech *NOUN* **figures of speech** a word or phrase used for special effect and not intended literally, e.g. *'a flood of letters'*

filament *NOUN* **filaments** a thread or thin wire, especially one in a light bulb

file [1] *NOUN* **files** a metal tool with a rough surface that is rubbed on things to shape them or make them smooth

file *VERB* **files, filing, filed** shape or smooth something with a file

file [2] *NOUN* **files** **1** a folder or box etc. for keeping papers in order **2** a collection of data stored under one name in a computer **3** a line of people one behind the other

file *VERB* **files, filing, filed** **1** put something into a file **2** walk in a file • *They filed out.*

filings *PLURAL NOUN* tiny pieces of metal rubbed off by a file • *iron filings*

Thesaurus

► passionate, ardent, intense, strong, powerful **4** *a fierce pain* ► acute, severe, strong, powerful, intense

fiery *ADJECTIVE* **1** *a fiery furnace* ► burning, blazing, flaming, raging, glowing, scorching, red-hot **2** *She remained calm, despite her fiery temperament.* ► passionate, ardent, fervent, excitable, spirited, lively, volatile, explosive, violent, hot-headed **3** *The sky was a fiery red.* ► bright, vivid, brilliant, intense, vibrant, rich, strong

fight *NOUN* **1** *He had got into a fight on the way home.* ► brawl, fracas, tussle, struggle **2** *She hated having fights with her boyfriend.* ► quarrel, argument, row, squabble, wrangle, contretemps, altercation, difference of opinion, (*more informal*) bust-up, (*more informal*) slanging match **3** *the fight for women's rights* ► struggle, battle, campaign, effort **4** *a championship fight* ► contest, match, bout, meeting, fixture

fight *VERB* **1** *Some men were fighting in the street.* ► brawl, tussle, struggle, grapple, wrestle, have a fight, exchange blows **2** *Her sons all fought in the war.* ► serve, be a soldier, join up, take up arms **3** *She and her boyfriend are always fighting.* ► quarrel, argue, row, squabble, wrangle **4** *The unions will fight any proposals to cut jobs.* ► oppose, resist, contest, challenge, defy, object to, combat, withstand **5** *women who fought for their basic freedoms* ► campaign, battle, strive, crusade

fighter *NOUN* *an enemy fighter* ► soldier, combatant, fighting man, fighting woman, warrior

figure *NOUN* **1** *The final figure was higher than last year.* ► total, sum, amount, number **2** *The third figure is an eight.* ► digit, numeral, character, number **3** *It's hard to put an exact figure on it.* ► amount, price, cost, sum **4** *Jane has a lovely figure.* ► shape, physique, build, proportions, body, frame **5** *By now she had become a public figure.* ► personality, character, celebrity, dignitary, person, individual, personage **6** *He did not want to be seen as a figure of fun.* ► symbol, personification, embodiment, epitome

figure *VERB* *an animal that figures in many ancient myths* ► feature, appear, play a role, have a place

file *NOUN* **1** *He keeps his business letters in A4 files.* ► folder, binder, portfolio, wallet, sleeve **2** *There is a file on these people at headquarters.* ► dossier, record, set of notes **3** *A file of soldiers was walking up the road.* ► line, column, string, train, procession, convoy, stream

file *VERB* **1** *Completed forms are filed by year in the top drawer.* ► classify, arrange, organize, put in order, enter, store, keep, archive **2** *She was sitting filing her nails.* ► smooth, shape, rub,

fill *VERB* **fills, filling, filled** **1** make or become full **2** block up a hole or cavity **3** hold a position, or appoint a person to a vacant post
▷ **filler** *NOUN*

fill *NOUN* enough to fill a person or thing • *We ate our fill*

filling station *NOUN* **filling stations** a place where petrol is sold from pumps

film *NOUN* **films** **1** a movie, such as those shown in cinemas or on television **2** a rolled strip or sheet of thin plastic coated with material that is sensitive to light, used for taking photographs or making a movie **3** a very thin layer • *a film of grease*

film *VERB* **films, filming, filmed** record something on film; make a film of a story etc.

filter *NOUN* **filters** **1** a device for holding back dirt or other unwanted material from a liquid or gas etc. that passes through it **2** a system for filtering traffic

filter *VERB* **filters, filtering, filtered** **1** pass through a filter **2** move gradually • *They filtered into the hall.* • *News began to filter out.* **3** (said about traffic) move in a particular direction while other traffic is held up

filth *NOUN* disgusting dirt

filthy *ADJECTIVE* **filthier, filthiest** **1** disgustingly dirty **2** obscene or offensive
▷ **filthiness** *NOUN*

fin *NOUN* **fins** **1** a thin flat part sticking out from a fish's body, that helps it to swim **2** a small part that sticks out on an aircraft or rocket etc., for helping its balance

final *ADJECTIVE* **1** coming at the end; last **2** that puts an end to an argument etc. • *You must go, and that's final!*
▷ **finally** *ADVERB* **finality** *NOUN*

final *NOUN* **finals** the last in a series of contests

finalist *NOUN* **finalists** a competitor in a final

finance *NOUN* **1** the use or management of money **2** the money used to pay for something
▷ **financial** *ADJECTIVE*
finances *PLURAL NOUN* money resources; funds

Thesaurus

polish **3** *The children filed through the door into the sunshine.* ► stream, troop, march, parade, walk in a line, proceed in a line

fill *VERB* **1** *She soon filled a suitcase with the things she needed.* ► pack, load **2** *Fill the holes and gaps before you start papering.* ► plug, stop, stop up, bung up, block up, seal **3** *With thirty guests we will fill the house.* ► crowd, throng, pack, pack into, congest **4** *A smell of coffee filled the room.* ► spread through, pervade, permeate, penetrate **5** *Recruits will fill the new posts by the end of the year.* ► occupy, take up, be appointed to, move into **6** *A bank loan will fill their needs for now.* ► fulfil, satisfy, meet, supply, furnish
fill in **1** *You have to fill in this form.* ► complete, fill out, answer **2** *I am filling in for Shirley while she is away.* ► deputize, cover, stand in, substitute **3** *Ken will fill us in on the details.* ► brief, inform (of), advise (of), apprise (of)

filling *NOUN* *The cushion was losing its filling.* ► stuffing, padding, wadding, insides, contents

filling *ADJECTIVE* *a filling meal* ► satisfying, nourishing, nutritious, ample, square, solid, substantial

film *NOUN* **1** *There was a film of dust on the table.* ► layer, covering, coat, coating, dusting, patina, sheet, veil, skin, screen **2** *The boys are going to see a film this evening.* ► movie, picture, feature, (*old-fashioned*) motion picture

filth *NOUN* *I needed a hose to get the filth off my boots.* ► dirt, muck, grime, mud, slime, sludge, garbage, excrement

filthy *ADJECTIVE* **1** *The house was filthy.* ► dirty, grubby, mucky, squalid, uncleaned, unwashed AN OPPOSITE IS clean **2** *Everyone agreed it was a filthy trick.* ► nasty, mean, vile, despicable, contemptible, disgusting, shabby **3** *They were accused of using filthy language.* ► rude, indecent, coarse, vulgar, lewd, improper, obscene OPPOSITES ARE clean, polite **4** *He was in a filthy mood.* ► bad, foul, bad-tempered, irritable

final *ADJECTIVE* **1** *the final month of their course* ► last, closing, concluding, finishing, end OPPOSITES ARE first, initial **2** *the final minutes of the match* ► last, closing, dying **3** *The judges' decision is final.* ► irrevocable, definitive, absolute, indisputable, unalterable, decisive, incontrovertible

finalize *VERB* *We can now finalize the arrangements for the trip.* ► complete, conclude, settle, clinch, resolve, decide, confirm, (*more informal*) wrap up

finally *ADVERB* *The bank finally agreed to loan the money.* ► eventually, ultimately, in the end, at length, at last

finance *NOUN* **1** *He needs to learn more about finance.* ► economics, money management, accounting, banking, fiscal matters **2** *The company is seeking longer-term finance.* ► funding, funds, capital, assets, revenue, income, financial backing **3** *His finances are in a fairly good state.* ► resources, assets, financial affairs, money affairs

A B C D E F G H I J K L M N O P Q R S T U V W X Y Z

finance *VERB* **finances, financing, financed** provide the money for something
▷ **financier** *NOUN*

find *VERB* **finds, finding, found** **1** get or see something by looking for it or by chance **2** learn something by experience • *He found that digging was hard work.* **3** decide and give a verdict • *The jury found him guilty.*
find out get or discover some information

find *NOUN* **finds** something found

findings *PLURAL NOUN* the conclusions reached from an investigation

fine[1] *ADJECTIVE* **1** of high quality; excellent **2** dry and clear; sunny • *fine weather* **3** very thin; consisting of small particles **4** in good health; well • *I'm fine*
▷ **finely** *ADVERB* **fineness** *NOUN*

fine *ADVERB* **1** finely • *chop it fine* **2** (*informal*) very well • *That will suit me fine.*

fine[2] *NOUN* **fines** money which has to be paid as a punishment

fine *VERB* **fines, fining, fined** make somebody pay a fine

finger *NOUN* **fingers** **1** one of the separate parts of the hand **2** a narrow piece of something • *fish fingers*

finger *VERB* **fingers, fingering, fingered** touch or feel something with your fingers

fingernail *NOUN* **fingernails** the hard covering at the end of a finger

fingerprint *NOUN* **fingerprints** a mark made by the tiny ridges on the fingertip, used as a way of identifying someone

finish *VERB* **finishes, finishing, finished** bring or come to an end

finish *NOUN* **finishes** **1** the last stage of something; the end **2** the surface or coating on woodwork etc.

finite (fy- nyt) *ADJECTIVE* limited; not infinite • *We have only a finite supply of coal.*

finicky *ADJECTIVE* very fussy

fir *NOUN* **firs** an evergreen tree with needle-like leaves, that produces cones

fire *NOUN* **fires** **1** the process of burning that produces light and heat **2** coal and wood etc. burning in a grate or furnace to give heat **3** a device using electricity or gas to heat a room **4** the shooting of guns • *Hold your fire!*

Thesaurus

finance *VERB* *Private sponsors will finance the venture.* ► fund, back, subsidize, support, provide money for, invest in, underwrite, pay for, sponsor

financial *ADJECTIVE* *financial affairs* ► monetary, fiscal, pecuniary, economic

find *VERB* **1** *I found some old coins in the cupboard.* ► discover, locate, retrieve, track down, come across, chance on, unearth, uncover **2** *We found it odd that there were so many complaints.* ► consider, think, believe, reckon, see as, regard as, look on as, view as **3** *You will find that it's helpful to number each paragraph.* ► realize, discover, learn, perceive, notice, become aware **4** *I hope you find the success you deserve.* ► achieve, attain, win, obtain, acquire, reach, secure, get
find out **1** *At last we will find out what happened.* ► learn, ascertain, discover, perceive **2** *The culprits were soon found out.* ► reveal, expose, unmask, uncover, (*more informal*) rumble

find *An ancient ship burial was among the exciting finds.* ► discovery, acquisition

fine *ADJECTIVE* **1** *It was a fine achievement.* ► excellent, outstanding, admirable, remarkable, exceptional, commendable, first-class, good **2** *The next day was fine.* ► bright, fair, dry, clear, sunny, warm, cloudless OPPOSITES ARE bad, wet, inclement **3** *He brought out the fine china.* ► delicate, fragile **4** *A pen with a fine tip.* ► thin, narrow, slender, slim **5** *a beach of fine warm sand* ► powdery, minute **6** *He likes fine clothes.* ► elegant, stylish, smart, chic, fashionable **7** *The mechanism needs a fine adjustment.* ► small, minor, subtle **8** *It's fine to write to me here.* ► all right, acceptable, suitable, agreeable

fine *NOUN* *He got a parking fine.* ► penalty, charge

finger *VERB* *He fingered the ring on his finger.* ► touch, feel, handle, stroke, rub, fondle, caress, twiddle

finish *NOUN* **1** *The race had an exciting finish.* ► ending, end, close, last stage, conclusion, result **2** *They went out to celebrate the finish of the work.* ► completion, conclusion, end, cessation, termination **3** *Mix the paint well for an even finish.* ► appearance, surface, texture, lustre, polish, shine, gloss, smoothness

finish *VERB* **1** *We have to finish the work today.* ► complete, conclude, end, finalize **2** *They never seem to finish complaining.* ► stop, cease, end **3** *We've finished the biscuits.* ► use up, eat, consume, devour, exhaust, (*more informal*) polish off **4** *The film finishes at ten.* ► end, conclude, terminate **5** *Another year of losses will finish the company.* ► destroy, ruin, overwhelm, overpower

fire *NOUN* **1** *The building was destroyed in a fire.* ► blaze, conflagration, inferno, flames, burning, combustion, holocaust, pyre **2** *She spoke with fire in her eyes.* ► passion, feeling, enthusiasm, intensity, vigour, fervour, ardour, dynamism, exuberance

on fire burning
set fire to start something burning

fire *VERB* **fires, firing, fired** **1** set fire to **2** bake pottery or bricks etc. in a kiln **3** shoot a gun; send out a bullet or missile **4** (*informal*) dismiss someone from a job **5** excite • *fire them with enthusiasm*
▷ **firer** *NOUN*

firearm *NOUN* **firearms** a small gun; a rifle, pistol, or revolver

fire brigade *NOUN* **fire brigades** a team of people organized to fight fires

fire engine *NOUN* **fire engines** a large vehicle that carries firefighters and equipment to put out large fires

fire escape *NOUN* **fire escapes** a special staircase by which people may escape from a burning building etc.

fire extinguisher *NOUN* **fire extinguishers** a metal cylinder from which water or foam can be sprayed to put out a fire

firefighter *NOUN* **firefighters** a member of a fire brigade

fireplace *NOUN* **fireplaces** an open structure for holding a fire in a room

firewood *NOUN* wood for use as fuel

firework *NOUN* **fireworks** a device containing chemicals that burn or explode attractively and noisily

firing squad *NOUN* **firing squads** a group of soldiers given the duty of shooting a condemned person

firm *NOUN* **firms** a business organization

firm *ADJECTIVE* **1** not giving way when pressed; hard or solid **2** steady; not shaking or moving **3** definite and not likely to change • *a firm belief*
▷ **firmly** *ADVERB* **firmness** *NOUN*

firm *VERB* **firms, firming, firmed** make something become firm

first *ADJECTIVE* coming before all others in time or order or importance
▷ **firstly** *ADVERB*

first *ADVERB* before everything else • *Finish this work first.*

first aid *NOUN* treatment given to an injured person before a doctor comes

first-class *ADJECTIVE* **1** using the best class of a service • *first-class post* **2** excellent

fish *NOUN* **fish** or **fishes** an animal with gills and fins that always lives and breathes in water

fish *VERB* **fishes, fishing, fished** **1** try to catch fish **2** search for something; try to get something • *He is only fishing for compliments.* [from Old English]

fisherman *NOUN* **fishermen** a person who tries to catch fish

fishmonger *NOUN* **fishmongers** a shopkeeper who sells fish

fishy *ADJECTIVE* **fishier, fishiest** **1** smelling or tasting of fish **2** (*informal*) causing doubt or suspicion • *a fishy excuse*
▷ **fishily** *ADVERB* **fishiness** *NOUN*

fission *NOUN* **1** splitting something **2** splitting the nucleus of an atom so as to release energy

fist *NOUN* **fists** a tightly closed hand with the fingers bent into the palm

fit[1] *ADJECTIVE* **fitter, fittest** **1** suitable or good enough • *a meal fit for a king* **2** healthy, in good physical condition • *Keep fit!* **3** ready or likely

Thesaurus

fire *VERB* **1** *The engine began to fire.* ► ignite, start, catch, (*more informal*) get going **2** *The guerrillas fired a rocket.* ► launch, discharge, shoot, detonate, set off, let off, let fly with **3** *The idea fired their imagination.* ► excite, stimulate, arouse, inspire, enliven, stir up **4** (*informal*) *They fired him for misconduct.* ► dismiss, discharge, sack, give someone notice, lay off

firm *ADJECTIVE* **1** *The ground is fairly firm at this point.* ► hard, solid, unyielding, hardened, compact, compressed, resistant, stable AN OPPOSITE IS soft **2** *The house lacked firm foundations.* ► secure, steady, strong, sturdy, fast, fixed, stable, tight, anchored **3** *Firm action is essential.* ► resolute, determined, decided, steadfast, adamant, dogged, obstinate, persistent, unshakeable, unwavering, unflinching **4** *We need a firm commitment.* ► definite, agreed, settled, unchangeable **5** *Sally was a firm friend of hers.* ► devoted, constant, faithful, loyal, reliable, dependable

firm *NOUN* *Dave joined an accountancy firm.* ► company, establishment, organization, business, concern, corporation

first *ADJECTIVE* **1** *Our first attempts didn't work.* ► initial, opening, preliminary **2** *The first inhabitants were hunters.* ► original, earliest, oldest, primeval, primitive **3** *The first consideration is the welfare of the children.* ► principal, prime, paramount, primary, main, chief, key, foremost, supreme, overriding

firstly *ADVERB* *Firstly, we must learn each other's names.* ► first, to begin with, to start with, at the outset, as a start

fishy *ADJECTIVE* (*informal*) *The price was so low it all seemed a bit fishy.* ► suspicious, dubious, doubtful, suspect, peculiar, strange, odd, queer, funny

fit *ADJECTIVE* **1** *She looked remarkably fit for a seventy-two-year-old.* ► healthy, well, able-

- *They worked till they were fit to collapse.*
▷ **fitness** NOUN

fit VERB **fits, fitting, fitted 1** be the right size and shape for something; be suitable **2** put something into place • *Fit a lock on the door.* **3** alter something to make it the right size and shape **4** make suitable for something • *His training fits him for the job.*
▷ **fitter** NOUN

fit NOUN the way something fits • *a good fit*

fit[2] NOUN **fits 1** a sudden illness, especially one that makes you move violently or become unconscious **2** an outburst • *a fit of rage*

fitful ADJECTIVE happening in short periods, not steadily
▷ **fitfully** ADVERB

fitting ADJECTIVE proper or appropriate • *This statue is a fitting memorial to an extraordinary woman.*

five ADJECTIVE, NOUN **fives** the number 5

fix VERB **fixes, fixing, fixed 1** fasten or place firmly **2** make permanent and unable to change **3** decide or arrange • *We fixed a date for the party.* **4** repair; put into working condition • *He is fixing my bike.*
▷ **fixer** NOUN

fix up arrange or organize something

fix NOUN **fixes 1** (*informal*) an awkward situation • *I'm in a fix* **2** finding the position of something, by using a compass, radar, etc. **3** (*informal*) an addict's dose of a drug

fixedly ADVERB with a fixed expression

fixture NOUN **fixtures 1** something fixed in its place **2** a sports event planned for a particular day

fizz VERB **fizzes, fizzing, fizzed** make a hissing or spluttering sound; produce a lot of small bubbles

fizzy ADJECTIVE (said about a drink) having a lot of small bubbles
▷ **fizziness** NOUN

flabby ADJECTIVE fat and soft, not firm
▷ **flabbily** ADVERB **flabbiness** NOUN

flag[1] NOUN **flags 1** a piece of cloth with a coloured pattern or shape on it, used as a sign or signal **2** a small piece of paper or plastic that looks like a flag
▷ **flagpole** NOUN **flagstaff** NOUN

Thesaurus

bodied, robust, hale and hearty, in good form OPPOSITES ARE unfit, unhealthy **2** *The vehicles are all fit for commercial use.* ► suitable, appropriate, prepared, equipped, ready, proper, right, correct OPPOSITES ARE unfit, unsuitable **3** *Do you think he is fit to be a parent?* ► competent, able, capable (of being), qualified, worthy OPPOSITES ARE unfit, incapable

fit NOUN **1** *He might have an epileptic fit at any time.* ► seizure, convulsion, paroxysm, spasm, attack **2** *She was having a fit of hysterics.* ► outbreak, outburst, spell, bout, attack, explosion

fit VERB **1** *It takes a long time to fit all the pieces together.* ► arrange, assemble, build, construct, dovetail, install, interlock, join, match, position, put in place, put together **2** *Make the punishment fit the crime.* ► suit, match, accord with, be appropriate to, correspond with *or* to, be fitting for, conform with

fitted ADJECTIVE **1** *He clearly isn't fitted for the job.* ► suited, suitable, right, equipped, appropriate **2** *It was a modern house with fitted cupboards everywhere you looked.* ► built-in, integral, incorporated, customized

fitting ADJECTIVE *The concert was a fitting tribute to a fine singer.* ► suitable, apt, appropriate, apposite, proper, timely, felicitous OPPOSITES ARE inappropriate, unsuitable

fittings PLURAL NOUN *The bathroom fittings were cheap and flimsy.* ► fixtures, fitments, equipment, accessories, furnishings

fix VERB **1** *You can fix the notice to a lamppost.* ► fasten, tie, pin, attach, affix, secure **2** *The farmer had fixed posts into the ground.* ► set, embed, cement, place, position **3** *I can fix it for you to get an invitation.* ► arrange, organize, manage **4** *Let's fix a date to meet.* ► set, decide on, agree on, arrange, settle, determine **5** *The television needs to be fixed.* ► mend, repair, put right

fix NOUN (*informal*) *I'm in a bit of a fix* ► difficulty, predicament, mess, plight, dilemma, (*informal*) hole, (*informal*) jam, quandary, corner

fixed ADJECTIVE *The licence is for a fixed period.* ► set, definite, decided, established, settled, predetermined, firm

fizz VERB *She dropped in a tablet and the water fizzed.* ► bubble, effervesce, foam, froth, fizzle, sizzle, hiss

fizzy ADJECTIVE *There are fizzy drinks in the garden.* ► sparkling, effervescent, bubbly, carbonated, foaming AN OPPOSITE IS still

flabbergasted ADJECTIVE *He just stood there, flabbergasted.* ► astonished, amazed, astounded, surprised, staggered, startled, disconcerted, dumbfounded, speechless, shocked, perplexed, stunned, stupefied, bewildered, (*more informal*) thunderstruck

flabby ADJECTIVE *When he took her hand in his, it was soft and flabby.* ► slack, limp, loose, floppy, flaccid, weak, feeble OPPOSITES ARE firm, stiff

flag NOUN *The route was decorated with flags.* ► banner, standard, ensign, pennant, pennon, streamer, bunting, colours

flag *VERB* **flags**, **flagging**, **flagged** **1** become weak; droop **2** signal with a flag or by waving

flag[2] *NOUN* **flags** a flat slab of stone used for paving

flagrant (flay- grant) *ADJECTIVE* very bad and noticeable • *flagrant disobedience*
▷ **flagrantly** *ADVERB* **flagrancy** *NOUN*

flagship *NOUN* **flagships** **1** a ship that carries an admiral and flies his flag **2** a company's best or most important product, store, etc.

flair *NOUN* a natural ability or talent • *Ian has a flair for languages.*
USAGE Do not confuse with **flare**.

flake *NOUN* **flakes** **1** a very light thin piece of something **2** a small flat piece of falling snow
▷ **flaky** *ADJECTIVE*

flamboyant *ADJECTIVE* very showy in appearance or manner

flame *NOUN* **flames** a tongue-shaped portion of fire or burning gas

flame *VERB* **flames**, **flaming**, **flamed** **1** produce flames **2** become bright red

flamingo *NOUN* **flamingoes** a wading bird with long legs, a long neck, and pinkish feathers

flammable *ADJECTIVE* able to be set on fire
▷ **flammability** *NOUN*
USAGE See note at **inflammable**.

flank *NOUN* **flanks** the side of something, especially an animal's body or an army

flannel *NOUN* **flannels** **1** a soft cloth for washing yourself **2** a soft woollen material

flap *VERB* **flaps**, **flapping**, **flapped** **1** wave about **2** (*informal*) panic or fuss about something

flap *NOUN* **flaps** **1** a part that is fixed at one edge on to something else, often to cover an opening **2** the action or sound of flapping **3** (*informal*) a panic or fuss • *Don't get in a flap.*

flare *VERB* **flares**, **flaring**, **flared** **1** blaze with a sudden bright flame **2** become angry suddenly **3** become gradually wider • *flaring nostrils*

flare *NOUN* **flares** **1** a sudden bright flame or light, especially one used as a signal **2** a gradual widening, especially in skirts or trousers
USAGE Do not confuse with **flair**.

flash *NOUN* **flashes** **1** a sudden bright flame or light **2** a device for making a sudden bright light for taking photographs **3** a sudden display of anger, wit, etc. **4** a short item of news

flash *VERB* **flashes**, **flashing**, **flashed** **1** make a flash **2** appear suddenly; move quickly • *The train flashed past us.*

flashback *NOUN* **flashbacks** going back in a film or story to something that happened earlier

flashy *ADJECTIVE* gaudy or showy

flask *NOUN* **flasks** **1** a bottle with a narrow neck **2** a vacuum flask

flat *ADJECTIVE* **flatter**, **flattest** **1** with no curves or bumps; smooth and level **2** spread out; lying at full length • *Lie flat on the ground.* **3** (said about a tyre) with no air inside **4** (said about feet) without the normal arch underneath

Thesaurus

flag *VERB* *Our energy was beginning to flag.* ► fade, fail, decline, diminish, dwindle, sink, disappear

flair *NOUN* **1** *He has a flair for games.* ► talent, aptitude, gift, ability, genius, faculty, capacity, adeptness **2** *She dresses with great flair.* ► style, elegance, taste, discernment, panache, finesse

flake *NOUN* *First remove any loose flakes of old paint.* ► scale, sliver, chip, splinter, shaving, bit, leaf, slice, wafer

flamboyant *ADJECTIVE* *He was well known for his flamboyant appearance.* ► ostentatious, showy, colourful, gaudy, brilliant, resplendent, extravagant

flap *VERB* **1** *The washing was flapping in the wind.* ► flutter, sway, swing, quiver, wave about **2** *The swan flapped its wings angrily.* ► beat, flutter, shake, agitate, quiver, thrash **3** (*informal*) *He tried hard to avoid flapping.* ► panic, fuss, become agitated, become flustered

flare *VERB* *The match flared in his cupped hands.* ► blaze, flame, flash, burn, erupt, sparkle

flare up **1** *This border war could flare up at any time.* ► break out, burst out, erupt, blow up, recur **2** *They annoyed her and she flared up at them.* ► lose your temper, lose control, fly into a rage, become angry

flash *VERB* *Lights flashed in the distance.* ► shine, blaze, flare, gleam, beam, glint, sparkle, spark

flash *NOUN* **1** *a flash of light* ► blaze, burst, flare, glare, gleam, glint, sparkle, flicker, twinkle, ray **2** *a flash of inspiration* ► burst, wave, surge, rush

flashy *ADJECTIVE* *Lily held out her hand with a flashy ring on one finger.* ► showy, gaudy, ostentatious, vulgar, (*more informal*) tacky

flat *ADJECTIVE* **1** *a flat surface* ► level, smooth, even, horizontal, plane OPPOSITES ARE bumpy, uneven **2** *She lay flat on the bed.* ► outstretched, prostrate, spread out, recumbent **3** *a flat sea* ► calm, still, smooth, waveless, tranquil OPPOSITES ARE rough, choppy **4** *His voice was flat and lifeless.* ► dull, monotonous, uninteresting, unexciting, tedious, boring, bland, dreary, insipid, colourless, featureless, unexpressive, weak AN OPPOSITE IS emotional **5** *The request met with a flat refusal.* ► outright, direct, straight, plain, absolute, positive

5 absolute • *a flat refusal* **6** dull; not changing **7** (said about a drink) no longer fizzy **8** (said about a battery) unable to produce any more electric current **9** (in music) one semitone lower than the natural note • *E flat*
▷ **flatly** ADVERB **flatness** NOUN

flat NOUN **flats** **1** a set of rooms for living in, usually on one floor of a building **2** (in music) a note one semitone lower than the natural note; the sign (♭) that indicates this **3** a punctured tyre

flatten VERB **flattens, flattening, flattened** make or become flat

flatter VERB **flatters, flattering, flattered** **1** praise somebody more than he or she deserves **2** make a person or thing seem better or more attractive than they really are
▷ **flatterer** NOUN **flattery** NOUN

flaunt VERB **flaunts, flaunting, flaunted** display something proudly in a way that annoys people; show it off • *He liked to flaunt his expensive clothes and cars.*
USAGE Do not confuse this word with **flout**, which has a different meaning.

flavour NOUN **flavours** the taste of something

flavour VERB **flavours, flavouring, flavoured** give something a flavour; season it
▷ **flavouring** NOUN

flaw NOUN **flaws** something that makes a person or thing imperfect
▷ **flawed** ADJECTIVE

flea NOUN **fleas** a small jumping insect that sucks blood

fleck NOUN **flecks** **1** a very small patch of colour **2** a particle; a speck • *flecks of dirt*
▷ **flecked** ADJECTIVE

fledged ADJECTIVE (said about young birds) having grown feathers and able to fly
fully-fledged ADJECTIVE fully trained • *a fully-fledged engineer*

fledgeling NOUN **fledgelings** a young bird that is just fledged

fleece NOUN **fleeces** **1** the woolly hair of a sheep or similar animal **2** a warm piece of clothing made from a soft fabric
▷ **fleecy** ADJECTIVE

fleece VERB **fleeces, fleecing, fleeced** **1** shear the fleece from a sheep **2** swindle a person out of some money

fleet NOUN **fleets** a number of ships, aircraft, or vehicles owned by one country or company

Thesaurus

flat NOUN *They lived in a small flat for several years.* ► apartment, maisonette, set of rooms, flatlet, penthouse

flatten VERB **1** *Tom flattened the crumpled paper against his knee.* ► smooth, press, even out, iron out, level out, roll OPPOSITES ARE roughen, crumple **2** *People had walked over the beds and flattened the plants.* ► squash, trample, crush, compress, run over **3** *The hurricane had flattened hundreds of buildings.* ► demolish, destroy, devastate, knock down, level, raze **4** (*informal*) *He's quite capable of flattening you with a single blow.* ► knock down, knock over, fell, prostrate, (*informal*) floor, (*informal*) lay out

flatter VERB **1** *He enjoyed teasing and flattering her.* ► praise, compliment, humour, fawn on, play up to, (*more informal*) sweet-talk, (*more informal*) butter up USAGE Note that to *flatter* is to compliment someone in an insincere way, whereas to *praise* is to pay genuine compliments. **2** *She wore a dress that flattered her small figure.* ► suit, enhance, set off, look good on, show to advantage

flattering ADJECTIVE **1** *flattering remarks* ► complimentary, favourable, appreciative, adulatory, effusive, obsequious, fawning, fulsome, ingratiating OPPOSITES ARE insulting, sincere **2** *a flattering outfit* ► becoming, fetching, enhancing

flattery NOUN *We succumb to flattery because it makes us feel good.* ► praise, compliments, adulation, blandishments, admiration, fawning, obsequiousness, servility
USAGE Note that *flattery* is always insincere, whereas *praise* is usually genuine.

flavour NOUN **1** *The food had a spicy flavour.* ► taste, tang, savour **2** *a story with an oriental flavour* ► character, quality, atmosphere, aura, ambience, mood, feel, style, feeling, aspect

flavour VERB *You can flavour the stew with mixed herbs.* ► season, spice, enliven, liven up, enrich

flavouring NOUN *Add some gentle flavouring.* ► seasoning, additive, spice, essence, extract

flaw NOUN *There is a flaw in this reasoning; a glass with a tiny flaw you can hardly see* ► defect, blemish, fault, imperfection, deficiency, weakness, failing, shortcoming

flawed ADJECTIVE *The argument was obviously flawed.* ► defective, unsound, faulty, imperfect, weak, deficient

flawless ADJECTIVE *Her skin was flawless.* ► perfect, faultless, immaculate, unblemished, unmarked, spotless

flee VERB *She left the others and fled to her room.* ► run off, bolt, fly, take off, clear off, hurry off, escape, disappear

fleet NOUN *A large fleet of ships sailed out.* ► flotilla, armada, naval force, convoy, navy, squadron, task force

fleeting *ADJECTIVE* passing quickly; brief

flesh *NOUN* **1** the soft substance of the bodies of people and animals, consisting of muscle and fat **2** the body as opposed to the mind or soul **3** the pulpy part of fruits and vegetables
▷ **fleshy** *ADJECTIVE*

flex *VERB* **flexes, flexing, flexed** bend or stretch something that is flexible • *Try flexing your muscles*

flex *NOUN* **flexes** flexible insulated wire for carrying electric current

flexible *ADJECTIVE* **1** easy to bend or stretch **2** able to be changed or adapted • *Our plans are flexible.*
▷ **flexibility** *NOUN*

flick *NOUN* **flicks** a quick light hit or movement

flick *VERB* **flicks, flicking, flicked** hit or move with a flick

flicker *VERB* **flickers, flickering, flickered** **1** burn or shine unsteadily **2** move quickly to and fro

flicker *NOUN* **flickers** a flickering light or movement

flight[1] *NOUN* **flights** **1** flying **2** a journey in an aircraft **3** a series of stairs **4** a group of flying birds or aircraft **5** the feathers or fins on a dart or arrow

flight[2] *NOUN* **flights** fleeing; an escape

flight recorder *NOUN* **flight recorders** an electronic device in an aircraft that records technical information about its flight. It is used after an accident to help find the cause

flimsy *ADJECTIVE* **flimsier, flimsiest** made of something thin or weak
▷ **flimsily** *ADVERB* **flimsiness** *NOUN*

flinch *VERB* **flinches, flinching, flinched** move or shrink back because you are afraid; wince
▷ **flinch** *NOUN*

fling *VERB* **flings, flinging, flung** throw something violently or carelessly

fling *NOUN* **flings** **1** a short time of enjoyment • *a final fling before the exams* **2** a brief romantic affair **3** a vigorous dance • *the Highland fling*

flint *NOUN* **flints** **1** a very hard kind of stone **2** a piece of flint or hard metal used to produce sparks
▷ **flinty** *ADJECTIVE*

flip *VERB* **flips, flipping, flipped** **1** flick **2** (*slang*) become crazy or very angry

flip *NOUN* **flips** a flipping movement

flippant *ADJECTIVE* not showing proper seriousness
▷ **flippantly** *ADVERB* **flippancy** *NOUN*

flirt *VERB* **flirts, flirting, flirted** behave as though you are sexually attracted to someone to amuse yourself
▷ **flirtation** *NOUN*

flirt *NOUN* **flirts** a person who flirts
▷ **flirtatious** *ADJECTIVE* **flirtatiously** *ADVERB*

Thesaurus

flesh *NOUN* *an animal's flesh* ► meat, muscle, tissue, carrion, fat USAGE Note that *carrion* is the decaying flesh of a dead animal.

flex *NOUN* *a flex for an electric iron* ► cable, lead, wire

flexible *ADJECTIVE* **1** *flexible working practices* ► adaptable, adjustable, variable, fluid, open OPPOSITES ARE inflexible, rigid **2** *a flexible rod used as an aerial* ► bendable, pliable, pliant, malleable, stretchable OPPOSITES ARE rigid, fixed

flick *VERB* *He flicked a finger lightly against her cheek.* ► stroke, wag, brush, wave, sweep, flip, jerk

flick *NOUN* **1** *The king dismissed his page with a flick of his head.* ► jerk, toss, flip, sweep **2** *He gave the table a few flicks with a duster.* ► dab, touch, brush, swipe, stroke

flight *NOUN* **1** *a short history of flight* ► flying, aviation, aeronautics, air travel **2** *the flight of a missile* ► path, trajectory, track **3** *the king's flight to safety* ► escape , getaway, retreat, fleeing

flimsy *ADJECTIVE* **1** *He moved the flimsy barrier and walked past.* ► fragile, rickety, shaky, makeshift, insubstantial, frail, weak AN OPPOSITE IS substantial **2** *She wore a flimsy nightdress.* ► light, lightweight, thin, fine, diaphanous, silky, filmy **3** *We heard the usual flimsy excuses.* ► feeble, weak, poor, thin, unconvincing, implausible

flinch *VERB* *She flinched as he put out his hand.* ► wince, recoil, start, shrink, pull back, draw back, shy away, shrink back
flinch from *He never flinches from his duty.* ► shrink from, shirk, avoid, evade, balk at

fling *VERB* *He flung the rope over the wall.* ► throw, hurl, toss, sling, cast, pitch, heave

flip *VERB* **1** *He flipped a coin in the air.* ► toss, flick, spin, throw **2** *The beetle flipped on to its back.* ► turn, spin, tip, topple **3 flip through** *She was flipping through the pages of a magazine.* ► flick through, thumb through, skim through, scan, peruse

flirt *VERB* **flirt with** **1** *He loves flirting with the girls.* ► tease, trifle with, lead on, make up to, (*more informal*) chat up **2** *an idea I had been flirting with for some time* ► consider, entertain, toy with, trifle with, dabble in

flit *VERB* *insects flitting from plant to plant* ► dart, flip, fly, flutter, whisk, skim, dance

A B C D E **F** G H I J K L M N O P Q R S T U V W X Y Z

float *VERB* **floats, floating, floated 1** stay or move on the surface of a liquid or in air **2** make something float **3** launch a business by getting financial support from the sale of shares
▷ **floater** *NOUN*

float *NOUN* **floats 1** a device designed to float **2** a vehicle with a platform used for delivering milk or for carrying a display in a parade etc. **3** a small amount of money kept for paying small bills or giving change etc.

flock *NOUN* **flocks** a group of sheep, goats, or birds

flock *VERB* **flocks, flocking, flocked** gather or move in a crowd

flog *VERB* **flogs, flogging, flogged 1** beat a person or animal hard with a whip or stick as a punishment **2** (*slang*) sell
▷ **flogging** *NOUN*

flood *NOUN* **floods 1** a large amount of water spreading over a place that is usually dry **2** a great amount • *a flood of requests* **3** the movement of the tide when it is coming in towards the land

flood *VERB* **floods, flooding, flooded 1** cover with a flood **2** come in great amounts • *Letters flooded in*

floodlight *NOUN* **floodlights** a lamp that makes a broad bright beam to light up a stage, stadium, important building, etc.
▷ **floodlit** *ADJECTIVE*

floor *NOUN* **floors 1** the part of a room that people walk on **2** a storey of a building; all the rooms at the same level
USAGE In Britain, the *ground floor* of a building is the one at street level, and the one above it is the *first floor*. In the USA, the *first floor* is the one at street level, and the one above it is the *second floor*.

floor *VERB* **floors, flooring, floored 1** put a floor into a building **2** knock a person down **3** baffle somebody [from Old English]

flop *VERB* **flops, flopping, flopped 1** fall or sit down clumsily **2** hang or sway heavily and loosely **3** (*informal*) be a failure
▷ **floppy** *ADJECTIVE*

floppy disk *NOUN* **floppy disks** a flexible disc holding data for use in a computer

flora *NOUN* the plants of a particular area or period COMPARE **fauna**

florist *NOUN* **florists** a shopkeeper who sells flowers

floss *NOUN* **1** silky thread or fibres **2** a soft medicated thread pulled between the teeth to clean them
▷ **flossy** *ADJECTIVE*

flotsam *NOUN* wreckage or cargo found floating after a shipwreck
flotsam and jetsam odds and ends

flounce *VERB* **flounces, flouncing, flounced** go in an impatient or annoyed manner • *She flounced out of the room.*
▷ **flounce** *NOUN*

Thesaurus

float *VERB* **1** *little boats floating on the water* ► sail, bob, drift **2** *A cloud floated across the sun.* ► drift, glide, hover, slip, slide, waft **3** *We want to float a few ideas.* ► suggest, propose, put forward, submit, raise, present, come up with, moot **4** *The company was floated on the Stock Market.* ► launch, set up, promote, initiate, offer

flock *NOUN* **1** *a flock of sheep* ► herd, drove, group **2** *a flock of birds* ► flight, group **3** *a flock of anxious relatives* ► crowd, throng, horde, gathering, bunch, huddle, mob, mass

flock *VERB* *People flocked from all quarters.* ► gather, collect, assemble, come together, congregate, crowd, convene, converge, muster

flog *VERB* *The executioner flogged the woman on her back.* ► whip, beat, flay, lash, scourge, thrash, flagellate, birch, cane

flood *NOUN* **1** *The flood cut off several villages.* ► inundation, deluge, torrent, downpour **2** *a flood of protests* ► succession, torrent, barrage, spate, storm, volley, excess, abundance, profusion, plethora AN OPPOSITE IS trickle

flood *VERB* **1** *The dam burst, flooding the town.* ► inundate, swamp, submerge, engulf, overwhelm, drown, deluge, immerse **2** *Light flooded the room.* ► fill, swamp, saturate **3** *The loo flooded yesterday.* ► overflow, run over, brim over **4** *The press flooded back into the courtroom.* ► pour, stream, surge, swarm, flock, crowd, throng

floor *NOUN* **1** *The floor was sopping wet.* ► ground, flooring, base **2** *Take the lift to the third floor.* ► level, storey, stage, landing

flop *VERB* **1** *His white hair flopped over his eyes.* ► dangle, droop, hang down, slump, flag, sag, wilt **2** *All she wanted was to flop into a chair.* ► drop, fall, sink, slump, collapse, tumble **3** (*informal*) *The idea flopped spectacularly.* ► fail, founder, misfire, be unsuccessful, fold

flop *NOUN* (*informal*) *The show was a flop.* ► failure, disaster, debacle, fiasco, (*more informal*) washout

floppy *ADJECTIVE* *a girl in pigtails, wearing a large floppy woollen hat* ► limp, droopy, drooping, dangling, loose, saggy, sagging, hanging AN OPPOSITE IS stiff

flounder *VERB* *The infantry floundered in the swampy ground. He was floundering in a situation of his own making.* ► struggle, falter, grope, wallow, stumble, fumble, stagger

flounder *VERB* **flounders, floundering, floundered** 1 move clumsily and with difficulty 2 make mistakes or become confused when trying to do something

flour *NOUN* a fine powder of wheat or other grain, used in cooking
▷ **floury** *ADJECTIVE*

flourish *VERB* **flourishes, flourishing, flourished** 1 grow or develop strongly 2 be successful; prosper 3 wave something about dramatically

flourish *NOUN* **flourishes** a showy or dramatic sweeping movement, curve, or passage of music

flout *VERB* **flouts, flouting, flouted** disobey a rule or instruction openly and scornfully • *She shaved her head one day, just because she loved to flout convention.*
USAGE Do not confuse this word with **flaunt**, which has a different meaning.

flow *VERB* **flows, flowing, flowed** 1 move along smoothly or continuously 2 gush out • *Water flowed from the tap* 3 hang loosely • *flowing hair* 4 (said about the tide) come in towards the land

flow *NOUN* **flows** 1 a flowing movement or mass 2 a steady continuous stream of something • *a flow of ideas* 3 the movement of the tide when it is coming in towards the land • *the ebb and flow of the tide*

flower *NOUN* **flowers** 1 the part of a plant from which seed and fruit develops 2 a blossom and its stem used for decoration, usually in groups

flower *VERB* **flowers, flowering, flowered** produce flowers

flowery *ADJECTIVE* 1 full of flowers 2 (said about language) elaborate, full of ornamental phrases

flu *NOUN* influenza

fluctuate *VERB* **fluctuates, fluctuating, fluctuated** rise and fall; vary • *Prices fluctuated.*
▷ **fluctuation** *NOUN*

fluent (floo- ent) *ADJECTIVE* 1 skilful at speaking clearly and without hesitating 2 able to speak a foreign language easily and well
▷ **fluently** *ADVERB* **fluency** *NOUN*

fluff *NOUN* a fluffy substance

fluffy *ADJECTIVE* having a mass of soft fur or fibres
▷ **fluffiness** *NOUN*

fluid *NOUN* **fluids** a substance that is able to flow freely as liquids and gases do

fluid *ADJECTIVE* 1 able to flow freely 2 not fixed • *My plans for Christmas are fluid.*
▷ **fluidity** *NOUN*

fluke *NOUN* **flukes** a success that you achieve by unexpected good luck

fluorescent (floo- er- ess- ent) *ADJECTIVE* creating light from radiation • *a fluorescent lamp*
▷ **fluorescence** *NOUN*

Thesaurus

flourish *VERB* 1 *Plants flourish in this good soil. The farmers flourished, aided by good weather.* ► thrive, prosper, bloom, blossom, succeed, boom, be strong, be vigorous, progress 2 *She went out, flourishing an umbrella.* ► brandish, wave, wield, swirl, swing, flaunt

flout *VERB* *He had no intention of flouting a court order.* ► disobey, defy, violate, contravene, infringe, break, spurn, scorn
OPPOSITES ARE respect, observe

flow *VERB* 1 *Water was flowing through the pipes.* ► run, stream, spurt, trickle, ooze, spurt, squirt, gush, flood, cascade 2 *Several issues flow from these proposals.* ► result, proceed, follow, arise, spring, emerge, emanate

flow *NOUN* 1 *Alcohol increases the flow of blood to the brain.* ► movement, circulation, stream, motion, course, current, passage, surge 2 *a steady flow of correspondence* ► stream, current, deluge, cascade, flood, gush, spate

flower *NOUN* 1 *Mandy picked flowers from the garden.* ► bloom, blossom, floret, bud 2 *the flower of a nation's youth* ► finest, best, pick, cream, choice, elite

fluctuate *VERB* *Their income fluctuates from year to year.* ► vary, change, alter, shift, differ, rise and fall

fluent *ADJECTIVE* 1 *She is fluent in five European languages.* ► articulate, able to speak 2 *It is important to speak in a fluent and interesting manner.* ► articulate, natural, expressive, eloquent, effortless, flowing, polished, ready, smooth, unhesitating, (*disapproving*) glib, (*disapproving*) facile AN OPPOSITE IS inarticulate

fluffy *ADJECTIVE* *She padded into the bedroom wrapped in a big fluffy towel.* ► furry, woolly, fleecy, fuzzy, downy, velvety, soft

fluid *ADJECTIVE* 1 *fluid substances* ► liquid, aqueous, flowing, watery, running, gaseous, liquefied, melted, molten, (*more informal*) runny AN OPPOSITE IS solid 2 *fluid movements* ► graceful, flowing, smooth 3 *My plans are still fairly fluid.* ► flexible, adaptable, adjustable, variable, open, changeable, unstable, indefinite, unsettled OPPOSITES ARE firm, fixed, definite USAGE Be careful when you use *changeable* or *indefinite*, because they have other meanings.

fluid *NOUN* *Drink lots of fluids and eat fibre-rich foods.* ► liquid, juice

fluke *NOUN* *By a lucky fluke she came along at that moment.* ► chance, accident, piece of luck, stroke of luck

fluoridation *NOUN* adding fluoride to drinking water in order to help prevent tooth decay

fluoride *NOUN* a chemical substance that is thought to prevent tooth decay

flurry *NOUN* **flurries 1** a sudden whirling gust of wind, rain, or snow **2** a short period of activity or excitement

flush[1] *VERB* **flushes, flushing, flushed 1** blush **2** clean or remove something with a fast flow of water

flush *NOUN* **flushes 1** a blush **2** a fast flow of water **3** (in card games) a hand of cards of the same suit

flush[2] *ADJECTIVE* **1** level with the surrounding surface • *The doors are flush with the walls* **2** (*informal*) having plenty of money

fluster *VERB* **flusters, flustering, flustered** make somebody nervous and confused
▷ **fluster** *NOUN*

flute *NOUN* **flutes** a musical instrument consisting of a long pipe with holes that are stopped by fingers or keys

flutter *VERB* **flutters, fluttering, fluttered 1** flap wings quickly **2** move or flap quickly and irregularly

flutter *NOUN* **flutters 1** a fluttering movement **2** a nervously excited condition **3** (*informal*) a small bet • *Have a flutter!*

fly[1] *NOUN* **flies 1** a small flying insect with two wings **2** a real or artificial fly used as bait in fishing

fly[2] *VERB* **flies, flying, flew, flown 1** move through the air by means of wings or in an aircraft **2** travel through the air or through space **3** wave in the air • *Flags were flying* **4** make something fly • *They flew model aircraft* **5** move or pass quickly • *Time flies* **6** flee from • *You must fly the country!*
▷ **flyer** *NOUN*

fly *NOUN* **flies** the front opening of a pair of trousers

flying saucer *NOUN* **flying saucers** a mysterious saucer-shaped object reported to have been seen in the sky and believed by some people to be an alien spacecraft

flyleaf *NOUN* **flyleaves** a blank page at the beginning or end of a book

flyover *NOUN* **flyovers** a bridge that carries one road or railway over another

flywheel *NOUN* **flywheels** a heavy wheel used to regulate machinery

foal *NOUN* **foals** a young horse

foam *NOUN* **1** a white mass of tiny bubbles on a liquid; froth **2** a spongy kind of rubber or plastic
▷ **foamy** *ADJECTIVE*

foam *VERB* **foams, foaming, foamed** form bubbles or froth

fob *VERB* **fobs, fobbing, fobbed**
fob off get rid of someone by an excuse or a trick

focal *ADJECTIVE* to do with or at a focus

focus *NOUN* **focuses** or **foci 1** the distance from an eye or lens at which an object appears clearest **2** the point at which rays etc. seem to meet **3** something that is a centre of interest or attention etc.
in focus appearing clearly
out of focus not appearing clearly

focus *VERB* **focuses, focusing, focused 1** adjust the focus of your eye or a lens so that objects

Thesaurus

flurry *NOUN* **1** *a snow flurry* ► swirl, whirl, gust **2** *a flurry of activity* ► spate, wave, burst, spell, stir, spurt, outbreak, commotion

flush *ADJECTIVE* **1** *He had just been paid and was feeling flush.* ► rich, wealthy, well off, prosperous **2** *The opening needs to be flush with the wall.* ► level, flat, even, square, true

flush *VERB* **1** *Nancy flushed with embarrassment.* ► blush, go red, redden, colour, glow **2** *Fruit helps flush toxins from the body.* ► cleanse, rinse out, wash out, swill **3** *The police tried to flush the suspects out.* ► chase out, drive out, expel, send up

flustered *ADJECTIVE* *She looked shocked and flustered.* ► confused, bewildered, bemused, perplexed, baffled, puzzled, mystified, disconcerted, confounded

fly *VERB* **1** *A flock of birds flew past.* ► glide, flit, flutter, hover, soar, wing **2** *A gull flew into the air.* ► rise, soar, ascend, mount **3** *He refused to fly the aircraft until it had been checked.* ► pilot, operate, take off in, travel in **4** *A flag was flying at half mast.* ► flutter, flap, wave **5** *The ship was flying a neutral flag.* ► display, show, exhibit
fly at *Charley flew at him, shaking his fist.* ► attack, assault, go for, set upon, weigh into, let fly at, hit out at, lash out at

foam *NOUN* **1** *The sea looked like white crests of foam.* ► froth, spume, surf, spray, lather, scum, suds **2** *There was at least an inch of foam on his beer.* ► head, bubbles, effervescence

foam *VERB* *The water heaved and foamed.* ► froth, fizz, seethe, ferment, bubble, effervesce, lather, boil

focus *NOUN* **1** *Get the camera into focus.* ► clarity, correct adjustment, sharpness **2** *The television has become a main focus of the living room.* ► centre, focal point, heart, hub, core, pivot

focus *VERB* **focus on** *We need to focus on the events of this coming week.* ► concentrate on, direct attention to, fix attention on, home in on, zero in on, spotlight, think about, aim at, centre on, look mainly at appear clearly **2** concentrate • *She focused her attention on the screen.*

fodder NOUN food for horses and farm animals

foetus (fee- tus) NOUN **foetuses** another spelling of **fetus**

fog NOUN thick mist
▷ **foggy** ADJECTIVE

foghorn NOUN **foghorns** a loud horn for warning ships in fog

foil [1] NOUN **foils** **1** a very thin sheet of metal • *cooking foil* **2** a person or thing that makes another look better in contrast

foil [2] NOUN **foils** a long narrow sword used in the sport of fencing

foil [3] VERB **foils, foiling, foiled** prevent something from being successful • *We foiled his evil plan*

foist VERB **foists, foisting, foisted** make a person accept something inferior or unwelcome • *They foisted the job on me*

fold VERB **folds, folding, folded** bend or move so that one part lies on another part

fold NOUN **folds** a line where something is folded

folder NOUN **folders** a folding cover for loose papers

folk NOUN people

folk dance NOUNS **folk dances** a dance in the traditional style of a country

folklore NOUN old beliefs and legends

folk song NOUN **folk songs** a song in the traditional style of a country

follow VERB **follows, following, followed** **1** go or come after **2** do a thing after something else **3** take a person or thing as a guide or example **4** take an interest in the progress of events or a sport or team etc. **5** understand • *Did you follow what he said?* **6** result from something
▷ **follower** NOUN

following PREPOSITION after, as a result of • *Following the burglary, we had new locks fitted.*

folly NOUN **follies** foolishness; a foolish action etc.

fond ADJECTIVE **1** loving or liking a person or thing **2** foolishly hopeful • *fond hopes*
▷ **fondly** ADVERB **fondness** NOUN

fondle VERB **fondles, fondling, fondled** touch or stroke lovingly

food NOUN **foods** any substance that a person or animal can eat in order to grow and be healthy

Thesaurus

foggy ADJECTIVE *Outside it was dull and foggy.*
► misty, smoggy, hazy, murky, gloomy, dingy, dim AN OPPOSITE IS clear

foil VERB *She foiled their efforts by walking in at the wrong moment.* ► thwart, frustrate, obstruct, impede, hamper, hinder, baffle, scotch, check, prevent, stop

fold VERB **1** *Fold the sheets and put them in a drawer.* ► double, double over, turn over, bend, tuck, overlap, crease, pleat **2** *She stood there, folding her arms.* ► clasp, wrap, cradle, enfold, enclose, embrace, entwine, envelop, hug **3** *I'll fold the chair and put it away.* ► close, collapse, let down, put down **4** *The business folded during the recession.* ► fail, collapse, crash, founder, close down

fold NOUN **1** *Neatly arrange the folds in the curtains.* ► pleat, crease, tuck, furrow, bend **2** *a fold for sheep* ► enclosure, pen, paddock, compound

folder NOUN *I need a folder for these papers.*
► file, binder, portfolio, wallet, sleeve

folk or **folks** PLURAL NOUN **1** *It was good news for the folk back home.* ► people, individuals, citizens, inhabitants **2** *She would visit her folks at the weekend.* ► family, parents, relatives, people, kinsfolk

follow VERB **1** *He followed them as far as the corner.* ► go after, come after, walk behind, tread on the heels of, trace the footsteps of **2** *She hoped to follow her father as chief executive of the company.* ► succeed, replace, take the place of, take over from, supplant, supersede, step into someone's shoes **3** *An undercover police officer followed him everywhere.* ► pursue, stalk, track, shadow, trail, go after, (*more informal*) tail **4** *Make sure you follow the instructions on the packet.* ► observe, comply with, adhere to, carry out, obey, note, heed, conform to, keep to **5** *Many benefits followed from their membership of the community.*
► result, ensue, emanate, arise, develop **6** *I found it hard to follow his meaning.*
► understand, comprehend, grasp, fathom, take in, catch **7** *Which team do you follow?* ► support, be a fan of

following ADJECTIVE *She went home on the following day.* ► next, ensuing, subsequent, succeeding OPPOSITES ARE preceding, previous

folly NOUN *It would be an act of folly to start a war.*
► foolishness, stupidity, senselessness, recklessness, silliness, madness, lunacy, idiocy

fond ADJECTIVE **1** *her fond father* ► loving, adoring, devoted, doting, caring, attentive, kind **2** *a fond hope* ► foolish, unrealistic, naive, vain, empty **3 be fond of** *She's fond of dancing. I'm very fond of Jo.* ► be keen on, be partial to, be attached to, like, love, (*more informal*) be hooked on, (*more informal*) be wild about, (*more informal*) be crazy about

fondle VERB *He stooped down to fondle the cat.*
► stroke, caress, pat, pet, cuddle, play with

food NOUN **1** *He had gone a week without food.*
► nourishment, sustenance, nutriment,

a b c d e f g h i j k l m n o p q r s t u v w x y z

food chain *NOUN* **food chains** a series of plants and animals each of which serves as food for the one above it in the series

fool *NOUN* **fools 1** a stupid person; someone who acts unwisely **2** a jester or clown • *Stop playing the fool.* **3** a creamy pudding with crushed fruit in it • *gooseberry fool*
fool's errand a useless errand
fool's paradise happiness that comes only from being mistaken about something

fool *VERB* **fools, fooling, fooled 1** behave in a joking way; play about **2** trick or deceive someone

foolish *ADJECTIVE* without good sense or judgement; unwise
▷ **foolishly** *ADVERB* **foolishness** *NOUN*

foolproof *ADJECTIVE* easy to use or do correctly

foot *NOUN* **feet 1** the lower part of the leg below the ankle **2** any similar part, e.g. one used by certain animals to move or attach themselves to things **3** the lowest part • *the foot of the hill* **4** a measure of length, 12 inches or about 30 centimetres • *a ten-foot pole;* • *it is ten feet long* **5** a unit of rhythm in a line of poetry, e.g. each of the four divisions in *Jack / and Jill / went up / the hill.*
on foot walking

foot-and-mouth disease *NOUN* a serious contagious disease that affects cattle, sheep, and other animals

football *NOUN* **footballs 1** a game played by two teams which try to kick an inflated leather ball into their opponents' goal **2** the ball used in this game
▷ **footballer** *NOUN*

foothill *NOUN* **foothills** a low hill near the bottom of a mountain or range of mountains

foothold *NOUN* **footholds 1** a place to put your foot when climbing **2** a small but firm position from which further progress can be made

footing *NOUN* **1** having your feet placed on something; a foothold • *He lost his footing and slipped.* **2** the status or nature of a relationship • *We are on a friendly footing with that country.*

footlights *PLURAL NOUN* a row of lights along the front of the floor of a stage

footnote *NOUN* **footnotes** a note printed at the bottom of the page

footpath *NOUN* **footpaths** a path for pedestrians

footprint *NOUN* **footprints** a mark made by a foot or shoe

footstep *NOUN* **footsteps 1** a step taken in walking or running **2** the sound of this

for *PREPOSITION* This word is used to show purpose or direction (*This letter is for you; We set out for home*), distance or time (*Walk for six miles or two hours*), price or exchange (*We bought it for £2; New lamps for old*), cause (*She was fined for speeding*), defence or support (*He fought for his country; Are you for us or against us?*), reference (*For all her wealth, she is bored*), similarity or correspondence (*We took him for a fool*)
for ever for all time; always

for *CONJUNCTION* because • *They hesitated, for they were afraid.*

forbear *VERB* **forbears, forbearing, forbore, forborne 1** refrain from something • *We forbore to mention it.* **2** be patient or tolerant
▷ **forbearance** *NOUN*

Thesaurus

subsistence RELATED ADJECTIVE alimentary
2 *Have you brought any food?* ► provisions, refreshments, eatables, something to eat, (*old use*) victuals, (*more informal*) grub

fool *NOUN* **1** *He was acting like a fool.* ► idiot, ass, halfwit, dimwit, blockhead, dunderhead, nincompoop, imbecile, moron, clown, buffoon, clot, chump, (*more informal*) dope, (*more informal*) prat, (*more informal*) ninny, (*more informal*) twit, (*more informal*) twerp **2** (*old-fashioned*) *a fool at the court of the king* ► jester, clown, buffoon, comic, stooge

fool *VERB* **1** *We easily fooled him.* ► deceive, trick, hoodwink, hoax, dupe **2** *I thought you were just fooling.* ► pretend, joke, jest, tease, make believe, put on an act
fool about *Some children were fooling about.* ► play about, lark about, misbehave USAGE You can use *around* instead of *about* in all these synonyms.

foolish *ADJECTIVE* *a foolish remark; She had been extremely foolish.* ► stupid, silly, ill-advised, unwise, crazy, mad, insane, (*more informal*) daft OPPOSITES ARE wise, sensible

foolishness *NOUN* *They shook their heads at her foolishness in going back to France.* ► stupidity, folly, senselessness, recklessness, silliness, madness, lunacy, idiocy

foolproof *ADJECTIVE* *The system is foolproof if you follow the instructions carefully.* ► infallible, unfailing, dependable, straightforward, simple, (*more informal*) idiot-proof

foot *NOUN* **1** *The animal had hurt its foot.* ► paw, hoof, trotter, claw **2** *The house was at the foot of the hill.* ► bottom, base

footprint *NOUN* *There were huge footprints in the snow.* ► footmark, footstep, track, print, trace, spoor USAGE You use *spoor* only when referring to an animal.

forbid *VERB* **forbids, forbidding, forbade, forbidden** **1** order someone not to do something **2** refuse to allow • *We shall forbid the marriage.*

forbidding *ADJECTIVE* looking stern or unfriendly

force *NOUN* **forces** **1** strength or power **2** (in science) an influence, which can be measured, that causes something to move **3** an organized group of police, soldiers, etc.
in *or* **into force** in or into effectiveness • *The new law comes into force next week.*
the forces a country's armed forces

force *VERB* **forces, forcing, forced** **1** use force in order to get or do something, or to make somebody obey **2** break something open by force **3** cause plants to grow or bloom earlier than is normal • *You can force them in a greenhouse.*

forceful *ADJECTIVE* strong and vigorous
▷ **forcefully** *ADVERB*

forcible *ADJECTIVE* done by force; forceful
▷ **forcibly** *ADVERB*

ford *NOUN* **fords** a shallow place where you can walk across a river

ford *VERB* **fords, fording, forded** cross a river at a ford

fore *ADJECTIVE, ADVERB* at or towards the front
• *fore and aft*

fore *NOUN* the front part
to the fore to or at the front; in or to a prominent position

forearm[1] *NOUN* **forearms** the arm from the elbow to the wrist or fingertips

forearm[2] *VERB* **forearms, forearming, forearmed** prepare in advance against possible danger

forecast *NOUN* **forecasts** a statement that tells in advance what is likely to happen

forecast *VERB* **forecasts, forecasting, forecast** make a forecast
▷ **forecaster** *NOUN*

forefinger *NOUN* **forefingers** the finger next to the thumb

foregone conclusion *NOUN* **foregone conclusions** a result that can be foreseen easily or is bound to happen

foreground *NOUN* the part of a scene, picture, or view that is nearest to you

forehand *NOUN* **forehands** a stroke made in tennis etc. with the palm of the hand turned forwards

forehead (for- hed, forrid) *NOUN* **foreheads** the part of the face above the eyes

foreign *ADJECTIVE* **1** belonging to or in another country **2** not belonging naturally to a place or to someone's nature • *Lying is foreign to her nature.*

Thesaurus

forbid *VERB* *She forbids the use of calculators in this exercise.* ► ban, prohibit, bar, disallow, rule out, exclude, proscribe, veto, outlaw, refuse, preclude OPPOSITES ARE permit, allow

forbidden *ADJECTIVE* **1** *Ball games are forbidden on the grass outside the building.* ► banned, prohibited, barred, disallowed, proscribed, illegal, against the law, outlawed, unauthorized, unlawful
AN OPPOSITE IS permissible **2** *This part of the house is forbidden to them.* ► out of bounds, restricted, closed

forbidding *ADJECTIVE* *The house has a dark, forbidding appearance.* ► grim, ominous, menacing, threatening, gloomy, stern, unfriendly, uninviting, unwelcoming
AN OPPOSITE IS friendly

force *NOUN* **1** *It needed some force to get the door open.* ► strength, might, vigour, effort, energy, muscle, power, drive, pressure, weight **2** *The force of the explosion was felt for miles.* ► intensity, impact, effect, shock, momentum **3** *They used force to get their way.* ► violence, coercion, compulsion, aggression, constraint, duress **4** *I could see the force of the argument.* ► strength, cogency, effectiveness, validity, persuasiveness, weight, rightness **5** *a peace-keeping force* ► body, group, corps, unit, team, detachment, troops, army

force *VERB* **1** *If necessary we will force them to do it.* ► compel, make, oblige, coerce, constrain, pressure, pressurize, order, impel, bulldoze, drive, press-gang **2** *The intruders had to force a door.* ► break open, burst open, prise open, smash, use force on, wrench **3** *They tried to force their opinions on us.* ► impose, inflict, thrust

forceful *ADJECTIVE* **1** *a forceful personality* ► strong, dynamic, powerful, assertive, commanding, self-assured, energetic **2** *forceful arguments* ► strong, cogent, compelling, convincing, potent, plausible, effective

foreign *ADJECTIVE* **1** *I like travelling to foreign countries.* ► overseas, distant, remote, exotic, faraway, far-flung **2** *the company's foreign branches* ► overseas, international, external AN OPPOSITE IS domestic **3** *Jealousy is foreign to her nature.* ► unknown, familiar, alien, strange AN OPPOSITE IS natural

A B C D E F G H I J K L M N O P Q R S T U V W X Y Z

foreigner *NOUN* **foreigners** a person from another country

foreman *NOUN* **foremen** **1** a worker in charge of a group of other workers **2** a member of a jury who is in charge of the jury's discussions and who speaks on its behalf

foremost *ADJECTIVE, ADVERB* first in position or rank; most important

forensic (fer-en-sik) *ADJECTIVE* to do with or used in lawcourts

forensic medicine *NOUN* medical knowledge used in legal matters or in solving crimes

forerunner *NOUN* **forerunners** a person or thing that comes before another; a sign of what is to come

foresee *VERB* **foresees, foreseeing, foresaw, foreseen** realize what is going to happen

foreshadow *VERB* **foreshadows, foreshadowing, foreshadowed** be a sign of something that is to come

foreshorten *VERB* **foreshortens, foreshortening, foreshortened** show an object in a drawing etc. with some lines shortened to give an effect of distance or depth

foresight *NOUN* the ability to foresee and prepare for future needs

forest *NOUN* **forests** trees and undergrowth covering a large area
▷ **forested** *ADJECTIVE*

forestry *NOUN* planting forests and looking after them
▷ **forester** *NOUN*

foretaste *NOUN* **foretastes** an experience of something that is to come in the future

foretell *VERB* **foretells, foretelling, foretold** tell in advance; prophesy

forethought *NOUN* careful thought and planning for the future

foreword *NOUN* **forewords** a preface

forfeit (for-fit) *VERB* **forfeits, forfeiting, forfeited** pay or give up something as a penalty
▷ **forfeiture** *NOUN*

forfeit *NOUN* **forfeits** something forfeited

forge[1] *NOUN* **forges** a place where metal is heated and shaped; a blacksmith's workshop

forge *VERB* **forges, forging, forged** **1** shape metal by heating and hammering **2** copy something in order to deceive people
▷ **forger** *NOUN* **forgery** *NOUN*

forge[2] *VERB* **forges, forging, forged**
forge ahead move forward by a strong effort

forget *VERB* **forgets, forgetting, forgot, forgotten** **1** fail to remember **2** stop thinking about • *Forget your troubles.*
forget yourself behave rudely or thoughtlessly

forgetful *ADJECTIVE* tending to forget
▷ **forgetfully** *ADVERB* **forgetfulness** *NOUN*

forgive *VERB* **forgives, forgiving, forgave, forgiven** stop feeling angry with somebody about something
▷ **forgiveness** *NOUN*

Thesaurus

foreigner *NOUN* *Many foreigners come to live in this city.* ► overseas visitor, visitor, immigrant alien, outsider, newcomer, stranger
AN OPPOSITE IS native

foremost *ADJECTIVE* *the foremost musicians of the day* ► leading, principal, chief, main, greatest, supreme, primary

foresight *NOUN* *She had the foresight to write a will.* ► forethought, prudence, perspicacity, far-sightedness, prescience, vision, circumspection, preparedness
AN OPPOSITE IS improvidence

forge *VERB* **1** *The smithy forged swords and knives for the army.* ► work, cast, make, mould, shape, hammer out, beat into shape **2** *He would have a go at forging the signature.* ► fake, falsify, counterfeit, imitate, copy, reproduce **3** *He had been highly successful in forging a strong team.* ► build, create, develop, establish, set up
forge ahead *The Persians forged ahead through Thrace.* ► advance, make progress

forgery *NOUN* *He thinks they sold him a forgery.* ► fake, copy, imitation, reproduction, replica, duplicate, hoax, sham, simulation, (*more informal*) phoney

forget *VERB* **1** *I forgot my passport.* ► leave behind, overlook, mislay
AN OPPOSITE IS remember **2** *She forgot to lock the door.* ► omit, neglect, fail
AN OPPOSITE IS remember **3** *This is not something we can easily forget.* ► ignore, disregard, overlook, dismiss, think no more of, stop thinking about

forgetful *ADJECTIVE* *As he grew older he became more forgetful.* ► absent-minded, inattentive, neglectful, abstracted, oblivious, vague, dreamy, lax, heedless

forgive *VERB* **1** *He found it hard to forgive them.* ► excuse, pardon, exonerate, absolve, let off, spare, (*more informal*) exculpate **2** *We cannot forgive such rudeness.* ► excuse, condone, overlook, ignore, disregard

forgiveness *NOUN* *He begged their forgiveness.* ► pardon, absolution, exoneration, understanding, tolerance, mercy

forgo *VERB* *They would have to forgo their morning swim.* ► do without, go without, miss, give up, sacrifice, eschew, abandon, renounce

fork *NOUN* **forks** **1** a small device with prongs for lifting food to your mouth **2** a large device with prongs used for digging or lifting things **3** a place where something separates into two or more parts • *a fork in the road*

fork *VERB* **forks, forking, forked** **1** lift or dig with a fork **2** form a fork by separating into two branches **3** follow one of these branches • *Fork left.*
fork out (*informal*) pay out money

fork-lift truck *NOUN* **fork-lift trucks** a truck with two metal bars at the front for lifting and moving heavy loads

forlorn *ADJECTIVE* left alone and unhappy
forlorn hope the only faint hope left

form *NOUN* **forms** **1** the shape, appearance, or condition of something **2** the way something exists • *Ice is a form of water* **3** a class in school **4** a bench **5** a piece of paper with spaces to be filled in

form *VERB* **forms, forming, formed** **1** shape or construct something; create **2** come into existence; develop • *Icicles formed*

formal *ADJECTIVE* **1** strictly following the accepted rules or customs; ceremonious • *a formal occasion* • *formal dress* **2** rather serious and stiff in your manner
▷ **formally** *ADVERB*

format *NOUN* **formats** **1** the shape and size of something **2** the way something is arranged or organized **3** (in computing) the way data is organized for processing or storage by a computer

formation *NOUN* **formations** **1** the act of forming something **2** a thing formed **3** a special arrangement or pattern • *flying in formation*

former *ADJECTIVE* of an earlier time
▷ **formerly** *ADVERB*
the former the first of two people or things just mentioned

formidable (for- mid- a- bul) *ADJECTIVE*
1 difficult to deal with or do • *a formidable task*
2 fearsome or frightening
▷ **formidably** *ADVERB*

formula *NOUN* **formulae** **1** a set of chemical symbols showing what a substance consists of **2** a rule or statement expressed in symbols or numbers **3** a list of substances needed for making something **4** a fixed wording for a ceremony etc. **5** one of the groups into which racing cars are placed according to the size of their engines • *Formula One*

formulate *VERB* **formulates, formulating, formulated** express an idea or plan clearly and exactly
▷ **formulation** *NOUN*

Thesaurus

fork *VERB* **1** *The road forks at the bottom of the hill.* ► branch, split, separate
fork out (*informal*) *If necessary they would just have to fork out the money.* ► pay, produce, (*informal*) cough up

form *NOUN* **1** *a form of blackmail* ► kind, type, sort, class, order, variety **2** *the human form* ► body, frame, shape, figure, build **3** *They wanted to know the correct form for these occasions.* ► etiquette, custom, protocol, usage, procedure, convention **4** *There is a form to fill in.* ► document, questionnaire, sheet **5** *Her son moved into a new form at school.* ► class, year, grade, set, group, stream **6** *The form of the landscape has hardly changed for centuries.* ► appearance, shape, formation, configuration, structure, outline, silhouette **7** *He exercised hard to get into good form.* ► condition, shape, health, fettle, fitness

form *VERB* **1** *We must form a plan.* ► devise, formulate, develop, prepare, draw up, put together, work out, conceive **2** *The pots were formed from clay.* ► make, fashion, shape, model **3** *The decided to form a club.* ► set up, establish, found, launch, institute, begin **4** *Ice was forming on the windows.* ► materialize, appear, take shape, develop, emerge, grow **5** *Six players form a team.* ► make up, constitute, compose, comprise

formal *ADJECTIVE* **1** *a formal manner* ► aloof, prim, staid, stiff, starchy, punctilious **2** *a formal occasion* ► solemn, official, ceremonious, conventional, dignified **3** *a formal education* ► prescribed, conventional, institutional

formality *NOUN* **1** *He behaved towards her with greater formality.* ► aloofness, remoteness, staidness, correctness, decorum, ceremony **2 formalities** *Certain formalities have to be observed.* ► procedures, conventions, rules, customs, protocol

former *ADJECTIVE* **1** *She met her former husband in town.* ► ex-, past, one-time, previous, late **2** *The fields were a lake in former times.* ► earlier, past, bygone, ancient

formerly *ADVERB* *The work had formerly been done by volunteers.* ► previously, in the past, at one time, once, earlier, hitherto

formula *NOUN* **1** *a legal formula* ► form of words, phrase, rubric **2** *a formula for success* ► recipe, prescription, blueprint, procedure, method, rule, way

formulate *VERB* *The party formulated a ten-point programme.* ► form, devise, develop, prepare, draw up, put together, work out, conceive

a b c d e f g h i j k l m n o p q r s t u v w x y z

fort *NOUN* **forts** a fortified building

forth *ADVERB* **1** out; into view **2** onwards or forwards • *from this day forth*
and so forth and so on

forthcoming *ADJECTIVE* **1** happening soon • *forthcoming events* **2** made available when needed • *Money for the trip was not forthcoming.* **3** willing to give information

forthright *ADJECTIVE* frank and outspoken

fortification *NOUN* **fortifications** **1** fortifying something **2** a wall or building constructed to make a place strong against attack

fortify *VERB* **fortifies, fortifying, fortified** **1** make a place strong against attack, especially by building fortifications **2** strengthen

fortnight *NOUN* **fortnights** a period of two weeks
▷ **fortnightly** *ADVERB, ADJECTIVE*

fortress *NOUN* **fortresses** a fortified building or town

fortunate *ADJECTIVE* lucky
▷ **fortunately** *ADVERB*

fortune *NOUN* **fortunes** **1** luck, especially good luck **2** a great amount of money
tell someone's fortune predict what will happen to them in the future

forty *ADJECTIVE, NOUN* **forties** the number 40
▷ **fortieth** *ADJECTIVE, NOUN*
forty winks a short sleep; a nap

forward *ADJECTIVE* **1** going forwards **2** placed in the front **3** having made more than the normal progress **4** too eager or bold
▷ **forwardness** *NOUN*

forward *ADVERB* forwards

forward *NOUN* **forwards** a player in the front line of a team in football, hockey, etc.

forwards *ADVERB* **1** to or towards the front **2** in the direction you are facing

fossil *NOUN* **fossils** the remains or traces of a prehistoric animal or plant that has been buried in the ground for a very long time and become hardened in rock
▷ **fossilized** *ADJECTIVE*

fossil fuel *NOUN* **fossil fuels** a natural fuel such as coal or gas formed in the geological past

foster *VERB* **fosters, fostering, fostered** **1** bring up someone else's child as if he or she was your own **2** help to grow or develop
▷ **foster child** *NOUN* **foster parent** *NOUN*

Thesaurus

fort *NOUN* *A small garrison was left to defend the fort.* ► fortress, fortification, stronghold, castle, citadel, tower

forthcoming *ADJECTIVE* **1** *He would be a candidate in the forthcoming election.* ► imminent, impending, approaching, coming, future, next **2** *She is not always particularly forthcoming.* ► communicative, talkative, expansive, informative, voluble, chatty, sociable
AN OPPOSITE IS uncommunicative **3** *No reply was forthcoming.* ► available, ready, on offer, at hand AN OPPOSITE IS unavailable

fortify *VERB* **1** *The knights fortified the citadel.* ► strengthen, reinforce, secure, defend, protect, garrison **2** *She fortified herself with a strong drink.* ► strengthen, support, sustain, invigorate, hearten, reassure, encourage, boost, cheer OPPOSITES ARE weaken, subdue

fortuitous *ADJECTIVE* *It was fortuitous that they arrived on the same day.* ► accidental, coincidental, unintentional, chance

fortunate *ADJECTIVE* **1** *He was fortunate not to be shown a red card.* ► lucky, favoured **2** *These events provided them with a fortunate opportunity.* ► favourable, advantageous, auspicious, providential, welcome, happy, lucky

fortune *NOUN* **1** *a major change of fortune* ► fate, destiny, luck **2** *By good fortune he was able to take up the offer.* ► chance, luck, accident, providence **3** *She decided she would leave her fortune to charity.* ► wealth, riches, property, possessions, (*more informal*) pile

fortune-teller *NOUN* *He had the solemn voice of a fortune-teller.* ► clairvoyant, crystal-gazer, soothsayer, palmist, prophet

forward *ADJECTIVE* **1** *The animal's long hind legs enable a fast forward movement.* ► onward, advancing, frontal, front, leading, progressive AN OPPOSITE IS backward **2** *forward planning* ► advance, future, early, prospective, forward-looking AN OPPOSITE IS retrospective. **3** *His manner on the phone had been a little too forward.* ► bold, brazen, barefaced, brash, audacious, daring, presumptuous, familiar, uninhibited, precocious, assertive, over-confident, cheeky, (*more informal*) fresh, (*more informal*) pushy OPPOSITES ARE shy, diffident

forward *VERB* **1** *Will you forward my letter?* ► send on, redirect **2** *The goods are forwarded by air.* ► dispatch, send, transport, transmit, convey, carry **3** *I will try to forward my plans during my visit.* ► advance, progress, develop, expedite, promote

forwards or **forward** *ADVERB* *The car shot forwards.* ► ahead, in front, onwards

foster *VERB* **1** *activities that foster good health* ► encourage, promote, cultivate, stimulate, nurture, advance, further **2** *The couple had fostered several children.* ► bring up, rear, raise,

A
B
C
D
E
F
G
H
I
J
K
L
M
N
O
P
Q
R
S
T
U
V
W
X
Y
Z

foul *ADJECTIVE* **1** disgusting; tasting or smelling unpleasant **2** (said about weather) rough; stormy **3** unfair; breaking the rules of a game **4** very disagreeable or unpleasant • *a foul mood*
▷ **foully** *ADVERB* **foulness** *NOUN*

foul *NOUN* **fouls** an action that breaks the rules of a game

foul *VERB* **fouls, fouling, fouled** **1** make or become foul • *Smoke had fouled the air* **2** commit a foul against a player in a game

found[1] *past tense* of **find**

found[2] *VERB* **founds, founding, founded** **1** establish; provide money for starting • *They founded a hospital* **2** base • *This novel is founded on fact*

foundation *NOUN* **foundations** **1** the solid base on which a building is built up **2** the basis for something **3** the founding of something **4** a fund of money set aside for a charitable purpose
▷ **foundation stone** *NOUN*

founder[1] *NOUN* **founders** a person who founds something • *the founder of the hospital*

founder[2] *VERB* **founders, foundering, foundered** **1** fill with water and sink • *The ship foundered* **2** stumble or fall **3** fail completely • *Their plans foundered*

fountain *NOUN* **fountains** an ornamental structure in which a jet of water shoots up into the air

four *ADJECTIVE, NOUN* **fours** the number 4
on all fours on hands and knees

fourteen *ADJECTIVE, NOUN* the number 14
▷ **fourteenth** *ADJECTIVE, NOUN*

fourth *ADJECTIVE* next after the third
▷ **fourthly** *ADVERB*

fourth *NOUN* **fourths** **1** the fourth person or thing **2** one of four equal parts; a quarter

fowl *NOUN* **fowls** a bird, especially one kept on a farm etc. for its eggs or meat

fox *NOUN* **foxes** a wild animal that looks like a dog with a long furry tail
▷ **foxy** *ADJECTIVE*

fraction *NOUN* **fractions** **1** a number that is not a whole number, e.g. ½, 0.5 **2** a tiny part
▷ **fractional** *ADJECTIVE* **fractionally** *ADVERB*

fracture *NOUN* **fractures** the breaking of something, especially of a bone

fracture *VERB* **fractures, fracturing, fractured** break

Thesaurus

care for, take care of, look after, nurture, parent, mother USAGE You can also use *adopt*, but it has a special legal meaning.

foul *ADJECTIVE* **1** *You can recognize the animal from its foul smell.* ► nasty, horrible, unpleasant, disgusting, revolting, repulsive, repellent, dreadful, terrible, vile AN OPPOSITE IS pleasant **2** *There was a foul mess on the floor.* ► dirty, filthy, unclean, nasty, mucky AN OPPOSITE IS clean **3** *He had committed a foul crime.* ► wicked, evil, vile, contemptible, despicable, obnoxious, shameful, abhorrent, repellent, loathsome AN OPPOSITE IS pleasant **4** *She had been subjected to taunts and foul language.* ► obscene, indecent, coarse, vulgar, offensive, crude, lewd AN OPPOSITE IS mild **5** *The game was spoilt by a series of foul tackles.* ► illegal, unfair, prohibited OPPOSITES ARE legal, fair **6** *The weather was foul all day.* ► unpleasant, bad, vile, disagreeable, inclement AN OPPOSITE IS fine **7** *He apologized for having been so foul to her.* ► unkind, unfriendly, unpleasant, disagreeable, bad-tempered OPPOSITES ARE kind, friendly

foul *VERB* **1** *Chemical waste was fouling the water.* ► pollute, contaminate, dirty, soil, sully, stain **2** *Silt was fouling the river mouth.* ► clog, choke, block, obstruct, stop up **3** *The ship had fouled its own nets.* ► entangle, snarl, catch, ensnare, twist

found *VERB* **1** *He founded the business in the 1880s.* ► establish, set up, start, create, begin, institute, inaugurate, initiate, organize, endow, fund **2** *Democracy is founded on the principle of free speech.* ► base, build, ground, construct, erect

foundation *NOUN* **1** *the foundation of the company in the eighteenth century* ► founding, establishment, institution, inauguration, initiation, setting up, starting, beginning **2** *There was no foundation for the claim.* ► basis, grounds, reason, justification, rationale **3 foundations** *The building had weak foundations.* ► base, substructure, footing, underpinning, basis, bottom, cornerstone, bedrock **4 foundations** *the foundations of the subject* ► fundamentals, rudiments, basic principles, elements, essentials, origins

founder *NOUN* *His grandfather had been the founder of the college.* ► originator, creator, initiator, benefactor

founder *VERB* *The scheme foundered for lack of money.* ► fail, collapse, miscarry, come to grief, come to nothing, (*more informal*) fold

fountain *NOUN* *The fountains are switched off in the cold months.* ► jet, spout, spray, spring, fount

fox *VERB* *The question completely foxed them.* ► baffle, confuse, perplex, bemuse, disconcert, confound, (*more informal*) flummox, (*more informal*) floor

A B C D E F G H I J K L M N O P Q R S T U V W X Y Z

fragile *ADJECTIVE* easy to break or damage
▷ **fragility** *NOUN*

fragment *NOUN* **fragments** **1** a small piece broken off **2** a small part
▷ **fragmentary** *ADJECTIVE* **fragmentation** *NOUN* **fragmented** *ADJECTIVE*

fragrant *ADJECTIVE* having a pleasant smell
▷ **fragrance** *NOUN*

frail *ADJECTIVE* **1** (said about people) not strong or healthy • *a frail old man* **2** (said about things) fragile
▷ **frailty** *NOUN*

frame *NOUN* **frames** **1** a holder that fits round the outside of a picture **2** a rigid structure that supports something **3** a human or animal body • *He has a small frame* **4** a single exposure on a cinema film
frame of mind the way you think or feel for a while

frame *VERB* **frames, framing, framed** **1** put a frame on or round **2** construct or form • *They framed the question badly.* **3** make an innocent person seem guilty by arranging false evidence

framework *NOUN* **frameworks** **1** a frame supporting something **2** a basic plan or system

franc *NOUN* **francs** a unit of money used in many countries and replaced in some by the euro in 2002

frank *ADJECTIVE* making your thoughts and feelings clear to people; candid
▷ **frankly** *ADVERB* **frankness** *NOUN*

frantic *ADJECTIVE* wildly agitated or excited
▷ **frantically** *ADVERB*

fraud *NOUN* **frauds** **1** the crime of swindling people **2** a dishonest trick **3** an impostor; a person or thing that is not what he, she, or it pretends to be
▷ **fraudulent** *ADJECTIVE* **fraudulently** *ADVERB* **fraudulence** *NOUN*

fray[1] *NOUN* **frays** a fight or conflict • *ready for the fray*

fray[2] *VERB* **frays, fraying, frayed** **1** make or become ragged so that loose threads show **2** (said about tempers or nerves) become strained or upset

Thesaurus

fragile *ADJECTIVE* **1** *She put away her fragile china.* ► breakable, brittle, delicate, weak, easily damaged AN OPPOSITE IS strong **2** *The fragile ceasefire was barely holding.* ► precarious, tenuous, insecure, flimsy, vulnerable, (*more informal*) dodgy

fragment *NOUN* (with the stress on *frag-*) *Fragments of broken pottery lay around.* ► piece, bit, particle, chip, sliver, scrap, shiver, shred, remnant, snippet, speck, atom, crumb, part

fragment *VERB* (with the stress on *-ment*) *The impact made the glass fragment.* ► break, shatter, splinter, split, disintegrate, shiver, crumble, come to pieces

fragmentary *ADJECTIVE* *They couldn't tell much from the fragmentary information available.* ► scrappy, incomplete, piecemeal, partial, disconnected, disjointed, bitty USAGE Be careful when you use *partial*, because it has other meanings.

frame *NOUN* **1** *The vehicle has a strong lightweight frame.* ► framework, shell, skeleton, chassis, structure, construction, bodywork **2** *a portrait in a gilt frame* ► surround, mount, mounting, border, setting, edging

frame *VERB* **1** *The artists frame their own pictures.* ► mount, surround, encase, set **2** *The lawyers will frame the proposals.* ► compose, formulate, draw up, plan

frank *ADJECTIVE* *At least he is frank about his opinions.* ► honest, candid, sincere, genuine, direct, open, forthright, ingenuous, straightforward, straight, truthful, unequivocal OPPOSITES ARE insincere, disingenuous

frantic *ADJECTIVE* **1** *Her parents were frantic about her safety.* ► anxious, agitated, worried, distraught, fraught, overwrought, (*more informal*) beside yourself OPPOSITES ARE calm, composed **2** *There were frantic attempts to locate the luggage.* ► hectic, feverish, frenzied, wild AN OPPOSITE IS calm

fraud *NOUN* **1** *He was accused of fraud.* ► fraudulence, swindling, cheating, sharp practice, deceit, deception **2** *The offer turned out to be a fraud.* ► swindle, deception, trick, hoax, sham **3** *They exposed him as a fraud.* ► impostor, charlatan, cheat, trickster, (*more informal*) phoney

fraudulent *ADJECTIVE* *fraudulent dealings on the stock exchange* ► dishonest, illegal, unlawful, illicit, corrupt, criminal, bogus, (*more informal*) crooked AN OPPOSITE IS honest

fraught *ADJECTIVE* *By the end of the day she looked tired and fraught.* ► anxious, apprehensive, agitated, tense, worried, concerned, nervous, fearful, uneasy, troubled, distressed AN OPPOSITE IS calm

freak *NOUN* **freaks** a very strange or abnormal person, animal, or thing
▷ **freakish** *ADJECTIVE*

freckle *NOUN* **freckles** a small brown spot on the skin
▷ **freckled** *ADJECTIVE*
[from Old Norse]

free *ADJECTIVE* **freer, freest 1** able to do what you want to do or go where you want to go **2** not costing anything **3** not fixed • *Leave one end free.* **4** not having or being affected by something • *The harbour is free of ice.* **5** available; not being used or occupied **6** generous • *She is very free with her money.*
▷ **freely** *ADVERB*

free *VERB* **frees, freeing, freed** set free

freedom *NOUN* **freedoms** being free; independence

freehand *ADJECTIVE* (said about a drawing) done without a ruler or compasses, or without tracing it • *Draw a circle freehand.*

free-range *ADJECTIVE* **1** free-range hens are not kept in small cages but are allowed to move about freely **2** free-range eggs are ones laid by these hens

freewheel *VERB* **freewheels, freewheeling, freewheeled** ride a bicycle without pedalling

freeze *VERB* **freezes, freezing, froze, frozen 1** turn into ice; become covered with ice **2** make or be very cold **3** keep wages or prices etc. at a fixed level **4** suddenly stand completely still

freezer *NOUN* **freezers** a refrigerator in which food can be frozen quickly and stored

freezing point *NOUN* **freezing points** the temperature at which a liquid freezes

Thesaurus

freak *ADJECTIVE* *The south of the country was battered by freak storms.* ► unusual, exceptional abnormal, untypical, anomalous, unpredictable, extraordinary
AN OPPOSITE IS normal

freak *NOUN* **1** *The animal is a genetically engineered freak.* ► oddity, aberration, abnormality, irregularity, anomaly, quirk, monster, monstrosity, mutant, malformation **2** *(informal) a weight-training freak* ► fanatic, devotee, enthusiast, admirer, lover, fan, addict, aficionado

free *ADJECTIVE* **1** *Tickets to the concert are free.* ► without charge, free of charge, gratis, complimentary, gratuitous, on the house
AN OPPOSITE IS to be paid for **2** *The people longed to be free.* ► independent, self-governing, autonomous, emancipated
OPPOSITES ARE subjugated, dependent **3** *The wanted man is still free.* ► at liberty, on the loose, at large, unrestrained
AN OPPOSITE IS captive **4** *We don't have much free time.* ► spare, available, idle, unused **5** *The bathroom is free now.* ► vacant, unoccupied, empty, available, not in use
OPPOSITES ARE occupied, engaged **6** *She is very free with her money.* ► generous, lavish, liberal, unstinting, bounteous OPPOSITES ARE mean, tight **7** *Are you free on Friday?* ► available, unoccupied, able to come AN OPPOSITE IS busy **8** *They are free to choose.* ► able, allowed, permitted, in a position, at leisure
AN OPPOSITE IS unable **9 free of** *We are free of any commitments now.* ► relieved of, unaffected by, unencumbered by, unhindered by, lacking, without AN OPPOSITE IS encumbered by **10** *the free movement of people and goods* ► unrestricted, unimpeded, unobstructed, unhindered, unlimited, clear, open
AN OPPOSITE IS obstructed

free *VERB* **1** *The new government freed all political prisoners.* ► release, liberate, set free, set at liberty, let loose, set loose, turn loose, deliver
OPPOSITES ARE confine, lock up **2** *The jury freed all three accused.* ► acquit, clear, exonerate, absolve, discharge, pardon
AN OPPOSITE IS condemn **3** *Firefighters managed to free the trapped victims.* ► rescue, release, extricate, remove, pull out, pull free **4** *She struggled hard to free her hand.* ► clear, loose, extricate, disentangle, disengage, untie, untangle AN OPPOSITE IS tangle

freedom *NOUN* **1** *The prisoners longed for their freedom.* ► liberty, liberation, release, deliverance OPPOSITES ARE captivity, confinement **2** *Only a revolution would give the country its freedom.* ► independence, self-government, self-determination
AN OPPOSITE IS dependence **3** *Parents should have the freedom to choose the education for their children.* ► ability, opportunity, chance, facility, power, licence, scope, leeway
AN OPPOSITE IS restriction

freely *ADVERB* *He found it hard to talk freely.* ► openly, candidly, frankly, plainly, honestly

freeze *VERB* **1** *In winter the river freezes.* ► ice over, become ice, become solid, solidify, harden **2** *We had no fire and were beginning to freeze.* ► feel cold, go numb with cold **3** *If you have too much fruit you can freeze it.* ► deep-freeze, dry-freeze, refrigerate, chill, preserve **4** *a government plan to freeze prices* ► fix, peg, hold, curb, limit, keep as they are

freight *NOUN* **1** *a mixture of passenger and freight services* ► cargo, goods, merchandise **2** *Air*

a b c d e f g h i j k l m n o p q r s t u v w x y z

French window *NOUN* **French windows** a long window that serves as a door on an outside wall

frenzy *NOUN* wild excitement or agitation
▷ **frenzied** *ADJECTIVE* **frenziedly** *ADVERB*

frequency *NOUN* **frequencies** **1** being frequent **2** how often something happens **3** the number of vibrations made each second by a wave of sound, radio, or light

frequent (freek-went) *ADJECTIVE* happening often
▷ **frequently** *ADVERB*

frequent (frik-went) *VERB* **frequents, frequenting, frequented** be in or go to a place often • *They frequented the club*

fresh *ADJECTIVE* **1** newly made or produced or arrived; not stale • *fresh bread* **2** not tinned or preserved • *fresh fruit* **3** cool and clean • *fresh air* **4** (said about water) not salty
▷ **freshly** *ADVERB* **freshness** *NOUN*

freshen *VERB* **freshens, freshening, freshened** make or become fresh

fret[1] *VERB* **frets, fretting, fretted** worry about something
▷ **fretful** *ADJECTIVE* **fretfully** *ADVERB*

fret[2] *NOUN* **frets** a bar or ridge on the fingerboard of a guitar etc.

friar *NOUN* **friars** a man who is a member of a Roman Catholic religious order and has vowed to live a life of poverty
▷ **friary** *NOUN*

friction *NOUN* **1** rubbing of one thing against another **2** bad feeling between people; quarrelling
▷ **frictional** *ADJECTIVE*

Friday *NOUN* the day of the week following Thursday [from Old English *Frigedaeg* = day of Frigga, a Norse goddess]

fridge *NOUN* **fridges** a refrigerator

friend *NOUN* **friends** **1** a person you like who likes you **2** a helpful or kind person

friendly *ADJECTIVE* **friendlier, friendliest** behaving like a friend
▷ **friendliness** *NOUN*

friendship *NOUN* **friendships** being friends

frieze (freez) *NOUN* **friezes** a strip of designs or pictures round the top of a wall

fright *NOUN* **frights** **1** sudden great fear **2** a person or thing that looks ridiculous

Thesaurus

freight charges are extremely high.
► transportation, shipment, carriage, conveyance

frenzy *NOUN* **1** *The audience was in a state of frenzy.* ► hysteria, fever, delirium, turmoil, agitation, mania, derangement **2** *a frenzy of anger* ► fit, spasm, outburst, paroxysm, ferment

frequent *ADJECTIVE* **1** *An airport bus leaves at frequent intervals.* ► regular, numerous, repeated, constant, recurring, continual **2** *Claire is a frequent visitor here.* ► habitual, constant, regular, common

fresh *ADJECTIVE* **1** *Good eating habits include fresh fruit and vegetables.* ► natural, raw **2** *The party needs new members and fresh ideas.* ► new, original, innovative, novel, recent, up-to-date **3** *The army has a batch of fresh recruits.*
► young, youthful, inexperienced, callow **4** *Next day was fresh and bright.* ► cool, crisp, refreshing, clear **5** *She was feeling fresh after her shower.* ► refreshed, rested, restored, revived, invigorated **6** *They walked out to a fresh wind.*
► cold, brisk, bracing, invigorating **7** *He told him not to get fresh.* ► impudent, impertinent, insolent, cheeky, saucy, familiar, disrespectful, forward

friend *NOUN* *He can stay with a friend while his parents are away.* ► acquaintance, companion, associate, (*more informal*) mate, (*more informal*) pal, (*more informal*) buddy, (*more informal*) chum

friendliness *NOUN* *They liked him for his friendliness and humour.* ► kindness, sociability, goodwill, hospitality, warmth

friendly *ADJECTIVE* **1** *The staff are very friendly and helpful.* ► pleasant, agreeable, kind, amiable, kindly, kind-hearted, well disposed, likeable, genial, congenial, sympathetic, approachable, receptive, sociable, outgoing **2** *Volunteers are on hand to give friendly advice. The hotel is small with a friendly atmosphere.* ► cordial, good-natured, sympathetic, amicable, warm, welcoming **3** *The girls had been friendly since their childhood.* ► close, affectionate, intimate, familiar, (*more informal*) chummy, (*more informal*) pally, (*more informal*) matey

friendship *NOUN* **1** *He thanked his colleagues for their friendship and support.* ► friendliness, affection, goodwill, comradeship, cordiality
OPPOSITES ARE hostility, enmity **2** *Their friendship grew over the coming months.*
► relationship, affection, intimacy, closeness, love, attachment

fright *NOUN* **1** *The blast gave everyone a fright.*
► scare, shock, surprise, start, turn, jolt **2** *Amy was overcome by fright.* ► fear, alarm, terror, trepidation, consternation, horror, dismay, dread, panic

frighten *VERB* **frightens, frightening, frightened** make someone afraid
be frightened of be afraid of

frightful *ADJECTIVE* awful; very great or bad
▷ **frightfully** *ADVERB*

frill *NOUN* **frills** **1** a decorative gathered or pleated trimming on a dress, curtain, etc. **2** something extra that is pleasant but unnecessary • *a simple life with no frills*
▷ **frilled** *ADJECTIVE* **frilly** *ADJECTIVE*

fringe *NOUN* **fringes** **1** a decorative edging with many threads hanging down loosely **2** a straight line of hair hanging down over the forehead **3** the edge of something
▷ **fringed** *ADJECTIVE*

frisk *VERB* **frisks, frisking, frisked** **1** jump or run about playfully **2** search somebody by running your hands over his or her clothes

frisky *ADJECTIVE* playful or lively
▷ **friskily** *ADVERB* **friskiness** *NOUN*

fritter[1] *NOUN* **fritters** a slice of meat or fruit or potato etc. coated in batter and fried

fritter[2] *VERB* **fritters, frittering, frittered** waste something gradually; spend money or time on trivial things

frivolous *ADJECTIVE* seeking pleasure in a light-hearted way; not serious
▷ **frivolously** *ADVERB* **frivolity** *NOUN*

frizzy *ADJECTIVE* (said about hair) in tight curls
▷ **frizziness** *NOUN*

fro *ADVERB*
to and fro backwards and forwards

frock *NOUN* **frocks** a girl's or woman's dress

frog *NOUN* **frogs** a small jumping animal that can live both in water and on land
a frog in your throat hoarseness

frolic *NOUN* **frolics** a lively cheerful game or entertainment
▷ **frolicsome** *ADJECTIVE*

frolic *VERB* **frolics, frolicking, frolicked** play about in a lively cheerful way

from *PREPOSITION* This word is used to show starting point in space or time or order (*We flew from London to Paris; We work from 9 to 5 o'clock; Count from one to ten*), source or origin (*Get water from the tap*), separation or release (*Take the gun from him; She was freed from prison*), difference (*Can you tell margarine from butter?*), cause (*I suffer from headaches*)

frond *NOUN* **fronds** a leaf-like part of a fern, palm tree, etc.

front *NOUN* **fronts** **1** the part or side that comes first or is the most important or furthest forward **2** a road or promenade along the seashore **3** the place where fighting is happening in a war **4** (in weather systems) the forward edge of an approaching mass of air
▷ **frontal** *ADJECTIVE*

Thesaurus

frighten *VERB* *The noises outside began to frighten them.* ► scare, startle, alarm, terrify, shock, agitate, disturb, fluster, panic, intimidate, disconcert AN OPPOSITE IS reassure

frightened *ADJECTIVE* *The children were tired and frightened.* ► scared, afraid, alarmed, terrified, petrified, fearful, shaken, shocked, panicky

frightening *ADJECTIVE* *a frightening experience* ► terrifying, alarming, fearsome, daunting, (*more informal*) scary

frightful *ADJECTIVE* **1** *We had to eat frightful food.* ► awful, terrible, dreadful, ghastly, appalling, horrible **2** *a scene of frightful devastation* ► shocking, horrible, terrible, gruesome, harrowing, hideous, grisly, horrid, macabre

frigid *ADJECTIVE* **1** *the frigid northern climate* ► bitter, bitterly cold, freezing, frozen, icy, arctic **2** *Leo glared back in frigid indignation.* ► stiff, stony, formal, unfeeling, austere, distant, aloof

frill *NOUN* **1** *a skirt with deep frills* ► fringe, ruff, ruffle, flounce **2** *a small hotel with no frills* ► extra, luxury, embellishment, extravagance

fringe *NOUN* **1** *a fringe round the edge of a curtain* ► border, edging, flounce, frill, gathering, trimming, valance **2** *on the fringe of the town* ► edge, outskirts, limits, periphery, perimeter, borders, margin AN OPPOSITE IS centre

fritter *VERB* *He frittered away all the money he had been given.* ► squander, waste, misspend, dissipate, get through

frivolous *ADJECTIVE* *They often made frivolous comments.* ► flippant, facetious, trivial, trifling, silly, shallow, stupid, foolish, jocular, flighty, ridiculous, superficial, unimportant, vacuous AN OPPOSITE IS serious

frock *NOUN* *a red cotton frock* ► dress, gown, shift, robe

frolic *VERB* *Lambs frolicked in the fields.* ► play, cavort, frisk, caper, leap, jump, sport, spring, bounce, gambol, skip, bound

front *NOUN* **1** *the front of the house* ► façade, facing, exterior AN OPPOSITE IS back **2** *the front of a boat* ► prow, bow, forepart OPPOSITES ARE back, stern **3** *the front of a car* ► nose, forepart AN OPPOSITE IS rear **4** *the front of the queue* ► head, start, beginning, lead OPPOSITES ARE back, end **5** *Young recruits were sent to the front.* ► front line, battle line, combat zone **6** *He managed to keep up a brave front.* ► appearance, manner, show, pose, bearing

front *ADJECTIVE* of the front; in front
frontier *NOUN* **frontiers** the boundary between two countries or regions
frontispiece *NOUN* **frontispieces** an illustration opposite the title page of a book
frost *NOUN* **frosts** **1** powdery ice that forms on things in freezing weather **2** weather with a temperature below freezing point
frosted *ADJECTIVE* covered with frost
frostbite *NOUN* harm done to the body by very cold weather
▷ **frostbitten** *ADJECTIVE*
frosty *ADJECTIVE* **frostier**, **frostiest** **1** cold with frost **2** unfriendly and unwelcoming • *a frosty look*
▷ **frostily** *ADVERB*
froth *NOUN* a white mass of tiny bubbles on a liquid
▷ **frothy** *ADJECTIVE*
frown *VERB* **frowns**, **frowning**, **frowned** wrinkle your forehead because you are angry or worried
frown *NOUN* **frowns** a frowning movement or look
fruit *NOUN* **fruits** or **fruit** **1** the seed container that grows on a tree or plant and is often used as food **2** the result of doing something • *the fruits of his efforts*
▷ **fruity** *ADJECTIVE*
fruit *VERB* **fruits**, **fruiting**, **fruited** produce fruit
fruitful *ADJECTIVE* producing good results
• *fruitful discussions*
▷ **fruitfully** *ADVERB*
fruitless *ADJECTIVE* producing no results
▷ **fruitlessly** *ADVERB*
frustrate *VERB* **frustrates**, **frustrating**, **frustrated** prevent somebody from doing something; prevent something from being successful • *A lack of money has frustrated our plans.*
▷ **frustration** *NOUN*
fry *VERB* **fries**, **frying**, **fried** cook something in very hot fat
▷ **fryer** *NOUN*
fudge *NOUN* a soft sugary sweet
fuel *NOUN* **fuels** something that is burnt to produce heat or power
fuel *VERB* **fuels**, **fuelling**, **fuelled** supply something with fuel
fugitive (few- jit- iv) *NOUN* **fugitives** a person who is running away from something
fulcrum *NOUN* **fulcrums** or **fulcra** the point on which a lever rests
fulfil *VERB* **fulfils**, **fulfilling**, **fulfilled** **1** do what is required; satisfy; carry out • *You must fulfil your promises* **2** make something come true • *It fulfilled an ancient prophecy.* **3** give you satisfaction
▷ **fulfilment** *NOUN*

Thesaurus

front *ADJECTIVE* *The front runners came into view.*
► first, leading, foremost, most advanced
AN OPPOSITE IS back
frosty *ADJECTIVE* **1** *a frosty autumn morning*
► freezing, bitter, ice-cold, crisp **2** *I'm afraid we'll get a frosty reception.* ► unfriendly, unwelcoming, unsympathetic, cool, stony
froth *NOUN* **1** *Claude wiped the champagne froth from his moustache.* ► foam, bubbles, effervescence, head **2** *He shook his hand in the water to make a froth.* ► lather, suds, foam
frown *VERB* *The woman frowned at them.*
► scowl, glower, glare, lour, grimace, knit your brow, look sullen, (*more informal*) give a dirty look
frown on *They frown on bad language.*
► disapprove of, view with disfavour, look askance at, object to, disfavour, dislike, discourage
frozen *ADJECTIVE* **1** *The lake is frozen.* ► iced over, ice-covered, ice-bound, solidified **2** *She felt frozen in the keen wind.* ► freezing, very cold, numbed
fruitful *ADJECTIVE* **1** *a fruitful crop* ► abundant, copious, productive, rich, prolific, fertile, plenteous, profuse AN OPPOSITE IS unproductive **2** *Talks have proved fruitful.* ► successful, productive, beneficial, profitable, useful, effective, worthwhile, gainful, rewarding
AN OPPOSITE IS fruitless
fruitless *ADJECTIVE* *three days of fruitless negotiations* ► futile, vain, abortive, unsuccessful, unfruitful, unproductive, profitless, unavailing, pointless, useless, disappointing, unprofitable, unrewarding
AN OPPOSITE IS fruitful
frustrate *VERB* **1** *The lack of progress was clearly frustrating them.* ► exasperate, discourage, dispirit, irritate OPPOSITES ARE satisfy, please
2 *Bad weather frustrated all attempts at a rescue.*
► thwart, foil, defeat, forestall, inhibit, prevent
fuel *NOUN* **1** *Vehicles were running out of fuel in the motorway jams.* ► petrol, propellant, diesel oil
2 *The inspectors' report added fuel to the war cause.* ► encouragement, provocation, incentive
fulfil *VERB* **1** *She was fulfilling her life's ambition of seeing the world.* ► achieve, realize, carry out, accomplish, succeed in, attain, effect, perform
2 *They have to work twelve hours a day to fulfil their obligations.* ► meet, complete, implement, execute, comply with, satisfy, respond to, answer, conform to
OPPOSITES ARE fail in, neglect

full *ADJECTIVE* **1** containing as much or as many as possible **2** having many people or things • *full of ideas* **3** complete • *the full story* **4** the greatest possible • *at full speed* **5** fitting loosely; with many folds • *a full skirt*
▷ **fully** *ADVERB* **fullness** *NOUN*
in full with nothing left out • *We have paid in full*

full *ADVERB* completely and directly • *It hit him full in the face.* [from Old English]

full-blown *ADJECTIVE* fully developed

full moon *NOUN* **full moons** the moon when you can see the whole of it as a bright disc

full stop *NOUN* **full stops** the dot used as a punctuation mark at the end of a sentence or an abbreviation

fully *ADVERB* completely

fumble *VERB* **fumbles, fumbling, fumbled** hold or handle something clumsily

fume *NOUN* or **fumes** *PLURAL NOUN* strong-smelling smoke or gas

fume *VERB* **fumes, fuming, fumed** **1** give off fumes **2** be very angry

fumigate (few- mig- ayt) *VERB* **fumigates, fumigating, fumigated** disinfect something by fumes
▷ **fumigation** *NOUN*

fun *NOUN* amusement or enjoyment
make fun of make people laugh at a person or thing

function *NOUN* **functions** **1** what somebody or something is there to do • *The function of a knife is to cut things.* **2** an important event or party **3** a basic operation in a computer or calculator **4** a variable quantity whose value depends on the value of other variable quantities • *X is a function of Y and Z.*

function *VERB* **functions, functioning, functioned** perform a function; work properly

fund *NOUN* **funds** **1** money collected or kept for a special purpose **2** a stock or supply

fund *VERB* **funds, funding, funded** supply with money

Thesaurus

full *ADJECTIVE* **1** *His glass was still full.* ► filled, loaded, topped up AN OPPOSITE IS empty **2** *The trains would be full on a Friday afternoon.* ► crowded, packed, crammed, congested, thronged, teeming, swarming, stuffed, mobbed, (*more informal*) jam-packed AN OPPOSITE IS empty **3** *By the end of the meal they were too full to talk.* ► well fed, satisfied, satiated, replete, sated, (*more informal*) bursting **4** *The bureau can give you a full list of local hotels and guest houses.* ► complete, comprehensive, exhaustive, thorough, copious **5** *The article did not tell the full story.* ► entire, complete, total, unabridged, unexpurgated **6** *She had led a full life and was looking forward to a period of quiet.* ► exciting, eventful, interesting, busy, lively, hectic **7** *The new piano had a full sound.* ► rich, resonant, sonorous, full-bodied, deep

fully *ADVERB* *We fully accept that there must be changes. I don't think you fully understand.* ► completely, entirely, wholly, totally, thoroughly, quite, altogether, positively, without reserve AN OPPOSITE IS partially

fumble *VERB* **1** *He fumbled for his wallet.* ► grope, feel about, fish, delve **2** *Without any light she could only fumble about.* ► stumble, blunder, flounder, lurch, stagger, totter **3** *Then, unfortunately, the keeper fumbled the ball.* ► mishandle, miss, drop, fail to catch, fail to keep

fumes *PLURAL NOUN* *fumes from an old tractor* ► exhaust, smoke, gases, vapour, fog, pollution, smog

fuming *ADJECTIVE* *Dad was pacing back and forth, fuming.* ► angry, furious, enraged, seething, raging, incensed

fun *NOUN* *After their exams they just wanted some fun.* ► enjoyment, entertainment, amusement, recreation, diversion, distraction, relaxation, jollity, play

function *NOUN* **1** *The organization has several functions.* ► role, responsibility, obligation, purpose, concern, use, job, task **2** *I had seen him at an official function.* ► event, occasion, party, gathering, reception, dinner, (*more informal*) do

function *VERB* **1** *To stop the machine functioning, switch it off.* ► work, operate, run, perform **2 function as** *The office also functions as an advice centre.* ► act as, serve as, operate as, constitute, form, have the role of

fund *NOUN* **1** *an emergency fund for refugees* ► pool, kitty, store, reserve, cache, source, supply **2 funds** *Funds are running low.* ► money, cash, capital, finances, assets, reserves, savings

fund *VERB* *Private capital will help fund the railways.* ► pay for, finance, capitalize, sponsor, subsidize, back, endow, maintain

A B C D E F G H I J K L M N O P Q R S T U V W X Y Z

fundamental *ADJECTIVE* basic
▷ **fundamentally** *ADVERB*

funeral *NOUN* **funerals** the ceremony when a dead person is buried or cremated

funfair *NOUN* **funfairs** a fair consisting of amusements and sideshows

fungus *NOUN* **fungi** (fung- I) a plant without leaves or flowers that grows on other plants or on decayed material, such as mushrooms and toadstools [from Latin]

funnel *NOUN* **funnels** **1** a metal chimney on a ship or steam engine **2** a tube that is wide at the top and narrow at the bottom to help you pour things into a narrow opening [from Latin *fundere* = pour]

funny *ADJECTIVE* **funnier, funniest** **1** making you laugh or smile **2** strange or odd • *a funny smell*
▷ **funnily** *ADVERB*

fur *NOUN* **furs** **1** the soft hair that covers some animals **2** animal skin with the fur on it, used for clothing; fabric that looks like animal fur

furious *ADJECTIVE* **1** very angry **2** violent or intense • *furious heat*
▷ **furiously** *ADVERB*

furnace *NOUN* **furnaces** a device in which great heat can be produced, e.g. for melting metals or making glass

furnish *VERB* **furnishes, furnishing, furnished** **1** provide a place with furniture **2** provide or supply with something

furniture *NOUN* tables, chairs, and other movable things that you need in a house or school or office etc.

furrow *NOUN* **furrows** **1** a long cut in the ground made by a plough or other implement **2** a groove **3** a deep wrinkle in the skin

furry *ADJECTIVE* like fur; covered with fur

further *ADVERB, ADJECTIVE* **1** at or to a greater distance; more distant **2** more; additional • *We made further enquiries.*
USAGE See the note at **farther**.

further *VERB* **furthers, furthering, furthered** help something to progress • *This success will further your career.*
▷ **furtherance** *NOUN*

further education *NOUN* education for people above school age

furthest *ADVERB, ADJECTIVE* at or to the greatest distance; most distant

fury *NOUN* **furies** wild anger; rage

fuse[1] *NOUN* **fuses** a safety device containing a short piece of wire that melts if too much electricity is passed through it

fuse *VERB* **fuses, fusing, fused** **1** stop working because a fuse has melted **2** blend together, especially through melting

fuse[2] *NOUN* **fuses** a length of material that burns easily, used for setting off an explosive

fusion *NOUN* **1** the action of blending or uniting things **2** the uniting of atomic nuclei, usually releasing energy

fuss *NOUN* **fusses** **1** unnecessary excitement or bustle **2** an agitated protest
make a fuss of treat someone with great kindness and attention

fuss *VERB* **fusses, fussing, fussed** make a fuss about something

Thesaurus

fundamental *ADJECTIVE* *fundamental political principles* ► basic, elementary, essential, primary, underlying, axiomatic, key, prime, principal, important, main, necessary
OPPOSITES ARE secondary, inessential

funny *ADJECTIVE* **1** *a funny story* ► amusing, humorous, comic, comical, witty, hilarious, facetious, droll, entertaining, silly, absurd, ridiculous AN OPPOSITE IS serious **2** *a funny coincidence* ► peculiar, strange, odd, curious, puzzling, queer, weird, bizarre

furious *ADJECTIVE* *She was furious when she found out.* ► angry, enraged, infuriated, incensed, fuming, annoyed, cross, displeased, irritated, irate, indignant, outraged
OPPOSITES ARE pleased, calm

furnish *VERB* *They have furnished the rooms tastefully.* ► decorate, appoint, fit out, fit up, equip

furniture *NOUN* *After the fire they had to buy new furniture.* ► furnishings, fitments, fittings, effects, household goods, equipment, movables, possessions

further *ADJECTIVE* *We need further information* ► more, additional, extra, fresh, new, supplementary

fury *NOUN* **1** *She could not hide her fury.* ► anger, rage, wrath, passion **2** *The storm hit the town with immense fury.* ► force, ferocity, fierceness, violence, turbulence, severity, savagery

fuss *NOUN* **1** *There was a lot of fuss about the missing money.* ► commotion, agitation, excitement, confusion, upset, worry **2** *He wanted to get the job done with as little fuss as possible.* ► bother, trouble, difficulty, inconvenience, effort, (*more informal*) hassle

fuss *VERB* *He begged her not to fuss.* ► fret, worry, get worked up, agitate, bother, complain, (*more informal*) flap, (*more informal*) create

fussy *ADJECTIVE* **fussier, fussiest 1** fussing; inclined to make a fuss **2** choosing very carefully; hard to please **3** full of unnecessary details or decorations
▷ **fussily** *ADVERB* **fussiness** *NOUN*

future *NOUN* **1** the time that will come; what is going to happen then **2** (in grammar) the tense of a verb that indicates something happening in the future, expressed by using 'shall', 'will', or 'be going to'

future *ADJECTIVE* belonging or referring to the future

fuzz *NOUN* something fluffy or frizzy

fuzzy *ADJECTIVE* **1** like fuzz; covered with fuzz **2** blurred; not clear
▷ **fuzzily** *ADVERB* **fuzziness** *NOUN*

Thesaurus

fussy *ADJECTIVE* **1** *They are both fussy about their food.* ► finicky, fastidious, particular, choosy, (*more informal*) picky **2** *The menu is a little fussy and over-rich.* ► fancy, elaborate, ornate, florid, detailed

futile *ADJECTIVE* *In the end the rebels abandoned the futile struggle.* ► fruitless, pointless, vain, ineffectual, unsuccessful, useless, abortive, unavailing, unproductive, barren
AN OPPOSITE IS fruitful

future *NOUN* **1** *There is a bright future for them.* ► outlook, prospects, expectations, destiny **2** *our plans for the future* ► time to come, time ahead AN OPPOSITE IS past

future *ADJECTIVE* *Future generations may find themselves living on a warmer planet.* ► later, following, coming, succeeding, subsequent, prospective, approaching, forthcoming, impending AN OPPOSITE IS past

fuzzy *ADJECTIVE* **1** *The baby had a large fuzzy head.* ► downy, frizzy, fluffy, woolly, fleecy, velvety, feathery **2** *good sound but a fuzzy picture* ► blurred, bleary, unfocused, ill-defined, indistinct, vague, hazy, shadowy, unclear, cloudy, dim, faint, misty OPPOSITES ARE clear, sharp

a b c d e f g h i j k l m n o p q r s t u v w x y z

A B C D E F **G** H I J K L M N O P Q R S T U V W X Y Z

Gg

gabble *VERB* **gabbles, gabbling, gabbled** talk so quickly that it is difficult to know what is being said

gadget *NOUN* **gadgets** any small useful tool
▷ **gadgetry** *NOUN*
[probably from French *gâchette*, = lock mechanism]

Gaelic (gay- lik) *NOUN* the Celtic languages of Scotland and Ireland

gag *NOUN* **gags 1** something put into a person's mouth or tied over it to prevent them from speaking **2** a joke

gag *VERB* **gags, gagging, gagged 1** put a gag on a person **2** prevent someone from making comments • *We cannot gag the press* **3** retch

gaggle *NOUN* **gaggles** a flock of geese

gaiety *NOUN* **1** cheerfulness **2** brightly coloured appearance

gaily *ADVERB* in a cheerful way

gain *VERB* **gains, gaining, gained 1** get something that you did not have before; obtain **2** a clock or watch gains when it becomes ahead of the correct time **3** reach; arrive at • *At last we gained the shore*
gain on come closer to a person or thing when chasing them or in a race

gain *NOUN* **gains** something gained; a profit or improvement
▷ **gainful** *ADJECTIVE*

galaxy *NOUN* **galaxies** a very large group of stars
▷ **galactic** (ga- lak- tik) *ADJECTIVE*

gale *NOUN* **gales** a very strong wind

gallant (gal- lant) *ADJECTIVE* **1** brave or heroic • *a gallant effort* **2** (gal- lant, ga- **lant**) courteous towards women
▷ **gallantly** *ADVERB* **gallantry** *NOUN*

gallery *NOUN* **galleries 1** a room or building for showing works of art **2** a platform jutting out from the wall in a church or hall **3** the highest balcony in a cinema or theatre **4** a long room or passage

Thesaurus

gadget *NOUN a kitchen full of gadgets* ► tool, utensil, appliance, contraption, contrivance, device, implement, machine, invention, instrument

gaffe *NOUN Anne was taking a day off trying to forget her gaffe.* ► mistake, blunder, error, slip, indiscretion

gag *NOUN His latest gag was quite funny for a change.* ► joke, jest, quip, funny remark, witticism, wisecrack

gag *VERB* **1** *The food had a strange taste that made her gag.* ► retch, choke, heave **2** *The regime found effective ways of gagging the press.* ► silence, muzzle, stifle, keep quiet, suppress, smother, restrain, prevent from speaking

gaiety *NOUN* **1** *There was gaiety in her voice.* ► cheerfulness, cheer, joy, happiness, merriment, jollity, delight **2** *They headed for the gaiety of a London bar.* ► festivity, fun, celebration, revelry, jollification

gaily *ADVERB* **1** *She waved gaily back.* ► merrily, cheerfully, cheerily, happily, joyfully, blithely OPPOSITES ARE sadly, drearily **2** *She wore a gaily coloured sari.* ► brightly, brilliantly, flamboyantly AN OPPOSITE IS drably **3** *There was Ben, gaily waving the traffic past.* ► casually, nonchalantly, heedlessly, airily, breezily, lightly, unthinkingly, uncaringly AN OPPOSITE IS anxiously

gain *VERB* **1** *She gained a huge income from her investments.* ► earn, gross, clear, bring in, obtain, acquire, procure **2** *They gained a wide reputation from the publicity.* ► earn, achieve, acquire, win, secure **3** *Trevor raised his head to gain a better view.* ► get, achieve, attain **4** *The car began to gain speed.* ► increase, gather, pick up USAGE You can also say *the car began to accelerate.*
gain on *We were gaining on the vehicle in front.* ► catch up with, draw nearer to, narrow the gap between, creep up on, approach

gain *NOUN* **1** *We are all motivated by the prospect of financial gain. There was no personal gain in it for me.* ► profit, earnings, income, advantage, benefit, return, reward, proceeds, yield, acquisition, asset, attainment, dividend, increase, winnings AN OPPOSITE IS loss **2 gain** *or* **gains** *Labour made modest gains in the local elections in the spring.* ► advances, progress, advancement, headway

gala *NOUN the annual summer gala* ► festival, carnival, jamboree, fête, fair, fiesta, celebration, revelry, party

gale *NOUN* **1** *Rain and gales are frequent.* ► storm, squall, high wind, hurricane **2** *She collapsed in gales of laughter.* ► outburst, burst, eruption, paroxysm, fit, peal, howl, hoot, roar

gallant *ADJECTIVE* **1** *a gallant band of soldiers* ► brave, courageous, valiant, daring, fearless, intrepid, heroic, doughty, noble, manly AN OPPOSITE IS cowardly **2** *A gallant gentleman at the next table came over to help her.* ► courteous, chivalrous, respectful, considerate, obliging, gracious OPPOSITES ARE discourteous, rude

gallon *NOUN* **gallons** a unit used to measure liquids, 8 pints or 4.546 litres

gallop *NOUN* **gallops** **1** the fastest pace that a horse can go **2** a fast ride on a horse

gallop *VERB* **gallops, galloping, galloped** go or ride at a gallop

gallows *NOUN* **gallows** a framework with a noose for hanging criminals

galoshes *PLURAL NOUN* a pair of waterproof shoes worn over ordinary shoes

galvanize *VERB* **galvanizes, galvanizing, galvanized** **1** stimulate someone into sudden activity **2** coat iron with zinc to protect it from rust
▷ **galvanization** *NOUN*

gambit *NOUN* **gambits** **1** a kind of opening move in chess **2** an action or remark intended to gain an advantage

gamble *VERB* **gambles, gambling, gambled** **1** bet on the result of a game, race, or other event **2** take great risks in the hope of gaining something
▷ **gambler** *NOUN*

gamble *NOUN* **gambles** **1** a bet or chance • *a gamble on the lottery* **2** a risky attempt

gambol *VERB* **gambols, gambolling, gambolled** jump or skip about in play

game *NOUN* **games** **1** a form of play or sport, especially one with rules • *a game of football;* • *a computer game* **2** a section of a long game such as tennis or whist **3** a scheme or plan; a trick • *Whatever his game is, he won't succeed.* **4** wild animals or birds hunted for sport or food
give the game away reveal a secret

game *ADJECTIVE* **1** able and willing to do something • *'Shall we swim to the island?' 'I'm game!'* **2** brave
▷ **gamely** *ADVERB*

gamekeeper *NOUN* **gamekeepers** a person employed to protect game birds and animals, especially from poachers

gamma *NOUN* the third letter of the Greek alphabet, = g

gamma rays *PLURAL NOUN* very short X-rays emitted by radioactive substances

gander *NOUN* **ganders** a male goose

gang *NOUN* **gangs** **1** a group of people who do things together **2** a group of criminals

gang *VERB* **gangs, ganging, ganged** join in a gang • *gang together*
gang up on form a group to fight or oppose someone

gangling *ADJECTIVE* tall, thin, and awkward-looking

gangplank *NOUN* **gangplanks** a plank placed so that people can walk into or out of a boat

gangrene (gang-green) *NOUN* decay of body tissue in a living person

gangster *NOUN* **gangsters** a member of a gang of violent criminals

gangway *NOUN* **gangways** **1** a gap left for people to pass between rows of seats or through a crowd **2** a movable bridge placed so that people can walk on to or off a ship

gaol (jayl) *NOUN* **gaols** a different spelling of **jail**
▷ **gaol** *VERB* **gaoler** *NOUN*

gap *NOUN* **gaps** **1** a break or opening in something continuous such as a hedge or fence **2** an interval **3** a wide difference in ideas

gape *VERB* **gapes, gaping, gaped** **1** have your mouth open **2** stare with your mouth open **3** be open wide

Thesaurus

gallop *VERB* *A horse galloped past.* ► race, run, canter, rush, dash, speed, sprint

gambit *NOUN* *It was a daring gambit and might just work.* ► plan, stratagem, tactic, ruse, move, manoeuvre, trick

gamble *VERB* **1** *He drinks and gambles and chases women.* ► bet, game, risk money, wager, (*more informal*) have a flutter **2** *We gambled and were lucky.* ► take a risk, take a chance, try your luck, speculate, venture

game *NOUN* **1** *The children were playing a new game.* ► pastime, diversion, amusement, entertainment, sport, activity **2** *I know how to deal with his little game.* ► scheme, trick, plot, plan, dodge **3** *It was the big game on Saturday.* ► match, contest, tournament, competition, event, meeting **4** *They were just playing a game on us.* ► joke, trick, prank, hoax

gang *NOUN* **1** *a gang of teenagers* ► band, group, crowd, pack, mob **2** *a gang working on the road* ► team, squad, troop, shift, detachment, working party **3** *I was never a part of his gang.* ► circle, set, group, ring, clan, clique

gang *VERB* **gang together** *or* **up** *They always gang up to get their way.* ► combine, conspire, cooperate, work together, team up

gaol *NOUN, VERB another spelling of* **jail**

gap *NOUN* **1** *a gap in a wall* ► opening, breach, break, chink, space, hole, cleft, crack, cranny, crevice, rift, void **2** *a gap in the fighting* ► pause, break, interruption, lull, intermission, interval **3** *the gap between rich and poor* ► divide, gulf, rift, chasm, disparity, imbalance

gape *VERB* *He gaped at her in surprise.* ► stare, gaze, goggle, (*more informal*) gawk, (*more informal*) gawp

garage (ga- rahzh, ga- rij) *NOUN* **garages** **1** a building in which a motor vehicle or vehicles may be kept **2** a place where motor vehicles are repaired or serviced and where petrol is sold

garbage *NOUN* rubbish, especially household rubbish

garble *VERB* **garbles, garbling, garbled** give a confused account of a story or message so that it is misunderstood

garden *NOUN* **gardens** a piece of ground where flowers, fruit, or vegetables are grown
▷ **gardener** *NOUN* **gardening** *NOUN*

gargle *VERB* **gargles, gargling, gargled** hold a liquid at the back of the mouth and breathe air through it to wash the inside of the throat
▷ **gargle** *NOUN*

gargoyle *NOUN* **gargoyles** an ugly or comical face or figure carved on a building, especially on a water spout

garland *NOUN* **garlands** a wreath of flowers worn or hung as a decoration
▷ **garland** *VERB*

garlic *NOUN* a plant with a bulb divided into smaller bulbs (**cloves**), which have a strong smell and taste and are used for flavouring food

garment *NOUN* **garments** a piece of clothing

garnish *VERB* **garnishes, garnishing, garnished** decorate something, especially food

garnish *NOUN* something used to decorate food or give it extra flavour

garret *NOUN* **garrets** an attic

garrison *NOUN* **garrisons** **1** troops who stay in a town or fort to defend it **2** the building they occupy
▷ **garrison** *VERB*

garter *NOUN* **garters** a band of elastic to hold up a sock or stocking

gas [1] *NOUN* **gases** **1** a substance that (like air) can move freely and is not liquid or solid at ordinary temperatures **2** a gas that can be burned, used for lighting, heating, or cooking

gas *VERB* **gasses, gassing, gassed** **1** kill or injure someone with gas **2** (*informal*) talk idly for a long time

gas [2] *NOUN* (*American*) gasoline

gaseous (gas- ee- us) *ADJECTIVE* in the form of a gas

gash *NOUN* **gashes** a long deep cut or wound

gash *VERB* **gashes, gashing, gashed** make a gash in something

gasoline *NOUN* (*American*) petrol

gasp *VERB* **gasps, gasping, gasped** **1** breathe in suddenly when you are shocked or surprised **2** struggle to breathe with your mouth open when you are tired or ill **3** speak in a breathless way
▷ **gasp** *NOUN*

gassy *ADJECTIVE* fizzy

gastric *ADJECTIVE* to do with the stomach

gastronomy (gas- **tron**- om- ee) *NOUN* the art or science of good eating
▷ **gastronomic** *ADJECTIVE*

gastropod *NOUN* **gastropods** an animal (e.g. a snail) that moves by means of a fleshy 'foot' on its stomach

gate *NOUN* **gates** **1** a movable barrier, usually on hinges, used as a door in a wall or fence **2** a barrier for controlling the flow of water in a dam or lock **3** a place where you wait before you board an aircraft **4** the number of people attending a football match etc.

gatecrash *VERB* **gatecrashes, gatecrashing, gatecrashed** go to a private party without being invited
▷ **gatecrasher** *NOUN*

Thesaurus

garage *NOUN* **1** *The house had a large garage, which the new owner turned into a study.* ► carport **2** *She had stopped to fill up the tank at a local garage.* ► filling station, petrol station, service station

garbled *ADJECTIVE* *The story seems garbled and may be nonsense.* ► confused, muddled, mixed up, twisted, jumbled, scrambled AN OPPOSITE IS clear

garden *NOUN* **1** *a house with a garden* ► plot, allotment, patch, yard **2** **gardens** *a walk through the gardens* ► grounds, park RELATED ADJECTIVE horticultural RELATED NOUN horticulture

gash *NOUN* *Blood was pouring from a gash on his head.* ► cut, slash, wound, injury, slit, laceration, abrasion

gash *VERB* *Frank gashed his hand on a broken glass.* ► cut, slash, lacerate, wound, injure, gouge

gasp *VERB* *She gasped and sat back, her face pale.* ► catch your breath, pant, choke, gulp, blow

gasp *NOUN* *The boy fell back with a gasp.* ► pant, heave, wheeze, puff, blow

gate *NOUN* *Some children came through the gate.* ► gateway, doorway, door, entrance, entry, exit, (*poetic*) portal

gateway *NOUN* **gateways 1** an opening containing a gate **2** a way to reach something • *The gateway to success*

gather *VERB* **gathers**, **gathering**, **gathered** **1** come or bring together **2** collect; obtain gradually • *We've been gathering information.* **3** collect as harvest; pluck • *Gather the corn when it is ripe.* • *gather flowers* **4** understand or learn • *I gather you've been on holiday.* **5** pull cloth into folds by running a thread through it **6** a sore gathers when it swells up and forms pus
gather speed move gradually faster

gathering *NOUN* **gatherings** an assembly or meeting of people; a party

gaudy *ADJECTIVE* too showy and bright
▷ **gaudily** *ADVERB* **gaudiness** *NOUN*

gauge (gayj) *NOUN* **gauges 1** a standard measurement **2** the distance between a pair of rails on a railway **3** a measuring instrument

gauge *VERB* **gauges**, **gauging**, **gauged** **1** measure **2** estimate; form a judgement

gaunt *ADJECTIVE* (said about a person) lean and haggard
▷ **gauntness** *NOUN*

gauntlet[1] *NOUN* **gauntlets** a glove with a wide cuff covering the wrist
throw down the gauntlet offer a challenge

gauntlet[2] *NOUN*
run the gauntlet have to suffer continuous severe criticism or risk

gauze *NOUN* **1** thin transparent woven material **2** fine wire mesh
▷ **gauzy** *ADJECTIVE*

gay *ADJECTIVE* **1** homosexual **2** cheerful **3** brightly coloured
▷ **gayness** *NOUN*
USAGE Nowadays the most common meaning of **gay** is 'homosexual'. The older meanings 'cheerful' and 'brightly coloured' can still be used but are becoming less and less common in everyday use. • *Gayness* is the noun from meaning 1 of **gay**. The noun that relates to the other two meanings is **gaiety**.

gaze *VERB* **gazes**, **gazing**, **gazed** look at something steadily for a long time

gaze *NOUN* **gazes** a long steady look

gazetteer (gaz- it- eer) *NOUN* **gazetteers** a list of place names

GCSE *ABBREVIATION* General Certificate of Secondary Education

gear *NOUN* **gears 1** a cogwheel, especially one of a set in a motor vehicle that turn power from the engine into movement of the wheels **2** equipment or apparatus • *camping gear*

gear *VERB* **gears**, **gearing**, **geared**
gear to make something match or be suitable for something else • *Health care should be geared to people's needs, not to whether they can pay.*

Thesaurus

gather *VERB* **1** *A crowd gathered near the entrance.* ► assemble, collect, come together, congregate, crowd round, convene, converge, flock, group, muster AN OPPOSITE IS disperse **2** *She spent some time gathering her books.* ► collect, assemble, accumulate, bring together, heap up **3** *They went into the garden to gather flowers and berries.* ► pick, pluck, garner, harvest **4** *I gather you have been unwell.* ► understand, believe, be told, be given to understand, learn, hear, be informed, deduce, infer, surmise **5** *You can gather the dress at the waist.* ► pleat, fold, crimp, ruffle, pucker

gaudy *ADJECTIVE* *She wore dull clothes, nothing gaudy.* ► garish, lurid, flashy, loud, glaring, vulgar OPPOSITES ARE sober, dull

gauge *NOUN* **1** *He checked the pressure gauge.* ► meter, instrument, dial, reading **2** *The track was the wrong gauge for the new rolling stock.* ► size, width, measure, standard **3** *The local elections will be seen as a gauge of public opinion.* ► measure, indicator, test, guide (to), touchstone, benchmark

gauge *VERB* **1** *A special scoring table will gauge which competitor does best.* ► assess, evaluate, appraise, calculate, reckon **2** *Instruments can gauge the distance precisely.* ► measure, calculate, compute, quantify, determine

gaunt *ADJECTIVE* *His arms were wrapped round his gaunt body.* ► haggard, drawn, lank, emaciated, wasted, skinny, scrawny, shrivelled, skeletal, cadaverous

gawky *ADJECTIVE* *She had been a thin, gawky adolescent.* ► awkward, ungainly, inelegant, ungraceful, graceless, gangling, gauche, inept, lumbering, bumbling, maladroit, uncoordinated AN OPPOSITE IS graceful

gay *ADJECTIVE* **1** *a club for gay people* ► homosexual, (*female*) lesbian **2** *He was so gay and lively.* ► cheerful, happy, carefree, lively, merry, jolly, jovial, glad

gaze *VERB* *He continued to gaze out of the window.* ► stare, look, gape

gear *NOUN* (*informal*) *You can put your gear in here.* ► equipment, paraphernalia, belongings, possessions, stuff, things, tackle

A B C D E F G H I J K L M N O P Q R S T U V W X Y Z

gear up get ready for • *We were all geared up to play cricket, but then it rained.*

Geiger counter (gy- ger) NOUN **Geiger counters** an instrument that detects and measures radioactivity

gel NOUN **gels** a jelly-like substance, especially one used to give a style to hair

gelatine NOUN a clear jelly-like substance made by boiling animal tissue and used to make jellies and other foods and in photographic film
▷ **gelatinous** (jil- at- in- us) ADJECTIVE

gem NOUN **gems** **1** a precious stone **2** an excellent person or thing

gender NOUN **genders** **1** the group in which a noun is classed in the grammar of some languages, e.g. masculine, feminine, or neuter **2** a person's sex • *Jobs should be open to all, regardless of race or gender.*

gene (jeen) NOUN **genes** the part of a living cell that controls which characteristics (such as the colour of hair or eyes) are inherited from parents

genealogy (jeen- ee- al- o- jee) NOUN **genealogies** **1** a list or diagram showing how people are descended from an ancestor **2** the study of family history and ancestors
▷ **genealogical** (jeen- ee- a- **loj**- ik- al) ADJECTIVE

genera (jen- e- ra) PLURAL NOUN plural of **genus**

general ADJECTIVE **1** to do with or involving most people or things • *This drug is now in general use.* **2** not detailed; broad • *I've got the general idea.* **3** chief or head • *the general manager*
in general as a general rule; usually

general NOUN **generals** a senior army officer

general election NOUN **general elections** an election of Members of Parliament for the whole country

generally ADVERB **1** usually **2** in a general sense; without regard to details • *I was speaking generally.*

general practitioner NOUN **general practitioners** a doctor who treats all kinds of diseases. He or she is the first doctor that people see when they are ill

generate VERB **generates, generating, generated** produce or create

generation NOUN **generations** **1** generating **2** a single stage in a family • *Three generations were included: children, parents, and grandparents.* **3** all the people born at about the same time • *our parents' generation*

generator NOUN **generators** **1** an apparatus for producing gases or steam **2** a machine for converting mechanical energy into electricity

generous ADJECTIVE **1** willing to give things or share them **2** given freely; plentiful • *a generous helping*
▷ **generously** ADVERB **generosity** NOUN

genetic (jin- et- ik) ADJECTIVE **1** to do with genes **2** to do with characteristics inherited from parents or ancestors
▷ **genetically** ADVERB

genetically modified (said about an animal or

Thesaurus

gem NOUN **1** *a tiara made of gems and pearls* ► jewel, precious stone, gemstone **2** *The anthology contains some real gems.* ► pearl, wonder, treasure, masterpiece, outstanding example

general ADJECTIVE **1** *The idea is sound in general terms.* ► broad, rough, sweeping, vague, loose, indefinite AN OPPOSITE IS specific **2** *This model is more suitable for general use.* ► widespread, universal, popular, regular, typical, normal, ordinary, everyday, conventional OPPOSITES ARE specialist, restricted **3** *a general pay increase* ► comprehensive, inclusive, overall, universal

generally ADVERB *It is generally a mistake to ignore these factors.* ► normally, as a rule, by and large, on the whole, broadly, mainly, mostly, in the main, predominantly, usually

generate VERB *a move to generate more business* ► create, produce, bring about, make, cause, give rise to, propagate, engender, beget, breed, (*more informal*) whip up

generation NOUN **1** *people of an earlier generation* ► age, age group **2** *the generation of new jobs* ► creation, production, origination, initiation, genesis

generosity NOUN *Thanks to the generosity of sponsors the games can continue.* ► kindness, munificence, liberality, philanthropy, benevolence, bounty, charity, largesse

generous ADJECTIVE **1** *a person of a good and generous nature* ► kind, kind-hearted, magnanimous, benevolent, unselfish, charitable, big-hearted, beneficent, philanthropic **2** *She was always generous on the children's birthdays.* ► bountiful, liberal, lavish, munificent, indulgent, bounteous **3** *a generous helping of pudding* ► large, lavish, ample, copious, plentiful, abundant

genius NOUN **1** *They have a genius for getting attention.* ► talent, gift, flair, aptitude, bent, intellect, knack **2** *It doesn't take a genius to work out his little game.* ► mastermind, great thinker, great brain, prodigy, past master, expert, intellectual

gentle ADJECTIVE **1** *The mild, gentle face looked back at him.* ► kind, kindly, tender, sympathetic, compassionate, warm-hearted,

plant) containing genes that have been artificially altered

genetics *NOUN* the study of genes and genetic behaviour

genial (jee- nee- al) *ADJECTIVE* kindly and cheerful
▷ **genially** *ADVERB* **geniality** (jee- nee- al- it- ee) *NOUN*

genital (jen- it- al) *ADJECTIVE* to do with animal reproduction or reproductive organs

genitals (jen- it- alz) *PLURAL NOUN* external sexual organs

genius *NOUN* **geniuses** **1** an unusually clever or creative person **2** a very great natural ability • *He has a real genius for music*

genocide (jen- o- syd) *NOUN* deliberate extermination of a race of people

gentle *ADJECTIVE* **1** mild or kind; not rough **2** not harsh or severe • *a gentle breeze*
▷ **gently** *ADVERB* **gentleness** *NOUN*

gentleman *NOUN* **gentlemen** **1** a well-mannered or honourable man **2** a man of good social position **3** (*in polite use*) a man

genuine *ADJECTIVE* real; not faked or pretending
▷ **genuinely** *ADVERB* **genuineness** *NOUN*

genus (jee- nus) *NOUN* **genera** (jen- er- a) a group of similar animals or plants • *Lions and tigers belong to the same genus.*

geography (jee- og- ra- fee) *NOUN* the study of the earth's surface and of its climate, peoples, and products
▷ **geographer** *NOUN* **geographical** *ADJECTIVE* **geographically** *ADVERB*
[from *geo-* = earth + *-graphy* = description]

geology (jee- ol- o- jee) *NOUN* the study of the structure of the earth's crust and its layers
▷ **geological** *ADJECTIVE* **geologically** *ADVERB* **geologist** *NOUN*

geometry (jee- om- it- ree) *NOUN* the study of lines, angles, surfaces, and solids in mathematics
▷ **geometric** *ADJECTIVE* **geometrical** *ADJECTIVE* **geometrically** *ADVERB*

gerbil (jer- bil) *NOUN* **gerbils** a small brown rodent with long hind legs, often kept as a pet

geriatric (je- ree- at- rik) *ADJECTIVE* to do with the care of old people and their health [from Greek *geras* = old age + *iatros* = doctor]

germ *NOUN* **germs** **1** a micro-organism, especially one that can cause disease **2** a tiny living structure from which a plant or animal may develop **3** part of the seed of a cereal plant [from Latin *germen* = seed or sprout]

German measles *NOUN* rubella

German shepherd dog *NOUN* **German shepherd dogs** a large strong dog, often used by the police

germinate *VERB* **germinates, germinating, germinated** when a seed germinates, it begins to develop, and roots and shoots grow from it
▷ **germination** *NOUN*

gesticulate (jes- tik- yoo- layt) *VERB* **gesticulates, gesticulating, gesticulated** make expressive movements with your hands and arms
▷ **gesticulation** *NOUN*

gesture (jes- cher) *NOUN* **gestures** **1** a movement that expresses what a person feels **2** an action that shows goodwill • *It would be a nice gesture to send her some flowers*

gesture *VERB* **gestures, gesturing, gestured** tell a person something by making a gesture • *She gestured me to be quiet.*

get *VERB* **gets, getting, got** This word has many different uses, including: **1** obtain or receive • *She got first prize* **2** become • *Don't get angry!* **3** reach a place • *We got there by midnight.* **4** put or move • *I can't get my shoe on.* **5** prepare • *Will you get the tea?* **6** persuade or order • *Get him to wash up.* **7** catch or suffer from an illness **8** (*informal*) understand • *Do you get what I mean?*

Thesaurus

soft-hearted, placid, calm OPPOSITES ARE unkind, harsh **2** *A gentle breeze was blowing.* ► light, faint, soft OPPOSITES ARE strong, fierce **3** *There was a gentle slope up to the house.* ► gradual, slight, easy AN OPPOSITE IS steep

genuine *ADJECTIVE* **1** *A genuine Picasso hung on the wall.* ► authentic, original, bona fide, actual, real, true, authenticated AN OPPOSITE IS fake **2** *She's a very genuine person.* ► sincere, honest, unaffected, frank, truthful, devout, candid, earnest, true AN OPPOSITE IS insincere

germ *NOUN* **1** *the germ of a great idea* ► beginning, nucleus, seed, start, genesis, embryo, cause, origin **2** *a cleaner that also kills germs* ► microbe, micro-organism, bacterium, (*more informal*) bug, virus

get *VERB* **1** *She got her degree at St Andrews.* ► obtain, receive, acquire, come by, achieve, procure **2** *It's getting cold.* ► become, turn, grow **3** *We'll get there soon.* ► arrive, reach, come to **4** *Will you get my book?* ► fetch, bring, collect, pick up **5** *I got a cold.* ► catch, come down with, develop

get across *It's hard to get the idea across.* ► communicate, convey, impart, transmit

get ahead *people who want to get ahead* ► succeed, prosper, flourish, get on well

get along **1** *They do seem to get along with each other.* ► agree, see eye to eye, be friendly, be compatible **2** *We are getting along quite well*

a b c d e f g h i j k l m n o p q r s t u v w x y z

A B C D E F G H I J K L M N O P Q R S T U V W X Y Z

get away with 1 escape with something 2 avoid being punished for what you have done
get by (*informal*) manage
get on 1 make progress 2 be friendly with somebody
get over recover from an illness etc.
get up 1 stand up 2 get out of your bed in the morning 3 prepare or organize • *We got up a concert.*
get your own back (*informal*) have your revenge
have got to must

geyser (gee- zer, gy- zer) NOUN **geysers** 1 a natural spring that shoots up columns of hot water 2 a kind of water heater [from **Geysir** = gusher, the name of a geyser in Iceland]

ghastly ADJECTIVE 1 very unpleasant or bad 2 looking pale and ill
▷ **ghastliness** NOUN
[from Old English *gaestan* = terrify]

ghost NOUN **ghosts** the spirit of a dead person that appears to the living
▷ **ghostly** ADJECTIVE

ghoulish (gool- ish) ADJECTIVE enjoying things that are grisly or unpleasant
▷ **ghoulishly** ADVERB **ghoulishness** NOUN
[from Arabic *gul* = a demon that eats dead bodies]

giant NOUN **giants** 1 (in myths or fairy tales) a creature like a huge man 2 a man, animal, or plant that is much larger than the usual size [via early French from Greek *gigas*]

gibberish (jib- er- ish) NOUN meaningless speech; nonsense

gibbet (jib- it) NOUN **gibbets** 1 a gallows 2 an upright post with an arm from which a criminal's body was hung after execution, as a warning to others

gibbon NOUN **gibbons** a small ape from south-east Asia. Gibbons have very long arms to help them swing through the trees where they live

giddy ADJECTIVE 1 feeling that everything is spinning round and that you might fall 2 causing this feeling • *We looked down from the giddy height of the cliff.*
▷ **giddily** ADVERB **giddiness** NOUN

Thesaurus

now. ► manage, cope, get on, make out, progress, advance
get at *What are you getting at?* ► suggest, imply, intend, insinuate, mean
get away *Tom and Fiona wanted to get away for the weekend.* ► escape, leave, (*more informal*) make off
get back *We won't get our money back.* ► recover, recoup, regain, retrieve
get by (*informal*) *We have enough money to get by.* ► survive, manage, cope, make do, muddle along, muddle through
get down *All the talk of war got them down.* ► depress, deject, dishearten, dispirit, sadden
get in *The train gets in at 7 o'clock.* ► arrive, come
get on 1 *We'd better get on the bus.* ► board, embark, mount, ascend 2 *How did they get on during their holiday?* ► cope, manage, fare, get along, make out
get out *Some of the prisoners had got out.* ► escape, break out, break free, get away, flee
get over 1 *She's just got over flu.* ► recover from, shake off, survive 2 *difficulties that we can never get over* ► overcome, surmount, deal with
get round 1 *a problem they tried to get round* ► avoid, evade, overcome, get the better of 2 *He always got round his mother when he needed something.* ► persuade, cajole, prevail on, win over, beguile
get together *Let's get together next week.* ► meet, meet up, see one another
get up 1 *She got up from her chair.* ► rise, stand, stand up 2 *They would have to get up early to leave for the airport.* ► rise, get out of bed

getaway NOUN *a quick getaway* ► escape, breakout, breakaway

ghastly ADJECTIVE 1 *a ghastly murder* ► terrible, frightful, horrible, horrific, horrifying, gruesome 2 *a ghastly time* ► unpleasant, disagreeable, nasty, horrid, revolting
AN OPPOSITE IS lovely

ghost NOUN 1 *They say there's a ghost in the house.* ► phantom, spectre, spirit, wraith, vision 2 *a ghost of a smile* ► trace, hint, suggestion, glimmer, semblance, shadow

ghostly ADJECTIVE *The ghostly figure seemed to belong to a dream.* ► unearthly, spectral, eerie, phantom, uncanny, weird, supernatural, (*informal*) spooky, (*informal*) creepy, (*informal*) scary

giant NOUN *A giant of a man stood in the doorway.* ► monster, colossus, titan, Goliath, ogre
AN OPPOSITE IS dwarf

giant ADJECTIVE *The thrust from the four giant engines pushed him back in his seat.* ► huge, enormous, gigantic, colossal, immense, massive, mighty, vast, large, elephantine, gargantuan, mammoth, monstrous, prodigious, titanic, (*more informal*) whopping, (*more informal*) jumbo, (*more informal*) king-size OPPOSITES ARE tiny, miniature

giddy ADJECTIVE *The heat of the sun made her giddy.* ► dizzy, faint, weak, light-headed, unsteady, wobbly, (*more informal*) woozy

gift *NOUN* **gifts** **1** a present **2** a natural talent • *She has a gift for music.*

gifted *ADJECTIVE* having a special talent

gig *NOUN* **gigs** (*informal*) a live performance by a musician, comedian, etc.

gigabyte (**gi**- ga- byt, **ji**- ga- byt) *NOUN* **gigabytes** (in computing) a unit of information equal to one thousand million bytes, or (more precisely) 2^{30} bytes

gigantic (jy- **gan**- tik) *ADJECTIVE* extremely large; huge

giggle *VERB* **giggles, giggling, giggled** laugh in a silly way

giggle *NOUN* **giggles** **1** a silly laugh **2** (*informal*) something amusing; a bit of fun

gild *VERB* **gilds, gilding, gilded** cover something with a thin layer of gold or gold paint

gills *PLURAL NOUN* the part of the body through which fish and certain other water animals breathe

gilt *NOUN* a thin covering of gold or gold paint

gimmick *NOUN* **gimmicks** something unusual or silly done or used just to attract people's attention

gin *NOUN* a colourless alcoholic drink flavoured with juniper berries

ginger *NOUN* **1** the hot-tasting root of a tropical plant, or a flavouring made from this root, used especially in drinks and Eastern cooking **2** liveliness or energy **3** a reddish-yellow colour
▷ **ginger** *ADJECTIVE*

ginger *VERB* **gingers, gingering, gingered** make something more lively • *This will ginger things up!* [via Old English, Latin, and Greek from Dravidian (a group of languages spoken in southern India)]

gingerly *ADVERB* cautiously

giraffe *NOUN* **giraffe** or **giraffes** an African animal with long legs and a very long neck, the world's tallest mammal [from Arabic]

girder *NOUN* **girders** a metal beam supporting part of a building or a bridge

girdle *NOUN* **girdles** **1** a belt or cord worn round the waist **2** a woman's elastic corset covering from the waist to the thigh

girl *NOUN* **girls** **1** a female child **2** a young woman
▷ **girlhood** *NOUN* **girlish** *ADJECTIVE*

girlfriend *NOUN* **girlfriends** a person's regular female companion in a romantic or sexual relationship

giro (**jy**- roh) *NOUN* a system of sending money directly from one bank account or post office account to another

gist (jist) *NOUN* the essential points or general sense of what someone says

give *VERB* **gives, giving, gave, given** **1** let someone have something **2** make or do something • *He gave a laugh.* **3** be flexible or springy; bend or collapse when pressed
▷ **giver** *NOUN*

Thesaurus

gift *NOUN* **1** *He made the library a generous gift.* ► present, donation, benefaction, contribution, largesse, handout, offering, grant, gratuity, bequest, endowment **2** *a gift for languages* ► talent, flair, aptitude, capacity, genius, knack, ability, bent, capability

gifted *ADJECTIVE* *a gifted young musician* ► talented, able, accomplished, capable, skilful, skilled

gigantic *ADJECTIVE* *a gigantic old building* ► huge, enormous, colossal, immense, massive, mighty, vast, large, giant, (*more informal*) whopping, (*more informal*) jumbo, (*more informal*) king-size

giggle *VERB* *The silly hat made them giggle.* ► snigger, titter, chuckle, laugh

girdle *NOUN* *They wore girdles round their waists.* ► belt, sash, band, waistband, corset

girl *NOUN* *a pretty little girl* ► lass, daughter, female child, (*literary*) maid, (*literary*) maiden

give *VERB* **1** *He would give them another hundred pounds.* ► provide with, present with, supply with, allow, award, bestow on, donate, make over **2** *Will you give her a message?* ► pass on, convey, communicate, transmit, send, deliver **3** *three brothers who had given their lives in the Great War* ► sacrifice, lose, relinquish, devote **4** *a note giving details of Christmas opening times* ► show, list, provide, display **5** *The boys gave no trouble.* ► cause, make, create, start **6** *The right herbs will give your food a better flavour.* ► afford, produce, yield, lend **7** *We are going to give a party.* ► hold, lay on, organize, arrange **8** *He saw her and gave a shout.* ► utter, emit, let out **9** *The roof was giving under the weight.* ► collapse, yield, break, fall in **10** *She would give them a warning.* ► issue, deliver, administer, impose on

give away *She tried not to give away their secret.* ► reveal, disclose, divulge, betray

give in *They had to give in after a while.* ► submit, surrender, capitulate, yield, succumb, comply

give off *The fire gave off grey fumes.* ► produce, emit, send out, discharge, exude, release

give out **1** *Please give out the books.* ► hand out, hand round, distribute, dole out, deal out **2** *The money gave out after four days.* ► run out, be used up, be exhausted, dry up

give in acknowledge that you are defeated; yield
give up **1** stop trying **2** end a habit

given *ADJECTIVE* named or stated in advance • *All the people in a given area.*

glacial (glay- shal) *ADJECTIVE* icy; made of or produced by ice
▷ **glacially** *ADVERB*

glacier (glas- ee- er) *NOUN* **glaciers** a mass of ice that moves very slowly down a mountain valley

glad *ADJECTIVE* **1** pleased; expressing joy **2** giving pleasure • *We brought the glad news.*
▷ **gladly** *ADVERB* **gladness** *NOUN*
glad of grateful for or pleased with something

gladden *VERB* **gladdens**, **gladdening**, **gladdened** make a person glad

glade *NOUN* **glades** an open space in a forest

gladiator (glad- ee- ay- ter) *NOUN* **gladiators** a man trained to fight for public entertainment in ancient Rome
▷ **gladiatorial** (glad- ee- at- or- ee- al) *ADJECTIVE* [from Latin *gladius* = sword]

glamorous *ADJECTIVE* excitingly attractive

glamour *NOUN* an attractive and exciting quality

glance *VERB* **glances**, **glancing**, **glanced** **1** look at something briefly **2** strike something at an angle and slide off it • *The ball glanced off his bat.*
▷ **glance** *NOUN*

gland *NOUN* **glands** an organ of the body that separates substances from the blood so that they can be used or secreted (passed out of the body)
▷ **glandular** *ADJECTIVE*

glare *VERB* **glares**, **glaring**, **glared** **1** shine with a bright or dazzling light **2** stare angrily or fiercely
▷ **glare** *NOUN*

glasnost *NOUN* the open reporting of news or giving of information, especially in the former Soviet Union [from Russian, = openness]

glass *NOUN* **glasses** **1** a hard brittle substance that is usually transparent **2** a container made of glass for drinking from **3** a mirror **4** a lens
▷ **glassy** *ADJECTIVE*

glasses *PLURAL NOUN* **1** a pair of lenses in a frame, worn over the eyes to help improve eyesight **2** binoculars

glaze *VERB* **glazes**, **glazing**, **glazed** **1** fit a window or building with glass **2** give a shiny surface to something **3** (said of a person's eyes) lose brightness and animation

gleam *NOUN* **gleams** **1** a beam of soft light, especially one that comes and goes **2** a small amount of hope, humour, etc.

gleam *VERB* **gleams**, **gleaming**, **gleamed** shine brightly, especially after cleaning or polishing

glee *NOUN* great delight
▷ **gleeful** *ADJECTIVE* **gleefully** *ADVERB*

glen *NOUN* **glens** a narrow valley, especially in Scotland [from Scottish Gaelic or Irish]

glib *ADJECTIVE* speaking or writing readily but not sincerely or thoughtfully
▷ **glibly** *ADVERB* **glibness** *NOUN*

glide *VERB* **glides**, **gliding**, **glided** **1** move along smoothly **2** fly without using an engine **3** birds glide when they fly without beating their wings
▷ **glide** *NOUN*

Thesaurus

give up *Don't give up now.* ► quit, stop, concede defeat, admit defeat, resign, despair

glad *ADJECTIVE* **1** *I am glad you came.* ► pleased, happy, delighted, thrilled, overjoyed **2** *They were glad to help.* ► pleased, willing, eager, keen

glamorous *ADJECTIVE* **1** *a glamorous woman* ► beautiful, elegant, captivating, alluring, gorgeous, smart, lovely, entrancing, stylish, fashionable USAGE Be careful when you use *smart*, because it has another important meaning. **2** *a glamorous lifestyle* ► exciting, colourful, dazzling, glittering, alluring, smart

glamour *NOUN* **1** *She offered that extra bit of glamour.* ► beauty, attractiveness, elegance, style, charm, seductiveness **2** *the glamour of living in a big city* ► appeal, excitement, attraction, allure, glitter, lustre, magic

glance *VERB* **1** *She glanced at her watch.* ► look, peek, peep, take a look at **2** **glance at** *or* **through** *I only had time to glance at the article.* ► scan, skim, read quickly, run your eye over

glance *NOUN* *He gave us a quick glance.* ► look, peek, peep, glimpse

glare *VERB* **1** *She glared at him.* ► stare angrily, glower, scowl, frown **2** *The lights of oncoming cars glared in the darkness.* ► dazzle, blaze, be blinding, flare, beam

glare *NOUN* **1** *an angry glare* ► stare, scowl, glower, frown, black look **2** *the glare of the lights* ► dazzle, shine, blaze, brilliance, beam, flare

glaring *ADJECTIVE* *a glaring error* ► obvious, conspicuous, blatant, flagrant, patent, plain, overt, inescapable

gleam *VERB* *The brass door knob gleamed in the moonlight.* ► glimmer, glint, glow, shine, flash, glisten, glitter, sparkle, shimmer

gleam *NOUN* *the gleam of lights in the distance* ► glimmer, glint, glow, glitter, sparkle, shimmer

glide *VERB* **1** *A boat glided past.* ► slide, move smoothly, slip, sail, coast, skim **2** *The gulls were*

glider *NOUN* **gliders** an aircraft without an engine that flies by floating on warm air currents called thermals

glimmer *NOUN* **glimmers** **1** a faint light **2** a small sign or trace of something • *a glimmer of hope*

glimmer *VERB* **glimmers, glimmering, glimmered** shine with a faint, flickering light

glimpse *NOUN* **glimpses** a brief view

glimpse *VERB* **glimpses, glimpsing, glimpsed** see something briefly

glint *NOUN* **glints** a very brief flash of light

glint *VERB* **glints, glinting, glinted** shine with a flash of light

glisten (glis- en) *VERB* **glistens, glistening, glistened** shine like something wet or oily

glitter *VERB* **glitters, glittering, glittered** shine with tiny flashes of light; sparkle

glitter *NOUN* tiny sparkling pieces used for decoration

gloat *VERB* **gloats, gloating, gloated** be pleased in an unkind way that you have succeeded or that someone else has been hurt or upset

global *ADJECTIVE* **1** to do with the whole world; worldwide **2** to do with the whole of a system ▷ **globally** *ADVERB*

global warming *NOUN* the increase in the temperature of the earth's atmosphere, caused by the greenhouse effect

globe *NOUN* **globes** **1** something shaped like a ball, especially one with a map of the whole world on it **2** the world • *She has travelled all over the globe* **3** a hollow round glass object

gloom *NOUN* **1** darkness **2** sadness or despair

gloomy *ADJECTIVE* **gloomier, gloomiest** **1** almost dark **2** depressed or depressing ▷ **gloomily** *ADVERB* **gloominess** *NOUN*

glorify *VERB* **glorifies, glorifying, glorified** **1** give great praise or great honour to **2** make a thing seem more splendid or attractive than it really is • *It is a film that glorifies war.* ▷ **glorification** *NOUN*

glorious *ADJECTIVE* splendid or magnificent ▷ **gloriously** *ADVERB*

glory *NOUN* **glories** **1** fame and honour **2** praise **3** beauty or magnificence

glory *VERB* **glories, glorying, gloried** rejoice; pride yourself • *They gloried in victory.*

Thesaurus

gliding overhead. ▶ drift, soar, wheel, hover, sail, float, fly

glimmer *VERB* *The moonlight glimmered on the great sweep of lawn.* ▶ gleam, glint, glow, shine, flash, glisten, glitter, sparkle, shimmer, twinkle

glimmer *NOUN* *There was a faint glimmer in his eyes.* ▶ gleam, glint, glow, glitter, sparkle, shimmer, twinkle

glimpse *VERB* *I glimpsed Auntie sitting on the bottom stair.* ▶ spot, spy, catch sight of, make out

glimpse *NOUN* *I caught a quick glimpse of the house.* ▶ glance, peep, look, sight, sighting, view, (*more informal*) squint

glint *VERB* *Her blue eyes glinted like ice.* ▶ gleam, glow, shine, flash, glisten, glitter, sparkle, shimmer

glint *NOUN* *a glint in the mirror* ▶ gleam, glimmer, glow, glitter, sparkle, shimmer

global *ADJECTIVE* **1** *global communications* ▶ worldwide, international, world, intercontinental, universal **2** *a global solution to the problem* ▶ total, comprehensive, general, all-inclusive, wide-ranging

globe *NOUN* **1** *people from all over the globe* ▶ world, earth, planet **2** *the shape of a globe* ▶ ball, orb, sphere, round

gloom *NOUN* **1** *They peered out into the gloom.* ▶ darkness, dimness, semi-darkness, murk, murkiness, shade, shadow, twilight, cloudiness, dullness, dusk, obscurity **2** *Her feeling of gloom lifted.* ▶ depression, dejection, despondency, low spirits, melancholy

gloomy *ADJECTIVE* **1** *They walked through the front door into a gloomy hall.* ▶ dark, dingy, dim, dismal, dreary, dull, shadowy, sombre, cheerless AN OPPOSITE IS bright **2** *a gloomy expression* ▶ miserable, downcast, downhearted, dejected, dispirited, glum, unhappy OPPOSITES ARE cheerful, happy **3** *a gloomy outlook for the economy* ▶ pessimistic, unfavourable, unpromising, depressing, bleak, downbeat OPPOSITES ARE optimistic, upbeat

glorious *ADJECTIVE* **1** *a glorious victory* ▶ magnificent, splendid, illustrious, celebrated, acclaimed, distinguished, renowned, great **2** *a glorious view across the hills* ▶ wonderful, spectacular, magnificent, superb, beautiful, stunning

glory *NOUN* **1** *the glory of competing for your country; successes that bring much glory* ▶ distinction, honour, renown, prestige, kudos, fame, credit, triumph, success **2** *glory to God* ▶ adoration, homage, praise, thanksgiving, veneration, worship **3** *the glories of New England in the autumn* ▶ beauty,

A B C D E F G H I J K L M N O P Q R S T U V W X Y Z

gloss [1] *NOUN* **glosses** the shine on a smooth surface

gloss *VERB* **glosses, glossing, glossed** make a thing glossy

gloss [2] *VERB* **glosses, glossing, glossed**
gloss over mention a fault or mistake etc. only briefly to make it seem less serious than it really is

glossary *NOUN* **glossaries** a list of difficult words with their meanings explained

glossy *ADJECTIVE* **glossier, glossiest** smooth and shiny
▷ **glossily** *ADVERB* **glossiness** *NOUN*

glove *NOUN* **gloves** a covering for the hand, usually with separate divisions for each finger and thumb
▷ **gloved** *ADJECTIVE*

glow *NOUN* **1** brightness and warmth without flames **2** a warm or cheerful feeling • *We felt a glow of pride*

glow *VERB* **glows, glowing, glowed** shine with a soft, warm light

glue *NOUN* **glues** a sticky substance used for joining things together
▷ **gluey** *ADJECTIVE*

glue *VERB* **glues, gluing, glued** **1** stick with glue **2** attach or hold closely • *His ear was glued to the keyhole*

glum *ADJECTIVE* miserable or depressed
▷ **glumly** *ADVERB* **glumness** *NOUN*

glut *NOUN* **gluts** an excessive supply

glutinous (gloo- tin- us) *ADJECTIVE* glue-like or sticky

glutton *NOUN* **gluttons** a person who eats too much
▷ **gluttonous** *ADJECTIVE* **gluttony** *NOUN*
glutton for punishment a person who seems to enjoy doing something difficult or unpleasant

gm *ABBREVIATION* gram

GMT *ABBREVIATION* Greenwich Mean Time

gnarled (narld) *ADJECTIVE* twisted and knobbly, like an old tree

gnash (nash) *VERB* **gnashes, gnashing, gnashed** grind your teeth together

gnat (nat) *NOUN* **gnats** a tiny fly that bites

gnaw (naw) *VERB* **gnaws, gnawing, gnawed** keep on biting something hard so that it wears away

gnome (nohm) *NOUN* **gnomes** a kind of dwarf in fairy tales, usually living underground

GNVQ *ABBREVIATION* General National Vocational Qualification

go *VERB* **goes, going, went, gone** This word has many uses, including: **1** move from one place to another • *Where are you going?* **2** leave • *I must go.* **3** lead from one place to another • *The road goes to Bristol.* **4** become • *The milk has gone sour.* **5** make a sound • *The gun went bang.* **6** belong in some place or position • *Plates go*

Thesaurus

magnificence, grandeur, majesty, radiance, splendour

gloss *NOUN* *The new paint has a fine gloss.*
► shine, sheen, brightness, brilliance, lustre, burnish, polish

glossy *ADJECTIVE* *a glossy tiled floor* ► bright, burnished, glassy, glazed, gleaming, lustrous, polished, reflective, shiny, silky, sleek, smooth
AN OPPOSITE IS dull

glow *VERB* **1** *Lights glowed from the windows.*
► shine, gleam, glimmer, flicker, flare **2** *She glowed with pleasure at having said the right thing.* ► shine, flush, blush, colour, redden

glow *NOUN* **1** *the glow of the street lights* ► shine, gleam, glimmer, radiance, luminosity, brilliance **2** *There was a distinct glow in her cheeks.* ► flush, blush, rosiness, pinkness, warmth **3** *We felt a glow of excitement.*
► ardour, fervour, enthusiasm, feeling, intensity, passion

glowing *ADJECTIVE* **1** *glowing street lights*
► bright, shining, luminous, radiant **2** *glowing cheeks* ► bright, rosy, red, pink, blushing, flushed **3** *a glowing report* ► complimentary, enthusiastic, highly favourable, fervent, admiring, eulogistic, ecstatic

glue *NOUN* *a tube of glue* ► adhesive, paste, gum, fixative, sealant, cement

glue *VERB* *Glue the pieces together.* ► fix, stick, fasten, affix, paste, cement, bond, gum, seal

glum *ADJECTIVE* *Tony looked glum.* ► miserable, downcast, downhearted, dejected, dispirited, gloomy, unhappy OPPOSITES ARE cheerful, happy

go *VERB* **1** *She started to go towards the entrance.*
► move, advance, proceed, walk, make your way, progress **2** *We are going to London on Friday.* ► travel, journey, make a trip **3** *Several of the guests had already gone.* ► leave, depart, go away, withdraw, make off, (*more informal*) clear off **4** *My purse had gone.* ► disappear, vanish, be taken, be stolen **5** *The path goes to the village.* ► lead, take you, continue, extend, stretch **6** *All the money goes to charity.* ► be given, be donated, be granted, be presented **7** *All our money has gone.* ► be used up, be spent, be exhausted **8** *His hair had gone grey.*
► turn, become, grow **9** *I hope things go well for them.* ► work out, turn out, develop **10** *The coat and hat don't go.* ► match, harmonize, blend, suit one another **11** *The car won't go.*
► start, work, function, operate, run **12** *Where*

on that shelf. **7** be sold • *The house went very cheaply.*
go off **1** explode **2** become stale or decayed **3** stop liking something
go on continue
go out stop burning or shining
go through experience something unpleasant or difficult

go *NOUN* **goes** **1** a turn or try • *May I have a go?* **2** (*informal*) energy or liveliness • *She is full of go.*
make a go of make a success of something
on the go active; always working or moving

goad *NOUN* **goads** a stick with a pointed end for prodding cattle to move onwards

goad *VERB* **goads, goading, goaded** stir into action by being annoying • *He goaded me into fighting.*

goal *NOUN* **goals** **1** the place where a ball must go to score a point in football, hockey, etc. **2** a point scored in this way **3** something that you are trying to reach or achieve

goalkeeper *NOUN* **goalkeepers** the player who stands in the goal to try and keep the ball from entering

goat *NOUN* **goats** a mammal with horns and a beard, closely related to the sheep. Domestic goats are kept for their milk [from Old English]

gobble *VERB* **gobbles, gobbling, gobbled** eat quickly and greedily [from early French *gober* = to swallow]

go-between *NOUN* **go-betweens** a person who acts as a messenger or negotiator between others

God *NOUN* the creator of the universe in Christian, Jewish, and Muslim belief

god *NOUN* **gods** a male being that is worshipped • *Mars was a Roman god.*

godchild *NOUN* **godchildren** a child that has a godparent
▷ **god-daughter** *NOUN* **godson** *NOUN*

goddess *NOUN* **goddesses** a female being that is worshipped

godparent *NOUN* **godparents** a person at a child's christening who promises to see that the child has a religious education
▷ **godfather** *NOUN* **godmother** *NOUN*

godsend *NOUN* **godsends** a piece of unexpected good luck

goggle *VERB* **goggles, goggling, goggled** stare with wide open eyes

going *present participle* of **go**
be going to do something be ready or likely to do it

gold *NOUN* **golds** **1** a precious yellow metal **2** a deep yellow colour **3** a gold medal, awarded as first prize
▷ **gold** *ADJECTIVE*

golden *ADJECTIVE* **1** made of gold **2** coloured like gold **3** precious or excellent • *a golden opportunity*

Thesaurus

do these books go? ► belong, be placed, be kept, have a place **13** *Has the bell gone?* ► sound, ring, chime, peal **14** *The time will go quickly.* ► pass, go by, elapse, lapse
go ahead *The plan will go ahead.* ► begin, proceed, continue, take place
go away *She wanted them all to go away.* ► leave, depart, (*more informal*) clear off
go back *I'll have to go back and look for it.* ► return, turn round
go down *Prices are expected to go down.* ► fall, drop, decrease, get lower
go for **1** *Which one will you go for?* ► choose, take, favour, prefer **2** *He went for her with a hammer.* ► attack, assault, set on, lunge at
go in for *We are going in for a competition.* ► enter, take part in, participate in
go into *The lawyers will go into it in detail.* ► discuss, consider, think about, investigate, probe, delve into, review
go off **1** *A bomb went off.* ► explode, detonate, blow up **2** *The milk's gone off.* ► go bad, go sour, turn
go on **1** *The programme went on for over two hours.* ► continue, extend, carry on, run **2** *She went on about how lucky we were.* ► chatter, witter, ramble, (*more informal*) rabbit
go over *Shall we go over the figures?* ► study, check, review, examine, analyse, scrutinize, investigate
go through *It's hard to comprehend what they must have gone through.* ► suffer, experience, undergo, endure, withstand
go with **1** *Will you go with them?* ► accompany, escort **2** *I'm not sure this tie goes with my shirt.* ► match, suit, harmonize with, blend with

goal *NOUN* *The overall goal is to promote the use of good English.* ► aim, objective, object, ambition, intention, purpose, target, aspiration, design, end

gobble *VERB* *He stopped talking to gobble his food.* ► guzzle, devour, bolt, gulp, eat

god or **goddess** *NOUN* *the gods and goddesses of ancient Olympus* ► deity, divinity, divine being, immortal RELATED ADJECTIVE divine

golden *ADJECTIVE* **1** *a golden carriage* ► gilt, gilded **2** *golden hair* ► blond, blonde, yellow **3** *a golden opportunity* ► excellent, unique, special, promising, auspicious, propitious

A B C D E F G H I J K L M N O P Q R S T U V W X Y Z

golden wedding *NOUN* **golden weddings** a couple's fiftieth wedding anniversary

goldfish *NOUN* **goldfish** a small red or orange fish, often kept as a pet

golf *NOUN* an outdoor game played by hitting a small white ball with a club into a series of holes on a specially prepared ground (a **golf course** or **golf links**) and taking as few strokes as possible
▷ **golfer** *NOUN* **golfing** *NOUN*

gong *NOUN* **gongs** a large metal disc that makes an echoing sound when it is hit

good *ADJECTIVE* **better, best** **1** having the right qualities; of the kind that people like • *a good book* **2** kind • *It was good of you to help us.* **3** well behaved • *Be a good boy.* **4** skilled or talented • *a good pianist* **5** healthy; giving benefit • *Exercise is good for you.* **6** thorough • *Give it a good clean.* **7** large; considerable • *It's a good distance from the shops.*

good *NOUN* **1** something good • *Do good to others.* **2** benefit • *It's for your own good.*
for good for ever
no good useless
USAGE In standard English, **good** cannot be used as an adverb. You can say *She's a good player* but not *She played good.* The adverb that goes with **good** is **well**.

goodbye *INTERJECTION* a word used when you leave somebody or at the end of a phone call

goods *PLURAL NOUN* **1** things that are bought and sold **2** things that are carried on trains or lorries

goose *NOUN* **geese** a long-necked water bird with webbed feet, larger than a duck

gooseberry *NOUN* **gooseberries** **1** a small green fruit that grows on a prickly bush **2** (*informal*) an unwanted extra person

goose pimples or **goosebumps** *PLURAL NOUN* skin that has turned rough with small bumps on it because a person is cold or afraid

Thesaurus

good *ADJECTIVE* **1** *She is basically a good person.* ► virtuous, exemplary, righteous, moral, honest, upright, worthy, trustworthy
OPPOSITES ARE bad, wicked, immoral **2** *Can you recommend a good hotel?* ► fine, high-quality, satisfactory, acceptable, excellent, superb, outstanding AN OPPOSITE IS poor **3** *The children were exceptionally good all evening.* ► well behaved, obedient, well mannered
AN OPPOSITE IS naughty **4** *That would be a good thing to do.* ► proper, right, correct, appropriate, auspicious AN OPPOSITE IS inappropriate **5** *He is not a good swimmer. She has always been good at music.* ► capable, able, proficient, accomplished, talented, skilled
OPPOSITES ARE poor, inept **6** *She was a good friend.* ► true, loyal, close, dear, trusty, reliable, trustworthy, dependable
AN OPPOSITE IS distant **7** *It was a good party.* ► enjoyable, pleasant, agreeable, pleasing **8** *Tom gave the car a good clean.* ► thorough, complete **9** *a good number of people* ► considerable, substantial, appreciable, sizeable, fair, ample **10** *It is good of you to come.* ► kind, generous, considerate, obliging
AN OPPOSITE IS unkind **11** *When is a good time to call?* ► convenient, suitable, appropriate, opportune, fitting OPPOSITES ARE bad, unsuitable **12** *food that is good for you* ► healthy, wholesome, nutritious, nourishing
OPPOSITES ARE bad, unhealthy **13** *a pub that serves good food* ► delicious, appetizing, tasty **14** *There are several good reasons for going.* ► valid, genuine, cogent, real, convincing
AN OPPOSITE IS poor

goodbye *NOUN* *Roddy said goodbye and left us.* ► farewell, (*more informal*) cheerio, (*French*) adieu, (*French*) au revoir, (*Italian*) ciao

good-humoured *ADJECTIVE* *He was patient and good-humoured.* ► genial, affable, cordial, congenial, amiable, easygoing AN OPPOSITE IS ill-humoured

good-looking *ADJECTIVE* *a good-looking woman* ► attractive, handsome, nice-looking, presentable, beautiful, pretty, lovely
AN OPPOSITE IS ugly

good-natured *ADJECTIVE* *He had a blunt good-natured face.* ► kind, kindly, gentle, warm-hearted, amiable, friendly, neighbourly, benevolent AN OPPOSITE IS ill-natured

goodness *NOUN* *There is a lot of goodness in these people, criminals though they are.* ► virtue, good, uprightness, generosity, goodwill, honesty AN OPPOSITE IS wickedness

goods *PLURAL NOUN* **1** *the supply of goods and services* ► merchandise, produce, products, articles, stock **2** *The dead man's goods did not amount to much.* ► property, possessions, effects, chattels

good-tempered *ADJECTIVE* *He remained patient and good-tempered despite the difficulties.* ► calm, placid, equable, unflustered, composed, self-possessed, tranquil
AN OPPOSITE IS bad-tempered

goodwill *NOUN* *People come here full of goodwill and good intentions.* ► kindness, benevolence, generosity, friendliness, consideration
OPPOSITES ARE hostility, ill will

gorge *NOUN* **gorges** a narrow valley with steep sides
gorge *VERB* **gorges, gorging, gorged** eat greedily; stuff with food
gorgeous *ADJECTIVE* magnificent or beautiful
▷ **gorgeously** *ADVERB*
gorilla *NOUN* **gorillas** a large powerful African ape, the largest of all the apes
USAGE Do not confuse with **guerrilla**, which can be pronounced in the same way.
gospel *NOUN*
the Gospels the first four books of the New Testament, telling of the life and teachings of Jesus Christ
gospel music *NOUN* a fervent style of black American religious singing
gossip *VERB* **gossips, gossiping, gossiped** talk a lot about other people
gossip *NOUN* **gossips** **1** talk, especially rumours, about other people **2** a person who enjoys gossiping
▷ **gossipy** *ADJECTIVE*
got *past tense of* **get**
have got possess • *Have you got a car?*
Gothic *NOUN* the style of building common in Europe in the 12th-16th centuries, with pointed arches and much decorative carving
gouge (gowj) *VERB* **gouges, gouging, gouged** scoop or force out by pressing
gourmet (goor- may) *NOUN* **gourmets** a person who understands and appreciates good food and drink
govern *VERB* **governs, governing, governed** be in charge of the public affairs of a country or region
governess *NOUN* **governesses** a woman employed to teach children in a private household
government *NOUN* **governments** **1** the group of people who are in charge of the public affairs of a country **2** the process of governing
▷ **governmental** *ADJECTIVE*
governor *NOUN* **governors** **1** a person who governs a state or a colony etc. **2** a member of the governing body of a school or other institution **3** the person in charge of a prison
gown *NOUN* **gowns** **1** a woman's long dress **2** a loose robe worn by lawyers, members of a university, etc.
GP *ABBREVIATION* general practitioner
grab *VERB* **grabs, grabbing, grabbed** take hold of something firmly or suddenly
grace *NOUN* **1** beauty, especially of movement **2** goodwill or favour **3** dignity or good manners • *At least he had the grace to apologize.* **4** a short prayer of thanks before or after a meal **5** the title of a duke, duchess, or archbishop • *His Grace the Duke of Kent.*
grace *VERB* **graces, gracing, graced** bring honour or dignity to something • *The mayor himself graced us with his presence.*

Thesaurus

gorgeous *ADJECTIVE* **1** *a gorgeous young woman* ► beautiful, lovely, glamorous, dazzling, pretty, stunning, striking **2** *a gorgeous view* ► magnificent, spectacular, splendid, superb, glorious
gossip *NOUN* **1** *He liked gossip and knew something about everybody.* ► idle talk, tittle-tattle, tattle, prattle, rumour, hearsay, chatter, scandal **2** *The sisters were both dreadful gossips.* ► scandalmonger, gossipmonger, talebearer, busybody, tattler
gossip *VERB* *The landlord was busy gossiping to the other customers.* ► chat, chatter, prattle, spread stories, (*informal*) natter, (*informal*) tattle
govern *VERB* **1** *A coalition was formed to govern the country.* ► run, rule, administer, be in charge of, conduct the affairs of, direct, manage, preside over **2** *the rules that govern the way we treat each other* ► regulate, determine, control, direct, affect, influence, shape
government *NOUN* **1** *The new government takes office next week.* ► administration, executive, regime, ministry **2** *a country that badly needs a period of stable government* ► rule, direction, leadership, management, guidance, regulation
governor *NOUN* **1** *a prison governor* ► administrator, director, principal, superintendent **2** *the governor of a province* ► ruler, overseer, viceroy, commissioner, administrator
grab *VERB* **1** *She grabbed him by his arm.* ► seize, grasp, catch, grip, take hold of, clutch at **2** *Someone grabbed her credit card while she wasn't looking.* ► snatch, steal, take, (*more informal*) nab, (*more informal*) pinch
grace *NOUN* **1** *The dancers moved with considerable grace.* ► elegance, poise, gracefulness, refinement **2** *He conceded the point with good grace.* ► courtesy, civility, decorum, decency, charm, generosity **3** *They did not want to see another president fall from grace.* ► favour, approval, esteem, regard, support **4** *by the grace of the monarch* ► generosity, favour, benevolence, indulgence, goodwill

graceful *ADJECTIVE* beautiful and elegant in movement or shape
▷ **gracefully** *ADVERB* **gracefulness** *NOUN*

gracious *ADJECTIVE* behaving kindly and honourably
▷ **graciously** *ADVERB* **graciousness** *NOUN*

grade *NOUN* **grades** **1** a step in a scale of quality or value or rank **2** a mark showing the quality of a student's work

grade *VERB* **grades**, **grading**, **graded** sort or divide into grades

gradient (gray- dee- ent) *NOUN* **gradients** a slope or the steepness of a slope

gradual *ADJECTIVE* happening slowly but steadily
▷ **gradually** *ADVERB*

graduate (grad- yoo- at) *NOUN* **graduates** a person who has a university or college degree

graduate (grad- yoo- ayt) *VERB* **graduates**, **graduating**, **graduated** be awarded a university or college degree

graffiti *NOUN* words or drawings scribbled or sprayed on a wall
USAGE Strictly speaking, this word is a plural noun (the singular is **graffito**), so it should be used with a plural verb: *There are graffiti all over the wall*. However, the word is widely used nowadays as if it were a singular noun and most people do not regard this as wrong: *There is graffiti all over the wall.*

graft *NOUN* **grafts** **1** a shoot from one plant or tree fixed into another to form a new growth **2** a piece of living tissue transplanted by a surgeon to replace what is diseased or damaged • *a skin graft*

graft *VERB* **grafts**, **grafting**, **grafted** insert or transplant as a graft

grain *NOUN* **grains** **1** a small hard seed or similar particle **2** cereal plants when they are growing or after being harvested **3** a very small amount • *a grain of truth* **4** the pattern of lines made by the fibres in a piece of wood or paper
▷ **grainy** *ADJECTIVE*

gram *NOUN* **grams** a unit of mass or weight in the metric system

grammar *NOUN* **grammars** **1** the rules for using words correctly **2** a book about these rules
▷ **grammatical** *ADJECTIVE*

grammar school *NOUN* **grammar schools** a secondary school for children with academic ability

grand *ADJECTIVE* **1** splendid and impressive **2** most important or highest-ranking **3** including everything; complete
▷ **grandly** *ADVERB* **grandness** *NOUN*

grandchild *NOUN* **grandchildren** the child of a person's son or daughter
▷ **granddaughter** *NOUN* **grandson** *NOUN*

grandeur (grand- yer) *NOUN* impressive beauty; splendour

grandfather *NOUN* **grandfathers** the father of a person's father or mother

Thesaurus

graceful *ADJECTIVE* *Mary's clothes were light and graceful.* ► elegant, flowing, stylish, tasteful, smooth, beautiful

grade *NOUN* **1** *She is trying for a higher grade in the exam.* ► mark, score, level, grading, assessment, standard **2** *a hotel in the top grade* ► class, category, classification **3** *officers in the lower grades* ► rank, level, status, echelon, step

grade *VERB* **1** *Eggs are graded according to size.* ► sort, classify, categorize, differentiate, group, range, arrange, rank **2** *An external examiner will grade the coursework.* ► mark, assess, evaluate, rank, rate

gradual *ADJECTIVE* **1** *a gradual change in the weather* ► steady, slow, moderate, progressive, continuous, regular, step-by-step AN OPPOSITE IS sudden **2** *a gradual slope* ► gentle, moderate, slight, easy AN OPPOSITE IS steep

gradually *ADVERB* *The colours fade gradually in the sunlight. Gradually she eased the drawer back in its place.* ► slowly, little by little, steadily, gently, cautiously, progressively, imperceptibly

grain *NOUN* **1** *a good grain harvest* ► corn, cereal, seed **2** *grains of sand* ► granule, particle, speck, crumb, fragment **3** *not a grain of truth in the story* ► trace, hint, ounce, scrap **4** *wood with a strong grain* ► texture, marking, surface, pattern

grand *ADJECTIVE* **1** *a grand palace* ► magnificent, splendid, majestic, glorious, stately, imposing **2** *a grand old lady* ► distinguished, illustrious, august, eminent, prominent, celebrated **3** (*informal*) *They are doing a grand job.* ► excellent, very good, fine, splendid, first-class, first-rate

grandeur *NOUN* *the grandeur of the royal ceremonies* ► splendour, magnificence, glory, resplendence, stateliness

grandiose (grand- ee- ohss) *ADJECTIVE* large and impressive; trying to seem impressive

grandmother *NOUN* **grandmothers** the mother of a person's father or mother

grandparent *NOUN* **grandparents** a grandfather or grandmother

grand piano *NOUN* **grand pianos** a large piano with the strings fixed horizontally

grandstand *NOUN* **grandstands** a building with a roof and rows of seats for spectators at a racecourse or sports ground

grand total *NOUN* the sum of other totals

granite *NOUN* a very hard kind of rock used for building

grant *VERB* **grants, granting, granted** **1** give or allow someone what they have asked for • *We have decided to grant your request.* **2** admit; agree that something is true
take for granted assume that something is true or will happen

grant *NOUN* **grants** something granted, especially a sum of money

Granth (grunt) *NOUN* the sacred scriptures of the Sikhs

grape *NOUN* **grapes** a small green or purple berry that grows in bunches on a vine. Grapes are used to make wine

grapefruit *NOUN* **grapefruit** a large round yellow citrus fruit

grapevine *NOUN* **grapevines** **1** a vine on which grapes grow **2** a way by which news spreads unofficially, with people passing it on from one to another

graph *NOUN* **graphs** a diagram showing how two quantities or variables are related

graphic *ADJECTIVE* **1** to do with drawing or painting • *a graphic artist* **2** giving a lively description
▷ **graphically** *ADVERB*

grapple *VERB* **grapples, grappling, grappled** **1** struggle or wrestle **2** seize or hold firmly **3** try to deal with a problem etc. • *I've been grappling with this essay all day.*

grasp *VERB* **grasps, grasping, grasped** **1** seize and hold firmly **2** understand

grasp *NOUN* **1** a person's understanding of something • *a good grasp of electronics* **2** a firm hold

grasping *ADJECTIVE* greedy for money or possessions

grass *NOUN* **grasses** **1** a plant with green blades and stalks **2** ground covered with grass; lawn
▷ **grassy** *ADJECTIVE*

grasshopper *NOUN* **grasshoppers** a jumping insect that makes a shrill noise

grass roots *PLURAL NOUN* the ordinary people in a political party or other group

grate [1] *NOUN* **grates** **1** a metal framework that keeps fuel in a fireplace **2** a fireplace

grate [2] *VERB* **grates, grating, grated** **1** shred something into small pieces by rubbing it on a rough surface **2** make an unpleasant noise by

Thesaurus

grant *VERB* **1** *The award body can grant you a scholarship.* ► give, award, allow, confer on you, pay, provide you with **2** *The court granted her request.* ► allow, consent to, accede to, permit **3** *We grant that the difference is small.* ► admit, concede, acknowledge, agree, accept, confess

grant *NOUN* **1** *They were given a local authority grant to repair their roof.* ► award, allowance, subsidy, subvention, endowment, contribution, donation, allocation **2** *a student grant* ► bursary, scholarship, sponsorship, loan

graph *NOUN* *a graph showing the rise in house prices* ► table, chart, diagram, grid, pie chart, column graph

graphic *ADJECTIVE* *a graphic description of the accident* ► vivid, explicit, striking, forceful, dramatic, lurid, detailed, colourful
AN OPPOSITE IS vague

grapple *VERB* **1** *They grappled for the gun on the wet grass.* ► struggle, wrestle, tussle, scuffle, brawl, fight **2** **grapple with** *The Prime Minister has a major problem to grapple with.* ► contend with, tackle, attend to, cope with, deal with, manage, handle, come to grips with, engage with, get involved with, try to solve, (*more informal*) have a go at AN OPPOSITE IS avoid

grasp *VERB* **1** *He got up and grasped her hand.* ► grip, clasp, clutch, grab, seize, catch, snatch, hold, get hold of, hang on to **2** *He got impatient if they failed to grasp a point.* ► understand, comprehend, follow, take in, apprehend, perceive, master, learn, realize, (*more informal*) cotton on to

grasp *NOUN* **1** *She managed to escape his grasp.* ► grip, hold, clutch, embrace, control **2** *His ultimate goal was within his grasp.* ► reach, power, command **3** *They now have a good grasp of the subject.* ► understanding, comprehension, perception, mastery, familiarity (with)

grass *NOUN* *A notice told them to keep off the grass.* ► lawn, turf, green

grate *VERB* **1** *She started to grate some cheese.* ► shred, grind, cut up, mince **2** *His whining voice began to grate.* ► irritate, jar, rankle, be irksome

rubbing **3** sound harshly
grate on have an irritating effect

grateful ADJECTIVE feeling or showing that you are thankful for something that has been done for you
▷ **gratefully** ADVERB

gratify VERB **gratifies, gratifying, gratified** **1** give pleasure **2** satisfy a feeling or desire • *May we gratify our curiosity and have a look?*
▷ **gratification** NOUN

grating NOUN **gratings** a framework of metal bars placed across an opening

gratitude NOUN being grateful

grave[1] NOUN **graves** the place where a dead body is buried

grave[2] ADJECTIVE serious or solemn
▷ **gravely** ADVERB

grave accent (rhymes with *starve*) NOUN **grave accents** a backward-sloping mark over a vowel, as in *vis-à-vis*

gravel NOUN small stones mixed with coarse sand, used to make paths
▷ **gravelled** ADJECTIVE **gravelly** ADJECTIVE

graveyard NOUN **graveyards** a burial ground

gravity NOUN **1** the force that pulls all objects in the universe towards each other **2** the force that pulls everything towards the earth **3** seriousness

gravy NOUN a hot brown sauce made from meat juices

graze VERB **grazes, grazing, grazed** **1** feed on growing grass **2** scrape your skin slightly • *I grazed my elbow on the wall.* **3** touch something lightly in passing

graze NOUN **grazes** a raw place where skin has been scraped

grease NOUN **1** any thick oily substance **2** melted fat
▷ **greasy** ADJECTIVE

grease VERB **greases, greasing, greased** put grease on something

great ADJECTIVE **1** very large; much above average **2** very important or talented • *a great composer* **3** (*informal*) very good or enjoyable • *It's great to see you again.* **4** older or younger by one generation • *great-grandfather*
▷ **greatly** ADVERB **greatness** NOUN

greed NOUN being greedy

Thesaurus

grateful ADJECTIVE *The families are grateful for all the support they have received.* ► thankful, appreciative (of), indebted, obliged
AN OPPOSITE IS ungrateful

gratitude NOUN *His letter expressed gratitude for the help he had been given.* ► thanks, appreciation (of), acknowledgement (of), indebtedness

grave ADJECTIVE **1** *a grave error; grave matters* ► serious, important, significant, crucial, critical, momentous, vital, acute, weighty AN OPPOSITE IS unimportant **2** *a grave offence* ► criminal, indictable, punishable AN OPPOSITE IS minor **3** *a grave expression* ► serious, solemn, sombre, earnest, severe, subdued, dignified, gloomy, thoughtful, unsmiling, grim, long-faced AN OPPOSITE IS happy

gravity NOUN **1** *the gravity of the situation* ► seriousness, severity, acuteness, magnitude, momentousness, danger, importance **2** *the gravity of his manner* ► solemnity, dignity, sobriety, earnestness, ceremony, pomp, sedateness **3** *the force of gravity* ► gravitation, pull, weight, heaviness, downward force

graze VERB **1** *She fell and grazed her knee.* ► scrape, cut, scratch, scuff, abrade **2** *Cattle grazed in the fields.* ► feed, browse, crop, ruminate, pasture

graze NOUN *a graze on his elbow* ► cut, abrasion, laceration, raw spot

greasy ADJECTIVE **1** *She had greasy hair and worried about her weight.* ► oily, shiny, waxy AN OPPOSITE IS dry **2** *His hand left greasy fingerprints on the glass.* ► fatty, oily, smeary, slimy, buttery

great ADJECTIVE **1** *A great hill rose before them.* ► large, huge, big, enormous, gigantic, massive, colossal AN OPPOSITE IS small **2** *Speaking a foreign language is a great advantage. She is a person of great courage.* ► considerable, special, much, extreme OPPOSITES ARE small, little **3** *He read through the list of great statesmen.* ► famous, eminent, celebrated, distinguished, honoured, renowned, acclaimed, prominent, revered, exalted, illustrious OPPOSITES ARE unknown, obscure **4** *The invasion proved a great mistake; a talk on the great advances in medicine* ► important, significant, crucial, critical, big, vital OPPOSITES ARE insignificant, unimportant **5** (*informal*) *We went to a great party.* ► excellent, enjoyable, marvellous, wonderful, fantastic, first-rate AN OPPOSITE IS poor

greed NOUN **1** *I ate my supper with undisguised greed.* ► hunger, gluttony, ravenousness, overeating, over-indulgence **2** *Material greed is not one of their faults.* ► avarice, acquisitiveness, covetousness, rapacity, cupidity, craving, desire, selfishness **3** *He was clearly motivated by a greed for power.* ► appetite, desire, urge, need, lust, longing, craving

greedy *ADJECTIVE* **greedier, greediest** wanting more food, money, or other things than you need
▷ **greedily** *ADVERB* **greediness** *NOUN*

green *NOUN* **greens** **1** the colour of grass, leaves, etc. **2** an area of grassy land • *the village green* • *a putting green*

green *ADJECTIVE* **1** of the colour green **2** concerned with protecting the natural environment **3** inexperienced and likely to make mistakes
▷ **greenness** *NOUN*

green belt *NOUN* **green belts** an area kept as open land round a city

greenery *NOUN* green leaves or plants

greengrocer *NOUN* **greengrocers** a person who keeps a shop that sells fruit and vegetables
▷ **greengrocery** *NOUN*

greenhouse *NOUN* **greenhouses** a glass building where plants are protected from cold

greenhouse effect *NOUN* the warming of the earth's surface when heat from the sun is trapped in the earth's atmosphere by gases such as carbon dioxide and methane

greens *PLURAL NOUN* green vegetables, such as cabbage and spinach

Greenwich Mean Time (gren- ich) *NOUN* the time on the line of longitude which passes through Greenwich in London, used as a basis for calculating time throughout the world

greet *VERB* **greets, greeting, greeted** **1** speak to a person who arrives **2** receive • *They greeted the song with applause.* **3** present itself to • *A strange sight greeted our eyes.*

greeting *NOUN* **greetings** words or actions used to greet somebody

grey *NOUN* **greys** the colour between black and white, like ashes or dark clouds
▷ **grey** *ADJECTIVE* **greyness** *NOUN*

greyhound *NOUN* **greyhounds** a slender dog with smooth hair, used in racing

grid *NOUN* **grids** **1** a framework or pattern of bars or lines crossing each other **2** a network of cables or wires for carrying electricity over a large area

grid reference *NOUN* **grid references** a set of numbers that allows you to describe the exact position of something on a map

grief *NOUN* deep sorrow, especially at a person's death
come to grief suffer a disaster

grievance *NOUN* **grievances** something that people are discontented about

grieve *VERB* **grieves, grieving, grieved** **1** feel deep sorrow, especially at a person's death **2** make a person feel very sad

grill *NOUN* **grills** **1** a heated element on a cooker, for sending heat downwards **2** food cooked under this **3** a grille

grill *VERB* **grills, grilling, grilled** **1** cook under a grill **2** question closely and severely • *The police grilled him for an hour.*

Thesaurus

greedy *ADJECTIVE* **1** *a greedy eater* ► gluttonous, ravenous, voracious, insatiable **2** *greedy for money* ► avaricious, covetous, acquisitive, mercenary, grasping **3** *greedy for power* ► eager, avid, longing, craving, (*more informal*) itching

green *ADJECTIVE* **1** *a green garden* ► leafy, grassy, verdant OPPOSITES ARE barren, bare **2** *green with envy* ► envious, covetous, jealous, resentful **3** *a green recruit* ► inexperienced, raw, naive, innocent, immature, untried, credulous, gullible OPPOSITES ARE experienced, worldly-wise **4** *green issues* ► environmental, ecological, conservationist

greet *VERB* *She greeted her visitors one by one.* ► welcome, say hello to, acknowledge, receive, give a greeting to, hail, salute

greeting *NOUN* **1** *She called out a greeting.* ► hello, salutation, welcome **2** **greetings** *birthday greetings* ► good wishes, best wishes, congratulations, compliments

gregarious *ADJECTIVE* *He is cheerful, hard-working, and gregarious.* ► sociable, outgoing, extrovert, friendly, convivial, companionable, affable

grey *ADJECTIVE* **1** *His grey beard had grown very long.* ► silver, silvery, slate-grey, whitish, greying, grizzled, grizzly, hoary **2** *Her face was grey with worry.* ► pale, ashen, leaden, wan, sallow, pasty, drawn **3** *The day began grey and dull.* ► cloudy, overcast, gloomy, dismal, dreary, bleak

grid *NOUN* **1** *He had broken the stone to which the iron grid was fixed.* ► grating, grille, lattice, mesh, framework **2** *The information is shown in the form of a grid.* ► graph, matrix, network

grief *NOUN* *His letters made her grief for her mother more bearable.* ► sadness, sorrow, mourning, bereavement, unhappiness, distress, misery, affliction, desolation
AN OPPOSITE IS joy

grieve *VERB* **1** *She grieved for her mother constantly.* ► mourn, sorrow, lament, weep, cry **2** *They were deeply grieved by the unkind newspaper reports.* ► hurt, wound, upset, sadden, distress

A B C D E F **G** H I J K L M N O P Q R S T U V W X Y Z

grim *ADJECTIVE* **grimmer**, **grimmest** **1** stern or severe **2** unpleasant or unattractive • *a grim prospect*
▷ **grimly** *ADVERB* **grimness** *NOUN*

grimace (grim- ayss, grim- as) *NOUN* **grimaces** a twisted expression on the face made in pain or disgust

grimace *VERB* **grimaces**, **grimacing**, **grimaced** make a grimace

grime *NOUN* dirt in a layer on a surface or on the skin
▷ **grimy** *ADJECTIVE*

grin *NOUN* **grins** a broad smile showing your teeth

grin *VERB* **grins**, **grinning**, **grinned** smile broadly showing your teeth

grind *VERB* **grinds**, **grinding**, **ground** **1** crush something into tiny pieces or powder **2** sharpen or smooth something by rubbing it on a rough surface **3** rub harshly together • *He ground his teeth in fury.*
▷ **grinder** *NOUN*
grind to a halt stop suddenly with a loud noise

grip *VERB* **grips**, **gripping**, **gripped** **1** hold something firmly **2** hold a person's attention • *The opening chapter really gripped me.*

grip *NOUN* **grips** **1** a firm hold **2** a handle, especially on a sports racket, bat, etc. **3** a travelling bag **4** control or power • *The country is in the grip of lottery fever.*
get to grips with begin to deal with successfully

gristle *NOUN* tough rubbery tissue in meat
▷ **gristly** *ADJECTIVE*

grit *NOUN* **1** tiny pieces of stone or sand **2** courage and endurance
▷ **gritty** *ADJECTIVE* **grittiness** *NOUN*

grit *VERB* **grits**, **gritting**, **gritted** **1** spread a road or path with grit **2** clench your teeth when in pain or trouble

grizzled *ADJECTIVE* streaked with grey hairs

grizzly bear *NOUN* **grizzly bears** a large fierce bear of North America

groan *VERB* **groans**, **groaning**, **groaned** **1** make a long deep sound in pain, distress, or disapproval **2** creak loudly under a heavy load
▷ **groan** *NOUN* **groaner** *NOUN*

grocer *NOUN* **grocers** a person who keeps a shop that sells food and household goods

groceries *PLURAL NOUN* goods sold by a grocer

groom *NOUN* **grooms** **1** a person whose job is to look after horses **2** a bridegroom

groom *VERB* **grooms**, **grooming**, **groomed** **1** clean and brush a horse or other animal **2** make something neat and trim **3** train a person for a certain job or position • *Evans is being groomed for the captaincy.*

groove *NOUN* **grooves** a long narrow furrow or channel cut in the surface of something
▷ **grooved** *ADJECTIVE*

grope *VERB* **gropes**, **groping**, **groped** feel about for something you cannot see

gross (grohss) *ADJECTIVE* **1** fat and ugly **2** very obvious or shocking • *gross stupidity* **3** having bad manners; vulgar **4** (*informal*) disgusting **5** total; without anything being deducted • *our gross income* (Compare **net** [2])
▷ **grossly** *ADVERB* **grossness** *NOUN*

Thesaurus

grim *ADJECTIVE* **1** *His face bore a grim expression.* ► stern, severe, harsh, dour, forbidding, sullen, morose, gloomy OPPOSITES ARE cheerful, pleasant **2** *the grim knowledge that she might die* ► unpleasant, dreadful, terrible, grisly, gruesome, macabre, distressing, fearsome, horrid, shocking **3** *a grim little mining town* ► dreary, bleak, dismal, gloomy, dingy

grimy *ADJECTIVE* *The other office was dark and grimy.* ► dirty, grubby, filthy, messy, smutty, soiled

grin *VERB* *She grinned at us and left the room.* ► smile, beam, smirk

grin *NOUN* *He had a silly grin on his face.* ► smile, smirk

grind *VERB* **1** *He ground the coffee into a fine powder.* ► crush, pound, grate **2** *The kitchen had a wheel for grinding knives.* ► sharpen, whet, hone, file

grip *VERB* **1** *He gripped Helen's hand.* ► grasp, clasp, clutch, grab, seize, catch, snatch, hold, get hold of, hang on to **2** *The story gripped everyone.* ► engross, enthral, absorb, captivate, fascinate, rivet, mesmerize

grip *NOUN* *She kept a firm grip on the back of the chair.* ► hold, grasp, clasp, clutch

groan *VERB* *She heard him groaning in his sleep.* ► moan, cry out, sigh, wail

groan *NOUN* *He let out a weary groan.* ► moan, sigh, cry, wail

groove *NOUN* *The water had worn a groove in the rock.* ► channel, furrow, hollow, rut, indentation, slot, track

gross *ADJECTIVE* **1** *a gross exaggeration* ► extreme, blatant, flagrant, glaring, obvious, conspicuous, sheer, outright **2** *gross indecency* ► coarse, vulgar, crude, obscene, lewd, improper **3** *He looked gross and he knew it.* ► obese, fat, corpulent, overweight, big **4** *gross income* ► total, inclusive, overall, aggregate, whole, full **5** *gross misshapen versions of the human form* ► disgusting, repellent, abhorrent, loathsome, sickening

gross *NOUN* **gross** twelve dozen (144) of something • *ten gross = 1440*

grotesque (groh- tesk) *ADJECTIVE* fantastically ugly or very strangely shaped
▷ **grotesquely** *ADVERB* **grotesqueness** *NOUN* [from Italian *pittura grottesca* = painting like one found in a grotto]

grotto *NOUN* **grottoes** a small pretty cave, especially an artificial one [from Italian]

ground[1] *past tense of* **grind**

ground[2] *NOUN* **grounds** **1** the solid surface of the earth **2** a sports field **3** land of a certain kind • *marshy ground* **4** the amount of a subject that is dealt with • *The course covers a lot of ground*

ground *VERB* **grounds, grounding, grounded** **1** prevent a plane from flying • *All aircraft are grounded because of the fog.* **2** stop a child from going out, as a punishment **3** give a good basic training to someone • *Ground them in the rules of spelling.* **4** base • *This theory is grounded on reliable evidence.*

grounds *PLURAL NOUN* **1** the gardens of a large house **2** solid particles that sink to the bottom • *coffee grounds* **3** reasons • *There are grounds for suspicion.*

group *NOUN* **groups** **1** a number of people, animals, or things that come together or belong together in some way **2** a band of musicians

group *VERB* **groups, grouping, grouped** put together or come together in a group or groups

grouse[1] *NOUN* **grouse** a bird with feathered feet, hunted as game

grouse[2] *VERB* **grouses, grousing, groused** (*informal*) grumble or complain
▷ **grouse** *NOUN* **grouser** *NOUN*

grove *NOUN* **groves** a group of trees; a small wood

grovel *VERB* **grovels, grovelling, grovelled** **1** crawl on the ground, especially in a show of fear or humility **2** act in an excessively humble way, for example by apologizing a lot
▷ **groveller** *NOUN*

grow *VERB* **grows, growing, grew, grown** **1** become bigger or greater **2** develop **3** cultivate; plant and look after • *She grows roses.* **4** become • *He grew rich.*
▷ **grower** *NOUN*
grow up become an adult

growl *VERB* **growls, growling, growled** make a deep angry sound in the throat
▷ **growl** *NOUN*

grown-up *NOUN* **grown-ups** an adult person
▷ **grown-up** *ADJECTIVE*

growth *NOUN* **growths** **1** growing or developing **2** something that has grown **3** a lump that has grown on or inside a person's body; a tumour

Thesaurus

ground *NOUN* **1** *The ground was wet and spongy.* ► earth, terrain, soil, turf, loam **2** *The little plane slowly rose from the ground.* ► land, surface **3 grounds** *a large house in its own grounds* ► land, estate, gardens, surroundings

groundless *ADJECTIVE* *Their fears proved to be groundless.* ► baseless, needless, unfounded, unjustified, unwarranted, unsubstantiated, uncalled for, false, gratuitous, imaginary, irrational AN OPPOSITE IS justifiable

group *NOUN* **1** *Divide the children into groups for a game.* ► set, circle, section **2** *The reading group meets once a month.* ► club, circle, society, association **3** *a small group of islands off the north-east coast* ► cluster, collection, formation, bunch, mass, clump **4** *A group of fans waited at the stage door.* ► crowd, band, body, gathering, flock, assembly, gang, pack **5** *They sorted the books into different groups.* ► category, class, type, sort, kind, set

group *VERB* **group together** **1** *Farmers began to group together to form cooperatives.* ► unite, join together, join forces, team up, come together **2** *Comfortable chairs are grouped around coffee tables.* ► arrange, organize, dispose, assemble, collect, cluster **3** *We group the books according to their size.* ► classify, categorize, sort, range, band

grow *VERB* **1** *The baby grew fast.* ► get bigger, get larger, increase in size, fill out, put on growth **2** *Their debts are growing.* ► increase, mount up, multiply AN OPPOSITE IS decrease **3** *She grows roses in her garden.* ► cultivate, produce, propagate, farm **4** *At about 4 o'clock it grows dark.* ► become, turn, come to be **5** *The business was growing.* ► expand, develop, flourish, thrive, prosper, succeed, boom OPPOSITES ARE decline, fail

growl *VERB* *The dog growled at him.* ► snarl, snap, yap

grown-up *ADJECTIVE* *Chris has a grown-up sister.* ► adult, fully grown, mature

grown-up *NOUN* *He wants to be treated like a grown-up.* ► adult, grown person, mature person, grown man *or* woman

growth *NOUN* **1** *a steady growth in population* ► increase, expansion, development OPPOSITES ARE decline, decrease **2** *hormones that aid growth* ► growing, development, maturing **3** *measures to increase economic growth* ► expansion, development, progress, advance AN OPPOSITE IS decline **4** *She has to have*

grub *NOUN* **grubs** **1** a tiny worm-like creature that will become an insect; a larva **2** (*slang*) food

grub *VERB* **grubs, grubbing, grubbed** **1** dig up by the roots **2** turn things over or move them about while looking for something; rummage

grubby *ADJECTIVE* **grubbier, grubbiest** rather dirty
▷ **grubbiness** *NOUN*

grudge *NOUN* **grudges** a feeling of resentment or ill will • *She isn't the sort of person who bears a grudge.*

grudge *VERB* **grudges, grudging, grudged** resent having to give or allow something

gruff *ADJECTIVE* having a rough or unfriendly voice or manner
▷ **gruffly** *ADVERB* **gruffness** *NOUN*

grumble *VERB* **grumbles, grumbling, grumbled** complain in a bad-tempered way
▷ **grumble** *NOUN* **grumbler** *NOUN*

grunt *VERB* **grunts, grunting, grunted** **1** make a pig's gruff snort **2** speak or say gruffly
▷ **grunt** *NOUN*

guarantee *NOUN* **guarantees** a formal promise to do something or to repair something you have sold if it breaks or goes wrong

guarantee *VERB* **guarantees, guaranteeing, guaranteed** **1** give a guarantee; promise **2** make it certain that something will happen • *Money does not guarantee happiness.*
▷ **guarantor** *NOUN*

guard *VERB* **guards, guarding, guarded** **1** protect; keep safe **2** watch over and prevent from escaping
guard against try to prevent something happening

guard *NOUN* **guards** **1** guarding; protection • *Keep the prisoners under close guard.* **2** someone who guards a person or place **3** a group of soldiers or police officers etc. acting as a guard **4** a railway official in charge of a train **5** a protecting device • *a fireguard*
on guard alert for possible danger or difficulty

guardian *NOUN* **guardians** **1** someone who guards **2** a person who is legally in charge of a child whose parents cannot look after him or her
▷ **guardianship** *NOUN*

Thesaurus

a growth removed. ► tumour, lump, swelling, cyst

grub *NOUN* *The fruit was riddled with grubs.* ► larva, maggot, caterpillar

grubby *ADJECTIVE* *He had not yet changed out of his grubby overalls.* ► dirty, filthy, grimy, soiled, messy

grudge *NOUN* *The letter was written by someone with a grudge.* ► grievance, resentment, umbrage, pique, bitterness, rancour, bad feelings

grudge *VERB* *He grudged the money he would have to pay out.* ► resent, begrudge, object to, be angry about

gruelling *ADJECTIVE* *a gruelling journey back from the Himalayas* ► exhausting, arduous, tiring, wearying, exacting, demanding, punishing, hard, taxing, strenuous, laborious, (*more informal*) killing AN OPPOSITE IS easy

gruesome *ADJECTIVE* *The gruesome remains had to be analysed.* ► grisly, gory, ghastly, bloody, horrific, repulsive, frightful, hideous, macabre, revolting, repellent

gruff *ADJECTIVE* **1** *His voice was gruff in the darkness.* ► harsh, rough, hoarse, husky, throaty **2** *his unique gruff manner* ► abrupt, brusque, curt, blunt, bad-tempered, churlish

grumble *VERB* *Everyone was grumbling about the heat.* ► complain, carp, protest, whine, grouch, moan, (*informal*) whinge, (*more informal*) bellyache, (*more informal*) gripe

grumble *NOUN* *constant grumbles about the weather* ► complaint, moan, groan, protest, objection

grumpy *ADJECTIVE* *I'm always grumpy early in the morning.* ► bad-tempered, irritable, irascible, testy, grouchy, touchy, crotchety, cantankerous, peevish, fractious, cross, (*more informal*) stroppy, (*more informal*) shirty OPPOSITES ARE good-humoured, good-tempered

guarantee *NOUN* **1** *Used cars come with a six-month guarantee.* ► warranty, warrant, covenant **2** *We cannot give a guarantee that these measures will succeed.* ► assurance, pledge, promise, commitment, surety, oath

guarantee *VERB* **1** *He could not guarantee that they would keep their jobs.* ► promise, swear, pledge, assure, certify, give a guarantee, give your word, vouch, vow **2** *You need a reservation to guarantee a seat.* ► secure, ensure, make sure of

guard *VERB* **1** *Troops guarded the house.* ► protect, stand guard over, watch over, shield, safeguard, defend, cover **2** *An escort guarded the prisoners.* ► supervise, watch over, control **3** **guard against** *Take care to guard against over-tiredness in the first few weeks.* ► beware of, be alert to, try to prevent

guard *NOUN* **1** *We were turned back by the guards at the border.* ► sentry, sentinel, custodian, lookout, patrol, watchman **2** *He felt the guard's hand on his shoulder.* ► jailer, prison officer,

guerrilla (ger- il- a) *NOUN* **guerrillas** a member of a small unofficial army who fights by making surprise attacks
USAGE Do not confuse with **gorilla**.

guess *NOUN* **guesses** an opinion or answer that you give without making careful calculations or without certain knowledge

guess *VERB* **guesses**, **guessing**, **guessed** make a guess
▷ **guesser** *NOUN*

guesswork *NOUN* something you think of or work out by guessing

guest *NOUN* **guests** **1** a person who is invited to visit or stay at another's house **2** a person staying at a hotel **3** a person who takes part in another's show as a visiting performer

guidance *NOUN* **1** guiding **2** advising or advice on problems

Guide *NOUN* **Guides** a member of the Girl Guides Association, an organization for girls

guide *NOUN* **guides** **1** a person who shows others the way or points out interesting sights **2** a book giving information about a place or subject

guide *VERB* **guides**, **guiding**, **guided** show someone the way or how to do something

guidebook *NOUN* **guidebooks** a book of information about places that tourists visit

guide dog *NOUN* **guide dogs** a dog trained to lead a blind person

guile (rhymes with *mile*) *NOUN* craftiness

guillotine (gil- ot- een) *NOUN* **guillotines** a machine with a heavy blade for beheading criminals, formerly used in France [named after Dr Guillotin, who suggested its use in France in 1789]

guilt *NOUN* **1** the fact that you have committed an offence **2** a feeling that you are to blame for something that has happened

guilty *ADJECTIVE* **1** having done wrong • *He was found guilty of murder* **2** feeling or showing guilt • *a guilty conscience*
▷ **guiltily** *ADVERB*

guinea pig *NOUN* **guinea pigs** **1** a small furry animal without a tail **2** a person who is used as the subject of an experiment

Thesaurus

warder, warden
off your guard *or* **off guard** *He was caught off guard for a moment and the water surged over him.* ► unprepared, unready, unsuspecting
on your guard *Thieves are operating in this area, so be on your guard.* ► alert, watchful, vigilant, heedful, circumspect, chary

guarded *ADJECTIVE* *Their reaction was guarded and unfriendly.* ► cautious, wary, chary, unenthusiastic, non-committal, discreet

guess *VERB* **1** *You have to guess the weight of a large cake.* ► estimate, reckon, judge, predict, gauge, determine **2** (*informal*) *I guess I should say sorry.* ► suppose, believe, think, imagine, expect, assume, consider, reckon

guess *NOUN* *My guess was he would head for the motorway.* ► theory, hypothesis, prediction, feeling, belief, opinion, conjecture, supposition, notion, idea, intuition

guest *NOUN* **1** *They joined their guests for dinner.* ► visitor, company, caller **2** *The hotel could take up to thirty guests.* ► resident, patron, client, lodger, boarder, customer, tenant

guidance *NOUN* *His supervisor offered him guidance.* ► advice, direction, instruction, help, counsel, teaching, support, pointers, guidelines

guide *VERB* **1** *I asked her to guide me back to the town.* ► lead, direct, show, show the way, take, accompany, escort, conduct **2** *The students have to be guided carefully through this stage of their work.* ► advise, counsel, direct, supervise, instruct, teach

guide *NOUN* **1** *Your guide will show you the way.* ► escort, leader, courier, navigator, pilot, attendant **2** *The sample is only meant to be a guide.* ► model, indication, example, gauge, guideline, pointer

guilt *NOUN* **1** *The jury was quite sure of his guilt.* ► guiltiness, culpability, liability, responsibility, blame, blameworthiness, wrongfulness, criminality AN OPPOSITE IS innocence **2** *There is no need to feel guilt about it.* ► shame, remorse, self-reproach, self-accusation, bad conscience, penitence, contrition, dishonour, guilty feelings, regret AN OPPOSITE IS virtue

guilty *ADJECTIVE* **1** *Brown was found guilty of assault.* ► culpable, blameworthy, at fault, liable, responsible, blameable, in the wrong, reprehensible AN OPPOSITE IS innocent **2** *She felt guilty about deceiving her friends.* ► ashamed, remorseful, sorry, repentant, regretful, contrite, penitent, conscience-stricken, shamefaced, sheepish AN OPPOSITE IS unrepentant

A B C D E F G H I J K L M N O P Q R S T U V W X Y Z

guitar *NOUN* **guitars** a musical instrument played by plucking its strings
▷ **guitarist** *NOUN*

gulf *NOUN* **gulfs** **1** a large area of the sea that is partly surrounded by land **2** a wide gap; a great difference

gull *NOUN* **gulls** a seagull [a Celtic word]

gullible *ADJECTIVE* easily deceived

gulp *VERB* **gulps, gulping, gulped** **1** swallow hastily or greedily **2** make a loud swallowing noise, especially because of fear

gulp *NOUN* **gulps** **1** the act of gulping **2** a large mouthful of liquid

gum[1] *NOUN* **gums** the firm flesh in which your teeth are rooted

gum[2] *NOUN* **gums** **1** a sticky substance produced by some trees and shrubs, used as glue **2** a sweet made with gum or gelatine • *a fruit gum* **3** chewing gum **4** a gum tree
▷ **gummy** *ADJECTIVE*

gum *VERB* **gums, gumming, gummed** cover or stick something with gum

gum tree *NOUN* **gum trees** a eucalyptus

gun *NOUN* **guns** **1** a weapon that fires shells or bullets from a metal tube **2** a starting pistol **3** a device that forces a substance out of a tube • *a grease gun*
▷ **gunfire** *NOUN* **gunshot** *NOUN*

gun *VERB* **guns, gunning, gunned**
gun down shoot someone with a gun

gunpowder *NOUN* an explosive made from a powdered mixture of potassium nitrate, charcoal, and sulphur

gurgle *VERB* **gurgles, gurgling, gurgled** make a low bubbling sound
▷ **gurgle** *NOUN*

guru *NOUN* **gurus** **1** a Hindu religious leader **2** an influential teacher; a mentor

gush *VERB* **gushes, gushing, gushed** **1** flow suddenly or quickly **2** talk too enthusiastically or emotionally
▷ **gush** *NOUN*

gust *NOUN* **gusts** a sudden rush of wind, rain, or smoke
▷ **gusty** *ADJECTIVE* **gustily** *ADVERB*

gust *VERB* **gusts, gusting, gusted** blow in gusts

gut *NOUN* **guts** the lower part of the digestive system; the intestine

gut *VERB* **guts, gutting, gutted** **1** remove the guts from a dead fish or other animal **2** remove or destroy the inside of something • *The fire gutted the factory.*

guts *PLURAL NOUN* **1** the digestive system; the insides of a person or thing **2** (*informal*) courage

gutted *ADJECTIVE* (*informal*) extremely disappointed or upset

gutter *NOUN* **gutters** a long narrow channel at the side of a street, or along the edge of a roof, for carrying away rainwater

gutter *VERB* **gutters, guttering, guttered** a candle gutters when it burns unsteadily so that melted wax runs down

Thesaurus

gulf *NOUN* **1** *Here ships turn into the gulf.* ► bay, inlet, creek, estuary, sound **2** *the gulf between rich and poor* ► gap, contrast, chasm, divergence, divide, rift, split, division

gullible *ADJECTIVE* *Wayne is very gullible when he's had too much to drink.* ► credulous, over-trusting, trustful, suggestible, easily taken in OPPOSITES ARE suspicious, astute

gulp *VERB* *Brian gulped his beer and stood to leave.* ► swallow, swill down, (*more informal*) swig, (*more informal*) knock back AN OPPOSITE IS sip

gulp *NOUN* *She finished her juice in one gulp.* ► swallow, mouthful, (*more informal*) swig

gum *NOUN* *You can stick the pictures in with gum.* ► glue, adhesive, paste

gum *VERB* *The photos were gummed to the page.* ► stick, glue, paste, fix

gun *NOUN* *He threatened her with a gun.* ► firearm, weapon, pistol, revolver, rifle, shotgun, (*more informal*) shooter

gush *VERB* **1** *Blood gushed from the wound in his head.* ► pour, spurt, squirt, stream, flow, rush, cascade, spout, surge OPPOSITES ARE trickle, ooze **2** *They gushed all afternoon about their holiday plans.* ► enthuse, rave, effuse, chatter, jabber, (*more informal*) go on

gush *NOUN* *Turning the tap slightly produced a gush of scalding water.* ► rush, spurt, surge, stream, torrent, cascade, flood, flow, jet, spout, squirt, burst

gut *NOUN* **1** **gut** or **guts** (*informal*) *He felt a sharp pain in his gut.* ► stomach, belly, bowels, intestines, innards, insides RELATED ADJECTIVE visceral **2** **guts** (*informal*) *It takes guts to say what you think.* ► courage, nerve, bravery, audacity, boldness, daring, (*informal*) bottle

gut *ADJECTIVE* *I had a gut feeling Eric was the right man for us.* ► instinctive, intuitive, deep-seated, spontaneous, innate, reflex

guttural (gut- er- al) *ADJECTIVE* throaty and harsh-sounding • *a guttural voice*

guy [1] *NOUN* **guys** **1** a figure representing Guy Fawkes, burnt on 5 November in memory of the Gunpowder Plot which planned to blow up Parliament on that day in 1605 **2** (*informal*) a man

guy [2] or **guy-rope** *NOUN* **guys** or **guy-ropes** a rope used to hold something in place, especially a tent

gym (jim) *NOUN* **gyms** (*informal*) **1** a gymnasium **2** gymnastics

gymkhana (jim- kah- na) *NOUN* **gymkhanas** a series of horse-riding contests and other sports events [from Urdu]

gymnasium *NOUN* **gymnasia** or **gymnasiums** a place equipped for gymnastics [from Greek *gymnasion*, from *gymnos* = naked (because Greek men exercised naked)]

gymnastics *PLURAL NOUN* exercises performed to develop the muscles or to show the performer's agility
▷ **gymnastic** *ADJECTIVE*

Gypsy *NOUN* **Gypsies** a member of a community of people, also called travellers, who live in caravans or similar vehicles and travel from place to place [from *Egyptian*, because gypsies were originally thought to have come from Egypt]

gyrate (jy- rayt) *VERB* **gyrates, gyrating, gyrated** revolve; move in circles or spirals
▷ **gyration** *NOUN*

gyroscope (jy- ro- skohp) *NOUN* **gyroscopes** a device used in navigation, which keeps steady because of a heavy wheel spinning inside it [from Greek *gyros* = a ring or circle + *skopein* = to look at (because gyroscopes were once used to study the earth's rotation)]

Thesaurus

guy *NOUN* (*informal*) *He's a clever guy.*
► (*informal*) bloke, chap, fellow, man, boy, individual

guzzle *VERB* *They came in and guzzled all the food.*
► gobble, gobble up, wolf, wolf down, devour, (*more informal*) scoff, (*more informal*) tuck into, (*more informal*) polish off

Hh

haberdashery *NOUN* small articles used in sewing, e.g. ribbons, buttons, and thread
▷ **haberdasher** *NOUN*

habit *NOUN* **habits** **1** something that you do without thinking because you have done it so often; a settled way of behaving **2** something that is hard to give up • *a smoking habit* **3** the long dress worn by a monk or nun
▷ **habitual** *ADJECTIVE* **habitually** *ADVERB*

habitat *NOUN* **habitats** where an animal or plant lives naturally

habitation *NOUN* **habitations** **1** a place to live in **2** inhabiting a place

hack *VERB* **hacks, hacking, hacked** **1** chop or cut roughly **2** (*informal*) break into a computer system
▷ **hacker** *NOUN*

hackles *PLURAL NOUN*
make someone's hackles rise make someone angry or indignant

haddock *NOUN* **haddock** a sea fish like cod but smaller, used as food

hadn't (*mainly spoken*) had not

haemoglobin (heem- a- **gloh**- bin) *NOUN* the red substance that carries oxygen in the blood

haemophilia (heem- o- **fil**- ee- a) *NOUN* a disease that causes people to bleed dangerously from even a slight cut
▷ **haemophiliac** *NOUN*

haemorrhage (**hem**- er- ij) *NOUN* bleeding, especially inside a person's body

hag *NOUN* **hags** an ugly old woman

haggard *ADJECTIVE* looking ill or very tired

haggis *NOUN* **haggises** a Scottish food made from sheep's offal

hail[1] *NOUN* frozen drops of rain
▷ **hail** *VERB* **hailstone** *NOUN* **hailstorm** *NOUN*

hail[2] *INTERJECTION* (*old use*) an exclamation of greeting

hail *VERB* **hails, hailing, hailed** call out to somebody
hail from come from • *He hails from Ireland*

hair *NOUN* **hairs** **1** a soft covering that grows on the heads and bodies of people and animals **2** one of the strands that make up this covering
▷ **hairbrush** *NOUN* **haircut** *NOUN* **hairstyle** *NOUN*
keep your hair on (*informal*) do not lose your temper
split hairs make petty or unimportant distinctions of meaning

hairdresser *NOUN* **hairdressers** a person whose job is to cut and arrange people's hair

hairpin *NOUN* **hairpins** a U-shaped pin for keeping hair in place

hairpin bend *NOUN* **hairpin bends** a sharp bend in a road

hair-raising *ADJECTIVE* terrifying

hairy *ADJECTIVE* **1** with a lot of hair **2** (*informal*) dangerous or risky

hajj *NOUN* the pilgrimage to Mecca which all Muslims are expected to make at least once

halal *NOUN* meat prepared according to Muslim law

halcyon (**hal**- see- on) *ADJECTIVE* happy and peaceful • *halcyon days*

Thesaurus

habit *NOUN* **1** *healthy eating habits* ► practice, custom, pattern, routine, tendency, way, rule **2** *her habit of twirling her hair as she spoke* ► mannerism, quirk, trick, gesture, custom, practice **3** *They stole money to fund their drug habit.* ► addiction, dependence, craving, fixation, compulsion, obsession, weakness **4** *a nun's habit* ► costume, robe, garment, outfit, attire, garb
in the habit of *He was in the habit of practising his flute when he went to bed.* ► used to, accustomed to, given to, inclined to

habitat *NOUN* *the panda's natural habitat* ► environment, surroundings, element, territory, terrain, haunt, domain

habitual *ADJECTIVE* **1** *She expected his habitual response to such suggestions.* ► usual, customary, normal, regular, characteristic, typical, fixed, routine, accustomed, established AN OPPOSITE IS unaccustomed **2** *their habitual criticism of everything we did* ► constant, persistent, continual, recurrent, incessant, interminable, unremitting, endless, relentless AN OPPOSITE IS infrequent **3** *habitual smokers* ► confirmed, regular, addicted, persistent, inveterate, hardened, compulsive, chronic AN OPPOSITE IS occasional

hair *NOUN* **1** *She ran her hand through her hair.* ► locks, tresses, curls, (*more informal*) mop **2** *a dog with short hair* ► coat, fur, hide

hairy *ADJECTIVE* *His shirt was open, revealing a hairy chest.* ► shaggy, fuzzy, bristly, downy, hirsute, fleecy, furry, long-haired, stubbly, woolly OPPOSITES ARE hairless, smooth-skinned

hall *NOUN* **1** *The meeting will be in the village hall.* ► assembly hall, meeting room, auditorium, concert hall, theatre **2** *You can leave your coat in the hall.* ► hallway, entrance hall, lobby, foyer, corridor, passage, vestibule

half *NOUN* **halves** one of the two equal parts or amounts into which something is or can be divided

half *ADVERB* partly; not completely • *This meat is only half cooked.*
not half (*slang*) extremely • *Was she cross? Not half!*

half-brother *NOUN* **half-brothers** a brother to whom you are related by one parent but not by both parents

half-hearted *ADJECTIVE* not very enthusiastic
▷ **half-heartedly** *ADVERB*

half-life *NOUN* **half-lives** the time taken for the radioactivity of a substance to fall to half its original value

half mast *NOUN* a point about halfway up a flagpole, to which a flag is lowered as a mark of respect for a person who has died

halfpenny (**hayp- nee**) *NOUN* **halfpennies** *for separate coins,* **halfpence** *for a sum of money* a former coin worth half a penny

half-sister *NOUN* **half-sisters** a sister to whom you are related by one parent but not by both parents

half-term *NOUN* **half-terms** a short holiday in the middle of a term

halfway *ADJECTIVE, ADVERB* between two others and equally distant from each

hall *NOUN* **halls** **1** a space or passage just inside the front entrance of a house **2** a very large room or building used for meetings, concerts, etc. **3** a large country house

Hallowe'en *NOUN* 31 October, traditionally a time when ghosts and witches are believed to appear

hallucination *NOUN* **hallucinations** something you think you can see or hear that is not really there
▷ **hallucinate** *VERB*

halo *NOUN* **haloes** a circle of light round something, especially round the head of a saint etc. in paintings

halt *VERB* **halts, halting, halted** stop

halt *NOUN* **halts** **1** a stop or standstill • *Work came to a halt* **2** a small stopping place on a railway

halve *VERB* **halves, halving, halved** **1** divide something into halves **2** reduce something to half its size

ham *NOUN* **hams** **1** meat from a pig's leg **2** (*informal*) an actor who overacts **3** (*informal*) someone who operates a radio to send and receive messages as a hobby

hamburger *NOUN* **hamburgers** a flat round cake of minced beef served fried, often in a bread roll

hammer *NOUN* **hammers** a tool with a heavy metal head used for driving nails in, breaking things, etc.

hammer *VERB* **hammers, hammering, hammered** **1** hit something with a hammer **2** knock loudly • *Someone was hammering on the door.* **3** (*informal*) defeat

hammock *NOUN* **hammocks** a bed made of a strong net or piece of cloth hung by cords [via Spanish from Taino (a South American language)]

hamper[1] *NOUN* **hampers** a large box-shaped basket with a lid

hamper[2] *VERB* **hampers, hampering, hampered** hinder; prevent from moving or working freely

hamster *NOUN* **hamsters** a small furry animal with cheek pouches for carrying grain

hamstring *NOUN* **hamstrings** any of the five tendons at the back of a person's knee

hand *NOUN* **hands** **1** the end part of the arm below the wrist **2** a pointer on a clock or dial **3** a worker; a member of a ship's crew • *All hands on deck!* **4** the cards held by one player in a card

Thesaurus

halt *VERB* **1** *A series of strikes halted production for several weeks.* ► stop, terminate, obstruct, arrest, impede, block, check, curb OPPOSITES ARE start, continue **2** *Traffic halted on the bridge.* ► stop, wait, come to a halt, come to rest, draw up, pull up OPPOSITES ARE start, continue **3** *Work on the building halted during the holiday period.* ► cease, stop, break off, end, terminate OPPOSITES ARE start, resume

halt *NOUN* **1** *The train came to a halt.* ► stop, standstill, break, interruption, pause, stoppage **2** *a halt in the output of spare parts* ► stoppage, cessation, break, interruption, pause

halve *VERB* **1** *Halve the pears and remove the cores.* ► cut in half, split in two, divide in two, bisect **2** *Their income halved over the next year.* ► lessen by half *or* by fifty percent, decrease by half *or* by fifty percent

hammer *NOUN* *He hit the nail with a hammer.* ► mallet, gavel

hammer *VERB* *The soldiers hammered on the door.* ► beat, batter, bash, pummel, pound, strike, knock

hamper *VERB* **1** *Bad weather hampered the rescue operation.* ► obstruct, hinder, hold up, interfere with, restrict, thwart, prevent, curb, curtail, foil AN OPPOSITE IS facilitate **2** *Her bandaged hand hampered her.* ► hinder, encumber, impede, restrain, entangle, handicap, hold back AN OPPOSITE IS aid

hand *NOUN* **1** *a person's hand* ► fist, palm RELATED ADJECTIVE manual **2** *the hand of a gauge*

A B C D E F G H I J K L M N O P Q R S T U V W X Y Z

game **5** side or direction • *the right-hand side* • *on the other hand* **6** help or aid • *Give me a hand with these boxes.*
at hand near
by hand using your hand or hands
give *or* **receive a big hand** applaud or be applauded
hands down winning easily
in good hands in the care or control of someone who can be trusted
in hand in your possession; being dealt with
on hand available
out of hand out of control

hand VERB **hands, handing, handed** give or pass something to somebody • *Hand it over.*
hand down pass something from one generation to another

handbag NOUN **handbags** a small bag for holding a purse and personal articles

handbook NOUN **handbooks** a small book that gives useful facts about something

handcuff NOUN **handcuffs** one of a pair of metal rings linked by a chain, for fastening a prisoner's wrists together

handcuff VERB **handcuffs, handcuffing, handcuffed** fasten with handcuffs

handful NOUN **handfuls** **1** as much as can be carried in one hand **2** a few people or things **3** (*informal*) a troublesome person or task

handicap NOUN **handicaps** **1** a disadvantage **2** a physical or mental disability
▷ **handicapped** ADJECTIVE

handkerchief NOUN **handkerchiefs** a small square of cloth for wiping the nose or face

handle NOUN **handles** the part of a thing by which it is held, carried, or controlled

handle VERB **handles, handling, handled** **1** touch or feel something with your hands **2** deal with; manage • *Will you handle the catering?*
▷ **handler** NOUN

handlebar NOUN or **handlebars** PLURAL NOUN the bar, with a handle at each end, that steers a bicycle or motorcycle etc.

handsome ADJECTIVE **1** good-looking **2** generous • *a handsome offer*
▷ **handsomely** ADVERB

Thesaurus

► pointer, indicator **3** *The factory took on more hands.* ► worker, employee, labourer **4** **hands** *The property came into his sister's hands.* ► possession, control, charge, custody, power, responsibility
at *or* **on** *or* **to hand** ► close by, handy, accessible, available, present, waiting, within reach
give somebody a hand *Let me give you a hand with the dinner.* ► help, assist

hand VERB *He handed her a letter.* ► give, offer, pass, present (her with a letter), submit (a letter to her), convey, deliver
hand down *The family property is handed down from one generation to the next.* ► pass down, pass on, bequeath, leave as a legacy, will
hand out *or* **round** *A flight attendant handed out forms.* ► distribute, circulate, give out, deal out, share out
hand over **1** *She handed over a large sum.* ► pay, donate, tender, surrender **2** *The prisoners were handed over to the local police.* ► deliver up, entrust, turn over

handful NOUN *a handful of complaining letters* ► small number, smattering, sprinkling, trickle

handicap NOUN *Their poor French was a handicap when travelling.* ► disadvantage, difficulty, drawback, shortcoming, hindrance, inconvenience, limitation, encumbrance, stumbling block, restriction, obstacle, problem, nuisance opposites are advantage, benefit

handicap VERB *They were handicapped by the fact that they had not been taught science.* ► hamper, impede, limit, disadvantage, restrict, hinder, hold back AN OPPOSITE IS help

handle NOUN *The head flew off the handle and cracked our only mirror.* ► haft, shank, stock, shaft, grip

handle VERB **1** *A notice asked visitors not to handle the exhibits.* ► touch, feel, hold, finger, fondle, pick up, grip, grasp **2** *It would not be easy to handle such a tense meeting. He was used to handling temperamental singers.* ► manage, deal with, cope with, control, tackle, contend with **3** *The firm handles a lot of overseas business.* ► deal in, trade in, market **4** *He needed a smaller car that he could handle more easily.* ► control, drive, manoeuvre, operate, steer

handsome ADJECTIVE **1** *a handsome man* ► good-looking, nice-looking, attractive, comely, personable, (*more informal*) dishy OPPOSITES ARE ugly, unattractive **2** *a handsome building* ► elegant, striking, imposing, stately, well-proportioned, attractive OPPOSITES ARE ugly, hideous **3** *a handsome profit* ► large, big, sizeable, substantial, considerable, ample AN OPPOSITE IS meagre **4** *a handsome offer* ► generous, gracious, liberal, magnanimous, munificent AN OPPOSITE IS mean

handstand *NOUN* **handstands** balancing on your hands with your feet in the air

handwriting *NOUN* writing done by hand; a person's style of writing
▷ **handwritten** *ADJECTIVE*

handy *ADJECTIVE* **handier, handiest**
1 convenient or useful **2** good at using the hands
▷ **handily** *ADVERB* **handiness** *NOUN*

hang *VERB* **hangs, hanging, hung 1** fix the top or side of something to a hook or nail etc.; be supported in this way **2** stick wallpaper to a wall **3** decorate with drapery or hanging ornaments etc. • *The tree was hung with lights.* **4** droop or lean • *People hung over the gate.* **5** remain in the air or as something unpleasant • *Smoke hung over the city.* • *The threat is still hanging over him.* **6** (with *past tense & past participle* **hanged**) execute someone by hanging them from a rope that tightens round the neck • *He was hanged in 1950.*
hang about (*informal*) **1** loiter **2** not go away
hang back hesitate to go forward or to do something
hang on 1 hold tightly **2** (*informal*) wait
hang up end a telephone conversation by putting back the receiver

hang *NOUN*
get the hang of (*informal*) learn how to do or use something

hang-glider *NOUN* **hang-gliders** a framework in which a person can glide through the air
▷ **hang-gliding** *NOUN*

hangover *NOUN* **hangovers** an unpleasant feeling after drinking too much alcohol

hank *NOUN* **hanks** a coil or piece of wool, thread, etc.

hanker *VERB* **hankers, hankering, hankered** feel a longing for something

haphazard *ADJECTIVE* done or chosen at random, not by planning

happen *VERB* **happens, happening, happened 1** take place; occur **2** do something by chance • *I happened to see him.*

happy *ADJECTIVE* **happier, happiest 1** pleased or contented **2** fortunate • *a happy coincidence* **3** willing • *I'd be happy to help.*
▷ **happily** *ADVERB* **happiness** *NOUN*

Thesaurus

handy *ADJECTIVE* **1** *The brush is handy for cleaning up stubborn dust.* ► useful, convenient, practical, helpful, effective **2** *He's handy with a screwdriver.* ► skilful, adept, dexterous, proficient, practical, able, deft **3** *Keep your timer handy.* ► accessible, available, ready, at *or* to hand, close by, nearby

hang *VERB* **1** *Baskets of flowers hung from the lamp posts.* ► be suspended, dangle, swing, sway **2** *Rich exotic curtains hang from every window.* ► drape, drop, droop, cascade, trail **3** *Make sure you hang the pictures at eye level.* ► fix, attach, fasten, display, suspend, stick **4** *A damp mist hung in the air.* ► float, hover, drift, linger, cling, remain
hang about (*informal*) *Don't hang about if you want to take advantage of this offer.* ► delay, wait, procrastinate
hang around (*informal*) *small groups hanging around coffee bars* ► linger in, loiter in, frequent, haunt
hang back *He hung back, afraid to go in.* ► hesitate, demur, hold back, recoil, shy away
hang on *If they can hang on a few more days it will help us.* ► stay, persevere, remain, continue, carry on, persist
hang on to *If you have cash, hang on to it.* ► keep, hold on to, retain, preserve
hang out (*informal*) *She enjoyed hanging out with members of the band.* ► associate, mix, spend time, keep company, fraternize, socialize

hang-up *NOUN* (*informal*) *Wally has a hang-up about his appearance.* ► fixation, obsession, neurosis, inhibition, anxiety, (*more informal*) thing

haphazard *ADJECTIVE* *the haphazard spray of machine-gun fire things strewn about in a haphazard fashion* ► random, indiscriminate, arbitrary, chaotic, disorderly, disorganized, casual, irregular, unmethodical AN OPPOSITE IS orderly

happen *VERB* **1** *The collision happened as the pursuing boat tried to turn. Something strange was happening that day.* ► occur, take place, come about, arise, result, ensue, transpire **2 happen to** *We never knew what happened to her.* ► become of, befall

happening *NOUN* *There is a record of all the happenings of that week.* ► event, incident, occurrence, circumstance, episode, affair

happiness *NOUN* *A feeling of great happiness filled her.* ► contentment, joy, joyfulness, gladness, pleasure, bliss, elation, ecstasy OPPOSITES ARE unhappiness, sorrow

happy *ADJECTIVE* **1** *a room full of happy faces* ► contented, cheerful, joyful, jolly, delighted, merry, smiling **2** *I will be happy to help.* ► pleased, glad, willing, disposed, delighted **3** *By a happy chance a film crew was there to record the scene.* ► fortunate, lucky, felicitous, favourable, fitting

a b c d e f g h i j k l m n o p q r s t u v w x y z

A B C D E F G **H** I J K L M N O P Q R S T U V W X Y Z

harangue (ha- rang) *VERB* **harangues**, **haranguing**, **harangued** make a long aggressive speech to somebody
▷ **harangue** *NOUN*

harass (ha- ras) *VERB* **harasses**, **harassing**, **harassed** trouble or annoy somebody often
▷ **harassment** (ha- ras- ment) *NOUN*

harbour *NOUN* **harbours** a place where ships can shelter or unload

harbour *VERB* **harbours**, **harbouring**, **harboured** **1** give shelter to somebody, especially a criminal **2** keep a strong or hostile thought in your mind • *I think she still harbours a grudge against them*

hard *ADJECTIVE* **1** firm or solid; not soft **2** difficult • *hard sums* **3** severe or stern **4** causing suffering • *hard luck* **5** using great effort • *a hard worker* **6** hard drugs are strong and addictive ones
▷ **hardness** *NOUN*
hard of hearing slightly deaf
hard up (*informal*) short of money

hard *ADVERB* **1** so as to be hard • *The ground froze hard* **2** with great effort; intensively • *We worked hard* • *It is raining hard* **3** with difficulty • *hard-earned*

hard disk *NOUN* **hard disks** a disk fixed inside a computer, able to store large amounts of data

harden *VERB* **hardens**, **hardening**, **hardened** make or become hard
▷ **hardener** *NOUN*

hardly *ADVERB* only just; only with difficulty • *She can hardly walk*
USAGE It is not acceptable in standard English to use 'not' with **hardly**, as in 'she can't hardly walk'.

hardship *NOUN* **hardships** difficult conditions that cause discomfort or suffering • *a life of hardship*

hardware *NOUN* **1** metal implements and tools etc.; machinery **2** the machinery of a computer as opposed to the software COMPARE **software**

hard water *NOUN* water containing minerals that prevent soap from making much lather

hardy *ADJECTIVE* **hardier**, **hardiest** able to endure cold or difficult conditions
▷ **hardiness** *NOUN*

hare *NOUN* **hares** an animal like a rabbit but larger

harm *VERB* **harms**, **harming**, **harmed** damage or injure

Thesaurus

harass *VERB The men continued to harass her.* ► pester, torment, badger, hound, persecute, trouble, harry, (*informal*) hassle, annoy, vex

harassed *ADJECTIVE good news for harassed mums and dads* ► stressed, harried, worn, troubled, exhausted AN OPPOSITE IS carefree

harbour *NOUN Boats bobbed up and down in the harbour.* ► port, dock, marina, mooring, quay, waterfront

harbour *VERB* **1** *He was arrested for harbouring a criminal.* ► hide, protect, shelter, conceal, shield, give refuge to, give asylum to, give sanctuary to **2** *Better not to harbour a grudge.* ► bear, hold, nurse, nurture, entertain, foster, cling to

hard *ADJECTIVE* **1** *The ground is too hard to play on.* ► solid, firm, unyielding, hardened, tough, compact AN OPPOSITE IS soft **2** *three weeks of hard work* ► strenuous, arduous, exhausting, fatiguing, demanding AN OPPOSITE IS easy **3** *a hard problem to solve* ► difficult, complicated, complex, involved, knotty, baffling, puzzling AN OPPOSITE IS simple **4** *a hard taskmaster* ► strict, harsh, firm, stern, demanding, severe OPPOSITES ARE mild, easy-going **5** *a hard blow* ► heavy, forceful, strong, powerful, violent AN OPPOSITE IS light

hard *ADVERB* **1** *She works hard at school.* ► diligently, industriously, steadily, earnestly, energetically **2** *It has been raining hard.* ► heavily, steadily, (*more informal*) cats and dogs **3** *She looked hard at them.* ► intently, intensely, closely, attentively, keenly

harden *VERB* **1** *The cement hardens after two hours.* ► set, solidify, become hard, stiffen **2** *These experiences hardened their determination to continue.* ► strengthen, reinforce, increase, intensify, fortify, toughen

hardly *ADVERB* **1** *It is hardly surprising that so many people have considered leaving.* ► not at all, by no means, barely, scarcely **2** *John said he hardly knew her.* ► scarcely, barely, only just, only slightly, only faintly

hardship *NOUN Drought caused the population much hardship.* ► suffering, privation, misery, misfortune, adversity, affliction, austerity, destitution, difficulty, need, trouble, unhappiness, want

hard-wearing *ADJECTIVE outdoor clothes that are hard-wearing* ► durable, strong, tough, resilient, lasting, sturdy, well made, stout OPPOSITES ARE flimsy, delicate

hardy *ADJECTIVE a good expedition for hardy walkers* ► fit, robust, sturdy, hearty, healthy, tough, vigorous, strong, resilient, rugged opposites are tender, delicate

harm *VERB* **1** *If they harmed any of the hostages the police would have to go in.* ► hurt, injure, maltreat, mistreat, ill-treat, wound, molest, abuse, (*more informal*) lay a finger on

harm *NOUN* damage or injury
▷ **harmful** *ADJECTIVE* **harmless** *ADJECTIVE*

harmonica *NOUN* **harmonicas** a mouth organ

harmonious *ADJECTIVE* **1** combining together in a pleasant, attractive, or effective way **2** sounding pleasant **3** peaceful and friendly

harmony *NOUN* **harmonies** **1** a pleasant combination, especially of musical notes **2** being friendly to each other

harness *NOUN* **harnesses** the straps put round a horse's head and neck for controlling it

harness *VERB* **harnesses, harnessing, harnessed** **1** put a harness on a horse **2** control and use something • *Could we harness the power of the wind?*

harp *NOUN* **harps** a musical instrument with strings stretched across a frame and plucked by the fingers
▷ **harpist** *NOUN*

harpoon *NOUN* **harpoons** a spear attached to a rope, used for catching whales etc.
▷ **harpoon** *VERB*

harrowing *ADJECTIVE* very upsetting or distressing

harsh *ADJECTIVE* **1** rough and unpleasant **2** severe or cruel
▷ **harshly** *ADVERB* **harshness** *NOUN*

harvest *NOUN* **harvests** **1** the time when farmers gather in the corn, fruit, or vegetables that they have grown **2** the crop that is gathered in

hash *NOUN* a mixture of small pieces of meat and vegetables, usually fried
make a hash of (*informal*) make a mess of something; bungle

hasn't (*mainly spoken*) has not

haste *NOUN* a hurry
make haste act quickly

hasten *VERB* **hastens, hastening, hastened** hurry

hasty *ADJECTIVE* hurried; done too quickly
▷ **hastily** *ADVERB* **hastiness** *NOUN*

hat *NOUN* **hats** a covering for the head, worn out of doors
keep something under your hat keep it a secret

hatch [1] *NOUN* **hatches** an opening in a floor, wall, or door, usually with a covering

Thesaurus

2 *chemicals that harm the environment* ► damage, spoil, ruin, hurt, do damage to, do harm to

harm *NOUN* **1** *a way of dealing with waste without causing any harm to the public* ► injury, damage, suffering, hurt, detriment, inconvenience AN OPPOSITE IS benefit **2** *We can't see any harm in their idea.* ► wrong, disadvantage, snag

harmful *ADJECTIVE* *the harmful effects of smoking* ► damaging, detrimental, injurious, dangerous, noxious, destructive, unhealthy OPPOSITES ARE harmless, beneficial

harmless *ADJECTIVE* **1** *a harmless substance* ► safe, innocuous, non-toxic, non-poisonous, benign AN OPPOSITE IS harmful **2** *It was just a bit of harmless fun.* ► safe, inoffensive, innocuous, unobjectionable, gentle AN OPPOSITE IS objectionable

harmony *NOUN* **1** *different ethnic groups living in harmony* ► friendship, agreement, concord, peace, amity, fellowship, goodwill, unity OPPOSITES ARE disagreement, enmity **2** *musical harmony* ► tunefulness, euphony, concord, melody AN OPPOSITE IS discord

harsh *ADJECTIVE* **1** *He spoke in a high, harsh voice.* ► shrill, grating, strident, grasping **2** *harsh measures to combat street crime* ► severe, punitive, strict, draconian **3** *They exchanged harsh words.* ► sharp, bitter, unfriendly, unkind **4** *the harsh rule of a tyrant* ► cruel, savage, brutal, despotic, hard, strict, intolerant

harvest *NOUN* *a bumper harvest* ► crop, yield, produce, return

harvest *VERB* *crops that have to be harvested by hand* ► gather, reap, take in, bring in, collect, garner, mow, pick

hassle *NOUN* **1** (*informal*) *It's always such a hassle trying to park.* ► bother, nuisance, inconvenience, struggle, difficulty **2** (*informal*) *She started getting hassle from the kids coming to her.* ► harassment, trouble, annoyance, argument, (*more informal*) aggravation

hassle *VERB* (*informal*) *Some of the passengers were hassling the driver.* ► harass, pester, badger, trouble, harry, annoy

haste *NOUN* *He was working with great haste.* ► speed, hurry, urgency, swiftness, rapidity, promptness, impetuosity

hasten *VERB* **1** *The king hastened back from Berwick.* ► hurry, rush, speed, make haste **2** *A rise in interest rates will hasten the ruin of many small businesses.* ► quicken, accelerate, speed up, bring nearer, precipitate

hasty *ADJECTIVE* **1** *They made a hasty retreat back to the house.* ► hurried, swift, rapid, brisk, quick, headlong **2** *The decision seemed hasty.* ► rash, precipitate, impulsive, imprudent, impetuous, reckless

hatch[2] *VERB* **hatches**, **hatching**, **hatched** **1** break out of an egg **2** keep an egg warm until a baby bird comes out **3** plan • *They hatched a plot*

hatchet *NOUN* **hatchets** a small axe

hate *VERB* **hates**, **hating**, **hated** dislike very strongly

hate *NOUN* extreme dislike

hatred *NOUN* extreme dislike

hat-trick *NOUN* **hat-tricks** achieving three goals, wickets, or victories one after the other

haughty *ADJECTIVE* **haughtier**, **haughtiest** proud of yourself and looking down on other people
▷ **haughtily** *ADVERB* **haughtiness** *NOUN*

haul *VERB* **hauls**, **hauling**, **hauled** pull or drag with great effort
▷ **haulage** *NOUN*

haul *NOUN* **hauls** **1** hauling **2** the amount obtained by an effort; booty • *The thieves' haul came to £2 million* **3** a distance to be covered • *a long haul*

haunt *VERB* **haunts**, **haunting**, **haunted** **1** (said about ghosts) appear often in a place or to a person **2** visit a place often **3** stay in your mind • *The memory haunts me still*
▷ **haunted** *ADJECTIVE*

haunt *NOUN* **haunts** a place that you often visit • *my favourite haunt*

have *VERB* **has**, **having**, **had** This word has many uses, including: **1** possess or own • *We have two dogs.* **2** contain • *This tin has sweets in it.* **3** be obliged to do something • *We have to go now.* **4** experience • *He had a shock.* **5** allow • *I won't have him bullied.* **6** receive or accept • *Will you have a sweet?* **7** get something done • *I'm having my watch mended.* **8** (*slang*) cheat or deceive • *We've been had!*
have somebody on (*informal*) fool him or her

have *AUXILIARY VERB* used to form the past tense of verbs, e.g. *He has gone*

haven *NOUN* **havens** a safe place or refuge

haven't (*mainly spoken*) have not

havoc *NOUN* great destruction or disorder
play havoc with disrupt something completely

hawk *NOUN* **hawks** a bird of prey with very strong eyesight

hawthorn *NOUN* **hawthorns** a thorny tree with small red berries (called **haws**)

hay *NOUN* dried grass for feeding to animals

hay fever *NOUN* irritation of the nose, throat, and eyes, caused by pollen or dust

Thesaurus

hate *VERB* **1** *The brothers hated each other.* ► loathe, detest, abhor, dislike, abominate, (*more informal*) can't bear, (*more informal*) can't stand **2** *I hate to bother them.* ► be sorry, hesitate, regret, be reluctant

hate *NOUN* **1** *feelings of hate* ► hatred, loathing, detestation, dislike, distaste, revulsion, abhorrence **2** *They made a list of their pet hates.* ► dislike, bugbear, bane, bête noire

hateful *ADJECTIVE* *I'll never come back to this hateful country.* ► detestable, loathsome, horrible, horrid, awful, nasty AN OPPOSITE IS lovable

hatred *NOUN* *The war left a legacy of fear and hatred.* ► hate, loathing, detestation, revulsion, repugnance, hostility, enmity, bad feeling OPPOSITES ARE love, liking

haughty *ADJECTIVE* *He walked out with a haughty toss of his head.* ► proud, arrogant, self-important, supercilious, disdainful, contemptuous, scornful, superior, lofty, overbearing AN OPPOSITE IS modest

haul *VERB* *A special locomotive is needed to haul these trains. She hauled him up from the floor.* ► pull, drag, heave, tug, tow AN OPPOSITE IS push

haunt *VERB* **1** *He likes to haunt old junk shops.* ► frequent, spend time in, keep returning to, visit frequently, (*more informal*) hang around in **2** *Her words came back to haunt her.* ► obsess, torment, trouble, worry, prey on

haunting *ADJECTIVE* *haunting and lyrical poetry* ► evocative, touching, emotive, memorable, poignant, nostalgic, wistful, plaintive AN OPPOSITE IS unmemorable

have *VERB* **1** *They have a house in France.* ► own, possess, be the owner of, boast, keep, enjoy AN OPPOSITE IS lack **2** *We have coffee at eleven.* ► drink, take **3** *What did you have for lunch?* ► eat, consume **4** *She had a letter from her boyfriend.* ► receive, get, be sent, obtain, acquire OPPOSITES ARE send, reject **5** *They are having a party next door.* ► hold, give, organize, arrange, throw, provide, lay on **6** *The apartment has five rooms.* ► contain, comprise, consist of, include, incorporate, be made up of **7** *We had trouble parking.* ► experience, encounter, undergo, meet with, run into, suffer, face **8** *I have a bad cold.* ► be suffering from, be afflicted by, be affected by, be troubled by **9** *The boys had a lot of fun.* ► enjoy, experience, go through **10** *Mike had guests at the weekend.* ► entertain, receive, be host to, cater for, invite **11** *Julia has had her baby.* ► give birth to, bear, produce, be delivered of, bring into the world

haven *NOUN* **1** *a haven for ships on the north coast* ► harbour, port, anchorage, mooring **2** *a safe haven in time of trouble* ► refuge, retreat, shelter, sanctuary, asylum

hazard *NOUN* **hazards** **1** a danger or risk **2** an obstacle
▷ **hazardous** *ADJECTIVE*

hazy *ADJECTIVE* **1** misty **2** vague or uncertain
▷ **hazily** *ADVERB* **haziness** *NOUN*

he *PRONOUN* **1** the male person or animal being talked about **2** a person (male or female) • *He who hesitates is lost*

head *NOUN* **heads** **1** the part of the body containing the brains, eyes, and mouth **2** your brains or mind; intelligence • *Use your head!* **3** a talent or ability • *She has a good head for figures.* **4** the side of a coin on which someone's head is shown • *Heads or tails?* **5** a person • *It costs £2 per head.* **6** the top or front of something • *a pinhead* • *at the head of the procession* **7** the chief; the person in charge **8** a headteacher
come to a head reach a crisis point
keep your head stay calm
off the top of your head without preparation or thinking carefully

head *VERB* **heads, heading, headed** **1** be at the top or front of something **2** hit a ball with your head **3** move in a particular direction • *We headed for the coast.* **4** force someone to turn aside by getting in front of them • *Let's see if we can head him off.* [from Old English]

headache *NOUN* **headaches** **1** a pain in the head **2** (*informal*) a worrying problem

heading *NOUN* **headings** a word or words put at the top of a piece of printing or writing

headland *NOUN* **headlands** a large piece of high land that sticks out into the sea

headlight *NOUN* **headlights** a powerful light at the front of a car, engine, etc.

headline *NOUN* **headlines** a heading in a newspaper
the headlines the main items of news

headlong *ADVERB, ADJECTIVE* **1** falling head first **2** in a hasty or thoughtless way

headmaster *NOUN* **headmasters** a male headteacher

headmistress *NOUN* **headmistresses** a female headteacher

head-on *ADVERB, ADJECTIVE* with the front parts colliding • *a head-on collision*

headquarters *NOUN* the place from which an organization is controlled

headstrong *ADJECTIVE* determined to do as you want

headteacher *NOUN* **headteachers** the person in charge of a school

headway *NOUN*
make headway make progress

heal *VERB* **heals, healing, healed** **1** make or become healthy flesh again • *The wound healed slowly.* **2** (*old use*) cure • *healing the sick*

health *NOUN* **1** the condition of a person's body or mind • *His health is bad.* **2** being healthy • *in sickness and in health*

Thesaurus

hazard *NOUN* *a serious health hazard* ► risk, threat, danger, menace

hazard *VERB* **1** *a business that is too risky to hazard money on* ► risk, chance, jeopardize **2** *I wouldn't want to hazard a guess about that.* ► offer, put forward, venture, advance

hazardous *ADJECTIVE* *He knew how hazardous the road could be in the dark.* ► dangerous, risky, perilous, precarious, uncertain, unpredictable, unsafe, chancy, (*more informal*) dicey
OPPOSITES ARE safe, secure

hazy *ADJECTIVE* **1** *The weather was good, if a little hazy.* ► misty, cloudy, foggy, smoky **2** *hazy memories of childhood* ► vague, indistinct, blurred, fuzzy, unclear, faint, dim

head *NOUN* **1** *He hit his head on a beam.* ► skull, crown, cranium, (*more informal*) nut, (*more informal*) bonce RELATED ADJECTIVE cephalic **2** *the head of a publishing firm* ► chief, chairman, chief executive, president, principal **3** *You need a good head for this work.* ► brain, intellect, intelligence, wit **4** *She has quite a head for figures.* ► aptitude, gift, talent, bent, knack
lose your head *Connie lost her head and ran off.* ► panic, lose control, go to pieces, (*more informal*) lose your cool
off your head (*informal*) *He was quite off his head, spouting complete nonsense.* ► mad, crazy, insane, out of your mind, unbalanced, demented, deranged

head *ADJECTIVE* *the head chef* ► chief, senior, principal, leading

head *VERB* **1** *She headed a team of researchers.* ► lead, be in charge of, be at the head of, manage, direct, oversee, supervise **2 head for** *They were heading for the station.* ► go *or* move towards, make for, aim for, point to

heading *NOUN* **1** *He turned the page and read the chapter heading.* ► title, headline, caption, rubric **2** *The subject is discussed under several headings.* ► category, division, section, class, group

heal *VERB* **1** *Madra's wounds began to heal.* ► get better, recover, knit, mend, unite **2** *an ointment to heal her injured finger* ► make better, cure, treat, remedy, restore **3** *The rift between father and son was never completely healed.* ► mend, repair, put right, settle, remedy, reconcile, patch up

health *NOUN* **1** *He is now in excellent health and back at work.* ► condition, shape, form, fettle, constitution **2** *Hormone levels are important to*

healthy *ADJECTIVE* **healthier, healthiest 1** being well; free from illness **2** producing good health • *Fresh air is healthy.*
▷ **healthily** *ADVERB* **healthiness** *NOUN*

heap *NOUN* **heaps** a pile, especially an untidy one
heaps *PLURAL NOUN* (*informal*) a great amount; plenty • *There's heaps of time.*

heap *VERB* **heaps, heaping, heaped 1** make things into a heap **2** to load heavily with • *She heaped the plate with food.*

hear *VERB* **hears, hearing, heard 1** take in sounds through the ears **2** receive news or information etc. **3** listen to and try a case in a lawcourt
▷ **hearer** *NOUN*
hear! hear! (in a debate) I agree
not hear of refuse to allow something • *He wouldn't hear of my paying for it.*

hearing *NOUN* **hearings 1** the ability to hear **2** a chance to be heard; a trial in a lawcourt

hearing aid *NOUN* **hearing aids** a device to help a deaf person to hear

heart *NOUN* **hearts 1** the organ of the body that makes the blood circulate **2** a person's feelings or emotions; sympathy **3** enthusiasm; courage • *Take heart.* **4** the middle or most important part **5** a curved shape representing a heart **6** a playing card with red heart shapes on it
break someone's heart make someone very unhappy
by heart memorized

heart attack *NOUN* **heart attacks** a sudden failure of the heart to work properly, which results in great pain or sometimes death

hearten *VERB* **heartens, heartening, heartened** make a person feel encouraged

heartfelt *ADJECTIVE* felt deeply

hearth *NOUN* **hearths** the floor of a fireplace, or the area in front of it

heartless *ADJECTIVE* without pity or sympathy

hearty *ADJECTIVE* **1** strong and vigorous **2** enthusiastic and sincere • *hearty congratulations* **3** (said about a meal) large
▷ **heartily** *ADVERB* **heartiness** *NOUN*

Thesaurus

health. ► fitness, well-being, healthiness, good health RELATED ADJECTIVE sanitary

healthy *ADJECTIVE* **1** *We try to promote a healthy lifestyle.* ► health-giving, wholesome, beneficial, bracing, invigorating **2** *I think I am fit, healthy, and looking good again.* ► well, in good health, in good condition, in good shape, in good trim **3** *a healthy respect for the opposite sex* ► sound, strong

heap *NOUN* **1** *a heap of old newspapers* ► pile, stack, mass, mound, mountain, collection, hoard **2 heaps** (*informal*) *We've got heaps of time.* ► plenty, a lot, a great deal, (*more informal*) lots, (*more informal*) masses, (*more informal*) piles

heap *VERB* **1** *She heaped more cakes on their plates.* ► pile, stack, mass, bank, collect **2** *The praise heaped on them was well deserved.* ► lavish, shower, bestow, confer

hear *VERB* **1** *You can hear the traffic in the distance.* ► make out, catch, listen to, perceive, discern, detect USAGE Note that all these words, except for *listen to*, can also be used about seeing, and so you might need to make the meaning clear by saying, for example, *You can make out the sound of traffic in the distance.* Note also that *listen to* implies something you try to do, whereas *hear* can refer to sounds that you might be aware of by chance. RELATED ADJECTIVE audible **2** *I heard that you were leaving.* ► be told, be informed, learn, gather, find out, discover **3** *A female judge heard the case.* ► try, judge, sit in judgement on

hearing *NOUN* **1** *He made the comment out of our hearing.* ► earshot, range, reach RELATED ADJECTIVE acoustic **2** *a judicial hearing* ► trial, court case, inquiry, investigation, tribunal, review, proceedings

heart *NOUN* **1** *His heart had stopped beating.* ► organ of circulation, (*more informal*) ticker RELATED ADJECTIVE cardiac **2** *an air link into the heart of the city* ► centre, middle, nucleus, core, hub, inside, kernel **3** *the heart of the problem* ► essence, nub, crux, root, focus **4** *He won't allow his heart to rule his head.* ► feelings, emotion, sentiment **5** *The lack of support made them lose heart.* ► enthusiasm, eagerness, courage, bravery, resolution, determination **6** *She may be stern but she has a lot of heart.* ► compassion, feeling, sympathy, tenderness, understanding, affection, humanity, kindness, love

heartbreaking *ADJECTIVE* *heartbreaking sobs from the bedroom* ► distressing, harrowing, pitiful, saddening, tragic, grievous, heart-rending

heartbroken *ADJECTIVE* *He was heartbroken at having to sell his home.* ► broken-hearted, inconsolable, devastated, grief-stricken, desolate, despairing AN OPPOSITE IS happy

hearty *ADJECTIVE* **1** *The remark brought a loud hearty laugh.* ► enthusiastic, sincere, warm, jovial, cordial, exuberant, cheerful, uninhibited **2** *Beth always had a hearty appetite.* ► big, healthy, strong, robust, vigorous **3** *They looked forward to a hearty meal and a good night's sleep.*

heat *NOUN* **heats 1** hotness or (in scientific use) the form of energy causing this **2** hot weather **3** strong feeling, especially anger **4** a race or contest to decide who will take part in the final
on heat (said about a female mammal) ready for mating

heat *VERB* **heats, heating, heated** make or become hot

heathen *NOUN* **heathens** a person who does not believe in any of the world's chief religions

heather *NOUN* an evergreen plant with small purple, pink, or white flowers

heatwave *NOUN* **heatwaves** a long period of hot weather

heave *VERB* **heaves, heaving, heaved 1** lift or move something heavy **2** (*informal*) throw **3** rise and fall **4** (said about the stomach) feel uncomfortable, making you want to vomit
▷ **heave** *NOUN*
heave a sigh utter a deep sigh

heaven *NOUN* **heavens 1** the place where God and angels are thought to live **2** a very pleasant place or condition
the heavens the sky

heavy *ADJECTIVE* **heavier, heaviest 1** weighing a lot; difficult to lift or carry **2** great in amount or force etc. • *heavy rain* • *a heavy penalty* **3** needing much effort • *heavy work* **4** full of sadness or worry • *with a heavy heart*
▷ **heavily** *ADVERB* **heaviness** *NOUN*

heavyweight *NOUN* **heavyweights 1** a heavy person **2** a boxer of the heaviest weight
▷ **heavyweight** *ADJECTIVE*

Hebrew *NOUN* the language of the Jews in ancient Palestine and modern Israel

hectare (**hek**- tair) *NOUN* **hectares** a unit of area equal to 10,000 square metres or nearly 2 acres

hedge *NOUN* **hedges** a row of bushes forming a barrier or boundary

hedgehog *NOUN* **hedgehogs** a small animal covered with long prickles

heed *NOUN*
take *or* **pay heed** give attention to something
▷ **heedful** *ADJECTIVE* **heedless** *ADJECTIVE*

heel *NOUN* **heels 1** the back part of the foot **2** the part round or under the heel of a sock or shoe etc.
take to your heels run away

Thesaurus

► substantial, generous, sizeable, solid, large, ample, wholesome

heat *NOUN* **1** *The fire gave out a lot of heat.* ► warmth, hotness, glow RELATED ADJECTIVE thermal, calorific **2** *The summer heat was exhausting.* ► hot weather, warmth, humidity, sultriness, swelter **3** *There is too much heat in these arguments.* ► passion, intensity, ardour, warmth, vehemence, anger, fury

heat *VERB* **1** *You can heat the food under the grill, if you prefer.* ► cook, heat up, reheat **2** *The room has two external walls and is difficult to heat.* ► keep warm, warm up

heated *ADJECTIVE* **1** *The discussion soon became heated.* ► passionate, vehement, animated, impassioned, bitter, tempestuous OPPOSITES ARE dispassionate, calm **2** *Rachel grew heated as she talked about her ordeal.* ► excited, roused, worked up, keyed up, animated, impassioned AN OPPOSITE IS calm

heave *VERB* *Two men heaved back the great iron gates.* ► haul, drag, pull, throw, draw, tow, tug, hoist, lift, lug, raise

heaven *NOUN* **1** *You might get your reward in heaven, if you are lucky.* ► paradise, the next world, the hereafter, the afterlife **2** *In that heat a cool drink was absolute heaven.* ► ecstasy, bliss, joy, rapture, delight AN OPPOSITE IS hell **3 the heavens** *The moon caused a glow in the heavens.* ► the sky, the skies, the firmament, the blue RELATED ADJECTIVE celestial

heavenly *ADJECTIVE* **1** *the sound of joyful, heavenly music* ► beautiful, celestial, divine, angelic, blissful, exquisite OPPOSITES ARE devilish, infernal **2** *They had a heavenly time.* ► delightful, marvellous, wonderful, lovely, pleasant

heavy *ADJECTIVE* **1** *too heavy to lift* ► weighty, massive, bulky, hefty **2** *a heavy man* ► large, fat, corpulent, overweight **3** *heavy smoking* ► excessive, immoderate, intensive, uncontrolled **4** *a heavy meal* ► substantial, hearty, filling, sizeable, solid, stodgy **5** *a heavy blow* ► hard, forceful, violent, powerful, hefty **6** *heavy losses; a heavy fine* ► large, substantial, considerable **7** *a heavy burden of responsibility* ► onerous, demanding, formidable, challenging, severe **8** *heavy work* ► arduous, strenuous, taxing **9** *heavy reading* ► serious, tedious, dull **10** *heavy rain* ► strong, intense, teeming, torrential

hectic *ADJECTIVE* *We spent three hectic days getting the house in order.* ► busy, frantic, feverish, frenzied, manic, chaotic OPPOSITES ARE leisurely, quiet

hefty *ADJECTIVE* *A hefty young man stood in their way.* ► burly, beefy, sturdy, well built, strapping, brawny, hulking, muscular, powerful, stocky, stout, athletic, big, heavy OPPOSITES ARE slight, thin

hefty *ADJECTIVE* **heftier, heftiest** large and strong
▷ **heftily** *ADVERB*

height *NOUN* **heights 1** how high something is; the distance from the base to the top or from head to foot **2** a high place **3** the highest or most intense part • *at the height of the holiday season*

heighten *VERB* **heightens, heightening, heightened** make or become higher or more intense

heir (*say as* air) *NOUN* **heirs** a person who inherits something

heiress (**air**- ess) *NOUN* **heiresses** a female heir, especially to great wealth

heirloom (**air**- loom) *NOUN* **heirlooms** a valued possession that has been handed down in a family for several generations

helicopter *NOUN* **helicopters** a kind of aircraft with a large horizontal propeller or rotor [from Greek *helix* = coil + Greek *pteron* = wing]

helium (**hee**- lee- um) *NOUN* a light colourless gas that does not burn

helix (**hee**- liks) *NOUN* **helices** (**hee**- liss- eez) a spiral [from Greek, = coil]

hell *NOUN* **1** a place where, in some religions, wicked people are thought to be punished after they die **2** a very unpleasant place or experience
hell for leather (*informal*) at high speed [from Old English]

hello *INTERJECTION* a word used to greet somebody or to attract their attention

helmet *NOUN* **helmets** a strong covering worn to protect the head

help *VERB* **helps, helping, helped 1** do part of another person's work for him or her **2** benefit; make something better or easier • *This will help you to sleep.* **3** if you cannot help doing something, you cannot avoid doing it • *I can't help coughing.* **4** serve food etc. to somebody • *just help yourself*
▷ **helper** *NOUN* **helpful** *ADJECTIVE* **helpfully** *ADVERB*

help *NOUN* **1** helping somebody **2** a person or thing that helps [from Old English]

helping *NOUN* **helpings** a portion of food

helpless *ADJECTIVE* not able to do things
▷ **helplessly** *ADVERB* **helplessness** *NOUN*

helpline *NOUN* **helplines** a telephone service giving advice on problems

Thesaurus

height *NOUN* **1** *We wanted to know the height of the tower.* ► tallness, highness, vertical measurement, elevation, altitude **2 heights** *reaching the mountain heights* ► summit, top, peak, crest, crown, tip **3** *They were at the height of their fame.* ► peak, high point, acme, climax, zenith OPPOSITES ARE nadir, low point

heighten *VERB* **1** *The architects proposed heightening the roof levels.* ► raise, make higher, lift up, elevate, build up AN OPPOSITE IS lower **2** *The presence of police heightened their sense of alarm.* ► increase, magnify, intensify, add to, sharpen, strengthen, augment, boost, enhance AN OPPOSITE IS lessen

hell *NOUN* **1** *religions that believe in a hell* ► netherworld, eternal punishment, infernal regions, lower regions AN OPPOSITE IS heaven RELATED ADJECTIVE infernal **2** *Living with Patrick must be hell.* ► agony, torture, a misery, a nightmare, an ordeal, a torment

hellish *ADJECTIVE* *It was a hellish experience they wanted never to repeat.* ► dreadful, ghastly, horrible, terrible, frightful

help *VERB* **1** *Will you help me move this bed?* ► assist, aid, lend a hand **2** *I couldn't help laughing.* ► prevent yourself, restrain yourself from, refrain from, resist **3** *A small donation will help those in need.* ► support, contribute to, encourage, promote **4** *Foreign visits will help your languages.* ► improve, enhance, bolster **5** *She took aspirin to help her headache.* ► relieve, reduce, ease, soothe, alleviate, remedy, lessen

help *NOUN* **1** *We could do with some help.* ► assistance, support, aid, guidance, cooperation, advice AN OPPOSITE IS hindrance **2** *Would a screwdriver be of help?* ► use, service, benefit, utility

helper *NOUN* **1** *A chain of helpers passed buckets of water along.* ► supporter, volunteer, worker **2** *All her helpers were away that day.* ► assistant, colleague, collaborator, subordinate, associate, co-worker

helpful *ADJECTIVE* **1** *The shop assistant was friendly and helpful.* ► obliging, willing, cooperative, thoughtful, considerate, sympathetic, eager to please, friendly **2** *A hammer might be helpful. A sceptical attitude won't be helpful.* ► useful, of use, beneficial, worthwhile, profitable, productive, constructive, valuable

helping *NOUN* *a good helping of pudding* ► portion, serving, plateful, bowlful, share, amount, ration, (*more informal*) dollop

helpless *ADJECTIVE* *She felt helpless and frustrated.* ► powerless, impotent, incapable, dependent, weak, forlorn, vulnerable, defenceless, destitute

hem *NOUN* *She lowered the hem of her skirt.* ► hemline, edge, border, fringe

hem *NOUN* **hems** the edge of a piece of cloth that is folded over and sewn down

hem *VERB* **hems, hemming, hemmed** put a hem on something
hem in surround and restrict

hemisphere *NOUN* **hemispheres** **1** half a sphere **2** half the earth • *Australia is in the southern hemisphere*
▷ **hemispherical** *ADJECTIVE*

hen *NOUN* **hens** **1** a female bird **2** a female fowl

hence *ADVERB* **1** henceforth **2** therefore **3** (*old use*) from here

henchman *NOUN* **henchmen** a trusty supporter

her *PRONOUN* the form of **she** used as the object of a verb or after a preposition

her *ADJECTIVE* belonging to her • *her book*

herald *NOUN* **heralds** an official in former times who made announcements and carried messages for a king or queen

heraldry *NOUN* the study of coats of arms
▷ **heraldic** (hir- al- dik) *ADJECTIVE*

herb *NOUN* **herbs** a plant used for flavouring or for making medicine
▷ **herbal** *ADJECTIVE*

herbivorous (her- biv- er- us) *ADJECTIVE* plant-eating COMPARE **carnivorous**
▷ **herbivore** *NOUN*

herd *NOUN* **herds** **1** a group of cattle or other animals that feed together **2** a mass of people; a mob
▷ **herdsman** *NOUN*

herd *VERB* **herds, herding, herded** **1** gather or move or send in a herd • *We all herded into the dining room.* **2** look after a herd of animals

here *ADVERB* in or to this place etc.
here and there in various places or directions

hereby *ADVERB* by this act or decree etc.

hereditary *ADJECTIVE* **1** inherited • *a hereditary disease* **2** inheriting a position • *Our Queen is a hereditary monarch.*

heredity (hir- ed- it- ee) *NOUN* the process of inheriting physical or mental characteristics from parents or ancestors

heresy (herri- see) *NOUN* **heresies** an opinion that disagrees with the beliefs generally accepted by the Christian Church or other authority

heretic (herri- tik) *NOUN* **heretics** a person who supports a heresy
▷ **heretical** (hi- ret- ik- al) *ADJECTIVE*

heritage *NOUN* the things that someone has inherited

hermetically *ADVERB* so as to be airtight • *The tin is hermetically sealed.*

hermit *NOUN* **hermits** a person who lives alone and keeps away from people

hero *NOUN* **heroes** **1** a man or boy who is admired for doing something very brave or great **2** the chief male character in a story etc.
▷ **heroic** *ADJECTIVE* **heroically** *ADVERB* **heroism** *NOUN*

heroin *NOUN* a very strong drug, made from morphine

heroine *NOUN* **heroines** **1** a woman or girl who is admired for doing something very brave or great **2** the chief female character in a story etc.

heron *NOUN* **herons** a wading bird with long legs and a long neck

herring *NOUN* **herring** or **herrings** a sea fish used as food

hers *POSSESSIVE PRONOUN* belonging to her • *Those books are hers*
USAGE It is incorrect to write *her's*.

herself *PRONOUN* she or her and nobody else. The word is used to refer back to the subject of a sentence (e.g. *She cut herself*) or for emphasis (e.g. *She herself has said it*)
by herself alone; on her own

hertz *NOUN* **hertz** a unit of frequency of electromagnetic waves, = one cycle per second

Thesaurus

hem *VERB* **hem in** *We were hemmed in by a group of tourist buses.* ▶ shut in, close in, box in, enclose, surround, confine, restrict

herd *NOUN* **1** *herds of farm animals* ▶ drove, pack, flock **2** *She cut her way through the herd of lunchtime drinkers.* ▶ crowd, mass, throng, horde, crush

herd *VERB* **1** *They herded the sheep into the pens.* ▶ drive, lead, guide, round, gather, collect **2** *We all herded into a meeting room.* ▶ crowd, pack, throng, flock, huddle, squash

hero *NOUN* **1** *His father had been decorated as a war hero.* ▶ champion, brave man **2** *James had always been her hero.* ▶ idol, star, ideal, paragon, favourite, darling **3** *The story had no real hero.* ▶ principal character, lead character, protagonist

heroic *ADJECTIVE* *All his heroic efforts might come to nothing.* ▶ brave, courageous, noble, valiant, bold, daring, gallant, intrepid AN OPPOSITE IS cowardly

heroine *NOUN* *the heroine of the film* ▶ leading *or* principal female character, female lead, female star, leading lady

hesitate *VERB* **hesitates, hesitating, hesitated** be slow or uncertain in speaking, moving, etc.
▷ **hesitant** *ADJECTIVE* **hesitation** *NOUN*

heterogeneous (het- er- o- jeen- ee- us) *ADJECTIVE* composed of people or things of different kinds

heterosexual *ADJECTIVE* attracted to people of the opposite sex; not homosexual
▷ **heterosexual** *NOUN*

hexagon *NOUN* **hexagons** a flat shape with six sides and six angles
▷ **hexagonal** *ADJECTIVE*

hibernate *VERB* **hibernates, hibernating, hibernated** spend the winter in a state like deep sleep
▷ **hibernation** *NOUN*
[from Latin *hiberna* = winter quarters]

hiccup *NOUN* **hiccups 1** a high gulping sound made when your breath is briefly interrupted **2** a brief hitch or setback
▷ **hiccup** *VERB* **hicups, hicupping, hicupped**

hide [1] *VERB* **hides, hiding, hid, hidden 1** get into a place where you cannot be seen **2** keep a person or thing from being seen **3** keep a thing secret

hide [2] *NOUN* **hides** an animal's skin

hide-and-seek *NOUN* a game in which one person looks for others who are hiding

hideous *ADJECTIVE* very ugly or unpleasant
▷ **hideously** *ADVERB*

hiding [1] *NOUN* being hidden • *She went into hiding*
▷ **hiding place** *NOUN*

hiding [2] *NOUN* **hidings** a thrashing or beating

hierarchy (hyr- ark- ee) *NOUN* **hierarchies** an organization that ranks people one above another according to the power or authority that they hold

hieroglyphics (hyr- o- glif- iks) *PLURAL NOUN* pictures or symbols used in ancient Egypt to represent words

hi-fi *NOUN* **hi-fis** (*informal*) **1** high fidelity **2** equipment for reproducing recorded sound with very little distortion

higgledy-piggledy *ADVERB, ADJECTIVE* completely mixed up; in great disorder

high *ADJECTIVE* **1** reaching a long way upwards • *high hills* **2** far above the ground or above sea level • *high clouds* **3** measuring from top to bottom • *two metres high* **4** above average level in importance, quality, amount, etc. • *high rank* • *high prices* **5** (said about meat) beginning to go bad **6** (*informal*) affected by a drug
it is high time it is already the time for something to happen • *It's high time we left.*

high *ADVERB* at or to a high level or position etc. • *They flew high above us.*

Thesaurus

hesitant *ADJECTIVE They were hesitant about what to do next. He took a hesitant step back.*
► uncertain, tentative, cautious, faltering, doubtful, half-hearted, irresolute, indecisive, undecided, dithering OPPOSITES ARE decisive, resolute

hesitate *VERB She hesitated before searching in her bag for her keys.* ► pause, delay, falter, dither, hold back, vacillate, waver, wait, have second thoughts

hesitation *NOUN He answered without any hesitation.* ► pause, delay, equivocation, reluctance, vacillation, misgivings, second thoughts, qualms, reservation, doubt, uncertainty

hidden *ADJECTIVE* **1** *a hidden entrance a hidden camera* ► concealed, secret, unseen, invisible, disguised, camouflaged, covered **2** *The message may have a hidden meaning.*
► unknown, obscure, cryptic, secret, abstruse, mysterious, ulterior

hide *VERB* **1** *Sam hid in a cupboard.* ► conceal yourself, take cover, keep hidden, lie low, keep out of sight **2** *Where did they hide the jewels?*
► conceal, secrete, store away, bury, (*more informal*) stash AN OPPOSITE IS expose **3** *Richard tried to hide his disapproval.* ► disguise, conceal, keep hidden, suppress, repress, mask OPPOSITES ARE disclose, flaunt **4** *Passing clouds hid the moon.* ► obscure, shadow, block out, conceal, obstruct AN OPPOSITE IS reveal

hide *NOUN an animal's hide* ► skin, pelt, coat, fur, leather

hideous *ADJECTIVE* **1** *His mouth was twisted in a hideous grin.* ► ugly, unsightly, repulsive, repellent, revolting, gruesome, disgusting, macabre AN OPPOSITE IS beautiful **2** *It is one of the most hideous experiences we have had in our lives.* ► horrible, ghastly, horrific, terrible, appalling, shocking, sickening, dreadful, frightful, grim, grisly, odious

hiding *NOUN I was given a good hiding.*
► beating, thrashing, caning, spanking, belting, whacking

high *ADJECTIVE* **1** *a high mountain; a high building*
► tall, lofty, elevated, towering OPPOSITES ARE low, short **2** *a high position in the government*
► senior, prominent, high-ranking, top-ranking, leading, distinguished, important, influential, powerful OPPOSITES ARE junior, low-ranking **3** *high moral principles* ► noble, lofty, honourable, high-minded AN OPPOSITE IS base

highbrow *ADJECTIVE* intellectual

higher education *NOUN* education at a university or college

high fidelity *NOUN* reproducing recorded sound with very little distortion

high jump *NOUN* an athletic contest in which competitors try to jump over a high bar

highlight *NOUN* **highlights 1** the most interesting part of something • *The highlight of the holiday was the trip to Pompeii.* **2** a light area in a painting etc. **3** a light-coloured streak in a person's hair

highly *ADVERB* **1** extremely • *highly amusing* **2** very favourably • *We think highly of her.*

Highness *NOUN* **Highnesses** the title of a prince or princess

high road *NOUN* **high roads** the main road

high school *NOUN* **high schools** a secondary school

high street *NOUN* **high streets** a town's main street

high tea *NOUN* a meal eaten in the late afternoon or early evening

highway *NOUN* **highways** a main road or route

highwayman *NOUN* **highwaymen** a man who robbed travellers on highways in former times

hijack *VERB* **hijacks, hijacking, hijacked** seize control of an aircraft or vehicle during a journey
▷ **hijack** *NOUN* **hijacker** *NOUN*

hike *NOUN* **hikes** a long walk
▷ **hike** *VERB* **hiker** *NOUN*

hilarious *ADJECTIVE* very funny
▷ **hilariously** *ADVERB* **hilarity** *NOUN*

hill *NOUN* **hills** a piece of land that is higher than the ground around it
▷ **hillside** *NOUN* **hilly** *ADJECTIVE*

hilt *NOUN* **hilts** the handle of a sword, dagger, or knife
to the hilt completely

him *PRONOUN* the form of **he** used as the object of a verb or after a preposition

himself *PRONOUN* he or him and nobody else
COMPARE **herself**

hind *ADJECTIVE* at the back • *the hind legs*

hinder *VERB* **hinders, hindering, hindered** get in someone's way or make things difficult for them
▷ **hindrance** *NOUN*

hindquarters *PLURAL NOUN* an animal's hind legs and rear parts

hindsight *NOUN* looking back on an event with knowledge or understanding that you did not have at the time

Hindu *NOUN* **Hindus** a person who believes in Hinduism, which is one of the religions of India

hinge *NOUN* **hinges** a joining device on which a lid or door etc. turns when it opens

hinge *VERB* **hinges, hinging, hinged 1** fix something with a hinge **2** depend • *Everything hinges on this meeting.*

Thesaurus

4 *high prices* ► inflated, excessive, exorbitant, top, costly AN OPPOSITE IS low **5** *the high notes* ► high-pitched, soprano, treble, shrill, sharp, piercing OPPOSITES ARE low, bass **6** *the highest standards* ► excellent, outstanding, exceptional, exemplary OPPOSITES ARE low, poor **7** *high winds* ► strong, powerful, violent, stiff, blustery AN OPPOSITE IS gentle **8** *I have a high opinion of them.* ► favourable, positive, good, approving OPPOSITES ARE low, unfavourable

highbrow *ADJECTIVE* *highbrow tastes in music* ► intellectual, sophisticated, cultivated, cultured, serious

highly *ADVERB* *a form of waste that is highly toxic* ► very, extremely, considerably, exceedingly, distinctly, decidedly, immensely

hijack *VERB* *A man was charged with hijacking a Russian plane to Stockholm.* ► seize, commandeer, take over, skyjack, expropriate

hike *VERB* *They hiked across the moors for several miles.* ► trek, go on foot, walk , ramble, tramp, trudge, traipse, slog

hike *NOUN* *a twenty-mile hike* ► trek, walk, ramble, tramp, trudge, slog

hilarious *ADJECTIVE* *A group clustered round a hilarious puppet show.* ► comical, funny, amusing, entertaining, uproarious, riotous, (*more informal*) hysterical, (*more informal*) side-splitting

hill *NOUN* **1** *the house at the top of the hill* ► high ground, elevation, hillock, ridge, peak, mount **2** *The car stalled on a steep hill.* ► slope, rise, gradient, incline, ascent

hinder *VERB* *Power failures have hindered production.* ► hamper, hold up, interfere with, obstruct, restrict, thwart, prevent, curb, curtail, foil AN OPPOSITE IS facilitate

hindrance *NOUN* *Our presence might be as much a hindrance to you as a help.* ► impediment, obstacle, obstruction, encumbrance, handicap, restriction, limitation, restraint, inconvenience, complication, disadvantage, drawback AN OPPOSITE IS help

hinge *VERB* *Everything hinges on next month's elections.* ► depend, rest, hang, revolve, turn

A B C D E F G H I J K L M N O P Q R S T U V W X Y Z

hint *NOUN* **hints 1** a slight indication or suggestion • *Give me a hint of what you want* **2** a useful idea or piece of advice • *household hints*

hint *VERB* **hints, hinting, hinted** make a hint

hip [1] *NOUN* **hips** the bony part at the side of the body between the waist and the thigh

hip [2] *NOUN* **hips** the fruit of the wild rose

hippopotamus *NOUN* **hippopotamuses** a very large African animal that lives near water

hire *VERB* **hires, hiring, hired 1** pay to borrow something **2** lend something for payment • *He hires out bicycles*
▷ **hirer** *NOUN*

hire *NOUN* hiring something • *bikes for hire*

hire purchase *NOUN* a system of buying something by paying for it in instalments

his *ADJECTIVE, POSSESSIVE PRONOUN* belonging to him • *That is his book* • *That book is his*

hiss *VERB* **hisses, hissing, hissed** make a sound like an *s* • *The snakes were hissing*
▷ **hiss** *NOUN*

histogram *NOUN* **histograms** a chart showing amounts as rectangles of varying sizes

historian *NOUN* **historians** a person who writes or studies history

historic *ADJECTIVE* famous or important in history; likely to be remembered • *a historic town* • *a historic meeting*
USAGE Do not confuse with **historical**.

historical *ADJECTIVE* **1** to do with history **2** that actually existed or took place in the past • *The novel is based on historical events*
USAGE Do not confuse with **historic**.

history *NOUN* **histories 1** what happened in the past **2** study of past events **3** a description of important events [from Greek *historia* = learning or finding out]

hit *VERB* **hits, hitting, hit 1** come forcefully against a person or thing; knock or strike **2** have a bad effect on • *Famine has hit the poor countries* **3** reach • *I can't hit that high note*
hit on discover something by chance

hit *NOUN* **hits 1** hitting; a knock or stroke **2** a shot that hits the target **3** a success **4** a successful song, show, etc.

hitch *VERB* **hitches, hitching, hitched 1** raise or pull with a slight jerk **2** fasten with a loop or hook etc. **3** hitch-hike

hitch *NOUN* **hitches 1** a slight difficulty causing delay **2** a hitching movement **3** a knot

hitch-hike *VERB* **hitch-hikes, hitch-hiking, hitch-hiked** travel by getting lifts from passing vehicles
▷ **hitch-hiker** *NOUN*

Thesaurus

hint *NOUN* **1** *She would drop a few casual hints about leaving. I can take a hint that I'm not wanted.* ► clue, sign, signal, indication, reminder, inkling, intimation **2** *His father kept turning up to offer handy hints.* ► tip, piece of advice, pointer **3** *There was a hint of sadness in her voice.* ► trace, tinge, touch, suggestion

hint *VERB* **1** *He hinted that a new project was being considered.* ► suggest, imply, indicate, intimate **2 hint at** *I'm not sure what she was hinting at.* ► allude to, refer to, imply, suggest

hire *VERB* **1** *We could hire a car and drive to London.* ► rent, lease, book, charter **2** *The new bosses want to hire more freelance workers.* ► employ, engage, recruit, appoint

hiss *VERB* **1** *She turned the tap until she heard the gas hiss.* ► fizz, fizzle, whistle **2** *The audience hissed and threw things on the stage.* ► jeer, boo, catcall

historic *ADJECTIVE a historic meeting of the heads of state* ► famous, notable, epoch-making, celebrated, momentous, significant, important
AN OPPOSITE IS unimportant

historical *ADJECTIVE a story based on historical events* ► real, real-life, true, actual, authentic, documented, attested, verifiable OPPOSITES ARE fictitious, fictional

history *NOUN* **1** *their interest in history* ► the past, former times, days of old, antiquity **2** *a history of the civil wars* ► chronicle, record, narrative

hit *VERB* **1** *He hit the tree with his fist.* ► strike, smack, slap, thump, whack, (*more informal*) slug **2** *Several lorries hit the central barrier.* ► crash into, run into, collide with, smash into **3** *The industry has been hit by lightning strikes.* ► affect, hurt, harm, damage **4** *It suddenly hit me that I should have confirmed the booking.* ► strike, occur to, dawn on, come to, cross your mind **5** *Contributions should hit the million mark.* ► reach, achieve

hit *NOUN* **1** *He got a hit on the head.* ► blow, punch, thump, knock, smack, slap, whack **2** *The party had been a huge hit.* ► success, triumph, winner, best-seller, (*more informal*) knockout

hitch *NOUN The moves all went without any hitch.* ► problem, difficulty, snag, setback, hindrance

hitch *VERB* **1** *The farmer hitched a tractor to the cart.* ► fasten, attach, hook, couple, connect **2** *Diana hitched up her skirts and entered the water.* ► pull, lift, raise, hoist, jerk, (*more informal*) hike

hi-tech *ADJECTIVE* using the most advanced technology, especially electronic devices and computers

hither *ADVERB* to or towards this place

hitherto *ADVERB* until this time

HIV *ABBREVIATION* human immunodeficiency virus; a virus that causes Aids

hive *NOUN* **hives 1** a beehive **2** the bees living in a beehive
hive of industry a place full of people working busily

hoard *NOUN* **hoards** a carefully saved store of money, treasure, food, etc.

hoard *VERB* **hoards, hoarding, hoarded** store something away
▷ **hoarder** *NOUN*
USAGE Do not confuse with **horde**.

hoarding *NOUN* **hoardings** a tall fence covered with advertisements

hoar frost *NOUN* a white frost

hoarse *ADJECTIVE* having a rough or croaking voice
▷ **hoarsely** *ADVERB* **hoarseness** *NOUN*

hoax *VERB* **hoaxes, hoaxing, hoaxed** deceive somebody as a joke
▷ **hoax** *NOUN* **hoaxer** *NOUN*

hobble *VERB* **hobbles, hobbling, hobbled** limp or walk with difficulty

hobby *NOUN* **hobbies** something you do for pleasure in your spare time

hobby horse *NOUN* **hobby horses 1** a stick with a horse's head, used as a toy **2** a subject that a person likes to talk about whenever he or she gets the chance

hobgoblin *NOUN* **hobgoblins** a mischievous or evil spirit

hockey *NOUN* a game played by two teams with curved sticks and a hard ball

hoe *NOUN* **hoes** a tool for scraping up weeds

hoe *VERB* **hoes, hoeing, hoed** scrape or dig with a hoe

hog *NOUN* **hogs 1** a male pig **2** (*informal*) a greedy person
go the whole hog (*informal*) do something completely or thoroughly

Hogmanay *NOUN* New Year's Eve in Scotland [perhaps from early French *aguillanneuf* = a gift at new year]

hoist *VERB* **hoists, hoisting, hoisted** lift something up, especially by using ropes or pulleys

hold *VERB* **holds, holding, held 1** have and keep, especially in your hands **2** have room for • *The jug holds two pints.* **3** support • *This plank won't hold my weight.* **4** stay the same; continue • *Will the fine weather hold?* **5** believe or consider • *We shall hold you responsible.* **6** cause something to take place • *hold a*

Thesaurus

hoard *NOUN* *The tomb contained a huge hoard of jewellery.* ► cache, store, stock, pile, stockpile, heap, supply, treasure trove

hoard *VERB* *The refugees had hoarded their supplies.* ► store, amass, accumulate, mass, put by, save, stockpile, pile up, collect, gather, keep, lay up, treasure, (*more informal*) stash away AN OPPOSITE IS squander

hoarse *ADJECTIVE* *a voice that was hoarse from shouting* ► rough, harsh, gruff, husky, throaty, rasping, croaking, grating, gravelly, growling, raucous

hoax *NOUN* *The virus warning was a hoax.* ► joke, practical joke, prank, trick, spoof, deception, fake, fraud, imposture, cheat, swindle, (*more informal*) leg-pull, (*more informal*) con

hobby *NOUN* *Kevin took up fishing as a hobby.* ► pastime, leisure activity, leisure pursuit, recreation, diversion, interest, relaxation

hoist *VERB* *The crew hoisted more cargo on deck.* ► raise, lift, pull up, heave, winch up

hoist *NOUN* *a hand-operated pneumatic hoist* ► crane, jack, pulley, winch, lift, lifting gear, block and tackle, davit, windlass, derrick

hold *VERB* **1** *He was holding a black briefcase.* ► clasp, clutch, grip, cling to, cling on to **2** *I wanted to hold her in my arms.* ► hug, embrace, clasp, fold, cradle **3** *Visitors must hold a valid passport.* ► possess, bear, have, own **4** *The society holds a general meeting in March.* ► call, convene, summon, conduct, assemble **5** *Police are holding him pending further investigation.* ► detain, keep in custody, imprison, lock up, arrest **6** *She held a senior position in a bank.* ► occupy, fill, (*more informal*) hold down **7** *The house holds six to eight people.* ► take, accommodate, have room for, have space for, contain **8** *The sect holds that killing animals is a sin.* ► believe, consider, maintain, contend, think, take the view **9** *I hope the good weather will hold.* ► continue, last, carry on, persist, endure
hold back 1 *Joe held back his anger.* ► suppress, control, restrain, curb, check, keep back, hold in AN OPPOSITE IS release **2** *The lack of information held us back.* ► hinder, hamper, inhibit, impede, thwart, restrain AN OPPOSITE IS help **3** *There is no need to hold back if you have things to say.* ► hesitate, pause, desist, shrink AN OPPOSITE IS proceed
hold forth *Ivor was holding forth about his adventures.* ► discourse, declaim, speak at length, spout, rant
hold off 1 *The rain held off until lunch time.*

meeting **7** restrain someone or stop them getting away • *The police are holding three men for the robbery.*
hold forth make a long speech
hold out refuse to give in
hold up **1** hinder **2** stop and rob somebody by threats or force
hold with approve of • *We don't hold with bullying.*
hold your tongue (*informal*) stop talking

hold NOUN **holds** **1** holding something; a grasp **2** something to hold on to for support **3** the part of a ship where cargo is stored, below the deck
get hold of **1** grasp **2** obtain **3** make contact with a person

hold-up NOUN **hold-ups** **1** a delay **2** a robbery with threats or force

hole NOUN **holes** **1** a hollow place; a gap or opening **2** a burrow **3** one of the small holes into which you have to hit the ball in golf **4** (*informal*) an unpleasant place
▷ **holey** ADJECTIVE
in a hole in an awkward situation

hole VERB **holes, holing, holed** **1** make a hole or holes in something **2** hit a golf ball into one of the holes

holiday NOUN **holidays** **1** a day or week etc. when people do not go to work or to school **2** a time when you go away to enjoy yourself

holiness NOUN being holy or sacred
His Holiness the title of the Pope

hollow ADJECTIVE with an empty space inside; not solid
▷ **hollowly** ADVERB

hollow NOUN **hollows** a hollow or sunken place

hollow VERB **hollows, hollowing, hollowed** make a thing hollow

holly NOUN **hollies** an evergreen bush with shiny prickly leaves and red berries

holocaust NOUN **holocausts** an immense destruction, especially by fire • *the nuclear holocaust*
the Holocaust the mass murder of the Jews by the Nazis from 1939 to 1945

hologram NOUN **holograms** a type of photograph made by laser beams that produces a three-dimensional image

holy ADJECTIVE **holier, holiest** **1** belonging or devoted to God **2** consecrated • *holy water*
▷ **holiness** NOUN

homage NOUN **homages** an act or expression of respect or honour • *We paid homage to his achievements.*

Thesaurus

► stay away, desist **2** *He held the attackers off as long as he could.* ► resist, fend off, ward off, stave off, repel, rebuff
hold out **1** *Supplies will not hold out much longer.* ► last, remain, continue AN OPPOSITE IS run out **2** *The garrison held out for a whole month.* ► resist, persevere, stand fast, hang on OPPOSITES ARE give in, yield
hold up **1** *The bridge is held up by concrete columns.* ► support, bear, shore up, carry, raise **2** *Work on the roof was held up by bad weather.* ► delay, detain, hinder, impede AN OPPOSITE IS facilitate

hold NOUN **1** *She released her hold on the handle.* ► grip, grasp, clutch **2** *Tim had some kind of hold over them.* ► influence, power, control, sway, (*more informal*) clout

holder NOUN **1** *She put the knife back in its holder.* ► case, container, receptacle, casing, cover, sheath, stand, rest **2** *holders of EU passports* ► bearer, possessor, owner

hole NOUN **1** *The work gang dug a large hole in the road.* ► opening, orifice, trench, ditch **2** *There were holes in the plaster caused by damp.* ► gap, split, cavity, crack, fissure, pit, puncture, hollow, depression, tear **3** *The animal crawled out of its hole.* ► burrow, lair, retreat **4** (*informal*) *We were out of money and in a bit of a hole.* ► predicament, mess, difficulty, tight corner, quandary, plight, crisis, emergency

holiday NOUN **1** *Her doctor told her she needed a holiday.* ► vacation, break, rest, time off, leave **2** *Monday is a public holiday.* ► bank holiday, festival, feast day

holiness NOUN *Her holiness affected everyone who saw her.* ► sanctity, devoutness, spirituality, piety, saintliness, godliness, righteousness

hollow ADJECTIVE **1** *a hollow space* ► empty, concave, sunken, deep, depressed AN OPPOSITE IS solid **2** *a hollow laugh* ► dull, low, flat, muffled, muted **3** *a hollow promise* ► insincere, artificial, false, empty, deceptive AN OPPOSITE IS sincere **4** *a hollow victory* ► worthless, futile, vain, meaningless, pointless, pyrrhic AN OPPOSITE IS worthwhile

hollow NOUN *an ancient theatre built in the hollow of a hillside* ► depression, cavity, dimple, dip, crater, hole, indentation, bowl, concavity, dent, dint, dish

holy ADJECTIVE **1** *holy men and women* ► saintly, godly, pious, devout, religious, spiritual, virtuous, pure **2** *a holy place* ► sacred, hallowed, consecrated, sanctified, revered, venerated

homage NOUN *an act of homage to the king* ► respect, recognition, acknowledgement, devotion, tribute, honour, admiration, esteem,

A B C D E F G H I J K L M N O P Q R S T U V W X Y Z

home *NOUN* **homes** **1** the place where you live **2** the place where you were born or where you feel you belong **3** a place where those who need help are looked after • *an old people's home* **4** the place to be reached in a race or in certain games

home *ADJECTIVE* **1** to do with your own home or country • *home industries* **2** played on a team's own ground • *a home match*

home *ADVERB* **1** to or at home • *Is she home yet?* **2** to the point aimed at • *Push the bolt home.* **bring something home to somebody** make him or her realize it

home *VERB* **homes, homing, homed** make for a target • *The missile homed in.*

home economics *NOUN* the study of cookery and how to run a home

homeless *ADJECTIVE* having no home

homely *ADJECTIVE* simple and ordinary • *a homely meal*
▷ **homeliness** *NOUN*

home-made *ADJECTIVE* made at home, not bought from a shop

homeopathy *NOUN* the treatment of disease by tiny doses of drugs that in a healthy person would produce symptoms of the disease
▷ **homeopathic** *ADJECTIVE*

home page *NOUN* **home pages** the first page of an Internet website, with a summary of all the information it gives

homesick *ADJECTIVE* sad because you are away from home
▷ **homesickness** *NOUN*

homeward *ADJECTIVE, ADVERB* going towards home
▷ **homewards** *ADVERB*

homework *NOUN* school work that has to be done at home

homicide *NOUN* **homicides** the killing of one person by another
▷ **homicidal** *ADJECTIVE*

homogeneous (**hom- o- jeen- ee- us**) *ADJECTIVE* formed of people or things of the same kind

homograph *NOUN* **homographs** a word that is spelt like another but has a different meaning or origin, e.g. *bat* (a flying animal) and *bat* (for hitting a ball)

homonym (**hom- o- nim**) *NOUN* **homonyms** a homograph or homophone

homophone *NOUN* **homophones** a word with the same sound as another, e.g. *son, sun*

Homo sapiens *NOUN* human beings regarded as a species of animal [Latin, = wise man or person]

homosexual *ADJECTIVE* attracted to people of the same sex
▷ **homosexual** *NOUN* **homosexuality** *NOUN*

honest *ADJECTIVE* not stealing or cheating or telling lies; truthful
▷ **honestly** *ADVERB* **honesty** *NOUN*

Thesaurus

deference, veneration
pay homage to *He paid homage to all who had sacrificed their lives in the war.* ► honour, praise, salute, acclaim, applaud

home *NOUN* **1** *People were forced to leave their homes.* ► house, dwelling, place of residence, address, accommodation RELATED ADJECTIVE domestic **2** *They had travelled thousands of miles from home.* ► native land, homeland, birthplace, motherland, fatherland **3** *He refused to go into a home.* ► institution, nursing home, residential home, hospice, shelter

homeless *ADJECTIVE* *increasing numbers of homeless people* ► destitute, vagrant, down-and-out, outcast, unhoused, wandering, evicted, forsaken, abandoned, itinerant, nomadic

homely *ADJECTIVE* *The hotel offers a warm welcome and a homely atmosphere.* ► friendly, informal, relaxed, easy-going, familiar, intimate, congenial, comfortable, cosy, natural, simple, unaffected, unpretentious AN OPPOSITE IS formal

honest *ADJECTIVE* **1** *He's a fair and honest man.* ► upright, honourable, virtuous, law-abiding, high-minded, scrupulous, moral, decent, principled, upstanding AN OPPOSITE IS dishonest **2** *business practices that are barely honest* ► legal, lawful, ethical, legitimate, above-board, (*more informal*) on the level AN OPPOSITE IS dishonest **3** *It was an honest mistake.* ► genuine, real, authentic, legitimate AN OPPOSITE IS deliberate **4** *Let us have your honest opinion. I've tried to be perfectly honest with you.* ► sincere, objective, candid, direct, open, frank, truthful, impartial, unbiased, unprejudiced, balanced OPPOSITES ARE insincere, untruthful, biased

honestly *ADVERB* **1** *He said he had come by the money honestly.* ► fairly, legally, lawfully, legitimately, honourably **2** *She could honestly say she had had nothing to do with the incident.* ► frankly, sincerely, truthfully, genuinely

honesty *NOUN* **1** *She demanded complete honesty from her staff.* ► truthfulness, trustworthiness, integrity, goodness, morality, honour, uprightness, veracity, fairness, probity, rectitude, reliability, scrupulousness AN OPPOSITE IS dishonesty **2** *They were encouraged to speak with complete honesty.* ► sincerity, candour, directness, frankness, straightforwardness, bluntness, outspokenness, plainness AN OPPOSITE IS insincerity

honey *NOUN* a sweet sticky food made by bees

honeycomb *NOUN* **honeycombs** a wax structure of small six-sided sections made by bees to hold their honey and eggs

honeycombed *ADJECTIVE* with many holes or tunnels

honeymoon *NOUN* **honeymoons** a holiday spent together by a newly married couple [from **honey** + **moon** (because the first intensely passionate feelings gradually wane like the moon)]

honeysuckle *NOUN* a climbing plant with fragrant yellow or pink flowers

honk *NOUN* **honks** a loud sound like that made by a goose or an old-fashioned car horn
▷ **honk** *VERB*

honorary *ADJECTIVE* **1** given or received as an honour • *an honorary degree* **2** unpaid • *the honorary treasurer of the club*
USAGE Do not confuse with **honourable**.

honour *NOUN* **honours** **1** great respect or reputation **2** a person or thing that brings honour **3** something a person is proud to do • *It is an honour to meet you.* **4** honesty and loyalty • *a man of honour* **5** an award for distinction
in honour of as an expression of respect for

honour *VERB* **honours, honouring, honoured** **1** feel or show honour for a person **2** keep to the terms of an agreement or promise

honourable *ADJECTIVE* deserving honour; honest and loyal
▷ **honourably** *ADVERB*
USAGE Do not confuse with **honorary**.

hood *NOUN* **hoods** **1** a covering of soft material for the head and neck **2** a folding roof or cover
▷ **hooded** *ADJECTIVE*

hoodwink *VERB* **hoodwinks, hoodwinking, hoodwinked** deceive

hoof *NOUN* **hoofs** or **hooves** the horny part of the foot of a horse etc.

hook *NOUN* **hooks** a bent or curved piece of metal etc. for hanging things on or for catching hold of something

hook *VERB* **hooks, hooking, hooked** **1** fasten something with or on a hook **2** catch a fish etc. with a hook **3** hit a ball in a curving path
be hooked on something (*slang*) be addicted to it

hooked *ADJECTIVE* hook-shaped

hooligan *NOUN* **hooligans** a rough and violent young person
▷ **hooliganism** *NOUN*

hoop *NOUN* **hoops** a ring made of metal or wood

hoot *NOUN* **hoots** **1** the sound made by an owl or a vehicle's horn or a steam whistle **2** a cry of scorn or disapproval **3** an outburst of laughter **4** (*informal*) something funny
▷ **hoot** *VERB* **hooter** *NOUN*

Thesaurus

honour *NOUN* **1** *He defended the President, calling him a man of honour.* ► honesty, integrity, morality, principle, distinction, decency, probity **2** *She received many honours from the film industry.* ► award, accolade, tribute, distinction, commendation, acknowledgement, recognition **3** *I appreciate the honour of speaking at this assembly.* ► privilege, distinction, cachet, kudos **4** *They were received with honour by the king.* ► praise, acclaim, homage, admiration, adulation

honour *VERB* **1** *a grand parade to honour the distinguished visitors* ► praise, applaud, acclaim, salute, celebrate, commend, pay homage to **2** *They intend to honour their commitment to the peace process.* ► fulfil, respect, observe, carry out, keep, discharge

honourable *ADJECTIVE* **1** *No one doubted that her motives were entirely honourable; honourable people who were fighting for the common good* ► honest, sincere, reputable, noble, worthy, just, straight, trustworthy, principled, virtuous, upright, proper **2** *a respected politician who has done honourable service in the Treasury* ► distinguished, illustrious, eminent, great

hoodwink *VERB* *The man had hoodwinked him into parting with a large sum of money.* ► deceive, trick, dupe, cheat, swindle, fool, mislead, delude, (*more informal*) take in

hook *NOUN* **1** *He hung his coat on one of the hooks.* ► peg, nail **2** *a dress fastened at the back with a hook and eye* ► fastener, fastening, clasp, clip, hasp **3** *a fishing hook* ► barb, snare

hook *VERB* **1** *David hooked a 64-pound carp.* ► catch, take, land, net, bag **2** *He hooked a trailer to the car.* ► hitch, fasten, attach, couple, connect

hoop *NOUN* *a hoop of metal* ► band, loop, ring, round, circle, circlet, girdle

hoot *VERB* **1** *An owl hooted.* ► screech, call, tu-whit tu-whoo **2** *The driver became impatient and hooted.* ► beep, toot, honk, sound the horn **3** *The audience hooted in derision.* ► shout, shriek, yell, jeer, call out

hoot *NOUN* **1** *the hoot of an owl* ► screech, call, tu-whit tu-whoo **2** *hoots of laughter* ► shriek, shout, scream, yell, jeer

A B C D E F G H I J K L M N O P Q R S T U V W X Y Z

hop[1] *VERB* **hops, hopping, hopped 1** jump on one foot **2** (said about an animal) spring from all feet at once **3** (*informal*) move quickly
• *Here's the car—hop in!*
hop it (*informal*) go away

hop *NOUN* **hops** a hopping movement

hop[2] *NOUN* **hops** a climbing plant used to give beer its flavour

hope *NOUN* **hopes 1** the feeling of wanting something to happen, and thinking that it will happen **2** a person or thing that gives hope
• *You are our only hope.*

hope *VERB* **hopes, hoping, hoped** feel hope; want and expect something

hopeful *ADJECTIVE* **1** feeling hope **2** likely to be good or successful

hopefully *ADVERB* **1** it is to be hoped; I hope that **2** in a hopeful way
USAGE Some people say it is incorrect to use **hopefully** to mean 'I hope that' or 'let's hope', and say that it should only be used to mean 'in a hopeful way'. This first use is very common in informal language but you should avoid it when you are writing or speaking formally.

hopeless *ADJECTIVE* **1** without hope **2** very bad at something
▷ **hopelessly** *ADVERB* **hopelessness** *NOUN*

hopscotch *NOUN* a game of hopping into squares drawn on the ground

horde *NOUN* **hordes** a large group or crowd
USAGE Do not confuse with **hoard**.

horizon *NOUN* **horizons** the line where the earth and the sky seem to meet

horizontal *ADJECTIVE* level, so as to be parallel to the horizon; going across from left to right (The opposite is **vertical**)
▷ **horizontally** *ADVERB*

hormone *NOUN* **hormones** a substance produced by glands in the body and carried by the blood to stimulate other organs in the body
▷ **hormonal** *ADJECTIVE*

horn *NOUN* **horns 1** a hard substance that grows into a point on the head of a bull, cow, ram, etc. **2** a pointed part **3** a brass instrument played by blowing **4** a device for making a warning sound
▷ **horned** *ADJECTIVE* **horny** *ADJECTIVE*

horoscope *NOUN* **horoscopes** an astrologer's forecast of future events

horrendous *ADJECTIVE* extremely unpleasant

horrible *ADJECTIVE* **1** horrifying **2** very unpleasant or nasty
▷ **horribly** *ADVERB*

horrid *ADJECTIVE* horrible
▷ **horridly** *ADVERB*

Thesaurus

hop *VERB He hopped along beside her. She hopped on a bus and went home.* ▸ jump, leap, skip, spring, trip, bound, dance, flit, prance, caper

hope *VERB* **1** *I hope to answer all your questions.* ▸ aim, intend, plan, have it in mind, aspire **2 hope for** *We are hoping for a quick response.* ▸ expect, look for, wish for, want USAGE It is better to avoid *anticipate* in this sense, because it has other meanings.

hope *NOUN* **1** *She has the hope of being in the national team.* ▸ ambition, aspiration, expectation, dream, desire, wish **2** *There's some hope of a better future.* ▸ prospect, expectation, likelihood, optimism, assumption

hopeful *ADJECTIVE* **1** *We are still hopeful about avoiding a conflict.* ▸ optimistic, confident, positive, expectant, sanguine AN OPPOSITE IS pessimistic **2** *hopeful signs of an economic recovery* ▸ promising, encouraging, favourable, heartening, reassuring, propitious, auspicious, cheering AN OPPOSITE IS discouraging

hopefully *ADVERB* **1** *'Are we going back,' she asked hopefully.* ▸ expectantly, optimistically, confidently, with hope AN OPPOSITE IS pessimistically **2** *Hopefully the work will be completed next week.* ▸ all being well, most likely, with luck, conceivably, probably

hopeless *ADJECTIVE* **1** *He looked at her in hopeless bewilderment.* ▸ despairing, desperate, dejected, downhearted, downcast, wretched, pessimistic **2** *The doctors regarded his case as hopeless.* ▸ impossible, incurable, irremediable, beyond hope, beyond recovery, lost, unattainable **3** *The situation seemed hopeless, now that the food had run out.* ▸ desperate, critical, serious, dire, impossible, beyond hope, useless, futile **4** *He is hopeless at board games.* ▸ incompetent, ineffective, ineffectual, poor, inept, (*more informal*) pathetic, (*more informal*) useless, (*more informal*) rubbish

horde *NOUN A horde of journalists waited outside the house.* ▸ crowd, throng, pack, mob, swarm, band, gang, group

horizon *NOUN A ship was visible on the horizon.* ▸ skyline, vista, range of view

horrible or **horrid** *ADJECTIVE* **1** *a horrible accident on the bypass* ▸ dreadful, horrific, horrifying, horrendous, frightful, fearful, terrible, ghastly, hideous, sickening **2** *Saturday was a wet, horrible day. The smell was horrid.* ▸ unpleasant, nasty, disagreeable, awful, beastly, dreadful, ghastly, revolting, terrible OPPOSITES ARE pleasant, agreeable **3** *Nora was a horrible person. The teachers were horrid to him.* ▸ nasty, disagreeable, odious, objectionable,

A B C D E F G H I J K L M N O P Q R S T U V W X Y Z

horrify VERB **horrifies, horrifying, horrified** **1** make somebody feel very afraid or disgusted **2** shock

horror NOUN **horrors** **1** great fear or disgust **2** a person or thing causing horror

horse NOUN **horses** **1** a large four-legged animal used for riding on and for pulling carts etc. **2** a framework for hanging clothes on to dry
on horseback mounted on a horse

horse chestnut NOUN **horse chestnuts** a large tree that produces dark-brown nuts (**conkers**)

horsepower NOUN a unit for measuring the power of an engine, equal to 746 watts

horseshoe NOUN **horseshoes** a U-shaped piece of metal nailed to a horse's hoof

horticulture NOUN the art of cultivating gardens
▷ **horticultural** ADJECTIVE

hose NOUN **hoses** **1** (also **hosepipe**) a flexible tube for taking water to something **2** (*old use*) breeches • *doublet and hose*

hospitable ADJECTIVE welcoming; liking to give hospitality
▷ **hospitably** ADVERB

hospital NOUN **hospitals** a place providing medical and surgical treatment for people who are ill or injured

hospitality NOUN welcoming guests or strangers and giving them food and entertainment

host [1] NOUN **hosts** **1** a person who has guests and looks after them **2** the presenter of a television or radio programme [from Latin *hospes*]

host [2] NOUN **hosts** a large number of people or things [from Latin *hostis* = enemy or army]

host [3] NOUN **hosts** the bread consecrated at Holy Communion [from Latin *hostia* = sacrifice]

hostage NOUN **hostages** a person who is held prisoner until the holder's demands are met

hostel NOUN **hostels** a building where travellers, students, or other groups can stay or live

hostess NOUN **hostesses** a woman who has guests and looks after them

hostile ADJECTIVE **1** unfriendly • *a hostile glance* **2** opposed to something **3** to do with an enemy • *hostile aircraft*
▷ **hostility** NOUN

Thesaurus

loathsome, hateful, offensive OPPOSITES ARE nice, kind

horrific ADJECTIVE *He died from horrific head injuries.* ► dreadful, appalling, horrifying, horrendous, frightful, fearful, terrible, hideous, ghastly, sickening

horrify VERB **1** *He wrote stories that horrified his readers.* ► terrify, frighten, scare, alarm, petrify, terrorize **2** *The news would have horrified her.* ► shock, appal, outrage, scandalize, offend, sicken, disgust, revolt, nauseate, unnerve, alarm OPPOSITES ARE please, delight

horror NOUN **1** *People screamed in horror.* ► terror, fear, fright, alarm **2** *Public opinion reacted with horror.* ► shock, outrage, disgust, revulsion, repugnance, consternation AN OPPOSITE IS delight **3** *Newspaper reports described the full horror of the attack.* ► ghastliness, awfulness, frightfulness, hideousness, savagery, barbarity

horse NOUN *a woman on a horse* ► (*for riding*) mount, (*small breed*) pony, (*adult male*) stallion, (*young male*) colt, (*large and strong*) cob, (*adult female*) mare, (*young female*) filly, (*new-born horse*) foal RELATED ADJECTIVES equestrian, equine

hospitable ADJECTIVE *a kind, hospitable family* ► friendly, sociable, welcoming, congenial, cordial, convivial, amicable, generous, gracious, receptive OPPOSITES ARE inhospitable, unfriendly

hospital NOUN *Joe was lying in a bed in the hospital.* ► infirmary, clinic, nursing home, sanatorium, medical institution, convalescent home, hospice

hospitality NOUN **1** *We needed hospitality for the night.* ► accommodation, catering, entertainment **2** *Thank you for your hospitality.* ► kindness, friendliness, sociability, welcome, conviviality, warm reception

host NOUN **1** *A host of people headed for the town.* ► crowd, throng, band, horde, swarm, group **2** *The host of the restaurant welcomed his guests.* ► proprietor, landlord **3** *the host of a television programme* ► presenter, compère, anchorman, anchorwoman, announcer, link person

hostage NOUN *The hijackers released some of the hostages.* ► captive, prisoner, detainee

hostile ADJECTIVE **1** *a hostile crowd; a hostile attack* ► aggressive, antagonistic, belligerent, confrontational, bellicose, pugnacious, angry, militant, unfriendly, malevolent, ill-disposed, warlike AN OPPOSITE IS friendly **2** *a hostile climate* ► harsh, unfavourable, adverse, inhospitable, bad, contrary, unpropitious AN OPPOSITE IS favourable **3** **hostile to** *They are hostile to the idea.* ► opposed to, averse to, unsympathetic to, antagonistic to, against

hostility NOUN **1** *They reacted with hostility.* ► antagonism, enmity, animosity, opposition, malice, hatred, ill will AN OPPOSITE IS friendship **2** *their hostility to our suggestion* ► opposition,

hot *ADJECTIVE* **hotter, hottest 1** having great heat or a high temperature **2** giving a burning sensation when tasted **3** passionate or excitable • *a hot temper*
▷ **hotly** *ADVERB* **hotness** *NOUN*
in hot water (*informal*) in trouble or disgrace

hotel *NOUN* **hotels** a building where people pay to have meals and stay for the night

hound *NOUN* **hounds** a dog used in hunting or racing [from Old English]

hour *NOUN* **hours 1** one twenty-fourth part of a day and night; sixty minutes **2** a time • *Why are you up at this hour?*
hours *PLURAL NOUN* a fixed period for work • *Office hours are 9 a.m. to 5 p.m.*

hourly *ADVERB, ADJECTIVE* every hour

house (howss) *NOUN* **houses 1** a building made for people to live in, usually designed for one family **2** a building or establishment for a special purpose • *the opera house* **3** a building for a government assembly; the assembly itself • *the House of Commons* • *the House of Lords* **4** one of the divisions of a school for sports competitions etc. **5** a family or dynasty • *the royal house of Tudor*

house (howz) *VERB* **houses, housing, housed** provide accommodation or room for someone or something [from Old English]

household *NOUN* **households** all the people who live together in the same house [from **house** + an old sense of **hold** = possession]

householder *NOUN* **householders** a person who owns or rents a house

housekeeper *NOUN* **housekeepers** a person employed to look after a household

housekeeping *NOUN* **1** looking after a household **2** (*informal*) the money for a household's food and other necessities

housemaid *NOUN* **housemaids** a woman servant in a house, especially one who cleans rooms

house-proud *ADJECTIVE* very careful to keep a house clean and tidy

house-trained *ADJECTIVE* (said about an animal) trained to be clean in the house

housewife *NOUN* **housewives** a woman who does the housekeeping for her family

housework *NOUN* the cleaning and cooking etc. done in housekeeping

housing *NOUN* **housings 1** accommodation; houses **2** a stiff cover or guard for a piece of machinery

housing estate *NOUN* **housing estates** a set of houses planned and built together in one area

hovel *NOUN* **hovels** a small shabby house

hover *VERB* **hovers, hovering, hovered 1** stay in one place in the air **2** wait about near someone or something

hovercraft *NOUN* **hovercraft** a vehicle that travels just above the surface of land or water, supported by a strong current of air sent downwards from its engines

how *ADVERB* **1** in what way; by what means • *How did you do it?* **2** to what extent or amount etc. • *How high can you jump?* **3** in what condition • *How are you?*
how about would you like • *How about a game of football?*
how do you do? a formal greeting

however *ADVERB* **1** in whatever way; to whatever extent • *You will never catch him,*

Thesaurus

antipathy, disapproval (of), aversion, antagonism

hot *ADJECTIVE* **1** *hot weather* ► warm, balmy, summery, boiling, blazing, roasting, scorching, sweltering, sultry OPPOSITES ARE cold, chilly **2** *What we need is a hot meal.* ► cooked, heated, piping, sizzling **3** *a hot dish with peppers* ► spicy, peppery, piquant, pungent AN OPPOSITE IS mild **4** *a hot temper* ► fierce, angry, raging, intense, violent, passionate

hotel *NOUN* *We stayed in a hotel by the river.* ► guest house, boarding house, inn, pension, motel

hound *VERB* *The reporters went on hounding her.* ► harass, pursue, harry, (*informal*) hassle, pester, persecute, trouble

house *NOUN* **1** *a row of terraced houses* ► home, dwelling, abode, residence **2** *the house of Stuart* ► dynasty, clan, family, tribe

house *VERB* *The cabins housed twenty people.* ► accommodate, provide room for, lodge, quarter, shelter, take in, billet, board, (*more informal*) put up

household *NOUN* *a large household with lots of children* ► family, home, ménage, establishment, (*more informal*) set-up

housing *NOUN* *an acute need for better housing* ► accommodation, houses, homes, habitation, shelter

hovel *NOUN* *The little cottage was not much better than a hovel.* ► shack, shanty, shed, slum, hut

hover *VERB* **1** *A police helicopter hovered above the crowd.* ► float, hang, flutter, drift, fly **2** *He hovered outside the room waiting to be called in.* ► linger, dally, pause, wait about, waver, loiter, hesitate, (*informal*) hang about

A B C D E F G H I J K L M N O P Q R S T U V W X Y Z

however hard you try **2** all the same; nevertheless • *Later, however, he decided to go.*

howl *NOUN* **howls** a long loud sad-sounding cry or sound, such as that made by a dog or wolf

howl *VERB* **howls, howling, howled** **1** make a howl **2** weep loudly

howler *NOUN* **howlers** (*informal*) a foolish mistake

HQ *ABBREVIATION* headquarters

hub *NOUN* **hubs** **1** the central part of a wheel **2** the central point of interest or activity

hubbub *NOUN* a loud confused noise of voices

huddle *VERB* **huddles, huddling, huddled** **1** crowd together with other people, often for warmth **2** curl your body closely
▷ **huddle** *NOUN*

huff *NOUN*
in a huff offended or sulking about something • *She went away in a huff*
▷ **huffy** *ADJECTIVE*

hug *VERB* **hugs, hugging, hugged** **1** clasp someone tightly in your arms **2** keep close to something • *The ship hugged the shore.*

hug *NOUN* **hugs** a tight embrace

huge *ADJECTIVE* extremely large; enormous
▷ **hugely** *ADVERB* **hugeness** *NOUN*

hulk *NOUN* **hulks** **1** the body or wreck of an old ship **2** a large clumsy person or thing
▷ **hulking** *ADJECTIVE*

hull *NOUN* **hulls** the framework of a ship

hullabaloo *NOUN* **hullabaloos** an uproar

hum *VERB* **hums, humming, hummed** **1** sing a tune with your lips closed **2** make a low continuous sound like that of a bee

human *ADJECTIVE* to do with human beings

human being *NOUN* **human beings** a man, woman, or child

humane (hew- **mayn**) *ADJECTIVE* kind-hearted and merciful
▷ **humanely** *ADVERB*

humanitarian *ADJECTIVE* concerned with people's welfare and the reduction of suffering
▷ **humanitarian** *NOUN*

humanity *NOUN* **1** human beings; people **2** being human **3** being humane
humanities *PLURAL NOUN* arts subjects such as history, literature, and music, not sciences

humble *ADJECTIVE* **1** modest; not proud or showy **2** of low rank or importance
▷ **humbly** *ADVERB* **humbleness** *NOUN*

Thesaurus

howl *VERB A dog howled in the distance.* ► yowl, bay, cry

howl *NOUN howls of laughter* ► shriek, hoot, roar, gale, scream, yell

hub *NOUN* **1** *He gripped the hub of the rear wheel.* ► centre, middle, pivot, axis **2** *The foyer will be the hub of activity in this part of the building.* ► focus, focal point, heart, pivot, nucleus

huddle *VERB* **1** *They huddled together in twos and threes.* ► crowd, gather, cluster, squeeze, pack, throng, flock, herd, pile, press AN OPPOSITE IS scatter **2** *He huddled under the duvet.* ► cuddle, curl up, nestle, snuggle

hue *NOUN* **1** *gloss paint in a range of hues* ► colour, shade, tone, tint, tinge **2** *people of all political hues* ► complexion, kind, type, nature, character

huffy *ADJECTIVE They didn't have an answer and became huffy when we asked.* ► irritable, irritated, annoyed, unfriendly, grumpy, prickly, piqued, testy, petulant AN OPPOSITE IS friendly

hug *VERB Mary was kissed and hugged by her workmates.* ► embrace, clasp, cuddle, squeeze, cling to, enfold, fold in your arms, hold close, nurse, snuggle against

hug *NOUN They met with tears and hugs.* ► embrace, clasp, cuddle, squeeze

huge *ADJECTIVE a huge building; a huge tax increase* ► enormous, gigantic, immense, massive, colossal, vast, large, big, great, giant, (*more informal*) whopping, (*more informal*) ginormous AN OPPOSITE IS tiny

hum *VERB The engine was still humming.* ► purr, whirr, drone, murmur, throb, vibrate

human *ADJECTIVE* **1** *the human race* ► anthropoid **2** *They are only human and make mistakes.* ► mortal, fallible, imperfect, weak **3** *a very human reaction to the problem* ► compassionate, humane, kind, considerate, understanding, sympathetic, merciful, philanthropic AN OPPOSITE IS inhuman
human beings ► men and women, humankind, humanity, mortals, people, folk

humane *ADJECTIVE a humane way to control the fox population* ► kind, compassionate, considerate, understanding, sympathetic, merciful

humanity *NOUN* **1** *If they have a shred of humanity in them they will hand over the suspects.* ► compassion, understanding, sensitivity, fellow feeling, sympathy, tolerance **2** *a decision that could affect the whole of humanity* ► humankind, the human race, mankind, mortals, people

humble *ADJECTIVE* **1** *He acted in a humble and contrite manner.* ► meek, self-effacing, unassuming, deferential, respectful,

humbug *NOUN* **humbugs 1** insincere or dishonest talk or behaviour **2** a hard peppermint sweet

humdrum *ADJECTIVE* dull and not exciting; commonplace

humid (hew- mid) *ADJECTIVE* (said about air) moist and damp
▷ **humidity** *NOUN*

humiliate *VERB* **humiliates, humiliating, humiliated** make a person feel disgraced or ashamed
▷ **humiliation** *NOUN*

humility *NOUN* being humble

hummingbird *NOUN* **hummingbirds** a small tropical bird that makes a humming sound by beating its wings rapidly

humorous *ADJECTIVE* full of humour; amusing

humour *NOUN* **1** being amusing; what makes people laugh **2** the ability to enjoy comical things • *a sense of humour* **3** a mood • *in a good humour*

humour *VERB* **humours, humouring, humoured** keep a person contented by doing what he or she wants

hump *NOUN* **humps 1** a rounded lump or mound **2** an abnormal outward curve at the top of a person's back

humpback bridge *NOUN* **humpback bridges** a small bridge that curves steeply upwards in the middle

humus (hew- mus) *NOUN* rich earth made by decayed plants

hunch[1] *NOUN* **hunches** a feeling that you can guess what is going to happen

hunch[2] *VERB* **hunches, hunching, hunched** bend your shoulders upward so that your back is rounded

hunchback *NOUN* **hunchbacks** someone with a hump on their back
▷ **hunchbacked** *ADJECTIVE*

hundred *NOUN, ADJECTIVE* **hundreds** the number 100
▷ **hundredth** *ADJECTIVE, NOUN*

hundredweight *NOUN* **hundredweight** a unit of weight equal to 112 pounds (about 50.8 kilograms)

hunger *NOUN* the feeling that you have when you have not eaten for some time; need for food

hunger strike *NOUN* **hunger strikes** refusing to eat, as a way of making a protest

hungry *ADJECTIVE* **hungrier, hungriest** feeling hunger
▷ **hungrily** *ADVERB*

Thesaurus

submissive AN OPPOSITE IS proud **2** *I live in a humble house in the suburbs.* ► modest, simple, plain, ordinary, unpretentious, unostentatious OPPOSITES ARE grand, pretentious **3** *She comes from a humble background.* ► lowly, undistinguished, poor, common, ordinary OPPOSITES ARE distinguished, noble

humid *ADJECTIVE* *a hot and humid day* ► muggy, clammy, sultry, sticky, damp, dank, moist, steamy, sweaty AN OPPOSITE IS fresh

humiliate *VERB* *He liked to humiliate them with constant reminders of their mistakes.* ► embarrass, humble, mortify, demean, shame, put to shame

humiliating *ADJECTIVE* *Rome inflicted a humiliating defeat on its neighbour.* ► embarrassing, mortifying, ignominious, degrading, demeaning, humbling, chastening, crushing, inglorious, discreditable, dishonourable, shaming, undignified AN OPPOSITE IS glorious

humiliation *NOUN* *At immigration he suffered the humiliation of a body search.* ► embarrassment, indignity, ignominy, mortification, shame, disgrace, degradation, dishonour

humility *NOUN* *I'm not sure I have the humility to admit my mistakes.* ► modesty, deference, humbleness, meekness, self-effacement, unpretentiousness, lowliness AN OPPOSITE IS pride

humorous *ADJECTIVE* *a love story with humorous episodes* ► amusing, funny, comic, comical, jocular, hilarious, entertaining

humour *NOUN* **1** *a conversation spiced with humour* ► wit, jocularity, badinage, repartee, jokes, jesting, hilarity, comedy, drollery **2** *in a bad humour* ► mood, temper, frame of mind, state of mind, disposition, spirits

hump *NOUN* *a hump in the road* ► bump, protuberance, bulge, mound, rise, curve, knob, lump, swelling

hunch *NOUN* *The theory was no more than a hunch.* ► feeling, intuition, inkling, guess, impression, suspicion, idea

hunch *VERB* *He sat in a corner and hunched his shoulders.* ► arch, curve, bend, hump, shrug, huddle, curl up

hunger *NOUN* **1** *She had no feelings of hunger that day.* ► appetite, desire for food **2** *He grew faint with hunger.* ► lack of food, malnutrition, starvation, deprivation, famine **3** *a hunger for knowledge* ► desire, yearning, longing, craving, appetite, thirst

hungry *ADJECTIVE* *I was hungry again by 3 o'clock.* ► in need of food, ravenous, famished, starving, (*more informal*) peckish

A B C D E F G H I J K L M N O P Q R S T U V W X Y Z

hunk *NOUN* **hunks** **1** a large piece of something **2** (*informal*) a muscular, good-looking man

hunt *VERB* **hunts, hunting, hunted** **1** chase and kill animals for food or as a sport **2** search for something
▷ **hunter** *NOUN* **huntsman** *NOUN*

hurdle *NOUN* **hurdles** **1** an upright frame to be jumped over in hurdling **2** an obstacle or difficulty

hurdling *NOUN* racing in which the runners jump over hurdles
▷ **hurdler** *NOUN*

hurl *VERB* **hurls, hurling, hurled** throw something with great force

hurray or **hurrah** *INTERJECTION* a shout of joy or approval; a cheer

hurricane *NOUN* **hurricanes** a storm with violent wind

hurry *VERB* **hurries, hurrying, hurried** **1** move quickly; do something quickly **2** try to make somebody or something be quick
▷ **hurried** *ADJECTIVE* **hurriedly** *ADVERB*

hurry *NOUN* hurrying; a need to hurry

hurt *VERB* **hurts, hurting, hurt** **1** cause pain or injury to someone **2** suffer pain • *My leg hurts.* **3** upset or offend • *I'm sorry if I hurt your feelings.*

hurt *NOUN* physical or mental pain or injury
▷ **hurtful** *ADJECTIVE*

hurtle *VERB* **hurtles, hurtling, hurtled** move rapidly • *The train hurtled along*

husband *NOUN* **husbands** the man to whom a woman is married [from Old Norse *husbondi* = master of the house]

hush *VERB* **hushes, hushing, hushed** make or become silent or quiet
hush up prevent something from becoming generally known

husk *NOUN* **husks** the dry outer covering of some seeds and fruits

Thesaurus

hunk *NOUN* *a hunk of bread* ► lump, chunk, block, wedge, piece, portion, slab

hunt *NOUN* *the hunt for clues* ► search, quest, pursuit (of), chase

hunt *VERB* **1** *They hunt foxes and deer.* ► chase, give chase to, stalk, track, trail, course, pursue **2** *She spent ages hunting for her keys.* ► search, look, rummage, scour, root around

hurdle *NOUN* **1** *He hit the last hurdle and fell.* ► fence, jump, barrier, obstacle **2** *There was one more hurdle to overcome before they could claim success.* ► obstacle, difficulty, handicap, problem, snag, stumbling block

hurl *VERB* *She hurled a book at Roger.* ► throw, fling, toss, cast, pitch, heave

hurried *ADJECTIVE* **1** *hurried attempts to change the venue* ► hasty, hectic, rushed, speedy, precipitate, swift, rapid **2** *He gave the paper a hurried read.* ► brief, cursory, superficial, swift, rapid

hurry *VERB* **1** *If I don't hurry I'll be late.* ► be quick, hurry up, hasten, make speed, move faster, (*more informal*) buck up, (*more informal*) shift, (*more informal*) step on it AN OPPOSITE IS dawdle **2** *Sarah hurried to the library.* ► rush, hasten, dash, speed, chase, hurtle, hustle, move quickly, (*more informal*) belt OPPOSITES ARE go slowly, amble **3** *She hurried the children into the bathroom.* ► hustle, hasten, push on, urge on, drive AN OPPOSITE IS delay

hurry *NOUN* *In our hurry we forgot the food.* ► haste, bustle, confusion, urgency, agitation

hurt *VERB* **1** *My arm hurts.* ► be sore, be painful, ache, throb, sting **2** *Derek hurt his leg.* ► injure, wound, maim, bruise, damage, disable **3** *The criticism hurt her deeply.* ► upset, distress, offend, grieve

hurt *NOUN* *She loved him in spite of the hurt he had caused her.* ► distress, suffering, pain, wrong, sadness, anguish, torment

hurt *ADJECTIVE* **1** *A hurt animal lay in the road.* ► injured, wounded, maimed, bruised, scarred **2** *He felt hurt by the words she had used.* ► upset, pained, distressed, wounded

hurtful *ADJECTIVE* *She forgot all the hurtful remarks and remembered the good times.* ► upsetting, distressing, unkind, spiteful, mean, cruel, malicious, wounding, painful OPPOSITES ARE kind, comforting

hurtle *VERB* **1** *A train was hurtling towards them.* ► speed, rush, race, career, charge, dash, fly, tear, chase, shoot **2** *The plane hurtled to the ground.* ► plunge, plummet, nosedive, drop

husband *NOUN* *Their husbands had taken their cars to the rally.* ► spouse, partner, (*more formal*) consort, (*more informal*) man, (*more informal*) mate, (*more informal*) better half

hush *NOUN* *A hush fell on the room.* ► silence, quiet, quietness, calm, stillness, tranquillity OPPOSITES ARE noise, clamour

hush *VERB* *She wanted to hush their fears.* ► calm, soothe, allay, ease, assuage, quieten
hush up *The government is accused of hushing up the dangers.* ► conceal, cover up, keep secret, keep quiet, hide, stifle, suppress

hush-hush *ADJECTIVE* *The news is still rather hush-hush.* ► secret, confidential, restricted, classified, (*more informal*) under wraps

husky *ADJECTIVE* **huskier, huskiest 1** hoarse **2** big and strong; burly
▷ **huskily** *ADVERB* **huskiness** *NOUN*

hustle *VERB* **hustles, hustling, hustled 1** hurry **2** push or shove rudely
▷ **hustle** *NOUN* **hustler** *NOUN*

hut *NOUN* **huts** a small roughly made house or shelter

hutch *NOUN* **hutches** a box-like cage for a pet rabbit etc.

hybrid *NOUN* **hybrids 1** a plant or animal produced by combining two different species or varieties **2** something that combines parts or characteristics of two different things

hydrant *NOUN* **hydrants** a special water tap to which a large hose can be attached for fire-fighting or street-cleaning etc.

hydraulic *ADJECTIVE* worked by the force of water or other fluid • *hydraulic brakes*

hydrochloric acid *NOUN* a colourless acid containing hydrogen and chlorine

hydroelectric *ADJECTIVE* using water power to produce electricity
▷ **hydroelectricity** *NOUN*

hydrogen *NOUN* a lightweight gas that combines with oxygen to form water

hydrogen bomb *NOUN* **hydrogen bombs** a very powerful bomb using energy created by the fusion of hydrogen nuclei

hyena *NOUN* **hyenas** a wild animal that looks like a wolf and makes a shrieking howl

hygiene (hy- jeen) *NOUN* keeping things clean in order to remain healthy and prevent disease
▷ **hygienic** *ADJECTIVE* **hygienically** *ADVERB*

hymn *NOUN* **hymns** a religious song, usually one praising God
▷ **hymn book** *NOUN*

hype *NOUN* (*informal*) extravagant publicity or advertising

hyperactive *ADJECTIVE* unable to relax and always moving about or doing things

hyperbola (hy- per- bol- a) *NOUN* **hyperbolas** a kind of curve

hyphen *NOUN* **hyphens** a short dash used to join words or parts of words together (e.g. in *hitch-hiker*)

hypnosis (hip- **noh**- sis) *NOUN* a condition like a deep sleep in which a person's actions may be controlled by someone else

hypnotize *VERB* **hypnotizes, hypnotizing, hypnotized** produce hypnosis in somebody
▷ **hypnotism** *NOUN* **hypnotic** *ADJECTIVE* **hypnotist** *NOUN*

hypochondriac (hy- po- **kon**- dree- ak) *NOUN* **hypochondriacs** a person who constantly imagines that he or she is ill
▷ **hypochondria** *NOUN*

hypocrite (**hip**- o- krit) *NOUN* **hypocrites** a person who pretends to be more virtuous than he or she really is
▷ **hypocrisy** (hip- **ok**- riss- ee) *NOUN* **hypocritical** *ADJECTIVE*

hypodermic *ADJECTIVE* injecting something under the skin • *a hypodermic syringe*

hypotenuse (hy- **pot**- i- newz) *NOUN* **hypotenuses** the side opposite the right angle in a right-angled triangle

hypothermia *NOUN* the condition of having a body temperature well below normal

hypothesis (hy- **poth**- i- sis) *NOUN* **hypotheses** a suggestion or guess that tries to explain something

hypothetical (hy- po- **thet**- i- kal) *ADJECTIVE* based on a theory or possibility, not on proven facts

hysteria *NOUN* wild uncontrollable excitement, panic, or emotion
▷ **hysterics** *NOUN*

hysterical *ADJECTIVE* **1** in a state of hysteria **2** (*informal*) extremely funny
▷ **hysterically** *ADVERB*

Thesaurus

hut *NOUN a hut in the woods* ► cabin, shack, shed, shelter, shanty, den, hovel

hybrid *NOUN a hybrid of two species* ► cross, cross-breed, mixed breed, blend, amalgam, combination, composite, compound, mixture, fusion

hybrid *ADJECTIVE hybrid roses* ► cross-bred, composite, mixed, compound, mongrel
AN OPPOSITE IS pure-bred

hygiene *NOUN acceptable standards of hygiene* ► cleanliness, sanitariness, sanitation, health, wholesomeness RELATED ADJECTIVE sanitary

hygienic *ADJECTIVE Hygienic conditions are essential.* ► sanitary, clean, germ-free, sterilized, sterile, aseptic, disinfected, healthy, pure, salubrious, unpolluted, wholesome
OPPOSITES ARE unhygienic, insanitary, dirty

hypnotize *VERB She was hypnotized by the flames of the camp fire.* ► mesmerize, bewitch, entrance, captivate, enthral, transfix, fascinate, dominate, magnetize, stupefy

hysterical *ADJECTIVE* **1** *The fans were screaming and hysterical.* ► overwrought, frenzied, uncontrollable, uncontrolled, crazed, berserk, delirious, demented, frantic, wild, raving, distraught **2** (*informal*) *A dog set off the security alarm with hysterical results.* ► hilarious, crazy, comical, funny, amusing, uproarious, (*informal*) killing, (*informal*) side-splitting

a b c d e f g **h** i j k l m n o p q r s t u v w x y z

A B C D E F G H I J K L M N O P Q R S T U V W X Y Z

Ii

I *PRONOUN* a word used by a person to refer to himself or herself

-ible SEE **-able**

ice *NOUN* **ices** **1** frozen water, a brittle transparent solid substance **2** an ice cream

ice age *NOUN* **ice ages** a period in the past when most of the earth's surface was covered with ice

iceberg *NOUN* **icebergs** a large mass of ice floating in the sea with most of it under water [from Dutch *ijs* = ice + *berg* = hill]

ice cream *NOUN* **ice creams** a sweet creamy frozen food

ice hockey *NOUN* a form of hockey played on ice

ice rink *NOUN* **ice rinks** a place made for skating

icicle *NOUN* **icicles** a pointed hanging piece of ice formed when dripping water freezes

icing *NOUN* a sugary substance for decorating cakes

icon (I-kon) *NOUN* **icons** **1** a sacred painting of a holy person **2** a small symbol or picture on a computer screen

icy *ADJECTIVE* **icier, iciest** **1** covered with ice **2** very cold
▷ **icily** *ADVERB* **iciness** *NOUN*

idea *NOUN* **ideas** **1** a plan or thought formed in the mind **2** an opinion or belief **3** a feeling that something is likely [from Greek, = form, pattern]

ideal *ADJECTIVE* perfect; completely suitable
▷ **ideally** *ADVERB*

ideal *NOUN* **ideals** a person or thing regarded as perfect or a standard worth trying to achieve

identical *ADJECTIVE* exactly the same
▷ **identically** *ADVERB*

identify *VERB* **identifies, identifying, identified** **1** recognize as being a certain person or thing **2** treat something as being identical to something else • *Don't identify wealth with happiness.* **3** think of yourself as sharing someone's feelings etc. • *We can identify with the hero of this play.*
▷ **identification** *NOUN*

identity *NOUN* **identities** **1** who or what a person or thing is **2** being identical; sameness **3** distinctive character

Thesaurus

icy *ADJECTIVE* **1** *An icy blast of air hit Dad full in the face.* ► freezing, biting, bitter, frosty, arctic, cold **2** *Few people had braved the icy streets.* ► frozen, frozen over, ice-covered, glacial, glassy, slippery, (*more informal*) slippy **3** *She looked at him with an icy stare.* ► unfriendly, hostile, cold, frosty, stony

idea *NOUN* **1** *The idea of an afterlife appeals to him.* ► concept, notion, conception, image, perception, hypothesis **2** *Our idea is to go abroad this year.* ► plan, intention, scheme, object, objective, aim, goal, proposal, project **3** *I have other ideas on that subject.* ► view, thought, opinion, viewpoint, theory, feeling **4** *Did you have an idea this might happen?* ► suspicion, feeling, fancy, inkling, impression, notion **5** *We need some idea of the cost.* ► estimate, estimation, approximation, guess, (*more informal*) guesstimate

ideal *ADJECTIVE* **1** *The conditions for skiing were ideal.* ► perfect, excellent, optimum, exemplary, suitable, best, classic, faultless, model **2** *Such things are only possible in an ideal world.* ► Utopian, visionary, unattainable, hypothetical, imaginary, unreal, impractical

ideal *NOUN* **1** *an ideal to aim at* ► model, example, pattern, standard, yardstick, epitome, paradigm, archetype **2** *a person of high ideals* ► principle, standard, value, belief, conviction

identical *ADJECTIVE* **1** *The two houses looked identical.* ► alike, similar, the same, indistinguishable **2** *Successive tests produced identical results.* ► the same, corresponding, matching, equal, equivalent

identification *NOUN* **1** *The Bank will need to see your identification.* ► ID, proof of identity, identity card, papers, credentials, documents **2** *An early identification of problems is important.* ► recognition, detection, diagnosis, discovery, classification, establishment **3** *their identification with independence struggles in Africa* ► association, sympathy, empathy, involvement, rapport, fellow feeling

identify *VERB* **1** *The suspect was identified by three witnesses.* ► recognize, pick out, single out, name **2** *The report identifies three areas for action.* ► establish, determine, recognize, diagnose, detect, discover, distinguish, pinpoint, spot
identify with *Readers can easily identify with the chief character in the story.* ► empathize with, relate to, feel for, sympathize with, (*informal*) put yourself in the shoes of

identity *NOUN* **1** *There was nothing to show the owner's identity.* ► name, ID **2** *a case of mistaken identity* ► identification, recognition,

idiom *NOUN* **idioms** a phrase that means something different from the meanings of the words in it, e.g. *in hot water* (= in disgrace), *hell for leather* (= at high speed)
▷ **idiomatic** *ADJECTIVE* **idiomatically** *ADVERB*
[from Greek *idios* = your own]

idiosyncrasy (id- ee- o- **sink**- ra- see) *NOUN* **idiosyncrasies** one person's own way of behaving or doing something [from Greek *idios* = your own + *syn-* = together + *krasis* = mixture]

idiot *NOUN* **idiots** a stupid or foolish person
▷ **idiocy** *NOUN* **idiotic** *ADJECTIVE* **idiotically** *ADVERB*
[from Greek *idiotes* = private citizen, uneducated person]

idle *ADJECTIVE* **1** doing no work; lazy **2** not in use • *The machines were idle.* **3** useless; with no special purpose • *idle gossip*
▷ **idly** *ADVERB* **idleness** *NOUN*

idol *NOUN* **idols 1** a statue or image that is worshipped as a god **2** a famous person who is widely admired [from Greek *eidolon* = image]

idolize *VERB* **idolizes, idolizing, idolized** admire someone greatly

i.e. *ABBREVIATION* that is • *The world's highest mountain (i.e. Mount Everest) is in the Himalayas.*
USAGE Do not confuse with **e.g.**

-ier SEE **-er**

if *CONJUNCTION* **1** on condition that; supposing that • *He will do it if you pay him.* **2** even though • *I'll finish this job if it kills me.* **3** whether • *Do you know if dinner is ready?*
if only I wish • *If only I were rich!*

ignite *VERB* **ignites, igniting, ignited** catch fire, or set on fire

ignition *NOUN* **ignitions 1** igniting **2** the part of a motor engine that starts the fuel burning

ignominious *ADJECTIVE* humiliating; bringing disgrace
▷ **ignominy** *NOUN*

ignorant *ADJECTIVE* **1** not knowing about something **2** knowing very little
▷ **ignorantly** *ADVERB* **ignorance** *NOUN*

ignore *VERB* **ignores, ignoring, ignored** take no notice of a person or thing

ilk *NOUN*
of that ilk (*informal*) of that kind

Thesaurus

picking out **3** *She might lose her identity if she married him.* ► individuality, character, personality, selfhood, uniqueness, distinctiveness, singularity

idiom *NOUN* **1** *He uses 'spiffing' and other outdated idioms.* ► expression, phrase, turn of phrase, choice of words, manner of speaking, colloquialism, usage **2** *the poet's idiom* ► language, mode of expression, style, usage, phraseology

idiomatic *ADJECTIVE* *idiomatic expressions* ► colloquial, natural, well phrased

idiot *NOUN* *The mistake made him feel an idiot.* ► fool, ass, dolt, imbecile, simpleton, blockhead, ignoramus, dunderhead, dunce, halfwit, moron, cretin, (*more informal*) dope, (*more informal*) dimwit, (*more informal*) nitwit, (*more informal*) chump, (*more informal*) ninny

idiotic *ADJECTIVE* *How idiotic it seemed for a man of his age to fall in love.* ► stupid, silly, foolish, absurd, senseless, nonsensical, (*more informal*) daft AN OPPOSITE IS sensible

idle *ADJECTIVE* **1** *The chief problem with Jack was that he was idle.* ► lazy, indolent, slothful, work-shy **2** *The computers had been idle all day.* ► out of use, unused, dormant, out of service, inoperative **3** *She refused to indulge in idle speculation.* ► futile, pointless, aimless, vain, meaningless, trivial, frivolous, fatuous

idle *VERB* **1** *Jane idled across the park.* ► saunter, amble, dawdle, wander **2** *Richard had finished his work and idled until it was time to go home.* ► do nothing, laze, take it easy, kill time, loaf, slack **3** *A car was idling in the driveway.* ► tick over
idle away *We idled away an hour or two.* ► fritter away, while away, pass, spend

idol *NOUN* **1** *a temple in which idols were worshipped* ► image, icon, statue, deity, god **2** *the newest pop idols* ► star, superstar, icon, hero, heroine, favourite

ignorance *NOUN* **1** *She seemed amused by Rashid's obvious ignorance of the subject.* ► unawareness, unfamiliarity (with), incomprehension, lack of knowledge, inexperience OPPOSITES ARE knowledge, familiarity (with) **2** *They could not hide their ignorance.* ► foolishness, unintelligence, naivety, stupidity

ignorant *ADJECTIVE* **1** *He called the man an ignorant peasant.* ► uneducated, illiterate, unread, unschooled, untaught, untutored, simple, stupid **2** *We are hopelessly ignorant of events in this part of the world.* ► unaware, uninformed (about), unenlightened (about), ill-informed, oblivious, (*more informal*) clueless (about)

ignore *VERB* **1** *The complaints are too serious to ignore.* ► disregard, overlook, take no notice of, neglect, pass over, set aside **2** *Helen had*

ill *ADJECTIVE* **1** unwell; in bad health **2** bad or harmful • *There were no ill effects.*

ill *ADVERB* badly • *She was ill-treated.*
ill at ease uncomfortable or embarrassed

illegal *ADJECTIVE* not legal; against the law
▷ **illegally** *ADVERB* **illegality** *NOUN*

illegible *ADJECTIVE* impossible to read
▷ **illegibly** *ADVERB* **illegibility** *NOUN*

illegitimate *ADJECTIVE* born of parents who are not married to each other
▷ **illegitimately** *ADVERB* **illegitimacy** *NOUN*

illiterate *ADJECTIVE* unable to read or write
▷ **illiterately** *ADVERB* **illiteracy** *NOUN*

illness *NOUN* **illnesses** **1** being ill **2** a particular form of bad health; a disease

illogical *ADJECTIVE* not logical; not reasoning correctly
▷ **illogically** *ADVERB* **illogicality** *NOUN*

illuminate *VERB* **illuminates, illuminating, illuminated** **1** light something up **2** decorate streets etc. with lights **3** decorate a manuscript with coloured designs **4** clarify or help to explain something
▷ **illumination** *NOUN*

illusion *NOUN* **illusions** **1** something that seems to be real or actually happening but is not, especially something that deceives the eye **2** a false idea or belief COMPARE **delusion**
▷ **illusive** *ADJECTIVE* **illusory** *ADJECTIVE*

illustrate *VERB* **illustrates, illustrating, illustrated** **1** show something by pictures, examples, etc. **2** put illustrations in a book
▷ **illustrator** *NOUN*

illustration *NOUN* **illustrations** **1** a picture in a book etc. **2** illustrating something **3** an example that helps to explain something

illustrious *ADJECTIVE* famous and distinguished

image *NOUN* **images** **1** a picture or statue of a person or thing **2** the appearance of something as seen in a mirror or through a lens etc. **3** a person or thing that is very much like another • *He is the image of his father.* **4** a word or phrase that describes something in an imaginative way **5** a person's public reputation

imaginary *ADJECTIVE* existing only in the imagination; not real

imagination *NOUN* **imaginations** the ability to imagine things, especially in a creative or inventive way
▷ **imaginative** *ADJECTIVE*

Thesaurus

ignored him, out of spite. ► snub, spurn, shun, give the cold shoulder to

ill *ADJECTIVE* **1** *Jenny began to feel ill in the taxi home.* ► sick, unwell, poorly, out of sorts, off colour, indisposed, ailing, peaky, queasy, nauseous **2** *She suffered no ill effects from her night out.* ► harmful, damaging, adverse

illegal *ADJECTIVE* *Under-age drinking is illegal.* ► unlawful, prohibited, criminal, wrong, forbidden, barred OPPOSITES ARE legal, lawful, permitted

illegible *ADJECTIVE* *The signature was illegible.* ► unreadable, indecipherable, unintelligible, indistinct, obscure, unclear OPPOSITES ARE legible, readable

illness *NOUN* *The doctors were unsure of the exact nature of the illness.* ► disease, disorder, sickness, infirmity, complaint, indisposition, ailment, malady, affliction

illogical *ADJECTIVE* *The conclusion, however illogical it seems, was correct.* ► irrational, unreasonable, fallacious, invalid, unsound, absurd, inconsequential, inconsistent, senseless AN OPPOSITE IS logical

illusion *NOUN* **1** *an illusion created by mirrors* ► hallucination, apparition, mirage, deception, delusion, fantasy, figment of the imagination, trick **2** *We have no illusions about the difficulty of the task.* ► delusion, misapprehension, misconception, fantasy

illustrate *VERB* **1** *The book is illustrated with photographs and drawings.* ► decorate, adorn, embellish **2** *A few examples will illustrate the argument.* ► clarify, elucidate, throw *or* shed light on, illuminate, clear up, enlighten, explain

illustration *NOUN* **1** *a children's book with beautiful illustrations* ► picture, drawing, plate, sketch, photograph, figure, depiction **2** *a good illustration of the difficulties involved* ► example, instance, specimen, demonstration, case

image *NOUN* **1** *There were images of the saints along the church walls.* ► picture, portrait, representation, likeness, icon, effigy, figure **2** *The image on the screen was a little fuzzy.* ► picture, reproduction **3** *The image the company gives is one of ruthless profiteering.* ► impression, perception, conception, idea, notion

imaginary *ADJECTIVE* *a story set in an imaginary country* ► imagined, fictitious, fictional, invented, made-up, make-believe, fanciful, unreal, non-existent, hypothetical, mythical, fabulous OPPOSITES ARE real, actual

imagination *NOUN* *The writing shows a great deal of imagination.* ► creativity, inventiveness, originality, inspiration, vision, ingenuity, insight, sensitivity, resourcefulness, artistry, cleverness, fancy, thought

imaginative *ADJECTIVE* *an imaginative dramatization for television* ► creative, inventive, original, inspired, ingenious, resourceful, enterprising, fanciful, clever AN OPPOSITE IS unimaginative

imagine *VERB* **imagines, imagining, imagined 1** form pictures or ideas in your mind **2** suppose or think • *I don't imagine there'll be any tickets left.*

imitate *VERB* **imitates, imitating, imitated** copy or mimic something
▷ **imitation** *NOUN* **imitator** *NOUN* **imitative** *ADJECTIVE*

immaculate *ADJECTIVE* **1** perfectly clean; spotless **2** without any fault or blemish
▷ **immaculately** *ADVERB*

immature *ADJECTIVE* not mature
▷ **immaturity** *NOUN*

immediate *ADJECTIVE* **1** happening or done without any delay **2** nearest; with nothing or no one between • *our immediate neighbours*
▷ **immediately** *ADVERB* **immediacy** *NOUN*

immense *ADJECTIVE* exceedingly great; huge
▷ **immensely** *ADVERB* **immensity** *NOUN*

immersion heater *NOUN* **immersion heaters** a device that heats up water by means of an electric element in the water in a tank etc.

immigrate *VERB* **immigrates, immigrating, immigrated** come into a country to live there
▷ **immigration** *NOUN* **immigrant** *NOUN*
USAGE See the note at **emigrate**.

imminent *ADJECTIVE* likely to happen at any moment • *an imminent storm*
▷ **imminence** *NOUN*

immobilize *VERB* **immobilizes, immobilizing, immobilized** stop a thing from moving or working
▷ **immobilization** *NOUN*

immoral *ADJECTIVE* morally wrong; wicked
▷ **immorally** *ADVERB* **immorality** *NOUN*

immortal *ADJECTIVE* **1** living for ever; not mortal **2** famous for all time
▷ **immortal** *NOUN* **immortality** *NOUN* **immortalize** *VERB*

immune *ADJECTIVE* safe from danger or attack, especially from disease • *immune from* (or *against* or *to*) *infection*
▷ **immunity** *NOUN*

immunize *VERB* **immunizes, immunizing, immunized** make a person immune from a disease etc., e.g. by vaccination
▷ **immunization** *NOUN*

Thesaurus

imagine *VERB* **1** *Can you imagine life on a desert island?* ► visualize, envisage, picture, conceive, conceptualize **2** *I imagine you'd like us to pay you now.* ► suppose, assume, presume, expect, take it

imitate *VERB* **1** *June liked to imitate her mother's social life.* ► copy, emulate, follow, model yourself on, echo **2** *He was good at imitating politicians.* ► mimic, impersonate, do an impression of, parody, caricature, send up, spoof

imitation *NOUN* **1** *a good imitation of the human voice* ► impersonation, impression, parody, travesty **2** *The stolen jewels turned out to be imitations.* ► copy, reproduction, replica, duplicate, fake, counterfeit

imitation *ADJECTIVE* *The weapon was an imitation firearm.* ► fake, artificial, simulated, sham, counterfeit, dummy, mock, model
OPPOSITES ARE real, genuine

immature *ADJECTIVE* *an immature young man behaving in a silly way* ► childish, babyish, inexperienced, callow

immediate *ADJECTIVE* **1** *We need to take immediate action.* ► instant, instantaneous, prompt, urgent, speedy, swift, quick, rapid, direct, pressing, top-priority OPPOSITES ARE delayed, low-priority **2** *our immediate neighbours* ► nearest, closest, close, near, adjacent, next AN OPPOSITE IS remote

immediately *ADVERB* **1** *I went back to London immediately.* ► straight away, at once, directly, forthwith, instantly, promptly, right away, unhesitatingly **2** *The wall has a damp patch immediately below the window.* ► directly, exactly, precisely, squarely, dead, close

immense *ADJECTIVE* *a cathedral with two immense towers* ► huge, great, enormous, gigantic, massive, colossal, vast, giant, (*more informal*) whopping, (*more informal*) ginormous
AN OPPOSITE IS tiny

immerse *VERB* *You need to immerse your hair in warm water.* ► plunge, submerge, submerse, bathe, dip, dunk, drench, douse, duck, lower

immersed *ADJECTIVE* *I was immersed in my work.* ► absorbed, engrossed, preoccupied (by), occupied (by), busy (with), involved, wrapped up, interested, engaged

imminent *ADJECTIVE* *An invasion of Crete seemed imminent.* ► close, near, at hand, in the offing, in the air, impending, threatening, about to happen, approaching, looming, coming, foreseeable

immoral *ADJECTIVE* *immoral behaviour* ► wrong, unethical, morally wrong, wrongful, disreputable, degenerate, sinful, wicked, unscrupulous, unprincipled, evil, bad
AN OPPOSITE IS moral

immortal *ADJECTIVE* *She might place her immortal soul in deadly peril.* ► eternal, undying, everlasting, ageless, timeless, deathless, endless, perpetual, unchanging AN OPPOSITE IS mortal

impact *NOUN* **impacts** **1** a collision; the force of a collision **2** an influence or effect • *the impact of computers on our lives*

impale *VERB* **impales, impaling, impaled** pierce or fix something on a sharp pointed object

impartial *ADJECTIVE* not favouring one side more than the other; not biased
▷ **impartially** *ADVERB* **impartiality** *NOUN*

impatient *ADJECTIVE* not patient; in a hurry
▷ **impatiently** *ADVERB* **impatience** *NOUN*

impel *VERB* **impels, impelling, impelled** **1** urge or drive someone to do something • *Curiosity impelled her to investigate.* **2** drive forward; propel

impending *ADJECTIVE* soon to happen; imminent

impenetrable *ADJECTIVE* **1** impossible to get through **2** incomprehensible

imperative *ADJECTIVE* **1** expressing a command **2** essential • *Speed is imperative.*

imperative *NOUN* **imperatives** a command; the form of a verb used in making commands (e.g. 'come' in *Come here!*)

imperceptible *ADJECTIVE* too small or gradual to be noticed

imperfect *ADJECTIVE* **1** not perfect **2** (said about a tense of a verb) showing a continuous action, e.g. *She was singing*
▷ **imperfectly** *ADVERB* **imperfection** *NOUN*

imperial *ADJECTIVE* **1** to do with an empire or its rulers **2** (said about weights and measures) formerly fixed by British law; non-metric
▷ **imperially** *ADVERB*

imperious *ADJECTIVE* haughty and bossy

impermeable *ADJECTIVE* not allowing liquid to pass through it

impersonal *ADJECTIVE* **1** not affected by personal feelings; showing no emotion **2** not referring to a particular person
▷ **impersonally** *ADVERB*

impersonal verb *NOUN* **impersonal verbs** a verb used only with 'it', e.g. in *It is raining*

impertinent *ADJECTIVE* insolent; not showing proper respect
▷ **impertinently** *ADVERB* **impertinence** *NOUN*

imperturbable *ADJECTIVE* not excitable; calm
▷ **imperturbably** *ADVERB*

impervious *ADJECTIVE* **1** not allowing water, heat, etc. to pass through • *impervious to water* **2** not able to be affected by something • *impervious to criticism*

Thesaurus

impact *NOUN* **1** *She suffered a broken ankle in the impact.* ► crash, collision, smash, clash, blow, jolt, bump, bang, knock **2** *High street technology is having a huge impact on modern life.* ► effect, influence, impression, repercussions, consequences (for)

impartial *ADJECTIVE* *Counsellors are on hand to give you free and impartial advice.* ► objective, unbiased, disinterested, dispassionate, balanced, detached, neutral, non-partisan, open-minded, equitable, even-handed, fair, fair-minded, just, unprejudiced AN OPPOSITE IS biased

impatience *NOUN* **1** *There was a tremor of impatience in her voice.* ► irritability, agitation, shortness, intolerance, brusqueness, frustration, nervousness **2** *his impatience to start work* ► eagerness, keenness, haste

impatient *ADJECTIVE* **1** *As time passed Michael grew impatient.* ► restless, agitated, fretful, irritated, tetchy, testy, anxious, ill at ease, keyed up, jumpy **2** *The army was impatient to engage the enemy.* ► anxious, eager, keen, avid

imperceptible *ADJECTIVE* *The movement was slow and imperceptible.* ► indiscernible, undetectable, indistinguishable, unnoticeable, infinitesimal, insignificant, negligible, slight, small, subtle AN OPPOSITE IS noticeable
USAGE You can also use *inaudible* when you are referring to sounds, and *invisible* when you are referring to sight.

imperfect *ADJECTIVE* *The goods were imperfect and had to be sent back.* ► faulty, defective, deficient, flawed, damaged, broken, incomplete, shop-soiled AN OPPOSITE IS perfect

imperfection *NOUN* *She handed over her work, hoping they would not notice its many imperfections.* ► defect, fault, deficiency, shortcoming, weakness, flaw, failing, blemish, inadequacy AN OPPOSITE IS perfection

imperil *VERB* *He did not wish to imperil their chances of success.* ► endanger, harm, risk, jeopardize, threaten, compromise

impersonal *ADJECTIVE* *His manner was brusque and impersonal.* ► detached, aloof, distant, formal, unemotional, unfriendly, unsympathetic, businesslike, remote, cold, cool AN OPPOSITE IS friendly

impertinence *NOUN* *They were unclear whether the remark was a joke or a piece of impertinence.* ► rudeness, cheek, insolence, impudence, effrontery, audacity, impoliteness, discourtesy, disrespect AN OPPOSITE IS politeness

impertinent *ADJECTIVE* *A question like that would seem impertinent from anyone else.* ► rude, impolite, insolent, impudent, disrespectful, audacious, brazen OPPOSITES ARE respectful, polite

impetuous *ADJECTIVE* acting hastily without thinking

impetus *NOUN* **1** the force that makes an object start moving and that keeps it moving **2** the influence that causes something to develop more quickly • *The ceasefire gave an impetus to peace talks*

implacable *ADJECTIVE* not able to be placated; relentless
▷ **implacably** *ADVERB*

implant *VERB* **implants, implanting, implanted** insert; fix something in
▷ **implantation** *NOUN*

implant *NOUN* **implants** an organ or piece of tissue inserted in the body

implement *NOUN* **implements** a tool

implicate *VERB* **implicates, implicating, implicated** involve a person in a crime etc.; show that a person is involved • *His evidence implicates his sister*

implication *NOUN* **implications 1** implicating **2** implying; something that is implied

implicit (im- pliss- it) *ADJECTIVE* **1** implied but not stated openly COMPARE **explicit 2** absolute; unquestioning • *She expects implicit obedience*
▷ **implicitly** *ADVERB*

implore *VERB* **implores, imploring, implored** beg somebody to do something

imply *VERB* **implies, implying, implied** suggest something without actually saying it
▷ **implication** *NOUN*

impolite *ADJECTIVE* not polite

import *VERB* **imports, importing, imported** bring in goods etc. from another country

import *NOUN* **imports 1** importing; something imported **2** (*formal*) meaning or importance • *The message was of great import*

important *ADJECTIVE* **1** having or able to have a great effect **2** having great authority or influence
▷ **importantly** *ADVERB* **importance** *NOUN*

impose *VERB* **imposes, imposing, imposed** put or inflict • *It imposes a strain upon us*
impose on somebody put an unfair burden on him or her

imposing *ADJECTIVE* impressive

Thesaurus

impetus *NOUN* **1** *Their enthusiasm began to lose impetus.* ► momentum, force, power, drive, motivation, stimulus, energy, impulse, incentive, push, spur **2** *A new product would give the sales campaign an added impetus.* ► boost, stimulus, inducement, incentive, push, spur

implausible *ADJECTIVE* *The suggestion seemed implausible.* ► unconvincing, improbable, unlikely, questionable, unreasonable, doubtful, dubious, far-fetched, incredible, fanciful, suspect, flimsy, weak, feeble AN OPPOSITE IS plausible

implication *NOUN* **1** *He did not like the implication that he had been dishonest.* ► suggestion, insinuation, intimation, imputation, innuendo USAGE Strictly, *inference* means 'a conclusion you draw' rather than 'a conclusion you suggest', so it is better to use one of the other words given here. **2** *They are suspected of implication in the crime.* ► involvement, association, connection, entanglement, incrimination

implore *VERB* *His family implored him to come home.* ► beg, entreat, urge, appeal to, call on, exhort, (*literary*) beseech

imply *VERB* **1** *He seemed to imply that we were wrong.* ► suggest, hint, insinuate, intimate, indicate USAGE You will sometimes see *infer* used as a synonym of *imply*, but *infer* properly means 'to draw a conclusion' rather than 'to suggest a conclusion', so it is better to use one of the other words given here. **2** *The traffic measures imply a need for better public transport.* ► entail, involve, point to, indicate, suggest, signify, necessitate

impolite *ADJECTIVE* *It would have been impolite to leave the party so early.* ► rude, bad-mannered, discourteous, disrespectful, inconsiderate, ungracious

importance *NOUN* **1** *an event of the greatest importance* ► significance, consequence, seriousness, import, substance, gravity, urgency **2** *a person of importance* ► power, influence, authority, prominence, status, distinction, eminence

important *ADJECTIVE* **1** *an important decision* ► significant, momentous, crucial, critical, vital, far-reaching, consequential, historic **2** *It is important to get there early.* ► crucial, vital, essential **3** *an important person* ► powerful, influential, prominent, distinguished, eminent

impose *VERB* *The library will impose a fine on the late return of books.* ► exact, enforce, introduce, fix, inflict, levy, prescribe, set, place
impose on *They were afraid they might be imposing on us.* ► intrude on, presume on, inconvenience, encroach on, obtrude on, force yourself on, take advantage of

imposing *ADJECTIVE* *an imposing mock-baronial building* ► grand, stately, impressive, magnificent, majestic, splendid, distinguished, striking, dignified, grandiose OPPOSITES ARE unimposing, modest

a b c d e f g h i j k l m n o p q r s t u v w x y z

imposition *NOUN* **impositions** **1** something imposed; an unfair burden or inconvenience **2** imposing something

impossible *ADJECTIVE* **1** not possible **2** (*informal*) very annoying; unbearable • *He really is impossible!*
▷ **impossibly** *ADVERB* **impossibility** *NOUN*

impostor *NOUN* **impostors** a person who dishonestly pretends to be someone else

impotent *ADJECTIVE* **1** powerless; unable to take action **2** (said about a man) unable to have sexual intercourse
▷ **impotently** *ADVERB* **impotence** *NOUN*

impoverish *VERB* **impoverishes, impoverishing, impoverished** **1** make a person poor **2** make a thing poor in quality • *impoverished soil*
▷ **impoverishment** *NOUN*

impracticable *ADJECTIVE* not able to be done in practice

impractical *ADJECTIVE* not practical

imprecise *ADJECTIVE* not precise

impregnable *ADJECTIVE* strong enough to be safe against attack

impregnate *VERB* **impregnates, impregnating, impregnated** **1** fertilize; make pregnant **2** saturate; fill throughout • *The air was impregnated with the scent.*
▷ **impregnation** *NOUN*

impress *VERB* **impresses, impressing, impressed** **1** make a person admire something or think it is very good **2** fix something firmly in the mind • *He impressed on them the need for secrecy.* **3** press a mark into something

impression *NOUN* **impressions** **1** an effect produced on the mind • *The book made a big impression on me.* **2** a vague idea **3** an imitation of a person or a sound etc. **4** a reprint of a book

impressionable *ADJECTIVE* easily influenced or affected

impressive *ADJECTIVE* making a strong impression; seeming to be very good

imprison *VERB* **imprisons, imprisoning, imprisoned** put someone in prison; shut someone up in a place
▷ **imprisonment** *NOUN*

improbable *ADJECTIVE* unlikely
▷ **improbably** *ADVERB* **improbability** *NOUN*

impromptu *ADJECTIVE, ADVERB* done without any rehearsal or preparation

Thesaurus

imposition *NOUN* **1** *the imposition of a windfall tax* ► introduction, levying, charging, exacting, enforcing, fixing, setting **2** *Asking for help might seem an imposition.* ► intrusion, encroachment, presumption, liberty, burden, encumbrance

impossible *ADJECTIVE* **1** *The tears made speaking impossible.* ► impractical, hopeless, inconceivable, unthinkable, out of the question, unachievable **2** *They had succeeded against impossible odds.* ► unrealistic, hopeless, overwhelming, insurmountable, implausible, unbelievable, preposterous, ludicrous, unattainable AN OPPOSITE IS possible

impostor *NOUN* *The official turned out to be an impostor.* ► impersonator, masquerader, charlatan, fraud, cheat, hoaxer, trickster, (*more informal*) phoney

imprecise *ADJECTIVE* *an imprecise description* ► vague, loose, inexact, inaccurate, hazy, woolly, equivocal OPPOSITES ARE precise, exact

impress *VERB* **1** *This evidence did not impress the jury.* ► move, stir, influence, affect, excite, make an impression on, have an impact on, (*more informal*) grab **2 impress on** *We must impress on Chris what good work he has done.* ► emphasize to, bring home to, instil in, inculcate in

impression *NOUN* **1** *We got the impression they were hiding something.* ► feeling, sense, suspicion, conviction, awareness, notion, idea, hunch, inkling **2** *The experience left a good impression on him.* ► effect, impact, influence **3** *He had formed a favourable impression of them.* ► opinion, view, perception, assessment, estimation, judgement, verdict **4** *She did a good impression of the Queen Mother.* ► imitation, impersonation, parody, caricature, (*more informal*) send-up **5** *The mug had left a circular impression in the cloth.* ► indentation, dent, hollow, stamp, mark, print, outline

impressive *ADJECTIVE* **1** *She has made an impressive concert debut.* ► striking, accomplished, masterly, first-class, exciting, stirring AN OPPOSITE IS insignificant **2** *The conference is held in an impressive building near the university.* ► magnificent, imposing, splendid, grand, stately, monumental

imprison *VERB* *The judge imprisoned him for five years.* ► jail, incarcerate, send to prison, put in prison, detain, lock up, confine, (*more informal*) put away, (*more informal*) send down

imprisonment *NOUN* *The penalty is life imprisonment.* ► incarceration, internment, detention, confinement, custody

improbable *ADJECTIVE* *The excuse was most improbable.* ► unlikely, implausible, incredible, doubtful, questionable, far-fetched, unbelievable, unconvincing, preposterous AN OPPOSITE IS probable

improper *ADJECTIVE* **1** unsuitable or wrong **2** indecent
▷ **improperly** *ADVERB* **impropriety** (im- pro- pry- it- ee) *NOUN*

improper fraction *NOUN* **improper fractions** a fraction that is greater than 1, with the numerator greater than the denominator, e.g. 7/5

improve *VERB* **improves, improving, improved** make or become better
▷ **improvement** *NOUN*

improvise *VERB* **improvises, improvising, improvised** **1** compose or perform something without any rehearsal or preparation **2** make something quickly with whatever is available
▷ **improvisation** *NOUN*

imprudent *ADJECTIVE* unwise or rash

impudent *ADJECTIVE* cheeky or disrespectful
▷ **impudently** *ADVERB* **impudence** *NOUN*

impulse *NOUN* **impulses** **1** a sudden desire to do something • *I did it on impulse.* **2** a push or impetus **3** (in science) a force acting for a very short time • *electrical impulses*

impulsive *ADJECTIVE* done or acting on impulse, not after careful thought
▷ **impulsively** *ADVERB* **impulsiveness** *NOUN*

impure *ADJECTIVE* not pure
▷ **impurity** *NOUN*

in *PREPOSITION* This word is used to show position or condition, e.g. **1** at or inside; within the limits of something (*in a box; in two hours*), **2** into (*He fell in a puddle.*), **3** arranged as; consisting of (*a serial in four parts*), **4** occupied with; a member of (*He is in the army.*), **5** by means of (*We paid in cash.*)
in all in total number; altogether

in *ADVERB* **1** so as to be in something or inside (*Get in*) **2** inwards (*The top caved in*) **3** at home; indoors (*Is anybody in?*) **4** in action; (in cricket) batting **5** having arrived (*The train is in*)
in for likely to get • *You're in for a shock*
in on (*informal*) aware of or sharing in • *I want to be in on this project.*

in- *PREFIX* (changing to **il-** before *l*, **im-** before *b, m, p*, **ir-** before *r*) **1** in; into; on; towards (as in *include, invade*) **2** not (as in *incorrect, indirect*)

Thesaurus

improper *ADJECTIVE* **1** *It would be improper to accept payment.* ► wrong , inappropriate, unsuitable, irregular, out of place, unacceptable, unprofessional, incorrect, inopportune, uncalled for, unwarranted **2** *In those days such behaviour would have been thought improper.* ► indecent, unseemly, indecorous, unbecoming, unfitting, shocking, vulgar AN OPPOSITE IS proper

improve *VERB* **1** *We are always looking for ways to improve the service.* ► make better, better, enhance, reform, upgrade, develop **2** *Relations between the employers and unions have improved markedly.* ► get better, progress, advance, develop, make headway, rally, (*more informal*) look up **3** *Reduce the dose as soon as the patient begins to improve.* ► recover, get better, recuperate, regain strength **4** *They are hoping to improve their offer shortly.* ► increase, raise, supplement, enlarge, augment, top up
improve on *It will be hard to improve on work of that quality.* ► surpass, outdo, do better than, exceed

improvement *NOUN* **1** *The weather showed a little improvement; an improvement in East–West relations* ► recovery, advance, upturn, progress, enhancement, amelioration, development, rectification, betterment, gain, rally, reformation **2** *We have carried out a lot of improvements to the house.* ► renovation, alteration, extension, modernization, modification, (*informal*) face-lift

impudence *NOUN* *They soon forgave him his impudence.* ► cheek, insolence, impertinence, effrontery, audacity, rudeness, impoliteness, discourtesy, disrespect AN OPPOSITE IS politeness

impudent *ADJECTIVE* *She thought him an impudent bully.* ► rude, insolent, impertinent, impolite, disrespectful, audacious, brazen OPPOSITES ARE respectful, polite

impulse *NOUN* **1** *His first impulse was to call the police.* ► instinct, urge, inclination, compulsion, whim, caprice, desire **2** *His actions were so often governed by impulse.* ► impetuosity, spontaneity, rashness, recklessness **3** *Emotion is one of the main impulses of poetry.* ► stimulus, inspiration, motivation

impulsive *ADJECTIVE* *With an impulsive gesture she flounced out of the room.* ► impetuous, spontaneous, rash, reckless, hasty, uninhibited, instinctive, passionate AN OPPOSITE IS deliberate

impure *ADJECTIVE* **1** *The water was found to be impure.* ► contaminated, polluted, tainted, unclean, foul, defiled, dirty, filthy, infected, unhygienic, unwholesome, adulterated **2** *impure thoughts* ► immoral, indecent, unclean, corrupt, wicked, degenerate

impurity *NOUN* **1** *An instrument measured the impurity of the air.* ► contamination, pollution, dirtiness, uncleanliness, foulness, filthiness **2** *water full of impurities* ► contaminant, pollutant, adulterant, foreign matter

inability *NOUN* being unable

inaccessible *ADJECTIVE* not able to be reached

inaccurate *ADJECTIVE* not accurate

inadequate *ADJECTIVE* **1** not enough **2** not able to cope or deal with something
▷ **inadequately** *ADVERB* **inadequacy** *NOUN*

inadvisable *ADJECTIVE* not advisable

inanimate *ADJECTIVE* **1** not living **2** showing no sign of life

inappropriate *ADJECTIVE* not appropriate

inarticulate *ADJECTIVE* **1** not able to speak or express yourself clearly • *inarticulate with rage* **2** not expressed in words • *an inarticulate cry*

inaudible *ADJECTIVE* not able to be heard
▷ **inaudibly** *ADVERB* **inaudibility** *NOUN*

inaugurate *VERB* **inaugurates, inaugurating, inaugurated** **1** start or introduce something new and important **2** formally establish a person in office • *inaugurate a new President*
▷ **inaugural** *ADJECTIVE* **inauguration** *NOUN* **inaugurator** *NOUN*

inborn *ADJECTIVE* present in a person or animal from birth • *an inborn ability*

inbred *ADJECTIVE* **1** inborn **2** produced by inbreeding

inbreeding *NOUN* breeding from closely related individuals

incalculable *ADJECTIVE* not able to be calculated or predicted

incandescent *ADJECTIVE* giving out light when heated; shining
▷ **incandescence** *NOUN*

incantation *NOUN* **incantations** a spoken spell or charm; the chanting of this

incapable *ADJECTIVE* not able to do something • *They seem incapable of understanding*

incapacitate *VERB* **incapacitates, incapacitating, incapacitated** make a person or thing unable to do something; disable

incarnate *ADJECTIVE* having a body or human form • *a devil incarnate*
▷ **incarnation** *NOUN*

the Incarnation the embodiment of God in human form as Jesus Christ

incautious *ADJECTIVE* rash

incendiary *ADJECTIVE* starting or designed to start a fire • *an incendiary bomb*

incentive *NOUN* **incentives** something that encourages a person to do something or to work harder

incest *NOUN* sexual intercourse between two people who are so closely related that they cannot marry each other
▷ **incestuous** *ADJECTIVE*

inch *NOUN* **inches** a measure of length, one-twelfth of a foot (about 2 centimetres)

inch *VERB* **inches, inching, inched** move slowly and gradually • *I inched along the ledge.* [from Old English]

incident *NOUN* **incidents** an event

Thesaurus

inability *NOUN* *their inability to agree on a single point* ► incapacity, incapability, impotence, powerlessness, lack of ability

inaccessible *ADJECTIVE* *More of the countryside is becoming inaccessible.* ► unreachable, cut off, out of reach, isolated, remote, godforsaken, hard to find, out-of-the-way, in the middle of nowhere, in the back of beyond, secluded, unfrequented, (*informal*) unget-at-able AN OPPOSITE IS accessible

inaccuracy *NOUN* *The information is marred by inaccuracies.* ► mistake, error, miscalculation, blunder, imprecision, fault, defect, flaw, slip, oversight OPPOSITES ARE accuracy, precision

inaccurate *ADJECTIVE* *The road map is very inaccurate.* ► inexact, imprecise, incorrect, erroneous, faulty, imperfect, defective, unsound

inactive *ADJECTIVE* **1** *Illness left me inactive for several weeks.* ► idle, immobile, inert, lethargic, listless, sluggish **2** *The alarm was inactive at the time of the break-in.* ► inoperative, idle, non-functioning, turned off, out of action, out of use

inappropriate *ADJECTIVE* *The police decided a prosecution would be inappropriate.* ► unsuitable, out of place, inapt, ill-suited, unfitting, untimely, ill-timed, improper, incongruous OPPOSITES ARE appropriate, suitable

inaudible *ADJECTIVE* *From that distance the voices were inaudible.* ► indistinct, hard to hear, unclear, quiet, silent, weak, undetectable, unidentifiable, muted, faint, low, muffled, mumbled AN OPPOSITE IS audible

incapable *ADJECTIVE* *Those who feel incapable in their work can get advice.* ► incompetent, ineffective, ineffectual, inadequate, impotent, inept, unable, useless, weak AN OPPOSITE IS capable

incessant *ADJECTIVE* *incessant noise from the road works outside* ► continuous, continual, constant, ceaseless, endless, unceasing, interminable, non-stop OPPOSITES ARE temporary, intermittent

incident *NOUN* **1** *He recalled an amusing incident from his childhood.* ► event, episode, occurrence, happening, occasion, affair, experience, activity, business, circumstance **2** *Police were called to an incident in the centre of town.* ► disturbance, commotion, fracas, scene, brawl, rumpus, fight

incidental *ADJECTIVE* happening as a minor part of something else • *incidental expenses*

incidentally *ADVERB* by the way

incinerate *VERB* **incinerates, incinerating, incinerated** destroy something by burning
▷ **incineration** *NOUN*

incinerator *NOUN* **incinerators** a device for burning rubbish

incision *NOUN* **incisions** a cut, especially one made in a surgical operation

incisive *ADJECTIVE* clear and sharp • *incisive comments*

incisor (in- sy- zer) *NOUN* **incisors** each of the sharp-edged front teeth in the upper and lower jaws

incite *VERB* **incites, inciting, incited** urge a person to do something; stir up • *They incited a riot*
▷ **incitement** *NOUN*

inclination *NOUN* **inclinations 1** a tendency **2** a liking or preference **3** a slope or slant

incline *VERB* **inclines, inclining, inclined**
1 lean or slope **2** bend the head or body forward, as in a nod or bow **3** cause or influence • *Her frank manner inclines me to believe her.* • *The door is inclined to bang.* • *I'm inclined to agree with you.*
be inclined have a tendency or willingness

include *VERB* **includes, including, included** make or consider something as part of a group of things
▷ **inclusion** *NOUN*

inclusive *ADJECTIVE* including everything; including all the things mentioned • *Read pages 20 to 28 inclusive.*

incoherent *ADJECTIVE* not speaking or reasoning in an orderly way

income *NOUN* **incomes** money received regularly from doing work or from investments

income tax *NOUN* tax charged on income

incomparable *ADJECTIVE* without an equal; not surpassed • *incomparable beauty*

incompatible *ADJECTIVE* not able to exist or be used together

incompetent *ADJECTIVE* not able or skilled enough to do something properly

incomplete *ADJECTIVE* not complete

incomprehensible *ADJECTIVE* not able to be understood
▷ **incomprehension** *NOUN*

Thesaurus

inclination *NOUN* **1** *He showed no inclination to leave.* ► readiness, desire, impulse, wish, disposition, predisposition, predilection AN OPPOSITE IS disinclination **2** *She had no inclination for work that day.* ► liking, partiality, appetite, taste, fondness, penchant AN OPPOSITE IS dislike

incline *VERB* *The uprights incline slightly to the right.* ► lean, slant, tilt, tip, slope, veer
be inclined *We are inclined to believe him.* ► be disposed, be minded, be willing, be ready

include *VERB* **1** *Sports activities include swimming and aerobics.* ► incorporate, involve, comprise, contain, embrace, encompass, consist of, take in, make room for, subsume **2** *The package includes flights, hotels costs, and all outings.* ► cover, allow for, take into account, add in AN OPPOSITE IS exclude

incoherent *ADJECTIVE* *The letter was long and incoherent.* ► unclear, confused, muddled, unintelligible, disorganized, incomprehensible, inarticulate, garbled, rambling, hard to follow, disjointed, disordered, illogical OPPOSITES ARE coherent, intelligible

income *NOUN* **1** *Her income has gone up significantly in the last year.* ► earnings, salary, pay, remuneration, wages, money **2** *taxes on business income* ► revenue, receipts, takings, profits, gains, proceeds, takeover OPPOSITES ARE expenditure, outgoings

incompetent *ADJECTIVE* *They were all either too lazy or too incompetent to do an honest day's work.* ► inept, incapable, unqualified, inefficient, unskilful, unfit, inadequate, unproficient, bungling, blundering, clumsy, ineffectual AN OPPOSITE IS competent

incomplete *ADJECTIVE* *They have to move into the house even though it's still incomplete.* ► unfinished, uncompleted, half-finished, not finished, unready

incomprehensible *ADJECTIVE* **1** *She made some incomprehensible remark.* ► unintelligible, incoherent, unfathomable, baffling, confusing, perplexing, obscure, cryptic, opaque, mysterious, inscrutable, enigmatic AN OPPOSITE IS comprehensible **2** *The writing was incomprehensible.* ► illegible, indecipherable, unintelligible OPPOSITES ARE intelligible, legible

inconceivable *ADJECTIVE* *It was inconceivable that the king would agree to these demands.* ► unimaginable, unthinkable, implausible, incredible, unbelievable, undreamed of, (*more informal*) mind-boggling OPPOSITES ARE conceivable, credible

inconclusive *ADJECTIVE* *The opinion polls are inconclusive.* ► unconvincing, indefinite, undecided, ambiguous, equivocal, indecisive, indeterminate, uncertain, unsettled, open AN OPPOSITE IS conclusive

a b c d e f g h i j k l m n o p q r s t u v w x y z

A B C D E F G H I J K L M N O P Q R S T U V W X Y Z

incongruous ADJECTIVE out of place or unsuitable
▷ **incongruously** ADVERB **incongruity** NOUN

inconsiderate ADJECTIVE not considerate towards other people

inconsistent ADJECTIVE not consistent
▷ **inconsistently** ADVERB **inconsistency** NOUN

inconspicuous ADJECTIVE not conspicuous
▷ **inconspicuously** ADVERB

incontinent ADJECTIVE not able to control the bladder or bowels
▷ **incontinence** NOUN

incontrovertible ADJECTIVE unable to be denied; indisputable

inconvenience NOUN **inconveniences** being inconvenient

inconvenience VERB **inconveniences, inconveniencing, inconvenienced** cause inconvenience or slight difficulty to someone

inconvenient ADJECTIVE not convenient

incorporate VERB **incorporates, incorporating, incorporated** include something as a part of something larger
▷ **incorporation** NOUN

incorporated ADJECTIVE (said about a business firm) formed into a legal corporation

incorrect ADJECTIVE not correct
▷ **incorrectly** ADVERB

incorruptible ADJECTIVE **1** not able to decay **2** not able to be bribed

increase VERB **increases, increasing, increased** make or become larger or more

increase NOUN **increases** increasing; the amount by which a thing increases

incredible ADJECTIVE unbelievable
▷ **incredibly** ADVERB **incredibility** NOUN
USAGE Do not confuse with **incredulous**.

Thesaurus

incongruous ADJECTIVE *the incongruous sound of an electric doorbell* ▶ inappropriate, out of place, discordant, unsuitable, ill-suited, incompatible, inconsistent, conflicting, odd, clashing, contrasting, ill-matched, uncoordinated, irreconcilable AN OPPOSITE IS appropriate

inconsiderate ADJECTIVE *inconsiderate behaviour; It was very inconsiderate of them.* ▶ thoughtless, insensitive, unthinking, uncaring, unkind, discourteous, impolite, unconcerned, tactless

inconsistent ADJECTIVE **1** *Their attitudes are inconsistent and hard to understand.* ▶ changeable, unreliable, erratic, capricious, unstable, variable, fickle, inconstant, unpredictable, (*more informal*) up-and-down **2** *There are several inconsistent versions of the legend.* ▶ conflicting, contradictory, incompatible, irreconcilable, discrepant, incongruous, at variance, clashing, contrasting, different AN OPPOSITE IS consistent

inconsolable ADJECTIVE *Lisa was inconsolable when she arrived back from the accident.* ▶ heartbroken, broken-hearted, devastated, grief-stricken, desolate, despairing

inconspicuous ADJECTIVE **1** *The building is small and inconspicuous.* ▶ unobtrusive, undistinguished, unremarkable, unostentatious, camouflaged, hidden, out of sight, insignificant, ordinary, invisible **2** *Jane did her best to remain inconspicuous.* ▶ retiring, self-effacing, unassuming, modest, restrained OPPOSITES ARE conspicuous, noticeable

inconvenience NOUN *The roadworks have caused a great deal of inconvenience.* ▶ trouble, bother, difficulty, disruption, awkwardness, nuisance, hindrance, irritation, fuss, upset, annoyance, disadvantage, drawback, encumbrance AN OPPOSITE IS convenience

inconvenience VERB *We hope the delay will not inconvenience you too much.* ▶ trouble, bother, disturb, put out, incommode, annoy, irritate, disadvantage, embarrass, (*informal*) put you out

inconvenient ADJECTIVE *Shirley arrived at an extremely inconvenient moment.* ▶ awkward, difficult, unsuitable, inappropriate, inopportune, untimely, ill-timed, embarrassing, annoying, bothersome, irritating, troublesome AN OPPOSITE IS convenient

incorporate VERB **1** *The peace treaty incorporated the region into Italy.* ▶ absorb, merge, assimilate, subsume, embody, include (in), contain (in) **2** *The leaflet incorporates a sponsorship form.* ▶ include, contain, embrace

incorrect ADJECTIVE *The next three answers were incorrect.* ▶ wrong, erroneous, mistaken, inaccurate, imprecise, inexact, false, untrue

increase NOUN *an increase in size an increase in demand* ▶ growth, rise, development, enlargement, expansion, swelling, intensification, upsurge, upturn AN OPPOSITE IS decrease

increase VERB **1** *Applications for jobs have increased.* ▶ rise, grow, swell, multiply, expand, spread, proliferate OPPOSITES ARE decrease, decline **2** *Prosperity increases consumer demand.* ▶ raise, heighten, boost, enhance, add to, strengthen, intensify, develop, expand, escalate, augment OPPOSITES ARE reduce, lower

incredible ADJECTIVE **1** *an incredible feat of engineering* ▶ magnificent, marvellous,

incredulous *ADJECTIVE* not believing somebody; showing disbelief
▷ **incredulously** *ADVERB* **incredulity** *NOUN*
USAGE Do not confuse with **incredible**.

incriminate *VERB* **incriminates, incriminating, incriminated** show a person to have been involved in a crime etc.
▷ **incrimination** *NOUN*

incubate *VERB* **incubates, incubating, incubated** **1** hatch eggs by keeping them warm **2** cause bacteria or a disease etc. to develop
▷ **incubation** *NOUN*

incubator *NOUN* **incubators** **1** a device in which a baby born prematurely can be kept warm and supplied with oxygen **2** a device for incubating eggs etc.

incur *VERB* **incurs, incurring, incurred** bring something on yourself • *I hope you don't incur too much expense.*

indebted *ADJECTIVE* owing money or gratitude to someone

indecent *ADJECTIVE* not decent; improper
▷ **indecently** *ADVERB* **indecency** *NOUN*

indecisive *ADJECTIVE* not decisive

indeed *ADVERB* **1** really; truly • *I am indeed surprised*; (used to strengthen a meaning) • *very nice indeed* **2** admittedly • *It is, indeed, his first attempt.*

indefensible *ADJECTIVE* unable to be defended or justified • *an indefensible decision*

indefinite *ADJECTIVE* not definite; vague

indefinite article *NOUN* **indefinite articles** (in grammar) the word 'a' or 'an'

indefinitely *ADVERB* for an indefinite or unlimited time

indelible *ADJECTIVE* impossible to rub out or remove
▷ **indelibly** *ADVERB*

indelicate *ADJECTIVE* **1** slightly indecent **2** tactless
▷ **indelicacy** *NOUN*

independent *ADJECTIVE* **1** not dependent on any other person or thing for help, money, or support **2** (said about a country) governing itself **3** (said about broadcasting) not financed by money from licences
▷ **independently** *ADVERB* **independence** *NOUN*

indestructible *ADJECTIVE* unable to be destroyed
▷ **indestructibility** *NOUN*

indeterminate *ADJECTIVE* not fixed or decided exactly; left vague

index *NOUN* **1** (**indexes**) an alphabetical list of things, especially at the end of a book **2** (**indexes**) a number showing how prices or wages have changed from a previous level **3** (**indices**) (in mathematics) the raised number etc. written to the right of another (e.g. 3 in 2^3) showing how many times the first one is to be multiplied by itself

Thesaurus

spectacular, remarkable, wonderful, extraordinary, amazing, astounding **2** *Their story is incredible.* ► unbelievable, implausible, far-fetched, improbable, unlikely, questionable, unreasonable, doubtful, dubious AN OPPOSITE IS credible

incur *VERB* *actions that might incur a penalty* ► earn, sustain, attract, provoke, run up, suffer, get, expose you to, bring on yourself

incurable *ADJECTIVE* **1** *an incurable illness* ► untreatable, inoperable, irremediable, irreparable, terminal, fatal, chronic, hopeless AN OPPOSITE IS curable **2** *Jenny is an incurable romantic.* ► inveterate, incorrigible, hardened, dyed-in-the-wool

indecision *NOUN* *She wanted to act, but indecision prevented her.* ► hesitation, irresolution, indecisiveness, uncertainty, doubt, ambivalence, vacillation, equivocation OPPOSITES ARE decisiveness, resolution

indecisive *ADJECTIVE* **1** *He came across as an indecisive leader.* ► hesitant, irresolute, tentative, equivocating, uncertain, weak, dithering **2** *The result of the tests was indecisive.* ► uncertain, doubtful, unsure

indefinite *ADJECTIVE* **1** *The inspectors are here for an indefinite period.* ► unspecified, unknown, uncertain, unlimited AN OPPOSITE IS definite **2** *a word like 'get', with an indefinite meaning* ► vague, unclear, unspecific, imprecise, hazy

indelible *ADJECTIVE* **1** *indelible ink* ► permanent, ineradicable, fixed, lasting, fast, ingrained **2** *The experience left an indelible impression on her.* ► unforgettable, ineradicable, lasting, enduring AN OPPOSITE IS erasable.

independence *NOUN* **1** *The country gained its independence in the 1950s.* ► self-government, autonomy, freedom, individualism, liberty, nonconformity AN OPPOSITE IS dependence **2** *The judges must be able to act with complete independence.* ► impartiality, neutrality, disinterest, detachment, objectivity, freedom

independent *ADJECTIVE* **1** *an independent country* ► autonomous, sovereign, self-governing **2** *an independent person* ► free, unconstrained, self-reliant, self-sufficient, free-thinking, liberated AN OPPOSITE IS dependent **3** *an independent opinion* ► impartial, unbiased, disinterested, objective

A B C D E F G H I J K L M N O P Q R S T U V W X Y Z

Indian ADJECTIVE **1** to do with India or its people **2** to do with Native Americans
▷ **Indian** NOUN
USAGE The preferred term for the descendants of the original inhabitants of North and South America is *Native American*. *American Indian* is usually acceptable but the term *Red Indian* is now regarded as offensive and should not be used.

india rubber NOUN **india rubbers** a rubber

indicate VERB **indicates, indicating, indicated**
1 point something out or make it known **2** be a sign of **3** when drivers indicate, they signal which direction they are turning by using their indicators
▷ **indication** NOUN

indicative ADJECTIVE giving an indication

indicative NOUN the form of a verb used in making a statement (e.g. 'he said' or 'he is coming'), not in a command or question, or wish

indicator NOUN **indicators** **1** a thing that indicates or points to something **2** a flashing light used to signal that a motor vehicle is turning **3** (in science) a chemical compound, such as litmus, that changes colour in the presence of a particular substance or condition

indifferent ADJECTIVE **1** not caring about something; not interested **2** not very good
• *an indifferent cricketer*
▷ **indifferently** ADVERB **indifference** NOUN

indigenous (in- dij- in- us) ADJECTIVE growing or originating in a particular country; native • *The koala bear is indigenous to Australia.*

indigestible ADJECTIVE difficult or impossible to digest

indigestion NOUN pain or discomfort caused by difficulty in digesting food

indignant ADJECTIVE angry at something that seems unfair or wicked
▷ **indignantly** ADVERB **indignation** NOUN

indignity NOUN **indignities** treatment that makes a person feel undignified or humiliated; an insult

indirect ADJECTIVE not direct
▷ **indirectly** ADVERB

indirect speech NOUN someone's words given in a changed form reported by someone else, as in *He said that he would come* (reporting the words 'I will come')

indiscreet ADJECTIVE **1** not discreet; revealing secrets **2** not cautious; rash
▷ **indiscreetly** ADVERB **indiscretion** NOUN

indiscriminate ADJECTIVE showing no discrimination; not making a careful choice
▷ **indiscriminately** ADVERB

indispensable ADJECTIVE not able to be dispensed with; essential
▷ **indispensability** NOUN

indisputable ADJECTIVE undeniable

Thesaurus

indicate VERB **1** *A linesman raised his flag to indicate a goal.* ► signify, denote, register, record, designate **2** *Good sales indicate the book's popularity.* ► show, demonstrate, be a sign of, testify to, suggest, imply, attest **3** *Indicate your choice of prize on the form.* ► specify, point out

indication NOUN **1** *His secretary could give no clear indication of when he was expected back.* ► clue, hint, inkling, intimation, suggestion, explanation **2** *Pain may be an indication of injury.* ► sign, indicator, symptom, mark, evidence, manifestation

indifference NOUN *He reacted with complete indifference to their predicament.* ► unconcern, apathy, coolness, disregard, nonchalance, inattention

indifferent ADJECTIVE **1** *His voice showed how indifferent he was.* ► unconcerned, apathetic, uncaring, nonchalant **2** *After an indifferent meal he went off to bed.* ► mediocre, ordinary, inferior, unexceptional, average

indignant ADJECTIVE *The newspaper received indignant letters from outraged readers.* ► irate, angry, affronted, aggrieved, incensed, outraged, resentful, offended, vexed, piqued, heated, furious, fuming

indignation NOUN *The false accusations filled him with indignation.* ► anger, fury, resentment, outrage, affront, umbrage, vexation

indirect ADJECTIVE **1** *The convoy took a quieter indirect route.* ► roundabout, circuitous, meandering, out-of-the-way **2** *It was an insult, if only an indirect one.* ► disguised, ambiguous, equivocal, oblique, implicit, implied, inexplicit
AN OPPOSITE IS direct

indiscreet ADJECTIVE *Her mum would never have done anything so indiscreet.* ► imprudent, unwise, injudicious, tactless, ill-advised, ill-considered, ill-judged, unthinking, impolite, impolitic, undiplomatic, careless, incautious, unguarded OPPOSITES ARE discreet, careful

indisputable ADJECTIVE *Charles returned in triumph, indisputable King of Aquitaine.* ► incontrovertible, incontestable, acknowledged, undeniable, indubitable, unassailable, unequivocal OPPOSITES ARE questionable, debatable

indistinct ADJECTIVE not distinct
▷ **indistinctly** ADVERB **indistinctness** NOUN

indistinguishable ADJECTIVE not able to be told apart; not distinguishable

individual ADJECTIVE **1** of or for one person **2** single or separate • *Count each individual word.*
▷ **individually** ADVERB

individual NOUN **individuals** one person, animal, or plant

individuality NOUN the things that make one person or thing different from another; distinctive identity

indivisible ADJECTIVE not able to be divided or separated
▷ **indivisibly** ADVERB

indoctrinate VERB **indoctrinates, indoctrinating, indoctrinated** fill a person's mind with particular ideas or beliefs, so that they come to accept them without thinking
▷ **indoctrination** NOUN

indomitable ADJECTIVE not able to be overcome or conquered

indoor ADJECTIVE used or placed or done etc. inside a building • *indoor games*

indoors ADVERB inside a building

induce VERB **induces, inducing, induced** **1** persuade **2** produce or cause • *Some substances induce sleep.* **3** if a pregnant woman is induced, labour is brought on artificially with drugs
▷ **induction** NOUN

indulge VERB **indulges, indulging, indulged** allow a person to have or do what they want
▷ **indulgence** NOUN **indulgent** ADJECTIVE
indulge in allow yourself to have or do something that you like

industrial ADJECTIVE to do with industry; working or used in industry
▷ **industrially** ADVERB

industrial action NOUN ways for workers to protest, such as striking or working to rule

industrialized ADJECTIVE (said about a country or district) having many industries
▷ **industrialization** NOUN

Industrial Revolution NOUN the rapid expansion of British industry by the use of machines during the late 18th and early 19th centuries

industrious ADJECTIVE working hard
▷ **industriously** ADVERB

industry NOUN **industries** **1** making or producing goods etc., especially in factories **2** a particular branch of this, or any business activity • *the motor industry;* • *the tourist industry* **3** being industrious

Thesaurus

indistinct ADJECTIVE **1** *In the photocopies, some of the letters were indistinct.* ► blurred, fuzzy, unclear, out of focus, ill-defined, dim, faint, hazy, misty, obscure, vague, shadowy, bleary **2** *She murmured, but her voice was indistinct.* ► muffled, muted, faint, weak, inaudible, slurred AN OPPOSITE IS distinct

indistinguishable ADJECTIVE *The boys are indistinguishable.* ► identical, interchangeable, alike, the same AN OPPOSITE IS different

individual ADJECTIVE **1** *music with an individual style* ► characteristic, distinctive, distinct, particular, special, specific, unique, peculiar, exclusive, idiosyncratic, private, personal **2** *Individual countries can make their own decisions.* ► separate, single, discrete AN OPPOSITE IS collective

individual NOUN *In the corner sat a strange individual.* ► person, being, human being, soul, mortal

indoctrinate VERB *With their psychological techniques they were able to indoctrinate large numbers of people.* ► brainwash, propagandize, re-educate, instruct, train, teach

induce VERB **1** *Their leaders induced them to continue fighting.* ► persuade, convince, prevail upon, press, urge, encourage **2** *Conversations like these induce close friendship.* ► bring about, cause, create, effect, instigate, engender, develop, produce, lead to, give rise to, arouse, kindle

inducement NOUN *Paying off student loans is an inducement to join the profession.* ► incentive, encouragement, enticement, stimulus, motivation, spur, lure, bait

indulge VERB **1** *She decided to indulge her passion for music.* ► satisfy, gratify, fulfil, pander to, go along with, humour **2** *She could not be accused of indulging her children.* ► spoil, pamper, cosset, mollycoddle
indulge in *Here we stopped and indulged in a cream tea.* ► enjoy, revel in

indulgent ADJECTIVE *He could see the looks of indulgent amusement on their faces.* ► tolerant, compliant, patient, permissive, easy-going, lenient, liberal, overgenerous, fond, genial, kind AN OPPOSITE IS strict

industrious ADJECTIVE *an industrious and studious youth* ► diligent, hard-working, conscientious, assiduous, enterprising, painstaking, energetic, active, keen, productive, zealous, sedulous, tireless OPPOSITES ARE lazy, indolent

industry NOUN **1** *the American oil industry* ► business, trade, commerce, manufacturing **2** *The garden looked a hive of industry.*

ineffective *ADJECTIVE* not effective; inefficient
▷ **ineffectively** *ADVERB*

ineffectual *ADJECTIVE* not achieving anything

inefficient *ADJECTIVE* not efficient
▷ **inefficiently** *ADVERB* **inefficiency** *NOUN*

inept *ADJECTIVE* lacking any skill; clumsy
▷ **ineptly** *ADVERB* **ineptitude** *NOUN*

inert *ADJECTIVE* not moving or reacting
▷ **inertly** *ADVERB*

inert gas *NOUN* **inert gases** a gas that almost never combines with other substances

inertia (in- er- sha) *NOUN* **1** inactivity; being inert or slow to take action **2** the tendency for a moving thing to keep moving in a straight line

inevitable *ADJECTIVE* unavoidable; sure to happen
▷ **inevitably** *ADVERB* **inevitability** *NOUN*

inexhaustible *ADJECTIVE* so great that it cannot be used up completely • *Ben has an inexhaustible supply of jokes.*

inexorable (in- eks- er- a- bul) *ADJECTIVE* **1** relentless **2** not able to be persuaded by requests or entreaties
▷ **inexorably** *ADVERB*

inexperience *NOUN* lack of experience
▷ **inexperienced** *ADJECTIVE*

infallible *ADJECTIVE* **1** never wrong **2** never failing • *an infallible remedy*
▷ **infallibly** *ADVERB* **infallibility** *NOUN*

infancy *NOUN* **1** early childhood; babyhood **2** an early stage of development

infant *NOUN* **infants** a baby or young child

infantile *ADJECTIVE* **1** to do with infants **2** very childish

infantry *NOUN* soldiers who fight on foot
COMPARE **cavalry**

infatuated *ADJECTIVE* filled with foolish or unreasoning love
▷ **infatuation** *NOUN*

infect *VERB* **infects, infecting, infected** pass on a disease or bacteria to a person, animal, or plant

infection *NOUN* **infections 1** infecting **2** an infectious disease or condition

infectious *ADJECTIVE* **1** (said about a disease) able to be spread by air or water etc. COMPARE **contagious 2** quickly spreading to others • *His fear was infectious.*

Thesaurus

► activity, hard work, industriousness, diligence, effort, toil, energy, vigour, application, commitment, determination, keenness, labour, perseverance, persistence, tirelessness, zeal OPPOSITES ARE laziness, indolence

ineffective *ADJECTIVE* **1** *The protests were quite ineffective.* ► unsuccessful, unproductive, useless, futile, vain, fruitless, unavailing, worthless OPPOSITES ARE effective, fruitful **2** *an ineffective leader* ► inadequate, ineffectual, weak, feeble, inept, incompetent AN OPPOSITE IS effective

inefficient *ADJECTIVE* **1** *He must be the world's most inefficient gardener.* ► ineffective, ineffectual, unproductive, disorganized, incompetent, inept, inexpert **2** *The wood stoves are extremely inefficient for cooking food.* ► uneconomical, unproductive, extravagant, wasteful, awkward, clumsy AN OPPOSITE IS efficient

inevitable *ADJECTIVE* *There have been the inevitable delays.* ► unavoidable, inescapable, obligatory, mandatory, ineluctable

inexperienced *ADJECTIVE* *School-leavers and inexperienced people often get jobs in riding schools.* ► inexpert, untrained, unskilled, unpractised, unaccustomed, immature, callow, amateur, fresh, green, raw AN OPPOSITE IS experienced.

infallible *ADJECTIVE* **1** *The idea works well, but it is not infallible.* ► foolproof, unfailing, guaranteed, perfect, certain AN OPPOSITE IS fallible **2** *Kate always adopted her infallible routine.* ► dependable, reliable, unerring, accurate

infant *NOUN* *an age at which infants are learning to walk* ► baby, child, tot, (*informal*) toddler

infect *VERB* **1** *The organism may infect the eye of the infant with a 'sticky eye'* ► cause an infection in, spread disease to **2** *The water supply had become infected.* ► contaminate, pollute, poison, taint, blight **3** *Her cheerful humour infects every one she meets.* ► affect, influence, inspire, animate, touch

infection *NOUN* **1** *a bladder infection* ► disease, virus, disorder, complaint **2** *The dressing will keep the wound free of infection.* ► contamination, contagion, bacteria, poisoning

infectious *ADJECTIVE* **1** *the conquest of infectious diseases* ► contagious, communicable, catching, transmissible, transmittable, spreading **2** *infectious laughter* ► contagious, irresistible, spreading

infer *VERB* *What can we infer from the table of results?* ► conclude, deduce, extrapolate, reason, gather, assume, work out, guess, understand USAGE See the note at *imply*.

inferior *ADJECTIVE* less good or less important; low or lower in position, quality, etc.
▷ **inferiority** *NOUN*

inferior *NOUN* **inferiors** a person who is lower in position or rank than someone else

infernal *ADJECTIVE* **1** to do with or like hell • *the infernal regions* **2** (*informal*) detestable or tiresome • *that infernal noise*
▷ **infernally** *ADVERB*

inferno *NOUN* **infernos** a raging fire

infertile *ADJECTIVE* not fertile
▷ **infertility** *NOUN*

infest *VERB* **infests, infesting, infested** (said about pests) be numerous and troublesome in a place
▷ **infestation** *NOUN*

infidelity *NOUN* unfaithfulness

infiltrate *VERB* **infiltrates, infiltrating, infiltrated** get into a place or organization gradually and without being noticed
▷ **infiltration** *NOUN* **infiltrator** *NOUN*

infinite *ADJECTIVE* **1** endless; without a limit **2** too great to be measured
▷ **infinitely** *ADVERB*

infinitesimal *ADJECTIVE* extremely small
▷ **infinitesimally** *ADVERB*

infinitive *NOUN* **infinitives** (in grammar) the form of a verb that does not change to indicate a particular tense or number or person, in English used with or without **to**, e.g. *go* in 'Let him go' or 'Allow him to go'

infinity *NOUN* an infinite number or distance or time

inflame *VERB* **inflames, inflaming, inflamed** **1** produce strong feelings or anger in people **2** cause redness, heat, and swelling in a body part

inflammable *ADJECTIVE* able to be set on fire
USAGE This word means the same as **flammable**. If you want to say that something is not able to be set on fire, use **non-flammable.**

inflammation *NOUN* painful redness or swelling in a part of the body

inflate *VERB* **inflates, inflating, inflated** **1** fill something with air or gas so that it expands **2** increase something too much **3** raise prices or wages etc. more than is justifiable

inflation *NOUN* **1** inflating **2** a general rise in prices and fall in the purchasing power of money
▷ **inflationary** *ADJECTIVE*

inflect *VERB* **inflects, inflecting, inflected** **1** change the ending or form of a word to show its tense or its grammatical relation to other words, e.g. *sing* changes to *sang* or *sung*; *child* changes to *children* **2** alter the voice in speaking

inflection *NOUN* **inflections** an ending or form of a word used to inflect, e.g. **-ed**

inflexible *ADJECTIVE* not able to be bent or changed or persuaded
▷ **inflexibly** *ADVERB* **inflexibility** *NOUN*

influence *NOUN* **influences** **1** the power to produce an effect **2** a person or thing with this power

influence *VERB* **influences, influencing, influenced** have influence on a person or thing

Thesaurus

inferior *ADJECTIVE* **1** *inferior rank* ► lesser, lower, subsidiary, subordinate, junior, secondary, second-class, ancillary, low, humble **2** *inferior quality* ► poor, mediocre, substandard, shoddy, tawdry, bad, cheap, indifferent

infinite *ADJECTIVE* **1** *You will need infinite patience in detailed work like this.* ► endless, limitless, boundless, immeasurable, unlimited, incalculable, immense, prodigious
OPPOSITES ARE limited, finite **2** *Along the roofs were infinite numbers of chimneys.* ► countless, innumerable, numberless, incalculable
OPPOSITES ARE limited, finite

inflammation *NOUN* *inflammation of the skin* ► swelling, redness, soreness, burning, tenderness, infection

inflate *VERB* **1** *We have ten minutes to inflate fifty balloons.* ► pump up, blow up, puff up, dilate, distend, swell **2** *News reports have greatly inflated the number of casualties.* ► exaggerate, magnify, overstate, overplay, overdramatize

inflict *VERB* **1** *He was determined to inflict some sort of penalty on them.* ► impose, administer (to), mete out (to), deal out (to), apply (to), perpetrate, wreak, enforce, force **2** *No one really wants an elderly relative inflicted on them for months.* ► impose, foist, thrust, saddle someone (with), burden someone (with)

influence *NOUN* *The local organizations can have a large influence on the party at national level.* ► effect, impact, control, sway, hold, pressure, pull, power (over), direction (over), authority (over), dominance (over)

influence *VERB* **1** *Parents influence their children enormously in the first few years.* ► affect, have an effect on, guide, exert an influence on, direct, control **2** *There had been several attempts to influence the jury.* ► sway, bias, coerce, pressurize, prejudice, suborn, lead astray, bribe, corrupt

influential *ADJECTIVE* having great influence

influenza *NOUN* an infectious disease that causes fever, catarrh, and pain

inform *VERB* **informs, informing, informed** give information to somebody
▷ **informant** *NOUN*

informal *ADJECTIVE* not formal
▷ **informally** *ADVERB* **informality** *NOUN*
USAGE In this dictionary, words marked *informal* are used in talking but not when you are writing or speaking formally.

information *NOUN* facts told or heard or discovered, or put into a computer etc.

informative *ADJECTIVE* giving a lot of useful information

informed *ADJECTIVE* knowing about something

infra-red *ADJECTIVE* below or beyond red in the colour spectrum

infuriate *VERB* **infuriates, infuriating, infuriated** make a person very angry

ingenious *ADJECTIVE* **1** clever at inventing things **2** cleverly made or thought out
▷ **ingeniously** *ADVERB* **ingenuity** *NOUN*

ingrained *ADJECTIVE* **1** (said about dirt) marking a surface deeply **2** (said about feelings or habits etc.) firmly fixed

ingratiate *VERB* **ingratiates, ingratiating, ingratiated**
ingratiate yourself get yourself into favour with someone, especially by flattering them or always agreeing with their ideas or opinions
▷ **ingratiation** *NOUN*

ingratitude *NOUN* lack of gratitude

ingredient *NOUN* **ingredients** one of the parts of a mixture; one of the things used in a recipe

inhabit *VERB* **inhabits, inhabiting, inhabited** live in a place
▷ **inhabitant** *NOUN*

inhale *VERB* **inhales, inhaling, inhaled** breathe in
▷ **inhalation** *NOUN*

inhaler *NOUN* **inhalers** a device used for relieving asthma etc. by inhaling

inherent (in- heer- ent) *ADJECTIVE* existing in something as one of its natural or permanent qualities
▷ **inherently** *ADVERB* **inherence** *NOUN*

inherit *VERB* **inherits, inheriting, inherited**
1 receive money, property, or a title etc. when its previous owner dies **2** get certain qualities etc. from parents or predecessors
▷ **inheritance** *NOUN* **inheritor** *NOUN*

Thesaurus

influential *ADJECTIVE* **1** *a respected and influential politician* ► important, authoritative, leading, powerful, dominant OPPOSITES ARE uninfluential, insignificant **2** *a piece of writing that has been highly influential* ► significant, persuasive, pivotal, seminal, crucial, effective, far-reaching, telling OPPOSITES ARE uninfluential, unimportant

inform *VERB* **1** *I'll inform them that we are ready to leave.* ► tell, notify, advise, let someone know, send word to, apprise **2 inform on** *No one wants to inform on a friend.* ► denounce, betray, report, incriminate, tell on, (*more informal*) shop

informal *ADJECTIVE* **1** *We were having an informal conversation.* ► casual, relaxed, natural, easy-going **2** *The style of the article was very informal.* ► colloquial, idiomatic, vernacular, demotic, popular **3** *You can wear informal clothes.* ► casual, everyday, comfortable, leisure

information *NOUN* *You can get more information from the website.* ► details, particulars, facts, data, guidance, material, documentation, advice, knowledge, (*more informal*) info

informative *ADJECTIVE* *The two-day course is too short to be informative.* ► instructive, useful, helpful, communicative, enlightening, revealing, illuminating, factual OPPOSITES ARE uninformative, uncommunicative

informed *ADJECTIVE* *She seems highly informed on the subject.* ► knowledgeable, enlightened, conversant (with), familiar (with), abreast (of), au fait (with) OPPOSITES ARE ill-informed, ignorant

infuriate *VERB* *His stubborn refusal began to infuriate her.* ► anger, enrage, exasperate, incense, annoy, irritate, vex, madden, aggravate, antagonize, displease, make angry, (*more informal*) needle, (*more informal*) rile OPPOSITES ARE placate, appease, please

ingenious *ADJECTIVE* *an ingenious solution to the difficulty* ► inventive, imaginative, creative, clever, original, cunning, resourceful, astute, shrewd, inspired, skilful, subtle AN OPPOSITE IS unimaginative

inhabit *VERB* *a cave complex that hermits used to inhabit* ► live in, occupy, dwell in, people, populate, settle in

inhabitant *NOUN* *the inhabitants of the town* ► resident, citizen, native, local, occupant, dweller, (*plural*) population, (*plural*) townsfolk

inherit *VERB* *His son will inherit the business on his death.* ► receive, be left, be bequeathed, succeed to

inheritance *NOUN* *She bought a house with her inheritance.* ► legacy, bequest, estate, fortune, heritage

inhibition *NOUN* **inhibitions** a feeling of embarrassment or worry that prevents you from doing something or expressing your emotions
▷ **inhibited** *ADJECTIVE*

inhospitable *ADJECTIVE* **1** unfriendly to visitors **2** (said about a place) not giving any shelter or good weather

inhuman *ADJECTIVE* cruel; without pity or kindness
▷ **inhumanity** *NOUN*

inimitable *ADJECTIVE* impossible to imitate

initial *NOUN* **initials** the first letter of a word or name

initial *ADJECTIVE* at the beginning • *the initial stages*
▷ **initially** *ADVERB*

initiative (in- ish- a- tiv) *NOUN* **1** the power or right to get something started **2** the ability to make decisions and take action on your own without being told what to do
take the initiative take action to start something happening

inject *VERB* **injects, injecting, injected** **1** put a medicine or drug into the body by means of a syringe **2** add a new quality • *Inject some humour into the story.*
▷ **injection** *NOUN*

injure *VERB* **injures, injuring, injured** harm or hurt someone
▷ **injury** *NOUN* **injurious** (in- joor- ee- us) *ADJECTIVE*

injustice *NOUN* **injustices** **1** lack of justice **2** an unjust action or treatment

ink *NOUN* **inks** a black or coloured liquid used in writing and printing

inkling *NOUN* **inklings** a slight idea or suspicion • *I had no inkling of your artistic talents.*

inky *ADJECTIVE* **1** stained with ink **2** black like ink • *inky darkness*

inland *ADJECTIVE, ADVERB* in or towards the interior of a country; away from the coast

Inland Revenue *NOUN* the government department responsible for collecting taxes and similar charges inland (not at a port)

in-laws *PLURAL NOUN* (*informal*) relatives by marriage

inlet *NOUN* **inlets** a strip of water reaching into the land from a sea or lake

inmost *ADJECTIVE* most inward

inn *NOUN* **inns** a hotel or public house, especially in the country
▷ **innkeeper** *NOUN*

innards *PLURAL NOUN* the internal organs of a person or animal; the inner parts of a machine

inner *ADJECTIVE* inside; nearer to the centre
▷ **innermost** *ADJECTIVE*

Thesaurus

inhibited *ADJECTIVE* *He felt inhibited about discussing money.* ► shy, reticent, embarrassed, awkward, self-conscious, reserved, diffident, bashful, (*more informal*) hung-up

inhibition *NOUN* **1** *The state places no inhibition on press freedom.* ► restraint, bar, check, barrier, interference, impediment
2 inhibitions *Not everyone can overcome their inhibitions so easily.* ► shyness, reticence, diffidence, reserve, self-consciousness, insecurity, repression, (*informal*) hang-ups

inhuman *ADJECTIVE* *the inhuman treatment of political prisoners* ► inhumane, brutal, cruel, barbaric, barbarous, harsh, callous, bestial, savage, merciless, pitiless, ruthless, unnatural, bloodthirsty, diabolical, fiendish, heartless
OPPOSITES ARE humane, compassionate

inhumane *ADJECTIVE* *It would be inhumane to take away their freedom.* ► cruel, inhuman, harsh, callous, sadistic, barbaric, barbarous, uncivilized AN OPPOSITE IS humane

initial *ADJECTIVE* **1** *Their initial reaction was one of anger.* ► first, original, provisional, earliest
OPPOSITES ARE final, eventual **2** *an initial payment of £100* ► opening, preliminary, starting, commencing, inaugural, introductory
OPPOSITES ARE final, closing

initiative *NOUN* **1** *Employers are looking for initiative in candidates for jobs.* ► enterprise, resourcefulness, drive, inventiveness, innovativeness, energy, dynamism, leadership, originality, ambition **2** *We are in danger of losing the initiative.* ► advantage, upper hand, edge, lead **3** *a new initiative for peace* ► proposal, plan, scheme, strategy, measure

injure *VERB* **1** *He was injured in a street fight.* ► hurt, harm, wound , maim, cripple, disfigure **2** *She injured her arm.* ► hurt, damage, break, crush

injury *NOUN* **1** *His hand injury had fully recovered.* ► wound, cut, damage, fracture, lesion **2** *The suit will protect you from personal injury.* ► harm, hurt, suffering

injustice *NOUN* **1** *He shook his head at the cruel injustice of the world.* ► unfairness, unjustness, inequality, inequity, oppression, discrimination, dishonesty, partiality, wrongness AN OPPOSITE IS justice **2** *She felt her treatment to be a grave injustice.* ► wrong, injury, affront, grievance, offence, crime, iniquity, outrage

inner *ADJECTIVE* **1** *the inner part of the building* ► interior, central, innermost, internal, inside
AN OPPOSITE IS outer **2** *She kept her inner feelings to herself.* ► private, secret, personal, intimate

A B C D E F G H I J K L M N O P Q R S T U V W X Y Z

innings *NOUN* **innings** the time when a cricket team or player is batting

innocent *ADJECTIVE* **1** not guilty **2** not wicked; lacking experience of evil **3** harmless
▷ **innocently** *ADVERB* **innocence** *NOUN*

innocuous *ADJECTIVE* harmless

innovation *NOUN* **innovations** **1** introducing new things or new methods **2** a newly introduced process or way of doing things
▷ **innovative** *ADJECTIVE* **innovator** *NOUN*

innumerable *ADJECTIVE* countless

inoculate *VERB* **inoculates, inoculating, inoculated** inject or treat someone with a vaccine or serum as a protection against a disease
▷ **inoculation** *NOUN*
USAGE Note the spelling of this word. It has one 'n' and one 'c'.

inoffensive *ADJECTIVE* harmless

inorganic *ADJECTIVE* not of living organisms; of mineral origin

input *NOUN* what is put into something, especially data put into a computer
▷ **input** *VERB* **inputs, inputting, inputted**

inquest *NOUN* **inquests** an official inquiry to find out how a person died

inquire *VERB* **inquires, inquiring, inquired** **1** investigate something carefully **2** ask for information
USAGE You can spell this word **inquire** or **enquire** in either of its meanings. It is probably more common for **inquire** to be used for 'investigate' and **enquire** to be used for 'ask for information', but there is no real need to follow this distinction.

inquiry *NOUN* **inquiries** **1** an official investigation **2** a question

inquisitive *ADJECTIVE* always asking questions or trying to find out things
▷ **inquisitively** *ADVERB*

inroads *PLURAL NOUN*
make inroads on *or* **into** use up large quantities of supplies or resources

insane *ADJECTIVE* not sane; mad
▷ **insanely** *ADVERB* **insanity** *NOUN*

insanitary *ADJECTIVE* unclean and likely to be harmful to health

insatiable (in- say- sha- bul) *ADJECTIVE* impossible to satisfy • *an insatiable appetite*

inscribe *VERB* **inscribes, inscribing, inscribed** write or carve words etc. on something

inscription *NOUN* **inscriptions** words written or carved on a monument, coin, stone, etc. or written in the front of a book

insect *NOUN* **insects** a small animal with six legs, no backbone, and a body divided into three parts (head, thorax, abdomen)

insecticide *NOUN* **insecticides** a substance for killing insects

insectivorous *ADJECTIVE* feeding on insects and other small invertebrate creatures
▷ **insectivore** *NOUN*

insecure *ADJECTIVE* **1** not secure or safe **2** lacking confidence about yourself
▷ **insecurely** *ADVERB* **insecurity** *NOUN*

inseminate *VERB* **inseminates, inseminating, inseminated** insert semen into the womb
▷ **insemination** *NOUN*

Thesaurus

innocent *ADJECTIVE* **1** *He always swore that he was innocent.* ► guiltless, blameless, free from blame AN OPPOSITE IS guilty **2** *At her age she looked so innocent.* ► pure, virtuous, chaste, fresh, childlike, trusting, guileless, artless **3** *They claimed it had just been innocent fun.* ► harmless, innocuous, inoffensive

input *NOUN* *They went to the meeting armed with input from their survey.* ► information, data, facts and figures, statistics

inquire *VERB* **inquire into** *The committee will inquire into all these matters.* ► investigate, look into, examine, probe, scrutinize, explore
USAGE Note that *enquire* is normally used in the meaning 'to ask for information', as in *She enquired about his health.*

inquiry *NOUN* *The government has set up a formal inquiry into the incident.* ► investigation, inquest, scrutiny, inquisition, inspection

inquisitive *ADJECTIVE* *Gareth possessed a sharp and inquisitive mind.* ► curious, questioning, inquiring, interested, probing, prying

insane *ADJECTIVE* **1** *She was declared insane on the recommendation of two doctors.* ► mad, deranged, crazy, demented, mentally ill **2** *It would be insane to think they could do the journey in a day.* ► crazy, foolish, stupid, senseless, ludicrous, absurd, mad

insanity *NOUN* **1** *Insanity ran in the family.* ► madness, mental disorder, mental illness, derangement, lunacy, dementia **2** *A loan at such a high rate of interest would be insanity.* ► folly, foolishness, stupidity, madness, lunacy

insect *NOUN* *Some insects are disguised as a leaf or a twig.* ► bug, pest, (*more informal*) creepy-crawly

insecure *ADJECTIVE* **1** *Police warned that the house was insecure.* ► unsafe, unprotected, ill-protected, vulnerable, exposed, ill-defended, defenceless **2** *All this bold talk made him feel*

insensitive *ADJECTIVE* not sensitive or thinking about other people's feelings
▷ **insensitively** *ADVERB* **insensitivity** *NOUN*

inseparable *ADJECTIVE* **1** not able to be separated **2** liking to be constantly together • *inseparable friends*
▷ **inseparably** *ADVERB*

insert *VERB* **inserts, inserting, inserted** put a thing into something else
▷ **insertion** *NOUN*

inside *NOUN* **insides** the inner side, surface, or part
inside out with the inside turned to face outwards
insides (*informal*) the organs in the abdomen; the stomach and bowels

inside *ADVERB, PREPOSITION* on or to the inside of something; in • *Come inside.* • *It's inside that box.*

insider *NOUN* **insiders** a member of a certain group, especially someone with access to private information

insight *NOUN* **insights** being able to perceive the truth about things; understanding

insignificant *ADJECTIVE* not important or influential
▷ **insignificance** *NOUN*

insincere *ADJECTIVE* not sincere
▷ **insincerely** *ADVERB* **insincerity** *NOUN*

insinuate *VERB* **insinuates, insinuating, insinuated** **1** hint something unpleasant **2** introduce a thing or yourself gradually or craftily into a place
▷ **insinuation** *NOUN*

insist *VERB* **insists, insisting, insisted** be very firm in saying or asking for something • *I insist on seeing the manager.*
▷ **insistent** *ADJECTIVE* **insistence** *NOUN*

insolent *ADJECTIVE* very rude and insulting
▷ **insolently** *ADVERB* **insolence** *NOUN*

insoluble *ADJECTIVE* **1** impossible to solve • *an insoluble problem* **2** impossible to dissolve
▷ **insolubility** *NOUN*

insomnia *NOUN* being unable to sleep
▷ **insomniac** *NOUN*

inspect *VERB* **inspects, inspecting, inspected** examine something carefully and critically
▷ **inspection** *NOUN*

inspector *NOUN* **inspectors** **1** a person whose job is to inspect or supervise things **2** a police officer ranking next above a sergeant

Thesaurus

insecure. ► anxious, worried, concerned, unconfident, diffident

insert *VERB* *He inserted a new film in the camera.* ► put, place, push, slip, install, locate

inside *ADJECTIVE* *The inside walls of the house were damp.* ► inner, interior, internal, innermost, indoor OPPOSITES ARE outside, outer, exterior

inside *NOUN* *The inside of the box should be lined with silver paper.* ► interior, inner surface, inner part, core

insignificant *ADJECTIVE* *The differences are mostly insignificant.* ► unimportant, negligible, trivial, trifling, small, footling, inconsequential, inconsiderable, irrelevant, meaningless AN OPPOSITE IS significant

insincere *ADJECTIVE* *He flashed a gleaming, insincere smile.* ► false, deceitful, dishonest, disingenuous, pretended, feigned, hypocritical, devious AN OPPOSITE IS sincere

insist *VERB* *He insisted he had done everything they had asked.* ► maintain, contend, assert, hold, aver, claim, declare, state, stress
insist on *parents who insist on an early bedtime* ► demand, enforce, require, stipulate

insistence *NOUN* **1** *her insistence that they should go with her* ► demand, requirement, entreaty, urging **2** *Jane's insistence that she loved him* ► assertion, declaration, contention, claim, avowal

insistent *ADJECTIVE* *There were insistent requests for financial support.* ► persistent, demanding, unrelenting, unremitting, urgent, emphatic, relentless, repeated, forceful, assertive

insolence *NOUN* *She accused him of insolence.* ► cheek, impertinence, impudence, effrontery, audacity, rudeness, impoliteness, discourtesy, disrespect

insolent *ADJECTIVE* *The boy was constantly insolent.* ► rude, impolite, impertinent, impudent, disrespectful, audacious, brazen OPPOSITES ARE respectful, polite

insoluble *ADJECTIVE* *one of the world's insoluble problems* ► unsolvable, unresolvable, inexplicable, unanswerable, unfathomable, incomprehensible, mysterious, mystifying, baffling, enigmatic, puzzling AN OPPOSITE IS soluble

inspect *VERB* *The houses had been inspected by a surveyor.* ► check, examine, investigate, scrutinize, supervise, oversee

inspection *NOUN* *The machinery needs a regular inspection.* ► examination, check, check-up, investigation, review, scrutiny, survey

inspector *NOUN* *Inspectors are sent out each week to assess the work done.* ► examiner, investigator, supervisor, tester, controller, official, superintendent

inspiration *NOUN* **inspirations 1** a sudden brilliant idea **2** inspiring; an inspiring influence

inspire *VERB* **inspires, inspiring, inspired** fill a person with enthusiasm or creative feelings or ideas • *The applause inspired us with confidence*

install *VERB* **installs, installing, installed 1** put something in position and ready to use • *They installed central heating.* **2** put a person into an important position with a ceremony • *He was installed as Pope.*
▷ **installation** *NOUN*

instalment *NOUN* **instalments** each of the parts in which something is given or paid for over a period of time • *an instalment of a serial* • *You can pay by instalments.*

instance *NOUN* **instances** an example • *a serious instance of corruption*
for instance for example

instant *ADJECTIVE* **1** happening immediately • *instant success* **2** (said about food) designed to be prepared quickly and easily • *instant coffee*
▷ **instantly** *ADVERB*

instant *NOUN* **instants** a moment • *not an instant too soon*

instantaneous *ADJECTIVE* happening immediately
▷ **instantaneously** *ADVERB*

instead *ADVERB* in place of something else

instinct *NOUN* **instincts** a natural tendency or ability • *Birds fly by instinct.*
▷ **instinctive** *ADJECTIVE* **instinctively** *ADVERB*

institute *NOUN* **institutes** a society or organization; the building used by this

institution *NOUN* **institutions 1** an institute; a public organization, e.g. a hospital or university **2** a habit or custom **3** instituting something
▷ **institutional** *ADJECTIVE*

instruct *VERB* **instructs, instructing, instructed 1** teach a person a subject or skill **2** inform **3** tell a person what he or she must do
▷ **instructive** *ADJECTIVE* **instructor** *NOUN*

instruction *NOUN* **instructions 1** teaching a subject or skill **2** an order or piece of information • *Follow the instructions carefully.*

Thesaurus

inspiration *NOUN* **1** *writing that relies on inspiration* ► creativity, imagination, inventiveness, ingenuity, enthusiasm, genius, influence **2** *The success proved an inspiration to everyone involved in the project.* ► stimulus, spur, motivation, boost **3** *Emma had a sudden inspiration.* ► idea, thought, brainwave, revelation

inspire *VERB* *a simple tune that inspired him to write a musical* ► stimulate, influence, motivate, prompt, encourage, enthuse, galvanize, spur, stir, animate, arouse, (*more informal*) egg on

install *VERB* **1** *We want to install central heating on all floors.* ► put in, establish, fix, introduce, set up **2 install yourself** *She installed herself in a sofa by the fire.* ► ensconce yourself, settle, place yourself, plant yourself, (*more informal*) park yourself

instalment *NOUN* **1** *You can pay for your licence in monthly instalments.* ► payment, part **2** *a serial in four instalments* ► episode, part, section

instance *NOUN* *We could not find a single instance of discrimination.* ► example, occurrence, case, illustration, sample

instant *ADJECTIVE* *The website gives you instant access to the information you need.* ► immediate, instantaneous, on-the-spot, prompt, fast, quick, rapid, speedy, direct, swift

instant *NOUN* *The incident was over in an instant.* ► moment, second, minute, flash, split second, (*more informal*) tick, (*more informal*) twinkling

instantly *ADVERB* *He fell asleep instantly.* ► immediately, at once, straight away, right away, there and then, in a trice, directly

instinct *NOUN* *Her instinct was to find out more about them.* ► impulse, inclination, intuition, hunch, feeling, presentiment, sixth sense, tendency, urge

instinctive *ADJECTIVE* *Their instinctive reaction is to find someone to blame.* ► intuitive, natural, innate, automatic, reflex OPPOSITES ARE deliberate, conscious

institution *NOUN* **1** *the institution of a new language course* ► introduction, establishment, setting up, formation, creation, launching, inauguration, inception, initiation, founding, opening **2** *He did not want to spend the rest of his life in an institution.* ► home, hospital, asylum **3** *an academic institution* ► establishment, school, academy, college **4** *A spring holiday has become a family institution.* ► custom, convention, tradition, routine, practice, ritual, habit

instruct *VERB* **1** *A private tutor instructed the children in French.* ► coach, educate, train, drill, ground, teach **2** *The officials instructed us to wait.* ► order, direct, command, require, call on, advise

instruction *NOUN* **1** *It is important to listen out for instructions.* ► direction, directive, order, command, guidance **2** *basic instruction in mathematics* ► education, tuition, teaching, schooling, coaching, tutoring, grounding

instrument *NOUN* **instruments** **1** a device for producing musical sounds **2** a tool used for delicate or scientific work **3** a measuring device

instrumental *ADJECTIVE* **1** performed on musical instruments, without singing **2** being the means of doing something • *She was instrumental in getting me a job.*

insubordinate *ADJECTIVE* disobedient or rebellious
▷ **insubordination** *NOUN*

insufferable *ADJECTIVE* unbearable

insular *ADJECTIVE* **1** to do with or like an island **2** narrow-minded

insulate *VERB* **insulates, insulating, insulated** cover or protect something to prevent heat, cold, or electricity etc. from passing in or out
▷ **insulation** *NOUN* **insulator** *NOUN*

insulin *NOUN* a substance that controls the amount of sugar in the blood. The lack of insulin causes diabetes

insult (in-sult) *VERB* **insults, insulting, insulted** hurt a person's feelings or pride

insult (in-sult) *NOUN* **insults** an insulting remark or action

insuperable *ADJECTIVE* unable to be overcome • *an insuperable difficulty*

insurance *NOUN* an agreement to compensate someone for a loss, damage, or injury etc., in return for a payment (called a **premium**) made in advance

insure *VERB* **insures, insuring, insured** protect with insurance • *Is your jewellery insured?*
USAGE Do not confuse with **ensure**.

intact *ADJECTIVE* not damaged; complete [from Latin *intactum* = not touched]

intake *NOUN* **intakes** **1** taking something in **2** the number of people or things taken in • *We have a high intake of students this year.*

integer *NOUN* **integers** a whole number (e.g. 0, 3, 19), not a fraction

integral (in-tig-ral) *ADJECTIVE* **1** being an essential part of a whole thing • *An engine is an integral part of a car.* **2** whole or complete

integrate *VERB* **integrates, integrating, integrated** **1** make parts into a whole; combine **2** bring people together harmoniously into a single community
▷ **integration** *NOUN*

integrity (in-teg-rit-ee) *NOUN* honesty

intellect *NOUN* **intellects** the ability to think and work things out with the mind

intellectual *ADJECTIVE* **1** to do with or using the intellect **2** having a good intellect and a liking for knowledge
▷ **intellectually** *ADVERB*

intellectual *NOUN* **intellectuals** an intellectual person

intelligence *NOUN* **1** being intelligent **2** information, especially of military value; the people who collect and study this information

Thesaurus

instrument *NOUN* *a sharp instrument*
► implement, tool, device, utensil, contrivance, contraption, apparatus, appliance, equipment, gadget, machine, mechanism

insult *NOUN* (with the stress on *in-*) *The two men threw insults at each other.* ► affront, abuse, indignity, slight, snub AN OPPOSITE IS compliment

insult *VERB* (with the stress on *-sult*) *She put her head out of the window to insult passers-by.*
► abuse, affront, malign, revile, offend, mock, snub, vilify, sneer at AN OPPOSITE IS compliment

insulting *ADJECTIVE* *They directed their insulting remarks at anyone they happened to see.*
► abusive, rude, offensive, disparaging, contemptuous, deprecatory, scornful, scurrilous, slanderous, insolent, condescending, mocking, patronizing, (*more informal*) snide OPPOSITES ARE polite, complimentary

intact *ADJECTIVE* *Several buildings remained intact despite heavy bombing.* ► whole, undamaged, untouched, unharmed, complete, entire

integral *ADJECTIVE* **1** *Speech is an integral part of human interaction.* ► essential, constituent, indispensable, intrinsic, irreplaceable, necessary, requisite AN OPPOSITE IS incidental
2 *The equipment is sold as an integral system.*
► complete, integrated, combined, indivisible, whole

integrity *NOUN* *No one doubts their integrity.*
► honesty, honour, morality, sincerity, reliability, virtue, fidelity, uprightness, honourableness, righteousness, goodness, incorruptibility, loyalty, principle AN OPPOSITE IS dishonesty

intellect *NOUN* *a story that appeals to the intellect rather than the emotions* ► mind, reason, intelligence, judgement, wits

intellectual *ADJECTIVE* **1** *intellectual powers*
► mental, cerebral, rational, cognitive, conceptual **2** *an intellectual person*
► intelligent, academic, cultured, scholarly, studious, thoughtful, highbrow

intellectual *NOUN* *Opposition to the regime is strongest among intellectuals.* ► academic, scholar, highbrow, thinker, member of the intelligentsia, intelligent person

intelligence *NOUN* **1** *a person of great intelligence* ► intellect, brainpower, powers of reasoning, perceptiveness, acumen, wisdom, wits, understanding, comprehension, (*more*

a b c d e f g h i j k l m n o p q r s t u v w x y z

intelligent *ADJECTIVE* able to learn and understand things; having great mental ability
▷ **intelligently** *ADVERB*

intend *VERB* **intends, intending, intended** **1** have something in mind as what you want to do **2** plan that something should be used or understood in a particular way

intense *ADJECTIVE* **1** very strong or great **2** feeling things very strongly and seriously • *He's a very intense young man*
▷ **intensely** *ADVERB* **intensity** *NOUN*

intent *NOUN* **intents** intention

intent *ADJECTIVE* with concentrated attention; very interested
▷ **intently** *ADVERB*
intent on eager or determined to do something

intention *NOUN* **intentions** what a person intends; a purpose or plan

intentional *ADJECTIVE* deliberate, not accidental
▷ **intentionally** *ADVERB*

interact *VERB* **interacts, interacting, interacted** have an effect upon one another
▷ **interaction** *NOUN*

interactive *ADJECTIVE* (in computing) allowing information to be sent immediately in either direction between a computer system and its user

interbreed *VERB* **interbreeds, interbreeding, interbred** breed with each other; cross-breed

intercept *VERB* **intercepts, intercepting, intercepted** stop or catch a person or thing that is going from one place to another
▷ **interception** *NOUN*

interchange *VERB* **interchanges, interchanging, interchanged** **1** put each of two things into the other's place **2** exchange things **3** alternate
▷ **interchangeable** *ADJECTIVE*

interchange *NOUN* **interchanges** **1** interchanging **2** a road junction where vehicles can move from one motorway etc. to another

intercourse *NOUN* **1** communication or dealings between people **2** sexual intercourse

interdependent *ADJECTIVE* dependent upon each other

interest *NOUN* **interests** **1** a feeling of wanting to know about or help with something **2** a thing that interests somebody • *Science fiction is one of my interests.* **3** an advantage or benefit • *She looks after her own interests.* **4** money paid regularly in return for money lent or deposited

Thesaurus

informal) nous AN OPPOSITE IS stupidity **2** *constant intelligence regarding terrorist attacks* ► information, report, warning, news, notification, data, facts, knowledge, (*more informal*) tip-off

intelligent *ADJECTIVE* *She is a highly intelligent writer.* ► clever, bright, acute, sharp, perceptive, profound, shrewd

intelligible *ADJECTIVE* *The message was barely intelligible.* ► understandable, comprehensible, coherent, decipherable, legible, clear, lucid, meaningful OPPOSITES ARE unintelligible, incomprehensible

intend *VERB* **1** *I intend to apply for a grant.* ► propose, mean, plan, have it in mind, have a mind, aim, contemplate (applying), determine, purpose **2** *The book is intended for learners of English.* ► design, destine, mean

intense *ADJECTIVE* *She was suffering from intense pain. The experience rouses intense emotions.* ► extreme, acute, severe, fierce, sharp, strong, powerful, profound, potent OPPOSITES ARE moderate, mild

intensify *VERB* **1** *The dizzy feeling in his head intensified.* ► increase, strengthen, grow, escalate AN OPPOSITE IS weaken **2** *We must intensify our efforts.* ► increase, escalate, step up, reinforce, sharpen, concentrate AN OPPOSITE IS reduce

intensive *ADJECTIVE* *Police have made an intensive search of the area.* ► thorough, exhaustive, comprehensive, rigorous, detailed, complete, full, all-out, concentrated

intent *ADJECTIVE* **1** *She was intent on visiting her friends in Spain.* ► keen (to), resolved (to), determined (to), bent, fixed AN OPPOSITE IS reluctant **2** *He had an intent look on his face.* ► attentive, engrossed, absorbed, preoccupied, steadfast OPPOSITES ARE vacant, blank

intention *NOUN* *Our intention is to accept the offer.* ► aim, purpose, objective, object, plan, ambition, design, end, goal

intentional *ADJECTIVE* *The remarks were intentional.* ► deliberate, premeditated, intended, planned, calculated, conscious, considered, meant, designed, prearranged, wilful AN OPPOSITE IS unintentional

interaction *NOUN* *the interaction of two influences* ► effect on each other, exchange, (*informal*) give and take, interplay, reciprocal effect, (*informal*) to and fro

interest *NOUN* **1** *a matter of great interest to both of them* ► importance, significance, consequence, moment, note, value **2** *Her interests include rock-climbing.* ► activity, pursuit, hobby, pastime, diversion, preoccupation
show interest in *John was showing interest in*

A B C D E F G H I J K L M N O P Q R S T U V W X Y Z

interest *VERB* **interests**, **interesting**, **interested** attract a person's interest
▷ **interested** *ADJECTIVE* **interesting** *ADJECTIVE*

interface *NOUN* **interfaces** (in computing) a connection between two parts of a computer system

interfere *VERB* **interferes**, **interfering**, **interfered** **1** take part in something that has nothing to do with you **2** get in the way; obstruct
▷ **interference** *NOUN*

interior *ADJECTIVE* inner

interior *NOUN* **interiors** the inside of something; the central or inland part of a country

interjection *NOUN* **interjections** a word or words exclaimed expressing joy or pain or surprise, such as *oh!* or *wow!* or *good heavens!*

interlude *NOUN* **interludes** **1** an interval **2** something happening in an interval or between other events

intermediate *ADJECTIVE* coming between two things in time, place, or order

interminable *ADJECTIVE* seeming to be endless; long and boring
▷ **interminably** *ADVERB*

intermission *NOUN* **intermissions** an interval, especially between parts of a film

intermittent *ADJECTIVE* happening at intervals; not continuous
▷ **intermittently** *ADVERB*

internal *ADJECTIVE* inside
▷ **internally** *ADVERB*

internal-combustion engine *NOUN* **internal-combustion engines** an engine that produces power by burning fuel inside the engine itself

international *ADJECTIVE* to do with or belonging to more than one country; agreed between nations
▷ **internationally** *ADVERB*

international *NOUN* **internationals** **1** a sports contest between teams representing different countries **2** a sports player who plays for his or her country

Internet *NOUN* a computer network that allows users all over the world to communicate and exchange information [from *inter* = among, between + *net*]

interplanetary *ADJECTIVE* between planets

interpolate *VERB* **interpolates**, **interpolating**, **interpolated** **1** interject a remark in a conversation **2** insert words; put terms into a mathematical series
▷ **interpolation** *NOUN*

interpose *VERB* **interposes**, **interposing**, **interposed** place something between two things

interpret *VERB* **interprets**, **interpreting**, **interpreted** **1** explain what something means **2** translate what someone says into another language orally **3** perform music etc. in a way that shows your feelings about its meaning
▷ **interpretation** *NOUN* **interpreter** *NOUN*

Thesaurus

the idea. ► take notice of, pay attention to, be concerned about, be curious about, have regard for, show involvement in, show commitment to

interest *VERB* *an idea that interests me* ► appeal to, attract, excite, fascinate, intrigue, engage, engross, concern, stimulate, arouse the curiosity of, capture the imagination of, divert, entertain, involve, (*more informal*) turn on
AN OPPOSITE IS bore

interested *ADJECTIVE* **1** *None of them appeared to be interested.* ► curious, enthusiastic, excited, keen, responsive, fascinated, absorbed, attentive, engrossed, intent AN OPPOSITE IS uninterested. **2** *At the meeting various problems were explained to the interested parties.* ► affected, involved, concerned, connected
AN OPPOSITE IS disinterested
be interested in *The owners were interested in the idea of selling off part of the land.* ► like, be attracted by, fancy

interesting *ADJECTIVE* *an interesting idea* ► attractive, appealing, engrossing, stimulating, exciting, intriguing, fascinating, thought-provoking

interfere *VERB* **1 interfere in** *She did not wish to interfere in her friends' lives.* ► intervene, intrude in, meddle in, butt into, pry into, snoop into, encroach on **2 interfere with** *A headache interfered with his thoughts.* ► inhibit, hinder, hamper, impede, get in the way of

interference *NOUN* *He would not tolerate any interference.* ► intrusion, intervention, meddling, snooping, involvement

interfering *ADJECTIVE* *She blamed his interfering brother.* ► meddlesome, meddling, nosy, prying, snooping, intrusive

internal *ADJECTIVE* **1** *The house was built round an internal courtyard.* ► inner, interior, inside, central AN OPPOSITE IS external **2** *the country's internal affairs* ► domestic, home, interior, local, civil

international *ADJECTIVE* *the growth of fast international travel* ► global, worldwide, intercontinental, universal

A B C D E F G H I J K L M N O P Q R S T U V W X Y Z

interrogate *VERB* **interrogates, interrogating, interrogated** question someone closely or formally
▷ **interrogation** *NOUN* **interrogator** *NOUN*

interrogative *ADJECTIVE* questioning; expressing a question
▷ **interrogatory** *ADJECTIVE*

interrupt *VERB* **interrupts, interrupting, interrupted** **1** break in on what someone is saying by inserting a remark **2** prevent something from continuing
▷ **interruption** *NOUN*

intersect *VERB* **intersects, intersecting, intersected** **1** divide a thing by passing or lying across it **2** (said about lines or roads etc.) cross each other
▷ **intersection** *NOUN*

interval *NOUN* **intervals** **1** a time between two events or parts of a play etc. **2** a space between two things
at intervals with some time or distance between each one
[from Latin *intervallum* = space between the ramparts of a fortification, from *vallum* = rampart]

intervene *VERB* **intervenes, intervening, intervened** **1** come between two events • *in the intervening years* **2** interrupt a discussion or fight etc. to try and stop it or change its result
▷ **intervention** *NOUN*

interview *NOUN* **interviews** a formal meeting with someone to ask him or her questions or to obtain information

interview *VERB* **interviews, interviewing, interviewed** hold an interview with someone
▷ **interviewer** *NOUN*

intestine *NOUN* **intestines** the long tube along which food passes while being absorbed by the body, between the stomach and the anus
▷ **intestinal** *ADJECTIVE*

intimate (in- tim- at) *ADJECTIVE* **1** very friendly with someone **2** private and personal • *intimate thoughts* **3** detailed • *an intimate knowledge of the country*
▷ **intimately** *ADVERB* **intimacy** *NOUN*

intimidate *VERB* **intimidates, intimidating, intimidated** frighten a person by threats into doing something
▷ **intimidation** *NOUN*

into *PREPOSITION* used to express **1** movement to the inside (*Go into the house.*), **2** change of condition or occupation etc. (*It broke into pieces; She went into politics.*), **3** (in division) *4 into 20* = 20 divided by 4

intolerable *ADJECTIVE* unbearable
▷ **intolerably** *ADVERB*

intoxicate *VERB* **intoxicates, intoxicating, intoxicated** make a person drunk or very excited
▷ **intoxication** *NOUN*

Thesaurus

interrogate *VERB* *The secret police wanted to interrogate them.* ► question, cross-examine, examine, investigate, (*more informal*) grill, (*more informal*) quiz

interrogation *NOUN* *The police interrogation continued all morning.* ► questioning, cross-examination, investigation, examination, (*more informal*) grilling

interrupt *VERB* **1** *He opened his mouth to interrupt.* ► butt in, break in, cut in, intervene **2** *People at the back of the hall began to interrupt her.* ► heckle, disrupt, butt in on, cut in on **3** *The news from home led them to interrupt their holiday.* ► suspend, break off, discontinue, delay, postpone, put off, defer **4** *The new building will interrupt the view.* ► break, break up, divide, disturb

interruption *NOUN* **1** *There were several interruptions during the speech.* ► intervention, intrusion, disruption, cutting in, disturbance **2** *A note through the letterbox warned of interruptions in the water supply.* ► break, disruption, suspension, pause, check, hiatus, stop

interval *NOUN* **1** *There will be an interval of 20 minutes halfway through the show.* ► intermission, interlude, break, pause **2** *The next class will be in a week's time and you can revise in the interval.* ► interim, meantime, meanwhile, pause, delay

intimate *ADJECTIVE* **1** *an intimate friendship* ► close, loving, affectionate, personal, familiar, friendly, informal, sexual **2** *an intimate atmosphere* ► friendly, welcoming, warm, informal, relaxed, cosy **3** *intimate thoughts* ► personal, private, secret, confidential **4** *an intimate knowledge of the area* ► detailed, exhaustive, profound, deep, in-depth

intimidate *VERB* *He wanted to get his way without appearing to intimidate them.* ► threaten, bully, frighten, coerce, browbeat, menace, persecute, scare, terrify, terrorize, cow, daunt, hector, make afraid

intolerable *ADJECTIVE* *The noise had become intolerable.* ► unbearable, unendurable, unacceptable, insufferable, insupportable, excruciating, impossible OPPOSITES ARE tolerable, bearable

intolerant *ADJECTIVE* *He was extremely intolerant about religion.* ► bigoted, dogmatic, narrow-minded, opinionated, prejudiced, chauvinistic, illiberal AN OPPOSITE IS tolerant

intransitive ADJECTIVE (said about a verb) used without a direct object after it, e.g. *hear* in *we can hear* (but not in *we can hear you*) COMPARE **transitive**
▷ **intransitively** ADVERB

intravenous (in- tra- veen- us) ADJECTIVE directly into a vein

intricate ADJECTIVE very complicated
▷ **intricately** ADVERB **intricacy** NOUN

intrigue (in- treeg) VERB **intrigues**, **intriguing**, **intrigued** **1** interest someone very much • *The subject intrigues me* **2** plot with someone in an underhand way

introduce VERB **introduces**, **introducing**, **introduced** **1** bring an idea or practice into use **2** make a person known to other people **3** announce a broadcast, speaker, etc.

introduction NOUN **introductions**
1 introducing somebody or something **2** an explanation put at the beginning of a book or speech etc.
▷ **introductory** ADJECTIVE

introvert NOUN **introverts** a shy person who does not like to talk about his or her own thoughts and feelings with other people (The opposite is **extrovert**)

intrude VERB **intrudes**, **intruding**, **intruded** come in or join in without being wanted
▷ **intrusion** NOUN **intrusive** ADJECTIVE

intruder NOUN **intruders** **1** someone who intrudes **2** a burglar

intuition NOUN the power to know or understand things without having to think hard or without being taught
▷ **intuitive** ADJECTIVE **intuitively** ADVERB

Inuit (in- yoo- it) NOUN **Inuit** **1** a member of a people living in northern Canada and Greenland **2** the language of the Inuit
USAGE This name is now preferred to *Eskimo*.

inundate VERB **inundates**, **inundating**, **inundated** flood or overwhelm a place • *We've been inundated with letters about the programme.*
▷ **inundation** NOUN

invade VERB **invades**, **invading**, **invaded** **1** attack and enter a country etc. **2** crowd into a place • *Tourists invade Oxford in summer.*
▷ **invader** NOUN

Thesaurus

intrepid ADJECTIVE *The four intrepid climbers had to turn back because of fierce winds.* ► bold, courageous, daring, brave, gallant, fearless, plucky, valiant

intricate ADJECTIVE *intricate designs; intricate relationships* ► complex, elaborate, ornate, detailed, complicated, convoluted, tangled, delicate, involved, sophisticated, tortuous
AN OPPOSITE IS simple

intrigue NOUN **1** *a leader vulnerable to jealousy and intrigue* ► conspiracy, plotting, scheming, machination, trickery, subterfuge **2** *a family abuzz with romantic intrigues* ► affair, liaison, amour, flirtation, dalliance, intimacy

intrigue VERB **1** *These stories have always intrigued young children.* ► interest, fascinate, engross, captivate, enthral, absorb, beguile **2** *The men were suspected of intriguing against the king.* ► plot, conspire, scheme, connive, manoeuvre

intriguing ADJECTIVE *an intriguing account of a trip round the world* ► interesting, fascinating, engrossing, captivating, enthralling, absorbing, beguiling

introduce VERB **1** *Jane introduced us to her husband.* ► present, make known, acquaint **2** *The new owners have introduced some new features.* ► bring in, institute, initiate, establish, set up, start, begin, create, offer, propose, suggest, pioneer **3** *a new star to introduce the show* ► present, host, compère, announce

introduction NOUN **1** *the introduction of a democratic government* ► institution, establishment, foundation, inauguration, beginning, development **2** *The author thanks his friends in the book's introduction.* ► foreword, preface, preamble, front matter, opening

introvert NOUN *He enjoyed a social life despite being an introvert.* ► shy person, reserved person AN OPPOSITE IS extrovert USAGE For other synonyms see the words in the next entry.

introverted ADJECTIVE *a quiet and introverted character* ► shy, reserved, retiring, introspective, inward-looking, thoughtful, meditative, withdrawn, contemplative, pensive, self-contained, unsociable
AN OPPOSITE IS extrovert

intrude VERB **intrude on** *No one has the right to intrude on a person's privacy in this way.* ► encroach on, break in on, interrupt, interfere with, butt in on, eavesdrop on, intervene in, gatecrash

intruder NOUN *Intruders had left the house in a mess.* ► trespasser, interloper, invader, burglar, housebreaker, prowler, robber, thief, raider

intuition NOUN **1** *He relied on his intuition to get him out of the difficulty.* ► instinct, intuitiveness, sixth sense, insight **2** *What you say confirms all my intuitions.* ► feeling, gut feeling, hunch, suspicion, premonition

invade VERB *The allies invaded the country from the south.* ► march into, occupy, enter,

A B C D E F G H **I** J K L M N O P Q R S T U V W X Y Z

invalid (in- va- lid) *NOUN* **invalids** a person who is ill or who is weakened by illness
▷ **invalidity** *NOUN*

invalid (in- val- id) *ADJECTIVE* not valid • *This passport is invalid* [from *in-* = not + Latin *validus* = strong or powerful]

invaluable *ADJECTIVE* having a value that is too great to be measured; extremely valuable

invariable *ADJECTIVE* not variable; never changing
▷ **invariably** *ADVERB*

invasion *NOUN* **invasions** attacking and entering a country etc.

invent *VERB* **invents, inventing, invented 1** be the first person to make or think of a particular thing **2** make up a false story • *She had to invent an excuse*
▷ **invention** *NOUN* **inventor** *NOUN* **inventive** *ADJECTIVE*

invertebrate *NOUN* **invertebrates** an animal without a backbone
▷ **invertebrate** *ADJECTIVE*

inverted commas *PLURAL NOUN* punctuation marks " " or ' ' put round quotations and spoken words

invest *VERB* **invests, investing, invested 1** use money to make a profit, e.g. by lending it in return for interest to be paid, or by buying stocks and shares or property **2** give somebody an honour, medal, or special title in a formal ceremony
▷ **investment** *NOUN* **investor** *NOUN*

investigate *VERB* **investigates, investigating, investigated** find out as much as you can about something; make a systematic inquiry
▷ **investigation** *NOUN* **investigator** *NOUN* **investigative** *ADJECTIVE*

invigilate *VERB* **invigilates, invigilating, invigilated** supervise candidates at an examination
▷ **invigilation** *NOUN* **invigilator** *NOUN*

invigorate *VERB* **invigorates, invigorating, invigorated** give a person strength or courage
COMPARE **vigour**

invincible *ADJECTIVE* not able to be defeated
▷ **invincibly** *ADVERB* **invincibility** *NOUN*

invisible *ADJECTIVE* not visible; not able to be seen
▷ **invisibly** *ADVERB* **invisibility** *NOUN*

Thesaurus

penetrate, overrun, raid, subdue, violate, attack, descend on, encroach on

invalid *ADJECTIVE* (With the stress on *-val-*) **1** *His licence would be invalid in America.* ► void, unacceptable, unusable, worthless, null and void AN OPPOSITE IS valid **2** *It was not difficult to prove the idea invalid.* ► false, fallacious, unfounded, unreasonable, unsound, incorrect, untrue, illogical, irrational, unconvincing, unscientific AN OPPOSITE IS valid

invalid *ADJECTIVE* (With the stress on *in-*) *Kate has an invalid husband.* ► sick, ailing, infirm, disabled, incapacitated, bedridden

invaluable *ADJECTIVE* *James is an invaluable member of the team.* ► crucial, indispensable, irreplaceable, precious, priceless, useful, valuable, incalculable, inestimable
AN OPPOSITE IS worthless USAGE Note that *invaluable* is not the opposite of *valuable*: for this you should use *valueless*.

invasion *NOUN* **1** *an air invasion of the island* ► attack (on), occupation, incursion, seizure, annexation, overrunning, onslaught, raid **2** *the annual invasion of tourists* ► influx, incursion, inundation, flood, horde, spate, stream, swarm, throng, infestation

invent *VERB* **1** *He invented a new board game.* ► create, devise, conceive, formulate, improvise, originate **2** *They invented any excuse to avoid going near the swimming pool.* ► make up, concoct, fabricate, manufacture, (*more informal*) cook up

invention *NOUN* **1** *the invention of printing* ► development, origination, creation, devising, innovation, pioneering **2** *writing that shows a lot of invention* ► originality, creativity, imagination, ingenuity, inventiveness, resourcefulness, inspiration **3** *The excuse was pure invention.* ► fabrication, fantasy, fiction, deceit, concoction

inventor *NOUN* *the inventor of the telephone* ► creator, originator, designer, discoverer, architect, author, maker

invert *VERB* *A storm inverted the little boat.* ► overturn, reverse, turn upside down, upset, capsize

investigate *VERB* *Police are investigating the discovery of a body.* ► inquire into, look into, follow up, probe, examine, explore, consider, study, gather evidence about, scrutinize, (*more informal*) go into

investigation *NOUN* *The problem needs further investigation. There will have to be an official investigation.* ► examination, inquiry, research, scrutiny, study, survey, inspection, inquisition, (*informal*) probing

invincible *ADJECTIVE* *the invincible power of the invading armies* ► unbeatable, unassailable, indestructible, indomitable, unconquerable, invulnerable, mighty

invisible *ADJECTIVE* *The house was invisible in the dark.* ► hidden, obscured, concealed, undetectable, unnoticeable, imperceptible,

invite *VERB* **invites, inviting, invited 1** ask a person to come or do something **2** be likely to cause something to happen • *You are inviting disaster*
▷ **invitation** *NOUN*

invoice *NOUN* **invoices** a list of goods sent or work done, with the prices charged

involuntary *ADJECTIVE* not deliberate; unintentional
▷ **involuntarily** *ADVERB*

involve *VERB* **involves, involving, involved 1** have as a part; make a thing necessary • *The job involves hard work.* **2** make someone share or take part in something • *They involved us in their charity work.*
▷ **involvement** *NOUN*

inward *ADJECTIVE* **1** on the inside **2** going or facing inwards

inward *ADVERB* inwards

inwards *ADVERB* towards the inside

iodine *NOUN* a chemical substance used as an antiseptic

ion *NOUN* **ions** an electrically charged particle

ionosphere (I- on- os- feer) *NOUN* a region of the upper atmosphere, containing ions

IQ *ABBREVIATION* intelligence quotient; a number showing how a person's intelligence compares with that of an average person

IRA *ABBREVIATION* Irish Republican Army

iridescent *ADJECTIVE* showing rainbow-like colours
▷ **iridescence** *NOUN*

iron *NOUN* **irons 1** a hard grey metal **2** a device with a flat base that is heated for smoothing clothes or cloth **3** a tool made of iron • *a branding iron*
▷ **iron** *ADJECTIVE*

iron *VERB* **irons, ironing, ironed** smooth clothes or cloth with an iron
iron out sort out a difficulty or problem

Iron Age *NOUN* the time when tools and weapons were made of iron

ironic (I- ron- ik) *ADJECTIVE* using irony; full of irony
▷ **ironical** *ADJECTIVE* **ironically** *ADVERB*

ironmonger *NOUN* **ironmongers** a shopkeeper who sells tools and other metal objects
▷ **ironmongery** *NOUN*

irony (I- ron- ee) *NOUN* **ironies 1** saying the opposite of what you mean in order to emphasize it, e.g. saying 'What a lovely day' when it is pouring with rain **2** an oddly contradictory situation • *The irony of it is that I tripped while telling someone else to be careful.*

irrational *ADJECTIVE* not rational; illogical
▷ **irrationally** *ADVERB*

Thesaurus

unnoticed, unseen, out of sight, covered, disguised, inconspicuous AN OPPOSITE IS visible

invitation *NOUN* **1** *an invitation to attend the conference* ► call, summons, request **2** *An open door is an invitation to any passing thief.* ► temptation, encouragement, enticement, lure, provocation, inducement

invite *VERB* **1** *They've invited us to dinner on Saturday.* ► ask, request the company of, welcome, summon **2** *Using emotive language might invite trouble.* ► provoke, cause, generate, engender, foster, elicit

inviting *ADJECTIVE* *the inviting sight of a buffet lunch* ► attractive, appealing, welcome, pleasant, enticing, agreeable, appetizing, seductive

involuntary *ADJECTIVE* *She gave an involuntary shudder.* ► reflex, automatic, unconscious, spontaneous, unthinking, unintentional, conditioned, impulsive, instinctive AN OPPOSITE IS deliberate

involve *VERB* **1** *Her job involves a lot of travel.* ► necessitate, entail, require, demand, mean **2** *These are decisions that involve everybody.* ► affect, concern, interest, include, embrace, take in, touch **3** *The project involved them in community work.* ► occupy, engage, absorb, engross **4** *A drug habit can rapidly involve them in crime.* ► implicate, associate, embroil, entangle

involved *ADJECTIVE* **1** *a long and involved story* ► complex, complicated, convoluted, elaborate, intricate, tangled, confusing, difficult, (*more informal*) knotty AN OPPOSITE IS straightforward **2** *She is totally involved in her work.* ► occupied, engrossed, absorbed, engaged, preoccupied, caught up, committed (to), dedicated (to) AN OPPOSITE IS uninvolved

involvement *NOUN* **1** *her involvement in charity work.* ► interest, participation, activity **2** *There was no doubting their involvement in the plot.* ► complicity, connivance, participation, entanglement, association

irate *ADJECTIVE* *The helpline has to deal with hundreds of irate callers.* ► angry, enraged, furious, incensed, infuriated, indignant, displeased, outraged

ironic *ADJECTIVE* **1** *The tone of Sarah's voice was sharply ironic.* ► sarcastic, ironical, satirical, wry, derisive, double-edged, mocking **2** *It is ironic that after criticizing London so much he should end up living there.* ► paradoxical, strange, peculiar, odd, weird, incongruous

irrational *ADJECTIVE* *an irrational fear of flying* ► illogical, baseless, unreasonable, senseless,

a b c d e f g h i j k l m n o p q r s t u v w x y z

A B C D E F G H I J K L M N O P Q R S T U V W X Y Z

irregular *ADJECTIVE* **1** not regular; uneven **2** against the rules or usual custom **3** (said about troops) not in the regular armed forces
▷ **irregularly** *ADVERB* **irregularity** *NOUN*

irrepressible *ADJECTIVE* unable to be repressed; always lively and cheerful
▷ **irrepressibly** *ADVERB*

irreproachable *ADJECTIVE* blameless or faultless
▷ **irreproachably** *ADVERB*

irresistible *ADJECTIVE* too strong or attractive to be resisted
▷ **irresistibly** *ADVERB*

irrespective *ADJECTIVE* not taking something into account • *Prizes are awarded to winners, irrespective of age.*

irresponsible *ADJECTIVE* not showing a proper sense of responsibility
▷ **irresponsibly** *ADVERB* **irresponsibility** *NOUN*

irrigate *VERB* **irrigates, irrigating, irrigated** supply land with water so that crops etc. can grow
▷ **irrigation** *NOUN*

irritable *ADJECTIVE* easily annoyed; bad-tempered
▷ **irritably** *ADVERB* **irritability** *NOUN*

irritate *VERB* **irritates, irritating, irritated** **1** annoy **2** cause itching
▷ **irritation** *NOUN* **irritant** *ADJECTIVE, NOUN*

Islam *NOUN* the religion of Muslims
▷ **Islamic** *ADJECTIVE*

island *NOUN* **islands** **1** a piece of land surrounded by water **2** something that resembles an island because it is isolated or detached • *a traffic island*

isn't (*mainly spoken*) is not

isobar (I- so- bar) *NOUN* **isobars** a line on a map connecting places that have the same atmospheric pressure

Thesaurus

arbitrary, unsound, absurd AN OPPOSITE IS rational

irregular *ADJECTIVE* **1** *an irregular surface* ► uneven, rough, coarse, bumpy, pitted **2** *an irregular heartbeat; an irregular pattern* ► variable, fluctuating, erratic, fitful, haphazard, unsystematic, intermittent **3** *Her appointment was most irregular.* ► improper, abnormal, unorthodox, anomalous, unconventional, against the rules

irrelevant *ADJECTIVE* *Don't waste time on irrelevant details.* ► inappropriate, unnecessary, inessential, extraneous, peripheral, immaterial, inapplicable, pointless, unconnected, unrelated AN OPPOSITE IS relevant

irreparable *ADJECTIVE* *A power failure can cause irreparable damage.* ► permanent, irretrievable, irreversible, irremediable, unrectifiable, lasting, irrecoverable, unalterable, incurable AN OPPOSITE IS reparable

irreplaceable *ADJECTIVE* *a work of art that is irreplaceable* ► unique, inimitable, indispensable, matchless, priceless, rare OPPOSITES ARE replaceable, common

irresistible *ADJECTIVE* **1** *The temptation to laugh was irresistible.* ► overpowering, overwhelming, inescapable, inexorable, powerful, seductive, unavoidable, compelling, persuasive **2** *She has an irresistible laugh.* ► attractive, appealing, enticing, alluring, seductive, fetching, captivating, beguiling

irresponsible *ADJECTIVE* **1** *an irresponsible attitude* ► reckless, rash, inconsiderate, thoughtless, careless, immoral, selfish, shiftless AN OPPOSITE IS responsible **2** *They sometimes behave like irresponsible teenagers.* ► immature, unreliable, feckless, unthinking, untrustworthy

irreverent *ADJECTIVE* *an irreverent approach to authority* ► disrespectful, discourteous, disdainful, insolent, impertinent, impudent, scornful, flippant, casual, rude OPPOSITES ARE reverent, respectful

irrevocable *ADJECTIVE* *an irrevocable decision* ► unalterable, unchangeable, irreversible, immutable, binding, final, firm, fixed, settled, hard and fast AN OPPOSITE IS reversible

irritable *ADJECTIVE* *Harry sat back with an irritable look on his face.* ► bad-tempered, irascible, grumpy, testy, grouchy, touchy, tetchy, crotchety, cantankerous, peevish, fractious, cross, (*more informal*) stroppy, (*more informal*) shirty OPPOSITES ARE good-tempered, good-humoured, affable

irritate *VERB* *I was letting silly things irritate me.* ► annoy, displease, anger, infuriate, enrage, exasperate, incense, peeve, vex, madden, aggravate, antagonize, inflame, make angry, (*more informal*) needle, (*more informal*) rile, (*more informal*) bug, (*more informal*) rub up the wrong way OPPOSITES ARE please, gratify

irritation *NOUN* *It was hard to hide our irritation at such rudeness.* ► annoyance, indignation, displeasure, exasperation, pique, chagrin, vexation

isolate *VERB* **isolates, isolating, isolated** place a person or thing apart or alone; separate ▷ **isolation** *NOUN*

isosceles (I-soss-il-eez) *ADJECTIVE* an isosceles triangle has two sides of equal length

isotope *NOUN* **isotopes** (in science) a form of an element that differs from other forms in the structure of its nucleus but has the same chemical properties as the other forms

ISP *ABBREVIATION* Internet service provider, a company providing individual users with a connection to the Internet

issue *VERB* **issues, issuing, issued 1** come or go out; flow out **2** supply; give out • *We issued one blanket to each refugee* **3** send out • *They issued a gale warning* **4** put out for sale; publish **5** come or go out; flow out

issue *NOUN* **issues 1** a subject for discussion or concern • *What are the real issues?* **2** a particular edition of a newspaper or magazine • *The Christmas issue of Radio Times* **3** issuing something • *The issue of passports is held up* **4** (*formal*) heirs • *He died without issue*
take issue with disagree with

isthmus (iss-mus) *NOUN* **isthmuses** a narrow strip of land connecting two larger pieces of land

IT *ABBREVIATION* information technology

it *PRONOUN* **1** the thing being talked about **2** the player who has to catch others in a game **3** used in statements about the weather or about circumstances etc. • *It is raining* • *It is six miles to York* **4** used as an indefinite object • *Run for it!* **5** used to refer to a phrase • *It is unlikely that she will fail*

italic (it-al-ik) *ADJECTIVE* printed with sloping letters (called **italics**) *like this*.

itch *VERB* **itches, itching, itched 1** have or feel a tickling sensation in the skin that makes you want to scratch it **2** long to do something

item *NOUN* **items 1** one thing in a list or group of things **2** one piece of news or article etc. in a newspaper or bulletin

its *POSSESSIVE PRONOUN* belonging to it • *The cat hurt its paw*
USAGE Do not put an apostrophe into *its* unless you mean 'it is' or 'it has' (see the next entry).

it's (*mainly spoken*) **1** it is • *It's very hot* **2** it has • *It's broken all records*
USAGE Do not confuse with **its**.

itself *PRONOUN* it and nothing else
by itself on its own; alone

ITV *ABBREVIATION* Independent Television

ivory *NOUN* **1** the hard creamy-white substance that forms elephants' tusks **2** a creamy-white colour

ivy *NOUN* **ivies** a climbing evergreen plant with shiny leaves

-ize or **-ise** *SUFFIX* forms verbs meaning 'bring or come into a certain condition' (e.g. *civilize*), or 'treat in a certain way' (e.g. *pasteurize*), or 'have a certain feeling' (e.g. *sympathize*)

Thesaurus

isolate *VERB* **1** *Their extreme political views tended to isolate them from their contemporaries.* ► separate, set apart, keep apart, cut off, segregate, detach, insulate, seclude, alienate, exclude, single out **2** *Sophisticated cameras can easily isolate offending vehicles.* ► identify, recognize, pick out, single out, pinpoint, distinguish

isolated *ADJECTIVE* **1** *an isolated town in eastern Malaysia* ► remote, outlying, secluded, solitary, inaccessible, out of the way, deserted
AN OPPOSITE IS accessible **2** *an isolated occurrence* ► unique, special, exceptional, untypical, abnormal

issue *NOUN* **1** *The society debates political issues.* ► matter, concern, subject, topic, affair, point, question, argument, controversy, dispute, problem **2** *a special issue of the magazine* ► edition, number, instalment, publication, printing

issue *VERB* **1** *Smoke issued from the top of the building.* ► emerge, emanate, erupt, flow out, rise, appear, come out, gush, leak, spring **2** *The ambassador issued a formal statement.* ► publish, publicize, release, circulate, distribute, give out, print, produce, send out

itch *NOUN* **1** *I have an itch on my back.* ► itchiness, tickle, tingling, irritation, need to scratch **2** *She felt an itch to start painting.* ► desire, hankering, longing, yearning, urge, wish, impulse, lust, need, ache, impatience, restlessness, (*more informal*) yen

itch *VERB* **1** *The warmth made my skin itch.* ► tickle, tingle, be irritated **2** *They were itching to leave.* ► long, hanker, yearn, be eager, be keen

item *NOUN* **1** *an item of equipment* ► article, bit, object, component, ingredient **2** *a news item* ► report, article, account, feature, notice, piece **3** *several items on the agenda* ► topic, subject

a b c d e f g h **i** j k l m n o p q r s t u v w x y z

Jj

jab *VERB* **jabs, jabbing, jabbed** poke roughly; push a thing into something

jack *NOUN* **jacks 1** a device for lifting something heavy off the ground **2** a playing card with a picture of a young man **3** a small white ball aimed at in bowls
jack of all trades someone who can do many different kinds of work

jackdaw *NOUN* **jackdaws** a kind of small crow

jacket *NOUN* **jackets 1** a short coat, usually reaching to the hips **2** a cover to keep the heat in a water tank etc. **3** a paper wrapper for a book **4** the skin of a potato that is baked without being peeled

jackpot *NOUN* **jackpots** an amount of prize money that increases until someone wins it
hit the jackpot 1 win a large prize **2** have remarkable luck or success

jacuzzi (ja-koo-zi) *NOUN* **jacuzzis** (*trademark*) a large bath in which underwater jets of water massage the body

jagged (jag-id) *ADJECTIVE* having an uneven edge with sharp points

jaguar *NOUN* **jaguars** a large fierce South American animal rather like a leopard [via Portuguese from Tupi (a South American language)]

jail *NOUN* **jails** a prison

Jain (jayn) *NOUN* **Jains** a believer in an Indian religion rather like Buddhism

jam *NOUN* **jams 1** a sweet food made of fruit boiled with sugar until it is thick **2** a lot of people, cars, or logs etc. crowded together so that movement is difficult
in a jam in a difficult situation

jam *VERB* **jams, jamming, jammed 1** make or become fixed and difficult to move • *The window has jammed.* **2** crowd or squeeze into a space **3** push something forcibly • *jam the brakes on* **4** block a broadcast by causing interference with the transmission

jamboree *NOUN* **jamborees** a large party or celebration

jangle *VERB* **jangles, jangling, jangled** make a loud harsh ringing sound
▷ **jangle** *NOUN*

janitor *NOUN* **janitors** a caretaker

January *NOUN* the first month of the year [named after *Janus*, a Roman god of gates and beginnings, usually shown with two faces that look in opposite directions]

jar[1] *NOUN* **jars** a container made of glass or pottery

jar[2] *VERB* **jars, jarring, jarred 1** cause an unpleasant jolt or shock **2** sound harshly • *Her voice really jars on me*

jar *NOUN* **jars** a jarring effect

jargon *NOUN* words or expressions used by a profession or group that are difficult for other people to understand • *computer jargon*

jaunt *NOUN* **jaunts** a short trip

Thesaurus

jab *VERB He laughed and jabbed his friend in the ribs.* ► poke, prod, dig, nudge, elbow, shove

jack *VERB* **jack up** *He got a passer-by to help him jack up the car and change the tyre.* ► lift, raise, hoist, lever up

jagged *ADJECTIVE He gashed his head against a jagged branch.* ► spiky, uneven, broken, irregular, ragged, rough, toothed, serrated, zigzag OPPOSITES ARE even, smooth

jail *NOUN a building that used to be the town jail* ► prison, jailhouse, guardhouse, (*more informal*) nick, (*more informal*) clink

jail *VERB If he's found guilty he'll be jailed.* ► send to prison, put in prison, imprison, give a custodial sentence to

jam *NOUN* **1** *a long jam on the motorway* ► tailback, hold-up, obstruction, blockage, bottleneck **2** *We're in a bit of a jam.* ► predicament, quandary, embarrassment, difficulty, dilemma, tight corner, trouble, plight, (*more informal*) fix, (*more informal*) hole **3** *Have some home-made jam.* ► preserve, conserve, jelly, marmalade

jam *VERB* **1** *They try to jam too many people in the lifts.* ► cram, pack, squeeze, stuff, crowd, crush, ram, squash **2** *Protesters jammed one side of the motorway.* ► block, clog, obstruct, congest **3** *I'll jam the door open with a newspaper.* ► prop, stick, wedge **4** *The window has jammed.* ► stick, become stuck, become wedged, become lodged, seize

jangle *VERB He jangled his keys as he walked to the door. Bracelets jangled on her wrists.* ► jingle, clink, tinkle, clang

jar *NOUN a jar of honey* ► pot, drum, glass, crock, container

jar *VERB* **1 jar on** *His whining voice jarred on me.* ► grate on, annoy, irritate, irk, exasperate, set your teeth on edge **2** *The fall jarred her whole body.* ► jolt, jerk, shake, shock, vibrate

jargon *NOUN The instructions are full of difficult jargon.* ► technical language, parlance, idiom, (*more informal*) gobbledegook

jaunt *NOUN a jaunt round the old city* ► trip, outing, excursion, tour, expedition, journey

jaunty *ADJECTIVE* **jauntier, jauntiest** lively and cheerful
▷ **jauntily** *ADVERB* **jauntiness** *NOUN*

javelin *NOUN* **javelins** a lightweight spear

jaw *NOUN* **jaws** **1** either of the two bones that form the framework of the mouth **2** the lower part of the face **3** something shaped like the jaws or used for gripping things **4** (*slang*) talking

jazz *NOUN* a kind of music with strong rhythm, often improvised
▷ **jazzy** *ADJECTIVE*

jealous *ADJECTIVE* **1** unhappy or resentful because you feel that someone is your rival or is better or luckier than yourself **2** careful in keeping something • *He is very jealous of his own rights.*
▷ **jealously** *ADVERB* **jealousy** *NOUN*

jeans *PLURAL NOUN* trousers made of strong cotton fabric

Jeep *NOUN* **Jeeps** (*trademark*) a small sturdy motor vehicle with four-wheel drive, especially one used in the army

jeer *VERB* **jeers, jeering, jeered** laugh or shout at somebody rudely or scornfully
▷ **jeer** *NOUN*

jelly *NOUN* **jellies** **1** a soft transparent food **2** any soft slippery substance
▷ **jellied** *ADJECTIVE*

jellyfish *NOUN* **jellyfish** a sea animal with a body like jelly

jerk *VERB* **jerks, jerking, jerked** **1** make a sudden sharp movement **2** pull something suddenly

jerk *NOUN* **jerks** **1** a sudden sharp movement **2** (*slang*) a stupid person
▷ **jerky** *ADJECTIVE* **jerkily** *ADVERB*

jerkin *NOUN* **jerkins** a sleeveless jacket

jersey *NOUN* **jerseys** **1** a pullover with sleeves **2** a plain machine-knitted material used for making clothes

jest *NOUN* **jests** a joke [from Middle English *gest* = a story]

jester *NOUN* **jesters** a professional entertainer at a royal court in the Middle Ages

jet *NOUN* **jets** **1** a stream of water, gas, flame, etc. shot out from a narrow opening **2** a spout or nozzle from which a jet comes **3** an aircraft driven by engines that send out a high-speed jet of hot gases at the back

jet lag *NOUN* extreme tiredness that a person feels after a long flight between different time zones

jettison *VERB* **jettisons, jettisoning, jettisoned** **1** throw something overboard **2** get rid of something that is no longer wanted **3** release or drop something from an aircraft or spacecraft in flight

Thesaurus

jazzy *ADJECTIVE* **1** *jazzy music* ► animated, lively, rhythmic, spirited, syncopated **2** *a jazzy colour scheme* ► bright, bold, colourful, gaudy, showy, loud, flashy OPPOSITES ARE sober, dull

jealous *ADJECTIVE* **1** *Jason was jealous of her ability to come up with good ideas.* ► envious, resentful, grudging, covetous, desirous OPPOSITES ARE proud, admiring **2** *the story of a beautiful woman who is locked away by her jealous lover* ► suspicious, distrustful, possessive, protective, dominating AN OPPOSITE IS trusting **3** *They are very jealous of their privileges.* ► protective, defensive, watchful, mindful AN OPPOSITE IS unconcerned (about)

jealousy *NOUN* **1** *He was overcome by jealousy at their good fortune.* ► envy, resentment, bitterness, discontent, covetousness **2** *She could no longer stand her lover's jealousy.* ► suspicion, distrust, mistrust, possessiveness

jeer *VERB* *The demonstrators were jeering the police.* ► mock, taunt, scoff, deride, sneer at, abuse, insult, barrack, heckle AN OPPOSITE IS cheer

jeer *NOUN* *comments that brought jeers from his schoolmates* ► taunt, sneer, jibe, insult, boo, hiss, ridicule, disapproval AN OPPOSITE IS cheer

jeopardize *VERB* *He wouldn't jeopardize his career by taking risks now.* ► threaten, endanger, put at risk, compromise, harm, imperil, expose

jeopardy *NOUN* **in jeopardy** *With the country at war the empire was in jeopardy* ► in danger, in peril, at risk, vulnerable, under threat AN OPPOSITE IS secure

jerk *VERB* **1** *She jerked her hand from his and turned away.* ► pull, tug, pluck, wrench, yank, tweak **2** *The car jerked forward.* ► jolt, lurch, bump, bounce

jerk *NOUN* **1** *He pulled away his hand with a jerk.* ► tug, pull, wrench, yank, twitch **2** *The bus stopped with a jerk.* ► jolt, lurch, start, bump, shock

jerky *ADJECTIVE* *Her voice had grown jerky and breathless.* ► fitful, spasmodic, convulsive, shaky, twitchy, jumpy, uncoordinated, incoherent OPPOSITES ARE steady, smooth

jest *NOUN* *The men talked and exchanged jests.* ► joke, witticism, quip, banter

jest *VERB* *He admitted that he had been jesting.* ► joke, fool, hoax, tease, (*more informal*) kid

jet *NOUN* **1** *a jet of water* ► stream, spurt, squirt, gush, spout, spray, flow, fountain, rush **2** *He pointed the jet at the flames.* ► nozzle, sprinkler

A B C D E F G H I J K L M N O P Q R S T U V W X Y Z

jetty *NOUN* **jetties** a small landing stage

Jew *NOUN* **Jews** a member of a people descended from the ancient tribes of Israel, or who practises the religion of this people
▷ **Jewish** *ADJECTIVE*

jewel *NOUN* **jewels** **1** a precious stone **2** an ornament containing precious stones
▷ **jewelled** *ADJECTIVE*
[from early French]

jewellery *NOUN* jewels and similar ornaments for wearing

jigsaw *NOUN* **jigsaws** **1** a picture cut into irregular pieces which are then shuffled and fitted together again for amusement **2** a saw that can cut curved shapes

jilt *VERB* **jilts, jilting, jilted** abandon a boyfriend or girlfriend, especially after promising to marry him or her

jingle *VERB* **jingles, jingling, jingled** make or cause to make a tinkling sound

jingle *NOUN* **jingles** **1** a jingling sound **2** a very simple verse or tune, especially one used in advertising

jitters *PLURAL NOUN* (*informal*) a feeling of extreme nervousness
▷ **jittery** *ADJECTIVE*

job *NOUN* **jobs** **1** work that someone does regularly to earn a living **2** a piece of work to be done **3** (*informal*) a difficult task • *You'll have a job to lift that box.* **4** (*informal*) a thing; a state of affairs • *It's a good job you're here*
just the job (*informal*) exactly what you want or need

jockey *NOUN* **jockeys** a person who rides horses in races

jodhpurs (**jod**- perz) *PLURAL NOUN* trousers for horse riding, fitting closely from the knee to the ankle [named after *Jodhpur*, a city in India, where similar trousers are worn]

jog *VERB* **jogs, jogging, jogged** **1** run or trot slowly, especially for exercise **2** give something a slight push
▷ **jogger** *NOUN*
jog someone's memory help someone to remember something

jogtrot *NOUN* a slow steady trot

join *VERB* **joins, joining, joined** **1** put or come together; fasten or connect **2** take part with others in doing something • *We all joined in the chorus.* **3** become a member of a group or organization etc. • *Join the Navy*
join up enlist in the armed forces

Thesaurus

jewel *NOUN* **1** *a tiara encrusted with jewels* ► gem, gemstone, precious stone **2** *His girlfriend was a jewel.* ► treasure, angel, paragon, pearl, wonder

jewellery *NOUN* *A street fair was selling ethnic jewellery.* ► gems, jewels, ornaments, (*more informal*) sparklers

jilt *VERB* *Perhaps Hugh had done her a favour by jilting her.* ► reject, desert, discard, abandon, (*more informal*) ditch

jingle *NOUN* **1** *He could hear the jingle of her bracelet.* ► jangle, clink, tinkle **2** *An advertising jingle kept coming into his head.* ► slogan, song, catchline, ditty, refrain

jingle *VERB* *The coins jingled in their pockets.* ► jangle, clink, tinkle, clang

jinx *NOUN* *They wondered whether the jinx would strike again.* ► curse, spell, evil eye, bad luck

jinxed *ADJECTIVE* *It was almost as if the house was jinxed.* ► cursed, bewitched, bedevilled, under a spell

jitters *PLURAL NOUN* (*informal*) *a fit of jitters* ► nervousness, nerves, anxiety, agitation, tension, edginess, restlessness

jittery *ADJECTIVE* *He felt jittery about meeting her again.* ► nervous, anxious, agitated, tense, edgy, fretful, restless, ill at ease

job *NOUN* **1** *The job involves some weekend work.* ► occupation, employment, position, situation, post, work, career **2** *Painting the house will be a long job.* ► task, piece of work, undertaking, operation, assignment, project, chore **3** *It's my job to lock up in the evenings.* ► responsibility, duty, task, concern, role, function **4** (*informal*) *We had a job finding the house.* ► problem, difficulty, difficult task, hard time, struggle

jobless *ADJECTIVE* *Two percent of the population is jobless.* ► unemployed, out of work, laid off, redundant OPPOSITES ARE employed, in work

jocular *ADJECTIVE* *a few jocular remarks* ► humorous, funny, witty, comical, amusing, droll, joking AN OPPOSITE IS serious
USAGE Remember that *funny* can mean 'peculiar' as well as 'jocular', and it is sometimes better to use another word.

jog *VERB* **1** *He jogged her elbow as he walked past.* ► nudge, prod, jolt, jar, bump, jostle **2** *I need a clue to jog my memory.* ► prompt, stir, arouse, stimulate, remind **3** *They were jogging through the park.* ► trot, run, jogtrot

join *VERB* **1** *Join the two pieces together.* ► connect, fasten, attach, couple, merge, stick, tie, glue **2** *Her son wanted to join the army.* ► enlist in, enrol in, sign up in, enter, volunteer for, become a member of **3** *We joined the peace march along the route.* ► follow, go along with, tag along with, accompany **4** *The two roads join here.* ► meet, come together, converge

join *NOUN* *You have to look hard to see the join.* ► joint, connection, seam, knot, link, mend

joint *NOUN* **joints** **1** a place where two things are joined **2** the place where two bones fit together **3** a large piece of meat cut ready for cooking **4** (*informal*) a cannabis cigarette

joint *ADJECTIVE* shared or done by two or more people, nations, etc. • *a joint project*
▷ **jointly** *ADVERB*

joke *NOUN* **jokes** something said or done to make people laugh

joke *VERB* **jokes, joking, joked** **1** make jokes **2** tease someone or not be serious • *I'm only joking*

joker *NOUN* **jokers** **1** someone who jokes **2** an extra playing card with a jester on it

jolly *ADJECTIVE* **jollier, jolliest** cheerful and good-humoured
▷ **jollity** *NOUN*

jolly *ADVERB* (*informal*) very • *jolly good*

jolt *VERB* **jolts, jolting, jolted** **1** shake or dislodge something with a sudden sharp movement **2** move along jerkily, e.g. on a rough road **3** give someone a shock

jolt *NOUN* **jolts** **1** a jolting movement **2** a shock

jostle *VERB* **jostles, jostling, jostled** push roughly, especially in a crowd

jot *VERB* **jots, jotting, jotted** write something quickly • *Let me jot down that phone number.*

jotter *NOUN* **jotters** a notepad or notebook

joule (jool) *NOUN* **joules** a unit of work or energy

journal *NOUN* **journals** **1** a newspaper or magazine **2** a diary

journalist *NOUN* **journalists** a person who writes for a newspaper or magazine
▷ **journalism** *NOUN* **journalistic** *ADJECTIVE*

journey *NOUN* **journeys** **1** going from one place to another **2** the distance or time taken to travel somewhere • *two days' journey*

journey *VERB* **journeys, journeying, journeyed** make a journey

jovial *ADJECTIVE* cheerful and good-humoured
▷ **jovially** *ADVERB* **joviality** *NOUN*

joy *NOUN* **joys** **1** a feeling of great pleasure or happiness **2** a thing that causes joy
▷ **joyful** *ADJECTIVE* **joyfully** *ADVERB* **joyfulness** *NOUN* **joyous** *ADJECTIVE* **joyously** *ADVERB*

joyride *NOUN* **joyrides** a drive in a stolen car for amusement
▷ **joyrider** *NOUN* **joyriding** *NOUN*

joystick *NOUN* **joysticks** **1** the control lever of an aircraft **2** a device for moving a cursor or image on a VDU screen, especially in computer games

JP *ABBREVIATION* Justice of the Peace

jubilant *ADJECTIVE* rejoicing or triumphant
▷ **jubilantly** *ADVERB* **jubilation** *NOUN*

Thesaurus

joint *NOUN* *the joint between the wall and the flat roof* ▶ join, connection, junction, seam

joint *ADJECTIVE* *The two artists are holding a joint exhibition.* ▶ combined, shared, common, collaborative, coordinated, cooperative, collective, communal, concerted, united, mutual OPPOSITES ARE separate, discrete, individual

joke *NOUN* *They sat all evening telling each other jokes.* ▶ funny story, jest, witticism, wisecrack, pleasantry, quip, (*more informal*) crack, (*more informal*) gag

joke *VERB* **1** *He laughed and joked with his friends.* ▶ tell jokes, crack jokes, jest, clown, have a laugh, be facetious **2** *From the look on her face I'd say she was only joking.* ▶ fool, tease, hoax, (*more informal*) kid

joker *NOUN* *She seems quite a joker, but she has her serious side.* ▶ jester, comedian, comic, humorist, wag, wit, clown

jolly *ADJECTIVE* *We had a jolly time. He was in a jolly mood when he came back.* ▶ cheerful, merry, cheery, happy, jovial, exuberant, hearty

jolt *VERB* **1** *The car jolted along the rough roads.* ▶ bump, bounce, jerk, jog, shake, shudder **2** *The fierceness of his remarks jolted her.* ▶ startle, surprise, shock, disturb, disconcert, upset, discompose, astonish, nonplus

jot *VERB* **jot down** *The man jotted down my details.* ▶ write down, note down, take down, scribble, make a note of

journal *NOUN* **1** *an academic journal* ▶ periodical, publication, magazine, gazette, digest **2** *She kept a journal of the voyage.* ▶ diary, log, record, chronicle, account

journalist *NOUN* *A journalist wanted to hear his story.* ▶ reporter, correspondent, columnist, feature-writer, contributor, writer

journey *NOUN* *The journey takes you through three countries.* ▶ trip, route, itinerary, travels, voyage, peregrination USAGE You normally use *voyage* to mean a long journey by sea.

joy *NOUN* *There was a look of joy on her face.* ▶ delight, bliss, pleasure, happiness, gladness, ecstasy, elation, joyfulness, exultation, rapture, euphoria, exuberance OPPOSITES ARE sorrow, misery

joyful *ADJECTIVE* *Kate set off with joyful enthusiasm.* ▶ cheerful, happy, joyous, jubilant, bright, sunny, lively, elated, animated, contented, buoyant, good-humoured, light-hearted, chirpy AN OPPOSITE IS sad

jubilant *ADJECTIVE* *Jubilant fans surged on to the pitch.* ▶ delighted, joyful, overjoyed, exultant, joyous, elated, ecstatic, thrilled

jubilee (joo- bil- ee) *NOUN* **jubilees** a special anniversary: *silver* (25th), *golden* (50th), and *diamond* (60th) *jubilee*

Judaism (joo- day- izm) *NOUN* the religion of the Jewish people

judge *NOUN* **judges 1** a person appointed to hear cases in a lawcourt and decide what should be done **2** a person deciding who has won a contest or competition **3** someone who is good at forming opinions or making decisions • *She's a good judge of character.*

judge *VERB* **judges, judging, judged 1** act as a judge **2** form and give an opinion **3** estimate • *He judged the distance carefully*

judgement *NOUN* **judgements 1** judging **2** the decision made by a lawcourt **3** someone's opinion **4** the ability to judge wisely **5** something considered as a punishment from God • *It's a judgement on you!*

judicial *ADJECTIVE* to do with lawcourts, judges, or judgements • *the British judicial system*
▷ **judicially** *ADVERB*
USAGE Do not confuse with **judicious**.

judicious (joo- dish- us) *ADJECTIVE* having or showing good sense or good judgement
▷ **judiciously** *ADVERB*
USAGE Do not confuse with **judicial**.

judo *NOUN* a Japanese method of self-defence without using weapons [from Japanese *ju* = gentle + *do* = way]

jug *NOUN* **jugs** a container for holding and pouring liquids, with a handle and a lip

juggernaut *NOUN* **juggernauts** a huge lorry [named after a Hindu god whose image was dragged in procession on a huge wheeled vehicle]

juggle *VERB* **juggles, juggling, juggled 1** toss and catch a number of objects skilfully for entertainment, keeping one or more in the air at any time **2** rearrange or alter things skilfully or in order to deceive people
▷ **juggler** *NOUN*

jugular *ADJECTIVE* to do with the throat or neck • *the jugular veins*

juice *NOUN* **juices 1** the liquid from fruit, vegetables, or other food **2** a liquid produced by the body • *the digestive juices*
▷ **juicy** *ADJECTIVE*

jukebox *NOUN* **jukeboxes** a machine that automatically plays a record you have selected when you put a coin in

July *NOUN* the seventh month of the year [named after Julius Caesar, who was born in this month]

jumble *VERB* **jumbles, jumbling, jumbled** mix things up into a confused mass

jumble *NOUN* a confused mixture of things; a muddle

jumble sale *NOUN* **jumble sales** a sale of second-hand goods

jumbo *NOUN* **jumbos 1** something very large; a jumbo jet **2** an elephant

jumbo jet *NOUN* **jumbo jets** a very large jet aircraft

jump *VERB* **jumps, jumping, jumped 1** move up suddenly from the ground into the air **2** go

Thesaurus

jubilee *NOUN a royal jubilee* ► anniversary, celebration, festival, gala, carnival, commemoration

judge *NOUN* **1** *The judges could not agree on a winner.* ► adjudicator, arbiter, arbitrator, assessor, moderator, referee, umpire **2** *a good judge of art* ► connoisseur, authority (on), expert (on), critic

judge *VERB* **1** *A magistrate will judge the case.* ► try, hear, sit in judgement on, adjudicate on, decide **2** *A panel of experts will judge the ten best entries.* ► assess, appraise, decide, evaluate, review, examine **3** *We judged that she had been misled.* ► conclude, decide, consider, believe, think, reckon, determine, come to the view, form the opinion

judgement *NOUN* **1** *the judgement of the court* ► verdict, decision, adjudication, ruling, finding, pronouncement, sentence **2** *He showed a lack of judgement.* ► understanding, discernment, perception, wisdom, sense, common sense, acumen, prudence **3** *my judgement of the situation* ► assessment, appraisal, evaluation, estimate, analysis, view, opinion, belief

jug *NOUN a jug of water* ► pitcher, carafe, flagon, ewer, crock, vessel

juice *NOUN Add the juice of a lemon.* ► liquid, fluid, extract, essence

juicy *ADJECTIVE* **1** *a juicy pear* ► succulent, tender, moist, soft, ripe AN OPPOSITE IS dry **2** *a juicy piece of gossip* ► interesting, lurid, spicy, colourful, racy

jumble *NOUN Clothes lay on the floor in a jumble.* ► muddle, hotchpotch, mess, clutter, chaos, confusion, disorder

jumble *VERB I'll try not to jumble the photographs.* ► muddle, disorganize, mix up, shuffle, confuse, disarrange, (*more informal*) mess up AN OPPOSITE IS organize

jump *VERB* **1** *A dog jumped off the chair.* ► leap, spring, bound, bounce, hop **2** *All the horses jumped the first fence.* ► vault, clear **3** *The children were jumping about in the garden.* ► skip, dance, frolic, prance, cavort **4** *A noise made him jump.* ► start, jerk, jolt, flinch, recoil

over something by jumping • *The horse jumped the fence* **3** pass over something; miss out part of a book etc. **4** move suddenly in surprise **5** pass quickly to a different place or level
jump at (*informal*) accept something eagerly
jump on (*informal*) start criticizing someone
jump the gun start before you should
jump the queue not wait your turn

jump NOUN **jumps** **1** a jumping movement **2** an obstacle to jump over **3** a sudden rise or change

jumper NOUN **jumpers** a jersey [from French *jupe* = tunic]

jumpy ADJECTIVE nervous and edgy

junction NOUN **junctions** **1** a join **2** a place where roads or railway lines meet

June NOUN the sixth month of the year [named after the Roman goddess Juno]

jungle NOUN **jungles** a thick tangled forest, especially in the tropics
▷ **jungly** ADJECTIVE
[from Hindi]

junior ADJECTIVE **1** younger **2** for young children • *a junior school* **3** lower in rank or importance • *junior officers* [from Latin, = younger]

junk NOUN rubbish; things of no value

junk food NOUN food that is not nourishing

junk mail NOUN unwanted advertising material sent by post

jury NOUN **juries** a group of people (usually twelve) appointed to give a verdict about a case in a lawcourt
▷ **juryman** NOUN **jurywoman** NOUN
[from Latin *jurare* = take an oath]

just ADJECTIVE **1** giving proper consideration to everyone's claims **2** deserved; right in amount etc. • *a just reward*
▷ **justly** ADVERB **justness** NOUN

just ADVERB **1** exactly • *It's just what I wanted.* **2** only; simply • *I just wanted to see him.* **3** barely; by only a small amount • *just below the knee* **4** at this moment or only a little while ago • *She has just gone.*

justice NOUN **justices** **1** being just; fair treatment **2** legal proceedings • *a court of justice* **3** a judge or magistrate [via early French from Latin *jus* = law]

justify VERB **justifies, justifying, justified** show that something is fair, just, or reasonable
▷ **justifiable** ADJECTIVE **justification** NOUN

jut VERB **juts, jutting, jutted** stick out

jute NOUN fibre from tropical plants, used for making sacks etc.

juvenile ADJECTIVE to do with or for young people

juvenile NOUN **juveniles** a young person, not old enough to be legally considered an adult

juvenile delinquent NOUN **juvenile delinquents** a young person who has broken the law

Thesaurus

5 *Attendance had jumped by more than 20 percent.* ► rise, increase, leap, go up, escalate

jump NOUN **1** *With a jump he reached the other side.* ► leap, bound, spring, vault, hop **2** *The horse cleared the last jump comfortably.* ► fence, hurdle, ditch, barrier, obstacle, gap, gate **3** *a huge jump in house prices* ► rise, increase, escalation, upturn **4** *She woke up with a jump.* ► start, jerk, jolt, shock, shudder, lurch

jumpy ADJECTIVE *He was tired and jumpy.* ► nervous, edgy, jittery, tense, anxious, agitated, apprehensive

junior ADJECTIVE *a junior official* ► low-ranking, lower-ranking, subordinate, subsidiary, younger, lesser, minor, secondary
AN OPPOSITE IS senior

junk NOUN *a cupboard full of old junk* ► rubbish, clutter, oddments, odds and ends, garbage, refuse, scrap, trash, waste

just ADJECTIVE **1** *a just ruler; a just settlement* ► fair, equitable, fair-minded, honourable, even-handed, unprejudiced, unbiased, neutral, non-partisan AN OPPOSITE IS unjust **2** *a just punishment* ► fair, fitting, deserved, merited, appropriate, suitable, reasonable, legitimate
OPPOSITES ARE undeserved, unfair

justice NOUN **1** *He appealed to their sense of justice.* ► fairness, justness, fair play, integrity, equity, honesty, impartiality, legality, right
AN OPPOSITE IS injustice **2** *the administration of justice* ► the law, legal proceedings

justifiable ADJECTIVE *a justifiable reaction* ► reasonable, justified, valid, legitimate, defensible, excusable, well founded, understandable, warranted, acceptable
AN OPPOSITE IS unjustifiable

justification NOUN **1** *There is no justification for such callousness.* ► excuse, reason, grounds, basis, warrant, foundation **2** *Such extreme measures call for some justification.* ► explanation, defence, vindication, argument, rationalization

justify VERB *Tiredness cannot justify this kind of reckless behaviour.* ► excuse, defend, absolve, mitigate, account for, vindicate, exonerate, warrant, validate, uphold, support

jut VERB **jut out** *A set of shelves jutted out on one wall.* ► project, protrude, stick out, extend, overhang, poke out

juvenile ADJECTIVE **1** *juvenile behaviour* ► immature, childish, babyish, infantile, puerile AN OPPOSITE IS mature **2** *juvenile novels* ► adolescent, young, youthful

juvenile NOUN *The people involved were all juveniles.* ► youth, young person, minor, under-age person

Kk

kaleidoscope (kal- I- dos- kohp) *NOUN* **kaleidoscopes** a tube that you look through to see brightly coloured patterns which change as you turn the end of the tube
▷ **kaleidoscopic** *ADJECTIVE*

kangaroo *NOUN* **kangaroos** an Australian animal that jumps along on its strong hind legs (See **marsupial**) [an Australian Aboriginal word]

karaoke *NOUN* (ka- ree- oh- ki) a form of entertainment in which people sing well-known songs against a pre-recorded backing [from Japanese, = empty orchestra]

karate (ka- rah- tee) *NOUN* a Japanese method of self-defence in which the hands and feet are used as weapons [from Japanese *kara* = empty + *te* = hand]

KB or **Kb** *ABBREVIATION* kilobyte(s)

keel *NOUN* **keels** the long piece of wood or metal along the bottom of a boat
on an even keel steady

keel *VERB* **keels, keeling, keeled**
keel over fall down or overturn • *The ship keeled over.*

keen *ADJECTIVE* **1** enthusiastic; very interested in or eager to do something • *a keen swimmer* **2** sharp • *a keen edge* **3** piercingly cold • *a keen wind*
▷ **keenly** *ADVERB* **keenness** *NOUN*

keep *VERB* **keeps, keeping, kept 1** have something and look after it or not get rid of it **2** stay or cause to stay in the same condition etc. • *keep still;* • *keep it hot* **3** do something continually • *She keeps laughing.* **4** last without going bad • *How long will this milk keep?* **5** respect and not break • *keep a promise* **6** make entries in • *keep a diary*
keep to observe or respect
keep up 1 make the same progress as others **2** continue something

keep *NOUN* **keeps 1** maintenance; the food etc. that you need to live • *She earns her keep.* **2** a strong tower in a castle
for keeps (*informal*) permanently; to keep • *Is this football mine for keeps?*

keeper *NOUN* **keepers 1** a person who looks after an animal, building, etc. • *the park keeper* **2** a goalkeeper or wicketkeeper

keeping *NOUN* care; looking after something • *in safe keeping*

keg *NOUN* **kegs** a small barrel

kelvin *NOUN* **kelvins** the SI unit of thermodynamic temperature

kennel *NOUN* **kennels** a shelter for a dog

kerb *NOUN* **kerbs** the edge of a pavement

kernel *NOUN* **kernels** the part inside the shell of a nut etc.

ketchup *NOUN* a thick sauce made from tomatoes and vinegar etc. [probably from Chinese *k'e chap* = tomato juice]

kettle *NOUN* **kettles** a container with a spout and handle, for boiling water in

kettledrum *NOUN* **kettledrums** a large drum shaped like a bowl

key *NOUN* **keys 1** a piece of metal shaped so that it will open a lock **2** a device for winding up a

Thesaurus

keen *ADJECTIVE* **1** *Competition is keen and a good honours degree is essential.* ► intense, acute, fierce, extreme, strong **2** *France was keen to attract more foreign investment.* ► eager, anxious, determined, impatient, ambitious, intent (on attracting) **3** *William is a keen devotee of science fiction.* ► enthusiastic, eager, avid, fervent, impassioned, committed, conscientious **4** *a knife with a keen cutting edge* ► sharp, sharp-edged, razor-sharp, honed **5** *Patience, nimble fingers, and keen eyesight are needed to operate the tool.* ► sharp, acute, clear, sensitive, strong, powerful **6** *She still displays a keen sense of humour.* ► sharp, piercing, incisive, penetrating, pungent, trenchant

keep *VERB* **1** *an in-flight magazine for you to read and keep* ► retain, hold on to, hang on to, possess **2** *They did their best to keep quiet.* ► remain, stay, continue to be, carry on being **3** *He keeps twitching his ears.* ► persist in, go on, continue, carry on **4** *We'll try not to keep you too long.* ► detain, delay, hold up, keep waiting **5** *These problems shouldn't keep you from continuing.* ► deter, constrain, hinder, impede, obstruct **6** *You must keep your promise.* ► observe, fulfil, comply with, obey, respect, keep faith with **7** *Where do you keep the coats?* ► store, put, stow, house **8** *Keeping a family can be expensive.* ► support, maintain, provide for, look after, care for, be responsible for

keeper *NOUN* **1** *the keeper of the museum* ► curator, custodian, administrator, superintendent **2** *the prisoners and their keeper* ► jailer, warden, guard, custodian **3** *He said he was not his brother's keeper.* ► guardian, protector, minder

key *NOUN* **1** *the key to a problem* ► clue, indicator, pointer, lead, secret, solution, answer, interpretation **2** *a key to a map* ► guide, legend, index, table, explanation, glossary

key *ADJECTIVE* *the key question* ► fundamental, crucial, vital, critical, essential, important

clock or clockwork toy etc. **3** a small lever to be pressed by a finger, e.g. on a piano, typewriter, or computer **4** a system of notes in music • *the key of C major* **5** a fact or clue that explains or solves something • *the key to the mystery* **6** a list of symbols used in a map or table, showing what they mean

key VERB **keys, keying, keyed**
key in type information into a computer using a keyboard

keyboard NOUN **keyboards** the set of keys on a piano, typewriter, computer, etc.

keyhole NOUN **keyholes** the hole through which a key is put into a lock

keyhole surgery NOUN surgery carried out through a very small cut in the patient's body, using special instruments

keypad NOUN **keypads** a small keyboard or set of buttons used to operate a telephone, television, etc.

kg ABBREVIATION kilogram(s)

khaki NOUN a dull yellowish-brown colour, used for military uniforms [from Urdu *khaki* = dust-coloured]

kibbutz NOUN **kibbutzim** a commune in Israel, especially for farming [from Hebrew *qibbus* = gathering]

kick VERB **kicks, kicking, kicked** **1** hit or move a person or thing with your foot **2** move your legs about vigorously **3** (said about a gun) recoil when fired
kick off **1** start a football match **2** (*informal*) start doing something
kick out get rid of; dismiss
kick up (*informal*) make a noise or fuss

kick NOUN **kicks** **1** a kicking movement **2** the recoiling movement of a gun **3** (*informal*) a thrill **4** (*informal*) an interest or activity • *He's on a health kick*

kick-off NOUN **kick-offs** the start of a football match

kid NOUN **kids** **1** (*informal*) a child **2** a young goat **3** fine leather made from goatskin

kidnap VERB **kidnaps, kidnapping, kidnapped** take someone away by force, especially in order to obtain a ransom
▷ **kidnapper** NOUN

kidney NOUN **kidneys** either of the two organs in the body that remove waste products from the blood and excrete urine into the bladder

kill VERB **kills, killing, killed** **1** make a person or thing die **2** destroy or put an end to something
▷ **killer** NOUN
kill time occupy time idly while waiting

killing NOUN **killings** an act causing death

kilo NOUN **kilos** a kilogram

kilogram NOUN **kilograms** a unit of mass or weight equal to 1,000 grams (about 22 pounds)

kilometre (kil- o- meet- er, kil- om- it- er) NOUN **kilometres** a unit of length equal to 1,000 metres (about of a mile)

kilowatt NOUN **kilowatts** a unit of electrical power equal to 1,000 watts

kilt NOUN **kilts** a kind of pleated skirt worn especially by Scotsmen
▷ **kilted** ADJECTIVE

kin PLURAL NOUN a person's family and relatives

Thesaurus

kick NOUN **1** *He gave the television a kick.* ► hit, boot, blow **2** (*informal*) *Some people might get a kick out of crossing the Atlantic in an old bath.* ► thrill, excitement, (*informal*) buzz

kick VERB **1** *Merv kicked the ball out.* ► boot, hit, drive, send, punt, heel **2** (*informal*) *a habit I have to kick* ► give up, quit, break, abandon, cease, desist from

kid VERB (*informal*) **1** *I think they were only kidding.* ► tease, fool, bluff, lie **2** *Are you kidding me?* ► hoodwink, pull your leg, have you on, deceive

kidnap VERB *The group was allegedly preparing to kidnap a businessman.* ► abduct, capture, seize, carry off, run away with, snatch

kill VERB **1** *The gang would not hesitate to kill the prisoners.* ► murder, put to death, slay, slaughter, dispatch, eliminate, exterminate, assassinate, (*more informal*) bump off USAGE You use *assassinate* to refer to an important person, especially a statesman or stateswoman. *Slay* and *dispatch* are literary words. **2** *The war killed all hopes of continuing archaeological investigation at the site.* ► end, destroy, put an end to, dash, extinguish, finish **3** *Take aspirin to kill the pain.* ► soothe, alleviate, assuage, deaden, suppress, dull, blunt, reduce, stifle, extinguish **4** (*informal*) *She complained that her back was killing her.* ► hurt, pain, torment, torture, give discomfort to, give pain to **5** *We arrived early and had an hour to kill.* ► occupy, fill up, while away, pass, spend **6** (*informal*) *She nearly killed herself getting the work finished in time.* ► exhaust, wear out, tire out, sap, debilitate

killer NOUN *A witness was able to identify the killers.* ► murderer, assassin, gunman, (*more informal*) hitman

killing NOUN *a brutal killing that shocked the community* ► murder, assassination, slaughter, massacre, execution USAGE Note that *slaughter* and *massacre* refer to the killing of a large number of people.

kind[1] *NOUN* **kinds** a class of similar things or animals; a sort or type
in kind (said about payment) made in goods or services and not in money
kind of (*informal*) in a way, to some extent • *I felt kind of sorry for him.*
USAGE Correct use is *this kind of thing* or *these kinds of things* (not 'these kind of things').

kind[2] *ADJECTIVE* friendly and helpful; considerate ▷ **kind-hearted** *ADJECTIVE* **kindness** *NOUN*

kindergarten *NOUN* **kindergartens** a school or class for very young children

kindle *VERB* **kindles, kindling, kindled 1** start a flame; set light to something **2** begin burning

kinetic *ADJECTIVE* to do with or produced by movement • *kinetic energy*

king *NOUN* **kings 1** a man who is the ruler of a country through inheriting the position **2** a person or thing regarded as supreme • *the lion is the king of beasts* **3** the most important piece in chess **4** a playing card with a picture of a king ▷ **kingly** *ADJECTIVE* **kingship** *NOUN*
[from Old English]

kingdom *NOUN* **kingdoms 1** a country ruled by a king or queen **2** a major division of the natural world • *the animal kingdom*

kingfisher *NOUN* **kingfishers** a small bird with blue feathers that dives to catch fish

kink *NOUN* **kinks 1** a short twist in a rope, wire, piece of hair, etc. **2** a peculiarity

kinky *ADJECTIVE* involving peculiar sexual behaviour

kiosk *NOUN* **kiosks 1** a telephone box **2** a small hut or stall where newspapers, sweets, etc. are sold

kiss *NOUN* **kisses** touching somebody with your lips as a sign of affection

kiss *VERB* **kisses, kissing, kissed** give somebody a kiss

kiss of life *NOUN* blowing air from your mouth into another person's to help the other person to start breathing again, especially after an accident

kit *NOUN* **kits 1** equipment or clothes for a particular occupation **2** a set of parts sold ready to be fitted together

kitchen *NOUN* **kitchens** a room in which meals are prepared and cooked

kite *NOUN* **kites 1** a light framework covered with cloth, paper, etc. and flown in the wind on the end of a long piece of string **2** a large hawk

kitten *NOUN* **kittens** a very young cat

kiwi *NOUN* **kiwis** a New Zealand bird that cannot fly [from a Maori word]

kleptomania *NOUN* an uncontrollable urge to steal things
▷ **kleptomaniac** *NOUN*

km *ABBREVIATION* kilometre(s)

knack *NOUN* a special skill • *There's a knack to putting up a deckchair.*

Thesaurus

kind *ADJECTIVE* *A kind friend helped him home. It was kind of her to ring.* ► caring, good, kind-hearted, kindly, considerate, sympathetic, thoughtful, obliging, tender-hearted, benevolent OPPOSITES ARE unkind, unfriendly

kind *NOUN* *a new kind of rock music* ► sort, type, style, form, variety, category, genre

kindle *VERB* **1** *Bonfires are kindled on Midwinter's Day.* ► light, burn, ignite, fire, set fire to **2** *These events kindled strong feelings.* ► stir up, stimulate, arouse, give rise to, evoke, induce, inflame, call forth

kindly *ADJECTIVE* *a kindly old man* ► kind, kind-hearted, benevolent, caring, good, considerate, sympathetic, thoughtful, obliging, tender-hearted

kindness *NOUN* *She had shown them much kindness over many years.* ► consideration, thoughtfulness, generosity, goodwill, benevolence, favour, understanding

king *NOUN* *After the war the country expelled its king.* ► ruler, monarch, sovereign, crowned head RELATED ADJECTIVES regal, royal

kingdom *NOUN* *a small kingdom in Asia Minor* ► monarchy, realm, dominion

kink *NOUN* **1** *a kink in the road.* ► bend, corner, angle **2** *kinks in the line* ► twist, curl, loop, knot, tangle

kiss *VERB* *She stooped to kiss the little boy.* ► caress, embrace, (*more informal*) peck

kiss *NOUN* *He gave her a long kiss.* ► caress, embrace, (*more informal*) peck, (*more informal*) snog

kit *NOUN* **1** *a tool kit* ► equipment, gear, implements, appliances, tackle **2** *They made the furniture from kits.* ► outfit, set of parts, self-assembly set, flatpack **3** *a football kit* ► outfit, strip, colours, clothes

knack *NOUN* *He has a knack of hitting the nail on the head.* ► gift, flair (for), talent (for), instinct (for), ability (to hit), skill (for)

knapsack *NOUN* **knapsacks** a bag carried on the back by soldiers, hikers, etc.

knave *NOUN* **knaves** **1** (*old use*) a dishonest man; a rogue **2** a jack in playing cards

knead *VERB* **kneads, kneading, kneaded** press and stretch something soft (especially dough) with your hands

knee *NOUN* **knees** the joint in the middle of the leg

kneecap *NOUN* **kneecaps** the small bone covering the front of the knee joint

kneel *VERB* **kneels, kneeling, knelt** be or get yourself in a position on your knees

knickers *PLURAL NOUN* underpants worn by women and girls

knife *NOUN* **knives** a cutting instrument consisting of a sharp blade set in a handle

knight *NOUN* **knights** **1** a man who has been given the rank that allows him to put 'Sir' before his name **2** (in the Middle Ages) a warrior of high social rank, usually mounted and in armour **3** a piece in chess, with a horse's head
▷ **knighthood** *NOUN*

knit *VERB* **knits, knitting, knitted** *or* **knit** make something by looping together wool or other yarn, using long needles or a machine
▷ **knitter** *NOUN* **knitting needle** *NOUN*
knit your brow frown

knob *NOUN* **knobs** **1** the round handle of a door, drawer, etc. **2** a round lump on something **3** a round button or switch on a dial or machine **4** a small round piece of something • *a knob of butter*
▷ **knobbly** *ADJECTIVE* **knobby** *ADJECTIVE*

knock *VERB* **knocks, knocking, knocked** **1** hit a thing hard or so as to make a noise **2** produce by hitting • *We need to knock a hole in the wall.* **3** (*informal*) criticize unfavourably • *People are always knocking this country.*
knock off **1** (*informal*) stop working **2** deduct something from a price **3** (*informal*) steal
knock out make a person unconscious, especially by a blow to the head

knockout *NOUN* **knockouts** **1** knocking someone out **2** a contest in which the loser in each round has to drop out **3** (*informal*) an amazing person or thing

knot *NOUN* **knots** **1** a place where a piece of string, rope, or ribbon etc. is twisted round itself or another piece **2** a tangle or lump **3** a round spot on a piece of wood where a branch joined it **4** a cluster of people or things **5** a unit for measuring the speed of ships and aircraft, equal to 2,025 yards (= 1,852 metres or 1 nautical mile) per hour

knot *VERB* **knots, knotting, knotted** **1** tie or fasten with a knot **2** entangle

know *VERB* **knows, knowing, knew, known** **1** have something in your mind that you have learned or discovered **2** recognize or be familiar with a person or place • *I've known him for years.* **3** understand • *She knows how to please us.*

Thesaurus

kneel *VERB* *She knelt by the bed to pray.* ► bend, bow, crouch, stoop, squat, fall to your knees, genuflect

knife *VERB* *The victim had been knifed repeatedly.* ► stab, gash, slash, pierce, cut, wound

knit *VERB* **knit together** *The new arrangements took a few months to knit together.* ► unite, become unified, come together, combine, connect

knob *NOUN* **1** *He held the door knob as he looked into the room.* ► handle **2** *The gnarled old tree was covered with knobs.* ► bump, lump, bulge, swelling, boss, projection, protuberance

knock *VERB* **1** *He swore as he knocked his knee on the edge of the desk.* ► bump, hit, strike, bang, crack, rap **2** *The man knocked on the door and waited.* ► bang, rap, tap, thump, pound
knock about (*informal*) *He knocks about with some lads from Walsall.* ► mix, associate, go around
knock down **1** *They are going to knock down the entire row of houses.* ► demolish, level, raze, destroy **2** *He knocked her down with one blow.* ► fell, topple, flatten, floor
knock off (*informal*) **1** *We knock off early tonight.* ► finish work, go home **2** *Someone had knocked off the vicar's car.* ► steal, take, (*informal*) pinch, (*informal*) nick
knock out **1** *I hit him and knocked him out.* ► stun, strike unconscious **2** (*informal*) *The long walk knocked us out.* ► exhaust, tire out, wear out **3** (*informal*) *music that knocked me out* ► overwhelm, amaze, astound

knock *NOUN* *The car has taken a few knocks.* ► blow, bump, bang, shock, collision, smash

knockout *NOUN* *The event was a knockout.* ► success, sensation, triumph, winner, hit

knot *NOUN* **1** *a knot in a rope* ► tie, twist, splice, hitch **2** *a knot of people* ► cluster, bunch, clump, group

knot *VERB* *She knotted a scarf round her neck.* ► tie, secure, bind, fasten, do up, entwine
OPPOSITES ARE unknot, untie

know *VERB* **1** *Does she know we are here?* ► realize, be aware, understand, appreciate **2** *I speak French but don't know any German.*

A B C D E F G H I J K L M N O P Q R S T U V W X Y Z

knowing *ADJECTIVE* showing that you know something • *a knowing look*

knowingly *ADVERB* **1** in a knowing way **2** deliberately

knowledge *NOUN* **1** knowing **2** all that a person knows **3** all that is known
to my knowledge as far as I know

knowledgeable *ADJECTIVE* well informed
▷ **knowledgeably** *ADVERB*

knuckle *NOUN* **knuckles** a joint in the finger

knuckle *VERB* **knuckles, knuckling, knuckled**
knuckle down begin to work hard
knuckle under yield or submit

koala (koh-ah-la) *NOUN* **koalas** an Australian animal that looks like a small bear [an Australian Aboriginal word]

Koran (kor-ahn) *NOUN* the sacred book of Islam, written in Arabic, believed by Muslims to contain the words of Allah revealed to the prophet Muhammad

kosher *ADJECTIVE* keeping to Jewish laws about the preparation of food • *kosher meat*

kw *ABBREVIATION* kilowatt(s)

Thesaurus

► understand, speak, have knowledge of, be familiar with, be conversant with, have a grasp of **3** *Gerry knows me from our student days.* ► be acquainted with, have met, be friendly with, have had dealings with **4** *He had known much better times.* ► experience, live through, go through, undergo

know-all *NOUN* *He's such a know-all he's bound to be able to tell us.* ► (*informal*) smart alec, (*informal*) wise guy, show-off, wiseacre, expert, pundit

know-how *NOUN* (*informal*) *technical know-how* ► expertise, knowledge, skill, proficiency, understanding

knowing *ADJECTIVE* **1** *She gave a knowing look.* ► meaningful, expressive, significant, suggestive, eloquent, shrewd, artful AN OPPOSITE IS innocent **2** *a knowing young woman* ► clever, astute, crafty, cunning

knowledge *NOUN* **1** *an extensive knowledge of the local history* ► understanding, comprehension, mastery, command, grasp **2** *technical knowledge* ► expertise, skill, proficiency, understanding, (*more informal*) know-how **3** *I have no knowledge of these people.* ► acquaintance (with), familiarity (with) **4** *people with a wide range of knowledge* ► learning, education, erudition, scholarship

knowledgeable *ADJECTIVE* **1** *a knowledgeable man* ► educated, erudite, learned, well informed **2** *knowledgeable about modern art* ► well informed, versed (in), acquainted (with), conversant (with), familiar (with), au fait (with) AN OPPOSITE IS ignorant

Ll

label *NOUN* **labels** a small piece of paper, cloth, or metal etc. fixed on or beside something to show what it is or what it costs, or its owner or destination, etc.

label *VERB* **labels, labelling, labelled** put a label on something

laboratory *NOUN* **laboratories** a room or building equipped for scientific experiments

laborious *ADJECTIVE* **1** needing or using a lot of hard work **2** explaining something at great length and with obvious effort
▷ **laboriously** *ADVERB*

Labour *NOUN* the Labour Party, a British political party formed to represent the interests of working people

labour *NOUN* **labours** **1** hard work **2** a task **3** working people **4** the contractions of the womb when a baby is being born

labour *VERB* **labours, labouring, laboured** **1** work hard **2** explain or discuss something at great length and with obvious effort • *I will not labour the point.*

labourer *NOUN* **labourers** a person who does hard manual work, especially outdoors

laburnum *NOUN* **laburnums** a tree with hanging yellow flowers

labyrinth *NOUN* **labyrinths** a complicated arrangement of passages or paths; a maze

lace *NOUN* **laces** **1** net-like material with decorative patterns of holes in it **2** a piece of thin cord or leather for fastening a shoe etc.

lack *NOUN* being without something

lack *VERB* **lacks, lacking, lacked** be without something • *He lacks courage.*

lacquer *NOUN* a hard glossy varnish
▷ **lacquered** *ADJECTIVE*

lacrosse *NOUN* a game in which players use a stick with a net on it (a **crosse**) to catch and throw a ball

lacy *ADJECTIVE* made of lace or like lace

lad *NOUN* **lads** a boy or youth

ladder *NOUN* **ladders** **1** two upright pieces of wood or metal etc. and crosspieces (**rungs**), used for climbing up or down **2** a vertical ladder-like flaw in a pair of tights etc. where a stitch has become undone

ladle *NOUN* **ladles** a large deep spoon with a long handle, used for lifting and pouring liquids

Thesaurus

label *NOUN* **1** *Always read the label on the packet.* ► tag, tab, sticker, ticket, docket, marker **2** *a new independent record label* ► brand, company, organization

label *VERB* *The authorities were too ready to label people as troublemakers.* ► identify, mark, categorize, class, classify, define, describe, regard, name, stamp, brand, call

laborious *ADJECTIVE* *Restoring your data is a long and laborious process.* ► arduous, hard, heavy, difficult, stiff, tough, exhausting, fatiguing, gruelling, wearisome, onerous, strenuous, burdensome, back-breaking, tiresome, uphill
OPPOSITES ARE easy, straightforward

labour *NOUN* **1** *Keeping the place clean involved a lot of labour.* ► work , toil, effort, exertion, industry, drudgery, donkey work, (*more informal*) grind, (*more informal*) sweat **2** *The company took on extra labour to cope with the seasonal rush.* ► staff, workers, employees, workforce, (*more informal*) hands **3** *Agnes went into labour about lunchtime.* ► childbirth, labour pains, contractions, delivery, (*technical*) parturition

labour *VERB* **1** *Levin laboured day and night on the project.* ► work, work hard, toil, drudge, grind, exert yourself, (*more informal*) beaver, (*more informal*) slave, (*more informal*) sweat **2** *As he laboured to get back on course another blast threw the boat lopsided.* ► struggle, strive, endeavour, work, do your utmost, go all out **3** *We have made our point and there is no need to labour it.* ► overdo, overemphasize, dwell on, elaborate, exaggerate, make heavy weather of

lace *NOUN* **1** *a cloth trimmed with lace* ► lacework, openwork, filigree, net, tatting **2** *One shoe had a lace missing.* ► shoelace, bootlace, shoestring, cord, string, thong

lace *VERB* **1** *He laced his shoes.* ► fasten, do up, tie up, secure **2** *She laced her fingers into his.* ► twine, entwine, intertwine, interweave

lack *NOUN* *suffering from a lack of vitamins* ► deficiency, shortage, want, scarcity, absence, dearth, paucity, deprivation, need, privation, famine OPPOSITES ARE sufficiency, abundance

lack *VERB* *The film lacks drama.* ► be without, be short of, be deficient in, miss, want, need, require

lacking *ADJECTIVE* **1** *a relationship lacking in affection* ► wanting, needing, without, missing, short of, weak in, deficient in, inadequate in, defective in **2** *Convincing arguments are lacking.* ► absent, missing, unavailable, non-existent

lad *NOUN* *a young lad of ten* ► boy, youth, youngster, schoolboy, fellow, (*more informal*) kid, (*more informal*) guy

A B C D E F G H I J K L M N O P Q R S T U V W X Y Z

lady *NOUN* **ladies 1** a well-mannered woman **2** a woman of good social position **3** (in polite use) a woman
▷ **ladylike** *ADJECTIVE* **ladyship** *NOUN*
Lady *NOUN* the title of a noblewoman
[from Old English *hlaefdige* = person who makes the bread (compare **lord**)]

ladybird *NOUN* **ladybirds** a small flying beetle, usually red with black spots

lag[1] *VERB* **lags, lagging, lagged** go too slowly and fail to keep up with others

lag[2] *VERB* **lags, lagging, lagged** wrap pipes or boilers etc. in insulating material (**lagging**) to prevent loss of heat

lager (lah- ger) *NOUN* **lagers** a light beer

lagoon *NOUN* **lagoons** a salt-water lake separated from the sea by sandbanks or reefs

laid *past tense of* **lay**

laid-back *ADJECTIVE* (*informal*) relaxed and calm

lain *past participle of* **lie**[2]

lair *NOUN* **lairs** a sheltered place where a wild animal lives

lake *NOUN* **lakes** a large area of water entirely surrounded by land [from Latin *lacus* = pool, lake]

lamb *NOUN* **lambs 1** a young sheep **2** meat from a lamb
▷ **lambswool** *NOUN*

lame *ADJECTIVE* **1** unable to walk normally **2** weak; not convincing • *a lame excuse*
▷ **lamely** *ADVERB* **lameness** *NOUN*

lament *NOUN* **laments** a statement, song, or poem expressing grief or regret

lament *VERB* **laments, lamenting, lamented** express grief or regret about something
▷ **lamentation** *NOUN*

lamentable (lam- in- ta- bul) *ADJECTIVE* regrettable or deplorable

lamp *NOUN* **lamps** a device for producing light from electricity, gas, or oil
▷ **lamplight** *NOUN* **lampshade** *NOUN*

lamp post *NOUN* **lamp posts** a tall post in a street etc., with a lamp at the top

lance *NOUN* **lances** a long spear

lance corporal *NOUN* **lance corporals** a soldier ranking between a private and a corporal

land *NOUN* **lands 1** the part of the earth's surface not covered by sea **2** the ground or soil; an area of country • *forest land* **3** the area occupied by a nation; a country

land *VERB* **lands, landing, landed 1** arrive or put on land from a ship or aircraft etc. **2** reach the ground after jumping or falling **3** bring a fish out of the water **4** obtain • *She landed an excellent job* **5** arrive or cause to arrive at a certain place or position etc. • *They landed up in jail.* **6** present with a problem • *He landed me with this task.* [from Old English]

landing *NOUN* **landings 1** the level area at the top of a flight of stairs **2** bringing or coming to land • *The pilot made a smooth landing.* **3** a place where people can get on and off a boat

landing stage *NOUN* **landing stages** a platform on which people and goods are taken on and off a boat

landlady *NOUN* **landladies 1** a woman who lets rooms to lodgers **2** a woman who runs a pub

landlord *NOUN* **landlords 1** a person who lets a house, room, or land to a tenant **2** a person who runs a pub

landmark *NOUN* **landmarks 1** an object that is easily seen in a landscape **2** an important event in the history or development of something

Thesaurus

lag *VERB* **1** *Some of the runners were lagging behind.* ► straggle, trail, fall behind, drop behind, hang back, linger, dally, dawdle, bring up the rear, come last, idle OPPOSITES ARE keep up, take the lead **2** *material for lagging water pipes* ► insulate, wrap up

laid-back *ADJECTIVE* (*informal*) *He took a laid-back attitude despite the difficulties.* ► relaxed, unruffled, nonchalant, philosophical, casual, easygoing, at ease, informal OPPOSITES ARE tense, uptight

lair *NOUN* **1** *an animal's lair* ► den, burrow, haunt, hole, earth **2** *a criminal's lair* ► hideaway, hideout, hiding place, refuge, retreat, shelter, sanctuary

lame *ADJECTIVE* **1** *The horse was lame and would not race that day.* ► crippled, limping **2** *As excuses went, this one was pretty lame.* ► feeble, weak, flimsy, thin, unconvincing, implausible, hard to believe OPPOSITES ARE convincing, persuasive

land *NOUN* **1** *a large house with several acres of land* ► grounds, ground, estate, property, farmland, open space **2** *Egypt is a land steeped in history.* ► country, nation, state, region **3** *The ship reached land at last.* ► dry land, terra firma, shore

land *VERB* **1** *Allied troops landed in Kuwait.* ► disembark, debark, go ashore, alight, arrive, berth, come ashore, dock, end a journey, reach landfall AN OPPOSITE IS embark **2** *The ship will land at Calais.* ► dock, berth, moor, anchor, reach shore OPPOSITES ARE set sail, put to sea **3** *The plane landed ten minutes ahead of schedule.* ► touch down, come in to land AN OPPOSITE IS take off

landmark *NOUN* **1** *The church steeple was a landmark visible for miles around.* ► feature,

landmine *NOUN* **landmines** an explosive mine laid on or just under the surface of the ground

landowner *NOUN* **landowners** a person who owns a large amount of land

landscape *NOUN* **landscapes** **1** a view of a particular area of countryside or town **2** a picture of the countryside

landslide *NOUN* **landslides** **1** a huge mass of soil and rocks sliding down a slope **2** an overwhelming victory in an election • *She won the general election by a landslide.*

lane *NOUN* **lanes** **1** a narrow road, especially in the country **2** a strip of road for a single line of traffic **3** a strip of track or water for one runner, swimmer, etc. in a race

language *NOUN* **languages** **1** words and their use **2** the words used in a particular country or by a particular group of people **3** a system of signs or symbols giving information, especially in computing

languid *ADJECTIVE* slow because of tiredness, weakness, or laziness
▷ **languidly** *ADVERB* **languor** *NOUN*

languish *VERB* **languishes, languishing, languished** **1** live in miserable conditions; be neglected • *He has been languishing in prison for three years.* **2** become weak or listless

lank *ADJECTIVE* (said about hair) long and limp

lanky *ADJECTIVE* **lankier, lankiest** awkwardly thin and tall
▷ **lankiness** *NOUN*

lantern *NOUN* **lanterns** a transparent case for holding a light and shielding it from the wind

lap[1] *NOUN* **laps** **1** the level place formed by the front of the legs above the knees when a person is sitting down **2** going once round a racecourse **3** one section of a journey • *the last lap*

lap *VERB* **laps, lapping, lapped** overtake another competitor in a race to become one or more laps ahead

lap[2] *VERB* **laps, lapping, lapped** **1** take up liquid by moving the tongue, as a cat does **2** make a gentle splash against something • *Waves lapped the shore*

lapel (la- pel) *NOUN* **lapels** a flap folded back at the front edge of a coat or jacket

lapse *NOUN* **lapses** **1** a slight mistake or failure • *a lapse of memory* **2** an amount of time elapsed • *after a lapse of six months*

lapse *VERB* **lapses, lapsing, lapsed** **1** pass or slip gradually • *He lapsed into unconsciousness.* **2** be no longer valid, through not being renewed • *My insurance policy has lapsed.*

laptop *NOUN* **laptops** a portable computer for use while travelling

larch *NOUN* **larches** a tall deciduous tree that bears small cones

lard *NOUN* a white greasy substance prepared from pig fat and used in cooking

larder *NOUN* **larders** a cupboard or small room for storing food

large *ADJECTIVE* of more than the ordinary or average size; big
▷ **largeness** *NOUN*

at large **1** free to roam about, not captured

Thesaurus

sight, spectacle, marker, high point **2** *a landmark in history* ► turning point, milestone, watershed, new era

landscape *NOUN* **1** *the landscape of the Scottish Highlands.* ► scenery, countryside, topography, terrain, environment, rural scene, scene **2** *a landscape painting* ► panorama, vista, view, outlook, prospect

lane *NOUN* *a country lane* ► road, byroad, byway, track, trail, path

language *NOUN* **1** *the language of the media* ► vocabulary, usage, style, speech **2** *The forms are written in plain language.* ► wording, phraseology, phrasing **3** *the grammar of language* ► speech, writing, communication, utterance, discourse **4** *How many languages do you know?* ► tongue RELATED ADJECTIVE linguistic

lanky *ADJECTIVE* *a lanky young man* ► tall, gangling, gaunt, gawky, lean, spindly, scraggy

lap *NOUN* **1** *A cat was sitting on her lap.* ► knee *or* knees, thighs **2** *They managed three laps of the track.* ► circuit, round, orbit, circle, loop, stretch, course

lap *VERB* **1** *Waves lapped against the rocks.* ► wash, splash, dash, beat, strike, surge, rush **2** *The dog lapped a bowl of water.* ► drink, sip, lick, slurp, gulp

lapse *NOUN* **1** *a temporary lapse of attention* ► failure, error, weakness, relapse, failing, fault, slip, mistake, omission, flaw, shortcoming **2** *a lapse into crime* ► decline, descent, fall, falling, deterioration **3** *The friends got back in touch after a lapse of ten years.* ► interval, gap, pause, break, interruption

lapse *VERB* **1** *They soon lapsed into their bad old habits.* ► slide, slip, drop, fall, decline, deteriorate, degenerate **2** *Membership will lapse at the end of the month.* ► expire, run out, finish, stop, terminate, become invalid

large *ADJECTIVE* **1** *a large house; elected with a large majority* ► big, great, huge, sizeable, substantial, enormous, gigantic, immense, massive, colossal, vast, giant, (*more informal*) whopping, (*more informal*) ginormous **2** *a large man* ► big, burly, hefty, bulky, stocky, hulking, strapping **3** *a large supply of food* ► plentiful, abundant, copious, generous, lavish, profuse,

A B C D E F G H I J K **L** M N O P Q R S T U V W X Y Z

• *The escaped prisoners are still at large.* **2** in general, as a whole • *She is respected by the country at large.*
[from Latin *largus* = abundant or generous]

largely ADVERB to a great extent • *You are largely responsible for the accident.*

lark[1] NOUN **larks** a small sandy-brown bird; the skylark

lark[2] NOUN **larks** (*informal*) something amusing; a bit of fun • *We did it for a lark.*

larva NOUN **larvae** an insect in the first stage of its life, after it comes out of the egg
▷ **larval** ADJECTIVE
[from Latin, = ghost or mask]

laser NOUN **lasers** a device that makes a very strong narrow beam of light or other electromagnetic radiation [from the initials of 'light amplification by stimulated emission of radiation']

lash NOUN **lashes** **1** a stroke with a whip or stick **2** the cord or cord-like part of a whip **3** an eyelash

lash VERB **lashes, lashing, lashed** **1** strike with a whip; beat violently **2** tie with cord etc. • *Lash the sticks together.*
lash down (said about rain) pour or beat down forcefully
lash out **1** speak or hit out angrily **2** spend money extravagantly

lass NOUN **lasses** a girl or young woman
▷ **lassie** NOUN

lasso NOUN **lassoes** or **lassos** a rope with a sliding noose at the end, used for catching cattle etc. [via Spanish *lazo* from Latin *laqueus* = noose]

last[1] ADJECTIVE, ADVERB **1** coming after all others; final **2** latest; most recent • *last night* **3** least likely • *She is the last person I'd have chosen.*
the last straw a final thing that makes problems unbearable

last NOUN **1** a person or thing that is last **2** the end • *He was brave to the last.*
at last or **at long last** finally; after much delay

last[2] VERB **lasts, lasting, lasted** **1** continue; go on existing or living or being usable **2** be enough for • *The food will last us for three days.*

lasting ADJECTIVE able to last for a long time • *a lasting peace.*

lastly ADVERB in the last place; finally

latch NOUN **latches** a small bar fastening a door or gate, lifted by a lever or spring
▷ **latchkey** NOUN

latch VERB **latches, latching, latched** fasten with a latch
latch onto **1** meet someone and follow them around all the time **2** understand something

late ADJECTIVE, ADVERB **1** after the usual or expected time **2** near the end • *late in the afternoon* **3** recent • *the latest news* **4** who has died recently • *the late king*
of late recently

lately ADVERB recently

latent heat NOUN the heat needed to change a solid into a liquid or vapour, or a liquid into a vapour, without a change in temperature

Thesaurus

ample, liberal **4** *large areas of conifers* ► widespread, extensive, wide-ranging, large-scale

largely ADVERB *She was largely responsible for getting us into this mess.* ► mainly, chiefly, principally, primarily, mostly, to a large extent

lark NOUN (*informal*) *It all seemed just a lark to them.* ► prank, bit of fun, joke, laugh, game, escapade, amusement

lash VERB **1** *Driving rain lashed down.* ► beat against, dash against, batter, pound **2** *She lashed the poor donkey with a belt.* ► whip, beat, thrash, lash out at **3** *The speaker lashed out at his critics.* ► attack, condemn, denounce, lambaste, castigate, censure

last ADJECTIVE **1** *There was none of the violence associated with the last protest.* ► previous, preceding, recent, former **2** *She realized she was still the last person in the queue.* ► final, rearmost, endmost OPPOSITES ARE first, leading **3** *She decided to have one last look.* ► final, concluding, ultimate OPPOSITES ARE initial, opening **4** *I am the last person to complain.* ► least likely, most unlikely OPPOSITES ARE first, most likely

last VERB *The storm lasted all night.* ► continue, carry on, keep on, persist, endure, linger, remain, stay, hold, hold out, live, survive OPPOSITES ARE stop, cease, fade

lasting ADJECTIVE *The reforms will produce lasting change.* ► permanent, enduring, continuing, long-lasting, long-standing, unceasing, undying, unending, long-term, long-lived, durable, indestructible, indissoluble, lifelong, stable, abiding AN OPPOSITE IS temporary

late ADJECTIVE **1** *The train was over an hour late.* ► overdue, delayed, slow, behind-hand, belated, dilatory, tardy, unpunctual AN OPPOSITE IS early **2** *her father, the late king* ► deceased, dead, departed, former **3** *He had taken part in the late conflict.* ► recent, previous, preceding, former

later ADJECTIVE *The issue would be dealt with at a later meeting.* ► subsequent, future, following, succeeding

later ADVERB *We will meet you later.* ► afterwards, in a while, subsequently, eventually, next

lathe (layth) *NOUN* **lathes** a machine for holding and turning pieces of wood while they are being shaped

lather *NOUN* a mass of froth

lather *VERB* **lathers, lathering, lathered** **1** cover with lather **2** form a lather

Latin *NOUN* the language of the ancient Romans

Latin America *NOUN* the parts of Central and South America where the main language is Spanish or Portuguese

latitude *NOUN* **latitudes** **1** the distance of a place from the equator, measured in degrees **2** freedom from restrictions on what people can do or believe

latrine (la- treen) *NOUN* **latrines** a lavatory in a camp or barracks etc.

latter *ADJECTIVE* later • *the latter part of the year*
the latter the second of two people or things just mentioned COMPARE **former**

lattice *NOUN* **lattices** a framework of crossed laths or bars with spaces between

laudable *ADJECTIVE* deserving praise
▷ **laudably** *ADVERB*

laugh *VERB* **laughs, laughing, laughed** make the sounds that show you are happy or think something is funny

laugh *NOUN* **laughs** the sound of laughing

laughable *ADJECTIVE* deserving to be laughed at

laughing stock *NOUN* **laughing stocks** a person or thing that is the object of ridicule and scorn

laughter *NOUN* the act, sound, or manner of laughing

launch[1] *VERB* **launches, launching, launched** **1** send a ship from the land into the water **2** send a rocket etc. into space **3** set a thing moving by throwing or pushing it **4** make a new product available for the first time • *Our new model will be launched in April.* **5** start into action • *launch an attack*

launch[2] *NOUN* **launches** a large motor boat

launderette *NOUN* **launderettes** a place fitted with washing machines that people pay to use

laundry *NOUN* **laundries** **1** a place where clothes etc. are washed and ironed for customers **2** clothes etc. needing to be washed or after being washed

laureate (lorri- at) *ADJECTIVE*
Poet Laureate a person appointed to write poems for national occasions

laurel *NOUN* **laurels** an evergreen shrub with smooth shiny leaves

lava *NOUN* molten rock that flows from a volcano; the solid rock formed when it cools

lavatory *NOUN* **lavatories** **1** a toilet **2** a room containing a toilet

lavender *NOUN* **1** a shrub with sweet-smelling purple flowers **2** a light-purple colour

lavish *ADJECTIVE* **1** generous **2** plentiful
▷ **lavishly** *ADVERB* **lavishness** *NOUN*

law *NOUN* **laws** **1** a rule or set of rules that everyone must obey **2** the profession of lawyers **3** (*informal*) the police **4** a scientific statement of something that always happens • *the law of gravity*

Thesaurus

latter *ADJECTIVE* *There are more games in the latter part of the month.* ▶ later, closing, concluding, last, recent, second AN OPPOSITE IS former

laugh *VERB* *Joe's antics began to make them laugh.* ▶ giggle, chuckle, chortle, snigger, titter, guffaw, (*more informal*) scream with laughter
laugh at *I didn't say anything in case the others laughed at me.* ▶ mock, ridicule, make fun of, scoff at, deride, jeer

laugh *NOUN* **1** *She gave a loud laugh.* ▶ chuckle, chortle, snigger, titter, guffaw **2** *Being with Henry was always a laugh.* ▶ joke, piece of fun, adventure, (*more informal*) scream

laughable *ADJECTIVE* **1** *The money they were offering was laughable.* ▶ absurd, ridiculous, ludicrous, preposterous, risible, derisory **2** *laughable attempts to steer the boat* ▶ funny, comic, comical, amusing, hilarious, farcical

laughter *NOUN* *sounds of conversation and laughter from the next room* ▶ laughing, mirth, laughs, chuckling, sniggering, hilarity, tittering, giggling, guffaws, merriment, (*more informal*) hysterics

launch *VERB* **1** *In its heyday the dockyard launched a ship every year.* ▶ float, set afloat, put in the water **2** *It was decided to launch the shuttle from a different site.* ▶ fire, propel, send off, blast off, set off **3** *The enemy launched a counter-offensive. A new business will be launched next year.* ▶ begin, start, initiate, open, set up, embark on, establish, found, inaugurate

lavatory *NOUN* *There's another lavatory downstairs.* ▶ toilet, cloakroom, convenience, (*more informal*) loo, (*old-fashioned*) WC

lavish *ADJECTIVE* *After the show there will be a lavish supper.* ▶ sumptuous, elaborate, copious, extravagant, luxurious, generous, liberal, abundant, plentiful, bountiful, munificent, opulent, unstinting AN OPPOSITE IS meagre

law *NOUN* **1** *a new law closing tax loopholes* ▶ regulation, statute, act, bill, ruling, rule, enactment, edict USAGE Note that a *bill* is a government's proposal for a law, and an *act* is the bill after it has been passed and received the royal assent. RELATED ADJECTIVE legal, judicial **2** *the laws of logic* ▶ rule, principle, precept,

a b c d e f g h i j k l m n o p q r s t u v w x y z

law-abiding *ADJECTIVE* obeying the law

lawcourt *NOUN* **lawcourts** a room or building in which a judge or magistrate hears evidence and decides whether someone has broken the law

lawful *ADJECTIVE* allowed or accepted by the law
▷ **lawfully** *ADVERB*

lawless *ADJECTIVE* **1** not obeying the law **2** without proper laws • *a lawless country*
▷ **lawlessly** *ADVERB* **lawlessness** *NOUN*

lawn *NOUN* **lawns** an area of closely cut grass in a garden or park

lawnmower *NOUN* **lawnmowers** a machine for cutting the grass of lawns

lawn tennis *NOUN* tennis played on an outdoor grass or hard court

lawsuit *NOUN* **lawsuits** a dispute or claim that is brought to a lawcourt to be settled

lawyer *NOUN* **lawyers** a person who is qualified to give advice in matters of law

laxative *NOUN* **laxatives** a medicine that stimulates the bowels to empty

lay[1] *VERB* **lays, laying, laid 1** put something down in a particular place or way **2** arrange things, especially for a meal • *Can you lay the table?* **3** place • *He laid the blame on his sister.* **4** form or prepare • *We laid our plans.* **5** produce an egg
lay off 1 stop employing somebody for a while **2** (*informal*) stop doing something
lay on supply or provide
lay out 1 arrange or prepare **2** (*informal*) knock a person unconscious **3** prepare a dead body for burial
USAGE Do not confuse **lay/laid/laying** = 'put down', with **lie/lay/lain/lying** = 'be in a flat position'. Correct uses are as follows: • *Go and lie down.* • *she went and lay down* • *please lay it on the floor.* 'Go and lay down' is incorrect.

lay[2] *past tense of* **lie**[2]

lay[3] *ADJECTIVE* **1** not belonging to the clergy • *a lay preacher* **2** not professionally qualified • *a lay magistrate*

lay-by *NOUN* **lay-bys** a place where vehicles can stop beside a main road

Thesaurus

prescription, guideline, tenet, maxim, doctrine **3** (*informal*) *on the run from the law* ► police, authorities

law-abiding *ADJECTIVE* *law-abiding citizens* ► well-behaved, respectable, honest, decent, orderly, peaceable, peaceful, compliant, disciplined, good, obedient OPPOSITES ARE lawless, criminal

lawful *ADJECTIVE* **1** *The police were making a lawful arrest.* ► legal, legitimate, permissible, permitted, allowable, allowed, just, right **2** *people going about their lawful business* ► legitimate, rightful, proper, valid, recognized, authorized, regular, legal, documented, prescribed AN OPPOSITE IS illegal

lawless *ADJECTIVE* *a lawless rabble* ► disorderly, unruly, riotous, mutinous, wild, rowdy, rebellious, disruptive, undisciplined, seditious, reckless, anarchic, anarchical, chaotic AN OPPOSITE IS law-abiding

lawyer *NOUN* *This is a matter for the lawyers.* ► solicitor, legal practitioner, legal adviser, barrister, QC, advocate, attorney USAGE A *barrister* is a lawyer who presents a case in a lawcourt, and an *advocate* is a name for a barrister in Scotland. A *QC* (= Queen's Counsel) is a specially appointed senior barrister. *Attorney* has special meanings in the USA.

lax *ADJECTIVE* *lax discipline in schools* ► slack, slipshod, casual, easy-going, lenient, permissive, careless, loose, neglectful, negligent, remiss, vague AN OPPOSITE IS strict

lay *VERB* **1** *He laid the map on the seat beside him.* ► put, place, set, set down, spread, deposit, leave **2** *We began to lay plans for a spring holiday.* ► form, make, devise, prepare, work out, hatch, concoct **3** *Be careful where you lay the blame for this.* ► assign, attach, attribute, ascribe, allot, apportion, fix, impute **4** *The landlady laid a table for breakfast.* ► arrange, set out, organize
lay in *The men laid in a supply of beer.* ► stock up with, put aside, put by, collect, store
lay into (*informal*) *His father laid into him when he got home.* ► scold, rebuke, berate, castigate, criticize, censure
lay off 1 (*informal*) *You really should lay off smoking.* ► give up, stop, cut out **2** *Over a hundred staff were laid off just before Christmas.* ► make redundant, dismiss, discharge, release, (*more informal*) sack
lay on *His mother laid on a marvellous tea.* ► provide, supply, furnish, give
lay out 1 *Richard laid out the plans on the table.* ► arrange, set out, spread, display **2** (*informal*) *The blow laid him out for an hour.* ► knock out, make unconscious, flatten

layabout *NOUN* *It's odd for such a lively lad to have a layabout for a brother.* ► idler, loafer, good-for-nothing, sluggard, (*more informal*) slob, (*more informal*) couch potato OPPOSITES ARE hard worker, beaver

layer *NOUN* **layers** a single thickness or coating

layman *NOUN* **laymen 1** a person who does not have specialized knowledge or training (e.g. as a doctor or lawyer) **2** a person who is not ordained as a member of the clergy

layout *NOUN* **layouts** an arrangement of parts of something according to a plan

lazy *ADJECTIVE* **lazier, laziest** not wanting to work; doing little work
▷ **lazily** *ADVERB* **laziness** *NOUN*

lead[1] (leed) *VERB* **leads, leading, led 1** take or guide someone, especially by going in front **2** be winning in a race or contest etc.; be ahead **3** be in charge of a group of people **4** be a way or route • *This path leads to the beach.* **5** play the first card in a card game **6** live or experience • *He leads a dull life.*
lead to result in; cause

lead (leed) *NOUN* **leads 1** a leading place or part or position • *She took the lead on the final bend.* **2** guidance or example • *We should be taking a lead on this issue.* **3** a clue to be followed **4** a strap or cord for leading a dog or other animal **5** an electrical wire attached to something

lead[2] (led) *NOUN* **leads 1** a soft heavy grey metal **2** the writing substance (graphite) in a pencil
▷ **lead** *ADJECTIVE*

leader *NOUN* **leaders 1** the person in charge of a group of people; a chief **2** the person who is winning **3** a newspaper article giving the editor's opinion
▷ **leadership** *NOUN*

leaf *NOUN* **leaves 1** a flat, usually green, part of a plant, growing out from its stem, branch, or root **2** the paper forming one page of a book **3** a very thin sheet of metal • *gold leaf* **4** a flap that makes a table larger
▷ **leafy** *ADJECTIVE* **leafless** *ADJECTIVE*
turn over a new leaf make a fresh start and improve your behaviour

leaflet *NOUN* **leaflets** a piece of paper printed with information

league[1] *NOUN* **leagues 1** a group of teams who compete against each other for a championship **2** a group of people or nations who agree to work together
in league with working or plotting together

league[2] *NOUN* **leagues** an old measure of distance, about 3 miles

Thesaurus

layer *NOUN* **1** *an extra layer of paint* ► coating, coat, covering, surface, film, sheet, skin, thickness **2** *a layer of rock* ► seam, stratum, substratum

layout *NOUN* *The layout of the house takes some getting used to.* ► arrangement, organization, design, plan, disposition, (*more informal*) set-up

laze *VERB* *Young girls lazed in the sun.* ► relax, idle, loaf, lounge, loll AN OPPOSITE IS work

laziness *NOUN* *His report mentioned lateness and laziness.* ► idleness, indolence, slothfulness, sloth, lethargy, loafing, lounging about, dilatoriness, inactivity, slowness, sluggishness AN OPPOSITE IS industry

lazy *ADJECTIVE* **1** *No one can accuse them of being lazy after all they've achieved.* ► idle, indolent, slothful, work-shy, inactive, lethargic, slack AN OPPOSITE IS industrious **2** *They headed for a lazy weekend in the country.* ► quiet, relaxing, peaceful

lead *NOUN* **1** *The older students provide a lead for the younger ones.* ► example, guidance, leadership, direction **2** *Detectives are following an important new lead.* ► clue, hint, tip, tip-off, line of inquiry **3** *One of the Ferrari team took the lead.* ► first place, front position, spearhead, vanguard **4** *She will play the lead in his new film.* ► principal role, chief part, starring role, title role **5** *The toaster needs a new lead.* ► cable, flex, wire **6** *He let the dog off the lead.* ► leash, tether, rein, chain, strap, cord

lead *VERB* **1** *She led her guests out on the terrace.* ► conduct, guide, show, escort, usher, marshal, shepherd, steer, pilot AN OPPOSITE IS follow **2** *Smith was appointed to lead the delegation.* ► head, be in charge of, be the leader of, preside over, direct, manage, command, govern, supervise, rule **3** *The Oxford boat was leading for most of the distance.* ► be in front, be in the lead, head the field AN OPPOSITE IS trail **4** *They have led a very happy life.* ► pass, spend, have, experience, undergo
lead to *Asking awkward questions might lead to trouble.* ► cause, bring about, result in, give rise to, produce, generate, create, precipitate, induce, stimulate
lead on *She was accused of leading them on.* ► mislead, deceive, entice, beguile, hoodwink, string along

leader *NOUN* **1** *the leader of the marketing team* ► head, chief, director, manager, principal, superior, (*more informal*) boss **2** *one of the country's former leaders* ► ruler, chief, governor

leading *ADJECTIVE* *The book is acknowledged as the leading authority on the subject.* ► principal, foremost, chief, major, key, main, primary, pre-eminent, outstanding, dominant, important, inspiring, prominent, well known

league *NOUN* **1** *The countries came together to form a league.* ► association, alliance, federation, confederation, confederacy, syndicate **2** *On Saturday they face the league leaders.* ► group, class, championship

leak *NOUN* **leaks 1** a hole or crack etc. through which liquid or gas accidentally escapes **2** the revealing of secret information
▷ **leaky** *ADJECTIVE*

leak *VERB* **leaks, leaking, leaked 1** get out or let out through a leak **2** reveal secret information
▷ **leakage** *NOUN*

lean[1] *ADJECTIVE* **1** with little or no fat • *lean meat* **2** thin • *a lean body*

lean[2] *VERB* **leans, leaning, leaned** *or* **leant 1** bend your body towards or over something **2** put or be in a sloping position **3** rest against something **4** rely or depend on someone for help

leaning *NOUN* **leanings** a tendency or preference

leap *VERB* **leaps, leaping, leaped** *or* **leapt** jump vigorously
▷ **leap** *NOUN*

leapfrog *NOUN* a game in which each player jumps with legs apart over another who is bending down

leap year *NOUN* **leap years** a year with an extra day in it (29 February)

learn *VERB* **learns, learning, learned** *or* **learnt 1** get knowledge or skill through study or training **2** find out about something

USAGE It is not acceptable in standard English to use **learn** to mean 'to teach'.

learned (ler- nid) *ADJECTIVE* having much knowledge obtained by study

learner *NOUN* **learners** a person who is learning something, especially to drive a car

learning *NOUN* knowledge obtained by study

lease *NOUN* **leases** an agreement to allow someone to use a building or land etc. for a fixed period in return for payment
▷ **leaseholder** *NOUN*
a new lease of life a chance to be healthy, active, or usable again

lease *VERB* **leases, leasing, leased** allow or obtain the use of something by lease

leash *NOUN* **leashes** a dog's lead

least *ADJECTIVE*, *ADVERB* very small in amount etc. • *the least bit*; • *the least expensive bike*
at least 1 not less than what is mentioned • *It will cost at least £40.* **2** anyway • *He's at home, or at least I think he is.*

leather *NOUN* material made from animal skins
▷ **leathery** *ADJECTIVE*

leave *VERB* **leaves, leaving, left 1** go away from a person or place **2** stop belonging to a group or stop working somewhere **3** cause or allow something to stay where it is or as it is • *You left*

Thesaurus

leak *VERB* **1** *Oil was leaking from the tank.* ► seep, escape, ooze, spill, trickle, drip, exude **2** *We still haven't discovered who leaked the information.* ► reveal, disclose, divulge, pass on, give away, let out, make known

leak *NOUN* **1** *several leaks in the roof* ► hole, opening, crack, drip, perforation, puncture **2** *a gas leak* ► escape, seepage, discharge **3** *a leak of information* ► disclosure, divulgence, revelation

leaky *ADJECTIVE* *a leaky roof* ► leaking, dripping, cracked, holed, perforated, punctured
AN OPPOSITE IS watertight

lean *ADJECTIVE* **1** *a tall lean figure* ► thin, spare, skinny, slender, slim, gaunt, lanky, wiry, bony, emaciated AN OPPOSITE IS fat **2** *a lean harvest* ► meagre, scanty, sparse, poor, mean, barren, inadequate

lean *VERB* **1** *The trees were leaning in the wind.* ► slant, incline, bend, tilt, tip, bank, heel over, list, loll, slope **2** *Mary leaned against the fence.* ► rest, support yourself, prop yourself up, recline
lean towards *We lean towards a peaceful solution.* ► favour, prefer, tend towards, incline towards

leap *VERB* **1** *The dog leapt over the gate.* ► jump, spring, vault, bound **2** *Claire leapt to her feet* ► spring, jump **3** *Prices have leapt in the last few months.* ► soar, rise, rocket, surge, increase
OPPOSITES ARE tumble, plummet, fall
leap at *He leapt at the opportunity.* ► seize, grasp, accept eagerly, (*more informal*) go for
OPPOSITES ARE turn down, reject

learn *VERB* **1** *It is important to learn the language when living in a foreign country.* ► master, acquire a knowledge of, acquire, understand, assimilate, pick up **2** *If I want to learn a poem I stick it on the fridge.* ► memorize, learn by heart, know

learned *ADJECTIVE* *a learned piece of writing* ► scholarly, erudite, intellectual, academic, cultured, educated, highbrow

learner *NOUN* *At this stage he is just a learner.* ► beginner, novice, apprentice, pupil, starter, newcomer, cadet, trainee, tiro

learning *NOUN* *a person of great learning* ► scholarship, erudition, knowledge, culture, education, schooling, wisdom, information

least *ADJECTIVE* **1** *I haven't the least idea what he means.* ► slightest, smallest, tiniest
AN OPPOSITE IS greatest **2** *Choose a place that involves the least travel.* ► minimum, minimal, smallest amount of OPPOSITES ARE maximum, most

leave *VERB* **1** *It is time to leave now.* ► depart, set off, go, go away, go out, take your leave, withdraw, retire, say goodbye, (*more informal*) disappear AN OPPOSITE IS arrive **2** *She left the*

the door open. **4** go away without taking something • *I left my book at home.* **5** let someone deal with something • *Leave the washing-up to me* **6** put something to be collected or passed on • *Would you like to leave a message?*
leave off cease
leave out omit; not include

leave *NOUN* **1** permission **2** official permission to be away from work; the time for which this permission lasts • *three days' leave* [from Old English]

lecture *NOUN* **lectures 1** a talk about a subject to an audience or a class **2** a long serious warning or reprimand given to someone

lecture *VERB* **lectures, lecturing, lectured** give a lecture
▷ **lecturer** *NOUN*
[from Latin *lectura* = reading, or something to be read]

led *past tense of* **lead**[1]

ledge *NOUN* **ledges** a narrow shelf • *a window ledge* • *a mountain ledge*

ledger *NOUN* **ledgers** an account book [probably from Dutch]

leech *NOUN* **leeches** a small blood-sucking worm that lives in water

leek *NOUN* **leeks** a long green and white vegetable of the onion family

leer *VERB* **leers, leering, leered** look at someone in a sly or unpleasant way
▷ **leer** *NOUN*

leeway *NOUN* **1** extra space or time available **2** a drift to leeward or off course
make up leeway make up lost time; regain a lost position

left[1] *ADJECTIVE, ADVERB* **1** on or towards the west if you think of yourself as facing north **2** (said about political groups) in favour of socialist or radical views
▷ **left-hand** *ADJECTIVE*

left *NOUN* the left-hand side or part etc. [from Old English *lyft* = weak]

left[2] *past tense of* **leave**

left-handed *ADJECTIVE* using the left hand in preference to the right hand

leg *NOUN* **legs 1** one of the limbs on a person's or animal's body, on which it stands or moves **2** the part of a piece of clothing covering a leg **3** each of the supports of a chair or other piece of furniture **4** one part of a journey **5** one of a pair of matches between the same teams [from Old Norse]

legacy *NOUN* **legacies 1** something left to a person in a will **2** something that results from what people have done in the past • *a legacy of distrust*

legal *ADJECTIVE* **1** lawful **2** to do with the law or lawyers
▷ **legally** *ADVERB* **legality** *NOUN*

legend *NOUN* **legends 1** an old story handed down from the past, which may or may not be true COMPARE **myth 2** a very famous person
▷ **legendary** *ADJECTIVE*
[from Latin *legenda* = things to be read]

legible *ADJECTIVE* clear enough to read
▷ **legibly** *ADVERB* **legibility** *NOUN*
[from Latin *legere* = to read]

Thesaurus

house that afternoon. ► depart from, quit, vacate **3** *His wife has left him.* ► desert, abandon, forsake **4** *He's going to leave his job at the end of the month.* ► quit, give up, resign from, relinquish **5** *I've left my case on the train.* ► lose, mislay, leave behind **6** *Leave it to me to sort out.* ► entrust, refer, hand over, consign **7** *When he died he left them the house.* ► bequeath, will, endow

leave *NOUN* **1** *The judge granted him leave to appeal against the verdict.* ► permission, consent, authorization, approval, liberty **2** *Greg was having some leave from the army.* ► free time, time off, holiday, absence, sabbatical, vacation

lecture *NOUN* **1** *a lecture on modern poetry* ► talk, discourse, speech, address, lesson **2** *He got a stern lecture about being late.* ► reprimand, scolding, rebuke, harangue

lecture *VERB* **1** *Anna lectures at the university.* ► teach, give lectures, give lessons, take students **2** *Professor Jones will lecture on advances in genetics.* ► give a lecture, speak, talk, discourse, (*more informal*) hold forth **3** *She lectured us on our bad manners.* ► reprimand, scold, rebuke, admonish, chide

leg *NOUN* **1** *the first leg of the journey* ► stage, part, phase, stretch, lap, step **2** *a table leg* ► support, upright, prop

legal *ADJECTIVE* **1** *legal advice* ► judicial, judiciary **2** *activity that is not legal* ► lawful, legitimate, licit, permissible, authorized, permitted, above board, allowable, allowed, rightful, proper, constitutional, valid AN OPPOSITE IS illegal

legend *NOUN* *legends from the past* ► myth, story, folk tale, fable, tradition

legible *ADJECTIVE* *The writing was barely legible.* ► readable, clear, decipherable, intelligible, distinct, neat, plain AN OPPOSITE IS illegible

a b c d e f g h i j k l m n o p q r s t u v w x y z

A B C D E F G H I J K L M N O P Q R S T U V W X Y Z

legion *NOUN* **legions 1** a division of the ancient Roman army **2** a group of soldiers or former soldiers

legislate *VERB* **legislates, legislating, legislated** make laws
▷ **legislation** *NOUN* **legislator** *NOUN*

legitimate *ADJECTIVE* **1** lawful **2** born when parents are married to each other
▷ **legitimately** *ADVERB* **legitimacy** *NOUN*

leisure *NOUN* time that is free from work, when you can do what you like
▷ **leisured** *ADJECTIVE* **leisurely** *ADJECTIVE*
at leisure having leisure; not hurried
at your leisure when you have time

lemming *NOUN* **lemmings** a small mouse-like animal of Arctic regions that migrates in large numbers and is said to run headlong into the sea and drown

lemon *NOUN* **lemons 1** an oval yellow citrus fruit with a sour taste **2** a pale yellow colour

lemonade *NOUN* a lemon-flavoured drink

lemur (lee-mer) *NOUN* **lemurs** a monkey-like animal

lend *VERB* **lends, lending, lent 1** allow a person to use something of yours for a short time **2** provide someone with money that they must repay, usually in return for payments (called **interest**) **3** give or add a quality • *She lent dignity to the occasion.*
▷ **lender** *NOUN*
lend a hand help somebody
USAGE Do not use **lend** to mean **borrow**.

length *NOUN* **lengths 1** how long something is **2** a piece of cloth, rope, wire, etc. cut from a larger piece **3** the distance of a swimming pool from one end to the other **4** the amount of thoroughness in an action • *They went to great lengths to make us comfortable.*
at length 1 after a long time **2** taking a long time; in detail

lengthen *VERB* **lengthens, lengthening, lengthened** make or become longer

lengthy *ADJECTIVE* going on for a long time
▷ **lengthily** *ADVERB*

lenient (lee-nee-ent) *ADJECTIVE* merciful; not severe
▷ **leniently** *ADVERB* **lenience** *NOUN*

lens *NOUN* **lenses 1** a curved piece of glass or plastic used to focus things **2** the transparent part of the eye, immediately behind the pupil [Latin, = lentil (because of its shape)]

Lent *NOUN* a time of fasting and penitence observed by Christians for about six weeks before Easter
▷ **Lenten** *ADJECTIVE*
[from Old English *lencten* = the spring]

lent *past tense of* **lend**

lentil *NOUN* **lentils** a kind of small bean

leopard (lep-erd) *NOUN* **leopards** a large spotted mammal of the cat family, also called a panther
▷ **leopardess** *NOUN*

leper *NOUN* **lepers** a person who has leprosy

leprosy *NOUN* an infectious disease that makes parts of the body waste away
▷ **leprous** *ADJECTIVE*

lesbian *NOUN* **lesbians** a homosexual woman [named after the Greek island of Lesbos (because Sappho, a poetess who lived there about 600 BC, wrote poetry about love between women)]

Thesaurus

legitimate *ADJECTIVE* **1** *They have legitimate reasons for the action they took.* ► valid, sound, cogent, admissible, well-founded, acceptable, justifiable **2** *The Duke lacked a legitimate heir.* ► lawful, legal, rightful, acknowledged, true, proper

leisure *NOUN* **1** *They lead a life of leisure.* ► ease, relaxation, enjoyment, inactivity, pleasure, amusement, recreation, retirement **2** *She never had enough leisure to do the things she wanted.* ► free time, spare time, time off, freedom, liberty, rest

leisurely *ADJECTIVE* *a leisurely stroll through the park* ► slow, gentle, unhurried, relaxed, relaxing, restful, sedate, comfortable, easy, lingering, peaceful OPPOSITES ARE brisk, hurried

lend *VERB* *He asked me to lend him the money.* ► loan, advance, let someone have
an opposite is borrow

length *NOUN* **1** *The snakes grew to a length of twenty feet or more.* ► extent, measurement, stretch, distance **2** *People began to grumble about the length of the wait.* ► duration, extent, protractedness, period, time

lengthen *VERB* **1** *The days begin to lengthen in March.* ► grow longer, get longer, draw out, stretch, enlarge, elongate, expand, extend, increase, prolong, pull out AN OPPOSITE IS shorten **2** *You will need to lengthen the cooking time.* ► extend, increase, prolong, continue
AN OPPOSITE IS shorten

lengthy *ADJECTIVE* *The family faced a lengthy journey.* ► long, protracted, drawn out, tedious, extended OPPOSITES ARE short, brief

lenient *ADJECTIVE* *He always said his mother had been too lenient with him.* ► soft, easy-going, tolerant, soft-hearted, indulgent, merciful, forgiving, mild, kind OPPOSITES ARE strict, severe

less *ADJECTIVE, ADVERB* smaller in amount; not so much • *Make less noise.* • *It is less important.* USAGE Do not use **less** when you mean **fewer**. You should use **fewer** when you are talking about a number of individual things, and **less** when you are talking about a quantity or mass of something: • *The less batter you make, the fewer pancakes you'll get.*

less *NOUN* a smaller amount

less *PREPOSITION* minus; deducting • *She earned £100, less tax.*

-less *SUFFIX* forms adjectives meaning 'without' (e.g. *colourless*) or 'unable to be ...' (e.g. *countless*)

lesser *ADJECTIVE* not so great as the other • *the lesser evil*

lesson *NOUN* **lessons** **1** an amount of teaching given at one time **2** something to be learnt by a pupil **3** an example or experience from which you should learn • *Let this be a lesson to you!* **4** a passage from the Bible read aloud as part of a church service

lest *CONJUNCTION* (*old use*) so that something should not happen • *Remind us, lest we forget.*

let *VERB* **lets, letting, let** **1** allow somebody or something to do something; not prevent or forbid • *Let me see it.* **2** cause to • *Let us know what happens.* **3** allow or cause to come or go or pass • *Let me out!* **4** allow someone to use a house or building etc. in return for payment (**rent**) **5** leave • *Let it alone.*
let down **1** deflate **2** disappoint somebody
let off **1** cause to explode **2** excuse somebody from a duty or punishment etc.
let on (*informal*) reveal a secret
let up (*informal*) relax

lethal (lee- thal) *ADJECTIVE* deadly; causing death
▷ **lethally** *ADVERB*

lethargy (leth- er- jee) *NOUN* extreme lack of energy or vitality
▷ **lethargic** (lith- ar- jik) *ADJECTIVE*

letter *NOUN* **letters** **1** a symbol representing a sound used in speech **2** a written message, usually sent by post
to the letter paying strict attention to every detail

letter box *NOUN* **letter boxes** **1** a slot in a door, through which letters are delivered **2** a postbox

lettering *NOUN* letters drawn or painted

lettuce *NOUN* **lettuces** a garden plant with broad crisp leaves used in salads

leukaemia (lew- kee- mee- a) *NOUN* a disease in which there are too many white corpuscles in the blood [from Greek *leukos* = white + *haima* = blood]

level *ADJECTIVE* **1** flat or horizontal **2** at the same height or position as something else

level *NOUN* **levels** **1** height, depth, position, or value etc. • *Fix the shelves at eye level.* **2** a level surface **3** a device that shows whether

Thesaurus

lessen *VERB* **1** *He took an aspirin to lessen the pain.* ► reduce, lower, decrease, deaden, alleviate, assuage, mitigate, make less, minimize, tone down **2** *Her love for him would never lessen.* ► diminish, decrease, abate, fade, dwindle, weaken, grow less, recede, shrink AN OPPOSITE IS increase

lesson *NOUN* **1** *a French lesson* ► class, period, lecture, seminar, tutorial, instruction **2** *The experience might be a lesson to all of them.* ► example, warning, deterrent, moral

let *VERB* **1** *His parents wouldn't let him go on the trip.* ► allow, permit, give permission, authorize, consent to, agree to USAGE If you use *allow, permit,* or *authorize* you have to add *to*, e.g. *His parents wouldn't allow him to go.* If you use *give permission*, you have to say *His parents wouldn't give him permission to go* or *His parents wouldn't give permission for him to go.* If you use *consent* or *agree* you have to say *His parents wouldn't agree or consent to his or him going.* OPPOSITES ARE prevent, forbid **2** *The landlord will let rooms for six months.* ► rent out, lease out, hire out AN OPPOSITE IS intensify
let down *They felt the manager had let them down.* ► fail, disappoint, betray, abandon, desert
let off *They decided to let him off with a warning.* ► pardon, forgive, excuse, spare, release
let up *The rain let up for a while.* ► ease, subside, abate, slacken, diminish

lethal *ADJECTIVE* *execution by lethal injection* ► deadly, fatal, mortal, poisonous

letter *NOUN* **1** *She wrote a letter to her MP.* ► message, note, communication, dispatch, missive, (*more formal*) epistle RELATED ADJECTIVE epistolary **2** *The wall was daubed with large letters.* ► character, figure, sign, symbol, device

level *ADJECTIVE* **1** *Make sure the surface is level before spreading the paper on it.* ► flat, even, smooth, uniform, flush, regular, horizontal, plane AN OPPOSITE IS uneven **2** *The scores were level at half time.* ► equal, even, matching, balanced, the same, (*more informal*) neck-and-neck

level *NOUN* **1** *Soon she was promoted to a senior level.* ► rank, status, position, class, echelon **2** *There is a high level of absenteeism.* ► amount, quantity, extent, degree, proportion **3** *The water rose to a dangerous level.* ► height, elevation, altitude **4** *There are offices on this level of the building.* ► floor, storey, tier

level *VERB* **1** *He piled on the earth, levelling it with his hands.* ► smooth, even out, flatten, rake

something is level
on the level (*informal*) honest

level *VERB* **levels, levelling, levelled 1** make or become level **2** aim a gun or missile **3** direct an accusation at a person

level crossing *NOUN* **level crossings** a place where a road crosses a railway at the same level

lever *NOUN* **levers 1** a bar that turns on a fixed point (the **fulcrum**) in order to lift something or force something open **2** a bar used as a handle to operate machinery etc. • *a gear lever*

lever *VERB* **levers, levering, levered** lift or move something by means of a lever

leverage *NOUN* **1** the force you need when you use a lever **2** influence

levity *NOUN* being humorous, especially at an unsuitable time

levy *VERB* **levies, levying, levied** impose or collect a tax or other payment by the use of authority or force

levy *NOUN* **levies** an amount of money paid in tax

liability *NOUN* **liabilities 1** being legally responsible for something **2** a debt or obligation **3** a disadvantage or handicap

liable *ADJECTIVE* **1** likely to do or suffer something • *She is liable to colds.* • *The cliff is liable to crumble.* **2** legally responsible for something

liaison (lee-ay-zon) *NOUN* **liaisons** **1** communication and cooperation between people or groups **2** a person who is a link or go-between **3** a sexual affair

liar *NOUN* **liars** a person who tells lies

libel (ly-bel) *NOUN* **libels** an untrue written, printed, or broadcast statement that damages a person's reputation COMPARE **slander**
▷ **libellous** *ADJECTIVE*

libel *VERB* **libels, libelling, libelled** make a libel against someone

liberal *ADJECTIVE* **1** giving generously **2** given in large amounts **3** not strict; tolerant
▷ **liberally** *ADVERB* **liberality** *NOUN*

Liberal Democrat *NOUN* **Liberal Democrats** a member of the Liberal Democrat political party

liberate *VERB* **liberates, liberating, liberated** set free
▷ **liberation** *NOUN* **liberator** *NOUN*

liberty *NOUN* **liberties** freedom
take liberties behave too casually or in too familiar a way

Thesaurus

2 *A series of violent tremors levelled the area.* ► raze, demolish, destroy, devastate, knock down, lay low **3** *His hand was shaking, making it difficult to level the gun.* ► aim, point, direct, train

level-headed *ADJECTIVE* *Belinda was too level-headed to fool herself in this way.* ► sensible, balanced, practical, prudent, realistic, self-possessed, commonsensical, judicious

lever *NOUN* *You push the lever down and leave it there.* ► switch, handle, knob, bar

lever *VERB* *He picked up a crowbar and levered open the window.* ► prise, force, wrench, heave

liability *NOUN* **1** *The driver of the other car admitted liability for the accident.* ► responsibility, blame, culpability, accountability **2** *Taking the dog with us could prove a liability.* ► nuisance, inconvenience, encumbrance, hindrance, burden, handicap, drawback, (*more informal*) drag

liable *ADJECTIVE* **1** *The company is not liable for any damage that might be caused.* ► responsible, accountable, answerable, to blame AN OPPOSITE IS exempt (from) **2** *The shaft is liable to break under pressure.* ► likely, apt, prone, inclined, given (to breaking), disposed, predisposed, ready AN OPPOSITE IS unlikely

liar *NOUN* *Parkin was either a coward or a liar, or both.* ► deceiver, fabricator, falsifier, (*more informal*) storyteller, (*more informal*) fibber

libel *NOUN* *He said the newspaper article amounted to libel.* ► defamation of character, misrepresentation, an insult, a slur, a smear USAGE You can also use *slander* when the insult is spoken rather than printed.

libellous *ADJECTIVE* *Lawyers check whether there is anything libellous in the writing.* ► defamatory, derogatory, false, insulting USAGE You can also use *slanderous* when the insult is spoken rather than printed.

liberal *ADJECTIVE* **1** *a liberal supply of liquid refreshment* ► copious, generous, plentiful, lavish, abundant, ample, bounteous, bountiful, munificent, unstinting AN OPPOSITE IS mean **2** *liberal social attitudes* ► broad-minded, tolerant, enlightened, moderate, easy-going, magnanimous, lenient, unbiased, unprejudiced, permissive, free AN OPPOSITE IS narrow-minded **3** *liberal political views* ► progressive, radical, forward-looking AN OPPOSITE IS conservative

liberate *VERB* *the intention to liberate all people from every kind of slavery* ► free, set free, release, discharge, deliver, rescue, save, emancipate, unfetter, loose, ransom, untie OPPOSITES ARE enslave, subjugate

liberty *NOUN* *You can enjoy the liberty to follow your own interests.* ► freedom, independence, emancipation, liberation, release
at liberty 1 *The escaped prisoners were at liberty for three months.* ► free, on the run, on the

librarian *NOUN* **librarians** a person in charge of or working in a library
▷ **librarianship** *NOUN*

library (ly- bra- ree) *NOUN* **libraries** **1** a place where books are kept for people to use or borrow **2** a collection of books, records, films, etc.

lice *plural of* **louse**

licence *NOUN* **licences** **1** an official permit to do or use or own something • *a driving licence* **2** special freedom to avoid the usual rules or customs

license *VERB* **licenses, licensing, licensed** give a licence to a person; authorize • *We are licensed to sell tobacco.*

lichen (ly- ken, lich- en) *NOUN* **lichens** a dry-looking plant that grows on rocks, walls, trees, etc.

lick *VERB* **licks, licking, licked** **1** move your tongue over something **2** (said about a wave or flame) move like a tongue; touch lightly **3** (*slang*) defeat
a lick of paint a light covering of paint
at a lick (*informal*) at a fast pace

lid *NOUN* **lids** **1** a cover for a box or pot etc. **2** an eyelid

lie[1] *NOUN* **lies** a statement that the person who makes it knows to be untrue

lie *VERB* **lies, lying, lied** tell a lie or lies; be deceptive

lie[2] *VERB* **lies, lying, lay, lain** **1** be or get in a flat or resting position • *He lay on the grass.* • *The cat has lain here all night.* **2** be or remain • *The island lies near the coast.* • *The machinery lay idle.*
lie low keep yourself hidden
USAGE See the note at **lay**[1].

lieutenant (lef- ten- ant) *NOUN* **lieutenants** **1** an officer in the army or navy **2** a deputy or chief assistant

life *NOUN* **lives** **1** the period between birth and death **2** being alive and able to function and grow **3** living things • *Is there life on Mars?* **4** liveliness • *full of life* **5** a biography **6** the length of time that something exists or functions • *The battery has a life of two years.*

lifebelt *NOUN* **lifebelts** a ring of material that will float, used to support someone's body in water

lifeboat *NOUN* **lifeboats** a boat for rescuing people at sea

life cycle *NOUN* **life cycles** the series of changes in the life of a living thing

lifeguard *NOUN* **lifeguards** someone whose job is to rescue swimmers who are in difficulty

life insurance *NOUN* insurance that pays out a sum of money when the insured person dies

life jacket *NOUN* **life jackets** a jacket of material that will float, used to support someone's body in water

lifeless *ADJECTIVE* **1** without life **2** unconscious
▷ **lifelessly** *ADVERB*

lifelike *ADJECTIVE* looking exactly like a real person or thing

lifestyle *NOUN* **lifestyles** the way of life of a person or a group of people

Thesaurus

loose **2** *She is at liberty to use her money as she wishes.* ► free, entitled, permitted, allowed, authorized AN OPPOSITE IS forbidden

licence *NOUN* **1** *I needed a licence to play music in my shop.* ► permit, certificate, document, authorization, warrant **2** *the licence to act as you see fit* ► authority, authorization, permission, entitlement, prerogative, privilege

lick *VERB* **1** *Tessa was licking a lollipop.* ► suck, taste **2** (*more informal*) *They licked the visiting side 4–0.* ► beat, defeat, overcome, trounce, rout, thrash **3** *By now the flames were licking the ceiling.* ► touch, reach, brush, flicker round, dance round

lid *NOUN* *The lid was stuck to the jar.* ► top, cap, stopper, cover, covering

lie *NOUN* *He can't help telling lies.* ► untruth, falsehood, falsification, fabrication, deception, invention, falsity, deceit, fiction, (*more informal*) fib OPPOSITES ARE truth, fact

lie *VERB* **1** *He lied about where he'd been.* ► tell an untruth, invent a story, dissemble, (*more informal*) fib **2** *She was lying on the bed.* ► recline, stretch out, rest, lounge, sprawl **3** *The town lies twenty miles from the coast.* ► be situated, be located, be placed, be found, be sited

life *NOUN* **1** *the joy of giving life* ► existence, breath, being **2** *Their dog still looked full of life.* ► vitality, energy, liveliness, vigour, verve, spirit, vivacity, zest, activity, (*more informal*) go **3** *He's reading a life of John Lennon.* ► biography, autobiography, life story **4** *The contract covers the life of the project.* ► duration, course, span, extent

lifeless *ADJECTIVE* **1** *The lifeless body fell into the grave.* ► dead, deceased, inanimate, defunct, comatose, inert AN OPPOSITE IS living **2** *a lifeless desert* ► barren, arid, bare, sterile AN OPPOSITE IS fertile **3** *The voice was dull and lifeless.* ► lacklustre, lethargic, unexciting, apathetic, tedious, boring, flat, slow AN OPPOSITE IS animated

lifelike *ADJECTIVE* *The new portrait was unusually lifelike.* ► realistic, true to life, authentic, natural, graphic, convincing, photographic AN OPPOSITE IS unrealistic

lifetime *NOUN* **lifetimes** the time for which someone is alive

lift *VERB* **lifts, lifting, lifted 1** raise or pick up something **2** rise or go upwards **3** remove or abolish something • *The ban has been lifted.* **4** (*informal*) steal

lift *NOUN* **lifts 1** lifting **2** a device for taking people or goods from one floor or level to another in a building **3** a free ride in somebody else's vehicle • *Can you give me a lift to the station?* [from Old Norse]

ligament *NOUN* **ligaments** a piece of the tough flexible tissue that holds your bones together [from Latin *ligare* = bind]

light[1] *NOUN* **lights 1** radiation that stimulates the sense of sight and makes things visible **2** something that provides light, especially an electric lamp **3** a flame
bring or **come to light** make or become known

light *ADJECTIVE* **1** full of light; not dark **2** pale • *light blue*

light *VERB* **lights, lighting, lit** *or* **lighted 1** start a thing burning; begin to burn **2** provide light for something
light up 1 put lights on, especially at dusk **2** make or become light or bright
USAGE Say *He lit the lamps; the lamps were lit* (not 'lighted'), but *She carried a lighted torch* (not 'a lit torch').

light[2] *ADJECTIVE* **1** having little weight; not heavy **2** small in amount or force etc. • *light rain* • *a light punishment* **3** needing little effort • *light work* **4** cheerful, not sad • *with a light heart* **5** not serious or profound • *light music*
▷ **lightly** *ADVERB* **lightness** *NOUN*

light *ADVERB* lightly; with only a small load • *We were travelling light* [from Old English *liht*]

lighten[1] *VERB* **lightens, lightening, lightened** make or become lighter or brighter

lighten[2] *VERB* **lightens, lightening, lightened** make or become lighter or less heavy

light-hearted *ADJECTIVE* **1** cheerful and free from worry **2** not serious

lighthouse *NOUN* **lighthouses** a tower with a bright light at the top to guide or warn ships

lightning *NOUN* a flash of bright light produced by natural electricity during a thunderstorm
like lightning with very great speed

lightning conductor *NOUN* **lightning conductors** a metal rod or wire fixed on a building to divert lightning into the earth

light year *NOUN* **light years** the distance that light travels in one year (about 95 million million km)

like[1] *VERB* **likes, liking, liked 1** think a person or thing is pleasant or satisfactory **2** wish • *I'd like to come.*

Thesaurus

lift *VERB* **1** *She lifted the twins into their special chairs.* ► raise, pick up, hoist, heave OPPOSITES ARE lower, drop **2** *The plane lifted off the ground.* ► rise, ascend, go up, soar OPPOSITES ARE land, touch down **3** *The sight of the sea lifted their spirits.* ► raise, boost, buoy up, revive, enliven, perk up OPPOSITES ARE lower, subdue **4** *The six-month ban has now been lifted.* ► cancel, revoke, rescind, remove, withdraw AN OPPOSITE IS impose **5** *By now the mist had lifted.* ► clear, disperse, disappear, vanish, dissolve, rise OPPOSITES ARE come down, appear

lift *NOUN* *She took the lift to the top floor.* ► elevator, escalator, hoist

light *ADJECTIVE* **1** *a light load* ► slight, lightweight, portable, insubstantial, weightless, flimsy, feathery AN OPPOSITE IS heavy **2** *a light blue* ► pale, faint, pastel, fair AN OPPOSITE IS dark **3** *a light meal* ► modest, frugal, simple, skimpy, insubstantial OPPOSITES ARE heavy, rich **4** *light music; a little light reading* ► entertaining, lightweight, diverting, undemanding, easy **5** *She looked light on her feet.* ► nimble, deft, agile, graceful

light *NOUN* **1** *The gas lamp did not give out much light.* ► brightness, illumination, radiance, luminescence, glow, lustre **2** *There was a light on in the bedroom.* ► lamp, lantern, torch, bulb **3** *She saw the problem in a new light.* ► aspect, complexion, angle, standpoint, point of view, slant, approach USAGE With the last five synonyms you use *from* instead of *in*, e.g. *She saw the problem from a new standpoint.* **4** *In an hour they would be working in the light.* ► daylight, light of day, daytime, sunlight

light *VERB* **1** *The boys wanted to light a fire.* ► kindle, ignite, set alight, set burning, put a match to, set fire to, switch on OPPOSITES ARE put out, extinguish **2** *Hundreds of searchlights lit the sky.* ► illuminate, light up, lighten, brighten, irradiate, floodlight, cast light on, shed light on, shine on AN OPPOSITE IS darken

lighten *VERB* **1** *Pale streaks lightened the sky.* ► light, light up, illuminate, brighten, irradiate AN OPPOSITE IS darken **2** *The sky lightened in the east.* ► brighten, grow lighter AN OPPOSITE IS darken **3** *The gift lightened their financial burden.* ► ease, reduce, relieve, alleviate, mitigate, moderate OPPOSITES ARE increase, intensify

light-hearted *ADJECTIVE* *His light-hearted banter had a serious side.* ► cheerful, carefree, jolly, playful, jovial, bright

like *VERB* **1** *I have always liked Rosamund.* ► be fond of, be attached to, care for, adore, admire,

like[2] *ADJECTIVE* similar; having some or all of the qualities of another person or thing • *They are as like as two peas.*

like *NOUN* a similar person or thing • *We shall not see his like again.*

like *PREPOSITION* **1** similar to; in the manner of • *He swims like a fish.* **2** in a suitable state for • *It looks like rain.* • *I feel like a cup of tea.*

likelihood *NOUN* being likely; probability

likely *ADJECTIVE* **likelier**, **likeliest** **1** probable; expected to happen or be true etc. • *Rain is likely.* **2** expected to be suitable or successful • *a likely spot*

liken *VERB* **likens**, **likening**, **likened** compare • *He likened the human heart to a pump.*

likeness *NOUN* **likenesses** **1** a similarity in appearance; a resemblance **2** a portrait

liking *NOUN* a feeling that you like something • *She has a liking for ice cream.*

lilac *NOUN* **1** a bush with fragrant purple or white flowers **2** pale purple

lilt *NOUN* **lilts** a light pleasant rhythm in a voice or tune
▷ **lilting** *ADJECTIVE*

lily *NOUN* **lilies** a garden plant with trumpet-shaped flowers, growing from a bulb

limb *NOUN* **limbs** **1** a leg, arm, or wing **2** a large branch of a tree
out on a limb isolated; without any support

limber *VERB* **limbers**, **limbering**, **limbered**
limber up do exercises in preparation for an athletic activity

lime[1] *NOUN* a white chalky substance (calcium oxide) used in making cement and as a fertilizer

lime[2] *NOUN* **limes** **1** a green fruit like a small round lemon **2** a drink made from the juice of this fruit

lime[3] *NOUN* **limes** a tree with yellow flowers

limelight *NOUN*
in the limelight receiving a lot of publicity and attention

limerick *NOUN* **limericks** a type of amusing poem with five lines [named after Limerick, a town in Ireland, possibly because people sang 'will you come up to Limerick' as a refrain]

limestone *NOUN* a kind of rock from which lime (calcium oxide) is obtained

limit *NOUN* **limits** **1** a line, point, or level where something ends **2** the greatest amount allowed • *the speed limit*

limit *VERB* **limits**, **limiting**, **limited** **1** keep something within certain limits **2** be a limit to something
▷ **limitation** *NOUN*

limited company *NOUN* **limited companies** a business company whose shareholders would have to pay only some of its debts if it went bankrupt

limp[1] *VERB* **limps**, **limping**, **limped** walk lamely

Thesaurus

respect, esteem, (*old-fashioned*) hold dear, (*more informal*) have a soft spot for, (*more informal*) take a shine to, (*more informal*) fancy **2** *Do you like dancing?* ► enjoy, care for, appreciate, be keen on, be partial to, (*more informal*) love, (*more informal*) fancy

like *ADJECTIVE* *The cousins are very like each other.* ► similar to, the same as, identical
AN OPPOSITE IS unlike

likeable *ADJECTIVE* *The person appointed needs to be likeable and a good mixer.* ► pleasant, personable, nice, friendly, attractive, charming, congenial, pleasing, endearing
AN OPPOSITE IS hateful

likely *ADJECTIVE* **1** *It was likely that there would be an inquiry.* ► probable, possible, expected, foreseeable, envisaged, (*more informal*) odds-on **2** *Try to think of a more likely explanation.* ► credible, believable, plausible, convincing, reasonable **3** *It was a likely place for them to meet.* ► suitable, appropriate, proper, apposite, promising, hopeful

likeness *NOUN* **1** *The painting was a good likeness of their mother.* ► representation, image, depiction, portrayal, picture, portrait, copy, replica **2** *The brothers' likeness is remarkable.* ► resemblance, similarity, affinity, correspondence AN OPPOSITE IS dissimilarity

liking *NOUN* *a liking for rock music* ► fondness, partiality, taste, desire, attraction, weakness, penchant, predilection, fancy OPPOSITES ARE dislike (of), aversion (to)

limber *VERB* **limber up** *She was limbering up for the next race.* ► warm up, loosen up, work out, prepare, get ready, exercise

limit *NOUN* **1** *There was a limit to what they could do to help. There is a limit of ten thousand tickets for away supporters.* ► restriction, maximum, ceiling, cut-off point, curb, restraint, limitation **2** *They drove out as far as the city limits.* ► boundary, border, edge, perimeter, confines

limit *VERB* *The organizers have to limit numbers in the interests of safety.* ► restrict, curb, put a limit on, restrain, check, control, circumscribe, demarcate, confine, fix

limited *ADJECTIVE* *Resources are limited.* ► restricted, circumscribed, finite, short, controlled, rationed, defined, determinate, fixed, inadequate, insufficient, narrow, reduced, small OPPOSITES ARE unlimited, limitless

limp *ADJECTIVE* *The man held out a limp hand.* ► soft, loose, flabby, drooping, slack, weak, sagging, wilting, bendy, flexible, pliable, yielding, floppy OPPOSITES ARE firm, rigid

a b c d e f g h i j k l m n o p q r s t u v w x y z

limp *NOUN* **limps** a limping walk

limp[2] *ADJECTIVE* **1** not stiff or firm **2** without strength or energy
▷ **limply** *ADVERB* **limpness** *NOUN*

limpet *NOUN* **limpets** a small shellfish that attaches itself firmly to rocks

line[1] *NOUN* **lines 1** a long thin mark **2** a row or series of people or things; a row of words **3** a length of rope, string, wire, etc. used for a special purpose • *a fishing line* **4** a railway; a line of railway track **5** a company operating a transport service of ships, aircraft, or buses **6** a way of doing things or behaving; a type of business **7** a telephone connection
in line 1 forming a straight line **2** conforming

line *VERB* **lines, lining, lined 1** mark something with lines • *Use lined paper.* **2** form something into a line or lines • *Line them up.*

line[2] *VERB* **lines, lining, lined** cover the inside of something

lineage (**lin**-ee-ij) *NOUN* **lineages** ancestry; a line of descendants from an ancestor

linear (**lin**-ee-er) *ADJECTIVE* **1** arranged in a line **2** to do with a line or length

linen *NOUN* **1** cloth made from flax **2** shirts, sheets, and tablecloths etc. (which were formerly made of linen)

liner *NOUN* **liners** a large passenger ship

linger *VERB* **lingers, lingering, lingered** stay for a long time, as if unwilling to leave; be slow to leave

lingerie (**lan**-*zher*-ee) *NOUN* women's underwear

linguistics *NOUN* the study of languages
▷ **linguistic** *ADJECTIVE*

lining *NOUN* **linings** a layer that covers the inside of something

link *NOUN* **links 1** one of the rings or loops of a chain **2** a connection or relationship

link *VERB* **links, linking, linked** join things together; connect
▷ **linkage** *NOUN*

links *PLURAL NOUN* a golf course, especially one near the sea

linoleum *NOUN* a stiff shiny floor covering

linseed *NOUN* the seed of flax, from which oil is obtained

lint *NOUN* a soft material for covering wounds

lion *NOUN* **lions** a large strong flesh-eating animal of the cat family found in Africa and India
▷ **lioness** *NOUN*

Thesaurus

limp *VERB She limped back into the house.*
► hobble, hop, falter, shuffle, stumble, totter

line *NOUN* **1** *A line of cars was waiting at the lights.* ► queue, row, file, column, procession, chain, string **2** *He drew a line under his signature. From their window they could see lines in the sand.* ► stroke, rule, underline, strip, band, bar, streak **3** *As she grew older the lines on her face increased.* ► crease, wrinkle, furrow, groove **4** *They walked in a straight line across the field.* ► direction, path, route, course, track **5** *The courts are taking a tough line with repeat offenders. Cabinet members are obliged to support the government line.* ► approach, course, course of action, procedure, policy, position, stance, tactic **6** *There aren't many opportunities in my line.* ► field, line of work, occupation, business, calling, speciality, trade, work, province, domain **7** *Mark attached a line to the post.* ► cord, rope, string, cable, wire, thread, flex **8** *the handsome lines of a classical building* ► shape, contour, profile, figure, features, silhouette **9** *The ball had not crossed the line.* ► limit, boundary, border, edge, demarcation **10** *She comes from a noble line related to the royal family.* ► ancestry, family, descent, lineage, extraction, pedigree, genealogy, stock, background

line *VERB* **1** *She lined the cat's box with blankets.* ► cover, face, pad, stuff, reinforce **2** *The drive was lined with trees.* ► border, edge, fringe, bound, skirt
line up *The children lined up by the door.* ► form a line, form a queue, queue, queue up, fall in, form a crocodile

linger *VERB* **1** *Most of the crowd leave promptly but some tend to linger.* ► wait around, lag behind, loiter, dally, tarry, hang on, stay put, delay **2** *An aroma of coffee lingered all morning.* ► persist, last, continue, remain, endure, stay

lining *NOUN a coat with a thick lining* ► padding, inner layer, interfacing, inlay, liner, interlining

link *NOUN* **1** *She fostered links between the two families.* ► bond, tie, relationship, attachment **2** *a rail link between the city centre and the airport* ► connection, communication, line **3** *an important link in the organization* ► element, component, constituent, piece **4** *a chain of hardened steel links* ► loop, ring, connector, connection

link *VERB* **1** *Police are linking this crime with a series of other robberies.* ► connect, associate, relate (to), draw a connection between **2** *The two trains were linked together.* ► couple, join, connect, attach, fasten

lip *NOUN* **lips** **1** either of the two fleshy edges of the mouth **2** the edge of something hollow, such as a cup or crater **3** the pointed part at the top of a jug etc., from which you pour things

lip-read *VERB* **lip-reads, lip-reading, lip-read** understand what a person says by watching the movements of their lips, not by hearing

lipstick *NOUN* **lipsticks** a stick of a waxy substance for colouring the lips

liqueur (lik-yoor) *NOUN* **liqueurs** a strong sweet alcoholic drink

liquid *NOUN* **liquids** a substance like water or oil that flows freely but (unlike a gas) has a constant volume

liquid *ADJECTIVE* **1** in the form of a liquid; flowing freely **2** easily converted into cash • *the firm's liquid assets*
▷ **liquidity** *NOUN*

liquor *NOUN* **1** alcoholic drink **2** juice produced in cooking; liquid in which food has been cooked

liquorice (lick-er-ish) *NOUN* **1** a black substance used in medicine and as a sweet **2** the plant from whose root this substance is obtained

lisp *NOUN* **lisps** a fault in speech in which *s* and *z* are pronounced like *th*
▷ **lisp** *VERB*

list *NOUN* **lists** a number of names, items, or figures etc. written or printed one after another

list *VERB* **lists, listing, listed** make a list of people or things

listen *VERB* **listens, listening, listened** pay attention in order to hear something
▷ **listener** *NOUN*

listless *ADJECTIVE* too tired to be active or enthusiastic
▷ **listlessly** *ADVERB* **listlessness** *NOUN*

lit *past tense of* **light**[1]

literacy *NOUN* the ability to read and write

literal *ADJECTIVE* **1** meaning exactly what is said, not metaphorical or exaggerated **2** word for word • *a literal translation*

literally *ADVERB* really; exactly as stated • *The noise made me literally jump out of my seat.*

literature *NOUN* books and other writings, especially those considered to have been written well

litigation *NOUN* **litigations** a lawsuit; the process of carrying on a lawsuit

litmus *NOUN* a blue substance that is turned red by acids and can be turned back to blue by alkalis

litmus paper *NOUN* paper stained with litmus

litre *NOUN* **litres** a measure of liquid, about 1.75 pints

litter *NOUN* **litters** **1** rubbish or untidy things left lying about **2** the young animals born to one mother at one time **3** absorbent material put down on a tray for a cat to urinate and defecate in indoors **4** a kind of stretcher

litter *VERB* **litters, littering, littered** make a place untidy with litter

Thesaurus

lip *NOUN* *Coffee poured over the lip of the jug.* ► rim, brim, brink, mouth, edge

liquid *NOUN* *The doctor says he can only take liquids for a few days.* ► fluid, liquid substance, juice, drink, solution

liquid *ADJECTIVE* *The pudding had become liquid in the heat.* ► runny, fluid, thin, watery, sloppy, sloshy, wet, aqueous, molten, running, flowing AN OPPOSITE IS solid

list *NOUN* *I had a list of over 7,000 names.* ► register, inventory, catalogue, index, file, roll, roster, schedule

list *VERB* **1** *We have listed names of contributors in alphabetical order.* ► record, register, itemize, enter, index, file, enumerate, catalogue **2** *The ship was listing in the heavy seas.* ► tilt, lean, lean over, tip, heel, pitch, keel over

listen *VERB* *I don't think they were listening.* ► pay attention, take notice
listen to *a doctor who listens to what his patients tell him* ► pay attention to, take notice of, hear, heed, attend to, concentrate on, (*old-fashioned*) hark AN OPPOSITE IS ignore

listless *ADJECTIVE* *a young woman clutching a pale, listless child* ► lethargic, sluggish, enervated, lackadaisical, torpid, inert, apathetic, unenthusiastic AN OPPOSITE IS lively

literal *ADJECTIVE* **1** *a literal translation* ► word-for-word, verbatim, faithful, strict, exact, close, plain, prosaic, unimaginative **2** *the literal truth of the Bible* ► strict, plain, bare, exact, precise, straightforward, unvarnished, narrow

literary *ADJECTIVE* **1** *a collection of literary works* ► written, printed, published, dramatic, poetic, imaginative **2** *a literary style of writing* ► formal, stylish, ornate, polished, sophisticated, imaginative, recognized as literature **3** *a group of literary friends* ► cultured, educated, literate, scholarly, refined, well read, widely read, erudite, learned

literature *NOUN* **1** *a class in English literature* ► writings, books **2** *We can pick up some literature about the place from the tourist office.* ► brochures, leaflets, pamphlets, handouts, circulars

litter *NOUN* **1** *It took days to clear up all the litter.* ► rubbish, refuse, junk, waste, debris, clutter, garbage, mess, scraps, bits and pieces, odds and ends, trash, jumble **2** *a litter of puppies* ► brood, family, (*more formal*) progeny

A B C D E F G H I J K L M N O P Q R S T U V W X Y Z

little *ADJECTIVE* **less, least** small in amount or size or intensity etc.; not great or big or much
a little **1** a small amount • *Have a little sugar.* **2** slightly • *I'm a little tired.*
little by little gradually; by a small amount at a time

little *ADVERB* not much • *He was little known in this country.*

live[1] (rhymes with *give*) *VERB* **lives, living, lived** **1** have life; be alive **2** have your home • *She lives in Glasgow.* **3** pass your life in a certain way • *He lived as a hermit.*
live down if you cannot live down a mistake or embarrassment, you cannot make people forget it
live on use something as food; depend on for your living

live[2] (rhymes with *hive*) *ADJECTIVE* **1** alive **2** connected to a source of electric current **3** broadcast while it is actually happening, not from a recording **4** burning • *live coals*

livelihood *NOUN* **livelihoods** a way of earning money or providing enough food to support yourself

lively *ADJECTIVE* **livelier, liveliest** full of life or action; vigorous and cheerful
▷ **liveliness** *NOUN*

liver *NOUN* **livers** **1** a large organ of the body, found in the abdomen, that processes digested food and purifies the blood **2** an animal's liver used as food

livestock *NOUN* farm animals

livid *ADJECTIVE* **1** bluish-grey • *a livid bruise* **2** furiously angry

living *NOUN* **1** being alive **2** the way that a person lives • *a good standard of living* **3** a way of earning money or providing enough food to support yourself

living room *NOUN* **living rooms** a room for general use during the day

lizard *NOUN* **lizards** a reptile with a rough or scaly skin, four legs, and a long tail

llama *NOUN* **llamas** a South American animal with woolly fur [via Spanish from Quechua (a South American language)]

Thesaurus

little *ADJECTIVE* **1** *a little book* ► small, tiny, minute, miniature, mini, petite, (*Scottish*) wee, (*more informal*) teeny **2** *a little person* ► small, slight, short, diminutive, (*Scottish*) wee **3** *in a little while* ► short, brief, fleeting, (*Scottish*) wee **4** *We have a little problem.* ► minor, trivial, unimportant, insignificant, inconsequential, negligible
a little *Add a little water.* ► some, a small amount of, a bit of, a touch of, a spot of, a taste of

little *NOUN* *You only need a little.* ► bit, dash, pinch, small amount, touch, modicum

little *ADVERB* *The singers are little known in this country.* ► scarcely, barely, hardly, slightly, not much

live *VERB* **1** *We live in Glasgow.* ► reside, have a home, dwell, lodge **2** *He hardly earns enough to live on.* ► exist, subsist, survive, endure, stay alive **3** *I'm not sure these plants will live much longer.* ► last, survive, stay alive **4** *She has led a happy life.* ► pass, spend, experience, undergo

live *ADJECTIVE* **1** *live animals* ► living, alive, breathing, animate **2** *a live show* ► real-time, actual, unrecorded **3** *a live rail* ► electrified, charged, powered, connected **4** *a live issue* ► topical, current, relevant, pertinent, contemporary, vital, controversial

livelihood *NOUN* *The printing business was his main livelihood.* ► income, source of income, means of support, living, subsistence, occupation, employment

lively *ADJECTIVE* **1** *The bars are lively late in the evening.* ► busy, hectic, bustling, crowded, swarming OPPOSITES ARE quiet, dead **2** *an attractive and lively young woman* ► vivacious, high-spirited, exuberant, animated, alert, active, spirited, exciting, cheerful OPPOSITES ARE lifeless, dull **3** *a lively colour scheme* ► bright, vivid, colourful, striking, bold OPPOSITES ARE dull, bland

liven *VERB* **liven up** *The room needed a few pictures to liven it up.* ► brighten up, animate, cheer up, vitalize, put life into, (*more informal*) perk up, (*more informal*) pep up

livery *NOUN* **1** *the pageboys in their blue livery* ► uniform, costume, outfit, suit, regalia, garb, (*more informal*) get-up **2** *railway coaches repainted in their old maroon livery* ► colours, colour scheme, paintwork

livid *ADJECTIVE* **1** *A row of livid bruises began to form on his skin.* ► bluish-grey, purplish, dark, discoloured **2** *He was livid with me.* ► furious, angry, fuming, seething, raging, enraged, infuriated

living *ADJECTIVE* *all living creatures* ► live, alive, breathing, animate, existing, vital, active, sentient, surviving, vigorous OPPOSITES ARE dead, extinct

living *NOUN* *He was washing cars for a living.* ► livelihood, income, source of income, means of support, subsistence, occupation, employment

living room *NOUN* *Music was playing in the living room.* ► sitting room, drawing room, lounge, reception room

load *NOUN* **loads 1** something carried; a burden **2** the quantity that can be carried **3** the total amount of electric current supplied
4 (*informal*) a large amount • *It's a load of nonsense.* • *You could earn loads of money.*
loads (*informal*) plenty • *We've got loads of time.*

load *VERB* **loads, loading, loaded 1** put a load in or on something **2** fill heavily **3** weight with something heavy • *loaded dice* **4** put a bullet or shell into a gun; put a film into a camera **5** enter programs or data into a computer

loaf[1] *NOUN* **loaves** a shaped mass of bread baked in one piece
use your loaf (*informal*) think; use common sense
[from Old English]

loaf[2] *VERB* **loafs, loafing, loafed** spend time idly; loiter or stand about
▹ **loafer** *NOUN*

loam *NOUN* rich soil containing clay, sand, and decayed leaves etc.
▹ **loamy** *ADJECTIVE*

loan *NOUN* **loans 1** something lent, especially money **2** lending; being lent • *These books are on loan from the library.*

loathe (rhymes with *clothe*) *VERB* **loathes, loathing, loathed** feel great hatred and disgust for something
▹ **loathing** *NOUN*

loathsome *ADJECTIVE* making you feel great hatred and disgust; repulsive

lob *VERB* **lobs, lobbing, lobbed** throw, hit, or kick a ball etc. high into the air, especially in a high arc

lobby *NOUN* **lobbies 1** an entrance hall **2** a group who lobby MPs etc. • *the anti-hunting lobby*

lobby *VERB* **lobbies, lobbying, lobbied** try to persuade an MP or other person to support your cause, by speaking to them in person or writing letters

lobster *NOUN* **lobsters** a large shellfish with eight legs and two long claws

local *ADJECTIVE* belonging to a particular place or a small area
▹ **locally** *ADVERB*

local *NOUN* **locals** (*informal*) **1** someone who lives in a particular district **2** a pub near a person's home [from Latin *locus* = a place]

local anaesthetic *NOUN* **local anaesthetics** an anaesthetic affecting only the part of the body where it is applied

Thesaurus

load *NOUN* **1** *a load of goods* ► cargo, consignment, freight, vanload, lorryload, truckload, shipment, boatload, (*more formal*) lading **2** *a heavy load of work* ► burden, commitment, obligation, weight
a load of (*informal*) *a load of rubbish* ► a lot of, a great deal of, a wealth

load *VERB* **1** *We loaded the luggage into the car.* ► pack, stow, store, stack, cram, heap, pile AN OPPOSITE IS unload (from) **2** *They've loaded me with more responsibilities.* ► burden, encumber, weigh down, saddle AN OPPOSITE IS relieve (of)

loaded *ADJECTIVE* **1** *He had a loaded gun in his hand.* ► primed, charged, filled, ready **2** *A loaded trolley trundled up the platform.* ► full, filled, laden, burdened, inundated, piled high, weighed down, crammed **3** *a loaded argument* ► one-sided, biased, tendentious, prejudiced, unfair, distorted, emotive, partial **4** (*informal*) *Their parents are loaded and can easily afford the fees.* ► wealthy, well-off, rich, affluent, prosperous, moneyed

loaf *VERB* *He can't go on loafing around any longer.* ► laze, idle, lounge, waste time, kill time OPPOSITES ARE work, toil

loafer *NOUN* (*informal*) *education that produces a generation of loafers* ► layabout, idler, lounger, shirker, wastrel, (*informal*) skiver, (*informal*) lazybones, (*informal*) good-for-nothing

loan *NOUN* *A bank loan would help develop the business.* ► advance, credit, mortgage

loan *VERB* **1** *We will loan you the money for a period of 5 years.* ► lend, advance, credit **2** *The gallery loans pictures all over the world.* ► lend, give on loan, provide on loan

loathe *VERB* *She loathed living in the suburbs.* ► hate, detest, abhor, abominate, dislike, despise OPPOSITES ARE love, like, adore

loathing *NOUN* *Loathing for the other woman rose in her chest.* ► hatred, detestation, abhorrence, repugnance (for), revulsion (for) AN OPPOSITE IS love

loathsome *ADJECTIVE* *a loathsome crime* ► detestable, horrible, horrid, awful, nasty OPPOSITES ARE pleasant, likeable

lob *VERB* *He lobbed the ball in the air.* ► throw, toss, hurl, pitch, fling, loft, shy, bowl, cast, chuck, sling

local *ADJECTIVE* **1** *the local library* ► nearby, neighbourhood, neighbouring **2** *Try the local cuisine.* ► regional, district, provincial, community OPPOSITES ARE national, global **3** *a local infection* ► confined, restricted, limited, localized, circumscribed AN OPPOSITE IS general

local *NOUN* (*informal*) *The restaurant is filled with locals.* ► inhabitant, resident, parishioner, native

A B C D E F G H I J K L M N O P Q R S T U V W X Y Z

localized *ADJECTIVE* restricted to a particular place • *localized showers*

locate *VERB* **locates, locating, located** discover where something is • *I have located the fault.*
be located be situated in a particular place • *The cinema is located in the High Street.*

location *NOUN* **locations 1** the place where something is situated **2** discovering where something is; locating
on location filmed in natural surroundings, not in a studio

lock[1] *NOUN* **locks 1** a fastening that is opened with a key or other device **2** a section of a canal or river fitted with sluice gates so that boats can be raised or lowered to the level beyond each gate **3** the distance that a vehicle's front wheels can turn **4** a wrestling hold that keeps an opponent's arm or leg from moving
lock, stock, and barrel completely

lock *VERB* **locks, locking, locked 1** fasten or secure something by means of a lock **2** store something away securely **3** become fixed in one place; jam

lock[2] *NOUN* **locks** a clump of hair

locker *NOUN* **lockers** a small cupboard or compartment where things can be stowed safely

locket *NOUN* **lockets** a small ornamental case for holding a portrait or lock of hair etc., worn on a chain round the neck

locks *PLURAL NOUN* a person's hair

locomotive *NOUN* **locomotives** a railway engine

locomotive *ADJECTIVE* to do with movement or the ability to move • *locomotive power*
▷ **locomotion** *NOUN*

locus (loh-kus) *NOUN* **loci** (loh-ky) **1** (in mathematics) the path traced by a moving point, or made by points placed in a certain way **2** the exact place of something

locust *NOUN* **locusts** a kind of grasshopper that travels in large swarms which eat all the plants in an area

lodge *NOUN* **lodges 1** a small house, especially at the gates of a park **2** a porter's room at the entrance to a college, factory, etc. **3** a beaver's or otter's lair

lodge *VERB* **lodges, lodging, lodged 1** stay somewhere as a lodger **2** provide a person with somewhere to live temporarily **3** become stuck or caught somewhere • *The ball lodged in the tree.*
lodge a complaint complain formally

lodger *NOUN* **lodgers** a person who pays to live in another person's house

lodgings *PLURAL NOUN* a room or rooms, not in a hotel, rented for living in

loft *NOUN* **lofts** a room or storage space under the roof of a house or barn etc.

lofty *ADJECTIVE* **1** tall **2** noble **3** haughty
▷ **loftily** *ADVERB* **loftiness** *NOUN*

log[1] *NOUN* **logs 1** a large piece of a tree that has fallen or been cut down; a piece cut off this **2** a detailed record kept of a voyage or flight, kept in a **logbook**

log *VERB* **logs, logging, logged** enter facts in a log
log in (*or* **on**) start using a computer
log out (*or* **off**) finish using a computer

log[2] *NOUN* **logs** a logarithm • *log tables*

logarithm *NOUN* **logarithms** one of a series of numbers set out in tables which make it possible to do sums by adding and subtracting instead of multiplying and dividing

loggerheads *PLURAL NOUN*
at loggerheads disagreeing or quarrelling

logic *NOUN* **1** reasoning; a system or method of reasoning **2** the principles used in designing a computer; the circuits involved in this

Thesaurus

locality *NOUN* **1** *There are several good schools in the locality.* ► region, area, neighbourhood, vicinity, location, district, community, parish **2** *new housing in an attractive locality* ► position, location, setting, situation, place

locate *VERB* **1** *He located the skylight window he had noticed from the outside.* ► find, discover, identify, pinpoint, track down, detect, light on **2** *The boiler room is located in the basement.* ► situate, site, position, place

location *NOUN* *The firm is moving to a new location.* ► position, site, locality, locale, place, point, situation, spot, venue, whereabouts

lock *NOUN* **1** *a lock on a door* ► fastening, latch, clasp **2** *a lock of hair* ► curl, tress, tuft

lock *VERB* *We lock the door at night.* ► fasten, secure, shut, bolt, close, seal
lock up *He was locked up for causing criminal damage.* ► jail, imprison, put behind bars

lodge *NOUN* *a hunting lodge* ► cabin, cottage, hut, chalet

lodge *VERB* **1** *The family lodged at a guest house for a few weeks.* ► board, stay, live, reside **2** *I will lodge a formal complaint.* ► submit, register, enter, place, present

lodger *NOUN* *Her husband had once been a lodger of hers.* ► boarder, paying guest, tenant, resident, inmate, guest

logic *NOUN* *We accept the logic of your case.* ► reasoning, rationale, sense, validity, argumentation, rationality, cogency

logical *ADJECTIVE* using logic; reasoning or reasoned correctly
▷ **logically** *ADVERB* **logicality** *NOUN*

logo (loh-goh, log-oh) *NOUN* **logos** a printed symbol used by a business company etc. as its emblem

loiter *VERB* **loiters, loitering, loitered** linger or stand about idly
▷ **loiterer** *NOUN*

lollipop *NOUN* **lollipops** a large round hard sweet on a stick

lonely *ADJECTIVE* **lonelier, loneliest 1** sad because you are on your own **2** solitary **3** far from inhabited places; not often visited or used • *a lonely road*
▷ **loneliness** *NOUN*

long[1] *ADJECTIVE* **1** measuring a lot from one end to the other **2** taking a lot of time • *a long holiday* **3** having a certain length • *The river is 10 miles long.*

long *ADVERB* **1** for a long time • *Have you been waiting long?* **2** at a long time before or after • *They left long ago.* **3** throughout a time • *all night long*
as long as or **so long as** provided that; on condition that
before long soon
no longer not any more

long[2] *VERB* **longs, longing, longed** feel a strong desire

long division *NOUN* dividing one number by another and writing down all the calculations

longing *NOUN* **longings** a strong desire

longitude *NOUN* **longitudes** the distance east or west, measured in degrees, from the Greenwich meridian

long jump *NOUN* an athletic contest in which competitors jump as far as possible along the ground in one leap

long-sighted *ADJECTIVE* able to see distant things clearly but not things close to you

long wave *NOUN* a radio wave of a wavelength above one kilometre and a frequency less than 300 kilohertz

long-winded *ADJECTIVE* talking or writing at great length

look *VERB* **looks, looking, looked 1** use your eyes; turn your eyes in a particular direction **2** face in a particular direction **3** have a certain appearance; seem • *You look sad.*
look after 1 protect or take care of someone **2** be in charge of something
look down on despise
look forward to be waiting eagerly for something you expect
look into investigate
look out be careful

Thesaurus

logical *ADJECTIVE The conclusions are logical.* ► rational, reasonable, cogent, coherent, clear, sound, valid, consistent, intelligent, methodical, sensible, systematic AN OPPOSITE IS illogical

loiter *VERB With so much to do there was no time to loiter in the shopping malls.* ► linger, dally, potter, dawdle, tarry, (*more informal*) loaf about, (*more informal*) mooch about

lone *ADJECTIVE a lone cyclist; a lone tree* ► solitary, single, solo, isolated, individual, unaccompanied, separate

lonely *ADJECTIVE* **1** *I walked through the garden feeling very lonely.* ► alone, solitary, friendless, abandoned, lonesome, neglected, forlorn AN OPPOSITE IS popular **2** *The cart drove along the lonely road* ► deserted, unfrequented, remote, secluded, isolated, abandoned, desolate, forsaken, out of the way, uninhabited, (*informal*) off the beaten track AN OPPOSITE IS crowded

long *ADJECTIVE* **1** *long blonde hair* ► flowing, shoulder-length, waist-length AN OPPOSITE IS short **2** *a long wait* ► lengthy, prolonged, extended, extensive, long-lasting OPPOSITES ARE short, brief

long *VERB* **long for** *We longed for the holidays.* ► yearn for, crave, dream of, hanker after, hunger for, pine for

longing *NOUN He felt a longing for his home.* ► yearning, hankering (after), craving desire, hunger, need, thirst, urge, wish, (*informal*) yen

long-lasting *ADJECTIVE We need long-lasting solutions to these problems.* ► enduring, abiding, long-running, durable, permanent, prolonged

long-standing *ADJECTIVE a long-standing arrangement* ► well-established, long-established, time-honoured, firm

look *VERB* **1** *Everywhere you look there are trees.* ► see, observe, regard, survey, glance, scrutinize, scan **2** *Things looked difficult that day.* ► seem, appear
look after *Jane had to look after her father during his last illness.* ► take care of, care for, tend, attend to, provide for, mind, nurse, supervise, watch over, (*more informal*) keep an eye on
look at *I knew if I looked at her we'd both start laughing.* ► glance at, watch, observe
look down on *The family looked down on all their neighbours.* ► despise, disdain, scorn, hold in contempt, sneer at, (*more informal*) look down your nose at
look for 1 *I was still looking for my wallet.* ► search for, hunt for, seek, try to find **2** *Behaviour like that is looking for trouble.* ► ask for, provoke, invite, attract, court, incite, tempt,

A B C D E F G H I J K L M N O P Q R S T U V W X Y Z

look up 1 search for information about something **2** improve in prospects • *Things are looking up.*
look up to admire or respect

look *NOUN* **looks 1** the act of looking; a gaze or glance **2** appearance • *I don't like the look of this place*

looking glass *NOUN* **looking glasses** a glass mirror

lookout *NOUN* **lookouts 1** looking out or watching for something **2** a place from which you can keep watch **3** a person whose job is to keep watch **4** a future prospect • *It's a poor lookout for us.* **5** (*informal*) a person's own fault or concern • *If he wastes his money, that's his lookout.*

loom[1] *NOUN* **looms** a machine for weaving cloth

loom[2] *VERB* **looms, looming, loomed** appear suddenly; seem large or close and threatening • *An iceberg loomed up through the fog.*

loop *NOUN* **loops** the shape made by a curve crossing itself; a piece of string, ribbon, wire, etc. made into this shape

loophole *NOUN* **loopholes** a way of avoiding a law or rule or promise etc. without actually breaking it

loose *ADJECTIVE* **1** not tight; not firmly fixed • *a loose tooth* **2** not tied up or shut in • *There's a lion loose!* **3** not packed in a box or packet etc. **4** not exact • *a loose translation*
▷ **loosely** *ADVERB* **looseness** *NOUN*
at a loose end with nothing to do
on the loose escaped or free

loosen *VERB* **loosens, loosening, loosened** make or become loose or looser

loot *NOUN* stolen things; goods taken from an enemy

loot *VERB* **loots, looting, looted 1** rob a place or an enemy, especially in a time of war or disorder **2** take something as loot
▷ **looter** *NOUN*
[from a Hindi word, = to rob]

lop *VERB* **lops, lopping, lopped** cut away branches or twigs; cut off

Thesaurus

cause, encourage, generate, (*more informal*) stir up
look into *The official said he would look into the complaint.* ▸ investigate, find out about, inquire into, study, explore, examine
look out *A ball can easily hit you if you don't look out.* ▸ beware, watch out, be careful, be vigilant, pay attention, keep your eyes open
look up 1 *You can look up the answer in an encyclopedia.* ▸ find, search for, research, track down **2** (*informal*) *We can look up some friends on our way home.* ▸ visit, call on, stop by, (*informal*) drop in on, (*informal*) look in on **3** *Things were beginning to look up.* ▸ improve, progress, show an improvement, revive
look up to *Susan looked up to her father.* ▸ admire, respect, esteem, revere, have a high regard for, have a high opinion of, think highly of

look *NOUN* **1** *We had a look at the house.* ▸ glance, glimpse, peek, peep, sight (of), observation (of), view (of), (*informal*) squint **2** *You could see he was angry from the look on his face.* ▸ expression, mien **3** *a house with a Tudor look* ▸ appearance, aspect, façade, guise, quality, atmosphere, semblance **4** *this year's new look* ▸ fashion, vogue, style, trend, craze, rage
looks *All the sisters enjoyed stunning good looks.* ▸ appearance, features

lookalike *NOUN* *a Madonna lookalike* ▸ double, twin, exact likeness, spitting image, replica, clone, (*more informal*) spit

lookout *NOUN* **1** *a lookout on the bridge* ▸ sentry, guard, sentinel, scout, watchman **2** *It might not work but that's their lookout.* ▸ concern, responsibility, business, affair, problem

loom *VERB* **1** *The cathedral loomed above them.* ▸ soar, tower, rise, appear, rear up **2** *Blurred shapes loomed out of the mist.* ▸ appear, emerge, come into view, reveal itself **3** *Without action, big problems loom.* ▸ threaten, impend, be imminent, menace, overshadow

loop *NOUN* *He slipped a loop of wire over the handle and pulled it tight.* ▸ coil, noose, ring, twist, curl, hoop, turn, bend, circle, kink

loop *VERB* *Loop a rope round the animal's neck.* ▸ coil, wind, twist, bend, curl, entwine, turn

loophole *NOUN* *a loophole in the regulations* ▸ means of escape, ambiguity, flaw, (*more informal*) get-out, (*more informal*) let-out

loose *ADJECTIVE* **1** *a loose screw* ▸ insecure, unfastened, untied, unfixed, wobbly OPPOSITES ARE tight, secure **2** *a wild animal loose in the grounds* ▸ free, at large, unconfined, on the loose, at liberty AN OPPOSITE IS confined **3** *loose trousers* ▸ baggy, slack, loose-fitting, roomy OPPOSITES ARE tight, close-fitting **4** *a loose translation* ▸ free, imprecise, vague, inexact OPPOSITES ARE literal, exact

loosen *VERB* **1** *He tried to loosen the knots.* ▸ ease, free, slacken, undo, untie, unfasten, release **2** *She loosened her grip.* ▸ weaken, relax, lessen AN OPPOSITE IS tighten

loot *NOUN* *a bag full of the thieves' loot* ▸ booty, spoils, plunder, haul, (*more informal*) swag

loot *VERB* *Soldiers looted the deserted buildings.* ▸ raid, plunder, pillage, ransack, rifle, rob, steal from

lopsided *ADJECTIVE* with one side lower or smaller than the other

lord *NOUN* **lords** **1** a nobleman, especially one who is allowed to use the title 'Lord' in front of his name **2** a master or ruler
▷ **lordly** *ADJECTIVE* **lordship** *NOUN*
[from Old English *hlaford* = person who keeps the bread (compare **lady**)]

lorry *NOUN* **lorries** a large strong motor vehicle for carrying heavy goods or troops

lose *VERB* **loses, losing, lost** **1** be without something that you once had, especially because you cannot find it **2** fail to keep or obtain something • *We lost control.* **3** be defeated in a contest or argument etc. **4** cause the loss of • *That one mistake lost us the game.* **5** (said about a clock or watch) become behind the correct time
▷ **loser** *NOUN*
be lost or **lose your way** not know where you are or which is the right path
lose your life be killed
lost cause an idea or policy etc. that is failing

loss *NOUN* **losses** **1** losing something **2** something lost
be at a loss not know what to do or say

lot *NOUN* **lots** **1** a large number or amount • *You have a lot of friends.* • *There's lots of time.* **2** one of a set of objects used in choosing or deciding something by chance • *We drew lots to see who should go first.* **3** a person's share or fate **4** something for sale at an auction **5** a piece of land
a lot very much • *I feel a lot better.*
the lot or **the whole lot** everything; all

lotion *NOUN* **lotions** a liquid for putting on the skin

lottery *NOUN* **lotteries** a way of raising money by selling numbered tickets and giving prizes to people who hold winning numbers, which are chosen by a method depending on chance
COMPARE **lot** 2

loud *ADJECTIVE* **1** easily heard; producing much noise **2** unpleasantly bright; gaudy • *loud colours*
▷ **loudly** *ADVERB* **loudness** *NOUN*

loudspeaker *NOUN* **loudspeakers** a device that changes electrical signals into sound, for reproducing music or voices

lounge *NOUN* **lounges** a sitting room

lounge *VERB* **lounges, lounging, lounged** sit or stand in a lazy and relaxed way

Thesaurus

lopsided *ADJECTIVE* *a tractor pulling a lopsided load* ► uneven, unbalanced, tilting, askew, asymmetrical, crooked, (*more informal*) cock-eyed

lord *NOUN* **1** *the lord of the manor* ► master, overlord, leader, chief, prince **2** *He has been made a lord.* ► peer, noble, baron, earl, duke

lordly *ADJECTIVE* **1** *lordly titles* ► noble, aristocratic, princely, courtly **2** *He spoke in a lordly manner.* ► haughty, imperious, disdainful, condescending, domineering, overbearing, high-handed

lose *VERB* **1** *I've lost my passport.* ► mislay, misplace, lose track of, forget AN OPPOSITE IS find **2** *We've already lost a lot of time. They lost money on the deal.* ► waste, use up, squander, dissipate, forfeit, exhaust OPPOSITES ARE gain, make **3** *The home side lost 3–0.* ► be beaten, be defeated, fail, suffer defeat AN OPPOSITE IS win

loser *NOUN* **1** *There are many losers and few winners in this game.* ► runner-up AN OPPOSITE IS winner **2** (*informal*) *He's a complete loser.* ► failure, non-achiever, nobody, (*informal*) no-hoper

loss *NOUN* **1** *The loss of all his money ruined the holiday.* ► losing, theft, deprivation, disappearance **2** *The loss of her husband devastated her.* ► death, demise, passing, decease **3** *The company faced a huge loss.* ► deficit, debit, debt, lack of profit **4** *Loss of the game was a major blow.* ► defeat (in), failure (in), forfeiture **5** *The army suffered heavy losses.* ► casualty, fatality, mortality, victim

lost *ADJECTIVE* **1** *The lost keys never turned up.* ► missing, mislaid, misplaced, vanished **2** *I became lost in the complications of the plot.* ► confused, baffled, bewildered, perplexed **3** *many lost opportunities* ► missed, neglected, wasted, squandered **4** *She appeared to be lost in thought.* ► absorbed, engrossed, preoccupied

lot *NOUN* **1 a lot of** *or* **lots of** *She has a lot of friends. We need lots of money.* ► many, plenty of, a large amount *or* number of, a great deal of **2** *On Monday a new lot of tourists arrives.* ► set, collection, group, batch, crowd **3** *He was not at all happy with his lot.* ► fate, destiny, fortune, future **4** *The money was divided into three lots.* ► share, portion, allocation, quota

lottery *NOUN* *She won a thousand pounds in a lottery.* ► draw, raffle, sweepstake, sweep, gamble

loud *ADJECTIVE* **1** *loud music* ► noisy, blaring, deafening, booming, thunderous AN OPPOSITE IS quiet **2** *loud colours* ► gaudy, garish, bold, lurid, flashy, showy AN OPPOSITE IS subdued

lounge *VERB* *Miranda lounged on the sofa all morning.* ► laze, loll, recline, relax, sprawl, slump, slouch, luxuriate, idle, waste time

lounge *NOUN* *We will have our drinks in the lounge.* ► living room, sitting room, drawing room, day room

louse *NOUN* **lice** a small insect that lives as a parasite on animals or plants

lousy *ADJECTIVE* **lousier**, **lousiest** **1** full of lice **2** (*informal*) very bad or unpleasant

lout *NOUN* **louts** a bad-mannered man

lovable *ADJECTIVE* easy to love

love *NOUN* **loves** **1** great liking or affection **2** sexual affection or passion **3** a loved person; a sweetheart **4** (in tennis) no score; nil
in love feeling strong love
make love have sexual intercourse

love *VERB* **loves**, **loving**, **loved** feel love for a person or thing
▷ **lover** *NOUN* **lovingly** *ADVERB*
[from Old English]

love affair *NOUN* **love affairs** a romantic or sexual relationship between two people in love

lovely *ADJECTIVE* **lovelier**, **loveliest** **1** beautiful **2** very pleasant or enjoyable
▷ **loveliness** *NOUN*

lover *NOUN* **lovers** **1** a person who someone is having a sexual relationship with but is not married to **2** someone who loves something • *an art lover*

lovesick *ADJECTIVE* longing for someone you love, especially someone who does not love you

low *ADJECTIVE* **1** only reaching a short way up; not high **2** below average in importance, quality, amount, etc. • *low prices* • *of low rank* **3** unhappy • *I'm feeling low.* **4** not high-pitched; not loud • *low notes* • *a low voice*
▷ **lowness** *NOUN*

low *ADVERB* at or to a low level or position etc. • *The plane was flying low*

lower *ADJECTIVE*, *ADVERB* less high

lower *VERB* **lowers**, **lowering**, **lowered** make or become lower

Thesaurus

lousy *ADJECTIVE* (*informal*) *He had been a lousy father.* ► awful, terrible, dreadful, atrocious, appalling, frightful, poor, bad OPPOSITES ARE wonderful, lovely

lout *NOUN* *a group of drunken louts* ► hooligan, hoodlum, ruffian, (*more informal*) yob

loutish *ADJECTIVE* *loutish behaviour* ► uncouth, rude, ill-mannered, coarse, crude, vulgar, (*more informal*) yobbish

lovable *ADJECTIVE* *a lovable little kitten* ► adorable, dear, sweet, charming, appealing, likeable, attractive, cuddly, enchanting, endearing, engaging, lovely, pleasing, taking, winning AN OPPOSITE IS hateful

love *VERB* **1** *She told him she loved him.* ► care for, feel deeply for, adore, cherish, hold dear, treasure OPPOSITES ARE hate, loathe, detest **2** *We all love the holidays.* ► like, like very much, enjoy, take pleasure in, appreciate, desire, look forward to, (*more informal*) fancy AN OPPOSITE IS dislike

love *NOUN* **1** *He gave her flowers to show his love.* ► fondness, affection, adoration, devotion, admiration, ardour, desire, friendship, infatuation, liking, passion **2** *Emma was his true love.* ► beloved, loved one, darling, dear, dearest, lover
in love with *He had been in love with her all his life.* ► devoted to, enamoured with, fond of, infatuated with RELATED ADJECTIVES amatory, erotic

loveless *ADJECTIVE* *a loveless marriage* ► passionless, unloving, unfeeling, heartless, unresponsive, cold, frigid, undemonstrative AN OPPOSITE IS loving

lovely *ADJECTIVE* **1** *a lovely young woman; You look lovely.* ► beautiful, attractive, good-looking, exquisite, pretty, enchanting, charming, delightful, appealing OPPOSITES ARE unattractive, hideous, ugly **2** *a lovely spring morning* ► pleasant, delightful, glorious, wonderful, fine OPPOSITES ARE horrible, unpleasant

lover *NOUN* *There is a rumour that she has a secret lover.* ► admirer, sweetheart, boyfriend, girlfriend, man friend, lady friend

loving *ADJECTIVE* *He adored her loving nature.* ► affectionate, tender, fond, friendly, kind, warm, amorous, ardent, demonstrative, devoted, doting, passionate AN OPPOSITE IS loveless

low *ADJECTIVE* **1** *a low wall* ► short, small, squat, shallow AN OPPOSITE IS high **2** *Prices are now low.* ► reasonable, cheap, inexpensive OPPOSITES ARE high, exorbitant **3** *Supplies were getting low.* ► sparse, scarce, meagre, inadequate, depleted, paltry OPPOSITES ARE plentiful, abundant **4** *He was feeling low that day.* ► depressed, dispirited, downcast, unhappy AN OPPOSITE IS happy **5** *a low trick* ► mean, base, despicable, shameful, contemptible AN OPPOSITE IS admirable **6** *a low rumbling sound* ► muted, soft, deep AN OPPOSITE IS loud

lower *VERB* **1** *The soldier lowered the flag.* ► bring down, drop, let down, take down OPPOSITES ARE raise, hoist **2** *a need to lower interest rates* ► reduce, decrease, bring down, lessen OPPOSITES ARE raise, increase

loyal *ADJECTIVE* always firmly supporting your friends or group or country etc.
▷ **loyally** *ADVERB* **loyalty** *NOUN*

lozenge *NOUN* **lozenges** **1** a small flavoured tablet, especially one containing medicine **2** a diamond shape

Ltd. *ABBREVIATION* limited

lubricant *NOUN* **lubricants** a lubricating substance

lubricate *VERB* **lubricates**, **lubricating**, **lubricated** oil or grease something so that it moves smoothly
▷ **lubrication** *NOUN*

lucid *ADJECTIVE* **1** clear and easy to understand **2** thinking clearly; not confused in your mind
▷ **lucidly** *ADVERB* **lucidity** *NOUN*

luck *NOUN* **1** the way things happen without being planned; chance **2** good fortune • *It will bring you luck.*

lucky *ADJECTIVE* **luckier**, **luckiest** having or bringing or resulting from good luck
▷ **luckily** *ADVERB*

ludicrous *ADJECTIVE* ridiculous or laughable
▷ **ludicrously** *ADVERB*

luggage *NOUN* suitcases and bags etc. holding things for taking on a journey

lukewarm *ADJECTIVE* **1** only slightly warm; tepid **2** not very enthusiastic • *lukewarm applause*

lull *VERB* **lulls**, **lulling**, **lulled** soothe or calm; send someone to sleep

lull *NOUN* **lulls** a short period of quiet or inactivity

lullaby *NOUN* **lullabies** a song that is sung to send a baby to sleep

lumbago *NOUN* pain in the muscles of the lower back

lumber *NOUN* **1** unwanted furniture etc.; junk **2** (*American*) timber

lumber *VERB* **lumbers**, **lumbering**, **lumbered** **1** leave someone with an unwanted or unpleasant task **2** move in a heavy clumsy way

luminous *ADJECTIVE* glowing in the dark
▷ **luminosity** *NOUN*

lump[1] *NOUN* **lumps** **1** a solid piece of something **2** a swelling
▷ **lumpy** *ADJECTIVE*

lump *VERB* **lumps**, **lumping**, **lumped** put or treat things together in a group because you regard them as alike in some way

lump[2] *VERB* **lumps**, **lumping**, **lumped**
lump it (*informal*) put up with something you dislike

lump sum *NOUN* **lump sums** a single payment, especially one covering a number of items

Thesaurus

loyal *ADJECTIVE* *a loyal friend* ► faithful, true, devoted, steadfast, staunch, constant, dependable, reliable, sincere AN OPPOSITE IS disloyal

loyalty *NOUN* *His first loyalty was to his family.* ► allegiance, faithfulness, fidelity, devotion, constancy, dependability, fealty, honesty, patriotism, reliability, staunchness, steadfastness, trustworthiness AN OPPOSITE IS disloyalty

luck *NOUN* **1** *They could not believe their luck.* ► good fortune, good luck, success **2** *She hopes her luck will change.* ► fate, fortune, lot, destiny **3** *It was luck that brought them here.* ► chance, accident, serendipity

lucky *ADJECTIVE* **1** *a lucky chance; a lucky guess* ► fortunate, auspicious, providential, opportune, expedient, timely **2** *He is lucky to have such a good friend as you.* ► fortunate, blessed, favoured, advantaged

ludicrous *ADJECTIVE* *a ludicrous suggestion* ► absurd, ridiculous, laughable, incredible, farcical, preposterous, risible, foolish, idiotic, (*more informal*) crazy, (*more informal*) daft, (*more informal*) barmy, (*more informal*) zany OPPOSITES ARE reasonable, sensible

lug *VERB* *He lugged his old suitcase up the hill.* ► drag, pull, haul, carry, heave, hump

luggage *NOUN* *Trevor put his luggage on the rack.* ► bags, cases, baggage, things, paraphernalia, belongings

lukewarm *ADJECTIVE* **1** *She pulled a face over her lukewarm tea.* ► tepid, warm **2** *a lukewarm response* ► unenthusiastic, indifferent, half-hearted, offhand, cool, apathetic

lull *NOUN* *a lull in the fighting* ► pause, respite, break, calm, gap, interval, rest, (*more informal*) let-up

lull *VERB* *The singing lulled her to sleep.* ► soothe, calm, subdue, hush, pacify, quell, quieten, tranquillize AN OPPOSITE IS agitate

lumber *VERB* **1** (*informal*) *We were lumbered with paying the bill.* ► saddle, burden, encumber, load **2** *Henry lumbered down the stairs.* ► shamble, trudge, tramp, plod, shuffle, blunder, move clumsily

lump *NOUN* **1** *a lump of bread* ► chunk, hunk, block, wedge, piece, portion, slab, wad **2** *The blow left a lump on his head.* ► swelling, bump, growth, protuberance

lump verb **1 lump together** *The newspaper reports lumped together several stories.* ► combine, amalgamate, merge, bunch **2 lump it** (*informal*) *We're not going and we'll just have to lump it.* ► accept it, put up with it, tolerate it, endure it

lunacy *NOUN* **lunacies** insanity or great foolishness

lunatic *NOUN* **lunatics** an insane person
▷ **lunatic** *ADJECTIVE*

lunch *NOUN* **lunches** a meal eaten in the middle of the day
▷ **lunch** *VERB*

lung *NOUN* **lungs** either of the two parts of the body, in the chest, used in breathing

lunge *VERB* **lunges, lunging, lunged** thrust the body forward suddenly
▷ **lunge** *NOUN*

lupin *NOUN* **lupins** a garden plant with tall spikes of flowers

lurch[1] *VERB* **lurches, lurching, lurched** stagger; lean suddenly to one side
▷ **lurch** *NOUN*

lurch[2] *NOUN*
leave somebody in the lurch leave somebody in difficulties

lure *VERB* **lures, luring, lured** tempt a person or animal into a trap; entice
▷ **lure** *NOUN*

lurid (lewr- id) *ADJECTIVE* **1** in very bright colours; gaudy **2** sensational and shocking • *the lurid details of the murder*
▷ **luridly** *ADVERB* **luridness** *NOUN*

lurk *VERB* **lurks, lurking, lurked** wait where you cannot be seen

luscious (lush- us) *ADJECTIVE* delicious
▷ **lusciously** *ADVERB* **lusciousness** *NOUN*

lush *ADJECTIVE* **1** growing thickly and strongly • *lush grass* **2** luxurious
▷ **lushly** *ADVERB* **lushness** *NOUN*

lust *NOUN* **lusts** powerful desire, especially sexual desire
▷ **lustful** *ADJECTIVE*

lust *VERB* **lusts, lusting, lusted** have a powerful desire for a person or thing • *people who lust after power*

lusty *ADJECTIVE* **lustier, lustiest** strong and vigorous
▷ **lustily** *ADVERB* **lustiness** *NOUN*

lute *NOUN* **lutes** a stringed musical instrument with a pear-shaped body, popular in the 14th-17th centuries

luxuriant *ADJECTIVE* growing abundantly
USAGE Do not confuse with **luxurious**.

luxurious *ADJECTIVE* expensive and comfortable
▷ **luxuriously** *ADVERB*
USAGE Do not confuse with **luxuriant**.

luxury *NOUN* **luxuries** **1** something expensive that you enjoy but do not really need **2** expensive and comfortable surroundings • *a life of luxury* [from Latin *luxus* = plenty]

Thesaurus

lunacy *NOUN* **1** *a scene of despair and lunacy* ► insanity, madness, mental disorder, mental illness, derangement, dementia **2** *It would be lunacy to try a rescue in this weather.* ► folly, foolishness, stupidity, madness, insanity

lunatic *NOUN* *a dangerous lunatic* ► maniac, madman, madwoman, (*more informal*) loony

lunge *VERB* *The man lunged at him.* ► thrust, charge, pounce, rush, throw yourself, dash, dive, lurch

lurch *VERB* *James lurched into the bathroom.* ► stagger, stumble, totter, reel, roll, list, lunge, sway, pitch, heave, lean, plunge, wallow

lure *VERB* *Advertising can lure people into debt.* ► tempt, entice, attract, induce, coax, seduce, draw, inveigle, invite, lead on, persuade

lurid *ADJECTIVE* **1** *window blinds of lurid colours* ► garish, gaudy, flashy, loud, glaring, vulgar OPPOSITES ARE sober, dull **2** *The report included all the lurid details.* ► sensational, melodramatic, graphic, salacious, gruesome, macabre

lurk *VERB* *lions lurking in shadows* ► skulk, loiter, lie in wait, lie low, crouch, hide

luscious *ADJECTIVE* *luscious fruit hanging from the trees* ► delicious, juicy, succulent, mouth-watering, appetizing

lush *ADJECTIVE* **1** *lush vegetation* ► rich, luxuriant, abundant, profuse, exuberant, prolific, flourishing **2** *a lush penthouse* ► luxurious, sumptuous, grand, opulent, lavish

lust *NOUN* *a lust for power* ► greed, desire, craving, longing, hunger, appetite, itch

luxurious *ADJECTIVE* *luxurious surroundings* ► sumptuous, grand, opulent, lavish, comfortable, lush, magnificent, plush, splendid
OPPOSITES ARE austere, simple, spartan

luxury *NOUN* *They led a life of luxury.* ► opulence, sumptuousness, splendour, affluence, extravagance, comfort, ease, enjoyment, indulgence, pleasure, relaxation, self-indulgence

-ly *SUFFIX* forms adjectives (e.g. *friendly, heavenly, sickly*), adverbs from adjectives (e.g. *boldly, sweetly, thoroughly*)

Lycra *NOUN* (*trademark*) a thin stretchy material used especially for sports clothing

lying *present participle of* **lie**[1] and **lie**[2]

lynch *VERB* **lynches**, **lynching**, **lynched** join together to execute or punish someone violently without a proper trial, especially by hanging them

lyric (li- rik) *NOUN* **lyrics** **1** a short poem that expresses thoughts and feelings **2** the words of a song
▷ **lyrical** *ADJECTIVE* **lyrically** *ADVERB*

Thesaurus

lying *ADJECTIVE* *He was just a lying schemer.* ► deceitful, dishonest, double-dealing, two-faced, false, untrustworthy, untruthful
AN OPPOSITE IS truthful

lying *NOUN* *She was no good at lying, even to save her own skin.* ► falsehood, untruthfulness, deceit, dishonesty, mendacity, (*more formal*) perjury

Mm

MA *ABBREVIATION* Master of Arts

mac *NOUN* **macs** (*informal*) a mackintosh

macaroni *NOUN* pasta in the form of short tubes [via Italian from Greek *makaria* = food made from barley]

macaroon *NOUN* **macaroons** a small sweet cake or biscuit made with ground almonds

machine *NOUN* **machines** something with parts that work together to do a job

machine gun *NOUN* **machine guns** a gun that can keep firing bullets quickly one after another

machinery *NOUN* **1** machines **2** the moving parts of a machine **3** an organized system for doing something • *the machinery of local government*

mackerel *NOUN* **mackerel** a sea fish used as food

mackintosh *NOUN* **mackintoshes** a raincoat

mad *ADJECTIVE* **madder, maddest 1** having something wrong with the mind; insane **2** extremely foolish **3** very keen • *He is mad about football.* **4** (*informal*) very excited or annoyed
▷ **madly** *ADVERB* **madness** *NOUN* **madman** *NOUN*
like mad (*informal*) with great speed, energy, or enthusiasm

madam *NOUN* a word used when speaking politely to a woman • *Can I help you, madam?*

mad cow disease *NOUN* BSE

madden *VERB* **maddens, maddening, maddened** make a person mad or angry
▷ **maddening** *ADJECTIVE*

mafia *NOUN* **1** a large organization of criminals in Italy, Sicily, and the United States of America **2** any group of people believed to act together in a sinister way

magazine *NOUN* **magazines 1** a paper-covered publication that comes out regularly, with articles, stories, or features by several writers **2** the part of a gun that holds the cartridges **3** a store for weapons and ammunition or for explosives **4** a device that holds film for a camera or slides for a projector [from Arabic *makhazin* = storehouses]

magenta (ma-**jen**-ta) *NOUN* a colour between bright red and purple [named after Magenta, a town in north Italy, where Napoleon III won a battle in the year when the dye was discovered (1859)]

maggot *NOUN* **maggots** the larva of some kinds of fly
▷ **maggoty** *ADJECTIVE*

magic *NOUN* **1** the art of making things happen by supernatural powers **2** mysterious tricks performed for entertainment **3** a mysterious and enchanting quality • *the magic of the East*
▷ **magic** *ADJECTIVE* **magical** *ADJECTIVE* **magically** *ADVERB*

Thesaurus

macabre *ADJECTIVE* *the macabre business of the switched bodies* ► gruesome, grisly, grim, gory, morbid, eerie, weird, lurid, dreadful, horrible, ghoulish

machine *NOUN* *The machine started to make a noise.* ► apparatus, appliance, contrivance, device, contraption, instrument, tool, gadget, mechanism RELATED ADJECTIVE mechanical

machinery *NOUN* **1** *a factory equipped with modern machinery* ► equipment, machines, plant, instruments, hardware, gear **2** *the agreed machinery for resolving disputes* ► procedure, organization, structure, system, constitution, method

macho *NOUN* *macho jobs like bricklaying* ► manly, male, masculine, virile, (*more informal*) butch, (*more informal*) laddish

mad *ADJECTIVE* **1** *He thought he was going mad.* ► insane, mentally ill, deranged, demented, crazy, (*more informal*) out of your mind, (*more informal*) off your head, (*more informal*) potty, (*more informal*) nutty, (*more informal*) nuts **2** *It was a mad idea but they liked it.* ► foolish, crazy, insane, absurd, senseless, wild, preposterous **3** (*informal*) *Is she still mad with you for ditching her?* ► angry, cross, furious, enraged, infuriated, irate **4** mad about(*informal*) *Jenny is mad about jazz.* ► keen on, crazy about, enthusiastic about, eager for, devoted to, addicted to

madden *VERB* *It's their pretence that maddens me most.* ► infuriate, exasperate, anger, enrage, incense, annoy, craze, irritate, vex, provoke

maddening *ADJECTIVE* *The traffic moved with maddening slowness.* ► infuriating, exasperating, irritating, annoying, vexing, irksome

madness *NOUN* **1** *There was a gleam of madness in his eyes.* ► insanity, dementia, lunacy, delirium, frenzy, hysteria, derangement, eccentricity, mania, mental illness, psychosis **2** *It is madness to let children roam about after dark.* ► foolishness, folly, stupidity, insanity, lunacy

magazine *NOUN* **1** *a pile of magazines on the dining-room table* ► journal, periodical, colour supplement, weekly, monthly, comic **2** *a magazine of weapons* ► arsenal, ammunition dump, storehouse, depot

magic *NOUN* **1** *It was so real it had to be magic.* ► sorcery, wizardry, witchcraft, devilry, the

magician *NOUN* **magicians** **1** a person who does magic tricks **2** a wizard

magistrate *NOUN* **magistrates** an official who hears and judges minor cases in a local court
▷ **magistracy** *NOUN*
[from Latin *magister* = master]

magnanimous (mag- nan- im- us) *ADJECTIVE* generous and forgiving, not petty-minded
▷ **magnanimously** *ADVERB* **magnanimity** *NOUN*

magnate *NOUN* **magnates** a wealthy influential person, especially in business

magnesium *NOUN* a silvery-white metal that burns with a very bright flame

magnet *NOUN* **magnets** a piece of iron or steel that can attract iron and that points north and south when it is hung up
▷ **magnetism** *NOUN*

magnetic *ADJECTIVE* **1** having the powers of a magnet **2** having the power to attract people • *a magnetic personality*
▷ **magnetically** *ADVERB*

magnetize *VERB* **magnetizes, magnetizing, magnetized** **1** make into a magnet **2** attract like a magnet
▷ **magnetization** *NOUN*

magneto (mag- neet- oh) *NOUN* **magnetos** a small electric generator using magnets

magnificent *ADJECTIVE* **1** grand or splendid in appearance etc. **2** excellent
▷ **magnificently** *ADVERB* **magnificence** *NOUN*
[from Latin *magnificus* = splendid]

magnify *VERB* **magnifies, magnifying, magnified** make something look or seem bigger than it really is
▷ **magnification** *NOUN* **magnifier** *NOUN*

magnifying glass *NOUN* **magnifying glasses** a lens that magnifies things

magnitude *NOUN* **magnitudes** **1** size or extent **2** importance

magpie *NOUN* **magpies** a noisy bird with black and white feathers, related to the crow [from **Mag** (short for Margaret) + an old word *pie* = magpie]

mahogany *NOUN* a hard brown wood

maid *NOUN* **maids** **1** a female servant **2** (*old use*) a girl
▷ **maidservant** *NOUN*

maiden *NOUN* **maidens** (*old use*) a girl
▷ **maidenhood** *NOUN*

maiden *ADJECTIVE* **1** not married • *a maiden aunt* **2** first • *a maiden voyage*

maiden name *NOUN* **maiden names** a woman's family name before she married

maiden over *NOUN* **maiden overs** a cricket over in which no runs are scored

mail[1] *NOUN* letters and parcels sent by post

mail[2] *NOUN* armour made of metal rings joined together • *a suit of chain mail*

mailing list *NOUN* **mailing lists** a list of names and addresses of people to whom an organization sends information from time to time

mail order *NOUN* a system for buying and selling goods by post

Thesaurus

black arts, the supernatural **2** *No children's party is complete without the magic.*
► conjuring, conjuring tricks, illusion, sleight of hand, (*technical*) prestidigitation **3** *The place had lost none of its magic.* ► charm, fascination, appeal, allure, glamour

magic *ADJECTIVE* *a magic spell* ► supernatural, magical, miraculous

magical *ADJECTIVE* *They would remember this magical day for the rest of their lives.*
► wonderful, marvellous, extraordinary, delightful, enchanting

magician *NOUN* *A magician would finish off the day's entertainment.* ► conjuror, entertainer, illusionist, wizard, sorcerer

magnificent *ADJECTIVE* **1** *a magnificent view*
► spectacular, splendid, impressive, imposing, noble, glorious, gorgeous, sumptuous **2** *a magnificent achievement* ► brilliant, masterly, superb, marvellous, wonderful, very fine

magnify *VERB* **1** *The device magnifies the image.*
► enlarge, maximize, amplify, make larger, augment, expand, increase, intensify, (*more informal*) blow up AN OPPOSITE IS reduce **2** *It is easy to magnify the difficulties involved.* (*informal*)
► exaggerate, inflate, maximize, overdo, overestimate, overstate, make too much of, blow up out of all proportion, dramatize
AN OPPOSITE IS minimize.

magnitude *NOUN* **1** *They realized the magnitude of the task* ► size, immensity, vastness, hugeness, extent, enormousness **2** *events of tragic magnitude* ► importance, significance, consequence, import, moment

maid *NOUN* *A maid cleared the room.* ► servant, serving girl, maidservant, domestic

mail *NOUN* *The letter came with the morning mail.*
► post, letters, delivery, packages, packets, parcels, correspondence

mail *VERB* *I'll mail you the package tomorrow.*
► post, send, dispatch, forward

maim *VERB* **maims, maiming, maimed** injure a person so that part of their body is made useless

main *ADJECTIVE* largest or most important

main *NOUN* **1** the main pipe or cable in a public system carrying water, gas, or (usually called **mains**) electricity to a building **2** (*old use*) the seas • *Drake sailed the Spanish main.*
in the main for the most part; on the whole

main clause *NOUN* **main clauses** a clause that can be used as a complete sentence COMPARE **subordinate clause**

mainland *NOUN* the main part of a country or continent, not the islands round it

mainly *ADVERB* **1** chiefly **2** almost completely **3** usually

mainstream *NOUN* the most widely accepted ideas or opinions about something • *Fascism is not in the mainstream of British politics.*

maintain *VERB* **maintains, maintaining, maintained** **1** cause something to continue; keep in existence **2** keep a thing in good condition **3** provide money for a person to live on **4** state that something is true

maintenance *NOUN* **1** maintaining or keeping something in good condition **2** money for food and clothing **3** money to be paid by a husband or wife to the other partner after a divorce

maize *NOUN* a tall kind of corn with large seeds on cobs

majestic *ADJECTIVE* **1** stately and dignified **2** imposing
▷ **majestically** *ADVERB*

majesty *NOUN* **majesties** **1** the title of a king or queen • *Her Majesty the Queen* **2** being majestic

major *ADJECTIVE* **1** greater; very important • *major roads* **2** of the musical scale that has a semitone after the 3rd and 7th notes COMPARE **minor**

major *NOUN* **majors** an army officer ranking next above a captain [from Latin, = larger, greater]

majority *NOUN* **majorities** **1** the greatest part of a group of people or things COMPARE **minority** **2** the amount by which the winner in an election beats the loser • *She had a majority of 25 over her opponent.* **3** the age at which a person becomes an adult according to the law (now usually 18) • *He has attained his majority.*

make *VERB* **makes, making, made** **1** bring something into existence, especially by putting things together **2** cause or compel • *Make him repeat it.* **3** gain or earn • *She makes £25,000 a year.* **4** achieve or reach • *He made 25 runs* • *The swimmer just made the shore.* **5** reckon • *What do you make the time?* **6** result in or add up to • *4 and 6 make 10* **7** perform an action etc. • *make an effort* **8** arrange for use • *make*

Thesaurus

maim *VERB* *Many people were killed or maimed in the attack.* ▸ injure, disable, mutilate, wound, disfigure, cripple, handicap

main *ADJECTIVE* *These are the main issues.* ▸ chief, principal, primary, prime, most important, overriding, foremost, fundamental, key, crucial, central, paramount, predominant, basic, essential

mainly *ADVERB* *The staff are mainly trainees.* ▸ chiefly, primarily, principally, mostly, predominantly, especially, essentially

maintain *VERB* **1** *The villagers pay to maintain the private road.* ▸ keep up, preserve, service, look after, take care of **2** *We need to maintain our links with industry.* ▸ sustain, continue, keep up, conserve, retain, preserve, prolong **3** *They maintain that they were never there.* ▸ assert, claim, affirm, insist, make out, declare, contend, argue

maintenance *NOUN* **1** *The buildings need a good deal of regular maintenance.* ▸ upkeep, repairs, preservation, care, servicing, conservation, looking after **2** *Absent fathers have to pay maintenance.* ▸ financial support, subsistence, alimony, allowance

majestic *ADJECTIVE* *a majestic range of mountains* ▸ magnificent, grand, spectacular, splendid, impressive, imposing, noble, glorious, gorgeous, sumptuous

majesty *NOUN* **1** *The procession continued with great majesty.* ▸ dignity, stateliness, solemnity, glory, splendour, grandeur, nobility **2** *the Queen's majesty* ▸ sovereignty, royalty, dominion, authority

major *ADJECTIVE* *a major achievement* ▸ important, considerable, significant, noteworthy, substantial, sizeable, appreciable

majority *NOUN* **1** *The majority of older people are poor.* ▸ greater number, preponderance, bulk **2** *the age of majority* ▸ adulthood, coming of age, manhood, maturity, womanhood
AN OPPOSITE IS minority
be in the majority ▸ predominate, preponderate, be greater, dominate, outnumber, prevail

make *VERB* **1** *He makes reproduction furniture.* ▸ build, construct, assemble, put together, manufacture, produce **2** *She made me tell her the whole story.* ▸ force, coerce, oblige, compel, prevail on, pressure, urge USAGE You need to use the word *to* after all these synonyms, e.g. *She forced me to tell her the whole story.* If you use prevail you have to say *She prevailed on me to tell her the whole story.* **3** *The*

the beds **9** cause to be successful or happy • *Her visit made my day.*
make do manage with something that is not what you really want
make for go towards
make love **1** have sexual intercourse **2** (*old use*) try to win someone's love
make off go away quickly
make out **1** manage to see, hear, or understand something **2** claim or pretend that something is true
make up **1** build or put together **2** invent a story etc. **3** be friendly again after a disagreement **4** compensate for something **5** put on make-up
make up your mind decide

make *NOUN* **makes** **1** making; how something is made **2** a brand of goods; something made by a particular firm

makeshift *ADJECTIVE* improvised or used because you have nothing better • *We used a box as a makeshift table.*

make-up *NOUN* **1** cosmetics **2** the way something is made up **3** a person's character

maladjusted *ADJECTIVE* unable to fit in or cope with other people or your own circumstances

malapropism *NOUN* **malapropisms** a comical confusion of words, e.g. using **hooligan** instead of **hurricane**

malaria *NOUN* a feverish disease spread by mosquitoes
▷ **malarial** *ADJECTIVE*

male *ADJECTIVE* **1** belonging to the sex that reproduces by fertilizing egg cells produced by the female **2** of men • *a male voice choir*

male *NOUN* **males** a male person, animal, or plant

male chauvinist *NOUN* **male chauvinists** a man who thinks that women are not as good as men

malevolent (ma- lev- ol- ent) *ADJECTIVE* wishing to harm people
▷ **malevolently** *ADVERB* **malevolence** *NOUN*

Thesaurus

animals make such a noise. ► cause, create, generate, engender, give rise to **4** *She made a little bow.* ► perform, execute, give, do, effect, carry out **5** *The town made him their mayor.* ► appoint, name, designate, nominate, elect, vote **6** *We seem to have made some mistakes.* ► commit, perpetrate, be responsible for, be guilty of **7** *The scheme is bound to make money.* ► earn, bring in, gain, acquire AN OPPOSITE IS lose **8** *James's mother went out to make the lunch.* ► prepare, get ready, cook, put together, concoct **9** *I make the total over £500.* ► estimate, calculate, work out USAGE You need to use the word *at* after all these synonyms, e.g. *I estimate the total at over £500.* **10** *We must make a decision.* ► reach, come to, arrive at, settle on **11** *I think she'll make a good leader.* ► be, constitute, act as, serve as
make off *The thieves made off with the money.* ► escape, run off, get away, leave, bolt, (*more informal*) clear off
make out **1** *We could make out a tower in the distance.* ► see, discern, distinguish, perceive, detect, recognize, catch sight of, glimpse **2** *They made out we owed them money.* ► maintain, assert, claim, affirm, insist, declare, contend, argue **3** *How did you make out at the interview?* ► manage, get on, get along, do, cope, (*more formal*) fare **4** *The old man had made out a will.* ► draw up, write, complete
make up **1** *Such a story is not something anyone could make up.* ► invent, fabricate, contrive, concoct, think up, devise, create, (*more informal*) cook up **2** *They decided to kiss and make up.* ► be friends again, make peace, settle your differences, bury the hatchet, mend fences AN OPPOSITE IS quarrel
make up for *The fine acting made up for all the problems with the production.* ► compensate for, offset, counterbalance, counteract, make amends for, redress

make *NOUN* *a new make of car* ► brand, marque, model, sort, kind, type, variety

make-believe *NOUN* *The secret garden was only make-believe.* ► fantasy, pretence, fiction, fancy, illusion, invention, imagination
AN OPPOSITE IS reality

make-believe *ADJECTIVE* *a make-believe world of elves and fairies* ► imaginary, fanciful, pretended, sham, simulated, unreal, feigned, made-up, mock, (*more informal*) pretend
AN OPPOSITE IS real

maker *NOUN* *a maker of toy cars*
► manufacturer, producer, creator, designer, originator, constructor, builder

makeshift *ADJECTIVE* *He arranged a row of chairs to form a makeshift bed.* ► temporary, standby, rough-and-ready, improvised, stopgap, pernicious, hurtful

make-up *NOUN* **1** *Ambition is an important part of his make-up.* ► character, nature, temperament, constitution, disposition **2** *Her make-up started to run.* ► cosmetics, powder, paint

malevolent *ADJECTIVE* *the malevolent gaze of his eyes* ► malicious, hostile, spiteful, baleful, malign, vindictive, malignant, pernicious, hurtful, offensive, venomous

malfunction *NOUN* **malfunctions** faulty functioning • *a malfunction in the computer*

malfunction *VERB* **malfunctions, malfunctioning, malfunctioned** fail to work properly

malice *NOUN* the desire to harm other people
▷ **malicious** *ADJECTIVE* **maliciously** *ADVERB*

malign (mal- I'n) *ADJECTIVE* **1** harmful • *a malign influence* **2** showing malice
▷ **malignity** (mal- ig- nit- ee) *NOUN*

malignant *ADJECTIVE* **1** (said about a tumour) growing uncontrollably **2** full of malice
▷ **malignantly** *ADVERB* **malignancy** *NOUN*

malleable *ADJECTIVE* **1** able to be pressed or hammered into shape **2** easy to influence; adaptable
▷ **malleability** *NOUN*

mallet *NOUN* **mallets** **1** a large hammer, usually made of wood **2** an implement with a long handle, used in croquet or polo for striking the ball

malnutrition *NOUN* bad health because you do not have enough food or the right kind of food
▷ **malnourished** *ADJECTIVE*

malt *NOUN* dried barley used in brewing, making vinegar, etc.
▷ **malted** *ADJECTIVE*

maltreat *VERB* **maltreats, maltreating, maltreated** ill-treat
▷ **maltreatment** *NOUN*

mammal *NOUN* **mammals** any animal of which the female gives birth to live babies which are fed with milk from her own body
▷ **mammalian** (mam- ay- lee- an) *ADJECTIVE*

mammoth *NOUN* **mammoths** an extinct elephant with a hairy skin and curved tusks

mammoth *ADJECTIVE* huge

man *NOUN* **men** **1** a grown-up male human being **2** an individual person **3** mankind **4** a piece used in chess or other board games

man *VERB* **mans, manning, manned** supply with people to work something • *Man the pumps!* [from Old English]

manacle *NOUN* **manacles** a fetter or handcuff

manacle *VERB* **manacles, manacling, manacled** fasten with manacles

manage *VERB* **manages, managing, managed** **1** be able to cope with something difficult **2** be in charge of a business or part of it, or a group of people
▷ **manageable** *ADJECTIVE*

management *NOUN* **1** managing **2** managers; the people in charge

Thesaurus

malice *NOUN* *actions prompted by malice*
► malevolence, ill will, spite, spitefulness, animosity

malicious *ADJECTIVE* *malicious remarks*
► malevolent, hostile, spiteful, baleful, malign, vindictive, malignant, mischievous, pernicious, offensive, hurtful, venomous OPPOSITES ARE benevolent, kind

malignant *ADJECTIVE* **1** *a malignant disease*
► fatal, incurable, terminal, virulent, destructive **2** *a malignant growth* ► cancerous, poisonous, non-benign, spreading AN OPPOSITE IS benign **3** *a malignant stare*
► malevolent, hostile, spiteful, baleful, malign, pernicious, offensive, hurtful, venomous OPPOSITES ARE benevolent, kind

maltreat *VERB* *He was a bully and often maltreated his wife.* ► ill-treat, mistreat, abuse, misuse, harm, injure, molest, (*more informal*) knock about

mammoth *ADJECTIVE* *It would be a mammoth task getting the house to rights again.* ► huge, enormous, gigantic, immense, massive, colossal, vast, large, big, giant, (*more informal*) whopping, (*more informal*) ginormous AN OPPOSITE IS tiny

man *NOUN* **1** *a man in a smart suit* ► male, gentleman, fellow, (*more informal*) chap, (*more informal*) bloke **2** *All men are fallible.* ► person, individual, human being **3** *the evolution of modern man* ► humanity, humankind, mankind, the human race, humans, Homo sapiens **4** *The men have gone on strike.*
► worker, employee RELATED ADJECTIVES male, masculine

man *VERB* *We need to man the reception desk from 8 till 5.* ► staff, provide personnel for, provide staff for, occupy

manage *VERB* **1** *She manages a team of 20.* ► be in charge of, run, head, lead, supervise, oversee, control **2** *a course in managing money*
► organize, administer, deal with, regulate **3** *I could only just manage the extra work I had to do.* ► undertake, accomplish, achieve, finish, complete, carry out **4** *I don't know how we'll manage without her.* ► cope, get along, survive, fare, make do **5** *a horse that's difficult to manage* ► control, handle, master, cope with, deal with

manageable *ADJECTIVE* **1** *a manageable task*
► achievable, doable, practicable, feasible, reasonable, attainable, viable AN OPPOSITE IS awkward **2** *a manageable horse* ► controllable, obedient, tractable, compliant, amenable, disciplined, docile OPPOSITES ARE unmanageable, disobedient

management *NOUN* **1** *The local cinema is under new management.* ► administration, control,

manager *NOUN* **managers** a person who manages something
▷ **manageress** *NOUN* **managerial** (man- a- jeer- ee- al) *ADJECTIVE*

mandarin *NOUN* **mandarins** **1** an important official **2** a kind of small orange

mane *NOUN* **manes** the long hair on a horse's or lion's neck

manganese *NOUN* a hard brittle metal

manger *NOUN* **mangers** a trough in a stable for horses or cattle to feed from

mangle *VERB* **mangles, mangling, mangled** damage something by crushing or cutting it roughly

mango *NOUN* **mangoes** a tropical fruit with yellow pulp

manhandle *VERB* **manhandles, manhandling, manhandled** treat or push roughly

manhole *NOUN* **manholes** a space or opening, usually with a cover, by which a person can get into a sewer or boiler etc. to inspect or repair it

manhood *NOUN* **1** the condition of being a man **2** manly qualities

mania *NOUN* **manias** **1** violent madness **2** great enthusiasm • *a mania for sport*
▷ **maniac** *NOUN* **manic** *ADJECTIVE*

manicure *NOUN* **manicures** care and treatment of the hands and nails
▷ **manicure** *VERB* **manicurist** *NOUN*

manifest *ADJECTIVE* clear and obvious
▷ **manifestly** *ADVERB*

manifesto *NOUN* **manifestos** a public statement of a group's or person's policy or principles

manifold *ADJECTIVE* of many kinds; very varied

manipulate *VERB* **manipulates, manipulating, manipulated** **1** handle or arrange something skilfully **2** get someone to do what you want by treating them cleverly
▷ **manipulation** *NOUN* **manipulator** *NOUN*

mankind *NOUN* human beings in general

manly *ADJECTIVE* **1** suitable for a man **2** brave and strong
▷ **manliness** *NOUN*

manner *NOUN* **1** the way something happens or is done **2** a person's way of behaving **3** a sort or type • *all manner of things*

mannerism *NOUN* **mannerisms** a person's own particular gesture or way of speaking

manners *PLURAL NOUN* how a person behaves with other people; politeness

manoeuvre (man- oo- ver) *NOUN* **manoeuvres** a difficult or skilful or cunning action

manoeuvre *VERB* **manoeuvres, manoeuvring, manoeuvred** move carefully and skilfully
▷ **manoeuvrable** *ADJECTIVE*

Thesaurus

direction, supervision, charge, care **2** *The union is in dispute with the management.*

manager *NOUN* *a meeting of departmental managers* ► director, administrator, head, executive, supervisor, principal, controller, boss, chief

mangle *VERB* *Henry was staring at the man's mangled hand.* ► maul, mutilate, maim, crush, damage, disfigure, injure, wound, lacerate, squash, tear

maniac *NOUN* *a homicidal maniac* ► lunatic, madman *or* madwoman, psychopath, (*more informal*) loony

manipulate *VERB* **1** *You need to know how to manipulate all the machine's knobs and levers.* ► operate, work, wield, control, negotiate, twiddle **2** *Governments try to manipulate the economy before elections.* ► influence, control, exploit **3** *It is not difficult to manipulate the data to get the result you want.* ► alter, distort, falsify, doctor, massage, tinker with, fiddle with, fudge, rig, (*more informal*) cook

mankind *NOUN* *They want to save nature from mankind.* ► humanity, humankind, the human race, humans, man, Homo sapiens

manly *ADJECTIVE* **1** *a manly physique* ► virile, masculine, muscular, sturdy, robust, well-built **2** *manly deeds* ► brave, courageous, bold, heroic, valiant, gallant, chivalrous

man-made *ADJECTIVE* *a man-made fibre* ► synthetic, artificial, manufactured, simulated, imitation AN OPPOSITE IS natural

manner *NOUN* **1** *They dealt with the problem in a very efficient manner.* ► way, fashion, style, method, means, procedure, process, mode **2** *I don't much like his unfriendly manner.* ► attitude, demeanour, disposition, air, look, bearing, behaviour, character, conduct, mien **3** *We've seen all manner of things there.* ► kind, sort, type, variety, category, class **4** manners *He needs to learn some manners.* ► politeness, refinement, civility, courtesy, etiquette, good behaviour, good conduct, breeding, gentility

manoeuvre *NOUN* **1** *She parked the car with a deft manoeuvre.* ► movement, move, action, operation **2** *a diplomatic manoeuvre* ► stratagem, strategy, tactic, move, plan, plot, ploy, ruse, dodge, gambit, trick **3** *military manoeuvres* ► exercise, movement, operation, training

manoeuvre *VERB* *He manoeuvred the trunk down the stairs.* ► manipulate, negotiate, move, engineer, guide, navigate, pilot, steer

A B C D E F G H I J K L **M** N O P Q R S T U V W X Y Z

manor *NOUN* **manors** **1** a manor house **2** the land belonging to a manor house
▷ **manorial** *ADJECTIVE*
[from early French, related to **mansion**]

manor house *NOUN* **manor houses** a large important house in the country

manpower *NOUN* the number of people who are working or needed or available for work on something

mansion *NOUN* **mansions** a large stately house [from Latin *mansio* = a place to stay, a dwelling]

manslaughter *NOUN* killing a person unlawfully but without meaning to

mantelpiece *NOUN* **mantelpieces** a shelf above a fireplace

mantle *NOUN* **mantles** **1** a cloak **2** a covering • *a mantle of snow*

manual *ADJECTIVE* worked by or done with the hands • *a manual typewriter; manual work*
▷ **manually** *ADVERB*

manual *NOUN* **manuals** a handbook containing instructions etc.

manufacture *VERB* **manufactures, manufacturing, manufactured** make things, especially on a large scale
▷ **manufacture** *NOUN* **manufacturer** *NOUN*

manure *NOUN* fertilizer, especially dung

manuscript *NOUN* **manuscripts** something written or typed but not printed

Manx *ADJECTIVE* to do with the Isle of Man

many *ADJECTIVE* **more, most** great in number; numerous • *many people*

many *NOUN* many people or things • *Many were found.*

Maori (rhymes with *flowery*) *NOUN* **Maoris** **1** a member of the aboriginal people of New Zealand **2** their language

map *NOUN* **maps** a diagram of part or all of the earth's surface or of the sky

map *VERB* **maps, mapping, mapped** make a map of an area
map out plan the details of something

marathon *NOUN* **marathons** a long-distance running race, especially one covering 26 miles 385 yards (42.195 km) [named after Marathon in Greece, from which a messenger is said to have run to Athens (about 40 kilometres) to announce that the Greeks had defeated the Persian army]

March *NOUN* the third month of the year [named after Mars, the Roman god of war]

marauding *ADJECTIVE* going about in search of plunder or prey
▷ **marauder** *NOUN*

marble *NOUN* **marbles** **1** a small glass ball used in games **2** a kind of limestone polished and used in sculpture or building

march *VERB* **marches, marching, marched** **1** walk with regular steps **2** make somebody walk somewhere • *He marched them up the hill.*
▷ **marcher** *NOUN*

march *NOUN* **marches** **1** marching **2** music suitable for marching to

mare *NOUN* **mares** a female horse or donkey

margarine (mar- ja- reen, mar- ga- reen) *NOUN* a substance used like butter, made from animal or vegetable fats

margin *NOUN* **margins** **1** an edge or border **2** the blank space between the edge of a page and the writing or pictures etc. on it **3** the difference between two scores or prices etc. • *She won by a narrow margin.*

Thesaurus

manual *ADJECTIVE* *manual work* ► labouring, physical, by hand

manual *NOUN* *a training manual* ► handbook, guide, guidebook, reference book

manufacture *VERB* *The country could manufacture a nuclear weapon within five years.* ► make, construct, create, build, prefabricate, assemble, fabricate, mass-produce, process, (*informal*) turn out

many *ADJECTIVE* *There are many reasons.* ► a lot of, plenty of, numerous, countless, various, copious, profuse, innumerable, umpteen, (*more informal*) lots of AN OPPOSITE IS few

map *NOUN* *a map of Europe* ► chart, diagram, plan RELATED ADJECTIVE cartographic RELATED NOUN cartography

map *VERB* *Aircraft were used to map the region.* ► chart, survey
map out *We mapped out a plan.* ► outline, set out, formulate, detail

mar *VERB* *His good looks were marred by stubble and red eyes.* ► spoil, impair, disfigure, ruin, deface, detract from, tarnish

march *VERB* *A company of soldiers marched past.* ► file, troop, parade, stride, pace, walk

march *NOUN* **1** *a three-day march* ► trek, hike, tramp, slog **2** *a protest march* ► procession, rally, demonstration, parade, (*more informal*) demo **3** *the march of time* ► advance, progress, progression, passage, evolution

margin *NOUN* **1** *the margin of the lake* ► edge, border, boundary, verge, perimeter, side **2** *They won by a narrow margin.* ► difference, gap, surplus

marginal *ADJECTIVE* **1** in a margin • *marginal notes* **2** very slight • *a marginal difference*
▷ **marginally** *ADVERB*

marginal seat *NOUN* **marginal seats** a constituency where an MP was elected with only a small majority and may be defeated in the next election

marine (ma- reen) *ADJECTIVE* to do with the sea; living in the sea

marine *NOUN* **marines** a member of the troops who are trained to serve at sea as well as on land

marionette *NOUN* **marionettes** a puppet worked by strings or wires

marital *ADJECTIVE* to do with marriage

maritime *ADJECTIVE* **1** to do with the sea or ships **2** found near the sea

mark[1] *NOUN* **marks** **1** a spot, dot, line, or stain etc. on something **2** a number or letter etc. put on a piece of work to show how good it is **3** a distinguishing feature **4** a sign or symbol • *They all stood as a mark of respect.* **5** a target
on your marks! a command to runners to get ready to begin a race
up to the mark of the normal or expected standard

mark *VERB* **marks, marking, marked** **1** put a mark on something **2** give a mark to a piece of work **3** pay attention to something • *Mark my words!* **4** keep close to an opposing player in football etc.
▷ **marker** *NOUN*
mark time **1** march on the spot without moving forward **2** occupy your time without making any progress

mark[2] *NOUN* **marks** a German unit of money replaced by the euro in 2002

marked *ADJECTIVE* noticeable • *a marked improvement*
▷ **markedly** *ADVERB*

market *NOUN* **markets** **1** a place where things are bought and sold, usually from stalls in the open air **2** demand for things • *Is there a market for typewriters now?*
▷ **marketplace** *NOUN*
on the market offered for sale

market research *NOUN* the study of what people need or want to buy

marksman *NOUN* **marksmen** an expert in shooting at a target
▷ **marksmanship** *NOUN*

marmalade *NOUN* jam made from oranges, lemons, or other citrus fruit

maroon *VERB* **maroons, marooning, marooned** abandon or isolate somebody in a deserted place; strand

marquee (mar- kee) *NOUN* **marquees** a large tent used for a party or exhibition etc.

marquis *NOUN* **marquises** a nobleman ranking next above an earl

marriage *NOUN* **marriages** **1** the state of being married **2** a wedding

marrow *NOUN* **marrows** **1** a large gourd eaten as a vegetable **2** the soft substance inside bones

Thesaurus

marginal *ADJECTIVE* *The extra cost is marginal.* ► negligible, minimal, insignificant, unimportant, borderline OPPOSITES ARE significant, important

mark *NOUN* **1** *a dirty mark* ► spot, stain, blot, blotch, smudge, blemish **2** *a mark of respect* ► sign, token, symbol, indication, proof, evidence, gesture **3** *Donations have passed the million mark.* ► stage, point, level **4** *a comment that hit the mark* ► target, objective, purpose, aim **5** *He got a better mark for French than for German.* ► grade, grading, score, assessment, evaluation

mark *VERB* **1** *She took great care not to mark her white dress.* ► stain, blemish, smudge, dirty, discolour, blot **2** *All possessions should be clearly marked.* ► label, tag **3** *The capture of the rebel stronghold marked a new stage in the war.* ► represent, signify, herald, denote, identify, characterize **4** *a festival to mark the Golden Jubilee* ► celebrate, recognize, observe, commemorate, remember **5** *Mark my words carefully.* ► heed, note, mind, take notice of, listen to, regard **6** *She had exam papers to mark that evening.* ► assess, grade, correct, evaluate, appraise

marked *ADJECTIVE* *a marked improvement in health* ► distinct, noticeable, decided, pronounced, plain, clear, emphatic, palpable AN OPPOSITE IS slight

market *NOUN* **1** *The local market is every Saturday.* ► bazaar, fair, sale, marketplace **2** *The market for second-hand cars is thriving.* ► demand, call, need, requirement

market *VERB* *The firm markets reproduction furniture.* ► sell, trade in, merchandise, retail

maroon *VERB* *a story about a group of boys marooned on a desert island* ► strand, cast away, abandon, isolate, leave, desert, forsake

marriage *NOUN* **1** *The couple will celebrate their 50 years of marriage.* ► matrimony, wedlock, partnership, union **2** *The marriage took place in the local register office.* ► wedding, wedding ceremony, match, nuptials RELATED ADJECTIVES conjugal, marital, matrimonial, nuptial

marry *VERB* **marries, marrying, married** **1** become a person's husband or wife **2** join two people as husband and wife; be in charge of a marriage ceremony

marsh *NOUN* **marshes** a low-lying area of very wet ground
▷ **marshy** *ADJECTIVE*

marshal *NOUN* **marshals** **1** an official who supervises a contest or ceremony etc. **2** an officer of very high rank • *a Field Marshal*

marshmallow *NOUN* **marshmallows** a soft spongy sweet, usually pink or white

marsupial (mar- soo- pee- al) *NOUN* **marsupials** an animal such as a kangaroo or wallaby The female has a pouch on the front of its body in which its babies are carried

martial *ADJECTIVE* to do with war; warlike

martial arts *PLURAL NOUN* fighting sports, such as judo and karate

martial law *NOUN* government of a country by the armed forces during a crisis

martyr *NOUN* **martyrs** a person who is killed or made to suffer because of his or her beliefs
▷ **martyrdom** *NOUN*

marvel *NOUN* **marvels** a wonderful thing
▷ **marvellous** *ADJECTIVE*

marzipan *NOUN* a soft sweet food made of ground almonds, eggs, and sugar

mascot *NOUN* **mascots** a person, animal, or thing that is believed to bring good luck

masculine *ADJECTIVE* **1** to do with men **2** typical of or suitable for men **3** (in some languages) belonging to the class of words which includes the words referring to men, such as *garçon* and *livre* in French
▷ **masculinity** *NOUN*

mash *VERB* **mashes, mashing, mashed** crush into a soft mass

mask *NOUN* **masks** a covering worn over the face to disguise or protect it

masochist (mas- ok- ist) *NOUN* **masochists** a person who enjoys things that seem painful or tiresome
▷ **masochism** *NOUN*

mason *NOUN* **masons** a person who builds or works with stone

masonry *NOUN* **1** the stone parts of a building; stonework **2** a mason's work

masquerade *NOUN* **masquerades** a pretence

masquerade *VERB* **masquerades, masquerading, masqueraded** pretend to be something • *He masqueraded as a policeman.*

Mass *NOUN* **Masses** the Communion service in a Roman Catholic church

mass *NOUN* **masses** **1** a large amount **2** a heap or other collection of matter **3** (in science) the

Thesaurus

marry *VERB* **1** *They never married.* ► get married, wed, (*more informal*) tie the knot OPPOSITES ARE separate, divorce **2** *He married Jessica in Italy.* ► wed, (*more informal*) get hitched to OPPOSITES ARE separate from, divorce **3** *The exhibition marries information with entertainment.* ► combine, unite, link, merge, connect, join, ally

marsh *NOUN* *The car had plunged into a marsh.* ► swamp, bog, marshland, wetland, mire, morass, quagmire, quicksands, fen

marshal *VERB* *The king marshalled a huge army. The police marshalled their evidence with great care.* ► gather, assemble, collect, organize, muster, set out, deploy, draw up, group, line up, arrange OPPOSITES ARE disperse, scatter

marvel *VERB* **marvel at** *Everyone marvelled at their courage.* ► admire, be amazed by, wonder at, applaud, praise, appreciate, respect, be astonished by, be surprised by

marvellous *ADJECTIVE* **1** *a marvellous achievement* ► remarkable, amazing, extraordinary, wonderful, magnificent, astonishing, astounding AN OPPOSITE IS ordinary **2** *We had a marvellous time.* ► excellent, wonderful, fantastic, splendid, lovely, delightful, smashing, (*more informal*) terrific OPPOSITES ARE awful, dreadful

masculine *ADJECTIVE* **1** *She wore a masculine shirt with rolled-up sleeves.* ► male, man's *or* men's, manlike AN OPPOSITE IS feminine **2** *a powerfully masculine man* ► manly, virile, muscular, well-built, strapping, vigorous OPPOSITES ARE weak, timid

mash *VERB* *Mash the potatoes and put them on top.* ► crush, pulp, cream, purée, pulverize, pound, smash, squash, grind, mangle, beat

mask *NOUN* *They wore masks to hide their faces.* ► disguise, veil, camouflage, cover, screen, shield, façade

mask *VERB* *A row of trees masked the view.* ► conceal, cover, obscure, screen, shield, hide, shroud, veil, blot out, camouflage, cloak, disguise

mass *NOUN* **1** *a mass of wet leaves* ► pile, heap, load, accumulation, collection, conglomeration **2** *a mass of cars heading for the coast* ► multitude, throng, crowd, troop, mob, quantity, large number **3** *The mass of people declined to vote at all.* ► majority, greater part, bulk, body **4** *an object having a large mass* ► weight, size, magnitude, bulk

quantity of physical matter that a thing contains

mass *ADJECTIVE* involving a large number of people • *mass murder*

massacre *NOUN* **massacres** the killing of a large number of people
▷ **massacre** *VERB*

massage (mas- ahzh) *VERB* **massages, massaging, massaged** rub and press the body to make it less stiff or less painful
▷ **massage** *NOUN* **masseur** *NOUN* **masseuse** *NOUN*

massive *ADJECTIVE* large and heavy; huge

mass media *NOUN* the main media of news information, especially newspapers and broadcasting

mass production *NOUN* manufacturing goods in large quantities
▷ **mass-produced** *ADJECTIVE*

mast *NOUN* **masts** a tall pole that holds up a ship's sails or a flag or an aerial

master *NOUN* **masters** **1** a man who is in charge of something **2** a male teacher **3** a great artist, composer, sportsman, etc. **4** something from which copies are made **5** (*old use*) a title put before a boy's name

masterful *ADJECTIVE* **1** domineering **2** very skilful
▷ **masterfully** *ADVERB*

master key *NOUN* **master keys** a key that will open several different locks

masterly *ADJECTIVE* very skilful

Master of Arts *NOUN* **Masters of Arts** a person who has taken the next degree after Bachelor of Arts

master of ceremonies *NOUN* **masters of ceremonies** a person who introduces the speakers at a formal event, or the entertainers at a variety show

Master of Science *NOUN* **Masters of Science** a person who has taken the next degree after Bachelor of Science

masterpiece *NOUN* **masterpieces** **1** an excellent piece of work **2** a person's best piece of work

mastery *NOUN* complete control or thorough knowledge or skill in something

mastiff *NOUN* **mastiffs** a large kind of dog

masturbate *VERB* **masturbates, masturbating, masturbated** get sexual pleasure by rubbing your genitals
▷ **masturbation** *NOUN*

mat *NOUN* **mats** **1** a small carpet **2** a doormat **3** a small piece of material put on a table to protect the surface

matador *NOUN* **matadors** a bullfighter who fights on foot

Thesaurus

mass *ADJECTIVE* *a mass protest* ► wholesale, universal, large-scale, widespread, comprehensive, general, popular
AN OPPOSITE IS small-scale

mass *VERB* *Spectators massed under the trees during the downpour.* ► gather, assemble, collect, flock

massacre *NOUN* *the massacre of innocent civilians* ► slaughter, killing, mass murder, extermination, butchery, carnage, annihilation

massacre *VERB* *The army massacred most of the population.* ► slaughter, butcher, exterminate, annihilate, murder, liquidate, eliminate

massive *ADJECTIVE* *a massive building; massive debts* ► huge, enormous, gigantic, immense, colossal, vast, large, big, giant, (*more informal*) whopping, (*more informal*) ginormous
AN OPPOSITE IS tiny

master *NOUN* **1** *He became master of the country after a bloody coup.* ► ruler, chief, head, lord, overlord, governor **2** *a dog's master* ► owner, keeper **3** *a master of disguises* ► expert (at), genius, past master, maestro, virtuoso

master *VERB* **1** *He managed to master his feelings.* ► control, restrain, check, contain, curb, confine, curb, keep in check, repress, subdue, suppress **2** *She mastered the language after a few months.* ► learn, grasp, acquire, be expert in, (*more informal*) get the hang of

masterful *ADJECTIVE* USAGE Do not confuse this word with *masterly*, which has a different meaning. *the most masterful sovereign in English history* ► authoritative, commanding, powerful, domineering, overbearing, arrogant, dictatorial, tyrannical, bossy

masterly *ADJECTIVE* USAGE Do not confuse this word with *masterful*, which has a different meaning. *a masterly survey of the subject* ► expert, skilful, adept, adroit, accomplished, consummate, intelligent, fine

mastermind *NOUN* *the mastermind behind the robbery* ► originator, planner, creator, engineer, prime mover, architect, inventor, manager, (*more informal*) brain, (*more informal*) brains

mastermind *VERB* *They brought him back to mastermind the new operation.* ► control, direct, plan, organize, coordinate, conduct, supervise, carry through

mastery *NOUN* **1** *a mastery of languages* ► command, knowledge, grasp, comprehension, understanding, proficiency (in) **2** *work done with great mastery*

match[1] *NOUN* **matches** a small thin stick with a head made of a substance that gives a flame when rubbed on something rough
▷ **matchbox** *NOUN* **matchstick** *NOUN*

match[2] *NOUN* **matches** **1** a game or contest between two teams or players **2** one person or thing that matches another **3** a marriage

match *VERB* **matches, matching, matched** **1** be equal or similar to another person or thing **2** put teams or players to compete against each other **3** find something that is similar or corresponding

mate[1] *NOUN* **mates** **1** a companion or friend **2** each of a mated pair of birds or animals **3** an officer on a merchant ship

mate *VERB* **mates, mating, mated** **1** come together or bring two together in order to breed **2** put things together as a pair or because they correspond

mate[2] *NOUN, VERB* (*in chess*) checkmate

material *NOUN* **materials** **1** anything used for making something else **2** cloth or fabric

materialize *VERB* **materializes, materializing, materialized** **1** become visible; appear • *The ghost didn't materialize.* **2** become a fact; happen • *The trip did not materialize.*
▷ **materialization** *NOUN*

maternal *ADJECTIVE* **1** to do with a mother **2** motherly
▷ **maternally** *ADVERB*

maternity *NOUN* motherhood

maternity *ADJECTIVE* to do with having a baby • *a maternity ward*

mathematics *NOUN* the study of numbers, measurements, and shapes
▷ **mathematical** *ADJECTIVE* **mathematically** *ADVERB* **mathematician** *NOUN*
[from Greek *mathema* = science, from *manthanein* = to learn]

matriarch (may- tree- ark) *NOUN* **matriarchs** a woman who is head of a family or tribe COMPARE **patriarch**
▷ **matriarchal** *ADJECTIVE* **matriarchy** *NOUN*

matrix (may- triks) *NOUN* **matrices** (may- tri- seez) **1** (in mathematics) a set of quantities arranged in rows and columns **2** a mould or framework in which something is made or allowed to develop

matron *NOUN* **matrons** **1** a mature married woman **2** a woman in charge of nursing in a school etc. or (formerly) of the nursing staff in a hospital
▷ **matronly** *ADJECTIVE*

matted *ADJECTIVE* tangled into a mass

matter *NOUN* **matters** **1** something you can touch or see, not spirit or mind or qualities etc. **2** a substance • *Peat consists mainly of vegetable matter.* **3** things of a certain kind • *printed matter.* **4** something to be thought about or done • *It's a serious matter.* **5** a quantity • *in a matter of minutes*

Thesaurus

► proficiency, capability, expertness, skill, adroitness, dexterity

match *NOUN* **1** *a cricket match* ► game, contest, competition, fixture, test match, tie, tournament **2** *The dress and shoes are a good match.* ► combination, pair **3** *She found a match for the tall vase.* ► copy, replica, complement, counterpart, duplicate, twin **4** *The enemy tanks were no match for ours in speed and range.* ► equal, rival, equivalent, counterpart **5** *a love match* ► marriage, union, friendship, partnership, relationship, alliance

match *VERB* **1** *The hat matches her dress.* ► go with, suit, harmonize with, tone with, blend with, complement **2** *The two versions of the story don't match.* ► agree, correspond, tally **3** *No one can match him at Scrabble.* ► equal, rival, compete with

matching *ADJECTIVE* *The curtains have a matching duvet cover.* ► corresponding, coordinating, equivalent, harmonizing, toning, complementing AN OPPOSITE IS incongruous

mate *NOUN* **1** *a plumber's mate* ► assistant, helper, apprentice, colleague **2** *He went to see a film with his mates.* ► friend, pal, chum, companion **3** *He's still looking for his ideal mate.*
► partner, wife *or* husband, spouse, lover, consort

mate *VERB* *The zoo is trying to get the pandas to mate.* ► breed, copulate, couple

material *NOUN* **1** *material for making curtains* ► fabric, cloth, textile, stuff **2** *organic material* ► matter, substance, stuff **3** *We are collecting material for an article on surfing.* ► data, information, facts, statistics, evidence, particulars

material *ADJECTIVE* **1** *the material world as distinct from the spiritual world* ► physical, corporeal, tangible, earthly, concrete OPPOSITES ARE spiritual, abstract **2** *information that is material to our enquiries* ► relevant, pertinent, applicable, germane OPPOSITES ARE irrelevant, immaterial

matter *NOUN* **1** *Excess vegetable matter can be kept in a separate waste bin.* ► material, substance, stuff **2** *The last sentence of his statement goes to the heart of the matter.* ► affair, business, subject, topic, issue, concern **3** *It's of little matter now.* ► importance, consequence, significance, moment

a matter of course the natural or expected thing • *I always lock my bike, as a matter of course.*
as a matter of fact in fact
no matter it does not matter
what is the matter? what is wrong?

matter *VERB* **matters, mattering, mattered** be important

matter-of-fact *ADJECTIVE* keeping to facts; not imaginative or emotional • *She talked about death in a very matter-of-fact way.*

mattress *NOUN* **mattresses** soft or springy material in a fabric covering, used on or as a bed

mature *ADJECTIVE* **1** fully grown or developed **2** grown-up
▷ **maturely** *ADVERB* **maturity** *NOUN*

mature *VERB* **matures, maturing, matured** make or become mature

maul *VERB* **mauls, mauling, mauled** injure by handling or clawing • *He was mauled by a lion.*

mauve (mohv) *NOUN* pale purple

maxim *NOUN* **maxims** a short saying giving a general truth or rule of behaviour, e.g. 'Waste not, want not'

maximize *VERB* **maximizes, maximizing, maximized** increase something to a maximum

maximum *NOUN* **maxima** or **maximums** the greatest possible number or amount (The opposite is **minimum**)

May *NOUN* the fifth month of the year [named after Maia, a Roman goddess]

may[1] *AUXILIARY VERB* **may, might** used to express permission (*You may go now*), possibility (*It may be true*), wish (*Long may she reign*), uncertainty (*whoever it may be*)
USAGE See note at **can**.

may[2] *NOUN* hawthorn blossom

maybe *ADVERB* perhaps; possibly

mayfly *NOUN* **mayflies** an insect that lives for only a short time, in spring

mayhem *NOUN* violent confusion or damage • *The mob caused mayhem.*

mayonnaise *NOUN* a creamy sauce made from eggs, oil, vinegar, etc., usually eaten with salad or in sandwiches

mayor *NOUN* **mayors** the person in charge of the council in a town or city
▷ **mayoral** *ADJECTIVE* **mayoress** *NOUN*
[from early French, related to **major**]

maze *NOUN* **mazes** a network of paths, especially one designed as a puzzle in which to try and find your way

Mb *ABBREVIATION* megabyte(s)

MD *ABBREVIATION* Doctor of Medicine

me *PRONOUN* the form of **I** used as the object of a verb or after a preposition

meadow (**med**- oh) *NOUN* **meadows** a field of grass

meagre *ADJECTIVE* scanty in amount; barely enough • *a meagre diet*

Thesaurus

matter *VERB Does it matter what I wear?* ► make a difference, be important, count, signify

mature *ADJECTIVE* **1** *a mature woman* ► adult, grown-up, grown, full-grown, advanced, well-developed OPPOSITES ARE immature, adolescent **2** *He seems very mature for his age.* ► responsible, sensible, dependable, reliable OPPOSITES ARE immature, childish **3** *mature cheese; mature fruit* ► mellow, ready, ripened, seasoned AN OPPOSITE IS unripe

mature *VERB* **1** *Bella had matured into a beautiful young woman.* ► grow, grow up, develop, blossom **2** *Their friendship matured rapidly.* ► develop, grow, blossom, bloom, flourish, thrive

maul *VERB* **1** *He pulled me to the ground and started mauling me on my back and neck.* ► savage, attack, claw, manhandle, molest, maltreat, ill-treat, mutilate, lacerate **2** *The new production was mauled by the critics.* ► criticize, attack, savage, pillory, lambaste, (*more informal*) hammer, (*more informal*) slam

maximum *ADJECTIVE a maximum speed of 80 kph* ► greatest, highest, top, full, utmost, extreme, fullest, largest, most, biggest, supreme AN OPPOSITE IS minimum

maximum *NOUN Production has reached its maximum.* ► upper limit, limit, peak, ceiling, highest point, pinnacle, top level AN OPPOSITE IS minimum

mayhem *NOUN I decided I'd caused enough mayhem for one day.* ► confusion, chaos, disorder, muddle, bedlam, pandemonium, anarchy, disorganization, lawlessness, shambles, tumult AN OPPOSITE IS order

maze *NOUN a maze of rooms and corridors* ► labyrinth, warren, network, web, tangle, confusion

meadow *NOUN sheep grazing in a meadow* ► field, paddock, pasture, (*poetic*) mead, (*poetic*) lea

meagre *ADJECTIVE* **1** *He had a few coins in his pocket, his meagre earnings for the day.* ► paltry, scanty, scant, sparse, negligible, pitiful, miserable, modest, (*more informal*) mingy, (*more informal*) measly OPPOSITES ARE plentiful, abundant **2** *a tall, meagre youth* ► thin, lean, skinny, scrawny, scraggy, lanky

meal[1] *NOUN* **meals** food served and eaten at one sitting [from Old English *mael*]

meal[2] *NOUN* coarsely ground grain
▷ **mealy** *ADJECTIVE*
[from Old English *melu*]

mean[1] *VERB* **means**, **meaning**, **meant** (ment) **1** have as an equivalent or explanation • *'Maybe' means 'perhaps'* **2** have as a purpose; intend • *I mean to win.* **3** indicate • *Dark clouds mean rain.* **4** have as a result • *It means I'll have to get the early train.*

mean[2] *ADJECTIVE* **meaner**, **meanest** **1** not generous; miserly **2** unkind or spiteful • *a mean trick* **3** poor in quality or appearance • *a mean little house*
▷ **meanly** *ADVERB* **meanness** *NOUN*

mean[3] *NOUN* **means** a point or number midway between two extremes; the average of a set of numbers

mean *ADJECTIVE* midway between two points; average

meander (mee-an-der) *VERB* **meanders**, **meandering**, **meandered** take a winding course; wander
▷ **meander** *NOUN*
[named after the Maeander, a river in south-west Turkey (now Mendere or Menderes)]

meaning *NOUN* **meanings** what something means
▷ **meaningful** *ADJECTIVE* **meaningless** *ADJECTIVE*

means *NOUN* a way of achieving something or producing a result • *a means of transport*
by all means certainly
by means of by this method; using this
by no means not at all

means *PLURAL NOUN* money or other wealth
live beyond your means spend more than you can afford

meantime *NOUN*
in the meantime in the time between two events or while something else is happening

meanwhile *ADVERB* in the time between two events or while something else is happening

measles *NOUN* an infectious disease that causes small red spots on the skin

measure *VERB* **measures**, **measuring**, **measured** **1** find the size, amount, or extent of something by comparing it with a fixed unit or with an object of known size **2** be a certain size • *The room measures 3 x 4 metres*
▷ **measurable** *ADJECTIVE* **measurement** *NOUN*

Thesaurus

meal *NOUN* *A meal would be waiting for them when they got home.* ► bite to eat, (*literary*) repast, (*more informal*) spread, (*more informal*) feed
RELATED ADJECTIVE prandial

mean *ADJECTIVE* **1** *He was too mean to leave a tip.* ► miserly, niggardly, stingy, parsimonious, (*more informal*) mingy, (*more informal*) tight-fisted, (*more informal*) penny-pinching **2** *It was mean of them to leave her like that.* ► unkind, nasty, shameful, unpleasant, callous, cruel, spiteful **3** *His room was a cold mean affair.* ► squalid, shabby, wretched, dismal, humble, lowly

mean *VERB* **1** *The sign means you have to stop.* ► indicate, signify, denote, convey, show **2** *What do you think they mean by these remarks?* ► intend, suggest, imply **3** *I mean to find him come what may.* ► intend, plan, aim, want, wish, propose, purpose, aspire **4** *Her promotion meant a lot more travel.* ► involve, entail, necessitate, lead to, result in **5** *Your help means a lot to me.* ► matter, be important, have importance

meaning *NOUN* **1** *I didn't understand the meaning of her remarks.* ► significance, sense, import, implication, force, thrust, connotation **2** *Some words have several meanings.* ► sense, definition, denotation, explanation **3** *Life has little meaning for them now.* ► value, worth, point, purpose, significance

meaningless *ADJECTIVE* **1** *a meaningless compliment* ► empty, worthless, insincere, hollow, fatuous, nonsensical AN OPPOSITE IS meaningful **2** *Life seemed meaningless.* ► pointless, senseless, worthless, inconsequential, insignificant

means *NOUN* **1** *modern means of communication* ► method, mode, way, medium, channel, vehicle, instrument, course **2** *I don't have the means for such a lifestyle.* ► resources, funds, money, wherewithal, income, finance **3** *a person of means* ► wealth, riches, substance, property

measly *ADJECTIVE* (*informal*) *All he could find was a measly ten-pence piece.* ► meagre, paltry, scanty, scant, sparse, negligible, pitiful, miserable, modest, (*more informal*) mingy
AN OPPOSITE IS generous

measure *NOUN* **1** *These successes earned them a measure of glory. Add three measures of liquid.* ► share, portion, amount, allocation, quota, ration **2** *personal income as a measure of success* ► gauge, criterion, yardstick, standard, touchstone, meter, test **3** *special measures to monitor noise levels* ► step, action, procedure, process, means, control, operation

measure *VERB* **1** *It's not easy to measure the effects of such a disaster.* ► evaluate, assess, gauge, appraise, determine, fathom
2 measure up to *attempts to measure up to the expected standards* ► achieve, meet, satisfy, match, comply with

measurement *NOUN* **1** *Measurements are given in metric units.* ► dimension, size, extent,

A B C D E F G H I J K L M N O P Q R S T U V W X Y Z

measure *NOUN* **measures** **1** a unit used for measuring • *A kilometre is a measure of length.* **2** a device used in measuring **3** the size or quantity of something **4** something done for a particular purpose • *We took measures to stop vandalism.*

meat *NOUN* **meats** animal flesh used as food
▷ **meaty** *ADJECTIVE*

mechanic *NOUN* **mechanics** a person who maintains or repairs machinery

mechanical *ADJECTIVE* **1** to do with machines **2** produced or worked by machines **3** done or doing things without thought
▷ **mechanically** *ADVERB*

mechanics *NOUN* **1** the study of movement and force **2** the study or use of machines

mechanism *NOUN* **mechanisms** **1** the moving parts of a machine **2** the way a machine works **3** the process by which something is done

medal *NOUN* **medals** a piece of metal shaped like a coin, star, or cross, given to a person for bravery or for achieving something

meddle *VERB* **meddles, meddling, meddled** **1** interfere **2** tinker • *Don't meddle with it.*
▷ **meddler** *NOUN* **meddlesome** *ADJECTIVE*

media *plural* of **medium** *NOUN*
the media newspapers, radio, and television, which convey information and ideas to the public (See **medium**)
USAGE This word is a plural. Although it is commonly used with a singular verb, this is not generally approved of. Say *The media are* (not 'is') *very influential.* It is incorrect to speak of one of them (e.g. television) as 'this media'.

mediate *VERB* **mediates, mediating, mediated** negotiate between the opposing sides in a dispute
▷ **mediation** *NOUN* **mediator** *NOUN*

medical *ADJECTIVE* to do with the treatment of disease
▷ **medically** *ADVERB*

medicine *NOUN* **medicines** **1** a substance, usually swallowed, used to try to cure a disease **2** the study and treatment of diseases
▷ **medicinal** (med- iss- in- al) *ADJECTIVE* **medicinally** *ADVERB*

medieval (med- ee- ee- val) *ADJECTIVE* belonging to or to do with the Middle Ages

mediocre (mee- dee- oh- ker) *ADJECTIVE* not very good; of only medium quality
▷ **mediocrity** *NOUN*

meditate *VERB* **meditates, meditating, meditated** think deeply and quietly
▷ **meditation** *NOUN* **meditative** *ADJECTIVE*

Mediterranean *ADJECTIVE* to do with the Mediterranean Sea (which lies between Europe and Africa) or the countries round it

medium *ADJECTIVE* neither large nor small; moderate

Thesaurus

proportions **2** *an instrument used in the measurement of air speed* ► calculation, computation, mensuration, evaluation, assessment

mechanical *ADJECTIVE* **1** *a mechanical doll* ► mechanized, automated, machine-driven, motor-driven, automatic AN OPPOSITE IS manual **2** *The voice sounded detached and mechanical.* ► unemotional, unfeeling, matter-of-fact, perfunctory, unthinking, cold, inhuman, lifeless, routine, soulless AN OPPOSITE IS thoughtful

mechanism *NOUN* **1** *A trigger mechanism activates the bolt.* ► apparatus, machine, device, appliance, system, tool **2** *Mechanisms are in place for correcting mistakes.* ► procedure, process, system, means, channel, structure

medal *NOUN* *Their son had won a medal for bravery.* ► medallion, honour, decoration, award, reward, trophy, prize

meddle *VERB* *We don't want them meddling in our affairs.* ► interfere, pry, intrude, poke, nose, snoop, (*more informal*) stick your nose in

medicine *NOUN* **1** *examples of how modern medicine has helped to prolong life* ► medical science, healing, surgery, therapeutics, treatment of diseases **2** *He poured a dose of the medicine into the glass.* ► medication, medicament, remedy, cure, drug, prescription, treatment RELATED ADJECTIVES clinical, pharmaceutical

mediocre *ADJECTIVE* *Fred turned a mediocre business into one that was thriving.* ► ordinary, commonplace, indifferent, average, undistinguished, middle-of-the-road, run-of-the-mill, unexceptional, middling, passable, tolerable, second-rate OPPOSITES ARE exceptional, outstanding

meditation *NOUN* *He fell silent for a while, as if in meditation.* ► contemplation, prayer, reflection, yoga

medium *ADJECTIVE* *She is of medium height.* ► average, middling, middle, normal, ordinary, standard, usual, intermediate, midway, moderate

medium *NOUN* **1** *Television is a powerful medium of communication.* ► method, means, channel, mode, way, vehicle, instrument, course **2** *a happy medium between quality and quantity* ► average, midpoint, middle way, middle ground, compromise **3** *I went to see a medium and she told me I would be rich one day.* ► clairvoyant, spiritualist, psychic

medium *NOUN* **media 1** a thing in which something exists, moves, or is expressed • *Air is the medium in which sound travels.* • *Television is used as a medium for advertising.* (See **media**) **2** (**mediums**) a person who claims to be able to communicate with the dead

medium wave *NOUN* a radio wave of a frequency between 300 kilohertz and 3 megahertz

meek *ADJECTIVE* **meeker, meekest** quiet and obedient
▷ **meekly** *ADVERB* **meekness** *NOUN*

meet *VERB* **meets, meeting, met 1** come together from different places • *We all met in London.* **2** get to know someone • *We met at a party.* **3** come into contact; touch **4** go to receive an arrival • *We will meet your train.* **5** pay a bill or the cost of something **6** satisfy or fulfil • *I hope this meets your needs.*

meet *NOUN* **meets** a gathering of riders and hounds for a hunt

meeting *NOUN* **meetings 1** coming together **2** a number of people who have come together for a discussion, contest, etc.

megabyte *NOUN* **megabytes** (in computing) a unit of information roughly equal to one million bytes

megalomania *NOUN* an exaggerated idea of your own importance
▷ **megalomaniac** *NOUN*

megaphone *NOUN* **megaphones** a funnel-shaped device for amplifying a person's voice

melancholy *ADJECTIVE* sad; gloomy

melancholy *NOUN* sadness or depression [from Greek *melas* = black + *chole* = bile Black bile in the body was once thought to cause this feeling]

mellow *ADJECTIVE* **mellower, mellowest 1** not harsh; soft and rich in flavour, colour, or sound **2** having become more kindly and sympathetic with age
▷ **mellowness** *NOUN*

mellow *VERB* **mellows, mellowing, mellowed** make or become mellow

melodious *ADJECTIVE* like a melody; pleasant to listen to

melodrama *NOUN* **melodramas** a play full of dramatic excitement and emotion
▷ **melodramatic** *ADJECTIVE*

melody *NOUN* **melodies** a tune, especially a pleasing tune

melt *VERB* **melts, melting, melted 1** make or become liquid by heating **2** disappear slowly • *The crowd just melted away.* **3** soften • *a pudding that melts in the mouth*

melting pot *NOUN* **melting pots** a place where people of many different races and cultures live and influence each other

member *NOUN* **members 1** a person or thing that belongs to a particular society or group **2** a part of something
▷ **membership** *NOUN*

Thesaurus

meek *ADJECTIVE She seemed meek but could be fiercely passionate.* ► gentle, mild, demure, submissive, compliant, modest, docile, unassuming, self-effacing, unassertive, forbearing AN OPPOSITE IS assertive

meet *VERB* **1** *She met an old friend in town.* ► encounter, come across, run across, run into, chance on , stumble on **2** *I'll meet you at the airport.* ► collect **3** *They met the challenge bravely.* ► face, undergo, encounter, experience, endure, suffer **4** *The equipment does not meet our requirements.* ► satisfy, fulfil, answer, measure up to, match up to, conform to **5** *The board meets every month.* ► gather, assemble, come together, convene, hold a meeting **6** *The two roads meet north of the city.* ► join, converge, merge, come together, connect, intersect

meeting *NOUN* **1** *He rushed back to be in time for the meeting.* ► gathering, assembly, conference, forum, convention **2** *He adored her from their very first meeting.* ► encounter, rendezvous, contact, assignation, get-together, date **3** *The town stands at the meeting of three mighty rivers.* ► convergence, coming together, junction, confluence, union, concourse

melancholy *ADJECTIVE* **1** *melancholy music* ► sad, sorrowful, mournful, reflective **2** *a melancholy mood* ► unhappy, downhearted, despondent, gloomy, dispirited, depressed, dejected, downcast OPPOSITES ARE joyful, happy, elated

melancholy *NOUN a feeling of melancholy* ► sadness, sorrow, dejection, unhappiness, depression, dejection, despondency, gloom OPPOSITES ARE joy, happiness, elation

mellow *ADJECTIVE* **1** *a mellow voice* ► smooth, melodious, dulcet, tuneful, sweet **2** *a mellow temperament* ► easy-going, tolerant, amiable, good-natured, affable, kind-hearted **3** *mellow fruit* ► ripe, mature, juicy, tender, sweet

melt *VERB The sun soon melted the snow. The ice was beginning to melt.* ► thaw, unfreeze, defrost, liquefy, soften, dissolve
melt away *The crowds rapidly melted away.* ► disperse, dissolve, dwindle, vanish, evaporate, disappear, fade

member *NOUN new members of the sports club* ► associate, subscriber, fellow, adherent

A B C D E F G H I J K L M N O P Q R S T U V W X Y Z

membrane *NOUN* **membranes** a thin skin or similar covering
▷ **membranous** *ADJECTIVE*

memoir (mem- wahr) *NOUN* **memoirs** a biography, especially one written by someone who knew the person

memorable *ADJECTIVE* **1** worth remembering **2** easy to remember
▷ **memorably** *ADVERB*

memorandum *NOUN* **memoranda** or **memorandums** **1** a note to remind yourself of something **2** a note from one person to another in the same firm

memorial *NOUN* **memorials** something to remind people of a person or event • *a war memorial*
▷ **memorial** *ADJECTIVE*

memorize *VERB* **memorizes, memorizing, memorized** get something into your memory

memory *NOUN* **memories** **1** the ability to remember things **2** something that you remember **3** the part of a computer where information is stored
in memory of in honour of a person or event remembered

menace *NOUN* **menaces** **1** a threat or danger **2** a troublesome person or thing

menace *VERB* **menaces, menacing, menaced** threaten with harm or danger

mend *VERB* **mends, mending, mended** **1** repair **2** make or become better; improve
▷ **mender** *NOUN*

mend *NOUN* **mends** a repair
on the mend getting better after an illness

menopause *NOUN* the time of life when a woman gradually ceases to menstruate

menstruate *VERB* **menstruates, menstruating, menstruated** bleed from the womb about once a month, as girls and women normally do from their teens until middle age
▷ **menstruation** *NOUN* **menstrual** *ADJECTIVE*

-ment *SUFFIX* used to make nouns, as in *amusement* and *oddments*

mental *ADJECTIVE* **1** to do with or in the mind **2** (*informal*) mad
▷ **mentally** *ADVERB*

mentality *NOUN* **mentalities** a person's mental ability or attitude

mention *VERB* **mentions, mentioning, mentioned** speak or write about a person or thing briefly; refer to

mention *NOUN* **mentions** an example of mentioning something • *Our school got a mention in the local paper.*

menu (men- yoo) *NOUN* **menus** **1** a list of the food available in a restaurant or served at a meal **2** (in computing) a list of possible actions, shown on a screen, from which you decide what you want a computer to do

MEP *ABBREVIATION* Member of the European Parliament

mercenary *ADJECTIVE* working only for money or some other reward

mercenary *NOUN* **mercenaries** a soldier hired to serve in a foreign army

Thesaurus

memorial *NOUN a memorial to victims of the war* ► monument, remembrance, shrine, cenotaph, plaque, tablet

memorize *NOUN Long numbers are hard to memorize.* ► remember, commit to memory, learn by heart, retain AN OPPOSITE IS forget

memory *NOUN* **1** *My mother always had a good memory.* ► recall, retention, ability to remember, recollection **2** *happy memories of a lovely occasion* ► reminiscence, recollection, remembrance, reminder, souvenir, impression **3** *a plaque in memory of local writers* ► commemoration, remembrance, tribute, honour, recognition

menace *NOUN* **1** *a menace to society* ► danger, threat, hazard, risk **2** *That child is a menace.* ► nuisance, pest, annoyance **3** *a situation full of menace* ► threat, ominousness, intimidation

mend *VERB* **1** *An electrician was mending faulty wiring.* ► repair, fix, restore, renovate AN OPPOSITE IS break **2** *a pile of socks to mend* ► patch, repair, darn **3** *a quarrel that a few kind words can mend* ► put right, resolve, sort out, straighten out, remedy, rectify, redress AN OPPOSITE IS make worse

menial *ADJECTIVE Someone has to do the menial tasks.* ► humble, lowly, routine, unskilled, low-grade, humdrum, inferior, degrading, demeaning OPPOSITES ARE skilled, important

mental *ADJECTIVE* **1** *The work calls for considerable mental concentration.* ► intellectual, cerebral, abstract, rational, cognitive, theoretical **2** *Your mental attitude affects your behaviour.* ► psychological, temperamental, emotional, subjective

mentality *NOUN They seem to have an ostrich-like mentality.* ► attitude, way of thinking, outlook, predisposition, disposition, frame of mind, character, temperament, personality, (*more informal*) make-up

mention *VERB* **1** *Nick mentioned that he would be here next week.* ► state, say, remark, observe, reveal, indicate, disclose, divulge **2** *Better not to mention the score.* ► refer to, allude to, touch on, speak about, comment on, disclose, hint at, let out, reveal, (*more informal*) let drop

A B C D E F G H I J K L M N O P Q R S T U V W X Y Z

merchandise *NOUN* goods for sale

merchant *NOUN* **merchants** a person involved in trade

merchant navy *NOUN* the ships and sailors that carry goods for trade

merciful *ADJECTIVE* showing mercy
▷ **mercifully** *ADVERB*

mercury *NOUN* a heavy silvery metal that is usually liquid, used in thermometers
▷ **mercuric** *ADJECTIVE*

mercy *NOUN* **mercies 1** kindness or pity shown in not punishing a wrongdoer severely or not harming a defeated enemy etc. **2** something to be thankful for
at the mercy of completely in the power of

mere *ADJECTIVE* not more than • *He's a mere child.*

merely *ADVERB* only; simply

merge *VERB* **merges, merging, merged** combine or blend

merger *NOUN* **mergers** the combining of two business companies etc. into one

meridian *NOUN* **meridians** a line on a map or globe from the North Pole to the South Pole The meridian that passes through Greenwich is shown on maps as 0° longitude

meringue (mer- ang) *NOUN* **meringues** a crisp cake made from egg white and sugar

merit *NOUN* **merits 1** a quality that deserves praise **2** excellence
▷ **meritorious** *ADJECTIVE*

mermaid *NOUN* **mermaids** a mythical sea creature with a woman's body but with a fish's tail instead of legs
▷ **merman** *NOUN*

merry *ADJECTIVE* **merrier, merriest** cheerful and lively
▷ **merrily** *ADVERB* **merriment** *NOUN*

merry-go-round *NOUN* **merry-go-rounds** a roundabout at a fair

mesh *NOUN* **meshes 1** the open spaces in a net, sieve, or other criss-cross structure **2** material made like a net

mesmerize *VERB* **mesmerizes, mesmerizing, mesmerized 1** (*old use*) hypnotize **2** fascinate or hold a person's attention completely
▷ **mesmerism** *NOUN* **mesmeric** *ADJECTIVE*

mess *NOUN* **messes 1** a dirty or untidy condition or thing **2** a difficult or confused situation; trouble **3** (in the armed forces) a dining room
make a mess of bungle

mess *VERB* **messes, messing, messed**
mess about behave stupidly or idly
mess up 1 make a thing dirty or untidy **2** bungle or spoil • *They've messed up our plans.*
mess with interfere or tinker with
[from early French *mes* = a portion of food]

Thesaurus

merciful *ADJECTIVE They believe in a merciful God.*
► compassionate, forgiving, humane, gracious, understanding, sympathetic, generous, beneficent OPPOSITES ARE merciless, cruel

merciless *ADJECTIVE a leader who was merciless to his enemies* ► cruel, pitiless, ruthless, heartless, unsparing, unforgiving, unrelenting, harsh, severe AN OPPOSITE IS merciful

mercy *NOUN* **1** *The prisoners begged for mercy.*
► clemency, compassion, leniency, pity, sympathy, forbearance, forgiveness, understanding AN OPPOSITE IS cruelty **2** *It is a mercy that more people weren't killed.*
► blessing, godsend, boon, favour, piece of good fortune

merge *VERB* **1** *It seems a good idea to merge the two organizations.* ► combine, amalgamate, integrate, unite, join together, consolidate, coalesce, blend, fuse, link up, put together **2** *The two parties have agreed to merge.* ► unite, join together, come together, amalgamate, unify, combine **3** *The motorways merge ahead.*
► join, meet, converge OPPOSITES ARE split, separate

merit *NOUN writers of merit* ► excellence, goodness, value, virtue, worth, importance, quality, credit, eminence

merit *VERB The idea certainly merits consideration.*
► deserve, warrant, be worth, be worthy of, be entitled to, justify, rate, earn, incur

merriment *NOUN They could hear bursts of laughter and ripples of merriment.* ► jollity, enjoyment, cheerfulness, mirth, festivity, conviviality, amusement, revelry, high spirits OPPOSITES ARE misery, gloom

merry *ADJECTIVE merry crowds of holidaymakers a merry ringing of bells* ► jolly, cheerful, light-hearted, carefree, joyful, joyous, festive, happy, gleeful

mess *NOUN* **1** *There's quite a mess in the kitchen.*
► muddle, untidiness, disarray, jumble, confusion, clutter, shambles **2** *It was a mess of his own making and he would have to find a way out.* ► predicament, quandary, difficulty, trouble, (*more informal*) fix
make a mess of *I'm afraid I've made a mess of the assignment.* ► ruin, spoil, botch, bungle, mishandle, mismanage, fluff, muff, mess up, (*more informal*) make a hash of, (*much more informal*) cock up, (*much more informal*) screw up OPPOSITES ARE succeed in, bring off

mess *VERB* **mess about** *or* **around** *They need to stop messing around and get on with something.*
► fool about *or* around, play about *or* around, (*more informal*) muck about *or* around

message *NOUN* **messages** **1** a piece of information etc. sent from one person to another **2** the main theme or moral of a book, film, etc.

messenger *NOUN* **messengers** a person who carries a message

Messiah (mis- I- a) *NOUN* **Messiahs** **1** the saviour of the world expected by the Jewish people **2** Jesus Christ, who Christians believe to be this saviour
▷ **Messianic** *ADJECTIVE*
[from Hebrew *mashiah* = anointed]

messy *ADJECTIVE* **messier, messiest** dirty and untidy
▷ **messily** *ADVERB* **messiness** *NOUN*

metabolism (mit- ab- ol- izm) *NOUN* the process by which food is built up into living material in a plant or animal, or used to supply it with energy
▷ **metabolic** *ADJECTIVE* **metabolize** *VERB*

metal *NOUN* **metals** a chemical substance, usually hard, that conducts heat and electricity and melts when it is heated, e.g. gold, silver, copper, iron, and uranium
▷ **metallic** *ADJECTIVE*

metamorphosis (met- a- mor- fo- sis) *NOUN* **metamorphoses** (met- a- mor- fo- seez) a change of form or character, especially one made by a living thing
▷ **metamorphose** *VERB*

metaphor *NOUN* **metaphors** using a word or phrase in a way that is not literal, e.g. 'The pictures of starving people *touched our hearts*'
▷ **metaphorical** *ADJECTIVE* **metaphorically** *ADVERB*

meteor (meet- ee- er) *NOUN* **meteors** a piece of rock or metal that moves through space and burns up when it enters the earth's atmosphere

meteorite *NOUN* **meteorites** the remains of a meteor that has landed on the earth

meter *NOUN* **meters** a device for measuring something, e.g. the amount supplied • *a gas meter*
▷ **meter** *VERB*
USAGE Do not confuse with **metre**.

methane (mee- thayn) *NOUN* an inflammable gas produced by decaying matter

method *NOUN* **methods** **1** a procedure or way of doing something **2** methodical behaviour; orderliness

methodical *ADJECTIVE* doing things in an orderly or systematic way
▷ **methodically** *ADVERB*

methylated spirit or **spirits** *NOUN* a liquid fuel made from alcohol

metre *NOUN* **metres** **1** a unit of length in the metric system, about 39 inches **2** rhythm in poetry
USAGE Do not confuse with **meter**.

metric *ADJECTIVE* **1** to do with the metric system **2** to do with metre in poetry
▷ **metrically** *ADVERB*

metric system *NOUN* a measuring system based on decimal units (the metre, litre, and gram)

metric ton *NOUN* **metric tons** 1,000 kilograms

metronome *NOUN* **metronomes** a device that makes a regular clicking noise to help a person keep in time when practising music

mew *VERB* **mews, mewing, mewed** make a cat's cry
▷ **mew** *NOUN*

mice *plural of* **mouse**

microbe *NOUN* **microbes** a microorganism

Thesaurus

mess up **1** *They had messed up the garden in less than ten minutes.* ► jumble, muddle, make a mess of, dirty, dishevel, disrupt, disarrange **2** *A new assignment: try not to mess this one up.* ► ruin, spoil, botch, bungle, mishandle, mismanage, fluff, muff, make a mess of, (*more informal*) make a hash of, (*much more informal*) cock up, (*much more informal*) screw up

message *NOUN* *Sarah sent a message with her brother.* ► communication, note, letter, word, memo, dispatch, missive

messenger *NOUN* *A messenger brought the news.* ► courier, emissary, go-between, envoy, runner, dispatch rider

messy *ADJECTIVE* **1** *All these jobs can be messy and produce a lot of debris.* ► dirty, filthy, mucky, grubby, grimy **2** *The bathroom had become very messy. Her hair was tangled and messy.* ► untidy, dishevelled, unkempt, disorganized, chaotic, sloppy OPPOSITES ARE tidy, neat, organized

metal *NOUN* a lump of metal ► ingot, nugget

method *NOUN* *a new method of gathering vital data* ► way, approach (to), procedure (for), manner, mode, technique (for), style, plan (for)

methodical *ADJECTIVE* *a methodical approach to working* ► organized, orderly, systematic, meticulous, painstaking, efficient, businesslike, meticulous, logical, tidy, precise, neat OPPOSITES ARE disorganized, inefficient

meticulous *ADJECTIVE* *He continued his meticulous inspection of the machine.* ► careful, methodical, scrupulous, diligent, painstaking, systematic, thorough, rigorous

a b c d e f g h i j k l m n o p q r s t u v w x y z

microchip NOUN **microchips** a very small piece of silicon etc. made to work like a complex wired electric circuit

microcosm NOUN **microcosms** a world in miniature; something regarded as resembling something else on a very small scale

microfilm NOUN a length of film on which written or printed material is photographed in greatly reduced size

micron NOUN **microns** a unit of measurement, one millionth of a metre

microphone NOUN **microphones** an electrical device that picks up sound waves for recording, amplifying, or broadcasting [from Greek *mikros* = small + *phone* = sound]

microprocessor NOUN **microprocessors** the central processing unit of a computer, consisting of one or more microchips

microscope NOUN **microscopes** an instrument with lenses that magnify tiny objects or details [from Greek *mikros* = small + *skopein* = to look at]

microscopic ADJECTIVE **1** extremely small; too small to be seen without the aid of a microscope **2** to do with a microscope

microwave NOUN **microwaves** **1** a very short electromagnetic wave **2** a microwave oven

microwave oven NOUN **microwave ovens** an oven that uses microwaves to heat or cook food very quickly

mid ADJECTIVE in the middle of • *mid-July* • *He's in his mid thirties*

midday NOUN the middle of the day; noon

middle NOUN **middles** **1** the place or part of something that is at the same distance from all its sides or edges or from both its ends **2** someone's waist

in the middle of during or halfway through a process or activity • *I'm just in the middle of cooking.*

middle ADJECTIVE **1** placed or happening in the middle **2** moderate in size or rank etc.

middle-aged ADJECTIVE aged between about 40 and 60

Middle Ages NOUN the period in history from about 1000 to 1400

middle class or **classes** NOUN the class of people between the upper class and the working class, including business and professional people such as teachers, doctors, and lawyers

▷ **middle-class** ADJECTIVE

Middle East NOUN the countries from Egypt to Iran inclusive

Middle English NOUN the English language from about 1150 to 1500

middle school NOUN **middle schools** a school for children aged from about 9 to 13

middling ADJECTIVE of medium size or quality

middling ADVERB fairly or moderately

midge NOUN **midges** a small insect like a gnat

midget NOUN **midgets** an extremely small person or thing

▷ **midget** ADJECTIVE

midland ADJECTIVE **1** to do with the middle part of a country **2** to do with the Midlands

Midlands PLURAL NOUN the central part of England

midnight NOUN twelve o'clock at night

midst NOUN

in the midst of in the middle of or surrounded by

in our midst among us

midsummer NOUN the middle of summer, about 21 June in the northern hemisphere

midway ADVERB halfway

midwife NOUN **midwives** a person trained to look after a woman who is giving birth to a baby

▷ **midwifery** (**mid- wif- ri**) NOUN

might[1] NOUN great strength or power

with all your might using all your strength and determination

might[2] AUXILIARY VERB used as the past tense of **may**[1] (*We told her she might go*), to express possibility (*It might be true*)

mighty ADJECTIVE very strong or powerful

▷ **mightily** ADVERB **mightiness** NOUN

Thesaurus

middle ADJECTIVE *Remove the middle pin.* ► central, midway, mean, medial, median, half-way, inner, inside

middle NOUN **1** *There was a large table in the middle of the room.* ► centre, midpoint OPPOSITES ARE edge, border **2** *a journey to the middle of the earth* ► centre, core, heart, kernel OPPOSITES ARE surface, circumference

middling ADJECTIVE *She speaks middling to good Japanese.* ► average, medium, fair, ordinary, moderate, everyday, modest, passable

midget ADJECTIVE *a midget car* ► miniature, baby, dwarf, small

miffed ADJECTIVE (*informal*) *She felt miffed at being ignored.* ► annoyed, irritated, angry, cross, displeased, vexed, infuriated, incensed, enraged, (*more informal*) put out

might NOUN *I hit it with all my might.* ► strength, force, power, energy, vigour

mighty ADJECTIVE *a mighty blow to the head* ► powerful, forceful, violent, vigorous, ferocious, hefty, savage AN OPPOSITE IS weak

migraine (mee- grayn, my- grayn) *NOUN* **migraines** a severe kind of headache

migrate *VERB* **migrates, migrating, migrated** **1** leave one place or country and settle in another **2** (said about birds or animals) move periodically from one area to another
▷ **migration** *NOUN* **migratory** *ADJECTIVE*

mild *ADJECTIVE* **milder, mildest** **1** gentle; not harsh or severe **2** (said about weather) quite warm and pleasant **3** (said about food) not strongly flavoured
▷ **mildly** *ADVERB* **mildness** *NOUN*

mildew *NOUN* a tiny fungus that forms a white coating on things kept in damp conditions
▷ **mildewed** *ADJECTIVE*

mile *NOUN* **miles** a measure of distance equal to 1,760 yards (about 16 kilometres) [from Latin *mille* = thousand A Roman mile was reckoned as 1,000 paces]

milestone *NOUN* **milestones** **1** a stone of a kind that used to be fixed beside a road to mark the distance between towns **2** an important event in life or history

militant *ADJECTIVE* **1** eager to fight **2** forceful or aggressive • *a militant protest*
▷ **militant** *NOUN* **militancy** *NOUN*

military *ADJECTIVE* to do with soldiers or the armed forces
the military a country's armed forces

milk *NOUN* **1** a white liquid that female mammals produce in their bodies to feed their babies **2** the milk of cows, sheep, or goats used as food by human beings **3** a milky liquid, e.g. that in a coconut

milk *VERB* **milks, milking, milked** get the milk from a cow or other animal [from Old English]

milkman *NOUN* **milkmen** a man who delivers milk to customers' houses

milkshake *NOUN* **milkshakes** a cold frothy drink made from milk whisked with sweet fruit flavouring

milky *ADJECTIVE* **milkier, milkiest** **1** like milk **2** white

Milky Way *NOUN* the broad band of stars formed by our galaxy

mill *NOUN* **mills** **1** machinery for grinding corn to make flour; a building containing this machinery **2** a grinding machine • *a pepper mill* **3** a factory for processing certain materials • *a paper mill*

millennium *NOUN* **millenniums** a period of 1,000 years

millennium bug *NOUN* a fault in older computer systems that made it impossible for programs to deal with dates later than 1999

million *NOUN* **millions** one thousand thousand (1,000,000)
▷ **millionth** *ADJECTIVE, NOUN*

millionaire *NOUN* **millionaires** a person who has at least a million pounds or dollars; an extremely rich person

millipede *NOUN* **millipedes** a small crawling creature with many legs

millstone *NOUN* **millstones** either of a pair of large circular stones between which corn is ground
a millstone around someone's neck a heavy responsibility or burden

mimic *VERB* **mimics, mimicking, mimicked** imitate someone, especially to amuse people
▷ **mimicry** *NOUN*

Thesaurus

mild *ADJECTIVE* **1** *She spoke in a mild voice.* ► gentle, soft, tender, calm, tender-hearted, easygoing, sympathetic AN OPPOSITE IS harsh **2** *The weather turned mild.* ► warm, calm, fair, temperate OPPOSITES ARE severe, cold

militant *ADJECTIVE* *militant opponents of the regime* ► belligerent, active, aggressive, combatant, assertive, positive OPPOSITES ARE restrained, peaceful

military *ADJECTIVE* *a military command; military units* ► fighting, service, armed, martial, belligerent, enlisted, uniformed AN OPPOSITE IS civilian

milk *VERB* *Unscrupulous moneylenders can milk unwary clients.* ► exploit, take advantage of, cash in on, squeeze, bleed

milky *ADJECTIVE* **1** *her beautiful milky skin* ► pale, white, cream, creamy **2** *a milky liquid* ► cloudy, chalky, misty, opaque, whitish AN OPPOSITE IS clear RELATED ADJECTIVE lactic

mill *NOUN* **1** *a paper mill* ► factory, plant, processing plant, works, workshop **2** *a pepper mill* ► grinder, crusher, roller

mill *VERB* *The wheat is milled into flour.* ► grind, crush, roll, pulverize, powder
mill about *or* **around** *Outside, people were still milling about.* ► throng, swarm, stream, surge, wander about, move aimlessly

mime *VERB* *She mimed a telephone conversation.* ► act out, mimic, simulate, gesture, impersonate

mimic *VERB* *She could mimic anyone after a few minutes listening to them.* ► imitate, impersonate, copy, ape, caricature, do an impression of, parody, parrot, pretend to be, simulate, (*more informal*) take off

A B C D E F G H I J K L **M** N O P Q R S T U V W X Y Z

mimic *NOUN* **mimics** a person who mimics others

mince *VERB* **minces, mincing, minced** **1** cut into very small pieces in a machine **2** walk in an affected way with short quick steps
▷ **mincer** *NOUN*
not to mince matters speak bluntly

mince *NOUN* minced meat

mincemeat *NOUN* a sweet mixture of currants, raisins, apple, etc. used in pies

mince pie *NOUN* **mince pies** a pie containing mincemeat, traditionally eaten at Christmas

mind *NOUN* **minds** **1** the ability to think, feel, understand, and remember, originating in the brain **2** a person's thoughts, opinion, or intention • *Have you made your mind up?* • *I changed my mind*
in two minds not able to decide
out of your mind insane

mind *VERB* **minds, minding, minded** **1** look after • *He was minding the baby.* **2** be careful about • *Mind the step.* **3** be sad or upset about something; object to • *We don't mind waiting.*
▷ **minder** *NOUN*

mindless *ADJECTIVE* done without thinking; stupid or pointless

mine[1] *POSSESSIVE PRONOUN* belonging to me

mine[2] *NOUN* **mines** **1** a place where coal, metal, precious stones, etc. are dug out of the ground **2** an explosive placed in or on the ground or in the sea etc. to destroy people or things that come close to it

mine *VERB* **mines, mining, mined** **1** dig from a mine **2** lay explosive mines in a place

minefield *NOUN* **minefields** **1** an area where explosive mines have been laid **2** something with hidden dangers or problems

miner *NOUN* **miners** a person who works in a mine

mineral *NOUN* **minerals** **1** a hard inorganic substance found in the ground **2** a cold fizzy non-alcoholic drink

mingle *VERB* **mingles, mingling, mingled** mix or blend

mingy *ADJECTIVE* **mingier, mingiest** (*informal*) not generous; mean

miniature *ADJECTIVE* **1** very small **2** copying something on a very small scale • *a miniature railway*

miniature *NOUN* **miniatures** **1** a very small portrait **2** a small-scale model

Thesaurus

mimic *NOUN* *He was entertaining and a good mimic.* ► impersonator, impressionist, imitator

mince *VERB* **1** *He took the meat and minced it.* ► grind, chop, dice, crumble, cube **2 not mince words** *She doesn't mince her words when she's angry.* ► speak plainly, speak straight, get to the point, not pull your punches

mind *NOUN* **1** *people with brilliant minds* ► brain, intellect, intelligence, sense, wits, understanding, mentality, power of reasoning, (*more informal*) grey matter RELATED ADJECTIVE mental **2** *It's hard to keep my mind on my work.* ► attention, concentration, thinking **3** *I couldn't get her words out of my mind.* ► memory, recollection, remembrance **4** *I've a mind to go and complain.* ► inclination, wish, desire, fancy, intention, disposition, tendency

mind *VERB* **1** *I'll mind your bags while you're gone.* ► look after, watch, guard, take care of, attend to, (*more informal*) keep an eye on **2** *You'd better mind what they say.* ► be careful of, beware of, heed, pay attention to, look out for, watch out for, take notice of, note, remember **3** *Will you mind if I eat my lunch?* ► care, object, bother, disapprove, grumble, take offence, worry, be resentful, complain

mindful *ADJECTIVE* **mindful of** *Rob flew with care, mindful of the lives of his crew.* ► aware of, conscious of, heedful of, alive to, attentive to, careful of OPPOSITES ARE heedless of, oblivious to

mindless *ADJECTIVE* **1** *The occasion was spoilt by incidents of mindless violence.* ► senseless, wanton, gratuitous, thoughtless **2** *People are reduced to mindless automatons, unable to think for themselves.* ► stupid, idiotic, brainless, witless, foolish

mine *NOUN* **1** *a coal mine* ► pit, colliery, coalfield, deposit, mineshaft **2** *He was killed by a mine.* ► landmine, explosive **3** *The book is a mine of information.* ► store, wealth, fund, treasury, repository, hoard, rich supply

mine *VERB* *Gold is mined in these hills.* ► excavate, extract, quarry, dig for, remove

mingle *VERB* **1** *Guests mingled in the gardens.* ► socialize, circulate, get together, merge, mix, fraternize, associate, move about, rub shoulders, intermingle **2** *Open air smells mingled with the aroma of food cooking.* ► combine, merge, fuse, unite, join, coalesce

mingy *ADJECTIVE* (*informal*) *All I got was a mingy five pounds.* ► meagre, measly, paltry, miserable, scanty, scant, sparse, negligible, pitiful, modest, (*informal*) mouldy
AN OPPOSITE IS generous

miniature *ADJECTIVE* *a miniature village* ► tiny, small-scale, scaled-down, diminutive, minute, baby, model

minim *NOUN* **minims** a note in music, lasting twice as long as a crotchet (written 𝅗𝅥)

minimize *VERB* **minimizes, minimizing, minimized** make something as small as possible

minimum *NOUN* **minima** or **minimums** the lowest possible number or amount (The opposite is **maximum**)
▷ **minimal** *ADJECTIVE*

minister *NOUN* **ministers 1** a person in charge of a government department **2** a member of the clergy
▷ **ministerial** *ADJECTIVE*

ministry *NOUN* **ministries 1** a government department • *the Ministry of Defence* **2** the work of the clergy

minnow *NOUN* **minnows** a tiny freshwater fish

minor *ADJECTIVE* **1** not very important, especially when compared to something else **2** to do with the musical scale that has a semitone after the second note COMPARE **major**

minor *NOUN* **minors** a person under the age of legal responsibility

minority *NOUN* **minorities 1** the smallest part of a group of people or things **2** a small group that is different from others COMPARE **majority**

minstrel *NOUN* **minstrels** a travelling singer and musician in the Middle Ages

mint[1] *NOUN* **mints 1** a plant with fragrant leaves that are used for flavouring things **2** peppermint or a sweet flavoured with this [from Latin *mentha* = mint]

mint[2] *NOUN* **mints** the place where a country's coins are made
in mint condition in perfect condition, as though it had never been used

mint *VERB* **mints, minting, minted** make coins [from Latin *moneta* = money]

minus *PREPOSITION* with the next number or thing subtracted • *Ten minus four equals six (10 - 4 = 6)*

minus *ADJECTIVE* less than zero • *temperatures of minus ten degrees* (-10°) [from Latin, = less]

minute[1] (**min**- it) *NOUN* **minutes 1** one-sixtieth of an hour **2** a very short time; a moment **3** a particular time • *Come here this minute!* **4** one-sixtieth of a degree (used in measuring angles)

minute[2] (**my- newt**) *ADJECTIVE* **1** very small • *a minute insect* **2** very detailed • *a minute examination*
▷ **minutely** *ADVERB*

minutes *PLURAL NOUN* a written summary of what was said at a meeting

miracle *NOUN* **miracles** something wonderful and good that happens, especially something believed to have a supernatural or divine cause
▷ **miraculous** *ADJECTIVE* **miraculously** *ADVERB*

Thesaurus

minimal *ADJECTIVE* *Increases in rent this year have been minimal.* ► very little, negligible, slight, least, smallest, minimum, token, nominal

minimize *VERB* **1** *They banned smoking to minimize the danger of fire.* ► reduce, keep down, cut down, lessen, curtail, diminish OPPOSITES ARE maximize, increase **2** *He should not minimizes the value of their contribution.* ► underestimate, gloss over, make light of, play down OPPOSITES ARE maximize, exaggerate

minimum *ADJECTIVE* *The pay is well above the minimum wage.* ► lowest, least, smallest, minimal, bottom

minimum *NOUN* *Costs are kept to a minimum.* ► lower limit, limit, base, lowest point, bottom level AN OPPOSITE IS maximum

minister *NOUN* **1** *a minister of the church* ► clergyman, clergywoman, cleric, parson, priest, vicar, preacher **2** *a government minister* ► official, office-holder, executive, secretary of state USAGE A *secretary of state* is a head of a government department (such as transport) and a member of the cabinet; not all ministers are secretaries of state.

minor *ADJECTIVE* *minor alterations to the treaty* ► small, trivial, unimportant, insignificant, inconsequential, negligible, secondary, lesser, trifling, petty AN OPPOSITE IS major

minority *NOUN* *A minority voted for a return to work.* ► small number, lesser number, smaller number
be in a minority ► be outnumbered, be less, be the smaller number

mint *ADJECTIVE* *in mint condition* ► brand new, pristine, immaculate, perfect, new, unblemished, unmarked, unused, fresh

mint *NOUN* (*informal*) *They made a mint from the deal.* ► fortune, heap, (*informal*) packet, (*informal*) pile, (*informal*) stack

mint *VERB* *Special coins were minted to celebrate the jubilee.* ► strike, cast, manufacture, stamp out, coin, forge, make

minute *ADJECTIVE* *a minute insect* ► tiny, minuscule, infinitesimal, diminutive, miniature

minute *NOUN* *I'll only be a minute.* ► moment, short while, second, (*more informal*) tick

miracle *NOUN* *a miracle of modern technology* ► marvel, wonder, sensation, phenomenon, feat

miraculous *ADJECTIVE* *a miraculous escape* ► amazing, astounding, astonishing, extraordinary, unbelievable, incredible,

a b c d e f g h i j k l m n o p q r s t u v w x y z

A B C D E F G H I J K L M N O P Q R S T U V W X Y Z

mirage (mi- rah*zh*) NOUN **mirages** an illusion; something that seems to be there but is not, especially when a lake seems to appear in a desert

mirror NOUN **mirrors** a device or surface of reflecting material, usually glass

mirror VERB **mirrors, mirroring, mirrored** reflect in or like a mirror

mis- PREFIX badly or wrongly COMPARE **amiss**

misbehave VERB **misbehaves, misbehaving, misbehaved** behave badly
▷ **misbehaviour** NOUN

miscalculate VERB **miscalculates, miscalculating, miscalculated** calculate incorrectly
▷ **miscalculation** NOUN

miscarriage NOUN **miscarriages 1** the birth of a baby before it has developed enough to live **2** failure to achieve the right result • *a miscarriage of justice*

miscellaneous (mis- el- ay- nee- us) ADJECTIVE of various kinds; mixed
▷ **miscellany** (mis- el- an- ee) NOUN

mischief NOUN **1** naughty or troublesome behaviour **2** trouble caused by this
▷ **mischievous** ADJECTIVE **mischievously** ADVERB

misconception NOUN **misconceptions** a mistaken idea

misconduct NOUN bad behaviour by someone in a responsible position • *professional misconduct*

miser NOUN **misers** a person who hoards money and spends as little as possible
▷ **miserly** ADJECTIVE **miserliness** NOUN

miserable ADJECTIVE **1** full of misery; very unhappy, poor, or uncomfortable **2** disagreeable or unpleasant • *miserable weather*
▷ **miserably** ADVERB

Thesaurus

inexplicable, marvellous, wonderful, mysterious

mirage NOUN *The lake turned out to be a mirage.* ► illusion, optical illusion, hallucination, vision, delusion

mirror NOUN **1** *She took a quick look in the mirror on her way out.* ► looking glass, glass, reflector **2** *art as a mirror of life* ► reflection, image, likeness, copy, double

mirror VERB *Jody's views mirrored her own.* ► reflect, correspond to, match, imitate, copy, echo

mirth NOUN *sounds of mirth from the terrace* ► merriment, amusement, revelry, jollity, enjoyment, cheerfulness, festivity, conviviality, high spirits OPPOSITES ARE misery, gloom

misbehave VERB *Little Mary was misbehaving again.* ► behave badly, be naughty, be disobedient, (*more informal*) play up, (*more informal*) fool about

misbehaviour NOUN *In those days any form of misbehaviour was punished.* ► bad behaviour, misconduct, naughtiness, disobedience, indiscipline, insubordination, mischief, mischief-making, wrongdoing

miscalculate VERB *We miscalculated the amount of fuel we would need.* ► misjudge, make a mistake over, get wrong, underestimate *or* overestimate, blunder over

miscalculation NOUN *The problem arises from miscalculations by officials.* ► mistake, error, error of judgement, blunder

miscellaneous ADJECTIVE *He made money from gardening and miscellaneous jobs.* ► various, varied, different, assorted, mixed, sundry, multifarious

mischief NOUN **1** *He was always plotting some mischief with his brother.* ► misbehaviour, naughtiness, bad behaviour, mischievousness, misconduct, disobedience, pranks **2** *A faulty fuel pipe can cause much mischief.* ► trouble, difficulty, harm, damage, injury, bother, nuisance

mischievous ADJECTIVE **1** *mischievous children* ► naughty, badly behaved, misbehaving, disobedient, insubordinate, troublesome, vexatious **2** *There was a mischievous grin on his face.* ► playful, impish, roguish, teasing **3** *The house was full of mischievous rumours.* ► malicious, malevolent, hostile, unfriendly, spiteful, vicious, pernicious

miser NOUN *an old miser who kept his money hidden under the floorboards* ► scrooge, penny-pincher, hoarder, niggard, (*informal*) skinflint AN OPPOSITE IS spendthrift

miserable ADJECTIVE **1** *She was too miserable to eat.* ► unhappy, sad, dejected, despondent, downcast, downhearted, down, disheartened, disconsolate, glum, melancholy, cast down **2** *The house was cramped and miserable.* ► dreary, dismal, gloomy, cheerless, joyless, squalid **3** *It was a miserable way to treat people.* ► contemptible, despicable, disgraceful, deplorable, shameful **4** *They kept us waiting for hours and all we got was a miserable cup of tea.* ► measly, paltry, meagre, wretched, niggardly, pitiful, (*more informal*) mingy, (*more informal*) mouldy

miserly ADJECTIVE *He was miserly for all his life and died rich as a result.* ► mean, niggardly, penny-pinching, parsimonious, tight, stingy AN OPPOSITE IS generous

misery *NOUN* **miseries** **1** great unhappiness or discomfort or suffering, especially lasting for a long time **2** (*informal*) a person who is always unhappy or complaining

misfire *VERB* **misfires**, **misfiring**, **misfired** **1** fail to fire **2** fail to function correctly or to have the required effect • *The joke misfired.*

misfit *NOUN* **misfits** a person who does not fit in well with other people or who is not well suited to his or her work

misfortune *NOUN* **misfortunes** **1** bad luck **2** an unlucky event or accident

misgiving *NOUN* **misgivings** a feeling of doubt or slight fear or mistrust

misguided *ADJECTIVE* guided by mistaken ideas or beliefs

mishap (mis- hap) *NOUN* **mishaps** an unlucky accident

misinterpret *VERB* **misinterprets**, **misinterpreting**, **misinterpreted** interpret incorrectly
▷ **misinterpretation** *NOUN*

mislay *VERB* **mislays**, **mislaying**, **mislaid** lose something for a short time because you cannot remember where you put it

mislead *VERB* **misleads**, **misleading**, **misled** give somebody a wrong idea or impression deliberately

misnomer *NOUN* **misnomers** an unsuitable name for something

misogynist (mis- oj- in- ist) *NOUN* **misogynists** a man who hates women
▷ **misogyny** *NOUN*

misplaced *ADJECTIVE* **1** placed wrongly **2** inappropriate • *misplaced loyalty*
▷ **misplacement** *NOUN*

misprint *NOUN* **misprints** a mistake in printing

misrepresent *VERB* **misrepresents**, **misrepresenting**, **misrepresented** represent in a false or misleading way
▷ **misrepresentation** *NOUN*

Miss *NOUN* **Misses** a title put before a girl's or unmarried woman's name [short for **mistress**]

miss *VERB* **misses**, **missing**, **missed** **1** fail to hit, reach, catch, see, hear, or find something **2** be sad because someone or something is not with you **3** notice that something has gone
miss out **1** leave out **2** not get the benefit

miss *NOUN* **misses** missing something • *Was that shot a hit or a miss?*

misshapen *ADJECTIVE* badly shaped

Thesaurus

misery *NOUN* **1** *the misery of unemployment* ▶ hardship, suffering, privation, affliction, distress, misfortune, tribulation, anguish **2** *She put her hands to her face in silent misery.* ▶ unhappiness, distress, wretchedness, despair, grief, suffering **3** (*more informal*) *He can be fun but a lot of the time he's a real misery.* ▶ spoilsport, killjoy, pessimist, (*more informal*) wet blanket

misfire *VERB* *The plan had misfired.* ▶ fail, fall through, founder, miscarry, go wrong, (*more informal*) flop AN OPPOSITE IS succeed

misfit *NOUN* *a bunch of misfits and weirdos* ▶ eccentric, nonconformist, maverick, dropout, individualist, (*more informal*) oddball

misfortune *NOUN* *Bruce had the misfortune to break a bone in his wrist. The family had suffered several generations of misfortune* ▶ bad luck, mischance, mishap, trouble, setback, tribulation, hardship AN OPPOSITE IS good luck

misgiving *NOUN* *We agreed to the proposal with several misgivings.* ▶ doubt, reservation, qualm, scruple, diffidence AN OPPOSITE IS confidence

misguided *ADJECTIVE* *a misguided policy on immigration* ▶ mistaken, misconceived, erroneous, fallacious, unsound, unfounded, ill-judged, ill-considered

mishap *NOUN* *an unfortunate mishap in the kitchen* ▶ accident, misfortune, misadventure, setback, problem, difficulty

misjudge *VERB* *He misjudged the distance and hit a parked car.* ▶ miscalculate, overestimate, underestimate, get wrong, guess wrongly, make a mistake about, misinterpret, misunderstand

mislay *VERB* *I seem to have mislaid my passport.* ▶ lose, misplace, lose track of, forget

mislead *VERB* *Colin had evidently tried to mislead her.* ▶ deceive, delude, fool, hoodwink, take in, misguide, misinform, lead astray

misleading *ADJECTIVE* *a misleading answer* ▶ confusing, deceptive, equivocal, ambiguous, evasive, dishonest, unreliable

mismanage *VERB* *The redundancies had been badly mismanaged.* ▶ mishandle, bungle, botch, ruin, spoil, fluff, muff, mess up, make a mess of, (*more informal*) make a hash of, (*much more informal*) cock up, (*much more informal*) screw up

miss *VERB* **1** *The bullet missed him by inches.* ▶ fail to hit, fall short of **2** *It was an easy catch but he still missed it.* ▶ drop, fumble, fail to catch, let slip, mishandle **3** *If we're not careful we'll miss the last train.* ▶ be too late for, fail to catch **4** *He was ill and had to miss the party.* ▶ be absent from, skip **5** *I will miss Debbie terribly.* ▶ pine for, long for, yearn for, feel the loss of **6** *He*

missile *NOUN* **missiles** a weapon or other object for firing or throwing at a target

missing *ADJECTIVE* **1** lost; not in the proper place **2** absent

mission *NOUN* **missions 1** an important job that somebody is sent to do or feels they must do **2** a place or building where missionaries work **3** a military or scientific expedition

missionary *NOUN* **missionaries** a person who is sent to another country to spread a religious faith

misspell *VERB* **misspells, misspelling, misspelt** *or* **misspelled** spell a word wrongly

mist *NOUN* **mists 1** damp cloudy air near the ground **2** condensed water vapour on a window, mirror, etc.
▷ **mist** *VERB*

mistake *NOUN* **mistakes 1** something done wrongly **2** an incorrect opinion

mistake *VERB* **mistakes, mistaking, mistook, mistaken 1** misunderstand • *Don't mistake my meaning.* **2** choose or identify wrongly • *We mistook her for her sister.*

mistaken *ADJECTIVE* **1** incorrect **2** having an incorrect opinion

mister *NOUN* (*informal*) a form of address to a man

mistletoe *NOUN* a plant with white berries that grows as a parasite on trees

mistress *NOUN* **mistresses 1** a woman who is in charge of something **2** a woman who is a man's lover but not his wife **3** a woman teacher **4** the woman owner of a dog or other animal

mistrust *VERB* **mistrusts, mistrusting, mistrusted** feel no trust in somebody or something
▷ **mistrust** *NOUN*

misty *ADJECTIVE* **mistier, mistiest 1** full of mist **2** not clear or distinct
▷ **mistily** *ADVERB* **mistiness** *NOUN*

misunderstand *VERB* **misunderstands, misunderstanding, misunderstood** get a wrong idea or impression of something
▷ **misunderstanding** *NOUN*

Thesaurus

swerved and managed to miss an oncoming car. ► avoid, dodge, evade, escape, circumvent **7** *Don't miss your chance.* ► let slip, let go, forfeit, pass by, pass up, disregard

missing *ADJECTIVE* *A few books are still missing.* ► lost, mislaid, misplaced, gone astray, straying, unaccounted for, absent, disappeared

mission *NOUN* **1** *a mission to Africa* ► expedition, assignment, operation, exploration, journey, sortie, voyage **2** *his mission in life* ► calling, vocation, goal, aim, purpose, function

mist *NOUN* **1** *The sun was breaking through the early morning mist.* ► haze, fog, vapour, cloud, mistiness **2** *She wiped a hole to peep through the mist on the windows.* ► condensation, film, steam

mistake *NOUN* *It's easy to make mistakes when you are tired.* ► error, slip, blunder, lapse, misjudgement, miscalculation, oversight, (*more informal*) gaffe

mistake *VERB* *I mistook the meaning of the instruction.* ► misunderstand, misinterpret, confuse, get wrong, misjudge, misread, misconstrue, (*informal*) get the wrong end of the stick about, mix up

mistaken *ADJECTIVE* *These conclusions are mistaken, in our view.* ► wrong , incorrect, erroneous, misguided, unfounded, unsound, ill-judged, inappropriate

mistreat *VERB* *Some of the prisoners had been mistreated.* ► ill-treat, maltreat, abuse, misuse, harm, injure, molest, (*more informal*) knock about

mistrust *VERB* *I mistrust their intentions.* ► distrust, suspect, be suspicious of, be sceptical about, have misgivings about, have qualms about, be wary of, disbelieve, doubt, question AN OPPOSITE IS trust

misty *ADJECTIVE* **1** *misty weather* ► hazy, foggy, murky, cloudy AN OPPOSITE IS clear **2** *a misty window* ► misted, clouded **3** *misty memories* ► indistinct, vague, hazy, unclear, obscure, nebulous OPPOSITES ARE sharp, distinct

misunderstand *VERB* *I must have misunderstood; I thought you were coming with us.* ► make a mistake, misapprehend, misinterpret, mishear, get it wrong, (*more informal*) get hold of the wrong end of the stick

misunderstanding *NOUN* **1** *The suggestion was based on a misunderstanding of the issues.* ► misapprehension, misconception, misinterpretation, misjudgement, false impression, delusion (about), (*informal*) mix-up **2** *It wasn't a row, just a slight misunderstanding.* ► difference of opinion, disagreement, dispute, quarrel , squabble, argument, contretemps

misuse (mis- yooz) *VERB* **misuses, misusing, misused** **1** use incorrectly **2** treat badly
▷ **misuse** (mis- yooss) *NOUN*

mitten *NOUN* **mittens** a kind of glove without separate parts for the fingers

mix *VERB* **mixes, mixing, mixed** **1** put different things together so that they are no longer distinct; blend or combine **2** (said about a person) get together with others
▷ **mixer** *NOUN*
mix up **1** mix thoroughly **2** confuse

mix *NOUN* **mixes** a mixture

mixed *ADJECTIVE* containing two or more kinds of things or people

mixture *NOUN* **mixtures** **1** something made of different things mixed together **2** the process of mixing

mnemonic (nim- on- ik) *NOUN* **mnemonics** a verse or saying that helps you to remember something [from Greek *mneme* = memory]

moan *VERB* **moans, moaning, moaned** **1** make a long low sound of pain or suffering **2** grumble
▷ **moan** *NOUN*

moat *NOUN* **moats** a deep wide ditch round a castle, usually filled with water
▷ **moated** *ADJECTIVE*

mob *NOUN* **mobs** **1** a large disorderly crowd **2** a gang

mobile *ADJECTIVE* moving easily
▷ **mobility** *NOUN*

mobile *NOUN* **mobiles** **1** a decoration for hanging up so that its parts move in currents of air **2** a mobile phone

mobile home *NOUN* **mobile homes** a large caravan permanently parked and used for living in

mobile phone *NOUN* **mobile phones** a phone you can carry about that uses a cellular radio system

mobilize *VERB* **mobilizes, mobilizing, mobilized** assemble people or things for a particular purpose, especially for war
▷ **mobilization** *NOUN*

mock *VERB* **mocks, mocking, mocked** **1** make fun of a person or thing **2** imitate someone or something to make people laugh
▷ **mockery** *NOUN*

Thesaurus

misuse *NOUN* **1** *the misuse of confidential information* ► wrong use, misappropriation, misapplication, exploitation **2** *the misuse of innocent people* ► ill-treatment, maltreatment, mistreatment **3** *the misuse of drugs* ► abuse, careless use, ill-use, mishandling

misuse *VERB* **1** *He was accused of misusing public money.* ► misapply, misemploy, embezzle, put to wrong use **2** *She had been misused by successive partners.* ► ill-treat, maltreat, mistreat, abuse, harm, injure, molest, (*more informal*) knock about

mix *VERB* **1** *Mix the ingredients together. Oil and water don't mix.* ► blend, mingle, combine, merge, fuse, unite, coalesce, amalgamate **2** *He mixes with all sorts of people.* ► associate, consort, fraternize, socialize, mingle, (*more informal*) hang about with
mix up *I've mixed up the two dates.* ► confuse, muddle, muddle up, jumble up, mistake

mixed *ADJECTIVE* **1** *a mixed collection* ► assorted, varied, diverse, miscellaneous, heterogeneous, different **2** *mixed ingredients* ► combined, integrated, amalgamated, united, composite, hybrid, joint **3** *Their reactions were mixed.* ► ambivalent, equivocal, uncertain, unsure, confused, muddled, ambiguous

mixture *NOUN* *a strange mixture of people* ► assortment, variety, medley, combination, blend, miscellany, jumble, hotchpotch, assemblage, gathering

moan *VERB* **1** *The injured man was moaning with pain.* ► groan, cry, howl, whimper **2** *Everyone moaned about the food.* ► complain, grumble, grouse, grouch, carp, whine, (*more informal*) whinge

moan *NOUN* **1** *moans of pain* ► groan, cry, howl, whimper **2** *moans about the awful food* ► complaint, grumble, grouse, grouch, carping, whining, (*more informal*) whinging

mob *NOUN* (*informal*) *An angry mob gathered at the gate.* ► crowd, throng, mass, horde, rabble, swarm, bunch, gang, group, herd, pack, riot

mob *VERB* *Her fans mobbed her all the way to her car.* ► crowd round, swarm round, throng round, jostle, surround, besiege, hem in, harass, hassle

mobile *ADJECTIVE* **1** *She was soon mobile again after her operation.* ► moving, walking, able to move **2** *The village is visited by a mobile library once a week.* ► travelling, itinerant, peripatetic, roving, wandering **3** *It helps to be mobile in furthering a career.* ► adaptable, flexible, versatile, adjustable

mobilize *VERB* **1** *The army was mobilized to fight the rebels.* ► summon, assemble, call up, enlist, levy, marshal, muster **2** *The spin doctors mobilize support for government policy.* ► rally, generate, activate, stir up, stimulate, promote, galvanize, organize

mock *VERB* *Her brother had grinned and mocked her behind her back.* ► ridicule, jeer, make fun

A B C D E F G H I J K L M N O P Q R S T U V W X Y Z

mock *ADJECTIVE* imitation, not real • *mock exams*

mock-up *NOUN* **mock-ups** a model of something, made in order to test or study it

mode *NOUN* **modes** **1** the way a thing is done **2** what is fashionable

model *NOUN* **models** **1** a copy of an object, usually on a smaller scale **2** a particular design **3** a person who poses for an artist or displays clothes by wearing them **4** a person or thing that is worth copying

model *VERB* **models, modelling, modelled** **1** make a model of something **2** design or plan something using another thing as an example **3** work as an artist's model or a fashion model

modem (moh- dem) *NOUN* **modems** a device that links a computer to a telephone line for transmitting data

moderate *ADJECTIVE* **1** medium; not extremely small or great or hot etc. • *a moderate climate* **2** not extreme or unreasonable • *moderate opinions*
▷ **moderately** *ADVERB*

moderate (mod- er- ayt) *VERB* **moderates, moderating, moderated** make or become moderate
▷ **moderation** *NOUN*
in moderation in moderate amounts

modern *ADJECTIVE* **1** belonging to the present or recent times **2** in fashion now
▷ **modernity** *NOUN*

modernize *VERB* **modernizes, modernizing, modernized** make a thing more modern
▷ **modernization** *NOUN*

modest *ADJECTIVE* **1** not vain or boastful **2** moderate in size or amount • *a modest income* **3** not showy or splendid **4** behaving or dressing decently or decorously
▷ **modestly** *ADVERB* **modesty** *NOUN*

modify *VERB* **modifies, modifying, modified** **1** change something slightly **2** describe a word or limit its meaning • *Adjectives modify nouns.*
▷ **modification** *NOUN*

modulate *VERB* **modulates, modulating, modulated** **1** adjust or regulate **2** vary in pitch or tone etc. **3** alter an electronic wave to allow signals to be sent
▷ **modulation** *NOUN* **modulator** *NOUN*

module *NOUN* **modules** **1** an independent part of a spacecraft, building, etc. **2** a unit; a section of a course of study
▷ **modular** *ADJECTIVE*

moist *ADJECTIVE* slightly wet
▷ **moistly** *ADVERB* **moistness** *NOUN*

Thesaurus

of, laugh at, taunt, scorn, sneer at, deride, disparage, tease

mock *ADJECTIVE* *He shook his head in mock disbelief.* ► pretend, imitation, simulated, false, fake, sham, feigned

mockery *NOUN* **1** *There was a note of mockery in her voice.* ► ridicule, derision, contempt, scorn, sarcasm, disdain **2** *The trial was a mockery of justice.* ► travesty, parody, caricature, sham

model *ADJECTIVE* **1** *a model railway* ► miniature, toy, replica **2** *a model pupil* ► ideal, perfect, exemplary, impeccable, faultless

model *NOUN* **1** *a working model of a high-speed train* ► replica, copy, representation, facsimile, imitation **2** *a model of good behaviour* ► ideal, paragon, epitome, personification **3** *laws based on the American model* ► pattern, example, type, standard, paradigm, prototype, version, mould

model *VERB* **1** *The artist modelled the figure in bronze.* ► form, make, fashion, mould, sculpt, design **2** *Characters who are modelled on real life.* ► base, draw (from), derive (from)

moderate *ADJECTIVE* **1** *a moderate success* ► average, modest, mediocre, tolerable, passable **2** *a moderate drinker; Prices are moderate this year.* ► reasonable, sensible, restrained, controlled, modest, fair

moderate *VERB* **1** *The wind has moderated.* ► abate, die down, ease off, subside, decrease, become less extreme **2** *Can we do something to moderate the noise?* ► control, curb, check, reduce, lessen, mitigate, alleviate, allay, subdue

modern *ADJECTIVE* **1** *modern art* ► contemporary, present-day, current **2** *She wears very modern clothes.* ► fashionable, stylish, modish, voguish, advanced

modernize *VERB* (*informal*) *The factory needs to modernize its production methods.* ► update, renovate, refurbish, regenerate, improve, rebuild

modest *ADJECTIVE* **1** *a modest increase in income* ► moderate, reasonable, limited, slight, small AN OPPOSITE IS large **2** *He is always modest about his achievements.* ► unassuming, unpretentious, humble, reserved, discreet, retiring, bashful AN OPPOSITE IS boastful

modesty *NOUN* *She shows admirable modesty about her abilities.* ► humility, reserve, reticence, discretion, self-effacement, shyness, lack of pretension

modify *VERB* *These events have led us to modify our views.* ► change, alter, amend, adapt, revise, adjust, reform

moist *ADJECTIVE* *He dug into the dark moist earth.* ► damp, soggy, clammy, wet, watery

moisten *VERB* **moistens, moistening, moistened** make or become moist

moisture *NOUN* water in the air or making a thing moist

moisturizer *NOUN* a cream used to make the skin less dry

mole[1] *NOUN* **moles** **1** a small furry animal that burrows under the ground **2** a spy working within an organization and passing information to another organization or country

mole[2] *NOUN* **moles** a small dark spot on skin

molecule *NOUN* **molecules** the smallest part into which a substance can be divided without changing its chemical nature; a group of atoms
▷ **molecular** (mo- lek- yoo- ler) *ADJECTIVE*

molehill *NOUN* **molehills** a small pile of earth thrown up by a burrowing mole

molest *VERB* **molests, molesting, molested** **1** annoy or pester **2** attack or abuse someone sexually

mollusc *NOUN* **molluscs** any of a group of animals including snails, slugs, and mussels, with soft bodies, no backbones, and sometimes external shells

molten *ADJECTIVE* melted; made liquid by great heat

moment *NOUN* **moments** **1** a very short time **2** a particular time • *Call me the moment she arrives.*

momentary *ADJECTIVE* lasting for only a moment
▷ **momentarily** *ADVERB*

momentous (mo- ment- us) *ADJECTIVE* very important

momentum *NOUN* **1** the ability something has to keep moving or developing **2** (in science) the quantity of motion of a moving object, measured as its mass multiplied by its velocity

monarch *NOUN* **monarchs** a king, queen, emperor, or empress ruling a country
▷ **monarchic** *ADJECTIVE*

monarchy *NOUN* **monarchies** a country ruled by a monarch
▷ **monarchist** *NOUN*

monastery *NOUN* **monasteries** a building where monks live and work
▷ **monastic** *ADJECTIVE*

Monday *NOUN* the day of the week following Sunday [from Old English *monandaeg* = day of the moon]

monetary *ADJECTIVE* to do with money

money *NOUN* **1** coins and banknotes **2** wealth

mongrel (mung- rel) *NOUN* **mongrels** a dog of mixed breeds

monitor *NOUN* **monitors** **1** a device for watching or testing how something is working **2** a screen that displays data and images produced by a computer **3** a pupil who is given a special responsibility in a school

monitor *VERB* **monitors, monitoring, monitored** watch or test how something is working

monk *NOUN* **monks** a member of a community of men who live according to the rules of a religious organization COMPARE **nun**

monkey *NOUN* **monkeys** **1** an animal with long arms, hands with thumbs, and often a tail **2** a mischievous person, especially a child

monocle *NOUN* **monocles** a lens worn over one eye, like half of a pair of glasses

monogram *NOUN* **monograms** a design made up of a letter or letters, especially a person's initials
▷ **monogrammed** *ADJECTIVE*

monolith *NOUN* **monoliths** a large single upright block of stone

Thesaurus

moisten *VERB* *Moisten the compost if it becomes dry.* ► dampen, wet, damp, soak, moisturize, make moist, humidify AN OPPOSITE IS dry

moisture *NOUN* *The windows were covered in moisture.* ► dampness, condensation, damp, humidity, liquid, steam, vapour, wetness, wet

molest *VERB* *The woman had been molested by a group of men.* ► harass, pester, beset, torment, persecute, harry

moment *NOUN* **1** *She waited for a moment before going in.* ► minute, second, little while, short time **2** *We can leave the moment the rain stops.* ► instant, minute, second, point **3** *These matters are of little moment to most people.* ► importance, import, significance, consequence, interest, weight, value

momentary *ADJECTIVE* *He had a momentary glimpse of her face.* ► brief, fleeting, passing, quick, temporary, transient, transitory AN OPPOSITE IS permanent

momentous *ADJECTIVE* *a momentous decision* ► important, significant, fateful, epoch-making, historic, critical, crucial, decisive AN OPPOSITE IS unimportant

momentum *NOUN* *The car began to gain momentum. a momentum for change* ► impetus, force, velocity, power, impulse, incentive, thrust

money *NOUN* **1** *I don't have enough money to buy it.* ► cash, means, funds, capital, finance, change, (*more informal*) dosh **2** *How much money shall we take on holiday?* ► currency, cash RELATED ADJECTIVES financial, monetary, pecuniary

monolithic *ADJECTIVE* **1** to do with or like a monolith **2** huge and difficult to move or change

monologue *NOUN* **monologues** a long speech by one person

monopolize *VERB* **monopolizes, monopolizing, monopolized** take the whole of something for yourself • *One girl monopolized my attention*
▷ **monopolization** *NOUN*

monopoly *NOUN* **monopolies** the exclusive right to own something or to provide a service

monosyllable *NOUN* **monosyllables** a word with only one syllable
▷ **monosyllabic** *ADJECTIVE*

monotone *NOUN* a level unchanging tone of voice in speaking or singing

monotonous *ADJECTIVE* boring because it does not change • *monotonous work*
▷ **monotonously** *ADVERB* **monotony** *NOUN*

monsoon *NOUN* **monsoons 1** a strong wind in and near the Indian Ocean, bringing heavy rain in summer **2** the rainy season brought by this wind

monster *NOUN* **monsters 1** a large frightening creature **2** a huge thing **3** a wicked or cruel person

monster *ADJECTIVE* huge

monstrosity *NOUN* **monstrosities** a monstrous thing

monstrous *ADJECTIVE* **1** like a monster; huge **2** very shocking or outrageous

month *NOUN* **months** each of the twelve parts into which a year is divided

monthly *ADJECTIVE, ADVERB* happening or done once a month

monument *NOUN* **monuments** a statue, building, or column etc. put up as a memorial of some person or event

monumental *ADJECTIVE* **1** built as a monument **2** very large or important

moo *VERB* **moos, mooing, mooed** make the low deep sound of a cow
▷ **moo** *NOUN*

mood *NOUN* **moods** the way someone feels • *She is in a cheerful mood.*

moody *ADJECTIVE* **moodier, moodiest 1** gloomy or sullen **2** having sudden changes of mood for no apparent reason
▷ **moodily** *ADVERB* **moodiness** *NOUN*

moon *NOUN* **moons 1** the natural satellite of the earth that can be seen in the sky at night **2** a satellite of any planet
▷ **moonbeam** *NOUN* **moonlight** *NOUN* **moonlit** *ADJECTIVE*

moor[1] *NOUN* **moors** an area of rough land covered with heather, bracken, and bushes
▷ **moorland** *NOUN*

moor[2] *VERB* **moors, mooring, moored** fasten a boat etc. to a fixed object by means of a cable

Thesaurus

monotonous *ADJECTIVE a monotonous piece of work* ► boring, tedious, dull, dreary, uninteresting, tiresome, wearisome, repetitive, repetitious OPPOSITES ARE interesting, varied

monotony *NOUN the monotony of their working lives* ► dullness, boredom, tedium, sameness, repetitiveness, repetitiousness, weariness, dreariness, routine, uniformity

monster *NOUN* **1** *a huge monster of a man* ► giant, colossus, mammoth, leviathan **2** *He was behaving like a monster.* ► beast, brute, fiend, savage, ogre

monster *ADJECTIVE She came in eating a monster ice cream. The film was a monster hit.* ► huge, enormous, massive, colossal, gigantic, immense, (*informal*) ginormous

monstrous *ADJECTIVE* **1** *A monstrous wave loomed over the ship.* ► huge, enormous, massive, colossal, gigantic, immense, (*informal*) ginormous **2** *a monstrous winged creature* ► grotesque, hideous, gruesome, horrible, grisly, repulsive **3** *a monstrous injustice* ► appalling, dreadful, shocking, outrageous, abominable, disgraceful, scandalous, hideous, wicked, vile, foul, evil

monument *NOUN* **1** *a monument to local heroes* ► memorial, obelisk, statue, shrine, mausoleum **2** *a monument over his grave* ► gravestone, headstone, tombstone **3** *The book is a monument to years of research.* ► testament, record, token, evidence

monumental *ADJECTIVE* **1** *a monumental plaque* ► commemorative, memorial **2** *a monumental task* ► huge, great, enormous, immense, awesome, grand, impressive

mood *NOUN* **1** *He was in a bad mood for most of the day.* ► temper, humour, disposition, spirit, frame of mind, state of mind, vein **2** *The music sets the right mood for the story.* ► atmosphere, feeling, tone, spirit, ambience

moody *ADJECTIVE Charles was quiet and moody, and this worried her.* ► changeable, temperamental, volatile, unpredictable, sulky, sullen, gloomy, morose

moon *NOUN by the light of a full moon* RELATED ADJECTIVE lunar

moon *VERB There was not much to do and the young ones were mooning about.* ► mope, loaf, idle, waste time, (*more informal*) mooch

mooring *NOUN* **moorings** a place where a boat can be moored

mop *NOUN* **mops** **1** a bunch or pad of soft material fastened on the end of a stick, used for cleaning floors etc. **2** a thick mass of hair

mop *VERB* **mops, mopping, mopped** clean or wipe with a mop etc.
mop up **1** wipe or soak up liquid **2** deal with the last parts of something • *The army is mopping up the last of the rebels.*

mope *VERB* **mopes, moping, moped** be sad

moped (moh- ped) *NOUN* **mopeds** a kind of small motorcycle

moral *ADJECTIVE* **1** connected with what is right and wrong in behaviour **2** good or virtuous
▷ **morally** *ADVERB* **morality** *NOUN*
moral support help in the form of encouragement

moral *NOUN* **morals** a lesson in right behaviour taught by a story or event
USAGE Do not confuse with **morale**.

morale (mor- ahl) *NOUN* the level of confidence and good spirits in a person or group of people • *Morale was high after the victory.*
USAGE Do not confuse with **moral**.

morals *PLURAL NOUN* standards of behaviour

morbid *ADJECTIVE* **1** thinking about gloomy or unpleasant things **2** (in medicine) unhealthy • *a morbid growth*
▷ **morbidly** *ADVERB* **morbidity** *NOUN*

more *ADJECTIVE* (comparative of **much** and **many**) greater in amount etc.

more *NOUN* a greater amount

more *ADVERB* **1** to a greater extent • *more beautiful* **2** again • *once more*
more or less **1** approximately **2** nearly or practically

moreover *ADVERB* besides; in addition to what has been said

Mormon *NOUN* **Mormons** a member of a religious group founded in the USA

morning *NOUN* **mornings** the early part of the day, before noon or before lunchtime

moron *NOUN* **morons** (*informal*) a very stupid person
▷ **moronic** *ADJECTIVE*

morose (mo- rohss) *ADJECTIVE* bad-tempered and miserable
▷ **morosely** *ADVERB* **moroseness** *NOUN*

Morse code *NOUN* a signalling code using short and long sounds or flashes of light (dots and dashes) to represent letters

morsel *NOUN* **morsels** a small piece of food

mortal *ADJECTIVE* **1** not living for ever • *All of us are mortal.* **2** causing death; fatal • *a mortal wound* **3** deadly • *mortal enemies*
▷ **mortally** *ADVERB* **mortality** *NOUN*

mortal *NOUN* **mortals** a human being, as compared to a god or immortal spirit

mortar *NOUN* **mortars** **1** a mixture of sand, cement, and water used in building to stick

Thesaurus

mop *VERB* *A man was mopping the floor.* ► wash, clean, sponge, wipe

mope *VERB* *She realized it was no use moping.* ► brood, fret, sulk, pine, be miserable, grieve

moral *ADJECTIVE* **1** *moral issues* ► ethical, social, behavioural **2** *a very moral person* ► good, honest, virtuous, upright, principled, honourable, decent, proper, pure, blameless, upstanding, responsible, trustworthy AN OPPOSITE IS immoral **3** *moral support* ► emotional, psychological

moral *NOUN* *There's a clear moral to this story.* ► lesson, message, meaning, point, significance, import, principle

morality *NOUN* *standards of morality* ► ethics, morals, ideals, principles, integrity, honesty, goodness, propriety, conduct, behaviour, manners AN OPPOSITE IS immorality

morbid *ADJECTIVE* **1** *a morbid obsession with death* ► macabre, ghoulish, unhealthy, gruesome, grisly, unwholesome **2** *The thought of old age made her morbid.* ► gloomy, depressed, dejected, melancholy, downhearted, pessimistic AN OPPOSITE IS cheerful

more *ADJECTIVE* *They want more money.* ► additional, extra, further, added, increased, fresh, supplementary, other AN OPPOSITE IS less

morning *NOUN* *It was nearly morning when they finally reached home.* ► daybreak, dawn, daylight, sunrise, first light

morose *ADJECTIVE* *Back home dad was looking very morose.* ► sullen, gloomy, bad-tempered, ill-tempered, glum, sour, surly, moody, tetchy, crabby AN OPPOSITE IS cheerful

morsel *NOUN* *a few morsels of food* ► bite, mouthful, nibble, taste, fragment, piece, scrap, crumb, titbit

mortal *ADJECTIVE* **1** *The coffins contained the mortal remains of the victims.* ► physical, bodily, corporeal, earthly, worldly, perishable **2** *She struck him a mortal blow.* ► deadly, fatal, lethal **3** *mortal enemies* ► deadly, bitter, irreconcilable **4** *living in mortal fear* ► extreme, intense, grave, dire

mortal *NOUN* *a tale of mortals battling with divine forces* ► human being, human, mortal creature, individual, person, man *or* woman, earthling

bricks together **2** a hard bowl in which substances are pounded with a pestle **3** a short cannon for firing shells at a high angle

mortgage (mor- gij) *NOUN* **mortgages** an arrangement to borrow money to buy a house, with the house as security for the loan

mortgage *VERB* **mortgages**, **mortgaging**, **mortgaged** offer a house etc. as security in return for a loan

mortify *VERB* **mortifies**, **mortifying**, **mortified** humiliate someone or make them feel very ashamed
▷ **mortification** *NOUN*

mortuary *NOUN* **mortuaries** a place where dead bodies are kept before being buried or cremated

mosaic (mo- zay- ik) *NOUN* **mosaics** a picture or design made from small coloured pieces of stone or glass

mosque (mosk) *NOUN* **mosques** a building where Muslims worship

mosquito *NOUN* **mosquitoes** a kind of gnat that sucks blood

moss *NOUN* **mosses** a plant that grows in damp places and has no flowers
▷ **mossy** *ADJECTIVE*

most *ADJECTIVE* (superlative of **much** and **many**) greatest in amount or degree • *Most people came by bus.*

most *NOUN* the greatest amount • *Most of the food was eaten.*

most *ADVERB* **1** to the greatest extent; more than any other • *most beautiful* **2** very or extremely • *most impressive*

mostly *ADVERB* mainly

motel *NOUN* **motels** a hotel providing accommodation for motorists and their cars

moth *NOUN* **moths** an insect rather like a butterfly, that usually flies at night

mother *NOUN* **mothers** a female parent
▷ **motherhood** *NOUN*

mother *VERB* **mothers**, **mothering**, **mothered** look after someone in a motherly way [from Old English]

mother-in-law *NOUN* **mothers-in-law** the mother of a married person's husband or wife

motherly *ADJECTIVE* kind and gentle like a mother
▷ **motherliness** *NOUN*

motion *NOUN* **motions** **1** a way of moving; movement **2** a formal statement to be discussed and voted on at a meeting

motion *VERB* **motions**, **motioning**, **motioned** signal by a gesture • *She motioned him to sit beside her.*

motivation *NOUN* what gives a person a reason for doing something
▷ **motivate** *VERB*

motive *NOUN* **motives** what makes a person do something • *a motive for murder*

motor *NOUN* **motors** a machine providing power to drive machinery etc.; an engine

motor *VERB* **motors**, **motoring**, **motored** go or take someone in a car

motorcycle or **motorbike** *NOUN* **motorcycles** or **motorbikes** a two-wheeled road vehicle with an engine
▷ **motorcyclist** *NOUN*

Thesaurus

mostly *ADVERB* *She reads books all day, mostly novels.* ► mainly, chiefly, predominantly, primarily, principally, normally, typically, usually, generally, largely OPPOSITES ARE rarely, hardly

mother *NOUN* *Her mother picked her up every day from school.* ► female parent, (*more informal*) mum, (*more informal*) mummy, (*more informal*) ma, (*old-fashioned*) mater RELATED ADJECTIVE maternal

mother *VERB* *She was fond of mothering the residents when they were sick.* ► look after, care for, nurse, comfort, pamper, protect, cherish, fuss over

motherly *ADJECTIVE* *a motherly woman* ► maternal, protective, caring, kind, loving

motion *NOUN* *The motion of the bus made her queasy.* ► movement, moving, action, shifting, progress RELATED ADJECTIVES dynamic, kinetic

motionless *ADJECTIVE* **1** *The traffic ahead was motionless.* ► static, stationary, immobile, still, at a standstill, at rest AN OPPOSITE IS moving **2** *They stood motionless for several minutes, neither wanting to speak first.* ► still, stock-still, immobile, unmoving, paralysed, rooted to the spot, frozen, inert OPPOSITES ARE moving, active

motivate *VERB* *Money is what motivated them most.* ► prompt, drive, urge, stimulate, provoke, influence, activate, incite, persuade, impel

motivation *NOUN* *the motivation to learn* ► incentive, stimulus, impulse, drive, inspiration, inducement, encouragement, spur

motive *NOUN* *The police could not establish any motive for the attacks.* ► reason, grounds, rationale, motivation, object, intention, purpose, thinking, aim, cause

motorist *NOUN* **motorists** a person who drives a car

motorway *NOUN* **motorways** a wide road for fast long-distance traffic

motto *NOUN* **mottoes** **1** a short saying used as a guide for behaviour • *Their motto is 'Who dares, wins'.* **2** a short verse or riddle etc. found inside a cracker

mould[1] *NOUN* **moulds** a hollow container of a particular shape, in which a liquid or soft substance is put to set into this shape

mould *VERB* **moulds, moulding, moulded** make something have a particular shape or character

mould[2] *NOUN* a furry growth of very small fungi
▷ **mouldy** *ADJECTIVE*

moulder *VERB* **moulders, mouldering, mouldered** rot away or decay into dust

moult *VERB* **moults, moulting, moulted** shed feathers, hair, or skin etc. while a new growth forms

mound *NOUN* **mounds** **1** a pile of earth or stones etc. **2** a small hill

mount *NOUN* **mounts** **1** a mountain • *Mount Everest* **2** something on which an object is mounted **3** a horse etc. for riding [from Latin *mons* = mountain]

mount *VERB* **mounts, mounting, mounted** **1** climb or go up; ascend **2** get on a horse or bicycle etc. **3** increase in amount • *Our costs mounted.* **4** place or fix in position for use or display • *Mount your photos in an album.*

mountain *NOUN* **mountains** **1** a very high hill **2** a large heap or pile or quantity
▷ **mountainous** *ADJECTIVE*

mountaineer *NOUN* **mountaineers** a person who climbs mountains
▷ **mountaineering** *NOUN*

mounted *ADJECTIVE* serving on horseback
• *mounted police*

mourn *VERB* **mourns, mourning, mourned** be sad, especially because someone has died
▷ **mourner** *NOUN*

mournful *ADJECTIVE* sad and sorrowful
▷ **mournfully** *ADVERB*

mouse *NOUN* **mice** **1** a small animal with a long thin tail and a pointed nose **2** (**mouses** or **mice**) a small device which you move around on a mat to control the movements of a cursor on a VDU screen
▷ **mousetrap** *NOUN* **mousy** *ADJECTIVE*

mousse (mooss) *NOUN* **mousses** **1** a creamy pudding flavoured with fruit or chocolate **2** a frothy creamy substance put on the hair so that it can be styled more easily

moustache (mus- tahsh) *NOUN* **moustaches** hair allowed to grow on a man's upper lip

Thesaurus

motto *NOUN* *Their guiding motto was 'You scratch my back, and I'll scratch yours'.* ► saying, maxim, watchword, dictum, proverb, adage, precept, slogan, axiom

mould *NOUN* **1** *The cheese had mould on it.* ► mildew, fungus, must, growth **2** *The molten metal is poured into a mould.* ► cast, die, form, matrix, template

mould *VERB* **1** *The figures are moulded in bronze.* ► shape, form, fashion, forge, model, create, sculpt **2** *Education helps to mould your character.* ► form, shape, influence, determine, direct

mouldy *ADJECTIVE* **1** *a hunk of mouldy bread* ► mildewed, mildewy, mouldering, decaying, musty, rotten, stale **2** (*informal*) *The prize was just a mouldy book token.* ► measly, paltry, miserable, meagre, wretched, niggardly, pitiful, (*informal*) mingy

mound *NOUN* **1** *a mound of dirty socks* ► pile, heap, stack **2** *The common had several mounds to climb.* ► hill, hillock, hummock, rise, ridge, embankment

mount *VERB* **1** *The gallery mounts a special exhibition every year.* ► put on, organize, present, display, show, exhibit **2** *June mounted her pony. The guest of honour mounted the platform.* ► climb on to, jump on to, get on, get up on, get astride OPPOSITES ARE get off, climb down from **3** *Our savings were mounting at last.* ► grow, increase, accumulate, pile up OPPOSITES ARE dwindle, decrease

mountain *NOUN* **1** *several mountains to climb in the area* ► peak, summit, height RELATED ADJECTIVE alpine **2** *a mountain of work to get through* ► heap, pile, load, mound, stack, mass, great deal, backlog

mountainous *ADJECTIVE* **1** *mountainous country* ► hilly, craggy, rocky, alpine, highland, precipitous **2** *mountainous waves* ► huge, enormous, gigantic, colossal, immense, towering, (*more informal*) ginormous

mourn *VERB* **1** *He hid himself away, mourning his dead wife.* ► grieve for, sorrow over, lament for, weep for, pine for **2** *We all mourn the loss of so many precious artefacts.* ► regret, deplore, bewail AN OPPOSITE IS rejoice over

mournful *ADJECTIVE* *mournful music; a mournful cry* ► sad, sorrowful, melancholy, unhappy, doleful, desolate, heartbroken, tragic, sombre

a b c d e f g h i j k l m n o p q r s t u v w x y z

A B C D E F G H I J K L **M** N O P Q R S T U V W X Y Z

mouth *NOUN* **mouths** **1** the opening through which food is taken into the body **2** the place where a river enters the sea **3** an opening or outlet
▷ **mouthful** *NOUN*

mouth organ *NOUN* **mouth organs** a small musical instrument that you play by blowing and sucking while passing it along your lips

mouthpiece *NOUN* **mouthpieces** the part of a musical instrument or other device that you put to your mouth

move *VERB* **moves, moving, moved** **1** take or go from one place to another; change a person's or thing's position **2** affect a person's feelings • *Their sad story moved us deeply.* **3** put forward a formal statement (a **motion**) to be discussed and voted on at a meeting
▷ **mover** *NOUN*

move *NOUN* **moves** **1** a movement or action **2** a player's turn to move a piece in chess or other games
get a move on (*informal*) hurry up
on the move moving or making progress

movement *NOUN* **movements** **1** moving or being moved **2** a group of people working together to achieve something **3** one of the main divisions of a symphony or other long musical work

mow *VERB* **mows, mowing, mowed, mown** cut down grass etc.
▷ **mower** *NOUN*
mow down knock down and kill

MP *ABBREVIATION* Member of Parliament

Mr (mist- er) *NOUN* **Messrs** a title put before a man's name

Mrs (mis- iz) *NOUN* **Mrs** a title put before a married woman's name

Ms (miz) *NOUN* a title put before a woman's name
USAGE You put **Ms** before the name of a woman if she does not wish to be called 'Miss' or 'Mrs', or if you do not know whether she is married.

M.Sc. *ABBREVIATION* Master of Science

Mt *ABBREVIATION* mount or mountain

much *ADJECTIVE* **more, most** existing in a large amount • *much noise*

much *NOUN* a large amount of something

much *ADVERB* **1** greatly or considerably • *much to my surprise* **2** approximately • *It is much the same.*

Thesaurus

mouth *NOUN* **1** *He opened his mouth.* ► jaws, lips, (*more informal*) gob RELATED ADJECTIVE oral **2** *the mouth of the cave* ► entrance, opening, entry, aperture **3** *the mouth of a river* ► outfall, outlet, estuary, firth

mouth *VERB* *Thank you, I answered, mouthing the words carefully.* ► utter, enunciate, pronounce, articulate, form, say

mouthful *NOUN* **1** *a mouthful of food* ► bite, taste, morsel, nibble, gobbet, spoonful, swallow **2** *a mouthful of water* ► gulp, draught, sip, swallow, (*more informal*) swig

move *VERB* **1** *He got up and moved to the bench under the tree.* ► go, walk, march, proceed, advance, stroll, amble **2** *The traffic moved slowly forward.* ► edge, creep, crawl, slide **3** *I'll move the chair closer to the table.* ► carry, take, shift, transport **4** *We need to move quickly to secure a place.* ► act, take action, take steps, make a move, take the initiative **5** *At long last things are starting to move.* ► progress, make progress, make headway, develop, (*more informal*) get somewhere **6** *She moved from London to the country last year.* ► relocate, move house, move home, migrate, decamp, depart **7** *The beautiful performance moved them deeply.* ► touch, affect, impress, disturb, agitate **8** *The language course moved her to find out about living abroad.* ► prompt, stimulate, motivate, persuade, rouse, impel, induce, inspire

move *NOUN* **1** *The group got together to talk over their next move.* ► step, action, initiative, tactic, ploy, ruse **2** *It's your move.* ► turn, go, opportunity, chance

movement *NOUN* **1** *the movement of goods and animals* ► transportation, carrying, relocation, conveyance, transferral, repositioning **2** *She joined a left-wing political movement in her student days.* ► party, organization, faction, group, grouping, campaign **3** *A movement in the bushes caught his eye.* ► motion, move, activity, action **4** *There has been little movement on our grant application.* ► progress, change, advance **5** *a movement towards equal pay for men and women* ► trend, tendency, swing, current

moving *ADJECTIVE* **1** *a moving train* ► travelling, mobile, active, on the move, under way OPPOSITES ARE stationary, motionless **2** *a moving story* ► touching, affecting, poignant, emotive, stirring, emotional, heart-warming, inspiring, exciting, stimulating AN OPPOSITE IS unemotional

much *NOUN* *We don't have much to do.* ► a lot, a great deal, plenty

much *ADJECTIVE* *Do you need much help?* ► a lot of, a great deal of, plenty of, considerable, substantial

muck *NOUN* **1** farmyard manure **2** (*informal*) dirt or filth **3** (*informal*) a mess
▷ **mucky** *ADJECTIVE*

muck *VERB*
muck about (*informal*) mess about
muck out clean out the place where an animal is kept
muck up (*informal*) **1** make dirty **2** make a mess of; spoil
[probably from a Scandinavian language]

mud *NOUN* wet soft earth
▷ **muddy** *ADJECTIVE* **muddiness** *NOUN*

muddle *VERB* **muddles, muddling, muddled**
1 jumble or mix things up **2** confuse
▷ **muddler** *NOUN*

muddle *NOUN* **muddles** a muddled condition or thing; confusion or disorder

mudguard *NOUN* **mudguards** a curved cover over the top part of the wheel of a bicycle etc. to protect the rider from the mud and water thrown up by the wheel

muff *NOUN* **muffs** a short tube-shaped piece of warm material into which the hands are pushed from opposite ends

muffin *NOUN* **muffins** **1** a flat bun eaten toasted and buttered **2** a small sponge cake, usually containing fruit, chocolate chips, etc.

muffle *VERB* **muffles, muffling, muffled**
1 cover or wrap something to protect it or keep it warm **2** deaden the sound of something • *a muffled scream*

muffler *NOUN* **mufflers** a warm scarf

mug *NOUN* **mugs** **1** a kind of large cup with straight sides **2** (*slang*) a fool; a person who is easily deceived **3** (*slang*) a person's face

mug *VERB* **mugs, mugging, mugged** attack and rob somebody in the street
▷ **mugger** *NOUN*

mule *NOUN* **mules** an animal that is the offspring of a donkey and a mare, known for being stubborn
▷ **mulish** *ADJECTIVE*

mull[1] *VERB* **mulls, mulling, mulled** heat wine or beer with sugar and spices, as a drink
• *mulled ale*

mull[2] *VERB* **mulls, mulling, mulled**
mull something over think about something carefully; ponder

Thesaurus

muck *NOUN* **1** *He went out to clean the muck off the windows.* ► dirt, grime, filth, slime, sludge, mess, mud, (*more informal*) gunge **2** *spreading muck in the fields* ► manure, dung

muck *VERB* **muck about** *or* **around** (*informal*) *John was mucking about with an old engine.*
► fool about *or* around, play about *or* around, tinker, (*informal*) mess about *or* around

mucky *ADJECTIVE* *She took off her mucky shoes.*
► dirty, messy, muddy, filthy, grubby, soiled, foul, grimy AN OPPOSITE IS clean

mud *NOUN* *He slipped and fell in the mud.*
► sludge, slime, slurry, clay, soil, dirt, mire, muck, ooze, silt

muddle *NOUN* **1** *a muddle over the time of the train* ► confusion, misunderstanding, mistake, mix-up **2** *Look at the muddle in the kitchen.* ► mess, shambles, jumble, clutter, chaos, untidiness, disorder, tangle

muddle *VERB* **1** *Her explanation merely muddled him.* ► confuse, bewilder, mix up, perplex, puzzle, disorientate, mislead AN OPPOSITE IS enlighten **2** *Don't muddle the papers on the desk.*
► disorganize, disarrange, mix up, mess up, jumble up, make a mess of, disorder
OPPOSITES ARE tidy, clear up

muddled *ADJECTIVE* *He felt muddled and couldn't think what to do.* ► confused, disorganized, bewildered, mixed up, perplexed, puzzled, disorientated

muddy *ADJECTIVE* **1** *They came in to change their muddy boots.* ► dirty, messy, mucky, filthy, grubby, soiled, foul, grimy AN OPPOSITE IS clean
2 *The ground was wet and muddy.*
► waterlogged, boggy, marshy, sodden, soft, spongy, sloppy **3** *The water looked muddy.*
► cloudy, misty, opaque, messy AN OPPOSITE IS clear

muffle *VERB* **1** **muffle up** *She went out, muffling herself up against the cold.* ► wrap up, cover up, envelop, swathe, enclose **2** *He muffled the sound of the gun with cushions.* ► deaden, dull, dampen, smother, soften, suppress, muzzle

muffled *ADJECTIVE* *a muffled cry* ► faint, indistinct, muted, deadened, dull, unclear
OPPOSITES ARE distinct, loud

mug *NOUN* **1** *We drank tea from mugs.* ► beaker, cup **2** *He was rather a mug to drive so fast.*
► fool, simpleton, idiot, clot

mug *VERB* *They were mugged on their way home.*
► attack, assault, molest, rob, steal from, set on, jump on
mug up *He's mugging up for his driving test.*
► study, learn, read up, cram

muggy *ADJECTIVE* *muggy weather* ► humid, close, clammy, sultry, oppressive, sticky, stuffy, airless

mull *VERB* **mull over** *a few suggestions to mull over*
► consider, ponder, think about, contemplate, reflect on, weigh up, turn over in your mind

multicultural *ADJECTIVE* made up of people of many different races, religions, and cultures

multilateral *ADJECTIVE* (said about an agreement or treaty) made between three or more people or countries etc.

multimedia *ADJECTIVE* using more than one medium ● *a multimedia show with pictures, lights, and music*

multimedia *NOUN* a computer program with sound and still and moving pictures linked to the text

multimillionaire *NOUN* **multimillionaires** a person with a fortune of several million pounds or dollars

multinational *NOUN* **multinationals** a large business company which works in several countries

multiple *ADJECTIVE* having many parts or elements

multiple *NOUN* **multiples** a number that contains another number (a **factor**) an exact amount of times with no remainder ● *8 and 12 are multiples of 4.*

multiple sclerosis *NOUN* a disease of the nervous system which makes a person unable to control their movements, and may affect their sight

multiply *VERB* **multiplies**, **multiplying**, **multiplied** **1** take a number a given quantity of times ● *Five multiplied by four equals twenty (5 x 4 = 20)*. **2** make or become many; increase
▷ **multiplication** *NOUN* **multiplier** *NOUN*

multiracial *ADJECTIVE* consisting of people of many different races

multitude *NOUN* **multitudes** a great number of people or things
▷ **multitudinous** *ADJECTIVE*

mumble *VERB* **mumbles**, **mumbling**, **mumbled** speak indistinctly so that you are not easy to hear
▷ **mumble** *NOUN* **mumbler** *NOUN*

mumbo-jumbo *NOUN* talk that sounds mysterious but has no real meaning

mummy *NOUN* **mummies** a corpse wrapped in cloth and treated with oils etc. before being buried so that it does not decay, as was the custom in ancient Egypt
▷ **mummify** *VERB*

mumps *NOUN* an infectious disease that makes the neck swell painfully

munitions *PLURAL NOUN* military weapons, ammunition, and equipment

mural *ADJECTIVE* on or to do with a wall

mural *NOUN* **murals** a picture painted on a wall

murder *VERB* **murders**, **murdering**, **murdered** kill a person unlawfully and deliberately
▷ **murderer** *NOUN* **murderess** *NOUN*

murder *NOUN* **murders** the murdering of somebody
▷ **murderous** *ADJECTIVE*

Thesaurus

multiply *VERB* **1** *The problems began to multiply.* ► increase, proliferate, grow, mount up, spread, become numerous OPPOSITES ARE decrease, diminish **2** *The hedgehogs multiplied rapidly.* ► breed, propagate, reproduce, procreate

multitude *NOUN* *a multitude of people; a multitude of questions to answer* ► mass, host, myriad, swarm, throng, lots, large number, legion

mumble *VERB* *She walked off, mumbling quietly.* ► mutter, murmur, whisper, burble

mumbo-jumbo *NOUN* *The form was covered in mumbo-jumbo.* ► jargon, gobbledegook, gibberish, nonsense

munch *VERB* *The children waited, munching their rolls.* ► chomp, crunch, eat, bite, chew, gnaw

mundane *ADJECTIVE* *She hoped such mundane matters would keep him occupied for a while.* ► everyday, routine, commonplace, day-to-day, humdrum, tedious, dull, boring, unexceptional OPPOSITES ARE extraordinary, exceptional

murder *NOUN* *Reports are coming in of a brutal murder.* ► killing , homicide, slaughter (= killing of many people), assassination (= killing of an important person), fratricide (= killing of a brother), infanticide (= killing of a child), matricide (= killing of a mother), parricide (= killing of a parent or close relative), patricide (= killing of a father), regicide (= killing of a king or queen)

murder *VERB* *A gang had tried to murder him.* ► kill, put to death, assassinate

murderer *NOUN* *The murderer was never caught.* ► killer, assassin

murderous *ADJECTIVE* *a murderous assault* ► homicidal, deadly, lethal, brutal, bloodthirsty, barbarous, savage, ferocious, vicious

murky *ADJECTIVE* **murkier**, **murkiest** dark and gloomy
▷ **murk** *NOUN* **murkiness** *NOUN*

murmur *VERB* **murmurs**, **murmuring**, **murmured** **1** make a low continuous sound **2** speak in a soft voice
▷ **murmur** *NOUN*

muscle *NOUN* **muscles** **1** a band or bundle of fibrous tissue that can contract and relax and so produce movement in parts of the body **2** the power of muscles; strength
▷ **muscular** *ADJECTIVE* **muscularity** *NOUN*

museum *NOUN* **museums** a place where interesting, old, or valuable objects are displayed for people to see [from Greek *mouseion* = place of the Muses, the goddesses of the arts and sciences]

mush *NOUN* soft pulp
▷ **mushy** *ADJECTIVE*

mushroom *NOUN* **mushrooms** an edible fungus with a stem and a dome-shaped top

music *NOUN* **1** a pattern of pleasant or interesting sounds made by instruments or by the voice **2** printed or written symbols which stand for musical sounds [from Greek *mousike tekhne* = art of the Muses (see **museum**)]

musical *ADJECTIVE* **1** to do with music **2** producing music **3** good at music or interested in it
▷ **musically** *ADVERB*

musical *NOUN* **musicals** a play or film containing a lot of songs

musician *NOUN* **musicians** someone who plays a musical instrument

Muslim *NOUN* **Muslims** a person who follows the religious teachings of Muhammad (who lived in about 570-632), set out in the Koran

must *AUXILIARY VERB* used to express **1** necessity or obligation (*You must go*), **2** certainty (*You must be joking!*)

mustard *NOUN* a yellow paste or powder used to give food a hot taste
mustard and cress small green plants eaten in salads

muster *NOUN* **musters** an assembly of people or things
pass muster be up to the required standard

mustn't (*mainly spoken*) must not

musty *ADJECTIVE* **mustier**, **mustiest** smelling or tasting mouldy or stale
▷ **mustiness** *NOUN*

mutation *NOUN* **mutations** a change in the form of a living creature because of changes in its genes
▷ **mutate** *VERB* **mutant** *NOUN*

mute *ADJECTIVE* **1** silent; not speaking or able to speak **2** not pronounced • *The g in 'gnat' is mute.*
▷ **mutely** *ADVERB* **muteness** *NOUN*

mutilate *VERB* **mutilates**, **mutilating**, **mutilated** damage something by breaking or cutting off part of it
▷ **mutilation** *NOUN*

mutineer *NOUN* **mutineers** a person who mutinies

mutiny *NOUN* **mutinies** rebellion against authority, especially refusal by members of the armed forces to obey orders
▷ **mutinous** *ADJECTIVE* **mutinously** *ADVERB*

mutiny *VERB* **mutinies**, **mutinying**, **mutinied** take part in a mutiny

mutter *VERB* **mutters**, **muttering**, **muttered** **1** speak in a low voice **2** grumble
▷ **mutter** *NOUN*

mutton *NOUN* meat from a sheep [from early French, probably from Celtic]

mutual (mew- tew- al) *ADJECTIVE* **1** given or done to each other • *mutual destruction* **2** shared by two or more people • *a mutual friend*
▷ **mutually** *ADVERB*

Thesaurus

murky *ADJECTIVE* *The sky was murky and drizzle was falling.* ► gloomy, grey, dark, overcast, leaden, misty, dim, dull, cloudy, foggy, sombre AN OPPOSITE IS clear

murmur *VERB* *He murmured an apology and left.* ► mutter, mumble, whisper, burble

muscular *ADJECTIVE* *He's tall and muscular.* ► brawny, muscly, athletic, strong, well built, beefy, strapping, sinewy

musical *ADJECTIVE* *musical sounds* ► tuneful, melodic, melodious, euphonious, harmonious, lyrical, pleasant, sweet-sounding AN OPPOSITE IS discordant

musician *NOUN* *A small group of musicians were playing on the terrace.* ► performer, player, instrumentalist

mutiny *NOUN* *a mutiny on board ship; a mutiny by government MPs* ► rebellion, revolt, protest, uprising, insurrection

mutiny *VERB* *The troops mutinied over pay.* ► rebel, revolt, rise up, protest, go on strike

mutter *VERB* *Her husband mutters in his sleep.* ► mumble, murmur, whisper, burble

mutual *ADJECTIVE* *an agreement based on mutual trust* ► joint, shared, reciprocal, reciprocated, common, complementary

A B C D E F G H I J K L M N O P Q R S T U V W X Y Z

muzzle *NOUN* **muzzles 1** an animal's nose and mouth **2** a cover put over an animal's nose and mouth so that it cannot bite **3** the open end of a gun

muzzle *VERB* **muzzles, muzzling, muzzled** **1** put a muzzle on an animal **2** silence; prevent a person from expressing opinions

my *ADJECTIVE* belonging to me

myself *PRONOUN* I or me and nobody else

mysterious *ADJECTIVE* full of mystery; puzzling
▷ **mysteriously** *ADVERB*

mystery *NOUN* **mysteries** something that cannot be explained or understood; something puzzling [from Greek *mysterion* = a secret thing or ceremony]

mystic *ADJECTIVE* **1** having a spiritual meaning **2** mysterious and filling people with wonder
▷ **mystical** *ADJECTIVE* **mystically** *ADVERB* **mysticism** *NOUN*

mystic *NOUN* **mystics** a person who seeks to obtain spiritual contact with God by deep religious meditation [from Greek *mystikos* = secret]

mystify *VERB* **mystifies, mystifying, mystified** puzzle or bewilder
▷ **mystification** *NOUN*

myth (mith) *NOUN* **myths 1** an old story containing ideas about ancient times or about supernatural beings COMPARE **legend 2** an untrue story or belief

mythical *ADJECTIVE* imaginary; found only in myths • *a mythical animal*

mythology *NOUN* myths or the study of myths
▷ **mythological** *ADJECTIVE*

Thesaurus

mysterious *ADJECTIVE His friends had disappeared in mysterious circumstances.*
► strange, puzzling, odd, peculiar, curious, weird, obscure, baffling, unexplained, unknown AN OPPOSITE IS straightforward

mystery *NOUN* **1** *Their disappearance remains a mystery.* ► puzzle, enigma, riddle, conundrum **2** *events surrounded in mystery* ► secrecy, obscurity, uncertainty, ambiguity

mystify *VERB The work he did mystified his contemporaries.* ► puzzle, perplex, baffle, bewilder, bamboozle, confuse

mythical *ADJECTIVE a story based on mythical events* ► legendary, mythological, imaginary, fabled, fabulous, fictional, invented, fanciful, make-believe AN OPPOSITE IS real

mythological *ADJECTIVE mythological gods and heroes* ► mythical, fabled, legendary, traditional

mythology *NOUN creatures in mythology*
► legend, myth, tradition, folklore

Nn

N. *ABBREVIATION* **1** north **2** northern

nag *VERB* **nags, nagging, nagged 1** pester a person by keeping on criticizing, complaining, or asking for things **2** keep on hurting or bothering you • *a nagging pain*

nail *NOUN* **nails 1** the hard covering over the end of a finger or toe **2** a small sharp piece of metal hammered in to fasten pieces of wood etc. together

nail *VERB* **nails, nailing, nailed 1** fasten with a nail or nails **2** (*informal*) catch; arrest

naked *ADJECTIVE* **1** without any clothes or coverings on **2** obvious; not hidden • *the naked truth*
▷ **nakedly** *ADVERB* **nakedness** *NOUN*

naked eye *NOUN* the eye when it is not helped by a telescope or microscope etc.

name *NOUN* **names 1** the word or words by which a person, animal, place, or thing is known **2** a person's reputation

name *VERB* **names, naming, named 1** give a name to **2** state the name or names of **3** say what you want something to be • *Name your price.*

name the day decide when something, especially a wedding, is to take place or happen • *Have you two named the day yet?*

namely *ADVERB* that is to say • *My two favourite subjects are sciences, namely chemistry and biology.*

nanny *NOUN* **nannies** a woman employed to look after young children

nap *NOUN* **naps** a short sleep
catch a person napping catch a person unprepared for something or not alert

napkin *NOUN* **napkins 1** a piece of cloth or paper used at meals to protect your clothes or for wiping your lips or fingers **2** (*old use*) a nappy

nappy *NOUN* **nappies** a piece of cloth or other fabric put round a baby's bottom

narcotic *NOUN* **narcotics** a drug that makes a person sleepy or unconscious
▷ **narcotic** *ADJECTIVE* **narcosis** *NOUN*
[from Greek *narke* = numbness]

narrative *NOUN* **narratives** a spoken or written account of something

narrow *ADJECTIVE* **1** not wide or broad **2** uncomfortably close; with only a small margin of safety • *a narrow escape*
▷ **narrowly** *ADVERB*

Thesaurus

nab *VERB* (*informal*) *A police car nabbed him on his way home.* ► catch, arrest, apprehend, take into custody

nag *VERB* *He's been nagging me about it for weeks.* ► harass, badger, pester, chivvy, hound, (*more informal*) keep on at, (*more informal*) go on at, (*more informal*) moan at

nail *NOUN* **1** *The nail's fallen out so I'll have to use a screw.* ► tack, pin, stud **2** *He broke his nail opening a carton.* RELATED ADJECTIVE ungual

nail *VERB* *Nail it to the wall.* ► hammer, pin, tack, fasten, attach, secure, fix

naive *ADJECTIVE* *I was very naive in those days but I've learned a lot since then.* ► innocent, ingenuous, unsophisticated, inexperienced, credulous, artless, raw, green
OPPOSITES ARE sophisticated, experienced, knowing

naked *ADJECTIVE* **1** *a naked statue* ► nude, bare, unclothed, uncovered, undressed, unclad
AN OPPOSITE IS clothed **2** *the naked truth* ► plain, undisguised, unadorned, unvarnished, simple, bald, unmitigated

name *NOUN* *His name is Carl.* ► first name, forename, (*more formal*) denomination, (*more formal*) appellation RELATED ADJECTIVES nominal, onomastic

name *VERB* **1** *Her father had wanted to name her Clio.* ► call, dub, style, christen, baptize **2** *The victim will not be be named until relatives have been notified.* ► identify, specify **3** *The king has to name a successor.* ► choose, designate, nominate, decide on, specify, appoint

nameless *ADJECTIVE* *pictures by a nameless artist* ► unnamed, unidentified, anonymous, unheard of

nap *NOUN* *He was on the sofa, having a nap.* ► snooze, doze, sleep, rest, lie-down, (*more informal*) forty winks

narrate *VERB* *The story is narrated by the governess.* ► tell, relate, recount, report, describe, unfold, detail, relay, chronicle

narrative *NOUN* *a chronological narrative of the events of the last five years* ► account, summary, narration, commentary, description, sketch

narrow *ADJECTIVE* **1** *a narrow path; She was elected by a narrow majority.* ► slim, thin, slender, fine **2** *a narrow space* ► tight, close, confined, cramped, enclosed, limited, constricting AN OPPOSITE IS wide **3** *a narrow point of view* ► narrow-minded, intolerant, conservative, illiberal, insular, parochial, small-minded, bigoted, hidebound
OPPOSITES ARE broad-minded, open-minded, tolerant

narrow-minded *ADJECTIVE* not tolerant of other people's beliefs and ways

nasal *ADJECTIVE* to do with the nose [from Latin *nasus* = nose]

nasty *ADJECTIVE* **nastier**, **nastiest** **1** unpleasant **2** unkind
▷ **nastily** *ADVERB* **nastiness** *NOUN*

nation *NOUN* **nations** a large community of people most of whom have the same ancestors, language, history, and customs, and who usually live in the same part of the world under one government
▷ **national** *ADJECTIVE*, *NOUN* **nationally** *ADVERB*

national anthem *NOUN* **national anthems** a nation's official song, which is played or sung on important occasions

national curriculum *NOUN* an official list of the subjects that must be taught by state schools

nationalist *NOUN* **nationalists** **1** a person who is very patriotic **2** a person who wants his or her country to be independent rather than being part of another country • *Scottish Nationalists*
▷ **nationalism** *NOUN* **nationalistic** *ADJECTIVE*

nationality *NOUN* **nationalities** the condition of belonging to a particular nation • *What is his nationality?*

nationalize *VERB* **nationalizes**, **nationalizing**, **nationalized** put an industry or business under state ownership or control
▷ **nationalization** *NOUN*

national park *NOUN* **national parks** an area of natural beauty which is protected by the government and which the public may visit

nationwide *ADJECTIVE* & *ADVERB* over the whole of a country

native *NOUN* **natives** a person born in a particular place • *He is a native of Sweden*

native *ADJECTIVE* **1** belonging to a person because of the place of his or her birth • *my native country* **2** grown or originating in a particular place • *a plant native to China* **3** natural; belonging to a person by nature • *native ability*

Native American *NOUN* **Native Americans** one of the original inhabitants of North and South America
USAGE See note at **Indian**.

natural *ADJECTIVE* **1** produced or done by nature, not by people or machines **2** normal; not surprising **3** having a quality or ability that you were born with • *a natural leader* **4** (said about a note in music) neither sharp nor flat
▷ **naturally** *ADVERB* **naturalness** *NOUN*

natural *NOUN* **naturals** **1** a person who is naturally good at something **2** a natural note in music; a sign (♮) that shows this

natural history *NOUN* the study of plants and animals

naturalist *NOUN* **naturalists** an expert in natural history

natural science *NOUN* the study of physics, chemistry, and biology

Thesaurus

narrow-minded *ADJECTIVE* *a narrow-minded outlook* ► small-minded, intolerant, narrow, bigoted, conservative, illiberal, insular, parochial, short-sighted, hidebound
OPPOSITES ARE broad-minded, open-minded, tolerant

nasty *ADJECTIVE* **1** *The pudding had a nasty taste* ► unpleasant, disagreeable, disgusting, horrible, repellent OPPOSITES ARE pleasant, nice, lovely **2** *He can be very nasty at times.* ► unkind, unfriendly, unpleasant, disagreeable, malicious, mean, spiteful, vindictive **3** *The weather turned nasty.* ► unpleasant, rough, squally OPPOSITES ARE fine, pleasant

nation *NOUN* **1** *The president will broadcast to the nation.* ► people, population, country, community, society **2** *the nations of the world* ► country, people, civilization, land, power, race, state RELATED ADJECTIVE ethnic

national *ADJECTIVE* **1** *a national strike* ► nationwide, countrywide, general, widespread **2** *national costume* ► ethnic, popular, domestic

national *NOUN* *an Italian national* ► citizen, subject, native, resident, inhabitant

nationalism *NOUN* *the surge of nationalism in Europe* ► patriotism, (*disapproving*) chauvinism, (*disapproving*) jingoism, (*disapproving*) xenophobia

native *ADJECTIVE* **1** *native inhabitants* ► original, aboriginal, indigenous **2** *a native instinct for politics* ► innate, inherent, inborn, inbred, natural, congenital, hereditary, inherited

native *NOUN* *a native of New York* ► inhabitant, resident, citizen, national

natter *VERB* *They nattered on for hours.* ► chatter, chat, prattle, blather, burble, talk

natural *ADJECTIVE* **1** *a natural tendency to self-preservation* ► innate, inborn, instinctive, intuitive, inherent **2** *Her manner is fresh and natural.* ► genuine, sincere, unaffected, uninhibited, ingenuous, open **3** *It was natural for them to want more information.* ► understandable, reasonable, logical, unsurprising, predictable **4** *Kim proved to be a natural leader.* ► born, spontaneous, untaught **5** *The bay forms a natural port on this side of the island.* ► ready-made

natural selection *NOUN* Darwin's theory that only the plants and animals suited to their surroundings will survive and breed

nature *NOUN* **natures** **1** everything in the world that was not made by people **2** the characteristics of a person or thing • *She has a loving nature.* **3** a kind or sort of thing • *He likes things of that nature.*

naughty *ADJECTIVE* **naughtier, naughtiest** **1** badly behaved or disobedient **2** slightly rude or indecent • *naughty pictures*
▷ **naughtily** *ADVERB* **naughtiness** *NOUN*

nausea (**naw**- zee- a) *NOUN* a feeling of sickness or disgust
▷ **nauseous** *ADJECTIVE* **nauseating** *ADJECTIVE*

nautical *ADJECTIVE* to do with ships or sailors

nautical mile *NOUN* **nautical miles** a measure of distance used at sea, equal to 2,025 yards (1852 kilometres)

naval *ADJECTIVE* to do with a navy [from Latin *navis* = ship]

navel *NOUN* **navels** the small hollow in the centre of the abdomen, where the umbilical cord was attached [from Old English]

navigate *VERB* **navigates, navigating, navigated** **1** sail in or through a river or sea etc. • *The ship navigated the Suez Canal.* **2** make sure that a ship, aircraft, or vehicle is going in the right direction
▷ **navigation** *NOUN* **navigator** *NOUN*

navy *NOUN* **navies** **1** a country's warships and the people trained to use them **2** (also **navy blue**) a very dark blue, the colour of naval uniform

Nazi (**nah**- tsee) *NOUN* **Nazis** a member of the National Socialist Party in Germany in Hitler's time, with fascist beliefs
▷ **Nazism** *NOUN*

NB *ABBREVIATION* take note that (Latin **nota bene** = note well)

NE *ABBREVIATION* **1** north-east **2** north-eastern

near *ADVERB, ADJECTIVE* not far away
near by not far away • *They live near by.*

near *PREPOSITION* not far away from • *near the shops*

nearby *ADJECTIVE* near • *a nearby house*

nearly *ADVERB* almost • *We have nearly finished.*

neat *ADJECTIVE* **neater, neatest** **1** simple and clean and tidy **2** skilful **3** undiluted • *neat whisky*
▷ **neatly** *ADVERB* **neatness** *NOUN*

neaten *VERB* **neatens, neatening, neatened** make or become neat

nebula *NOUN* **nebulae** a bright or dark patch in the sky, caused by a distant galaxy or a cloud of dust or gas

nebulous *ADJECTIVE* indistinct or vague • *nebulous ideas*

Thesaurus

nature *NOUN* **1** *the beauties of nature* ► the natural world, the living world, the environment, the countryside, the landscape **2** *It's not in his nature to make complaints.* ► character, personality, temperament, disposition, constitution, make-up **3** *decisions that by their nature cause resentment* ► essence, characteristics **4** *coins, medals, and things of that nature* ► kind, type, sort, category, description

naughty *ADJECTIVE* *a naughty child* ► badly behaved, mischievous, misbehaving, disobedient, insubordinate, troublesome, vexatious

nausea *NOUN* *He had a bad headache and a feeling of nausea.* ► sickness, queasiness, biliousness, retching, vomiting

nauseating *ADJECTIVES* *She disliked his nauseating self-importance.* ► sickening, disgusting, revolting, repulsive, repellent, loathsome, offensive

nautical *ADJECTIVE* *eating seafood in a nautical atmosphere* ► maritime, naval, marine, seafaring, seagoing

navy *NOUN* *an officer in the navy* ► fleet, armada, convoy, flotilla, naval force

near *ADJECTIVE* **1** *She is a near neighbour of ours.* ► nearby, close, adjacent, adjoining, next-door, bordering, connected, neighbouring OPPOSITES ARE distant, faraway **2** *A decision is near.* ► close, approaching, imminent, coming, forthcoming, impending, (*more informal*) round the corner **3** *near relatives* ► close, dear, familiar, intimate AN OPPOSITE IS distant

nearby *ADVERB* *Her children all live nearby.* ► close by, not far away, at hand, within reach, in the vicinity

nearly *ADVERB* *The work is nearly finished.* ► almost, practically, virtually, about, more or less, as good as, just about, around

neat *ADJECTIVE* **1** *The room was neat and newly decorated.* ► tidy, orderly, trim, spick-and-span, spruce, immaculate OPPOSITES ARE untidy, messy **2** *hair tied in a neat bun at the back* ► compact, elegant, trim, well formed, simple OPPOSITES ARE clumsy, awkward **3** *neat writing* ► regular, precise, well formed, elegant **4** *a neat solution to the problem* ► clever, ingenious, adroit, deft, inventive, resourceful, slick AN OPPOSITE IS inept **5** *a glass of neat whisky* ► undiluted, straight, pure, unmixed, unadulterated AN OPPOSITE IS diluted

A B C D E F G H I J K L M N O P Q R S T U V W X Y Z

necessary *ADJECTIVE* not able to be done without; essential
▷ **necessarily** *ADVERB*

necessity *NOUN* **necessities** **1** need • *the necessity of buying food and clothing* **2** something necessary

neck *NOUN* **necks** **1** the part of the body that joins the head to the shoulders **2** the part of a garment round the neck **3** a narrow part of something, especially of a bottle
neck and neck almost exactly together in a race or contest

necklace *NOUN* **necklaces** an ornament worn round the neck

necktie *NOUN* **neckties** a strip of material worn passing under the collar of a shirt and knotted in front

need *VERB* **needs**, **needing**, **needed** **1** be without something you should have; require • *We need two more chairs.* **2** (as an *auxiliary verb*) have to do something • *You need not answer.*

need *NOUN* **needs** **1** something needed; a necessary thing **2** a situation where something is necessary • *There is no need to cry.* **3** great poverty or hardship
▷ **needful** *ADJECTIVE* **needless** *ADJECTIVE*

needle *NOUN* **needles** **1** a very thin pointed piece of steel used in sewing **2** something long and thin and sharp • *a knitting needle* • *pine needles* **3** the pointer of a meter or compass

needlework *NOUN* sewing or embroidery

needy *ADJECTIVE* **needier**, **neediest** very poor; lacking things necessary for life
▷ **neediness** *NOUN*

negative *ADJECTIVE* **1** that says 'no' • *a negative answer* **2** looking only at the bad aspects of a situation • *Don't be so negative.* **3** showing no sign of what is being tested for • *Her pregnancy test was negative.* **4** less than nought; minus **5** (in science) to do with the kind of electric charge carried by electrons
▷ **negatively** *ADVERB*
USAGE The opposite of sense 1 is **affirmative**, and of senses 2, 3, 4 **positive**.

negative *NOUN* **negatives** **1** a negative statement **2** a photograph on film with the dark parts light and the light parts dark, from which a positive print (with the dark and light or colours correct) can be made

neglect *VERB* **neglects**, **neglecting**, **neglected** **1** not look after or pay attention to a person or thing **2** not do something; forget • *He neglected to shut the door.*

Thesaurus

necessary *ADJECTIVE* *necessary repairs to the bridge* ► essential, indispensable, vital, unavoidable, requisite, needed, needful, obligatory, imperative, compulsory, mandatory AN OPPOSITE IS unnecessary

necessitate *VERB* *Measures as drastic as these would necessitate legislation.* ► require, involve, entail, demand, call for, mean, compel

necessity *NOUN* **1** *A mobile phone is now regarded as a necessity by most people.* ► essential, requirement, prerequisite **2** *Necessity compelled thousands to emigrate.* ► need, poverty, hardship, destitution, penury, deprivation **3** *the necessity for caution* ► need, demand, indispensability (of)

need *VERB* **1** *The room needs redecorating.* ► require, want, be in need of, demand, call for **2** *We need more milk.* ► require, want, be short of, lack **3** *He needed her so much now.* ► yearn for, long for, pine for, crave, depend on, rely on **4 need to** *Do we need to come?* ► have to, be obliged to, be required to, be compelled to, be under an obligation to

need *NOUN* **1** *There is no need to say anything.* ► necessity, obligation, call, requirement **2** *basic human needs like food and water* ► requirement, essential, necessity, want, prerequisite

needless *ADJECTIVE* *a lot of needless expense* ► unnecessary, unwanted, inessential, unneeded, gratuitous, superfluous, pointless

needy *ADJECTIVE* *day centres for the frail and needy* ► poor, deprived, destitute, impoverished, underprivileged, penniless

negate *VERB* *The decision negates years of hard work.* ► nullify, invalidate, undo, reverse, cancel, neutralize, abrogate, countermand

negative *ADJECTIVE* **1** *a negative response* ► dissenting, saying 'no', rejecting, refusing OPPOSITES ARE affirmative, positive **2** *They have been criticized for their negative attitudes.* ► pessimistic, unenthusiastic, uncooperative, defeatist, dismissive, antipathetic AN OPPOSITE IS positive

neglect *VERB* **1** *He'd been neglecting his work for the past week.* ► pay no attention to, ignore, let slide, shirk, skip, disregard, overlook, forget, leave alone AN OPPOSITE IS concentrate on **2** *She neglected her son and had a succession of boyfriends.* ► fail to take care of, fail to look after, abandon, spurn, forsake AN OPPOSITE IS look after **3** *He was being neglected by all his friends.* ► ignore, disregard, abandon, rebuff, disdain, slight AN OPPOSITE IS appreciate

neglect *NOUN* neglecting or being neglected
▷ **neglectful** *ADJECTIVE*

negligence *NOUN* lack of proper care or attention; carelessness
▷ **negligent** *ADJECTIVE* **negligently** *ADVERB*

negligible *ADJECTIVE* not big enough or important enough to be worth bothering about

negotiable *ADJECTIVE* able to be changed after being discussed • *The salary is negotiable.*

negotiate *VERB* **negotiates**, **negotiating**, **negotiated** **1** bargain or discuss with others in order to reach an agreement **2** arrange after discussion • *They negotiated a treaty.* **3** get over an obstacle or difficulty
▷ **negotiation** *NOUN* **negotiator** *NOUN*

neigh *VERB* **neighs**, **neighing**, **neighed** make the high-pitched cry of a horse
▷ **neigh** *NOUN*

neighbour *NOUN* **neighbours** a person who lives next door or near to another
▷ **neighbouring** *ADJECTIVE* **neighbourly** *ADJECTIVE*
[from Old English *neahgebur* = near dweller]

neighbourhood *NOUN* **neighbourhoods** **1** the surrounding district or area **2** a part of a town where people live • *a quiet neighbourhood*

neither (ny-*ther*nee-*ther*) *ADJECTIVE, PRONOUN* not either
USAGE Correct use is *Neither of them likes it. Neither he nor his children like it.* Use a singular verb (e.g. *likes*) unless one of its subjects is plural (e.g. *children*).

neither *ADVERB, CONJUNCTION*
neither ... nor not one thing and not the other • *She neither knew nor cared*
USAGE Say *I don't know that either* (not 'neither').

neolithic (nee- o- **lith**- ik) *ADJECTIVE* belonging to the later part of the Stone Age

neon *NOUN* a gas that glows when electricity passes through it, used in glass tubes to make illuminated signs

nephew *NOUN* **nephews** the son of a person's brother or sister

nerve *NOUN* **nerves** **1** any of the fibres in the body that carry messages to and from the brain, so that parts of the body can feel and move **2** courage; calmness in a dangerous situation • *Don't lose your nerve* **3** impudence • *You've got a nerve!*
get on someone's nerves irritate someone
nerves *PLURAL NOUN* nervousness

nerve *VERB* **nerves**, **nerving**, **nerved** give strength or courage to someone

nervous *ADJECTIVE* **1** easily upset or agitated; excitable **2** slightly afraid; timid **3** to do with the nerves • *a nervous illness*
▷ **nervously** *ADVERB* **nervousness** *NOUN*

Thesaurus

neglect *NOUN* *The building had suffered from years of neglect.* ► negligence, carelessness, dereliction of duty, inattention, indifference, slackness OPPOSITES ARE attention, care

neglected *ADJECTIVE* **1** *The back of the house overlooked a neglected garden.* ► untended, uncared for, derelict, dilapidated, run-down, ramshackle, overgrown

negligible *ADJECTIVE* *The difference in price is negligible.* ► tiny, trifling, trivial, insignificant, unimportant, inconsequential, imperceptible, inconsiderable, minor, slight, small
OPPOSITES ARE considerable, significant

negotiate *VERB* **1** *We would like to negotiate a better deal.* ► work out, hammer out, agree on, reach agreement on, settle, transact **2** *The other side refused to negotiate.* ► consult, confer, discuss terms, deal, talk, parley **3** *The road has several sharp bends to negotiate.* ► get round, clear, pass round, deal with, overcome

negotiation *NOUN* *The negotiations will begin in Rome next week.* ► discussion, consultation, bargaining, arbitration, mediation, conciliation, transaction, debate, diplomacy

neighbourhood *NOUN* *a quiet neighbourhood* ► district, area, locality, vicinity, region, place, community, environs, surroundings, zone

neighbouring *ADJECTIVE* *The neighbouring buildings have parking facilities.* ► nearby, adjacent, adjoining, nearest, closest, next-door, bordering, close OPPOSITES ARE distant, remote

neighbourly *ADJECTIVE* *a neighbourly offer of help* ► friendly, amiable, obliging, considerate, kind, helpful, genial, sociable, companionable

nerve *NOUN* **1** *The manoeuvre takes some nerve and a good sense of timing. He lost his nerve at the last moment and couldn't go through with it.* ► courage, bravery, boldness, daring, gallantry, determination, fearlessness, fortitude, heroism, (*more informal*) bottle, (*more informal*) grit, (*more informal*) guts, (*more informal*) pluck, (*much more informal*) spunk **2** *They had the nerve to ask for more money.* ► cheek, audacity, effrontery, temerity, impertinence, impudence, insolence, presumptuousness, shamelessness, (*more informal*) sauce **3** *the nerves in your body*
RELATED ADJECTIVE neural

nervous *ADJECTIVE* **1** *a nervous girl who always wore black* ► highly-strung, nervy, anxious, excitable **2** *He was getting a little nervous out there, all by himself.* ► anxious, worried,

A B C D E F G H I J K L M N O P Q R S T U V W X Y Z

nervous breakdown *NOUN* **nervous breakdowns** a state of severe depression and anxiety, so that the person cannot cope with life

nervous system *NOUN* **nervous systems** the system, consisting of the brain, spinal cord, and nerves, which sends electrical messages from one part of the body to another

-ness *SUFFIX* forming nouns from adjectives (e.g. *kindness, sadness*)

nest *NOUN* **nests** **1** a structure or place in which a bird lays its eggs and feeds its young **2** a place where some small creatures (e.g. mice or wasps) live **3** a set of similar things that fit inside each other • *a nest of tables*

nest *VERB* **nests, nesting, nested** **1** have or make a nest **2** fit inside something

nest egg *NOUN* **nest eggs** a sum of money saved up for future use

nestle *VERB* **nestles, nestling, nestled** curl up comfortably

net[1] *NOUN* **nets** **1** material made of pieces of thread, cord, or wire etc. joined together in a criss-cross pattern with holes between **2** something made of this
the Net the Internet

net *VERB* **nets, netting, netted** cover or catch with a net

net[2] *ADJECTIVE* remaining when nothing more is to be deducted • *The net weight, without the box, is 100 grams.* COMPARE **gross**

net *VERB* **nets, netting, netted** obtain or produce as net profit

netball *NOUN* a game in which two teams try to throw a ball into a high net hanging from a ring

netting *NOUN* a piece of net

nettle *NOUN* **nettles** a wild plant with leaves that sting when they are touched

nettle *VERB* **nettles, nettling, nettled** annoy or provoke someone

network *NOUN* **networks** **1** a net-like arrangement or pattern of intersecting lines or parts • *the railway network* **2** an organization with many connecting parts that work together • *a spy network* **3** a group of radio or television stations which broadcast the same programmes **4** a set of computers which are linked to each other

neuron or **neurone** *NOUN* **neurons** or **neurones** a cell that is part of the nervous system and sends impulses to and from the brain

neurotic (newr- ot- ik) *ADJECTIVE* always very worried about something

neuter *ADJECTIVE* **1** neither masculine nor feminine **2** (in some languages) belonging to the class of words which are neither masculine nor feminine, such as *Fenster* in German

neuter *VERB* **neuters, neutering, neutered** remove an animal's sex organs so that it cannot breed

neutral *ADJECTIVE* **1** not supporting either side in a war or quarrel **2** not very distinctive • *a neutral colour such as grey* **3** neither acid nor alkaline
▷ **neutrally** *ADVERB* **neutrality** *NOUN*

neutral gear *NOUN* a gear that is not connected to the driving parts of an engine

neutron *NOUN* **neutrons** (in science) a particle of matter with no electric charge

never *ADVERB* **1** at no time; not ever **2** not at all

nevertheless *ADVERB, CONJUNCTION* in spite of this; although this is a fact

new *ADJECTIVE* not existing before; just made, invented, discovered, or received etc.
▷ **newly** *ADVERB* **newness** *NOUN*

new *ADVERB* newly • *newborn;* • *new-laid*

Thesaurus

apprehensive, agitated, concerned, (*more informal*) jumpy, (*more informal*) jittery

nestle *VERB* *The children nestled together in the back of the car.* ► huddle, cuddle, nuzzle, snuggle, curl up, lie comfortably

net *NOUN* *The gardener put nets on the trees to catch falling fruit.* ► mesh, netting, webbing, lattice

nettle *VERB* *remarks that began to nettle him* ► annoy, irritate, displease, anger, infuriate, enrage, exasperate, incense, vex, madden, aggravate, antagonize, inflame, make angry, (*more informal*) needle, (*more informal*) rile, (*more informal*) bug, (*more informal*) rub up the wrong way

network *NOUN* **1** *a network of tiny tubes* ► web, grid, mesh, net, netting, crisscross pattern, labyrinth, lattice, maze, tracery **2** *a computer network; the rail network* ► system, complex, organization

neutral *ADJECTIVE* **1** *He would be the perfect neutral umpire.* ► impartial, unbiased, objective, disinterested, uprejudiced, even-handed OPPOSITES ARE biased, prejudiced **2** *neutral colours* ► dull, indefinite, indeterminate, intermediate, characterless, colourless, middle AN OPPOSITE IS distinctive

new *ADJECTIVE* **1** *new ways of beating crime* ► modern, recent, up-to-date, advanced **2** *We need some new ideas.* ► fresh, original, innovative, novel, creative, different **3** *The school has had some new labs built.* ► additional, extra, more, further, supplementary, fresh **4** *After the operation I felt a new person.* ► changed, improved, restored, revived, invigorated

newcomer NOUN **newcomers** a person who has arrived recently

newfangled ADJECTIVE disliked because it is new in method or style

newly ADVERB **1** recently **2** in a new way

new moon NOUN **new moons** the moon at the beginning of its cycle, when only a thin crescent can be seen

news NOUN **1** information about recent events or a broadcast report of this **2** a piece of new information • *That's news to me.*

newsagent NOUN **newsagents** a shopkeeper who sells newspapers

newspaper NOUN **newspapers** **1** a daily or weekly publication on large sheets of paper, containing news reports, articles, etc. **2** the sheets of paper forming a newspaper • *Wrap it in newspaper.*

newt NOUN **newts** a small animal rather like a lizard, that lives near or in water [from Old English: originally *an ewt*]

newton NOUN **newtons** a unit for measuring force

New Year's Day NOUN 1 January

next ADJECTIVE nearest; coming immediately after • *on the next day*

next ADVERB **1** in the next place **2** on the next occasion • *What happens next?*

next door ADVERB, ADJECTIVE in the next house or room

nib NOUN **nibs** the pointed metal part of a pen

nibble VERB **nibbles**, **nibbling**, **nibbled** take small, quick, or gentle bites

nice ADJECTIVE **nicer**, **nicest** **1** pleasant or kind **2** precise or careful • *Dictionaries make nice distinctions between meanings of words.*
▷ **nicely** ADVERB **niceness** NOUN

nick NOUN **nicks** **1** a small cut or notch **2** (*informal*) a police station or prison
in good nick (*informal*) in good condition
in the nick of time only just in time

nickel NOUN **nickels** **1** a silvery-white metal **2** (*American*) a 5-cent coin

nickname NOUN **nicknames** a name given to a person instead of his or her real name

nicotine NOUN a poisonous substance found in tobacco [from the name of J Nicot, who introduced tobacco into France in 1560]

niece NOUN **nieces** the daughter of a person's brother or sister

niggardly ADJECTIVE mean or stingy
▷ **niggardliness** NOUN

night NOUN **nights** **1** the dark hours between sunset and sunrise **2** a particular night or evening • *the first night of the play*

nightclub NOUN **nightclubs** a place that is open at night where people go to drink and dance

nightdress NOUN **nightdresses** a loose dress that girls or women wear in bed

nightingale NOUN **nightingales** a small brown bird that sings sweetly

nightmare NOUN **nightmares** **1** a frightening dream **2** an unpleasant experience • *The journey was a nightmare.*
▷ **nightmarish** ADJECTIVE
[from **night** + Middle English *mare* = an evil spirit thought to lie on people asleep and suffocate them]

nil NOUN nothing or nought

nimble ADJECTIVE able to move quickly; agile
▷ **nimbly** ADVERB

nine ADJECTIVE, NOUN **nines** the number 9
▷ **ninth** ADJECTIVE, NOUN

Thesaurus

news NOUN *The news of his death stunned his colleagues.* ► report, announcement, story, account, tidings, information (about), disclosure (about), statement, revelation

next ADJECTIVE **1** *Her friend lived in the next street.* ► adjacent, neighbouring, adjoining, connecting, closest, nearest
AN OPPOSITE IS distant **2** *The next train is not for another hour.* ► following, soonest, succeeding, subsequent
AN OPPOSITE IS previous

nibble VERB *She nibbled her sandwich while she waited.* ► munch, pick at, gnaw, eat

nice ADJECTIVE **1** *We had a nice time in Greece.* ► pleasant, agreeable, enjoyable, marvellous, wonderful, delightful, splendid **2** *They are such nice people.* ► pleasant, likeable, agreeable, personable, friendly, congenial, genial

nick VERB **1** *He had nicked his skin while shaving.* ► cut **2** (*informal*) *Someone nicked my pen.* ► steal, take, (*informal*) pinch

nick NOUN **1** *a nick in the wood* ► cut, notch, chip, groove, scar **2** (*informal*) *The car is in good nick.* ► condition, shape, repair, order, trim, fettle

nickname NOUN *Her nickname is 'Posh'.* ► pet name, sobriquet, tag, alias

night NOUN *It had rained in the night.* ► night-time, dark RELATED ADJECTIVE nocturnal

nightmare NOUN **1** *After the accident he had a series of nightmares.* ► bad dream **2** *Getting the tyre fixed had been a nightmare.* ► ordeal, trial, torment

nimble ADJECTIVE *He was surprisingly light and nimble on his feet.* ► agile, lithe, lively, sprightly, deft, quick, graceful, (*informal*) nippy

nineteen *NOUN, ADJECTIVE* the number 19
▷ **nineteenth** *ADJECTIVE, NOUN*

ninety *ADJECTIVE, NOUN* **nineties** the number 90
▷ **ninetieth** *ADJECTIVE, NOUN*

nip *VERB* **nips, nipping, nipped** **1** pinch or bite quickly **2** (*informal*) go quickly

nip *NOUN* **nips** **1** a quick pinch or bite **2** sharp coldness • *There's a nip in the air.* **3** a small drink of a spirit • *a nip of brandy*

nippers *PLURAL NOUN* pincers

nipple *NOUN* **nipples** the small part that sticks out at the front of a person's breast, from which babies suck milk

nirvana *NOUN* (in Buddhism and Hinduism) the highest state of knowledge and understanding, achieved by meditation [from Sanskrit]

nit *NOUN* **nits** a parasitic insect or its egg, found in people's hair

nit-picking *NOUN* pointing out very small faults

nitrate *NOUN* **nitrates** **1** a chemical compound containing nitrogen **2** potassium or sodium nitrate, used as a fertilizer

nitrogen (**ny**- tro- jen) *NOUN* a gas that makes up about four-fifths of the air

no *ADJECTIVE* not any • *We have no money.*

no *ADVERB* **1** used to deny or refuse something • *Will you come? No.* **2** not at all • *She is no better.*

No. or **no.** *ABBREVIATION* **Nos.** or **nos.** number

noble *ADJECTIVE* **nobler, noblest** **1** of high social rank; aristocratic **2** having a very good character or qualities • *a noble king* **3** stately or impressive • *a noble building*
▷ **nobly** *ADVERB* **nobility** *NOUN*

noble *NOUN* **nobles** a person of high social rank
▷ **nobleman** *NOUN* **noblewoman** *NOUN*

nobody *PRONOUN* no person; no one

nobody *NOUN* **nobodies** (*informal*) an unimportant or unimpressive person; a nonentity

nocturnal *ADJECTIVE* **1** happening at night **2** active at night • *Badgers are nocturnal animals.*

nod *VERB* **nods, nodding, nodded** **1** move the head up and down, especially as a way of agreeing with somebody or as a greeting **2** be drowsy
▷ **nod** *NOUN*

noise *NOUN* **noises** a sound, especially one that is loud or unpleasant
▷ **noisy** *ADJECTIVE* **noisily** *ADVERB* **noiseless** *ADJECTIVE*

nomad *NOUN* **nomads** a member of a tribe that moves from place to place looking for pasture for their animals
▷ **nomadic** *ADJECTIVE*

no man's land *NOUN* an area that does not belong to anybody, especially the land between opposing armies

nominate *VERB* **nominates, nominating, nominated** propose someone as a candidate in an election or to be appointed to a post
▷ **nomination** *NOUN* **nominator** *NOUN*

non- *PREFIX* not

Thesaurus

nip *VERB* **1** *The dog nipped her leg.* ► bite, peck, snap at, pinch, tweak **2** (*informal*) *I'll nip round and see how he's getting on.* ► go, dash, drop, (*informal*) pop

nippy *ADJECTIVE* **1** (*informal*) *She drives a nippy two-seater.* ► speedy, fast, nimble, quick, rapid **2** (*informal*) *The weather's quite nippy for June.* ► chilly, cold, raw

nobility *NOUN* **1** *actions that showed true nobility* ► honour, dignity, nobleness, uprightness, virtue, worthiness, greatness, integrity, magnanimity, morality **2** *The king had the support of the nobility.* ► aristocracy, gentry, nobles, lords, peerage

noble *ADJECTIVE* **1** *He came from a noble family.* ► aristocratic, high-born, patrician, princely, (*informal*) blue-blooded AN OPPOSITE IS humble **2** *a noble deed* ► honourable, virtuous, worthy, brave, chivalrous, courageous, gallant, glorious, heroic, magnanimous
AN OPPOSITE IS ignoble **3** *a noble building* ► imposing, impressive, magnificent, elegant, grand, majestic, splendid, stately, dignified, distinguished, great
AN OPPOSITE IS unimpressive

noble *NOUN* *War was the principal activity of many of the nobles in Edward's reign.* ► aristocrat, nobleman, noblewoman, lord, peer, grandee, lady, peers

nod *VERB* **1** *She nodded to him to go in.* ► signal, gesture, indicate, sign **2** *He nodded his head in agreement.* ► incline, bob, dip, lower
nod off *She nodded off and started to snore.* ► fall asleep, go to sleep, doze off, drop off

nod *NOUN* *He gave us a discreet nod.* ► signal, gesture, cue

noise *NOUN* *The noise from below battered her eardrums.* ► sound, din, clamour, racket, uproar, tumult, commotion, crash, clatter, clash, (*more informal*) hullabaloo
AN OPPOSITE IS silence

noisy *ADJECTIVE* **1** *He loved this noisy, busy city.* ► loud, clamorous, rackety, tumultuous, turbulent, deafening **2** *The plane completed its noisy take-off.* ► loud, deafening, ear-splitting, thunderous **3** *They were disturbed by the noisy argument going on in the next room.* ► loud, vociferous, raucous, rowdy, strident, shouting, shrieking

non-commissioned officer *NOUN* **non-commissioned officers** a member of the armed forces, such as a corporal or sergeant, who has not been commissioned as an officer but has been promoted from the ranks of ordinary soldiers

non-committal *ADJECTIVE* not committing yourself; not showing what you think

nondescript *ADJECTIVE* having no special or distinctive qualities and therefore difficult to describe

none *PRONOUN* **1** not any **2** no one • *None can tell.*
USAGE It is better to use a singular verb (e.g. *None of them is here*), but the plural is not incorrect (e.g. *None of them are here*).

nonentity (non- en- tit- ee) *NOUN* **nonentities** an unimportant person

non-existent *ADJECTIVE* not existing or unreal

non-fiction *NOUN* writings that are not fiction; books about real people and things and true events

non-flammable *ADJECTIVE* not able to be set on fire
USAGE See note at **inflammable**.

nonplussed *ADJECTIVE* puzzled or confused

nonsense *NOUN* **1** words put together in a way that does not mean anything **2** stupid ideas or behaviour
▷ **nonsensical** (non- sens- ik- al) *ADJECTIVE*

non-stop *ADJECTIVE, ADVERB* **1** not stopping • *They talked non-stop for hours.* **2** not stopping between two main stations • *a non-stop train*

noodles *PLURAL NOUN* pasta made in narrow strips, used in soups etc. [from German *Nudel*]

nook *NOUN* **nooks** a sheltered corner; a recess

noon *NOUN* twelve o'clock midday

no one *NOUN* no person; nobody

noose *NOUN* **nooses** a loop in a rope that gets smaller when the rope is pulled

nor *CONJUNCTION* and not • *She cannot do it; nor can I.*

normal *ADJECTIVE* **1** usual or ordinary **2** natural and healthy; without a physical or mental illness
▷ **normally** *ADVERB* **normality** *NOUN*

Norman *NOUN* **Normans** a member of the people of Normandy in northern France, who conquered England in 1066
▷ **Norman** *ADJECTIVE*

Thesaurus

nonchalant *ADJECTIVE* *Kate leant back, trying to look nonchalant.* ► unconcerned, detached, relaxed, indifferent, dispassionate, unemotional, unruffled, blasé, calm, casual, cool, (*more informal*) laid-back
AN OPPOSITE IS anxious

non-committal *ADJECTIVE* *He held up a hand in a non-committal gesture.* ► guarded, cautious, wary, discreet, (*more informal*) cagey

nondescript *ADJECTIVE* *The town was a nondescript, cheerless place.* ► ordinary, undistinguished, commonplace, average, dull, uninspiring OPPOSITES ARE distinctive, remarkable

non-existent *ADJECTIVE* *The danger was non-existent.* ► imaginary, fictitious, mythical, supposed, unreal, hypothetical, imagined, legendary, made-up AN OPPOSITE IS existing

nonplussed *ADJECTIVE* *The confusion left us feeling nonplussed.* ► surprised, disconcerted, astonished, astounded, bewildered, stunned, flummoxed, stupefied, perplexed, (*more informal*) thunderstruck

nonsense *NOUN* **1** *They're talking nonsense.* ► rubbish, balderdash, gibberish, claptrap, drivel, gobbledegook, (*more informal*) rot, (*more informal*) twaddle **2** *The idea was a complete nonsense.* ► absurdity, folly, mistake, inanity

nonsensical *ADJECTIVE* *The suggestion was nonsensical and shouldn't be taken seriously.* ► absurd, ludicrous, meaningless, ridiculous, senseless, unreasonable, incomprehensible, foolish, crazy, laughable, silly, stupid, fatuous, inane, illogical, irrational AN OPPOSITE IS sensible

non-stop *ADJECTIVE* **1** *non-stop fun and laughter* ► continuous, constant, endless, uninterrupted, unending, never-ending, ceaseless

non-stop *ADVERB* **1** *We worked non-stop to get the job finished.* ► continuously, all the time, unceasingly, incessantly, steadily, round the clock

norm *NOUN* *Society imposes its own norms of behaviour.* ► standard, principle, yardstick, benchmark, pattern, basis, guide (to)

normal *ADJECTIVE* **1** *They seem like a perfectly normal couple.* ► ordinary, average, typical, run-of-the-mill, standard, conventional, everyday **2** *During the holidays you can borrow books in the normal way.* ► usual, customary, standard, regular, routine, habitual, established

normality *NOUN* *The household returned to something like normality.* ► routine, regularity, typicality, usualness

normally *ADVERB* **1** *Reminders are normally sent out at the beginning of the month.* ► usually, ordinarily, customarily, typically
AN OPPOSITE IS exceptionally **2** *They just wanted*

a b c d e f g h i j k l m n o p q r s t u v w x y z

north *NOUN* **1** the direction to the left of a person who faces east **2** the northern part of a country, city, etc.

north *ADJECTIVE, ADVERB* towards or in the north
▷ **northerly** *ADJECTIVE* **northern** *ADJECTIVE* **northerner** *NOUN* **northernmost** *ADJECTIVE*

north-east *NOUN, ADJECTIVE, & ADVERB* midway between north and east
▷ **north-easterly** *ADJECTIVE* **north-eastern** *ADJECTIVE*

northward *ADJECTIVE, ADVERB* towards the north
▷ **northwards** *ADVERB*

north-west *NOUN, ADJECTIVE, & ADVERB* midway between north and west
▷ **north-westerly** *ADJECTIVE* **north-western** *ADJECTIVE*

Nos. or **nos.** *plural of* **No.** or **no**

nose *NOUN* **noses** **1** the part of the face that is used for breathing and for smelling things **2** the front end or part

nosedive *NOUN* **nosedives** a steep downward dive, especially of an aircraft
▷ **nosedive** *VERB*

nostalgia (nos- tal- ja) *NOUN* sentimental remembering or longing for the past
▷ **nostalgic** *ADJECTIVE* **nostalgically** *ADVERB*

nostril *NOUN* **nostrils** either of the two openings in the nose

nosy *ADJECTIVE* **nosier, nosiest** inquisitive
▷ **nosily** *ADVERB* **nosiness** *NOUN*

not *ADVERB* used to change the meaning of something to its opposite or absence

notation *NOUN* **notations** a system of symbols representing numbers, quantities, musical notes, etc.

notch *NOUN* **notches** a small V-shape cut into a surface

note *NOUN* **notes** **1** something written down as a reminder or as a comment or explanation **2** a short letter **3** a banknote • *a £5 note* **4** a single sound in music **5** any of the black or white keys on a piano etc. (see **key** 3) **6** a sound or quality that indicates something • *a note of warning* **7** notice or attention • *Take note*

note *VERB* **notes, noting, noted** **1** make a note about something; write down **2** notice or pay attention to • *Note what we say.*

notebook *NOUN* **notebooks** a book with blank pages on which to write notes

notepaper *NOUN* paper for writing letters

nothing *NOUN* **1** no thing; not anything **2** no amount; nought
for nothing **1** without payment, free **2** without a result

notice *NOUN* **notices** **1** something written or printed and displayed for people to see **2** attention • *It escaped my notice.* **3** warning that something is going to happen **4** formal information that you are about to end an agreement or a person's employment etc. • *We gave him a month's notice.*

Thesaurus

to be able to live normally again. ► as normal, in the normal way

nose *NOUN* **1** *He stood scratching the side of his nose.* ► nostrils, (*technical*) proboscis, snout
RELATED ADJECTIVE nasal **2** *The nose of a boat appeared at the harbour entrance.* ► prow, bow, front

nose *VERB* *He nosed the car into a gap in the traffic.* ► ease, inch, edge, move, manoeuvre

nosy *ADJECTIVE* *He always wanted to help, but sometimes he seemed too nosy for his own good.* ► inquisitive, prying, intrusive, curious, (*more informal*) snoopy

notable *ADJECTIVE* **1** *Musicians (with some notable exceptions) are highly practical people.* ► significant, noteworthy, remarkable, important, memorable
AN OPPOSITE IS insignificant **2** *a notable American statesman* ► prominent, famous, distinguished, noted, eminent, illustrious
OPPOSITES ARE obscure, unknown

note *NOUN* **1** *Leave me a note before you go.* ► message, communication, letter, memo, line **2** *I'll make a note of her new address.* ► record, entry, reminder **3** *Someone had written notes in the margin.* ► comment, annotation, gloss, remark **4** *a writer of some note* ► importance, distinction, renown, eminence, acclaim

note *VERB* **1** *Note the new cafeteria built since our last visit.* ► observe, notice, see, remark **2** *I'll be happy to note your suggestion.* ► consider, heed, bear in mind, make a note of, take into account **3** *Note the dates in your diary.* ► write down, jot down, enter, record, scribble

notebook *NOUN* *She wrote the details in a notebook.* ► exercise book, jotter, writing book, diary

noted *ADJECTIVE* *a noted local celebrity* ► famous, well-known, renowned, notable
OPPOSITES ARE obscure, unknown

noteworthy *ADJECTIVE* *a noteworthy addition to his collection* ► important, significant, notable, remarkable, striking
OPPOSITES ARE insignificant, unimportant

notice *NOUN* **1** *There was a notice pinned on the classroom door.* ► announcement, message, note, information sheet, poster, sticker, sign, placard, warning **2** *Nothing escaped her notice that day.* ► attention, observation, awareness, perception, heed
take no notice of *Take no notice of the shouting.*

notice *VERB* **notices, noticing, noticed** see or become aware of something

noticeable *ADJECTIVE* easily seen or noticed
▷ **noticeably** *ADVERB*

notion *NOUN* **notions** an idea, especially one that is vague or incorrect

notorious *ADJECTIVE* well-known for something bad
▷ **notoriously** *ADVERB* **notoriety** (noh- ter- I- it- ee) *NOUN*

notwithstanding *PREPOSITION* in spite of

nought (nawt) *NOUN* **1** the figure 0 **2** nothing

noun *NOUN* **nouns** a word that stands for a person, place, or thing. *Common nouns* are words such as *boy, dog, river, sport, table,* which are used of a whole kind of people or things; *proper nouns* are words such as *Charles, Thames,* and *London* which name a particular person or thing

nourish *VERB* **nourishes, nourishing, nourished** keep a person, animal, or plant alive and well by means of food
▷ **nourishing** *ADJECTIVE* **nourishment** *NOUN*

novel *NOUN* **novels** a story that fills a whole book

novel *ADJECTIVE* of a new and unusual kind • *a novel experience* [from Latin *novus* = new]

novelist *NOUN* **novelists** a person who writes novels

novelty *NOUN* **novelties** **1** newness and originality **2** something new and unusual **3** a cheap toy or ornament

November *NOUN* the eleventh month of the year [from Latin *novem* = nine, because it was the ninth month of the ancient Roman calendar]

novice *NOUN* **novices** **1** a beginner **2** a person preparing to be a monk or nun

now *ADVERB* **1** at this time **2** by this time **3** immediately • *You must go now.* **4** I wonder, or I am telling you • *Now why didn't I think of that?*
now and again or **now and then** sometimes; occasionally

now *CONJUNCTION* as a result of or at the same time as something • *Now that you have come, we'll start.*

now *NOUN* this moment • *They will be at home by now.*

nowadays *ADVERB* at the present time, as contrasted with years ago

nowhere *ADVERB* not anywhere

nowhere *NOUN* no place • *Nowhere is as beautiful as Scotland.*

Thesaurus

► ignore, disregard, pay no attention to, pass over

notice *VERB* **1** *Did you notice the window was open?* ► observe, perceive, see, spot **2** *I noticed a smell of gas in the kitchen.* ► detect, perceive, note

noticeable *ADJECTIVE* *a noticeable reduction in the cost* ► perceptible, appreciable, observable, conspicuous, recognizable, distinct, marked, significant, unmistakable
AN OPPOSITE IS imperceptible

notify *VERB* *Parents will be notified of any changes.* ► inform, advise, tell, apprise, let somebody know

notion *NOUN* **1** *Paul was a dreamer, his head full of wild notions.* ► idea, belief, concept, thought, image, perception, opinion **2** *He had no notion of what her words meant.* ► understanding, idea, knowledge, clue

notional *ADJECTIVE* *the notional line along the horizon* ► theoretical, hypothetical, conjectural, putative, imaginary

nought *NOUN* **1** *Her card number has a lot of noughts in it.* ► zero, nil, O **2** *One of the contestants scored a resounding nought.* ► nil, zero, nothing, (*more informal*) zilch

nourish *VERB* *They had just enough money to nourish their children.* ► feed, provide for, support, sustain, maintain

nourishing *ADJECTIVE* *a nourishing diet* ► nutritious, wholesome, sustaining, healthy, nutritive, beneficial, health-giving

nourishment *NOUN* *the nourishment that elderly people require* ► sustenance, nutriment, nutrition, diet, food, subsistence, goodness

novel *ADJECTIVE* *a novel idea for its time* ► new, original, innovative, unconventional, unfamiliar, unusual, fresh, imaginative, different, singular, surprising, uncommon
OPPOSITES ARE familiar, common, hackneyed

novelty *NOUN* **1** *the beauty and novelty of the poetry* ► freshness, originality, unfamiliarity, unconventionality, imaginativeness, newness **2** *a little shop selling sweets and novelties* ► knick-knack, trinket, souvenir, bauble, curiosity, gimmick

now *ADVERB* **1** *You need to decide now.* ► immediately, straight away, here and now, on the spot, without delay **2** *The box office is closed now.* ► at present, at the moment, at the minute, currently

a b c d e f g h i j k l m n o p q r s t u v w x y z

nozzle *NOUN* **nozzles** the spout of a hose, pipe, or tube

nuclear *ADJECTIVE* **1** to do with a nucleus, especially of an atom **2** using the energy that is created by reactions in the nuclei of atoms • *nuclear power* • *nuclear weapons*

nucleus *NOUN* **nuclei** **1** the part in the centre of something, round which other things are grouped **2** the central part of an atom or of a seed or a biological cell

nude *ADJECTIVE* not wearing any clothes; naked
▷ **nudity** *NOUN*

nudge *VERB* **nudges, nudging, nudged** **1** poke a person gently with your elbow **2** push slightly or gradually
▷ **nudge** *NOUN*

nugget *NOUN* **nuggets** **1** a rough lump of gold or platinum found in the earth **2** a small but useful fact

nuisance *NOUN* **nuisances** an annoying person or thing

numb *ADJECTIVE* unable to feel or move
▷ **numbly** *ADVERB* **numbness** *NOUN*

number *NOUN* **numbers** **1** a symbol or word indicating how many; a numeral or figure **2** a numeral given to a thing to identify it • *a telephone number* **3** a quantity of people or things • *the number of people present* **4** one issue of a magazine or newspaper **5** a song or piece of music
USAGE Note that *a number of*, meaning 'several', should be followed by a plural verb: *A number of problems remain.*

number *VERB* **numbers, numbering, numbered** **1** mark with numbers **2** count **3** amount to • *The crowd numbered 10,000.*

numeral *NOUN* **numerals** a symbol that represents a certain number; a figure

numerate (new- mer- at) *ADJECTIVE* having a good basic knowledge of mathematics
▷ **numeracy** *NOUN*

numerator *NOUN* **numerators** the number above the line in a fraction, showing how many parts are to be taken, e.g. 2 in $\frac{2}{5}$ COMPARE **denominator**

numerical (new- merri- kal) *ADJECTIVE* to do with or consisting of numbers • *in numerical order*
▷ **numerically** *ADVERB*

numerous *ADJECTIVE* many

nun *NOUN* **nuns** a member of a community of women who live according to the rules of a religious organization COMPARE **monk**

nunnery *NOUN* **nunneries** a convent

nurse *NOUN* **nurses** **1** a person trained to look after people who are ill or injured **2** (*old use*) a woman employed to look after young children

nurse *VERB* **nurses, nursing, nursed** **1** look after someone who is ill or injured **2** feed a baby at the breast **3** have a feeling for a long time • *She's been nursing a grudge against him for years.* **4** hold carefully

nursemaid *NOUN* **nursemaids** (*old use*) a young woman employed to look after young children

Thesaurus

nub *NOUN* *Money is the nub of the problem.* ► crux, essence, central point, core, gist

nucleus *NOUN* *These three chapters form the nucleus of the description.* ► heart, core, centre, kernel

nude *ADJECTIVE* *Nude bathing is forbidden.* ► naked, unclothed, undressed, uncovered, bare

nudge *VERB* *Every time he laughed she nudged him in his side.* ► poke, prod, shove, jog, jolt, bump, hit , touch

nuisance *NOUN* **1** *What a nuisance for you, having to go back into hospital.* ► inconvenience, annoyance, bother, bore, trial, irritant, irritation, worry, pest, vexation, trouble, (*more informal*) pain **2** *I'm sorry if I'm being a nuisance.* ► pest, bother, trial, burden

numb *ADJECTIVE* *My hands were numb with cold.* ► dead, frozen, numbed, benumbed, insensitive, unfeeling AN OPPOSITE IS sensitive

numb *VERB* *Sheer terror had numbed her senses.* ► deaden, paralyse, desensitize, freeze, immobilize, make numb, anaesthetize

number *NOUN* **1** *The paper had a line of numbers written on it.* ► figure, numeral, integer, digit, unit RELATED ADJECTIVE numerical **2** *a large number of children* ► quantity, amount, collection, sum, total, crowd, multitude, aggregate **3** *The film included a few musical numbers.* ► item, piece, song **4** *the spring number of the magazine* ► issue, edition, publication, impression, printing

number *VERB* *Visitors to the city this year numbered over ten million.* ► total, add up to, amount to, come to

numeral *NOUN* *Items over a hundred are written in numerals.* ► figure, digit, integer, number

numerous *ADJECTIVE* *Numerous reasons have been given to justify the invasion.* ► many, several, a lot of, plenty of, copious, abundant, profuse, multitudinous, diverse, sundry
AN OPPOSITE IS few

nurse *VERB* **1** *She nursed her old father for years.* ► look after, care for, take care of, tend, treat

nursery *NOUN* **nurseries** **1** a place where young children are looked after or play **2** a place where young plants are grown and are usually for sale

nursery rhyme *NOUN* **nursery rhymes** a simple rhyme or song of the kind that young children like

nursery school *NOUN* **nursery schools** a school for children below primary school age

nursing home *NOUN* **nursing homes** a small hospital or home for invalids

nut *NOUN* **nuts** **1** a fruit with a hard shell **2** a kernel **3** a small piece of metal with a hole in the middle, for screwing onto a bolt **4** (*slang*) the head **5** (*slang*) a mad or eccentric person
▷ **nutty** *ADJECTIVE*

nutcrackers *PLURAL NOUN* pincers for cracking nuts

nutrition (new- trish- on) *NOUN*
1 nourishment **2** the study of what nourishes people
▷ **nutritional** *ADJECTIVE* **nutritionally** *ADVERB*

nutritious (new- trish- us) *ADJECTIVE* nourishing; giving good nourishment
▷ **nutritiousness** *NOUN*

nutshell *NOUN* **nutshells** the shell of a nut
in a nutshell stated very briefly

nuzzle *VERB* **nuzzles, nuzzling, nuzzled** rub gently with the nose

NVQ *ABBREVIATION* National Vocational Qualification

NW *ABBREVIATION* **1** north-west **2** north-western

nylon *NOUN* a synthetic, strong, lightweight cloth or fibre

NZ *ABBREVIATION* New Zealand

Thesaurus

2 *A woman was nursing a baby.* ► breastfeed, feed, suckle **3** *hopes that have to be nursed until they become reality* ► preserve, sustain, support, cherish, maintain, encourage **4** *They went on nursing their grievance all their lives.* ► harbour, foster, bear

nutritious *ADJECTIVE* *nutritious food* ► nourishing, wholesome, sustaining, healthy, nutritive, beneficial, health-giving

Oo

O *INTERJECTION* oh

oaf *NOUN* **oafs** a stupid lout

oak *NOUN* **oaks** a large deciduous tree with seeds called acorns
▷ **oaken** *ADJECTIVE*

oar *NOUN* **oars** a pole with a flat blade at one end, used for rowing a boat
▷ **oarsman** *NOUN* **oarsmanship** *NOUN*

oasis (oh- ay- sis) *NOUN* **oases** a fertile place in a desert, with a spring or well of water

oath *NOUN* **oaths** **1** a solemn promise to do something or that something is true, sometimes appealing to God as witness **2** a swear word
on *or* **under oath** having sworn to tell the truth in a lawcourt

oats *PLURAL NOUN* a cereal used to make food (*oats* for horses, *oatmeal* for people)

obedient *ADJECTIVE* doing what you are told; willing to obey
▷ **obediently** *ADVERB* **obedience** *NOUN*

obey *VERB* **obeys, obeying, obeyed** do what you are told to do by a person, law, etc.

obituary *NOUN* **obituaries** an announcement in a newspaper of a person's death, often with a short account of his or her life

object (ob- jikt) *NOUN* **objects** **1** something that can be seen or touched **2** a purpose or intention **3** a person or thing to which some action or feeling is directed • *She has become an object of pity.* **4** (in grammar) the word or words naming who or what is acted upon by a verb or by a preposition, e.g. *him* in *the dog bit him* and *against him*

object (ob- jekt) *VERB* **objects, objecting, objected** say that you are not in favour of something or do not agree; protest
▷ **objector** *NOUN*

objection *NOUN* **objections** **1** objecting to something **2** a reason for objecting

objectionable *ADJECTIVE* unpleasant or nasty
▷ **objectionably** *ADVERB*

objective *NOUN* **objectives** what you are trying to reach or do; an aim

objective *ADJECTIVE* **1** real or actual • *Is there any objective evidence to prove his claims?* **2** not influenced by personal feelings or opinions • *an objective account of the quarrel* COMPARE **subjective**
▷ **objectively** *ADVERB* **objectivity** *NOUN*

Thesaurus

oaf *NOUN* *She called him a loud-mouthed oaf.* ► lout, fool, dolt, ass, idiot, clod, clot

oath *NOUN* **1** *The nobles refused to take the oath of allegiance to the king.* ► vow, pledge, promise, affirmation, avowal **2** *He uttered a terrible oath.* ► swear word, profanity, expletive, imprecation, curse, obscenity

obedient *ADJECTIVE* *She was described as a good girl, always obedient.* ► dutiful, compliant, deferential, respectful, well-behaved, subservient, submissive, acquiescent, amenable, biddable, tractable AN OPPOSITE IS disobedient

obese *ADJECTIVE* *The proportion of obese men has risen to 8 percent.* ► fat, overweight, outsize, corpulent, rotund

obey *VERB* **1** *I obeyed him without question.* ► do what someone says, take orders from, submit to, defer to **2** *He was not too good at obeying orders.* ► follow, carry out, perform, discharge, execute **3** *Her legs wouldn't obey her brain's command to move.* ► respond to, respect, abide by

object *NOUN* **1** *It's an object I found on the beach.* ► article, body, item, thing **2** *Research is published regularly with the object of providing the most up-to-date findings.* ► objective, purpose, intention, aim, point, target, end, goal, intent

object *VERB* **1** *I'll open a window if you don't object.* ► mind, protest, demur **2** **object to** *I hope they don't object to us coming.* ► oppose, protest against, be against, disapprove of, take exception to

objection *NOUN* *The scheme went ahead despite many objections.* ► protest, protestation, challenge, complaint, exception, dissent, disapproval, opposition, remonstration

objectionable *ADJECTIVE* *He can be objectionable when he wants to be. There was an objectionable smell in the room.* ► unpleasant, offensive, disagreeable, obnoxious, intolerable, unacceptable, nasty, repellent, distasteful

objective *ADJECTIVE* **1** *The case lacks objective evidence.* ► impartial, unbiased, disinterested, neutral, detached, dispassionate AN OPPOSITE IS subjective **2** *a research programme based on objective investigation* ► factual, scientific, rational

objective *NOUN* *The main objective is to build a strong business.* ► object, purpose, intention, aim, point, target, end, goal, intent

obligation *NOUN* **obligations** **1** being obliged to do something **2** what you are obliged to do; a duty
under an obligation owing gratitude to someone who has helped you

obligatory (ob- lig- a- ter- ee) *ADJECTIVE* compulsory, not optional

oblige *VERB* **obliges, obliging, obliged** **1** force or compel **2** help and please someone • *Can you oblige me with a loan?*
be obliged to someone feel gratitude to a person who has helped you

obliging *ADJECTIVE* polite and helpful

oblique (ob- leek) *ADJECTIVE* **1** slanting **2** not saying something straightforwardly • *an oblique reply*
▷ **obliquely** *ADVERB*

obliterate *VERB* **obliterates, obliterating, obliterated** blot out; destroy and remove all traces of something
▷ **obliteration** *NOUN*

oblong *ADJECTIVE* rectangular in shape and longer than it is wide
▷ **oblong** *NOUN*

obnoxious *ADJECTIVE* very unpleasant; objectionable

oboe *NOUN* **oboes** a high-pitched woodwind instrument
▷ **oboist** *NOUN*

obscene (ob- seen) *ADJECTIVE* indecent in a very offensive way
▷ **obscenely** *ADVERB* **obscenity** *NOUN*

obscure *ADJECTIVE* **1** difficult to see or to understand; not clear **2** not well-known
▷ **obscurely** *ADVERB* **obscurity** *NOUN*

obscure *VERB* **obscures, obscuring, obscured** make a thing obscure; darken or conceal • *Clouds obscured the sun.*

observant *ADJECTIVE* quick at observing or noticing things
▷ **observantly** *ADVERB*

observation *NOUN* **observations** **1** observing or watching **2** a comment or remark

observatory *NOUN* **observatories** a building with telescopes etc. for observing the stars or weather

observe *VERB* **observes, observing, observed** **1** see and notice; watch carefully **2** obey a law **3** keep or celebrate a custom or religious festival etc. **4** make a remark
▷ **observer** *NOUN*

Thesaurus

obligation *NOUN* *She believed she had an obligation to help.* ► responsibility, duty, liability, commitment, requirement, need

obligatory *ADJECTIVE* *Use of seat-belts in the back seats is now obligatory.* ► compulsory, mandatory, binding, required, stipulated, unavoidable, de rigueur, imperative, imposed, incumbent, inescapable, official AN OPPOSITE IS optional

oblige *VERB* *We cannot oblige them to agree, but we can persuade them.* ► force, compel, require, constrain, make

obliged *ADJECTIVE* *We'd be obliged if you would let us know when you arrive.* ► grateful, indebted, gratified, appreciative, thankful

obliging *ADJECTIVE* *Richard is an obliging sort of chap.* ► helpful, accommodating, considerate, cooperative, thoughtful, willing, agreeable, civil, courteous, friendly, kind, neighbourly, polite OPPOSITES ARE disobliging, unhelpful

obliterate *VERB* *The explosion might obliterate the entire building.* ► destroy, demolish, wipe out, ruin, wreck, devastate, shatter, blow up

obscene *ADJECTIVE* *obscene literature* ► pornographic, indecent, improper, immodest, immoral, depraved, salacious, shocking, suggestive

obscenity *NOUN* **1** *laws against obscenity* ► indecency, immodesty, impurity, impropriety, pornography, licentiousness, grossness, indelicacy **2** *The crime was an obscenity.* ► atrocity, abomination, outrage, enormity, evil **3** *louts uttering obscenities* ► swear word, profanity, curse, expletive

obscure *ADJECTIVE* *He was suffering from an obscure disease that made his hand shaky.* ► unknown, little-known, unheard-of, mysterious, dubious

obscure *VERB* **1** *Clouds obscured the sun.* ► hide, conceal, cover, veil, shroud, mask, envelop **2** *Their evidence has merely obscured the issues.* ► confuse, complicate, muddle, obfuscate

observant *ADJECTIVE* *Her observant eye took in every detail.* ► alert, attentive, vigilant, watchful, perceptive, percipient, eagle-eyed, sharp-eyed, heedful, quick AN OPPOSITE IS inattentive

observation *NOUN* **1** *He was sent to hospital for observation.* ► monitoring, scrutiny, examination, inspection, surveillance, attention **2** *Put any further observations on a separate sheet of paper.* ► remark, comment, statement, opinion

observe *VERB* **1** *She observed her friends over by the bar.* ► notice, see, perceive, discern, spot, descry, behold **2** *James observed that Rachel looked unhappy.* ► remark, comment, mention, note, declare, announce, state

A B C D E F G H I J K L M N O P Q R S T U V W X Y Z

obsolescent *ADJECTIVE* becoming obsolete; going out of use or fashion
▷ **obsolescence** *NOUN*

obsolete *ADJECTIVE* not used any more; out of date

obstacle *NOUN* **obstacles** something that stands in the way or obstructs progress

obstinate *ADJECTIVE* **1** keeping firmly to your own ideas or ways, even though they may be wrong **2** difficult to overcome or remove • *an obstinate problem*
▷ **obstinately** *ADVERB* **obstinacy** *NOUN*

obstreperous (ob- strep- er- us) *ADJECTIVE* noisy and unruly

obstruct *VERB* **obstructs, obstructing, obstructed** stop a person or thing from getting past; hinder
▷ **obstruction** *NOUN* **obstructive** *ADJECTIVE*

obtain *VERB* **obtains, obtaining, obtained** get or be given something
▷ **obtainable** *ADJECTIVE*

obtrusive *ADJECTIVE* unpleasantly noticeable
▷ **obtrusiveness** *NOUN*

obtuse angle *NOUN* **obtuse angles** an angle of more than 90° but less than 180° COMPARE **acute angle**

obvious *ADJECTIVE* easy to see or understand
▷ **obviously** *ADVERB*

occasion *NOUN* **occasions** **1** the time when something happens **2** a special event **3** a suitable time; an opportunity
on occasion from time to time

occasional *ADJECTIVE* **1** happening from time to time but not regularly or frequently **2** for special occasions • *occasional music*
▷ **occasionally** *ADVERB*

Thesaurus

3 *From her window she could observe what was going on in the street.* ► watch, view, survey, regard, monitor, witness, scrutinize

observer *NOUN Brian was merely an observer and took no part in the action.* ► spectator, onlooker, looker-on, bystander, viewer, watcher, commentator, eye-witness, witness

obsess *VERB* **1** *Thoughts of death obsessed him.* ► preoccupy, dominate, haunt, prey on, engross, possess, take a hold on **2 be obsessed with** *or* **by** *I was totally obsessed with food and controlling my weight.* ► be fixated with *or* by, be preoccupied with *or* by, (*more informal*) be hung up on

obsession *NOUN These memories rapidly became an obsession.* ► fixation, preoccupation, mania, passion, infatuation, compulsion, addiction

obsessive *ADJECTIVE His jealousy was becoming obsessive.* ► compulsive, consuming, all-consuming, dominating, controlling, fanatical, addictive

obsolete *ADJECTIVE The machinery installed in the 1990s had become obsolete.* ► out of date, outdated, outmoded, anachronistic, antiquated, extinct, superseded, old-fashioned, passé, disused, dated, primitive OPPOSITES ARE current, up to date

obstacle *NOUN a major obstacle in the peace process* ► barrier, hurdle, hindrance, stumbling block, obstruction, drawback, difficulty, impediment, problem, snag, bar, interference

obstinate *ADJECTIVE They were too obstinate to see the advantages of the scheme.* ► stubborn, inflexible, intractable, immovable, intransigent, unbending, unyielding, dogged, headstrong OPPOSITES ARE amenable, open-minded

obstruct *VERB* **1** *The opposite side of the road was obstructed by cars.* ► block, jam, clog up, choke up **2** *He was charged with obstructing the course of justice.* ► impede, hinder, hamper, frustrate, thwart, hold up, inhibit, retard, interfere with OPPOSITES ARE assist, further

obstruction *NOUN an obstruction to learning* ► barrier, hurdle, hindrance, stumbling block, drawback, difficulty, impediment, problem, snag, bar, interference

obstructive *ADJECTIVE He accused her of being deliberately obstructive.* ► uncooperative, unhelpful, awkward, difficult, disobliging, stalling OPPOSITES ARE helpful, cooperative

obtain *VERB You will need to obtain the necessary permission. I obtained the books at half price.* ► get, acquire, secure, procure, come by, achieve

obvious *ADJECTIVE It's obvious that she's keen on Bill. He spoke with an obvious French accent.* ► clear, plain, evident, self-evident, patent, apparent, glaring, perceptible AN OPPOSITE IS imperceptible

obviously *ADVERB She was obviously very upset.* ► clearly, plainly, patently, evidently, discernibly, indubitably, manifestly, unmistakably, without doubt

occasion *NOUN* **1** *She had spoken to him on several occasions.* ► instance, point, time, moment **2** *His eighteenth birthday would be a special occasion.* ► event, affair, celebration **3** *I'll mention it if the occasion arises.* ► opportunity, chance, opening, right moment **4** *I've never had any occasion to complain.* ► reason, cause, grounds, excuse, need, justification, pretext

occasional *ADJECTIVE There were still occasional air raids.* ► intermittent, periodic, sporadic,

occult *ADJECTIVE* to do with the supernatural or magic • *occult powers*

occupation *NOUN* **occupations** **1** a person's job or profession **2** something you do to pass your time **3** capturing a country etc. by military force

occupational *ADJECTIVE* caused by an occupation • *an occupational disease*

occupational therapy *NOUN* creative work designed to help people to recover from certain illnesses

occupy *VERB* **occupies, occupying, occupied** **1** live in a place; inhabit **2** fill a space or position **3** capture a country etc. and place troops there **4** keep somebody busy
▷ **occupier** *NOUN*

occur *VERB* **occurs, occurring, occurred** **1** happen or exist **2** be found; appear • *These plants occur in ponds.* **3** come into a person's mind • *An idea occurred to me.*

ocean *NOUN* **oceans** the seas that surround the continents of the earth, especially one of the large named areas of this • *the Pacific Ocean*
▷ **oceanic** *ADJECTIVE*

o'clock *ADVERB* by the clock • *Lunch is at one o'clock.*

octagon *NOUN* **octagons** a flat shape with eight sides and eight angles
▷ **octagonal** *ADJECTIVE*

octave *NOUN* **octaves** the interval of eight steps between one musical note and the next note of the same name above or below it

October *NOUN* the tenth month of the year [from Latin *octo* = eight, because it was the eighth month of the ancient Roman calendar]

octopus *NOUN* **octopuses** a sea creature with eight long tentacles [from Greek *okto* = eight + *pous* = foot]

oculist *NOUN* **oculists** a doctor who treats diseases of the eye

odd *ADJECTIVE* **1** strange or unusual **2** (said about a number) not able to be divided exactly by 2; not even **3** left over from a pair or set • *I've got one odd sock.* **4** of various kinds; not regular • *odd jobs*
▷ **oddly** *ADVERB* **oddness** *NOUN*

oddity *NOUN* **oddities** a strange person or thing

Thesaurus

infrequent, irregular, isolated, odd, rare, random

occasionally *ADVERB* *Tess turned her head occasionally to look at him.* ► sometimes, from time to time, now and then, every so often, intermittently, periodically, sporadically, infrequently, irregularly

occupant *NOUN* *The apartment had two occupants at the time.* ► resident, inhabitant, tenant, occupier, lodger, householder

occupation *NOUN* **1** *Passports no longer specify your occupation.* ► job, profession, work, line of work, walk of life, employment, business **2** *The occupation of the country continued for much longer than predicted.* ► invasion, annexation, seizure, takeover, occupancy, possession **3** *a house built for multiple occupation* ► occupancy, residence, habitation, tenancy, possession, use **4** *Swiming is my favourite leisure occupation.* ► pastime, hobby, interest, activity, diversion

occupy *VERB* **1** *Colin occupies the top floor.* ► live in, inhabit, be the tenant of, reside in, lodge in, possess, have possession of, own **2** *These problems occupied her mind for several days.* ► absorb, engage, hold, preoccupy, engross, divert **3** *The army occupied the country in the spring.* ► capture, seize, invade, take over, take possession of, overrun, annex, conquer, garrison

occur *VERB* **1** *We need to know everything that occurred that morning.* ► happen, take place, come about **2** *The disease occurs only in tropical climates.* ► be found, exist, be prevalent, appear, show itself, manifest itself **3 occur to** *It occurred to him that she might still be waiting there. It never occurred to us that we'd have to pay extra.* ► cross your mind, enter your head

occurrence *NOUN* *Bicycle theft has become a common occurrence.* ► event, happening, incident, experience, circumstance, affair, occasion, phenomenon

odd *ADJECTIVE* **1** *It was an odd thing to do.* ► strange, peculiar, weird, unusual, bizarre, curious, eccentric **2** *His friends thought him quite odd.* ► eccentric, strange, peculiar, abnormal, weird **3** *the odd numbers* ► uneven **4** *Do you have any odd change you could give him?* ► spare, leftover, miscellaneous, sundry, available **5** *She noticed he was wearing odd socks.* ► unmatched, different, unpaired, clashing

oddity *NOUN* **1** *people remembered chiefly for their oddity* ► strangeness, abnormality, peculiarity, idiosyncrasy, quirkiness **2** *He is regarded as a bit of an oddity.* ► eccentric, crank, misfit, maverick, curiosity, character

oddments PLURAL NOUN scraps or pieces left over from a larger piece or set

odds PLURAL NOUN **1** the chances that a certain thing will happen **2** the proportion of money that you will win if a bet is successful • *When the odds are 10 to 1, you will win £10 if you bet £1*
odds and ends oddments

odious (oh-dee-us) ADJECTIVE extremely unpleasant; hateful
▷ **odiously** ADVERB **odiousness** NOUN

odour NOUN **odours** a smell, especially an unpleasant one
▷ **odorous** ADJECTIVE **odourless** ADJECTIVE

odyssey (od-iss-ee) NOUN **odysseys** a long adventurous journey

o'er PREPOSITION, ADVERB (*poetic*) over

oesophagus (ee-sof-a-gus) NOUN **oesophagi** (ee-sof-a-gI) the tube leading from the throat to the stomach; the gullet

oestrogen (ees-tro-jen) NOUN a hormone which develops and maintains female sexual and physical characteristics

of PREPOSITION (used to indicate relationships) belonging to • *the mother of the child;* concerning; about • *news of the disaster;* made from • *built of stone;* from • *north of the town*

off PREPOSITION **1** not on; away or down from • *He fell off the ladder* **2** not taking or wanting • *She is off her food* **3** deducted from • *£5 off the price*

off ADVERB **1** away or down from something • *His hat blew off.* **2** not working or happening • *The heating is off.* • *The match is off because of snow.* **3** to the end; completely • *Finish it off.* **4** as regards money or supplies • *How are you off for cash?* **5** behind or at the side of a stage • *There were noises off.* **6** (said about food) beginning to go bad • *The milk was going off.*

offal NOUN the organs of an animal (e.g. liver or kidneys) sold as food

off-colour ADJECTIVE slightly unwell

offence NOUN **offences** **1** an illegal action **2** a feeling of annoyance or resentment
give offence hurt someone's feelings
take offence be upset by something said or done

offend VERB **offends, offending, offended**
1 cause offence to someone; hurt a person's feelings **2** do wrong or commit a crime
▷ **offender** NOUN

offensive ADJECTIVE **1** causing offence; insulting **2** disgusting • *an offensive smell* **3** used in attacking • *offensive weapons*
▷ **offensively** ADVERB **offensiveness** NOUN

offensive NOUN **offensives** an attack
take the offensive be the first to attack

Thesaurus

oddments PLURAL NOUN *oddments left over from a jumble sale* ► bits and pieces, odds and ends, scraps, fragments, remnants, leftovers, offcuts

odds PLURAL NOUN *The odds are that they have left the country.* ► likelihood, probability, chances
usage If you use *likelihood* or *probability* you should use a singular verb, e.g. *The likelihood is that they have left the country.*

odious ADJECTIVE *odious methods of dealing with their political opponents* ► hateful, offensive, repulsive, repellent, obnoxious, unpleasant, abhorrent, detestable, abominable

off ADJECTIVE **1** *The milk is off.* ► bad, rotten, putrid **2** *The game is now off.* ► postponed, cancelled **3** *I think their remarks were a bit off, to put it mildly.* ► unacceptable, objectionable, unsatisfactory, disappointing

offbeat ADJECTIVE *an offbeat humour*
► unconventional, unorthodox, idiosyncratic, strange, weird, bizarre, quirky

off colour ADJECTIVE *He was feeling a bit off colour and decided to stay at home.* ► unwell, poorly, ill, queasy, peaky, nauseous

offence NOUN **1** *The company might even be guilty of a criminal offence.* ► crime, misdemeanour, wrong, wrongdoing, misdeed, fault, transgression **2** *We don't want to cause any offence.* ► annoyance, anger, resentment, hard feelings, indignation, irritation, upset, displeasure, disgust
take offence *She made it clear she had taken offence.* ► be *or* feel offended, be upset, be *or* feel aggrieved, be *or* feel affronted, take umbrage

offend VERB **1** *I didn't mean to offend you.* ► give *or* cause offence to, upset, hurt, displease, annoy, affront, insult, anger, irritate, disgust, make angry, outrage, provoke, rile, vex **2** *A large percentage of prisoners released early went on to offend again.* ► break the law, commit a crime, do wrong, transgress **be *or* feel offended** ► take offence, be upset, be *or* feel aggrieved, be *or* feel affronted, take umbrage

offensive ADJECTIVE *The remarks were clearly offensive.* ► insulting, derogatory, depreciatory, disrespectful, abusive, objectionable, provocative, discourteous, insolent, uncivil, rude OPPOSITES ARE complimentary, courteous

offer *VERB* **offers, offering, offered** **1** present something so that people can accept it if they want to **2** say that you are willing to do or give something or to pay a certain amount

offer *NOUN* **offers** **1** offering something **2** an amount of money offered **3** a specially reduced price

offhand *ADJECTIVE* **1** said or done without preparation **2** (said about a remark etc.) rather casual and rude; curt
▷ **offhanded** *ADJECTIVE*

office *NOUN* **offices** **1** a room or building used for business; the people who work there **2** a government department • *the Foreign and Commonwealth Office* **3** an important job or position
be in office hold an official position

officer *NOUN* **officers** **1** a person who is in charge of others, especially in the armed forces **2** an official **3** a member of the police

official *ADJECTIVE* **1** done or said by someone with authority **2** done as part of your job or position • *official duties*
▷ **officially** *ADVERB*

official *NOUN* **officials** a person who holds a position of authority

offing *NOUN*
in the offing likely to happen soon

off-licence *NOUN* **off-licences** a shop with a licence to sell alcoholic drinks to be drunk away from the shop

off-putting *ADJECTIVE* making you less keen on something; disconcerting

offshoot *NOUN* **offshoots** **1** a side shoot on a plant **2** a by-product

offside *ADJECTIVE, ADVERB* (said about a player in football etc.) in a position where the rules do not allow him or her to play the ball

often *ADVERB* many times; in many cases

ogre *NOUN* **ogres** **1** a cruel giant in fairy tales **2** a terrifying person

oh *INTERJECTION* an exclamation of pain, surprise, delight, etc., or used for emphasis • *Oh yes I will!*

ohm *NOUN* **ohms** a unit of electrical resistance

Thesaurus

offer *VERB* **1** *Counsellors are on hand to offer advice and support.* ► provide, give, extend, make available, put forward, hold out, suggest **2** *Many local people offered to help in the search.* ► volunteer, come forward, present yourself, show willing **3** *The job offers good career prospects.* ► provide, afford, present, hold out, involve, entail

offer *NOUN* **1** *a business offer* ► bid, proposal, tender, proposition, submission **2** *kind offers of help* ► proposal, proposition, overture

offering *NOUN* *an offering of a few silver coins* ► contribution, donation, gift, benefaction, present

offhand *ADJECTIVE* *His manner was most offhand.* ► casual, indifferent, cool, cavalier, brusque, abrupt, aloof, curt, uncooperative, perfunctory
OPPOSITES ARE polite, courteous

office *NOUN* **1** *Her office was just a few blocks away.* ► workplace, place of work, place of business, bureau **2** *The new Prime Minister took up his office immediately.* ► post, position, appointment, function, task, duty, responsibility, situation

officer *NOUN* *The trade union had few full-time officers.* ► official, functionary, office-holder, representative, executive, administrator

official *ADJECTIVE* **1** *There were calls for an official inquiry into the matter. a member of an official organization* ► authorized, accredited, approved, proper, authentic, authenticated, certified, formal **2** *They were dressed for an official function.* ► formal, ceremonial

official *NOUN* *An official came down to escort us to the president's office.* ► officer, functionary, office-holder, representative, executive, administrator

officious *ADJECTIVE* *An officious waiter led us to a table in a poky corner.* ► self-important, bumptious, bossy, over-zealous, dictatorial, interfering, meddling, (*more informal*) pushy

off-putting *ADJECTIVE* *She tried to think of some off-putting remark to make them go away.* ► discouraging, unpleasant, intimidating, unnerving, unsettling, disconcerting, unappealing, unattractive, disagreeable, distasteful

offshoot *NOUN* *The business has offshoots all over Europe.* ► branch, subsidiary, (*more informal*) spin-off

offspring *NOUN* **1** *the core of the family: parents and their offspring* ► children, sons and daughters, progeny, family **2** *Their latest offspring was playing in the garden.* ► child, baby, infant, little one, son, daughter, youngster

often *ADVERB* *She often asks about you.* ► frequently, regularly, repeatedly, constantly, again and again, many times, time after time

A B C D E F G H I J K L M N O P Q R S T U V W X Y Z

oil NOUN **oils** **1** a thick slippery liquid that will not dissolve in water **2** a kind of petroleum used as fuel **3** oil paint

oil VERB **oils, oiling, oiled** put oil on something, especially to make it work smoothly

oilfield NOUN an area where oil is found

oil rig NOUN **oil rigs** a structure with equipment for drilling for oil

oil well NOUN **oil wells** a hole drilled in the ground or under the sea to get oil

oily ADJECTIVE **1** containing or like oil; covered or soaked with oil **2** behaving in an insincerely polite way
▷ **oiliness** NOUN

ointment NOUN **ointments** a cream or slippery paste for putting on sore skin and cuts

OK or **okay** ADVERB, ADJECTIVE (*informal*) all right

old ADJECTIVE **1** not new; born or made or existing from a long time ago **2** of a particular age • *I'm ten years old.* **3** former or original • *in its old place* **4** (*informal*) used casually or for emphasis • *good old mum!*
▷ **oldness** NOUN
[from Old English]

old age NOUN the time when a person is old

Old English NOUN the English language from about 700 to 1150, also called **Anglo-Saxon**

old-fashioned ADJECTIVE of the kind that was usual a long time ago; no longer fashionable

Old Norse NOUN the language spoken by the Vikings, the ancestor of modern Scandinavian languages

olive NOUN **olives** **1** an evergreen tree with a small bitter fruit **2** this fruit, from which an oil (**olive oil**) is made **3** a shade of green like an unripe olive

olive branch NOUN **olive branches** something you do or offer that shows you want to make peace [from a story in the Bible, in which a dove brings Noah an olive branch as a sign that God is no longer angry with the human race]

Olympic Games or **Olympics** PLURAL NOUN a series of international sports contests held every four years in a different part of the world

omega (oh- meg- a) NOUN the last letter of the Greek alphabet, a long **o**

omelette NOUN **omelettes** eggs beaten together and cooked in a pan, often with a filling

omen NOUN **omens** an event regarded as a sign of what is going to happen

ominous ADJECTIVE suggesting that trouble is coming
▷ **ominously** ADVERB

omit VERB **omits, omitting, omitted** **1** miss something out **2** fail to do something
▷ **omission** NOUN

omnibus NOUN **omnibuses** **1** a single book, television programme, etc., containing several instalments that were previously published or broadcast separately **2** (*old use*) a bus

omniscient (om- niss- ee- ent) ADJECTIVE knowing everything
▷ **omniscience** NOUN

omnivorous (om- **niv**- er- us) ADJECTIVE feeding on all kinds of food COMPARE **carnivorous, herbivorous**

on PREPOSITION **1** supported by; covering; added or attached to • *the sign on the door* **2** close to; towards • *The army advanced on Paris.* **3** during; at the time of • *on my birthday* **4** by reason of • *Arrest him on suspicion of murder.*

Thesaurus

oil VERB *She went to the shed to oil her bike.* ► lubricate, grease

oily ADJECTIVE **1** *oily skin; an oily substance* ► greasy, oleaginous, slimy **2** *an oily manner* ► smooth, unctuous, fawning, ingratiating, obsequious, (*more informal*) smarmy

OK or **okay** ADJECTIVE (*informal*) *Is everything OK now? The film is OK.* ► all right, satisfactory, fine, in order, acceptable, adequate, reasonable

OK or **okay** INTERJECTION (*informal*) *OK, I'll go with you.* ► all right, very well, very good, right you are, right, fine

OK or **okay** NOUN (*informal*) *The manager gave his OK.* ► permission, approval, consent, authorization, agreement, assent

OK or **okay** VERB (*informal*) *Get a parent to okay your proposal.* ► agree to, approve, authorize, consent to, endorse, ratify

old ADJECTIVE **1** *an old man* ► elderly, aged, advanced in years, senile **2** *old buildings* ► antiquated, dilapidated, ramshackle, ruined, historic **3** *old clothes* ► worn, shabby, threadbare, frayed, moth-eaten **4** *in the old days* ► past, former, bygone, early, ancient, olden **5** *an old practice* ► long-standing, time-honoured, traditional, established, familiar **6** *an old joke* ► hackneyed, stale, tired, overworked

old-fashioned ADJECTIVE *a big old-fashioned bathroom with noisy pipes* ► outdated, out of date, outmoded, antiquated, obsolescent OPPOSITES ARE up to date, modern, fashionable

omit VERB **1** *Someone had omitted her name from the list.* ► leave out, miss out, exclude, ignore, cut, drop, overlook, edit out, eliminate OPPOSITES ARE include, add, insert **2** *I omitted to tell you.* ► forget, neglect, fail AN OPPOSITE IS remember

5 concerning • *a book on butterflies* **6** in a state of; using or showing • *The house was on fire.*

on ADVERB **1** so as to be on something • *Put it on* **2** further forward • *Move on* **3** working; in action • *Is the heater on?*
on and off not continually

once ADVERB **1** for one time or on one occasion only • *They came only once.* **2** formerly • *They once lived here.*

once NOUN one time • *Once is enough.*

once CONJUNCTION as soon as • *You can go once I have taken your names.*

oncoming ADJECTIVE approaching; coming towards you • *oncoming traffic*

one ADJECTIVE **1** single **2** individual or united

one NOUN **1** the smallest whole number, 1 **2** a person or thing alone
one another each other

one PRONOUN any person or thing • *I need a pen but I can't find one.* • *One likes to help.*
▷ **oneself** PRONOUN

one-sided ADJECTIVE **1** with one side or person in a contest, conversation etc. being much stronger or doing a lot more than the other • *a one-sided match* **2** showing only one point of view in an unfair way • *This is a very one-sided account of the conflict.*

onion NOUN **onions** a round vegetable with a strong flavour
▷ **oniony** ADJECTIVE

onlooker NOUN **onlookers** a spectator

only ADJECTIVE being the one person or thing of a kind; sole • *my only wish*
only child a child who has no brothers or sisters

only ADVERB no more than; and that is all • *There are only three cakes left.*

only CONJUNCTION but then; however • *He makes promises, only he never keeps them.*

onomatopoeia (on- om- at- o- pee- a) NOUN the formation of words that imitate what they stand for, e.g. *cuckoo*, *plop*
▷ **onomatopoeic** ADJECTIVE

onshore ADJECTIVE from the sea towards the land • *an onshore breeze*

onslaught NOUN **onslaughts** a fierce attack

onto PREPOSITION to a position on

onward ADVERB, ADJECTIVE going forward; further on
▷ **onwards** ADVERB

ooze VERB **oozes**, **oozing**, **oozed** **1** flow out slowly; trickle **2** allow something to flow out slowly • *The wound oozed blood.*

ooze NOUN mud at the bottom of a river or sea

opal NOUN **opals** a kind of stone in which small points of shifting colour can be seen
▷ **opalescent** ADJECTIVE

opaque (o- **payk**) ADJECTIVE not able to be seen through; not transparent or translucent

open ADJECTIVE **1** allowing people or things to go in and out; not closed or fastened **2** not covered or blocked up **3** spread out; unfolded **4** not limited or restricted • *an open*

Thesaurus

once ADVERB *We were good friends once.* ▸ at one time, in the past, formerly, previously

one-sided ADJECTIVE **1** *a one-sided account of the conflict* ▸ biased, prejudiced, partisan, partial, preferential, slanted, unfair OPPOSITES ARE impartial, fair **2** *a one-sided argument* ▸ unequal, uneven, unbalanced AN OPPOSITE IS even

ongoing ADJECTIVE **1** *an ongoing problem with noisy neighbours* ▸ continuous, continuing, persistent, constant, ceaseless **2** *A road improvement programme is ongoing.* ▸ under way, in progress, developing, progressing, evolving, continuing, current, extant, existing

only ADJECTIVE *She is their only child.* ▸ sole, single, solitary, lone, unique

ooze VERB *Blood oozed from a wound on his arm.* ▸ seep, leak, issue, exude, escape, flow, dribble

opaque ADJECTIVE *The glass of the bottle was opaque so the contents could not be seen.* ▸ cloudy, non-transparent, obscure, blurred, misty, dark, hazy, unclear OPPOSITES ARE clear, transparent

open ADJECTIVE **1** *an open door* ▸ unclosed, ajar, unlocked AN OPPOSITE IS closed **2** *an open box* ▸ uncovered, unfastened, unsealed, lidless OPPOSITES ARE closed, fastened **3** *open access* ▸ free, unrestricted, clear, unobstructed, wide, available AN OPPOSITE IS restricted **4** *open country* ▸ sweeping, rolling, broad, extensive, unenclosed **5** *an open secret* ▸ plain, evident, overt, obvious, conspicuous, noticeable AN OPPOSITE IS closed **6** *an open question* ▸ unresolved, unsettled, undecided, debatable, moot AN OPPOSITE IS closed **7** *open about his feelings* ▸ frank, honest, candid, unreserved, natural OPPOSITES ARE reserved, guarded **8** *a procedure open to abuse* ▸ vulnerable, subject, susceptible, liable

open VERB **1** *A young woman opened the door.* ▸ unfasten, unlock, unbolt **2** *He started to open the packet.* ▸ unwrap, undo, untie, unseal **3** *A new superstore will open next month.* ▸ start trading **4** *The story opens with a train journey.* ▸ begin, start, (*more formal*) commence **5** *The chairman then opened the meeting.* ▸ begin, start, inaugurate, set in motion

championship **5** letting in visitors or customers **6** with wide empty spaces • *open country* **7** honest and frank; not secret or secretive • *Be open about the danger.* **8** willing to listen to other ideas • *an open mind* • *I'm open to suggestions.*
▷ **openness** NOUN
in the open air not inside a house or building

open VERB **opens, opening, opened** **1** make or become open or more open **2** begin
▷ **opener** NOUN

opencast ADJECTIVE (said about a mine) worked by removing layers of earth from the surface, not underground

opening NOUN **openings** **1** a space or gap; a place where something opens **2** the beginning of something **3** an opportunity

openly ADVERB without secrecy

opera NOUN **operas** a drama set to music, with singers acting the story
▷ **operatic** ADJECTIVE

operate VERB **operates, operating, operated** **1** make a machine work **2** be in action; work **3** perform a surgical operation on somebody
▷ **operable** ADJECTIVE

operating system NOUN **operating systems** (in computing) the software that controls a computer's basic functions

operation NOUN **operations** **1** a piece of work or method of working **2** something done to a patient's body to take away or repair a damaged part **3** a planned military activity
▷ **operational** ADJECTIVE
in operation working or in use • *When does the new system come into operation?*

operator NOUN **operators** a person who works something, especially a telephone switchboard or exchange

opinion NOUN **opinions** what you think of something; a belief or judgement

opinion poll NOUN **opinion polls** an estimate of what people think, made by questioning a sample of them

opium NOUN a drug made from the juice of certain poppies, used in medicine

opponent NOUN **opponents** a person or group opposing another in a contest or war

opportunist NOUN **opportunists** a person who is quick to seize opportunities
▷ **opportunism** NOUN

opportunity NOUN **opportunities** a good chance to do a particular thing

oppose VERB **opposes, opposing, opposed** **1** argue or fight against; resist **2** contrast • *'Soft' is opposed to 'hard'.*

Thesaurus

opening NOUN **1** *an opening in the wall* ► doorway, gateway, entry, aperture, breach, chink, crack, cleft, hole, fissure **2** *looking for openings in accountancy* ► opportunity, chance, (*more informal*) break

opening ADJECTIVE *the opening line of the poem* ► first, initial, beginning, introductory, inaugural AN OPPOSITE IS final

operate VERB **1** *The alarms had been switched off and were not operating.* ► work, function, run, act, perform, be operative, go **2** *a machine that's difficult to operate* ► work, use, utilize, handle, manage, deal with, drive **3** *X-rays will show whether doctors will need to operate on him.* ► perform surgery, carry out an operation

operation NOUN **1** *There are few other business operations the size of ours.* ► enterprise, undertaking, procedure, proceeding, process, transaction **2** *Military operations have been delayed by the weather.* ► campaign, exercise, action, activity, manoeuvre, movement, effort **3** *a committee to ensure the smooth operation of the system* ► running, functioning, working, direction, control, management **4** *a surgical operation* ► biopsy, surgery, transplant

operative ADJECTIVE *Perhaps you're right: the operative word is 'perhaps'.* ► key, significant, important, principal, relevant, crucial, effective

opinion NOUN *You can have an opinion but you must back it up with facts or reasons.* ► belief, judgement, view, point of view, viewpoint, thought, attitude, standpoint, stance, idea, notion, feeling

opponent NOUN **1** *He threw the ball at an opponent's head.* ► adversary, opposer, rival, antagonist, competitor, contestant, enemy, foe, opposition OPPOSITES ARE ally, partner **2** *an opponent of reform* ► objector (to), opposer, dissident, dissenter

opportune ADJECTIVE *It was an opportune moment to speak out.* ► appropriate, suitable, timely, auspicious, convenient, favourable, propitious, advantageous, lucky, right OPPOSITES ARE unsuitable, inconvenient

opportunity NOUN (*informal*) *This was a good opportunity to make some money.* ► chance, occasion, possibility, moment, opening, time, (*more informal*) break

oppose VERB **1** *There was a large group of protesters who opposed the plans for a new runway.* ► object to, be against, protest against, disapprove of, take exception to OPPOSITES ARE support, defend **2** *If you want to go I shan't oppose you.* ► resist, counter, withstand, take issue with, defy, confront

opposed ADJECTIVE **opposed to** *The village was opposed to the scheme for a new hostel.* ► against, hostile to, antagonistic to, antipathetic to, unsympathetic to

as opposed to in contrast with
be opposed to be strongly against • *We are opposed to parking in the town centre.*

opposite ADJECTIVE **1** placed on the other or further side; facing • *on the opposite side of the road* **2** moving away from or towards each other • *The trains were travelling in opposite directions.* **3** completely different • *opposite characters*

opposite NOUN **opposites** an opposite person or thing

opposite PREPOSITION opposite to • *They live opposite the school.*

opposition NOUN **1** opposing something; resistance **2** the people who oppose something
the Opposition the chief political party opposing the one that is in power

oppress VERB **oppresses**, **oppressing**, **oppressed** **1** govern or treat somebody cruelly or unjustly **2** weigh somebody down with worry or sadness
▷ **oppression** NOUN **oppressive** ADJECTIVE **oppressor** NOUN

opt VERB **opts**, **opting**, **opted** choose
opt out decide not to take part in something

optical ADJECTIVE to do with sight; aiding sight • *optical instruments*
▷ **optically** ADVERB

optical illusion NOUN **optical illusions** a deceptive appearance that makes you think you see something that is not really there

optician NOUN **opticians** a person who tests people's eyesight and makes or sells glasses and contact lenses

optimist NOUN **optimists** a person who expects that things will turn out well COMPARE **pessimist**
▷ **optimism** NOUN **optimistic** ADJECTIVE **optimistically** ADVERB

optimum ADJECTIVE best; most favourable
▷ **optimum** NOUN **optimal** ADJECTIVE

option NOUN **options** **1** the right or power to choose something **2** something chosen or that may be chosen

optional ADJECTIVE that you can choose, not compulsory
▷ **optionally** ADVERB

Thesaurus

opposite ADJECTIVE **1** *She lived in a house opposite the church.* ► facing, across from **2** *There is a long mirror on the opposite wall.* ► opposing, facing **3** *They were brothers who had fought on opposite sides in the civil war.* ► rival, opposing, conflicting, contrary, enemy AN OPPOSITE IS allied

opposite NOUN *He always says one thing and does the opposite.* ► contrary, reverse, other extreme, antithesis, converse AN OPPOSITE IS same

opposition NOUN **1** *The suggestion met with fierce opposition.* ► resistance, hostility, antagonism, disapproval, scepticism, unfriendliness, competition AN OPPOSITE IS support **2** *In the argument she quickly won over the opposition.* ► opponents, opposing side, other side

oppress VERB **1** *He could not get rid of the gloomy feelings that oppressed him.* ► depress, cast down, weigh down, burden, hang over, dispirit **2** *a people that had been oppressed by successive invaders* ► persecute, abuse, maltreat, tyrannize, repress, suppress, subjugate, subdue, keep down

oppressed ADJECTIVE *oppressed minorities in the community* ► persecuted, downtrodden, repressed, abused, maltreated, tyrannized, suppressed AN OPPOSITE IS privileged

oppressive ADJECTIVE **1** *an oppressive dictatorship* ► dictatorial, autocratic, authoritarian, despotic, brutal, cruel, harsh, repressive, tyrannical **2** *oppressive weather* ► humid, muggy, sultry, stuffy, airless, close, hot, stifling, heavy

oppressor NOUN *The angry mob thirsted for the blood of its oppressors.* ► persecutor, intimidator, tormentor, despot, tyrant, autocrat

optimism NOUN *Despite the difficulties he tried to keep up a note of optimism.* ► confidence, hopefulness, hope, positiveness, cheerfulness, good cheer AN OPPOSITE IS pessimism

optimistic ADJECTIVE **1** *I am really optimistic about winning the match tomorrow.* ► cheerful, confident, positive, hopeful, upbeat, sanguine, cheerful, buoyant AN OPPOSITE IS pessimistic **2** *The accounts included an optimistic assessment of the financial outlook.* ► favourable, encouraging, hopeful, upbeat, bright, rosy AN OPPOSITE IS pessimistic

optimum ADJECTIVE *The announcement is timed to have the optimum effect.* ► best, maximum, most favourable, most advantageous, highest, ideal, perfect AN OPPOSITE IS worst

option NOUN *We had little option but to agree.* ► choice, alternative, possibility

optional ADJECTIVE *The exam consists of two compulsory questions and an optional essay.* ► voluntary, discretionary, non-compulsory, elective OPPOSITES ARE compulsory, obligatory

A B C D E F G H I J K L M N O P Q R S T U V W X Y Z

or *CONJUNCTION* used to show that there is a choice or an alternative • *Do you want a bun or a biscuit?*

-or *SUFFIX* forms nouns meaning 'a person or thing that does something' (e.g. *tailor*, *refrigerator*)

oracle *NOUN* **oracles** **1** a shrine where the ancient Greeks consulted one of their gods for advice or a prophecy **2** a wise or knowledgeable adviser
▷ **oracular** (or- ak- yoo- ler) *ADJECTIVE*

oral *ADJECTIVE* **1** spoken, not written **2** to do with or using the mouth
▷ **orally** *ADVERB*
USAGE Do not confuse with **aural**.

orange *NOUN* **oranges** **1** a round juicy citrus fruit with reddish-yellow peel **2** a reddish-yellow colour

orangeade *NOUN* an orange-flavoured drink

orang-utan *NOUN* **orang-utans** a large ape of Borneo and Sumatra

orator *NOUN* **orators** a person who is good at making speeches in public
▷ **oratorical** *ADJECTIVE* **oratory** *NOUN*

orbit *NOUN* **orbits** **1** the curved path taken by something moving round a planet, moon, or star **2** the range of someone's influence or control
▷ **orbital** *ADJECTIVE*

orbit *VERB* **orbits, orbiting, orbited** move in an orbit round something • *The satellite has been orbiting the earth since 1986.*

orchard *NOUN* **orchards** a piece of ground planted with fruit trees

orchestra *NOUN* **orchestras** a large group of people playing various musical instruments together
▷ **orchestral** *ADJECTIVE*
[from Greek, = the space where the chorus danced during a play]

orchid *NOUN* **orchids** a kind of plant with brightly coloured, often unevenly shaped, flowers

ordain *VERB* **ordains, ordaining, ordained** **1** make a person a member of the clergy in the Christian Church • *He was ordained in 2001.* **2** declare or order something by law

ordeal *NOUN* **ordeals** a difficult or horrific experience

order *NOUN* **orders** **1** a command **2** a request for something to be supplied **3** the way things are arranged • *in alphabetical order* **4** a neat arrangement; a proper arrangement or condition • *in working order* **5** obedience to rules or laws • *law and order* **6** a kind or sort • *She showed courage of the highest order.* **7** a group of monks or nuns who live by certain religious rules
in order that or **in order to** for the purpose of

order *VERB* **orders, ordering, ordered** **1** command **2** ask for something to be supplied **3** put something into order; arrange neatly

orderly *ADJECTIVE* **1** arranged neatly or well; methodical **2** well-behaved and obedient
▷ **orderliness** *NOUN*

ordinal number *NOUN* **ordinal numbers** a number that shows a thing's position in a series, e.g. first, fifth, twentieth, etc. COMPARE **cardinal number**

Thesaurus

oral *ADJECTIVE* *Witnesses give oral evidence to the inquiry.* ► spoken, unwritten, verbal, by mouth, said AN OPPOSITE IS written

orbit *NOUN* **1** *the earth's orbit round the sun* ► course, path, circuit, track, trajectory, rotation, revolution **2** *This question is outside the orbit of the ordinary officials.* ► domain, sphere, range, scope, ambit

orbit *VERB* *other planets that orbit the sun* ► circle, go round, travel round

ordeal *NOUN* *She helped nurse him back to health after his four-year ordeal as a captive.* ► trial, tribulation, suffering, difficulty, test, torture, unpleasant experience, nightmare

order *NOUN* **1** *He gave the order to charge.* ► command, directive, instruction, direction, decree, edict **2** *It would not be easy to restore order.* ► peace, control, calm, quiet, law and order, discipline, harmony **3** *The plants were put in in a set order.* ► sequence, arrangement, disposition **4** *I've put in an order for a hundred storage boxes.* ► request, requisition, booking, demand, application **5** *the lowest orders in society* ► class, rank, hierarchy **6** *an ancient order of craftsmen* ► association, society, guild, company, lodge, brotherhood, sisterhood **7** *skills of a very high order* ► type, kind, sort, nature, variety, category out of order **1** *The ticket machine was, as usual, out of order.* ► broken, not working, inoperative **2** *Remarks like that would be ruled out of order.* ► improper, uncalled-for, unacceptable, irregular, unwarranted

order *VERB* **1** *She ordered them to leave the room.* ► instruct, command, direct, charge, enjoin **2** *I ordered the tickets on the Internet.* ► book, reserve, apply for, requisition **3** *He tried hard to order his thoughts.* ► arrange, organize, sort out, set in order, regulate

orderly *ADJECTIVE* **1** *The army began an orderly withdrawal.* ► methodical, systematic, ordered, regular, well organized, well regulated AN OPPOSITE IS disorganized **2** *The children were told to form an orderly queue.* ► neat, tidy,

ordinary *ADJECTIVE* normal or usual; not special
▷ **ordinarily** *ADVERB*
out of the ordinary unusual

ordination *NOUN* **ordinations** ordaining or being ordained as a member of the clergy

Ordnance Survey *NOUN* an official survey organization that makes detailed maps of the British Isles

ore *NOUN* **ores** rock with metal or other useful substances in it • *iron ore*

organ *NOUN* **organs** **1** a musical instrument from which sounds are produced by air forced through pipes, played by keys and pedals **2** a part of the body with a particular function • *the digestive organs*

organic *ADJECTIVE* **1** to do with the organs of the body • *organic diseases* **2** to do with or formed from living things • *organic matter* **3** organic food is grown or produced without the use of chemical fertilizers, pesticides, etc. • *organic farming*
▷ **organically** *ADVERB*

organism *NOUN* **organisms** a living thing; an individual animal or plant

organist *NOUN* **organists** a person who plays the organ

organization *NOUN* **organizations** **1** an organized group of people, such as a business, charity, government department, etc. **2** the organizing of something
▷ **organizational** *ADJECTIVE*

organize *VERB* **organizes, organizing, organized** **1** plan and prepare something • *We organized a picnic.* **2** form people into a group to work together **3** put things in order
▷ **organizer** *NOUN*

orgasm *NOUN* **orgasms** the climax of sexual excitement

orgy *NOUN* **orgies** **1** a wild party that involves a lot of drinking and sex **2** an extravagant activity • *an orgy of spending*

oriental *ADJECTIVE* to do with the countries east of the Mediterranean Sea, especially China and Japan

orientate *VERB* **orientates, orientating, orientated** **1** place something or face in a certain direction **2** get your bearings • *I'm just trying to orientate myself.*
▷ **orientation** *NOUN*

origami (o- rig- ah- mee) *NOUN* folding paper into decorative shapes [from Japanese *ori* = fold + *kami* = paper]

origin *NOUN* **origins** **1** the start of something; the point or cause from which something began **2** a person's family background • *a man of humble origins* **3** the point where two or more axes on a graph meet [from Latin *oriri* = to rise]

Thesaurus

controlled, well behaved AN OPPOSITE IS disorderly

ordinary *ADJECTIVE* **1** *just an ordinary day's work* ► usual, normal, typical, habitual, customary OPPOSITES ARE unusual, abnormal **2** *Susan is not like ordinary women.* ► average, normal, typical, conventional OPPOSITES ARE abnormal, unconventional **3** *My life seemed so ordinary; I needed a change.* ► routine, humdrum, run-of-the-mill, dull, routine, unremarkable, uninteresting, unexceptional, unexciting, commonplace OPPOSITES ARE exceptional, unique

organic *ADJECTIVE* **1** *an organic substance* ► natural, animate, live, living, biological AN OPPOSITE IS inorganic **2** *organic foods* ► natural, additive-free, pesticide-free, non-chemical **3** *society as an organic whole* ► integrated, organized, structured, coherent, systematic, harmonious AN OPPOSITE IS disparate

organization *NOUN* **1** *Sara is responsible for the organization of trips and visits.* ► planning, administration, coordination, running **2** *Organization is an important aspect of essay writing.* ► structure, planning, arrangement, composition **3** *an international organization with branches throughout the world* ► institution, enterprise, operation, company, (*more informal*) outfit, (*more informal*) set-up

organize *VERB* **1** *The protesters used mobile phones and the Internet to organize a demonstration.* ► arrange, coordinate, plan, make arrangements for, assemble, bring together, run **2** *Try to organize your ideas on paper.* ► order, marshal, structure, assemble, develop, coordinate, establish, systematize, put in order, form, shape

organized *ADJECTIVE* *a well organized sales promotion* ► systematic, coordinated, efficient, well ordered, well planned, well run, meticulous, methodical, orderly, scientific, structured OPPOSITES ARE disorganized, inefficient

orient or **orientate** *VERB* **1** *After her dad left she had to orientate herself to a new way of life.* ► adapt, adjust, accommodate, familiarize, acclimatize, accustom **2 orient** *or* **orientate yourself** *They looked out for landmarks to orient themselves.* ► get your bearings, get the lie of the land

oriental *ADJECTIVE* *oriental countries* ► eastern, Far Eastern, Asian, Asiatic

origin *NOUN* **1** *a discussion of the origin of the universe* ► beginning, start, birth, genesis, dawning, emergence, inception, source

A B C D E F G H I J K L M N O P Q R S T U V W X Y Z

original *ADJECTIVE* **1** existing from the start; earliest • *the original inhabitants* **2** new in its design etc.; not a copy **3** producing new ideas; inventive
▷ **originally** *ADVERB* **originality** *NOUN*

originate *VERB* **originates, originating, originated 1** cause something to begin; create **2** have its origin • *The quarrel originated in rivalry.*
▷ **origination** *NOUN* **originator** *NOUN*

ornament *NOUN* **ornaments** an object displayed or worn as a decoration
▷ **ornamental** *ADJECTIVE*

ornament *VERB* **ornaments, ornamenting, ornamented** decorate something with beautiful things
▷ **ornamentation** *NOUN*

ornithology *NOUN* the study of birds
▷ **ornithologist** *NOUN* **ornithological** *ADJECTIVE*

orphan *NOUN* **orphans** a child whose parents are dead

orthodox *ADJECTIVE* **1** holding beliefs that are correct or generally accepted **2** conventional or normal
▷ **orthodoxy** *NOUN*

Orthodox Church *NOUN* the Christian Churches of eastern Europe

orthopaedics (orth- o- pee- diks) *NOUN* the treatment of deformities and injuries to bones and muscles
▷ **orthopaedic** *ADJECTIVE*
[from Greek *orthos* = straight+ *paideia* = rearing of children (because the treatment was originally of children)]

oscillate *VERB* **oscillates, oscillating, oscillated 1** move to and fro like a pendulum; vibrate **2** waver or vary
▷ **oscillation** *NOUN* **oscillator** *NOUN*

osmosis *NOUN* the passing of fluid through a porous partition into another more concentrated fluid

ostentatious *ADJECTIVE* making a showy display of something to impress people
▷ **ostentatiously** *ADVERB* **ostentation** *NOUN*

osteopath *NOUN* **osteopaths** a person who treats certain medical conditions, diseases, etc. by manipulating a patient's bones and muscles
▷ **osteopathy** *NOUN* **osteopathic** *ADJECTIVE*

ostrich *NOUN* **ostriches** a large long-legged African bird that can run very fast but cannot fly. It was said to bury its head in the sand when pursued, in the belief that it cannot then be seen.

other *ADJECTIVE* **1** different • *some other tune* **2** remaining • *Try the other shoe.* **3** additional • *my other friends* **4** just recent or past • *I saw him the other day.*

other *PRONOUN, NOUN* **others** the other person or thing • *Where are the others?*

otherwise *ADVERB* **1** if things happen differently; if you do not • *Write it down, otherwise you'll forget.* **2** in other ways • *It rained, but otherwise the holiday was good.* **3** differently • *We could not do otherwise.*

otter *NOUN* **otters** a fish-eating animal with webbed feet, a flat tail, and thick brown fur, living near water [from Old English]

Thesaurus

OPPOSITES ARE end, conclusion **2** *a man of Irish origins* ► descent, ancestry, parentage, extraction, family, pedigree, background, stock

original *ADJECTIVE* **1** *the original inhabitants of North America* ► earliest, first, indigenous, native, aboriginal, initial AN OPPOSITE IS recent **2** *an original idea for a story* ► new, creative, innovative, novel, fresh, unfamiliar, unique, unusual, first-hand, imaginative, inventive, unconventional OPPOSITES ARE unoriginal, commonplace **3** *an original painting by Picasso* ► authentic, genuine, real

originate *VERB* **1** *Where did the rumour originate?* ► arise, start, begin, emerge, emanate, evolve, be born, crop up **2** *It is not clear who originated the idea.* ► conceive, invent, create, initiate, introduce, inaugurate, discover, inspire, pioneer, be the inventor of, give birth to, institute, launch

ornament *NOUN* **1** *a plain style of clothing without ornament* ► decoration, adornment, embellishment, trimming, accessory, filigree, frill, frippery, finery, garnish, jewel, tracery **2** *a shelf covered with ornaments* ► trinket, knick-knack, bauble, gewgaw

ornamental *ADJECTIVE* *an ornamental ceiling* ► decorative, fancy, attractive, ornate, ornamented, showy

ornate *ADJECTIVE* **1** *an ornate mirror over the fireplace* ► ornamented, decorated, elaborate, showy AN OPPOSITE IS plain **2** *ornate language* ► elaborate, florid, fancy, grandiose, affected, pretentious

orthodox *ADJECTIVE* *He has orthodox views on most things.* ► conventional, mainstream, established, conservative, standard, traditional, conformist OPPOSITES ARE unorthodox, unconventional

ostentatious *ADJECTIVE* *Their ostentatious attempts to look busy fools nobody.* ► showy, pretentious, conspicuous, flamboyant, obtrusive, vulgar, theatrical, overdone AN OPPOSITE IS modest

ought *AUXILIARY VERB* expressing duty (*We ought to feed them*), rightness or advisability (*You ought to take more exercise*), or probability (*At this speed, we ought to be there by noon*)

oughtn't (*mainly spoken*) ought not

ounce *NOUN* **ounces** a unit of weight equal to one sixteenth of a pound (about 28 grams)

our *ADJECTIVE* belonging to us

ours *POSSESSIVE PRONOUN* belonging to us • *These seats are ours.*

USAGE It is incorrect to write *our's*.

ourselves *PRONOUN* we or us and nobody else

oust *VERB* **ousts, ousting, ousted** drive a person out from a position or office

out *ADVERB* **1** away from or not in a particular place or position or state etc.; not at home **2** into the open; into existence or sight etc. • *The sun came out.* **3** no longer burning or shining **4** in error • *Your estimate was 10% out.* **5** to or at an end; completely • *sold out* • *tired out* **6** without restraint; boldly or loudly • *Speak out!* **7** (in cricket) no longer batting

be out for or **out to** be seeking or wanting • *They are out to make trouble.*

be out of have no more of something left

out of date **1** old-fashioned **2** not valid any more

out of doors in the open air

out of the way remote

USAGE Use hyphens when *out of date* is used as an adjective before a noun, e.g. *out-of-date information* (but *The information is out of date*).

out and out *ADJECTIVE* thorough or complete • *an out and out villain*

outboard motor *NOUN* **outboard motors** a motor fitted to the outside of a boat's stern

outbreak *NOUN* **outbreaks** the start of a disease or war or anger etc.

outburst *NOUN* **outbursts** a sudden bursting out of anger or laughter etc.

outcast *NOUN* **outcasts** a person who has been rejected by family, friends, or society

outcrop *NOUN* **outcrops** a piece of rock from a lower level that sticks out on the surface of the ground

outcry *NOUN* **outcries** a strong protest

outdo *VERB* **outdoes, outdoing, outdid, outdone** do better than another person

outdoors *ADVERB* in the open air

outer *ADJECTIVE* outside or external; nearer to the outside

▷ **outermost** *ADJECTIVE*

outer space *NOUN* the universe beyond the earth's atmosphere

outfit *NOUN* **outfits** **1** a set of clothes worn together **2** a set of equipment **3** (*informal*) a team or organization

Thesaurus

oust *VERB* *The president knew that his opponent would never unite to oust him.* ► depose, overthrow, remove, drive out, expel, unseat, defeat

out-and-out *ADJECTIVE* *an out-and-out success* ► complete, utter, outright, thoroughgoing, downright, absolute, thorough, unmitigated

outbreak *NOUN* **1** *an outbreak of Sars; new outbreaks of violence* ► eruption, upsurge, outburst, epidemic, rash, spate **2** *the outbreak of war* ► start, beginning, onset

outburst *NOUN* *At this there was a loud outburst of laughter.* ► eruption, burst, explosion, outbreak, surge, spasm

outcast *NOUN* *a social outcast* ► reject, pariah, leper, outsider, exile, outlaw, castaway

outclass *VERB* *She won every game, outclassing every rival.* ► surpass, outdo, outstrip, outshine, beat, exceed, eclipse, excel, be better than

outcome *NOUN* *speculation about the outcome of the next election* ► result, consequence, conclusion, upshot, issue, conclusion

outcry *NOUN* *an outcry about the state of the railways* ► protest, complaint, furore, clamour, tumult

outdated *ADJECTIVE* *an outdated road network* ► out-of-date, obsolete, old-fashioned, dated, decrepit, antiquated, ancient

outdo *VERB* *Everyone tried to outdo each other with stories of how exciting their holidays had been.* ► surpass, outstrip, outshine, exceed, eclipse, excel, be better than, outclass, beat

outdoor *ADJECTIVE* *an outdoor sport such as archery* ► open-air, outside, alfresco

outer *ADJECTIVE* **1** *It was so hot they began to shed their outer clothing.* ► outermost, exterior, external, outside, outward, surface, superficial **2** *superstores built in the outer areas of cities* ► outlying, distant, remote, peripheral, further, suburban AN OPPOSITE IS inner

outfit *NOUN* **1** *a complete photography outfit* ► equipment, kit, apparatus, (*more informal*) gear, (*more informal*) set-up **2** *The weather was still too cold for summer outfits.* ► costume, ensemble, suit, dress, clothing, (*informal*) get-up, (*informal*) turn-out, (*more informal*) gear, (*more informal*) togs

outgoing *ADJECTIVE* **1** *She was in a bright, outgoing mood that day.* ► sociable, friendly, amiable, genial, congenial, demonstrative, pleasant, agreeable, kind, kindly, kind-hearted, well-disposed, sympathetic, likeable, approachable, receptive **2** *the outgoing*

outgrow *VERB* **outgrows**, **outgrowing**, **outgrew**, **outgrown** **1** grow out of clothes or habits etc. **2** grow faster or larger than another person or thing

outhouse *NOUN* **outhouses** a small building (e.g. a shed or barn) that belongs to a house but is separate from it

outing *NOUN* **outings** a journey for pleasure

outlandish *ADJECTIVE* looking or sounding strange or foreign

outlast *VERB* **outlasts**, **outlasting**, **outlasted** last longer than something else

outlaw *NOUN* **outlaws** a person who is punished by being excluded from legal rights and the protection of the law, especially a robber or bandit

outlay *NOUN* **outlays** what is spent on something

outlet *NOUN* **outlets** **1** a way for something to get out **2** a way of expressing strong feelings **3** a place from which goods are sold or distributed

outline *NOUN* **outlines** **1** a line round the outside of something, showing its boundary or shape **2** a summary

outlook *NOUN* **outlooks** **1** a view on which people look out **2** a person's mental attitude to something **3** future prospects • *The outlook is bleak.*

outlying *ADJECTIVE* far from the centre; remote • *the outlying districts*

outmoded *ADJECTIVE* out of date

outnumber *VERB* **outnumbers**, **outnumbering**, **outnumbered** be more numerous than another group

outpatient *NOUN* **outpatients** a person who visits a hospital for treatment but does not stay there

outpost *NOUN* **outposts** a distant settlement

output *NOUN* **outputs** **1** the amount produced **2** the information or results produced by a computer

outrage *NOUN* **outrages** **1** something that shocks people by being very wicked or cruel **2** great anger
▷ **outrageous** *ADJECTIVE* **outrageously** *ADVERB*

outrage *VERB* **outrages**, **outraging**, **outraged** shock and anger people greatly

Thesaurus

president ► departing, leaving, retiring, former, ex- AN OPPOSITE IS incoming

outing *NOUN* *family outings to the coast* ► trip, excursion, jaunt, expedition, drive, run, ride, joyride

outlandish *ADJECTIVE* *We could dream up all sorts of outlandish ideas.* ► weird, strange, extraordinary, odd, queer, eccentric, bizarre, quirky

outlaw *NOUN* *those notorious outlaws Jesse and Frank James* ► bandit, brigand, fugitive, desperado, renegade, robber, marauder, criminal, outcast

outlaw *VERB* *The state in effect outlawed political opposition.* ► ban, prohibit, bar, forbid, disallow, banish, embargo, condemn, veto

outlet *NOUN* **1** *The boiler has an outlet for fumes.* ► vent, duct, channel, opening, orifice, exit, mouth, way out **2** *We need a better outlet for complaints.* ► channel, process, means **3** *High Street outlets for these goods* ► shop, store, retailer, market

outline *NOUN* **1** *the outline of a low building* ► profile, silhouette, shape, form, contour, shadow, figure **2** (*informal*) *He sat down and wrote an outline of his essay.* ► summary, sketch, framework, skeleton, plan, draft, rough idea, bare bones

outlook *NOUN* **1** *The house has a glorious outlook over the downs.* ► view, vista, prospect, panorama, aspect, vantage point **2** *The sisters were totally different in character and outlook.* ► attitude, way of thinking, standpoint, viewpoint, frame of mind, point of view **3** *Lower interest rates will improve the economic outlook.* ► prospects, expectations, forecast, hopes, future, prognosis, prediction, (*more informal*) lookout

outnumber *VERB* *On these occasions males usually outnumber females.* ► exceed, be more than, outstrip

out-of-date *ADJECTIVE* **1** *He handed over an out-of-date passport.* ► expired, lapsed, invalid, void **2** *She was using a machine that was totally out of date.* ► old-fashioned, outdated, obsolete, dated, obsolescent

out-of-the-way *ADJECTIVE* *out-of-the-way places* ► distant, outlying, faraway, remote, isolated, far-flung, far-off

output *NOUN* *a marked increase in industrial output* ► production, productivity, product, yield, manufacture

outrage *NOUN* **1** *I was outraged by the way he spoke to me.* ► anger, indignation, fury, disgust, affront, horror **2** *The country's suffering is an outrage.* ► scandal, disgrace, atrocity, enormity, barbarity, infamy

outrageous *ADJECTIVE* **1** *an outrageous slur on his character* ► disgraceful, shocking, scandalous, appalling, monstrous, shameful, dreadful, intolerable, wicked, heinous AN OPPOSITE IS mild **2** *We were invited to tell outrageous stories*

outright *ADVERB* **1** completely; not gradually • *This drug should be banned outright.* **2** frankly • *We told him this outright.*

outright *ADJECTIVE* thorough or complete • *an outright fraud*

outrun *VERB* **outruns, outrunning, outran, outrun** run faster or further than another

outset *NOUN* the beginning of something • *from the outset of his career*

outside *NOUN* **outsides** the outer side, surface, or part
at the outside at the most • *a mile at the outside*

outside *ADJECTIVE* **1** on or coming from the outside • *the outside edge* **2** greatest possible • *the outside price* **3** remote or slight • *an outside chance*

outside *ADVERB* on or to the outside; outdoors • *Leave it outside* • *It's cold outside*

outside *PREPOSITION* on or to the outside of • *Leave it outside the door.*

outside broadcast *NOUN* **outside broadcasts** a broadcast made on location and not in a studio

outsider *NOUN* **outsiders** **1** a person who does not belong to a certain group **2** a horse or person thought to have no chance of winning a race or competition

outsize *ADJECTIVE* much larger than average

outskirts *PLURAL NOUN* the outer parts or districts, especially of a town

outspoken *ADJECTIVE* speaking or spoken very frankly

outstanding *ADJECTIVE* **1** extremely good or distinguished **2** not yet paid or dealt with

outstrip *VERB* **outstrips, outstripping, outstripped** **1** run faster or further than another; outrun **2** surpass in achievement or success

outward *ADJECTIVE* **1** going outwards **2** on the outside
▷ **outwardly** *ADVERB* **outwards** *ADVERB*

outwit *VERB* **outwits, outwitting, outwitted** deceive somebody by being crafty

ova *plural of* **ovum**

oval *ADJECTIVE* shaped like a 0, rounded and longer than it is broad
▷ **oval** *NOUN*

ovary *NOUN* **ovaries** **1** either of the two organs in which ova or egg cells are produced in a woman's or female animal's body **2** part of the pistil in a plant, from which fruit is formed

oven *NOUN* **ovens** a closed space in which things are cooked or heated

over *PREPOSITION* **1** above **2** more than • *It's over a mile away.* **3** concerning • *They quarrelled over money.* **4** across the top of; on or to the other side of • *They rowed the boat over the lake.* **5** during • *We can talk over dinner.* **6** in

Thesaurus

about people we knew. ► far-fetched, extravagant, preposterous, unlikely, questionable, dubious AN OPPOSITE IS reasonable **3** *If you're not careful about the extras the cost can become outrageous.* ► excessive, exorbitant, extortionate

outright *ADJECTIVE* *By now it was clear the whole story was an outright fabrication.* ► complete, utter, out-and-out, thoroughgoing, downright, absolute, thorough, unmitigated AN OPPOSITE IS indefinite

outside *ADJECTIVE* **1** *An outside light will improve security.* ► exterior, external, outer, outdoor, outward AN OPPOSITE IS inside **2** *We must resist all outside interference.* ► external, extraneous, foreign, alien AN OPPOSITE IS inside **3** *There is an outside chance of thunder.* ► slight, remote, slender, slim, faint, negligible

outside *NOUN* *The outside of the building is covered in ivy.* ► exterior, facade, surface, outer surface, shell, skin AN OPPOSITE IS inside

outsider *NOUN* *I still felt an outsider after years of living in the village.* ► stranger, visitor, foreigner, alien, newcomer, incomer, interloper, intruder, immigrant, non-resident, outcast AN OPPOSITE IS insider

outskirts *PLURAL NOUN* *a group of buildings on the outskirts of the city* ► outer areas, outlying districts, edge, fringe, suburbs, margin, periphery, purlieus OPPOSITES ARE centre, heart

outspoken *ADJECTIVE* *some outspoken remarks* ► frank, forthright, candid, direct, blunt, plain-speaking, straightforward, unequivocal OPPOSITES ARE guarded, diplomatic

outstanding *ADJECTIVE* **1** *She is an outstanding musician.* ► excellent, exceptional, superb, superlative, fine, extraordinary, distinguished, celebrated OPPOSITES ARE mediocre, unexceptional **2** *All outstanding questions will be answered.* ► unresolved, unsettled, remaining, pending

outweigh *VERB* *The benefits of the scheme have to outweigh the costs.* ► exceed, be better than, be greater than, prevail over, override, have the edge on

outwit *VERB* *The besieged garrison managed to outwit the enemy.* ► outsmart, dupe, fool, hoodwink, hoax, cheat, deceive, trick, (*more informal*) take in, (*more informal*) outfox

oval *ADJECTIVE* *an oval lawn* ► egg-shaped, elliptical, ovoid

a b c d e f g h i j k l m n o p q r s t u v w x y z

superiority or preference to • *their victory over United*

over ADVERB **1** out and down from the top or edge; from an upright position • *He fell over.* **2** so that a different side shows • *Turn it over.* **3** at or to a place; across • *Walk over to our house.* **4** remaining • *There is nothing left over.* **5** all through; thoroughly • *Think it over.* **6** at an end • *The lesson is over.*
over and over many times; repeatedly

over NOUN **overs** a series of six balls bowled in cricket [from Old English]

overact VERB **overacts, overacting, overacted** (said about an actor) act in an exaggerated manner

overall ADJECTIVE including everything; total • *the overall cost*

overalls PLURAL NOUN a piece of clothing like a shirt and trousers combined, worn over other clothes to protect them

overarm ADJECTIVE, ADVERB with the arm lifted above shoulder level and coming down in front of the body • *bowling overarm*

overawe VERB **overawes, overawing, overawed** overcome a person with awe

overbalance VERB **overbalances, overbalancing, overbalanced** lose balance and fall over

overbearing ADJECTIVE domineering

overblown ADJECTIVE **1** exaggerated or pretentious **2** (said about a flower) too fully open; past its best

overboard ADVERB from in or on a ship into the water • *She jumped overboard.*

overcast ADJECTIVE covered with cloud

overcoat NOUN **overcoats** a warm outdoor coat

overcome VERB **overcomes, overcoming, overcame, overcome 1** win a victory over somebody; defeat **2** have a strong physical or emotional effect on someone and make them helpless • *He was overcome by the fumes.* **3** find a way of dealing with a problem etc.

overdo VERB **overdoes, overdoing, overdid, overdone 1** do something too much **2** cook food for too long

overdose NOUN **overdoses** too large a dose of a drug

overdraft NOUN **overdrafts** the amount by which a bank account is overdrawn

overdraw VERB **overdraws, overdrawing, overdrew, overdrawn** draw more money from a bank account than the amount you have in it

overdue ADJECTIVE late; not paid or arrived etc. by the proper time

overhaul VERB **overhauls, overhauling, overhauled 1** examine something thoroughly and repair it if necessary **2** overtake
▷ **overhaul** NOUN

overhead ADJECTIVE, ADVERB **1** above the level of your head **2** in the sky

overheads PLURAL NOUN the expenses of running a business

overhear VERB **overhears, overhearing, overheard** hear something accidentally or without the speaker intending you to hear it

overjoyed ADJECTIVE filled with great joy

overlap VERB **overlaps, overlapping, overlapped 1** lie across part of something **2** happen partly at the same time
▷ **overlap** NOUN

overlay VERB **overlays, overlaying, overlaid** cover with a layer; lie on top of something

Thesaurus

overall ADJECTIVE *It was a good overall result.* ► general, all-inclusive, all-embracing, comprehensive, inclusive AN OPPOSITE IS specific

overall ADVERB *Things have improved overall.* ► generally, in general, generally speaking, altogether, all in all, for the most part, on the whole, in the main, on balance, on average

overcome VERB **1** *Neither army was strong enough to overcome the other.* ► defeat, beat, conquer, overpower, vanquish, overwhelm, trounce **2** *It would be be easy to overcome his fear of flying.* ► control, master, get the better of, repress, subdue

overdo VERB *She spoilt her case by overdoing the emotion.* ► exaggerate, overstate, overplay, overemphasize, overdramatize OPPOSITES ARE underplay, play down

overdue ADJECTIVE **1** *The train is overdue.* ► late, delayed, behind time, tardy, unpunctual, slow AN OPPOSITE IS early **2** *Our phone bill is overdue.* ► unpaid, unsettled, outstanding, owing, in arrears

overeat VERB *The food was so dreadful at least there was no danger of them overeating.* ► overindulge, eat too much, be greedy, gorge, guzzle, binge, (*more informal*) stuff yourself, (*more informal*) make a pig of yourself OPPOSITES ARE diet, fast, undereat

overflow VERB *The water tank overflowed, causing damage to the roof.* ► spill over, flow over, pour over, run over, brim over, flood

overjoyed ADJECTIVE *Brian was overjoyed at the birth of his daughter.* ► thrilled, delighted, ecstatic, pleased, excited, happy, glad OPPOSITES ARE dejected, disappointed

overload *VERB* **overloads**, **overloading**, **overloaded** put too great a load on someone or something

overlook *VERB* **overlooks**, **overlooking**, **overlooked** **1** not notice or consider something **2** deliberately ignore something wrong; not punish an offence **3** have a view over something

overpower *VERB* **overpowers**, **overpowering**, **overpowered** defeat someone by greater strength or numbers

overpowering *ADJECTIVE* very strong

overrate *VERB* **overrates**, **overrating**, **overrated** have too high an opinion of something

override *VERB* **overrides**, **overriding**, **overrode**, **overridden** **1** overrule **2** be more important than • *Safety overrides all other considerations.*
▷ **overriding** *ADJECTIVE*

overrule *VERB* **overrules**, **overruling**, **overruled** reject a suggestion etc. by using your authority • *We voted for having a disco but the headteacher overruled the idea.*

overrun *VERB* **overruns**, **overrunning**, **overran**, **overrun** **1** spread over and occupy or harm something • *Mice overran the place.* **2** go on for longer than it should • *The broadcast overran by ten minutes.*

oversee *VERB* **oversees**, **overseeing**, **oversaw**, **overseen** watch over or supervise people working
▷ **overseer** *NOUN*

oversight *NOUN* **oversights** a mistake made by not noticing something

overtake *VERB* **overtakes**, **overtaking**, **overtook**, **overtaken** **1** pass a moving vehicle or person etc. **2** catch up with someone

overthrow *VERB* **overthrows**, **overthrowing**, **overthrew**, **overthrown** remove someone from power by force • *They overthrew the king.*

overtime *NOUN* time spent working outside the normal hours; payment for this

overture *NOUN* **overtures** **1** a piece of music written as an introduction to an opera, ballet, etc. **2** a friendly attempt to start a discussion • *They made overtures of peace.*

overturn *VERB* **overturns**, **overturning**, **overturned** **1** turn over or upside down **2** reverse a legal decision

Thesaurus

overlook *VERB* **1** *a mistake we are willing to overlook* ► ignore, disregard, take no notice of, pay no attention to, discount, overlook, pass over, let pass, excuse, forget, make light of, brush aside, (*more informal*) turn a blind eye to AN OPPOSITE IS penalize **2** *The house overlooks a car park.* ► look out on, have a view of, look on to, look over, face, front

overpowering *ADJECTIVE* **1** *an overpowering feeling of sorrow* ► overwhelming, irrepressible, irresistible, uncontrollable, oppressive, intense OPPOSITES ARE slight, weak **2** *The smell was overpowering.* ► stifling, suffocating, nauseating, sickening, pungent AN OPPOSITE IS mild **3** *overpowering evidence of their guilt* ► compelling, irrefutable, undeniable, incontrovertible, conclusive, forceful, powerful, strong OPPOSITES ARE unconvincing, inconclusive

overrule *VERB* *A higher court overruled the decision.* ► overturn, override, revoke, reverse, cancel, rescind, quash, set aside, countermand OPPOSITES ARE confirm, endorse, allow

oversight *NOUN* *The delay was caused by oversight.* ► omission, lapse, carelessness, neglect, error

overtake *VERB* **1** *Huge lorries were overtaking one another.* ► pass, pull ahead of, go past, overhaul, catch up with **2** *Fruit had overtaken oil as the country's main export.* ► outstrip, exceed, surpass, outdo **3** *Another disaster overtook the family.* ► befall, overwhelm, overpower, strike, hit, afflict, engulf

overthrow *VERB* *The emperor was finally overthrown by his own guard.* ► depose, oust, remove, drive out, expel, unseat, defeat

overthrow *NOUN* *the overthrow of the tyrant* ► downfall, defeat, removal, fall, collapse, deposing, ousting, expulsion, unseating

overtone *NOUN* *The word 'compulsory' has threatening overtones.* ► connotation, association, implication, undertone, undercurrent, reverberation, suggestion

overturn *VERB* **1** *The boat overturned in a squall.* ► capsize, turn over, tip over, keel over, turn turtle, overbalance **2** *Someone had overturned a box of tools over the garage floor.* ► upset, spill, knock over, tip over, topple **3** *The decision was overturned in the House of Lords.* ► overrule, override, revoke, reverse, cancel, rescind, quash, set aside, countermand

overweight *ADJECTIVE* *I had put on two stone and was noticeably overweight.* ► fat, obese, corpulent, gross OPPOSITES ARE underweight, undernourished

overwhelm *VERB* **overwhelms, overwhelming, overwhelmed 1** bury or drown beneath a huge mass **2** overcome completely
▷ **overwhelming** *ADJECTIVE*

ovum (oh- vum) *NOUN* **ova** a female cell that can develop into a new individual when it is fertilized [from Latin, = egg]

owe *VERB* **owes, owing, owed 1** have a duty to pay or give something to someone, especially money **2** have something because of the action of another person or thing • *They owed their lives to the pilot's skill.*
owing to because of; caused by
USAGE The use of *owing to* as a preposition meaning 'because of' is entirely acceptable, unlike this use of *due to*, which some people object to. See note at **due**.

owl *NOUN* **owls** a bird of prey with large eyes, usually flying at night

own *ADJECTIVE* belonging to yourself or itself
get your own back get revenge
on your own alone

own *VERB* **owns, owning, owned 1** possess; have something as your property **2** acknowledge or admit something • *I own that I made a mistake.*
own up confess; admit guilt

owner *NOUN* **owners** the person who owns something
▷ **ownership** *NOUN*

own goal *NOUN* **own goals** a goal scored by a member of a team against their own side

ox *NOUN* **oxen** a large animal kept for its meat and for pulling carts

oxide *NOUN* **oxides** a compound of oxygen and one other element

oxygen *NOUN* a colourless odourless tasteless gas that exists in the air and is essential for living things

oyster *NOUN* **oysters** a kind of shellfish whose shell sometimes contains a pearl

ozone *NOUN* a form of oxygen with a sharp smell

ozone layer *NOUN* a layer of ozone high in the atmosphere, protecting the earth from harmful amounts of the sun's radiation

Thesaurus

overwhelm *VERB* **1** • *The home side overwhelmed the visitors in the league game.* ► defeat, overcome, crush, overpower, rout, trounce, win against, conquer, vanquish, subdue, get the better of, (*more informal*) thrash **2** • *Monsoons would soon overwhelm the region.* ► overrun, inundate, submerge, engulf, flood, deluge, bury **3** • *She bent her head, overwhelmed by grief.* ► overcome, overpower, strike, crush

overwhelming *ADJECTIVE* **1** *The campaign received overwhelming support.* ► strong, massive, formidable, sweeping, forceful, powerful **2** *The army suffered another overwhelming defeat.* ► crushing, devastating, great, overpowering

owing *ADJECTIVE* *There is a small amount of money still owing.* ► due, outstanding, unpaid, payable, owed, unsettled, overdue
owing to *He would not use the lifts, owing to his claustrophobia.* ► because of, as a result of, on account of, as a consequence of, by reason of, thanks to

own *VERB* *Many more people own their own house.* ► possess, be the owner of, have, hold
own up to *He was waiting for a good moment to own up to the mistake.* ► confess, admit, acknowledge, tell the truth about, (*more informal*) come clean about, (*more informal*) make a clean breast of

owner *NOUN* **1** *Maintenance of the service road is the responsibility of the properties' owners.* ► possessor, proprietor, freeholder, landlord, landlady **2** *Dog owner should not let their pets foul the pavements.* ► keeper, master, mistress

Pp

p *ABBREVIATION* penny or pence

p. *ABBREVIATION* **pp.** page

pace *NOUN* **paces** **1** one step in walking, marching, or running **2** speed • *He set a fast pace.*

pacemaker *NOUN* **pacemakers** **1** a person who sets the pace for another in a race **2** an electrical device to keep the heart beating

pacifist (pas- if- ist) *NOUN* **pacifists** a person who believes that war is always wrong
▷ **pacifism** *NOUN*

pacify *VERB* **pacifies ,pacifying ,pacified** **1** calm a person down **2** bring peace to a country or to people who are fighting
▷ **pacification** *NOUN*

pack *NOUN* **packs** **1** a bundle or collection of things wrapped or tied together **2** a set of playing cards (usually 52) **3** a bag carried on your back **4** a large amount • *a pack of lies* **5** a group of hounds or wolves etc. **6** a group of people; a group of Brownies or Cub Scouts

pack *VERB* **packs ,packing ,packed** **1** put things into a suitcase, bag, or box etc. in order to move or store them **2** crowd together; fill tightly
pack off (*informal*) send a person away
send a person packing (*informal*) dismiss him or her

package *NOUN* **packages** **1** a parcel or packet **2** a number of things offered or accepted together
▷ **packaging** *NOUN*

package holiday *NOUN* **package holidays** a holiday with all the travel and accommodation arranged and included in the price

packet *NOUN* **packets** a small parcel

pack ice *NOUN* a mass of pieces of ice floating in the sea

pad *NOUN* **pads** **1** a soft thick mass of material, used e.g. to protect or stuff something **2** a piece of soft material worn to protect your leg in cricket and other games **3** a set of sheets of paper fastened together at one edge **4** the soft fleshy part under an animal's foot or the end of a finger or toe **5** a flat surface from which rockets are launched or where helicopters take off and land

Thesaurus

pace *NOUN* **1** *She moved back a few paces.* ► step, stride **2** *The traffic was moving at a slow pace.* ► speed, rate, velocity, movement, quickness, gait, (*informal*) lick **3** *They quickened their pace to a run.* ► stride, gait, tread, walk, march, speed, progress

pace *VERB* *Richard paced up and down for ages before going in.* ► walk, stride, tread, march

pacify *VERB* *It was too late to pacify her now, and she stormed off.* ► appease, placate, calm, conciliate, mollify, soothe, assuage, propitiate, quieten AN OPPOSITE IS anger

pack *NOUN* **1** *The bookshelves come in a self-assembly pack. A pack of cigarettes lay on the table.* ► package, packet, container, carton, box, parcel, bundle **2** *a group of walkers with packs on their backs* ► backpack, rucksack, knapsack, kitbag **3** *a pack of wolves* ► group, herd, troop **4** *a pack of youths* ► group, crowd, band, gang, set, throng, horde, mob

pack *VERB* **1** *The children helped to pack the hamper.* ► fill, load, stuff, put things in **2** *She decided to pack her belongings and leave.* ► bundle, parcel, wrap, stow, store **3** *On rainy days visitors pack the local museums.* ► throng, crowd into, cram into, squash into, squeeze into, fill, jam
pack in (*informal*) *James has decided to pack in his job.* ► give up, leave, resign from, (*informal*) quit, (*informal*) chuck in
pack up **1** (*informal*) *The microwave chose that very moment to pack up.* ► break down, stop working, go wrong, fail, develop a fault, (*more formal*) malfunction, (*informal*) play up, (*informal*) act up **2** (*informal*) *If you're not having a good time perhaps it's time to pack up.* ► stop, break off, call it a day

package *NOUN* *A strange package arrived by special delivery.* ► parcel, packet, container, consignment

packed *a packed room* ► crowded, full, crammed, jam-packed, chock-a-block

packet *NOUN* **1** *a packet of sugar* ► pack, carton, bag, box, container **2 a packet** (*informal*) *new shoes that cost a packet* ► a fortune, a small fortune, a huge amount, a king's ransom, (*informal*) an arm and a leg

pact *NOUN* *The two countries signed a non-aggression pact.* ► treaty, alliance, agreement, settlement, truce, protocol, understanding

pad *NOUN* **1** *Take a pad to sit on as the seats are hard.* ► cushion, pillow, padding, squab, bolster, wad **2** *She made notes on a small pad.* ► notebook, notepad, jotter, sketchbook

a b c d e f g h i j k l m n o p q r s t u v w x y z

pad VERB **pads, padding, padded** put a pad on or in something
pad out make a book, speech, etc. longer than it needs to be

padding NOUN material used to pad things

paddle[1] VERB **paddles, paddling, paddled** walk about in shallow water
▷ **paddle** NOUN

paddle[2] NOUN **paddles** a short oar with a broad blade; something shaped like this

paddle VERB **paddles, paddling, paddled** move a boat along with a paddle or paddles; row gently

paddock NOUN **paddocks** a small field where horses are kept

padlock NOUN **padlocks** a detachable lock with a metal loop that passes through a ring or chain etc.
▷ **padlock** VERB

paediatrics (peed- ee- at- riks) NOUN the study of children's diseases
▷ **paediatric** ADJECTIVE **paediatrician** NOUN
[from Greek *paidos* = of a child + *iatros* = doctor]

pagan (pay- gan) NOUN **pagans** a person who does not believe in one of the chief religions; a heathen
▷ **pagan** ADJECTIVE
[from Latin *paganus* = country dweller, civilian. In Christian Latin the word was used of anyone who was a civilian in the sense of not being in the 'army' of Christ.]

page[1] NOUN **pages** a piece of paper that is part of a book or newspaper etc.; one side of this

page[2] NOUN **pages 1** a boy or man employed to go on errands or be an attendant **2** a young boy attending a bride at a wedding

pageant NOUN **pageants 1** a play or entertainment about historical events and people **2** a procession of people in costume as an entertainment
▷ **pageantry** NOUN

pagoda (pag- **oh**- da) NOUN **pagodas** a Buddhist tower, or a Hindu temple shaped like a pyramid, in India and the Far East [via Portuguese from Persian]

paid *past tense* of **pay**
put paid to (*informal*) put an end to someone's activity or hope etc.

pail NOUN **pails** a bucket

pain NOUN **pains 1** an unpleasant feeling caused by injury or disease **2** suffering in the mind
▷ **painful** ADJECTIVE **painfully** ADVERB **painless** ADJECTIVE
take pains make a careful effort with work etc.

Thesaurus

pad VERB **1** *You can pad the cushion with plastic foam.* ► stuff, pack, fill, line, upholster **2** *He padded along to the bathroom.* ► walk, creep, tiptoe
pad out *Try not to pad out your letter with irrelevant detail.* ► expand, inflate, fill out, elaborate, lengthen, spin out, stretch out

padding NOUN **1** *The sofa burst open and masses of grey padding fell out.* ► stuffing, wadding, filling, cushioning **2** *The story could be much shorter but for all the tedious padding.* ► verbiage, verbosity, prolixity, wordiness, (*informal*) waffle

paddle NOUN *You'll need to use the paddle to reach the shore.* ► oar, scull

paddle VERB **1** *We paddled furiously to get to safety.* ► row, scull, pull **2** *You can paddle a long way out at low tide.* ► dabble, wade, splash about

pagan NOUN *pagans who worshipped nature* ► heathen, infidel, non-believer, unbeliever
USAGE You should only use *pagan* with reference to people in the past. It is an unfavourable term used by Christians and other believers in God to refer to non-believers. It is not an ordinary equivalent to words such as *atheist*, which is a more neutral term for someone who believes there is no God.

pagan ADJECTIVE *pagan festivals* ► heathen, infidel, ungodly, atheistic, godless, idolatrous, irreligious, unchristian
USAGE See the note at the previous entry.

page NOUN **1** *He had written a whole page by the time she returned.* ► side, sheet, folio, leaf **2** *Clare's little brother had been a page at her friend's wedding.* ► pageboy, attendant, train-bearer

pain NOUN **1** *The pain in his tooth was fading.* ► ache, soreness, hurt, tenderness, throb, discomfort **2** *How could anyone be expected to put up with so much pain?* ► suffering, discomfort, agony, affliction **3** *the pain of losing a child* ► grief, sorrow, distress, torment, anguish, misery, trauma **4** (*informal*) *Younger brothers could be a pain at times like this.* ► nuisance, pest, bother, bore, trial, tribulation, inconvenience

pain VERB *It pained him to think of all the trouble they had been through.* ► hurt, sadden, grieve, distress, mortify

painful ADJECTIVE **1** *The knight had a painful wound in his side.* ► sore, hurting, tender, agonizing, excruciating **2** *The journey had been a painful experience.* ► unpleasant, traumatic, disagreeable, bitter, wretched
OPPOSITES ARE pleasant, agreeable

painkiller *NOUN* **painkillers** a medicine or drug that relieves pain

painstaking *ADJECTIVE* very careful and thorough

paint *NOUN* **paints** a liquid substance put on something to colour it
▷ **paintbox** *NOUN* **paintbrush** *NOUN*

paint *VERB* **paints, painting, painted** **1** put paint on something **2** make a picture with paints

painting *NOUN* **paintings** **1** a painted picture **2** using paints to make a picture

pair *NOUN* **pairs** **1** a set of two things or people; a couple **2** something made of two joined parts • *a pair of scissors*

pair *VERB* **pairs, pairing, paired** put two things together as a pair
pair off *or* **up** form a couple

palace *NOUN* **palaces** a mansion where a king, queen, or other important person lives

palatable *ADJECTIVE* tasting pleasant

palate *NOUN* **palates** **1** the roof of your mouth **2** a person's sense of taste

pale [1] *ADJECTIVE* **1** almost white • *a pale face* **2** not bright in colour or light • *pale green* • *the pale moonlight*
▷ **palely** *ADVERB* **paleness** *NOUN*

pale [2] *NOUN* **pales** a boundary
beyond the pale beyond the limits of good taste or behaviour etc.

palindrome *NOUN* **palindromes** a word or phrase that reads the same backwards as forwards, e.g. *radar* or *Madam, I'm Adam* [from Greek *palindromos* = running back again]

paling *NOUN* **palings** a fence made of wooden posts or railings; one of its posts

pall [1] (pawl) *NOUN* **palls** **1** a cloth spread over a coffin **2** a dark covering • *A pall of smoke lay over the town.*

pall [2] (pawl) *VERB* **palls, palling, palled** become uninteresting or boring to someone • *The novelty of the new computer game soon began to pall.*

palliative *NOUN* **palliatives** something that lessens pain or suffering
▷ **palliative** *ADJECTIVE*

palm *NOUN* **palms** **1** the inner part of the hand, between the fingers and the wrist **2** a palm tree
palm off deceive a person into accepting something

palm tree *NOUN* **palm trees** a tropical tree with large leaves and no branches

palpitate *VERB* **palpitates, palpitating, palpitated** **1** (said about the heart) beat hard and quickly **2** (said about a person) quiver with fear or excitement
▷ **palpitation** *NOUN*

pampas *NOUN* wide grassy plains in South America

pamper *VERB* **pampers, pampering, pampered** treat or look after someone very kindly and indulgently

Thesaurus

paint *NOUN* *They chose a bright paint for the walls.* ► colour, pigment, tint, colouring, stain

paint *VERB* **1** *Kim couldn't make up her mind whether to paint the room or paper it.* ► colour, tint, use paint on, coat with paint, apply paint to, decorate **2** *The article paints a vivid picture of life in rural Wales.* ► describe, depict, portray, present, sketch, outline, delineate

painting *NOUN* *She was eager to buy one of his larger paintings.* ► picture, oil painting, watercolour

pair *NOUN* **1** *a pair of earrings* ► set, set of two **2** *The guests drank to the happy pair.* ► couple, partners, husband and wife, man and wife **3** *The pair sang, one standing and the other at the piano.* ► couple, duo, two, twosome

pal *NOUN* (*informal*) *The boys had been pals since primary school.* ► friend, companion, (*informal*) mate, (*informal*) buddy, (*informal*) chum

palace *NOUN* *a royal palace open to the public* ► official residence, château, mansion, stately home, castle RELATED ADJECTIVE palatial

pale *ADJECTIVE* **1** *He frowned and turned pale.* ► pallid, white, wan, ashen, anaemic, sallow AN OPPOSITE IS flushed **2** *a pale shade of pink* ► light, soft, muted, pastel, faint, weak OPPOSITES ARE dark, strong **3** *a pale light* ► dim, weak, watery, feeble OPPOSITES ARE bright, strong

pally *ADJECTIVE* *The two men had become quite pally over the years.* ► friendly, close, on good terms, intimate, (*informal*) matey, (*informal*) chummy

palm *VERB* **palm off** *They palmed off the worst wines on their visitors.* ► foist, fob off, get rid of, dispose of, offload, (*more informal*) unload

paltry *ADJECTIVE* *All he gave was a paltry five pounds.* ► meagre, negligible, pitiful, miserable, modest, scanty, scant, sparse, (*more informal*) mingy, (*more informal*) measly OPPOSITES ARE generous, extravagant

pamper *VERB* *His mother tended to pamper him.* ► spoil, indulge, overindulge, cosset, mollycoddle, coddle, humour, pander to

a b c d e f g h i j k l m n o p q r s t u v w x y z

A B C D E F G H I J K L M N O P Q R S T U V W X Y Z

pamphlet *NOUN* **pamphlets** a leaflet or booklet giving information on a subject [from *Pamphilet*, the name of a long 12th-century poem in Latin]

pan *NOUN* **pans** **1** a wide container with a flat base, used for cooking etc. **2** something shaped like this **3** the bowl of a lavatory

pancake *NOUN* **pancakes** a thin round cake of batter fried on both sides

panda *NOUN* **pandas** a large bear-like black-and-white animal found in China

pandemonium *NOUN* uproar and complete confusion [from *Pandemonium*, John Milton's name for the capital of hell in his poem 'Paradise Lost', from *pan-* = all + **demon**]

pane *NOUN* **panes** a sheet of glass in a window

panel *NOUN* **panels** **1** a long flat piece of wood, metal, etc. that is part of a door, wall, piece of furniture, etc. **2** a flat board with controls or instruments on it **3** a group of people chosen to discuss or decide something
▷ **panelled** *ADJECTIVE* **panelling** *NOUN*

pang *NOUN* **pangs** a sudden sharp pain

panic *NOUN* sudden uncontrollable fear
▷ **panic-stricken** *ADJECTIVE* **panicky** *ADJECTIVE*

panic *VERB* **panics**, **panicking**, **panicked** fill or be filled with panic

panorama *NOUN* **panoramas** a view or picture of a wide area
▷ **panoramic** *ADJECTIVE*

pant *VERB* **pants**, **panting**, **panted** take short quick breaths, usually after running or working hard

panther *NOUN* **panthers** a leopard, especially a black one

pantomime *NOUN* **pantomimes** **1** a Christmas entertainment, usually based on a fairy tale **2** mime

pantry *NOUN* **pantries** a small room for storing food; a larder

pants *PLURAL NOUN* (*informal*) **1** underpants or knickers **2** (*American*) trousers

paper *NOUN* **papers** **1** a substance made in thin sheets from wood, rags, etc. and used for writing or printing or drawing on or for wrapping things **2** a newspaper **3** wallpaper **4** a document **5** a set of examination questions • *a history paper*

paper *VERB* **papers**, **papering**, **papered** cover a wall or room with wallpaper

paperback *NOUN* **paperbacks** a book with a thin flexible cover

papier mâché (pap- yay **mash**- ay) *NOUN* paper made into pulp and moulded to make models, ornaments, etc.

parable *NOUN* **parables** a story told to teach people something, especially one of those told by Jesus Christ

parabola (pa- **rab**- ol- a) *NOUN* **parabolas** a curve like the path of an object thrown into the air and falling down again
▷ **parabolic** *ADJECTIVE*

Thesaurus

pamphlet *NOUN a pamphlet on bee-keeping* ► leaflet, brochure, booklet, handout, folder, notice

pan *NOUN Fry the mushrooms and onions in a large pan.* ► frying-pan, saucepan, container, vessel, pot

pan *VERB* (*informal*) *The reviews all panned the film mercilessly.* ► criticize, attack, lambaste, censure, (*informal*) hammer, (*informal*) take apart, (*informal*) knock OPPOSITES ARE praise, commend, recommend

panache *NOUN Julian produced the flowers with all the panache of a successful conjuror.* ► confidence, enthusiasm, flourish, spirit, style, verve, zest

pandemonium *NOUN The meeting ended in pandemonium.* ► chaos, uproar, bedlam, mayhem, confusion, disorder, muddle

pander *VERB*
pander to *Susan was prepared to pander to some of their foibles, but there were limits.* ► gratify, indulge, satisfy, cater to

panel *NOUN* **1** *He stared at the control panel, looking for the right switch.* ► console, fascia, board **2** *The case will be decided by a panel of judges.* ► group, team, body, board, council, commission

panic *NOUN They rushed out in panic.* ► alarm, fright, fear, trepidation, consternation, horror, terror, frenzy

panic *VERB There is no need to panic yet.* ► be alarmed, take fright, lose your head, lose your nerve, overreact, (*more informal*) flap

panicky *ADJECTIVE Her voice became breathless and panicky.* ► panic-stricken, alarmed, frantic, hysterical, frightened, overexcited, terror-stricken, unnerved AN OPPOSITE IS calm

pants *NOUN a pair of pants* ► underpants, briefs, trunks, shorts, (*for men*) boxer shorts, (*for men*) Y-fronts, (*for women*) panties, (*for women*) knickers

paper *NOUN* **1** *They had to show their papers at the border.* ► document, credentials, identification, authorization, certificate **2** *I'll go and buy a paper.* ► newspaper, daily, broadsheet (= large newspaper), tabloid (= small newspaper), magazine **3** *Her father was writing a paper for a medical journal.* ► article, essay, study, lecture, dissertation, thesis

parachute *NOUN* **parachutes** an umbrella-like device on which people or things can float slowly to the ground from an aircraft
▷ **parachute** *VERB* **parachutist** *NOUN*

parade *NOUN* **parades** **1** a procession that displays people or things **2** an assembly of troops for inspection, drill, etc.; a ground for this **3** a public square, promenade, or row of shops

parade *VERB* **parades, parading, paraded** **1** move in a parade **2** assemble for a parade

paradise *NOUN* **1** heaven; a heavenly place **2** the Garden of Eden

paradox *NOUN* **paradoxes** a statement that seems to contradict itself but is in fact true
▷ **paradoxical** *ADJECTIVE* **paradoxically** *ADVERB*

paraffin *NOUN* a kind of oil used as fuel

paragraph *NOUN* **paragraphs** one or more sentences on a single subject, forming a section of a piece of writing and beginning on a new line, usually slightly in from the margin of the page

parallel *ADJECTIVE* **1** (said about lines etc.) side by side and the same distance apart from each other for their whole length, like railway lines **2** similar or corresponding • *When petrol prices rise there is a parallel rise in bus fares.*
▷ **parallelism** *NOUN*

parallel *NOUN* **parallels** **1** something similar or corresponding **2** a comparison • *You can draw a parallel between the two situations.* **3** a line that is parallel to another **4** a line of latitude
USAGE Take care with the spelling of this word: one 'r', two 'l's, then one 'l'.

parallelogram *NOUN* **parallelograms** a quadrilateral with its opposite sides equal and parallel

paralyse *VERB* **paralyses, paralysing, paralysed** **1** cause paralysis in a person etc. **2** make something be unable to move • *She was paralysed with fear.*

paralysis *NOUN* being unable to move, especially because of a disease or an injury to the nerves
▷ **paralytic** (pa- ra- lit- ik) *ADJECTIVE*

paramedic *NOUN* **paramedics** a person who is trained to do medical work, especially emergency first aid, but is not a fully qualified doctor

parameter (pa- ram- it- er) *NOUN* **parameters** a quantity, quality, or factor that is variable and affects other things by its changes
USAGE Do not confuse with **perimeter**.

paramount *ADJECTIVE* more important than anything else • *Secrecy is paramount.*

parapet *NOUN* **parapets** a low wall along the edge of a balcony, bridge, roof, etc.

paraphernalia *NOUN* numerous pieces of equipment, belongings, etc.

paraphrase *VERB* **paraphrases, paraphrasing, paraphrased** give the meaning of something by using different words
▷ **paraphrase** *NOUN*

parasite *NOUN* **parasites** an animal or plant that lives in or on another, from which it gets its food
▷ **parasitic** *ADJECTIVE*
[from Greek *parasitos* = guest at a meal]

paratroops *PLURAL NOUN* troops trained to be dropped from aircraft by parachute
▷ **paratrooper** *NOUN*

parcel *NOUN* **parcels** something wrapped up to be sent by post or carried

Thesaurus

parade *NOUN a military parade* ► procession, march, cavalcade, spectacle, display, pageant, review, show

parade *VERB* **1** *The teams will parade through the city.* ► process, troop, march past **2** *He paraded up and down in the corridor.* ► stride, strut, walk **3** *She was eager to parade her knowledge.* ► display, show off, demonstrate, exhibit, make a show of

paradise *NOUN* **1** *non-Christian theories about Paradise* ► heaven, Utopia, Eden, Elysium, nirvana **2** *Their holiday had been absolute paradise.* ► bliss, heaven, joy, delight, ecstasy

parallel *VERB Their lives parallel each other in many respects.* ► resemble, match, be similar to, compare with, correspond to

paralyse *VERB* **1** *The injury paralysed his right leg for a time.* ► disable, immobilize, cripple, incapacitate, deaden **2** *The country was paralysed by a wave of strikes.* ► bring to a standstill, immobilize, bring to a halt, cripple, halt, freeze

paralysed *ADJECTIVE I had a paralysed right arm.* ► disabled, handicapped, incapacitated, immobilized, crippled, lame, unusable

paralysis *NOUN* **1** *a disease that can cause paralysis* ► immobility, incapacity, paraplegia **2** *paralysis of the country's transport system* ► shutdown, immobilization, stopping, standstill

parameter *NOUN It is important to define the parameters for this research.* ► criterion, guideline, framework, limit, boundary

paramount *ADJECTIVE an issue of paramount importance* ► supreme, prime, primary, central, pre-eminent, highest, cardinal, foremost, utmost

parcel *NOUN a parcel of food* ► package, packet, pack, consignment, bale, bundle, carton

A B C D E F G H I J K L M N O P Q R S T U V W X Y Z

parcel VERB **parcels, parcelling, parcelled**
1 wrap something up as a parcel **2** divide something into portions • *parcel out the work* [from old French, related to **particle**]

parched ADJECTIVE very dry or thirsty

parchment NOUN **parchments** a kind of heavy paper, originally made from animal skins [from the city of Pergamum, now in Turkey, where parchment was made in ancient times]

pardon NOUN **1** forgiveness **2** the cancelling of a punishment • *a free pardon*

pardon VERB **pardons, pardoning, pardoned**
1 forgive or excuse somebody **2** cancel a person's punishment
▷ **pardonable** ADJECTIVE **pardonably** ADVERB

pardon INTERJECTION used to mean 'I didn't hear or understand what you said'

parent NOUN **parents 1** a father or mother; a living thing that has produced others of its kind **2** a source from which others are derived • *the parent company*
▷ **parenthood** NOUN **parenting** NOUN
parental (pa-rent-al) ADJECTIVE

parenthesis (pa-ren-thi-sis) NOUN **parentheses 1** something extra that is inserted in a sentence, usually between brackets or dashes **2** either of the pair of brackets (like these) used to mark off words from the rest of a sentence
▷ **parenthetical** ADJECTIVE

parish NOUN **parishes** a district with its own church
▷ **parishioner** NOUN
[from Greek *paroikia* = neighbourhood]

park NOUN **parks 1** a large garden or recreation ground for public use **2** an area of grassland or woodland belonging to a country house

park VERB **parks, parking, parked** leave a vehicle somewhere for a time

parliament NOUN **parliaments** the assembly that makes a country's laws
▷ **parliamentary** ADJECTIVE
[from early French *parlement* = speaking]

parlour NOUN **parlours** (*old use*) a sitting room

parody NOUN **parodies** an amusing imitation of the style of a writer, composer, literary work, etc.

parody VERB **parodies, parodying, parodied** make or be a parody of a person or thing

parole NOUN the release of a prisoner before the end of his or her sentence on condition of good behaviour • *He was on parole.*
▷ **parole** VERB

paroxysm (pa-roks-izm) NOUN **paroxysms** a sudden outburst of rage, jealousy, laughter, etc.

parrot NOUN **parrots** a brightly coloured tropical bird that can learn to repeat words etc.

parsley NOUN a plant with crinkled green leaves used to flavour and decorate food

parsnip NOUN **parsnips** a plant with a pointed pale yellow root used as a vegetable

parson NOUN **parsons** a member of the clergy, especially a rector or vicar

part NOUN **parts 1** some but not all of a thing or number of things; anything that belongs to something bigger **2** the character played by an actor or actress **3** the words spoken by a character in a play **4** how much a person or thing is involved in something • *She played a huge part in her daughter's success.* **5** one side in

Thesaurus

parcel VERB **parcel out** *Land was parcelled out in small plots.* ► divide up, distribute, share out, apportion, portion out, split up

pardon VERB **1** *The king would pardon them if they admitted their guilt.* ► forgive, excuse, absolve, grant a pardon to, reprieve, amnesty, acquit AN OPPOSITE IS punish **2** *These are faults we can forgive and even admire.* ► forgive, excuse, condone

pardon NOUN *A pardon was offered to the rebels.* ► amnesty, reprieve, release, discharge

parent NOUN *She had an elderly parent to look after.* ► mother *or* father, guardian

parentage NOUN *a young man of Indian parentage* ► origin, ancestry, lineage, pedigree, extraction, descent, heredity, roots, stock, derivation, blood, ancestors, forebears

park NOUN *The children went off to play in the park.* ► recreation ground, public gardens, playground, parkland

park VERB *She parked the car outside her friend's house.* ► leave, position, station, stop, place

parliament NOUN *The country's parliament dates back to the Middle Ages.* ► legislature, congress, assembly, council, government, senate, conclave, convocation

parody NOUN **1** *He swivelled his hips in a parody of the belly dance.* ► caricature, lampoon, comic imitation, mimicry, mockery, skit, (*more informal*) take-off, (*more informal*) spoof, (*more informal*) send-up **2** *The article was no more than a parody of the truth.* ► travesty, distortion, mockery, caricature

parson NOUN *The parson shook hands outside the church.* ► clergyman, clergywoman, cleric, minister, priest, vicar, preacher

part NOUN **1** *This is only one part of the story.* ► bit, piece, portion, segment, section, episode, chapter, constituent
OPPOSITES ARE whole, entirety **2** *A part of the house had been closed off.* ► section, portion

an agreement or in a dispute or quarrel
take in good part not be offended at something
take part join in an activity

part *VERB* **parts, parting, parted** separate or divide
part with give away or get rid of something

part exchange *NOUN* giving something that you own as part of the price of what you are buying

partial *ADJECTIVE* **1** not complete or total • *a partial eclipse* **2** favouring one side more than the other; biased or unfair
▷ **partially** *ADVERB* **partiality** *NOUN*
be partial to be fond of something

participate *VERB* **participates, participating, participated** take part or have a share in something
▷ **participant** *NOUN* **participation** *NOUN* **participator** *NOUN*

participle *NOUN* **participles** a word formed from a verb (e.g. *gone, going; guided, guiding*) and used with an auxiliary verb to form certain tenses (e.g. *It has gone. It is going.*) or the passive (e.g. *We were guided to our seats*), or as an adjective (e.g. *a guided missile; a guiding light*) The **past participle** (e.g. *gone, guided*). describes a completed action or past condition. The **present participle** (which ends in **-ing**) describes a continuing action or condition.

particle *NOUN* **particles** a very small piece or amount

particular *ADJECTIVE* **1** of this one and no other; individual • *This particular stamp is very rare.* **2** special • *Take particular care of it.* **3** giving something close attention; choosing carefully • *He is very particular about his clothes.*
▷ **particularly** *ADVERB* **particularity** *NOUN*

particular *NOUN* **particulars** a detail or single fact • *Can you give me some particulars of the job?*
in particular 1 especially • *We liked this one in particular.* **2** special • *We did nothing in particular.*

parting *NOUN* **partings 1** leaving or separation **2** a line where hair is combed away in different directions

partisan *NOUN* **partisans 1** a strong supporter of a party or group etc. **2** a member of an

Thesaurus

3 *The washing machine has broken and needs a new part.* ► component, element, unit **4** *Deborah would take the lead part in the school play.* ► role, character **5** *Her parents lived in another part of town.* ► region, district, neighbourhood, quarter, section, sector **6** *Their part in the affair had not been very distinguished.* ► involvement, role, function, concern, responsibility, contribution (to)

part *VERB* **1** *They did not want to part on such bad terms.* ► separate, leave, say goodbye, say farewell, break up, go away OPPOSITES ARE meet, reunite **2** *The authorities are anxious not to part the children.* ► separate, divide, split
part with *advertising designed to persuade shoppers to part with their money.* ► give up, relinquish, hand over, let go of, give up, forgo, surrender, discard

partial *ADJECTIVE* **1** *The economic collapse was followed by a partial recovery.* ► incomplete, qualified, limited, restricted, imperfect, unfinished AN OPPOSITE IS complete
be partial to *She had always been partial to a cream tea.* ► like, love, enjoy, be fond of, have a fondness for, be keen on, appreciate, (*more informal*) go for

particle *NOUN* *There was not a single particle of food left.* ► bit, piece, morsel, scrap, shred, crumb, drop, fragment, grain, iota, jot, sliver, speck

particular *ADJECTIVE* **1** *The article criticized a particular group of companies.* ► specific, certain, distinct, definite, discrete **2** *This is a matter of particular interest to us.* ► special, exceptional, marked, unusual, uncommon, noteworthy, remarkable **3** *He was not too particular about the methods they used.* ► fussy, discriminating, finicky, fastidious, (*more informal*) choosy

particulars *PLURAL NOUN* *A police officer will call to take your particulars.* ► details, facts, information, circumstances

particularly *ADVERB* *The river trip is particularly enjoyable.* ► especially, exceptionally, remarkably, unusually, distinctly, notably

parting *NOUN* **1** *It will be an emotional parting.* ► farewell, goodbye, departure, leaving OPPOSITES ARE meeting, reunion **2** *They would tell their son and daughter that evening about their intended parting.* ► separation, breakup, split-up, divorce AN OPPOSITE IS reconciliation

partisan *NOUN* *The country was swarming with Tito's partisans.* ► supporter, follower, adherent, devotee, champion, guerrilla, fighter

partisan *ADJECTIVE* *the bitterly partisan nature of the debate* ► biased, one-sided, prejudiced, coloured, partial, slanted, factional

a b c d e f g h i j k l m n o p q r s t u v w x y z

organization resisting the authorities in a conquered country

partition *NOUN* **partitions** **1** a thin wall that divides a room or space **2** dividing something, especially a country, into separate parts

partition *VERB* **partitions**, **partitioning**, **partitioned** **1** divide something into separate parts **2** divide a room or space by means of a partition

partly *ADVERB* to some extent but not completely

partner *NOUN* **partners** **1** one of a pair of people who do something together, such as dancing or playing a game **2** a person who jointly owns a business with one or more other people **3** the person that someone is married to or is having a sexual relationship with
▷ **partnership** *NOUN*

part of speech *NOUN* **parts of speech** any of the groups (also called **word classes**) into which words are divided in grammar (noun, pronoun, adjective, verb, adverb, preposition, conjunction, and interjection)

partridge *NOUN* **partridges** a game bird with brown feathers

part-time *ADJECTIVE*, *ADVERB* working for only some of the normal hours
▷ **part-timer** *NOUN*

party *NOUN* **parties** **1** a gathering of people to enjoy themselves • *a birthday party* **2** a group working or travelling together **3** an organized group of people with similar political beliefs • *the Labour Party* **4** a person who is involved in an action or lawsuit etc. • *the guilty party*

pass *VERB* **passes**, **passing**, **passed** **1** go past something; go or move in a certain direction **2** move something in a certain direction • *Pass the cord through the ring.* **3** give or transfer something to another person • *Could you pass the butter?* **4** (in ball games) kick or throw the ball to another player of your own side **5** be successful in a test or examination **6** approve or accept • *They passed a law.* **7** occupy time • *They passed several hours chatting together.* **8** happen • *We heard what passed when they met.* **9** come to an end **10** utter • *Pass a remark.* **11** (in a game, quiz, etc.) let your turn go by or choose not to answer
pass out **1** complete your military training **2** faint

pass *NOUN* **passes** **1** passing something **2** a success in an examination **3** (in ball games)

Thesaurus

partition *NOUN* **1** *the partition of the country after the war* ▸ division, dividing, splitting, breaking-up **2** *A partition separated the two parts of a room.* ▸ screen, panel, divider, barrier, dividing wall

partition *VERB* *A UN resolution partitioned the country into two states.* ▸ divide, split, subdivide, separate

partly *ADVERB* *The work was now partly finished* ▸ partially, in part, to some extent, up to a point

partner *NOUN* **1** *Jack had been his business partner for many years.* ▸ colleague, associate, collaborator, ally, confederate, comrade, companion **2** *Staff were encouraged to bring their partners to the party.* ▸ girlfriend *or* boyfriend, husband *or* wife, spouse, consort, mate

partnership *NOUN* **1** *a business partnership* ▸ company, firm, corporation, organization, syndicate, alliance, combination, cooperative, affiliation **2** *a partnership between nations* ▸ cooperation, association, coalition, collaboration

party *NOUN* **1** *a flat-warming party* ▸ celebration, gathering, festivity, function, merrymaking, (*humorous*) jollification, (*more informal*) get-together, (*more informal*) do **2** *a political party* ▸ faction, group, grouping, league, alliance, association, cabal, coalition **3** *a search party* ▸ team, crew, squad, company, group

pass *VERB* **1** *Lots of heavy traffic passed through the village.* ▸ drive, go, move, stream, progress **2** *She went to pass him the sugar and spilled it.* ▸ hand, give, deliver **3** *Eventually the storm passed.* ▸ blow over, go away, fade, fade away, disappear, come to an end **4** *As time passed he gradually forgot her.* ▸ elapse, go by, advance, progress, tick by
pass away *He passed away in his sleep.* ▸ die, pass on, lose your life, meet your end, breathe your last, expire
pass off *The meeting passed off without any trouble.* ▸ happen, take place, go off, occur, turn out
pass out *She must have passed out.* ▸ faint, lose consciousness, black out, (*more informal*) flake out
pass over *Perhaps we can pass over these mistakes.* ▸ disregard, overlook, ignore, forget, take no notice of, pay no attention to, discount
pass up *He was not one to pass up a chance of a free holiday.* ▸ forgo, reject, refuse, turn down, miss out on

pass *NOUN* **1** *a pass through the mountains* ▸ route, way, defile, gap, gorge, ravine, canyon **2** *Your pass will get you into all the city's museums.* ▸ permit, ticket, warrant, authority, authorization, licence

kicking or throwing the ball to another player of your own side **4** a permit to go in or out of a place **5** a route through a gap in a range of mountains **6** a critical state of affairs • *Things have come to a pretty pass!*

passage *NOUN* **passages 1** a way through something; a corridor **2** a journey by sea or air **3** a section of a piece of writing or music **4** passing • *the passage of time*
▷ **passageway** *NOUN*

passenger *NOUN* **passengers** a person who is driven or carried in a car, train, ship, or aircraft etc.

passer-by *NOUN* **passers-by** a person who happens to be going past something

passion *NOUN* **passions 1** strong emotion **2** great enthusiasm
the Passion the sufferings of Jesus Christ at the Crucifixion
[from Latin *passio* = suffering]

passionate *ADJECTIVE* full of passion
▷ **passionately** *ADVERB*

passive *ADJECTIVE* **1** not resisting or fighting against something **2** acted upon and not active **3** (in grammar, said about a form of a verb) used when the subject of the sentence receives the action, e.g. *was hit* in 'She was hit on the head'. COMPARE **active 4** (said about an activity) that you get the effect of because other people are doing it • *passive smoking*
▷ **passively** *ADVERB* **passiveness** *NOUN* **passivity** *NOUN*

Passover *NOUN* a Jewish religious festival commemorating the freeing of the Jews from slavery in Egypt [from *pass over*, because according to the Bible God spared the Jews from the fate which affected the Egyptians]

passport *NOUN* **passports** an official document that entitles the person holding it to travel abroad

password *NOUN* **passwords 1** a secret word or phrase used to distinguish friends from enemies **2** a word you need to key in to gain access to certain computer files

past *ADJECTIVE* of the time gone by • *during the past week*

Thesaurus

passable *ADJECTIVE* **1** *The food was no more than passable.* ► adequate, acceptable, satisfactory, tolerable, moderate, ordinary, sufficient, all right, fair, mediocre, middling, (*more informal*) so-so AN OPPOSITE IS unacceptable **2** *The road is passable again after being closed because of floods.* ► traversable, navigable, open, usable, unblocked, clear AN OPPOSITE IS impassable

passage *NOUN* **1** *the passage of time* ► passing, advance, course, march, progress, progression, moving on **2** *a sea passage* ► crossing, journey, voyage, trip, cruise, sail **3** *a narrow passage leading to the garden* ► corridor, passageway, walkway, thoroughfare, hallway, way through **4** *a passage between the two houses* ► alley, alleyway, path, pathway, way, lane, track **5** *a passage from The Amber Spyglass* ► excerpt, extract, section, episode, scene, paragraph, piece, quotation

passenger *NOUN* *Passengers were told to get out at the next station.* ► traveller, commuter, voyager, rider

passer-by *NOUN* *Passers-by stopped and looked.* ► bystander, onlooker, observer, spectator, watcher, witness, eyewitness

passing *ADJECTIVE* *a passing feeling of regret* ► brief, temporary, short-lived, transient, momentary, cursory, short

passion *NOUN* **1** *You could talk about your passion for hang-gliding.* ► fondness, enthusiasm, eagerness, keenness (on), mania, appetite, interest (in), fanaticism, zeal, craving, commitment (to) OPPOSITES ARE indifference (to), apathy **2** *He recalled the passion with which she had kissed him.* ► feeling, ardour, intensity, emotion, fervour, love, longing, craving, desire, excitement, fire, heat AN OPPOSITE IS detachment **3** *He spoke with a fierce passion.* ► emotion, feeling, vehemence, anger, rage, fury, frenzy, paroxysm OPPOSITES ARE coolness, indifference

passionate *ADJECTIVE* **1** *a passionate appeal for help* ► impassioned, emotional, heartfelt, intense, ardent, fervent, impulsive OPPOSITES ARE half-hearted, cool **2** *a passionate embrace* ► loving, amorous, sensual, (*more informal*) steamy AN OPPOSITE IS cold **3** *His passionate temperament got the better of him.* ► excitable, hot-blooded, intense, fiery, wild, violent OPPOSITES ARE placid, phlegmatic

passive *ADJECTIVE* **1** *a passive acceptance of hardship* ► submissive, resigned, compliant, impassive, docile, long-suffering, non-violent, indifferent, patient, unresisting OPPOSITES ARE active, lively **2** *Tim had played a passive role in the affair.* ► inactive, uninvolved, non-participating OPPOSITES ARE active, assertive

past *ADJECTIVE* *memories of past happiness* ► bygone, former, previous, earlier, ended, finished, gone, (*more informal*) over and done with OPPOSITES ARE present, future

A B C D E F G H I J K L M N O P Q R S T U V W X Y Z

past *NOUN* the time gone by

past *PREPOSITION* **1** beyond • *Walk past the school.* **2** after • *It is past midnight.*
past it (*slang*) too old to be able to do something

paste *NOUN* **pastes** **1** a soft, moist, and sticky substance **2** a glue, especially for paper **3** a soft edible mixture • *tomato paste* **4** a hard glassy substance used to make imitation jewellery

paste *VERB* **pastes**, **pasting**, **pasted** **1** stick something onto a surface by using paste **2** coat something with paste **3** (*slang*) beat or thrash someone

pastel *NOUN* **pastels** **1** a crayon that is like chalk **2** a light delicate colour

pasteurize *VERB* **pasteurizes**, **pasteurizing**, **pasteurized** purify milk by heating and then cooling it [named after Louis Pasteur, a 19th-century French scientist who invented the process]

pastille *NOUN* **pastilles** a small flavoured sweet for sucking

pastime *NOUN* **pastimes** something you do to make time pass pleasantly; a hobby or game

pastoral *ADJECTIVE* to do with country life • *a pastoral scene*

pastry *NOUN* **pastries** **1** dough made with flour, fat, and water, rolled flat and baked **2** something made of pastry

pasture *NOUN* **pastures** land covered with grass etc. that cattle, sheep, or horses can eat

pasture *VERB* **pastures**, **pasturing**, **pastured** put animals to graze in a pasture

pasty [1] (pas- tee) *NOUN* **pasties** pastry with a filling of meat and vegetables, baked without a dish to shape it

pasty [2] (pay- stee) *ADJECTIVE* looking pale and unhealthy

pat *VERB* **pats**, **patting**, **patted** tap gently with the hand open or with something flat

pat *NOUN* **pats** **1** a patting movement or sound **2** a small piece of butter or other soft substance
a pat on the back praise

patch *NOUN* **patches** **1** a piece of material or metal etc. put over a hole or damaged place **2** an area that is different from its surroundings **3** a piece of ground • *the cabbage patch* **4** a small area or piece of something • *There are patches of fog.*
not a patch on (*informal*) not nearly as good as

patch *VERB* **patches**, **patching**, **patched** put a patch on something
patch up **1** repair something roughly **2** settle a quarrel

patchwork *NOUN* needlework in which small pieces of different cloth are sewn edge to edge

patchy *ADJECTIVE* occurring in patches; uneven
▷ **patchily** *ADVERB* **patchiness** *NOUN*

Thesaurus

past *NOUN* *She was trying hard to forget the past.* ► antiquity, days gone by, history, old days, olden days, past times OPPOSITES ARE present, future

paste *NOUN* **1** *He used paste to fix his photos in an album.* ► glue, gum, adhesive, fixative **2** *Mix the ingredients into a smooth paste.* ► purée, spread, mixture, pulp

paste *VERB* *She was busy pasting wallpaper.* ► fix, fasten, glue, gum, hang

pastime *NOUN* *a time when art was a rich man's pastime* ► hobby, activity, recreation, diversion, amusement, entertainment, occupation, game, sport, relaxation

pastoral *ADJECTIVE* **1** *a pastoral scene of trees and cows* ► rural, rustic, country, outdoor, agrarian, bucolic, farming, idyllic
AN OPPOSITE IS urban **2** *the pastoral duties of a vicar's wife* ► ecclesiastical, priestly, parochial, ministerial, caring

pasty *ADJECTIVE* *a row of people with pasty faces* ► pale, pallid, white, wan, sickly, anaemic, unhealthy OPPOSITES ARE healthy, ruddy

pat *VERB* *Les leaned forward to pat her hand.* ► tap, touch, dab, stroke, rub, fondle

pat *ADJECTIVE* *His answers sounded pat, as if he'd rehearsed them.* ► glib, slick, facile, simplistic, smooth, unconvincing, perfunctory, superficial

pat *ADVERB* **1** *She trotted out her suggestion pat.* ► opportunely, at the right moment, in a timely way
off pat *They have the right language off pat.* ► by heart, by rote, word for word, parrot-fashion

patch *NOUN* **1** *old jeans covered in patches* ► mend, repair **2** *The family was going through a difficult patch.* ► period, time, spell, phase, stretch **3** *Harry had a vegetable patch up the road.* ► plot, piece of ground, strip, row, area

patch *VERB* *He had got someone to patch his jacket at the elbow.* ► mend, repair, reinforce, put a patch on, cover, darn, fix, sew up, stitch up

patchy *ADJECTIVE* **1** *They drove through stretches of patchy fog.* ► irregular, uneven, sporadic, intermittent, variable, erratic, inconsistent, unpredictable, bitty, changeable
AN OPPOSITE IS constant **2** *a piece of patchy grass* ► uneven, speckled, mottled, dappled, multicoloured **3** *Their story was patchy and confusing.* ► fragmentary, deficient, variable,

pâté (pat- ay) *NOUN* **pâtés** paste made of meat or fish

pâté de foie gras (pat- ay der fwah grah) *NOUN* a rich paste made from goose liver

patent (pat- ent, pay- tent) *NOUN* **patents** the official right given to an inventor to make or sell his or her invention and to prevent other people from copying it

patent *VERB* **patents, patenting, patented** get a patent for something

patent *ADJECTIVE* obvious
▷ **patently** *ADVERB*

paternal *ADJECTIVE* **1** to do with a father **2** fatherly
▷ **paternally** *ADVERB*

paternalistic *ADJECTIVE* treating people in a paternal way; providing for people's needs but giving them no responsibility
▷ **paternalism** *NOUN*

paternity *NOUN* **1** fatherhood **2** being the father of a particular baby

path *NOUN* **paths** **1** a narrow way along which people or animals can walk **2** a line along which a person or thing moves **3** a course of action

pathetic *ADJECTIVE* **1** making you feel pity or sympathy **2** miserably inadequate or useless
• *a pathetic attempt*
▷ **pathetically** *ADVERB*

pathos (pay- thoss) *NOUN* a quality of making people feel pity or sympathy

patience *NOUN* **1** being patient **2** a card game for one person

patient *ADJECTIVE* able to wait or put up with trouble or inconvenience without becoming anxious or angry
▷ **patiently** *ADVERB*

patient *NOUN* **patients** a person who has treatment from a doctor or dentist etc.

patio *NOUN* **patios** a paved area beside a house [from Spanish, = courtyard]

patriarch (pay- tree- ark) *NOUN* **patriarchs** **1** the male who is head of a family or tribe **2** a bishop of high rank in the Orthodox Christian churches
▷ **patriarchal** *ADJECTIVE*

patriot (pay- tree- ot, pat- ree- ot) *NOUN* **patriots** a person who loves his or her country and supports it loyally
▷ **patriotic** *ADJECTIVE* **patriotically** *ADVERB* **patriotism** *NOUN*

patrol *VERB* **patrols, patrolling, patrolled** walk or travel regularly over an area in order to guard it and see that all is well

patrol *NOUN* **patrols** **1** a patrolling group of people, ships, aircraft, etc. **2** a group of Scouts or Guides
on patrol patrolling

patron (pay- tron) *NOUN* **patrons** **1** someone who supports a person or cause with money or encouragement **2** a regular customer
▷ **patronage** (pat- ron- ij) *NOUN*

Thesaurus

limited, inadequate
OPPOSITES ARE comprehensive, complete

path *NOUN* **1** *a path by the railway line* ► footpath, pathway, track, alley, lane **2** *His path was blocked by the barricades.* ► way, route, course, passage, progress

pathetic *ADJECTIVE* **1** *a pathetic wave of the hand* ► pitiful, pitiable, poignant, plaintive, sad, touching, moving, affecting, distressing, heartrending, lamentable, wretched
2 (*informal*) *He added up his pathetic savings.* ► inadequate, paltry, meagre, feeble, derisory, miserable, wretched, worthless

patience *NOUN* **1** *Great care and patience is needed to avoid damaging the plants.* ► diligence, perseverance, persistence, self-control, stoicism, endurance, fortitude **2** *Will's behaviour was stretching their patience to the limit.* ► toleration, forbearance, composure, calmness, restraint, equanimity, resignation

patient *ADJECTIVE* **1** *She tried to be patient while her husband hunted for the key.* ► composed, calm, self-controlled, restrained, forbearing, indulgent, tolerant, lenient, understanding, forbearing, philosophical
OPPOSITES ARE impatient, intolerant **2** *The task called for a great deal of patient work.* ► diligent, persistent, persevering, tenacious, determined, dogged, resolved, purposeful

patient *NOUN* *the relation between doctor and patient* ► invalid, sick person, sufferer, case

patriotic *ADJECTIVE* *Many of his patriotic songs have a stirring lilt.* ► nationalistic, loyal, flag-waving, (*disapproving*) jingoistic, (*disapproving*) chauvinistic

patrol *NOUN* **1** *Security guards remain on patrol all night.* ► surveillance, watch, guard, duty **2** *A four-man patrol set off through the jungle.* ► guard, lookout, party, task force, convoy, detail

patrol *VERB* *Guards with dogs patrol the estate.* ► police, tour, inspect, keep watch on, be on patrol on, go the rounds of

patron *NOUN* **1** (*informal*) *a patron of the arts* ► sponsor, supporter, benefactor, champion, backer, defender **2** *Parking outside the shops is for patrons only.* ► client, customer, (*more informal*) regular

patronize (pat- ron- I'z) VERB **patronizes**, **patronizing**, **patronized** **1** be a regular customer of a particular shop, restaurant, etc. **2** talk to someone in a way that shows you think they are stupid or inferior to you

patter [1] NOUN a series of light tapping sounds

patter VERB **patters**, **pattering**, **pattered** make light tapping sounds • *Rain pattered on the window panes.*

patter [2] NOUN the quick talk of a comedian, conjuror, salesperson, etc. [originally = recite a prayer: from Latin *pater noster* = Our Father, the first words of a Christian prayer]

pattern NOUN **patterns** **1** a repeated arrangement of lines, shapes, or colours etc. **2** a thing to be copied in order to make something • *a dress pattern* **3** the regular way in which something happens • *Our French classes follow a set pattern.* **4** an excellent example or model
▷ **patterned** ADJECTIVE

paunch NOUN **paunches** a large belly

pauper NOUN **paupers** a person who is very poor

pause NOUN **pauses** a temporary stop in speaking or doing something

pause VERB **pauses**, **pausing**, **paused** **1** stop speaking or doing something for a short time **2** temporarily interrupt the playing of a CD, videotape, etc.

pave VERB **paves**, **paving**, **paved** lay a hard surface on a road or path etc.
▷ **paving stone** NOUN
pave the way prepare for something

pavement NOUN **pavements** a paved path along the side of a street

pavilion NOUN **pavilions** **1** a building for use by players and spectators etc., especially at a cricket ground **2** an ornamental building or shelter used for dances, concerts, exhibitions, etc.

paw NOUN **paws** the foot of an animal that has claws

paw VERB **paws**, **pawing**, **pawed** touch or scrape something with a hand or foot

pawn [1] NOUN **pawns** **1** the least valuable piece in chess **2** a person whose actions are controlled by somebody else

pawn [2] VERB **pawns**, **pawning**, **pawned** leave something with a pawnbroker as security for a loan

pawnbroker NOUN **pawnbrokers** a shopkeeper who lends money to people in return for objects that they leave as security
▷ **pawnshop** NOUN

Thesaurus

patronize VERB **1** *The parents of girls like Sally patronized the little shop.* ► do business with, be a customer of, frequent, shop at, buy from, deal with **2** *The nobility patronized music and the arts.* ► sponsor, support, finance, back, foster, encourage **3** *She accused them of patronizing her.* ► condescend to, talk down to, look down on, put down

patronizing ADJECTIVE *The British should learn to adopt a less patronizing tone.* ► condescending, supercilious, superior, disdainful, haughty, lofty, paternalistic, snobbish
OPPOSITES ARE humble, modest

patter VERB **1** *Rain pattered against the window.* ► beat, tap, rattle, clatter, pitter-patter **2** *The children pattered up to their rooms.* ► scurry, scamper, scuttle

patter NOUN **1** *the patter of feet* ► pattering, pitter-patter, scurrying, scuttling **2** *a salesman's patter* ► chatter, babble, line, (*more informal*) spiel

pattern NOUN **1** *patterns drawn in the sand* ► design, device, figure, motif, shape, figuration, arrangement, decoration, ornamentation **2** *Their actions might set a pattern* ► example, model, standard, guide, norm, original, precedent, archetype, criterion, prototype, sample, specimen **3** *The insects have a special behaviour pattern.* ► system, order, method, scheme

pauper NOUN *The revolution left the family almost paupers.* ► beggar, bankrupt, insolvent, down and out

pause VERB *She paused for a moment before going in.* ► hesitate, wait, stop, delay, halt, waver, hang back, break off, rest, have a pause

pause NOUN *There was a short pause while the band regrouped.* ► break, interruption, interval, delay, rest, wait, interlude, intermission, lull, stoppage, respite, stop, suspension, (*more informal*) breather

pave VERB *She decided to pave part of the garden to put a table on.* ► cover, concrete, flag, tile, asphalt
pave the way for *Tax cuts paved the way for an economic recovery.* ► prepare for, lay the foundations for, clear the way for, herald, precede

pavement NOUN *A parked car was blocking the pavement.* ► footpath, path, walkway, (*American*) sidewalk

paw NOUN *She stroked the cat's paw.* ► foot, pad

pay *VERB* **pays, paying, paid** **1** give money in return for goods or services **2** give what is owed • *pay your debts* • *pay the rent* **3** be profitable or worthwhile • *It pays to advertise* **4** give or express • *Try to pay attention* • *It's time we paid them a visit* • *He doesn't often pay people compliments* **5** suffer a penalty **6** let out a rope by loosening it gradually
▷ **payer** *NOUN*
pay off **1** pay in full what you owe **2** be worthwhile or have good results • *All the preparation she did really paid off.*
pay up pay the full amount you owe

pay *NOUN* salary or wages

payable *ADJECTIVE* that must be paid

payment *NOUN* **payments** **1** paying **2** money paid

payphone *NOUN* **payphones** a public telephone operated by coins or a card

PC *ABBREVIATION* **1** personal computer **2** police constable

PE *ABBREVIATION* physical education

pea *NOUN* **peas** the small round green seed of a climbing plant, growing inside a pod and used as a vegetable; the plant bearing these pods

peace *NOUN* **1** a time when there is no war, violence, or disorder **2** quietness and calm

peaceable *ADJECTIVE* fond of peace; not quarrelsome or warlike
▷ **peaceably** *ADVERB*

peaceful *ADJECTIVE* quiet and calm
▷ **peacefully** *ADVERB* **peacefulness** *NOUN*

peach *NOUN* **peaches** **1** a round soft juicy fruit with a pinkish or yellowish skin and a large stone **2** (*informal*) an extremely good thing • *a peach of a shot*

peacock *NOUN* **peacocks** a large male bird with a long brightly coloured tail that it can spread out like a fan
▷ **peahen** *NOUN*

peak *NOUN* **peaks** **1** a pointed top, especially of a mountain **2** the highest or most intense part of something • *Traffic reaches its peak at 5 p.m.* **3** the part of a cap that sticks out in front
▷ **peaked** *ADJECTIVE*

peak *VERB* **peaks, peaking, peaked** reach its highest point or value

peal *NOUN* **peals** **1** the loud ringing of a bell or set of bells **2** a loud burst of thunder or laughter

peal *VERB* **peals, pealing, pealed** (said about bells) ring loudly

Thesaurus

pay *NOUN* *Her pay would go up in April.* ► income, earnings, salary, wages, payment, (*more formal*) remuneration, (*more formal*) emolument

pay *VERB* **1** *I'd rather pay more and get a better machine.* ► spend, expend, pay out, part with, (*more informal*) shell out, (*more informal*) dish out **2** *He said he'd pay me for the broken window.* ► reimburse, recompense, refund, repay, pay back **3** *Stella is trying to pay her debts.* ► discharge, settle, pay off, meet, clear, honour **4** *I'll make them pay for this.* ► suffer, make amends, atone, answer **5** *It would pay us to wait until the new model comes out.* ► benefit, profit, be an advantage to

payment *NOUN* **1** *You can settle in six or twelve monthly payments.* ► instalment, contribution, remittance **2** *There is a discount for prompt payment.* ► settlement, remittance **3** *You get extra payment for working late.* ► pay, wages, income, remuneration

peace *NOUN* **1** *It's not easy to get any peace in this house.* ► tranquillity, calm, quiet, silence, relaxation, hush OPPOSITES ARE disturbance, noise **2** *The country longed for peace after years of civil unrest.* ► order, harmony, harmoniousness, non-violence AN OPPOSITE IS disorder **3** *A peace will be signed and the war ended.* ► armistice, truce, ceasefire, treaty, agreement, concord

peaceable *ADJECTIVE* *a peaceable nation* ► peace-loving, unwarlike, non-violent, pacific, peaceful, placid, conciliatory, cooperative, friendly, harmonious OPPOSITES ARE aggressive, warlike, belligerent

peaceful *ADJECTIVE* **1** *a peaceful part of the country* ► quiet, restful, serene, tranquil, secluded, undisturbed, unruffled, untroubled, calm, still, pleasant, relaxing, balmy OPPOSITES ARE noisy, troubled **2** *The country wants to resolve the dispute in a peaceful manner.* ► calm, cordial, amicable, friendly, orderly **3** *Tanya had a peaceful temperament.* ► serene, calm, placid, amicable, friendly, unruffled, pacific, gentle OPPOSITES ARE turbulent, agitated

peak *NOUN* **1** *the peaks of the mountains* ► summit, tip, top, crest, pinnacle, crown, point **2** *Ruth had reached the peak of her career.* ► height, highest point, zenith, acme, climax, culmination OPPOSITES ARE nadir, trough

peaky *ADJECTIVE* *Josh had been looking peaky all morning, and stayed at home.* ► pale, pallid, pasty, unwell, sickly, poorly, queasy, out of sorts

peal *NOUN* *a peal of bells* ► chime, carillon, ringing, clang

peal *VERB* *The bells pealed* ► chime, ring, toll, resound, resonate

a b c d e f g h i j k l m n o p q r s t u v w x y z

peanut *NOUN* **peanuts** a small round nut that grows in a pod in the ground

pear *NOUN* **pears** a juicy fruit that gets narrower near the stalk

pearl *NOUN* **pearls** a small shiny white ball found in the shells of some oysters and used as a jewel
▷ **pearly** *ADJECTIVE*

peasant *NOUN* **peasants** a person who belongs to a farming community, especially in poor areas of the world
▷ **peasantry** *NOUN*
[from Latin *paganus* = country dweller]

peat *NOUN* rotted plant material that can be dug out of the ground and used as fuel or in gardening
▷ **peaty** *ADJECTIVE*
[from Latin *peta*, probably from a Celtic word]

pebble *NOUN* **pebbles** a small round stone
▷ **pebbly** *ADJECTIVE*

peck *VERB* **pecks, pecking, pecked** **1** bite at something quickly with the beak **2** kiss someone lightly on the cheek

peck *NOUN* **pecks** **1** a quick bite by a bird **2** a light kiss on the cheek

peckish *ADJECTIVE* (*informal*) hungry

peculiar *ADJECTIVE* **1** strange or unusual **2** belonging to a particular person, place, or thing; restricted • *This custom is peculiar to this tribe.*
▷ **peculiarly** *ADVERB* **peculiarity** *NOUN*

pedal *NOUN* **pedals** a lever pressed by the foot to operate a bicycle, car, machine, etc. or in certain musical instruments

pedal *VERB* **pedals, pedalling, pedalled** use a pedal; move or work something, especially a bicycle, by means of pedals

pedantic *ADJECTIVE* too concerned with minor details or with sticking strictly to formal rules
▷ **pedantically** *ADVERB*

peddle *VERB* **peddles, peddling, peddled** **1** go from house to house selling goods **2** sell illegal drugs **3** try to get people to accept an idea, way of life, etc.

pedestal *NOUN* **pedestals** the raised base on which a statue or pillar etc. stands
put someone on a pedestal admire him or her greatly

pedestrian *NOUN* **pedestrians** a person who is walking

pedestrian *ADJECTIVE* ordinary and dull

pedestrian crossing *NOUN* **pedestrian crossings** a place where pedestrians can cross the road safely

pedigree *NOUN* **pedigrees** a list of a person's or animal's ancestors, especially to show how well an animal has been bred [from early French *pé de grue* = crane's foot (from the shape made by the lines on a family tree)]

pedlar *NOUN* **pedlars** a person who goes from house to house selling small things [from Middle English *ped* = a hamper or basket (in which a pedlar carried his goods)]

peel *NOUN* **peels** the skin of certain fruits and vegetables

peel *VERB* **peels, peeling, peeled** **1** remove the peel or covering from something **2** come off in strips or layers **3** lose a covering or skin

Thesaurus

peasant *NOUN* **1** *There were rows of peasants picking tomatoes in the fields.* ► countryman, rustic, farmhand, yokel **2** (*informal*) *He became angry and called them a bunch of peasants.* ► lout, oaf, bumpkin

peculiar *ADJECTIVE* **1** *Something peculiar was happening to her computer.* ► strange, odd, unusual, weird, curious, funny, extraordinary, bizarre, abnormal OPPOSITES ARE normal, ordinary **2** *By that stage of the journey we were all feeling a bit peculiar.* ► unwell, ill, sick, poorly, queasy, out of sorts **3** *Norman had his own peculiar way of doing things.* ► special, characteristic, distinctive, individual, particular, singular, unique, idiosyncratic, (*more informal*) wacky, (*more informal*) screwy

peculiarity *NOUN* **1** *Find out about the peculiarities of the local weather when you go abroad. He had a strange physical peculiarity.* ► oddity, peculiar *or* special feature, abnormality, foible, idiosyncrasy, quirk, trait, characteristic, eccentricity **2** *We will have to accept the peculiarity of this arrangement.* ► strangeness, abnormality, oddness, oddity, eccentricity, bizarreness

pedantic *ADJECTIVE* **1** *He has a pedantic style of writing.* ► academic, bookish, formal, humourless, learned, old-fashioned, pompous, scholarly, schoolmasterly, stilted AN OPPOSITE IS informal **2** *a pedantic application of the rules* ► inflexible, precise, strict, over-scrupulous, unimaginative, (*more informal*) nit-picking AN OPPOSITE IS flexible

peek *VERB* *A face peeked round the doorway.* ► peep, peer, glance, look

peek *NOUN* *He took a quick peek at the recipe.* ► peep, glance, glimpse, look

peel *NOUN* *Orange peel lay in a spiral on the table.* ► rind, skin, covering, zest

peel *VERB* *Jeff peeled an apple.* ► pare, skin, strip

peelings *PLURAL NOUN* strips of skin peeled from potatoes etc.

peep *VERB* **peeps, peeping, peeped** **1** look quickly or secretly **2** look through a narrow opening **3** come slowly or briefly into view • *The moon peeped out from behind the clouds.*
▷ **peep** *NOUN* **peephole** *NOUN*

peer[1] *VERB* **peers, peering, peered** look at something closely or with difficulty

peer[2] *NOUN* **peers** **1** a noble **2** someone who is equal to another in rank, merit, or age etc.
• *She had no peer.*
▷ **peeress** *NOUN* **peerage** *NOUN*

peer group *NOUN* **peer groups** a group of people of roughly the same age or status

peerless *ADJECTIVE* without an equal; better than the others

peevish *ADJECTIVE* irritable

peg *NOUN* **pegs** a piece of wood or metal or plastic for fastening things together or for hanging things on

peg *VERB* **pegs, pegging, pegged** **1** fix something with pegs **2** keep wages or prices at a fixed level
peg away work diligently; persevere
peg out (*slang*) die

Pekinese or **Pekingese** *NOUN* **Pekinese** or **Pekingese** a small kind of dog with short legs, a flat face, and long silky hair [from **Peking**, the old name of Beijing, the capital of China (where the breed came from)]

pelican *NOUN* **pelicans** a large bird with a pouch in its long beak for storing fish

pelican crossing *NOUN* **pelican crossings** a place where pedestrians can cross a street safely by operating lights that signal traffic to stop

pellet *NOUN* **pellets** a tiny ball of metal, food, paper, etc.

pelt[1] *VERB* **pelts, pelting, pelted** **1** throw a lot of things at someone **2** run fast **3** rain very hard
at full pelt as fast as possible

pelt[2] *NOUN* **pelts** an animal skin, especially with the fur still on it

pen[1] *NOUN* **pens** an instrument with a point for writing with ink

pen[2] *NOUN* **pens** an enclosure for cattle, sheep, hens, or other animals

pen *VERB* **pens, penning, penned** shut animals etc. into a pen or other enclosed space

penalize *VERB* **penalizes, penalizing, penalized** punish; give someone a penalty
▷ **penalization** *NOUN*

penalty *NOUN* **penalties** **1** a punishment **2** a point or advantage given to one side in a game when a member of the other side has broken a rule, e.g. a free kick at goal in football

pence *PLURAL NOUN* SEE **penny**

pencil *NOUN* **pencils** an instrument for drawing or writing, made of a thin stick of graphite or coloured chalk etc. enclosed in a cylinder of wood or metal

pendant *NOUN* **pendants** an ornament worn hanging on a cord or chain round the neck

pending *PREPOSITION* **1** until • *Please take charge, pending his return.* **2** during • *pending these discussions*

pending *ADJECTIVE* **1** waiting to be decided or settled **2** about to happen

Thesaurus

peep *VERB* *Jane peeped through the keyhole.* ► peek, peer, glance, look

peep *NOUN* *Have a peep at the baby.* ► peek, glance, glimpse, look

peer *VERB* *A woman peered at us from a corner of the room.* ► gaze, look, glance, squint, peep, peek

peeved *ADJECTIVE* *Paula still felt peeved about it.* ► annoyed, irritated, angry, cross, displeased, vexed, infuriated, incensed, enraged, (*more informal*) miffed, (*more informal*) put out
AN OPPOSITE IS pleased

peg *NOUN* *She put her coat on a peg.* ► hook, pin, spike, knob

peg *VERB* **1** *Make sure you peg the tent to the ground.* ► fasten, fix, secure, attach **2** *Prices will be pegged for six months.* ► fix, hold, hold down, keep down, freeze, control

pelt *VERB* **1** *The men were pelting each other with snowballs.* ► bombard, shower, attack, assail, batter **2** *It was pelting down outside.* ► pour, teem, rain cats and dogs **3** *The players pelted back to the dressing room.* ► rush, dash, run, hurry, sprint, charge, streak

pen *NOUN* **1** *sheep in a pen* ► enclosure, compound, paddock, stockade **2** *He wrote it down with a pen.* ► ballpoint, biro, felt-tipped pen, fountain pen

penalty *NOUN* *a fixed penalty for illegal parking* ► punishment, fine, forfeit
AN OPPOSITE IS reward

pendulum *NOUN* **pendulums** a weight hung so that it can swing to and fro, especially in the works of a clock

penetrate *VERB* **penetrates, penetrating, penetrated** make or find a way through or into something; pierce
▷ **penetration** *NOUN* **penetrative** *ADJECTIVE*

penfriend *NOUN* **penfriends** a friend you write to regularly without meeting

penguin *NOUN* **penguins** an Antarctic seabird that cannot fly but uses its wings as flippers for swimming

penicillin *NOUN* an antibiotic obtained from mould

peninsula *NOUN* **peninsulas** a piece of land that is almost surrounded by water
▷ **peninsular** *ADJECTIVE*
[from Latin *paene* = almost + *insula* = island]

penis (**peen**- iss) *NOUN* **penises** the part of the body with which a male urinates and has sexual intercourse

penitence *NOUN* regret for having done wrong
▷ **penitent** *ADJECTIVE* **penitently** *ADVERB*

penknife *NOUN* **penknives** a small folding knife

pen-name *NOUN* **pen-names** a name used by an author instead of his or her real name

penniless *ADJECTIVE* having no money; very poor

penny *NOUN* **pennies** *for separate coins,* **pence** *for a sum of money* **1** a British coin worth one hundredth of a pound **2** a former coin worth of a shilling

pension *NOUN* **pensions** an income consisting of regular payments made to someone who is retired, widowed, or disabled

pensioner *NOUN* **pensioners** a person who receives a pension

pentagon *NOUN* **pentagons** a flat shape with five sides and five angles
▷ **pentagonal** (pent- ag- on- al) *ADJECTIVE*
the Pentagon a five-sided building in Washington, headquarters of the leaders of the American armed forces
[from Greek *pente* = five + *gonia* = angle]

pentameter *NOUN* **pentameters** a line of verse with five rhythmic beats [from Greek *pente* = five + *metron* = measure]

pentathlon *NOUN* **pentathlons** an athletic contest consisting of five events [from Greek *pente* = five + *athlon* = contest]

Pentecost *NOUN* **1** the Jewish harvest festival, fifty days after Passover **2** Whit Sunday [from Greek *pentekoste* = fiftieth (day)]

pent-up *ADJECTIVE* shut in • *pent-up feelings*

penultimate *ADJECTIVE* last but one

peony *NOUN* **peonies** a plant with large round red, pink, or white flowers

people *PLURAL NOUN* human beings; persons, especially those belonging to a particular country, area, or group etc.

people *NOUN* **peoples** a community or nation • *a warlike people* • *the English-speaking peoples*

pepper *NOUN* **peppers** **1** a hot-tasting powder used to flavour food **2** a bright green, red, or yellow vegetable
▷ **peppery** *ADJECTIVE*

Thesaurus

penetrate *VERB* **1** *Make sure the screws do not penetrate the top surface of the shelf.* ► pierce, puncture, perforate, bore through, make a hole in **2** *An advance force penetrated the city's outer defences.* ► infiltrate, enter, get through, slip through, probe **3** *Damp had penetrated the stone-work.* ► impregnate, permeate, pervade, seep into

penetrating *ADJECTIVE* **1** *She looked away from his penetrating dark eyes.* ► piercing, probing, staring, sharp, keen **2** *The students asked some penetrating questions.* ► perceptive, sharp, acute, intelligent, incisive, profound, searching **3** *The silence was interrupted by a penetrating scream.* ► shrill, piercing, strident, ear-splitting, deafening

penniless *ADJECTIVE* *Epstein was a penniless student in Paris.* ► poor, impoverished, destitute, poverty-stricken, moneyless, (*more informal*) skint

people *NOUN* **1** *By mid-afternoon many people were hungry. People like to read books like these.* ► persons, individuals, human beings, humans, folk, mortals, humanity, humankind, mankind USAGE Note that *humanity, humankind,* and *mankind* are all singular nouns and you use a singular verb with them, e.g. *Humankind likes to read books like these.* **2** *The government will appeal to the people in a general election.* ► nation, electorate, voters, electors, community **3** *a shopping centre that serves the people of the area; a proud and brave people* ► populace, population, citizens, inhabitants, public, society, common people, community, electorate, nation RELATED ADJECTIVES ethnic, national **4** *Her people live in Ireland.* ► family, relatives, relations, parents, clan, kith and kin usage Note that *family* and *clan* are singular verbs but you can use a singular or plural verb with them, e.g. *Her family lives in Scotland* or *Her family live in Scotland.*

pep *NOUN* *The project needed a lot more pep.* ► energy, vigour, vitality, spirit, verve, exuberance, fizz

pep *VERB*
pep up *He added some herbs to pep up the flavour.* ► liven up, vitalize, enhance, intensify

pepper *VERB* **peppers, peppering, peppered** **1** sprinkle with pepper **2** pelt with many small objects

peppermint *NOUN* **peppermints** **1** a kind of mint used for flavouring **2** a sweet flavoured with this mint

per *PREPOSITION* for each • *The charge is £2 per person.*

perceive *VERB* **perceives, perceiving, perceived** see, notice, or understand something

per cent *ADVERB* for or in every hundred • *three per cent* (3%)

percentage *NOUN* **percentages** an amount or rate expressed as a proportion of 100

perceptible *ADJECTIVE* able to be seen or noticed
▷ **perceptibly** *ADVERB* **perceptibility** *NOUN*

perception *NOUN* **perceptions** the ability to see, notice, or understand something

perceptive *ADJECTIVE* quick to notice or understand things

perch[1] *NOUN* **perches** **1** a place where a bird sits or rests **2** a seat high up

perch *VERB* **perches, perching, perched** rest or place on a perch

perch[2] *NOUN* **perch** an edible freshwater fish

percolate *VERB* **percolates, percolating, percolated** flow through small holes or spaces
▷ **percolation** *NOUN*

percolator *NOUN* **percolators** a pot for making coffee, in which boiling water percolates through coffee grounds

percussion *NOUN* **1** musical instruments (e.g. drums or cymbals) played by being struck or shaken **2** the striking of one thing against another
▷ **percussive** *ADJECTIVE*

perdition *NOUN* eternal damnation

peregrine *NOUN* **peregrines** a kind of falcon

perennial *ADJECTIVE* lasting for many years; keeping on recurring
▷ **perennially** *ADVERB*

perennial *NOUN* **perennials** a plant that lives for many years

perfect (per- fikt) *ADJECTIVE* **1** so good that it cannot be made any better **2** complete • *a perfect stranger* **3** (in grammar, said about a tense of a verb) showing a completed action, e.g. *He has arrived.*
▷ **perfectly** *ADVERB*

perfect (per- **fekt**) *VERB* **perfects, perfecting, perfected** make a thing perfect
▷ **perfection** *NOUN*
to perfection perfectly

Thesaurus

perceive *VERB* **1** *Those in the room perceived voices outside.* ► hear, discern, distinguish, make out, notice, recognize, become aware of **2** *Some animals cannot perceive colour.* ► see, discern, distinguish, recognize, observe, identify **3** *I began to perceive her meaning.* ► understand, comprehend, apprehend, grasp, realize, sense, deduce, gather, know **4** *We all perceive the world in different ways.* ► regard, consider, view, judge, deem, think of, look on

perception *NOUN* **1** *The public's perception of the government's honesty has changed.* ► impression, consciousness, apprehension, sense, view, awareness, cognition, comprehension, understanding, recognition, sensation **2** *She speaks with great perception on these problems.* ► insight, perceptiveness, discernment, understanding, perspicacity, astuteness, shrewdness, intelligence, observation

perceptive *ADJECTIVE* *A few perceptive questions can liven up the interview.* ► discerning, astute, shrewd, intelligent, insightful, perspicacious OPPOSITES ARE obtuse, inept

perch *VERB* *A monkey came in and perched on a table.* ► sit, settle, rest, balance, alight

perfect *ADJECTIVE* (with the stress on *per-*) **1** *It was the start to a perfect day.* ► superb, excellent, superlative, wonderful, marvellous, idyllic, blissful **2** *a second-hand book in perfect condition* ► impeccable, flawless, immaculate, spotless, pristine OPPOSITES ARE imperfect, flawed **3** *a copy so perfect you can't tell it from the original* ► exact, precise, faithful, accurate, true, close AN OPPOSITE IS inaccurate **4** *A digital radio will make a perfect birthday present.* ► ideal, suitable, fitting, apt, appropriate, OPPOSITES ARE unsuitable, inappropriate **5** *He felt a perfect fool. They had never met; they were perfect strangers.* ► complete, absolute, utter, total, entire, thoroughgoing

perfect *VERB* (with the stress on *-fect*) *He is spending some time perfecting his speech.* ► improve, make perfect, refine, complete, finish, fulfil, realize

perfection *NOUN* **1** *the perfection of her complexion* ► faultlessness, flawlessness, excellence, beauty, completeness, ideal, wholeness AN OPPOSITE IS imperfection **2** *the perfection of their plans* ► completion, consummation, fulfilment, realization, accomplishment, fruition, achievement

a b c d e f g h i j k l m n o p q r s t u v w x y z

A B C D E F G H I J K L M N O P Q R S T U V W X Y Z

perfectionist *NOUN* **perfectionists** a person who is only satisfied if something is done perfectly

perforate *VERB* **perforates, perforating, perforated** **1** make tiny holes in something, especially so that it can be torn off easily **2** pierce
▷ **perforated** *ADJECTIVE* **perforation** *NOUN*

perform *VERB* **performs, performing, performed** **1** do something in front of an audience • *The school will perform a play.* **2** do or carry out something • *Surgeons had to perform an emergency operation.*
▷ **performance** *NOUN* **performer** *NOUN*

perfume *NOUN* **perfumes** **1** a pleasant smell **2** a liquid for giving something a pleasant smell; scent
▷ **perfume** *VERB* **perfumery** *NOUN*
[originally used of pleasant-smelling smoke from something burning: via French from old Italian *parfumare* = to smoke through]

perfunctory *ADJECTIVE* done without much care or interest • *a perfunctory glance*
▷ **perfunctorily** *ADVERB*

perhaps *ADVERB* it may be; possibly

peril *NOUN* **perils** danger
▷ **perilous** *ADJECTIVE* **perilously** *ADVERB*
at your peril at your own risk

perimeter *NOUN* **perimeters** **1** the outer edge or boundary of something **2** the distance round the edge
USAGE Do not confuse with **parameter**.

period *NOUN* **periods** **1** a length of time **2** the time allowed for a lesson in school **3** the time when a woman menstruates **4** (in punctuation) a full stop

periodic *ADJECTIVE* occurring at regular intervals
▷ **periodically** *ADVERB*

periodical *NOUN* **periodicals** a magazine published at regular intervals (e.g. monthly)

periodic table *NOUN* a table in which the chemical elements are arranged in order of increasing atomic number

periscope *NOUN* **periscopes** a device with a tube and mirrors with which a person in a trench or submarine etc. can see things that are otherwise out of sight

Thesaurus

perfectionist *NOUN* *He was such a perfectionist he wouldn't allow any mistakes.* ► idealist, purist, precisionist, (*more informal*) stickler

perfectly *ADVERB* **1** *He brought in a perfectly baked cake.* ► superbly, impeccably, faultlessly, flawlessly, beautifully, excellently **2** *I'm perfectly happy to let them use the house. He can be perfectly horrid at times.* ► absolutely, completely, entirely, totally, utterly **3** *You know perfectly well what I mean.* ► very, quite, full, (*more informal*) jolly

perform *VERB* **1** *The two devices perform the same function. She has her duties to perform.* ► fulfil, exercise, carry out, execute, discharge, accomplish, achieve **2** *The company formed the new play in London.* ► present, stage, put on, produce, mount **3** *The speakers perform best at a fairly high volume.* ► function, operate, work, behave

performance *NOUN* **1** *the performance of their duties* ► execution, carrying out, discharge, accomplishment, fulfilment, completion, implementation **2** *The music received a fine performance.* ► rendition, interpretation, rendering, account **3** *The review praised the new range of cars for their performance.* ► operation, running, functioning, behaviour **4** *He made a huge performance of thanking them.* ► fuss, exhibition, act, scene, parade

performer *NOUN* *The song was sung by the original performers.* ► singer, entertainer, artist, artiste, musician, player, star, actor, actress

perfume *NOUN* **1** *With a final spray of exotic perfume she left the room.* ► scent, toilet water, eau de cologne **2** *the fresh, sweet perfume of roses* ► smell , scent, fragrance, aroma, odour, whiff

perfunctory *ADJECTIVE* *They greeted each other with perfunctory grunts.* ► cursory, desultory, fleeting, casual, hurried, offhand, half-hearted, unthinking, mechanical, automatic
OPPOSITES ARE enthusiastic, careful

perhaps *ADVERB* *Perhaps they took the train to Glasgow.* ► maybe, possibly, conceivably, feasibly

peril *NOUN* **1** *the perils of the sea* ► danger, hazard, risk, menace, uncertainty
OPPOSITES ARE security, safety
in peril *The climbers found themselves in great peril.* ► in danger, at risk, in jeopardy

perimeter *NOUN* **1** *The airport perimeter is closely guarded.* ► boundary, periphery, confines, edge, fringe, border, margin, borderline, bounds, circumference **2** *The perimeter is about twelve miles.*
► circumference, outer edge

period *NOUN* **1** *They suffered from several long periods of separation.* ► spell, interval, stretch, term, bout, run, span, phase, session **2** *the Hanoverian period of English history* ► age, era, years, epoch, time **3** *There was a double period of maths on Monday.* ► lesson, class, session

perish *VERB* **perishes, perishing, perished**
1 die; be destroyed **2** rot • *The rubber ring has perished.*
▷ **perishable** *ADJECTIVE*

perjure *VERB* **perjures, perjuring, perjured**
perjure yourself commit perjury

perjury *NOUN* telling a lie while you are on oath to speak the truth

perk[1] *VERB* **perks, perking, perked**
perk up make or become more cheerful

perk[2] *NOUN* **perks** (*informal*) something extra given to a worker • *Free bus travel is one of the perks of the job.*

perky *ADJECTIVE* lively and cheerful
▷ **perkily** *ADVERB*

perm or **permanent wave** *NOUN*
permanent waves treatment of the hair to give it long-lasting waves

permafrost *NOUN* a permanently frozen layer of soil in polar regions

permanent *ADJECTIVE* lasting for always or for a very long time
▷ **permanently** *ADVERB* **permanence** *NOUN*

permeate *VERB* **permeates, permeating, permeated** spread into every part of something; pervade • *Smoke had permeated the hall.*
▷ **permeation** *NOUN*

permissible *ADJECTIVE* permitted or allowed

permission *NOUN* the right to do something, given by someone in authority; authorization

permissive *ADJECTIVE* letting people do what they wish; tolerant or liberal

permit (per- mit) *VERB* **permits, permitting, permitted** give permission or consent or a chance to do something; allow

permit (per- mit) *NOUN* **permits** written or printed permission to do something or go somewhere

permutation *NOUN* **permutations**
1 changing the order of a set of things **2** a changed order • *3, 1, 2 is a permutation of 1, 2, 3*

peroxide *NOUN* a chemical used for bleaching hair

perpendicular *ADJECTIVE* upright; at a right angle (90°) to a line or surface

perpetrate *VERB* **perpetrates, perpetrating, perpetrated** commit or be guilty of
• *perpetrate a crime*
▷ **perpetration** *NOUN* **perpetrator** *NOUN*

perpetual *ADJECTIVE* lasting for a long time; continual
▷ **perpetually** *ADVERB*

perplex *VERB* **perplexes, perplexing, perplexed** bewilder or puzzle somebody
▷ **perplexity** *NOUN*

Thesaurus

perish *VERB* **1** *Many people perished in the floods.* ► die, be killed, lose your life, pass away **2** *The tyres had started to perish.* ► decay, decompose, disintegrate, crumble away, rot

perk *NOUN* (*informal*) *company cars and other perks* ► benefit, extra, bonus, (*more formal*) perquisite, (*more informal*) plus

perk up *VERB* *He perked up when he saw Susan coming.* ► cheer up, liven up, brighten, take heart, pick up, bounce back

permanent *ADJECTIVE* **1** *We are looking for a permanent solution to the problem.* ► continuing, lasting, durable, fixed, long-term, unchangeable, irreversible, everlasting, perpetual, eternal **2** *Leslie has got his first permanent job.* ► stable, fixed, established, secure, firm

permission *NOUN* *We will need permission to miss the afternoon classes.* ► authorization, authority, leave, consent, approval, agreement, licence, assent, clearance, dispensation, (*more informal*) the go-ahead, (*informal*) the green light

permit *VERB* **1** *The authorities would not permit release of the documents.* ► allow, authorize, endorse, agree to, consent to, approve of, give permission for, sanction, license, tolerate OPPOSITES ARE prohibit, prevent, ban **2** *His club will permit him to play in the national side.* ► allow, authorize, give an opportunity, make it possible
OPPOSITES ARE forbid, prohibit (from)

permit *NOUN* *The warden asked to see his permit.* ► authorization, licence, pass, warrant, certification, passport, visa, charter

perpetual *ADJECTIVE* **1** *The Arctic is in almost perpetual daylight.* ► continuous, everlasting, eternal, non-stop AN OPPOSITE IS temporary **2** *the perpetual evolution of humanity* ► constant, permanent, continuous, ceaseless, eternal, unending, uninterrupted OPPOSITES ARE transitory, temporary **3** *Their perpetual rows upset the children.* ► continual, interminable, incessant, constant, eternal, endless, ceaseless OPPOSITES ARE occasional, intermittent

perplex *VERB* *a helpline that answers any questions that perplex you* ► baffle, bewilder, puzzle, mystify, confuse, bemuse, disconcert, confound, fox, (*more informal*) flummox, (*more informal*) floor

A B C D E F G H I J K L M N O P Q R S T U V W X Y Z

persecute *VERB* **persecutes**, **persecuting**, **persecuted** be continually cruel to somebody, especially because you disagree with his or her beliefs
▷ **persecution** *NOUN* **persecutor** *NOUN*

persevere *VERB* **perseveres**, **persevering**, **persevered** go on doing something even though it is difficult
▷ **perseverance** *NOUN*

Persian *ADJECTIVE* to do with Persia, a country in the Middle East now called Iran

Persian *NOUN* the language of Persia

persist *VERB* **persists**, **persisting**, **persisted** **1** continue firmly or obstinately • *She persists in breaking the rules.* **2** continue to exist • *The custom persists in some countries.*
▷ **persistent** *ADJECTIVE* **persistently** *ADVERB* **persistence** *NOUN* **persistency** *NOUN*

person *NOUN* **people** or **persons** **1** a human being; a man, woman, or child **2** (in grammar) any of the three groups of personal pronouns and forms taken by verbs The **first person** (= **I**, **me**, **we**, **us**) refers to the person(s) speaking; the **second person** (= **you**) refers to the person(s) spoken to; the **third person** (= **he**, **him**, **she**, **her**, **it**, **they**, **them**) refers to the person(s) spoken about
in person being actually present oneself • *She hopes to be there in person.*
[from Latin *persona* = mask used by an actor]

personal *ADJECTIVE* **1** belonging to, done by, or concerning a particular person • *personal belongings* **2** private • *We have personal business to discuss.* **3** criticizing a person's appearance, character, or private affairs • *making personal remarks*
▷ **personally** *ADVERB*
USAGE Do not confuse with **personnel**.

personal computer *NOUN* **personal computers** a small computer designed to be used by one person at a time

personality *NOUN* **personalities** **1** a person's character • *She has a cheerful personality.* **2** a well-known person • *a TV personality*

personify *VERB* **personifies**, **personifying**, **personified** represent a quality or idea etc. as a person
▷ **personification** *NOUN*

personnel *NOUN* the people employed by a firm or other large organization
USAGE Do not confuse with **personal**.

Thesaurus

persecute *VERB* **1** *In Rome, Christians were being persecuted by the Emperor Nero.* ► oppress, victimize, martyr, discriminate against, maltreat, ill-treat, tyrannize **2** *He thought everyone was persecuting him.* ► harass, hound, pester, pursue, bother, plague, torment, intimidate, bully, terrorize

persecution *NOUN* *victims of political persecution* ► oppression, victimization, discrimination, harassment, maltreatment, martyrdom, tyranny, abuse

perseverance *NOUN* *The job required perseverance and patience.* ► persistence, tenacity, determination, resolve, doggedness, diligence, dedication, application, commitment, endurance, stamina

persevere *VERB* *He decided to persevere, in spite of some early failures.* ► persist, continue, keep going, carry on, press on, endure, (*more informal*) soldier on, (*more informal*) hang on, (*more informal*) keep at it, (*informal*) stick at it, (*more informal*) plug away OPPOSITES ARE give up, stop

persist *VERB* **1** *The officer persisted with his questions.* ► persevere, continue, keep going, carry on, press on, endure, (*more informal*) soldier on, (*more informal*) hang on, (*more informal*) keep at it, (*informal*) stick at it, (*more informal*) plug away
OPPOSITES ARE desist, give up, stop **2** *If the pain persists, you should see a doctor.* ► continue, carry on, keep on, go on, linger, last, remain AN OPPOSITE IS cease **3 persist in** *He would persist in interrupting her.* ► keep on, insist on

persistent *ADJECTIVE* **1** *The company should respond to its more persistent critics.* ► determined, tenacious, persevering, resolute, single-minded **2** *They were interrupted by a persistent knocking at the door.* ► continuing, constant, steady, incessant, endless, non-stop

person *NOUN* *We must find the person responsible. She was the first person to arrive. There was not a person to be seen.* ► individual, man *or* woman, being, human being, soul, body

personal *ADJECTIVE* **1** *a story based on the author's personal experiences* ► own, individual, particular, special, exclusive
OPPOSITES ARE general, public **2** *The letter was marked 'personal'.* ► private, confidential, secret

personality *NOUN* **1** *He has a warmth of personality and a generous nature.* ► character, nature, disposition, temperament, identity, individuality, (*more informal*) make-up **2** *a television personality* ► celebrity, star, superstar, name

perspective *NOUN* **perspectives** **1** the impression of depth and space in a picture or scene **2** a person's point of view
in perspective giving a well-balanced view of things

perspire *VERB* **perspires, perspiring, perspired** sweat
▷ **perspiration** *NOUN*

persuade *VERB* **persuades, persuading, persuaded** make someone believe or agree to do something
▷ **persuasion** *NOUN* **persuasive** *ADJECTIVE*

pert *ADJECTIVE* cheeky
▷ **pertly** *ADVERB* **pertness** *NOUN*

perturb *VERB* **perturbs, perturbing, perturbed** worry someone
▷ **perturbation** *NOUN*

pervade *VERB* **pervades, pervading, pervaded** spread all through something
▷ **pervasion** *NOUN* **pervasive** *ADJECTIVE*

perverse *ADJECTIVE* obstinately doing something different from what is reasonable or required
▷ **perversely** *ADVERB* **perversity** *NOUN*

pervert (per- vert) *VERB* **perverts, perverting, perverted** **1** turn something from the right course of action • *By giving false evidence they perverted the course of justice.* **2** make a person behave wickedly or abnormally
▷ **perversion** *NOUN*

pervert (per- vert) *NOUN* **perverts** a person whose sexual behaviour is thought to be unnatural or disgusting

pessimist *NOUN* **pessimists** a person who expects that things will turn out badly COMPARE **optimist**
▷ **pessimism** *NOUN* **pessimistic** *ADJECTIVE* **pessimistically** *ADVERB*

pest *NOUN* **pests** **1** a destructive insect or animal, such as a locust or a mouse **2** a nuisance

pester *VERB* **pesters, pestering, pestered** keep annoying someone by frequent questions or requests

pesticide *NOUN* **pesticides** a substance for killing harmful insects and other pests

pestilence *NOUN* **pestilences** a deadly epidemic

pestle (pes- el) *NOUN* a heavy tool with a rounded end, used for crushing substances in a mortar [from Latin *pinsere* = to pound]

Thesaurus

perspective *NOUN* *Since the war we see history from a different perspective.* ► outlook, viewpoint, point of view, slant, view, angle
in perspective *To put this in perspective, ten percent of buyers admitted to being dissatisfied with what they had bought.* ► in context, in proportion

persuade *VERB* *Will you be able to persuade Susie to go back to England?* ► prevail on *or* upon, induce, coax, convince, make, entice, influence, pressure, pressurize, tempt, urge, bring round, cajole, inveigle, talk into
AN OPPOSITE IS dissuade

persuasion *NOUN* **1** *I shall need a lot of persuasion to change my mind.* ► persuading, coaxing, coercion, convincing, inducement, exhortation, cajolery, enticement, argument **2** *people with a wide range of political persuasions* ► belief, conviction, view, opinion, faith

persuasive *ADJECTIVE* *There's a lot of persuasive talk but not much action.* ► convincing, compelling, cogent, sound, valid, plausible, reasonable, forceful, strong, telling, credible, effective, eloquent, influential, logical, watertight OPPOSITES ARE unconvincing, unpersuasive

perverse *ADJECTIVE* *He has the perverse habit of calling all young girls 'madam' and all older women girls.* ► contrary, wayward, awkward, unreasonable, tiresome, capricious, wilful, obstinate, stubborn, unhelpful, rebellious
OPPOSITES ARE reasonable, obliging

pessimism *NOUN* *His pessimism prevented him from taking any risks.* ► despondency, fatalism, negativeness, hopelessness, gloom, despair, resignation, unhappiness, cynicism
AN OPPOSITE IS optimism

pessimistic *ADJECTIVE* *Manufacturers are pessimistic about the economic future.* ► negative, fatalistic, gloomy, downbeat, downhearted, unhopeful, defeatist, despairing, despondent, resigned, unhappy, cynical AN OPPOSITE IS optimistic

pest *NOUN* **1** *Vincent's demands for attention were becoming a pest.* ► nuisance, bother, annoyance, irritation, curse, trial, bore, bane, vexation, (*more informal*) pain, (*more informal*) pain in the neck **2** *the rise in crop pests* ► insect, bug, parasite, (*more informal*) creepy-crawly

pester *NOUN* *Claire was nice and didn't pester him with silly questions.* ► badger, harass, annoy, bother, irritate, nag, harry, chivvy, hound, trouble, besiege, (*more informal*) hassle, (*more informal*) bug, (*more informal*) keep on at, (*more informal*) go on at

pet *NOUN* **pets** **1** a tame animal kept for companionship and pleasure **2** a person treated as a favourite • *a teacher's pet*

pet *ADJECTIVE* favourite • *my pet subject*

pet *VERB* **pets, petting, petted** treat or fondle someone affectionately

petal *NOUN* **petals** one of the separate coloured outer parts of a flower

peter *VERB* **peters, petering, petered**
peter out become gradually less and cease to exist

petition *NOUN* **petitions** a formal request for something, especially a written one signed by many people

petrify *VERB* **petrifies, petrifying, petrified**
1 make someone so terrified that he or she cannot move **2** turn to stone
▷ **petrifaction** *NOUN*

petrol *NOUN* a liquid made from petroleum, used as fuel for engines

petroleum *NOUN* an oil found underground that is refined to make fuel (e.g. petrol or paraffin) or for use in dry-cleaning etc.

petticoat *NOUN* **petticoats** a woman's or girl's dress-length piece of underwear worn under a skirt or dress

petting *NOUN* affectionate touching or fondling

petty *ADJECTIVE* **pettier, pettiest** **1** unimportant or trivial • *petty regulations* **2** mean and small-minded
▷ **pettily** *ADVERB* **pettiness** *NOUN*

petty cash *NOUN* cash kept by an office for small payments

pew *NOUN* **pews** a long wooden seat, usually fixed in rows, in a church

pewter *NOUN* a grey alloy of tin and lead

pH *NOUN* a measure of the acidity or alkalinity of a solution Pure water has a pH of 7, acids have a pH between 0 and 7, and alkalis have a pH between 7 and 14

phantom *NOUN* **phantoms** **1** a ghost **2** something that does not really exist

Pharaoh (fair- oh) *NOUN* **Pharaohs** the title of the king of ancient Egypt

pharmacy *NOUN* **pharmacies** **1** a shop selling medicines; a dispensary **2** the job of preparing medicines

phase *NOUN* **phases** a stage in the progress or development of something

phase *VERB* **phases, phasing, phased** do something in stages, not all at once • *a phased withdrawal*

Ph.D. *ABBREVIATION* Doctor of Philosophy; a university degree awarded to someone who has done advanced research in their subject

pheasant (fez- ant) *NOUN* **pheasants** a game bird with a long tail

phenomenal *ADJECTIVE* amazing or remarkable
▷ **phenomenally** *ADVERB*

phenomenon *NOUN* **phenomena** an event or fact, especially one that is remarkable
USAGE Note that **phenomena** is a plural. It is incorrect to say 'this phenomena' or 'these phenomenas'.

Thesaurus

pet *NOUN* (*informal*) *They teased him and called him teacher's pet.* ► favourite, darling, treasure, blue-eyed boy *or* girl

pety *ADJECTIVE* **1** *Whoever heard of a pet rattlesnake?* ► tame, domestic **2** *The shop was very much his own pet scheme.* ► favourite, cherished, prized, precious, special, personal

pet *VERB* **1** *Kim sat holding the kitten and petting it.* ► pat, stroke, pamper, caress, cuddle, fondle, kiss, touch **2** *She wouldn't let boys pet her on their first date.* ► fondle, caress, kiss and cuddle

peter out *VERB* *The traffic began to peter out.* ► dwindle, diminish, decrease, subside, disappear, fall off, die out, wane, shrink

petition *NOUN* *a petition protesting at the new building plans* ► appeal, list of signatures, application, supplication, entreaty, plea

petty *ADJECTIVE* **1** *The meeting was called for petty reasons.* ► trivial, minor, trifling, unimportant, insignificant, slight, secondary, paltry **2** *The criticisms were unfair and petty.* ► spiteful, small-minded, vindictive, mean, ungenerous, grudging

petulant *ADJECTIVE* *He sounded as petulant as an obstinate child.* ► peevish, bad-tempered, irritable, fractious, irascible, fretful, touchy, sullen, snappy, crotchety OPPOSITES ARE good-humoured, agreeable

phantom *NOUN* **1** *a phantom that appeared at night* ► ghost, spectre, spirit, apparition, wraith, (*more informal*) spook **2** *He realized that what he had seen had been a phantom of his own mind.* ► hallucination, figment, illusion, delusion, vision **3** *a phantom pregnancy* ► imaginary, imagined, false, unreal

phase *NOUN* **1** *the final phase of the war* ► stage, part, period, step, chapter **2** *The marriage was going through a difficult phase.* ► period, stage, spell, time, state

phenomenal *ADJECTIVE* *Lutyens had a phenomenal memory for detail.* ► remarkable, extraordinary, outstanding, amazing, astonishing, astounding, staggering, sensational, breathtaking
OPPOSITES ARE ordinary, run-of-the-mill

phial *NOUN* **phials** a small glass bottle

philanthropy *NOUN* concern for fellow human beings, especially as shown by kind and generous acts that benefit large numbers of people
▷ **philanthropist** *NOUN* **philanthropic** *ADJECTIVE*

philistine (fil- ist- I'n) *NOUN* **philistines** a person who dislikes art, poetry, etc.

philosopher *NOUN* **philosophers** an expert in philosophy

philosophical *ADJECTIVE* **1** to do with philosophy **2** calm and not upset after a misfortune or disappointment • *Be philosophical about losing.*
▷ **philosophically** *ADVERB*

philosophy *NOUN* **philosophies** **1** the study of truths about life, morals, etc. **2** a set of ideas or principles or beliefs

phobia (foh- bee- a) *NOUN* **phobias** great or abnormal fear of something

phone *NOUN* **phones** a telephone

phone *VERB* **phones, phoning, phoned** telephone

phone-in *NOUN* **phone-ins** a radio or television programme in which people telephone the studio and take part in a discussion

phonetic (fon- et- ik) *ADJECTIVE* **1** to do with speech sounds **2** representing speech sounds
▷ **phonetically** *ADVERB*

phosphorus *NOUN* a chemical substance that glows in the dark

photo *NOUN* **photos** a photograph

photograph *NOUN* **photographs** a picture made by the effect of light or other radiation on film or special paper, using a camera

photograph *VERB* **photographs, photographing, photographed** take a photograph of a person or thing
▷ **photographer** *NOUN*

photography *NOUN* taking photographs
▷ **photographic** *ADJECTIVE*

photosynthesis *NOUN* the process by which green plants use sunlight to turn carbon dioxide and water into complex substances, giving off oxygen

phrase *NOUN* **phrases** **1** a group of words that form a unit in a sentence or clause, e.g. *in the garden* in 'The Queen was in the garden' **2** a short section of a tune

physical *ADJECTIVE* **1** to do with the body rather than the mind or feelings **2** to do with things that you can touch or see **3** to do with physics
▷ **physically** *ADVERB*

Thesaurus

philosophical *ADJECTIVE* **1** *a new approach to old philosophical ideas* ▸ theoretical, analytical, rational, reasoned, abstract, academic, metaphysical, ideological, intellectual, learned, logical, wise, erudite **2** *He felt in a philosophical mood.* ▸ thoughtful, reflective, contemplative, meditative, introspective, studious, ruminative **3** *Jane was philosophical about life's problems.* ▸ calm, composed, collected, resigned, unemotional, unruffled, stoical, self-possessed, patient
AN OPPOSITE IS emotional

philosophy *NOUN* **1** *a student of philosophy* ▸ thinking, reasoning, metaphysics, wisdom, knowledge, logic **2** *Taylor spent his life promoting his philosophy.* ▸ convictions, beliefs, ideology, principles, theories, credo, attitudes, viewpoint

phobia *NOUN* *He has a phobia about noise.* ▸ aversion (to), dread (of), fear (of) , anxiety, obsession, neurosis, revulsion, dislike (of), hatred (of), horror, (*more informal*) hang-up, (*more informal*) thing

phone *VERB* *She tried to phone home on her mobile.* ▸ call, ring, telephone, reach, dial

phoney *ADJECTIVE* *He gave a phoney name.* ▸ false, bogus, sham, fake, made-up, invented, fictitious, assumed, spurious
OPPOSITES ARE genuine, authentic

phoney *NOUN* *The lawyer was a phoney.* ▸ impostor, sham, fraud, fake, charlatan, swindler

photograph *NOUN* *She published her best photographs in a magazine.* ▸ photo, picture, snapshot, snap, image, print, slide, transparency

photograph *VERB* *I photographed them as people first and models second.* ▸ shoot, snap, take a picture of

phrase *NOUN* *He searched in his mind for the right phrase to describe his feelings.* ▸ expression, wording, group of words, form of words, construction, idiom

phrase *VERB* *She thought about how to phrase the question.* ▸ express, word, put in words, formulate, couch, frame, present

physical *ADJECTIVE* **1** *It is hard to describe his physical appearance* ▸ bodily, corporal, corporeal, carnal AN OPPOSITE IS mental **2** *our physical existence* ▸ earthly, material, mortal, terrestrial, tangible, fleshly, substantial
AN OPPOSITE IS spiritual

physical education or **physical training** *NOUN* exercises and sports done to keep the body healthy

physician *NOUN* **physicians** a doctor, especially one who is not a surgeon

physicist (fiz- i- sist) *NOUN* **physicists** an expert in physics

physics (fiz- iks) *NOUN* the study of the properties of matter and energy (e.g. heat, light, sound, movement) [from Greek *physikos* = natural]

physiotherapy (fiz- ee- o- therra- pee) *NOUN* the treatment of a disease or weakness by massage, exercises, etc.
▷ **physiotherapist** *NOUN*

physique (fiz- eek) *NOUN* **physiques** a person's build

pi *NOUN* the symbol (p) for the ratio of the circumference of a circle to its diameter The value of pi is approximately 3.14159

pianist *NOUN* **pianists** a person who plays the piano

piano *NOUN* **pianos** a large musical instrument with a keyboard

piccolo *NOUN* **piccolos** a small high-pitched flute

pick[1] *VERB* **picks, picking, picked 1** separate a flower or fruit from its plant • *We picked apples.* **2** choose; select carefully **3** pull bits off or out of something **4** open a lock by using something pointed, not with a key
pick a quarrel deliberately provoke a quarrel with somebody
pick holes in find fault with
pick on single someone out for criticism or unkind treatment
pick someone's pocket steal from it
pick up 1 lift or take up **2** collect **3** take someone into a vehicle **4** manage to hear something **5** get better or recover

pick *NOUN* **1** choice • *take your pick* **2** the best of a group

pick[2] *NOUN* **picks 1** a pickaxe **2** a plectrum

pickaxe *NOUN* **pickaxes** a heavy pointed tool with a long handle, used for breaking up hard ground etc.

picket *NOUN* **pickets 1** a striker or group of strikers who try to persuade other people not to go into a place of work during a strike **2** a pointed post as part of a fence

picket *VERB* **pickets, picketing, picketed** stand outside a place of work to try to persuade other people not to go in during a strike

pickle *NOUN* **pickles 1** a strong-tasting food made of pickled vegetables **2** (*informal*) a mess

pickle *VERB* **pickles, pickling, pickled** preserve food in vinegar or salt water

pickpocket *NOUN* **pickpockets** a thief who steals from people's pockets or bags

pick-up *NOUN* **pick-ups 1** an open truck for carrying small loads **2** the part of a record player that holds the stylus

picnic *NOUN* **picnics** a meal eaten in the open air away from home

picnic *VERB* **picnics, picnicking, picnicked** have a picnic
▷ **picnicker** *NOUN*

picture *NOUN* **pictures 1** a representation of a person or thing made by painting, drawing, or photography **2** a film at the cinema **3** how something seems; an impression
in the picture fully informed about something

picture *VERB* **pictures, picturing, pictured 1** show in a picture **2** imagine

Thesaurus

pick *VERB* **1** *We spent the afternoon picking fruit.* ► gather, collect, pluck, harvest, garner **2** *He picked a card and held it to his chest. Pick a time and place that suit you.* ► choose, select, take, decide on, opt for, settle on, fix on, single out
pick on *They are always picking on Freddie.* ► victimize, bully, persecute, tease, (*more informal*) get at
pick out *It was difficult to pick anything out in the fog.* ► see, discern, spot, distinguish, make out, recognize, identify
pick up 1 *It was too heavy to pick up.* ► lift, raise, take up, hoist **2** *You can pick up a bargain at the car-boot sales.* ► find, discover, obtain, acquire, get hold of, buy, purchase **3** *Lisa picked up some Spanish during her stay abroad.* ► learn, acquire, absorb, get to know, master **4** *He offered to pick up the children from school.* ► collect, fetch, go to get, call for **5** *The weather began to pick up.* ► improve, recover, get better, brighten **6** *Be careful you don't pick up an infection.* ► catch, contract, get, come down with

pick *NOUN* **1** *Take your pick.* ► choice, preference, selection, option **2** *the pick of the bunch* ► best, finest, prime, top, cream, choicest, élite

picture *NOUN* **1** *the famous picture of Bubbles* ► painting, portrait, likeness, portrayal, representation, depiction, profile, image **2** *Kevin wanted to take a picture of them.* ► photograph, snapshot, snap, shot

picture *VERB* **1** *Charles is pictured on the right receiving his prize.* ► depict, show, portray, illustrate, represent, delineate, outline **2** *I can picture him now, a thin tall figure smoking his pipe.* ► visualize, imagine, call to mind, see in your mind, conceive, envisage, think up

picturesque *ADJECTIVE* **1** forming an attractive scene • *a picturesque village* **2** vividly described; expressive • *picturesque language*
▷ **picturesquely** *ADVERB*

pie *NOUN* **pies** a baked dish of meat, fish, or fruit covered with pastry

piece *NOUN* **pieces** **1** a part or portion of something; a fragment **2** a separate thing or example • *a fine piece of work* **3** something written, composed, or painted etc. • *a piece of music* **4** one of the objects used to play a game on a board • *a chess piece* **5** a coin • *a 50p piece*

piece *VERB* **pieces, piecing, pieced** put pieces together to make something

piecemeal *ADJECTIVE, ADVERB* done or made one piece at a time

pie chart *NOUN* **pie charts** a circle divided into sectors to represent the way in which a quantity is divided up

pier *NOUN* **piers** **1** a long structure built out into the sea for people to walk on **2** a pillar supporting a bridge or arch

pierce *VERB* **pierces, piercing, pierced** make a hole through something; penetrate

piety *NOUN* being very religious and devout; piousness

pig *NOUN* **pigs** **1** a fat animal with short legs and a blunt snout, kept for its meat **2** (*informal*) someone greedy, dirty, or unpleasant
▷ **piggy** *ADJECTIVE, NOUN*

pigeon *NOUN* **pigeons** a bird with a fat body and a small head

pigeonhole *NOUN* **pigeonholes** a small compartment above a desk etc., used for holding letters or papers

piggyback *ADVERB* carried on somebody else's back or shoulders
▷ **piggyback** *NOUN*

pig-headed *ADJECTIVE* obstinate

piglet *NOUN* **piglets** a young pig

pigment *NOUN* **pigments** a substance that colours something
▷ **pigmented** *ADJECTIVE* **pigmentation** *NOUN*

pigsty *NOUN* **pigsties** **1** a partly covered pen for pigs **2** a filthy room or house

pigtail *NOUN* **pigtails** a plait of hair worn hanging at the back of the head

pike *NOUN* **pikes** **1** a heavy spear **2** (**pike**) a large freshwater fish

pile[1] *NOUN* **piles** **1** a number of things on top of one another **2** (*informal*) a large quantity; a lot of money **3** (*informal*) a large impressive building

pile *VERB* **piles, piling, piled** put things into a pile; make a pile

Thesaurus

picturesque *ADJECTIVE* **1** *He had spent the morning painting picturesque views of his master.* ► attractive, pretty, beautiful, charming, pleasant, scenic AN OPPOSITE IS ugly **2** *She was trying to find a more picturesque way to describe it.* ► colourful, graphic, descriptive, expressive, vivid, imaginative, poetic AN OPPOSITE IS prosaic

piece *NOUN* **1** *a piece of cheese; a piece of stone* ► bit, chunk, lump, hunk, portion, fragment, morsel, particle **2** *a piece of furniture* ► item, article **3** *She wrote a piece for the local newspaper.* ► article, story, feature, essay, account

piece *VERB* **piece together** *It is difficult to piece the evidence together into a convincing case.* ► assemble, compose, fit together, join together

pied *ADJECTIVE* ► dappled, flecked, mottled, particoloured, piebald, spotted, variegated

pier *NOUN* **1** *Boats were tied up at the pier.* ► jetty, quay, wharf, dock, landing stage, breakwater **2** *Immense piers supported a high vault.* ► column, pillar, support, buttress, upright, pile

pierce *VERB* *a spear that could pierce the thickest armour* ► penetrate, puncture, perforate, make a hole in, probe, enter, transfix, impale

piercing *ADJECTIVE* **1** *From the wood comes a piercing screech.* ► shrill, sharp, penetrating, shattering, ear-splitting, high-pitched, strident, deafening, loud **2** *a piercing wind* ► freezing, bitter, biting, wintry, stinging **3** *a piercing pain* ► stabbing, intense, excruciating, agonizing, stinging

piety *NOUN* *a priest respected for his piety* ► devoutness, devotion, piousness, holiness, godliness, saintliness, sanctity, religion, faith AN OPPOSITE IS impiety

pig *NOUN* **1** (*informal*) *He was always a bit of a pig when it came to food.* ► glutton, guzzler, gourmand, (*informal*) greedy guts **2** *Her husband can be a real pig at times.* ► brute, monster, beast, fiend, animal, demon

pile *NOUN* **1** *a pile of stones* ► heap, stack, mass, mound, mountain, collection, hoard **2** *We have piles of work to do.* ► plenty, a lot, a great deal, (*more informal*) lots, (*more informal*) masses, (*more informal*) heaps

pile *VERB* **1** *They piled everything into a corner.* ► heap, stack, pack, jam, accumulate, amass, load, mass, store, collect, gather, hoard
pile up *Problems were beginning to pile up.* ► build up, mount up, increase, grow, accumulate

A B C D E F G H I J K L M N O P Q R S T U V W X Y Z

pile [2] *NOUN* **piles** a heavy beam made of metal, concrete, or timber driven into the ground to support something

pile [3] *NOUN* a raised surface on fabric, made of upright threads • *a carpet with a thick pile*

pile-up *NOUN* **pile-ups** a road accident that involves a number of vehicles

pilfer *VERB* **pilfers, pilfering, pilfered** steal small things
▷ **pilferer** *NOUN* **pilferage** *NOUN*

pilgrim *NOUN* **pilgrims** a person who travels to a holy place for religious reasons
▷ **pilgrimage** *NOUN*

pill *NOUN* **pills** a small solid piece of medicine for swallowing
the pill a contraceptive pill

pillage *VERB* **pillages, pillaging, pillaged** carry off goods using force, especially in a war; plunder
▷ **pillage** *NOUN*

pillar *NOUN* **pillars** a tall stone or wooden post

pillar box *NOUN* **pillar boxes** a postbox standing in a street

pillion *NOUN* **pillions** a seat behind the driver on a motorcycle

pillow *NOUN* **pillows** a cushion for a person's head to rest on, especially in bed [from Latin *pulvinus* = cushion]

pillowcase or **pillowslip** *NOUN* **pillowcases** or **pillowslips** a cloth cover for a pillow

pilot *NOUN* **pilots** **1** a person who works the controls for flying an aircraft **2** a person qualified to steer a ship in and out of a port or through a difficult stretch of water **3** a guide

pilot *VERB* **pilots, piloting, piloted** **1** be pilot of an aircraft or ship **2** guide or steer

pilot *ADJECTIVE* testing on a small scale how something will work • *a pilot scheme* [from Greek *pedon* = oar or rudder]

pilot light *NOUN* **pilot lights** **1** a small flame that lights a larger burner on a gas cooker etc. **2** an electric indicator light

pimp *NOUN* **pimps** a man who gets clients for prostitutes and lives off their earnings

pimple *NOUN* **pimples** a small round raised spot on the skin
▷ **pimply** *ADJECTIVE*

PIN *ABBREVIATION* personal identification number; a number used as a person's password so that he or she can use a cash dispenser, computer, etc.

pin *NOUN* **pins** **1** a short thin piece of metal with a sharp point and a rounded head, used to fasten pieces of cloth or paper etc. together **2** a pointed device for fixing or marking something
pins and needles a tingling feeling in the skin

pin *VERB* **pins, pinning, pinned** **1** fasten something with a pin or pins **2** make a person or thing unable to move • *He was pinned under the wreckage.* **3** fix blame or responsibility on someone • *They pinned the blame on her sister.*

pincer *NOUN* **pincers** the claw of a shellfish such as a lobster

pincers *PLURAL NOUN* a tool with two parts that are pressed together for gripping and holding things

pinch *VERB* **pinches, pinching, pinched** **1** squeeze something tightly or painfully between two things, especially between the finger and thumb **2** (*informal*) steal

pinch *NOUN* **pinches** **1** a pinching movement **2** the amount that can be held between the tips of the thumb and forefinger • *a pinch of salt*
at a pinch in time of difficulty; if necessary
feel the pinch suffer from lack of money

pincushion *NOUN* **pincushions** a small pad into which pins are stuck to keep them ready for use

Thesaurus

pilfer *VERB* *People were pilfering bricks from building sites.* ► steal, take, snatch, pinch, filch, (*more informal*) swipe, (*more informal*) nick, (*more informal*) knock off

pillar *NOUN* *A row of pillars supports the roof.* ► column, pier, support, buttress, upright, pile

pillow *NOUN* *She rested her head on a pillow.* ► cushion, bolster, headrest, pad

pilot *NOUN* **1** *the pilot of an aircraft* ► airman *or* airwoman, (*old-fashioned*) aviator **2** *a harbour pilot* ► navigator, helmsman, steersman, coxswain, guide

pilot *ADJECTIVE* *a pilot scheme* ► experimental, trial, test, sample, model

pilot *VERB* *He piloted the little plane to the island.* ► fly, guide, lead, navigate, steer, direct, drive

pimple *NOUN* *a face covered in pimples* ► spot, blackhead, swelling, (*more informal*) zit

pin *NOUN* *The notice was attached by a pin.* ► tack, nail, spike, brad, skewer

pin *VERB* *She pinned a badge on him.* ► fasten, attach, fix, stick

pinch *VERB* **1** *She pinched his arm.* ► nip, squeeze, crush, tweak **2** *Someone has pinched my pen.* ► steal, take, pilfer, snatch, filch, (*more informal*) swipe, (*more informal*) nick, (*more informal*) knock off

pine[1] *NOUN* **pines** an evergreen tree with needle-shaped leaves

pine[2] *VERB* **pines, pining, pined** **1** feel an intense longing for somebody or something **2** become weak through longing for somebody or something

pineapple *NOUN* **pineapples** a large tropical fruit with a tough prickly skin and yellow flesh

ping-pong *NOUN* table tennis

pinion *NOUN* **pinions** a bird's wing, especially the outer end

pinion *VERB* **pinions, pinioning, pinioned** **1** clip a bird's wings to prevent it from flying **2** hold or fasten someone's arms or legs in order to prevent them from moving

pink *ADJECTIVE* pale red
▷ **pinkness** *NOUN*

pink *NOUN* **pinks** **1** a pink colour **2** a garden plant with fragrant flowers, often pink or white

pinnacle *NOUN* **pinnacles** **1** a pointed ornament on a roof **2** a high pointed piece of rock **3** the highest point of something • *It was the pinnacle of her career.*

pinpoint *ADJECTIVE* exact or precise • *with pinpoint accuracy*

pinpoint *VERB* **pinpoints, pinpointing, pinpointed** find or identify something precisely

pinstripe *NOUN* **pinstripes** one of the very narrow stripes that form a pattern in cloth
▷ **pinstriped** *ADJECTIVE*

pint *NOUN* **pints** a measure for liquids, equal to one-eighth of a gallon

pin-up *NOUN* **pin-ups** (*informal*) a picture of an attractive or famous person for pinning on a wall

pioneer *NOUN* **pioneers** one of the first people to go to a place or do or investigate something
▷ **pioneer** *VERB*

pious *ADJECTIVE* very religious; devout
▷ **piously** *ADVERB* **piousness** *NOUN*

pip *NOUN* **pips** **1** a small hard seed of an apple, pear, orange, etc. **2** one of the stars on the shoulder of an army officer's uniform **3** a short high-pitched sound • *She heard the six pips of the time signal on the radio.*

pip *VERB* **pips, pipping, pipped** (*informal*) defeat someone by a small amount

pipe *NOUN* **pipes** **1** a tube through which water or gas etc. can flow from one place to another **2** a short narrow tube with a bowl at one end in which tobacco can burn for smoking **3** a tube forming a musical instrument or part of one
the pipes bagpipes

pipe *VERB* **pipes, piping, piped** **1** send something along pipes **2** transmit music or other sound by wire or cable **3** play music on a pipe or the bagpipes **4** decorate a cake with thin lines of icing, cream, etc.
pipe down (*informal*) be quiet
pipe up begin to say something

pipe dream *NOUN* **pipe dreams** an impossible wish

pipeline *NOUN* **pipelines** a pipe for carrying oil or water etc. a long distance
in the pipeline in the process of being made or organized

piping *NOUN* **1** pipes; a length of pipe **2** a decorative line of icing, cream, etc. on a cake or other dish **3** a long narrow pipe-like fold decorating clothing, upholstery, etc.

piping *ADJECTIVE* shrill • *a piping voice*
piping hot very hot

pirate *NOUN* **pirates** **1** a person on a ship who attacks and robs other ships at sea **2** someone who produces or publishes or broadcasts illegally • *a pirate radio station* • *pirate videos*
▷ **piratical** *ADJECTIVE* **piracy** *NOUN*

Thesaurus

pine *VERB* *He thinks you were pining from love.*
► languish, wither, fade, droop, sicken
pine for *The Smiths were pining for their home.*
► long for, yearn for, hanker after, miss, crave

pioneer *NOUN* **1** *pioneers of the American West*
► settler, colonist, colonizer, discoverer, explorer **2** *a pioneer of birth control*
► developer, innovator, originator, pathfinder, groundbreaker

pioneer *VERB* *a scientist who pioneered genetic fingerprinting* ► develop, introduce, evolve, create, discover, invent, originate, initiate, spearhead

pious *ADJECTIVE* **1** *His second wife was a remarkably pious woman.* ► religious, devout, devoted, spiritual, dutiful
OPPOSITES ARE impious, irreligious **2** *The remark was no more than a pious platitude.*
► sanctimonious, insincere, self-righteous
AN OPPOSITE IS sincere

pipe *NOUN* *a water pipe* ► duct, channel, tube, conduit, hose, pipeline

pipe *VERB* **1** *The liquid is piped into containers.*
► channel, funnel, siphon, carry, run **2** *birds piping* ► chirp, cheep, tweet, trill, peep, chirrup, sing
pipe down *informal He got annoyed and told them to pipe down.* ► be quiet, be silent, quieten down, stop talking, hush

pirate *NOUN* *Pirates attacked the ship.*
► freebooter, marauder, privateer, (*historical*) buccaneer, (*old-fashioned*) corsair

A B C D E F G H I J K L M N O **P** Q R S T U V W X Y Z

pirouette (pir- oo- et) *NOUN* **pirouettes** a spinning movement of the body made while balanced on the point of the toe or on one foot
▷ **pirouette** *VERB*
[from French, = spinning top]

pistil *NOUN* the female organs of a flower

pistol *NOUN* **pistols** a small handgun

piston *NOUN* **pistons** a disc or cylinder that fits inside a tube in which it moves up and down as part of an engine or pump etc.

pit *NOUN* **pits** **1** a deep hole **2** a hollow **3** a coal mine **4** the part of a race circuit where racing cars are refuelled and repaired during a race

pit *VERB* **pits, pitting, pitted** **1** make holes or hollows in something • *The ground was pitted with craters.* **2** put somebody in competition with somebody else • *He was pitted against the champion in the final.*
▷ **pitted** *ADJECTIVE*

pitch[1] *NOUN* **pitches** **1** a piece of ground marked out for cricket, football, or another game **2** the highness or lowness of a voice or a musical note **3** intensity or strength • *Excitement was at fever pitch.* **4** the steepness of a slope • *the pitch of the roof*

pitch *VERB* **pitches, pitching, pitched** **1** throw or fling **2** set up a tent or camp **3** fall heavily • *He pitched forward as the bus braked suddenly.* **4** move up and down on a rough sea **5** set something at a particular level • *They pitched their hopes high.* **6** (said about a bowled ball in cricket) strike the ground
pitch in (*informal*) start working or doing something vigorously

pitch[2] *NOUN* a black sticky substance rather like tar
pitch-black or **pitch-dark** *ADJECTIVES* very black or very dark

pitched battle *NOUN* **pitched battles** a battle between troops in prepared positions

pitcher *NOUN* **pitchers** a large jug

pitchfork *NOUN* **pitchforks** a large fork with two prongs, used for lifting hay

pitchfork *VERB* **pitchforks, pitchforking, pitchforked** **1** lift something with a pitchfork **2** put a person somewhere suddenly

pitfall *NOUN* **pitfalls** an unsuspected danger or difficulty

pitiable *ADJECTIVE* making you feel pity

pitiful *ADJECTIVE* **1** making you feel pity **2** very bad or inadequate
▷ **pitifully** *ADVERB*

pity *NOUN* **1** the feeling of being sorry because someone is in pain or trouble **2** a cause for regret • *It's a pity that you can't come.*
take pity on feel sorry for someone and help them

pity *VERB* **pities, pitying, pitied** feel pity for someone

Thesaurus

pit *NOUN* **1** *A deep pit had been dug in the ground.* ► hole, ditch, trench, shaft, hollow, depression, trough, cavity, chasm, abyss **2** *increasing pit closures* ► mine, coal mine, colliery, quarry, shaft, working

pitch *NOUN* **1** *Their voices rose in pitch with the excitement.* ► tone, timbre, key, modulation **2** *His anger reached such a pitch that he became almost violent.* ► level, point, height, degree, intensity **3** *the pitch of the roof* ► steepness, angle, gradient, incline, slope, slant, tilt **4** *The referee ordered the players off the pitch.* ► playing field, field, park, ground

pitch *VERB* **1** *This is where we pitch our tents for the night.* ► put up, raise, fix, erect, set up **2** *She picked up the ball and pitched it into the neighbouring garden.* ► throw, fling, toss, hurl, lob, sling, bowl, heave, cast, (*more informal*) bung, (*more informal*) chuck **3** *Several lads pitched into the water.* ► plunge, dive, plummet, drop, topple **4** *The boat was pitching in the storm.* ► lurch, toss, wallow, rock, roll, reel, flounder, dip up and down

pitfall *NOUN* *Drama producers no longer need to fear the pitfalls of live television.* ► hazard, snag, trap, danger, peril, snare, difficulty, drawback, catch

pitiful *ADJECTIVE* **1** *She was a pitiful sight, still lying where she had fallen.* ► pathetic, pitiable, sad, sorrowful, wretched, touching, affecting, distressing, heartbreaking, heartrending **2** *He trudged off with the pitiful few pounds he had made that day.* ► meagre, negligible, paltry, miserable, modest, scanty, scant, sparse, (*more informal*) mingy, (*more informal*) measly
OPPOSITES ARE generous, extravagant

pitiless *ADJECTIVE* *Dinah did not break under the pitiless criticism.* ► merciless, relentless, ruthless, unrelenting, callous, cruel, hard, heartless, inexorable, unfeeling
OPPOSITES ARE merciful, compassionate

pity *NOUN* **1** *He had never felt pity for anyone in his life.* ► compassion, sympathy, commiseration, tenderness, understanding, feeling, forbearance, mercy, forgiveness, humanity, kindness OPPOSITES ARE indifference, animosity **2 a pity** *It's a pity it was dark and we couldn't see the garden.* ► a shame, unfortunate, a piece of bad luck, a cause for regret

pity *VERB* *He always pitied people who had to ask for money.* ► feel sorry for, feel pity for, feel for, sympathize with, commiserate with, take pity on

pivot *NOUN* **pivots** a point or part on which something turns or balances
▷ **pivotal** *ADJECTIVE*

pivot *VERB* **pivots, pivoting, pivoted** turn or place something to turn on a pivot

pixel (piks- el) *NOUN* **pixels** one of the tiny dots on a computer display screen from which the image is formed [short for *picture element*]

pixie *NOUN* **pixies** a small fairy; an elf

pizza (peets- a) *NOUN* **pizzas** an Italian food that consists of a layer of dough baked with a savoury topping [from Italian, = pie]

pizzicato (pits- i- kah- toh) *ADJECTIVE, ADVERB* plucking the strings of a musical instrument

placard *NOUN* **placards** a poster or notice, especially one carried at a demonstration [from early French *plaquier* = to lay flat]

placate *VERB* **placates, placating, placated** make someone feel calmer and less angry

place *NOUN* **places** **1** a particular part of space, especially where something belongs; an area or position **2** a seat • *Save me a place.* **3** a job; employment **4** a building; a home • *Come round to our place.* **5** a duty or function • *It's not my place to interfere.* **6** a point in a series of things • *In the first place, the date is wrong.*
in place **1** in the right position **2** suitable
in place of instead of
out of place **1** in the wrong position **2** unsuitable

place *VERB* **places, placing, placed** put something in a particular place
▷ **placement** *NOUN*

placid *ADJECTIVE* calm and peaceful; not easily made anxious or upset
▷ **placidly** *ADVERB* **placidity** *NOUN*

plagiarize (play- jee- er- I'z) *VERB* **plagiarizes, plagiarizing, plagiarized** take someone else's writings or ideas and use them as if they were your own
▷ **plagiarism** *NOUN* **plagiarist** *NOUN*

plague *NOUN* **plagues** **1** a dangerous illness that spreads very quickly **2** a large number of pests • *a plague of locusts*

plague *VERB* **plagues, plaguing, plagued** pester or annoy • *We've been plagued by wasps all afternoon.*

plain *ADJECTIVE* **1** simple; not decorated or elaborate **2** not beautiful **3** easy to see or hear or understand **4** frank and straightforward
▷ **plainly** *ADVERB* **plainness** *NOUN*

plain *NOUN* **plains** a large area of flat country
USAGE Do not confuse with **plane**.

Thesaurus

place *NOUN* **1** *She rose quietly from her place at the table.* ► seat, chair, position, space **2** *They would choose a foreign place for their next holiday.* ► locality, region, resort, city, town, village **3** *Seaview is the ideal place to write and work quietly.* ► locale, location, venue, spot, point **4** *They badly wanted a place of their own.* ► home, house, residence, dwelling, property, flat, apartment, establishment, accommodation **5** *She was offered a place on the company's board.* ► position, post, appointment, situation **6** *I know my place and won't interfere.* ► status, position, station, standing, rank

place *VERB* **1** *He placed the shopping on the table.* ► put, set, lay, deposit, leave, (*more informal*) stick, (*more informal*) dump, (*more informal*) plonk **2** *The judges placed her second overall.* ► rank, grade, position **3** *The face was familiar but I couldn't quite place it.* ► recognize, identify, remember

plague *NOUN* **1** *a study of the effects of the plague on two major cities* ► pestilence, blight, epidemic, contagion, infestation, outbreak **2** *a plague of flies* ► infestation, invasion, nuisance, scourge, swarm **3** *the plague of street crime in the area* ► bane, curse, blight, scourge, affliction, cancer

plague *VERB* **1** *The fears which had menaced her before returned to plague her.* ► afflict, bedevil, beset, torment, hound, torture, persecute **2** *He was being plagued with questions.* ► pester, badger, harass, trouble, annoy, bother, disturb, irritate, molest, vex, worry, (*more informal*) nag

plain *ADJECTIVE* **1** *The forms are written in plain English.* ► clear, simple, straightforward, understandable, intelligible, direct
OPPOSITES ARE obscure, unclear **2** *It was plain that someone had been in the house before them.* ► obvious, clear, evident, apparent, manifest **3** *They thought some plain speaking was needed.* ► frank, candid, outspoken, blunt, direct, explicit, unequivocal **4** *The house had a rather plain appearance.* ► unattractive, ordinary, unprepossessing, ugly AN OPPOSITE IS attractive **5** *The room was decorated in a plain style.* ► simple, basic, restrained, unadorned, unembellished, unelaborate, unpretentious
OPPOSITES ARE elaborate, fancy

plain *NOUN* *the movement of wildebeest across the plains of Africa* ► grassland, flatland, prairie, savannah, steppe

plain *ADVERB* *Many people are just plain scared of making the change.* ► downright, completely, totally, utterly, really, thoroughly, absolutely, simply

A B C D E F G H I J K L M N O P Q R S T U V W X Y Z

plain clothes *NOUN* civilian clothes worn instead of a uniform, e.g. by police

plaintiff *NOUN* **plaintiffs** the person who brings a complaint against somebody else to a lawcourt COMPARE **defendant**

plaintive *ADJECTIVE* sounding sad • *a plaintive cry*

plait (plat) *VERB* **plaits, plaiting, plaited** weave three or more strands of hair or rope to form one length

plait *NOUN* **plaits** a length of hair or rope that has been plaited

plan *NOUN* **plans 1** a way of doing something thought out in advance **2** a drawing showing the arrangement of parts of something **3** a map of a town or district

plan *VERB* **plans, planning, planned** make a plan for something
▷ **planner** *NOUN*

plane[1] *NOUN* **planes 1** an aeroplane **2** a tool for making wood smooth by scraping its surface **3** a flat or level surface

plane *VERB* **planes, planing, planed** smooth wood with a plane

plane *ADJECTIVE* flat or level • *a plane surface*
USAGE Do not confuse with **plain**.

plane[2] *NOUN* **planes** a tall tree with broad leaves

planet *NOUN* **planets** one of the bodies that move in an orbit round the sun. The main planets are Mercury, Venus, Earth, Mars, Jupiter, Saturn, Uranus, Neptune, and Pluto
▷ **planetary** *ADJECTIVE*

plank *NOUN* **planks** a long flat piece of wood

plankton *NOUN* microscopic plants and animals that float in the sea, lakes, etc.

plant *NOUN* **plants 1** a living thing that cannot move, makes its food from chemical substances, and usually has a stem, leaves, and roots **2** a small plant, not a tree or shrub **3** a factory or its equipment **4** (*informal*) something deliberately placed for other people to find, usually to mislead people or cause trouble

plant *VERB* **plants, planting, planted 1** put something in soil for growing **2** fix something firmly in place **3** place something where it will be found, usually to mislead people or cause trouble
▷ **planter** *NOUN*

plantation *NOUN* **plantations 1** a large area of land where cotton, tobacco, or tea etc. is planted **2** a group of planted trees

plaque (plak) *NOUN* **plaques 1** a flat piece of metal or porcelain fixed on a wall as an ornament or memorial **2** a filmy substance that forms on teeth and gums, where bacteria can live

plaster *NOUN* **plasters 1** a small covering put over the skin around a cut or wound to protect it **2** a mixture of lime, sand, and water etc. for covering walls and ceilings **3** plaster of Paris, or a cast made of this to hold broken bones in place

plaster *VERB* **plasters, plastering, plastered 1** cover a wall etc. with plaster **2** cover something thickly; daub

Thesaurus

plan *NOUN* **1** (*informal*) *a plan of the building* ► chart, diagram, map, layout, blueprint, representation **2** *a clever plan for raising money* ► scheme, idea, proposal, project, programme, strategy, suggestion, proposition

plan *VERB* **1** *She began planning tomorrow's journey.* ► organize, arrange, work out, think out, prepare **2** *some tips for anyone planning a new garden* ► design, devise, contrive, sketch out **3** *We plan to go abroad this year.* ► intend, propose, aim, mean, envisage, contemplate, be thinking of USAGE If you use any of the last three synonyms, you need to say *going* instead of *to go*, e.g. *We envisage going abroad this year.*

plane *NOUN* **1** *The plane rose gently in the air.* ► aeroplane, aircraft, jet, airliner, craft **2** *The thought that came to her now was on a more creative plane.* ► level, stage, degree, position

planet *NOUN* *the population of the planet* ► globe, world, orb

plank *NOUN* *a plank of wood* ► board, floorboard, beam, timber

plant *NOUN* **1 plants** ► greenery, growth, flora, undergrowth, vegetation **2** *industrial plant* ► machinery, machines, equipment, apparatus **3** *a plant of British intelligence* ► informer, informant, spy, agent, infiltrator, mole

plant *VERB* **1** *Plant the seeds in September.* ► sow, bury, set out, put in the ground **2** *Someone had planted the idea in her mind.* ► establish, introduce, fix, put, lodge, impress, instil, imprint

plaster *NOUN* **1** *He stripped the wall down to the plaster.* ► plasterwork, mortar, stucco **2** *A nurse put a plaster on the cut.* ► dressing, sticking plaster, bandage

plaster *VERB* *The floor was plastered with mud.* ► cover, daub, coat, smother, smear, spread

plaster of Paris *NOUN* a white paste used for making moulds or for casts round a broken leg or arm

plastic *NOUN* **plastics** a strong light synthetic substance that can be moulded into a permanent shape

plastic *ADJECTIVE* **1** made of plastic **2** soft and easy to mould • *Clay is a plastic substance.*
▷ **plasticity** *NOUN*
[from Greek *plastos* = moulded or formed]

plastic surgery *NOUN* surgery to repair deformed or injured parts of the body
▷ **plastic surgeon** *NOUN*

plate *NOUN* **plates** **1** an almost flat usually circular object from which food is eaten or served **2** a thin flat sheet of metal, glass, or other hard material **3** an illustration on special paper in a book
▷ **plateful** *NOUN*

plate *VERB* **plates, plating, plated** **1** coat metal with a thin layer of gold, silver, tin, etc. **2** cover something with sheets of metal

plateau (plat- oh) *NOUN* **plateaux** (plat- ohz) a flat area of high land

platform *NOUN* **platforms** **1** a flat raised area along the side of a line at a railway station **2** a flat surface above the level of the floor, especially one from which someone speaks to an audience **3** the policies that a political party puts forward

platinum *NOUN* a valuable silver-coloured metal that does not tarnish

platitude *NOUN* **platitudes** a trite or over-used remark
▷ **platitudinous** *ADJECTIVE*

plausible *ADJECTIVE* seeming to be honest or worth believing but perhaps deceptive • *a plausible excuse*
▷ **plausibly** *ADVERB* **plausibility** *NOUN*

play *VERB* **plays, playing, played** **1** take part in a game, sport, or other amusement **2** make music or sound with a musical instrument, record player, etc. **3** perform a part in a play or film
▷ **player** *NOUN*
play about or **play around** have fun or be mischievous
play down give people the impression that something is not important
play up (*informal*) tease or annoy someone

play *NOUN* **plays** **1** a story acted on a stage or on radio or television **2** playing or having fun
[from Old English]

Thesaurus

plastic *ADJECTIVE* *They were drinking warm beer from plastic tumblers.* ► PVC, polystyrene, polyurethane, celluloid

plate *NOUN* **1** *She helped herself to a plate of food.* ► dish, platter, dinner plate, plateful, helping, serving, portion, bowl **2** *Someone had removed the plates from the end of the book.* ► illustration, picture, print, photograph, lithograph **3** *There was a brass plate by the front door.* ► plaque, nameplate, sign

platform **1** *A speaker addressed the audience from the platform.* ► dais, rostrum, podium, stand, stage **2** *the Liberal Democrats' election platform* ► policy, programme, manifesto, plan, party line

plausible *ADJECTIVE* **1** *He knew he had presented a plausible explanation.* ► credible, reasonable, believable, convincing, persuasive, tenable, likely, feasible, probable, possible, acceptable, conceivable AN OPPOSITE IS implausible **2** *He had the sort of plausible charm that Georgina was wary of.* ► smooth, smooth-talking, glib, specious

play *NOUN* **1** *a balance between work and play* ► amusement, entertainment, relaxation, recreation, enjoyment, leisure, pleasure, diversion, fun **2** *a play by Shakespeare* ► drama, theatrical work, stage play, tragedy, comedy, production, performance, show **3** *There was some play in the mechanism.* ► movement, freedom of movement, looseness, flexibility, latitude, leeway

play *VERB* **1** *The children were playing in the garden.* ► amuse yourself, have fun, enjoy yourself, play games, romp, frolic, caper **2** *I enjoy playing indoor sports.* ► take part in, engage in, participate in, join in, compete in **3** *The two sides play each other next week.* ► compete against, take on, challenge, oppose, vie with **4** *We need someone to play Hamlet.* ► act, perform, portray, act the part of, play the part of, take the role of **5** *He regretted not being able to play a musical instrument.* ► perform on, make music on
play down *The Government played down the effect of the tax increases.* ► minimize, make light of, gloss over, underplay
OPPOSITES ARE exaggerate, play up
play on *advertising that plays on people's anxieties* ► exploit, take advantage of, make use of, capitalize on, trade on
play up **1** *Some of the children began to play up.* ► misbehave, behave badly, be naughty, cause trouble **2** *The newspapers played up the scandal.* ► emphasize, accentuate, exaggerate, underline, highlight, give prominence to, stress
OPPOSITES ARE minimize, play down

player *NOUN* **1** *The team has bought some new players.* ► team member, sportsman *or* sportswoman, competitor, contestant **2** *players on stage* ► actor *or* actress,

playful *ADJECTIVE* **1** wanting to play; full of fun **2** done in fun; not serious
▷ **playfully** *ADVERB* **playfulness** *NOUN*

playground *NOUN* **playgrounds** a piece of ground for children to play on

playgroup *NOUN* **playgroups** a group of very young children who play together regularly, supervised by adults

playing card *NOUN* **playing cards** each of a set of cards (usually 52) used for playing games

playing field *NOUN* **playing fields** a field used for outdoor games

playmate *NOUN* **playmates** a person you play games with

play-off *NOUN* **play-offs** an extra match that is played to decide a draw or tie

plaything *NOUN* **playthings** a toy

playwright *NOUN* **playwrights** a person who writes plays

PLC or **p.l.c.** *ABBREVIATION* public limited company

plea *NOUN* **pleas** **1** a request or appeal • *a plea for mercy* **2** an excuse • *He stayed at home on the plea of a headache.* **3** a formal statement of 'guilty' or 'not guilty' made in a lawcourt by someone accused of a crime

plead *VERB* **pleads, pleading, pleaded** **1** beg someone to do something **2** state formally in a lawcourt that you are guilty or not guilty of a crime **3** give something as an excuse • *She didn't come on holiday with us, pleading poverty.*

pleasant *ADJECTIVE* pleasing; giving pleasure
▷ **pleasantly** *ADVERB* **pleasantness** *NOUN*

please *VERB* **pleases, pleasing, pleased** **1** make a person feel satisfied or glad **2** (used to make a request or an order polite) • *Please ring the bell.* **3** like; think suitable • *Do as you please.*

pleasure *NOUN* **pleasures** **1** a feeling of satisfaction or gladness; enjoyment **2** something that pleases you

plectrum *NOUN* **plectra** a small piece of metal or bone etc. for plucking the strings of a musical instrument

pledge *NOUN* **pledges** **1** a solemn promise **2** a thing handed over as security for a loan or contract

pledge *VERB* **pledges, pledging, pledged** **1** promise solemnly to do or give something **2** hand something over as security

Thesaurus

performer, artist, entertainer **3** *players in an orchestra* ► musician, performer, instrumentalist, soloist, artist

playful *ADJECTIVE* **1** *She came back from the party in a playful mood.* ► frisky, lively, jolly, spirited **2** *a few playful remarks* ► light-hearted, joking, teasing, jocular, frivolous

playground *NOUN* *a playground behind the school* ► play area, recreation ground, amusement park

playing field *NOUN* *The train passed a playing field where a game was going on.* ► sports ground, ground, pitch, recreation ground

plea *NOUN* **1** *a plea for mercy* ► appeal, petition, request, entreaty, supplication, invocation, prayer **2** *His plea was that he had been ill.* ► claim, excuse, defence, justification, pretext

plead *VERB* *The prisoners pleaded for their lives.* ► beg, implore, entreat, petition, request, solicit, appeal, ask, importune

pleasant *ADJECTIVE* **1** *It was a pleasant afternoon.* ► enjoyable, pleasing, agreeable, satisfying, delightful, lovely, nice AN OPPOSITE IS unpleasant **2** *The assistants are all very pleasant.* ► friendly, agreeable, congenial, likeable, personable, good-humoured, nice OPPOSITES ARE unpleasant, disagreeable

please *VERB* **1** *She did her best to please them.* ► make happy, satisfy, give pleasure to, gladden, gratify, amuse, content, delight, entertain **2** *Do what you please* ► want, like, wish, desire, feel like

pleased *ADJECTIVE* *We were so pleased to see you.* ► happy, glad, delighted, satisfied, overjoyed, thrilled OPPOSITES ARE displeased, annoyed

pleasing *ADJECTIVES* *a very pleasing result* ► pleasant, agreeable, gratifying, satisfying, welcome, acceptable

pleasure *NOUN* **1** *She found great pleasure in fashionable clothes.* ► enjoyment, gratification, happiness, satisfaction, amusement, contentment, fulfilment, delight, comfort, entertainment, gladness, joy, solace **2** *the pleasures that children bring* ► joy, delight, enjoyment

pledge *NOUN* **1** *Labour's pledge to spend billions on education.* ► promise, undertaking, assurance, commitment, guarantee **2** *She gave her rings as a pledge.* ► surety, security, bond, deposit, bail

pledge *VERB* *They all pledged their loyalty to the Queen.* ► promise, swear, vow, guarantee, undertake

plentiful *ADJECTIVE* *a plentiful supply of fruit* ► abundant, copious, ample, liberal, profuse, generous, lavish, rich, bountiful, prolific, inexhaustible OPPOSITES ARE sparse, scarce
be plentiful *The flowers are plentiful at this time of year.* ► abound, proliferate, be abundant, flourish, thrive

plenty *NOUN* quite enough; as much as is needed or wanted

plenty *ADVERB* (*informal*) quite or fully • *It's plenty big enough.*

pliable *ADJECTIVE* **1** easy to bend; flexible **2** easy to influence or control
▷ **pliability** *NOUN*

pliers *PLURAL NOUN* pincers that have jaws with flat surfaces for gripping things

plight *NOUN* **plights** a difficult or dangerous situation

plimsoll *NOUN* **plimsolls** a canvas sports shoe with a rubber sole [same origin as **Plimsoll line** (because the thin sole reminded people of a Plimsoll line)]

Plimsoll line *NOUN* **Plimsoll lines** a mark on a ship's side showing how deeply it may legally go down in the water when loaded [named after an English politician, S. Plimsoll, who in the 1870s protested about ships being overloaded]

PLO *ABBREVIATION* Palestine Liberation Organization

plod *VERB* **plods, plodding, plodded 1** walk slowly and heavily **2** work slowly but steadily
▷ **plodder** *NOUN*

plop *NOUN* **plops** the sound of something dropping into water
▷ **plop** *VERB*

plot *NOUN* **plots 1** a secret plan **2** the story in a play, novel, or film **3** a small piece of land

plot *VERB* **plots, plotting, plotted 1** make a secret plan **2** make a chart or graph of something • *We plotted the ship's route on our map.*

plough *NOUN* **ploughs** a farming implement for turning the soil over, in preparation for planting seeds

plough *VERB* **ploughs, ploughing, ploughed 1** turn over soil with a plough **2** go through something with great effort or difficulty • *He ploughed through the book.*
▷ **ploughman** *NOUN*
plough back reinvest profits in the business that produced them

pluck *VERB* **plucks, plucking, plucked 1** pick a flower or fruit **2** pull the feathers off a bird **3** pull something up or out **4** pull a string (e.g. on a guitar) and let it go again
pluck up courage summon up courage and overcome fear

pluck *NOUN* courage or spirit

plucky *ADJECTIVE* **pluckier, pluckiest** brave or spirited
▷ **pluckily** *ADVERB*

Thesaurus

plenty *NOUN* **1** *a time of plenty* ► affluence, prosperity, wealth, opulence, luxury, well-being, comfort **2 plenty of** *There is plenty of time before they arrive.* ► a lot of, a great deal of, much, enough, (*more informal*) lots of, (*more informal*) heaps of, (*more informal*) loads of, (*more informal*) masses of

pliable *ADJECTIVE* **1** *a pliable material* ► flexible, bendable, pliant, supple, plastic, springy, (*more informal*) bendy AN OPPOSITE IS stiff **2** *a pliable mind* ► adaptable, impressionable, responsive, suggestible, compliant, flexible, tractable, biddable, accommodating
AN OPPOSITE IS rigid

plight *NOUN* *the plight of the homeless* ► difficulty, predicament, danger, trouble, extremity, quandary, straits

plod *VERB* **1** *Mary plodded up the path.* ► trudge, tramp, lumber, stomp **2** *It will take hours to plod through the whole book.* ► plough, wade, trawl, labour, persevere, grind on

plot *NOUN* **1** *He grew vegetables in a plot behind the house.* ► piece of ground, patch, allotment, smallholding, lot **2** *The novel has a complicated plot.* ► storyline, story, outline, action, thread, scenario, narrative **3** *A plot was revealed against the government.* ► conspiracy, intrigue, plan, scheme, cabal, machination

plot *VERB* **1** *The president's brother was plotting his downfall.* ► plan, scheme, concoct, devise, hatch **2** *He was accused of plotting against the government.* ► conspire, scheme, intrigue **3** *They plotted their course on the map.* ► chart, mark, map

plough *VERB* **1** *Farmers ploughed the fields.* ► cultivate, till, work, turn over **2** *A van had ploughed into a shop window.* ► plunge, crash, career, smash, bulldoze

ploy *NOUN* *It was just a ploy to get rid of Doreen.* ► ruse, trick, move, device, stratagem, manoeuvre

pluck *NOUN* *It must have taken a lot of pluck to walk along a path marked 'danger'.* ► courage, daring, nerve, audacity, boldness, heroism, (*more informal*) bottle, (*more informal*) grit, (*more informal*) guts

pluck *VERB* **1** *She began to pluck hairs off her skirt.* ► pick, pull, take off, snatch **2** *He sang and plucked a guitar.* ► pick, twang, strum, finger **3** *The girls stood plucking fruit from the trees.* ► pick, gather, collect, harvest, garner

plucky *ADJECTIVE* *a plucky young woman's tale of escape* ► brave, courageous, bold, daring, intrepid, valiant, resolute OPPOSITES ARE timid, cowardly

A B C D E F G H I J K L M N O **P** Q R S T U V W X Y Z

plug *NOUN* **plugs** **1** something used to stop up a hole • *a bath plug* **2** a device that fits into a socket to connect wires to a supply of electricity **3** (*informal*) a piece of publicity for something

plug *VERB* **plugs, plugging, plugged** **1** stop up a hole **2** (*informal*) publicize something
plug in put a plug into an electrical socket

plum *NOUN* **plums** **1** a soft juicy fruit with a pointed stone in the middle **2** a reddish-purple colour **3** (*informal*) something very good • *a plum job*

plumb *VERB* **plumbs, plumbing, plumbed** **1** measure how deep something is **2** get to the bottom of a matter • *We could not plumb the mystery.* **3** fit a room or building with a plumbing system

plumb *ADJECTIVE* exactly upright; vertical • *The wall was plumb*

plumb *ADVERB* (*informal*) exactly • *It fell plumb in the middle.*

plumber *NOUN* **plumbers** a person who fits and mends plumbing

plumbing *NOUN* **1** the water pipes, water tanks, and drainage pipes in a building **2** the work of a plumber

plumb line *NOUN* a line with a heavy object tied to it, used for finding a vertical line on an upright surface or for testing the depth of water

plume *NOUN* **plumes** **1** a large feather **2** something shaped like a feather • *a plume of smoke*

plummet *NOUN* **plummets** a plumb line or the weight on its end

plummet *VERB* **plummets, plummeting, plummeted** **1** drop downwards quickly **2** decrease rapidly in value • *Prices have plummeted.*

plump [1] *ADJECTIVE* slightly fat; rounded
▷ **plumpness** *NOUN*

plump *VERB* **plumps, plumping, plumped** make something rounded • *plump up a cushion*

plump [2] *VERB* **plumps, plumping, plumped**
plump for (*informal*) choose

plunder *VERB* **plunders, plundering, plundered** rob a person or place using force, especially during a war or riot
▷ **plunderer** *NOUN*

plunder *NOUN* **1** plundering **2** goods etc. that have been plundered

plunge *VERB* **plunges, plunging, plunged** **1** go or push forcefully into something; dive **2** fall or go downwards suddenly **3** go or force into action etc. • *They plunged the world into war.*

plunge *NOUN* **plunges** a sudden fall or dive
take the plunge start a bold course of action

plural *NOUN* **plurals** the form of a noun or verb used when it stands for more than one person or thing • *The plural of 'child' is 'children'.*
COMPARE **singular**
▷ **plural** *ADJECTIVE* **plurality** *NOUN*

plus *PREPOSITION* with the next number or thing added • *2 plus 2 equals four* (2 + 2 = 4) [from Latin, = more]

plush *NOUN* a thick velvety cloth used in furnishings
▷ **plushy** *ADJECTIVE*

Thesaurus

plug *NOUN* **1** *He put a plug in the top of the bottle.* ► stopper, cork, bung **2** (*informal*) *They put in a plug for their new song.* ► advertisement, piece of publicity, mention, (*informal*) puff, (*informal*) boost

plug *VERB* **1** *The first thing to do was plug the leak.* ► seal, stop up, block up, close **2** (*informal*) *He wanted to plug the new film.* ► publicize, promote, advertise, mention frequently
plug away *He plugged away at the work he had to do.* ► toil, labour, soldier on, plod on

plumb *ADVERB* *The arrow hit the target plumb in the middle.* ► exactly, precisely, dead, (*more informal*) slap

plumb *VERB* *They seem to have plumbed the depths of despair.* ► penetrate, probe, sound, explore, measure

plummet *VERB* *A stone came loose and plummeted to the ground.* ► plunge, fall, hurtle, drop, crash, dive

plump *ADJECTIVE* *a plump little boy* ► chubby, podgy, tubby, fat, dumpy, rotund, round, overweight, stout, portly, pudgy
OPPOSITES ARE thin, slim, skinny

plump *VERB* *Jill plumped down on the sofa and fell asleep.* ► sink, drop, flop, fall, collapse
plump for *I'm going to plump for the vegetarian meal.* ► choose, opt for, go for, pick, decide on

plunder *VERB* *Pirates plundered towns and villages near the coast.* ► despoil, loot, pillage, raid, ransack, ravage, rifle, rob, sack, steal from

plunder *NOUN* *The army was bent on plunder and murder.* ► looting, robbery, pillage, pillaging, marauding

plunge *VERB* **1** *The plane plunged to the ground.* ► dive, plummet, fall, hurtle, drop, crash, dive, swoop, nosedive **2** *I plunged into the lake.* ► dive, leap, jump, throw yourself, hurl yourself **3** *He plunged the knife into the ripe fruit.* ► thrust, force, stab, shove, stick, push **4** *She plunged a hand in the water.* ► dip, immerse, submerge, sink

plutonium *NOUN* a radioactive substance used in nuclear weapons and reactors [named after the planet Pluto]

ply [1] *NOUN* **plies** **1** a thickness or layer of wood or cloth etc. **2** a strand in yarn • *4-ply wool*

ply [2] *VERB* **plies, plying, plied** **1** use or wield a tool or weapon **2** work at • *Tailors plied their trade.* **3** keep offering • *They plied her with food or with questions.* **4** go regularly • *The boat plies between the two harbours.* **5** drive or wait about looking for custom • *Taxis are allowed to ply for hire.*

plywood *NOUN* strong thin board made of layers of wood glued together

PM *ABBREVIATION* Prime Minister

p.m. *ABBREVIATION* after noon

pneumatic (new- **mat**- ik) *ADJECTIVE* filled with or worked by compressed air • *a pneumatic drill*
▷ **pneumatically** *ADVERB*
[from Greek *pneuma* = wind]

pneumonia (new- **moh**- nee- a) *NOUN* a serious illness caused by inflammation of one or both lungs [from Greek *pneumon* = lung]

PO *ABBREVIATION* **1** Post Office **2** postal order

poach *VERB* **poaches, poaching, poached** **1** cook an egg (removed from its shell) in or over boiling water **2** cook fish or fruit etc. in a small amount of liquid **3** steal game or fish from someone else's land or water **4** take something unfairly • *One club was poaching members from another.*
▷ **poacher** *NOUN*

pocket *NOUN* **pockets** **1** a small bag-shaped part, especially in a piece of clothing **2** a person's supply of money • *The expense is beyond my pocket.* **3** an isolated part or area • *small pockets of rain*
▷ **pocketful** *NOUN*
be out of pocket have spent more money than you have gained

pocket *ADJECTIVE* small enough to carry in a pocket • *a pocket calculator*

pocket *VERB* **pockets, pocketing, pocketed** put something into a pocket [from old French *pochet* = little pouch]

pocket money *NOUN* money given to a child to spend as he or she likes

pod *NOUN* **pods** a long seed container of the kind found on a pea or bean plant

poem *NOUN* **poems** a piece of poetry

poet *NOUN* **poets** a person who writes poetry
▷ **poetess** *NOUN*

poetry *NOUN* writing arranged in short lines, usually with a particular rhythm and sometimes with rhymes
▷ **poetic** *ADJECTIVE* **poetical** *ADJECTIVE* **poetically** *ADVERB*

poignant (**poin**- yant) *ADJECTIVE* very distressing; affecting the feelings • *poignant memories*
▷ **poignancy** *NOUN*

point *NOUN* **points** **1** the narrow or sharp end of something **2** a dot • *the decimal point* **3** a particular place or time • *At this point she was winning.* **4** a detail or characteristic • *He has his good points.* **5** the important or essential idea • *Keep to the point!* **6** purpose or value • *There is no point in hurrying.* **7** an electrical socket **8** a device for changing a train from one track to another

Thesaurus

poach *VERB* *The new company was poaching staff from its rivals.* ► steal, purloin, filch, (*more informal*) pinch, (*more informal*) nick

pocket *NOUN* *There were some pockets of resistance to the new regime.* ► area, patch, centre, cluster

pocket *VERB* • *The management was accused of pocketing all the profits.* ► appropriate, steal, help yourself to, take for yourself

podgy *ADJECTIVE* *She looked a bit podgy.* ► plump, chubby, tubby, fat , dumpy, rotund, round, overweight, pudgy OPPOSITES ARE thin, slim, skinny

poem *NOUN* *He read her some of his poems.* ► verse, rhyme, poetry

poet *NOUN* *She wrote stories and was a poet.* ► writer of verse, rhymester, rhymer, lyricist, versifier, bard

poetic *ADJECTIVE* *poetic language* ► expressive, lyrical, poetical, emotive, metrical, imaginative AN OPPOSITE IS prosaic

poetry *NOUN* *a book of poetry* ► poems, verses, rhymes

point *NOUN* **1** *the point of the needle* ► tip, end, sharp end, spike, extremity **2** *points of light* ► spot, speck, dot, fleck **3** *At this point, the door opened.* ► moment, instant, time, stage **4** *I wish they would get to the point.* ► essence, crux, meaning, thrust **5** *a few points of detail* ► detail, item, issue, factor, consideration, particular, facet, feature **6** *She admitted he had some good points.* ► characteristic, feature, attribute, aspect, peculiarity, side **7** *There didn't seem much point in staying.* ► purpose, reason, object, aim, goal, advantage, benefit **8** *They could get on the train at a point further up the line.* ► place, position, location, spot, site, locality

A B C D E F G H I J K L M N O P Q R S T U V W X Y Z

point *VERB* **points, pointing, pointed** **1** show where something is, especially by holding out a finger etc. towards it **2** aim or direct • *She pointed her finger at me.* **3** fill in the parts between bricks with mortar or cement
point out draw attention to something

point-blank *ADJECTIVE* **1** aimed or fired from close to the target **2** direct and straightforward • *a point-blank refusal*

point-blank *ADVERB* in a point-blank manner • *He refused point-blank.*

pointed *ADJECTIVE* **1** with a point at the end **2** clearly directed at a person • *a pointed remark*
▷ **pointedly** *ADVERB*

pointer *NOUN* **pointers** **1** a stick, rod, or mark etc. used to point at something **2** a dog that points with its muzzle towards birds that it scents **3** an indication or hint

pointless *ADJECTIVE* without a point; with no purpose
▷ **pointlessly** *ADVERB*

poise *VERB* **poises, poising, poised** balance

poise *NOUN* **1** a dignified self-confident manner **2** balance

poison *NOUN* **poisons** a substance that can harm or kill a living thing if swallowed or absorbed into the body
▷ **poisonous** *ADJECTIVE*

poison *VERB* **poisons, poisoning, poisoned** **1** give poison to; kill somebody with poison **2** put poison in something **3** corrupt or spoil something • *He poisoned their minds.*
▷ **poisoner** *NOUN*
[via early French from Latin *potio* = potion]

poke *VERB* **pokes, poking, poked** **1** prod or jab **2** push out or forward; stick out **3** search • *I was poking about in the attic.*
poke fun at ridicule

poke *NOUN* **pokes** a poking movement; a prod

poker [1] *NOUN* **pokers** a stiff metal rod for poking a fire

poker [2] *NOUN* a card game in which players bet on who has the best cards

Thesaurus

point *VERB* **1 point** *or* **point to** *An official pointed the way. He pointed to a picture on the stairs.* ► indicate, point out, draw attention to, show, signal **2** *She saw the man was pointing a gun at her.* ► aim, direct, level, train **3** *I'll point you in the right direction.* ► direct, guide, lead, steer

point-blank *ADJECTIVE* **1** *The gun was fired at point-blank range.* ► close **2** *Their request met with a point-blank refusal.* ► blunt, direct, straight, plain, frank, open, explicit, forthright

point-blank *ADVERB* *She told him point-blank that it was over.* ► bluntly, directly, straight, straight out, frankly, openly, plainly, clearly, forthrightly

pointed *ADJECTIVE* **1** *He used the pointed end of a stick.* ► sharp, tapered, spiky **2** *Kathleen greeted this pointed remark with a smile.* ► cutting, biting, trenchant, caustic, acerbic, scathing, barbed, sharp, insinuating, hurtful
AN OPPOSITE IS bland

pointless *ADJECTIVE* *The country was being dragged into a pointless military conflict. It was pointless to try to catch them now.* ► futile, senseless, fruitless, useless, needless, vain, aimless, meaningless, unprofitable
OPPOSITES ARE useful, valuable

poise *NOUN* *Claudia admired her poise.* ► composure, calmness, equanimity, aplomb, assurance, self-confidence, self-control, coolness, dignity, elegance, equilibrium

poised *ADJECTIVE* **1** *Both forces were poised to take the city.* ► prepared, ready, set, waiting, keyed up **2** *She gave a poised performance.* ► assured, self-assured, self-confident, dignified, composed, graceful, elegant

poison *NOUN* **1** *A gram of the poison is enough to kill a man.* ► toxin, venom **2** *a poison in society* ► blight, contamination, contagion, cancer

poison *VERB* **1** *to poison someone* ► kill **2** *Chemicals are poisoning the country's rivers.* ► pollute, contaminate, infect, foul, taint **3** *The media were accused of trying to poison people's minds.* ► prejudice, subvert, corrupt, embitter, colour, warp, affect, pervert

poisonous *ADJECTIVE* **1** *a poisonous insect* ► venomous, deadly, virulent **2** *a cloud of poisonous gases* ► toxic, lethal, noxious, fatal, mortal **3** *a poisonous remark* ► malicious, malevolent, hostile, vicious, spiteful, vitriolic

poke *VERB* *They poked burning sticks at him. He poked her with his elbow.* ► prod, dig, jab, nudge, thrust, stab, shove, stick
poke about *or* **around** *Someone was poking about in the cupboard.* ► search, rummage, root around
poke fun at *They laughed and poked fun at him.* ► ridicule, mock, make fun of, jeer at
poke out *A hand was poking out of the back window.* ► protrude, stick out, jut out, peek, project

poke *NOUN* *Amy gave him a poke.* ► prod, dig, jab, nudge, shove

poky *ADJECTIVE* *a poky room with one chair* ► confined, cramped, tiny, small, uncomfortable, restrictive
AN OPPOSITE IS spacious

polar *ADJECTIVE* **1** to do with or near the North Pole or South Pole **2** to do with either pole of a magnet
▷ **polarity** *NOUN*

polar bear *NOUN* **polar bears** a white bear living in Arctic regions

polarize *VERB* **polarizes, polarizing, polarized 1** keep vibrations of light waves etc. to a single direction **2** divide into two groups of completely opposite extremes of feeling or opinion • *Opinions had polarized.*
▷ **polarization** *NOUN*

Polaroid camera *NOUN* **Polaroid cameras** (*trade mark*) a camera that takes a picture and produces the finished photograph a few seconds later

pole[1] *NOUN* **poles** a long slender rounded piece of wood or metal

pole[2] *NOUN* **poles 1** a point on the earth's surface that is as far north (**North Pole**) or as far south (**South Pole**) as possible **2** either of the ends of a magnet **3** either terminal of an electric cell or battery

pole star *NOUN* the star above the North Pole

pole vault *NOUN* an athletic contest in which competitors jump over a high bar with the help of a long flexible pole

police *NOUN* the people whose job is to catch criminals and make sure that the law is kept
▷ **policeman** *NOUN* **police officer** *NOUN* **policewoman** *NOUN*

police *VERB* **polices, policing, policed** keep order in a place by means of police

policy[1] *NOUN* **policies** the aims or plan of action of a person or group

policy[2] *NOUN* **policies** a document stating the terms of a contract of insurance

polish *VERB* **polishes, polishing, polished 1** make a thing smooth and shiny by rubbing **2** make a thing better by making corrections and alterations
▷ **polisher** *NOUN*
polish off finish off

polish *NOUN* **polishes 1** a substance used in polishing **2** a shine **3** elegance of manner

polite *ADJECTIVE* having good manners
▷ **politely** *ADVERB* **politeness** *NOUN*

political *ADJECTIVE* connected with the governing of a country or region
▷ **politically** *ADVERB*

politician *NOUN* **politicians** a person who is involved in politics

politics *NOUN* political matters; the business of governing a country or region

poll (rhymes with *pole*) *NOUN* **polls 1** voting or votes at an election **2** an opinion poll **3** (*old use*) the head

Thesaurus

pole *NOUN* **1** *The fence was held up by a series of poles.* ► post, pillar, stake, stick, upright, support, shaft, spar **2** *Their opinions are at opposite poles.* ► extreme, extremity, limit
poles apart *Our political views are poles apart.* ► completely different, worlds apart, like chalk and cheese, irreconcilable, incompatible

police *NOUN* *The police soon arrived at the scene.* ► police force, constabulary, (*more informal*) the Law, (*more informal*) the Fuzz, (*more informal*) the Bill

police *VERB* *It would be difficult to police such a large area.* ► control, supervise, watch over, monitor, patrol, keep in order, keep the peace at, provide a police presence at

policeman or **policewoman** *NOUN* ► police officer, officer, constable, (*more informal*) bobby, (*more informal*) cop, (*more informal*) copper

policy *NOUN* **1** *the school's policy on truancy* ► strategy, code of practice, approach (to), procedure **2** *It's always a good policy to read the instructions carefully.* ► practice, habit, custom, rule

polish *VERB* **1** *I must polish my shoes.* ► shine, brush up, clean, buff up, burnish, brighten, rub down, rub up, wax
polish off *The boys polished off a plate of burgers.* ► finish, eat up
polish up *She sat down to polish up her essay.* ► improve, refine, enhance, brush up

polish *NOUN* **1** *The table had a lovely bright polish.* ► shine, sheen, gloss, lustre, patina, finish **2** *His years abroad had given him polish.* ► refinement, sophistication, suavity, urbanity, class, finesse, grace, style, elegance

polished *ADJECTIVE* **1** *a polished table* ► shiny, shining, bright, glossy, gleaming, lustrous, burnished, glassy OPPOSITES ARE dull, tarnished **2** *polished manners* ► refined, sophisticated, suave, urbane, polite, cultured, elegant, gracious, perfected, (*more informal*) posh OPPOSITES ARE rough, crude **3** *a polished performance* ► accomplished, skilful, masterly, expert, flawless, faultless

polite *ADJECTIVE* *They were too polite to complain.* ► well-mannered, courteous, respectful, civil, well behaved, considerate, cultivated
AN OPPOSITE IS rude

poll *NOUN* **1** *There would have to be a second poll to decide the winner.* ► ballot, vote, election **2** *The store organized a poll to determine views on smoking.* ► survey, opinion poll, sampling, census, plebiscite, referendum

a b c d e f g h i j k l m n o p q r s t u v w x y z

poll *VERB* **polls, polling, polled 1** vote at an election **2** receive a stated number of votes in an election
▷ **polling booth** *NOUN* **polling station** *NOUN*

pollen *NOUN* powder produced by flowers, containing male cells for fertilizing other flowers

pollen count *NOUN* **pollen counts** a measurement of the amount of pollen in the air, given as a warning for people who are allergic to pollen

pollinate *VERB* **pollinates, pollinating, pollinated** fertilize a plant with pollen
▷ **pollination** *NOUN*

poll tax *NOUN* **poll taxes** a tax that every adult has to pay regardless of income

pollute *VERB* **pollutes, polluting, polluted** make the air, water, etc. dirty or impure
▷ **pollutant** *NOUN* **pollution** *NOUN*

polygamy (pol- ig- a- mee) *NOUN* having more than one wife at a time
▷ **polygamous** *ADJECTIVE* **polygamist** *NOUN*

polygon *NOUN* **polygons** a shape with many sides. Hexagons and octagons are polygons
▷ **polygonal** *ADJECTIVE*

polyhedron *NOUN* **polyhedrons** a solid shape with many sides

polytechnic *NOUN* **polytechnics** a college giving instruction in many subjects at degree level or below. In 1992 the British polytechnics were able to change their names and call themselves universities

polythene *NOUN* a lightweight plastic used to make bags, wrappings, etc.

pomegranate *NOUN* **pomegranates** a tropical fruit with many seeds [from Latin *pomum* = apple + *granatum* = having many seeds]

pomp *NOUN* the ceremonial splendour that is traditional on important public occasions

pompous *ADJECTIVE* full of excessive dignity and self-importance
▷ **pompously** *ADVERB* **pomposity** *NOUN*

pond *NOUN* **ponds** a small lake

ponder *VERB* **ponders, pondering, pondered** think deeply and seriously

ponderous *ADJECTIVE* **1** heavy and awkward **2** laborious and dull • *He writes in a ponderous style.*
▷ **ponderously** *ADVERB*

pontificate *VERB* **pontificates, pontificating, pontificated** give your opinions in a pompous way
▷ **pontification** *NOUN*

pony *NOUN* **ponies** a small horse

ponytail *NOUN* **ponytails** a bunch of long hair tied at the back of the head

poodle *NOUN* **poodles** a dog with thick curly hair

pool[1] *NOUN* **pools 1** a pond **2** a puddle **3** a swimming pool

pool[2] *NOUN* **pools 1** the fund of money staked in a gambling game **2** a group of things shared by several people **3** a game resembling billiards **the pools** gambling based on the results of football matches

pool *VERB* **pools, pooling, pooled** put money or things together for sharing

poor *ADJECTIVE* **1** with very little money or other resources **2** not good; inadequate • *a poor piece of work* **3** unfortunate; deserving pity • *Poor fellow!*
▷ **poorness** *NOUN*

poorly *ADVERB* in a poor way • *We've played poorly this season.*

poorly *ADJECTIVE* rather ill • *You look poorly.*

pop[1] *NOUN* **pops 1** a small explosive sound **2** a fizzy drink

Thesaurus

pompous *ADJECTIVE He sounded so pompous I couldn't help giggling.* ► self-important, grandiose, overbearing, haughty, arrogant, conceited, pretentious, puffed up, condescending, domineering
AN OPPOSITE IS modest

ponder *VERB* **ponder** *or* **ponder about** *It was a good time to ponder the events of the last week.* ► consider, think about, contemplate, reflect on, meditate on, review, mull over

ponderous *ADJECTIVE* **1** *He spoke in a slow ponderous way.* ► clumsy, awkward, lumbering, cumbersome, ungainly
OPPOSITES ARE elegant, graceful

pool *NOUN* **1** *a pool of water* ► pond, puddle, lake, mere, tarn **2** *a pool of hire cars* ► supply, stock, reserve

poor *ADJECTIVE* **1** *The scheme was intended to rehouse poor families.* ► impoverished, poverty-stricken, badly off, impecunious, hard-up, destitute, penniless OPPOSITES ARE rich, wealthy **2** *The workmanship was of poor quality.* ► inferior, substandard, deficient, defective, unsatisfactory, mediocre, second-rate, shoddy OPPOSITES ARE superior, fine **3** *The poor man had to wait ten hours for a train.* ► unfortunate, unlucky, luckless, wretched, pitiful, unhappy OPPOSITES ARE fortunate, lucky

poorly *ADJECTIVE She began to feel poorly in the taxi home.* ► ill, unwell, sick, out of sorts, off colour, indisposed, ailing, peaky, queasy, nauseous

pop *NOUN the pop of an air rifle* ► crack, bang, explosion, burst, snap

pop *VERB* **pops, popping, popped 1** make a pop **2** (*informal*) go or put quickly • *Pop down to the shop.* • *I'll just pop this pie into the microwave.*

pop[2] *NOUN* modern popular music

Pope *NOUN* **Popes** the leader of the Roman Catholic Church

pop-eyed *ADJECTIVE* with bulging eyes

poplar *NOUN* **poplars** a tall slender tree

poppadom *NOUN* **poppadoms** a thin crisp biscuit made of lentil flour, eaten with Indian food

poppy *NOUN* **poppies** a plant with large red flowers

popular *ADJECTIVE* **1** liked or enjoyed by many people **2** believed by many people • *popular opinion* **3** intended for the general public
▷ **popularly** *ADVERB* **popularity** *NOUN*

populate *VERB* **populates, populating, populated** supply with a population; inhabit

population *NOUN* **populations** the people who live in a district or country; the total number of these people

porcelain *NOUN* the finest kind of china

porch *NOUN* **porches** a shelter outside the entrance to a building

porcupine *NOUN* **porcupines** a small animal covered with long prickles

pore[1] *NOUN* **pores** a tiny opening on the skin through which moisture can pass in or out

pore[2] *VERB* **pores, poring, pored**
pore over study with close attention • *He was poring over his books.*
USAGE Do not confuse with **pour**.

pork *NOUN* meat from a pig [from Latin *porcus* = pig]

pornography (porn- og- ra- fee) *NOUN* obscene pictures or writings
▷ **pornographic** *ADJECTIVE*

porpoise (por- pus) *NOUN* **porpoises** a sea animal rather like a small whale

porridge *NOUN* a food made by boiling oatmeal to a thick paste [from an old word *pottage* = soup]

port[1] *NOUN* **ports 1** a harbour **2** a city or town with a harbour **3** the left-hand side of a ship or aircraft when you are facing forward COMPARE **starboard** [from Latin *portus* = harbour]

port[2] *NOUN* a strong red Portuguese wine [from the city of Oporto in Portugal]

portable *ADJECTIVE* able to be carried [from Latin *portare* = carry]

portcullis *NOUN* **portcullises** a strong heavy vertical grating that can be lowered in grooves to block the gateway to a castle [from early French *porte coleice* = sliding door]

porter[1] *NOUN* **porters** a person whose job is to carry luggage or other goods [from Latin *portare* = carry]

porter[2] *NOUN* **porters** a person whose job is to look after the entrance to a large building [from Latin *porta* = gate]

porthole *NOUN* **portholes** a small window in the side of a ship or aircraft

portion *NOUN* **portions** a part or share given to somebody

Thesaurus

pop *VERB* *Corks were popping everywhere.*
► crack, go bang, explode, go off, burst, snap

poppycock *NOUN* (*informal*) *They rejected the charges as poppycock.* ► nonsense, rubbish, claptrap, gibberish, drivel

popular *ADJECTIVE* **1** *a popular student* ► well-liked, favoured, favourite, liked, admired, accepted **2** *a popular line in women's fashion* ► modish, sought-after, well-known, current, (*more informal*) trendy

popularize *VERB* **1** *to popularize a new product* ► make popular, bring into vogue *or* fashion, promote, spread **2** *There are several good books that popularize the subject.* ► simplify, make accessible, make easy, present in a popular way, universalize

population *NOUN* *the population of the country* ► inhabitants, people, populace, residents, citizens, occupants, community

pore *VERB* **pore over** *She was poring over a map of Greece.* ► study, peruse, scan, scrutinize, be absorbed in, be engrossed in

port *NOUN* *A large liner had entered the port.* ► harbour, seaport, marina, anchorage, dock, dockyard, haven

portable *ADJECTIVE* *a portable computer* ► transportable, mobile, movable, lightweight, compact, easy to carry, handy, light, manageable, small

porter *NOUN* **1** *The apartment block had its own porter.* ► caretaker, doorkeeper, doorman, janitor, commissionaire, concierge **2** *A porter helped her with her luggage.* ► baggage-carrier, baggage-handler, baggage-attendant, bearer, carrier

portion *NOUN* **1** *a large portion of rice* ► helping, serving, plateful, bowlful, share, amount, ration, (*more informal*) dollop **2** *Use the rear portion of the train.* ► section, part, segment **3** *Her portion of the inheritance came to several millions.* ► share, allocation, quota, division, ration, percentage

A B C D E F G H I J K L M N O P Q R S T U V W X Y Z

portion VERB **portions, portioning, portioned** divide something into portions • *Portion it out.*

portly ADJECTIVE **portlier, portliest** rather fat
▷ **portliness** NOUN

portrait NOUN **portraits 1** a picture of a person or animal **2** a description in words

pose NOUN **poses 1** a position or posture of the body, e.g. for a portrait or photograph **2** a way of behaving that someone adopts to give a particular impression

pose VERB **poses, posing, posed 1** take up a pose **2** put someone into a pose **3** pretend **4** put forward or present • *It poses several problems for us.*

posh ADJECTIVE (*informal*) **1** very smart; high-class • *a posh restaurant* **2** upper-class • *a posh accent*

position NOUN **positions 1** the place where something is or should be **2** the way a person or thing is placed or arranged • *in a sitting position* **3** a situation or condition • *I am in no position to help you.* **4** paid employment; a job
▷ **positional** ADJECTIVE

positive ADJECTIVE **1** definite or certain • *Are you positive you saw him?* • *We have positive proof that he is guilty.* **2** agreeing; saying 'yes' • *We received a positive reply.* **3** confident and hopeful **4** showing signs of what is being tested for • *Her pregnancy test was positive.* **5** greater than nought **6** to do with the kind of electric charge that lacks electrons **7** (in grammar, said about an adjective or adverb) in the simple form, not comparative or superlative • *The positive form is 'big', the comparative is 'bigger', the superlative is 'biggest'.*
▷ **positively** ADVERB
USAGE The opposite of senses 1-4 is **negative**

possess VERB **possesses, possessing, possessed 1** have or own something **2** control someone's thoughts or behaviour • *I don't know what possessed you to do such a thing!*
▷ **possessor** NOUN

Thesaurus

portrait NOUN *a portrait of the Prince Regent*
► painting, picture , drawing, portrayal, depiction, representation, image, likeness

portray VERB **1** *The artist portrayed her in profile.* ► paint, draw, sketch, depict, show **2** *The novel portrays London life in Victorian England.* ► depict, describe, picture , characterize, represent, illustrate, show, delineate, evoke

pose VERB **1** *River levels pose a threat at this time of year.* ► present, constitute, create, produce **2** *The article poses a number of important questions.* ► raise, put forward, advance, offer, posit, broach, suggest **3** *She posed for a local artist on Saturday afternoons.* ► sit, model, be a model **4** *From his manner it was clear he was only posing.* ► pretend, put on an act, strike a pose, put on airs, feign, masquerade **5 pose as** *He decided to pose as a police officer.*
► impersonate, pretend to be, masquerade as, pass yourself off as

pose NOUN **1** *a model in a suggestive pose*
► attitude, position **2** *His behaviour was only a pose.* ► pretence, act, affectation, façade, show, front, masquerade, posture

poser NOUN **1** (*informal*) *How to get home in time was a bit of a poser.* ► problem, difficulty, dilemma, puzzle **2** (*informal*) *The bar was full of posers showing off to the girls.* ► exhibitionist, poseur, (*informal*) phoney, (*informal*) pseud, (*informal*) show-off

posh ADJECTIVE (*informal*) *The car was parked outside a posh hotel.* ► smart, stylish, high-class, luxury, luxurious, fashionable, elegant, plush, showy, (*informal*) classy, (*informal*) swanky, (*informal*) snazzy, (*informal*) swish

position NOUN **1** *The map shows the position of the house.* ► location, situation, setting, locality, site, point **2** *She rose to a standing position.* ► posture, pose, stance, attitude **3** *His lack of money left him in an awkward position.* ► situation, circumstances, predicament, plight **4** *They well knew their position in society.* ► status, standing, level, role, rank, grade **5** *advertisements for positions in banking* ► job, post, situation, appointment, vacancy **6** *the opposition's position on the war* ► point of view, viewpoint, attitude, policy, stand, standpoint, stance, outlook

position VERB *Chairs had been positioned along the walls.* ► put, arrange, deploy, dispose, locate, place, settle, situate, stand, station

positive ADJECTIVE **1** *I was positive they would come back.* ► certain, sure, convinced, confident, satisfied, assured
OPPOSITES ARE uncertain, unsure **2** *The case lacked positive proof.* ► definite, conclusive, categorical, unequivocal, incontrovertible, irrefutable, indisputable, clear, explicit
OPPOSITES ARE doubtful, unclear **3** *The criticism was positive.* ► helpful, constructive, practical, useful AN OPPOSITE IS negative **4** *a positive advantage* ► definite, conclusive, clear, unmistakable, emphatic, unequivocal, undeniable AN OPPOSITE IS vague **5** *a positive attitude* ► optimistic, confident, hopeful, assured AN OPPOSITE IS pessimistic **6** *The journey was a positive nightmare.* ► absolute, utter, complete, sheer, perfect

possess VERB **1** *The family possessed a house in France.* ► own, have, be in possession of **2** *Foreign armies possessed the country* ► seize,

possessed *ADJECTIVE* seeming to be controlled by strong emotion or an evil spirit • *He fought like a man possessed.*

possession *NOUN* **possessions 1** something you possess or own **2** owning something

possessive *ADJECTIVE* **1** wanting to possess and keep things for yourself **2** (in grammar) showing that somebody owns something • *a possessive pronoun* (see **pronoun**)

possibility *NOUN* **possibilities 1** being possible **2** something that may exist or happen etc.

possible *ADJECTIVE* able to exist, happen, be done, or be used

possibly *ADVERB* **1** in any way • *I can't possibly do it.* **2** perhaps

post[1] *NOUN* **posts 1** an upright piece of wood, concrete, or metal etc. set in the ground **2** the starting point or finishing point of a race • *He was left at the post.*

post *VERB* **posts, posting, posted** put up a notice or poster etc. to announce something

post[2] *NOUN* **1** the collecting and delivering of letters, parcels, etc. **2** these letters and parcels etc.

post *VERB* **posts, posting, posted** put a letter or parcel etc. into a postbox for collection
keep me posted keep me informed

post[3] *NOUN* **posts 1** a position of paid employment; a job **2** the place where someone is on duty • *a sentry post* **3** a place occupied by soldiers, traders, etc.

post *VERB* **posts, posting, posted** place someone on duty • *We posted sentries.*

postage *NOUN* the charge for sending something by post

postage stamp *NOUN* **postage stamps** a stamp for sticking on things to be posted, showing the amount paid

postal *ADJECTIVE* to do with or by the post

postal order *NOUN* **postal orders** a document bought from a post office for sending money by post

postbox *NOUN* **postboxes** a box into which letters are put for collection

postcard *NOUN* **postcards** a card for sending messages by post without an envelope

postcode *NOUN* **postcodes** a group of letters and numbers included in an address to help in sorting the post

poster *NOUN* **posters** a large sheet of paper announcing or advertising something, for display in a public place

Thesaurus

occupy, take over, acquire, control, dominate, govern, rule **3** *A strange feeling possessed him.* ► preoccupy, obsess, dominate, haunt, consume

possession *NOUN* **1** *She came into possession of the fortune.* ► ownership, control, title, tenure, custody **2 possessions** *She put her few possessions in the van.* ► belongings, things, property, chattels, effects, assets, goods, bits and pieces

possessive *ADJECTIVE* *He was very possessive and grew angry when she wanted to leave.* ► proprietorial, overprotective, clinging, domineering, jealous, selfish

possibility *NOUN* **1** *There was still a possibility they might come.* ► chance, likelihood, probability, prospect, hope, fear **2** *the possibility of starting their own business* ► feasibility, practicality, capability, potentiality **3** *They even considered the possibility of going to war.* ► option, alternative, choice

possible *ADJECTIVE* **1** *An improvement next year might be possible.* ► feasible, practicable, achievable, attainable, viable, workable AN OPPOSITE IS impossible **2** *There is another possible explanation.* ► conceivable, imaginable, plausible, likely, believable, tenable, credible OPPOSITES ARE unlikely, inconceivable **3** *He is regarded as a possible party leader.* ► potential, prospective, probable, promising, likely OPPOSITES ARE unlikely, improbable

possibly *ADVERB* **1** *Possibly Jane will be there too.* ► maybe, perhaps, conceivably **2** *Could you possibly bring some food?* ► conceivably, by any chance, at all

post *NOUN* **1** *a flat roof supported by wooden posts* ► pole, pillar, stake, stick, upright, support, shaft, spar **2** *The post hasn't come yet.* ► mail, letters, delivery **3** *The post will be advertised in the local newspaper.* ► job, position, situation, appointment, vacancy

post *VERB* **1** *An announcement had been posted on all notice boards.* ► display, pin up, put up, stick up, advertise, announce **2** *I must go and post a letter.* ► mail, send, dispatch, put in the post, send off, get off

posterity *NOUN* future generations of people • *These letters and diaries should be preserved for posterity*

postman *NOUN* **postmen** a person who delivers or collects letters etc.

postmark *NOUN* **postmarks** an official mark put on something sent by post to show where and when it was posted

post-mortem *NOUN* **post-mortems** an examination of a dead body to discover the cause of death

posthumous (poss- tew- mus) *ADJECTIVE* coming after a person's death • *a posthumous award for bravery*
▷ **posthumously** *ADVERB*

post office *NOUN* **post offices** **1** a building or room where postal business is carried on **2** the national organization responsible for postal services

postpone *VERB* **postpones, postponing, postponed** fix a later time for something • *They postponed the meeting for a fortnight.*
▷ **postponement** *NOUN*

postscript *NOUN* **postscripts** something extra added at the end of a letter (after the writer's signature) or at the end of a book

posture *NOUN* **postures** a particular position of the body, or the way in which a person stands, sits, or walks

post-war *ADJECTIVE* happening during the time after a war

pot[1] *NOUN* **pots** **1** a deep, usually round, container **2** (*informal*) a lot of something • *He has got pots of money.*
go to pot (*informal*) lose quality; be ruined
take pot luck (*informal*) take whatever is available

pot *VERB* **pots, potting, potted** put into a pot

pot[2] *NOUN* (*informal*) cannabis

potassium *NOUN* a soft silvery-white metal substance that is essential for living things

potato *NOUN* **potatoes** a starchy white tuber growing underground, used as a vegetable [via Spanish from a Caribbean word]

potentate (poh- ten- tayt) *NOUN* **potentates** a powerful monarch or ruler

potential (po- ten- shal) *ADJECTIVE* capable of happening or being used or developed • *a potential winner*
▷ **potentially** *ADVERB* **potentiality** *NOUN*

potential *NOUN* **1** the ability of a person or thing to develop in the future **2** (in science) the voltage between two points

pothole *NOUN* **potholes** **1** a deep natural hole in the ground **2** a hole in a road

potion *NOUN* **potions** a liquid for drinking as a medicine etc.

potted *ADJECTIVE* **1** shortened or abridged • *a potted account of the story* **2** preserved in a pot • *potted shrimps*

potter[1] *NOUN* **potters** a person who makes pottery

potter[2] *VERB* **potters, pottering, pottered** work or move about in a leisurely way • *I spent the afternoon pottering around in the garden.*

pottery *NOUN* **potteries** **1** cups, plates, ornaments, etc. made of baked clay **2** the craft of making these things **3** a place where a potter works

pouch *NOUN* **pouches** **1** a small bag **2** a fold of skin in which a kangaroo etc. keeps its young **3** something shaped like a bag

poultry *NOUN* birds (e.g. chickens, geese, and turkeys) kept for their eggs and meat

pounce *VERB* **pounces, pouncing, pounced** jump or swoop down quickly on something
▷ **pounce** *NOUN*

Thesaurus

postpone *VERB The game was postponed for a fortnight.* ► put off, defer, delay, put back, adjourn, hold over, suspend, put on ice

posture *NOUN He bent his head forward in a posture of respect.* ► position, stance, pose, attitude, bearing, deportment

posy *NOUN a posy of violets and freesias* ► bouquet, bunch, spray, nosegay, buttonhole, corsage

pot *NOUN a pot of stew* ► pan, saucepan, vessel, casserole, cauldron, stewpot, stockpot, crock, urn

potent *ADJECTIVE* **1** *a potent drug* ► strong, powerful, pungent, intoxicating **2** *a potent influence* ► strong, powerful, vigorous, compelling, impressive, dominant, overpowering, weighty

potty *ADJECTIVE* **1** (*informal*) *Maybe I'm going potty.* ► mad, insane, crazy, (*informal*) round the bend, (*informal*) bonkers **2** **potty about** *She's potty about her two sons.* ► devoted to, infatuated with, smitten with, mad about, crazy about

pounce *VERB* **pounce on** *The animal pounced on its prey.* ► jump on, spring on, leap on, swoop on, bound at, lunge at, attack, ambush

pound[1] *NOUN* **pounds 1** a unit of money (in Britain = 100 pence) **2** a unit of weight equal to 16 ounces or about 454 grams [from Old English *pund*]

pound[2] *NOUN* **pounds 1** a place where stray animals are taken **2** a public enclosure for vehicles officially removed [origin unknown]

pound[3] *VERB* **pounds, pounding, pounded 1** hit something often, especially in order to crush it **2** run or go heavily • *He pounded down the stairs.* **3** thump • *My heart was pounding.* [from Old English *punian*]

pour *VERB* **pours, pouring, poured 1** flow or make something flow **2** rain heavily • *It poured all day.* **3** come or go in large amounts • *Letters poured in.*
▷ **pourer** *NOUN*
USAGE Do not confuse with **pore**.

pout *VERB* **pouts, pouting, pouted** push out your lips when you are annoyed or sulking
▷ **pout** *NOUN*

poverty *NOUN* **1** being poor **2** a lack or scarcity • *a poverty of ideas*

powder *NOUN* **powders 1** a mass of fine dry particles of something **2** a medicine or cosmetic etc. made as a powder **3** gunpowder
▷ **powdery** *ADJECTIVE*

powder *VERB* **powders, powdering, powdered 1** put powder on something **2** make something into powder

power *NOUN* **powers 1** strength or energy **2** the ability to do something • *the power of speech* **3** political authority or control **4** a powerful country, person, or organization **5** mechanical or electrical energy; the electricity supply • *There was a power failure after the storm.* **6** (in science) the rate of doing work, measured in watts or horsepower **7** (*in mathematics*) the product of a number multiplied by itself a given number of times • *The third power of 2 = 2 x 2 x 2 = 8*
▷ **powered** *ADJECTIVE* **powerless** *ADJECTIVE*

powerful *ADJECTIVE* having great power, strength, or influence
▷ **powerfully** *ADVERB*

power station *NOUN* **power stations** a building where electricity is produced

pp. *ABBREVIATION* pages

practicable *ADJECTIVE* able to be done
USAGE Do not confuse with **practical**.

practical *ADJECTIVE* **1** able to do or make useful things • *a practical person* **2** likely to be useful • *a very practical invention* **3** actually doing something, rather than just learning or thinking about it • *She has had practical experience.*
▷ **practicality** *NOUN*
USAGE Do not confuse with **practicable**.

Thesaurus

pound *VERB* **1** *Hans pounded his huge fists on the desk and glared.* ► beat, strike, thump, thud, batter, bang, bash **2 pound on** *He pounded on the gates, shouting wildly.* ► batter, beat, thump, pummel, bang on, strike, hit **3** *Her heart was pounding.* ► throb, pulsate, thump, thud, race **4** *Pound the garlic with a little salt.* ► crush, grind, powder, mash, pulverize

pour *VERB* **1** *Blood poured from his wound.* ► spill, issue, stream, run, discharge, flow, gush, spout **2** *She poured milk from the jug.* ► serve, tip, decant

poverty *NOUN* *The region suffered from years of poverty.* ► want, penury, privation, destitution, hardship, shortage, need, necessity AN OPPOSITE IS wealth

powdery *ADJECTIVE* *a white powdery deposit* ► dusty, sandy, grainy, chalky, crumbly, fine, granular, loose, pulverized

power *NOUN* **1** *His father had a stroke and lost the power of speech.* ► faculty, property, capability, capacity, ability, competence **2** *Who knows where the real power lies.* ► control, authority, influence, dominance, mastery, domination **3** *The governor has the power to impose a curfew.* ► right, prerogative, authorization, authority **4** *a speech of great power* ► force, strength, potency, vigour, intensity, energy AN OPPOSITE IS weakness

powerful *ADJECTIVE* **1** *a powerful blow* ► violent, hard, strong, forceful AN OPPOSITE IS weak **2** *a powerful ruler* ► dominant, commanding, forceful, strong, vigorous, effective OPPOSITES ARE weak, ineffective **3** *a powerful physique* ► strong, muscular, sturdy, hefty, mighty, solid, burly OPPOSITES ARE weak, puny **4** *a powerful argument* ► strong, convincing, compelling, cogent, overwhelming OPPOSITES ARE weak, unconvincing

powerless 1 *We felt powerless in the face of such determination.* ► impotent, helpless, ineffectual, ineffective, incapable, defenceless, feeble, weak OPPOSITES ARE powerful, strong **2** *The police were powerless to act.* ► unable, incapable (of acting), without power

practicable *ADJECTIVE* *Such a detailed plan would not be practicable.* ► realistic, feasible, viable, workable, achievable, attainable, possible, sensible, practical OPPOSITES ARE impracticable, impractical

practical *ADJECTIVE* **1** *You need practical experience of the work before you apply for the job.* ► real, actual, hands-on, empirical, relevant

practical *NOUN* **practicals** a lesson or examination in which you actually do or make something rather than reading or writing about it • *a chemistry practical*

practical joke *NOUN* **practical jokes** a trick played on somebody

practically *ADVERB* **1** in a practical way **2** almost • *I've practically finished.*

practice *NOUN* **practices** **1** doing something repeatedly in order to become better at it • *Have you done your piano practice?* **2** actually doing something; action, not theory • *It works well in practice.* **3** the professional business of a doctor, dentist, lawyer, etc. **4** a habit or custom • *It is his practice to work until midnight.*
out of practice no longer skilful because you have not practised recently
USAGE See the note on **practise.**

practise *VERB* **practises, practising, practised** **1** do something repeatedly in order to become better at it **2** do something actively or habitually • *Practise what you preach.* **3** work as a doctor, dentist, or lawyer
USAGE Note the spelling: **practice** is a noun, **practise** is a verb.

practised *ADJECTIVE* experienced or expert

prairie *NOUN* **prairies** a large area of flat grass-covered land in North America

praise *VERB* **praises, praising, praised** **1** say that somebody or something is very good **2** honour God in words

praise *NOUN* words that praise somebody or something
▷ **praiseworthy** *ADJECTIVE*

pram *NOUN* **prams** a four-wheeled carriage for a baby, pushed by a person walking

prance *VERB* **prances, prancing, pranced** move about in a lively or happy way

prank *NOUN* **pranks** a trick played for mischief; a practical joke
▷ **prankster** *NOUN*

prattle *VERB* **prattles, prattling, prattled** chatter like a young child
▷ **prattle** *NOUN*

prawn *NOUN* **prawns** an edible shellfish like a large shrimp

pray *VERB* **prays, praying, prayed** **1** talk to God **2** ask earnestly for something **3** (*formal*) please • *Pray be seated.*

prayer *NOUN* **prayers** praying; words used in praying

pre- *PREFIX* before (as in *prehistoric*)

preach *VERB* **preaches, preaching, preached** give a religious or moral talk
▷ **preacher** *NOUN*

Thesaurus

AN OPPOSITE IS theoretical **2** *We can't think of any practical alternatives.* ► workable, feasible, realistic, viable, reasonable, sensible, possible, achievable AN OPPOSITE IS impractical **3** *Let's be practical and not try far-fetched ideas.* ► pragmatic, sensible, realistic, down-to-earth, commonsensical, hard-headed AN OPPOSITE IS impractical **4** *a cute little gadget but also practical* ► handy, functional, useful, serviceable, utilitarian
OPPOSITES ARE impractical, useless

practically *ADVERB* *The place was practically deserted.* ► almost, nearly, virtually, just about, more or less, close to

practice *NOUN* **1** *It has become a common practice to use robots to disarm devices.* ► custom, procedure, convention, policy, routine, method, system **2** *It takes a lot of practice to play that well.* ► training, rehearsal, preparation, exercise, drill **3** *He was better at the theory than the practice of medicine.* ► application, exercise, use, execution, implementation **4** **in practice** *The idea is good but probably won't work in practice.* ► in real life, for real, in reality, in actuality, in effect, in operation

practise *VERB* **1** *They practised these pieces for weeks.* ► do exercises, drill, exercise, prepare, rehearse, train, warm up **2** *These customs are still practised in some parts of the world.* ► follow, carry out, perform, put into practice, observe, apply, engage in

praise *VERB* **1** *The judge praised her for her bravery.* ► commend, applaud, pay tribute to, express approval of, compliment, congratulate, admire, acclaim, acknowledge, eulogize **2** *They praised God for the good harvest.* ► worship, glorify, honour, exalt, adore

praise *NOUN* **1** *The rescue services deserve all our praise.* ► approval, acclaim, admiration, commendation, applause, adulation, recognition, tribute **2** *Give praise to God.* ► homage, honour, worship, thanks, thanksgiving, glory, adoration

praiseworthy *ADJECTIVE* *a praiseworthy attempt to put things right* ► commendable, laudable, admirable, creditable, worthy, estimable, exemplary, deserving, honourable, meritorious OPPOSITES ARE deplorable, blameworthy

prank *NOUN* *It had been a prank that had gone tragically wrong.* ► escapade, trick, practical joke, game, hoax, stunt, (*more informal*) lark

pray *VERB* **pray to** *The village prayed to God for a good harvest.* ► ask, beg, call upon, entreat, beseech, invoke, supplicate, say prayers to

prayer *NOUN* *The priest murmured some prayers.* ► invocation, devotion, supplication, entreaty

precarious (pri- kair- ee- us) *ADJECTIVE* not very safe or secure
▷ **precariously** *ADVERB*

precaution *NOUN* **precautions** something done to prevent future trouble or danger
▷ **precautionary** *ADJECTIVE*

precede *VERB* **precedes, preceding, preceded** come or go before someone or something else
USAGE Do not confuse with **proceed.**

precedence (press- i- dens) *NOUN* the right of someone or something to be first
take precedence have priority

precedent (press- i- dent) *NOUN* **precedents** a previous case that is taken as an example to be followed

precinct (pree- sinkt) *NOUN* **precincts** **1** the area round a place, especially round a cathedral **2** a part of a town where traffic is not allowed • *a shopping precinct*

precious *ADJECTIVE* **1** very valuable **2** greatly loved
▷ **preciousness** *NOUN*

precious *ADVERB* (*informal*) very • *We have precious little time.*

precipice *NOUN* **precipices** a very steep place, such as the face of a cliff

précis (pray- see) *NOUN* **précis** (pray- seez) a summary

precise *ADJECTIVE* exact; clearly stated
▷ **precisely** *ADVERB* **precision** *NOUN*

precocious (prik- oh- shus) *ADJECTIVE* (said about a child) very advanced or developed for his or her age
▷ **precociously** *ADVERB* **precocity** *NOUN*

predator (pred- a- ter) *NOUN* **predators** an animal that hunts or preys upon others
▷ **predatory** *ADJECTIVE*

predecessor (pree- dis- ess- er) *NOUN* **predecessors** an earlier person or thing, e.g. an ancestor or the former holder of a job

predicate *NOUN* **predicates** the part of a sentence that says something about the subject, e.g. 'is short' in *life is short*

predicative (prid- ik- a- tiv) *ADJECTIVE* forming part of the predicate, e.g. *old* in • *The dog is old.*
COMPARE **attributive**
▷ **predicatively** *ADVERB*

predict *VERB* **predicts, predicting, predicted** say what will happen in the future; foretell or prophesy
▷ **predictable** *ADJECTIVE* **prediction** *NOUN* **predictor** *NOUN*

predispose *VERB* **predisposes, predisposing, predisposed** make you likely to be in favour of something • *We are predisposed to help them.*
▷ **predisposition** *NOUN*

predominate *VERB* **predominates, predominating, predominated** be the largest or most important or most powerful
▷ **predominant** *ADJECTIVE* **predominance** *NOUN*

pre-eminent *ADJECTIVE* excelling others; outstanding
▷ **pre-eminently** *ADVERB* **pre-eminence** *NOUN*

preen *VERB* **preens, preening, preened** (said about a bird) smooth its feathers with its beak
preen yourself smarten your appearance

preface (pref- as) *NOUN* **prefaces** an introduction at the beginning of a book or speech
▷ **preface** *VERB*

prefect *NOUN* **prefects** **1** a senior pupil in a school, given authority to help to keep order **2** a regional official in France, Japan, and other countries

Thesaurus

precaution *NOUN* *As an extra precaution, tell a neighbour when you are going to be away.*
► safeguard, safety measure, insurance, protection, defence, provision

precious *ADJECTIVE* **1** *a collection of precious paintings* ► valuable, priceless, choice, costly, inestimable, rare **2** *The ring was her most precious possession.* ► treasured, cherished, valued, prized, favourite, dearest, beloved **3** *This action gained them a few precious minutes.* ► valuable, priceless, vital

precise *ADJECTIVE* **1** *I don't know the precise time. Here are the precise measurements of the room.* ► exact, accurate, correct, detailed, definite OPPOSITES ARE imprecise, approximate, rough **2** *The train stopped at that precise moment.* ► exact, particular, specific, actual **3** *The workmanship is very precise.* ► meticulous, careful, exact, detailed, finicky, punctilious, scrupulous AN OPPOSITE IS careless

precisely *ADVERB* **1** *The plane took off at three o'clock precisely.* ► exactly, on the dot, promptly **2** *The house is precisely what we are looking for.* ► exactly, absolutely, entirely, altogether, in every way

predict *VERB* *The polls predicted a landslide victory.* ► forecast, prophesy, foretell, foresee, divine, forewarn, anticipate, envisage

predictable *ADJECTIVE* *David's reaction was entirely predictable.* ► foreseeable, to be expected, likely, probable, certain
AN OPPOSITE IS unpredictable

A B C D E F G H I J K L M N O P Q R S T U V W X Y Z

prefer VERB **prefers, preferring, preferred**
1 like one person or thing more than another **2** (*formal*) put forward • *They preferred charges of forgery against him.*
▷ **preference** NOUN

preferable (pref- er- a- bul) ADJECTIVE liked better; more desirable
▷ **preferably** ADVERB

prefix NOUN **prefixes** a word or syllable joined to the front of a word to change or add to its meaning, as in *dis*order, *out*stretched, *un*happy

pregnant ADJECTIVE having a baby developing in the womb
▷ **pregnancy** NOUN

prehensile ADJECTIVE (said about an animal's foot or tail etc.) able to grasp things

prehistoric ADJECTIVE belonging to very ancient times, before written records of events were made
▷ **prehistory** NOUN

prejudice NOUN **prejudices** an unfavourable opinion or dislike formed without examining the facts fairly
▷ **prejudiced** ADJECTIVE

preliminary ADJECTIVE coming before an important action or event and preparing for it

prelude NOUN **preludes 1** a thing that introduces or leads up to something else **2** a short piece of music, especially one that introduces a longer piece

premature ADJECTIVE too early; coming before the usual or proper time
▷ **prematurely** ADVERB

premeditated ADJECTIVE planned beforehand • *a premeditated crime*

premier NOUN **premiers** a prime minister or other head of government

première (prem- yair) NOUN **premières** the first public performance of a play or film

premises PLURAL NOUN a building and its grounds

premium NOUN **premiums 1** an amount or instalment paid to an insurance company **2** an extra charge or payment
at a premium in demand but scarce

Premium Bond NOUN **Premium Bonds** a savings certificate that gives the person who holds it a chance to win a prize of money

premonition NOUN **premonitions** a feeling that something is about to happen, especially something bad

preoccupied ADJECTIVE having your thoughts completely busy with something
▷ **preoccupation** NOUN

prep NOUN (*informal*) homework

preparation NOUN **preparations 1** getting something ready **2** something done in order to get ready for an event or activity • *last-minute preparations*

Thesaurus

prefer VERB **1** *I prefer tea thanks.* ► like better, would rather have, favour, go for, opt for, plump for **2 prefer to** *We'd prefer to travel by car.* ► would rather, would sooner, would like better

preferable ADJECTIVE *Many people find self-catering preferable.* ► advantageous, better, more desirable, more suitable, superior, nicer, advisable, preferred
OPPOSITES ARE disadvantageous, undesirable

preference NOUN **1** *Our preference is for winter holidays.* ► liking, choice, inclination, option, partiality, predilection, leaning, wish, fancy **2** *Preference will be given to applicants with a foreign language.* ► precedence, priority, favour, advantage

pregnant ADJECTIVE *It is probably best to cut out alcohol altogether when pregnant.* ► expecting a baby, carrying a child, expectant, (*more informal*) expecting

prejudice NOUN *They were the victims of widespread prejudice.* ► bigotry, bias, discrimination, partisanship, chauvinism, favouritism, intolerance, racialism, racism, sexism AN OPPOSITE IS tolerance

prejudice VERB **1** *He feared the accused's attitude might prejudice the jury.* ► influence, bias, sway, predispose, colour **2** *The reports might prejudice his election chances.* ► damage, harm, injure, be detrimental to, adversely affect, undermine

prejudiced ADJECTIVE **1** *Racially prejudiced attitudes are thought to be widespread.* ► biased, discriminatory, chauvinistic, intolerant, partial **2** *The staff seemed prejudiced against the poor.* ► biased, intolerant (of), partial, conditioned

preoccupied ADJECTIVE **1** *He looked anxious and preoccupied.* ► pensive, thoughtful, lost in thought, absent-minded, rapt **2 preoccupied with** *Sarah became more and more preoccupied with her child.* ► engrossed in, absorbed in, obsessed with, involved with, taken up with, concerned with, wrapped up in, engaged in, immersed in

preparation NOUN **1** *They devoted the next week to the preparation of plans.* ► devising, drawing up, putting together, development, formulation **2** *More staff were taken on to help with the preparations for the hotel's opening.* ► arrangements, plans, provisions, preliminaries, groundwork

preparatory school *NOUN* **preparatory schools** a school that prepares pupils for a higher school

prepare *VERB* **prepares, preparing, prepared** get ready; make something ready
be prepared to be willing to do something

preposition *NOUN* **prepositions** a word used with a noun or pronoun to show place, position, time, or means, e.g. *at* home, *in* the hall, *on* Sunday, *by* train

preposterous *ADJECTIVE* completely absurd or ridiculous

prep school *NOUN* **prep schools** a preparatory school

Presbyterian (prez- bit- eer- ee- an) *NOUN* **Presbyterians** a member of a Christian Church governed by elders who are all of equal rank, especially the national Church of Scotland

prescribe *VERB* **prescribes, prescribing, prescribed 1** advise a person to use a particular medicine or treatment etc. **2** say what should be done

prescription *NOUN* **prescriptions 1** a doctor's written order for a medicine **2** the medicine prescribed **3** prescribing

presence *NOUN* **1** being present in a place • *Your presence is required.* **2** a person's impressive appearance or manner

presence of mind *NOUN* the ability to act quickly and sensibly in an emergency

present[1] *ADJECTIVE* **1** in a particular place • *No one else was present.* **2** belonging or referring to what is happening now; existing now • *the present Queen*

present *NOUN* present times or events
at present now, for the time being

present[2] *NOUN* **presents** something given or received without payment; a gift

present (priz- ent) *VERB* **presents, presenting, presented 1** give something, especially with a ceremony • *Who is to present the prizes?*
2 introduce someone to another person
3 introduce a radio or television programme to an audience **4** put on a play or other

Thesaurus

prepare *VERB* **1** *Students have to prepare their presentations well in advance.* ► draw up, write, compose, construct, put together, get ready, make ready **2** *The cooks have to start preparing the food early each morning.* ► make ready, get ready, make, assemble, cook **3** *We should begin to prepare for the future.* ► plan, make arrangements, make provision *or* provisions, get ready

prepared *ADJECTIVE* **1** *We are prepared to wait for the right person to be found.* ► willing, ready, disposed, predisposed, inclined, able, set AN OPPOSITE IS unwilling **2** *His solicitor read out a prepared statement.* ► pre-arranged, arranged, agreed, organized

preposterous *ADJECTIVE* *Anyone who maintained such a preposterous theory would be considered mad.* ► absurd, ridiculous, ludicrous, laughable, incredible, farcical, risible, foolish, idiotic, (*more informal*) crazy, (*more informal*) daft, (*more informal*) barmy, (*more informal*) zany OPPOSITES ARE reasonable, sensible

prerequisite *ADJECTIVE* *prerequisite qualifications for entry to college* ► compulsory, indispensable, mandatory, necessary, prescribed, required, requisite, specified, stipulated AN OPPOSITE IS **optional**

prescribe *NOUN* **1** *The doctor decided to prescribe penicillin.* ► write a prescription for, authorize, advise, recommend **2** *The teachers would prescribe the topics to be dealt with.* ► stipulate, specify, lay down, assign, fix, impose, ordain, dictate

prescription *NOUN* **1** *Some of these medicines can be bought without a prescription.* ► authorization, order, instruction, direction **2** *She ran to the chemist to fetch her prescription before closing time.* ► medicine, medication, mixture, pills, tablets, drug

presence *NOUN* **1** *She could not explain the presence of Richard's car outside her flat.* ► existence, being there **2** *He requested the presence of a solicitor.* ► attendance, company, appearance, support **3** *She had a strong presence which gave her added authority.* ► aura, air, demeanour, bearing, manner, appearance, charisma **4** *the presence of her family in the area* ► proximity, nearness, closeness, vicinity **5** *They felt some sort of presence in the room* ► spirit, ghost, spectre, phantom

present *ADJECTIVE* (with the stress on *pres-*) **1** *A police officer should be present whenever possible.* ► in attendance, at hand, nearby, attending, available, there *or* here AN OPPOSITE IS absent **2** *The shares are not expected to maintain their present high value.* ► current, present-day, existing, prevailing, contemporary
at present *or* **at the present time** *We have no plans to increase taxes at present.* ► just now, right now, at the moment, at this time, currently

present *NOUN* (with the stress on *pres-*) **1** *a history of the family from the sixteenth century to the present* ► present day, modern times, today **2** *She let him keep the pen as a present.* ► gift, donation, gratuity, contribution, offering

present *VERB* (with the stress on *-sent*) **1** *She presented a prize to the winners.* ► hand out, give out, hand over, award, grant, bestow (on) **2** *The committee has presented its report.*

a b c d e f g h i j k l m n o p q r s t u v w x y z

entertainment **5** show **6** cause or provide a problem or difficulty
▷ **presentation** *NOUN* **presenter** *NOUN*

presently *ADVERB* **1** soon • *I shall be with you presently.* **2** now • *the person who is presently in charge*

preservative *NOUN* **preservatives** a substance added to food to preserve it

preserve *VERB* **preserves, preserving, preserved** keep something safe or in good condition
▷ **preserver** *NOUN* **preservation** *NOUN*

preserve *NOUN* **preserves 1** jam made with preserved fruit **2** an activity that belongs to a particular person or group

preside *VERB* **presides, presiding, presided** be in charge of a meeting etc.

president *NOUN* **presidents 1** the person in charge of a club, society, or council etc. **2** the head of a republic
▷ **presidency** *NOUN* **presidential** *ADJECTIVE*

press *VERB* **presses, pressing, pressed 1** put weight or force steadily on something; squeeze **2** make something by pressing **3** make clothes smooth by ironing them **4** urge; make demands • *They pressed for an increase in wages.*

press *NOUN* **presses 1** a device for pressing things • *a trouser press* **2** a machine for printing things **3** a firm that prints or publishes books etc. • *Oxford University Press* **4** newspapers; journalists

pressing *ADJECTIVE* needing immediate action; urgent • *a pressing need*

press-up *NOUN* **press-ups** an exercise in which you lie face downwards and press down with your hands to lift your body

pressure *NOUN* **pressures 1** continuous pressing **2** the force with which something presses **3** the force of the atmosphere on the earth's surface • *a band of high pressure* **4** an influence that persuades or compels you to do something

prestige (pres- teej) *NOUN* good reputation
▷ **prestigious** *ADJECTIVE*
[from Latin *praestigium* = an illusion, glamour]

presumably *ADVERB* according to what you may presume

presume *VERB* **presumes, presuming, presumed 1** suppose; assume something to be true • *I presumed that they were dead.* **2** (*formal*) take the liberty of doing something; venture • *May we presume to advise you?*
▷ **presumption** *NOUN*

presumptuous *ADJECTIVE* too bold or confident
▷ **presumptuously** *ADVERB*

Thesaurus

► submit, tender, hand in, offer, proffer, publish **3** *The situation presents some novel features.* ► show, demonstrate, display, exhibit **4** *A compère presented each act.* ► introduce, announce

presently *ADVERB* **1** *We'll be there presently.* ► shortly, soon, directly, in a while, (*more informal*) in a bit **2** *The family is presently abroad.* ► currently, at present, at the moment, now

preserve *VERB* **1** *Local action can also preserve wildlife.* ► safeguard, secure, protect, conserve, maintain, sustain, uphold, defend, guard OPPOSITES ARE endanger, neglect **2** *She wanted to preserve him from harm.* ► protect, defend, guard, safeguard, shield **3** *special containers for preserving fruit* ► conserve, bottle, store, keep, save

preside *VERB* *We elect a chairman to preside at the meeting.* ► officiate, take charge, be in charge, take the chair
preside over *The finance director presides over the annual budget review.* ► be in charge of, direct, have responsibility for, manage, be in control of

press *VERB* **1** *She pressed his hand.* ► squeeze, grip, clutch, clinch **2** *He pressed some clothes into a suitcase.* ► squash, stuff, cram, push, squeeze, force **3** *Donna needed time to press her clothes.* ► iron, smooth, smooth out, flatten **4** *The next process is to press the grapes.* ► crush, squeeze, compress, mash, pulp **5** *People pressed round to see what was going on.* ► gather, cluster, crowd, swarm, throng **6** *You must press them to give you an answer.* ► urge, pressure, persuade, compel, plead with, force, insist on USAGE If you use *insist on* you say *You must insist on them giving (or their giving) you an answer.*

pressure *NOUN* **1** *The pressure on the foundations caused them to crack.* ► force, load, weight, burden, strain, stress **2** *The team is working under severe pressure.* ► stress, strain, difficulty, (*more informal*) hassle **3** *She was under a lot of pressure to accept the offer.* ► constraint, coercion, duress, harassment, compulsion, intimidation

prestige *NOUN* *Achieving an agreement would bring the president added prestige.* ► status, reputation, standing, credit, kudos, renown, esteem, fame, glory, honour, importance

presume *VERB* **1** *We presume there will be a call-out charge.* ► assume, expect, suppose, imagine, take it, dare say, guess, conjecture, surmise, believe **2** *Don't presume to take charge yourself.* ► venture, dare, have the nerve, have the temerity, have the audacity, be so bold as, go so far as

presumptuous *ADJECTIVE* *It was presumptuous to make a decision without consulting us.* ► arrogant, audacious, forward, bold,

presuppose *VERB* **presupposes, presupposing, presupposed** suppose or assume something beforehand
▷ **presupposition** *NOUN*

pretence *NOUN* **pretences** an attempt to pretend that something is true
false pretences pretending to be something that you are not in order to deceive people
• *You've invited me here under false pretences.*

pretend *VERB* **pretends, pretending, pretended** behave as if something is true or real when you know that it is not, either in play or so as to deceive people

pretender *NOUN* **pretenders** a person who claims a throne or title

pretentious *ADJECTIVE* **1** trying to impress by claiming greater importance or merit than is actually the case **2** showy or ostentatious
▷ **pretentiously** *ADVERB* **pretentiousness** *NOUN*

pretext *NOUN* **pretexts** a reason put forward to conceal the true reason

pretty *ADJECTIVE* **prettier, prettiest** attractive in a delicate way
▷ **prettily** *ADVERB* **prettiness** *NOUN*

pretty *ADVERB* (*informal*) quite • *It's pretty cold.* [from Old English]

prevent *VERB* **prevents, preventing, prevented 1** stop something from happening **2** stop a person from doing something
▷ **preventable** *ADJECTIVE* **prevention** *NOUN* **preventive** *ADJECTIVE*

preview *NOUN* **previews** a showing of a film or play etc. before it is shown to the general public

previous *ADJECTIVE* coming before this; preceding
▷ **previously** *ADVERB*

prey (rhymes with *pray*) *NOUN* an animal that is hunted or killed by another for food

prey *VERB* **preys, preying, preyed**
prey on 1 hunt or take as prey **2** cause to worry • *The problem preyed on his mind.*

price *NOUN* **prices 1** the amount of money for which something is bought or sold **2** what

Thesaurus

impudent, insolent, bumptious, unwarranted, conceited, impertinent, overconfident, shameless, (*more informal*) pushy, (*more informal*) cheeky

pretence *NOUN* *Their self-confidence turned out to be just a pretence.* ► make-believe, act, show, display, front, affectation, deception, posturing, façade, masquerade, charade, subterfuge, falsehood, sham, pose, ruse, bluff, cover, faking, dissembling

pretend *VERB* **1** *She pretended to understand, but we were all confused.* ► affect, profess, claim, purport **2** *Let's pretend we're ghosts.* ► imagine, make believe, suppose, play being

pretend *ADJECTIVE* (*informal*) *He made his room into a pretend cave.* ► imaginary, make-believe, fantasy, fanciful, mythical, pretended

pretentious *ADJECTIVE* *The best food can often be found in smaller, less pretentious restaurants.* ► ostentatious, showy, affected, conspicuous, flashy, grandiose, extravagant
OPPOSITES ARE modest, unassuming

pretty *ADJECTIVE* *a pretty little garden* ► attractive, lovely, good-looking, beautiful, charming, appealing, pleasing, (*more informal*) cute OPPOSITES ARE plain, ugly, hideous

pretty *ADVERB* (*informal*) *It was a pretty daft thing to do.* ► rather, quite, somewhat, fairly, moderately, (*more informal*) kind of

prevail *VERB* **1** *attitudes that prevailed in the 1960s* ► exist, hold, obtain, be prevalent, be current **2** *Common sense prevailed in the end.* ► win, win through, triumph, reign, rule, predominate **3** *The Greek army prevailed against all the odds.* ► be victorious, triumph, win
prevail on or **upon** *Can you prevail on her to change her mind?* ► persuade, induce, urge, pressure, pressurize, tempt

prevent *VERB* **1** *It was too late to prevent the accident.* ► stop, avert, avoid, head off, forestall, frustrate, hinder **2** *I'll try to prevent them from coming in before you're ready.* ► stop, restrain, check, inhibit, block, bar

previous *ADJECTIVE* *a review of the previous three years* ► preceding, foregoing, antecedent, last, earlier, former, prior
AN OPPOSITE IS following

previously *ADVERB* *Previously she had worked in a chemist.* ► formerly, earlier, in the past, at one time, before this *or* that, hitherto

prey *NOUN* *Lions are often slower than their prey.* ► quarry, victim, game, kill

prey *VERB* **prey on 1** *Wild dogs will also prey on cattle.* ► hunt, catch, kill, eat, feed on **2** *The thought kept preying on his mind.* ► trouble, oppress, disturb, distress, haunt, beset, burden, weigh down, worry

price *NOUN* **1** *The price of your holiday is fully guaranteed.* ► cost, terms, rate, amount, charge (for), outlay (on) **2** *What price should you charge?* ► amount, figure, sum, fee, rate,

a b c d e f g h i j k l m n o p q r s t u v w x y z

must be given or done in order to achieve something

priceless *ADJECTIVE* **1** very valuable **2** (*informal*) very amusing

prick *VERB* **pricks, pricking, pricked 1** make a tiny hole in something **2** hurt somebody with a pin or needle etc.
▷ **prick** *NOUN*
prick up your ears start listening suddenly

prickle *NOUN* **prickles 1** a small thorn **2** a sharp spine on a hedgehog or cactus etc. **3** a feeling that something is pricking you
▷ **prickly** *ADJECTIVE*

prickle *VERB* **prickles, prickling, prickled** feel or cause a pricking feeling

pride *NOUN* **prides 1** a feeling of deep pleasure or satisfaction when you have done something well **2** something that makes you feel proud **3** dignity or self-respect **4** too high an opinion of yourself **5** a group of lions
pride of place the most important or most honoured position

pride *VERB* **prides, priding, prided**
pride yourself on be proud of

priest *NOUN* **priests 1** a member of the clergy in certain Christian Churches **2** a person who conducts religious ceremonies in a non-Christian religion
▷ **priestess** *NOUN* **priesthood** *NOUN* **priestly** *ADJECTIVE*

prig *NOUN* **prigs** a self-righteous person
▷ **priggish** *ADJECTIVE*

prim *ADJECTIVE* **primmer, primmest** formal and correct in manner; disliking anything rough or rude
▷ **primly** *ADVERB* **primness** *NOUN*

primary *ADJECTIVE* first; most important COMPARE **secondary**
▷ **primarily** (pry- mer- il- ee) *ADVERB*

primary colour *NOUN* **primary colours** one of the colours from which all others can be made by mixing (red, yellow, and blue for paint; red, green, and violet for light)

primary school *NOUN* **primary schools** a school for the first stage of a child's education

primate (pry- mayt) *NOUN* **primates**
1 an animal of the group that includes human beings, apes, and monkeys **2** an archbishop

Thesaurus

charge, levy **3** *Isolation was one price of their peaceful existence.* ► consequence, result, penalty, sacrifice, downside

priceless *ADJECTIVE* **1** *a priceless collection of watercolours; a priceless away goal* ► precious, valuable, irreplaceable, inestimable, treasured, prized, costly **2** (*informal*) *a priceless remark that made them all laugh* ► hilarious, riotous, uproarious, funny, (*more informal*) hysterical

prick *VERB* **1** *He pricked the lid and put it in the microwave.* ► pierce, puncture, perforate, make a hole in, stab, jab, punch **2** *The smoke made my eyes start to prick.* ► sting, smart, prickle, hurt **3** *His conscience was pricking him.* ► trouble, worry, disturb, distress, oppress, torment, afflict

prickle *NOUN* **1** *The bush was covered with prickles.* ► thorn, spike, needle, spine, quill, barb **2** *The shuffling sound outside sent a prickle down my spine.* ► tingle, tingling, prickling, chill, thrill

prickle *VERB* *The grass prickled their legs.* ► sting, prick, tickle

prickly *ADJECTIVE* **1** *a prickly bush* ► spiky, spiny, thorny, bristly, scratchy, sharp **2** (*informal*) *He's quite a prickly character.* ► irritable, irascible, peevish, testy, edgy, touchy, grumpy, short-tempered, fractious

pride *NOUN* **1** *Pride prevented him from accepting the offer.* ► conceit, vanity, arrogance, snobbery **2** *She took great pride in her work.* ► satisfaction, pleasure, delight, joy, comfort, sense of achievement **3** *Their victory was a source of great pride to them.* ► self-esteem, self-respect, gratification, honour, dignity

priest *NOUN* ► clergyman *or* clergywoman, minister, pastor, vicar, padre RELATED ADJECTIVE sacerdotal

priggish *ADJECTIVE* *She too was in danger of seeming priggish and opinionated.* ► self-righteous, smug, sanctimonious, sententious, prudish, prim, strait-laced, stuffy, starchy

prim *ADJECTIVE* *She sat behind her desk looking prim.* ► demure, proper, formal, strait-laced, prissy, prudish, starchy, fastidious
AN OPPOSITE IS broad-minded

primarily *ADVERB* *The work is primarily funded by a grant from the Lottery Fund.* ► chiefly, principally, mainly, mostly, predominantly, basically, in the main

primary *ADJECTIVE* **1** *Their primary aim was to make money.* ► main, chief, principal, key, prime, paramount, overiding, ultimate, supreme **2** *the primary cause of the infection* ► original, initial, first

prime *ADJECTIVE* **1** *The prime reason for his decision was a wish for change.* ► main, chief, principal,

prime *ADJECTIVE* **1** chief; most important • *the prime cause* **2** excellent; first-rate • *prime beef*

prime *NOUN* the best time or stage of something • *in the prime of life*

prime *VERB* **primes, priming, primed** **1** prepare something for use or action **2** put a coat of liquid on something to prepare it for painting **3** equip a person with information

prime minister *NOUN* **prime ministers** the leader of a government

prime number *NOUN* **prime numbers** a number (e.g. 2, 3, 5, 7, 11) that can be divided exactly only by itself and one

primeval (pry- mee- val) *ADJECTIVE* belonging to the earliest times of the world

primitive *ADJECTIVE* **1** at an early stage of civilization **2** at an early stage of development; not complicated or advanced • *primitive technology*

primrose *NOUN* **primroses** a pale yellow flower that blooms in spring [from Latin *prima rosa* = first rose]

prince *NOUN* **princes** **1** the son of a king or queen **2** a man or boy in a royal family
▷ **princely** *ADJECTIVE*

princess *NOUN* **princesses** **1** the daughter of a king or queen **2** a woman or girl in a royal family **3** the wife of a prince

principal *ADJECTIVE* chief; most important
▷ **principally** *ADVERB*

principal *NOUN* **principals** the head of a college or school [from Latin *principalis* = first or chief]
USAGE Do not confuse with **principle**.

principle *NOUN* **principles** **1** a general truth, belief, or rule • *She taught me the principles of geometry.* **2** a rule of conduct • *Cheating is against his principles.*
in principle as a general idea, without going into details
on principle because of your principles of behaviour
[from Latin *principium* = source]
USAGE Do not confuse with **principal**.

print *VERB* **prints, printing, printed** **1** put words or pictures on paper by using a machine **2** write with letters that are not joined together **3** press a mark or design etc. on a surface **4** make a picture from the negative of a photograph

print *NOUN* **prints** **1** printed lettering or words **2** a mark made by something pressing on a surface **3** a printed picture, photograph, or design
in print available from a publisher
out of print no longer available from a publisher

Thesaurus

key, primary, paramount, overriding, ultimate, supreme **2** *a hundred acres of prime agricultural land* ► best, choice, select, superior, first-class, high-grade, top-quality

primitive *ADJECTIVE* **1** *primitive peoples* ► ancient, early, earliest, prehistoric
AN OPPOSITE IS developed **2** *primitive tools* ► crude, basic, rudimentary, simple, undeveloped, elementary, rough
OPPOSITES ARE sophisticated, advanced

principal *ADJECTIVE* *Traffic noise is the principal objection to the new road scheme.* ► chief, main, primary, prime, most important, overriding, foremost, fundamental, key, crucial, central, paramount, predominant, basic, essential

principally *ADVERB* *The place was full of foreigners, principally Americans.* ► chiefly, mainly, primarily, mostly, predominantly, especially, essentially

principle *NOUN* **1** *a woman of principle* ► honour, integrity, morality, ideals, conscience, scruples, decency, virtue **2** *a basic principle of physics* ► rule, law, formula, canon, dictum, axiom, tenet
in principle *In principle the idea is a good one.* ► in theory, theoretically, in general, in the main, by and large

principles *PLURAL NOUN* **1** *They were praised for sticking to their principles.* ► morals, values, morality, standards, moral standards, code of behaviour **2** *the first principles of a subject* ► essentials, fundamentals, basics, elements, laws

print *VERB* **1** *The company logo is printed at the top of each page.* ► mark, stamp, imprint, impress, engrave, reproduce **2** *The books are printed in the Far East.* ► set in print, run off, produce, reproduce, manufacture **3** *The publishers plan to print ten thousand copies of the book.* ► issue, publish, produce **4** *Print your name at the top of the form.* ► write in capital letters *or* large letters

print *NOUN* **1** *The print was difficult to read.* ► type, typeface, printing, lettering, letters, characters **2** *There were prints of feet in the sand* ► impression, imprint, mark, indentation, stamp **3** *A print would be less costly than an original painting.* ► reproduction, engraving, lithograph, copy, duplicate, photograph

priority *NOUN* **1** *Traffic from the right has priority.* ► right of way, precedence

printed circuit *NOUN* **printed circuits** an electric circuit made by pressing thin metal strips on to a board

printer *NOUN* **printers** **1** a machine that prints on paper from data in a computer **2** someone who prints books or newspapers

printout *NOUN* **printouts** information etc. produced in printed form by a computer

priority *NOUN* **priorities** **1** being earlier or more important than something else; precedence **2** something considered more important than other things • *Safety is a priority.*

prise *VERB* **prises, prising, prised** lever something out or open • *Prise the lid off the crate.*

prism (prizm) *NOUN* **prisms** **1** a solid shape with ends that are triangles or polygons which are equal and parallel **2** a glass prism that breaks up light into the colours of the rainbow
▷ **prismatic** *ADJECTIVE*

prison *NOUN* **prisons** a place where criminals are kept as a punishment [from early French]

prisoner *NOUN* **prisoners** **1** a person kept in prison **2** a captive

private *ADJECTIVE* **1** belonging to a particular person or group • *private property* **2** confidential • *private talks* **3** quiet and secluded **4** not holding public office • *a private citizen* **5** independent or commercial; not run by the government • *private education* • *a private hospital*
▷ **privately** *ADVERB* **privacy** (priv- a- see) *NOUN*
in private where only particular people can see or hear; not in public

private *NOUN* **privates** a soldier of the lowest rank

privatize *VERB* **privatizes, privatizing, privatized** transfer the running of a business or industry from the state to private owners
▷ **privatization** *NOUN*

privilege *NOUN* **privileges** a special right or advantage given to one person or group
▷ **privileged** *ADJECTIVE*

Privy Council *NOUN* a group of distinguished people who advise the sovereign

prize *NOUN* **prizes** **1** an award given to the winner of a game or competition etc. **2** something taken from an enemy

prize *VERB* **prizes, prizing, prized** value something greatly

pro *NOUN* **pros** (*informal*) a professional

probable *ADJECTIVE* likely to happen or be true
▷ **probably** *ADVERB* **probability** *NOUN*

probation *NOUN* the testing of a person's character and abilities, e.g. to see whether they are suitable for a job they have recently started
▷ **probationary** *ADJECTIVE*
on probation being supervised by a probation officer instead of being sent to prison

Thesaurus

2 *Education will have priority at this year's conference.* ► precedence, preference, first place, first importance, primacy, predominance

prison *NOUN* *They would spend the next three years in prison.* ► jail, confinement, detention, custody, place of detention, penitentiary

prisoner *NOUN* *The prisoners staged a demonstration on the prison roof.* ► detainee, convict, captive, hostage, inmate, internee, (*more informal*) jailbird

privacy *NOUN* *The little room gave her some privacy.* ► seclusion, solitude, tranquillity, peace and quiet, quietness, secrecy, isolation

private *ADJECTIVE* **1** *He had amassed a huge private fortune.* ► personal, exclusive, individual, special **2** *Private talks were held at Chequers.* ► confidential, secret, covert, clandestine OPPOSITES ARE public, open **3** *She had her own private thoughts on the matter.* ► personal, secret, hidden, intimate **4** *They needed somewhere private to talk.* ► secluded, undisturbed, out of the way, isolated, solitary, quiet, peaceful, tranquil AN OPPOSITE IS busy **5** *John is a very private sort of person.* ► reserved, withdrawn, intimate, reticent, unsocial

privilege *NOUN* **1** *Full members enjoy special privileges.* ► benefit, entitlement, advantage, prerogative, concession, right **2** *It had been a privilege to meet them.* ► honour, pleasure

privileged *ADJECTIVE* *He enjoyed a privileged social position.* ► advantaged, affluent, prosperous, wealthy, favoured, fortunate, special, superior, élite, powerful OPPOSITES ARE disadvantaged, underprivileged

prize *NOUN* *Helen won the prize three years in a row.* ► award, reward, trophy, honour, accolade

prize *VERB* *They prize their freedom above all else.* ► value, appreciate, cherish, esteem, treasure, hold dear, regard, rate, approve of, revere, like

probable *ADJECTIVE* *Engine failure was the most probable cause of the crash. It is probable that this road was heavily guarded.* ► likely, plausible, credible, feasible, believable, expected, possible, predictable, presumed, (*more informal*) odds-on, (*more informal*) on the cards OPPOSITES ARE improbable, unlikely

probe *VERB* **1** *The inquiry will probe the circumstances of the accident.* ► investigate,

probation officer *NOUN* **probation officers** an official who supervises the behaviour of a convicted criminal who is not in prison

probe *NOUN* **probes 1** a long thin instrument used to look closely at something such as a wound **2** an unmanned spacecraft used for exploring **3** an investigation

probe *VERB* **probes, probing, probed** **1** explore something with a probe **2** investigate

problem *NOUN* **problems 1** something difficult to deal with or understand **2** something that has to be done or answered
▷ **problematic** *ADJECTIVE*

procedure *NOUN* **procedures** an orderly way of doing something

proceed *VERB* **proceeds, proceeding, proceeded 1** go forward or onward **2** continue; go on to do something • *She proceeded to explain the plan.*
USAGE Do not confuse with **precede**.

proceedings *PLURAL NOUN* **1** things that happen; activities **2** a lawsuit

proceeds *PLURAL NOUN* the money made from a sale or event

process (proh- sess) *NOUN* **processes** a series of actions for making or doing something
in the process of in the course of doing something

process *VERB* **processes, processing, processed** put something through a manufacturing or other process • *processed cheese*

procession *NOUN* **processions** a number of people or vehicles etc. moving steadily forward following each other

processor *NOUN* **processors 1** a machine that processes things **2** the part of a computer that controls all its operations

proclaim *VERB* **proclaims, proclaiming, proclaimed** announce something officially or publicly
▷ **proclamation** *NOUN*

prod *VERB* **prods, prodding, prodded 1** poke **2** stimulate someone into action
▷ **prod** *NOUN*

Thesaurus

examine, inquire into, look into, scrutinize, analyse, study, go into **2** *Unmanned underwater vehicles probed the ocean depths.* ► sound, plumb, penetrate, explore, feel

probe *NOUN* **1** *a space probe* ► exploration, expedition **2** *a police probe* ► inquiry, investigation, examination, study, research, scrutiny

problem *NOUN* **1** *He gave them a page of problems to solve.* ► puzzle, question, riddle, conundrum, enigma, mystery, (*more informal*) brainteaser, (*more informal*) poser **2** *Money was becoming a big problem for them.* ► burden, complication, difficulty, dilemma, dispute, (*informal*) headache, predicament, quandary, set-back, snag, trouble, worry

problematic *ADJECTIVE* *Unravelling this argument can be problematic.* ► difficult, complicated, complex, problematical, intractable, tricky, thorny, knotty, taxing, involved, enigmatic, controversial
OPPOSITES ARE straightforward, simple, easy

procedure *NOUN* *There is a special procedure for dealing with complaints.* ► course of action, process, routine, system, policy, strategy, approach, proceeding

proceed *VERB* **1** *We still don't know how to proceed.* ► begin, make a start, act, take action, make a move, progress **2** *They turned off the main road and proceeded as far as the village.* ► advance, continue, progress, make your way, carry on, press on
proceed with *Despite opposition, they decided to proceed with the changes.* ► implement, carry out, go ahead with, put into effect

process *NOUN* **1** *Sending email attachments is a simple process.* ► operation, procedure, activity, exercise, affair **2** *a new process for producing colour pictures* ► system, method, technique, procedure **3** *The learning process continues for many years.* ► progression, course, development, experience, evolution

process *VERB* **1** *Officials hope to process asylum claims more quickly.* ► deal with, attend to, handle, expedite, treat, see to, sort out **2** *The crude oil is processed at this refinery.* ► refine, convert, make usable, prepare, transform, treat

procession *NOUN* *A procession passed through the town.* ► parade, march, cavalcade, spectacle, display, pageant, review, show

proclaim *VERB* **1** *She proclaimed her love for him.* ► declare, announce, profess, make known, affirm, assert, give out, pronounce **2** *The president proclaim the day a public holiday.* ► decree, declare, pronounce

proclamation *NOUN* *The Queen issues a proclamation dissolving Parliament.* ► decree, edict, order, command, ruling, announcement, declaration

prod *VERB* **1** *The cook grumbled as he prodded the potatoes. He continued to prod her palms with the needle.* ► jab, poke, stab, dig, nudge, push **2** *He always needs someone to prod him into action.* ► goad, spur, stir, rouse, prompt, urge, stimulate, egg on, incite, provoke

a b c d e f g h i j k l m n o p q r s t u v w x y z

prodigal *ADJECTIVE* wasteful or extravagant
▷ **prodigally** *ADVERB* **prodigality** *NOUN*

prodigious *ADJECTIVE* wonderful or enormous
▷ **prodigiously** *ADVERB*

prodigy *NOUN* **prodigies 1** a person with wonderful abilities **2** a wonderful thing

produce *VERB* **produces, producing, produced 1** make or create something; bring something into existence **2** bring something out so that it can be seen **3** organize the performance of a play, making of a film, etc. **4** supervise the making of a musical recording
▷ **producer** *NOUN*

produce (**prod**- yooss) *NOUN* things produced, especially by farmers

product *NOUN* **products 1** something produced **2** the result of multiplying two numbers COMPARE **quotient**

production *NOUN* **productions 1** the process of making or creating something **2** the amount produced • *Oil production increased last year*

productive *ADJECTIVE* producing a lot of useful things or results
▷ **productivity** *NOUN*

profanity *NOUN* **profanities** words or language that show disrespect for religion

profession *NOUN* **professions 1** an occupation that needs special education or training, such as medicine or law **2** a declaration • *They made professions of loyalty.* [from Latin *professio* = public declaration]

professional *ADJECTIVE* **1** to do with a profession **2** doing a certain kind of work as a full-time job for payment, not as an amateur • *a professional footballer* **3** done with a high standard of skill
▷ **professional** *NOUN* **professionally** *ADVERB*

professor *NOUN* **professors** a university lecturer of the highest rank
▷ **professorship** *NOUN*

profile *NOUN* **profiles 1** a side view of a person's face **2** a short description of a person's character or career
keep a low profile try not to attract attention [from early Italian *profilare* = draw in outline]

profit *NOUN* **profits 1** the extra money obtained by selling something for more than it cost to buy or make **2** an advantage gained by doing something
▷ **profitable** *ADJECTIVE* **profitably** *ADVERB*

Thesaurus

prod *NOUN* **1** *She gave him a prod that woke him up.* ► jab, poke, stab, dig, nudge, shove, push **2** *The phone call was a prod to remind him to put the bins out that night.* ► prompt, reminder, stimulus

produce *VERB* (with the stress on -*duce*) **1** *The remark produced a wave of sniggers through the room.* ► cause, give rise to, occasion, provoke, bring about, result in, generate, effect **2** *He had failed to produce an essay for the third week running.* ► present, submit, offer, hand in, supply, provide **3** *He put his hand in his pocket and produced his passport.* ► show, display, present, bring out, take out **4** *It would be difficult to produce the required output that year.* ► yield, supply, deliver, provide **5** *The company produced Hamlet at the Edinburgh Festival.* ► stage, mount, present, put on, show

produce *NOUN* (with the stress on *prod-*) *an increase in organically grown produce* ► food, crops, harvest, output, products, commodities, yield, fruit, vegetables

product *NOUN* **1** *The company will announce its new product at the trade fair.* ► commodity, output, production, artefact, produce, end-product, goods, merchandise **2** *The story was the product of a vivid imagination.* ► result, consequence, outcome, effect, fruit, upshot

productive *ADJECTIVE* **1** *He still had years of productive work ahead.* ► useful, valuable, worthwhile, constructive, creative, effective, gainful, profitable, profitmaking, rewarding, beneficial, busy OPPOSITES ARE unproductive, fruitless **2** *a productive area of land* ► fertile, fruitful, rich, prolific, lush
OPPOSITES ARE unproductive, barren

profession *NOUN* **1** *She was no longer attracted by the teaching profession.* ► career, occupation, vocation, line of work, business, calling, employment, work **2** *a profession of loyalty* ► declaration, acknowledgement, affirmation, avowal, confession, statement, protestation

professional *ADJECTIVE* **1** *the study of modern languages as a preparation for professional life* ► working, business, executive **2** *the use of professional judgement* ► expert, qualified, skilled, trained, competent, efficient, proficient **3** *The plays were recorded in a studio with professional actors.* ► paid, salaried, full-time OPPOSITES ARE amateur, voluntary **4** *He was a thoroughly professional journalist.* ► conscientious, businesslike, proficient, dutiful, responsible
AN OPPOSITE IS unprofessional

profile *NOUN* **1** *a beautiful woman with a perfect profile* ► shape, side view, contour, figure, outline, silhouette **2** *a profile of John F Kennedy* ► biography, sketch, portrait, study, account **3** *The company has raised its profile in Eastern Europe.* ► influence, presence, image

profit *NOUN* **1** *The company made a modest profit in the last financial year.* ► return, surplus, yield, excess **2** **profits** *Two percent of profits contribute to the social fund.* ► revenue, income, takings, earnings, proceeds **3** *There would be no*

profit *VERB* **profits, profiting, profited** gain an advantage or benefit from something

profiteer *NOUN* **profiteers** a person who makes a great profit unfairly
▷ **profiteering** *NOUN*

profound *ADJECTIVE* **1** very deep or intense • *We take a profound interest in it.* **2** showing considerable knowledge or thought • *a profound remark*
▷ **profoundly** *ADVERB* **profundity** *NOUN*

prognosis (prog- noh- sis) *NOUN* **prognoses** a forecast or prediction, especially about a disease
▷ **prognostication** *NOUN*

program *NOUN* **programs** (in computing) a series of coded instructions for a computer to carry out

program *VERB* **programs, programming, programmed** put instructions into a computer by means of a program
▷ **programmer** *NOUN*

programme *NOUN* **programmes** **1** a list of planned events **2** a leaflet giving details of a play, concert, match, etc. **3** a show, play, or talk etc. on radio or television

progress (proh- gress) *NOUN* **1** forward movement; an advance **2** a development or improvement
in progress taking place

progress (pro- gress) *VERB* **progresses, progressing, progressed** **1** move forward **2** improve
▷ **progression** *NOUN* **progressive** *ADJECTIVE*

prohibit *VERB* **prohibits, prohibiting, prohibited** forbid or ban • *Smoking is prohibited.*
▷ **prohibition** *NOUN*

prohibitive *ADJECTIVE* **1** prohibiting **2** (said about prices) so high that people will not buy things

project (proj- ekt) *NOUN* **projects** **1** a plan or scheme **2** the task of finding out as much as you can about something and writing about it

project (pro- jekt) *VERB* **projects, projecting, projected** **1** stick out **2** show a picture on a screen **3** give people a particular impression • *He likes to project an image of absent-minded brilliance.*
▷ **projection** *NOUN*

Thesaurus

profit in continuing. ► advantage, benefit, value, use, gain, point, purpose

profit *VERB* **1** *It would profit us to wait for a while.* ► benefit, advantage, be an advantage to, pay, help **2** **profit by** *or* **from** *No one profited from these changes.* ► benefit from, gain advantage from, do well out of

profitable *ADJECTIVE* *a profitable undertaking* ► moneymaking, profitmaking, remunerative, lucrative, paying, productive, fruitful, gainful, rewarding, advantageous, beneficial, commercial, useful, valuable, worthwhile
AN OPPOSITE IS unprofitable

profound *ADJECTIVE* **1** *I offered my profound sympathy.* ► sincere, deep, heartfelt, intense
AN OPPOSITE IS insincere. **2** *a profound disagreement* ► complete, total, utter, absolute, extreme **3** *a profound argument* ► learned, wise, erudite, intelligent, perceptive, penetrating, thoughtful

programme *NOUN* **1** *a varied programme of events* ► schedule, agenda, timetable, calendar, listing, plan, order, scheme, (*more informal*) line-up **2** *a television programme* ► broadcast, transmission, performance, production, show

progress *NOUN* (with the stress on *pro-*) **1** *major progress in medical research* ► advance, development, headway, improvement, movement, progression, breakthrough, (*more informal*) step forward **2** *The heavy rain made further progress difficult.* ► travel, headway, advance, movement

progress *VERB* (with the stress on *-gress*) *The plans are progressing slowly.* ► advance, develop, move forward, make progress, make headway, proceed, prosper, mature, improve, (*more informal*) come on OPPOSITES ARE regress, deteriorate

progressive *ADJECTIVE* **1** *a progressive improvement in health* ► continuous, continuing, steady, increasing, ongoing, accelerating, growing, escalating
OPPOSITES ARE faltering, fluctuating, unsteady
2 *a party leader with progressive ideas* ► liberal, advanced, radical, modern, go-ahead, forward-looking, enlightened, avant-garde, contemporary, enterprising, up-to-date
AN OPPOSITE IS conservative

prohibit *VERB* **1** *a law prohibiting the advertising of tobacco products.* ► forbid, ban, disallow, proscribe, outlaw, make illegal **2** *Her commitments prohibited her from attending the funeral.* ► prevent, preclude, rule out, restrict, impede, obstruct

project *NOUN* (with the stress on *proj-*) **1** *a project to create more conservation areas* ► scheme, undertaking, plan, proposal, venture, enterprise, idea **2** *They're doing a history project.* ► assignment, piece of research, piece of work, activity, task

project *VERB* (with the stress on *-ject*) **1** *Balconies project from the upstairs windows.* ► protrude,

a b c d e f g h i j k l m n o **p** q r s t u v w x y z

projectile *NOUN* **projectiles** a missile

projector *NOUN* **projectors** a machine for showing films or photographs on a screen

prolific *ADJECTIVE* producing a lot • *a prolific author*
▷ **prolifically** *ADVERB*

prologue (proh- log) *NOUN* **prologues** an introduction to a poem or play etc.

prolong *VERB* **prolongs, prolonging, prolonged** make a thing longer or make it last for a long time
▷ **prolongation** *NOUN*

prom *NOUN* **proms** (*informal*) **1** a promenade **2** a promenade concert

promenade (prom- in- ahd) *NOUN* **promenades 1** a place suitable for walking, especially beside the seashore **2** a leisurely walk
▷ **promenade** *VERB*

promenade concert *NOUN* **promenade concerts** a concert where part of the audience may stand or walk about

prominent *ADJECTIVE* **1** easily seen; conspicuous • *The house stood in a prominent position.* **2** sticking out **3** important
▷ **prominently** *ADVERB* **prominence** *NOUN*

promiscuous *ADJECTIVE* **1** having many casual sexual relationships **2** indiscriminate
▷ **promiscuously** *ADVERB* **promiscuity** *NOUN*

promise *NOUN* **promises 1** a statement that you will definitely do or not do something **2** an indication of future success or good results • *His work shows promise.*

promise *VERB* **promises, promising, promised** make a promise

promote *VERB* **promotes, promoting, promoted 1** move a person to a higher rank or position **2** help the progress of something • *He has done much to promote the cause of peace.*
▷ **promoter** *NOUN* **promotion** *NOUN*

prompt *ADJECTIVE* **1** without delay • *a prompt reply* **2** punctual
▷ **promptly** *ADVERB* **promptness** *NOUN* **promptitude** *NOUN*

Thesaurus

stand out, stick out, extend, jut out, overhang, bulge **2** *The torch projected a strong beam.* ▸ cast, throw, throw out, flash, shine **3** *You can project the year's income from these monthly figures.* ▸ estimate, reckon, forecast, predict, extrapolate

proliferate *VERB* *The problems proliferated.* ▸ multiply, increase, escalate, build up, mushroom, intensify, snowball, spread

prolific *ADJECTIVE* **1** *a prolific crop of vegetables* ▸ plentiful, abundant, copious, profuse, productive, rich, bountiful, fertile, fruitful AN OPPOSITE IS unproductive **2** *a prolific writer* ▸ productive, creative, inventive

prolong *VERB* *She didn't want to prolong the argument.* ▸ lengthen, protract, extend, continue, perpetuate, spin out, draw out, increase, make longer, stretch out OPPOSITES ARE shorten, curtail

prominent *ADJECTIVE* **1** *a prominent member of the government* ▸ important, well known, leading, eminent, distinguished, notable, noteworthy, celebrated

promise *VERB* **1** *He promised to pay for the damage.* ▸ undertake, guarantee, agree, contract **2** *He promised she'd be there.* ▸ give your word, say, pledge, swear **3** *The bright sky promised a fine day* ▸ indicate, presage, suggest, signify, augur, predict

promiscuous *ADJECTIVE* *She was promiscuous in her younger days.* ▸ licentious, loose, immoral, dissolute, abandoned, wanton, casual OPPOSITES ARE moral, chaste

promise *NOUN* **1** *You have my promise.* ▸ assurance, word, word of honour, pledge, undertaking, commitment, guarantee, oath, vow **2** *a group of pupils showing outstanding promise* ▸ potential, ability, aptitude, talent, capability

promising *ADJECTIVE* **1** *There are promising signs of an improvement.* ▸ encouraging, hopeful, favourable, auspicious, propitious, talented **2** *a promising young talent* ▸ budding, gifted, up-and-coming, able

promote *VERB* **1** *She was promoted in the recent cabinet reshuffle.* ▸ upgrade, move up, give a promotion to, advance, honour **2** *He will promote his new novel on the television.* ▸ advertise, publicize, push, sponsor, boost, (*more informal*) plug **3** *an organization promoting equal opportunities* ▸ champion, further, advance, sponsor, encourage, stimulate, foster, nurture, boost

promotion *NOUN* **1** *He is hoping for a promotion next year.* ▸ advancement, upgrading, elevation, preferment, rise **2** *the promotion of her new film* ▸ marketing, publicity, advertising, backing, selling, pushing, (*more informal*) plugging

prompt *ADJECTIVE* *We hope for a prompt response.* ▸ quick, swift, rapid, speedy, early, punctual, immediate, expeditious OPPOSITES ARE late, slow

prompt *VERB* **prompts, prompting, prompted** **1** cause or encourage a person to do something **2** remind an actor or speaker of words when he or she has forgotten them
▷ **prompter** *NOUN*

prone *ADJECTIVE*
be prone to be likely to do or suffer from something • *He is prone to jealousy*

prong *NOUN* **prongs** one of the spikes on a fork
▷ **pronged** *ADJECTIVE*

pronoun *NOUN* **pronouns** a word used instead of a noun. **Demonstrative pronouns** are *this, that, these, those*; **interrogative pronouns** are *who?, what?, which?*, etc.; **personal pronouns** are *I, me, we, us, thou, thee, you, ye, he, him, she, her, it, they, them*; **possessive pronouns** are *mine, yours, theirs*, etc.; **reflexive pronouns** are *myself, yourself*, etc.; **relative pronouns** are *who, what, which, that*

pronounce *VERB* **pronounces, pronouncing, pronounced** **1** say a sound or word in a particular way • *'Two' and 'too' are pronounced the same.* **2** declare something formally • *I now pronounce you man and wife.*

pronounced *ADJECTIVE* noticeable • *This street has a pronounced slope.*

pronunciation *NOUN* **pronunciations** the way a word is pronounced
USAGE Note the spelling; this word should not be written or spoken as 'pronounciation'.

proof *NOUN* **proofs** **1** a fact or thing that shows something is true **2** a printed copy of a book or photograph etc. made for checking before other copies are printed

proof *ADJECTIVE* able to resist something or not be penetrated • *a bulletproof jacket*

prop[1] *NOUN* **props** a support, especially one made of a long piece of wood or metal

prop *VERB* **props, propping, propped** support something by leaning it against something else

prop[2] *NOUN* **props** an object or piece of furniture used on a theatre stage or in a film

propaganda *NOUN* biased or misleading publicity intended to make people believe something

propel *VERB* **propels, propelling, propelled** push something forward

propeller *NOUN* **propellers** a device with blades that spin round to drive an aircraft or ship

proper *ADJECTIVE* **1** suitable or right • *the proper way to hold a bat* **2** respectable • *prim and*

Thesaurus

prompt *VERB* **1** *We are not sure what prompted such an angry outburst.* ► cause, give rise to, bring about, occasion, lead to, produce, bring on, precipitate, trigger, spark off
OPPOSITES ARE deter, prevent **2** *A noise prompted her to turn round.* ► cause, lead, induce, stimulate, prod, provoke
AN OPPOSITE IS discourage (from) **3** *He forgot what to say and his wife had to prompt him.* ► remind, cue, prod, jog the memory

prone *ADJECTIVE* **1** *A man was lying prone on the floor* ► face down, on your front, prostrate
AN OPPOSITE IS upright **2** *People here are prone to exaggerate.* ► apt, inclined, susceptible, predisposed, disposed, given, liable
OPPOSITES ARE resistant, immune

prong *NOUN* *the prong of a fork* ► point, spike, spur, tine

pronounce *VERB* **1** *The name is difficult to pronounce.* ► say, enunciate, articulate, sound, speak, utter, get your tongue round **2** *The doctor pronounced me well.* ► declare, proclaim, judge, announce, affirm, assert USAGE If you use *affirm* or *assert* you say *The doctor affirmed* or *asserted that I was well.*

pronunciation *NOUN* *The key to pronunciation of long words is often the stress.* ► enunciation, articulation, intonation, accent, diction, elocution, inflection

proof *NOUN* *If there is a problem, return the goods with proof of purchase.* ► evidence, confirmation, verification, authentication, certification, corroboration, demonstration

prop *NOUN* **1** *The bridge is supported by steel props.* ► post, strut, upright, support, buttress, bolster **2** *She had become the family's emotional prop.* ► support, mainstay, pillar, anchor, backbone

prop *VERB* *He propped his bike against the wall.* ► lean, rest, stand
prop up *The old tree was propped up with posts.* ► support, hold up, brace, strengthen, reinforce, shore up, buttress

propagate *VERB* **1** *They were accused of propagating false reports.* ► spread, transmit, disseminate, pass on, communicate, put about, circulate, proliferate **2** *The plants are propagated in large greenhouses.* ► breed, grow, cultivate, generate **3** *Wild flowers thrive and propagate.* ► reproduce, multiply, proliferate, procreate

propel *VERB* **1** *He propelled the ball high into the air.* ► throw, toss, fling, hurl, pitch, launch, shoot, kick, punt **2** *The little craft was propelled by a small outboard motor.* ► drive, move, power, impel, set in motion, push

proper *ADJECTIVE* **1** *It was about time he found a proper job.* ► real, genuine, bona fide **2** *She doesn't think it proper that the children all share a room.* ► right, correct, decent, respectable, decorous **3** *You have to apply through the proper channels.* ► correct, right, appropriate, official,

proper **3** (*informal*) complete or thorough • *You're a proper nuisance!*
▷ **properly** ADVERB

proper fraction NOUN **proper fractions** a fraction that is less than 1, with the numerator less than the denominator, e.g. $\frac{1}{2}$

proper noun NOUN **proper nouns** the name of an individual person or thing, e.g. *Mary, London, Spain*, usually written with a capital first letter

property NOUN **properties** **1** a thing or things that belong to somebody **2** a building or someone's land **3** a quality or characteristic • *It has the property of becoming soft when heated.*

prophecy NOUN **prophecies** **1** a statement that prophesies something **2** the action of prophesying

prophesy VERB **prophesies, prophesying, prophesied** say what will happen in the future; foretell

prophet NOUN **prophets** **1** a person who makes prophecies **2** a religious teacher who is believed to be inspired by God
▷ **prophetess** NOUN **prophetic** ADJECTIVE
the Prophet Muhammad, who founded the Muslim faith

proportion NOUN **proportions** **1** a part or share of a whole thing **2** a ratio **3** the correct relationship in size, amount, or importance between two things • *You've drawn his head out of proportion.*
▷ **proportional** ADJECTIVE **proportionally** ADVERB **proportionate** ADJECTIVE
proportions PLURAL NOUN size • *a ship of large proportions*

proportional representation NOUN a system in which each political party has a number of Members of Parliament in proportion to the number of votes for all its candidates

proposal NOUN **proposals** **1** something that is proposed; a formal suggestion **2** an offer of marriage

propose VERB **proposes, proposing, proposed** **1** suggest an idea or plan etc. **2** plan or intend to do something **3** ask a person to marry you

proposition NOUN **propositions** **1** a suggestion or offer **2** a statement **3** (*informal*) an undertaking or problem • *a difficult proposition*

proprietor NOUN **proprietors** the owner of a shop or business
▷ **proprietress** NOUN

prosaic ADJECTIVE plain or dull and ordinary
▷ **prosaically** ADVERB

prose NOUN writing or speech that is not in verse

prosecute VERB **prosecutes, prosecuting, prosecuted** **1** make someone go to a lawcourt to be tried for a crime **2** continue with something; pursue • *prosecuting their trade*
▷ **prosecution** NOUN **prosecutor** NOUN

prospect NOUN **prospects** **1** a possibility or expectation of something • *There is no prospect of success.* **2** a wide view

prospect (pro- spekt) VERB **prospects, prospecting, prospected** explore in search of gold or some other mineral
▷ **prospector** NOUN

Thesaurus

established, usual **4** (*informal*) *He felt a proper fool.* ► complete, utter, perfect, absolute, positive

property NOUN **1** *He left all his property to his nephew.* ► possessions, belongings, assets, worldly goods, wealth, valuables, chattels, effects, fortune **2** *Brits looking for property to buy abroad.* ► buildings, premises, houses, estate **3** *the medicinal properties of garlic* ► quality, attribute, characteristic, power, peculiarity, trait, feature

prophet NOUN *an Old Testament prophet* ► seer, soothsayer, clairvoyant, oracle, forecaster, fortune teller

proportion NOUN **1** *the proportion of girls to boys in a class* ► ratio, balance, relationship, distribution **2** *A large proportion of the country is forested.* ► part, portion, amount, quantity, percentage, section, share, piece, quota
proportions *a building of huge proportions* ► dimensions, measurements, size, magnitude

proposal NOUN *There is a proposal to build a ring road.* ► plan, scheme, proposition, suggestion, project, bid, motion, offer, recommendation

propose VERB **1** *Charles proposed Greece for their next holiday.* ► suggest, put forward, recommend, offer, come up with, submit, ask for, present AN OPPOSITE IS withdraw **2** *How do you propose to find the money?* ► plan, intend, mean, aim, have in mind **3** *Six candidates have been proposed for election.* ► nominate, put up

proposition NOUN **1** *They discussed the proposition that war was inevitable.* ► theory, hypothesis, premiss, notion, idea **2** *a business proposition* ► proposal, plan, scheme, suggestion, project

prosecute VERB *The police are going to prosecute him for dangerous driving.* ► charge, prefer charges against, institute legal proceedings against, bring to trial, take legal proceedings against, indict

prospect NOUN **1** *She went to India with every prospect of a long stay.* ► chance, expectation,

prospective *ADJECTIVE* expected to be or to happen; possible • *prospective customers*

prospectus *NOUN* **prospectuses** a booklet describing and advertising a school, business company, etc.

prosperous *ADJECTIVE* successful or rich
▷ **prosperity** *NOUN*

prostitute *NOUN* **prostitutes** a person who takes part in sexual acts for payment
▷ **prostitution** *NOUN*

protect *VERB* **protects, protecting, protected** keep safe from harm or injury
▷ **protection** *NOUN* **protective** *ADJECTIVE* **protector** *NOUN*

protein *NOUN* **proteins** a substance that is found in all living things and is an essential part of the food of animals

protest (proh- test) *NOUN* **protests** a statement or action showing that you disapprove of something

protest (pro- test) *VERB* **protests, protesting, protested 1** make a protest **2** declare firmly • *They protested their innocence.*
▷ **protestation** *NOUN*

Protestant *NOUN* **Protestants** a member of any of the western Christian Churches that are separate from the Roman Catholic Church

proton *NOUN* **protons** a particle of matter with a positive electric charge

prototype *NOUN* **prototypes** the first model of something, from which others are copied or developed

protractor *NOUN* **protractors** a device for measuring angles, usually a semicircle marked off in degrees

protrude *VERB* **protrudes, protruding, protruded** stick out from a surface

proud *ADJECTIVE* **1** very pleased with yourself or with someone else who has done well • *We are all so proud of you.* **2** causing pride • *This is a proud moment for us.* **3** full of self-respect and independence • *They were too proud to ask for help.* **4** having too high an opinion of yourself
▷ **proudly** *ADVERB*
[via Old English from old French *prud* = brave]

Thesaurus

likelihood, possibility, probability, promise, hope **2** *There is a magnificent prospect from the penthouse apartment.* ▶ view, vista, outlook, panorama, landscape, perspective, scene, sight, spectacle **3 prospects** *His job prospects were looking good.* ▶ future, potential, outlook, possibilities, hopes

prosper *VERB* *The market in mobiles continues to prosper.* ▶ thrive, do well, flourish, boom, blossom, expand, succeed, progress, make progress

prosperity *NOUN* *The future prosperity of inner cities depends on how safe they are to live in.* ▶ success, welfare, wealth, affluence, growth, plenty, profitability

prosperous *ADJECTIVE* *She took out a dress she had bought in more prosperous times.* ▶ thriving, prospering, flourishing, affluent, well-off, well-to-do, wealthy, fortunate, successful, booming, buoyant, profitable, rich
AN OPPOSITE IS unsuccessful

protect *VERB* **1** *The men were anxious to protect their women and children. The city fought a war to protect its democracy.* ▶ defend, safeguard, keep safe, preserve, secure, shield, guard, save **2** *An armed guard protected the convoy.* ▶ escort, guard, accompany, defend, cover, shield

protection *NOUN* **1** *They looked for some form of protection from the wind and rain.* ▶ shelter, refuge, security, shield **2** *Military strength would be no protection against terrorist activities of that sort.* ▶ barrier, buffer, screen, bulwark, security, insurance

protective *ADJECTIVE* **1** *protective clothing* ▶ protecting, insulating, shielding, sheltering, defensive **2** *Her parents had always been protective towards her.* ▶ caring, solicitous, watchful, vigilant, jealous, defensive, possessive

protest *NOUN* (with the stress on *pro-*) **1** *The violence shown in the programme caused a wave of protests.* ▶ complaint, objection, outcry, protestation, remonstrance, cry of disapproval **2** *There will be a large protest in the town square.* ▶ demonstration, rally, march, sit-in, (*more informal*) demo

protest *VERB* (with the stress on *-test*) **1** *People protested against the export of animals.* ▶ demonstrate, object, make a protest, remonstrate, express disapproval (of) **2** *The neighbours protested that the music was too loud.* ▶ complain, object, grumble, expostulate, fulminate, argue, take exception **3** *He continued to protest his innocence.* ▶ maintain, insist on, claim, profess, proclaim, assert, contend

proud *ADJECTIVE* **1** *He's too proud to admit his mistake.* ▶ conceited, arrogant, vain, big-headed, self-important, full of yourself, presumptuous, boastful OPPOSITES ARE modest, unassuming, humble **2** *They are a proud people.* ▶ noble, dignified, honourable, self-respecting **3 proud of** *Anna was so proud of her garden.* ▶ pleased with, delighted with, thrilled with, satisfied with, happy about, glad about, gratified at, fond of AN OPPOSITE IS ashamed of

prove *VERB* **proves, proving, proved 1** show that something is true **2** turn out • *The forecast proved to be correct.*
▷ **provable** *ADJECTIVE*

proverb *NOUN* **proverbs** a short well-known saying that states a truth, e.g. 'Many hands make light work'

proverbial *ADJECTIVE* **1** referred to in a proverb **2** well known

provide *VERB* **provides, providing, provided 1** make something available; supply **2** prepare for something • *Try to provide for emergencies.*
▷ **provider** *NOUN*

provided *CONJUNCTION* on condition • *You can stay provided that you help.*

providing *CONJUNCTION* provided

province *NOUN* **provinces 1** a section of a country **2** the area of a person's special knowledge or responsibility • *I'm afraid carpentry is not my province.*
▷ **provincial** *ADJECTIVE*
the provinces the parts of a country outside its capital city

provision *NOUN* **provisions 1** providing something **2** a statement in a document • *the provisions of the treaty*

provisional *ADJECTIVE* arranged or agreed upon temporarily but possibly to be altered later
▷ **provisionally** *ADVERB*

provisions *PLURAL NOUN* supplies of food and drink

provoke *VERB* **provokes, provoking, provoked 1** make a person angry **2** cause or give rise to something • *The joke provoked laughter.*
▷ **provocation** *NOUN* **provocative** *ADJECTIVE*

prow *NOUN* **prows** the front end of a ship

prowl *VERB* **prowls, prowling, prowled** move about quietly or cautiously, like a hunter
▷ **prowl** *NOUN* **prowler** *NOUN*

proxy *NOUN* **proxies** a person authorized to represent or act for another person • *I will be abroad, so I have arranged to vote by proxy.*

prude *NOUN* **prudes** a person who is easily shocked
▷ **prudish** *ADJECTIVE* **prudery** *NOUN*

prudent *ADJECTIVE* careful, not rash or reckless
▷ **prudently** *ADVERB* **prudence** *NOUN* **prudential** *ADJECTIVE*

prune[1] *NOUN* **prunes** a dried plum

prune[2] *VERB* **prunes, pruning, pruned** cut off unwanted parts of a tree or bush etc.

pry *VERB* **pries, prying, pried** look into or ask about someone else's private business

PS *ABBREVIATION* postscript

Thesaurus

prove *VERB* **1** *The new evidence proves your innocence.* ► confirm, corroborate, demonstrate, establish, substantiate, attest, authenticate, bear out, show to be true, verify AN OPPOSITE IS disprove **2** *The story proved to be true.* ► turn out, happen, be found

proverb *NOUN* *the old proverb about too many cooks* ► saying, maxim, adage, dictum, byword, catchphrase

provide *VERB* **1** *The hotel can provide a picnic.* ► supply, furnish, serve, produce, present, contribute, lay on, arrange for **2 provide for** *He now made enough money to provide for his family.* ► support, maintain, feed, keep, sustain, provide food for **3 provide for** *The agreement provides for arbitration in the case of disputes.* ► allow for, make provision for, stipulate, specify, require, call for, arrange for

provincial *ADJECTIVE* **1** *the provincial government* ► local, regional, district, territorial **2** *the provincial attitudes of the middle classes* ► unsophisticated, insular, parochial, suburban, small-town, narrow-minded, dreary, dull

provisional *ADJECTIVE* *The provisional total is over a million dollars.* ► interim, temporary, tentative, conditional, stopgap OPPOSITES ARE definite, permanent

provisions *PLURAL NOUN* ► supplies, food and drink, foodstuff, stores, subsistence, rations, groceries, requirements

provocation *NOUN* *He refused to react despite extreme provocation.* (*informal*) ► annoyance, goading, aggravation, irritation, harassment, taunting, incitement, inducement, grounds, justification, motivation

provoke *VERB* **1** *Plans for a new ring road have provoked a lot of interest.* ► arouse, rouse, prompt, cause, kindle, instigate, spark off, stimulate, stir up, (*more informal*) whip up AN OPPOSITE IS allay **2** *She was provoked into making comments that she later regretted.* ► goad, spur, prick, sting **3** *Better not to provoke him while he's in a good mood.* ► annoy, irritate, anger, incense, offend, tease, taunt

prudent *ADJECTIVE* **1** *It's not always prudent to speak to strangers.* ► wise, advisable, sensible, shrewd AN OPPOSITE IS unwise **2** *a prudent attitude to money* ► cautious, careful, shrewd, far-sighted, thoughtful, wary

pry *VERB* *I didn't mean to pry, I was just curious.* ► delve, interfere, meddle, poke about, nose about, ferret about, be inquisitive, snoop, (*informal*) stick your nose in

psalm (sahm) *NOUN* **psalms** a religious song, especially one from the Book of Psalms in the Bible
▷ **psalmist** *NOUN*

pseudonym *NOUN* **pseudonyms** a false name used by an author

psychiatrist (sy- ky- a- trist) *NOUN* **psychiatrists** a doctor who treats mental illnesses
▷ **psychiatry** *NOUN* **psychiatric** *ADJECTIVE*

psychic (sy- kik) *ADJECTIVE* **1** supernatural **2** having supernatural powers, especially being able to predict the future **3** to do with the mind or soul
▷ **psychical** *ADJECTIVE*

psychoanalysis *NOUN* investigation of a person's mental processes, especially in the treatment of mental illness
▷ **psychoanalyst** *NOUN*

psychology *NOUN* the study of the mind and how it works
▷ **psychological** *ADJECTIVE* **psychologist** *NOUN*

PT *ABBREVIATION* physical training

pterodactyl (te- ro- dak- til) *NOUN* **pterodactyls** an extinct flying reptile

PTO *ABBREVIATION* please turn over

pub *NOUN* **pubs** a building licensed to serve alcoholic drinks to the public

puberty (pew- ber- tee) *NOUN* the time when a young person is developing physically into an adult

public *ADJECTIVE* belonging to or known by everyone, not private
▷ **publicly** *ADVERB*

public *NOUN* people in general
in public openly, not in private

publication *NOUN* **publications** **1** publishing **2** a published book or newspaper etc.

public house *NOUN* **public houses** (*formal*) a pub

publicity *NOUN* public attention; doing things (e.g. advertising) to draw people's attention to something

public school *NOUN* **public schools** **1** a secondary school that charges fees **2** (in Scotland and the USA) a school run by a local authority or by the state

publish *VERB* **publishes, publishing, published** **1** have something printed and sold to the public **2** announce something in public
▷ **publisher** *NOUN*

pucker *VERB* **puckers, puckering, puckered** wrinkle

pudding *NOUN* **puddings** **1** a cooked sweet food eaten at the end of a meal **2** the sweet course of a meal **3** a savoury food made with suet and flour

puddle *NOUN* **puddles** a shallow patch of liquid, especially of rainwater on a road

Thesaurus

psychic *ADJECTIVE* *She seemed to have psychic powers and knew exactly what would happen.* ► clairvoyant, telepathic, extrasensory, supernatural, mystic, occult, psychical

psychological *ADJECTIVE* *The effects are mostly psychological.* ► mental, subconscious, emotional, subjective, irrational
AN OPPOSITE IS physical

public *ADJECTIVE* **1** *public gardens* ► communal, open, free, community, unrestricted
AN OPPOSITE IS private **2** *a public figure* ► prominent, well known, celebrated, leading, eminent, important, distinguished, notable, famous OPPOSITES ARE unknown, obscure **3** *This is all public knowledge by now.* ► general, common, recognized, widely known, open

public *NOUN* *houses open to the public* ► people, the populace, the community, the country, the nation, citizens

publication *NOUN* **1** *Publication of the report will be in July.* ► issuing, appearance, publishing, printing, production, dissemination **2** *a list of the latest publications* ► book, volume, title, work, tome, opus, newspaper, magazine

publicity *NOUN* **1** *The film was launched in a blaze of publicity.* ► attention, media attention, public interest, exposure **2** *Publicity will include television advertising.* ► promotion, marketing, advertising, (*more informal*) hype

publicize *VERB* *The event is being publicized weeks in advance.* ► advertise, make known, announce, report, (*more informal*) plug
OPPOSITES ARE suppress, conceal

publish *VERB* **1** *A sequel to the story was published last year.* ► issue, bring out, produce, print **2** *The letters should be published as soon as possible.* ► make public, make known, publicize, disseminate, put out, make available

pucker *VERB* *She felt her lips pucker and her eyes grow moist.* ► wrinkle, screw up, crease, purse, tighten, compress

pudding *NOUN* *When Steve arrived the others were starting their pudding.* ► dessert, sweet, (*more informal*) afters

puddle *NOUN* *He woke up to find a puddle of water on his sleeping bag.* ► pool, splash, spill

puff *NOUN* **puffs 1** a short blowing of breath, wind, or smoke etc. **2** a soft pad for putting powder on the skin **3** a cake of very light pastry filled with cream

puff *VERB* **puffs, puffing, puffed 1** blow out puffs of smoke etc. **2** breathe with difficulty; pant **3** inflate or swell something • *He puffed out his chest.*

puffy *ADJECTIVE* puffed out; swollen
▷ **puffiness** *NOUN*

pugnacious *ADJECTIVE* wanting to fight; aggressive
▷ **pugnaciously** *ADVERB* **pugnacity** *NOUN*

puke *VERB* **pukes, puking, puked** (*informal*) vomit

pull *VERB* **pulls, pulling, pulled 1** make a thing come towards or after you by using force on it **2** move by a driving force • *The car pulled out into the road.*
▷ **pull** *NOUN*
pull a face make a strange face
pull in 1 (said about a vehicle) move to the side of the road and stop **2** (said about a train) come to a station and stop
pull somebody's leg tease him or her
pull off achieve something
pull through recover from an illness
pull up (said about a vehicle) stop abruptly
pull yourself together become calm or sensible

pulley *NOUN* **pulleys** a wheel with a rope, chain, or belt over it, used for lifting or moving heavy things

pullover *NOUN* **pullovers** a knitted piece of clothing for the top half of the body

pulp *NOUN* **1** the soft moist part of fruit **2** any soft moist mass
▷ **pulpy** *ADJECTIVE*

pulpit *NOUN* **pulpits** a small enclosed platform for the preacher in a church or chapel

pulsate *VERB* **pulsates, pulsating, pulsated** expand and contract rhythmically; vibrate
▷ **pulsation** *NOUN*

pulse[1] *NOUN* **pulses 1** the rhythmical movement of the arteries as blood is pumped through them by the beating of the heart • *The pulse can be felt in a person's wrists.* **2** a throb

pulse *VERB* **pulses, pulsing, pulsed** throb or pulsate

pulse[2] *NOUN* **pulses** the edible seed of peas, beans, lentils, etc.

pulverize *VERB* **pulverizes, pulverizing pulverized** crush something into powder
▷ **pulverization** *NOUN*

puma *NOUN* **pumas** a large brown animal of western America; a mountain lion [via Spanish from Quechua (a South American language)]

Thesaurus

puff *NOUN* **1** *a puff of wind* ► gust, blast, breath, rush, draught, flurry **2** *a puff of grey smoke* ► cloud, whiff

puff *VERB* *He was puffing when he reached the top of the stairs.* ► gasp, pant, wheeze, breathe heavily, blow
puff out *The curtains puffed out in the draught.* ► swell, distend, become inflated, billow, rise

puke *VERB* *She had eaten something that upset her and went off to puke.* ► vomit, be sick, retch, heave, (*informal*) throw up

pull *VERB* **1** *She pulled another chair to where she was sitting.* ► drag, draw, tug, heave, (*more informal*) yank **2** *Cars were pulling trailers and caravans.* ► tow, haul, lug, drag, trail **3** *The match will pull huge crowds.* ► attract, draw, bring in, entice, allure, tempt **4** *He had pulled a muscle and was forced to withdraw.* ► strain, sprain, wrench, dislocate **5** *A dentist might need to pull the tooth.* ► extract, take out, remove, pull out
pull apart *Only pull the machine apart if you know how to put it together again.* ► dismantle, take apart, take to pieces, dismember, separate
pull down *A row of houses will be pulled down to make space for the new complex.* ► demolish, knock down, tear down, bulldoze, dismantle
pull someone's leg *They stopped pulling his leg when they realized he was upset.* ► tease, rag, make fun of, play tricks on
pull off *The gang have pulled off another bank robbery.* ► achieve, accomplish, manage, carry out, bring off, succeed in
pull out *The army will pull out by the end of the year.* ► withdraw, retreat, leave, depart, quit, move out
pull through *She is likely to pull through despite severe injuries.* ► recover, get better, improve, come through, recuperate
pull together *Everyone has to pull together if we are going to succeed.* ► cooperate, work together, work as a team, collaborate

pull *NOUN* **1** *He gave the handle a pull.* ► tug, jerk, heave, (*more informal*) yank **2** *The beauty of the place exerted quite a pull.* ► attraction, lure, draw, influence, enticement

pulp *NOUN* *a fruit with a juicy pulp* ► flesh, mash, mush, paste, pap

pulse *NOUN* *The music lacked a regular pulse.* ► beat, rhythm, throb, oscillation, vibration

pump[1] *NOUN* **pumps** a device that pushes air or liquid into or out of something, or along pipes

pump *VERB* **pumps, pumping, pumped** **1** move air or liquid with a pump **2** (*informal*) question a person to obtain information
pump up inflate

pump[2] *NOUN* **pumps** a canvas sports shoe with a rubber sole

pumpkin *NOUN* **pumpkins** a very large round fruit with a hard orange skin [from Greek *pepon*, a kind of large melon]

pun *NOUN* **puns** a joking use of a word sounding the same as another, e.g. 'Deciding where to bury him was a *grave* decision'.

punch[1] *VERB* **punches, punching, punched** **1** hit someone with your fist **2** make a hole in something

punch *NOUN* **punches** **1** a hit with a fist **2** a device for making holes in paper, metal, leather, etc. **3** vigour

punch[2] *NOUN* a drink made by mixing wine or spirits and fruit juice in a bowl

punchline *NOUN* **punchlines** words that give the climax of a joke or story

punctual *ADJECTIVE* doing things exactly at the time arranged; not late
▷ **punctually** *ADVERB* **punctuality** *NOUN*

punctuate *VERB* **punctuates, punctuating, punctuated** **1** put punctuation marks into something **2** put something in at intervals
• *His speech was punctuated with cheers.*

punctuation *NOUN* marks such as commas, full stops, and brackets put into a piece of writing to make it easier to read

puncture *NOUN* **punctures** a small hole made by something sharp, especially in a tyre

puncture *VERB* **punctures, puncturing, punctured** make a puncture in something

pungent (pun- jent) *ADJECTIVE* **1** having a strong taste or smell **2** (said about remarks) sharp
▷ **pungently** *ADVERB* **pungency** *NOUN*

punish *VERB* **punishes, punishing, punished** make a person suffer because he or she has done something wrong
▷ **punishable** *ADJECTIVE* **punishment** *NOUN*

punk *NOUN* **punks** **1** (also **punk rock**) a loud aggressive style of rock music **2** a person who likes this music

punt[1] *NOUN* **punts** a flat-bottomed boat, usually moved by pushing a pole against the bottom of a river while standing in the punt

punt *VERB* **punts, punting, punted** move a punt with a pole

punt[2] *VERB* **punts, punting, punted** kick a football after dropping it from your hands and before it touches the ground

pupa (pew- pa) *NOUN* **pupae** a chrysalis

pupil *NOUN* **pupils** **1** someone who is being taught by a teacher, especially at school **2** the opening in the centre of the eye

puppet *NOUN* **puppets** **1** a kind of doll that can be made to move by fitting it over your hand or working it by strings or wires **2** a person whose actions are controlled by someone else
▷ **puppetry** *NOUN*

puppy *NOUN* **puppies** a young dog

purchase *VERB* **purchases, purchasing, purchased** buy
▷ **purchaser** *NOUN*

purchase *NOUN* **purchases** **1** something bought **2** buying **3** a firm hold or grip

Thesaurus

pump *VERB* *The crew rushed to pump the water out of the boat.* ► drain, draw off, empty, force, drive, raise, siphon
pump up *We'd better pump up the tyres.* ► inflate, blow up, fill

pun *NOUN* ► double meaning, wordplay, play on words

punch *VERB* **1** *Ken punched him in the stomach.* ► hit, strike, bash, thump, box, sock, clout, jab, poke, prod, beat, cuff, slog **2** *He punched a hole in the wall.* ► pierce, puncture, perforate

punch *NOUN* *a punch on the nose* ► blow, bash, thump, box, poke

punctual *ADJECTIVE* *We're expected to be punctual.* ► on time, prompt, in good time, (*more informal*) on the dot OPPOSITES ARE unpunctual, late

puncture *NOUN* *Her bike had a puncture on the way home.* ► flat tyre, burst tyre, (*more informal*) flat

puncture *VERB* *Vandals had punctured her tyres.* ► make a hole in, pierce, rupture, let down, deflate

punish *VERB* *The culprits would be punished.* ► penalize, discipline, correct, chastise, scold, make an example of

punishment *NOUN* *The punishment has to be reasonable.* ► penalty, discipline, correction, chastisement RELATED ADJECTIVE penal

puny *ADJECTIVE* *He looked small and puny for his age.* ► weak, feeble, frail, sickly, undersized, undernourished, stunted OPPOSITES ARE sturdy, strong

pupil *NOUN* *She is an able pupil.* ► student, scholar, schoolgirl *or* schoolboy, learner

A B C D E F G H I J K L M N O P Q R S T U V W X Y Z

pure *ADJECTIVE* **1** not mixed with anything else • *pure olive oil* **2** clean or clear • *pure spring water* **3** free from evil or sin **4** mere; nothing but • *pure nonsense*
▷ **purely** *ADVERB* **pureness** *NOUN* **purity** *NOUN*

purée (pewr-ay) *NOUN* **purées** fruit or vegetables made into pulp

purge *VERB* **purges, purging, purged** get rid of unwanted people or things
▷ **purge** *NOUN*

purify *VERB* **purifies, purifying, purified** make a thing pure
▷ **purification** *NOUN* **purifier** *NOUN*

Puritan *NOUN* **Puritans** a Protestant in the 16th and 17th centuries who wanted simpler religious ceremonies and strictly moral behaviour

purple *NOUN* a deep reddish-blue colour

purpose *NOUN* **purposes 1** what you intend to do; a plan or aim **2** determination • *walk with purpose*
▷ **purposeful** *ADJECTIVE* **purposefully** *ADVERB*
on purpose by intention, not by accident

purr *VERB* **purrs, purring, purred** make the low murmuring sound that a cat does when it is pleased
▷ **purr** *NOUN*

purse *NOUN* **purses** a small pouch for carrying money

purse *VERB* **purses, pursing, pursed**
purse your lips draw them tightly together because you are annoyed or frustrated

pursue *VERB* **pursues, pursuing, pursued**
1 chase someone in order to catch them
2 continue with something; work at • *We are pursuing our enquiries.*
▷ **pursuer** *NOUN*

pursuit *NOUN* **pursuits 1** pursuing **2** a regular activity

pus *NOUN* a thick yellowish substance produced in inflamed or infected tissue, e.g. in an abscess or boil

push *VERB* **pushes, pushing, pushed 1** make a thing go away from you by using force on it **2** move yourself by using force • *He pushed in front of me.* **3** try to force someone to do or use something; urge
push off (*informal*) go away

Thesaurus

pure *ADJECTIVE* **1** *pure gold* ► unalloyed, unmixed, genuine, natural
OPPOSITES ARE impure, adulterated **2** *places where the air is pure* ► clean, fresh, clear, untainted, unpolluted, uncontaminated
OPPOSITES ARE impure, polluted **3** *a pure mind* ► virtuous, moral, chaste, good, innocent, righteous, blameless OPPOSITES ARE immoral, dirty

purely *ADVERB* *The lights are purely for show.* ► simply, only, solely, entirely, totally, completely, exclusively

purity *NOUN* **1** *the purity of the water* ► cleanliness, clearness, freshness, naturalness, wholesomeness **2** *the purity of their thoughts* ► virtue, morality, goodness, rightness, uprightness, integrity, honesty

purpose *NOUN* **1** *They made their purpose clear.* ► intention, motive, justification **2** *I can't see any purpose in doing that.* ► point, advantage, benefit, gain **3** *Their actions show a lot of purpose.* ► determination, resolution, resolve, single-mindedness, tenacity, enthusiasm
on purpose *He says it was an accident but I'm sure he did it on purpose.* ► deliberately, intentionally, purposely, consciously, knowingly

purse *NOUN* **1** *Keep your foreign money in a separate purse.* ► pouch, wallet, money bag, bag **2** *activities that are paid for out of the public purse* ► fund *or* funds, resources, money, kitty, finances, resources, exchequer

pursue *VERB* **1** *I pursued a fox to the end of the lane.* ► chase, go after, run after, follow, track **2** *It was an ambitious objective to pursue.* ► strive for, work towards, aim at, aspire to **3** *She is determined to pursue a career in politics.* ► follow, undertake, take up, engage in **4** *He pursues a number of interests in his spare time.* ► carry on, maintain, follow, continue, devote yourself to

pursuit *NOUN* **1** *Police gave up the pursuit when they lost the trail in London.* ► chase, hunt, search, tracking **2** *The family enjoy their outdoor pursuits.* ► activity, pastime, diversion, amusement **3** *the pursuit of knowledge* ► search (for), quest (for), striving (for), aim, goal, objective

push *VERB* **1** *She pushed a chair against the door.* ► shove, thrust, press, propel, nudge
AN OPPOSITE IS pull **2** *I pushed a few things into a bag.* ► pack, cram, squash, squeeze, jam, ram, crush, put, insert **3** *He tried to push his way through the crowd.* ► force, thrust, shove, elbow, jostle, shoulder, prod, press **4** *Better not to push them to come if they don't want to.* ► press, pressure, pressurize, put pressure on, urge, persuade, cajole, browbeat, coerce, bully, compel, (*more informal*) lean on **5** *Each software company wants to push its own product.* ► promote, publicize, advertise, popularize, make known, market, (*more informal*) plug
push around *He was fed up with being pushed around.* ► bully, domineer, boss about *or*

push *NOUN* **pushes** a pushing movement or effort
at a push if necessary but only with difficulty
get the push (*informal*) be dismissed from a job
pushchair *NOUN* **pushchairs** a folding chair on wheels, for pushing a young child along
pusher *NOUN* **pushers** a person who sells illegal drugs
pushy *ADJECTIVE* unpleasantly self-confident and eager to do things
puss *NOUN* (*informal*) a cat
put *VERB* **puts, putting, put** **1** move a person or thing to a place or position • *Put the lamp on the table.* **2** make a person or thing do or experience something or be in a certain condition • *Put the light on.* • *The news put me in a good mood.* **3** express in words • *She put it tactfully.*
be hard put have difficulty in doing something
put off **1** postpone **2** dissuade **3** stop someone wanting something • *The smell puts me off.*
put out **1** stop a fire from burning or a light from shining **2** annoy or inconvenience • *Our lateness has put her out.*
put up **1** construct or build **2** raise **3** give someone a place to sleep • *Can you put me up for the night?*
put up with endure or tolerate

Thesaurus

around, trample on, mistreat
push for *Trade unions are pushing for the repeal of some of these laws.* ► demand, insist on, press for, urge
push off (*informal*) *She was busy and told us to push off.* ► go away, leave, be off, run along, depart, (*informal*) beat it, (*informal*) scram

push *NOUN* **1** *She felt a push in her back.* ► shove, thrust, prod, nudge, jolt, poke, knock **2** *The enemy's push was aimed at reaching the coast.* ► advance, thrust, drive, offensive, onslaught, assault

pushy *ADJECTIVE* *He needed to appear in control without seeming too pushy.* ► assertive, dominating, dominant, aggressive, forceful, officious

put *VERB* **1** *He put the case on the table. They put a guard on the door.* ► place, leave, set, deposit, position, stand, settle, station, post **2** *I wanted to say something but I wasn't sure how to put it.* ► express, word, phrase, formulate, couch **3** *The government will put a tax on it.* ► impose, inflict, levy, apply (to), assign (to) **4** *They put the cost at over a million.* ► estimate, reckon, calculate, assess, evaluate, measure, judge **5** *We have some ideas to put to you.* ► submit, present, propose, advance, offer, suggest
put across *The government needs to put its message across clearly.* ► communicate, convey, get across, spell out, make clear, express
put aside *We have put aside some money.* ► save, set aside, put by, keep, keep in reserve, reserve
put away **1** *The judge put him away for life.* ► jail, imprison, send to prison, lock up, put behind bars, incarcerate, commit **2** *Did you see how much food they put away?* ► eat, consume, devour
put back **1** *I'll put the book back.* ► replace, return **2** *The meeting has been put back for a week.* ► postpone, defer, delay, hold over
AN OPPOSITE IS bring forward
put by *She wanted to put something by each week for emergencies.* ► save, set aside, keep, earmark
put down **1** *I'd better put down some details.* ► write down, record, enter, note down, make a note of **2** *The army quickly put down the rebellion.* ► suppress, crush, quell, quash, defeat **3** *He enjoyed putting people down, especially in public.* ► criticize, belittle, disparage, humiliate, mortify **4** *You can put it down to laziness.* ► attribute, ascribe, blame (on)
put forward *Stella put forward a new suggestion.* ► advance, offer, propose, suggest, present, submit AN OPPOSITE IS withdraw
put in *You have to put in a new ink cartridge* ► insert, install, fit OPPOSITES ARE remove, take out
put off **1** *The noise put her off.* ► deter, discourage, disconcert, unnerve, repel, distract, intimidate AN OPPOSITE IS attract **2** *We'd better put off a decision.* ► postpone, defer, delay, hold over, shelve, reschedule AN OPPOSITE IS bring forward
put on **1** *He put on an air of importance.* ► assume, affect, simulate, feign, sham **2** *The gallery is putting on a special exhibition.* ► mount, organize, stage, produce, present
put out **1** *Nina was put out by this criticism.* ► offend, annoy, anger, irritate, affront, insult **2** *I hope it won't put you out if I stay a few days.* ► inconvenience, bother, trouble, impose on **3** *The BBC put out an appeal.* ► announce, publish, broadcast, circulate
put up **1** *He put up a shed in the garden.* ► erect, build, construct, assemble OPPOSITES ARE take down, demolish **2** *We can put you up for a few days.* ► accommodate, house, lodge, take in, give a bed to, shelter **3** *They have put up their prices.* ► increase, raise, lift, (*more informal*) bump up
put up with *She is not prepared to put up with*

A B C D E F G H I J K L M N O P Q R S T U V W X Y Z

putt *VERB* **putts, putting, putted** hit a golf ball gently towards the hole
▷ **putt** *NOUN* **putter** *NOUN* **putting green** *NOUN*

putty *NOUN* a soft paste that sets hard, used for fitting the glass into a window frame

puzzle *NOUN* **puzzles 1** a difficult question or problem **2** a game or toy that sets a problem to solve or a difficult task to complete **3** a jigsaw puzzle

puzzle *VERB* **puzzles, puzzling, puzzled 1** give someone a problem so that they have to think hard **2** think patiently about how to solve something
▷ **puzzlement** *NOUN*

pygmy (pig- mee) *NOUN* **pygmies 1** a very small person or thing **2** a member of certain unusually short peoples in parts of Africa

pyjamas *PLURAL NOUN* a loose jacket and trousers worn in bed [from Persian or Urdu *pay* = leg + *jamah* = clothing]

pylon *NOUN* **pylons** a tall framework made of strips of steel, supporting electric cables [from Greek, = monumental gateway, which a modern pylon resembles in shape]

pyramid *NOUN* **pyramids 1** a structure with a square base and with sloping sides that meet in a point at the top **2** an ancient Egyptian tomb shaped like this
▷ **pyramidal** (pir- am- id- al) *ADJECTIVE*

python *NOUN* **pythons** a large snake that kills its prey by coiling round and crushing it [from the name of a large serpent or monster in Greek legend, killed by Apollo]

Thesaurus

such behaviour. ► tolerate, stand for, accept, bear, take, endure, stomach

puzzle *NOUN* *It is a hard puzzle to solve.*
► problem, riddle, question, enigma, paradox

puzzle *VERB* **1** *Mike's angry response puzzled me.*
► confuse, perplex, baffle, mystify, bewilder, disconcert, confound, fox, (*more informal*) flummox
puzzle out *She was trying to puzzle out who the caller might have been.* ► work out, figure out, resolve, decide, get to the bottom of, make sense of

puzzled *ADJECTIVE* *Freda had a puzzled look on her face.* ► confused, baffled, perplexed, mystified, bewildered, at a loss, nonplussed, (*more informal*) stumped

puzzling *ADJECTIVE* *There was something puzzling about the shape of the house.* ► confusing, baffling, bewildering, perplexing, mystifying, mysterious, inexplicable, extraordinary
OPPOSITES ARE straightforward, comprehensible

Qq

QC *ABBREVIATION* Queen's Counsel

QED *ABBREVIATION* quod erat demonstrandum (Latin, = which was the thing that had to be proved)

quack[1] *VERB* **quacks, quacking, quacked** make the harsh cry of a duck
▷ **quack** *NOUN*
[imitating the sound]

quack[2] *NOUN* **quacks** a person who falsely claims to have medical skill or have remedies to cure diseases [from Dutch *quacken* = to boast]

quadratic equation *NOUN* **quadratic equations** an equation that involves quantities or variables raised to the power of two, but no higher than two

quadrilateral *NOUN* **quadrilaterals** a flat geometric shape with four sides

quadruped *NOUN* **quadrupeds** an animal with four feet

quagmire (kwog-mire) *NOUN* **quagmires** a bog or marsh

quail[1] *NOUN* **quail** or **quails** a bird related to the partridge

quail[2] *VERB* **quails, quailing, quailed** feel or show fear

quaint *ADJECTIVE* attractively odd or old-fashioned
▷ **quaintly** *ADVERB* **quaintness** *NOUN*

quake *VERB* **quakes, quaking, quaked** tremble; shake with fear

Quaker *NOUN* **Quakers** a member of a religious group called the Society of Friends, founded by George Fox in the 17th century [originally an insult, probably from George Fox's saying that people should 'tremble at the name of the Lord']

qualification *NOUN* **qualifications** **1** a skill or ability that makes someone suitable for a job **2** an exam that you have passed or a course of study that you have completed **3** something that qualifies a remark or statement

qualify *VERB* **qualifies, qualifying, qualified** **1** make or become able to do something through having certain qualities or training, or by passing an exam **2** make a remark or statement less extreme; limit its meaning **3** (in grammar, said about an adjective) add meaning to a noun

quality *NOUN* **qualities** **1** how good or bad something is **2** a characteristic; something that is special in a person or thing

qualm (kwahm) *NOUN* **qualms** a misgiving or scruple

quandary *NOUN* **quandaries** a difficult situation where you are uncertain what to do

quantity *NOUN* **quantities** **1** how much there is of something; how many things there are of one sort **2** a large amount

quantum leap or **quantum jump** *NOUN* **quantum leaps** or **quantum jumps** a sudden large increase or advance

quarantine *NOUN* keeping a person or animal isolated in case they have a disease which could spread to others [from Italian *quaranta* = forty (because the original period of isolation was 40 days)]

Thesaurus

quaint *ADJECTIVE* *a quaint little shop that served teas* ► charming, picturesque, antiquated, strange, sweet, old-world, (*more informal*) twee

qualification *NOUN* **1** *You need a professional qualification in social work.* ► certificate, diploma, degree, training, skill, competence, eligibility, fitness **2** *He agreed without any qualification.* ► reservation, hesitation, restriction, exception, condition, modification

qualified *ADJECTIVE* **1** *His two sons were both qualified doctors.* ► certified, chartered, skilled, trained, professional, graduate, competent AN OPPOSITE IS unqualified **2** *She could only give the idea qualified approval.* ► limited, modified, conditional, cautious, guarded, reserved, restricted, equivocal, half-hearted OPPOSITES ARE unqualified, unconditional

qualify *VERB* **1** *The course qualifies you to teach young children.* ► authorize, permit, allow, entitle, prepare, equip, fit AN OPPOSITE IS disqualify (from) **2** *I may qualify for a discount.* ► be eligible, be entitled (to), be allowed **3** *He qualified his conclusion with a few reservations.* ► moderate, modify, restrict, mitigate, limit

quality *NOUN* **1** *work of a high quality* ► standard, calibre, class, grade, rank, sort, value, condition, excellence **2** *He has many good qualities.* ► characteristic, feature, attribute, point, aspect, peculiarity, property, trait

quantity *NOUN* *A huge quantity of stolen goods was recovered.* ► amount, number, total, volume, lot, portion, proportion, consignment

A B C D E F G H I J K L M N O P Q R S T U V W X Y Z

quarrel *NOUN* **quarrels** an angry disagreement

quarrel *VERB* **quarrels, quarrelling, quarrelled** have a quarrel
▷ **quarrelsome** *ADJECTIVE*

quarry[1] *NOUN* **quarries** an open place where stone or slate is dug or cut out of the ground

quarry *VERB* **quarries, quarrying, quarried** dig or cut from a quarry

quarry[2] *NOUN* **quarries** an animal etc. being hunted or pursued

quart *NOUN* **quarts** two pints, a quarter of a gallon

quarter *NOUN* **quarters** **1** each of four equal parts into which a thing is or can be divided **2** three months, one-fourth of a year **3** a district or region • *People came from every quarter.*
at close quarters very close together
give no quarter show no mercy

quarter *VERB* **quarters, quartering, quartered** **1** divide something into quarters **2** put soldiers etc. into lodgings

quarter-final *NOUN* **quarter-finals** each of the matches or rounds before a semi-final, in which there are eight contestants or teams

quarters *PLURAL NOUN* lodgings

quartet *NOUN* **quartets** **1** a group of four musicians **2** a piece of music for four musicians **3** a set of four people or things

quartz *NOUN* a hard mineral, often in crystal form [via German from a Polish dialect word *kwardy* = hard]

quaver *VERB* **quavers, quavering, quavered** tremble or quiver

quaver *NOUN* **quavers** **1** a quavering sound **2** a note in music (♩) lasting half as long as a crotchet

quay (kee) *NOUN* **quays** a landing place where ships can be tied up for loading and unloading; a wharf
▷ **quayside** *NOUN*

queasy *ADJECTIVE* feeling slightly sick
▷ **queasily** *ADVERB* **queasiness** *NOUN*

queen *NOUN* **queens** **1** a woman who is the ruler of a country through inheriting the position **2** the wife of a king **3** a female bee or ant that produces eggs **4** an important piece in chess **5** a playing card with a picture of a queen on it
▷ **queenly** *ADJECTIVE*
[from Old English]

Queen's Counsel *NOUN* **Queen's Counsels** a senior barrister

queer *ADJECTIVE* **1** strange or eccentric **2** slightly ill or faint
▷ **queerly** *ADVERB* **queerness** *NOUN*

queer *VERB* **queers, queering, queered**
queer a person's pitch spoil his or her chances beforehand
[perhaps from German *quer* = perverse]

Thesaurus

quarrel *NOUN* *A quarrel developed in which Kemp was struck over the head.* ▸ argument, row, disagreement, altercation, difference of opinion, dispute, squabble, clash, tiff
OPPOSITES ARE agreement, reconciliation

quarrel *VERB* **1** *They were always quarelling.* ▸ argue, disagree, row, have a row, squabble, bicker, fall out, tiff, fight AN OPPOSITE IS agree **2 quarrel with** *I can't quarrel with your version of what happened.* ▸ disagree with, find fault with, criticize, oppose

quarrelsome *ADJECTIVE* *He didn't want to stay with such a quarrelsome family.* ▸ argumentative, contentious, belligerent, disputatious, aggressive, factious, confrontational, ill-tempered
AN OPPOSITE IS peaceable

quarter *NOUN* **1** *a house in the poor quarter of the city* ▸ district, locality, neighbourhood, vicinity, area, region, part, sector **2** *There was help from an unexpected quarter.* ▸ source, direction, point, location

quash *VERB* **1** *The Court of Appeal may quash the sentence.* ▸ overrule, revoke, rescind, overturn, set aside, cancel, retract, repeal, nullify **2** *The rebellion was brutally quashed. The statement failed to quash rumours.* ▸ put an end to, stamp out, suppress, crush, quell, subdue, overthrow

quaver *VERB* *She broke off as her voice began to quaver.* ▸ tremble, quiver, waver, shake, flutter, vibrate, pulsate

quay *NOUN* *Overlooking the quay was a small hotel.* ▸ dock, wharf, pier, harbour, jetty, landing-stage, berth

queasy *ADJECTIVE* *He had been feeling tired and queasy for the past few days.* ▸ nauseous, bilious, sick, unwell, poorly, queer, out of sorts

queen *NOUN* *She knew she would be queen one day.* ▸ ruler, monarch, sovereign, crowned head
RELATED ADJECTIVES regal, royal

queer *ADJECTIVE* **1** *There was something queer going on.* ▸ odd, strange, unusual, weird, peculiar, funny, curious, bizarre, puzzling, mysterious, remarkable OPPOSITES ARE ordinary, normal **2** *I was feeling a bit queer.* ▸ sick, unwell, poorly, queasy, out of sorts, nauseous, bilious, faint, dizzy

quell *VERB* **quells, quelling, quelled 1** crush a rebellion **2** stop yourself from feeling fear, anger etc.; suppress

quench *VERB* **quenches, quenching, quenched 1** satisfy your thirst by drinking **2** put out a fire or flame

query (kweer- ee) *NOUN* **queries 1** a question **2** a question mark

query *VERB* **queries, querying, queried** question whether something is true or correct [from Latin *quaere* = ask!]

quest *NOUN* **quests** a long search for something • *the quest for gold*

question *NOUN* **questions 1** a sentence asking something **2** a problem to be discussed or solved • *Parliament debated the question of education.* **3** doubt • *Whether we shall win is open to question.*
in question being discussed or disputed • *His honesty is not in question.*
out of the question impossible

question *VERB* **questions, questioning, questioned 1** ask someone questions **2** say that you are doubtful about something
▷ **questioner** *NOUN*

questionable *ADJECTIVE* causing doubt; not certainly true or honest or advisable

question mark *NOUN* **question marks** the punctuation mark ? placed after a question

questionnaire *NOUN* **questionnaires** a written set of questions asked to provide information for a survey

queue (kew) *NOUN* **queues** a line of people or vehicles waiting for something

queue *VERB* **queues, queueing, queued** wait in a queue [via French from Latin *cauda* = tail. *Queue* originally meant 'an animal's tail' as a term in heraldry.]

quibble *NOUN* **quibbles** a trivial complaint or objection

quibble *VERB* **quibbles, quibbling, quibbled** make trivial complaints or objections

quick *ADJECTIVE* **1** taking only a short time to do something **2** done in a short time **3** able to notice or learn or think quickly **4** (*old use*) alive • *the quick and the dead*
▷ **quickly** *ADVERB* **quickness** *NOUN*

Thesaurus

quell *VERB* *Troops were sent in to quell the rising.* ► suppress, put an end to, stamp out, crush, quash, subdue, overthrow

query *NOUN* *Please send a stamped addressed envelope with any queries.* ► question, enquiry, problem, doubt, uncertainty

query *VERB* *She had to query the wisdom of such a plan.* ► question, doubt, suspect, have doubts about, have reservations about, feel uneasy about, challenge, dispute AN OPPOSITE IS accept

quest *NOUN* *a quest to find Iron-Age remains* ► expedition, mission, search, hunt, crusade

question *NOUN* **1** *You haven't answered the question.* ► enquiry, query, problem AN OPPOSITE IS answer **2** *There is the question of all his debts.* ► issue, matter, business, point, subject, problem **3** *There's some question about who will be in charge.* ► uncertainty, doubt, misgiving, argument, reservation, debate, dispute, controversy, objection
out of the question *Sending them more money was out of the question.* ► impossible, inconceivable, unthinkable, unrealistic, not feasible, impractical, (*more informal*) not on OPPOSITES ARE possible, feasible

question *VERB* **1** *A man is being questioned at Gloucester police station.* ► interrogate, interview, cross-examine, investigate, (*more informal*) quiz, (*more informal*) grill, (*more informal*) pump **2** *She never questioned his right to be there.* ► query, doubt, suspect, have doubts about, have reservations about, feel uneasy about, challenge, dispute

questionable *ADJECTIVE* *All these arguments are highly questionable.* ► debatable, doubtful, dubious, suspect, unreliable, disputable, uncertain, unclear, unprovable, (*more informal*) iffy, (*more informal*) shady
OPPOSITES ARE unquestionable, indisputable, acceptable

queue *NOUN* **1** *To my surprise there was no queue at the Post Office.* ► line, line of people **2** *There were traffic queues all down the motorway.* ► jam, tailback, file, column, procession

queue *VERB* *They queued for hours to be sure of tickets.* ► line up, form a queue, wait in a queue

quibble *VERB* *He accepted the offer without quibbling.* ► complain, find fault, carp, cavil, object , equivocate, split hairs, nit-pick

quibble *NOUN* *Her only quibble was about the cost.* ► objection, complaint, reservation, doubt, query, criticism

quick *ADJECTIVE* **1** *She gave a quick glance at her watch.* ► hasty, brief, cursory, furtive, fleeting, rapid OPPOSITES ARE long, careful **2** *He was always a quick worker.* ► fast, swift, rapid, speedy, lively, sprightly, prompt
AN OPPOSITE IS slow **3** *There is no quick solution to the problem.* ► instant, instantaneous, ready, sudden **4** *Kevin wasn't as quick as some of the others in the class.* ► bright, clever, intelligent, gifted, able, sharp, alert, acute, (*more informal*) on the ball AN OPPOSITE IS dull

quicksand *NOUN* **quicksands** an area of loose wet deep sand that sucks in anything resting or falling on top of it [from **quick** in the old sense 'alive' (because the sand moves as if it were alive and 'eats' things)]

quid *NOUN* **quid** (*informal*) £1

quiet *ADJECTIVE* **1** silent • *Be quiet!* **2** with little sound; not loud or noisy **3** calm and peaceful; without disturbance • *a quiet life* **4** (said about colours) not bright
▷ **quietly** *ADVERB* **quietness** *NOUN*

quiet *NOUN* quietness

quieten *VERB* **quietens, quietening, quietened** make or become quiet

quill *NOUN* **quills 1** a large feather **2** a pen made from a large feather **3** one of the spines on a hedgehog

quilt *NOUN* **quilts** a padded bedcover [from Latin *culcita* = mattress or cushion]

quintet *NOUN* **quintets 1** a group of five musicians **2** a piece of music for five musicians

quirk *NOUN* **quirks 1** a peculiarity of a person's behaviour **2** a trick of fate
▷ **quirky** *ADJECTIVE*

quit *VERB* **quits, quitting, quitted** *or* **quit 1** leave or abandon **2** (*informal*) stop doing something
▷ **quitter** *NOUN*

quite *ADVERB* **1** completely or entirely • *I am quite all right.* **2** somewhat; to some extent • *She is quite a good swimmer.* **3** really • *It's quite a change.*

quits *ADJECTIVE* even or equal after retaliating or paying someone back • *I think you and I are quits now.*

quiver[1] *NOUN* **quivers** a container for arrows

quiver[2] *VERB* **quivers, quivering, quivered** tremble
▷ **quiver** *NOUN*

quiz *NOUN* **quizzes** a series of questions, especially as an entertainment or competition

quiz *VERB* **quizzes, quizzing, quizzed** (*informal*) qestion someone closely

Thesaurus

quicken *VERB* **1** *The pace quickened.* ► speed up, accelerate, get *or* go faster, hasten, hurry OPPOSITES ARE slow, slow down **2** *The programme quickened their interest in archaeology.* ► arouse, rouse, stimulate, excite, revive, galvanize AN OPPOSITE IS dull

quickly *ADVERB* **1** *She began to walk more quickly.* ► fast, swiftly, rapidly, speedily AN OPPOSITE IS slowly **2** *We quickly realized they had gone.* ► soon, at once, straight away, right away, rapidly, immediately, instantly, directly, suddenly

quiet *ADJECTIVE* **1** *The house is in a quiet village near the river.* ► peaceful, tranquil, secluded, isolated, calm, restful, pleasant OPPOSITES ARE noisy, busy **2** *He spoke in a quiet voice.* ► soft, low, muted, muffled OPPOSITES ARE loud, raised **3** *Can we have a quiet word together?* ► private, confidential, secret **4** *Fiona's a lovely, quiet person.* ► shy, reserved, private, subdued, taciturn, withdrawn, calm, placid, serene, composed, untroubled, unruffled AN OPPOSITE IS outgoing **5** *It's hard to keep rumours like that quiet.* ► secret, silent, private, confidential, undisclosed AN OPPOSITE IS public

quieten *VERB* **1** *The audience quietened when the curtain went up.* ► go quiet, fall silent, grow silent, hush, shush, (*more informal*) shut up **2** *He was so excited it was impossible to quieten him.* ► calm, calm down, pacify, mollify, appease, assuage

quirk *NOUN* *One of his quirks is that he checks things over and over again.* ► peculiarity, oddity, idiosyncrasy, foible, whim, caprice

quit *VERB* **1** *She's much too determined to quit now.* ► give up, stop, leave, depart, go, cease **2** (*informal*) *It's time you quit smoking.* ► give up, stop, cease, discontinue, drop, (*more informal*) pack in **3** *He decided to quit his job and go abroad.* ► leave, resign from, retire from, renounce, forsake, abandon

quite *ADVERB* **1** *The two sisters are quite different in appearance.* ► completely, totally, wholly, entirely, utterly **2** *It was quite late by now.* ► rather, fairly, a bit, somewhat, comparatively, relatively, (*more informal*) pretty

quits *ADJECTIVE* *After four games we were quits.* ► level, even, square, equal

quiver *VERB* *The trees quivered in the wind. I sat quivering with fright.* ► shake, tremble, shudder, shiver, quaver, flutter

quiz *NOUN* *The day ended with a quiz between the two teams.* ► competition, questionnaire, test, examination, questioning

quiz *VERB* (*informal*) *The police are quizzing a suspect.* ► question, interrogate, interview, cross-examine, investigate

quoit (koit) *NOUN* **quoits** a ring thrown at a peg in the game of **quoits**

quota *NOUN* **quotas 1** a fixed share that must be given or received or done **2** a limited amount

quotation *NOUN* **quotations 1** quoting **2** something quoted **3** a statement of the price of goods or services that can be supplied

quotation marks *PLURAL NOUN* inverted commas, used to mark a quotation

quote *VERB* **quotes, quoting, quoted 1** repeat words that were first written or spoken by someone else **2** mention something as proof **3** state the price of goods or services that you can supply

quote *NOUN* **quotes** a quotation

quotient (kwoh- shent) *NOUN* **quotients** the result of dividing one number by another COMPARE **product** [from Latin *quotiens* = how many times?]

Thesaurus

quotation *NOUN* **1** *a quotation from Shakespeare* ► citation, quote, reference, excerpt, extract, piece, passage **2** *First we need a quotation for the work.* ► estimate, price, quote, figure, tender

quote *VERB* **1** *She quoted a few lines from a poem.* ► cite, recite, recall, repeat, mention, refer to **2** *The figure the builder quoted was too high.* ► estimate, offer, tender, bid, specify

Rr

rabbi (rab- I) *NOUN* **rabbis** a Jewish religious leader

rabbit *NOUN* **rabbits** a furry animal with long ears that digs burrows

rabble *NOUN* **rabbles** a disorderly crowd or mob

rabid (rab- id) *ADJECTIVE* **1** fanatical • *a rabid tennis fan* **2** suffering from rabies

rabies (ray- beez) *NOUN* a fatal disease that affects dogs, cats, etc. and can be passed to humans by the bite of an infected animal

race[1] *NOUN* **races 1** a competition to be the first to reach a particular place or to do something **2** a strong fast current of water • *the tidal race*

race *VERB* **races, racing, raced 1** compete in a race **2** move very fast
▷ **racer** *NOUN*
[from Old Norse]

race[2] *NOUN* **races** a very large group of people thought to have the same ancestors and with physical characteristics (e.g. colour of skin and hair, shape of eyes and nose) that differ from those of other groups
▷ **racial** *ADJECTIVE*
[via French from Italian *razza*]

racehorse *NOUN* **racehorses** a horse bred or kept for racing

racetrack *NOUN* **racetracks** a track for horse or vehicle races

racism (ray- sizm) *NOUN* **1** belief that a particular race of people is better than others **2** discrimination against or hostility towards people of other races
▷ **racist** *NOUN*

rack[1] *NOUN* **racks 1** a framework used as a shelf or container **2** a bar or rail with cogs into which the cogs of a gear or wheel etc. fit **3** an ancient device for torturing people by stretching them

rack *VERB* **racks, racking, racked** torment • *He was racked with guilt.*
rack your brains think hard in trying to solve a problem

rack[2] *NOUN*
go to rack and ruin gradually become worse in condition from neglect
[a different spelling of **wreck**]

racket[1] *NOUN* **rackets** a bat with strings stretched across a frame, used in tennis, badminton, and squash [from Arabic *rahat* = palm of the hand]

racket[2] *NOUN* **rackets 1** a loud noise; a din **2** (*informal*) a dishonest or illegal business • *a drugs racket* [perhaps imitating the sound of clattering]

racy *ADJECTIVE* **racier, raciest** lively and slightly shocking in style • *She gave a racy account of her travels.*

radar *NOUN* a system or apparatus that uses radio waves to show on a screen etc. the position of objects that cannot be seen because of darkness, fog, distance, etc.

radiant *ADJECTIVE* **1** radiating light or heat etc. **2** radiated • *radiant heat* **3** looking very bright and happy
▷ **radiantly** *ADVERB* **radiance** *NOUN*

radiate *VERB* **radiates, radiating, radiated 1** send out light, heat, or other energy in rays **2** give out a strong feeling or quality • *She radiated confidence.* **3** spread out from a central point like the spokes of a wheel

radiation *NOUN* **1** light, heat, or other energy radiated **2** the energy or particles sent out by a radioactive substance **3** the process of radiating

Thesaurus

rabble *NOUN He was met by a rabble of angry, noisy youths.* ► crowd, throng, horde, mob, gang, group, herd, swarm

race *NOUN* **1** *people of many different races* ► ethnic group, nation, people, clan, tribe RELATED ADJECTIVES ethnic, racial **2** *Donald won the race easily.* ► contest, competition, chase, heat, event

race *VERB* **1** *The children were racing each other in the garden.* ► have a race with, run against, compete with, try to beat **2** *She raced towards the house.* ► dash, rush, shoot, sprint, streak, dart, hare, hasten, hurry, run, tear, zoom, career, fly, gallop, move fast **3** *All kinds of thoughts raced through my mind.* ► rush, dart, fly, shoot, zoom

racial *ADJECTIVE laws against racial discrimination* ► ethnic, national, cultural

racism *NOUN the struggle to end racism in all its forms* ► discrimination, racialism, racial hatred, intolerance, prejudice, xenophobia, bigotry, chauvinism

racist *ADJECTIVE racist attitudes* ► discriminatory, racialist, intolerant, prejudiced, xenophobic, biased, bigoted, chauvinist
OPPOSITES ARE tolerant, unbiased

rack *NOUN a vegetable rack; a luggage rack* ► stand, shelf, support, framework, frame

racket *NOUN* **1** *The machines make a frightful racket.* ► noise, din, commotion, hubbub, clamour, tumult, rumpus, uproar **2** (*informal*) *He was involved in a stolen car racket.* ► swindle, fraud, dodge, fiddle, deception, (*more informal*) con, (*informal*) scam

radiant *ADJECTIVE* **1** *a radiant moon* ► bright, shining, brilliant OPPOSITES ARE dark, dull **2** *a*

radiator *NOUN* **radiators 1** a device that gives out heat, especially a metal case that is heated electrically or through which steam or hot water flows **2** a device that cools the engine of a motor vehicle

radical *ADJECTIVE* **1** basic and thorough • *radical changes* **2** wanting to make great reforms • *a radical politician*
▷ **radically** *ADVERB*

radical *NOUN* **radicals** a person who wants to make great reforms

radio *NOUN* **radios 1** the process of sending and receiving sound or pictures by means of electromagnetic waves **2** an apparatus for receiving sound (a **receiver**) or sending it out (a **transmitter**) in this way **3** sound broadcasting [from Latin *radius* = a spoke or ray]

radioactive *ADJECTIVE* having atoms that break up spontaneously and send out radiation which produces electrical and chemical effects and penetrates things
▷ **radioactivity** *NOUN*

radiocarbon dating *NOUN* the use of a kind of radioactive carbon that decays at a steady rate, to find out how old something is

radio telescope *NOUN* **radio telescopes** an instrument that can detect radio waves from space

radiotherapy *NOUN* the use of radioactive substances in treating diseases such as cancer

radish *NOUN* **radishes** a small hard round red vegetable, eaten raw in salads

radium *NOUN* a radioactive metal, often used in radiotherapy [from Latin *radius* = a spoke or ray]

radius *NOUN* **radii** or **radiuses 1** a straight line from the centre of a circle or sphere to the circumference; the length of this line **2** a range or distance from a central point • *The school takes pupils living within a radius of ten kilometres.*

radon *NOUN* a radioactive gas used in radiotherapy

raffle *NOUN* **raffles** a kind of lottery, usually to raise money for a charity

raffle *VERB* **raffles, raffling, raffled** offer something as a prize in a raffle

raft *NOUN* **rafts** a flat floating structure made of wood etc., used as a boat

rafter *NOUN* **rafters** any of the long sloping pieces of wood that hold up a roof

rag[1] *NOUN* **rags 1** an old or torn piece of cloth **2** a piece of ragtime music

rag[2] *NOUN* **rags** a series of entertainments and activities held by students to collect money for charity

rag *VERB* **rags, ragging, ragged** (*slang*) tease

rage *NOUN* **rages** great or violent anger
all the rage very popular or fashionable for a time

rage *VERB* **rages, raging, raged 1** be very angry **2** continue violently or with great force • *A storm was raging.*

ragged *ADJECTIVE* **1** torn or frayed **2** wearing torn clothes **3** irregular or uneven • *a ragged performance* [from Old Norse *roggvathr* = tufted]

raid *NOUN* **raids 1** a sudden attack **2** a surprise visit by police etc. to arrest people or seize illegal goods

raid *VERB* **raids, raiding, raided** make a raid on a place
▷ **raider** *NOUN*

Thesaurus

radiant smile ► beautiful, glowing, dazzling, sparkling, beaming, joyful, elated, happy
OPPOSITES ARE faint, weak

radical *ADJECTIVE* **1** *a radical course of action* ► fundamental, drastic, thoroughgoing, thorough, comprehensive, sweeping, rigorous, complete, basic AN OPPOSITE IS superficial **2** *a government committed to radical change* ► revolutionary, extreme, extremist, militant
OPPOSITES ARE moderate, conservative

raffle *NOUN* *She won a prize in a raffle.* ► draw, lottery, tombola, sweepstake

rage *NOUN* **1** *He stormed out of the room in a burst of rage.* ► anger, fury, temper, outrage, passion, pique, exasperation **2** *the rage for portable DVD players* ► craze, vogue, trend, fashion, passion

rage *VERB* **1** *He raged on for a while about loyalty.* ► fume, storm, seethe, rant, fulminate, be angry **2** *A fierce blizzard raged for days.* ► blow, storm, thunder, rampage

ragged *ADJECTIVE* **1** *She spent the morning mending ragged clothes.* ► tattered, torn, frayed, threadbare, ripped, shabby, tatty, unkempt, worn out **2** *He drilled his ragged collection of men.* ► disorganized, disordered, disorderly, erratic, irregular, uneven

raid *NOUN* **1** *Sentries watched out for any air raids.* ► attack, assault, strike, swoop, blitz, foray, sortie, onslaught, invasion **2** *He had killed a guard during a bank raid.* ► robbery, burglary, break-in, hold-up, (*more informal*) heist

raid *VERB* **1** *The army raided towns on the border.* ► pillage, loot, plunder, ransack, maraud, assault, attack, storm, descend on **2** *Burglars raided local jewellers for the second time.* ► rob, hold up, burgle, break into **3** *Police raided*

A B C D E F G H I J K L M N O P Q R S T U V W X Y Z

rail[1] *NOUN* **rails** **1** a level or sloping bar for hanging things on or forming part of a fence, banisters, etc. **2** a long metal bar forming part of a railway track
by rail on a train
[from old French; related to **rule**]

rail[2] *VERB* **rails, railing, railed** protest angrily or bitterly [via French from Latin *rugire* = to bellow]

railings *PLURAL NOUN* a fence made of metal bars

railway *NOUN* **1** the parallel metal bars that trains travel on **2** (**railways**) a system of transport using rails

rain *NOUN* drops of water that fall from the sky
▷ **rainy** *ADJECTIVE*

rain *VERB* **rains, raining, rained** **1** fall as rain or like rain **2** send down like rain • *They rained blows on him.*

rainbow *NOUN* **rainbows** an arch of all the colours of the spectrum formed in the sky when the sun shines through rain

rainfall *NOUN* the amount of rain that falls in a particular place or time

rainforest *NOUN* **rainforests** a dense tropical forest in an area of very heavy rainfall

raise *VERB* **raises, raising, raised** **1** move something to a higher place or an upright position **2** increase the amount or level of something • *We are trying to raise standards.* **3** collect; manage to obtain • *They raised £100 for charity.* **4** bring up young children or animals • *She had to raise her family alone.* **5** rouse or cause • *He raised a laugh with his joke.* **6** put forward • *We raised objections.* **7** end a siege [from Old Norse]

raisin *NOUN* **raisins** a dried grape [from French, = grape]

rake *NOUN* **rakes** a gardening tool with a row of short spikes fixed to a long handle

rake *VERB* **rakes, raking, raked** **1** gather or smooth with a rake **2** search
rake up **1** collect **2** remind people of an old scandal etc. that would be best forgotten • *Don't rake that up.*

rally *NOUN* **rallies** **1** a large meeting to support something or share an interest **2** a competition to test skill in driving • *the Monte Carlo Rally* **3** a series of strokes in tennis before a point is scored **4** a recovery

rally *VERB* **rallies, rallying, rallied** **1** bring or come together for a united effort • *They rallied support.* • *People rallied round.* **2** revive; recover strength

RAM *ABBREVIATION* (in computing) random-access memory, with contents that can be retrieved or stored directly without having to read through items already stored

ram *NOUN* **rams** **1** a male sheep **2** a device for ramming things

ram *VERB* **rams, ramming, rammed** push one thing hard against another

Ramadan *NOUN* the ninth month of the Muslim year, when Muslims do not eat or drink between dawn and sunset [Arabic, from *ramida* = to be parched]

ramble *NOUN* **rambles** a long walk in the country

Thesaurus

homes and offices in the area. ► search, swoop on

railings *PLURAL NOUN* *A notice had been put on the railings.* ► fence, paling, barrier

railway *NOUN* *They were warned not to cross the railway.* ► track, line, rails

rain *NOUN* *The rain had started again.* ► rainfall, wet weather, drizzle, shower, downpour, cloudburst, raindrops, rainstorm, squall, deluge, (*more formal*) precipitation

rain *VERB* *It rained all afternoon.* ► pour, bucket, teem, pelt, drizzle, spit

rainy *ADJECTIVE* *a rainy day* ► wet, showery, drizzly, damp AN OPPOSITE IS dry

raise *VERB* **1** *Ben raised his hand.* ► put up, lift **2** *A crane will raise the load to the top of the building.* ► lift, hoist **3** *The company was forced to raise its prices.* ► increase, put up, push up, lift **4** *United will need to raise their game for the away match.* ► improve, enhance, strengthen, heighten, boost, step up, put more life into **5** *We need to raise five thousand pounds.* ► collect, get, obtain, gather, net, amass, scrape together, yield, assemble **6** *This good news raised their hopes.* ► arouse, rouse, excite, increase, improve, encourage **7** *She raised three children on her own.* ► bring up, provide for, nurture, look after, educate **8** *Charles raised several objections to the idea.* ► present, bring up, introduce, advance, put forward, pose, offer **9** *The incident raises questions about rail safety.* ► give rise to, occasion, cause, bring about, produce, engender

rally *NOUN* *an anti-war rally* ► demonstration, meeting, protest, march, (*more informal*) demo

rally *VERB* **1** *The king rallied his troops at the border. They tried to rally support for the election.* ► muster, assemble, marshal, amass, gather, round up, organize **2** *Our spirits rallied.* ► recover, improve, pick up, get better, look up, perk up

ram *VERB* *The getaway van rammed a police car.* ► hit, strike, smash into, be in collision with, slam into, collide with, crash into

ramble *VERB* **rambles, rambling, rambled** **1** go for a ramble; wander **2** talk or write a lot without keeping to the subject
▷ **rambler** *NOUN*

ramifications *PLURAL NOUN* **1** the branches of a structure **2** the many effects of a plan or action

ramp *NOUN* **ramps** a slope joining two different levels [from French *ramper* = to climb]

rampage *VERB* **rampages, rampaging, rampaged** rush about wildly or destructively
on the rampage rampaging

rampant *ADJECTIVE* **1** growing or spreading uncontrollably • *Disease was rampant in the poorer districts.* **2** (said about an animal on coats of arms) standing upright on a hind leg • *a lion rampant*

rampart *NOUN* **ramparts** a wide bank of earth built as a fortification or a wall on top of this

ramshackle *ADJECTIVE* badly made and rickety • *a ramshackle hut*

ranch *NOUN* **ranches** a large cattle farm in America

rancid *ADJECTIVE* smelling or tasting unpleasant like stale fat

random *NOUN*
at random using no particular order or method • *numbers chosen at random*

random *ADJECTIVE* done or taken at random • *a random sample*

range *NOUN* **ranges 1** a set of different things of the same type • *a wide range of backgrounds* • *a lovely range of colours* **2** the limits between which things exist or are available; an extent • *the age range 15 to 18* **3** the distance that a gun can shoot, an aircraft can travel, a sound can be heard, etc. **4** a place with targets for shooting practice **5** a line or series of mountains or hills **6** a large open area of grazing land or hunting ground **7** a kitchen fireplace with ovens

range *VERB* **ranges, ranging, ranged 1** exist between two limits; extend • *Prices ranged from £1 to £50* **2** arrange **3** move over a wide area; wander

ranger *NOUN* **rangers** someone who looks after or patrols a park, forest, etc.

rank[1] *NOUN* **ranks 1** a line of people or things **2** a place where taxis stand to await customers **3** a position in a series of different levels • *He holds the rank of sergeant.*

rank *VERB* **ranks, ranking, ranked 1** put things in order according to their rank **2** have a certain rank or place • *She ranks among the greatest novelists.*

rank[2] *ADJECTIVE* **ranker, rankest 1** growing too thickly and coarsely **2** smelling very unpleasant **3** unmistakably bad • *rank injustice*
▷ **rankly** *ADVERB* **rankness** *NOUN*

rank and file *NOUN* the ordinary people or soldiers, not the leaders

ransack *VERB* **ransacks, ransacking, ransacked 1** search thoroughly or roughly **2** rob or pillage a place

ransom *NOUN* **ransoms** money that has to be paid for a prisoner to be set free
hold to ransom hold someone captive or in your power and demand a ransom

Thesaurus

ramble *VERB* **1** *We spent a week rambling in the countryside.* ► walk, roam, trek, tramp, hike, rove, stroll **2** *He was rambling on about his schooldays.* ► chatter, blather, prattle, drift, run, maunder, (*more informal*) rabbit, (*more informal*) witter

rambling *ADJECTIVE* **1** *a long rambling speech* ► verbose, long-winded, diffuse, disjointed, disconnected, incoherent, roundabout, digressive

ramp *NOUN* *There's a ramp for wheelchairs.* ► slope, incline, gradient, rise, sloping surface

ramshackle *ADJECTIVE* *a ramshackle old house* ► dilapidated, tumbledown, derelict, decrepit, rickety, shaky, unsafe, broken down, ruined, tottering, crumbling AN OPPOSITE IS sturdy

random *ADJECTIVE* *Her house came up in a random sample of houses in the area.* ► indiscriminate, arbitrary, chance, haphazard, casual, unplanned, accidental, unconsidered, unpremeditated, fortuitous, irregular AN OPPOSITE IS systematic

range *NOUN* **1** *a range of mountains* ► chain, row, line, series, string, file **2** *a wide range of food* ► variety, assortment, selection, array, scope, choice, spectrum, extent **3** *an age range between 20 and 30* ► span, scope, compass, radius

range *VERB* **1** *Prices range between £100 and £600.* ► extend, vary, differ, fluctuate, reach **2** *Sheep ranged over the hills.* ► roam, rove, wander, stray, travel **3** *Pupils are ranged by ability.* ► classify, class, categorize, rank, order, group

rank *NOUN* **1** *She was promoted to the rank of assistant manager.* ► level, grade, position, status, standing, station, title, class, degree **2** *a family of rank* ► high standing, distinction, importance, nobility, aristocracy **3** *The front rank began to move forward.* ► row, line, file, column

rank *VERB* *He's ranked number two in the world.* ► grade, class, categorize, classify, designate, list

ransom VERB **ransoms**, **ransoming**, **ransomed** **1** free someone by paying a ransom **2** get a ransom for someone

rant VERB **rants**, **ranting**, **ranted** speak loudly and violently [from Dutch *ranten* = talk nonsense]

rap VERB **raps**, **rapping**, **rapped** **1** knock loudly **2** (*informal*) reprimand **3** (*informal*) chat **4** perform rap music

rap NOUN **raps** **1** a rapping movement or sound **2** (*informal*) blame or punishment • *take the rap* **3** (*informal*) a chat **4** a type of popular music in which words are spoken rhythmically to an instrumental backing

rapacious (ra- pay- shus) ADJECTIVE **1** greedy **2** using threats or force to get everything you can
▷ **rapaciously** ADVERB **rapacity** NOUN

rape[1] NOUN **rapes** the act of having sexual intercourse with a person without their consent

rape VERB **rapes**, **raping**, **raped** force someone to have sexual intercourse against their will
▷ **rapist** NOUN
[from Latin *rapere* = take by force]

rape[2] NOUN a plant with bright yellow flowers, grown as food for sheep and for its seed from which oil is obtained [from Latin *rapum* = turnip (to which it is related)]

rapid ADJECTIVE moving very quickly; swift
▷ **rapidly** ADVERB **rapidity** NOUN

rapids PLURAL NOUN part of a river where the water flows very quickly

rapt ADJECTIVE very intent and absorbed
▷ **raptly** ADVERB

rapture NOUN very great delight
▷ **rapturous** ADJECTIVE **rapturously** ADVERB

rare[1] ADJECTIVE **rarer**, **rarest** **1** unusual; not often found or happening **2** (said about air) thin; below normal pressure
▷ **rarely** ADVERB **rareness** NOUN **rarity** NOUN

rare[2] ADJECTIVE (said about meat) only lightly cooked; undercooked

rarefied ADJECTIVE **1** (said about air) rare **2** remote from everyday life • *the rarefied atmosphere of the university*

rascal NOUN **rascals** a dishonest or mischievous person; a rogue
▷ **rascally** ADJECTIVE

rash[1] ADJECTIVE doing something or done without thinking of the possible risks or effects
▷ **rashly** ADVERB **rashness** NOUN

rash[2] NOUN **rashes** **1** an outbreak of spots or patches on the skin **2** a number of (usually unwelcome) events happening in a short time • *a rash of accidents*

rasher NOUN **rashers** a slice of bacon

rasp NOUN **rasps** **1** a file with sharp points on its surface **2** a rough grating sound

rasp VERB **rasps**, **rasping**, **rasped** **1** scrape roughly **2** make a rough grating sound or effect

raspberry NOUN **raspberries** a small soft red fruit

Rastafarian NOUN **Rastafarians** a member of a religious group that started in Jamaica

rat NOUN **rats** **1** an animal like a large mouse **2** (*informal*) an unpleasant or treacherous person

rate NOUN **rates** **1** speed • *The train travelled at a great rate.* **2** a measure of cost, value, etc. • *Postage rates went up.* **3** quality or standard • *first-rate*
at any rate anyway

Thesaurus

ransom NOUN *The ransom was set at four million dollars.* ► pay-off, release money, payment, price

ransom VERB *The kidnappers demanded a million pounds to ransom the girl.* ► obtain the release of, release, redeem, liberate, free

rap VERB **rap on** *He rapped on the big oak door.* ► knock on, strike, tap, hit

rapid ADJECTIVE *They made rapid progress.* ► fast, quick, swift, speedy, brisk, lively, smooth, sharp, prompt, headlong OPPOSITES ARE slow, leisurely

rare ADJECTIVE **1** *a rare moment of peace* ► infrequent, uncommon, scarce, occasional, sporadic, odd, singular OPPOSITES ARE frequent, common **2** *a person of rare abilities* ► exceptional, remarkable, incomparable, unusual, uncommon, special, abnormal

rascal NOUN **1** *One of the rascals had stolen money from the till.* ► rogue, scoundrel, ne'er-do-well **2** *Dad asked, 'What's the little rascal been up to?'* ► scamp, scallywag, monkey, mischief-maker, wretch, monster

rash ADJECTIVE *He regretted making such a rash promise.* ► reckless, impulsive, impetuous, foolhardy, hasty, precipitate, imprudent, incautious, injudicious, indiscreet, ill-advised, ill-considered, headstrong, unthinking, heedless, hot-headed, hurried OPPOSITES ARE cautious, considered, prudent

rash NOUN **1** *Her skin broke out in a rash.* ► spots, eruption, hives **2** *a rash of break-ins in the area* ► outbreak, spate, series, succession

rate NOUN **1** *They were pedalling at a furious rate.* ► speed, pace, tempo, velocity, (*more informal*) lick **2** *You can hire a boat for a reasonable daily rate.* ► charge, amount, price, cost, payment, fare, fee, figure

rate *VERB* **rates, rating, rated** **1** put a value on something **2** regard as • *He rated me among his friends*

rates *PLURAL NOUN* a local tax paid by owners of commercial land and buildings

rather *ADVERB* **1** slightly or somewhat • *It's rather dark* **2** preferably or more willingly • *I would rather not go* **3** more exactly; instead of • *He is lazy rather than stupid* **4** (*informal*) definitely, yes • *'Will you come?' 'Rather!'*

rating *NOUN* **ratings** **1** the way something is rated **2** a sailor who is not an officer

ratio (ray- shee- oh) *NOUN* **ratios** **1** the relationship between two numbers, given by the quotient • *The ratio of 2 to 10* = $2{:}10 = \frac{2}{10} = \frac{1}{5}$ **2** proportion • *Mix flour and butter in the ratio of two to one* (= two measures of flour to one measure of butter)

ration *NOUN* **rations** an amount allowed to one person

ration *VERB* **rations, rationing, rationed** share something out in fixed amounts

rational *ADJECTIVE* **1** reasonable or sane **2** able to reason
▷ **rationally** *ADVERB* **rationality** *NOUN*

rationalize *VERB* **rationalizes, rationalizing, rationalized** **1** make a thing logical and consistent • *Attempts to rationalize English spelling have failed.* **2** justify something by inventing a reasonable explanation for it • *They rationalized their meanness by calling it economy.* **3** make an industry etc. more efficient by reorganizing it
▷ **rationalization** *NOUN*

rations *PLURAL NOUN* a fixed daily amount of food issued to a soldier etc.

rattle *VERB* **rattles, rattling, rattled** **1** make a series of short sharp hard sounds **2** make a person nervous or flustered
rattle off say or recite rapidly

rattle *NOUN* **rattles** **1** a rattling sound **2** a device or baby's toy that rattles

rattlesnake *NOUN* **rattlesnakes** a poisonous American snake with a tail that rattles

raucous (raw- kus) *ADJECTIVE* loud and harsh • *a raucous voice*

ravages *PLURAL NOUN* damaging effects • *the ravages of war*

rave *VERB* **raves, raving, raved** **1** talk wildly or angrily or madly **2** talk enthusiastically about something

rave *NOUN* **raves** a large party or event with dancing to loud fast electronic music

Thesaurus

rate *VERB* **1** *They do not rate our chances very highly.* ► assess, evaluate, appraise, judge, regard, value, count, weigh, estimate, calculate, consider, measure **2** *The suggestion only rated a brief mention.* ► merit, deserve, warrant, be worthy of **3** (*informal*) *I don't rate this stuff like you do.* ► think much of, think highly of, admire, value, enjoy

rather *ADVERB* **1** *It sounds rather difficult.* ► fairly, somewhat, quite, slightly, moderately, relatively, (*more informal*) pretty **2** *I'd rather leave it until the weekend.* ► sooner, preferably

ratio *NOUN* *The ratio of men to women has changed.* ► proportion, balance, relationship, correlation, correspondence

ration *NOUN* *They decided not to increase their daily ration of biscuits.* ► allowance, allocation, quota, share, measure, helping, portion
rations *The expedition might soon run out of rations.* ► supplies, provisions, stores, food, necessaries, necessities

ration *VERB* *Fuel is strictly rationed in wartime.* ► control, limit, restrict, conserve, allocate, allot, apportion

rational *ADJECTIVE* **1** *Feelings are so high it's difficult to have a rational discussion.* ► reasoned, logical, sensible, coherent, cogent, reasonable, balanced, sane, intelligent, judicious, lucid, normal OPPOSITES ARE irrational, illogical **2** *In the last year of his life he was often barely rational.* ► lucid, coherent, sane, intelligible, in your right mind

rattle *VERB* **1** *He rattled the coins in his purse.* ► jangle, clink, clunk **2** *A row of trucks rattled along the track.* ► clatter, jolt, shake, bounce **3** *The wind rattled at the doors and windows* ► shake, batter, beat **4** *This news had rattled her badly.* ► disconcert, disturb, unnerve, fluster, shake, discomfit, (*more informal*) throw
rattle off *He rattled off the words he had learned.* ► recite, run through, reel off, repeat, list

rattle *NOUN* *the rattle of crockery in the kitchen* ► clatter, clattering, clank, clanking

raucous *ADJECTIVE* *the raucous clamour of alarm bells* ► harsh, shrill, strident, jarring, grating, noisy, loud, rough

rave *VERB* **1** *He was raving and swearing at them.* ► rage, rant, shout, roar, bellow, storm **2** **rave about** *Everyone raved about Leeds that day.* ► praise, idolize, be ecstatic about, go into raptures over

rave *ADJECTIVE* *The film got a rave review.* ► enthusiastic, rapturous, glowing, ecstatic, wonderful

a b c d e f g h i j k l m n o p q **r** s t u v w x y z

ravenous *ADJECTIVE* very hungry
▷ **ravenously** *ADVERB*

ravine (ra-veen) *NOUN* **ravines** a deep narrow gorge or valley

ravishing *ADJECTIVE* very beautiful

raw *ADJECTIVE* **1** not cooked **2** in the natural state; not yet processed • *raw materials* **3** without experience • *raw recruits* **4** with the skin removed • *a raw wound* **5** cold and damp • *a raw morning*
▷ **rawness** *NOUN*
a raw deal (*informal*) unfair treatment

raw material *NOUN* **raw materials** natural substances used in industry • *rich in iron ore, coal, and other raw materials*

ray *NOUN* **rays 1** a thin line of light, heat, or other radiation **2** each of a set of lines or parts extending from a centre **3** a slight trace of something • *a ray of hope*

raze *VERB* **razes, razing, razed** destroy a building or town completely • *The fort was razed to the ground.*

razor *NOUN* **razors** a device with a very sharp blade, especially one used for shaving

re- *PREFIX* **1** again (as in *rebuild*) **2** back again, to an earlier condition (as in *reopen*) **3** in return; to each other (as in *react*) **4** against (as in *rebel*) **5** away or down (as in *recede*)

reach *VERB* **reaches, reaching, reached 1** go as far as; arrive at a place or thing **2** stretch out your hand to get or touch something **3** succeed in achieving something • *The cheetah can reach a speed of 70 m.p.h.* • *Have you reached a decision?*
▷ **reachable** *ADJECTIVE*

reach *NOUN* **reaches 1** the distance a person or thing can reach **2** a distance you can easily travel • *We live within reach of the sea.* **3** a straight stretch of a river or canal [from Old English]

react *VERB* **reacts, reacting, reacted 1** respond to something; have a reaction **2** (in science) undergo a chemical change

reaction *NOUN* **reactions 1** an effect or feeling etc. produced in one person or thing by another **2** (in science) a chemical change caused when substances act upon each other

reactionary *ADJECTIVE* opposed to progress or reform

reactor *NOUN* **reactors** an apparatus for producing nuclear power in a controlled way

read *VERB* **reads, reading, read** (red) **1** look at something written or printed and understand it or say it aloud **2** (in computing) copy, search, or extract data **3** indicate or register • *The thermometer reads 20° Celsius.*
▷ **readable** *ADJECTIVE*

reader *NOUN* **readers 1** a person who reads **2** a book that helps you learn to read

Thesaurus

raw *ADJECTIVE* **1** *She ate a piece of raw onion.* ► uncooked, fresh **2** *the high cost of raw materials* ► natural, untreated, unprocessed, basic **3** *His skin had become raw.* ► sore, inflamed, red, tender **4** *You could sense the raw passion.* ► strong, intense, powerful, fervent, unrestrained **5** *They walked against the raw wind.* ► cold, bitter, biting, freezing, piercing, chilly

ray *NOUN* **1** *A ray of light shone through the branches.* ► beam, shaft, stream, streak, finger, glint, glimmer **2** *There was one ray of hope left.* ► glimmer, flicker, gleam, spark, trace, sign, hint, indication

reach *VERB* **1** *After a while the walkers reached a village.* ► arrive at, get to, come to, go as far as, (*more informal*) end up at, (*more informal*) make it to **2** *The Government has not reached any of its major targets yet.* ► achieve, attain, succeed in, (*more informal*) hit, (*more informal*) make **3** *I can't reach the switch.* ► get hold of, grasp, get your hand to, take, touch **4** *You can reach me on my mobile.* ► contact, get in touch with, communicate with
reach out *She reached out her hand.* ► stretch out, stick out, hold out, put out, extend, raise

reach *NOUN* **1** *The station is within easy reach.* ► distance, range, compass, scope **2** *The fugitives were now beyond the reach of the law.* ► jurisdiction, authority, control, sway, command **3** *Aim at achievements that are within your reach.* ► capabilities, abilities, capacity

react *VERB* *Zoe wondered how he would react if she told him everything.* ► respond, reply, answer, behave, take it, act

reaction *NOUN* *His reaction had puzzled her.* ► response, manner of response, reply, answer, rejoinder, retort, behaviour

read *VERB* **1** *He sat on the sofa, reading the papers.* ► peruse, study, scan, skim, glance at, pore over, dip into **2** *She promised to read them a story.* ► read out, tell, say aloud, recite **3** *The writing is not hard to read.* ► decipher, make out, make sense of, understand, decode

readable *ADJECTIVE* **1** *a readable book* ► enjoyable, entertaining, interesting, well written, compulsive, gripping
OPPOSITES ARE boring, unreadable **2** *readable handwriting* ► legible, clear, decipherable, understandable, neat, plain
AN OPPOSITE IS illegible

readily (red- il- ee) *ADVERB* **1** willingly **2** easily; without any difficulty

reading *NOUN* **readings 1** reading books **2** the figure shown on a meter, gauge, or other instrument **3** a gathering of people at which something is read aloud • *a poetry reading*

ready *ADJECTIVE* **readier, readiest** able or willing to do something or be used immediately; prepared
▷ **readiness** *NOUN*
at the ready ready for use or action

ready *ADVERB* beforehand • *This meat is ready cooked*
▷ **ready-made** *ADJECTIVE*

real *ADJECTIVE* **1** existing or true; not imaginary **2** genuine; not an imitation • *real pearls* **3** (said about food or drink) regarded as superior because it is produced by traditional methods • *real ale*

realism *NOUN* seeing or showing things as they really are
▷ **realist** *NOUN*

realistic *ADJECTIVE* **1** true to life; showing things as they really are **2** sensible and practical about what is possible
▷ **realistically** *ADVERB*

reality *NOUN* **realities 1** what is real • *You must face reality.* **2** something real • *Her worst fears had become a reality.*

realize *VERB* **realizes, realizing, realized 1** be fully aware of something; accept something as true **2** make a hope or plan etc. happen • *She realized her ambition to become a racing driver.* **3** obtain money in exchange for something by selling it
▷ **realization** *NOUN*

really *ADVERB* **1** truly or in fact **2** very • *She's really clever*

realm (relm) *NOUN* **realms 1** a kingdom **2** an area of knowledge, interest, etc. • *in the realms of science*

Thesaurus

readily *ADVERB* **1** *Janet readily agreed.* ► willingly, gladly, happily, unhesitatingly, promptly, eagerly, freely, voluntarily AN OPPOSITE IS reluctantly **2** *The town is readily reached from the shore.* ► easily, quickly, without difficulty

reading *NOUN* **1** *He gave the letters a hurried reading.* ► study, perusal, scrutiny, scan, browse, glance, look through **2** *This is our reading of the evidence.* ► interpretation, understanding, construal, reconstruction

ready *ADJECTIVE* **1** *We are ready to leave. He wasn't ready for the answer he got.* ► prepared, set, primed, (*more informal*) psyched up **2** *They were more than ready to take us to the station.* ► willing, prepared, happy, pleased, eager, keen, agreeable, disposed **3** *Everything was ready to start the game.* ► prepared, in place **4 ready to** *By the time she got home she was ready to collapse.* ► about to, close to, likely to, on the point of, on the verge of, on the brink of **5** *He has a ready answer to all criticisms.* ► prompt, quick, immediate, telling, perceptive, sharp, astute

real *ADJECTIVE* **1** *Is that real cream?* ► genuine, natural, authentic, bona fide, (*German*) echt OPPOSITES ARE false, artificial **2** *Some viewers treat characters in soaps as if they were real people.* ► actual, physical, existing, unimaginary OPPOSITES ARE imaginary, made-up **3** *'Carl' is not his real name.* ► true, actual, proper AN OPPOSITE IS assumed **4** *She began to feel real remorse for what had happened.* ► sincere, genuine, honest, heartfelt AN OPPOSITE IS insincere **5** (*informal*) *I felt a real idiot.* ► complete, utter, absolute, total, (*informal*) right, (*informal*) proper

realistic *ADJECTIVE* **1** *The film was meant to be a realistic portrayal of the events.* ► authentic, truthful, true to life, faithful, lifelike, natural, genuine, convincing, recognizable, representational, graphic OPPOSITES ARE fictional, imaginary **2** *To stand any chance the plan has to be realistic.* ► practical, sensible, pragmatic, reasonable, commonsensical OPPOSITES ARE impractical, idealistic **3** *Wage rises have to be realistic.* ► reasonable, moderate, acceptable, adequate, fair, justifiable OPPOSITES ARE unrealistic, excessive

reality *NOUN* *He sometimes finds it hard to distinguish reality from fantasy.* ► truth, fact, actuality, certainty, the real world AN OPPOSITE IS fantasy

realize *VERB* **1** *I realized it was going to be difficult.* ► understand, grasp, register, comprehend, appreciate, recognize, accept, (*more informal*) twig **2** *They will realize their life's ambition at last.* ► achieve, accomplish, fulfil, attain, bring about, bring off, complete **3** *The picture could realize thousands at auction.* ► fetch, sell for, be sold for, earn, bring in, produce

realm *NOUN* **1** *the defence of the realm* ► kingdom, monarchy, state, empire, principality **2** *the realm of scientific research* ► sphere, domain, field, area, activity, department

a b c d e f g h i j k l m n o p q r s t u v w x y z

reams *PLURAL NOUN* a large quantity of writing

reap *VERB* **reaps**, **reaping**, **reaped** **1** cut down and gather corn when it is ripe **2** obtain as the result of something done • *They reaped great benefit from their training* .
▷ **reaper** *NOUN*

rear[1] *NOUN* the back part

rear *ADJECTIVE* placed at the rear

rear[2] *VERB* **rears**, **rearing**, **reared** **1** bring up young children or animals **2** rise up; raise itself on hind legs • *The horse reared in fright.* **3** (said of a building) appear very large or high

rearguard *NOUN* **rearguards** troops protecting the rear of an army
fight a rearguard action go on defending or resisting something even though you are losing

rearrange *VERB* **rearranges**, **rearranging**, **rearranged** arrange in a different way or order
▷ **rearrangement** *NOUN*

reason *NOUN* **reasons** **1** a cause or explanation of something **2** reasoning; common sense • *You must listen to reason.*
USAGE Do not use the phrase *the reason is* with the word **because** (which means the same thing). Correct usage is *We cannot come. The reason is that we both have flu* (not 'The reason is because ...').

reason *VERB* **reasons**, **reasoning**, **reasoned** **1** use your ability to think and draw conclusions **2** try to persuade someone by giving reasons • *We reasoned with the rebels.*

reasonable *ADJECTIVE* **1** ready to use or listen to reason; sensible or logical **2** fair or moderate; not expensive • *reasonable prices* **3** acceptable or fairly good • *a reasonable standard of living*
▷ **reasonably** *ADVERB*

reassure *VERB* **reassures**, **reassuring**, **reassured** restore someone's confidence by removing doubts and fears
▷ **reassurance** *NOUN*

rebel (rib- el) *VERB* **rebels**, **rebelling**, **rebelled** refuse to obey someone in authority, especially the government; fight against the rulers of your own country

rebel (reb- el) *NOUN* **rebels** someone who rebels against the government, or against accepted standards of behaviour [from *re-* = again + Latin *bellum* = war (originally referring to a defeated enemy who began to fight again)]

Thesaurus

rear *NOUN* **1** *There is a door at the rear of the house.* ► back, back part, other end, other side **2** *We went to the rear of the queue.* ► end, tail, back **3** *He gave the horse a slap on the rear.* ► bottom, backside, behind, rump, buttocks, (*more informal*) bum

rear *ADJECTIVE* *The animal had hurt one of its rear legs.* ► back, hind, hindmost, rearmost
AN OPPOSITE IS front

rear *VERB* *I was born and reared in Liverpool.* ► bring up, raise, educate, care for, nurture

reason *NOUN* **1** *Money was his main reason for changing jobs.* ► cause, ground *or* grounds, justification, excuse, pretext, case, motive, explanation, apology, argument, incentive, occasion, rationale **2** *arguments based on reason rather than emotion* ► reasoning, logic, sense, rationality, intellect, judgement, common sense **3** *She was terrified of losing her reason.* ► sanity, mind, mental faculties, senses, wits, (*more informal*) marbles RELATED ADJECTIVE rational

reason *VERB* **1** *John reasoned that it was too late to reach home in time now.* ► calculate, conclude, come to the conclusion, work out, deduce, judge, consider, infer **2** *Her husband tried to reason with her.* ► persuade, talk round, bring round, prevail on, debate with, argue with, remonstrate with, discuss with

reasonable *ADJECTIVE* **1** *Any reasonable person would have to agree with you.* ► sensible, rational, logical, fair-minded
OPPOSITES ARE unreasonable, irrational **2** *It was a reasonable explanation.* ► logical, cogent, convincing, compelling, sound, credible, plausible, viable OPPOSITES ARE unreasonable, illogical **3** *They charge a reasonable fee for this service.* ► modest, moderate, acceptable, tolerable OPPOSITES ARE unreasonable, excessive

reasoning *NOUN* *I couldn't follow his reasoning.* ► thinking, logic, train of thought, rationality, rationale, argumentation, arguments, hypothesis, interpretation

reassure *VERB* *Danny tried hard to reassure us.* ► comfort, calm, hearten, support, encourage, assure, bolster up, inspirit, give confidence to OPPOSITES ARE unnerve, disconcert

rebel *NOUN* (with the stress on *reb-*) *The rebels took control of the region.* ► revolutionary, insurgent, revolutionist, guerrilla, dissenter, malcontent, mutineer, renegade

rebel *ADJECTIVE* (with the stress on *reb-*) *Rebel forces captured the town.* ► insurgent, revolutionary, rebellious, mutinous

rebel *VERB* (with the stress on *-bel*) *The people of the south rebelled.* ► revolt, mutiny, riot, rise up, mount a rebellion

rebellion *NOUN* **rebellions** organized armed resistance to the government; a revolt
▷ **rebellious** *ADJECTIVE*

reboot *VERB* **reboots, rebooting, rebooted** switch a computer off and then on again

rebound *VERB* **rebounds, rebounding, rebounded** bounce back after hitting something
▷ **rebound** *NOUN*

rebuff *NOUN* **rebuffs** an unkind refusal; a snub
▷ **rebuff** *VERB*
[from *re-* = again + Italian *buffo* = a gust]

rebuke *VERB* **rebukes, rebuking, rebuked** speak severely to a person who has done wrong
▷ **rebuke** *NOUN*

recalcitrant *ADJECTIVE* disobedient or uncooperative
▷ **recalcitrance** *NOUN*
[from Latin *recalcitrare* = to kick back]

recall *VERB* **recalls, recalling, recalled 1** bring back into the mind; remember **2** ask a person to come back **3** ask for something to be returned
▷ **recall** *NOUN*

recapitulate *VERB* **recapitulates, recapitulating, recapitulated** state again the main points of what has been said
▷ **recapitulation** *NOUN*

recapture *VERB* **recaptures, recapturing, recaptured 1** capture again **2** bring or get back a mood or feeling
▷ **recapture** *NOUN*

recede *VERB* **recedes, receding, receded** go back from a certain point • *The floods have receded.*

receipt (ris- eet) *NOUN* **receipts 1** a written statement that money has been paid or something has been received **2** receiving something [via early French from Latin *recipire* = to receive]

receive *VERB* **receives, receiving, received 1** take or get something that is given or sent to you **2** experience something • *He received injuries to his face and hands.* **3** greet someone who comes

receiver *NOUN* **receivers 1** a person or thing that receives something **2** a person who buys and sells stolen goods **3** an official who takes charge of a bankrupt person's property **4** a radio or television set that receives broadcasts **5** the part of a telephone that receives the sound and is held to a person's ear

recent *ADJECTIVE* happening or made or done a short time ago
▷ **recently** *ADVERB*

reception *NOUN* **receptions 1** the way a person or thing is received **2** a formal party to receive guests • *a wedding reception* **3** a place in a hotel or office etc. where visitors are received and registered **4** the first class in an infant school **5** the quality of television or radio signals

receptionist *NOUN* **receptionists** a person whose job is to greet and deal with visitors, clients, patients, etc.

receptive *ADJECTIVE* quick or willing to receive ideas etc.

recess *NOUN* **recesses 1** a small space set back in a wall **2** a time when work or business is stopped for a while

Thesaurus

rebellion *NOUN* *Troops were sent in to crush the rebellion.* ► uprising, revolt, rising, insurrection, insurgency, sedition, mutiny, insubordination, resistance, revolution

rebellious *ADJECTIVE* **1** *rebellious troops* ► mutinous, insurgent, rebel, rebelling, mutinying, subversive **2** *rebellious staff* ► defiant, insubordinate, unruly, ungovernable, unmanageable, uncontrollable, recalcitrant, obstreperous

rebound *VERB* **1** *The ball rebounded off the wall.* ► bounce, bounce back, ricochet, recoil, boomerang **2** *His devious tactics rebounded on him.* ► backfire, misfire, recoil, boomerang, come back

recall *VERB* *She could not recall what he had said.* ► remember, recollect, call to mind, think, cast your mind back to AN OPPOSITE IS forget

receipt *NOUN* **1** *Make sure you keep the receipt.* ► sales slip, proof of purchase, bill, ticket, counterfoil, stub **2** *Receipt of your tickets is guaranteed within three working days.* ► delivery, arrival, receiving

receipts *receipts from the sale of council houses* ► income, proceeds, revenue, earnings, profits, takings, gains

receive *VERB* **1** *He received an award for gallantry.* ► be given, earn, get, accept, collect, obtain, gain, take, acquire, be sent OPPOSITES ARE give, present **2** *He received some minor injuries in the accident.* ► sustain, suffer, experience, undergo, bear AN OPPOSITE IS inflict **3** *She received the news in complete silence.* ► hear, listen to, respond to, react to, take, greet

recent *ADJECTIVE* *Recent events have caused them to change their minds.* ► new, current, fresh, latest, present-day, up-to-date, contemporary, modern, novel OPPOSITES ARE old, earlier

reception *NOUN* **1** *We got a friendly reception.* ► greeting, welcome **2** *A reception will be held at the local hotel.* ► party, function, gathering, celebration, get-together, social event, (*more informal*) do

recession *NOUN* **recessions** **1** a reduction in a country's trade or prosperity **2** receding from a point

recharge *VERB* **recharges, recharging, recharged** refill or reload something, especially put an electric charge into a used battery

recipe (ress- ip- ee) *NOUN* **recipes** instructions for preparing or cooking food

reciprocal (ris- ip- rok- al) *ADJECTIVE* given and received; mutual • *reciprocal help*
▷ **reciprocally** *ADVERB* **reciprocity** *NOUN*

reciprocal *NOUN* **reciprocals** a reversed fraction, $\frac{3}{2}$ *is the reciprocal of* $\frac{2}{3}$

recital *NOUN* **recitals** **1** reciting something **2** a musical entertainment given by one performer or group

recite *VERB* **recites, reciting, recited** say a poem etc. aloud from memory
▷ **recitation** *NOUN*

reckless *ADJECTIVE* rash; ignoring risk or danger
▷ **recklessly** *ADVERB* **recklessness** *NOUN*

reckon *VERB* **reckons, reckoning, reckoned** **1** calculate or count up **2** have as an opinion; feel confident • *I reckon we shall win.*
reckon with think about or deal with • *We didn't reckon with the train strike when we planned our journey.*

reclaim *VERB* **reclaims, reclaiming, reclaimed** **1** claim or get something back **2** make a thing usable again • *reclaimed land*
▷ **reclamation** *NOUN*

recognize *VERB* **recognizes, recognizing, recognized** **1** know who someone is or what something is because you have seen that person or thing before **2** realize • *She recognized the truth of what he was saying.* **3** accept something as genuine, welcome, or lawful etc. • *Nine countries recognized the island's new government.*
▷ **recognition** *NOUN* **recognizable** *ADJECTIVE*

recoil *VERB* **recoils, recoiling, recoiled** **1** move back suddenly in shock or disgust **2** (said about a gun) jerk backwards when it is fired

recollect *VERB* **recollects, recollecting, recollected** remember
▷ **recollection** *NOUN*

recommend *VERB* **recommends, recommending, recommended** say that a person or thing would be good or suitable for a particular job or purpose
▷ **recommendation** *NOUN*

Thesaurus

recipe *NOUN* **1** *She would try out her new soufflé recipe.* ► method, procedure, directions, instructions **2** *The measures might prove to be a recipe for disaster.* ► prescription, formula, procedure, likely cause (of)

recital *NOUN* **1** *She gave her first piano recital at the age of eight.* ► concert, public performance, programme **2** *a recital of poems* ► recitation, rendering, saying aloud, delivery, narration

recite *VERB* **1** *She announced that she would recite a poem.* ► say aloud, read out, deliver, perform, declaim **2** *It would take too long to recite all the events of the week.* ► list, enumerate, detail, recount, relate, repeat, run through, reel off, specify

reckless *ADJECTIVE* *For such a mild man he could be amazingly reckless behind the wheel of a car.* ► rash, careless, heedless, mindless, thoughtless, negligent, foolhardy, daredevil

reckon *VERB* **1** *They reckoned the cost at about three thousand pounds.* ► assess, estimate, calculate, work out, figure out, gauge, evaluate, count, add up, compute, total **2** (*informal*) *I reckon she's keen on him.* ► think, believe, suspect, consider, dare say, have an idea, fancy, guess **3** *These animals are reckoned the most dangerous.* ► consider, regard as, deem, judge, count
reckon on *We didn't reckon on such stiff opposition.* ► expect, foresee, plan for, bargain for, figure on

reckoning *NOUN* *By my reckoning we should make a small profit.* ► calculation, estimation, estimate, judgement, evaluation

reclaim *VERB* **1** *You can reclaim your travelling expenses.* ► get back, claim back, recover, (*more informal*) put in for **2** *an area of land reclaimed from the sea* ► recover, restore, save, make usable, regenerate

recognize *VERB* **1** *I didn't recognize him in his smart suit.* ► identify, place, know, remember, recall, call to mind, put a name to **2** *They recognize his abilities without liking his work very much.* ► acknowledge, admit, accept, concede, grant, allow, appreciate, confess, realize **3** *The qualification is not recognized in Britain.* ► approve, acknowledge, accept, accredit, admit, endorse, support

recoil *VERB* **1** *She recoiled instinctively as he put his hand out.* ► flinch, draw back, shy away, jerk back, start, wince, shrink back **2** *Their deception will recoil on them.* ► rebound, backfire, misfire, boomerang, come back

recollect *VERB* *I don't recollect any such promise.* ► remember, recall, call to mind, think, cast your mind back to AN OPPOSITE IS forget

recollection *NOUN* *She had no recollection of what happened.* ► memory, remembrance, recall, impression

recommend *VERB* **1** *His doctor recommended surgery.* ► advise, counsel, propose, advocate, suggest, urge, prescribe **2** *This book is*

reconcile *VERB* **reconciles, reconciling, reconciled 1** make people who have quarrelled become friendly again **2** persuade a person to put up with something • *New frames reconciled him to wearing glasses.* **3** make things agree • *I cannot reconcile what you say with what you do.*
▷ **reconciliation** *NOUN*

recondition *VERB* **reconditions, reconditioning, reconditioned** overhaul and repair

reconnaissance (rik- on- i- suns) *NOUN* an exploration of an area, especially in order to gather information about it for military purposes

reconstruct *VERB* **reconstructs, reconstructing, reconstructed 1** construct or build something again **2** create or act past events again • *Police reconstructed the robbery.*
▷ **reconstruction** *NOUN*

record (rek- ord) *NOUN* **records 1** information kept in a permanent form, e.g. written or printed **2** a disc on which sound has been recorded **3** the best performance in a sport etc., or the most remarkable event of its kind • *He holds the record for the high jump.* **4** facts known about a person's past life or career etc. • *She has a good school record.*

record (rik- ord) *VERB* **records, recording, recorded 1** put something down in writing or other permanent form **2** store sounds or scenes (e.g. television pictures) on a disc or magnetic tape etc. so that you can play or show them later

recorder *NOUN* **recorders 1** a kind of flute held downwards from the player's mouth **2** a person or thing that records something

recover *VERB* **recovers, recovering, recovered 1** get something back again after losing it; regain **2** get well again after being ill or weak
▷ **recovery** *NOUN*

recreation *NOUN* **recreations 1** refreshing or entertaining yourself with an enjoyable activity **2** a game or hobby etc. that is an enjoyable pastime
▷ **recreational** *ADJECTIVE*

recruit *NOUN* **recruits 1** a person who has just joined the armed forces **2** a new member of a society, company, or other group

Thesaurus

recommended by teachers. ► approve of, advocate, endorse, commend, suggest, praise, speak well of, vouch for, (*more informal*) plug

recommendation *NOUN* **1** *The governors accepted the main recommendation of the committee.* ► advice, counsel, guidance, proposal, suggestion **2** *She supported him with her personal recommendation.*
► commendation, endorsement, advocacy, testimonial, reference, blessing

reconnoitre *VERB* *Helicopters reconnoitred the area ahead of ground troops.* ► survey, patrol, scout, spy out, explore, investigate, scan, examine, gather intelligence about, inspect

reconstruct *VERB* **1** *They will have to reconstruct a large part of the building.* ► rebuild, renovate, restore, reassemble AN OPPOSITE IS demolish
2 *Police will reconstruct the incident using actors.*
► recreate, re-enact

record *NOUN* (with the stress on *rec-*) **1** *You should keep a record of everything they say.*
► account, report, note, log **2 records** *There are more historical records for these years.*
► documents, archives, evidence, accounts, documentation, annals **3** *She stayed in listening to records.* ► CD, disc, compact disc, album, recording, LP **4** *There is not a single mistake to tarnish his record.* ► background, career, CV
5 *The new time was a world record.* ► best performance, fastest time

record *VERB* (with the stress on *-cord*) **1** *He recorded everything he heard in a notebook.*
► note, register, enter, put down, set down, write down, transcribe, log, minute **2** *They wanted to record the song and send it in.* ► tape, tape-record, make a recording of, video, preserve, keep

recover *VERB* **1** *She was recovering from a mild stroke.* ► recuperate, convalesce, get better, improve, heal, mend, rally, revive, pull round *or* through, (*more informal*) be on the mend
2 *Police say they have recovered some of the stolen property.* ► trace, find, get back, track down, retrieve, reclaim, recoup, repossess, salvage

recovery *NOUN* **1** *Her recovery is proving slow.*
► recuperation, convalescence, return to health, improvement, healing, cure **2** *The economy is showing signs of recovery.*
► improvement, revival, upturn, picking up
3 *A reward will be paid on recovery of the stolen paintings.* ► retrieval, repossession, restoration, recapture, reclamation, salvaging

recreation *NOUN* *a study of the use of the countryside for recreation* ► relaxation, amusement, diversion, enjoyment, pleasure, leisure, entertainment, fun, play, games, pastime

recruit *NOUN* **1** *The Army is trying to attract more recruits.* ► initiate, new member, conscript
2 *Many recruits to the industry turn out to be unsuitable.* ► new entrant, trainee, apprentice, novice, new member, newcomer

A B C D E F G H I J K L M N O P Q R S T U V W X Y Z

recruit *VERB* **recruits, recruiting, recruited** enlist recruits
▷ **recruitment** *NOUN*

rectangle *NOUN* **rectangles** a shape with four sides and four right angles
▷ **rectangular** *ADJECTIVE*

rector *NOUN* **rectors** a member of the Church of England clergy in charge of a parish

rectum *NOUN* **rectums** the last part of the large intestine, ending at the anus

recuperate *VERB* **recuperates, recuperating, recuperated** get better after an illness
▷ **recuperation** *NOUN*

recur *VERB* **recurs, recurring, recurred** happen again; keep on happening
▷ **recurrent** *ADJECTIVE* **recurrence** *NOUN*

recurring decimal *NOUN* **recurring decimals** (in mathematics) a decimal fraction in which a digit or group of digits is repeated indefinitely, e.g. 0.666 ...

recycle *VERB* **recycles, recycling, recycled** convert waste material into a form in which it can be reused

red *ADJECTIVE* **redder, reddest 1** of the colour of blood or a colour rather like this **2** to do with communists; favouring communism
▷ **redness** *NOUN*

red *NOUN* **1** red colour **2** a communist
in the red in debt (because debts were entered in red in account books)
see red become suddenly angry

redden *VERB* **reddens, reddening, reddened** make or become red

redeem *VERB* **redeems, redeeming, redeemed 1** buy something back or pay off a debt **2** save a person from damnation
• *Christians believe that Christ redeemed us all.*
3 make up for faults • *His one redeeming feature is his kindness.*
▷ **redeemer** *NOUN* **redemption** *NOUN*

red-handed *ADJECTIVE*
catch red-handed catch while actually committing a crime

red herring *NOUN* **red herrings** something that draws attention away from the main subject; a misleading clue

red-hot *ADJECTIVE* very hot; so hot that it has turned red

Red Indian *NOUN* **Red Indians** (*old use*) a Native American from North America
USAGE See note at **Indian**.

red tape *NOUN* use of too many rules and forms in official business

reduce *VERB* **reduces, reducing, reduced 1** make or become smaller or less **2** force someone into a condition or situation • *She was reduced to tears.*
▷ **reduction** *NOUN*

redundant *ADJECTIVE* no longer needed, especially for a particular job
▷ **redundancy** *NOUN*

Thesaurus

recruit *VERB* **1** *The services recruit a high proportion of graduates.* ► enlist, enrol, draft, conscript **2** *The Company provides training for the staff it has recruited.* ► hire, employ, enrol, engage, take on, advertise for
OPPOSITES ARE dismiss, lay off, make redundant

recur *VERB* *The problem is certain to recur if we don't do something about it.* ► return, happen again, reappear, come again, be repeated, persist

recycle *VERB* *The department is advising customers on how to recycle their waste.* ► reuse, reprocess, reclaim, recover, salvage, use again

red *ADJECTIVE* **1** *She wore a red dress.* ► scarlet, vermilion, ruby, crimson, cherry, claret, maroon, flame-coloured **2** *He was red in the face with embarrassment.* ► flushed, blushing, flaming, ruddy, florid, glowing, inflamed, rosy, rubicund **3** *The chemicals in the water made his eyes red.* ► bloodshot, inflamed, swollen, sore

redeem *VERB* **1** *Freddie had to redeem his oboe from the pawnbroker's.* ► reclaim, retrieve, recover, repossess, buy back **2** *You can redeem your voucher at any branch of the store.*
► exchange, cash in, exchange for cash, return, trade in
redeem yourself *He failed the first test but redeemed himself in the second.* ► vindicate, absolve

reduce *VERB* **1** *The goal is to reduce carbon emissions by 20 percent.* ► lessen, lower, decrease, bring down, curtail, moderate
OPPOSITES ARE increase, enlarge **2** *The novel has been greatly reduced in the television adaptation.*
► shorten, abridge, condense
AN OPPOSITE IS expand **3** *The father's gambling debts reduced the family to poverty.* ► drive, force, bring to the point of

reduction *NOUN* **1** *a reduction in pollution*
► decrease, drop, fall, lessening, lowering, diminution AN OPPOSITE IS increase **2** *a series of price reductions* ► cut, discount, (*more informal*) slash AN OPPOSITE IS increase

redundant *ADJECTIVE* *There are three redundant churches in the area.* ► unnecessary, unwanted, superfluous, surplus, excessive, too many
an opposite is necessary
make someone redundant *They plan to make twenty members of the workforce redundant just before Christmas.* ► lay off, dismiss, sack, discharge

re-echo *VERB* **re-echoes, re-echoing, re-echoed** echo; go on echoing

reed *NOUN* **reeds** **1** a tall plant that grows in water or marshy ground **2** a thin strip that vibrates to make the sound in a clarinet, saxophone, oboe, etc.

reef *NOUN* **reefs** a ridge of rock, coral, or sand, especially one near the surface of the sea

reek *VERB* **reeks, reeking, reeked** smell strongly or unpleasantly
▷ **reek** *NOUN*

reel *NOUN* **reels** **1** a round device on which cotton, thread, film, etc. is wound **2** a lively Scottish dance

reel *VERB* **reels, reeling, reeled** **1** wind something on to or off a reel **2** stagger **3** feel giddy or confused • *I am still reeling from the shock.*
reel off say something quickly

refer *VERB* **refers, referring, referred** pass a problem etc. to someone else • *My doctor referred me to a specialist.*
▷ **referral** *NOUN*
refer to **1** mention or speak about • *I wasn't referring to you.* **2** look in a book etc. for information • *We referred to our dictionary.*

referee *NOUN* **referees** someone appointed to see that people keep to the rules of a game

reference *NOUN* **references** **1** referring to something • *There was no reference to recent events.* **2** a direction to a book or page or file etc. where information can be found **3** a letter from a previous employer describing someone's abilities and qualities
in or **with reference to** concerning or about

reference book *NOUN* **reference books** a book (such as a dictionary or encyclopedia) that gives information systematically

referendum *NOUN* **referendums** or **referenda** a vote on a particular question by all the people of a country [from Latin, = something to be referred]

refill *VERB* **refills, refilling, refilled** fill again

refill *NOUN* **refills** a container holding a substance which is used to refill something • *This pen needs a refill.*

refine *VERB* **refines, refining, refined** **1** purify **2** improve something, especially by making small changes [from *re-* = again + Middle English *fine* = make pure]

refined *ADJECTIVE* **1** purified **2** having good taste or good manners

refinement *NOUN* **refinements** **1** the action of refining **2** being refined **3** something added to improve a thing

refinery *NOUN* **refineries** a factory for refining something • *an oil refinery*

reflect *VERB* **reflects, reflecting, reflected** **1** send back light, heat, or sound etc. from a surface **2** form an image of something as a mirror does **3** think something over; consider **4** be a sign of something; be influenced by something • *Prices reflect the cost of producing things.*
▷ **reflection** *NOUN* **reflective** *ADJECTIVE* **reflector** *NOUN*

Thesaurus

reel *VERB* *A woman reeled towards him clutching a half-eaten burger.* ▶ stagger, stumble, sway, totter, lurch, swerve
reel from *When the worst happens you reel from it and the shock is enormous.* ▶ be shaken by, be shocked by, be stunned by, be staggered by, be aghast at
reel off *He reeled off one joke after another.* ▶ recite, rattle off, fire off, run off

refer *VERB* **1** *His GP referred him to a specialist. The manager referred the matter to head office.* ▶ pass, send, transfer, direct, entrust, hand on, send on **2** **refer to** *The police officer referred to her notes.* ▶ consult, look up, turn to, look in, search in **3** **refer to** *The third paragraph of the article refers to new publications.* ▶ mention, detail, list, touch on, describe, allude to, cite

referee *NOUN* **1** *The referee blew his whistle.* ▶ umpire, judge, adjudicator, arbitrator, (*more informal*) ref **2** *Your CV must include the names of two referees.* ▶ supporter, character witness, backer, advocate

reference *NOUN* **1** *The title 'Brave New World' is a reference to Shakespeare.* ▶ allusion, quotation (from), citation (from), example (of), illustration (from), instance (of), mention (of) **2** *His teacher had given him a glowing reference.* ▶ testimonial, recommendation, endorsement, backing
with reference to *She spoke to him with reference to his recent conduct.* ▶ about, with regard to, in relation to, a propos of, on the subject of

refined *ADJECTIVE* **1** *refined sugar* ▶ purified, pure, processed, clarified, distilled, concentrated **2** *a refined man* ▶ cultivated

reflect *VERB* **1** *The window reflected their faces staring in.* ▶ mirror, send back, shine back, throw back **2** *The looks on their faces reflected their feelings.* ▶ indicate, show, reproduce, demonstrate, correspond to, echo, exhibit, match, reveal, bear witness to
reflect on *She reflected on the promises she had made to her friends.* ▶ think about, consider, contemplate, meditate on, ponder, brood on, ruminate on, mull over, muse on, reminisce about, (*more informal*) chew over

reflection *NOUN* **1** *We could see our reflections in the water.* ▶ image, likeness **2** *The test will provide an accurate reflection of a child's ability.*

a b c d e f g h i j k l m n o p q **r** s t u v w x y z

A B C D E F G H I J K L M N O P Q R S T U V W X Y Z

reflex NOUN **reflexes** a movement or action done without any conscious thought

reflexive pronoun NOUN **reflexive pronouns** any of the pronouns **myself**, **herself**, **himself**, etc. (as in 'She cut *herself*'), which refer back to the subject of the verb

reflexive verb NOUN **reflexive verbs** a verb in which the subject and the object are the same person or thing, as in 'They *hurt themselves*', 'The cat *washed itself*'

reform VERB **reforms, reforming, reformed** **1** make changes in something in order to improve it **2** give up a criminal or immoral lifestyle, or make someone do this
▷ **reformer** NOUN **reformative** ADJECTIVE **reformatory** ADJECTIVE

reform NOUN **reforms** **1** reforming **2** a change made in order to improve something

reformation NOUN reforming
the Reformation a religious movement in Europe in the 16th century intended to reform certain teachings and practices of the Roman Catholic Church, which resulted in the establishment of the Reformed or Protestant Churches

refract VERB **refracts, refracting, refracted** bend a ray of light at the point where it enters water or glass etc. at an angle
▷ **refraction** NOUN **refractor** NOUN **refractive** ADJECTIVE

refrain[1] VERB **refrains, refraining, refrained** stop yourself from doing something • *Please refrain from talking.*

refrain[2] NOUN **refrains** the chorus of a song

refresh VERB **refreshes, refreshing, refreshed** make a tired person etc. feel fresh and strong again
refresh someone's memory remind someone of something by going over previous information

refreshing ADJECTIVE **1** producing new strength • *a refreshing sleep* **2** pleasantly different or unusual • *refreshing honesty*

refreshments PLURAL NOUN drinks and snacks provided at an event

refrigerator NOUN **refrigerators** a cabinet or room in which food is stored at a very low temperature

refuge NOUN **refuges** a place where a person is safe from pursuit or danger
take refuge go somewhere or do something so that you are protected

refugee NOUN **refugees** someone who has had to leave their home or country and seek refuge elsewhere, e.g. because of war or persecution or famine

refund VERB **refunds, refunding, refunded** pay money back

refund NOUN **refunds** money paid back

Thesaurus

► indication, demonstration, manifestation, expression, evidence, echo, result **3** *After some reflection, he decided to accept the offer.*
► deliberation, consideration, contemplation, thought, thinking, meditation, rumination, pondering, musing

reform VERB **1** *He realized he would have to reform.* ► mend your ways, turn over a new leaf, improve, do better **2** *Everyone agrees on the need to reform the prison system.*
► reconstitute, regenerate, remodel, reorganize, revolutionize, purge

reform NOUN *the need for reform*
► improvement, betterment, change, adjustment, reorganization, (*more informal*) shake-up

refrain VERB **refrain from** *Please refrain from shouting comments during the speeches.* ► desist from, avoid, do without, forgo, abstain from, eschew, forbear, (*more informal*) quit, (*more informal*) leave off, stop

refresh VERB **1** *A bit of air will refresh us.*
► invigorate, cool, freshen, revive, revitalize, restore, enliven, renew **2** *Revisiting the scene might refresh my memory.* ► prompt, jog, stimulate, remind, prod

refreshing ADJECTIVE **1** *a refreshing drink: a refreshing breeze* ► invigorating, revitalizing, reviving, enlivening, stimulating, bracing, exhilarating, cool, restorative, thirst-quenching, tingling **2** *a refreshing change*
► welcome, stimulating, different, interesting, fresh, new, original

refreshments PLURAL NOUN *You can get some refreshments in the interval.* ► food and drink, sustenance, snacks, (*more informal*) eats, (*more informal*) nibbles

refuge NOUN **1** *The homeless seek refuge in doorways and under bridges.* ► shelter, protection, safety, sanctuary, security, cover, hideout, hiding place, retreat **2** *The mountains provide a refuge for the freedom fighters.*
► sanctuary, shelter, haven, retreat, hideaway, hideout, hiding place, (*more informal*) bolt-hole

refusal NOUN **1** *There have been two refusals to the invitation so far.* ► rejection, negative reply, non-acceptance, regrets, no
AN OPPOSITE IS acceptance **2** *Her refusal to see him again caused great distress.*
► unwillingness, disinclination, reluctance, aversion

refuse (ri- fewz) *VERB* **refuses, refusing, refused** say that you are unwilling to do or give or accept something
▷ **refusal** *NOUN*

refuse (ref- yooss) *NOUN* waste material • *Lorries collected the refuse.*

regain *VERB* **regains, regaining, regained** **1** get something back after losing it **2** reach a place again

regalia (rig- ayl- i- a) *PLURAL NOUN* the emblems of royalty or rank • *The royal regalia include the crown, sceptre, and orb.*

regard *VERB* **regards, regarding, regarded** **1** think of in a certain way; consider to be • *We regard the matter as serious.* **2** look or gaze at

regard *NOUN* **1** a gaze **2** consideration or heed • *You acted without regard to people's safety.* **3** respect • *We have a great regard for her.* **4** a gaze
with regard to concerning

regarding *PREPOSITION* concerning • *There are laws regarding drugs.*

regardless *ADVERB* without considering something • *Do it, regardless of the cost.*

regards *PLURAL NOUN* kind wishes sent in a message • *Give him my regards.*

regatta *NOUN* **regattas** a meeting for boat or yacht races

regenerate *VERB* **regenerates, regenerating, regenerated** give new life or strength to something
▷ **regeneration** *NOUN*

regent *NOUN* **regents** a person appointed to rule a country while the monarch is too young or unable to rule

reggae (reg- ay) *NOUN* a West Indian style of music with a strong beat

regime (ray- *zheem*) *NOUN* **regimes** a system of government or organization • *a Fascist regime*

regiment *NOUN* **regiments** an army unit, usually divided into battalions or companies
▷ **regimental** *ADJECTIVE*

region *NOUN* **regions** an area; a part of a country or of the world • *in tropical regions*
▷ **regional** *ADJECTIVE* **regionally** *ADVERB*
in the region of near • *The cost will be in the region of £100.*

register *NOUN* **registers** **1** an official list of things or names etc. **2** a book in which information about school attendances is recorded **3** the range of a voice or musical instrument

register *VERB* **registers, registering, registered** **1** list something in a register **2** indicate; show • *The thermometer registered 100°.* **3** make an impression on someone's mind **4** pay extra for a letter or parcel to be sent with special care
▷ **registration** *NOUN*

Thesaurus

refuse *VERB* (with the stress on *-fuse*) **1** *He refused several invitations that week.* ► decline, turn down, reject, say no to, rebuff, spurn, baulk at, give a negative reply to
AN OPPOSITE IS accept **2** *The local council refused permission for the building to go ahead.* ► withhold, deny, not grant, deprive of
AN OPPOSITE IS grant

regard *VERB* **1** *She regarded them closely for a while.* ► look at, observe, eye, gaze at, stare at, watch, contemplate, scrutinize, view
AN OPPOSITE IS disregard **2** *We regard these paintings as the best from the 11–14 age group.* ► consider, look on, view, judge, rate, deem, reckon, account, esteem, value

regard *NOUN* **1** *Good planning must have due regard for the costs involved.* ► attention, care, concern, consideration, deference, heed, notice, respect, thought **2** *They have a high regard for your opinions.* ► respect, esteem, appreciation (of), approval (of), estimation (of), admiration, affection

regardless *ADVERB* **1** *The cliff walk was dangerous, but we carried on regardless.* ► anyway, anyhow, nonetheless, nevertheless, even so, just the same **2** **regardless of** *Dinghy sailing has something to offer everyone, regardless of age or fitness.* ► irrespective of, without regard to, disregarding, no matter OPPOSITES ARE mindful of, taking account of

regime *NOUN* **1** *members of the former military regime* ► government, administration, rule, reign, jurisdiction, command **2** *Slimmers usually start a new health regime on a Monday.* ► programme, plan, system, arrangement, scheme, diet

region *NOUN* *The family came from the coastal region.* ► district, area, territory, neighbourhood, locality, sector, quarter, zone, terrain, land
in the region of *It will cost in the region of five million dollars.* ► about, approximately, roughly, in the neighbourhood of

register *NOUN* *The local authority keeps a register of disabled people.* ► list, official list, directory, record, index, file

register *VERB* **1** *We wish to register a protest. The car is registered in his wife's name.* ► record, put on record, file, log, list, enter, submit, report **2** *You can still register for a place on the course.* ► enrol, enlist, put your name down, check in, apply, enter **3** *Their faces registered relief.*

a b c d e f g h i j k l m n o p q r s t u v w x y z

A B C D E F G H I J K L M N O P Q R S T U V W X Y Z

register office *NOUN* **register offices** an office where marriages are performed and records of births, marriages, and deaths are kept
USAGE The name *registry office* is also used, and is the official name in Scotland.

regret *NOUN* **regrets** a feeling of sorrow or disappointment about something that has happened or been done
▷ **regretful** *ADJECTIVE* **regretfully** *ADVERB*

regret *VERB* **regrets**, **regretting**, **regretted** feel regret about something
▷ **regrettable** *ADJECTIVE* **regrettably** *ADVERB*

regular *ADJECTIVE* **1** always happening or doing something at certain times • *Try to eat regular meals.* **2** even or symmetrical • *regular teeth* **3** normal, standard, or correct • *the regular procedure* **4** belonging to a country's permanent armed forces • *a regular soldier*
▷ **regularly** *ADVERB* **regularity** *NOUN*

regulate *VERB* **regulates**, **regulating**, **regulated** **1** control, especially by rules **2** make a machine work at a certain speed
▷ **regulator** *NOUN*

regulation *NOUN* **1** regulating **2** a rule or law

rehabilitation *NOUN* restoring a person to a normal life or a building etc. to a good condition
▷ **rehabilitate** *VERB*

rehearse *VERB* **rehearses**, **rehearsing**, **rehearsed** practise something before performing to an audience
▷ **rehearsal** *NOUN*

reign *VERB* **reigns**, **reigning**, **reigned** **1** rule a country as king or queen **2** be supreme; be the strongest influence • *Silence reigned*

reign *NOUN* the time when someone reigns

reimburse *VERB* **reimburses**, **reimbursing**, **reimbursed** repay money that has been spent • *Your travelling expenses will be reimbursed.*
▷ **reimbursement** *NOUN*

rein *NOUN* **reins** a strap used to guide a horse

reincarnation *NOUN* being born again into a new body

reindeer *NOUN* **reindeer** a kind of deer that lives in Arctic regions

reinforce *VERB* **reinforces**, **reinforcing**, **reinforced** strengthen by adding extra people or supports etc.

Thesaurus

► show, display, express, indicate, exhibit, betray, manifest

regret *VERB* **1** *You may come to regret your decision.* ► be sorry about, repent, rue, deplore **2** *She said how much she regretted her uncle's death.* ► lament, mourn, grieve over, feel sorrow for, be upset about

regret *NOUN* **1** *Both men expressed regret for their actions.* ► remorse, sorrow, shame, contrition, repentance, guilt **2** *We left our old home with a feeling of regret.* ► sadness, sorrow, unhappiness, disappointment

regretful *ADJECTIVE* *She was regretful about what had happened.* ► sorry, remorseful, apologetic, repentant, contrite, penitent, ashamed, sorrowful, disappointed, sad
OPPOSITES ARE unrepentant, happy

regrettable *ADJECTIVE* *It was a regrettable thing to say but it was too late to change it.*
► undesirable, unfortunate, unwelcome, ill-advised, inappropriate, unsuitable, distressing, upsetting, lamentable, shameful
OPPOSITES ARE fortunate, suitable

regular *ADJECTIVE* **1** *She had a regular route to work each morning.* ► routine, habitual, customary, typical, usual, normal, established **2** *There were regular complaints about the noise.* ► frequent, periodic, constant, continual, persistent OPPOSITES ARE rare, occasional **3** *a regular procedure for dealing with enquiries* ► systematic, methodical, efficient, well organized, established, approved, conventional AN OPPOSITE IS haphazard

regulate *VERB* **1** *a body that regulates the railways* ► supervise, oversee, monitor, administer, manage, control, (*more informal*) keep an eye on **2** *The clocks need to be regulated every so often.* ► control, manage, adjust, alter, change, moderate

regulation *NOUN* **1** *A copy of the regulations about working hours is pinned on the notice board.* ► rule, ruling, law, order, requirement, procedure, ordnance, statute, decree, edict **2** *the regulation of traffic in the city centre* ► control, management, supervision, direction, monitoring, overseeing, administration

rehearse *VERB* *We need to rehearse the last scene a bit more.* ► practise, go over *or* through, run through, try out, prepare, (*informal*) run over

reign *VERB* *Victoria reigned for sixty-four years.* ► rule, be queen *or* king, be on the throne, wear the crown, govern, be in power RELATED ADJECTIVE regnal

reign *NOUN* *She had a long and successful reign.* ► rule, monarchy, sovereignty

reinforce *VERB* **1** *Two stone supports reinforce the old wall. These events reinforced all our suspicions.* ► strengthen, fortify, support, bolster, buttress, underpin, prop up, hold up, stiffen, toughen, back up, give strength to **2** *Two more legions were sent to reinforce the army on the Rhine.* ► strengthen, supplement, increase, augment

reinforcements *PLURAL NOUN* extra troops or ships etc. sent to strengthen a force

reiterate *VERB* **reiterates, reiterating, reiterated** say something again or repeatedly
▷ **reiteration** *NOUN*

reject (ri-jekt) *VERB* **rejects, rejecting, rejected** **1** refuse to accept a person or thing **2** throw away or discard
▷ **rejection** *NOUN*

reject (ree-jekt) *NOUN* **rejects** a person or thing that is rejected, especially because of being faulty or poorly made

rejoice *VERB* **rejoices, rejoicing, rejoiced** feel or show great joy

rejuvenate *VERB* **rejuvenates, rejuvenating, rejuvenated** make a person seem young again
▷ **rejuvenation** *NOUN*

relapse *VERB* **relapses, relapsing, relapsed** return to a previous condition; become worse after improving
▷ **relapse** *NOUN*

relate *VERB* **relates, relating, related** **1** narrate **2** connect or compare one thing with another **3** understand and get on well with • *Some people cannot relate to animals.*

related *ADJECTIVE* belonging to the same family

relation *NOUN* **relations** **1** a relative **2** the way one thing is related to another

relationship *NOUN* **relationships** **1** how people or things are related **2** how people get on with each other **3** an emotional or sexual association between two people

relative *NOUN* **relatives** a person who is related to another

relative *ADJECTIVE* connected or compared with something; compared with the average • *They live in relative comfort.*
▷ **relatively** *ADVERB*

relative pronoun see **pronoun**

relax *VERB* **relaxes, relaxing, relaxed** **1** stop working; rest **2** become less anxious or worried **3** make a rule etc. less strict or severe **4** make a limb or muscle less stiff or tense
▷ **relaxation** *NOUN*

relay (ri-lay) *VERB* **relays, relaying, relayed** pass on a message or broadcast

relay (re-lay) *NOUN* **relays** **1** a fresh group taking the place of another • *The firemen worked in relays.* **2** a relay race **3** a device for relaying a broadcast

relay race *NOUN* **relay races** a race between teams in which each person covers part of the distance

Thesaurus

reinforcements *PLURAL NOUN* *The police unit badly needed reinforcements.* ► support, back-up, additional help

reject *VERB* **1** *The union rejected the new offer.* ► turn down, refuse, decline, say no to, dismiss, veto AN OPPOSITE IS accept **2** *Although she loved him, in the end she rejected him.* ► rebuff, spurn, jilt, repudiate, cast aside, (*more informal*) dump

rejection *NOUN* **1** *Their leaders urged rejection of the offer.* ► refusal, non-acceptance, dismissal, turning down AN OPPOSITE IS acceptance **2** *Her rejection of Clive hurt him deeply.* ► spurning, repudiation, rebuff, shunning, (*more informal*) dumping

rejoice *VERB* *Scientists rejoiced at the new discovery.* ► celebrate, delight, exult, revel, be happy OPPOSITES ARE lament, be sad

rejoicing *NOUN* *It was a time for rejoicing.* ► celebration, festivity, jubilation, euphoria, gladness, happiness AN OPPOSITE IS mourning

relate *VERB* **1** *They have many stories to relate about their adventures abroad.* ► tell, recount, narrate, report, present, describe, recite **2** *Police are relating the two crimes.* ► link, connect, associate, see a connection between **3** **relate to** *The questions relate to an incident that took place the previous week.* ► refer to, concern, have to do with, apply to, bear on, pertain to, involve **4** **relate to** *They wanted a worker who could communicate with the young and relate to them.* ► identify with, sympathize with, understand, feel for, have a rapport with

relationship *NOUN* **1** *the relationship between religion and politics* ► connection, relation, link, association, correlation, correspondence, affinity **2** *Her relationship with her stepmother had deteriorated.* ► rapport, friendship, understanding, attachment, closeness

relative *ADJECTIVE* **1** *Assess the relative importance of each fact.* ► comparative, respective, corresponding **2** **relative to** *evidence relative to the incident* ► related to, relevant to, pertinent to, connected with, germane to, associated with

relative *NOUN* *She's a relative of mine.* ► relation, member of the same family, (*more formal*) kinsman *or* kinswoman

relax *VERB* **1** *Yoga helps you to relax.* ► unwind, unbend, ease up, let up, take it easy **2** *She relaxed her grip on the handle.* ► loosen, slacken, loose, let go, weaken, reduce **3** *His presence helped to relax her.* ► calm, calm down, soothe, pacify

relaxation *NOUN* *a few hours left for relaxation* ► recreation, relaxing, rest, unwinding, enjoyment, loosening up

a b c d e f g h i j k l m n o p q r s t u v w x y z

A B C D E F G H I J K L M N O P Q R S T U V W X Y Z

release VERB **releases, releasing, released** **1** set free or unfasten **2** let a thing fall or fly or go out **3** make a film or record etc. available to the public

release NOUN **releases** **1** being released **2** something released, such as a new film or CD **3** a device that unfastens something

relegate VERB **relegates, relegating, relegated** **1** put into a less important place **2** put a sports team into a lower division of a league
▷ **relegation** NOUN

relent VERB **relents, relenting, relented** become less severe or more merciful

relentless ADJECTIVE not stopping or relenting; pitiless
▷ **relentlessly** ADVERB

relevant ADJECTIVE connected with what is being discussed or dealt with (The opposite is **irrelevant**)
▷ **relevance** NOUN

reliable ADJECTIVE able to be relied on; trustworthy
▷ **reliably** ADVERB **reliability** NOUN

relic NOUN **relics** something that has survived from an earlier period of history

relief NOUN **reliefs** **1** the ending or lessening of pain, trouble, boredom, etc. **2** something that gives relief or help **3** help given to people in need • *a relief fund for the tsunami victims* **4** a person who takes over a turn of duty when another finishes **5** a method of making a design etc. that stands out from a surface

relief map NOUN **relief maps** a map that shows hills and valleys by shading or moulding

relieve VERB **relieves, relieving, relieved** give relief to a person or thing
relieve of take something from a person • *The thief relieved him of his wallet*

religion NOUN **religions** **1** what people believe about God or gods, and how they worship **2** a particular system of beliefs and worship

religious ADJECTIVE **1** to do with religion **2** believing firmly in a religion and taking part in its customs
▷ **religiously** ADVERB

relish NOUN **relishes** **1** great enjoyment **2** a tasty sauce or pickle that adds flavour to plainer food

relish VERB **relishes, relishing, relished** enjoy greatly

Thesaurus

release VERB **1** *The guerrillas promised to release one hostage.* ► free, liberate, let go
OPPOSITES ARE imprison, detain **2** *The names of the victims were released when the families had been informed.* ► make public, make known, publish, reveal, divulge, disclose, publicize, circulate, communicate
OPPOSITES ARE withhold, keep secret

relevant ADJECTIVE *Take a note of any relevant information.* ► pertinent, applicable, significant, apposite, material, suitable
AN OPPOSITE IS irrelevant

reliable ADJECTIVE **1** *The case lacked any reliable evidence.* ► dependable, valid, trustworthy, sound, genuine, authentic
AN OPPOSITE IS unreliable **2** *John was his most reliable friend.* ► trustworthy, dependable, faithful, devoted, staunch, constant, true, good

relic NOUN **1** *The book was a relic of her schooldays.* ► survival (from), souvenir, memento, remnant, reminder, token, vestige **2 relics** *a saint's relics* ► remains, sacred objects

relief NOUN **1** *It was a relief to find the village after miles of empty countryside.* ► reassurance, consolation, comfort, solace **2** *The medicine offered some relief from the pain.* ► alleviation (of), easing (of), lessening (of), remedy (for), assuagement (of), mitigation (of)
AN OPPOSITE IS intensification **3** *He needed a little light relief from his work.* ► respite, diversion, release, recreation, amusement, entertainment **4** *Aircraft brought relief to the beleaguered inhabitants.* ► help, aid, assistance, succour, deliverance

relieve VERB **1** *The pills helped to relieve her headache.* ► alleviate, ease, lessen, assuage, mitigate, diminish **2** *A video might relieve the boredom of the afternoon.* ► reduce, counteract, lighten, dispel **3** *It relieved us to know she was safely home.* ► reassure, comfort, console, soothe, please, gladden **4** *The army sent in supplies to relieve the townspeople.* ► help, aid, support, assist, sustain **5** *Her spell of duty was nearly over and a colleague would soon relieve her.* ► replace, take over from, stand in for

religion NOUN *the country's official religion* ► faith, belief, form of worship

religious ADJECTIVE **1** *religious beliefs; religious music* ► spiritual, sacred, holy, theological
AN OPPOSITE IS secular **2** *a religious person* ► devout, pious, reverent, holy, saintly, God-fearing AN OPPOSITE IS irreligious

relish NOUN *He ate his meal with relish.* ► appetite, delight, enjoyment, enthusiasm, gusto, zest OPPOSITES ARE disgust, dislike

relish VERB *He was relishing his moment of triumph.* ► enjoy, delight in, revel in, take pleasure in, savour, appreciate, like, love

relive *VERB* **relives, reliving, relived** remember something that happened very vividly, as though it was happening again

reluctant *ADJECTIVE* unwilling or not keen
▷ **reluctantly** *ADVERB* **reluctance** *NOUN*

rely *VERB* **relies, relying, relied**
rely on 1 trust a person or thing to help or support you **2** be dependent on something • *Many people rely on this local bus service.*

remain *VERB* **remains, remaining, remained**
1 be there after other parts have gone or been dealt with; be left over **2** continue to be in the same place or condition; stay

remainder *NOUN* **1** the remaining part or people or things **2** the number left after subtraction or division

remains *PLURAL NOUN* **1** all that is left over after other parts have been removed or destroyed **2** ancient ruins or objects; relics **3** a dead body

remand *VERB* **remands, remanding, remanded** send a prisoner back into custody while further evidence is being gathered
▷ **remand** *NOUN*
on remand in prison while waiting for a trial

remark *NOUN* **remarks** something said; a comment

remark *VERB* **remarks, remarking, remarked**
1 make a remark; say **2** notice

remarkable *ADJECTIVE* unusual or extraordinary
▷ **remarkably** *ADVERB*

remedial *ADJECTIVE* **1** helping children who learn slowly **2** helping to cure an illness or deficiency

remedy *NOUN* **remedies** something that cures or relieves a disease etc. or that puts a matter right

remember *VERB* **remembers, remembering, remembered 1** keep something in your mind **2** bring something back into your mind
▷ **remembrance** *NOUN*

remind *VERB* **reminds, reminding, reminded**
1 help or make a person remember something • *Remind me to buy some stamps.* **2** make a

Thesaurus

reluctant *ADJECTIVE* *I was reluctant to admit where I had been.* ► unwilling, disinclined, averse, hesitant (about), resistant, opposed, loath
OPPOSITES ARE willing, ready, eager

rely *VERB* *We can rely on them to help us.*
► depend on, count on, trust, have confidence in, (*more informal*) bank on

remain *VERB* **1** *He remained in hospital for several weeks.* ► stay, continue, stop, linger **2** *Even after the revolution the chief of police remained in power.* ► survive, continue, persist, prevail, endure **3** *By the end of the evening only a handful of guests remained.* ► be left, be present, survive, stay around

remainder *NOUN* **1** *They were excused duties for the remainder of the day.* ► rest, residue, balance **2** *Finish what you can and do the remainder tomorrow.* ► rest, extra, difference, remnant, residue, what is left

remaining *ADJECTIVE* **1** *She wanted to remove any remaining doubts.* ► persisting, surviving, lingering, abiding, continuing, residual **2** *Melt the remaining butter and brush it over the pastry.* ► left over, unused, surplus, extra

remains *PLURAL NOUN* **1** *He ate the remains of his sandwich in one huge mouthful.* ► remainder, rest, residue, remnant **2** *The saint's remains are in the crypt.* ► body, corpse, ashes, relics

remark *NOUN* *We had the usual conversational remarks about the weather.* ► comment, observation, thought, utterance, reflection, statement, word, opinion

remark *VERB* **1** *He remarked that it was very quiet in the room.* ► comment, observe, mention, note, say, state, declare, reflect **2** *We did not remark anything unusual.* ► note, mark, notice, observe, heed, see, perceive

remarkable *ADJECTIVE* **1** *They were bubbling with excitement after their remarkable journey.*
► extraordinary, amazing, astonishing, memorable, unforgettable, wonderful, marvellous, breathtaking, fantastic, strange, incredible, astounding, startling, staggering, stunning AN OPPOSITE IS ordinary **2** *It was certainly a remarkable achievement.*
► outstanding, striking, impressive, noteworthy, exceptional, memorable, phenomenal, distinguished

remedy *NOUN* **1** *a flu remedy* ► cure, treatment, medicine, medication, relief, antidote **2** *He suggested a day out as a remedy for their boredom.* ► answer, solution, cure, relief, corrective, palliative

remedy *VERB* *The government will pass a bill to remedy the problem.* ► put right, correct, rectify, solve, resolve, fix, deal with, sort out, redress, counteract

remember *VERB* **1** *a lot of facts to remember*
► memorize, learn, commit to memory **2** *Do you remember my cousin Alice? I can't remember where I put my keys.* ► recall, recollect, recognize **3** *Remember that she won't be here for several days yet.* ► bear in mind, keep in mind, take into account, not forget **4** *They sat on the terrace remembering their childhoods.*
► reminisce about, recall, recollect, look back on, muse on, be nostalgic about

remind *VERB* **1** *A note on the fridge reminded me to feed the cat.* ► prompt, nudge, hint at, tell
2 remind you of something *The music reminded me of my holiday.* ► make you think of, take you back to

A B C D E F G H I J K L M N O P Q R S T U V W X Y Z

person think of someone or something because of being similar • *She reminds me of my history teacher.*
▷ **reminder** NOUN

reminisce (rem- in- iss) VERB **reminisces, reminiscing, reminisced** think or talk about things that you remember
▷ **reminiscence** NOUN **reminiscent** ADJECTIVE

remiss ADJECTIVE negligent; careless about doing what you ought to do

remnant NOUN **remnants** a part or piece left over from something

remonstrate VERB **remonstrates, remonstrating, remonstrated** make a protest • *We remonstrated with him about his behaviour.*

remorse NOUN deep regret for having done wrong
▷ **remorseful** ADJECTIVE **remorsefully** ADVERB

remote ADJECTIVE **1** far away or isolated **2** some but very little; unlikely • *a remote chance*
▷ **remotely** ADVERB **remoteness** NOUN

remote control NOUN controlling something from a distance, usually by electricity or radio

removal NOUN removing or moving something

remove VERB **removes, removing, removed** take something away or off

remove NOUN **removes** a distance or degree away from something • *That is several removes from the truth.*

Renaissance (ren- ay- sans) NOUN the revival of classical styles of art and literature in Europe in the 14th-16th centuries [from French, = new birth]

rename VERB **renames, renaming, renamed** give a new name to a person or thing

render VERB **renders, rendering, rendered** **1** cause to become • *This news rendered us speechless.* **2** give or perform something • *The local community was quick to render help to the victims.*

rendezvous (rond- ay- voo) NOUN **rendezvous** (rond- ay- vooz) **1** a meeting with somebody **2** a place arranged for this [from French, = present yourselves]

renew VERB **renews, renewing, renewed** **1** restore something to its original condition or replace it with something new **2** begin or make or give again • *We renewed our request.*
▷ **renewal** NOUN

renewable resource NOUN **renewable resources** a resource (such as power from the sun, wind, or waves) that can never be used up, or which can be renewed

renounce VERB **renounces, renouncing, renounced** give up or reject
▷ **renunciation** NOUN

Thesaurus

reminder NOUN **1** *She forgot about him and needed a reminder to phone.* ► prompt, nudge, cue, hint, suggestion **2** *The photo was a reminder of a happy time.* ► memento, souvenir

remorse NOUN *He was filled with remorse for the harm he had done.* ► contrition, guilt, shame, sorrow, repentance, penitence, compunction, regret, bad conscience

remote ADJECTIVE **1** *The works would be sited at a remote place for safety.* ► isolated, outlying, secluded, out-of-the-way, distant, faraway, inaccessible, cut-off AN OPPOSITE IS central **2** *There was a remote chance the decision would be overruled.* ► slight, small, slim, slender, faint, unlikely, doubtful, improbable, negligible AN OPPOSITE IS strong **3** *His manner was remote and unfriendly.* ► aloof, detached, distant, withdrawn, reserved, stand-offish, uncommunicative OPPOSITES ARE warm, friendly

removal NOUN **1** *A local company would take care of the removal.* ► relocation, transfer, transportation **2** *The nail took some removal.* ► extraction, withdrawal, taking out, drawing **3** *The king insisted on the Prime Minister's removal from office.* ► dismissal, expulsion, displacement, elimination, ejection, ousting OPPOSITES ARE restoration, appointment

remove VERB **1** *It took ten minutes to remove the tooth.* ► extract, pull out, take out, withdraw **2** *She decided to remove the last sentence from her letter.* ► delete, erase, expunge, efface, rub out, strike out AN OPPOSITE IS restore (to) **3** *He tidied up the garden and removed some dead branches.* ► cut off, pull off, detach, strip off **4** *Karen went into the bathroom and removed her clothes.* ► take off, peel off, slip out of, shed, cast off AN OPPOSITE IS put on **5** *The more severe penalties had been removed.* ► abolish, get rid of, eliminate, withdraw, do away with, (*more informal*) axe OPPOSITES ARE impose, restore

render VERB **1** *The blow rendered him unconscious.* ► make, leave, cause to be **2** *People were eager to render assistance.* ► offer, give, provide, tender, furnish, supply **3** *Scholars rendered the Latin original into modern English.* ► translate, transcribe, adapt

renew VERB **1** *It was time to renew her interest in the countryside.* ► refresh, revive, restore, revitalize, resurrect, awaken **2** *I'll have to renew my passport next month.* ► extend, prolong **3** *The interior of the building was completely renewed in the eighteenth century.* ► renovate, restore, rebuild, modernize, refurbish, revamp, reconstruct, redecorate, make over, recondition, overhaul, transform

renovate *VERB* **renovates, renovating, renovated** repair a thing and make it look new
▷ **renovation** *NOUN*

renowned *ADJECTIVE* well known or famous

rent[1] *NOUN* **rents** a regular payment for the use of something, especially a house that belongs to another person

rent *VERB* **rents, renting, rented** have or allow the use of something in return for rent

rent[2] *NOUN* **rents** a torn place; a split

reorganize *VERB* **reorganizes, reorganizing, reorganized** change the way in which something is organized
▷ **reorganization** *NOUN*

repair *VERB* **repairs, repairing, repaired** put something into good condition after it has been damaged or broken etc.
▷ **repairable** *ADJECTIVE*

repair *NOUN* **repairs** **1** repairing • *closed for repair* **2** a mended place • *The repair is hardly visible.*
in good repair in good condition; well maintained

repartee *NOUN* witty replies and remarks

repatriate *VERB* **repatriates, repatriating, repatriated** send a person back to his or her own country
▷ **repatriation** *NOUN*

repeal *VERB* **repeals, repealing, repealed** cancel a law officially
▷ **repeal** *NOUN*

repeat *VERB* **repeats, repeating, repeated** **1** say or do the same thing again **2** tell another person about something told to you
▷ **repeatedly** *ADVERB*

repeat *NOUN* **repeats** **1** the action of repeating **2** something that is repeated, especially a television programme

repel *VERB* **repels, repelling, repelled** **1** drive back or away • *They fought bravely and repelled the attackers.* **2** push something away from itself by means of a physical force • *One north magnetic pole repels another.* **3** disgust somebody
▷ **repellent** *ADJECTIVE, NOUN*

repent *VERB* **repents, repenting, repented** be sorry for what you have done
▷ **repentance** *NOUN* **repentant** *ADJECTIVE*

repercussion *NOUN* **repercussions** a result or reaction produced indirectly by something

repertoire (rep- er- twahr) *NOUN* a stock of songs or plays etc. that a person or company knows and can perform

repetition *NOUN* **repetitions** **1** repeating **2** something repeated
▷ **repetitious** *ADJECTIVE*

repetitive *ADJECTIVE* full of repetitions
▷ **repetitively** *ADVERB*

Thesaurus

renovation *NOUN* *the renovation of an old building* ► improvement, modernization, overhaul, reconditioning, redevelopment, refit, refurbishment, renewal, repair, restoration, transformation, updating

rent *VERB* **1** *You can rent a car at the airport.* ► hire, lease, charter **2** *They rent out their apartment during the Festival.* ► let, lease, sublet

repair *VERB* *Public money will be spent to repair the damage. He longed to get back with Maggie and repair their broken marriage.* ► mend, fix, put right, rectify, overhaul, patch up, renew, renovate

repair *NOUN* **1** *The engine is in dire need of repair.* ► mending, fixing, overhaul, maintenance, renovation **2** *The building is in good repair.* ► condition, state, shape, fettle

repay *VERB* **1** *The debt has been completely repaid.* ► pay off, pay back, settle, expunge, extinguish **2** *We must repay your train fare.* ► refund, reimburse, pay back, recompense, compensate, remunerate, settle **3** *He was eager to repay their kindness.* ► reciprocate, return, recompense, requite

repeat *VERB* **1** *Neither of them had any wish to repeat their experience.* ► have again, do again, redo, re-experience, reproduce, duplicate **2** *The tale became more colourful every time someone repeated it.* ► say again, restate, reiterate, reproduce, recite, relate

repeat *NOUN* **1** *We are hoping for a repeat of last week's successes.* ► repetition, repeating, recurrence, reiteration, rerun, return **2** *I watched a repeat of the programme.* ► replay, rerun, reshowing, rebroadcast, repetition

repel *VERB* **1** *The invaders were repelled at the border.* ► repulse, drive back, beat back, push back, ward off, parry, put to flight **2** *a device for repelling cats* ► deter, keep away, scare off
AN OPPOSITE IS attract **3** *Such selfishness repelled me.* ► revolt, disgust, sicken, offend, nauseate
OPPOSITES ARE delight, please

repellent *ADJECTIVE* *Reviewers found the programme repellent.* ► revolting, disgusting, sickening, repulsive, offensive, repugnant, nauseating

repetition *NOUN* *The authorities do not want to see any repetition of last week's incident.* ► repeat, repeating, recurrence, reiteration, rerun, return, reappearance, duplication

repetitive *ADJECTIVE* *To him fixing tiles was repetitive and boring.* ► monotonous, tedious, boring, humdrum, mechanical, repetitious,

replace *VERB* **replaces, replacing, replaced** **1** put a thing back in its place **2** take the place of another person or thing **3** put a new or different thing in place of something
▷ **replacement** *NOUN*

replay *NOUN* **replays** **1** a sports match played again after a draw **2** the playing or showing again of a recording
▷ **replay** *VERB*

replica *NOUN* **replicas** an exact copy [from Italian]

reply *NOUN* **replies** something said or written to deal with a question, letter, etc.; an answer

reply *VERB* **replies, replying, replied** give a reply to; answer

report *VERB* **reports, reporting, reported** **1** describe something that has happened or that you have done or studied **2** make a complaint or accusation against somebody **3** go and tell somebody that you have arrived or are ready for work

report *NOUN* **reports** **1** a description or account of something **2** a regular statement of how someone has worked or behaved, e.g. at school **3** an explosive sound

reported speech *NOUN* indirect speech

reporter *NOUN* **reporters** a person whose job is to collect and report news for a newspaper, radio or television programme, etc.

repose *NOUN* calm, rest, or sleep

repose *VERB* **reposes, reposing, reposed** rest or lie somewhere

repossess *VERB* **repossesses, repossessing, repossessed** take something back because it has not been paid for

reprehensible *ADJECTIVE* extremely bad and deserving blame or rebuke

represent *VERB* **represents, representing, represented** **1** help someone by speaking or doing something on their behalf **2** symbolize or stand for • *In Roman numerals, V represents 5.* **3** be an example or equivalent of something **4** show a person or thing in a picture or play etc. **5** describe a person or thing in a particular way
▷ **representation** *NOUN*

representative *NOUN* **representatives** a person or thing that represents another or others

representative *ADJECTIVE* **1** representing others **2** typical of a group

Thesaurus

unchanging, unvaried, (*more informal*) samey
AN OPPOSITE IS varied

replace *VERB* **1** *She replaced the book on the shelf.* ► put back, return, reinstate, restore **2** *He did not need to look far for someone to replace him when he left.* ► succeed, follow, take over from, take the place of, supersede, supplant, be a substitute for, come after **3** *a scheme to replace dying trees* ► renew, change, provide a substitute for

replacement *NOUN* *Thomas had lost his mobile and bought a replacement.* ► substitute, alternative, successor, surrogate, stand-in

replica *NOUN* *Katie wore a replica of her sister's dress.* ► copy, duplicate, imitation, reproduction, likeness, double, clone, facsimile, model, reconstruction

reply *VERB* **1** *She replied that they would just have to wait.* ► answer, respond, retort, counter **2 reply to** *He never replies to letters.* ► answer, acknowledge, give a reply to, respond to, react to

reply *NOUN* *My letter called for a reply.* ► answer, response, acknowledgement, reaction, rejoinder, retort

report *VERB* **1** *She threatened to report him to the police.* ► inform on, make a complaint against **2** *You must report for duty at 9 o'clock.* ► present yourself, arrive, appear, turn up, check in, clock in **3** *The government has reported an increase in exports.* ► announce, proclaim, declare, communicate, notify, relate, recount, note

report *NOUN* **1** *There is a full report of the incident in today's newspaper.* ► account, description, review, article, announcement, record, statement, story, (*more informal*) write-up **2** *We heard the report of a gun.* ► bang, blast, crack, noise, explosion, detonation, pop

reporter *NOUN* *A group of reporters waited outside the house.* ► journalist, correspondent, newspaperman *or* newspaperwoman

represent *VERB* **1** *The picture represents a winter scene.* ► depict, describe, portray, show, illustrate, delineate, draw, paint, picture, exhibit, enact **2** *Each character in the play represents a particular human quality.* ► embody, stand for, symbolize, typify, personify, epitomize, exemplify **3** *They chose a spokesperson to represent their views.* ► speak for, express, present, be an example of

representation *NOUN* *a representation of a young woman* ► portrayal, depiction, likeness, image, picture, portrait, resemblance, delineation

representative *ADJECTIVE* **1** *a representative sample of British society* ► typical, characteristic, average, archetypal, illustrative, normal AN OPPOSITE IS abnormal **2** *The Greeks devised forms of representative government.* ► democratic, elected, elective, popular, chosen

representative *NOUN* **1** *the queen's representative abroad* ► ambassador, delegate, deputy, consul, diplomat, spokesperson,

repress *VERB* **represses, repressing, repressed 1** keep down; control by force **2** restrain or suppress
▷ **repression** *NOUN* **repressive** *ADJECTIVE*

reprieve *NOUN* **reprieves** postponement or cancellation of a punishment etc., especially the death penalty

reprimand *NOUN* **reprimands** a rebuke, especially a formal or official one

reprimand *VERB* **reprimands, reprimanding, reprimanded** give someone a reprimand

reprisal *NOUN* **reprisals** an act of revenge

reproach *VERB* **reproaches, reproaching, reproached** tell someone you are upset and disappointed by something he or she has done
▷ **reproach** *NOUN* **reproachful** *ADJECTIVE* **reproachfully** *ADVERB*

reproduce *VERB* **reproduces, reproducing, reproduced 1** cause to be seen or heard or happen again **2** make a copy of something **3** produce offspring
▷ **reproduction** *NOUN* **reproductive** *ADJECTIVE*

reprove *VERB* **reproves, reproving, reproved** rebuke or reproach
▷ **reproof** *NOUN*

reptile *NOUN* **reptiles** a cold-blooded animal that has a backbone and very short legs or no legs at all, e.g. a snake, lizard, crocodile, or tortoise [from Latin *reptilis* = crawling]

republic *NOUN* **republics** a country that has a president, especially one who is elected
COMPARE **monarchy**
▷ **republican** *ADJECTIVE*
[from Latin *res publica* = public affairs]

repudiate *VERB* **repudiates, repudiating, repudiated** reject or deny
▷ **repudiation** *NOUN*

repulsive *ADJECTIVE* **1** disgusting **2** repelling things (The opposite is **attractive**)
▷ **repulsively** *ADVERB* **repulsiveness** *NOUN*

reputable (rep- yoo- ta- bul) *ADJECTIVE* having a good reputation; respected
▷ **reputably** *ADVERB*

reputation *NOUN* **reputations** what people say about a person or thing

Thesaurus

spokesman *or* spokeswoman, proxy, stand-in **2** *a sales representative* ► agent, salesperson, salesman *or* saleswoman, (*informal*) rep

reprimand *VERB* *They were reprimanded for their bad behaviour.* ► rebuke, admonish, reprove, reproach, upbraid, censure, scold, chide, criticize, reprehend, (*more informal*) tell off, (*more informal*) tick off OPPOSITES ARE praise, commend

reprimand *NOUN* *The police gave them a formal reprimand.* ► rebuke, admonishment, admonition, reproof, scolding, (*more informal*) telling-off, (*more informal*) ticking-off, (*more informal*) talking-to

reproachful *ADJECTIVE* *She gave him a reproachful frown.* ► disapproving, reproving, scornful, accusatory, censorious, critical, withering
AN OPPOSITE IS approving

reproduce *VERB* **1** *The drawings are reproduced in beautiful colour illustrations.* ► copy, reprint, duplicate, transcribe, print, simulate, reissue, repeat, photocopy **2** *These animals reproduce in large numbers.* ► breed, bear young, produce offspring, multiply, propagate, procreate, spawn, increase

reproduction *NOUN* **1** *methods of reproduction in fish* ► breeding, propagation, procreation, multiplying **2** *The portrait is only a reproduction.* ► copy, replica, duplicate, facsimile, imitation, fake, forgery, likeness, print
AN OPPOSITE IS original

reproof *NOUN* *He tutted at her in mild reproof.* ► reprimand, rebuke, admonishment, admonition, censure AN OPPOSITE IS approval

repudiate *VERB* **1** *He repudiated all the charges made against him.* ► dispute, rebuff, reject, deny, disagree with, renounce, refute OPPOSITES ARE accept, acknowledge **2** *She did not want to repudiate their agreement.* ► disown, go back on, recant, rescind, retract, reverse, revoke

repugnant *ADJECTIVE* *Polygamy may seem repugnant to us.* ► abhorrent, repulsive, revolting, repellent, offensive, disgusting, loathsome

repulse *VERB* **1** *The rebels attacked and were repulsed.* ► repel, drive back, beat back, push back, ward off, parry, put to flight **2** *He showed her affection but was repulsed.* ► reject, rebuff, spurn, snub, jilt

repulsive *ADJECTIVE* *His appearance was repulsive.* ► revolting, disgusting, repugnant, repellent, loathsome, obnoxious, hideous
AN OPPOSITE IS attractive

reputable *ADJECTIVE* *Make sure you get a reputable builder to do the work.* ► dependable, reliable, highly regarded, well thought of, tried and trusted, respectable, respected, trustworthy, creditable AN OPPOSITE IS disreputable

reputation *NOUN* *His reputation had been damaged by the affair.* ► good name, name, standing, stature, character, esteem, honour, repute, image, prestige

reputed *ADJECTIVE* said or thought to be something • *This is reputed to be the best hotel.*
▷ **reputedly** *ADVERB*

request *VERB* **requests, requesting, requested** **1** ask for a thing **2** ask a person to do something

request *NOUN* **requests** **1** asking for something **2** a thing asked for

require *VERB* **requires, requiring, required** **1** need **2** make somebody do something; oblige • *Drivers are required to pass a test.*

requirement *NOUN* **requirements** what is required; a need

rescue *VERB* **rescues, rescuing, rescued** save from danger, harm, etc.; free from captivity
▷ **rescuer** *NOUN*

rescue *NOUN* **rescues** the action of rescuing

research *NOUN* careful study or investigation to discover facts or information

research (ri- serch) *VERB* **researches, researching, researched** do research into something [from early French *recerche* = careful search]

resemblance *NOUN* **resemblances** likeness or similarity

resemble *VERB* **resembles, resembling, resembled** be like another person or thing

resent *VERB* **resents, resenting, resented** feel indignant about or insulted by something
▷ **resentful** *ADJECTIVE* **resentfully** *ADVERB* **resentment** *NOUN*

reservation *NOUN* **reservations** **1** reserving **2** something reserved • *a hotel reservation* **3** an area of land kept for a special purpose **4** a limit on how far you agree with something • *I believe most of his story, but I have some reservations.*

reserve *VERB* **reserves, reserving, reserved** **1** keep or order something for a particular person or a special use **2** postpone • *reserve judgement*

reserve *NOUN* **reserves** **1** a person or thing kept ready to be used if necessary **2** an extra player chosen in case a substitute is needed in a team

Thesaurus

request *NOUN* *Our request for assistance has been accepted.* ► appeal, plea, petition, entreaty, application, call, supplication

request *VERB* **1** *We requested immediate help.* ► ask for, appeal for, call for, seek, plead for, require, solicit **2** *They requested us to stop.* ► ask, call on, require, implore, beseech

require *VERB* **1** *One of the victims required immediate surgery.* ► need, have to have **2** *The situation required extreme care.* ► call for, need, necessitate, involve, entail **3** *An official required me to show my passport.* ► order, instruct, direct, command, oblige, request

requirement *NOUN* *One of the requirements for this work is a quiet place to go and do it.* ► need, necessity, essential, requisite, prerequisite, stipulation, condition, proviso

rescue *VERB* **1** *In a few hours someone would come and rescue them.* ► set free, free, release, save, liberate, deliver, extricate, ransom **2** *I went back to the house to rescue some of my belongings.* ► recover, retrieve, salvage, get back, bring away

rescue *NOUN* *The news was all about a dramatic sea rescue.* ► saving, rescuing, recovery, release, deliverance, liberation

research *NOUN* *More research is needed into the causes of violent crime.* ► investigation, experimentation, testing, exploration, inquiry, analysis, searching, study

research *VERB* *The disease has been widely researched.* ► investigate, study, inquire into, explore, probe, look into

resemblance *NOUN* *There is a close resemblance between the two accounts.* ► similarity, correspondence, conformity, agreement, comparison, equivalence, likeness
OPPOSITES ARE difference, dissimilarity

resemble *VERB* *The garden resembled a wilderness.* ► look like, be like, remind you of, be similar to, mirror AN OPPOSITE IS differ from

resent *VERB* *Jack resented his mother's interference.* ► begrudge, take exception to, take umbrage at, object to, be annoyed about, be resentful of, dislike

resentful *ADJECTIVE* *Her parents' constant complaining left her feeling resentful.* ► aggrieved, indignant, disgruntled, discontented, offended, bitter, hurt, irritated, antagonistic, sour, jealous, (*more informal*) put out, (*more informal*) peeved, (*more informal*) miffed

resentment *NOUN* *The appointment of an outsider caused intense resentment among the workforce.* ► indignation, discontent, bad feelings, disgruntlement, rancour, antagonism, irritation

reservation *NOUN* **1** *You will need to make a reservation if you come on a Friday.* ► booking, advance booking, prior arrangement **2** *Some members of the group had reservations about the plan.* ► misgiving, doubt, scepticism, unease, scruple, qualification, hesitation, qualm

reserve *VERB* **1** *Demand will be high so make sure your newsagent reserves you a copy.* ► keep, put aside, set aside, hold, retain, earmark **2** *Chuck reserved a room at the local hotel.* ► book, secure, arrange for, order

reserve *NOUN* **1** *Her reserve of money was running out.* ► supply, fund, stock, store,

3 an area of land kept for a special purpose • *a nature reserve* **4** shyness; being slow to reveal opinions or emotions

reservoir (rez- er- vwar) NOUN **reservoirs** a place where water is stored, especially an artificial lake

residence NOUN **residences** a place where a person lives

resident NOUN **residents** a person living in a particular place
▷ **resident** ADJECTIVE

residential ADJECTIVE **1** containing people's homes • *a residential area* **2** providing accommodation • *a residential course*

residue NOUN **residues** what is left over
▷ **residual** ADJECTIVE

resign VERB **resigns, resigning, resigned** give up your job or position
▷ **resignation** NOUN

be resigned or **resign yourself to something** accept that you must put up with it

resist VERB **resists, resisting, resisted** oppose; fight or act against something

resistance NOUN **1** resisting • *The troops came up against armed resistance.* **2** the ability of a substance to hinder the flow of electricity
▷ **resistant** ADJECTIVE

resolute ADJECTIVE showing great determination
▷ **resolutely** ADVERB

resolution NOUN **resolutions 1** being resolute **2** something you have resolved to do • *New Year resolutions* **3** a formal decision made by a committee etc. **4** the solving of a problem etc.

Thesaurus

reservoir, hoard, accumulation **2** *a wildlife reserve* ► preserve, reservation, sanctuary, park **3** *His reserve prevented him from joining in the fun.* ► reticence, shyness, diffidence, timidity, restraint, modesty, aloofness
AN OPPOSITE IS openness

reserved ADJECTIVE *As a young man he had been rather reserved.* ► shy, reticent, diffident, retiring, unforthcoming, quiet, timid, restrained, distant, aloof
OPPOSITES ARE forthcoming, outgoing

reside VERB **reside in** *Most students reside in halls during their first year.* ► live in, stay in, have a room in, dwell in, lodge in, settle in, occupy, have as a home, inhabit

residence NOUN *They spent the summer in their country residence.* ► home, house, dwelling, domicile, abode, address, mansion, quarters, habitation

resident NOUN **1** *the residents of Boston* ► inhabitant, citizen, townsman *or* townswoman, denizen, native **2** *The hotel's first duty is to ensure the safety of its residents.* ► guest, boarder, lodger, client, occupant
AN OPPOSITE IS non-resident

resign VERB **1** *The manager resigned at the end of the season.* ► leave, stand down, step down, give in your notice, (*informal*) quit, (*more informal*) call it a day, give up **2** *She resigned all her rights in the matter.* ► renounce, relinquish, abandon, surrender, cede, give up, forsake
AN OPPOSITE IS take up

resignation NOUN **1** *They faced an uncertain future with resignation.* ► patience, forbearance, tolerance, stoicism, endurance, fortitude, sufferance, acceptance, fatalism **2** *There would be many resignations from the right wing of the party.* ► departure, notice, standing down, retirement, relinquishment

resilient ADJECTIVE **1** *Use a resilient material for harder wear.* ► flexible, supple, pliable, pliant, durable, tough, elastic, springy
AN OPPOSITE IS inflexible **2** *She was still young and resilient.* ► adaptable, buoyant, irrepressible, tough, hardy, strong OPPOSITES ARE vulnerable, sensitive

resist VERB **1** *He resisted all our attempts to persuade him.* ► oppose, withstand, stand up to, defy, balk at, fend off, confront, fight
OPPOSITES ARE yield to, submit to **2** *a hard varnish that resists wear for years* ► withstand, be proof against, combat, weather, endure, keep out AN OPPOSITE IS be susceptible to **3** *The temptation was so strong he was unable to resist any longer.* ► hold out, desist, restrain yourself, forbear OPPOSITES ARE yield, give in

resistant ADJECTIVE **1 resistant to** *a material that is resistant to heat* ► impervious to, proof against, repellent to, immune to, unaffected by
AN OPPOSITE IS susceptible to **2 resistant to** *He was always resistant to change.* ► opposed to, averse to, hostile to, suspicious of
OPPOSITES ARE receptive to, attracted to

resolute ADJECTIVE *The local people put up a resolute resistance.* ► determined, purposeful, resolved, firm, steadfast, staunch, tenacious, unflinching, undaunted
OPPOSITES ARE irresolute, half-hearted, feeble

resolution NOUN **1** *They showed great resolution in the face of danger.* ► determination, resolve, spirit, boldness, courage, firmness, fortitude, commitment, perseverance, doggedness, staunchness, steadfastness, tenacity, will power **2** *The committee passed the resolution by a large majority.* ► motion, proposal, proposition, declaration, decision, judgement **3** *Let's hope financial aid can be a resolution of the country's difficulties.* ► settlement, solution, answer (to)

resolve *VERB* **resolves, resolving, resolved** **1** decide firmly or formally **2** solve a problem etc. **3** overcome doubts or disagreements

resolve *NOUN* **1** something you have decided to do; a resolution **2** great determination

resort *VERB* **resorts, resorting, resorted** turn to or make use of something • *They resorted to violence.*

resort *NOUN* **resorts** **1** a place where people go for relaxation or holidays **2** resorting • *without resort to cheating*
the last resort something to be tried when everything else has failed

resounding *ADJECTIVE* **1** loud and echoing **2** very great; outstanding • *a resounding victory*

resource *NOUN* **resources** **1** something that can be used; an asset • *The country's natural resources include coal and oil.* **2** an ability; ingenuity

resourceful *ADJECTIVE* clever at finding ways of doing things
▷ **resourcefully** *ADVERB* **resourcefulness** *NOUN*

respect *NOUN* **respects** **1** admiration for a person's or thing's good qualities **2** politeness or consideration • *Have respect for people's feelings.* **3** a detail or aspect • *In this respect he is like his sister.* **4** reference • *The rules with respect to bullying are quite clear.*

respect *VERB* **respects, respecting, respected** have respect for a person or thing

respectable *ADJECTIVE* **1** having good manners and character etc. **2** fairly good • *a respectable score*
▷ **respectably** *ADVERB* **respectability** *NOUN*

respectful *ADJECTIVE* showing respect
▷ **respectfully** *ADVERB*

respective *ADJECTIVE* belonging separately to each one of several • *We went to our respective rooms*

respectively *ADVERB* in the same order as the people or things already mentioned • *Ruth and Emma finished first and second respectively.*

respiration *NOUN* breathing
▷ **respiratory** *ADJECTIVE*

respirator *NOUN* **respirators** **1** a device that fits over a person's nose and mouth to purify air before it is breathed **2** an apparatus for giving artificial respiration

Thesaurus

resolve *VERB* **1** *It will take months to resolve the matter completely.* ► settle, sort out, work out, solve, put right, straighten out, rectify, deal with **2** *The boys resolved to keep going until dark.* ► determine, decide, make up your mind, take a decision

resolve *NOUN* *Opposition to his ideas only strengthened his resolve.* ► resolution, determination, firmness of purpose, steadfastness, tenacity
OPPOSITES ARE indecision, hesitancy

resort *NOUN* **1** *Going on strike would be a last resort.* ► option, choice, alternative, course of action, expedient, recourse, refuge **2** *a seaside resort on the south coast* ► holiday town, tourist spot, retreat, spa

resort *VERB* **resort to** *I don't want to have to resort to threats.* ► have recourse to, fall back on, make use of, turn to, adopt, utilize, use, sink to, stoop to

resound *VERB* *Thunder resounded in the hills.* ► resonate, reverberate, ring, echo, boom, vibrate

resounding *ADJECTIVE* **1** *His fist hit the table with a resounding thump.* ► resonant, vibrant, reverberating, clear, ringing, echoing, booming **2** *The show had been a resounding success.* ► decided, emphatic, decisive, thorough, complete, outstanding, tremendous, great

resourceful *ADJECTIVE* *They were resourceful in using the few materials available.* ► imaginative, enterprising, inventive, creative, ingenious, innovative, original, talented, clever
AN OPPOSITE IS unimaginative

resources *PLURAL NOUN* *The business had to survive on limited resources.* ► assets, funds, wealth, money, riches, capital, reserves

respect *NOUN* **1** *He showed the respect due to such a great writer.* ► esteem, regard, honour, deference, homage, admiration, awe, reverence, veneration, consideration **2** *The conclusions were correct in every respect.* ► aspect, regard, particular, point, characteristic, detail, facet, feature, way

respect *VERB* **1** *We respected them for their honesty.* ► admire, esteem, think well of, appreciate, regard, commend
AN OPPOSITE IS despise **2** *She promised to respect her father's wishes.* ► comply with, abide by, observe, honour, obey, follow, conform to, adhere to

respectable *ADJECTIVE* **1** *He came from a respectable family in New England.* ► reputable, honourable, respected, upright, worthy, decent AN OPPOSITE IS disreputable **2** *She found a job and now earns a respectable income.* ► decent, reasonable, substantial, considerable, sizeable

respectful *ADJECTIVE* *Two chambermaids were standing at a respectful distance.* ► deferential, courteous, polite, dutiful, reverential, gracious, civil OPPOSITES ARE disrespectful, rude

respective *ADJECTIVE* *We handed the horses back to their respective lads.* ► separate, individual, own, various, particular, several

resplendent *ADJECTIVE* brilliant with colour or decorations

respond *VERB* **responds, responding, responded 1** reply **2** act in answer to, or because of, something; react

response *NOUN* **responses 1** a reply **2** a reaction

responsibility *NOUN* **responsibilities 1** being responsible **2** something for which a person is responsible

responsible *ADJECTIVE* **1** looking after a person or thing and having to take the blame if something goes wrong **2** reliable and trustworthy **3** with important duties • *a responsible job* **4** causing something • *His carelessness was responsible for their deaths.*
▷ **responsibly** *ADVERB*

rest[1] *NOUN* **rests 1** a time of sleep or freedom from work as a way of regaining strength **2** a support • *a chin rest* **3** an interval of silence between notes in music

rest *VERB* **rests, resting, rested 1** have a rest; be still **2** allow to rest • *Sit down and rest your feet.* **3** lean or place something so it is supported; be supported • *Rest the ladder against the wall.* **4** be left without further investigation etc. • *And there the matter rests.*

rest[2] *NOUN*
the rest the remaining part; the others

rest *VERB* **rests, resting, rested** remain • *Rest assured, it will be a success.*
rest with be left to someone to deal with • *It rests with you to suggest a date.*

restaurant *NOUN* **restaurants** a place where you can buy a meal and eat it

restful *ADJECTIVE* giving rest or a feeling of rest

restive *ADJECTIVE* restless or impatient because of delay, boredom, etc.

restless *ADJECTIVE* unable to rest or keep still
▷ **restlessly** *ADVERB*

restore *VERB* **restores, restoring, restored 1** put something back to its original place or condition **2** clean and repair a work of art or building etc. so that it looks as good as it did originally
▷ **restoration** *NOUN*

Thesaurus

respond *VERB* **respond to** *He responded to each question with a shrug.* ▸ answer, react to, reply to, acknowledge, greet, counter

response *NOUN* *The comment brought an angry response.* ▸ answer, reply, retort, reaction, rejoinder, riposte, acknowledgement, counter, (*more informal*) comeback

responsible *ADJECTIVE* **1** *He is responsible for the day-to-day running of the computer system.* ▸ accountable, answerable, in charge of **2** *Kim was responsible for the damage.* ▸ culpable, guilty, liable **3** *Mr Jones was one of her most responsible tenants.* ▸ trustworthy, reliable, dependable, conscientious, honest, sensible AN OPPOSITE IS irresponsible **4** *She has a responsible position in a city bank.* ▸ important, powerful, influential, authoritative, executive

responsive *ADJECTIVE* *Educational institutions must become more responsive to the needs of students.* ▸ alert, alive, aware, impressionable, interested, open, perceptive, receptive, sympathetic, warm-hearted, willing OPPOSITES ARE insensitive, apathetic

rest *NOUN* **1** *The rest of the group went to visit a gallery.* ▸ remainder, balance, remains, others **2** *You need a rest, Fran, you look tired.* ▸ break, breathing space, time off, lie-down, nap, snooze, respite, pause, (*more informal*) breather **3** *alternating periods of rest and exercise* ▸ relaxation, leisure, respite, inactivity, ease, calm, tranquillity

rest *VERB* **1** *She went to rest in her room.* ▸ relax, take a rest, lie down, ease up, have a sleep, have a nap, have a snooze **2** *Her hand rested on his shoulder.* ▸ lie, be laid **3** *She rested her bike against the wall.* ▸ prop, lean, stand, support, place, put **4** *The success of the idea rests on the financial support they can bring in.* ▸ depend, rely, hang, hinge

restaurant *NOUN* *She wondered if the restaurant had a sushi bar.* ▸ eating place, eating house, (*more informal*) noshery

restful *ADJECTIVE* *He enjoyed the most restful night he could remember.* ▸ relaxing, soothing, calm, peaceful, placid, quiet, tranquil, leisurely, untroubled OPPOSITES ARE restless, disturbed

restless *ADJECTIVE* **1** *My mother was restless, waiting for the family to return.* ▸ agitated, anxious, edgy, nervous, restive, fidgety, impatient, jittery, jumpy, worried AN OPPOSITE IS relaxed. **2** *a restless night of tossing and turning* ▸ sleepless, disturbed, troubled, uncomfortable, unsettled, interrupted AN OPPOSITE IS restful

restore *VERB* **1** *The interim government wished to restore democracy as soon as possible.* ▸ reinstate, bring back, reinstitute, reinstall, give back, put back, replace, return AN OPPOSITE IS abolish **2** *We must restore the property to its rightful owners.* ▸ return, give back, hand back, take back, replace AN OPPOSITE IS retain **3** *The building has been beautifully restored.* ▸ renovate, repair, rebuild, recondition, reconstruct, refurbish, clean, (*more informal*) do up, renew

restrain *VERB* **restrains, restraining, restrained** hold a person or thing back; keep under control
▷ **restraint** *NOUN*

restrict *VERB* **restricts, restricting, restricted** keep within certain limits
▷ **restriction** *NOUN* **restrictive** *ADJECTIVE*

result *NOUN* **results 1** something produced by an action or condition etc.; an effect or consequence **2** the score or situation at the end of a game, competition, or race etc. **3** the answer to a sum or calculation

result *VERB* **results, resulting, resulted 1** happen as a result **2** have a particular result • *The match resulted in a draw.*
▷ **resultant** *ADJECTIVE*

resurrect *VERB* **resurrects, resurrecting, resurrected** bring back into use or existence • *It is time to resurrect this old custom.*

resurrection *NOUN* **1** coming back to life after being dead **2** the revival of something
the Resurrection in the Christian religion, the resurrection of Jesus Christ three days after his death

resuscitate *VERB* **resuscitates, resuscitating, resuscitated** revive a person from unconsciousness or apparent death
▷ **resuscitation** *NOUN*

retail *NOUN* selling to the general public COMPARE **wholesale**
▷ **retailer** *NOUN*

retain *VERB* **retains, retaining, retained 1** continue to have something; keep in your possession or memory etc. **2** hold something in place

retaliate *VERB* **retaliates, retaliating, retaliated** repay an injury or insult etc. with a similar one; attack someone in return for a similar attack
▷ **retaliation** *NOUN*

reticent (ret- i- sent) *ADJECTIVE* not telling people what you feel or think; discreet
▷ **reticence** *NOUN*

retina *NOUN* **retinas** a layer of membrane at the back of the eyeball, sensitive to light

retinue *NOUN* **retinues** a group of people accompanying an important person

Thesaurus

AN OPPOSITE IS neglect **4** *An operation was needed to restore the girl's sight.* ► bring back, re-establish, rehabilitate, reinstate, reintroduce, revive

restrain *VERB* **1** *The dogs were restrained by leads.* ► bind, fetter, confine, restrict, tie, shackle **2** *She found it hard to restrain her laughter.* ► control, hold back, suppress, check, curb, prevent OPPOSITES ARE encourage, stimulate **3** *He had to restrain himself from jumping up and looking out of the window.* ► stop, keep, prevent, hold back AN OPPOSITE IS force

restrained *ADJECTIVE* *He was unusually restrained and conventional.* ► self-controlled, muted, unemotional, undemonstrative, inhibited, quiet, discreet, reserved, reticent, repressed, subdued AN OPPOSITE IS uninhibited

restrict *VERB* **1** *A busy working life restricted her opportunities to get away.* ► limit, constrain, impede, hinder, hamper, restrain, curtail AN OPPOSITE IS increase **2** *The prisoners were restricted to their cells.* ► confine, restrain, enclose, imprison, keep, shut AN OPPOSITE IS free

restriction *NOUN* **1** *There is a restriction on the number of places available.* ► limit, limitation, constraint, control, curb, restraint, check **2** *a society that imposes restrictions on personal freedom* ► limitation, reduction, diminution, curtailment, cutback

result *NOUN* **1** *The water shortage is a result of the hot weather.* ► consequence, effect, outcome, sequel, repercussion, upshot, fruit, issue, product, end-product **2** *the result of a trial* ► verdict, decision, judgement **3** *the result of an exam* ► mark, grade, score, assessment, ranking **4** *the result of a calculation* ► answer, solution

result *VERB* *What resulted from your interview?* ► arise, come about, culminate, develop, emanate, emerge, ensue, eventuate, follow, happen, issue, occur, proceed, spring, stem, take place, turn out
result in *The accident resulted in serious injuries.* ► end in, cause, involve, bring about, lead to, give rise to, achieve, provoke

resume *VERB* *It is essential to resume talks to reach an agreement.* ► restart, reopen, recommence, continue, begin again, start again, carry on, proceed with, reconvene

retain *VERB* **1** *When he retired he retained his shares in the company.* ► keep, hold on to, hang on to, preserve AN OPPOSITE IS surrender **2** *She retained her composure despite much provocation.* ► keep control of, maintain, preserve AN OPPOSITE IS lose **3** *Some students are good at retaining facts from their reading.* ► remember, memorize, keep in mind, learn, recall, recollect AN OPPOSITE IS forget

retaliate *VERB* *After the attack the Egyptians were powerless to retaliate.* ► fight back, strike back, hit back, respond, reciprocate, take revenge, get even

retaliation *NOUN* *The best safeguard is the power to threaten retaliation.* ► reprisal, retribution, revenge, counter-attack, vengeance

retire *VERB* **retires, retiring, retired 1** give up your regular work when you reach a certain age **2** retreat or withdraw **3** go to bed or to your private room
▷ **retirement** *NOUN*

retiring *ADJECTIVE* shy; avoiding company

retort *NOUN* **retorts 1** a quick or witty or angry reply **2** a glass bottle with a long downward bent neck, used in distilling liquids **3** a receptacle used in making steel etc.

retort *VERB* **retorts, retorting, retorted** make a quick, witty, or angry reply

retract *VERB* **retracts, retracting, retracted 1** pull back or in • *The snail retracts its horns.* **2** withdraw an offer or statement
▷ **retraction** *NOUN* **retractable** *ADJECTIVE*

retreat *VERB* **retreats, retreating, retreated** go back after being defeated or to avoid danger or difficulty etc.; withdraw

retreat *NOUN* **retreats 1** retreating **2** a quiet place to which someone can withdraw

retribution *NOUN* **retributions** a deserved punishment

retrieve *VERB* **retrieves, retrieving, retrieved 1** bring or get something back **2** rescue
▷ **retrievable** *ADJECTIVE* **retrieval** *NOUN*

retriever *NOUN* **retrievers** a kind of dog that is often trained to retrieve game

retrograde *ADJECTIVE* **1** going backwards **2** becoming less good

retrospect *NOUN*
in retrospect when you look back at what has happened

retrospective *ADJECTIVE* **1** looking back on the past **2** applying to the past as well as the future • *The law could not be made retrospective.*
▷ **retrospection** *NOUN*

return *VERB* **returns, returning, returned 1** come back or go back **2** bring, give, put, or send back **3** elect to parliament

return *NOUN* **returns 1** returning **2** something returned **3** profit • *He gets a good return on his savings.* **4** a return ticket

Thesaurus

retire *VERB* **1** *She retired two years ago after a long career in teaching.* ► stop working, give up work **2** *Jane retired to her room for the evening.* ► withdraw, adjourn, retreat, decamp **3 retire from** *He intended to retire from Parliament at the next election.* ► resign from, withdraw from, give up, leave, quit

retort *NOUN* *She intended to make a sharp retort.* ► response, answer, reply, riposte, rejoinder, comeback, counter

retort *VERB* *'It's worth a try, surely,' Jenkins retorted.* ► reply, answer, respond, counter, react, snap back

retract *VERB* **1** *The landing gear is retracted on takeoff.* ► pull in, draw in, pull back **2** *She apologized and retracted the accusations.* ► withdraw, take back, abandon, rescind, reverse, revoke, recant, renounce, cancel, disclaim, disown, repeal, repudiate

retreat *NOUN* **1** *Before he could say anything I made a hasty retreat.* ► departure, withdrawal, escape, exit, flight **2** *The family had a holiday retreat in the hills.* ► refuge, resort, haven, hideaway, hideout, sanctuary, shelter

retreat *VERB* **1** *The army retreated in disarray.* ► withdraw, retire, draw back, fall back, move back, back away, depart, go away, leave, (*more informal*) run away, (*more informal*) turn tail AN OPPOSITE IS advance **2** *The tide retreated rapidly.* ► recede, shrink back, go out, ebb, flow back AN OPPOSITE IS come in **3** *The management had to retreat over their modernization plan.* ► back down, climb down, change your mind, backtrack, do a U-turn, withdraw AN OPPOSITE IS persevere

retrieve *VERB* **1** *She went next door to retrieve her ball.* ► get back, fetch back, bring back, recover, regain, rescue, find, reclaim, repossess, track down, salvage, save, trace **2** *It would not be easy to retrieve such an awkward situation.* ► put right, set right, rectify, remedy, sort out, straighten out, put to rights

return *VERB* **1** *They returned to Paris the next day.* ► go back, come back, get back, depart (for), set off (for), set out (for) **2** *I'll see you when I return.* ► come back, get back, arrive back, come home, get home, reappear **3** *She had found a stray cat and wanted to return it to its owner.* ► give back, send back, take back, restore, deliver, reunite (with) **4** *Things will soon return to their normal state.* ► go back, be back, revert **5** *After a while the headaches returned.* ► happen again, recur, reappear **6** *Neil came to return the money I had lent him.* ► give back, repay, refund, reimburse **7** *Jenny was eager to repay the favour.* ► reciprocate, repay, requite, recompense

return *NOUN* **1** *Their return was delayed by bad weather.* ► setting off back, departure **2** *We look forward to your return.* ► arrival, homecoming, reappearance **3** *the country's return to normality after the war* ► reversion, restoration (of), re-establishment (of) **4** *There is every danger of a return of the problem.* ► recurrence, reappearance, repetition **5** *We all want a good return on our investments.* ► income, profit, gain, interest **6** *There was a notice requesting the return of all library books.* ► replacement, bringing back, giving back, restitution

A B C D E F G H I J K L M N O P Q R S T U V W X Y Z

return match NOUN **return matches** a second match played between the same teams

return ticket NOUN **return tickets** a ticket for a journey to a place and back again

reunion NOUN **reunions** **1** reuniting **2** a meeting of people who have not met for some time

reunite VERB **reunites, reuniting, reunited** unite again after being separated

reuse VERB **reuses, reusing, reused** use something again
▷ **reusable** ADJECTIVE

reuse NOUN using something again

reveal VERB **reveals, revealing, revealed** let something be seen or known

revel VERB **revels, revelling, revelled** **1** take great delight in something **2** hold revels
▷ **reveller** NOUN

revelation NOUN **revelations** **1** revealing **2** something revealed, especially something surprising

revels PLURAL NOUN lively and noisy festivities

revenge NOUN harming somebody in return for harm that they have done to you

revenge VERB **revenges, revenging, revenged**
revenge yourself take vengeance

revenue NOUN **revenues** **1** a country's income from taxes etc., used for paying public expenses **2** a company's income

reverberate VERB **reverberates, reverberating, reverberated** resound or re-echo
▷ **reverberation** NOUN

reverence NOUN a feeling of awe and deep or religious respect

Reverend NOUN the title of a member of the clergy • *the Reverend John Smith*
USAGE Do not confuse with **reverent**.

reverent ADJECTIVE feeling or showing reverence
▷ **reverently** ADVERB
USAGE Do not confuse with **Reverend**.

reverie (rev- er- ee) NOUN **reveries** a daydream

reversal NOUN **reversals** **1** reversing or being reversed **2** a piece of bad luck; a reverse

reverse ADJECTIVE opposite in direction, order, or manner etc.

reverse NOUN **reverses** **1** the reverse side, order, manner, etc. **2** a piece of misfortune • *They suffered several reverses.*
in reverse the opposite way round

Thesaurus

reveal VERB **1** *Kenny revealed the truth at last.* ► admit, confess, impart, divulge, tell, disclose, communicate, expose
OPPOSITES ARE hide, conceal **2** *The police were unwilling to reveal the man's whereabouts.* ► disclose, divulge, publicize, broadcast, publish, betray OPPOSITES ARE conceal, keep secret **3** *He removed the cloth to reveal a beautiful bronze statuette.* ► expose, display, exhibit, show, uncover, unveil
AN OPPOSITE IS cover

revenge NOUN **1** *The family is seeking revenge for Nino's killing.* ► vengeance, retribution, retaliation, reprisal, satisfaction **2** *They shot Maria's brother out of revenge.* ► vengefulness, vindictiveness, spite, malice, maliciousness, hatred

revenge VERB *He was determined to revenge his brother's ill-treatment.* ► avenge, take revenge for, retaliate for, have satisfaction for, repay, (*more informal*) get your own back for
be revenged *He would be revenged on them before the year was out.* ► take revenge on, have revenge on, retaliate against, get even with

revenue NOUN *The government is looking to increase its revenue from taxes on tobacco.* ► income, proceeds, receipts, return, yield, gain, profits, takings, money

reverberation NOUN **1** *The hall had a long reverberation period, making it unsuitable for their music.* ► resonance, resounding, echo, echoing, re-echoing, ringing **2** *The scandal had reverberations for years.* ► repercussion, ramification, consequence, result, aftermath

revere VERB *They still revere him as a national hero.* ► respect, honour, esteem, admire, venerate, pay homage to, idolize, exalt, feel reverence for AN OPPOSITE IS despise

reverence NOUN *a deep reverence for their country's heroic past* ► respect, esteem, veneration, awe, homage, admiration, adoration (of), devotion (to), deference (to)
OPPOSITES ARE disrespect, contempt

reverent ADJECTIVE *A reverent silence fell on the room.* ► respectful, reverential, deferential, awestruck, awed, solemn, devout, dutiful, pious OPPOSITES ARE irreverent, disrespectful

reverse NOUN **1** *The story turned out to be the reverse of the truth.* ► opposite, contrary, converse, inverse, antithesis **2** *Last year saw a mixture of successes and reverses.* ► failure, misfortune, setback, defeat, reversal, upset

reverse *VERB* **reverses, reversing, reversed**
1 turn in the opposite direction or order etc.; turn something inside out or upside down **2** move backwards **3** cancel a decision or decree
▷ **reversible** *ADJECTIVE*

reverse gear *NOUN* a gear that allows a vehicle to be driven backwards

review *NOUN* **reviews 1** an inspection or survey **2** a published description and opinion of a book, film, play, etc.

review *VERB* **reviews, reviewing, reviewed**
1 write a review of a book, film, play, etc. **2** reconsider **3** inspect or survey
▷ **reviewer** *NOUN*
USAGE Do not confuse with **revue**.

revise *VERB* **revises, revising, revised 1** go over work that you have already done, especially in preparing for an examination **2** alter or correct something
▷ **revision** *NOUN*

revive *VERB* **revives, reviving, revived** come or bring back to life, strength, activity, or use etc.
▷ **revival** *NOUN*

revolt *VERB* **revolts, revolting, revolted**
1 rebel **2** disgust somebody

revolt *NOUN* **revolts** a rebellion

revolting *ADJECTIVE* disgusting

revolution *NOUN* **revolutions 1** a rebellion that overthrows the government **2** a complete change **3** revolving or rotation; one complete turn of a wheel, engine, etc.
▷ **revolutionary** *ADJECTIVE*

revolve *VERB* **revolves, revolving, revolved**
1 turn in a circle round a central point **2** have something as the most important element
• *Her life revolves around her work*

Thesaurus

reverse *VERB* **1** *We can reverse the order of events if you like.* ► turn round, swap round, change round, transpose, invert, alter **2** *He reversed the car into a tree. The lorry reversed into the opening.* ► back, go *or* drive backwards **3** *The referee refused to reverse his decision.* ► rescind, retract, revoke, undo, countermand, negate, overturn, repeal

review *NOUN* **1** *a review of the year's achievements* ► survey, report, reappraisal, study, analysis, reassessment, look back (at) **2** *On Saturday the paper has book reviews.* ► criticism, critique, notice, appreciation, (*informal*) write-up **3** *The research is described in a scientific review.* ► journal, periodical, magazine, publication **4** *a military review* ► inspection, parade, display, demonstration

review *VERB* **1** *Let's review the situation and decide what to do.* ► consider, survey, assess, evaluate, appraise, weigh up, go over, study, reconsider, re-examine, scrutinize **2** *She reviewed the book on a television arts programme.* ► criticize, discuss, assess, evaluate

revise *VERB* **1** *I am not about to revise my opinion.* ► reconsider, reassess, rethink, change, alter **2** *She spent the weekend revising for her exam.* ► study, read up, cram, (*more informal*) swot, (*more informal*) bone up

revival *NOUN* *a revival of interest in politics* ► resurgence, reawakening, renewal, recovery, restoration, resurrection, upsurge, rebirth, renaissance, return, revitalization
AN OPPOSITE IS decline

revive *VERB* **1** *The man was unconscious but soon revived.* ► regain consciousness, recover, come round, come to, awake **2** *Hot drinks soon revived us.* ► reinvigorate, revitalize, resuscitate, refresh, freshen up, renew, restore, bring back to life

revoke *VERB* *The new regime revoked his passport.* ► cancel, withdraw, rescind, abrogate, invalidate, retract, nullify

revolt *VERB* **1** *The island revolted against Athenian rule.* ► rebel, rise up, defect, mutiny **2** *Their cruelty revolted us.* ► disgust, sicken, shock, outrage, offend, repel, nauseate

revolt *NOUN* *a revolt in the Netherlands* ► rebellion, uprising, revolution, defection, mutiny

revolting *ADJECTIVE* *There was a revolting mess on the floor.* ► disgusting, repulsive, nauseating, offensive, sickening, loathsome, repugnant, unpleasant

revolution *NOUN* **1** *A revolution brought the democrats to power again.* ► rebellion, revolt, rising, uprising, coup, coup d'état, mutiny, civil war **2** *a revolution of the earth* ► rotation, circuit, cycle, orbit, turn **3** *a revolution in information technology* ► transformation, dramatic change, sea change, shift

revolutionary *ADJECTIVE* **1** *Revolutionary forces attacked the city.* ► rebel, rebellious, renegade, seditious, subversive, extremist **2** *a revolutionary idea for traffic control* ► original, innovative, innovatory, radical, novel, new, unconventional, progressive, inventive, advanced, experimental, avant-garde, challenging AN OPPOSITE IS conservative

revolve *VERB* **1** *The ceiling fan began to revolve.* ► turn, go round, rotate, spin, whirl **2** *The moon revolves round the earth.* ► circle, orbit, gyrate **3** **revolve around** *Their lives revolved around their dogs.* ► concentrate on, centre on, focus on *or* be focused on, be absorbed in, be preoccupied with

revolver *NOUN* **revolvers** a pistol with a revolving mechanism that makes it possible to fire it a number of times without reloading

revue *NOUN* **revues** an entertainment consisting of songs, sketches, etc., often about current events
USAGE Do not confuse with **review**.

revulsion *NOUN* a feeling of disgust

reward *NOUN* **rewards** **1** something given in return for something good you have done **2** a sum of money offered for help in catching a criminal or finding lost property

reward *VERB* **rewards, rewarding, rewarded** give a reward to someone

rewarding *ADJECTIVE* giving satisfaction and a feeling of achievement • *a rewarding job*

rewind *VERB* **rewinds, rewinding, rewound** wind a cassette or videotape back to or towards the beginning

rhetorical question *NOUN* **rhetorical questions** a question asked for dramatic effect and not intended to get an answer, e.g. 'Who cares?' (= nobody cares)

rheumatism *NOUN* a disease that causes pain and stiffness in joints and muscles
▷ **rheumatic** *ADJECTIVE* **rheumatoid** *ADJECTIVE* [from Greek *rheuma*, a substance in the body which was once believed to cause rheumatism]

rhino *NOUN* **rhino** or **rhinos** (*informal*) a rhinoceros

rhinoceros *NOUN* **rhinoceros** or **rhinoceroses** a large heavy animal with a horn or two horns on its nose [from Greek *rhinos* = of the nose + *keras* = horn]

rhizome *NOUN* **rhizomes** a thick underground stem which produces roots and new plants

rhododendron *NOUN* **rhododendrons** an evergreen shrub with large trumpet-shaped flowers [from Greek *rhodon* = rose + *dendron* = tree]

rhombus *NOUN* **rhombuses** a shape with four equal sides but no right angles, like the diamond on playing cards

rhubarb *NOUN* a plant with thick reddish stalks that are cooked and eaten as fruit

rhyme *NOUN* **rhymes** **1** a similar sound in the endings of words, e.g. *bat/fat/mat* or *batter/fatter/matter* **2** a poem with rhymes **3** a word that rhymes with another

rhyme *VERB* **rhymes, rhyming, rhymed** **1** form a rhyme **2** have rhymes

rhythm *NOUN* **rhythms** a regular pattern of beats, sounds, or movements
▷ **rhythmic** *ADJECTIVE* **rhythmical** *ADJECTIVE* **rhythmically** *ADVERB*

rib *NOUN* **ribs** **1** each of the curved bones round the chest **2** a curved part that looks like a rib or supports something • *the ribs of an umbrella*
▷ **ribbed** *ADJECTIVE*

ribbon *NOUN* **ribbons** **1** a narrow strip of silk or nylon etc. used for decoration or for tying something **2** a long narrow strip of inked material used in a typewriter etc.

rice *NOUN* a cereal plant grown in flooded fields in hot countries, or its seeds

Thesaurus

revulsion *NOUN* *a feeling of revulsion against the savagery of these acts* ► disgust, repulsion, abhorrence, repugnance, horror, loathing, nausea, contempt (for)

reward *NOUN* **1** *a reward for years of loyal service* ► honour, award, remuneration, prize, bonus, return, decoration, medal **2** *The dog's owners have offered a reward for its safe return.* ► recompense, payment, compensation, inducement, present, bounty
AN OPPOSITE IS punishment

reward *VERB* **1** *All three soldiers were rewarded for their bravery.* ► decorate, honour, recognize AN OPPOSITE IS punish **2** *You will be well rewarded for your work.* ► recompense, remunerate, pay, repay, compensate, give a reward to AN OPPOSITE IS punish

rewarding *ADJECTIVE* *The trip proved to be a rewarding experience.* ► satisfying, worthwhile, pleasing, gratifying, fulfilling, fruitful, valuable OPPOSITES ARE unrewarding, thankless

reword *VERB* *Do you think you should reword the last sentence?* ► rephrase, recast, rewrite, put another way, express differently, revise, redraft, edit

rhetoric *NOUN* **1** *a statesman renowned for his rhetoric* ► oratory, eloquence, power of speech **2** *Ignore the rhetoric and there are some interesting things in these speeches.* ► pomposity, bombast, extravagant language, grandiloquence, verbosity, wordiness, exaggeration, hyperbole

rhetorical *ADJECTIVE* *His manner of speaking tends to be rhetorical.* ► extravagant, grandiloquent, bombastic, oratorical, high-flown, ornate, artificial, pretentious, verbose, wordy, flowery
OPPOSITES ARE plain, direct

rhyme *NOUN* *She tried to remember the words of the rhyme.* ► poem, verse, ditty, ode, song, jingle

rhythm *NOUN* **1** *the rhythm of the poem* ► metre, measure, accent, flow **2** *the heavy rhythm of the rock music upstairs* ► beat, throb, pulse

rhythmic *ADJECTIVE* *the rhythmic beat of the music* ► pulsing, rhythmical, metrical, throbbing, steady, regular, lilting AN OPPOSITE IS irregular

rich *ADJECTIVE* **1** having a lot of money or property; wealthy **2** having a large supply of something • *The country is rich in natural resources.* **3** (said about colour, sound, or smell) pleasantly deep or strong **4** (said about food) containing a lot of fat, butter, eggs, etc. **5** expensive or luxurious
▷ **richness** *NOUN*

richly *ADVERB* **1** in a rich or luxurious way **2** fully or thoroughly • *This award is richly deserved.*

rickety *ADJECTIVE* shaky; likely to break or fall down

rickshaw *NOUN* **rickshaws** a two-wheeled carriage pulled by one or more people, used in the Far East [from Japanese *jin-riki-sha* = person-power-vehicle]

ricochet (rik-osh-ay) *VERB* **ricochets, ricocheting, ricocheted** bounce off something; rebound • *The bullets ricocheted off the wall.*
▷ **ricochet** *NOUN*
[from French, = the skipping of a flat stone on water]

ricotta *NOUN* a kind of soft Italian cheese made from sheep's milk [from Italian]

rid *VERB* **rids, ridding, rid** make a person or place free from something unwanted • *He rid the town of rats.*
get rid of remove something or throw it away

riddle[1] *NOUN* **riddles** a puzzling question, especially as a joke

riddle[2] *VERB* **riddles, riddling, riddled** pierce with many holes • *The car was riddled with bullets.*

ride *VERB* **rides, riding, rode, ridden** **1** sit on a horse, bicycle, etc. and be carried along on it **2** travel in a car, bus, train, etc. **3** float or be supported on something • *The ship rode the waves.*

ride *NOUN* **rides** **1** a journey on a horse, bicycle, etc. or in a vehicle **2** a roundabout etc. that you ride on at a fair or amusement park

ridge *NOUN* **ridges** **1** a long narrow part higher than the rest of something **2** a long narrow range of hills or mountains
▷ **ridged** *ADJECTIVE*

ridicule *VERB* **ridicules, ridiculing, ridiculed** make fun of a person or thing
▷ **ridicule** *NOUN*

ridiculous *ADJECTIVE* so silly that it makes people laugh or despise it
▷ **ridiculously** *ADVERB*

rifle *NOUN* **rifles** a long gun with spiral grooves (called **rifling**) inside the barrel that make the bullet spin and so travel more accurately

Thesaurus

rich *ADJECTIVE* **1** *Rich people pay higher rates of tax.* ► wealthy, affluent, moneyed, well-off, well-to-do, prosperous, opulent, (*more informal*) flush, (*more informal*) loaded
OPPOSITES ARE poor, impoverished **2** *a room of rich furnishings* ► sumptuous, opulent, luxurious, ornate, lavish, costly, fine, gorgeous, elaborate, splendid **3** *acres of rich agricultural land* ► fertile, productive, fruitful, lush
OPPOSITES ARE infertile, unproductive **4** *a rich output of music dramas* ► plentiful, abundant, copious, prolific, profuse, plenteous, ample, teeming **5** *the rich colours of autumn* ► deep, full, strong, intense, vibrant, vivid, warm
AN OPPOSITE IS pale

riches *PLURAL NOUN* *He spoke dreamily of the riches of America.* ► wealth, money, affluence, fortune, treasure, assets, means, property

rickety *ADJECTIVE* *a small wild garden with a rickety greenhouse* ► shaky, unsteady, unstable, wobbly, flimsy, decrepit, ramshackle, dilapidated, broken-down

rid *VERB* *The builders should rid the house of asbestos and all dangerous substances.* ► clear, free, strip, purge, cleanse
get rid of *Scotland had got rid of its usurper.* ► dispose of, expel, remove, eject, evict, throw out, dispense with, (*more informal*) dump

riddle *NOUN* *The authorities want to solve the riddle of the man's identity.* ► enigma, mystery, puzzle, question, problem, conundrum, (*more informal*) poser

riddle *VERB* **1** *The gunman riddled the door with holes.* ► perforate, puncture, pepper, pierce **2** *Her body was riddled with arthritis.* ► overrun, infest, permeate, pervade, cripple

ride *VERB* **1** *I'm learning to ride a horse.* ► control, handle, manage, sit on **2** *She rode through the town on a bicycle.* ► travel, pedal, drive, steer, progress

ride *NOUN* *The house is a short ride from the city centre.* ► journey, trip, drive, run, jaunt, outing, (*more informal*) spin

ridicule *NOUN* *We will be open to ridicule if we get things wrong.* ► derision, mockery, scorn, contempt, taunting, jeering, banter, teasing

ridicule *VERB* *I did not ridicule him as the others did.* ► deride, mock, make fun of, laugh at, jeer at, sneer at, scoff at, humiliate, taunt

ridiculous *ADJECTIVE* *It was ridiculous to feel so worried.* ► absurd, preposterous, ludicrous, senseless, silly, stupid, unreasonable, nonsensical, incredible, irrational, insane, mad

rife *ADJECTIVE* *Terror and torture were rife then.* ► widespread, common, prevalent, general, universal, endemic, abundant

a b c d e f g h i j k l m n o p q r s t u v w x y z

A B C D E F G H I J K L M N O P Q R S T U V W X Y Z

rifle *VERB* **rifles, rifling, rifled** search and rob • *They rifled his desk.*

rift valley *NOUN* **rift valleys** a steep-sided valley formed where the land has sunk

rig[1] *VERB* **rigs, rigging, rigged 1** provide a ship with ropes, spars, sails, etc. **2** set something up quickly or out of makeshift materials • *We managed to rig up a shelter for the night.*
rig out provide with clothes or equipment

rig *NOUN* **rigs 1** a framework supporting the machinery for drilling an oil well **2** the way a ship's masts and sails etc. are arranged **3** (*informal*) an outfit of clothes [probably from a Scandinavian language]

rig[2] *VERB* **rigs, rigging, rigged** arrange the result of an election or contest dishonestly [origin unknown]

rigging *NOUN* the ropes etc. that support a ship's mast and sails

right *ADJECTIVE* **1** on or towards the east if you think of yourself as facing north **2** correct; true • *the right answer* **3** morally good; fair or just • *Is it right to cheat?* **4** (said about political groups) conservative; not in favour of socialist reforms
▷ **right-hand** *ADJECTIVE* **rightly** *ADVERB* **rightness** *NOUN*

right *ADVERB* **1** on or towards the right-hand side • *Turn right here.* **2** straight • *Go right on.* **3** completely • *Turn right round.* **4** exactly • *right in the middle* **5** correctly or appropriately • *Did I do that right?*
right away immediately

right *NOUN* **rights 1** the right-hand side or part etc. **2** what is morally good or fair or just **3** something that people are allowed to do or have • *People over 18 have the right to vote in elections.*

right *VERB* **rights, righting, righted 1** make a thing right or upright • *They righted the boat.* **2** put right • *The fault might right itself.*

right angle *NOUN* an angle of 90°

rightful *ADJECTIVE* deserved or proper • *in her rightful place*
▷ **rightfully** *ADVERB*

right hand *NOUN* **right hands** the hand that most people use more than the left, on the right side of the body

right-handed *ADJECTIVE* using the right hand in preference to the left hand

right of way *NOUN* **rights of way 1** a public path across private land **2** the right of one vehicle to pass or cross a junction etc. before another

rigid *ADJECTIVE* **1** stiff or firm; not bending • *a rigid support* **2** strict • *rigid rules*
▷ **rigidly** *ADVERB* **rigidity** *NOUN*

rigmarole *NOUN* **rigmaroles 1** a long rambling statement **2** a complicated procedure

rigorous *ADJECTIVE* **1** strict or severe **2** careful and thorough
▷ **rigorously** *ADVERB*

Thesaurus

rift *NOUN* **1** *a rift in the ice* ► crack, fault, flaw, fracture, split, break, fissure **2** *a rift between the two leaders* ► breach, division, disagreement, difference of opinion, falling-out, estrangement, schism, alienation

rig *NOUN* **1** *He was wearing the rig of an army captain.* ► uniform, dress, outfit, livery **2** *She was busy setting up the recording rig for the afternoon.* ► equipment, apparatus, machinery, gear, system, kit, tackle

rig *VERB* *They were accused of rigging the election.* ► manipulate, falsify, tamper with, interfere with, gerrymander, influence

right *ADJECTIVE* **1** *What is the right thing to do? Are you sure he's the right person for the job?* ► proper, appropriate, suitable, fitting, ideal OPPOSITES ARE wrong, unsuitable **2** *She gave the right answer.* ► correct, accurate, exact, precise, true, actual, real, apposite, appropriate, apt, factual, genuine, proper OPPOSITES ARE wrong, incorrect **3** *It's not right for them to be treated in this way.* ► fair, just, equitable, lawful, ethical, honourable, moral AN OPPOSITE IS unjust

right *NOUN* **1** *Everyone should have the right to say what they believe.* ► entitlement, prerogative, freedom, liberty, privilege (of saying), facility **2** *We believe we have right on our side.* ► justice, virtue, fairness, goodness, legality, integrity, morality, honesty

right *VERB* *We will do our best to right the situation.* ► remedy, rectify, put right, set right, redress, repair, resolve, correct, sort out, make amends for

rightful *ADJECTIVE* **1** *The car was returned to its rightful owner.* ► lawful, legal, legitimate, genuine, approved, authorized, proper, real, true, valid AN OPPOSITE IS wrongful **2** *He felt he had been denied his rightful place in the company.* ► deserved, due, merited, earned, proper, fitting, just, right

rigid *ADJECTIVE* **1** *It's best to keep your lunch in a rigid container.* ► stiff, hard, firm, inflexible **2** *He had not yet established a rigid routine for his work.* ► fixed, set, firm, definite, unvarying, hard-and-fast **3** *She had a reputation as a rigid disciplinarian.* ► strict, stern, severe, harsh, uncompromising, unyielding AN OPPOSITE IS flexible

rigorous *ADJECTIVE* **1** *a rigorous attention to detail* ► meticulous, thorough, careful, scrupulous, painstaking, conscientious, diligent, fastidious,

rim *NOUN* **rims** the outer edge of a cup, wheel, or other round object

rind *NOUN* the tough skin on bacon, cheese, or fruit

ring[1] *NOUN* **rings** **1** a circle **2** a thin circular piece of metal worn on a finger **3** the space where a circus performs **4** a square area in which a boxing match or wrestling match takes place

ring *VERB* **rings, ringing, ringed** put a ring round something; encircle

ring[2] *VERB* **rings, ringing, rang, rung** **1** cause a bell to sound **2** make a loud clear sound like that of a bell **3** be filled with sound • *The hall rang with cheers* **4** telephone • *Please ring me tomorrow.*
▷ **ringer** *NOUN*

ring *NOUN* **rings** the act or sound of ringing
give someone a ring (*informal*) telephone someone

ringleader *NOUN* **ringleaders** a person who leads others in rebellion, mischief, crime, etc.

ringmaster *NOUN* **ringmasters** the person in charge of a performance in a circus ring

ring road *NOUN* **ring roads** a road that runs around the edge of a town so that traffic does not have to go through the centre

rink *NOUN* **rinks** a place made for skating

rinse *VERB* **rinses, rinsing, rinsed** **1** wash something lightly **2** wash in clean water to remove soap

rinse *NOUN* **rinses** **1** rinsing **2** a liquid for colouring the hair

riot *NOUN* **riots** wild or violent behaviour by a crowd of people
run riot behave or spread in an unruly or uncontrolled way

riot *VERB* **riots, rioting, rioted** take part in a riot

riotous *ADJECTIVE* **1** disorderly or unruly **2** boisterous • *riotous laughter*

RIP *ABBREVIATION* may he or she (or they) rest in peace

rip *VERB* **rips, ripping, ripped** **1** tear roughly **2** rush
rip off (*informal*) swindle or charge too much

rip *NOUN* a torn place

ripe *ADJECTIVE* **riper, ripest** **1** ready to be harvested or eaten **2** ready and suitable • *The time is ripe for revolution.*
▷ **ripeness** *NOUN*
a ripe old age a great age

ripen *VERB* **ripens, ripening, ripened** make or become ripe

rip-off *NOUN* **rip-offs** (*informal*) a swindle or excessive charge

ripple *NOUN* **ripples** a small wave or series of waves

ripple *VERB* **ripples, rippling, rippled** form ripples

Thesaurus

stringent OPPOSITES ARE lax, careless **2** *a rigorous climate* ► harsh, severe, inclement, extreme, inhospitable, unfriendly, unpleasant AN OPPOSITE IS mild

rile *VERB* (*informal*) *His companions seemed determined to rile him.* ► irritate, annoy, anger, enrage, exasperate, incense, upset, peeve, vex, (*more informal*) needle, (*more informal*) bug, (*more informal*) rub up the wrong way

rim *NOUN* *They stared over the rim of the crater.* ► brim, edge, lip, border, brink, verge, circumference

rind *NOUN* *the rind of a lemon* ► peel, skin, husk, crust, outer layer

ring *NOUN* **1** *A ring of fire would protect her.* ► circle, loop, round, circuit, halo **2** *a spy ring* ► network, organization, syndicate, association, gang, group, cell, cartel **3** *a ring of spectators* ► circle, band, group, crowd, throng **4** *a circus ring* ► arena, enclosure RELATED ADJECTIVE annular

ring *VERB* **1** *Riot police ringed the area.* ► surround, circle, encircle, confine, enclose, encompass, form a ring round **2** *Church bells rang all morning.* ► peal, chime, toll, clang, resound, jangle, reverberate **3** *I'll ring you tomorrow evening.* ► phone, call, telephone, ring up, (*informal*) give a buzz

rinse *VERB* *Campers were rinsing their plates in the stream.* ► wash, wash out, swill, bathe, clean, sluice

riot *NOUN* *The authorities were reluctant to make arrests for fear of sparking a riot.* ► uproar, insurrection, uprising, rising, tumult, commotion, brawl, street fight, fracas

riot *VERB* *The crowd rioted and pulled down the gates.* ► rampage, run riot, create a riot, run amok, go berserk, revolt, rise up, mutiny, rebel

riotous *ADJECTIVE* *a riotous party* ► wild, lively, boisterous, roisterous, loud, noisy, uproarious, rollicking OPPOSITES ARE orderly, restrained

rip *VERB* *She read the note and ripped it into little pieces. The travellers ripped a way through the foliage.* ► tear, slash, cut, rend, gash

ripe *ADJECTIVE* **1** *a ripe melon* ► mature, ripened, tender, juicy OPPOSITES ARE unripe, green **2** *an area ripe for development* ► ready, suitable, fit AN OPPOSITE IS unsuitable

ripen *VERB* *The apples need time to ripen.* ► become ripe, mature, develop, mellow

A B C D E F G H I J K L M N O P Q R S T U V W X Y Z

rise *VERB* **rises, rising, rose, risen 1** go upwards **2** increase • *Prices are expected to rise.* **3** get up from lying, sitting, or kneeling **4** get out of bed **5** rebel • *They rose in revolt against the tyrant.* **6** (said about bread or cake etc.) swell up by the action of yeast **7** (said about a river) begin its course **8** (said about the wind) begin to blow more strongly

rise *NOUN* **rises 1** the action of rising; an upward movement **2** an increase in amount etc. or in wages **3** an upward slope
give rise to cause

rising *NOUN* **risings** a revolt

risk *NOUN* **risks** a chance of danger or loss

risk *VERB* **risks, risking, risked 1** take the chance of damaging or losing something • *They were risking their lives.* **2** accept the risk of something unpleasant happening • *He risks injury.*

risky *ADJECTIVE* **riskier, riskiest** full of risk

rissole *NOUN* **rissoles** a fried cake of minced meat or fish

ritual *NOUN* **rituals** the series of actions used in a religious or other ceremony
▷ **ritual** *ADJECTIVE* **ritually** *ADVERB*

rival *NOUN* **rivals** a person or thing that competes with another or tries to do the same thing
▷ **rivalry** *NOUN*
[from Latin *rivalis* = someone using the same stream (from *rivus* = stream)]

river *NOUN* **rivers** a large stream of water flowing in a natural channel

rivet *NOUN* **rivets** a strong nail or bolt for holding pieces of metal together. The end opposite the head is flattened to form another head when it is in place

rivet *VERB* **rivets, riveting, riveted 1** fasten with rivets **2** hold firmly • *He stood riveted to the spot.* **3** fascinate • *The concert was riveting.*
▷ **riveter** *NOUN*

road *NOUN* **roads 1** a level way with a hard surface made for traffic to travel on **2** a way or course • *the road to success* [from Old English]

roadblock *NOUN* **roadblocks** a barrier across a road, set up by the police or army to stop and check vehicles

road rage *NOUN* violent or aggressive behaviour by a driver towards other drivers

roadworthy *ADJECTIVE* safe to be used on roads

roam *VERB* **roams, roaming, roamed** wander
▷ **roam** *NOUN*

roar *NOUN* **roars** a loud deep sound like that made by a lion

Thesaurus

rise *VERB* **1** *The little plane rose into the air.* ► ascend, go up, fly up, climb OPPOSITES ARE fall, descend **2** *The castle walls rose above us.* ► tower, soar, loom, reach up **3** *Incomes have risen by an average 3 percent.* ► increase, grow, go up, get higher, escalate **4** *She rose from her chair.* ► stand up, get up, jump up, leap up

rise *NOUN* **1** *We walked up the rise to the castle.* ► slope, incline, elevation, ascent, hill, ramp, bank **2** *another rise in interest rates* ► increase, jump, leap, upturn

risk *NOUN* **1** *She faced the risk of being stopped by the police.* ► chance, likelihood, possibility, danger **2** *Travelling at such a high speed involved risk.* ► hazard, peril, danger, speculation, uncertainty, gamble

risk *VERB* **1** *He didn't want to risk leaving her alone.* ► chance, dare, venture **2** *She risked everything to meet him again.* ► endanger, jeopardize, put at risk, put in peril, chance, imperil, hazard

risky *ADJECTIVE* **1** *Any project involving rockets is always risky.* ► dangerous, hazardous, unsafe, perilous, (*more informal*) dodgy AN OPPOSITE IS safe **2** *Farming is a risky business.* ► precarious, uncertain, chancy, touch-and-go AN OPPOSITE IS secure

ritual *NOUN* **1** *a religious ritual* ► ceremony, rite, ceremonial, observance, service, liturgy **2** *The Sunday outing had become something of a ritual.* ► custom, tradition, habit, formality

rival *NOUN* *Leo was his main rival for the job.* ► competitor, adversary, challenger, opponent, contender, contestant

rival *ADJECTIVE* *A rival supermarket has opened.* ► competing, competitive, opposing

rival *VERB* *Few countries rival Greece for its beauty.* ► compete with, contend with, compare with, equal, match, be as good as, emulate, vie with

rivalry *NOUN* *There was growing rivalry between the two teams.* ► competitiveness, competition, contention, opposition, conflict, antagonism AN OPPOSITE IS cooperation

river *NOUN* *a trip down the river* ► stream, waterway, watercourse, brook, rivulet, creek

road *NOUN* *a busy road* ► roadway, route, way, highway, motorway, street, avenue, boulevard

roadworthy *ADJECTIVE* *a roadworthy vehicle* ► safe, usable

roam *VERB* *People like to roam over the hills.* ► wander, rove, ramble, stroll, amble, walk, meander, travel, stray, range

roar *NOUN* *the roars of the crowd* ► yell, shout, clamour, bellow, howl

roar *VERB* **roars, roaring, roared 1** make a roar **2** laugh loudly
do a roaring trade do very good business

roast *VERB* **roasts, roasting, roasted 1** cook meat etc. in an oven or by exposing it to heat **2** make or be very hot

roast *ADJECTIVE* roasted • *roast beef*

roast *NOUN* **roasts 1** meat for roasting **2** roast meat [from early French]

rob *VERB* **robs, robbing, robbed** take or steal from somebody • *He robbed me of my watch.*
▷ **robber** *NOUN* **robbery** *NOUN*

robe *NOUN* **robes** a long loose garment

robin *NOUN* **robins** a small brown bird with a red breast [from early French, = Robert]

robot *NOUN* **robots 1** a machine that looks or acts like a person **2** a machine operated by remote control
▷ **robotic** *ADJECTIVE*
[from Czech *robota* = forced labour]

robust *ADJECTIVE* strong and vigorous
▷ **robustly** *ADVERB* **robustness** *NOUN*

rock[1] *NOUN* **rocks 1** a large stone or boulder **2** the hard part of the earth's crust, under the soil **3** a hard sweet usually shaped like a stick and sold at the seaside

rock[2] *VERB* **rocks, rocking, rocked 1** move gently backwards and forwards while supported on something **2** shake violently • *The earthquake rocked the city.*

rock *NOUN* **1** a rocking movement **2** rock music

rock and roll or **rock 'n' roll** *NOUN* a kind of popular dance music with a strong beat, originating in the 1950s

rock-bottom *ADJECTIVE* at the lowest level
• *rock-bottom prices*

rockery *NOUN* **rockeries** a mound or bank in a garden, where plants are made to grow between large rocks

rocket *NOUN* **rockets 1** a firework that shoots high into the air **2** a structure that flies by expelling burning gases, used to send up a missile or a spacecraft

rocket *VERB* **rockets, rocketing, rocketed** move quickly upwards or away

rocking horse *NOUN* **rocking horses** a model of a horse that can be rocked by a child sitting on it

rock music *NOUN* popular music with a heavy beat

rocky[1] *ADJECTIVE* **rockier, rockiest 1** like rock **2** full of rocks

rocky[2] *ADJECTIVE* **rockier, rockiest** unsteady
▷ **rockiness** *NOUN*

rod *NOUN* **rods 1** a long thin stick or bar **2** a stick with a line attached for fishing

rodent *NOUN* **rodents** an animal that has large front teeth for gnawing things. Rats, mice, and squirrels are rodents

Thesaurus

roar *VERB* **1** *Bill roared at them to stop.* ► bellow, yell, shout, bawl, clamour, shriek **2** *A motorbike roared past.* ► speed, zoom, whizz, flash **3** *He had the audience roaring.* ► guffaw, howl, hoot, (*more informal*) split your sides, (*more informal*) kill yourself laughing

rob *VERB* **1** *The gang had robbed banks all over the south-east.* ► burgle, hold up, steal from, break into, raid, loot, rifle **2** *She was attacked and robbed on her way home that evening.* ► mug, steal from, hold up **3** *They thought they had been robbed of their victory.* ► deprive, cheat, defraud, swindle

robber *NOUN* *Robbers attacked the travellers on the road north.* ► thief, brigand, bandit, raider, highwayman, marauder USAGE You can also use *burglar* and *housebreaker* for robbers who steal from buildings, and *mugger* for robbers who attack people in the street.

robbery *NOUN* *a wave of robberies and other crimes* ► burglary, theft, thieving, stealing, housebreaking, shoplifting, pilfering, hold-up, mugging, (*more informal*) stick-up

robot *NOUN* ► automaton, computerized machine, automated machine, android

robust *ADJECTIVE* **1** *a man with a robust physique* ► strong, vigorous, hardy, muscular, powerful, rugged, athletic, brawny, healthy, sound **2** *The tools will need to be very robust.* ► sturdy, durable, strong, tough, serviceable
AN OPPOSITE IS fragile

rock *NOUN* **1** *a castle high up on a rock* ► cliff, crag, outcrop **2** *Rocks were strewn across the road.* ► boulder, stone

rock *VERB* **1** *The woman rocked gently in her chair.* ► sway, swing, move gently **2** *The ship rocked in the storm.* ► toss, lurch, sway, pitch, plunge, roll **3** *News of the disaster rocked the nation.* ► stun, shake, stagger, astound, astonish, startle, dumbfound

rocket *VERB* *Prices have rocketed under this government.* ► shoot up, soar, escalate, spiral, increase rapidly, (*more informal*) go through the roof

rocky *ADJECTIVE* **1** *a rocky hillside* ► stony, rock-strewn, craggy, shingly, pebbly, rugged **2** *The table is rocky.* ► unsteady, shaky, wobbly, rickety, tottery **3** *The marriage had become decidedly rocky.* ► precarious, difficult, problematic, unstable

rod *NOUN* **1** *an iron rod* ► bar, pole, baton, staff, shaft, sceptre **2** *He was beaten with a rod.* ► cane, switch

rodeo (roh- di- oh) *NOUN* **rodeos** a display of cowboys' skill in riding, controlling horses, etc.

roe[1] *NOUN* a mass of eggs or reproductive cells in a fish's body

roe[2] *NOUN* **roes** or **roe** a kind of small deer of Europe and Asia. The male is called a **roebuck**

rogue *NOUN* **rogues 1** a dishonest person **2** a mischievous person
▷ **roguery** *NOUN*

role *NOUN* **roles 1** a performer's part in a play or film etc. **2** someone's or something's purpose or function • *the role of computers in education*

role model *NOUN* **role models** a person admired by others as an example of how to behave

roll *VERB* **rolls, rolling, rolled 1** move along by turning over and over, like a ball or wheel **2** form something into the shape of a cylinder or ball **3** flatten something by rolling a rounded object over it **4** rock from side to side **5** pass steadily • *The years rolled on.* **6** make a long vibrating sound • *The thunder rolled.*

roll *NOUN* **rolls 1** a cylinder made by rolling something up **2** a small individual portion of bread baked in a rounded shape **3** an official list of names **4** a long vibrating sound • *a drum roll*

roll-call *NOUN* **roll-calls** the calling of a list of names to check that everyone is present

roller *NOUN* **rollers 1** a cylinder for rolling over things, or on which something is wound **2** a long swelling sea wave

Rollerblade *NOUN* **Rollerblades** (*trade mark*) a boot like an ice-skating boot, with a line of wheels in place of the skate, for rolling smoothly on hard ground
▷ **rollerblading** *NOUN*

roller coaster *NOUN* **roller coasters** a type of railway used for amusement at fairgrounds etc. with a series of alternate steep descents and ascents

roller skate *NOUN* **roller skates** a framework with wheels, fitted under a shoe so that the wearer can roll smoothly over the ground
▷ **roller-skating** *NOUN*

rolling pin *NOUN* a heavy cylinder for rolling over pastry to flatten it

ROM *ABBREVIATION* (in computing) read-only memory, a type of memory with contents that can be searched or copied but not changed

Roman *ADJECTIVE* to do with ancient or modern Rome or its people
▷ **Roman** *NOUN*

Roman alphabet *NOUN* the alphabet used by the ancient Romans, in which most European languages are written

Roman Catholic *ADJECTIVE* belonging to or to do with the Christian Church that has the Pope as its leader

Roman Catholic *NOUN* **Roman Catholics** a member of this Church

romance (ro- manss) *NOUN* **romances 1** tender feelings, experiences, and qualities connected with love **2** a love story **3** a love affair **4** an imaginative story about the adventures of heroes • *a romance of King Arthur's court*

Roman numerals *PLURAL NOUN* letters that represent numbers (I = 1, V = 5, X = 10, etc.), used by the ancient Romans COMPARE **arabic numerals**

romantic *ADJECTIVE* **1** to do with love or romance **2** sentimental or idealistic; not realistic or practical
▷ **romantically** *ADVERB*

Thesaurus

rogue *NOUN In the story, everyone is either a fool or a rogue.* ► villain, scoundrel, rascal, good-for-nothing, reprobate, crook

role *NOUN* **1** *The director took a small role in the film.* ► part, character, portrayal **2** *He spoke in his role of government adviser.* ► capacity, function, position, office, post, job

roll *NOUN* **1** *a roll of film* ► reel, spool, cylinder, drum, scroll **2** *an electoral roll* ► register, list, record, index, catalogue, schedule, inventory

roll *VERB* **1** *The can rolled into the gutter. The huge wheels began to roll.* ► rotate, revolve, turn, spin, whirl, gyrate **2** *She rolled the paper into a ball.* ► wind, fold, coil, twist, curl, screw **3** *The ship began to roll.* ► rock, sway, lurch, pitch, toss, reel **4** *He was in the kitchen, rolling pastry.* ► smooth, flatten, level, even out **5** *Thunder rolled in the distance.* ► rumble, boom, resound, reverberate, thunder
roll up (*informal*) • *He rolled up with some friends just as we were leaving.* ► arrive, appear, come, show your face, (*informal*) turn up, (*informal*) show up

romance *NOUN* **1** *a historical romance* ► love story, romantic novel, fantasy **2** *the romance of travel* ► glamour, excitement, adventure, fascination, mystique **3** *Romance was in the air.* ► love, passion, ardour **4** *They were having a wild romance.* ► love affair, relationship, attachment

romantic *ADJECTIVE* **1** *He was handsome and romantic.* ► amorous, passionate, loving, tender-hearted, affectionate **2** *romantic stories set in the Far East* ► imaginary, fanciful, sentimental, (*more informal*) soppy **3** *a pretty village in a romantic landscape* ► idyllic, picturesque, fairy-tale **4** *Their notions about life were highly romantic.* ► idealistic, idealized, starry-eyed, unrealistic, visionary, utopian, fanciful, dreamy

romp *VERB* **romps**, **romping**, **romped** play in a lively way
▷ **romp** *NOUN*

roof *NOUN* **roofs** **1** the part that covers the top of a building, shelter, or vehicle **2** the top inside surface of something • *the roof of the mouth*

rook[1] *NOUN* **rooks** a black crow that nests in large groups

rook *VERB* **rooks**, **rooking**, **rooked** (*informal*) swindle; charge people an unnecessarily high price

rook[2] *NOUN* **rooks** a chess piece shaped like a castle

room *NOUN* **rooms** **1** a part of a building with its own walls and ceiling **2** enough space • *Is there room for me?*
▷ **roomful** *NOUN*

roost *VERB* **roosts**, **roosting**, **roosted** (said about birds) perch or settle for sleep

roost *NOUN* **roosts** a place where birds roost

root[1] *NOUN* **roots** **1** that part of a plant that grows under the ground and absorbs water and nourishment from the soil **2** a source or basis • *The love of money is the root of all evil* **3** a number in relation to the number it produces when multiplied by itself • *9 is the square root of 81 (9 x 9 = 81)*
take root **1** grow roots **2** become established

root *VERB* **roots**, **rooting**, **rooted** **1** take root; cause something to take root **2** fix firmly • *Fear rooted us to the spot*
root out get rid of something

root[2] *VERB* **roots**, **rooting**, **rooted** **1** (said about an animal) turn up ground in search of food **2** rummage; find something by doing this • *I've managed to root out some facts and figures.*

rope *NOUN* **ropes** a strong thick cord made of twisted strands of fibre
show someone the ropes show him or her how to do something

rope *VERB* **ropes**, **roping**, **roped** fasten with a rope
rope in persuade a person to take part in something

rose[1] *NOUN* **roses** **1** a shrub that has showy flowers, often with thorny stems **2** a deep pink colour **3** a nozzle with many holes, e.g. on a watering can or hosepipe

rose[2] *past tense* of **rise**

Rosh Hashanah or **Rosh Hashana** *NOUN* the Jewish New Year

roster *NOUN* **rosters** a list showing people's turns to be on duty etc.

rosy *ADJECTIVE* **rosier**, **rosiest** **1** deep pink **2** hopeful or cheerful • *a rosy future*
▷ **rosiness** *NOUN*

rot *VERB* **rots**, **rotting**, **rotted** go soft or bad and become useless; decay

rot *NOUN* **1** rotting or decay **2** (*informal*) nonsense

rota (roh-ta) *NOUN* **rotas** a list of people to do things or of things to be done in turn

rotate *VERB* **rotates**, **rotating**, **rotated** **1** go round like a wheel; revolve **2** arrange or happen in a series; take turns at doing something
▷ **rotation** *NOUN* **rotary** *ADJECTIVE* **rotatory** *ADJECTIVE*

rote *NOUN*
by rote from memory or by routine, without full understanding of the meaning • *We used to learn French songs by rote.*

rotor *NOUN* **rotors** a rotating part of a machine or helicopter

Thesaurus

romp *VERB* *The children romped in the garden.* ► cavort, caper, leap about, run about, skip about, bound about, frisk, frolic, gambol

room *NOUN* **1** *There wasn't enough room for a bed.* ► space, capacity, volume **2** *We need more room to live our own lives.* ► freedom, latitude, leeway, allowance, elbow room **3** *There's always room for improvement.* ► scope, capacity, margin, opportunity

roomy *ADJECTIVE* *The apartment was bright and roomy.* ► spacious, capacious, large, sizeable, extensive, commodious, voluminous
OPPOSITES ARE cramped, poky

root *NOUN* **1** *The plant had long stringy roots.* ► tuber, radicle, rhizome, rootlet **2** *Money is the root of the problem.* ► source, origin, cause, basis, starting point, seed, germ

root *VERB* **root out** *The magistrates were determined to root out corruption.* ► discover, unearth, dig out, ferret out, remove, eliminate, extirpate

rope *NOUN* *A rope attached the boat to the quayside.* ► cable, cord, line, halyard, hawser, lanyard

rot *NOUN* **1** *The surveyor found traces of rot in the roof timbers.* ► decay, decomposition, mould, mildew, dry rot, wet rot **2** (*informal*) *You're talking rot* ► nonsense, rubbish, gibberish, drivel, codswallop, claptrap

rot *VERB* *The floorboards had begun to rot.* ► decay, decompose, perish, become rotten, degenerate, deteriorate, crumble, disintegrate

rotate *VERB* *The arms of the windmill were rotating.* ► revolve, turn round, go round, move round, spin, gyrate, twirl, swivel, roll

A B C D E F G H I J K L M N O P Q R S T U V W X Y Z

rotten *ADJECTIVE* **1** rotted • *rotten apples* **2** (*informal*) very bad or unpleasant • *rotten weather*
▷ **rottenness** *NOUN*

rouble (roo- bul) *NOUN* **roubles** the unit of money in Russia

rouge (roozh) *NOUN* a reddish cosmetic for colouring the cheeks
▷ **rouge** *VERB*

rough *ADJECTIVE* **rougher, roughest** **1** not smooth; uneven **2** not gentle or careful; violent • *a rough push* **3** not exact • *a rough guess* **4** (said about weather or the sea) wild and stormy
▷ **roughly** *ADVERB* **roughness** *NOUN*

rough *VERB* **roughs, roughing, roughed**
rough it do without ordinary comforts
rough out draw or plan something roughly
rough up (*slang*) treat a person violently

roughen *VERB* **roughens, roughening, roughened** make or become rough

round *ADJECTIVE* **1** shaped like a circle or ball or cylinder; curved **2** full or complete • *a round dozen* **3** returning to the start • *a round trip*
▷ **roundness** *NOUN*
in round figures approximately, without giving exact units

round *ADVERB* **1** in a circle or curve; round something • *Go round to the back of the house.* **2** in every direction or to every person • *Hand the cakes round.* **3** in a new direction • *Turn your chair round.* **4** to someone's house or office etc. • *Go round after dinner.*
come round become conscious again
round about **1** near by **2** approximately

round *PREPOSITION* **1** on all sides of • *Put a fence round the field.* **2** in a curve or circle at an even distance from • *The earth moves round the sun.* **3** to all parts of • *Show them round the house.* **4** on the further side of • *The shop is round the corner.*

round *NOUN* **rounds** **1** a series of visits made by a doctor, postman, etc. **2** one section or stage in a competition • *Winners go on to the next round.* **3** a shot or volley of shots from a gun; ammunition for this **4** a whole slice of bread; a sandwich made with two slices of bread **5** a song in which people sing the same words but start at different times **6** a set of drinks bought for all the members of a group

round *VERB* **rounds, rounding, rounded** **1** make or become round **2** travel round • *The car rounded the corner.*
round off finish something
round up gather people or animals together

Thesaurus

rotten *ADJECTIVE* **1** *Some of the wood looked rotten.* ► decayed, decaying, decomposed, crumbling, disintegrating **2** *the stench of rotten meat* ► mouldy, mouldering, putrid, decayed, decaying, foul, tainted AN OPPOSITE IS fresh **3** (*informal*) *They had a rotten time.* ► unpleasant, disagreeable, terrible, bad OPPOSITES ARE pleasant, good **4** (*informal*) *The builders had done a rotten job. He would make a rotten teacher.* ► poor, inferior, inadequate, bad, low-grade, (*informal*) crummy, (*informal*) ropy, (*informal*) lousy OPPOSITES ARE fine, good

rough *ADJECTIVE* **1** *She picked her way over the rough ground.* ► bumpy, rugged, uneven, broken, irregular, rocky, stony, coarse, craggy AN OPPOSITE IS even **2** *rough skin* ► dry, chapped, coarse, hairy, bristly, shaggy, unshaven AN OPPOSITE IS smooth **3** *rough treatment; It was pretty rough on your mother.* ► harsh, severe, hard, tough, stern **4** *a rough sea; the ability to withstand rough weather* ► choppy, turbulent, agitated, stormy, tempestuous, violent, wild AN OPPOSITE IS calm **5** *a rough voice* ► harsh, grating, gruff, rasping, hoarse, husky AN OPPOSITE IS soft **6** *She doesn't like rough kids.* ► rowdy, boisterous, disorderly, unrestrained AN OPPOSITE IS polite **7** *The tower is of rough workmanship.* ► amateurish, careless, clumsy, crude, hasty, imperfect, inept, (*informal*) rough and ready, unfinished, unpolished, unskilful AN OPPOSITE IS skilful **8** *This gives you a rough idea of what we mean.* ► approximate, imprecise, inexact, estimated, hazy, crude, vague AN OPPOSITE IS exact **9** *He went home. He was feeling rough.* ► ill, unwell, sick, poorly, out of sorts, queasy, off colour, (*more informal*) lousy, (*more informal*) grotty OPPOSITES ARE well, fit

roughly *ADVERB* **1** *There were roughly equal numbers of men and women.* ► about, around, approximately, nearly, close to **2** *Geoffrey pulled his arm roughly away.* ► violently, forcefully, forcibly, abruptly

round *ADJECTIVE* **1** *a round window* ► spherical, circular, bulbous, curved, cylindrical, globular **2** *a man with a short round figure* ► rounded, plump, chubby, rotund, ample, full, fat

round *NOUN* **1** *the most exciting tie of the second round* ► stage, game, series, sequence, contest **2** *an endless round of radio and television interviews* ► cycle, series, succession, sequence

round *VERB* *A large van rounded the corner.* ► travel round, skirt, turn
round off *We rounded the evening off with some drinks.* ► end, finish, complete, conclude, cap, top
round on *Jo rounded on her. 'You're supposed to be looking after this place.'* ► turn on, snap at, attack, weigh into, let fly at

roundabout *NOUN* **roundabouts 1** a road junction where traffic has to pass round a circular structure in the road **2** a circular revolving ride at a fair

roundabout *ADJECTIVE* indirect; not using the shortest way of going or of saying or doing something • *I heard the news in a roundabout way.*

rounders *NOUN* a game in which players try to hit a ball and run round a circuit

round-the-clock *ADJECTIVE* lasting or happening all day and all night

round trip *NOUN* **round trips** a trip to one or more places and back to where you started

round-up *NOUN* **round-ups 1** a gathering-up of cattle or people • *a police round-up of suspects* **2** a summary • *a round-up of the news*

rouse *VERB* **rouses, rousing, roused 1** make or become awake **2** cause to become active or excited

rousing *ADJECTIVE* loud or exciting • *three rousing cheers*

rout *VERB* **routs, routing, routed** defeat and chase away an enemy
▷ **rout** *NOUN*

route (root) *NOUN* **routes** the way taken to get to a place

routine (roo- teen) *NOUN* **routines** a regular way of doing things
▷ **routinely** *ADVERB*

rove *VERB* **roves, roving, roved** roam or wander
▷ **rover** *NOUN*

row[1] (rhymes with *go*) *NOUN* **rows** a line of people or things

row[2] (rhymes with *go*) *VERB* **rows, rowing, rowed** make a boat move by using oars
▷ **rower** *NOUN* **rowing boat** *NOUN*

row[3] (rhymes with *cow*) *NOUN* **rows 1** a loud noise **2** a quarrel

rowdy *ADJECTIVE* **rowdier, rowdiest** noisy and disorderly
▷ **rowdiness** *NOUN*

royal *ADJECTIVE* to do with a king or queen
▷ **royally** *ADVERB*
[via early French from Latin *regalis*]

royalty *NOUN* **1** being royal **2** a royal person or people • *in the presence of royalty* **3** (**royalties**) a payment made to an author or composer etc. for each copy of a work sold or for each performance

Thesaurus

round up *His dog, Nell, rounded up 300 sheep.* ► herd, drive together, muster, marshal, assemble

roundabout *ADJECTIVE* *He reached the town square by a roundabout route.* ► indirect, circuitous, devious, winding, rambling, meandering, tortuous, twisting, long
AN OPPOSITE IS direct

roundabout *NOUN* **1** *Let's play on the roundabout.* ► merry-go-round, carousel **2** *Turn right at the next roundabout.* ► traffic circle, rotary

rouse *VERB* **1** *Next morning he was roused by the clanging of church bells.* ► arouse, awaken, wake up **2** *His words roused feelings of sympathy in her.* ► arouse, provoke, stir up, trigger, spark off, kindle, cause **3** *He can be violent when he's roused.* ► anger, annoy, provoke, incite, inflame, incense, work up

rousing *ADJECTIVE* *a rousing speech* ► stirring, inspiring, moving, stimulating, exciting

rout *VERB* *They went on to rout the Royalist forces.* ► crush, defeat, overwhelm, trounce, thrash, put to flight, drive off, (*more informal*) hammer

route *NOUN* *This route is direct but gets tedious in the later stages.* ► way, road, course, direction, path, passage, itinerary, journey

routine *NOUN* **1** *Their evening routine never varied.* ► procedure, pattern, way, method, course of action, practice, system, custom, drill, habit **2** *I've been practising a new dance routine.* ► act, performance, programme, number, turn

routine *ADJECTIVE* *It is now a fairly routine operation done under local anaesthetic.* ► standard, normal, ordinary, everyday, run-of-the-mill

row *NOUN* (rhymes with *crow*) *a row of small plants* ► line, string, chain, series, sequence, cordon, file

row (rhymes with *cow*) **1** *She and Paul had had a row.* ► quarrel, argument, squabble, fight, scrap, altercation, disagreement, dispute, (*more informal*) slanging match
AN OPPOSITE IS reconciliation **2** *The crowd was making a dreadful row.* ► noise, racket, rumpus, tumult, din, disturbance, uproar, commotion

row *VERB* (rhymes with *cow*) *They had been shouting and rowing all evening.* ► quarrel, argue, wrangle, bicker, squabble, fight, scrap

rowdy *ADJECTIVE* *a bunch of rowdy men* ► unruly, disorderly, riotous, noisy, badly behaved, rough, wild, disruptive, boisterous
OPPOSITES ARE quiet, peaceful

royal *ADJECTIVE* **1** *the royal family* ► regal, imperial, kingly, princely, queenly, majestic, stately **2** *We received a royal welcome* ► magnificent, splendid, excellent, fine

RSVP *ABBREVIATION* répondez s'il vous plaît [French, = please reply]

rub *VERB* **rubs, rubbing, rubbed** move something backwards and forwards while pressing it on something else
▷ **rub** *NOUN*
rub out remove something by rubbing

rubber *NOUN* **rubbers 1** a strong elastic substance used for making tyres, balls, hoses, etc. **2** a piece of rubber for rubbing out pencil or ink marks
▷ **rubbery** *ADJECTIVE*

rubbish *NOUN* **1** things that are worthless or not wanted **2** nonsense

rubble *NOUN* broken pieces of brick or stone

rubella (roo- bel- la) *NOUN* an infectious disease which causes a red rash, and which can damage a baby if the mother catches it early in pregnancy [from Latin *rubellus* = reddish]

ruby *NOUN* **rubies** a red jewel [from Latin *rubeus* = red]

rucksack *NOUN* **rucksacks** a bag on straps for carrying on the back [from German *Rücken* = back + *Sack* = bag, sack]

rudder *NOUN* **rudders** a hinged upright piece at the back of a ship or aircraft, used for steering

ruddy *ADJECTIVE* **ruddier, ruddiest** red and healthy-looking • *a ruddy complexion*

rude *ADJECTIVE* **ruder, rudest 1** impolite **2** indecent or improper **3** roughly made; crude • *a rude shelter* **4** vigorous and hearty • *in rude health*
▷ **rudely** *ADVERB* **rudeness** *NOUN*

rudimentary *ADJECTIVE* **1** to do with rudiments; elementary **2** not fully developed • *Penguins have rudimentary wings.*

rudiments (rood- i- ments) *PLURAL NOUN* the basic principles of a subject • *She taught me the rudiments of chemistry*

ruff *NOUN* **ruffs 1** a starched pleated frill worn round the neck in the 16th century **2** a collar-like ring of feathers or fur round a bird's or animal's neck

ruffian *NOUN* **ruffians** a violent lawless person
▷ **ruffianly** *ADJECTIVE*

ruffle *VERB* **ruffles, ruffling, ruffled 1** disturb the smoothness of a thing **2** upset or annoy someone

ruffle *NOUN* **ruffles** a gathered ornamental frill

rug *NOUN* **rugs 1** a thick mat for the floor **2** a piece of thick fabric used as a blanket

rugby or **rugby football** *NOUN* a kind of football game using an oval ball that players may carry or kick [named after Rugby School in Warwickshire, where it was first played]

Thesaurus

rub *VERB* **1** *John rubbed the back of his leg.*
► stroke, knead, massage, caress, smooth
2 *She rubbed lotion on the children's backs.*
► apply (to), smear, smooth, spread, put on
3 *His new shoes were rubbing dreadfully.*
► chafe, pinch, abrade, graze, scrape, hurt
4 *Stella rubbed the table with polish.* ► polish, buff, shine, wipe
rub out *Someone had rubbed out his name.*
► erase, remove, delete, efface, expunge, blot out

rubbish *NOUN* **1** *Household rubbish is collected on Wednesdays.* ► refuse, waste, garbage, debris, junk, leavings, litter, trash **2** *They are talking rubbish.* ► nonsense, balderdash, gibberish, claptrap, drivel, gobbledegook, (*more informal*) rot, (*more informal*) twaddle

rubble *NOUN* *Often he had to clear away piles of rubble before he could continue.* ► debris, ruins, remains, wreckage, fragments

rude *NOUN* **1** *He was sometimes rude, but always honest.* ► impolite, discourteous, disrespectful, impertinent, impudent, insolent, ill-mannered, ill-bred, uncivil, offensive, abusive OPPOSITES ARE polite, civil **2** *a rude joke*
► vulgar, coarse, dirty, smutty, filthy
AN OPPOSITE IS clean

rudeness *NOUN* *'You,' she called, with uncharacteristic rudeness.* ► discourtesy, disrespect, impoliteness, bad manners, incivility, impertinence, impudence, insolence, churlishness, cheek

rudimentary *ADJECTIVE* **1** *You'll need a rudimentary knowledge of first aid.* ► simple, basic, elementary, primitive, fundamental, crude AN OPPOSITE IS advanced **2** *The pelycosaurs tended to develop rudimentary teeth.*
► incomplete, embryonic, primitive **3** *a rudimentary language course* ► introductory, basic, elementary, preliminary, initial

ruffian *NOUN* *A group of ruffians assaulted a university student on his way home.* ► thug, hoodlum, hooligan, lout, rogue, scoundrel, brute, bully, villain, mugger, (*more informal*) tough, (*more informal*) yob

ruffle *VERB* **1** *A light wind ruffled the leaves of the trees.* ► stir, agitate, ripple, disturb **2** *Isobel took off her scarf and ruffled her hair.* ► rumple, tousle, run your fingers through, dishevel, mess up AN OPPOSITE IS smooth **3** *Don't let their stupid remarks ruffle you.* ► annoy, upset, unsettle, disconcert, fluster, irritate, vex, worry, (*more informal*) nettle, (*more informal*) rattle AN OPPOSITE IS calm

rug *NOUN* **1** *The children sat on a rug on the floor.*
► mat, runner, matting **2** *She was wrapped in a rug to keep out the cold.* ► blanket, coverlet, throw

rugged *ADJECTIVE* **1** having an uneven surface or outline; craggy **2** sturdy

rugger *NOUN* rugby football

ruin *NOUN* **ruins 1** severe damage or destruction to something **2** a building that has fallen down

ruin *VERB* **ruins, ruining, ruined** damage or destroy a thing so severely that it is useless
▷ **ruination** *NOUN*

ruinous *ADJECTIVE* **1** causing ruin **2** in ruins; ruined

rule *NOUN* **rules 1** something that people have to obey **2** ruling; governing • *under French rule* **3** a carpenter's ruler
as a rule usually; more often than not

rule *VERB* **rules, ruling, ruled 1** govern or reign **2** make a decision • *The referee ruled that it was a foul.* **3** draw a straight line with a ruler or other straight edge [from early French]

ruler *NOUN* **rulers 1** a person who governs **2** a strip of wood, metal, or plastic with straight edges, used for measuring and drawing straight lines

ruling *NOUN* **rulings** a judgement

rum *NOUN* a strong alcoholic drink made from sugar or molasses

rumble *VERB* **rumbles, rumbling, rumbled** make a deep heavy continuous sound like thunder
▷ **rumble** *NOUN*

ruminant *ADJECTIVE* ruminating

ruminant *NOUN* **ruminants** an animal that chews the cud (see **cud**)

ruminate *VERB* **ruminates, ruminating, ruminated 1** chew the cud **2** meditate or ponder
▷ **rumination** *NOUN* **ruminative** *ADJECTIVE*

rummage *VERB* **rummages, rummaging, rummaged** turn things over or move them about while looking for something
▷ **rummage** *NOUN*

rumour *NOUN* **rumours** information that spreads to a lot of people but may not be true

rumour *VERB*
be rumoured be spread as a rumour
[from Latin *rumor* = noise]

Thesaurus

rugged *ADJECTIVE* **1** *a Spanish village nestling in rugged hills* ► rough, uneven, rocky, craggy, stark, bumpy, jagged, irregular
OPPOSITES ARE smooth, gentle **2** *The only softness about his rugged face was in his lips.* ► strong, sturdy, rough, tough, robust, hardy, burly, husky, muscular, weather-beaten

ruin *NOUN* **1** *They now face financial ruin.* ► bankruptcy, insolvency, failure, breakdown, collapse, downfall, ruination, undoing **2** *It was the ruin of all their hopes.* ► destruction, disintegration, devastation, overthrow, failure, undoing, ruination **3** *Crackpot Hall is a sad ruin in a beautiful location.* ► remnant, shell, group of remains **4 ruins** *They explored the ruins of the castle.* ► remains, rubble, debris, wreckage

ruin *VERB* **1** *Once again the rain has ruined what promised to be a good contest.* ► spoil, wreck, destroy, shatter, blight, wreak havoc on, torpedo, (*more informal*) mess up
OPPOSITES ARE save, rescue **2** *He would be ruined if he had to pay.* ► bankrupt, impoverish, financially cripple

ruined *ADJECTIVE* *the gateway to a ruined fortress* ► derelict, dilapidated, ramshackle, ruined, tumbledown, crumbling

ruinous *ADJECTIVE* **1** *activity that has a ruinous effect on the environment* ► disastrous, catastrophic, devastating, calamitous, destructive, cataclysmic, dire, fatal **2** *They found the building in a ruinous condition.* ► ruined, dilapidated, derelict

rule *NOUN* **1** *the rules governing procedures in case of fire* ► regulation, law, code, convention, precept, principle, routine, practice, custom **2** *British rule had ended in 1947.* ► jurisdiction, control, administration, sovereignty, mastery, command, domination, dominion, authority, government, supremacy, sway **3** *The normal rule is to apply for tickets by letter.* ► procedure, practice, protocol, form, custom, convention

rule *VERB* **1** *How could a city-state like Rome rule an empire?* ► govern, administer, manage, run, control, direct, command, dominate, lead, reign over **2** *The king's successor ruled for less than a year.* ► reign, be ruler, be in power, be monarch **3** *The judge ruled that the defendant should be awarded the costs of the case.* ► decree, order, direct, pronounce, resolve, decide, determine, adjudicate, determine, find, judge
rule out *We cannot rule out suicide as a cause of death.* ► exclude, discount, reject, eliminate, dismiss, preclude, disregard

ruler *NOUN* *a much-respected ruler* ► leader, sovereign, overlord, governor, dynast, monarch, president (of a republic), head of state

ruling *NOUN* *A ruling came from the president himself.* ► decision, pronouncement, resolution, decree, judgement, adjudication, order, command, instruction

rumble *VERB* *Thunder rumbled in the distance.* ► boom, reverberate, resound, echo

rumour *NOUN* **1** *A rumour had started that the company would close.* ► report, story, piece of gossip, whisper **2** *The suggestion was only rumour.* ► gossip, hearsay, talk, tittle-tattle

a b c d e f g h i j k l m n o p q r s t u v w x y z

rump *NOUN* **rumps** the hind part of an animal

rumple *VERB* **rumples, rumpling, rumpled** crumple; make a thing untidy

rump steak *NOUN* **rump steaks** a piece of meat from the rump of a cow

rumpus *NOUN* **rumpuses** (*informal*) an uproar; an angry protest

run *VERB* **runs, running, ran, run 1** move with quick steps so that both or all feet leave the ground at each stride **2** go or travel; flow • *Tears ran down his cheeks.* **3** produce a flow of liquid • *Run some water into it.* **4** work or function • *The engine was running smoothly.* **5** manage or organize • *She runs a corner shop.* **6** compete in a contest • *He ran for President.* **7** extend • *A fence runs round the estate.* **8** go or take in a vehicle • *I'll run you to the station.*
run a risk take a chance
run away leave a place secretly or quickly
run down 1 run over **2** stop gradually; decline **3** (*informal*) say unkind or unfair things about someone
run into 1 collide with **2** happen to meet
run out 1 have used up your stock of something **2** knock over the wicket of a running batsman
run over knock down or crush with a moving vehicle
run through examine or rehearse

run *NOUN* **runs 1** the action of running; a time spent running • *I went for a run* **2** a point scored in cricket or baseball **3** a continuous series of events, etc. • *She had a run of good luck.* **4** an enclosure for animals • *a chicken run* **5** a series of damaged stitches in a pair of tights or stockings **6** a track • *a ski run*
on the run running away, especially from the police
[from Old English]

runaway *NOUN* **runaways** someone who has run away

runaway *ADJECTIVE* **1** having run away or out of control **2** won easily • *a runaway victory*

run-down *ADJECTIVE* **1** tired and in bad health **2** in bad condition; dilapidated

rung[1] *NOUN* **rungs** one of the crossbars on a ladder

rung[2] *past participle of* **ring**[2]

runner *NOUN* **runners 1** a person or animal that runs, especially in a race **2** a stem that grows away from a plant and roots itself **3** a groove, rod, or roller for a thing to move on; each of the long strips under a sledge **4** a long narrow strip of carpet or covering

runner bean *NOUN* **runner beans** a kind of climbing bean with long green pods which are eaten

Thesaurus

rumpus *NOUN* *A terrible rumpus was going on outside.* ► commotion, uproar, racket, tumult, hullabaloo, hubbub, fracas, furore, upheaval, agitation, excitement

run *VERB* **1** *We ran across the field.* ► sprint, race, jog, tear, dash, rush, hasten, speed, streak, bolt, scamper, scoot **2** *The buses don't run on Sundays.* ► operate, function, go, provide a service **3** *The car has been running erratically.* ► function, perform, work, behave **4** *His car was stolen because he had left the engine running.* ► operate, tick over, go **5** *Water ran down the wall.* ► stream, trickle, flow, flood, pour, spill, gush, cascade, dribble, leak **6** *She was running a small business in Leeds.* ► manage, be in charge of, direct, control, administer, conduct, supervise, govern, look after, maintain, rule **7** *He could no longer afford to run a car.* ► maintain, keep, own, use, drive **8** *She ran me back to my house.* ► drive, take, bring, ferry, give a lift to **9** *It is important to run exhaustive tests.* ► carry out, perform, complete, do, fulfil **10** *A sharp pain ran up her arm.* ► pass, move, shoot, travel, go **11** *The road runs north.* ► extend, reach, stretch, go, continue
run across *I ran across your sister in Paris.* ► meet, encounter, come across, run into, chance on
run after *Jill ran after him with his keys.* ► chase, pursue, follow
run away *He threw down his shield and ran away.* ► escape, flee, bolt, abscond, (*more informal*) make off
run down 1 *A dog ran into the road and he ran it down.* ► run over, knock over, hit, struck **2** (*informal*) *She didn't want to run him down in public.* ► criticize, denigrate, disparage, belittle, find fault with
run into *Did you run into any of your friends?* ► meet, encounter, come across, run across, chance on
run out *My subscription runs out in December.* ► expire, terminate, end, come to an end, cease, dry up

run *NOUN* **1** *a run across the park* ► jog, dash, sprint, spurt, trot, gallop, canter, race **2** *a run in the car* ► drive, ride, trip, excursion, journey, (*more informal*) spin **3** *a run of bad luck* ► sequence, stretch, series, chain, course **4** *a chicken run* ► enclosure, compound, coop, pen

runaway *NOUN* *a safe house for young runaways* ► fugitive, escapee, refugee, absconder

runner *NOUN* **1** *There are seven runners in the next race.* ► competitor, entrant, participant, athlete **2** *The commanding officer sent a runner to headquarters.* ► courier, messenger

runner-up *NOUN* **runners-up** someone who comes second in a competition

running *present participle* of **run**
in the running competing and with a chance of winning

running *ADJECTIVE* continuous or consecutive; without an interval • *It rained for four days running.*

runny *ADJECTIVE* **runnier, runniest 1** flowing like liquid • *runny honey* **2** producing a flow of liquid • *a runny nose*

runway *NOUN* **runways** a long hard surface on which aircraft take off and land

rural *ADJECTIVE* to do with or belonging to the countryside

ruse *NOUN* **ruses** a deception or trick

rush[1] *VERB* **rushes, rushing, rushed 1** move or do something quickly **2** make someone hurry **3** attack or capture by dashing forward suddenly

rush *NOUN* **rushes 1** a hurry **2** a sudden movement towards something **3** a sudden great demand for something

rush[2] *NOUN* **rushes** a plant with a thin stem that grows in marshy places

rush hour *NOUN* **rush hours** the time when traffic is busiest

rusk *NOUN* **rusks** a kind of hard, dry biscuit, especially for feeding babies

rust *NOUN* **1** a red or brown substance that forms on iron or steel exposed to damp and corrodes it **2** a reddish-brown colour

rust *VERB* **rusts, rusting, rusted** make or become rusty

rustic *ADJECTIVE* **1** rural **2** made of rough timber or branches • *a rustic bridge*

rustle *VERB* **rustles, rustling, rustled 1** make a sound like paper being crumpled **2** (*American*) steal horses or cattle • *cattle rustling*
▷ **rustle** *NOUN* **rustler** *NOUN*
rustle up (*informal*) produce • *rustle up a meal*

rusty *ADJECTIVE* **rustier, rustiest 1** coated with rust **2** weakened by lack of use or practice • *My French is a bit rusty.*
▷ **rustiness** *NOUN*

rut *NOUN* **ruts 1** a deep track made by wheels in soft ground **2** a settled and usually dull way of life • *We are getting into a rut.*
▷ **rutted** *ADJECTIVE*

ruthless *ADJECTIVE* pitiless, merciless, or cruel
▷ **ruthlessly** *ADVERB* **ruthlessness** *NOUN*
[from Middle English *ruth* = pity]

rye *NOUN* a cereal used to make bread, biscuits, etc.

Thesaurus

running *NOUN* **1** *A private company has taken over the running of the school.* ► administration, management, direction, controlling, supervision **2** *These measures will ensure the smooth running of the organization.* ► operation, working, functioning

runny *ADJECTIVE* *a runny mixture of egg and milk* ► watery, thin, fluid, liquid, free-flowing OPPOSITES ARE solid, viscous

rural *ADJECTIVE* *The majority lived in rural communities outside London.* ► country, rustic, pastoral, agricultural, agrarian, countrified AN OPPOSITE IS urban

rush *VERB* *She rushed into the garden.* ► hurry, hasten, dash, run, sprint, race, tear, streak, bolt OPPOSITES ARE dawdle, saunter

rush *NOUN* **1** *a frantic rush to put out the flames* ► hurry, haste, dash, race, scramble **2** *It stopped the rush of water for a time.* ► flood, gush, spate, cataract **3** *There was a sudden rush for the doors.* ► charge, stampede, surge (towards)

rust *VERB* *a special coating to prevent the iron from rusting* ► corrode, become rusty, oxidize, crumble away, decay, rot

rustic *ADJECTIVE* **1** *a house in rustic surroundings* ► rural, country, pastoral, agricultural, agrarian, countrified AN OPPOSITE IS urban **2** *She sat down on a rustic wooden seat.* ► plain, simple, crude, rough, artless, unsophisticated

rusty *ADJECTIVE* **1** *Nothing causes more blisters than using a rusty trowel.* ► corroded, rusted, oxidized, rotten, tarnished, discoloured **2** *My French is a little rusty.* ► unpractised, neglected, below par, deficient, weak, unused, (*more informal*) creaky

ruthless 1 *a ruthless dictator* ► merciless, pitiless, brutal, cruel, callous, unfeeling, heartless, vicious, violent, ferocious, fierce AN OPPOSITE IS compassionate **2** *He carried out his instructions with ruthless efficiency.* ► relentless, unrelenting, inexorable, unremitting, intense, implacable

a b c d e f g h i j k l m n o p q r s t u v w x y z

Ss

S. *ABBREVIATION* **1** south **2** southern

sabbath *NOUN* **sabbaths** a weekly day for rest and prayer, Saturday for Jews, Sunday for Christians [from Hebrew *shabat* = rest]

sabotage *NOUN* deliberate damage or disruption to hinder an enemy, employer, etc.
▷ **sabotage** *VERB* **saboteur** *NOUN*
[from French *saboter* = make a noise with *sabots* (= wooden clogs)]

saccharin (sak- er- in) *NOUN* a very sweet substance used as a substitute for sugar

sack[1] *NOUN* **sacks** a large bag made of strong material
▷ **sacking** *NOUN*
the sack (*informal*) dismissal from a job • *He got the sack.*

sack *VERB* **sacks, sacking, sacked** (*informal*) dismiss someone from a job [via Old English and Latin from Greek *sakkos*]

sack[2] *VERB* **sacks, sacking, sacked** (*old use*) plunder a captured town in a violent destructive way
▷ **sack** *NOUN*
[from French *mettre à sac* = put (booty) in a sack]

sacrament *NOUN* **sacraments** an important Christian religious ceremony such as baptism or Holy Communion

sacred *ADJECTIVE* holy; to do with God or a god

sacrifice *NOUN* **sacrifices 1** an offering to a god of a killed animal or other special thing **2** giving up a thing you value, so that something good may happen **3** a thing sacrificed
▷ **sacrificial** *ADJECTIVE*

sacrifice *VERB* **sacrifices, sacrificing, sacrificed** offer something or give it up as a sacrifice

sacrilege (sak- ril- ij) *NOUN* disrespect or damage to something people regard as sacred
▷ **sacrilegious** *ADJECTIVE*

sad *ADJECTIVE* **sadder, saddest** unhappy; showing or causing sorrow
▷ **sadly** *ADVERB* **sadness** *NOUN*
[from Old English]

Thesaurus

sabotage *NOUN* *The crash was probably caused by engine failure and not sabotage.* ► wilful damage, deliberate destruction, vandalism, wrecking, disruption, treachery

sabotage *VERB* **1** *A gang had sabotaged the cash machines in the shopping mall.* ► wreck, deliberately damage, destroy, disable, put out of action, cripple, vandalize **2** *Are you telling me he deliberately set out to sabotage your work?* ► wreck, ruin, spoil, thwart, undermine, disrupt

sack *NOUN* **1** *The flour was in an open sack on the floor.* ► bag, pack, pouch **2** *When she complained she promptly got the sack.* ► notice, dismissal, discharge, your cards, (*more informal*) the boot

sack *VERB* **1** *Unbelievably, he sacked his son-in-law and replaced him with Trevor.* ► dismiss, give notice to, get rid of, lay someone off, let someone go, (*more informal*) fire, (*more informal*) kick out **2** *Edward I had sacked the town in 1296.* ► destroy, raid, loot, plunder, pillage, ravage

sacred *ADJECTIVE* **1** *The new pope was enthroned in the most sacred place in the basilica.* ► holy, blessed, consecrated, sanctified, hallowed, dedicated, venerated
AN OPPOSITE IS unconsecrated **2** *The recital mixed operatic arias with traditional sacred melodies.* ► religious, spiritual, devotional, ecclesiastical AN OPPOSITE IS secular

sacrifice *NOUN* **1** *The festival involved a sacrifice of a ram and seven lambs.* ► offering, ritual slaughter, votive offering, oblation **2** *The building was rebuilt with some sacrifice of its earlier features.* ► loss, abandonment, discarding, rejection, surrender, giving up, yielding, renunciation, renouncing

sacrifice *VERB* **1** *They have sacrificed their principles and lost their good name. a memorial to the bomber crews who sacrificed their lives in the war* ► give up, forfeit, relinquish, surrender, forgo, go without **2** *The goat had been sacrificed at the shrine.* ► offer up, kill, slaughter, immolate

sacrilege *NOUN* *Wearing armour in a holy place was sacrilege.* ► blasphemy, desecration, impiety, profanity, irreverence, disrespect, ungodliness OPPOSITES ARE piety, respect

sad *ADJECTIVE* **1** *Everyone was sad to be leaving. He looked at her sad face.* ► unhappy, sorrowful, dejected, downcast, despondent, downhearted, depressed, miserable, glum, in low spirits **2** *I told my brother and sister the sad news. The story is sadder than we realized.* ► distressing, upsetting, depressing, grave, tragic, unfortunate, regrettable, serious, heart-rending **3** *This sad state of affairs does not have to continue.* ► sorry, wretched, unfortunate, regrettable, shameful, disgraceful **4** (*informal*) *They live in a sad little house.* ► pathetic, pitiful, inadequate

A B C D E F G H I J K L M N O P Q R S T U V W X Y Z

sadden *VERB* **saddens, saddening, saddened** make a person sad

saddle *NOUN* **saddles** **1** a seat for putting on the back of a horse or other animal **2** the seat of a bicycle **3** a ridge of high land between two peaks

saddle *VERB* **saddles, saddling, saddled** put a saddle on a horse etc..
saddle someone with burden someone with a task or problem

sadist (say- dist) *NOUN* **sadists** a person who enjoys hurting or humiliating other people
▷ **sadism** *NOUN* **sadistic** *ADJECTIVE*
[named after an 18th-century French novelist, the Marquis de Sade, noted for the cruelties in his stories]

safari *NOUN* **safaris** an expedition to see or hunt wild animals [from Arabic *safar* = a journey]

safari park *NOUN* **safari parks** a park where wild animals are kept in large enclosures to be seen by visitors

safe *ADJECTIVE* **1** not in danger **2** not dangerous • *a safe speed*
▷ **safely** *ADVERB* **safeness** *NOUN* **safety** *NOUN*

safe *NOUN* **safes** a strong cupboard or box in which valuables can be locked safely

safeguard *NOUN* **safeguards** a protection

safe sex *NOUN* sexual activity using a condom or other precautions to prevent the spread of infection

safety pin *NOUN* **safety pins** a U-shaped pin with a clip fastening over the point

sag *VERB* **sags, sagging, sagged** hang or go down in the middle from its own weight or because something heavy is pressing on it
▷ **sag** *NOUN*

saga (sah- ga) *NOUN* **sagas** a long story with many episodes or adventures

sage[1] *NOUN* a kind of herb used in cooking and formerly used in medicine

sage[2] *ADJECTIVE* wise
▷ **sagely** *ADVERB*

sage *NOUN* **sages** a wise and respected person

sago *NOUN* a starchy white food used to make puddings

said *past tense of* **say**

sail *NOUN* **sails** **1** a large piece of strong cloth attached to a mast etc. to catch the wind and make a ship or boat move **2** a short voyage **3** an arm of a windmill
set sail start on a voyage in a ship

sail *VERB* **sails, sailing, sailed** **1** travel in a ship or boat **2** start a voyage • *We sail at noon.* **3** control a ship or boat **4** move quickly and smoothly
▷ **sailing ship** *NOUN*

sailboard *NOUN* **sailboards** a flat board with a mast and sail, used in windsurfing

sailor *NOUN* **sailors** a person who sails; a member of a ship's crew or of a navy

Thesaurus

sadden *VERB* *That brief reminder of her husband saddened her.* ► dispirit, distress, upset, grieve, dishearten AN OPPOSITE IS cheer up

sadistic *ADJECTIVE* *a sadistic killer* ► callous, cruel, brutal, brutish, pitiless, cold-blooded, ruthless, merciless, vile

sadness *NOUN* *She could not hide her sadness.* ► unhappiness, sorrow, dejection, misery, melancholy, low spirits, depression, regret

safe *ADJECTIVE* **1** *The building was safe from attack.* ► secure, protected, guarded, invulnerable, impregnable **2** *The missing children were all safe.* ► unharmed, unhurt, uninjured, out of danger **3** *She is a safe driver. Better safe than sorry.* ► prudent, cautious, circumspect, attentive **4** *He's a safe person to be with.* ► trustworthy, reliable, responsible, sensible, level-headed, upright **5** *a medicine that is safe for young children* ► harmless, innocuous, proven

safeguard *NOUN* *Burglar alarms are an additional safeguard.* ► protection, defence, guard, shield, precaution, security, assurance

safeguard *VERB* *The charter safeguards your human rights.* ► protect, preserve, defend, secure, look after, shield, guard

safety *NOUN* **1** *The safety of passengers is paramount.* ► security, protection, welfare, well-being AN OPPOSITE IS danger **2** *The refugees looked for a place of safety.* ► refuge, shelter, sanctuary, protection

safety-belt *NOUN* ► safety-harness, seat-belt

sag *VERB* **1** *The ceiling sags in the middle.* ► hang down, sink, slump, dip, droop, fall **2** *His spirits were beginning to sag.* ► falter, fade, weaken, wilt, shrivel

saga *NOUN* *They longed to tell the saga of their day's adventures.* ► tale, story, catalogue, rigmarole

sail *VERB* **1** *John loves sailing his boat.* ► pilot, navigate, skipper, steer, captain **2** *We had a holiday sailing in the Mediterranean.* ► cruise, voyage, boat, yacht, go sailing, navigate **3** *The ferry sails at midday.* ► put to sea, set sail, leave harbour, weigh anchor

sailor *NOUN* *He did not make a very good sailor.* ► seaman, seafarer, mariner, boatman, yachtsman *or* yachtswoman

saint *NOUN* **saints** a holy or very good person
▷ **saintly** *ADJECTIVE* **saintliness** *NOUN*

sake *NOUN*
for the sake of so as to help or please a person, get a thing, etc.
for someone's sake so as to help or please them • *Don't go to any trouble for my sake.*

salad *NOUN* **salads** a mixture of vegetables eaten raw or cold

salary *NOUN* **salaries** a regular wage, usually for a year's work, paid in monthly instalments
▷ **salaried** *ADJECTIVE*

sale *NOUN* **sales** **1** selling **2** a time when things are sold at reduced prices
for sale or **on sale** available to be bought

salient (say- lee- ent) *ADJECTIVE* most important or noticeable • *the salient features of the plan*

saliva *NOUN* the natural liquid in a person's or animal's mouth
▷ **salivary** *ADJECTIVE*

sallow *ADJECTIVE* (said about the skin) slightly yellow
▷ **sallowness** *NOUN*

salmon (sam- on) *NOUN* **salmon** a large edible fish with pink flesh

salon *NOUN* **salons** **1** a large elegant room **2** a room or shop where a hairdresser etc. receives customers

saloon *NOUN* **saloons** **1** a car with a hard roof and a separate boot **2** a comfortable room in a pub or bar

salt *NOUN* **salts** **1** sodium chloride, the white substance that gives sea water its taste and is used for flavouring food **2** a chemical compound of a metal and an acid
▷ **salty** *ADJECTIVE*

salt *VERB* **salts, salting, salted** flavour or preserve food with salt

salt cellar *NOUN* **salt cellars** a small dish or perforated pot holding salt for use at meals

salute *VERB* **salutes, saluting, saluted** **1** raise your right hand to your forehead as a sign of respect **2** greet **3** say that you respect or admire something • *We salute this achievement.*

salute *NOUN* **salutes** **1** the act of saluting **2** the firing of guns as a sign of greeting or respect

salvage *VERB* **salvages, salvaging, salvaged** save or rescue something such as a damaged ship's cargo so that it can be used again
▷ **salvage** *NOUN*

salvation *NOUN* **1** saving from loss or damage etc. **2** (in Christian teaching) saving the soul from sin and its consequences

same *ADJECTIVE* **1** of one kind, exactly alike or equal **2** not changing; not different
▷ **sameness** *NOUN*

samosa *NOUN* **samosas** a triangular, thin pastry case filled with spicy meat or vegetables, fried and eaten as a snack

sample *NOUN* **samples** a small amount that shows what something is like; a specimen

sample *VERB* **samples, sampling, sampled** **1** take a sample of something **2** try part of something

sanatorium *NOUN* **sanatoriums** or **sanatoria** a hospital for treating long-term diseases or people recovering from diseases

sanctimonious *ADJECTIVE* making a show of being virtuous or pious

Thesaurus

saintly *ADJECTIVE* *a saintly priest* ► holy, godly, pious, devout, spiritual, God-fearing, blessed, virtuous AN OPPOSITE IS unholy

sake *NOUN* **for the sake of** *He did it for the sake of his family.* ► for the good of, in the interests of, for the benefit of, for the advantage of, on behalf of

sale *NOUN* *laws to control the sale of drugs* ► selling, marketing, trading (in), dealing (in), traffic (in), disposal AN OPPOSITE IS purchase

salty *ADJECTIVE* *a thick salty paste used for flavouring* ► salt, salted, piquant, saline, briny, tangy, spicy OPPOSITES ARE fresh, bland

salute *VERB* **1** *You call me 'sir' but you don't salute me, OK?* ► greet, acknowledge, hail, address, welcome **2** *I salute them for having the courage to admit their mistakes.* ► pay tribute to, acknowledge, celebrate, recognize, honour

salute *NOUN* *He gave a quick salute.* ► greeting, acknowledgement, salutation, wave

same *ADJECTIVE* **1** *Is that the same person?* ► actual, identical, selfsame **2 the same** *The witnesses' versions were all essentially the same.* ► similar, identical, alike, comparable, equivalent, matching, indistinguishable OPPOSITES ARE different, unalike **3 the same** *The timetable tends to remain the same from year to year.* ► unchanged, constant, unvarying, identical **4** *Let's celebrate again on the same day next year.* ► corresponding, analogous

sample *NOUN* **1** *Finalists will submit samples of their photographic work.* ► specimen, example, representative piece, selection, demonstration, illustration, indication, instance, model, pattern **2** *The survey was based on a sample of a thousand voters.* ► cross section, sampling

sample *VERB* *Guests will sample some of the great wines of the world with their dinner.* ► try out, try, test, check out, inspect, taste

sanctimonious *ADJECTIVE* *What happened to all the sanctimonious talk about putting his family*

sanction *NOUN* **sanctions 1** action taken against a nation that is considered to have broken an international law etc. • *Sanctions against that country include refusing to trade with it.* **2** a penalty for disobeying a law **3** permission or authorization

sanction *VERB* **sanctions, sanctioning, sanctioned** permit or authorize

sanctity *NOUN* being sacred; holiness

sanctuary *NOUN* **sanctuaries 1** a safe place; a refuge **2** an area where wildlife is protected • *a bird sanctuary* **3** a sacred place; the part of a church where the altar stands

sand *NOUN* the tiny particles that cover the ground in deserts, seashores, etc.

sand *VERB* **sands, sanding, sanded** smooth or polish with sandpaper or some other rough material
▷ **sander** *NOUN*

sandal *NOUN* **sandals** a lightweight shoe with straps over the foot
▷ **sandalled** *ADJECTIVE*

sandpaper *NOUN* strong paper coated with sand or a similar substance, rubbed on rough surfaces to make them smooth

sandwich *NOUN* **sandwiches** two or more slices of bread with jam, meat, or cheese etc. between them

sandwich *VERB* **sandwiches, sandwiching, sandwiched** put a thing between two other things [named after the Earl of Sandwich (1718-92), who invented them so that he could eat while gambling]

sandy *ADJECTIVE* **1** like sand **2** covered with sand **3** yellowish-red • *sandy hair*
▷ **sandiness** *NOUN*

sane *ADJECTIVE* **1** having a healthy mind; not mad **2** sensible
▷ **sanely** *ADVERB* **sanity** *NOUN*

sanitary *ADJECTIVE* **1** free from germs and dirt; hygienic **2** to do with sanitation

sanitary towel *NOUN* **sanitary towels** an absorbent pad worn by women during menstruation

sanitation *NOUN* arrangements for drainage and the disposal of sewage

sanity *NOUN* being sane

Sanskrit *NOUN* an ancient language of India

sap *NOUN* the liquid inside a plant, carrying food to all its parts

sap *VERB* **saps, sapping, sapped** take away a person's strength gradually

sapling *NOUN* **saplings** a young tree

sapphire *NOUN* **sapphires** a bright blue jewel

sarcastic *ADJECTIVE* saying amusing or contemptuous things that hurt someone's feelings
▷ **sarcastically** *ADVERB* **sarcasm** *NOUN*

sardine *NOUN* **sardines** a small sea fish, usually sold in tins, packed tightly in oil

sari *NOUN* **saris** a length of cloth worn wrapped round the body as a dress, especially by Indian women and girls [from Hindi]

sash *NOUN* **sashes** a strip of cloth worn round the waist or over one shoulder [from Arabic *shash* = turban]

satchel *NOUN* **satchels** a bag worn on the shoulder or the back, especially for carrying books to and from school [from Latin *saccellus* = little sack]

satellite *NOUN* **satellites 1** a spacecraft put in orbit round a planet to collect information or transmit communications signals **2** a moon moving in an orbit round a planet **3** a country

Thesaurus

first? ► self-righteous, holier-than-thou, smug, superior, moralizing, priggish, mealy-mouthed, pious, unctuous
AN OPPOSITE IS **modest**

sanctions *PLURAL NOUN* *The UN will vote on whether to lift the sanctions.* ► restrictions, penalties, embargo, boycott, prohibition

sanctuary *NOUN* *an escape route provided by sanctuary north of the border* ► protection, refuge, asylum, safety, security, shelter

sand *NOUN* *The children played on the sand for hours.* ► beach, sands, shore, seaside, strand

sane *ADJECTIVE* *Humour was what helped keep them sane.* ► rational, lucid, normal, balanced, reasonable, sensible, (*informal*) compos mentis, level-headed, sound, stable
AN OPPOSITE IS **mad**

sanity *NOUN* *He was not sure enough of his own sanity to take these risks.* ► reason, senses, rationality, balance of mind, mental health, lucidity

sap *VERB* *a fever that sapped his strength and depressed his mind* ► drain, exhaust, deplete, erode, bleed, wear away

sarcasm *NOUN* *She spoke with more than a hint of sarcasm in her voice.* ► ridicule, derision, mockery, irony, scorn, scoffing

sarcastic *ADJECTIVE* *If bosses are sarcastic, try not to react.* ► sardonic, ironic, derisive, scornful, scathing, scoffing, sneering, withering

sash *NOUN* *She wore a girlish blue sash round her waist.* ► girdle, belt, band, waistband, cummerbund

that is under the influence of a more powerful country

satellite dish *NOUN* **satellite dishes** a bowl-shaped aerial for receiving broadcasting signals transmitted by satellite

satin *NOUN* a silky material that is shiny on one side
▷ **satiny** *ADJECTIVE*
[from an Arabic word = 'from Tsinkiang', a town in China]

satire *NOUN* **satires** **1** using humour or exaggeration to criticize people in authority **2** a play or sketch that does this
▷ **satirical** *ADJECTIVE* **satirically** *ADVERB* **satirist** *NOUN* **satirize** *VERB*

satisfaction *NOUN* **1** satisfying a need or want **2** a feeling of pleasure arising from having what you need or want **3** something that satisfies a desire etc.

satisfactory *ADJECTIVE* good enough; sufficient
▷ **satisfactorily** *ADVERB*

satisfy *VERB* **satisfies, satisfying, satisfied** **1** give someone what they need or want **2** make someone feel certain; convince • *The police are satisfied that the death was accidental.* **3** fulfil • *You have satisfied all our requirements.*

saturate *VERB* **saturates, saturating, saturated** **1** make a thing very wet **2** make something take in as much as possible of a substance or goods etc.
▷ **saturation** *NOUN*

Saturday *NOUN* the day of the week following Friday [from Old English *Saeternesdaeg* = day of Saturn, a Roman god]

sauce *NOUN* **sauces** **1** a thick liquid served with food to add flavour **2** (*informal*) being cheeky; impudence [from Latin *salsus* = salted]

saucepan *NOUN* **saucepans** a metal cooking pan with a handle at the side

saucer *NOUN* **saucers** a small shallow object on which a cup etc. is placed [from early French *saussier* = container for sauce]

saucy *ADJECTIVE* **saucier, sauciest** cheeky or impudent
▷ **saucily** *ADVERB* **sauciness** *NOUN*

sauna *NOUN* **saunas** a room or compartment filled with steam, used as a kind of bath [from Finnish]

saunter *VERB* **saunters, sauntering, sauntered** walk slowly and casually
▷ **saunter** *NOUN*

sausage *NOUN* **sausages** a tube of skin or plastic stuffed with minced meat and other filling [from early French; related to **sauce**]

savage *ADJECTIVE* wild and fierce; cruel
▷ **savagely** *ADVERB* **savageness** *NOUN* **savagery** *NOUN*

savage *NOUN* **savages** **1** a savage person **2** (*old use*) a member of a people thought of as primitive or uncivilized

Thesaurus

satire *NOUN* *a smutty satire about marriage*
► parody, lampoon, burlesque, caricature, invective, irony, mockery, (*more informal*) spoof, (*more informal*) send-up, (*more informal*) take-off

satirical *ADJECTIVE* *a satirical cartoon series.*
► ironical, irreverent, mocking, critical, disparaging, disrespectful, sarcastic

satirize *VERB* *an attempt to satirize films and film-makers* ► mock, parody, ridicule, caricature, burlesque, criticize, deride, lampoon, travesty, make fun of, (*more informal*) send up, (*more informal*) take off

satisfaction *NOUN* **1** *This year, she thought with satisfaction, she was well-prepared. Job satisfaction tends to be high.* ► contentment, comfort, happiness, pleasure, pride, self-satisfaction, sense of achievement, enjoyment, fulfilment, gratification
AN OPPOSITE IS dissatisfaction **2** *They may have to turn to the courts for satisfaction.* ► settlement, reparation, compensation, recompense, reparation, amends, justice, redress

satisfactory *ADJECTIVE* *There was no satisfactory method of dealing with trivial complaints.*
► adequate, acceptable, satisfying, suitable, reasonable, tolerable, fair, passable, sufficient, (*more informal*) all right, (*informal*) up to scratch AN OPPOSITE IS unsatisfactory

satisfy *VERB* **1** *There are not enough terminals to satisfy demand.* ► fulfil, gratify, answer, meet, fill, service, provide for AN OPPOSITE IS frustrate **2** *Neither place had fully satisfied him.*
► content, make happy
AN OPPOSITE IS dissatisfy

saturate *VERB* *Heavy rainfall had saturated the ground. The Colombian cartel saturated the market with cocaine.* ► soak, drench, impregnate, permeate, suffuse, steep, wet

saturated *ADJECTIVE* **1** *Saturated soil lacks air.*
► soaked, sodden, waterlogged, steeped (in)
2 *Her clothes had become saturated in the downpour.* ► soaked, soaking wet, sopping, drenched, wringing

saucy *ADJECTIVE* **1** *saucy postcards* ► titillating, suggestive, rude, lewd **2** *a saucy child*
► cheeky, impudent, insolent, impertinent, disrespectful, pert, brazen, cocky, presumptuous OPPOSITES ARE polite, respectful

savage *ADJECTIVE* **1** *savage peoples of the past*
► primitive, uncivilized, barbarian, uncultivated, uneducated

savage *VERB* **savages, savaging, savaged** attack by biting or wounding • *The sheep had been savaged by a dog.*

save *VERB* **saves, saving, saved 1** keep safe; free a person or thing from danger or harm **2** keep something, especially money, so that it can be used later **3** avoid wasting something • *This will save time.* **4** (in computing) keep data by storing it in the computer's memory or on a disk **5** (in sports) prevent an opponent from scoring
▷ **save** *NOUN* **saver** *NOUN*

savings *PLURAL NOUN* money saved

saviour *NOUN* **saviours** a person who saves someone
the or **our Saviour** (in Christianity) Jesus Christ

savoury *ADJECTIVE* **1** tasty but not sweet **2** having an appetizing taste or smell

saw[1] *NOUN* **saws** a tool with a zigzag edge for cutting wood or metal etc.

saw *VERB* **saws, sawing, sawed, sawn 1** cut something with a saw **2** move to and fro as a saw does [from Old English]

saw[2] *past tense of* **see**

sawdust *NOUN* powder that comes from wood cut by a saw

saxophone *NOUN* **saxophones** a brass wind instrument with a reed in the mouthpiece
▷ **saxophonist** *NOUN*
[named after a 19th-century Belgian instrument maker, Adolphe Sax, who invented it]

say *VERB* **says, saying, said 1** speak or express something in words **2** give an opinion

say *NOUN* the power to decide something • *I have no say in the matter.*

saying *NOUN* **sayings** a well-known phrase or proverb or other statement

scab *NOUN* **scabs** a hard crust that forms over a cut or graze while it is healing
▷ **scabby** *ADJECTIVE*
[from Old Norse]

scaffold *NOUN* **scaffolds** a platform on which criminals are executed

scaffolding *NOUN* a structure of poles or tubes and planks making platforms for workers to stand on while building or repairing a house etc.

scald *VERB* **scalds, scalding, scalded 1** burn yourself with very hot liquid or steam **2** heat milk until it is nearly boiling **3** clean pans etc. with boiling water
▷ **scald** *NOUN*

scale[1] *NOUN* **scales 1** a series of units, degrees, or qualities etc. for measuring something **2** a series of musical notes going up or down in a fixed pattern **3** proportion or ratio • *The scale of this map is one centimetre to the kilometre.* **4** the relative size or importance of something • *They organize parties on a large scale.*
to scale with the parts in the same proportions as those of an original • *The architect's plans were drawn to scale.*

Thesaurus

AN OPPOSITE IS civilized **2** *Savage dogs roamed the streets.* ► fierce, wild, ferocious, vicious, untamed AN OPPOSITE IS tame **3** *a savage assault* ► fierce, ferocious, brutal, cruel, sadistic AN OPPOSITE IS humane **4** *The speech was a savage attack.* ► fierce, scathing, vitriolic, harsh, blistering, searing

save *VERB* **1** *They wanted to save money for a holiday.* ► put by, set aside, store up, conserve, reserve, retain, scrape together, (*more informal*) stash away OPPOSITES ARE waste, squander **2** *Try to save petrol during the fuel crisis.* ► economize on, cut back on, be sparing with, use wisely AN OPPOSITE IS waste **3** *The crew managed to save all the passengers after an emergency landing.* ► rescue, free, release, liberate, recover, retrieve, salvage, set free **4** *A bit of help would have saved me from exhausting myself.* ► prevent, preserve, protect, safeguard, defend, guard, shield

saving *NOUN* *a saving of 20% on the regular price* ► reduction, cut, discount
savings *With all his savings gone he could not afford to work for nothing.* ► nest egg, funds, reserves, resources

savoury *ADJECTIVE* *Sun-dried tomatoes give a pizza a savoury taste.* ► piquant, spicy, appetizing, mouth-watering, delectable, delicious, luscious

say *VERB* **1** *She could not say his name.* ► speak, utter, voice, articulate, enunciate **2** *'It's snowing,' he said* ► observe, remark, declare, state, announce, answer, reply, respond **3** *Hugh says he didn't do it.* ► maintain, claim, assert, insist, contend **4** *He lit a candle and said a prayer.* ► recite, utter, speak **5** *What are you trying to say?* ► express, put into words, communicate, make known **6** *We cannot say what might happen.* ► guess, foretell, imagine, judge, estimate

saying *NOUN* *You know the saying about too many cooks?* ► proverb, adage, maxim, dictum, aphorism

scale *NOUN* **1** *people at different ends of the social scale* ► hierarchy, ladder, spectrum, ranking, sequence, progression **2** *the scale of a map* ► proportion, ratio, measure, relative size **3** *the scale of the tragedy* ► extent, size, scope, magnitude, degree, range

a b c d e f g h i j k l m n o p q r s t u v w x y z

scale *VERB* **scales, scaling, scaled** climb • *She scaled the ladder.*
scale down or **up** reduce or increase at a fixed rate, or in proportion to something else
[from Latin *scala* = ladder]

scale[2] *NOUN* **scales 1** each of the thin overlapping parts on the outside of fish, snakes, etc.; a thin flake or part like this **2** a hard substance formed in a kettle or boiler by hard water, or on teeth
▷ **scaly** *ADJECTIVE*

scale *VERB* **scales, scaling, scaled** remove scales or scale from something [from old French; related to scales]

scale model *NOUN* **scale models** a model of something, made to scale

scales *PLURAL NOUN* a device for weighing things [from Old Norse *skal* = bowl]

scalp *NOUN* **scalps** the skin on the top of the head

scamp *NOUN* **scamps** a rascal

scamper *VERB* **scampers, scampering, scampered** run quickly, lightly, or playfully
▷ **scamper** *NOUN*

scan *VERB* **scans, scanning, scanned 1** look at every part of something **2** glance at something **3** count the beats of a line of poetry; be correct in rhythm • *This line doesn't scan.* **4** sweep a radar or electronic beam over an area to examine it or in search of something **5** (in computing) use a scanner to convert printed text or pictures into digital form for storing in a computer

scan *NOUN* **scans 1** scanning **2** an examination using a scanner • *a brain scan*

scandal *NOUN* **scandals 1** something shameful or disgraceful **2** gossip about people's faults and wrongdoings
▷ **scandalous** *ADJECTIVE*
[from Greek *skandalon* = stumbling block]

scandalize *VERB* **scandalizes, scandalizing, scandalized** shock a person by something considered shameful or disgraceful

scanner *NOUN* **scanners 1** a machine that examines things by means of light or other rays **2** a machine that converts printed text, pictures, etc. into a form that can be stored in a computer

scant *ADJECTIVE* barely enough or adequate • *We paid scant attention.*

scanty *ADJECTIVE* **scantier, scantiest** small in amount or extent; meagre • *a scanty harvest*
▷ **scantily** *ADVERB* **scantiness** *NOUN*

scapegoat *NOUN* **scapegoats** a person who is made to bear the blame or punishment for what others have done [from *escape* and *goat*, after the goat which the ancient Jews allowed to escape into the desert after the priest had symbolically laid the people's sins upon it]

scar *NOUN* **scars 1** the mark left by a cut or burn etc. after it has healed **2** a lasting bad effect left by an unpleasant experience

Thesaurus

scale *VERB The intruders had to scale a 10-foot fence.* ► climb, ascend, clamber up, scramble up, shin up, go up, go over, mount

scamp *NOUN He was an idle young scamp in those days.* ► rascal, scallywag, devil, monkey, imp

scamper *VERB Sam scampered off and waited at the gate.* ► scurry, scuttle, dash, dart, scoot, run, rush, hasten, hurry
scamper about *Dogs scampered about the churchyard.* ► gambol, frisk, frolic, run about, romp

scan *VERB* **1** *We scanned the trees and caught sight of a magpie.* ► study, examine, regard, view, watch, gaze at, look at, scrutinize, survey, search, stare at **2** *Mungo scanned the books to see what Vic might like.* ► skim, glance through, flick through, have a look at

scandal *NOUN* **1** *The tabloids loved reporting scandal.* ► gossip, rumour, aspersions, notoriety, sensation, slander, calumny, (*more informal*) tittle-tattle **2** *The college had been involved in a drugs scandal.* ► wrongdoing, affair, business **3** *It's a scandal that the hospital has to close.* ► disgrace, outrage, injustice, affront, insult, shame

scandalize *VERB behaviour that scandalized polite society* ► shock, outrage, horrify, disgust, appal, sicken, insult

scandalous *ADJECTIVE* **1** *This is a scandalous way to treat people who have risked their lives for the sake of their country.* ► shameful, disgraceful, shocking, outrageous, monstrous, appalling, wicked **2** *This was scandalous behaviour and the Palace gave her a firm warning.* ► discreditable, disreputable, improper, shameful **3** *The scandalous rumours had been quickly forgotten.* ► scurrilous, malicious, libellous, slanderous, defamatory

scanty *ADJECTIVE* **1** *a conclusion based on scanty evidence* ► meagre, sparse, scant, paltry, minimal, negligible, pitiful, miserable, modest, (*more informal*) mingy, (*more informal*) measly AN OPPOSITE IS plentiful **2** *They looked bored and cold in their scanty dresses.* ► skimpy, revealing, insubstantial, short, thin

scar *NOUN a scar on his left cheek* ► mark, injury, wound , disfigurement, blemish, cicatrix

scar *VERB* **scars, scarring, scarred** make a scar or scars on skin etc.

scarce *ADJECTIVE* **scarcer, scarcest 1** not enough to supply people **2** rare
▷ **scarcity** *NOUN*
make yourself scarce (*informal*) go away; keep out of the way

scarcely *ADVERB* only just; only with difficulty • *She could scarcely walk.*

scare *VERB* **scares, scaring, scared** frighten

scare *NOUN* **scares 1** a fright **2** a sudden widespread sense of alarm about something • *a bomb scare* [from Old Norse]

scarecrow *NOUN* **scarecrows** a figure of a person dressed in old clothes, set up to frighten birds away from crops

scarf *NOUN* **scarves** a strip of material worn round the neck or head

scarlet *ADJECTIVE, NOUN* bright red

scary *ADJECTIVE* (*informal*) frightening

scathing (skayth- ing) *ADJECTIVE* severely criticizing a person or thing

scatter *VERB* **scatters, scattering, scattered 1** throw or send or move in various directions **2** run or leave quickly in all directions

scavenge *VERB* **scavenges, scavenging, scavenged 1** search for useful things amongst rubbish **2** (said about a bird or animal) search for decaying flesh as food
▷ **scavenger** *NOUN*

scene *NOUN* **scenes 1** the place where something has happened • *the scene of the crime* **2** a part of a play or film **3** a view as seen by a spectator **4** an angry or noisy outburst • *He made a scene about the money.* **5** stage scenery **6** an area of activity • *the local music scene*

scenery *NOUN* **1** the natural features of a landscape **2** things put on a stage to make it look like a place

Thesaurus

scar *VERB* **1** *The wound scarred his face.* ► disfigure, mark, leave a scar on, deface, brand, damage, spoil **2** *He was scarred for life by his mother's early death.* ► traumatize, disturb, distress, upset, damage

scarce *ADJECTIVE* (*informal*) *When money became scarce, he tried to go on welfare.* ► sparse, meagre, in short supply, hard to find, hard to come by, scanty, at a premium, rare, lacking, deficient AN OPPOSITE IS plentiful

scarcely *ADVERB* *There was scarcely enough to go round.* ► barely, hardly, only just

scarcity *NOUN* *a scarcity of good job opportunities* ► shortage, dearth, deficiency, want, paucity, inadequacy, insufficiency, lack
OPPOSITES ARE abundance, surplus

scare *VERB* **1** *I didn't mean to scare you. I just wanted to talk.* ► alarm, startle, shake, unnerve, dismay, shock AN OPPOSITE IS calm **2** *The bogeyman could not scare him any more.* ► frighten, intimidate, terrorize, threaten, make afraid, menace, panic, bully, cow
AN OPPOSITE IS reassure

scare *NOUN* *Finding the door unlocked gave her a scare.* ► fright, shock, start, turn, jolt, alarm

scared *ADJECTIVE* *Many of us are too scared to go out alone.* ► frightened, afraid, fearful, anxious, alarmed, terrified, panic-stricken

scary *ADJECTIVE* *It's not so scary now with all these people around.* ► frightening, scaring, alarming, eerie, spooky, creepy, terrifying, chilling, spine-chilling, intimidating

scathing *ADJECTIVE* *There followed a scathing attack on the government for its lack of action.* ► critical, scornful, cutting, withering, caustic, vitriolic, devastating, harsh
AN OPPOSITE IS complimentary

scatter *VERB* **1** *The crowd quickly scattered.* ► disperse, break up, disband, separate, disintegrate, dissolve, go off in all directions **2** *She scattered breadcrumbs across the path.* ► strew, sprinkle, spread, throw, fling, toss, shower AN OPPOSITE IS gather

scatterbrained *ADJECTIVE* *She was scatterbrained about such things and left everything to Tod.* ► absent-minded, disorganized, forgetful, dreamy, feather-brained, muddled, empty-headed, unsystematic, vague, (*more informal*) scatty

scene *NOUN* **1** *Police were called to the scene of the accident.* ► location, site, place, position, point, spot, setting, locale, locality, whereabouts **2** *a beautiful scene by the lake* ► view, vista, outlook, prospect, panorama, landscape, picture, tableau, sight, spectacle **3** ► backdrop, scenery, set, stage **4** *The last scene of the novel is set in France.* ► part, section, episode, sequence **5** *He lost his money and there was a scene at the checkout.* ► fuss, commotion, disturbance, outburst, row, contretemps, exhibition, argument, quarrel, drama, (*more informal*) to-do, (*more informal*) carry-on

scenery *NOUN* *They stopped to admire the scenery.* ► landscape, terrain, panorama, scene, vista, outlook, surroundings

scenic *ADJECTIVE* *There is a scenic route through the mountains.* ► picturesque, panoramic, pretty, pleasing, attractive, beautiful, lovely, spectacular, striking

scent *NOUN* **scents** **1** a pleasant smell **2** a liquid perfume **3** an animal's smell that other animals can detect
▷ **scented** *ADJECTIVE*

sceptical (skep- tik- al) *ADJECTIVE* inclined to question things; not believing easily
▷ **sceptically** *ADVERB* **scepticism** *NOUN*

sceptre (sep-ter) *NOUN* **sceptres** a rod carried by a king or queen as a symbol of power

schedule (shed- yool) *NOUN* **schedules** a programme or timetable of planned events or work

schematic (skee- mat- ik) *ADJECTIVE* in the form of a diagram or chart

scheme *NOUN* **schemes** a plan of action

scheme *VERB* **schemes, scheming, schemed** make plans; plot
▷ **schemer** *NOUN*

scholar *NOUN* **scholars** **1** a person who has studied a subject thoroughly **2** a person who has been awarded a scholarship
▷ **scholarly** *ADJECTIVE*

scholarship *NOUN* **scholarships** **1** a grant of money given to someone to help to pay for his or her education **2** scholars' knowledge or methods; advanced study

school[1] *NOUN* **schools** **1** a place where teaching is done, especially of pupils aged 5-18 **2** the pupils in a school **3** the time when teaching takes place in a school • *School begins at 9 a.m.* **4** a group of people who have the same beliefs or style of work etc.

school *VERB* **schools, schooling, schooled** teach or train • *She was schooling her horse for the competition.* [from Greek *skhole*]

school[2] *NOUN* **schools** a shoal of fish or whales etc. [from early German or Dutch *schole* = a troop]

schoolchild *NOUN* **schoolchildren** a child who goes to school
▷ **schoolboy** *NOUN* **schoolgirl** *NOUN*

schooling *NOUN* **1** training **2** education, especially in a school

schoolteacher *NOUN* **schoolteachers** a person who teaches in a school
▷ **schoolmaster** *NOUN* **schoolmistress** *NOUN*

science *NOUN* the study of the physical world by means of observation and experiment [from Latin *scientia* = knowledge]

science fiction *NOUN* stories about imaginary scientific discoveries or space travel and life on other planets

science park *NOUN* **science parks** an area set up for industries using science or for organizations doing scientific research

Thesaurus

scent *NOUN* **1** *The scent of rose water hung in the air.* ► smell , odour, perfume, fragrance, aroma, redolence **2** *a bottle of scent* ► perfume, toilet water, lavender water, cologne **3** *The dogs picked up the scent.* ► trail, track

sceptical *ADJECTIVE* *He was initially sceptical about her abilities but soon changed his mind.* ► dubious, doubtful, distrustful, mistrustful, disbelieving, incredulous, suspicious, uncertain, unconvinced, unsure, cynical
AN OPPOSITE IS confident

scepticism *NOUN* *Others expressed scepticism about using this method.* ► distrust, mistrust, disbelief, suspicion, doubt, incredulity, lack of confidence, cynicism AN OPPOSITE IS confidence

schedule *NOUN* *There was hardly any spare time in her busy schedule. I will organize a schedule of visits.* ► timetable, agenda, programme, scheme, calendar, diary, list, plan

scheme *NOUN* **1** *Pitt proposed a national scheme of cash allowances for children.* ► plan, project, proposal, programme, venture, enterprise, strategy, system, blueprint, idea, method, procedure **2** *a scheme to steal the jewels* ► plot, conspiracy, intrigue, secret plan, ruse, ploy, (*more informal*) racket, (*more informal*) scam **3** *a bright colour scheme* ► design, arrangement, pattern, layout

scheme *VERB* *The emperor's wife schemed to exercise power through her son.* ► plot, intrigue, connive, conspire, collude, plan

scholar *NOUN* *a leading classical scholar* ► academic, authority, expert, savant, intellectual, intellect, man *or* woman of letters

scholarly *ADJECTIVE* *a serious, scholarly woman* ► intellectual, learned, erudite, academic, lettered, knowledgeable

scholarship *NOUN* **1** *a music scholarship worth £2,000 a year* ► award, grant, bursary, exhibition **2** *a person of great scholarship* ► learning, erudition, knowledge, wisdom, academic achievement, intellectual attainment

school *NOUN* *Have you asked them what makes a good school?* ► college, academy, educational institution, centre of learning, institute

schooling *NOUN* *the last two years of schooling* ► education, instruction, tuition, teaching, training, coaching

science *NOUN* *the science of forensic medicine* ► technology, discipline, field, technique, art

scientific *ADJECTIVE* **1** to do with science or scientists **2** studying things systematically and testing ideas carefully
▷ **scientifically** *ADVERB*

scientist *NOUN* **scientists 1** an expert in science **2** someone who uses scientific methods

scintillating *ADJECTIVE* **1** shining brightly; sparkling **2** very lively and witty

scissors *PLURAL NOUN* a cutting instrument used with one hand, with two blades pivoted so that they can close against each other

scoff *VERB* **scoffs, scoffing, scoffed 1** jeer; speak contemptuously **2** (*informal*) eat greedily
▷ **scoffer** *NOUN*

scold *VERB* **scolds, scolding, scolded** speak angrily; tell someone off
▷ **scolding** *NOUN*

scone (skon, skohn) *NOUN* **scones** a soft flat cake, usually eaten with butter

scoop *NOUN* **scoops 1** a kind of deep spoon for serving ice cream etc. **2** a deep shovel for lifting grain, sugar, etc. **3** a scooping movement **4** an important piece of news published by only one newspaper

scoop *VERB* **scoops, scooping, scooped** lift or hollow something out with a scoop

scoot *VERB* **scoots, scooting, scooted 1** propel a bicycle or scooter by sitting or standing on it and pushing it along with one foot **2** (*informal*) run or go away quickly

scooter *NOUN* **scooters 1** a kind of motorcycle with small wheels **2** a board with wheels and a long handle, which you ride on by scooting

scope *NOUN* **1** opportunity or possibility for something. ● *There is scope for improvement.* **2** the range or extent of a subject

scorch *VERB* **scorches, scorching, scorched** make something go brown by burning it slightly

scorched-earth policy *NOUN* the burning of crops and destruction of anything that might be useful to an opposing army

score *NOUN* **scores** *or, in sense 2,* **score 1** the number of points or goals made in a game; a result **2** (*old use*) twenty ● *'Three score years and ten' means 3 x 20 + 10 = 70 years.* **3** written or printed music
on that score for that reason, because of that ● *You needn't worry on that score.*

score *VERB* **scores, scoring, scored 1** get a point or goal in a game **2** keep a count of the score **3** mark with lines or cuts **4** write out a musical score
▷ **scorer** *NOUN*
[from Old Norse]

scores *PLURAL NOUN* many; a large number

scorn *NOUN* contempt
▷ **scornful** *ADJECTIVE* **scornfully** *ADVERB*

scorn *VERB* **scorns, scorning, scorned 1** treat someone with contempt **2** refuse something scornfully

Thesaurus

scientific *ADJECTIVE* **1** *scientific research* ► science-based, technical, technological **2** *Our methods are not scientific enough.* ► systematic, methodical, analytical, organized, precise, rigorous, thorough, regulated

scientist *NOUN* *the accusation that scientists are 'playing God'* ► researcher, scientific expert, technologist, (*more informal*) boffin

scoff *VERB* **scoff at 1** *Experts are inclined to scoff at such theories.* ► mock, ridicule, sneer at, jeer at, scorn, deride, make fun of, poke fun at **2** (*informal*) *You feel guilty when you scoff a sherry trifle.* ► eat up, guzzle, gobble up, wolf, wolf down, devour, (*more informal*) tuck into, (*more informal*) polish off

scold *VERB* *Busy young mothers scolded their children.* ► reprimand, rebuke, admonish, reprove, reproach, upbraid, censure, chide, criticize, reprehend, (*more informal*) tell off, (*more informal*) tick off OPPOSITES ARE praise, commend

scoop *VERB* **1 scoop out** *They would scoop out holes in the sand.* ► gouge, dig, scrape, excavate, hollow, cut **2 scoop out** *Scoop out the flesh of the pineapple halves.* ► remove, take out, scrape out, spoon out, extract **3 scoop up** *She scooped up her things and left hurriedly.* ► pick up, gather up, grab, collect

scope *NOUN* **1** *issues that are beyond the scope of the inquiry* ► extent, limit, range, competence, terms of reference, remit, ambit, capacity, compass, sphere, reach **2** *There is plenty of scope for new ideas.* ► opportunity, chance, latitude, leeway, freedom, room, space

scorch *VERB* *Some of the walls had been scorched by fire.* ► burn, singe, char, blacken

score *NOUN* **1** *The final score did not reflect the balance of the game.* ► result, tally, total, mark, number of points **2** *They had a score to settle.* ► debt, grievance

score *VERB* **1** *a move that scored double points* ► earn, win, gain, achieve, make, (*more informal*) chalk up **2** *A pattern had been scored in the surface.* ► cut, engrave, incise, mark, gouge, scratch, scrape, slash

scorn *NOUN* *She treated that remark with the scorn it deserved.* ► contempt, disdain, derision, disparagement, ridicule, mockery
AN OPPOSITE IS admiration

scorn *VERB* *Their haircuts are severe and they scorn make-up.* ► deride, despise, scoff at, ridicule,

scorpion *NOUN* **scorpions** an animal that looks like a tiny lobster, with a poisonous sting

Scot *NOUN* **Scots** a person who comes from Scotland

scotch[1] *NOUN* whisky made in Scotland

scotch[2] *VERB* **scotches, scotching, scotched** put an end to an idea or rumour etc.

scot-free *ADJECTIVE* without harm or punishment

Scots *ADJECTIVE* from or belonging to Scotland
USAGE See note at **Scottish**.

Scottish *ADJECTIVE* to do with or belonging to Scotland
USAGE **Scottish** is the most widely used word for describing things to do with Scotland: *Scottish education, Scottish mountains*. **Scots** is less common and is mainly used to describe people: *a Scots girl*. **Scotch** is only used in fixed expressions like *Scotch terrier*, a breed of terrier with rough hair.

scoundrel *NOUN* **scoundrels** a wicked or dishonest person

scour[1] *VERB* **scours, scouring, scoured 1** rub something until it is clean and bright **2** clear a channel or pipe by the force of water flowing through it
▷ **scourer** *NOUN*

scour[2] *VERB* **scours, scouring, scoured** search thoroughly

scourge (skerj) *NOUN* **scourges 1** a whip for flogging people **2** something that inflicts suffering or punishment

Scout *NOUN* **Scouts** a member of the Scout Association, an organization for boys

scout *NOUN* **scouts** someone sent out to collect information

scout *VERB* **scouts, scouting, scouted 1** act as a scout **2** search an area thoroughly

scowl *NOUN* **scowls** a bad-tempered frown

scowl *VERB* **scowls, scowling, scowled** make a scowl

scrabble *VERB* **scrabbles, scrabbling, scrabbled 1** scratch or claw at something with the hands or feet **2** grope or struggle to get something

scraggy *ADJECTIVE* thin and bony

scramble *VERB* **scrambles, scrambling, scrambled 1** move quickly and awkwardly **2** struggle to do or get something **3** (said about aircraft or their crew) hurry and take off quickly **4** cook eggs by mixing them up and heating them in a pan **5** mix things together **6** alter a radio or telephone signal so that it cannot be used without a decoding device
▷ **scrambler** *NOUN*

scramble *NOUN* **scrambles 1** a climb or walk over rough ground **2** a struggle to do or get

Thesaurus

mock, spurn, look down on, dismiss
AN OPPOSITE IS admire

scornful *ADJECTIVE* *Richard was prepared to put up with the scornful disapproval of Eve and Ted.* ► contemptuous, derisive, disdainful, supercilious, scathing, disparaging, mocking, scoffing, sneering, withering
OPPOSITES ARE admiring, respectful

scotch *VERB* *Hopes of trying a first kiss were scotched when she fell asleep the moment she got into the car.* ► end, bring to an end, put paid to, frustrate, shatter, wreck, destroy, scupper

scot-free *ADJECTIVE* *You wouldn't want to see the real villains getting off scot-free.* ► unpunished, unscathed, unharmed, unhurt, safe

scoundrel *NOUN* *It wasn't her fault she had a scoundrel for a grandson.* ► rascal, rogue, ruffian, ne'er-do-well, good-for-nothing, villain, knave, scallywag, scamp

scour *VERB* **1** *They were made to scrub kitchen floors and scour out pans.* ► scrub, clean, scrape, wash, buff up, burnish, polish, rub **2** *Rita scoured the junk shops for second-hand pieces to fill the rooms.* ► ransack, rummage through, search, comb, forage through, hunt through

scourge *NOUN* *High interests were the scourge of those years.* ► affliction, bane, curse, misfortune, torment

scout *NOUN* *Scouts came back with information about the enemy positions.* ► lookout, outrider, advance guard, spy

scout *VERB* **scout about** *or* **around** *I asked Claire to scout around to find him a place to stay.* ► look about, reconnoitre, search, explore, hunt, investigate, cast about, get information

scowl *VERB* *She scowled at him and told him to go away.* ► glower, frown, glare, grimace

scrabble *VERB* *She scrabbled about in her pockets until she found her glasses.* ► rummage, grope, root, fumble, claw, dig

scraggy *ADJECTIVE* *She kept out of the way of her sister's scraggy old cat.* ► scrawny, skinny, thin, lanky, gaunt, lean, bony, emaciated, underfed
OPPOSITES ARE plump, fat

scram *VERB* (*informal*) *Scram or I'll call the police.* ► go away, leave, get going, get moving, (*informal*) beat it, (*informal*) shove off, (*informal*) clear off

scramble *NOUN* *Getting there in time proved quite a scramble.* ► struggle, rush, hustle, dash

scramble *VERB* **1** *I scrambled down the slope towards the car. Daniel scrambled to his feet and*

something **3** a motorcycle race over rough ground

scrap[1] *NOUN* **scraps 1** a small piece **2** rubbish; waste material, especially metal that is suitable for reprocessing

scrap *VERB* **scraps, scrapping, scrapped** get rid of something that is useless or unwanted

scrap[2] *NOUN* **scraps** (*informal*) a fight

scrap *VERB* **scraps, scrapping, scrapped** (*informal*) fight

scrape *VERB* **scrapes, scraping, scraped**
1 clean or smooth or damage something by passing something hard over it **2** make a harsh sound by rubbing against a rough or hard surface **3** remove by scraping • *Scrape the mud off your shoes.* **4** get something by great effort or care • *They scraped together enough money for a holiday.*
▷ **scraper** *NOUN*
scrape through only just succeed, pass an exam, etc.

scrape *NOUN* **scrapes 1** a scraping movement or sound **2** a mark etc. made by scraping **3** (*informal*) an awkward situation caused by mischief or foolishness

scrappy *ADJECTIVE* **1** made of scraps or bits or disconnected things **2** carelessly done
▷ **scrappiness** *NOUN*

scratch *VERB* **scratches, scratching, scratched**
1 mark or cut the surface of a thing with something sharp **2** rub the skin with fingernails or claws because it itches **3** withdraw from a race or competition

scratch *NOUN* **scratches 1** a mark made by scratching **2** the action of scratching
▷ **scratchy** *ADJECTIVE*
start from scratch start from the beginning or with nothing prepared
up to scratch up to the proper standard

scratch card *NOUN* **scratch cards** a lottery card on which you scratch off part of the surface to see if you have won a prize

scrawl *NOUN* **scrawls** untidy handwriting

scrawl *VERB* **scrawls, scrawling, scrawled** write in a scrawl

scrawny *ADJECTIVE* scraggy

scream *NOUN* **screams 1** a loud cry of pain, fear, anger, or excitement **2** a loud piercing sound **3** (*informal*) a very amusing person or thing

scream *VERB* **screams, screaming, screamed** make a scream

screech *NOUN* **screeches** a harsh high-pitched scream or sound
▷ **screech** *VERB*

screen *NOUN* **screens 1** a special surface for displaying films, television pictures, or computer data **2** a movable panel used to hide, protect, or divide something **3** a vehicle's windscreen

Thesaurus

left the room. ► clamber, climb, crawl, scrabble, move awkwardly **2** *She saw the two men scramble for the fallen gun.* ► scuffle, struggle, tussle, fight, jostle **3** *They quickly scrambled into the plane.* ► dash, hasten, hurry, run, rush

scrap *NOUN* **1** *There were a few scraps of food on the table.* ► bit, piece, morsel, particle, crumb, speck, fragment, mouthful **2** *Not a scrap of evidence could be found.* ► shred, speck, iota, jot, ounce, trace **3** *a lorry loaded with scrap* ► junk, refuse, rubbish, salvage, waste, litter, odds and ends **4** *He wanted to avoid a scrap with Kevin.* ► fight, quarrel, disagreement, tussle, brawl

scrap *VERB* **1** *Local residents want the road plan to be scrapped.* ► abandon, cancel, discard, (*informal*) ditch, drop, give up, jettison, throw away, write off **2** *The younger children are always scrapping.* ► fight, quarrel, argue, brawl

scrape *VERB* **1** *Elaine had scraped her skin against the wall.* ► graze, scratch, scuff, abrade, bark, lacerate **2** *He scraped his boots before going inside.* ► scrub, scour, rub, clean
scrape together *We scraped enough money together to get home* ► collect, amass, rake together, dredge up

scrape *NOUN* *Try not to get into any scrapes* ► predicament, difficulty, tight spot, mischief, trouble

scrappy *ADJECTIVE* *The game turned out to be a scrappy affair.* ► disorganized, disjointed, uneven, slipshod, unsatisfactory
AN OPPOSITE IS well-organized

scratch *VERB* **1** *Be careful not to scratch the table top.* ► scrape, mark, score, gash, cut, damage the surface of, gouge **2** *The thorns were scratching his legs.* ► graze, chafe, prick, cut, lacerate

scratch *NOUN* **1** *There were scratches in the paintwork.* ► gash, groove, line, mark, scoring, scrape **2** *He had a long scratch down one side of his face.* ► graze, laceration, wound , cut
up to scratch *The work was not up to scratch.* ► satisfactory, adequate, acceptable, good enough, passable, all right

scream *VERB* *She screamed at them to stop.* ► yell, shriek, shout, bawl, screech, roar, howl, wail

scream *NOUN* *He let out a scream of pain.* ► yell, shriek, shout, screech, roar, howl, wail

screen *NOUN* **1** *a computer with a 17-inch screen* ► monitor, display, VDU *or* visual display unit **2** *A screen divided the room in two.* ► partition, divider, curtain, blind

A B C D E F G H I J K L M N O P Q R S T U V W X Y Z

screen *VERB* **screens, screening, screened** **1** protect, hide, or divide with a screen **2** show a film or television pictures on a screen **3** carry out tests on someone to find out if they have a disease **4** check whether a person is suitable for a job

screenplay *NOUN* **screenplays** the script of a film, with instructions to the actors etc.

screw *NOUN* **screws** **1** a metal pin with a spiral ridge (the **thread**) round it, holding things together by being twisted in **2** a twisting movement **3** something twisted **4** a propeller, especially for a ship or motor boat

screw *VERB* **screws, screwing, screwed** **1** fasten with a screw or screws **2** fit or turn something by twisting

screwdriver *NOUN* **screwdrivers** a tool for turning screws

scribble *VERB* **scribbles, scribbling, scribbled** **1** write quickly or untidily or carelessly **2** make meaningless marks
▷ **scribble** *NOUN*

script *NOUN* **scripts** **1** handwriting **2** the text of a play, film, broadcast talk, etc.

scripture *NOUN* **scriptures** **1** sacred writings **2** (in Christianity) the Bible

scroll *NOUN* **scrolls** **1** a roll of paper or parchment used for writing on **2** a spiral design

scroll *VERB* **scrolls, scrolling, scrolled** move the display on a computer screen up or down to see what comes before or after it

scrounge *VERB* **scrounges, scrounging, scrounged** get something without paying for it
▷ **scrounger** *NOUN*

scrub[1] *VERB* **scrubs, scrubbing, scrubbed** **1** rub with a hard brush, especially to clean something **2** (*informal*) cancel
▷ **scrub** *NOUN*

scrub[2] *NOUN* **1** low trees and bushes **2** land covered with these

scruff *NOUN* the back of the neck

scruffy *ADJECTIVE* shabby and untidy
▷ **scruffily** *ADVERB* **scruffiness** *NOUN*

scrum *NOUN* **scrums** **1** (also **scrummage**) a group of players from each side in rugby football who push against each other and try to kick back the ball when it is thrown between them **2** a crowd pushing against each other

scruple *NOUN* **scruples** a feeling of doubt or hesitation when your conscience tells you that an action would be wrong

scruple *VERB* **scruples, scrupling, scrupled** have scruples • *He would not scruple to betray us.* [from Latin *scrupum*, literally = rough pebble]

scrupulous *ADJECTIVE* **1** very careful and conscientious **2** strictly honest or honourable
▷ **scrupulously** *ADVERB*

Thesaurus

screen *VERB* **1** *A low hedge screened the dustbins.* ► hide, conceal, mask, shield, shelter **2** *Staff are regularly screened in the interests of security.* ► vet, scrutinize, examine, investigate

screw *VERB* **1** *She screwed the lid on the jar.* ► fasten, tighten, twist, turn **2** *James screwed the piece of paper into a tight ball.* ► twist, wind, wring **3** *The last thing to do was screw the boards back down.* ► fix, fasten, secure **4** (*informal*) *He was not going to let them screw him for money like that again.* ► cheat, swindle, defraud, pressurize, extort, squeeze USAGE If you use *extort* or *squeeze* you have to say (for example) *He was not going to let them extort money from him like that again.*

scribble *VERB* *He quickly scribbled a shopping list.* ► scrawl, dash off, jot down, write

scribe *NOUN* *He would need to get a scribe to write his letter for him.* ► copyist, clerk, transcriber, amanuensis, scrivener, secretary

script *NOUN* **1** *The note had been written in an elegant script.* ► handwriting, hand, autograph **2** *The film was spoilt by a poor script.* ► screenplay, text, dialogue

scrounge *VERB* *Street urchins scrounged money from the tourists.* ► beg, cadge, sponge

scrounger *NOUN* *He was neither a scrounger nor a misfit.* ► cadger, sponger, parasite

scrub *VERB* **1** *She decided to scrub the bathroom floor.* ► scour, wash, clean, rub, brush **2** (*informal*) *If interest rates went up again they would have to scrub their holiday.* ► cancel, scrap, go without, do without, call off, drop, abandon, (*informal*) ditch

scruffy *ADJECTIVE* **1** *He had worn scruffy jeans and a T-shirt to his Downing Street breakfast.* ► shabby, worn, ragged, worn-out, dirty AN OPPOSITE IS smart **2** *He was standing in a bar, scruffy and long-haired.* ► unkempt, untidy, dishevelled, ungroomed, messy, bedraggled AN OPPOSITE IS tidy

scrupulous *ADJECTIVE* **1** *The story had been written with a scrupulous attention to historical accuracy.* ► conscientious, diligent, fastidious, meticulous, minute, painstaking, precise, punctilious, rigorous, strict, systematic, thorough **2** *The accounts will be reviewed by the most scrupulous auditor.* ► honest, honourable, upright, upstanding, principled, right-minded, fair-minded, ethical AN OPPOSITE IS unscrupulous

scrutinize *VERB* **scrutinizes, scrutinizing, scrutinized** look at something carefully
▷ **scrutiny** *NOUN*

scuba diving *NOUN* swimming underwater using a tank of air strapped to your back [from the initials of *self-contained underwater breathing apparatus*]

scuff *VERB* **scuffs, scuffing, scuffed 1** drag your feet while walking **2** scrape with your foot; mark or damage something by doing this

scuffle *NOUN* **scuffles** a confused fight or struggle

scuffle *VERB* **scuffles, scuffling, scuffled** take part in a scuffle [probably from a Scandinavian language]

scullery *NOUN* **sculleries** a room where dishes etc. are washed up

sculptor *NOUN* **sculptors** a person who makes sculptures
▷ **sculpt** *VERB*

sculpture *NOUN* **sculptures 1** making shapes by carving wood or stone or casting metal **2** a shape made in this way
▷ **sculpture** *VERB*

scum *NOUN* **1** froth or dirt on top of a liquid **2** worthless people

scuttle[1] *NOUN* **scuttles** a bucket or container for coal in a house

scuttle[2] *VERB* **scuttles, scuttling, scuttled** scurry; hurry away

scuttle[3] *VERB* **scuttles, scuttling, scuttled** sink a ship deliberately by letting water into it

scythe *NOUN* **scythes** a tool with a long curved blade for cutting grass or corn

scythe *VERB* **scythes, scything, scythed** cut with a scythe

SE *ABBREVIATION* **1** south-east **2** south-eastern

sea *NOUN* **seas 1** the salt water that covers most of the earth's surface; a part of this **2** a large lake • *the Sea of Galilee* **3** a large area of something • *a sea of faces*
at sea 1 on the sea **2** not knowing what to do

sea anemone *NOUN* **sea anemones** a sea creature with short tentacles round its mouth

seaboard *NOUN* **seaboards** a coastline or coastal region

seafaring *ADJECTIVE, NOUN* working or travelling on the sea
▷ **seafarer** *NOUN*

seafood *NOUN* fish or shellfish from the sea eaten as food

seagull *NOUN* **seagulls** a seabird with long wings

seal[1] *NOUN* **seals** a sea mammal with thick fur or bristles, that breeds on land [from Old English]

seal[2] *NOUN* **seals 1** a piece of metal with an engraved design for pressing on a soft substance to leave an impression **2** an impression made on a piece of wax **3** something designed to close an opening and prevent air or liquid etc. from getting in or out **4** a confirmation or guarantee • *a seal of approval*

seal *VERB* **seals, sealing, sealed 1** close something by sticking two parts together **2** close securely; stop up **3** press a seal on something **4** settle or decide • *His fate was sealed.*
seal off prevent people getting to an area [from early French; related to **sign**]

sea level *NOUN* the level of the sea halfway between high and low tide

sealing wax *NOUN* a substance that is soft when heated but hardens when cooled, used

Thesaurus

scuff *VERB The toe was scuffed and the shoes would need mending.* ► scrape, scratch, rub, graze, brush

scuffle *NOUN There was a scuffle and the sound of people running.* ► fight, fracas, brawl, struggle, tussle, scrap, rumpus, commotion, argument

scuffle *VERB Three teenage boys were scuffling and messing around.* ► fight, brawl, struggle, tussle, scrap, come to blows

sculpture *NOUN a marble sculpture of Venus* ► carving, figure, statue, effigy, image USAGE A small sculpture is called a *statuette*. A *bust* is a sculpture of the top part of a person.

scum *NOUN The water had a thick scum on it.* ► froth, foam, film, impurities

scurry *VERB Officials scurried about.* ► scamper, scuttle, dash, dart, rush, hurry

sea *ADJECTIVE sea creatures; a sea voyage; a sea port* ► aquatic, marine, maritime, nautical, naval, oceangoing, oceanic, saltwater, seafaring, seagoing

sea *NOUN* **1** *They caught sight of the sea in the distance.* ► water, ocean, waves RELATED ADJECTIVES marine, maritime, nautical, naval **2** *sea creatures* ► aquatic, marine, seafaring, ocean, salt **3** *a sea of friendly faces* ► mass, host, multitude, profusion

seal *NOUN the queen's seal* ► emblem, crest, insignia, symbol, stamp

seal *VERB* **1** *She folded the letter and sealed the envelope.* ► stick down, close, fasten, secure **2** *He filled the jar and sealed it.* ► stop up, close, plug, stopper **3** *He held out a hand to seal the agreement.* ► confirm, clinch, complete, secure, (*more informal*) sew up
seal off *Police sealed off the city centre.*

A B C D E F G H I J K L M N O P Q R S T U V W X Y Z

for sealing documents or for marking with a seal

sea lion *NOUN* **sea lions** a kind of large seal that lives in the Pacific Ocean

seam *NOUN* **seams** **1** the line where two edges of cloth or wood etc. join **2** a layer of coal in the ground

seamanship *NOUN* skill in seafaring

seamy *ADJECTIVE*
seamy side the less attractive side or part • *Police see a lot of the seamy side of life* [originally, the 'wrong' side of a piece of sewing, where the rough edges of the seams show]

sear *VERB* **sears, searing, seared** scorch or burn the surface of something

search *VERB* **searches, searching, searched** look very hard or carefully in order to find something
▷ **search** *NOUN* **searcher** *NOUN*

search engine *NOUN* **search engines** (in computing) a program that searches for data, especially on the Internet

searchlight *NOUN* **searchlights** a light with a strong beam that can be turned in any direction

search party *NOUN* **search parties** a group of people organized to search for a missing person or thing

search warrant *NOUN* **search warrants** an official document giving the police permission to search private property

seasick *ADJECTIVE* sick because of the movement of a ship
▷ **seasickness** *NOUN*

seaside *NOUN* a place by the sea where people go for holidays

season *NOUN* **seasons** **1** each of the four main parts of the year (spring, summer, autumn, and winter) **2** the time of year when something happens • *the football season*
in season available and ready for eating • *Strawberries are in season in the summer.*

season *VERB* **seasons, seasoning, seasoned** **1** give extra flavour to food by adding salt, pepper, or other strong-tasting substances **2** dry and treat timber etc. to make it ready for use

seasonable *ADJECTIVE* suitable for the season • *Hot weather is seasonable in summer.*
▷ **seasonably** *ADVERB*
USAGE Do not confuse with **seasonal.**

seasonal *ADJECTIVE* **1** for or to do with a season **2** happening in a particular season • *Fruit-picking is seasonal work.*
▷ **seasonally** *ADVERB*
USAGE Do not confuse with **seasonable.**

seasoning *NOUN* **seasonings** a substance used to season food

season ticket *NOUN* **season tickets** a ticket that can be used as often as you like throughout a period of time

seat *NOUN* **seats** **1** a thing made or used for sitting on **2** the right to be a member of a council, committee, parliament, etc. • *She won the seat ten years ago.* **3** the buttocks; the part of a skirt or trousers covering these **4** the place where something is based or located • *London is the seat of our government.*

seat *VERB* **seats, seating, seated** **1** place in or on a seat **2** have seats for • *The theatre seats 3,000 people.*

seat belt *NOUN* **seat belts** a strap to hold a person securely in a seat

seating *NOUN* **1** the seats in a place • *seating for 400* **2** the arrangement of seats • *a seating plan*

sea urchin *NOUN* **sea urchins** a sea animal with a round shell covered in sharp spikes

seaweed *NOUN* a plant or plants that grow in the sea

Thesaurus

search *VERB* **1** *We searched for clues.* ► explore, ferret about, hunt, look, nose about, poke about, prospect, pry, seek **2** *Security staff will search passengers and their luggage.* ► check, examine, investigate, scrutinize, inspect, (*more informal*) frisk **3** *I searched the house for my keys.* ► scour, comb, ransack, rummage through, forage through, hunt through

search *NOUN* *We began our search for a place to eat.* ► hunt, quest, exploration, investigation, look, check

seaside *NOUN* *a trip to the seaside* ► coast, beach, seashore, shore RELATED ADJECTIVE littoral

season *NOUN* *The holiday season lasts until October these days.* ► period, time of year, time, phase

season *VERB* **1** *herbs for seasoning fish* ► flavour, spice, salt, add seasoning to **2** *The wood should be well seasoned.* ► mature, age, temper, condition

seat *NOUN* **1** *There were not enough seats for everyone to sit on.* ► chair, bench, stool, pew, place **2** *The capital city is not always the seat of government.* ► centre, headquarters, location, site, base, nucleus, heart, hub **3** *a country seat in Scotland* ► residence, ancestral, mansion, abode, stately home

seat *VERB* **1** *She seated her guests round a large oval table.* ► place, position, put, settle **2** *The smaller cinema seats thirty.* ► accommodate, hold, take, have seats for, sit

seaworthy *ADJECTIVE* (said about a ship) fit for a sea voyage
▷ **seaworthiness** *NOUN*

secateurs *PLURAL NOUN* clippers held in the hand for pruning plants

secluded *ADJECTIVE* quiet or sheltered from view • *a secluded beach*
▷ **seclusion** *NOUN*

second[1] *ADJECTIVE* **1** next after the first **2** another • *a second chance* **3** less good • *second quality*
▷ **secondly** *ADVERB*
have second thoughts wonder whether a decision you have made was the right one

second *NOUN* **seconds 1** a person or thing that is second **2** an attendant of a fighter in a boxing match, duel, etc. **3** a thing that is not of the best quality, often sold cheaply **4** one-sixtieth of a minute of time or of a degree used in measuring angles

second *VERB* **seconds, seconding, seconded** **1** assist someone **2** support a proposal, motion, etc.
▷ **seconder** *NOUN*

second[2] (sik-ond) *VERB* **seconds, seconding, seconded** transfer a person temporarily to another job or department etc.
▷ **secondment** *NOUN*

secondary *ADJECTIVE* **1** coming after or from something **2** less important **3** (said about education etc.) for children of more than about 11 years old • *a secondary school* COMPARE **primary**

second-hand *ADJECTIVE* **1** bought or used after someone else has owned it **2** selling used goods • *a second-hand shop*

second nature *NOUN* behaviour that has become automatic or a habit • *Lying is second nature to him.*

second-rate *ADJECTIVE* inferior; not very good

secret *ADJECTIVE* **1** that must not be told or shown to other people **2** not known by everybody **3** working secretly
▷ **secretly** *ADVERB* **secrecy** *NOUN*

secret *NOUN* **secrets** something secret

secretary (sek-rit-ree) *NOUN* **secretaries 1** a person whose job is to help with letters, answer the telephone, and make business arrangements for a person or organization **2** the chief assistant of a government minister or ambassador
▷ **secretarial** *ADJECTIVE*
[from Latin *secretarius* = an officer or servant allowed to know his employer's secrets]

secrete (sik-reet) *VERB* **secretes, secreting, secreted 1** hide something **2** produce a substance in the body • *Saliva is secreted in the mouth.*
▷ **secretion** *NOUN*

secretive (seek-rit-iv) *ADJECTIVE* liking or trying to keep things secret
▷ **secretively** *ADVERB* **secretiveness** *NOUN*

secret service *NOUN* a government department responsible for espionage

Thesaurus

secede *VERB* **secede from** *The southern states seceded from the Union.* ► withdraw from, separate from, break away from, leave, quit, split with

second *ADJECTIVE* **1** *There won't be a second chance.* ► another, further, additional, repeated, alternative, extra **2** *We keep a second set of data in another building.* ► spare, extra, alternative, backup

second *NOUN* **1** *They were only gone for a second.* ► moment, instant, bit, flash, (*more informal*) jiffy, (*more informal*) tick **2** *Chris was acting as his second.* ► assistant, attendant, supporter, right-hand man *or* woman, helper

secondary *ADJECTIVE* **1** *issues that are regarded as secondary* ► subsidiary, subordinate, minor, lesser, lower, inferior, second-rate **2** *A secondary action was started in support of the main attack.* ► ancillary, auxiliary, supplementary, supportive, reinforcing, extra, second, reserve

second-hand *ADJECTIVE* **1** *a second-hand car* ► used, pre-owned, old AN OPPOSITE IS new **2** *She was relying on second-hand information.* ► indirect, secondary, derivative AN OPPOSITE IS personal.

second-rate *ADJECTIVE* *a second-rate holiday camp entertainer* ► second-class, second-best, substandard, mediocre, middling, ordinary, below par, commonplace, indifferent, inferior, low-grade

secret *ADJECTIVE* **1** *secret information* ► confidential, classified, restricted, (*more informal*) hush-hush AN OPPOSITE IS public **2** *They met at a secret location.* ► private, secluded, hidden, isolated, remote, unknown, undisclosed OPPOSITES ARE public, well-known **3** *a secret operation* ► clandestine, covert, undercover, surreptitious AN OPPOSITE IS overt

secretary *NOUN* *She called in her secretary to take notes of the meeting.* ► assistant, personal assistant *or* PA, clerk, typist

secretive *ADJECTIVE* *He was being very secretive about his intentions.* ► uncommunicative, unforthcoming, reticent, tight-lipped, cagey, close, withdrawn AN OPPOSITE IS communicative

A B C D E F G H I J K L M N O P Q R **S** T U V W X Y Z

sect *NOUN* **sects** a group of people whose beliefs differ from others in the same religion

section *NOUN* **sections** **1** a part of something **2** a cross-section

sector *NOUN* **sectors** **1** one part of an area **2** a part of something • *the private sector of industry* **3** (in mathematics) a section of a circle between two lines drawn from its centre to its circumference

secular *ADJECTIVE* to do with worldly affairs, not spiritual or religious matters

secure *ADJECTIVE* **1** safe, especially against attack **2** certain not to slip or fail **3** reliable
▷ **securely** *ADVERB*

secure *VERB* **secures, securing, secured** **1** make a thing secure **2** fasten something firmly **3** obtain • *We secured two tickets for the show.*

security *NOUN* **securities** **1** being secure; safety **2** precautions against theft or spying etc. **3** something given as a guarantee that a promise will be kept or a debt repaid **4** investments such as stocks and shares

sedate *ADJECTIVE* calm and dignified
▷ **sedately** *ADVERB* **sedateness** *NOUN*

sedate *VERB* **sedates, sedating, sedated** give a sedative to
▷ **sedation** *NOUN*

sedative (sed- a- tiv) *NOUN* **sedatives** a medicine that makes a person calm

sedentary (sed- en- ter- ee) *ADJECTIVE* done sitting down • *sedentary work*

Seder (say-der) *NOUN* **Seders** (in Judaism) a ritual and a ceremonial meal to mark the beginning of Passover

sedge *NOUN* a grass-like plant growing in marshes or near water

sediment *NOUN* fine particles of solid matter that float in liquid or sink to the bottom of it

sedimentary *ADJECTIVE* formed from particles that have settled on a surface • *sedimentary rocks*

sedition *NOUN* speeches or actions intended to make people rebel against the authority of the State
▷ **seditious** *ADJECTIVE*

seduce *VERB* **seduces, seducing, seduced** **1** persuade a person to have sexual intercourse **2** attract or lead astray by offering temptations
▷ **seducer** *NOUN* **seduction** *NOUN* **seductive** *ADJECTIVE*

see *VERB* **sees, seeing, saw, seen** **1** perceive with the eyes **2** meet or visit somebody • *See a doctor about your cough.* **3** understand • *She saw what I meant.* **4** imagine • *Can you see yourself as a teacher?* **5** consider • *I will see what can be done.* **6** make sure • *See that the windows are shut.* **7** discover • *See who is at the door* **8** escort • *See her to the door.*
see through not be deceived by something
see to attend to

Thesaurus

section *NOUN* **1** *You must complete every section of the application form* ► part, division, portion, paragraph **2** *the reference section of your local library* ► department, part, division

secular *ADJECTIVE* *secular music; a secular ceremony* ► non-religious, temporal, worldly, earthly, civil, lay OPPOSITES ARE sacred, religious

secure *ADJECTIVE* **1** *Check that all doors and windows are secure.* ► locked, sealed, closed tight, impregnable, invulnerable OPPOSITES ARE insecure, vulnerable **2** *We felt secure indoors during the storm.* ► protected, safe, unharmed, unhurt, unscathed OPPOSITES ARE exposed, in danger **3** *The ladder needs to be made secure.* ► stable, steady, firm, fast, fixed, immovable OPPOSITES ARE insecure, unsteady

secure *VERB* **1** *Secure the front door when you leave.* ► fasten, close, lock, shut, seal, bolt **2** *a charter that secures the rights of the individual* ► ensure, assure, guarantee, protect, confirm **3** *Jenny secured a senior post in the company.* ► obtain, acquire, gain, get, be given

security *NOUN* **1** *The first priority is the security of passengers.* ► safety, protection, care, guarding, freedom from harm AN OPPOSITE IS vulnerability **2** *The president's visit called for unprecedented levels of security.* ► safety measures, safeguards, protection, surveillance

sedate *ADJECTIVE* **1** *The procession moved forward at a sedate pace.* ► steady, unhurried, deliberate, gentle, easy-going, comfortable, slow OPPOSITES ARE brisk, lively **2** *They enjoyed their sedate suburban life and didn't hanker after the bright lights.* ► calm, staid, prim, sober, seemly, demure, dignified, serene

sedentary *ADJECTIVE* *People with sedentary lifestyles need to take exercise.* ► seated, sitting, desk-bound, immobile, inactive AN OPPOSITE IS active

seductive *ADJECTIVE* **1** *Lori gave him one of her most seductive smiles.* ► sexy, alluring, captivating, ravishing, bewitching, appealing, attractive, enticing, irresistible, provocative, tempting OPPOSITES ARE repulsive, repellent **2** *the seductive warmth of a coal fire* ► attractive, appealing, enticing, comforting

see *VERB* **1** *She saw Eve waiting for her. Did you see who got into the car with him?* ► discern, perceive, glimpse, make out, pick out, recognize, identify, distinguish RELATED

seed *NOUN* **seeds** or **seed 1** a fertilized part of a plant, capable of growing into a new plant **2** (*old use*) descendants **3** a seeded player

seed *VERB* **seeds, seeding, seeded 1** plant or sprinkle seeds in something **2** name the best players and arrange for them not to play against each other in the early rounds of a tournament

seedling *NOUN* **seedlings** a very young plant growing from a seed

seedy *ADJECTIVE* **seedier, seediest 1** full of seeds **2** shabby and disreputable
▷ **seediness** *NOUN*

seeing *CONJUNCTION* considering • *Seeing that we have all finished, let's go.*

seek *VERB* **seeks, seeking, sought 1** search for **2** try to do or obtain something • *to seek fame*

seem *VERB* **seems, seeming, seemed** give the impression of being something • *She seems worried about her work.*
▷ **seemingly** *ADVERB*

seemly *ADJECTIVE* (*old use*) (said about behaviour etc.) proper or suitable
▷ **seemliness** *NOUN*
[from an old sense of **seem** = be suitable]

seep *VERB* **seeps, seeping, seeped** ooze slowly out or through something
▷ **seepage** *NOUN*

see-saw *NOUN* **see-saws** a plank balanced in the middle so that two people can sit, one on each end, and make it go up and down

seethe *VERB* **seethes, seething, seethed 1** bubble and surge like water boiling **2** be very angry or excited

segment *NOUN* **segments** a part that is cut off or separates naturally from other parts • *the segments of an orange*
▷ **segmented** *ADJECTIVE*

segregate *VERB* **segregates, segregating, segregated 1** separate people of different religions, races, etc. **2** isolate a person or thing
▷ **segregation** *NOUN*

seismic (sy- zmik) *ADJECTIVE* to do with earthquakes or other vibrations of the earth

seize *VERB* **seizes, seizing, seized 1** take hold of a person or thing suddenly or forcibly **2** take possession of something by force or by legal

Thesaurus

ADJECTIVE visible **2** *She could see how difficult it might be.* ► understand, follow, know, comprehend, realize, recognize, take in, grasp, appreciate, fathom **3** *I can see trouble ahead.* ► foresee, envisage, picture, visualize, predict, imagine, anticipate, conceive **4** *We'll see what we can do.* ► consider, think about, reflect on, weigh up, decide, investigate **5** *They are going to see the game on Saturday.* ► watch, attend, be a spectator at **6** *Is she still seeing Stephen?* ► go out with, be dating, meet, visit **7** *Keith offered to see her home.* ► escort, accompany, take, conduct **8** *Stuart went to see the doctor about his leg.* ► visit, consult, confer with, talk to, speak to **9** *I saw an old friend in town.* ► encounter, meet by chance, run into, run across, chance on, (*more informal*) bump into **10** *I must go and see what the dog is up to.* ► find out, discover, ascertain, establish
see to *Will you see to the repairs?* ► attend to, deal with, take care of, look after, sort out, organize, manage

seed *NOUN* **1** *The male provides the seed to fertilize the female egg.* ► sperm, semen, seminal fluid **2** *The birds feed on insects, seed, and shoots.* ► grains **3** *The fruit was full of seeds.* ► pip, stone **4** *The conflict was the seed for all future troubles.* ► source, origin, cause, basis RELATED ADJECTIVE seminal

seedy *ADJECTIVE* *a seedy hotel on the seafront* ► sleazy, squalid, shabby, run-down, sordid, seamy, rough

seek *VERB* **1** *The fleet sailed south to seek the enemy.* ► look for, search for, pursue, follow, try to find, hunt **2** *They will need to seek advice from a lawyer.* ► call on, ask for, get **3** *Spain is seeking the extradition of the suspects.* ► request, solicit, try to obtain **4** *We seek to please our customers.* ► try, attempt, endeavour, strive, aspire

seem *VERB* *The woman seemed too afraid to speak.* ► appear, look, sound, give the impression of being

seep *VERB* *Smoke seeped into the auditorium.* ► leak, ooze, escape, exude, flow, trickle, dribble

seething *ADJECTIVE* *Rose was seething about what had happened.* ► fuming, furious, angry, livid, infuriated, incensed, outraged

segregate *VERB* *The school agreed to segregate them for swimming lessons.* ► separate, isolate, keep apart, set apart, put apart, exclude, cut off

segregation *NOUN* **1** *Racial segregation has been outlawed.* ► apartheid, discrimination, separation **2** *the segregation of smokers and non-smokers in public places* ► isolation, separation, keeping apart

seize *VERB* **1** *He seized the remote and turned up the volume.* ► grab, snatch, take hold of OPPOSITES ARE release, let go of **2** *Rebels have seized an outpost in the jungle.* ► capture, take, take possession of, take over, overrun OPPOSITES ARE abandon, relinquish **3** *Customs officers seized a large cache of drugs.*

authority • *Customs officers seized a lot of smuggled goods.* **3** take eagerly • *Seize your chance!* **4** have a sudden effect on • *Panic seized us.*

seize up become jammed, especially because of friction or overheating

seizure NOUN **seizures 1** seizing **2** a sudden fit, as in epilepsy or a heart attack

seldom ADVERB rarely; not often

select VERB **selects, selecting, selected** choose a person or thing
▷ **selector** NOUN

select ADJECTIVE **1** carefully chosen • *a select group* **2** (said about a club etc.) choosing its members carefully; exclusive

selection NOUN **selections 1** selecting; being selected **2** a person or thing selected **3** a group selected from a larger group **4** a range of goods from which to choose

self NOUN **selves 1** a person as an individual **2** a person's particular nature • *She has recovered and is her old self again.* **3** a person's own advantage • *He always puts self first.*

self-assured ADJECTIVE confident

self-catering NOUN catering for yourself (instead of having meals provided)

self-centred ADJECTIVE selfish

self-confident ADJECTIVE confident of your own abilities

self-conscious ADJECTIVE embarrassed or unnatural because you know that people are watching you

self-contained ADJECTIVE (said about accommodation) complete in itself; containing all the necessary facilities

self-control NOUN the ability to control your own behaviour
▷ **self-controlled** ADJECTIVE

self-denial NOUN deliberately going without things you would like to have

self-determination NOUN a country's right to rule itself and to choose its own method of government

self-employed ADJECTIVE working independently, not for an employer

self-esteem NOUN your own opinion of yourself and your own worth

self-evident ADJECTIVE obvious and not needing proof or explanation

self-important ADJECTIVE pompous

selfish ADJECTIVE doing what you want and not thinking of other people; keeping things for yourself
▷ **selfishly** ADVERB **selfishness** NOUN

selfless ADJECTIVE unselfish

self-made ADJECTIVE rich or successful because of your own efforts

self-pity NOUN too much sorrow and pity for yourself and your own problems

self-possessed ADJECTIVE calm and dignified

self-raising ADJECTIVE (said about flour) making cakes rise without needing to have baking powder etc. added

Thesaurus

► confiscate, appropriate, impound
OPPOSITES ARE return, give back **4** *Bandits seized his wife and children.* ► kidnap, abduct, take prisoner, capture, (*more informal*) snatch
OPPOSITES ARE release, let go

seldom ADVERB *She was seldom away from home for long.* ► rarely, not often, hardly ever, infrequently AN OPPOSITE IS often

select VERB *The committee met to select a chairperson.* ► choose, pick, appoint, name, elect, vote for, nominate, decide on

selection NOUN **1** *There's a wide selection of food to choose from.* ► range, variety, assortment **2** *Mike put a coin in the machine and made his selection.* ► choice, pick, option

selective ADJECTIVE *She's very selective in her reading.* ► discerning, discriminating, particular, careful, (*more informal*) choosy
AN OPPOSITE IS indiscriminate

self-confident ADJECTIVE *In self-confident mood, Franco pressed ahead with this plans.*
► self-assured, self-possessed, sure of yourself, confident, positive, assertive, assured, poised
AN OPPOSITE IS diffident

self-conscious ADJECTIVE *He felt self-conscious about having to borrow money from his father.*
► embarrassed, bashful, diffident, uneasy, awkward, uncomfortable, unnatural, coy, shy, ill at ease, nervous OPPOSITES ARE natural, confident

self-control NOUN *He lost self-control and shouted at her.* ► composure, restraint, self-discipline, calmness, coolness, self-command

selfish ADJECTIVE *People are seen as being more selfish and less tolerant.* ► self-centred, egocentric, inconsiderate, self-absorbed, self-obsessed OPPOSITES ARE unselfish, considerate, generous, selfless

selfishness NOUN *They were motivated by greed and selfishness.* ► egotism, self-obsession, self-interest, thoughtlessness, meanness
OPPOSITES ARE unselfishness, generosity

selfless ADJECTIVE *He made a selfless sacrifice for his country.* ► generous, magnanimous, unselfish

self-respect *NOUN* your own proper respect for yourself

self-righteous *ADJECTIVE* smugly sure that you are behaving virtuously

self-service *ADJECTIVE* where customers help themselves to things and pay a cashier for what they have taken

self-sufficient *ADJECTIVE* able to produce or provide what you need without help from others

self-supporting *ADJECTIVE* earning enough to keep yourself without needing money from others

sell *VERB* **sells, selling, sold 1** exchange something for money **2** be on sale at a certain price • *It sells for £5.99.*
▷ **seller** *NOUN*
sell out 1 sell all your stock of something **2** (*informal*) betray someone **3** abandon your principles for reasons of convenience because it suits you

sell *NOUN*
hard sell putting pressure on someone to buy something
sell-by date a mark on the packaging of food showing the date by which it must be sold
soft sell selling by gentle persuasion

sell-out *NOUN* **sell-outs** an entertainment, sporting event, etc. for which all the tickets have been sold

selves *plural of* **self**

semaphore *NOUN* a system of signalling by holding flags out with your arms in positions that indicate letters of the alphabet

semen (seem- en) *NOUN* a white liquid produced by males and containing sperm

semibreve *NOUN* **semibreves** the longest musical note normally used (𝅝), lasting four times as long as a crotchet

semicircle *NOUN* **semicircles** half a circle
▷ **semicircular** *ADJECTIVE*

semicolon *NOUN* **semicolons** a punctuation mark (;) used to mark a break that is more than that marked by a comma

semiconductor *NOUN* **semiconductors** a substance that can conduct electricity but not as well as most metals do

semi-detached *ADJECTIVE* (said about a house) joined to another house on one side

semifinal *NOUN* **semifinals** a match or round whose winner will take part in the final

seminar *NOUN* **seminars** a meeting for advanced discussion and research on a subject

semiquaver *NOUN* **semiquavers** a note in music (𝅘𝅥𝅯), equal in length to one quarter of a crotchet

Semitic (sim- it- ik) *ADJECTIVE* to do with the Semites, the group of people that includes the Jews and Arabs
▷ **Semite** (see- my't) *NOUN*

semitone *NOUN* **semitones** half a tone in music

semolina *NOUN* hard round grains of wheat used to make milk puddings and pasta

senate *NOUN* **senates 1** the governing council in ancient Rome **2** the upper house of the parliament of the United States, France, and certain other countries
▷ **senator** *NOUN*

send *VERB* **sends, sending, sent 1** make a person or thing go or be taken somewhere **2** cause to become • *The noise is sending me crazy.*
▷ **sender** *NOUN*
send for order a person or thing to come or be brought to you
send up (*informal*) make fun of something by imitating it

Thesaurus

self-respect *NOUN* *Under the new president, the country prospered and recovered its self-respect.* ► pride, dignity, self-confidence, self-esteem

self-righteous *ADJECTIVE* *He called her a stuck-up, self-righteous Miss Perfect.* ► sanctimonious, holier-than-thou, priggish, smug, self-satisfied, moralizing, unctuous

self-satisfied *ADJECTIVE* *Hilary relaxed and gave a little self-satisfied smile.* ► smug, complacent, self-congratulatory

sell *VERB* **1** *The corner shop sells basic provisions.* ► stock, trade in, deal in, retail, handle, peddle **2** *They are having problems selling their house.* ► dispose of, put on the market, (*more formal*) vend

seller *NOUN* *sellers of household goods* ► supplier, trader (in), dealer (in), vendor, retailer, stockist, purveyor

send *VERB* **1** *I'll send you a letter.* ► dispatch, post, mail, convey, forward **2** *She sent John a message.* ► transmit, fax, email, wire **3** *The space programme will be sending a satellite into orbit.* ► launch, propel, shoot, direct, fire **4** *It's the sort of remark that sends you mad.* ► make, drive, cause to be
send for *They decided to send for the police.* ► call, fetch, summon, ask to come

senile (seen- I'll) *ADJECTIVE* weak or confused and forgetful because of old age
▷ **senility** *NOUN*

senior *ADJECTIVE* **1** older than someone else **2** higher in rank **3** for older children • *a senior school*
▷ **seniority** *NOUN*

senior *NOUN* **seniors 1** a person who is older or higher in rank than you are • *He is my senior.* **2** a member of a senior school

senior citizen *NOUN* **senior citizens** an elderly person, especially a pensioner

sensation *NOUN* **sensations 1** a feeling • *a sensation of warmth* **2** a very excited condition; something causing this • *The news caused a great sensation.*

sensational *ADJECTIVE* **1** causing great excitement, interest, or shock **2** (*informal*) very good; wonderful
▷ **sensationally** *ADVERB*

sense *NOUN* **senses 1** the ability to see, hear, smell, touch, or taste things **2** the ability to feel or appreciate something • *a sense of guilt* • *a sense of humour* **3** the power to think or make wise decisions • *Hasn't he got the sense to come in out of the rain?* **4** meaning • *The word 'run' has many senses*
make sense 1 have a meaning **2** be a sensible idea

sense *VERB* **senses, sensing, sensed 1** feel; get an impression • *I sensed that she did not like me.* **2** detect something • *This device senses radioactivity.*

senseless *ADJECTIVE* **1** stupid; not showing good sense **2** unconscious

senses *PLURAL NOUN* sanity • *He is out of his senses.*

sensible *ADJECTIVE* wise; having or showing good sense
▷ **sensibly** *ADVERB*

sensitive *ADJECTIVE* **1** affected by something • *Photographic paper is sensitive to light* **2** receiving impressions quickly and easily • *sensitive fingers* **3** easily hurt or offended • *She is very sensitive about her age.* **4** considerate about other people's feelings **5** needing to be dealt with tactfully • *a sensitive subject*
▷ **sensitively** *ADVERB* **sensitivity** *NOUN*

Thesaurus

senile *ADJECTIVE* *Her husband was becoming senile and difficult to cope with.* ► old, aged, doddering, infirm, feeble, decrepit, (*more informal*) past it AN OPPOSITE IS in his *or* her prime

senior *ADJECTIVE* **1** *a senior pupil* ► older, elder **2** *a senior official* ► high-ranking, superior, chief OPPOSITES ARE junior, subordinate

sensation *NOUN* **1** *She felt a sensation of floating.* ► feeling, sense, awareness, impression **2** *The affair caused a sensation.* ► commotion, excitement, stir, furore, outrage, scandal, surprise, thrill

sensational *ADJECTIVE* **1** *a sensational murder trial* ► shocking, horrifying, lurid, scandalous, thrilling, blood-curdling, breathtaking, exciting, hair-raising **2** *Her singing was sensational.* ► amazing, extraordinary, remarkable, wonderful, fabulous, fantastic, magnificent, great, marvellous, spectacular, superb

sense *NOUN* **1** *She has a strong sense of rhythm.* ► sensation, feeling, perception **2** *He felt a sense of guilt.* ► awareness, feeling, sensation, perception **3** *They had the sense to get out in time.* ► wisdom, common sense, intelligence, wit, shrewdness **4** *I couldn't see the sense of leaving then.* ► point, purpose, advantage, benefit **5** *I didn't grasp the sense of their message.* ► meaning, significance, substance, implication, import, drift, gist, point
make sense of *It's hard to make sense of these remarks.* ► understand, grasp, comprehend

sense *VERB* *We sensed that they didn't trust us.* ► discern, feel, suspect, perceive, realize, get the impression, appreciate, guess, notice, be aware, detect

senseless *ADJECTIVE* **1** *It was a senseless crime.* ► pointless, futile, needless, aimless, absurd, nonsensical, foolish, stupid **2** *They found him in the morning, senseless but alive.* ► unconscious, comatose, stunned, out cold

sensible *ADJECTIVE* **1** *Joanna was sensible enough to listen. Everyone agreed that this was a sensible decision.* ► prudent, thoughtful, far-sighted, shrewd, wise, judicious, intelligent, pragmatic, responsible, realistic, rational, level-headed OPPOSITES ARE foolish, unwise **2** *She liked to wear sensible clothes.* ► practical, functional, comfortable, useful, (*informal*) no-nonsense OPPOSITES ARE impractical, fashionable

sensitive *ADJECTIVE* **1** *The human eye is very sensitive to green.* ► responsive, reactive, susceptible, affected (by), conscious (of) AN OPPOSITE IS insensitive **2** *The problem needs sensitive handling.* ► tactful, thoughtful, considerate, sympathetic, understanding, perceptive OPPOSITES ARE insensitive, tactless **3** *She's a very sensitive girl, so take care what you say.* ► emotional, easily offended, easily upset, volatile, thin-skinned, touchy AN OPPOSITE IS thick-skinned **4** *Take care in the sun if you have a fair sensitive skin.* ► delicate, soft, tender, fragile, fine OPPOSITES ARE tough, resilient **5** *The court ruling comes at a sensitive time for the government.* ► awkward, tricky,

sensor *NOUN* **sensors** a device or instrument for detecting a physical property such as light, heat, or sound

sentence *NOUN* **sentences 1** a group of words that express a complete thought and form a statement, question, exclamation, or command **2** the punishment announced to a convicted person in a lawcourt

sentence *VERB* **sentences, sentencing, sentenced** give someone a sentence in a lawcourt • *The judge sentenced him to a year in prison.* [from Latin *sententia* = opinion]

sententious *ADJECTIVE* giving moral advice in a pompous way

sentiment *NOUN* **sentiments 1** an opinion **2** sentimentality

sentimental *ADJECTIVE* showing or arousing tenderness or romantic feeling or foolish emotion
▷ **sentimentally** *ADVERB* **sentimentality** *NOUN*

sentinel *NOUN* **sentinels** a guard or sentry

sentry *NOUN* **sentries** a soldier guarding something

separate *ADJECTIVE* **1** not joined to anything **2** not shared
▷ **separately** *ADVERB*

separate *VERB* **separates, separating, separated 1** make or keep separate; divide **2** become separate **3** stop living together as a married couple
▷ **separation** *NOUN* **separator** *NOUN*

September *NOUN* the ninth month of the year [from Latin *septem* = seven, because it was the seventh month of the ancient Roman calendar]

septic *ADJECTIVE* infected with harmful bacteria that cause pus to form

Thesaurus

controversial, delicate
AN OPPOSITE IS uncontroversial

sentence *NOUN* **1** *The judge will decide on a sentence next week.* ► judgement, ruling, decision, verdict **2** *Her husband is serving a three-year sentence for robbery.* ► prison term, (*more informal*) stretch

sentence *VERB* *The men will be sentenced at a later date.* ► pass judgement on, pronounce sentence on, punish

sentiment *NOUN* **1** *I agree with the sentiments expressed in your letter.* ► view, opinion, belief, thought, attitude, idea, judgement **2** *There's not much room for sentiment in this kind of business.* ► sentimentality, emotionalism, finer feelings, sensibility, soft-heartedness, mawkishness

sentimental *ADJECTIVE* **1** *The family held a sentimental attachment to their old home.* ► nostalgic, emotional, affectionate, tender, romantic, soft-hearted **2** *a sentimental story about separated twins* ► maudlin, mawkish, over-emotional, sickly, saccharine, syrupy, indulgent, gushing, corny, (*more informal*) soppy, (*more informal*) mushy, (*more informal*) treacly OPPOSITES ARE unsentimental, realistic

sentry *NOUN* *A sentry was on duty at the gate.* ► guard, sentinel, lookout, watchman, patrol, picket

separable *ADJECTIVE* *The components are separable and can be replaced individually. Teaching and research are not completely separable activities.* ► separate, distinct, detachable, divisible, removable, distinguishable

separate *ADJECTIVE* **1** *The guards took care to keep the two groups separate.* ► apart, segregated, cut off, divided, divorced, fenced off, isolated OPPOSITES ARE together, united **2** *You may prefer to have the kitchen separate from the dining area. The reports may have been referring to two separate events.* ► distinct, detached, different, discrete, unattached (to), unconnected (to)
AN OPPOSITE IS joined

separate *VERB* **1** *They were arguing so fiercely it was difficult to separate them. The war separated us for many years.* ► divide, part, break up, split up, segregate AN OPPOSITE IS unite **2** *Only a short distance separated them.* ► divide, come between AN OPPOSITE IS unite **3** *We separated at the station and I went home.* ► part company, go different ways, split up AN OPPOSITE IS meet **4** *The path separated and went up the hill.* ► diverge, fork, branch off AN OPPOSITE IS merge **5** *Separate the yolks of the eggs from the whites.* ► extract, remove, isolate, abstract, filter out AN OPPOSITE IS mix **6** *When his parents separated he lived with his mother.* ► split up, break up, divorce, part, become estranged, part company **7 separate from** *She separated herself from the company and formed her own business.* ► withdraw from, break away from, leave, quit, dissociate yourself from
AN OPPOSITE IS join

separation *NOUN* **1** *the separation of church and state* ► division, splitting, dissociation, severance, detachment, disconnection, parting, isolation, removal, segregation, cutting off OPPOSITES ARE merging, unification **2** *The separation of the prince and princess has been formally announced.* (*informal*) ► break-up, split, parting, rift, estrangement
AN OPPOSITE IS marriage

septic *ADJECTIVE* *One of her toes looked septic.* ► infected, poisoned, putrefying, festering, putrid, inflamed, purulent, suppurating

a b c d e f g h i j k l m n o p q r **s** t u v w x y z

sepulchre (sep- ul- ker) NOUN **sepulchres** a tomb

sequel NOUN **sequels 1** a book or film etc. that continues the story of an earlier one **2** something that follows or results from an earlier event

sequence NOUN **sequences 1** the following of one thing after another; the order in which things happen **2** a series of things

seraph NOUN **seraphim** or **seraphs** a kind of angel

serenade NOUN **serenades** a song or tune of a kind played by a man under his lover's window

serenade VERB **serenades, serenading, serenaded** sing or play a serenade to someone

serene ADJECTIVE calm and cheerful
▷ **serenely** ADVERB **serenity** NOUN

serf NOUN **serfs** a farm labourer who worked for a landowner in the Middle Ages, and who was not allowed to leave
▷ **serfdom** NOUN

sergeant (sar- jent) NOUN **sergeants** a soldier or policeman who is in charge of others

sergeant major NOUN **sergeant majors** a soldier who is one rank higher than a sergeant

serial NOUN **serials** a story or film etc. that is presented in separate parts
USAGE Do not confuse with **cereal**.

serial killer NOUN **serial killers** a person who commits a series of murders

serial number NOUN **serial numbers** a number put onto an object, usually by the manufacturers, to distinguish it from other identical objects

series NOUN **series 1** a number of things following or connected with each other **2** a number of games or matches between the same competitors **3** a number of separate radio or television programmes with the same characters or on the same subject

serious ADJECTIVE **1** solemn and thoughtful; not smiling **2** sincere; not casual or light-hearted • *a serious talk* • *a serious attempt* **3** causing anxiety, not trivial • *a serious accident*
▷ **seriously** ADVERB **seriousness** NOUN

sermon NOUN **sermons** a talk given by a preacher, especially as part of a religious service

serpent NOUN **serpents** a snake

serried ADJECTIVE arranged in rows close together • *serried ranks of troops*

servant NOUN **servants** a person whose job is to work or serve in someone else's house

serve VERB **serves, serving, served 1** work for a person or organization or country etc. **2** sell things to people in a shop **3** give out food to people at a meal **4** spend time in something; undergo • *He has served a prison sentence.* **5** be

Thesaurus

sequel NOUN **1** *The immediate sequel was a riot in the capital.* ► consequence, result, outcome, upshot **2** *a sequel to Daphne du Maurier's 'Rebecca'.* ► continuation, (*more informal*) follow-up

sequence NOUN **1** *A similar sequence of events occurred in the Baltic States.* ► succession, order, course, progression, series, chain, cycle **2** *Here is a short sequence from her new film.* ► excerpt, scene, clip, extract, section, episode

serene ADJECTIVE *Her eyes lit up, and a serene smile spread across her face.* ► calm, composed, contented, untroubled, unruffled, placid, tranquil, peaceful, imperturbable, quiet
AN OPPOSITE IS agitated

series NOUN **1** *Guerrillas carried out a series of kidnappings.* ► succession, sequence, string, chain, wave, spate, rash, outbreak, run **2** *Filming has started on a six-part drama series.* ► serial, run of programmes

serious ADJECTIVE **1** *She wore a serious expression.* ► solemn, grave, earnest, thoughtful, pensive, sombre, unsmiling, grim, dour
OPPOSITES ARE jovial, cheerful **2** *A serious disagreement arose between them.* ► important, significant, momentous, critical, urgent, weighty, crucial, grave
OPPOSITES ARE unimportant, frivolous **3** *She suffered serious injuries when she fell from her horse. robbery, assault, theft, and other serious crimes* ► severe, critical, bad, acute, shocking, terrible, appalling, dreadful, grave, grievous
AN OPPOSITE IS trivial **4** *He said he was only interested in serious literature.* ► profound, intellectual, scholarly, learned, highbrow, (*more informal*) heavy **5** *Are you serious about leaving?* ► sincere, in earnest, genuine, committed, wholehearted
AN OPPOSITE IS uncommitted

seriously ADVERB **1** *He looked at her seriously, frowning deeply.* ► solemnly, earnestly, thoughtfully, sternly, dourly **2** *The baby was seriously ill in hospital.* ► severely, critically, badly, acutely, gravely **3** *Do you seriously expect me to believe you?* ► really, actually, honestly

servant NOUN *A servant appeared, carrying a tray.* ► attendant, retainer, domestic, valet, butler, maid, menial, helper, (*more informal*) skivvy, (*more informal*) flunkey

serve VERB **1** *They served their masters well.* ► attend, assist, look after, minister to, work for **2** *He claimed to use his business skills to serve the public interest.* ► further, advance, benefit, advantage, support **3** *The book served as a useful guide to the city's attractions. a slogan that would*

suitable for something • *This will serve our purpose.* **6** start play in tennis etc. by hitting the ball

▷ **server** *NOUN*

it serves you right you deserve it

serve *NOUN* **serves** a service in tennis etc.

service *NOUN* **services 1** working for a person or organization or country etc. **2** something that helps people or supplies what they want • *a bus service* **3** the army, navy, or air force • *the armed services* **4** a religious ceremony **5** providing people with goods, food, etc. • *The service at the restaurant was slow.* **6** a set of dishes and plates etc. for a meal • *a dinner service* **7** the servicing of a vehicle or machine etc. **8** the action of serving in tennis etc.

service *VERB* **services, servicing, serviced 1** repair or keep a vehicle or machine etc. in working order **2** supply with services

serviceable *ADJECTIVE* usable; suitable for ordinary use or wear

service station *NOUN* **service stations** a place beside a major road where motorists can stop for fuel, light meals, etc.

serviette *NOUN* **serviettes** a piece of cloth or paper used to keep your clothes or hands clean at a meal

serving *NOUN* **servings** a helping of food

session *NOUN* **sessions 1** a meeting or series of meetings • *The Queen will open the next session of Parliament.* **2** a time spent doing one thing • *a recording session*

set *VERB* **sets, setting, set 1** put or fix• *Set the vase on the table.* • *They've set a date for the wedding.* **2** make ready to work • *I'd better set the alarm.* **3** make or become firm or hard• *Leave the jelly to set.* **4** give someone a task• *This sets us a problem.* **5** put into a condition• *Set them free.* **6** go down below the horizon• *The sun was setting.*

set about 1 start doing something **2** (*informal*) attack somebody

set off 1 begin a journey **2** start something happening **3** cause something to explode

set out 1 begin a journey **2** display or make known

set sail begin a voyage

set to 1 begin doing something vigorously **2** begin fighting or arguing

set up 1 place in position **2** arrange or establish • *set up house* **3** cause or start • *set up a din*

set *NOUN* **sets 1** a group of people or things that belong together **2** a radio or television receiver **3** (in mathematics) a collection of things that have a common property **4** the way something is placed • *the set of his jaw* **5** the scenery or stage for a play or film **6** a group of games in a tennis match **7** a badger's burrow

set *ADJECTIVE* **1** fixed or arranged in advance • *a set time* **2** ready or prepared to do something

set on determined about doing something

Thesaurus

serve for the whole range of products ► function, be adequate, be useful **4** *a tool that serves a special purpose* ► fulfil, answer, perform, satisfy, complete, discharge **5** *At that point he went in to serve the food.* ► give out, dish up, distribute, provide **6** *Molly spent the summer serving in a local shop.* ► assist, be an assistant, sell **7 serve on** *He had served on the committee for ten years.* ► work on, be a member of, sit on, contribute to

service *NOUN* **1** *The contract lists the terms of service.* ► employment, work, business, labour, duty **2** *They have done us quite a service.* ► favour, benefit, assistance, kindness, good turn **3** *products that will give years of service* ► use, usage, utility **4** *She took the car in for a service.* ► overhaul, maintenance check **5** *a church service* ► ceremony, worship, ritual, rite, observance

service *VERB* *A local garage services their car.* ► overhaul, maintain, repair, check, mend

serving *NOUN* *a large serving of pasta* ► portion, helping, plateful, plate, share, amount, ration, (*more informal*) dollop

session *NOUN* **1** *The council held its first session in October.* ► meeting, sitting, assembly, conference, discussion, hearing **2** *More practice sessions were needed.* ► period, time, spell, bout

set *NOUN* **1** *There was a set of keys on the table. The government will announce a set of new proposals on human rights.* ► collection, group , series, batch, bunch, assortment, array **2** *She belonged to a fashionable London set.* ► circle, clique, group, crowd, coterie, company **3** *a television set* ► apparatus, receiver **4** *a chemistry set* ► kit, outfit, apparatus **5** *The production boasted a spectacular set and lavish costumes.* ► staging, setting, scenery, stage furniture

set *VERB* **1** *She set the bags on a bench in the porch.* ► put, place, deposit, position, stand, leave, settle, station, post **2** *We should set a date for the next meeting.* ► fix, decide on, agree on, establish, choose, select, name, arrange, schedule **3** *She set the alarm for five the next morning.* ► adjust, regulate, programme, synchronize **4** *The sun was setting.* ► go down, sink, subside, vanish, disappear **5** *Leave the jelly in the fridge to set.* ► harden, solidify, thicken, stiffen, gel

set about 1 *He set about the task with gusto.*

a b c d e f g h i j k l m n o p q r s t u v w x y z

setback *NOUN* **setbacks** something that stops progress or slows it down

set book *NOUN* **set books** a book that must be studied for a literature examination

set square *NOUN* **set squares** a device shaped like a right-angled triangle, used in drawing lines parallel to each other etc.

settee *NOUN* **settees** a long soft seat with a back and arms

setter *NOUN* **setters** a dog of a long-haired breed that can be trained to stand rigid when it scents game

setting *NOUN* **settings 1** the way or place in which something is set **2** music for the words of a song etc. **3** a set of cutlery or crockery for one person at a meal

settle *VERB* **settles, settling, settled 1** arrange; decide or solve something • *That settles the problem.* **2** make or become calm or comfortable or orderly; stop being restless • *Stop chattering and settle down!* **3** go and live somewhere • *They settled in Canada.* **4** sink; come to rest on something • *Dust had settled on his books.* **5** pay a bill or debt

settlement *NOUN* **settlements 1** settling something **2** the way something is settled **3** a small number of people or houses established in a new area

settler *NOUN* **settlers** one of the first people to settle in a new country

set-up *NOUN* (*informal*) the way something is organized or arranged

seven *NOUN, ADJECTIVE* **sevens** the number 7
▷ **seventh** *ADJECTIVE, NOUN*

seventeen *NOUN, ADJECTIVE* the number 17
▷ **seventeenth** *ADJECTIVE, NOUN*

Thesaurus

► begin, start, make a start on, get down to, embark on, tackle **2** *A gang set about them in a dark alley.* ► attack, assault, assail, fall on, lay into

set aside 1 *Daphne set aside money each month towards her holiday.* ► save, put by, keep, earmark **2** *The decision was set aside in the Appeal Court.* ► overrule, overturn, reverse, revoke, quash, annul

set off or **out** *We set off early for the airport.* ► set out, start out, leave, depart

set out *He set out his collection of coins.* ► lay out, arrange, display, exhibit, present

set up 1 *A statue will be set up in the main square.* ► erect, put up, raise, construct **2** *The company plans to set up a branch in New York.* ► establish, found, start, institute **3** *Her secretary set up a meeting for the following week.* ► organize, arrange, fix, schedule

setback *NOUN He had survived a whole series of setbacks.* ► difficulty, problem, hitch, delay, hold-up, obstacle, reverse, snag, blow, upset, disappointment, complication, misfortune, (*more informal*) glitch, (*more informal*) hiccup
OPPOSITES ARE advance, breakthrough

setting *NOUN* **1** *a relaxing holiday in a quiet setting* ► surroundings, location, position, site, background, environment, locale **2** *diamonds in a silver setting* ► mounting, mount, fixture, surround **3** *a drama in a historical setting* ► backdrop, context, (*French*) mise en scène, scene, set

settle *VERB* **1** *Further talks will be held today in an attempt to settle the dispute.* ► resolve, conclude, clear up, put an end to, find a solution to, reach an agreement about **2** *The solicitors will settle their affairs.* ► arrange, organize, sort out, put in order, order, complete **3** *We can settle the bill in the morning.* ► pay, square, clear **4** *Jack settled into an armchair by the fire.* ► sink, fall, drop, subside **5** *A bird settled on a branch.* ► land, alight, descend **6** *He needed something to settle his nerves.* ► calm, soothe, compose, pacify, quell
AN OPPOSITE IS agitate

settle down *Why can't you settle down?* ► calm down, quieten down, be quiet, be still, relax

settle down to *Rachel wanted her to settle down to something.* ► get down to, apply yourself to, concentrate on, focus on

settle for *Shelby wasn't a man to settle for a dull life.* ► agree to, accept, acquiesce in, compromise on

settle in *After the war the family settled in Liverpool.* ► set up home, make your home, move to, establish yourself in

settle on *It was high time they settled on a date for the wedding.* ► decide, choose, fix, agree on, name, arrange, organize, schedule

settlement *NOUN* **1** *a legal settlement* ► agreement, deal, arrangement, treaty, contract **2** *The dispute is no nearer settlement.* ► resolution, solution, sorting out, settling **3** *an Iron-Age settlement near the modern trunk road* ► community, colony, encampment, commune, town, village

set-up *NOUN a modern communications set-up; a new constitutional set-up for the EU* ► system, arrangement, framework, organization, business, operation

sever *VERB* **1** *The arm had been severed at the shoulder.* ► cut off , cut, chop off, hack off, shear off, slice off, separate, amputate, disconnect, remove **2** *Henry VIII severed his relationship with the Church of Rome.* ► break off, cut off, terminate, disconnect, cease

seventy *NOUN, ADJECTIVE* **seventies** the number 70
▷ **seventieth** *ADJECTIVE, NOUN*

several *ADJECTIVE, NOUN* more than two but not many

severe *ADJECTIVE* **1** strict; not gentle or kind **2** intense or forceful • *severe gales* **3** very plain • *a severe style of dress*
▷ **severely** *ADVERB* **severity** *NOUN*

sew *VERB* **sews, sewing, sewed, sewn** *or* **sewed** **1** join things together by using a needle and thread **2** work with a needle and thread or with a sewing machine
USAGE Do not confuse with **sow**.

sewage (soo- ij) *NOUN* liquid waste matter carried away in drains

sewer (soo- er) *NOUN* **sewers** a large underground drain for carrying away sewage

sewing machine *NOUN* **sewing machines** a machine for sewing things

sex *NOUN* **sexes** **1** each of the two groups (*male* and *female*) into which living things are placed according to their functions in the process of reproduction **2** the instinct that causes members of the two sexes to be attracted to one another **3** sexual intercourse

sexism *NOUN* discrimination against people of a particular sex, especially women
▷ **sexist** *ADJECTIVE, NOUN*

sexual *ADJECTIVE* **1** to do with sex or the sexes **2** (said about reproduction) happening by the fusion of male and female cells
▷ **sexually** *ADVERB* **sexuality** *NOUN*

sexual intercourse *NOUN* an intimate act between two people, in which the man puts his penis into the woman's vagina, to express love, for pleasure, or to conceive a child

sexy *ADJECTIVE* **sexier, sexiest** (*informal*) **1** sexually attractive **2** concerned with sex

SF *ABBREVIATION* science fiction

shabby *ADJECTIVE* **shabbier, shabbiest** **1** in a poor or worn-out condition; dilapidated **2** poorly dressed **3** unfair or dishonourable • *a shabby trick*
▷ **shabbily** *ADVERB* **shabbiness** *NOUN*

shack *NOUN* **shacks** a roughly built hut

Thesaurus

several *ADJECTIVE* **1** *The cable is split into several strands. He had admitted the murder several times.* ▶ a number of, many, some, a few **2** *There are several ways of looking at the problem.* ▶ various, miscellaneous, a number of, sundry, assorted

severe *ADJECTIVE* **1** *The region faced a severe threat of mass starvation. Wreckage covered the road, causing severe traffic disruption.* ▶ serious, acute, grave, extreme, critical, dire, grievous AN OPPOSITE IS minor **2** *Many birds were found injured or dead after the severe weather.* ▶ harsh, hard, extreme, turbulent, stormy AN OPPOSITE IS mild **3** *Oliver developed a severe stomach ulcer. The pains could be severe and disruptive.* ▶ acute, intense, painful, excruciating AN OPPOSITE IS slight **4** *The expedition will be a severe test of their stamina.* ▶ demanding, hard, formidable, difficult, onerous, burdensome OPPOSITES ARE simple, easy **5** *She did not expect the criticism to be so severe.* ▶ fierce, harsh, sharp, scathing, caustic AN OPPOSITE IS mild **6** *More severe penalties were needed for hit-and-run drivers. They deplored the imposition of such severe censorship.* ▶ strict, harsh, draconian, ruthless AN OPPOSITE IS mild **7** *It was described as neoclassical architecture in a severe style.* ▶ plain, simple, spare, stark, unadorned OPPOSITES ARE ornate, elaborate

sew *VERB* *His aunt sewed the badge on his sleeve.* ▶ stitch, tack, attach, fasten OPPOSITES ARE unpick, remove
sew up *You need to sew up the hole in your sleeve.* ▶ darn, stitch, mend, patch, repair

sex *NOUN* **1** *The disease affects children of both sexes.* ▶ gender **2** *There is nothing wrong in asking questions about sex.* ▶ the facts of life, sexual activity, reproduction, sexual reproduction **3** *Unsafe sex in this age group was increasing.* ▶ sexual intercourse, intercourse, making love, lovemaking, sexual relations
have sex *Derek said they'd been having sex.* ▶ have sexual intercourse, make love, go to bed together, (*more informal*) go all the way

sexual *ADJECTIVE* **1** *A bit of petting had been the only sexual activity.* ▶ erotic, physical, sensual, carnal, sexy **2** *A diagram of the sexual organs might help.* ▶ reproductive, procreative, genital

sexy *ADJECTIVE* **1** *'You're young,' he said coolly, 'beautiful, sexy, and intelligent.'* ▶ sexually attractive, desirable, seductive, sensual **2** *Louise stripped to her sexy lace underwear.* ▶ titillating, erotic, suggestive, salacious, lewd, racy, sexually explicit, (*more informal*) steamy

shabby *ADJECTIVE* **1** *Florrie straightened the lapel of her shabby coat.* ▶ worn, scruffy, ragged, tattered **2** *She went into a shabby coffee bar in the centre of town.* ▶ run-down, scruffy, dilapidated, seedy, dingy, dirty, poky, tatty **3** *He hated resorting to such shabby lying.* ▶ shameful, mean, cheap, contemptible, despicable, rotten

shack *NOUN* *a shack in the woods* ▶ hut, cabin, shanty, shed, hovel

shackle *NOUN* **shackles** an iron ring for fastening a prisoner's wrist or ankle to something

shackle *VERB* **shackles, shackling, shackled** put shackles on a prisoner

shade *NOUN* **shades 1** slight darkness produced where something blocks the sun's light **2** a device that reduces or shuts out bright light **3** a colour; how light or dark a colour is **4** a slight difference • *The word had several shades of meaning.* **5** (*poetical*) a ghost

shade *VERB* **shades, shading, shaded 1** shelter something from bright light **2** make part of a drawing darker than the rest **3** move gradually from one state or quality to another • *evening shading into night*

shadow *NOUN* **shadows 1** the dark shape that falls on a surface when something is between the surface and a light **2** an area of shade **3** a slight trace • *a shadow of doubt*
▷ **shadowy** *ADJECTIVE*

shadow *VERB* **shadows, shadowing, shadowed 1** cast a shadow on something **2** follow a person secretly

Shadow Cabinet *NOUN* members of the Opposition in Parliament who each have responsibility for a particular area of policy

shady *ADJECTIVE* **shadier, shadiest 1** giving shade • *a shady tree* **2** in the shade • *a shady place* **3** (*informal*) not completely honest; disreputable • *a shady deal*

shaft *NOUN* **shafts 1** a long slender rod or straight part • *the shaft of an arrow* **2** a ray of light **3** a deep narrow hole • *a mine shaft*

shaggy *ADJECTIVE* **shaggier, shaggiest 1** having long rough hair or fibre **2** rough, thick, and untidy • *shaggy hair*

shake *VERB* **shakes, shaking, shook, shaken 1** move quickly up and down or from side to side **2** shock or upset • *The news shook us.* **3** tremble; be unsteady • *His voice was shaking.*
▷ **shaker** *NOUN*
shake hands clasp a person's right hand with yours in greeting or parting or as a sign of agreement

shake *NOUN* **shakes** shaking; a shaking movement
▷ **shaky** *ADJECTIVE* **shakily** *ADVERB*
in two shakes very soon

Thesaurus

shade *NOUN* **1** *They spend most of the day lying in the shade.* ► shadow, shelter, cover **2** *The shades of evening drew on.* ► darkness, twilight, gloominess, dimness, obscurity, shadow **3** *She pulled the shade down over the window.* ► blind, screen, curtain, awning, canopy **4** *a mass-produced shirt in a harsh shade of blue* ► hue, tinge, tint, tone, colour **5** *There was a shade of distrust in her voice.* ► hint, trace, dash, suggestion, suspicion, tone, nuance **6** *All shades of opinion were represented.* ► variety, variation, form, nuance, subtlety **7 a shade** *Silvio laughed a shade too heartily.* ► a little, a bit, a touch, rather, (*more informal*) a tad

shade *VERB* **1** *A tall fence shaded most of the garden.* ► overshadow, cast a shadow over, screen, shield, shroud, veil, conceal, obscure, mask, protect **2** *You can shade the background with a dark pencil.* ► colour in, darken, block in

shadow *NOUN* **1** *He lingered in the shadow of the corridor outside the room.* ► shade, darkness, dimness, semi-darkness, gloom **2** *She saw a shadow on the wall.* ► silhouette, outline, shape, profile, contour **3** *There's not a shadow of doubt that they were there at the time of the crime.* ► trace, slightest bit, scrap, shred, crumb, ounce, particle, iota, jot **4** *There was a shadow of a smile across her face.* ► hint, flicker, suspicion, trace, suggestion, sign

shadow *VERB* *He continued to shadow the van until forced to return.* ► follow, trail, track, stalk, pursue

shadowy *ADJECTIVE* **1** *They made out a shadowy form in front of them.* ► indistinct, hazy, vague, blurred, blurry, nebulous, unsubstantial, indeterminate, indistinguishable, unrecognizable **2** *She let herself out into the shadowy hall.* ► dark, shady, shaded

shady *ADJECTIVE* **1** *Mrs Halliday took Dot down a shady footpath.* ► shaded, shadowy, sheltered, dark, shrouded, sunless OPPOSITES ARE sunny, bright **2** *Blake had been authorized to do shady deals with Russian intelligence.* ► dubious, suspect, suspicious, disreputable, unethical, dishonest, untrustworthy, (*more informal*) fishy, (*more informal*) dodgy, (*more informal*) shifty AN OPPOSITE IS honest

shaft *NOUN* **1** *a wooden shaft* ► pole, rod, stick, staff, shank, post **2** *The shaft of a pickaxe lay on the ground.* ► handle, stem, stock **3** *The first shaft of light broke through the window.* ► ray, beam, gleam, bar, finger **4** *a shaft in a mine* ► passage, mineshaft, tunnel, duct

shaggy *ADJECTIVE* *The dog had a shaggy coat. The big shaggy head turned to look at me.* ► hairy, bushy, thick, woolly, fleecy, unkempt, dishevelled, unshorn, hirsute
OPPOSITES ARE smooth, sleek

shake *VERB* **1** *The whole building seemed to shake. We were shaking with fear.* ► tremble, quiver, shudder, shiver, convulse, judder, heave,

shall AUXILIARY VERB **1** used with **I** and **we** to refer to the future • *I shall arrive tomorrow* **2** used with **I** and **we** in questions when making a suggestion or offer or asking for advice • *Shall I shut the door?* **3** (*old-fashioned use*) used with words other than **I** and **we** in promises or to express determination • *Trust me, you shall have a party.*

shallow ADJECTIVE **shallower, shallowest 1** not deep • *shallow water* **2** not capable of deep feelings • *a shallow character*
▷ **shallowness** NOUN

sham NOUN **shams** something that is not genuine; a pretence
▷ **sham** ADJECTIVE

sham VERB **shams, shamming, shammed** pretend

shamble VERB **shambles, shambling, shambled** walk or run in a lazy or awkward way

shame NOUN **1** a feeling of great sorrow or guilt because you have done wrong **2** dishonour or disgrace **3** something you regret; a pity • *It's a shame that it rained.*
▷ **shameful** ADJECTIVE **shamefully** ADVERB

shame VERB **shames, shaming, shamed** make a person feel ashamed

shameless ADJECTIVE not feeling or looking ashamed
▷ **shamelessly** ADVERB

shampoo NOUN **shampoos 1** a liquid substance for washing the hair **2** a substance for cleaning a carpet etc. or washing a car **3** a wash with shampoo • *a shampoo and set*

shampoo VERB **shampoos, shampooing, shampooed** wash or clean with a shampoo [originally = to massage: from Hindi *champo* = press]

shan't (*mainly spoken*) shall not

shanty[1] NOUN **shanties** a shack [from Canadian French]

shanty[2] NOUN **shanties** a sailors' song with a chorus [probably from French *chanter* = sing]

shanty town NOUN **shanty towns** a settlement consisting of shacks

Thesaurus

wobble **2** *The wind shook the window frame.* ► rattle, vibrate **3** *She shook her umbrella at an approaching taxi.* ► wave, waggle, wag, brandish, flourish, jiggle, joggle **4** *The news shook them.* ► shock, startle, unnerve, unsettle, upset, alarm, distress, disturb, frighten, perturb
shake something off *Bobby finally shook off his flu and was able to play again.* ► get over, recover from, get rid of, (*more informal*) see the back of
shake someone off *He looked round to see if he had shaken off his pursuer.* ► escape, elude, get away from, leave behind, give someone the slip

shaky ADJECTIVE **1** *They sat at a shaky table.* ► unsteady, flimsy, wobbly, rickety, rocky, weak, frail, ramshackle **2** *She let out a deep, shaky breath.* ► trembling, shaking, faltering, quivering **3** *His voice was shaky with emotion.* ► faltering, nervous, quavering, tremulous, unsteady AN OPPOSITE IS steady **4** *He had to admit it was a shaky alibi, but he got away with it.* ► precarious, uncertain, unpromising, doubtful, unsound

shallow ADJECTIVE **1** *I do not agree with that shallow view of the situation.* ► superficial, facile, oversimplified, simplistic, narrow, flimsy, lightweight, surface
OPPOSITES ARE profound, deep

sham NOUN *The lad's appearance and manner could be a sham.* ► pretence, act, fake, fraud, fiction, lie AN OPPOSITE IS real thing

sham ADJECTIVE *She felt trapped in a sham marriage.* ► false, fake, bogus, pretended, simulated, imitation AN OPPOSITE IS genuine

sham VERB *He wasn't shamming, he was obviously injured.* ► pretend, fake, dissemble

shambles NOUN (*informal*) *The room was a shambles. The loans scheme had degenerated into a shambles.* ► mess, muddle, chaos, confusion, disorder

shame NOUN **1** *He couldn't face the shame of being found out.* ► humiliation, opprobrium, dishonour, disgrace, stigma, remorse, guilt, embarrassment, ignominy, mortification, degradation, discredit OPPOSITES ARE honour, pride **2 a shame** *It's a shame he didn't stick to chess instead of cards.* ► a pity, unfortunate, a piece of bad luck, a cause for regret
OPPOSITES ARE fortunate, lucky

shame VERB **1** *He had been shamed in public.* ► humiliate, mortify, humble, chasten, embarrass, (*more informal*) show up **2** *You have shamed your family name. He would have shamed an angel with his table manners.* ► disgrace, dishonour, discredit, degrade, taint, tarnish
OPPOSITES ARE honour, do credit to

shameful ADJECTIVE *The scheme had been a shameful waste of money.* ► disgraceful, deplorable, contemptible, outrageous, reprehensible, scandalous, unworthy, wicked, vile AN OPPOSITE IS honourable

shameless ADJECTIVE **1** *People said he was a shameless sponger.* ► brazen, bold, audacious, forward, incorrigible, abandoned
OPPOSITES ARE reticent, bashful **2** *They knew it was a shameless lie.* ► flagrant, blatant, barefaced, unashamed, overt

shape *NOUN* **shapes** **1** a thing's outline; the appearance an outline produces **2** proper form or condition • *Get it into shape.* **3** the general form or condition of something • *the shape of British industry*

shape *VERB* **shapes, shaping, shaped** **1** make into a particular shape **2** develop • *The plan is shaping up nicely.* [from Old English]

shapeless *ADJECTIVE* having no definite shape

shapely *ADJECTIVE* **shapelier, shapeliest** having an attractive shape

share *NOUN* **shares** **1** a part given to one person or thing out of something that is being divided **2** each of the equal parts forming a business company's capital, giving the person who holds it the right to receive a portion (a **dividend**) of the company's profits

share *VERB* **shares, sharing, shared** **1** give portions of something to two or more people **2** have or use or experience something jointly with others • *She shared a house with me.*

shark *NOUN* **sharks** a large sea fish with sharp teeth

sharp *ADJECTIVE* **1** with an edge or point that can cut or make holes **2** quick at noticing or learning things • *sharp eyes* **3** steep or pointed; not gradual • *a sharp bend* **4** forceful or severe • *a sharp frost* **5** distinct; loud and shrill • *a sharp cry* **6** slightly sour **7** (in music) one semitone higher than the natural note • *C sharp*
▷ **sharply** *ADVERB* **sharpness** *NOUN*

sharp *ADVERB* **1** sharply • *Turn sharp right here* **2** punctually • *I'll see you at six o'clock sharp* **3** (in music) above the correct pitch • *You were singing sharp.*

sharp *NOUN* **sharps** (in music) a note one semitone higher than the natural note; the sign (#) that indicates this

sharpen *VERB* **sharpens, sharpening, sharpened** make or become sharp
▷ **sharpener** *NOUN*

sharp practice *NOUN* dishonest or barely honest dealings in business

Thesaurus

shape *NOUN* **1** *The shape of their bodies changes with astonishing speed.* ► form, figure, configuration, physique, outline, profile, silhouette, pattern **2** *For his age he was in pretty good shape.* ► condition, health, state, trim, fettle, (*more informal*) nick

shape *VERB* *She shaped the clay into a tall pot. A number of factors have shaped their ideas.* ► form, fashion, mould, cast, make, sculpt

shapeless *ADJECTIVE* **1** *This shapeless mass was my dinner.* ► amorphous, formless, indeterminate, irregular, nebulous, undefined, unformed, vague AN OPPOSITE IS defined. **2** *Gladys removed a shapeless cardigan and hung it over the chair.* ► baggy, saggy, sagging, unshapely, formless, dumpy AN OPPOSITE IS shapely

shapely *ADJECTIVE* *advertisements full of shapely hips and pretty faces* ► well-proportioned, elegant, graceful, attractive, trim AN OPPOSITE IS shapeless

share *NOUN* *We will get a share of the profits.* ► portion, part, division, quota, allocation, allowance

share *VERB* **1** *Member countries will have to share the costs.* ► divide, split, deal out, distribute, ration out, share out, apportion, allocate, allot, go halves with **2** *She had to share a room with two other people.* ► use jointly, live in **3 share in** *It is important for everyone to share in the decision-making process.* ► be involved in, take part in, participate in, join in, cooperate in

sharp *ADJECTIVE* **1** *A sharp knife is essential.* ► keen-edged, keen, pointed, spiky AN OPPOSITE IS blunt **2** *Kittens can strike out with their sharp claws.* ► pointed, jagged, cutting **3** *She felt a sharp pain in her arm.* ► acute, piercing, intense, fierce, stabbing, severe OPPOSITES ARE gentle, mild **4** *a cheese with a sharp flavour* ► strong, piquant, pungent, bitter OPPOSITES ARE mild, mellow **5** *There was a sharp cry from outside. There was a series of sharp raps on the door.* ► loud, piercing, shrill, high-pitched AN OPPOSITE IS soft **6** *A sharp wind blew outside.* ► cold, chilly, bitter, keen, brisk, biting, cutting OPPOSITES ARE gentle, warm **7** *If he disapproves there will be frowns and sharp words.* ► harsh, bitter, cutting, scathing, caustic, acerbic, tart **8** *She adjusted the focus to make the image sharper.* ► distinct, clear, crisp OPPOSITES ARE blurred, indistinct **9** *There could be a sharp drop in prices.* ► abrupt, rapid, steep, sudden AN OPPOSITE IS gradual **10** *His sharp eyes spotted something moving.* ► keen, perceptive, observant, keen-sighted, acute AN OPPOSITE IS weak **11** *He had a quick wit and a sharp mind.* ► perceptive, incisive, discerning, percipient OPPOSITES ARE dull, slow

sharpen *VERB* *You will need to sharpen the knife.* ► make sharp, whet, hone, grind, strop, file AN OPPOSITE IS blunt

shatter *VERB* **shatters, shattering, shattered** **1** break violently into small pieces **2** destroy • *It shattered our hopes.* **3** upset greatly • *We were shattered by the news.*

shave *VERB* **shaves, shaving, shaved** **1** scrape growing hair off the skin with a razor **2** cut or scrape a thin slice off something
▷ **shaven** *ADJECTIVE* **shaver** *NOUN*

shave *NOUN* **shaves** the act of shaving the face
close shave (*informal*) a narrow escape

shavings *PLURAL NOUN* thin strips shaved off a piece of wood or metal

shawl *NOUN* **shawls** a large piece of material worn round the shoulders or head or wrapped round a baby [from Persian or Urdu]

she *PRONOUN* the female person or animal being talked about

sheaf *NOUN* **sheaves** **1** a bundle of cornstalks tied together **2** a bundle of arrows, papers, etc. held together

shear *VERB* **shears, shearing, sheared** *or, in sense 1,* **shorn** **1** cut or trim; cut the wool off a sheep **2** break because of a sideways or twisting force • *One of the bolts sheared off.*
▷ **shearer** *NOUN*
USAGE Do not confuse with **sheer**.

shears *PLURAL NOUN* a cutting tool shaped like a very large pair of scissors and worked with both hands

sheath *NOUN* **sheaths** **1** a cover for the blade of a knife or sword etc. **2** a close-fitting cover **3** a condom

shed[1] *NOUN* **sheds** a simply made building used for storing things or sheltering animals, or as a workshop

shed[2] *VERB* **sheds, shedding, shed** **1** let something fall or flow • *The tree shed its leaves.* • *We shed tears.* **2** give off • *The candle shed soft light on the table.* **3** get rid of • *The company has shed 200 workers.*

sheen *NOUN* a shine or gloss

sheep *NOUN* **sheep** an animal that eats grass and has a thick fleecy coat, kept in flocks for its wool and its meat [from Old English]

sheepdog *NOUN* **sheepdogs** a dog trained to guard and herd sheep

sheepish *ADJECTIVE* **1** bashful **2** embarrassed or shamefaced
▷ **sheepishly** *ADVERB* **sheepishness** *NOUN*

sheer[1] *ADJECTIVE* **1** complete or thorough • *sheer stupidity* **2** vertical, with almost no slope • *a sheer drop* **3** (said about material) very thin; transparent

sheer[2] *VERB* **sheers, sheering, sheered** swerve; move sharply away
USAGE Do not confuse with **shear**.

sheet *NOUN* **sheets** **1** a large piece of lightweight material used on a bed to sleep under **2** a whole flat piece of paper, glass, or metal **3** a wide area of water, ice, flame, etc.

sheikh (shayk, sheek) *NOUN* **sheikhs** the leader of an Arab tribe or village

shelf *NOUN* **shelves** **1** a flat piece of wood, metal, or glass etc. fixed to a wall or in a piece of furniture so that things can be placed on it **2** a flat level surface that sticks out; a ledge

Thesaurus

shatter *VERB* **1** *The blast was loud enough to shatter windows. The glass shattered like an eggshell.* ► break, smash, blow out, splinter, crack **2** *The silence was shattered by a warning shout from the alley.* ► destroy, wreck, ruin, dash, overturn, upset

shattered *ADJECTIVE* **1** *She seemed shattered by the refusal.* ► upset, devastated, stunned, shocked, staggered, distraught **2** *By the time he reached home he felt shattered.* ► exhausted, tired out, worn out, weary, fatigued, (*more informal*) dead tired, (*more informal*) played out, (*more informal*) washed out

shave *VERB* *His shot shaved the near post.* ► brush, graze, touch, glance off
shave off *Michael shaved off his moustache.* ► cut off, snip off, crop

shed *NOUN* *Marion kept her rabbits in a garden shed.* ► hut, shack, shelter, storehouse, lean-to, outhouse, potting shed

shed *VERB* **1** *A lorry had shed its load on the inside lane.* ► spill, throw off, drop, scatter, cast off, discard, let fall, shower **2** *We went indoors and shed our coats.* ► take off, discard, peel off, slip out of

sheen *NOUN* *Using the right polish will give the surface a delicate sheen.* ► shine, gloss, lustre, brightness, gleam, patina, burnish, polish

sheer *ADJECTIVE* **1** *It was sheer chance that Beverley had been to the same hotel. The offence was an act of sheer desperation.* ► utter, complete, absolute, total, pure, unmitigated, unqualified, out-and-out **2** *A few yards ahead was a sheer drop.* ► precipitous, vertical, abrupt, perpendicular **3** *Sheer fabrics look great in a bathroom setting.* ► diaphanous, fine, gauzy, flimsy, see-through, transparent, thin

sheet *NOUN* **1** *a sheet of paper* ► piece, leaf, page, folio **2** *a sheet of ice* ► layer, film, covering, strip, expanse, surface **3** *a sheet of glass* ► pane, panel, place

shelf *NOUN* *She put the vase back on the shelf.* ► ledge, mantelpiece, sill, rack

A B C D E F G H I J K L M N O P Q R S T U V W X Y Z

shell NOUN **shells 1** the hard outer covering of an egg, nut, etc., or of an animal such as a snail, crab, or tortoise **2** the walls or framework of a building, ship, etc. **3** a metal case filled with explosive, fired from a large gun

shell VERB **shells, shelling, shelled 1** take something out of its shell **2** fire explosive shells at something
shell out (*informal*) pay out money

shellfish NOUN **shellfish** a sea animal that has a shell

shelter NOUN **shelters 1** something that protects people from rain, wind, danger, etc. • *The bus stop has a shelter beside it.*
2 protection • *The villagers sought shelter from the storm.*

shelter VERB **shelters, sheltering, sheltered 1** provide with shelter **2** protect **3** find a shelter • *They sheltered under the trees.*

shelve VERB **shelves, shelving, shelved 1** put things on a shelf or shelves **2** fit a wall or cupboard etc. with shelves **3** postpone or reject a plan etc. **4** slope • *The bed of the river shelves steeply.*

shepherd NOUN **shepherds** a person whose job is to look after sheep

shepherd VERB **shepherds, shepherding, shepherded** guide or direct people

sheriff NOUN **sheriffs** the chief law officer of a county, whose duties vary in different countries

sherry NOUN **sherries** a kind of strong wine

Shetland pony NOUN **Shetland ponies** a kind of small, strong, shaggy pony, originally from the Shetland Isles

shield NOUN **shields 1** a large piece of metal, wood, etc. carried to protect the body **2** a model of a triangular shield used as a trophy **3** a protection

shield VERB **shields, shielding, shielded** protect from harm or from being discovered

shift VERB **shifts, shifting, shifted 1** move or cause to move **2** (said about an opinion or situation) change slightly
shift for yourself manage without help; rely on your own efforts

shift NOUN **shifts 1** a change of position or condition etc. **2** a group of workers who start work as another group finishes; the time when they work • *the night shift* **3** a straight dress with no waist

shifty ADJECTIVE evasive, not straightforward; untrustworthy
▷ **shiftily** ADVERB **shiftiness** NOUN

shilling NOUN **shillings** a former British coin, equal to 5p

shilly-shally VERB **shilly-shallies, shilly-shallying, shilly-shallied** be unable to make up your mind

Thesaurus

shell NOUN **1** *an insect that has no hard shell to protect it* ► pod, casing, case, crust, husk, hull **2** *All that was left of the building was its shell.* ► skeleton, frame, framework, hull

shelter NOUN **1** *Their house provided shelter for countless escapees.* ► protection, refuge, sanctuary, safety, cover, haven, lee, asylum **2** *We set up a shelter against the wind.* ► shield, screen, barrier, cover **3** *She ran a shelter for the homeless.* ► sanctuary, refuge, haven, safe haven, retreat

shelter VERB **1** *The hut sheltered us from the storm.* ► protect, keep safe, shield, cover, safeguard, screen, guard **2** *The walkers sheltered in doorways.* ► take shelter, take refuge, seek protection, take cover **3** *His family took it in turns to shelter him.* ► harbour, accommodate, give shelter to, hide

sheltered ADJECTIVE **1** *a sheltered spot behind the sand dunes* ► protected, enclosed, screened, shielded, covered, calm, quiet, windless
AN OPPOSITE IS exposed. **2** *She had led a sheltered life.* ► secluded, withdrawn, cloistered, reclusive, isolated, unadventurous, unexciting
AN OPPOSITE IS adventurous

shelve VERB *The plans had to be shelved for the time being.* ► postpone, defer, put off, put to one side, suspend, abandon, mothball, (*more informal*) put on ice, (*more informal*) put on the back burner OPPOSITES ARE implement, revive

shield NOUN *One coating will afford the metal a shield against corrosion.* ► protection, safeguard, guard, screen, shelter, barrier, defence, bulwark

shield VERB *She tried to shield her eyes from the glare of the sun.* ► protect, shade, screen, cover, defend, guard, keep safe, safeguard, shelter

shift VERB **1** *Les shifted the furniture to make more space.* ► move, rearrange, reposition, relocate, adjust, transfer, switch round, haul, lug **2** *It wouldn't be easy to shift all that dirt.* ► remove, dislodge, budge **3** *Their opinions had shifted somewhat.* ► change, alter, modify, vary, fluctuate

shift NOUN **1** *constant shifts in public opinion* ► change, alteration, variation, fluctuation **2** *His mum was working on the night shift.* ► period, stint, stretch

shifty ADJECTIVE *She had seen that shifty look before.* ► untrustworthy, dishonest, deceitful, furtive, underhand, shady, wily, scheming, dubious
AN OPPOSITE IS straightforward

shimmer *VERB* **shimmers, shimmering, shimmered** shine with a quivering light • *The sea shimmered in the moonlight.*
▷ **shimmer** *NOUN*

shin *NOUN* **shins** the front of the leg between the knee and the ankle

shin *VERB* **shins, shinning, shinned** climb by using the arms and legs, not on a ladder

shine *VERB* **shines, shining, shone** *or, in sense 4,* **shined** **1** give out or reflect light; be bright **2** be excellent • *He doesn't shine in maths.* **3** aim a light • *Shine your torch on it.* **4** polish • *Have you shined your shoes?*

shingle *NOUN* pebbles on a beach

shingles *NOUN* a disease caused by the chicken pox virus, producing a painful rash

shiny *ADJECTIVE* **shinier, shiniest** shining or glossy

ship *NOUN* **ships** a large boat, especially one that goes to sea

ship *VERB* **ships, shipping, shipped** transport goods etc., especially by ship

-ship *SUFFIX* forms nouns meaning 'condition' (e.g. *friendship, hardship*), position (e.g. *chairmanship*), or skill (e.g. *seamanship*)

shipping *NOUN* **1** ships • *Britain's shipping* **2** transporting goods by ship

shipshape *ADJECTIVE* in good order; tidy

shipwreck *NOUN* **shipwrecks** **1** the wrecking of a ship by storm or accident **2** a wrecked ship
▷ **shipwrecked** *ADJECTIVE*

shipyard *NOUN* **shipyards** a place where ships are built or repaired

shire *NOUN* **shires** a county
the Shires the country areas of (especially central) England, away from the cities

shirk *VERB* **shirks, shirking, shirked** avoid a duty or work etc. selfishly or unfairly
▷ **shirker** *NOUN*
[probably from German *Schurke* = scoundrel]

shirt *NOUN* **shirts** a piece of clothing for the top half of the body, made of light material and with a collar and sleeves
in your shirtsleeves not wearing a jacket over your shirt

shiver *VERB* **shivers, shivering, shivered** tremble with cold or fear
▷ **shiver** *NOUN* **shivery** *ADJECTIVE*

shoal[1] *NOUN* **shoals** a large number of fish swimming together

shoal[2] *NOUN* **shoals** **1** a shallow place **2** an underwater sandbank

shock[1] *NOUN* **shocks** **1** a sudden unpleasant surprise **2** great weakness caused by pain or injury etc. **3** the effect of a violent shake or knock **4** an effect caused by electric current passing through the body

shock *VERB* **shocks, shocking, shocked** **1** give someone a shock; surprise or upset a person greatly **2** seem very improper or scandalous to a person

shock[2] *NOUN* **shocks** a bushy mass of hair

Thesaurus

shimmer *VERB* *The lights shimmered on the surface of the water.* ► glimmer, glint, gleam, glow, glisten, glitter, sparkle, shine, flash

shine *VERB* **1** *The sun shone through the windows.* ► beam, gleam, glow, glisten, glint, sparkle, flash **2** *He had forgotten to shine his shoes.* ► polish, brush, buff, brighten **3** *There was one thing they all shone at.* ► excel, stand out, be outstanding

shine *NOUN* *a shine on the furniture* ► polish, sheen, lustre, patina, burnish, gleam

shining *ADJECTIVE* **1** *a knight in shining armour* ► gleaming, brilliant, radiant, glittering, glowing, luminous, shiny, sparkling **2** *a shining example* ► conspicuous, outstanding, splendid, eminent, glorious, praiseworthy, resplendent

shiny *ADJECTIVE* *He liked her shiny black boots.* ► bright, glossy, gleaming, shining, glistening, polished, burnished, lustrous
OPPOSITES ARE dull, matt

ship *NOUN* *Another very big wave hit the ship.* ► vessel, craft, boat, liner, steamer

ship *VERB* *Twenty flamingoes were shipped from Tanzania to London.* ► send, consign, transport, post, mail

shipment *NOUN* *There's a grain shipment due out tomorrow.* ► load, cargo, consignment, freight, vanload, lorryload, truckload, boatload, (*more formal*) lading

shirk *VERB* *We've got responsibilities, and we can't shirk them.* ► dodge, duck, evade, avoid, shun, get out of, shrink from, neglect

shiver *VERB* *Maria stood at the door shivering.* ► tremble, quiver, shake, shudder, palpitate, flutter

shock *NOUN* **1** *the shock of an explosion* ► blow, vibration, impact, collision, concussion, jolt **2** *The news came as a shock.* ► blow, upset, surprise, bombshell, bolt from the blue **3** *The state of the room always gave her a shock.* ► surprise, fright, scare, jolt, start, (*more informal*) turn **4** *She was in a state of shock for several days.* ► trauma, distress,

shock *VERB* *The brutal attack shocked the whole community.* ► horrify, appal, stun, stagger, alarm, outrage, dismay, scandalize, repel, offend, disgust, sicken, revolt

shocking *ADJECTIVE* **1** causing indignation or disgust **2** (*informal*) very bad • *shocking weather*

shock wave *NOUN* **shock waves** a sharp change in pressure in the air around an explosion or an object moving very quickly

shod *past tense of* **shoe**

shoddy *ADJECTIVE* **shoddier, shoddiest** of poor quality; badly made or done • *shoddy work*
▷ **shoddily** *ADVERB* **shoddiness** *NOUN*

shoe *NOUN* **shoes 1** a strong covering for the foot **2** a horseshoe **3** something shaped or used like a shoe
be in somebody's shoes be in his or her situation

shoe *VERB* **shoes, shoeing, shod** fit with a shoe or shoes

shoelace *NOUN* **shoelaces** a cord for lacing up and fastening a shoe

shoot *VERB* **shoots, shooting, shot 1** fire a gun or missile etc. **2** hurt or kill by shooting **3** move or send very quickly • *The car shot past us* **4** kick or hit a ball at a goal **5** (said about a plant) put out buds or shoots **6** slide the bolt of a door into or out of its fastening **7** film or photograph something • *The film was shot in Africa.*

shoot *NOUN* **shoots 1** a young branch or new growth of a plant **2** an expedition for shooting animals

shooting star *NOUN* **shooting stars** a meteor

shop *NOUN* **shops 1** a building or room where goods or services are on sale to the public **2** a workshop **3** talk that is about your own work or job • *She is always talking shop.*

shop *VERB* **shops, shopping, shopped** go and buy things at shops
▷ **shopper** *NOUN*
shop around compare goods and prices in several shops before buying

shop floor *NOUN* **1** the workers in a factory, not the managers **2** the place where they work

shopkeeper *NOUN* **shopkeepers** a person who owns or manages a shop

shoplifter *NOUN* **shoplifters** a person who steals goods from a shop after entering as a customer
▷ **shoplifting** *NOUN*

shopping *NOUN* **1** buying goods in shops **2** the goods bought

shore[1] *NOUN* **shores** the land along the edge of a sea or of a lake [from early German or Dutch *schore*]

shore[2] *VERB* **shores, shoring, shored** prop something up with a piece of wood etc. [from early German or Dutch *schoren*]

shorn *past participle of* **shear**

short *ADJECTIVE* **1** not long; occupying a small distance or time • *a short walk* **2** not tall • *a short person* **3** not enough; not having enough of something • *Water is short in hot weather* • *We are short of water* **4** bad-tempered or curt **5** (said about pastry) rich and crumbly because it contains a lot of fat
▷ **shortness** *NOUN*
for short as an abbreviation • *Raymond is called Ray for short.*
short for an abbreviation of • *'Ray' is short for Raymond.*
short of without going to the length of • *I'll do anything to help, short of breaking the law*

short *ADVERB* suddenly • *She stopped short.*

Thesaurus

shocking *ADJECTIVE* **1** *Next day they heard the whole shocking story.* ► horrifying, horrific, appalling, alarming, distressing, terrible, dreadful, awful, frightening, upsetting **2** *Their language was quite shocking.* ► offensive, disgusting, outrageous

shoddy *ADJECTIVE* **1** *the shoddy state of our national services* ► inferior, poor-quality, second-rate, cheap, trashy, rubbishy, (*more informal*) tacky AN OPPOSITE IS well-made **2** *The workmanship was noticeably shoddy.* ► careless, slapdash, slipshod, sloppy
OPPOSITES ARE painstaking, careful

shoot *VERB* **1** *The gunman had been daring the police to shoot him.* ► hit, kill, gun down, snipe at, pick off **2** *A motorcycle shot past.* ► race, dash, zoom, career, fly, rush, streak, hare **3** *They plan to shoot the outdoor scenes on location in Africa.* ► film, make, capture

shop *NOUN* *His father opened a shop in the town.* ► store, retail store, outlet, emporium

shopping *NOUN* *She put her shopping in the back of the car.* ► goods, purchases

shore *NOUN* *They stopped for a picnic near the shore.* ► seashore, beach, sands, coast, foreshore, seaboard, shingle, bank, strand
RELATED ADJECTIVE littoral

short *ADJECTIVE* **1** *a short piece of string* ► small, little AN OPPOSITE IS long **2** *a short person* ► small, little, petite, squat, stocky, diminutive AN OPPOSITE IS tall **3** *a short account of the voyage* ► brief, concise, succinct, pithy
OPPOSITES ARE long, elaborate, lengthy **4** *Take a short look at this.* ► brief, cursory, fleeting, momentary OPPOSITES ARE prolonged, lengthy **5** *Supplies were short.* ► low, meagre, scant, deficient, inadequate, insufficient
OPPOSITES ARE plentiful, abundant **6** *She was rather short with me.* ► curt, abrupt, sharp, blunt, brusque, snappy, impatient
OPPOSITES ARE courteous, patient

shortage *NOUN* **shortages** lack or scarcity of something; insufficiency

shortbread *NOUN* a rich sweet biscuit, made with butter

short circuit *NOUN* **short circuits** a fault in an electrical circuit in which current flows along a shorter route than the normal one
▷ **short-circuit** *VERB*

shortcoming *NOUN* **shortcomings** a fault or failure to reach a good standard

short cut *NOUN* **short cuts** a route or method that is quicker than the usual one

shorten *VERB* **shortens, shortening, shortened** make or become shorter

shorthand *NOUN* a set of special signs for writing words down as quickly as people say them

short-handed *ADJECTIVE* not having enough workers or helpers

shortly *ADVERB* **1** in a short time; soon • *They will arrive shortly.* **2** in a few words **3** curtly

shorts *PLURAL NOUN* trousers with legs that do not reach to the knee

short-sighted *ADJECTIVE* **1** unable to see things clearly when they are further away **2** lacking imagination or foresight

short-tempered *ADJECTIVE* easily becoming angry

short wave *NOUN* a radio wave of a wavelength between 10 and 100 metres and a frequency of about 3 to 30 megahertz

shot[1] *past tense* of **shoot**

shot[2] *NOUN* **shots** **1** the firing of a gun or missile etc.; the sound of this **2** something fired from a gun; lead pellets for firing from small guns **3** a person judged by skill in shooting • *He's a good shot.* **4** a heavy metal ball thrown as a sport **5** a stroke in tennis, cricket, billiards, etc. **6** a photograph; a filmed scene **7** (*informal*) an attempt • *Have a shot at the crossword.* **8** an injection of a drug or vaccine

shot *ADJECTIVE* (said about fabric) woven so that different colours show at different angles • *shot silk*

should *AUXILIARY VERB* **1** used for saying what someone ought to do • *You should have told me.* **2** used for saying what someone expects • *They should be here by ten o'clock.* **3** used for saying what might happen • *If you should happen to see him, tell him to come.* **4** used with **I** and **we** to make a polite statement (*I should like to come*) or in a conditional clause (*If they had supported us we should have won*)
USAGE In sense 4, although **should** is strictly correct, many people nowadays use **would** and this is not regarded as wrong.

shoulder *NOUN* **shoulders** **1** the part of the body between the neck and the arm, foreleg, or wing **2** a side that juts out • *the shoulder of the bottle*

shoulder *VERB* **shoulders, shouldering, shouldered** **1** take something on your shoulder or shoulders **2** push with your shoulder **3** accept responsibility or blame

shoulder blade *NOUN* **shoulder blades** either of the two large flat bones at the top of your back

shouldn't (*mainly spoken*) should not

shout *NOUN* **shouts** a loud cry or call

shout *VERB* **shouts, shouting, shouted** give a shout; speak or call loudly

shove *VERB* **shoves, shoving, shoved** push roughly
▷ **shove** *NOUN*
shove off (*informal*) go away

Thesaurus

shortage *NOUN* *a shortage of water* ► scarcity, sparseness, dearth, deficiency, insufficiency, lack, want, paucity, shortfall
AN OPPOSITE IS abundance

shortcoming *NOUN* *He was well aware of his own shortcomings.* ► defect, failing, fault, imperfection, weakness, drawback, foible, vice
AN OPPOSITE IS strength

shorten *VERB* *The composer shortened the work for a concert performance.* ► cut down, reduce, condense, compress, cut, trim, abridge
OPPOSITES ARE lengthen, expand

shortly *ADVERB* *A note arrived shortly afterwards.* ► soon, presently, directly, before long, by and by

short-sighted *ADJECTIVE* *The media tend to be short-sighted when dealing with the arts.* ► narrow-minded, narrow, improvident, intolerant, conservative, illiberal, insular, parochial, small-minded

shot *NOUN* **1** *A shot rang out.* ► report, bang, blast, explosion **2** *This is a shot of us on the beach.* ► photo, photograph, snap, snapshot **3** *He managed a winning shot.* ► stroke, hit, strike, throw **4** (*informal*) *He wanted a shot at driving the car.* ► attempt, try, go, (*informal*) bash

shout *VERB* *'Come on,' she shouted.* ► cry, call, yell, exclaim, shriek, scream, bawl

shove *VERB* **1** *She shoved the boy into the back of the van.* ► push, thrust, drive, propel, force **2** *Several large men shoved past them.* ► push, barge, elbow, jostle, hustle, shoulder, crowd

A B C D E F G H I J K L M N O P Q R S T U V W X Y Z

shovel *NOUN* **shovels** a tool like a spade with the sides turned up, used for lifting coal, earth, snow, etc.

shovel *VERB* **shovels, shovelling, shovelled** **1** move or clear with a shovel **2** scoop or push roughly • *He was shovelling food into his mouth*

show *VERB* **shows, showing, showed, shown** **1** allow or cause something to be seen • *Show me your new bike.* **2** make a person understand; demonstrate • *Show me how to use it.* **3** guide • *Show him in.* **4** treat in a certain way • *She showed us much kindness.* **5** be visible • *That scratch won't show.* **6** prove your ability to someone • *We'll show them!*
show off **1** show something proudly **2** try to impress people
show up **1** make or be clearly visible; reveal a fault etc. **2** (*informal*) arrive

show *NOUN* **shows** **1** a display or exhibition • *a flower show* **2** an entertainment **3** (*informal*) something that happens or is done • *He runs the whole show.*

showdown *NOUN* **showdowns** a final test or confrontation

shower *NOUN* **showers** **1** a brief fall of rain or snow **2** a lot of small things coming or falling like rain • *a shower of stones* **3** a device or cabinet for spraying water to wash a person's body; a wash in this

shower *VERB* **showers, showering, showered** **1** fall or send things in a shower **2** wash under a shower

showman *NOUN* **showmen** **1** a person who presents entertainments **2** someone who is good at attracting attention
▷ **showmanship** *NOUN*

show-off *NOUN* **show-offs** (*informal*) a person who tries to impress people boastfully

showpiece *NOUN* **showpieces** a fine example of something for people to see and admire

showy *ADJECTIVE* **showier, showiest** likely to attract attention; brightly or highly decorated
▷ **showily** *ADVERB* **showiness** *NOUN*

shrapnel *NOUN* pieces of metal scattered from an exploding shell

shred *NOUN* **shreds** **1** a tiny piece torn or cut off something **2** a small amount • *There is not a shred of evidence.*

shred *VERB* **shreds, shredding, shredded** cut into shreds
▷ **shredder** *NOUN*

shrew *NOUN* **shrews** **1** a small mouse-like animal **2** (*old use*) a bad-tempered woman who is constantly scolding people
▷ **shrewish** *ADJECTIVE*

shrewd *ADJECTIVE* having common sense and good judgement; clever
▷ **shrewdly** *ADVERB* **shrewdness** *NOUN*

shriek *NOUN* **shrieks** a shrill cry or scream

shriek *VERB* **shrieks, shrieking, shrieked** give a shriek

Thesaurus

show *NOUN* **1** *Thousands came to watch the show.* ► entertainment, performance, production, presentation, spectacle, pageant **2** *They had to put on a show of strength.* ► display, exhibition, demonstration, appearance, impression, facade, pretence, illusion, affectation

show *VERB* **1** *Shall I show you how to do it?* ► demonstrate, explain, point out, clarify **2** *There's a hole in the sleeve but it won't show.* ► be visible, be seen, be obvious, appear **3** *This shows you what you can achieve with limited resources.* ► demonstrate, reveal, illustrate, prove, exemplify **4** *They are showing his watercolours at the local gallery.* ► exhibit, display **5** *Finn began to show her impatience.* ► reveal, manifest, convey, indicate, communicate, expose **6** *A girl showed them to their seats.* ► escort, accompany, take, conduct, walk

shower *NOUN* **1** *a shower of rain* ► fall, drizzle, downpour **2** *a shower of compliments* ► spate, wave, flood, rush, volley, barrage, torrent, flurry

shower *VERB* **1** *A passing lorry showered mud over the pavement.* ► spray, spatter, splash, sprinkle, rain **2** *The awards committee showered praise on the winners.* ► lavish, pour, heap, load

show-off *NOUN* *a show-off with a big flashy car* ► exhibitionist, boaster, poser, bragger, egotist

showy *ADJECTIVE* *showy fake jewellery* ► ostentatious, pretentious, gaudy, flashy, flamboyant, conspicuous, garish, tawdry, (*more informal*) tacky OPPOSITES ARE sober, restrained

shred *NOUN* *Not a shred of evidence could be found.* ► scrap, speck, iota, jot, ounce, trace
shreds *The dress had been torn to shreds.* ► tatters, ribbons, rags, strips

shrewd *ADJECTIVE* *a shrewd politician; a shrewd sense of timing* ► astute, sharp, acute, canny, prudent, clever, intelligent, quick-witted, perceptive, discerning, crafty, wily AN OPPOSITE IS stupid

shriek *VERB* *The audience shrieked with laughter. 'Come and see, quick!' Mary shrieked.* ► scream, screech, squeal, roar, howl, bellow, yell

shrill *ADJECTIVE* sounding very high and piercing
▷ **shrilly** *ADVERB* **shrillness** *NOUN*

shrimp *NOUN* **shrimps** a small shellfish, pink when boiled

shrine *NOUN* **shrines** an altar, chapel, or other sacred place

shrink *VERB* **shrinks, shrinking, shrank, shrunk 1** make or become smaller **2** move back to avoid something **3** avoid doing something because of fear, conscience, embarrassment, etc.
▷ **shrinkage** *NOUN* **shrunken** *ADJECTIVE*

shrivel *VERB* **shrivels, shrivelling, shrivelled** make or become dry and wrinkled

shroud *NOUN* **shrouds 1** a cloth in which a dead body is wrapped **2** each of a set of ropes supporting a ship's mast

Shrove Tuesday *NOUN* the day before Lent, when pancakes are eaten, originally to use up fat before the fast

shrub *NOUN* **shrubs** a woody plant smaller than a tree; a bush
▷ **shrubby** *ADJECTIVE*

shrubbery *NOUN* **shrubberies** an area planted with shrubs

shrug *VERB* **shrugs, shrugging, shrugged** raise your shoulders as a sign that you do not care, do not know, etc.
▷ **shrug** *NOUN*
shrug something off treat it as unimportant

shudder *VERB* **shudders, shuddering, shuddered 1** shiver violently with horror, fear, or cold **2** make a strong shaking movement
▷ **shudder** *NOUN*

shuffle *VERB* **shuffles, shuffling, shuffled 1** walk without lifting the feet from the ground **2** slide playing cards over each other to get them into random order **3** shift or rearrange
▷ **shuffle** *NOUN*

shun *VERB* **shuns, shunning, shunned** avoid; deliberately keep away from something

shunt *VERB* **shunts, shunting, shunted 1** move a train or wagons on to another track **2** divert to a less important place or position
▷ **shunt** *NOUN* **shunter** *NOUN*

shut *VERB* **shuts, shutting, shut 1** move a door, lid, or cover etc. so that it blocks an opening; make or become closed **2** bring or fold parts together • *Shut the book.*
shut down 1 stop something working **2** stop business
shut up 1 shut securely **2** (*informal*) stop talking or making a noise

shutter *NOUN* **shutters 1** a panel or screen that can be closed over a window **2** the device in a camera that opens and closes to let light fall on the film
▷ **shuttered** *ADJECTIVE*

Thesaurus

shrill *ADJECTIVE* *'That's not true!' she protested in a shrill voice.* ► piercing, penetrating, high-pitched, screaming, sharp, strident, screechy OPPOSITES ARE soft, gentle

shrink *VERB* **1** *Your sweater has shrunk in the wash* ► become smaller, contract, dwindle, shrivel, wither AN OPPOSITE IS expand **2** *The woman shrank in alarm.* ► draw back, cower, cringe, flinch, hang back, back off, recoil

shrivel *VERB* *The plants were shrivelling in the heat.* ► shrink, wilt, wither, droop, become parched, dehydrate, dry up, wrinkle

shroud *NOUN* *a shroud of mist over the sea; The outfit operates behind a shroud of secrecy.* ► covering, blanket, mantle, pall, veil

shroud *VERB* *A mist shrouded the seafront.* ► cover, envelop, wrap, blanket, cloak, enshroud, hide, mask, conceal, screen, swathe, veil

shrug *VERB* **shrug off** *She shrugged off suggestions that she had been unfair.* ► dismiss, disregard, ignore, take no notice of, pay no heed to, set aside

shudder *VERB* *She still shuddered at the thought of what had happened.* ► quiver, shake, shiver, tremble, be horrified, convulse, quake, squirm

shudder *NOUN* *Another mighty shudder passed through the ship.* ► tremor, spasm, convulsion, trembling, tremble, quiver

shuffle *VERB* **1** *He shuffled over to the fireplace.* ► shamble, hobble, scuffle, stumble, teeter, totter **2** *She shuffled the cards and began dealing.* ► mix, mix up, jumble, rearrange, reorganize

shun *VERB* *The group shunned all forms of publicity.* ► avoid, shy away from, stay clear of, evade, steer clear of, keep away from

shut *VERB* *I'll shut the window.* ► close, fasten, latch, lock, push to, bolt, seal, secure
shut down *They will have to shut down the operation in South Africa.* ► close down, discontinue, terminate, cease, suspend OPPOSITES ARE open up, activate
shut in *or* **up** *She closed the door to shut the dogs in.* ► keep in, confine, detain, enclose, imprison, incarcerate
shut off *They had been shut off without food for two days.* ► cut off, isolate, separate, segregate
shut out 1 *He shut them out of the house by mistake.* ► lock out, keep out, exclude AN OPPOSITE IS let in **2** *She tried to shut out those bad memories.* ► exclude, keep out, suppress, forget AN OPPOSITE IS recall

A B C D E F G H I J K L M N O P Q R S T U V W X Y Z

shuttle *NOUN* **shuttles 1** a holder carrying the weft thread across a loom in weaving **2** a train, bus, or aircraft that makes frequent short journeys between two points

shuttle *VERB* **shuttles, shuttling, shuttled** move, travel, or send backwards and forwards

shy *ADJECTIVE* **shyer, shyest** afraid to meet or talk to other people; timid
▷ **shyly** *ADVERB* **shyness** *NOUN*

shy *VERB* **shies, shying, shied** jump or move suddenly in alarm

SI *NOUN* an internationally recognized system of metric units of measurement, including the metre and kilogram

Siamese cat *NOUN* **Siamese cats** a cat with short pale fur with darker face, ears, tail, and feet

Siamese twins *PLURAL NOUN* twins who are born with their bodies joined together

sick *ADJECTIVE* **1** ill; physically or mentally unwell **2** vomiting or likely to vomit ● *I feel sick.* **3** distressed or disgusted **4** making fun of death, disability, or misfortune in an unpleasant way
sick of tired of

sicken *VERB* **sickens, sickening, sickened** **1** begin to be ill **2** make or become distressed or disgusted ● *Vandalism sickens us all.*
▷ **sickening** *ADJECTIVE*

sickle *NOUN* **sickles** a tool with a narrow curved blade, used for cutting corn etc.

sickly *ADJECTIVE* **1** often ill; unhealthy **2** making people feel sick ● *a sickly smell* **3** weak ● *a sickly smile*

sickness *NOUN* **sicknesses 1** illness **2** a disease **3** vomiting

side *NOUN* **sides 1** a surface, especially one joining the top and bottom of something **2** a line that forms part of the boundary of a triangle, square, etc. **3** either of the two halves into which something can be divided by a line down its centre **4** the part near the edge and away from the centre **5** the place or region next to a person or thing ● *He stood at my side.* **6** one aspect or view of something ● *Study all sides of the problem.* **7** one of two groups or teams etc. who oppose each other
on the side as a sideline
side by side next to each other
take sides support one person or group in a dispute or disagreement and not the other

side *VERB* **sides, siding, sided**
side with take a person's side in an argument

side effect *NOUN* **side effects** an effect, especially an unpleasant one, that a medicine has on you as well as the effect intended

sidelight *NOUN* **sidelights 1** a light at the side of a vehicle or ship **2** light from one side

sideline *NOUN* **sidelines 1** something done in addition to your main work or activity **2** each of the lines on the two long sides of a sports pitch

sidelong *ADJECTIVE* towards one side; sideways ● *a sidelong glance*

Thesaurus

shy *ADJECTIVE He was too shy to say his name.* ► coy, reserved, diffident, bashful, sheepish, inhibited, embarrassed, modest, self-conscious, hesitant, timid, retiring
OPPOSITES ARE assertive, forward, bold, confident

sick *ADJECTIVE* **1** *He had been sick and had to stay at home.* ► ill, unwell, poorly, out of sorts, off colour, indisposed, ailing, peaky, queasy, nauseous **2 be sick of** *We are all sick of having to wait so long.* ► be fed up with, be tired of, be weary of, have had enough of

sicken *VERB It sickened us to see so much waste.* ► make someone sick, disgust, revolt, nauseate, repel, put off

sickening *ADJECTIVE The stench of burnt fuel oil is sickening. There was a sickening sound of tearing metal.* ► nauseating, revolting, disgusting, offensive, repulsive, repellent, appalling

sickly *ADJECTIVE* **1** *He was a sickly child with a bad chest.* ► unhealthy, poorly, sick, ill, infirm, frail, feeble, weak **2** *She had a sickly complexion.* ► pale, wan, pasty, sallow, pallid, ashen **3** *The walls were painted a sickly green.* ► insipid, pale, wan

sickness *NOUN* **1** *She was away because of sickness.* ► illness, disease, ailment, disorder **2** *The spells of sickness lasted four or five days.* ► biliousness, nausea, queasiness, vomiting

side *NOUN* **1** *The box has an address label on one side.* ► surface, face, facet, elevation, flank **2** *A hut stood by the side of the lake.* ► edge, border, verge, boundary, margin, fringe, brink, limit, perimeter, rim **3** *He was driving over the limit on the wrong side of the road.* ► half, part, carriageway **4** *I could see both sides in the argument.* ► point of view, aspect, perspective, standpoint, opinion, stance, angle, view, viewpoint, slant **5** *The family had backed the winning side in the civil war.* ► faction, camp, army, team **6** *The home side was one player short.* ► team, squad, lineup
RELATED ADJECTIVE lateral

side *VERB* **side with** *They didn't know who to side with.* ► support, favour, prefer, take the side of, agree with

sidetrack *VERB* **sidetracks, sidetracking, sidetracked** take someone's attention away from the main subject or problem

sideways *ADVERB, ADJECTIVE* **1** to or from one side • *Move it sideways.* **2** with one side facing forwards • *We sat sideways in the bus.*

siding *NOUN* **sidings** a short railway line by the side of a main line

siege *NOUN* **sieges** the surrounding of a place in order to capture it or force someone to surrender
lay siege to begin a siege of a place

sieve (siv) *NOUN* **sieves** a device made of mesh or perforated metal or plastic, used to separate the smaller or soft parts of something from the larger or hard parts

sieve *VERB* **sieves, sieving, sieved** put something through a sieve

sift *VERB* **sifts, sifting, sifted 1** sieve **2** examine and analyse facts or evidence etc. carefully
▷ **sifter** *NOUN*

sigh *NOUN* **sighs** a sound made by breathing out heavily when you are sad, tired, relieved, etc.

sigh *VERB* **sighs, sighing, sighed** make a sigh

sight *NOUN* **sights 1** the ability to see **2** a thing that can be seen or is worth seeing • *Our garden is a lovely sight in May.* **3** something ugly or ridiculous to look at • *You do look a sight in those clothes!* **4** a device looked through to help aim a gun or telescope etc.
at sight or **on sight** as soon as a person or thing has been seen
catch sight of to see or glimpse for a moment
in sight 1 visible **2** clearly near • *Victory was in sight.*
USAGE Do not confuse with **site**.

sight *VERB* **sights, sighting, sighted 1** see or observe something **2** aim a gun or telescope etc. [from Old English]

sighted *ADJECTIVE* able to see; not blind

sight-reading *NOUN* playing or singing music at sight, without preparation

sightseeing *NOUN* visiting interesting places in a town etc.
▷ **sightseer** *NOUN*

sign *NOUN* **signs 1** something that shows that a thing exists • *There are signs of decay.* **2** a mark, device, or notice etc. that gives a special meaning • *a road sign* **3** an action or movement giving information or a command etc. **4** any of the twelve divisions of the zodiac, represented by a symbol

sign *VERB* **signs, signing, signed 1** make a sign or signal **2** write your signature on something; accept a contract etc. by doing this **3** use signing
sign on 1 accept a job etc. by signing a contract **2** sign a form to say that you are unemployed and want to claim benefit

signal *NOUN* **signals 1** a device, gesture, or sound etc. that gives information or a command **2** a message made up of such things **3** a sequence of electrical impulses or radio waves

Thesaurus

sieve *NOUN Use a sieve to strain the fruit.*
► strainer, sifter, colander, filter, riddle, screen

sieve *VERB Sieve the mixture into a bowl.* ► strain, sift, filter, riddle, screen

sift *VERB* **1** *Sift the flour over the eggs and milk.* ► sieve, strain, filter, riddle, screen **2 sift through** *Police have been sifting through piles of evidence.* ► examine, inspect, sort out, analyse, scrutinize, investigate, review

sigh *VERB* **1** *She sighed with relief.* ► breathe out, exhale **2** *'Not again,' he sighed.* ► moan, complain, lament, grumble

sight *NOUN* **1** *His sight was failing.* ► eyesight, vision, seeing, visual perception RELATED ADJECTIVES visual, optic *or* optical **2** *The enemy was almost in sight.* ► range, view, field of vision **3** *In the early afternoon they had their first sight of land.* ► view, glimpse, appearance, look (at), glance (at) **4** *Thousands of visitors enjoy the sights every year.* ► place of interest, landmark **5** *The fireworks were an impressive sight.* ► spectacle, display, show, exhibition, showpiece, scene

sight *VERB A spotter plane sighted the survivors.* ► spot, discern, make out, glimpse, notice, observe, perceive, distinguish, recognize, see, behold

sign *NOUN* **1** *There are no signs yet of a change in the weather.* ► indication, intimation, hint, warning, forewarning, promise, threat, omen, pointer, portent, presage, augury **2** *He gave the sign to begin.* ► signal, cue, gesture , nod **3** *There were signs of a much earlier occupation at the site.* ► trace, vestige, clue, proof, reminder **4** *Cards are sent as a sign of affection.* ► token, marker, manifestation, symptom **5** *We'll have to put a sign in the window.* ► notice, placard, poster, publicity, signboard, advertisement **6** *The walls were daubed with signs and pictures.* ► symbol, mark, device, emblem, insignia, badge, logo, cipher, trademark

sign *VERB* **1** *She signed her name at the bottom of the page.* ► autograph, inscribe, write, initial, endorse
sign up 1 *The brothers all signed up in the army.* ► enlist, enrol, register, join **2** *The company has signed up many more clerical staff.* ► enrol, enlist, recruit, engage, take on, hire

signal *NOUN* **1** *The captain gave the signal to move forward.* ► sign, gesture, wave, prompt, cue,

signal *VERB* **signals, signalling, signalled** make a signal to somebody
▷ **signaller** *NOUN*
USAGE Do not use this word in mistake for **single** in the phrase *to single out*.

signal box *NOUN* **signal boxes** a building from which railway signals, points, etc. are controlled

signature *NOUN* **signatures** **1** a person's name written by himself or herself **2** (in music) a set of sharps and flats after the clef in a score, showing the key the music is written in (the **key signature**), or the sign, often a fraction such as (the **time signature**), showing the number of beats in the bar and their rhythm

signature tune *NOUN* **signature tunes** a special tune always used to announce a particular programme, performer, etc.

significant *ADJECTIVE* **1** having a meaning; full of meaning **2** important • *a significant event*
▷ **significantly** *ADVERB* **significance** *NOUN*

signing or **sign language** *NOUN* a way of communicating by using movements of the arms and hands, used mainly by and for deaf people

signpost *NOUN* **signposts** a sign at a road junction etc. showing the names and distances of places down each road

Sikh (seek) *NOUN* **Sikhs** a member of a religion founded in northern India, believing in one God and accepting some Hindu and some Islamic beliefs
▷ **Sikhism** *NOUN*

silence *NOUN* **silences** absence of sound or speaking
in silence without speaking or making a sound

silence *VERB* **silences, silencing, silenced** make a person or thing silent

silencer *NOUN* **silencers** a device for reducing the sound made by a gun or a vehicle's exhaust system etc.

silent *ADJECTIVE* **1** without any sound **2** not speaking
▷ **silently** *ADVERB*

silhouette (sil- oo- et) *NOUN* **silhouettes** a dark shadow seen against a light background
▷ **silhouette** *VERB*

silicon *NOUN* a substance found in many rocks, used in making transistors, chips for microprocessors, etc.

silk *NOUN* **silks** **1** a fine soft thread or cloth made from the fibre produced by silkworm caterpillars for making their cocoons **2** a length of silk thread used for embroidery
▷ **silken** *ADJECTIVE* **silky** *ADJECTIVE*

Thesaurus

nod, (*more informal*) go-ahead **2** *The city mob took Edward's flight as the signal for an orgy of destruction.* ► cue, prompt, occasion, excuse, stimulus

signal *VERB* **1** *A police officer signalled to him to stop.* ► gesture, indicate, motion, sign, wave, beckon, communicate, flag, gesticulate, give a signal **2** *The pointed gun signalled his intentions very clearly.* ► indicate, express, reveal, announce, proclaim, declare, show

significance *NOUN* *He thought hard about the significance of her remarks.* ► importance, import, force, purport, implication, meaning, relevance, sense, point, signification, message
AN OPPOSITE IS insignificance

significant *ADJECTIVE* **1** *The tests produced some significant results.* ► meaningful, revealing, informative, important, indicative, expressive, (*more informal*) tell-tale **2** *The measures would have a significant effect on prices.* ► considerable, important, noteworthy, serious, sizeable, remarkable, influential, big
AN OPPOSITE IS insignificant

signify *VERB* **1** *Red signifies danger.* ► mean, denote, symbolize, represent, indicate, stand for, imply **2** *Signify your agreement by signing your name at the bottom of the letter.* ► indicate, express, show, declare

silence *NOUN* **1** *There was silence for a time, while they thought.* ► quiet, quietness, stillness, tranquillity, peace, peacefulness, calm, hush
AN OPPOSITE IS noise **2** *The criticism reduced him to silence.* ► speechlessness, dumbness, muteness, reticence, taciturnity, uncommunicativeness OPPOSITES ARE speech, verbosity

silence *VERB* **1** *The menace in his voice silenced them.* ► quieten, keep quiet, make silent, suppress, muzzle, shut up, gag **2** *A special muffler helps to silence exhaust noise* ► deaden, muffle, quieten, mute

silent *ADJECTIVE* **1** *George was silent until they reached the car park.* ► speechless, quiet, unspeaking, voiceless, dumb, mute, taciturn, reticent **2** *It was totally silent in the kitchen.* ► quiet, hushed, peaceful, tranquil, noiseless, soundless

silhouette *NOUN* *I made out the long silhouette of a tall man.* ► outline, profile, contour, shape, figure, form, features

silky *ADJECTIVE* *She ran her fingers through her dark silky hair.* ► smooth, soft, sleek, velvety, glossy, fine, satiny

silly *ADJECTIVE* **sillier**, **silliest** foolish or unwise
▷ **silliness** *NOUN*

silt *NOUN* sediment laid down by a river or sea etc.

silt *VERB* **silts**, **silting**, **silted**
silt up block or clog or become blocked with silt

silver *NOUN* **1** a shiny white precious metal **2** the colour of silver **3** coins or objects made of silver or silver-coloured metal **4** a silver medal, usually given as second prize
▷ **silver** *ADJECTIVE* **silvery** *ADJECTIVE*

silver *VERB* **silvers**, **silvering**, **silvered** make or become silvery

silver wedding *NOUN* **silver weddings** a couple's 25th wedding anniversary

similar *ADJECTIVE* **1** nearly the same as another person or thing; of the same kind **2** (in mathematics) having the same shape but not the same size • *similar triangles*
▷ **similarly** *ADVERB* **similarity** *NOUN*

simile (sim- il- ee) *NOUN* **similes** a comparison of one thing with another (e.g. *He is as strong as a horse* or *We ran like the wind.*)

simmer *VERB* **simmers**, **simmering**, **simmered** boil very gently
simmer down calm down

simper *VERB* **simpers**, **simpering**, **simpered** smile in a silly affected way
▷ **simper** *NOUN*

simple *ADJECTIVE* **simpler**, **simplest** **1** easy • *a simple question* **2** not complicated or elaborate **3** plain, not showy • *a simple cottage* **4** without much sense or intelligence **5** not of high rank; ordinary • *a simple countryman*
▷ **simplicity** *NOUN*

simple-minded *ADJECTIVE* not having much intelligence

simplify *VERB* **simplifies**, **simplifying**, **simplified** make a thing simple or easy to understand
▷ **simplification** *NOUN*

simply *ADVERB* **1** in a simple way • *Explain it simply.* **2** without doubt; completely • *It's simply marvellous.* **3** only or merely • *It's simply a question of time.*

simulator *NOUN* **simulators** a machine or device for simulating actual conditions or events, often used for training • *a flight simulator*

simultaneous (sim- ul- tay- nee- us) *ADJECTIVE* happening at the same time
▷ **simultaneously** *ADVERB*

Thesaurus

silly *ADJECTIVE* **1** *'I'm not quite as silly as you think,' she said.* ► stupid, foolish, crazy, mad, (*more informal*) daft **2** *People often do silly things.* ► foolish, unwise, stupid, imprudent, rash, reckless, foolhardy, senseless, idiotic, (*more informal*) daft

simian *ADJECTIVE* ► monkey-like

similar *ADJECTIVE* **1** *The boys are similar in appearance.* ► alike, identical, indistinguishable, close, like, the same
OPPOSITES ARE dissimilar, different **2** *hills and similar features* ► comparable, analogous, equivalent **3** **similar to** *Her views are similar to my own.* ► like, comparable to, close to
OPPOSITES ARE unlike, dissimilar to, different from

similarity *NOUN* *There is a startling similarity between them.* ► resemblance, likeness, affinity, closeness, correspondence, congruity, similitude, sameness, uniformity
AN OPPOSITE IS difference

simple *ADJECTIVE* **1** *a simple method of fixing up shelving* ► straightforward, easy, uncomplicated, elementary, undemanding
OPPOSITES ARE complicated, difficult **2** *The forms are written in simple language.* ► clear, plain, straightforward, unambiguous, direct **3** *They led simple, honest lives. He is a simple sort of guy.* ► unpretentious, unsophisticated, ordinary, unassuming, innocent, artless

simplicity *NOUN* **1** *The solution was amazing for its simplicity.* ► straightforwardness, simpleness, ease AN OPPOSITE IS difficulty **2** *The house appealed because of the simplicity of its style.* ► plainness, unpretentiousness, restraint, purity, austerity
AN OPPOSITE IS ornateness

simplify *VERB* *The rules are difficult to apply and need to be simplified.* ► make simple, clarify, disentangle, streamline
AN OPPOSITE IS complicate

simply *ADVERB* **1** *It was simply impossible to tell the difference.* ► wholly, absolutely, completely, utterly **2** *She did it simply because we asked her to.* ► merely, just, purely, solely, only **3** *It is important to dress simply and avoid flamboyance.* ► plainly, soberly, without fuss, without frills, with restraint **4** *He writes simply and effectively.* ► clearly, plainly, straightforwardly, intelligibly **5** *They lived simply.* ► modestly, unpretentiously, naturally, quietly

simultaneous *ADJECTIVE* *There were three simultaneous bomb attacks in the city.* ► concurrent, coinciding, synchronized, synchronous, contemporaneous, parallel

sin *NOUN* **sins 1** the breaking of a religious or moral law **2** a very bad action

sin *VERB* **sins, sinning, sinned** commit a sin
▷ **sinner** *NOUN*

since *CONJUNCTION* **1** from the time when • *Where have you been since I last saw you?* **2** because • *Since we have missed the bus we must walk home.*

since *PREPOSITION* from a certain time • *She has been here since Christmas*

since *ADVERB* between then and now • *He ran away and hasn't been seen since.*

sincere *ADJECTIVE* without pretence; truly felt or meant • *my sincere thanks*
▷ **sincerely** *ADVERB* **sincerity** *NOUN*
Yours sincerely SEE **yours**

sine *NOUN* **sines** (in a right-angled triangle) the ratio of the length of a side opposite one of the acute angles to the length of the hypotenuse
COMPARE **cosine**

sinew *NOUN* **sinews** strong tissue that connects a muscle to a bone
▷ **sinewy** *ADJECTIVE*

sinful *ADJECTIVE* **1** guilty of sin **2** wicked
▷ **sinfully** *ADVERB* **sinfulness** *NOUN*

sing *VERB* **sings, singing, sang, sung 1** make musical sounds with the voice **2** perform a song
▷ **singer** *NOUN*

singe (sinj) *VERB* **singes, singeing, singed** burn something slightly

single *ADJECTIVE* **1** one only; not double or multiple **2** suitable for one person • *single beds* **3** separate • *We sold every single thing.* **4** not married **5** for the journey to a place but not back again • *a single ticket*
▷ **singly** *ADVERB*

single *NOUN* **singles 1** a single person or thing **2** a single ticket **3** a record with one short piece of music on each side

single *VERB* **singles, singling, singled**
single out pick out or distinguish from other people or things

single file *NOUN*
in single file in a line, one behind the other

single-handed *ADJECTIVE* without help

single-minded *ADJECTIVE* with your mind set on one purpose only

singsong *ADJECTIVE* having a monotonous tone or rhythm • *a singsong voice*

singular *NOUN* **singulars** the form of a noun or verb used when it stands for only one person or thing • *The singular is 'man', the plural is 'men'*

singular *ADJECTIVE* **1** to do with the singular **2** uncommon or extraordinary • *a woman of singular courage*
▷ **singularly** *ADVERB* **singularity** *NOUN*

sinister *ADJECTIVE* **1** looking evil or harmful **2** wicked • *a sinister motive* [from Latin, = on the left (which was thought to be unlucky)]

sink *VERB* **sinks, sinking, sank, sunk 1** go or cause to go under the surface or to the bottom of the sea etc. • *The ship sank.* • *They sank the ship.* **2** go or fall slowly downwards • *He sank to his knees.* **3** push something sharp deeply into something soft • *The dog sank its teeth into my*

Thesaurus

sin *NOUN* **1** *It was a sin against their gods.* ► offence, wrong, transgression, evil, iniquity **2** *a powerful sermon on the dangers of sin* ► wickedness, wrongdoing, sinfulness, immorality, evil AN OPPOSITE IS virtue

sin *VERB* *He confessed he had sinned and incurred the wrath of his God.* ► do wrong, be guilty of sin, transgress, err, go astray, offend

sincere *ADJECTIVE* **1** *Their praise was completely sincere.* ► heartfelt, honest, candid, genuine, truthful, wholehearted, open AN OPPOSITE IS insincere **2** *Jane is a very sincere person.* ► honest, genuine, truthful, straightforward, ingenuous, artless

sincerity *NOUN* *I trust the sincerity of their intentions.* ► honesty, genuineness, integrity, openness, straightforwardness, trustworthiness, truthfulness

sinful *ADJECTIVE* *Such behaviour was sinful.* ► wicked, wrong, evil, iniquitous, unrighteous, ungodly AN OPPOSITE IS virtuous

sing *VERB* *To cheer herself up she began to sing.* ► chant, croon, hum, intone, trill

single *ADJECTIVE* **1** *All the chocolates were gone apart from a single orange cream.* ► solitary, lone, sole, isolated AN OPPOSITE IS plural. **2** *He had remained single all his life.* ► unattached, unmarried, a bachelor, unwedded AN OPPOSITE IS married **3** *She listened to every single word.* ► individual, particular

single *VERB* **single out** *It would be invidious to single out any individual for praise.* ► pick out, choose, select, fix on, separate out

singular *ADJECTIVE* *They acted with singular determination.* ► extraordinary, remarkable, exceptional, uncommon, unusual, conspicuous, notable

sinister *His words had a sinister undertone.* ► menacing, threatening, ominous, disturbing, alarming, disquieting, malevolent, baleful, (*more informal*) scary, (*more informal*) creepy

sink *VERB* **1** *The sun sank below the horizon.* ► descend, dip, fall, drop, disappear, vanish AN OPPOSITE IS rise **2** *Their hopes began to sink.* ► dwindle, fade, flag, fail, weaken, lessen,

leg. **4** dig or drill • *They sank a well.* **5** invest money in something

sink in become understood

sink NOUN **sinks** a fixed basin with a drainpipe and usually a tap or taps to supply water

sip VERB **sips, sipping, sipped** drink in small mouthfuls

▷ **sip** NOUN

siphon NOUN **siphons** **1** a pipe or tube in the form of an upside-down U, arranged so that liquid is forced up it and down to a lower level **2** a bottle containing soda water which is released through a tube

siphon VERB **siphons, siphoning, siphoned** flow or draw out through a siphon

sir NOUN **1** a word used when speaking politely to a man • *Please sir, may I go?* **2 Sir** the title given to a knight or baronet • *Sir John Moore*

siren NOUN **sirens** **1** a device that makes a long loud sound as a signal **2** a dangerously attractive woman [named after the Sirens in Greek legend, women who by their sweet singing lured seafarers to shipwreck on the rocks]

sissy NOUN **sissies** (*informal*) a timid or cowardly person [from *sis*, a shortening of *sister*]

sister NOUN **sisters** **1** a daughter of the same parents as another person **2** a woman who is a fellow member of an association etc. **3** a nun **4** a senior hospital nurse, especially one in charge of a ward

▷ **sisterly** ADJECTIVE

[from Old English]

sister-in-law NOUN **sisters-in-law** **1** the sister of a married person's husband or wife **2** the wife of a person's brother

sit VERB **sits, sitting, sat** **1** rest with your body supported on the buttocks; occupy a seat • *We were sitting in the front row.* **2** seat; cause someone to sit **3** (said about birds) perch; stay on the nest to hatch eggs **4** be a candidate for an examination **5** be situated; stay **6** (said about Parliament or a lawcourt etc.) be assembled for business

sitcom NOUN **sitcoms** (*informal*) a radio or television comedy based on characters reacting to unusual or comic situations [short for *situation comedy*]

site NOUN **sites** the place where something happens or happened or is built etc. • *a camping site* [from Latin *situs* = position]

USAGE Do not confuse with **sight**.

sit-in NOUN **sit-ins** a protest in which people sit down or occupy a public place and refuse to move

sitter NOUN **sitters** a person who looks after children, pets, or a house while the owners are away

sitting NOUN **sittings** the time when people are served a meal or when an official body of people does business

sitting room NOUN **sitting rooms** a room with comfortable chairs for sitting in

situation NOUN **situations** **1** a position, with its surroundings **2** a state of affairs at a certain time • *The police faced a difficult situation.* **3** a job

six NOUN, ADJECTIVE **sixes** the number 6

▷ **sixth** ADJECTIVE, NOUN

at sixes and sevens in disorder or disagreement

sixteen NOUN, ADJECTIVE the number 16

▷ **sixteenth** ADJECTIVE, NOUN

Thesaurus

subside, collapse AN OPPOSITE IS revive **3** *The ship sank with the loss of many lives.* ► founder, go under, submerge, capsize OPPOSITES ARE rise, float

sip VERB *She sat sipping tea.* ► drink slowly, taste, sample, (*more informal*) slurp

sip NOUN *He took another sip of his beer.* ► mouthful, drink, drop, taste, (*more informal*) slurp

sister NOUN ► sibling RELATED ADJECTIVE sororal

sit VERB **1** *Julian sat in an armchair.* ► settle, perch, flop, ensconce yourself **2** *The hall sat about a hundred people.* ► seat, accommodate, have seats for, hold, take, has room for **3** *Parliament sits again in a week's time.* ► meet, assemble, convene, gather, be in session **4** *She sits her exams this year.* ► take, go in for, be a candidate in

site NOUN *the site for the new hospital* ► location, situation, setting, spot, plot, locality, ground

site VERB *Bus stops are sited at intervals of no more than half a mile.* ► position, place, situate, locate, erect, station, install

sitting NOUN *a sitting of Parliament* ► session, assembly, meeting, period

sitting room NOUN ► living room, drawing room, lounge, front room, reception room

situated ADJECTIVE *a hypermarket situated near the bypass* ► located, positioned, sited, built, placed, established

situation NOUN **1** *new houses in a pleasant situation* ► locality, location, position, setting, site, spot, place **2** *Their financial situation had improved significantly.* ► circumstances, position, state, state of affairs, condition, plight, predicament USAGE You use *plight* and *predicament* about bad situations **3** *She applied for a situation with an estate agent.* ► job, position, post, employment

sixth form *NOUN* **sixth forms** a form for students aged 16-18 in a secondary school

sixth sense *NOUN* the ability to know something by instinct rather than by using any of the five senses; intuition

sixty *NOUN, ADJECTIVE* **sixties** the number 60
▷ **sixtieth** *ADJECTIVE, NOUN*

size *NOUN* **sizes** **1** the measurements or extent of something **2** any of the series of standard measurements in which certain things are made • *a size eight shoe*

size *VERB* **sizes, sizing, sized** arrange things according to their size
size up 1 estimate the size of something **2** form an opinion or judgement about a person or thing

sizeable *ADJECTIVE* large or fairly large

sizzle *VERB* **sizzles, sizzling, sizzled** make a crackling or hissing sound

skate *NOUN* **skates 1** a boot with a steel blade attached to the sole, used for sliding smoothly over ice **2** a roller-skate

skate *VERB* **skates, skating, skated** move on skates
▷ **skater** *NOUN*

skateboard *NOUN* **skateboards** a small board with wheels, used for standing and riding on as a sport
▷ **skateboarder, skateboarding** *NOUNS*

skein *NOUN* **skeins** a coil of yarn or thread

skeleton *NOUN* **skeletons 1** the framework of bones of the body **2** the shell or other hard part of a crab etc. **3** a framework, e.g. of a building
▷ **skeletal** *ADJECTIVE*
[from Greek *skeletos* = dried-up]

sketch *NOUN* **sketches 1** a rough drawing or painting **2** a short account of something **3** a short amusing play

sketch *VERB* **sketches, sketching, sketched** make a sketch

sketchy *ADJECTIVE* rough and not detailed or careful

skewer *NOUN* **skewers** a long pin pushed through meat to hold it together while it is being cooked
▷ **skewer** *VERB*

ski (skee) *NOUN* **skis** each of a pair of long narrow strips of wood, metal, or plastic fixed under the feet for moving quickly over snow

ski *VERB* **skies, skiing, skied** travel on skis
▷ **skier** *NOUN*
[from Norwegian]

skid *VERB* **skids, skidding, skidded** slide accidentally

skid *NOUN* **skids 1** a skidding movement **2** a runner on a helicopter, for use in landing
[probably from Old Norse *skith* = ski]

ski jump *NOUN* **ski jumps** a steep slope with a sharp drop where it levels out at the bottom, for skiers to jump off as a sport

skilful *ADJECTIVE* having or showing great skill
▷ **skilfully** *ADVERB*

skill *NOUN* **skills** the ability to do something well
▷ **skilled** *ADJECTIVE*
[from Old Norse]

Thesaurus

size *NOUN* **1** *the vast size of the main bedroom* ► dimensions, proportions, scale, magnitude, area, volume **2** *the size of the job* ► scale, extent, scope, range, immensity

sizeable *ADJECTIVE* *A sizeable reward is being offered.* ► large, substantial, considerable, significant, decent, generous, worthwhile, (*more informal*) tidy

sizzle *VERB* *Food sizzled in the pan.* ► crackle, frizzle, hiss, sputter

skeleton *NOUN* **1** *the skeleton of a building* ► framework, frame, bones, structure **2** *a skeleton of the plan* ► outline, draft, abstract, blueprint, sketch

sketch *NOUN* **1** *She drew a sketch of the scene.* ► drawing, outline, picture , diagram, plan **2** *a biographical sketch* ► description, portrait, profile, cameo **3** *a brief sketch of the main events* ► outline, summary, synopsis, rundown **4** *a comic sketch from the television series* ► scene, skit, turn, routine, number

sketch *VERB* *He decided to sketch the garden instead of taking a photograph.* ► draw, make a drawing of, portray, depict, rough out, represent
sketch out *We will sketch out our plan.* ► outline, describe, summarize, rough out, draft, give the gist of

sketchy *ADJECTIVE* *The information was too sketchy to act on.* ► incomplete, imperfect, perfunctory, bitty, scrappy, skimpy, meagre, rough, vague, imprecise, scanty
OPPOSITES ARE detailed, comprehensive

skilful *ADJECTIVE* *a skilful negotiator; a skilful use of the materials* ► expert, skilled, able, capable, accomplished, proficient, adroit, deft, talented, clever, masterly, consummate
AN OPPOSITE IS incompetent

skill *NOUN* *work that needs a lot of skill* ► expertise, ability, skillfulness, aptitude, adeptness, dexterity, competence, talent
AN OPPOSITE IS incompetence

skilled *ADJECTIVE* *a skilled engineer* ► experienced, trained, qualified, skilful, proficient, accomplished, expert, practised, versed OPPOSITES ARE unskilled, inexperienced

skim *VERB* **skims, skimming, skimmed** **1** remove something from the surface of a liquid; take the cream off milk **2** move quickly over a surface or through the air **3** read something quickly [from early French *escume* = scum]

skimp *VERB* **skimps, skimping, skimped** supply or use less than is needed • *Don't skimp on the food.*

skimpy *ADJECTIVE* **skimpier, skimpiest** scanty or too small

skin *NOUN* **skins** **1** the flexible outer covering of a person's or animal's body **2** an outer layer or covering, e.g. of a fruit **3** a skin-like film formed on the surface of a liquid

skin *VERB* **skins, skinning, skinned** take the skin off something

skinny *ADJECTIVE* **skinnier, skinniest** very thin

skip[1] *VERB* **skips, skipping, skipped** **1** move along lightly, especially by hopping on each foot in turn **2** jump with a skipping rope **3** go quickly from one subject to another **4** miss something out • *You can skip chapter six.*

skip *NOUN* **skips** a skipping movement [probably from Scandinavian]

skip[2] *NOUN* **skips** a large metal container for taking away builders' rubbish etc. [from Old Norse *skeppa* = basket]

skipping rope *NOUN* **skipping ropes** a rope, usually with a handle at each end, that is swung over your head and under your feet as you jump

skirt *NOUN* **skirts** **1** a piece of clothing for a woman or girl that hangs down from the waist **2** the part of a dress below the waist

skirt *VERB* **skirts, skirting, skirted** go round the edge of something

skittish *ADJECTIVE* frisky; lively and excitable

skulk *VERB* **skulks, skulking, skulked** loiter stealthily

skull *NOUN* **skulls** the framework of bones of the head

skunk *NOUN* **skunks** a North American animal with black and white fur that can spray a bad-smelling fluid [from a Native American word]

sky *NOUN* **skies** the space above the earth, appearing blue in daylight on fine days [from Old Norse]

skylight *NOUN* **skylights** a window in a roof

skyline *NOUN* **skylines** the outline of buildings etc. against the sky

skyscraper *NOUN* **skyscrapers** a very tall building

slab *NOUN* **slabs** a thick flat piece

slack *ADJECTIVE* **1** not pulled tight **2** not busy; not working hard
▷ **slackly** *ADVERB* **slackness** *NOUN*

slack *VERB* **slacks, slacking, slacked** avoid work; be lazy
▷ **slacker** *NOUN*

slacken *VERB* **slackens, slackening, slackened** make or become slack

Thesaurus

skim *VERB* **1** *The boat skim across the water.* ► glide, skate, plane, slide, float, coast **2** **skim through** *He skimmed through a picture book.* ► scan, skip through, flick through, look through, riffle through, read quickly

skimp *VERB* *Despite the low price you won't skimp on comfort here.* ► stint on, be frugal with, economize on, cut corners on

skimpy *ADJECTIVE* *I'd rather have my clothes too long than looking skimpy.* ► scanty, short, flimsy, low-cut

skin *NOUN* **1** *The animal has a tough skin.* ► hide, pelt **2** *the skin of an apple* ► peel, rind, outside

skin *VERB* *She skinned three tomatoes.* ► peel, pare, strip

skinny *ADJECTIVE* *We have to find skinny people to try our designs on.* ► thin, scrawny, scraggy, lean, lanky, spindly, emaciated

skip *VERB* **1** *Cathy skipped along the path.* ► prance, trip, frisk **2** *We can skip these details.* ► pass over, ignore, omit, leave out, miss out, dispense with, forget **3** *We skipped school to go on the demo.* ► miss, be absent from, play truant from, absent yourself from, cut

sky *NOUN* *Suddenly the whole sky around them was filled with birds.* ► heavens, atmosphere, blue yonder RELATED ADJECTIVE celestial

slab *NOUN* *slabs of rock cut from the quarries* ► block, piece, tablet, chunk, hunk, lump, slice

slack *ADJECTIVE* **1** *The rope suddenly went slack.* ► limp, loose AN OPPOSITE IS tight **2** *A slack defence let in several goals.* ► disorganized, negligent, careless, undisciplined, inattentive, lax, lazy, listless, easygoing OPPOSITES ARE alert, diligent. **3** *Business tends to be slack just after Christmas.* ► sluggish, slow, quiet, inactive, slow-moving, depressed OPPOSITES ARE brisk, busy

slack *VERB* *This was no time for slacking.* ► idle, shirk, be lazy, (*more informal*) skive

slacken *VERB* **1** *The boat lurched as he slackened his grip on the wheel.* ► loosen, relax, release, ease off AN OPPOSITE IS tighten **2** *The rain might just have slackened by now.* ► decrease, ease, lessen, abate, lower, moderate, reduce, slow down

slacker *NOUN* *There was no room for slackers.* ► layabout, idler, shirker, loafer, malingerer, sluggard

A B C D E F G H I J K L M N O P Q R S T U V W X Y Z

slacks *PLURAL NOUN* trousers for informal occasions

slag *NOUN* waste material separated from metal in smelting

slag heap *NOUN* **slag heaps** a mound of waste matter from a mine etc.

slain *past participle* of **slay**

slake *VERB* **slakes, slaking, slaked** quench • *slake your thirst*

slam *VERB* **slams, slamming, slammed** **1** shut loudly **2** hit violently
▷ **slam** *NOUN*

slander *NOUN* **slanders** a spoken statement that damages a person's reputation and is untrue COMPARE **libel**
▷ **slanderous** *ADJECTIVE*

slander *VERB* **slanders, slandering, slandered** make a slander against someone
▷ **slanderer** *NOUN*

slang *NOUN* words that are used very informally to add vividness or humour to what is said, especially those used only by a particular group of people • *teenage slang*
▷ **slangy** *ADJECTIVE*

slant *VERB* **slants, slanting, slanted** **1** slope **2** present news or information etc. from a particular point of view

slap *VERB* **slaps, slapping, slapped** **1** hit with the palm of the hand or with something flat **2** put forcefully or carelessly • *We slapped paint on the walls.*
▷ **slap** *NOUN*

slapdash *ADJECTIVE* hasty and careless

slapstick *NOUN* comedy with people hitting each other, falling over, etc.

slash *VERB* **slashes, slashing, slashed** **1** make large cuts in something **2** cut or strike with a long sweeping movement **3** reduce greatly • *Prices were slashed.*

slash *NOUN* **slashes** **1** a slashing cut **2** a slanting line (/) used in writing and printing

slate *NOUN* **slates** **1** a kind of grey rock that is easily split into flat plates **2** a piece of this rock used in covering a roof or (formerly) for writing on
▷ **slaty** *ADJECTIVE*

slate *VERB* **slates, slating, slated** **1** cover a roof with slates **2** (*informal*) criticize severely

slaughter *VERB* **slaughters, slaughtering, slaughtered** **1** kill an animal for food **2** kill people or animals ruthlessly or in great numbers
▷ **slaughter** *NOUN*

slaughterhouse *NOUN* **slaughterhouses** a place where animals are killed for food

Thesaurus

slam *VERB* **1** *He stormed out and slammed the door.* ► bang, shut, fling shut, crash

slander *NOUN* *He'd sue me for slander if I made the accusations publicly.* ► defamation, misrepresentation, calumny, libel, slur, aspersion, malicious gossip, scandalmongering OPPOSITES ARE compliment, praise

slander *VERB* *She discovered that her friend had been slandering her behind her back.* ► defame, libel, smear, vilify, besmirch

slanderous *ADJECTIVE* *The truth can often be slanderous if you put it in a certain way.* ► defamatory, libellous, disparaging, pejorative, scurrilous, malicious, abusive

slant *NOUN* **1** *The floor seemed to be on a slant.* ► slope, angle, incline, diagonal, gradient, list, rake, ramp, pitch, tilt **2** *The Youth Theatre brings a new slant to Christmas shows.* ► point of view, viewpoint, standpoint, angle, perspective, emphasis, bias

slant *VERB* **1** *The handwriting slants to the right. Joe slanted his gaze towards the door.* ► tilt, lean, slope, incline, be at an angle, be skewed **2** *He slanted his version of the story to avoid awkward admissions.* ► bias, distort, twist, warp, weight, colour, prejudice

slanting *ADJECTIVE* *The slanting sunlight cast long shadows.* ► oblique, sloping, angled, inclined, diagonal, listing, raked, askew, skewed, slantwise, tilted OPPOSITES ARE straight, level

slap *VERB* **1** *Anne was at the end of her patience and wanted to slap him.* ► smack, strike, hit, clout, whack, spank **2** *She had slapped a parking ticket on his Mercedes.* ► fling, throw, toss, hurl **3** *Slap some varnish on to seal the surface.* ► daub, plaster, spread, apply

slap *NOUN* *He heard the sound of a slap from the next room.* ► smack, clout, whack, blow, thump

slash *VERB* **1** *Someone had slashed the tyres.* ► cut, slit, gash, rip, tear, knife **2** *Prices will be slashed out of the high season.* ► reduce, cut, drop

slash *NOUN* *He had a deep slash across his arm.* ► cut, gash, laceration, wound, injury

slate *VERB* (*informal*) *The critics all slated the production, though they liked the music.* ► criticize, pillory, lambaste, revile, (*informal*) pan

slaughter *NOUN* *The senseless slaughter of dolphins takes place merely to catch a few extra tuna.* ► massacre, carnage, killing, butchery, murder, bloodshed

slaughter *VERB* *A whole legion was ambushed and slaughtered.* ► massacre, butcher, kill, annihilate, eliminate, murder, slay

slave *NOUN* **slaves** a person who is owned by another and obliged to work for him or her without being paid
▷ **slavery** *NOUN*

slave *VERB* **slaves, slaving, slaved** work very hard [from Latin *sclavus* = captive]

slavish *ADJECTIVE* **1** like a slave **2** showing no independence or originality

slay *VERB* **slays, slaying, slew, slain** (*poetical*) kill

sledge *NOUN* **sledges** a vehicle for travelling over snow, with strips of metal or wood instead of wheels
▷ **sledging** *NOUN*

sledgehammer *NOUN* **sledgehammers** a very large heavy hammer

sleek *ADJECTIVE* smooth and shiny

sleep *NOUN* the condition or time of rest in which the eyes are closed, the body relaxed, and the mind unconscious
go to sleep (said about part of the body) become numb
put to sleep kill an animal painlessly, e.g. with an injection of a drug

sleep *VERB* **sleeps, sleeping, slept** have a sleep
sleep with have sexual intercourse with [from Old English]

sleeper *NOUN* **sleepers 1** someone who is asleep **2** each of the wooden or concrete beams on which the rails of a railway rest **3** a railway carriage with beds or berths for passengers to sleep in; a place in this

sleepwalker *NOUN* **sleepwalkers** a person who walks about while asleep
▷ **sleepwalking** *NOUN*

sleepy *ADJECTIVE* feeling a need or wish to sleep
▷ **sleepily** *ADVERB* **sleepiness** *NOUN*

sleet *NOUN* a mixture of rain and snow or hail

sleeve *NOUN* **sleeves 1** the part of a piece of clothing that covers the arm **2** the cover of a record
up your sleeve hidden but ready for you to use

sleight (rhymes with *slight*) *NOUN*
sleight of hand skill in using the hands to do conjuring tricks etc.

slender *ADJECTIVE* **1** slim and graceful **2** slight or small • *a slender chance*
▷ **slenderness** *NOUN*

sleuth (slooth) *NOUN* **sleuths** a detective [from Old Norse *sloth* = a track or trail]

slew *past tense of* **slay**

slice *NOUN* **slices 1** a thin piece cut off something **2** a portion

Thesaurus

slave *NOUN* *Most of the work was done by slaves at that time.* ► serf, thrall, vassal, drudge, servant
RELATED ADJECTIVE servile

slave *VERB* *That's all the thanks you get for slaving over a hot stove all morning.* ► toil, labour, grind, sweat, work , drudge, exert yourself, work your fingers to the bone, (*more informal*) work your socks off OPPOSITES ARE relax, skive

slavery *NOUN* *They were being sent back to torture, slavery, and death.* ► bondage, enslavement, servitude, captivity, serfdom
AN OPPOSITE IS freedom

slay *VERB* *Thousands of men and women were slain in the reprisals.* ► kill, slaughter, massacre, butcher, murder, put to death, exterminate, annihilate, cut down, (*informal*) finish off

sleazy *ADJECTIVE* *a sleazy little cafe on the edge of town* ► dirty, squalid, shabby, run-down, sordid, seamy, rough

sleek *ADJECTIVE* **1** *She combed her sleek dark hair.* ► silky, glossy, shiny, smooth, brushed, soft, velvety, well-groomed AN OPPOSITE IS dull **2** *a sleek sports car* ► streamlined, graceful, elegant, aerodynamic **3** *a group of sleek young men in smart suits* ► stylish, well-groomed, prosperous AN OPPOSITE IS unkempt

sleep *NOUN* *She often had a sleep in the afternoon.* ► snooze, nap, rest, doze, catnap, siesta, (*more informal*) kip, (*more informal*) forty winks

sleep *VERB* *He had slept for about an hour.* ► snooze, doze, rest, slumber, (*more informal*) kip, (*more informal*) drop off, (*more informal*) nod off, (*more informal*) doss down

sleepy *ADJECTIVE* **1** *I wasn't sleepy, so I decided to walk round for a bit.* ► drowsy, somnolent, lethargic, weary, tired, torpid, sluggish, soporific, heavy-eyed, (*informal*) dopey, ready to sleep AN OPPOSITE IS awake **2** *a sleepy little town near the border* ► quiet, peaceful, tranquil, inactive, dull, unexciting
OPPOSITES ARE lively, busy

slender *ADJECTIVE* **1** *a slender youth with dark hair* ► slim, lean, slight, thin, graceful, svelte
AN OPPOSITE IS fat **2** *a slender thread* ► fine, fragile, tenuous, feeble AN OPPOSITE IS strong **3** *slender hopes* ► faint, slim, remote, flimsy **4** *a verdict based on slender evidence* ► meagre, scanty, flimsy, tenuous, inadequate
AN OPPOSITE IS adequate

slice *NOUN* *a slice of bread* ► piece, sliver (=thin slice), chunk (= thick slice), hunk (= thick slice), tranche, slab

a b c d e f g h i j k l m n o p q r s t u v w x y z

A B C D E F G H I J K L M N O P Q R S T U V W X Y Z

slice *VERB* **slices, slicing, sliced** **1** cut into slices **2** cut from a larger piece • *Slice the top off the egg.* **3** cut cleanly • *The knife sliced through the apple.*

slick *ADJECTIVE* **1** done or doing things quickly and cleverly **2** slippery

slick *NOUN* **slicks** **1** a large patch of oil floating on water **2** a slippery place

slide *VERB* **slides, sliding, slid** **1** move or cause to move smoothly on a surface **2** move quietly or secretly • *The thief slid behind a bush.*

slide *NOUN* **slides** **1** a sliding movement **2** a smooth surface or structure on which people or things can slide **3** a photograph that can be projected on a screen **4** a small glass plate on which things are placed to be examined under a microscope **5** a fastener to keep hair tidy

slight *ADJECTIVE* very small; not serious or important
▷ **slightly** *ADVERB* **slightness** *NOUN*

slim *ADJECTIVE* **slimmer, slimmest** **1** thin and graceful **2** small; hardly enough • *a slim chance*
▷ **slimness** *NOUN*

slim *VERB* **slims, slimming, slimmed** make yourself thinner, especially by dieting
▷ **slimmer** *NOUN*

slime *NOUN* unpleasant wet slippery stuff
▷ **slimy** *ADJECTIVE* **sliminess** *NOUN*

sling *NOUN* **slings** **1** a loop or band placed round something to support or lift it • *He had his arm in a sling.* **2** a looped strap used to throw a stone etc.

sling *VERB* **slings, slinging, slung** **1** hang or support something so that it hangs loosely **2** (*informal*) throw carelessly

slink *VERB* **slinks, slinking, slunk** move in a stealthy or guilty way
▷ **slinky** *ADJECTIVE*

slip *VERB* **slips, slipping, slipped** **1** slide accidentally; lose your balance by sliding **2** move or put quickly and quietly • *Slip it in your pocket.* • *We slipped away from the party.* **3** escape from • *The dog slipped its leash. It slipped my memory.*
slip up make a mistake

slip *NOUN* **slips** **1** an accidental slide or fall **2** a mistake **3** a small piece of paper **4** a petticoat **5** a pillowcase
give someone the slip escape or avoid someone skilfully

slipper *NOUN* **slippers** a soft comfortable shoe to wear indoors

slippery *ADJECTIVE* smooth or wet so that it is difficult to stand on or hold
▷ **slipperiness** *NOUN*

slipshod *ADJECTIVE* careless; not systematic

slipstream *NOUN* **slipstreams** a current of air driven backward as an aircraft or vehicle is propelled forward

slit *NOUN* **slits** a narrow straight cut or opening

slit *VERB* **slits, slitting, slit** make a slit or slits in something

slither *VERB* **slithers, slithering, slithered** slip or slide unsteadily

Thesaurus

slice *VERB* *She sliced the cheese into thin pieces.* ► cut, cut up, chop, carve, divide

slick *ADJECTIVE* *a slick marketing campaign* ► smooth, efficient, smart, polished, streamlined, skilful, professional
AN OPPOSITE IS inept

slide *VERB* *The spoon slid across the table.* ► glide, slither, skim, skid, slip

slight *ADJECTIVE* **1** *There was a slight problem with this plan.* ► small, modest, tiny, imperceptible, insignificant, negligible, slim, minor, trivial **2** *her slight figure* ► slim, slender, delicate, dainty, graceful, petite, svelte
AN OPPOSITE IS big

slightly *ADVERB* *The new models are slightly bigger. He was slightly taken aback by this.* ► a little, a bit, rather, somewhat, a shade, moderately
AN OPPOSITE IS very

slim *ADJECTIVE* **1** *She is tall, slim, and dignified.* ► slender, lean, slight, thin, graceful, svelte **2** *a slim chance of winning* ► faint, slender, remote, flimsy

slimy *ADJECTIVE* *He slid helplessly down the slimy walls.* ► slithery, slippery, sticky, oozy, greasy

sling *VERB* *He slung his coat on a chair.* ► throw, hurl, toss, fling, cast, pitch, heave

slink *VERB* *He slunk round to the back of the house.* ► creep, sneak, slip, steal, edge, sidle

slip *VERB* **1** *People were slipping on the icy ground.* ► slide, slither, fall, trip, stumble **2** *He got up and slipped quietly out of the door.* ► creep, sneak, slink, steal, edge, sidle **3** *He slipped some money into his pocket.* ► put, tuck, stick, shove, stuff

slip *NOUN* **1** *a slip of paper* ► piece, scrap, chit, sheet **2** *Did you mean to write 'yes' or was that a slip?* ► mistake, error, gaffe, lapse, blunder

slippery *ADJECTIVE* **1** *The floor was wet and slippery.* ► slithery, greasy, slimy, slippy **2** *a slippery character* ► devious, unreliable, dishonest, crafty, cunning

slit *NOUN* **1** *He peeped through a slit in a fence.* ► opening, chink, gap, crack, aperture, slot **2** *She made a slit in the side of the box.* ► cut, incision, gash, tear, slash

slit *VERB* *Henry looked for a knife to slit open his letter.* ► cut, tear, rip, slice

sliver (sliv- er) *NOUN* **slivers** a thin strip of wood or glass etc.

slog *VERB* **slogs, slogging, slogged 1** hit hard **2** work or walk hard and steadily
▷ **slog** *NOUN* **slogger** *NOUN*

slogan *NOUN* **slogans** a phrase used to advertise something or to sum up the aims of a campaign etc. • *Their slogan was 'Ban the bomb!'* [from Scottish Gaelic *sluagh-ghairm* = battle-cry]

slope *VERB* **slopes, sloping, sloped** lie or turn at an angle; slant
slope off (*informal*) go away

slope *NOUN* **slopes 1** a sloping surface **2** the amount by which something slopes

sloppy *ADJECTIVE* **sloppier, sloppiest 1** liquid and splashing easily **2** careless or slipshod • *sloppy work* **3** weakly sentimental • *a sloppy story*
▷ **sloppily** *ADVERB* **sloppiness** *NOUN*

slot *NOUN* **slots** a narrow opening to put things in
▷ **slotted** *ADJECTIVE*

slot *VERB* **slots, slotting, slotted** put something into a place where it fits

sloth (rhymes with *both*) *NOUN* **sloths 1** laziness **2** a South American animal that lives in trees and moves very slowly
▷ **slothful** *ADJECTIVE*

slot machine *NOUN* **slot machines** a machine worked by putting a coin in the slot

slouch *VERB* **slouches, slouching, slouched** stand, sit, or move in a lazy awkward way, not with an upright posture
▷ **slouch** *NOUN*

slovenly (sluv- en- lee) *ADJECTIVE* careless or untidy
▷ **slovenliness** *NOUN*

slow *ADJECTIVE* **1** not quick; taking more time than is usual **2** showing a time earlier than the correct time • *Your watch is slow.* **3** not clever; not able to understand quickly or easily
▷ **slowly** *ADVERB* **slowness** *NOUN*

slow *ADVERB* slowly • *Go slow.*

slow *VERB* **slows, slowing, slowed** go more slowly; cause to go more slowly • *The storm slowed us down.*

slow-worm *NOUN* **slow-worms** a small European legless lizard that looks like a snake, and gives birth to live young

sludge *NOUN* thick mud

slug *NOUN* **slugs 1** a small slimy animal like a snail without a shell **2** a pellet for firing from a gun

sluggish *ADJECTIVE* slow-moving; not alert or lively

sluice gate *NOUN* **sluice gates** a sliding barrier for controlling a flow of water

slum *NOUN* **slums** an area of dirty overcrowded houses

slumber *VERB* **slumbers, slumbering, slumbered** sleep
▷ **slumber** *NOUN* **slumberer** *NOUN* **slumberous** or **slumbrous** *ADJECTIVE*

slump *VERB* **slumps, slumping, slumped** fall heavily or suddenly

Thesaurus

slog *NOUN* (*informal*) *The work was a year's hard slog.* ► toil, labour, struggle, work, (*informal*) grind

slope *NOUN* **1** *A flat roof must have a slope for drainage.* ► incline, gradient, slant, angle, pitch **2** *They had their picnic on a grassy slope.* ► hillock, hill, bank, rise

slope *VERB* *The garden slopes gently away from the house.* ► slant, fall *or* rise, fall away, shelve, bank, incline

sloppy *ADJECTIVE* **1** *The cement mixture was much too sloppy.* ► liquid, runny, slushy, watery, messy, wet AN OPPOSITE IS solid **2** *sloppy work* ► careless, slovenly, slapdash, slipshod AN OPPOSITE IS careful

slosh *VERB* **1** *Michael threatened to slosh anyone else who said anything.* ► hit, thump, bash, clout **2** *Water was sloshing about.* ► splash, slop, spill, splatter

slot *NOUN* **1** *She put another coin in the slot and waited.* ► slit, chink, aperture, opening **2** *a weekly radio slot for listeners' comments* ► spot, time, place, space

slovenly *ADJECTIVE* **1** *He was criticized for his slovenly appearance.* ► untidy, scruffy, messy, dishevelled, frowzy AN OPPOSITE IS careful **2** *The work is slovenly and needs to be redone.* ► careless, slapdash, slipshod, untidy, thoughtless

slow *ADJECTIVE* **1** *They walked on at a slow pace.* ► leisurely, unhurried, measured, moderate, steady, deliberate, plodding **2** *It was slow work.* ► lengthy, prolonged, protracted, tedious **3** *He could be extremely slow at times.* ► obtuse, stupid, slow-witted, dim, (*more informal*) dense

slow *VERB* *The huge vehicle slowed to a halt.* ► decelerate, go slower, slow down, reduce speed, brake OPPOSITES ARE accelerate, speed up

sluggish *ADJECTIVE* *He woke up feeling sluggish after a sleepless night.* ► lethargic, lifeless, listless, torpid, unresponsive, dull, idle, lazy, slothful OPPOSITES ARE lively, vigorous

slump *VERB* **1** *House values have slumped in the last few months.* ► decline, drop, fall off, collapse, plummet, plunge, sink, worsen

slump *NOUN* **slumps** a sudden great fall in prices or trade

slur *VERB* **slurs, slurring, slurred 1** pronounce words indistinctly by running the sounds together **2** mark with a slur in music

slur *NOUN* **slurs 1** a slurred sound **2** something that harms a person's reputation **3** (in music) a curved line placed over notes to show that they are to be sung or played smoothly without a break

slurp *VERB* **slurps, slurping, slurped** eat or drink with a loud sucking sound
▷ **slurp** *NOUN*

slush *NOUN* partly melted snow on the ground
▷ **slushy** *ADJECTIVE*

sly *ADJECTIVE* **slyer, slyest 1** unpleasantly cunning or secret **2** mischievous and knowing • *a sly smile*
▷ **slyly** *ADVERB* **slyness** *NOUN*

smack[1] *NOUN* **smacks 1** a slap **2** a loud sharp sound • *It hit the wall with a smack.* **3** (*informal*) a loud kiss

smack *VERB* **smacks, smacking, smacked 1** slap **2** smash into
smack your lips close and then part them noisily in enjoyment

smack *ADVERB* (*informal*) forcefully or directly • *The ball went smack through the window.*

smack[2] *NOUN* **smacks** a slight flavour of something; a trace

smack *VERB* **smacks, smacking, smacked** have a slight flavour or trace • *His manner smacks of conceit.*

small *ADJECTIVE* **1** not large; less than the usual size **2** not important or significant
▷ **smallness** *NOUN*
the small of the back the lower part of a person's back, where the spine curves in

smallholding *NOUN* **smallholdings** a small area of land used for farming
▷ **smallholder** *NOUN*

small hours *PLURAL NOUN* the early hours of the morning, after midnight

small-minded *ADJECTIVE* selfish; petty

smallpox *NOUN* a serious contagious disease that causes a fever and produces spots that leave scars on the skin

smarmy *ADJECTIVE* (*informal*) trying to win someone's favour by being friendly in an insincere or exaggerated way

smart *ADJECTIVE* **1** neat and elegant; dressed well **2** clever **3** forceful; brisk • *She ran at a smart pace.*
▷ **smartly** *ADVERB* **smartness** *NOUN*

smart card *NOUN* **smart cards** a card like a credit card, which stores information or enables you to use a cash machine etc.

Thesaurus

OPPOSITES ARE soar, rise **2** *Joanna slumped into a chair.* ► flop, loll, droop, sag, slouch, collapse **3** *He slumped to the ground, clutching his leg.* ► fall, sink, collapse, drop

slump *NOUN* *a financial crisis and a slump in world trade* ► decline, depression, downturn, collapse, drop, fall, tumble, crash, trough AN OPPOSITE IS boom

slur *NOUN* *This is a slur on one of our great national heroes.* ► insult, slight, slander, libel, defamation

sly *ADJECTIVE* *The master was a devious, sly man.* ► cunning, crafty, clever, wily, foxy, canny, knowing, shifty, sneaky, furtive, scheming, conniving

smack *VERB* *She smacked the dog.* ► slap, strike, hit, clout, whack, spank

smack *NOUN* *It was a hard smack smack.* ► slap, clout, whack, blow, thump

small *ADJECTIVE* **1** *A small packet lay on the mat.* ► little, tiny, minute, compact, baby, diminutive, minuscule AN OPPOSITE IS large **2** *His mother was a small woman.* ► short, little, slight, petite OPPOSITES ARE big, large, tall **3** *We will need to make some small changes.* ► minor, trivial, trifling, insignificant, unimportant, negligible OPPOSITES ARE major, substantial **4** *They wanted to complain about the small portions.* ► meagre, inadequate, paltry, insufficient OPPOSITES ARE large, generous, ample

small-minded *ADJECTIVE* *a lot of small-minded chauvinists* ► narrow-minded, intolerant, narrow, bigoted, conservative, illiberal, insular, parochial, short-sighted, hidebound OPPOSITES ARE broad-minded, open-minded, tolerant

smarmy *ADJECTIVE* *His manner was over-polite and smarmy.* ► smooth, oily, unctuous, obsequious, fawning

smart *ADJECTIVE* **1** *He looked smart in his new suit.* ► elegant, well dressed, stylish, spruce, trim, chic, fashionable AN OPPOSITE IS scruffy **2** *Jenny had always been the smart member of the family.* ► clever, bright, intelligent, sharp, shrewd, astute AN OPPOSITE IS stupid **3** *They would stay in a smart hotel and eat out every night.* ► fashionable, high-class, exclusive, fancy, (*more informal*) posh AN OPPOSITE IS low-class **4** *They set off at a smart pace.* ► brisk, fast, quick, lively, spirited AN OPPOSITE IS slow

smart *VERB* *The smoke made her eyes smart.* ► sting, tingle, prickle, prick, hurt

smarten *VERB* **smartens, smartening, smartened** make or become smarter

smash *VERB* **smashes, smashing, smashed** **1** break noisily into pieces **2** hit or move with great force **3** destroy or defeat completely

smash *NOUN* **smashes** **1** the action or sound of smashing **2** a collision between vehicles

smash hit *NOUN* **smash hits** (*informal*) a very successful song, show, etc.

smashing *ADJECTIVE* (*informal*) excellent or beautiful
▷ **smasher** *NOUN*

smear *VERB* **smears, smearing, smeared** **1** rub something greasy or sticky or dirty on a surface **2** try to damage someone's reputation
▷ **smeary** *ADJECTIVE*

smear *NOUN* **smears** **1** smearing; something smeared **2** material smeared on a slide to be examined under a microscope **3** a false accusation **4** a smear test

smear test *NOUN* **smear tests** the taking and examination of a sample of the cervix lining, to check for faulty cells which may cause cancer

smell *VERB* **smells, smelling, smelt** *or* **smelled** **1** be aware of something by means of the sense organs of the nose • *I can smell smoke.* **2** give out a smell

smell *NOUN* **smells** **1** something you can smell; a quality in something that makes people able to smell it **2** an unpleasant quality of this kind **3** the ability to smell things
▷ **smelly** *ADJECTIVE*

smile *NOUN* **smiles** an expression on the face that shows pleasure or amusement, with the lips stretched and turning upwards at the ends

smile *VERB* **smiles, smiling, smiled** give a smile

smirk *NOUN* **smirks** a self-satisfied smile

smirk *VERB* **smirks, smirking, smirked** give a smirk

smite *VERB* **smites, smiting, smote, smitten** (*old use*) hit hard

smith *NOUN* **smiths** **1** a person who makes things out of metal **2** a blacksmith

smithereens *PLURAL NOUN* small fragments [from Irish]

smock *NOUN* **smocks** **1** an overall shaped like a very long shirt **2** a loose top with the upper part gathered into stitched pleats

smog *NOUN* a mixture of smoke and fog

smoke *NOUN* **1** the mixture of gas and solid particles given off by a burning substance **2** a period of smoking tobacco • *He wanted a smoke.*
▷ **smoky** *ADJECTIVE*

smoke *VERB* **smokes, smoking, smoked** **1** give out smoke **2** have a lighted cigarette, cigar, or pipe between your lips and draw its smoke into your mouth; do this as a habit **3** preserve meat or fish by treating it with smoke • *smoked haddock*
▷ **smoker** *NOUN*

smokescreen *NOUN* **smokescreens** **1** a mass of smoke used to hide the movement of troops **2** something that conceals what is happening

Thesaurus

smarten *VERB* **1 smarten up** *The house had been smartened up before it was put on the market.* ► refurbish, renovate, do up, improve, redecorate **2 smarten yourself up** *Eleanor went to smarten herself up for dinner.* ► dress, spruce yourself up, freshen yourself up, make yourself smart

smash *VERB* **1** *He dropped the glass and smashed it.* ► break, shatter, crack **2 smash into** *A car had smashed into the lamppost.* ► crash into, collide with, smack into, bash into, thump into, hit

smashing *ADJECTIVE* *They had a smashing time.* ► marvellous, excellent, wonderful, splendid, lovely, delightful, (*more informal*) terrific

smear *VERB* **1** *He smeared grease on the bearings.* ► daub, spread, wipe, plaster, rub, dab, smudge **2** *The canvas was smeared with paint.* ► cover, coat, rub, streak **3** *The newspapers tried to smear his reputation.* ► sully, besmirch, tarnish, blacken, defame, malign, vilify

smear *NOUN* **1** *a smear of paint* ► streak, smudge, daub, mark **2** *smears about them in the press* ► slander, libel, defamation, imputation, false report

smell *NOUN* **1** *the fresh smells of spring* ► fragrance, scent, perfume, aroma **2** *a smell of cooking* ► aroma, odour **3** *a bad smell* ► odour, stench, stink, reek, (*more informal*) pong, (*more informal*) niff RELATED ADJECTIVE olfactory

smell *VERB* **1** *Smell the flowers.* ► scent, sniff **2** (*informal*) *The milk was starting to smell.* ► stink, whiff, pong, reek

smelly *ADJECTIVE* *The room was damp and smelly.* ► smelling, stinking, malodorous, reeking, foul, putrid, (*more informal*) pongy

smile *VERB* *Jo smiled at her.* ► beam, grin, simper, smirk, leer USAGE Note that *smirk* and *leer* are unpleasant expressions.

smoke *VERB* **1** *The fire was smoking.* ► smoulder, emit smoke, fume, reek **2** *He was smoking a cigar.* ► puff on, draw on, inhale

A B C D E F G H I J K L M N O P Q R S T U V W X Y Z

smooth *ADJECTIVE* **1** having a surface without any lumps, wrinkles, roughness, etc. **2** moving without bumps or jolts etc. **3** not harsh • *a smooth flavour* **4** without problems or difficulties
▷ **smoothly** *ADVERB* **smoothness** *NOUN*

smooth *VERB* **smooths, smoothing, smoothed** make a thing smooth

smote *past tense of* **smite**

smother *VERB* **smothers, smothering, smothered** **1** suffocate **2** put out a fire by covering it **3** cover thickly • *The buns were smothered in sugar.* **4** restrain or conceal • *She smothered a smile.*

smoulder *VERB* **smoulders, smouldering, smouldered** **1** burn slowly without a flame **2** feel an emotion strongly without showing it • *He was smouldering with jealousy*

smudge *NOUN* **smudges** a dirty mark made by rubbing something
▷ **smudgy** *ADJECTIVE*

smudge *VERB* **smudges, smudging, smudged** make a smudge on something; become smudged

smug *ADJECTIVE* self-satisfied; too pleased with your own good fortune or abilities
▷ **smugly** *ADVERB* **smugness** *NOUN*

smuggle *VERB* **smuggles, smuggling, smuggled** bring something into a country etc. secretly or illegally
▷ **smuggler** *NOUN*

snack *NOUN* **snacks** **1** a small meal **2** food eaten between meals

snag *NOUN* **snags** **1** an unexpected difficulty **2** a sharp or jagged part sticking out from something **3** a tear in material that has been caught on something sharp

snail *NOUN* **snails** a small animal with a soft body and a shell

snake *NOUN* **snakes** a reptile with a long narrow body and no legs
▷ **snaky** *ADJECTIVE*

snap *VERB* **snaps, snapping, snapped** **1** break suddenly or with a sharp sound **2** bite suddenly or quickly **3** say something quickly and angrily **4** take something or move quickly **5** take a snapshot of something
snap your fingers make a sharp snapping sound with your thumb and a finger

Thesaurus

smooth *ADJECTIVE* **1** *a smooth road* ► even, level, flat, horizontal OPPOSITES ARE uneven, rough **2** *a smooth surface* ► shiny, polished, glossy, silky AN OPPOSITE IS dull **3** *a smooth sea* ► calm, still, tranquil, placid, serene, glassy AN OPPOSITE IS rough **4** *a smooth talker* ► suave, articulate, glib, slick, smarmy, plausible, persuasive AN OPPOSITE IS awkward **5** *the smooth running of the engine* ► regular, steady, rhythmic, flowing, fluent OPPOSITES ARE irregular, jerky **6** *a smooth operation* ► straightforward, efficient, well-run, trouble-free, untroubled OPPOSITES ARE troubled, fraught

smooth *VERB* **1** *He took his clothes out of the bag and smoothed them before putting them away.* ► flatten, press, iron **2** *Use sandpaper to smooth the surface.* ► plane, sand, polish, level **3** *Extra support would smooth their progress.* ► ease, facilitate, help, assist, expedite

smother *VERB* **1** *He tried to smother the flames with his coat.* ► put out, extinguish, snuff out, damp down, dampen, douse **2** *A young mother was accused of smothering her baby.* ► suffocate, stifle, asphyxiate, strangle, choke

smudge *NOUN* *His thumb left a smudge on the paper.* ► smear, mark, stain, blot, streak

smudge *VERB* **1** *Her hand slipped and she smudged the writing.* ► blur, smear, streak **2** *The wall was smudged with heavy drops of rain.* ► mark, stain, blot, dirty

smug *ADJECTIVE* *He tried not to look smug when the results were announced.* ► self-satisfied, conceited, superior, self-righteous, complacent, priggish AN OPPOSITE IS humble

smutty *ADJECTIVE* *They had been telling each other smutty jokes.* ► dirty, rude, filthy, crude, indecent, coarse, obscene

snack *NOUN* *They had a quick snack before leaving.* ► bite, bite to eat, light meal, refreshments, (*more informal*) nibble

snag *NOUN* *The snag was that nobody wanted to make the first move.* ► disadvantage, catch, hitch, obstacle, problem, setback, complication, hindrance, difficulty, (*informal*) stumbling-block

snap *VERB* **1** *The rope snapped and the trailer slipped backwards.* ► break, split, separate **2** *The dogs were snapping at them.* ► snarl, growl, bark, bite **3** *'I wasn't there,' Ginny snapped.* ► retort, bark, snarl, say angrily, rejoin **4** *After years of suffering she finally snapped.* ► crack, lose control, go to pieces, (*more informal*) lose your cool, (*more informal*) freak out

snap *NOUN* **snaps** **1** the action or sound of snapping **2** a snapshot **3 Snap** a card game in which players shout 'Snap!' when they see two similar cards

snappy *ADJECTIVE* **1** snapping at people **2** quick and lively
▷ **snappily** *ADVERB*

snapshot *NOUN* **snapshots** an informal photograph

snare *NOUN* **snares** **1** a trap for catching birds or animals **2** something that attracts someone but is a trap or a danger

snare *VERB* **snares, snaring, snared** catch in a snare

snarl *VERB* **snarls, snarling, snarled** **1** growl angrily **2** speak in a bad-tempered way
▷ **snarl** *NOUN*
[imitating the sound]

snatch *VERB* **snatches, snatching, snatched** seize; take quickly, eagerly, or by force

snatch *NOUN* **snatches** **1** snatching **2** a short and incomplete part of a song, conversation, etc.

sneak *VERB* **sneaks, sneaking, sneaked** **1** move quietly and secretly **2** (*informal*) take secretly • *He sneaked a biscuit from the tin.* **3** (*informal*) tell tales

sneak *NOUN* **sneaks** (*informal*) a telltale

sneaky *ADJECTIVE* dishonest or deceitful
▷ **sneakily** *ADVERB* **sneakiness** *NOUN*

sneer *VERB* **sneers, sneering, sneered** speak or behave in a scornful way
▷ **sneer** *NOUN*

sneeze *VERB* **sneezes, sneezing, sneezed** send out air suddenly and uncontrollably through the nose and mouth in order to get rid of something irritating the nostrils
▷ **sneeze** *NOUN*
[from Old English *fneosan*, imitating the sound]

sniff *VERB* **sniffs, sniffing, sniffed** **1** make a sound by drawing in air through the nose **2** smell something
▷ **sniff** *NOUN* **sniffer** *NOUN*

sniffle *VERB* **sniffles, sniffling, sniffled** **1** sniff slightly **2** keep on sniffing
▷ **sniffle** *NOUN*

snigger *VERB* **sniggers, sniggering, sniggered** giggle slyly
▷ **snigger** *NOUN*

snip *VERB* **snips, snipping, snipped** cut with scissors or shears in small quick cuts
▷ **snip** *NOUN*

snipe *VERB* **snipes, sniping, sniped** **1** shoot at people from a hiding place **2** attack someone with critical remarks
▷ **sniper** *NOUN*

snippet *NOUN* **snippets** a small piece of news, information, etc.

snivel *VERB* **snivels, snivelling, snivelled** cry or complain in a whining way

Thesaurus

snap *NOUN* **1** *He closed the case with a snap.* ► click, crack **2** *There is often a cold snap just after Christmas.* ► spell, period, interval, stretch **3** *She showed us her holiday snaps.* ► photo, photograph, picture, image

snap *ADJECTIVE* *a snap decision* ► instant, on-the-spot, off-the-cuff, abrupt

snappy *ADJECTIVE* **1** *We need a snappy answer.* ► quick, prompt, brisk **2** *a snappy dresser* ► smart, stylish, fashionable, chic, (*more informal*) trendy **3** *The campaign needs a slogan that's snappy.* ► pithy, crisp, memorable

snarl *VERB* *'Leave me alone,' he snarled.* ► growl, snap, bark, say angrily

snatch *VERB* *Thieves had snatched her handbag near the station.* ► steal, seize, grab, take, grasp, pluck, wrench away, wrest away

sneak *VERB* **1** *The boys sneaked in when nobody was about.* ► creep, steal, slink, slip, sidle **2 sneak on** (*informal*) *Someone must have sneaked on me.* ► inform on *or* against, report, tell tales about, (*informal*) grass on

sneaking *ADJECTIVE* **1** *She has a sneaking fondness for Turkish delight.* ► secret, private, hidden, concealed, inward, unexpressed **2** *Claudia had a sneaking feeling that Myra could be right.* ► nagging, niggling, lingering, lurking

sneaky *ADJECTIVE* (*informal*) *a sneaky trick* ► sly, cunning, crafty, clever, wily, foxy, canny, knowing, shifty, sneaky, furtive, scheming, conniving OPPOSITES ARE honest, open

sneer *VERB* **sneer at** *It is easy to sneer at their first efforts.* ► scoff at, mock, scorn, ridicule, deride, jeer at, laugh at, look down on

snide *ADJECTIVE* *His snide remarks became irritating.* ► disparaging, deprecating, sarcastic, scornful, sneering, spiteful, mocking, nasty AN OPPOSITE IS complimentary

snigger *VERB* *They might snigger at him behind his back.* ► snicker, giggle, laugh, titter, chuckle, sneer

snip *VERB* **1** *She snipped the ends off the stalks.* ► cut, clip, trim, crop, chop, dock **2** *The inspector snipped our tickets.* ► clip, nick, notch, snick

snippet *NOUN* *snippets of information* ► piece, scrap, bit, morsel, fragment, particle, shred, snatch

snivel *VERB* *If you get caught, don't snivel about the consequences.* ► complain, grizzle, moan, grouse, whine, make a fuss, (*more informal*) whinge

A B C D E F G H I J K L M N O P Q R S T U V W X Y Z

snob *NOUN* **snobs** a person who despises those who have not got wealth, power, or particular tastes or interests
▷ **snobbery** *NOUN* **snobbish** *ADJECTIVE*

snooker *NOUN* a game played with cues and 21 balls on a special cloth-covered table

snoop *VERB* **snoops, snooping, snooped** pry; ask or look around secretly
▷ **snooper** *NOUN*

snooze *NOUN* **snoozes** (*informal*) a short sleep
▷ **snooze** *VERB*

snore *VERB* **snores, snoring, snored** breathe very noisily while sleeping
▷ **snore** *NOUN*

snort *VERB* **snorts, snorting, snorted** make a rough sound by breathing forcefully through the nose
▷ **snort** *NOUN*

snout *NOUN* **snouts** an animal's projecting nose and jaws

snow *NOUN* frozen drops of water that fall from the sky in small white flakes

snow *VERB* **snows, snowing, snowed** come down as snow
be snowed under be overwhelmed with a mass of letters or work etc.

snowball *NOUN* **snowballs** a ball of snow pressed together for throwing

snowball *VERB* **snowballs, snowballing, snowballed** grow quickly in size or intensity

snowdrop *NOUN* **snowdrops** a small white flower that blooms in early spring

snowdrift *NOUN* **snowdrifts** a large heap or bank of snow piled up by the wind

snowflake *NOUN* **snowflakes** a flake of snow

snowshoe *NOUN* **snowshoes** a frame rather like a tennis racket for walking on soft snow

snowstorm *NOUN* **snowstorms** a storm in which snow falls

snub *VERB* **snubs, snubbing, snubbed** treat in a scornful or unfriendly way

snub *NOUN* **snubs** scornful or unfriendly treatment

snub-nosed *ADJECTIVE* having a short turned-up nose

snuff[1] *NOUN* powdered tobacco for taking into the nose by sniffing

snuff[2] *VERB* **snuffs, snuffing, snuffed** put out a candle by covering or pinching the flame
▷ **snuffer** *NOUN*

snuffle *VERB* **snuffles, snuffling, snuffled** sniff in a noisy way
▷ **snuffle** *NOUN*

snug *ADJECTIVE* **snugger, snuggest** **1** cosy **2** fitting closely
▷ **snugly** *ADVERB* **snugness** *NOUN*

snuggle *VERB* **snuggles, snuggling, snuggled** curl up in a warm comfortable place

so *ADVERB* **1** in this way; to such an extent • *Why are you so cross?* **2** very • *Cricket is so boring.* **3** also • *I was wrong but so were you.*
and so on and other similar things
or so or about that number
so far up to now
so long! (*informal*) goodbye
so what? (*informal*) that is not important

so *CONJUNCTION* for that reason • *They threw me out, so I came here.*

soak *VERB* **soaks, soaking, soaked** make a person or thing very wet
▷ **soak** *NOUN*
soak up take in a liquid in the way that a sponge does

Thesaurus

snobbery *NOUN* *Forget the snobbery and mystique that is associated with choosing wine.* ► snobbishness, snootiness, arrogance, affectation, pretension, superciliousness

snobbish *ADJECTIVE* *She dislikes the snobbish and materialistic attitudes of many people.* ► snooty, snobby, pretentious, superior, condescending, (*more informal*) stuck up, (*more informal*) toffee-nosed AN OPPOSITE IS unpretentious

snoop *VERB* *You shouldn't snoop into our affairs.* ► pry, meddle (in *or* with), nose, sneak, (*informal*) stick your nose (in *or* into)

snooze *VERB* (*informal*) *There he was snoozing by the fire.* ► sleep, doze, rest, nap, take a nap, catnap

snub *VERB* *They snubbed the hosts by leaving the party early.* ► insult, affront, offend, rebuff, reject, scorn, (*more informal*) put down

snug *ADJECTIVE* **1** *The cottage was warm and snug.* ► cosy, comfortable, homely, cheerful, welcome, reassuring, (*more informal*) comfy OPPOSITES ARE forbidding, unwelcoming **2** *She wore a snug long dress.* ► close-fitting, tight, figure-hugging

soak *VERB* **1** *You need to soak the beans overnight in liquid.* ► immerse, steep, wet, submerge **2** *Days of rain had soaked the ground.* ► drench, saturate, swamp, inundate
soak into *Ink had soaked into the paper.* ► permeate, penetrate, saturate
soak up *A sponge soaks up water.* ► absorb, take up, draw up, suck up

soaking *ADJECTIVES* *By the time they returned their clothes were soaking.* ► drenched, soaked, wet through, dripping, wringing, sodden, sopping AN OPPOSITE IS dry

soap *NOUN* **soaps 1** a substance used with water for washing and cleaning things **2** a soap opera
▷ **soapy** *ADJECTIVE*

soap opera *NOUN* **soap operas** a television serial about the everyday lives of a group of people [originally American, where the serials were sponsored by soap manufacturers]

soar *VERB* **soars, soaring, soared 1** rise high in the air **2** increase by a lot • *Prices are soaring.*

sob *VERB* **sobs, sobbing, sobbed** make a gasping sound when crying
▷ **sob** *NOUN*
[probably from early Dutch]

sober *ADJECTIVE* **1** not drunk **2** serious and calm **3** (said about colour) not bright or showy
▷ **soberly** *ADVERB* **sobriety** (so- **bry**- it- ee) *NOUN*

sober *VERB* **sobers, sobering, sobered** make or become sober

so-called *ADJECTIVE* named in what may be the wrong way • *This so-called gentleman slammed the door.*

soccer *NOUN* Association football [short for **Association**]

sociable *ADJECTIVE* liking to be with other people; friendly
▷ **sociably** *ADVERB* **sociability** *NOUN*

social *ADJECTIVE* **1** living in a community, not alone • *Bees are social insects.* **2** to do with life in a community • *social science* **3** concerned with people's welfare • *a social worker* **4** helping people to meet each other • *a social club* **5** sociable
▷ **socially** *ADVERB*
[from Latin *sociare* = unite, associate]

socialism *NOUN* a political system where wealth is shared equally between people, and the main industries and trade etc. are controlled by the government COMPARE **capitalism**

socialist *NOUN* **socialists** a person who believes in socialism

social security *NOUN* money and other assistance provided by the government for those in need through being unemployed, ill, or disabled

social services *PLURAL NOUN* welfare services provided by the government, including schools, hospitals, and pensions

society *NOUN* **societies 1** a community; people living together in a group or nation • *We live in a multiracial society.* **2** a group of people organized for a particular purpose • *the school dramatic society* **3** company or companionship • *We enjoy the society of our friends.*

sock *NOUN* **socks** a piece of clothing that covers your foot and the lower part of your leg [from Old English]

socket *NOUN* **sockets 1** a hollow into which something fits • *a tooth socket* **2** a device into which an electric plug or bulb is put to make a connection

soda water *NOUN* water made fizzy with carbon dioxide, used in drinks

sodden *ADJECTIVE* made very wet

sodium *NOUN* a soft white metal

sodium bicarbonate *NOUN* a soluble white powder used in fire extinguishers and fizzy drinks, and to make cakes rise

sofa *NOUN* **sofas** a long soft seat with a back and arms [from Arabic *suffa* = long stone bench]

Thesaurus

soar *VERB* **1** *Birds soared overhead.* ► climb, ascend, wing, glide, drift **2** *Prices have continued to soar.* ► rise, escalate, rocket

sob *VERB* *He turned his face to the wall and began to sob.* ► weep, cry, shed tears, blubber, snivel

sober *ADJECTIVE* **1** *Matt craved a drink but knew he had to stay sober.* ► temperate, abstemious, not drunk AN OPPOSITE IS drunk **2** *After sober reflection I decided to stay the way I was.* ► serious, thoughtful, calm, level-headed, sensible, sombre, grave, earnest, down-to-earth, commonsensical AN OPPOSITE IS light-hearted **3** *She dressed in a sober style.* ► subdued, sombre, austere, severe, staid AN OPPOSITE IS flamboyant

sociable *ADJECTIVE* *She had been a lively, bright, and sociable girl before the accident.* ► friendly, outgoing, companionable, convivial, gregarious, clubbable, cordial, affable, amicable OPPOSITES ARE unsociable, unfriendly

social *ADJECTIVE* **1** *Ants are social creatures.* ► gregarious, organized, civilized, collaborative AN OPPOSITE IS solitary **2** *a range of cultural and social interests* ► communal, community, public, group AN OPPOSITE IS individual

social *NOUN* *The club has a social every month.* ► party, gathering, function

society *NOUN* **1** *In our society, men historically have occupied the positions of power.* ► civilization, nation, culture, community **2** *We must remember our position in society.* ► the community, the population, the public **3** *They enjoy the society of their friends.* ► company, fellowship, friendship, companionship, camaraderie **4** *He joined a local history society.* ► association, club, group, organization, circle, fraternity

A B C D E F G H I J K L M N O P Q R S T U V W X Y Z

soft *ADJECTIVE* **1** not hard or firm; easily pressed **2** smooth, not rough or stiff **3** gentle; not loud **4** (said about drugs) not likely to be addictive
▷ **softly** *ADVERB* **softness** *NOUN*

soft drink *NOUN* **soft drinks** a cold drink that is not alcoholic

soften *VERB* **softens, softening, softened** make or become soft or softer
▷ **softener** *NOUN*

software *NOUN* (in computing) programs and data, which are not part of the machinery of a computer COMPARE **hardware**

soggy *ADJECTIVE* **soggier, soggiest** very wet and heavy • *soggy ground* [from a dialect word *sog* = swamp]

soil *NOUN* **soils 1** the loose earth in which plants grow **2** territory • *on British soil* [from early French]

solar panel *NOUN* **solar panels** a panel designed to catch the sun's rays and use their energy for heating or to make electricity

solar power *NOUN* electricity or other forms of power derived from the sun's rays

solar system *NOUN* the sun and the planets that revolve round it

soldier *NOUN* **soldiers** a member of an army

sole[1] *NOUN* **soles 1** the bottom surface of a foot or shoe **2** a flat edible sea fish

sole *VERB* **soles, soling, soled** put a sole on a shoe

sole[2] *ADJECTIVE* single; only • *She was the sole survivor.*
▷ **solely** *ADVERB*

solemn *ADJECTIVE* **1** not smiling or cheerful **2** dignified or formal
▷ **solemnly** *ADVERB* **solemnity** *NOUN*

solicit *VERB* **solicits, soliciting, solicited** ask for or try to obtain • *I've been soliciting opinions from rail users.*

solicitor *NOUN* **solicitors** a lawyer who advises clients, prepares legal documents, etc.

solid *ADJECTIVE* **1** not hollow; with no space inside **2** keeping its shape; not liquid or gas **3** continuous • *for two solid hours* **4** firm or strongly made; not flimsy • *a solid foundation* **5** showing solidarity; unanimous
▷ **solidly** *ADVERB* **solidity** *NOUN*

solid *NOUN* **solids 1** a solid thing **2** a shape that has three dimensions (length, width, and height or depth)

solids *PLURAL NOUN* solid food; food that is not liquid • *Is your baby eating solids yet?*

Thesaurus

soft *ADJECTIVE* **1** *a soft pillow* ► supple, pliable, springy, yielding, flexible, malleable, squashy AN OPPOSITE IS hard **2** *soft ground* ► squelchy, swampy, marshy, boggy, heavy AN OPPOSITE IS firm **3** *soft music* ► gentle, soothing, melodious AN OPPOSITE IS harsh **4** *a soft voice* ► quiet, low, faint, muted, subdued AN OPPOSITE IS loud **5** *soft colours* ► pale, pastel, muted, subtle OPPOSITES ARE bright, lurid **6** *a soft fabric* ► velvety, silky, smooth, downy, fleecy **7** *Some teachers are too soft with their pupils.* ► lenient, easygoing, indulgent, permissive, forbearing OPPOSITES ARE strict, severe

soften *VERB* **1** *Lower interest rates might soften the effect of the tax increases.* ► moderate, temper, alleviate, ease, relieve, assuage AN OPPOSITE IS intensify **2** *The butter softened in the warmth of the kitchen.* ► melt, liquefy, go soft AN OPPOSITE IS harden

soft-hearted *ADJECTIVE* *You were always too soft-hearted to tell them what you thought.* ► kind, kind-hearted, gentle, easygoing, generous, charitable

soggy *ADJECTIVE* *a pile of soggy clothes* ► sodden, sopping, saturated, soaked, drenched, wet through AN OPPOSITE IS dry

soil *NOUN* **1** *The tiny eggs can also be picked up in garden soil.* ► earth, loam, ground, humus, topsoil **2** *English troops withdrew from Scottish soil.* ► territory, land, space, jurisdiction

soil *VERB* *Try not to soil your clothes.* ► dirty, make dirty, stain, tarnish, contaminate, defile, pollute

soldier *NOUN* *The town was surrounded by enemy soldiers.* ► serviceman *or* servicewoman, fighting man *or* woman, trooper RELATED ADJECTIVE military

sole *ADJECTIVE* *The sole intention is to raise money.* ► one, only, single, solitary, exclusive, singular, individual, unique

solemn *ADJECTIVE* **1** *He was tall with a thin, solemn face.* ► serious, earnest, sombre, staid, sober, thoughtful, reverential, glum, grave, grim AN OPPOSITE IS cheerful **2** *The ceremony was a solemn occasion.* ► dignified, formal, grand, stately, majestic, impressive, pompous, awe-inspiring, ceremonious, imposing AN OPPOSITE IS frivolous

solid *ADJECTIVE* **1** *The floor was of solid concrete. The metal below him was quite solid.* ► hard, firm, dense, rigid, fixed, unyielding OPPOSITES ARE liquid, gaseous, hollow **2** *a solid sort of person* ► dependable, reliable, trustworthy, honest, upright, level-headed OPPOSITES ARE unreliable, dishonest **3** *The police*

soliloquy (sol- il- ok- wee) *NOUN* **soliloquies** a speech in which a person speaks his or her thoughts aloud when alone or without addressing anyone
▷ **soliloquize** *VERB*
[from Latin *solus* = alone + *loqui* = speak]

solitary *ADJECTIVE* **1** alone, without companions **2** single • *a solitary example*

solitary confinement *NOUN* a form of punishment in which a prisoner is kept alone in a cell and not allowed to talk to others

solo *NOUN* **solos** something sung, played, danced, or done by one person
▷ **solo** *ADJECTIVE, ADVERB* **soloist** *NOUN*

soluble *ADJECTIVE* **1** able to be dissolved **2** able to be solved
▷ **solubility** *NOUN*

solution *NOUN* **solutions 1** a liquid in which something is dissolved **2** the answer to a problem or puzzle

solve *VERB* **solves, solving, solved** find the answer to a problem or puzzle [from Latin *solvere* = unfasten]

solvent *ADJECTIVE* **1** having enough money to pay all your debts **2** able to dissolve another substance
▷ **solvency** *NOUN*

solvent *NOUN* **solvents** a liquid used for dissolving something

sombre *ADJECTIVE* dark and gloomy

some *ADJECTIVE* **1** a few; a little • *some apples* • *some money* **2** an unknown person or thing • *Some fool left the door open.* **3** about • *We waited some 20 minutes.*
some time 1 quite a long time • *I've been wondering about it for some time.* **2** at some point in time • *You must come round for a meal some time.*

some *PRONOUN* a certain number or amount that is less than the whole • *Some of them were late.*

somebody *PRONOUN* **1** some person **2** an important or impressive person

somehow *ADVERB* in some way

someone *PRONOUN* somebody

somersault *NOUN* **somersaults** a movement in which you turn head over heels before landing on your feet
▷ **somersault** *VERB*
[from Latin *supra* = above + *saltus* = a leap]

something *NOUN* some thing; a thing which you cannot or do not want to name
something like 1 rather like • *It's something like a rabbit.* **2** approximately • *It cost something like £10.*

sometimes *ADVERB* at some times but not always • *We sometimes walk to school.*

somewhat *ADVERB* to some extent • *He was somewhat annoyed.*

somewhere *ADVERB* in or to some place

son *NOUN* **sons** a boy or man who is someone's child

sonata *NOUN* **sonatas** a piece of music for one instrument or two, in several movements

song *NOUN* **songs 1** a tune for singing **2** singing • *He burst into song.*
a song and dance (*informal*) a great fuss
for a song bought or sold very cheaply

sonic boom *NOUN* **sonic booms** a loud noise caused by the shock wave of an aircraft travelling faster than the speed of sound

son-in-law *NOUN* **sons-in-law** a daughter's husband

Thesaurus

needed solid evidence. ► real, genuine, substantial **4** *a ring of solid gold* ► pure, genuine, unalloyed AN OPPOSITE IS alloyed **5** *He can expect solid support from a third of the delegates.* ► firm, united, unanimous
AN OPPOSITE IS divided

solidify *VERB* *As the liquid cools it rapidly solidifies.* ► harden, set, thicken, stiffen, congeal, clot, coagulate AN OPPOSITE IS liquefy

solitary *ADJECTIVE* **1** *He leads a solitary existence.* ► lonely, unsociable, friendless, isolated, cloistered, companionless
AN OPPOSITE IS sociable **2** *a solitary survivor* ► single, sole, one, only **3** *a few solitary villages dotted on the landscape* ► isolated, out-of-the-way, remote, secluded, hidden, sequestered, unfrequented, desolate

solution *NOUN* **1** *There is no easy solution to the problem.* ► answer, resolution, key, solving (of), explanation (of) **2** *a solution of ammonia in water* ► mixture, mix, blend, compound

solve *VERB* *This will solve our immediate problem.* ► resolve, answer, settle, sort out, put right, deal with

sombre *ADJECTIVE* **1** *sombre colours* ► dark, dull, sober, drab, dreary, gloomy
AN OPPOSITE IS cheerful **2** *His face bore a sombre expression.* ► solemn, thoughtful, reverential, glum, grave

sometimes *ADVERB* *He sometimes seems preoccupied.* ► occasionally, from time to time, at times, now and then, now and again

song *NOUN* *She sang an old song.* ► air, strain, melody, tune, number

sonnet *NOUN* **sonnets** a kind of poem with 14 lines [from Italian *sonetto* = a little sound]

soon *ADVERB* **1** in a short time from now **2** not long after something
as soon as willingly • *I'd just as soon stay here.*
as soon as at the moment that
sooner or later at some time in the future

soot *NOUN* the black powder left by smoke in a chimney or on a building etc.
▷ **sooty** *ADJECTIVE*

soothe *VERB* **soothes, soothing, soothed** **1** calm or comfort **2** ease pain or distress
▷ **soothingly** *ADVERB*

sop *VERB* **sops, sopping, sopped**
sop up soak up liquid like a sponge

sophisticated *ADJECTIVE* **1** having refined tastes or experienced about the world **2** complicated • *a sophisticated machine*
▷ **sophistication** *NOUN*

sopping *ADJECTIVE* very wet; drenched

soppy *ADJECTIVE* **1** very wet **2** (*informal*) sentimental in a silly way

soprano *NOUN* **sopranos** a woman, girl, or boy with a high singing voice

sorcerer *NOUN* **sorcerers** a person who can perform magic
▷ **sorceress** *NOUN* **sorcery** *NOUN*

sordid *ADJECTIVE* **1** dirty and nasty **2** dishonourable; selfish and mercenary • *sordid motives*
▷ **sordidly** *ADVERB* **sordidness** *NOUN*

sore *ADJECTIVE* **1** painful or smarting **2** (*informal*) annoyed or offended **3** serious or distressing • *in sore need*
▷ **soreness** *NOUN*

sore *NOUN* **sores** a sore place

sorrow *NOUN* **sorrows** **1** unhappiness or regret caused by loss or disappointment **2** something that causes this
▷ **sorrowful** *ADJECTIVE* **sorrowfully** *ADVERB*

sorry *ADJECTIVE* **sorrier, sorriest** **1** feeling regret • *I'm sorry I forgot your birthday.* **2** feeling pity or sympathy **3** wretched • *His clothes were in a sorry state.*

sort *NOUN* **sorts** a group of things or people that are similar; a kind or variety
out of sorts slightly unwell or depressed
sort of (*informal*) rather; to some extent • *I sort of expected it.*
USAGE Correct use is *this sort of thing* or *these sorts of things* (not 'these sort of things').

Thesaurus

soon *ADVERB* *We'll be there soon.* ► shortly, presently, quickly, before long, in a while, in a moment *or* minute

soothe *VERB* *She patted him gently to soothe him.* ► calm, comfort, console, pacify, mollify, settle, subdue, quiet, still OPPOSITES ARE agitate, disturb

soothing *ADJECTIVE* **1** *a soothing ointment* ► palliative, comforting, emollient, balmy, healing, mild **2** *soothing words* ► calming, relaxing, restful, gentle, peaceful, pleasant

sophisticated *ADJECTIVE* **1** *sophisticated techniques for crime detection* ► advanced, developed, complex, elaborate **2** *a sophisticated person* ► urbane, worldly, experienced, cultivated, refined

soppy *ADJECTIVE* (*informal*) **1** *a soppy story* ► sentimental, mawkish, maudlin, sugary, corny **2** *a soppy child* ► silly, daft, feeble, soft, foolish

sorcerer or **sorceress** *NOUN* *Come and see the sorcerer's workshop.* ► wizard *or* witch, magician, conjuror, enchanter *or* enchantress, warlock, witch doctor

sorcery *NOUN* *She was charged with sorcery by his successor, Richard III, and made to do public penance.* ► magic *or* black magic, charms, witchcraft, wizardry, conjuring, magic, voodoo

sore *ADJECTIVE* **1** *a sore arm* ► painful, hurting, aching, smarting, tender, stinging, burning, injured, wounded **2** (*informal*) *They were sore at us for leaving them like that.* ► annoyed, angry, upset, aggrieved, peeved (with), (*more informal*) miffed (with)

sore *NOUN* *There were sores all down his leg.* ► swelling, inflammation, abscess, laceration, contusion, lesion, boil, carbuncle, ulcer

sorrow *NOUN* **1** *The loss caused him great sorrow.* ► sadness, unhappiness, regret, misery, grief, distress, anguish, heartbreak, tribulation AN OPPOSITE IS joy **2** *He related all the sorrows of his life.* ► trouble, difficulty, affliction, problem

sorrowful *ADJECTIVE* *She gave a sorrowful smile.* ► sad, unhappy, dejected, miserable, despondent, disconsolate OPPOSITES ARE happy, cheerful

sorry *ADJECTIVE* **1** *He called his parents to say he was sorry for what he had done.* ► apologetic, ashamed (of), penitent, regretful, remorseful, repentant, conscience-stricken, contrite **2** *He felt rather sorry for his father.* ► sympathetic, compassionate, full of pity, pitying, understanding **3** *The house was in a sorry state* ► pitiful, pitiable, wretched, unfortunate, pathetic, dismal

sort *NOUN* **1** *What sort of films do you like to see?* ► type, kind, variety, category, class, genre, style, nature

A B C D E F G H I J K L M N O P Q R S T U V W X Y Z

sort *VERB* **sorts, sorting, sorted** arrange things in groups according to their size, kind, etc.
▷ **sorter** *NOUN*
sort out 1 deal with and solve a problem or difficulty **2** (*informal*) deal with and punish someone

sortie *NOUN* **sorties 1** an attack by troops coming out of a besieged place **2** an attacking expedition by a military aircraft [from French *sortir* = go out]

SOS *NOUN* **SOSs** an urgent appeal for help [the international Morse code signal of extreme distress, chosen because it is easy to recognize, but often said to stand for 'Save Our Souls']

sought *past tense of* **seek**

soul *NOUN* **souls 1** the invisible part of a person that is believed to go on living after the body has died **2** a person's mind and emotions etc. **3** a person • *There isn't a soul about.* **4** a kind of popular music that originated in gospel music

sound[1] *NOUN* **sounds 1** vibrations that travel through the air and can be detected by the ear; the sensation they produce **2** sound reproduced in a film etc. **3** a mental impression • *We don't like the sound of his plans.*

sound *VERB* **sounds, sounding, sounded 1** produce or cause to produce a sound **2** give an impression when heard • *He sounds angry.* **3** test by noting the sounds heard • *A doctor sounds a patient's lungs with a stethoscope.* [from Latin *sonus*]

sound[2] *VERB* **sounds, sounding, sounded** test the depth of water beneath a ship
sound out try to find out what a person thinks or feels about something
[from Latin *sub* = under + *unda* = a wave]

sound[3] *ADJECTIVE* **1** in good condition; not damaged **2** healthy; not diseased **3** reasonable or correct • *His ideas are sound.* **4** reliable or secure • *a sound investment* **5** thorough or deep • *a sound sleep*
▷ **soundly** *ADVERB* **soundness** *NOUN*
[from Old English *gesund* = healthy]

sound barrier *NOUN* the resistance of the air to objects moving at speeds near the speed of sound

sound bite *NOUN* **sound bites** a short piece taken from a speech or statement because it has a special interest

sound effects *PLURAL NOUN* sounds produced artificially to make a play, film, etc. seem more realistic

soundtrack *NOUN* **soundtracks** the sound that goes with a cinema film

soup *NOUN* **soups** liquid food made from stewed bones, meat, fish, vegetables, etc.
in the soup (*informal*) in trouble
[from early French *soupe* = broth poured on bread, from Latin *suppa*]

sour *ADJECTIVE* **1** tasting sharp like unripe fruit **2** stale and unpleasant, not fresh • *sour milk* **3** bad-tempered
▷ **sourly** *ADVERB* **sourness** *NOUN*

source *NOUN* **sources 1** the place from which something comes **2** the starting point of a river

sour grapes *PLURAL NOUN* pretending that something you want is no good because you know you cannot have it

south *NOUN* **1** the direction to the right of a person who faces east **2** the southern part of a country, city, etc.

Thesaurus

sort *VERB The eggs are sorted by size and colour.* ► class, grade, group, categorize, classify, divide
sort out *It took a long time to sort out the difficulties.* ► resolve, settle, put right, deal with

soul *NOUN* **1** *the immortality of the soul* ► psyche, spirit, inner being **2** (*informal*) *The poor soul had to wait for hours to be seen.* ► person, individual, creature

sound *NOUN They could hear the sound of traffic in the street.* ► noise, din, hubbub, racket, tone
RELATED ADJECTIVES aural, acoustic, sonic

sound *VERB* **1** *A signal sounded.* ► be heard, become audible, resound, resonate, reverberate, make a noise **2** *Opening a door or window will sound the alarm.* ► set off, operate, blast **3** *He sounded angry.* ► seem, appear, give the impression of being **4** *You can sound the depth of a river with a pole.* ► measure, gauge, plumb, determine, probe, test, try

sound out *The survey will sound out public opinion.* ► canvass, measure, gauge, test, investigate

sound *ADJECTIVE* **1** *sound advice* ► valid, well-founded, reasonable, dependable
AN OPPOSITE IS unsound **2** *The foundations seem sound.* ► firm, sturdy, solid, well built, substantial, stable AN OPPOSITE IS unsafe **3** *a sound investment* ► wise, judicious, well chosen
AN OPPOSITE IS unwise **4** *She fell into a sound sleep.* ► deep, prolonged, unbroken, uninterrupted OPPOSITES ARE light, shallow

sour *ADJECTIVE* **1** *a sour taste* ► sharp, acid, tart, bitter **2** *a sour look* ► embittered, resentful, peevish, acrimonious, disagreeable

source *NOUN* **1** *the source of the problem* ► origin, originator, initiator, author, cause, fount, root, derivation, starting point **2** *the source of the river* ► spring, origin, head, beginning, start

A B C D E F G H I J K L M N O P Q R S T U V W X Y Z

south *ADJECTIVE, ADVERB* towards or in the south
▷ **southerly** (suth- er- lee) *ADJECTIVE* **southern** *ADJECTIVE* **southerner** *NOUN* **southernmost** *ADJECTIVE*

south-east *NOUN, ADJECTIVE, & ADVERB* midway between south and east
▷ **south-easterly** *ADJECTIVE* **south-eastern** *ADJECTIVE*

southward *ADJECTIVE, ADVERB* towards the south
▷ **southwards** *ADVERB*

south-west *NOUN, ADJECTIVE, & ADVERB* midway between south and west
▷ **south-westerly** *ADJECTIVE* **south-western** *ADJECTIVE*

souvenir (soo- ven- eer) *NOUN* **souvenirs** something that you keep to remind you of a person, place, or event

sovereign *NOUN* **sovereigns** **1** a king or queen who is the ruler of a country; a monarch **2** an old British gold coin, originally worth £1

sow[1] (rhymes with *go*) *VERB* **sows, sowing, sowed, sown** *or* **sowed** **1** put seeds into the ground so that they will grow into plants **2** cause feelings or ideas to develop • *Her words sowed doubt in my mind.*
▷ **sower** *NOUN*
[from Old English *sawan*]
USAGE Do not confuse with **sew**.

sow[2] (rhymes with *cow*) *NOUN* **sows** a female pig [from Old English *sugu*]

soy sauce or **soya sauce** *NOUN* a Chinese or Japanese sauce made from fermented **soya beans** [from Chinese words meaning 'salted beans' and 'oil']

space *NOUN* **spaces** **1** the whole area outside the earth, where the stars and planets are **2** an area or volume • *This table takes too much space.* **3** an empty area; a gap **4** an interval of time • *within the space of an hour*

space *VERB* **spaces, spacing, spaced** arrange things with spaces between • *Space them out.*

spacecraft *NOUN* **spacecraft** a vehicle for travelling in outer space

spaceship *NOUN* **spaceships** a spacecraft, especially one carrying people

space shuttle *NOUN* **space shuttles** a spacecraft for repeated use to and from outer space

space station *NOUN* **space stations** a satellite which orbits the earth and is used as a base by scientists and astronauts

spacious *ADJECTIVE* providing a lot of space; roomy
▷ **spaciousness** *NOUN*

spade[1] *NOUN* **spades** a tool with a long handle and a wide blade for digging

spade[2] *NOUN* **spades** a playing card with black shapes like upside-down hearts on it, each with a short stem

spaghetti *NOUN* pasta made in long thin sticks [from Italian, = little strings]

span *NOUN* **spans** **1** the length from end to end or across something **2** the part between two uprights of an arch or bridge **3** the length of a period of time **4** the distance from the tip of the thumb to the tip of the little finger when the hand is spread out

span *VERB* **spans, spanning, spanned** reach from one side or end to the other • *A bridge spans the river.*

spaniel *NOUN* **spaniels** a kind of dog with long ears and silky fur [from early French *espaigneul* = Spanish (because the dog originally came from Spain)]

spank *VERB* **spanks, spanking, spanked** smack a person several times on the bottom as a punishment

spanner *NOUN* **spanners** a tool for gripping and turning the nut on a bolt etc. [from German **spannen** = tighten]

spar[1] *NOUN* **spars** a strong pole used for a mast or boom etc. on a ship [from Old Norse]

spar[2] *VERB* **spars, sparring, sparred** **1** practise boxing **2** quarrel or argue [from Old English]

spare *VERB* **spares, sparing, spared** **1** afford to give something or do without it • *Can you spare a moment?* **2** be merciful towards someone;

Thesaurus

sow *VERB* *Sow the seeds in parallel rows.* ► plant, scatter, spread, distribute, put in the ground

space *NOUN* **1** *A minibus would have space for ten people.* ► room, capacity, accommodation, seating, seats, volume **2** *The city has very few green spaces left.* ► area, stretch, expanse **3** *There are spaces between the houses.* ► gap, interval, opening, aperture

spacious *ADJECTIVE* *A spacious hallway leads to the living rooms.* ► roomy, sizeable, ample, capacious, commodious, extensive, generous, large, big OPPOSITES ARE cramped, poky

span *VERB* *An old iron bridge spans the river.* ► cross, straddle, bridge, pass over, reach over, stretch over, extend across, traverse, arch over

spank *VERB* *She warned him that next time she would spank him.* ► smack, slap, chastise, give someone a spanking

spare *VERB* **1** *We can't spare all that money.* ► afford, manage, part with, do without **2** *The captors would not spare any of the hostages.* ► pardon, show mercy to, let off, be lenient with, leave unharmed *or* unhurt

spare *ADJECTIVE* **1** *Our neighbours have a spare set of house keys.* ► extra, additional,

not hurt or harm a person or thing **3** avoid making a person suffer something • *Spare me the details.* **4** use or treat economically • *No expense will be spared.*
to spare left over without being needed • *We arrived with five minutes to spare.*

spare ADJECTIVE **1** not used but kept ready in case it is needed; extra • *a spare wheel* **2** thin; lean
▷ **sparely** ADVERB **spareness** NOUN
go spare (*slang*) become very annoyed

spare time NOUN time not needed for work

sparing (**spair-** ing) ADJECTIVE careful or economical; not wasteful
▷ **sparingly** ADVERB

spark NOUN **sparks 1** a tiny glowing particle **2** a flash produced electrically **3** a trace • *a spark of hope*

spark VERB **sparks, sparking, sparked** give off a spark or sparks

sparkle VERB **sparkles, sparkling, sparkled 1** shine with tiny flashes of light **2** show brilliant wit or liveliness
▷ **sparkle** NOUN

sparkler NOUN **sparklers** a hand-held firework that gives off sparks

spark plug NOUN **spark plugs** a device that makes a spark to ignite the fuel in an engine

sparrow NOUN **sparrows** a small brown bird

sparse ADJECTIVE thinly scattered; not numerous • *a sparse population*
▷ **sparsely** ADVERB **sparseness** NOUN

spasm NOUN **spasms 1** a sudden involuntary movement of a muscle **2** a sudden brief spell of activity etc. [from Greek *spasmos*, from *span* = to pull]

spasmodic ADJECTIVE happening or done at irregular intervals
▷ **spasmodically** ADVERB

spastic NOUN **spastics** (*offensive*) a person suffering from spasms of the muscles and jerky movements, especially caused by cerebral palsy

spat *past tense of* **spit**[1]

spate NOUN **spates** a sudden flood or rush

spatter VERB **spatters, spattering, spattered 1** scatter in small drops **2** splash • *spattered with mud*
▷ **spatter** NOUN

spawn NOUN **1** the eggs of fish, frogs, toads, or shellfish **2** the thread-like matter from which fungi grow

spawn VERB **spawns, spawning, spawned 1** produce spawn **2** be produced from spawn **3** produce something in great quantities

speak VERB **speaks, speaking, spoke, spoken 1** say something; talk **2** talk or be able to talk in a foreign language • *Do you speak French?*
speak up 1 speak more loudly **2** give your opinion

speaker NOUN **speakers 1** a person who is speaking **2** someone who makes a speech **3** a loudspeaker

Thesaurus

supplementary, alternative, backup **2** *Do you have any spare paper?* ► surplus, leftover, odd, unwanted, superfluous, unused, unnecessary **3** *a spare figure* ► slender, slim, lean, slight, thin AN OPPOSITE IS fat
go spare (*informal*) *They'll go spare if they find out.* ► lose your temper, be *or* become angry, go wild, (*informal*) hit the roof, (*informal*) go bananas, (*informal*) go ballistic

spark NOUN *a spark of light* ► flash, gleam, glint, flicker, sparkle, twinkle

spark VERB *The comments sparked a furious row.* ► cause, give rise to, bring about, occasion, set off, stir up, provoke, stimulate, precipitate

sparkle VERB *Lights sparkled in the distance.* ► glitter, glint, glisten, glimmer, twinkle, gleam, shimmer

sparkling ADJECTIVE **1** *sparkling jewellery* ► glittering, glinting, glistening, twinkling, flashing, scintillating, brilliant, shining, shiny AN OPPOSITE IS dull **2** *a sparkling drink* ► effervescent, fizzy, bubbly, bubbling, aerated, carbonated, foaming OPPOSITES ARE still, flat

sparse ADJECTIVE *an area of sparse vegetation* ► meagre, sparse, scarce, scant, paltry, minimal, negligible AN OPPOSITE IS dense

spartan ADJECTIVE *They led a spartan life.* ► austere, harsh, frugal, ascetic, arduous, stringent, strict, stern OPPOSITES ARE luxurious, opulent

spasm NOUN **1** *a spasm of coughing* ► fit, attack, outbreak, eruption, seizure **2** *a muscular spasm* ► convulsion, contraction, twitch

spasmodic ADJECTIVE *The night was interrupted by spasmodic gunfire.* ► intermittent, fitful, sporadic, occasional, irregular, erratic OPPOSITES ARE regular, continuous

spate NOUN *a spate of burglaries* ► series, succession, run, string, outbreak, wave AN OPPOSITE IS trickle

speak VERB **1** *She left before anyone could speak. He refused to speak about the incident.* ► talk, say anything, converse, communicate **2** *We must speak the truth.* ► tell, utter, express, declare, voice **3** *The chairman spoke for an hour.* ► declaim, lecture, give a speech, hold forth **4 speak to** *She promised to speak to them soon. He did not speak to her for six months after that.*

A B C D E F G H I J K L M N O P Q R S T U V W X Y Z

the Speaker the person who controls the debates in the House of Commons or a similar assembly

spear *NOUN* **spears** a weapon for throwing or stabbing, with a long shaft and a pointed tip

special *ADJECTIVE* **1** not ordinary or usual; exceptional • *a special occasion;* • *Take special care of it* **2** meant for a particular person or purpose • *You need a special tool for this job.*

special effects *PLURAL NOUN* illusions created for films or television by using props, trick photography, or computer images

specialist *NOUN* **specialists** an expert in one subject • *a skin specialist*

speciality *NOUN* **specialities 1** something in which a person specializes **2** a special product, especially a food

specialize *VERB* **specializes, specializing, specialized** give particular attention or study to one subject or thing • *She specialized in biology.*
▷ **specialization** *NOUN*

special needs *PLURAL NOUN* educational needs resulting from special reasons such as learning difficulties or physical disability

species (spee- shiz) *NOUN* **species** a group of animals or plants that are very similar

specific *ADJECTIVE* definite or precise; of or for a particular thing • *The money was given for a specific purpose.*
▷ **specifically** *ADVERB*

specific gravity *NOUN* the weight of something as compared with the same volume of water or air

specimen *NOUN* **specimens 1** a sample **2** an example • *a fine specimen of an oak tree*

speck *NOUN* **specks** a small spot or particle

speckle *NOUN* **speckles** a small spot or mark
▷ **speckled** *ADJECTIVE*

spectacle *NOUN* **spectacles 1** an impressive sight or display **2** a ridiculous sight

spectacles *PLURAL NOUN* a pair of glasses
▷ **spectacled** *ADJECTIVE*

spectacular *ADJECTIVE* impressive or striking

spectator *NOUN* **spectators** a person who watches a game, show, incident, etc. [from Latin *spectare* = to look at]

spectre *NOUN* **spectres** a ghost
▷ **spectral** *ADJECTIVE*

spectrum *NOUN* **spectra 1** the bands of colours seen in a rainbow **2** a wide range of things, ideas, etc.

speculate *VERB* **speculates, speculating, speculated 1** form opinions without having any definite evidence **2** invest in stocks, property, etc. in the hope of making a profit but with the risk of loss
▷ **speculation** *NOUN* **speculator** *NOUN* **speculative** *ADJECTIVE*

sped *past tense of* **speed**

Thesaurus

► communicate with, say something *or* anything, converse with, contact

special *ADJECTIVE* **1** *a special occasion* ► important, exceptional, significant, particular, remarkable, extraordinary **2** *a perfume with a special smell* ► distinct, distinctive, characteristic, peculiar, unique, exclusive

specific *ADJECTIVE There is no specific evidence to support the allegations.* ► definite, particular, explicit, precise, special, clear-cut, detailed, exact AN OPPOSITE IS general

specify *VERB He would not specify the source of his information.* ► name, identify, state, mention, spell out, indicate, designate, detail, be specific about

specimen *NOUN They asked for a specimen of his handwriting.* ► sample, illustration, example, demonstration, instance, model, pattern, copy

speck *NOUN a speck of dust* ► particle, bit, fleck, grain, speckle, spot, trace, dot

speckled *ADJECTIVE a speckled brown egg* ► flecked, speckly, spotted, freckly, freckled, mottled

spectacle *NOUN* **1** *The parade proved quite a spectacle.* ► display, show, performance, pageant, extravaganza, exhibition **2** *The group did look quite an odd spectacle.* ► sight, scene, vision, picture **3** *I think we're making a spectacle of ourselves.* ► exhibition, laughing stock, fool

spectacular *ADJECTIVE a spectacular display* ► magnificent, splendid, impressive, sensational, dazzling, showy, stunning, outstanding

spectator *NOUN Spectators lined the streets.* ► onlooker, watcher, viewer, observer, bystander, looker-on

speculate *VERB* **1** *His colleagues tended to speculate about his private life.* ► conjecture, theorize, wonder, hypothesize, make guesses, meditate, reflect, muse **2** *People have been speculating on the stock exchange.* ► gamble, venture, hazard

speculative *ADJECTIVE* **1** *Their conclusions are merely speculative.* ► conjectural, theoretical, hypothetical, notional, tentative **2** *a series of speculative investments* ► risky, hazardous, unpredictable, unsafe, unsound

speech NOUN **speeches** **1** the action or power of speaking **2** a talk to an audience **3** a group of lines spoken by a character in a play

speechless ADJECTIVE unable to speak because of great emotion

speed NOUN **speeds** **1** a measure of the time in which something moves or happens
2 quickness or swiftness
at speed quickly

speed VERB **speeds, speeding, sped** *(in sense 3* **speeded)** **1** go quickly • *The train sped by.* **2** make or become quicker • *This will speed things up.* **3** drive faster than the legal limit

speed camera NOUN **speed cameras** a camera by the side of a road which automatically photographs any vehicle which is going too fast

speed limit NOUN **speed limits** the maximum speed at which vehicles may legally travel on a particular road

speedometer NOUN **speedometers** a device in a vehicle, showing its speed

speedy ADJECTIVE **speedier, speediest** quick or swift
▷ **speedily** ADVERB

spell[1] NOUN **spells** a saying or action etc. supposed to have magical power [from Old English *spel* = speech, story]

spell[2] NOUN **spells** **1** a period of time **2** a period spent doing a certain task or activity etc. [from Old English *spelian* = take someone's place, take over a task]

spell[3] VERB **spells, spelling, spelled** *or* **spelt**
1 put letters in the right order to make a word or words **2** (said about letters) form a word • *C-A-T spells 'cat'.* **3** have as a result • *Wet weather spells ruin for crops.*
▷ **speller** NOUN
[from early French]

spellbound ADJECTIVE entranced as if by a magic spell

spend VERB **spends, spending, spent** **1** use money to pay for things **2** use up • *Don't spend too much time on it.* **3** pass time • *We spent a holiday in Spain.*

sperm NOUN **sperms** *or* **sperm** the male cell that fuses with an ovum to fertilize it [from Greek *sperma* = seed]

Thesaurus

speech NOUN **1** *the power of speech* ► speaking, talking, verbal communication RELATED ADJECTIVES oral, phonetic **2** *His speech was slurred.* ► diction, articulation, enunciation, utterance, elocution, delivery **3** *an after-dinner speech* ► talk, address, lecture, oration, discourse

speechless ADJECTIVE *She was speechless with rage.* ► dumbfounded, dumbstruck, thunderstruck, aghast, tongue-tied OPPOSITES ARE talkative, verbose

speed NOUN **1** *It's important to check your speed on this piece of road.* ► velocity, pace, rate, tempo **2** *They completed the work with amazing speed.* ► rapidity, swiftness, alacrity, celerity, quickness, expeditiousness, promptness, fleetness, dispatch

speed VERB **1** *We sped back home* ► hurry, hasten, rush, dash, chase, hurtle, hustle, move quickly, (*more informal*) belt OPPOSITES ARE go slowly, amble **2** *He was over the limit and speeding.* ► break the speed limit, go *or* drive too fast
speed up *He called to them to speed up.* ► hurry up, go faster, increase speed, get a move on, quicken, accelerate

speedy ADJECTIVE *We got a speedy response.* ► quick, rapid, swift, fast, prompt, immediate, brisk

spell NOUN **1** *a magic spell* ► incantation, charm, magic formula, bewitchment, sorcery, witchcraft, conjuration, conjuring, enchantment **2** *She cast her spell on all around her.* ► allure, charm, magic, fascination, influence, glamour **3** *a spell of dry weather* ► period, interval, stretch, run, patch, turn, stint

spell VERB *Lack of rain has spelt disaster for the natural life of the region.* ► mean, lead to, result in, signal, signify, presage, herald, foretell, indicate, suggest
spell out *Let me spell out what I plan to do.* ► explain, elucidate, clarify, make plain, set out, specify, detail

spellbound ADJECTIVE *The audience was spellbound by the performance.* ► enthralled, entranced, captivated, enchanted, transfixed, mesmerized, gripped, bewitched, charmed, fascinated, hypnotized, transported

spend VERB **1** *You needn't spend more than £50 on it.* ► pay, pay out, expend, disburse, fritter, squander, (*more informal*) fork out, (*more informal*) shell out **2** *They spent all their time arguing.* ► pass, occupy, fill, while away

spendthrift NOUN *He was a spendthrift and lived luxuriously.* ► big spender, profligate, prodigal, wastrel, squanderer OPPOSITES ARE miser, scrooge, skinflint

sphere *NOUN* **spheres** **1** a perfectly round solid shape; the shape of a ball **2** a field of action or interest etc. • *That country is in Russia's sphere of influence.*
▷ **spherical** *ADJECTIVE*

sphinx *NOUN* **sphinxes** a stone statue with the body of a lion and a human head, especially the huge one (almost 5,000 years old) in Egypt [named after the Sphinx in Greek mythology, a winged creature with a woman's head and a lion's body]

spice *NOUN* **spices** **1** a strong-tasting substance used to flavour food, often made from dried parts of plants **2** something that adds interest or excitement • *Variety is the spice of life.*
▷ **spicy** *ADJECTIVE*

spick and span *ADJECTIVE* neat and clean [*span* is from Old Norse; *spick* is probably from early Dutch]

spider *NOUN* **spiders** a small animal with eight legs that spins webs to catch insects on which it feeds [from Old English *spithra* = spinner]

spike *NOUN* **spikes** a pointed piece of metal; a sharp point
▷ **spiky** *ADJECTIVE*

spill *VERB* **spills, spilling, spilt** *or* **spilled** **1** let something fall out of a container • *Try not to spill your drink.* **2** become spilt • *The coins came spilling out.*
▷ **spillage** *NOUN*

spin *VERB* **spins, spinning, spun** **1** turn round and round quickly **2** make raw wool or cotton into threads by pulling and twisting its fibres **3** (said about a spider or silkworm) make a web or cocoon out of threads from its body
spin a yarn tell a story
spin out make something last as long as possible

spinach *NOUN* a vegetable with dark green leaves [via early French from Persian]

spinal cord *NOUN* **spinal cords** the thick cord of nerves enclosed in the spine, that carries impulses to and from the brain

spindly *ADJECTIVE* thin and long or tall

spin doctor *NOUN* **spin doctors** a person who works for a political party and publishes information in a way that shows it in the best possible light

spine *NOUN* **spines** **1** the line of bones down the middle of the back **2** a thorn or prickle **3** the back part of a book where the pages are joined together

spineless *ADJECTIVE* **1** without a backbone **2** lacking in determination or strength of character

spinney *NOUN* **spinneys** a small wood or thicket

spin-off *NOUN* **spin-offs** something extra produced while making something else

spinster *NOUN* **spinsters** a woman who has not married [the original meaning was 'someone who spins' Many unmarried women used to earn their living by spinning, which could be done at home]

spiny *ADJECTIVE* covered with spines; prickly

spiral *ADJECTIVE* going round and round a central point and becoming gradually closer to it or further from it; twisting continually round a central line or cylinder etc.
▷ **spirally** *ADVERB*

spiral *NOUN* **spirals** a spiral line or course

spiral *VERB* **spirals, spiralling, spiralled** **1** move in a spiral **2** increase or decrease

Thesaurus

sphere *NOUN* **1** *A glass sphere hung from the ceiling.* ► ball, globe, orb, spheroid, globule **2** *She has a lot of experience in this sphere* ► domain, field, milieu, area, department, scope, subject, province, range, territory

spice *NOUN* **1** *Add some spices to liven up your dish.* ► herb, seasoning, flavouring **2** *The risk of getting caught added spice to the adventure.* ► excitement, interest, zest, colour

spiel *NOUN* (*informal*) *He gave the usual spiel about raising standards.* ► speech, monologue, rigmarole, patter, line

spike *NOUN* *She tore her dress on a spike.* ► prong, point, barb, stake, skewer, spit

spike *VERB* *He spiked another pea with his fork.* ► pierce, spear, skewer, impale

spill *VERB* **1** *Keith slipped and spilled his drink.* ► knock over, tip over, upset, slop, overturn, splash about **2** *Water spilled over the top of the bath.* ► overflow, flow, brim, run, pour **3** *A lorry had spilled its load.* ► shed, tip, scatter, discharge, drop **4** *People spilled into the streets.* ► stream, pour, surge, swarm, throng

spin *VERB* **1** *A wheel spins on an axle.* ► rotate, revolve, gyrate, turn, whirl, twirl **2** *My head was spinning.* ► reel, swim, whirl, go round

spindle *NOUN* *The yarn is spun on a spindle.* ► axle, rod, shaft

spine *NOUN* **1** *The posture puts an unnecessary stress on the spine.* ► backbone, spinal column, vertebrae **2** *the spines of a hedgehog* ► needle, quill, spike, bristle, point

spiral *ADJECTIVE* *a spiral column of smoke* ► coiled, curling, winging, corkscrew, turning

spiral *NOUN* *a spiral of smoke* ► coil, twist, whorl, corkscrew, screw

spiral *VERB* **1** *Costs continued to spiral.* ► soar, rise, mount, escalate, shoot up **2** *Feelings of anger and jealousy can spiral violently out of*

continuously and quickly • *Prices are spiralling* [from Greek *speira* = winding]

spire *NOUN* **spires** a tall pointed part on top of a church tower

spirit *NOUN* **spirits** **1** the soul **2** a person's mood or mind and feelings • *He was in good spirits.* **3** a ghost or a supernatural being **4** courage or liveliness • *She answered with spirit.* **5** a kind of quality in something • *the romantic spirit of the book* **6** a strong distilled alcoholic drink

spirit *VERB* **spirits, spiriting, spirited** carry off quickly and secretly • *They spirited her away.*

spirit level *NOUN* **spirit levels** a device consisting of a tube of liquid with an air bubble in it, used to find out whether something is level

spiritual *ADJECTIVE* **1** to do with the human soul; not physical **2** to do with religion
▷ **spiritually** *ADVERB* **spirituality** *NOUN*

spiritual *NOUN* **spirituals** a religious folk song, originally sung by black Christians in America

spiritualism *NOUN* the belief that the spirits of dead people communicate with living people
▷ **spiritualist** *NOUN*

spit[1] *VERB* **spits, spitting, spat** *or* **spit** **1** send out drops of liquid etc. forcibly from the mouth • *He spat at me.* **2** fall lightly • *It's spitting with rain.*

spit *NOUN* saliva

spit[2] *NOUN* **spits** **1** a long thin metal spike put through meat or vegetables to hold them together while they are being roasted **2** a narrow strip of land sticking out into the sea

spite *NOUN* a desire to hurt or annoy somebody
▷ **spiteful** *ADJECTIVE* **spitefully** *ADVERB* **spitefulness** *NOUN*
in spite of not being prevented by • *We went out in spite of the rain.*

spitting image *NOUN* an exact likeness

splash *VERB* **splashes, splashing, splashed** **1** make liquid fly about in drops **2** (said about liquid) fly about in drops **3** make wet by splashing • *The bus splashed us.*

splash *NOUN* **splashes** **1** the action or sound or mark of splashing **2** a bright patch of colour or light
make a splash attract a lot of attention

splay *VERB* **splays, splaying, splayed** spread or slope apart

Thesaurus

control. ► deteriorate, decline, degenerate, worsen, nosedive

spirit *NOUN* **1** *a philosophy of reconciling the body and the spirit* ► soul, psyche, inner self, inner being **2** *They went about their task with a good deal of spirit.* ► enthusiasm, vigour, energy, vivacity, ardour, zest, keenness, eagerness, liveliness, animation, resolution **3** *There is a legend of spirits haunting the place.* ► ghost, spectre, phantom, apparition, wraith, shadow **4** *We need to approach this challenge with a positive spirit.* ► attitude, frame of mind, outlook **5** *My spirit was dampened by these setbacks.* ► mood, morale, temperament, disposition, humour **6** *an action that breaks the spirit of the law if not the letter* ► substance, essence, true meaning

spirited *ADJECTIVE* *The team gave a spirited performance; an attractive and spirited young person* ► lively, vivacious, vibrant, animated, energetic, high-spirited, vigorous, dynamic, sparkling, vital OPPOSITES ARE timid, lifeless

spiritual *ADJECTIVE* **1** *a spiritual existence* ► non-material, incorporeal, unworldly, other-worldly, metaphysical OPPOSITES ARE physical, material **2** *spiritual music* ► religious, sacred, holy, divine, devotional

spit *VERB* *Don't spit in public.* ► expectorate, hawk
spit out *He spat out a lemon pip.* ► eject, spew

spit *NOUN* *He wiped the spit from his face.* ► spittle, saliva, dribble, sputum

spite *NOUN* *He publicly criticized her out of spite.* ► malice, maliciousness, spitefulness, animosity, vindictiveness, rancour, ill will, ill feeling, resentment, malevolence

spiteful *ADJECTIVE* *The speech contained many spiteful remarks.* ► malicious, malevolent, ill-natured, hostile, hurtful, vicious, venomous, wounding, unkind, snide, cruel, nasty

splash *VERB* **1** *A passing van splashed water over us.* ► splatter, spray, shower, spatter, slosh, slop, sprinkle, squirt, wash **2** *Children splashed about in the water.* ► paddle, wade, dabble, wallow, slosh **3** *The newspapers splashed the story across their front pages.* ► blazon, display, spread, flaunt, trumpet, plaster, publicize
splash out (*informal*) *He was tempted to splash out on a Porsche.* ► spend money, splurge, be extravagant

splash *NOUN* **1** *a splash of colour* ► spot, patch, splodge, speck, burst, touch, dash **2** *The scandal made quite a splash.* ► effect, impact, display

A B C D E F G H I J K L M N O P Q R S T U V W X Y Z

splendid ADJECTIVE **1** magnificent; full of splendour **2** excellent
▷ **splendidly** ADVERB

splendour NOUN a brilliant display or appearance

splint NOUN **splints** a straight piece of wood or metal etc. tied to a broken arm or leg to hold it firm

splinter NOUN **splinters** a thin sharp piece of wood, glass, stone, etc. broken off a larger piece

splinter VERB **splinters, splintering, splintered** break into splinters

split VERB **splits, splitting, split** **1** break apart, especially along the length of something **2** divide something into parts
split up **1** end a marriage or other relationship **2** go in different directions

split NOUN **splits** **1** the splitting or dividing of something **2** a place where something has split
the splits an acrobatic position in which the legs are stretched widely in opposite directions

split second NOUN a very brief moment of time; an instant

splutter VERB **splutters, spluttering, spluttered** **1** make a quick series of spitting sounds **2** speak quickly but not clearly
▷ **splutter** NOUN
[imitating the sound]

spoil VERB **spoils, spoiling, spoilt** *or* **spoiled** **1** damage something and make it useless or unsatisfactory **2** make someone selfish by always letting them have what they want

spoke[1] NOUN **spokes** each of the bars or rods that go from the centre of a wheel to its rim

spoke[2] *past tense of* **speak**

spokesperson NOUN **spokespersons** a person who speaks on behalf of a group of people
▷ **spokesman** NOUN **spokeswoman** NOUN

sponge NOUN **sponges** **1** a sea creature with a soft porous body **2** the skeleton of this creature, or a piece of a similar substance, used for washing or padding things **3** a soft lightweight cake or pudding
▷ **spongy** ADJECTIVE

sponge VERB **sponges, sponging, sponged** **1** wipe or wash something with a sponge **2** (*informal*) get money or food off other people without giving anything in return,
• *He's always sponging off his friends.*
▷ **sponger** NOUN

Thesaurus

splendid ADJECTIVE **1** *The roses can be enjoyed in a splendid park setting.* ► magnificent, impressive, imposing, noble, glorious, spectacular, gorgeous, sumptuous **2** *He is a splendid police officer.* ► distinguished, outstanding, remarkable, exceptional, celebrated, acclaimed **3** *He had clearly had a splendid day out.* ► wonderful, marvellous, excellent, lovely, delightful

splendour NOUN *the classical splendour of the viceroy's palace* ► magnificence, grandeur, sumptuousness, brilliance, resplendence, majesty, richness, pomp, spectacle, stateliness

splice VERB *The cables were spliced in mid-ocean* ► join, unite, connect, interweave, mesh, entwine

splinter NOUN *a splinter of wood; small splinters of glass* ► sliver, chip, flake, shard, fragment, shaving, shiver

splinter VERB *She had a voice that could splinter a glass.* ► shatter, shiver, crack, fracture, chip, smash, split

split NOUN **1** *There was a large split in the rock.* ► crack, fissure, crevice, breach, break, cleft **2** *His t-shirt was stained and had a split in the side.* ► tear, rip, cut, slash, slit **3** *The policy might produce a split in the party.* ► division, schism, rift, breach AN OPPOSITE IS union **4** *After the split with her partner she moved to London.* ► break-up, separation (from), parting, estrangement (from)

split VERB **1** *The child had pulled the curtain and split it.* ► tear, rip, slash, slit **2** *He split the log with an axe.* ► chop, cut, hew, break, cleave **3** *They worked out a system for splitting the proceeds.* ► divide, share, distribute, allocate, apportion **4** *Further on the paths split.* ► fork, divide, diverge, branch AN OPPOSITE IS merge **5** *The proposal would split the Party.* ► divide, disunite
split up *Her parents had split up when she was small.* ► separate, break up, part, divorce

spoil VERB **1** *She stayed off the beach because she didn't want to spoil her shoes.* ► damage, harm, mar, hurt, blemish, disfigure, deface OPPOSITES ARE improve, enhance **2** *An emergency at a time like this could spoil everything.* ► ruin, wreck, upset, mess up, destroy, undo, scupper, sabotage, scotch AN OPPOSITE IS further **3** *She decided to spoil herself with a vintage champagne.* ► indulge, pamper, cosset AN OPPOSITE IS neglect

sponge VERB **1** *He asked his nephew to sponge the windows.* ► wash, clean, swab, mop, rinse, swill, wipe **2** **sponge on** *He didn't want to be sponging on his parents any longer.* ► live off, impose on, cadge from, scrounge from

spongy ADJECTIVE *The material was light and spongy.* ► soft, springy, squashy, cushioned, absorbent, porous OPPOSITES ARE solid, hard

sponsor *NOUN* **sponsors** **1** a person or organization that provides money for an arts or sports event or for a broadcast in return for advertising **2** someone who gives money to a charity in return for something achieved by another person
▷ **sponsorship** *NOUN*

sponsor *VERB* **sponsors, sponsoring, sponsored** be a sponsor for a person or thing [from Latin *sponsum* = promised]

spontaneous (spon- tay- nee- us) *ADJECTIVE* happening or done naturally; not forced or suggested by someone else
▷ **spontaneously** *ADVERB* **spontaneity** *NOUN*

spool *NOUN* **spools** a rod or cylinder on which something is wound

spoon *NOUN* **spoons** a small device with a rounded bowl on a handle, used for lifting things to the mouth or for stirring or measuring things
▷ **spoonful** *NOUN* **spoonfuls**

spoonerism *NOUN* **spoonerisms** an accidental exchange of the initial letters of two words, e.g. by saying *a boiled sprat* instead of *a spoiled brat* [named after Canon Spooner (1844-1930), who made mistakes of this kind]

spore *NOUN* **spores** a tiny reproductive cell of a plant such as a fungus or fern

sport *NOUN* **sports** **1** an athletic activity; a game or pastime, especially outdoors **2** games of this kind • *Are you keen on sport?* **3** (*informal*) a person who behaves fairly and generously • *Thanks for being such a good sport.*

sporting chance *NOUN* a reasonable chance of success

sports car *NOUN* **sports cars** an open low-built fast car

sportsman *NOUN* **sportsmen** **1** a man who takes part in sport **2** a person who shows sportsmanship

sportsmanship *NOUN* behaving fairly and generously to rivals

sportswoman *NOUN* **sportswomen** **1** a woman who takes part in sport **2** a woman who shows sportsmanship

spot *NOUN* **spots** **1** a small round mark **2** a pimple **3** a small amount • *We had a spot of trouble.* **4** a place **5** a drop • *a few spots of rain*
on the spot without delay or change of place; under pressure to take action • *This really puts him on the spot!*
spot on (*informal*) exactly right or accurate

spot *VERB* **spots, spotting, spotted** **1** mark with spots **2** (*informal*) notice or recognize • *We spotted her in the crowd.* **3** watch for and take note of • *trainspotting*
▷ **spotter** *NOUN*

spotlight *NOUN* **spotlights** **1** a strong light that can shine on one small area **2** public attention • *The Royal Family are used to being in the spotlight.*

spotty *ADJECTIVE* marked with spots

Thesaurus

spontaneous *ADJECTIVE* **1** *The March Revolution was a spontaneous uprising.* ► unplanned, unpremeditated, unprepared, unrehearsed, voluntary, impromptu, impulsive, unconstrained, unforced
AN OPPOSITE IS premeditated **2** *The verdict was announced to cheers and spontaneous applause.* ► involuntary, automatic, natural, reflex, instinctive **3** *She always seems to friendly and spontaneous.* ► natural, uninhibited, unaffected, open, genuine
AN OPPOSITE IS inhibited

spooky *ADJECTIVE* *I bet this place is really spooky late at night.* ► eerie, sinister, creepy, frightening, ghostly, weird, (*more informal*) scary

sport *NOUN* **1** *They showed a lot of interest in sport.* ► games, competitive games, physical recreation, physical exercise

sporting *ADJECTIVE* *It was sporting of them to pay the bill.* ► generous, considerate, decent, sportsmanlike AN OPPOSITE IS unsporting

sporty *ADJECTIVE* *They look sporty in their jogging suits.* ► athletic, fit, healthy, energetic

spot *NOUN* **1** *There was a dirty spot in the middle of the carpet.* ► stain, mark, smudge, blotch, smear **2** *He had a small spot on the side of his nose.* ► pimple, freckle, mole, blemish **3** *a bright fabric with small spots* ► dot, speck, fleck **4** *We stopped at a quiet spot near the sea.* ► place, position, location, locality, setting, site **5** *Money problems left them in a bit of a spot.* ► predicament, difficulty, plight, mess, corner, trouble, awkward situation, quandary, dilemma, (*more informal*) jam, (*more informal*) fix

spot *VERB* **1** *My apron was spotted with splashes of grease.* ► stain, mark, smudge, spatter, speckle, streak, blot, discolour, fleck, mottle **2** *She spotted Jack weeding in the garden.* ► notice, observe, glimpse, spy, see, make out, discern, detect

spotless *ADJECTIVE* **1** *He was wearing his spotless white shirt.* ► unmarked, perfectly clean, immaculate, gleaming **2** *They had a spotless reputation for fair dealing.* ► unblemished, unsullied, untarnished, blameless, faultless, pure, immaculate, irreproachable, pure, (*more informal*) whiter than white

spotty *ADJECTIVE* *a spotty face* ► pimply, pimpled, potmarked, spotted, blotchy, freckled

a b c d e f g h i j k l m n o p q r **s** t u v w x y z

spouse *NOUN* **spouses** a person's husband or wife

spout *NOUN* **spouts** **1** a pipe or similar opening from which liquid can pour **2** a jet of liquid

spout *VERB* **spouts, spouting, spouted** **1** come or send out as a jet of liquid **2** (*informal*) speak for a long time

sprain *VERB* **sprains, spraining, sprained** injure a joint by twisting it
▷ **sprain** *NOUN*

sprawl *VERB* **sprawls, sprawling, sprawled** **1** sit or lie with the arms and legs spread out loosely **2** spread out loosely or untidily
▷ **sprawl** *NOUN*

spray[1] *VERB* **sprays, spraying, sprayed** scatter tiny drops of liquid over something

spray *NOUN* **sprays** **1** tiny drops of liquid sent through the air **2** a device for spraying liquid **3** a liquid for spraying • *fly spray*

spray[2] *NOUN* **sprays** **1** a single shoot with its leaves and flowers **2** a small bunch of flowers

spread *VERB* **spreads, spreading, spread** **1** open or stretch something out to its full size • *The bird spread its wings.* **2** make something cover a surface • *We spread jam on the bread.* **3** become longer or wider • *The stain was spreading.* **4** make or become more widely known or felt or distributed etc. • *We spread the news* • *The story quickly spread round the village.*

spread *NOUN* **spreads** **1** the action or result of spreading **2** a thing's breadth or extent **3** a paste for spreading on bread **4** (*informal*) a large or grand meal

spreadeagled *ADJECTIVE* with arms and legs stretched out • *He lay spreadeagled on the bed* [A *spread eagle* was originally a picture of an eagle with legs and wings stretched out, used as an emblem in heraldry]

spreadsheet *NOUN* **spreadsheets** (in computing) a program for handling information, especially figures, displayed in a table

spree *NOUN* **sprees** something you do with a lot of freedom and enjoyment • *a shopping spree*

sprig *NOUN* **sprigs** a small branch; a shoot [from early German]

sprightly *ADJECTIVE* **sprightlier, sprightliest** lively and full of energy

spring *VERB* **springs, springing, sprang, sprung** **1** jump; move quickly or suddenly • *He sprang to his feet.* **2** originate or develop • *The trouble has sprung from carelessness.* • *Weeds have started to spring up.* **3** present or produce suddenly • *They sprang a surprise on us.*

spring *NOUN* **springs** **1** a springy coil or bent piece of metal **2** a springing movement **3** a place where water comes up naturally from the ground **4** the season when most plants begin to grow [from Old English]

Thesaurus

spout *NOUN* *Water poured from the spout.* ► nozzle, outlet, jet, sprinkler

spout *VERB* **1** *Molten lava was spouting from the crater.* ► spurt, gush, spew, pour, stream, shoot, surge, discharge, issue **2** *He spouted endlessly about how much better life used to be.* ► hold forth, sound off, go on, pontificate, declaim, (*more informal*) mouth off, (*more informal*) rabbit on

sprain *VERB* SEE **wound** *VERB*

sprawl *VERB* **1** *He sprawled on a huge armchair.* ► stretch out, lounge, recline, slump, slouch, flop **2** *The woods sprawled across the hillside.* ► spread, stretch, straggle, be scattered

spray *NOUN* **1** *a fine spray of water* ► shower, sprinkling, fountain, splash, mist **2** *a spray of flowers* ► bouquet, bunch, posy, nosegay, garland **3** *a paint spray* ► aerosol, atomizer, spray gun, sprinkler

spray *VERB* **1** *A sprinkler was spraying water over the grass.* ► sprinkle, spread, shower, disperse, diffuse **2** *Water sprayed into the air.* ► spout, gush, spurt, shoot

spread *NOUN* **1** *the spread of civilization* ► expansion, extension, growth, proliferation, diffusion, advance **2** *a vast spread of open country* ► stretch, expanse, extent, sweep, span **3** (*informal*) *There was a good spread on the table.* ► meal, feast

spread *VERB* **1** *He sat back and spread his arms.* ► extend, stretch **2** *I found a map and spread it on the table.* ► open out, unfurl, unroll, display **3** *She spread seeds along the edge of the flower bed.* ► scatter, strew, diffuse **4** *new ways of spreading information* ► diffuse, communicate, propagate, broadcast, transmit, circulate, advertise **5** *These feelings of resentment were beginning to spread.* ► grow, increase, proliferate, escalate, develop, broaden

sprightly *ADJECTIVE* *He's very sprightly for his age.* ► lively, active, spry, agile, nimble, spirited, vivacious, vigorous OPPOSITES ARE doddering, lethargic

spring *NOUN* **1** *With a sudden spring he was out of the door.* ► leap, jump, bound, vault **2** *The cushion had lost its spring.* ► bounce, springiness, resilience, elasticity, flexibility

spring *VERB* **1** *Steve sprang to his feet.* ► leap, jump, bound, bounce **2** *Some of these ideas spring from earlier research.* ► originate, derive, arise, develop, come
spring up *New hotels are springing up all along the coast.* ► appear, develop, emerge, shoot up

springboard *NOUN* **springboards** a springy board from which people jump in diving and gymnastics

spring-clean *VERB* **spring-cleans, spring-cleaning, spring-cleaned** clean a house thoroughly in springtime

springy *ADJECTIVE* **springier, springiest** able to spring back easily after being bent or squeezed
▷ **springiness** *NOUN*

sprinkle *VERB* **sprinkles, sprinkling, sprinkled** make tiny drops or pieces fall on something
▷ **sprinkler** *NOUN*

sprint *VERB* **sprints, sprinting, sprinted** run very fast for a short distance
▷ **sprint** *NOUN* **sprinter** *NOUN*
[from Old Norse]

sprout *VERB* **sprouts, sprouting, sprouted** start to grow; put out shoots

sprout *NOUN* **sprouts** **1** a shoot of a plant **2** a Brussels sprout

spruce [1] *NOUN* **spruces** a kind of fir tree

spruce [2] *ADJECTIVE* neat and trim; smart

spruce *VERB* **spruces, sprucing, spruced** smarten • *Spruce yourself up.*

spry *ADJECTIVE* **spryer, spryest** active, nimble, and lively

spur *NOUN* **spurs** **1** a sharp device worn on the heel of a rider's boot to urge a horse to go faster **2** a stimulus or incentive **3** a ridge that sticks out from a mountain
on the spur of the moment on an impulse; without planning

spur *VERB* **spurs, spurring, spurred** urge on; encourage

spurious *ADJECTIVE* not genuine

spurn *VERB* **spurns, spurning, spurned** reject scornfully

spurt *VERB* **spurts, spurting, spurted** **1** gush out **2** increase your speed suddenly

spurt *NOUN* **spurts** **1** a sudden gush **2** a sudden increase in speed or effort

spy *NOUN* **spies** someone who works secretly for one country, person, etc. to find out things about another

spy *VERB* **spies, spying, spied** **1** be a spy **2** keep watch secretly • *Have you been spying on me?* **3** see or notice • *She spied a house in the distance.* [from early French *espier* = catch sight of]

squabble *VERB* **squabbles, squabbling, squabbled** quarrel or bicker
▷ **squabble** *NOUN*

squad *NOUN* **squads** a small group of people working or being trained together

squadron *NOUN* **squadrons** part of an army, navy, or air force

squalid *ADJECTIVE* dirty and unpleasant
▷ **squalidly** *ADVERB* **squalor** *NOUN*

squall *NOUN* **squalls** **1** a sudden storm or gust of wind **2** a baby's loud cry

squall *VERB* **squalls, squalling, squalled** (said about a baby) cry loudly

Thesaurus

springy *ADJECTIVE* **1** *The floor felt springy under their feet.* ► elastic, stretchy, pliable, resilient, spongy, supple, bendy, flexible
AN OPPOSITE IS rigid **2** *He walked on with a springy step.* ► jaunty, bouncy, buoyant, lively, light

sprinkle *VERB* **1** *He sprinkled sugar over his cereal.* ► scatter, strew, shower **2** *Sprinkle the grass with seed.* ► dust, powder, pepper

sprint *VERB* *She sprinted up the road.* ► run, dash, tear, shoot, dart, (*more informal*) belt

sprout *VERB* *The seeds began to sprout.* ► grow, germinate, shoot up, spring up, bud, develop, emerge

spur *NOUN* *Music can become a spur to our imaginations.* ► stimulus, incentive, impetus, encouragement, enticement, filip
on the spur of the moment *He decided to go with her on the spur of the moment.* ► on impulse, impulsively, impetuously, spontaneously, all of a sudden

spur *VERB* *The boy's frantic calls spurred her to action.* ► stimulate, encourage, drive, prompt, goad, incite

spurt *VERB* *Blood spurted from his finger and he swore.* ► squirt, gush, shoot, stream, pour, spew, erupt, surge

spy *NOUN* *He had never thought of himself as a traitor, or a spy.* ► secret agent, undercover agent, double agent, (*more informal*) plant, (*more informal*) mole

spy *VERB* **1 spy on** *She sent you to spy on me.* ► snoop on, keep a watch on, watch, shadow, trail **2** *We heard a rustle and spied a baby adder slithering away.* ► notice, observe, glimpse, spot, see, make out, discern, detect

squabble *VERB* *Every evening a crowd gathered to squabble over politics.* ► argue, quarrel, bicker, wrangle, dispute, clash, fight

squalid *ADJECTIVE* **1** *a depressing mixture of cheap housing and squalid surroundings* ► dirty, filthy, grimy, grubby, sordid, seedy, dingy
AN OPPOSITE IS clean **2** *squalid attempts to rig the election* ► improper, shameful, sordid, dishonest, corrupt AN OPPOSITE IS honourable

A B C D E F G H I J K L M N O P Q R S T U V W X Y Z

squander *VERB* **squanders, squandering, squandered** spend money or time etc. wastefully

square *NOUN* **squares 1** a flat shape with four equal sides and four right angles **2** an area surrounded by buildings • *Leicester Square* **3** the result of multiplying a number by itself • *9 is the square of 3* (9 = 3 x 3)

square *ADJECTIVE* **1** having the shape of a square **2** forming a right angle • *The desk has square corners.* **3** equal or even • *The teams are all square with six points each.*
▷ **squarely** *ADVERB* **squareness** *NOUN*

square foot, square metre etc. the area of a surface with sides that are one foot or one metre etc. long

square *VERB* **squares, squaring, squared 1** make a thing square **2** multiply a number by itself • *5 squared is 25* **3** match; make or be consistent • *His story doesn't square with yours.* **4** settle or pay

square deal *NOUN* a deal that is honest and fair

square meal *NOUN* **square meals** a good satisfying meal

square root *NOUN* **square roots** the number that gives a particular number if it is multiplied by itself • *3 is the square root of 9* (3 x 3 = 9)

squash *VERB* **squashes, squashing, squashed 1** press something so that it becomes flat or out of shape **2** force into a small space; pack tightly **3** suppress or quash

squash *NOUN* **squashes 1** a crowded condition **2** a fruit-flavoured soft drink **3** a game played with rackets and a soft ball in a special indoor court

squat *VERB* **squats, squatting, squatted 1** sit on your heels; crouch **2** live in an unoccupied building without permission
▷ **squat** *NOUN* **squatter** *NOUN*

squat *ADJECTIVE* short and fat

squawk *VERB* **squawks, squawking, squawked** make a loud harsh cry
▷ **squawk** *NOUN*

squeak *VERB* **squeaks, squeaking, squeaked** make a short high-pitched cry or sound
▷ **squeak** *NOUN* **squeaky** *ADJECTIVE* **squeakily** *ADVERB*

squeal *VERB* **squeals, squealing, squealed** make a long shrill cry or sound
▷ **squeal** *NOUN*

squeamish *ADJECTIVE* easily disgusted or shocked
▷ **squeamishness** *NOUN*

squeeze *VERB* **squeezes, squeezing, squeezed 1** press something from opposite sides, especially to get liquid out of it **2** force into or through a place • *We squeezed through a gap in the hedge.*
▷ **squeezer** *NOUN*

Thesaurus

squander *VERB The servant girl he married squandered every penny of his.* ► waste, misspend, fritter away, dissipate, (*more informal*) blow AN OPPOSITE IS save

square *ADJECTIVE* **1** *They sat at a square table.* ► rectangular, right-angled, quadrilateral **2** *The sides were still square at full time.* ► level, even, neck and neck **3** *All they wanted was a square deal.* ► fair, honest, just, equitable, genuine, above-board, (*more informal*) on-the-level

square *NOUN* **1** *They arranged to meet in the town square.* ► piazza, plaza **2** (*informal*) *He must have seemed such a square to them.* ► old fogy, conservative, traditionalist, conformist, conventional person, (*informal*) stick-in-the-mud

square *VERB* **1** *He went in to square his bill.* ► settle, pay, clear, discharge **2** *He needed to square a few things with his dad.* ► resolve, settle, sort out, clear up, put right, remedy, reconcile **3** *These facts don't quite square with the accepted version of what happened.* ► agree, tally, accord, harmonize

squash *VERB* **1** *Someone had squashed the flowers in the garden.* ► crush, flatten, press, mangle, trample on, compress **2** *He squashed a few things into his case.* ► stuff, force, cram, ram, pack **3** *The uprising was ruthlessly squashed.* ► suppress, quash, quell, put down **4** *He meanly squashed them in front of everyone.* ► humiliate, humble, show up, put down, mortify, snub

squat *VERB The children squatted on the floor to listen.* ► crouch, stoop, sit

squawk *VERB A bird squawked overhead.* ► screech, shriek, squeal, cry, call

squeak *VERB* **1** *The door squeaked.* ► creak, grate, rasp **2** *The bird squeaked in its cage.* ► chirp, peep, cheep

squeal *VERB She squealed with pain.* ► cry, yell, yelp, screech, scream, shriek

squeamish *ADJECTIVE Her father had always been squeamish about changing nappies.* ► queasy, nauseated, fastidious, finicky, fussy, choosy, particular, prim, prissy

squeeze *VERB* **1** *Katherine squeezed her daughter's hand affectionately.* ► clasp, press, grip, hug, squash, wring, compress, crush, embrace, enfold **2** *She put her arm round him and squeezed him.* ► hug, embrace, cuddle, hold, clasp **3** *They squeezed the audience into a room that was obviously too small. She squeezed herself into a bright red minidress.* ► cram, push,

squeeze *NOUN* **squeezes 1** the action of squeezing **2** a drop of liquid squeezed out • *Add a squeeze of lemon.* **3** a time when money is difficult to get or borrow

squelch *VERB* **squelches, squelching, squelched** make a sound like someone treading in thick mud
▷ **squelch** *NOUN*

squid *NOUN* **squids** a sea animal with eight short tentacles and two long ones

squint *VERB* **squints, squinting, squinted 1** be cross-eyed **2** peer; look with half-shut eyes at something
▷ **squint** *NOUN*

squire *NOUN* **squires 1** the man who owns most of the land in a country parish or district **2** a young nobleman in the Middle Ages who served a knight

squirm *VERB* **squirms, squirming, squirmed** wriggle about, especially when you feel embarrassed

squirrel *NOUN* **squirrels** a small animal with a bushy tail and red or grey fur, living in trees [via early French from Greek *skia* = shade + *oura* = tail]

squirt *VERB* **squirts, squirting, squirted** send or come out in a jet of liquid
▷ **squirt** *NOUN*

St. or **St** *ABBREVIATION* **1** Saint **2** Street

stab *VERB* **stabs, stabbing, stabbed** pierce or wound with something sharp

stab *NOUN* **stabs 1** the action of stabbing **2** a sudden sharp pain • *She felt a stab of fear.* **3** (*informal*) an attempt • *I'll have a stab at it.*

stability *NOUN* being stable

stable[1] *ADJECTIVE* **1** steady and firmly fixed **2** not likely to change or end suddenly • *a stable relationship* **3** sensible and dependable
▷ **stably** *ADVERB*

stable[2] *NOUN* **stables** a building where horses are kept

stable *VERB* **stables, stabling, stabled** put or keep in a stable

stack *NOUN* **stacks 1** a neat pile **2** a haystack **3** (*informal*) a large amount • *I have a stack of work to do.* **4** a single tall chimney; a group of small chimneys

stack *VERB* **stacks, stacking, stacked** pile things up [from Old Norse]

stadium *NOUN* **stadiums** a sports ground surrounded by seats for spectators [via Latin from Greek *stadion*]

staff *NOUN* **staffs** *or, in sense 4,* **staves 1** the people who work in an office, shop, etc. **2** the teachers in a school or college **3** a stick or pole used as a weapon or support or as a symbol of authority **4** a set of five horizontal lines on which music is written

staff *VERB* **staffs, staffing, staffed** provide with a staff of people • *The centre is staffed by volunteers.*

stag *NOUN* **stags** a male deer

Thesaurus

ram, shove, stuff, thrust, crowd, wedge **4** *Two elderly Americans squeezed past her chair.* ► push, force your way **5** *The government seems determined to squeeze as much money out of the motorist as it can.* ► wring, wrest, extort, extract, force, milk

squeeze *NOUN* **1** *He gave her hand a squeeze.* ► press, pinch, grip, grasp, clasp **2** *Three of us in the back of the car was quite a squeeze.* ► crush, jam, huddle, crowd

squirt *VERB* **1** *The first bite made jam squirt down my chin.* ► spurt, shoot, gush, spout, spray, erupt, surge **2** *She squirted me with water.* ► splash, spray, shower, spatter, splatter, sprinkle

stab *NOUN* **1** *He got a stab in the leg.* ► wound, wounding, blow, jab, cut, prick, thrust **2** *She felt a brief stab of pain.* ► twinge, pang, sting, throb, spasm **3** (*informal*) *I'll have a stab at it.* ► try, go, attempt, (*informal*) bash, (*informal*) shot

stab *VERB* **1** *One of the gang stabbed him in the arm.* ► knife, spear, pierce, jab, stick, thrust, wound **2** *She stabbed at the ground with a spade.* ► thrust, jab, prod, lunge, poke

stable *ADJECTIVE* **1** *Make sure the equipment is stable.* ► steady, firm, secure, balanced, fixed, solid OPPOSITES ARE unstable, flimsy **2** *Their power and authority depend on a stable regime.* ► well-founded, well-established, secure, firm, enduring, durable, lasting, sound, strong OPPOSITES ARE unstable, changeable

stack *NOUN* **1** *The publisher had a stack of unsold copies on his hands.* ► heap, pile, mound, mass, load, accumulation, stockpile, mountain **2** *a stack of hay* ► rick, stook, haycock

stack *VERB* *The boxes were stacked on desks and tables.* ► pile, heap, load, mass, assemble, collect, accumulate, build up, gather

staff *NOUN* **1** *We have extra staff on duty over the busy period.* ► personnel, assistants, employees, workers, workforce, crew, officers, team **2** *Magistrates carried a staff as a sign of their authority* ► cane, crosier, pole, rod, sceptre, stave, stick

stage *NOUN* **stages** **1** a platform for performances in a theatre or hall **2** a point or part of a process, journey, etc. • *Now for the final stage.*
the stage the profession of acting or working in the theatre

stage *VERB* **stages, staging, staged** **1** present a performance on a stage **2** organize • *We decided to stage a protest.*

stagecoach *NOUN* **stagecoaches** a horse-drawn coach that formerly ran regularly from one point to another along the same route

stage manager *NOUN* **stage managers** the person in charge of the scenery, lighting, sound, etc. in a theatre during a performance

stagger *VERB* **staggers, staggering, staggered** **1** walk unsteadily **2** amaze or shock deeply • *We were staggered at the price.* **3** arrange things so that they do not all happen together • *Please stagger your holidays so that there is always someone here.*
▷ **stagger** *NOUN*

stagnant *ADJECTIVE* **1** not flowing **2** not active or developing • *business is stagnant*

stain *NOUN* **stains** **1** a dirty mark on something **2** a blemish on someone's character or past record **3** a liquid used for staining things

stain *VERB* **stains, staining, stained** **1** make a stain on something **2** colour with a liquid that sinks into the surface [from an old word *distain* = dye]

stained glass *NOUN* pieces of coloured glass held together in a lead framework to make a picture or pattern

stainless steel *NOUN* steel that does not rust easily

stair *NOUN* **stairs** each of the fixed steps in a series that lead from one level or floor to another in a building

staircase *NOUN* **staircases** a set of stairs

stake *NOUN* **stakes** **1** a thick pointed stick to be driven into the ground **2** the post to which people used to be tied for execution by being burnt alive **3** an amount of money bet on something **4** an investment that gives a person a share or interest in a business etc.
at stake being risked

stake *VERB* **stakes, staking, staked** **1** fasten, support, or mark out with stakes **2** bet or risk money etc. on an event
stake a claim claim or obtain a right to something

stalactite *NOUN* **stalactites** a stony spike hanging like an icicle from a cave roof [from Greek *stalaktos* = dripping]
USAGE See note at **stalagmite**.

stalagmite *NOUN* **stalagmites** a stony spike standing like a pillar on the floor of a cave [from Greek *stalagma* = a drop]
USAGE Remember that a **stalagmite** stands up from the ground, while a **stalactite** hangs down from the ceiling.

stale *ADJECTIVE* **1** not fresh **2** bored and not having any good ideas
▷ **staleness** *NOUN*

stalemate *NOUN* **1** a drawn position in chess when a player cannot make a move without putting his or her king in check **2** a deadlock; a situation in which neither side in an argument will give way

Thesaurus

stage *NOUN* **1** *They faced the long last stage of their journey.* ► part, section, phase, portion, stretch, lap **2** *The treaty marks a new stage in relations between the two countries.* ► point, phase, step, juncture

stage *VERB* **1** *They even staged an opera.* ► mount, put on, present, perform, arrange **2** *Workers staged a two-hour strike on 5 November.* ► organize, mount, set up, go through with

stagger *VERB* **1** *He staggered up the stairs to bed.* ► totter, stumble, lurch, reel, sway, falter, walk unsteadily, waver, wobble **2** *Rory was staggered by his answer.* ► astonish, amaze, astound, surprise, dumbfound, flabbergast, shock, startle, stun, stupefy

stain *NOUN* **1** *Her eyes alighted on a milk stain on the tablecloth.* ► mark, spot, smear, blemish, smudge, blot, blotch, discoloration **2** *It was not seen as a stain on their character.* ► blemish, taint, blot, slur, disgrace, discredit

stain *VERB* **1** *Sweat had stained his shirt.* ► discolour, mark, blemish, dirty, sully, spoil, blacken **2** *There is a product that will stain and varnish in one go.* ► dye, colour, tinge, tint, paint

stake *NOUN* **1** *The soldier had been speared with a wooden stake.* ► pole, post, spike, stave, stick, paling, pile **2** *The multinational has bought a 40% stake in the company.* ► share, interest, involvement **3** *If you win, you get your stake back plus ten times its value.* ► bet, pledge, wager

stale *ADJECTIVE* **1** *You can make the pudding with stale bread and milk.* ► dry, hard, old, musty, mouldy **2** *The war had already become stale news.* ► worn out, jaded, hackneyed, out-of-date, uninteresting, unoriginal, overused AN OPPOSITE IS fresh

stalemate *NOUN* *The negotiations ended in a stalemate.* ► deadlock, impasse, standstill

stalk[1] *NOUN* **stalks** a stem of a plant etc.

stalk[2] *VERB* **stalks, stalking, stalked** **1** track or hunt stealthily **2** walk in a stiff or dignified way

stall *NOUN* **stalls** **1** a table or counter from which things are sold **2** a place for one animal in a stable or shed

stall *VERB* **stalls, stalling, stalled** **1** delay things or avoid giving an answer to give yourself more time **2** stop suddenly from lack of power • *The car engine stalled.* **3** put an animal into a stall

stallion *NOUN* **stallions** a male horse

stalls *PLURAL NOUN* the seats in the lowest level of a theatre

stalwart *ADJECTIVE* strong and faithful • *my stalwart supporters*

stamen *NOUN* **stamens** the part of a flower bearing pollen [from Latin, = thread]

stamina *NOUN* strength and ability to endure hard effort over a long time [from Latin, plural of **stamen** (referring to the threads of life spun by the Fates, three mythological godesses who were believed to determine each person's birth and death)]

stammer *VERB* **stammers, stammering, stammered** keep repeating the same syllables when you speak
▷ **stammer** *NOUN*

stamp *NOUN* **stamps** **1** a small piece of gummed paper with a special design on it; a postage stamp **2** a small device for pressing words or marks on something; the words or marks made by this **3** a distinctive characteristic • *His story bears the stamp of truth.*

stamp *VERB* **stamps, stamping, stamped** **1** bang your foot heavily on the ground **2** walk with loud heavy steps **3** stick a postage stamp on a letter or packet **4** press a mark or design etc. on something
stamp out **1** put out a fire by stamping **2** stop something • *We have stamped out bullying.*

stampede *NOUN* **stampedes** a sudden rush by animals or people
▷ **stampede** *VERB*
[from Spanish *estampida* = crash, uproar]

stand *VERB* **stands, standing, stood** **1** be on your feet without moving • *We were standing at the back of the hall.* **2** rise to your feet • *Please all stand now.* **3** set or be upright; place • *We stood the vase on the table.* **4** stay the same • *My offer still stands.* **5** be a candidate for election • *She stood for Parliament.* **6** tolerate or endure • *I can't stand that noise.* **7** provide and pay for • *I'll stand you a drink.*
it stands to reason it is reasonable or obvious
stand by be ready for action
stand for **1** represent • *'US' stands for 'United States'.* **2** tolerate
stand in for take someone's place
stand out be clear or obvious
stand up for support or defend
stand up to **1** resist bravely **2** stay in good condition in spite of prolonged use

Thesaurus

stalk *NOUN* *the stalk of a plant* ► stem, shoot, branch, trunk, twig

stalk *VERB* **1** *The cat began to stalk her through the long grass.* ► track, trail, hunt, pursue, shadow, tail, follow **2** *He rose and stalked out of the door.* ► stride, strut, march, flounce, sweep

stall *NOUN* *The school will have a stall at Fun in the Parks.* ► stand, booth, kiosk

stall *VERB* *He clearly believed she was only stalling.* ► procrastinate, prevaricate, temporize, play for time, delay, hang back

stamp *NOUN* **1** *The licence needs an official stamp to be valid.* ► mark, seal, brand, imprint **2** *She left her stamp on history as an inspired visionary.* ► mark, impression **3** *The new head was of a different stamp from her predecessor.* ► type, kind, sort, brand, character

stamp *VERB* **1** *'Bad girl,' she said and stamped her foot.* ► strike, bring down, thump **2** *Sir George had stamped his authority firmly on the subject.* ► imprint, mark, print, brand, engrave, impress
stamp on *Ellie moved forward and stamped on the creature.* ► tread on, crush, trample
stamp out *The police are trying to stamp out racism.* ► eliminate, eradicate, extinguish, end, put an end to, suppress

stampede *NOUN* *In the stampede that follows, the young elephants can easily get trampled.* ► charge, rush, dash, rout, panic

stampede *VERB* *The audience panicked and stampeded for the exit.* ► dash, bolt, charge, rush, flee

stand *VERB* **1** *The choir stood for the final chorus.* ► rise, get to your feet, get up **2** *A house once stood on this spot.* ► be situated, be located, be sited, exist, sit, be **3** *She stood the packet on the table.* ► put, place, set, deposit, position, situate, station, locate, (*more informal*) plonk **4** *The offer still stands.* ► remain in force, remain valid, be unchanged, stay, continue **5** *Her heart could not stand the strain.* ► withstand, endure, handle, cope with **6** *I can't stand noise.* ► bear, abide, endure, tolerate, put up with, suffer, (*more informal*) stick, (*more informal*) stomach, (*more informal*) wear
stand by *He was determined to stand by his friends.* ► support, defend, stand *or* stick up for, be faithful to, be loyal to, adhere to, stay with, stick to OPPOSITES ARE betray, let down

stand *NOUN* **stands** **1** something made for putting things on • *a music stand* **2** a stall where things are sold or displayed **3** a grandstand **4** a stationary condition or position • *He took his stand near the door.* **5** resistance to attack • *The time has come to make a stand.*

standard *NOUN* **standards** **1** how good something is • *a high standard of work* **2** a thing used to measure or judge something else **3** a special flag • *the royal standard* **4** an upright support

standard *ADJECTIVE* **1** of the usual or average quality or kind **2** regarded as the best and widely used • *the standard book on spiders*

standby *NOUN*
on standby ready to be used if needed

stand-in *NOUN* **stand-ins** a deputy or substitute

standing order *NOUN* **standing orders** an instruction to a bank to make regular payments, or to a trader to supply something regularly

stand-offish *ADJECTIVE* cold and formal; not friendly

standpoint *NOUN* **standpoints** a point of view

standstill *NOUN* a stop; an end to movement or activity

staple[1] *NOUN* **staples** **1** a small piece of metal pushed through papers and clenched to fasten them together **2** a U-shaped nail
▷ **staple** *VERB* **stapler** *NOUN*

staple[2] *ADJECTIVE* main or usual • *Rice is their staple food.*
▷ **staple** *NOUN*

star *NOUN* **stars** **1** a large mass of burning gas that is seen as a speck of light in the sky at night **2** a shape with points or rays sticking out from it; an asterisk **3** an object or mark of this shape showing rank or quality • *a five-star hotel* **4** a famous performer; one of the chief performers in a play, film, or show

star *VERB* **stars, starring, starred** **1** be one of the main performers in a film or show **2** have someone as a main performer **3** mark with an asterisk or star symbol

starboard *NOUN* the right-hand side of a ship or aircraft when you are facing forward COMPARE **port**[1] [from Old English *steor* = paddle for steering (usually mounted on the right-hand side), + **board**]

starch *NOUN* **starches** **1** a white carbohydrate in bread, potatoes, etc. **2** this or a similar substance used to stiffen clothes
▷ **starchy** *ADJECTIVE*

starch *VERB* **starches, starching, starched** stiffen with starch

stare *VERB* **stares, staring, stared** look at something intensely
▷ **stare** *NOUN*

starfish *NOUN* **starfish** or **starfishes** a sea animal shaped like a star with five points

Thesaurus

stand down *He would have to accept responsibility and stand down.* ► resign, step down, retire, (*more informal*) quit
stand for *What do the initials stand for?* ► mean, represent, signify, denote, indicate, symbolize, be a sign for
stand in for *She stood in for the lead singer who was unwell.* ► replace, substitute for, take over from, be a substitute for, deputize for, cover for, understudy
stand out *He stands out in that suit.* ► be prominent, be obvious, catch the eye, show, stick out
stand up for *It is important to stand up for our principles.* ► support, defend, champion, stand *or* stick by, be faithful to, be loyal to, adhere to, stay with, stick to AN OPPOSITE IS betray
stand up to *The little band stood up bravely to the attack.* ► resist, withstand, confront, face up to, defy, oppose OPPOSITES ARE give in to, succumb to

stand *NOUN* **1** *a large vase on a stand* ► base, pedestal, support, tripod, trivet, rack **2** *a newspaper stand* ► stall, booth, kiosk **3** *They are taking a bold stand.* ► attitude, stance, viewpoint, position, policy, posture

standard *ADJECTIVE* *The fee is subject to VAT at the standard rate. The council said the letter was part of their standard procedure.* ► normal, usual, typical, customary, conventional

standard *NOUN* **1** *The standard of music-making can be very high indeed.* ► quality, level, calibre, grade, excellence **2** *a standard of behaviour* ► norm, principle, yardstick, criterion, benchmark, example **3** *Next day at dawn they raised the regimental standard for the last time.* ► flag, banner, pennant, colours, ensign

standing *NOUN* *The superintendent has to be a medical practitioner of high standing.* ► reputation, distinction, status, repute, rank, stature, seniority, eminence

star *NOUN* **1** *a sky full of stars* ► celestial body, heavenly body RELATED ADJECTIVES astral, stellar **2** *She was an international star by the age of nineteen.* ► celebrity, famous person, public figure, big name, idol

stare *VERB* *She seemed stunned and sat staring in front of her.* ► gaze, gape, glare, goggle, look fixedly, peer
stare at *Simon was staring at him.* ► gaze at, eye, scrutinize, study, watch, contemplate, examine

stark *ADJECTIVE* **1** complete or unmistakable • *stark nonsense* **2** desolate and bare • *the stark lunar landscape*
▷ **starkly** *ADVERB* **starkness** *NOUN*

stark *ADVERB* completely • *stark naked*

starling *NOUN* **starlings** a noisy black bird with speckled feathers

starry *ADJECTIVE* full of stars

starry-eyed *ADJECTIVE* made happy by foolish dreams or unrealistic hopes

start *VERB* **starts, starting, started 1** begin or cause to begin **2** make an engine or machine begin running, • *I'll start the car.* **3** begin a journey **4** make a sudden movement because of pain or surprise
▷ **starter** *NOUN*

start *NOUN* **starts 1** the beginning; the place where a race starts **2** an advantage that someone starts with • *We gave the young ones ten minutes' start.* **3** a sudden movement

startle *VERB* **startles, startling, startled** surprise or alarm someone

starve *VERB* **starves, starving, starved 1** suffer or die from lack of food; cause to do this **2** deprive someone of something they need, • *She was starved of love.*
▷ **starvation** *NOUN*

starving *ADJECTIVE* (*informal*) very hungry

state *NOUN* **states 1** the quality of a person's or thing's characteristics or circumstances; condition **2** an organized community under one government (*the state of Israel*) or forming part of a republic (*the 50 states of the USA*) **3** a country's government • *Help for the earthquake victims was provided by the state.* **4** a grand style • *She arrived in state* **5** (*informal*) an excited or upset condition • *Don't get into a state about the robbery.*

state *VERB* **states, stating, stated** express something in spoken or written words

Thesaurus

stark *ADJECTIVE* **1** *Those who survived had the stark choice of submitting or fleeing into exile.* ► grim, blunt, harsh, plain, bald **2** *Their barracks are a stark contrast to the brightness elsewhere.*
► absolute, complete, utter, total, sheer

start *VERB* **1** *The film starts at 8.* ► begin, (*more formal*) commence **2** *She wants to start a reading group.* ► set up, establish, found, launch, begin, institute, originate, activate, create, embark on, inaugurate, initiate, instigate, introduce, open AN OPPOSITE IS finish **3** *The bus was ready to start.* ► depart, leave, move off, set off, set out, (*more informal*) get going AN OPPOSITE IS stop **4** *We'd better start if we are going to finish in time.* ► make a start, begin, (*more informal*) get going, (*more informal*) get cracking **5** *A crash in the kitchen made us start.* ► jump, recoil, flinch, spring up, blench, jerk, twitch, wince
start out *They would have to start out before breakfast.* ► set off, set out, set forth, make a start, depart, leave, (*more informal*) get going, (*more informal*) hit the road

start *NOUN* **1** *It was the start of a long process.* ► beginning, outset, inception, birth, dawn, initiation, inauguration OPPOSITES ARE end, conclusion **2** *A good education gives you a start in life.* ► advantage, opportunity, encouragement, helping hand **3** *This was the start of all our problems.* ► origin, cause, source, starting point OPPOSITES ARE end, culmination **4** *The doorbell rang, giving me a start* ► shock, jump, surprise

startle *VERB* *Some caterpillars manage to startle their attackers by raising themselves up like small snakes.* ► alarm, frighten, scare, surprise, give you a start, take by surprise, catch unawares, make you start, shake, shock
AN OPPOSITE IS calm

startling *ADJECTIVE* *It was startling to see hundreds of people toiling up and down the hill. The letter contained some startling news.* ► surprising, astonishing, amazing, staggering, disconcerting, unsettling

starvation *NOUN* *The civil war left most of the population facing starvation.* ► hunger, malnutrition, undernourishment, malnourishment, deprivation, famine

starve *VERB* *Many starved in the famine.* ► die of starvation, go hungry, go without, perish

starving *ADJECTIVE* **1** *She devoted her energies to helping the starving children of the world.*
► starved, underfed, undernourished, emaciated **2** *Let's go and eat, I'm starving.*
► very hungry, famished, ravenous

state *NOUN* **1** *The closure reflects the state of the town's economy.* ► condition, situation, shape, circumstances, predicament, position, health **2** *a sovereign state* ► country, nation, land, (*more formal*) polity
in a state *Try not to get in a state.* ► agitated, flustered, anxious, panicky, frenzied, (*more informal*) uptight

state *VERB* *In the speech she stated her company's objectives.* ► declare, express, communicate, voice, utter, tell, say, affirm, make known, reveal, disclose, divulge

a b c d e f g h i j k l m n o p q r s t u v w x y z

A B C D E F G H I J K L M N O P Q R S T U V W X Y Z

stately *ADJECTIVE* **statelier, stateliest** dignified, imposing, or grand
▷ **stateliness** *NOUN*

statement *NOUN* **statements 1** words stating something **2** a formal account of facts • *The witness made a statement to the police.* **3** a written report of a financial account • *a bank statement*

state school *NOUN* **state schools** a school which is funded by the government and which does not charge fees to pupils

statesman *NOUN* **statesmen** a person, especially a man, who is important or skilled in governing a country
▷ **statesmanship** *NOUN* **stateswoman** *NOUN*

static *ADJECTIVE* not moving or changing

static electricity *NOUN* electricity that is present in something, not flowing as current

station *NOUN* **stations 1** a stopping place for trains, buses, etc. with platforms and buildings for passengers and goods **2** a building equipped for people who serve the public or for certain activities • *the police station* **3** a broadcasting company with its own frequency **4** a place where a person or thing stands or is stationed; a position [from Latin *statio* = a stand, standing]

stationary *ADJECTIVE* not moving • *The car was stationary when the van hit it.*
USAGE Do not confuse with **stationery**.

stationery *NOUN* paper, envelopes, and other articles used in writing or typing
USAGE Do not confuse with **stationary**.

statistician (stat- is- tish- an) *NOUN* **statisticians** an expert in statistics

statistics *NOUN* **1** the study of information based on the numbers of things **2** facts obtained from studying statistics

statue *NOUN* **statues** a model made of stone or metal etc. to look like a person or animal

statuette *NOUN* **statuettes** a small statue

stature *NOUN* **1** the natural height of the body **2** greatness gained by ability or achievement

status (stay- tus) *NOUN* **statuses 1** a person's or thing's position or rank in relation to others **2** high rank or prestige

statute *NOUN* **statutes** a law passed by a parliament
▷ **statutory** *ADJECTIVE*

staunch *ADJECTIVE* firm and loyal • *our staunch supporters*
▷ **staunchly** *ADVERB*

stave *VERB* **staves, staving, staved** *or* **stove** dent or break a hole in something • *The collision stove in the front of the ship.*
stave off keep something away • *We staved off the disaster.*

stave *NOUN* **staves** a set of five horizontal lines on which music is written

stay *VERB* **stays, staying, stayed 1** continue to be in the same place or condition; remain **2** spend time in a place as a visitor **3** satisfy temporarily • *We stayed our hunger with a sandwich.* **4** pause **5** show endurance in a race or task
stay put (*informal*) remain in place

Thesaurus

stately *ADJECTIVE* *a stately procession through the town* ► dignified, majestic, ceremonious, grand, splendid, imposing, noble

statement *NOUN* *The minister issued a brief statement.* ► announcement, declaration, account, report, communication, utterance

static *ADJECTIVE* **1** *a static display of work and photographs* ► stationary, immobile, motionless, fixed, still, unmoving
AN OPPOSITE IS mobile **2** *Prices have remained static for several years.* ► unchanged, steady, stable, constant, invariable, stagnant
AN OPPOSITE IS variable

station *NOUN* **1** *a nuclear power station in Armenia; a research station funded by the EU* ► establishment, facility, base, depot, post, plant, headquarters, office **2** *a radio station* ► channel, transmitter, wavelength, company **3** *It's one of the busiest railway stations in the world.* ► stopping place, terminus, halt, platform **4** *a grand station in life* ► standing, status, position, rank, situation, calling

station *VERB* *She used to date John when he was stationed in Berlin.* ► post, base, assign (to), deploy, locate, establish

stationary *ADJECTIVE* *One moment we were stationary, the next moving forward smoothly.* ► still, at a standstill, motionless, standing, immobile, at rest, halted, static
AN OPPOSITE IS moving

statistics *NOUN* *a comprehensive volume of facts, records, and statistics* ► data, figures, information, numbers

statue *NOUN* *a bronze statue of a Roman emperor* ► figure, sculpture, effigy, carving, bronze

stay *VERB* **1** *The officer told him to stay where he was.* ► wait, remain, continue, (*more informal*) hang on OPPOSITES ARE leave, depart **2** *It was vital to stay calm.* ► remain, keep, continue, carry on being **3** *He said it would be better to stay in a hotel.* ► live, lodge, reside, settle, board, dwell, be accommodated, be a guest, be housed, sojourn, stop, visit

stay *NOUN* **stays** **1** a time spent somewhere • *We made a short stay in Rome.* **2** a postponement • *a stay of execution*

stead *NOUN*
in a person's or **thing's stead** instead of this person or thing
stand a person in good stead be very useful to him or her

steadfast *ADJECTIVE* firm and not changing • *a steadfast refusal*

steady *ADJECTIVE* **steadier, steadiest** **1** not shaking or moving; firm **2** regular; continuing the same • *a steady pace*
▷ **steadily** *ADVERB* **steadiness** *NOUN*

steak *NOUN* **steaks** a thick slice of meat (especially beef) or fish [from Old Norse]

steal *VERB* **steals, stealing, stole, stolen** **1** take and keep something that does not belong to you; take secretly or dishonestly **2** move secretly or without being noticed • *He stole out of the room.*

stealthy (stelth-ee) *ADJECTIVE* **stealthier, stealthiest** quiet and secret, so as not to be noticed
▷ **stealth** *NOUN* **stealthily** *ADVERB* **stealthiness** *NOUN*

steam *NOUN* **1** the gas or vapour that comes from boiling water; this used to drive machinery **2** energy • *He ran out of steam.*
▷ **steamy** *ADJECTIVE*

steam *VERB* **steams, steaming, steamed** **1** give off steam **2** move by the power of steam • *The ship steamed down the river.* **3** cook or treat by steam • *a steamed pudding*
steam up be covered with mist or condensation

steam engine *NOUN* **steam engines** an engine driven by steam

steamroller *NOUN* **steamrollers** a heavy vehicle with a large roller used to flatten surfaces when making roads [so called because the first ones were powered by steam]

steed *NOUN* **steeds** (*old or poetical use*) a horse [from Old English]

steel *NOUN* **steels** **1** a strong metal made from iron and carbon **2** a steel rod for sharpening knives

steel *VERB* **steels, steeling, steeled**
steel yourself find courage to face something difficult

steely *ADJECTIVE* **1** like or to do with steel **2** cold, hard, and severe • *a steely glare*

steep[1] *ADJECTIVE* **1** sloping very sharply, not gradually **2** (*informal*) unreasonably high • *a steep price*
▷ **steeply** *ADVERB* **steepness** *NOUN*
[from Old English]

steep[2] *VERB* **steeps, steeping, steeped** soak thoroughly; saturate
be steeped in be completely filled or familiar

Thesaurus

stay *NOUN* **1** *I had several suitcases, in preparation for a long stay.* ► visit, stop, stopover, break, holiday, sojourn

steady *ADJECTIVE* **1** *The ladder doesn't look steady.* ► secure, stable, settled, fixed, balanced, fast, firm, solid, safe AN OPPOSITE IS unsteady. **2** *The Middle East has provided Wimpey with a steady stream of work.* ► continuous, regular, constant, even, reliable, uninterrupted, consistent, dependable, ceaseless, non-stop AN OPPOSITE IS intermittent **3** *Talk in a firm steady voice without shouting.* ► regular, even, invariable, rhythmic, smooth, uniform **4** *He didn't then have a steady girlfriend.* ► regular, habitual, settled, established, devoted, faithful, loyal, serious, steadfast

steady *VERB* **1** *Alec steadied himself as the ground shook again.* ► stabilize, balance, brace, make steady, secure **2** *I needed something to steady my nerves.* ► calm, soothe, settle, quieten, quell, control

steal *VERB* **1** *He rushed in to help when a mugger tried to steal a fan's camera. He had been caught stealing from a friend.* ► thieve, pilfer, purloin, appropriate, rob, run off with, (*more informal*) filch, (*more informal*) pinch, (*more informal*) nick, (*more informal*) swipe, (*more informal*) snaffle **2** *I stole quietly out of the room.* ► creep, slink, sneak, move stealthily, tiptoe **3** *Carson stole sideways glances at his passenger.* ► snatch, sneak, take

stealing *NOUN* *They were convicted of stealing.* ► theft, thieving, robbery, burglary, pilfering, shoplifting

stealthy *ADJECTIVE* *a lot of stealthy movement from one room to another* ► furtive, secretive, covert, secret, surreptitious, sneaking, sly, slinky, clandestine AN OPPOSITE IS blatant

steam *NOUN* *The kitchen was full of steam.* ► vapour, condensation, moisture, haze, mist

steamy *ADJECTIVE* **1** *The windows were steamy.* ► misty, cloudy, hazy **2** *the hot steamy jungle* ► humid, muggy, sticky, close, sultry, sweaty, damp, moist

steep *ADJECTIVE* **1** *steep cliffs overlooking the sea* ► precipitous, sheer, abrupt, perpendicular, vertical, sudden, sharp AN OPPOSITE IS gentle **2** *The costs seem rather steep.* ► expensive, dear, costly, exorbitant, extortionate, (*more informal*) pricey, (*more informal*) stiff OPPOSITES ARE reasonable, moderate

with something, • *The story is steeped in mystery.*
[probably from a Scandinavian language]

steepen *VERB* **steepens, steepening, steepened** make or become steeper

steeple *NOUN* **steeples** a church tower with a spire on top

steer *VERB* **steers, steering, steered** make a car, ship, or bicycle etc. go in the direction you want; guide
▷ **steersman** *NOUN*
steer clear of take care to avoid

steering wheel *NOUN* **steering wheels** a wheel for steering a car, boat, etc.

stem[1] *NOUN* **stems 1** the main central part of a tree, shrub, or plant **2** a thin part on which a leaf, flower, or fruit is supported **3** a thin upright part, e.g. the thin part of a wineglass between the bowl and the foot **4** the main part of a verb or other word, to which endings are attached **5** the front part of a ship • *from stem to stern*

stem *VERB* **stems, stemming, stemmed**
stem from arise from; have as its source
[from Old English]

stem[2] *VERB* **stems, stemming, stemmed** stop the flow of something [from Old Norse]

stench *NOUN* **stenches** a very unpleasant smell

stencil *NOUN* **stencils** a piece of card, metal, or plastic with pieces cut out of it, used to produce a picture or design etc.

step *NOUN* **steps 1** a movement made by lifting the foot and setting it down **2** the sound of a person putting down their foot when walking or running **3** a level surface for placing the foot on in climbing up or down **4** each of a series of things done in some process or action • *The first step is to find somewhere to practise.*
in step 1 stepping in time with others in marching or dancing **2** in agreement
watch your step be careful

step *VERB* **steps, stepping, stepped** tread or walk
step in intervene
step on it (*informal*) hurry
step up increase something

stepfather *NOUN* **stepfathers** a man who is married to your mother but is not your natural father

stepladder *NOUN* **stepladders** a folding ladder with flat treads

stepmother *NOUN* **stepmothers** a woman who is married to your father but is not your natural mother

stepping stone *NOUN* **stepping stones 1** each of a line of stones put into a shallow stream so that people can walk across **2** a way of achieving something, or a stage in achieving it • *good exam results can be a stepping stone to a career*

stereo *NOUN* **stereos 1** stereophonic sound or recording **2** a stereophonic CD player, record player, etc.

stereophonic *ADJECTIVE* using sound that comes from two different directions to give a natural effect

stereotype *NOUN* **stereotypes** a fixed idea or image of a person or thing • *The stereotype of a hero is one who is tall, strong, brave, and good-looking.*
▷ **stereotypical** *ADJECTIVE*

sterile *ADJECTIVE* **1** not fertile; barren **2** free from germs
▷ **sterility** *NOUN*

Thesaurus

steer *VERB* *She steered the huge vehicle into the garage.* ► direct, drive, guide, navigate, control, pilot
steer clear of *The rickety old barn was a place to steer clear of.* ► avoid, keep away from, give a wide berth to

step *NOUN* **1** *She took a step backwards.* ► pace, stride, footstep **2** *Anyone seeking political asylum is taking a major step.* ► decision, move, action, course, measure **3** *This was a good first step towards retaining her title.* ► phase, stage, action, measure, manoeuvre **4** *an important step towards achieving peace* ► advance, movement, progress, progression **5 steps** *I climbed the steps and knocked on the door.* ► stairs, staircase

step *VERB* *I stepped over several mounds of brick and rubble.* ► tread, put your foot, walk, stamp, trample
step down *The minister would step down at the next election.* ► resign, stand down, retire, (*more informal*) quit
step up *The army stepped up the attack.* ► intensify, increase, escalate, augment, boost

sterile *ADJECTIVE* **1** *sterile soil* ► infertile, barren, unproductive, arid, dry, lifeless
AN OPPOSITE IS fertile **2** *a sterile bandage* ► sterilized, antiseptic, aseptic, clean, disinfected, germ-free, hygienic, uninfected
AN OPPOSITE IS unsterilized **3** *a sterile discussion* ► fruitless, unfruitful, pointless, unprofitable, useless, abortive, hopeless
AN OPPOSITE IS fruitful

sterilize *VERB* **sterilizes, sterilizing, sterilized** **1** make a thing free from germs, e.g. by heating it **2** make a person or animal unable to reproduce
▷ **sterilization** *NOUN* **sterilizer** *NOUN*

sterling *NOUN* British money

sterling *ADJECTIVE* **1** genuine • *sterling silver* **2** excellent; of great worth • *her sterling qualities*

stern[1] *ADJECTIVE* strict and severe, not lenient or kindly
▷ **sternly** *ADVERB* **sternness** *NOUN*

stern[2] *NOUN* **sterns** the back part of a ship

stew *VERB* **stews, stewing, stewed** cook slowly in liquid

stew *NOUN* **stews** a dish of stewed food, especially meat and vegetables
in a stew (*informal*) very worried or agitated

steward *NOUN* **stewards** **1** a man whose job is to look after the passengers on a ship or aircraft **2** an official who keeps order or looks after the arrangements at a large public event

stewardess *NOUN* **stewardesses** a woman whose job is to look after the passengers on a ship or aircraft

stick[1] *NOUN* **sticks** **1** a long thin piece of wood **2** a walking stick **3** the implement used to hit the ball in hockey, polo, etc. **4** a long thin piece of something • *a stick of rock*

stick[2] *VERB* **sticks, sticking, stuck** **1** push a thing into something • *Stick a pin in it.* **2** fix or be fixed by glue or as if by this • *Stick stamps on the parcel.* **3** become fixed and unable to move • *The drawer keeps sticking.* **4** (*informal*) endure or tolerate • *I can't stick that noise!*
stick out **1** come or push out from a surface; stand out from the surrounding area **2** be very noticeable
stick to **1** remain faithful to a friend or promise etc. **2** keep to and not alter • *He stuck to his story.*
stick together **1** stay together **2** support each other
stick up for (*informal*) stand up for
be stuck with (*informal*) be unable to avoid something unwelcome

stickler *NOUN* **sticklers** a person who insists on something • *a stickler for punctuality*

sticky *ADJECTIVE* **stickier, stickiest** **1** able or likely to stick to things **2** (said about weather) hot and humid, causing perspiration **3** (*informal*) difficult or awkward • *a sticky situation*
▷ **stickily** *ADVERB* **stickiness** *NOUN*
come to a sticky end (*informal*) die or end in a painful or unpleasant way

Thesaurus

sterilize *VERB* **1** *The room should be clean but you don't have to sterilize everything.* ▸ disinfect, fumigate, decontaminate, make sterile, pasteurize, purify, clean, cleanse OPPOSITES ARE contaminate, infect **2** *In the poorest families both husband and wife have been sterilized.* ▸ make infertile, give a hysterectomy *or* vasectomy to

stern *ADJECTIVE* **1** *Their father looked stern for a while, but soon went to them.* ▸ severe, strict, harsh, grim, grave, serious, austere, authoritarian, dour OPPOSITES ARE genial, kindly **2** *Stern measures were needed.* ▸ strict, severe, stringent, rigorous, harsh, drastic, tough OPPOSITES ARE lenient, lax

stew *NOUN* *stew for dinner* ▸ casserole, hot-pot, ragout, goulash, hash

stick *NOUN* **1** *a pile of dry sticks* ▸ twig, branch, stalk **2** *She threatened him with a stick.* ▸ rod, cane

stick *VERB* **1** *Iris stuck her fork in the earth.* ▸ poke, prod, dig, jab, stab, thrust **2** *He stuck a message on her computer screen.* ▸ affix, attach, fasten, fix, glue, paste, pin **3** *The plastic seats stuck to her skin.* ▸ adhere, cling, bond, fuse **4** (*informal*) *I've got some stewed fruit I stuck in the freezer.* ▸ put, place, leave, deposit, drop, (*informal*) bung, (*informal*) dump **5** *The wheels stuck in the soft mud.* ▸ become trapped, jam **6** *A particular memory stuck in his mind.* ▸ remain, linger, persist, stay **7** (*informal*) *I couldn't stick it any longer.* ▸ tolerate, put up with
stick at (*informal*) *If you want to learn a language, you'll have to stick at it.* ▸ persevere with, persist with, keep at, work hard at
stick out *He had his hands on his hips and his chin stuck out.* ▸ jut out, protrude, project
stick to *She advises her staff to stick to six basic safety guidelines.* ▸ abide by, adhere to, keep, hold to, fulfil
stick up *The monument sticks up above the trees.* ▸ rise, stand out, loom, tower
stick up for *I was born here and I try to stick up for Britain.* ▸ support, defend, stand up for

sticky *ADJECTIVE* **1** *She tied up the package with sticky tape.* ▸ adhesive, gummed, self-adhesive, glued **2** *There was a patch of sticky fluid on the carpet.* ▸ gluey, tacky, gummy, treacly, (*more informal*) gooey AN OPPOSITE IS dry **3** *It was a hot sticky afternoon.* ▸ humid, muggy, sultry, clammy, close OPPOSITES ARE fresh, cool

stiff *ADJECTIVE* **1** not bending or moving or changing its shape easily **2** not fluid; hard to stir • *a stiff dough* **3** difficult • *a stiff examination* **4** formal in manner; not friendly **5** severe or strong • *a stiff breeze*
▷ **stiffly** *ADVERB* **stiffness** *NOUN*

stiffen *VERB* **stiffens, stiffening, stiffened** make or become stiff
▷ **stiffener** *NOUN*

stifle *VERB* **stifles, stifling, stifled 1** suffocate **2** suppress • *She stifled a yawn.*

stigma *NOUN* **stigmas 1** a mark of disgrace **2** part of a flower's pistil that receives the pollen [from Greek]

stile *NOUN* **stiles** an arrangement of steps or bars for people to climb over a fence

stiletto heel *NOUN* **stiletto heels** a high pointed shoe heel

still *ADJECTIVE* **1** not moving • *still water* **2** silent **3** not fizzy
▷ **stillness** *NOUN*

still *ADVERB* **1** without moving • *Stand still.* **2** up to this or that time • *He was still there.* **3** in a greater amount or degree • *You can do still better.* **4** nevertheless • *They've lost. Still, they tried, and that was good.*

stillborn *ADJECTIVE* born dead

still life *NOUN* **still lifes** a painting of lifeless things such as ornaments and fruit

stilted *ADJECTIVE* stiffly formal

stilts *PLURAL NOUN* a pair of poles with supports for the feet so that the user can walk high above the ground

stimulate *VERB* **stimulates, stimulating, stimulated 1** make someone excited or enthusiastic **2** cause or arouse • *The programme has stimulated a lot of interest in her work.*
▷ **stimulant** *NOUN* **stimulation** *NOUN*

sting *NOUN* **stings 1** a sharp-pointed part of an animal or plant, often containing a poison, that can cause a wound **2** a painful wound caused by this part

sting *VERB* **stings, stinging, stung 1** wound or hurt with a sting **2** feel a sharp pain **3** make someone feel upset or hurt • *I was stung by this criticism.* **4** (*slang*) cheat a person by overcharging; extort money from someone

stingy (**stin**-jee) *ADJECTIVE* **stingier, stingiest** mean, not generous; giving or given in small amounts
▷ **stingily** *ADVERB* **stinginess** *NOUN*

Thesaurus

stiff *ADJECTIVE* **1** *You'll need a sheet of stiff cardboard.* ► rigid, firm, hard OPPOSITES ARE limp, flexible **2** *Make a stiff paste.* ► thick, firm, semi-solid, viscous **3** *Her muscles were stiff. I was so stiff it was difficult to climb upstairs.* ► achy, aching, arthritic, painful, immovable, rheumatic, taut, tight AN OPPOSITE IS supple **4** *a long stiff climb up the hillside* ► arduous, strenuous, difficult, tough, exacting, hard, tiring AN OPPOSITE IS easy **5** *We will face some stiff competition later this year.* ► strong, powerful, severe **6** *His manner was stiff and aloof.* ► formal, reserved, unfriendly, cool, awkward AN OPPOSITE IS relaxed **7** *The judge handed out stiff sentences.* ► harsh, severe, punitive, strict, hard, swingeing AN OPPOSITE IS lenient **8** *A stiff breeze made it hard going.* ► fresh, strong, brisk AN OPPOSITE IS gentle **9** *They all needed a stiff drink.* ► strong, potent, alcoholic AN OPPOSITE IS weak

stifle *VERB* **1** *The heat can stifle you.* ► suffocate, choke, smother **2** *Margaret stifled a cough. The policy has stifled realistic thinking.* ► suppress, check, smother, restrain, muffle, curb

still *ADJECTIVE* **1** *Paul stood still and looked around.* ► motionless, immobile, stationary, unmoving, static, inert, lifeless AN OPPOSITE IS moving **2** *The evening was warm and still* ► quiet, calm, silent, soundless, noiseless, wind-free OPPOSITES ARE windy, stormy

stimulate *VERB* **1** *The literature course stimulated their interest in modern fiction.* ► trigger, activate, kindle, rouse, arouse, stir, increase, enhance AN OPPOSITE IS discourage **2** *The right words from you might stimulate them to keep trying.* ► encourage, prompt, motivate, inspire, provoke

stimulating *ADJECTIVE* *a stimulating lecture by Professor Smithers* ► thought-provoking, interesting, entertaining, challenging, exciting, rousing, stirring, exhilarating, inspiring, invigorating, provoking OPPOSITES ARE boring, dull

stimulus *NOUN* *Cash is the best stimulus to economic development in the region.* ► spur, stimulant, encouragement, incentive, inducement, impetus, fillip AN OPPOSITE IS deterrent

sting *NOUN* **1** *an ointment to soothe a wasp sting* ► bite, prick, wound **2** *He felt the sting of the wound still.* ► smarting, stinging, pain, burn, pricking

sting *VERB* **1** *an insect that stings.* ► bite, nip, prick **2** *The salt water began to sting.* ► smart, tingle, hurt, burn

stingy *ADJECTIVE* *Derek was notoriously stingy.* ► mean, miserly, niggardly, penny-pinching, parsimonious, (*more informal*) tight-fisted AN OPPOSITE IS generous

stink *NOUN* **stinks** **1** an unpleasant smell **2** (*informal*) an unpleasant fuss or protest

stink *VERB* **stinks, stinking, stank** *or* **stunk** have an unpleasant smell

stint *NOUN* **stints** **1** a fixed amount of work to be done **2** limitation of a supply or effort • *They gave help without stint.*

stint *VERB* **stints, stinting, stinted** be sparing; restrict to a small amount • *Don't stint on the cream.*

stir *VERB* **stirs, stirring, stirred** **1** mix a liquid or soft mixture by moving a spoon etc. round and round in it **2** move slightly; start to move **3** excite or stimulate • *They stirred up trouble.*

stir *NOUN* **1** the action of stirring **2** a disturbance; excitement • *The news caused a stir.*

stir-fry *VERB* **stir-fries, stir-frying, stir-fried** cook by frying quickly over a high heat while stirring and tossing
▷ **stir-fry** *NOUN*

stirrup *NOUN* **stirrups** a metal part that hangs from each side of a horse's saddle, for a rider to put his or her foot in

stitch *NOUN* **stitches** **1** a loop of thread made in sewing or knitting **2** a method of arranging the threads • *cross stitch* **3** a sudden sharp pain in the side of the body, caused by running

stitch *VERB* **stitches, stitching, stitched** sew or fasten with stitches

stoat *NOUN* **stoats** a kind of weasel

stock *NOUN* **stocks** **1** a number of things kept ready to be sold or used **2** livestock **3** a line of ancestors • *a man of Irish stock* **4** a number of shares in a company's capital **5** liquid made by stewing meat, fish, or vegetables, used for making soup etc. **6** the main stem of a tree or plant **7** the base, holder, or handle of an implement, weapon, etc. **8** a garden flower with a sweet smell **9** a kind of cravat

stock *VERB* **stocks, stocking, stocked** **1** keep goods in stock **2** provide a place with a stock of something
stock up buy a supply of goods etc.

stockade *NOUN* **stockades** a fence made of stakes

stockbroker *NOUN* **stockbrokers** a broker who deals in stocks and shares

stock exchange *NOUN* **stock exchanges** a country's central place for buying and selling stocks and shares

stocking *NOUN* **stockings** a piece of clothing covering the foot and part or all of the leg

stock market *NOUN* **stock markets** **1** a stock exchange **2** the buying and selling of stocks and shares

stockpile *NOUN* **stockpiles** a large stock of things kept in reserve
▷ **stockpile** *VERB*

stocks *PLURAL NOUN* a wooden structure in which people used to be locked as a public punishment

stock-still *ADJECTIVE* quite still

stocktaking *NOUN* the counting, listing, and checking of the amount of stock held by a shop or business

stocky *ADJECTIVE* **stockier, stockiest** short and solidly built • *a stocky man*

stodgy *ADJECTIVE* **stodgier, stodgiest** **1** (said about food) heavy and filling **2** dull and boring • *a stodgy book*
▷ **stodginess** *NOUN*

Thesaurus

stink *VERB* **1** *The room stank of smoke.* ► reek, smell, (*more informal*) pong

stink *NOUN* *The stink hits you as soon as you open the door.* ► stench, reek, foul smell, odour, (*more informal*) pong, (*more informal*) niff

stint *NOUN* *a three-month stint on night duty* ► spell, stretch, period, term, turn, shift, run, session

stir *NOUN* *The arrival of the royal car caused quite a stir.* ► commotion, fuss, excitement, disturbance, sensation, to-do

stir *VERB* **1** *Use a wooden spoon to stir the mixture.* ► mix, blend, beat, agitate, whisk, fold in **2** *Mary stirred in her sleep.* ► quiver, tremble, twitch, move slightly **3** *A gentle breeze stirred.* ► rustle, shake, flutter **4** *a thought to stir our imaginations* ► kindle, rouse, arouse, stimulate, excite, inspire, trigger, activate
stir up *These remarks stirred up considerable anger.* ► whip up, work up, rouse, arouse, trigger, spark off, provoke

stitch *VERB* *He stitched a patch on his jeans.* ► sew, tack, darn, mend, repair

stock *NOUN* **1** *a stock of fuel; a stock of jokes* ► supply, store, hoard, reserve, quantity, cache, fund **2** *During winter the stock is kept in sheds.* ► livestock, farm animals, cattle, beasts **3** *The shop will be closed for a day to review its stock.* ► merchandise, goods, wares, commodities, **4** *He is descended from Italian stock.* ► descent, ancestry, origins, parentage, pedigree, heritage

stodgy *ADJECTIVE* **1** *a rich stodgy pudding* ► starchy, indigestible, heavy, lumpy, soggy, solid, filling AN OPPOSITE IS light **2** *a stodgy story about his childhood* ► boring, dull, tedious, turgid, unexciting, unimaginative, uninteresting, stuffy OPPOSITES ARE lively, exciting

A B C D E F G H I J K L M N O P Q R S T U V W X Y Z

stoical (stoh- ik- al) *ADJECTIVE* bearing pain or difficulties etc. calmly without complaining
▷ **stoically** *ADVERB* **stoicism** *NOUN*

stoke *VERB* **stokes, stoking, stoked** put fuel in a furnace or on a fire
▷ **stoker** *NOUN*

stole *past tense of* **steal**

stolid *ADJECTIVE* not showing much emotion or excitement
▷ **stolidly** *ADVERB* **stolidity** *NOUN*

stomach *NOUN* **stomachs** **1** the part of the body where food starts to be digested **2** the abdomen

stomach *VERB* **stomachs, stomaching, stomached** endure or tolerate

stone *NOUN* **stones** **1** a piece of rock **2** stones or rock as material, e.g. for building **3** a jewel **4** the hard case round the kernel of plums, cherries, etc. **5** a unit of weight equal to 14 pounds (635 kg) • *She weighs 8 stone.*

stone *VERB* **stones, stoning, stoned** **1** throw stones at somebody **2** remove the stones from fruit [from Old English]

Stone Age *NOUN* the earliest period of human history, when tools and weapons were made of stone

stone-cold *ADJECTIVE* extremely cold

stone-deaf *ADJECTIVE* completely deaf

stony *ADJECTIVE* **1** full of stones **2** like stone; hard **3** unfriendly and not answering • *a stony silence*

stool *NOUN* **stools** **1** a movable seat without arms or a back **2** a footstool **3** a lump of faeces

stoop *VERB* **stoops, stooping, stooped** **1** bend your body forwards and down **2** lower yourself • *He would not stoop to cheating.*
▷ **stoop** *NOUN*

stop *VERB* **stops, stopping, stopped** **1** bring or come to an end; no longer do something **2** be no longer moving or working • *A car stopped in front of us.* **3** prevent or obstruct something **4** stay for a short time **5** fill a hole

stop *NOUN* **stops** **1** stopping; a pause or end **2** a place where a bus or train etc. regularly stops **3** a punctuation mark, especially a full stop **4** a lever or knob that controls pitch in a wind instrument or allows organ pipes to sound

stopcock *NOUN* **stopcocks** a valve controlling the flow of liquid or gas in a pipe

stopgap *NOUN* **stopgaps** a temporary substitute

stoppage *NOUN* **stoppages** **1** an interruption in the work of a factory etc. **2** a blockage **3** an amount taken off someone's wages

stopper *NOUN* **stoppers** a plug for closing a bottle etc.

stopwatch *NOUN* **stopwatches** a watch that can be started and stopped when you wish, used for timing races etc.

store *NOUN* **stores** **1** a supply of things kept for future use **2** a place where things are kept until they are needed **3** a shop, especially a large one
in store **1** being stored **2** going to happen • *There's a surprise in store for you.*
set store by something value it greatly

store *VERB* **stores, storing, stored** keep things until they are needed
▷ **storage** *NOUN*

Thesaurus

stomach *NOUN* *I was hungry and my stomach started to rumble.* ► gut, belly, abdomen, (*more informal*) tummy RELATED ADJECTIVE gastric

stone *NOUN* **1** *A gang threw stones.* ► rock, pebble, boulder **2** *a ring with a bright red stone* ► gem, gemstone, jewel **3** *A memorial stone stood by the grave.* ► gravestone, headstone, tombstone, tablet

stony *ADJECTIVE* **1** *a stony path* ► rocky, pebbly, rough, shingly **2** *a stony silence* ► unfriendly, cold, chilly, frosty, icy, hostile, stern, severe, unfeeling, heartless AN OPPOSITE IS friendly

stoop *VERB* **1** *Fred stooped to pick up the dog.* ► crouch, bend, kneel, lean, squat, bow, duck **2** *I would never stoop to accepting such an idea.* ► lower yourself, sink, descend, condescend, deign

stop *VERB* **1** *measures taken to stop tax fraud* ► check, prevent, thwart, frustrate, reduce, put and end to, put a stop to OPPOSITES ARE start, encourage **2** *He wanted to stop smoking.* ► give up, discontinue, cease, desist from, refrain from, quit OPPOSITES ARE begin, start, resume **3** *The bus stopped near the corner.* ► halt, come to a stop, come to a halt, pull up, draw up, pull in, come to rest **4** *He tried to stop her leaving the house.* ► prevent, intercept, hinder, obstruct, bar **5** *a special dressing to stop the escape of blood* ► stem, staunch, check, restrict, block, arrest

stop *NOUN* **1** *Business came to a stop for the day.* ► halt, end, finish, standstill, conclusion, stoppage, cessation **2** *They had a short stop at the motorway services.* ► break, pause, stopover, rest

store *NOUN* **1** *a store of food* ► supply, stock, hoard, reserve, quantity, cache, fund **2** *the coal store* ► storeroom, storehouse, repository, depository **3** *a DIY store* ► shop, outlet, retail business, retailers, supermarket, mart

store *VERB* *a place to store food for the winter* ► stow, keep, save, put aside, hoard, accumulate, amass, lay by, deposit, (*more informal*) stash

storehouse *NOUN* **storehouses** a building for storing goods

storey *NOUN* **storeys** one whole floor of a building
USAGE Do not confuse with **story**.

stork *NOUN* **storks** a large bird with long legs and a long beak

storm *NOUN* **storms** **1** a very strong wind usually with rain, snow, etc. **2** a violent attack or outburst • *a storm of protest*
▷ **stormy** *ADJECTIVE*
a storm in a teacup a great fuss over something unimportant

storm *VERB* **storms, storming, stormed** **1** move or behave violently or angrily • *He stormed out of the room.* **2** suddenly attack and capture a place • *They stormed the castle.*

story *NOUN* **stories** **1** an account of a real or imaginary event **2** the plot of a play or novel etc. **3** (*informal*) a lie • *Don't tell stories!* [from Latin *historia* = history]
USAGE Do not confuse with **storey**.

stout *ADJECTIVE* **1** rather fat **2** thick and strong **3** brave and determined • *a stout defender of human rights*
▷ **stoutly** *ADVERB* **stoutness** *NOUN*

stove[1] *NOUN* **stoves** **1** a device containing an oven or ovens **2** a device for heating a room

stove[2] *past tense of* **stave**

stow *VERB* **stows, stowing, stowed** pack or store something away
▷ **stowage** *NOUN*
stow away hide on a ship or aircraft so as to travel without paying **stowaway** *NOUN*

straddle *VERB* **straddles, straddling, straddled** have a position across or astride something

straggle *VERB* **straggles, straggling, straggled** **1** grow or spread in an untidy way **2** lag behind; wander on your own
▷ **straggler** *NOUN* **straggly** *ADJECTIVE*

straight *ADJECTIVE* **1** going continuously in one direction; not curving or bending **2** level or upright • *Is the picture straight?* **3** tidy; in proper order **4** honest and frank • *a straight answer*
▷ **straightness** *NOUN*

straight *ADVERB* **1** in a straight line or manner **2** directly; without delay • *Go straight home.*
straight away immediately
USAGE Do not confuse with **strait**.

straighten *VERB* **straightens, straightening, straightened** make or become straight

Thesaurus

storm *NOUN* **1** *A storm blew up out at sea.* ► tempest, gale, squall, hurricane, typhoon, deluge **2** *a storm of protest* ► outburst, outcry, uproar, clamour, commotion, furore

storm *VERB* **1** *Police decided to storm the building.* ► attack, assault, rush, charge **2** *He stormed out in a rage.* ► march, stomp, stalk, flounce

stormy *ADJECTIVE* **1** *The weather was wet and stormy.* ► blustery, squally, tempestuous, turbulent, gusty, wild AN OPPOSITE IS calm

story *NOUN* **1** *the dramatic story of a rescue at sea; What happened that night turned out to be a long story.* ► tale, account, narrative, history, yarn, (*more informal*) spiel **2** *a novel with a gripping story* ► plot, storyline, scenario **3** *She read the newspaper stories.* ► news item, report, article, feature, piece

stout *ADJECTIVE* **1** *You'll need a stout pair of boots.* ► sturdy, strong, substantial, robust, solid, thick, tough, reliable, sound AN OPPOSITE IS flimsy **2** *The small stout man marched on ahead.* ► fat, plump, stocky, portly, beefy, bulky, burly, chubby, heavy, tubby, well-built OPPOSITES ARE thin, slender **3** *The defenders put up a stout resistance.* ► brave, courageous, determined, spirited, valiant, strong, forceful, staunch, resolute, firm AN OPPOSITE IS feeble

stow *VERB* *He left her to stow the shopping in the fridge.* ► store, load, put, stack, (*more informal*) stuff, (*more informal*) stash

straight *ADJECTIVE* **1** *They were driving along a straight stretch of road* ► direct, smooth, undeviating, unswerving OPPOSITES ARE winding, crooked **2** *I'll make the room straight for our visitors.* ► tidy, neat, orderly, shipshape, organized, right AN OPPOSITE IS untidy **3** *They have staged something of a comeback with three straight victories.* ► consecutive, continuous, unbroken, uninterrupted, non-stop **4** *John is a straight character and very much his own man. I'll give you a straight answer if I can.* ► honest, direct, frank, straightforward AN OPPOSITE IS evasive

straight *ADVERB* *We would be walking straight into a trap. She looked straight into his face.* ► directly, squarely, plumb, (*more informal*) slap bang
straight away *He went to see her straight away when he got the news.* ► at once, directly, immediately, instantly, now, without delay

straighten *VERB* *Rick straightened his tie.* ► adjust, arrange, put straight, neaten, order
straighten out *It will take a while to straighten out all the confusion.* ► sort out, put right,

straightforward ADJECTIVE **1** easy, not complicated **2** honest and frank

strain[1] VERB **strains, straining, strained** **1** injure or weaken something by stretching or working it too hard **2** stretch tightly **3** make a great effort **4** put something through a sieve or filter to separate liquid from solid matter

strain NOUN **strains** **1** straining; the force of straining **2** an injury caused by straining **3** something that uses up strength, patience, resources, etc. **4** exhaustion **5** a part of a tune

strain[2] NOUN **strains** **1** a breed or variety of animals, plants, etc.; a line of descent **2** an inherited characteristic • *There's an artistic strain in the family.*

strait NOUN **straits** a narrow stretch of water connecting two seas
USAGE Do not confuse with **straight**.

straits PLURAL NOUN **1** a strait • *the Straits of Dover* **2** a difficult condition • *We were in dire straits when we lost our money.*

strand[1] NOUN **strands** **1** each of the threads or wires etc. twisted together to form a rope, yarn, or cable **2** a single thread or hair **3** one idea or theme of several in a story

strand[2] VERB **strands, stranding, stranded** **be stranded** **1** (said about a boat) run onto sand or rocks in shallow water **2** be left in a difficult or helpless position • *We were stranded when our car broke down.*

strange ADJECTIVE **1** unusual or surprising **2** not known or seen or experienced before
▷ **strangely** ADVERB **strangeness** NOUN

stranger NOUN **strangers** a person you do not know, or who is in a place they do not know

strangle VERB **strangles, strangling, strangled** **1** kill by squeezing the throat to prevent breathing **2** restrict something so that it does not develop
▷ **strangler** NOUN

strap NOUN **straps** a flat strip of leather or cloth etc. for fastening things or holding them in place

strap VERB **straps, strapping, strapped** fasten with a strap or straps; bind

strapping ADJECTIVE tall and healthy-looking • *a strapping lad*

strata (strah-ta, stray-ta) PLURAL NOUN layers or levels, especially of rock

Thesaurus

settle, disentangle, make straight, clear up, tidy, unbend, untwist

straightforward ADJECTIVE *It is hard to resist one straightforward conclusion. They seem straightforward enough.* ► blunt, candid, direct, easy, forthright, frank, genuine, honest, intelligible, lucid, open, plain, simple, sincere, straight, truthful, uncomplicated
AN OPPOSITE IS devious

strain VERB **1** *The dog strained at its leash.* ► tug, pull, stretch, haul, tighten **2** *Martha strained to hear but heard only faint sounds.* ► strive, struggle, make an effort, endeavour, exert yourself, attempt, try **3** *Try not to strain yourself.* ► weaken, wear out, exhaust, tire out, weary **4** *She had strained a muscle in the last race.* ► pull, sprain, twist, wrench, rick, damage, hurt, injure **5** *Strain the liquid to remove impurities.* ► sieve, sift, filter, separate

strain NOUN *the strain of doing jobs for which they are unsuited* ► stress, pressure, tension, worry, anxiety, burden, difficulty, effort

strained ADJECTIVE *the strained relations between Russia and Japan; The dark gaze was intent on her strained face.* ► tense, awkward, uneasy, fraught, uncomfortable, troubled
AN OPPOSITE IS relaxed

strand NOUN *Sibyl frowned, absent-mindedly twirling a strand of hair round her fingers.* ► fibre, filament, string, thread, wire

stranded ADJECTIVE **1** *marks left by jellyfish stranded on the beach* ► grounded, run aground, marooned, beached **2** *The waiting rooms were filled with stranded passengers.* ► helpless, abandoned, deserted, forsaken, lost

strange ADJECTIVE **1** *I heard a strange noise outside.* ► odd, unusual, weird, peculiar, curious, funny, extraordinary, unexplained AN OPPOSITE IS ordinary **2** *They wear strange clothes.* ► weird, eccentric, bizarre, unconventional, idiosyncratic, (*more informal*) oddball, (*more informal*) wacky AN OPPOSITE IS normal **3** *He found it hard to get to sleep in a strange house.* ► unfamiliar, unknown, new, alien AN OPPOSITE IS familiar **4** *She began to feel a little strange and went to the bathroom.* ► unwell, ill, sick, poorly, indisposed, (*more informal*) funny AN OPPOSITE IS well

stranger NOUN *They were strangers in the town.* ► newcomer, outsider, visitor, alien, foreigner, guest

strangle VERB **1** *The bird had been strangled by the wire fence.* ► throttle, asphyxiate, choke, suffocate, strangulate **2** *She strangled a cry of alarm.* ► suppress, smother, stifle, restrain, choke back

strap NOUN *The package was tied with straps.* ► thong, tie, belt, cord

strap VERB *He strapped the bag to his bicycle.* ► fasten, secure, tie, bind, lash

strategy *NOUN* **strategies** **1** a plan or policy to achieve something • *our economic strategy* **2** the planning of a war or campaign COMPARE **tactics** [from Greek *strategos* = a general]

stratosphere *NOUN* a layer of the atmosphere between about 10 and 60 kilometres above the earth's surface

straw *NOUN* **straws** **1** dry cut stalks of corn **2** a narrow tube for drinking through [from Old English]

strawberry *NOUN* **strawberries** a small red juicy fruit, with its seeds on the outside

stray *VERB* **strays, straying, strayed** leave a group or proper place and wander; get lost

stray *ADJECTIVE* that has become lost or separated • *a stray cat* • *a stray sock*
▷ **stray** *NOUN*

streak *NOUN* **streaks** **1** a long thin line or mark **2** a trace • *a streak of cruelty* **3** a spell of success, luck, etc. • *on a winning streak*
▷ **streaky** *ADJECTIVE*

streak *VERB* **streaks, streaking, streaked** **1** mark with streaks **2** move very quickly **3** run naked in a public place for fun or to get attention
▷ **streaker** *NOUN*

stream *NOUN* **streams** **1** water flowing in a channel; a brook or small river **2** a flow of liquid or of things or people **3** a group in which children of similar ability are placed in a school

stream *VERB* **streams, streaming, streamed** **1** move in or like a stream **2** produce a stream of liquid **3** arrange schoolchildren in streams according to their ability

streamline *VERB* **streamlines, streamlining, streamlined** **1** give something a smooth shape that helps it to move easily through air or water **2** organize something so that it works more efficiently
▷ **streamlined** *ADJECTIVE*

street *NOUN* **streets** a road with houses beside it in a city or village [via Old English from Latin *strata via* = paved way]

strength *NOUN* **strengths** **1** how strong a person or thing is; being strong **2** an ability or good quality • *Patience is your great strength.*

strengthen *VERB* **strengthens, strengthening, strengthened** make or become stronger

stress *NOUN* **stresses** **1** a force that acts on something, e.g. by pressing, pulling, or twisting it; strain **2** emphasis, especially the extra force with which you pronounce part of a word or phrase **3** distress caused by having too many problems or too much to do

Thesaurus

stray *VERB* **1** *The aircraft had strayed into unauthorized airspace.* ► wander, drift, roam, meander **2** *We are rather straying from the main point.* ► digress, diverge, drift, wander, deviate, be sidetracked

streak *NOUN* **1** *His hair had several streaks of white.* ► strip, stripe, vein, band, line, smear, stain **2** *She admits to having a competitive streak in her.* ► element, trace, component

streak *VERB* **1** *Their dirty faces were streaked with tears.* ► stain, smear, smudge, daub **2** *Huge lorries streaked past him.* ► hurtle, rush, speed, tear, flash, zoom, whistle

streaky *ADJECTIVE* *The windows were streaky from the rain.* ► smeary, smudged, streaked, lined, stripy, veined

stream *NOUN* **1** *a mountain stream* ► brook, burn, beck, rill, river, rivulet, watercourse, channel **2** *a stream of water* ► jet, flow, rush, gush, surge, spurt, spout

stream *VERB* *Rain streamed through the hole.* ► flow, pour, gush, surge, spurt, flood

street *NOUN* *The streets are deserted at this time of night.* ► road, avenue, boulevard, thoroughfare

strength *NOUN* **1** *Physical strength is important.* ► power, brawn, muscle, toughness, sturdiness, robustness, vigour, might AN OPPOSITE IS weakness **2** *She has enormous strength of character.* ► courage, firmness, resolution, spirit, commitment AN OPPOSITE IS feebleness

strengthen *VERB* **1** *The exercises will help strengthen your back.* ► build up, fortify, toughen, make stronger, harden, tone up AN OPPOSITE IS weaken **2** *Stone supports strengthen the massive walls.* ► bolster, reinforce, support, brace, buttress, prop up **3** *The police want to strengthen their links with the local communities.* ► consolidate, reinforce, substantiate, bolster, fortify, enhance, back up, increase, invigorate AN OPPOSITE IS undermine

strenuous *ADJECTIVE* **1** *Success was the result of three years' strenuous work.* ► hard, tough, demanding, arduous, taxing, gruelling, exhausting **2** *He has made strenuous efforts to get to know the area.* ► vigorous, determined, resolute, energetic, active, forceful

stress *NOUN* **1** *She was obviously under a lot of stress.* ► anxiety, difficulty, hardship, pressure, strain, tension, trauma, worry **2** *We need to lay*

A B C D E F G H I J K L M N O P Q R S T U V W X Y Z

stress VERB **stresses, stressing, stressed** **1** emphasize a point or idea • *I must stress the importance of arriving on time.* **2** pronounce part of a word or phrase with extra emphasis **3** cause stress to someone

stretch VERB **stretches, stretching, stretched** **1** pull something or be pulled so that it becomes longer or wider or larger **2** extend or be continuous • *The wall stretches right round the estate.* **3** push out your arms and legs as far as you can **4** make use of all your ability or intelligence • *This course should really stretch you.*
stretch out lie down with your arms and legs at full length

stretch NOUN **stretches** **1** the action of stretching **2** a continuous period of time or area of land or water

stretcher NOUN **stretchers** a framework for carrying a sick or injured person

strict ADJECTIVE **1** demanding obedience and good behaviour • *a strict teacher* **2** complete or exact • *in strict confidence* • *the strict truth*
▷ **strictly** ADVERB **strictness** NOUN

stride VERB **strides, striding, strode, stridden** walk with long steps

stride NOUN **strides** **1** a long step when walking or running **2** progress
get into your stride settle into a fast and steady pace of working
take something in your stride manage or deal with something without difficulty

strife NOUN conflict; fighting or quarrelling

strike VERB **strikes, striking, struck** **1** hit **2** attack suddenly • *Plague struck the village.* **3** make an impression on someone's mind • *She strikes me as truthful.* **4** light a match by rubbing it against a rough surface **5** refuse to work as a protest against pay or conditions **6** produce by pressing or stamping something • *They are striking some special coins.* **7** sound • *The clock struck ten.* **8** find gold or oil etc. by digging or drilling **9** go in a certain direction • *We struck north through the forest.*
strike off or **out** cross out
strike up **1** begin playing or singing **2** start a friendship or conversation

strike NOUN **strikes** **1** a hit **2** an attack • *an air strike* **3** refusing to work as a way of making a protest **4** a sudden discovery of gold or oil etc.
on strike (said about workers) striking

striking ADJECTIVE attractive or impressive
▷ **strikingly** ADVERB

string NOUN **strings** **1** thin cord made of twisted threads, used to fasten or tie things; a piece of this or similar material **2** a piece of wire or cord etc. stretched and vibrated to produce

Thesaurus

greater stress on accuracy. ► accent, beat, emphasis, importance, weight

stress VERB *I stressed the importance of a balanced diet.* ► accentuate, assert, emphasize, insist on, lay stress on, put the stress on, repeat, underline

stressful ADJECTIVE *She'd had an extremely stressful day.* ► anxious, difficult, tense, traumatic, worrying AN OPPOSITE IS **easy**

stretch NOUN **1** *a five-hour stretch on duty* ► spell, stint, period, run, term, time **2** *a fine stretch of moorland* ► expanse, sweep, spread, tract, area

stretch VERB **1** *He stretched the rubber until it snapped.* ► pull, strain, tighten, extend, lengthen AN OPPOSITE IS compress **2** *The road stretched into the distance.* ► extend, continue, spread **3** **stretch to** *My money won't stretch to a two-week holiday.* ► be enough for, cover, reach to
stretch out *She stretched out on a couch.* ► recline, lean back, lie down, sprawl, relax

strict ADJECTIVE **1** *Their parents could be too strict at times.* ► severe, stern, harsh, authoritarian, rigid, austere AN OPPOSITE IS lenient **2** *strict controls on public spending* ► stringent, rigorous, severe, tough, extreme AN OPPOSITE IS liberal **3** *a strict interpretation of the rule* ► exact, precise, scrupulous, rigid, rigorous AN OPPOSITE IS loose

strident ADJECTIVE *a strident voice* ► harsh, shrill, jarring, grating, raucous, rasping, screeching, loud OPPOSITES ARE soft, quiet

strike NOUN *The dispute ended in a prolonged strike.* ► stoppage, withdrawal of labour, industrial action, work-to-rule, walkout

strike VERB **1** *I struck my head on the low ceiling.* ► hit, knock, bump, smack, thump **2** *The commandos struck without warning.* ► attack, raid, pounce **3** *The two sides struck a deal at the last moment.* ► agree, agree on, reach, endorse, settle on, sign **4** (*informal*) *The workforce threatened to strike.* ► down tools, stop work, come out, take industrial action, withdraw your labour

striking ADJECTIVE *She has a striking resemblance to her sister.* ► noticeable, conspicuous, outstanding, prominent, distinctive, impressive, memorable, obvious, stunning, telling, unmistakable
AN OPPOSITE IS inconspicuous

string NOUN **1** *a piece of string* ► twine, cord, line, rope **2** *a string of vehicles* ► row, succession, series, file, line, procession, queue **3** *a string of misfortunes* ► sequence, series, chain, progression

sounds in a musical instrument **3** a line or series of things • *a string of cars*

string *VERB* **strings, stringing, strung 1** fit or fasten with string **2** thread on a string **3** remove the tough fibre from beans
string along mislead someone over a period of time
string out 1 spread out in a line **2** cause something to last a long time

strings *PLURAL NOUN* musical instruments with strings

stringy *ADJECTIVE* **1** like string **2** containing tough fibres

strip[1] *VERB* **strips, stripping, stripped 1** take a covering or layer off something **2** undress **3** deprive a person of something

strip *NOUN* the distinctive clothes worn by a sports team while playing

strip[2] *NOUN* **strips** a long narrow piece or area

strip cartoon *NOUN* **strip cartoons** a series of drawings telling a story

stripe *NOUN* **stripes 1** a long narrow band of colour **2** a strip of cloth worn on the sleeve of a uniform to show the wearer's rank
▷ **striped** *ADJECTIVE* **stripy** *ADJECTIVE*

striptease *NOUN* **stripteases** an entertainment in which a person slowly undresses

strive *VERB* **strives, striving, strove, striven 1** try hard to do something **2** carry on a conflict

stroke[1] *NOUN* **strokes 1** a hit **2** a movement; a style of swimming **3** an action or effort • *a stroke of genius* **4** the sound made by a clock striking **5** a sudden illness that often causes paralysis

stroke[2] *VERB* **strokes, stroking, stroked** move your hand gently along something
▷ **stroke** *NOUN*

stroll *VERB* **strolls, strolling, strolled** walk in a leisurely way
▷ **stroll** *NOUN* **stroller** *NOUN*

strong *ADJECTIVE* **1** having great power, energy, or effect **2** not easy to break, damage, or defeat **3** great in intensity • *strong feelings* **4** having a lot of flavour or smell **5** having a certain number of members • *an army 5,000 strong*
▷ **strongly** *ADVERB*
be going strong be making good progress

stronghold *NOUN* **strongholds 1** a fortified place **2** an area where many people live or think in a particular way • *a Tory stronghold*

strove *past tense of* **strive**

structure *NOUN* **structures 1** something that has been constructed or built **2** the way something is constructed or organized
▷ **structural** *ADJECTIVE* **structurally** *ADVERB*

Thesaurus

string *VERB Lights had been strung across the road.* ► hang, link, thread, connect, join, line up

strip *NOUN* **1** *a strip of paper; a narrow strip of land* ► slip, band, ribbon, belt, sliver, narrow piece, stripe, swathe, lath, line, shred, slat **2** *The team were sporting a new strip.* ► outfit, kit

strip *VERB* **1** *He stripped and climbed into the shower.* ► undress, take off your clothes, remove your clothes, (*more informal*) peel off **2** *Thieves had completely stripped the house.* ► empty, clear out, ransack, loot, pillage, burgle
strip down *Mechanics were busy stripping down the engine.* ► dismantle, take to pieces, take apart, disassemble
strip off *First you must strip off the old paint.* ► peel off, remove, take off, scrape off, flake off

stripe *NOUN tracksuit bottoms with a stripe down the side* ► line, strip, band, bar, flash

stroke *NOUN* **1** *a swift stroke of the axe* ► blow, swipe, hit, knock **2** *a stroke of genius* ► feat, accomplishment, achievement, attainment **3** *She gave the cat a gentle stroke.* ► pat, rub, caress

stroke *VERB You can stroke the dog if you like.* ► pat, caress, fondle, touch, brush, pass your hand over, pet

stroll *VERB They strolled together round the grounds.* ► saunter, amble, wander, meander, ramble, dawdle

stroll *NOUN There was time for a stroll in the woods.* ► saunter, amble, ramble, walk, turn

strong *ADJECTIVE* **1** *a strong lad of nineteen* ► tough, muscular, powerful, brawny, well built, strapping, burly OPPOSITES ARE weak, puny **2** *The door needs a strong lock* ► robust, sturdy, firm, durable, sound, secure AN OPPOSITE IS weak **3** *She had a strong interest in what they were doing.* ► keen, eager, deep, dedicated, passionate, fervent, zealous AN OPPOSITE IS feeble **4** *a cup of strong coffee* ► highly flavoured, pungent, piquant AN OPPOSITE IS weak **5** *We have a strong case to make.* ► forceful, persuasive, convincing, cogent, effective OPPOSITES ARE weak, unconvincing

stroppy *ADJECTIVE* (*informal*) *I hope he doesn't get stroppy with us.* ► bad-tempered, irritable, grumpy, cross, peevish, truculent, sulky

structure *NOUN a tall structure of five storeys* ► construction, edifice, building, erection, pile

struggle *VERB* **struggles, struggling, struggled** **1** move your arms, legs, etc. in trying to get free **2** make strong efforts to do something **3** try to overcome an opponent or a problem etc.

struggle *NOUN* **struggles** the action of struggling; a hard fight or great effort

strum *VERB* **strums, strumming, strummed** sound a guitar by running your fingers across its strings

strut *VERB* **struts, strutting, strutted** walk proudly or stiffly

strut *NOUN* **struts** **1** a bar of wood or metal strengthening a framework **2** a strutting walk

stub *NOUN* **stubs** **1** a short stump left when the rest has been used or worn down **2** a counterfoil of a cheque, ticket, etc.

stub *VERB* **stubs, stubbing, stubbed** bump your toe painfully
stub out put out a cigarette by pressing it against something hard

stubble *NOUN* **1** the short stalks of corn left in the ground after the harvest is cut **2** short hairs growing after shaving

stubborn *ADJECTIVE* **1** determined not to change your ideas or ways; obstinate **2** difficult to remove or deal with • *stubborn stains*
▷ **stubbornly** *ADVERB* **stubbornness** *NOUN*

stubby *ADJECTIVE* short and thick

stuck-up *ADJECTIVE* (*informal*) conceited or snobbish

stud *NOUN* **studs** **1** a small curved lump or knob **2** a device like a button on a stalk, used to fasten a detachable collar to a shirt

student *NOUN* **students** a person who studies a subject, especially at a college or university

studio *NOUN* **studios** **1** the room where a painter or photographer etc. works **2** a place where cinema films are made **3** a room from which radio or television broadcasts are made or recorded

studious *ADJECTIVE* keen on studying; studying hard
▷ **studiously** *ADVERB* **studiousness** *NOUN*

study *VERB* **studies, studying, studied** **1** spend time learning about something **2** look at something carefully

study *NOUN* **studies** **1** the process of studying **2** a subject studied; a piece of research **3** a room used for studying or writing **4** a piece of music for playing as an exercise **5** a drawing done for practice or in preparation for another work

Thesaurus

struggle *VERB* **1** *We struggled to get free.* ► strive, strain, toil, try, work hard, endeavour, exert yourself, labour, wrestle, make an effort, move violently, wriggle about, writhe about **2** *They had to struggle with a determined enemy.* ► fight, contend, battle, grapple, wrestle, vie **3** *She struggled over the wet rocks.* ► scramble, flounder, stumble, labour

struggle *NOUN* **1** *It was a struggle to finish the work in time.* ► effort, challenge, difficulty, endeavour, exertion, labour, problem **2** *The police arrested the gang without a struggle.* ► fight, scuffle, brawl, fracas, affray

stub *NOUN* **1** *a cigarette stub* ► butt, end, (*more informal*) dog-end **2** *the stub of a ticket* ► counterfoil, slip

stubborn *ADJECTIVE* *He was too stubborn to admit he was wrong.* ► obstinate, obdurate, strong-willed, headstrong, wilful, pig-headed
OPPOSITES ARE compliant, yielding

stuck *ADJECTIVE* **1** *The door was stuck and wouldn't open.* ► jammed, fixed, fast, immovable **2** *He admitted he was stuck and needed help.* ► baffled, beaten, at a loss, bewildered, (*more informal*) stumped

stuck-up *ADJECTIVE* *a bunch of stuck-up businessmen* ► arrogant, conceited, snobbish, snobby, haughty, supercilious, overweening, (*more informal*) snooty, (*more informal*) uppish, (*more informal*) toffee-nosed

student *NOUN* **1** *a student at the university* ► undergraduate, postgraduate, scholar **2** *a student at the local school* ► pupil, schoolboy *or* schoolgirl, schoolchild, scholar **3** *a nursing student* ► learner, novice, trainee

studied *ADJECTIVE* *He spoke with studied politeness.* ► deliberate, intentional, considered, calculated, affected, thoughtful

studio *NOUN* *the artist's studio* ► workroom, workshop, atelier

studious *ADJECTIVE* *a studious young pupil* ► scholarly, serious-minded, hard-working, diligent, industrious, thoughtful, intellectual, academic, bookish, brainy, earnest

study *NOUN* **1** *two years of study in the sixth form* ► learning, education, schooling, reading, academic work, (*informal*) cramming **2** *a study of the causes of conflict* ► investigation (into), inquiry (into), survey, examination, research (into) **3** *The study deals with all aspects of the subject.* ► essay, article, report, review

study *VERB* **1** *She studied the information carefully.* ► examine, analyse, survey, consider, investigate, inspect, scrutinize, look into, peruse **2** *They both wanted to study languages.* ► learn, work at, be taught, read **3** *Alan had studied hard at school.* ► work, apply yourself

stuff *NOUN* **1** a substance or material **2** things • *Leave your stuff outside.*

stuff *VERB* **stuffs, stuffing, stuffed 1** fill tightly **2** fill with stuffing **3** push a thing into something • *He stuffed the notebook into his pocket.* **4** (*informal*) eat greedily

stuffing *NOUN* **1** material used to fill the inside of something; padding **2** a savoury mixture put into meat or poultry etc. before cooking

stuffy *ADJECTIVE* **stuffier, stuffiest 1** badly ventilated; without fresh air **2** with blocked breathing passages • *a stuffy nose* **3** formal and boring
▷ **stuffily** *ADVERB* **stuffiness** *NOUN*

stumble *VERB* **stumbles, stumbling, stumbled 1** trip and lose your balance **2** speak or do something hesitantly or uncertainly
▷ **stumble** *NOUN*
stumble across or **on** find accidentally

stumbling block *NOUN* **stumbling blocks** an obstacle; something that causes difficulty

stump *NOUN* **stumps 1** the bottom of a tree trunk left in the ground when the rest has fallen or been cut down **2** something left when the main part is cut off or worn down **3** each of the three upright sticks of a wicket in cricket

stump *VERB* **stumps, stumping, stumped 1** put a batsman out by knocking the bails off the stumps while they are out of the crease **2** be too difficult or puzzling for somebody • *The last question stumped everyone.*
stump up (*informal*) produce the money to pay for something

stumpy *ADJECTIVE* short and thick
▷ **stumpiness** *NOUN*

stun *VERB* **stuns, stunning, stunned 1** knock a person unconscious **2** daze or shock • *She was stunned by the news.*

stunt[1] *VERB* prevent a thing from growing or developing normally • *a stunted tree* [from a dialect word meaning 'foolish' or 'stubborn']

stunt[2] *NOUN* **stunts** something unusual or difficult done as a performance or part of a film, or to attract attention [originally American: origin unknown]

stupendous *ADJECTIVE* amazing or tremendous
▷ **stupendously** *ADVERB*

stupid *ADJECTIVE* **1** not clever or thoughtful **2** without reason or common sense
▷ **stupidly** *ADVERB* **stupidity** *NOUN*

Thesaurus

stuff *NOUN* **1** *There was some wet stuff on the floor.* ► matter, substance **2** *The skirt was made of a tough lightweight stuff.* ► material, fabric, cloth, textile **3** *I'll put all my stuff in a suitcase.* ► belongings, effects, possessions, things, (*more informal*) gear

stuff *VERB* **1** *I stuffed everything in a drawer.* ► pack, push, cram, ram, shove, squeeze, force, jam **2** *Use foam to stuff the cushions.* ► fill, pad, pack
stuff yourself *They had been stuffing themselves all day and were no longer hungry.* ► gorge, guzzle, cram, overindulge, eat

stuffy *ADJECTIVE* **1** *a stuffy atmosphere* ► airless, close, muggy, sultry, musty, stifling, oppressive, unventilated AN OPPOSITE IS airy **2** *a stuffy lecture on citizenship* ► staid, prim, strait-laced, pompous, conventional, stodgy, dull, boring AN OPPOSITE IS informal

stumble *VERB* **1** *She stumbled on a loose paving stone.* ► trip, totter, tumble, lose your balance **2** *He stumbled back to his house.* ► stagger, totter, lumber, lurch, blunder, bumble, hobble **3** *The speaker stumbled through the rest of the speech.* ► stammer, stutter, falter, flounder, hesitate

stump *VERB* *One of the questions stumped us.* ► baffle, puzzle, perplex, mystify, bewilder, outwit, confound, confuse, defeat, (*more informal*) flummox

stun *VERB* **1** *A hard blow had stunned him.* ► daze, knock out, knock senseless, make unconscious **2** *The election results stunned everyone.* ► amaze, astonish, astound, stagger, stupefy, shock, dumbfound, flabbergast, bewilder, confound

stunning *ADJECTIVE* **1** *a stunning victory* ► remarkable, sensational, spectacular, extraordinary, staggering, incredible **2** *She looked stunning in a red dress.* ► beautiful, dazzling, gorgeous, ravishing, sensational, lovely AN OPPOSITE IS unattractive

stunt *NOUN* *a circus stunt* ► trick, exploit, feat, turn, performance

stupendous *ADJECTIVE* *a stupendous achievement* ► amazing, astounding, astonishing, extraordinary, remarkable, wonderful, staggering, breathtaking, (*more informal*) mind-boggling AN OPPOSITE IS ordinary

stupid *ADJECTIVE* **1** *They are not as stupid as they seem.* ► foolish, silly, foolhardy, unintelligent, dim-witted, half-witted, empty-headed, vacuous, dim, dumb, thick OPPOSITES ARE intelligent, wise **2** *It was a stupid thing to do.* ► foolish, silly, unwise, senseless, mindless, idiotic, crass, absurd, ridiculous, ludicrous AN OPPOSITE IS sensible

stupidity *NOUN* *Their stupidity had been breathtaking.* ► foolishness, folly, silliness, irresponsibility, ineptitude, idiocy OPPOSITES ARE wisdom, intelligence

a b c d e f g h i j k l m n o p q r s t u v w x y z

sturdy *ADJECTIVE* **sturdier, sturdiest** strong and vigorous or solid
▷ **sturdily** *ADVERB* **sturdiness** *NOUN*

stutter *VERB* **stutters, stuttering, stuttered** stammer
▷ **stutter** *NOUN*

style *NOUN* **styles** **1** the way something is done, made, said, or written **2** fashion or elegance
▷ **stylistic** *ADJECTIVE*

stylish *ADJECTIVE* in a fashionable style

subconscious *ADJECTIVE* to do with mental processes of which we are not fully aware but which influence our actions
▷ **subconscious** *NOUN*

subdivide *VERB* **subdivides, subdividing, subdivided** divide again or into smaller parts
▷ **subdivision** *NOUN*

subdue *VERB* **subdues, subduing, subdued** **1** overcome or bring under control **2** make quieter or gentler
▷ **subdued** *ADJECTIVE*

subject *NOUN* **subjects** **1** the person or thing being talked or written about or dealt with **2** something that is studied **3** (in grammar) the word or words naming who or what does the action of a verb, e.g. *'the book'* in • *The book fell off the table.* **4** someone who is ruled by a monarch or government

subject *ADJECTIVE* ruled by a monarch or government; not independent

subject to **1** having to obey **2** liable to • *Trains are subject to delays during fog.* **3** depending upon • *Our decision is subject to your approval.*

subject (sub- jekt) *VERB* **subjects, subjecting, subjected** **1** make a person or thing undergo something • *They subjected him to torture.* **2** bring a country under your control
▷ **subjection** *NOUN*
[from Latin *subicere* = bring under, include under a heading]

subjective *ADJECTIVE* **1** existing in a person's mind and not produced by things outside it **2** depending on a person's own taste or opinions etc. COMPARE **objective**

subjunctive *NOUN* **subjunctives** the form of a verb used to indicate what is imagined or wished or possible There are only a few cases where it is commonly used in English, e.g. *'were'* in *'if I were you'* and *'save'* in *'God save the Queen'*.

sublime *ADJECTIVE* **1** noble or impressive **2** extreme; not caring about the consequences • *with sublime carelessness*

submarine *ADJECTIVE* under the sea • *We laid a submarine cable.*

submarine *NOUN* **submarines** a ship that can travel under water

submerge *VERB* **submerges, submerging, submerged** go under or put under water
▷ **submergence** *NOUN* **submersion** *NOUN*

Thesaurus

sturdy *ADJECTIVE* **1** *a sturdy and handsome young man* ► strapping, strong, big, brawny, well-built, muscular AN OPPOSITE IS weak **2** *He packed a sturdy pair of shoes for the walk.* ► stout, strong, substantial, robust, solid, thick, tough, reliable, sound
AN OPPOSITE IS flimsy

style *NOUN* **1** *an old-fashioned style of writing* ► manner, technique, mode, method, fashion, tone, way **2** *the latest styles in the fashion magazines* ► design, pattern, fashion, mode, vogue, cut, taste **3** *She always dresses with style.* ► elegance, refinement, flair, panache, stylishness, smartness, sophistication, refinement, taste

stylish *ADJECTIVE* *stylish clothes* ► chic, fashionable, modish, trendy, snappy, elegant, smart, (*more informal*) snazzy
OPPOSITES ARE unfashionable, dowdy

subdue *VERB* **1** *The army quickly subdued all opposition.* ► overcome, defeat, quell, suppress, crush, overpower **2** *It was difficult to subdue their excitement.* ► restrain, suppress, check, curb, repress, hold back, keep under, quieten

subdued *ADJECTIVE* **1** *Sylvie was in a subdued mood.* ► sombre, downcast, restrained, serious, silent, sober, solemn, depressed, grave, reflective, thoughtful AN OPPOSITE IS lively **2** *They spoke in subdued tones.* ► hushed, muted, quiet, soft, low, faint, calm
AN OPPOSITE IS loud

subject *NOUN* **1** *a British subject* ► citizen, national, passport-holder **2** *a subject for discussion* ► theme, topic, affair, business, issue, matter, point, question **3** *a subject of study* ► discipline, field, branch, course, area

subject *ADJECTIVE* **1** *subject nations* ► subjugated, dependent, subservient, tributary AN OPPOSITE IS independent **2** *The trains are subject to constant delays.* ► liable, prone, disposed, vulnerable **3 subject to** *The decision is subject to approval by the board.* ► dependent on, contingent on, conditional on

subjective *ADJECTIVE* *It is difficult to build a theory on such subjective criteria.* ► biased, prejudiced, personal, individual, intuitive, idiosyncratic
OPPOSITES ARE objective, unbiased

submerge *VERB* **1** *The utter darkness submerged them.* ► inundate, overwhelm, immerse, engulf, inundate, flood, swamp, cover, drown **2** *Submerge the vegetables in cold water.*

submit *VERB* **submits, submitting, submitted** 1 let someone have authority over you; surrender 2 put forward for consideration, testing, etc. • *Submit your plans to the committee*
▷ **submission** *NOUN*

subnormal *ADJECTIVE* below normal

subordinate *ADJECTIVE* 1 less important 2 lower in rank

subordinate *NOUN* **subordinates** a person working under someone's authority or control

subordinate *VERB* **subordinates, subordinating, subordinated** treat as being less important than another person or thing
▷ **subordination** *NOUN*

subordinate clause *NOUN* **subordinate clauses** a clause which adds details to the main clause of the sentence, but cannot be used as a sentence by itself

sub-plot *NOUN* **sub-plots** a secondary plot in a play etc.

subscribe *VERB* **subscribes, subscribing, subscribed** 1 pay regularly in order to be a member of a society, receive a periodical, have the use of a telephone, etc. 2 contribute money to a project or charity etc. 3 apply to take part in something• *The course is already fully subscribed.* 4 say that you agree • *We cannot subscribe to this theory.*
▷ **subscriber** *NOUN* **subscription** *NOUN*

subsequent *ADJECTIVE* coming after in time or order; later
▷ **subsequently** *ADVERB*

subside *VERB* **subsides, subsiding, subsided** 1 sink into the ground 2 become quieter or less intense • *Her fear subsided.*
▷ **subsidence** *NOUN*

subsidiary *ADJECTIVE* 1 less important; secondary 2 (said about a business) controlled by another • *a subsidiary company*
▷ **subsidiary** *NOUN*

subsidize *VERB* **subsidizes, subsidizing, subsidized** pay a subsidy to a person or firm etc.

subsidy *NOUN* **subsidies** money paid to an industry etc. that needs help, or to keep down the price at which its goods etc. are sold to the public

subsoil *NOUN* soil lying just below the surface layer

substance *NOUN* **substances** 1 matter of a particular kind 2 the main or essential part of something • *We agree with the substance of your report but not with its details.*

substantial *ADJECTIVE* 1 of great size, value, or importance • *a substantial sum of money*

Thesaurus

► immerse, dip, plunge, dunk 3 *The submarine had no time to submerge.* ► dive, go down

submission *NOUN* 1 *Complete submission was the key point of women in the eighteen-forties.* ► compliance, submissiveness, acquiescence, passivity, docility, meekness 2 *The enemy's submission was only a matter of time.* ► surrender, capitulation, defeat 3 *There was an alternative submission that the money had been paid under duress.* ► contention, claim, proposal, argument, suggestion, theory

submissive *ADJECTIVE* *Be polite, but not submissive.* ► acquiescent, compliant, servile, deferential, ingratiating, subservient, docile, uncomplaining, humble, meek, passive
OPPOSITES ARE domineering, assertive

submit *VERB* 1 *She had only submitted under duress.* ► give in, yield, accede, back down, surrender, capitulate, relent, succumb, comply, (*more informal*) knuckle under 2 *The union agreed to submit their disagreement to arbitration.* ► present, offer, tender, put forward, suggest, propose
submit to *We refuse to submit to political pressure. Applicants have to submit to a full medical examination.* ► accept, agree to, succumb to, undergo, tolerate, endure, comply with, conform to, defer to, bow to, keep to, obey

subordinate *ADJECTIVE* *It would not be easy to accept a subordinate role.* ► inferior, lower, lesser, secondary, subservient, subsidiary, minor, junior

subordinate *NOUN* *There stood the manager with her three subordinates.* ► assistant, junior, inferior, dependant, employee, (*more informal*) underling AN OPPOSITE IS superior

subscribe *VERB* **subscribe to** 1 *There are so many good causes to subscribe to.* ► contribute to, support, donate to, give to 2 *How many magazines do they subscribe to?* ► buy regularly, pay a subscription to, take, read 3 *I don't subscribe to that view at all.* ► agree with, accept, endorse, support, approve of, believe in, advocate, give your blessing to

subside *VERB* 1 *We'd better wait for the storm to subside.* ► abate, diminish, moderate, slacken, die down, quieten, ease up, let up
AN OPPOSITE IS intensify 2 *The flood waters had begun to subside.* ► recede, fall back, ebb 3 *Paul subsided into a chair.* ► collapse, sink, settle, drop AN OPPOSITE IS rise

substance *NOUN* 1 *a strange sticky substance* ► material, matter, stuff, chemical 2 *The substance of the story is not hard to follow.* ► essence, gist, theme, meaning, content, subject-matter 3 *We may wonder how much*

2 solidly built • *substantial houses*
▷ **substantially** ADVERB

substitute NOUN **substitutes** a person or thing that acts or is used instead of another

substitute VERB **substitutes, substituting, substituted** put or use a person or thing as a substitute
▷ **substitution** NOUN

subterranean ADJECTIVE underground

subtitle NOUN **subtitles** **1** a secondary or additional title **2** words shown on the screen during a film, e.g. to translate a foreign language

subtle (sut- el) ADJECTIVE **1** faint or delicate • *a subtle perfume* **2** slight and difficult to detect or describe • *a subtle distinction* **3** ingenious; not immediately obvious • *a subtle joke*
▷ **subtly** ADVERB **subtlety** NOUN

subtract VERB **subtracts, subtracting, subtracted** deduct; take away a part, quantity, or number from a greater one
▷ **subtraction** NOUN

suburb NOUN **suburbs** a district with houses that is outside the central part of a city
▷ **suburban** ADJECTIVE

subway NOUN **subways** an underground passage for pedestrians

succeed VERB **succeeds, succeeding, succeeded** **1** do or get what you wanted or intended **2** come after another person or thing; become the next king or queen • *She succeeded to the throne.* • *Edward VII succeeded Queen Victoria.*

success NOUN **successes** **1** doing or getting what you wanted or intended **2** a person or thing that does well • *The show was a great success.*

successful ADJECTIVE having success; being a success
▷ **successfully** ADVERB

Thesaurus

substance there was in many of the accusations. ► meaning, force, weight, significance

substantial ADJECTIVE **1** *a substantial building* ► strong, sturdy, hefty, solid, well-made, durable, sound AN OPPOSITE IS flimsy **2** *If you make substantial improvements to your home they might increase its value.* ► significant, sizeable, worthwhile, big, considerable, generous, large AN OPPOSITE IS trivial

substitute ADJECTIVE *a substitute teacher* ► acting, replacement, deputy, relief, reserve, standby, surrogate, temporary

substitute NOUN **1** *There is no substitute for practical experience.* ► replacement, alternative (to) **2** *Nurses can often be effective substitutes for doctors.* ► alternative, replacement, stand-in, proxy, surrogate

substitute VERB **1** *You can substitute yoghurt for cream cheese in this recipe.* ► change, exchange, interchange, swop, switch, replace USAGE If you use *replace*, you have to say *You can replace cream cheese with yoghurt.* **2** *Maggie agreed to substitute for her boss for few days.* ► deputize, stand in, act as a substitute

subtle ADJECTIVE **1** *Add a subtle yet striking change to your hair.* ► mild, slight, faint, delicate, elusive, unobtrusive **2** *a subtle hint* ► gentle, tactful, indirect, understated AN OPPOSITE IS tactless **3** *subtle colours* ► muted, subdued, delicate, faint, pale AN OPPOSITE IS lurid **4** *a subtle distinction* ► fine, nice, precise, tenuous AN OPPOSITE IS crude

subtract VERB *Half a pint of skimmed milk supplies 100 calories, which must be subtracted from your daily total.* ► deduct, take away, remove, debit AN OPPOSITE IS add

suburban ADJECTIVE *The couple disappeared from their suburban house about two weeks ago.* ► residential, outlying, provincial, outer

succeed VERB **1** *For some people, happiness is to compete and succeed no matter how.* ► be successful, do well, prosper, thrive, flourish, triumph, be victorious, accomplish your objective, (*more informal*) get on, (*more informal*) make it **2** *The scheme might still succeed.* ► be effective, produce results, work, (*more informal*) catch on AN OPPOSITE IS fail **3** *Kim's ambition to succeed Roh as President* ► replace, take the place of, take over from, supersede, come after, follow AN OPPOSITE IS precede

success NOUN **1** *The criteria for judging success would not be the same for all pupils.* ► accomplishment, achievement, attainment, fame, prosperity AN OPPOSITE IS failure **2** *Links with industry are essential for the success of the programme.* ► effectiveness, successful outcome, completion OPPOSITES ARE failure, collapse **3** (*informal*) *Her first novel was an instant success.* ► triumph, hit, sensation, victory, (*more informal*) winner OPPOSITES ARE failure, disaster **4** *This performance alone might well have made him a success.* ► celebrity, star, big name, household name, sensation

successful ADJECTIVE **1** *Blazer, the successful menswear chain* ► flourishing, prosperous, thriving, effective, profitable, fruitful, lucrative, productive, profit-making OPPOSITES ARE unsuccessful, unprofitable **2** *He had been a successful prize fighter at the time. This wooden aeroplane was one of the most successful*

succession *NOUN* **successions** **1** a series of people or things **2** the process of following in order **3** succeeding to the throne; the right of doing this
in succession one after another

successive *ADJECTIVE* following one after another • *on five successive days*
▷ **successively** *ADVERB*

succumb (suk- um) *VERB* **succumbs, succumbing, succumbed** give way to something overpowering

such *ADJECTIVE* **1** of the same kind; similar • *Cakes, biscuits, and all such foods are fattening.* **2** of the kind described • *There's no such person.* **3** so great or intense • *It gave me such a fright!*
such as for example

such-and-such *ADJECTIVE* particular but not now named • *He promises to come at such-and-such a time but is always late.*

suck *VERB* **sucks, sucking, sucked** **1** take in liquid or air through the mouth with the lips almost closed **2** squeeze something in your mouth by using your tongue • *sucking a toffee* **3** draw in • *The canoe was sucked into the whirlpool.*
▷ **suck** *NOUN*
suck up to (*informal*) flatter someone in the hope of winning their favour

sucker *NOUN* **suckers** **1** an organ or device that can stick to a surface by suction **2** a shoot coming up from a root or underground stem **3** (*informal*) a person who is easily deceived

suckle *VERB* **suckles, suckling, suckled** feed on milk at the mother's breast or udder

suction *NOUN* **1** sucking **2** producing a vacuum so that things are sucked into the empty space • *Vacuum cleaners work by suction.*

sudden *ADJECTIVE* happening or done quickly or without warning
▷ **suddenly** *ADVERB* **suddenness** *NOUN*

suds *PLURAL NOUN* froth on soapy water

sue *VERB* **sues, suing, sued** start a lawsuit to claim money from somebody

suet *NOUN* hard fat from cattle and sheep, used in cooking

suffer *VERB* **suffers, suffering, suffered** **1** feel pain or sadness **2** experience something bad • *The house suffered some damage.* • *She suffers from hay fever.* **3** be badly affected • *She's not sleeping and her work is suffering.* **4** (*old use*) allow or tolerate
▷ **sufferer** *NOUN* **suffering** *NOUN*

suffice *VERB* **suffices, sufficing, sufficed** be enough for someone's needs

sufficient *ADJECTIVE* enough
▷ **sufficiently** *ADVERB* **sufficiency** *NOUN*

suffix *NOUN* **suffixes** a letter or set of letters joined to the end of a word to make another word (e.g. in forget*ful*, lion*ess*, rust*y*) or a form of a verb (e.g. sing*ing*, wait*ed*)

suffocate *VERB* **suffocates, suffocating, suffocated** **1** make it difficult or impossible for someone to breathe **2** suffer or die because breathing is prevented
▷ **suffocation** *NOUN*

sugar *NOUN* a sweet food obtained from the juices of various plants, such as sugar cane or sugar beet
▷ **sugar** *VERB* **sugary** *ADJECTIVE*
[via early French from Arabic]

Thesaurus

aircraft of all time. ► victorious, triumphant, winning, effective OPPOSITES ARE unsuccessful, ineffective

succession *NOUN* *He drifted into a succession of menial jobs.* ► sequence, series, string, chain, run, line, cycle, course, progression

suck *VERB* **1** *The boys sat sucking their drinks.* ► sip, sup, slurp, drink **2** *Extra roads can suck people away from buses and trains.* ► draw, entice, attract, pull
suck up *He fetched a cloth to suck up the water.* ► soak up, absorb, draw up, pull up
suck up to (*informal*) *They suck up to him, hanging on his every word.* ► flatter, grovel to, kowtow to, behave obsequiously towards

sudden *ADJECTIVE* **1** *Lydia emitted a sudden giggle. a sudden increase in student numbers* ► unexpected, startling, abrupt, sharp, unforeseen, unlooked for, impulsive, quick, rash OPPOSITES ARE expected, gradual

suffer *VERB* **1** *She loved him too much to see him suffer.* ► feel pain, hurt, be in pain, be in distress **2** *England suffered a humiliating defeat.* ► undergo, experience, meet with, receive, be subjected to, sustain, encounter **3** *Dustin's relationship with Anne did suffer.* ► deteriorate, decline, be damaged, be impaired

suffering *NOUN* *Damage and suffering are inflicted on the population.* ► hardship, distress, misery, anguish, pain, unhappiness, sorrow, grief

sugary *ADJECTIVE* *a rather sugary Broadway musical* ► sentimental, cloying, mawkish, sickly, saccharine, (*more informal*) soppy

suggest *VERB* **suggests, suggesting, suggested** **1** put forward an idea or plan for someone to consider **2** cause an idea or possibility to come into the mind
▷ **suggestion** *NOUN* **suggestive** *ADJECTIVE*

suicide *NOUN* **suicides** **1** killing yourself deliberately • *He committed suicide.* **2** a person who deliberately kills himself or herself
▷ **suicidal** *ADJECTIVE*

suit *NOUN* **suits** **1** a matching jacket and trousers, or a jacket and skirt, that are meant to be worn together **2** a set of clothing for a particular activity • *a diving suit* **3** any of the four sets of cards (clubs, hearts, diamonds, and spades) in a pack of playing cards **4** a lawsuit
USAGE Do not confuse with **suite**.

suit *VERB* **suits, suiting, suited** **1** be suitable or convenient for a person or thing **2** make a person look attractive

suitable *ADJECTIVE* satisfactory or right for a particular person, purpose, or occasion etc.
▷ **suitably** *ADVERB* **suitability** *NOUN*

suitcase *NOUN* **suitcases** a rectangular container for carrying clothes, usually with a hinged lid and a handle

suite (rhymes with *sweet*) *NOUN* **suites** **1** a set of furniture **2** a set of rooms **3** a set of short pieces of music
USAGE Do not confuse with **suit**.

sulk *VERB* **sulks, sulking, sulked** be silent and bad-tempered because you are not pleased
▷ **sulks** *PLURAL NOUN* **sulky** *ADJECTIVE* **sulkily** *ADVERB* **sulkiness** *NOUN*

sullen *ADJECTIVE* sulking and gloomy
▷ **sullenly** *ADVERB* **sullenness** *NOUN*

sulphur *NOUN* a yellow chemical used in industry and in medicine
▷ **sulphurous** *ADJECTIVE*

sultry *ADJECTIVE* **1** hot and humid • *sultry weather* **2** suggesting passion or sexual desire • *her sultry smile*
▷ **sultriness** *NOUN*

sum *NOUN* **sums** **1** a total **2** a problem in arithmetic **3** an amount of money

sum *VERB* **sums, summing, summed**
sum up give a summary at the end of a talk etc.

summarize *VERB* **summarizes, summarizing, summarized** make or give a summary of something

summary *NOUN* **summaries** a statement of the main points of something said or written

summary *ADJECTIVE* **1** brief **2** done or given hastily, without delay • *summary punishment*
▷ **summarily** *ADVERB*

summer *NOUN* **summers** the warm season between spring and autumn
▷ **summery** *ADJECTIVE*

summer house *NOUN* **summer houses** a small building providing shade in a garden or park

summit *NOUN* **summits** **1** the top of a mountain or hill **2** a meeting between the leaders of powerful countries • *a summit conference*

Thesaurus

suggest *VERB* **1** *Connie suggested an outing to the lake.* ► propose, recommend, advise, propound, put forward, raise, advocate, moot, move **2** *The evidence suggests we could be right.* ► imply, indicate, hint, intimate, mean, signal

suggestion *NOUN* **1** *We have a few suggestions to consider.* ► proposal, proposition, recommendation, idea, plan **2** *There has been no suggestion of dishonesty.* ► hint, trace, suspicion, sign, implication, insinuation

suit *NOUN* *He wore a dark suit with a cream shirt.* ► outfit, set of clothes, ensemble, clothing

suit *VERB* **1** *credit terms to suit all pockets* ► accommodate, be suitable for, please, satisfy, gratify, fit **2** *Black doesn't really suit me.* ► look attractive on, look right on, become, flatter

suitable *ADJECTIVE* **1** *Would tomorrow afternoon be a suitable time?* ► convenient, appropriate, fitting, acceptable, satisfactory, apposite
AN OPPOSITE IS unsuitable **2** *a film that is considered suitable for all age groups* ► appropriate (to), suited (to), right, relevant (to)

sulk *VERB* *Dave was sulking in his room.* ► mope, brood, be sullen, pout

sulky *ADJECTIVE* *A row of sulky faces greeted him.* ► sullen, surly, moody, morose, glum, moping, pouting, disgruntled
AN OPPOSITE IS cheerful

sum *NOUN* **1** *a large sum of money* ► amount, quantity **2** *a sum you can do in your head* ► calculation, problem **3** *These books were the sum of her life's work.* ► total, entirety, totality, sum total, whole, aggregate

summarize *VERB* *The ideas can be summarized very easily.* ► sum up, outline, review, precis

summary *NOUN* **1** *There is a summary of the main arguments at the end of the article.* ► resumé, review, summing-up, summation, outline, recapitulation, abstract, digest **2** *a summary of a story* ► synopsis, precis, abridgement

summit *NOUN* *This year thirty-two people reached the summit of Everest.* ► top, peak, crest, crown, apex, pinnacle OPPOSITES ARE foot, bottom

summon *VERB* **summons, summoning, summoned** **1** order someone to come or appear **2** call people together • *A meeting of the governors was quickly summoned.*
summon up gather together your strength in order to do something • *She summoned up all her courage and knocked on the door.*

sumptuous *ADJECTIVE* splendid and expensive-looking
▷ **sumptuously** *ADVERB*

sun *NOUN* **suns** **1** the star round which the earth travels **2** light and warmth from the sun • *Go and sit in the sun.* **3** any star in the universe round which planets travel

sun *VERB* **suns, sunning, sunned**
sun yourself sit or lie in the sunshine

sunbathe *VERB* **sunbathes, sunbathing, sunbathed** expose your body to the sun, especially to get a tan

sunbeam *NOUN* **sunbeams** a ray of sun

sunburn *NOUN* redness of the skin caused by too much exposure to the sun
▷ **sunburnt** *ADJECTIVE*

sundae (**sun**-day) *NOUN* **sundaes** a mixture of ice cream and fruit, nuts, cream, etc.

Sunday *NOUN* the first day of the week, observed by Christians as a day of rest and worship [from Old English *sunnandaeg* = day of the sun]

sundial *NOUN* **sundials** a device that shows the time by a shadow on a dial

sundry *ADJECTIVE* various or several
all and sundry everyone

sunglasses *PLURAL NOUN* dark glasses to protect your eyes from strong sunlight

sunken *ADJECTIVE* sunk deeply into a surface • *Their cheeks were pale and sunken.*

sunlamp *NOUN* **sunlamps** a lamp which uses ultraviolet light to give people an artificial tan

sunlight *NOUN* light from the sun
▷ **sunlit** *ADJECTIVE*

sunny *ADJECTIVE* **sunnier, sunniest** **1** full of sunshine **2** cheerful • *She was in a sunny mood.*
▷ **sunnily** *ADVERB*

sunrise *NOUN* **sunrises** the rising of the sun; dawn

sunset *NOUN* **sunsets** the setting of the sun

sunshade *NOUN* **sunshades** a parasol or other device to protect people from the sun

sunshine *NOUN* sunlight with no cloud between the sun and the earth

sunstroke *NOUN* illness caused by being in the sun too long

suntan *NOUN* **suntans** a brown colour of the skin caused by the sun
▷ **suntanned** *ADJECTIVE*

super *ADJECTIVE* (*informal*) excellent or superb

superb *ADJECTIVE* magnificent or excellent
▷ **superbly** *ADVERB*

superficial *ADJECTIVE* **1** on the surface • *a superficial cut* **2** not deep or thorough • *a superficial knowledge of French*
▷ **superficially** *ADVERB* **superficiality** *NOUN*

Thesaurus

summon *VERB* **1** *Coleman was summoned to Washington for a final briefing.* ► send for, call, order, command, demand, invite **2** *The lawyers then summoned a meeting.* ► convene, assemble, convoke, gather together, call, announce

sun *NOUN* *Enjoy the sun while you can.* ► sunlight, sunshine RELATED ADJECTIVE solar

sunbathe *VERB* *Jill was sunbathing on the beach.* ► sun yourself, bask, get a tan

sunburnt *ADJECTIVE* *His neck and shoulders were sunburnt.* ► burnt, inflamed, peeling, red, blistered AN OPPOSITE IS pale

sunny *ADJECTIVE* **1** *It will be a day of sunny spells and showers.* ► bright, clear, fine, cloudless, summery, sunlit AN OPPOSITE IS dull **2** *There was rage beneath the sunny smile.* ► cheerful, happy, joyful, joyous, smiling, beaming, bright, jolly OPPOSITES ARE miserable, gloomy

sunrise *NOUN* *A farmer's day begins at sunrise.* ► dawn, daybreak, daylight, crack of dawn

sunset *NOUN* *Walk along the beach at sunset.* ► dusk, twilight, sundown, evening, close of day, half-light, (*literary*) gloaming

super *ADJECTIVE* *There is a super kitchen with a traditional tiled stove.* ► excellent, superb, superlative, first-class, first-rate, marvellous, magnificent, wonderful, splendid, fine, remarkable, (*more informal*) brilliant, (*more informal*) fantastic, (*more informal*) terrific, (*more informal*) awesome

superb *ADJECTIVE* *The large bay has a superb backdrop of mountains.* ► excellent, superlative, marvellous, magnificent, wonderful, splendid, fine, remarkable, (*more informal*) fantastic, (*more informal*) awesome

superficial *ADJECTIVE* **1** *He sustained superficial injuries which soon disappeared. Time spent on repairing superficial damage is well worthwhile.* ► surface, exterior, external, slight, moderate OPPOSITES ARE severe, deep **2** *These similarities are purely superficial.* ► apparent, cosmetic, slight, shallow, specious OPPOSITES ARE significant, meaningful **3** *At a superficial level these categories appear to be the same.* ► shallow, surface AN OPPOSITE IS deep **4** *It was no more than a superficial examination of the subject.* ► cursory, casual, perfunctory,

superfluous ADJECTIVE more than is needed
▷ **superfluity** NOUN

superhuman ADJECTIVE **1** beyond ordinary human ability • *their superhuman strength* **2** higher than human; divine

superimpose VERB **superimposes, superimposing, superimposed** place a thing on top of something else
▷ **superimposition** NOUN

superintend VERB **superintends, superintending, superintended** supervise

superintendent NOUN **superintendents 1** a supervisor **2** a police officer above the rank of inspector

superior ADJECTIVE **1** higher in position or rank • *She is your superior officer.* **2** better than another person or thing **3** showing conceit
▷ **superiority** NOUN

superior NOUN **superiors** a person who is higher in position or rank than someone else

superlative ADJECTIVE of the highest degree or quality • *superlative skill*
▷ **superlatively** ADVERB

superlative NOUN **superlatives** the form of an adjective or adverb that expresses 'most' • *The superlative of 'great' is 'greatest'.*
COMPARE **positive** & **comparative**

supermarket NOUN **supermarkets** a large self-service shop that sells food and other goods

supermodel NOUN **supermodels** a very successful and famous fashion model

supernatural ADJECTIVE not belonging to the natural world or having a natural explanation • *supernatural beings such as ghosts*

superpower NOUN **superpowers** one of the most powerful nations of the world, such as the USA

supersede VERB **supersedes, superseding, superseded** take the place of something

supersonic ADJECTIVE faster than the speed of sound

superstition NOUN **superstitions** a belief or action that is not based on reason or evidence, e.g. the belief that it is unlucky to walk under a ladder
▷ **superstitious** ADJECTIVE

supervise VERB **supervises, supervising, supervised** be in charge of a person or thing and inspect what is done
▷ **supervision** NOUN **supervisor** NOUN **supervisory** ADJECTIVE

supper NOUN **suppers** a meal eaten in the evening

supple ADJECTIVE bending easily; flexible
▷ **supplely** ADVERB **suppleness** NOUN

Thesaurus

desultory, hurried, lightweight
OPPOSITES ARE thorough, rigorous

superfluous ADJECTIVE **1** *Superfluous material can be trimmed from around the edges.* ► excess, surplus, spare, redundant, unwanted **2** *This is so obvious that at first sight it might seem superfluous to state it.* ► unnecessary, needless, pointless, gratuitous, redundant

superior ADJECTIVE **1** *Lewis watched, aware of his superior status.* ► senior, higher, higher-level, higher-ranking, greater, more important
OPPOSITES ARE inferior, lower **2** *Superior rooms are all recently renovated. The Americans have superior technology.* ► first-class, first-rate, high-quality, top-quality, better, exclusive, choice, fine, select, surpassing
OPPOSITES ARE inferior, low-quality **3** *He found her cold and superior.* ► haughty, arrogant, disdainful, condescending, patronizing, supercilious, self-important, stuck-up, (*informal*) snooty, (*informal*) hoity-toity
OPPOSITES ARE modest, approachable

superiority *The professional troops soon proved their technical superiority over the poorly trained local forces.* ► advantage, supremacy, dominance, predominance, ascendancy, pre-eminence, edge, lead
AN OPPOSITE IS inferiority

supersede VERB *Steel began to supersede iron in the 1880s.* ► replace, supplant, take the place of, displace, oust, succeed

superstition NOUN *the old superstition that seagulls were the souls of dead sailors* ► myth, superstitious belief, delusion, illusion, old wives' tale

superstitious ADJECTIVE **1** *a haze of superstitious beliefs and practices* ► irrational, mythical, traditional, unfounded, unprovable, groundless, illusory OPPOSITES ARE rational, factual, scientific **2** *I'm not superstitious like some people I could mention.* ► credulous, gullible AN OPPOSITE IS sceptical

supervise VERB *People are needed during the summer to supervise children and organize activities.* ► oversee, watch over, superintend, be in charge of, be responsible for, direct, manage

supervision NOUN *These tasks should be carried out under the supervision of a senior member of staff.* ► oversight, surveillance, control, direction, care, charge, oversight, management

supervisor NOUN *The housewife is her own supervisor.* ► manager, director, overseer, superintendent, controller, boss

supplement *NOUN* **supplements**
1 something added as an extra **2** an extra section added to a book or newspaper • *the colour supplement*
▷ **supplementary** *ADJECTIVE*

supplement *VERB* **supplements, supplementing, supplemented** add to something • *She supplements her pocket money by working on Saturdays.*

supply *VERB* **supplies, supplying, supplied** give or sell or provide what is needed or wanted
▷ **supplier** *NOUN*

supply *NOUN* **supplies** **1** an amount of something that is available for use when needed **2** the action of supplying something

support *VERB* **supports, supporting, supported** **1** keep a person or thing from falling or sinking; hold something up **2** give strength, help, or encouragement to someone • *Support your local team.* **3** provide with the necessities of life • *She has two children to support.*
▷ **supporter** *NOUN* **supportive** *ADJECTIVE*

support *NOUN* **supports** **1** the action of supporting **2** a person or thing that supports

suppose *VERB* **supposes, supposing, supposed** **1** think that something is likely to happen or be true **2** assume; consider as a suggestion • *Suppose the world were flat.*
▷ **supposedly** *ADVERB* **supposition** *NOUN*
be supposed to be expected to do something; have as a duty

Thesaurus

supplement *NOUN* **1** *A supplement is payable for rooms with a sea view.* ► surcharge, additional payment, excess **2** *the newspaper's new travel supplement* ► insert, pull-out, addendum, addition

supplement *VERB* *the need to supplement the family income* ► augment, increase, boost, enlarge, swell, add to, top up, complement, reinforce

supply *NOUN* *As a breeder, I give one week's supply of food with each puppy.* ► stock, store, quantity, amount, stockpile, reserve
supplies *Many people use their cars to buy a whole week's supplies.* ► provisions, stores, rations, materials, shopping, food, necessities

supply *VERB* **1** *studios set up to supply cheaply-made films* ► produce, provide, purvey, sell, contribute **2** *The reservoir supplies water to an area of about five hundred square miles.* ► serve, provide, furnish **3** *They were unable to supply us with what we needed.* ► equip, provide, furnish **4** *A supermarket that supplies all your needs.* ► provide, fulfil, fill

support *NOUN* **1** *The group offers emotional support to members in times of stress.* ► encouragement, solace, comfort, succour, relief, strength, friendship, protection **2** *The Arts Council eventually withdrew all financial support.* ► backing, funding, funds, aid, subsidy, donations, money **3** *The shelf was resting on three supports.* ► prop, brace, bracket, pillar, foundation

support *VERB* **1** *The walls were too weak to support the weight of the roof. He supported the old man over to his bed.* ► carry, bear, sustain, hold up, prop up, provide a support for, underpin **2** *She was determined to support Alice during these difficult weeks.* ► comfort, be a support to, sustain, encourage, hearten, console, fortify, reassure, succour
AN OPPOSITE IS abandon **3** *His land was not fertile enough to support his family.* ► maintain, nourish, provide for, sustain, feed, keep
AN OPPOSITE IS neglect **4** *The company supports research into the causes of back pain.* ► sponsor, subsidize, fund, patronize, contribute to, encourage AN OPPOSITE IS discourage **5** *They both support some sort of fees. The Socialist Party agreed to support the bill. There is no evidence to support such a notion.* ► advocate, endorse, promote, substantiate, uphold, agree with, argue for, confirm, corroborate, defend, justify
AN OPPOSITE IS oppose

supporter *NOUN* **1** *The perpetrators were unlikely to be genuine rugby supporters.* ► enthusiast, follower, devotee, fan **2** *The United States became an important supporter of the project.* ► champion, advocate, adherent, defender, seconder, upholder, apologist (for) **3** *Labour's supporters in business* ► backer, adherent, ally, sponsor, henchman

supportive *ADJECTIVE* *Alan and Ian were the most supportive friends in her life.* ► encouraging, helpful, caring, concerned, reassuring, sympathetic, understanding, protective, interested, kind, loyal, positive
OPPOSITES ARE unhelpful, discouraging

suppose *VERB* **1** *I suppose it would be nice for you to earn a little pin money.* ► assume, expect, guess, infer, dare say, presume, imagine, fancy, surmise, suspect, think, conclude, conjecture, judge **2** *just suppose I saw her again* ► imagine, pretend, hypothesize, fancy, assume

supposed *ADJECTIVE* *Where is this supposed cousin of yours?* ► alleged, assumed, presumed, rumoured, reputed, imagined, conjectural, hypothetical, reported, putative
be supposed to *You are supposed to read the whole book.* ► be meant to, be expected to, be required to, be obliged to, have to, need to, ought to

A B C D E F G H I J K L M N O P Q R **S** T U V W X Y Z

suppress *VERB* **suppresses, suppressing, suppressed 1** put an end to something forcibly or by authority • *Troops suppressed the rebellion.* **2** keep something from being known or seen • *They suppressed the truth.*
▷ **suppression** *NOUN* **suppressor** *NOUN*

supreme *ADJECTIVE* **1** most important or highest in rank **2** greatest • *supreme courage*
▷ **supremely** *ADVERB* **supremacy** *NOUN*

sure *ADJECTIVE* **1** completely confident that you are right; feeling no doubt **2** certain to happen or do something • *Our team is sure to win.* **3** reliable; undoubtedly true
▷ **sureness** *NOUN*
for sure definitely
make sure 1 find out exactly **2** make something happen or be true • *Make sure the door is locked.*

surely *ADVERB* **1** in a sure or certain way **2** I feel sure • *Surely we met last year.*

surf *NOUN* the white foam of waves breaking on a rock or shore

surf *VERB* **surfs, surfing, surfed 1** go surfing **2** browse through the Internet

surface *NOUN* **surfaces 1** the outside of something **2** any of the sides of an object, especially the top part **3** an outward appearance • *On the surface he was a kindly man.*

surfboard *NOUN* **surfboards** a board used in surfing

surfeit (ser-fit) *NOUN* too much of something
▷ **surfeited** *ADJECTIVE*

surfing *NOUN* balancing yourself on a board that is carried to the shore on the waves
▷ **surfer** *NOUN*

surf-riding *NOUN* surfing
▷ **surf-rider** *NOUN*

surge *VERB* **surges, surging, surged 1** move forwards or upwards like waves **2** increase suddenly and powerfully
▷ **surge** *NOUN*

surgeon *NOUN* **surgeons** a doctor who treats disease or injury by removing or repairing the affected parts of the body

surgery *NOUN* **surgeries 1** the work of a surgeon **2** the place where a doctor or dentist etc. regularly gives advice and treatment to patients **3** the time when patients can visit the doctor etc.
▷ **surgical** *ADJECTIVE* **surgically** *ADVERB*

surly *ADJECTIVE* **surlier, surliest** bad-tempered and unfriendly
▷ **surliness** *NOUN*

surname *NOUN* **surnames** the name held by all members of a family

surpass *VERB* **surpasses, surpassing, surpassed** do or be better than all others; excel

Thesaurus

supposition *NOUN* *Terry had gone to bed happy in the supposition that he would get revenge.* ► belief, assumption, presumption, notion, suspicion, expectation, conjecture, idea, hunch, feeling

suppress *VERB* **1** *The National Guard was established to suppress anti-government demonstrations.* ► quash, quell, crush, subdue, overcome, overthrow, conquer, put an end to, put down, stamp out, stop **2** *She had been advised to suppress all critical remarks. McGuire made a conscious effort to suppress his emotions.* ► conceal, hide, restrain, stifle, repress, control, contain, hold back, smother, silence, cover up, bottle up, choke back

sure *ADJECTIVE* **1** *I'm sure Dan will be perfectly safe.* ► certain, convinced, confident, positive, assured, definite, persuaded, satisfied, decided, resolute OPPOSITES ARE doubtful, uncertain **2** *He's sure to ask us what we were doing.* ► bound, certain, likely, destined, compelled, obliged, required AN OPPOSITE IS unlikely **3** *He left in the sure knowledge that he would be returning. He was pacing the floor, a sure sign of anxiety.* ► clear, undoubted, indisputable, inescapable, undeniable, undisputed, guaranteed, convincing, precise, proven, inevitable, accurate, true OPPOSITES ARE uncertain, doubtful, unsure **4** *James was always a sure friend.* ► dependable, steadfast, steady, reliable, faithful, firm, solid, trusty, trustworthy, effective, loyal, safe, secure, unfailing, unswerving OPPOSITES ARE fickle, unreliable.

surf *VERB* *surfing the Internet* ► browse, explore, search, probe, research, survey, scrutinize

surface *NOUN* **1** *The surface of the door had become rotten.* ► outside, exterior, facade, veneer, covering, face AN OPPOSITE IS inside **2** *A cube has six surfaces.* ► face, side, facet, plane

surface *VERB* *A submarine surfaced in the loch. A new idea has surfaced* ► come up, rise, appear, emerge, materialize, come to light, (*informal*) pop up AN OPPOSITE IS dive

surge *NOUN* **1** *a surge of water* ► gush, rush, sweep, flow, wave **2** *a surge of excitement* ► outburst, upsurge, outpouring, rush, gush, increase, onrush

surge *VERB* **1** *Water surged into people's houses.* ► gush, rush, stream, flow, swirl, roll **2** *The crowd surged forward* ► rush, sweep, push, stampede

surplus *NOUN* **surpluses** an amount left over after spending or using all that was needed
▷ **surplus** *ADJECTIVE*

surprise *NOUN* **surprises** **1** something unexpected **2** the feeling caused by something that was not expected
take someone by surprise happen to someone unexpectedly

surprise *VERB* **surprises, surprising, surprised** **1** be a surprise; make someone feel surprise **2** come upon or attack somebody unexpectedly
▷ **surprisingly** *ADVERB*

surrender *VERB* **surrenders, surrendering, surrendered** **1** stop fighting and give yourself up to an enemy **2** hand something over to another person, especially when compelled to do so
▷ **surrender** *NOUN*

surreptitious (su- rep- tish- us) *ADJECTIVE* stealthy
▷ **surreptitiously** *ADVERB*

surrogate mother *NOUN* **surrogate mothers** a woman who agrees to conceive and give birth to a baby for a woman who cannot do so herself, using a fertilized egg of the other woman or sperm from the other woman's partner

surround *VERB* **surrounds, surrounding, surrounded** come or be all round a person or thing • *Police surrounded the building.*

surroundings *PLURAL NOUN* the conditions or area around a person or thing

survey (ser- vay) *NOUN* **surveys** **1** a general look at something **2** an inspection of an area, building, etc.

survey (ser- vay) *VERB* **surveys, surveying, surveyed** make a survey of something; inspect
▷ **surveyor** *NOUN*

Thesaurus

surplus *NOUN* *a fruit surplus* ► excess, surfeit, glut, superfluity, oversupply, oversufficiency, superabundance, profusion

surprise *NOUN* **1** *Alice looked at him in surprise.* ► amazement, astonishment, incredulity, wonder, alarm, consternation, bewilderment, dismay **2** *This might come as a surprise to you.* ► shock, revelation, bolt from the blue, (*more informal*) bombshell, (*more informal*) eye-opener

surprise *VERB* **1** *Here's a piece of information that will surprise you.* ► astonish, amaze, astound, shock, stupefy, dumbfound, stagger, disconcert, flabbergast, nonplus, take your breath away, take aback, (*more informal*) bowl over, (*more informal*) gobsmack **2** *He surprised an intruder, who ran off.* ► discover, take unawares, take by surprise, come upon, catch out, catch in the act, catch red-handed, detect

surprised *ADJECTIVE* *I was surprised to see Lisa sitting up in bed reading.* ► astonished, amazed, astounded, dumbfounded, flabbergasted, nonplussed, shocked, speechless, staggered, disconcerted, incredulous, startled, stunned, taken aback, taken by surprise, thunderstruck, (*more informal*) gobsmacked

surprising *ADJECTIVE* *They completed the task with surprising speed.* ► astonishing, amazing, astounding, unexpected, extraordinary, remarkable, incredible, staggering, startling, stunning OPPOSITES ARE predictable, unsurprising

surrender *VERB* **1** *The rebels surrendered after months of fierce fighting.* ► capitulate, submit, yield, succumb, give up, resign, (*more informal*) throw in the towel **2** *We are being asked to surrender personal freedoms in the national interest.* ► relinquish, give up, forgo, cede, abandon, renounce, waive

surround *VERB* **1** *The garden surrounds the ruins of a fourteenth-century castle.* ► encircle, ring, skirt, encompass **2** *Anabelle found herself surrounded by angry faces.* ► besiege, beset, engulf, girdle, hedge in, hem in

surroundings *NOUN* *The hotel is set in the beautiful surroundings of a country park.* ► environment, location, setting, vicinity, neighbourhood, background, ambience, milieu

surveillance *NOUN* *Police surveillance prevented us from contacting your sister-in-law.* ► check, observation, scrutiny, supervision, vigilance, watch

survey *NOUN* **1** *In our main survey, people were asked where they would go for a loan.* ► poll, investigation, appraisal, inquiry, census, count, evaluation, study, assessment, examination, inspection, scrutiny, (*technical*) triangulation **2** *a survey of recent work on the subject* ► review, overview, synopsis, summary **3** *Be sure to get a survey of the house before making an offer.* ► inspection, assessment, appraisal, examination, valuation

survey *VERB* **1** *Those who wish can survey the scene from a panoramic tower.* ► observe, view, look at, look over **2** *The artist stood back to survey his work.* ► examine, inspect, study, scrutinize, consider, review **3** *Engineers arrived to survey the area.* ► do a survey of, reconnoitre, plot, map out, plan out, measure, (*technical*) triangulate

survival *NOUN* **survivals 1** surviving; the likelihood of surviving **2** something that has survived from an earlier time

survive *VERB* **survives, surviving, survived 1** stay alive; continue to exist **2** remain alive after an accident or disaster • *Only two people survived the crash.* **3** continue living after someone has died
▷ **survivor** *NOUN*

susceptible (sus- ept- ib- ul) *ADJECTIVE* likely to be affected by something • *She is susceptible to colds.*
▷ **susceptibility** *NOUN*

suspect (sus- pekt) *VERB* **suspects, suspecting, suspected 1** think that a person is not to be trusted or has committed a crime; distrust **2** have a feeling that something is likely or possible

suspect (sus- pekt) *NOUN* **suspects** a person who is suspected of a crime etc.
▷ **suspect** *ADJECTIVE*

suspend *VERB* **suspends, suspending, suspended 1** hang something up **2** postpone; stop something temporarily **3** remove a person from a job or position for a time **4** keep something from falling or sinking in air or liquid, • *Particles are suspended in the fluid.*

suspender *NOUN* **suspenders** a fastener to hold up a sock or stocking by its top

suspense *NOUN* an anxious or uncertain feeling while waiting for something to happen or become known

suspension *NOUN* **1** suspending **2** the springs etc. in a vehicle that lessen the effect of rough road surfaces **3** a liquid containing small pieces of solid material which do not dissolve

suspicion *NOUN* **suspicions 1** suspecting or being suspected; distrust **2** a slight belief

suspicious *ADJECTIVE* feeling or causing suspicion
▷ **suspiciously** *ADVERB*

sustain *VERB* **sustains, sustaining, sustained 1** keep someone alive **2** keep something happening **3** undergo or suffer • *We sustained another defeat.* **4** support or uphold
▷ **sustainable** *ADJECTIVE*

Thesaurus

survive *VERB* **1** *They had enough water to survive until help came.* ► remain alive, live, last, carry on, keep going, sustain yourself, continue, endure AN OPPOSITE IS perish **2** *Some of the workers' cottages still survive.* ► remain, exist **3** *Six people survived the crash.* ► withstand, come through, live through, weather AN OPPOSITE IS succumb to **4** *She is survived by her husband and three sons.* ► outlast, outlive

susceptible *ADJECTIVE* *Network cables are susceptible to electrical interference.* ► vulnerable, prone, liable, subject, sensitive, inclined, predisposed OPPOSITES ARE resistant, immune

suspect *ADJECTIVE* *Two suspect packages stood by the door.* ► suspicious, doubtful, dubious, questionable, (*more informal*) fishy, (*more informal*) dodgy

suspect *VERB* **1** *The plan's only going to be successful if they don't suspect anything.* ► distrust, mistrust, call into question, have doubts about, doubt **2** *I suspect another visit may not be possible.* ► expect, surmise, presume, assume, imagine, dare say, think, fancy, guess, infer, conclude, conjecture, judge

suspend *VERB* **1** *Long sacks were suspended from hooks on the wall.* ► hang, sling, swing, dangle, drape **2** *The Stock Exchange decided to suspend trading.* ► adjourn, discontinue, interrupt, break off, postpone, put off, defer, delay **3** *Two directors were suspended for a year.* ► exclude, debar, remove, dismiss, expel

suspense *NOUN* *There is an art to building up suspense.* ► tension, uncertainty, doubt, anticipation, expectation, expectancy, excitement, apprehension, drama

suspicion *NOUN* **1** *The KGB did not need proof; suspicion was more than enough.* ► intuition, conjecture, speculation, supposition, belief, caution, wariness **2** *As we drank our coffee I outlined my suspicions about Martinez.* ► misgiving, doubt, qualm, uncertainty, reservation **3** *A suspicion of a grin appeared on her face.* ► trace, hint, glimmer, shadow, suggestion, tinge, touch

suspicious *ADJECTIVE* **1** *It was clear that he was increasingly suspicious of his visitor.* ► doubtful, distrustful, mistrustful, unsure, sceptical, apprehensive, wary, chary, disbelieving, incredulous, unconvinced (about), uneasy (about) OPPOSITES ARE trusting, credulous **2** *He's a highly suspicious character and we haven't spoken for years. At first the police treated the case as a suspicious death.* ► questionable, suspect, dubious, disreputable, unreliable, untrustworthy, peculiar, irregular, (*more informal*) fishy, (*more informal*) shady OPPOSITES ARE straightforward, innocent

sustain *VERB* **1** *The country would have to sustain a large population.* ► maintain, keep, continue, preserve, provide for, nurture **2** *She had some bread and cheese to sustain her.* ► nourish, feed **3** *They were sustained by these happy memories.* ► comfort, support, encourage, succour, hearten, (*more informal*) buck up **4** *It was doubtful whether the structure could sustain the increased weight.* ► support, bear, carry

SW *ABBREVIATION* **1** south-west **2** south-western

swab (swob) *NOUN* **swabs 1** a mop or pad for cleaning or wiping something; a small pad for cleaning a wound **2** a specimen of fluid from the body taken on a swab for testing

swab *VERB* **swabs, swabbing, swabbed** clean or wipe with a swab

swagger *VERB* **swaggers, swaggering, swaggered** walk or behave in a conceited way; strut
▷ **swagger** *NOUN*

swallow[1] *VERB* **swallows, swallowing, swallowed 1** make something go down your throat **2** believe something that ought not to be believed
▷ **swallow** *NOUN*
swallow up take in and cover; engulf • *She was swallowed up in the crowd.*
[from Old English *swelgan*]

swallow[2] *NOUN* **swallows** a small bird with a forked tail and pointed wings [from Old English *swealwe*]

swamp *NOUN* **swamps** a marsh
▷ **swampy** *ADJECTIVE*

swamp *VERB* **swamps, swamping, swamped 1** flood **2** overwhelm with a great mass or number of things

swan *NOUN* **swans** a large white water bird with a long neck

swank *VERB* **swanks, swanking, swanked** (*informal*) boast or swagger; show off

swank *NOUN* (*informal*) showing yourself or your possessions off in a conceited way

swansong *NOUN* **swansongs** a person's last performance or work

swap *VERB* **swaps, swapping, swapped** (*informal*) exchange one thing for another
▷ **swap** *NOUN*
[formerly = seal a bargain by slapping each other's hands; imitating the sound]

swarm *NOUN* **swarms** a large number of insects or birds etc. flying or moving about together

swarm *VERB* **swarms, swarming, swarmed 1** gather or move in a swarm **2** be crowded with people etc. • *The town is swarming with tourists in the summer.*

swarthy *ADJECTIVE* having a dark complexion
▷ **swarthiness** *NOUN*

swastika *NOUN* **swastikas** an ancient symbol formed by a cross with its ends bent at right angles, adopted by the Nazis as their sign [from Sanskrit *svasti* = well-being, luck]

swat *VERB* **swats, swatting, swatted** hit or crush a fly etc.
▷ **swatter** *NOUN*

swathe (swayth) *VERB* **swathes, swathing, swathed** wrap in layers of bandages, paper, or clothes etc.

swathe *NOUN* **swathes** a broad strip or area • *vast swathes of countryside*

sway *VERB* **sways, swaying, swayed 1** move or swing gently from side to side **2** influence • *His speech swayed the crowd.*
▷ **sway** *NOUN*

swear *VERB* **swears, swearing, swore, sworn 1** make a solemn promise • *She swore to tell the truth.* **2** make a person take an oath • *We swore him to secrecy.* **3** use curses or coarse words in anger or surprise etc.
swear by have great confidence in something

Thesaurus

swallow *VERB* **1** *He was finding it hard to swallow food.* ► eat, drink, consume, devour, gulp down, guzzle **2** *I was a little surprised when they swallowed my story.* ► accept, believe, (*more informal*) buy
swallow up *The darkness swallowed them up.* ► engulf, enfold, envelop, absorb, enclose

swamp *NOUN* *The rains had turned the fields into a huge swamp.* ► marsh, bog, quagmire, mire, fen, marshland, morass, wetland, slough

swamp *VERB* **1** *A tidal wave swamped the coastal regions.* ► flood, inundate, overwhelm, engulf, drench, saturate, submerge, waterlog **2** *Journalists had swamped the unfortunate village.* ► overrun, overwhelm, besiege, beset

swap *VERB* *Helen swapped her Spanish stamps for some Belgian ones she didn't have.* ► exchange, barter, bargain, switch

swarm *NOUN* *There were swarms of police everywhere.* ► crowd, horde, mass, throng, multitude, host

swarm *VERB* *Reporters were swarming all over the place.* ► crowd, throng, flock, mass, cluster, congregate
be swarming with *The beaches were swarming with tourists.* ► be overrun with, be crawling with, be teeming, be full of, be infested with, be invaded by, abound in

sway *VERB* **1** *The branches swayed in the breeze.* ► swing, bend, rock, wave, lurch, lean from side to side, move to and fro, oscillate **2** *Many people are swayed by what they read in the newspapers.* ► influence, persuade, affect, govern **3** *She would not sway in her resolve to go through with it.* ► fluctuate, waver, swerve, vacillate, hesitate, veer, divert, go off course

swear *VERB* **1** *He swore he had told the truth.* ► vow, pledge, promise, give your word, affirm, attest, declare, state on oath, take an oath, testify **2** *She spilled her drink and swore.* ► blaspheme, curse, use bad language

swearword *NOUN* *In those days you never heard a swear word on television.* ► expletive,

A B C D E F G H I J K L M N O P Q R S T U V W X Y Z

sweat (swet) *NOUN* moisture given off by the body through the pores of the skin; perspiration
▷ **sweaty** *ADJECTIVE*

sweat *VERB* **sweats, sweating, sweated** give off sweat; perspire

sweater *NOUN* **sweaters** a jersey or pullover

sweatshirt *NOUN* **sweatshirts** a thick cotton jersey worn for sports or casual wear

sweep *VERB* **sweeps, sweeping, swept 1** clean or clear with a broom or brush etc. **2** move or remove quickly • *The floods swept away the bridge.* **3** go smoothly and quickly • *She swept out of the room.* **4** spread quickly over an area • *A new craze is sweeping the country.*
▷ **sweeper** *NOUN*

sweep *NOUN* **sweeps 1** the process of sweeping • *Give this room a good sweep.* **2** a sweeping movement **3** a chimney sweep **4** a sweepstake

sweeping *ADJECTIVE* general or wide-ranging • *He made sweeping changes.*

sweet *ADJECTIVE* **1** tasting as if it contains sugar; not bitter **2** very pleasant • *a sweet smell* **3** charming or delightful
▷ **sweetly** *ADVERB* **sweetness** *NOUN*
a sweet tooth a liking for sweet things

sweet *NOUN* **sweets 1** a small shaped piece of sweet food made with sugar, chocolate, etc. **2** a pudding; the sweet course in a meal **3** a beloved person

sweeten *VERB* **sweetens, sweetening, sweetened** make or become sweet
▷ **sweetener** *NOUN*

sweetheart *NOUN* **sweethearts** a person you love very much

swell *VERB* **swells, swelling, swelled, swollen** *or* **swelled 1** make or become larger • *My ankle was starting to swell.* **2** increase in amount, volume, or force

swell *NOUN* **swells 1** the process of swelling **2** the rise and fall of the sea's surface

swelling *NOUN* **swellings** a swollen place

swerve *VERB* **swerves, swerving, swerved** turn to one side suddenly
▷ **swerve** *NOUN*

swift *ADJECTIVE* quick or rapid
▷ **swiftly** *ADVERB* **swiftness** *NOUN*

swift *NOUN* **swifts** a small bird rather like a swallow

swill *VERB* **swills, swilling, swilled** pour water over or through something; wash or rinse

Thesaurus

obscenity, profanity, curse, oath, four-letter word
swearwords ► bad language, foul language, profanity, swearing

sweat *VERB He had begun to sweat in the heat.* ► perspire, swelter, exude

sweat *NOUN* **1** *By now he was drenched in sweat.* ► perspiration, moisture, dampness **2** (*informal*) *We were in a sweat to get away.* ► panic, fluster, state of agitation, state of anxiety **3** (*informal*) *Taking all the children home had been quite a sweat.* ► chore, task, labour, ordeal

sweaty *ADJECTIVE He shook Karl's sweaty hand.* ► sweating, perspiring, sticky, clammy, damp, moist

sweep *VERB* **1** *It was time to sweep the kitchen floor.* ► brush, clean, scrub, wipe, hoover **2** *Another bus swept past them.* ► sail, glide, streak, tear, hurtle, whizz

sweet *ADJECTIVE* **1** *The tea was too sweet.* ► sweetened, sugary, saccharine, honeyed, cloying **2** *the sweet perfume of roses* ► fragrant, aromatic, sweet-smelling, balmy, scented **3** *She sang a sweet song.* ► melodious, lyrical, mellifluous, sweet-toned **4** *Life can be sweet.* ► pleasant, pleasing, enjoyable, satisfying, delightful, agreeable **5** *the sweet air of the mountains* ► fresh, pure, wholesome, clear, clean **6** *a sweet little baby* ► cute, pretty, delightful **7** *Dora has a sweet nature.* ► loving, appealing, affectionate, adorable, lovely, charming

sweeten *VERB* **1** *You may need to sweeten the juice a little.* ► make sweeter, sugar **2** *She was furious and he had no idea how to sweeten her.* ► mollify, pacify, calm, soothe, appease, mellow

swell *VERB* **1** *He could almost feel his stomach swelling.* ► expand, dilate, distend, enlarge, bloat, bulge, balloon, inflate, puff up, billow
OPPOSITES ARE contract, shrink **2** *The droning in her head swelled and faded.* ► intensify, increase, heighten, surge **3** *The population swelled with immigration after the war.* ► increase, enlarge, expand, grow *or* get bigger, build up, extend
OPPOSITES ARE decrease, decline

swell *NOUN a heavy swell in the Channel* ► surge, roll, billow, undulation

swerve *VERB The car swerved to avoid a squirrel.* ► turn aside, deviate, swing, weave, change direction, veer, take avoiding action

swift *ADJECTIVE* **1** *Her letter brought a swift reply.* ► quick, rapid, prompt, immediate, instant, speedy, fast, instantaneous, punctual
AN OPPOSITE IS slow **2** *They all made swift progress.* ► rapid, quick, speedy, fast, brisk, lively

swim VERB **swims, swimming, swam, swum** **1** move the body through the water; be in the water for pleasure **2** cross by swimming • *She swam the Channel.* **3** float **4** be covered with or full of liquid • *Our eyes were swimming with tears.* **5** feel dizzy • *His head swam.*
▷ **swimmer** NOUN

swim NOUN **swims** the action of swimming • *We went for a swim.*
▷ **swimsuit** NOUN

swimming bath NOUN **swimming baths** a public swimming pool

swimming pool NOUN **swimming pools** an artificial pool for swimming in

swindle VERB **swindles, swindling, swindled** cheat a person in business etc.
▷ **swindle** NOUN **swindler** NOUN
[from German *Schwindler* = a fool, a cheat]

swine NOUN **swine** **1** a pig **2** (*informal*) a very unpleasant person

swing VERB **swings, swinging, swung** **1** move back and forth while hanging **2** move or turn in a curve • *The door swung open.* **3** change from one opinion or mood etc. to another

swing NOUN **swings** **1** a swinging movement **2** a seat hung on chains or ropes etc. so that it can be moved backwards and forwards **3** the amount by which votes or opinions etc. change from one side to another **4** a kind of jazz music
in full swing at the height of activity

swipe VERB **swipes, swiping, swiped** **1** hit with a swinging blow **2** (*informal*) steal something **3** pass a credit card through an electronic reading device when making a payment
▷ **swipe** NOUN

swirl VERB **swirls, swirling, swirled** move round quickly in circles
▷ **swirl** NOUN
[probably from early German or Dutch]

swish VERB **swishes, swishing, swished** move with a hissing sound
▷ **swish** NOUN

Swiss roll NOUN **Swiss rolls** a thin sponge cake spread with jam or cream and rolled up

switch NOUN **switches** **1** a device that is pressed or turned to start or stop something working, especially by electricity **2** a change of opinion, policy, or methods **3** a mechanism for moving the points on a railway track **4** a flexible rod or whip

switch VERB **switches, switching, switched** **1** turn something on or off by means of a switch **2** change or replace something

switchback NOUN **switchbacks** a railway at a fair, with steep slopes up and down alternately

switchboard NOUN **switchboards** a panel with switches etc. for making telephone connections or operating electric circuits

swivel VERB **swivels, swivelling, swivelled** turn round

swivel NOUN **swivels** a device joining two things so that one can revolve without turning the other

swollen *past participle of* **swell**

Thesaurus

swindle VERB *The company had been swindled out of a large sum of money.* ► cheat, defraud, trick, fleece, dupe, deceive, (*more informal*) con, (*more informal*) diddle, (*more informal*) do, (*more informal*) bamboozle

swindle NOUN *an insurance swindle* ► fraud, fiddle, racket, deception, sham, (*more informal*) con

swindler NOUN *Thousands of pensioners had fallen victim to the swindlers.* ► fraudster, confidence trickster, confidence man, trickster, imposter, cheat, charlatan, (*more informal*) con man

swing VERB **1** *The inn sign swung in the wind.* ► sway, flap, dangle, hang loose, rock, swivel, oscillate, turn, wave about **2** *The van swung across the carriageway.* ► swerve, veer, turn aside, deviate, weave **3** *Public opinion was swinging in favour of the war.* ► fluctuate, shift, change, waver, move, alter, oscillate

swing NOUN **1** *a huge swing in public opinion* ► shift, fluctuation, movement, change, oscillation, variation **2** *a swing of the pendulum* ► oscillation

swipe VERB **1** *He threatened to swiped at her with the towel.* ► hit, strike **2** (*informal*) *Someone swiped my pen.* ► steal, take, filch, snatch, (*informal*) nick, (*informal*) pinch

swipe NOUN *She took a playful swipe at his face.* ► blow, strike, swing, slap, smack, clout, hit

switch NOUN *Whitlock activated the switch on the dashboard.* ► button, control, key, lever, handle

switch VERB *She managed to switch places so she was sitting next to Neil.* ► change, swap, exchange, replace, shift, substitute
switch on *or* **off** *The user must not switch off the computer before this option is chosen.* ► turn on *or* off, put on *or* off, activate *or* deactivate, power up *or* down

swollen ADJECTIVE *I climbed the ladder despite my swollen foot.* ► inflamed, distended, bloated, enlarged, puffed up, puffy, tumescent
OPPOSITES ARE shrunken, shrivelled

A B C D E F G H I J K L M N O P Q R S T U V W X Y Z

swoon *VERB* **swoons, swooning, swooned** (*old use or poetical*) faint
▷ **swoon** *NOUN*

swoop *VERB* **swoops, swooping, swooped**
1 come down with a rushing movement
2 make a sudden attack or raid
▷ **swoop** *NOUN*

sword (sord) *NOUN* **swords** a weapon with a long pointed blade fixed in a handle or hilt
▷ **swordsman** *NOUN*

swordfish *NOUN* **swordfish** a large sea fish with a long sword-like upper jaw

sworn *ADJECTIVE* **1** given under oath, • *sworn testimony* **2** determined to remain so • *They are sworn enemies.*

swot *VERB* **swots, swotting, swotted** (*slang*) study hard
▷ **swot** *NOUN*
[originally a dialect word for **sweat**]

sycamore *NOUN* **sycamores** a tall tree with winged seeds, often grown for its timber

syllable *NOUN* **syllables** a word or part of a word that has one vowel sound when you say it • *'Cat' has one syllable, 'el-e-phant' has three syllables.*
▷ **syllabic** *ADJECTIVE*

syllabus *NOUN* **syllabuses** a summary of the things to be studied by a class or for an examination etc. [via Latin from Greek *sittuba* = label The *tt* was misread in Latin as *ll*]

symbol *NOUN* **symbols** **1** a thing used as a sign • *The crescent is a symbol of Islam.* **2** a mark or sign with a special meaning (e.g. +, -, and x, in mathematics)
USAGE Do not confuse with **cymbal**.

symbolic *ADJECTIVE* acting as a symbol of something; representing something
▷ **symbolical** *ADJECTIVE* **symbolically** *ADVERB*

symbolize *VERB* **symbolizes, symbolizing, symbolized** make or be a symbol of something

symmetrical *ADJECTIVE* able to be divided into two halves which are exactly the same but the opposite way round
▷ **symmetrically** *ADVERB* **symmetry** *NOUN*

sympathize *VERB* **sympathizes, sympathizing, sympathized** show or feel sympathy
▷ **sympathizer** *NOUN*

sympathy *NOUN* **sympathies** **1** the sharing or understanding of other people's feelings, opinions, etc. **2** a feeling of pity or tenderness towards someone who is hurt, sad, or in trouble
▷ **sympathetic** *ADJECTIVE* **sympathetically** *ADVERB*

symphony *NOUN* **symphonies** a long piece of music for an orchestra
▷ **symphonic** *ADJECTIVE*

symptom *NOUN* **symptoms** a sign that a disease or condition exists • *Red spots are a symptom of measles.*
▷ **symptomatic** *ADJECTIVE*

Thesaurus

swoop *VERB* *Wagtails swooped across my path.* ► dive, sweep, plunge, plummet, drop, descend, fly down, lunge
swoop on *Fifty police officers swooped on a group of farm buildings.* ► descend on, pounce on, raid, besiege, search

sword *NOUN* *James had armed himself with the sword of Robert the Bruce.* ► blade, foil, rapier, sabre, broadsword, cutlass, scimitar

symbol *NOUN* **1** *Snakes were seen as symbols of sexuality.* ► emblem, token, sign, image, figure, representation, mark **2** *Too many symbols make the timetable difficult to use if you are in a hurry.* ► sign, character, hieroglyph **3** *The Red Cross symbol was painted on the roof of the vehicle.* ► logo, badge, mark, crest, insignia

sympathetic *ADJECTIVE* **1** *She managed a sympathetic smile.* ► commiserating, comforting, supportive, understanding, appreciative, consoling, caring, compassionate, considerate, tender
OPPOSITES ARE unsympathetic, unfeeling
2 sympathetic to *All the parents felt very sympathetic to what their daughters were going through.* ► understanding of, appreciative of, concerned about, well-disposed towards
3 sympathetic to *Some of the republics seem to have been sympathetic to this idea.* ► in favour of, in sympathy with, in agreement with, supportive of, receptive to

sympathize *VERB* **sympathize with** **1** *We sympathize with the views of the people living in the area.* ► understand, agree with, approve of, support, commend, appreciate **2** *Many trade unionists instinctively sympathized with the plight of the miners.* ► commiserate with, show sympathy for, be sympathetic towards, be sorry for, identify with, empathize with, feel for, side with, pity

sympathy *NOUN* *Friends expressed sympathy for those who died or were injured. Don't waste your sympathy on them.* ► commiseration, pity, compassion, condolences, feeling, fellow-feeling, tenderness, understanding, consideration, empathy

symptom *NOUN* **1** *Several patients suffered from symptoms such as nausea and vomiting.* ► manifestation, indicator, indication, feature **2** *The first symptom of a frozen waste pipe is that the water won't flow out.* ► sign, evidence, indication, warning, testimony

synagogue (sin- a- gog) *NOUN* **synagogues** a place where Jews meet for worship

syndicate *NOUN* **syndicates** **1** a group of people or firms who work together in business **2** a group of people who buy something together, or who gamble together, sharing the cost and any gains

syndrome *NOUN* **syndromes** a set of signs that are characteristic of a condition, especially of a disease

synonym (sin- o- nim) *NOUN* **synonyms** a word that means the same or almost the same as another word • *'Large' and 'great' are synonyms of 'big'.*
▷ **synonymous** (sin- on- im- us) *ADJECTIVE*

syntax (sin- taks) *NOUN* the way words are arranged to make phrases or sentences
▷ **syntactic** *ADJECTIVE* **syntactically** *ADVERB*

synthesizer *NOUN* **synthesizers** an electronic musical instrument that can make a large variety of sounds

synthetic *ADJECTIVE* artificially made; not natural
▷ **synthetically** *ADVERB*

syringe *NOUN* **syringes** a device for sucking in a liquid and squirting it out [from Greek *syrinx* = pipe, tube]

syrup *NOUN* a thick sweet liquid
▷ **syrupy** *ADJECTIVE*
[from Arabic *sharab* = a drink]

system *NOUN* **systems** **1** a set of parts, things, or ideas that are organized to work together **2** a way of doing something • *a new system of training motorcyclists*

systematic *ADJECTIVE* methodical; carefully planned
▷ **systematically** *ADVERB*

Thesaurus

synthetic *ADJECTIVE* *The whole pitch has been replaced by a synthetic surface.* ► artificial, imitation, manufactured, simulated, substitute, man-made, unnatural, concocted, mock, ersatz, fabricated, fake
OPPOSITES ARE natural, real, genuine

system *NOUN* **1** *a reform of the criminal justice system* ► organization, structure, framework, network, institution, (*informal*) set-up **2** *a system for recording accidents at work* ► procedure, process, routine, scheme, arrangement, means (of), method, methodology, plan, structure, set of rules **3** *a system of government that commands the confidence of all the people* ► philosophy, regime, science, constitution, principles

systematic *ADJECTIVE* *Citizenship should be taught in every school in a systematic way.* ► methodical, ordered, orderly, organized, structured, planned, systematized, coherent, scientific, logical AN OPPOSITE IS unsystematic

Tt

tab *NOUN* **tabs** a small flap or strip that sticks out

tabby *NOUN* **tabbies** a grey or brown cat with dark stripes

table *NOUN* **tables** **1** a piece of furniture with a flat top supported on legs **2** a list of facts or figures arranged in order **3** a list of the results of multiplying a number by other numbers • *multiplication tables*

tablecloth *NOUN* **tablecloths** a cloth for covering a table, especially at meals

tablespoon *NOUN* **tablespoons** a large spoon for serving food
▷ **tablespoonful** *NOUN*

tablet *NOUN* **tablets** **1** a pill **2** a solid piece of soap **3** a flat piece of stone or wood etc. with words carved or written on it

table tennis *NOUN* a game played on a table divided by a net, over which you hit a small ball with bats

taboo *ADJECTIVE* not to be done or used or talked about
▷ **taboo** *NOUN*
[from Tongan (South Pacific) *tabu* = sacred]

tack[1] *NOUN* **tacks** **1** a short nail with a flat top **2** a tacking stitch **3** (in sailing) the direction taken when tacking **4** a course of action or policy • *I think we need to change tack.*

tack *VERB* **tacks, tacking, tacked** **1** nail something down with tacks **2** fasten material together with long stitches **3** sail a zigzag course to take advantage of what wind there is
tack on (*informal*) add an extra thing

tack[2] *NOUN* harness, saddles, etc.

tackle *VERB* **tackles, tackling, tackled** **1** try to do something that needs doing **2** try to get the ball from someone else in a game of football or hockey **3** talk to someone about a difficult or awkward matter

tackle *NOUN* **tackles** **1** equipment, especially for fishing **2** a set of ropes and pulleys **3** tackling someone in football or hockey

tacky *ADJECTIVE* sticky, not quite dry • *The paint is still tacky.*
▷ **tackiness** *NOUN*

tact *NOUN* skill in not offending people
▷ **tactful** *ADJECTIVE* **tactfully** *ADVERB* **tactless** *ADJECTIVE* **tactlessly** *ADVERB*

tactics *NOUN* **1** the method of arranging troops etc. skilfully for a battle **2** the methods you use to achieve something or gain an advantage
▷ **tactical** *ADJECTIVE* **tactically** *ADVERB* **tactician** *NOUN*
[from Greek *taktika* = things arranged]
USAGE *Strategy* is a general plan for a whole campaign; *tactics* is for one part of this.

Thesaurus

table *NOUN* **1** *He put the glasses on the table.* ► dining table, kitchen table, worktop, working surface, coffee table **2** *The table on page three shows monthly rainfall in the region.* ► chart, diagram, graph, list

tablet *NOUN* **1** *There is a stone tablet over the doorway.* ► plaque, slab, plate, sign **2** *She rang reception and asked for another tablet of soap.* ► bar, piece, block, chunk, slab **3** *He went to his room and took a headache tablet.* ► pill, capsule, caplet

taboo *NOUN* *There is a taboo against doing business on the sabbath.* ► ban, prohibition, proscription, veto, restriction, anathema

taboo *ADJECTIVE* *Politics were a taboo subject at the dinner table.* ► forbidden, prohibited, banned, proscribed, unacceptable, disapproved of, unmentionable

tack *NOUN* **1** *The carpet was held down with a row of tacks.* ► pin, drawing-pin, nail, tin tack **2**

tack *VERB* **1** *He tacked a photo to the notice board.* ► pin, nail, fix **2** *She tacked the hem and tried it on for length.* ► stitch, sew
tack on *A few maps and plans are tacked on at the back of the book.* ► attach, add, append

tackle *NOUN* **1** *He wanted to buy new fishing tackle.* ► gear, equipment, apparatus, implements, kit, outfit, paraphernalia, rig, tools **2** *The referee penalized him for a late tackle.* ► challenge, interception, attack, block

tackle *VERB* **1** *The Government is determined to tackle the issue of tax avoidance.* ► deal with, grapple with, address yourself to, confront, cope with, face up to, sort out, handle, manage, attend to, combat, set about, undertake **2** *An opposing player tackled him near the touchline.* ► challenge, intercept, stop, confront, attack, take on **3** *Lettie decided to tackle him directly about her pay.* ► confront, approach, challenge, address

tacky *ADJECTIVE* **1** *The paint was still tacky.* ► sticky, wet, gluey AN OPPOSITE IS dry **2** *tacky quizzes and game shows* ► vulgar, coarse, crude, tawdry, garish, trashy
AN OPPOSITE IS tasteful

tact *NOUN* *A police officer told her the news with great tact.* ► discretion, consideration, sensitivity, tactfulness, delicacy, diplomacy, thoughtfulness, understanding
OPPOSITES ARE indiscretion, tactlessness

tactful *ADJECTIVE* *Molly gave them a tactful reminder about the rent.* ► discreet, judicious, considerate, polite, delicate, diplomatic,

tadpole *NOUN* **tadpoles** a young frog or toad that has developed from the egg and lives entirely in water

tag[1] *NOUN* **tags 1** a label tied on or stuck into something **2** a metal or plastic point at the end of a shoelace

tag *VERB* **tags, tagging, tagged 1** label something with a tag **2** add as an extra thing • *A postscript was tagged on to her letter.* **3** (*informal*) go with other people • *Her sister tagged along.*

tag[2] *NOUN* a game in which one person chases the others

tail *NOUN* **tails 1** the part that sticks out from the rear end of the body of a bird, fish, or animal **2** the part at the end or rear of something **3** the side of a coin opposite the head • *Heads or tails?*

tail *VERB* **tails, tailing, tailed 1** remove stalks etc. from fruit • *top and tail gooseberries* **2** (*informal*) follow someone closely
tail off become fewer, smaller, or slighter etc.; cease gradually

tailor *NOUN* **tailors** a person who makes men's clothes

taint *NOUN* **taints** a small amount of decay, pollution, or a bad quality that spoils something

taint *VERB* **taints, tainting, tainted** give something a taint

take *VERB* **takes, taking, took, taken 1** get something into your hands or possession or control etc. • *Take this cup.* • *We took many prisoners.* **2** carry or convey • *Take this parcel to the post.* **3** make use of • *Shall we take a taxi?* **4** indulge in or undertake • *You need to take a holiday.* **5** perform or deal with • *When do you take your music exam?* **6** study or teach a subject • *Who takes you for maths?* **7** make an effort • *Thanks for taking the trouble to see me.* **8** experience a feeling • *Don't take offence.* **9** accept or endure • *I'll take a risk.* **10** require • *It takes a strong man to lift this.* **11** write down • *take notes* **12** make a photograph **13** subtract • *take 4 from 10* **14** assume • *I take it that you agree.*
▷ **taker** *NOUN*
take after be like a parent etc.
take in deceive somebody
take leave of say goodbye to
take off (said about an aircraft) leave the ground and become airborne

Thesaurus

sensitive, thoughtful OPPOSITES ARE tactless, indiscreet

tactless *ADJECTIVE She was plainly upset by his tactless remark.* ► indiscreet, insensitive, thoughtless, unthinking, indelicate, clumsy OPPOSITES ARE tactful, discreet

tag *VERB Each bottle was tagged with a different coloured label.* ► label, mark, identify, ticket
tag on *A note was tagged on at the end of the letter.* ► add, attach, append, tack on
tag along *Sometimes he let me tag along.* ► follow, go along, accompany

tail *NOUN They waited at the tail of the queue.* ► back, end, rear, extremity, tail end

tail *VERB A squad of reporters had tailed him for five years.* ► follow, shadow, stalk, pursue, track, trail
tail off *Her words tailed off at the expression in his eyes.* ► fade, wane, ebb, peter out, drop away, subside, dwindle, decline, decrease, lessen, reduce, slacken

taint *NOUN free from the taint of corruption* ► stain, smear, hint, trace, blight, contamination

taint *VERB* **1** *an area tainted by pollution* ► contaminate, pollute, poison, soil, adulterate, dirty, infect **2** *These unhappy events tainted their reputation for ever.* ► tarnish, stain, sully, besmirch, blacken, dishonour, smear, ruin, slander

take *VERB* **1** *Many prisoners were taken.* ► catch, seize, capture, take captive, arrest **2** *He took her hand gently.* ► clasp, clutch, grasp, grab, grip, take hold of, lay hold of **3** *Someone had taken his car.* ► steal, remove, make off with, appropriate, (*more informal*) pinch, (*more informal*) nick, (*more informal*) filch, (*more informal*) swipe **4** *Take ten percent from the total.* ► subtract, deduct, knock off, discount **5** *It takes a long time to recover from an illness like this.* ► need, require, call for, necessitate **6** *The pain was more than he could take.* ► bear, put up with, endure, tolerate, suffer, stomach **7** *I'll take you home.* ► accompany, drive, bring, convey, conduct, escort, guide, transport, carry
be taken with *Tanya was rather taken with the idea.* ► be interested in, be attracted by, be captivated by, be fascinated by, be delighted by, be enchanted by
take aback *This suggestion took us aback.* ► surprise, astonish, astound
take apart *a cot that can be easily taken apart* ► dismantle, take to pieces, disassemble
take back *I took back everything I had said.* ► withdraw, retract, disown, recant, repudiate, deny
take down *A police officer took down the details.* ► write down, note, jot down, record
take in 1 *a confidence trick that took everyone in* ► fool, deceive, mislead, dupe, trick, hoodwink, cheat **2** *It was too much information*

A B C D E F G H I J K L M N O P Q R S T U V W X Y Z

take on 1 begin to employ someone **2** play or fight against someone **3** (*informal*) show that you are upset
take over take control
take place happen or occur
take up 1 start something **2** occupy space or time etc. **3** accept an offer
[from Old Norse]

takeaway *NOUN* **takeaways 1** a place that sells cooked meals for customers to take away **2** a meal from this

tale *NOUN* **tales** a story [from Old English]

talent *NOUN* **talents** a special or very great ability
▷ **talented** *ADJECTIVE*
[from Greek *talanton* = sum of money. The meaning in English is based on the use of the word in a parable in the New Testament (Matthew 25:14-30), in which a man gives his servants 'talents' of money to put to good use]

talk *VERB* **talks, talking, talked** speak; have a conversation
▷ **talker** *NOUN*

talk *NOUN* **talks 1** a conversation or discussion **2** an informal lecture

talkative *ADJECTIVE* talking a lot

tall *ADJECTIVE* **1** higher than the average • *a tall tree* **2** measured from the bottom to the top • *It is 10 metres tall.*
▷ **tallness** *NOUN*

tall story *NOUN* **tall stories** (*informal*) a story that is hard to believe

tally *VERB* **tallies, tallying, tallied** correspond or agree with something else • *Does your list tally with mine?*

talon *NOUN* **talons** a strong claw

tambourine *NOUN* **tambourines** a circular musical instrument with metal discs round it, tapped or shaken to make it jingle

Thesaurus

to take in at once. ► understand, comprehend, grasp, absorb, assimilate, digest **3** *a cruise that takes in the main Greek islands* ► include, incorporate, encompass, comprise, cover
take it *I take it you want to stay.* ► assume, infer, deduce
take off 1 *I took off my shoes before going in.* ► remove, shed, throw off, discard **2** *a plan that might never take off* ► succeed, do well, catch on **3** *The man took off at a run.* ► run off, run away, leave, escape, depart, disappear
take on *She took on more responsibilities that year.* ► accept, assume, undertake, acquire, shoulder
take up 1 *She took up painting in her forties.* ► engage in, practise, become interested in **2** *a cupboard that takes up a lot of space* ► occupy, absorb, use up, fill

take-off *NOUN* **1** *The flight was bumpy for a while after take-off.* ► lift-off, departure, ascent **2** *The sketch is a take-off of the American President.* ► parody, imitation, pastiche, satire, lampoon

tale *NOUN* *a tale about dragons and heroes* ► story, narrative, narration, history, account, yarn

talent *NOUN* *a talent for playing the violin* ► gift, aptitude, ability, accomplishment, flair, genius, skill, capacity, expertise, knack, prowess

talented *ADJECTIVE* *a talented young player* ► gifted, able, accomplished, skilful, skilled, artistic, brilliant, clever, distinguished, expert
OPPOSITES ARE inept, unskilful

talk *VERB* **1** *I was talking to a friend.* ► speak, chat, converse (with) **2** *They were talking complete rubbish.* ► speak, utter, express, articulate, communicate **3** *They looked for a quiet spot to talk.* ► have a talk, have a chat, converse, confer, speak to one another, communicate with one another **4** *He refused to talk.* ► give information, confess, admit anything **5** *People were beginning to talk.* ► gossip, spread rumours, make remarks, pass comments
talk of *She talked of leaving and settling abroad.* ► speak about, mention, refer to
talk to *He talked to an eager audience.* ► speak to, address, lecture

talk *NOUN* **1** *too much talk and not enough action* ► conversation, speaking, chatter, discussion, dialogue, (*more informal*) yakking **2** *There was talk of an affair.* ► rumour, gossip (about), (*more informal*) tittle-tattle **3** *a talk in the village hall* ► lecture, address, speech, presentation, discourse **4 talks** *Peace talks will resume next week.* ► negotiations, discussions, consultations

talkative *ADJECTIVE* *He had chanced on an unusually talkative taxi driver* ► chatty, loquacious, garrulous, voluble, effusive, vocal, communicative, forthcoming, articulate
OPPOSITES ARE taciturn, unforthcoming

talking-to *NOUN* (*informal*) *He was given a severe talking-to and told not to come back.* ► reprimand, lecture, scolding, (*informal*) telling-off, (*informal*) dressing-down

tall *ADJECTIVE* **1** *a tall man* ► large, big **2** *a tall building* ► high, lofty, towering, soaring, elevated

tally *NOUN* *a final tally of twenty goals scored during the season* ► total, count, reckoning, account

tally *VERB* *Her explanation did not tally with the evidence before their eyes.* ► agree, accord, correspond (with to), concur, fit

tame *ADJECTIVE* **1** (said about animals) gentle and not afraid of people; not wild or dangerous **2** not exciting; dull
▷ **tamely** *ADVERB* **tameness** *NOUN*

tame *VERB* **tames, taming, tamed** make an animal become tame
▷ **tamer** *NOUN*

tamper *VERB* **tampers, tampering, tampered** meddle or interfere with something

tampon *NOUN* **tampons** a plug of soft material that a woman puts into her vagina to absorb the blood during her period

tan *NOUN* **tans 1** a light brown colour **2** a brown colour in skin that has been exposed to sun

tan *VERB* **tans, tanning, tanned 1** make or become brown by exposing skin to the sun **2** make an animal's skin into leather by treating it with chemicals

tandem *NOUN* **tandems** a bicycle for two riders, one behind the other
in tandem one behind another; together
[Latin, = at length]

tang *NOUN* **tangs** a strong flavour or smell

tangent *NOUN* **tangents** a straight line that touches the outside of a curve or circle
go off at a tangent move away suddenly from a subject or line of thought being considered

tangerine *NOUN* **tangerines** a kind of small orange

tangle *VERB* **tangles, tangling, tangled** make or become twisted into a confused mass
▷ **tangle** *NOUN*

tango *NOUN* **tangos** a ballroom dance with gliding steps

tank *NOUN* **tanks 1** a large container for a liquid or gas **2** a heavy armoured vehicle used in war

tankard *NOUN* **tankards** a large mug for drinking beer from, usually made of silver or pewter

tanker *NOUN* **tankers 1** a large ship for carrying oil **2** a large lorry for carrying a liquid

tantalize *VERB* **tantalizes, tantalizing, tantalized** tease or torment a person by showing him or her something good but keeping it out of reach

tantrum *NOUN* **tantrums** an outburst of bad temper

Thesaurus

tame *ADJECTIVE* **1** *The animal was so tame that it shinned up his leg and dived into a deep pocket.* ▸ domesticated, gentle, manageable, disciplined, trained, meek, obedient, safe, subdued, submissive, tractable
AN OPPOSITE IS wild **2** *Aren't you Joe's tame reporter?* ▸ cooperative, willing, amenable, biddable AN OPPOSITE IS uncooperative **3** *It turned out to be a tame evening after all.* ▸ dull, tedious, boring, unexciting, uninteresting, humdrum, bland, feeble, flat, lifeless, uninspiring, unadventurous
AN OPPOSITE IS exciting

tame *VERB* **1** *Wild rabbits can be tamed in captivity.* ▸ domesticate, break in, train, discipline, house-train, master **2** *She made strenuous efforts to tame her behaviour.* ▸ control, subdue, curb, conquer, master, moderate, mitigate, quell, repress, subjugate, suppress, temper

tamper *VERB*
tamper with *A student was able to enter the cockpit of an empty aircraft and tamper with the controls.* ▸ interfere with, meddle with, tinker with, alter, change, adjust, play about with, fiddle about with, make adjustments to

tan *ADJECTIVE* *a tan overcoat* ▸ light brown, pale brown, tawny

tangible *ADJECTIVE* *The experiment brought no tangible results.* ▸ definite, solid, substantial, concrete, actual, real, material, positive, discernible AN OPPOSITE IS intangible

tangle *NOUN* *a tangle of wires and cables* ▸ mass, muddle, jumble, confusion, maze, jungle, knot, twist

tangle *VERB* **1** *She had managed to tangle her hair.* ▸ entangle, knot, twist, ravel
OPPOSITES ARE untangle, disentangle **2** *A dolphin had become tangled in the net.* ▸ trap, ensnare, entrap, catch, enmesh **3** *Better not to tangle with people like that.* ▸ become involved with, come into conflict with, confront, quarrel with, cross swords with

tangled *ADJECTIVE* **1** *Later they emigrated, but could never escape their tangled past.* ▸ complicated, complex, confused, convoluted, involved, entangled, intricate
AN OPPOSITE IS straightforward **2** *an undergrowth of tangled bushes and trees* ▸ knotted, matted, convoluted, dishevelled, tousled, unkempt, untidy AN OPPOSITE IS tidy

tangy *ADJECTIVE* *Citrus adds a tangy taste to all sorts of savoury dishes.* ▸ sharp, pungent, piquant, appetizing, spicy, strong, tart, fresh, refreshing OPPOSITES ARE insipid, bland

tank *NOUN* **1** *a hot water tank* ▸ container, cistern, reservoir, basin **2** *a tank of fish* ▸ aquarium, bowl

tantrum *NOUN* *He threw a tantrum and rolled on the floor, kicking and screaming.* ▸ fit of rage, fit of temper, scene, outburst, (*more informal*) paddy, (*more informal*) wobbly

tap[1] *NOUN* **taps** a device for letting out liquid or gas in a controlled flow

tap *VERB* **taps, tapping, tapped** **1** take liquid out of something, especially through a tap **2** obtain supplies or information etc. from a source **3** fix a device to a telephone line so that you can overhear conversations on it

tap[2] *NOUN* **taps** a quick light hit; the sound of this

tap *VERB* **taps, tapping, tapped** hit a person or thing quickly and lightly

tape *NOUN* **tapes** **1** a narrow strip of cloth, paper, plastic, etc. **2** a narrow plastic strip coated with a magnetic substance and used for making recordings **3** a tape recording **4** a tape measure

tape *VERB* **tapes, taping, taped** **1** fix, cover, or surround something with tape **2** record something on magnetic tape
get or **have something taped** (*slang*) know or understand it; be able to deal with it

tape measure *NOUN* **tape measures** a long strip marked in centimetres or inches for measuring things

taper *VERB* **tapers, tapering, tapered** **1** make or become thinner towards one end **2** make or become gradually less

tape recorder *NOUN* **tape recorders** a machine for recording music or sound on magnetic tape and playing it back
▷ **tape recording** *NOUN*

tapestry *NOUN* **tapestries** a piece of strong cloth with pictures or patterns woven or embroidered on it

tapeworm *NOUN* **tapeworms** a long flat worm that can live as a parasite in the intestines of people and animals

tar *NOUN* a thick black liquid made from coal or wood etc. and used in making roads

target *NOUN* **targets** something aimed at; a thing that someone tries to hit or reach

tariff *NOUN* **tariffs** a list of prices or charges

tarmac *NOUN* an area surfaced with a mixture of tar and broken stone (called **tarmacadam**), especially on an airfield

tarnish *VERB* **tarnishes, tarnishing, tarnished** **1** make or become less shiny • *The silver had tarnished.* **2** spoil or blemish • *The scandal tarnished his reputation.*
▷ **tarnish** *NOUN*

tarpaulin *NOUN* **tarpaulins** a large sheet of waterproof canvas

tarry[1] (tar- ee) *ADJECTIVE* covered with or like tar

tarry[2] (ta- ree) *VERB* **tarries, tarrying, tarried** (*old use*) stay for a while longer; linger

tart[1] *NOUN* **tarts** an open pastry case with a sweet filling

tart[2] *ADJECTIVE* **1** sour **2** sharp in manner • *a tart reply*
▷ **tartly** *ADVERB* **tartness** *NOUN*

tartan *NOUN* a pattern with coloured stripes crossing each other, especially one that is used by a Scottish clan

tartar[1] *NOUN* **tartars** a person who is fierce or difficult to deal with

tartar[2] *NOUN* **tartars** a hard chalky deposit that forms on teeth

task *NOUN* **tasks** a piece of work to be done
take a person to task rebuke him or her

tassel *NOUN* **tassels** a bundle of threads tied together at the top and used to decorate something
▷ **tasselled** *ADJECTIVE*

Thesaurus

tap *NOUN* **1** *a water tap* ► faucet, stopcock, valve **2** *There was a tap at the window.* ► knock, rap, knocking, touch

tap *VERB* **1** *She tapped on the door.* ► knock, rap, strike **2** *I leaned forward to tap her shoulder.* ► pat, touch, poke, nudge

tape *NOUN* **1** *The parcel was bound with tape.* ► band, binding, strip, braid, ribbon **2** *They listened to music on tapes.* ► cassette, tape recording

tape *VERB* *I'll tape up the parcel.* ► bind, tie, seal

taper *VERB* **1** *The leaves taper to a point.* ► narrow, thin, become narrower **2** *Their enthusiasm soon tapered off.* ► decrease, lessen, dwindle, wane, diminish, die down, peter out

target *NOUN* **1** *a target of £100,000* ► goal, objective, aim, ambition, end, intention **2** *the target of attacks* ► victim, butt, object, quarry, prey

tart *ADJECTIVE* **1** *the tart taste of cooked apples* ► sharp, sour, acid, tangy, piquant, pungent
OPPOSITES ARE sweet, bland **2** *He regretted his rather tart response.* ► acerbic, sharp, biting, cutting, caustic, scathing

task *NOUN* *Finishing the book in time proved a daunting task.* ► job, undertaking, enterprise, exercise, chore, duty, charge, burden, labour, work, mission, requirement
take to task *He took his advisers to task for misleading him.* ► criticize, rebuke, reproach, reprove, upbraid, censure, admonish

taste *VERB* **tastes, tasting, tasted 1** take a small amount of food or drink to try its flavour **2** be able to perceive flavours **3** have a certain flavour

taste *NOUN* **tastes 1** the feeling caused in the tongue by something placed on it **2** the ability to taste things **3** the ability to enjoy beautiful things or to choose what is suitable • *She shows good taste in her choice of clothes.* **4** a liking • *I've developed quite a taste for skiing.* **5** a very small amount of food or drink

tasteful *ADJECTIVE* showing good taste
▷ **tastefully** *ADVERB* **tastefulness** *NOUN*

tasteless *ADJECTIVE* **1** having no flavour **2** showing poor taste
▷ **tastelessly** *ADVERB* **tastelessness** *NOUN*

tasty *ADJECTIVE* **tastier, tastiest** having a strong pleasant taste

tattered *ADJECTIVE* badly torn; ragged

tatters *PLURAL NOUN* rags; badly torn pieces
in tatters torn to pieces • *My coat was in tatters.*

tattoo[1] *VERB* **tattoos, tattooing, tattooed** mark a person's skin permanently with a picture or pattern by using a needle and dye

tattoo *NOUN* **tattoos** a tattooed picture or pattern [from a Polynesian (South Pacific) language]

tattoo[2] *NOUN* **tattoos 1** a drumming or tapping sound **2** an entertainment consisting of military music, marching, etc. [from Dutch *taptoe* = close the tap of a cask]

taunt *VERB* **taunts, taunting, taunted** jeer at or insult someone
▷ **taunt** *NOUN*

taut *ADJECTIVE* stretched tightly
▷ **tautly** *ADVERB* **tautness** *NOUN*

tautology *NOUN* **tautologies** saying the same thing again in different words, e.g. *You can get the book free for nothing* (where *free* and *for nothing* mean the same)

tavern *NOUN* **taverns** (*old use*) an inn or public house

tawny *ADJECTIVE* brownish-yellow

tax *NOUN* **taxes 1** money that people or business firms have to pay to the government, to be used for public purposes **2** a strain or burden • *The long walk was a tax on his strength*

tax *VERB* **taxes, taxing, taxed 1** put a tax on something **2** charge someone a tax **3** pay the tax on something • *I have taxed the car up to June.* **4** put a strain or burden on a person or thing • *This will tax your strength.* **5** accuse • *I taxed him with leaving the door open.*
▷ **taxable** *ADJECTIVE* **taxation** *NOUN*

taxi *NOUN* **taxis** a car that carries passengers for payment, usually with a meter to record the fare to be paid
▷ **taxicab** *NOUN*

taxi *VERB* **taxies, taxiing, taxied** (said about an aircraft) move along the ground or water, especially before or after flying

tea *NOUN* **teas 1** a drink made by pouring hot water on the dried leaves of an evergreen shrub **2** these dried leaves **3** a drink made with the leaves of other plants • *camomile tea* **4** a meal in the afternoon or early evening
▷ **teacup** *NOUN* **tea leaf** *NOUN* **teatime** *NOUN*
[via Dutch from Chinese]

tea bag *NOUN* **tea bags** a small bag holding about a teaspoonful of tea

Thesaurus

taste *NOUN* **1** *I don't much like the taste of raisins.* ► flavour, savour, character **2** *Would you like a taste of my pudding?* ► mouthful, bite, morsel, nibble, bit, piece, sample **3** *a millionaire with a taste for travel* ► liking, appreciation, fondness, desire, inclination, preference **4** *Hilary is a person of taste. The decoration was done with taste.* ► judgement, discernment, discretion, discrimination, perception, refinement, sensitivity, style

taste *VERB* *Anna tasted her drink and smiled.* ► sample, test, try, sip, check

tasteful *ADJECTIVE* *a plain and tasteful decor* ► discriminating, refined, restrained, sensitive, smart, stylish, well-judged, elegant, fashionable, in good taste, judicious, fastidious, proper AN OPPOSITE IS tasteless

tasteless *ADJECTIVE* **1** *The vegetables were overcooked and tasteless.* ► flavourless, bland, insipid, weak, watery, characterless, mild, uninteresting AN OPPOSITE IS tasty **2** *a tasteless remark* ► crude, indelicate, uncouth, vulgar, tactless, crass, injudicious, unseemly OPPOSITES ARE tasteful, delicate

tasty *ADJECTIVE* *a tasty meal* ► delicious, appetizing, luscious, mouth-watering, (*more informal*) yummy, (*more informal*) scrumptious

taunt *VERB* *People taunted him about his marriage.* ► tease, torment, jeer at, mock, ridicule, bait

taut *ADJECTIVE* *The rope should be taut.* ► tight, tense, firm, rigid, stretched AN OPPOSITE IS slack

tax *NOUN* *The new government immediately imposed a tax on imports.* ► duty, tariff, charge, imposition, levy RELATED ADJECTIVE fiscal

tax *VERB* **1** *It seems unfair to many people to tax pensions.* ► impose a tax on, levy a tax on **2** *The long walk taxed them severely.* ► tire, strain, exhaust, burden, make heavy demands on

teach *VERB* **teaches, teaching, taught 1** give a person knowledge or skill; train **2** give lessons, especially in a particular subject **3** show someone what to do or avoid • *That will teach you not to meddle!*

teacher *NOUN* **teachers** a person who teaches others, especially in a school

team *NOUN* **teams 1** a set of players forming one side in certain games and sports **2** a set of people working together **3** two or more animals harnessed to pull a vehicle or a plough etc.

teapot *NOUN* **teapots** a pot with a lid and a handle, for making and pouring tea

tear[1] (teer) *NOUN* **tears** a drop of the water that comes from the eyes when a person cries
▷ **teardrop** *NOUN*
in tears crying

tear[2] (tair) *VERB* **tears, tearing, tore, torn**
1 pull something apart, away, or into pieces
2 become torn • *Newspaper tears easily.*
3 (*informal*) run or travel hurriedly

tear *NOUN* **tears** a split made by tearing

tear gas *NOUN* a gas that makes people's eyes water painfully

tease *VERB* **teases, teasing, teased 1** amuse yourself by deliberately annoying or making fun of someone **2** pick threads apart into separate strands

tease *NOUN* **teases** a person who often teases others

teaspoon *NOUN* **teaspoons** a small spoon for stirring tea etc.
▷ **teaspoonful** *NOUN*

tea towel *NOUN* **tea towels** a cloth for drying washed dishes, cutlery, etc.

technical *ADJECTIVE* **1** to do with technology **2** to do with a particular subject and its methods • *the technical terms of chemistry* **3** using language that only experts can understand
▷ **technically** *ADVERB*

technical college *NOUN* **technical colleges** a college where technical subjects are taught

technicality *NOUN* **technicalities 1** being technical **2** a technical word, phrase, or detail

technician *NOUN* **technicians** a person whose job is to look after scientific equipment and do practical work in a laboratory

technique *NOUN* **techniques** the method of doing something skilfully

technology *NOUN* **technologies** the study of machinery, engineering, and how things work
▷ **technological** *ADJECTIVE* **technologist** *NOUN*

teddy bear *NOUN* **teddy bears** a soft furry toy bear

tedious *ADJECTIVE* annoyingly slow or long; boring
▷ **tediously** *ADVERB* **tediousness** *NOUN* **tedium** *NOUN*

tee *NOUN* **tees 1** the flat area from which golfers strike the ball at the start of play for each hole **2** a small piece of wood or plastic on which a golf ball is placed for being struck

teem *VERB* **teems, teeming, teemed** be full of something • *The river was teeming with fish.*

teenage *ADJECTIVE* to do with teenagers

Thesaurus

teach *VERB* **1** *He taught me to swim in the holidays.* ► instruct, train, coach **2** *She teaches children with special needs.* ► educate, tutor, instruct, coach

teacher *NOUN* *He had been a teacher all his working life.* ► educator, tutor, instructor, schoolteacher, schoolmaster schoolmistress, pedagogue, academic RELATED ADJECTIVE pedagogic pedagogical

team *NOUN* **1** *the local cricket team* ► squad, side, line-up **2** *the BBC's production team* ► group, crew, company, body, gang

team *VERB* **team up** *She teamed up with her fellow artists for a joint exhibition.* ► join forces, collaborate, cooperate, get together, band together, work together, combine, unite

tear *NOUN* USAGE rhymes with *fearThere was a tear in his eyes.* ► teardrop, droplet
tears *She was so upset she was close to tears.* ► crying, weeping, sobbing, blubbering

tear *VERB* (rhymes with *bear*) **1** *Take care you don't tear your clothes.* ► rip, slit, snag, split **2** *She tore the packet open.* ► rip, pull **3** *He tore the book from my hands.* ► snatch, grab, seize, wrench, wrest **4** (*informal*) *James tore round to the shop.* ► rush, hurry, race, speed, sprint, shoot, bolt AN OPPOSITE IS stroll

tear *NOUN* (rhymes with *bear*) *There's a tear in my jeans.* ► rip, hole, split, slit, rent, gash

tearful *ADJECTIVE* **1** *Glenda was tearful.* ► in tears, crying, weeping, close to tears, upset OPPOSITES ARE cheerful, happy **2** *a tearful farewell* ► emotional, distressing, upsetting, sorrowful, sad, heartbreaking

tease *VERB* *His friends teased him about his hair.* ► make fun of, poke fun at, laugh at, mock, taunt, provoke, torment

tedious *ADJECTIVE* *The work is tedious and time-consuming.* ► dull, boring, monotonous, uninteresting, dreary, humdrum, laborious, irksome, tiresome, unexciting, wearisome OPPOSITES ARE interesting, exciting

teem *VERB* **teem with** *The pond teemed with fish.* ► be full of, abound in, seethe with, swarm with, be infested with, be crawling with

A B C D E F G H I J K L M N O P Q R S T U V W X Y Z

teenager NOUN **teenagers** a person in his or her teens

teens PLURAL NOUN the time of life between 13 and 19 years of age

teething NOUN (said about a baby) having its first teeth beginning to grow through the gums

teetotal ADJECTIVE never drinking alcohol
▷ **teetotaller** NOUN

telecommunications PLURAL NOUN communications over a long distance, e.g. by telephone, telegraph, radio, or television

telegram NOUN **telegrams** a message sent by telegraph

telegraph NOUN a way of sending messages by using electric current along wires or by radio
▷ **telegraphic** ADJECTIVE **telegraphy** NOUN

telepathy (til- ep- ath- ee) NOUN communication of thoughts from one person's mind to another without speaking, writing, or gestures
▷ **telepathic** ADJECTIVE

telephone NOUN **telephones** a device or system using electric wires or radio etc. to enable one person to speak to another who is some distance away

telephone VERB **telephones, telephoning, telephoned** speak to a person on the telephone

telescope NOUN **telescopes** an instrument using lenses to magnify distant objects
▷ **telescopic** ADJECTIVE

telescope VERB **telescopes, telescoping, telescoped** **1** make or become shorter by sliding overlapping sections into each other **2** compress or condense something so that it takes less space or time [from Greek *tele-* = far + *skopein* = look at]

televise VERB **televises, televising, televised** to show a programme on television

television NOUN **televisions** **1** a system using radio waves to reproduce a view of scenes, events, or plays etc. on a screen **2** an apparatus for receiving these pictures **3** televised programmes [from Greek *tele-* = far + **vision**]

tell VERB **tells, telling, told** **1** make a thing known to someone, especially by words **2** speak • *Tell the truth.* **3** order • *Tell them to wait.* **4** reveal a secret • *Promise you won't tell.* **5** decide or distinguish • *Can you tell the difference between butter and margarine?* **6** produce an effect • *The strain began to tell on him.*
all told in all, all together • *There are ten of them, all told.*
tell off (*informal*) reprimand
tell tales report something wrong or bad that someone has done

telling ADJECTIVE having a strong effect or meaning • *It was a telling reply.*

tell-tale ADJECTIVE revealing or indicating something • *There was a tell-tale spot of jam on his chin.*

temper NOUN **tempers** **1** a person's mood • *He is in a good temper.* **2** an angry mood • *She was in a temper.*
lose your temper become angry

temper VERB **tempers, tempering, tempered** **1** harden or strengthen metal etc. by heating and cooling it **2** moderate or soften the effects of something • *Justice needs to be tempered with mercy.*

Thesaurus

tell VERB **1** *Tell me what happened.* ► inform, advise, notify (of), let know, acquaint (with) **2** *She told us there would be another train in an hour.* ► assure, promise, advise, inform **3** *I'll tell you a secret.* ► disclose, reveal, confess, admit **4** *He became more and more excited as he told his story.* ► recount, narrate, relate, describe, communicate, speak **5** *Colin told us to leave.* ► order, instruct, command, direct, call on **6** *It's not easy to tell them apart.*
► distinguish, differentiate, identify, recognize, discern
tell off (*informal*) *He told them off for being late.*
► reprimand, scold, rebuke, upbraid, censure, berate, (*informal*) tick off

telling ADJECTIVE *The argument is expressed in a few telling phrases.* ► revealing, forceful, striking, persuasive, potent, compelling, effective AN OPPOSITE IS insignificant

telling-off NOUN (*informal*) *They were lucky to escape with a mild telling-off.* ► reprimand, scolding, rebuke, caution, admonishment, (*informal*) ticking-off

temper NOUN **1** *He walked out in a temper.*
► rage, fury, fit of rage, passion, tantrum **2** *Jenny's temper flared.* ► anger, fury, rage, annoyance, irritation, irritability, petulance **3** *Both children had a calm temper.*
► temperament, disposition, nature, character, personality
lose your temper *Diana was capable of losing her temper.* ► become angry, fly into a rage, lose control, blow up, go berserk, (*more informal*) go mad, (*more informal*) go crazy, (*more informal*) go bananas, (*more informal*) fly off the handle, (*more informal*) go through the roof, (*more informal*) have a fit, (*more informal*) see red

A B C D E F G H I J K L M N O P Q R S T U V W X Y Z

temperament NOUN **temperaments** a person's nature as shown in the way he or she usually behaves • *a nervous temperament*

temperamental ADJECTIVE **1** likely to become excitable or moody suddenly **2** to do with a person's temperament
▷ **temperamentally** ADVERB

temperate ADJECTIVE neither extremely hot nor extremely cold • *Britain has a temperate climate.*

temperature NOUN **temperatures 1** how hot or cold a person or thing is **2** an abnormally high temperature of the body

tempest NOUN **tempests** a violent storm

template NOUN **templates** a thin sheet of shaped metal, plastic, etc. used as a guide for cutting or shaping things

temple[1] NOUN **temples** a building where a god is worshipped [from Latin *templum* = consecrated place]

temple[2] NOUN **temples** the part of the head between the forehead and the ear [from Latin *tempora* = sides of the head]

tempo NOUN **tempos** or **tempi** the speed or rhythm of something, especially of a piece of music [Italian, from Latin *tempus* = time]

temporary ADJECTIVE lasting for a limited time only; not permanent
▷ **temporarily** ADVERB

tempt VERB **tempts, tempting, tempted** try to persuade or attract someone, especially into doing something wrong or unwise
▷ **temptation** NOUN **tempter** NOUN **temptress** NOUN

ten NOUN, ADJECTIVE **tens** the number 10

tenacious (ten- ay- shus) ADJECTIVE **1** holding or clinging firmly to something **2** obstinate and persistent
▷ **tenaciously** ADVERB **tenacity** NOUN

tenant NOUN **tenants** a person who rents a house, building, or land etc. from a landlord
▷ **tenancy** NOUN

tend[1] VERB **tends, tending, tended** be inclined or likely to do something • *Prices tend to rise.*

tend[2] VERB **tends, tending, tended** look after • *Shepherds were tending their sheep.*

tendency NOUN **tendencies** the way a person or thing is likely to behave • *She has a tendency to be lazy.*

tender[1] ADJECTIVE **1** easy to chew; not tough or hard **2** easily hurt or damaged; sensitive or delicate • *tender plants* **3** (said about a part of the body) painful when touched **4** gentle and loving • *a tender smile*
▷ **tenderly** ADVERB **tenderness** NOUN

tender[2] VERB **tenders, tendering, tendered** offer something formally • *He tendered his resignation.*

tender NOUN **tenders** a formal offer to supply goods or carry out work at a stated price • *The council asked for tenders to build a school.*
legal tender kinds of money that are legal for

Thesaurus

temperamental ADJECTIVE **1** *The new king proved to be a temperamental despot.* ► moody, excitable, emotional, volatile, unpredictable, highly-strung, sensitive, capricious, mercurial, touchy, neurotic OPPOSITES ARE placid, phlegmatic **2** *He had a strong temperamental dislike of all conflict.* ► natural, inherent, innate, inborn, characteristic, congenital, constitutional

temporary ADJECTIVE *The restrictions on imports were a temporary measure only.* ► short-term, interim, provisional, stop-gap, short-lived, transitory, momentary, transient, ephemeral AN OPPOSITE IS permanent

tempt VERB *Window displays tempt shoppers into their stores.* ► entice, lure, allure, attract, persuade, coax, woo, inveigle, seduce OPPOSITES ARE deter, repel, discourage

temptation NOUN **1** *She had to resist the temptation to call him from her mobile.* ► urge, desire, impulse, inclination **2** *I could see the dangers in the temptations of life in London.* ► attraction, appeal, lure, pull, fascination, seduction, allurement, draw, enticement

tempting ADJECTIVE *It was a tempting package, and I bought the whole deal.* ► attractive, enticing, appealing, beguiling, tantalizing, irresistible

tenable ADJECTIVE *This theory is disproved by modern science and is no longer tenable.* ► credible, defensible, plausible, reasonable, sensible, viable, sound, feasible, justifiable, arguable, legitimate, logical, rational OPPOSITES ARE untenable, indefensible

tend VERB **1** *She spends many hours in the garden tending her flowers.* ► look after, attend to, manage, take care of, care for, cultivate, mind **2** *Nurses tend the sick and wounded in the field hospitals.* ► look after, attend to, care for, minister to, treat, nurse **3** **tend to** *At this time of year, our appetites tend to favour rich, stodgy puddings.* ► be inclined to, be apt to, be liable to, have a tendency to, be disposed to

tendency NOUN *John has a tendency to put his foot in it.* ► propensity, proclivity, readiness, susceptibility, predilection, predisposition, disposition, inclination, liability, partiality, penchant, trend

tender ADJECTIVE **1** *She liked him tender, gentle like this.* ► kind, caring, compassionate, considerate, humane, affectionate, sensitive, warm-hearted OPPOSITES ARE hard-hearted,

making payments • *Pound notes are no longer legal tender.*

tendril NOUN **tendrils** **1** a thread-like part by which a climbing plant clings to a support **2** a thin curl of hair etc.

tennis NOUN a game played with rackets and a ball on a court with a net across the middle

tenor NOUN **tenors** **1** a male singer with a high voice **2** the general meaning or drift of something • *What was the tenor of her speech?*

tenpin bowling NOUN a game in which players try to knock over ten skittles set up at the end of a track by rolling hard balls down it

tense[1] NOUN **tenses** the form of a verb that shows when something happens, e.g. he *came* (**past tense**), he *comes* or *is coming* (**present tense**), he *will come* (**future tense**)

tense[2] ADJECTIVE **1** tightly stretched **2** nervous or worried and unable to relax **3** making people tense • *a tense moment*
▷ **tensely** ADVERB **tenseness** NOUN

tense VERB **tenses, tensing, tensed** make or become tense

tension NOUN **tensions** **1** how tightly stretched a rope or wire is **2** a feeling of anxiety or nervousness about something that is just about to happen **3** voltage • *high-tension cables*

tent NOUN **tents** a shelter made of canvas or other material

tentacle NOUN **tentacles** a long flexible part of the body of certain animals (e.g. snails or octopuses), used for feeling or grasping things or for moving

tentative ADJECTIVE cautious; trying something out • *a tentative suggestion*
▷ **tentatively** ADVERB

tenth ADJECTIVE, NOUN next after the ninth

tenuous ADJECTIVE very slight or thin • *tenuous threads* • *a tenuous connection*

tepid ADJECTIVE only slightly warm; lukewarm • *tepid water*

term NOUN **terms** **1** the period of weeks when a school or college is open **2** a definite period • *a term of imprisonment* **3** a word or expression • *technical terms*

term VERB **terms, terming, termed** name; call something by a certain term • *This music is termed jazz.*

terminal NOUN **terminals** **1** the place where something ends; a terminus **2** a building where air passengers arrive or depart **3** a place where a wire is connected in an electric circuit or battery etc. **4** a monitor and keyboard used for putting data into a computer, or for receiving it

terminal ADJECTIVE **1** to do with or at the end or boundary of something **2** (said of a disease) leading to death
▷ **terminally** ADVERB

terminate VERB **terminates, terminating, terminated** end; stop finally
▷ **termination** NOUN

Thesaurus

callous, uncaring **2** *He pressed a tender loving kiss on her fingertips.* ► fond, loving, affectionate **3** *In my tender pre-teen years, I hadn't yet learned to be critical.* ► young, youthful, early, callow, immature, green, inexperienced, impressionable
OPPOSITES ARE advanced, mature **4** *Alan's voice cut into the tender little scene coldly. This is one of the author's most tender passages.* ► romantic, touching, moving, poignant **5** *Cook the rice in boiling salted water until tender.* ► soft, succulent, juicy, fleshy OPPOSITES ARE hard, tough **6** *He lifted her up with tender care, holding her head to his cheek.* ► gentle, fond, loving **7** *Her ankle felt tender.* ► sore, painful, sensitive, inflamed, raw

tense ADJECTIVE **1** *The muscles in his neck were tense.* ► taut, tight, strained, stretched
AN OPPOSITE IS slack **2** *Angela was feeling tense and nervy.* ► anxious, nervous, edgy, on edge, strained, stressed, agitated, apprehensive, jittery, fidgety, ill at ease, jumpy, (*more informal*) uptight OPPOSITES ARE calm, relaxed **3** *There was a tense atmosphere in the room.* ► fraught, uncomfortable, strained, charged
AN OPPOSITE IS relaxed

tension NOUN **1** *the tension of the ropes* ► tightness, tautness, strain, stretching
AN OPPOSITE IS slackness **2** *The tension was unbearable.* ► stress, strain, anxiety, suspense, apprehension, excitement, nervousness, unease, worry AN OPPOSITE IS relaxation.

tentative ADJECTIVE **1** *This conclusion can only be tentative.* ► provisional, unconfirmed, cautious, diffident, doubtful, halfhearted **2** *a few tentative steps* ► hesitant, indecisive, indefinite, nervous, timid, uncertain
AN OPPOSITE IS decisive

tenuous ADJECTIVE *a tenuous argument* ► slight, insubstantial, flimsy, thin , weak, unconvincing
AN OPPOSITE IS strong

term NOUN **1** *a technical term* ► word, expression, name, designation **2** *a five-year term of office* ► period, duration, interval, spell, session

terminal ADJECTIVE *a terminal illness* ► incurable, untreatable, inoperable, fatal, mortal, lethal, deadly

terminology NOUN **terminologies** the technical terms of a subject
▷ **terminological** ADJECTIVE

terminus NOUN **termini** or **terminuses** the last station on a railway or bus route

termite NOUN **termites** a small insect that is very destructive to timber

terms PLURAL NOUN **1** a relationship between people • *They remained on friendly terms.* **2** conditions offered or accepted • *peace terms*
come to terms with become reconciled to a difficulty or unwelcome situation

terrace NOUN **terraces** **1** a level area on a slope or hillside **2** a paved area beside a house **3** a row of houses joined together **4** a series of steps for spectators at a sports ground
▷ **terraced** ADJECTIVE

terrestrial ADJECTIVE to do with the earth or land

terrible ADJECTIVE very bad; awful
▷ **terribly** ADVERB

terrier NOUN **terriers** a kind of small lively dog

terrific ADJECTIVE (*informal*) **1** very great • *a terrific storm* **2** excellent
▷ **terrifically** ADVERB

terrify VERB **terrifies, terrifying, terrified** fill someone with terror

territory NOUN **territories** an area of land, especially one that belongs to a country or person
▷ **territorial** ADJECTIVE

terror NOUN **terrors** **1** very great fear **2** a terrifying person or thing

terrorist NOUN **terrorists** a person who uses violence for political purposes
▷ **terrorism** NOUN

terrorize VERB **terrorizes, terrorizing, terrorized** fill someone with terror; frighten someone by threatening them
▷ **terrorization** NOUN

test NOUN **tests** **1** a short examination **2** a way of discovering the qualities, abilities, or presence of a person or thing • *a test for radioactivity* **3** a test match

Thesaurus

terms PLURAL NOUN **1** *She was on good terms with all her staff.* ► relations, standing, footing **2** *The two kings came to terms.* ► agreement, understanding, deal **3** *The terms of the contract prevented this.* ► conditions, provisos, stipulations, specifications **4** *The hotel offers good terms out of season.* ► rates, prices, tariff, charges

terrestrial ADJECTIVE *one of the factors that give rise to intelligent terrestrial life* ► earthly, worldly, mundane, earthbound, ordinary
OPPOSITES ARE heavenly, extraterrestrial
USAGE *Mundane* has the special meaning 'ordinary'. Also, be careful how you use the opposite word *heavenly*, which has a common second meaning 'wonderful'.

terrible ADJECTIVE **1** *I had a terrible fall which left me with two broken legs.* ► dreadful, frightful, horrible, awful, fearful, ghastly, hideous, shocking, frightening, terrifying **2** *There was a terrible smell in the kitchen.* ► disgusting, nasty, unpleasant, dreadful, horrible

terribly ADVERB **1** *This is terribly important.* ► very, extremely, exceptionally, exceedingly, dreadfully, awfully **2** *In the next game they played dreadfully.* ► badly, atrociously, awfully, appallingly, dismally

terrific ADJECTIVE **1** *We heard a terrific thud.* ► tremendous, huge, mighty, massive, colossal, enormous, gigantic **2** *The novel provides the basis for a terrific movie.* ► excellent, wonderful, marvellous, outstanding, magnificent, superb, splendid, first-class, first-rate

terrified ADJECTIVE *She gave them a terrified glance, and then bolted.* ► petrified, frightened, scared, alarmed, terror-stricken, horror-stricken, panic-stricken

terrify VERB *The prospect of all that responsibility terrified him.* ► frighten, petrify, scare, horrify, appal, dismay, shock, unnerve

terrifying ADJECTIVE *Water was pouring in with terrifying speed.* ► frightening, horrifying, petrifying, dreadful, hair-raising, blood-curdling, spine-chilling, appalling, unnerving, (*more informal*) scary

territory NOUN **1** *France sought to locate the launching site on French territory.* ► land, country, terrain, ground **2** *a Dutch territory in the East* ► domain, state, dependency, dominion, colony, possession

terror NOUN *Men were driven to do these things by hunger and terror.* ► fear , extreme fear, alarm, fright, horror, panic, shock, trepidation

terrorize VERB *In the 1820s, Romney Marsh was openly terrorized by armed gangs of smugglers.* ► threaten, intimidate, torment, tyrannize, menace, persecute, victimize, oppress, terrify, frighten

test NOUN **1** *They will have to pass a test to continue to be paid for the work.* ► exam, examination, appraisal, assessment, evaluation **2** *We'll be conducting a series of scientific tests.* ► trial, experiment, study, evaluation, investigation, analysis, probe

test *VERB* **tests, testing, tested** carry out a test on a person or thing
▷ **tester** *NOUN*

testament *NOUN* **testaments 1** a written statement **2** either of the two main parts of the Bible, the Old Testament or the New Testament

testicle *NOUN* **testicles** either of the two glands where semen is produced

testify *VERB* **testifies, testifying, testified 1** give evidence; swear that something is true **2** be evidence or proof of something [from Latin *testis* = witness]

testimonial *NOUN* **testimonials 1** a letter describing someone's abilities, character, etc. **2** a gift presented to someone as a mark of respect

test match *NOUN* **test matches** a cricket or rugby match between teams from different countries

testosterone (test- ost- er- ohn) *NOUN* a male sex hormone

test tube *NOUN* **test tubes** a tube of thin glass with one end closed, used for experiments in chemistry etc.

tether *VERB* **tethers, tethering, tethered** tie an animal so that it cannot move far

tether *NOUN* **tethers** a rope for tethering an animal
at the end of your tether unable to endure something any more

tetrahedron *NOUN* **tetrahedrons** a solid with four triangular sides (i.e. a pyramid with a triangular base)

text *NOUN* **texts 1** the words of something written or printed **2** a sentence from the Bible used as the subject of a sermon etc.

textbook *NOUN* **textbooks** a book that teaches you about a subject

text message *NOUN* **text messages** a written message sent on a mobile phone

texture *NOUN* **textures** the way that the surface of something feels

than *CONJUNCTION* compared with another person or thing • *His brother is taller than he is or taller than him.*

thank *VERB* **thanks, thanking, thanked** tell someone that you are grateful to him or her
thank you an expression of thanks

thankful *ADJECTIVE* grateful

thankfully *ADVERB* **1** in a grateful way **2** fortunately • *Thankfully, John remembered to bring some money.*

thankless *ADJECTIVE* not likely to win thanks from people • *a thankless task*

Thesaurus

test *VERB* **1** *Psychologists have developed experiments to test their ideas.* ► check, appraise, evaluate, validate, examine, analyse, assess, study, screen, try out **2** *Here's a chance to test your DIY skills.* ► try out, put to the test, explore, trial **3** *These demands tested his patience to breaking point.* ► strain, tax, put a strain on, stretch, make demands on, sap, drain

testify *VERB* **1** *I may be called on to testify in court.* ► give evidence, be a witness, go into the dock **2** *He testified that he had not been present at the time of the incident.* ► swear, state on oath, attest, declare, affirm, give evidence **3 testify to** *The latest finds testify to the great wealth of the city in antiquity.* ► confirm, attest to, demonstrate, substantiate

testy *ADJECTIVE* *I would get very testy if things weren't exactly right.* ► irritable, bad-tempered, irascible, grumpy, grouchy, touchy, tetchy, crotchety, cantankerous, peevish, fractious, cross, (*more informal*) stroppy, (*more informal*) shirty AN OPPOSITE IS good-humoured

text *NOUN* **1** *Supplying material on disk saves having to retype the text.* ► words, wording, content **2** *a literary text* ► piece of writing, work, book, textbook **3** *a text from the Bible* ► passage, extract, reading, quotation

texture *NOUN* *The dough should have a soft spongy texture.* ► consistency, composition, quality, feel, constitution, structure, touch

thank *VERB* **1** *I want to thank all those people who have supported us over the years.* ► acknowledge, express thanks to, show or express gratitude to, express appreciation of, recognize **2** *He only had himself to thank for the mess he was in.* ► blame, hold responsible

thankful *ADJECTIVE* *She was thankful for the moonlight, without which she would never have found her way.* ► grateful, appreciative (of), pleased (about), relieved (about), happy (about) OPPOSITES ARE disappointed, ungrateful
USAGE Note that *thankful* and *thankless* are not opposites: *thankful* is normally used about a person, whereas *thankless* is used about an activity.

thankless *ADJECTIVE* *America inherited Britain's thankless task of maintaining stability in the region.* ► unenviable, unappreciated, unrecognized, unrewarding, fruitless
OPPOSITES ARE worthwhile, rewarding
USAGE See the note at **thankful**.

a b c d e f g h i j k l m n o p q r s t u v w x y z

A B C D E F G H I J K L M N O P Q R S T U V W X Y Z

thanks PLURAL NOUN **1** statements of gratitude **2** (*informal*) thank you
thanks to as a result of; because of • *Thanks to your help, we succeeded.*

that ADJECTIVE, PRONOUN **those** the one there • *That book is mine* • *Whose is that?*

that ADVERB to such an extent • *I'll come that far but no further.*

that RELATIVE PRONOUN which, who, or whom • *This is the record that I wanted.* • *We liked the people that we met on holiday.*

that CONJUNCTION used to introduce a wish, reason, result, etc. • *I hope that you are well* • *The puzzle was so hard that no one could solve it.*

thatch NOUN straw or reeds used to make a roof

thatch VERB **thatches, thatching, thatched** make a roof with thatch
▷ **thatcher** NOUN

thaw VERB **thaws, thawing, thawed** melt; stop being frozen

thaw NOUN **thaws** a period of warm weather that thaws ice and snow [from Old English]

the ADJECTIVE (called the *definite article*) a particular one; that or those

theatre NOUN **theatres 1** a building where plays etc. are performed to an audience **2** the writing, acting, and producing of plays **3** a special room where surgical operations are done • *the operating theatre* [from Greek *theatron* = place for seeing things]

theatrical ADJECTIVE **1** to do with plays or acting **2** (said about a person's behaviour) exaggerated and done for showy effect
▷ **theatrically** ADVERB

thee PRONOUN (*old use*) you (referring to one person and used as the object of a verb or after a preposition)

theft NOUN **thefts** stealing

their ADJECTIVE **1** belonging to them • *Their coats are over there* **2** belonging to a person • *Somebody has left their coat on the bus.* [from Old Norse] USAGE Do not confuse with **there** or **they're**.

theirs POSSESSIVE PRONOUN belonging to them • *These coats are theirs*
USAGE It is incorrect to write *their's*.

them PRONOUN the form of **they** used as the object of a verb or after a preposition • *We saw them.*

theme NOUN **themes 1** the subject about which a person speaks, writes, or thinks **2** a melody

themselves PRONOUN they or them and nobody else

then ADVERB **1** at that time • *We were younger then.* **2** after that; next • *Make the tea, then pour it out.* **3** in that case • *If this is yours, then this must be mine.*

theology NOUN the study of religion
▷ **theological** ADJECTIVE **theologian** NOUN [from Greek *theos* = a god]

theorem NOUN **theorems** a mathematical statement that can be proved by reasoning

theoretical ADJECTIVE based on theory not on practice or experience
▷ **theoretically** ADVERB

theory NOUN **theories 1** an idea or set of ideas put forward to explain something • *Darwin's theory of evolution.* **2** the principles of a subject rather than its practice
in theory according to what should happen rather than what may in fact happen

Thesaurus

thanks NOUN *Julia smiled her thanks and then turned to accept David's invitation.* ► gratitude, appreciation, acknowledgement, recognition, thanksgiving

thaw VERB *The snow was beginning to thaw.* ► melt, unfreeze, soften, liquefy, defrost
AN OPPOSITE IS freeze

theatre NOUN **1** *This is a work that needs to be heard in a theatre.* ► playhouse, auditorium **2** *What made you take up the theatre?* ► acting, drama, theatricals, performing

theatrical ADJECTIVE **1** *She wanted a theatrical career.* ► dramatic, acting, stage, thespian **2** *'My dear,' cried Ruby making a theatrical gesture.* ► affected, exaggerated, ostentatious, melodramatic, showy, stagy, stilted, unnatural AN OPPOSITE IS natural USAGE In the first meaning, be careful how you use *dramatic*, which has a common second meaning 'sudden and exciting'.

theft NOUN *a report of the theft of jewels from a hotel room* ► robbery, stealing, thieving, pilfering, burglary

theme NOUN **1** *Public services have become the dominant theme of domestic politics.* ► topic, issue, subject, concern, question, matter **2** *The theme is played by the orchestra and then picked up by the soloist.* ► melody, motif, subject, tune, air

theoretical ADJECTIVE **1** *theoretical physics* ► conceptual, pure, abstract, academic OPPOSITES ARE practical, applied **2** *a theoretical possibility* ► hypothetical, notional, conjectural, suppositional, speculative, postulated OPPOSITES ARE concrete, actual, real

theory NOUN **1** *His theories are based on observations and experiments.* ► argument, assumption, belief, conjecture, explanation, guess, hypothesis, idea, notion, speculation, supposition, surmise, thesis, view **2** *the theory*

therapy *NOUN* **therapies** a way of treating a physical or mental illness, especially without using surgery or medicines
▷ **therapeutic** *ADJECTIVE*

there *ADVERB* **1** in or to that place etc. **2** used to call attention to something (*There's a good boy!*) or to introduce a sentence where the verb comes before its subject (*There was plenty to eat*)
USAGE Do not confuse with **their** or **they're**.

thereabouts *ADVERB* near there

therefore *ADVERB* for that reason

thermodynamics *NOUN* the science dealing with the relation between heat and other forms of energy

thermometer *NOUN* **thermometers** a device for measuring temperature

thermostat *NOUN* **thermostats** a piece of equipment that automatically keeps the temperature of a room or piece of equipment steady
▷ **thermostatic** *ADJECTIVE* **thermostatically** *ADVERB*

thesaurus (thi- sor- us) *NOUN* **thesauruses** or **thesauri** a kind of dictionary containing sets of words grouped according to their meaning [from Greek *thesauros* = storehouse, treasury]

these *plural of* **this**

they *PRONOUN* **1** the people or things being talked about **2** people in general • *They say the show is a great success.* **3** he or she; a person • *I am never angry with anyone unless they deserve it.*

they're (*mainly spoken*) they are
USAGE Do not confuse with **their** or **there**.

thick *ADJECTIVE* **1** measuring a lot between opposite surfaces **2** measuring from one side to the other • *The wall is ten centimetres thick.* **3** (said about a line) broad, not fine **4** crowded with things; dense • *a thick forest* • *thick fog* **5** fairly stiff, not flowing easily • *thick cream* **6** (*informal*) stupid
▷ **thickly** *ADVERB* **thickness** *NOUN*

thicken *VERB* **thickens, thickening, thickened** make or become thicker

thicket *NOUN* **thickets** a number of shrubs and small trees etc. growing close together

thief *NOUN* **thieves** a person who steals things
▷ **thievish** *ADJECTIVE* **thievery** *NOUN* **thieving** *NOUN*

thigh *NOUN* **thighs** the part of the leg between the hip and the knee

thimble *NOUN* **thimbles** a small metal or plastic cap worn on the end of the finger to push the needle in sewing

Thesaurus

of quantum physics ► laws, principles, rules, science AN OPPOSITE IS practice

therefore *ADVERB* *This is only a story and therefore you shouldn't believe a word of it.* ► consequently, accordingly, for this or that reason, as a result, as a consequence, so, thus, hence

thesis *NOUN* **1** *The facts do not bear out his thesis.* ► theory, hypothesis, argument, premise or premiss, proposition, idea **2** *Her research was presented in her PhD thesis.* ► dissertation, monograph, paper, treatise

thick *ADJECTIVE* **1** *He was stuffing a thick wad of notes into his jacket pocket. The thick felt curtains were closely fastened.* ► fat, chunky, broad, wide, hefty, bulky, solid, stout, sturdy, substantial AN OPPOSITE IS thin **2** *The lava deposit was no more than a few metres thick. He was a good-looking man with a head of thick black hair.* ► deep, heavy **3** *The collision occurred in thick fog. The path wound through thick oak and pine forests.* ► dense, solid, impenetrable OPPOSITES ARE sparse, clear, open **4** *The shallow water was thick with paddling children.* ► crowded, filled, packed, swarming, teeming, covered **5** *Beat the mixture into a thick smooth paste.* ► stiff, heavy, concentrated, condensed, clotted, coagulated, viscous OPPOSITES ARE thin, watery **6** (*informal*) *'Some of these councillors are so thick,' said the woman.* ► stupid, foolish, dull, slow, dim-witted, brainless OPPOSITES ARE clever, bright

thicken *VERB* *Put a little flour in to thicken the sauce.* ► stiffen, concentrate, condense, reduce, set AN OPPOSITE IS thin out

thickness *NOUN* **1** *You can use paper of similar thickness.* ► breadth, width, bulk **2** *The thickness of the smoke made it impossible to see.* ► density, denseness, murkiness **3** *Great thicknesses of pumice and ash had piled up on the slopes of Vesuvius.* ► layer, coating, stratum, seam

thick-skinned *ADJECTIVE* *He was too thick-skinned to notice the insult.* ► insensitive, unfeeling, hardened, tough, (*informal*) hard-boiled OPPOSITES ARE sensitive, thin-skinned

thief *NOUN* *The 28-year-old thief was arrested when he returned to collect his dog.* ► robber, burglar, housebreaker, shoplifter, pilferer, bandit

thieving *NOUN* *a life of thieving* ► theft, robbery, stealing, pilfering, burglary

a b c d e f g h i j k l m n o p q r s t u v w x y z

thin *VERB* **thins, thinning, thinned** make or become less thick
▷ **thinner** *NOUN*
thin out make or become less dense or crowded

thin *ADJECTIVE* **thinner, thinnest 1** not thick; not fat **2** feeble • *a thin excuse*
▷ **thinly** *ADVERB* **thinness** *NOUN*

thine *ADJECTIVE, POSSESSIVE PRONOUN* (*old use*) yours (referring to one person)

thing *NOUN* **things** an object; something which can be seen, touched, thought about, etc.

think *VERB* **thinks, thinking, thought 1** use your mind; form connected ideas **2** have as an idea or opinion • *Do you think we have enough time?*
▷ **think** *NOUN* **thinker** *NOUN*

third *ADJECTIVE* next after the second
▷ **thirdly** *ADVERB*

third *NOUN* **thirds 1** the third person or thing **2** one of three equal parts of something

Third World *NOUN* the poorer countries of Asia, Africa, and South America, also called 'developing countries'

thirst *NOUN* **1** a feeling of dryness in the mouth and throat, causing a desire to drink **2** a strong desire • *a thirst for adventure*
▷ **thirsty** *ADJECTIVE* **thirstily** *ADVERB*

thirteen *NOUN, ADJECTIVE* the number 13
▷ **thirteenth** *NOUN, ADJECTIVE*

thirty *NOUN, ADJECTIVE* **thirties** the number 30
▷ **thirtieth** *ADJECTIVE, NOUN*

this *ADJECTIVE, PRONOUN* **these** the one here • *This house is ours.* • *Whose is this?*

Thesaurus

thin *VERB* *Thin the paint with water before use.*
► dilute, water down, weaken
thin out *The crowds began to thin out.*
► decrease, diminish, dwindle, disperse, scatter

thin *ADJECTIVE* **1** *Frankie was small and thin for his age. He wore a silk shirt with a cravat tucked in round his thin neck.* ► slim, slender, lean, slight, skinny AN OPPOSITE IS fat **2** *She was clad only in a thin nightgown. Thermal underwear keeps you warm by trapping a thin layer of air in its fibres.*
► fine, delicate, light, filmy, flimsy, diaphanous, insubstantial, wispy
OPPOSITES ARE thick, heavy **3** *When the paint is nearly dry, apply another thin coat.* ► light, runny, watery, dilute, flowing, fluid
OPPOSITES ARE thick, heavy **4** *a thin spread of butter* ► sparse, meagre, scanty, scarce
AN OPPOSITE IS thick **5** *The soft thin mist gave a mysterious air to the scene.* ► light, rarefied
AN OPPOSITE IS dense **6** *'Get on with it,' said a thin, peevish voice.* ► weak, faint, feeble
OPPOSITES ARE strong, loud **7** *a thin excuse*
► feeble, tenuous, unconvincing, implausible
AN OPPOSITE IS convincing

thing *NOUN* **1** *The cupboard was full of weird things.* ► object, item, artefact, article, body, device, entity, implement **2** *A strange thing happened today.* ► event, occurrence, incident, eventuality, happening, phenomenon, affair, circumstance, deed **3** *He didn't have a single thing to add.* ► idea, point, statement, thought, concept, detail, fact, factor **4** *There's a thing we have to do.* ► job, task, deed, act, action **5** (*informal*) *He's got this thing about wasps.* ► obsession, preoccupation, phobia, fear (of), terror (of), dislike (of), (*informal*) hang-up
things 1 *Susan put her things in the back of the car.* ► belongings, possessions, baggage, clothing, luggage, equipment, (*more informal*) gear, (*more informal*) stuff **2** *Things improved once I had a job.* ► circumstances, conditions, life

think *VERB* **1** *Do you think Molly will come? We thought Rose must have gone home.* ► believe, expect, imagine, consider, surmise, conclude **2** *Jennifer thought hard for a few moments.*
► concentrate, ponder, contemplate, deliberate, cogitate, reflect, muse
think about *It was time to start thinking about. the future.* ► consider, contemplate, weigh up, deliberate about
think of *He thought of all the good times they had had together.* ► recall, remember, recollect, call to mind
think over *Think over what we have said.*
► consider, reflect on, muse on, ponder, mull over, (*more informal*) chew over
think to be *She was thought to be worthy of high office.* ► consider, deem, judge, hold, reckon
think up *We tried to think up a convincing excuse.* ► concoct, invent, contrive, devise

thin-skinned *ADJECTIVE* *He is thin-skinned and hates criticism.* ► sensitive, touchy, defensive, paranoid AN OPPOSITE IS insensitive

thirst *NOUN* **1** *We needed a drink to quench our raging thirst.* ► dehydration, thirstiness, dryness **2** *their thirst for knowledge* ► appetite, hunger, longing, love (of), yearning, craving, hankering, desire, eagerness, passion

thirst *VERB* **thirst for** *They thirsted for power.*
► be thirsty for, crave, strive after, long for, have a thirst for, hunger after, yearn for

thirsty *ADJECTIVE* **1** *The boys were hot and thirsty after their run.* ► dehydrated, dry, parched, (*more informal*) gasping (for a drink), (*more informal*) panting **2** *They were thirsty for adventure.* ► eager, hungry, yearning, greedy, itching, longing, avid

this *ADVERB* to such an extent • *I'm surprised he got this far.*

thistle *NOUN* **thistles** a prickly wild plant with purple, white, or yellow flowers

thong *NOUN* **thongs** a narrow strip of leather etc. used for fastening things

thorn *NOUN* **thorns** **1** a small pointed growth on the stem of a plant **2** a thorny tree or shrub

thorny *ADJECTIVE* **thornier, thorniest** **1** having many thorns; prickly **2** difficult • *a thorny problem*

thorough *ADJECTIVE* **1** done or doing things carefully and in detail **2** complete in every way • *a thorough mess*
▷ **thoroughly** *ADVERB* **thoroughness** *NOUN*

thoroughbred *ADJECTIVE* bred of pure or pedigree stock
▷ **thoroughbred** *NOUN*

thoroughfare *NOUN* **thoroughfares** a public road or path that is open at both ends

those *plural of* **that**

thou *PRONOUN* *(old use)* you (referring to one person)

though *CONJUNCTION* in spite of the fact that; even if • *We can try phoning her, though she's probably left by now.*

though *ADVERB* however • *She's right, though.*

thought[1] *NOUN* **thoughts** **1** something that you think; an idea or opinion **2** the process of thinking • *She was deep in thought.*

thought[2] *past tense of* **think**

thoughtful *ADJECTIVE* **1** thinking a lot **2** showing thought for other people's needs; considerate
▷ **thoughtfully** *ADVERB* **thoughtfulness** *NOUN*

thoughtless *ADJECTIVE* **1** careless; not thinking of what may happen **2** inconsiderate
▷ **thoughtlessly** *ADVERB* **thoughtlessness** *NOUN*

thousand *NOUN, ADJECTIVE* **thousands** the number 1,000
▷ **thousandth** *ADJECTIVE, NOUN*

thrash *VERB* **thrashes, thrashing, thrashed** **1** beat someone with a stick or whip; keep hitting very hard **2** defeat someone thoroughly **3** move violently • *The crocodile thrashed its tail.*
thrash something out discuss a matter thoroughly

thread *NOUN* **threads** **1** a thin length of any substance **2** a length of spun cotton, wool, or nylon etc. used for making cloth or in sewing or knitting **3** the spiral ridge round a screw **4** a

Thesaurus

thorny *ADJECTIVE* **1** *They had to scramble through thorny undergrowth.* ► prickly, bristly, sharp, spiky, spiny, scratchy, barbed **2** *the thorny question of who would pay* ► tricky, difficult, problematic, awkward, delicate

thorough *ADJECTIVE* **1** *a thorough inquiry* ► rigorous, exhaustive, thoroughgoing, detailed, in-depth AN OPPOSITE IS superficial. **2** *He was slow but very thorough.* ► meticulous, scrupulous, conscientious, assiduous, methodical, diligent **3** *He's being a thorough nuisance.* ► utter, complete, downright, absolute, perfect, thoroughgoing, total

thought *NOUN* **1** *She appeared to be lost in thought. It only needs a moment's thought.* ► thinking, contemplation, deliberation, meditation, reflection, pondering, regard, consideration, introspection **2** *I had a sudden thought.* ► idea, notion, belief, concept, conception, perception, conjecture, conviction, opinion **3** *We've given up all thought of extending the project.* ► hope, expectation, intention, aspiration, aim, plan, purpose, design, objective **4** *They seem to have no thought for others.* ► consideration, sympathy, regard, concern, caring, understanding, compassion

thoughtful *ADJECTIVE* **1** *The thoughtful look on his face did not change.* ► pensive, reflective, contemplative, introspective, absorbed, preoccupied OPPOSITES ARE blank, vacant **2** *Members of the audience added thoughtful comments after the lecture.* ► profound, studious, intelligent, scrupulous, thorough, diligent, meticulous AN OPPOSITE IS superficial **3** *It was thoughtful of you to visit.* ► considerate, kind, caring, attentive, helpful, concerned, friendly, good-natured, unselfish AN OPPOSITE IS thoughtless

thoughtless *ADJECTIVE* **1** *She realized it was thoughtless of her to rush off like that.* ► inconsiderate, insensitive, unthinking, unkind, unfeeling, uncaring AN OPPOSITE IS considerate **2** *One thoughtless remark can prompt a feeling of depression.* ► unthinking, careless, unmindful, injudicious, ill-considered, unwise, rash AN OPPOSITE IS thoughtful

thrash *VERB* **1** *The boy was thrashed by his exasperated mother.* ► punish, beat, whip, flog, spank, cane, strap, birch **2** *She thrashed her arms, attempting to swim towards him.* ► jerk, toss, flail **3** *(informal) They were thrashed by six wickets in the final.* ► defeat, beat, trounce, overwhelm
thrash out *I must thrash things out with him over the next few months.* ► resolve, settle, sort out, clarify

thread *NOUN* **1** *He sewed it up with a needle and thread in his girlfriend's flat.* ► cotton, yarn, fibre, strand, twine **2** *I lost the thread of the argument.* ► train of thought, line of thought,

theme or idea running through a story, argument, etc. • *I'm afraid I've lost the thread.*

thread VERB **threads, threading, threaded** **1** put a thread through the eye of a needle **2** pass a strip of film etc. through or round something **3** put beads on a thread

threadbare ADJECTIVE (said about cloth) with the surface worn away so that the threads show

threat NOUN **threats** **1** a warning that you will punish, hurt, or harm a person or thing **2** a sign of something undesirable **3** a person or thing causing danger

threaten VERB **threatens, threatening, threatened** **1** make threats against someone **2** be a threat or danger to a person or thing

three NOUN, ADJECTIVE **threes** the number 3

three-dimensional ADJECTIVE having three dimensions (length, width, and height or depth)

threshold NOUN **thresholds** **1** a slab of stone or board etc. forming the bottom of a doorway; the entrance **2** the point at which something begins to happen or change • *We are on the threshold of a great discovery.*

thrift NOUN **1** careful spending or management of money or resources **2** a plant with pink flowers
▷ **thrifty** ADJECTIVE **thriftily** ADVERB

thrill NOUN **thrills** a feeling of excitement

thrill VERB **thrills, thrilling, thrilled** have or give a feeling of excitement
▷ **thrilling** ADJECTIVE

thriller NOUN **thrillers** an exciting story, play, or film, usually about crime

thrive VERB **thrives, thriving, throve, thrived** *or* **thriven** grow strongly; prosper or be successful [from Old Norse, = grasp, get hold of]

throat NOUN **throats** **1** the tube in the neck that takes food and drink down into the body **2** the front of the neck [from Old English]

throb VERB **throbs, throbbing, throbbed** beat or vibrate with a strong rhythm • *My head throbbed with pain.*
▷ **throb** NOUN

thrombosis NOUN the formation of a clot of blood in the body

throne NOUN **thrones** **1** a special chair for a king, queen, or bishop at ceremonies **2** the position of being king or queen • *the heir to the throne*

Thesaurus

drift, tenor, continuity, course, direction, theme

threadbare ADJECTIVE *He inched his way along the threadbare strip of carpet.* ► worn, frayed, ragged, shabby, tattered, tatty

threat NOUN **1** *We got bomb threats against our building.* ► warning, ultimatum, menace **2** *It is a brutal regime that poses a threat to world peace.* ► danger, risk, hazard, menace

threaten VERB **1** *When they came in they threatened us.* ► intimidate, menace, make threats against, browbeat, bully, terrorize, frighten, pressurize **2** *The freedom fighters threatened reprisals. A mass of rain clouds threatened a dramatic change in the weather.* ► warn of, forebode, foreshadow, forewarn of, give warning of, portend, presage, indicate **3** *Dumping waste here will threaten the safety and well-being of the region.* ► endanger, imperil, jeopardize, put at risk

threatening ADJECTIVE *The dog was baring its teeth in threatening snarls.* ► ominous, menacing, sinister, forbidding, grim, minatory, stern, unfriendly AN OPPOSITE IS comforting

thrill NOUN *Just to work with him was a thrill.* ► adventure, excitement, sensation, pleasure, tingle, tremor, (*more informal*) buzz, (*more informal*) kick

thrill VERB *She knew he was hers and it thrilled her.* ► excite, delight, rouse, stimulate, exhilarate, stir, electrify, titillate AN OPPOSITE IS bore

thrilling ADJECTIVE *a thrilling boat ride to the base of Niagara falls* ► exciting, electrifying, riveting, gripping, stirring, rousing, sensational, spectacular, stimulating, (*more informal*) hair-raising OPPOSITES ARE unexciting, boring

thrive VERB *Plants often thrive when the same species are massed together. Two-year-olds thrive on attention.* ► flourish, burgeon, grow, prosper, succeed, be vigorous, develop strongly, do well OPPOSITES ARE decline, wither

thriving ADJECTIVE *By Tudor times distilling was a thriving industry in Scotland.* ► flourishing, growing, prosperous, booming, burgeoning, vigorous, developing, expanding, successful, healthy, affluent, lively, profitable OPPOSITES ARE failing, dying

throaty ADJECTIVE *Lucinda's smile gave way to a throaty laugh.* ► gruff, guttural, deep, hoarse, husky, croaky, gravelly, rasping, rough, thick

throb NOUN *the annoying dull throb of a neighbour's stereo* ► beat, rhythm, pulsation, pounding, thud, thump, thrum, vibration

throb VERB *A vein started to throb in his forehead.* ► pound, pulsate, pulse, beat, thump, palpitate

throng *NOUN* **throngs** a crowd of people

throng *VERB* **throngs, thronging, thronged** crowd • *People thronged the streets.*

throttle *NOUN* **throttles** a device that controls the flow of fuel to an engine; an accelerator

throttle *VERB* **throttles, throttling, throttled** strangle
throttle back or **down** reduce the speed of an engine by partially closing the throttle

through *PREPOSITION* **1** from one end or side to the other end or side of • *Climb through the window.* **2** by means of; because of • *We lost it through carelessness.* **3** at the end of; having finished successfully • *He is through his exam.*

through *ADVERB* **1** through something • *We squeezed through.* **2** with a telephone connection made • *I'll put you through to the president.* **3** finished • *Wait till I'm through with these papers.*

through *ADJECTIVE* **1** going through something • *no through road* **2** going all the way to a destination • *a through train*

throughout *PREPOSITION, ADVERB* all the way through; from beginning to end

throve *past tense of* **thrive**

throw *VERB* **throws, throwing, threw, thrown 1** send a person or thing through the air **2** put something in a place carelessly or hastily **3** move part of your body quickly • *He threw his head back and laughed.* **4** put someone in a certain condition etc. • *It threw us into confusion.* **5** confuse or upset • *Your question threw me.* **6** move a switch or lever in order to operate it **7** shape a pot on a potter's wheel **8** hold a party
▷ **throw** *NOUN* **thrower** *NOUN*
throw away 1 get rid of something because it is useless or unwanted **2** waste • *You threw away an opportunity.*
throw up (*informal*) vomit

thrush *NOUN* **thrushes** a songbird with a speckled breast

thrust *VERB* **thrusts, thrusting, thrust** push hard
▷ **thrust** *NOUN*

thud *VERB* **thuds, thudding, thudded** make the dull sound of a heavy knock or fall
▷ **thud** *NOUN*

thug *NOUN* **thugs** a rough and violent person
▷ **thuggery** *NOUN*

thumb *NOUN* **thumbs** the short thick finger set apart from the other four
be under a person's thumb be completely under his or her influence

Thesaurus

throng *NOUN* *Vehicles mingled with the throng of foot passengers.* ► crowd, mass, horde, mob, crush

throng *VERB* *Tourists thronged the streets and canals.* ► pack, cram, fill, press into, squeeze into

throttle *VERB* *You're lucky Lewis didn't throttle you.* ► strangle, choke, stifle, smother, suffocate, asphyxiate

throw *VERB* **1** *They asked her to throw their ball back.* ► toss, fling, hurl, pitch, lob, cast, (*more informal*) chuck, (*more informal*) sling **2** *He threw a quick glance at them.* ► direct, cast, send, shoot, dart **3** *The horse threw its rider.* ► unseat, dislodge, upset, bring down **4** *The torch threw a beam of light across the passage.* ► cast, project, send, emit, radiate
throw away *He cleared out his room and threw lots of stuff away.* ► discard, throw out, dispose of, get rid of, (*more informal*) ditch
throw off *He hoped he had thrown off his pursuers.* ► shake off, escape, elude, give the slip to, get away from
throw out *He tried to get in the house but was thrown out. The government might be thrown out at the next election.* ► eject, expel, remove, force out, oust, get rid of
throw up *He was tempted to throw up his job and go abroad.* ► abandon, relinquish, give up, (*more informal*) quit, (*more informal*) chuck in

throw *NOUN* *With one mighty throw the ball went over the fence.* ► heave, fling, toss, lob, pitch

thrust *VERB* **1** *He thrust a mug of tea into my hands.* ► push, shove, force, press, stick, poke **2** *His attacker thrust at him with a knife.* ► lunge, jab, prod, stab, plunge, poke, stick

thrust *NOUN* **1** *He gave the door a firm thrust.* ► shove, push, prod, poke **2** *I strongly support the thrust of your argument.* ► gist, substance, drift, burden, force

thud *VERB* *Heavy footsteps thudded across the front porch.* ► thump, clump, stomp, crash

thud *NOUN* *He was hammering on the door, thud after thud.* ► thump, bang, rap, clunk, clonk, crash

thug *NOUN* (*informal*) *A fight broke out between two armies of thugs.* ► ruffian, hoodlum, tough, bully

thumb *VERB* *She thumbed through her notes.* ► browse, flick, flip, leaf, riffle, scan

thump *VERB* **thumps, thumping, thumped** **1** hit or knock something heavily **2** punch
▷ **thump** *NOUN*

thunder *NOUN* **1** the loud noise that is heard with lightning **2** a similar noise • *a thunder of applause*
▷ **thunderous** *ADJECTIVE* **thunderstorm** *NOUN* **thundery** *ADJECTIVE*

thunder *VERB* **thunders, thundering, thundered** **1** sound with thunder **2** make a noise like thunder; speak loudly

thunderbolt *NOUN* **thunderbolts** a lightning flash thought of as a destructive missile

Thursday *NOUN* the day of the week following Wednesday [from Old English *thuresdaeg* = day of thunder, named after Thor, the Norse god of thunder]

thus *ADVERB* **1** in this way • *Hold the wheel thus.* **2** therefore

thwart *VERB* **thwarts, thwarting, thwarted** frustrate; prevent someone from achieving something

thy *ADJECTIVE* (*old use*) your (referring to one person)

tiara (tee-**ar**-a) *NOUN* **tiaras** a woman's jewelled crescent-shaped ornament worn like a crown

tic *NOUN* **tics** an unintentional twitch of a muscle, especially of the face

tick[1] *NOUN* **ticks** **1** a mark (usually) put by something to show that it is correct or has been checked **2** a regular clicking sound, especially that made by a clock or watch **3** (*informal*) a moment • *I won't be a tick.*

tick *VERB* **ticks, ticking, ticked** **1** put a tick by something **2** make the sound of a tick
tick off (*informal*) reprimand someone

tick[2] *NOUN* **ticks** a bloodsucking insect

ticket *NOUN* **tickets** **1** a printed piece of paper or card that allows a person to travel on a bus or train, see a show, etc. **2** a label showing a thing's price

tickle *VERB* **tickles, tickling, tickled** **1** touch a person's skin lightly in order to produce a slight tingling feeling and laughter **2** (said about a part of the body) have a slight tingling or itching feeling **3** amuse or please somebody

ticklish *ADJECTIVE* **1** likely to laugh or wriggle when tickled **2** awkward or difficult • *a ticklish situation*

tidal wave *NOUN* **tidal waves** a huge sea wave

tide *NOUN* **tides** **1** the regular rise and fall in the level of the sea which usually happens twice a day **2** (*old use*) a time or season • *Christmas-tide*

tide *VERB* **tides, tiding, tided**
tide a person over provide him or her with what is needed, for a short time

tidy *ADJECTIVE* **tidier, tidiest** **1** with everything in its right place; neat and orderly **2** (*informal*) fairly large • *It costs a tidy sum.*
▷ **tidily** *ADVERB* **tidiness** *NOUN*

Thesaurus

thump *NOUN* **1** *He sat down with a painful thump on the floor.* ► thud, bang, clunk, clonk, crash **2** *The heavy thump of acid house music was everywhere.* ► beat, rhythm, pulsation, pounding, throb, thud, thrum, vibration

thump *VERB* *The woman thumped the table with her fist.* ► bang, hit, strike, pound, beat, rap, batter, wallop, knock

thunder *NOUN* *Her musings were interrupted by the thunder of hooves.* ► rumble, rumbling, boom, booming, roar, roaring, thud, thump, ringing

thunder *VERB* *Fighter aircraft thundered overhead.* ► roar, boom, rumble, blast

thunderous *ADJECTIVE* *The speech was greeted by thunderous applause and standing ovations.* ► deafening, tumultuous, resounding, loud, booming

thwart *VERB* *He stayed in power as long as he could, just to thwart his main rival.* ► frustrate, hinder, impede, foil, obstruct, prevent, stand in the way of, stop OPPOSITES ARE help, further

tick *NOUN* **1** *Put a tick in the box marked 'no'.* ► mark, stroke, dash, line **2** *They heard the tick of a clock.* ► ticking, clicking
in a tick (*informal*) *I'll be back in a tick.* ► in a moment, in a minute, in a second, in a trice, very soon, very shortly, (*informal*) in a jiffy

tick *VERB* **1** *It was so quiet I could hear my watch ticking.* ► click, make a tick, beat **2** *Tick the box against your preferred method of payment.* ► mark, check off, indicate
tick off (*informal*) *She ticked off the children for making a noise.* ► tell off, scold, reprimand, admonish, rebuke

ticket *NOUN* **1** *a ticket to the game* ► pass, permit, token, voucher, coupon **2** *a price ticket* ► label, tag, sticker, marker, slip, tab

tickle *VERB* **1** *He tickled her toes until she gurgled happily.* ► touch, stroke, pet **2** *The little story tickled us.* ► amuse, entertain, delight, cheer

ticklish *ADJECTIVE* **1** *'It's lucky I'm not ticklish,' she squealed.* ► giggly, wriggly, sensitive **2** *He had the ticklish problem of explaining where he had been all night.* ► tricky, awkward, delicate, thorny, difficult, hazardous, risky, touchy, (*more informal*) dodgy

tide *NOUN* *The tide of opinion was turning against the government.* ► trend, tendency, current, course, drift, movement

tidy *ADJECTIVE* **1** *Each desk should be tidy and have a place card.* ► neat, orderly, uncluttered,

tidy *VERB* **tidies, tidying, tidied** make a place tidy

tie *VERB* **ties, tying, tied 1** fasten something with string, ribbon, etc. **2** arrange something into a knot or bow **3** make the same score as another competitor
be tied up be busy

tie *NOUN* **ties 1** a strip of material worn passing under the collar of a shirt and knotted in front **2** a result when two or more competitors have equal scores **3** one of the matches in a competition **4** a close connection or bond • *the ties of friendship*

tier (teer) *NOUN* **tiers** each of a series of rows or levels etc. placed one above the other
▷ **tiered** *ADJECTIVE*

tiff *NOUN* **tiffs** a slight quarrel

tiger *NOUN* **tigers** a large wild animal of the cat family, with yellow and black stripes [from Greek *tigris*]

tight *ADJECTIVE* **1** fitting very closely **2** firmly fastened **3** fully stretched; tense **4** in short supply • *Money is tight at the moment.* **5** stingy • *He is very tight with his money.* **6** severe or strict • *tight security* **7** (*slang*) drunk
▷ **tightly** *ADVERB* **tightness** *NOUN*

tighten *VERB* **tightens, tightening, tightened** make or become tighter

tightrope *NOUN* **tightropes** a tightly stretched rope high above the ground, on which acrobats perform

tights *PLURAL NOUN* a piece of clothing that fits tightly over the feet, legs, and lower part of the body

tile *NOUN* **tiles** a thin square piece of baked clay or other hard material, used in rows for covering roofs, walls, or floors
▷ **tiled** *ADJECTIVE*

till[1] *PREPOSITION, CONJUNCTION* until [from Old English *til* = to]
USAGE It is better to use **until** rather than **till** when the word stands first in a sentence (e.g. *Until last year we had never been abroad.*) or when you are speaking or writing formally.

till[2] *NOUN* **tills** a drawer or box for money in a shop; a cash register [origin unknown]

tilt *VERB* **tilts, tilting, tilted** move into a sloping position

tilt *NOUN* a sloping position
at full tilt at full speed or force

Thesaurus

shipshape, smart, spick and span
OPPOSITES ARE untidy, messy **2** *He tried to be tidy in his new apartment.* ► methodical, meticulous, organized, systematic, house-proud OPPOSITES ARE untidy, disorganized **3** (*informal*) *All those books will cost a tidy sum.* ► sizeable, considerable, substantial, appreciable, large, (*informal*) hefty

tidy *VERB* *The girls started to wash up and tidy.* ► clean up, put in order, set straight, arrange, smarten, spruce up, neaten, straighten
OPPOSITES ARE untidy, muddle

tie *VERB* **1** *The dog was tied to a lamppost.* ► fasten, secure, attach, tether, bind, hitch
AN OPPOSITE IS untie **2** *Her new job tied her to the office.* ► restrict, limit, confine, restrain **3** *The home side tied its next game.* ► draw, finish level
tie up 1 *He tied up the boat at the jetty.* ► moor, tether, fasten, attach **2** *We were keen to tie up the deal.* ► complete, finalize, conclude, settle **3 be tied up** *The manager is still tied up I'm afraid.* ► be busy, be occupied, be engaged

tie *NOUN* *Family ties are important.* ► bond, connection, link, attachment, relationship, association

tight *ADJECTIVE* **1** *The rope was pulled tight.* ► taut, stretched, rigid, stiff, tense
OPPOSITES ARE slack, loose **2** *Her grip was tight.* ► firm, fast, secure, clenched
AN OPPOSITE IS relaxed **3** *The joint was completely tight.* ► sealed, airtight, impervious
AN OPPOSITE IS leaking **4** *The bed had to fit into a tight space.* ► small, compact, constricted, snug, poky **5** *He can be very tight with his money.* ► mean, stingy, niggardly, miserly, parsimonious, (*more informal*) tight-fisted, (*more informal*) penny-pinching
AN OPPOSITE IS generous **6** *There is tight security at the airport.* ► strict, stringent, rigorous, severe, tough, scrupulous AN OPPOSITE IS lax

tighten *VERB* **1** *Jane tightened her grip on the rail.* ► strengthen, squeeze, tense, stiffen, increase
OPPOSITES ARE loosen, relax **2** *You need to tighten your shoelaces.* ► make tight, pull tighter, tauten, stretch AN OPPOSITE IS slacken **3** *Tighten all screws when the chair is assembled.* ► make tighter, screw up, give another turn to
AN OPPOSITE IS loosen
tighten up *Security will be tightened up during the peak season.* ► increase, heighten, strengthen, intensify, escalate

tight-fisted *ADJECTIVE* *We were too tight-fisted to pay a motorway toll.* ► mean, stingy, niggardly, miserly, parsimonious, (*more informal*) penny-pinching

tilt *VERB* *He tilted his hat to one side. The wall tilted alarmingly.* ► lean, slant, slope, tip, angle

tilt *NOUN* *The tray was on a tilt.* ► slant, slope, incline, angle
at full tilt *They ran at full tilt down the bank.* ► headlong, pell-mell, at full speed, at full pelt, at a gallop, fast

a b c d e f g h i j k l m n o p q r s t u v w x y z

A B C D E F G H I J K L M N O P Q R S T U V W X Y Z

timber *NOUN* **timbers** **1** wood for building or making things **2** a wooden beam

time *NOUN* **times** **1** all the years of the past, present, and future; the continuous existence of the universe **2** a particular point or portion of time **3** an occasion • *the first time I saw him* **4** a period suitable or available for something • *Is there time for a cup of tea?* **5** a system of measuring time • *Greenwich Mean Time* **6** (in music) rhythm depending on the number and stress of beats in the bar **7** (**times**) multiplied by • *Five times three is 15 (5 x 3 = 15)*
at times or **from time to time** sometimes; occasionally
in time **1** not late **2** eventually
on time punctual

time *VERB* **times, timing, timed** **1** measure how long something takes **2** arrange when something is to happen
▷ **timer** *NOUN*
[from Old English]

timeless *ADJECTIVE* not affected by the passage of time; eternal

timely *ADJECTIVE* happening at a suitable or useful time • *a timely warning*

timetable *NOUN* **timetables** a list showing the times when things will happen, e.g. when buses or trains will arrive and depart, or when school lessons will take place

timid *ADJECTIVE* easily frightened
▷ **timidly** *ADVERB* **timidity** *NOUN*

timing *NOUN* **1** the choice of time to do something **2** the time when something happens

timpani *PLURAL NOUN* kettledrums

tin *NOUN* **tins** **1** a silvery-white metal **2** a metal container for food

tinge *VERB* **tinges, tingeing, tinged** **1** colour something slightly **2** add a slight amount of another feeling • *Our relief was tinged with sadness.*
▷ **tinge** *NOUN*

tingle *VERB* **tingles, tingling, tingled** have a slight pricking or stinging feeling
▷ **tingle** *NOUN*

tinker *VERB* **tinkers, tinkering, tinkered** work at something casually, trying to improve or mend it

tinkle *VERB* **tinkles, tinkling, tinkled** make a gentle ringing sound
▷ **tinkle** *NOUN*

tinny *ADJECTIVE* **1** like tin **2** (said about a sound) unpleasantly thin and high-pitched

tinsel *NOUN* strips of glittering material used for decoration

tint *NOUN* **tints** a shade of colour, especially a pale one

tint *VERB* **tints, tinting, tinted** colour something slightly

tiny *ADJECTIVE* **tinier, tiniest** very small

Thesaurus

timber *NOUN* *Houses built of timber and mud would be very damp.* ► wood, planks, planking, beams, laths, boarding, boards, logs, lumber, trees

time *NOUN* **1** *in the time of Queen Mary* ► age, era, period, generation **2** *He lived here for a time.* ► while, period, spell **3** *It took a long time to fix the problem.* ► while, interval, duration, **4** *When is the best time to come? I didn't know what to do at that time.* ► moment, point, juncture, stage, date, occasion RELATED ADJECTIVES temporal, chronic, chronological

time *VERB* **1** *She had timed her arrival for half an hour after the party was due to start.* ► regulate, choose, fix, set, schedule **2** *The nurse timed ten minutes.* ► measure, count

timely *ADJECTIVE* *The incident was a timely reminder of how dangerous these waters had become.* ► opportune, fitting, suitable, appropriate, apt, prompt

timetable *NOUN* *They established a timetable for elections and political reform.* ► schedule, agenda, programme, calendar, diary, roster, rota

timid *ADJECTIVE* *Elaine handed him her bag with a timid smile.* ► shy, diffident, bashful, modest, timorous, faint-hearted, weak, fearful OPPOSITES ARE bold, brazen

tinge *NOUN* **1** *The light took on a green tinge.* ► tint, shade, hue, colour **2** *There was a tinge of amusement on his face.* ► trace, touch, note, suggestion, flavour, streak

tingle *NOUN* **1** *There was a strange tingle in her fingers.* ► prickling, stinging, tickle, tickling, itch, itching, pins and needles **2** *Melissa felt a tingle of excitement.* ► quiver, tremor, thrill, sensation, shiver

tingle *VERB* *His shoes were so tight they made his feet tingle.* ► itch, prickle, sting, tickle

tinker *VERB* *He watched Nathan tinkering with his bike.* ► fiddle, play, meddle, tamper, dabble, trifle, interfere, (*more informal*) mess about, (*more informal*) play about

tint *NOUN* *smooth glossy paper with a yellowish tint* ► tinge, shade, hue, colour

tiny *ADJECTIVE* **1** *We've got a tiny pond in the front garden.* ► minute, miniature, diminutive, midget, mini, very small, (*more informal*) teeny, (*more informal*) titchy AN OPPOSITE IS huge **2** *These man-made gases are present in the atmosphere only tiny amounts.* ► minute, insignificant, negligible, paltry, meagre

tip[1] *NOUN* **tips** the part right at the top or end of something

tip *VERB* **tips, tipping, tipped** put a tip on something

tip[2] *NOUN* **tips 1** a small present of money given to someone who has helped you **2** a small but useful piece of advice; a hint

tip *VERB* **tips, tipping, tipped 1** give a person a tip **2** name someone as a likely winner • *Which team would you tip to win the championship?*
▷ **tipper** *NOUN*
tip off give a warning or special information about something

tip[3] *VERB* **tips, tipping, tipped 1** tilt or topple **2** empty rubbish somewhere

tip *NOUN* **tips 1** the action of tipping something **2** a place where rubbish etc. is tipped

tipsy *ADJECTIVE* slightly drunk

tiptoe *VERB* **tiptoes, tiptoeing, tiptoed** walk on your toes very quietly or carefully
on tiptoe walking or standing on your toes

tire *VERB* **tires, tiring, tired** make or become tired
▷ **tiring** *ADJECTIVE*

tired *ADJECTIVE* feeling that you need to sleep or rest
be tired of have had enough of something and feel impatient or bored with it

tireless *ADJECTIVE* having a lot of energy; not tiring easily

tiresome *ADJECTIVE* annoying

tissue *NOUN* **tissues 1** tissue paper **2** a paper handkerchief **3** the substance forming any part of the body of an animal or plant • *bone tissue*

tissue paper *NOUN* very thin soft paper used for wrapping and packing things

tit[1] *NOUN* **tits** a kind of small bird

tit[2] *NOUN*
tit for tat something equal given in return; retaliation

titbit *NOUN* **titbits** a nice little piece of something, e.g. of food, gossip, or information

titillate *VERB* **titillates, titillating, titillated** stimulate or excite you pleasantly
▷ **titillation** *NOUN*

title *NOUN* **titles 1** the name of a book, film, song, etc. **2** a word used to show a person's rank or position, e.g. *Dr, Lord, Mrs* **3** a championship in sport • *the world heavyweight title* **4** a legal right to something

Thesaurus

tip *NOUN* **1** *He ran the tip of his finger along the handlebar. The tip of the arrow couldn't be far into the tree.* ► end, point, extremity, sharp end, nib **2** *The tip of a mountain was visible above the clouds.* ► summit, peak, pinnacle, top, apex, cap, crown, head **3** *He paid his bill, left a good tip, and walked home.* ► gratuity, gift **4** *My tip is to go for really good-quality ski pants.* ► hint, suggestion, advice, clue, information, warning **5** *To most people the rubbish tip is an eyesore.* ► dump, heap, pit

tip *VERB* **1** *He tipped his head back to look. The van was tipping to one side.* ► lean, incline, list, slant, slope, tilt, keel over **2** *She tipped the fish into the sink and began to clean them.* ► empty, dump, pour out, spill, unload **3** *He decided to tip the driver after all.* ► give a tip to, remunerate, reward
tip over *A whale is capable of tipping over a small boat.* ► overturn, capsize, topple, turn over, upset, knock over

tip-off *NOUN* (*informal*) *The police received a tip-off about a shipment of cocaine.* ► alert, clue, prompt, piece of information

tire *VERB* *The long walk tired us.* ► exhaust, fatigue, weary, tire out, wear out, drain
OPPOSITES ARE refresh, invigorate

tired *ADJECTIVE* **1** *He was tired from his hectic battle with the goblins.* ► exhausted, fatigued, wearied, worn out OPPOSITES ARE energetic, refreshed **2** *tired old debates about nature and nurture* ► stale, hackneyed, overworked, banal
OPPOSITES ARE fresh, new
tired of *They grew tired of waiting.* ► bored with, fed up with, sick of, impatient with

tireless *ADJECTIVE* *a tireless campaigner on behalf of chimpanzees in the wild* ► vigorous, energetic, determined, unflagging, untiring, indefatigable, persistent, zealous, diligent, sedulous, unceasing AN OPPOSITE IS lazy
USAGE Note that *tireless* and *tiresome* are not opposites.

tiresome *ADJECTIVE* *Richard was back from work after a tiresome day.* ► irritating, annoying, wearisome, troublesome, trying, irksome, bothersome, vexing, distracting, exasperating
OPPOSITES ARE stimulating, exciting
USAGE See the note at *tireless*.

tiring *ADJECTIVE* *Infant care can be tiring.*
► exhausting, exacting, taxing, wearying, fatiguing, demanding, difficult, hard
AN OPPOSITE IS refreshing

title *NOUN* **1** *The title of the picture was printed underneath.* ► caption, heading, name
2 *Specify the title you want to be known by.*
► form of address, designation, appellation, rank, status, office, position **3** *He sought to prove his title to the land.* ► right, entitlement, claim, ownership (of), tenure (of)

titter *VERB* **titters, tittering, tittered** giggle
▷ **titter** *NOUN*

to *PREPOSITION* This word is used to show direction or arrival at a position (*We walked to school. He rose to power*), limit (*from noon to two o'clock*), comparison (*We won by six goals to three*), receiving or being affected by something (*Give it to me. Be kind to animals*) Also used before a verb to form an infinitive (*I want to see him*) or to show purpose etc. (*He does that to annoy us*), or alone when the verb is understood (*We meant to go but forgot to*)

to *ADVERB* **1** to or in the proper or closed position or condition • *Push the door to.* **2** into a state of activity • *We set to and cleaned the kitchen.*
to and fro backwards and forwards

toad *NOUN* **toads** a frog-like animal that lives mainly on land

toadstool *NOUN* **toadstools** a fungus (usually poisonous) with a round top on a stalk

toast *VERB* **toasts, toasting, toasted 1** heat bread etc. to make it brown and crisp **2** warm something in front of a fire etc. **3** drink in honour of someone

toast *NOUN* **toasts 1** toasted bread **2** the call to drink in honour of someone; the person honoured in this way

tobacco *NOUN* the dried leaves of certain plants prepared for smoking in cigarettes, cigars, or pipes or for making snuff [via Spanish from a Central American language]

toboggan *NOUN* **toboggans** a small sledge used for sliding downhill
▷ **tobogganing** *NOUN*
[via Canadian French from a Native American language]

today *NOUN* this present day • *Today is Monday.*

today *ADVERB* on this day • *Have you seen him today?*

toddler *NOUN* **toddlers** a young child who has only recently learnt to walk
▷ **toddle** *VERB*

to-do *NOUN* **to-dos** a fuss or commotion

toe *NOUN* **toes 1** any of the separate parts (five in humans) at the end of each foot **2** the part of a shoe or sock etc. that covers the toes
on your toes alert

toffee *NOUN* **toffees** a sticky sweet made from heated butter and sugar

together *ADVERB* with another person or thing; with each other • *They went to the party together.*

toil *VERB* **toils, toiling, toiled 1** work hard **2** move slowly and with difficulty
▷ **toiler** *NOUN*

toil *NOUN* hard work

toilet *NOUN* **toilets 1** a bowl-like object, connected by pipes to a drain, which you use to get rid of urine and faeces **2** a room containing a toilet **3** the process of washing, dressing, and tidying yourself

token *NOUN* **tokens 1** a piece of metal or plastic that can be used instead of money **2** a voucher or coupon that can be exchanged for goods **3** a sign or signal of something • *a token of our friendship*

tolerable *ADJECTIVE* able to be tolerated
▷ **tolerably** *ADVERB*

Thesaurus

toast *VERB* **1** *They toasted bread by the fire.* ► grill, brown, heat, warm **2** *The guests then toasted their host.* ► drink a toast to, drink the health of, raise your glass to, salute, honour

together *ADVERB* **1** *They were all speaking together.* ► simultaneously, at the same time, at once, collectively, concurrently, in chorus, in unison, jointly OPPOSITES ARE independently, separately **2** *Naim and I work together.* ► jointly, with each other, in concert, side by side OPPOSITES ARE separately, alone **3** *Nothing happened for days together.* ► in a row, in succession, continuously, consecutively

toil *NOUN* *years of hardship and toil* ► work, labour, donkey work, slaving, drudgery, effort, exertion, industry

toil *VERB* *The team needed to toil all day.* ► work, labour, slave, sweat, struggle, (*more informal*) slog, (*more informal*) grind away

toilet *NOUN* **1** *There is a toilet on the first floor.* ► lavatory, WC, convenience, facilities, privy, (*more informal*) loo **2** *She was taking ages over her toilet.* ► washing, bathing

token *NOUN* **1** *Saladin's ring was sent as a token of good faith.* ► symbol, sign, mark, expression, testimony, evidence, indication, proof, reminder **2** *He had her name tattooed on his arm as a token of their love.* ► memento, souvenir, record, keepsake **3** *a book token* ► voucher, coupon, counter

token *ADJECTIVE* **1** *She did the work for a token fee.* ► nominal, minimal, trivial, slight AN OPPOSITE IS substantial **2** *The garrison offered only token resistance.* ► perfunctory, insignificant, superficial, symbolic AN OPPOSITE IS considerable

tolerable *ADJECTIVE* **1** *The pain was barely tolerable.* ► bearable, acceptable, endurable, sufferable, supportable AN OPPOSITE IS intolerable **2** *He was fond of music and had a tolerable voice.* ► adequate, passable, middling, ordinary, satisfactory, fair, mediocre, indifferent

tolerant *ADJECTIVE* willing to accept or tolerate other people's behaviour and opinions even if you do not agree with them
▷ **tolerantly** *ADVERB* **tolerance** *NOUN*

tolerate *VERB* **tolerates, tolerating, tolerated** **1** allow something even if you do not approve of it **2** bear or put up with something unpleasant
▷ **toleration** *NOUN*

toll[1] (rhymes with *hole*) *NOUN* **tolls** **1** a charge made for using a road, bridge, etc. **2** loss or damage caused • *The death toll in the earthquake is rising.*

toll[2] (rhymes with *hole*) *VERB* **tolls, tolling, tolled** ring a bell slowly
▷ **toll** *NOUN*

tom *NOUN* **toms** a male cat
▷ **tomcat** *NOUN*

tomato *NOUN* **tomatoes** a soft round red fruit eaten as a vegetable [via French, Spanish, or Portuguese from Nahuatl (a Central American language)]

tomb (toom) *NOUN* **tombs** a place where someone is buried; a monument built over this

tomboy *NOUN* **tomboys** a girl who enjoys rough noisy games etc.

tombstone *NOUN* **tombstones** a memorial stone set up over a grave

tomorrow *NOUN, ADVERB* the day after today

ton *NOUN* **tons** **1** a unit of weight equal to 2,240 pounds or about 1,016 kilograms **2** a large amount • *There's tons of room.* **3** (*slang*) a speed of 100 miles per hour

tone *NOUN* **tones** **1** a sound in music or of the voice **2** each of the five larger intervals between notes in a musical scale (the smaller intervals are **semitones**) **3** a shade of a colour **4** the quality or character of something • *a cheerful tone*
▷ **tonal** *ADJECTIVE* **tonally** *ADVERB*

tone *VERB* **tones, toning, toned** **1** give a particular tone or quality to something **2** be harmonious in colour
tone down make a thing quieter or less bright or less harsh
[from Greek *tonos* = tension]

tongs *PLURAL NOUN* a tool with two arms joined at one end, used to pick up or hold things

tongue *NOUN* **tongues** **1** the long soft muscular part that moves about inside the mouth **2** a language **3** the leather flap on a shoe or boot underneath the laces **4** a pointed flame [from Old English]

tongue-tied *ADJECTIVE* too shy to speak

tonic *NOUN* **tonics** **1** a medicine etc. that makes a person healthier or stronger **2** anything that makes a person more energetic or cheerful **3** a fizzy mineral water with a bitter taste, often mixed with gin **4** a keynote in music
▷ **tonic** *ADJECTIVE*

Thesaurus

tolerance *NOUN* *He has always preached tolerance for people of whatever religion.*
► toleration, forbearance, sufferance, acceptance, open-mindedness, broad-mindedness, liberalism, understanding, permissiveness

tolerant *ADJECTIVE* *He's a tolerant chap who didn't seem to mind if I got it wrong.* ► understanding, open-minded, long-suffering, forbearing, sympathetic, fair, magnanimous, charitable
OPPOSITES ARE intolerant, unsympathetic

tolerate *VERB* **1** *At work she will not tolerate interference.* ► put up with, bear, endure, stand, abide, stomach, suffer, take, (*more informal*) stick **2** *This sort of behaviour is difficult to tolerate.* ► accept, condone, countenance, admit, brook, make allowances for, permit, sanction

toll *NOUN* **1** *a road toll* ► charge, fee, levy, tariff, payment, duty, tax **2** *the death toll from the accident* ► count, tally, total, reckoning

toll *VERB* *We heard a bell toll.* ► ring, peal, chime, sound

tomb *NOUN* *the tomb of Ramesses II* ► burial chamber, burial place, sepulchre, grave, catacomb, crypt, mausoleum RELATED ADJECTIVE sepulchral

tone *NOUN* **1** *He objected to the arrogant tone of the letter.* ► manner, mood, spirit, attitude, tenor, quality **2** *She called out in an angry tone of voice.* ► expression, timbre, quality, sound, modulation, intonation **3** *emulsion paint with a rosy tone* ► tint, tinge, hue, shade, blush, colour

tone *VERB* **tone with** *The pastel shades of the wallpaper tone beautifully with the light wood of the furniture.* ► harmonize with, coordinate with, match, go well with, suit
tone down *He was unwilling to tone down his criticisms of the management.* ► moderate, modify, temper, mitigate, soften, restrain, dampen, subdue, play down
AN OPPOSITE IS intensify

tongue *NOUN* *He spoke in a foreign tongue.*
► language, vernacular, idiom, talk, speech, utterance

tongue-tied *ADJECTIVE* *He is often tongue-tied in company.* ► lost for words, inarticulate, dumbstruck, speechless, mute, silent

tonight NOUN, ADVERB this evening or night

tonne NOUN **tonnes** a metric ton (1,000 kilograms)

too ADVERB **1** also • *Take the others too.* **2** more than is wanted or allowed etc. • *That's too much sugar for me.*

tool NOUN **tools 1** a device that helps you to do a particular job • *A saw is a tool for cutting wood or metal.* **2** a thing used for a particular purpose • *An encyclopedia is a useful study tool.*

tooth NOUN **teeth 1** one of the hard white bony parts that are rooted in the gums, used for biting and chewing things **2** one of a row of sharp parts • *the teeth of a saw*
▷ **toothache** NOUN **toothbrush** NOUN **toothed** ADJECTIVE
fight tooth and nail fight very fiercely

toothpaste NOUN **toothpastes** a paste for cleaning your teeth

top[1] NOUN **tops 1** the highest part of something **2** the upper surface **3** the covering or stopper of a bottle, jar, etc. **4** a piece of clothing for the upper part of the body
on top of in addition to something

top ADJECTIVE highest • *at top speed*

top VERB **tops, topping, topped 1** put a top on something **2** be at the top of something • *She tops the list* **3** remove the top of something
top up fill up something that is half empty • *top up your glass*

top[2] NOUN **tops** a toy that can be made to spin on its point

top hat NOUN **top hats** a man's tall stiff black or grey hat worn with formal clothes

top-heavy ADJECTIVE too heavy at the top and likely to overbalance

topic NOUN **topics** a subject to write, learn, or talk about

topical ADJECTIVE connected with things that are happening now • *a topical film*
▷ **topically** ADVERB **topicality** NOUN

topmost ADJECTIVE highest

topple VERB **topples, toppling, toppled 1** fall over; totter and fall **2** make something fall; overthrow

top secret ADJECTIVE extremely secret • *top secret information*

topsy-turvy ADVERB, ADJECTIVE upside down; muddled

torch NOUN **torches 1** a small electric lamp that you can carry in your hand **2** a stick with burning material on the end, used as a light

torment VERB **torments, tormenting, tormented 1** make someone suffer greatly **2** tease; keep annoying someone
▷ **tormentor** NOUN

torment NOUN **torments** great suffering

tornado (tor- nay- doh) NOUN **tornadoes** a violent storm or whirlwind

Thesaurus

tool NOUN **1** *a set of garden tools* ► implement, utensil, device, gadget, appliance, contraption **2** *The tabloid press became a tool of the government.* ► dupe, pawn, puppet, creature, stooge, minion, (*more informal*) poodle

top NOUN **1** *The top of the mountain was still covered in snow.* ► summit, peak, pinnacle, tip, apex, cap, crown, head AN OPPOSITE IS foot **2** *The top of the jar was stuck.* ► lid, cap, cover, covering AN OPPOSITE IS bottom

top ADJECTIVE **1** *an office on the top floor* ► highest, topmost, uppermost, upper OPPOSITES ARE bottom, lowest **2** *some of the world's top golf professionals* ► leading, finest, foremost, principal, chief, pre-eminent, prime **3** *the top Paris restaurants* ► best, prime, superior, leading, foremost, finest AN OPPOSITE IS inferior

top VERB **1** *The cake can be topped with chopped nuts.* ► cover, cap, decorate, finish off, garnish, crown **2** *Sales are expected to top the million mark.* ► exceed, beat, be higher than, outdo, surpass, better, cap, excel

topic NOUN *An article on this topic appeared last month.* ► subject, theme, issue, matter, question, talking-point

topical ADJECTIVE *Choose a news item of topical interest each week.* ► current, contemporary, recent, up-to-date, up-to-the-minute, newsworthy

topple VERB **1** *The heavy winds toppled several pylons, causing power cuts.* ► knock down, overturn, tip over, throw down, upset **2** *She saw a man topple sideways into the gutter. If kangaroos had no tails, they would topple over.* ► fall, overbalance, tumble **3** *A party revolt had toppled the conservative leadership.* ► bring down, overthrow, oust, unseat, depose

topsy-turvy ADJECTIVE *The carts lay in a topsy-turvy heap at the bottom of the hill. My emotions are all topsy-turvy.* ► disordered, confused, mixed up, muddled, jumbled, untidy, higgledy-piggledy OPPOSITES ARE ordered, neat

torment VERB **1** *The urge to express her feelings tormented her. Sometimes, he was tormented by jealousy.* ► afflict, torture, distress, persecute, plague, bedevil, bother, be a torment to, pain, vex **2** *Marjory loved tormenting her younger brother.* ► tease, bait, pester, harass, annoy, bully, victimize

torpedo *NOUN* **torpedoes** a long tube-shaped missile that can be fired under water to destroy ships

torrent *NOUN* **torrents** **1** a rushing stream; a great flow **2** a heavy downpour of rain
▷ **torrential** *ADJECTIVE*

torso *NOUN* **torsos** the trunk of the human body

tortoise *NOUN* **tortoises** a slow-moving animal with a shell over its body

tortoiseshell (**tort**- as- shell) *NOUN* **tortoiseshells** **1** the mottled brown and yellow shell of certain turtles, used for making combs etc. **2** a cat or butterfly with mottled brown colouring

torture *VERB* **tortures, torturing, tortured** make a person feel great pain or worry
▷ **torture** *NOUN* **torturer** *NOUN*

Tory *NOUN* **Tories** a Conservative
▷ **Tory** *ADJECTIVE*

toss *VERB* **tosses, tossing, tossed** **1** throw something, especially up into the air **2** spin a coin to decide something according to which side of it is upwards after it falls **3** move restlessly or unevenly from side to side
▷ **toss** *NOUN*

toss-up *NOUN* **toss-ups** **1** the tossing of a coin **2** an even chance

tot[1] *NOUN* **tots** **1** a small child **2** (*informal*) a small amount of spirits • *a tot of rum*

tot[2] *VERB* **tots, totting, totted**
tot up (*informal*) add up

total *ADJECTIVE* **1** including everything • *the total amount* **2** complete • *total darkness*
▷ **totally** *ADVERB*

total *NOUN* **totals** the amount you get by adding everything together

total *VERB* **totals, totalling, totalled** **1** add up the total **2** amount to something • *The cost of the damage totalled £500.*

totalitarian *ADJECTIVE* using a form of government where people are not allowed to form rival political parties

totem pole *NOUN* **totem poles** a pole carved or painted by Native Americans with the symbols (**totems**) of their tribes or families

totter *VERB* **totters, tottering, tottered** walk unsteadily; wobble
▷ **tottery** *ADJECTIVE*

touch *VERB* **touches, touching, touched** **1** put your hand or fingers etc. on something lightly **2** be or come together so that there is no space between **3** come into contact with something or hit it gently **4** move or meddle with something **5** reach • *The thermometer touched 30° Celsius.* **6** affect someone's feelings, e.g. by making them feel sympathy • *The sad story touched our hearts.*
touch and go an uncertain situation
touch down **1** (said about an aircraft) land **2** (in rugby football) touch the ball on the ground behind the goal line
touch on discuss a subject briefly
touch up improve something by making small additions or changes

Thesaurus

torrent *NOUN* **1** *The sky opened and a heavy torrent fell down.* ► downpour, deluge, flood, shower, flow AN OPPOSITE IS trickle **2** *These points are lost to the reader in a torrent of words.* ► cascade, gush, rush, outburst, spate, stream, tide

torture *NOUN* **1** *Human rights groups claimed that torture of prisoners had taken place.* ► maltreatment, persecution, cruelty, torment, humiliation, degradation, inquisition **2** *The rest of the journey was torture.* ► agony, torment, misery, affliction

torture *VERB* **1** *They were out to torture their victims.* ► persecute, inflict pain on, inflict suffering on, be cruel to, degrade, humiliate, hurt, torment **2** *I was having thoughts that tortured me.* ► afflict, torment, distress, persecute, plague, bedevil, bother, be a torment to, pain, vex

toss *VERB* **1** *He tossed a ball high in the air.* ► throw, fling, hurl, cast, pitch, heave **2** *The boat was tossing about in shallow water.* ► lurch, pitch, reel, rock, roll, bob, shake, wallow, welter, writhe **3** *Marion tossed restlessly in bed.* ► twist and turn, move restlessly, flail, thrash about, wriggle, fidget

toss *NOUN* *a toss of a coin* ► flip, fling, throw, jerk, heave

tot *VERB* **tot up** *He was totting up some figures.* ► add up, calculate, count, total, find the total of, reckon up, totalize, work out

total *ADJECTIVE* **1** *The total volume of sales reached five million.* ► complete, comprehensive, entire, full, gross, overall, whole **2** *A senior fire officer said it was total carnage.* ► sheer, utter, absolute, downright, thorough, unmitigated, unqualified, perfect, out-and-out

total *NOUN* *The airport will handle a total of a million passengers in the week before Christmas.* ► sum, totality, aggregate, amount, whole

total *VERB* *The cash bag totalled £1,200.* ► amount to, come to, add up to, make, reach

total up *Total up your scores.* ► add up, calculate, count, tot up, find the total of, reckon up, totalize, work out

touch *VERB* **1** *She touched his arm and he turned.* ► pat, brush, contact, feel, rub, stroke, tap, caress, dab **2** *Their sorrow touched him.*

touch *NOUN* **touches** **1** the action of touching **2** the ability to feel things by touching them **3** a small amount; a small thing done • *the finishing touches* **4** a special skill or style of workmanship • *She hasn't lost her touch.* **5** communication with someone • *We lost touch with him* **6** the part of a football field outside the playing area

touching *ADJECTIVE* causing you to have kindly feelings such as pity or sympathy

touchline *NOUN* **touchlines** one of the lines that mark the side of a sports pitch

touchstone *NOUN* **touchstones** a test by which the quality of something is judged

touchy *ADJECTIVE* **touchier, touchiest** easily offended
▷ **touchily** *ADVERB* **touchiness** *NOUN*

tough *ADJECTIVE* **1** strong; difficult to break or damage **2** difficult to chew **3** able to stand hardship; not easily hurt **4** firm or severe **5** difficult • *a tough decision*
▷ **toughly** *ADVERB* **toughness** *NOUN*

toughen *VERB* **toughens, toughening, toughened** make or become tough

tour *NOUN* **tours** a journey visiting several places

tour *VERB* **tours, touring, toured** make a tour

tourism *NOUN* the industry of organizing holidays and visits to places of interest

tourist *NOUN* **tourists** a person who makes a tour or visits a place for pleasure

tournament *NOUN* **tournaments** a series of games or contests

tow (rhymes with *go*) *VERB* **tows, towing, towed** pull something along behind you
▷ **tow** *NOUN*
on tow being towed

toward *PREPOSITION* towards

towards *PREPOSITION* **1** in the direction of • *She walked towards the sea.* **2** in relation to;

Thesaurus

► move, affect, concern, disturb, influence, inspire, stir, upset **3** *Their speed touched 100 m.p.h.* ► reach, rise to, attain **4** (*informal*) *Nothing could touch them for good value.* ► equal, match, compare with, rival, come up to, parallel
touch on *The programme touched on recent concerns.* ► refer to, deal with, mention, treat, raise, cover
touch up *The room had been touched up and given a new carpet.* ► improve, repaint, renovate, refurbish, redecorate

touch *NOUN* **1** *Animals communicate by touch.* ► feeling, touching, contact **2** *She jumped under his touch.* ► pat, stroke, tap, caress, contact, dab **3** *Funny speeches need a bubbly, light touch.* ► manner, style, technique, flair, knack, feel, sensitivity **4** *There was a touch of genius in the way he talked that night.* ► hint, suggestion, suspicion, tinge, trace **5** *A gift of flowers can be a nice touch.* ► feature, detail, extra **6** *He and Carol kept in touch.* ► contact, communication, correspondence RELATED ADJECTIVE tactile

touched *ADJECTIVE* *I was touched by their generosity.* ► moved, affected, impressed, stirred, responsive (to)

touching *ADJECTIVE* *She was beautiful, her face crossed by a touching sadness.* ► moving, affecting, poignant, emotional, tender

touchy *ADJECTIVE* *Like most tired children she was touchy and uncooperative.* ► irritable, bad-tempered, irascible, grumpy, grouchy, testy, tetchy, crotchety, cantankerous, peevish, fractious, cross, (*more informal*) stroppy, (*more informal*) shirty AN OPPOSITE IS good-humoured

tough *ADJECTIVE* **1** *It was my first outing in my tough new boots.* ► strong, stout, durable, hard-wearing, indestructible, lasting, unbreakable, well-made OPPOSITES ARE flimsy, delicate **2** *He is tall with a tough physique.*(*informal*) ► sturdy, muscular, strong, beefy, brawny, burly, hardy, robust, stalwart AN OPPOSITE IS weak **3** *They proved to be tough rivals. She's a tough, single-minded woman.* ► determined, tenacious, unyielding, resilient, resolute, resistant, stiff, stubborn AN OPPOSITE IS weak. **4** *The meat was overcooked and tough.* ► chewy, leathery, gristly, rubbery, hard, uneatable AN OPPOSITE IS tender **5** *There was a tough climb ahead.* ► difficult, arduous, strenuous, exacting, exhausting, gruelling, stiff, hard, laborious AN OPPOSITE IS easy **6** *They had some tough questions to answer.* ► difficult, baffling, intractable, puzzling, perplexing, (*more informal*) thorny, (*more informal*) knotty AN OPPOSITE IS easy

toughen *VERB* *ways of toughening wood* ► harden, strengthen, make tougher, reinforce AN OPPOSITE IS weaken

tour *NOUN* *a tour round the castles of southern Bavaria* ► journey, expedition, trip, ride, drive, outing, excursion

tour *VERB* *The town is well situated for touring the area.* ► travel round, visit, explore, sightsee, go round, make a tour of

tourist *NOUN* *Tribal dances are performed for the tourists.* ► sightseer, holidaymaker, visitor, tripper, traveller

tournament *NOUN* *He was due to take part in a celebrity golf tournament.* ► competition, contest, championship, match, meeting, series

tow *VERB* *The rope seemed too slender to tow the forty-foot barge.* ► pull, drag, tug, draw, haul, transport, trail

regarding • *He behaved kindly towards his children.* **3** as a contribution to • *Put the money towards a new bicycle.* **4** near • *towards four o'clock*

towel *NOUN* **towels** a piece of absorbent cloth for drying things
▷ **towelling** *NOUN*

tower *NOUN* **towers** a tall narrow building

tower *VERB* **towers, towering, towered** be very high; be taller than others • *Skyscrapers towered over the city.*

town *NOUN* **towns** a place with many houses, shops, offices, and other buildings

town hall *NOUN* **town halls** a building with offices for the local council and usually a hall for public events

towpath *NOUN* **towpaths** a path beside a canal or river, originally for use when a horse was towing a barge etc.

toxic *ADJECTIVE* poisonous; caused by poison
▷ **toxicity** *NOUN*

toy *NOUN* **toys** a thing to play with

toy *ADJECTIVE* **1** made as a toy **2** (said about a dog) of a very small breed • *a toy poodle*

toy *VERB* **toys, toying, toyed**
toy with handle a thing or consider an idea casually

trace *NOUN* **traces 1** a mark left by a person or thing; a sign • *There was no trace of the thief.* **2** a very small amount

trace *VERB* **traces, tracing, traced 1** copy a picture or map etc. by drawing over it on transparent paper **2** follow the traces of a person or thing; find • *The police have been trying to trace her.*
▷ **tracer** *NOUN*

tracery *NOUN* a decorative pattern of holes in stone, e.g. in a church window

track *NOUN* **tracks 1** a mark or marks left by a moving person or thing **2** a rough path made by being used **3** a road or area of ground specially prepared for racing **4** a set of rails for trains or trams etc. **5** one of the songs or pieces of music on a CD, tape, etc. **6** a continuous band round the wheels of a tank or tractor etc.
keep *or* **lose track of** keep or fail to keep yourself informed about where something is or what someone is doing

track *VERB* **tracks, tracking, tracked 1** follow the tracks left by a person or animal **2** follow or observe something as it moves
▷ **tracker** *NOUN*
track down find a person or thing by searching

tract[1] *NOUN* **tracts 1** an area of land **2** a series of connected parts along which something passes • *the digestive tract* [from Latin *tractus* = drawing, draught]

tract[2] *NOUN* **tracts** a pamphlet containing a short essay, especially about religion or politics [via Old English from Latin]

Thesaurus

tower *NOUN* *We passed two abbeys, one with a tower and one without.* ► steeple, turret, column, pillar, belfry

tower *VERB* *Clouds towered on every side. He stood up, and he towered above her.* ► loom, rear, rise, dominate, stand out, stick up, ascend

towering *ADJECTIVE* *towering crags and cliffs* ► tall, high, lofty, soaring, mighty, colossal, gigantic, imposing

town *NOUN* *The family moved to an industrial town.* ► conurbation, urban area, borough, city, municipality, settlement RELATED ADJECTIVE urban, civic, municipal

toxic *ADJECTIVE* *You have two minutes to get out before the heat and toxic fumes overcome you.* ► poisonous, noxious, lethal, deadly, dangerous, harmful OPPOSITES ARE harmless, safe

toy *ADJECTIVE* *giant toy animals* ► model, imitation, make-believe, simulation, (*more informal*) pretend

toy *NOUN* *The children can bring their favourite toy.* ► plaything, game, doll

toy *VERB* **toy with 1** *She picked up her fork and toyed with her food.* ► play with, fiddle with, fidget with, tinker with, peck at, pick at **2** *He toyed with the idea of walking to the station to meet her.* ► think about, play with, consider

trace *NOUN* **1** *'No,' he said with a trace of irritation.* ► hint, touch, suggestion, suspicion **2** *The animal had left no trace.* ► trail, track, mark, sign, spoor, indication **3** *The investigators could find no trace of blood.* ► sign, remnant, remains, vestige

trace *VERB* **1** *Police are trying to trace the owner of the car.* ► track down, find, discover, uncover, unearth, detect **2** *It would be best to trace the map from an atlas.* ► copy, draw, outline, mark out, sketch, make a copy of

track *NOUN* **1** *An animal had left clear tracks.* ► trace, trail, mark, scent, spoor, footmark, footprint **2** *a track across the fields* ► path, way, pathway, footpath, route, lane, trail **3** *a racing track* ► course, circuit, dirt-track, race-track **4** *Passengers were seen walking along the tracks.* ► rail, line

track *VERB* *He tracked a bear all day.* ► follow, trail, pursue, stalk, chase, hunt, dog, shadow, trace
track down *It took years to track everyone down.* ► discover, trace, find, detect, recover, retrieve

tractor *NOUN* **tractors** a motor vehicle for pulling farm machinery or other heavy loads

trade *NOUN* **trades** **1** buying, selling, or exchanging goods **2** business of a particular kind; the people working in this **3** an occupation, especially a skilled craft

trade *VERB* **trades, trading, traded** buy, sell, or exchange things
▷ **trader** *NOUN*
trade in give a thing as part of the payment for something new • *He traded in his motorcycle for a car.*

trade mark *NOUN* **trade marks** a firm's registered symbol or name used to distinguish its goods etc. from those of other firms

tradesman *NOUN* **tradesmen** a person employed in trade, especially one who sells or delivers goods

trade union *NOUN* **trade unions** a group of workers organized to help and protect workers in their own trade or industry

tradition *NOUN* **traditions** **1** the passing down of beliefs or customs etc. from one generation to another **2** something passed on in this way
▷ **traditional** *ADJECTIVE* **traditionally** *ADVERB*

traffic *NOUN* **1** vehicles, ships, or aircraft moving along a route **2** trading, especially when it is illegal or wrong • *drug traffic*

traffic lights *PLURAL NOUN* coloured lights used as a signal to traffic at road junctions etc.

traffic warden *NOUN* **traffic wardens** an official who assists police to control the movement and parking of vehicles

tragedy *NOUN* **tragedies** **1** a play with unhappy events or a sad ending **2** a very sad or distressing event [from Greek *tragos* = goat + *oide* = song The connection with goats is not known]

tragic *ADJECTIVE* **1** very sad or distressing **2** to do with tragedies • *a great tragic actor*
▷ **tragically** *ADVERB*

trail *NOUN* **trails** **1** a track, scent, or other sign left where something has passed **2** a path or track made through the countryside or a forest

trail *VERB* **trails, trailing, trailed** **1** follow the trail of something; track **2** drag or be dragged along behind; lag behind **3** follow someone more slowly or wearily **4** hang down or float loosely **5** become fainter • *Her voice trailed away.*

trailer *NOUN* **trailers** **1** a truck or other container pulled along by a vehicle **2** a short piece from a film or television programme, shown in advance to advertise it

train *NOUN* **trains** **1** a railway engine pulling a line of carriages or trucks that are linked together **2** a number of people or animals

Thesaurus

trade *NOUN* **1** *international trade* ► commerce, buying and selling, dealing, trading, traffic, transactions, barter, business, marketing RELATED ADJECTIVE mercantile **2** *He wanted to be trained in a trade.* ► craft, occupation, job, career, profession, calling, pursuit, line of work

trade *VERB* **1** *The family traded in diamonds.* ► deal, traffic, buy and sell, do business **2** *She traded her old car for a new model.* ► exchange, part-exchange, barter, swap, switch

trader *NOUNS* *local high-street traders* ► dealer, merchant, retailer, tradesman, shopkeeper, stockist, supplier, vendor

tradition *NOUN* *the old tradition of first-footing* ► custom, practice, convention, institution, observance, habit, routine

traditional *ADJECTIVE* **1** *a traditional white wedding* ► conventional, customary, established, accustomed, familiar, time-honoured, typical, orthodox, regular, usual AN OPPOSITE IS unconventional **2** *traditional beliefs* ► popular, folk, oral, unwritten, historical OPPOSITES ARE modern, contemporary

traffic *NOUN* **1** *Road traffic is not allowed in the park.* ► vehicles, cars, transport **2** *goods traffic* ► transport, transportation, movement **3** *illegal traffic in antiquities* ► trade, trading, dealing, commerce, peddling

tragedy *NOUN* *the tragedy of their son's death* ► disaster, calamity, catastrophe, affliction, blow, misfortune, misadventure

tragic *ADJECTIVE* **1** *a tragic accident* ► disastrous, catastrophic, calamitous, dreadful, fatal, appalling, terrible, unfortunate AN OPPOSITE IS fortunate **2** *a tragic expression on her face* ► sad, sorrowful, woeful, wretched, distressed, grief-stricken, hurt, pathetic, piteous, pitiful AN OPPOSITE IS comic

trail *NOUN* **1** *The fox followed the trail of its prey.* ► track, footprints, mark, scent, signs, spoor, traces **2** *a nature trail* ► path, pathway, route, track, road **3** *They left a trail of clues.* ► series, string, stream, chain, line

trail *VERB* **1** *The car was trailing a large caravan.* ► draw, haul, drag, pull, tow **2** *His feet were trailing in the water.* ► dangle, hang **3** *She suspected someone was trailing her.* ► follow, pursue, shadow, stalk, track, trace, tail, chase **4** *The smaller children were trailing behind.* ► straggle, linger, lag, fall behind, dawdle, dally

train *NOUN* **1** *a strange train of events* ► chain, series, sequence, succession **2** *The minister had a train of attendants.* ► entourage, retinue, cortège, following, suite

moving in a line • *a camel train* **3** a series of things • *a train of events* **4** part of a long dress or robe that trails on the ground at the back

train *VERB* **trains, training, trained 1** give a person instruction or practice so that they become skilled **2** practise, especially for a sporting event • *She was training for the race.* **3** make something grow in a particular direction • *We'd like to train roses up the walls.* **4** aim a gun or camera etc.

trainer *NOUN* **trainers 1** a person who trains people or animals **2** a soft rubber-soled shoe of the kind worn for running or by athletes etc. while exercising

traitor *NOUN* **traitors** a person who betrays his or her country or friends
▷ **traitorous** *ADJECTIVE*

tram *NOUN* **trams** a public passenger vehicle running on rails in the road

tramp *NOUN* **tramps 1** a person without a home or job who walks from place to place **2** a long walk **3** the sound of heavy footsteps

tramp *VERB* **tramps, tramping, tramped 1** walk with heavy footsteps **2** walk for a long distance

trample *VERB* **tramples, trampling, trampled** tread heavily on something; crush something by treading on it

trampoline *NOUN* **trampolines** a large piece of canvas joined to a frame by springs, used by gymnasts for jumping on

trance *NOUN* **trances** a dreamy or unconscious state rather like sleep

tranquil *ADJECTIVE* calm and quiet
▷ **tranquilly** *ADVERB* **tranquillity** *NOUN*

tranquillizer *NOUN* **tranquillizers** a medicine used to make a person feel calm

transatlantic *ADJECTIVE* across or on the other side of the Atlantic Ocean

transcript *NOUN* **transcripts** a written copy

transfer *VERB* **transfers, transferring, transferred 1** move a person or thing to another place **2** hand over
▷ **transferable** *ADJECTIVE* **transference** *NOUN*

transfer *NOUN* **transfers 1** the transferring of a person or thing **2** a picture or design that can be transferred onto another surface

transfigure *VERB* **transfigures, transfiguring, transfigured** change the appearance of something greatly
▷ **transfiguration** *NOUN*

transfix *VERB* **transfixes, transfixing, transfixed 1** make a person or animal unable to move because of fear or surprise etc. **2** pierce and fix with something pointed

transform *VERB* **transforms, transforming, transformed** change the form or appearance

Thesaurus

train *VERB* **1** *Now she had three assistants to train.* ► teach, instruct, tutor, coach, educate, prepare **2** *The team was training hard.* ► practise, exercise, prepare yourself, get fit, (*more informal*) work out **3** *The guns were trained on a position in the hills.* ► aim (at), point (at), direct (at), level (at)

trainer *NOUN* *a fitness trainer* ► instructor, coach, teacher, tutor, mentor

training *NOUN* *Next week he would report for training.* ► exercise, exercises, physical exercise, fitness routine, (*more informal*) working out

traitor *NOUN* *Thousands of students denounced Kim as a traitor.* ► betrayer, defector, deserter, double-crosser, apostate, blackleg, turncoat, collaborator, informer, quisling, renegade

tramp *NOUN* **1** *the ritual tramp across Ilkley Moor* ► trek, trudge, march, walk, (*more informal*) slog **2** *He remembered an old tramp he used to see by the tube station.* ► beggar, vagrant, homeless person, destitute person, (*more informal*) dosser, (*more informal*) down and out

tramp *VERB* *We tramped across the wet grass and bracken.* ► trudge, trek, traipse, hike, march, plod, stride, toil

trample *VERB* **trample on** *Her dog had trampled on his tulips.* ► tread on, stamp on, walk over, crush, flatten, squash

trance *NOUN* *She was lost in a trance.* ► daze, dream, hypnotic state, reverie, day-dream, ecstasy, spell

tranquil *ADJECTIVE* **1** *the tranquil and pretty hamlet of Blore* ► peaceful, quiet, calm, restful, placid, serene, still, undisturbed, unruffled
OPPOSITES ARE noisy, busy **2** *He felt relaxed and tranquil.* ► calm, placid, sedate, sober, unemotional, unexcited, untroubled, collected, composed, dispassionate, (*more informal*) laid-back AN OPPOSITE IS excited

transfer *VERB* (with the stress on *-fer*) *The books will be transferred to the central library.* ► move, remove, shift, relocate, take over, take across, convey, transmit

transfer *NOUN* (with the stress on *trans-*) *the transfer of rights to the new owner* ► change, changeover, shift, shifting, handover, transferral, transmission

transform *VERB* *The new owners transformed the property into a lovely family house.* ► convert, change, alter, develop, renovate, reorganize, (*more formal*) metamorphose

A B C D E F G H I J K L M N O P Q R S T U V W X Y Z

or character of a person or thing
▷ **transformation** *NOUN*

transformer *NOUN* **transformers** a device used to change the voltage of an electric current

transfusion *NOUN* **transfusions** putting blood taken from one person into another person's body
▷ **transfuse** *VERB*

transistor *NOUN* **transistors** **1** a tiny semiconductor device that controls a flow of electricity **2** (also **transistor radio**) a portable radio that uses transistors
▷ **transistorized** *ADJECTIVE*

transit *NOUN* the process of travelling from one place to another • *The goods were damaged in transit.*

transition *NOUN* **transitions** the process of changing from one condition or form etc. to another
▷ **transitional** *ADJECTIVE*

transitive *ADJECTIVE* (said about a verb) used with a direct object after it, e.g. *change* in *change your shoes* (but not in *change into dry shoes*) COMPARE **intransitive**
▷ **transitively** *ADVERB*

translate *VERB* **translates, translating, translated** put something into another language
▷ **translatable** *ADJECTIVE* **translation** *NOUN* **translator** *NOUN*

transliterate *VERB* **transliterates, transliterating, transliterated** write a word in the letters of a different alphabet or language
▷ **transliteration** *NOUN*

translucent (tranz-loo-sent) *ADJECTIVE* allowing some light to shine through but not transparent

transmission *NOUN* **transmissions** **1** transmitting something **2** a broadcast **3** the gears by which power is transmitted from the engine to the wheels of a vehicle

transmit *VERB* **transmits, transmitting, transmitted** **1** send or pass on from one person or place to another **2** send out a signal or broadcast etc.
▷ **transmitter** *NOUN*

transmute *VERB* **transmutes, transmuting, transmuted** change something from one form or substance into another
▷ **transmutation** *NOUN*

transparent *ADJECTIVE* able to be seen through

transplant *VERB* **transplants, transplanting, transplanted** **1** remove a plant and put it to grow somewhere else **2** transfer a part of the body to another person or animal
▷ **transplantation** *NOUN*

transplant *NOUN* **transplants** **1** the process of transplanting **2** something transplanted

transport *VERB* **transports, transporting, transported** take a person, animal, or thing from one place to another
▷ **transportation** *NOUN* **transporter** *NOUN*

transport *NOUN* the process or means of transporting people, animals, or things • *The city has a good system of public transport.*

transpose *VERB* **transposes, transposing, transposed** **1** change the position or order of something **2** put a piece of music into a different key
▷ **transposition** *NOUN*

trap *NOUN* **traps** **1** a device for catching and holding animals **2** a plan or trick for capturing, detecting, or cheating someone **3** a two-wheeled carriage pulled by a horse **4** a bend in a pipe, filled with water to prevent gases from rising up from a drain

Thesaurus

transformation *NOUN There was a transformation in her attitude.* ► change, conversion, alteration, improvement, revolution, transfiguration, transition, (*more formal*) metamorphosis, (*more informal*) turn-about

translate *VERB a poem by Goethe translated into English* ► render, convert, interpret, express, paraphrase, transcribe

translation *NOUN an English translation of the Iliad* ► version, rendering, transcription, interpretation, gloss, paraphrase

transmission *NOUN The programme was scheduled for transmission after 9 o'clock.* ► broadcast, relaying, diffusion, dissemination, sending out

transmit *VERB* **1** *The broadcast will be transmitted next Saturday.* ► broadcast, relay, send out **2** *Short-wave radios are used to transmit messages.* ► communicate, convey, dispatch, disseminate, emit, pass on
AN OPPOSITE IS receive

transparent *ADJECTIVE a transparent fabric* ► see-through, translucent, diaphanous, clear, sheer, filmy, gauzy, limpid, pellucid

transport *VERB* (with the stress on *-port*) *The larger components will be transported by rail.* ► take, carry, convey, ship, transfer, bring, fetch, haul, move, shift

transport *NOUN* (with the stress on *trans-*) *The village has limited access to public transport.* ► conveyance, haulage, shipping, transportation

trap *NOUN* **1** *Some kinds of animal traps are illegal.* ► snare, noose, net, gin **2** *The cavalry rode straight into a trap* ► ambush, lure, decoy,

trap *VERB* **traps, trapping, trapped 1** catch or hold a person or animal in a trap **2** prevent someone from escaping • *The driver was trapped in the wreckage.*
▷ **trapper** *NOUN*

trapdoor *NOUN* **trapdoors** a door in a floor, ceiling, or roof

trapeze *NOUN* **trapezes** a bar hanging from two ropes as a swing for acrobats

trapezium *NOUN* **trapeziums** or **trapezia** a quadrilateral in which two opposite sides are parallel and the other two are not

trash *NOUN* rubbish or nonsense
▷ **trashy** *ADJECTIVE*

trauma (traw- ma) *NOUN* **traumas** a shock that produces a lasting effect on a person's mind
▷ **traumatic** *ADJECTIVE* **traumatize** *VERB*

travel *VERB* **travels, travelling, travelled** move from place to place
▷ **travel** *NOUN*

traveller *NOUN* **travellers 1** a person who is travelling or who often travels **2** a gypsy, or a person who does not settle in one place

traveller's cheque *NOUN* **traveller's cheques** a cheque for a fixed amount of money that is sold by banks and that can be exchanged for money in foreign countries

trawl *VERB* **trawls, trawling, trawled** fish by dragging a large net along the seabed

trawler *NOUN* **trawlers** a boat used in trawling

tray *NOUN* **trays 1** a flat piece of wood, metal, or plastic, usually with raised edges, for carrying cups, plates, food, etc. **2** an open container for holding letters etc. in an office

treacherous *ADJECTIVE* **1** betraying someone; disloyal **2** dangerous or unreliable • *It's snowing and the roads are treacherous.*
▷ **treacherously** *ADVERB* **treachery** *NOUN*

treacle *NOUN* a thick sticky liquid produced when sugar is purified
▷ **treacly** *ADJECTIVE*
[originally = ointment for an animal bite; from Greek *therion* = wild or poisonous animal]

tread *VERB* **treads, treading, trod, trodden** walk or put your foot on something

tread *NOUN* **treads 1** a sound or way of walking **2** the top surface of a stair; the part you put your foot on **3** the part of a tyre that touches the ground

treadmill *NOUN* **treadmills 1** a wide mill wheel turned by the weight of people or animals treading on steps fixed round its edge **2** monotonous routine work

treason *NOUN* betraying your country
▷ **treasonable** *ADJECTIVE* **treasonous** *ADJECTIVE*

Thesaurus

ambuscade **3** *The last question might be a trap.* ► trick, ploy, deception, artifice

trap *VERB* **1** *They had to find a way of trapping the fox before it did any more damage.* ► snare, capture, catch, ensnare, entrap, corner **2** *The question was designed to trap them.* ► trick, deceive, fool, dupe

trash *NOUN* **1** *The cleaners shake out your carpets and empty your trash.* ► rubbish, waste, refuse, garbage, litter **2** *He despised himself for having to write such trash.* ► rubbish, nonsense, drivel, gibberish, junk

trash *VERB* *He went to a phone box but it had been trashed.* ► vandalize, wreck, ruin, destroy

trashy *ADJECTIVE* *(informal) a trashy horror movie from the sixties* ► inferior, poor-quality, second-rate, rubbishy, worthless

traumatic *ADJECTIVE* *She talked about her traumatic divorce from Ronnie.* ► distressing, stressful, disturbing, shocking, upsetting, hurtful, painful AN OPPOSITE IS soothing

travel *NOUN* *When he retired he had much more time for travel.* ► travelling, touring, tourism, journeying, sightseeing, excursions, globetrotting

travel *VERB* *With this ticket you can travel as many miles as you wish.* ► journey, go, ramble, wander, rove, tour, move, proceed, progress

traveller *NOUN* **1** *refreshments for the weary traveller* ► voyager, passenger, tourist, tripper, holidaymaker, sightseer **2** *ground set aside for travellers' camps* ► gypsy, itinerant, nomad

treacherous *ADJECTIVE* **1** *She did not believe him capable of such treacherous behaviour.* ► traitorous, disloyal, deceitful, faithless, false, unfaithful, perfidious, double-dealing, duplicitous AN OPPOSITE IS loyal **2** *There was a mile of deep treacherous water separating him from the mainland.* ► dangerous, hazardous, perilous, unsafe, unreliable, deceptive, misleading, risky, shifting, unpredictable, unstable OPPOSITES ARE safe, reliable

treachery *NOUN* *His resignation from the party would be seen as an act of treachery.* ► betrayal, disloyalty, infidelity, perfidy, treason, dishonesty, double-dealing, duplicity, faithlessness, untrustworthiness
AN OPPOSITE IS loyalty

tread *VERB* *There is erosion along the route and walkers should tread carefully.* ► step, walk, proceed, pace, stride
tread on *His father accidentally trod on a model boat he'd been making.* ► step on, walk on, trample, crush, squash, stamp on

treason *NOUN* *In July 1540 he was beheaded for treason.* ► treachery, betrayal, sedition,

A B C D E F G H I J K L M N O P Q R S T U V W X Y Z

treasure *NOUN* **treasures 1** a store of precious metals or jewels **2** a precious thing or person

treasure *VERB* **treasures, treasuring, treasured** value greatly something that you have

treasurer *NOUN* **treasurers** a person in charge of the money of a club, society, etc.

treasury *NOUN* **treasuries** a place where money and valuables are kept
the Treasury the government department in charge of a country's income

treat *VERB* **treats, treating, treated 1** behave in a certain way towards a person or thing **2** deal with a subject etc. **3** give medical care in order to cure a person or animal **4** put something through a chemical or other process • *The fabric has been treated to make it waterproof.* **5** pay for someone else's food, drink, or entertainment • *I'll treat you to an ice cream.*

treat *NOUN* **treats 1** something special that gives pleasure **2** the process of treating someone to food, drink, or entertainment [from Latin *tractare* = to handle or manage]

treatment *NOUN* **treatments 1** the process or manner of dealing with a person, animal, or thing **2** medical care

treaty *NOUN* **treaties** a formal agreement between two or more countries

treble *ADJECTIVE* three times as much or as many

treble *NOUN* **trebles 1** a treble amount **2** a person with a high-pitched or soprano voice

treble *VERB* **trebles, trebling, trebled** make or become three times as much or as many [from early French; related to **triple**]

tree *NOUN* **trees** a tall plant with a single very thick hard stem or trunk that is usually without branches for some distance above the ground [from Old English]

trek *NOUN* **treks** a long walk or journey

trek *VERB* **treks, trekking, trekked** go on a long walk or journey [from South African Dutch *trekken* = to pull, to travel]

trellis *NOUN* **trellises** a framework with crossing bars of wood or metal etc. to support climbing plants

tremble *VERB* **trembles, trembling, trembled** shake gently, especially with fear
▷ **tremble** *NOUN*

tremendous *ADJECTIVE* **1** very large; huge **2** excellent
▷ **tremendously** *ADVERB*

tremor *NOUN* **tremors 1** a shaking or trembling movement **2** a slight earthquake

Thesaurus

rebellion, mutiny OPPOSITES ARE loyalty, allegiance

treasure *NOUN* **1** *The treasure sank to the bottom of the sea, along with the ship that held it.* ► hoard, cache, jewels, riches, fortune, gold, treasure trove, valuables, wealth **2** *Rosie was a treasure who had brought happiness to the house.* ► gem, paragon, angel, prize, star

treasure *VERB* *It's a very special photo and we'll treasure it for ever.* ► prize, value, cherish, esteem, guard, keep safe, adore, appreciate, love

treat *NOUN* **1** *Add some prawns to the dish for a special treat.* ► indulgence, extravagance **2** *She would give the children a birthday treat next year.* ► celebration, surprise, entertainment, outing **3** *The ballet is a treat to the eye.* ► pleasure, delight, joy, thrill

treat *VERB* **1** *They didn't treat her badly, but she was made to feel a nuisance.* ► behave towards, deal with, look after, care for, use, serve, attend to **2** *The lectures treat all broad aspects of the subject.* ► deal with, discuss, cover, consider, tackle **3** *attempts to treat illness by radiation* ► cure, heal, medicate, dress, tend **4** *People tend to treat the videos as entertainment rather than information.* ► regard, consider, view **5** *If you like, I'll treat you to a film.* ► give, pay for, provide for, entertain

treatment *NOUN* **1** *She found it difficult to accept his treatment of her.* ► care, handling, management, behaviour (towards), conduct (towards), dealing (with), use **2** *He was responding well to the treatment.* ► therapy, medical care, medication, nursing, healing **3** *The book's treatment of this topic is extremely thorough.* ► coverage, handling, explanation, analysis, discussion

treaty *NOUN* *The two countries signed a treaty of mutual support.* ► agreement, settlement, pact, deal, entente, alliance, compact, concordat, convention, protocol, understanding

trek *NOUN* *a long trek through the hills* ► journey, trip, expedition, march, hike, slog, tramp, trudge, walk

trek *VERB* *They've trekked all over the Greek mainland.* ► hike, tramp, march, journey, walk, slog

tremble *VERB* **1** *His hands were trembling.* ► shake, shiver, quake, quaver, quiver **2** *Heavy traffic outside makes the ornaments tremble.* ► vibrate, shake, wobble, shudder, waver

tremendous *ADJECTIVE* **1** *It had been a tremendous achievement.* ► great, wonderful, marvellous, sensational, stupendous, extraordinary, considerable, significant, immense OPPOSITES ARE insignificant, trivial **2** *There was a tremendous crash.* ► terrible,

trench NOUN **trenches 1** a long narrow hole cut in the ground **2** a ditch dug by troops to protect them from enemy fire

trench VERB dig a trench or trenches

trend NOUN **trends** the general direction in which something is going

trendy ADJECTIVE (*informal*) fashionable; following the latest trends
▷ **trendily** ADVERB **trendiness** NOUN

trespass VERB **trespasses, trespassing, trespassed 1** go on someone's land or property unlawfully **2** (*old use*) do wrong; sin
▷ **trespasser** NOUN

trespass NOUN **trespasses** (*old use*) wrongdoing; sin

tress NOUN **tresses** a lock of hair

trestle NOUN **trestles** each of a set of supports on which a board is rested to form a table
▷ **trestle table** NOUN

trial NOUN **trials 1** the process of examining the evidence in a lawcourt to decide whether a person is guilty of a crime **2** testing a thing to see how good it is **3** a test of qualities or ability **4** an annoying person or thing; a hardship
on trial 1 being tried in a lawcourt **2** being tested
trial and error trying out different methods of doing something until you find one that works

triangle NOUN **triangles 1** a flat shape with three sides and three angles **2** a percussion instrument made from a metal rod bent into a triangle
▷ **triangular** ADJECTIVE

tribe NOUN **tribes 1** a group of families living in one area as a community, ruled by a chief **2** a set of people
▷ **tribal** ADJECTIVE **tribally** ADVERB **tribesman** NOUN **tribeswoman** NOUN

tribunal (try- bew- nal) NOUN **tribunals** a committee appointed to hear evidence and give judgements when there is a dispute

tributary NOUN **tributaries** a river or stream that flows into a larger one or into a lake

tribute NOUN **tributes 1** something said, done, or given to show respect or admiration **2** payment that one country or ruler was formerly obliged to pay to a more powerful one

trice NOUN (*old use*)
in a trice in a moment
[from early Dutch *trisen* = to pull quickly, to tug]

trick NOUN **tricks 1** a crafty or deceitful action; a practical joke • *Let's play a trick on Jo.* **2** a skilful action, especially one done for entertainment • *magic tricks* **3** the cards picked up by the winner after one round of a card game such as whist

Thesaurus

terrific, frightful, awful, fearful, fearsome, alarming, appalling, frightening, horrifying, shocking OPPOSITES ARE faint, slight

trend NOUN **1** *a downward trend in unemployment* ► tendency, movement, shift, bias, leaning, direction, inclination **2** *the latest trend in rock music* ► fashion, vogue, craze, rage, mode, style, fad, way

trendy ADJECTIVE (*informal*) *trendy clothes* ► fashionable, stylish, up-to-date, contemporary, latest, modern, (*more informal*) cool, (*more informal*) in
AN OPPOSITE IS unfashionable

trial NOUN **1** *The trial will last about a month.* ► lawsuit, court case, hearing, tribunal, proceedings, examination **2** *The latest model is undergoing trials.* ► test, testing, experiment, pilot, try-out **3** *Such a long meeting was a real trial.* ► ordeal, problem, tribulation, difficulty, trouble, burden, worry, affliction, hardship **4** *Joan can be a trial at times.* ► nuisance, pest, bother, (*more informal*) pain

tribe NOUN *nomadic tribes* ► people, race, nation, group, horde, stock, clan

tribute NOUN **1** *Tributes came in from friends and colleagues.* ► praise, accolade, eulogy, testimonial, appreciation, commendation, recognition, compliment, panegyric **2** *Their eventual success was a tribute to their courage and determination.* ► testimony, evidence (of), proof (of) **3** *The city had to pay an annual tribute to the king.* ► tax, payment, levy, duty, contribution
pay tribute to *She paid tribute to her staff for their hard work.* ► praise, commend, applaud, celebrate, honour, pay homage to, respect

trick NOUN **1** *He entertained the children with conjuring tricks* ► feat, stunt, illusion, magic **2** *He saw through every trick she used.* ► ruse, scheme, stratagem, deceit, deception, subterfuge, manoeuvre, ploy, pretence, fraud, wile, cheat, (*more informal*) con **3** *My favourite trick was to hide above everyone and jump on them. Who else would play a trick like that on me?* ► joke, practical joke, prank, stunt, (*informal*) leg-pull **4** *The essential trick is to think backwards and write forwards.* ► knack, secret, skill, device, dodge, technique, art, craft, expertise, gimmick, (*informal*) know-how

trick *VERB* **tricks, tricking, tricked 1** deceive or cheat someone by a trick **2** decorate • *The building was tricked out with little flags.*

trickery *NOUN* the use of tricks; deception

trickle *VERB* **trickles, trickling, trickled** flow or move slowly
▷ **trickle** *NOUN*

tricky *ADJECTIVE* **trickier, trickiest 1** difficult; needing skill • *a tricky job* **2** cunning or deceitful
▷ **trickiness** *NOUN*

tricycle *NOUN* **tricycles** a vehicle like a bicycle but with three wheels

trifle *NOUN* **trifles 1** a pudding made of sponge cake covered in custard, fruit, cream, etc. **2** a very small amount **3** something that has very little importance or value

trifle *VERB* **trifles, trifling, trifled** treat a person or thing without seriousness or respect • *She is not a woman to be trifled with.*

trifling *ADJECTIVE* small in value or importance

trigger *NOUN* **triggers** a lever that is pulled to fire a gun

trigger *VERB* **triggers, triggering, triggered**
trigger off start something happening

trigonometry (trig- on- **om**- it- ree) *NOUN* the calculation of distances and angles by using triangles

trill *VERB* **trills, trilling, trilled** make a quivering musical sound
▷ **trill** *NOUN*

trillion *NOUN* **trillions 1** a million million **2** (*old use*) a million million million

trim *ADJECTIVE* neat and orderly
▷ **trimly** *ADVERB* **trimness** *NOUN*

trim *VERB* **trims, trimming, trimmed 1** cut the edges or unwanted parts off something **2** decorate a hat or piece of clothing by adding lace, ribbons, etc. **3** arrange sails to suit the wind

trim *NOUN* **trims 1** cutting or trimming • *Your beard needs a trim.* **2** lace, ribbons, etc. used to decorate something
in good trim in good condition; fit

Trinity *NOUN* God regarded as three persons (Father, Son, and Holy Spirit)

trinket *NOUN* **trinkets** a small ornament or piece of jewellery

trio *NOUN* **trios 1** a group of three people or things **2** a group of three musicians or singers **3** a piece of music for three musicians

trip *VERB* **trips, tripping, tripped 1** catch your foot on something and fall; make someone do this **2** move with quick light steps **3** operate a switch
trip up 1 stumble **2** make a mistake **3** cause a person to stumble or make a mistake

Thesaurus

trick *VERB* *He was furious with himself for being tricked so easily.* ► fool, deceive, cheat, dupe, hoodwink, swindle, trap, outwit, hoax, bluff, mislead, catch out, defraud, (*informal*) con, (*informal*) bamboozle

trickery *NOUN* *The excuses he makes sound like the old trickery.* ► deception, pretence, cheating, chicanery, deceit, mischief, dishonesty, bluffing, fraud, (*informal*) monkey business, (*informal*) jiggery-pokery, (*informal*) shenanigans

trickle *VERB* *Sweat trickled down his sides despite the cold.* ► drip, dribble, seep, ooze, leak, flow slowly, percolate, run OPPOSITES ARE pour, gush

trickle *NOUN* *She saw a trickle of blood flow over her fingers.* ► dribble, seepage, thin stream OPPOSITES ARE flood, gush

trickster *NOUN* *I shall reveal you for the sly trickster that you are.* ► cheat, swindler, fraud, fraudster, impostor, charlatan, deceiver, dissembler

tricky *ADJECTIVE* **1** *Tony was a tricky individual.* ► cunning, crafty, wily, artful **2** *Tricky negotiations were taking place.* ► difficult, complicated, awkward, delicate, sensitive

trifle *NOUN* *It cost a mere trifle.* ► small amount, next to nothing, pittance, (*more informal*) peanuts
a trifle *He looked a trifle embarrassed.* ► a little, a bit, somewhat, a touch, a spot

trifling *ADJECTIVE* *We shouldn't bother them with such a trifling matter.* ► trivial, unimportant, insignificant, inconsequential, minor, petty

trim *VERB* **1** *He had trimmed his hair and beard.* ► cut, crop, clip, tidy, shape, shear **2** *The Chancellor will have either to increase taxes or trim his budget.* ► reduce, cut, prune, scale down **3** *The silk curtains were trimmed with gold.* ► decorate, embellish

trim *ADJECTIVE* **1** *a housing estate with trim gardens* ► neat, tidy, orderly, smart, spruce, well-groomed, well-kept AN OPPOSITE IS untidy **2** *Trousers help to accentuate a trim figure.* ► slim, slender, lean

trip *VERB* **1** *Angela tripped along in her red mac and hood.* ► run, skip, walk **2** *She tripped over and gashed her knee.* ► stumble, totter, tumble, catch your foot, fall, stagger

trip *NOUN* **trips 1** a journey or outing **2** the action of tripping; a stumble **3** (*informal*) hallucinations caused by taking a drug

tripe *NOUN* **1** part of an ox's stomach used as food **2** (*slang*) nonsense

triple *ADJECTIVE* **1** consisting of three parts **2** involving three people or groups • *a triple alliance* **3** three times as much or as many
▷ **triply** *ADVERB*

triple *VERB* **triples, tripling, tripled** make or become three times as much or as many

triplet *NOUN* **triplets** each of three children or animals born to the same mother at one time

triplicate *NOUN*
in triplicate as three identical copies

tripod (try- pod) *NOUN* **tripods** a stand with three legs, e.g. to support a camera

trite (rhymes with *kite*) *ADJECTIVE* worn out by constant repetition; unoriginal • *a few trite remarks*

triumph *NOUN* **triumphs 1** a great success or victory; a feeling of joy at this **2** a celebration of a victory
▷ **triumphal** *ADJECTIVE* **triumphant** *ADJECTIVE* **triumphantly** *ADVERB*

triumph *VERB* **triumphs, triumphing, triumphed 1** be successful or victorious **2** rejoice in success or victory

trivia *PLURAL NOUN* unimportant details or pieces of information

trivial *ADJECTIVE* small in value or importance
▷ **trivially** *ADVERB* **triviality** *NOUN*

troll (rhymes with *hole*) *NOUN* **trolls** (in Scandinavian mythology) a supernatural being, either a giant or a friendly but mischievous dwarf [originally = witch: from Old Norse]

trolley *NOUN* **trolleys 1** a small table on wheels or castors **2** a small cart or truck **3** a basket on wheels, used in supermarkets

trombone *NOUN* **trombones** a large brass musical instrument with a sliding tube

troop *NOUN* **troops 1** an organized group of soldiers, Scouts, etc. **2** a number of people moving along together
USAGE Do not confuse with **troupe**.

troop *VERB* **troops, trooping, trooped** move along as a group or in large numbers • *They all trooped in.* [from Latin *troppus* = herd]

trooper *NOUN* **troopers** a soldier in the cavalry or in an armoured unit

troops *PLURAL NOUN* armed forces

trophy *NOUN* **trophies 1** a cup etc. given as a prize for winning a competition **2** something taken in war or hunting as a souvenir of success

tropic *NOUN* **tropics** a line of latitude about 23° north of the equator (**tropic of Cancer**) or 23° south of the equator (**tropic of Capricorn**)
the tropics the hot regions between these two latitudes

tropical *ADJECTIVE* to do with the tropics • *tropical fish*

Thesaurus

trip *NOUN* *He met the Czar during a trip to Russia in 1908.* ► journey, visit, voyage, excursion, expedition, holiday, jaunt, outing, tour

trite *ADJECTIVE* *However trite it may sound, there is joy to be found in a spring day.* ► banal, commonplace, ordinary, hackneyed, clichéd, stale

triumph *NOUN* **1** *He was a key figure in the party's election triumph.* ► victory, win, conquest, (*informal*) walkover
AN OPPOSITE IS defeat **2** *She smiled in triumph.* ► celebration, joy, exultation, jubilation, elation **3** *The visit to Wales had been a triumph.* ► success, accomplishment, achievement, master stroke, (*more informal*) hit

triumph *VERB* **triumph over** *He had triumphed over disease and misfortune.* ► overcome, defeat, conquer, prevail over, succeed against, be victorious over, win over

triumphant *ADJECTIVE* **1** *The communists emerged triumphant from the revolution.* ► successful, victorious, dominant, conquering, winning
AN OPPOSITE IS unsuccessful **2** *He gave her a knowing, triumphant look.* ► exultant, jubilant, boastful, joyful, elated, gleeful, gloating, immodest, proud OPPOSITES ARE modest, humble

trivial *ADJECTIVE* *The offence was regarded as trivial.* ► insignificant, unimportant, inconsequential, minor, trifling, incidental
OPPOSITES ARE important, significant

troop *NOUN* *A troop of tourists crossed the square.* ► group, party, band, body, company

troop *VERB* *Rod looked up as Sara and the others trooped in.* ► march, file, flock, parade, straggle

trophy *NOUN* **1** *trophies of war* ► souvenir, memento, reward, spoils, booty, loot **2** *a sports trophy* ► award, cup, medal, prize

tropical *ADJECTIVE* *tropical areas such as East Africa* ► equatorial, hot, humid, sultry, torrid

A B C D E F G H I J K L M N O P Q R S T U V W X Y Z

trot *VERB* **trots, trotting, trotted** **1** (said about a horse) run, going faster than when walking but more slowly than when cantering **2** run gently with short steps
trot out (*informal*) produce or repeat • *He trotted out the usual excuses.*

trot *NOUN* a trotting run
on the trot (*informal*) one after the other without a break • *She worked for ten days on the trot.*

trouble *NOUN* **troubles** **1** difficulty, inconvenience, or distress **2** a cause of any of these
take trouble take great care in doing something

trouble *VERB* **troubles, troubling, troubled** **1** cause trouble to someone **2** give yourself trouble or inconvenience etc. • *Nobody troubled to ask if he needed help.*

troublesome *ADJECTIVE* causing trouble or annoyance

trough (trof) *NOUN* **troughs** **1** a long narrow open container, especially one holding water or food for animals **2** a channel for liquid **3** the low part between two waves or ridges **4** a long region of low air pressure

troupe (rhymes with *troop*) *NOUN* **troupes** a company of actors or other performers
USAGE Do not confuse with **troop**.

trousers *PLURAL NOUN* a piece of clothing worn over the lower half of the body, with a separate part for each leg [from Irish or Scottish Gaelic]

trout *NOUN* **trout** a freshwater fish that is caught as a sport and for food

trowel *NOUN* **trowels** **1** a small garden tool with a curved blade for lifting plants or scooping things **2** a small tool with a flat blade for spreading mortar etc. [from Latin *trulla* = scoop]

truant *NOUN* **truants** a child who stays away from school without permission
▷ **truancy** *NOUN*
play truant be a truant
[from early French, = criminal]

truce *NOUN* **truces** an agreement to stop fighting for a while

Thesaurus

trot *VERB* *Danny trotted into the house.* ▶ run, scurry, scamper, scuttle, hurry

trouble *NOUN* **1** *See what trouble you've caused.* ▶ difficulty, bother, problems, inconvenience, distress, anxiety **2** *He recounted his troubles and asked for advice.* ▶ problem, misfortune, difficulty, tribulation, trial, affliction, suffering, hardship **3** *We took some trouble to help them.* ▶ care, effort, bother, exertion, pains **4** *I hope I wasn't a trouble to you.* ▶ nuisance, bother, irritation **5** *The trouble with these machines is the lack of spare parts.* ▶ problem, difficulty, disadvantage, weakness, failing
OPPOSITES ARE advantage, benefit **6** *There was crowd trouble after the match.* ▶ disturbance, disorder, unrest, conflict, fighting, violence
OPPOSITES ARE order, peace **7** *She suffered from back trouble.* ▶ ailment, disorder, complaint, illness, disability

trouble *VERB* **1** *Something was troubling him.* ▶ bother, worry, distress, concern, pain, vex, torment, upset **2** *I'm very sorry to trouble you.* ▶ disturb, interrupt, bother, inconvenience

troubled *ADJECTIVE* **1** *Tara looked troubled.* ▶ anxious, worried, bothered, concerned, disturbed, perturbed, uneasy, unhappy, vexed, restless OPPOSITES ARE untroubled, peaceful **2** *We live in troubled times.* ▶ difficult, unsettled, uncertain

troublemaker *NOUN* *She was branded a troublemaker for complaining about a colleague who harassed her.* ▶ mischief-maker, agitator, rabble-rouser, ringleader, wrongdoer

troublesome *ADJECTIVE* **1** *Craig was recovering from a troublesome knee injury.* ▶ annoying, irritating, irksome, tiresome, trying, bothersome, vexing, distressing, inconvenient, upsetting OPPOSITES ARE trouble-free, harmless **2** *The younger boy was being particularly troublesome.* ▶ badly behaved, naughty, unruly, disobedient, disorderly, uncooperative, rowdy

trousers *NOUN* *He was wearing a pair of pale trousers.* ▶ pants, slacks

truancy *NOUN* *We are determined to crack down on truancy.* ▶ absenteeism, malingering, shirking, (*more informal*) skiving
AN OPPOSITE IS attendance

truant *NOUN* *I was a truant from a Youth Custody Centre.* ▶ absentee, non-attender, runaway, malingerer, shirker, (*more informal*) skiver
play truant *52 percent admitted to playing truant for the odd lesson now and then.* ▶ be absent, stay away, desert, malinger, (*more informal*) skive off

truce *NOUN* *The enemy broke the truce and resumed the war.* ▶ ceasefire, armistice, moratorium, pact, peace, suspension of hostilities, treaty

truck[1] *NOUN* **trucks 1** a lorry **2** an open container on wheels for transporting loads; an open railway wagon **3** an axle with wheels attached, fitted under a skateboard

truck[2] *NOUN*
have no truck with refuse to have dealings with • *I'll have no truck with fortune tellers!*

trudge *VERB* **trudges, trudging, trudged** walk slowly and heavily

true *ADJECTIVE* **truer, truest 1** representing what has really happened or exists • *a true story* **2** genuine or proper; not false • *He was the true heir.* **3** accurate **4** loyal or faithful • *Be true to your friends.*
▷ **trueness** *NOUN*
come true actually happen as hoped or predicted

truffle *NOUN* **truffles 1** a soft sweet made with chocolate **2** a fungus that grows underground and is valued as food because of its rich flavour

truly *ADVERB* **1** truthfully **2** sincerely or genuinely • *We are truly grateful.* **3** accurately **4** loyally or faithfully
Yours truly see **yours**

trump *NOUN* **trumps** a playing card of a suit that ranks above the others for one game

trump *VERB* **trumps, trumping, trumped** beat a card by playing a trump
trump up invent an excuse or an accusation etc.

trumpet *NOUN* **trumpets 1** a metal wind instrument with a narrow tube that widens near the end **2** something shaped like this

trumpet *VERB* **trumpets, trumpeting, trumpeted 1** blow a trumpet **2** (said about an elephant) make a loud sound with its trunk **3** shout or announce something loudly
▷ **trumpeter** *NOUN*

truncheon *NOUN* **truncheons** a short thick stick carried as a weapon, especially by police

trundle *VERB* **trundles, trundling, trundled** roll along heavily • *He was trundling a wheelbarrow.* • *A bus trundled up.*

trunk *NOUN* **trunks 1** the main stem of a tree **2** an elephant's long flexible nose **3** a large box with a hinged lid for transporting or storing clothes etc. **4** the human body except for the head, arms, and legs

trunk road *NOUN* **trunk roads** an important main road

trunks *PLURAL NOUN* shorts worn by men and boys for swimming, boxing, etc.

truss *NOUN* **trusses 1** a framework of beams or bars supporting a roof or bridge etc. **2** a bundle of hay etc.

truss *VERB* **trusses, trussing, trussed 1** tie up a person or thing securely **2** support a roof or bridge etc. with trusses

trust *VERB* **trusts, trusting, trusted 1** believe that a person or thing is good, truthful, or strong **2** let a person have or use something in the belief that they will behave responsibly • *Don't trust him with your CD player!* **3** hope • *I trust that you are well.*
trust to rely on • *We're trusting to luck.*

Thesaurus

truck *NOUN* *The truck was skidding all over the motorway.* ► lorry, heavy goods vehicle, juggernaut

true *ADJECTIVE* **1** *The story turned out to be true.* ► correct, right, accurate, factual, authentic, confirmed, proper, veracious, veritable
OPPOSITES ARE untrue, false **2** *The document was certified as a true copy.* ► exact, faithful, genuine, real, actual AN OPPOSITE IS false
3 *Anne, true friend though she was, would never give in to him.* ► loyal, faithful, devoted, firm, constant, sincere, steady, trustworthy, dependable, honest, honourable
OPPOSITES ARE false, unfaithful **4** *He was acting under the authority of the property's true owner.* ► legal, legitimate, rightful, authorized, valid **5** *Such studies do not give a true reflection of people's needs.* ► accurate, precise, exact, perfect, unerring AN OPPOSITE IS inaccurate

truly *ADVERB* **1** *a truly remarkable woman* ► really, absolutely, extremely, very **2** *I'm truly glad for you.* ► sincerely, genuinely, honestly **3** *Tell us truly what you think.* ► truthfully, frankly, candidly, honestly

trumpet *NOUN* *a part for solo trumpet* ► bugle, clarion, cornet
blow your own trumpet *He was blowing his own trumpet and promoting his new show.* ► boast, brag, sing your own praises, congratulate yourself, show off, swank

trunk *NOUN* **1** *A squirrel leapt on a branch and ran up the trunk.* ► stem, bole, stock **2** *A slit in his shirt revealed his powerful trunk.* ► torso, frame, body **3** *He locked the trunk and stored it in a shed.* ► chest, case, coffer, box, crate, suitcase

trust *VERB* **1** *He doesn't trust me not to do it again.* ► believe in, have confidence in, have faith in, rely on, be sure of, bank on, count on, depend on **2** *We trust they will be here soon.* ► hope, expect, presume, suppose, assume, imagine, surmise AN OPPOSITE IS doubt

trust *NOUN* **trusts** **1** the belief that a person or thing can be trusted **2** responsibility; being trusted • *Being a prefect is a position of trust.* **3** a legal arrangement in which money is entrusted to a person with instructions about how to use it
▷ **trustful** *ADJECTIVE* **trustfully** *ADVERB*

trustworthy *ADJECTIVE* able to be trusted; reliable

trusty *ADJECTIVE* (*old use*) trustworthy or reliable • *my trusty sword*

truth *NOUN* **truths** **1** something that is true **2** the quality of being true

truthful *ADJECTIVE* **1** telling the truth • *a truthful boy* **2** true • *a truthful account of what happened*
▷ **truthfully** *ADVERB* **truthfulness** *NOUN*

try *VERB* **tries, trying, tried** **1** make an effort to do something; attempt **2** test something by using or doing it • *Try sleeping on your back.* **3** examine the evidence in a lawcourt to decide whether a person is guilty of a crime **4** be a strain on • *You are trying my patience.*
try on put on clothes etc. to see if they fit
try out use something to see if it works

try *NOUN* **tries** **1** an attempt **2** (in rugby football) putting the ball down behind the opponents' goal line in order to score points

trying *ADJECTIVE* putting a strain on someone's patience; annoying

T-shirt or **tee shirt** *NOUN* **T-shirts** or **tee-shirts** a short-sleeved casual shirt

tub *NOUN* **tubs** a round open container holding liquid, ice cream, soil for plants, etc.

tubby *ADJECTIVE* **tubbier, tubbiest** short and fat
▷ **tubbiness** *NOUN*

tube *NOUN* **tubes** **1** a long hollow piece of metal, plastic, rubber, glass, etc., especially for liquids or air etc. to pass along **2** a container made of flexible material with a screw cap • *a tube of toothpaste* **3** the underground railway in London

tuber *NOUN* **tubers** a short thick rounded root (e.g. of a dahlia) or underground stem (e.g. of a potato) that produces buds from which new plants will grow

tuberculosis *NOUN* a disease of people and animals, producing small swellings in the parts affected by it, especially in the lungs
▷ **tubercular** *ADJECTIVE*

tuck *VERB* **tucks, tucking, tucked** **1** push a loose edge into something so that it is hidden or held in place **2** put something away in a small space • *Tuck this in your pocket.*
tuck in (*informal*) eat heartily
tuck someone in *or* **up** make someone comfortable in bed by folding the edges of the bedclothes tightly

tuck *NOUN* **tucks** **1** a flat fold stitched in a piece of clothing **2** (*informal, dated*) food, especially

Thesaurus

trust *NOUN* **1** *I am grateful to you for your trust.* ► confidence, faith, belief, reliance, certainty, credence **2** *She enjoyed a position of trust in the City.* ► responsibility, obligation

trusting *ADJECTIVE* *The trouble with me is I'm too trusting.* ► trustful, credulous, gullible, unquestioning, unsuspecting, ingenuous, innocent OPPOSITES ARE suspicious, cynical

trustworthy *ADJECTIVE* *Harriet was always trustworthy and hard-working.* ► reliable, dependable, responsible, honest, upright, steadfast OPPOSITES ARE untrustworthy, deceitful

truth *NOUN* **1** *He doubted the truth of some of these statements.* ► veracity, accuracy, validity, truthfulness, correctness, candour, honesty, authenticity, reliability AN OPPOSITE IS falseness **2** *Elizabeth had been telling the truth.* ► fact facts, reality, actuality **3** *an acknowledged truth* ► fact, axiom, maxim, certitude, truism AN OPPOSITE IS lie

truthful *ADJECTIVE* **1** *Clive had been less than truthful.* ► honest, sincere, candid, frank, reliable, straight, forthright, credible, straightforward, trustworthy, veracious **2** *The truthful answer has to be 'no'.* ► proper, right, accurate, correct, true, valid AN OPPOSITE IS dishonest

try *VERB* **1** *Always try to respond positively.* ► aim, attempt, endeavour, essay, exert yourself, make an effort, strain, strive, struggle, venture **2** *Why not try another school?* (*informal*) ► check out, evaluate, examine, experiment with, investigate, test, try out, undertake

try *NOUN* *I'll have another try.* ► attempt, endeavour, effort, experiment, test, trial, (*more informal*) bash, (*more informal*) go, (*more informal*) shot

trying *ADJECTIVE* **1** *This could be quite a trying evening.* ► difficult, stressful, taxing, frustrating, troublesome, vexatious **2** *Clare can be very trying.* ► annoying, irritating, tiresome, exasperating, infuriating

tub *NOUN* **1** *Corbett bathed in the guest house's one and only tub.* ► bath, bathtub **2** *a plastic tub of sandwiches* ► pot, barrel, drum, cask, keg, vat

tubby *ADJECTIVE* (*informal*) *A short tubby man was waiting at the front door.* ► chubby, podgy, plump, fat, dumpy, rotund, round, overweight, stout, portly, pudgy OPPOSITES ARE thin, slim, skinny

tuck *VERB* *He tucked his shirt into his jeans.* ► push, ease, insert, stuff, shove, cram, (*more*

sweets and cakes etc. that children enjoy
▷ **tuck shop** NOUN

tug VERB **tugs, tugging, tugged** **1** pull something hard or suddenly **2** tow a ship

tug NOUN **tugs** **1** a hard or sudden pull **2** a small powerful boat used for towing others

tug of war NOUN a contest between two teams pulling a rope from opposite ends

tuition NOUN teaching, especially when given to one person or a small group

tulip NOUN **tulips** a large cup-shaped flower on a tall stem growing from a bulb [from Persian *dulband* = turban (because the flowers are this shape)]

tumble VERB **tumbles, tumbling, tumbled** **1** fall or roll over suddenly or clumsily **2** move or push quickly and carelessly
▷ **tumble** NOUN
tumble to (*informal*) realize what something means

tumbler NOUN **tumblers** **1** a drinking glass with no stem or handle **2** a part of a lock that is lifted when a key is turned to open it **3** an acrobat

tummy NOUN **tummies** (*informal*) the stomach

tumour (tew-mer) NOUN **tumours** an abnormal lump growing on or in the body

tumult (tew-mult) NOUN an uproar; a state of noisy confusion and agitation
▷ **tumultuous** ADJECTIVE

tune NOUN **tunes** a short piece of music; a pleasant series of musical notes
▷ **tuneful** ADJECTIVE **tunefully** ADVERB
in tune at the correct musical pitch

tune VERB **tunes, tuning, tuned** **1** put a musical instrument in tune **2** adjust a radio or television set to receive a certain channel **3** adjust an engine so that it runs smoothly
▷ **tuner** NOUN
tune up (said about an orchestra) bring the instruments to the correct pitch

tunic NOUN **tunics** **1** a jacket worn as part of a uniform **2** a piece of clothing reaching from the shoulders to the hips or knees

tunnel NOUN **tunnels** an underground passage

tunnel VERB **tunnels, tunnelling, tunnelled** make a tunnel [from early French *tonel* = barrel]

turban NOUN **turbans** a covering for the head made by wrapping a strip of cloth round a cap

turbine NOUN **turbines** a machine or motor driven by a flow of water, steam, or gas

turbulence NOUN violent and uneven movement of air or water • *We experienced turbulence during the flight.*

turbulent ADJECTIVE **1** moving violently and unevenly • *turbulent seas* **2** involving much change and disagreement or violence • *a turbulent period of history*
▷ **turbulently** ADVERB

turf NOUN **turfs** or **turves** **1** short grass and the earth round its roots **2** a piece of this cut from the ground
the turf horse racing

turkey NOUN **turkeys** a large bird kept for its meat

turmoil NOUN wild confusion or agitation • *Her mind was in turmoil.*

Thesaurus

informal) pop
tuck into *We tucked into plates of fish and chips.* ► eat up, consume, devour, gobble up, wolf down

tug VERB **1** *Lee tugged the rope.* ► pull, heave, drag, draw, haul, lug, tow **2 tug at** *A litte boy tugged at her skirt.* ► jerk, pluck, twitch, wrench, yank

tumble VERB **1** *He let out a yell as he tumbled into the water.* ► topple, collapse, pitch, stumble, plummet, drop, fall, flop, trip up **2** *Most of the audience then tumbled out of the room.* ► hurry, rush, pile, scramble

tumult NOUN *His voice could not be heard above the tumult.* ► noise, din, commotion, hubbub, clamour, racket, rumpus, uproar

tumultuous ADJECTIVE *John Knox returned to a tumultuous welcome.* ► loud, excited, uproarious, boisterous, unrestrained, deafening, passionate, tempestuous, hectic, turbulent, wild AN OPPOSITE IS restrained

tune NOUN *She sang a tune to the baby.* ► melody, song, air, strain, theme

tuneful ADJECTIVE *She spoke in a quiet, tuneful voice.* ► musical, melodious, mellifluous, pleasant, sweet, rhythmical, catchy
OPPOSITES ARE tuneless, discordant

tunnel NOUN *a tunnel under the Thames* ► underpass, passage, passageway, subway, shaft, gallery

tunnel VERB *A dog had tunnelled under the fence.* ► burrow, dig, excavate, mine, penetrate

turbulent ADJECTIVE **1** *Her turbulent feelings got the better of her.* ► passionate, excited, violent, volatile, seething, unrestrained **2** *an increasingly turbulent part of the world* ► unstable, unsettled, troubled, restless, explosive, anarchic AN OPPOSITE IS peaceful **3** *The ship was in turbulent waters.* ► rough, stormy, tempestuous, choppy, violent, wild
AN OPPOSITE IS calm

turmoil NOUN (*informal*) *Her mind was in state of turmoil.* ► confusion, chaos, disorder,

turn *VERB* **turns, turning, turned** **1** move round; move to a new direction **2** change in appearance etc.; become • *He turned pale.* **3** make something change • *You can turn milk into butter.* **4** move a switch or tap etc. to control something • *Turn that radio off.* **5** pass a certain time • *It has turned midnight.* **6** shape something on a lathe

turn down **1** fold down **2** reduce the flow or sound of something **3** reject • *We offered her a job but she turned it down.*

turn out **1** send out **2** empty something, especially to search or clean it **3** happen **4** prove to be • *The visitor turned out to be my uncle.*

turn up **1** appear or arrive **2** increase the flow or sound of something

turn *NOUN* **turns** **1** the action of turning; a turning movement **2** a change; the point where something turns **3** an opportunity or duty etc. that comes to each person in succession • *It's your turn to wash up.* **4** a short performance in an entertainment **5** (*informal*) an attack of illness; a nervous shock • *It gave me a nasty turn.*

a good turn a helpful action

in turn in succession; one after another

turning *NOUN* **turnings** a place where one road meets another, forming a corner

turnip *NOUN* **turnips** a plant with a large round white root used as a vegetable

turnout *NOUN* **turnouts** the number of people who attend a meeting, vote at an election, etc. • *Despite the rain, there was a pretty good turnout.*

Thesaurus

upheaval, turbulence, agitation, disruption, disturbance, mayhem, unrest, upset OPPOSITES ARE calm, peace

turn *VERB* **1** *The big wheel started to turn.* ► go round, revolve, rotate, whirl, roll **2** *The gates turned on a set of massive hinges.* ► swivel, hinge **3** *She turned to return home.* ► change direction, change course, turn round **4** *The van turned the corner and disappeared.* ► go round, negotiate, take **5** *The path turned to the right.* ► bend, curve, twist, loop, snake **6** *Ellie turned pale.* ► become, go, grow **7** *The house will be turned into luxury apartments.* ► convert, adapt, transform, modify, change, rebuild **8** *The milk had turned.* ► go off, go sour, curdle **9** **turn to** *She turned to her neighbour for help.* ► resort to, appeal to, approach, have recourse to, apply to

turn away *Reporters were turned away from the house.* ► send away, dismiss, rebuff, reject AN OPPOSITE IS admit (to)

turn down *The panel turned down her application.* ► reject, refuse, decline, dismiss, spurn AN OPPOSITE IS approve

turn in **1** *I decided to turn in early.* ► go to bed, retire **2** *He was ordered to turn in his passport* ► hand in, hand over, surrender, submit

turn off **1** *They had to turn off the motorway.* ► leave, branch off, deviate from AN OPPOSITE IS join **2** *She turned off the lights and left the building.* ► switch off, turn out, put out, extinguish OPPOSITES ARE turn on, switch on **3** *The violence in the film turned many people off.* ► deter, put off, discourage, disconcert, unnerve, repel, distract OPPOSITES ARE appeal to, attract

turn on **1** *She turned on the radio.* ► switch on, put on AN OPPOSITE IS turn off **2** *Rick always turned her on.* ► excite, arouse, stimulate, titillate AN OPPOSITE IS turn off

turn out **1** *Her father might well turn her out of the house.* ► throw out, expel, evict, eject, drive out OPPOSITES ARE admit (to), welcome (to) **2** *It was a relief that things turned out so well.* ► occur, happen, evolve, develop, end up, come out, work out **3** *Don't forget to turn out the light.* ► switch off, turn off, put out, extinguish OPPOSITES ARE turn on, switch on

turn over **1** *The car skidded and turned over.* ► overturn, roll over, keel over, capsize **2** *I've been turning it over in my mind.* ► consider, ponder, deliberate, think about, weigh up, mull over, chew over

turn up **1** *Several guests failed to turn up.* ► arrive, appear, put in an appearance **2** *A gardener in Oxfordshire has turned up a hoard of ancient coins.* ► discover, unearth, uncover, bring to light, dig up, find **3** *The voices are inaudible unless you turn the sound up.* ► increase, raise, amplify

turn *NOUN* **1** *hot water at the turn of a tap* ► twist, spin, twirl, whirl, rotation, revolution, circle, cycle **2** *The car came to a turn in the road.* ► bend, corner, curve, angle, deviation, hairpin bend, junction, loop, twist **3** *an unexpected turn of events* ► reversal, shift, change of direction, turning point **4** *It's your turn to speak.* ► chance, opportunity, occasion, time, stint, spell **5** *She was trying to do James a good turn.* ► favour, support **6** *a comic turn in a concert* ► act, performance, show **7** *His sudden appearance gave her quite a turn.* ► shock, start, surprise, fright, scare, jolt

in turn *The Eastern capital in turn influenced the culture of Venice.* ► in succession, successively

turning *NOUN* *Take the second turning on the right.* ► turn-off, turn, exit

turnover *NOUN* **turnovers** **1** the amount of money received by a firm selling things **2** the rate at which goods are sold or workers leave and are replaced **3** a small pie made by folding pastry over fruit, jam, etc.

turnstile *NOUN* **turnstiles** a revolving gate that lets one person in at a time

turntable *NOUN* **turntables** a circular revolving platform or support, e.g. for the record in a record player

turquoise *NOUN* **turquoises** **1** a sky-blue or greenish-blue colour **2** a blue jewel

turret *NOUN* **turrets** **1** a small tower on a castle or other building **2** a revolving structure containing a gun
▷ **turreted** *ADJECTIVE*

turtle *NOUN* **turtles** a sea animal that looks like a tortoise
turn turtle capsize

turtle dove *NOUN* **turtle doves** a wild dove

tusk *NOUN* **tusks** a long pointed tooth that sticks out from the mouth of an elephant, walrus, etc.

tussle *NOUN* **tussles** a struggle or conflict over something

tussock *NOUN* **tussocks** a tuft or clump of grass

tutor *NOUN* **tutors** **1** a private teacher, especially of one pupil or a small group **2** a teacher of students in a college or university

TV *ABBREVIATION* television

twain *NOUN, ADJECTIVE* (*old use*) two

twang *VERB* **twangs, twanging, twanged** make a sharp sound like that of a wire when plucked
▷ **twang** *NOUN*

tweak *VERB* **tweaks, tweaking, tweaked** pinch and twist or pull something sharply
▷ **tweak** *NOUN*

tweed *NOUN* thick woollen twill, often woven of mixed colours

tweet *NOUN* **tweets** the chirping sound made by a small bird
▷ **tweet** *VERB*

tweezers *PLURAL NOUN* small pincers for picking up or pulling very small things

twelve *NOUN, ADJECTIVE* **twelves** the number 12
▷ **twelfth** *ADJECTIVE, NOUN*

twenty *NOUN, ADJECTIVE* **twenties** the number 20
▷ **twentieth** *ADJECTIVE, NOUN*

twice *ADVERB* **1** two times; on two occasions **2** double the amount

twiddle *VERB* **twiddles, twiddling, twiddled** turn something round or over and over in an idle way • *He tried twiddling the knob on the radio.*
▷ **twiddle** *NOUN* **twiddly** *ADJECTIVE*
twiddle your thumbs have nothing to do

twig *NOUN* **twigs** a small shoot on a branch or stem of a tree or shrub

twilight *NOUN* dim light from the sky just after sunset or just before sunrise

twin *NOUN* **twins** **1** either of two children or animals born to the same mother at one time **2** either of two things that are exactly alike

twin *VERB* **twins, twinning, twinned** **1** put things together as a pair **2** if a town is twinned with a town in a different country, the two towns exchange visits and organize cultural events together

twine *VERB* **twines, twining, twined** twist or wind together or round something

twinge *NOUN* **twinges** a sudden pain or unpleasant feeling

twinkle *VERB* **twinkles, twinkling, twinkled** shine with tiny flashes of light; sparkle
▷ **twinkle** *NOUN*

Thesaurus

tussle *NOUN His glasses were broken in the tussle.* ► fight, scuffle, fracas, brawl, struggle, scrap, rumpus, commotion, argument

tussle *NOUN Some of the crowd tussled with police.* ► fight, scuffle, brawl, struggle, scrap, come to blows

tweak *VERB She tweaked Peter's ear.* ► twist, pinch, nip, pull, squeeze

twiddle *VERB Link your fingers in your lap so you're not tempted to twiddle them.* ► fiddle with, fidget with, twirl, twist

twig *VERB* (*informal*) *I finally twigged where they had come from.* ► realize, understand, grasp, comprehend

twin *ADJECTIVE twin towers on the French pattern* ► identical, matching, balancing, corresponding, duplicate, paired, similar, symmetrical, indistinguishable

twin *NOUN Fiona drove her own car, the twin of Harry's.* ► double, duplicate, clone, match, (*more informal*) lookalike

twinge *NOUN* **1** *I was getting sharp twinges in one knee.* ► pain, stab, spasm **2** *She felt a twinge of sadness.* ► pang, prick, qualm

twinkle *VERB I could see Beverly Hills twinkling in the distance.* ► glimmer, glitter, glint, glow, shine, flash, glisten, gleam, sparkle, shimmer

twinkle *NOUN the twinkle of a thousand lights* ► sparkle, glimmer, glitter, glint, glow, shimmer

A B C D E F G H I J K L M N O P Q R S T U V W X Y Z

twirl *VERB* **twirls, twirling, twirled** twist quickly
▷ **twirl** *NOUN*

twist *VERB* **twists, twisting, twisted 1** turn the ends of something in opposite directions **2** turn round or from side to side • *The road twisted through the hills.* **3** bend something out of its proper shape **4** pass threads or strands round something or round each other **5** distort the meaning of something • *You're twisting my words.*
▷ **twister** *NOUN*

twist *NOUN* **twists** a twisting movement or action
▷ **twisty** *ADJECTIVE*

twitch *VERB* **twitches, twitching, twitched** move or pull with a slight jerk
▷ **twitch** *NOUN*

twitter *VERB* **twitters, twittering, twittered** make quick chirping sounds
▷ **twitter** *NOUN*

two *NOUN, ADJECTIVE* **twos** the number 2
be in two minds be undecided about something

two-faced *ADJECTIVE* insincere or deceitful

tycoon *NOUN* **tycoons** a rich and influential business person [from Japanese *taikun* = great prince]

tying *present participle of* **tie**

type *NOUN* **types 1** a kind or sort **2** letters or figures etc. designed for use in printing

type *VERB* **types, typing, typed** write something by using a typewriter
▷ **typist** *NOUN*

typewriter *NOUN* **typewriters** a machine with keys that are pressed to print letters or figures etc. on a piece of paper
▷ **typewritten** *ADJECTIVE*

typhoon *NOUN* **typhoons** a violent hurricane in the western Pacific or East Asian seas [from Chinese *tai fung* = great wind]

typical *ADJECTIVE* **1** having the usual characteristics or qualities of a particular type of person or thing • *a typical school playground*

Thesaurus

twirl *VERB* **1** *They twirled round the room arm in arm.* ► spin, turn, twist, whirl, wheel, gyrate, pirouette, revolve, rotate **2** *He twirled his empty glass in his hands.* ► twiddle, twist, play with

twist *VERB* **1** *Huge girders had been twisted in the explosion.* ► crush, buckle, mangle, misshape, deform **2** *He twisted a strand of her hair round his fingers.* ► coil, curl, wind, entwine, twine **3** *Twist the cork slowly as you pull it.* ► turn, screw, revolve **4** *She fell off her bike and twisted her ankle.* ► sprain, wrench, rick **5** *He accused the newspaper of twisting his words.* ► distort, change, alter, misrepresent, garble, contort, pervert

twist *NOUN* **1** *Give the lid a firm twist.* ► turn, screw, jerk, spin **2** *a twist in the rope* ► coil, curl, loop, kink, tangle, knot **3** *a twist in the road* ► bend, turn, zigzag **4** *There was an unexpected twist to the story.* ► development, surprise, quirk, oddity

twisted *ADJECTIVE* **1** *A mass of twisted metal barred the way.* ► crumpled, buckled, crushed, mangled, distorted, misshapen, deformed, warped **2** *It seemed to be the product of a twisted mind* ► perverted, depraved, warped, deviant, corrupt

twit *NOUN* (*informal*) *You're an ignorant little twit.* ► fool, idiot, clot, ass, halfwit, dimwit, blockhead, dunderhead, nincompoop

twitch *NOUN* *She suppressed an involuntary twitch of her lip.* ► spasm, jerk, tremor, tic, blink, convulsion, flutter, jump

twitch *VERB* *The bushes twitched again.* ► start, tremble, jerk, jump, fidget, flutter

two-faced *ADJECTIVE* *I consider you have been a two-faced liar.* ► deceitful, insincere, double-dealing, dishonest, duplicitous, hypocritical
OPPOSITES ARE sincere, honest

tycoon *NOUN* *a newspaper advertisement sponsored by an oil tycoon* ► magnate, mogul, industrialist, baron, supremo, big businessman

type *NOUN* **1** *This type of injury could happen to any player at any time.* ► kind, sort, category, class, form, variety, classification, description, designation, genre, group, species **2** *Footnotes are printed in small type.* ► print, characters, typeface, font, letters

typhoon *NOUN* *aid for victims of the typhoon* ► cyclone, tornado, hurricane, whirlwind

typical *ADJECTIVE* **1** *Decorative carving is a typical feature of late Gothic architecture.* ► characteristic, distinctive, particular, representative, special OPPOSITES ARE untypical, uncharacteristic **2** *It had been a fairly typical week.* ► average, ordinary, normal, usual, conventional, orthodox, predictable, standard, unsurprising OPPOSITES ARE untypical, unusual
USAGE There is a slight difference in meaning between *untypical* and *atypical*: *untypical* means 'not typical, unusual', whereas *atypical* means 'not belonging to this type'.

2 usual in a particular person or thing • *He worked with typical carefulness.*
▷ **typically** ADVERB

tyranny (tirran- ee) NOUN **tyrannies**
1 government by a tyrant **2** the way a tyrant behaves towards people
▷ **tyrannical** ADJECTIVE **tyrannous** ADJECTIVE

tyrant (ty- rant) NOUN **tyrants** a person who rules cruelly and unjustly; someone who insists on being obeyed [from Greek *tyrannos* = ruler with full power]

tyre NOUN **tyres** a covering of rubber fitted round a wheel to make it grip the road and run more smoothly

Thesaurus

typify VERB *The village typifies the beauty of the Lake District.* ► epitomize, exemplify, characterize, embody, represent

tyrannical ADJECTIVE *His father is portrayed as a stern, tyrannical disciplinarian.* ► authoritarian, autocratic, despotic, dictatorial, domineering, oppressive, overbearing, cruel, brutal, harsh, imperious, ruthless, severe, tyrannous, unjust
OPPOSITES ARE liberal, tolerant, easygoing

tyrannize VERB *He tyrannized his family.*
► dominate, domineer over, oppress, bully, intimidate

tyranny NOUN *the injustice, cruelty, and tyranny in the world* ► despotism, autocracy, dictatorship, oppression

tyrant NOUN *She was a tyrant to the girls.*
► despot, autocrat, dictator, oppressor, slave-driver

Uu

ubiquitous (yoo- **bik**- wit- us) *ADJECTIVE* found everywhere • *Mobile phones are ubiquitous these days.*
▷ **ubiquity** *NOUN*

udder *NOUN* **udders** the bag-like part of a cow, ewe, female goat, etc. from which milk is taken

ugly *ADJECTIVE* **uglier, ugliest 1** unpleasant to look at; not beautiful **2** hostile and threatening • *The crowd was in an ugly mood.*
▷ **ugliness** *NOUN*
[from Old Norse *uggligr* = frightening]

UK *ABBREVIATION* United Kingdom

ulcer *NOUN* **ulcers** a sore on the inside or outside of the body
▷ **ulcerated** *ADJECTIVE* **ulceration** *NOUN*

ulterior *ADJECTIVE* beyond what is obvious or stated • *an ulterior motive*

ultimate *ADJECTIVE* furthest in a series of things; final • *Our ultimate destination is London.*
▷ **ultimately** *ADVERB*
[from Latin *ultimus* = last]

ultimatum (ul- tim- ay- tum) *NOUN* **ultimatums** a final demand or statement that unless something is done by a certain time action will be taken or war will be declared

ultramarine *NOUN* a deep bright blue [from Latin *ultra mare* = beyond the sea (because it was originally imported 'across the sea' from the East)]

ultrasound *NOUN* sound of a frequency beyond the range of human hearing, used in medical examinations

ultraviolet *ADJECTIVE* (said about light rays) beyond the violet end of the spectrum and so not visible to the human eye

umbilical cord *NOUN* **umbilical cords** the tube through which a baby receives nourishment before it is born, connecting its body with the mother's womb

umbrella *NOUN* **umbrellas 1** a circular piece of material stretched over a folding frame with a central stick used as a handle, or a central pole, which you open to protect yourself from rain or sun **2** a general protection [from Italian *ombrella* = a little shade]

umpire *NOUN* **umpires** a referee in cricket, tennis, and some other games

umpire *VERB* **umpires, umpiring, umpired** act as an umpire

UN *ABBREVIATION* United Nations

un- *PREFIX* **1** not (as in *uncertain*) **2** (before a verb) reversing the action (as in *unlock* = release from being locked) *Many words beginning with this prefix are not listed here if their meaning is obvious.*

unable *ADJECTIVE* not able to do something

unaccountable *ADJECTIVE* **1** unable to be explained • *For some unaccountable reason I completely forgot your birthday.* **2** not accountable for what you do
▷ **unaccountably** *ADVERB*

unanimous (yoo- **nan**- im- us) *ADJECTIVE* with everyone agreeing • *a unanimous decision*
▷ **unanimously** *ADVERB* **unanimity** (yoo- nan- im- it- ee) *NOUN*
[from Latin *unus* = one + *animus* = mind]

Thesaurus

ugly *ADJECTIVE* **1** *He may be ugly, but at least he writes good songs.* ► unattractive, unsightly, deformed, repulsive, hideous, plain, grisly, unpleasant, monstrous
AN OPPOSITE IS attractive **2** *an ugly iron bedstead* ► unsightly, hideous, inelegant, tasteless, unattractive, unpleasant, displeasing, inartistic, plain AN OPPOSITE IS beautiful **3** *There were a number of ugly scenes behind the goalposts.* ► angry, dangerous, threatening, ominous, unpleasant, sinister, unfriendly, forbidding, hostile, menacing AN OPPOSITE IS pleasant

ultimate *ADJECTIVE* *the decline and ultimate disappearance of the city-state* ► eventual, final, consequent

ultimately *ADVERB* *Perhaps these problems will ultimately prove too great.* ► eventually, finally, in the end, in the long run, in time

umbrage *NOUN*
take umbrage *He amused them without taking umbrage when they laughed at him.* ► take offence, take exception, be offended, be annoyed, be aggrieved, be insulted, bridle

umpire *NOUN* *They all abided by the umpire's decision.* ► referee, adjudicator, arbiter, judge, linesman, arbitrator, moderator, (*more informal*) ref

umpteen *ADJECTIVE* (*informal*) *He had to tell the story umpteen times.* ► many, numerous, plenty of, countless, innumerable

unacceptable *ADJECTIVE* *Public opinion has rejected this strategy as shortsighted and unacceptable.* ► intolerable, unsatisfactory, inadmissible, inappropriate, unsuitable, inadequate OPPOSITES ARE acceptable, satisfactory

unaided *ADJECTIVE* *by your own unaided efforts* ► single-handed, alone, by yourself, without help, independently

unanimous *ADJECTIVE* *The resulting decision was unanimous.* ► united, harmonious, of one mind

unassuming ADJECTIVE modest; not arrogant or pretentious

unavoidable ADJECTIVE not able to be avoided

unawares ADVERB unexpectedly; without warning • *His question caught me unawares.*

unbearable ADJECTIVE not able to be endured
▷ **unbearably** ADVERB

unbeaten ADJECTIVE not defeated or surpassed

unbecoming ADJECTIVE **1** not making a person look attractive **2** not suitable or fitting

unbelievable ADJECTIVE not able to be believed; incredible
▷ **unbelievably** ADVERB

unbend VERB **unbends, unbending, unbent** **1** change from a bent position; straighten up **2** relax and become friendly

unblock VERB **unblocks, unblocking, unblocked** remove an obstruction from something

unborn ADJECTIVE not yet born

unbroken ADJECTIVE not broken or interrupted

uncalled for ADJECTIVE not justified or necessary • *Such rudeness was quite uncalled for.*

uncanny ADJECTIVE **uncannier, uncanniest** strange or mysterious • *an uncanny coincidence*
▷ **uncannily** ADVERB **uncanniness** NOUN

uncertain ADJECTIVE **1** not known certainly **2** not sure about something **3** not reliable • *His aim is rather uncertain.*
▷ **uncertainly** ADVERB **uncertainty** NOUN
in no uncertain terms clearly and forcefully

uncharitable ADJECTIVE making unkind judgements of people or actions
▷ **uncharitably** ADVERB

Thesaurus

unarmed ADJECTIVE *Troops shot at unarmed civilians.* ► defenceless, undefended, weaponless, unprotected, exposed, vulnerable
AN OPPOSITE IS armed

unassuming ADJECTIVE *Sparks was an unassuming and kindly man.* ► modest, retiring, humble, self-effacing, unobtrusive

unavoidable ADJECTIVE *Job losses are unavoidable.* ► inevitable, inescapable, certain, necessary, obligatory, mandatory
opposites are avoidable, unnecessary

unaware ADJECTIVE *They seemed to be unaware of everything that had happened.* ► ignorant, oblivious, unconscious, unmindful, heedless
OPPOSITES ARE aware, conscious

unbalanced ADJECTIVE **1** *We must not give an unbalanced picture.* ► unfair, unjust, biased, one-sided, partial, partisan, prejudiced
OPPOSITES ARE balanced, fair **2** *She said her husband had become unbalanced and capable of doing nasty things.* ► unstable, disturbed, deranged, demented, crazy, insane

unbearable ADJECTIVE *The pain was unbearable.* ► unendurable, intolerable, excruciating, agonizing, insufferable, unmanageable
OPPOSITES ARE bearable, tolerable

unbeatable ADJECTIVE **1** *When in good form the side is unbeatable.* ► invincible, unassailable, indestructible, indomitable, unconquerable, matchless, supreme **2** *As a flavour enhancer, lemon is unbeatable.* ► incomparable, unrivalled, unsurpassed, matchless, supreme

unbelievable ADJECTIVE **1** *You may find the story bizarre, even unbelievable.* ► incredible, improbable, implausible, far-fetched, unconvincing, preposterous **2** *He acted with unbelievable recklessness.* ► incredible, unimaginable, inconceivable, unthinkable

unbiased ADJECTIVE *Every effort is made to obtain an unbiased opinion.* ► impartial, objective, dispassionate, neutral, independent
OPPOSITES ARE biased, partial

unbroken ADJECTIVE **1** *an unbroken night's sleep* ► continuous, uninterrupted, constant **2** *a world record that remains unbroken* ► unbeaten, unsurpassed, unequalled, unrivalled

uncalled-for ADJECTIVE *Such strict rules are totally uncalled-for.* ► unnecessary, gratuitous, needless, inappropriate, unwarranted, unjustified, unreasonable, unwelcome
OPPOSITES ARE opportune, appropriate

uncanny ADJECTIVE **1** *The silence was uncanny.* ► eerie, unnatural, weird, creepy, unreal, ghostly, unaccountable AN OPPOSITE IS normal

uncertain ADJECTIVE **1** *The side effects of the treatment are uncertain.* ► unknown, unclear, indefinite, undetermined, unforeseeable, unresolved, undecided, inconclusive, ambiguous, imprecise, indeterminate, speculative OPPOSITES ARE known, definite **2** *I was uncertain what to say.* ► unsure, undecided, doubtful, unconvinced (about), ambivalent (about), dubious (about), hazy (about), wavering (about), in two minds (about) **3** *Workers in the industry face an uncertain future.* ► changeable, variable, erratic, unpredictable, unreliable, precarious
AN OPPOSITE IS certain

uncertainty NOUN **1** *He tried to disguise his uncertainty.* ► doubt, misgiving, apprehension, qualm, hesitation, scruple
OPPOSITES ARE certainty, positiveness **2** *Some degree of uncertainty is bound to ensue.* ► unpredictability, unreliability, changeability, risk, danger
OPPOSITES ARE certainty, assurance

A B C D E F G H I J K L M N O P Q R S T U V W X Y Z

uncivilized ADJECTIVE not civilized; not having much culture

uncle NOUN **uncles** the brother of your father or mother; your aunt's husband

uncomfortable ADJECTIVE not comfortable
▷ **uncomfortably** ADVERB

uncommon ADJECTIVE not common; unusual

uncompromising (un- komp- rom- I- zing) ADJECTIVE not allowing a compromise; inflexible

unconcerned ADJECTIVE not caring about something; not worried

unconditional ADJECTIVE without any conditions; absolute • *unconditional surrender*
▷ **unconditionally** ADVERB

unconscious ADJECTIVE **1** not conscious **2** not aware of things
▷ **unconsciously** ADVERB **unconsciousness** NOUN

uncouth (un- kooth) ADJECTIVE rude and rough in manner

uncover VERB **uncovers, uncovering, uncovered 1** remove the covering from something **2** reveal or expose • *They uncovered a plot to kill the king.*

undecided ADJECTIVE **1** not yet settled; not certain **2** not having made up your mind yet

Thesaurus

uncivilized ADJECTIVE *I am sorry to see such uncivilized behaviour.* ► uncouth, primitive, barbaric, rough, boorish, antisocial, barbaric, barbarous, uncultured, uneducated, unenlightened, unsophisticated, wild OPPOSITES ARE civilized, respectable

unclear ADJECTIVE **1** *The answers are all very unclear.* ► vague, obscure, ambiguous, equivocal, puzzling, opaque, cryptic, hazy, imprecise OPPOSITES ARE clear, straightforward, unambiguous **2** *It was unclear whether the move was backed by the government.* ► uncertain, debatable, unsure, unsettled, doubtful, dubious OPPOSITES ARE clear , obvious

uncomfortable ADJECTIVE **1** *The lecture room had uncomfortable plastic chairs.* ► hard, cramped, restrictive, stiff, tight, ill-fitting, tight-fitting, lumpy AN OPPOSITE IS comfortable **2** *Carrying the bike over your shoulder is uncomfortable in the extreme.* ► painful, disagreeable, excruciating, inconvenient **3** *British workers felt uncomfortable about the slogans common in Japanese factories.* ► uneasy, embarrassed, awkward, troubled, worried, distressed, nervous, restless

uncommon ADJECTIVE *Two or three nights without sleep were not uncommon.* ► unusual, infrequent, rare, exceptional, abnormal OPPOSITES ARE common, usual

unconditional ADJECTIVE *All four offered their unconditional support.* ► unqualified, unrestricted, unlimited, unreserved, unquestioning, total, outright, absolute, complete AN OPPOSITE IS conditional

unconnected ADJECTIVE *The two events were unconnected. She has since died from causes unconnected with the incident.* ► unrelated (to), distinct (from), irrelevant (to), independent, discrete, disparate

unconscious ADJECTIVE **1** *My mother was still unconscious in hospital.* ► concussed, knocked out, insensible, senseless, comatose **2 unconscious of** *He ranted on, unconscious of the danger.* ► unaware of, heedless, ignorant of, disregardful of, disregarding, ignoring, impervious to **3** *He carries with him an unconscious guilt for his little sister's death.* ► subconscious, repressed, suppressed, involuntary, latent, subliminal, instinctive

unconventional ADJECTIVE *A wide range of colours can be used to create unconventional patterns.* ► unusual, unorthodox, unfamiliar, innovative, original, experimental, individual OPPOSITES ARE conventional, orthodox

unconvincing ADJECTIVE *They found that an unconvincing explanation. She put on a smile, but it was unconvincing.* ► dubious, doubtful, implausible, incredible, strained, forced, feeble, weak

uncooperative ADJECTIVE *The lawyers were proving to be uncooperative.* ► unhelpful, disobliging, awkward, obstructive, unaccommodating, inflexible, unwilling AN OPPOSITE IS cooperative

uncouth ADJECTIVE *They were rough uncouth men with the air of outcasts.* ► coarse, rude, ill-mannered, uncivilized, unrefined AN OPPOSITE IS refined

uncover VERB **1** *The earth had to be scraped away to uncover a trap door.* ► reveal, disclose, expose, lay bare, exhibit, show, strip, unmask, unveil, unwrap OPPOSITES ARE cover, conceal **2** *The intention was to uncover the causes of human social behaviour.* ► detect, discover, locate, unearth, expose, make known, come across, make public, dig up OPPOSITES ARE conceal, cover up

undecided ADJECTIVE **1** *The question of where to hold the trial remained undecided.* ► uncertain, unresolved, undetermined, unsettled, unclear, indefinite OPPOSITES ARE decided, settled **2** *She stood undecided in the rain, wanting to find Simon but not daring to step inside.* ► hesitant, wavering, indecisive, unsure, uncertain, dithering, in two minds AN OPPOSITE IS certain

undeniable *ADJECTIVE* impossible to deny; undoubtedly true
▷ **undeniably** *ADVERB*

under *PREPOSITION* **1** below or beneath • *Hide it under the desk.* **2** less than • *under 5 years old* **3** governed or controlled by • *The country prospered under his rule.* **4** in the process of; undergoing • *The road is under repair.* **5** using • *He writes under the name of 'Lewis Carroll'.* **6** according to the rules of • *This is permitted under our agreement.*
under way in motion or in progress

under *ADVERB* in or to a lower place or level or condition • *Slowly the diver went under.*

under *ADJECTIVE* lower • *the under layers*

undercarriage *NOUN* **undercarriages** an aircraft's landing wheels and their supports

undercover *ADJECTIVE* done or doing things secretly • *an undercover agent*

undercurrent *NOUN* **undercurrents 1** a current that is below the surface or below another current **2** an underlying feeling or influence • *an undercurrent of fear*

undercut *VERB* **undercuts, undercutting, undercut** sell something for a lower price than someone else sells it

underdone *ADJECTIVE* not thoroughly done; undercooked

underestimate *VERB* **underestimates, underestimating, underestimated** make too low an estimate of a person or thing

undergo *VERB* **undergoes, undergoing, underwent, undergone** experience or endure something; be subjected to • *The new aircraft underwent intensive tests.*

undergraduate *NOUN* **undergraduates** a student at a university who has not yet taken a degree

underground *ADJECTIVE, ADVERB* **1** under the ground **2** done or working in secret

underground *NOUN* a railway that runs through tunnels under the ground

undergrowth *NOUN* bushes and other plants growing close together, especially under trees

underhand *ADJECTIVE* done or doing things in a sly or secret way

underline *VERB* **underlines, underlining, underlined 1** draw a line under a word etc. **2** emphasize something

underlying *ADJECTIVE* **1** forming the basis or explanation of something • *the underlying causes of the trouble* **2** lying under something • *the underlying rocks*

undermine *VERB* **undermines, undermining, undermined** weaken something gradually

underneath *PREPOSITION, ADVERB* below or beneath

underpants *PLURAL NOUN* a piece of men's underwear covering the lower part of the body, worn under trousers

underprivileged *ADJECTIVE* having less than the normal standard of living or rights in a community

Thesaurus

undeniable *ADJECTIVE The undeniable fact is that chlorine is building up in the atmosphere.* ► indisputable, irrefutable, unquestionable, incontrovertible, undoubted, proven, certain OPPOSITES ARE questionable, debatable

undercover *ADJECTIVE Undercover agents are suspected of the assassination.* ► secret, covert, clandestine, underground, surreptitious, hidden, furtive

underestimate *VERB* **1** *Radiation fallout was underestimated by 40 times.* ► misjudge, miscalculate, set too low OPPOSITES ARE overestimate, exaggerate **2** *Sara puzzled him; he had underestimated her.* ► underrate, undervalue, misjudge, belittle, disparage, minimize, dismiss OPPOSITES ARE overestimate, overrate

undergo *VERB He may have to undergo more surgery.* ► experience, endure, go through, submit to, be subjected to, put up with, face, bear, suffer, withstand

underground *ADJECTIVE* **1** *the waters of an underground river* ► subterranean, buried, sunken AN OPPOSITE IS surface **2** *The two main underground opposition groups have decided to unite.* ► secret, clandestine, covert, surreptitious, undercover, unofficial

underline *VERB The killings underlined the need for political talks to resume.* ► emphasize, highlight, stress, accentuate, point up OPPOSITES ARE minimize, play down

undermine *VERB He denied that the change would undermine local democracy.* ► weaken, subvert, threaten, compromise, enfeeble, sap, wear away, destroy, ruin OPPOSITES ARE support, enhance, boost

underprivileged *ADJECTIVE Many children from underprivileged families have been able to join youth clubs.* ► needy, deprived, disadvantaged, impoverished, destitute, poor OPPOSITES ARE privileged, wealthy

underrate *VERB Most of us have a tendency to underrate our own skills.* ► underestimate, undervalue, belittle, disparage, minimize, dismiss, misjudge OPPOSITES ARE overrate, exaggerate

understand *VERB* **understands, understanding, understood 1** know what something means or how it works or why it exists **2** know and tolerate a person's ways **3** have been told • *I understand that you would like to speak to me.* **4** take something for granted • *Your expenses will be paid, that's understood*
▷ **understandable** *ADJECTIVE* **understandably** *ADVERB*

understanding *NOUN* **1** the power to understand or think; intelligence **2** sympathy or tolerance **3** agreement in opinion or feeling • *a better understanding between nations*

understatement *NOUN* **understatements** an incomplete or very restrained statement of facts or truth • *To say they disagreed is an understatement: they had a violent quarrel*

understudy *NOUN* **understudies** an actor who learns a part in order to be able to play it if the usual performer is ill or absent

undertake *VERB* **undertakes, undertaking, undertook, undertaken 1** agree or promise to do something **2** take on a task or responsibility

undertaker *NOUN* **undertakers** a person whose job is to arrange funerals and burials or cremations

undertone *NOUN* **undertones 1** a low or quiet tone • *They spoke in undertones.* **2** an underlying quality or feeling etc. • *His letter has a threatening undertone.*

underwear *NOUN* clothes worn next to the skin, under indoor clothing

underweight *ADJECTIVE* not heavy enough

underwent *past tense of* **undergo**

underworld *NOUN* **1** the people who are regularly involved in crime **2** (in myths and legends) the place for the spirits of the dead, under the earth

undeveloped *ADJECTIVE* not yet developed

undo *VERB* **undoes, undoing, undid, undone 1** unfasten or unwrap **2** cancel the effect of something • *He has undone all our careful work.*

Thesaurus

understand *VERB* **1** *They were unusually quiet, and I could not understand why. He began to understand the story in its full horror.*
► comprehend, grasp, perceive, discern, apprehend, fathom, follow, take in **2** *Do they not understand how much people like me love Morrissey?* ► appreciate, realize, recognize, acknowledge **3** *We understand that the university doesn't have a science park.* ► believe, think, suppose, conclude, surmise, fancy

understanding *NOUN* **1** *Coins can contribute to our understanding of the past.* ► knowledge, comprehension, perception, grasp
AN OPPOSITE IS ignorance **2** *We should look on them with deep understanding.* ► compassion, sympathy, feeling, consideration
AN OPPOSITE IS indifference **3** *My understanding was that there is a three-year guarantee.*
► belief, perception, conviction, notion, idea, conclusion **4** *She is a woman of acute understanding.* ► intelligence, intellect, intuition, discernment, judgement **5** *The various groups had come to an understanding.*
► agreement, arrangement, deal, settlement, pact, treaty, entente

understate *VERB* *The level of complaints received may well understate the scale of the problem.*
► play down, underplay, minimize, belittle, make light of, soft-pedal
OPPOSITES ARE overstate, exaggerate

undertake *VERB* **1** *He undertook to guarantee her son's safety.* ► agree, promise, guarantee, pledge, consent **2** *Some students undertake an industrial placement in their third year.* ► begin, commence, embark on, take on, take up, engage in, take responsibility for, manage, handle

undertaking *NOUN* **1** *Finding a suitable site is a difficult undertaking.* ► enterprise, venture, project, operation, endeavour, business, task, affair, scheme **2** *Booksellers agreed to sign an undertaking not to sell the book.* ► agreement, commitment, pledge, assurance

undervalue *VERB* *He seemed to undervalue his own work.* ► underestimate, underrate, misjudge, belittle, disparage, minimize, dismiss OPPOSITES ARE overestimate, overrate

underwater *ADJECTIVE* *Underwater sonar equipment was used to test for the presence of Nessie.* ► undersea, subaquatic, submarine, submerged, immersed

undesirable *ADJECTIVE* **1** *These undesirable side effects cannot be disregarded.* ► unpleasant, unwelcome, unwanted, disagreeable
OPPOSITES ARE desirable, pleasant **2** *Adam had allowed some undesirable people access to the place.* ► nasty, repellent, objectionable, disagreeable, distasteful
OPPOSITES ARE pleasant, agreeable

undivided *ADJECTIVE* *Be prepared to give your undivided attention and listen carefully.*
► complete, unqualified, unreserved, unbroken, full, total, whole, absolute
OPPOSITES ARE divided, partial

undo *VERB* **1** *She hardly had time to undo her safety belt and get out of the car.* ► unfasten, release, untie, unbutton, unlock, unhitch, loosen OPPOSITES ARE fasten, tie up **2** *Human error undid years of endeavour in a few seconds.*

undoing *NOUN*
be someone's undoing be the cause of their ruin or failure

undress *VERB* **undresses, undressing, undressed** take your clothes off

undue *ADJECTIVE* excessive; too great
▷ **unduly** *ADVERB*

undulate *VERB* **undulates, undulating, undulated** move like a wave or waves; have a wavy appearance
▷ **undulation** *NOUN*

undying *ADJECTIVE* everlasting

unearth *VERB* **unearths, unearthing, unearthed** **1** dig something up; uncover something by digging **2** find something by searching

unearthly *ADJECTIVE* **1** unnatural; strange and frightening **2** (*informal*) very early or inconvenient • *We had to get up at an unearthly hour.*

uneasy *ADJECTIVE* **1** worried or anxious **2** uncomfortable
▷ **uneasily** *ADVERB* **uneasiness** *NOUN*

unemployed *ADJECTIVE* without a job
▷ **unemployment** *NOUN*

unequal *ADJECTIVE* **1** not equal in amount, size, or value **2** not giving the same opportunities to everyone • *an unequal society*
▷ **unequalled** *ADJECTIVE* **unequally** *ADVERB*

Thesaurus

► undermine, subvert, overturn, nullify, scupper, sabotage **3** *A higher court might undo this decision.* ► reverse, overturn, revoke, overrule, disallow, rescind, annul

undoing *NOUN* *At this point fear was his undoing.* ► ruin, downfall, ruination, destruction, overthrow, weakness, failing

undoubtedly *ADVERB* *There will undoubtedly be things you do well already.* ► definitely, doubtless, indubitably, certainly, of course, surely, undeniably, unquestionably
AN OPPOSITE IS possibly

undress *VERB* *The patient has to undress slowly and carefully.* ► take off your clothes, strip, disrobe, (*more informal*) peel off
AN OPPOSITE IS dress

undressed *ADJECTIVE* *She was half undressed when the doorbell rang.* ► naked, unclothed, disrobed, nude, stripped, bare

undue *ADJECTIVE* *If people are under undue stress, they make mistakes.* ► excessive, extreme, unwarranted, unreasonable, disproportionate, unnecessary OPPOSITES ARE due, appropriate

unduly *ADVERB* *Perhaps you think me unduly harsh to express these things so openly.* ► excessively, unreasonably, inordinately, immoderately, unnecessarily

unearth *VERB* *They have done all they can to unearth the truth.* ► uncover, detect, discover, expose, make known, make public, dig up
OPPOSITES ARE conceal, cover up

unearthly *ADJECTIVE* **1** *She was a lady of unearthly beauty.* ► eerie, uncanny, strange, supernatural, otherworldly, weird
OPPOSITES ARE ordinary, mundane **2** (*informal*) *I had a job that involved getting up at an unearthly hour.* ► unreasonable, abnormal, unusual, (*informal*) ungodly OPPOSITES ARE reasonable, comfortable

uneasy *ADJECTIVE* **1** *The uneasy peace lasted a few months.* ► precarious, insecure, unsettled
AN OPPOSITE IS comfortable **2** *Moore was uneasy about the coat.* ► anxious, nervous, apprehensive, troubled, worried, concerned, fearful, jittery AN OPPOSITE IS confident **3** *There was an uneasy atmosphere in the room.* ► tense, awkward, fraught, strained, edgy, uncomfortable

uneducated *ADJECTIVE* *The superstition was by no means confined to uneducated people.* ► ill-educated, untaught, ignorant, ill-informed, uninformed, uncultured, unsophisticated
OPPOSITES ARE educated, learned

unemployed *ADJECTIVE* *I don't know what his job is; is he unemployed at the moment?* ► out of work, jobless, on the dole, not working, redundant OPPOSITES ARE employed, working, in work

unending *ADJECTIVE* *Her work seemed to be unending.* ► endless, interminable, never-ending, everlasting, unceasing, incessant

unenthusiastic *ADJECTIVE* *He was distinctly unenthusiastic about the idea.* ► indifferent, apathetic, half-hearted, lukewarm

unenviable *ADJECTIVE* *The job of being a project leader is an unenviable one.* ► unpleasant, disagreeable, undesirable, unwelcome, thankless

unequal *ADJECTIVE* **1** *The chair had four legs of unequal length.* ► different, differing, varying, uneven, dissimilar, disparate
AN OPPOSITE IS equal **2** *the unequal distribution of power and resources in society* ► unfair, unjust, inequitable, disproportionate
OPPOSITES ARE fair, equitable **3** *Should I give up the unequal struggle?* ► unbalanced, uneven, unfair, ill-matched, one-sided
OPPOSITES ARE equal, well-balanced **4** **unequal to** *Melanie felt unequal to the task she had been given.* ► inadequate for, incapable of, unqualified for, not up to, (*more informal*) not cut out for

a b c d e f g h i j k l m n o p q r s t u v w x y z

unerring (un- er- ing) *ADJECTIVE* making no mistake • *unerring accuracy*

uneven *ADJECTIVE* **1** not level or regular **2** not equally balanced • *an uneven contest*
▷ **unevenly** *ADVERB* **unevenness** *NOUN*

unfair *ADJECTIVE* not fair; unjust
▷ **unfairly** *ADVERB* **unfairness** *NOUN*

unfaithful *ADJECTIVE* not faithful; disloyal

unfamiliar *ADJECTIVE* not familiar
▷ **unfamiliarity** *NOUN*

unfasten *VERB* **unfastens, unfastening, unfastened** open the fastenings of something

unfavourable *ADJECTIVE* not favourable
▷ **unfavourably** *ADVERB*

unfeeling *ADJECTIVE* not caring about other people's feelings; unsympathetic

unfit *ADJECTIVE* **1** unsuitable **2** not in perfect health from lack of exercise

unfold *VERB* **unfolds, unfolding, unfolded** **1** open; spread out **2** make or become known slowly • *as the story unfolds*

Thesaurus

unequalled *ADJECTIVE* *Gregory of Tours provides evidence of unequalled richness.* ► incomparable, unmatched, unparalleled, unrivalled, unsurpassed, inimitable, supreme, surpassing, matchless, peerless

uneven *ADJECTIVE* **1** *Be careful when wheeling a trolley over uneven ground.* ► bumpy, rough, rutted, undulating, bent, broken, crooked, irregular, jagged, jerky, pitted, wavy AN OPPOSITE IS smooth **2** *The demand for electricity is uneven throughout the day.* ► inconsistent, variable, spasmodic, unpredictable, varying, erratic, fitful, fluctuating AN OPPOSITE IS consistent. **3** *Uneven steps led down to a rocky cove.* ► irregular, unsteady, lopsided, unbalanced **4** *He soon gave up the uneven contest.* ► unequal, unfair, ill-matched, one-sided, unbalanced AN OPPOSITE IS balanced

unexpected *ADJECTIVE* *An unexpected error had occurred.* ► unforeseen, accidental, unpredictable, chance, fortuitous, sudden, surprising, unhoped for, unlooked for, unplanned, unusual OPPOSITES ARE expected, predictable

unfair *ADJECTIVE* **1** *It was so unfair that she could never see him.* ► unjust, unreasonable, inequitable OPPOSITES ARE fair, just **2** *It seemed to Watson a cruel, unfair remark. He claims I have unfair advantages.* ► undeserved, unwarranted, uncalled-for, unreasonable, unjustified, unwarranted OPPOSITES ARE fair, justified **3** *The law was placing an unfair burden on small businesses.* ► unreasonable, discriminatory OPPOSITES ARE reasonable, legitimate **4** *The rules relating to unfair play need to be tightened up.* ► illegal, unsporting, dishonourable, illegitimate OPPOSITES ARE fair, honourable

unfaithful *ADJECTIVE* *He could not deny that he had been an unfaithful husband.* ► adulterous, disloyal, untrustworthy, deceitful, duplicitous, faithless OPPOSITES ARE faithful, loyal

unfamiliar *ADJECTIVE* *An unfamiliar smell was drifting from the flat.* ► strange, unusual, curious, novel, different

unfashionable *ADJECTIVE* *Now they were unfashionable, maybe it would be OK to get a personal organizer.* ► old-fashioned, outmoded, out of date, passé, obsolete OPPOSITES ARE fashionable, trendy

unfavourable *ADJECTIVE* **1** *A new head would face unfavourable comparison with his predecessor.* ► critical, hostile, unfriendly, adverse, negative, uncomplimentary, unsympathetic OPPOSITES ARE favourable, positive **2** *A high cost of living and unfavourable exchange rates ate into their holiday funds.* ► bad, adverse, unsatisfactory, undesirable, unenviable OPPOSITES ARE favourable, advantageous

unfeeling *ADJECTIVE* *He smiled, but it was a cool, unfeeling smile.* ► insensitive, heartless, hard-hearted, callous, uncaring OPPOSITES ARE sensitive, sympathetic

unfinished *ADJECTIVE* *The work remained unfinished on his death.* ► incomplete, uncompleted, imperfect, rough, sketchy, unpolished AN OPPOSITE IS complete

unfit *ADJECTIVE* **1** *The house was rapidly becoming unfit for habitation. They were unfit to pass judgement on modern architecture.* ► unsuited, ill-equipped, inadequate, unsatisfactory, useless, incapable (of) **2** *Kevin was also unfit, leaving the defence weakened.* ► out of condition, out of shape, unhealthy, feeble OPPOSITES ARE fit, healthy

unfold *VERB* **1** *Mick unfolded the space blanket.* ► open out, spread out, straighten out, unfurl AN OPPOSITE IS fold up **2** *Come and see history unfold before your eyes.* ► happen, evolve, develop, take place, progress, emerge

unforeseen *ADJECTIVE* *Many of the long-term results were unforeseen.* ► unexpected, unpredicted, unthought of, surprising, unanticipated OPPOSITES ARE foreseen, predictable

unfortunate ADJECTIVE **1** unlucky **2** unsuitable or regrettable • *an unfortunate remark*
▷ **unfortunately** ADVERB

unfounded ADJECTIVE not based on facts

unfriendly ADJECTIVE not friendly
▷ **unfriendliness** NOUN

unfurl VERB **unfurls, unfurling, unfurled** unroll; spread out • *They unfurled a large flag.*

ungainly ADJECTIVE awkward-looking or clumsy
▷ **ungainliness** NOUN

ungodly ADJECTIVE **1** not giving reverence to God; not religious **2** (*informal*) outrageous; very inconvenient • *She woke me at an ungodly hour.*
▷ **ungodliness** NOUN

unguarded ADJECTIVE **1** not guarded **2** without thought or caution; indiscreet • *He said this in an unguarded moment.*

unhappy ADJECTIVE **1** not happy; sad **2** unfortunate or unsuitable • *an unhappy coincidence*
▷ **unhappily** ADVERB **unhappiness** NOUN

unhealthy ADJECTIVE not healthy
▷ **unhealthiness** NOUN

unheard of ADJECTIVE never known or done before; extraordinary

unhinge VERB **unhinges, unhinging, unhinged** cause a person's mind to become unbalanced

unicorn NOUN **unicorns** (in legends) an animal that is like a horse with one long straight horn growing from its forehead

Thesaurus

unforgettable ADJECTIVE *The recreation park will provide hours of fun and an unforgettable experience.* ► memorable, striking, noteworthy, remarkable, impressive, distinctive OPPOSITES ARE forgettable, unexceptional

unforgivable ADJECTIVE *Losing your temper with him was unforgivable.* ► inexcusable, reprehensible, shameful, unjustifiable, unpardonable, unwarrantable
AN OPPOSITE IS forgivable

unfortunate ADJECTIVE **1** *Some of these unfortunate prisoners were later found to be innocent.* ► unlucky, hapless, wretched, poor, unhappy, ill-fated, luckless **2** *The incident led to the most unfortunate disagreement between the Allies.* ► disastrous, disadvantageous, unwelcome, inopportune, harmful, regrettable, lamentable, deplorable **3** *He said it would be most unfortunate if one year's results were regarded as typical.* ► regrettable, inappropriate, unsuitable

unfriendly ADJECTIVE *He glowered back in an unfriendly manner.* ► hostile, aggressive, disagreeable, unpleasant, antagonistic, unsociable, standoffish, aloof
OPPOSITES ARE friendly, amiable

ungainly ADJECTIVE *A kangaroo must use a lot of energy in its lopsided and ungainly walk.*
► awkward, clumsy, ungraceful, graceless, inelegant OPPOSITES ARE elegant, graceful

ungrateful ADJECTIVE *I'm going to seem so ungrateful if I refuse the offer.* ► unappreciative, unthankful, ungracious, ill-mannered, selfish
OPPOSITES ARE grateful, thankful

unhappy ADJECTIVE **1** *Her absence made Thomas unhappy.* ► sad, sorrowful, melancholy, miserable, dejected, despondent, dispirited, depressed OPPOSITES ARE happy, pleased **2** *One person at least had benefited from these unhappy events.* ► unlucky, unfortunate, luckless, ill-fated AN OPPOSITE IS fortunate **3** *Clearly it has been an unhappy compromise.* ► inappropriate, unsuitable, inapt, unsatisfactory, unfortunate
OPPOSITES ARE happy, satisfactory **4** *Graham was very unhappy with his performance.*
► dissatisfied, disappointed, displeased, discontented

unharmed ADJECTIVE *Almost all the population seem to have escaped unharmed.* ► safe, safe and sound, uninjured, unhurt, unscathed, intact
OPPOSITES ARE harmed, injured

unhealthy ADJECTIVE **1** *He was looking tired and unhealthy.* ► sickly, ill-looking, ailing, unwell, poorly, frail, weak OPPOSITES ARE healthy, well **2** *They lived in an unhealthy environment.*
► insalubrious, dirty, insanitary, polluted, unhygienic, unwholesome
OPPOSITES ARE healthy, salubrious **3** *As a nurse I knew it was unhealthy to be so overweight.*
► harmful, unnatural, deleterious
AN OPPOSITE IS healthy

unheard of ADJECTIVE *It was unheard of in those days for anyone to get so much money.*
► unprecedented, inconceivable, unimaginable, exceptional, extraordinary, unusual, uncommon AN OPPOSITE IS common

unhelpful ADJECTIVE *The bank cashier had been unhelpful.* ► uncooperative, disobliging, inconsiderate, uncivil, unwilling, negative, slow
OPPOSITES ARE helpful, obliging

unidentified ADJECTIVE *An unidentified vandal drew a Hitler moustache on the portrait.*
► unknown, unnamed, nameless, unrecognized, unspecified, anonymous, incognito, unfamiliar OPPOSITES ARE identified, known, named

uniform *NOUN* **uniforms** special clothes showing that the wearer is a member of a certain organization, school, etc.

uniform *ADJECTIVE* always the same; not varying • *The desks are of uniform size.* ▷ **uniformly** *ADVERB* **uniformity** *NOUN*

unilateral *ADJECTIVE* done by one person or group or country etc. • *a unilateral decision*

uninhabitable *ADJECTIVE* unfit to live in

union *NOUN* **unions** **1** the joining of things together; uniting **2** a trade union

Union Jack *NOUN* **Union Jacks** the flag of the United Kingdom

unique (yoo- neek) *ADJECTIVE* being the only one of its kind • *This jewel is unique.*
▷ **uniquely** *ADVERB*
[from French, from Latin *unicus* = one and only]

unison *NOUN*
in unison **1** with all sounding or singing the same tune etc. together, or speaking in chorus **2** in agreement

unit *NOUN* **units** **1** an amount used as a standard in measuring or counting things • *Centimetres are units of length.* **2** a group, device, piece of furniture, etc. regarded as a single thing but forming part of a larger group or whole • *an army unit* • *a sink unit* **3** (in mathematics) any whole number less than 10

unite *VERB* **unites, uniting, united** join together; make or become one thing

Thesaurus

uniform *ADJECTIVE* *A thermostat will maintain a uniform temperature.* ► regular, consistent, unvarying, homogeneous, identical, indistinguishable, similar, single
OPPOSITES ARE varying, inconsistent

uniform *NOUN* *He had never worn a uniform in his life.* ► outfit, livery, regalia, costume

unify *VERB* *He was concerned to unify the country.* ► unite, integrate, harmonize, bring together, combine, consolidate, amalgamate, bind, fuse, join, merge, weld together
OPPOSITES ARE divide, separate, split

unimaginable *ADJECTIVE* *He was motivated by the promise of unimaginable rewards.* ► inconceivable, unbelievable, incredible, unthinkable, unheard of, untold, mind-boggling

unimaginative *ADJECTIVE* *The drawings were flat and unimaginative.* ► boring, dull, uninspired, uncreative, uninventive, uninteresting, unexciting, unoriginal, pedestrian, prosaic, stale, trite, banal, derivative, ordinary
OPPOSITES ARE imaginative, creative

unimportant *ADJECTIVE* *The size of the power supply is unimportant.* ► insignificant, inconsequential, immaterial, irrelevant, trivial, trifling, minor, of no account, of no consequence, of no moment
AN OPPOSITE IS important

uninhabited *ADJECTIVE* *The centre of the island is vast and uninhabited.* ► empty, unoccupied, unpeopled, unsettled, deserted, depopulated, deserted, uncolonized, vacant
AN OPPOSITE IS inhabited

unintelligible *ADJECTIVE* *The conversation was unintelligible to Gina.* ► incomprehensible, incoherent, unfathomable, baffling, perplexing, obscure, cryptic, opaque, mysterious, confusing, inscrutable, enigmatic
OPPOSITES ARE intelligible, comprehensible

unintentional *ADJECTIVE* *Sometimes the harassment may be unintentional.* ► unintended, inadvertent, accidental, involuntary, unconscious, unplanned, unwitting, fortuitous AN OPPOSITE IS intentional

uninterrupted *ADJECTIVE* *A few extra hours of uninterrupted sleep can remedy the situation.* ► continuous, unbroken, undisturbed, constant, sustained, consecutive
OPPOSITES ARE interrupted, intermittent, broken

union *NOUN* **1** *A union was formed to fight the war with Persia.* ► alliance, coalition, league, federation, confederation, confederacy **2** *The company was formed from the union of three smaller firms.* ► merger, merging, amalgamation, fusion, combination, unification, uniting, joining

unique *ADJECTIVE* **1** *Each file has got a unique name.* ► distinctive, special, individual, peculiar, single, singular, (*more informal*) one-off AN OPPOSITE IS common **2** *The production was a unique opportunity to hear the music in its original form.* ► remarkable, outstanding, incomparable, extraordinary, unparalleled, unprecedented, unusual
AN OPPOSITE IS unremarkable

unit *NOUN* *The family is a fundamental unit of society.* ► component, constituent, element, entity, item, portion, section, segment

unite *VERB* **1** *They tried to unite the population in a common war effort against the English.* ► unify, integrate, combine, bring together, bind, join AN OPPOSITE IS divide **2** *Police and publicans united to solve the problem.* ► combine, join forces, cooperate, collaborate **3** *Mother and son were united after the war.* ► bring together, join

unity *NOUN* **1** being united; being in agreement **2** something whole that is made up of parts **3** (in mathematics) the number one

universal *ADJECTIVE* to do with or including or done by everyone or everything
▷ **universally** *ADVERB*

universe *NOUN* everything that exists, including the earth and living things and all the stars and planets

university *NOUN* **universities** a place where people go to study at an advanced level after leaving school [from Latin *universitas*, literally = the universe, and later = a community of teachers and students]

unjust *ADJECTIVE* not fair or just

unkempt *ADJECTIVE* looking untidy or neglected [from *un-* = not + an old word *kempt* = combed]

unkind *ADJECTIVE* not kind
▷ **unkindly** *ADVERB* **unkindness** *NOUN*

unleaded *ADJECTIVE* (said about petrol) without added lead

unleash *VERB* **unleashes, unleashing, unleashed** **1** set a dog free from a leash **2** let a strong feeling or force be released

unless *CONJUNCTION* except when; if ... not • *We cannot go unless we are invited.*

unlike *PREPOSITION* not like • *Unlike me, she enjoys cricket.*

unlike *ADJECTIVE* not alike; different • *The two children are very unlike*

unlikely *ADJECTIVE* **unlikelier, unlikeliest** not likely to happen or be true

unlimited *ADJECTIVE* not limited; very great or very many

unload *VERB* **unloads, unloading, unloaded** remove the load of things carried by a ship, aircraft, vehicle, etc.

Thesaurus

united *ADJECTIVE* *the potential power of a united Germany* ► unified, integrated, merged, amalgamated, combined
an opposite is disunited
be united *They were united on this one issue.*
► agree, be in agreement, be in accord, be unanimous, be of the same mind, have the same opinion OPPOSITES ARE be disunited, disagree

unity *NOUN* **1** *Creating national unity is a fundamental task for our people.* ► agreement, harmony, accord, consensus, concord OPPOSITES ARE discord, disagreement **2** *the issue of European unity* ► union, unification, federation OPPOSITES ARE division, disunity

universal *ADJECTIVE* *A sudden fall in house prices is a universal fear.* ► common, general, ubiquitous, widespread, worldwide, global, all-embracing, all-round OPPOSITES ARE restricted, local

unjust *ADJECTIVE* **1** *She was still smarting from her unjust dismissal.* ► unfair, unjustified, undeserved, unmerited, unreasonable, unwarranted, unlawful, wrong, wrongful, indefensible, inequitable OPPOSITES ARE just, justified **2** *The report was widely criticized for being unjust.* ► unfair, biased, one-sided, partial, partisan, prejudiced, bigoted OPPOSITES ARE just, fair, balanced

unkind *ADJECTIVE* *He says unkind things that cause her pain.* ► cruel, thoughtless, unfeeling, callous, uncharitable, unpleasant, inconsiderate, unfriendly, malicious, malevolent, spiteful, harsh OPPOSITES ARE kind, considerate

unknown *ADJECTIVE* **1** *Some of the civilians were transferred to unknown destinations. For some unknown reason, the blinds were always drawn. The date of their marriage is unknown.*
► unspecified, unidentified, unnamed, undisclosed, mysterious, strange, unrecognized, anonymous, nameless
AN OPPOSITE IS named **2** *Lowell began a search for this unknown planet.* ► undiscovered, unfamiliar, unexplored, unmapped, uncharted, alien, foreign AN OPPOSITE IS familiar **3** *The part was taken by the then unknown Maria.*
► unheard of, obscure, little known, undistinguished, lowly, inconsequential, insignificant, unimportant
AN OPPOSITE IS famous

unlikely *ADJECTIVE* **1** *It is unlikely that they will attend, being so busy.* ► doubtful, improbable, dubious AN OPPOSITE IS likely **2** *They would hardly believe such an unlikely explanation.*
► implausible, improbable, far-fetched, incredible, suspect, suspicious, dubious, questionable, unbelievable, unconvincing
AN OPPOSITE IS likely

unlimited *ADJECTIVE* **1** *The President emphasized that the USA did not have unlimited funds.*
► limitless, inexhaustible, infinite, unbounded, boundless, bottomless
OPPOSITES ARE limited, finite **2** *All parts carry a 12-month unlimited mileage warranty.*
► unrestricted, unqualified, unconditional, open, unhindered, clear OPPOSITES ARE limited, restricted

unload *VERB* **1** *Unload the box of essential items first.* ► remove, take off, offload, drop off, unpack, discharge AN OPPOSITE IS load **2** *About thirty men would be needed to unload the ship.*
► unpack, empty, unburden

unlock *VERB* **unlocks, unlocking, unlocked** open something by undoing a lock

unlucky *ADJECTIVE* not lucky; having or bringing bad luck
▷ **unluckily** *ADVERB*

unmask *VERB* **unmasks, unmasking, unmasked 1** remove a person's mask **2** reveal what a person or thing really is

unmentionable *ADJECTIVE* too bad or embarrassing to be spoken of

unmistakable *ADJECTIVE* not able to be mistaken for another person or thing
▷ **unmistakably** *ADVERB*

unmitigated *ADJECTIVE* absolute • *an unmitigated disaster*

unnatural *ADJECTIVE* not natural or normal
▷ **unnaturally** *ADVERB*

unnecessary *ADJECTIVE* not necessary; more than is necessary

unorthodox *ADJECTIVE* not generally accepted • *an unorthodox method*

unpack *VERB* **unpacks, unpacking, unpacked** take things out of a suitcase, bag, box, etc.

unpaid *ADJECTIVE* **1** not yet paid • *an unpaid bill* **2** not receiving payment for work you do

unpick *VERB* **unpicks, unpicking, unpicked** undo the stitching of something

unpleasant *ADJECTIVE* not pleasant
▷ **unpleasantly** *ADVERB* **unpleasantness** *NOUN*

unpopular *ADJECTIVE* not popular

unprecedented (un- press- id- en- tid) *ADJECTIVE* that has never happened before

Thesaurus

unlock *VERB* *He took the keys from his pocket and unlocked the boot.* ► open, release, unfasten, undo OPPOSITES ARE lock, fasten

unlucky *ADJECTIVE* **1** *You could be ruined as a result of some unlucky accident.* ► chance, untimely, unfortunate, unintended, disastrous, dreadful, tragic, calamitous, unwelcome OPPOSITES ARE lucky, timely, fortunate **2** *Miss Hill was unlucky not to get a medal. Phil was again unlucky with injuries.* ► unfortunate, hapless, luckless, unhappy, unsuccessful, wretched OPPOSITES ARE lucky, fortunate **3** *The 13th proved to be unlucky for one American skier.* ► inauspicious, ominous, unfavourable, jinxed, cursed, ill-fated, ill-omened, ill-starred OPPOSITES ARE lucky, auspicious

unmistakable *ADJECTIVE* *Then came the unmistakable sound of a shot.* ► distinct, distinctive, clear, plain, obvious, unambiguous, telltale OPPOSITES ARE uncertain, unclear

unnatural *ADJECTIVE* **1** *It was an unnatural crime: was the man mad? He was uneasy in this unnatural silence.* ► abnormal, unusual, uncanny, weird, bizarre, strange, odd, unaccountable, inexplicable, extraordinary AN OPPOSITE IS normal **2** *Her voice sounded unnatural.* ► affected, self-conscious, mannered, stilted, theatrical, unspontaneous, feigned, (*more informal*) put on OPPOSITES ARE natural, normal **3** *The white fur looked unnatural.* ► artificial, fabricated, imitation, man-made, manufactured, simulated, synthetic OPPOSITES ARE natural, genuine

unnecessary *ADJECTIVE* **1** *Don't let's take any unnecessary risks.* ► inessential, non-essential, needless, uncalled-for, unjustified, unneeded, unwanted, excessive, extra OPPOSITES ARE necessary, essential **2** *A deposit is unnecessary with this order.* ► superfluous, dispensable, redundant OPPOSITES ARE necessary, obligatory

unofficial *ADJECTIVE* **1** *She acted as an unofficial bank, cashing cheques for customers.* ► informal, casual, private, personal, unauthorized OPPOSITES ARE official, formal **2** *Unofficial figures put the dead and wounded at over 300.* ► unconfirmed, unauthenticated, unsubstantiated OPPOSITES ARE official, confirmed

unpaid *ADJECTIVE* **1** *There were unpaid bills spread all over the table.* ► outstanding, overdue, unsettled, owing, due OPPOSITES ARE paid, settled **2** *Some staff also did unpaid charity work.* ► voluntary, unremunerative OPPOSITES ARE paid, professional

unpleasant *ADJECTIVE* **1** *It reminded him of an earlier unpleasant experience.* ► disagreeable, distressing, distasteful, nasty, horrible, horrid, uncomfortable OPPOSITES ARE pleasant, agreeable **2** *They were the most unpleasant people I had ever met.* ► unlikable, disagreeable, objectionable, unattractive, unfriendly, obnoxious, repugnant, repulsive, revolting, repellent, ill-natured OPPOSITES ARE friendly, agreeable **3** *substances that give rise to unpleasant odours* ► repulsive, revolting, unappealing OPPOSITES ARE pleasant, appealing

unpopular *ADJECTIVE* **1** *The tax proved deeply unpopular and was later abolished.* ► hated, disliked, detested, unwelcome, unwanted, rejected, despised AN OPPOSITE IS popular **2** *He was unpopular at school.* ► disliked, friendless, unliked, shunned

unpredictable *ADJECTIVE* **1** *The weather is unpredictable in the hills.* ► changeable, variable, erratic, uncertain, unreliable, unforeseeable, unexpected AN OPPOSITE IS predictable **2** *She was unpredictable and likely to say anything.*

unprepared *ADJECTIVE* not prepared beforehand; not ready or equipped

unprintable *ADJECTIVE* too rude or indecent to be printed

unprofessional *ADJECTIVE* not professional; not worthy of a member of a profession

unqualified *ADJECTIVE* **1** not officially qualified to do something **2** not limited • *We gave it our unqualified approval.*

unravel *VERB* **unravels, unravelling, unravelled 1** disentangle **2** undo something that is knitted **3** investigate and solve a mystery etc.

unready *ADJECTIVE* not ready; hesitating
USAGE In the title of the English king *Ethelred the Unready* the word means 'lacking good advice or wisdom'.

unreal *ADJECTIVE* not real; existing in the imagination only
▷ **unreality** *NOUN*

unreasonable *ADJECTIVE* **1** not reasonable **2** excessive or unjust
▷ **unreasonably** *ADVERB*

unrelieved *ADJECTIVE* without anything to vary it • *unrelieved gloom*

unreserved *ADJECTIVE* **1** not reserved **2** without restriction; complete • *unreserved loyalty*
▷ **unreservedly** *ADVERB*

unrest *NOUN* trouble or rioting caused because people are dissatisfied

unroll *VERB* **unrolls, unrolling, unrolled** open something that has been rolled up

Thesaurus

► unreliable, fickle, erratic, volatile, capricious, moody, unstable AN OPPOSITE IS predictable

unqualified *ADJECTIVE* **1** *Too many nursing lectures are given by unqualified lecturers.* ► untrained, inexperienced, incapable, incompetent, unsuitable, ineligible OPPOSITES ARE qualified, competent **2** *The experiment was an unqualified success.* ► absolute, unreserved, complete, outright, total, utter, unmitigated OPPOSITES ARE qualified, partial

unravel *VERB* **1** *He cut the climbing rope and started to unravel its strands.* ► disentangle, untangle, unwind, untwist, undo, separate AN OPPOSITE IS entangle **2** *the sequence of events that archaeologists attempt to unravel* ► resolve, sort out, solve, puzzle out, interpret, explain, elucidate, clarify

unreal *ADJECTIVE* *It is a curiously unreal state of affairs.* ► false, artificial, fake, sham, illusory, imaginary OPPOSITES ARE real, genuine

unrealistic *ADJECTIVE* *It would be unrealistic to think of removing road congestion entirely.* ► impractical, unreasonable, unworkable, fanciful, impracticable, over-ambitious, idealistic, impossible OPPOSITES ARE realistic, practical, pragmatic

unreasonable *ADJECTIVE* **1** *I knew I was being unreasonable.* ► unfair, unjust, unhelpful, uncooperative, obstructive OPPOSITES ARE reasonable, helpful, fair **2** *It was unreasonable of him to expect her to know the answer.* ► irrational, illogical, perverse, unwarranted, absurd OPPOSITES ARE reasonable, sensible **3** *They were making unreasonable demands.* ► excessive, immoderate, exorbitant, extortionate OPPOSITES ARE reasonable, moderate

unrecognizable *ADJECTIVE* *He's unrecognizable as the boy we once knew.* ► unidentifiable, unknowable, changed (from), altered (from) AN OPPOSITE IS recognizable

unrelated *ADJECTIVE* **1** *Two men had been charged after the match in unrelated incidents.* ► separate, distinct, unconnected **2** *He was assigned to a menial post unrelated to his abilities.* ► irrelevant, unconnected (with), dissimilar

unrelenting *ADJECTIVE* *Success came through unrelenting hard work.* ► constant, continuous, relentless, remorseless, persistent, unremitting, unflagging, merciless, ruthless AN OPPOSITE IS intermittent

unreliable *ADJECTIVE* **1** *The official figures are unreliable for gauging levels of unemployment.* ► inaccurate, misleading, deceptive, suspect, false, implausible, unconvincing OPPOSITES ARE reliable, accurate **2** *The more he defended himself, the more unreliable he sounded.* ► untrustworthy, irresponsible, undependable, changeable, inconsistent, unpredictable, unsound, unstable, fallible, fickle OPPOSITES ARE reliable, dependable

unrivalled *ADJECTIVE* *From the hotel you look out on unrivalled views of Venice.* ► incomparable, unequalled, unmatched, unparalleled, unsurpassed, inimitable, supreme, surpassing, matchless, peerless

unruffled *ADJECTIVE* *Matthew's unruffled manner had evidently soothed them.* ► calm, composed, collected, self-possessed, cool, poised, unperturbed, unflustered, unbothered, untroubled, (*more informal*) unflappable, (*more informal*) laid-back opposites are excited, anxious, upset

A B C D E F G H I J K L M N O P Q R S T U V W X Y Z

unruly ADJECTIVE difficult to control; disorderly
▷ **unruliness** NOUN

unsavoury ADJECTIVE unpleasant or disgusting

unscrew VERB **unscrews**, **unscrewing**, **unscrewed** unfasten something by twisting it or loosening screws

unscrupulous ADJECTIVE having no scruples about wrongdoing

unseemly ADJECTIVE not proper or suitable; indecent

unseen ADJECTIVE not seen; invisible

unseen NOUN **unseens** a passage for translation without previous preparation

unsettled ADJECTIVE **1** not settled or calm **2** (said about weather) likely to change

unshakeable ADJECTIVE not able to be shaken; firm

unshaven ADJECTIVE (said about a man) not recently shaved

unsightly ADJECTIVE not pleasant to look at; ugly
▷ **unsightliness** NOUN

unskilled ADJECTIVE not having or not needing special skill or training

unsolicited ADJECTIVE not asked for • *unsolicited advice*

unsound ADJECTIVE **1** nor reliable or firm **2** not healthy

unspeakable ADJECTIVE too bad to be described; very objectionable

unstable ADJECTIVE not stable; likely to change or become unbalanced

Thesaurus

unruly ADJECTIVE *A military unit had been stoned by a hungry and unruly mob.* ► disorderly, rowdy, wild, rebellious, disruptive, undisciplined, disobedient, boisterous, rough
OPPOSITES ARE orderly, disciplined

unsafe ADJECTIVE **1** *They agreed it would be unsafe to try to get a message to London.* ► dangerous, risky, hazardous, precarious, insecure
OPPOSITES ARE safe, harmless *The verdicts were unsafe because they were based entirely on confessions.* ► unreliable, unsound, insecure, doubtful, unstable OPPOSITES ARE safe, reliable, secure

unsatisfactory ADJECTIVE *It was an unsatisfactory conclusion to an otherwise useful visit.* ► disappointing, dissatisfying, unacceptable, unhappy, displeasing, inadequate, unworthy, poor, unsatisfying
AN OPPOSITE IS satisfactory

unscathed ADJECTIVE *Richard walked away unscathed from the wreckage of his car.*
► unharmed, unhurt, uninjured, safe, intact
OPPOSITES ARE injured, hurt

unscrupulous ADJECTIVE *He showed himself to be a cunning and unscrupulous politician.*
► dishonest, dishonourable, unprincipled, unethical, immoral, improper, self-interested, shameless OPPOSITES ARE honest, principled

unseen ADJECTIVE *The magician made the box disappear as though by unseen hands.* ► hidden, concealed, invisible, unnoticed, obscured, imperceptible OPPOSITES ARE visible, seen

unselfish ADJECTIVE *They were motivated by entirely unselfish motives.* ► kind, selfless, thoughtful, altruistic, disinterested, magnanimous, charitable, considerate, caring, generous, humanitarian, philanthropic
AN OPPOSITE IS selfish

unsettled ADJECTIVE **1** *Unsettled weather makes a long painting session impossible.* ► changeable, variable, changing, unreliable, unpredictable, unsteady OPPOSITES ARE settled, calm **2** *He looked anxious and unsettled.* ► disturbed, upset, troubled, agitated, restless, uneasy, flustered OPPOSITES ARE settled, composed

unsociable ADJECTIVE *He was grumpy and unsociable.* ► unfriendly, aloof, distant, taciturn, reclusive, uncommunicative, uncongenial OPPOSITES ARE sociable, friendly

unsound ADJECTIVE **1** *Many of the older buildings were structurally unsound.* ► unsafe, unstable, unsteady, flimsy, weak OPPOSITES ARE sound, strong **2** *These arguments are obviously unsound.*
► untenable, flawed, erroneous, defective, ill-founded, fallacious OPPOSITES ARE sound, cogent

unspeakable ADJECTIVE *The gang was guilty of the most unspeakable acts.* ► indescribable, awful, dreadful, appalling, repellent, frightful, unutterable, inexpressible, monstrous

unstable ADJECTIVE **1** *The buildings are highly unstable.* ► unsteady, shaky, rickety, wobbly, flimsy, insecure, unsafe, precarious **2** *an emotionally unstable young student named Karl*
► unbalanced, disturbed, insecure, deranged, demented **3** *The country has a history of unstable government.* ► unreliable, changeable, erratic, unsettled, volatile

unsteady ADJECTIVE **1** *She balanced her cup on an unsteady iron table. He smelled of alcohol and was unsteady on his feet.* ► shaky, rickety, unstable, wobbly, insecure, unsafe, precarious
OPPOSITES ARE steady, firm **2** *She took a deep unsteady breath.* ► irregular, uneven, changeable, erratic, inconstant, intermittent, variable OPPOSITES ARE steady, regular **3** *He read by the unsteady light of a candle.* ► flickering, fluctuating, wavering, quavering, quivering, trembling, tremulous AN OPPOSITE IS steady

unstuck *ADJECTIVE*
come unstuck **1** cease to stick **2** (*informal*) fail or go wrong

unsure *ADJECTIVE* not sure or confident

unthinkable *ADJECTIVE* too bad or too unlikely to be worth considering

unthinking *ADJECTIVE* thoughtless

untidy *ADJECTIVE* **untidier, untidiest** not tidy
▷ **untidily** *ADVERB* **untidiness** *NOUN*

untie *VERB* **unties, untying, untied** undo something that has been tied

until *PREPOSITION, CONJUNCTION* up to a particular time or event [from an Old Norse word *und* = as far as, added to *till*]
USAGE See the note on **till**[1].

untold *ADJECTIVE* **1** not told **2** too much or too many to be counted • *untold wealth*

untruth *NOUN* **untruths** an untrue statement; a lie
▷ **untruthful** *ADJECTIVE* **untruthfully** *ADVERB*

unused *ADJECTIVE* **1** (un-yoozd) not yet used • *an unused stamp* **2** (un-yoost) not accustomed • *He is unused to eating meat.*

unusual *ADJECTIVE* not usual; strange or exceptional
▷ **unusually** *ADVERB*

unveil *VERB* **unveils, unveiling, unveiled** **1** remove a veil or covering from something **2** reveal

unwarranted *ADJECTIVE* not justified; uncalled for

Thesaurus

unsuccessful *ADJECTIVE He was the leader of an unsuccessful military coup against the previous government.* ► failed, abortive, fruitless, futile, ill-fated, vain, ineffective, ineffectual, unproductive, unsatisfactory, useless
OPPOSITES ARE successful, effective

unsuitable *ADJECTIVE I think the proposed new site is unsuitable.* ► inappropriate, unsuited, ill-suited, inapt, unsatisfactory, unfitting, unfit, out of keeping, ill-chosen, ill-judged, mistaken, inapposite OPPOSITES ARE suitable, appropriate

unsure *ADJECTIVE I was unsure of my welcome when I visited the cottage the next afternoon.*
► uncertain, doubtful, dubious, sceptical, suspicious, mistrustful, distrustful
AN OPPOSITE IS confident
unsure of yourself *She was still a little unsure of herself in formal society.* ► unconfident, hesitant, diffident, timid, timorous
OPPOSITES ARE sure of yourself, self-confident

unsympathetic *ADJECTIVE* **1** *The planning authority showed an unsympathetic attitude to applications for new homes.* ► uncaring, unconcerned, unresponsive, indifferent, insensitive, unfeeling, hostile, antagonistic
AN OPPOSITE IS sympathetic **2 unsympathetic to** *The new assembly was quite unsympathetic to these views.* ► opposed to, hostile to, unconcerned about, antagonistic towards, ill-disposed towards OPPOSITES ARE sympathetic to, understanding of

unsystematic *ADJECTIVE Their use of data was unsystematic.* ► disorganized, unmethodical, disorderly, haphazard, muddled, jumbled, unstructured, indiscriminate, inconsistent
AN OPPOSITE IS systematic

unthinkable *ADJECTIVE In a free society such a ban would be unthinkable.* ► inconceivable, unimaginable, unbelievable, undreamed of, incredible, absurd, preposterous, implausible
OPPOSITES ARE conceivable, plausible

untidy *ADJECTIVE* **1** *He staggered out of his untidy bedroom. The handwriting was untidy.*
► disorganized, messy, cluttered, muddled, disordered, chaotic OPPOSITES ARE tidy, orderly
2 *Her hair looked untidy.* ► dishevelled, scruffy, bedraggled, uncombed, ungroomed, unkempt, rumpled, shabby, tangled, tousled, uncared for OPPOSITES ARE tidy, neat

untie *VERB She began to untie the string around the box.* ► undo, loosen, unfasten, unknot, release, unbind, disentangle, free, untether
AN OPPOSITE IS tie up

untrue *ADJECTIVE The claims were completely untrue.* ► wrong, false, inaccurate, erroneous, incorrect, mistaken, unfounded, fallacious
OPPOSITES ARE true, correct

unusual *ADJECTIVE* **1** *The town had electric lighting, unusual in those days.* ► uncommon, rare, unfamiliar OPPOSITES ARE usual, common
2 *It was an unusual story.* ► strange, odd, curious, weird, queer, bizarre, peculiar, exceptional, unconventional
OPPOSITES ARE normal, conventional **3** *Vera was a woman of unusual quality.* ► remarkable, exceptional, extraordinary, untypical
AN OPPOSITE IS typical

unwanted *ADJECTIVE* **1** *Lila kept guard dogs to ward off unwanted visitors.* ► unwelcome, undesirable, undesired, unsolicited, uninvited, rejected OPPOSITES ARE welcome, wanted, desirable **2** *The ants will bring dead ants and unwanted rubbish from their nests.*
► superfluous, discarded, redundant, unused
OPPOSITES ARE needed, useful, wanted

unwary *ADJECTIVE Deep potholes can bring down an unwary rider and his horse.* ► careless, unthinking, inattentive, absent-minded, thoughtless, unguarded, incautious
OPPOSITES ARE wary, attentive

unwelcome *ADJECTIVE* **1** *As she went downstairs, an unwelcome voice reached her ears.*

unwell *ADJECTIVE* not in good health

unwholesome *ADJECTIVE* not wholesome

unwieldy *ADJECTIVE* awkward to move or control because of its size, shape, or weight
▷ **unwieldiness** *NOUN*

unwind *VERB* **unwinds, unwinding, unwound 1** unroll **2** (*informal*) relax after a time of work or strain

unwise *ADJECTIVE* not wise; foolish
▷ **unwisely** *ADVERB*

unworthy *ADJECTIVE* not worthy or deserving

unwrap *VERB* **unwraps, unwrapping, unwrapped** open something that is wrapped

up *ADVERB* **1** to or in a higher place or position or level • *Prices have gone up.* **2** so as to be upright • *Stand up* **3** out of bed • *It's time to get up.* **4** completely • *Eat up your carrots.* **5** finished • *Your time is up.* **6** (*informal*) happening • *Something is up.*
up against 1 close to **2** (*informal*) faced with difficulties, dangers, etc.
ups and downs alternate good and bad luck
up to 1 until **2** busy with or doing something • *What are you up to?* **3** capable of • *I don't think I'm up to it.* **4** needed from • *It's up to us to help her.*
up to date 1 modern or fashionable **2** giving recent information etc.
USAGE Use hyphens when this is used as an adjective before a noun, e.g. *up-to-date information* (but *The information is up to date*).

up *PREPOSITION* upwards through or along or into • *Water came up the pipes.* [from Old English]

upbringing *NOUN* the way someone is trained during childhood

update *VERB* **updates, updating, updated** bring a thing up to date
▷ **update** *NOUN*

upgrade *VERB* **upgrades, upgrading, upgraded** improve a machine by installing new or better parts in it
▷ **upgrade** *NOUN*

upheaval *NOUN* **upheavals** a sudden violent change or disturbance

uphill *ADVERB* up a slope

uphill *ADJECTIVE* **1** going up a slope **2** difficult • *It was an uphill struggle.*

uphold *VERB* **upholds, upholding, upheld** support or maintain a decision or belief etc.

upholster *VERB* **upholsters, upholstering, upholstered** put a soft padded covering on furniture
▷ **upholstery** *NOUN*

upkeep *NOUN* keeping something in good condition; the cost of this

uplifting *ADJECTIVE* making you feel more cheerful

upon *PREPOSITION* on

Thesaurus

► disagreeable, unacceptable, undesirable, unwanted AN OPPOSITE IS welcome **2** *He had been made to feel unwelcome.* ► unwanted, unpopular, excluded, spurned, uninvited

unwell *ADJECTIVE She told the ambulance service she was feeling unwell.* ► ill, sick, poorly, indisposed, out of sorts, under the weather OPPOSITES ARE well, in good health

unwieldy *ADJECTIVE He would also need to transport some unwieldy equipment.* ► awkward, cumbersome, clumsy, bulky, unmanageable, ungainly, heavy, massive OPPOSITES ARE manageable, handy

unwilling *ADJECTIVE* **1** *He called together his group of unwilling helpers.* ► unenthusiastic, grudging, reluctant, uncooperative, half-hearted, hesitant OPPOSITES ARE willing, keen **2** *A spokesman was unwilling to give a precise date.* ► reluctant, disinclined, averse, loath OPPOSITES ARE willing, ready

unwind *VERB* **1** *Kittie unwound balls of pink and blue wool.* ► unroll, unreel, unravel, untwist, undo, uncoil, untwine **2** *He found the farm a place to unwind and let himself go.* ► relax, ease up, loosen up

unwise *ADJECTIVE You would be unwise to ignore the warning signs.* ► foolish, stupid, silly, ill-advised, crazy, mad, insane, (*more informal*) daft OPPOSITES ARE wise, sensible

unworthy *ADJECTIVE* **1** *His was an unworthy remark.* ► shameful, discreditable, dishonourable, undeserving, unsuitable, despicable, disreputable, ignoble, inappropriate AN OPPOSITE IS worthy **2** *Such claims are unworthy of consideration.* ► undeserving, unfit (for), ineligible (for) OPPOSITES ARE worthy, deserving

update *VERB You should continually update your information.* ► review, amend, upgrade, bring up to date, correct, revise, modernize

upgrade *VERB You can upgrade our system free of charge.* ► improve, enhance, update, make better, renovate, expand

upheaval *NOUN Further changes could be made without major upheaval.* ► disruption, commotion, disturbance, confusion, disorder, turmoil

uphill *ADJECTIVE We are all facing an uphill struggle.* ► hard, arduous, strenuous, taxing, tough, difficult, exhausting, gruelling, laborious, stiff AN OPPOSITE IS easy

upper *ADJECTIVE* higher in place or rank etc.

upper class *NOUN* **upper classes** the highest class in society, especially the aristocracy ▷ **upper-class** *ADJECTIVE*

uppermost *ADJECTIVE* highest

uppermost *ADVERB* on or to the top or the highest place • *Keep the painted side uppermost.*

upright *ADJECTIVE* **1** vertical or erect **2** strictly honest or honourable

upright *NOUN* **uprights** a post or rod etc. placed upright, especially as a support

uprising *NOUN* **uprisings** a rebellion or revolt

uproar *NOUN* an outburst of noise or excitement or anger

uproot *VERB* **uproots, uprooting, uprooted** **1** remove a plant and its roots from the ground **2** make someone leave the place where he or she has lived for a long time

upset *VERB* **upsets, upsetting, upset** **1** overturn; knock something over **2** make a person unhappy or distressed **3** disturb the normal working of something; disrupt • *This has really upset my plans.*

upset *ADJECTIVE* **1** unhappy or distressed **2** slightly ill • *an upset stomach*

upset *NOUN* **upsets** **1** a slight illness • *a stomach upset* **2** an unexpected result or setback • *There has been a major upset in the quarter-finals.*

upshot *NOUN* **upshots** the eventual outcome

upside down *ADVERB, ADJECTIVE* **1** with the upper part underneath instead of on top **2** in great disorder; very untidy • *Everything had been turned upside down.*

upstairs *ADVERB, ADJECTIVE* to or on a higher floor

upstart *NOUN* **upstarts** a person who has risen suddenly to a high position, especially one who then behaves arrogantly

uptake *NOUN*
quick on the uptake quick to understand
slow on the uptake slow to understand

uptight *ADJECTIVE* (*informal*) tense and nervous or annoyed

Thesaurus

upper *ADJECTIVE* *There are lifts to the upper floors of the building.* ► higher, upstairs, raised, elevated, superior

upright *ADJECTIVE* **1** *Crude figures are incised on upright stones.* ► perpendicular, vertical, erect **2** *upright Victorians with a strong sense of family pride* ► honourable, honest, respectable, reputable, righteous, upstanding, moral, principled, virtuous, trustworthy OPPOSITES ARE dishonourable, corrupt

uprising *NOUN* *The uprising was soon suppressed by the army.* ► rebellion, revolt, rising, insurrection, insurgence, revolution, mutiny usage You use *mutiny* about members of the armed forces.

uproar *NOUN* **1** *There was an uproar when the council refused to hear the delegation.* ► outcry, clamour, protest, furore, rumpus **2** *They found the place in uproar.* ► turmoil, confusion, disorder, pandemonium, mayhem, commotion

uproot *VERB* **1** *He always imagined himself as some great monster uprooting trees.* ► pull up, tear up, rip out, root out, weed out, remove, destroy, (*more formal*) extirpate AN OPPOSITE IS plant **2** *Building a dam would uproot over a million people.* ► displace, disrupt, remove

upset *VERB* **1** *I would never want to upset anyone.* ► distress, trouble, agitate, disturb, unsettle, disquiet, disconcert, unnerve, dismay, grieve, perturb, fluster, confuse OPPOSITES ARE reassure, put at ease **2** *Grazing sheep is prohibited so as not to upset the natural balance.* ► disrupt, disturb, interfere with, affect, throw out, ruin OPPOSITES ARE maintain, restore **3** *He upset a pot of soup.* ► tip over, knock over, spill, overturn

upset *NOUN* *The youngsters put the upset behind them.* ► distress, worry, trouble, upheaval, bother, anxiety

upset *ADJECTIVE* **1** *She was upset about missing all the excitement.* ► distressed, dismayed, disturbed, troubled, unsettled, disconcerted, worried, anxious, grieved **2** *He rang in to say he had an upset stomach.* ► queasy, disordered, (*more informal*) gippy

upside-down *ADJECTIVE* **1** *I could read the writing upside-down on his desk.* ► the wrong way up, inverted, topsy-turvy, upturned OPPOSITES ARE upright, the right way up **2** *Somebody broke in and turned the place upside-down. It is traumatic having one's life turned upside-down like this.* ► into disarray, into chaos, into a muddle, untidy, chaotic AN OPPOSITE IS tidy

uptight *ADJECTIVE* (*informal*) *When Ian gets uptight it can affect his game.* ► tense, anxious, nervous, edgy, on edge, strained, stressed, agitated, apprehensive, jittery, fidgety, ill at ease, jumpy OPPOSITES ARE calm, relaxed

up-to-date *ADJECTIVE* **1** *None of the disks contained up-to-date programs.* ► current, latest, recent, new, modern, present-day, advanced AN OPPOSITE IS out-of-date **2** *Use the Internet to keep yourself up to date on this topic.* ► informed (about), in touch (with), conversant (with), (*more informal*) up to speed AN OPPOSITE IS uninformed

A B C D E F G H I J K L M N O P Q R S T U V W X Y Z

upward *ADJECTIVE, ADVERB* going towards what is higher
▷ **upwards** *ADVERB*

uranium *NOUN* a heavy radioactive grey metal used as a source of nuclear energy [named after the planet Uranus]

urban *ADJECTIVE* to do with a town or city [from Latin *urbis* = of a city]

urchin *NOUN* **urchins 1** a poorly dressed or mischievous boy **2** a sea urchin [via early French from Latin *hericius* = hedgehog]

urge *VERB* **urges, urging, urged 1** try to persuade a person to do something **2** drive people or animals onward **3** recommend or advise

urge *NOUN* **urges** a strong desire or wish

urgent *ADJECTIVE* needing to be done or dealt with immediately
▷ **urgently** *ADVERB* **urgency** *NOUN*

urinate (yoor- in- ayt) *VERB* **urinates, urinating, urinated** pass urine out of your body
▷ **urination** *NOUN*

urine (yoor- in) *NOUN* waste liquid that collects in the bladder and is passed out of the body
▷ **urinary** *ADJECTIVE*

urn *NOUN* **urns 1** a large metal container with a tap, in which water is heated **2** a container shaped like a vase, usually with a foot, especially a container for holding the ashes of a cremated person

US *ABBREVIATION* United States (said about America)

us *PRONOUN* the form of **we** used when it is the object of a verb or after a preposition

USA *ABBREVIATION* United States of America

use (yooz) *VERB* **uses, using, used** perform an action or job with something • *Use soap for washing.*
▷ **user** *NOUN*
used to 1 was or were in the habit of doing • *We used to go by train.* **2** accustomed to or familiar with • *I'm used to his strange behaviour.*
use up use all of something

use (yooss) *NOUN* **uses 1** the action of using something; being used • *the use of computers in schools* **2** the purpose for which something is used • *Can you find a use for this crate?* **3** the quality of being useful • *These scissors are no use at all.* [via early French from Latin *uti*]

Thesaurus

urban *ADJECTIVE* *greenfield sites on the edge of urban areas* ► built-up, town, city, densely populated, metropolitan, suburban, municipal

urge *VERB* **1** *We would urge people to be aware and alert with fireworks.* ► encourage, entreat, exhort, advise, counsel, appeal to, entreat, beg, press, plead with, beseech, implore, recommend OPPOSITES ARE deter, discourage **2** *The working group urged caution in implementing any changes.* ► advise, recommend, counsel, advocate, suggest **3** *He urged his crew on through the mountainous waves.* ► drive, spur, press, force, compel, impel, propel, push

urge *NOUN* *The urge to give him a hug was almost impossible to resist.* ► desire, wish, need, impulse, inclination, eagerness, compulsion, craving, fancy, instinct, longing, yearning, (*more informal*) itch, (*more informal*) yen

urgent *ADJECTIVE* **1** *The buildings are in urgent need of renovation.* ► immediate, pressing, acute, grave, dire, desperate, critical, serious, essential, drastic, extreme, instant, top-priority **2** *He was roused from sleep by the urgent calls of his mother.* ► insistent, persistent, earnest, determined, eager, pleading
AN OPPOSITE IS casual

usable *ADJECTIVE* **1** *a thousand square metres of usable floor space* ► functional, working, available, practical, serviceable, fit for use, functioning, operating, operational
AN OPPOSITE IS unusable. **2** *The ticket is usable at all the country's museums and galleries.*
► valid, acceptable, current
AN OPPOSITE IS invalid

use *NOUN* **1** *What's the use of arguing?* ► point, advantage, purpose, benefit, value, sense, usefulness, reason (for) **2** *There isn't much use for mechanical calculators any more.* ► need, call, demand, necessity, reason, justification **3** *There was trial and error in the use of video equipment.* ► utilization, employment, operation, application, usage **4** *People have to make the best use of their time.* ► application, utilization, employment, exercise

use *VERB* **1** *They use the garden like an extra room.* ► utilize, make use of, employ, avail yourself of, put to use **2** *He learned to use a word processor.* ► work, operate, utilize, handle, manage, make use of **3** *You will need to use all your judgement.* ► exercise, apply, employ, draw on, make use of, implement **4** *How much milk did you use?* ► use up, consume, exhaust, waste
to use up *By now Billy had used up all his money.* ► spend, get through, exhaust, deplete, squander, consume USAGE You use *squander* when you are talking about wasting something

used *ADJECTIVE* not new; second-hand • *used cars*

useful *ADJECTIVE* able to be used a lot or to do something that needs doing
▷ **usefully** *ADVERB* **usefulness** *NOUN*

useless *ADJECTIVE* not useful; producing no effect • *Their efforts were useless.*
▷ **uselessly** *ADVERB* **uselessness** *NOUN*

user-friendly *ADJECTIVE* designed to be easy to use

usher *NOUN* **ushers** a person who shows people to their seats in a cinema, theatre, or church

usher *VERB* **ushers, ushering, ushered** lead someone in or out; escort someone as an usher [via early French from Latin *ostiarius* = doorkeeper]

usherette *NOUN* **usherettes** a woman who shows people to their seats in a cinema or theatre

usual *ADJECTIVE* such as happens or is done or used etc. always or most of the time
▷ **usually** *ADVERB*

utensil (yoo- **ten**- sil) *NOUN* **utensils** a tool, device, or container, especially one for use in the house • *cooking utensils*

utilitarian *ADJECTIVE* designed to be useful rather than decorative or luxurious; practical

utility *NOUN* **utilities 1** usefulness **2** an organization that supplies water, gas, electricity, etc. to the community

utilize *VERB* **utilizes, utilizing, utilized** use; find a use for something
▷ **utilization** *NOUN*

utmost *ADJECTIVE* extreme or greatest • *Look after it with the utmost care.*
▷ **utmost** *NOUN*
do your utmost do the most that you are able to

Utopia (yoo- **toh**- pee- a) *NOUN* **Utopias** an imaginary place or state of things where everything is perfect
▷ **Utopian** *ADJECTIVE*

utter[1] *VERB* **utters, uttering, uttered** say or speak; make a sound with your mouth
▷ **utterance** *NOUN*
[from early Dutch]

utter[2] *ADJECTIVE* complete or absolute • *utter misery*
▷ **utterly** *ADVERB*
[from Old English *uttra* = outer]

uttermost *ADJECTIVE, NOUN* utmost

U-turn *NOUN* **U-turns 1** a U-shaped turn made in a vehicle so that it then travels in the opposite direction **2** a complete change of policy

Thesaurus

or using it extravagantly. You use *consume* when you are talking about food.
used to *He was used to being woken up in the middle of the night.* i accustomed to, familiar with, in the habit of, no stranger to

used *ADJECTIVE* *They always bought used cars.*
► second-hand, pre-owned, nearly new, old
OPPOSITES ARE unused, new

useful *ADJECTIVE* **1** *These specialists can offer useful advice and practical support.* ► helpful, beneficial, worthwhile, valuable, profitable, advantageous, positive, constructive, good, invaluable OPPOSITES ARE useless, unhelpful **2** *This is a useful tool for working in tight spaces.* ► handy, practical, convenient, effective, efficient, powerful, productive, utilitarian OPPOSITES ARE useless, awkward **3** *They had some useful players.* ► skilful, talented, competent, capable, proficient, effective, successful OPPOSITES ARE useless, incompetent

useless *ADJECTIVE* **1** *I'm full of useless bits of knowledge like that. Further inquiries would be useless.* ► worthless, pointless, futile, fruitless, vain, hopeless, unavailing, unprofitable, unsuccessful OPPOSITES ARE useful, helpful, practical **2** *It was a useless suggestion.* ► impractical, unusable, unworkable, ineffective, hopeless, (*more informal*) dud OPPOSITES ARE useful, positive **3** *She's useless at spelling.* ► bad, inept, no good, incompetent, ineffective, untalented, incapable (of)
OPPOSITES ARE useful, competent

usual *ADJECTIVE* *Today he didn't take his usual route home.* ► normal, customary, habitual, regular, routine, typical, familiar, accustomed, conventional, traditional, standard, orthodox
OPPOSITES ARE unusual, exceptional

usually *ADVERB* *Usually he lingered by the stream to throw in stones.* ► normally, generally, habitually, as a rule, customarily, routinely, regularly, often OPPOSITES ARE exceptionally, seldom, rarely

utter *ADJECTIVE* *Amy stared at him in utter disbelief.* ► absolute, complete, total, sheer, positive, thorough, outright, downright, out-and-out, unmitigated

utter *VERB* *They were all too stunned to utter a word.* ► say, speak, express, voice, articulate, enunciate

utterly *ADVERB* *The whole exercise seems utterly pointless.* ► absolutely, completely, totally, perfectly, quite, unquestionably, unreservedly

U-turn *NOUN* *It had been the most dramatic U-turn of her political career.* ► change of mind, reversal of policy, volte-face, about-face, about-turn, shift

Vv

vacant *ADJECTIVE* **1** empty; not filled or occupied • *a vacant seat* • *a vacant post* **2** without expression; blank • *a vacant stare*
▷ **vacantly** *ADVERB* **vacancy** *NOUN*
[from Latin *vacans* = being empty]

vacation (vak- ay- shun) *NOUN* **vacations** **1** a holiday, especially between the terms at a university **2** vacating a place etc.

vaccinate (vak- sin- ayt) *VERB* **vaccinates, vaccinating, vaccinated** inoculate someone with a vaccine
▷ **vaccination** *NOUN*

vaccine (vak- seen) *NOUN* **vaccines** a substance used to give someone immunity against a disease [from Latin *vacca* = cow (because serum from cows was used to protect people from the disease smallpox)]

vacuum *NOUN* **vacuums** **1** a completely empty space; a space without any air in it **2** (*informal*) a vacuum cleaner

vacuum *VERB* **vacuums, vacuuming, vacuumed** to clean a floor with a vacuum cleaner

vacuum cleaner *NOUN* **vacuum cleaners** an electrical device that sucks up dust and dirt etc.

vagabond *NOUN* **vagabonds** a person with no settled home or regular work; a vagrant

vagina (va- jy- na) *NOUN* **vaginas** the passage that leads from the vulva to the womb

vagrant (vay- grant) *NOUN* **vagrants** a person with no settled home or regular work; a tramp
▷ **vagrancy** *NOUN*

vague *ADJECTIVE* **1** not definite or clear **2** not thinking clearly or precisely
▷ **vaguely** *ADVERB* **vagueness** *NOUN*

vain *ADJECTIVE* **1** conceited, especially about your appearance **2** useless • *They made vain attempts to save her.*
▷ **vainly** *ADVERB*
in vain with no result; uselessly
USAGE Do not confuse with **vane** or **vein**.

valency *NOUN* **valencies** (in science) the power of an atom to combine with other atoms, measured by the number of hydrogen atoms it is capable of combining with

valentine *NOUN* **valentines** **1** a card sent on St Valentine's day (14 February) to someone you are fond of **2** the person you send this card to

valiant *ADJECTIVE* brave or courageous
▷ **valiantly** *ADVERB*

valid *ADJECTIVE* **1** legally able to be used or accepted • *a valid passport* **2** (said about reasoning) sound and logical
▷ **validity** *NOUN*

valley *NOUN* **valleys** **1** a long low area between hills **2** an area through which a river flows • *the Nile valley*

Thesaurus

vacant *ADJECTIVE* **1** *There is a plan to build offices on a vacant site in the city centre.* ► unused, unoccupied, unfilled, empty, bare, blank, clear, free, available AN OPPOSITE IS occupied **2** *Guns and ammunition were found in a planned search of a vacant house.* ► empty, unoccupied, deserted AN OPPOSITE IS occupied **3** *She maintained a vacant expression.* ► blank, expressionless, deadpan, absent-minded, vacuous, abstracted, inattentive, dreamy, far away OPPOSITES ARE attentive, alert

vacate *VERB* *They must vacate the premises by the end of the month.* ► leave, evacuate, quit, withdraw from, abandon, depart from, give up AN OPPOSITE IS occupy

vacation *NOUN* *Although I'm officially on vacation, I'm actually working.* ► holiday, leave, time off

vague *ADJECTIVE* **1** *He was full of vague promises.* ► indefinite, imprecise, inexact, unspecific, ill-defined, generalized OPPOSITES ARE specific, definite **2** *Vague shapes could be made out in the distance.* ► hazy, unclear, indistinct, indefinite, blurred OPPOSITES ARE distinct, clear **3** *He always seemed vague about money.* ► uncertain, unclear, unsure, confused, indecisive, uninformed OPPOSITES ARE certain, informed **4** *Our plans are fairly vague at this stage.* ► unsettled, uncertain, inexact, open, unsure, indefinite OPPOSITES ARE firm, definite

vain *ADJECTIVE* **1** *They are vain and ostentatious by nature.* ► conceited, arrogant, self-satisfied, self-important, boastful, egotistical AN OPPOSITE IS modest **2** *Dr Neil made vain attempts to stop the bleeding.* ► unsuccessful, ineffective, futile, abortive, fruitless, unavailing OPPOSITES ARE successful, effective

valid *ADJECTIVE* **1** *This may be a valid conclusion.* ► legitimate, reasonable, rational, sound, cogent, convincing, acceptable OPPOSITES ARE invalid, spurious **2** *Make sure you have a valid passport and a visa if necessary.* ► current, up-to-date, legal, certified, approved, authorized, official, suitable, bona fide, genuine AN OPPOSITE IS invalid

valley *NOUN* *Pupils will be taught in the school across the valley.* ► dale, glen, dell, vale, hollow, gorge, gulch

valour *NOUN* *The medals are awarded for acts of valour.* ► bravery, courage, daring, gallantry, heroism AN OPPOSITE IS cowardice

valuable *ADJECTIVE* worth a lot of money; of great value
▷ **valuably** *ADVERB*

valuables *PLURAL NOUN* valuable things

value *NOUN* **values** **1** the amount of money etc. that is considered to be the equivalent of something, or for which it can be exchanged **2** how useful or important something is • *They learned the value of regular exercise.* **3** (in mathematics) the number or quantity represented by a figure etc. • *What is the value of x?*

value *VERB* **values, valuing, valued** **1** think that something is valuable **2** estimate the value of a thing ▷ **valuation** *NOUN* **valuer** *NOUN*

valve *NOUN* **valves** **1** a device for controlling the flow of gas or liquid through a pipe or tube **2** a structure in the heart or in a blood vessel allowing blood to flow in one direction only **3** a device that controls the flow of electricity in old televisions, radios, etc. **4** each piece of the shell of oysters etc.
▷ **valvular** *ADJECTIVE*

vampire *NOUN* **vampires** a dead creature that is supposed to leave its grave at night and suck blood from living people [from Hungarian *vampir*, perhaps from a Turkish word *uber* = witch]

van *NOUN* **vans** **1** a covered vehicle for carrying goods **2** a railway carriage for luggage or goods, or for the use of the guard [short for **caravan**]

vandal *NOUN* **vandals** a person who deliberately breaks or damages things, especially public property
▷ **vandalism** *NOUN*
[named after the Vandals, a Germanic people who invaded the Roman Empire in the 5th century, destroying many books and works of art]

vandalize *VERB* **vandalizes, vandalizing, vandalized** damage things as a vandal

vane *NOUN* **vanes** **1** a weathervane **2** the blade of a propeller, sail of a windmill, or other device that acts on or is moved by wind or water [from Old English]
USAGE Do not confuse with **vain** or **vein.**

vanilla *NOUN* a flavouring obtained from the pods of a tropical plant [from Spanish *vainilla* = little pod]

vanish *VERB* **vanishes, vanishing, vanished** disappear completely

vanity *NOUN* conceit; being vain

vanquish *VERB* **vanquishes, vanquishing, vanquished** defeat thoroughly

vantage point *NOUN* **vantage points** a place from which you have a good view of scenery or something interesting [from Middle English *vantage* = advantage]

vaporize *VERB* **vaporizes, vaporizing, vaporized** change or be changed into vapour
▷ **vaporization** *NOUN* **vaporizer** *NOUN*

vapour *NOUN* **vapours** a visible gas to which some substances can be converted by heat; steam or mist

Thesaurus

valuable *ADJECTIVE* **1** *You need separate insurance cover for the more valuable jewellery.* ► costly, high-priced, expensive, precious, priceless, dear OPPOSITES ARE valueless, worthless **2** *The work provided them with valuable experience.* ► helpful, beneficial, advantageous, constructive, invaluable, positive, profitable, useful, valued, worthwhile, good
AN OPPOSITE IS worthless USAGE Note that *invaluable* is not an opposite of *valuable*, but means 'too great to be valued', i.e. 'extremely valuable', as in *an invaluable member of the team.*

value *NOUN* **1** *Houses in the area have practically doubled in value.* ► price, cost, worth, market value **2** *The value of regular exercise cannot be overestimated.* ► importance, merit, benefit, advantage, significance, usefulness, use

value *VERB* **1** *The vineyard is valued at £160 million.* ► assess, evaluate, price, cost, estimate the value of, (*more informal*) put a figure on **2** *His honesty endeared him to many who valued his wise advice.* ► appreciate, prize, rate highly, esteem, hold in high regard, have a high opinion of, set store by
OPPOSITES ARE neglect, disregard

values *PLURAL NOUN* *Each generation has its special values.* ► principles, standards, morality, morals, moral code, code of behaviour

vanish *VERB* **1** *Maria had vanished into the garden.* ► disappear, leave, withdraw, clear off
OPPOSITES ARE appear, reappear **2** *All thoughts of her vanished in the excitement.* ► evaporate, melt away, dissolve, end, come to an end, dwindle, fade, go away, disperse, pass
OPPOSITES ARE materialize, endure

vanity *NOUN* *A divorce would hit her vanity and her pocket.* ► pride, self-regard, self-admiration, conceit, arrogance, egoism
AN OPPOSITE IS modesty

vapour *NOUN* *His breath formed a vapour on the air.* ► mist, haze, fog, smoke, steam, fumes, gas, miasma

variable *ADJECTIVE* likely to vary; changeable
▷ **variably** *ADVERB* **variability** *NOUN*

variable *NOUN* **variables** something that varies or can vary; a variable quantity

variant *ADJECTIVE* differing from something
• *'Gipsy' is a variant spelling of 'gypsy'.*
▷ **variant** *NOUN*

variation *NOUN* **variations** **1** varying; the amount by which something varies **2** a different form of something

varied *ADJECTIVE* of different sorts; full of variety

variegated (vair- ig- ay- tid) *ADJECTIVE* with patches of different colours
▷ **variegation** *NOUN*

variety *NOUN* **varieties** **1** a quantity of different kinds of things **2** the quality of not always being the same; variation **3** a particular kind of something • *There are several varieties of spaniel.* **4** an entertainment that includes short performances of various kinds

various *ADJECTIVE* **1** of several kinds; unlike one another • *for various reasons* **2** several • *We met various people.*
▷ **variously** *ADVERB*

varnish *NOUN* **varnishes** a liquid that dries to form a hard, shiny, clear coating

varnish *VERB* **varnishes, varnishing, varnished** coat something with varnish

vary *VERB* **varies, varying, varied** **1** make or become different; change **2** be different

vase *NOUN* **vases** an open, usually tall, container used for holding cut flowers or as an ornament

vast *ADJECTIVE* very great, especially in area • *a vast expanse of water*
▷ **vastly** *ADVERB* **vastness** *NOUN*

VAT *ABBREVIATION* value added tax; a tax on goods and services

vat *NOUN* **vats** a very large container for holding liquid

vault *VERB* **vaults, vaulting, vaulted** jump over something, especially while supporting yourself on your hands or with the help of a pole

vault *NOUN* **vaults** **1** a vaulting jump **2** an arched roof **3** an underground room used to store things **4** a room for storing money or valuables **5** a burial chamber

vaulted *ADJECTIVE* having an arched roof

vaunt *VERB* **vaunts, vaunting, vaunted** (*old use or poetical*) boast
▷ **vaunt** *NOUN*

VCR *ABBREVIATION* video cassette recorder

VDU *ABBREVIATION* visual display unit

veal *NOUN* calf's flesh used as food

vector *NOUN* **vectors** (in mathematics) a quantity that has size and direction, such as velocity (which is speed in a certain direction)
▷ **vectorial** *ADJECTIVE*
[from Latin, = carrier, traveller]

veer *VERB* **veers, veering, veered** change direction; swerve

vegetable *NOUN* **vegetables** a plant that can be used as food [from Latin *vegetare* = enliven, animate]

vegetarian *NOUN* **vegetarians** a person who does not eat meat
▷ **vegetarianism** *NOUN*

Thesaurus

variable *ADJECTIVE* *The photos are of variable quality.* ► changing, varying, changeable, fluctuating, irregular, inconsistent, unpredictable, vacillating, unstable, unsteady, temperamental OPPOSITES ARE constant, uniform

variation *NOUN* **1** *There was considerable regional variation in these findings.* ► diversity, deviation, diversification, disparity, inequality, difference, discrepancy **2** *Prices are subject to variation.* ► change, alteration, adjustment, modification

varied *ADJECTIVE* *There is a varied choice of restaurants and tavernas.* ► diverse, assorted, wide-ranging, miscellaneous, mixed, sundry, motley, (*more formal*) heterogeneous

variety *NOUN* **1** *It is hard work, but the variety makes it stimulating.* ► diversity, variation, diversification, change, many-sidedness, unpredictability **2** *one-day courses on a variety of cookery themes* ► assortment, array, miscellany, mixture, multiplicity, range, collection, medley **3** *The list offers sixteen varieties of drinking chocolate.* ► kind, sort, type, form, brand, category, class, strain, make, species, breed

various *ADJECTIVE* **1** *The job can be done in various ways.* ► different, differing, diverse, distinct, varying, varied, assorted, dissimilar, miscellaneous AN OPPOSITE IS similar **2** *An uneasy truce existed between the various political parties.* ► numerous, many, several, innumerable, countless, multifarious, sundry

vary *VERB* **1** *Prices vary enormously for group holidays.* ► differ, fluctuate, range, change, shift, go up and down, (*more formal*) oscillate OPPOSITES ARE be static, be fixed **2** *The routine never varies.* ► change, alter, differ, deviate, diverge, fluctuate **3** *You can vary the size of your pictures.* ► alter, adapt, adjust, modify, diversify AN OPPOSITE IS fix

vast *ADJECTIVE* **1** *The birds fly over vast distances.* ► huge, great, extensive, enormous, immense, colossal, tremendous OPPOSITES ARE small, short **2** *The vast majority of patients are elderly.* ► great, huge, large

vegetation *NOUN* **1** plants that are growing **2** vegetating

vehement (vee- im- ent) *ADJECTIVE* showing strong feeling • *a vehement refusal*
▷ **vehemently** *ADVERB* **vehemence** *NOUN*

vehicle *NOUN* **vehicles** a means of transporting people or goods, especially on land

veil *NOUN* **veils** a piece of thin material worn to cover the face or head
take the veil become a nun

veil *VERB* **veils, veiling, veiled 1** cover something with a veil **2** partially conceal something • *veiled threats*

vein *NOUN* **veins 1** any of the tubes that carry blood from all parts of the body to the heart COMPARE **artery 2** a line or streak on a leaf, rock, insect's wing, etc. **3** a long deposit of mineral or ore in the middle of a rock **4** a mood or manner • *She spoke in a serious vein.*
USAGE Do not confuse with **vain** or **vane**.

velocity *NOUN* **velocities** speed in a given direction

velvet *NOUN* a woven material with very short soft furry fibres on one side
▷ **velvety** *ADJECTIVE*

vendetta *NOUN* **vendettas** a long-lasting bitter quarrel; a feud [from Italian, from Latin *vindicta* = vengeance]

vending machine *NOUN* **vending machines** a slot machine from which you can obtain drinks, chocolate, cigarettes, etc.

veneer *NOUN* **veneers 1** a thin layer of good wood covering the surface of a cheaper wood in furniture etc. **2** an outward show of some good quality • *a veneer of politeness*

venerable *ADJECTIVE* worthy of respect or honour, especially because of great age

venerate *VERB* **venerates, venerating, venerated** honour with great respect or reverence
▷ **veneration** *NOUN*

venereal disease *NOUN* **venereal diseases** a disease passed on by sexual intercourse

vengeance *NOUN* revenge
with a vengeance with great intensity

venison *NOUN* deer's flesh as food

Venn diagram *NOUN* **Venn diagrams** (in mathematics) a diagram in which circles are used to show the relationships between different sets of things

venom *NOUN* **1** the poisonous fluid produced by snakes, scorpions, etc. **2** strong bitterness or spitefulness
▷ **venomous** *ADJECTIVE*

vent *NOUN* **vents** an opening in something, especially to let out smoke or gas etc.
give vent to express your feelings openly

vent *VERB* **vents, venting, vented 1** make a vent in something **2** give vent to feelings

ventilate *VERB* **ventilates, ventilating, ventilated** let air move freely in and out of a room etc.
▷ **ventilation** *NOUN* **ventilator** *NOUN*

ventriloquist *NOUN* **ventriloquists** an entertainer who makes his or her voice sound as if it comes from another source
▷ **ventriloquism** *NOUN*
[from Latin *venter* = abdomen + *loqui* = speak]

venture *NOUN* **ventures** something you decide to do that is risky

Thesaurus

vehement *ADJECTIVE We are quite vehement in our pursuit of safety procedures. Opposition to the whale hunt drew vehement criticism from the islanders.* ► fierce, passionate, forceful, impassioned, intense, ardent, eager, fervent, vigorous, violent, enthusiastic, animated, excited, heated, strong, powerful, urgent
OPPOSITES ARE mild, apathetic

vehicle *NOUN Vehicles are not allowed in the town centre.* ► motor vehicle, car, automobile, wheeled transport

vengeance *NOUN He swore vengeance when he was banished four years ago.* ► revenge, retribution, retaliation, reprisal

vengeful *ADJECTIVE He felt vengeful towards his attackers.* ► revengeful, unforgiving, spiteful, bitter, avenging, vindictive, rancorous
AN OPPOSITE IS forgiving

venom *NOUN* **1** *Snake venom is usually clear yellow.* ► poison, toxin **2** *She was told to leave with such venom she recoiled.* ► malice, malevolence, rancour, ill-will, acrimony, animosity, bitterness, vitriol, virulence, hatred

venomous *ADJECTIVE* **1** *The only mammals with venomous bites are certain moles and shrews.* ► poisonous, toxic, noxious, deadly
AN OPPOSITE IS harmless **2** *He wrote a venomous criticism of their work.* ► vicious, spiteful, malicious, malevolent, vindictive, baleful, vitriolic, rancorous AN OPPOSITE IS friendly

venture *NOUN This new venture holds great promise for the future.* ► enterprise, undertaking, project, scheme, endeavour, operation, adventure

venture *VERB* **1** *Harry ventured an opinion.* ► put forward, suggest, offer, dare, risk, chance **2** *We venture to ask you for your permission.* ► dare, presume, be so bold as to **3** *When darkness came he ventured out.* ► journey, set forth, proceed, dare to go, risk going

a b c d e f g h i j k l m n o p q r s t u v w x y z

venture *VERB* **ventures, venturing, ventured** dare or be bold enough to do or say something or to go somewhere • *We ventured out into the snow.*

venturesome *ADJECTIVE* ready to take risks; daring

veracity (ver- as- it- ee) *NOUN* truth
▷ **veracious** (ver- ay- shus) *ADJECTIVE*

veranda *NOUN* **verandas** a terrace with a roof along the side of a house [via Hindi from Portuguese *varanda* = railing, balcony]

verb *NOUN* **verbs** a word that shows what a person or thing is doing, e.g. *bring, came, sing, were* [from Latin *verbum* = word]

verbal *ADJECTIVE* **1** to do with or in words; spoken, not written • *a verbal statement* **2** to do with verbs
▷ **verbally** *ADVERB*

verdict *NOUN* **verdicts** a judgement or decision made after considering something, especially that made by a jury

verge *NOUN* **verges** a strip of grass along the edge of a road or path
on the verge of very nearly doing something • *I was on the verge of tears.*

verge *VERB* **verges, verging, verged**
verge on border on something; be close to something • *This puzzle verges on the impossible.*

veritable *ADJECTIVE* real; rightly named • *a veritable villain*
▷ **veritably** *ADVERB*

vermin *PLURAL NOUN* animals or insects that damage crops or food or carry disease, such as rats and fleas
▷ **verminous** *ADJECTIVE*

vernacular (ver- nak- yoo- ler) *NOUN* **vernaculars** the language of a country or district, as distinct from an official or formal language

versatile *ADJECTIVE* able to do or be used for many different things
▷ **versatility** *NOUN*

verse *NOUN* **verses 1** writing arranged in short lines, usually with a particular rhythm and often with rhymes; poetry **2** a group of lines forming a unit in a poem or song **3** each of the short numbered sections of a chapter in the Bible [via Old English from Latin *versus* = a line of writing]

version *NOUN* **versions 1** a particular person's account of something that happened **2** a translation • *modern versions of the Bible* **3** a special or different form of something • *the latest version of this car*

versus *PREPOSITION* against; competing with • *The final was Germany versus Brazil.*

vertebra *NOUN* **vertebrae** each of the bones that form the backbone

vertebrate *NOUN* **vertebrates** an animal that has a backbone (The opposite is **invertebrate**)

vertical *ADJECTIVE* at right angles to something horizontal; upright
▷ **vertically** *ADVERB*

vertigo *NOUN* a feeling of dizziness and loss of balance, especially when you are very high up

verve *NOUN* enthusiasm and liveliness

Thesaurus

verbal *ADJECTIVE A verbal exchange was recorded between two people.* ► spoken, oral, word-of-mouth, unwritten AN OPPOSITE IS written

verbose *ADJECTIVE Parts of the speech were repetitive and verbose.* ► wordy, loquacious, diffuse, effusive, garrulous, talkative, long-winded, rambling AN OPPOSITE IS succinct

verdict *NOUN The verdict was suicide, but many people thought he was murdered.* ► judgement, decision, finding, ruling, adjudication, assessment, conclusion, opinion

verge *NOUN* **1** *Cars were parked on the grass verge.* ► edge, bank, kerb, margin, border, roadside, shoulder, side, wayside **2** *The country was on the verge of bankruptcy.* ► brink, point, threshold

verge *VERB* **verge on** *By this time the urgency verged on desperation.* ► border on, tend towards, approach, come close to

verify *VERB There was no one around to verify what happened.* ► prove, support, confirm, substantiate, establish, uphold, show the truth of, validate, authenticate, corroborate, check out, ascertain AN OPPOSITE IS refute

versatile *ADJECTIVE* **1** *She was a gifted and versatile teacher.* ► adaptable, many-sided, all-round, flexible, resourceful, talented, skilful **2** *The property offers spacious and versatile accommodation.* ► flexible, adaptable, modifiable, all-purpose
AN OPPOSITE IS restricted

verse *NOUN a story written in verse* ► rhyme, lines, lyrics, metre, stanza

version *NOUN* **1** *Would you like to tell us your version of the story?* ► account, record, explanation, interpretation, rendering **2** *a new version of the machine* ► form, type, model, design

vertical *ADJECTIVE* **1** *Pull the lever back to its vertical position.* ► upright, perpendicular, standing, erect AN OPPOSITE IS horizontal **2** *The passageway ended with a vertical drop into darkness.* ► sheer, steep, precipitous

very *ADVERB* **1** to a great amount or intensity; extremely • *It was very cold.* **2** (used to emphasize something) • *on the very next day* • *the very last drop*

very *ADJECTIVE* **1** exact or actual • *It's the very thing we need.* **2** extreme • *at the very end*

vessel *NOUN* **vessels 1** a ship or boat **2** a container, especially for liquid **3** a tube carrying blood or other liquid in the body of an animal or plant

vest *NOUN* **vests** a piece of underwear covering the trunk of the body

vest *VERB* **vests, vesting, vested 1** give something as a right • *The power to make laws is vested in Parliament.* **2** (*old use*) clothe

vested interest *NOUN* **vested interests** a strong reason for wanting something to happen, usually because you will benefit from it

vet *NOUN* **vets** a person trained to give medical and surgical treatment to animals

vet *VERB* **vets, vetting, vetted** make a careful check of a person or thing, especially of someone's background before employing them

veteran *NOUN* **veterans** a person who has long experience, especially in the armed forces

veterinary (vet- rin- ree) *ADJECTIVE* to do with the medical and surgical treatment of animals • *a veterinary surgeon*

veto (vee- toh) *NOUN* **vetoes 1** a refusal to let something happen **2** the right to prohibit something

veto *VERB* **vetoes, vetoing, vetoed** refuse or prohibit something [from Latin, = I forbid]

vex *VERB* **vexes, vexing, vexed** annoy; cause somebody worry
▷ **vexation** *NOUN* **vexatious** *ADJECTIVE*

VHF *ABBREVIATION* very high frequency

via (vy- a) *PREPOSITION* through; by way of • *The train goes from London to Exeter via Bristol.* [from Latin, = by way of]

viable *ADJECTIVE* able to work or exist successfully • *a viable plan*
▷ **viability** *NOUN*

viaduct *NOUN* **viaducts** a long bridge, usually with many arches, carrying a road or railway over a valley or low ground [from Latin *via* = road + *ducere* = to lead]

vibrant *ADJECTIVE* full of energy; lively

vibrate *VERB* **vibrates, vibrating, vibrated 1** shake very quickly to and fro **2** make a throbbing sound
▷ **vibration** *NOUN*

Thesaurus

very *ADVERB He felt very ashamed.* ► extremely, highly, deeply, exceedingly, acutely, truly, (*more informal*) terribly AN OPPOSITE IS slightly

very *ADJECTIVE* **1** *The key on the floor was the very one he had lost the week before. Those were her very words.* ► actual, same, selfsame, identical, exact, precise **2** *The very thought of it made him tremble.* ► mere, sheer, simple

vessel *NOUN* **1** *Pour the liquid into a sterile vessel.* ► container, receptacle, flask, bottle, jar, jug, holder **2** *Small vessels were bobbing about in the harbour.* ► craft, boat, ship USAGE Note that *craft* can be singular or plural (e.g. *a small craft was bobbing about* or *small craft were bobbing about*).

vet *VERB Peter vetted all the outfits and knew exactly what would suit Tara.* ► inspect, examine, screen, assess, evaluate, appraise, scrutinize, investigate, check out

veteran *ADJECTIVE He handled it all like a veteran superstar.* ► established, seasoned, mature, hardened, master, expert

veto *NOUN He had in effect acquired a right of veto over all sales of land.* ► rejection, refusal, embargo, prohibition, ban, (*more informal*) thumbs down AN OPPOSITE IS approval

veto *VERB The government had vetoed the proposal in late July.* ► reject, turn down, overrule, rule out, throw out, disallow, refuse, dismiss, ban, bar, blackball, forbid, prohibit, say no to, vote against AN OPPOSITE IS approve

vex *VERB His remarks had vexed her deeply.* ► annoy, irritate, displease, anger, infuriate, enrage, exasperate, incense, madden, aggravate, nettle, antagonize, inflame, make angry, (*more informal*) needle, (*more informal*) rile, (*more informal*) bug, (*more informal*) rub up the wrong way OPPOSITES ARE please, gratify

vexed *ADJECTIVE* **1** *She was still vexed with me for bringing Frankie.* ► annoyed, irritated, angry, cross, displeased, peeved, infuriated, incensed, enraged, (*more informal*) miffed, (*more informal*) put out AN OPPOSITE IS pleased **2** *The note was about the vexed question of sexism.* ► controversial, difficult, contentious, disputed, thorny, knotty

vibrant *ADJECTIVE* **1** *Green plants provide splashes of vibrant colour.* ► bright, vivid, brilliant, intense, striking OPPOSITES ARE dull, pale **2** *She made the most of her cheerful and vibrant personality.* ► vivacious, spirited, dynamic, alert, alive, energetic, electric OPPOSITES ARE restrained, reserved

vibrate *VERB* **1** *The room was vibrating from the sounds of rock music.* ► reverberate, throb, pulsate, resonate, resound, thud, ring, boom **2** *The machinery began to vibrate alarmingly.*

vicar *NOUN* **vicars** a member of the Church of England clergy who is in charge of a parish

vice[1] *NOUN* **vices** **1** evil or wickedness **2** an evil or bad habit; a bad fault

vice[2] *NOUN* **vices** a device for gripping something and holding it firmly while you work on it

vice versa *ADVERB* the other way round • *Which do you prefer-blue spots on a yellow background or vice versa?* [from Latin, = the position being turned round]

vicinity *NOUN* the area near or round a place • *Is there a newsagent in the vicinity?* [from Latin *vicinus* = neighbouring, a neighbour]

vicious *ADJECTIVE* **1** cruel and aggressive **2** severe or violent
▷ **viciously** *ADVERB* **viciousness** *NOUN*

vicious circle *NOUN* **vicious circles** a situation in which a problem produces an effect which in turn makes the problem worse

victim *NOUN* **victims** someone who is injured, killed, robbed, etc.

victimize *VERB* **victimizes, victimizing, victimized** single someone out for cruel or unfair treatment
▷ **victimization** *NOUN*

victor *NOUN* **victors** the winner

Victorian *ADJECTIVE* belonging to the time of Queen Victoria (1837-1901)
▷ **Victorian** *NOUN*

victory *NOUN* **victories** success won against an opponent in a battle, contest, or game
▷ **victorious** *ADJECTIVE*

video *NOUN* **videos** **1** the recording on tape of pictures and sound **2** a video recorder or cassette **3** a television programme or a film recorded on a video cassette

video *VERB* **videos, videoing, videoed** record something on videotape [from Latin, = I see]

video cassette recorder *NOUN* **video cassette recorders** a device for recording television programmes on videotape and for playing video cassettes

videotape *NOUN* **videotapes** magnetic tape suitable for recording television programmes

vie *VERB* **vies, vying, vied** compete; carry on a rivalry • *vying with each other*

view *NOUN* **views** **1** what can be seen from one place, e.g. beautiful scenery **2** sight; range of vision • *The ship sailed into view.* **3** an opinion • *She has strong views about politics.*
in view of because of

Thesaurus

► tremble, shake, shudder, judder, quiver, oscillate, rattle, shiver, wobble, quake

vibration *NOUN* *The special smoke detector produces vibration as well as flashing light.*
► reverberation, oscillation, pulsation, throbbing, trembling, juddering, quivering, rattling, shaking, shivering, shuddering, tremor, wobbling

vice *NOUN* **1** *They are determined to put an end to vice and prostitution.* ► immorality, depravity, corruption, wickedness, wrongdoing, degeneracy, evil-doing, evil, sin, (*more formal*) venality, (*more formal*) iniquity
AN OPPOSITE IS virtue **2** *Cowardice isn't the worst vice.* ► failing, fault, weakness, shortcoming, bad habit, blemish, defect, deficiency, imperfection OPPOSITES ARE virtue, strength

vicinity *NOUN* *There are several castles and abbeys in the vicinity.* ► neighbourhood, area, district, locality, region, locale, environs, outskirts, proximity

vicious *ADJECTIVE* **1** *He was finally captured in the vicious street fighting in Berlin in 1945.* ► brutal, savage, fierce, ferocious, wild, barbaric
OPPOSITES ARE gentle, humane **2** *He hadn't the vicious streak that showed in his brother.* ► cruel, malicious, spiteful, malevolent, vindictive, sadistic, brutish, callous, heartless, cold-blooded, aggressive, pitiless, ruthless, merciless, inhuman, vile OPPOSITES ARE kind, benevolent

victim *NOUN* **1** *It's thought she was the victim of a random attack by a thief. He is the third victim of this tough new policy.* ► target, casualty, sufferer, injury, fatality, scapegoat USAGE You use *fatality* about someone who has died as a result of an incident. **2** *At their feet, a white-clad sacrificial victim, was the body.* ► offering, martyr, prey, sacrifice

victimize *VERB* *The company had been victimizing workers for reporting safety concerns.*
► discriminate against, persecute, intimidate, oppress, mistreat, harass, treat unfairly, bully, terrorize, torment, (*more informal*) pick on

victorious *ADJECTIVE* *He emerged victorious in the second round of voting.* ► triumphant, successful, first, top, winning, leading, prevailing, undefeated, unbeaten
OPPOSITES ARE defeated, unsuccessful

victory *NOUN* *Her well-deserved victory in this year's Olympics was a boost for the British team.*
► win, success, triumph, conquest, knockout, mastery, superiority, achievement, (*more informal*) walkover AN OPPOSITE IS defeat

view *NOUN* **1** *From the top floor you get a magnificent view across the city.* ► outlook, prospect, panorama, perspective, vista, scene, aspect, picture, landscape, scenery, spectacle **2** *She caught a brief view of her top half in the mirror.* ► look, sight, glance, peek, vision **3** *Luke came into view.* ► sight, vision, range of vision, perspective **4** *He declined to give any*

on view displayed for inspection
with a view to with the hope or intention of

view *VERB* **views, viewing, viewed 1** look at something **2** consider or regard • *He viewed us with suspicion.* ▷ **viewer** *NOUN*

viewpoint *NOUN* **viewpoints** an opinion or point of view

vigorous *ADJECTIVE* full of strength and energy
▷ **vigorously** *ADVERB*

Viking *NOUN* **Vikings** a Scandinavian trader and pirate in the 8th-10th centuries [from Old Norse]

vile *ADJECTIVE* **1** extremely disgusting **2** very bad or wicked
▷ **vilely** *ADVERB* **vileness** *NOUN*

villa *NOUN* **villas** a house, especially a holiday home abroad [from Latin, = country house]

village *NOUN* **villages** a group of houses and other buildings in a country district, smaller than a town and usually having a church
▷ **villager** *NOUN*
[from early French; related to **villa**]

villain *NOUN* **villains** a wicked person or a criminal
▷ **villainous** *ADJECTIVE* **villainy** *NOUN*

vindicate *VERB* **vindicates, vindicating, vindicated 1** clear a person of blame or suspicion **2** prove something to be true or worthwhile
▷ **vindication** *NOUN*

vine *NOUN* **vines** a climbing or trailing plant whose fruit is the grape

vinegar *NOUN* a sour liquid used to flavour food or in pickling

vintage *NOUN* **vintages 1** the harvest of a season's grapes; the wine made from this **2** the period from which something comes

vintage car *NOUN* **vintage cars** a car made between 1917 and 1930

viola (vee- oh- la) *NOUN* **violas** a musical instrument like a violin but slightly larger and with a lower pitch

violate *VERB* **violates, violating, violated 1** break a promise, law, or treaty etc. **2** treat a

Thesaurus

official view of the situation. ► opinion, viewpoint, point of view, belief, judgement, notion, perception, idea, thought, attitude, conviction
in view of *In view of the length of time since the incident, no action was taken.* ► because of, on account of, considering, as a result of, as a consequence of, owing to, due to

view *VERB* **1** *He set out at ten and viewed as many houses as possible. A drop from a pond, viewed through a microscope, swarms with tiny organisms.* ► look at, inspect, survey, examine, observe, behold, eye, scan, gaze at, stare at **2** *She viewed him with dislike.* ► regard, contemplate, consider, perceive, behold **3** *Some of the guests were viewing a television programme.* ► watch, look at, see

vigilant *ADJECTIVE* *Everyone should be vigilant and report anything of a suspicious nature.* ► watchful, observant, alert, attentive, awake, on the lookout, on your guard, on the watch, sharp-eyed, eagle-eyed, careful, wide-awake, (*more informal*) on your toes
AN OPPOSITE IS negligent

vigorous *ADJECTIVE* **1** *Regular vigorous exercise can help to reduce blood pressure.* ► strenuous, energetic, animated, brisk, full-blooded
AN OPPOSITE IS feeble **2** *The child is strong and vigorous.* ► healthy, in good health, energetic, vivacious, active, lively, lusty, virile, vital **3** *He made a vigorous case for controlling the money supply.* ► strong, spirited, forceful, effective, robust, energetic, dynamic, active

vigour *NOUN* **1** *Geoffrey supported his wife's cause with vigour.* ► energy, force, forcefulness, spirit, vitality, gusto, verve, animation, dynamism **2** *He recovered from the illness with renewed vigour.* ► energy, fitness, vitality, stamina, robustness, life, strength, health, resilience, potency

vile *ADJECTIVE* **1** *It's ironic that such a fine building should house so vile an organization.* ► wicked, evil, foul, contemptible, despicable, obnoxious, shameful, abhorrent, repellent, loathsome
AN OPPOSITE IS pleasant **2** *I drank three cups of vile, greyish coffee.* ► nasty, horrible, foul, unpleasant, disgusting, revolting, repulsive, repellent, dreadful, terrible
AN OPPOSITE IS pleasant **3** *The vile weather had emptied the streets.* ► unpleasant, bad, foul, disagreeable, inclement AN OPPOSITE IS fine

villain *NOUN* *Did not two of history's greatest villains come from beautiful surroundings?* ► wrongdoer, evil-doer, rogue, scoundrel, criminal, reprobate, (*more formal*) malefactor, (*more formal*) miscreant

vindicate *VERB* **1** *He left claiming that history would vindicate him.* ► clear, exonerate, absolve, acquit, excuse, endorse, support, rehabilitate OPPOSITES ARE blame, censure **2** *She was desperate to vindicate her decision to be an artist.* ► justify, uphold, defend, sustain, maintain, assert AN OPPOSITE IS compromise

violate *VERB* **1** *Uses of these weapons against civilian targets violate international law.* ► breach, break, contravene, infringe, transgress, flout, defy, disobey, disregard,

person or place with disrespect and violence
▷ **violation** *NOUN* **violator** *NOUN*

violence *NOUN* **1** physical force that does harm or damage **2** strength or intensity • *the violence of the storm*
▷ **violent** *ADJECTIVE* **violently** *ADVERB*

violet *NOUN* **violets** **1** a small plant with purple or blue flowers **2** purple

violin *NOUN* **violins** a musical instrument with four strings, played with a bow
▷ **violinist** *NOUN*
[from Italian *violino* = small viola]

viper *NOUN* **vipers** a small poisonous snake

virgin *NOUN* **virgins** a person, especially a girl or woman, who has never had sexual intercourse
▷ **virginal** *ADJECTIVE* **virginity** *NOUN*

virgin *ADJECTIVE* not yet touched or used • *virgin snow*

virtual *ADJECTIVE* being something in effect though not strictly in fact • *His silence was a virtual admission of guilt.*

virtually *ADVERB* nearly or almost

virtual reality *NOUN* a computer image or environment that is so realistic it appears to be real

virtue *NOUN* **virtues** **1** moral goodness, or a particular form of this • *Honesty is a virtue.* **2** a good quality or advantage • *Jamie's plan has the virtue of simplicity.*
▷ **virtuous** *ADJECTIVE* **virtuously** *ADVERB*
by virtue of because of

virtuoso (ver- tew- oh- soh) *NOUN* **virtuosos** or **virtuosi** a person with outstanding skill, especially in singing or playing music
▷ **virtuosity** *NOUN*
[from Italian, = skilful]

virus *NOUN* **viruses** **1** a very tiny living thing, smaller than a bacterium, that can cause disease **2** a disease caused by a virus **3** a hidden set of instructions in a computer program that is designed to destroy data

visa (vee- za) *NOUN* **visas** an official mark put on someone's passport by officials of a foreign country to show that the holder has permission to enter that country

viscount (vy- kownt) *NOUN* **viscounts** a nobleman ranking below an earl and above a baron
▷ **viscountess** *NOUN*

visibility *NOUN* the distance you can see clearly • *Visibility is down to 20 metres.*

visible *ADJECTIVE* able to be seen or noticed • *The ship was visible on the horizon.*
▷ **visibly** *ADVERB*
USAGE Do not confuse with **visual**.

vision *NOUN* **visions** **1** the ability to see; sight **2** something seen in a person's imagination or in a dream **3** foresight and wisdom in planning

Thesaurus

ignore AN OPPOSITE IS comply with **2** *Several of the royal tombs had been violated.* ► desecrate, defile, vandalize, deface **3** *I did not like having my privacy violated.* ► invade, disturb, encroach on, interfere with, abuse AN OPPOSITE IS respect **4** *He set out to trap and violate women.* ► rape, abuse, indecently assault, sexually assault, molest, interfere with

violation *NOUN* *the violation of human rights throughout the world* ► contravention, breach, infringement, flouting, defiance, transgression, offence (against)

violence *NOUN* **1** *A whole generation had been brought up in violence.* ► brutality, brute force, savagery, cruelty, barbarity, destructiveness **2** *The violence of the blow made him reel.* ► force, forcefulness, strength, power, might, ferocity

violent *ADJECTIVE* **1** *There were violent clashes between police and demonstrators.* ► brutal, vicious, rough, aggressive, forceful AN OPPOSITE IS mild **2** *Too often violent criminals do not get sent to prison as they should.* ► rough, brutal, wild, fierce, vicious, aggressive, bloodthirsty, headstrong AN OPPOSITE IS gentle **3** *He felt a rush of violent jealousy.* ► intense, extreme, acute, forceful, devastating AN OPPOSITE IS weak

virtually *ADVERB* *Once on, paint is virtually impossible to remove.* ► effectively, in effect, practically, as good as, almost

virtue *NOUN* **1** *the virtue of a simple life* ► goodness, righteousness, virtuousness, rectitude, integrity, honesty, dignity, uprightness, worthiness, decency, morality, honour, nobility, principle, rectitude AN OPPOSITE IS iniquity **2** *I can see no virtue in such an arrangement.* ► merit, advantage, benefit, point AN OPPOSITE IS disadvantage **3** *Punctuality is not one of her virtues.* ► strength, quality, good point, redeeming feature OPPOSITES ARE failing, weakness

virtuous *ADJECTIVE* *Sam's virtuous and superior tone was beginning to irritate him.* ► moral, righteous, upright, worthy, honourable, exemplary, high-minded, right-minded, high-principled OPPOSITES ARE wicked, sinful

visible *ADJECTIVE* *There is no visible pattern in the paper. Kim received the news without any visible signs of emotion.* ► noticeable, perceptible, discernible, obvious, apparent, conspicuous, recognizable, evident, manifest, clear, detectable, distinct AN OPPOSITE IS invisible

vision *NOUN* **1** *Symptoms include blurred vision and sensitivity to bright lights.* ► eyesight, sight, seeing **2** *The Great Society remained more a*

vocational *ADJECTIVE* teaching you the skills you need for a particular job or profession • *vocational training*

vodka *NOUN* **vodkas** a strong alcoholic drink very popular in Russia

vogue *NOUN* **vogues** the current fashion • *Very short hair for women seems to be the vogue.*
in vogue in fashion • *Stripy dresses are definitely in vogue.*

voice *NOUN* **voices** **1** sounds formed by the vocal cords and uttered by the mouth, especially in speaking, singing, etc. **2** the ability to speak or sing • *She has lost her voice.* **3** someone expressing a particular opinion about something • *Emma's the only dissenting voice.* **4** the right to express an opinion or desire • *I have no voice in this matter.* [via early French *vois* from Latin *vox*]

void *ADJECTIVE* **1** empty **2** having no legal validity

void *NOUN* **voids** an empty space or hole

volatile (vol- a- tyl) *ADJECTIVE* **1** evaporating quickly • *a volatile liquid* **2** changing quickly from one mood or interest to another
▷ **volatility** *NOUN*

volcano *NOUN* **volcanoes** a mountain or hill with an opening at the top from which lava, ashes, and hot gases from below the earth's crust are or have been thrown out
▷ **volcanic** *ADJECTIVE*

vole *NOUN* **voles** a small animal like a mouse [from Norwegian *vollmus* = field mouse]

volley *NOUN* **volleys** **1** a number of bullets or shells etc. fired at the same time **2** hitting back the ball in tennis etc. before it touches the ground

volley *VERB* **volleys, volleying, volleyed** send or hit something in a volley or volleys

volt *NOUN* **volts** a unit for measuring electric force

voltage *NOUN* **voltages** electric force measured in volts

volume *NOUN* **volumes** **1** the amount of space filled by something **2** an amount or quantity • *The volume of work has increased.* **3** the strength or power of sound **4** a book, especially one of a set [from Latin *volumen* = a roll (because ancient books were made in the form of rolled parchment)]

voluntary *ADJECTIVE* **1** done or doing something willingly, not because you are forced to do it **2** unpaid • *voluntary work*
▷ **voluntarily** *ADVERB*

voluntary *NOUN* **voluntaries** an organ solo, often improvised, played before or after a church service

volunteer *VERB* **volunteers, volunteering, volunteered** give or offer something of your own accord, without being asked or forced to

volunteer *NOUN* **volunteers** a person who volunteers to do something, e.g. to serve in the armed forces

vomit *VERB* **vomits, vomiting, vomited** bring up food etc. from the stomach and out through the mouth; be sick
▷ **vomit** *NOUN*

voodoo *NOUN* a form of witchcraft and magical rites, especially in the West Indies [from a West African language]

vote *VERB* **votes, voting, voted** show which person or thing you prefer by putting up your

Thesaurus

vogue *NOUN* *Small-scale farming is enjoying a new vogue.* ► fashion, mode, trend, style, craze, rage, taste
in vogue *Suddenly it was in vogue to have an all-over tan.* ► fashionable, in fashion, stylish, modish, smart, chic, (*more informal*) trendy, (*more informal*) all the rage, (*more informal*) cool, (*more informal*) hip

voice *NOUN* **1** *There was no emotion in his voice.* ► speaking, speech, utterance, tone, inflection **2** *They were able to have a voice in choosing the chairman.* ► opinion, view, say, input, vote

luntary *ADJECTIVE* **1** *Voluntary work tends to rry higher prestige than paid work.*
optional, unpaid, willing AN OPPOSITE IS paid *e pay cuts will be voluntary.* ► optional, etionary, unforced
TES ARE obligatory, compulsory **3** *Her had been a voluntary act.* ► deliberate, us, intentional, intended, wilful

AN OPPOSITE IS involuntary USAGE Note that *involuntary* is an opposite of *voluntary* only in the third meaning.

volunteer *VERB* *Having promised his help, he had better volunteer at least.* ► offer your services, present yourself, step forward, make an offer, propose yourself, show willing

vomit *VERB* *He rushed towards the drain before the urge to vomit overcame him.* ► be sick, regurgitate, retch, heave, bring up, spew up, (*more informal*) throw up, (*more informal*) puke

vote *NOUN* *People suspected the vote of being rigged.* ► ballot, poll, election, plebiscite, referendum, show of hands

vote *VERB* **1** *Less than a third of the electorate voted in the last election.* ► cast a vote, go to the polls, ballot **2** *I vote we play another round.* ► suggest, propose, recommend, move
vote for *You may vote for one candidate only.* ► choose, pick, select, opt for, nominate

things **4** a person or thing that is beautiful to see

visionary *ADJECTIVE* extremely imaginative or fanciful

visionary *NOUN* **visionaries** a person with extremely imaginative ideas and plans

visit *VERB* **visits, visiting, visited** **1** go to see a person or place **2** stay somewhere for a while
▷ **visitor** *NOUN*

visit *NOUN* **visits** **1** going to see a person or place **2** a short stay somewhere

vista *NOUN* **vistas** a pleasing view [from Italian, = view]

visual *ADJECTIVE* to do with or used in seeing; to do with sight
▷ **visually** *ADVERB*
USAGE Do not confuse with **visible**.

visual aid *NOUN* **visual aids** a picture, slide, film, etc. used as an aid in teaching

visual display unit *NOUN* **visual display units** a device that looks like a television screen and displays data being received from a computer or fed into it

visualize *VERB* **visualizes, visualizing, visualized** form a mental picture of something
▷ **visualization** *NOUN*

vital *ADJECTIVE* **1** connected with life; necessary for life to continue • *vital functions such as breathing* **2** essential; very important
▷ **vitally** *ADVERB*

vitality *NOUN* liveliness or energy

vitamin (vit- a- minvy- ta- min) *NOUN* **vitamins** any of a number of substances that are present in various foods and are essential to keep people and animals healthy

vivacious (viv- ay- shus) *ADJECTIVE* happy and lively
▷ **vivaciously** *ADVERB* **vivacity** *NOUN*

vivid *ADJECTIVE* **1** bright and strong or clear • *vivid colours* • *a vivid description* **2** active and lively • *her vivid imagination*
▷ **vividly** *ADVERB* **vividness** *NOUN*

vivisection *NOUN* doing surgical experiments on live animals

vixen *NOUN* **vixens** a female fox [from Old English]

vocabulary *NOUN* **vocabularies** **1** all the words used in a particular subject or language, or that an individual person uses **2** a list of words with their meanings

vocal cords *PLURAL NOUN* two strap-like membranes in the throat that can be made to vibrate and produce sounds

vocalist *NOUN* **vocalists** a singer, especially in a pop group

vocation *NOUN* **vocations** **1** a person's job or occupation **2** a strong desire to do a particular kind of work, or a feeling of being called by God to do something

Thesaurus

vision than a reality. ► ideal, fantasy, apparition, illusion, mirage, phantasm, daydream, delusion, ghost, hallucination, phantom, spectre **3** *The plan made sense but lacked vision.* ► foresight, farsightedness, insight, imagination

visit *NOUN* **1** *Mrs Curdle paid her final visit to the place.* ► call, stay **2** *It was their first visit to Rome.* ► trip, outing, excursion, day out

visit *VERB* **1** *He was ten years old when he first started visiting the old woman.* ► call on, come to see, make a visit to, pay a call on, stay with, descend on, (*more informal*) drop in on, go to see, (*more informal*) look up **2** *The chairman of the airline recently visited Moscow.* ► travel to, make a trip to, spend time in, stay in

visitor *NOUN* **1** *Edward was a frequent and welcome visitor.* ► guest, caller **2** *The site will attract visitors during the festival.* ► tourist, holidaymaker, sightseer, tripper, globetrotter

visualize *VERB* *I like to visualize the mood of the song and take it from there.* ► picture, imagine, envisage, conceive, dream up

vital *ADJECTIVE* **1** *It's vital to keep momentum going. The college is expected to play a vital role in promoting these languages.* ► essential, crucial, fundamental, imperative, important, necessary, indispensable
OPPOSITES ARE unimportant, inessential **2** *He was a vital force in British music.* ► dynamic, lively, energetic, vibrant, vigorous, vivacious, life-giving, invigorating, exuberant, sparkling, spirited, animated, sprightly, zestful
AN OPPOSITE IS lifeless

vitality *NOUN* *For all her vitality, Faye was only five feet four inches tall.* ► energy, vivacity, vigour, spirit, gusto, verve, dynamism, exuberance, zest, (*more informal*) go
AN OPPOSITE IS lethargy

vivid *ADJECTIVE* **1** *a bouquet with four vi[…] flowers* ► bright, brilliant, colourf[…] showy, striking, gaudy AN OPPO[…] **2** *Wilson's autobiography give[…] his experiences.* ► clear, gr[…] lively, powerful, evocati[…] imaginative, lifelike, r[…]
AN OPPOSITE IS lifele[…]

vocal *ADJECTIVE* **1** […]
► voiced, sp[…] *students were* […] *reform.* ► outsp[…] plain-spoken, cand[…]

hand, making a mark on a paper, etc.
▷ **voter** *NOUN*

vote *NOUN* **votes** **1** the action of voting **2** the right to vote

vouch *VERB* **vouches, vouching, vouched**
vouch for guarantee that something is true or certain • *I will vouch for his honesty.*

voucher *NOUN* **vouchers** a piece of paper that can be exchanged for certain goods or services; a receipt

vow *NOUN* **vows** a solemn promise, especially to God or a saint

vow *VERB* **vows, vowing, vowed** make a vow

vowel *NOUN* **vowels** any of the letters a, e, i, o, u, and sometimes y, which represent sounds in which breath comes out freely COMPARE **consonant**

voyage *NOUN* **voyages** a long journey on water or in space

voyage *VERB* **voyages, voyaging, voyaged** make a voyage
▷ **voyager** *NOUN*

VSO *ABBREVIATION* Voluntary Service Overseas

vulgar *ADJECTIVE* rude; without good manners
▷ **vulgarly** *ADVERB* **vulgarity** *NOUN*
[from Latin *vulgus* = the common or ordinary people]

vulnerable *ADJECTIVE* able to be hurt or harmed or attacked
▷ **vulnerability** *NOUN*
[from Latin *vulnus* = wound]

vulture *NOUN* **vultures** a large bird that feeds on dead animals

vulva *NOUN* **vulvas** the outer parts of the female genitals

vying *present participle of* **vie**

Thesaurus

vouch *VERB* **vouch for** *I can vouch for the accuracy of these figures.* ► guarantee, verify, affirm, attest to, testify to, corroborate, endorse, confirm, support, speak for

voucher *NOUN* *You get a wallet of vouchers to pay for the various parts of your holiday.* ► coupon, ticket, token, certificate

vow *NOUN* *The monks take a vow of silence.* ► pledge, oath, promise, commitment, avowal, assurance, guarantee, undertaking, word of honour

vow *VERB* *She vowed to do better.* ► promise, pledge, swear, take an oath, give an assurance, give your word, guarantee

voyage *NOUN* *The voyage lasted two weeks.* ► journey, passage, crossing, trip, expedition, excursion

vulgar *ADJECTIVE* **1** *She sent him a postcard with a vulgar picture on the back.* ► rude, indecent, lewd, suggestive, racy, risqué **2** *The decor was new and vulgar.* ► tasteless, gaudy, garish, tawdry, flashy, (*more informal*) tacky **3** *He was a bit too vulgar for her taste. It was considered vulgar to smoke in public.* ► ill-mannered, unrefined, unseemly, impolite, indecorous, coarse, ill-bred

vulnerable *ADJECTIVE* **1** *We are most vulnerable when we are asleep.* ► defenceless, exposed, unguarded, unprotected, at risk, weak, wide open AN OPPOSITE IS invulnerable **2 vulnerable to** *More people are vulnerable to age discrimination.* ► in danger of, at risk of, exposed to, open to, liable to, prone to, susceptible to AN OPPOSITE IS immune to

Ww

W. *ABBREVIATION* **1** west **2** western

wad (wod) *NOUN* **wads** a pad or bundle of soft material or banknotes, papers, etc. [from Dutch]

waddle *VERB* **waddles, waddling, waddled** walk with short steps, swaying from side to side, as a duck does
▷ **waddle** *NOUN*

wade *VERB* **wades, wading, waded** walk through water or mud etc.
▷ **wader** *NOUN*
[from Old English]

wafer *NOUN* **wafers** a kind of thin biscuit [from early French]

waffle[1] (wof- el) *NOUN* **waffles** a small cake made of batter and eaten hot [from Dutch]

waffle[2] (wof- el) *NOUN* (*informal*) vague wordy talk or writing
▷ **waffle** *VERB*
[from a dialect word *waff* = to bark or yelp]

waft (woft) *VERB* **wafts, wafting, wafted** carry or float gently through the air or over water [originally = escort a ship: from early German or Dutch]

wag[1] *VERB* **wags, wagging, wagged** move quickly to and fro • *a dog wagging its tail*
▷ **wag** *NOUN*
[from Old English]

wag[2] *NOUN* **wags** a person who makes jokes [from an old word *waghalter* = someone likely to be hanged]

wage *NOUN* or **wages** *PLURAL NOUN* a regular payment to someone in return for his or her work

wage *VERB* **wages, waging, waged** carry on a war or campaign

wager (way- jer) *NOUN* **wagers** a bet
▷ **wager** *VERB*

waggle *VERB* **waggles, waggling, waggled** move quickly to and fro
▷ **waggle** *NOUN*

wagon *NOUN* **wagons** **1** a cart with four wheels, pulled by a horse or an ox **2** an open railway truck, e.g. for coal

waif *NOUN* **waifs** a homeless and helpless person, especially a child

wail *VERB* **wails, wailing, wailed** make a long sad cry
▷ **wail** *NOUN*

wainscot or **wainscoting** *NOUN* wooden panelling on the wall of a room near the floor

waist *NOUN* **waists** the narrow part in the middle of your body
USAGE Do not confuse with **waste**.

waistcoat *NOUN* **waistcoats** a short close-fitting jacket without sleeves, worn over a shirt and under a jacket

waistline *NOUN* **waistlines** the amount you measure around your waist, which indicates how fat or thin you are

wait *VERB* **waits, waiting, waited** **1** stay somewhere or postpone an action until something happens; pause **2** be left to be dealt with later • *This question must wait until next week.* **3** wait on people
wait on **1** hand food and drink to people at a meal **2** be an attendant to someone

wait *NOUN* an act or time of waiting • *We had a long wait for the train.*

Thesaurus

wad *NOUN* **1** *He took a wad of notes from his pocket and began to count them.* ► bundle, roll, pad, (*more informal*) wodge **2** *I needed a wad of cotton wool.* ► lump, mass, chunk, hunk

wadding *NOUN* *sleeping bags insulated with wadding* ► padding, lining, packing, filling, stuffing

waffle *NOUN* (*informal*) *My panic reduced the interview to waffle.* ► blather, prattle, nonsense, verbosity, wordiness, evasiveness, padding, prevarication

waffle *VERB* (*informal*) *She waffled on for a while about things that didn't matter.* ► blather, prattle, ramble, babble, chatter on, gibber, gabble

wag *VERB* **1** *The dog's tail began to wag frantically.* ► shake, swing, wave, waggle **2** *'You see what I mean,' Eleanor said, wagging her finger.* ► wave, shake, waggle, brandish

wage *VERB* *The country lacks any means to wage war.* ► carry on, conduct, engage in, fight, undertake

wages *PLURAL NOUN* *He was pleased to be earning regular wages at last.* ► earnings, income, pay , recompense

wail *VERB* *He was tearing at his hair and wailing 'Why me?'* ► howl, bawl, weep, moan, sob, shriek, whimper, snivel, cry, lament, yowl

wail *NOUN* *Tom let out a wail.* ► howl, bawl, moan, sob, shriek, cry, whimper, yowl

wait *NOUN* *The photos were ready after a short wait.* ► interval, pause, delay, hold-up, break, hiatus, halt, hesitation, rest, stay

wait *VERB* *She left the room and waited outside. I can't wait for you any longer.* ► remain, rest, linger, stay, stop, halt, delay, mark time, stand by, hold back, pause, hesitate, (*old-fashioned*) tarry, (*more informal*) hang about
AN OPPOSITE IS proceed

waiter *NOUN* **waiters** a man who serves people with food and drink in a restaurant

waiting list *NOUN* **waiting lists** a list of people waiting for something to become available

waiting room *NOUN* **waiting rooms** a room provided for people who are waiting for something

waitress *NOUN* **waitresses** a woman who serves people with food and drink in a restaurant

wake[1] *VERB* **wakes, waking, woke, woken** **1** stop sleeping • *I woke when I heard the bell.* **2** make someone stop sleeping • *You have woken the baby.*

wake *NOUN* **wakes** (in Ireland) a party held after a funeral [from Old English]

wake[2] *NOUN* **wakes** **1** the track left on the water by a moving ship **2** currents of air left behind a moving aircraft
in the wake of following or coming after [probably from an Old Norse word = opening in the ice (made by a ship)]

wakeful *ADJECTIVE* unable to sleep

waken *VERB* **wakens, wakening, wakened** wake

walk *VERB* **walks, walking, walked** move along on your feet at an ordinary speed
▷ **walker** *NOUN*

walk *NOUN* **walks** **1** a journey on foot **2** the manner of walking **3** a path or route for walking

walking stick *NOUN* **walking sticks** a stick used as a support while walking

walk of life *NOUN* **walks of life** a person's occupation or social position

walkover *NOUN* **walkovers** an easy victory

wall *NOUN* **walls** **1** a continuous upright structure, usually made of brick or stone, forming one of the sides of a building or room or supporting something or enclosing an area **2** the outside part of something • *the stomach wall*

wall *VERB* **walls, walling, walled** enclose or block something with a wall • *a walled garden*

wallet *NOUN* **wallets** a small flat folding case for holding banknotes, credit cards, documents, etc.

wallflower *NOUN* **wallflowers** a garden plant with fragrant flowers, blooming in spring

wallop *VERB* **wallops, walloping, walloped** (*informal*) hit or beat someone
▷ **wallop** *NOUN*

wallow *VERB* **wallows, wallowing, wallowed** **1** roll about in water, mud, etc. **2** get great pleasure by being surrounded by something • *a week wallowing in luxury*
▷ **wallow** *NOUN*
[from Old English]

wallpaper *NOUN* **wallpapers** paper used to cover the inside walls of rooms

walnut *NOUN* **walnuts** **1** an edible nut with a wrinkled surface **2** the wood from the tree that bears this nut, used for making furniture

walrus *NOUN* **walruses** a large Arctic sea animal with two long tusks [probably from an Old Norse word = horse-whale]

waltz *NOUN* **waltzes** a dance with three beats to a bar

Thesaurus

wake *VERB* **1** *Sara woke to find Rodney's arm round her. When I woke up I was in the back of a car.* ► awake, awaken, waken, become conscious, come round, stir, get up, rise **2** *Be careful not to wake the baby.* ► waken, rouse, disturb, stir, awaken, arouse
wake up to *Parliament finally woke up to the electronic age.* ► become aware of, appreciate, comprehend, realize
USAGE See the note at **awake** *VERB*

walk *NOUN* **1** *Go for short walks near your home.* ► stroll, ramble, saunter, march, hike, tramp, trek **2** *There is a pretty walk round the cathedral.* ► path, pathway, walkway, lane, alley, footway, promenade **3** *He observed her elegant walk.* ► gait, tread, carriage, stride
walk of life *There are cheats in every walk of life.* ► sphere, class, field, calling, profession, activity

walk *VERB* **1** *She decided to save her bus fare and walk to work.* ► go on foot, travel on foot, be a pedestrian **2** *They walked together along the sands, and talked.* ► stroll, amble, saunter, stride, pace, trudge, proceed, promenade **3** *I'll walk the children home.* ► accompany, escort, take, see, show
walk all over (*informal*) *You don't want to let the cops walk all over you.* ► take advantage of, make use of, exploit, impose on, manipulate
walk away or **off with** (*informal*) *Someone had walked off with his wallet.* ► steal, pilfer, purloin, filch, take
walk out on (*informal*) *He had just walked out on his girlfriend.* ► leave, abandon, desert, run out on, (*informal*) jilt

wall *NOUN* *There was a noticeboard on the wall.* ► partition, screen, room divider*The east wall of the castle had been breached.* ► fortification, rampart, barricade, palisade, barrier, bulwark, stockade RELATED ADJECTIVE mural

wallet *NOUN* *The wallet contained some money in euros.* ► purse, notecase, pouch, pocketbook

wallop *VERB* *She walloped his back with her hand.* ► thump, hit, strike, pound, beat, bang, rap, batter, knock

waltz *VERB* **waltzes, waltzing, waltzed** dance a waltz

wand *NOUN* **wands** a thin rod, especially one used by a magician

wander *VERB* **wanders, wandering, wandered** **1** go about without trying to reach a particular place **2** leave the right path or direction; stray **3** be distracted or digress • *He let his attention wander.*
▷ **wanderer** *NOUN*

wane *VERB* **wanes, waning, waned** **1** (said about the moon) show a bright area that becomes gradually smaller after being full (The opposite is **wax**) **2** become less, smaller, or weaker • *His popularity waned.*

wangle *VERB* **wangles, wangling, wangled** (*informal*) get or arrange something by trickery or clever planning • *He's managed to wangle himself a trip to Paris.*
▷ **wangle** *NOUN*

want *VERB* **wants, wanting, wanted** **1** wish to have something **2** need • *Your hair wants cutting.* **3** be without something; lack

want *NOUN* **wants** **1** a wish to have something **2** lack or need of something [from Old Norse]

wanted *ADJECTIVE* (said about a suspected criminal) that the police wish to find or arrest

WAP *ABBREVIATION* Wireless Application Protocol, a means of enabling a mobile phone to be connected to the Internet

war *NOUN* **wars** **1** fighting between nations or groups, especially using armed forces **2** a serious struggle or effort against crime, disease, poverty, etc.
at war taking part in a war
war crime a crime committed during a war that breaks the international rules of war

warble *VERB* **warbles, warbling, warbled** sing with a trilling sound, as some birds do
▷ **warble** *NOUN*

ward *NOUN* **wards** **1** a room with beds for patients in a hospital **2** a child looked after by a guardian **3** an area electing a councillor to represent it

ward *VERB* **wards, warding, warded**
ward off keep something away

warden *NOUN* **wardens** an official who is in charge of a hostel, college, etc., or who supervises something

warder *NOUN* **warders** an official in charge of prisoners in a prison

wardrobe *NOUN* **wardrobes** **1** a cupboard to hang clothes in **2** a stock of clothes or costumes

warhead *NOUN* **warheads** the head of a missile or torpedo etc., containing explosives

warlike *ADJECTIVE* **1** fond of making war **2** threatening war

warm *ADJECTIVE* **1** fairly hot; not cold or cool **2** keeping the body warm • *a warm coat* **3** friendly or enthusiastic • *a warm welcome* **4** close to the right answer, or to something hidden • *You're getting warm now.*

Thesaurus

wand *NOUN* *No magic wand can solve these problems.* ► baton, stick, rod, staff, sceptre

wander *VERB* **1** *We spent the day wandering about the old town.* ► ramble, roam, meander, range, rove, stray, walk, wind **2** *She had wandered away from the main group.* ► stray, deviate, digress, drift, veer **3 wander off** *I've told you not to wander off like that.* ► go away, drift off, leave, get lost

want *NOUN* **1** *The client always has wants and feelings.* ► demand, desire, need, requirement, wish **2** *The bridge is decaying for want of repair.* ► absence, lack, need

want *VERB* **1** *A clever alien wants to steal the spaceship.* ► wish, desire, hope, long **2** *That is exactly what he wanted.* ► wish for, desire, long for, yearn for, hanker after, crave, covet, fancy, hunger for, thirst for **3 want to** (*informal*) *You want to keep an eye on them.* ► need to, ought to, should

war *NOUN* **1** *During the war he joined the police force. They had been badly affected by the chaos of war.* ► conflict, fighting, hostilities, struggle, warfare, action, military action, strife RELATED ADJECTIVES martial, belligerent **2** *a war against drugs* ► campaign, crusade, battle, fight, struggle

ward *VERB* **ward off** 1 • *Garlands of garlic are worn to ward off evil spirits.* i fend off, drive away, beat off, repel, avert, stave off, thwart, turn aside, repulse 2 • *He brought up his arm to ward off the blow.* i deflect, parry, block, check

wardrobe *NOUN* **1** *Large areas of wardrobe doors can look plain.* ► cupboard, clothes cupboard, closet, cabinet **2** *Her mother organized her wedding and her wardrobe.* ► clothes, outfit, attire

warfare *NOUN* *thirty years of continuous warfare* ► fighting, hostilities, war, conflict, combat, bloodshed, action, battle, arms RELATED ADJECTIVES martial, belligerent

warlike *ADJECTIVE* *Tethlis was another warlike ruler.* ► belligerent, aggressive, warmongering, warring, combative, pugnacious AN OPPOSITE IS peaceable

warm *ADJECTIVE* **1** *She strolled in warm winter sunshine towards San Marco. The sun was already warm on their backs.* ► hot, balmy, summery, sultry, sunny, temperate, tropical, warmish AN OPPOSITE IS cold **2** *the warm waters of the*

▷ **warmly** *ADVERB* **warmness** *NOUN* **warmth** *NOUN*

warm *VERB* **warms, warming, warmed** make or become warm

warm-blooded *ADJECTIVE* having blood that remains warm permanently

warn *VERB* **warns, warning, warned** tell someone about a danger or difficulty that may affect them, or about what they should do • *I warned you to take your boots.*
▷ **warning** *NOUN*
warn off tell someone to keep away or to avoid a thing

warp (worp) *VERB* **warps, warping, warped** **1** bend or twist out of shape, e.g. by dampness **2** distort a person's ideas, judgement, etc. • *Jealousy warped his mind.*

warrant *NOUN* **warrants** a document that authorizes a person to do something (e.g. to search a place) or to receive something

warrant *VERB* **warrants, warranting, warranted** **1** justify • *Nothing can warrant such rudeness.* **2** guarantee

warren *NOUN* **warrens** **1** a piece of ground where there are many burrows in which rabbits live and breed **2** a building or place with many winding passages

warrior *NOUN* **warriors** a person who fights in battle; a soldier

warship *NOUN* **warships** a ship used in war

wart *NOUN* **warts** a small hard lump on the skin, caused by a virus

wary (wair- ee) *ADJECTIVE* cautious; looking carefully for possible danger or difficulty
▷ **warily** *ADVERB* **wariness** *NOUN*

wash *VERB* **washes, washing, washed** **1** clean something with water or other liquid **2** suitable for washing • *Cotton washes easily.* **3** flow against or over something • *Waves washed over the deck.* **4** carry along by a moving liquid • *A wave washed him overboard.* **5** (*informal*) be accepted or believed • *That excuse won't wash.*
be washed out (*informal*) (said about an event) be abandoned because of rain
wash up wash dishes and cutlery etc. after use
▷ **washing-up** *NOUN*

wash *NOUN* **washes** **1** the action of washing **2** clothes etc. being washed **3** the disturbed water behind a moving ship **4** a thin coating of colour

Thesaurus

western Mediterranean ► heated, lukewarm, tepid **3** *She was dressed in warm clothes.* ► thick, cosy, woolly, thermal, winter **4** *He gave them a warm welcome.* ► friendly, cordial, amiable, enthusiastic, affable, genial, affectionate, loving, sympathetic, warm-hearted, pleasant OPPOSITES ARE cool, unfriendly

warm *VERB* **1** *She was in the kitchen warming some soup.* ► heat (up), reheat, thaw OPPOSITES ARE cool, chill **2 warm to** *Anne was by now warming to her theme.* ► take to, become enthusiastic about, get on with, feel attracted by

warm-hearted *ADJECTIVE* *She is a generous, warm-hearted person.* ► kind, caring, good, kind-hearted, kindly, considerate, sympathetic, thoughtful, obliging, tender-hearted, benevolent OPPOSITES ARE unkind, unfriendly

warmth *NOUN* **1** *Despite the warmth of the fire, Isabel began to shiver.* ► heat, warmness, comfort AN OPPOSITE IS coldness **2** *The warmth of their welcome took them by surprise.* ► friendliness, cordiality, geniality, enthusiasm AN OPPOSITE IS hostility

warn *VERB* *The manufacturers had failed to warn doctors of the possible side effects.* ► advise, alert, notify, inform, caution, remind, forewarn, give a warning about, (*more informal*) tip off

warning *NOUN* **1** *The changes were announced without warning.* ► notice, advance notice, forewarning, hint, indication, omen, premonition, presage, sign, signal, threat, augury, (*informal*) tip-off **2** *The remarks were a warning of what might be in store.* ► omen, sign, signal, presage, portent, premonition, foreboding, prediction, token **3** *The warning in his voice was clear.* ► caution, reservation, caveat, doubt **4** *England received their third and final warning.* ► caution, reprimand, admonition

warrior *NOUN* *a mighty warrior* ► fighter, soldier, fighting man, combatant

wary *ADJECTIVE* *She had been wary of making known her name.* ► cautious, chary, careful, circumspect, suspicious, apprehensive, vigilant (about), watchful (about), alert (to), distrustful, heedful OPPOSITES ARE unwary, heedless

wash *NOUN* **1** *I said I needed to go for a wash.* ► bath, shower, rinse, shampoo **2** *They give all the cars a wash each morning.* ► clean, shampoo, hosing-down

wash *VERB* **1** *She took a couple of minutes to wash her face and comb her hair. Wash all fruit and vegetables thoroughly before use.* ► clean, cleanse, rinse, scrub, shampoo, mop, sluice, swill, wipe OPPOSITES ARE dirty, soil **2** *It was time to wash the dog.* ► soap down, sponge down, swab down, hose down **3** *He found the soap and began to wash.* ► bath, bathe, shower **4** *She washed, dried, and ironed the clothes.* ► launder, clean, scrub, rinse, sponge

washable *ADJECTIVE* able to be washed without becoming damaged

washbasin *NOUN* **washbasins** a small sink for washing your hands etc.

washer *NOUN* **washers** **1** a small ring of rubber or metal etc. placed between two surfaces (e.g. under a bolt or screw) to fit them tightly together **2** a washing machine

washing *NOUN* clothes etc. that need washing or have just been washed

washing machine *NOUN* **washing machines** a machine for washing clothes etc.

wasn t (*mainly spoken*) was not

wasp *NOUN* **wasps** a stinging insect with black and yellow stripes round its body

wastage *NOUN* loss of something by waste

waste *VERB* **wastes, wasting, wasted** **1** use something in an extravagant way or without getting enough results **2** fail to use something • *You are wasting a good opportunity.* **3** become gradually weaker or thinner from lack of nourishment

waste *ADJECTIVE* **1** left over or thrown away because it is not wanted **2** not used; not usable • *waste land*

lay waste destroy the crops and buildings etc. of an area

waste *NOUN* **wastes** **1** wasting a thing, not using it well • *a waste of time* **2** things that are not wanted or not used **3** an area of waste land • *the wastes of the Sahara Desert*

▷ **wasteful** *ADJECTIVE* **wastefully** *ADVERB* **wastefulness** *NOUN*

USAGE Do not confuse with **waist**.

watch *VERB* **watches, watching, watched** **1** look at a person or thing for some time **2** be on guard or ready for something to happen • *Watch for the traffic lights to change.* **3** pay careful attention to something • *Watch where you put your feet.* **4** take care of something • *His job is to watch the sheep.*

▷ **watcher** *NOUN*

watch *NOUN* **watches** **1** a device like a small clock, usually worn on the wrist **2** the action of watching **3** a turn of being on duty in a ship

watchful *ADJECTIVE* watching closely; alert

▷ **watchfully** *ADVERB* **watchfulness** *NOUN*

watchman *NOUN* **watchmen** a person employed to look after an empty building etc., especially at night

watchtower *NOUN* **watchtowers** a tall tower used as an observation post

water *NOUN* **waters** **1** a colourless liquid that is a compound of hydrogen and oxygen **2** a lake or sea **3** the tide • *at high water*

pass water urinate

Thesaurus

wash your hands of something *They cannot wash their hands of social problems.* ► disown, renounce, have nothing to do with, disclaim, reject, abandon AN OPPOSITE IS embrace

washing *NOUN* *Even the washing hanging from the windows seemed to be fluttering a welcome.* ► laundry, clothes, wash

waste *VERB* *He didn't want to waste money on a taxi fare.* ► squander, fritter away, misspend, misuse, throw away, lavish, consume, exhaust, dissipate, use wastefully, use up

AN OPPOSITE IS conserve

waste away *Many people wasted away from disease and malnutrition.* ► wither, become emaciated, become weaker, decline, pine, weaken AN OPPOSITE IS thrive

waste *ADJECTIVE* **1** *Energy savings are achieved by recycling waste materials.* ► unwanted, discarded, superfluous, unused, extra **2** *There was a patch of waste ground for them to play on.* ► bare, wild, empty, overgrown, barren, derelict, undeveloped, run-down, uncared for, uncultivated

waste *NOUN* **1** *Sewage and industrial waste still enter the North Sea.* ► refuse, rubbish, debris, effluent, garbage, dross, detritus, trash, junk, litter, scraps **2** *The trip had been a waste of time and money.* ► squandering, misuse, frittering away, misspending, dissipation

wasteful *ADJECTIVE* *a wasteful use of resources* ► extravagant, prodigal, profligate, spendthrift, lavish, reckless, thriftless, excessive, improvident, imprudent, uneconomical, needless

AN OPPOSITE IS economical

watch *NOUN* **1** *David checked the time by his new watch.* ► wristwatch, pocket watch, timepiece, chronometer, clock, timer **2** *One of us should keep watch at the back of the house.* ► guard, vigil, lookout, surveillance, heed

on the watch *Be on the watch for jellyfish.* ► alert, vigilant, attentive

watch *VERB* **1** *She watched him as he cleaned the room.* ► look at, observe, keep your eyes on, contemplate, eye, gaze at, survey, heed, regard, see, stare at, take notice of, view, pay attention to, concentrate on, attend to, mark, note **2** *We need someone to watch the children for a few hours.* ► look after, mind, supervise, keep an eye on, keep watch on, care for, tend, guard, protect, safeguard, shield

watch out *Watch out for snakes.* ► look out for, be alert, be vigilant, be attentive, (*more informal*) keep an eye open for

water *NOUN* **1** *a glass of water* ► drinking water, tap water, mineral water **2** *a picnic by the water* ► river, lake, sea, ocean, loch, pond, pool

RELATED ADJECTIVES aquatic, hydraulic

A B C D E F G H I J K L M N O P Q R S T U V W X Y Z

water *VERB* **waters, watering, watered**
1 sprinkle or supply something with water **2** produce tears or saliva • *It makes my mouth water.*
water down dilute

watercolour *NOUN* **watercolours** **1** paint made with pigment and water (not oil) **2** a painting done with this kind of paint

waterfall *NOUN* **waterfalls** a place where a river or stream flows over the edge of a cliff or large rock

waterlogged *ADJECTIVE* completely soaked or swamped in water

waterproof *ADJECTIVE* that keeps out water • *a waterproof jacket*
▷ **waterproof** *VERB*

waterskiing *NOUN* the sport of skimming over the surface of water on a pair of flat boards (**waterskis**) while being towed by a motor boat

watertight *ADJECTIVE* **1** made or fastened so that water cannot get in or out **2** so carefully put together that it cannot be changed or set aside or proved to be untrue • *a watertight excuse*

waterworks *PLURAL NOUN* a place with pumping machinery etc. for supplying water to a district

watery *ADJECTIVE* **1** like water **2** full of water **3** containing too much water

watt *NOUN* **watts** a unit of electric power

wave *NOUN* **waves** **1** a ridge moving along the surface of the sea etc. or breaking on the shore **2** a curling piece of hair **3** (in science) the wave-like movement by which heat, light, sound, or electricity etc. travels **4** the action of waving

wave *VERB* **waves, waving, waved** **1** move your hand to and fro as a greeting or signal etc. **2** move loosely to and fro or up and down **3** make a thing wavy **4** be wavy

wavelength *NOUN* **wavelengths** the size of a sound wave or electromagnetic wave

waver *VERB* **wavers, wavering, wavered** **1** be unsteady; move unsteadily **2** hesitate; be uncertain

wavy *ADJECTIVE* full of waves or curves
▷ **wavily** *ADVERB* **waviness** *NOUN*

wax[1] *NOUN* **waxes** **1** a soft substance that melts easily, used to make candles, crayons, and polish **2** beeswax
▷ **waxy** *ADJECTIVE*

wax *VERB* **waxes, waxing, waxed** coat or polish something with wax

wax[2] *VERB* **waxes, waxing, waxed** **1** (said about the moon) show a bright area that

Thesaurus

water *VERB* *She went out to water the plants.*
► sprinkle, wet, moisten, dampen, hose, soak, douse, drench, flood, irrigate, souse
water something down **1** *He asked her to water down his drink.* ► dilute, add water to, weaken, thin **2** *The proposals had to be watered down to stand any chance of success.*
► moderate, tone down, soften, mitigate, temper, mellow, weaken

waterfall *NOUN* *They looked down from the top of the waterfall.* ► cascade, cataract, shower, torrent, falls, rapids, chute

waterproof *ADJECTIVE* *a waterproof jacket*
► water-repellent, water-resistant, weatherproof, watertight, damp-proof, impermeable, impervious

watertight *ADJECTIVE* **1** *Use a watertight container.* ► sealed, hermetic, sound, waterproof AN OPPOSITE IS leaky **2** *a watertight excuse* ► foolproof, unassailable, flawless, conclusive, perfect AN OPPOSITE IS flawed

watery *ADJECTIVE* **1** *a bowl of watery porridge*
► runny, sloppy, thin, watered down, weak, insipid, liquid, tasteless, (*more informal*) wishy-washy **2** *His eyes looked watery.* ► damp, moist, tear-filled, tearful, wet

wave *NOUN* **1** *Surfers were riding the waves.*
► breaker, roller, billow, crest, ridge, surf, white horse **2** *A wave of panic seemed to grip the crowd.* ► surge, upsurge, outbreak, current, flood, rash, sweep, stream, swell **3** *She gave a wave of her hand as he sped past.* ► gesture, shake, signal, flourish, gesticulation **4** *Her hair flowed in long waves.* ► curl, twist, kink

wave *VERB* **1** *Jill waved at us to go over.*
► beckon, gesture, signal, motion, indicate **2** *He waved his umbrella at them.* ► shake, brandish, flourish, waggle, wiggle, wag **3** *A flag waved in the breeze.* ► flap, flutter, ripple, quiver, move to and fro
wave aside *All these objections were waved aside.* ► dismiss, reject, disregard, ignore, discount, brush aside, shrug off

wavelength *NOUN* *Tune your radio to the right wavelength.* ► channel, station, waveband

waver *VERB* **1** *Her voice began to waver and she looked faint.* ► tremble, falter, quaver, quiver, become unsteady, change, quake, shake, shiver, shudder, sway, teeter, totter, wobble **2** *He could see I was wavering.* ► hesitate, be undecided, be indecisive, dither, equivocate, vacillate **3** *the wavering light from the candle*
► flicker, quiver, tremble, glimmer

wavy *ADJECTIVE* *She ran her hand through her wavy hair.* ► curly, curling, curving, rippling, sinuous, undulating, winding, zigzag
AN OPPOSITE IS straight

A B C D E F G H I J K L M N O P Q R S T U V W X Y Z

becomes gradually larger (The opposite is **wane**) **2** become stronger or more important

waxwork *NOUN* **waxworks** a model of a person etc. made in wax

way *NOUN* **ways 1** how something is done; a method or style **2** a manner • *She spoke in a kindly way* **3** a line of communication between places, e.g. a path or road **4** a route or direction **5** a distance to be travelled • *Is it a long way away?* **6** a respect • *It's a good idea in some ways.* **7** a condition or state • *Things were in a bad way.*
get or **have your own way** make people let you do what you want
give way 1 collapse **2** let somebody else move first **3** yield
in the way forming an obstacle or hindrance
no way (*informal*) that is impossible!
under way see **under**

waylay *VERB* **waylays, waylaying, waylaid** lie in wait for a person or people, especially in order to talk to them or rob them

wayside *NOUN*
fall by the wayside fail to continue doing something

wayward *ADJECTIVE* disobedient; wilfully doing what you want

we *PRONOUN* a word used by a person to refer to himself or herself and another or others

weak *ADJECTIVE* **1** having little power, energy, or effect **2** easy to break, damage, or defeat **3** not great in intensity
▷ **weakness** *NOUN*

weaken *VERB* **weakens, weakening, weakened** make or become weaker

weakling *NOUN* **weaklings** a weak person or animal

wealth *NOUN* **1** a lot of money or property; riches **2** a large quantity • *The book has a wealth of illustrations.*

Thesaurus

way *NOUN* **1** *His engine overheated on the way home.* ► road, route, journey, direction **2** *There was a long way to go.* ► distance, length, measurement **3** *It was the best way of dealing with the problem.* ► method, means, manner, approach, mode, procedure, process, avenue, course, system, technique, mechanism **4** *He knew he had to change his ways.* ► habit, practice, routine, custom, fashion, style, tradition **5** *The arts benefit society in several ways.* ► respect, particular, aspect, circumstances, detail, feature

way-out *ADJECTIVE* (*informal*) *He introduced some way-out visual ideas that no one had tried before.* ► unconventional, offbeat, eccentric, quirky, bizarre, weird, odd, (*informal*) wacky

weak *ADJECTIVE* **1** *The bridge was weak as a result of metal fatigue.* ► unsafe, unsound, fragile, unsteady, rickety, shaky, flimsy, decrepit, substandard AN OPPOSITE IS strong **2** *He was still too weak to get up by himself.* ► frail, feeble, poorly, ill, infirm, sickly, debilitated, helpless, delicate, enervated, exhausted, listless, puny AN OPPOSITE IS strong **3** *A weak man, when provoked, is often more dangerous than a violent one.* ► timid, timorous, irresolute, spineless, ineffectual, pusillanimous, cowardly, fearful, impotent, indecisive, ineffective OPPOSITES ARE strong, brave **4** *His mistakes had put him in a weak position.* ► vulnerable, exposed, defenceless, unguarded, unprotected OPPOSITES ARE strong, powerful **5** *The weak joke fell hollowly.* ► feeble, lame, unconvincing, unsatisfactory **6** *She sipped the sweet, weak tea and began to feel better.* ► watery, diluted, watered down, insipid, bland, thin, tasteless AN OPPOSITE IS strong **7** *The light was becoming weak.* ► dim, pale, faint, feeble OPPOSITES ARE strong, bright

weaken *VERB* **1** *Their purpose was to weaken the unions' power.* ► reduce, sap, enfeeble, erode, impair, lessen, diminish, lower, debilitate, destroy, emasculate, enervate, make weaker, ruin, soften, undermine OPPOSITES ARE strengthen, boost **2** *Our resolve had weakened.* ► dwindle, ebb, fade, flag, wane, abate, become weaker, decline, decrease, give way OPPOSITES ARE strengthen, increase, intensify

weakness *NOUN* **1** *There is an obvious weakness in your argument.* ► fault, flaw, defect, imperfection, weak point, blemish, error, failing, mistake, shortcoming OPPOSITES ARE strength, strong point **2** *The economy is showing signs of weakness.* ► fragility, frailty, flimsiness, inadequacy, softness **3** *Her illness left her with a permanent physical weakness.* ► infirmity, debility, feebleness, illness, impotence, lassitude, vulnerability OPPOSITES ARE strength, vigour **4** *He has a weakness for chocolate cake.* ► liking, fondness, inclination, penchant, predilection, (*more informal*) soft spot

wealth *NOUN* **1** *We want to see wealth passed down from generation to generation.* ► affluence, assets, opulence, property, prosperity, capital, fortune, money, possessions, riches AN OPPOSITE IS poverty **2** *You realize the wealth of information inside the government.* ► abundance, profusion, plethora, store, plenty

wealthy *ADJECTIVE* **wealthier, wealthiest** having wealth; rich
▷ **wealthiness** *NOUN*

wean *VERB* **weans, weaning, weaned** make a baby take food other than its mother's milk
wean off make someone give up a habit etc. gradually

weapon *NOUN* **weapons** something used to harm or kill people in a battle or fight
▷ **weaponry** *NOUN*

wear *VERB* **wears, wearing, wore, worn**
1 have clothes, jewellery, etc. on your body **2** have a certain look on your face • *She wore a frown.* **3** damage something by rubbing or using it often; become damaged in this way • *The carpet has worn thin.* **4** last while in use • *It has worn well.*
▷ **wearable** *ADJECTIVE* **wearer** *NOUN*
wear off 1 be removed by wear or use **2** become less intense
wear on pass gradually • *The night wore on.*
wear out 1 use or be used until it becomes weak or useless **2** exhaust

wear *NOUN* **1** what you wear; clothes • *evening wear* **2** (also **wear and tear**) gradual damage done by rubbing or using something

weary *ADJECTIVE* **wearier, weariest 1** tired **2** tiring • *It's weary work.*
▷ **wearily** *ADVERB* **weariness** *NOUN*

weary *VERB* **wearies, wearying, wearied** make or become weary

weasel *NOUN* **weasels** a small fierce animal with a slender body and reddish-brown fur

weather *NOUN* the rain, snow, wind, sunshine etc. at a particular time or place
under the weather feeling ill or depressed

weather *VERB* **weathers, weathering, weathered 1** expose something to the effects of the weather **2** come through something successfully • *The ship weathered the storm.*

weathercock or **weathervane** *NOUN* **weathercocks** or **weathervanes** a pointer, often shaped like a cockerel, that turns in the wind and shows from which direction it is blowing

weave *VERB* **weaves, weaving, wove, woven**
1 make material or baskets etc. by crossing threads or strips under and over each other **2** put a story together • *She wove a thrilling tale.* **3** (*past tense & past participle* **weaved**) twist and turn • *He weaved through the traffic.*
▷ **weaver** *NOUN*

weave *NOUN* **weaves** a style of weaving • *a loose weave*

Thesaurus

wealthy *ADJECTIVE Her mother was a very wealthy woman.* ► rich, affluent, prosperous, well-off, well-to-do, moneyed, comfortable, (*more informal*) flush, (*more informal*) loaded
OPPOSITES ARE poor, impoverished

wear *VERB* **1** *Did you have to wear any special kind of clothing? Ruth wore a pale lavender cotton dress. He often wore dark glasses to hide the bags under his eyes.* ► dress in, be dressed in, clothe yourself in, put on, have on, present yourself in, wrap up in, don **2** *He wore his usual benign expression.* ► show, assume, present, exhibit **3** *Years of passing footsteps had badly worn the carpet.* ► damage, fray, scuff, mark, weaken **4** *The tyres have worn well.* ► last, endure, survive, hold up, (*more informal*) stand the test of time
wear away *Most of the grass had been worn away by the spectators.* ► rub away, erode, grind down, abrade, corrode, eat away
wear off *The effect of the tranquillizers was wearing off.* ► fade, subside, dwindle, reduce, lessen, diminish, peter out, disappear
wear out 1 *His shoes wear out twice as fast when he's working.* ► become worn, deteriorate, become damaged, become scuffed **2** *They cheered until their lungs were worn out.* ► exhaust, fatigue, tire out

wear *NOUN* **1** *Repairs were made necessary by heavy wear.* ► use, service, utility, wearing **2** *The brakes showed signs of wear.* ► damage, deterioration, friction, erosion, wear and tear **3** *The guests were dressed in formal wear.* ► dress, clothes, clothing, costume, outfit

wearing *ADJECTIVE The care of others can be a wearing business.* ► tiring, exhausting, tiresome, fatiguing, wearying, wearisome, trying, taxing AN OPPOSITE IS refreshing

weary *ADJECTIVE I have been too sad and too weary to write anything.* ► tired, exhausted, fatigued, wearied, worn out, sapped, drained, spent, (*more informal*) knackered

weather *NOUN She was tempted to use the weather as an excuse to postpone her visit. All farmers are exposed to the vagaries of the weather.* ► climate, the elements, meteorological conditions, atmospheric conditions
under the weather *She felt under the weather and went to rest.* ► unwell, poorly, indisposed, out of sorts, ill, sick OPPOSITES ARE well, in good health RELATED ADJECTIVE meteorological

weave *VERB* **1** *The design had been woven into the carpet.* ► intertwine, interweave, knit, plait, sew, entwine, interlace **2** *Victorian novelists weave romances round great houses. She wove a spell over him, so that he slept for ever and never grew old.* ► create, compose, make, plot, put together **3** *He dragged himself out of bed and*

web *NOUN* **webs** **1** a cobweb **2** a network
the Web the World Wide Web
[from Old English *webb* = a piece of woven cloth]

webbed or **web-footed** *ADJECTIVE* having toes joined by pieces of skin, as ducks and frogs do

website *NOUN* **websites** a place on the Internet where you can get information about a subject, company, etc.

wed *VERB* **weds, wedding, wedded** **1** marry **2** unite two different things

wedding *NOUN* **weddings** the ceremony when a man and woman get married

wedge *NOUN* **wedges** **1** a piece of wood or metal etc. that is thick at one end and thin at the other It is pushed between things to force them apart or prevent something from moving **2** a wedge-shaped thing

wedge *VERB* **wedges, wedging, wedged** **1** keep something in place with a wedge **2** pack tightly together • *Ten of us were wedged in the lift.*

Wednesday *NOUN* the day of the week following Tuesday [from Old English *Wodnesdaeg* = day of Woden or Odin, the chief Norse god]

weed *NOUN* **weeds** a wild plant that grows where it is not wanted

weed *VERB* **weeds, weeding, weeded** remove weeds from the ground

weedy *ADJECTIVE* **weedier, weediest** **1** full of weeds **2** thin and weak

week *NOUN* **weeks** a period of seven days, especially from Sunday to the following Saturday

weekday *NOUN* **weekdays** a day other than Saturday or Sunday

weekend *NOUN* **weekends** Saturday and Sunday

weekly *ADJECTIVE, ADVERB* happening or done once a week

weep *VERB* **weeps, weeping, wept** **1** shed tears; cry **2** ooze moisture in drops
▷ **weep** *NOUN* **weepy** *ADJECTIVE*

weeping *ADJECTIVE* (said about a tree) having drooping branches • *a weeping willow*

weigh *VERB* **weighs, weighing, weighed** **1** measure the weight of something **2** have a certain weight • *What do you weigh?* **3** be important or have influence • *Her evidence weighed with the jury.*
weigh anchor raise the anchor and start a voyage
weigh down **1** keep something down by its weight **2** depress or trouble somebody
weigh up estimate or assess something

weight *NOUN* **weights** **1** how heavy something is; the amount that something weighs **2** a piece of metal of known weight, especially one used on scales to weigh things **3** a heavy object

Thesaurus

weaved his way to the bathroom. ► thread, wind, work, dodge, zigzag

web *NOUN* **1** *The webs are built to a definite pattern.* ► mesh, net, netting, network, crisscross, lattice **2** *Their lives were caught up in a web of deception.* ► network, nexus, maze, complex

wedding *NOUN* *The wedding went ahead with two hundred guests.* ► marriage, marriage ceremony, nuptials, union RELATED ADJECTIVE nuptial, bridal

wedge *NOUN* **1** *He put a huge wedge of gleaming white pudding on her plate.* ► slice, segment, triangle, chunk, lump **2** *The window was held open with a wedge.* ► chock, block, door stop

wedge *VERB* *She wedged the string bag between her feet and took out a book. The children were wedged so tightly that it was difficult to move.* ► squeeze, jam, cram, push, force, thrust, stick, push, fasten, (*more informal*) shove

weedy *ADJECTIVE* **1** *I walked up through the weedy garden.* ► untidy, unweeded, overgrown, unkempt, wild, rank **2** (*informal*) *He was short and physically weedy.* ► weak, puny, feeble, frail

weep *VERB* *I began to weep, burying my face in my hands.* ► cry, sob, shed tears, whimper, blubber, snivel, wail

weigh *VERB* **1** *The man weighed some vegetables and put them in a bag.* ► measure the weight of, measure out, put on the scales **2** *I weigh the same now as when I married.* ► have a weight of, tip the scales at **3** **weigh** *or* **weigh up** *These were considerations that she weighed carefully. I weighed up my chances and decided to go.* ► consider, evaluate, assess, examine, think about, give thought to, ponder, study, mull over, meditate on **4** *Two other matters weigh in their favour.* ► be important, count, have weight
weigh down **1** *No one wants to be weighed down with heavy gear.* ► burden, weight, saddle, load, overload **2** *She walked to her room, mentally weighed down by her thoughts.* ► depress, oppress, trouble, bother, beset, afflict, prey on

weight *NOUN* **1** *The supports could no longer sustain the weight of the bridge, and it collapsed.* ► heaviness, load, burden, mass, pressure, strain **2** *The Prime Minister has attached a lot of weight to the scheme.* ► importance,

4 importance or influence
▷ **weighty** *ADJECTIVE* **weightless** *ADJECTIVE*

weight *VERB* **weights, weighting, weighted** put a weight on something

weir (weer) *NOUN* **weirs** a small dam across a river or canal to control the flow of water

weird *ADJECTIVE* very strange; uncanny
▷ **weirdly** *ADVERB* **weirdness** *NOUN*
USAGE When spelling this word, note that the 'e' comes before the 'i', not the other way round.

welcome *NOUN* **welcomes** a greeting or reception, especially a kindly one

welcome *ADJECTIVE* **1** that you are glad to receive or see • *a welcome gift* **2** allowed or invited to do or take something • *You are welcome to come.*

welcome *VERB* **welcomes, welcoming, welcomed 1** show that you are pleased when a person or thing arrives **2** be glad to receive or hear of something • *We welcome this decision.*

weld *VERB* **welds, welding, welded 1** join pieces of metal or plastic by heating and pressing or hammering them together **2** unite people or things into a whole

welfare *NOUN* people's health, happiness, and comfort

welfare state *NOUN* a system in which a country's government provides money to pay for health care, social services, benefits, etc.

well[1] *NOUN* **wells 1** a deep hole dug to bring up water or oil from underground **2** a deep space, e.g. containing a staircase

well *VERB* **wells, welling, welled** rise or flow up • *Tears welled up in our eyes.*

well[2] *ADVERB* **better, best 1** in a good or suitable way • *She swims well.* **2** thoroughly • *Polish it well.* **3** probably or reasonably • *This may well be our last chance.*
well off 1 fairly rich **2** in a good situation

well *ADJECTIVE* **1** in good health • *He is not well.* **2** satisfactory • *All is well.*

well-being *NOUN* good health, happiness, and comfort

wellingtons *PLURAL NOUN* rubber or plastic waterproof boots

Thesaurus

seriousness, significance, authority, emphasis, gravity, substance

weight *VERB* **1** *Driftwood can be sealed and weighted in the same way.* ► weigh down, make heavy, ballast, hold down, keep down, load **2** *The odds were weighted against them.* ► bias, load, slant, balance

weighty *ADJECTIVE* **1** *A pile of books can be very weighty.* ► heavy, bulky, cumbersome, massive, clumsy **2** *The weighty question, what is happiness?* ► serious, important, significant, momentous, far-reaching, consequential **3** *It is a weighty responsibility to be given.* ► demanding, onerous, exacting, taxing, troublesome

weird *ADJECTIVE* **1** *Some pretty weird things seemed to be happening.* ► uncanny, eerie, unearthly, unnatural, ghostly, mysterious, scary, supernatural, unaccountable, (*more informal*) spooky, (*more informal*) creepy
OPPOSITES ARE normal, ordinary **2** *They wouldn't make those weird garden ornaments if they'd ever seen a real gnome. The fridge made some really weird noises yesterday.* ► strange, peculiar, bizarre, grotesque, odd, curious, eccentric, outlandish, queer, unusual, abnormal, quirky, unconventional, (*more informal*) wacky, (*more informal*) freaky, (*more informal*) way-out
AN OPPOSITE IS conventional

welcome *ADJECTIVE* *We've received some welcome news.* ► pleasant, pleasing, gratifying, encouraging, good, nice
OPPOSITES ARE unwelcome, disappointing

welcome *NOUN* *Make for the Visitors' Centre, where you can be sure of a warm welcome.* ► reception, greeting, hospitality

welcome *VERB* **1** *Sophie welcomed her warmly and pulled out a chair.* ► greet, receive, hail, meet **2** *His colleagues welcomed his cheerfulness.* ► appreciate, approve of, delight in, like, want, accept

welfare *NOUN* *the safety and welfare of people at work* ► well-being, good, security, prosperity, comfort, benefit, happiness, health, interests

well *ADJECTIVE* *Mary was looking well.* ► healthy, in good health, fit, fine, sound, strong, thriving, flourishing, hearty, lively, robust, vigorous

well *ADVERB* **1** *They behaved well.* ► satisfactorily, correctly, nicely, properly AN OPPOSITE IS badly **2** *She sings well.* ► ably, skilfully, expertly
OPPOSITES ARE badly, poorly **3** *Mix the ingredients well.* ► thoroughly, fully, completely, rigorously AN OPPOSITE IS lightly **4** *You have been working well.* ► carefully, diligently, conscientiously, attentively
OPPOSITES ARE badly, poorly **5** *He has made enough money to live well.* ► comfortably, in comfort, prosperously

well *VERB* *The tears welled in her eyes.* ► flow, stream, spring, course, surge, flood, gush, rise, run, trickle

well-behaved *ADJECTIVE* *You will have to be quiet and well-behaved.* ► well-mannered, polite, obedient, respectful, courteous, cooperative, good, dutiful, nice AN OPPOSITE IS naughty

well-being *NOUN* *The medical staff are responsible for the well-being of the patients.*

A B C D E F G H I J K L M N O P Q R S T U V W X Y Z

▷ **wellies** PLURAL NOUN (*informal*) [named after the first Duke of Wellington (1769-1852), who wore long leather boots]

well known ADJECTIVE known to many people

well-mannered ADJECTIVE having good manners

well-meaning ADJECTIVE having good intentions

well-read ADJECTIVE having read a lot of good books

well-to-do ADJECTIVE fairly rich

weren't (*mainly spoken*) were not

werewolf NOUN **werewolves** (in legends and stories) a person who sometimes changes into a wolf [from Old English *wer* = man + **wolf**]

west NOUN **1** the direction where the sun sets, opposite east **2** the western part of a country, city, etc.

west ADJECTIVE **1** situated in the west • *the west coast* **2** coming from the west • *a west wind*

west ADVERB towards the west • *We sailed west.*

westerly ADJECTIVE to or from the west

western ADJECTIVE of or in the west

western NOUN **westerns** a film or story about cowboys or American Indians in western North America during the 19th and early 20th centuries

westward ADJECTIVE, ADVERB towards the west
▷ **westwards** ADVERB

wet ADJECTIVE **wetter, wettest 1** soaked or covered in water or other liquid **2** not yet dry • *wet paint* **3** rainy • *wet weather*
▷ **wetly** ADVERB **wetness** NOUN

wet VERB **wets, wetting, wet** or **wetted** make a thing wet

whale NOUN **whales** a very large sea animal
a whale of a (*informal*) very good or great • *We had a whale of a time.*

whaling NOUN hunting whales

what ADJECTIVE used to ask the amount or kind of something (*What kind of bike have you got?*) or to say how strange or great a person or thing is (*What a fool you are!*)

what PRONOUN **1** what thing or things • *What did you say?* **2** the thing that • *This is what you must do.*
what's what (*informal*) which things are important or useful

whatever PRONOUN **1** anything or everything • *Do whatever you like.* **2** no matter what • *Keep calm, whatever happens.*

whatever ADJECTIVE of any kind or amount • *Take whatever books you need.* • *There is no doubt whatever.*

wheat NOUN a cereal plant from which flour is made
▷ **wheaten** ADJECTIVE

wheedle VERB **wheedles, wheedling, wheedled** persuade by coaxing or flattering

wheel VERB **wheels, wheeling, wheeled 1** push a bicycle or trolley etc. along on its wheels **2** move in a curve or circle; change direction and face another way • *He wheeled round in astonishment.*

Thesaurus

► welfare, good, security, prosperity, comfort, benefit, happiness, health, interests

well-dressed ADJECTIVE *A well-dressed young woman came in.* ► smart, stylish, elegant, fashionable, well-groomed, chic, trim

well-known ADJECTIVE **1** *They played well-known types such as the domineering wife and the henpecked husband.* ► familiar, widely known, popular, common, typical **2** *She came from a well-known North London family.* ► famous, notable, prominent, leading, distinguished, eminent

well-off ADJECTIVE *dream gardens of well-off homeowners* ► rich, wealthy, well-to-do, affluent, moneyed, prosperous, opulent AN OPPOSITE IS poor

wet ADJECTIVE **1** *Her jacket was soaking and clung to her like a wet tea towel.* ► damp, soaked, saturated, drenched, moistened, sopping, dripping AN OPPOSITE IS dry **2** *The mowers could not be used because the ground was too wet.* ► waterlogged, sodden, boggy, soggy, spongy, swampy, squelchy OPPOSITES ARE dry, firm **3** *They were unlucky enough to meet wet weather at harvest time.* ► rainy, raining, drizzly, showery, pouring, humid, misty OPPOSITES ARE dry, fine **4** *The paint was still wet.* ► runny, sticky, tacky OPPOSITES ARE dry, set **5** (*informal*) *Some of the trainees seemed a bit wet.* ► feeble, weak, silly, soft, (*informal*) weedy, (*informal*) wimpish OPPOSITES ARE tough, strong

wet NOUN *The front wheels were prone to locking in the wet.* ► rain, dampness, wet weather, damp weather, drizzle

wet VERB *There is no need to wet your hair first.* ► dampen, damp, douse, drench, soak, spray, sprinkle, water, steep, irrigate, moisten, saturate AN OPPOSITE IS dry

whack VERB *I saw him take a stick and whack his dog.* ► hit, strike, smack, slap, thump, (*more informal*) slug

whack NOUN *She gave him a hefty whack across his shoulders.* ► blow, hit, slap, punch, thump, knock, smack

wheel VERB **1** *He grabbed a trolley and began to wheel the luggage away.* ► push, trundle, roll **2** *A flock of birds wheeled above them.* ► circle, gyrate, turn, orbit

wheel *NOUN* **wheels 1** a round device that turns on a shaft that passes through its centre **2** a horizontal revolving disc on which clay is made into a pot

wheelbarrow *NOUN* **wheelbarrows** a small cart with one wheel at the front and legs at the back, pushed by handles

wheelchair *NOUN* **wheelchairs** a chair on wheels for a person who cannot walk

wheeze *VERB* **wheezes, wheezing, wheezed** make a hoarse whistling sound as you breathe
▷ **wheeze** *NOUN* **wheezy** *ADJECTIVE*

when *ADVERB* at what time; at which time • *When can you come to tea?*

when *CONJUNCTION* **1** at the time that • *The bird flew away when I moved.* **2** although; considering that • *Why do you smoke when you know it's dangerous?*

whence *ADVERB* from where; from which

whenever *CONJUNCTION* at whatever time; every time • *Whenever I see it, I smile*

where *ADVERB* in or to what place or that place • *Where did you put it? Leave it where it is.*

whereabouts *ADVERB* in or near what place • *Whereabouts are you going?*

whereabouts *PLURAL NOUN* the place where something is • *Do you know the whereabouts of my radio?*

whereas *CONJUNCTION* but in contrast • *Some people enjoy sport, whereas others hate it.*

whereupon *CONJUNCTION* after which; and then

wherever *ADVERB* in or to whatever place

whet *VERB* **whets, whetting, whetted**
whet your appetite stimulate it
USAGE Do not confuse with **wet**

whether *CONJUNCTION* as one possibility; if • *I don't know whether to believe her or not.*

which *ADJECTIVE* what particular • *Which way did he go?*

which *PRONOUN* **1** what person or thing • *Which is your desk?* **2** the person or thing referred to • *The film, which is a western, will be shown on Saturday.*

whichever *PRONOUN, ADJECTIVE* no matter which; any which • *Take whichever you like.*

whiff *NOUN* **whiffs** a puff or slight smell of smoke, gas, etc.

while *CONJUNCTION* **1** during the time that; as long as • *Whistle while you work.* **2** although; but • *She is dark, while her sister is fair.*

while *NOUN* a period of time • *a long while*

while *VERB* **whiles, whiling, whiled**
while away pass time • *We whiled away the afternoon on the river.*

whim *NOUN* **whims** a sudden wish to do or have something

whimper *VERB* **whimpers, whimpering, whimpered** cry or whine softly
▷ **whimper** *NOUN*

whimsical *ADJECTIVE* quaint and playful
▷ **whimsically** *ADVERB* **whimsicality** *NOUN*

whine *VERB* **whines, whining, whined 1** make a long high miserable cry or a shrill sound **2** complain in a petty or feeble way
▷ **whine** *NOUN*

whip *NOUN* **whips 1** a cord or strip of leather fixed to a handle and used for hitting people or animals **2** an official of a political party in Parliament **3** a pudding made of whipped cream and fruit or flavouring

whip *VERB* **whips, whipping, whipped 1** hit a person or animal with a whip **2** beat cream until it becomes thick **3** move or take something suddenly • *He whipped out his pen.* **4** (*informal*) steal something

Thesaurus

wheel round *Elinor wheeled round, a look of horror on her face.* ► turn, swing round, change direction, swerve, veer

whereabouts *NOUN* *Despite inquiries, his whereabouts remain unknown.* ► location, position, situation, vicinity, address, site

whiff *NOUN* **1** *He caught a whiff of expensive perfume.* ► scent, aroma, smell, breath, puff, odour USAGE You normally use *odour* when you mean an unpleasant smell. **2** *At the slightest whiff of trouble he takes to his bed.* ► hint, trace, suggestion, suspicion, intimation

whim *NOUN* *It was silly to waste a whole morning on a foolish whim.* ► impulse, notion, urge, fancy, caprice, desire, quirk

whimper *VERB* *He began to whimper with fear.* ► snivel, wail, moan, cry, groan, weep, (*more informal*) grizzle

whimper *NOUN* *The dog made off with a whimper.* ► whine, cry, snivel

whine *NOUN* *There was a whine from the engines.* ► drone, whimper, hum

whine *VERB* **1** *Mosquitos whined in my ears.* ► drone, hum **2** (*informal*) *I'm sick of him whining to me about you.* ► grumble, complain, carp, grouch, moan, beef, (*informal*) whinge

whip *NOUN* *He threatened to use a whip on any intruders.* ► lash, scourge, cat, cat-o'-nine-tails, horsewhip, riding-crop, switch

whip *VERB* **1** *He whipped the boys and sent them away.* ► thrash, beat, flog, lash, scourge **2** *Why can you whip cream but not milk?* ► whisk, beat, stir vigorously **3** (*informal*) *She whipped a piece of paper out of her pocket.* ► pull, whisk, pluck, tug, take **4** (*informal*) *I can always whip round to the corner shop.* ► dash, hurry, shoot, run, sprint, rush, race, tear

whip up stir up people's feelings etc. • *She whipped up support for her plans.*

whirl *VERB* **whirls, whirling, whirled** turn or spin very quickly
▷ **whirl** *NOUN*

whirlpool *NOUN* **whirlpools** a whirling current of water

whirlwind *NOUN* **whirlwinds** a strong wind that whirls round a central point

whirr *VERB* **whirrs, whirring, whirred** make a continuous buzzing sound
▷ **whirr** *NOUN*

whisk *VERB* **whisks, whisking, whisked** **1** move or brush something away quickly and lightly • *A waiter whisked away our plates.* **2** beat eggs etc. until they are frothy

whisk *NOUN* **whisks** **1** a kitchen tool used for whisking things **2** a whisking movement [from Old Norse]

whisker *NOUN* **whiskers** **1** a hair of those growing on a man's face, forming a beard or moustache if not shaved off **2** a long bristle growing near the mouth of a cat etc.
▷ **whiskery** *ADJECTIVE*

whisky *NOUN* **whiskies** a strong alcoholic drink [from Scottish Gaelic *uisge beatha* = water of life]

whisper *VERB* **whispers, whispering, whispered** **1** speak very softly **2** talk secretly
▷ **whisper** *NOUN*

whist *NOUN* a card game usually for four people

whistle *VERB* **whistles, whistling, whistled** make a shrill or musical sound, especially by blowing through your lips
▷ **whistler** *NOUN*

whistle *NOUN* **whistles** **1** a whistling sound **2** a device that makes a shrill sound when air or steam is blown through it

white *NOUN* **whites** **1** the very lightest colour, like snow or salt **2** the transparent substance (**albumen**) round the yolk of an egg, which turns white when it is cooked **3** a person with a light-coloured skin

white *ADJECTIVE* **1** of the colour white **2** (said of a person) having light-coloured skin **3** very pale from the effects of illness or fear etc. **4** (said about coffee) with milk
▷ **whiteness** *NOUN*

white elephant *NOUN* **white elephants** a useless possession, especially one that is expensive to keep

white-hot *ADJECTIVE* extremely hot; so hot that heated metal looks white

white lie *NOUN* **white lies** a harmless or trivial lie that you tell in order to avoid hurting someone's feelings

whiten *VERB* **whitens, whitening, whitened** make or become whiter

whitewash *NOUN* **1** a white liquid containing lime or powdered chalk, used for painting walls and ceilings etc. **2** concealing mistakes or other unpleasant facts so that someone will not be punished
▷ **whitewash** *VERB*

whither *ADVERB* (*old use*) to what place
USAGE Do not confuse with **wither**.

whittle *VERB* **whittles, whittling, whittled** **1** shape wood by trimming thin slices off the surface **2** reduce something by removing various things from it • *We need to whittle down the cost.*

whizz or **whiz** *VERB* **whizzes, whizzing, whizzed** **1** move very quickly **2** sound like something rushing through the air

who *PRONOUN* which person or people; the particular person or people • *This is the boy who stole the apples.*

whoever *PRONOUN* **1** any or every person who **2** no matter who

whole *ADJECTIVE* **1** complete **2** not injured or broken

Thesaurus

whirl *NOUN* **1** *His mind was in a whirl and he was worried.* ► daze, spin, muddle, stupor, state of confusion **2** (*informal*) *The only way to find out was to give it a whirl.* ► try, test, (*informal*) shot, (*informal*) bash

whirl *VERB* *The dancers appear to whirl round with their hands on their hips.* ► circle, gyrate, twirl, spin, rotate, pirouette, reel, revolve, swivel, turn, twist, wheel

whisk *VERB* **1** *Whisk the sugar and eggs together.* ► beat, mix, stir, whip **2** *You will be whisked off to a studio for a photo session.* ► rush, speed, hurry, sweep, shoot, hurtle **3** *He whisked a blanket off the nearest trolley.* ► pull, pluck, tug, take, (*more informal*) whip

whisper *VERB* *Anne whispered something in his ear.* ► murmur, breathe, mutter, mumble
AN OPPOSITE IS shout

whisper *NOUN* **1** *He spoke in a whisper.* ► murmur, mutter, undertone, hushed voice **2** *I heard a whisper that he's left the country.* ► rumour, report, piece of gossip, piece of hearsay

white *ADJECTIVE* **1** *He rested his fingers on the white keys.* ► ivory, snowy, chalky, pale, snow-white, cream **2** *Her face was white with fear.* ► pale, pallid, ashen, colourless, bloodless

whole *ADJECTIVE* **1** *I don't have time to read the whole book.* ► entire, complete, full, total, full-length, unabridged, uncut, unexpurgated

A B C D E F G H I J K L M N O P Q R S T U V W X Y Z

whole NOUN **1** the full amount **2** a complete thing
on the whole considering everything; mainly
wholefood NOUN food that is free of additives and has been processed as little as possible
wholehearted ADJECTIVE without doubts or reservations • *You have my wholehearted support.*
wholemeal ADJECTIVE made from the whole grain of wheat
whole number NOUN **whole numbers** a number without fractions
wholesale NOUN selling goods in large quantities to be resold by others COMPARE **retail**
▷ **wholesaler** NOUN
wholesale ADJECTIVE, ADVERB **1** on a large scale; including everybody or everything • *wholesale destruction* **2** in the wholesale trade
wholesome ADJECTIVE good for health; healthy • *wholesome food*
▷ **wholesomeness** NOUN
wholly ADVERB completely or entirely
whom PRONOUN the form of **who** used when it is the object of a verb or comes after a preposition, as in • *the boy whom I saw* or *to whom we spoke*
whoop (woop) NOUN **whoops** a loud cry of excitement
▷ **whoop** VERB
whooping cough (**hoop**- ing) NOUN an infectious disease that causes spasms of coughing and gasping for breath
whopper NOUN **whoppers** (*slang*) something very large
whopping ADJECTIVE (*slang*) very large or remarkable • *a whopping lie*
who's (*mainly spoken*) who is; who has
USAGE Do not confuse with **whose**.
whose PRONOUN belonging to what person or people; of whom; of which • *Whose house is that?*
USAGE Do not confuse with **who's**.
why ADVERB for what reason or purpose; the particular reason on account of which • *This is why I came.*
wick NOUN **wicks** **1** the string that goes through the middle of a candle and is lit **2** the strip of material that you light in a lamp or heater etc. that uses oil
wicked ADJECTIVE **1** morally bad or cruel **2** mischievous • *a wicked smile* **3** (*informal*) very good
▷ **wickedly** ADVERB **wickedness** NOUN
wicket NOUN **wickets** **1** a set of three stumps and two bails used in cricket **2** the strip of ground between the wickets
wicketkeeper NOUN **wicketkeepers** the fielder in cricket who stands behind the batsman's wicket
wide ADJECTIVE **1** measuring a lot from side to side; not narrow **2** measuring from side to side • *The cloth is one metre wide.* **3** covering a great range • *a wide knowledge of birds* **4** fully open • *eyes wide with excitement* **5** missing the target • *The shot was wide of the mark.*
▷ **widely** ADVERB **wideness** NOUN

Thesaurus

OPPOSITES ARE incomplete, partial **2** *The archaeologists uncovered a Greek vase that turned out to be whole.* ► intact, in one piece, unbroken, undamaged, unharmed, unscathed, perfect OPPOSITES ARE broken, fragmentary
wholehearted ADJECTIVE *You have our wholehearted support.* ► total, complete, unreserved, unqualified, committed, absolute, outright, utter OPPOSITES ARE half-hearted, partial
whopping ADJECTIVE *The bill came to a whopping £500.* ► huge, enormous, gigantic, mammoth, immense, massive, colossal
wicked ADJECTIVE **1** *a wicked person a wicked act* ► evil, bad, sinful, base, immoral, corrupt, depraved, heinous, iniquitous
OPPOSITES ARE moral, good, upright **2** *It was wicked of you to say such things.* ► naughty, wrong, nasty, mischievous, unkind
OPPOSITES ARE good, kind **3** *There was a wicked gleam in his eye.* ► mischievous, playful, rascally, impish, devilish, cheeky **4** (*informal*) *He makes a wicked fruit salad.* ► excellent, marvellous, wonderful, superb
AN OPPOSITE IS lousy
wickedness NOUN *the sheer wickedness of their plan* ► evil , enormity, iniquity, vileness, baseness, foulness, heinousness, immorality, infamy, sinfulness, villainy, turpitude, wrong, wrongdoing AN OPPOSITE IS goodness
wide ADJECTIVE **1** *The river was fast and wide. Players are spread over a wide area.* ► broad, expansive, extensive, vast, large, spacious, spread out, outspread AN OPPOSITE IS narrow **2** *There is a wide choice of dinner menu. The programmes reach a wide audience.* ► extensive, comprehensive, wide-ranging, inclusive, all-embracing, broad, ample, universal OPPOSITES ARE narrow, limited **3** *Wide trousers became fashionable again.* ► baggy, loose, full, flared OPPOSITES ARE narrow, tight **4** *The shot went wide.* ► off course, off target, off the mark AN OPPOSITE IS on target
wide ADVERB *Her eyes opened wide.* ► fully, completely

a b c d e f g h i j k l m n o p q r s t u v w x y z

A B C D E F G H I J K L M N O P Q R S T U V **W** X Y Z

wide *ADVERB* **1** to the full extent; far apart • *Open wide.* **2** missing the target • *The shot went wide.* **3** over a large area • *She travelled far and wide.*

widen *VERB* **widens, widening, widened** make or become wider

widespread *ADJECTIVE* existing in many places or over a wide area • *a widespread belief*

widow *NOUN* **widows** a woman whose husband has died

widowed *ADJECTIVE* made a widow or widower

widower *NOUN* **widowers** a man whose wife has died

width *NOUN* **widths** how wide something is; wideness

wield *VERB* **wields, wielding, wielded 1** hold and use a weapon or tool • *wielding a sword* **2** have and use power or influence

wife *NOUN* **wives** the woman to whom a man is married [from Old English *wif* = woman]

wig *NOUN* **wigs** a covering for the head, made of real or artificial hair

wiggle *VERB* **wiggles, wiggling, wiggled** move from side to side

wigwam *NOUN* **wigwams** a tent formerly used by Native Americans, made by fastening skins or mats over poles

wild *ADJECTIVE* **1** living or growing in its natural state, not looked after by people **2** not cultivated • *a wild landscape* **3** not civilized • *the Wild West* **4** not controlled; very violent or excited **5** very foolish or unreasonable • *You do have wild ideas.*
▷ **wildly** *ADVERB* **wildness** *NOUN*

wilderness *NOUN* **wildernesses** a wild uncultivated area; a desert

wildfire *NOUN*
spread like wildfire (said about rumours etc.) spread very fast

wildlife *NOUN* wild animals in their natural setting

wilful *ADJECTIVE* **1** obstinately determined to do what you want • *a wilful child* **2** deliberate • *wilful murder*
▷ **wilfully** *ADVERB* **wilfulness** *NOUN*

will[1] *AUXILIARY VERB* used to express the future tense, questions, or promises • *They will arrive soon.* • *Will you shut the door?* • *I will get my*

Thesaurus

widen *VERB* **1** *There are plans to widen parts of the motorway.* ► broaden, make wider, expand, enlarge, extend, open out, spread, stretch AN OPPOSITE IS narrow **2** *Her smile widened.* ► broaden, become wider, spread AN OPPOSITE IS narrow **3** *They must widen the scope of the inquiry.* ► expand, extend, broaden, enlarge, increase OPPOSITES ARE narrow, restrict, limit

widespread *ADJECTIVE* **1** *These incidents provoked widespread protest.* ► general, extensive, universal, wholesale, far-reaching, global AN OPPOSITE IS uncommon **2** *Death and disease were widespread in these years.* ► rife, prevalent, endemic, pervasive, common

width *NOUN* *Two white lines should be drawn across the width of the pitch.* ► breadth, span, girth, diameter

wife *NOUN* *His new wife is a Parisian.* ► spouse, partner, (*more formal*) consort, (*more informal*) woman, (*more informal*) mate, (*more informal*) better half

wiggle *VERB* *He removed his shoes and wiggled his toes.* ► wriggle, waggle, jiggle

wild *ADJECTIVE* **1** *He began attacking me like a wild animal.* ► fierce, feral, ferocious, untamed, undomesticated AN OPPOSITE IS tame **2** *There are many wild flowers that can be legally picked.* ► natural, uncultivated, indigenous AN OPPOSITE IS cultivated **3** *Even seemingly wild ideas may be aired at this point.* ► crazy, ridiculous, madcap, absurd, foolish, silly, outrageous, extravagant, impractical, rash, foolhardy OPPOSITES ARE sensible, practical **4** *A wild urge rose up inside her to tell everything.* ► reckless, rash, intense, extreme OPPOSITES ARE gentle, mild **5** *My father liked these wild people.* ► primitive, savage, barbarous, uncivilized, uncultured AN OPPOSITE IS civilized **6** *She said she was sorry for her wild behaviour.* ► unruly, rowdy, violent, disorderly, uncontrolled, unrestrained, undisciplined, unconstrained, unbridled OPPOSITES ARE calm, restrained **7** *The parties involve loud music and wild dancing.* ► lively, flamboyant, boisterous, exuberant, animated AN OPPOSITE IS restrained **8** *Don't plan to go out in really wild weather.* ► rough, stormy, tempestuous, blustery, foul, inclement AN OPPOSITE IS calm **9** *the beautiful wild scenery of the Highlands* ► rugged, rough, desolate, uncultivated, unpopulated, barren **10** *His team mates were wild with joy.* ► excited, ecstatic, delirious, frantic, frenzied **11** *Without knowing the answer I decided to risk a wild guess.* ► arbitrary, random, haphazard, hit-or-miss AN OPPOSITE IS considered **12** (*informal*) *Being disturbed at this time made him wild.* ► furious, angry, enraged, irate, cross, livid, (*more informal*) hopping mad AN OPPOSITE IS pleased **13 wild about** (*informal*) *I'm not wild about the music.* ► keen on, enthusiastic about, (*informal*) mad about, (*informal*) crazy about

wilful *ADJECTIVE* **1** *He was charged with wilful damage and assault.* ► deliberate, intentional, premeditated, intended, planned, calculated, conscious, voluntary AN OPPOSITE IS accidental

revenge. [from Old English]USAGE See the entry for **shall**.

will [2] *NOUN* **wills** **1** the mental power to decide and control what you do **2** a desire; a chosen decision • *I wrote the letter against my will.* **3** determination to do something • *They set to work with a will.* **4** a written statement of how a person's possessions are to be disposed of after his or her death

at will whenever you like • *You can come and go at will.*

will *VERB* **wills, willing, willed** use your will power; influence something by doing this • *I was willing you to win!* [from Old English *willa*]

willing *ADJECTIVE* ready and happy to do what is wanted

▷ **willingly** *ADVERB* **willingness** *NOUN*

willow *NOUN* **willows** a tree or shrub with flexible branches, usually growing near water

will power *NOUN* strength of mind to control what you do

willy-nilly *ADVERB* whether you want to or not

wilt *VERB* **wilts, wilting, wilted** lose freshness or strength

wily (wy- lee) *ADJECTIVE* cunning or crafty

▷ **wiliness** *NOUN*

win *VERB* **wins, winning, won** **1** defeat your opponents in a battle, game, or contest **2** get or achieve something by a victory or by using effort or skill etc. • *She won the prize.*

win over gain someone's favour or support • *By the end he had won over the audience.*

win *NOUN* **wins** a victory

wince *VERB* **winces, wincing, winced** make a slight movement because of pain or embarrassment etc.

wind [1] (rhymes with *tinned*) *NOUN* **winds** **1** a current of air **2** gas in the stomach or intestines that makes you feel uncomfortable **3** breath used for a purpose, e.g. for running or speaking **4** the wind instruments of an orchestra

get or **have the wind up** (*informal*) feel frightened

get wind of hear a rumour of something

wind *VERB* **winds, winding, winded** put a person out of breath • *The climb had winded us.*

wind [2] (rhymes with *find*) *VERB* **winds, winding, wound** **1** go or turn something in twists, curves, or circles **2** make a clock or watch work by tightening its spring

▷ **winder** *NOUN*

wind up **1** make a clock or watch work by tightening its spring **2** close a business

Thesaurus

2 *She checked her wilful and impulsive self.* ► headstrong, self-willed, strong-willed, obstinate, stubborn, perverse, determined, dogged, intransigent, obdurate AN OPPOSITE IS amenable

will *NOUN* **1** *Corruption exists when politicians have lost the will to enforce the law.* ► determination, resolve, resolution, intention, purpose, aim, desire, inclination, volition, will-power, wish **2** *I don't think it's the will of the people.* ► desire, wish, choice, preference **3** *She had died without making a will.* ► testament, last wishes

will *VERB* **1** *He willed them not to panic.* ► encourage, inspire, influence, wish **2** *She willed her money equally to all her nephews and nieces.* ► bequeath, leave, pass on

willing *ADJECTIVE* **1** *Let us know if you are willing to make cakes or prepare sandwiches.* ► prepared, ready, disposed, agreeable, eager, inclined, content, pleased, (*more informal*) game OPPOSITES ARE unwilling, reluctant, disinclined **2** *You'd be surprised what can be achieved by willing hands eager to do good turns.* ► enthusiastic, helpful, obliging, cooperative, amenable, compliant, consenting OPPOSITES ARE unwilling, unhelpful

wilt *VERB* **1** *The flowers had begun to wilt.* ► droop, fade, shrivel, wither, become limp, flop, languish, sag OPPOSITES ARE thrive, revive, perk up **2** *Their joy soon wilted.* ► fail, flag, wane, dwindle, evaporate, weaken, diminish, sink AN OPPOSITE IS grow

wily *ADJECTIVE* *He was constantly in danger of being outwitted by his wily opponents.* ► clever, crafty, shrewd, artful, astute, cunning, devious, guileful, knowing, scheming, shifty, foxy, sly, underhand AN OPPOSITE IS naive

win *VERB* **1** *She had a good chance of winning.* ► be victorious, be the winner, succeed, triumph, come first, finish first, prevail, conquer, overcome AN OPPOSITE IS lose **2** *Next year they would win first prize.* ► achieve, receive, acquire, (*more informal*) carry off, (*more informal*) come away with, (*more informal*) pick up, (*more informal*) walk away with **3** *Charles II managed to win the support of the Scots.* ► gain, secure, obtain, earn, deserve, get

win *NOUN* *His win ended eleven years of American domination of the championship.* ► victory, triumph, success, conquest AN OPPOSITE IS defeat

wind *NOUN* (rhymes with *pinned*) *She shivered in the chill wind.* ► breeze, air current, gust, blast, puff, breath, draught, gale, squall

wind *VERB* (rhymes with *mind*) **1** *He wound the cord tightly.* ► coil, loop, twist, twine, curl, curve, furl, turn, roll **2** *The Saigon River begins to wind like a serpent.* ► twist, snake, bend, curve,

3 (*informal*) end up in a place or condition • *He wound up in jail.*

windfall NOUN **windfalls 1** a piece of unexpected good luck, especially a sum of money **2** a fruit blown off a tree by the wind

wind instrument NOUN **wind instruments** a musical instrument played by blowing, e.g. a trumpet

windmill NOUN **windmills** a mill worked by the wind turning its sails

window NOUN **windows 1** an opening in a wall or roof etc. to let in light and often air, usually filled with glass **2** the glass in this opening **3** (in computing) an area on a VDU screen used for a particular purpose [from Old Norse *vind* = wind, air + *auga* = eye]

windpipe NOUN **windpipes** the tube by which air passes from the throat to the lungs

windscreen NOUN **windscreens** the window at the front of a motor vehicle

windsurfing NOUN surfing on a board that has a sail fixed to it

▷ **windsurfer** NOUN

windy ADJECTIVE with much wind • *It's windy outside.*

wine NOUN **wines 1** an alcoholic drink made from grapes or other plants **2** a dark red colour

wing NOUN **wings 1** one of the pair of parts used by a bird, bat, or insect for flying **2** one of the pair of long flat parts that stick out from the side of an aircraft and support it while it flies **3** a part of a large building that extends from the main part **4** the part of a motor vehicle's body above a wheel **5** a player whose place is at one of the far ends of the forward line in football or hockey etc. **6** a section of a political party, with more extreme opinions than the others

on the wing flying

take wing fly away

under your wing under your protection

the wings the sides of a theatre stage out of sight of the audience

wing VERB **wings, winging, winged 1** fly; travel by means of wings • *The bird winged its way home.* **2** wound a bird in the wing or a person in the arm

winged ADJECTIVE having wings

wink VERB **winks, winking, winked 1** close and open your eye quickly, especially as a signal to someone **2** (said about a light) flicker or twinkle

wink NOUN **winks 1** the action of winking **2** a very short period of sleep • *I didn't sleep a wink.*

winkle VERB **winkles, winkling, winkled**

winkle out extract or obtain something with difficulty • *I managed to winkle out some information.*

winner NOUN **winners 1** a person or animal etc. that wins **2** something very successful • *Her latest book is a winner.*

winnings PLURAL NOUN money won

winter NOUN **winters** the coldest season of the year, between autumn and spring

▷ **wintry** ADJECTIVE

wipe VERB **wipes, wiping, wiped** dry or clean something by rubbing it

▷ **wipe** NOUN

wipe out 1 cancel • *wipe out the debt* **2** destroy something completely

wiper NOUN **wipers** a device for wiping something, especially on a vehicle's windscreen

Thesaurus

meander, ramble, twist and turn, zigzag

wind up (*informal*) *We could wind up paying the whole lot.* ► end up, finish up, land up, find yourself

wind someone up (*informal*) *I'm sure he's just doing it to wind me up.* ► tease, annoy, disconcert, trick

windy ADJECTIVE **1** *It was too cold and windy to sit and wait.* ► blowy, breezy, blustery, gusty, squally, boisterous, draughty, stormy AN OPPOSITE IS calm

wing NOUN **1** *The maternity department is in the north wing of the hospital.* ► section, annexe, end, extension **2** *the military wing of the organization* ► section, faction, branch, group

wink VERB *The red light winked.* ► flash, gleam, flicker, sparkle, twinkle

wink NOUN *Then, in a wink, it all turned to dust.* ► instant, moment, second, flash

winner NOUN *The points system produces an overall winner.* ► victor, champion, conqueror, first, prizewinner AN OPPOSITE IS loser

winning ADJECTIVE **1** *For the fourth time her was on the winning side.* ► victorious, successful, triumphant, champion, conquering, prevailing, leading, top-scoring AN OPPOSITE IS losing **2** *The show lacks a really winning song.* ► appealing, attractive, fetching, charming, engaging

winnings NOUN *She used part of her winnings to buy a new house.* ► prize money, gains, money AN OPPOSITE IS losses

wintry ADJECTIVE *He opened a window, letting in damp wintry air.* ► chilly, frosty, cold, bleak, freezing, icy, biting, snowy

wipe VERB *She wiped the table with a damp cloth. Nathan wiped the crumbs from his mouth.* ► rub, brush, clean, mop, sponge, swab, wash

wipe out *Two hurricanes almost wiped out the flourishing egg industry.* ► destroy, obliterate, annihilate, eradicate, exterminate, demolish

wire *NOUN* **wires** **1** a strand or thin flexible rod of metal **2** a piece of wire used to carry electric current **3** a fence etc. made from wire **4** a telegram

wire *VERB* **wires, wiring, wired** **1** fasten or strengthen something with wire **2** fit or connect something with wires to carry electric current

wireless *NOUN* **wirelesses** (*old use*) a radio

wiring *NOUN* the system of wires carrying electricity in a building or in a device

wiry *ADJECTIVE* **1** like wire **2** lean and strong

wisdom *NOUN* **1** being wise **2** wise sayings or writings

wisdom tooth *NOUN* **wisdom teeth** a molar tooth that may grow at the back of the jaw of a person aged about 20 or more

wise *ADJECTIVE* knowing or understanding many things, and making good judgements
▷ **wisely** *ADVERB*

wish *VERB* **wishes, wishing, wished** **1** feel or say that you would like to have or do something or would like something to happen **2** say that you hope someone will get something • *Wish me luck!*

wish *NOUN* **wishes** **1** something you wish for; a desire **2** the action of wishing • *Make a wish when you blow out the candles.*

wishbone *NOUN* **wishbones** a forked bone between the neck and breast of a chicken or other bird

wishful thinking *NOUN* believing something because you want it to be true rather than because it is likely

wisp *NOUN* **wisps** **1** a few strands of hair or bits of straw etc. **2** a small streak of smoke or cloud etc.
▷ **wispy** *ADJECTIVE*

wistful *ADJECTIVE* sadly longing for something
▷ **wistfully** *ADVERB* **wistfulness** *NOUN*

wit *NOUN* **wits** **1** intelligence or cleverness • *Use your wits.* **2** a clever kind of humour **3** a witty person
at your wits' end not knowing what to do
keep your wits about you stay alert

witch *NOUN* **witches** a person, especially a woman, who uses magic to do things

witchcraft *NOUN* the use of magic, especially for evil purposes

witch-hunt *NOUN* **witch-hunts** a campaign to find and punish people who hold views that are considered to be unacceptable or dangerous

with *PREPOSITION* used to indicate being in the company or care etc. of (*Come with me*), having (*a man with a beard*), using (*Hit it with a hammer*), because of (*shaking with laughter*), feeling or showing (*We heard it with pleasure*), towards or concerning (*I was angry with him*), in opposition to; against (*Don't argue with your father*), being separated from (*We had to part with it*)

withdraw *VERB* **withdraws, withdrawing, withdrew, withdrawn** **1** take back or away; remove • *She withdrew money from the bank.* **2** go away from a place or people • *The troops withdrew from the frontier.*

withdrawal *NOUN* **withdrawals** **1** taking something out, especially money from a bank

Thesaurus

wisdom *NOUN* *He would persuade them of the wisdom of adopting this course.* ► sense, prudence, common sense, good sense, intelligence, judgement, astuteness, sagacity, discernment, insight, reason

wise *ADJECTIVE* **1** *Wise parents are able to give support and advice.* ► sensible, prudent, shrewd, perceptive, intelligent, sagacious, sage, clever, astute, informed, judicious, discerning, enlightened OPPOSITES ARE unwise, foolish **2** *The action they took seemed wise and reasonable.* ► sensible, prudent, advisable, appropriate, proper, fair, just, right, sound OPPOSITES ARE unwise, foolish, ill-advised

wish *NOUN* **1** *It was her parents' dearest wish that she should be happy.* ► desire, ambition, objective, want, longing, inclination, aim, aspiration, craving, fancy, hankering, hope, yearning **2** *He had no wish to appear impolite.* ► desire, inclination **3** *We will respect your wishes.* ► request, bidding, direction, will, order

wish *VERB* *If guests wish to eat out, there are several pubs in the village.* ► want, hope
wish for *I wish for a really good night's sleep.* ► desire, want, long for, yearn for, crave, fancy, hanker after

wit *NOUN* **1** *The speech was improved by moments of great wit.* ► humour, wittiness, banter, repartee, drollery, badinage, facetiousness, ingenuity, comedy, jokes **2** *Jack was regarded as the club wit.* ► joker, comedian, wag, comic, humorist, jester **3** *She was a woman of great wit and wisdom.* ► intelligence, shrewdness, wisdom, cleverness, sense, understanding

witch *NOUN* **1** *She must look for the witch's hat.* ► sorceress, enchantress **2** *What are you talking about, you stupid witch?* ► hag, crone, harpy

withdraw *VERB* **1** *She withdrew the photo abruptly and returned it to the folder.* ► take back, remove, snatch **2** *All the objections were eventually withdrawn.* ► retract, rescind, revoke, take back, cancel, remove, disclaim, renounce, take away AN OPPOSITE IS introduc

A B C D E F G H I J K L M N O P Q R S T U

2 the process of stopping taking addictive drugs • *withdrawal symptoms*

withdrawn ADJECTIVE very shy or reserved

wither VERB **withers, withering, withered** **1** shrivel or wilt **2** make something shrivel or wilt

USAGE Do not confuse with **whither**.

withering ADJECTIVE scornful or sarcastic • *a withering remark*

withhold VERB **withholds, withholding, withheld** refuse to give or allow information or permission

within PREPOSITION, ADVERB inside; not beyond something

without PREPOSITION **1** not having • *without food* **2** free from • *without fear* **3** (*old use*) outside • *without the city wall*

without ADVERB (*old use*) outside • *We looked at the house from within and without.*

withstand VERB **withstands, withstanding, withstood** endure something successfully; resist

witness NOUN **witnesses** **1** a person who sees or hears something happen • *There were no witnesses to the accident.* **2** a person who gives evidence in a lawcourt

witness VERB **witnesses, witnessing, witnessed** **1** be a witness of something • *Did anyone witness the accident?* **2** sign a document to confirm that it is genuine

witticism NOUN **witticisms** a witty remark

witty ADJECTIVE **wittier, wittiest** clever and amusing; full of wit
▷ **wittily** ADVERB **wittiness** NOUN

wizard NOUN **wizards** **1** a male witch; a magician **2** a person with amazing abilities
▷ **wizardry** NOUN

wobble VERB **wobbles, wobbling, wobbled** move unsteadily from side to side; shake slightly
▷ **wobble** NOUN **wobbly** ADJECTIVE

woe NOUN **woes** **1** sorrow **2** misfortune
▷ **woeful** ADJECTIVE **woefully** ADVERB

woebegone ADJECTIVE looking unhappy

wok NOUN **woks** a Chinese cooking pan shaped like a large bowl [from Chinese]

wolf NOUN **wolves** a fierce wild animal of the dog family, often hunting in packs

wolf VERB **wolfs, wolfing, wolfed** eat something greedily

woman NOUN **women** a grown-up female human being
▷ **womanhood** NOUN
[from Old English]

womanly ADJECTIVE having qualities that are thought to be typical of women

womb (woom) NOUN **wombs** the hollow organ in a female's body where babies develop before they are born

Thesaurus

3 *The rebels were forced to withdraw into the hills.* ► retreat, retire, draw back, move back, fall back AN OPPOSITE IS advance **4** *One of the representatives decided to withdraw from future discussions.* ► pull out, back out, drop out, secede, (*more informal*) cry off AN OPPOSITE IS enter

wither VERB *The flowers had withered in the strong sun.* ► wilt, droop, become limp, dehydrate, dry up, sag, shrivel, waste away, flag, flop AN OPPOSITE IS thrive

withhold VERB *He had deliberately withheld the fact that he couldn't sail.* ► suppress, repress, onceal, hide, hold back, keep back, keep cret, retain

stand VERB *The boat must be strong enough hstand the roughest weather.* ► resist, hold out against, last out against, bear st, stand up to, survive, tolerate, e with AN OPPOSITE IS succumb to

The only witness was the office erver, bystander, onlooker, vitness, looker-on, watcher

e *aid he has witnessed several utality.* ► see, observe, be present at, be a witness to, notice, view, watch, attend, behold, look on

witty ADJECTIVE *Dolly is witty and entertaining.* ► humorous, amusing, funny, quick-witted, sharp-witted, waggish, droll, comic, facetious, sparkling AN OPPOSITE IS dull

wizard NOUN **1** *We were still under the wizard's spell.* ► magician, sorcerer, enchanter, warlock **2** *He's an absolute wizard with engines.* ► expert, genius, adept, master, (*more informal*) star

wobble VERB **1** *She reached out and caught it without so much as wobbling.* ► shake, sway, teeter, totter, be unsteady, oscillate, quake **2** *Once more the glass wobbled.* ► tremble, shake, quiver, vibrate, rock

wobbly ADJECTIVE **1** *The table had a wobbly leg.* ► unsteady, loose, rickety, rocky, unstable, shaky, insecure, unbalanced, unsafe AN OPPOSITE IS steady **2** *He felt wobbly and had to sit down.* ► giddy, dizzy, faint, groggy, unsteady

woman NOUN *The car pulled up and a woman got out.* ► female, lady, girl RELATED ADJECTIVES female, feminine

X Y Z

women's lib or **women's liberation** *NOUN* the freedom of women to have the same rights, opportunities, and status as men

wonder *NOUN* **wonders** **1** a feeling of surprise and admiration or curiosity **2** something that causes this feeling; a marvel
no wonder it is not surprising

wonder *VERB* **wonders, wondering, wondered** **1** feel that you want to know; try to decide • *We are still wondering what to do next.* **2** feel wonder

wonderful *ADJECTIVE* marvellous or excellent
▷ **wonderfully** *ADVERB*

won't (*mainly spoken*) will not

woo *VERB* **woos, wooing, wooed** (*old use*) **1** court a woman **2** seek someone's favour or support
▷ **wooer** *NOUN*

wood *NOUN* **woods** **1** the substance of which trees are made **2** many trees growing close together

wooded *ADJECTIVE* covered with growing trees

wooden *ADJECTIVE* **1** made of wood **2** stiff and showing no expression or liveliness
▷ **woodenly** *ADVERB*

woodlouse *NOUN* **woodlice** a small crawling creature with seven pairs of legs, living in rotten wood or damp soil etc.

woodpecker *NOUN* **woodpeckers** a bird that taps tree trunks with its beak to find insects

woodwind *NOUN* wind instruments that are usually made of wood, e.g. the clarinet and oboe

woodwork *NOUN* **1** making things out of wood **2** things made out of wood

woodworm *NOUN* **woodworms** the larva of a kind of beetle that bores into wood; the damage done by this

woody *ADJECTIVE* **1** like wood; consisting of wood **2** full of trees

wool *NOUN* **wools** **1** the thick soft hair of sheep and goats etc. **2** thread or cloth made from this

woollen *ADJECTIVE* made of wool

woolly *ADJECTIVE* **1** covered with wool or wool-like hair **2** like wool; woollen **3** not thinking clearly; vague or confused • *woolly ideas*
▷ **woolliness** *NOUN*

word *NOUN* **words** **1** a set of sounds or letters that has a meaning, and when written or printed has no spaces between the letters **2** a brief conversation • *Can I have a word with you?* **3** a promise • *He kept his word.* **4** a command or spoken signal • *Run when I give the word.* **5** a message; information • *We sent word of our safe arrival.*
have words quarrel
word for word in exactly the same words

word *VERB* **words, wording, worded** express something in words • *Word the question carefully.*

Thesaurus

wonder *NOUN* **1** *We were speechless with wonder.* ► awe, admiration, amazement, wonderment, astonishment, fascination, respect, reverence, surprise **2** *a wonder of nature* ► marvel, miracle, sensation, spectacle, prodigy **3** *It's a wonder there were no casualties.* ► marvel, miracle, extraordinary thing

wonder *VERB* *I was beginning to wonder if they would ever come.* ► ponder, speculate, ask yourself, be curious about, reflect on
wonder at *We wondered at such bravery.* ► marvel at, admire, be amazed by, feel wonder at, stand in awe of

wonderful *ADJECTIVE* *We had a wonderful time.* ► excellent, marvellous, fantastic, splendid, lovely, delightful, smashing, (*more informal*) terrific OPPOSITES ARE awful, dreadful

wood *NOUN* **1** *There is a nature trail through the wood.* ► forest, woodland, woods, trees, coppice, copse, thicket, grove, spinney RELATED ADJECTIVE sylvan **2** *a little cabin made from wood* ► timber, planks, planking, lumber RELATED ADJECTIVE ligneous

wooded *ADJECTIVE* *a wooded valley* ► tree-covered, forested afforested, woody, timbered, (*poetic*) sylvan

wooden *ADJECTIVE* **1** *wooden furniture* ► timber, wood **2** *The acting and production were wooden.* ► stiff, unnatural, stilted, lifeless, leaden, deadpan, emotionless, unemotional, expressionless, awkward, clumsy, graceless AN OPPOSITE IS lively

woolly *ADJECTIVE* **1** *a woolly hat* ► woollen, wool, fleecy **2** *a sheep's woolly coat* ► fleecy, furry, downy, fuzzy, hairy, shaggy, soft **3** *woolly thinking* ► vague, ill-defined, unfocused, unclear, imprecise, confused, muddled, blurry, hazy, foggy

word *NOUN* **1** *She wanted to find another word for 'chuckle'.* ► expression, term, locution RELATED ADJECTIVES verbal, lexical **2** *Have you had any word from the hospital?* ► news, information, communication, report, comment, advice **3** *I'll have a word with them in private.* ► talk, conversation, chat, discussion, consultation, exchange of views, tête-à-tête USAGE Note that *tête-à-tête* is normally used about a personal conversation between two people. **4** *I gave her my word.* ► promise, guarantee, pledge, assurance, word of honour, oath

word *VERB* *The book has advice on how to word your CV.* ► phrase, express, construct, formulate, frame, couch, write, say, put

word class *NOUN* **word classes** any of the groups (also called **parts of speech**) into which words are divided in grammar (noun, pronoun, adjective, verb, adverb, preposition, conjunction, and interjection)

wording *NOUN* the way something is worded

word of honour *NOUN* a solemn promise

word-perfect *ADJECTIVE* having memorized every word perfectly • *He was word-perfect at the rehearsal.*

word processor *NOUN* **word processors** a type of computer or program used for editing and printing letters and documents

wordy *ADJECTIVE* using too many words; not concise

wore *past tense of* **wear**

work *NOUN* **works 1** something you have to do that needs effort or energy • *Digging is hard work.* **2** a job; employment **3** something produced by work • *The teacher marked our work.* **4** (in science) the result of applying a force to move an object **5** a piece of writing, painting, music, etc. • *the works of William Shakespeare*

at work working

out of work having no work; unable to find paid employment

work *VERB* **works, working, worked 1** do work **2** have a job; be employed • *She works in a bank* **3** act or operate correctly or successfully • *Is the lift working?* **4** make something act; operate • *Can you work the lift?* **5** shape or press etc. • *Work the mixture into a paste.* **6** gradually move into a particular position or state • *The screw had worked loose.*

work out 1 find an answer by thinking or calculating **2** have a particular result

work up make people become excited; arouse

workable *ADJECTIVE* that can be used or will work

worker *NOUN* **workers 1** a person who works **2** a member of the working class **3** a bee or ant etc. that does the work in a hive or colony but does not produce eggs

workforce *NOUN* **workforces** the number of people who work in a particular factory, industry, country, etc.

Thesaurus

wording *NOUN The wording of the contract was unclear.* ► phrasing, phraseology, language, choice of words, mode of expression, terminology, style, diction

wordy *ADJECTIVE a wordy essay; a wordy speaker* ► long-winded, verbose, diffuse, rambling, repetitious, protracted, prolix, garrulous, loquacious, talkative OPPOSITES ARE brief, succinct USAGE You would normally use the last three synonyms about a person.

work *NOUN* **1** *The plastering will be several days' work.* ► labour, effort, exertion, toil, industry, (*more informal*) slog **2** *Stella's looking for work abroad.* ► employment, a job, an occupation, a career, business **3** *He had finished all his work by lunchtime.* ► tasks, jobs, assignments, projects, commissions **4** *He has written a new work for mixed choir.* ► composition, piece, opus, oeuvre, production **5** *It is a fine literary work.* ► creation, achievement, accomplishment

... *VERB* **1** *Some staff were still working at nine ... evening.* ► labour, toil, exert yourself, be ... desk, slave, (*more informal*) keep at it ... IS rest **2** *Margaret works in a bank.* ... , be employed, earn a living **3** *The ... is working again, thank goodness.* ... erate, perform, run, in working ... (*more informal*) behave ... k down **4** *He showed me how ... achine.* ► operate, use, ... *n had worked.* ► succeed, be successful, work out, take effect, (*more informal*) pay off, (*more informal*) do the trick AN OPPOSITE IS fail **6** *farmers who work the land* ► cultivate, till, dig, farm **7** *You can work miracles with the right ingredients.* ► achieve, accomplish, produce, perform, bring about, cause, (*more informal*) pull off **8** *Work the mixture into a thick dough.* ► knead, form, mould, mix, blend, stir, shape

work out 1 *The idea should work out.* ► succeed, be successful, work, (*more informal*) pay off, (*more informal*) do the trick AN OPPOSITE IS fail **2** *Things didn't quite work out as expected.* ► turn out, occur, happen, evolve, develop, end up, come out

work out at *The cost worked out at over a million dollars.* ► amount to, add up to, come to, total, reach

work something out 1 *Let's work out a plan.* ► devise, draw up, formulate, prepare, put together **2** *I can't work out the answer.* ► calculate, determine, reckon up, resolve, solve **3** *We're trying to work out what all this means.* ► understand, comprehend, make sense of, puzzle out, figure out, clear up

work up *It's hard to work up any enthusiasm.* ► raise, rouse, generate, stimulate, stir up

worker *NOUN* **1** *A strike by clerical workers brought the system to a standstill.* ► employee, member of staff, operative, working person **2** *She was a tireless worker for the party.* ► labourer, campaigner, supporter

working class *NOUN* **working classes** people who work for wages, especially in manual or industrial work

workman *NOUN* **workmen** a man employed to do manual labour

workmanship *NOUN* a person's skill in working; the result of this

work of art *NOUN* **works of art** a fine picture, building, etc.

workout *NOUN* **workouts** a session of physical exercise or training

works *PLURAL NOUN* **1** the moving parts of a machine **2** a factory or industrial site

workshop *NOUN* **workshops** a place where things are made or mended

world *NOUN* **worlds** **1** the earth with all its countries and peoples **2** all the people on the earth; everyone • *He felt that the world was against him.* **3** a planet • *creatures from another world* **4** everything to do with a certain subject or activity • *the world of sport* **5** a very great amount • *It will do him a world of good.*

worldwide *ADJECTIVE & ADVERB* over the whole world

World Wide Web *NOUN* an international information system that connects related sites and documents which can be accessed using the Internet

worm *NOUN* **worms** **1** a small animal with a long thin soft body **2** (*informal*) an unpleasant person
▷ **wormy** *ADJECTIVE*

worm *VERB* **worms, worming, wormed** move along by wriggling or crawling
worm out gradually get someone to tell you something by constantly and cleverly questioning them • *We eventually managed to worm the truth out of them.*

worn *past participle of* **wear**

worn-out *ADJECTIVE* **1** exhausted **2** damaged by too much use

worried *ADJECTIVE* feeling or showing worry

worry *VERB* **worries, worrying, worried** **1** be troublesome to someone; make a person feel slightly afraid **2** feel anxious **3** hold something in the teeth and shake it • *The dog was worrying a rat.*
▷ **worrier** *NOUN*

worry *NOUN* **worries** **1** the condition of worrying; being uneasy **2** something that makes a person worry

Thesaurus

working *ADJECTIVE* **1** *extra support for working mothers* ► employed, in work, salaried, waged AN OPPOSITE IS unemployed **2** *a working model of a steam engine* ► functioning, operational, operating, running, usable, going, in use, in working order AN OPPOSITE IS non-functioning

workmanship *NOUN* *The quality of workmanship is of a high standard.*
► craftsmanship, artistry, handiwork, technique, expertise, skill

works *NOUN* **1** *Visitors can explore the glass works and blacksmith's shop.* ► factory, workshop, foundry, plant **2** *The works of the clock needed cleaning.* ► mechanism, movement, action, parts, machinery, insides

world *NOUN* **1** *The university has links with academic institutions around the world.* ► earth, globe, planet **2** *Representatives came from the world of high finance* ► sphere, domain, field, area, realm, circle, milieu **3** *The world knows that these people need help.* ► everyone, everybody, people, humankind, humanity

worldly *ADJECTIVE* **1** *He had no ambitions for worldly power.* ► earthly, terrestrial, temporal, physical, material, materialistic, mundane, avaricious, greedy, selfish
AN OPPOSITE IS spiritual **2** *She was worldly enough to understand what was going on.*
► sophisticated, experienced, worldly-wise, knowing AN OPPOSITE IS naive

worn *ADJECTIVE* *His coat was old and worn.*
► shabby, threadbare, tattered, frayed, worn out, moth-eaten, ragged, scruffy, (*more informal*) tatty AN OPPOSITE IS smart
worn out *By the time they got home they were all worn out.* ► exhausted, tired out, weary, fatigued, shattered, (*more informal*) dead tired, (*more informal*) played out, (*more informal*) washed out

worried *ADJECTIVE* **1** *She had a worried look on her face. You seem worried about something.*
► anxious, troubled, disturbed, uneasy, distraught, apprehensive, bothered, tense, strained, nervous **2** *I was worried that our money would run out.* ► afraid, fearful, concerned, frightened, scared

worry *VERB* **1** *Try not to worry Dad while he's working.* ► bother, pester, disturb, annoy **2** *A dog had been worrying the sheep.* ► attack, torment, savage **3** *I was trying not to worry.*
► be anxious, be troubled, be disturbed, fret, panic AN OPPOSITE IS be unconcerned
4 *Something was worrying her.* ► trouble, bother, disturb, distress, upset, concern

worry *NOUN* **1** *I was too affected by worry to concentrate on the work.* ► anxiety, agitation apprehension, unease, distress, fear, misgiving, tension **2** *Each day seems to brin another worry.* ► problem, difficulty, trou concern, care, burden, misgiving

worse *ADJECTIVE, ADVERB* more bad or more badly; less good or less well
worse off less fortunate or well off

worship *VERB* **worships, worshipping, worshipped** **1** give praise or respect to God or a god **2** love or respect a person or thing greatly
▷ **worshipper** *NOUN*

worship *NOUN* **worships** **1** worshipping; religious ceremonies **2** a title of respect for a mayor or certain magistrates • *His Worship the Mayor*

worst *ADJECTIVE, ADVERB* most bad or most badly; least good or least well

worth *ADJECTIVE* **1** having a certain value • *This stamp is worth £100.* **2** deserving something; good or important enough for something • *That book is worth reading.*

worth *NOUN* **1** value or usefulness **2** the amount that a certain sum will buy • *a pound's worth of stamps*

worthwhile *ADJECTIVE* important or good enough to deserve the time or effort needed • *a worthwhile job*

worthy *ADJECTIVE* having great merit; deserving respect or support • *a worthy cause*
▷ **worthiness** *NOUN*
worthy of deserving • *This charity is worthy of your support.*

would *AUXILIARY VERB* **1** used as the past tense of **will**[1] (*We said we would do it.*), in questions (*Would you like to come?*), and in polite requests (*Would you come in, please?*) **2** used instead of **should** with **I** and **we** and the verbs **like, prefer** *be glad*, etc. (e.g. *I would like to come. We would be glad to help.*) **3** used of something to be expected *(That's just what he would do!)*
USAGE For sense 2, see the note on **should** 4.

would-be *ADJECTIVE* wanting or pretending to be • *a would-be comedian*

wouldn't (*mainly spoken*) would not

wound[1] (woond) *NOUN* **wounds** **1** an injury done by a cut, stab, or hit **2** an injury to a person's feelings

wound *VERB* **wounds, wounding, wounded** **1** cause a wound to a person or animal **2** hurt a person's feelings • *She was wounded by these remarks.*

wound[2] (wownd) *past tense of* **wind**[2]

Thesaurus

worrying *ADJECTIVE* *There was a worrying smell of gas.* ► alarming, disturbing, worrisome, disquieting, distressing, perturbing, troublesome AN OPPOSITE IS reassuring

worsen *VERB* **1** *Development of the site would worsen traffic problems.* ► aggravate, exacerbate, make worse, intensify, magnify, increase AN OPPOSITE IS improve **2** *The economic situation was beginning to worsen.* ► get or become worse, deteriorate, decline, degenerate, weaken, slide
OPPOSITES ARE improve, recover

worship *NOUN* *Christianity forbade the worship of these deities.* ► adoration, veneration, reverence (for), adulation, exaltation, devotion (to), idolatry

worship *VERB* **1** *They worshipped the sun as the giver of life.* ► revere, reverence, venerate, glorify, exalt, laud, pray to **2** *a materialistic ...ety that worships consumer goods* ► idolize, ...e, adore, dote on, be devoted to, look up ... AN OPPOSITE IS despise

...UN **1** *She knows her own worth.* ...merit, excellence, worthiness, quality, ...nts, strengths **2** *He was forced to sell ...action of its true worth.* ► value, ...ce

...VE **1** *The certificate turned out* ...valueless, of no value ...le **2** *Their advice proved* ...futile, ineffective, ...PPOSITES ARE useful, ...*him as a worthless slob.*

► good-for-nothing, useless, contemptible, despicable, miserable, wretched, vile, (*more informal*) no-good AN OPPOSITE IS worthy

worthwhile *ADJECTIVE* **1** *I've never done anything worthwhile like writing a book.* ► useful, valuable, worthy, meaningful, significant, positive, productive, important, invaluable
OPPOSITES ARE worthless, useless **2** *It might be worthwhile to join a local archaeology society.* ► advantageous, beneficial, helpful, useful, profitable, rewarding OPPOSITES ARE pointless, useless

worthy *ADJECTIVE* **1** *Our support extends to worthy causes around the country.* ► worthwhile, praiseworthy, deserving, creditable, honourable, reputable, commendable, respectable, admirable
OPPOSITES ARE unworthy, disreputable **2** *a worthy member of society* ► virtuous, honourable, honest, upright, moral, decent
OPPOSITES ARE unworthy, disreputable
3 worthy of *The site yielded pottery worthy of study and publication.* ► deserving, meriting, warranting, good enough for

wound *NOUN* **1** *There was a deep wound in the animal's forehead.* ► injury, scar, gash, cut, abrasion, disfigurement, hurt **2** *She survived these wounds inflicted by fate.* ► blow, insult, trauma, slight, affront, hurt

wound *VERB* *He was trying to rescue a colleague who had been wounded.* ► injure, hurt, harm, maim, disable, damage, disfigure

wrap *VERB* **wraps, wrapping, wrapped** put paper or cloth etc. round something as a covering
wrap up put on warm clothes
wrapper *NOUN* **wrappers** a piece of paper etc. wrapped round something
wrapping *NOUN* **wrapping** paper or other material for wrapping things in
wreath (reeth) *NOUN* **wreaths 1** flowers or leaves etc. fastened into a circle • *wreaths of holly* **2** a curving line of mist or smoke
wreathe (reeth) *VERB* **wreathes, wreathing, wreathed 1** surround or decorate something with a wreath **2** cover • *Their faces were wreathed in smiles.* **3** move in a curve • *Smoke wreathed upwards.*
wreck *VERB* **wrecks, wrecking, wrecked** damage or ruin something so badly that it cannot be used again
wreck *NOUN* **wrecks 1** a wrecked ship or building or car etc. **2** a person who is in a very bad state • *a nervous wreck* **3** the wrecking of something
wreckage *NOUN* the pieces of a wreck
wren *NOUN* **wrens** a very small brown bird
wrench *VERB* **wrenches, wrenching, wrenched** twist or pull something violently
wrench *NOUN* **wrenches 1** a wrenching movement **2** pain caused by parting • *Leaving home was a great wrench.* **3** an adjustable tool rather like a spanner, used for gripping and turning bolts, nuts, etc.
wrestle *VERB* **wrestles, wrestling, wrestled 1** take part in a fight in which opponents grapple with each other and try to throw each other to the ground **2** struggle with a problem etc.
▷ **wrestle** *NOUN* **wrestler** *NOUN*
wretch *NOUN* **wretches 1** a person who is very unhappy or who you pity **2** a person who is disliked
wretched *ADJECTIVE* **1** miserable or unhappy **2** of bad quality **3** not satisfactory; causing a nuisance • *This wretched car won't start.*
▷ **wretchedly** *ADVERB* **wretchedness** *NOUN*
wriggle *VERB* **wriggles, wriggling, wriggled** move with short twisting movements
▷ **wriggle** *NOUN* **wriggly** *ADJECTIVE*
wriggle out of avoid work or blame etc. cunningly
wring *VERB* **wrings, wringing, wrung 1** twist and squeeze a wet thing to get water etc. out of it **2** squeeze something firmly or forcibly **3** get something by a great effort • *We wrung a promise out of him.*
▷ **wring** *NOUN*
wringing wet so wet that water can be squeezed out of it
wrinkle *NOUN* **wrinkles 1** a small furrow or ridge in the skin **2** a small crease in something

Thesaurus

wrap *VERB* **1** *She wrapped a rug round her legs.* ► fold, swathe, wind, pack, place **2** *Harry wrapped himself in a towel.* ► cover, swathe, envelop, sheathe, enfold **3** *I'll wrap the sandwiches in foil.* ► cover, pack, fold, enclose
wrapper *NOUN* *The chocolate bar had 'extra value' printed on its wrapper.* ► wrapping, cover, packaging
wreck *NOUN* **1** *The wreck of an ancient gallery was discovered off Sicily.* ► wreckage, shipwreck, remains, hulk, skeleton **2** *It was the wreck of all their hopes.* ► ruin, destruction, undoing, demolition, devastation, overthrow, termination
wreck *VERB* **1** *The ship had been wrecked in a storm.* ► shipwreck, sink, destroy, break up **2** *He had wrecked his car when it skidded off the road.* ► crash, smash, demolish, shatter, crumple, crush, (*more informal*) write off **3** *A freak virus wrecked their holiday plans.* ► ruin, spoil, disrupt, undo, dash, put an end to
wreckage *NOUN* **1** *One person had to be cut from the wreckage by firemen.* ► wreck, debris, rubble, remains, ruin **2** *Wreckage from the aircraft was scattered for miles.* ► debris, fragments, remains, detritus, pieces, relics
wrench *NOUN* **1** *With a wrench he tore himself free.* ► jerk, jolt, pull, tug, twist, (*informal*) yank **2** *It was a wrench leaving the children behind with Polly.* ► trauma, painful experience
wrench *VERB* *Charlotte heard her wrench the door open.* ► pull, jerk, tug, force, prise, lever, wrest, (*informal*) yank
wretch *NOUN* **1** *He was a lonely, miserable wretch.* ► poor creature, down and out, beggar, pauper **2** *He had been mugged by some wretches in the park.* ► ruffian, scoundrel, rogue, villain, rascal, delinquent
wretched *ADJECTIVE* **1** *She had seldom felt so tired or so wretched.* ► miserable, unhappy, sad, despondent, melancholy, cast down, unwell, poorly **2** *The weather was wretched all week. The family had to endure wretched living conditions.* ► atrocious, appalling, dreadful, dismal, bleak
wriggle *VERB* **1** *He wriggled further back on the bed till he was leaning up against the wall.* ► twist, writhe, squirm, waggle, wiggle, worm
wriggle out of *He tried to wriggle out of work, as usual.* ► avoid, shirk, dodge, evade, escape from
wring *VERB* **1** *He went to the sink to wring out the socks.* ► squeeze, twist, compress, crush, press **2** *They managed to wring more money out of the government.* ► extract, coerce, force, wrest, exact, extort **3** *The look on his face wrung her heart.* ► stab, tear, pierce, rend, distress, pain, hurt

wrinkle *VERB* **wrinkles, wrinkling, wrinkled** make wrinkles in something; form wrinkles

wrist *NOUN* **wrists** the joint that connects the hand and arm

wristwatch *NOUN* **wristwatches** a watch for wearing on the wrist

write *VERB* **writes, writing, wrote, written** **1** put letters or words etc. on paper or another surface **2** be the author or composer of something **3** send a letter to somebody **4** (in computing) enter data into a computer memory
▷ **writer** *NOUN*
write off think something is lost or useless
write up write an account of something

writhe *VERB* **writhes, writhing, writhed** **1** twist your body because of pain **2** wriggle **3** suffer because of great shame

writing *NOUN* **writings** something you write; the way you write

wrong *ADJECTIVE* **1** incorrect; not true • *the wrong answer* **2** not fair or morally right • *It is wrong to cheat.* **3** not working properly • *There's something wrong with the engine.*
▷ **wrongly** *ADVERB* **wrongness** *NOUN*

wrong *ADVERB* wrongly • *You guessed wrong*

wrong *NOUN* **wrongs** something morally wrong; an injustice
in the wrong having done or said something wrong

wrong *VERB* **wrongs, wronging, wronged** do wrong to someone; treat a person unfairly

wry *ADJECTIVE* **wryer, wryest** **1** slightly mocking or sarcastic • *a wry smile* **2** twisted or bent out of shape COMPARE **awry**
▷ **wryly** *ADVERB* **wryness** *NOUN*

Thesaurus

wrinkle *NOUN* *Despite being carefully ironed the shirt was full of wrinkles. The wrinkles on her neck moved when she swallowed.* ► crease, fold, pucker, crinkle, ridge, furrow, dimple, gather, line, pleat

wrinkle *VERB* *You have to wrinkle your nose to break the spell.* ► crease, crinkle, pucker up, crumple, fold, furrow, ridge, ruck up, rumple AN OPPOSITE IS smooth

wrinkled *ADJECTIVE* *His hands were white and very wrinkled.* ► creased, wrinkly, crinkly, crumpled, furrowed, shrivelled, lined, pleated, ridged, rumpled, wavy, wizened

write *VERB* **1** *He wrote the details in a notebook.* ► write down, jot down, take down, put down, record, transcribe, make a note of, note down, scribble, register **2** *After a while she stopped writing to him.* ► communicate (with), send letters, keep in touch **3** *The music was written one summer at the lakeside retreat.* ► compose, create, set down, compile, pen, draft
write off *He wrote off for a free voucher.* ► apply, send off, send away
write something off **1** *The Inland Revenue wrote off millions of pounds in unpaid taxes.* ► disregard, cancel, delete, annul **2** (*informal*) *He wrote off his car on a Belgian motorway.* ► crash, smash, wreck

writer *NOUN* *one of the great writers of the 20th century* ► author, novelist, dramatist, essayist, wordsmith

writhe *VERB* *I tossed and writhed on the hard bed.* ► wriggle, squirm, thrash about, toss, flail, struggle, twist, contort

writing *NOUN* **1** *Her writing is neater than mine.* ► handwriting, penmanship, calligraphy, script, letters, longhand, scribble, scrawl **2** *She took up writing in old age.* ► composition, literature, letters
writings *His political views are clearly reflected in his writings.* ► literary texts, literature, texts, works

wrong *ADJECTIVE* **1** *It was wrong to take the books without asking.* ► bad, dishonest, blameworthy, reprehensible, sinful, wicked AN OPPOSITE IS right **2** *The law lays down limits and it is wrong to exceed them.* ► unlawful, illegal, criminal, delinquent OPPOSITES ARE lawful, legal **3** *She knew she had given a wrong answer. The visitor pressed the wrong buzzer.* ► incorrect, erroneous, inaccurate, mistaken OPPOSITES ARE correct, right **4** *I must have said something wrong.* ► inappropriate, unsuitable, inapt, ill-advised, ill-judged, unfitting AN OPPOSITE IS appropriate **5** *There's something wrong with the equipment.* ► faulty, defective, amiss, broken down, out of order, unusable AN OPPOSITE IS right

wrong *NOUN* **1** *He had done many wrongs that needed putting right.* ► misdeed, bad deed, offence, crime, injury, injustice AN OPPOSITE IS good deed **2** *We know the difference between right and wrong.* ► immorality, badness, sinfulness, wickedness, evil OPPOSITES ARE goodness, virtue

wrong *VERB* *She was determined to forget the man who had wronged her.* ► mistreat, abuse, be unfair to, maltreat, ill-treat, treat unfairly, cheat, do an injustice to, harm, hurt, misrepresent, traduce

wrongful *ADJECTIVE* *She is claiming damages for wrongful dismissal.* ► unjust, unfair, unlawful, unjustified, unwarranted, undeserved, unreasonable, uncalled-for OPPOSITES ARE rightful, fair

wry *ADJECTIVE* **1** *Robbie sipped his drink and pulled a wry face.* ► twisted, distorted, contorted, crooked, uneven, bent **2** *Lawrence allowed himself a wry smile.* ► mocking, sardonic, derisive, dry, ironic, droll

Xx

Xmas *NOUN* (*informal*) Christmas

X-ray *NOUN* **X-rays** a photograph or examination of the inside of something, especially a part of the body, made by a kind of radiation (called **X-rays**) that can penetrate solid things

X-ray *VERB* **X-rays, X-raying, X-rayed** make an X-ray of something

xylophone (zy- lo- fohn) *NOUN* **xylophones** a musical instrument made of wooden bars that you hit with small hammers [from Greek *xylon* = wood + *phone* = sound]

Thesaurus

xenophobia *NOUN* *Feelings of xenophobia can so easily be whipped up.* ► nationalism, jingoism, racism

xenophobic *ADJECTIVE* *the triumphs of xenophobic right-wing parties* ► nationalistic, jingoistic, racist

Yy

yacht (yot) *NOUN* **yachts** **1** a sailing boat used for racing or cruising **2** a private ship
▷ **yachting** *NOUN* **yachtsman** *NOUN* **yachtswoman** *NOUN*
[from Dutch *jaghtschip* = fast pirate ship]

yak *NOUN* **yaks** an ox with long hair, found in central Asia [from Tibetan]

yank *VERB* **yanks, yanking, yanked** (*informal*) pull something strongly and suddenly
▷ **yank** *NOUN*

Yankee *NOUN* **Yankees** (*informal*) an American, especially of the northern USA

yap *VERB* **yaps, yapping, yapped** bark shrilly
▷ **yap** *NOUN*

yard[1] *NOUN* **yards** **1** a measure of length, 36 inches or about 91 centimetres **2** a long pole stretched out from a mast to support a sail [from Old English *gerd*]

yard[2] *NOUN* **yards** an enclosed area beside a building or used for a certain kind of work • *a timber yard* [from Old English *geard*]

yarn *NOUN* **yarns** **1** thread spun by twisting fibres together, used in knitting etc. **2** (*informal*) a tale or story

yawn *VERB* **yawns, yawning, yawned** **1** open the mouth wide and breathe in deeply when feeling sleepy or bored **2** form a wide opening • *A pit yawned in front of us.*
▷ **yawn** *NOUN*

ye *PRONOUN* (*old use*) you (referring to two or more people)

year *NOUN* **years** **1** the time the earth takes to go right round the sun, about 365 days **2** the time from 1 January to 31 December; any period of twelve months **3** a group of students of roughly the same age
▷ **yearly** *ADJECTIVE, ADVERB*

yearn *VERB* **yearns, yearning, yearned** long for something

yeast *NOUN* a substance that causes alcohol and carbon dioxide to form as it develops, used in making beer and wine and in baking bread etc.

yell *VERB* **yells, yelling, yelled** give a loud cry; shout
▷ **yell** *NOUN*

yellow *NOUN* **yellows** the colour of buttercups and ripe lemons

yellow *ADJECTIVE* **1** of yellow colour **2** (*informal*) cowardly
▷ **yellowness** *NOUN*

yellow pages *PLURAL NOUN* a special telephone directory giving addresses and telephone numbers of businesses, arranged according to what services they provide

yelp *VERB* **yelps, yelping, yelped** give a shrill bark or cry
▷ **yelp** *NOUN*

yen[1] *NOUN* **yen** a unit of money in Japan [from Japanese *en* = round]

yen[2] *NOUN* **yens** a longing for something [from Chinese]

yes *ADVERB* used to agree to or accept something or as an answer meaning 'I am here'

yesterday *NOUN, ADVERB* the day before today

yet *ADVERB* **1** up to this time; by this time • *The post hasn't come yet.* **2** eventually • *I'll get even with him yet!* **3** in addition; even • *She became yet more excited.*

yet *CONJUNCTION* nevertheless • *It is strange, yet it is true.*

yew *NOUN* **yews** an evergreen tree with dark green needle-like leaves and red berries

yield *VERB* **yields, yielding, yielded** **1** give in or surrender **2** agree to do what is asked or

Thesaurus

yank *VERB* *(informal) He yanked the door open and stumbled inside.* ▸ pull, force, jerk, tug, wrench, prise, wrest

yap *VERB* *A dog yapped frantically somewhere inside.* ▸ yelp, bark, woof

yard *NOUN* *A pony stood in the middle of the yard.* ▸ court, courtyard, enclosure, quadrangle, (*more informal*) quad

yardstick *NOUN* *They regard the family as the yardstick to measure values by.* ▸ standard, criterion, benchmark, gauge, guideline, measure

yarn *NOUN* **1** *This is a lovely soft yarn.* ▸ thread, wool, fibre, strand, twine **2** (*informal*) *He rang with a yarn about problems at his hotel.* ▸ story, tale, rigmarole, anecdote, narrative

yearn *VERB* *They yearned to be home.* ▸ long, crave, pine, desire, hanker, wish

yearning *NOUN* *She had always had a yearning to play the piano.* ▸ longing, desire, craving, hankering, wish, (*more informal*) yen

yell *VERB* *He yelled at them to stop.* ▸ shout, cry out, call, shriek, scream, bawl, exclaim

yell *NOUN* *She gave a yell of pain.* ▸ cry, shriek, scream, screech

yelp *VERB* *He yelped with delight.* ▸ squeal, squawk, shriek, scream, howl, yell

yelp *NOUN* *The dog let out a yelp.* ▸ yap, bark, woof

yield *VERB* **1** *The contest continues until one side yields.* ▸ surrender, succumb, capitulate, submit, give in, give way, concede defeat,

A B C D E F G H I J K L M N O P Q R S T U V W X

Zz

zap *VERB* **zaps, zapping, zapped** (*slang*) **1** attack or destroy something forcefully, especially in electronic games **2** use a remote control to change television channels quickly

zeal *NOUN* enthusiasm or keenness
▷ **zealous** (zel- us) *ADJECTIVE* **zealously** *ADVERB*

zebra (zeb- ra) *NOUN* **zebras** an African animal of the horse family, with black and white stripes all over its body [from Italian, Spanish, or Portuguese]

zebra crossing *NOUN* **zebra crossings** a place for pedestrians to cross a road safely, marked with broad white stripes

zero *NOUN* **zeros** **1** nought; the figure 0 **2** the point marked 0 on a thermometer etc. [from Arabic *sifr* = cipher]

zero hour *NOUN* the time when something is planned to start

zest *NOUN* **1** great enjoyment or interest **2** the coloured part of orange or lemon peel
▷ **zestful** *ADJECTIVE* **zestfully** *ADVERB*

zigzag *NOUN* **zigzags** a line or route that turns sharply from side to side

zigzag *VERB* **zigzags, zigzagging, zigzagged** move in a zigzag

zinc *NOUN* a white metal [from German *Zink*]

zip *NOUN* **zips** **1** a zip fastener **2** a sharp sound like a bullet going through the air **3** liveliness or vigour
▷ **zippy** *ADJECTIVE*

zip *VERB* **zips, zipping, zipped** **1** fasten something with a zip fastener **2** move quickly with a sharp sound

zip fastener or **zipper** *NOUN* **zip fasteners** or **zippers** a fastener consisting of two strips of material, each with rows of small teeth that interlock when a sliding tab brings them together

zodiac (zoh- dee- ak) *NOUN* a strip of sky where the sun, moon, and main planets are found, divided into twelve equal parts (called **signs of the zodiac**), each named after a constellation [from Greek *zoidion* = image of an animal]

zone *NOUN* **zones** an area of a special kind or for a particular purpose • *a war zone* • *a no-parking zone* [from Greek, = girdle]

zoo *NOUN* **zoos** a place where wild animals are kept so that people can look at them or study them

zoology (zoh- ol- o- jee) *NOUN* the scientific study of animals
▷ **zoological** *ADJECTIVE* **zoologist** *NOUN*
[from Greek *zoion* = animal]

zoom *VERB* **zooms, zooming, zoomed** **1** move very quickly, especially with a deep buzzing sound **2** rise quickly • *Prices had zoomed.* **3** (in photography) use a zoom lens to change from a distant view to a close-up
▷ **zoom** *NOUN*
[imitating the sound]

zoom lens *NOUN* **zoom lenses** a camera lens that can be adjusted continuously to make things appear close up or far away

Thesaurus

zany *ADJECTIVE* *a zany thriller about ecological disaster* ► crazy, weird, bizarre, eccentric
OPPOSITES ARE serious, sensible

zeal *NOUN* *a zeal to improve society* ► enthusiasm, fervour, ardour, zest, passion, devotion, keenness, eagerness, dedication

zealous *ADJECTIVE* *Bran was a zealous patriot and served his country well.* ► keen, fervent, enthusiastic, fanatical, passionate, conscientious, committed, diligent, eager, earnest AN OPPOSITE IS apathetic

zenith *NOUN* *The country was then at the zenith of its power.* ► peak, pinnacle, height, top, acme, apex, climax AN OPPOSITE IS nadir

zero *NOUN* *Opportunities for further education might be reduced to zero.* ► nothing, nought, nil

zest *NOUN* *After his recovery he had a renewed zest for life.* ► eagerness, energy, enjoyment, enthusiasm, zeal, liveliness, pleasure

zigzag *ADJECTIVE* *Some escaping animals take a zigzag course.* ► winding, meandering, serpentine, twisting, weaving, bendy, crooked

zigzag *VERB* *A narrow path zigzagged steeply down to the shore.* ► wind, meander, snake, twist, weave, curve, bend

zone *NOUN* *He decided to leave the war zone and get back to his family.* ► area, sector, section, region, sphere, district, vicinity, locality, neighbourhood, territory, tract

zoom *VERB* (*informal*) *A motorbike zoomed across their path.* ► race, rush, speed, dash, hurry, hurtle, (*informal*) whiz, (*informal*) zip

ordered; give way • *He yielded to persuasion.* **3** produce as a crop or as profit etc.

yoga (yoh- ga) *NOUN* a Hindu system of meditation and self-control; a system of physical exercises based on this

yoghurt (yog- ert) *NOUN* milk thickened by the action of certain bacteria, giving it a sharp taste [from Turkish]

yoke *NOUN* **yokes** **1** a curved piece of wood put across the necks of animals pulling a cart or plough etc. **2** a shaped piece of wood fitted across a person's shoulders, with a pail or load hung at each end **3** a close-fitting upper part of a piece of clothing, from which the rest hangs

yoke *VERB* **yokes, yoking, yoked** harness or join things by means of a yoke [from Old English]
USAGE Do not confuse with **yolk**.

yolk (rhymes with *coke*) *NOUN* **yolks** the round yellow part inside an egg
USAGE Do not confuse with **yoke**.

yonder *ADJECTIVE, ADVERB* over there

you *PRONOUN* **1** the person or people being spoken to • *Who are you?* **2** anyone or everyone; one • *You can't tell what will happen next.*

young *ADJECTIVE* having lived or existed for only a short time; not old

youngster *NOUN* **youngsters** a young person; a child

your *ADJECTIVE* belonging to you
USAGE Do not confuse with **you're.**

you're (*mainly spoken*) you are
USAGE Do not confuse with **your.**

yours *POSSESSIVE PRONOUN* belonging to you
Yours faithfully, Yours sincerely ways of ending a letter before you sign it (*Yours faithfully* is more formal than *Yours sincerely*)
USAGE It is incorrect to write *your's*.

yourself *PRONOUN* **yourselves** you and nobody else

youth *NOUN* **youths** **1** being young; the time when you are young **2** a young man **3** young people
▷ **youthful** *ADJECTIVE* **youthfulness** *NOUN*

youth hostel *NOUN* **youth hostels** a place where young people can stay cheaply when they are hiking or on holiday

yo-yo *NOUN* **yo-yos** a round wooden or plastic toy that moves up and down on a string that you hold [probably from a language spoken in the Philippines]

Yule *NOUN* (*old use*) the Christmas festival, also called **Yuletide** [originally the name of a pagan festival: from Old English or Old Norse]

Thesaurus

(*more informal*) cave in, (*informal*) throw in the towel, (*informal*) throw up the sponge **2** *The allotment yields a fine crop of root vegetables.* ► produce, grow, bear, supply **3** *an investment yielding a high interest* ► earn, generate, provide, return, pay, attract

yield *NOUN* **1** *The farm has produced a good yield.* ► crop, harvest, produce, product **2** *I'm looking for a savings bond with a high yield.* ► return, interest, earnings, income, profit

yob *NOUN* *A gang of yobs were making a nuisance of themselves.* ► hooligan, hoodlum, lout, ruffian, troublemaker, vandal, thug, bully, delinquent, tough, rough, tearaway

young *ADJECTIVE* **1** *She enjoyed working with young people.* ► youthful, juvenile, teenage, adolescent OPPOSITES ARE old, elderly **2** *They seem young for their age.* ► immature, childish, babyish AN OPPOSITE IS mature

young *NOUN* **1** *Parents have an instinct to protect their young* ► offspring, family, progeny, brood, issue, litter **2 the young** *They enjoyed talking to the young.* ► young people, youths, youngsters, juveniles, minors RELATED ADJECTIVE juvenile

youth *NOUN* **1** *She had spent most of her youth abroad.* ► early life, early years, teenage years, adolescence, boyhood girlhood, childhood, infancy, (*informal*) teens **2** *a group of youths* ► young person, teenager, youngster, adolescent, boy girl, juvenile, (*more informal*) kid, (*more informal*) lad

youthful *ADJECTIVE* **1** *They sang before a youthful audience.* ► young **2** *He had a youthful appearance.* ► young-looking, fresh, lively, sprightly, vigorous, well-preserved